47TH EDITION

KOVELS'
Antiques &
Collectibles
PRICE GUIDE 2015

BLACK DOG
& LEVENTHAL
PUBLISHERS

Published by
Black Dog & Leventhal Publishers, Inc.
151 W. 19th Street
New York, NY 10011

Distributed by
Workman Publishing Company
225 Varick Street
New York, NY 10014

Designed by Sheila Hart Design, Inc.
Manufactured in the United States of America

ISBN-978-157912-977-4
Library of Congress Cataloging-in-Publication Data is available on file at
the offices of the publisher.

Paperback
b d f h g e c a

Front cover photographs, from top to bottom:
Furniture, chair, V. Kagan, lounge, walnut, adjustable, stainless steel
Daum, vase, lake scene, trees, shoreline
Toy, cat, velvet, glass eyes, wheels, Steiff

On the spine:
Sewing, scissors, embossed handle, cast white metal

Back cover photographs, from top to bottom:
Tiffany, lamp, mosaic, Black-Eyed Susan, 3-light
Scheier, vase, faces, magnetized volcanic glaze
Advertising, pin, Ocean Wave Washer, Voss Bro's., celluloid

Authors' photographs © Molly Nook (top) and Alex Montes de Oca (bottom)

BOOKS BY RALPH AND TERRY KOVEL

American Country Furniture, 1780–1875

A Directory of American Silver, Pewter, and Silver Plate

Kovels' Advertising Collectibles Price List

Kovels' American Antiques 1750–1900

Kovels' American Art Pottery

Kovels' American Collectibles 1900–2000

Kovels' American Silver Marks, 1650 to the Present

Kovels' Antiques & Collectibles Fix-It Source Book

Kovels' Antiques & Collectibles Price Guide

Kovels' Bid, Buy, and Sell Online

Kovels' Book of Antique Labels

Kovels' Bottles Price List

Kovels' Collector's Guide to American Art Pottery

Kovels' Collector's Guide to Limited Editions

Kovels' Collectors' Source Book

Kovels' Depression Glass & Dinnerware Price List

Kovels' Dictionary of Marks— Pottery and Porcelain, 1650 to 1850

Kovels' Guide to Selling, Buying, and Fixing Your Antiques and Collectibles

Kovels' Guide to Selling Your Antiques & Collectibles

Kovels' Illustrated Price Guide to Royal Doulton

Kovels' Know Your Antiques

Kovels' Know Your Collectibles

Kovels' New Dictionary of Marks— Pottery and Porcelain, 1850 to the Present

Kovels' Organizer for Collectors

Kovels' Price Guide for Collector Plates, Figurines, Paperweights, and Other Limited Edition Items

Kovels' Quick Tips: 799 Helpful Hints on How to Care for Your Collectibles

Kovels' Yellow Pages: A Resource Guide for Collectors

The Label Made Me Buy It: From Aunt Jemima to Zonkers— The Best-Dressed Boxes, Bottles, and Cans from the Past

BOOKS BY TERRY KOVEL AND KIM KOVEL

Kovels' Antiques & Collectibles Price Guide

INTRODUCTION

CHANGES IN PRICES, INFLATION, AND THE ECONOMY

The past year has been another year of the weak "collecting economy" that started in 2008. However, this year, prices are once again a little better than last and many record prices were set as bidders fought for the best of the best, especially the best of collectibles and art made after 1950. (See page vii for a list of this year's record prices.) It was another year of great changes in the way antiques are collected, thanks to the Internet, cell phones, tablet computers, and other electronic ways to buy and sell. Since 1953, the year we published our first book, the antiques world went from one or two antiques shows in a city per year to one almost every week. But with so many new online ways to buy and sell antiques—and the weak economy—many shows have been discontinued. Some cities have lost shows that were important annual events for 40 years. Auctions of expensive antiques used to be held in a few large cities; small towns had "farm auctions" often held outside a farmhouse. Or a local auctioneer who sold antiques sold the stuff in the barn, too. There were no antiques malls and no Internet shops, sales, or auctions. Collectors went on antiquing trips to look for the furniture, pottery, or glass they found in a few shops in each town, so buying was limited to a small geographic area and a few items. Today the New York City auction houses run regular sales at their galleries along with online auctions that reach buyers in every country. And major auctions are also online from London, Paris, Hong Kong, and sometimes from the sale site of a special collection. You can even watch live auctions and bid from your computer or phone.

When we wrote our first book, *Kovels' Dictionary of Marks: Pottery & Porcelain*, it was one of just 60 titles about antiques announced that year. In 1969, there were about 200. Then several publishers started to offer picture-price books about a single type of collectible. Soon hundreds of books for collectors filled shelves at bookstores across the country. Now fewer new books about collectibles and antiques are published, but old and new information is found on the Internet. And much of the information found in old books, even old company catalogs and advertisements, can be found by searching online. Our out-of-print newspaper columns, newsletters, special reports, books of marks, and other writings are now easily found on our website, Kovels.com, or via an Internet search.

The economic problems that started with the stock market crash and housing bust late in 2008 spread to other investments, including antiques and collectibles. There is still a myth that if you buy antiques, they will go up in value every year and therefore are a good investment. That is only half true. If you buy the right antiques and sell at the right time, they sell for higher prices than you paid, even when you factor in inflation. Consider this: Our first price book lists a Diamond Dyes cabinet for $50. In the early months of 2008, the same cabinet sold for $1,112 to $2,633. In 2012, two Diamond Dyes cabinets were listed in the Advertising category, one at $540 and the other at $550—very low prices. In 2013, the most common Diamond Dyes cabinets in good condition were $407, $1,320, and $1,540. In 2014, the Diamond Dyes cabinet featuring Children with Balloons was $896, the one picturing the Governess was $1,560, and the Washer Woman was $720. In this book, the Diamond Dyes cabinets listed are Evolution of Women, $360; Maypole, $1,596; Children with Balloons, $2,400; and Blond Fairy, $1,112. There are twelve old designs for these cabinets.

While the ongoing worldwide recession is still affecting the values of antiques, show organizers are seeing better attendance, and there are many more auction bidders—because most auctions today are online and international. But final prices show that the average auction may end with many unsold lots. Prices for items offered by people on eBay are still low, and many items do not sell at all. In 2012, prices had gone up for some things with international appeal, like Chinese porcelain and ivory. But in 2013 and 2014, Chinese bidding slowed down for all but

top-quality pieces. Hummel and Royal Doulton figurines, "country furniture" with peeling paint, and "brown furniture" like period Chippendale desks have gone way down in value. However, 1890s oak dining tables that had been hard to sell are starting to attract more buyers. Prices for Japanese antiques are down because buyers in Japan are showing less interest in Satsuma, Nippon, and other Japanese porcelains. But a new interest, Western-style Japanese paintings, prints, ceramics, and wood carvings, are being shown in museum exhibits and attracting new buyers. Prices for large advertising signs and rock 'n' roll posters are up. Through it all, malls, shows, and shops have seen fewer buyers and lower prices than they could get six years ago. But we talk to collectors and dealers, and most agree that "good stuff sells" and well-run shows, shops, and sales are doing "OK." Usable furniture in good condition and "smalls" are selling for expected prices, and the "best" of every type of antique or collectible is still in demand. Some auctions get prices that are closer to retail than they were before. But easy-to-find antiques are at about one-third of retail because of the large, worldwide supply. A shop must be able to triple the cost to cover the expenses of rent, travel, etc., and still make money.

One influence in this decade's market was the demand for Asian antiques. Jade, ivory, and cloisonné made in China, Japan, Korea, and other Asian countries were selling for many times estimates until about 2012. That has changed because China's economy is suffering and laws protecting endangered species are being enforced. Laws forbid the sale of elephant ivory, rhinoceros horns, eagle feathers, tiger skins, and even some types of turtle shells. An auction that advertises top-quality Asian items often is visited by buyers and appraisers who travel to the United States from China to see pieces at previews before bidding way over estimated prices. Do Asian buyers know more than Americans about the age and quality of these pieces? Or are they eager to bring their culture back home, no matter what the price? A few items estimated to be worth thousands have sold for millions of dollars. Unfortunately, there is a growing problem with bids from China. Some Chinese bidders refuse to honor their bids and instead ask for a large price reduction—or just don't pay for and pick up a piece. Often this "sale" is reported at the time of the auction, but there is rarely a public announcement that the bid was not honored. The highest bids now seem to be from Russian millionaires or a few overseas buyers opening museums.

Kovels' Antiques & Collectibles Price Guide 2015 still has current, reliable information, plus edited content. The book has 2,500 new color photographs and 35,000 prices. You will also find more than two hundred facts of interest and tips about care and repair. Each photograph is shown with a complete caption that includes the price and the source. The book has color tabs and color-coded paragraphs that make it easy to find listings, and it uses a modern, readable typestyle. More than seven hundred paragraphs that introduce price categories give history and descriptions that help identify an unknown piece. We make some changes in the paragraphs every year to indicate new owners, new distributors, or new information about production dates. This year we made more than twenty updates to paragraphs, many of which tell of the sale or closing of a company, and added three new categories: Bottle Stoppers, Mardi Gras, and Stainless Steel. All of the antiques and collectibles priced here were offered for sale during the past year, most of them in the United States. Other prices came from sales that accepted bids from all over the world. Almost all auction prices given include the buyer's premium, because that is part of what the buyer paid. Very few include local sales tax.

READ THIS FIRST

This is a book for the buyer and the seller. We check prices, visit shops, shows, and flea markets, read hundreds of publications and catalogs, check Internet sales and other online services, and decide which antiques and collectibles are of most interest to most collectors. We concentrate on the average pieces in any category. Sometimes high-priced items are included so you can see that special rarities are very valuable. Prices of some items were very high because major collections of top-quality pieces were auctioned. Auction houses like to have huge sales of things that belonged to one major collector or expert. This year's sales featured collections by authors: a sale of Hummel figurines owned by Robert L. Miller, who wrote the first Hummel price book, and dollhouses owned by Flora Gill Jacobs, the author of several books on dollhouses. Another sale featured 200 "catty" antiques, from

paintings and figurines to necklaces that belonged to the owner of the Cat Book Center, a store that featured rare books about cats. Rare and expensive sewing tools like a tape measure shaped like a carriage ($1,456) and a porcelain needle case in the shape of a lady's leg ($840) were from a famous Viennese collection. The fame of the owner is recorded as part of the provenance and makes the items more valuable.

Carved figure of Santa Claus: $875,000

Most listed pieces cost less than $10,000. The highest price in this book is $875,000 for a carved figure of Santa Claus made by Samuel A. Robb of New York in 1923. The lowest price, $2, is for a celluloid button with a rhinestone center made for a dress. The largest antique is a wooden and marble backbar with four columns, mirrors, and cast-iron trim. The 150-by-117-inch bar sold for $18,000. The smallest is a micro-mosaic glass button picturing a building. The ⅜-inch button sold for $14. Many unusual, unique, and weird things are included. This year, we list a patent model of an artificial leg ($1,304), another of a corpse cooler and preserver with a viewing window made in 1874 ($3,259), an Amish wood carving used by a spirit chaser ($300), and a pair of wooden tattooed arms, 30 ½ inches long, used as trade signs for a tattoo parlor ($300). A French Provincial dog's bed with a canopy and curved rails made about 1800, 29 by 24 inches, sold for $1,722. Taxidermy is very popular, but four boxes showing boxing squirrels made by William Hart in about 1850 surprised bidders when they sold for prices ranging from $17,700 to $22,420. Unique pieces like a sofa made from the tail end of a 1966 Corvette ($604) and a medical model of a human left foot made in the 1960s ($295) prove that collectors want rare "treasures."

There are still bargains to be had, some that have been emerging as "collectibles" over the last six years. Most are in newer categories, like modernist jewelry and twentieth-century studio pottery. Big is still "big." Small sets of figurines or plates are very hard to sell. But large-scale accent pieces with colors and lines that blend in with modern furnishings—pieces like huge crocks, floor vases, centerpieces, and garden statuary—attract decorators as well as the owners of large homes. Blue and white, the colors favored in the 17th and 18th centuries, are back; and orange, the stand-out color of 1920s Czechoslovakian glass and pottery, is a popular color this year. So decorators are buying big and blue and orange. Anything from clothes and glass to ceramics and furniture that was in the "newest style" between the 1950s and the 1990s is hot. Also wanted are very large beige pots from the 1960s that can be displayed on the floor, modernist and Mexican jewelry, and some old standbys, like toy cars, mechanical banks, shaving mugs, maps, and war and political memorabilia. They are all going up in price and attracting new, younger buyers. Of major interest today are antique guns and ammunition and anything made of iron, like bookends and doorstops. But costume jewelry is the most popular item we see selling at shows. Prices for pieces marked with important makers' names can sell for as much as $1,500. A few very popular collectibles of the past, like Roseville pottery and wicker furniture, have come down in price. The biggest change is silver tableware. The meltdown price of sterling silver made it profitable to melt some pieces. Hundreds of coin silver items, especially spoons, and no-name sterling serving dishes and flatware disappeared in the meltdown craze. Sterling by well-known companies or designers like Tiffany, Georg Jensen, or Paul Storr gets top dollar. Quality sells high—because collectors consider it an "investment" that will increase in value.

Kovels' Antiques & Collectibles Price Guide seems to have gotten younger over the past forty-seven years. Most items in our original book were made before 1860, so they were more than a century old. Today we list pieces made as recently as the twenty-first century, and there is great interest in furniture, glass, ceramics, and good design made since 1950.

The book is more than 670 pages long and crammed full of prices and photographs. We try to have a balanced format—not too many items that sell for over $5,000. We list a few very expensive pieces so you can realize that a great paperweight may cost $10,000 but an average one only $25. Nearly all the prices are from the American market for the American market. Only a few European sales are reported. We don't include prices we think result from "auction fever." We do list verified bargains.

The index is computer-generated. Use it often. It includes categories and much more. For example, there is a category for Celluloid. Most celluloid will be there, but a toy made of celluloid will be listed under Toy and also indexed under Celluloid. There are also cross-references in the listings and in the paragraphs. But some searching must be done. For example, Barbie dolls are in the Doll category; there is no Barbie category. And when you look at "doll, Barbie," you find a note that "Barbie" is under "doll, Mattel, Barbie" because Mattel makes Barbie dolls and most dolls are listed by maker.

All photographs and prices are new. Antiques and collectibles pictured are items that were offered for sale or sold for the amount listed in 2013–2014. Auction prices include the buyer's premium. Wherever we had extra space on a page, we filled it with tips about the care of collections and other useful information. Don't discard this book. Old Kovels' price guides can be used for future reference and for tax, estate, and appraisal information.

The prices in this book are reports of the general antiques market. As we said, every price in the book is new. We do not estimate or "update" prices. Prices are either realized prices from auctions or completed sales or they're asking prices. We know that a buyer may have negotiated an asking price to a lower selling price, but we report asking prices. We do not pay dealers, collectors, or experts to estimate prices. If the price is from an auction, it includes the buyer's premium if one was charged; but nearly all the prices do not include sales tax. If a price range is given, at least two identical items were offered for sale at different prices. Price ranges are found only in categories like Pressed Glass, where identical items can be identified. Some prices in *Kovels' Antiques & Collectibles Price Guide* may seem high and some low because of regional variations, but each price is one you could have paid for the object somewhere in the United States. Internet prices from sellers' ads or listings are avoided. Because so many non-collectors sell online but know little about the objects they are describing, there can be inaccuracies in descriptions. Sales from well-known Internet sites, shops, and sales, carefully edited, are included.

If you are selling your collection, do not expect to get retail value unless you are a dealer. Wholesale prices for antiques are 30 to 40 percent of retail prices. The antiques dealer must make a profit or go out of business. Internet auction prices are less predictable—because of an international audience and "auction fever," prices can be higher or lower than retail.

RECORD PRICES

Record prices for antiques and collectibles make news every year. We report those that relate to the entries in this book. We do not include record prices for works of art that are often seen in museums, like oil paintings, antique sculptures, or very recent work by modern artists unless the artist also worked in decorative arts. Our list is a snapshot of the collectors' market.

CLOCKS

E. Howard clock: $277,300 for an E. Howard & Co. No. 68 floor standing astronomical regulator clock, carved walnut case, with arched crest, scrolled seashell over carved maiden's head, silvered 14-in. bronze dial, brass, 8-day, 2 weights, time-only movement, signed, 1884, 105 in. h. x 33 in. w. Fontaine's Auction Gallery, Pittsfield, Mass.

Rolex wristwatch: $1,145,000 for a Rolex wristwatch, reference 8171 "Padellone," stainless steel and diamond-set, automatic, triple calendar, moon phases and 2-tone silvered dial, c.1953. Christie's, New York.

DECOY

Eider duck: $767,000 for an Eider drake duck, solid body, with inlet head & bill carving, original paint, maker unknown, c.1900, 8 x 7 ¾ x 16 in. Sotheby's, New York.

FOLK ART

Any Robb figure: $875,000 for a wooden carved figure of Santa Claus by Samuel A. Robb, painted with mica flakes for his daughter Elizabeth in 1923 as a Christmas present, inscribed on the underside of the base in ink, "This Is the Last Figure Made by Samuel A. Robb about 1923, Elizabeth W. Robb, May 16, 1966," 38 ¾ x 16 x 15 ⅞ in. Sotheby's, New York.

FURNITURE

Paul Evans furniture: $269,000 for the "Sculpture Front" cabinet by Paul Evans, lacquered and gilt steel, sculptured panels on a hinged door, placed on a chair base of 3 legs, 1969, 80 ½ x 42 x 24 ¾ in. Sotheby's, New York.

GLASS & BOTTLES

Alfredo Barbini: $11,900 for an Alfredo Barbini for Pauly Murano clear form glass "Aquarium Block," with bubbles and 3 iridescent blown glass squid inside, base etched "Pauly A. Barbini," c.1955, 9 x 8 ½ in. Clars Auction Gallery, Oakland, Calif.

MISCELLANEOUS

Cigar Store figure: $747,500 for an Indian Princess cigar store carved figure, holding bundle of cigars in one hand, tobacco leaves in the other, bold colors glazed with varnish, attributed to Samuel Robb or Thomas Brooks, c.1880, 83 x 23 x 14 in. Guyette, Schmidt & Deeter, St. Michaels, Md.

The Beatles Sgt. Pepper's Album: $290,500 for The Beatles *Sgt. Pepper's Lonely Hearts Club Band* Mono UK Gatefold cover (Parlophone PMC 7027, 1967), autographed by all four Beatles. Heritage Auctions, Dallas.

PAINTINGS & PRINTS

Andy Warhol painting: $105,445,000 for the Andy Warhol 2-part silkscreen ink & silver spray paint on canvas, "Silver Car Crash," signed, 1963, 8 x 13 ft. Sotheby's, New York.

Most expensive work of art ever sold at auction: $142,400,000 for the oil-on-canvas Francis Bacon triptych, "Three Studies of Lucian Freud," Lucian perched on a wooden chair, 1969, 78 x 58 in. Christie's, New York.

Hofman, Charles C., Alms-House painting: $545,100 for the Charles C. Hofman oil-on-tin view of buildings & surroundings of the Berks County, Pa., Alms-House, central oval view of the complex surrounded by 8 smaller vignettes of the outbuildings and the State Seal of Pennsylvania, signed "Charles Hofman, painter, 1878," original walnut frame, 32 ½ x 29 ½ in. Pook & Pook, Downingtown, Pa.

PAPER

Book sold at auction: $14,165,000 for the *Bay Psalm Book*, published in 1640, translated by the Puritans from Hebrew and first printed in English in the United States, also the first book turned out by a printing press shipped from England. Sotheby's, New York.

This issue comic book in any grade: $275,000 for comic book, *Journey Into Mystery* No. 83, first appearance of Thor, August 1962, graded 9.4. ComicLink.com.

Any page of interior comic art and tied as any page of American comic art: $657,250 for the original artwork for the first appearance of Wolverine on the final page of *The Incredible Hulk* No. 180 (1974) by Herb Trimpe and Jack Abel. Heritage Auctions, Dallas.

POTTERY & PORCELAIN

New York State pottery: $195,500 for a tapered jar incised with federal eagle & shield, olive branch & arrows, reverse side incised with flower & leaves, inscribed "NEW YORK/Octr 25/1802," highlighted in cobalt blue, handles, 5 ½ in. Crocker Farm, Sparks, Md.

John Bell Redware: $42,550 for a pair of glazed redware seated spaniels, molded, each with incised eyes, muzzle, teeth & paws, manganese over light yellow clay, stamped "John Bell," 9 ¼ in. Crocker Farm, Sparks, Md.

Virginia pottery: $115,000 for a pair of Shenandoah Valley redware whippets in a resting position, incised

details, painted black with white & red eyes, green-painted bases with incised borders, signed "Samuel Bell/Winchester Sept 21 1841," 9 ¾ in. Crocker Farm, Sparks, Md.

Baltimore stoneware, Maryland stoneware: $230,000 for a Morgan water cooler (William Morgan, Baltimore, 1822–27), tapered shoulders, rounded rim, large handles, with incised birds feeding in a flowering tree, cobalt blue highlights, signed, 6 gal., 17 in. Crocker Farm, Sparks, Md.

Hamilton & Jones stoneware crock: $20,700 for a 6-gallon stoneware crock from Greensboro, Pa., with brushed designs of a freehand eagle, flowers & leaves, stenciled "HAMILTON & JONES/6." Crocker Farm, Sparks, Md.

Martin Brothers: $101,492 for a Martinware stoneware bird jar & cover with outstretched wings, staring eyes, broad beak, blue, green & ocher glaze, incised head & base, sculpted by Robert Wallace Martin, 1891, 16 ½ in. Woolley & Wallis, Salisbury, Wiltshire, England.

Moorcroft for Shreve: $32,130 for a silver-overlaid loving cup in the Claremont pattern, signed W. Moorcroft/Shreve & Co., San Francisco, c.1905, 7 ½ x 7 in. Clars Auction Gallery, Oakland, Calif.

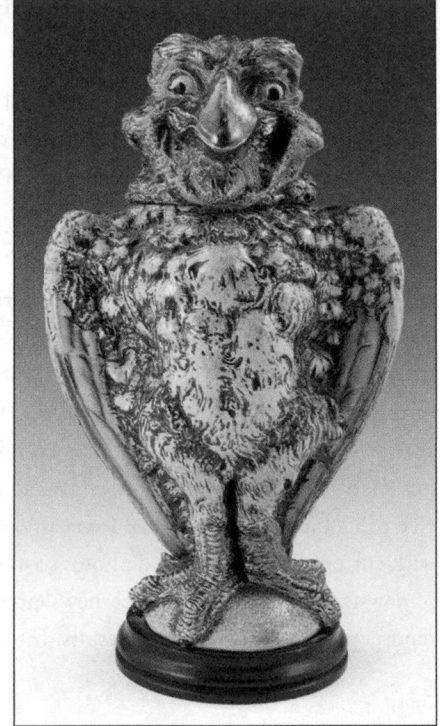

Martinware bird jar & cover: $101,492

American art pottery by Frederick Hurten Rhead: $570,000 for a Frederick Hurten Rhead vase incised with a peacock, tail feathers in blue and three shades of green on a brown & buff colored ground, with stylized tree branches, 1910, 17 ½ in. John Moran Auctioneers, California.

American art pottery by Margaret Kelly Cable: $43,200 for a Margaret Kelly Cable art pottery vase with brown glaze, cylindrical form, repeated patterns of stylized wheat stalks and ground squirrel on their haunches, inscribed, "M. Cable/1929," 13 x 7 ½ in. John Moran Auctioneers, Altadena, Calif.

Anna Pottery pig bottle: $35,650 for an Anna Pottery stoneware razorback hog flask, incised with inscriptions and map of Midwest, hand-modeled and incised facial features, opening at rear, signed "The Springfield Hog, from Kirkpatrick, Anna, Ills May 21, 1871," 8 ¾ in. Crocker Farm, Sparks, Md.

TEXTILE

Hermès Kelly bag: $125,000 for a one-of-a-kind Hermès Kelly handbag, made of pink crocodile and black Togo leather with built-in feet, made in 2010. Heritage Auctions, Dallas.

TOYS, DOLLS & BANKS

Tabby Bank by J. & E. Stevens & Co.: $5,750 for the cast-iron Tabby Bank with nodding chick, original paint, by J. & E. Stevens Co., Cromwell, Conn., c.1885, 4 ½ in. Jeffrey S. Evans & Associates, Crawford, Va.

Coasting Bank by J. & E. Stevens Co.: $266,500 for a one-of-a-kind, painted cast-metal mechanical Coasting Bank, by J. & E. Stevens Co., Cromwell, Conn., c.1884, 5 ¾ x 9 ½ x 2 ½ in. Freeman's Auction, Philadelphia.

Radicon Robot: $37,200 for a toy Radicon Robot from Masudaya's "Gang of Five" series, battery-operated, gray textured metal, with original remote control made in Japan, 14 ¾ in. Morphy Auctions, Denver, Pa.

Doll sold at auction: $300,000 for a French character doll by Albert Marque, with bisque socket head, amber brown glass paperweight eyes and brunette mohair wig, wearing an original signed costume, inscribed as No. 27, c.1916, 22 in. Theriault's, Annapolis, Md.

KOVELS OFFER EVEN MORE PRICE INFORMATION SOURCES

Website: Kovels.com

Join the community of collectors at Kovels.com to keep up on more in the buy-sell world of antiques. Register, but there is no charge for most of the information on the site, including our directory of services for collectors and dealers, years of answers to questions from collectors who read our newspaper column, and over 900,000 searchable prices from past years. Other information, including a database of pottery and porcelain marks and makers and another of silver marks and makers, is available for a fee.

Newsletter: *Kovels on Antiques and Collectibles*

You already know this is a great overall price guide for antiques and collectibles. Each entry is current, every photograph is new, and all prices are accurate. There is also another Kovel publication designed to keep you up-to-the-minute in the world of collecting. Things change quickly. Important sales produce new record prices. Fakes appear. Rarities are discovered. To keep up with developments, you can read *Kovels on Antiques and Collectibles*, our monthly newsletter. It is now available by subscription in two forms, a print edition that is mailed and an electronic format that is available via an online subscription at Kovels.com. Both provide the identical newsletter, with current information and photos so useful to collectors. The electronic edition gives you access to several years of newsletter archives, too. Each newsletter is filled with color photographs, about forty per issue. The newsletter reports prices, trends, auction results, Internet sales, and other news for collectors (see back page to order).

HOW TO USE THIS BOOK

There are a few rules for using this book. Each listing is arranged in the following manner: CATEGORY (such as silver), OBJECT (such as vase), DESCRIPTION (as much information as possible about size, age, color, and pattern). Some types of glass, pottery, and silver are exceptions to this rule. These are listed CATEGORY, PATTERN, OBJECT, DESCRIPTION. All items are presumed to be in good condition and undamaged, unless otherwise noted. In most sections, if a maker's name is easily recognized, like Gustav Stickley, we include it near the beginning of the entry. If the maker is obscure, the name may be near the end.

- You will find silver flatware in either Silver Flatware Plated or Silver Flatware Sterling. There is also a section for Silver Plate, which includes coffeepots, trays, and other plated hollowware. Most solid or sterling silver is listed by country, so look for Silver-American, Silver-Danish, Silver-English, etc. Silver jewelry is listed under Jewelry. Most pottery and porcelain is listed by factory name, such as Weller; by item, such as Calendar Plate; in sections like Dinnerware or Kitchen; or in a special section, such as Pottery-Art, Pottery-Contemporary, Pottery-Midcentury, etc.

- Sometimes we make arbitrary decisions. Fishing has its own category, but hunting is part of the larger category called Sports. We have omitted most guns except toy guns; these are listed in the Toy category. It is not legal to sell weapons without a special license, so guns are not part of the general antiques market. Air guns, BB guns, rocket guns, and others are listed in the Toy section. Everything is listed according to the computer alphabetizing system.

- We have made several editorial decisions. A butter dish is a "butter." A salt dish is called a "salt" to differentiate it from a saltshaker. It is always "sugar and creamer," never "creamer and sugar." Where one dimension is given, it is the height; or if the object is round, it's the diameter. The height of a picture is listed before width. Glass is clear unless a color is indicated.

- Some antiques terms, such as "Sheffield" or "Pratt," have two meanings. Read the paragraph headings to know the definition being used. All category headings are based on the vocabulary of the average person, and we use terms like "mud figures" even if not technically correct. Some categories are known by several names. Pressed glass is also called pattern glass or EAPG (Early American pattern glass). We use the name "pressed glass" because many old books and articles use that name.

- This book does not include price listings for fine art paintings, antiquities, stamps, coins, or most types of books. Comic books are listed only in special categories like Superman, but original comic art and cels are listed in their own categories.
- Prices for items pictured can be found in the appropriate category. Look for the matching entry with the abbreviation "Illus." The color photograph will be nearby.
- Thanks to computers, the book can be produced quickly. The last entries are added in June; the book is available in August. But human help finds prices and checks accuracy. We read everything at least five times, sometimes more. We edit more than 50,000 entries down to the 35,000 entries found here. We correct spelling, remove incorrect data, write category paragraphs, and decide on new categories. We proofread copy and prices many times, but there will always be some misspelled words and other errors. Information in the paragraphs is updated each year, and this year more than twenty updates and additions were made.
- Prices are reported from all parts of the United States, Canada, Europe, and Asia, converted to U.S. dollars at the time of the sale. The average rate of exchange in June 2014 was $1 U.S. to about $1.09 Canadian, €0.73 (euro), and £0.60 (British pound). Prices are from auctions, shops, Internet sales, shows, and even some flea markets. Every price is checked for accuracy, but we are not responsible for errors. We cannot answer your letters asking for price information, but please write if you have any requests for categories to be included or any corrections to the paragraphs or prices. You may find the answers to your other questions at Kovels.com.
- When you see us at shows, auctions, house sales, and flea markets, please stop and say hello. Don't be surprised if we ask for your suggestions. You can write to us at P.O. Box 22192-K, Beachwood, OH 44122, or visit us on our website, www.Kovels.com.

TERRY KOVEL AND KIM KOVEL
July 2014

ACKNOWLEDGMENTS

Our publisher, Black Dog & Leventhal, and its president, J.P. Leventhal, have continued to suggest and implement improvements to this book. There are also improvements in design and technology that add to the speed of production and ease of use. Thanks to J.P. Leventhal; Lisa Tenaglia, our editor; Pamela Schechter, production editor; and Stephanie Sorenson, publicity. Mary Flower, Robin Perlow, and Cynthia Schuster Eakin did copyediting and proofreading for the entire book and found the tiniest of errors.

Thanks to Sheila Hart and her assistants, Jonathan Botero and Bhavika Naghandi, who put all the prices, photographs, and paragraphs together and created the look and layout of *Kovels' Antiques & Collectibles Price Guide 2015*.

The details and hard work required to record prices, assemble photos and information, check accuracy and spelling, and solve many other problems are all done by our Kovel staff. We thank Mary Ellen Brennan, Marcia Goldberg, Katie Karrick, Liz Lillis, Tina McBean, Renee McRitchie, Erika Risley, and Cherrie Smrekar. Special thanks to Carmie Amata, who helped with the Charlie Chaplin and Movie categories, and Lee Markley, who helped proofread the glass categories, including Carnival Glass. Photographs came from many sources, and were edited by our photo editors and house photographers, Janet Dodrill and Darlene Craven. Gay Hunter, our in-house editor, always worries the most about the book. She kept detailed records and made sure all of us were on task and on schedule. She read and reviewed pages of prices, corrected spelling errors, and handled computer problems. Together we updated paragraph information when a company closed or was purchased and we added almost two hundred tips and sidebars of information. We have what we are sure is our best book ever. We know that the book is possible only because of the group effort, even though it is our names that appear on the cover.

The world of antiques and collectibles is filled with people who have answered our every request for help. Dealers, auction houses, and shops have given advice and opinions, supplied photographs and prices, and made suggestions for changes. Special thanks to all of them:

Photographs were furnished by: Allard Auctions, Anderson Americana, Aspire Auctions, Auction Team Breker, Bertoia Auctions, Brian Lebel's Old West Show & Auction, Brunk Auctions, Clars Auction Gallery, Conestoga Auction Co., Copake Auction, Corkscrews Online, Cottone Auctions, Cowan's Auctions, Crescent City Auction Gallery, Crocker Farm, Dirk Soulis Auctions, DuMouchelles Art Gallery, Early Auction Co., Fox Auctions, Garth's Auctioneers, Glass Works Auctions, Gray's Auctioneers, Hake's Americana, Hudson Valley Auctioneers, Humler & Nolan, Ivey-Selkirk Auctioneers, Jackson's International Auctioneers, James D. Julia Auctioneers, Jeffery S. Evans & Associates, Leighton Galleries, Leland Little Auction, Leslie Hindman Auctioneers, Locati Auctions, Los Angeles Modern Auctions, Manor Auctions, Martin Auction Co., Michaan's Auctions, Morphy Auctions, Neal Auction Co., New Orleans Auction Galleries, Norman C. Heckler & Co., Old Barn Auction, Palm Beach Modern Auctions, Phoebus Auction Gallery, Pook & Pook, Potter & Potter Auctions, Rachel Davis Fine Arts, Rago Arts & Auction Center, Regency-Superior Auctions, Roland Antiques, RSL Auction, Ruby Lane, Seeck Auctions, Serious Toyz, Showtime Auction Services, Skinner Auctioneers, Stanton Auctions, The Stein Auction Co., Susanin's Auctioneers, Swann Auction Galleries, Theriault's, Tom Hall Auctions, Tom Harris Auctions, Treadway Toomey Galleries, Victorian Casino Antiques, William H. Bunch Auctions, Wm. Morford Auction, Willis Henry Auctions, Woody Auction, and Wright.

To the others who knowingly or unknowingly contributed to this book, we say thank you: A.N. Abell Auction Co., Alderfer Auction, American Bottle Auctions, American Marble Auctions, Americana Auctions, Antique Bottle & Glass Collector, Apple Tree Auction Center, Auction Gallery of the Palm Beaches, Augusta Auctions,

Belhorn Auction, Bonhams, Boston Harbor Auctions, Breweriana Collector, Burchard Galleries, Butterfly Net, Capo Auction, Cast Iron Online, Chandler's Auction, Charlton Hall Auctions, Chesapeake Auction House, Collection Liquidators, Cowan's+Clark+DelVecchio, CRN Auctions, Crown Jewels of the Wire, Dallas Auction Gallery, Dan Ripley's Antique Helper, Don Presley Auction, Doyle New York, Early American History Auctions, Eldred's Auction Gallery, Eutaw Antiques, Faganarms, Fontaine's Auction Gallery, Freeman's Auctioneers, Great Gatsby's, Harlow Auctions, Heisey Collectors of America, Heritage Auction Galleries, Hollywood Poster Auction, Just Art Pottery, Kamelot Auctions, Keystone Auctions, Matthews Auction Co., McMasters Harris Auction Co., Morton Kuehnert Auctioneers, Nancy's Silver Shop, Noel Barrett Auctions, Northeast Auctions, O'Gallerie Auctioneers, Old Sleepy Eye Collectors Club, Old Toy Soldier Auctions, Old World Auctions, Passion for Perfume, Perfume Bottles Auction, Philip Weiss Auctions, Pole Top Discoveries, Potteries Specialist Auctions, Purcell's Auction Gallery, Quinn & Farmer Auctions, Quinn's Auction Galleries, R.G. Munn Auction, Richard Opfer Auctioneering, Robert Edward Auctions, San Rafael Auction Gallery, Simpson Galleries, Sloans & Kenyon, Sotheby's, Sparkle Plenty Glass, Stair Galleries, Stevenson's Auction, Stony Ridge Auction, Strawser Auctions, Team's Tiffany Treasures, Time and Again Galleries, U.S. Americana Auctions, Vary Vintage Antiques, Vectis Auctions, Vintage Jewelry Online, Waterford's Art & Antiques, Weschler's Auctioneers, William J. Jenack Auctioneers, Woodbury Auction, and other sites.

A. WALTER made pate-de-verre glass under contract at the Daum glassworks from 1908 to 1914. He decorated pottery during his early years in his studio in Sevres, where he also developed his formula for pale, translucent pate-de-verre. He started his own firm in Nancy, France, in 1919. Pieces made before 1914 are signed *Daum, Nancy* with a cross. After 1919 the signature is *A. Walter Nancy*.

Bowl, Vide Poche, Blue Nude Woman, Curled Up, Pate-De-Verre, Signed A. Fonot, c.1940, 9 In. ..	6875
Dish, Beetle, Translucent Green, Pate-De-Verre, c.1905, 4 In.	1080
Dish, Green, Applied Seahorse, Signed E. Royer, 5 x 4 In.	1020
Dish, Triangular, Yellow, Orange Mottled, Bumblebee, Signed, 4 ¼ In.	1304
Figurine, Rabbit, Resting, Pate-De-Verre, c.1910, 3 In.	984
Paperweight, Frog On Rock, 1920s, 1 ¾ x 2 In.	688
Paperweight, Lizard On Leaf, Brown, Frosted Glass, Signed, 8 ½ x 1 ½ In.	625
Paperweight, Multicolor Butterfly, Oval Base, Engraved, 4 In.	3000
Paperweight, Nude, Crouched On Knees, Smoky Quartz, Signed, 5 ½ x 3 In.	1586
Paperweight, Nude, Outstretched, Yellow, Orange, Tan, Signed, 10 x 2 ½ In.	976
Paperweight, Nude, Reclining, Blond, Rose, Rectangular Base, 5 ½ x 1 ½ In.	976
Paperweight, Scarab, Black, Brown, Amber Glass, Signed, 1 ¾ In.	830
Paperweight, Scarab, Molded Monogram AWN, 1 x 2 ⅛ In. ....*illus*	748
Sculpture, Nude, Outstretched, In Waves, Green, Brown, Signed, 10 x 3 In.	875
Tray, Frosted, Blue Glass, Pond, Swimming Fish, Round, Signed, 6 In.	729
Tray, Multicolor Flowers, Purple, Yellow, Green, Moth, Signed, 13 x 7 In.	9184
Tray, Vide Poche, Free-Form, Green Shaded To White, Serpent, 7 x 4 ½ In.	1294
Tray, Vide Poche, Nude, Reclining, Rose, Signed, 5 ½ x 1 ½ In.	1000
Tray, Vide Poche, Yellow, Brown Hermit Crab, Green Claws, Seaweed, 3 ½ x 9 ½ In.	4740
Vase, Berries & Leaves, Art Deco Design Flowers On Base, Signed, 6 ½ In. ....*illus*	3555

ABC plates, or children's alphabet plates, were most popular from 1780 to 1860 but are still being made. The letters on the plate were meant as teaching aids for children learning to read. The plates were made of pottery, porcelain, metal, or glass. Mugs and other items were also made with alphabet decorations.

Dish, Little Bo Peep, Marigold, Carnival Glass	185
Mug, Birds, Twigs, Leaves, Nest, Sterling Silver, Gorham, c.1906, 2 ⅝ In.	375
Mug, City Of Madrid, Brownhills Pottery, c.1880, 2 ¾ In.	150
Plate, Aluminum, Raised Rim, 6 ½ In.	10
Plate, Children, Dog, Green, Red, Blue, Transfer, c.1850, 6 In.	128
Plate, Fox Hunt Scene, Staffordshire, c.1840, 6 In.	175
Plate, Kittens In Yarn, Tin, Ohio Art Co., 4 ¼ In.	24
Plate, Mary Had A Little Lamb, Die Stamped, Tin, c.1900, 7 ¾ In.	100
Plate, Robinson Crusoe, On Raft, Brownhills Pottery, c.1872, 8 In.	155
Plate, Robinson Crusoe, Viewing Island, Brownhills Pottery, c.1887, 7 ¼ In.	145
Plate, Sancho Panza, Dapple, Glass, Gillinder & Sons, 1880s, 6 In.	55

ABINGDON POTTERY was established in 1908 by Raymond E. Bidwell as the Abingdon Sanitary Manufacturing Company. The company started making art pottery in 1934. The factory ceased production of art pottery in 1950.

Candleholder, Double, Curled Scroll, Art Deco, Pink, 4 x 3 In.	32
Console, Bouquet Border, Gilt Trim, 12 In. Diam.	42
Dish, Shell Shape, Cream, Flowers, Gilt Trim, 12 x 8 x 2 In.	50
Flowerpot, Attached Saucer, Ribbed, White, 3 ¼ In.	26
Planter, Pink Matte Glaze, 14 x 9 x 2 In.	19
Planter, Pink, Star Flower, Footed, 2 Handles, c.1947, 6 ¼ In.	35
Planter, Yellow, Flat Ends, Rounded Sides, 1960s, 10 x 6 x 2 In.	22
Vase, Jonquil Pattern, Black, Yellow Interior, 10 x 8 In.	121
Vase, Ships, Ribbed Sides, Green, 7 In.	18
Wall Pocket, Open Book Shape, Cookbook, Raised Blue Letters, 7 x 6 x 4 In.	75

ADAMS china was made by William Adams and Sons of Staffordshire, England. The firm was founded in 1769 and became part of the Wedgwood Group in 1966. The name *Adams* appeared on various items through 1998. All types of tablewares and useful wares were made. Other pieces of Adams may be found listed under Flow Blue and Tea Leaf Ironstone.

Dish, 3 Shaped Bowls, Pink Flowers, Green Shading, Gilt, England, 11 x 12 ¼ In.	34
Jardiniere, Relief Scene, 20 Women Dancers, Blue & White, 7 ½ x 9 In.	59
Mug, Rose, Rabbits & Frog, Tapered, Loop Handle, Spatterware, c.1900, 5 ½ In.	301
Pitcher, Blue & White, Flowers, Wide Wavy Spout, Loop Handle, 1800s	240

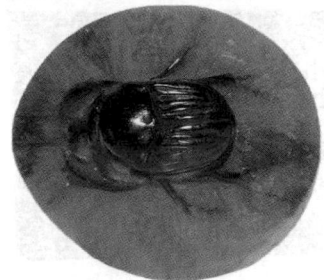

A. Walter, Paperweight, Scarab, Molded Monogram AWN, 1 x 2 ⅛ In.
$748

Humler & Nolan

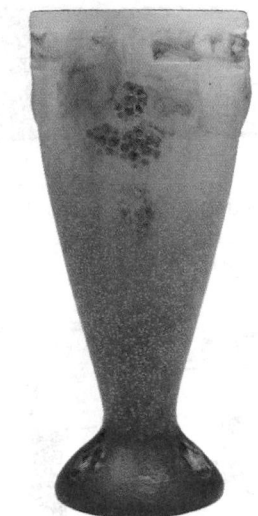

A. Walter, Vase, Berries & Leaves, Art Deco Design Flowers On Base, Signed, 6 ½ In.
$3,555

James D. Julia Auctioneers

Adams, Plate, American Eagle, Patriotic Ware, Tunstall, England, 9 ¾ In.
$94

Conestoga Auction Co., Inc.

Advertising, Ad, Wrigley's Premium Chewing Gum, Frame, 20 x 16 In.
$201

Victorian Casino Antiques

Advertising, Banner, Bull Durham Tobacco, Frame, Plexiglas, 1910-15, 58 ½ x 24 ¼ In.
$720

Morphy Auctions

Advertising, Bench, Buy Your Clothing & Gent's Furnishings Of Is. Oppenheim, c.1910, 60 In.
$780

Garth's Auctioneers & Appraisers

Advertising, Bin, R.A. Bartley, May Picking Japan Tea, Toledo, Ohio, Tin, 20 ½ x 21 In.
$1,020

Showtime Auction Services

Pitcher, Cream, Rose, Blue & Purple, Helmet Shape, Loop Handle, Spatterware, 5 In.	354
Plate, American Eagle, Patriotic Ware, Tunstall, England, 9 ¾ In. *illus*	94
Punch Bowl, Ship Caroline, Shipwright Arms, Black Transfer, Pink Luster, c.1896, 10 In.	510

ADVERTISING containers and products sold in the old country store are now all collectibles. These stores, with crackers in a barrel and a potbellied stove, are a symbol of an earlier, less hectic time. Listed here are many advertising items. Other similar pieces may be found under the product name, such as Planters Peanuts. We have tried to list items in logical places, so enameled tin dishes will be found under Graniteware, auto-related items in the Auto category, paper items in the Paper category, etc. Store fixtures, cases, signs, and other items that have no advertising as part of the decoration are listed in the Store category. The early Dr Pepper logo included a period after "Dr," but it was dropped in 1950. We list all Dr Pepper items without a period so they alphabetize together. For more prices, go to kovels.com.

Ad, Schwinn, Photographic Collage, White Highlights, Frame, c.1960, 19 ½ x 17 ¼ In.	144
Ad, Wrigley's Premium Chewing Gum, Frame, 20 x 16 In. *illus*	201
Ashtray Stand, Moxie Maid, Logo On Dress, Black, White Paint, Wood, 39 In.	330
Bag Holder, KC Baking Powder, 28 x 42 In.	684
Bag, Shipping, Pure Buckwheat Flour, Cobleskill Milling Co., 5-10 Lb. Sacks	30
Banner, Bull Durham Tobacco, Frame, Plexiglas, 1910-15, 58 ½ x 24 ¼ In. *illus*	720
Banner, Evan's Beverage, Red, White, Yellow, Cloth, c.1900, 30 x 24 In.	150
Banner, Gold Dust Washing Powder, Cardboard, 8 x 16 In. Letters, 132 In.	2565
Banner, Princeton 1920, Black Felt, Orange, U.S.A., c.1920, 82 x 31 In.	252
Banner, Star Brand Shoes Are Better, Velvet, Yellow On Burgundy, 46 In.	71
Bench, Buy Your Clothing & Gents' Furnishings Of Is. Oppenheim, c.1910, 60 In. *illus*	780
Bin, Luxury Coffee, Pine, Painted, Stenciled, Slant Top, c.1850, 32 x 22 In.	510
Bin, McLaughlin's Coffee, No. 99, Multicolor, 18 x 23 In.	798
Bin, R.A. Bartley, May Picking Japan Tea, Toledo, Ohio, Tin, 20 ½ x 21 In. *illus*	1020
Bin, Sweet Cuba Fine Cut, Tin, 8 x 10 In. *illus*	236
Biscuit Box, Havenner's Celebrated, Orange, Black, Green Label, Wood, 21 ¾ In.	480
Biscuit Box, Young & Larabee, Black, Yellow Label, Wood, 24 In.	180
Books may be included in the Paper category.	
Boot, Stamped J.R. Palmenberg & Sons, White, Black, Cast Iron, 8 ½ In.	390
Bootjack, Musselman's, Plug Tobacco, Embossed, Cast Iron, 9 ⅞ x 3 ½ In.	253
Bottle & Cap, Centlivre Brewing Co., Fort Wayne, Indiana, Nickel Plate Beer, 12 Oz.	400
Bottles are listed in their own category.	
Bottle Openers are listed in their own category.	
Bottle Topper, Cocoa-Crush, Man, Winking, Cardboard, Frame, c.1925, 13 x 9 ½ In.	270
Box, see also Box category.	
Box, Aircraft Rolled Oats, Cardboard, Cylindrical, 3 Lb., 9 ⅝ x 5 ⅜ In. *illus*	161
Box, Akron Cracker Co., Wood, Hinged Top, 10 x 14 x 17 In.	106
Box, Bear Brand Men's Hosiery, Original Box	200
Box, Cereal, Corn-Fetti, Sugar Corn-Fetti, Captain Jolly, Post, 1950s, 7 x 9 ½ In., Pair *illus*	422
Box, Cereal, Kellogg's Frosted Flakes, Dick Dastardly, Unopened, 1969, 8 ¾ In. *illus*	115
Box, Cereal, Kellogg's Pep, Pin Premium, Comic Strip Panel, 1948, 8 ½ In. *illus*	463
Box, Cereal, Kellogg's Raisin Bran, 3-D Baseball Card, Mays, 1971, 11 x 15 ¾ In.	253
Box, Cereal, Kellogg's Raisin Bran, Babe Ruth Premium, Plastic Ring Offer, 1950, 8 In. *illus*	209
Box, Display, Colgate's Fab, Detergent Waves, Sun, 1930s, 12 x 17 x 5 In.	115
Box, Duke Cameo Cigarettes, Cardboard, 7 ½ x 8 ¼ In.	912
Box, Fergus Rolled Oats, Cardboard, Beall & McGowan Co., 9 ¾ x 5 In. *illus*	161
Box, Gum, Adams Brand Tutti Frutti, Girl Wearing Hat, Red, Cardboard, 10 x 4 In.	161
Box, Gum, Silver Gem, Wood, Figures, Multicolor, 7 ½ x 8 In.	150
Box, Hollick's Aphrodisiac Remedy, Nude Goddess, Brass, Round, 2 ⅜ x ⅜ In.	1380
Box, Kangaroo Brand Castile Soap, Standing Kangaroo, Wood, 16 x 16 ¾ In.	173
Box, Mustard, Slade's Pure, Oxford, Flowers, Sailboats, 14 x 19 In.	253
Box, Red Coon Tobacco, Sun Cured, Wood, 1926, 6 x 6 ¾ In.	150
Box, Sambo Chimney Sweeper, Round, c.1915, 3 ¾ In.	150
Box, Soap, Wonderful Brand, Women Doing Laundry, Paper Label, 16 x 16 In.	253
Broom Holder, Chas. Brown Grocery Co., Cincinnati, Ohio, 21 x 40 In. *illus*	314
Cabinet, Belding's Spool Silk, Decals, Display, 21 x 9 x 15 In.	660
Cabinet, Bohsemeem Choice Spices, Marquee, Drawers, Victorian, 35 x 21 In. *illus*	708
Cabinet, Bread, Ward's, Glass, Wood, 31 In.	600
Cabinet, Crowley's Embroidery Forms, Oak, Stencils, Glass Front, 26 x 7 x 21 In.	1482
Cabinet, Diamond Dyes, Blond Fairy, Paneled Sliding Doors, Tin, 24 x 30 In.	1112
Cabinet, Diamond Dyes, Children With Balloon, Tin, 15 x 24 In.	2400
Cabinet, Diamond Dyes, Evolution Of Woman, 30 x 28 In. *illus*	360

Advertising, Bin, Sweet Cuba Fine Cut, Tin, 8 x 10 In.
$236

Showtime Auction Services

Advertising, Box, Aircraft Rolled Oats, Cardboard, Cylindrical, 3 Lb., 9 ⅝ x 5 ⅜ In.
$161

Wm Morford Auctions

Advertising, Box, Cereal, Corn-Fetti, Sugar-Corn-Fetti, Captain Jolly, Post, 1950s, 7 x 9 ½ In., Pair
$422

Hake's Americana & Collectibles

Advertising, Box, Cereal, Kellogg's Frosted Flakes, Dick Dastardly, Unopened, 1969, 8 ¾ In.
$115

Hake's Americana & Collectibles

Advertising, Box, Cereal, Kellogg's Pep, Pin Premium, Comic Strip Panel, 1948, 8 ½ In.
$463

Hake's Americana & Collectibles

Advertising, Box, Cereal, Kellogg's Raisin Bran, Babe Ruth Premium, Plastic Ring Offer, 1950, 8 In.
$209

Hake's Americana & Collectibles

Advertising, Box, Fergus Rolled Oats, Cardboard, Beall & McGowan Co., 9 ¾ x 5 In.
$161

Wm Morford Auctions

Advertising, Broom Holder, Chas. Brown Grocery Co., Cincinnati, Ohio, 21 x 40 In.
$314

Showtime Auction Services

Advertising, Cabinet, Bohsemeem Choice Spices, Marquee, Drawers, Victorian, 35 x 21 In.
$708

Conestoga Auction Co., Inc.

Advertising, Cabinet, Diamond Dyes, Evolution Of Woman, 30 x 28 In.
$360

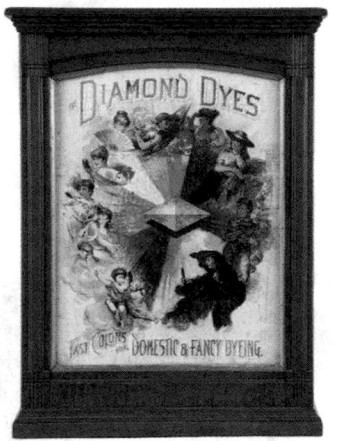

Morphy Auctions

Advertising, Cabinet, Diamond Dyes, Maypole, Oak, Embossed Tin, 23 x 30 In.
$1,596

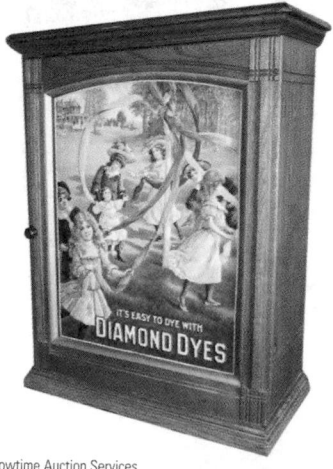

Showtime Auction Services

Advertising, Cabinet, Dr. Daniels' Veterinary Medicines, Embossed Tin, 21 ½ x 18 ½ In.
$2,850

Showtime Auction Services

Advertising, Cabinet, Freihofer's Quality Cakes, Display, c.1935, 27 In.
$330

Morphy Auctions

Advertising, Cabinet, Putnam Dyes & Tints, Tin, Horse, Soldier, 19 x 14 ½ x 7 ¾ In.
$342

Showtime Auction Services

Advertising, Dispenser, Drink Hires Root Beer, It Is Pure, Ceramic, Pump
$1,265

Victorian Casino Antiques

Advertising, Dispenser, Paper, E.O. Bulman Mfg. Co. Inc. Wire & Metal, Countertop, 25 In.
$83

Conestoga Auction Co., Inc.

Advertising, Dispenser, Ward's Orange Crush, Figural, Embossed, Pump, 15 In.
$1,020

Victorian Casino Antiques

Cabinet, Diamond Dyes, Maypole, Oak, Embossed Tin, 23 x 30 In.	*illus*	1596
Cabinet, Display, L. Paulle, Candy, Oak, Floor Model, c.1890, 30 x 64 x 21 In.		1026
Cabinet, Dr. Daniels' Veterinary Medicines, Embossed Tin, 21 ½ x 18 ½ In.	*illus*	2850
Cabinet, Dr. Lesure's Famous Remedies, Horse's Head, Wood, Door, Tin Panel, 29 x 18 In.		805
Cabinet, Dy-O-La Dye, Tin Front, 14 x 17 In.		285
Cabinet, Freihofer's Quality Cakes, Display, c.1935, 27 In.	*illus*	330
Cabinet, Heminway Silks, Oak, Glass Panel Door, 2 Drawers, Revolving, 28 x 17 In.		819
Cabinet, Humphrey's Veterinary Specifics, Embossed Composition Door, 21 x 33 In.		3990
Cabinet, Humphrey's Veterinary Specifics, Wood, Glass, Back Opening, 28 x 22 In.		345
Cabinet, Merrick's Six Cord Spool Cotton, 17 x 22 In.		1710
Cabinet, Perfection Dyes, Oak, Tin Litho, W. Cushing & Co., Foxcroft, Maine, 17 x 25 In.		720
Cabinet, Putnam Dyes & Tints, Tin, Horse, Soldier, 19 x 14 ½ x 7 ¾ In.	*illus*	342
Cabinet, Putnam Dyes, Tints, Mounted Soldier, Firing Weapon Label, Wood, Metal		180
Cabinet, Putnam Fadeless Dye, Tin, Dye Packets, 19 x 15 In.		420
Cabinet, Ribbon, General Store, Duvall's Mercantile, Columbia Falls, Mont., 28 x 38 x 23 In.		1080
Cabinet, Spool, Brannerd & Armstrong Co., Wood, 4 Glass Drawers, Door, 11 ½ x 20 In.		266
Cabinet, Spool, Clark's O.N.T., 2 Drawers, Oak, Ruby Cut Glass Inserts, 21 ¾ x 15 In.		148
Cabinet, Spool, Clark's O.N.T., 7 Columns, Curved Glass Doors, Tambour Doors, 17 x 21 In.		237
Cabinet, Spool, Clark's, 2 Drawers, Walnut, Glass Front, 16 x 8 In.		137
Cabinet, Spool, Clark's, Mahogany, 6 Drawers, Etched Red Glass Labels, c.1890, 21 x 30 In.		2242
Cabinet, Spool, Clark's O.N.T., 6 Glass Front Drawers, c.1900, 29 x 19 x 22 In.		690
Cabinet, Spool, Corticelli, 12 Drawers, Glass Front, Hardware, 21 x 31 x 19 In.		741
Cabinet, Spool, J. & P. Coats', Wood, 6 Drawers, 22 x 26 In.		1944
Cabinet, Spool, J. & P. Coats' Best Six Cord Spool Cotton, 4 Drawers, Wood, 22 x 18 In.		406
Cabinet, Spool, J. & P. Coats' Best Six Cord, 4 Drawers, Cherry, Turned, Brass Pulls		585
Cabinet, Spool, J. & P. Coats', Cotton, Oak, Glass Panels, Tambour Doors, 28 x 17 In.		468
Cabinet, Wellmade Hair Pins, Celluloid, Display, 12 x 7 In.		114
Cabinet, Woolson Spice Company, Oak, Atlas Brand Spice Fronts, Decal, 34 x 25 x 9 In.		2700
Calendars are listed in their own category.		
Can, Mammy Black Enamel Paint, 4 In.		240
Can, Mobiloil Marine, Gargoyle, Metal, Square, Gal.		295
Can, Mobiloil Marine, Small Pegasus, Round, Metal, Qt.		177
Can, Motor Oil, Red Indian Aviation, Round, Metal, Imperial Qt.		100
Can, Motor Oil, Vacuum Marine, Standing Gargoyle, Metal, Square, 2 Qt.		767
Can, Plymouth Rock Oyster, Jas. Hubbard & Son, Balt., Md., c.1925, 7 In.		403
Canisters, see introductory paragraph to Tins in this category.		
Cards are listed in the Card category.		
Case, Display, Corliss-Coon Collar, Decals, Collars, Statesville Showcase Co., 21 x 34 In.		1368
Case, Display, Sanford's Inks, Oak, Glass, Stencils, 11 Product Bottles, 12 x 16 In.		1800
Cereal Set, Ranger Joe, Ranch Mug, Round-Up Bowl, Milk Glass, Red Graphics		12
Change Receiver, see also Tip Tray in this category.		
Charger, Old English Curb Cut Tobacco, Old Man, Smoking, Red Jacket, 24 In.		780
Cigar Box, Lid, Planet, Multicolor, Wood, 11 x 7 ¼ In.		173
Cigar Box, Nixey Nit, Wood, Dome Top, Women Smoking Cigars, 8 ½ x 6 ½ In.		150
Cigar Box, Yellow Kid, Smoking Cigar, Smoke From Ears, Wood, 5 ¼ x 9 ½ In.		443
Cigarette Box, Richfield Oil, Racecar Shape, Patinated Plaster, c.1920, 5 x 10 In.		507
Clocks are listed in their own category.		
Cooler, Moxie, Red, White, Wood, Tin, Floor Model, c.1925, 30 x 32 In.		540
Crock, H.J. Heinz Co., Pickling & Preserving Works, Pittsburgh, Salt Glaze, 6 In.		748
Dispenser, Always Drink Fowler's Cherry Smash, Round, Porcelain, Footed, Pump, 14 In.		1029
Dispenser, Buckeye Root Beer, Cleveland Fruit Juice Co., Porcelain, Transfer		393
Dispenser, Drink Hires Root Beer, It Is Pure, Ceramic, Pump	*illus*	1265
Dispenser, Drink Howel's Orange-Julep, Round, Spigot, Iron Footed Base, 1920s, 18 In.		360
Dispenser, Drink Red Keg, Refreshing, 5 Cents, Ceramic, Barrel, Red, Black Bands, 15 In.		1363
Dispenser, Eskimo Pie, Magic Jar, Blue, Tin Lithograph, Brass Lid, 3 Eskimo Feet, 16 In.		1815
Dispenser, Kentucky Fried Chicken, Fresh Brewed Tea, Unsweetened, Stoneware, 20 In.		152
Dispenser, Lash's Orangeade, Pottery, Round, Nickeled Silver Top, 15 In.		390
Dispenser, Liberty Root Beer, 5 Cents, Wood, Figural, Footed, 14 x 9 In.		1553
Dispenser, Naboth Grape Juice, Grape Cluster, Cylindrical, Glass, Lid, 12 x 7 In.		431
Dispenser, Pall Mall Cigarettes, Gray Metal, Coin Slot, Turn Handle, 34 ½ In.		270
Dispenser, Paper, E.O. Bulman Mfg. Co. Inc. Wire & Metal, Countertop, 25 In.	*illus*	83
Dispenser, Syrup, Mission Fruit Orange, Grapefruit, Porcelain		3420
Dispenser, Syrup, Ward's Lime Crush, Lime Shape, Flower Base, c.1910		9625
Dispenser, U.S. Postage, Uncle Sam, Porcelain, White, Red, Blue, c.1950, 20 In.		120
Dispenser, Vernors Ginger Ale, Pictorial, Multicolor Porcelain Sides, 16 x 19 x 21 In.		2106
Dispenser, Ward's Lemon Crush, Lemon Form, Flowers, Pump, 1920s, 12 In.		960

Advertising, Display, Figural, High-Top Shoe, Canvas, Metal Eyelets, Chalkware, c.1970, 25 In.
$210

Morphy Auctions

Advertising, Display, Georges' Patent Corn & Bunion Shields, Foot, Chalkware, 10 In.
$600

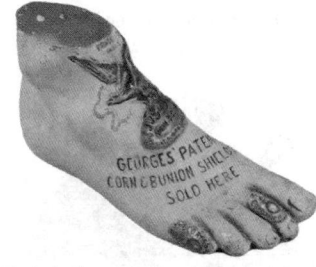

Morphy Auctions

Advertising, Display, Madame Grace, Folding, Cardboard, 39 ¾ x 27 ½ In.
$390

Morphy Auctions

Advertising, Sign, McK & R, 3-Panel Screen, Salesman's Sample, 1910-20, 24 ½ In.
$330

Morphy Auctions

Cures & Remedies

The Food and Drug Administration passed laws about cures and remedies and the claims made for the products in ads and on packaging in 1906. Proof of the accuracy was required. So it is assumed that an American bottle with the word *cure* or *remedy* embossed on the side was probably made before 1906.

Advertising, Display, National Mazda Lamps, Lightbulbs, Tin, Wood, Light-Up, 27 x 17 In.
$1,680

Victorian Casino Antiques

Advertising, Display, Yello-Bole $1.00, Pipe, Cardboard, Easel Back, 7 ¼ In.
$330

Morphy Auctions

Advertising, Door Push, Chocolate Milk, Delicious, Try A Bottle, Tin Litho, 11 ½ x 3 ½ In.
$288

Wm Morford Auctions

Dispenser, Ward's Lime Crush, Lime Shape, Ceramic Ball Pump, 13 In. 2074

Dispenser, Ward's Orange Crush, Figural, Ceramic, Raised Letters, 14 In. 1210

Dispenser, Ward's Orange Crush, Figural, Embossed, Pump, 15 In. *illus* 1020

Dispenser, Wolverine Potato Chips, 6-Sided, Metal Lift, 20 ½ In. 270

Display, Athlo Medicines, Searles Remedy, Lithograph, Trifold, Stand-Up, 19 x 29 In. 776

Display, B.R. Baker Co., Top Hat, Beaver Skin, 22 ½ In. 1368

Display, Bottle, Ice Cold Moxie, Purple, Yellow Lettering, c.1900, 35 ½ In. 6000

Display, Boye Spring Curtain Holder, Tin, Wood, 9 ¾ x 8 x 7 ½ In. 399

Display, Domes Of Silence, Perfect Furniture Footwear, Product, 10 ¾ x 11 ½ In. 228

Display, Dr. Morse's Indian Root Pills, Cardboard, Folding, c.1940, 27 x 42 In. 72

Display, Edison Mazda Lamps, GE, Woman Holding Bulb, 12 Lights, Metal, 28 In. 885

Display, Edison Mazda Lamps, Metal, 2 Glass Panels, 8 Multicolor Bulbs, 20 x 13 In. 1007

Display, El Vampire Bug Killer, Product 399

Display, Figural, High-Top Shoe, Canvas, Metal Eyelets, Chalkware, c.1970, 25 In. *illus* 210

Display, Figural, Old Crow Whiskey, Crow, Top Hat, Cane, Plastic 212

Display, Georges' Patent Corn & Bunion Shields, Foot, Chalkware, 10 In. *illus* 600

Display, Harmless Secret Ringun, c.1950, 13 x 10 ⅗ In. 240

Display, Heinz 57, Papier-Mache, Painted, 42 In. 3420

Display, Hills Bros. Coffee, Cardboard, Die Cut, Easel Back, 24 x 61 In. 1254

Display, Ideal Pocket Knife, Always A Sharp Buy, Card With 12 Knives, 11 x 9 In. 259

Display, J.B.F. Champlin & Son Scissors, 15 x 34 x 15 In. 7410

Display, Knight's Castile Soap, Wood, Glass, 3 Columns, 29 x 9 In. 242

Display, Kwik-Lite, Quality Flashlight, Wood, Slanted Glass Front, c.1918, 42 x 21 In. 593

Display, Madame Grace, Folding, Cardboard, 39 ¾ x 27 ½ In. *illus* 390

Display, Majestic Radio Tubes, Tin, Brochures 1320

Display, McK & R, 3-Panel Screen, Salesman's Sample, 1910-20, 24 ½ In. *illus* 330

Display, Miracle Dyes, Product, 10 x 6 In. 660

Display, Munsingwear, 3 Union Suits, Tin, Die Cut, 36 x 44 x 9 In. 2850

Display, Munyon's Homeopathic, Tin, Drawers, America Art Works, Coshocton, 15 x 14 In. 1053

Display, Mystery Edge Razor Blade, Cardboard, Easel Back, 13 x 10 In. 77

Display, National Mazda Lamps, Lightbulbs, Tin, Wood, Light-Up, 27 x 17 In. *illus* 1680

Display, National Mazda Lamps, Tin, Light-Up, 11 Different Lamps, 28 x 13 In. 2040

Display, Phillip Morris, Johnny Ashtray, Wood, Paint, 37 In. 234

Display, Poll-Parrot Shoes, Chalk Ware, Painted, 15 In. 741

Display, Rat Bis-Kit, Papier-Mache, Rat, Eating Biscuit, 13 x 20 In. 5700

Display, Red Goose Shoes, Chalkware, Painted, Child's Shoes, 9 x 12 In. 1596

Display, Sapolin Paint, Tin Lithograph, 8 Drawers, c.1920, 20 In. 330

Display, Suit, 3-D, Wood Frame, Painted Well-Dressed Man, c.1900, 60 x 22 x 15 In. 533

Display, Syrup, Vin Fiz, Glass, Label, Display Bottle, Metal Cap, 12 x 3 In. 2415

Display, Towle's Log Cabin Syrup, Wood Log Cabin, Early 1900s, 31 x 40 In. 470

Display, Winchester Guns & Ammunition, Better Trapshooting, 4 Men, 5 Sections, 40 In. 1140

Display, Window, Wrigley's, Die Cut, Cardboard, Dimensional, 37 x 29 In. 1920

Display, Yello-Bole $1.00, Pipe, Cardboard, Easel Back, 7 ¼ In. *illus* 330

Dog Dish, Hudson's Soap, White, Black Paint, Cast Iron, c.1910, 16 In. 156

Dolls are listed in their own category.

Door Handle, Eat Dairimaid Ice Cream, Brass, Embossed Red Letters, 18 ½ In. 145

Door Handle, Enjoy Empress, Queen Of Ice Creams, Metal, Plastic, Blue & White, 13 In. 218

Door Pull, Old Gold Cigarettes, Dancing Cigarette Packs, Legs, 1950s, 4 x 12 In. 280

Door Push, Canada Dry, A Beverage Mixer, Chaser, Bottle, Tin Lithograph, 9 x 3 In. 127

Door Push, Chesterfield Cigarettes, They Satisfy, Logo, Porcelain, 9 x 4 In. 207

Door Push, Chocolate Milk, Delicious, Try A Bottle, Tin Litho, 11 ½ x 3 ½ In. *illus* 288

Door Push, Come In, Vicks Va-Tro-Nol, Helps Prevent Colds, Porcelain, 7 x 4 In. 489

Door Push, Dr. Daniels' Medicines, Embossed, Tin Lithograph, 9 x 3 ¼ In. *illus* 1898

Door Push, Dukes Mixture, The Roll Of Fame, Sheet Metal, U.S.A., c.1915, 8 x 5 In. 150

Door Push, Hires Refreshes Right, Logo, Tin Bar, 1950s, 32 In. 120

Door Push, King Cole Tea, Coffee, Porcelain Bar, 1940s, 32 In. 84

Door Push, King Cole, Tea & Coffee, Porcelain, Lithograph, 3 x 8 In. 1422

Door Push, Read & White, Dress Clothing, Black & White, Porcelain, 6 x 3 ½ In. 276

Door Push, Recruit Little Cigars, All Tobacco Yet-Mild, Porcelain, 8 ½ x 4 In. 2013

Door Push, Red Rose Tea, Porcelain, Art Deco Style, Red, Black, Green, White, 3 x 9 In. 608

Door Push, Salada Tea, Delicious Flavor, Porcelain Bar, c.1950, 32 In. 72

Door Push, Senate Beer, Bottle, Blue & Yellow, Tin Lithograph, 11 x 3 ⅜ In. 184

Door Push, White Rock Beverages, Drink The Best, Bottle, Tin Lithograph, 14 ¾ x 4 In. 316

Fans are listed in their own category.

Figure, Bear, Hamm's Beer, Serving, White, Black, Red Base, Styrofoam, 60 In. 210

Figure, Drum Major, General Electric Radio, Ball Jointed, Maxfield Parrish, 1920s, 19 In. 1180

Advertising, Door Push, Dr. Daniels' Medicines, Embossed, Tin Lithograph, 9 x 3 ¼ In.
$1,898

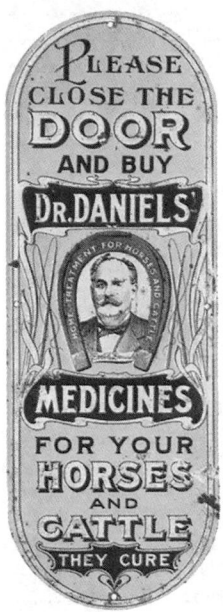

Wm Morford Auctions

Advertising, Figure, Radio Man, G.E., Wood, Composition, Arm Stringing, Cameo Co., 19 In.
$830

James D. Julia Auctioneers

Advertising, Label, Cigar Box, Dewey, Signed, O.L. Schwencke, Lith, New York, 8 ⅛ x 6 In.
$90

Morphy Auctions

Advertising, Label, Cigar Box, Frontier, Embossed, American Lithographic, 1899, 8 ½ x 6 In.
$106

Showtime Auction Services

Advertising, Label, Cigar Box, Gold Hunter, Signed, Geo Schlegel, 4 ½ x 4 ¾ In.
$390

Morphy Auctions

Advertising, Label, Cigar Box, Hoffman, Embossed, 8 x 4 ⅞ In.
$180

Showtime Auction Services

TIP

Fray Check, a product found in sewing supply shops, is useful for repairing tears in cardboard signs.

Advertising, Label, Heinz's Mustard Dressing, Paper Lithograph, 11 ½ x 9 ½ In.
$80

Wm Morford Auctions

Advertising, Label, Tobacco, Big Chunk, Framed Under Glass, 14 ¾ x 14 ¾ In.
$1,140

Morphy Auctions

Advertising, Label, Tobacco, Calvert Lith Co., Detroit, Paper, Horse Race, 13 ¼ x 10 ¾ In.
$86

Showtime Auction Services

Advertising, Label, Tobacco, Welcome Nugget, 6 ¾ x 13 ⅜ In.
$60

Morphy Auctions

Advertising, Mirror, Betsy Ross, Locke Shoe Co., Celluloid, Pocket, 2 ¾ In.
$4,255

Wm Morford Auctions

Figure, Fruit Of The Loom, Nude Woman's Shape, 1950s, 30 In.	270
Figure, Jack Daniel, Man Standing, White, c.1975, 33 In.	150
Figure, Jacquin's Cordials, Man In Tuxedo, Bulging Eyes, 2 Bottles, 14 In.	240
Figure, Jax Beer Server, Man, White Hair, Mustache, Plastic, 17 In.	240
Figure, Lamb Knit, Papier-Mache, 16 x 15 In.	1926
Figure, Moxie Car, Horse & Rider Driving, White, Chalkware, c.1925, 9 In.	420
Figure, Old Crow Whiskey, Formal Suit, Top Hat, Plastic, 31 In.	90
Figure, Radio Man, G.E., Wood, Composition, Arm Stringing, Cameo Co., 19 In. ....*illus*	830
Figure, Sea Siren Bathing Caps, Woman In Bikini & Cap, Rubber, 11 ¼ In.	1150
Figure, Torso, Life Bra, Formfit, Rubber Composition, 1940s	60
Figure, Undergarment, Formfit, Hard Rubber Composition, Wood Base, 32 In.	1920
Figure, William Penn Cigars, Stump, 10 Cents, Figural, Fiberboard, Hollow, 1920s, 41 In.	270
Hat, Harley-Davidson, Wings Logo, Braided Brim, 1950s, 7 ¼ In.	153
Hot Dog Cooker, Moxie, Miracle Appliance Co, 1940s, 25 In.	660
Jar, Bunker Hill Gherkins, Embossed, Amber, Paper Label, Skilton, Foote & Co., 8 ½ In.	210
Jar, Heinz Horseradish, Glass, Embossed, Horse Head Finial, Lid, c.1870, 5 x 3 In.	490
Keg, American Powder Mills Gunpowder, Wood, AW Pollard & Co., 1861, 10 In.	356
Knife Sharpener, Kent's Country Store, Iron, Oak, Paper Label, Instructions, 19 x 20 In.	741
Label, Cigar Box, Andy Gump, Tops Em All, Andy Smoking Cigar Cartoon, 4 ⅞ x 4 ⅞ In.	120
Label, Cigar Box, Dewey, Signed, O.L. Schwencke, Lith, New York, 8 ⅛ x 6 In. ....*illus*	90
Label, Cigar Box, Frontier, Embossed, American Lithographic, 1899, 8 ½ x 6 In. ....*illus*	106
Label, Cigar Box, Gold Hunter, Signed, Geo. Schlegel, 4 ½ x 4 ¾ In. ....*illus*	390
Label, Cigar Box, Golden Buck, Sample, Signed Geo. Schlegel, Frame, 6 x 9 ¼ In.	60
Label, Cigar Box, Hoffman, Embossed, 8 x 4 ⅞ In. ....*illus*	180
Label, Cigar Box, Kit Carson, Sample, Signed Geo. Schlegel, 5 ¾ x 9 ¼ In.	480
Label, Cigar Box, Los Inmortales, Washington, Lincoln, Grant, Eagle, 5 x 4 ½ In.	30
Label, Cigar Box, Natives Graded, Sample, Signed Geo. Schlegel, 6 x 9 In.	480
Label, Cigar Box, Old Abe, Lincoln's Portrait, c.1930, 6 ½ x 2 ¼ In.	10
Label, Cigar Box, Straight 5 Brand, Playing Cards, Hearts, O.L. Schwencke, 6 x 10 In.	330
Label, Cigar Box, White Prince, Elephant, Riders, Sample, Signed Geo. Schlegel, 6 x 8 ¾ In.	780
Label, Crate, Hoosier Brand, Sugar Corn, Squirrel Eating Corn, 11 x 12 In.	138
Label, Heinz Mustard Dressing, Paper Lithograph, 11 ½ x 9 ½ In. ....*illus*	80
Label, Tobacco, Big Chunk, Framed Under Glass, 14 ¾ x 14 ¾ In. ....*illus*	1140
Label, Tobacco, Calvert Lith Co., Detroit, Paper, Horse Race, 13 ¼ x 10 ¾ In. ....*illus*	86
Label, Tobacco, Captain Cook, Portrait, Sackett & Wilhelms Litho Co., 1800s, 12 x 12 In.	900
Label, Tobacco, Derby, Horse Race, Frame, 1800s, 16 x 16 In.	450
Label, Tobacco, Lion Brand, Lion Paw On Box, 1800s, 12 x 12 In.	660
Label, Tobacco, Oneida, Indian Princess, Paper, 13 ½ x 6 ¾ In.	219
Label, Tobacco, Stonewall Jackson, Portrait Of General Jackson, 1800s, 12 x 12 In.	1440
Label, Tobacco, Welcome Nugget, 6 ¾ x 13 ⅜ In. ....*illus*	60
Lamps are listed in the Lamp category.	
Lunch Boxes are also listed in their own category.	
Menu Board, Orange Crush, Blackboard, 1960s, 27 x 19 In.	72
Menu Board, Orange Crush, Bottles, Sandwich, Cardboard, 1940s, 26 x 17 In.	450

Advertising mirrors of all sizes are listed here. Pocket mirrors range in size from 1 ½ to 5 inches in diameter. Most of these mirrors were given away as advertising promotions and include the name of the company in the design.

Mirror, Baby Brand Butterine, Ammon & Person, Child, Oval, 2 ¾ x 1 ¾ In.	265
Mirror, Bailey's Pure Rye, Multicolor, Figures, Celluloid, Oval, 1 ¾ x 2 ¾ In.	546
Mirror, Beatrice Creamery Co., Woman, Cream Separator, Celluloid, Round, 2 In.	518
Mirror, Berry Bros. Varnishes, Boy, Dog In Wagon, Celluloid, Oval, 1 ¾ x 2 ¾ In.	276
Mirror, Betsy Ross, Locke Shoe Co., Celluloid, Pocket, 2 ¾ In. ....*illus*	4255
Mirror, Brotherhood Overalls, Topless Woman, Celluloid, Round, 2 ⅛ In.	403
Mirror, Continental Cubes, Pipe Tobacco, Saloon Girl, Celluloid, 3 x 2 In.	345
Mirror, Cooking Oil, A Pure Healthful Vegetable Oil, Family, Celluloid, 2 ¼ In.	950
Mirror, Cream Dove Shortening, Peanut Butter, Boy, Can, Celluloid, Round, 3 x 2 In.	431
Mirror, Finck's Detroit Special Overalls, Large Pig, Oval, 2 ¾ In.	231
Mirror, Fuller's Chocolates, Seated Woman, Cherub, Celluloid, Oval, 2 ¾ x 2 In.	374
Mirror, Garrett's XXXX Baker Rye, Nude Woman, Lounging, Celluloid, Oval, 3 x 2 In.	403
Mirror, Keystone Overalls, Masquerader, Seminude Woman, Oval, 2 ¾ In.	381
Mirror, Kolf's, Cafe & Restaurant, Ladies & Gents, Black Cat, Celluloid, 1 ¾ In.	403
Mirror, Lily White Flour, Children Baking, Oval, Celluloid, 1 ⅝ x 2 ⅜ In.	345
Mirror, Louisville Oil Co., Women In Kitchen, Celluloid, Oval, 1 ¾ x 2 ¾ In.	661
Mirror, O & S Gasoline Engines, Made In Reading, Engine, Oval, Pocket, 3 In.	150
Mirror, Oxford Chocolates, Woman, Graduation Clothing, Oval, 1900s, 2 ¾ In.	95

Mirror, Philadelphia Amusement Park, City Scape, Celluloid, Round, 2 ⅛ In.	86
Mirror, Sucrene, Happy Cow-What Makes You Laugh?, Calf, Celluloid, Pocket.	518
Mirror, Terre Haute Brewing Company, Topless Girl, Bottle, Celluloid, 2 ⅛ In.	863
Mirror, Victrola, Enrico Caruso, Record Shape, Red & Black, Celluloid, Pocket	253
Moving Picture Machine, Pillsbury, 3 Stooges, Cardboard, Columbia Pictures, 1937, 7 x 7 In.	569
Mug, Good Cheer Cigar, Without A Peer, Tin, Hinged Lid, 5 ½ In.	81
Mug, Health & Cheer, Hires Rootbeer, Man, Raising Hand In Toast, Mettlach, c.1900, 5 In.	120
Mug, Keegan's Irish Whiskey, Belfast, O.P., Cranberry Glass, Enamel, Spout, 6 In.	450
Napkin, Heinz, Story Of The 57, 7 x 7 In.	29
Nodder, Red Goose, Goose Form, Composition, Electric, c.1950, 27 In.	330
Oil Dispenser, Triangle Handle, S-Spout, Flared Rim, Tapered, Metal, 4 x 4 ½ In.	374
Pail, Albany Grease, Tin Litho, Yellow, Black, Lid, Bail Handle, 6 ¾ x 5 ½ In.	104
Pail, Bunny Brand Peanut Butter, Tin Lithograph, Handle, 3 x 3 ⅝ In. ....*illus*	546
Pail, Granger Twins Tobacco, Wood, 14 In.	180
Pail, Jo Beth Co. Peanut Butter, Children, School Room, Bail Handle, 3 x 3 ½ In.	431
Pail, Lovell & Covel Co. Candy, Historical Series, Bail Handle, 3 x 3 In.	184
Pail, Queen Of Hearts Candy, Poem, Bail Handle, 2 ¾ In. ....*illus*	840
Pail, Red Indian Cut Plug, Tobacco, Tin, Painted, 8 x 4 ¼ x 5 In.	1200
Pail, Squirrel Peanut Butter, Squirrel Eating Peanut, Orange, Lid, 4 ⅞ x 5 ⅛ In.	265
Pail, Tobacco, Board Of Trade, Power & Stuart, Wood, Glass Window, 10 x 12 In.	403
Pail, Uncle Wiggily Candy, Kiddie Confections, St. Joseph, Mo., At Seashore, 3 ½ In.	840
Pamphlet, Marble's Outing Equipment, Lithograph, Moose, Wolf, Mountains, c.1942, 7 x 4 In.	35
Peanut Roaster, Hot Peanuts, Kingery Mfg. Co., Tin, Paint, c.1905, 65 In.	360
Pen Wipe, Fleet Cat, White, Pennsylvania, c.1900, 6 ½ x 8 ½ In.	570
Pennant, Drink Blud Wine, Red, White, Felt, c.1915, 28 ½ x 11 In.	60
Pin, Ask For A Crush, Logo, Orange, Round, Celluloid, 9 In.	236
Pin, Babe Ruth Champions, Portrait, Quaker Cereals, 1935, ¹⁵⁄₁₆ In.	158
Pin, Badge, Watchman, Dain Mfg. Co., Star, Nickel Plated, c.1900, 2 ⅝ In.	804
Pin, Cleveland Brewing Co., Starlight, Indian, Centennial, c.1900, 1 ½ In.	86
Pin, Euclid Beach Park, Cleveland, Strollers, Pier, Beach, Bastian Paper, c.1920, 1 ⅝ In. .....*illus*	86
Pin, League Of American Wheelman, Man Riding Bike, c.1896, 1 ¼ In.	175
Pin, Morrell's Iowa's Pride Meats, Man, Apron, Celluloid, 2 ⅛ In. ....*illus*	135
Pin, Ocean Wave Washer, Voss Bro's., Celluloid, W&H, c.1908, 4 In. ....*illus*	873
Pitcher, Clinton Club Rye Whiskey, White Lettering, Polished Rim, Applied Handle, 5 ¼ In.	200
Plaque, Builder's, GE, Brass, Round, Raised Script, 4 Mounting Holes, 12 In.	360
Purse, Moxie, Farmer, Dog, Moxie Bag, Mesh, c.1920, 6 ½ In.	4800
Rack, Butler, Moxie, Painted, Logos, 1920s-30s, 28 ¾ In. ....*illus*	720
Ring, Action, Franken Berry Monster, Looking In Mirror, Premium, Box, 1972, 12 x 18 In.	705
Runner, Table, RCA, Woven, Flowers, Nipper, Master's Voice, c.1929, 13 x 42 In.	253
Salt & Pepper Shakers are listed in their own category.	
Scales are listed in their own category.	
Screen Door Sign, 7Up, Fresh Up, Green, White, Red, 8 x 10 In.	168
Service Board, Suburban Chauffeur, Gold, Chalk Tray, Masonite, 1900s, 24 x 16 In.	180
Shoehorn, Red Raven Splits, Ask The Man, Bird & Bottle, Tin Lithograph, c.1904, 5 x 2 In.	345
Sign, 66 Lithiated Lemon Soda, Peps You Up-Clears Your Head, Embossed, Tin, 12 x 29 In.	207
Sign, 7Up, Policeman, School Crossing, Base, 1950s, 62 In. ....*illus*	1440
Sign, ABC Beverage, Bottle Graphics, Yellow, Red, Embossed, Tin, 20 x 28 In.	177
Sign, Ace Beer, Sioux City Brewing Co., Always Ace High, Plastic, Light-Up, 16 x 3 In.	2835
Sign, Acme Beer, Black Face Waiter, Bottle, Glass, Tray, Frame, c.1925, 12 x 15 In.	150
Sign, Adams' Chewing Gum, Magician, Tricks, Paper Lithograph, 2-Sided, 6 x 13 In. ....*illus*	253
Sign, Aircraft Oil, No. 2 Heavy Medium, Paddle Shape, 2-Sided, Porcelain, 12 x 8 In.	708
Sign, Alka-Seltzer, Be Wise-Alkalize, Metallic Letters, Glass, 8 ⅞ x 20 ⅞ In.	403
Sign, American Beauty, Creamery Butter, Rose, Tin Litho, Cardboard, 6 ⅜ x 11 ⅜ In.	345
Sign, Anheuser-Busch, Woman, Eagle, Paper, Frame, Glass, 20 x 30 In. ....*illus*	5100
Sign, Anheuser-Busch-Budweiser, Eagle, Red, Green, Porcelain, 1920s, 13 In.	348
Sign, Armour's Meats, Star Hams & Bacon, Woman, Boy, Tin Lithograph, 31 ½ x 25 In.	4025
Sign, Ask For Doctors Special, Finest Old Scotch Whisky, Porcelain, 6 x 14 In.	891
Sign, Ask For Orange Crush, Orange, White, Tin, Embossed, 1937, 39 x 27 In.	1800
Sign, Aunt Jemima Pancake Flour, Die Cut, String Hanger, 9 ¼ x 17 In.	428
Sign, Aunt Jemima's, Old Plantation Pancakes, 3 For 1 Cent, Paper, 13 x 25 In.	1265
Sign, Austin, Britain's Dependable Eight, Red Car, Linen Mount, 121 x 161 In.	708
Sign, Banner, Canada's Traditional Favorite Conklin Shows, F. Johnson, c.1950, 94 x 117 In.	1875
Sign, Bay State Paints, Logo, Green, White, 2-Sided, Porcelain, Die Cut, 34 x 34 In.	1003
Sign, Beacon Coal, Coal, Lighthouse Graphics, Round, Tin, 14 In.	413
Sign, Beaumal Topcoat, Couple, Car, Cardboard, McClelland & Barclay, c.1925, 24 x 16 In.	150

Advertising, Pail, Bunny Brand Peanut Butter, Tin Lithograph, Handle, 3 x 3 ⅝ In.
$546

Wm Morford Auctions

Advertising, Pail, Queen Of Hearts Candy, Poem, Bail Handle, 2 ¾ In.
$840

Morphy Auctions

Tin Trays
The tin advertising tray was first used in the 1880s and is still popular.

Advertising, Pin, Euclid Beach Park, Cleveland, Strollers, Pier, Beach, Bastian Paper, c.1920, 1 ⅝ In.
$86

Advertising, Pin, Morrell's Iowa's Pride Meats, Man, Apron, Celluloid, 2 ⅛ In.
$135

Advertising, Pin, Ocean Wave Washer, Voss Bro's., Celluloid, W&H, c.1908, 4 In.
$873

Sign, Bee Soap, Save The Coupons, Colgate Co., Tin Lithograph, 9 ¼ x 15 ½ In.	863
Sign, Beeman's Gum, Tin, Embossed, Cardboard, c.1905, 9 x 13 In.	270
Sign, Betsy Ross Bread, Halloween Pumpkin, Boy, Dillon, 42 x 20 In.	300
Sign, Black Bunnie Lounge, Plexiglas, Painted, Multicolor, Chicago Southside, 40 x 22 In.	1440
Sign, Black Lake Fishing Club, Wood, Painted Fish, Lettering, 15 x 37 In.	180
Sign, Black Star, Great Northern Brewing Co., Neon, Bottle Cap Shape, 28 In. Diam.	645
Sign, Bond Bread, Home-Like Loaf, Yellow & Black, Porcelain, 8 x 22 ½ In.	403
Sign, Bookends, Kellogg's, Cardboard, Die Cut, 14 x 63 In.	2850
Sign, Boraxine, Soap, Woman Washing, Children, Dog, Cardstock, 7 ½ x 6 ½ In.	161
Sign, Breinig's Pure Paints, Navy, White, 2-Sided, Enameled Porcelain, 20 x 12 In.	711
Sign, Briar Pipe Tobacco, Black Baby, Bonnet, Cardboard, Frame, 1890s, 16 x 13 In.	120
Sign, Brooke's Kleenaline, Monkey, Playing Guitar, Paper, Frame, 36 x 16 In.	518
Sign, Budweiser, Tin, Oak Frame, Cans, Bottles, 70 x 34 In.	960
Sign, Burma Shave, Red, White, Wood, 40 x 12 In.	240
Sign, Butter Nut Bread, 2 Girls Carrying Loaves, Frame, 17 x 27 In.	84
Sign, C.M. Funk Confectionery, 2-Sided, 2 Parts, Wood, c.1900, 56 In. ....*illus*	764
Sign, Cab, London Tavern Ale, El Dorado Brewing Co., Light-Up, 13 x 7 x 5 In.	2200
Sign, Campbell's Soup, 21 Kinds, Tin, H.D. Beach, Ohio, 39 ½ x 27 ½ In. ....*illus*	40250
Sign, Campbell's Soup, Tin, Cans Arranged In U.S. Flag Pattern, 40 x 28 In.	54000
Sign, Capital Airlines, Bird Logo, Red, White, Round, Porcelain, 12 In.	236
Sign, Carnival, The Moon Rocket Ride, Hold Onto Your Hat, Canvas, 38 x 31 In.	65
Sign, Cascaret, Black Man Eating Watermelon, Is'e Not Afraid, Paper, 16 x 10 In.	780
Sign, Cavanaugh's Wonder Colic Remedy, Tin, Black, Yellow, c.1915, 14 x 20 In.	388
Sign, Centlivre Brewing Co., Tonic, Cardboard, Framed Under Glass, 22 x 12 In. ....*illus*	371
Sign, Charter Oak Stoves, Cobalt Blue, White, Wood, Paint, 5 ½ x 47 ⅝ In.	345
Sign, Chase & Miles, Applied Raised Letters, Wood, Gilt, c.1900, 15 x 116 In. ......*illus*	264
Sign, Cherry Blush Soda, Cherries Only Rival, Cardboard, Green Red, 6 x 9 In.	403
Sign, Cincinnati Stove Works, Horse, Woman Riding Side Saddle, Iron, c.1903, 28 x 42 In.	5100
Sign, City Of New York Fire Insurance Co., Harbor Scene, Tin, Frame, 30 x 22 In.	1560
Sign, Cleveland Leader, Tin, Flange, 2-Sided, 18 ½ x 9 In.	351
Sign, Clipper Beer, Celluloid, Airplane, Renner Brewing Co., 9 In. Diam.	788
Sign, Clothes Dryer, Horseshoe Brand, Hanging, Fold-Out, Wood, 25 x 7 In.	138
Sign, Colgan's Mint Chips, Woman, Plumed Hat, Green Border, Round, Cardboard, 10 In.	3900
Sign, Colgan's Violet Chips Gum, Woman, In Hat, Pink Border, Round, Cardboard, 10 In.	2400
Sign, Columbia Records, Black, Blue, White Label, Disc Shape, Porcelain, c.1910, 24 In.	444
Sign, Commercial Club Maple Syrup, Tin, Embossed, 13 x 6 In.	120
Sign, Continental Insurance Co., Soldier, Tin, Self-Framed, c.1915, 30 ¼ x 20 ¼ In. ....*illus*	720
Sign, Conway 2014, Men's & Women's Wear, 2-Sided, c.1900, 31 In. ....*illus*	646
Sign, Cook's Goldblume, Beer Bottle, Horseshoe, Tin Lithograph, 14 ½ x 11 ¾ In.	431
Sign, Cooper Sisters, Dress Making & Hair Work, Wood, Paint, c.1885, 25 x 33 In.	960
Sign, Cunard Line, Travellers' Checks Cashed, Ship, Mauretania, Tin Lithograph, 10 In.	384
Sign, Curlee Clothes, Cardboard, c.1925, 26 x 16 In.	90
Sign, Dake's Delicious Ice Cream, Tin, Frame, 25 x 16 ½ In.	144
Sign, Dakota Candy Co., Fine Candies, Mildred Model, Frame, c.1907, 14 In.	319
Sign, Danger High Pressure, Magnolia Pipe Line, Pegasus, Enamel, 1900s, 8 x 15 In.	90
Sign, Daybreak Field Seeds, Round, Red, White, Porcelain, 10 ½ In.	354
Sign, DeLaval Cream Separators, Cow, Embossed, Cardboard, Frame, 18 x 28 In. ....*illus*	259
Sign, DeLaval Cream Separators, Paper, Frame, 31 ½ x 22 ½ In. ....*illus*	570
Sign, DeLaval Cream Separators, Tin, Mother, Child, H.D. Beach Co., 25 ½ In. ....*illus*	4148
Sign, Delighted With Clothes Sold By Ethan Allen Clothier Marshall, Tin, c.1905, 36 In.	125
Sign, Deschutes Brewery, Bend, Oregon, Light-Up, 20 In. Diam.	257
Sign, Dr Pepper, Vim Vigor & Vitality, Framed Under Glass, 1905-10, 16 x 21 In. ....*illus*	12000
Sign, Dr. Daniels' Horse Remedies, Porcelain, Black, Yellow, 2 ½ x 20 In.	805
Sign, Dr. Meyer's Foot Soap, 10 Cents, Paper, 25 x 38 In. ....*illus*	114
Sign, Dr. P. Hall's Celebrated Catarrh Remedy, Paper, Cardboard, 1890-1900, 42 x 28 In.	240
Sign, Drink Brownie, If You Like Chocolate Soda, Cardboard, M.C.A., 21 x 60 In. ....*illus*	5700
Sign, Drink Hires, 2 Women Sipping Soda, Oval, Tin, Harry Morse Meyers, c.1915, 24 In.	4200
Sign, Drink Hires, Root Beer Bottle, Tin, Embossed, Rolled Edge, 11 x 32 In.	236
Sign, Drink Moxie, Man, White Coat, Pointing, Cutout, 2-Sided, Tin, 6 x 6 In.	600
Sign, Drink Moxie, Soda Jerk, Sitting, Pointing, Cardboard, Die Cut, c.1914, 41 In.	948
Sign, Drink Orange Crush, Green Lattice, Tin, Embossed, 36 x 30 In.	4800
Sign, Drink Schell's Carbonated Mead, Paper, Women In Touring Car, c.1908, 20 x 27 In.	4148
Sign, Drink Wine-Dip, Red, White, Tin, c.1925, 47 x 23 In.	210
Sign, Drink, Noxie Kola, Tin, Embossed, Yellow, Black, c.1925, 11 ¾ x 23 In.	210
Sign, Duck Head Overalls, Porcelain, Green Duck Head Logo, Blue, White, 14 x 12 In.	3792
Sign, Duffy's Cough Syrup, It's Best, Tin, Black & Yellow, c.1915, 10 x 14 In.	182

Advertising, Rack, Butler, Moxie, Painted, Logos, 1920s-30s, 28 ¾ In.
$720

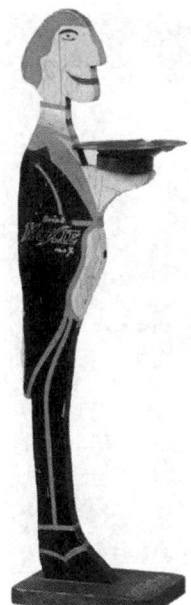

Morphy Auctions

Advertising, Sign, 7Up, Policeman, School Crossing, Base, 1950s, 62 In.
$1,440

Morphy Auctions

Advertising, Sign, Adams' Chewing Gum, Magician, Tricks, Paper Lithograph, 2-Sided, 6 x 13 In.
$253

Wm Morford Auctions

Advertising, Sign, Anheuser-Busch, Woman, Eagle, Paper, Frame, Glass, 20 x 30 In.
$5,100

Showtime Auction Services

Advertising, Sign, C.M. Funk Confectionery, 2-Sided, 2 Parts, Wood, c.1900, 56 In.
$764

Garth's Auctioneers & Appraisers

Advertising, Sign, Campbell's Soup, 21 Kinds, Tin, H.D. Beach, Ohio, 39 ½ x 27 ½ In.
$40,250

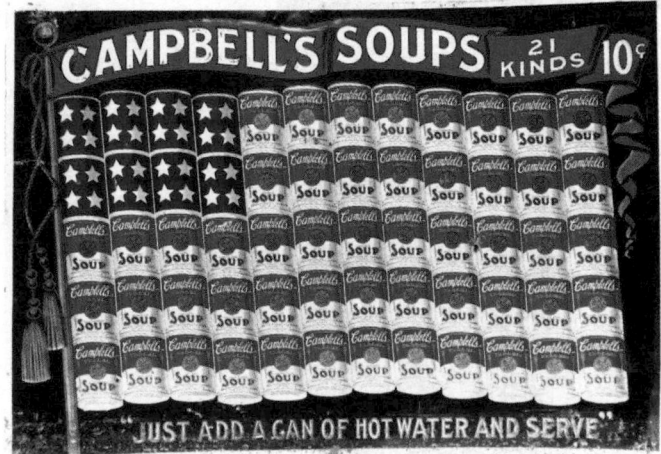

Showtime Auction Services

Advertising, Sign, Centlivre Brewing Co., Tonic, Cardboard, Framed Under Glass, 22 x 12 In.
$371

Showtime Auction Services

Advertising, Sign, Chase & Miles, Applied Raised Letters, Wood, Gilt, c.1900, 15 x 116 In.
$264

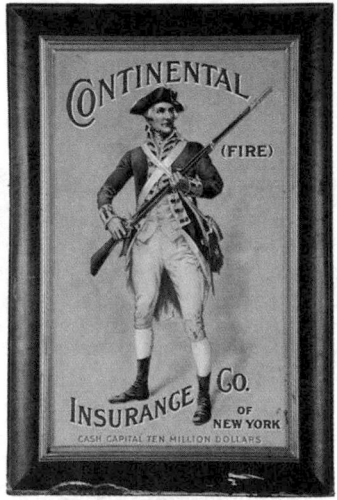

Garth's Auctioneers & Appraisers

Advertising, Sign, Continental Insurance Co., Soldier, Tin, Self-Framed, c.1915, 30 ¼ x 20 ¼ In.
$720

Morphy Auctions

Advertising, Sign, Conway 2014, Men's & Women's Wear, 2-Sided, c.1900, 31 In.
$646

Garth's Auctioneers & Appraisers

Advertising, Sign, DeLaval Cream Separators, Cow, Embossed, Cardboard, Frame, 18 x 28 In.
$259

Victorian Casino Antiques

Advertising, Sign, DeLaval Cream Separators, Paper, Frame, 31 ½ x 22 ½ In.
$570

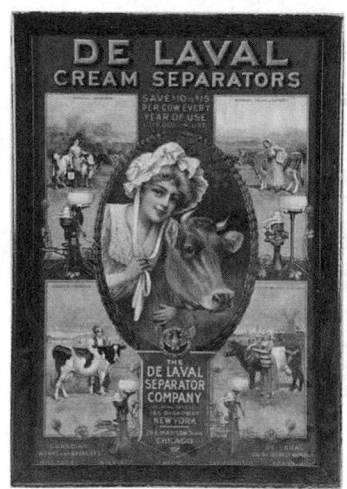

Morphy Auctions

Advertising, Sign, DeLaval Cream Separators, Tin, Mother, Child, H.D. Beach Co., 25 ½ In.
$4,148

James D. Julia Auctioneers

Sign, Dutch Paint, Dependable, Paint Bucket Shape, Porcelain, 26 x 21 In.	489
Sign, Eagle Iron Works, Carved, Eagle, Spread Wings, Gilt, Red Paint, 42 x 66 In.	1625
Sign, Edgar H. Herr Upholstery, 2-Sided, Wood, Painted, c.1900, 26 In. ....*illus*	470
Sign, Eisenlohr's Cinco Cigars, Philadelphia, Reverse Glass, Frame, 27 ½ x 21 ½ In. ....*illus*	780
Sign, Eldredge B Sewing Machine, Wood, c.1900, 13 x 72 In. ....*illus*	705
Sign, Elgin Watches, Tom Sawyer, Wearing Watch, Wood, 22 ⅛ x 15 In.	604
Sign, Enameline Stove Polish, Girl, Blue Dress, Stove, Frame, 1900, 27 x 16 In.	360
Sign, Farms, Auto, Perkin Insurance, Bird, 2-Sided, Blue, Orange, Porcelain, 17 x 21 In.	420
Sign, Fehr's Brewing Co., Malt Tonic, Topless Girl, Cherubs, Tin Lithograph, 29 x 22 In.	2645
Sign, Fellow Citizens, Cigars, Green, Glass, Foil Letters, Lee & Grant, Chain, 7 x 16 In.	708
Sign, Finck's Overalls, Detroit-Special, Wear Like A Pig's Nose, Porcelain, 12 x 17 In. ....*illus*	138
Sign, Fire Association Of Philadelphia, Reverse Glass, F.A. 1817, Oak Frame, 35 x 23 In.	720
Sign, Fireman's Fund Insurance, Gesso, Dimensional, Home Office Building, 27 x 36 In.	3990
Sign, Fitch's Shampoo, More Hair Skating Away From Dan Dandruff, Cardboard, 24 x 18 In.	480
Sign, Flour Perfection, American Beauty, Rose, Bag, Celluloid, Tin, 12 ⅝ x 8 ½ In.	489
Sign, Follow The Plane, Aer-O-Plane Stores, Bi-Wing Plane, Red & White, 7 x 20 In.	345
Sign, For Sale, M.S. Way & Son, Pine, Painted, West Chester, Pa., 21 x 26 In.	178
Sign, Forests For The Future, Stop Woods Fires, Maryland Forestry, Tin, 1930, 22 In.	236
Sign, Frazer Axle Grease, Horse, Wagon, Tin, Self-Framed, Meek Co., 25 x 38 In. ....*illus*	4800
Sign, Fresh Strawberry Whipped Cream Pie, Horn & Hardart, Frame, c.1950, 28 x 22 In.	313
Sign, Friskies For Your Dog, Metal, 2-Sided, Stout Sign Co., St. Louis, 18 x 17 In. ....*illus*	403
Sign, Fun-To-Wash Washing Powder, Mammy, Yellow, Frame, Canada, c.1900, 17 x 13 In.	240
Sign, G. Thornton Stable, Tin, Running Horse, Black, Gold Paint, 22 x 26 In.	425
Sign, G.L. Dana Farm Produce, Painted, Wood, Braces, c.1900, 15 ½ x 84 In. ....*illus*	588
Sign, Geisha Crab, Girl, Fish, Die Cut, Cardboard, Japan, 15 x 10 In.	120
Sign, Gem Damaskeene Blades, 7 For 50 Cents, Man Shaving, Cardboard, 5 x 13 In.	242
Sign, Genesee Beer, Fishing, Beer Case, Man, Woman, Light-Up, 1960s, 19 In.	90
Sign, George's Shoes, Keep Normal Feet Normal, Foot, Light-Up, 1940s, 10 x 12 In.	360
Sign, Gilt Edge Oil, Shoe Dressing, Reverse Glass, Denzi & Phillip, 35 x 33 In. ....*illus*	2700
Sign, Gold Dust Washing Powder, Boxes, 7 ½ x 10 ½ In.	570
Sign, Gold-En Girl Cola, Sun Drop, Refreshing As Cup Of Coffee, Tin Litho, 12 x 28 In.	374
Sign, Gollam's Ice Cream, Lebanon, Glass, Red Metal, Light-Up, 20 x 30 In.	1936
Sign, Grape-Nuts, Girl, St. Bernard Dog, Tin, Self-Framed, 1910-15, 30 x 20 In. ....*illus*	6000
Sign, Grapette Soda, Woman In Pool, Cardboard, Wood Frame, c.1950s, 21 x 33 In.	150
Sign, Great American Insurance Co., Uncle Sam, Porcelain, Jan., 1917, 17 x 23 In.	360
Sign, Great Majestic, Range With A Reputation, Paper, 59 x 25 In.	86
Sign, Great Northern Hotel, Paint, c.1900, 28 x 62 In.	403
Sign, Greyhound Lines Ticket Office, Dog, Bus, Porcelain, 2-Sided, 31 x 25 In.	2950
Sign, Guaranteed Pure Milk, Blue, Red, Yellow, Porcelain, Shield Shape, 19 x 14 In.	180
Sign, H. Disston & Sons, Saw, Painted Gold & Red, 41 ½ In.	863
Sign, H. McDonald, Anvil, Blacksmith, 2-Sided, Wood, Paint, 1800s, 19 x 43 In.	840
Sign, H.H. Gibbs, Jeweler, Pocket Watch Shape, 2-Sided, Paint, Zinc, 18 x 12 In.	1800
Sign, H.J. Vaughan, Clear Havana Cigars, Reverse Painted Glass, Frame, 24 x 36 In.	540
Sign, Hamm's Beer, Porcelain, One Sided, Neon, Theo. Hamm Brewing Co., 54 x 36 In.	2565
Sign, Hamm's Beer, Stars Twinkle, Beer Glasses Appear, Light-Up, 21 ½ In.	420
Sign, Hanger, Drink Cherry-Cheer, 5 Cent, Cherries, Woman Drinking, Litho, 11 x 7 In.	1200
Sign, Hanger, Grandpa's Wonder Soap, Figure, Cardboard, 2-Sided, c.1890, 13 x 7 In.	316
Sign, Hanger, Polar Bear Tobacco, 2-Sided, Die Cut, 14 ¼ In. ....*illus*	5700
Sign, Hanger, Post Toasties, Cardboard, Die Cut, 18 x 29 In.	1254
Sign, Hanger, The Home Of Rosebud Beer, Keg Shape, Chain, Felt Cloth, 13 x 11 In.	489
Sign, Hanover Fire Insurance Co., Eagle, Coat Of Arms, Reverse On Glass, 12 x 20 In.	330
Sign, Harley-Davidson, 2.50 Down Buys A Harley, Cardboard, 1924, 11 x 21 In.	690
Sign, Harmonica Shape, M. Hoener Marine Band, Plastic, Wood, c.1950, 6 x 24 x 4 In.	204
Sign, Hartford Fire Insurance, Elk, In Oval Reserve, Tin, 24 x 20 In.	330
Sign, Hartford Fire Insurance, Gesso, Dimensional, Elk, Org. 1794, Incorp. 1810, 33 x 26 In.	7410
Sign, Havana Cigars, Mildred Model, Portrait, Profile, Round, Tin Lithograph, Frame, 14 In.	682
Sign, Headlight Union Made Overalls, Light-Up, Neon, Glass, Metal, 26 x 14 In. ....*illus*	1920
Sign, Hedy Lamarr, Lucky Strike, Never A Rough Puff, Cardboard, 12 x 14 In.	115
Sign, Heileman's Special Export Beer, Bottle, Logo, 30 x 8 In.	53
Sign, Helmer Turkish Cigarettes, Woman, Hat, Tan, Brown, Red, Tin, c.1910, 23 x 28 In.	900
Sign, Hensler's Beer Ale, Bottles, Banner, Gold Lettering, Tin, Cardboard, 13 x 9 In.	460
Sign, Hershey's Ice Cream, The Purest Kind, Red, Yellow, Porcelain, 12 x 20 In.	1610
Sign, Hickman-Ebbert Wagons, Apple Tree, Tin, Self-Framed, 37 ½ x 25 ½ In. ....*illus*	1482
Sign, Hires Root Beer, Round, Metal, Plastic Front, Light-Up, c.1950, 15 ½ In.	180
Sign, Hires Root Beer, Yellow, Black, Cardboard, c.1905, 20 x 12 In.	780

Advertising, Sign, Dr. Meyer's Foot Soap, 10 Cents, Paper, 25 x 38 In.
$114

Showtime Auction Services

Advertising, Sign, Dr Pepper, Vim Vigor & Vitality, Framed Under Glass, 1905-10, 16 x 21 In.
$12,000

Morphy Auctions

Advertising, Sign, Drink Brownie, If You Like Chocolate Soda, Cardboard, M.C.A., 21 x 60 In.
$5,700

Victorian Casino Antiques

A

Advertising, Sign, Edgar H. Herr Upholstery, 2-Sided, Wood, Painted, c.1900, 26 In.
$470

Advertising, Sign, Eisenlohr's Cinco Cigars, Philadelphia, Reverse Glass, Frame, 27 ½ x 21 ½ In.
$780

Advertising, Sign, Eldredge B Sewing Machine, Wood, c.1900, 13 x 72 In.
$705

Advertising, Sign, Finck's Overalls, Detroit-Special, Wear Like A Pig's Nose, Porcelain, 12 x 17 In.
$138

Sign, Hires, It Hits The Spot, Tin Lithograph, Soda Jerk, 1914, 9 x 17 ¾ In. ....*illus*	1725
Sign, Holland-Amerika Line, Agentur, Ship, Porcelain, Fischer, 19 x 16 In.	1652
Sign, Homes Furnished Complete, Rosenbury & Sons, c.1950, 36 x 72 In. ....*illus*	2820
Sign, Hood, Rubber Canvas Footwear, Man, Red Suit, Flag, Die Cut, 13 ¾ In.	960
Sign, Hood's Sarsaparilla, Easel Back, Puppy On Crate, Cardboard, 18 x 11 In.	2185
Sign, Horse Shoe Brand, Toy Wringer, Gem, Girl, Clothes, Cardboard, 25 x 17 In.	805
Sign, Horsehead Cement, Yellow Bag Shape, 2-Sided, Porcelain, Cutout, 28 x 20 In.	390
Sign, Horvis Tea Cakes, Rule Of The Road, Paint, Wood, Iron, c.1930, 35 x 34 In.	219
Sign, I.W. Harper Whiskey, Here's Happy Days, Bernheim Dist., 1909, 18 x 24 In. ....*illus*	2015
Sign, Illinois Watch Co., Lithograph On Canvas, R. Bohunek, 1913, 11 x 14 In. ....*illus*	120
Sign, Imperial Beer, Wagner Brewing, 3 Pleasures Of Life, Tin, 22 x 28 In. ....*illus*	1540
Sign, Imperial Ice Cream, Neon, Metal Wire, Franceformer Transformer, 24 x 12 In. ....*illus*	196
Sign, Iroquois Indian Head Beer & Ale, Paper, Frame, 22 ½ x 26 ½ In.	428
Sign, Jas. E. Pepper & Co. Whiskey, Building, Reverse Glass, 27 x 19 In. ....*illus*	3990
Sign, John Dough Raised On Fleischmann's Yeast, 2-Sided, Tin Lithograph, 12 x 8 In.	5060
Sign, John Ruskin Best & Biggest, Cigar, Yellow Ground, c.1900, 10 x 30	270
Sign, John Smith Justice Of The Peace, Paint, Wood, 24 x 26 In.	374
Sign, Jos. S. Hayes Auto Painting & Trimming, Pine, Paint, c.1910, 24 x 91 In.	3840
Sign, Kayo, Tops In Taste, It's Real Chocolate Flavor, Tin Lithograph, 27 ½ x 14 In.	184
Sign, Kellogg's Corn Flakes, 2-Sided, American Art Works, Ohio, 1910, 19 In. ....*illus*	2040
Sign, Kelly Barb Wire, Wood, 49 x 5 ¾ In.	1824
Sign, Kerr's Thread, Spool Cotton, Girl & Dog, Cardboard, 19 ⅝ x 14 ⅝ In.	776
Sign, Kingman's Reliable Ham, Man & Sea Image, Frame, 15 x 21 In.	798
Sign, Korbel Champagne, Woman Holding Grapes, Bottle, Tin, Frame, 13 x 19 In.	108
Sign, L.A. Lyne Horse-Shoeing, Painted, Wood, c.1900, 25 x 72 In. ....*illus*	1763
Sign, L.E. Frazier & Co., Rexall, Black, Yellow Paint, Wood, 11 ½ x 60 ¼ In.	460
Sign, Lash's Bitters, Tine, Self-Framed, Embossed, Satisfied Customer Image, 20 ¼ x 24 In.	1823
Sign, Learn To Drink Moxie, Soda Case, Yellow, Red, Tin, Embossed, 1920s, 14 x 20 In.	1320
Sign, Lee Pants, Black, Yellow Ground, Tin, Embossed, Wood Frame, c.1945, 36 x 60 In.	480
Sign, LeRoy Little Cigar, Man, Smoking, Green, Blue, Red, Black, Tin, Embossed, 12 x 8 In.	300
Sign, Lime Kiln Club Bagley's Smoking Tobacco, Mat, Frame, 1904, 21 x 15 In. ....*illus*	3600
Sign, Limey, Delicious Flavor Of Real Limes, 5 Cent, Tin, Frame, 10 x 12 In.	236
Sign, Lion Brand Meats, Tin Lithograph, Oval, Mayer & Lavenson, 17 ¼ x 14 ¼ In.	1422
Sign, London & Lancashire Fire Insurance, Reverse On Glass, c.1900, 26 x 22 In. ....*illus*	150
Sign, Lone Star Beer, Bullet Shape, Light-Up, 14 In.	2445
Sign, Lookout Biscuits, Child, Lantern, Folding, Die Cut, Cardstock, 9 ½ x 14 ½ In.	138
Sign, Lorelei Beer, Kessler Brewing Co., Rocks & Sea Scene, Frame, 27 x 21 In.	3900
Sign, Lu Lu Biscuits, Le Fevre-Utile, Color Lithograph, 1897, 67 x 44 ¾ In.	688
Sign, Mandeville & King Flower Seed, Dutch Woman Watering Flower, 16 x 25 In.	119
Sign, Marine Products, Pegasus, Shield Shape, Tin, 2-Sided, 1955, 11 x 12 In.	1062
Sign, Marquee, Electro Freeze, Ice Cream Cone, Metal, Reticulated, 13 x 15 In.	145
Sign, Mavis Chocolate, Woman, Drinking Soda, Cutout, Cardboard, Webb, 1920s, 34 x 23 In.	1560
Sign, Mayo's Cut Plug, Smoking Cock O' The Walk, Porcelain, 1920s, 6 ½ x 13 In.	711
Sign, Mayo's Plug Tobacco, Paper, Frame, 60 x 24 In.	371
Sign, Mazda Lamps, Car With 1 Headlight, Don't Drive One-Eyed, Paper, Frame, 34 In.	1180
Sign, Meats, Korosec's Groceries, Scalloped, Yellow Black Paint, Wood, c.1865, 12 x 60 In.	403
Sign, Medicinal Gin, Watermelon, Doctor, 3 Women, Cardboard, 16 x 20 In.	288
Sign, Member Lehigh Valley Egg Producer, Blue & White, Porcelain, 10 x 13 In.	184
Sign, Midwest Ice Cream America's Favorite, Blue, Yellow, Porcelain, Die Cut, 38 x 48 In.	177
Sign, Mobilgas Marine, Pegasus, Shield Shape, Porcelain, 13 x 12 In.	2124
Sign, Mobiloil Marine, Pegasus, Waves, Porcelain, 36 x 60 In.	2650
Sign, Monarch Paint, 2-Sided, Wood, Arm, Holding Paint Bucket Pedestal, 18 x 15 In.	4600
Sign, Motorola Radio & Home Radio, Black, Yellow, Red, Vertical, Tin, 61 x 12 In.	443
Sign, Moxie Boy, Die Cut Embossed, Tin Lithograph, Chain, c.1910, 6 ¾ In.	450
Sign, Moxie, It's So Delicious, So Strengthening, Woman, Bike, Cardboard, 11 x 4 In.	575
Sign, Moxie, Teddy Roosevelt, Cardboard, Early 1900s, 22 ¼ x 27 ¾ In. ....*illus*	2700
Sign, Moxie, Woman In Tennis Outfit, White, Blue, Walt Otto, Cutout, 1940s, 34 x 27 In.	360
Sign, Muriel Senators Cigar, Box, Lamp, Fruit Bowl, Ashtray, Frame, 27 x 21 In.	330
Sign, Musik-Stadt Klingenthal, Black Forest, Basswood, c.1950, 33 x 21 In. ....*illus*	1320
Sign, Mutual Of New York, Indian Brave, Round, Reverse On Glass, Frame, c.1900, 20 In.	450
Sign, National Accident Society, Paper, Currier & Ives, Frame, Copyright 1884, 25 x 19 In.	1080
Sign, National Fire Insurance, Copper, Brass, Beveled Edge, 34 x 44 In.	542
Sign, Natural Chilean Soda, Flange, Bearded Black Man, Green Label, 1940s, 15 x 22 In.	450
Sign, Natural Chilean Soda, Yassuh!, Uncle Natchel, Black Man, Tin, Flange, 15 x 22 In.	413 to 767
Sign, Naturally It Tastes Better, Couple On Beach Towel, Cardboard, 1950s, 21 x 27 In.	600
Sign, Nehi Soda, Bottle, Woman's Legs, Green, Yellow, Cardboard, 13 ½ x 21 In.	374

Advertising, Sign, Frazer Axle Grease, Horse, Wagon, Tin, Self-Framed, Meek Co., 25 x 38 In.
$4,800

Morphy Auctions

Advertising, Sign, Friskies For Your Dog, Metal, 2-Sided, Stout Sign Co., St. Louis, 18 x 17 In.
$403

Victorian Casino Antiques

Advertising, Sign, G.L. Dana Farm Produce, Painted, Wood, Braces, c.1900, 15 ½ x 84 In.
$588

Garth's Auctioneers & Appraisers

Advertising, Sign, Gilt Edge Oil, Shoe Dressing, Reverse Glass, Denzi & Phillip, 35 x 33 In.
$2,700

Showtime Auction Services

Advertising, Sign, Grape-Nuts, Girl, St. Bernard Dog, Tin, Self-Framed, 1910-15, 30 x 20 In.
$6,000

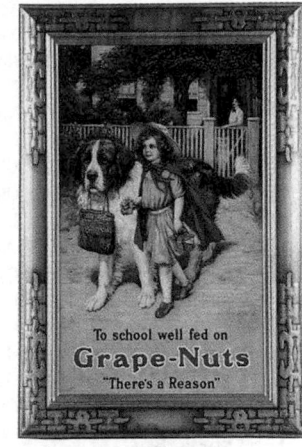

Morphy Auctions

Advertising, Sign, Hanger, Polar Bear Tobacco, 2-Sided, Die Cut, 14 ¼ In.
$5,700

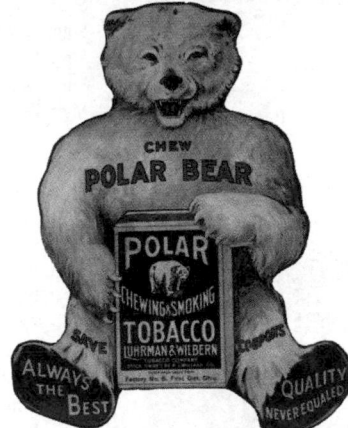

Morphy Auctions

Advertising, Sign, Headlight Union Made Overalls, Light-Up, Neon, Glass, Metal, 26 x 14 In.
$1,920

Victorian Casino Antiques

Advertising, Sign, Hickman-Ebbert Wagons, Apple Tree, Tin, Self-Framed, 37 ½ x 25 ½ In.
$1,482

Showtime Auction Services

A

Advertising, Sign, Hires, It Hits The Spot, Tin Lithograph, Soda Jerk, 1914, 9 x 17 ¾ In.
$1,725

Wm Morford Auctions

Advertising, Sign, Homes Furnished Complete, Rosenbury & Sons, c.1950, 36 x 72 In.
$2,820

Garth's Auctioneers & Appraisers

Advertising, Sign, I.W. Harper Whiskey, Here's Happy Days, Bernheim Dist., 1909, 18 x 24 In.
$2,015

James D. Julia Auctioneers

Advertising, Sign, Illinois Watch Co., Lithograph On Canvas, R. Bohunek, 1913, 11 x 14 In.
$120

Showtime Auction Services

Sign, Nehi, Take A Good Look, Bottle, Woman's Legs, Wood Frame, 36 x 60 In. ....*illus*	780
Sign, New York Fire Insurance Co., Brass, Copper, Applied Letters, 36 x 26 In.	485
Sign, New York Plate Glass Insurance Co., Reverse Painted, 24 x 18 In. ....*illus*	6270
Sign, Niagara Fire Insurance Co., Reverse On Glass, Frame, 33 x 26 In.	1320
Sign, Northrup Grown Seed Corn, Northern King & Co., Frame, 1912, 33 x 25 In. ....*illus*	1920
Sign, Northwestern Mutual Life Insurance, Milwaukee Building, Tin, Die Cut, 41 x 31 In.	390
Sign, NuGrape, Cardboard, Cutout, Framed Under Glass, 1950s, 20 x 16 In.	210
Sign, Old Dutch Cleanser, 10 Cents, Porcelain, B.S. Co., 22 x 32 In. ....*illus*	4500
Sign, Old Gold Cigarettes, Woman, Seated On Box, Cardboard, Stand-Up, 1930s, 31 x 43 In.	153
Sign, Old Harvest Whiskey, Tin, Embossed Self-Framed, c.1890, 16 x 22 In.	469
Sign, Old Hickory, Overalls, Shirts, Pants, Tin Over Cardboard, Easel Back, 9 x 13 In.	316
Sign, Old Line Maryland Rye, Mammy, Man, Umbrella, Meyer Cord, Wood, 21 x 15 In.	600
Sign, Old Reliable Coffee, Paper, Frame, 10 x 20 In.	57
Sign, Omar Cigarettes, 2 Men, Cardboard, Frame, 1910-20, 34 ½ x 26 In. ....*illus*	210
Sign, Omega Pocket Watch, Red, Gold Paint, Enameled Porcelain, 20 x 13 In.	326
Sign, Orange Crush, Logo Man, Bottle, Masonite, 1942, 48 x 18 In.	1680
Sign, Osborne Farm Machinery, Parade, Arc De Triomphe, c.1900, 22 x 15 In.	1422
Sign, Our Cigars Are Good Cigars, A. Hussey & Co., Nude Woman, 17 x 13 In.	2415
Sign, Overland Service Briggs Bros. Homer, Embossed, Porcelain, 10 x 28 In.	325
Sign, Owl Cigar, Now 5 Cents, Owl Perched On Cigar, Cardboard, 12 x 8 In.	891
Sign, Ox-Heart Chocolates, Long's, Cherry, Blue & White, Porcelain, 5 x 25 In.	2128
Sign, Paige, Sales & Service Entrance, Steel, Blue, White, Frame, c.1915, 38 x 61 In.	403
Sign, Pairpoint Co., Woman On Staircase, Roses, Die Cut, Cardboard, 23 x 18 ½ In.	316
Sign, Paul E. Wirt, Fountain Pens, Script, Gold, Red, Painted Tin, 6 ¼ x 9 ¾ In.	115
Sign, Pears Soap, Flowers Of The East, W.S. Coleman, Canvas, Lithograph, 1895, 18 x 27 In.	533
Sign, Pecheurs Reunis, Fishwife, Ethnic Attire, Adrien Barrer, France, 46 x 63 In.	1440
Sign, Pen Supreme Ice Cream, Tin, c.1935, 38 x 33 In.	360
Sign, Penn. Fire Insurance, Gesso, Raised, Rearing Horses, Org. 1825, Frame, 32 x 27 In.	4560
Sign, Phebus, Bicycle, Muted Color, France, 47 x 33 ½ In.	518
Sign, Phoenix Insurance Co., Gesso, Raised, Phoenix, In Crown, Est. 1857, 30 x 43 In.	1800
Sign, Phoenix Insurance Co., Hartford Co., Shield, Phoenix, Shadowbox Frame, 34 x 27 In.	960
Sign, Pioneer Food Store, Round, Stagecoach Logo, Porcelain, 16 In.	826
Sign, Pittsburg Underwriters Of Pennsylvania, Reverse Glass, Frame, 32 x 24 In.	171
Sign, Plenty Of Eggs Coconut Custard Pie, Horn & Hardart, Frame, c.1950, 28 x 22 In.	375
Sign, Plume Motor Spirit, 2 Red Plumes, Vacuum Oil Co., Porcelain, Flange, 15 x 24 In.	1770
Sign, Pocahontas Coal Co., Tin Litho, Indian Princess, Black & Gold, 14 x 12 In.	1150
Sign, Prairie Farms Butter 92 Score, Yellow, Navy, Porcelain, 21 x 33 In.	1770
Sign, Prince Albert, Chief Joseph, Headdress, Tin, R.J. Reynolds, 19 x 25 In. ....*illus*	7200
Sign, R. Brandt, Wood & Photo Engraving, Wood, Paint, Shield Shape, 12 x 11 In.	661
Sign, R.L. Maxwell Pharmacist, Wood, Paint, 37 x 8 In.	136
Sign, R.S. Denton, Inn, Shaped Crest, Tree Field, 1800s, 49 ½ x 36 ½ In.	3120
Sign, Raven's Horse, Cattle & Poultry Food, 14 x 22 In.	570
Sign, Red Fox Ginger Ale, Time To Get Acquainted, Woman In Masquerade, 35 In.	420
Sign, Reddy Kilowatt, I Work For Pennies, Cardboard, 1954, 28 x 22 In. ....*illus*	390
Sign, Redfern Rubber Heels & Soles For All Repairs, Yellow, Porcelain, 20 x 48 In.	413
Sign, Regatta Yacht Paint, Sailboats, Tin, c.1950, 23 x 35 In.	360
Sign, Remington Arms, Man In Rocker, Dogs, Tribute To A Dog Text, Frame, 1929, 22 In.	304
Sign, REO Motor Car, Side Image, Black & White, May 24, 1916, Frame, 14 ½ x 23 ½ In.	23
Sign, Research Brand Products, Microscope, Book, Tin Lithograph, Shank Sign Co., 19 In.	300
Sign, Rex Flour, Porcelain, Red Ground, White & Green Lettering, 40 x 8 In.	371
Sign, R-La Root Beer, Tin, Embossed, 1950s, 25 x 12 In.	210
Sign, Rolling Rock Beer, 2-Sided, Plastic, Light-Up, Metal Base, c.1975, 20 In.	390
Sign, Rooney's Malt Whiskey, Rooster, Tin, Self-Framed, c.1908, 24 ¼ x 20 ¼ In. ....*illus*	1560
Sign, Roselawn Milk, c.1950, 40 x 15 In.	300
Sign, Royal Tailors Chicago-New York, Tiger, Tin Litho, Die Cut, c.1910, 9 x 19 ½ In.	523
Sign, Rubber Products By Whitall Tatum Co., Water Bottle, Tin Over Cardboard, 19 In.	72
Sign, Ryan Aeronautical Co., Sales, Service, Porcelain Over Steel, Plane, c.1940, 9 x 12 In.	295
Sign, Rye Straw Bee Skep, Wood Hook, Silver Paint, c.1880, 23 x 18 In.	3080
Sign, Samuel Woodside Co., O., Laugh At Cigars, Saloon, Lithograph, 28 x 22 In. ....*illus*	6000
Sign, Sand, Household Sewing Machine, Wood, c.1890, 72 x 13 In.	1596
Sign, Sand, Jersey Creamery, Wood, 1890, 69 x 18 In.	2052
Sign, Satin Skin Products, Cutout, Cardboard, c.1900, 30 ¾ x 27 In.	180
Sign, Scarlet Glo, More Heat Per Dollar, Tin, Black, White, Orange, 10 x 24 In.	200
Sign, Scenerama, Hamm's Beer, Born In The Land Of Sky Blue Waters, 19 x 34 In.	1121
Sign, Selz Shoes, Make Your Feet Glad, Blue, White, Porcelain, c.1900, 24 x 36 In.	510
Sign, Shawnee Insurance Co., White, Blue, Porcelain, 12 x 18 In.	390

Sign, Sherwin-Williams Paint, Covers The Earth, Transfer, Wood, 20 x 13 ¾ In. ....*illus*	690
Sign, Sherwin-Williams Paint, Spilling On World Logo, Porcelain, Flange, 48 x 33 In.	472
Sign, Sherwin-Williams Paints, Porcelain, Relief Die Cut, Logo, Cover The Earth, 19 x 35 In......	652
Sign, Sherwin-Williams, Covers The Earth, Paint On Globe, Porcelain, Die Cut, 63 In.	649
Sign, Shoe Trade, Inscribed W.H. Vandy Shoe Shop, 1800s, 26 x 22 In.......................	3318
Sign, Sinclair Aircraft, Single Engine Airplane, Porcelain, 2-Sided, 48 In.	8260
Sign, Smith Detective Agency, Enamel, Red, White, Black, c.1950, 13 x 18 In.	150
Sign, Smith's Confectionery, Girl With Dog, Flowers, Paper Lithograph, 23 x 16 ¾ In.	374
Sign, Star Tobacco, 3-Way, Tin Litho, Tobacco Plug, Star, Black, Gold, 4 x 19 In...........	3105
Sign, Stewartgraph Stoves, W.M. Pasco, Wood, Paint, 5 ¾ x 36 In......................	489
Sign, Stickney & Poor Spice Co., 3 Boxes, Red, Gold Letters, Tin Litho, c.1900, 27 x 19 In.	1121
Sign, Stroh's, Beer, Script, Neon, 23 In.	60
Sign, Sun Insurance Office Limited Agency, Glowing Sun, Porcelain, 14 x 20 In. ....*illus*	660
Sign, Sun Paste Stove Polish, Black Woman, Child, Stove, Sun, Cardboard, 1890s, 9 x 12 In.	390
Sign, Sunflower Petroleum, Vacuum Oil Co., R.T., Porcelain, Flange, 16 x 24 In.	1475
Sign, Sweet Wheat Chewing Gum, The Best Of All, Girl, Roses, Cardboard, 12 x 9 In.	160
Sign, Sweet-Orr Overalls, Union Made, Porcelain, Tug-Of-War, Blue, Yellow, c.1910, 20 x 14 In. .	1541
Sign, Swim Easy Bathing Suits, Forest Outing Garments, Tin Lithograph, 3 x 10 In..............	345
Sign, Take Hood's Sarsaparilla, To Purify The Blood, Cardboard, Round, 8 ¾ In.	230
Sign, Tallman Boot & Shoe Co., Woman, Among Apple Blossoms, Utica, N.Y., 15 x 20 In.	89
Sign, Tavern, Colonial Figures, Pillars, Painted, 1800s, 23 ½ x 17 ½ In...............	201
Sign, Tavern, Plough Bullards, Shaped, Painted, 2-Sided, c.1950, 42 x 33 In.	711
Sign, Taxi, Light-Up, Wood Mount, 12 x 17 x 5 In.......................	177
Sign, Taylor's Milk, Protect Your Body, Tin Lithograph, Orange, Black, 1920s, 10 x 14 In........	115
Sign, Terrot Dijon Cycles & Motorcycles, Paper, Linen, 1906, 39 x 54 In.	2160
Sign, That Sleepy Eye Flour, Indian, Tin Lithograph, 19 ⅛ x 13 ½ In. ....*illus*	1495
Sign, The Lookout, Sailor, Telescope, Carved, Multicolor Paint, 1900s, 32 x 41 In..........	3375
Sign, The Ohio Dairy Co., Cash For Cream & Eggs, Wood, c.1900, 24 x 105 In.	1998
Sign, The Old Oaken Bucket, Owl, Parrot, 2 Wells, Wood, Paint, c.1920, 8 x 23 In............	3480
Sign, Thomas' Inks & Mucilage, Ask For Me, Ink Bottles, Tin, Embossed, 17 x 23 In.	4130
Sign, Timken Roller Bearing, Porcelain, 30 x 18 In.	203
Sign, Tom Turner Watch Repairing, Frame, c.1900, 18 x 37 ½ In...............	173
Sign, Top Hat Red Paint, Zinc, Inscribed Pineau, c.1890, 25 In...........	1422
Sign, Trolley, RC Cola Does Taste Best, Gene Tierney, Bottle, Cardboard, c.1950, 11 x 28 In.........	420
Sign, Unadilla Silo Seeps Silage Prime, Tin, 40 x 13 ½ In.	150
Sign, Uncle John's Golden Tree Syrup, Cardboard, Hanging, Bracket, 12 ½ x 20 ¾ In.	314
Sign, Use Mrs. Winslow's Soothing Syrup, Country Store, Paint, Wood, 6 x 36 In.	776
Sign, Use White Star Furnace Oil, Cardboard, Embossed, 10 x 14 In.	89
Sign, Van Dyck Cigars, Reverse Painted Glass, Frame, 24 x 32 In.....................	660
Sign, Velvet The Smoothest Tobacco, Red, Yellow, Enamel, Metal, c.1950, 12 x 9 In............	330
Sign, Vermont Mutual Fire Insurance, Tin, Self-Framed, Embossed, Streetscape, 20 x 24 In........	533
Sign, Violin Instructor, Violin, Open Book Of Music, Paint, U.S.A., 1800s, 19 x 24 In.	960
Sign, W.E. Peterson Veterinarian, Wood, Paint, 22 x 6 ½ In.......................	238
Sign, Waitt & Bond, Blackstone Cigar, Black, Yellow, Embossed, Porcelain, 12 x 36 In............	266
Sign, We Sell Star Tobacco, Blue, White, Porcelain, Flange, 8 x 18 In........................	384
Sign, We Use The DeLaval Separator, Black, Yellow, Porcelain, 16 x 12 In.	177
Sign, Welch's Stoves, 2-Sided, Tin, Wood Frame, c.1900, 29 x 65 In. ....*illus*	881
Sign, Western Pacific, Porcelain, Black, White, Red Feather, 41 x 46 In.	390
Sign, Westinghouse Light & Power Plant, Tin, Embossed, L.E. Madison, Conn., 24 x 23 In.	684
Sign, Wheatlet Cereal, Uncle Sam, Die Cut, Stand-Up, c.1895, 6 ½ x 3 ¾ In.	11
Sign, Whipped Cream Cottage Cheese, Mickey Mouse, Cardboard, 28 x 32 In. ....*illus*	460
Sign, Whistle Soda, Tin, Thirsty?, Just Get The Handy Bottle, Easel Back, 1920s, 9 x 6 In.	972
Sign, White Label Cigar, Tin, Sentenne & Green, 14 x 10 In.	180
Sign, White May & Royal Standard Lamp Oils, Sun, BP, Porcelain, Flange, 12 x 18 In............	443
Sign, Whitney Baby Coaches, Cardboard, Embossed, 1920s, 23 x 15 ½ In. ....*illus*	450
Sign, Wiedemann's Beer, Glass, Light-Up, 13 ½ x 7 In.	300
Sign, Wiedemann's Beer, Lake Scene, Ducks, Wood, Aluminum, Signed Eddy Cole, 1941, 35 In...	120
Sign, Wild Cherry Bitters, Reverse Glass, 8 x 15 ¾ In.	660
Sign, Wilkins Coffee, Celluloid, Over Tin, Smiling Waiter, Holding Tray, 1914, 9 x 12 In.........	1778
Sign, Wilkins Submarine, Boy Holding Toy, Multicolor, Paper Lithograph, 11 x 14 In...............	719
Sign, Winchester Rifle Always On Target, Flashlights & Batteries, Round, 2-Sided, Tin, 18 In......	500
Sign, Winchester Rifle, Hunter, Donkey, Dead Game, Cutout, Cardboard, c.1910, 12 x 7 In.......	3600
Sign, Winchester Rifle, Shell, Dog, Quails, Cardboard, Cutout, c.1910, 12 x 7 In.....................	2700
Sign, Winchester, Pheasant, Paper, 1955, 28 x 24 In.......................	270
Sign, Winchester, Squirrel, Paper, 1955, 28 x 42 In.......................	360
Sign, Wyandotte Cleaner, Cleanser, Indian With Shooting Arrow, Frame, 48 x 26 In.....................	1920

Advertising, Sign, Imperial Beer, Wagner Brewing, 3 Pleasures Of Life, Tin, 22 x 28 In.
$1,540

James D. Julia Auctioneers

Advertising, Sign, Imperial Ice Cream, Neon, Metal Wire, Franceformer Transformer, 24 x 12 In.
$196

Victorian Casino Antiques

Advertising, Sign, Jas. E. Pepper & Co. Whiskey, Building, Reverse Glass, 27 x 19 In.
$3,990

Showtime Auction Services

Advertising, Sign, Kellogg's Corn Flakes, 2-Sided, American Art Works, Ohio, 1910, 19 In.
$2,040

Morphy Auctions

Advertising, Sign, L.A. Lyne Horse-Shoeing, Painted, Wood, c.1900, 25 x 72 In.
$1,763

Garth's Auctioneers & Appraisers

Advertising, Sign, Lime Kiln Club Bagley's Smoking Tobacco, Mat, Frame, 1904, 21 x 15 In.
$3,600

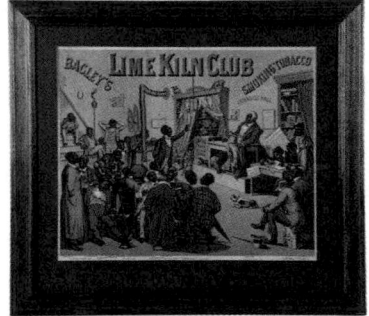

Morphy Auctions

Advertising, Sign, London & Lancashire Fire Insurance, Reverse On Glass, c.1900, 26 x 22 In.
$150

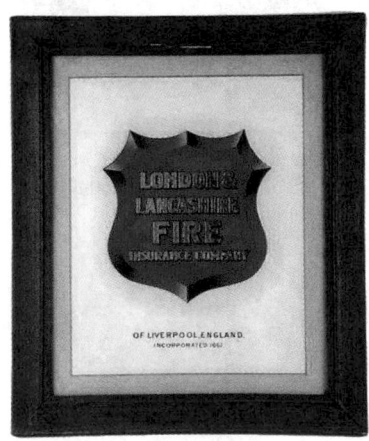

Morphy Auctions

Advertising, Sign, Moxie, Teddy Roosevelt, Cardboard, Early 1900s, 22 ¼ x 27 ¾ In.
$2,700

Morphy Auctions

Advertising, Sign, Musik-Stadt Klingenthal, Black Forest, Basswood, c.1950, 33 x 21 In.
$1,320

The Stein Auction Co.

Advertising, Sign, Nehi, Take A Good Look, Bottle, Woman's Legs, Wood Frame, 36 x 60 In.
$780

Morphy Auctions

Advertising, Sign, New York Plate Glass Insurance Co., Reverse Painted, 24 x 18 In.
$6,270

Showtime Auction Services

Advertising, Sign, Northrup Grown Seed Corn, Northern King & Co., Frame, 1912, 33 x 25 In.
$1,920

Morphy Auctions

Mail Pouch Ads on Barns
Mail Pouch tobacco used signs painted on barns as huge ads from the beginning of the twentieth century until the 1990s.

Sign, Yankee Label Bread, Heydt Bakery, Uncle Sam, Porcelain, c.1915, 16 x 32 In.	720
Sign, Yeast Foam, Black Woman, Watermelon, Cardboard, Die Cut, 1900, 18 x 12 In.	420
Sign, Yellow Cab, 5 Cent Cigar, Takes The Right Of Way, Tin Litho, Traffic Cop, 7 x 20 In.	891
Stand, Reddy Kilowatt, Bulb, Neon Orange, Plastic Composition Base, 12 x 10 In. ......*illus*	1778
Strawholder, Jersey Creme, Clear Glass, House Shape, Hinged Metal Lid, 10 In.	908
Stringholder, 7Up, Logo, Take Some Home, 1940s, 16 ¾ x 12 ¾ In.	270
Stringholder, Dutch Boy Paint Store, Die Cut Tin, 2-Sided, Grommet In Hand, 14 x 20 In.	2963
Stringholder, Lipton Tea, 13 ¾ x 20 In.	2565
Tap Knob, Alaskan Amber, Life Ring, Light, Battery Operated, Alaskan Brewing Co., 13 In.	70
Tap Knob, Ballantine, Milk Glass, Flat Top, P. Ballantine & Sons, 1 ⅜ In.	665
Tap Knob, Blitz Weinhard, Blitz Weinhard Co., Portland, Oregon	393
Tap Knob, Bohemian Stroh's Beer, Celluloid, Plastic, Round, 2 ⅜ x 2 In.	207
Thermometers are listed in their own category.	

Advertising tin cans or canisters were first used commercially in the United States in 1819 and were called tins. Today the word *tin* is used by most collectors to describe many types of containers, including food tins, biscuit boxes, roly poly tobacco containers, gunpowder cans, talcum powder sprinkle-top cans, cigarette flat-fifty tins, and more. Beer Cans are listed in their own category. Things made of undecorated tin are listed under Tinware.

Tin, Alcazar Cigar, Famous Race Horse, Round, Multicolor, 5 In.	19200
Tin, American Eagle Chewing Tobacco, Detroit, Woman On Eagle, Blue, Peach, 3 ¾ In.	3300
Tin, Aunt Jemima Sugar Cream, Lid, Handle, Color Litho Label, c.1905, 3 ½ In.	420
Tin, Baker Cocoa, Woman Holding Tray, Apron, Multicolor, 5 ¾ x 3 ¼ In.	403
Tin, Banner Fine Cut Chewing Tobacco, Woman Wrapped In U.S. Flag, Yellow, 3 ¾ In.	1080
Tin, Between The Acts Cigarettes, Actress Minnie Cummings, Gold, c.1890, 3 In.	780
Tin, Bingo Cut Plug, Tobacco, United States Tobacco Co., c.1890, 3 ¾ In. ......*illus*	1200
Tin, Biscuit, Agricultural Scene, Scalloped, Hinged Lid, Scroll, 3 ¾ x 7 ⅛ In.	374
Tin, Biscuit, Jubilee, Women In Native Costume, Hinged Lid, 6 ⅜ x 5 In.	230
Tin, Biscuit, Log Cabin, Cowboy, Horse, Embossed, Henderson Co., 5 x 6 ½ In. ......*illus*	374
Tin, Biscuit, National Biscuit Company, Glass Panel, 10 ½ x 11 ½ In.	79
Tin, Black & White Roll Cut, Tobacco, Vertical, Pocket, 4 ⅜ In.	178
Tin, Blanke's Mojave Coffee, Green, 2 Lb., 7 ½ In.	45
Tin, Blanke-Wenneker Candy, Beach Pail, Kids At Shore Scene, Bail Handle, 12 In.	148
Tin, Bright Eye Baking Powder, Cardboard, Metal Base & Lid, Baby, 5 ⅛ In.	207
Tin, Brown Bear Coffee, Brown & White, Bear Walking, Lid, 5 ⅛ x 4 ⅞ In.	115
Tin, Brunswick Cocoanut, Warner & Merritt, Yellow, Black, Square, 6 x 3 ¼ In.	173
Tin, Cardinal Cut Plug, Tobacco, Red Cardinal, Gold Ground, Vertical, Pocket, 4 ½ In.	1896
Tin, Century, Tobacco, Flowers, Black Ground, Pocket, c.1895, 3 ¾ In.	780
Tin, Century, Tobacco, Spinning Dial, P. Lorillard, Factory Scene, Pocket, c.1885, 3 ½ In.	600
Tin, Charm Of The West, Tobacco, Spaulding & Merrick, Woman, Horse, Dog, c.1885, 4 In.	390
Tin, Cheerio Coffee, Bird On Branch, Yellow, Blue, Tin Lithograph, 4 x 5 ⅛ In.	230
Tin, Cigar, Black Fox, 50 Count, MacDonald Mfg. Co., 5 ¼ x 5 ¼ In.	960
Tin, Cigar, Francis Lee, 50 Count, Liberty Can Co. ......*illus*	1140
Tin, Cigar, John Storm, 5 Cents, Man's Portrait, 5 ½ x 6 ¼ In.	69
Tin, Cigar, Splendid, 50 Count, National Can Co., 5 ¼ x 4 ¾ In.	120
Tin, Cigar, Tobacco Girl, 50 Count, Liberty Can Co., Lancaster, Pa., 5 ½ x 6 ¼ In.	540
Tin, Cigar, Totem Union Made, 25 Cents, 5 ⅜ x 3 In.	840
Tin, Columbia Allspice, Miss Columbia Profile, Yellow, Red, Blue, 3 ¾ x 2 ¼ In.	127
Tin, Comfort Powder, Cylindrical, 2 Young Girls, Nurse, Blue, Yellow, 4 x 2 ¼ In.	138
Tin, Congress Cut Plug, Tobacco, Round, Gold Letters, 1 Lb., 6 ½ In.	300
Tin, Continental Cubes Tobacco, 5 ¼ In.	1560
Tin, DeLuxe Fire Marshmallows, Blue Ground, Round, 13 In.	180
Tin, Derbies Condoms, Racing Theme Logo, Rounded Square, 1 ¾ x 2 ⅛ In.	115
Tin, Diamond Match Co., Black Family, Racial Humor Quote, 1880s, 4 ½ In.	510
Tin, Dixie Queen Plug Cut, Tobacco, Pretty Woman Wearing Hat, 6 x 5 In.	142
Tin, E.T. Pilkington, Tobacco, Virginia, Multicolor Fruits, Flowers Oval, 4 ½ In.	450
Tin, Fine Cut Bagley Tobacco, Pheasants, J. Bagley & Co., 8 x 11 In.	295
Tin, Forest & Stream, Tobacco, Men Fishing, Dog, Canoe, Pocket, 4 ⅛ x 3 In.	633
Tin, Gaiety Tobacco, Cut Plug, Woman's Portrait, Red & White, 2 ¾ x 4 ⅝ In.	345
Tin, George Washington Cut Plug, Bail Handle, 8 x 5 In.	79
Tin, Giant Salted Peanuts, Man With Mace, 11 In.	150
Tin, Gold Dust Gunpowder, Yellow Paint, Shield, 6 ¾ x 3 In.	138
Tin, Golden Pheasant Condoms, Bird On Branch, Rounded Corners, 1 ¾ x 2 ¼ In.	184
Tin, Great Atlantic & Pacific Tea Co., Yellow, 11 In.	51
Tin, Hiawatha Tobacco, Yellow Ground, 5 In.	360
Tin, His Master's Choice Cigars, 50 Count, Paper Label, 5 x 5 ¼ In.	450

Advertising, Sign, Old Dutch Cleanser, 10 Cents, Porcelain, B.S. Co., 22 x 32 In. $4,500

Showtime Auction Services

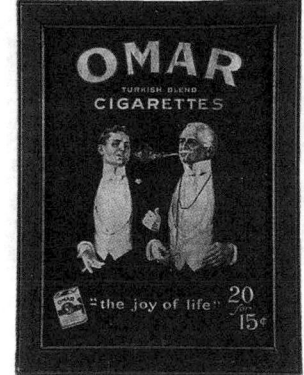

Advertising, Sign, Omar Cigarettes, 2 Men, Cardboard, Frame, 1910-20, 34 ½ x 26 In. $210

Morphy Auctions

Advertising, Sign, Prince Albert, Chief Joseph, Headdress, Tin, R.J. Reynolds, 19 x 25 In. $7,200

Showtime Auction Services

This is an edited listing of current prices. Visit **Kovels.com** to check thousands of prices from previous years and sign up for free information on trends, tips, reproductions, marks, and more.

Advertising, Sign, Reddy Kilowatt,
I Work For Pennies, Cardboard, 1954,
28 x 22 In.
$390

Morphy Auctions

Advertising, Sign, Rooney's Malt
Whiskey, Rooster, Tin, Self-Framed,
c.1908, 24 ¼ x 20 ¼ In.
$1,560

Morphy Auctions

Advertising, Sign, Samuel Woodside Co.,
O., Laugh At Cigars, Saloon, Lithograph,
28 x 22 In.
$6,000

Showtime Auction Services

Flat Fifties

The "flat fifties" cigarette tin
was popular with consumers
in the 1940s–1970s because
they could be carried in a jacket
pocket or a clutch purse.

Tin, Home Brand Coffee, House, Yellow, Red, Black, Bail Handle, 8 ¾ x 7 ½ In.	661
Tin, J. Monroe Taylor's Soda & Saleratus, Wood, Cardboard, Canister, 19 In. *illus*	354
Tin, Jack Frost Baking Powder, Cylindrical, Multicolor, 5 ½ x 3 ⅛ In.	242
Tin, Kentucky Smile, J.B. Pace Tobacco Co., Smiling Woman, Yellow, Green, c.1890, 3 In.	300
Tin, King Cole Coffee, Multicolor, King, Drinking Coffee, Lid, 5 ⅞ x 4 ¼ In.	219
Tin, Long Tom Tobacco, Yellow, Black, Canada, c.1900, 5 In.	600
Tin, Lorillard Fine Cut Rose Leaf Chewing Tobacco, Ginna, 3 ¾ In.	1560
Tin, Mallard Brand Coffee, Flying Duck, Paper Label, Cylindrical, 6 x 4 In.	345
Tin, Mammy's Favorite Brand Coffee, Cylindrical, Bail Handle, 10 ¾ In.	210 to 265
Tin, May Queen, Tobacco, J.G. Flint, Milwaukee, Woman Lolling, Blue, Black, 3 ¾ In.	840
Tin, Monadnock Peanut Butter, Bail Handle, Multicolor, 3 ½ x 3 ⅞ In.	115
Tin, Morning Glory Stogies, 50 Count, National Can Co., 6 x 4 ¾ In.	599
Tin, Morning Joy, Pure Coffee, Bird, Sun, Green, Yellow, 4 ⅜ x 5 ⅛ In.	265
Tin, Mother Dawson Spice, Paprika, Pure Household Spices, 3 ¾ x 2 ⅜ In. *illus*	69
Tin, North Carolina Plug Cut Tobacco, 2 Women, 6 ½ In.	210
Tin, North Star, Tobacco, Dayton, Ohio, Woman, Cherubs, Sepia, Flat Pocket, 3 ¾ In.	360
Tin, Ojibwa Tobacco, Indian, Hand Raised, River, Rectangular, 11 In.	5100
Tin, Old Glory Coffee, Knob Top, Flag Waving, Round, Norton Bros., Chicago, 7 ½ In.	2040
Tin, Old Glory, Tobacco, Spaulding & Merrick, Eagle, Old Man, Boy, Red, Black, 3 ¾ In.	1440
Tin, Orcico, Cigars, 2 For 5 Cents, Indian Chief, Multicolor, Lid, 5 ½ x 6 ⅛ In.	431
Tin, Paul Jones Clean Cut, Tobacco, John Paul Jones, Ship, Vertical, Pocket, 4 ⅜ In.	547
Tin, Pomade, The Champ, Boxer, Oval, Red & Yellow, 3 ½ x 2 ⅜ In.	138
Tin, Prexy, For Pipe & Cigarette, Tobacco, Graduate In Cap & Gown, Red, 4 ½ In.	1185
Tin, Rat Chips, Exterminator, Rounded Square, Yellow, Red, Rodent, 3 x 3 In.	184
Tin, Reuter's Jumbo Peanuts, Civil War Veteran, Uniform, Yellow, 8 ¾ x 5 ⅞ In.	288
Tin, Roly Poly, Mayo Tobacco, Store Keeper, Lithograph, 7 x 6 ½ In. *illus*	604
Tin, Roly Poly, Mayo's Cut Plug Tobacco, Dutchman, 7 ½ In.	960
Tin, Roly Poly, Mayo's Cut Plug Tobacco, Inspector, 7 ½ In.	1680
Tin, Roly Poly, Mayo's Cut Plug Tobacco, Mammy, Pipe, Lithograph, 7 x 6 ½ In. *illus*	891
Tin, Roly Poly, Mayo's Cut Plug Tobacco, Singing Waiter, 7 ½ In.	780
Tin, Roly Poly, Mayo's Cut Plug Tobacco, Storekeeper, 7 ½ In.	1080
Tin, Roly Poly, Red Indian Tobacco, Mammy, Pipe In Mouth, 7 x 6 ½ In.	1840
Tin, Roly Poly, Red Indian Tobacco, Singing Waiter, 7 x 6 ½ In.	690
Tin, Rose Leaf Chewing Tobacco, P. Lorillard & Co., Rosebuds, Leaves, c.1875, 3 ½ In.	480
Tin, Rosemary Spice, Woman Holding Flowers, Yellow, Blue, 2 ¼ x 2 ¼ In.	196
Tin, Royal Dutch Coffee, Children Playing, Sepia, 1890s, 10 ½ In.	240
Tin, S.B. Fields Wonderful Herb Hair Grower, Long Haired Woman, 3 x ⅞ In.	92
Tin, Samsoun Square Corner Tobacco, Man & Woman, Square, 3 ⅜ x 4 ½ In.	1668
Tin, Sanitary Roach Trap, Bugs, Yellow Ground, Mesh Side, 5 x 5 In.	360
Tin, Shield Condoms, Round, Tin Litho, Shield, Candles, 1 ⅝ In. Diam.	719
Tin, Silver-Tex Condom, Gold & Black, 1 ⅛ x 2 ¼ In.	604
Tin, Smith Bros., Cough Drops, Brothers Portraits, Round, Lid, 3 x 4 ¼ In.	207
Tin, Spaulding & Merrick Sweet Cuba Fine Cut Tobacco, Paint, 7 ¾ x 8 In.	122
Tin, Spice, Cayenne Pepper, W.M. Hoyt Co., Chicago, 7 x 9 ½ x 5 In.	180
Tin, Squirrel Peanut Butter, Squirrel In Tree, Yellow, Red, Lid, Bail Handle, 3 ½ x 4 In.	184
Tin, Stanley Woods Candy, Toffee, Clover, Motorcycle, 9 ⅜ x 9 ¼ In.	489
Tin, Stay Ready Additive, Petro, Woman Riding Goose, Can, 4 x 3 ⅜ In.	184
Tin, Sweet Clover, Tobacco, Lovell & Buffington, Kentucky, Clover, Blue, White, 3 ¾ In.	390
Tin, Sweet Cuba, Tobacco, Lithograph, Green, Red Lettering, Medallion, 8 x 8 x 11 In.	153
Tin, Sweet Tip Top, Tobacco, Horse-Drawn Fire Pumper, Lattice, 6 x 5 In.	115
Tin, Talc, Zanol, Baby Mine Nursery Powder, Lithograph, 5 ⅜ x 2 ⅝ In. *illus*	138
Tin, Taxi Crimp Cut Tobacco, Embossed Roll Top, Pocket, 4 ¼ In. *illus*	3792
Tin, Terrace Club, Country Club Building, 6 x 4 ⅛ In.	242
Tin, Tiger Chewing Tobacco, 15 Cents, Running Tiger, Tin Lithograph, Pocket, 3 x 3 In.	161
Tin, Tiger Chewing Tobacco, Tiger Face, Gold Black, Red, c.1880, 3 ½ In.	2400
Tin, Tobacco, Sweet Cuba Fine Cut, 5 Cent, 10 ¼ In.	120
Tin, Tobacco, Uncle Sam Smoking, Red, White & Blue Shield, 4 ½ In.	911
Tin, Turkey Coffee, Cylindrical, Green, Red, Wild Turkey, Lid, 1 Lb., 5 ¾ In.	420
Tin, Universal Blend Coffee, Uncle Sam, Sunrise, E.B. Miller & Co., Chicago, 7 In.	173
Tin, Vantine's Talc, Sana-Dermal Talcum, Woman & Baby, Cylindrical, 5 x 2 ½ In.	150
Tin, Veterinary, Poultry Tonic, Dr. David Roberts, Cylindrical, Cardboard, 7 x 3 In.	150
Tin, Wagon Wheel, Pipe & Cigarette, Tobacco, Covered Wagon, Vertical, Pocket, 4 ⅜ In.	296
Tin, Welcome Guest Coffee, Black Butler, Lid, Red, Yellow, 6 x 4 ¼ In.	276
Tin, Wheel Of Fortune, Burger & Lee, Numbered Dial, Yellow, Black, c.1885, 3 ¼ In.	450
Tin, White Witch, Nude Kneeling Woman, Cleansing Powder, 2 ¼ x 1 ¼ In.	104
Tin, Winner Cut Plug Tobacco, Auto Race, Rectangular, Top Handle, 8 In.	1560

Advertising, Sign, Sherwin-Williams Paint, Covers The Earth, Transfer, Wood, 20 x 13 ¾ In.
$690

Wm Morford Auctions

Advertising, Sign, Sun Insurance Office Limited Agency, Glowing Sun, Porcelain, 14 x 20 In.
$660

Morphy Auctions

Advertising, Sign, That Sleepy Eye Flour, Indian, Tin Lithograph, 19 ⅛ x 13 ½ In.
$1,495

Wrn Morford Auctions

Advertising, Sign, Welch's Stoves, 2-Sided, Tin, Wood Frame, c.1900, 29 x 65 In.
$881

Garth's Auctioneers & Appraisers

Advertising, Sign, Whipped Cream Cottage Cheese, Mickey Mouse, Cardboard, 28 x 32 In.
$460

Hake's Americana & Collectibles

Advertising, Sign, Whitney Baby Coaches, Cardboard, Embossed, 1920s, 23 x 15 ½ In.
$450

Morphy Auctions

Advertising, Stand, Reddy Kilowatt, Bulb, Neon Orange, Plastic Composition Base, 12 x 10 In.
$1,778

James D. Julia Auctioneers

Advertising, Tin, Bingo Cut Plug, Tobacco, United States Tobacco Co., c.1890, 3 ¾ In.
$1,200

Morphy Auctions

Advertising, Tin, Biscuit, Log Cabin, Cowboy, Horse, Embossed, Henderson Co., 5 x 6 ½ In.
$374

Wm Morford Auctions

Advertising, Tin, Cigar, Francis Lee, 50 Count, Liberty Can Co.
$1,140

Showtime Auction Services

Advertising, Tin, J. Monroe Taylor's Soda & Saleratus, Wood, Cardboard, Canister, 19 In.
$354

Bertoia Auctions

Advertising, Tin, Mother Dawson Spice, Paprika, Pure Household Spices, 3 ¾ x 2 ⅜ In.
$69

Wm Morford Auctions

Advertising, Tin, Roly Poly, Mayo Tobacco, Store Keeper, Lithograph, 7 x 6 ½ In.
$604

Wm Morford Auctions

Advertising, Tin, Roly Poly, Mayo's Cut Plug Tobacco, Mammy, Pipe, Lithograph, 7 x 6 ½ In.
$891

Wm Morford Auctions

Advertising, Tin, Talc, Zanol, Baby Mine Nursery Powder, Lithograph, 5 ⅜ x 2 ⅝ In.
$138

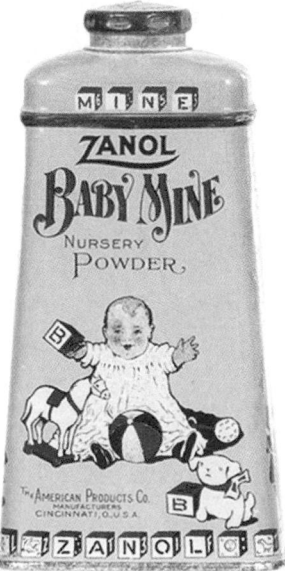

Wm Morford Auctions

Advertising, Tin, Taxi Crimp Cut Tobacco, Embossed Roll Top, Pocket, 4 ¼ In.
$3,792

James D. Julia Auctioneers

Advertising, Tip Tray, Blue Bell Dry Cleaning Co., Jolly Comrade, 6 ½ x 4 ½ In.
$600

Morphy Auctions

Advertising, Tip Tray, I Just Love Moxie Don't You, Young Woman, Glass, Tin Lithograph, 6 ⅛ In.
$288

Wm Morford Auctions

Tin, Yacht Tobacco, Cut Plug, Boat, Anchors, 2 ⅝ x 4 ⅝ In.	150
Tin, Yankee Boy Plug Cut, Tobacco, Burley At Bat, Checkerboard Ground, Pocket, 4 In.	444

Advertising tip trays are decorated metal trays less than 5 inches in diameter. They were placed on the table or counter to hold either the bill or the coins that were left as a tip. Change receivers could be made of glass, plastic, or metal. They were kept on the counter near the cash register and held the money passed back and forth by the cashier. Related items may be listed in the Advertising category under Change Receiver.

Tip Tray, American Can Co., Louisiana Purchase Exposition, Tin Lithograph, 1904, 4 In.	207
Tip Tray, Blue Bell Dry Cleaning Co., Jolly Comrade, 6 ½ x 4 ½ In. ....*illus*	600
Tip Tray, Deacon Brown Phosphates, Girl, Drinking, Red Stripe Top, 5 In.	3000
Tip Tray, Drink Moxie, Very Healthful, Script Style, Yellow Red, 6 In.	431
Tip Tray, G. Hupfel Brewing, New York City, J. Christopher Tin, 4 ½ In.	720
Tip Tray, I Just Love Moxie Don't You, Young Woman, Glass, Tin Lithograph, 6 ⅛ In. ....*illus*	288
Tip Tray, Lakeside Club Bouquet Whiskey, William Drueke Co., Grand Rapids, 4 In. ....*illus*	720
Tip Tray, Moxie, Tin, H.D. Beach Litho Co., 6 ½ In.	114
Tip Tray, Old Reliable Coffee, Dayton, Ohio, Woman, Coat, Hat, Flower Border, 4 ¼ In.	60
Tip Tray, Pin, W.B. Boyer Druggist, Woman In Sailor Suit, Round, Brass Rim, 3 ⅛ In.	90
Tip Tray, Pippins Cigar, 5 Cents, Round, Red Apple, 5 ½ In.	300
Tip Tray, Rothert & Co., York, Pa., 2 Women Lounging, 5 x 7 In. ....*illus*	173
Tip Tray, Treasure Line Stoves, D. Moore Co., Hamilton, Canada, 4 ¼ x 7 ½ In. ....*illus*	570
Tip Tray, White Rock, The World's Best Table Water, Tin, Winged Woman, 4 ⅜ In.	242
Tip Tray, Williams Ice Cream, Scranton, Pa., Take Home A Wrapped Brick, Tin, Red, 4 In.	363
Tip Tray, Wrigley's Soap, Cat Seated On Soap Bars, Round, Tin Lithograph, 3 ½ In.	374
Tobacco Cutter, Hiawatha Tobacco Works, Cast Iron, 16 ¼ In.	420
Tobacco Jar, Boch Habana, Dog Pulling Sled, Humidor, 10 In.	210
Top Hat, Smoother Than Silk, Kessler's Whiskey, Papier-Mache, Black, White, 12 In.	59
Trade Stimulator, Black Man, Top Hat, Mouth Moves, Composition, Wood, Wire, 23 In.	2950
Tray, Anheuser-Busch, Cherubs, Oval, c.1900, 17 In.	270
Tray, Arctic Ice Cream, The Cream Supreme, Polar Bear On Ice, Tin Lithograph, 13 In.	272
Tray, Bartholmay Brewing, Woman On Winged Wheel, Clouds, 12 In.	770
Tray, Cunningham's Ice Cream, Oval, Tin Lithograph, c.1910, 15 x 19 In.	570
Tray, Drink Koch's Beer, Round, Red, White, Blue, 13 In.	48
Tray, Granite City Ice Cream, It's A Food Not A Fad, Ice Cream, Tin Lithograph, 13 In.	109
Tray, Green Seal Beer, Tin, Buckeye Bottling Works Co., 12 In.	1350
Tray, Hall Co., Finest Ice Cream In Binghamton, Woman, 6 Children, Tin Lithograph, 13 In.	666
Tray, Hellman, Woman With Horse, Rectangular, Tin Lithograph, 17 ¼ x 12 In.	242
Tray, Hermes, All Cream Ice Cream, Woman, Flower In Hair, Gold Rim, Tin, Oval, 17 In.	484
Tray, Hires 5 Cents, Just What The Doctor Ordered, Soda Jerk, Tin Litho, 13 In. ....*illus*	2070
Tray, Hires, 5 Cents, Hires Are Still A Nickel A Trickle, Fountain, 13 In. Diam.	891
Tray, Hires, Man Serving Root Beer, Round, Tin, 1915, 13 In.	1020
Tray, Moxie I Like It, Woman's Face, Round, Glass, Handles, c.1915, 10 In.	1920
Tray, Moxie, Our Idol, Tin Lithograph, Mr. Moxie On Side, 11 ⅝ In.	295
Tray, Ranier Beer, From A Chinese Honeymoon With Evelyn Nesbitt, Round, c.1903, 13 In.	486
Tray, Tip, see Tip Trays in this category.	
Tray, Walker's Ice Cream, Celebrated IXL, Girl Eating, Sepia Tones, Round, 13 In.	272
Water Cooler, Allen Germ Proof, Barrel Shape, Blue & White Sponge, 29 x 22 In.	288
Window, Iroquois Brewery, Indian Chief, Reverse Paint, Glass, 21 x 31 ½ In.	4600
Windsock, Harley-Davidson, Logo, 1939, 11 In.	4400

AGATA glass was made by Joseph Locke of the New England Glass Company of Cambridge, Massachusetts, after 1885. A metallic stain was applied to New England Peachblow, which the company called Wild Rose, and the mottled design characteristic of agata appeared. There are a few known items made of opaque green with the mottled finish.

Bowl, Folded Rim, Mauve To Peach, Metallic Designs, 2 ½ x 5 ¼ In.	288
Celery Vase, Purple, Amber Stain, Bulbous, Square Mouth, New England, 6 In.	374
Creamer, Rose To Pink, Mottled Amber, Pontil, New England Glass, c.1885, 4 ½ In. ....*illus*	649
Cruet, Amber & Purple Stain, Stopper, New England, 6 ½ In. ....*illus*	1380
Cup, Lemonade, Amber & Purple Stain, Cylindrical, Loop Handle, New England, 5 In.	1380
Finger Bowl, Rose To Pink, Mottled Amber Stain, Tooled Rim, c.1880, 21 ½ x 5 ¼ In.	325
Tumbler, Glossy Finish, New England, 3 ¾ In.	115
Tumbler, Intaglio Etched Ferns, New England, 3 ½ In.	403
Vase, Lily, Trifold Rim, Purple, Amber Stain, Trumpet Shape, New England, 8 In.	403
Vase, Rose To Pink, Mottled Amber, Fluted, Pinched Tooled Rim, New England, 1800s, 4 In.	561
Vase, Satin, Free Flowing Purple Stain Cloud, Bulbous, New England, 9 In.	1438

Advertising, Tip Tray, Lakeside Club Bouquet Whiskey, William Drueke Co., Grand Rapids, 4 In.
$720

Morphy Auctions

Advertising, Tip Tray, Rothert & Co., York, Pa., 2 Women Lounging, 5 x 7 In.
$173

Wm Morford Auctions

Advertising, Tip Tray, Treasure Line Stoves, D. Moore Co., Hamilton, Canada, 4 ¼ x 7 ½ In.
$570

Morphy Auctions

Early Transistor Radios
The first American transistor radio was the Regency TR-1 made in 1954. These early transistor radios sell for about $300 to $1,000. The most expensive are red or black, ant the least expensive are ivory or gray.

Advertising, Tray, Hires 5 Cents, Just What The Doctor Ordered, Soda Jerk, Tin Litho, 13 In.
$2,070

Agata, Creamer, Rose To Pink, Mottled Amber, Pontil, New England Glass, c.1885, 4 ½ In.
$649

Agata, Cruet, Amber & Purple Stain, Stopper, New England, 6 ½ In.
$1,380

TIP

If you have a smelly tin, try filling it with fragrant peppermint tea for a few weeks. When you empty it, the tin will still smell, but like peppermint.

AKRO AGATE glass was founded in Akron, Ohio, in 1911 and moved to Clarksburg, West Virginia, in 1914. The company made marbles and toys. In the 1930s it began making other products, including vases, lamps, flowerpots, candlesticks, and children's dishes. Most of the glass is marked with a crow flying through the letter *A*. The company was sold to Clarksburg Glass Co. in 1951. Akro Agate marbles are listed in this book in the Marble category.

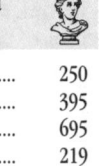

Ashtray, Ellipsoid, Green, 4 ¾ x 1 In.	12
Cup & Saucer, Stippled Band, Jade Trans Optic, c.1936	17
Cup, Concentric Ring, Apple Green, 1 ¼ In.	7
Cup, Interior Panel, Green Luster	20
Dish, Leaf Shape, Blue, Marbleized, 1930s, 4 In.	24
Flowerpot, Green, Marbleized, Concentric Ring, 2 ½ In.	10
Flowerpot, Ivory, Marbleized, Scalloped Top, 3 ½ In.	18
Planter, Jade Green, Scalloped Edge, Oval, 6 In.	35
Planter, Lilies, Footed, White, Green & Orange Streaks, 5 ½ x 2 In.	21
Planter, Royal Blue, Medium Blue, Marbleized, Rectangular, 8 In.	40
Plate, Concentric Ring, Apple Green, 3 ¼ In.	8
Powder Jar, Figural, Colonial Woman, Blue, Marbleized, 6 ¼ In.	95
Powder Jar, Figural, Colonial Woman, Light Blue Opaque	150
Saucer, Interior Panel, Green Luster, 2 ¾ In.	10
Teapot, Interior Panel, Green Luster	45
Tumbler, Paneled, Green, 1940s, 2 In., 6 Piece	30

ALABASTER is a very soft form of gypsum, a stone that resembles marble. It was often carved into vases or statues in Victorian times. There are alabaster carvings being made even today.

Bowl, Pedestal, Green, Gold, Italy, c.1940, 10 x 5 ½ In.	250
Box, Gilt Mounts, Lift Clasp, Hinged, 5 x 3 x 4 In.	395
Bust, Anne Of Cleves, Headdress, Rose, Pink Cast, Italy, Marked, c.1875, 9 ¼ In.	695
Bust, David, Marble Base, 6 ½ x 4 ½ In.	219
Bust, David, Marble, Italy, c.1920, 6 In.	219
Bust, Gypsy, Patterned Cap & Shawl, Veined Plinth, c.1900, 9 In.	246
Bust, Madonna, Pedestal, Italy, 19th Century, 13 ½ In.	1800
Bust, Musician, Female, Lyre, Signed O. Scheggia, 15 In.	885
Bust, Pensive Young Woman, Upswept Hair, Looking Down, 9 x 7 In.	119
Bust, Spanish Woman, Hair Comb, Marble Base, Italy, c.1900, 8 ¼ In.	450
Bust, Warrior, Female, Justice, Helmet, Lion's Head, Scale, Broken Column Base, 29 In.	700
Bust, Woman, Bonnet, Signed A. Bati, c.1900, 28 In.	1062
Bust, Woman, Coiled Hair, White, 18 In.	294
Bust, Woman, Curly Hair, V-Neck Dress, Round Socle, 21 In.	294
Bust, Woman, Hair Tied Back, Pedestal Base, 58 In.	313
Bust, Woman, Headband, Curly Hair, c.1895, 24 In.	500
Bust, Woman, Victorian Style Bonnet, Marble Stepped Base, 21 ½ In.	469
Chandelier, Relief Carved Shade, 4 Brass Rope Twist Rods, 36 x 17 ½ In.	826
Figurine, Boy, Headband, Sitting On Pedestal, Reading, c.1900, 17 In.	1250
Figurine, Chick, On Cracked Egg, 4 ½ In.	55
Figurine, Cupid, Standing, Playing Lute, c.1900, 21 x 14 In.	308
Figurine, Dante & Beatrice, Renaissance Style, Giuseppe Gambogi, c.1900, 24 In., Pair	1230
Figurine, Girl, Dancing, Playing Lyre, Onyx Base, c.1930, 21 In.	1140
Figurine, Girl, Folded Hands, Closed Eyes, Marble Base, Goldscheider, 1800s, 9 In.	1330
Figurine, Maiden, Standing, Green Robe, Hand Over Head, c.1900, 35 In.	780
Figurine, Maiden, With Wheat Sheaf, Putto, Swirled Base, c.1900, 28 In.	720
Figurine, Napoleon II, Standing, In Uniform, Continental, 20 ½ In.	313
Figurine, Napoleon, Standing, Winter Uniform, Continental, 23 ½ In.	1250
Figurine, Renaissance Woman, High Collar, Flower, Braids, Italy, Signed, c.1900, 38 In.	615
Figurine, Venus, Nude, Holding Apple, Leaning Against Tree Stump, 1900s, 35 In.	960
Figurine, Woman, With Sickle, Basket Of Wheat, c.1900, 25 In.	369
Font, Cross Shape, Enamel, Flowers, 19th Century, 7 x 4 In.	251
Jar, Egg Shape, Square Handles, Round Foot, Lid, Ball Finial, c.1900, 14 x 6 In.	96
Lamp, Birds, Round Etched Globe, Pull Chain, c.1940, 12 ½ x 7 x 4 In.	399
Lamp, Electric, Carved, Seated Woman, Pillar, Italy, c.1910, 18 x 9 In.	270
Lamp, Electric, Figural, Carved, Woman, Light Post, Continental, c.1890, 31 x 9 In. *illus*	956
Obelisk, On Pedestal, Italy, 20th Century, 15 ⅜ In., Pair	150
Pedestal, Octagonal Top & Base, Stepped, Italy, c.1870, 29 In., 4 Piece	1650
Pendant Planter, Bas Relief Putti Handles, c.1900, 16 ½ x 17 ¼ x 8 ¾ In.	1722
Sculpture, Beatrice, Standing, Reading, Long Dress, Stepped Base, c.1900, 23 In.	1180

Sculpture, Boy, Writing In Book, Italy, 1900s, 17 In.	2350
Sculpture, Head, Roman Emperor, Nerva, Vespasian, Cylindrical Marble Base, 10 In., Pair	2629
Sculpture, Neoclassical Woman, Carrying Urn On Shoulder, Italy, c.1900, 18 ½ In.	390
Sculpture, Thinker Style, Marble Base, Italy, 1900s, 11 In.	295
Sculpture, Venus, Entering Bath, Nude, Italy, c.1890, 29 ½ In.	4720
Trinket Box, Flowers, Gemstones, Hinged, Italy, 3 x 1 ½ In.	46
Urn, Black Plinth, 12 x 9 In.	145

ALUMINUM was more expensive than gold or silver until the 1850s. Chemists learned how to refine bauxite to get aluminum. Jewelry and other small objects were made of the valuable metal until 1914, when an inexpensive smelting process was invented. The aluminum collected today dates from the 1930s through the 1950s. Hand-hammered pieces are the most popular.

Airplane, Model, Art Deco Style, Chrome Metal Base, 15 x 26 In.	3125
Cocktail Set, Tray, Shaker, 6 Cups, Plastic, Chrome Trim, Wood Handles, Faberware	563
Hat Rack, Stetson Hats, Mounted On Wood Frame, 30 x 8 In.	371
Panel, Wall, Radiating, Brushed, Ebonized Particle Board, Signed O. Ciullini, 1975, 24 x 5 In.	1125
Planter, Shell Form, Reeded Support, Square Base, 2 Scroll Handles, 13 x 20 In., Pair	296
Scissors, c.1960, 35 ½ In.	273
Sculpture, Alligator, Brushed Finish, Signed Donald Drumm, 1997, 14 ½ x 55 ½ In.	1375
Sculpture, Checkpoint, Signed Menashe Kadishman, Israel, 1972, 7 x 16 In.	2000
Sculpture, Free-Form, Mounted On Marble Plinth, 14 ½ In.	295
Sculpture, Seuil Configuration, Brushed, Abstract Cutout, J. Arp, 1966, 7 In.	1875
Stool, Lattice Back & Seat, Curled Arms, Swivel, 48 x 21 x 19 In., Pair	43
Whirligig, Policeman, Blue, White Paint, Wood Stand, c.1920, 7 ½ In.	246

AMBER, *see Jewelry category.*

AMBER GLASS is the name of any glassware with the proper yellow-brown shading. It was a popular color just after the Civil War and many pressed glass pieces were made of amber glass. Depression glass of the 1930s–50s was also made in shades of amber glass. Other pieces may be found in the Depression Glass, Pressed Glass, and other glass categories. All types are being reproduced.

Figurine, Turtle, Clear Body, Amber Shell, Etched, 2 x 6 In.	288
Ornament, Enclosed Beetle, Egg Shape, Round Stand, 2 ½ x 1 ½ In.	357
Shade, Hurricane, Shaded, Swollen Center, Rolled Rims, 18 x 6 ½ In., Pair	922
Urn, Dome Lid, Finial, Diamond Pattern, Tapered, Square Base, 1800s, 16 In., Pair	1708

AMBERINA, a two-toned glassware, was originally made from 1883 to about 1900. It was patented by Joseph Locke of the New England Glass Company, but was also made by other companies and is still being made. The glass shades from red to amber. Similar pieces of glass may be found in the Baccarat, Libbey, Plated Amberina, and other categories. Glass shaded from blue to amber is called *Blue Amberina* or *Bluerina.*

Berry Bowl, Master, Daisy & Button, Canoe Shape, Hobbs, Brockunier, 10 In.	86
Butter, Coin Spot Cover, Hobbs, Brockunier, 6 ¾ In.	115
Candlestick, Block & Star, Triangle Base, c.1950, 5 In., Pair	50
Carafe, Bottle Shape, Optic Diamond, Amber Rigaree Bands, Side Prints, 8 ½ In.	460
Carafe, Water, Bulbous, Optic Diamond, 6 Dimples, Rigaree Collar, New England, 9 In.	201
Celery Vase, Blown, New England Glass Co., c.1886, 6 ¼ In.	2950
Clock, Daisy & Button, Pressed, Hobbs, Brockunier, 7 In. ......*illus*	230
Cruet, Inverted Thumbprint, Faceted Stopper, Amber, 6 ¾ In.	290
Decanter, Acanthus Leaf, Flower Dollop Optic, Amber Faceted Stopper, 12 In.	288
Lampshade, Open Lattice, 5 In.	115
Lemonade Set, Swirl Molded, Signed, Baccarat, c.1900, 9 ¾-In. Pitcher, 10 5-In. Glasses	615
Pitcher, Coin Spot, Cranberry Rim, 6 ¼ In.	115
Pitcher, Inverted Thumbprint, Tricornered Spout, Amber Ribbed Handle, 8 ½ In.	89
Pitcher, Water, Spiral Rib, Spot Optic, Reeded Handle, c.1890, 8 ½ In.	184
Sugar, Squat, Ruffled Rim, Applied Finger Handles, 3 In.	1121
Syrup, Reverse Coinspot, Silver Plate Flip Lid, Handle, 5 ½ In.	460
Toothpick Holder, Hobbs, Daisy & Button, c.1885, 2 ⅞ In.	127
Toothpick Holder, Venetian Diamond, Fuchsia To Yellow, c.1885, 2 ½ In.	104 to 115
Vase, Lily, Opalescent Amber Shaded To Purple, Trumpet Shape, Footed, Trifold Rim, 7 In.	4025
Vase, Lily, Optic Ribbed, Trifold Rim, Ruby Foot Wrap, 12 In.	460
Vase, Optic Ribbed, Trumpet Shape, Jack-In-The-Pulpit Rim, Rigaree Waist, 7 ½ In.	144
Vase, Squat, Trumpet Shape, Ruffled Rim, Amber To Red, c.1880, 5 In. Diam.	72
Vase, Stork In Reeds, Pressed, Hobbs, Brockunier, 4 ½ In. ......*illus*	920

Alabaster, Lamp, Electric, Figural, Carved, Woman, Light Post, Continental, c.1890, 31 x 9 In.
$956

Neal Auction Co.

Amberina, Clock, Daisy & Button, Pressed, Hobbs, Brockunier, 7 In.
$230

Early Auction Co.

Amberina, Vase, Stork In Reeds, Pressed, Hobbs, Brockunier, 4 ½ In.
$920

Early Auction Co.

25

Amethyst Glass, Bowl, Ormolu, Leaves, Grapevines Pedestal, Continental, 1800s, 14 In. $1,046

Cowan's Auctions

Amethyst Glass, Vase, Turned Out Rim, Rings, Polished Interior, Matte Exterior, 6 In. $24

Clars Auction Gallery

Animal Trophy, Black Bear, Standing On Hind Legs, America, 1900s, 47 In. $450

Garth's Auctioneers & Appraisers

Water Bottle, Daisy & Button, Pressed, Faceted Neck, 9 ½ In.	4370
Water Set, Diamond Optic, 9-In. Tankard, 7 Piece	378

AMERICAN DINNERWARE, see Dinnerware.

AMERICAN ENCAUSTIC TILING COMPANY was founded in Zanesville, Ohio, in 1875. The company planned to make a variety of tiles to compete with the English tiles that were selling in the United States for use in fireplaces and other architectural designs. The first glazed tiles were made in 1880, embossed tiles in 1881, faience tiles in the 1920s. The firm closed in 1935 and reopened in 1937 as the Shawnee Pottery.

Figurine, Seminude, Kneeling, Bowl On Shoulder, 12 In.	75
Fireplace Surround, Relief Busts, Napoleon, Josephine, Deep Red, 12 Tiles, 6 In.	237
Tile, Man, Profile, Mustache, Beard, Ribboned Collar Shirt, Green Glaze, 6 x 6 In.	95
Tile, Nude Woman, Kneeling, Squeezebag Decorated, 9 In.	1000
Tile, Portrait, Man, Stern Look, Green Glaze, c.1900, 6 x 6 In.	89
Tile, Portrait, Old Man, Sad Look, Green Glaze, c.1900, 6 x 6 In.	89
Tile, Woman, Profile, Bonnet, Green Glaze, c.1900, 6 x 6 In.	125
Trivet, Flower, Yellow, Blue, 7 In. Diam.	55

AMETHYST GLASS is any of the many glasswares made in the dark purple color of the gemstone amethyst. Included in this category are many pieces made in the nineteenth and twentieth centuries. Very dark pieces are called *black amethyst* and are listed under that heading.

Bowl, Ormolu, Leaves, Grapevines Pedestal, Continental, 1800s, 14 In.	*illus*	1046
Pitcher, Water, Shaded To Clear, Gold Lyre, Flowers, Lobed, Ruffled, 9 In.		35
Salt, Flared Sides, Flattened Foot, Pontil, 2 ¼ In.		345
Vase, Brass Band, Tapered Cylinder, Signed, 13 ¾ In.		840
Vase, Tulip Shape, Petal Rim, Footed, New England, c.1860, 10 In.		1560
Vase, Turned Out Rim, Rings, Polished Interior, Matte Exterior, 6 In.	*illus*	24

AMPHORA pieces are listed in the Teplitz category.

ANDIRONS and related fireplace items are included in the Fireplace category.

ANIMAL TROPHIES, such as stuffed animals, rugs made of animal skins, and other similar collectibles made from animal, fish, or bird parts, are listed in this category. Collectors should be aware of the endangered species laws that make it illegal to buy and sell some of these items. Any eagle feathers, many types of pelts or rugs (such as leopard), ivory, and many forms of tortoiseshell can be confiscated by the government. Related trophies may be found in the Fishing category. Ivory items may be found in the Scrimshaw or Ivory categories.

American Bison, Shoulder Mount, Custom Wood Stand, 1900s, 80 In.		1800
Bison, Half Shoulder Mount, 38 x 43 In.		2160
Black Bear, Head Mount, 1900s		360
Black Bear, Standing On Hind Legs, America, 1900s, 47 In.	*illus*	450
Boar, Standing, Full Body, Landscaped Mount, Wheels, Russia, 1900s, 60 In.	*illus*	300
Cedar Waxwing Group, Taxidermy, Shadowbox, Molded, Gilt Frame, Round, c.1890, 29 In.		510
Coyote, Table Top Mount, 1900s, 21 In.		240
Elk, Brown, 60 x 36 In.		319
Elk, Full Shoulder Mount, 26 In.		1020
Moose, 45-In. Rack		390
Ring-Necked Pheasant, In Flight, 1900s		62
Rug, Zebra, Mane, Tail, Stitch Down Ears, Hide, Burchell, 111 x 67 In.		800
Squirrels, Boxing, Glass, Wood, William Hart, c.1850s, 15 x 19 In., 4 Piece	*illus*	22420
Swordfish, Bill, Ends Mounted With Brass Bands, 38 ¾ In.		118
Tiger, Skull, Smoking Set, Silver, Applied Insets, Siam, 10 x 13 In.		1298
Zebra, Shoulder Mount, Wood Pedestal, Africa, c.1975, 37 x 19 In.	*illus*	861

ANIMATION ART collectibles include cels that are painted drawings on celluloid needed to make animated cartoons shown in movie theaters or on TV. Hundreds of cels were made, then photographed in sequence to make a cartoon showing moving figures. Early examples made by the Walt Disney Studios are popular with collectors today. Original sketches used by the artists are also listed here. Modern animated cartoons are made using computer-generated pictures. Some of these are being produced as cels to be sold to collectors. Other cartoon art is listed in Comic Art and Disneyana.

Cel, 3 Little Pigs, Practical Pig, Disney, 1937, 8 ½ x 13 In.	2607

Cel, Adventures Of Raggedy Ann, Andy, Bear, Dog, CBS, Frame, 12 x 15 In.	60
Cel, Alice In Wonderland, White Rabbit, Running, Double Mat, Frame, 13 x 14 ½ In.	443
Cel, Condorman, 9 ½ x 13 ¼ In.	71
Cel, Donald Duck In Mathmagic Land, Gouache On Celluloid, Disney, 1959, 15 x 16 In.	375
Cel, Donald Duck, Jiminy Cricket, Caveman, Mat, 11 x 13 In. *illus*	173
Cel, Donald's Penguin, Donald Duck, Gun, Penguin, Gouache, Disney, 1938, 8 In.	1000
Cel, Figaro & Frankie, Minnie Mouse, Disney, 1947	1625
Cel, How The Grinch Stole Christmas, Chuck Jones, Mat, Frame, 1966, 18 x 20 In. *illus*	1150
Cel, How The Grinch Stole Christmas, Dr. Seuss, Chuck Jones, Frame, 1966, 16 x 19 In. *illus*	1970
Cel, Jetsons, George, Jane, Elroy, Astro, Color Ground, Mat, Frame, 1960s, 12 ¼ x 15 ¾ In.	230
Cel, Jiminy Cricket, Butterfly, Courvoisier Galleries Frame, c.1939, 3 x 3 ½ In.	1150
Cel, Jungle Book, Mowgli, Balancing Jug On Head, Frame, 1967, 13 x 15 ½ In.	316
Cel, Lucy, It's Your First Kiss, Charlie Brown, Schultz, Bill Melendez Studios, 10 x 12 In.	600
Cel, Ludwig Von Drake, Navy Uniform, Frame, 1964, 7 ⅞ x 9 ⅞ In. *illus*	154
Cel, Minnie Loves Mickey, Mickey's Surprise Party, Serigraph, Mat, Frame, 9 ¼ x 13 In.	138
Cel, Mulan, Disney, 1998, 13 x 19 In.	687
Cel, Peter Pan, Hook's Ship Color Background, Mat, Frame, 1953, 17 x 21 In.	4025
Cel, Pink Panther, Background, Walking Behind Little Man, Frame, 1960s, 14 x 17 ¾ In.	291
Cel, Snow White, Disney, Signed, 5 ½ In.	2415
Drawing, 1 Little Pig, Initialed SW, 8 x 11 In.	58
Original Concept Art, Fantasia, Waltz Of The Flowers, Pastels, Elmer Plummer, 10 x 12 In.	575
Production Drawing, Mickey Mouse, Steamboat Willie, Ub Iwerks, Pencil, 1928, 4 ½ In.	4668
Production Drawing, Pinocchio, Figaro, Lead & Color Pencil, Mat, 7 ¾ x 9 ¼ In.	261
Production Drawing, Popeye, Olive Oyl, Dizzy Drivers, Pencil, 1935, 8 ⅜ x 11 In.	228
Production Drawing, Snow White & Seven Dwarfs, Doc, Bashful, Lead, Red Pencil, 10 x 12 In.	261
Sericel, Taz, Tazmanian Devil, Authentication Seal, Frame, 14 ¼ x 11 ¼ In.	115

ANNA POTTERY was started in Anna, Illinois, in 1859 by Cornwall and Wallace *Anna Pottery* Kirkpatrick. They made many types of utilitarian wares, bricks, drain tiles, and giftware. The most collectible pieces made by the pottery are the pig-shaped bottles and jugs with special inscriptions, applied animals, and figures. The pottery closed in 1894.

Bottle, Pig, Incised Maps, Mississippi, Railroad Stops, Kirkpatrick, 3 x 6 ¾ In.	8125
Flask, Incised Route To California, Applied Ears, 3 ¾ x 7 ¼ In.	2990
Flask, Pig, Incised Midwest Landmarks, Original Package, Signed, 1891, 7 In.	7475
Flask, Pig, Railroad, River Guide, 1888, 7 ½ In.	6518
Inkwell, Frog, On Bust-Of-Man Reservoir, Incised Blue Marks, 1884, 4 In.	10073
Inkwell, Frog, On Clamshell, Kirkpatrick, 1880s, 3 ½ x 3 ⅝ In. *illus*	5520
Jug, Etched Little Brown Jug Letters, Snake Handles, 1876, 5 ½ x 4 ½ In.	4945
Jug, Glazed, Little Brown Jug, Incised, W.A. Arms, Signed, 1877, 5 ¼ x 4 In.	1000
Paperweight, Frog, Green, Cold Painted, Incised Base, Signed, 1887, 3 In.	1093

APPLE PEELERS *are listed in the Kitchen category under Peeler, Apple.*

ARABIA began producing ceramics in 1874. The pottery was established in Helsinki, Finland, by Rörstrand, a Swedish pottery that wanted to export porcelain, earthenware, and other pottery from Finland to Russia. Most of the early workers at Arabia were Swedish. Arabia started producing its own models of tiled stoves, vases, and tableware c.1900. Rörstrand sold its interest in Arabia in 1916. By the late 1930s, Arabia was the largest producer of porcelain in Europe. Most of its products were exported. A line of stoneware was introduced in the 1960s. Arabia worked in cooperation with Rörstrand from 1975 to 1977. Arabia was bought by Hackman Group in 1990 and Hackman was bought by Iittala Group in 2004. Arabia is now a brand owned by Iittala Group.

ARABIA FINLAND

Coffeepot, Ruija, 8 ½ In.	50
Pitcher, Bull, Green, 6 ½ In.	65
Plate, Dinner, Finn Flower Blue, 10 ¼ In.	25
Plate, Scandinavian Scene, Square, 7 ⅞ In.	50
Platter, Finn Flower Blue, Blue & White, Oval, 16 In.	65
Platter, Rosmarin, Brown, 1960s, 13 In.	70

ARC-EN-CIEL is the French word for rainbow. A pottery factory named Arc-en-ciel was founded in Zanesville, Ohio, in 1903. The company made art pottery for a short time, then became the Brighton Pottery in 1905.

ARC-EN-CIEL POTTERY

Vase, Leaves At Rim, Swirling Stems, Gold Luster, Purple Highlights, Impressed, 6 ½ In. *illus*	58

Animal Trophy, Boar, Standing, Full Body, Landscaped Mount, Wheels, Russia, 1900s, 60 In.
$300

Garth's Auctioneers & Appraisers

Animal Trophy, Squirrels, Boxing, Glass, Wood, William Hart, c.1850s, 15 x 19 In., 4 Piece
$22,420

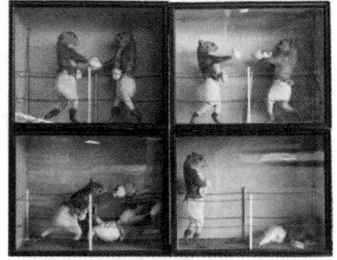

Rachel Davis Fine Arts

Animal Trophy, Zebra, Shoulder Mount, Wood Pedestal, Africa, c.1975, 37 x 19 In.
$861

Garth's Auctioneers & Appraisers

TIP
Do not clean a mounted animal that has fur. It could become bald.

A

Animation Art, Cel, Donald Duck, Jiminy Cricket, Caveman, Mat, 11 x 13 In. $173

Hake's Americana & Collectibles

Animation Art, Cel, How The Grinch Stole Christmas, Chuck Jones, Mat, Frame, 1966, 18 x 20 In. $1,150

Hake's Americana & Collectibles

Animation Art, Cel, How The Grinch Stole Christmas, Dr. Seuss, Chuck Jones, Frame, 1966, 16 x 19 In. $1,970

Hake's Americana & Collectibles

Animation Art, Cel, Ludwig Von Drake, Navy Uniform, Frame, 1964, 7 ⅞ x 9 ⅞ In. $154

Hake's Americana & Collectibles

ARCHITECTURAL antiques include a variety of collectibles, usually very large, that have been removed from buildings. Hardware, backbars, doors, paneling, and even old bathtubs are now wanted by collectors. Pieces of the Victorian, Art Nouveau, and Art Deco styles are in greatest demand.

Backbar, Wood, 4 Columns, Cast Iron Trim, Applied Detail, Mirrors, Marble, 150 x 117 In.	18000
Bank Teller Booth, Quarter Sawn Oak, Iron, Etched Glass Window, 136 x 85 x 56 In.	12000
Bathtub, Victorian, Iron, Cast Legs, Floral Detail, Wood Rail Rim, Oval, 27 x 60 In.	201
Bell Push, Door, Silver, Enamel, c.1950, 3 ¾ In.	1375
Bracket, Bronze, Flowers, Scrolls, c.1910, 14 ½ x 18 In., Pair	344
Bracket, Carved, White Paint, Gold Trim, c.1905, 38 x 13 In., Pair	104
Bracket, Georgian Rococo, Giltwood, Pierced, Scrolled, 16 ¾ In.	1680
Bracket, Giltwood, Carved Ribbons, Ferns, Flowers, c.1865, 15 x 16 In., Pair	4375
Bracket, Wall, Eagle, On Fruit, Carved, Gilded, c.1850, 19 In.	500
Bracket, Wall, Gilt, Serpentine, Plume Carved, Continental, c.1780, 15 In.	563
Bracket, Wood, Carved Scrolls, Gilt, White Ground, c.1900, 12 x 33 In.	184
Column, Ionic, Copper, Applied Verdigris, c.1900, 40 ½ In., 4 Piece	1024
Cornice, Galvanized Tin, Scrolled Bracket, Iowa Plaque, c.1890, 23 x 37 In.	2750
Crest, Coat-Of-Arms, Griffins, Walnut, Carved, Painted, 50 In.	3600
Door Grille, Wrought & Gilt Iron, Enamel, Scrolled Medallions, 54 x 17 In., Pair	1188
Door Handle, Wrought Iron, 14 In.	207
Door Hardware, Bronze, Monogram, Marked Massachusetts Motto, 1900s	288
Door Panel, Arched, Gilt, Painted, Molded Cherubs, Scroll, 1800s, 56 x 26 In., Pair	2988
Door Panel, Pine, Carved, Music Trophee, Molded Arch Frame, 86 x 40 In., Pair	4183
Door, Carved Panel, Elderly Couple, Painted, Continental, c.1900, 36 x 27 In., Pair	374
Door, Casing, Mixed Wood, 4 Panels, Blue Paint, Arched Cornice, White Paint, 95 x 50 In.	360
Door, Hardwood, Brass Inlay, Leaves, Flowers, Ring Handle, 90 x 27 In., Pair	1375
Door, Oak, Window Panel, Leaded, Beveled Glass, Jewels, 87 x 47 In.	4500
Door, Painted, Girl, Taking Bow, Stage Curtains, Signed E. Welch, 1934, 77 x 30 In.	510
Door, Pine, Red Grain Paint, Iron Latch, Pa., 1800s, 76 ¾ x 33 ½ In.	326
Door, Relief Carved, Krishna, Radha, Moldings, Rosehead Nails, c.1800, 77 x 34 In.	590
Door, Rococo Style, Oak, Carved Leaves, Scrolling, Limed, 123 x 27 In., Pair	1000
Door, Swinging, Walnut, Paneled, Etched Glass, 52 x 44 In., Pair	912
Door, Walnut, Carved Panels, Iron Hardware, Spain, c.1780, 78 x 25 In., Pair	118
Doorknob, Double Handled, Cut Glass, Crosscut Diamond, Brass, Steel Fittings, 8 In.	118
Doorknocker, Birdhouse Scene, Painted, Embossed, Marked, 4 In. *illus*	177
Doorknocker, Brass, Federal, Eagle, Shield, Bail Handle, 1800, 7 ½ In.	594
Doorknocker, Bronze, Mermaids, Dolphins, Clam Shape Wood Plaque, c.1865, 20 x 15 In.	1125
Doorknocker, Bronze, Woman, Horseshoe, c.1900, 4 x 9 x 8 In.	937
Doorknocker, Bunch Of Grapes On Vine, Purple, Gold Accents, 3 ½ In.	443
Doorknocker, Iron, Flowers In Vase, Pastel Colors, Yellow Ribbon, Cast, 4 In.	148
Doorknocker, Iron, Girl On Rope Swing, Hanging From Leafy Branch, Hubley, 3 ½ In.	148
Doorknocker, Iron, Ivy In Yellow Vase, Hubley, 4 ½ In.	177
Doorknocker, Iron, Pear, Flower Surround, 3 ½ In.	89
Doorknocker, Iron, Zinnias, Blue, Gold Trim, 3 ¾ In.	89
Doorknocker, Metal, Figural, Reclining Nude, P. Burnett, 1900s, 9 In., Pair	390
Element, Temple, Carved Stone, Standing Goddess, Animal Figures, India, 25 x 19 In.	2337
Element, Wood, Classical Figures, Carved, Arched, c.1865, 33 x 29 In.	345
Elevator Panel, Prairie Design, Iron, Chicago, W. Jenney, 1891, 13 x 79 In.	2125
Elevator Panel, Scrolled Prairie Design, Cast Iron, Chicago, W.L. Jenney, 12 x 79 In.	2100
Fan, Wood, Gray Paint, c.1860, 35 x 18 ½ In.	345
Finial, Building Shape, 2 Spires, Copper, Verdigris, c.1920, 19 x 13 In., 3 Piece	1020
Finial, Carved, Scrolled, Painted, c.1920, 35 x 24 In.	230
Finial, Copper, Pineapple Shape, Scroll Leaves, Dome Base, c.1885, 18 x 13 In.	3240
Finial, Copper, Scrolled Arms, Leaves, Verdigris, c.1880, 37 In.	1250
Finial, Gate Post, Eagle, Spread Wings, Black Paint, Cast Iron, 22 x 50 In., Pair	1180
Finial, Pineapple, Pine, Carved, White Paint, c.1910, 22 In.	470
Finial, Urn Shape, Copper, 55 In.	1080
Fireboard, 2 Panels, Applied Leaves, Carved, Green, Red Paint, 34 x 36 In.	780
Fireboard, Pine, Brick Fireplace Painted, c.1850, 31 x 31 In.	1920
Fireplace Surround, Carrara Marble, Louis XV Style, Carved, c.1890, 42 x 63 In. *illus*	5904
Fireplace Surround, Classical, Marble, Palmettes, Dentil Molding, 55 x 72 In.	2337
Fireplace Surround, Gray Marble, Scroll Carved, 43 x 56 In.	2000
Frieze, Figures Dancing, Plaster, Clement Barnhorn, 1901, 28 x 85 In. *illus*	360
Gate Post, Iron, Ball Finial, 44 In.	460
Gate, Drive, Cast Iron, Fleur-De-Lis Pickets, Post Ends, Cone Finials, 76 x 140 In., Pair	1355

Gate, Garden, Wood, Slated, Turned, Carved, 47 x 48 In.	144
Gate, Iron, Flower, Scroll Borders, 93 x 126 In.	2057
Gate, Iron, French Style, Scrolls, Leaves, Black Paint, 93 x 26 In., Pair	2000
Gate, Iron, Scroll Crest, Hinged Door, Paint, Gilt, 1800s, 146 x 56 In.	2280
Gate, Pine, 2 Doors, Star Carved Crest, Circle Opening, White Paint, c.1905, 87 x 62 In.	510
Gate, Steel, Iron, Arched, Scrolls, Handles & Latches, 1900s, 99 In., Pair	598
Hinge, Iron, Tulip Style, 15 ¼ In., Pair	295
Lion's Head, Roaring, Copper, Patina, c.1900, 19 x 15 In., Pair ......*illus*	1230
Lion's Head, Copper, Attaches To Downspout, Wood Base, c.1910, 15 In. ......*illus*	150
Lions, Paws In Front, Zinc, Signed, J.W. Fiske, 15 x 26 x 9 In., Pair ......*illus*	1380
Louver, ½ Round, Wood, Painted White, 19th Century, 50 x 66 In.	23
Mailbox, Arts & Crafts, Copper, Repousse Designs, Slant Lid, c.1920, 7 x 10 In.	450
Mailbox, House Shape, Iron, J.W. Fiske, N.Y., 1877, 17 In.	425
Mantel Cornice, Swag, Circle Carved, Painted, c.1850, 9 ½ x 60 In.	246
Mantel, Arched, Scalloped Top, Blue & White Paint, 1800s, 49 x 50 In.	264
Mantel, Federal, Blue Paint, c.1850, 45 ½ x 50 In.	415
Mantel, Federal, Mixed Wood, Carved Sunbursts, Columns, Painted White, 61 x 82 In.	1560
Mantel, Federal, Pine, Carved, c.1805, 54 x 68 In.	504
Mantel, Federal, Pine, Paint, Virginia, c.1815, 61 x 66 In.	711
Mantel, Federal, Pine, Paint, Virginia, c.1815, 55 x 67 In.	444
Mantel, Fireplace, Walnut, Carved, Atlas Figures, Mythological Beasts, 69 x 82 In. ......*illus*	8700
Mantel, Gray Milk Paint, Picture Frame Molding, Maryland, c.1800, 52 x 62 ½ In.	115
Mantel, Paneled, Blue Paint, New England, 60 x 65 In.	360
Mantel, Pine, Plaster, Carved, c.1800, 50 x 65 In.	504
Mantel, Softwood, Whitewash, c.1850, 50 x 73 In.	125
Mantel, Walnut, Paneled Design, Block Columns, 1800s, 54 x 57 In.	235
Mantel, Wood, Flowers, Basket, Fruit, Faux Paint, Red Marble, c.1850, 40 x 45 In.	354
Mask, Lion's Head, Zinc, 33 x 26 ½ In.	1265
Mask, Lion's Head, Zinc, c.1900, 12 ½ x 12 ½ In., Pair	403
Model, Barn, Post & Beam Frame, Early 20th Century, 15 ½ x 24 ½ In.	270
Model, Neuschwanstein Castle, Die Cut Paper Litho, Glass Dome, Victorian, 50 x 22 In.	1920
Model, Staircase, Double Spiral, Mahogany, Carved, c.1890, 21 ½ x 12 In. ......*illus*	5900
Ornament, Grotesque Mask, Leaves, Earthenware, 48 x 15 In.	69
Overmantel Mirror, Classical, Giltwood, Carved, Molded Cornice, c.1810, 24 x 63 In. ......*illus*	270
Overmantel Mirror, Federal, Giltwood, Eglomise Panel, c.1810, 28 x 43 In. ......*illus*	625
Overmantel Mirror, George II, Walnut, Gilt, Divided Plate, 2 Glass Candle Arms, 20 x 60 In.	2000
Overmantel Mirror, Giltwood, Eglomise Panels, Gilt Ribbons, Musical Trophies, 41 x 68 In.	1920
Overmantel Mirror, Giltwood, Eglomise, Columns, 3 Panes, 24 x 49 In.	2000
Overmantel Mirror, Giltwood, Ogee Frame, 3 Divided Panels, c.1875, 24 x 58 In.	293
Overmantel Mirror, Neoclassical, Painted, Electric Brass Wall Sconces, 1800s, 61 x 52 In.	120
Panel, Black Glass, Art Deco Revival, Bird, Flower Etched, D. Abbe, c.1990, 50 x 47 In.	1625
Panel, Carved Women's Faces, Glazed Stoneware, Gres De Bogot, c.1900, 11 ½ x 20 In.	5000
Panel, Overdoor, Neoclassical Style, Oil On Wood, Monkey, Xylophone, 1800s, 14 x 41 In.	1722
Panel, Rococo, Parcel Gilt, Chinoiserie, Painted, 19 x 29 In.	420
Panel, Victorian, Oak, Carved Leaves, Scrolls, Woman's Head, 55 x 17 In.	104
Panel, Wall, Carved, Red Paint, Chinese, c.1900, 36 x 17 In.	177
Panel, Wood, Painted, Arched Frame, Hindu Vignettes, Multicolor, 72 x 36 In.	1195
Panel, Zinc, Fan Shape, Arched Pine Frame, Gray Paint, c.1900, 22 x 40 In.	529
Pediment, Applied Moldings, c.1950, 16 x 55 In.	345
Pediment, Zinc Sheet, Acanthus Leaves, Pine Frame, Dentil Molding, 1800s, 51 x 100 In.	235
Plaque, Eagle, Terra-Cotta, 17 x 16 In.	173
Plaque, Giltwood, Carved Putti Heads, Leaves, 43 x 20 In.	316
Plaque, Giltwood, Carved Scrolls, Leaves, c.1850, 55 x 15 In.	230
Plaque, Giltwood, Carved Swags, Leaves, Instruments Of War, France, c.1820, 27 In.	738
Plaque, Giltwood, Scrolls, Continental, c.1800, 50 x 13 In.	414
Plaque, Running Nude, Plaster, Caproni, Boston, 29 x 20 In.	690
Plaque, Shield, Lions Fighting, French Text, Cast Iron, c.1850, 33 x 31 In.	510
Plaque, Wood, Carved Mary, Jesus, Cherubs, c.1850, 17 x 27 In.	518
Post Office, Oak, Boxes, Cupboards, 2 Windows, Florence, Mont., c.1895, 139 x 81 In.	9600
Post Office, Teller Station, Oak, Yale & Towne, Stamford, Conn., 45 x 34 In.	826
Railing, Geometric Design, Wrought Iron, 117 x 54 In.	4100
Santa Door, Wood, Painted, Mud, Jimmy Lee Sudduth, c.1988, 24 x 80 In.	360
Screens are also listed in the Fireplace and Furniture categories.	
Scupper, Dragon's Head, Metal, Waterspout Mouth, 1900s, 14 In. ......*illus*	180
Silo, Pine, Red Paint, Salesman's Sample, 25 In.	1007
Spire, Sheet Metal, Urn Shape, Petals, Sphere, Crossed Arrows, 1800s, 103 In. ......*illus*	840

Anna Pottery, Inkwell, Frog, On Clamshell, Kirkpatrick, 1880s, 3 ½ x 3 ⅝ In.
$5,520

Crocker Farm, Inc.

Arc-En-Ciel, Vase, Leaves At Rim, Swirling Stems, Gold Luster, Purple Highlights, Impressed, 6 ½ In.
$58

Humler & Nolan

Architectural, Doorknocker, Birdhouse Scene, Painted, Embossed, Marked, 4 In.
$177

Bertoia Auctions

Architectural, Fireplace Surround, Carrara Marble, Louis XV Style, Carved, c.1890, 42 x 63 In.
$5,904

New Orleans Auction Galleries, Inc.

Architectural, Frieze, Figures Dancing, Plaster, Clement Barnhorn, 1901, 28 x 85 In.
$360

Cowan's Auctions

Architectural, Lion's Head, Roaring, Copper, Patina, c.1900, 19 x 15 In., Pair
$1,230

New Orleans Auction Galleries, Inc.

Architectural, Lion's Head, Copper, Attaches To Downspout, Wood Base, c.1910, 15 In.
$150

Garth's Auctioneers & Appraisers

Architectural, Lions, Paws In Front, Zinc, Signed, J.W. Fiske, 15 x 26 x 9 In., Pair
$1,380

Cottone Auctions

Architectural, Mantel, Fireplace, Walnut, Carved, Atlas Figures, Mythological Beasts, 69 x 82 In.
$8,700

Gray's Auctioneers LLC

Architectural, Model, Staircase, Double Spiral, Mahogany, Carved, c.1890, 21 ½ x 12 In.
$5,900

Brunk Auctions

Architectural, Overmantel Mirror, Classical, Giltwood, Carved, Molded Cornice, c.1810, 24 x 63 In.
$270

Cowan's Auctionss

Architectural, Overmantel Mirror, Federal, Giltwood, Eglomise Panel, c.1810, 28 x 43 In.
$625

Leslie Hindman Auctioneers

TIP

It pays to get to know dealers. If you discuss what you collect, the dealer will try to find something for you. Many dealers travel to the same shows every year and bring things for returning customers.

Stair Baluster, Curved, Iron, Board Of Trade Bldg., Burnham & Root, 1888, 15 x 27 In.	813
Tabernacle, Wrought Iron, Scrolling Design, Arch, 32 x 16 In.	299
Teller Cage Front, Casino, Brass, 2 Sections, 19 x 31 In.	456
Ticket Booth, Train Depot, Marble Top, Iron Cage, 67 x 69 x 24 In.	2700
Window Shade, Hudson River Scenes, Tents, Military, 51 x 33 In., Pair	1440

AREQUIPA POTTERY was produced from 1911 to 1918 by the patients of the Arequipa Sanatorium in Marin County, north of San Francisco. The patients were trained by Frederick Hurten Rhead, who had worked at the Roseville Pottery.

Vase, Arts & Crafts, Pair Of Roses, Green Matte Glaze, 3 ½ In.	531
Vase, California Landscape, Carved, Glazed, Incised, 1911-13, 4 ½ x 3 ¾ In.	3125
Vase, Green Matte Glaze, 2-Tone Geometric Designs, Squeezebag, Signed, 4 x 7 ¼ In.	10000
Vase, Heart Shape Leaves, Squeezebag, Gray Purple Ground, F. Rhead, 7 x 4 In.	3750
Vase, Landscape, Carved, Brown Glaze, Bulbous, c.1911, 4 ½ x 3 ¾ In.	3125
Vase, Oval, Brown Matte Glaze, c.1915, 7 ½ x 4 In.	406
Vase, Squat, Green Matte Glaze, Signed, 1912, 3 x 7 In. ....*illus*	1000
Vase, Tapered, Applied Shoulder Design, Green Multitone Matte Glaze, 3 ½ x 6 In.	11875
Vase, Wreath Of Leaves, Squeezebag, Green Feathered Ground, Oval, c.1911, 8 x 5 In.	11250

ARGY-ROUSSEAU, *see G. Argy-Rousseau category.*

ARITA is a port in Japan. Porcelain was made there from about 1616. Many types of decorations were used, including the popular Imari designs, which are listed under Imari in this book.

Ashtray, Pinecones, Gold, 2 In., Pair	38
Charger, Blue & White, 7 Sages Of Bamboo Grove, Attendants, Stand, 18 In. Diam.	179
Jar, Dresser, Lid, Orange, Blue Green, Flowers, 4 In.	125
Plate, Paneled, Lotus Medallion, Fruit, Blue & White, Brown Rim, c.1900, 8 ⅝ In.	359
Plate, Vines, Flowers, Birds, Dragon, Green, Orange, Scalloped, 19th Century, 9 In., Pair ...	268
Vase, Stick Neck, Reticulated, Multicolor, Flowers, Scrolls, 8 In.	180
Whirligig, Pine, Star Shape, Red, White, Blue Paint, c.1920, 52 In.	900
Whirligig, Wood, Airplane, Prop, Stand, 22 x 12 In.	173

ART DECO, or Art Moderne, a style started at the Paris Exposition of 1925, is characterized by linear, geometric designs. All types of furniture and decorative arts, jewelry, book bindings, and even games were designed in this style. Additional items may be found in the Furniture category or in various glass and pottery categories, etc.

Ashtray, Black Onyx, Enamel Cylinder, Jade, Diamond, Sapphire Plaque, c.1920, 3 ¾ x 3 ½ In..	12500
Box, Nephrite, Platinum & Diamond Hinges & Clasp, Asprey, London, 3 x 2 x ½ In.	13200
Parasol, Silk, Bamboo Shaft, Silvered Knob, Enamel Leaves, Wiener Werkstatte, 35 In.	625

ART GLASS, *see Glass-Art category.*

ART NOUVEAU is a style of design that was at its most popular from 1895 to 1905. Famous designers, including Rene Lalique and Emile Galle, produced furniture, glass, silver, metalwork, and buildings in the new style. Ladies with long flowing hair and elongated bodies were among the more easily recognized design elements. Copies of this style are being made today. Many modern pieces of jewelry can be found. Additional Art Nouveau pieces may be found in Furniture or in various glass categories.

Figurine, Woman, Seminude, Dress Folds Into Bowl, Austria, c.1900, 18 In.	1701
Vase, Metal, Embossed Vine, Flowers, Handles, 10 In.	79

ART POTTERY *see Pottery-Art category*

AURENE *pieces are listed in the Steuben category.*

AUSTRIA *is a collecting term that covers pieces made by a wide variety of factories. They are listed in this book in categories such as Royal Dux or Porcelain.*

AUTO parts and accessories are collectors' items today. Gas pump globes and license plates are part of this specialty. Prices are determined by age, rarity, and condition. Signs and packaging related to automobiles may also be found in the Advertising category. Lalique hood ornaments will be listed in the Lalique category.

Air Pump, Eco Tireflator, Free Standing, 50 In.	1017

Architectural, Scupper, Dragon's Head, Metal, Waterspout Mouth, 1900s, 14 In.
$180

Cowan's Auctions

Architectural, Spire, Sheet Metal, Urn Shape, Petals, Sphere, Crossed Arrows, 1800s, 103 In.
$840

Cowan's Auctions

Arequipa, Vase, Squat, Green Matte Glaze, Signed, 1912, 3 x 7 In.
$1,000

Rago Arts & Auction Center

Auto, Button, Minneapolis Auto Show, Mar. 2-9 '07, Art Nouveau Style, 1907, 1 ½ In.
$278

Hake's Americana & Collectibles

Auto, Can, Marathon Motor Oil, Oil Well Shape, Tin Lithograph, Gal., 15 ¼ x 6 ½ In.
$4,830

Wm Morford Auctions

Auto, Display, Figural, Michelin Man, Hard Plastic, 19 In.
$330

Victorian Casino Antiques

Auto, Display, Stand, Sunoco Motor Oil, Bottles In Carriers, Porcelain Sides, Light-Up
$3,600

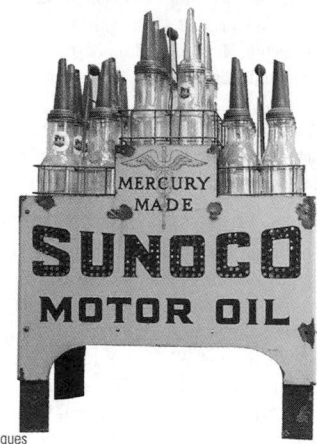

Victorian Casino Antiques

Auto, Gas Pump Globe, Mobilgas Special, Red Pegasus, Milk Glass, 2-Sided, 17 In.
$780

Victorian Casino Antiques

Auto, Gas Pump Globe, Red Crown, Figural, Milk Glass, 17 In.
$660

Showtime Auction Services

TIP
Don't ignore vintage transistor radios (1955–1963) if you see them at house sales or flea markets. The interest in radios is growing and the supply of old radios is shrinking.

Air Pump, Eco Tireflator, Wall Mount, 17 In.	961
Ashtray, Texaco, Boston Division Organization Meeting, Gas Station, 1965, 7 x 7 In.	10
Banner, Tydol Gasoline, Woman Driving, Steering Wheel, 1940s	660
Bottle, Phillips 66, Jay Rhodes Motor Oil, Glass, Metal Spout, Qt.	443
Button, Minneapolis Auto Show, Mar. 2-9, '07, Art Nouveau Style, 1907, 1 ½ In. ....*illus*	278
Cabin Car, Teardrop Travel Trailer, Wood, Upholstery, Carpet, Fleet Mfg., 1947, 14 Ft.	11400
Cabinet, Display, Standard Oil Company, Wood, Glass, 18 x 22 In.	1239
Cabinet, Display, Tung-Sol Auto Bulbs, Tin, 19 x 20 ½ In.	570
Can, Airman Motor Oil, Plane, Red, White, Blue, Tin Litho, 5 ⅝ x 4 In.	489
Can, Badger Automobile Oil Wadham, Squat, Gal.	177
Can, Beaver Penn Motor Oil, Metal, Rectangular, 2 Gal.	118
Can, Bingham's Cardinal Round, Metal, 5 Gal.	24
Can, Capitan Motor Oil, Car Logo, Rectangular, 2 Gal.	384
Can, Duplex Gear Grease, Tin Litho, Black, Yellow, Lid, 7 x 7 x 7 In.	288
Can, En-Ar-Co Motor Oil, Boy, Slate, Metal, Round, Rocker, 5 Gal.	236
Can, Four-State Motor Oil, Metal, Round, Qt.	590
Can, Freedom Perfect Oil, Bulldog, Metal, Round, Qt.	325
Can, General Petroleum Corp., Green, Tan, Metal, Gal.	325
Can, Hippo Oil, Bellowing Hippo Graphics, Rectangular, Metal, Canada, Gal.	325
Can, Keynoil, White Eagle Motor Oil, ½ Gal.	207
Can, Keynoil, White Eagle Motor Oil, Metal, Gal.	1298
Can, Lubrite Motor Oil, Metal, Round, Qt.	207
Can, Marathon Motor Oil, Oil Well Shape, Tin Lithograph, Gal., 15 ¼ x 6 ½ In. ....*illus*	4830
Can, Mobiloil A, Gargoyle Process, Gargoyle, Metal, Round, Qt.	354
Can, Mobiloil A, Gargoyle, Metal, Square, Wooden Box, Qt.	413
Can, Mobiloil Aero, Pegasus, Gray Band, Round, Metal, Qt.	236
Can, Mobiloil Aero, Pegasus, Green Band, Round, Metal, Qt.	413
Can, Mobiloil AF, Refinery Scene, Metal, Tapered Cone Shape.	413
Can, Mobiloil Arctic, Polar Bear Logo, Metal, Tapered Cone Shape	354
Can, Mobiloil BB, Greek Key, Round, Metal, Qt.	295
Can, Mobiloil D, Gargoyle, Metal, Triangle Shape, Lid	325
Can, Paragon, Petolene Motor Oil, Metal, Flat, Gal.	266
Can, Polarine Motor Oil, Polar Bear Logo, Standard Oil, Gal.	1593
Can, Pure Oil, Metal, Handle, 5 Gal.	113
Can, Socony 990 Motor Oil, For Ford Cars, Metal, Flat, Handle, Gal.	354
Can, Socony Motor Oil, Logo, White, Metal, Gal.	767
Can, Socony Regular Motor Oil, Metal, Flat, Gal.	159
Can, Standard Oil Of New York Axle Grease, Metal, Handle	30
Can, Texaco, Logo, Black T, Metal, Green, Elongated Pour Spout, Qt.	266
Can, Tiona Automobile Oil, Logo, Squat, Metal, Gal.	118
Can, Valvoline Motor Light Motor Oil, Metal, Squat, Qt.	738
Can, Valvoline Motor Oil, Metal, Flat, Gal.	443
Can, Vico Motor Oil, Round, Rocker, Metal, 5 Gal.	30
Can, Vulcan Motor Oil, Red V, Metal, Round, Qt.	130
Can, Wadhams Graphite Axle Grease, Logo, Red, Black, Round, Lb.	124
Can, Wadhams Motor Oil, Red, Yellow, Squat, Gal.	89
Can, Wadhams Tempered Grease, Black, Yellow, Round, Lb.	218
Can, Wadhams Tempered Motor Oil, Red, White, Gal.	266
Can, Wadhams Tempered Motor Oil, Square, Tip, Gal.	118
Can, Wings Grease, Tin Litho, Red, White, Blue, Flying Geese, Clouds, 4 ⅝ x 3 ⅜ In.	161
Car Seat, Steering Wheel, Pressed Steel, 1950s, Child's	85
Carrier, Mobiloil AF, 4 Filproof Bottles, Metal Caps, Tin, 23 x 19 In.	944
Cover, Spare Tire, RPM, First Choice Motor Oil, Blue, Red, White, Oilcloth, 32 In. Diam.	115
Coveralls, Cloth, Soco Patch, Standard Oil Brass Buttons, Size 42	24
Display, Auto Lite Spark Plug, Metal Cabinet, 19 x 14 In.	679
Display, Baum's Wonderful Polish, Cardboard, 13 x 10 In.	53
Display, Delco Battery, Rack, 56 x 40 In.	147
Display, Figural, Michelin Man, Hard Plastic, 19 In. ....*illus*	330
Display, Mazda Super Auto Lamps, Blue, Hinged Door, c.1950, 16 x 8 In.	120
Display, Stand, Sunoco Motor Oil, Bottles In Carriers, Porcelain Sides, Light-Up ....*illus*	3600
Display, Trico Wiper Blade, Refills, Lighted, Umbrella, Rain, 1960s, 16 ½ x 16 ½ In.	144
Display, Willard Batteries, Metal, 38 x 34 In.	59
First Aid Kit, Magnolia, With Pegasus, Cone Shape.	384
Fuel Pump, United Motors Service, Yellow, Red Paint, Tin, 1920s, 61 x 19 In.	1582
Gas Pump Globe, American Gas, Blue, Red, White, Glass Inserts, Steel Collar, 15 In.	456

Auto, Gas Pump, Mobilgas, Model 519, Restored, Wayne
$4,600

Victorian Casino Antiques

Auto, Hood Ornament, Figural, Mercury, Winged Helmet, Patina, 3 ⅞ x 6 ½ In.
$1,121

Wm Morford Auctions

Auto, Sign, Firestone, Tin, Self-Framed, Marked, Made In USA, 72 x 23 In.
$944

Victorian Casino Antiques

Auto, Sign, Highway, Minnesota 55, Metal, Reflective, 24 x 24 In. $120

MINNESOTA 55

Victorian Casino Antiques

Auto, Sign, Mobil, Pegasus, Enamel, Figural, 39 x 39 In. $840

Showtime Auction Services

Auto, Sign, Mobil, Pegasus, Winged Horse, Enamel, Iron Bracket, c.1935, 25 x 32 In. $3,000

Skinner Auctioneers & Appraisers

Modern Packages
Many products have had packaging that changed often. The logos were modernized, hair-dos and clothes were updated, cars resembled the latest models, slogans changed, and the wording was updated to follow the latest laws about health, nutrition, side effects, country of origin, and alcohol and drug content. All of these changes help determine the age of the product.

Gas Pump Globe, American, Red & White Stripes, Metal Globe, Lenses, 15 In.	708
Gas Pump Globe, Ashland Fuel Oil, Capco Globe, Single Lens, 13 ½ In.	472
Gas Pump Globe, Ashland Go-Mix Outboard Fuel, Capco Globe, Single Lens, 13 ½ In.	1298
Gas Pump Globe, Freedom, Iron Cross Logo, Blue, Yellow, White, Metal, Lenses, 15 In.	1888
Gas Pump Globe, Gold Crown, Milk Glass, 15 x 17 In.	424
Gas Pump Globe, Husky Hi-Power, Dog, Metal Globe, Single Lens, 15 In.	3835
Gas Pump Globe, Husky, Dog Logo Capco, 13 ½ In.	2596
Gas Pump Globe, Indian Gasoline, Green, 72 In.	1140
Gas Pump Globe, Mobilgas Special, Red Pegasus, Milk Glass, 2-Sided, 17 In. *illus*	780
Gas Pump Globe, Pan-Am, Orange Gasoline, Metal Globe, Lenses, 15 In.	1298
Gas Pump Globe, Pure Gas, High-Speed, Milk Glass Lenses, Plastic Sleeve, 13 ½ In.	171
Gas Pump Globe, Red Crown Gasoline, Ethyl Logo, Green Burst, Porcelain, Metal, 15 In.	590
Gas Pump Globe, Red Crown, Figural, Milk Glass, 17 In. *illus*	660
Gas Pump Globe, Richfield Ethyl, Art Deco Bird, Glass, Lenses, 13 ½ In.	443
Gas Pump Globe, Shell, Figural, White, Red, 17 ½ In.	570
Gas Pump Globe, Signal Gasoline, Orange, Black, 74 In.	1920
Gas Pump Globe, Standard Oil, Red Crown, Cast, Metal Screw Base	826
Gas Pump Globe, Super-Shell Ethyl, Milk Glass Globe, Shell Shape	708
Gas Pump Globe, Tama County Oil, Milk Glass	1416
Gas Pump Globe, Texaco, Glass Shade, Black T, White Round, 9 x 13 In.	472
Gas Pump Globe, Texas Rose, Ethyl Logo, Red, White, Capco, Single Lens, 13 ½ In.	2065
Gas Pump Globe, Tropical Gas, Palm Trees, Round, c.1925, 19 In.	36000
Gas Pump Globe, Valvoline, Capco Globe Body, Lenses, 13 ½ In.	649
Gas Pump Globe, White Eagle, Blunt Nose, Milk Glass, Cast, 20 ½ In.	885
Gas Pump Globe, White Eagle, Milk Glass, Cast, 20 ½ In.	2124
Gas Pump Globe, White Rose, Ethyl Logo In Yellow Burst, Glass Globe, 13 ½ In.	649
Gas Pump Globe, White Star Gasoline, Blue, White, Metal, Lens, 15 In.	2301
Gas Pump Plate, Texaco Fire Chief, Red Helmet, Porcelain, 1963, 18 x 12 In.	120
Gas Pump, Bowser Phillips 66, Electric Globe, Red, Orange, 76 In.	1413
Gas Pump, Capco Globe Body, Hose, Computing, Wayne Model 60, 77 In.	2040
Gas Pump, Marathon, Tokheim, Electric Globe, Porcelain, 74 In.	1074
Gas Pump, Mobilgas, Model 519, Restored, Wayne *illus*	4600
Gas Pump, Saucony, 96 ½ In.	396
Gas Pump, Shell Gravity, Globe, Cylinder, 120 In.	1752
Gas Pump, Texaco Gravity, Globe, Cylinder, Red, White, 120 In.	2260
Grease Testing Kit, Rat Trap, Conoco, Round, Salesman's Sample, 11 In.	148
Grill Badge, Marching Chevroliers, Enameled Bronze, GM, Box, 1930s, 4 ¾ In.	150
Hood Ornament, Action Twins, Cranking Fan, Chrome, Action Ornament Co., 9 In.	677
Hood Ornament, Figural, Mercury, Winged Helmet, Patina, 3 ⅞ x 6 ½ In. *illus*	1121
Hood Ornament, Greyhound, Running, Lincoln, 1920s, 4 ¾ x 8 ¾ In.	604
Hood Ornament, Policeman, Metal, Paint, Raised Arm, Whirligig Rotating Arms, 7 x 4 In.	345
Hood Ornament, Pontiac, Indian, Chrome, Mounted On Wood, c.1948, 11 x 19 In.	179
Hood Ornament, Running Indian Warrior, Spear, Eagle Wings, Chromed Metal, 7 ½ x 10 In.	268
Lens, General Petroleum Regular, Round, On Glass Globe Body, 13 ½ In.	1180
License Plate Attachment, Freedom, Bulldog, Tin, Die Cut, 5 ¼ x 4 ¾ In.	207
License Plate Attachment, Mobil, Pegasus Shape, Tin, Die Cut, 5 x 6 In.	177 to 236
License Plate Attachment, Mobile, California World's Fair, Pegasus, 5 ½ x 6 ½ In.	295
License Plate Attachment, St. Louis Cardinals, Bird On Bat, Metal, c.1927, 4 x 6 In.	173
License Plate Topper, Lake George, N.Y., Aluminum, Indian Chief, Cannon, 3 ½ x 12 ⅝ In.	253
License Plate Topper, Motorcycle, Stone Harbor, N.J., Nude Silhouette, 4 x 6 In.	230
License Plate, 21525, Porcelain, Ohio, 1908-09	396
License Plate, 32, Porcelain, Ohio, 1908	1525
License Plate, Ohio, 1916	45
Lubester, Richfield, Blue & White Eagle, Yellow, 40 Gal., 53 In.	360
Meter, Boyce Moto, Metal, Round, 4 In.	96
Moto Meter, Buick	175
Movie Window Speakers, Valley Drive-In, Cardboard Poster	226
Oil Filler Pump, National, Dayton, Ohio, 74 In.	339
Padlock, Texaco, Star Logo, Brass, Key	65
Paperweight, Lanigan Automobile Sales Co., Auto Photo, Glass, 3 x 4 ½ In.	230
Pin, Buick, Simplicity-Durability, Power, Automobile, Black & White, ⅞ In.	75
Pin, Buy A Moyer, Automobile Image, Red & White, c.1910, 1 In.	95
Pin, New Ford, Automobile, Celluloid, c.1915, ⅞ In.	104
Pump Plate, Clock, Time Super Gasoline, Porcelain, Die Cut, Electric, 14 x 9 In.	826
Pump Plate, Golden Eagle, Orange, Blue, Gold, 13 x 13 In.	236

Pump Plate, Mobilgas, Pegasus, Red, White, Black, Shield Shape, 1947, 12 x 12 In........................	295
Pump Plate, Pacer Hi-Test, Red, Black, White, Porcelain, 14 x 9 In..	767
Pump Plate, Signal Ethyl Gasoline, Logo, Round, Porcelain, Red, Pink, Black, 12 In..................	561
Pump Plate, Texaco, Sky Chief Gasoline, Porcelain, Curved, 18 x 12 In.	148
Pump Plate, Texaco, Sky Chief, Petrox, Green, Red, White, Porcelain, 1959, 18 x 12 In.	177
Radiator Cap, Indian Hood Ornament, Headdress, Thermometer, A. Buand, Paris, 6 In.	900
Road Map, Pennsylvania, Auto Trails, Mobiloil, Metro Gas, 1924	130
Sign, 76 Union, Royal Gasoline, Porcelain, Embossed, 18 x 14 In.	206
Sign, 1956 Woody Chevrolet Nomad Station Wagon, Oak Panel, 22 x 48 In.	65
Sign, 1958 Ford Truck, Cloth Banner, 34 x 10 In..	295
Sign, 1984 Corvette, Paper, Frame, 27 x 40 In.	59
Sign, AC Delco, Spark Plug, Plastic, Light-Up, Electric, 21 x 18 In.	266
Sign, Aeroshell Lubricating Oil Stocked Here, Wings, Shell, Porcelain, 38 x 20 In..................	708
Sign, Akron Tire Co., Vacation In A Ford, Car On Beach, 1923, 41 x 27 In.............................	1410
Sign, Akron Tire Co., Your Family Deserves A Ford, Family At Window, 1923, 41 x 27 In.	1410
Sign, Alemite Products, 2-Sided, Flange Mount, Metal, 25 ½ x 9 In.	107
Sign, Amalie, Pennsylvania Motor Oil, Flange, Tin, Red, Gold, Oval, 1946, 20 x 30 In.	1200
Sign, American Oil Co., Mighty Amoco Step Ahead, Drum Major, Cardboard, 28 x 62 In.............	70
Sign, Approved Clean Rest Rooms, Embossed, Porcelain, 20 x 29 In., Pair	384
Sign, Approved Willys Service, Round, 42 In..	1534
Sign, Armstrong Tires, Rhino-Flex, Porcelain, Die Cut, 40 x 58 In......................................	649
Sign, Ask For A Bear Safety Headlight Test Today, Paper, Frame, 20 x 40 In.	443
Sign, Ask For Wolf's Head Oil 7 Lubes, Logo, Round, Tin Flange, 22 x 16 In.	472
Sign, Authorized Nash Service, Blue, Black, 2-Sided, Enameled Porcelain, 36 x 22 In.	1659
Sign, Autolite Batteries, Vertical, Embossed, Tin, 60 x 18 In.	443
Sign, Autolite Battery Service, Blue, Gold, Metal, 15 ½ x 54 In.	367
Sign, Bartles Bonded Oils & Greases, Red, White, Blue, Round, Embossed, Tin, 10 x 28 In.	2596
Sign, Bear Car Conditioning Service, Die Cut Bear, Tin, Embossed, 40 x 28 In.	472
Sign, Bear Wheel Alignment Balancing Service, Yellow Bear Holding Sign, 36 x 52 In.	840
Sign, Billboard, White Eagle, Wood, Die Cut, 46 x 24 In.	531
Sign, Blue Sunoco, Yellow, Blue, Porcelain, Diamond Shape, 8 x 12 In..............................	384
Sign, Brake Service, With Arrow, 2-Sided, Porcelain, 35 x 34 In.......................................	531
Sign, Briggs & Stratton Engines, Sales & Service, Embossed, Tin, 24 x 30 In.	266
Sign, Buick 8, Forward!, March, And April, Car, Clouds, Frame, 1936, 31 x 24 In.	71
Sign, Buick, Quick Service, Red, White, Blue, Porcelain, 2-Sided, 16 x 26 In.	1770
Sign, Burd Hi Speed Piston Rings, Eagle Graphics, Tin, Die Cut, 12 x 18 In..........................	1770
Sign, Cabinet, Ask Here For Mobil Gargoyle Authorized Service, Porcelain, 24 x 20 In.	1534
Sign, Cadillac Dealer, Raised Crest, Wood, 47 x 47 In..	328
Sign, Cadillac Service, Crest Logo, Round, 2-Sided, Porcelain, 42 In..................................	3540
Sign, Champion Spark Plugs, When We Change Oil Let Us Check Plugs, Paper, 44 x 28 In.	41
Sign, Chevrolet Service, Aluminum, 1970s, 20 x 48 In..	330
Sign, Chevrolet, Genuine Parts, Bowtie Logo, 2-Sided, Porcelain, Die Cut, 20 x 24 In.	4400
Sign, Chevrolet, Logo, Sales & Service, Blue, Porcelain, 2-Sided, 28 x 40 In.	1593
Sign, Chicago Motor Club, AAA Bonded Service Station, 2-Sided, Porcelain, 44 x 36 In.............	767
Sign, Chrysler Plymouth Approved Service, Round, 2-Sided, Porcelain, Die Cut, 42 x 44 In........	4956
Sign, Chrysler Service, Ribbon Shape, 2-Sided Porcelain, Die Cut, 23 x 25 In.	7080
Sign, Cities Service Once, Always Koolmotor, Tin, 2-Sided, Sidewalk, 28 x 20 In....................	236
Sign, Cities Services, Premium Koolmotor Oil, 1940s Cars, Wood Back, 28 x 58 In.	2650
Sign, Clean Rest Rooms, Award, Torch, Die Cut, Porcelain, 2-Sided, Standard Oil, 51 x 15 In.	4130
Sign, Conoco, Triangular, Porcelain, Die Cut, 8 ½ x 7 ½ In.	236
Sign, Cooper Tire, Armored Cord, Tin, 17 ¼ x 71 In..	960
Sign, Corduroy, Extra Quality Tires, 2-Sided, Tin, 20 x 28 In.	206
Sign, CP, Derrick Logo, Porcelain, Truck Door, Round, 12 In.	325
Sign, Curb, Penn Drake Motor Oil, Derrick Logo, 2-Sided, Shield, Tin, Iron Stand, 28 x 20 In.	413
Sign, Curb, Pierce Pennant Gasoline, Oval, 2-Sided, Tin, Cast Iron Base, 14 x 20 In.	620
Sign, Curb, Tiolene Pure Oil Company, Round, 2-Sided Porcelain, Strap Base, 30 In.	3540
Sign, Curb, Wolf's Head Motor Oil, Wolf Logo, Red, White, Oval, Iron Base, 20 x 34 In.	826
Sign, Danger Look Out For Cars, Round, 2-Sided, Porcelain, 36 In.	283
Sign, Delco Batteries With Six Volt Battery, Vertical, Tin, Wood Back, 71 x 18 In.	826
Sign, Delco Batteries, Red, White, Tin, 1947, 12 x 34 In.	493
Sign, Delco Battery Service, United Motors Logo, 2-Sided, Porcelain, 24 x 48 In.	1770
Sign, Delco Dry Charge 12 Volt Battery, 2-Sided, Tin, Blue, Yellow, White, 20 x 28 In.	266
Sign, Delco Parts & Service, 2-Sided, Tin, 24 x 18 In.	236
Sign, Dependable Delco-Light, Embossed, Tin, 12 x 23 In.	207
Sign, Derby Gasoline, Star Logo, Porcelain, Round, 2-Sided, 30 In......................................	708

Auto, Sign, Mobilgas, Pegasus, Porcelain, Figural, Die Cut, 92 x 69 In.
$3,000

Victorian Casino Antiques

Auto, Sign, Wise Man, Ford, Chromolitho, Model T, Akron Tire Display, 1923, 41 x 27 In.
$1,410

Cowan's Auctions

Auto, Traffic Light, 3-Light-Hanging, Yellow Paint, Eagle Signal Corp., 30 In.
$450

Victorian Casino Antiques

Baccarat, Paperweight, Anemone, Blue & White Flowers, Leaves, Star Cut Base, 3 In.
$608

James D. Julia Auctioneers

Baccarat, Paperweight, Multicolor Flower Canes, Signed, Dated 28-8-1973, 3 x 3 ½ In.
$431

Cottone Auctions

TIP
Rub tartar-control toothpaste on your scratched snow dome paperweights. It will remove the smaller scratches.

Badge, Sheriff, Greenlee County, Arizona, Brass, Embossed, Enamel Letters, 2 x 2 ½ In.
$600

Showtime Auction Services

Sign, Diamond Tires, Logo, Red, Black, Tin, 20 x 60 In.	1180
Sign, Dunlop Tire, 2-Sided, Paint, Metal, 48 x 12 In.	102
Sign, Embassy Tires & Tubes, Tin, Wood Frame, 16 x 48 In.	389
Sign, Esso Credit Cards Honored, 2-Sided, Porcelain, 14 x 18 In.	295
Sign, Fina, Hypower Gasoline, Porcelain, Die Cut, 13 x 11 In.	590
Sign, Firestone Safety Champion, Red, White, 2-Sided, Tin, Die Cut, 18 x 28 In.	207
Sign, Firestone, Painted, Metal, 36 x 106 In.	452
Sign, Firestone, Tin, Self-Framed, Marked, Made In USA, 72 x 23 In. *illus*	944
Sign, Firestone, Tire & Battery Service, Arrow, Tin, 2-Sided, 23 x 48 In.	679
Sign, Firestone, Vertical, Black, Orange, Porcelain, 18 x 96 In.	424
Sign, Fleet Wing Credit Cards Honored, Tin, Flange, 14 x 18 In.	295
Sign, Flying A Motor Diesel Fuel, Wing Logo, Round, Porcelain, 2-Sided, 48 In.	885
Sign, FoMoCo, Genuine Ford Parts, Red, White, Tin, 2-Sided, 14 x 18 In.	236
Sign, Ford Tractor, Ferguson Systems, Masonite, 11 x 22 In.	153
Sign, Gas Pump, Atlantic Refining Company, Crossed Arrows, Porcelain, 1930s, 9 ¼ In.	133
Sign, Gasoline, Wood, 1920s, 39 x 8 In.	1560
Sign, General Motors Parts, Porcelain, Neon, 30 x 58 In.	5025
Sign, General Petroleum Gasoline & Lubricants, Round, Porcelain, 2-Sided, 30 In.	2360
Sign, General Tire, Porcelain, Baltimore Enamel Co., 78 x 18 In.	826
Sign, Gillette Tires-Batteries-Accessories A Bear For Wear, 1949, 73 x 18 In.	1180
Sign, GMC Trucks, Sales & Service, Round, Orange, Blue, 2-Sided, 42 In.	2950
Sign, Golden Penn Motor Oil, 2-Sided, Masonite, Yellow, 15 x 24 In.	266
Sign, Golden State Automobile Club Service, Logo, Porcelain, 2-Sided, 27 x 14 In.	295
Sign, Goodrich De Luxe Truck Tires, Porcelain, Rectangular, 36 In.	1062
Sign, Goodrich Tires, Logo, Tin, Die Cut, Embossed, 16 x 30 In.	443
Sign, Goodrich Tires, Silvertown Cords Best In Long Run, Porcelain, 20 x 60 In.	708
Sign, Goodrich, Logo, Blue, White, Porcelain, Vertical, 78 x 18 In.	1534
Sign, Goodyear Service Station, World In Tire Logo, Porcelain, Flange, 30 x 26 In.	826
Sign, Goodyear Tire & Rubber Co., Chromolithograph, Cardboard Mount, 1901, 25 x 20 In.	443
Sign, Goodyear Tires, 4 Miles, Garage Machine Shop, Tin, 12 x 34 In.	531
Sign, Goodyear Tires, Logo, Porcelain, Wood Frame, 24 x 66 In.	1180
Sign, Goodyear Tires, Tire & Battery Service, Logo, Tin, Embossed, 15 x 36 In.	679
Sign, Goodyear Tires, Winged Foot Logo, Porcelain, 34 x 94 In.	826
Sign, Goodyear, Winged Foot, White, Black, Porcelain, 12 x 31 In.	472
Sign, Gulf No Nox, Knockproof, Porcelain, Round, 10 ½ In.	148
Sign, Gulf Oil, Oil Of Untold Uses, Tin, Die Cut, Orange, Blue, 7 x 6 In.	295
Sign, Gulf Supreme Oil, Porcelain, Black, White, Orange, Green, c.1935, 30 x 72 In	660
Sign, Gulf Tires, Right Brand On All Fours, Cowboy, Branding Iron, 1950s, 42 In.	165
Sign, Gulf, Service Station Panel, Orange, White, Blue, Plastic, 48 x 48 In.	96
Sign, Harbor Petroleum Products, Seaplane, Porcelain, Die Cut, 39 x 35 In.	8850
Sign, Havoline Motor Oil, Keeps Your Engine Clean, Tin Lithograph, 1940s, 11 x 22 In.	196
Sign, Henry Ford, Seated, Holding Model T, Hand Painted, 2-Sided, 1930s, 48 x 38 In.	5400
Sign, Hercules Tires, Vertical, Red, White, Tin, 72 x 14 In.	177
Sign, Highway, Minnesota 55, Metal, Reflective, 24 x 24 In. *illus*	120
Sign, Hood Tires, Man With Bowtie Logo, Vertical, Tin, Wood Frame, 78 x 18 In.	1534
Sign, Hudson Dealer, Neon, Wood Crate, 34 x 179 x 6 ½ In.	9120
Sign, Hudson Essex Service, 2-Sided, Porcelain, 60 x 30 In.	649
Sign, Humble, Top Rated Rest Rooms, 2-Sided, Tin, Die Cut, 30 x 30 In.	207
Sign, Husky Dog Logo, Porcelain, Die Cut, 41 x 36 In.	2006
Sign, Hyvis Motor Oil Super Refined, Logo, Porcelain, 15 x 40 In.	826
Sign, Independent Gasoline, Ethyl Logo, Red, White, Blue, Round, 2-Sided, 30 In.	708
Sign, International Trucks, Ward Truck Sales, Blue, White, Porcelain, 54 x 73 In.	443
Sign, John Deere, Logo, Green, Yellow, 2-Sided, Aluminum, c.1975, 28 x 32 In.	295
Sign, John Deere, Quality Farm Equipment, Leaping 4-Legged Logo, Porcelain, 24 x 72 In.	2006
Sign, Keep To Right, California AAA Logo, Reflectors, Black, White, Porcelain, 24 x 18 In.	266
Sign, Kelly Tire, Woman Waving, Multicolor, Tin, Round, 24 In.	17100
Sign, Kendall Motor Oil, The Dealer Sign Of Quality, Red & White, 1961, 12 x 72 In.	480
Sign, Keynoil Motor Oil, White Eagle, Oval, Red, White, Porcelain, 2-Sided, 20 x 28 In.	3540
Sign, Life Ethyl Gasoline, Logo, Tin, 10 x 8 In.	2950
Sign, Magnolia Gasoline, Sold At This Station, Porcelain, 10 x 15 In.	1180
Sign, Manhattan Gasoline, Porcelain, Painted, Flange, Round, 22 In.	2400
Sign, Mansfield Tires, Extra Mileage, Embossed, Tin, 18 x 71 In.	797
Sign, Marathon Ethyl, Man Running Logo, Round, Porcelain, 2-Sided, 30 In.	1003
Sign, Marathon Running Man Logo, Ohio Oil Co., Tin, 24 x 36 In.	207
Sign, Mastermobile Western Oil, Embossed, Tin, 13 x 39 In.	236

Sign, Mazda Lamps, Keep Your Car Up, Don't Drive A One-Eyed Auto, Paper, Frame, 34 In.	1180
Sign, Miller Tires, Geared To The Road, Tin, Wood Frame, Reflective Paint, 12 x 72 In.	590
Sign, Mobil, Key, Locked For Your Protection, Key In Office, Porcelain, 4 x 9 In.	443
Sign, Mobil, Pegasus, Die Cut, Porcelain, 30 x 60 In.	1495
Sign, Mobil, Pegasus, Enamel, 39 x 39 In. ...illus	840
Sign, Mobil, Pegasus, Red, White, Porcelain, Flat, Die Cut, 34 x 44 In.	4130
Sign, Mobil, Pegasus, Weather Vane Topper, Red, Porcelain, 2-Sided, 28 x 28 In.	1180
Sign, Mobil, Pegasus, Winged Horse, Enamel, Iron Bracket, c.1935, 25 x 32 In. ...illus	3000
Sign, Mobil, Winter Front, Pegasus, Black, Red, 11 x 17 In.	89
Sign, Mobilfuel Diesel, Pegasus, Shield Shape, Porcelain, 12 x 12 In.	1092
Sign, Mobilgas Special Gasoline, Pegasus Drop Leg Logo, Shield Shape, Porcelain, 9 x 9 In.	1534
Sign, Mobilgas, Aircraft, Pegasus, Shield Shape, Porcelain, 12 x 12 In.	2655
Sign, Mobilgas, Diesel, Pegasus, Shield Shape, Porcelain, 12 x 12 In.	3540
Sign, Mobilgas, Pegasus, Porcelain, Figural, Die Cut, 92 x 69 In. ...illus	3000
Sign, Mobilgas, Pegasus, Shield Shape, Porcelain, 12 x 12 In.	236
Sign, Mobilgas, Red Pegasus, Porcelain, Round, 11 ¾ In.	210
Sign, Mobilgas, Red Pegasus, Round, Plastic, Metal, 58 In.	450
Sign, Mobilgas, Red, White, Porcelain, Side Rivets, 9 x 38 In.	748
Sign, Mobilgas, Restroom Pledge, Pegasus, Shield Shape, Porcelain, 8 x 8 In.	708
Sign, Mobiloil A, Gargoyle, Refuse Can If Seal Is Broken, Can Shape, Porcelain, 16 In.	1062
Sign, Mobiloil D, Recommended For All Motor Cycle Engines, Porcelain, 12 x 12 In.	1083
Sign, Mobiloil E, Certified Service, Gargoyle, Porcelain, Round, 8 In.	885
Sign, Mobiloil, Arctic Special, Spinner, Neon Lights, 8-Sided, 18 x 18 x 7 In.	413
Sign, Mobiloil, C For Gears, With Gargoyle, Paddle Shape, Porcelain, 2-Sided, 11 x 9 In.	531
Sign, Mobiloil, Gargoyle, Thermometer, Porcelain, 25 x 19 In.	1652
Sign, Mobiloil, Pegasus, 2-Sided, Porcelain, Socony Base, White, Red, Black, 65 x 30 In.	4025
Sign, Never Nox, Ethyl Logo, Round, Red, Cream, Porcelain, 30 In.	915
Sign, OK Used Cars, Chevrolet, Red, Yellow, Blue, 53 ¼ In.	3000
Sign, OK, Chevrolet, Porcelain, Red, Yellow, Blue, Round, 36 In.	1888 to 2006
Sign, Oldsmobile Service, Rocket Logo, Porcelain, Round, 2-Sided, 60 In.	3800
Sign, Oldsmobile Service, Rocket Shape, Porcelain, Die Cut, 2-Sided, 10 x 59 In.	9440
Sign, Oldsmobile Service, World Logo, Porcelain, Round, 2-Sided, 60 In.	2065
Sign, Pan-Am Motor Oils, Porcelain, Teal, Red, White, Black, Round, 15 In.	1888
Sign, Pan-Am Quality Gasoline, Painted, Metal, 17 x 13 In.	325
Sign, Pennzip Gasoline, Painted, Metal, 46 x 25 In.	147
Sign, Pennzoil Safe Lubrication With Brown Bell, Round, Porcelain, 2-Sided, 24 In.	826
Sign, Pennzoil Safe Lubrication, Red Bell Logo, Oval, Tin, Die Cut, 2-Sided, 22 x 31 In.	295
Sign, Pennzoil, Safe Lubrication, With Red Bell, Oval, Porcelain, 2-Sided, 18 x 31 In.	708
Sign, Pennzoil, Sound Your Horn We'll Open, Tin, 15 x 32 In.	118
Sign, Phillips 66, Orange, Black Paint, Shield Shape, Metal, 11 x 11 In.	283
Sign, Phillips 66, Red, White, Shield Shape, 2-Sided, 48 x 48 In.	1416
Sign, Plume Motor Spirit, Vacuum Oil Co., 2 Red Plumes, Porcelain, Flange, 15 x 24 In.	1770
Sign, Pneus Dominion Tires, Red, Gray, Enameled Porcelain, 24 x 80 In.	119
Sign, Pontiac Goodwill Used Cars, Feather Indian Logo, Round, Tin, Die Cut, 2-Sided, 42 In.	767
Sign, Pontiac, Full Feather Indian, Porcelain, Die Cut, 36 x 53 In.	1888
Sign, Porsche, Stuttgart, Shield, Heraldic Emblems, Porcelain, Die Cut, 18 x 13 In.	4130
Sign, Price, Weed Tire Chains, Tire With Chains, Gasoline Today, Tin, Wood, 24 x 17 In.	590
Sign, Quaker State Motor Oil, Green, White, Tin, Vertical, 72 x 12 In.	472
Sign, Quaker State Racing Oil, Logo, Tin, 2-Sided, 5 x 26 In.	207
Sign, Red Crown, World's Greatest Mileage Test, Logo, Cloth Banner, 105 x 35 In.	236
Sign, Registered Rest Room, Texaco, Tin, 2-Sided, 38 x 30 In.	207
Sign, Replace With Genuine Wagner Lockheed Brake Parts, Light-Up, Metal, 10 x 18 In.	384
Sign, Restroom, Ladies, Supertest, Black, White, Porcelain, 2-Sided, 8 x 13 In.	148
Sign, Restroom, Sunoco, Ladies, Woman Silhouette, Porcelain, 3 x 7 In.	443
Sign, Richfield, Gasoline Of Power, Eagle Logo, Shield Shape, Blue, White, 48 x 48 In.	2360
Sign, Roi-Tan Cigars, Auto A Day Is Given Away, Red Chevy, Tin Lithograph, Box, 1939, 5 In.	472
Sign, Royal Petroleum, Flying A Logo, Red, Porcelain, Die Cut, 28 x 66 In.	1770
Sign, Saxon Motor Oil Cars, 2-Sided, Horned Logo, Porcelain, 18 x 18 In.	10030
Sign, School, Drive Slowly Crossing Guard, Red, Yellow, Tin, Die Cut, 58 x 18 In.	2242
Sign, Shell Gasoline, Rozane Logo, Shell, Tin, Die Cut, Flange, 20 x 23 In.	2360
Sign, Shell Motor Oil, Shell Shape, Enamel, Yellow, Red, U.S.A., c.1950, 25 x 24 In.	338
Sign, Shell Motor Oil, Shell Shape, Porcelain, Metal Strap Base, 24 x 24 In.	4720
Sign, Sinclair Gasoline, Dinosaur Logo, Porcelain, 14 x 12 In.	207
Sign, Sinclair Opaline Motor Oil, Flat Stripe Can Logo, Porcelain, 20 x 48 In.	767
Sign, Sinclair Opaline, Stripe Logo, Green, White, Red, Porcelain, 12 x 12 In.	354 to 708

Bank, Building, First Presbyterian Church, Painted, Cast Iron, U.S.A., c.1895, 15 ¾ In.
$19,600

RSL Auction

Bank, Building, Independence Hall, Cast Iron, Enterprise Mfg. Co., Philadelphia, c.1875
$2,328

RSL Auction

Bank, Building, Westminster Abbey, Cast Iron, Sydenham & McOustra, England, c.1902
$3,675

RSL Auction

Bank, Eiffel Tower, Cast Iron, Sydenham & McOustra, England, c.1908
$2,328

RSL Auction

Bank, General Butler, Frog Body, Cast Iron, Painted, J. & E. Stevens, 6 ½ In.
$10,030

Bertoia Auctions

Bank, Hansel & Gretel House, Spelter, Heart Shape Lock, Germany, c.1910, 2 ⅞ x 3 ⅛ In.
$2,083

RSL Auction

Sign, Sinclair, Truck Door, Dino, Green, White, Red, 9 x 12 In.	885
Sign, Socony 990 Motor Oil, For Ford Cars, Lubster, 2-Sided, Porcelain, 12 x 8 In.	325
Sign, Socony Motor Oil, Logo, Curved, Round, Porcelain, 15 In.	885
Sign, Sohio, Operated By, Red, White, Porcelain, 2-Sided, 24 x 36 In.	59
Sign, Sonic Tires, Tires Of The Future, Embossed Tin, Red, White, Blue, 59 In.	540
Sign, Speedwell Motor Oil, Running Made Easy, Logo, Porcelain Flange, 16 x 24 In.	1357
Sign, Standard Credit Cards Honored, 2-Sided Porcelain, 36 x 24 In.	531
Sign, Standard Oil Co. Of New York, Tiger, Yellow, Black, Porcelain, Flange, 14 x 18 In.	885
Sign, Standard Oil Company, Embossed, Porcelain, 12 x 120 In.	502
Sign, Standard Oil Of Indiana, Elephant Logo, Porcelain, Flange, 20 x 30 In.	354
Sign, Standard Oil Of New York, Matchless Liquid Gloss, Tin, Cardboard Back, 7 x 9 In.	207
Sign, Standard Oil, Greatest Go On Earth, Man On Tiger, Crown, Cardboard, 56 x 40 In.	413
Sign, Standard Oil, Safety First, No Cars Filled While Motor Is Running, Porcelain, 18 x 12 In.	295
Sign, Stop, California AAA Logo, Reflectors, 8-Sided, Porcelain, Die Cut, 24 x 24 In.	236
Sign, Studebaker Authorized Sales & Service, Lazy S Logo, Round, Porcelain, 2-Sided, 42 In.	4130
Sign, Studebaker Service Station, Gray, White Paint, Porcelain, 30 x 14 In.	396
Sign, Sunflower Petroleum, Vacuum Oil Company, Porcelain, Flange, 16 x 24 In.	1475
Sign, Sunoco Motor Oil, Car Graphic, Cloth, 36 x 54 In.	531
Sign, Sunoco Motor Oil, Cleveland, Ohio, Orange, Black, Embossed, Tin, 15 x 20 In.	266
Sign, Super Chevrolet Service, Porcelain, Die Cut, Neon, 42 x 46 In.	5000
Sign, Superior Auto Parts, Gray, White, Metal, Paint, 1950s, 120 x 16 In.	102
Sign, Superlube Gear Lubricant, Tin, 29 x 17 In.	443
Sign, Texaco Fire Chief Gasoline, 1948, 12 x 18 In.	158
Sign, Texaco Fire Chief Gasoline, Red Helmet, Porcelain, 1957, 18 x 12 In.	180
Sign, Texaco Gasoline Motor Oil, Black-T, Porcelain, 42 In.	3776
Sign, Texaco Motor Oil, Can Logo, Porcelain, 2-Sided, 30 x 30 In.	354
Sign, Texaco, Clean Clear, Golden Motor Oil, Can Pouring, Porcelain, 15 x 16 In.	2596
Sign, Texaco, Diesel Chief, Logo With White T, Porcelain, 18 x 12 In.	531
Sign, Texaco, Easy Pour Can Motor Oil, Black T, Logo, Porcelain, Qt., 16 x 15 In.	472
Sign, Texaco, Logo With Black T, Porcelain, Round, 10 In.	472
Sign, Texaco, Porcelain, Round, Star, Red, White, Green, 15 In. Diam.	460
Sign, Texaco, Round, Red, White, Porcelain, 2-Sided, 42 In.	170
Sign, Texaco, Service You Can Trust, Thermometer, Tin, 14 x 5 In.	413
Sign, Trico Wiper Blades, Logo, Red, White, Tin, 9 ½ x 17 In.	148
Sign, Tru-Penn, Oiler Oil, Tin, 2-Sided, Sidewalk Stand, 27 x 20 In.	207
Sign, Union Gasoline, Shield Shape, Paint, Metal, 26 x 32 In.	158
Sign, Valvoline Motor Oil, Original Pennsylvania Oil, Porcelain, Rolled Edge, 20 x 16 In.	413
Sign, Valvoline, Original Pennsylvania Motor Oil, 35 Cents, Tin, Embossed, 10 x 14 In.	826
Sign, Valvoline, Pennsylvania, Motor Oils, Logo, Round, Tin, 2-Sided, 30 In.	3540
Sign, Veedol, 10-30 Motor Oil, Flying A Logo, Tin, Flange, 19 x 12 In.	177
Sign, Veedol, Change Now, Boy & Dog Graphics, Canvas Banner, 60 x 36 In.	472
Sign, Veedol, Motor Oil, Porcelain, Round, Convex, Notched, 20 In.	354
Sign, Viscoline Motor Oils & Greases, Tin, Flange, 20 x 21 In.	295
Sign, Wagner Automotive Brake Products Dealer, Embossed, Tin, 30 x 36 In.	325
Sign, We Use Genuine Chevrolet Parts, Tin, Flange, 18 x 19 In.	1534
Sign, Whitaker Automotive, Cable Service, Tin, Die Cut, 13 x 17 In.	89
Sign, White Eagle Gasoline, Balance With Ethyl Logo, Round, Porcelain, 2-Sided, 30 In.	2478
Sign, Wise Man, Ford, Chromolitho, Model T, Akron Tire Display, 1923, 41 x 27 In. *illus*	1410
Sign, Wolf's Head Motor Oil, Vertical, Tin Front, Wood Back, 82 x 12 In.	708
Sign, Wolf's Head Oil, Metal, Red, Cream, Howling Wolf, 2-Sided, 10 ½ x 18 In.	1438
Sofa, Tail End Of 1966 Corvette, Cut Into, Red, Cream, Fiberglass, Leather, 36 x 84 In.	604
Tin, AC Spark Plugs, The Standard Spark Plug Of The World, Blue, Red, Gold, 3 x 8 In.	30
Traffic Button, Embossed Stop, Dome Shape, Raised Feet, Cast Iron, c.1920, 14 In.	250
Traffic Light, 3-Light-Hanging, Yellow Paint, Eagle Signal Corp., 30 In. *illus*	450
Traffic Light, 4-Way, Metal	452
Traffic Light, Plastic, Metal Frame, 45 In.	120
Tray, Havoline Motor Oil, Cans, Bottles, 11 x 13 In.	6
Tray, Standard Vacuum Oil Company, Embossed Elephant, Metal, Oval	59

AUTUMN LEAF pattern china was made for the Jewel Tea Company beginning in 1933. Hall China Company of East Liverpool, Ohio, Crooksville China Company of Crooksville, Ohio, Harker Potteries of Chester, West Virginia, and Paden City Pottery, Paden City, West Virginia, made dishes with this design. Autumn Leaf has remained popular and was made by Hall China Company until 1978. Some other pieces in the Autumn Leaf pattern are still being made. For more prices, go to kovels.com.

Bowl, Vegetable, Oval, 10 ⅜ In.	15
Butter, Cover, Lb., 8 ¾ x 5 ⅝ x 4 In.	99

Casserole, 1 ¼ Qt.	25
Creamer	15
Cup & Saucer	9
Custard Cup, 2 ⅛ In.	5
Drip Jar, Lid, 5 In.	19
Jug, Ball, 6 ½ In.	65
Marmalade, Underplate, 4 ¾ x 2 ½ In.	35
Nesting Bowls, Ribbed, 3 Piece	85
Pitcher, 32 Oz.	21
Plate, Bread & Butter, 6 ⅛ In.	5
Plate, Dinner, 10 ⅛ In.	36
Platter, Oval, 11 ¼ In.	35
Salt & Pepper, Handles	45
Salt & Pepper, Ruffled Bottom, 2 ½ In.	48
Serving Bowl, 9 In.	18
Soup, Dish, Rimmed, 8 ½ In.	12
Sugar	18
Teapot, Aladdin Shape, 11 x 6 In.	60
Teapot, Donut Shape, 7 ½ In.	29
Vase, Oval, Footed, 5 ¾ In.	140
Vase, Pinched Neck, 5 ¾ In.	230

AVON *bottles are listed in the Bottle category under Avon.*

AZALEA dinnerware was made for Larkin Company customers from 1918 to 1941. Larkin, the soap company, was in Buffalo, New York. The dishes were made by Noritake China Company of Japan. Each piece of the white china was decorated with pink azaleas.

Bonbon, Loop Handle, 6 ⅝ In.	43
Bowl, Vegetable, Oval, 9 In.	37
Bowl, Vegetable, Round, 10 In.	49
Bowl, Vegetable, Round, Divided, 10 In.	176
Butter, Cover, Round	64
Celery Dish, Open Handle, 12 ¾ In.	21
Creamer, 2 ¾ In.	18
Cup & Saucer	19
Eggcup, 3 ⅛ In.	20
Gravy Boat, Underplate	40
Grill Plate, 3 Sections, 10 ½ In.	138
Plate, Bread & Butter, 6 ½ In.	9
Plate, Dinner, 9 ⅞ In.	24
Plate, Luncheon, 8 ½ In.	15
Plate, Salad, 7 ⅝ In.	10
Platter, 10 In.	125
Platter, Oval, 16 In.	369
Relish, 2 Sections, 8 ⅜ In.	36
Relish, 4 Sections, Loop Handle, 10 ⅜ In.	108
Salt & Pepper, Bulbous	35
Sugar, Lid, 3 In.	16
Teapot, Lid, 3 Cup	109
Toothpick Holder, 6-Sided, 2 ½ In.	46

BACCARAT glass was made in France by La Compagnie des Cristalleries de Baccarat, located 150 miles from Paris. The factory was started in 1765. The firm went bankrupt and began operating again about 1822. Cane and millefiori paperweights were made during the 1845 to 1880 period. The firm is still working near Paris making paperweights and glasswares.

Bowl, Boat Shape, Coil Interior Base, 16 x 11 ½ In.	118
Bowl, Clear, Vertical, Horizontal Bands, 16 x 7 In.	1452
Champagne Coupe, Narcissus, Pattern, Acid Etched, 1900s, 5 ½ x 3 ¾ In., 14 Piece	1293
Champagne Flute, Capri, Optic, Acid Etched Mark, 7 ¼ In., 5 Piece	184
Champagne Flute, Vega Flutissimo, Marked, 11 ¼ In., Pair	121
Cookie Jar, Cameo Cut, Chrysanthemum, Etched, Yellow, Bronze Handle, c.1900, 6 In.	1200
Decanter, Globular, Narrow Neck, Faceted Stopper, 13 In.	150
Goblet, Water, Capri, Optic, Acid Etched Mark, 7 In., 14 Piece	575
Goblet, Water, Cased Cranberry, Cut Panel, Clear Panel Stem, Colored Base, 5 ½ In.	118

Bank, Mechanical, Boy & Bulldog, Cast Iron, H.L. Judd
$4,200

Morphy Auctions

Bank, Mechanical, Building, Panorama, Cast Iron, J. & E. Stevens, 6 ½ In.
$1,944

Pook & Pook, Inc.

Bank, Mechanical, Bulldog, Seated, Glass Eyes, Cast Iron, J. & E. Stevens, 7 ⅝ In.
$163

Leslie Hindman Auctioneers

This is an edited listing of current prices. Visit Kovels.com to check thousands of prices from previous years and sign up for free information on trends, tips, reproductions, marks, and more.

Bank, Mechanical, Dinah, Black Woman, John Harper
$334

Pook & Pook, Inc.

Bank, Mechanical, Eagle & Eaglets, Cast Iron, J. & E. Stevens
$365

Pook & Pook, Inc.

Bank, Mechanical, Elephant & Howdah, Cast Iron, 6 ¼ In.
$330

Morphy Auctions

Bank, Mechanical, Fishing Bears, Put Fish In Bucket, Tin Litho, Battery, Japan, 7 In.
$600

Victorian Casino Antiques

Mustard, Lid, Spoon, Shaped & Paneled Sides	75
Paperweight, Anemone, Blue & White Flowers, Leaves, Star Cut Base, 3 In. *illus*	608
Paperweight, Black Monkey, Green Carpet Ground Canes, Animal Canes, 1975, 3 In.	360
Paperweight, Close Packed Millefiori, 1859, 2 ¾ In.	1033
Paperweight, Concentric Millefiori, 2 ½ In.	356
Paperweight, Dog, Rose, Cobalt Blue Petals, White Trim, Green Leaves, Stems, 2 ¾ x 2 In.	547
Paperweight, Flowers, Box, 1971, 3 x 2 In.	415
Paperweight, Millefiori Garlands, Clear Ground, 2 ¾ In.	486
Paperweight, Millefiori, Concentric, White, Blue, 1 ¾ In.	91
Paperweight, Millefiori, Packed Closely, 1846, 3 In.	1599
Paperweight, Millefiori, Purple, White Concentric, 2 In.	119
Paperweight, Multicolor Flower Canes, Signed, Dated 28-8-1973, 3 x 3 ½ In. *illus*	431
Paperweight, Mushroom Millefiori, 3 In.	415
Paperweight, Orange, White Flower, Blue Ground, 1974, 2 ¾ In.	182
Paperweight, Packed Millefiori, Zodiac Silhouettes, 1978, 3 In.	668
Paperweight, Pansy, Bud, Leaves, Stem, Clear Ground, Star Cut Base, 3 x 2 ⅜ In.	332
Paperweight, Pansy, Purple, Amber, Striping, 2 ⅜ x 2 In.	593
Paperweight, Pink, Blue Flowers, White Honeycomb Ground, 1986, 3 In.	395
Paperweight, Pink, White Primrose, Clear Ground, 2 ½ In.	356
Paperweight, Scattered Millefiori, White Muslin Ground, Silhouette Canes, c.1848, 2 In.	1200
Paperweight, Scrambled Canes, 2 ½ In.	59
Sculpture, Tete De Cerf, Marked, 1900s, 16 x 23 In.	3750
Vase, Clear, Flared, Fluted Sides, 15 x 8 ½ In.	590
Vase, Clear, Waisted, Applied Angled Rods, 10 In.	177
Vase, Club, Square Panel Design, Square Plinth, Bombe Flair, Narrow Neck, 10 In.	115
Vase, Flowers, Painted, White Opaline Ground, Flared, Rim, c.1870, 13 ¾ In., Pair	2500
Vase, Grasshopper, Opaque, Fan Shape Base, Molded Flower Stem, 1900s, 8 ½ In., Pair	480
Vase, Oceanic, Millefiori Fitted Roller, Clear, Shaped Square, 1900s, 8 x 8 In.	295

BADGES have been used since before the Civil War. Collectors search for examples of all types, including law enforcement and company identification badges. Well-known prison or law enforcement badges are most desirable. Most are made of nickel or brass. Many recent reproductions have been made.

Constable, Lincoln Nebr., Lancaster Co., Silver, 6-Point Star, Blue Enamel, 3 ¼ In.	1062
Deputy Sheriff, Jackson County, No. 36, 5-Point Ball Tip Star, Gold Metal, 2 ⅜ In.	472
Fireman, Captain, Truck 218, Freeport, Leather, 5 ½ In.	69
G-Men, Eagle, Wings, 1930s, 2 x 2 In.	175
Gold Cross & Food Physician, Enamel, Metal, c.1915, 3 In.	100
Honorary Jr. Clerk State Senate, Southwest Stamp Co., 1949	225
Junior Forest Fire Fighting, Boy, Portrait, Protect Our Trees, 1940s, 2 x 1 In.	50
Marshal, City Of Greenville, Ga., R.W. Maffett, Sterling Silver, Shield Shape, 1890	708
Police, Pittston, Pa., No. 10, Nickel, c.1900, 2 ½ x 2 ½ In.	345
Police, Washington, D.C., Truman, Inaugural, Metal, c.1945, 3 ⅛ In.	403
Prescott Fire Dept., Hose, Helmet Ribbon, Fire Tools, Ladder In Circle, Gold, T Pin, 2 ¾ In.	354
Press, World Series, Cleveland, Indian, Teepee, 1954, 1 ⁵⁄₁₆ In.	268
Sheriff, Greenlee County, Arizona, Brass, Embossed, Enamel Letters, 2 x 2 ½ In. *illus*	600
Sheriff, Tolland Co., Conn., 14K Yellow Gold, 1915	4500
Trainman, Delaware & Hudson, Crest Style, Silver, Blue	125

BANKS of metal have been made since 1868. There are still banks, mechanical banks, and registering banks (those that show the total money deposited on the face of the bank). Many old iron or tin banks have been reproduced since the 1950s in iron or plastic. Some old reproductions marked *Book of Knowledge, John Wright,* or *Capron* may be listed. Pottery, glass, and plastic banks are also listed here. Mickey Mouse and other Disneyana banks are listed in Disneyana. We have added the M numbers based on *The Penny Bank Book: Collecting Still Banks* by Andy and Susan Moore and the R numbers based on *Coin Banks by Banthrico* by James L. Redwine. There were several auctions of major collections of banks this year. Banks in excellent condition sold for very high prices. We have listed prices for the exceptional banks as well as prices for average banks.

Alphabet, Stacked Blocks, Cast Iron, M 1604, 3 ⅞ In.	3792
Anvil, Silver Paint, Cast Iron, 6 x 10 In.	30
Bank Building, 4 Towers, Cast Iron, 6 In.	450
Bank Building, 4 Towers, Japanned, J. & E. Stevens, M 1121, 6 In.	177
Bank Building, City Bank, Cast Iron, M 1111, 4 In.	210
Bank Building, Columbia, Cast Iron, Kenton, M 1070, 5 ½ In.	360

Bank, Mechanical, Football Player, Cast Iron, 7 In.
$300

Morphy Auctions

Bank, Mechanical, Galloping Cowboy, Tin, Battery Operated, Cragstan, Japan, 7 x 8 In.
$336

Victorian Casino Antiques

Bank, Mechanical, Humpty Dumpty, Coin Deposits In Mouth, Shepard Hardware, Pat. 1882
$1,121

Bertoia Auctions

Bank, Mechanical, Initiating Bank 2nd Degree, Goat, Frog, Man, Mechanical Novelty, 7 ½ In.
$2,400

Morphy Auctions

Bank, Mechanical, Magician, Cast Iron, J. & E. Stevens
$5,103

Pook & Pook, Inc.

Bank, Mechanical, Monkey, Organ Grinder, Light Green Base, Hubley, 1933, 9 In.
$360

Morphy Auctions

Bank, Mechanical, Organ, Monkey, Dancing Cat & Dog, Kyser & Rex, Pat. 1882
$472

Bertoia Auctions

Bank, Mechanical, Owl, Turns Head, Cast Iron, J. & E. Stevens
$516

Pook & Pook, Inc.

Bank, Mechanical, Parrot & Monkey, Tin, 6 In.
$270

Morphy Auctions

Bank, Mechanical, Praying Figure, Komm Heruber Und Hilf Uns, Tin, Germany, 9 In.
$577

Pook & Pook, Inc.

Bank, Mechanical, Punch & Judy, Cast Iron, Shepard Hardware, Pat. 1884
$1,298

Bertoia Auctions

Bank, Mechanical, Tammany Hall, Pockets Coin, J. & E. Stevens, Pat. 1873, 5 ¾ In.
$148

Bertoia Auctions

Bank, Mechanical, Trenton Trust, 75th Anniversary, 8 In.
$390

Morphy Auctions

Bank, Mechanical, Trick Dog, Cast Iron, Repainted, 8 ½ In.
$150

Morphy Auctions

Bank, Mechanical, Uncle Sam & Arab Oil, 11 In.
$96

Morphy Auctions

Bank, Mechanical, Uncle Sam, Coin In Satchel, Shepard Hardware, Pat. 1886, 11 In.
$1,298

Bertoia Auctions

Bank, Mechanical, William Tell, Cast Iron, J. & E. Stevens, c.1896
$941

RSL Auction

Bank, Multiplying, Green Paint, Glass, Cast Iron, J. & E. Stevens, c.1883
$20,213

RSL Auction

Bank Building, Cupola, Yellow, Blue, Red, Cast Iron, J. & E. Stevens, M 1145, 5 ½ In.	118
Bank Building, Emigrant Industrial Savings, Eagle, Spread Wings, 7 ½ In.	35
Bank Building, Home Savings, Cast Iron, M 1126, 6 In.	210
Bank Building, House, Cast Iron, White, Red, Green Trim, 5 ½ In.	510
Bank Building, Pagoda, Cast Iron, M 1153, 5 In.	480
Bank Building, Painted, Cast Iron, J. & E. Stevens, 6 ½ In.	540
Battleship, Kentucky, Cast Iron, White Paint, J. & E. Stevens, c.1901, 10 ¼ In.	1003
Bean Pot, Nickel Register, Red Paint, Cast Iron, M 951, 2 ¾ In.	119
Black Boy, 2 Faces, Cast Iron, A.C. Williams, M 83, c.1901, 4 In.	250
Building, Columbia Tower, Cast Iron, Grey Iron Casting, M 1118, 6 In.	122
Building, First Presbyterian Church, Painted, Cast Iron, U.S.A., c.1895, 15 ¾ In. ....*illus*	19600
Building, Independence Hall, Cast Iron, Enterprise Mfg. Co., Philadelphia, c.1875 ....*illus*	2328
Building, Independence Hall, Cast Iron, Enterprise, M 1242, 10 In.	326
Building, Independence Hall, Red Paint, Cast Iron, 9 In.	474
Building, Independence Tower, Cast Iron, Eagle Finial, Enterprise, M 1202, 9 ¾ In.	561
Building, Palace, Gold Cupola, Ives, M 116, c.1885, 7 ½ x 8 In.	1888
Building, Space Heater, Bird, Cast Iron, England, M 1087, 6 ½ In.	360
Building, State House, Cast Iron, Painted, A.C. Williams, 6 In.	240
Building, Stollwerck Chocolates, Savings Bank, Glass Window, Tin Litho, 6 ½ x 3 In.	253
Building, Swiss Cottage, Tin Litho, Script On Railing, Cologne, Germany, Stollwerck, 3 ¼ In.	177
Building, Westminster Abbey, Cast Iron, Sydenham & McOustra, England, c.1902 ....*illus*	3675
Building, With Roof, Cast Iron, Japanned, Grey Iron Casting, M 1124, 5 ⅜ In.	413
Camel, Saddle, Black Paint, Cast Iron, A.C. Williams, M 767, 7 ½ x 6 ½ In.	161
Captain Kidd, Cast Iron, Shovel, Tree Trunk, Ives, M 38, 1901	950
Cash Register, Your Savings National, Cast Iron, Cold Paint, 6 ¾ In.	207
Devil, 2 Faces, Grinning, Cast Iron, Painted, A.C. Williams, M 31, 4 ½ In.	660
Dog, Seated, Cast Iron, c.1900, 4 ½ x 5 ¼ In.	259
Dresser, Empire Style, Redware, Tan, Spattered Manganese Glaze, 6 ½ x 6 ¾ In.	259
Duck, On Tub, Save For A Rainy Day, Cast Iron, Hubley, M 616, 5 ⅝ In.	354
Duck, Round, Cast Iron, Painted Blue, Kenton, c.1936, 4 In.	84
Eiffel Tower, Cast Iron, Sydenham & McOustra, England, c.1908 ....*illus*	2328
Elephant, Circus, Cast Iron, Trunk Up, Gray, Spotted Costume, Hat, Hubley, M 462, 4 In.	413
General Butler, Frog Body, Cast Iron, Painted, J. & E. Stevens, 6 ½ In. ....*illus*	10030
Globe, On Arc, Red Paint, Cast Iron, M 789, 5 In.	119
Goodyear Zeppelin, Hanger, Cast Aluminum, 2 ⅜ x 7 ⅜ In.	374
Hansel & Gretel House, Spelter, Heart Shape Lock, Germany, c.1910, 2 ⅞ x 3 ⅛ In. ....*illus*	2083
Helmet, Brass, Embossed Plum & Dragon, 4 ½ In.	119
Ice Cream Freezer, Save Your Money & Freeze It, Grey Iron Casting, M 1371, 4 In.	150
John Brown's Hideout, House Shape, Yellowware, 2 ½ x 2 ½ In.	92
Mary & Little Lamb, Cast Iron, White, M 164, 4 ⅜ In.	354

Mechanical banks were first made about 1870. Any bank with moving parts is considered mechanical. The metal banks made before World War I are the most desirable. Copies and new designs of mechanical banks have been made in metal or plastic since the 1920s. The condition of the paint on the old banks is important. Worn paint can lower a price by 90 percent.

Mechanical, Acrobat, Paint, Cast Iron, J. & E. Stevens, c.1885	3792
Mechanical, Alms Bowl, Nodding Child, Multicolor, Composition, 14 In.	237
Mechanical, Artillery, Cast Iron, J. & E. Stevens, 8 In.	148 to 660
Mechanical, Atlas, Globe On Back, Paint, Cast Iron, 8 In.	12000
Mechanical, Atomic Bank, Duro, Box, 8 ¼ In.	177
Mechanical, Bad Accident, Child Scares Mule, Cast Iron, J. & E. Stevens, 10 In.	948
Mechanical, Baseball Player, Painted, Cast Iron, A.C. Williams, 5 ½ In.	89
Mechanical, Bird On Roof, Black, Cast Iron, J. & E. Stevens	593
Mechanical, Black Girl, Kneeling, Praying, House, German Text, Germany, 9 In.	577
Mechanical, Boy & Bulldog, Cast Iron, H.L. Judd ....*illus*	4200
Mechanical, Boy On Trapeze, Paint, Cast Iron, Barton & Smith, 9 ½ In.	3300
Mechanical, Boy Robbing Bird's Nest, Yellow & Brown, Iron, J. & E. Stevens, c.1910, 7 In.	2430
Mechanical, Boy Scout Camp, Tent, Paint, Cast Iron, J. & E. Stevens, 9 ½ In.	7800
Mechanical, Boys Stealing Watermelon, Paint, Cast Iron, Kyser & Rex, 6 ½ In.	2673 to 4200
Mechanical, Building, Panorama, Cast Iron, J. & E. Stevens, 6 ½ In. ....*illus*	1944
Mechanical, Bulldog, Pull Tail, Blue Blanket, Paint, Cast Iron, 7 ¾ In.	480
Mechanical, Bulldog, Red Blanket, J. & E. Stevens, 1880s, 8 In.	1700
Mechanical, Bulldog, Seated, Glass Eyes, Cast Iron, J. & E. Stevens, 7 ⅝ In. ....*illus*	163
Mechanical, Calamity, 3 Football Players, Paint, Cast Iron, J. & E. Stevens, c.1904	2607

Bank, Palace, Multicolor Version, Cast Iron, Ives, Blakeslee Co., c.1885
$39,200

RSL Auction

Barber, Chair, Koken, Sea Foam Green, Chrome
$660

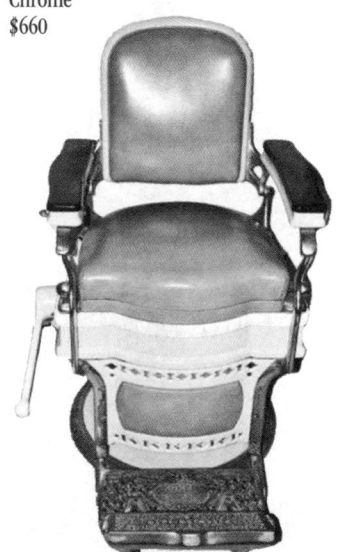

Morphy Auctions

Barber, Pole, Ice Cream Cone Shape, Light, 28 In.
$2,280

Showtime Auction Services

Barber, Pole, Pine, Carved, Turned, Tapered, Ball & Knob Finial, Painted, c.1865, 32 In.
$1,458

James D. Julia Auctioneers

Mechanical, Cat & Mouse, Paint, Cast Iron, J. & E. Stevens, 8 ½ In.	3000
Mechanical, Chief Big Moon, Frog, Indian, Paint, Cast Iron, J. & E. Stevens, 10 In.	729 to 1416
Mechanical, Circus Ticket Collector, Nods Head, Paint, Cast Iron, H.L. Judd, c.1890	486
Mechanical, Circus, Pony Kicks, Clown Gestures, Cast Iron, Shepard Hardware	2360
Mechanical, Clown On Globe, Yellow Base, Cast Iron, J. & E. Stevens, 9 In.	1200
Mechanical, Coasting Bank, Child, On Sled, Arms Out, Lead, Iron, J. & E. Stevens, 6 x 10 In.	266500
Mechanical, Confederate Soldier Shoots, Southern Comfort Bottle, Brass, 6 x 9 In.	59
Mechanical, Creedmoor, Paint, Cast Iron, J. & E. Stevens, 10 In.	900
Mechanical, Darktown Battery, Cast Iron, J. & E. Stevens, 1888, 9 ½ In.	3259 to 3318
Mechanical, Dinah, Black Woman, John Harper ....*illus*	334
Mechanical, Dog On Turntable, Building, Cast Iron, H.L. Judd, 4 ½ In.	360
Mechanical, Eagle & Eaglets, Cast Iron, 6 x 6 ¾ In.	1298
Mechanical, Eagle & Eaglets, Cast Iron, J. & E. Stevens ....*illus*	365
Mechanical, Elephant & 3 Clowns, Paint, Cast Iron, J. & E. Stevens, 6 In.	2160
Mechanical, Elephant & Howdah, Cast Iron, 6 ¼ In. ....*illus*	330
Mechanical, Fidelity Trust, Cashier Clock, Cast Iron, 6 ½ In.	1020
Mechanical, Fishing Bears, Put Fish In Bucket, Tin Litho, Battery, Japan, 7 In. ....*illus*	600
Mechanical, Football Player, Cast Iron, 7 In. ....*illus*	300
Mechanical, Football, English, Paint, Cast Iron, John Harper, 10 In.	2700
Mechanical, Frog On Round Base, Lattice, Green & Yellow Paint, Cast Iron, J. & E. Stevens	119
Mechanical, Galloping Cowboy, Tin, Battery Operated, Cragstan, Japan, 7 x 8 In. ....*illus*	336
Mechanical, Giant In Tower, Cast Iron, John Harper, 1892, 8 ½ In.	711
Mechanical, Giant In Tower, Red & Yellow Paint, Cast Iron, John Harper, c.1890, 9 ½ In.	16800
Mechanical, Girl Skipping Rope, Squirrel, Cast Iron, Key Wind, J. & E. Stevens, 1890, 8 In.	7670
Mechanical, Hall's Excelsior, Cast Iron, Painted, J. & E. Stevens, c.1910, 5 ½ In.	1446
Mechanical, Hall's Excelsior, Cast Iron, Red & White, J. & E. Stevens	472
Mechanical, Hall's Liliput, Man, Paint, Iron, J. & E. Stevens, 4 ½ In.	243 to 3600
Mechanical, Humpty Dumpty, Coin Deposits In Mouth, Shepard Hardware, Pat. 1882 ....*illus*	1121
Mechanical, I Always Did 'Spise A Mule, Cast Iron, c.1880, 10 In.	281
Mechanical, Indian Shooting Bear, Nodding, Iron, J. & E. Stevens, 10 ½ In.	1823 to 3000
Mechanical, Initiating Bank 2nd Degree, Goat, Frog, Man, Mechanical Novelty, 7 ½ In. ....*illus*	2400
Mechanical, Jolly Nigger, Cast Iron, Red & Black Paint, J. & E. Stevens, 6 ½ In.	450
Mechanical, Jonah & The Whale, Paint, Shepard Hardware, 10 ½ In.	1185 to 3600
Mechanical, Leap Frog, 2 Boys, Tree, Paint, Iron, Shepard Hardware, 7 ½ In.	1003 to 1140
Mechanical, Lion & 2 Monkeys, Up A Tree, Paint, Iron, Kyser & Rex, c.1885, 9 In.	472 to 1185
Mechanical, Lion, Monkeys, Small Peanut Variety, Paint, Cast Iron, 9 In.	1680
Mechanical, Magic Bank, Cast Iron, Painted, Blue, White, Red, J. & E. Stevens, 5 ¼ In.	507
Mechanical, Magician, Cast Iron, J. & E. Stevens ....*illus*	5103
Mechanical, Mason, Hod Carrier, Chimney, Paint, Shepard Hardware, 1890, 7 ½ In.	1094 to 2040
Mechanical, Monkey & Coconut, Paint, Cast Iron, J. & E. Stevens & Co., 8 ½ In.	3000
Mechanical, Monkey, Organ Grinder, Light Green Base, Hubley, 1933, 9 In. ....*illus*	360
Mechanical, Monkey, Red, Orange, Green Paint, Cast Iron, Hubley, 8 ¾ In.	1800
Mechanical, Mule Entering Barn, Paint, Cast Iron, J. & E. Stevens, 8 ½ In.	1080
Mechanical, Novelty Bank, Brown, Green Paint, Cast Iron, J. & E. Stevens, 6 ½ In.	450 to 840
Mechanical, Organ, Monkey, Dancing Cat & Dog, Kyser & Rex, Pat. 1882 ....*illus*	472
Mechanical, Owl, Turns Head, Cast Iron, J. & E. Stevens ....*illus*	516
Mechanical, Parrot & Monkey, Tin, 6 In. ....*illus*	270
Mechanical, Peg-Leg Beggar, Paint, Cast Iron, Black, Gold Coat, H.L. Judd, c.1880, 5 In.	2530
Mechanical, Pelican, Man Thumbs Nose, Black Paint, Cast Iron, 8 In.	11400
Mechanical, Pelican, Rabbit In Beak, Black Paint, Cast Iron, Trenton Lock & Hardware	1185
Mechanical, Perfection, Registering, Woman, Dog, Soldier, Paint, Iron, J. & E. Stevens, 5 ½ In..	10800
Mechanical, Praying Figure, Komm Heruber Und Hilf Uns, Tin, Germany, 9 In. ....*illus*	577
Mechanical, Presto Bank, Cast Iron, Japanned, Red Door & Roof, Kyser & Rex, 4 ½ In.	266
Mechanical, Professor Pug Frog, Paint, Iron, J. & E. Stevens, 10 ½ In.	3245 to 6000
Mechanical, Punch & Judy, Cast Iron, Shepard Hardware, Pat. 1884 ....*illus*	1298
Mechanical, Punch & Judy, Large Letter Variety, Paint, Cast Iron, 7 ½ In.	1560
Mechanical, Rabbit, Eating Cabbage, Paint, Cast Iron, Kilgore, 4 ½ In.	180
Mechanical, Reclining Chinese Man, Blue Pants, Cast Iron, J. & E. Stevens, 8 In.	4200
Mechanical, Red Riding Hood, Grandmother, Reproduction, Paint, Cast Iron, c.1940s, 8 In.	1800
Mechanical, Rooster, Black, Red Paint, 6 In.	780
Mechanical, Santa Claus, Chimney, Gray Coat, Paint, Iron, Shepard Hardware, c.1890, 6 In.	1440
Mechanical, Speaking Dog, Girl, Red Dress, Paint, Shepard Hardware, 8 In.	395 to 2160
Mechanical, Tammany Hall, Black, Yellow Paint, Cast Iron, 5 ½ In.	354
Mechanical, Tammany Hall, Pockets Coin, J. & E. Stevens, Pat. 1873, 5 ¾ In. ....*illus*	148
Mechanical, Tammany, Cast Iron, J. & E. Stevens	30

Mechanical, Toad On Stump, Black Paint, Cast Iron, J. & E. Stevens..................................	296
Mechanical, Trenton Trust, 75th Anniversary, 8 In. ....*illus*	390
Mechanical, Trick Dog, Cast Iron, Repainted, 8 ½ In. ....*illus*	150
Mechanical, Trick Dog, Jumps Through Hoop, Cast Iron, Shepard Hardware	270 to 649
Mechanical, Trick Pony, Brown, Silver Paint, Cast Iron, Shepard Hardware....................	516
Mechanical, Trick Pony, Paint, Cast Iron, Shepard Hardware, 7 In.	330 to 1416
Mechanical, Uncle Remus, Policeman, Chicken Coop, Paint, Cast Iron, Kyser & Rex, 6 In.	5400
Mechanical, Uncle Sam & Arab Oil, 11 In. ....*illus*	96
Mechanical, Uncle Sam, Coin In Satchel, Shepard Hardware, Pat. 1886, 11 In. ....*illus*	1298
Mechanical, William Tell, Cast Iron, J. & E. Stevens, c.1896 ....*illus*	941
Mechanical, William Tell, Rifle, Paint, Cast Iron, J. & E. Stevens, 10 ½ In.	472 to 720
Mechanical, Zoo, Cast Iron, Red, Green Shutters, Kyser & Rex, c.1894................................	1652
Money Bag, 100,000 Dollars, Cinched Top, Silver, Gold Paint, Cast Iron, M 1262, 3 ½ In.	49
Mosque, Domed, Combination Lock Door, Painted, Cast Iron, M 1176, 5 In.	59
Multiplying, Green Paint, Glass, Cast Iron, J. & E. Stevens, c.1883 ....*illus*	20213
Palace, Multicolor Version, Cast Iron, Ives, Blakeslee Co., c.1885 ....*illus*	39200
Pig, Seated, Gold Paint, Cast Iron, 4 ¾ In.	36
Polar Bear, Gold Bronze Finish, Red Mouth, Arcade, M 716, c.1912, 5 ¼ In.	150
Prudential Registering, Nickel, Silver Paint, Cast Iron, c.1880, 7 ¼ In.	152
Register, Penny & Nickel, Lighthouse, 1895, 12 In.	1500
Rhino, Black Paint, Cast Iron, Arcade, M 721, 5 In.	178
Safe, American Bank, Cast Iron, Nickeled, Scrolls, Combination Dial Door, Arcade, 4 In.............	561
Safe, Bank Of Columbia, M 906, Cast Iron, Arcade, 5 In.	360
Safe, Bank Of Industry, Blacksmith, Red, Nickeled Door, Kenton, 5 ⅜ In.........................	240 to 295
Safe, Chicago Savings, Cast Iron, 2 Doors, 2 Locks, Latticework, Kenton, c.1896...................	561
Safe, Cupid, Cast Iron, Nickel Finish, Flower Handle, Kenton, c.1911, 4 ⅝ In.......................	118
Safe, Diamond Safe, Cast Iron, Nickel Plated, Embossed Diamonds, Key, 6 ⅜ In......................	236
Safe, Grand Jewel Safe, Star, Cast Iron, Electroplated, Double Combination Lock, 5 ¼ In.	443
Safe, Home Savings, Cast Iron, 5 ½ In.	240
Safe, Iron, Key, Painted, Black, Green, White, 4 ¼ In..	83
Safe, Puzzle Try Me, Cast Iron, Green Paint, Gold Trim, M 871, c.1868, 2 ½ In.	1416
Safe, Wells Fargo Company Express, Wall, Cast Iron, Dodge City, Kansas, 10 x 13 x 16 In.	3705
Safe, White City Puzzle Safe, Electroplated, Buildings, Ferris Wheel, Nicol, M 910, 4 In.............	89
Santa With Tree, Red, White Paint, Cast Iron, Hubley, M 61, 5 ¾ In.................................	652
Shell Out, White Paint, Cast Iron, J. & E. Stevens, M 1622, 2 ½ x 5 In...............................	237
Taft-Sherman, Peaceful Bill, Smiling Jim, 2 Faces, John Harper, M 109, c.1908, 4 In.	1770
Top Hat, Handle, Paint, Tin, 4 ¼ In..	61
U.S. Mail, Silver, Red Paint, Cast Iron, 7 In.	652
Windmill, Metal, 8 ½ In.	96
Yellow Cab, Cast Iron, Orange & Black Paint, Arcade, 8 In..	1920
Young America, M 881, Japanned, Boy On Bicycle, Kyser & Rex, c.1882, 4 ⅜ In.	148

BARBER collectibles range from the popular red and white striped pole that used to be found in front of every shop to the small scissors and tools of the trade. Barber chairs are wanted, especially the older models with elaborate iron trim.

Cabinet, Mug, 12 Slots, Wood, c.1960, 24 x 27 In., Pair..	150
Chair Booster Seat, Tan Leather Cushion, Handles, Child's..	84
Chair, Adjustable Headrest, Reclining, Relief Carved Swan Arms, c.1865, 49 x 23 In.	238
Chair, Cast Iron, Oak, Leather, Adjustable, Harvard Co., Canton, Ohio, Victorian....................	1599
Chair, Horse Head, Carved Wood, Porcelain Base, Leather Seat, Koken, Child's....................	2166
Chair, Koken, Head Rest, Foot Rest, Velvet Covering, 1890..	960
Chair, Koken, Porcelain, Leather, Foot Rest, Hydraulic Pump, Salesman's Sample, 16 In.	35550
Chair, Koken, Sea Foam Green, Chrome ....*illus*	660
Chair, Round Seat, Back, Quartersawn Oak, Black Leather, Nickel Plating, Berninghaus............	5100
Chair, Walnut, Swan Neck Arms, Leather Upholstery, Eugene Berninghaus, Oh., Victorian..........	213
Chair, White Metal, Black Leather, Koken..	173
Chair, White Metal, Spread Base, Lattice Footrest, Red Leather, Emil J. Paidar	288
Globe, Leaded Glass, Cast Iron, Wall Bracket, 15 ½ x 11 ½ In.	900
Pole Plaque, Red, White, Wood, c.1910, 36 In.	210
Pole, Glass, Cast Iron, Red, White, Blue Spiral, Electrified, Wall Bracket, Koken, 24 x 11 In.........	365
Pole, Ice Cream Cone Shape, Light, 28 In. ....*illus*	2280
Pole, Pine, Carved, Red, White, Blue Stripes, Paint, Ball Finial, c.1910, 70 x 5 ½ In....................	708
Pole, Pine, Carved, Turned, Tapered, Ball & Knob Finial, Painted, c.1865, 32 In. ....*illus*	1458
Pole, Pine, Red, White, Blue Paint, Turned, Floor Standing, 45 In....................................	1680

Barber, Pole, Rounded Ends, Stripes, Koken, 1940s-50s, 25 In.
$330

Morphy Auctions

Barber, Tin, Powder, Sykes After Shaving, Comfort Powder Co., Boston, Mass., 4 ½ In.
$3,420

Showtime Auction Services

Barometer, Stick, Charles Wilder, Mahogany, Woodruff's Patent, 1860, 37 ¾ x 4 ½ In.
$594

Rago Arts & Auction Center

B

Barometer, Stick, J.E. Paxton, Silvered Dial, Thermometer, 1800s, 38 In. $299

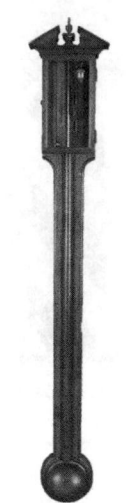

Neal Auction Co.

Barometer, Thermometer, Louis XVI, Giltwood, L. Eng & Chevallier Opt., c.1785, 36 In. $5,412

New Orleans Auction Galleries, Inc.

Barometer, Wheel, J. Ronchetti, Mahogany, Hygrometer, Thermometer, Level, c.1835, 40 In. $450

Cowan's Auctions

Pole, Pine, Turned, Multicolor Paint, Gilt, Wall Mount, c.1910, 24 In.	960
Pole, Porcelain, Red, White, Blue, White Globe, Theo Koch's Co., Chicago, 82 x 16 In.	1920
Pole, Red, White, Blue Base & Ball Top, c.1910, 65 In.	270
Pole, Red, White, Blue, Light-Up, Geometric Glass Globe, Metal Flange, 27 In.	180
Pole, Rounded Ends, Stripes, Koken, 1940s-50s, 25 In. ....*illus*	330
Pole, Wall Mount, Red, White, Blue, Wood, 25 In.	288
Pole, Wood, Carved, Painted Red, White, Blue, Acorn Shape Finial, c.1900, 88 x 4 In.	570
Pole, Wood, Glass, Metal Ends, Lighted, Early 1900s, 30 In.	240
Pole, Wood, Red & White Spiral, Tapered, Ball Center & Ends, Flush Wall Mount, 25 In.	474
Pole, Wood, Red, White, Ball Top & Bottom, c.1880, 60 In.	210
Pole, Wood, Red, White, Blue Paint, c.1860, 35 In.	719
Pole, Wood, Red, White, c.1900, 67 In.	240
Pole, Wood, Turned, Red, White Blue, Scissors, Wrought Iron Bracket, 35 x 11 In.	1185
Rack, Shaving Mug, 60 Pigeon Holes, Oak, Drawers, Lower Cupboard Doors, 41 x 89 In.	1482
Razor, Straight, Carved Bone Handle, Geo. Washington, B. Franklin, Wilson, 6 ⅜ In.	300
Sign, Hair Stylist, Plastic, 2-Sided, Light-Up, Red, White, Blue, Metal Flange, 16 x 17 In.	210
Sign, Straight Razor, Figural, Wood, Bolted, Blade Pivots, 19th Century, 26 In.	89
Sign, W.C. Scott Upstairs, Red, White, Blue Stripe, c.1925, 36 x 14 In.	240
Strop, Silver Plate, Embossed, Attached To Chair, Retracting Leather, 5 ½ In.	210
Tin, Powder, Sykes After Shaving, Comfort Powder Co., Boston, Mass., 4 ½ In. ....*illus*	3420
Tin, Safety Razor, Mohican, Indian Image, Yellow Ground, 2 ½ x 1 ¼ In.	741
Towel Steamer, Antiseptic Disinfectant, Nickel Plated Copper, Eagle Finial, PAZ, 61 In.	228

BAROMETERS are used to forecast the weather. Antique barometers with elaborate wooden cases and brass trim are the most desirable. Mercury column barometers are also popular with collectors. It is difficult to find someone to repair a broken one, so be sure your barometer is in working condition.

Aneroid, Oak Case, Ormolu Mounts, Thermometer, 1800s, 43 In.	236
Aneroid, Porcelain Face, Mahogany, Carved, c.1900, 7 ¼ In. Diam.	325
Aneroid, Thermometer, Hardwood, Carved, c.1900, 33 x 12 In.	1475
Anthemia, Scrollwork, Medallions, Wheel Face, Pierced, Carved, Gilt, c.1825, 35 x 22 In.	1045
Banjo, Gothic Style, Knott & Co., Paper Label, Mahogany, c.1850, 36 In.	300
Banjo, Mahogany, Broken Swan Crest, England, c.1850, 39 In.	182
Banjo, Mahogany, Inlaid, Tognietti & Co., England, c.1820, 38 x 10 ¼ In.	236
Banjo, Mahogany, Inscribed Anone & Co., 38 ¼ In.	510
Banjo, Mahogany, Shell Patera, Rosette Inlay, Ireland, 1800s, 37 ½ x 10 In.	236
Banjo, Mahogany, Signed A. Peduzzi, England, c.1850, 38 In.	237
Banjo, Rosewood, c.1850, 37 ¾ In.	243
Banjo, Rosewood, Panzeni & Valli, 39 ½ In.	267
Banjo, Thermometer Mahogany, Inlays, Humidity Dial, England, c.1845, 47 In.	2242
Banjo, Thermometer, Mahogany, Flower, Shell Inlays, Farelli, Eng., 38 In.	600
Barograph, Richard Frered, Paris, Wood Case, Glass Panels, 19th Century	540
Cast Iron, Inscribed S.C. Bowen, N.Y., c.1890, 37 In.	89
D.B. & Sons, Brass, Gilt & Silvered, Leaves, Drum Form, 8 In.	923
Diamond Shape, Swift & Anderson, Hardwood, 1950s, 16 x 9 x 2 In.	39
Flugelhorn Shape, Brass, Leather, Germany, 10 In.	34
Giltwood, Ornate Carving, France, c.1820, 31 ½ In.	2066
Louis XVI Style, Giltwood, Scientific Theme Carvings, Square, 37 x 23 In.	3125
Mixed Wood, Octagonal, Gilt Frame, Hand Lettered, Plastered Board, 1800s, 36 In.	470
Pocket, Compass, Brass, Silvered Dial, Fleur-De-Lis North, John Browning, London, 1800s	360
Rosewood, Mother-Of-Pearl Inlay, Leafy Scroll, Bird, J. Hancock, 40 ½ In.	469
Stick, Burl Walnut, Stepped Cornice, Thermometer Dial, 38 In.	450
Stick, C. Wilder, Bird's-Eye Maple, Acorn Finial, 1860, 39 In.	3120
Stick, Charles Wilder, Mahogany, Woodruff's Patent, 1860, 37 ¾ x 4 ½ In. ....*illus*	594
Stick, Federal, Mahogany, Signed Bros., Kendal N. Lebanon, 35 ½ In.	1080
Stick, George III, Mahogany, Thermometer, Silvered Dial, T. Bragonzi, 39 In.	390
Stick, Hepplewhite, Mahogany, Line Inlays, Eagle, Signed P.G. Cranbrook, c.1800, 40 In.	1422
Stick, J.E. Paxton, Silvered Dial, Thermometer, 1800s, 38 In. ....*illus*	299
Stick, L. Balernal, Mahogany, Scrolls, Flowers, Bust, Bone Dials, 47 In.	1920
Stick, Mahogany, Arch Top, Thomson, London, 1700s, 36 In.	3540
Stick, Mahogany, Brass Gimbaled Mount, Chas. Jones, Liverpool, c.1800, 37 In.	4320
Stick, Mahogany, Brass Gimbaled Mount, England, c.1810, 37 In.	4320
Stick, Mahogany, Charles Wilder, Peterboro, New Hampshire, 37 In.	356
Stick, Mahogany, Dome Top, Ball Base, Thermometer, Chadburn Bros., Eng., c.1850, 36 In.	1770

Stick, Mahogany, Hinged Glazed Door, Engraved Silvered Brass Dial, Thermometer, c.1825, 39 In.	472
Stick, Mahogany, James Foster Jr., Signed, c.1950, 38 ½ x 6 x 2 ¼ In.	687
Stick, Mahogany, W. Watkins, Charing Cross, England, 36 In.	1080
Stick, Molded Cornice, Silvered Engraved Scales, Frederick Pool, Boston, 39 In.	3000
Stick, S. & A. Calderara, Mahogany, Carved Scrolled Crest, London, c.1880, 41 ½ In.	840
Stick, Spencer Browning Co., Rosewood, Inlaid, Bone Scale, 37 In.	1560
Stick, Storm King, Walnut, Telescope Shape, Molded Crest, E.C. Spooner, c.1850, 42 In.	900
Stick, U.S. Navy, W.M. Welch, Brass, Silvered Dials, Case, 43 In.	1200
Stick, Wood, Ivory Markings, Dome Top, Ball Shape, James Gargory, England, c.1810, 35 In.	472
Thermometer, Admiral Fitzroy's, Oak, Mercury Tube, Atmospheric Gauge, 1800s, 40 ½ In.	295
Thermometer, Banjo, Edwardian, Inlaid Mahogany, J. Lizars, 38 In.	360
Thermometer, Hygrometer, Mahogany, Butler's Mirror, Weather Dial, 1800s, 42 In.	359
Thermometer, Hygrometer, Steel, Bronze, Marble Plinth, Handle, c.1875, 9 x 9 In.	2570
Thermometer, Louis Philippe, Giltwood, Lyre Shape Surmount, c.1840, 33 In.	2629
Thermometer, Louis XVI, Giltwood, L. Eng & Chevallier Opt., c.1785, 36 In. *illus*	5412
Thermometer, Metal, Fretwork, Eiffel Tower, France, 21 ½ In.	750
Thermometer, Naudet Petuis Hulot, Carved Wood Frame, c.1898, 34 ½ x 20 In.	276
Thermometer, Oak, Carved Case, Spiral Columns, Victorian, 45 In.	360
Thermometer, Oak, Weather Dial, Carved & Incised, c.1885, 40 x 13 ½ In.	615
Thermometer, Plaques, Scale, Woman, Farmer, Pewter Scrolls, Finials, c.1775, 40 x 10 In.	1476
Thermometer, Tiger Oak, Carved Flowers, Art Deco, c.1930, 14 x 8 In.	125
Victorian, Mahogany, Admiral Fitzroys, C. Cordeaux, Clifton, 46 In.	1452
Wheel, D. Fagioli & Son, Mahogany, Inlaid, Silvered Dial, 39 In.	180
Wheel, J. Ronchetti, Mahogany, Hygrometer, Thermometer, Level, c.1835, 40 In. *illus*	450
Wheel, J.B. Dancer, Quartersawn Oak, Thermometer, England, c.1880, 50 In. *illus*	540
Wheel, Mahogany, Inlays, Steel Dial, Thermometer, Pike & Sons, N.Y., c.1850, 37 x 10 In.	344
Wheel, Mahogany, Line Inlay, John Pensa, England, c.1810, 39 x 12 In.	502
Wheel, P. Ramos, Mahogany, Broken Pediment, Thermometer, Silvered Scale, 1700s, 39 In.	510
Wheel, Thermometer, Hyde, Mahogany, Engraved, Bristol, 37 x 10 In. *illus*	413
Wheel, Thermometer, Hygrometer, Mahogany Case, Swan Neck Pediment, Inlay, 40 x 10 In.	450
Wheel, Thermometer, Hygrometer, Mahogany, Arch Top, Steel Dial, L. Smeldley, c.1850, 38 In.	325
Wheel, Thermometer, Inlaid Mahogany, Urn Finial, Rosettes, Shells, c.1815, 39 In.	360

BASEBALL *collectibles are in the Sports category, except for baseball cards, which are listed under Baseball in the Card category.*

BASKETS of all types are popular with collectors. American Indian, Japanese, African, Nantucket, Shaker, and many other kinds of baskets can be found. Of course, baskets are still being made, so a collector must learn to judge the age and style of a basket to determine its value. Also see Purse.

Adirondack, Bentwood Handle, Brown & Green Paint, U.S.A., c.1915, 10 ½ x 9 In.	294
Apple, Bentwood Handles, Ribbed Construction, Rim, Metal Center Band, 14 x 20 In.	60
Bee Skep, Finial, France, c.1860, 25 In.	851
Bee Skep, Rye Straw, 12 x 17 In.	90
Bee Skep, Rye Straw, 16 x 13 In.	210
Bent Twig, Square Base, Painted Red, Silver, Blue, c.1910, 23 In.	24
Buttocks, Underwoven Pattern, Oval Opening, c.1900, 15 In.	75
Cane On Split, White Oak, Rib, Round, Bentwood Swing Handle, 6 x 8 In.	59
Chitimacha, Rivercane, Weave, Red, Black, Natural, Bull's-Eye Design, c.1900, 4 x 13 In.	1673
Egg, Oak, Handle, Kidney Shape, Ribbed, Double Rim, c.1940, 6 x 5 In.	196
Egg, Splint, Oak, Arch Handle, Kidney Shape, White Paint, c.1890, 6 x 8 In.	259
Egg, Splint, Oak, Arch Handle, Ribbed, Wide Rim, Appalachia, c.1960, 6 ½ x 6 In.	184
Egg, Splint, Oak, Kidney Shape, Ribbed, Green Paint, c.1850, 7 x 4 In.	1955
Egg, Splint, Oak, Kidney Shape, Ribbed, Shelton Sisters, North Carolina, c.1925, 6 x 4 In.	633
Egg, Splint, Oak, Round, X-Wrapped Rim, White, Shenandoah Valley, c.1910, 8 x 9 In.	173
Egg, Splint, White Oak, Arch Handle, Round, X-Wrapped Rim, Green, Va., c.1910, 9 x 5 In.	489
Eskimo, Sea Grass, Seal Gut, Lid, Coiled, 1950s, 8 x 9 In.	475
Gathering, Splint, Oak, Bentwood Handle, God's-Eye Support, 13 x 13 ½ In. *illus*	83
Gathering, Woven Splint, White Oak, Round, Ribbed, Bentwood Handle, Patina, 9 x 10 In.	71
Hamper, Rye Straw, Lid, c.1860, 27 In.	89
Hamper, Splint, 2 Handles, Rectangular, N.C., 13 ¾ x 35 ½ In.	236
Horse Feeding, 1800s, 14 In.	70
Market, Splint, White Oak, Bentwood Handle, Buttocks, Round Rim, Ribbed, 9 x 11 In.	118
Market, Split, White Oak, Bentwood Handle, Rectangular, 15 ¼ In.	47

Barometer, Wheel, J.B. Dancer, Quartersawn Oak, Thermometer, England, c.1880, 50 In. $540

Skinner Auctioneers & Appraisers

Barometer, Wheel, Thermometer, Hyde, Mahogany, Engraved, Bristol, 37 x 10 In. $413

Brunk Auctions

TIP
Let your baskets share the bathroom with you when you take a shower. The hot, moist air is good for the basket. Then let it dry.

Basket, Gathering, Splint, Oak, Bentwood Handle, God's-Eye Support, 13 x 13 ½ In.
$83

Conestoga Auction Co., Inc.

Basket, Picnic, Solid Top, Sidney Gage & Co., B & MRR Co., 12 x 7 In.
$600

Showtime Auction Services

Basket, Tobacco Drying, Split Ash, Double Wrapped Rim, Painted, c.1850, 50 ½ x 34 In.
$1,778

James D. Julia Auctioneers

Batman, Mask, Batman, Plastic, Die Cut, Translucent Green Eye Holes, Japan, Bag, 1966, 3 ¾ x 7 In.
$8,602

Hake's Americana & Collectibles

Melon, Split, White Oak, Oval, 6 ¾ x 13 In.	59
Mending, Bow Handles, Demijohn Bottom, c.1900, 24 In.	75
Nantucket, Friendship Purse, Oval Mahogany Panel, Ivory Sea Gull, Handle, 9 x 6 In.	1920
Nantucket, Ivory Whale Plaque, Swing Handle, Nantucket Map, c.1960, 5 x 8 x 6 In.	4425
Nantucket, Lightship, Applied Whale On Lid, Swing Handle, Oval, c.1974, 12 x 10 In.	780
Nantucket, Lightship, Handles, c.1860, 5 x 10 In.	652
Nantucket, Lightship, Handles, c.1910, 2 ⅜ x 6 ½ In.	1896
Nantucket, Lightship, Ivory Whale Plaque, Swing Handle, Jose F. Reyes, c.1965, 5 x 6 In.	4425
Nantucket, Lightship, Squared Handle, Paper Label Mitchell Ray, 5 ½ x 12 In.	474
Nantucket, Lightship, Swing Handle, c.1915, 4 x 8 ¾ In.	711
Nantucket, Lightship, Swing Handle, c.1915, 5 x 7 ½ In.	652
Nantucket, Oval, Swing Handle, Brass Pin Mounts, William D. Appleton, c.1900, 7 ¼ x 6 In.	1725
Nantucket, Oval, Swing Handle, Ferdinand Sylvaro, 8 x 12 In.	840
Nantucket, Oval, Swing Handle, Ferdinand Sylvaro, c.1915, 9 ½ x 9 In.	1320
Nantucket, Oval, Swing Handle, Wood Base, 11 ½ In.	649
Nantucket, Oval, Swing Handles, Signed, AAH 1987, Arnold A. Howard, 9 ½ x 17 ½ In.	531
Nantucket, Rattan, Carved Ash Handles, Round, c.1900, 12 x 14 ½ In.	1200
Nantucket, Round, 2 Carved Hardwood Handles, c.1912, 10 ¼ In. Diam.	2040
Nantucket, Round, Carved Hardwood Swing Handle, c.1900, 7 ½ In. Diam.	510
Nantucket, Round, Edge Handle, A.D. Williams, c.1910, 12 x 14 In.	1875
Nantucket, Round, Swing Handle, Brass Pin Mounts, S.P. Boyer Label, 2 ⅝ x 3 In.	920
Nantucket, Round, Swing Handle, Ferdinand Sylvaro, 9 x 4 In.	240
Nantucket, Round, Swing Handle, Stamped Boyer, 6 ½ x 5 ½ In.	3360
Nantucket, Round, Tight Weave, Swing Handle, 3 x 6 ¾ In.	590
Picnic, Solid, Top, Sidney Gage & Co., B & MRR Co., 12 x 7 In. ....*illus*	600
Picnic, Wicker, Brexton Collection, Complete Picnic Items, 15 x 15 x 8 In.	90
Rye Straw, Lid, Handles, Pennsylvania, c.1850, 18 x 26 In.	160
Service, White Oak, Notch Carved Handle, 13 ½ x 22 ½ In.	443
Service, White Oak, Round, Notched Out Handles, Square Bottom, 17 x 16 ½ In.	153
Sewing, Red Flowers, Green, Yellow Ground, Drawer, Inscribed J.J.F., 1838, 4 ½ In.	2015
Sewing, Splint, Oak, Arched Side Handles, Green Paint, Shenandoah Valley, c.1930, 4 x 11 In.	138
Sewing, Walnut, Pierced Tulip, Bobbin Support, Pincushion, Drawer, c.1825, 16 x 13 In.	1185
Splint, Ash, Demilune, Side Mount, Notched Handles, Arch Handle, c.1920, 10 x 15 In.	92
Splint, Coil Lid, Rye, Oak, Round, Mid-Atlantic, 1800s, 6 ½ x 14 In.	150
Splint, Green Milk Paint Interior, c.1900, 5 x 11 In.	62
Splint, Hickory, Oval, Highlanders Shop, Gatlinburg, Tenn., 1900s, 14 ½ In.	24
Splint, Oak, Blue Gray Paint, 11 ½ x 10 ½ In.	770
Splint, Oak, Gathering, Arch Handle, Double Rim, c.1900, 15 x 9 ½ In.	127
Splint, Oak, Handle, Double Wrap Rim, Shenandoah, c.1940, 15 x 9 In.	81
Splint, Oak, Kidney Shape, Low Arch Handle, Shenandoah, c.1945, 2 x 1 ¾ In.	259
Splint, Oak, Low Arch Handle, Shenandoah, c.1940, 11 ½ x 9 ¾ In.	161
Splint, Oak, Round, Carved Bail Handle, c.1900, 18 x 9 In.	196
Splint, Oak, Round, Carved Swing Handle, Domed Bottom, U.S.A., 18 In. Diam.	570
Splint, Oak, Salmon Paint, Bentwood Handle, c.1900, 11 ½ x 13 In.	360
Splint, Oak, Square Shape, Double Rim, Appalachia, c.1920, 5 x 8 In.	138
Splint, Oval, Ash Swing Handle, Maple Rim, c.1850, 11 ½ x 13 In.	570
Splint, Round Over Square, Carved Wood Handles, Paint, c.1900, 8 In. Diam.	123
Splint, Storage, Carved Ash Handles, U.S.A., 1800s, 22 x 40 In.	480
Split, White Oak, Round, Swing Handle, Carved Stirrups, 6 ¾ x 11 ¼ In.	267
Storage, Rye Straw, Oval, c.1900, 26 In.	570
Tobacco Drying, Split Ash, Double Wrapped Rim, Painted, c.1850, 50 ½ x 34 In. ....*illus*	1778
Wall, Splint, Oak, Demilune, Red Curlicues, Handles, Appalachia, c.1920, 13 x 5 In.	35

BATCHELDER products are made from California clay. Ernest Batchelder established a tile studio in Pasadena, California, in 1909. He went into partnership with Frederick Brown in 1912 and the company became Batchelder and Brown. In 1920 he built a larger factory with a new partner. The Batchelder-Wilson Company made all types of architectural tiles, garden pots, and bookends. The plant closed in 1932. In 1936 Batchelder opened Batchelder Ceramics, also in Pasadena, and made bowls, vases, and earthenware pots. He retired in 1951 and died in 1957. Pieces are marked *Batchelder Pasadena* or *Batchelder Los Angeles*.

BATCHELDER LOS ANGELES

Tile, Birds, Green, Marked, 5 ¾ x 5 ¾ In.	83
Tile, Carved Medieval Scene, Geometric Border, 13 ½ x 18 ¼ In.	594
Tile, Fish Shape Frame, Fountain, Brown Glaze, c.1915, 16 x 9 In.	188

BATMAN and Robin are characters from a comic strip by Bob Kane that started in 1939. In 1966, the characters became part of a popular television series. There have been radio and movie serials that featured the pair. The first full-length movie was made in 1989.

Action Figure,	Penguin, Posable, Brown Mailer Box, 1973, 8 In.	165
Belt,	Go-Go, Leather, Bat Symbol, c.1966, 42 In.	173
Bib,	The Penguin, Terry Cloth, Vinyl, 1966, 8 x 10 In.	115
Bookends,	Batman, Robin, Figural, Ceramic, c.1966, 6 ½ In.	190
Bullhorn,	Plastic, Red, Black, Box, Bayshore Industries Inc., 1966, 10 In.	196
Button,	Joker, Cesar Romero, Photo Portrait, c.1966, 6 In. Diam.	115
Candy Container,	PEZ, Batman, Cape, Blue, Logo, c.1966, 4 In.	205
Card,	Movie Window, Photo Images, Adam West, 1966, 14 x 22 In.	173
Comic Book Page,	Catwoman, Artboard, c.1989, 11 x 17 In.	1202
Comic Book,	Number 11, Joker & Penguin, Batman & Robin, Joker Cover, Cards, 1942	1800
Comic Book,	Number 20, First Batmobile Cover, Dec. 1943-Jan. 1944	886
Game,	Shooting Arcade Target, Batman, Robin, Plastic, Marx, c.1966, 5 x 7 x 3 In.	862
Jar,	Creamy Peanut Butter, Batman & Robin On Label, Holy Batwiches Sandman!, 5 In.	173
Marionette,	Batman, Plastic, Hazelle, Window Box, 1966, 16 In.	379
Mask,	Batman, Plastic, Die Cut, Translucent Green Eye Holes, Japan, Bag, 1966, 3 ¾ x 7 In. *illus*	8602
Montage Art,	Ink, Marker, Swooping, Moon, Bats, Goldwood Frame, 1997, 31 x 38 In.	1725
Pen,	Ballpoint, Metal Batman End, On Card, WOW!, 1 Dollar, Empire, 1966, 9 In.	108
Printing Plate,	The Joker, Comic Book, Star City, Bridge, 1975, 6 ½ x 10 ½ In.	199
Watch,	Round Dial, Batman Image, Box, Superheroes, Dabs, 6 In.	139

BATTERSEA enamels, which are enamels painted on copper, were made in the Battersea district of London from about 1750 to 1756. Many similar enamels are mistakenly called Battersea.

Basket,	Reticulated, Crown, Heart, Flowers, Phrase, Green, 3 x 2 ½ x 1 ¼ In.	685
Bodkin Case,	Vignettes, Pastures, Blue, c.1760, 5 ¼ x 1 In.	745
Box,	Bird Shape, Orange Breast, Black & Gray Wings, Hinged Base	531
Box,	Bird Shape, Yellow & Brown Speckled, Hinged Base, Pink Flower	472
Box,	Bulldog's Head, Scrolling Silver Mount, Hinged Lid, Woman In Garden, 2 ½ In.	1169
Box,	Chinoiserie, Figures, Trees, Scrolled Cartouches, Pink, White, Silver Bezel, 2 ½ In.	316
Box,	Dome Lid, Small Token Of Friendship, Oval, Urn, Flowers, 1700s, 1 ½ x ¾ In.	342
Box,	Fat Cherub, Under Tree, Cobalt Blue, c.1800, 1 In. Diam.	500
Box,	Flowers, A Token Of Esteem, Blue Ground, Beaded Oval, Mirror, 1 x 1 ¾ In.	300
Box,	Hot Air Balloon, Spectators, Multicolor, 2 ½ x 1 ¼ In.	135
Box,	Lid, Flowers, Sailboat, Lake, House, Green, White, Metal Rim, c.1780, 1 ¼ x 2 ½ In.	115
Box,	Men Playing Golf, Black & White, Round, Cinched, Hinged Lid, 1 x 2 In.	92
Box,	Sampan Rig On Water, House, Trees, Scrolls, Beads, Teal Ground, 1 ¼ x 2 ½ In.	115
Candlestick,	Pasture Scene Base, Gilt Trim, Purple, White, c.1780, 6 ¼ In.	950
Etui,	Pink, Purple & Blue Flowers, Green Leaves, Copper Ring, ¾ x 4 ¾ In.	61
Patch Box,	Figural, Bird, Blue, Green, Black, Hinged, 1 ¾ In.	750
Patch Box,	Lake, Men Fishing, Houses, Trees, 2 ¼ x 1 ⅝ In.	325
Patch Box,	Radcliffe Library, Oxford University, Pink, Oval, c.1790, 2 In.	800
Patch Box,	Windsor Castle, Pink, Oval, c.1790, 1 ¾ In.	500
Snuffbox,	Egg Shape, Figures, In Meadow, Trees, 18th Century	995
Snuffbox,	Flowers In Reserves, Cobalt Blue Ground, White Lattice, Oval, Hinged, 2 In.	121
Snuffbox,	Fruit, Pink, c.1770, 1 In., Diam.	425
Snuffbox,	Horse & Rider, Raised Sword, 18th Century, 1 ½ x 1 In.	245
Tieback,	Doves, Sitting On Pillar, Flowers, c.1775, 1 ¾ In., Pair	165

BAUER pottery is a California-made ware. J.A. Bauer bought Paducah Pottery in Paducah, Kentucky, in 1885. He moved the pottery to Los Angeles, California, in 1909. The company made art pottery after 1912 and introduced dinnerware marked *Bauer* in 1930. The factory went out of business in 1962 and the molds were destroyed. Since 1998, a new company, Bauer Pottery Company of Los Angeles, has been making Bauer pottery using molds made from original Bauer pieces. The pottery is now made in Highland, California. Most pieces are marked "2000." Original pieces of Bauer pottery are listed here. See also the Russel Wright category.

Cal-Art,	Figure, Duck, Green Matte Glaze, Head Down, 5 In.	70
Cal-Art,	Jardiniere, Satin Ivory, 8 In.	125
Cal-Art,	Vase, Pink Matte Glaze, Footed, Ribbed, 5 ⅛ In.	75
Jar,	Oil, Yellow Glaze, Oval, Wrought Iron Base, 18 x 28 In.	1342
Ring,	Carafe, Orange, Wood Handle, 8 In.	120
Ring,	Creamer, Gray, 3 ¾ x 5 ¼ In.	42

Bavaria, Cake Stand, Wild Rose, Gold Trim, Pedestal, Schumann Arzberg, 11 ¾ x 5 ½ In.
$65

Ruby Lane, Inc.

Beatles, Bank, George Harrison, Yellow Submarine, Rubber Trap, Pride Creations, 7 ¾ In.
$411

Hake's Americana & Collectibles

Beatles, Display, Bobbin' Head Set, Decal, Japan, Car Mascots Inc., 1964, 14 To 15 In.
$11,005

Hake's Americana & Collectibles

Beatles, Hangers, Figural, George, John, Paul, Ringo, 15 x 16 In., 4 Piece
$780

Palm Beach Modern Auctions

Beatles, Ticket Stub, Aug. 28, 1964,
Forest Hills Music Festival, N.Y.,
1 ½ x 1 ¾ In.
$115

Hake's Americana & Collectibles

Beatles, Wristwatch, Yellow Submarine-
Love, Leather Band, Sheffield Watch,
Case, 1968
$854

Hake's Americana & Collectibles

Beehive, Urn, Lid, Orpheus, Eurydice,
Handles, Royal Vienna, c.1890,
14 ½ In., Pair
$2,242

Brunk Auctions

Ring, Mixing Bowl, No. 12, Chartreuse	100
Ring, Pitcher Set, Jade, 3 Graduated Sizes, 6 x 5 ½ In.	123
Ring, Punch Bowl, Ivory, Footed, 11 ⅜ x 5 ⅜ In.	250
Ring, Vase, Light Blue, Cylindrical, 6 ⅛ In.	90
Salt & Pepper, Cobalt Blue, 4 ¾ x 3 In.	48

BAVARIA is a region in Europe where many types of porcelain were made. In the nineteenth century, the mark often included the word *Bavaria*. After 1871, the words *Bavaria, Germany*, were used. Listed here are pieces that include the name *Bavaria* in some form, but major porcelain makers, such as Rosenthal, are listed in their own categories.

Cake Stand, Wild Rose, Gold Trim, Pedestal, Schumann Arzberg, 11 ¾ x 5 ½ In. ....*illus*	65
Charger, Gilt Center Medallion, Gilt Rocaille Border, c.1925, 11 In., 8 Piece	154
Pitcher, Lemonade, Cherries On Branches, Gold Trim, Scalloped Rim, 7 In.	93
Plate, Gold Border, Rose Painted 2 Drawers, Center, 11 In., 6 Piece	102
Plate Set, Scrolled Gilt Border, Multicolor Flower Center, 10 ½ In., 12 Piece	144

BEADED BAGS *are included in the Purse category.*

BEATLES collectors search for any items picturing the four members of the famous music group or any of their recordings. Because these items are so new, the condition is very important and top prices are paid only for items in mint condition. The Beatles first appeared on American network television in 1964. The group disbanded in 1971. Ringo Starr and Paul McCartney are still performing. John Lennon died in 1980. George Harrison died in 2001.

Advertising Display, Red Telephone Booth, John, Paul, George & Ringo Images, 84 In.	978
Animation Cel, Yellow Submarine, John Lennon With 4 Green Fish, 11 ½ x 15 In.	437
Bank, George Harrison, Yellow Submarine, Rubber Trap, Pride Creations, 7 ¾ In. ....*illus*	411
Button, I'm A Beatles Fan, Portraits, Tin Litho, Green Duck Co., 1964, 4 In.	95
Button, John Lennon, Photo, Round, c.1964, ⅞ In.	95
Cel, Yellow Submarine, George & Paul, With Blue Meanie, 1968	738
Disk-Go-Case, Holds 45 RPM Records, Red, Yellow, Blue, Plastic, 7 In. Diam, 3 Piece	214
Display Box, Hair Pomade, Beatles Graphics, 100 Packages Of Hair Gel, 1960s, 7 In.	138
Display, Bobbin' Head Set, Decal, Japan, Car Mascots Inc., 1964, 14 To 15 In. ....*illus*	11005
Display, Die Cut, Cardboard, Here They Are, EMI, England, 1963, 18 x 22 In.	1496
Hangers, Figural, George, John, Paul, Ringo, 15 x 16 In., 4 Piece	780
Lithograph, Yesterday, Muhammad Ali, Posing, Beatles, Boxing Ring Floor, 1960s, 28 x 33 In.	921
Lunch Box, Pressed Steel, Portraits, Signatures, Thermos, Aladdin, 1965	214 to 411
Megaphone, Plastic, Yellow, Green, Portraits, Yell-A-Phone, 1965, 7 In.	1037
Model Kit, Yellow Submarine, Plastic Pieces, Wind-Up, Cardboard Box, 1968	281
Photograph, Lennon, McCartney, No. 32/275, Frame, 17 x 22 In.	63
Poster, A Hard Day's Night, 1964, 22 x 14 In.	483
Poster, John Lennon, Psychedelic Portrait By Richard Avedon, Cowles, 1967, 31 x 22 In.	109
Poster, Ringo Starr, Psychedelic Portrait By Richard Avedon, Cowles, 1967, 31 x 22 In.	75
Poster, Sgt. Pepper's Lonely Hearts Club Band, UK Fan Club, 1968, 30 x 20 In.	150
Record Player, 45 RPM Record, 1965	2583
Ticket Stub, Aug. 28, 1964, Forest Hills Music Festival, N.Y., 1 ½ x 1 ¾ In. ....*illus*	115
Ticket Stub, Philadelphia, Concert, Aug. 6, 1966, Photos Of Beatles, 4 ½ In.	483
Toy, Arthur A-Go-Go Drummer, Ringo Starr, Unlicensed, Battery, Alps, Japan, Box, 10 x 7 In.	3000
Wristwatch, Yellow Submarine-Love, Leather Band, Sheffield Watch, Case, 1968 ....*illus*	854

BEEHIVE, Austria, or Beehive, Vienna, are terms used in English-speaking countries to refer to the many types of decorated porcelain bearing a mark that looks like a beehive. The mark is actually a shield, viewed upside down. It was first used in 1744 by the Royal Porcelain Manufactory of Vienna. The firm made what collectors call Royal Vienna porcelains until it closed in 1864. Many other German, Austrian, and Japanese factories have reproduced Royal Vienna wares, complete with the original shield or beehive mark. This listing includes the expensive, original Royal Vienna porcelains and many other types of beehive porcelain. The Royal Vienna pieces include that name in the description.

Canister, Lid, Gilt, Paint, Square, Women, Seated, Tree, Marked, c.1900, 4 ½ In.	354
Charger, Woman, Turquoise Dress, Gilt Cartouches, Signed E. Vettori, Vienna, c.1925, 12 In.	69
Figurine, Woman, Naked, In Seashell, Ernst Wahliss, Royal Vienna, c.1904, 7 ½ In.	450
Plaque, Madonna, Jesus, St. John, Giltwood Frame, Shield Mark, 16 x 13 In.	5500
Plate, Apollo Chasing Daphne, Pink Band, Gold Filigree, Frame, 9 ½ In.	830
Plate, Cabinet, Ariadne, Gilt, Jeweled Border, Blue Underglaze, Frame, 17 x 17 In.	989
Plate, Classical Woman, Blue Border, Gilt Urns, Scrolls, Fritsclz, Vienna, 1873, 8 ⅝ In.	138
Plate, Clio Profile, Scrolls, Gilt Border, Cabinet, Royal Vienna, Wagner, c.1905, 9 ½ In.	1495

Plate, Farmer, Hat, Looking At Field, Gilt Scrolls, Blue Border, Vienna, c.1890, 8 ¾ In.	69
Plate, Gilt, Paint, Hector Departing For Battle, Rosettes, Grapevine, 10 In..................................	338
Plate, Graziella, Painted, Woman In Center, Gilt Rim, Beehive Mark, Bauerz, 9 ½ In..............	990
Plate, La Fiammetta, Woman, Florentine Style, Blue, Gilt, Royal Vienna, c.1900, 10 In.	489
Plate, Portrait, Marchen, Fairy Tale, Girl, In Forest, Gilt Border, Signed Wagner, 9 ½ In.	1652
Urn, Lid, Gilded Handles, Leaf Borders, Signed, 12 ¼ In., Pair...	600
Urn, Lid, Gilt, Flowers, Trophy Shape, Square Handles, Pedestal, 1800s, 25 x 11 In.	738
Urn, Lid, Orpheus, Eurydice, Handles, Royal Vienna, c.1890, 14 ½ In., Pair ....*illus*	2242
Urn, Stand, Allegorical Scenes, Gilt Highlights, Cobalt Blue Ground, 27 In.	3300
Vase, Oval, Maidens, Blue Ground, Marked, 21 ½ In...	3250
Vase, Pierced Lid, Wreath Finial, Gilt Handles, Figures, Marked, c.1890, 13 In., Pair	2640
Vase, Woman Holding Flowers, Oval Reserve, Gilt, Signed Prell, Royal Vienna, c.1900, 7 In........	590
Vase, Woman Smelling Flower, Oval Reserve, Brown, Gilt, Wagner, Royal Vienna, c.1900, 6 In....	1180

BEER BOTTLES *are listed in the Bottle category under Beer.*

Arrow Imperial Lagered Beer, Flat Top, Red, Black, Gold..	103
Beverwyck Cream Ale, Green, White, Shamrock, Cone Top	175
Griesedieck Bros. Light Lager Beer, Flat Top, Oklahoma...	25
Krueger Finest Beer, Cone Top, c.1945, 12 Oz...	88

BELL collectors collect all types of bells. Favorites include glass bells, figural bells, school bells, and cowbells. Bells have been made of porcelain, china, or metal through the centuries.

Brass, 3 Bells, Harness, Spread Wing Eagle Finial, Leather, 9 ¾ x 6 ¾ In........................	144
Brass, Cast Iron Harp, 2 Handles, Shaped Wooden Base, 8 ¼-In. Bell	365
Brass, Cast Iron Yoke, Stand, Lakeside Foundry, Chicago, c.1910, 12 In.	390
Brass, Cast Iron, Boxing, Inscribed Bevin, 12 In.	154
Brass, School, Iron Hook, Dong, G & J, 19th Century, 13 ¾ x 10 ½ In.	138
Brass, Sleigh, Graduated, 15 Sizes, Leather Strap, 71 In..	443
Brass, Sleigh, Graduated, Leather Strap, c.1890...	267
Bronze, Applied Flags, Swedish-American Liner Kungsholm, Wood Stand, c.1933, 22 ½ In.........	2400
Bronze, Cast Iron Framework, Joseph Bernhard, Philadelphia, 1856, 15 x 18 In. ....*illus*	2000
Bronze, Cast, Hanger, Embossed Gillett & Johnston, Croydon 1910, 15 x 18 In.	1230
Bronze, Chain, Figural, Disc, Bells, Shaped Hooks, Birds, Leaves, Temple, 72 In.	368
Bronze, Cicada Design, Dragon Finial, Japan, 1800s, 7 In.	492
Bronze, Hammer, Dragon Shape Handles, Dome Shape, Temple, Japan, c.1900, 7 ½ x 5 In.	708
Bronze, Knobs, Masks, Dragons, 2-Headed Dragon, Chinese, c.1900, 15 x 12 In. ....*illus*	1778
Bronze, Plantation, Iron Supports, Clapper, 1800s, 17 In.	2271
Bronze, Plantation, Stand, Buckeye Bell Foundry, c.1875, 24 x 30 In.	9225
Bronze, Temple, Reticulated Dragon Shape Handle, Wood Carved Stand, Japan, 22 x 11 In.......	330
Bronze, Yoke, Pierced Round Top, Tapered Base, Chinese, 5 In., Pair	1476
Cast Iron, Flared, Mount, 17 ½ x 15 In.	117
Glass, Wedding, Amber, Clear Handle, c.1880, 10 ¾ In.	240
Glass, Wedding, Dark Blue, Clear Handle, c.1880, 10 ¼ In...	240
Glass, Wedding, Green Ribbed, Clear Handle, c.1880, 11 ¾ In...	180
Glass, Wedding, Green, Clear Handle, c.1880, 10 ¾ In..	180
Horse Parade, 3 Bells, 2 Open, 1 Closed, Shaped Metal Frame, 6 Spur Dingers, 8 x 15 In.	70
Iron, Farm, Red Paint, Indiana, c.1920, 16 x 25 In...	59
Iron, Monastery Doorbell, Figural, Monk Ringer, c.1850, 35 ½ In......................................	1541
Iron, Mounting Extension, 10 ½ x 7 ¼ In.	29
Iron, New Remington Carbon Metal, 14 ½ In.	144
Iron, School, Goodville, 1800s, 12 ½ In.	62
Iron, School, Painted Black, 40-In. Chain, Omega Shape Armature, 16 x 15 In...........................	115
Iron, Weathered Patina, Marked Yolk, C.S. Bell & Co., Hillsboro, 12 x 16 In.	417
Metal, Hotel Bell, Snail, Windup, White Button On Shell Top, Wooden Base, 2 ¾ x 4 ½ In. .*illus*	460
On Carriage, Painted, Cast Iron, Gong Bell Company, 7 ¾ In..	182
Porcelain, Figural, Girl, Blond Hair, Holding Fan, Multicolor, 4 x 2 In...............................	18
Prize Fight, Spring Iron Hammer, Iron Wall Mount, c.1945, 15 x 12 In..............................	384
Railroad, Iron Clapper, Frame, c.1900, 12 ½ x 16 In.	1180

Bell, Bronze, Cast Iron Framework, Joseph Bernhard, Philadelphia, 1856, 15 x 18 In.
$2,000

Rago Arts & Auction Center

Bell, Bronze, Knobs, Masks, Dragons, 2-Headed Dragon, Chinese, c.1900, 15 x 12 In.
$1,778

James D. Julia Auctioneers

Bell, Metal, Hotel Bell, Snail, Windup, White Button On Shell Top, Wooden Base, 2 ¾ x 4 ½ In.
$460

Wm Morford Auctions

TIP
Use opaque window shades or drapes so the contents of your rooms can't be seen from outside.

Bell, Zinc, Hotel, Chinese Man, Umbrella Bell, Patina, 7 In.
$150

Victorian Casino Antiques

Belleek, Figurine, Meditation, Classical Maiden, Black Mark, 1891-1926, 14 ¾ In.
$594

Leslie Hindman Auctioneers

Silver, Push, Guilloche, Mother-Of-Pearl Enamel, Ivory Button, France, 1900, 1 ¾ In.	250
Wrought Iron, Brass, Double Door, c.1800, 12 ½ In.	420
Zinc, Hotel, Chinese Man, Umbrella Bell, Patina, 7 In. ....*illus*	150

BELLEEK china was made in Ireland, other European countries, and the United States. The glaze is creamy yellow and appears wet. The first Belleek was made in 1857. All pieces listed here are Irish Belleek. The mark changed through the years. The first mark, black, dates from 1863 to 1890. The second mark, black, dates from 1891 to 1926 and includes the words *Co. Fermanagh, Ireland*. The third mark, black, dates from 1926 to 1946 and has the words *Deanta in Eirinn*. The fourth mark, same as the third mark but green, dates from 1946 to 1955. The fifth mark (second green mark) dates from 1955 to 1965 and has an R in a circle added in the upper right. The sixth mark (third green mark) dates from 1965 to 1981 and the words *Co. Fermanagh* have been omitted. The seventh mark, gold, was used from 1981 to 1992 and omits the words *Deanta in Eirinn*. The eighth mark, used from 1993 to 1996, is similar to the second mark but is printed in blue. The ninth mark, blue, includes the words *Est. 1857* and the words *Co. Fermanagh, Ireland* are omitted. The tenth mark, black, is similar to the ninth mark but includes the words *Millennium 2000* and *Ireland*. It was used only in 2000. The eleventh mark, similar to the millennium mark but green, was introduced in 2001. The twelfth mark, black, is similar to the eleventh mark but has a banner above the mark with the words *"Celebrating 150 Years."* It was used in 2007. The thirteenth trademark, used from 2008 to 2010, is similar to the twelfth but is brown and has no banner. The fourteenth mark, the Classic Belleek trademark, is similar to the twelfth but includes Belleek's website address. The Belleek Living trademark was introduced in 2010 and is used on items from that giftware line. The word *Belleek* is now used only on the pieces made in Ireland even though earlier pieces from other countries were sometimes marked *Belleek*. These early pieces are listed by manufacturer, such as Ceramic Art Co., Haviland, Lenox, Ott & Brewer, and Willets.

Basket, Applied Border Flowers, Round, Side Handles, Ireland, 12 ½ In.	638
Basket, Applied Rim Flowers, Openwork Design, Doubled Handle, Ireland, 10 ¼ In.	696
Basket, Applied Roses, Yellow, Tan, Loop Rim, Black Mark, Ireland, 2 In.	97
Basket, Lid, Oval, Applied Roses, Thistles, Clover, Marked, 1800s, 12 ¼ In.	750
Basket, Oval, Ribbons, Flower Garlands, 9 ½ In.	531
Basket, Pierced, Round, Applied Flowers To Rim, Low Handles, Ireland, 2¼ x 7 ½ In.	58
Bowl, Handles, 3 Legs, Round, 5 In.	102
Candelabrum, 3-Light, Boy, Coraline Arms, Round Beaded Base, c.1875, 15 ¼ In.	688
Compote, Shell Form, Dolphin Pedestal, Green Trim, Black Mark, 3 ½ x 10 In.	93
Creamer, Latticework Ground, Dragonfly, Leaves, 3 ½ In.	52
Creamer, Shell Shape, Coral, Base, Sea Plant Handle, Ireland, 4 In.	186
Creamer, Textured, Off-White, Yellow Handle, Black Mark, 4 ¼ In.	12
Figurine, Affection, Woman, Standing, Draped, Round Base, Black Mark, Ireland, 15 In.	375 to 435
Figurine, Meditation, Classical Maiden, Black Mark, 1891-1926, 14 ¾ In. ....*illus*	594
Figurine, Venus, Crouching, On Shell, Bronzed, Gilt, Arm Bands, Black Mark, c.1885, 18 In.	4500
Jardiniere, Swirled Scalloped Shape, Applied Flowers, Leaves, 1900s, 8 ¼ In.	360
Mask, Bulldog Head, Collar, Brown, Tan, Black Mark, c.1885, 8 In.	2000
Mirror, Lily Of The Valley, Beaded Frame, Applied Flowers, Black Mark, 16 x 13 In. ....*illus*	625
Mug, Barrel Shape, Gold Trim, Signed, 5 ½ In.	59
Salt, Pink Rim, Shell Shape, Raised Barnacle, Ireland, 3 ½ In.	104
Sugar & Creamer, Lotus, Cob Luster, 2nd Black Mark, c.1905, 3 ¾ x 2 In.	13
Tea Set, Teapot, Creamer, Open Sugar, Pink Rim, Black Mark, Ireland, 3 Piece	174
Tea Urn, Lid, Opposing Dragon Spouts, Reptile Feet, Marked, c.1875, 13 In.	1250
Teapot, Chinese Design, Dragon Shape Spout, Gilt Highlights, c.1875, 9 ¾ In.	2375
Tray, Angel Faces, Grapes, Double Loop Handles, Oval, Ireland, 13 In.	162
Tray, Artichoke, Tinted Leaves, Gilt, c.1875, 18 In.	1188
Tray, Chinese Design, Dragon Chasing Pearl, Stars, Clouds, Iron Red, c.1875, 15 In.	1125
Tray, Shell, Textured, Wave Edge, Parian, 1st Mark, Black, 17 In.	288
Urn, Lid, Urn Shape, Ulysses Discovers Achilles, Hector & Paris, Painted, Gilt, Royal Vienna, 20 x 7 ¼ In.	2750
Vase, Coral, Triple, Ruffled Rims, Black Mark, 5 x 8 ½ In.	151
Vase, Imperial Shell, Openwork Coralene Base, 8 ¼ In.	250
Vase, Lily, Entwined Lizard, Parian, 1st Mark, Black, 9 In.	288
Vase, Triple Tulip, Flower Blossoms, Basket Shape Base, Marked, c.1875, 13 In.	1188
Vase, Trumpet, Flared, Brick Wall Base With Flowers, 3rd Mark, Black, 12 In.	374

BENNINGTON ware was the product of two factories working in Bennington, Vermont. Both the Norton Company and Lyman Fenton & Company were out of business by 1896. The wares include brown and yellow mottled pottery, Parian, scroddled ware, stoneware, graniteware, yellowware, and Staffordshire-type vases. The name is also a generic term for mottled brownware of the type made in Bennington.

Bottle, Boot Form, 6 ½ x 7 In.	71

Belleek, Mirror, Lily Of The Valley, Beaded Frame, Applied Flowers, Black Mark, 16 x 13 In.
$625

Leslie Hindman Auctioneers

Bennington, Figurine, Cat, 1800s, 11 x 10 x 7 ½ In.
$431

Locati Auctions

Bennington, Jug, Stoneware, Cobalt Blue Deer, J. & E. Norton & Co., c.1850, 2 Gal.
$3,450

Crocker Farm, Inc.

TIP
Re-key all locks when you move to a new house or apartment or if you lose a key.

Bicycle, Huffy, Radio Bike, Boy's, Radio, Battery, Powerpak, Delta Head Light, c.1957
$3,300

Victorian Casino Antiques

Bicycle, Monark, Deluxe, Balloon, Twin-Spring Fork, c.1941
$518

Conestoga Auction Co., Inc.

Bicycle, Murray, Tank Model, Woman's, Front Suspension, c.1953
$748

Conestoga Auction Co., Inc.

Bicycle, Raleigh, Folding, 3-Speed, Sturmey-Archer Gear, c.1970
$375

Conestoga Auction Co., Inc.

Bicycle, Schwinn, Black Phantom, Front Drum Brake, c.1950
$2,185

Conestoga Auction Co., Inc.

Bicycle, Schwinn, Tandem, Man-Woman, Drum Brakes, Gillette Balloon Tires, c.1954
$661

Conestoga Auction Co., Inc.

Bing & Grondahl, Vase, Maple Pods, Hegermann-Lindencrone, c.1900, 4 x 3 In.
$4,063

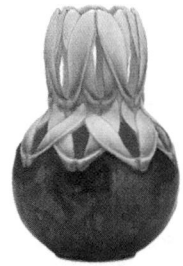

Rago Arts & Auction Center

Birdcage, Arts & Crafts, Wood, Galvanized Pullout Tray, 11 ½ x 16 In.
$90

Showtime Auction Services

Birdcage, Bamboo, Rectangular, Plaques, Animal Shapes, Fruit, Chinese, 16 In.
$397

Clars Auction Gallery

Candlestick, Flint Enamel, Mottled Brown, Yellow & Green, Blue Flecks, 8 In.	159
Creamer, Cow Shape, Rockingham Glaze, 1849-58, 5 In.	120
Crock, Stoneware, Cobalt Blue Flower Basket, J. & E. Norton, c.1850, 4 Gal., 11 In.	1007
Figurine, Cat, 1800s, 11 x 10 x 7 ½ In. *illus*	431
Figurine, Dog, Poodle, Fruit Basket In Mouth, Rockingham Glaze, c.1855, 8 ½ In. 764 to 1440	
Jar, Stoneware, Deer, Reclining, Hill, Fences, Cobalt Blue, J. & E. Norton, Vt., 4 Gal.	1265
Jar, Stoneware, Leaf, Dots, Cobalt Blue, E. & L.P. Norton, Lug Handles, 2 Gal.	230
Jug, Stoneware, Cobalt Blue Deer, J. & E. Norton & Co., c.1850, 2 Gal. *illus*	3450
Jug, Stoneware, Cobalt Blue Pheasant On Stump, J. & E. Norton, c.1855, 3 Gal.	9200
Pitcher, Basin, Flint, Enamel, Impressed Lyman, Fenton & Co., Pitcher 13 In., Basin, 13 x 5 In.	304
Pitcher, Flint Enamel, Scalloped Rib, Green, Cream, Brown, Orange, c.1850, 12 ¾ In.	1140
Pitcher, Milk, Scalloped Rib, Flint Enamel, Brown & Cream Mottled, Blue Ribs, 5 ½ In.	330
Soap Dish, Dome Lid, Mottled Brown, Lined, Canted Corners, c.1850, 4 ¾ In.	104
Vase, Tulip Shape, 8-Petal Rim, Flint Enamel, Hexagon Base, Brown, Blue, c.1850, 9 In.	575
Washbowl, Flint Enamel, Blue Flecks, Impressed Flowers, Scalloped Rim, 13 In.	542

BERLIN, a German porcelain factory, was started in 1751 by Wilhelm Kaspar Wegely. In 1763, the factory was taken over by Frederick the Great and became the Royal Berlin Porcelain Manufactory. It is still in operation today. Pieces have been marked in a variety of ways.

Figurine, Reclining Nude, White Glaze, Oval Base, Marked, c.1900, 16 In.	738
Plaque, Oval, Profile Of Napoleon, Giltwood Frame, 16 x 13 In.	1000
Vase, Cobalt Blue, Raised Gold Leaves, Coral & Turquoise, Marked, c.1890, 6 ⅝ In.	1020

BESWICK started making earthenware in Staffordshire, England, in 1936. The company is now part of Royal Doulton Tableware, Ltd. Figurines of animals, especially dogs and horses, Beatrix Potter animals, and other wares are still being made.

Beatrix Potter, Figurine, Aunt Pettitoes, BP 3B, 3 ⅝ In.	75
Beatrix Potter, Figurine, Benjamin Bunny, BP 3B, 4 In.	249
Beatrix Potter, Figurine, Duchess With Pie, BP 3B	235
Beatrix Potter, Figurine, Lady Mouse, BP 3B, 3 ¾ In.	75
Beatrix Potter, Figurine, Miss Moppet, BP 1A	275
Beatrix Potter, Figurine, Nutkin, BP 3B, 4 In.	139
Beatrix Potter, Figurine, Samuel Whiskers, BP 1B	197
Beatrix Potter, Figurine, Timmy Tiptoes, BP 1A	100
Beatrix Potter, Figurine, Tommy Brock, BP 1A	746
Figurine, Atlantic Salmon, No. 1233	158
Figurine, Bird, Hummingbird, In Flight, Blue, Green, Yellow, No. 1023	73
Figurine, Highland Bull, No. 2008	158
Figurine, Highland Pony, Mackionneach, No. 1644	89
Figurine, Magpie, No. 2305	60
Figurine, Persian Cat, Sitting, Ginger Stripes, Cream, No. 1867, 8 In.	180
Figurine, Siamese Cat, No. 1882, 9 ½ In.	68
Group, Birds, Spread Wings, On Branch, No. 926, 5 ½ In.	115
Group, Siamese Cats, Curled Up, Blue Eyes, No. 1296, 2 ¾ x 4 ¼ In.	52
Jug, Cream, Micawber, No. 674, 3 ½ In.	39
Plaque, Horse Head, Palomino, No. 1384, 4 x 2 In.	74
Teapot, Sairey Gamp, Polka Dot Tie, Umbrella, No. 691, 5 ½ In.	175
Toby Mug, Mister Pickwick, No. 1119, 3 ¼ In.	79
Vase, Ballerina, Trumpet Shape, 4-Sided, Peach, Mint Green, No. 1287, 11 In.	115
Vase, Pineapple, 3 Lobes, Footed, Green, No. 1306, 9 In.	65

BETTY BOOP, the cartoon figure, first appeared on the screen in 1931. Her face was modeled after the famous singer Helen Kane and her body after Mae West. In 1935, a comic strip was started. Her dog was named Bimbo. Although the Betty Boop cartoons ended by 1938, there was a revival of interest in the Betty Boop image in the 1980s and new pieces are being made.

Ashtray, Betty & Bimbo, Coney Island, 1930s, 2 ¾ x 2 ½ In.	190
Book, How To Make Movie Cartoons, Color Covers, 1930s, 9 x 12 In., 32 Pages	127
Carnival Statue, Plaster, Paint, Standing, Short Dress, Heart Garter, 1930s, 14 In.	391
Fan, Die Cut, Cardstock, Large Head, 1930s, 5 x 9 In.	172
Figure, Celluloid, Movable Arms, Holding Cello Rings, Tilt Head, 1930s, 4 In.	178
Pencil Holder, Betty, Rabbit, Round Base, Celluloid, Black, Red, 1930s, 3 ⅜ x 3 In.	696
Pin, Betty Posing, Black Dress, Curtains, Fleischer Studios, 1 ¼ In.	192

BICYCLES were invented in 1839. The first manufactured bicycle was made in 1861. Special ladies' bicycles were made after 1874. The modern safety bicycle was not produced until 1885. Collectors search for all types of bicycles and tricycles. Bicycle-related items are also listed here.

Arnold Schwinn, X-Caliber, Man's, Rear Fender Rack, Stand, 1930s	649
Brightwood, Pneumatic Safety, Wood & Metal, c.1898	5175
BSA, Pneumatic, Track Racer, Split Tube Frame, Major Taylor Handle Extender, c.1920	2070
Columbia, Boy's, Saddle Bags, White Metal, 1952	424
Columbia, Superb, Model 7, Chainless, c.1918	1840
Companion, Famous Fox Flyer, Wood Handlebars, Bell, Lake View Cycle, c.1898	9488
Elgin, Skylark, Girl's, Pink Paint, c.1930	1701
Elliot Hickory Safety, Hard Tires, c.1891, 20-In. Front, 27-In. Rear Tire	5750
Huffy, Radio Bike, Boy's, Radio, Battery, Powerpak, Delta Headlight, c.1957 *illus*	3300
J.C. Higgins, Color Flow, Girl's, Blue, Dart Whitewalls, Carlisle Tire & Rubber, Sears, 1953	798
Lamp, Bracket, C.T. Ham Mfg.	316
Model, 1820 Draisene, Running Machine, White, Wood, Steel Wheels, Base, Replica, 70 x 40 In.	625
Monark, Deluxe, Balloon, Twin-Spring Fork, c.1941 *illus*	518
Murray, Tank Model, Woman's, Front Suspension, c.1953 *illus*	748
Pan American, Chainless, New Departure Hub Brake, Nickel Plate, c.1901, 22 In.	8625
Pierce, Racing Tandem, Model 162/164, c.1912, 23 x 79 In.	747
Raleigh, Folding, 3-Speed, Sturmey-Archer Gear, c.1970 *illus*	375
Schwinn, Black Phantom, Front Drum Brake, c.1950 *illus*	2185
Schwinn, Black Phantom, Model B-17, 1949-1995 Centennial, Advertisements, Box, 1995	1080
Schwinn, Green Phantom, Girl's, Balloon Tires, 1950s	575
Schwinn, Tandem, Man-Woman, Drum Brakes, Gillette Balloon Tires, c.1954 *illus*	661
Shelby, Special Airflow, Balloon, Cadet Speedometer, Fender Lamp, c.1960	259
Stand, Lawn Cycle, Wood, Pat. March 31, 1896, Morristown, N.J., 44 x 13 x 32 In.	172
Tricycle, Bamboo, Yellow Paint, Basket	144
Tricycle, Fairy, Metal, Colson, c.1905	312
Tricycle, Metal, Wood, Handle Grips, 27 In.	120
Tricycle, Murray, Fire Patrol, Eng. Co. 2, Pressed Steel, White & Red, Nickel Bell, 39 In.	236
Tricycle, Sears & Roebuck, Air Flow Fenders, White Paint, Horn, 1937, 40 x 32 In.	1140
Tricycle, Tiller Style, Tube Iron Frame, Spoke Wheels, Wood Plank Seat, c.1890, 20 x 36 In.	149
Velocipede, Tricycle, Wood, c.1870	345
Victor Roadster, Name Badge, c.1886, 52 In.	6900

BING & GRONDAHL is a famous Danish factory making fine porcelains from 1853 to the present. Underglaze blue decoration was started in 1886. The annual Christmas plate series was introduced in 1895. Dinnerware, stoneware, and figurines are still being made today. The firm has used the initials *B & G* and a stylized castle as part of the mark since 1898. The company became part of Royal Copenhagen in 1987.

Figurine, 2 Jesters, Brown Tunics, Axel Locher, 1910, 15 x 8 In.	461
Figurine, Boy With Shoe, No. 2275, 5 In.	24
Figurine, Cobbler, Repairing Shoe, 5 x 6 x 9 In.	145
Figurine, Fisherwoman, Baskets Of Fish, 21 In.	220
Figurine, Ida's Flowers, 1969, 5 ½ In.	260
Figurine, Maiden, Milking Cow, Cat, 7 In.	130
Figurine, Siamese Cat, No. 2308, 5 ½ In.	35
Figurine, Young Sparrow, No. 1852A, 2 ¾ In.	12
Plate, Christmas, 1895, Behind The Frozen Window, City Scape, 7 In.	2000
Plate, Christmas, 1899, Crows Enjoying Christmas, 7 In.	200
Plate, Christmas, 1905, Anxiety Of The Coming Christmas Night, Deer, 7 In.	85
Plate, Christmas, 1922, Star Of Bethlehem, 7 ¼ In.	55
Plate, Christmas, 1934, Church Bell In Tower, 7 ¼ In.	88
Plate, Christmas, 1942, Danish Farm On Christmas Night, 6 ⅞ In.	195
Plate, Christmas, 1958, Santa Claus, Girl At Front Door, 7 In.	45
Plate, Christmas, 1966, Home For Christmas, 7 ¼ In.	18
Plate, Christmas, 1971, Christmas At Home	10
Plate, Christmas, 1979, White Christmas, 7 ¼ In.	12
Plate, Eskimos, Village, Jubilee, 1895-1950, 8 ¾ In.	179
Plate, Mother's Day, 1974, Polar Bears, Bear, Cubs, 6 In.	32
Plate, Oyster, Sea Gull, Blue Sky Inside, Garde, Denmark, c.1948, 3 x 3 ½ In., 4 Piece	88
Vase, Dandelion, Bulbous, Green 3 Tower Mark, 9 ¾ In.	59
Vase, Maple Pods, Hegermann-Lindencrone, c.1900, 4 x 3 In. *illus*	4063

Birdcage, Brass, George III Style, Door, 2 Perches, Copper Bowls, Pedestal Base, 79 x 23 In.
$671

Clars Auction Gallery

Birdcage, Brass, Round, Swinging Perch & Bottom Perch, Door, 4 Pierced Feet, 21 x 13 In.
$184

DuMouchelles Art Gallery

Birdcage, Brass, Wood, Chinese Style, 6-Sided, Door, c.1900s, 28 x 13 In.
$71

Manor Auctions LLC

Birdcage, Metal, Victorian, Pagoda Shape, White & Blue Paint, Stand, Without Base 65 x 34 In.
$5,250

Leslie Hindman Auctioneers

Birdcage, Wire, Double Dome Top, Paint, 34 x 28 In.
$87

Pook & Pook, Inc.

Birdcage, Wood, Glass Bird, Perch, Trough, 6 x 6 ¼ x 5 In.
$58

Tom Hall Auctions

BINOCULARS of all types are wanted by collectors. Those made in the eighteenth and nineteenth centuries are favored by serious collectors. The small, attractive binoculars called opera glasses are listed in their own category.

Anchor Optical Corp., World War II, US Navy, 7 x 3 x 7 In.	243
Bell & Howell, 8x40, Black, Plastic, Leather Case, 1960s	25
Brass, Hinged, Early 19th Century, 10 In.	554
Case, Busch, World War II, 1940s	27
Empire World's Best, 7x25, Leather Strap & Case, 1965	104
Legendre Grands Oculaires, Night Hawk, 7x24, 1940s	30
Ross Of London, Brown Leather, Case, c.1900, 6 x 5 In.	115
Tank, Green Metal, Leather Eye Caps, World War II	210
Thomas Armstrong & Brother, 8x30, Pre World War I, 4 x 2 x 4 In.	120
Tripod, Mahogany, Aluminum, Brass, SRPI Puteaux, Germany, World War II, 19 To 46 In.	3250

BIRDCAGES are collected for use as homes for pet birds and as decorative objects of folk art. Elaborate wooden cages of the past centuries can still be found. The brass or wicker cages of the 1930s are popular with bird owners.

Arts & Crafts, Wood, Galvanized Pullout Tray, 11 ½ x 16 In. ....*illus*	90
Bamboo, Rectangular, Plaques, Animal Shapes, Fruit, Chinese, 16 In. ....*illus*	397
Bamboo, Wood, Natural Color, Building Shape, Pitched Roofs, Swinging Perch, 19 x 15 In.	12
Brass, George III Style, Door, 2 Perches, Copper Bowls, Pedestal Base, 79 x 23 In. ....*illus*	671
Brass, Round, Swinging Perch & Bottom Perch, Door, 4 Pierced Feet, 21 x 13 In. ....*illus*	184
Brass, Spherical, Swing Perch, 4 Pierced Feet, Suspended Dishes, Hanging Ring, 21 x 13 In.	180
Brass, Wood, Chinese Style, 6-Sided, Door, c.1900s, 28 x 13 In. ....*illus*	71
Hardwood, Zinc, Center Spire, Finial, 4 Corner Turrets, Green, Asia, c.1900, 30 x 28 In.	450
Mahogany, Bone Finials, Barber Pole Inlay, Arched Pediment, c.1885, 22 x 15 ¼ In.	649
Mahogany, Wire, Dome Top, Acorn Finial, Square, Green, Turnip Feet, c.1820, 14 x 21 In.	144
Mahogany, Wirework, Rectangular, Stand, X-Stretcher, Cabriole Legs, 51 In.	1375
Metal, Victorian, Pagoda Shape, White & Blue Paint, Stand, Without Base 65 x 34 In. ....*illus*	5250
Tole, Wire, Pagoda Shape, Painted Salmon, Cream, Frame, France, 1900s, 87 x 33 In.	2688
Victorian, Hinged Door, Green, Gilt Paint, Octagonal, 86 x 49 In.	12500
Wire, Double Dome Top, Paint, 34 x 28 In. ....*illus*	87
Wire, Wood, Carved Brass Dragon Handle, Figures, Porcelain Feeders, Chinese, 29 In.	790
Wire, Wood, Double Dome Top, Red, Green Yellow Paint, 26 x 28 In.	720
Wire, Wood, Paint, c.1905, 27 ½ x 30 ½ In.	213
Wood, Carved, Pagoda Shape, Sliding Wood Door, Porcelain Feeders, 23 x 13 In.	173
Wood, Flared Shape, 4 Finials, Perch, 29 In.	82
Wood, Glass Bird, Perch, Trough, 6 x 6 ¼ x 5 In. ....*illus*	58
Wood, Octangular Base Fence, Multicolor Paint, c.1900, 19 In.	230
Wood, Paint, Pierced, Turned Perch, Brass Hook, c.1900, 38 ¼ x 17 ¼ In.	307
Wood, Red Stain, Pagoda Style, Steps, Chinese, 30 x 19 In.	281

BISQUE is an unglazed baked porcelain. Finished bisque has a slightly sandy texture with a dull finish. Some of it may be decorated with various colors. Bisque gained favor during the late Victorian era when thousands of bisque figurines were made. It is still being made. Additional bisque items may be listed under the factory name.

Figurine, Bathing Beauty, Nude, Crawling, Mohair Wig, Germany, c.1915, 4 ½ In. ....*illus*	2128
Figurine, Bathing Beauty, Painted Face, Galluba & Hoffman, c.1910, 3 ½ In. ....*illus*	684
Figurine, Cherub, Seated, Flowers, Urn, Gilt Metal Base, Boizot, 6 ½ x 6 ½ In., Pair	242
Figurine, Girl, 18th Century Clothing, Holding Feather Duster, Continental, c.1870, 17 In.	42
Figurine, Little Nemo Series, Movable Arms, Germany, c.1914, 4 In. To 5 In., 5 Piece ....*illus*	11480
Figurine, Man & Woman, Formal Dress, Hand Painted, 1800s, 23 In., Pair ....*illus*	1063
Figurine, Masquerade, Painted, Parcel Gilt, Chantilly, Continental, c.1890, 21 ½ In., Pair	240
Figurine, Women Water Carriers, Amphora On Shoulder, Porcelain, 1800s, 19 In., Pair	1020
Spill Vase, 2 Women, Tree, Leaves, c.1890, 12 ½ In.	30
Toothpick Holder, Figural, Gray Cat Head, Pink Bow, 2 In.	59

BLACK memorabilia has become an important area of collecting since the 1970s. The best material dates from past centuries, but many recent items are also of interest. F & F is the mark used on plastic made by Fiedler & Fiedler Mold & Die Works, Inc. in the 1930s and 1940s. Objects that picture a black person may also be listed in this book under Advertising, Sign; Bank; Bottle Opener; Cookie Jar; Doll; Salt & Pepper; Sheet Music; Toy; etc.

Automaton, Dancer, Automatic Toy Works, Patented Sept. 23 1873, 9 ½ In.	851
Automaton, Dancer, Carved, Jointed, Composition Head, Wood Base, Key Wind, c.1850, 10 In.	688

Automaton, Women's Rights, Molded Head, Glass Eyes, Walnut, Key Wind, c.1885, 10 In.		3500
Bell, Mammy, Steel, Wood Handle, Cloth Dress, 1950s, 4 In.		16
Bottle, Golliwog, Smiling Head, Paper Label, France, 5 ½ In.		90
Bottle, Moody's Quick Shine Stove Polish, Black Boy On Label, c.1915, 6 In.		210
Box, Nigger Brand Sahara Dates, Oval, France, c.1915, 8 ¾ In.		180
Bust, Man, Wood, Carved, 17 In.		960
Candy Box, Heide's Colored Coons, Men, Women, Fine Clothes, Licorice, Cardboard, 10 x 7 In.		400
Candy Box, Women Holding, Rabbit, Rooster, Easter Egg Shape, Multicolor, 4 In.		120
Cane, Ebony, Man's Head, Twisted, Carved Shaft, 22 ¾ In.		113
Carving, Slave, Folk Art, Whipping & Slashing Marks, 17 In.		44
Christmas Ornament, Minstrel, Pressed Cotton, Crepe Paper Suit, Top Hat, Germany, 6 In.		649
Cigar Cutter, Boy, On Mound, Cigar In Mouth, Press Arm, Iron, Slate, 1885, 7 In.		486
Container, Man, Smiling, Barefoot, Well Dressed, Plaster, 1920s, 5 ⅜ In.		126
Cookie Jars are listed in the Cookie Jar category.		
Deed, Manumission, V. Labadie, Freedom, Mulatto Slaves, Leather Folio, 1850, 16 x 13 In.		1968
Doll, Blackamoor, Bisque Head, Painted Face, Hair, Cloth Body, Red Felt Coat, 5 In.		537
Doll, Brad, Sculpted Black Hair, Bendable Legs, Jacket, Shorts, Box, Mattel, 1970, 12 In.		168
Doll, Character, Bisque Socket Head, Mohair Braids, Composition & Wood Body, 14 In.		1680
Doll, Character, Bisque, Mohair Wig, Composition, Wood, Simon & Halbig, c.1910, 22 In. *illus*		8400
Doll, Christie, Talking, Short Black Hair, Brown Eyes, Mattel, 1970, 11 In.		224
Doll, Cloth, Embroidered, Googly Eyes, Sewn Red Lips, Boy, Girl, 13 In., Pair		60
Doll, Cloth, Straw Filled, Painted Face, Jointed, Boy, Girl, 9 ½ & 10 ½ In., Pair		11
Doll, Curtis, Moving Sculpted Black Hair, Brown Eyes, Sport Suit, Mattel, 1975, 12 In.		168
Doll, Francie, Twist 'n Turn, Brown Hair, Bendable Knees, Swimsuit, Box, Mattel, 1967, 11 In.		728
Doll, Girl, Chubby, Felt, Seamed Face, Sewn Eyes, Mouth, Yarn Hair, Dress, Hat, 17 In.		60
Doll, Julia, Brunette, Bendable Legs, Twist 'n Turn Body, Box, Mattel, 1968, 11 In.		392
Doll, Kestner, 134, Bisque Head, Mohair Wig, Composition, Hat, Pink Dress, 8 ½ In.		311
Doll, Little Black Sambo, Celluloid, Jointed, Story Book, Johnny Gruelle, Box, 5 In.		72
Doll, Rag, Red Dress, Striped Stockings, 15 In.		83
Figure, Blackamoor, Gondolier, Holding Paddle & Cornucopia, Painted Gilt, c.1900, 33 In.		1168
Figure, Blackamoor, Woman, Turban, Fruit, Urn, Serpentine Plinth, Carving, 68 In., Pair		4780
Figure, Boy, Seated, Arm On Knee, Striped Pants, Bronze, Painted, 2 ½ x 3 x 3 In.		360
Figure, Jazz Band Group, 4 Seated Musicians, Paint, Bisque, 1930s, 3 ½ In., 4 Piece		63
Figure, Mammy, Red, Black Paint, Chalkware, 10 ½ In.		24
Figure, Man, Smiling, Holding Pole, Black Paint, Wood Carving, c.1890, 26 In.		1185
Figure, Man's Head, Redware, Black Paint, c.1860, 6 In.		3792
Figure, Slave On Pedestal, Col. T.B Parker, Auctioneer, Slave Trader, Wood, c.1900, 70 In.		1375
Figure, Soldier, Pine, Carved, Red, Gold, Black Paint, 1800s, 27 In.		948
Game, Basketball, Man Holding Ball, Wood Ball On String, Ruddell Mfg., Box, 1929, 7 x 5 In.		180
Game, Carnival Bean Toss, 2 Black Face Targets, Wood, Barrel Shape, c.1910, 42 In.		688
Game, Jolly Darkie Target Game, McLoughlin Bro's., Box, 13 x 7 In.		240
Game, Sambo Ring Toss, Cutout, Wood, 5 Cardboard Rings, Parker Bros., Box, 11 x 6 In.		150
Game, Twin Targets Ball Toss Game, Paper Lithograph, Milton Bradley, c.1900, 13 x 13 In.		125
Game, Watch On De Rind Catapult, Launcher, Balls, All-Fair, Box, 1931, 12 x 12 In.		300
Humidor, Black Man, Blue Hat, Marked Elizabeth, 8 In.		360
Humidor, Boy, Seated On Barrel, Playing Accordion, Majolica, c.1890, 8 ½ In.		125
Humidor, Boy, Seated, Watermelon, c.1890, 9 ¾ In.		281
Humidor, Copper, Sugar Barrel, Watch Cat, Boy Trying To Sneak A Taste, c.1880, 11 In.		594
Mask, Old Virginia Catsup, Mammy Face, c.1920, 10 x 9 In.		120
Paint Can, Black-O-Lene, Black Man Playing Banjo, Jet Black Enamel, c.1923, 3 ½ In.		139
Pipe Shelf, Hanging, Aunt Jemima, Uncle Mose Kissing, Moon Face, Wood, c.1910, 23 In.		250
Poster, American Negro Exposition, July 4 To Sept. 2, 1940, Chicago Coliseum, 21 In.		863
Poster, Circus, Greater Sheesley Shows, Donaldson Lithograph, c.1910, 42 x 28 In.		563
Poster, Primrose & West's Minstrels, Evolution Of Song & Dance, c.1880, 28 x 38 In.		2400
Poster, Theater, Little Eva's Temptation, Uncle Tom, Eva, D.L. Co., Frame, c.1900, 29 x 20 In.		344
Poster, Uncle Tom's Cabin, American Show Print Co., c.1915, 54 x 41 In.		63
Statue, Kneeling Man, Holding Spreadwing Eagle, Gilt, Stone Eyes, Italy, 1800s, 43 In.		5192
Stringholder, Mammy, Yellow Dress, Green Stripes, 7 In.		150
Stringholder, Mammy, Yellow Dress, Red Scarf, Occupied Japan, 6 ¼ In.		185

BLENKO GLASS COMPANY is the 1930s successor to several glassworks founded by William John Blenko in Milton, West Virginia. In 1933, his son, William H. Blenko Sr., took charge. The company made tablewares and vases in classical shapes. In the late 1940s it hired talented designers and made innovative pieces. The company made a line of reproductions for Colonial Williamsburg. It is still in business and is best known today for its decorative wares and stained glass. All products are made to order.

Ashtray, Cobalt Blue, Waffle Bottom, 1969, 8 ¼ In. 30

Bisque, Figurine, Bathing Beauty, Nude, Crawling, Mohair Wig, Germany, c.1915, 4 ½ In.
$2,128

Theriault's

Bisque, Figurine, Bathing Beauty, Painted Face, Galluba & Hoffman, c.1910, 3 ½ In.
$684

Theriault's

Bisque, Figurine, Little Nemo Series, Movable Arms, Germany, c.1914, 4 In. To 5 In., 5 Piece
$11,480

Hake's Americana & Collectibles

Book Rooms
Books and bookshelves are part of a new decorating trend. A recent "shelter" magazine pictured bookcases floor to ceiling in every featured house.

Bisque, Figurine, Man & Woman, Formal Dress, Hand Painted, 1800s, 23 In., Pair
$1,063

Rago Arts & Auction Center

Black, Doll, Character, Bisque, Mohair Wig, Composition, Wood, Simon & Halbig, c.1910, 22 In.
$8,400

Theriault's

Boch Freres, Vase, Stags, Crackleware, Black Catteau Stamp, 1920s, 12 x 7 ½ In.
$1,625

Rago Arts & Auction Center

Bottle, Water, Thumbprint Star Design, Emerald Green, Square, 9 In.	67
Bowl, Amber, Scalloped, 1960s, 11 ¼ x 4 In.	35
Bowl, Ruby, Low Flared, c.1940, 10 x 3 In.	250
Candleholder, Amber, Abstract, Sticker, 6 In.	20
Decanter, Blue, Tapered, Clear Stopper, 23 In.	34
Decanter, Gray, Clear Stopper, Pinched, 12 In.	28
Decanter, Squat, Amber, Lollipop Stopper, 10 x 5 ½ In.	99
Decanter, Stopper, Amber, Tapered, 22 In.	113
Decanter, Stopper, Cranberry, Long Neck, 13 In.	90
Ice Bucket, Top Hat Shape, Concave Bottom, Clear, 6 ½ x 12 In.	120
Paperweight, Owl, Cobalt Blue, Foil Label, c.1971, 5 In.	39
Pitcher, Crackle, Charcoal, 7 In.	95
Rose Bowl, Amber Crackle, Pinched, 4 In.	20
Vase, Amethyst, Tapered, Bulbous, 17 In.	45
Vase, Amethyst, Triangle Cylindrical, 12 In.	51
Vase, Applied Rosettes, Crackle, Flared Rim, 9 In.	95
Vase, Applied Threading, Amethyst, Stick Neck, 7 ¾ In.	95
Vase, Aqua, Clear Applied Handles, 13 In.	184
Vase, Blue, Fish Shape, 11 In.	79
Vase, Crimped Ruffled Rim, Ball Stem, Footed, Emerald Green, 7 ¾ In.	48
Vase, Emerald Green, Crackle, Flaring Cylinder, 8 In.	65
Vase, Green, Wavy Rim, 8 ½ In.	23
Vase, Yellow, Fish Shape, 11 ½ In.	42

BLOWN GLASS, *see Glass-Blown category.*

BLUE GLASS, *see Cobalt Blue category.*

BLUE ONION, *see Onion category.*

BLUE WILLOW, *see Willow category.*

BOCH FRERES factory was founded in 1841 in La Louviere in eastern Belgium. The wares resemble the work of Villeroy & Boch. The factory closed in 1985. M.R.L. Boch took over the production of tableware but went bankrupt in 1988. Le Hodey took over Boch Freres in 1989, using the name Royal Boch Manufacture S.A. It went bankrupt in 2009. A new managing director is now running the company.

Bowl, Keramis Majolica, Cherub On Dolphin, Dolphin Heads, 10 ½ x 20 In.	295
Box, Geometric Designs, Enamel, Blue, Bronze Mounts, c.1915, 5 x 4 x 2 In.	195
Plate, Napoleon Battle Scenes, Black, White Transfer, 8 In., 6 Piece	88
Plate, Working Peasants, Oxen, Blue & White, Marked, 11 In.	220
Tile, Village, Stylized Tree, Green, c.1900, 6 x 6 In.	45
Vase, Blue Vertical Stripes, Yellow Flowers, White Ground, Art Deco, C. Catteau, c.1925, 13 In.	1200
Vase, Grazing Deer, Blue, Art Deco, Craquelure, Turquoise, Signed, c.1935, 12 x 8 ½ In.	1045
Vase, Leaf & Berry, Metallic Glaze, Handles, c.1915, 6 In.	447
Vase, Stags, Craquelure, Black Catteau Stamp, 1920s, 12 x 7 ½ In. *illus*	1625
Vase, Teal To Red Slip Glaze, Gilt Brass Mounts, Tapered To Base, 8 ½ In.	177

BOEHM is the collector's name for the porcelains of Edward Marshall Boehm. In 1953 the Osso China Company was reorganized as Edward Marshall Boehm, Inc. The company is still working in England and New Jersey. In the early days of the factory, dishes were made, but the elaborate and lifelike bird figurines are the best-known ware. Edward Marshall Boehm, the founder, died in 1969, but the firm has continued to design and produce porcelain. Today, the firm makes both limited and unlimited editions of figurines and plates.

Alec's Red Rose, 7 x 8 In.	950
Baby Buntings, Cuddled In Nest, 4 In.	300
Baby Chickadee, 4 x 3 ¼ In.	80
Baby Chickadee, Black Capped, Pinecones, 3 ¼ x 3 ¼ x 3 In.	250
Baby Goldfinch, Sitting On Branch, Purple Flower, 4 In.	66
Baby Grouse, Threesome, 3 ½ x 5 In.	195
Baby Wood Thrush, 4 ½ x 3 ½ x 3 ¾ In.	125
Birds On Flowering Branch, Limited Edition, 8 ¾ x 12 In.	780
Black Capped Chickadee, Sitting On Holly, 8 ⅜ In.	60

Bobwhite, Quail, 10 x 14 x 9 In.	176
Box, Lid, Owl's Head, Belleek Type Porcelain, Yellow & Black Eyes, Oval, 3 x 5 In.	153
Bridal Rose, Flower, White Roses, Baby's Breath, Our Love Forever, 4 x 6 In.	60
Cedar Waxwing, 8 ½ x 8 In.	330
Chipmunk, Sitting, Holding Nut, c.1975, 3 In.	175
Chrysanthemum & Daisies, Bisque, Metal, 9 ½ x 10 ½ In.	480
Cygnet, Sitting On Leaf, 6 x 4 ½ In.	200
Eastern Meadowlark, 7 ½ x 6 ¾ In.	210
Fawn, 6 ½ x 4 ¼ In.	165
Gardenia, White, On Rocks, 5 x 5 ¼ In.	299
Great Egret, White, Signed Helen Boehm, 13 In.	432
Hummingbird, Paphiopedilum, 5 ½ x 7 In.	210
Kingfisher, Snow Covered Rock, 5 ⅞ x 4 In.	65
Magpie, 5 ½ x 4 In.	125
Mourning Doves, Perched, Leafy Branch, 14 ½ In.	360
Panda, Eating Bamboo, Multicolor, 6 ⅛ In.	90
Polo Player, Horse, Front Legs Up, 13 ½ In.	720
Ptamigan, Free-Form Rocky Base, Limited Edition, 1900s, 13 ¾ In., Pair	475
Royal Blessing, Pink Rose, Baby's Breath, 4 x 5 In.	83
Saw-Whet Owl, 6 ¼ x 4 ½ In.	210
Sparrow, On Branch, 8 In.	450
White Mouse, 4 In.	175
Whooping Crane, Wings Out, National Audubon Society, Signed Helen Boehm, 1984, 18 In.	384
Yellow Throated Warbler, Sitting On Trumpet Shape Flower, 9 ⅝ In.	120

BOOKENDS have probably been used since books became inexpensive. Early libraries kept books in cupboards, not on open shelves. By the 1870s bookends appeared, especially homemade fret-carved wooden examples. Most bookends listed in this book date from the twentieth century. Bookends are also listed in other categories by manufacturer or material. All bookends listed here are pairs.

Bison Head, Brass, Square Base, Bradley & Hubbard, Stamped, c.1900, 6 ½ x 5 In.	531
Building Facade, Door, Steps, Mt. Pleasant, Gilt Iron, Bradley & Hubbard, 5 ½ In.	58
Bust, Oliver Wendell Holmes, Arched, Patinated Iron, Holmes On Base, 6 In.	46
Cinnabar Plaque, Pewter, Stamped Potter Studio, Art Deco, 4 ¼ x 5 ¾ In.	127
Country House, Trees, Bronze Cast Iron, Bradley & Hubbard, c.1925, 5 x 3 In.	185
Dog, Scottie, On Hind Legs, Bronze, Marguerite Kirmse, c.1925, 7 ½ In.	4130
Eagle, Cast Iron, 7 x 6 In.	127
Elf, Seated, Reading Book, Green Suit, Black Base, Metal, Art Deco Style, 6 In.	170
End Of Trail, Dejected Cowboy On Horse, Bronze, Armor, 7 In.	35
End Of Trail, Indian On Horse, Cast Iron, 5 ¼ x 7 ¼ In.	371
Faun, Seated, Cast Spelter, Painted, McClelland Barklay, 6 ¾ In.	46
Fisherman, Black Hat & Coat, White Beard, Paint, Cast Iron, 6 ½ In.	48
Flowers, Repousse, Hammered Copper, Roycroft, c.1905, 5 x 3 x 4 In.	150
Frog, Brass, 8 In.	115
Horse, Rearing, Crystal Glass, L.E. Smith	98
Indian Chiefs, Brown Patina, Charles Henry Humphriss, Roman Bronze Works, N.Y., 9 ¼ In.	30000
Leather Clad, Silver Relief Plaque, Arched Top, Italy, 6 ½ x 4 ½ In.	40
Leda & The Swan, Bezel, Cast Steel, Polished, Art Deco, 7 ½ x 2 x 3 ¾ In.	351
Lincoln Memorial, Bronze, 7 In.	173
Lincoln, Seated, Bronze, Ronson, 4 ½ In.	144
Lion, Roaring, Against Book, Rosewood, 4 In.	59
Marley Horse, Bronze, Rosewood, c.1900, 9 In.	270
Men, Nude, Pushing, Bronze, Gorham Co., 1912, 7 ⅜ In.	7500
Moses, Isaiah, Patinated Metal, L. Gudebrod, 7 ½ x 5 In.	113
Native American Chief, Cast Iron, Gold Wash, 4 ¾ x 6 x 3 In. ....*illus*	86
Old Salt, Cape Cod Fishermen, Paint, Cast Iron, Connecticut Foundry Co., 1928, 5 ½ In.	212
Open Book Shape, Brown, Fulper, Marked, 5 x 4 ¾ In.	225
Owl, Bronze, Rocky Outcropping, Incised Heinrich W. Hirschler, Austria, 5 In.	500
Patinated Brass, C. Aubock, Austria, c.1940, 5 In.	1188
Punch & Judy, Painted, Cast Iron, England, c.1900, 12 In.	840 to 885
Pushing Men, Bronze, Harriet Whitney Frishmuth, Gorham Co., 1912, 7 ½ In.	16250
Seahorse, Brass, c.1890, 11 In.	413
Thinker, Bronze Coated, Pillars, Arched Background	72
Women, Seated, Green Paint, Spelter, Marble Base, J.R. Hirsch, 7 In.	144

Bookends, Native American Chief, Cast Iron, Gold Wash, 4 ¾ x 6 x 3 In.
$86

Showtime Auction Services

Bottle, Barber, Bay Rum Milk Glass, Blue, Reverse Glass Label, Risque Woman, 10 In.
$265

Bertoia Auctions

Bottle, Beer, W C & J & G. Willson, Sarsaparilla Mead, Stoneware, Salt Glaze, c.1865, 9 ¾ In.
$316

Glass Works Auctions

B

Bottle, Bininger, 19 Broad St., Old
London Dock Gin, Yellow Olive Green,
c.1860, 10 In.
$460

Glass Works Auctions

Bottle, Bitters, Bennett & Carrol,
Pittsburg Barrel, Yellow Amber, Applied
Collar, c.1860
$1,725

Glass Works Auctions

Bottle, Bitters, California Wine, Rennert,
Prosch & Co., Lady's Leg, Amber, c.1885,
12 ⅞ In.
$633

Glass Works Auctions

BOOKMARKS were originally made of parchment, cloth, or leather. Soon woven silk
ribbon, thin cardboard, celluloid, wood, silver, tortoiseshell, and metals were used.
Examples made before 1850 are scarce, but there are many to be found dating before 1920.

Aluminum, Heart Shape, Psalm 23, 2 ½ x 1 In.	24
Beaded, Geometric Designs, Multicolor, Navy Ground, c.1890, 6 ½ In.	15
Bone, Carved, Elephant, Chinese, 1930s, 4 In.	59
Brass, Castle, Boats, Enamel, Hjo, Sweden, 3 ½ x 1 In.	49
Celluloid, Cloisonne Enamel Handle, Multicolor, 1920s, 11 ½ In.	40
Celluloid, Passion Flower, c.1910, 5 ⅝ x 1 ⅞ In.	18
Chromolithograph, Embossed, Couple, A Pair Of Spoons, 6 ⅜ x 2 In.	10
Die Cut, Girl, Lilacs, Embossed, Lavender, 6 x 2 In.	18
Felt, Scottie Dog, Black, String, 1950s, 12 In.	10
Leather, Palm Trees, Books Like Friends Should Be Well Chosen, 8 ½ In.	16
Metal, Yellowstone Park, Deer Head, 2 ½ In.	16
Needlepoint On Perforated Paper, Holy Bible, Orange, Brown, 7 x 2 In.	22
Paper, Cross Shape, Embossed, Lord Bless Thee, Violets, Dove, Die Cut, 1910, 4 x 2 In.	24
Paper, Lilacs, Girl, Verse, Embossed, Die Cut, 6 x 2 In.	12
Ribbon, Flowers, Virgin Mary, Jesus, Hand Painted, c.1930, 7 ¼ In.	65
Ribbon, Red, Brass Shakespeare Portrait, 10 ¼ In.	22
Silk, Happy May Your Birthday Bee, Bee On Flowers, Stevens, c.1875, 9 ¼ In.	85
Silk, Piper, Auld Lang Syne, Castle, Red Tassel, 9 x 2 In.	25
Silk, The Old Arm Chair, Bible, Stevengraph, c.1871, 10 ¾ x 2 In.	45
Sterling Silver, Celtic Design, David Andersen, c.1900, 3 x 1 In.	95
Sterling Silver, Flowers, Repousse, S. Kirk & Son, 2 ½ x 1 In.	40
Sterling Silver, Hand, 1930s, 2 ¾ In.	130
Sterling Silver, Heart Shape, James Avery, 1 ¾ x 1 ¾ In.	54
Sterling Silver, Maple Leaf, Tiffany & Co., 3 ⅛ x 1 ⅛ In.	75
Sterling Silver, Maple Leaf, Tiffany & Co., Box, 3 x 1 In.	89
Sterling Silver, Mayan Figure, Blue Enamel, Mexico, 3 ⅞ In.	60
Sterling Silver, Repousse, Kirk Stieff, 2 ⅝ In.	95
Sterling Silver, Rose, Repousse, S. Kirk & Son, 2 ½ In.	45
Sterling Silver, Teddy Bear, Tiffany & Co., 2 x 1 ½ In.	110
Sterling Silver, William Shakespeare, Red Ribbon, 10 In.	22
Sterling Silver, Windmill, Dutch, c.1920, 3 ⅜ In.	75
Sterling Silver, Winston Churchill, England, 4 ⅜ In.	68

BOSSONS character wall masks (heads), plaques, figurines, and other decorative pieces
were made by W.H. Bossons, Limited, of Congleton, England. The company was founded in
1946 and closed in 1996. Dates shown are the date the item was introduced.

BOSSONS

Wall Mask, Abdul, 7 x 5 ½ In.	87
Wall Mask, Cavalier, c.1962, 7 ½ In.	40
Wall Mask, Drummer Boy, 5 ½ In.	55
Wall Mask, Mr. Bumble, 5 In.	40
Wall Mask, Mr. Micawber, c.1964, 5 ½ In.	35
Wall Mask, Scrooge, 5 ½ x 3 ¼ In.	55
Wall Mask, Smuggler, 5 ½ In.	45
Wall Mask, Tyrolean, 1960s, 6 In.	100
Wall Plaque, Custer & Sitting Bull, Paper Label	249
Wall Plaque, Dog, English Boxer, Buckle Collar, 4 In.	95
Wall Plaque, Dog, Scottie, c.1969, 5 x 3 ¼ In.	75
Wall Plaque, Koalas, 10 In.	115

BOSTON & SANDWICH CO. *pieces may be found in the Sandwich Glass category.*

BOTTLE collecting has become a major American hobby. There are several general
categories of bottles, such as historic flasks, bitters, household, and figural. ABM means the
bottle was made by an automatic bottle machine after 1903. Pyro is the shortened form of the
word *pyroglaze,* an enameled lettering used on bottles after the mid-1930s. This form of decoration is
also called ACL or applied color label. For more prices, go to kovels.com.

Apothecary, Porcelain, Eagle, Cornucopias, Cartouche, Inscription, Gilt Borders, 10 In.	115
Barber, Bay Rum Milk Glass, Blue, Reverse Glass Label, Risque Woman, 10 In. *illus*	265
Barber, Bay Rum, Cranberry Cut To Clear, Thumbprint Base, Elongated Neck, 7 ½ In.	69
Barber, Coral Reef, Clear Opalescent, Square, Tapered, c.1900, 8 x 2 ½ In.	259
Barber, Coral Reef, Cranberry Opalescent, Round, Tapered, Stopper, Hobbs, c.1900, 7 In.	518

Bottle, Bitters, Doctor Fisch's, W.H. Ware, Fish, Amber, c.1870, 11 ½ In.
$345

Bottle, Bitters, Greeley's Bourbon Whiskey, Strawberry Puce, Applied Mouth, c.1870, 9 In.
$920

Bottle, Bitters, Herb's Pure Wild Cherry Bark, Wertz & Field, Pa., Glass Label, c.1900, 8 In.
$3,163

Bottle, Bitters, Holtzermann's Patent Stomach, Cabin, Amber, Applied Collar, 9 ⅝ In.
$1,380

Bottle, Bitters, Tippecanoe, H.H. Warner & Co., Log, Amber, Cork, Metal Pull, c.1890
$1,093

Bottle, Cologne, Diamond Daisy Over Flutes, Amethyst, Flask, Stiegel Type, c.1770, 6 In.
$4,025

Bottle, Cologne, Fountain, Opalescent, Sapphire Blue, Pontil, 4 ¾ In.
$805

Bottle, Cure, Asthma, Shaker, Cork, Paper Label, Multicolor Box, Sliding Tin Top
$2,242

Bottle, Decanter, 25 Ribs, Swirled To Right, Blue Aqua, Pittsburgh, 1815-35, 8 ⅛ In.
$265

Bottle, Figural, Man, Shake Me Well Before Using, Japanese Polish, Amber, c.1895, 6 ¾ In.

$374

Glass Works Auctions

Bottle, Flask, Fish, Moravian, Scales, Earthenware, Green Copper, Manganese, 9 ¾ In.

$23,000

Crocker Farm, Inc.

Bottle, Flask, Jenny Lind & Glasshouse, Calabash, Sapphire Blue, Iron Pontil, Blob Top, c.1860

$7,480

Glass Works Auctions

TIP

Clean the inside of a bottle with detergent powder and a Water Pik.

Barber, Opaline Brocade, Cranberry Opalescent, Pinched, Stopper, Northwood, c.1900, 8 In.	3105
Barber, Swirl, Ruby Opalescent, Round, Silver Stopper, Hobbs, c.1888, 8 x 3 In.	219
Beer, Bayview Brewing Co., Seattle, Wash., Green, Sloping Collar, Qt.	350
Beer, Columbia Weiss Beer Brewery, St. Louis, Amber, Porcelain Stopper	18
Beer, DeFrest Lemon Beer, Stamped, Cobalt Dip, Tapered Neck & Spout	144
Beer, Dr. Brown's Lemon, Stoneware, Gray, Blue Shoulder, 9 In.	246
Beer, E. Ferris, Stoneware, Gray Glaze, Blue Shoulder, 10 In.	246
Beer, Geo. Bader Bottler, Newark, Oh., Amber	18
Beer, H.H.P. & Co., New York, Sapphire Blue, 10-Sided, Sloping Collar, 1855-65, 9 In.	2530
Beer, Philadelphia, XXX, Porter & Ale, Flip Hat, Blue Green, 2 ¼ x 5 ¼ In.	1495
Beer, S. Liebmann's Sons, Wagner NH, Aqua, Bail	20
Beer, W C & J & G. Willson, Sarsaparilla Mead, Stoneware, Salt Glaze, c.1865, 9 ¾ In. ....*illus*	316
Beer, Weiss Beer Co., St. Louis, Mo., Embossed In Arch, Aqua, Blob Top, 1860	68
Bininger, 19 Broad St., N.Y., Peep-O-Day, Amber, Double Collar, Flask, c.1865, 7 ⅝ In.	748
Bininger, 19 Broad St., Old London Dock Gin, Yellow Olive Green, c.1860, 10 In. ....*illus*	460
Bininger, A.M. & Co., 19 Broad St., New York, Olive Green, Jug, Double Collar, 8 In.	4600
Bininger, A.M. & Co., Gin, Amber, Embossed, c.1860, 9 ⅞ In.	58
Bininger, Old Kentucky Bourbon, 1848, Barrel, Yellow Amber, Double Collar, 9 ½ In.	805
Bitters, A.T. & Co., Amber, Turned Neck, Sloping Double Collar, 3-Piece Mold, 10 ¼ In.	1800
Bitters, A.T. & Co., Yellow, Green Tint, Turned Neck, Sloping Double Collar, 10 ¼ In.	2800
Bitters, Alpine Herb, Amber, Monogram On Reverse, Case, Sloping Collar, 9 ⅝ In.	800
Bitters, Amber, Cabin, Embossed Cannons, Sabers & Tent, Sloping Collar, 10 In.	3163
Bitters, Baker's Orange Grove, Plum, Roped Corners, Sloping Collar, 9 ⅜ In.	1200
Bitters, Baker's Orange Grove, Yellow Green, Roped Corners, Sloping Collar, 9 ½ In.	1400
Bitters, Bennett & Carrol, Pittsburg Barrel, Yellow Amber, Applied Collar, c.1860 ....*illus*	1725
Bitters, Bitter Witch, Horseshoe, Yellow Olive, Arched Shoulders, Double Roll Collar	2600
Bitters, Bourbon Whiskey, Barrel, Cherry Puce, Flattened Lip, 9 ¼ In.	805
Bitters, Brady's Nerve, Blue Aqua, Indented Panels, Double Collar, 9 ¼ In.	1725
Bitters, Bryant's Stomach, 8 Panels, Lady's Leg Neck, Yellow Green, Sloping Collar, 12 In.	3400
Bitters, Buhrer's Gentian, Yellow Amber, Indented Panels, Sloping Collar, 8 ⅜ In.	546
Bitters, California Wine, Rennert, Prosch & Co., Lady's Leg, Amber, c.1885, 12 ⅞ In. ....*illus*	633
Bitters, Catawba, Embossed Grapes, Emerald Green, Applied Mouth, Calif., c.1860, 9 ⅝ In.	4600
Bitters, Curtis, Calisaya, Great Stomach, 1866, 1900, Yellow Amber, Tapered, 11 ⅝ In.	978
Bitters, Doctor Fisch's, W.H. Ware, Fish, Amber, c.1870, 11 ½ In. ....*illus*	345
Bitters, Doyles Hop, Semi-Cabin, 1872, Amber	45
Bitters, Dr. A.W. Coleman's Anti Dyspeptic, Alabama, Green, Applied Mouth, c.1850, 9 In.	4025
Bitters, Dr. Boyce's Tonic, Waterbury, Vt., Aqua, Round, 12 Panels	125
Bitters, Dr. C.W. Roback's Stomach, Cincinnati, O., Yellow Olive Amber, 9 ¼ In.	431
Bitters, Dr. F. Fleschhut's Celebrated Stomach, Blue Aqua, Arched Panels, 8 ½ In.	1955
Bitters, Dr. Goodhue's Root & Herb, Salem, Ma.	95
Bitters, Dr. Henley's Wild Grape Root, IXL In Oval, Blue Aqua, Applied Ring, 12 ½ In.	250
Bitters, Dr. Henley's Wild Grape Root, IXL, Blue Green, Applied Ring, 12 In.	1035
Bitters, Dr. Henley's Wild Grape Root, IXL, Green Aqua, Applied Ring, 12 ½ In.	750
Bitters, Dr. Lyford's, C.P. Herrick, Tilton, N.H., Aqua, Oval, 8 ¼ In.	175
Bitters, Dr. Renz's Herb, Yellow Olive, Case, Arched Sides, Ring Collar, c.1870, 9 ¾ In.	600
Bitters, Dr. Soule's Hop, Embossed Hops, Light Green, Applied Collar, 9 ½ In.	450
Bitters, Dr. Stephen Jewett's Celebrated Health Restoring, Rindge, N.H., Olive, 7 ¼ In.	5265
Bitters, Dr. Tompkin, Vegetable, Teal Blue, Tooled Lip, c.1875, 9 In.	1150
Bitters, Dr. Walkinshaw's Curative, Batavia, N.Y., Yellow Amber, Sloping Collar, 10 In.	748
Bitters, Dr. Wonser's U.S.A. Indian Root, Root Beer Amber, Fluted Shoulder	11500
Bitters, Dr. Wonser's U.S.A., Teal, Case, Sloping Collar, 9 In.	805
Bitters, Dr. Zabriskies, Moonstone, Rectangular, Indented Panels, Flared Lip, c.1845, 6 In.	1560
Bitters, Dr. Zadoc Porter's Medicated Stomach, Aqua, Label, 5 ½ In.	275
Bitters, Drake's Plantation, 1860, Cabin, Topaz, Applied Collar, 9 ¾ In.	410
Bitters, Drake's Plantation, 6 Log, Cabin, Golden Amber, 10 In.	650
Bitters, Drake's Plantation, 6 Log, Cabin, Purple Amber, 10 In.	600
Bitters, Drake's Plantation, 6 Log, Cabin, Yellow Olive, 10 In.	1300
Bitters, Excelsior, Amber, Indented Panels, Sloping Collar, 8 ¾ In.	600
Bitters, Figural, Oriental Man, Beard, Letters DK, Aqua, Applied Ring Mouth, c.1870, 10 In.	1380
Bitters, Foerster's Teutonic, Chicago, Orange Amber, Jug, Ring Mouth, Handle, 6 ¾ In.	10925
Bitters, Greeley's Bourbon Whiskey, Strawberry Puce, Applied Mouth, c.1870, 9 In. ....*illus*	920
Bitters, Greeley's Bourbon, Barrel, Copper Puce, Square Collar, 9 In.	644
Bitters, Greeley's Bourbon, Barrel, Olive Amber, Square Collar, 9 ¼ In.	1400
Bitters, Greeley's Bourbon, Barrel, Smoky Puce, Square Collar, 9 ½ In.	950
Bitters, Greeley's Bourbon, Barrel, Smoky Topaz, Applied Mouth, Partial Label, c.1860, 9 ⅜ In.	2530
Bitters, H. Pharazyn, Phila., Indian Queen, Shaded Amber, Rolled Lip	2400

Bitters, H.P. Herb Wild Cherry, Reading, Pa., Cabin, Roped Corners, Orange Amber, 10 In.	500
Bitters, H.P. Herb Wild Cherry, Reading, Pa., Tree, Semi-Cabin, Golden Amber, 10 In.	293
Bitters, Hall's, E.E. Hall, New Haven, Barrel, Yellow Olive, Flattened Collar, 9 ⅜ In.	1035
Bitters, Herb's Pure Wild Cherry Bark, Wertz & Field, Pa., Glass Label, c.1900, 8 In. ....*illus*	3163
Bitters, Hibernia, Golden Amber, Case, Sloping Collar, 10 In.	850
Bitters, Highland, Scotch Tonic, Barrel, Yellow Amber, Flattened Lip, 9 ⅝ In.	863
Bitters, Holtzermann's Patent Stomach, Cabin, Amber, Applied Collar, 9 ⅝ In. ....*illus*	1380
Bitters, Jackson's Aromatic Life, Olive Green, Indented Panels, Sloping Collar	5500
Bitters, John Moffat, Phoenix, Aqua.	80
Bitters, Kimball's Jaundice, Troy, N.H., Backward S, Amber Shaded To Apricot, 7 In.	1300
Bitters, Lacour's Sarsapariphere, Amber, Indented Panels, Stepped & Tapered Top	3200
Bitters, Lash's Kidney & Liver, Best Cathartic, Blood Purifier, Red Amber, Case	325
Bitters, Lediard's Celebrated Stomach, Emerald Green, Double Collar, Pontil, 10 In.	2070
Bitters, Manitou, Indian Head, Amber, Ringed Lip, 7 ⅞ In.	805
Bitters, Mills', A.M. Gilman Sole Proprietor, Yellow Amber, Lady's Leg Neck, 11 ¼ In.	2645
Bitters, Mist Of The Morning, S.M. Barnett & Company, Barrel, Amber, 10 In.	500
Bitters, National, Ear Of Corn, Patent 1867, Apricot, Ring Collar, 12 ½ In.	1200
Bitters, National, Ear Of Corn, Patent 1867, Yellow Amber, 12 ⅜ In.	460
Bitters, National, Ear Of Corn, Patent 1867, Yellow, Green Tint, Ring Collar, 12 In.	2600
Bitters, Newman's Golden Fruit, Amber, Sloping Collar, 10 ¾ In.	633
Bitters, Old Dr. Townsend's Celebrated Stomach, Amber, Chestnut, Ringed Mouth, 8 ½ In.	7020
Bitters, Old Homestead Wild Cherry, Cabin, Golden Amber, Sloping Collar, 9 ¾ In.	1300
Bitters, Old Homestead Wild Cherry, Cabin, Yellow Lime, Sloping Collar, 9 ¾ In.	2800
Bitters, Old Sachem & Wigwam Tonic, Barrel, Amber, Square Collar, 9 In.	351 to 450
Bitters, Old Sachem & Wigwam Tonic, Barrel, Aqua, Iron Pontil, c.1860, 9 ⅜ In.	3162
Bitters, Pineapple, W & Co., N.Y., Green, Double Collar, Iron Pontil, 8 ½ In.	4200 to 5500
Bitters, Plantation X, Apricot Puce, Cabin, Applied Sloping Collar, 10 In.	995
Bitters, Polo Club Stomach, Amber.	155
Bitters, Purdy's Cottage, Amber, Applied Double Collar, c.1860, 9 ½ In.	1955
Bitters, Rohrer's Expectoral Wild Cherry Tonic, Golden Amber, Tapered, Roped, Arched.	1000
Bitters, Russ' St. Domingo, Cherry Puce, Beveled Corners, Sloping Collar, 10 In.	644
Bitters, Schiedam, New York, Amber, Arched Panels, Sloping Collar	200
Bitters, Segur's Golden Seal, Springfield, Mass., Aqua, Beveled Edge, Pontil, 8 ½ In.	375
Bitters, Solomon's Strengthening & Invigorating, Savannah, Ga., Blue, Sloping Collar	1200
Bitters, Suffolk, Philbrook & Tucker, Boston, Pig, Shaded Amber, Double Collar, 10 In.	1053
Bitters, Suffolk, Philbrook & Tucker, Boston, Yellow Amber, Pig, Ground Lip, c.1870, 9 ½ In.	748
Bitters, Tippecanoe, H.H. Warner & Co., Log, Amber, Cork, Metal Pull, c.1890.................*illus*	1093
Bitters, Tippecanoe, H.H. Warner & Co., Log, Golden Amber, Cylindrical, Mushroom Top	210
Bitters, Warner's Safe, Rochester, N.Y., Safe, Red Amber, Oval, Double Collar, 9 ½ In.	995
Bitters, Wheeler's Genuine, Apple Green, Sloping Collar, 9 ⅝ In.	345
Bitters, Woodgate's Plantation, Cabin, Amber, Sloping Collar, 10 ¼ In.	9775
Bitters, Wormser Bros., San Francisco, Barrel, Horizontal Rings, Amber, Sloping Collar	1700
Blown, Aqua, Swirl Design, c.1820, 7 In.	130
Blown, Beehive, 16 Ribs, Swirled To Right, Shaded Aqua, Rolled Lip, Midwestern, 8 In.	130
Blown, Globular, Straw Yellow, Olive Tone, Outward Rolled Lip, Paddle Marks, c.1800, 7 ¾ In.	805
Blown, Jenny Lind, Aqua, c.1860, 10 In.	62
Blown, Olive Green, c.1785, 10 ½ In.	326
Blown, Olive, Squat, Long Neck, c.1800, 7 ¼ In.	150
Coca-Cola bottles are listed in the Coca-Cola category.	
Cologne, 8-Sided, Amethyst, Pinched Waist, Flared Rim, 5 ¾ In.	380
Cologne, 8-Sided, Hourglass, Canary Yellow, Flared Mouth, 4 ¾ In.	761
Cologne, 8-Sided, Hourglass, Cobalt Blue, Inward Rolled Lip, 1855-70, 7 In.	1035
Cologne, 12-Sided, Tapered, Midnight Blue, Flared Mouth, 11 In.	410
Cologne, Blue Opalescent, Square, Tapered, Sawtooth Corners, Thumbprint Panels, 7 ½ In.	936
Cologne, Cobalt Blue, Beaded Flute, Tapered, Flared Flattened Rim, 10 ¼ In.	748
Cologne, Cobalt Blue, Square, Tapered, Herringbone Corners, Thumbprint Panels, 5 ½ In.	410
Cologne, Cut Glass, Florence Star, American Brilliant, Meriden, 6 ½ In.	125
Cologne, Diamond Daisy Over Flutes, Amethyst, Flask, Stiegel Type, c.1770, 6 In. ....*illus*	4025
Cologne, Fountain, Opalescent, Sapphire Blue, Pontil, 4 ¾ In. ....*illus*	805
Cologne, Lavender, Ribs, Swirled To Left, Flared Lip, Tam-O'-Shanter Stopper, 6 ½ In.	2106
Cologne, Monument, Grass Green, Brickwork, Tapered, Flared Rim, Stopper, 14 In.	12870
Cologne, Monument, Square, Tapered, Amethyst, Flared Mouth, 6 ½ In.	1287
Cologne, Monument, Square, Tapered, Cobalt Blue, Flared Lip, 8 In.	644
Cologne, Obelisk, Canary Yellow, Paneled, Vertical Ribs, Flared Mouth, 5 ¾ In.	1521
Cologne, Obelisk, Lavender Vertical Ribs, Flared Mouth, c.1875, 8 In.	497
Cologne, Obelisk, Teal Blue, Paneled, Vertical Ribs, Flared Mouth, 5 ⅜ In.	761

Bottle, Flask, Pale Sherry Wine, Cornucopia, Olive Amber, Open Pontil, c.1830, Pt.
$460

Glass Works Auctions

Bottle, Flask, Scroll & Louisville, Amber, Iron Pontil, 1840-50, Pt.
$4,025

Glass Works Auctions

Bottle, Flask, Scroll, Cobalt Blue, Iron Pontil, Sheared Lip, Pt.
$2,185

Glass Works Auctions

This is an edited listing of current prices. Visit **Kovels.com** to check thousands of prices from previous years and sign up for free information on trends, tips, reproductions, marks, and more.

Bottle, Flask, Washington & Sailing Ship, Yellow, Iron Pontil, c.1850, Pt. $11,115

Norman C. Heckler & Company

Bottle, Flask, Washington & Taylor, Emerald Green, Top Hat Mouth, Open Pontil, c.1850, Qt. $1,265

Glass Works Auctions

Bottle, Flask, Washington & Taylor, Light Blue Green, Dyottville Glass Works, c.1830, ½ Pt. $1,287

Norman C. Heckler & Company

Cologne, Plum Amethyst, Square, Tapered, Herringbone Corners, Thumbprint Panels, 6 In.	702
Cologne, Sapphire Blue, Floral & Scroll, Ribbed Shoulders, Sheared Lip, 4 In.	1495
Cologne, Sapphire Blue, Gray Tint, Gothic Arches, Knight, Inward Rolled Lip, 4 In.	1287
Cologne, Solon Palmer Perfumer, Green, Oval, 7 In.	35
Cordial, L.Q.C. Wishart's Pine Tree Tar, Phila, Green, Sloping Collar, c.1870, 9 ½ In.	316
Cosmetic, Dr. Kennedy's Hair Tea, Roxbury, Ma., Clear, 7 In.	125
Cosmetic, Farr's For Gray Hair, Boston, Dark Amber	12
Cosmetic, Lyon's Kathairon For The Hair, New York, Pontil, 6 In.	28
Cosmetic, Mrs. Allen's Hair Restorer, Amber, Label	80
Cosmetic, R.P. Hall's Improved Preparation For The Hair, Cobalt Blue, Box, 7 ½ In.	1521
Cure, Arctic Frost Bite, Aqua, Square, Cylindrical Neck, Flared Rim	18
Cure, Asthma, Shaker, Cork, Paper Label, Multicolor Box, Sliding Tin Top ....*illus*	2242
Cure, Faith Whitcomb's Balsam, Cures Coughs & Colds & Consumption, Aqua	155
Cure, Halls Catarrh, Aqua, 4 ½ In.	8
Cure, Otto's, For Throat & Lungs, Label, 6 In.	24
Cure, Rev. T. Hill's Vegetable Remedy, Aqua, Oval, Rolled Lip, 4 ¾ In.	431
Cure, Rhodes' Fever & Ague, Antidote To Malaria, Aqua, Sloping Collar, 8 ¼ In.	345
Cure, Warner's Safe Cure, Frankfurt, A/M, Safe, Yellow Olive, Blob Top, 9 ⅜ In.	230
Cure, Warner's, Log Cabin Hops & Buchu Remedy, Amber, 6 Indented Panels, 10 In.	219
Cure, Wynkoop & Co.'s Tonic Mixture, Warranted To Cure, Cobalt Blue, 6 ⅜ In.	8050
Decanter, 25 Ribs, Swirled To Right, Blue Aqua, Pittsburgh, 1815-35, 8 ⅛ In. ....*illus*	265
Decanter, Cobalt Blue, 6 Indented Panels, Pinched Waist, Applied Collar, Pontil, 10 In.	1170
Decanter, Diamond Diaper Band, Sunburst, Yellow Olive, 3-Piece Mold, Sheared Mouth, Pt.	936
Decanter, Old Crow, Top Hat, Yellow, Waistcoat, Royal Doulton, Label, 13 ¼ In.	109
Demijohn, Amber, Open Pontil, ½ Gal.	200
Demijohn, Emerald Green, Loaf Of Bread, Sloping Collar, Pontil, 8 x 9 x 5 ¾ In.	403
Demijohn, Golden Yellow, Tooled Lip, 15 In.	140
Figural, Fish, Yellow Amber, Tooled Mouth, Stopper, 1890-1900, 2 ⅞ In.	585
Figural, Man, Shake Me Well Before Using, Japanese Polish, Amber, c.1895, 6 ¾ In. ....*illus*	374
Figural, Pig, Beiser & Fisher, N.Y., Yellow Amber, Double Collar, 9 In.	1150
Flask, 10 Diamond, Blue Green, Sheared Mouth, Zanesville, c.1830, 4 ½ In.	702
Flask, 10 Diamond, Golden Amber, Rounded Lip, Zanesville, c.1830, 5 In.	1404
Flask, 18 Diamond, Sea Green, Inward Rolled Mouth, Pocket, 6 x 5 In.	558
Flask, 16 Ribs, Vertical, Amethyst, Pinched Sides, Sheared Mouth, Pocket, 6 ½ In.	497
Flask, 18 Ribs, Vertical, Cobalt Blue, Pumpkinseed, Sheared, Pontil, Pocket, 7 In.	936
Flask, 24 Ribs, Vertical, Amber, Pocket, Sheared Lip, Pontil, 1800-35, 5 In.	220
Flask, Amethyst, Diamond Daisy, Sheared Mouth, Pocket, c.1774, 5 In.	3510
Flask, Amethyst, Diamond Daisy, Sheared, Pontil, Pocket, 5 ¼ In.	4388
Flask, Anchor & Phoenix, Resurgam, Eagle, Yellow Topaz, Sheared Lip, Pontil, Pt.	550
Flask, Bryan & Eagle, Yellow Amber, Coin Form, Ribbing, ½ Pt.	761
Flask, Byron & Scott, Olive Amber, Sheared Mouth, Pontil, ½ Pt.	468
Flask, Byron & Scott, Yellow Olive Amber, Sheared Mouth, Pontil, ½ Pt.	374
Flask, Cannon, A Little More Grape, Aqua, ½ Pt.	585
Flask, Cannon, A Little More Grape, Green, Sheared Mouth, ½ Pt.	6435
Flask, Chestnut, Amber, Bubbles, Applied Lip, Pontil, c.1820, 8 ½ In.	475
Flask, Chestnut, Lime Green, Applied Lip, Pontil, c.1820, 5 ¼ In.	220
Flask, Chestnut, Olive Green, Applied Lip, Open Pontil, c.1800, 8 ¼ In.	345
Flask, Chestnut, Olive Green, Applied Lip, Pontil, 6 ¾ In.	374
Flask, Chestnut, Yellow Amber, Applied Lip, New England, c.1800, 8 ½ In.	805
Flask, Chestnut, Yellow Olive, Applied Lip, Pontil, c.1820, 7 In.	275
Flask, Chestnut, Yellow, Applied Lip, Pontil, c.1800, 8 ¾ In.	633
Flask, Corn For The World, Baltimore Monument, Peacock Blue, Qt.	1380
Flask, Corn For The World, Monument, Golden Topaz, Applied Band, Qt.	1100
Flask, Cornucopia & Urn, Light Green, Sheared Mouth, Iron Pontil, Pt.	702
Flask, Cornucopia & Urn, Light Green, Sheared Mouth, Pontil, ½ Pt.	748
Flask, Cornucopia & Urn, Stoneware, Mottled Yellow & Brown, ½ Pt.	690
Flask, Daisy In Hex, Amethyst, Sheared Mouth, American Flint Glass Manufactory, 4 ½ In.	2574
Flask, Daisy, Amethyst, American Flint Glass Manufactory, Pocket, 5 In.	4095
Flask, Double Eagle, Blue Aqua, Sheared Lip, Pontil, Pt.	325
Flask, Double Eagle, Eagle With Snake, Apple Green, Sheared, Pontil, Pt.	10530
Flask, Double Eagle, Sapphire Blue, Sheared Mouth, Pontil, Pt.	4888
Flask, Double Eagle, Yellow Olive, Ring Mouth, Pittsburgh, Pt.	468
Flask, Double Eagle, Yellow Olive, Sheared Mouth, Pontil, Pt.	53820
Flask, Eagle & Anchor, Citron, Double Collar, ½ Pt.	863
Flask, Eagle & Banner, Green, Calabash, Tapered Collar, Iron Pontil, c.1860, Qt.	863
Flask, Eagle & Cornucopia, Amber, 1800s, 6 ¾ In.	106

Flask, Eagle & Cornucopia, Aqua, Sheared, Pontil, ½ Pt.	819
Flask, Eagle & Cornucopia, Teal, Sheared Lip, Pontil, ½ Pt.	1100
Flask, Eagle & Louisville, Vertical Ribs, Amber, ½ Pt.	400
Flask, Eagle & Louisville, Vertical Ribs, Grass Green, Mouth Ring, Qt.	5436
Flask, Eagle & Morning Glory, Ice Blue, Sheared Mouth, Pt.	439
Flask, Eagle & Oak Tree, Amber, Sheared, ½ Pt.	2800
Flask, Eagle & Oak Tree, Aqua, Sheared, ½ Pt.	1300
Flask, Eagle & Oak Tree, Clambroth, Sheared, ½ Pt.	2200
Flask, Eagle & Oak Tree, Deep Tobacco Amber, Sheared, ½ Pt.	2600
Flask, Eagle & Oak Tree, Root Beer Amber, Sheared, Pontil, ½ Pt.	2223
Flask, Eagle & Willington, Golden Amber, Olive Tone, Double Collar, Qt.	1404
Flask, Eagle & Willington, Green, c.1865, 8 In.	502
Flask, Eagle & Willington, Green, Sheared Lip, Pontil, ½ Pt.	650
Flask, Eagle & Willington, Olive Green, 1800s, 6 In.	266
Flask, Eagle & Willington, Yellow Green, Olive Tone, Sloping Collar, Qt.	1404
Flask, Fish, Moravian, Scales, Earthenware, Green Copper, Manganese, 9 ¾ In. ....*illus*	23000
Flask, For Pike's Peak, Prospector, Hunter Shooting Stag, Yellow Amber, Pt.	761
Flask, Green, Ribbed, Bulbous Body, Broken Pontil, c.1810, 5 In.	94
Flask, Hanlen's Pure Wine & Liquor Products, Sherry, Sole Man'fs, Label, Pat. 1902, 11 In.	2875
Flask, Horseman & Hound, Yellow Amber, Pt.	2415
Flask, Hunter & Fisherman, Calabash, Strawberry Puce, Sloping Collar	690
Flask, Hunter & Fisherman, Calabash, Teal Blue, Tapered Collar, c.1860	863
Flask, Hunter & Stag, Blue Aqua, Ring Mouth, Pt.	644
Flask, Isabella, Anchor & Glasshouse, Blue Green, Sheared Mouth, Pontil, ½ Pt.	3218
Flask, Jackson & Flowers, Blue Aqua, Sheared Lip, Pontil, Pt.	4000
Flask, Jenny Lind & Glasshouse, Calabash, Blue Green, Sloping Collar, Qt.	2106
Flask, Jenny Lind & Glasshouse, Calabash, Green, Tapered Double Collar, c.1855, Qt.	2875
Flask, Jenny Lind & Glasshouse, Calabash, Sapphire Blue, Iron Pontil, Blob Top, c.1860 ....*illus*	7480
Flask, Jenny Lind & Glasshouse, Calabash, Teal, Sloping Collar	546
Flask, Jenny Lind & Glasshouse, Calabash, Yellow Olive, Sloping Collar	1093
Flask, Jenny Lind & Glasshouse, Cornflower Blue, Blob Top	316
Flask, Lafayette & Clinton, Olive Green, Horizontal Ribs, ½ Pt.	3738
Flask, Lafayette & Eagle, Blue Green, Sheared Mouth, Pontil, Pt.	5265
Flask, Lafayette & Liberty, Yellow Olive, Amber Tone, Pontil, ½ Pt.	920
Flask, Lafayette & Liberty, Yellow Olive, Sheared Mouth, Pontil, ½ Pt.	1287
Flask, Log Cabin & Flag, Hard Cider, Blue Aqua, Sheared Mouth, Pontil, Pt.	2223
Flask, Lowell Railroad & Eagle, Olive Green, ½ Pt.	633
Flask, Masonic & Eagle, Amber, Bubbles, Sheared Lip, Pontil, Pt.	425
Flask, Masonic & Eagle, Amethyst, Shaded To Cobalt Blue, Pontil, Pt.	15500
Flask, Masonic & Eagle, Aqua, Sheared Lip, Pontil, Pt.	350
Flask, Masonic & Eagle, Blue Green, Sheared Mouth, Pontil, Pt.	585
Flask, Masonic & Eagle, Olive Amber, Sheared, Pontil, Pt.	351
Flask, Masonic & Eagle, Shaded Blue Green, Sheared Mouth, Pontil, Pt.	558
Flask, Masonic & Eagle, Yellow Lime Green, Pt.	805
Flask, Masonic & Eagle, Yellow Olive, Sheared, ½ Pt.	468
Flask, Masonic & Seeing Eye, 6-Point Star, Golden Amber, Blown, 7 ½ In.	240
Flask, Masonic & Seeing Eye, Yellow Olive, Sloping Collar, Pt.	439
Flask, Monte Carlo, Parker & Clifford, Bakersfield, Cal., Pumpkinseed, ½ Pt.	650
Flask, Olive Amber, Granite Glass Co., Stoddard, N.H., Double Collar, Pt.	556
Flask, Olive Green, Presidents' Busts, c.1830, 6 ⅞ In.	420
Flask, Pale Sherry Wine, Cornucopia, Olive Amber, Open Pontil, c.1830, Pt. ....*illus*	460
Flask, Pitkin Type, 36 Broken Ribs, Swirled To Left, Yellow Amber, Tooled Lip, c.1820, 6 In.	690
Flask, Pitkin Type, 36 Broken Ribs, Swirled To Right, Green, Tooled Lip, c.1820, 7 ⅜ In.	489
Flask, Pitkin Type, 21 Ribs, Swirled To Right, Sea Green, Applied Rolled Collar, 6 In.	1872
Flask, Pitkin Type, 32 Ribs, Swirled To Left, Turquoise, 6 ¾ In.	550
Flask, Pitkin Type, 32 Ribs, Swirled To Right, Amber, Olive Tint, 5 ½ In.	600
Flask, Pitkin Type, 36 Ribs, Swirled To Left, Light Olive Yellow, Sheared, Pontil, 5 In.	995
Flask, Pitkin Type, 36 Ribs, Swirled To Left, Yellow Amber, 1783-1820, 5 In.	600
Flask, Pitkin Type, 36 Ribs, Swirled To Right, Light Olive Yellow, Sheared, Pontil, 6 ¼ In.	1638
Flask, S.F. Rose, Straight Goods From The Wood, Vallejo, Cal., Pumpkinseed, ½ Pt.	600
Flask, Scroll & Louisville, Amber, Iron Pontil, 1840-50, Pt. ......*illus*	4025
Flask, Scroll, Amethyst, Rolled Rim, J.R. & Son, ½ Pt.	24570
Flask, Scroll, Apple Green, Sheared Mouth, Pt.	748
Flask, Scroll, Aqua, Pinched Waist, Sheared Lip, Pontil, Pt.	1500
Flask, Scroll, Blue Aqua, Pinched Waist, Sheared Lip, Pontil, Pt.	900
Flask, Scroll, Blue Aqua, Pinched Waist, Sheared Mouth, Pt.	1265

Flask Shapes

The calabash flask looks like the calabash gourd.

The chestnut flask is almost round. It is named for the nut from chestnut trees.

The Pitkin-type flask is named for the Pitkin Glassworks of East Hartford, Connecticut. The glass blower added glass to make the sides of the flask thicker. The bottle was blown into a ribbed mold. The finished bottle could have vertical or swirled ribs.

Bottle, Fruit Jar, Ludlow's Patent, Aqua, Glass Lid, Cast Iron Yoke, c.1860, Pt. $690

Glass Works Auctions

Bottle, Fruit Jar, Trademark Lightning, Putnam 181, Yellow Olive, Lid, Wire Bail, c.1890, Qt. $173

Glass Works Auctions

Bottle, Ink, Teakettle, 8-Sided, Blue
Opalescent, Pinched Waist, 2 ⅛ In.
$345

Glass Works Auctions

Bottle, Ink, Teakettle, 8-Sided, Grass Green,
Brass Neck Ring, Hinged Lid, c.1885, 2 ⅛ In.
$1,610

Glass Works Auctions

Bottle, Ink, Teakettle, 8-Sided, Milk Glass,
Opalescent, Polished Lip, c.1885, 2 ⅜ In.
$288

Glass Works Auctions

Bottle, Ink, Wood's, Black, Portland, Cone,
Aqua, c.1870, 2 ½ In.
$760

Norman C. Heckler & Company

Bottle, Medicine, Dr. O.B. Osborn's Genuine
Golden Ointment, Aqua, c.1850, 2 ¼ In.
$431

Glass Works Auctions

Bottle, Medicine, J. Grout, Pain Extractor, Blue
Green, Wide Mouth, Label, c.1860, 3 In.
$497

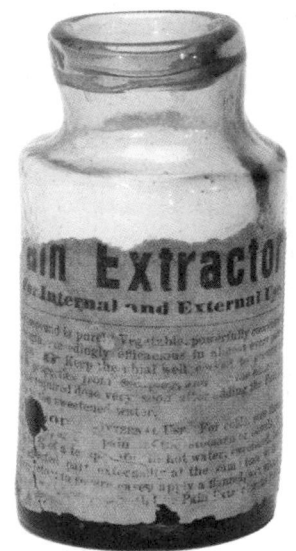

Norman C. Heckler & Company

Bottle, Medicine, Lindsey's Blood Searcher,
Hollidaysburg, Yellow Olive, c.1870, 9 ¼ In.
$3,510

Norman C. Heckler & Company

Bottle, Medicine, Phelps's Arcanum, Worcester,
Mass., Olive, Double Collar, 8 ⅞ In.
$1,955

Glass Works Auctions

Bottle, Medicine, Warner's Log Cabin Extract,
Rochester, N.Y., Patd. Sept 6, 1887, Amber, 8 In.
$1,035

Glass Works Auctions

Bottle, Milk, East End Dairy, Green, 9 ½ In.
$1,800

Morphy Auctions

Flask, Scroll, Cobalt Blue, Iron Pontil, Sheared Lip, Pt. ....*illus*	2185
Flask, Scroll, Cobalt Blue, Sheared Mouth, Iron Pontil, Qt.	2875
Flask, Scroll, Cobalt Blue, Tooled Lip, Iron Pontil, c.1845, Qt.	3450
Flask, Scroll, Hearts & Flowers, Blue Aqua, Sheared Mouth, Qt............................	6325
Flask, Scroll, J.R. & Son, Ice Green, Pinched Waist, Sheared Lip, Pontil, Pt.	1500
Flask, Scroll, Olive Amber, Sheared Mouth, Pontil, Pt.	878
Flask, Scroll, Yellow Green, Sheared Mouth, Pontil, Qt.	9775
Flask, Scroll, Yellow, Olive Tone, Sheared & Tooled Lip, Open Pontil, c.1845, Qt.	1495
Flask, Sloop & Star, Sapphire Blue, Sheared Mouth, Pontil, ½ Pt.	28750
Flask, Spirits, Orange Amber, Paneled, Beveled Corners, Sheared, Pewter Collar, 6 ⅝ In.	2925
Flask, Spirits, Purple Amethyst, White Loopings, Rectangular, Beveled Corners, 7 ½ In.	3218
Flask, Spring Garden & Anchor, Apricot, Applied Double Collar, ½ Pt.	1521
Flask, Success To The Railroad, Amber, c.1830, 7 ½ In.	1440
Flask, Success To The Railroad, Horse, Wagon, Olive Green, 6 ½ In.	212
Flask, Success To The Railroad, Olive Amber, Sheared, Pontil, Pt.	819
Flask, Success To The Railroad, Teal, Sheared Lip, Pontil, Pt.	3000
Flask, Success To The Railroad, Yellow Amber, Pt.	805
Flask, Success To The Railroad, Yellow Olive, Sheared, Pontil, Pt.	819
Flask, Sunburst, Amber, Sheared & Tooled Lip, Pontil, Coventry Glass Works, c.1820, Pt..........	2185
Flask, Sunburst, Aqua, M'Carty & Torreyson, Wellsburg, Va., Sheared Lip, c.1850....	2070
Flask, Sunburst, Blue Green, Elliptical, Sheared Mouth, Pt..............................	805
Flask, Sunburst, Forest Green, Sheared Mouth, Pontil, ½ Pt.	995
Flask, Sunburst, Yellow Olive, Sheared Mouth, ½ Pt.	863
Flask, Sunburst, Yellow Olive, Sheared Mouth, Pontil, Pt.	1755
Flask, T.J. Flack & Sons, Premium, Baltimore, Golden Amber, Double Collar, Pt., 7 ¼ In.	242
Flask, Taylor & Monument, Shaded Moss Green, Sheared, Pt.	3510
Flask, Taylor Never Surrenders, Cannon, A Little More Grape, Aqua, Pt.	556
Flask, Traveler's Companion & Star, Ravenna, Tobacco Amber, Pt.	1265
Flask, Union, Clasped Hands & Eagle, 13 Stars, Aqua, Qt.	110
Flask, Union, Clasped Hands & Eagle, Light Green, Qt..................................	700
Flask, Union, Clasped Hands & Eagle, Sapphire Blue, Sheared, ½ Pt.	8775
Flask, Union, Clasped Hands & Eagle, Yellow, Sloping Collar, Qt.	1872
Flask, Washington & Eagle, Adams, Jefferson, Teal, Sheared, Pontil, Pt.	9360
Flask, Washington & Eagle, Medial Ribs, Aqua, Sheared Lip, Pontil, Pt.	500
Flask, Washington & Monument, Fells Point, Pink Amethyst, Pt.	4972
Flask, Washington & Sailing Ship, Aqua, Sheared Mouth, Pontil, Pt.	878
Flask, Washington & Sailing Ship, Dark Chocolate Amber, Pontil, Pt.	3163
Flask, Washington & Sailing Ship, Yellow, Iron Pontil, c.1850, Pt. ....*illus*	11115
Flask, Washington & Taylor, A Little More Grape, Cobalt Blue, Qt.............	5175
Flask, Washington & Taylor, Bright Green, Pontil, Pt.	14040
Flask, Washington & Taylor, Cobalt Blue, Sheared Mouth, Pontil, Qt.	5558
Flask, Washington & Taylor, Emerald Green, Top Hat Mouth, Open Pontil, c.1850, Qt. ....*illus*	1265
Flask, Washington & Taylor, Ginger Ale Yellow, Sheared, Pontil, Qt...............	9360
Flask, Washington & Taylor, Light Blue Green, Dyottville Glass Works, c.1830, ½ Pt. ....*illus*	1287
Flask, Washington & Taylor, Light Yellow, Sheared, Pt..................................	14040
Flask, Washington & Taylor, Yellow, Olive Tone, Sheared, Pontil, ½ Pt.	5265
Flask, Washington, Father Of His Country, Blue Green, Ring Mouth, Pt...........	281
Flask, Washington, Father Of His Country, Blue Green, Sheared, Pontil, Qt.	819
Flask, Will You Take A Drink?, Will A Duck Swim?, Duck, Aqua, Mouth Ring, Pt.	585
Food, Cottage Cheese, Lassig Dairy, Rhinelander, Wis., Red ACL, Cylindrical	35
Food, Maple Sap & Boiled Cider Vinegar, C.I. Co., Cobalt Blue, Fluted Shoulder, 11 In.............	1638
Food, Mustard, Moutarde Diaphane, Louit Freres & Co., Green, Rolled Rim, Pontil, 5 In.	60
Food, Red Amber, Cylindrical, Outward Rolled Mouth, Stoddard, 8 x 3 ½ In.....	644
Food, Salt, Olive Green, Clark & White, New York, Wide Mouth, Qt..............	9775
Fruit Jar, Automatic Sealer, Patd. Sept. 15, 1885, Aqua, Dome Lid, Clayton Bottle Works, Pt.......	374
Fruit Jar, Canton Electric, Cobalt Blue, Cylindrical, Wire Closure, Qt.	4888
Fruit Jar, Cunningham & Co., Pittsburgh, Sapphire Blue, Squared Rim, Qt.	6325
Fruit Jar, Electric, Aqua, Notched Glass Lid, Wire Bail, ½ Gal.	345
Fruit Jar, Kline, Blue Green, Shaded, Cylindrical, Outward Rolled Mouth, Stopper, Qt.	351
Fruit Jar, Ludlow's Patent, Aqua, Glass Lid, Cast Iron Yoke, c.1860, Pt. ....*illus*	690
Fruit Jar, Mason's CFJCo. Patent Nov. 30th, 1858, Aqua, Lid, Midget	32
Fruit Jar, Mason's CFJCo. Patent Nov. 30th 1858, Golden Amber, Zinc Lid, Qt.............	199
Fruit Jar, Mason's CFJCo. Patent Nov. 30th 1858, Yellow Amber, Zinc Lid, Qt..........	234
Fruit Jar, Mason's CFJCo., Monogram, Improved Butter Jar, Aqua, Wide Mouth, Qt.........	173
Fruit Jar, Mason's Patent Nov. 30th 1858, Keystone, Yellow Amber, Zinc Lid, ½ Gal.	585
Fruit Jar, Ne Plus Ultra Air Tight, Bodine & Bros., Aqua, Squared Rim, ½ Gal., 9 ¼ In.	1100

Bottle, Milk, Polar Bear Ice Cream, Painted Label, Garden Farm Dairy, Denver, Col., 9 In.
$949

Wm Morford Auctions

Bottle, Mineral Water, W. Eagle's, Superior, Green, Iron Pontil, c.1850, 6 ¾ In.
$374

Glass Works Auctions

Bottle, Pickle, Cathedral, 6-Sided, Emerald Green, 12 ¾ In.
$1,265

Glass Works Auctions

Bottle, Pickle, Cathedral, Apple Green, Outward Rolled Lip, c.1865, 11 ¾ In. $253

Glass Works Auctions

Bottle, Poison, Coffin, Embossed Poison, Cobalt Blue, Norwich, 7 ½ In. $748

Glass Works Auctions

Bottle, Poison, Embossed Poison, Moss Green, Horizontal Ribs, 7 ⅞ In. $3,450

Glass Works Auctions

Fruit Jar, Petal, Olive Green, Cylindrical, 8 Shoulder Panels, Pontil, Qt.	1265
Fruit Jar, Trademark Lightning, Putnam 181, Yellow Olive, Lid, Wire Bail, c.1890, Qt. *illus*	173
Gin, Booth & Sedgwick's, London, Emerald Green, Sloping Collar, 9 ⅞ In.	1093
Gin, Case, Cobalt Blue, Tapered, Blob Top, 10 ¼ In.	374
Gin, Case, London Jockey Club House, Horse & Rider, Amber, Sloping Collar, 9 ½ In.	5000
Gin, Case, London Jockey Club House, Horse & Rider, Aqua, Sloping Collar, 9 ½ In.	2200
Gin, Case, London Jockey Club House, Horse & Rider, Green, Sloping Collar, 9 ½ In.	2800
Gin, Case, Olive Green, Crude Rounded Spout, Dutch, c.1790, 18 ⅛ In.	1150
Gin, Centaur Case, Olive Green, L.M. & Co. Seal, Blue & White Label, 9 ¾ In.	403
Gin, Charles London Cordial, Emerald Green, Embossed, c.1850, 9 ½ In.	115
Gin, Daniel Visser, Schiedam, Seal, Olive Green, Pinched Waist, 10 ¾ In.	58
Gin, H.H.S. & Co. Imperial, Orange Amber, Tapered, Sloping Collar, 9 ⅝ In.	288
Gin, Hol Genever, Embossed Buffalo, Olive Green, c.1900, 8 ⅝ In.	29
Gin, John L. Linnenbrink, Olive Tree, Embossed, Olive Green, c.1870, 9 ⅝ In.	288
Gin, Manya Ofu, Embossed Seated Cat, Olive Green, Africa, c.1900, 8 ⅝ In.	35
Gin, W.S.C., Club House, Yellow Olive, Tapered Case, 9 ½ In.	431
Go-With, Target Ball Thrower, Cast Iron, Wood Handle, c.1890, 28 In.	1725
Ink, 12-Sided, Olive Green, Inward Rolled Lip, Open Pontil, c.1850, 2 In.	1265
Ink, Barrel, S.I. Comp, Milk Glass, 2 ¼ In.	374
Ink, Cabin, Embossed, Applied Mouth, c.1880, 2 ½ In.	2070
Ink, Carters, Cathedral, Cobalt, Qt.	90
Ink, Cone, Blue Aqua, Inward Rolled Lip, 2 In.	374
Ink, Cone, Cobalt Blue, Inward Rolled Lip, 2 ½ In.	978
Ink, Cone, Draped, Sapphire Blue, Rolled Lip, 2 ⅛ In.	2185
Ink, Cone, Emerald Green, Inward Rolled Lip, 2 ½ In.	748
Ink, Cone, M & P, New York, Umbrella, 8-Sided, Blue Green, Inward Rolled Lip, 2 ½ In.	518
Ink, Cone, Olive Green, Tooled Lip, Pontil, New England Glass House, c.1850, 2 ¼ In.	748
Ink, Cone, Pitkin Type, 36 Ribs, Swirled To Left, Cone, Yellow Olive, Tooled Lip, 2 ⅜ In.	3803
Ink, Cone, Yellow Amber, Olive Tone, Sheared Mouth, 2 ¼ In.	518
Ink, Cottage, Blue Aqua, Applied Mouth, Patd Mar 14, 1871, 2 ½ In.	460
Ink, Cottage, S.I. Comp, Milk Glass, 2 ⅞ In.	288
Ink, Cylindrical, Sapphire Blue, Raised Diamonds, Disc Mouth, 3-Piece Mold, 1 ¾ In.	5850
Ink, Cylindrical, Sea Green, Raised Diamonds, 3-Piece Mold, Flared Mouth, 1 ¾ In.	2340
Ink, E.S. Curtis, Warranted Superior, Olive Amber, Cylindrical, Spout, Master, 9 ½ In.	527
Ink, G. & R.'s American Writing Fluid, Cone, Aqua, Rolled Lip, 2 ½ In.	633
Ink, Gaylord's Superior Record, Boston, Olive Amber, Cylindrical, Flared Lip, Master, 6 In.	3450
Ink, Geometric, Blue, Tooled Rim, Open Pontil, Keene Glass Works, c.1820, 1 ¾ In.	242
Ink, Gross & Robinson's, Writing Fluid, Horizontal Lines, Master, 6 In.	1100
Ink, Harrison's Colombian, 8-Sided, Apple Green, Rolled Mouth, Pontil, 1 ⅜ In.	585
Ink, Harrison's Columbian, 12-Sided, Aqua, Pontil, Master, 7 In.	219
Ink, Harrison's Columbian, Blue Green, Applied Mouth, c.1860, 5 ¾ In.	1495
Ink, Harrison's Columbian, Cobalt Blue, Cylindrical, Squat, Inward Rolled Lip, 2 In.	1035
Ink, Harrison's Columbian, Sapphire Blue, Flared Lip, Pontil, 4 ⅝ In.	878
Ink, Igloo, Black Amethyst, Sheared & Ground Lip, 1875-90, 2 In.	863
Ink, Igloo, Blue Green, 2 ¼ In.	207
Ink, Jones' Empire, N.Y., 12-Sided, Emerald Green, Flattened Lip, Master, 5 ⅞ In.	6325
Ink, Jones' No. 1, Aqua, Vertical Ribs, Flared Lip, 2 ⅞ In.	288
Ink, Lauglins & Bushfield, Wheeling, Va., 8-Sided, Aqua, Rolled Lip, 2 ⅞ In.	316
Ink, Locomotive, Clear, 2 ¾ x 2 ¾ In.	265
Ink, Lyons, Green Aqua, Square, Vertical Ribs, Pen Rest, 1 ¾ x 2 In.	50
Ink, Pitkin Type, 36 Ribs, Swirled To Left, Cone, Olive Green, 1 ⅝ x 2 ¼ In.	2106
Ink, Stafford's, Cobalt Blue, 16 Oz.	40
Ink, T.P. Spencer & Co., Perfumers, N.Y., School House, Dog, Clear, 3 In.	316
Ink, Teakettle, 8 Sided, Concave Cobalt Blue, Sheared Mouth, 2 In.	196
Ink, Teakettle, 8-Sided, Amethyst, Sheared Mouth, 2 In.	316
Ink, Teakettle, 8-Sided, Bisque, White Glaze, Sheaf Of Grain, Fish Neck, c.1890, 2 In.	431
Ink, Teakettle, 8-Sided, Blue Opalescent, Pinched Waist, 2 ⅛ In. *illus*	345
Ink, Teakettle, 8-Sided, Cobalt Blue, 3 Vertical Ribs, 2 ⅛ In.	345
Ink, Teakettle, 8-Sided, Deep Amethyst, Sheared Mouth, Brass Neck Ring, 1 ⅞ In.	374
Ink, Teakettle, 8-Sided, Grass Green, Brass Neck Ring, Hinged Lid, c.1885, 2 ⅛ In. *illus*	1610
Ink, Teakettle, 8-Sided, Milk Glass, Opalescent, Polished Lip, c.1885, 2 ⅝ In. *illus*	288
Ink, Teakettle, Barrel, Pink Amethyst, Sheared, Ground Lip, Brass Neck Ring, c.1880	1150
Ink, Umbrella, 8-Sided, Amber, Rolled Lip, Pontil, New England Glass House, c.1850, 2 In.	230
Ink, Umbrella, 8-Sided, Blue Green, Rolled Lip, Iron Pontil	120
Ink, Umbrella, 8-Sided, Deep Cobalt Blue, Inward Rolled Mouth, Pontil, 2 ½ In.	1755
Ink, Umbrella, 8-Sided, Olive Green, Rolled Lip, Pontil	250

Ink, Umbrella, 8-Sided, Yellow Amber, Inward Rolled Lip, 2 ½ In.	489
Ink, Umbrella, J.S. Dunham, 8-Sided, Blue Aqua, Outward Rolled Lip, 2 ½ In.	265
Ink, Umbrella, Waters, Troy, NY, Aqua, Inward Rolled Mouth, Pontil, c.1850, 2 ¾ In.	761
Ink, Warrens Congress, 8-Sided, Yellow Olive, Cylindrical Neck, Rolled Rim, 3 In.	1989
Ink, Wood's, Black, Portland, Cone, Aqua, c.1870, 2 ½ In. ...illus	760
Medicine, Acker's English Remedy, Cobalt Blue, W.H. Hooker & Co., 2 x 5 ½ In.	70
Medicine, Alden's, Extract Of Coffee, Blue Green, Applied Mouth, Crimped Spout, c.1850, 6 In.	575
Medicine, Allan's Anti-Fat Botanic, Buffalo, N.Y., Steel Blue, Indented Panels, 7 ½ In.	500
Medicine, American Liniment, Auburn, N.Y., Aqua, Rolled Lip, Pontil, 5 In.	1000
Medicine, American Medicinal Oil, Burkesville, Ky., Aqua, Indented Panels, 6 ¼ In.	920
Medicine, Aromatic Salts, G. Watts, 5 Stars, Baltimore, Pink Amethyst, 2 In.	489
Medicine, Beekman's Pulmonic Syrup, New York, Yellow Olive, 8-Sided, Sloping Collar, 7 In.	2340
Medicine, Briswell's Bromopepsin Cures Headache, Amber, Full Label, Contents	28
Medicine, C. Brinkerhoff's Health Restorative, Price $1.00, New York, Yellow Olive, 7 In.	995
Medicine, C. Brinkerhoff's Health Restorative, Price $1.00, Yellow Olive, 7 ½ In.	1300
Medicine, Carter's Spanish Mixture, Yellow Olive, Sloping Double Collar, 8 In.	920
Medicine, Clemens' Indian Tonic, Prepared By Geo. W. House, Indian, Aqua, 6 In.	498
Medicine, Dr. Clark, N. York, 3-Ring Chain, Emerald Green, Sloping Collar, 9 ¼ In.	920
Medicine, Dr. Davis's Depurative, Blue Green, Applied Mouth, Iron Pontil, c.1850, 9 ¾ In.	1610
Medicine, Dr. E. Hogg, Veterinarian, Wilkes-Barre, Pa., 2 Oz.	8
Medicine, Dr. Geo. W. Blocksom Druggist, Zanesville, Aqua, 12-Sided, Square Collar, 8 In.	497
Medicine, Dr. Hartshorne's, Olive Amber, Oval, 6 In.	978
Medicine, Dr. J. Watson's Cancer & Scrofula Syrup, Fulton, N.Y., Aqua, 9 ½ In.	190
Medicine, Dr. Jackson's Pile Embrocation, Phila., Aqua, Wide Mouth, Flattened Lip, 4 In.	920
Medicine, Dr. Kilmet's Ocean Weed Heart Remedy, Embossed Heart, 7 In.	175
Medicine, Dr. O.B. Osborn's Genuine Golden Ointment, Aqua, c.1850, 2 ¼ In. ...illus	431
Medicine, Dr. Rose's Antidispeptic Vermifuge, Philada, Aqua, Sloping Collar, c.1850, 5 ½ In.	316
Medicine, Duff Gordon Sherry, Medical Department, U.S.A., Olive Amber, 9 ⅞ In.	575
Medicine, Dunbar & Co.'s Wormwood Cordial, Boston, Emerald Green, Case, 9 ⅝ In.	633
Medicine, E.A. Buckhout's Dutch Liniment, Man, Saratoga, Aqua, Rolled Rim, 4 ⅝ In.	409
Medicine, Gargling Oil, Green, Label, Lockport, N.Y.	25
Medicine, Geo. W. Laird & Co. Oleo-Chyle, Sapphire Blue, Sloping Shoulder	550
Medicine, Hopkins Chalybeate, Baltimore, Teal Green	155
Medicine, Horse Liniment, Prepared By David Scott, Worcester, Mass., Olive, c.1850, 7 In.	6325
Medicine, Hyatt's Infallible Life Balsam, N-Y, Emerald Green, Recessed Panels, 10 In.	2223
Medicine, I. Covert's Balm Of Life, Yellow Olive, Beveled Corners, Sloping Collar, 6 In.	2340
Medicine, J. Grout, Pain Extractor, Blue Green, Wide Mouth, Label, c.1860, 3 In. ...illus	497
Medicine, Lindsey's Blood Searcher, Hollidaysburg, Yellow Olive, c.1870, 9 ¼ In. ...illus	3510
Medicine, Liquid, Opodeldoc, Aqua, Flipped Hat Shape, Pontil, 2 ½ In.	748
Medicine, Log Cabin Scalpine, Rochester, N.Y., Amber, 6 Indented Panels, Blob Top, 9 In.	575
Medicine, Louden & Co.'s Female Elixir, Philada., Aqua, Flared Lip, 4 In.	1035
Medicine, Morse's Celebrated Syrup, Prov., R.I., Green, Rounded Shoulders, 9 In.	1500
Medicine, N. Wood, Portland, Me., Yellow Amber, 8-Sided, 7 ¼ In.	2530
Medicine, Nuttall's Syriacum, Confirmed, Consumption, Blue Aqua, Flattened Lip, 6 ¼ In.	748
Medicine, Oriental Life Elixir, Blue Aqua, Sloping Collar, 7 In.	450
Medicine, Palmer Lavender Salts, Green, Square, 2 ½ In.	21
Medicine, Phelps's Arcanum, Worcester, Mass., Olive, Double Collar, 8 ⅞ In. ...illus	1955
Medicine, Rexford's Chamomile Cordial, Ogdensburg, N.Y., Green, Square, 9 ½ In.	6435
Medicine, Rush's Buchu & Iron, Aqua, A.H. Flanders, M.D., New York	30
Medicine, S.M. Kier Petroleum, Pittsburgh, Aqua, Indented Sides, Sloping Collar, 6 ½ In.	160
Medicine, Sanderson's Blood Renovator, Milton, Vt., Aqua, Round Collar, Pontil, 8 In.	1287
Medicine, Scarpa's Oil For Deafness, Aqua, 6-Sided, Flared Lip, 2 ⅜ In.	1035
Medicine, Schenck's Pulmonic Syrup, Octagonal, Aqua, Pontil, 7 ¼ In.	140
Medicine, Scott's Emulsion, Cod Liver Oil, Label	30
Medicine, Seaver's Joint & Nerve Liniment, Olive, Tooled Mouth, Stoddard, c.1850, 4 In.	4095
Medicine, Shaker Syrup No. 1, Canterbury, N.H., Aqua, Indented Panels, 7 ⅜ In.	230
Medicine, Smelling Salts, Gray Blue, White Striations, 8-Sided, Pinched Waist, Cap, 3 In.	140
Medicine, Swaim's Panacea, Philada, Aqua, Rectangular, Arched Sides, Sloping Collar, 8 In.	800
Medicine, Swaim's Panacea, Philada, Light Green, Round, Vertical Panels, 7 ¾ In.	325
Medicine, Swaim's Panacea, Philada, Olive Green, Vertical Panels, Sloping Collar, 7 ½ In.	643
Medicine, Tombstone Shape, Dr. J.S. Woods Elixir, Albany, N.Y., Yellow Emerald, 8 ½ In.	11700
Medicine, Tonisan, Tones The Nerves, Cobalt Blue, Tooled Lip, c.1890, 9 ¾ In.	690
Medicine, U.S.A. Hosp. Dept., Olive Amber, Double Collar, 9 ½ In.	1400
Medicine, University Free Medicine, Philada, Aqua, 6 Panels, Label, Contents, 5 ½ In.	475
Medicine, Warner's Log Cabin Extract, Rochester, N.Y., Patd. Sept 6, 1887, Amber, 8 In. ...illus	1035
Medicine, Warner's Safe Nervine, Frankfurt, Safe, Green, 7 In.	1035

Bottle, Seal, E.P. Middleton & Bro., 1825, Wheat Whiskey, Yellow Green, ½ Gal.
$489
Glass Works Auctions

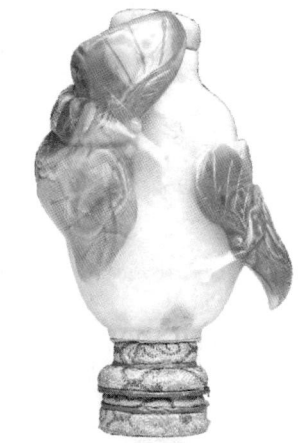
Bottle, Snuff, Agate, Butterflies, Carved, Brocade Stand & Box, c.1800, 2 ¼ In.
$2,074
James D. Julia Auctioneers

Bottle, Snuff, Cloisonne, Pa Pao Hsiang, Precious Items, Marked, Chinese, c.1900, 2 In.
$577
James D. Julia Auctioneers

Bottle, Snuff, Jade, Mottled, Pear Shape, Mask & Faux Ring Handles, c.1900, 2 ½ In. **$3,286**

Neal Auction Co.

Bottle, Soda, C & K Eagle Works, Sac City, Cobalt Blue, Sloping Collar, 7 ¼ In. **$518**

Glass Works Auctions

Bottle, Soda, J.T. Brown, Chemist, Boston, Green, Torpedo, Blob Top, 8 ½ In. **$316**

Glass Works Auctions

Medicine, Youatt's Gargling Oil, Comstock & Brother, N.Y., Aqua, Applied Lip, 9 In.	80
Medicine, Zoa-Phora Woman's Friend, Aqua, Kalamazoo, Mich.	18
Milk, Bentley's Dairy, Fall River, Mass., Cop The Cream, It Whips, Red ACL, Cop Top, Qt.	200
Milk, Borden's Morning Glory, Red ACL, Qt.	100
Milk, Carnation Dairy Products, Bottle, Fresh, Red ACL, Qt.	75
Milk, City Dairy, St. Paul, Minn., Skyline, Safe For Baby, Green & Black ACL, Qt.	200
Milk, Cloverleaf Dairy, Progress, Pa., Clover, Protected, Orange & Black ACL, Qt.	70
Milk, Crescent Milk, Reno, Nev., Crescent, Red ACL, Qt.	85
Milk, Dierdorf's Dairy, Rock Island, Ill., Baby Holding Bottle, Blue & Orange ACL, Qt.	105
Milk, Douglaston Manor Farm, Pulaski, New York, Flying Goose, Black ACL, Qt.	100
Milk, Earl's Dairy Products, Wilmington, Del., Cow, Build Your Health, Black ACL, Qt.	100
Milk, East End Dairy, Green, 9 ½ In. ....*illus*	1800
Milk, Fred H. Rabe & Sons Dairy, Elmhurst, Ill., Bottle, Rays, Yellow & Red ACL, Qt.	110
Milk, Frink, Denver, Eagle, Patriot, Make America Strong, Red ACL, Qt.	100
Milk, Garden Dairy Farm, Denver, Polar Ice Cream, Sunrise, Red & Blue ACL, Qt.	105
Milk, Holstein Holsom, Johnson Bros. Milk, Virginia, Minn., Yellow & Black ACL, Qt.	125
Milk, London Milk Co., London, Ky., Baby, Yours To Love, Ours To Protect, Blue ACL, Qt.	85
Milk, Mac Kenzie Dairy Farm, Cow's Head, Keene, N.H., Lattice, Tapered Neck, ½ Pt.	35
Milk, Michigan State College Creamery, Green ACL, Qt.	120
Milk, Pevely, St. Louis, Mo., ¼ Pt.	12
Milk, Pike's Peak Farm, Washington, Pa., Good For You & Baby Too, Red ACL, Qt.	55
Milk, Polar Bear Ice Cream, Painted Label, Garden Farm Dairy, Denver, Col., 9 In. ....*illus*	949
Milk, Price's Creamery, Roswell, N.M., Sunrise, Orange ACL, Qt.	70
Milk, Roddey Dairies, Guernsey, Columbia, S.C., Logo, Orange & Black ACL, Qt.	105
Milk, Schuyler's Dairy, Savanna, Illinois, Store Bottle, 5 Cents, Green ACL, Qt.	80
Milk, Shrum's Dairy, Jeanette, Pa., Eagle, War Slogan, Green ACL, Qt.	115
Milk, St. Louis Dairy, St. Louis, Mo., ¼ Pt.	12
Milk, Use Ohleen's Milk, Minneapolis, Dairy Farm, War Slogan, Red & Green ACL, Qt.	200
Milk, Westminster Farm Dairy, Vermont, Cow, Cop The Cream, Orange ACL, Cop Top, Qt.	250
Milk, Young's Dairy, Twin Falls, Idaho, Red ACL, Cylindrical, Creamer, 1 Oz.	30
Mineral Water, Adirondack Spring Co., Whitehall, N.Y., Emerald Green, Double Collar, Pt.	196
Mineral Water, Alex Eagle, 1861, Aqua, Blob Top	100
Mineral Water, B & G, San Francisco, Superior, Teal, Mineralization, Blob Top	650
Mineral Water, Congress & Empire Spring Co., E, Saratoga, N.Y., Honey Amber, Qt.	439
Mineral Water, Congress & Empire Spring Co., Hotchkiss Sons, C, Amber, Pt.	210
Mineral Water, Congress & Empire Spring Co., Hotchkiss Sons, E, Green, Pt.	500
Mineral Water, Congress & Empire Spring Co., Saratoga, N.Y., Green, c.1870, Pt. .... 1150 to 1265	
Mineral Water, Excelsior Spring, Saratoga, N.Y., Yellow Olive, Sloping Double Collar, Pt.	245
Mineral Water, Franklin Spring, Ballston Spa, Saratoga, N.Y., Yellow Olive, Pt.	1150
Mineral Water, Frost's, Magnetic Spring, Eaton Rapids, Mich., Amber, Applied Mouth, c.1875	1840
Mineral Water, G.W. Weston & Co., New York, Applied Mouth, 3-Piece Mold, Green, c.1850	5750
Mineral Water, Gardner & Brown, Grass Green, Torpedo, Sloping Collar, 8 ¾ In.	1035
Mineral Water, Haskin's Spring Co., H, Shutesbury, Mass., Emerald Green, Collar, Pt.	1404
Mineral Water, Highrock Congress Spring, Rock, Saratoga, N.Y., Teal, Double Collar, Qt.	4600
Mineral Water, Indian Medical Spring Water Co., Indian Head, Cobalt Blue, 10 ½ In.	2300
Mineral Water, Iodine Spring Water, L, South Hero, Vt., Golden Amber, Double Collar, Qt.	2457
Mineral Water, J. & A. Dearborn, New York, Sapphire Blue, Cylindrical, Blob Top, ½ Pt.	269
Mineral Water, John Boardman, New York, 8-Sided, Sapphire Blue, Applied Mouth, c.1850, 7 In.	920
Mineral Water, John Clarke, New York, Olive Green, Applied Mouth, c.1855	345
Mineral Water, John H. Gardner & Son, Sharon Springs, N.Y., Sulphur, Blue Green, Pt.	316
Mineral Water, Lynch & Clarke, New York, Dark Olive Green, Sloping Collar, 7 ¼ In.	800
Mineral Water, Lynch & Clarke, New York, Olive Green, Sloping Collar, Pt.	3450
Mineral Water, Magnetic Spring, Henniker, N.H., Honey Amber, Sloping Collar, Qt.	936
Mineral Water, Massena Spring, Monogram, Blue Green, Sloping Double Collar, Qt.	322
Mineral Water, Oak Orchard Acid Springs, H.W. Bostwick, Yellow Olive, Double Collar, Qt.	575
Mineral Water, P & U.S. Spring Co., P, Saratoga, N.Y., Pavilion, Emerald Green, ½ Pt.	4680
Mineral Water, Pacific Congress Springs, Black Glass, Sloping Collar, Pt.	1989
Mineral Water, Pavilion & United States Spring Co., Saratoga, Emerald Green, Pt.	265
Mineral Water, Pavilion & United States Spring Co., Saratoga, N.Y., Blue Green, Pt.	978
Mineral Water, Round Lake, Saratoga Co., N.Y., Orange Amber, Double Collar, Qt.	6325
Mineral Water, Round Lake, Saratoga Co., N.Y., Yellow Amber, Applied Mouth, c.1870, Qt.	2875
Mineral Water, S. Smith's, Knickerbocker, New York, Aqua, Applied Mouth, Iron Pontil, 6 In.	978
Mineral Water, Sage's Pacific Congress Springs, Jumping Deer, Green, Collar, 8 In.	3000
Mineral Water, Saratoga Vichy Spouting Spring, Amber, Applied Mouth, c.1870, Pt.	243
Mineral Water, Star Spring, 5-Pointed Star, Saratoga, N.Y., Emerald Green, Pt.	460

Mineral Water, TJ Sutton's, Balt., Ginger Ale Yellow, Cylindrical, Sloping Collar, 6 ¾ In.	2340
Mineral Water, W. Eagle's, Superior, Green, Iron Pontil, c.1850, 6 ¾ In. ....*illus*	374
Mineral Water, Washington Spring Co., Bust Of Washington, Emerald Green, Pt.	1840
Mineral Water, Wm. A. Carpenter's, Hudson, N.Y., Green, 8-Sided, 7 In.	489
Mineral Water, Wm. P. Davis & Co., Excelsior, Brooklyn, Blue, 8-Sided, Blob Top, c.1850, 7 In. ...	1495
Perfume bottles are listed in their own category.	
Pickle, Aqua, Wreaths, Applied Mouth, Iron Pontil, c.1850, 11 In..	345
Pickle, Cathedral, 6-Sided, Emerald Green, 12 ¾ In. ....*illus*	1265
Pickle, Cathedral, 6-Sided, Shaded Teal, Outward Rolled Lip, 13 ¼ In.	288
Pickle, Cathedral, Amber, 4-Sided, Arched, Tapered, Willington, c.1850, 8 ¼ In.	2000
Pickle, Cathedral, Apple Green, Outward Rolled Lip, c.1865, 11 ¾ In. ....*illus*	253
Pickle, Cathedral, Aqua, Fleur-De-Lis, Applied Lip, c.1870, 13 In..	207
Pickle, Cathedral, Aqua, Outward Rolled Lip, Willington, Pt.	1150
Pickle, Cathedral, Blue Aqua, Beveled Corners, Outward Rolled Lip, 11 ⅞ In.	257
Pickle, Cathedral, Blue Aqua, Flame Design In Arches, 9 ½ In.	575
Pickle, Cathedral, Blue Aqua, Nested Arches, Clamshell Embossing On Shoulder, 8 ⅝ In.	161
Pickle, Cathedral, Blue Green, Outward Rolled Lip, Willington, 8 ¾ In.	1610
Pickle, Cathedral, Blue Green, Square, Beveled Corners, Round Collar, Iron Pontil, 9 In.	936
Pickle, Cathedral, Emerald Green, Outward Rolled Lip, c.1875, 11 In.	1380
Pickle, Cathedral, Light Apple Green, Lattice In Arches, Rolled Lip, 8 ¾ In.	489
Pickle, Cathedral, Shaded Blue Green, Trefoils Over Arches, 11 ¾ In.	489
Pickle, E.H.V.B., N.Y., Cathedral, 6-Sided, Blue Aqua, Rolled Lip, 7 ⅞ In.	316
Pickle, J. McCollick & Co., New York, Cathedral, Aqua, Rolled Lip, Iron Pontil, c.1860, 8 In........	1380
Pickle, Yellow Amber, 14 In.	235
Poison, Coffin, Embossed Poison, Cobalt Blue, Norwich, 7 ½ In. ....*illus*	748
Poison, Embossed Poison & Skull, Pat. June 26th 1891, Cobalt Blue, Flat Lip, 3 In.	1380
Poison, Embossed Poison, Moss Green, Horizontal Ribs, 7 ⅞ In. ....*illus*	3450
Poison, Paine Drug Co., Rochester, N.Y., Grass Green, 6-Sided, Horizontal Ribs, 7 ¾ In..............	690
Sarsaparilla, Dr. Guysott's Compound Extract Of Yellow Dock, Yellow Olive, Square, 9 In.	4388
Sarsaparilla, Dr. Guysott's Yellow Dock, John D. Park, Cincinnati, O., Aqua...............................	78
Sarsaparilla, Dr. Myer's Vegetable Extract, Cherry Dandelion, Panels, Aqua, 9 In......................	293
Sarsaparilla, Dr. Townsend's, Albany, N.Y., Green, Sloping Collar, 9 In.	350
Sarsaparilla, Dr. Wynkoop's, Katharismic Honduras, New York, Cobalt, Pontil, c.1850, 10 In.....	4888
Sarsaparilla, F. Brown, Boston, Sarsaparilla & Tomato Bitters, Aqua, Double Collar...................	375
Sarsaparilla, Geo. C. Hubbel & Co., Semi-Cabin, Aqua...	185
Sarsaparilla, J.V. Babcock Gold Medal, Amber..	125
Sarsaparilla, Log Cabin, Rochester, N.Y., Chocolate Amber..	145
Sarsaparilla, Old Dr. J. Townsend's, Green, Sloping Collar, 9 In..	644
Sarsaparilla, Rackley's, B.F. Rackley Apothecary, Dover, N.H., Recessed Panels	300
Sarsaparilla, Wetherell's, For The Body, Clear, Small Dose	40
Sarsaparilla, Yager's, Amber..	65
Scent, Cobalt Blue, Concentric Rings, Horizontal Ribs On Sides, Pontil, 2 In............................	633
Scent, Cobalt Blue, Ribs, Swirled To Right, Straight Neck, Ball-Shaped Bottom, 1 ⅞ In.	345
Scent, Enamel, Blue, Gold Strapwork, Round, Footed, Stopper, 2 x 1 ¼ In.	472
Scent, Purple Amethyst, Ribs, Swirled To Right, Teardrop, Stiegel Type, Pontil, 2 ⅝ In.	431
Scent, Sunburst, Cobalt Blue, Diamond Pattern On Reverse, Oval, 2 ½ In.	748
Scent, Sunburst, Cobalt Blue, Elliptical, Flattened, Sheared Mouth, 2 ½ In.	1093
Seal, Anchor, Yellow Olive, Cylindrical, String Lip, Pontil, 6 ¼ In.	585
Seal, B.F. & Co., N.Y., Amber, 26 Ribs, Swirled Left, Tapered Jug, Spout, 9 ½ In.	5265
Seal, Crown, N, Black Glass, Yellow Olive, String Lip, England, 9 x 5 In.	2808
Seal, D P Brechva 1774, 5 Dots, Black Glass, Yellow Olive, String Lip, 9 x 4 ½ In.	1989
Seal, E.H., 1796, Olive Green, Cylindrical, Pontil, String Lip, 10 ¾ In.	690
Seal, E.P. Middleton & Bro., 1825, Wheat Whiskey, Yellow Green, ½ Gal. ....*illus*	489
Seal, H.F. & B., N.Y., Pink Amethyst, Melon Ribbed, Sloping Double Collar, 9 ¼ In.	978
Seal, John Andrews, Wine, Dark Olive Amber, Sloping Collar With Ring, Pontil, 8 ¾ In.	556
Seal, P.C. Brooks, 1820, Wine, Dark Olive Green, Cylindrical, Sloping Collar, 9 ½ In....................	1404
Seal, R.P.A., 1779, Wine, Deep Yellow Olive, Cylindrical, Sheared, String Rim, 10 ½ In.	1404
Seal, S.M. & Co., N.Y., Decanter, Amber, Tapered, Curled Handle, 3 Ridges, 8 In.	1200
Seal, W.R.T., Wine, Aqua, Sloping Collar, c.1876, 12 In.	1638
Seal, Wine, Charles Ludlow, Deep Yellow Olive, Sheared Mouth, String Lip, 10 ¾ In.	468
Snuff, Agate, Banded, 3 In.	60
Snuff, Agate, Butterflies, Carved, Brocade Stand & Box, c.1800, 2 ¼ In. ....*illus*	2074
Snuff, Agate, Red Stopper, Chinese, c.1890, 3 In..	362
Snuff, Agate, Shadow, Pebble Shape, Gray, Abstract Markings, 1900s, 2 ½ In.	720
Snuff, Amber, Buddha, Seated, On Lotus, Folded Hands, 2 ¾ In.	936
Snuff, Amber, Koi Fish, Carved, Stopper In Mouth, 3 ½ In...	410

Bitters

Bitters was a mixture of herbs, roots, spices, and barks blended with alcohol. Some ingredients, like opium or marijuana, are dangerous and illegal today. Bitters was considered medicine and was taken by the spoonful or more. It was considered a wonder cure in the days before penicillin.

Bottle, Stiegel Type, 12 Diamond, Amethyst, Pontil, Pocket, c.1770, 5 ¼ In. $8,775

Norman C. Heckler & Company

Bottle, Target Ball, For Hockey's Patent Trap, Green, Sheared Lip, 2 ½ In. $1,150

Glass Works Auctions

Bottle, Target Ball, N.B. Glass Works, Perth, Blue, Sheared Lip, c.1890, 2 ⅝ In. $196

Glass Works Auctions

Bottle, Whiskey, E.G. Booz's Old Cabin, Cabin, Amber, Sloping Collar, 8 In. $1,610

Glass Works Auctions

Bottle, Whiskey, Old Quaker Rye, Corning & Company Distillers, Label, c.1915, Qt. $960

Garth's Auctioneers & Appraisers

TIP

To dry antique bottles, try this. Buy an aquarium pump and a short length of plastic hose. Clean the bottle and let it drain upside down for about 15 minutes. Insert the aquarium hose and plug it in. The bottle will be safely dried inside in less than an hour.

Snuff, Cinnabar, Flattened Spade Shape, Carved, Elder & Child, Trees, Stopper, 2 ⅞ In.	351
Snuff, Cinnabar, Inlaid Stone, Chinese, 20th Century, 2 ¾ In.	176
Snuff, Cloisonne, Pa Pao Hsiang, Precious Items, Marked, Chinese, c.1900, 2 In. ....*illus*	577
Snuff, Enamel, Flowers, Yellow, Round, Flattened, Stopper, 3 In.	176
Snuff, Fish, Carved, Chinese, 18th Century, 1 ¼ In.	2938
Snuff, Glass, Amber, Square, Open Pontil, Flared Lip, c.1810, 5 x 3 In.	161
Snuff, Glass, Cherry Amber, Carved, Flattened Oval, Round Stopper, Chinese, 2 ½ In.	210
Snuff, Glass, E. Roome, Troy, New York, Shaded Olive Green, Flared Lip, Pontil, 4 ⅜ In.	650
Snuff, Glass, E. Roome, Troy, New York, Yellow Olive, Rectangular, Beveled Corners, 4 In.	380
Snuff, Glass, Reverse Painted, Signed, Le Yuan, Chinese, c.1890, 2 ¼ In.	964
Snuff, Horn Bill, Carved Flowers, Chinese, c.1800, 2 In.	1145
Snuff, Ivory, Frog On Lily Leaf, Carved, 1 ¼ x 2 ½ In.	351
Snuff, Ivory, Man, Long Robe, Multicolor, 2 ½ In.	60
Snuff, Jade, Carved, Green Stopper, Chinese, 19th Century, 2 ½ In.	844
Snuff, Jade, Gray, Tan Symbols, Carved, Flowering Branch, Magnum, 3 ½ x 2 In.	466
Snuff, Jade, Green, Eggplant Shape, Chinese, c.1900, 3 In.	603
Snuff, Jade, Mottled, Pear Shape, Mask & Faux Ring Handles, c.1900, 2 ½ In. ....*illus*	3286
Snuff, Jade, Spinach, Oval, Footed, Chinese, 2 ½ In.	29
Snuff, Jade, White, Carved, Quartz Stopper, Chinese, c.1800, 3 In.	2585
Snuff, Marble, Dyed, Rounded Oval, Coral Stopper, Chinese, 3 ⅞ x 3 In.	98
Snuff, Moss Agate, Egg Shape, Ball Finial, Spoon, Pierced Wood Base, Chinese, 3 ⅝ In.	875
Snuff, Moss Agate, Twin, 2 Buddhas' Hand Citrons, Bamboo, Carved, 1900s, 3 In.	300
Snuff, Peet's, Salem, Mass., Glass, Olive Green, Rectangular, Flared Rim, Label, c.1830, 5 In.	1170
Snuff, Peking Glass, Hawks, Flowering Trees, Cameo, Red Over White, 1900s, 2 ¾ In.	296
Snuff, Pink Quartz, Trellis Diaper Ground, Green Jade Stopper, Flask Shape, Chinese, 3 ¼ In.	1320
Snuff, Porcelain, Blue, White, Red, Flattened Circle, Stopper, Chinese, 3 ½ In.	480
Snuff, Porcelain, Celadon Glaze, Flask Shape, Handles At Neck, Red Stopper, 2 ¾ In.	234
Snuff, Porcelain, Famille Rose, 2 Spotted Deer, Monkey, Honey Tree, Baluster, Chinese, 3 ⅛ In...	123
Snuff, Porcelain, Figural, Acrobat, Woman, Tunic, Flowers, Red Trousers, Foot Stopper, 4 In.	2640
Snuff, Porcelain, Horses, Chinese, 19th Century, 2 ¾ In.	241
Snuff, Porcelain, White, Blue Chinese Characters, Design, 1821-50, 3 In.	5581
Snuff, Red Jasper, Flattened, Agate, Dome Lid, Spoon, 3 In.	325
Snuff, Rock Crystal, Rooster, Brown, Chestnut Shape, Spoon, Chinese, c.1900, 4 In.	2500
Snuff, Rose Quartz, Leaves, Vase Shape, Fluted Stopper, Chinese, 1800s, 3 In.	1659
Snuff, Smoky Quartz, Carved Leaves, Chestnut Flask Shape, Ball Stopper, 2 ¼ In.	410
Snuff, Tiger's-Eye, Flattened Oval, Tiger's Eye Top, Brass Spoon, 3 In.	354
Snuff, Turquoise, Matrix, Silver, Enamel & Coral Top, 2 ¾ In.	676
Soda, B.J. McGee, Benicia, Teal, Blob Top, 7 ¼ In.	500
Soda, Bonanza Bottling Co., N.W.T., Aqua, Blob Top, Hutchinson, 7 ¾ In.	800
Soda, Byrd Beverages, Panama City, Florida, Brown & White ACL, 8 Oz.	10
Soda, C & K Eagle Works, Sac City, Cobalt Blue, Sloping Collar, 7 ¼ In. ....*illus*	518
Soda, C. Shields, St. Louis, Mo., Aqua, Deep Kick Up, Blob Top, Pontil	85
Soda, Cairns Timmermann Block, St. Louis Soda Co., Pittsburgh, Aqua, Blob Top	45
Soda, Castle Beverages, Food For Thirst, Castle, Red & White ACL, 7 Oz.	9
Soda, Classic City Beverages, Athens, Georgia, Train, Bus, City, Red & White ACL, 6 ½ Oz.	52
Soda, Crystal Soda Works, Honolulu, Hi., Light Blue, Rounded Cylinder, Blob Top	375
Soda, Dad's Root Beer, Big Jr., Amber, Blue & Yellow ACL, 1952, 10 Oz.	11
Soda, Double Cola Jr., Seminole, Okla., Red ACL, Horizontal Rings, 7 ½ Oz.	5
Soda, Eureka-California, Soda Water Co., S.F., Eagle, Amethyst, Hutchinson, 6 ¾ In.	650
Soda, F & B, Boston, A.D.C. Co., New Haven, Ct., Pat Jan. 5th 1864, Aqua, Bulbous	500
Soda, F. Gleason, Rochester, N.Y., Light Cobalt Blue, Iron Pontil, Blob Top, 7 ½ In.	460
Soda, F. Knebel, 1860, Brooklyn, N.Y., Script K, Aqua, Olive Streak, Blob Top, 7 ½ In.	160
Soda, F.R. Goosman & Co., Root Beer, Cincinnati, Sapphire, 12-Sided, Sloping Collar	1989
Soda, G. Andrae, Port Huron, Mich., Sapphire Blue, Blob Top, 6 ¾ In.	110
Soda, Geo. Gemenden, Savannah, Geo., Flag, Eagle, Teal, Blob Top	550
Soda, Ghirardelli's, Branch, Oakland, Blue, Blob Top, 7 ½ In.	475
Soda, Hill Billy Brew, 'Lil Brown Jug, Hillbilly, Still, Green, Red & White ACL, 10 Oz.	10
Soda, J. Zeisler & Co., St. Charles, Mo., Tombstone, Slug Plate, Hutchinson	38
Soda, J.T. Brown, Chemist, Boston, Double Soda, Blue Green, Torpedo, 8 ⅜ In.	1380
Soda, J.T. Brown, Chemist, Boston, Green, Torpedo, Applied Lip	400
Soda, J.T. Brown, Chemist, Boston, Green, Torpedo, Blob Top, 8 ½ In. ....*illus*	316
Soda, Kickapoo Joy Juice, Original Dogpatch Recipe, Green, Red & Yellow ACL, 10 Oz.	8
Soda, Kimball & Co., Flip Hat, Cobalt Blue, 3 ¼ x 5 ⅝ In.	489
Soda, King Orange, Crown, Shield, Blue ACL, 12 Oz.	14
Soda, Koca Nola, J. Esposito, Philada, Yellow Amber, Blob Top, Hutchinson, 7 ¾ In.	1000
Soda, Leland Ice & Cold Storage Co., Leland, Miss., Light Blue, Blob Top, 7 ¼ In.	80

Soda, Luke Beard, Green, Tenpin, 7 ¼ In.	196
Soda, M.T. Crawford, Hartford, Ct., Cobalt Blue, Mug Base	275
Soda, Maui Soda, Wailuku, Maui, Island, No Ka Oi, Red & White ACL, 7 Oz.	14
Soda, Moriarity & Carroll, Waterbury, Conn., Amber, Blob Top, Hutchinson, ½ Pt.	234
Soda, Nehi Beverages, Embossed Shoulder & Base, Red & Yellow ACL, 7 Oz.	8
Soda, Niagara Dry, Niagara Falls, Green, White ACL, 7 Oz.	24
Soda, Owen Casey, Eagle Soda Works, Steel Blue, Blob Top, 7 In.	300
Soda, Pioneer Soda Works, Smith & Brian, Reno, Nev., Aqua, Hutchinson	395
Soda, Pokagon, Indian Head, Angola, Ind., Red & White ACL, 1966, 12 Oz.	6
Soda, Quality Beverages, Manitowoc, Wis., Parrot, Palm Trees, Red & White ACL, 7 Oz.	54
Soda, Randall & Co., Monument Square, Balt., Sea Green, Tenpin, Sloping Collar, 9 In.	3510
Soda, Re-O Cola, Liberty Bottling Co., Memphis, Blue, White ACL, 1942, 8 Oz.	11
Soda, Richmond Soda Works, RSW, Aqua, Blob Top, Hutchinson, 1902-15, 7 In.	425
Soda, Robertson's Beverages, Mount Forest, Since 1875, Green, White ACL, 7 Oz.	17
Soda, Royal Crown Cola, Logo On Top Of Diamond, Green, Red & White ACL, 10 Oz.	28
Soda, Royal Crown Cola, Pyramids, Red & Yellow ACL, Tapered, 12 Oz.	33
Soda, S. Smith, Auburn, N.Y., Cobalt Blue, Sloping Collar, Iron Pontil, 7 ½ In.	633
Soda, S.S. Knickerbocker, 10-Sided, Sapphire Blue, Iron Pontil, c.1850, 7 ½ In.	978
Soda, Snort, Drinksation Of The Nation, London, Ont., Green, White ACL, 12 Oz.	18
Soda, Steam Bottling Work, Shawnee, O.T., Anchor, Blob Top, Hutchinson, 6 ¾ In.	650
Soda, Swallow's Keg Root Beer, Keg, Muncie, Ind., Red & White ACL, 12 Oz.	5
Soda, Ukiah Soda Works, Ukiah, Cal., Aqua, Blob Top, Hutchinson, 7 In.	120
Soda, Union Soda Works, B & B, Amber, Shaded, Blob Top	2400
Soda, W. Eagle, New York, Union Glass Works, Blue, Mug Base, 7 ½ In.	805
Soda, W.P. Knickerbocker, Cobalt Blue, 10-Sided, Blob Top, 7 ¼ In.	1265
Stiegel Type, 12 Diamond, Amethyst, Pontil, Pocket, c.1770, 5 ¼ In. ....*illus*	8775
Stiegel Type, Scent, Seahorse, Cobalt Blue, Clear Rigaree, Pontil, c.1830, 2 In.	431
Storage, Cobalt Blue, Dip Mold, Wide Mouth, Flared Lip, Pontil, 10 ¾ x 5 ¾ In.	690
Target Ball, Bogardus, Pat'd Apr 10 1877, Diamond Lattice, Yellow Amber, 3 In.	500
Target Ball, Bogardus, Pat'd April 10 1877, Diamonds, Yellow Amber, 2 ⅝ In.	374
Target Ball, Cobalt Blue, 7 Horizontal Rings, Sheared Mouth, 2 ⅝ In.	345
Target Ball, For Hockey's Patent Trap, Green, Sheared Lip, 2 ½ In. ....*illus*	1150
Target Ball, J.H. Johnston Great Western Gun Works, Pittsburgh, Purple, 2 ¾ In.	11500
Target Ball, Man, Shooting, Lattice, Green, 2 ⅝ In.	403
Target Ball, Man, Shooting, Lattice, Pink Amethyst, 2 ⅝ In.	403
Target Ball, N.B. Glass Works, Perth, Blue, Sheared Lip, c.1890, 2 ⅝ In. ....*illus*	196
Target Ball, Yellow Amber, Patent Appl'd For, 8-Sided, Sheared Mouth, 2 ⅞ In.	5450
Tonic, Dr. Jones, Red Clover, Amber, 3-Leaf Clover, 9 In.	100
Tonic, Schenck's Seaweed, Aqua, Indented Sides, Sloping Collar, 8 ½ In.	90
Tonic, Wynkoop & Co.'s Mixture, New York, Dark Blue, Contents, 6 ½ In.	7500
Utility, Peach Puce, 12-Sided, Inward Rolled Mouth, Pontil, 5 In.	1872
Utility, Yellow Olive Amber, Chestnut Form, Sloping Collar, Pontil, 9 ⅛ In.	431
Water, Embossed White House Vinegar, Cameo, Green, Owens-Illinois, 1930s	30
Water, Forest Green, Embossed Water Label, Owens-Illinois, 8 ½ In.	25
Whiskey, Amber, Bell Form, Double Collar, Handle, 8 ½ In.	633
Whiskey, B.F. & Co., N.Y., Seal On Handle, Amber, Tapered, Vertical Ribs, 9 In.	978
Whiskey, Backbar, Mammoth Cave, Cave & Forest Scene, Enamel, Pinched, Stopper, 6 In.	345
Whiskey, Backbar, Rum, Cobalt Blue, Label Under Glass, Woman, Mouth Ring, 12 In.	920
Whiskey, Backbar, Target, Maryland Rye, Amber, Raised White Enamel Letters, 12 In.	920
Whiskey, Barrel, Golden Amber, Flattened Lip, Pontil 10 In.	1840
Whiskey, Boulevard Bourbon, Buneman Mercantile Co., SF, Cal., Amber, Fifth	230
Whiskey, Bucklye's Little Brown Jug, Stoneware, Pinched, M. Perine, Baltimore, 4 In.	115
Whiskey, Casper's, Made By Honest North Carolina People, Cobalt Blue, Fluted Neck, Qt.	600
Whiskey, Chapin & Gore, Sour Mash, Barrel, Yellow Amber, Internal Threads, 8 ½ In.	230
Whiskey, Charles White, Rectifier, No 255 W. 15th St., N.Y., Amber, Shaded, Jug, 9 ⅝ In.	230
Whiskey, Chestnut Grove, C.W., Red Amber, Flattened Chestnut, Ring Mouth, Handle, 9 In.	316
Whiskey, E.G. Booz's Old Cabin, Cabin, Amber, Sloping Collar, 8 In. ....*illus*	1610
Whiskey, Flask, Citron, Embossed Wreath, Coffin Shape, Knife Edge, Pt.	316
Whiskey, G.W. Chesley & Co., SF, Olive Amber, c.1875, Fifth	4600
Whiskey, Gold Dust, Kentucky Bourbon, Barkhouse Bros. & Co., Amber, Horse, Backbar, 11 In.	8850
Whiskey, Goudie & McKelvy Pepper Tree Saloon, Amber, Coffin Flask, c.1905, ½ Pt.	1600
Whiskey, Greybeard, Black Transfer, White Ground, Jug, 8 In.	96
Whiskey, Griffith Hyatt & Co., Baltimore, Amber, Applied Mouth, Handle, c.1865, 7 In.	345
Whiskey, Griffith Hyatt & Co., Baltimore, Olive Green, Applied Mouth, Handle, c.1860, 7 In.	863
Whiskey, Griffith Hyatt & Co., Baltimore, Yellow Olive, Jug, Flattened Lip, 7 ⅜ In.	4600
Whiskey, I. W. Harper, Black Transfer, Jug, 1880s, 7 ½ In.	240

Bottle, Whiskey, That's The Stuff, Barrel, Yellow Amber, Pontil, c.1850, 9 ¾ In. $1,404

Norman C. Heckler & Company

TIP
Never display bottles with labels in a sunny window. The labels will fade.

Bottle Stopper, Wood, Kissing Couple, Push Lever, Anri
$46

Corkscrews Online

Bottle Stopper, Wood, Woman, Swings Rolling Pin, Pull Lever, Anri
$84

Corkscrews Online

Box, Band, Pine, Maple, Flowers, Lid, Massachusetts, c.1830, 2 ½ x 4 ¾ x 6 In. $2,760

Skinner Auctioneers & Appraisers

Box, Bonbon, Velvet, Gold Tooled Paper, 6-Sided, Drawstrings, Tassels, France, 7 In. $342

Theriault's

Box, Gold, Enamel, Medallion, Flowers, Leaves, Marked, Continental, c.1800, 3 In. $9,600

Skinner Auctioneers & Appraisers

Dual Purpose

Many older bottle openers have a small square hole called a "Prest-O-Lite-Key." It was used to turn the valve on automobile gas headlights from about 1910 through the early 1930s, before electric headlights were used.

Whiskey, Jas. Durkin Wines & Liquors, Spokane, Wash., Amber, Tapered, 13 In.	184
Whiskey, Jug, Forest Green, Pear Shape, Curled Ear Handle, Sloping Collar, c.1865, 8 In.	761
Whiskey, Lilienthal & Co. Distillers, Monogram, Amber, Coffin Flask, Tooled Top	400
Whiskey, Louis Taussig & Co., S.F., Golden Amber, Knife Edge Flask, Rolled Lip, Pt., 7 In.	600
Whiskey, Mist Of The Morning, Barrel, Yellow Olive, Sloping Double Collar, 9 ⅞ In.	5175
Whiskey, Mist Of The Morning, S.M. Barnett & Co., Barrel, Yellow Amber, 10 In.	431
Whiskey, Mist Of The Morning, S.M. Barnett, Barrel, Golden Amber, Sloping Collar, 10 In.	585
Whiskey, Mohawk Pure Rye, Indian Queen Holding Shield, Pat Feb 11, 1868, Rolled Lip	3600
Whiskey, Nabob In Oval, Yellow, Applied Collar, c.1885, 10 ¾ In.	425
Whiskey, Old Gilt Edge OK Bourbon, Wichman & Lutgen & Co., Crown, Amber, Fifth	1000
Whiskey, Old Judge, KY Bourbon, M. Gruenberg & Co., San Francisco, Amber, c.1880, Fifth	350
Whiskey, Old Pioneer, Wm. H. Spears & Co., Sole Agents, Bear, Yellow Amber, Fifth	6000
Whiskey, Old Pioneer, Wm. H. Spears, Brown, Bear, Backbar, 11 In.	3835
Whiskey, Old Quaker Rye, Corning & Company Distillers, Label, c.1915, Qt. .....*illus*	960
Whiskey, Old Valley, Cook & Bernheimer Co., Amber, Cylindrical, Sloping Collar, 26 In.	351
Whiskey, Phoenix, Raised Eagle, Naber, Alfs & Bruce, Amber, Backbar, 12 In.	354
Whiskey, R.B. Cutters, Pure Bourbon, Honey Amber, Jug, Sloping Collar, 8 ½ In.	1380
Whiskey, S.S. Smith Jr. & Co., Cincinnati, O., Cabin, Blue, Sloping Collar, 9 ¾ In.	3738
Whiskey, Seminole Club, Topless Indian Maiden, Gold Letters, Fluted Base, Backbar, 10 In.	210
Whiskey, Simmond's Nabob, Amber, Applied Collar, 1879-85, 10 ¾ In.	110
Whiskey, Simmond's Nabob, Pure KY Bourbon, Man Being Served, Amber, Fifth	900
Whiskey, Smoky Copper, Globular, Blob Top, Handle, c.1865, 6 ½ In.	748
Whiskey, Superior Bourbon, Old Extra Fine, Amber, Applied Mouth, Handle, 8 ¾ In.	374
Whiskey, Teakettle Old Bourbon, Embossed Teakettle, Amber, Ring Collar, Fifth	1400
Whiskey, Teakettle Old Bourbon, Embossed Teakettle, Yellow Amber, Ring Collar, Fifth	1600
Whiskey, That's The Stuff, Barrel, Yellow Amber, Pontil, c.1850, 9 ¾ In. ....*illus*	1404
Whiskey, Thos. H. Jacobs & Co., Blue Green, Applied Collar, Seal, c.1850, 11 In.	3160
Whiskey, Wharton's, 1850, Chestnut Grove, Cobalt Blue, Teardrop, Double Collar, 5 ½ In.	345
Whiskey, Wine, Otard Dupuy, Cognac, Seal, Cylindrical, Olive Amber, Mouth Ring, 11 In.	3510
Whiskey, Yellow Amber, 26 Ribs, Swirled To Right, Flattened, Handle, 8 ¼ In.	633
Wine, Globular, Shaft & Globe, Yellow Olive, Elongated Neck, String Lip, 7 ½ x 4 In.	5850
Wine, Jas. Durkin Wines & Liquors, Amber, 8-Sided Base, Tapered, c.1900, 13 In.	230
Wine, Jas. Durkin, Wholesale, Retail, Sprague & Wall, Spokane, Amber, Tapered, c.1895, 13 In.	316
Wine, Olive Amber, Dip Mold, Applied String Lip, c.1750, Magnum, 11 ¼ In.	288
Wine, Olive Green, Bladder, String Lip, Pontil, 5 ¾ In.	978
Wine, Shaft & Globe, Blue Green, Sheared Mouth, String Rim, Pontil Scar, c.1660, 4 ³⁄₁₆ In.	1521
Wine, Yellow Olive, 8-Sided, Sheared Mouth, String Lip, 8 ¾ In.	5158
Zanesville, 24 Ribs, Swirled To Left, Yellow Amber, Globular, Rolled Lip, 9 In.	575
Zanesville, 24 Ribs, Swirled To Left, Yellow Olive, Globular, Rolled Mouth, 7 In.	1521
Zanesville, 24 Ribs, Swirled To Right, Yellow Green, Beehive, Applied Collar, 7 ¾ In.	246

BOTTLE CAPS for milk bottles are the printed cardboard caps used since the 1920s. Crown caps, used after 1892 on soda bottles, are also popular collectibles. Unusual mottoes, graphics, and caps from bottlers that are out of business bring the highest prices.

Brass, Steel Liner, Georg Jensen, 1981, 2 ¾ In.	40
Cardboard, Allumbaugh Dairy, Phone 438, Cream, Boise, Idaho, Blue, White, 1 ⅝ In.	5
Metal, Adolph Coors, Golden Colorado, Mountain, Red, Yellow, Cork Lined	10
Metal, Felix, Orange Dry, Cat, Orange, Black, 1 ¼ In.	20
Paper, Amber-Glo, Milk, Pasteurized, Grade A, Yellow, Red, 2 In.	4
Paper, Hoffman Coffee Cream, Decoursey, Ky., Red, White	6
Paper, Winona Dairy, Pasteurized Light Cream, Lebanon, N.H., Red, Green, 1940s	4
Porcelain, Rieber & Bretz, Phila., Pa., Black, Red, White Ground	6

BOTTLE OPENERS are needed to open many bottles. As soon as the commercial bottle was invented, the opener to be used with the new types of closures became a necessity. Many types of bottle openers can be found, most dating from the twentieth century. Collectors prize advertising and comic openers.

Antler, Silver Cap, 7 ¼ In.	145
Black Forest Wood Spirit, Hardwood, Painted, Germany, 7 ½ In.	48
Butterfly, Elk, Enamel, Brass, Rhodes, 3 ¾ x 2 ³⁄₁₆ In.	16
Cactus Design, Sterling Silver, Georg Jensen, 4 ¾ In.	108
Canada Goose, Black, White, Cast Iron, 3 ¾ x 1 ¾ In.	95
Clown Shape, Paint, Cast Iron, 4 x 4 In.	21
Dolphin, Chrome Plated, 6 ½ In.	12
Drunk Man, Lamp Post, Cast Iron	75

Drunk, On Signpost, Bourbon Street New Orleans, Cast Iron, 1950s, 4 ¼ In.	15
Elephant, Pink, Cast Iron, John Wright, c.1930	115
Embossed Leafy Stems, Iron, Made In U.S.A., Screw, Wood Handle, Victorian...................	270
Flower Handle, Sterling Silver, Web, 6 ⅞ In.	97
Man's Head, 4 Blue Eyes, Mustache, Cast Iron, Wall Mount, Wilton, 1940s, 3 x 3 In.	125
Pabst Blue Ribbon, Tin, Bottle Shape, 1950s, 4 In.	22
Parrot On Perch, Yellow, Cast Iron, John Wright, c.1930	95
Pelican, Cast Iron, John Wright, c.1940, 4 In.	40

BOTTLE STOPPERS are made of glass, metal, plastic, and wood. Decorative and figural stoppers are used to replace the original cork stoppers and are collected today.

Wood, Kissing Couple, Push Lever, Anri ....*illus*	46
Wood, Newspaper Reader, Eyeglasses, Anri	76
Wood, Violinist, Anri..	76
Wood, Woman, Swings Rolling Pin, Pull Lever, Anri ....*illus*	84

BOXES of all kinds are collected. They were made of thin strips of inlaid wood, metal, tortoiseshell, embroidery, or other material. Additional boxes may be listed in other sections, such as Advertising, Battersea, Ivory, Shaker, Tinware, and various Porcelain categories. Tea Caddies are listed in their own category.

Apple, Pine, Flared, Yellow Grained Paint, Pa., c.1820, 6 x 12 In.	1541
Art Nouveau, Oak, Brass Inlay, Latch, Canted Sides, Openwork Brackets, 2 x 5 ¼ In.	330
Ballot, Walnut, Lift Lid, Detachable Handle, c.1900, 4 x 14 ¾ In.	295
Bandbox, Cardboard, Wallpaper, Stag Chased By Dogs, Lid, U.S.A., c.1845, 12 x 18 In.	470
Bandbox, Floral Multicolor Wallpaper, Lined, 1835 Vermont Phoenix Newspaper, c.1840, 3 x 6 In.	570
Bandbox, Flowers, Blue, Green, Oval, Lid, Hannah Davis, 8 x 13 In.	840
Bandbox, House Landscape, Blue Ground, Wallpaper, S.M. Hurlbert, 11 x 16 In.	1920
Bandbox, Les Trois Jours, Three Days, Figures, Blue Ground, Oval, Lid, 15 x 20 In...........	660
Bandbox, Pine, Maple, Flowers, Lid, Massachusetts, c.1830, 2 ½ x 4 ¾ x 6 In. .....*illus*	2760
Bandbox, Toast To The Ladies, Lovers, Seated Outside, Lid, Hannah Davis, 16 x 20 In.	1440
Bandbox, Wallpaper, Bentwood, Oberlin Evangelist Lining, Hannah Davis, c.1800, 10 x 18 In. ..	264
Bandbox, Wallpaper, Wood, Oval, Lid, Marker's Label, Hannah Davis, 1853, 13 x 16 In...........	450
Bentwood, Heart, Flowering Urn, White, Red Borders, Initials, 1799, 9 ¾ x 4 ¾ In.	805
Bentwood, Painted Black, Splint Binding, Oval, Carved Lid, 19th Century, 22 x 16 In.	115
Bible, Chippendale, Walnut, Bracket Feet, Pa., c.1775, 8 x 22 In.	575
Bible, Oak, Carved Leaves & Arches, England, c.1805, 9 x 26 In.	363
Bible, Pine, Brown, Leaf, Scroll Carved, Pilgrim Century, 9 ½ x 30 In.......................	3600
Bible, Red Paint, Interior Till, Molded Lid & Base, c.1800, 9 ⅜ x 24 In.....................	3900
Bonbon, Louis XVI, Gold, Round, Husk, Leaf, Flowers, Paris 1789, 3 In.......................	7500
Bonbon, Velvet, Gold Tooled Paper, 6-Sided, Drawstrings, Tassels, France, 7 In. ....*illus*	342
Brass, Wood, Embossed Figures, Landscape, Side Handles, c.1890, 27 x 33 In..................	207
Bride's, Bentwood, 2 Stags, Oval, Red Rim, Painted, 7 ½ x 18 In.............................	660
Bride's, Bentwood, Embracing Man & Woman, Paint, Lid, Continental, c.1830, 6 ¾ x 11 In.	1701
Bride's, Bentwood, Flowers, Multicolor Paint, Oval, Continental, c.1820, 7 x 18 ½ In.	593
Bride's, Bentwood, Folksy Women, Painted, Scandinavia, Oval, 6 x 18 In......................	600
Bride's, Bentwood, Laced Seams, Blue Ground, Flowers, Couple On Lid, Germany, 7 x 19 In......	240
Bride's, Bentwood, Laced Seams, Flowers, Bear, Bear Trainer, Germany, c.1720, 6 ½ x 19 In.....	492
Bride's, Bentwood, Laced Seams, Painted, Stag Chased By Dogs, Oval, c.1860, 8 x 18 ½ In.......	1645
Bride's, Bentwood, Laced Seams, Salmon Ground, Woman, Verse, Germany, c.1830, 6 x 14 In....	480
Bride's, Bentwood, Oval, Flowers, Woman Standing, Painted, c.1820, 6 x 17 In................	474
Bride's, Bentwood, Sewn Lap Joints, Nail Construction, Shaped Top, Locking, 16 x 18 In.	106
Bride's, Painted, c.1850, 6 x 19 In..	326
Bride's, Painted, Oval, Angel Lid, Continental, c.1820, 5 x 15 ½ In.	652
Bride's, Paper Covered, Bentwood, Flowers, Leaves, Vines, Pa., c.1800, 15 x 9 In............	3245
Bride's, Poplar, Oblong, Lapped Seam, Arabesque Design, Dots, Lid, c.1820, 4 x 13 In.	3075
Bugle, Pine, Painted, Initials BRL, c.1850, 8 ½ x 15 In.....................................	207
Bureau, Softwood, Hearts, Clutching Hands, Divided Interior, Hinged Lid, c.1941, 4 x 13 In.....	94
Burl, Inlays, Desk Shape, 3 Drawers, Brass Ball Feet, Lift Lid, c.1900, 7 ¾ x 8 In.	374
Cake, Bentwood, Round, Stenciled Flowers, Yellow, Threaded Lid, Pa., c.1890, 6 x 12 In.	1410
Candle, Beech, Lollipop Hanger, Slide Lid, England, c.1800, 20 x 5 ½ In.....................	178
Candle, Cherry, Punched Pinwheel Design, Slide Lid, Pa., 5 x 10 ¾ In........................	1415
Candle, Cylindrical, Dome Sides, Shaped Backsplash, Rings, Hinged Lid, 8 ½ x 11 ½ In........	266
Candle, Mahogany, Interior Till, Finger Notch, Slide Lid, 5 ¾ x 16 ¼ In.....................	71
Candle, Oak, Linenfold Slide Lid, Carved, England, c.1760, 5 x 19 In.	385
Candle, Oak, Slide Lid, c.1800, 7 x 10 In...	480

Box, Jewelry, Brass, Opaline, Portrait Of Woman, Gilt, Guilloche, c.1900, 3 x 6 ½ In.
$522

Box, Knife, Walnut, Inlaid, Divided, Maple & Ebony Handle, c.1890, 7 ¼ x 12 In.
$1,560

Box, Malachite, Lid, Bronze Mounts, Plaques, Buildings In Rome, 16 ½ x 10 ½ In.
$3,690

Box, Vanity, Lid, Child Kneeling, Porcelain, Kimono, Germany, c.1925, 6 ½ In.
$114

Box, Vanity, Pincushion Doll, Woman On Lid, Sevres, Dressel Kister, c.1910, 10 In. $912

Theriault's

Box, Watch Hutch, Tall Clock, Mahogany, Ivory, Bone, 1800s, 14 ½ x 4 In. $1,920

Skinner Auctioneers & Appraisers

Box, Writing, Walnut, Inlay, Geometric, Inscription, Pen Tray, Compartments, 10 x 20 In. $89

James D. Julia Auctioneers

Candle, Pine, Painted Ship Design, Slide Lid, Continental, 18 x 8 In.	178
Candle, Pine, Painted, Flowers, Multicolor, Slide Lid, c.1850, 4 x 6 ¾ In.	608
Candle, Pine, Slide Top, Red, Green Paint, c.1855, 11 ½ In.	240
Candle, Poplar, Flowers, Red, Green Paint, Carved, Connecticut, c.1750, 10 ½ x 7 ¼ In.	17500
Candle, Softwood, Red Varnish, Finger Notches, Slide Lid, Brass Handle, 9 ½ x 18 ½ In.	201
Candle, Tiger Maple, c.1850, 2 x 9 In.	334
Candle, Tiger Maple, Heart Cutout, Scrolled Crest, Heart Shape Hanger, c.1715, 18 In.	6518
Candle, Wall, Mahogany, Low Drawer, Lift Lid, England, c.1860, 19 x 8 ½ In.	185
Candle, Wall, Walnut, Cutout Back, Divided Drawer, Slant Lid, c.1820, 14 x 14 In.	805
Casket, Steel, Leaves, Calligraphy, Relief, Bracket Feet, Lid, Middle East, 8 x 7 In.	1968
Cherry, Slide Lid, Tulip Inlays, Pa., 2 ½ x 5 ¼ In.	770
Cigar, Gilt Bronze, Louis XIV Style, Hinged Lid, Marked, France, c.1935, 2 x 6 In.	553
Cigar, Lacquer, New York City Shoreline Lithograph, Oval, 3 x 5 ½ In.	911
Cigar, Wood, Tobacco Plants, Monkey Smoking Pipe, Shelf, Marked, E.M.W., 1880, 11 x 10 In.	127
Cigarette, 14K Tricolor Gold, Woven, Line Engraved Lid, Sapphire Thumbpiece, 3 In.	1476
Cobalt Blue Glass, Silver Overlay, 6 x 4 ½ In.	170
Coffer, Copper, Brass, Silver, Geometric Designs, Wood Lined, Lid, Middle Eastern, 5 x 3 In.	115
Collar, Studs, Black, Oval Front, 8 In.	57
Copper, Hammered, Lid, 3 x 5 In.	89
Cutlery, Federal, Mahogany, String Inlays, Slant Top, c.1800, 15 x 9 In.	3186
Cutlery, Walnut, Pine, 2-Part, Heart Cutout Handle, Shenandoah Valley, c.1820, 9 x 14 In.	690
Desk, Bronze, People Fishing, Grape & Wheat Harvesting, 1800s, 2 ¾ x 6 ½ In.	179
Desk, Lap, Mahogany, Fitted Interior, Felt Slope, Hinged Lid, 7 x 21 x 10 In.	117
Desk, Pine, Dovetailed, Brass Escutcheon, Hinged, Cleated Lid, c.1715, 9 ¾ x 25 ¼ In.	3240
Document, Green Putty Design, Yellow Border, Hinged Lid, c.1815, 5 x 8 In.	540
Document, Green Sponge Grain Paint, Dome Lid, c.1845, 24 In.	344
Document, Pine, Brown, Tan Grained Paint, Sponged Fans, Dome Lid, c.1825, 6 x 12 In.	325
Document, Pine, Dovetail, Brass Ring, c.1850, 7 x 16 x 11 In.	180
Document, Pine, Dovetailed, Green Vinegar Graining, Signed GK 84, c.1870, 4 ½ x 12 In.	240
Document, Pine, Stencil, Black, Green, Yellow, Red Striping, Maine, c.1850, 2 ½ x 10 ½ In.	411
Document, Poplar, Brown Vinegar Sponging, Mustard Ground, Brass Ring, c.1860, 5 x 13 In.	353
Document, Poplar, Hinged, Stenciled, Freehand, Multicolor Paint, c.1830, 7 x 12 In.	138
Document, Rosewood, Urn, Flower Painted Top, 5 ½ x 19 ½ In.	1320
Document, Softwood, Painted Red Panels, Yellow Highlights, Brown Borders, 12 x 17 In.	71
Document, Tulips, Daisies, Red, Green, Dome Lid, Conn. River Valley, c.1829, 7 x 16 In.	1750
Document, Wood, Chip Carved, Wrought Iron Hinges, Footed, 17th Century, 9 x 17 In.	497
Document, Wood, Decorated Interior, Grain Paint, Dome Lift Lid, c.1820, 10 x 24 In.	502
Dome Top, Pine, Flowers, Swags, Tole, Paper Lined Interior, Mass., c.1860, 5 x 12 In.	4797
Dore Bronze, Repousse Classical Figures, 20th Century, 6 ¾ In.	360
Dresser, Bird's-Eye Maple, c.1850, 6 ½ x 10 ¾ In.	504
Dresser, Book Shape, Painted Album, Landscape, c.1890, 4 12 x 12 In.	356
Dresser, Burl Veneer, Inlaid Star, 6 x 10 In.	148
Dresser, Burl, Dome Lid, c.1820, 5 x 10 In.	948
Dresser, Burl, England, c.1850, 6 x 11 ½ In.	119
Dresser, Burl, Geometric Inlays, 2 Doors, Continental, c.1850, 14 x 12 In.	215
Dresser, L. Stickley, Mahogany, Drawer, Brass Pulls, 1952, 4 x 17 In.	250
Dresser, Mahogany, Grand Piano Shape, Ivory Inlaid Keys, 5 ¾ x 7 ½ In.	178
Dresser, Pine, Carved, Green, Red Fruit, Paw Feet, Cornucopia Apron, 7 ¾ x 12 In.	1541
Dresser, Pine, Dovetailed, Drawers, Stenciled Flowers, Pineapple, Dome Lid, 7 x 18 In.	1410
Dresser, Pine, Swivel Lid, Bird Finials, Pinprick Decoration, Initials F.J., c.1930, 7 ½ In.	240
Dresser, Poplar, Flowers, Green, Yellow Paint, Pa., c.1860, 5 x 8 In.	415
Dresser, Wallpaper, Cut Paper Heart Shape, Blue, Rusty Red Paint, c.1850, 1 ¾ x 3 In.	972
Dresser, Wallpaper, Green, Black, Peach Design, Lid, c.1850, 3 ¼ x 4 ½ In.	415
Dresser, Wood, Hinged Lid, Panel Doors, Drawers, Brass Handles, 13 x 8 In.	3120
Glove, Mahogany Veneer, Inlay, Cornucopia, Stringing, Velvet Lining, c.1810, 3 x 11 x 5 In.	150
Gold, 18K, Bicolor, Textured, Basket Weave Design, Hinged, 2 x 1 ¼ x ½ In.	1722
Gold, Enamel, Medallion, Flowers, Leaves, Marked, Continental, c.1800, 3 In. ....*illus*	9600
Hat, Bolt's New Hotel, New York Skyline, Blue, Oval, Lid, 12 x 16 In.	2250
Hat, Floral Wallpaper, Oval, 19th Century, 11 x 14 In.	59
Hat, Parrot, Flowers, Pink, Brown, Blue Border, Oval, Lid, 10 ½ x 15 ½ In.	330
Hat, Rural Landscape, Buildings, Oval, Lid, 11 ½ x 16 In.	840
Hat, Squirrels, Trees, Blue Ground, Rounded, Painted, Lid, 13 x 19 ½ In.	1020
Hat, Stag Hunt, Running Deer, Tan, Brown, Lid, 11 x 18 In.	1080
Hat, U.S. Capitol Building, Flag, Troops, Charioteer, Lion, 10 x 15 In.	4800
Hat, Wallpaper, Beaver, Trees, c.1850, 9 ½ x 13 ¾ In.	790
Hat, Wallpaper, Inscribed E.S. & S. Updike Fashionable Hat, Cap Store, c.1850, 8 x 12 ¾ In.	900

Hat, Wesleyan University Campus, Blue Ground, Lid, 12 x 15 ½ In..........................	2880
Hat, Wild Bull Hunt, Horseman, Spear, Tan, Blue, 9 x 14 In.	540
Hepplewhite, Mahogany, Shell Inlays, 6 Gilt Etched Bottles, Stoppers, c.1800, 10 x 12 In.	900
Ink, Porcelain, Peach Bloom, 6 Character Blue Mark, Chinese, 1 ¼ In...................	3013
Jewelry, Brass, Opaline, Portrait Of Woman, Gilt, Guilloche, c.1900, 3 x 6 ½ In. ....*illus*	522
Jewelry, Elizabethan Revival, Walnut, Brass, Fitted Trays, Strapwork, Satin Lined, 12 x 9 In.	461
Jewelry, Embossed Woman, Flowing Hair, Flowers, Hinged Lid, Spelter, 4 x 3 ½ In........................	59
Jewelry, Envelope Shape, Sterling, Gold, 2 Square Sapphires, France, c.1915, 3 x 2 ⅜ In.............	885
Jewelry, Gilt Metal, Beveled Glass, Openwork Scroll, Footed, France, c.1950, 4 x 6 x 8 In.	48
Jewelry, Gilt Metal, Hinged Lid, Cartouche, Putti, Flowers, Leaf Scrolls, Top Shape Feet, 9 In.	563
Jewelry, Mahogany, 2 Drawers, Turned Knobs, Ogee Bracket Feet, 8 x 18 In.	300
Jewelry, Mahogany, Metal Plaque, Hindenburg, Attached Lid, 1938, 10 x 6 x 2 In.	325
Jewelry, Mahogany, Rounded Corners, Turned Columns, Interior Drawers, c.1825, 6 x 11 In......	240
Jewelry, Mixed Wood, Brass, Ebony Inlays, Hinged Top, Drawer Door, Lobed, Footed, 1800s, 14 x 16 In.	2500
Jewelry, Wood, Metal Bound, Drawer, 9 x 10 In...	153
Keepsake, Walnut, Heart Shape, Lid, c.1815, 2 ¾ x 4 In.	948
Knife, George III, Mahogany, Inlays, c.1790, 15 ½ x 9 In., Pair	1541
Knife, George III, Mahogany, String & Starburst Inlay, c.1800, Pair........................	1610
Knife, Georgian Style, Mahogany, Slotted, Fitted Interior, Hinged Lid, c.1920, 15 In., Pair	805
Knife, Georgian, Mahogany, Inlaid, 15 ½ x 9 In..	246
Knife, Hepplewhite, Mahogany, Inlays, Serpentine Front, Fitted Interior, 14 In., Pair	4560
Knife, Hepplewhite, Mahogany, Inlays, Serpentine, England, c.1790........................	224
Knife, Inlaid Mahogany, Serpentine Front, Barber Pole Inlay, Crossbanding, c.1800, 14 x 9 In. ..	492
Knife, Inlaid Mahogany, Serpentine Front, Shells, Star, Slant Lid, c.1815, 14 x 9 In.	461
Knife, Mahogany, Barber Pole Inlays, Serpentine, Fitted Interior, c.1820, 14 In., Pair	2375
Knife, Mahogany, Inlaid Trim, Star, Shaped Front, Slant Lid, 1800s, 13 x 9 x 9 In., Pair	4000
Knife, Mahogany, Oval Fan Inlays, Banded, Serpentine Sloped Lid, c.1850, 12 ½ In.	625
Knife, Mahogany, Swag Carved, Urn Shape, c.1920, 26 In., Pair........................	1215
Knife, Maple, Dovetail, Scroll Cutout Handle, Geometric Inlay, c.1850, 5 x 13 In.	630
Knife, Maple, Inlays, Fitted Interior, Shaped Slant Lid, 15 In., Pair	2432
Knife, Pine, Cutout Handle, Red Paint, 1800s, 7 x 14 In.................................	264
Knife, Wall, Mahogany, Tapered, Scroll Pierced Pediment, Hinged Lid, 18 x 6 In.	215
Knife, Walnut, Inlaid, Divided, Maple & Ebony Handle, c.1890, 7 ¼ x 12 In. ....*illus*	1560
Leather Clad, Stand, Painted, Carp Swimming Among Lily Pads, 12 ¼ x 17 ¼ In.	92
Leather, Shoe Shape, Stacked Heel, Stitched Sole, Hinged Upper Lid, c.1860, 3 x 2 In.	46
Ledger, Poplar, Pine, Brass Side Handles, Blue Paint, Virginia, c.1925, 13 x 23 In.	259
Letter, Mahogany, Slant Lid, New York, c.1830, 7 x 15 ½ In.	308
Letter, Marquetry, Porcelain Insert, Flowers, Leaves, Center Plaque, Painted Musicians, 12 In....	390
Letter, Regency Style, Red Leather, Velvet Lined, Serpentine Lid, 4 ¼ x 11 ¼ In...............	307
Letter, Rosewood, Line Inlay, Slant Lid, France, c.1900, 6 x 10 In.	236
Letter, Rosewood, Shell Inlays, 2 Slots, Divided Interior, Hinged Lid, c.1875, 4 x 4 In.	52
Letter, Victorian, Slant Front, Burl Walnut, Calendar, Drawers, c.1885, 12 x 12 ¾ In.	540
Lock, Baroque, Iron, Lid, Spain, c.1700, 6 ½ x 12 ½ In.	826
Lock, Flowers, Hearts, Paint, Top Handle, Pa., 6 x 11 In.................................	2133
Lock, Mahogany, Brass Fittings, England, c.1850, 13 x 13 In.	150
Lock, Mahogany, Brass Mounts, Bail Handles, Hinged Lid, 25 ½ In.	500
Lock, Mahogany, Brass, Top Ring Handle, Triangular Lid, 7 ½ x 11 ¾ In.	207
Lock, Mother-Of-Pearl, Walnut, c.1850, 12 ½ x 25 In.	1185
Lock, Oak, Carved Pinwheels, 5 ½ x 13 In.	207
Lock, Pine, Green Trim, Flowers, Red, Black Grain, Handle, c.1830, 7 x 17 In.	240
Lock, Pine, Lid, Star, Painted, 8 ½ x 14 In.	400
Lock, Pine, Top Handle, Grain Painted, New England, 1829, 7 x 18 ½ In.	365
Lock, Walnut, Footed, Pa., c.1850, 11 x 21 In.	444
Lock, Walnut, Lid Inlaid Heart, Vines, Date 1803, Pa., 10 x 22 In.	5451
Lock, Wood, Inscribed Dr. H. R. Painter, Painted, c.1850, 7 x 13 In.	180
Mahogany, Blanket Chest Shape, Bootjack Ends, 5 x 10 In.	600
Malachite, Lid, Bronze Mounts, Plaques, Buildings In Rome, 16 ½ x 10 ½ In. ....*illus*	3690
New England, Framingham Common View, Vine, Schoolgirl Maker, c.1810, 4 x 12 In.	10000
Oak, Applied Embossed, Metal Coins Animal Designs, Handles, Chinese, c.1850, 9 x 9 In........	420
Opium, Foo Dog, Telescopic Eyes, Octagonal, Immortal Emblems, Lid, Chinese, 1800s, 2 In......	948
Painted, Asian Scenes, Orange Ground, Venice, 5 ½ x 14 In.	1080
Painted, Bonaparte Crossing The Alps, Green Ground, Signed A.P. Painter, 1838........................	8125
Painted, Flowers, Dianthus, c.1835, 22 x 20 In.	780
Perfume, Lid, 2 Bottles, Printed Scenes, Blue Opaline, Brass Mount, 1800s, 5 In.........................	861
Pine, 2 Parts, Cutout Center Divider, Shenandoah Valley, c.1850, 8 x 12 In.	259
Pine, Blue Paint, Dome Lid, Shenandoah Valley, c.1950, 12 x 21 In...........................	518

Brass, Box, White Jade Cabochon, Mahogany Lining, Horace Potter, c.1915, 2 x 6 ¾ In.
$1,875

Los Angeles Modern Auctions (LAMA)

Brass, Stencil, Alphabets, Numbers, Fractions, Symbols, Rotating, 1800s, 13 In.
$360

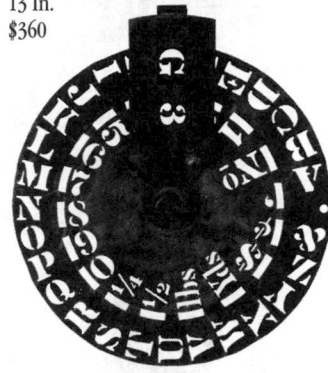

Garth's Auctioneers & Appraisers

Brass, Tazza, Empire Style, Snake Handles, Black Marble, Square Base, France, c.1890, 11 In., Pair
$354

Brunk Auctions

TIP

If your piece of old brass is covered with a protective coat of lacquer, it should not be cleaned. Test a darkened area with a dab of brass polish. If it stays dark, it has been lacquered and cannot be cleaned until the lacquer is removed from the entire piece.

Bride's Basket, Mauve Over Opal, Crimped Edge, Derby Silver Co. Frame, 8 x 12 In.
$75

Early Auction Co.

Bronze, Bust, Gutierrez, G., Maiden, Hat, Collar, Marble Base, 19 In.
$625

Leslie Hindman Auctioneers

Boom!
Watch out for exploding antiques! Guns, shells, powder cans, nitrate movie film, and some chemicals left in old bottles or cans are dangerous. If you don't know about these items, contact your local police or fire department for help.

Pine, Compass Designs, Red, White, Dome Lid, Lancaster County, Pa., c.1820, 8 ¾ x 12 In.	62500
Pine, Dome Lid, Painted, Continental, c.1850, 8 x 13 In.	92
Pine, Grisaille Street Scenes, Yellow Ground, New York, c.1830, 7 ⅝ x 14 ⅜ In.	8750
Pine, Iron Latch, Grain Paint, Dome Lid, New England, 9 ½ x 21 In.	120
Pine, Lift Lid, Inscribed D.S. Sears, East Dennis, Mass., c.1900, 11 ½ In.	106
Pine, Maple, Heart, Bird Geometric Designs, Multicolor, Round, G. Lawton, c.1845, 2 x 7 In.	209000
Pine, Maple, Mahogany, Lift Lid, c.1850, 5 ¾ x 10 In.	295
Pine, Monogram WP, Red Paint, Dome Lid, New England, c.1845, 14 ¾ x 29 In.	89
Pine, Open Compartment, Gray Paint, c.1890, 34 x 30 In.	266
Pine, Orange Flower Painted, Metal Lock, Dome Lid, c.1865, 9 x 5 In.	489
Pine, Painted Fruit, Geometric Designs, Till, Dome Lid, Sweden, A.S. Anno 1793, 13 x 21 In.	354
Pine, Painted Leaves, Cream Ground, Turquoise Interior, Hinged Lid, 1800s, 7 x 16 In.	330
Pine, Salt, Cutout Heart Gallery, Blue Paint, 1800s, 7 x 12 In.	600
Pine, Slide Lid, Blue Green Paint, J.R. 1870-71, 12 x 22 x 14 In.	277
Pine, Stenciled, Fruit Basket, Black Ground, Albany, N.Y., c.1830, 7 ¾ x 16 In.	338
Pine, Striated Multicolor Designs, S. Stenciled Lid, Octagonal, c.1830, 4 ¾ x 12 ¾ In.	12500
Pine, Yellow, Brown Grain Painted, Dome Lid, New England, c.1850, 11 ½ x 30 In.	182
Pipe, Hanging, Maple, Cutout Back, Drawer, 1900s, 16 ½ x 5 In.	161
Pipe, Hanging, Pine, Paint, Pierced Backboard, Drawer, Shaped Sides, c.1815, 23 x 6 In.	1020
Pipe, Mahogany, Hanging Cutout, Carved Frame, 2 Drawers, 19 x 6 In.	300
Poplar, Grain Paint, Serpentine Shape, Fitted Interior, Hinged Lid, c.1855, 14 x 8 In.	173
Poplar, Open, Chip Carved, c.1830, 6 ¾ x 11 ½ In.	460
Poplar, Scroll, Shield, Black, Yellow, Red Painted, J.P. Initials, 5 x 12 In.	1200
Poplar, Slide Lid, Fitted Interior, Black Trim, Bittersweet, c.1850, 3 x 10 In.	441
Poplar, Yellow, Red Paint, Slide Lid, Pa., c.1820, 3 ½ x 11 In.	711
Pottery, Blue, Brown Glaze, Dragonfly, Round, Max Claudet, France, c.1875, 5 x 2 ½ In.	427
Prayer, Copper, Tiger's Eye Cabochon, Silk Tassel, Hinged Lid, Tibet, c.1900, 4 ½ x 25 In.	123
Rosary, Leather, Beaded, Agarwood, Round, Flowers, Foo Dog, c.1900, 8 In. Diam.	3081
Rosewood, Carved, Applied Silver Flowers, 7 ½ x 3 In.	130
Rosewood, Ebonized, Satinwood Inlays, Stars, Leaves, Apple, Sailor Made, c.1860, 3 x 10 In.	1440
Rosewood, Mother-Of-Pearl, Whale Ivory, Gentleman, Lady, Stars, Mass., c.1845, 41 x 11 In.	18750
Salt, Open, Wall, Shaped Crest, Molding, Black Paint Trace, Lift Lid, 20 ½ x 10 In.	705
Salt, Pine, Deer & Tree Crest, Carved, New England, 12 ¾ x 10 In.	420
Salt, Pine, Wall, Shaped Crest, Yellow Paint, Lift Lid, c.1830, 14 ½ x 9 In.	353
Salt, Softwood, Wall, Lollipop Backboard, Swivel Lid Upper Well, Drawer, 1800s, 17 x 9 In.	1062
Salt, Wall, Mahogany, Scalloped Backsplash, Cutout, Slant Lid, 12 x 9 In.	474
Salt, Wall, Walnut, Pa., c.1845, 9 ¾ x 13 In.	563
Seed, Pine, Wall, Red Stain, Pa., c.1850, 10 ¾ x 14 In.	415
Seed, Wall, Arched Backsplash, Hanging Hold, Scalloped Supports, 6 Drawers, 12 x 8 In.	3540
Shibayama, Flowers, Mother-Of-Pearl, Lacquered Wood Base, 1800s, 2 ½ x 4 In.	4920
Shoeshine, Pine, Canted Sides, Handle, Compartment Door, Blue Paint, 11 x 13 In.	542
Shrine, Silver, Copper, Repousse, Arched Box, Buddhist Emblems, Tibet, 1900s, 4 ¾ In.	150
Silver, Enamel, Grid, Circles, Bead & Star Designs, Austria-Hungary, 3 x 2 ½ In.	780
Stamp, Arts & Crafts, Brass, Footed, Art Crafts Shop, Buffalo, N.Y., c.1910, 4 ½ x 2 In.	313
Storage, 6-Board, Inlaid Walnut, Tiger Maple, Hinged Overhang Lid, 9 x 16 In.	180
Storage, Bamboo, 4 Drawers, Footed, Bat, Endless Knot, Fluted Borders, 12 x 12 In.	9000
Storage, Bentwood, Yellow Flowers, Red Ground, Round, Pa., c.1820, 3 ¾ x 8 In.	2370
Storage, Camphorwood, Dragons, Phoenixes, Loop Handles, Hinged Lid, c.1900, 8 x 15 In.	295
Storage, Inlaid Walnut, Shield, Diamonds, Stars, Overhanging Lid, c.1885, 6 x 15 In.	615
Storage, Leather, Poplar, Divided Interior, Round, Virginia, c.1850, 1 ½ x 7 In.	748
Storage, Maple, Ash, Tin, Yellow, Black Flowers, Red, Painted, Round, Lid, Pa., 1853, 3 x 4 In.	25000
Storage, Pine, Basswood, Black & Red Paint, Dovetailed, Dome Lid, c.1835, 12 x 24 In.	323
Storage, Pine, Blue Paint, Lapped Seam, Iron Nails, Lid, 1800s, 4 x 16 In.	1680
Storage, Pine, Brown & Yellow Paint, Dovetailed, Dome Lid, c.1850, 13 x 28 In.	470
Storage, Pine, Inlay, Geometric Design, Birds & Hearts, U.S.A., c.1855, 8 x 14 In.	382
Storage, Pine, Paint, Geometric Design, Stars, Hinged Lid, c.1850, 6 x 14 In.	3690
Storage, Pine, Painted, Flat Top, Leather Straps, c.1815, 13 ½ x 30 In.	210
Storage, Pine, White & Gray Paint, Trestle Feet, Beaded Lift Lid, c.1820, 22 x 67 In.	2640
Storage, Poplar, Blue Grained Paint, Lift Lid, c.1870, 25 x 17 In.	572
Storage, Poplar, Compass Designs, Blue, Red, Dome Lid, Susanna Shrulb 1800, 7 x 11 In.	31250
Storage, Poplar, Red & Black Paint, Dome Lid, U.S.A., c.1850, 13 x 26 In.	470
Storage, Putty Design, Divided Interior, Black, Green, Dome Lid, 1800s, 5 x 13 ½ In.	861
Storage, Rosewood, Marquetry, Drop Front, Shapes, Leaves, Ball Feet, 1900s, 8 x 22 In.	240
Storage, Satinwood, Mahogany, Ebony Inlay, Drawer, Dome Lid, c.1800, 9 ½ x 16 In.	1955
Storage, Silver, Lotus, Watergrass, Birds, Dragonflies, Repousse, Hinged Lid, 1900s, 9 x 6 In.	2280
Storage, Stacked Books Shape, Gilded, London Journal, Hinged Lid, 1800s, 6 x 14 In.	270

Storage, Stand, Blue Paint, Deep Well, Stretcher, Tapered Legs, Lift Lid, c.1815, 38 x 34 In.		984
Storage, Wall, Pine, Brown Stain, Iron Hinges, Drawer, Slant Lid, 1900, 25 x 14 In.		83
Storage, Wood, Black Paint, Gilt Stencil, Leaves, Blossoms, Hinged Lid, c.1815, 8 x 13 In.		185
Storage, Wood, Sponge Painted, Dome Lid, 9 ½ x 22 In.		540
Store, Storage, Wood, 54 Drawers, Handles, 16 x 38 ½ In.		3750
Straw Work, Flowers, Prisoner Of War, Lid, Round Lid Cartouche, Turkey, 1888, 4 x 12 In.		1888
Strong, Cast Iron, Trunk Shape, Medallion, Handles, France, c.1865, 10 ½ x 17 In.		2440
Strong, Oak, Brass, England, 11 x 18 In.		2625
Sugar, Maple, Drawer, Hinged Lid, Square, 1800s, 8 x 14 ½ In.		472
Sugar, Walnut, Pine, Dovetailed, Cutout Bracket Base, c.1780, 13 x 19 In.		502
Sunfish Shape, Silver Metal, Lift Lid, Jennings Brothers, Bridgeport, Conn., 3 ½ In.		182
Tin, Dome Lid, Wire Handle, Flower Banding, 1800s, 3 ⅝ x 6 ¾ In.		1320
Tin, Heart Shape, Hinged Lid, Solder Joints, 2 x 7 x 6 ½ In.		47
Tinder, Cylindrical, Ring Handle, Lid With Candleholder, Tin, c.1815, 4 x 6 In.		1560
Tinder, Round, Embossed Stars, Applied Handle, Candle Socket Lid, Striker, Flint, Lid		59
Tinder, Sheet Iron, Bone Plaque, Engraved, c.1775, 2 x 2 ¾ In.		215
Tinder, Tin, Oval, Candle Socket On Lid, Iron Striker, U.S.A., 1800s, 4 ½ In.		353
Tobacco, Carved Sailing Ship, City Background, Seated Dragon, 10 In.		360
Trinket, Agate, Jeweled, Egg Shape, Footed, Engraved Scroll Design, 1899, 3 x 2 ½ In.		1121
Trinket, Cut Glass, Gilt Bronze, Globular, Lift Lid, Swan Finial, Dolphin Supports, 12 In.		813
Trinket, Flower, Turned Designs, Watercolor, Cantered Corners, Pasteboard, 6 x 4 ¾ In.		9375
Trinket, Gilt Metal, Pietra Dura, Textured Flowers, Velvet, 2 Compartments, 1 ½ x 1 ½ In.		178
Trinket, Gold, Enamel, Jeweled, Diamond Accent, Persian Style, 1 ⅛ x 2 ¾ In.		5900
Trinket, Lead, Octagonal, Lid, Oval Finial, 5 x 4 ½ In.		180
Trinket, Lid, Turquoise, Round, Carved, Bats, Shou Character, Chinese, 1900s, 3 ½ In. Diam.		2880
Trinket, Mahogany, Rosewood, Inlaid, George III, Hinged Lid, England, c.1815, 6 x 12 In.		236
Trinket, Marquetry Inlaid, Geometric Designs, 5 ½ x 10 ¾ In.		443
Trinket, Painted, Angel, Heart, Flowers, Birds, Flowers, J. Murphy, Lancaster, Pa., 3 x 5 In.		47
Trinket, Painted, Green & Black, Leather Hinges, Lid, c.1815, 4 x 7 In.		711
Trinket, Parquetry, Georgian Building Shape, Hinged Lid, England, c.1820, 12 x 18 In.		3120
Trinket, Pine, Inlaid, Paint, Hinged Lid, Sperm Whale, Ivory Heart, c.1885, 2 ⅞ x 8 In.		1440
Trinket, Pine, Red, Gold, Black Tulip Design, Painted, c.1815, 2 ½ x 5 ½ In.		2607
Trinket, Quartz, Lapis, Cylindrical, Gold Mount, Lid, 2 ½ x 1 ¾ In.		295
Trinket, Softwood, Yellow Ground, Brown Sponge Paint, Molded Lid, 3 ¾ x 8 ½ In.		384
Trinket, Zitan, Carved, Dragon, Lid, Chinese, 7 x 11 In.		720
Utensil, Walnut, Cutout Handle, Divided, Pa., c.1850, 6 ¼ x 15 ¼ In.		390
Vanity, Lid, Child Kneeling, Porcelain, Kimono, Germany, c.1925, 6 ½ In.	*illus*	114
Vanity, Pincushion Doll, Woman On Lid, Sevres, Dressel Kister, c.1910, 10 In.	*illus*	912
Wall, Carved, Half Barrel Shaped, Hinged Lid, Shaped Hanging Plate, 10 ½ In.		239
Wall, Cutout Door, Stag Design, Carved, Painted, 15 ¾ x 10 ¾ In.		563
Wall, Oak, Slide Lid, England, c.1850, 4 x 17 ½ In.		207
Wall, Pine, Arrows, Curved Shape, Green, Yellow Paint, c.1910, 11 x 10 In.		273
Wall, Pine, Blue Paint, Slant Front, Arch Top, Lift Lid, Drawer, c.1850, 12 x 9 In.		1175
Wall, Pine, Open, Lower Rod, Carved, Sheaf Of Wheat, Continental, c.1870, 22 x 9 ½ In.		88
Wall, Pine, Paint, Cutout Back, c.1820, 13 x 9 ¼ In.		1185
Wall, Pine, Scrolls, Heart Pendant, Carved, Painted, c.1920, 23 x 12 In.		104
Wall, Poplar, Red Paint, Pa., 11 x 10 ½ In.		415
Wall, Softwood, Red Paint, Arched Backboard, Hole, Hinged Slant Lids, 1800s, 13 x 14 In.		708
Wall, Walnut, Drawer, Cutout Hanger, Slant Lid, c.1850, 11 x 12 In.		474
Wall, Walnut, Punched Designs, Blue, Green Paint, c.1850, 28 x 11 ½ In.		207
Wall, Wood, Shaped Backsplash, Red Paint, Lid, 12 x 8 ½ In.		259
Wall, Wooden, Paint, Pierced Shaped Back, Red Guilloche Design, 12 x 11 In.		900
Wallpaper, Flowers, Blue, White, Oval, 10 x 11 In.		450
Wallpaper, Flowers, Lid, Pennsylvania, c.1850, 4 ½ x 6 ½ In.		330
Wallpaper, Fruit Basket, Figures, Landscape, Oval, 10 x 15 In.		1140
Wallpaper, New York City Hall, Blue Ground, c.1895, 12 ¾ x 17 In.		480
Wallpaper, Portrait, Lafayette, c.1850, 2 x 4 ½ In.		676
Wallpaper, Urn, Buildings, Blue Seascape Ground, Oval, 12 x 15 In.		540
Wallpaper, Wood, Parrot Scene, Yellow Ground, c.1835, 10 x 17 In.		540
Watch Hutch, Tall Clock, Mahogany, Ivory, Bone, 1800s, 14 ½ x 4 In.	*illus*	1920
Whalebone, Brass Tack Design, Loop Handle, 1 ½ x 1 ¾ In.		236
Wood, Carved Tavern Figures, Dogs, Sheep, c.1850, 6 In.		688
Wood, Divided, Blue Paint, Bronze, 5 ¾ x 8 ½ In.		100
Wood, Eagle Carved, Shaped Back, Footed, Lift Lid, 20 In.		720
Wood, Flower Band, 2 Coat Of Arms, Yellow Paint, 7 ½ x 12 ½ In.		600
Wood, Flower, Scroll, Deep Red Ground, Paint, Initials A.D., Dome Lid		10200

Bronze, Bust, Lady Liberty, Crown, Ormolu Bars, Eagle Support, Continental, 10 In.
$1,673

Neal Auction Co.

Bronze, Cannon, 50 Cal. Barrel, Inscriptions, Wood, Japan, c.1850, 6 ¾ x 10 In.
$593

James D. Julia Auctioneers

Bronze, Censer, Archaic Style, Cicada Design, Inscription, Chinese, 1800s, 4 ¾ In.
$122

James D. Julia Auctioneers

B

Bronze, Container, Ice, Jian, Lion Head Handles, Incised Mark, Chinese, 1900s, 10 In.
$29,520

Neal Auction Co.

Bronze, Ewer, Cupid, Standing On Turtle, Shell Shape Jug, Renaissance Style, c.1900, 19 In.
$1,045

New Orleans Auction Galleries, Inc.

Bronze, Planter, Elephant Handles, Chinese, 8 x 24 x 16 In.
$575

Cottone Auctions

Wood, Grain Painted, Domed Hinged Lid, Wrought Metal Lock, 9 x 24 x 12 In.	146
Wood, Green Paint, Dome Lid, c.1845, 24 x 25 In.	403
Wood, Hexagon, Red, Applied Hearts, Cream, Heart Shape Finial, Wreath, 6 x 10 In.	201
Wood, Painted Birds, Flowers, Eggs, Pale Green Ground, Dome Lid, c.1905, 9 x 10 In.	236
Wood, Parquetry, Inlaid Artwork, Velvet Lined, U.S.A., c.1900, 5 ½ x 12 In.	176
Wood, Silver Wrap, Tooled Line, Dot Lid Pattern, Marked T. Fres, France, c.1930, 7 x 1 ½ In.	300
Writing, Calamander, Brass, Rectangular, Opens To Velvet Slope, Fitted, England, 6 x 14 In.	234
Writing, Satinwood, Painted Shells, Seaweed, Roses, Fruit, Sawtooth Borders, 3 x 10 In.	120
Writing, Sea Captain's, Bird's-Eye Maple, Hinged Lid, Brass Handles, Drawer, 8 x 22 In.	475
Writing, Walnut, Inlay, Geometric, Inscription, Pen Tray, Compartments, 10 x 20 In. .....*illus*	89

BOY SCOUT collectibles include any material related to scouting, including patches, manuals, and uniforms. The Boy Scout movement in the United States started in 1910. The first Jamboree was held in 1937. Girl Scout items are listed under their own heading.

Bank, Plastic, Upper Torso, A Cub Scout Saves, Embossed, 6 ¾ In.	60
Bolo, Cub Scout, Wolf, Paw Print, Diamond Shape, Brass, Black Cord, 1960s, 1 x 1 In.	22
Canteen, Cloth Cover, Mirror Co., c.1960	20
Cap Badge, Patrol Leader, Be Prepared, Brass, Silver Finish, 1920s, 2 x 1 In.	95
Cub Master's Pack Book, Green, 309 Pages, 1943, 4 ½ x 7 In.	15
Good Turn Token, Logo, Motto, Pledge, Bronze, 1950s, 1 In. Diam.	15
Handbook, Norman Rockwell, Bill Harcourt, 1985	18
Handkerchief, Scout, Kneeling, Scouting Scenes, Cotton, c.1915, 15 x 15 In.	43
Kerchief Clasp, Metal, Insignia, Rope Like Design, Green, 1950s, 1 ¼ x 1 ¼ In.	10
Medal, Jamboree, Irvine Ranch, Calif., Covered Wagon, July, 1953, 1 ½ In.	10
Patch, Camporee, Log Cabins, Pine Trees, Brown, Green, 1960s, 2 ⅞ In.	7
Pin, Fleur-De-Lis, Enameled, Red, Heart Shape, Eagle, Be Prepared, ⅝ x ⅝ In.	40
Plaque, Composition, Scout Oath, Insignia, Brown, 1950s, 5 ¼ x 3 ¼ In.	25
Pocket Knife, Folding, 3 Blades, Logo, Imperial Co., Opens To 5 ½ In.	22

BRADLEY & HUBBARD is a name found on many metal objects. Walter Hubbard and his brother-in-law, Nathaniel Lyman Bradley, started making cast iron clocks, tables, frames, andirons, bookends, doorstops, lamps, chandeliers, sconces, and sewing birds in 1854 in Meriden, Connecticut. The company became Bradley & Hubbard Manufacturing Company in 1875. Charles Parker Company bought the firm in 1940. Bradley & Hubbard items may be found in other sections that include metal.

Candlestick, Finger, Brass, Arts & Crafts, 5 In.	74
Lamp, 16 Panels, Cast Socket Cluster, Slag Glass, 8 Panels, Ribbed, 25 In.	1350
Lamp, Copper, Hammered, Mica Shade, c.1920, 22 x 8 In.	492
Lamp, Double Student Brass, Green Glass Shades, Paint, c.1890, 21 ½ In.	246
Lamp, Double Student Brass, White Glass Shades, Paint, c.1890, 21 In.	180
Lamp, Floor, Oil, 4-Footed, Mums, Painted, 66 In.	2195
Lamp, Gourd Base, Paneled Shade, Reverse Painted Flower Urns & Swags, 24 In.	518
Lamp, Octagonal Panel Shade, Metal Poinsettia Overlay, Brass Base, 16 x 21 In.	1098
Lamp, Oil, Cherub, Butterfly, Birds, Ball Shade, c.1880, 22 In.	895
Lamp, Sconce, Candle, Patinated Metal, Smoke Caps, c.1900, 14 x 6 ½ In., Pair	100
Lamp, Student, 2-Light, Brass, Double Arm, 25 In.	273
Letter Holder, Brass, Footed, 3 x 4 In.	28
Letter Holder, Stag Jumping Over Fence, Dogs, 9 ¼ x 5 x 6 In.	229
Match Safe, Brass, Striker Pad, Geometric Design, Square Base, 3 In.	185
Paperweight, Mouse On Biscuit, Bronze, Cold Paint, c.1870, 4 x 2 In.	295
Plaque, Woman With Cape, Hollyberry Headband, 8 In.	150 to 450
Rack, Book, Brass, Signed, 13 x 9 In.	57
Snuffbox, Bronze, Brown Patina, Round Edges, c.1900, 3 x 1 ⅝ In.	85

BRASS has been used for decorative pieces and useful tablewares since ancient times. It is an alloy of copper, zinc, and other metals. Additional brass items may be found under Bell, Candlestick, Tool, or Trivet.

Bar Cart, Bamboo Style Legs & Handle, 2 Glass Shelves, Caster Wheels, France, 1960s, 29 In.	875
Basin, Dovetailed, England, c.1815, 16 In. Diam.	276
Basket, Secessionist Style, Cold Paint Birch Bark Design, Handle, c.1907, 8 x 11 In.	625
Bath Fixture, Spout, Swan Head, Curved, Swivel Arm, Soap Dish, Art Deco, 22 In.	413
Bed Warmer, Engraved Design, Turned Wood Handle, 1700s, 46 x 11 In.	240
Bed Warmer, Flower Engraved Lid, Wood Handle, 45 In.	118
Bed Warmer, Hinged Lid, Flowers, Scrolling Turned Wood Handle, 44 In.	47
Bed Warmer, Hinged Lid, Pierced, Engraved, Flower Urn, Baluster Handle, c.1790, 46 x 12 In.	450

Bed Warmer, Square, Punched Side Design, c.1850, 22 x 4 ¾ In.	92
Bed Warmer, Tree Punched Lid, Wood Handle, c.1800	300
Bed Warmer, Turned Wood Handle, Engraved Design, 1700s, 46 x 11 In.	239
Bed Warmer, William & Mary, Star Pierced, Iron, Wood Handle, c.1690, 44 ½ In.	360
Box, Renaissance Revival Style, Cast, Hinged Lid, Faux Lock, Wood Lined, 5 x 4 In.	86
Box, Tobacco, Scrolls, Reclining Nude, Octagonal, Pierced Lid, Dutch, c.1700, 6 x 2 ¼ In.	531
Box, Tortoise Shape, Fish Shape Knops, Oval Lid, Gadrooned Bezel, 10 ¾ x 24 ½ In.	2337
Box, White Jade Cabochon, Mahogany Lining, Horace Potter, c.1915, 2 x 6 ¾ In. ....*illus*	1875
Box, Wood, Mottled Green, Brown, Yellow Pinstripe, Dome Lid, New Eng., c.1830, 7 x 12 In.	360
Bucket, Kindling, Copper, Repousse Scene, Lion's Head Handles, 3 Paw Feet, c.1900, 17 In.	1075
Bucket, Wine, Oval, Lion's Head Ring Handles, 4 Tall Paw Feet, England, 11 x 19 x 14 In.	207
Card Tray, Angels, Fruit, Raised Devil Masks, Porcelain Plate, Cherubs, Garland, 8 x 11 In.	116
Cartridge Box, Crown & Shield On Flap, Round Suspension Rings, c.1800, 7 x 4 In.	180
Chocolate Pot, Hinged Lid, Wood Handle, Baluster, Banding, Curved Legs, c.1760, 10 In.	360
Coat Rack, Victorian, Bent Pole, Curved, 5 Hooks, 77 In.	240
Cocktail Set, Manhattan, N.B. Gedes, 6 Goblets, Shaker, c.1938, Tray 15 x 12 In., 8 Piece	15000
Collar, Dog, Engraved Horse, Coach Scenes, Text, England, c.1820, 5 In.	1320
Crucifix, Enameled, Cyrillic Text, Yellow, Blue, Russia, 6 ⅜ In.	200
Door Push Plate, Pelican, American Shield, Crest, Eagle, Paul Revere Co., 10 x 4 In., Pair	270
Ewer, Beaker Shape, Dish Foot, Angled Handle, Lid, Russia, 13 ½ In.	180
Figurine, Lion, Chinese, Paw On Ball, Ornate Base, 20 In., Pair	960
Figurine, Lion, Fused Glass Eyes, Mexico, Signed Pal Kepenyes, c.1950, 7 x 6 ½ In.	563
Figurine, Rooster, Mouth Open Wide, Mexico, 24 In.	750
Hourglass, Mahogany, Stamped Unsworth Warrington, England, c.1850, 12 In.	770
Kaleidoscope, Oak Base, Nickel Plated Standard, Brass Barrel, Rings, c.1910, 12 x 11 In.	461
Lectern, Eagle, Lion Feet, Turned Pedestal, Stamped, c.1900, 78 In.	5000
Lectern, Gothic Revival, Book Stand, Tripod Base, Openwork Scroll, c.1900, 57 x 18 In.	354
Magazine Rack, Swan Shape, France, c.1965, 19 ¾ x 26 ½ In.	938
Mortar & Pestle, Square Handles, 12 ½ In.	31
Ornament, Wall, Cast, Rococo Style, Leaf Scrolling, Woman's Mask, 13 ¾ In., Pair	69
Pail, Spun, Ansonia, Ct., 1851, 13 In.	59
Samovar, Russia, Wood Handle, 1859, 17 In.	59
Samovar, Square, Footed, Spout, Handles, Russia, 20 x 10 In.	210
Samovar, Undertray, 4-Footed, Pedestal Base, Russia, 1800s, 19 In.	438
Samovar, Urn Shape, Swivel Side Handles, Detachable Smokestack, Russia, 1800s, 21 In.	180
Sculpture, Butterfly Shape, Signed C. Jere 1978, 36 x 36 In., Pair	1500
Sculpture, Giraffe, Stamped Hagenauer, Austria, 7 ¼ x 17 ¼ In.	1500
Sculpture, Puzzle, Portrait Of Michelle, Miguel Berrocal, Spain, 1969, 4 x 3 In.	563
Sculpture, Sailor Courting Farm Maiden, Gilt Patina, Pilet, 1900, 27 In.	813
Sculpture, Wall, Bird, Signed C. Jere, 1966, 59 x 20 In.	225
Smoking Set, Alabaster Cigarette Holder, Octagonal, 9 ½ x 8 In.	215
Smoking Set, Victorian, Marble Cup, Candle Holder, Ornate Embossed, 7 ½ In.	113
Stencil, Alphabets, Numbers, Fractions, Symbols, Rotating, 1800s, 13 In. ....*illus*	360
Stirrups, Marked FF 50, Drain Hole, Engraved Strap, 10 ½ x 5 In., Pair	120
Tazza, Empire Style, Snake Handles, Black Marble, Square Base, France, c.1890, 11 In., Pair *illus*	354
Teakettle, Stand, Swing Handle, Dome Lid, Bulbous Body, Gooseneck Spout, 1700s, 11 In.	240
Teapot, Hunters, Horseback, Scroll, Bottle Shape, Loop Handle, Dome Lid, 18 ½ In.	584
Tobacco Box, Honesty, Coin Slot, Button, Handle, Ball Feet, c.1850, 7 x 9 In.	330
Umbrella Stand, 4 Lion Mask And Ring Handles, c.1890, 23 ¾ In.	313
Vase, Champleve, Foo Dog Handles, Multicolor Enamel, Flowers, Leaves, Shields, 13 ½ In.	47
Vase, Engraved, Flowers, Inscribed Superintendent, Found Beach, N.C., India, c.1900, 22 In.	144
Vase, Stick, Foo Dog, Holder On Back, 9 In., Pair	480

BRASTOFF, *see Sascha Brastoff category.*

BREAD PLATE, *see various silver categories, porcelain factories, and pressed glass patterns.*

BRIDE'S BOWLS OR BASKETS were usually one-of-a-kind novelties made in American and European glass factories. They were especially popular about 1880 when the decorated basket was often given as a wedding gift. Cut glass baskets were popular after 1890. All bride's bowls lost favor about 1905. Bride's bowls and baskets may also be found in other glass sections. Check the index at the back of the book.

Blue On White, Bristol Glass, Scalloped Rim, Flowers, Middletown Plate Frame, 12 In.	173
Blue Opalescent, Hobnail, Ruffled, Meriden Silver Plate, 4-Footed, 6 x 10 In.	400
Cranberry Glass, Multicolor Flowers, Rib Optic, Clear Rim, c.1890, 4 x 9 ¼ In.	207

Bronze, Planter, Elephants, Japan, Late 19th Century, 16 x 21 In.
$9,200

Cottone Auctions

Bronze, Sculpture, Arab, Shield, Sword, Palm Tree, Cold Paint, Geschutzt, c.1900, 8 x 3 In.
$1,215

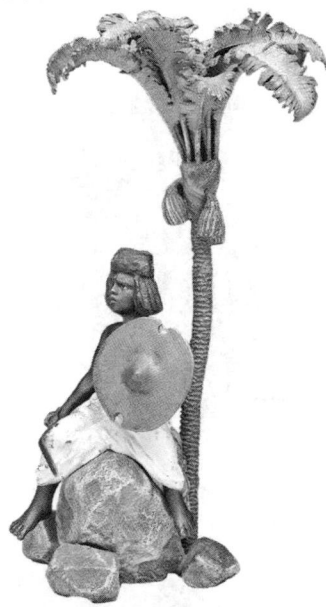

James D. Julia Auctioneers

Bronze, Sculpture, Barye, Antoine Louis, Lion, Stamped, 1800s, 9 x 15 ½ In.
$2,875

Rago Arts & Auction Center

B

Bronze, Sculpture, Bergman, Arab, Sable
Antelope Head, 1838-94, 5 x 5 ½ In.
$2,015

James D. Julia Auctioneers

Bronze, Sculpture, Bodhisattva, Seated,
Lotus Stalk, Nepal, c.1800s, 7 ¼ In.
$2,520

Skinner Auctioneers & Appraisers

Bronze, Sculpture, Bouret, E., Boy
Standing On Turtle, Late 1800s, 9 ½ In.
$748

Early Auction Co.

Cranberry, Ruffled Rim, Coin Spot, Silver Plated, 13 In.		63
Cranberry, White Glass, Enameled Flowers, Ruffled Rim, Metal Handle, 11 ½ In.		162
Mauve Over Opal, Crimped Edge, Derby Silver Co. Frame, 8 x 12 In.	*illus*	75
Milk Glass, Cranberry Rim, Wavy, Victorian, 12 In.		79
Milk Glass, Purple Rim, Wavy, Victorian, 12 In.		68
Mother-Of-Pearl, Squared, Ruffled Rim, Pink Satin Diamond Quilt, Plated Frame, 10 In.		150
Pink & White Cased Bowl, Wilcox Silver Plated Frame, 10 x 10 In.		236
Rose, Shaded, Ruffled Rim, Gilt, Enameled Flowers, Metal Frame, Rogers, Smith & Co., 11 In.		288
Rubina Verde, Ruffled, Silver Plated Scrolled Frame, E. Webster, 12 x 14 In.		215
Satin Glass, Purple, Ruffled Rim, Gold Scrolling, Blue Daisies, 8 ½ In.		86
Silver Plate, Scalloped, Leaf Border, 12 x 10 x 10 In.		145
Spatter Glass, Cranberry Opal Flakes, Pinched Clear Rim, 4 ½ x 7 ½ In.		230
Swirled, Pink Cased, Silver Plated Frame, Footed, 2 Handles, 6 ½ x 13 In.		175
Victorian, Swallows, Violets, Scalloped Rim, Green, Purple, Metal Frame, 15 x 12 In.		152
Yellow Overlay Glass Quilted Cup, Silver Plated Frame, 12 ½ In.		158

BRISTOL glass was made in Bristol, England, after the 1700s. The Bristol glass most often seen today is a Victorian, lightweight opaque glass that is often blue. Some of the glass was decorated with enamels.

Decanter, Green, Blown, Applied Strawberry Prunts, Rummerform Hock Glass, 11 ½ In.		492
Vase, Asian Man Sitting Under Tree By River, Orange & Gray Flowers, Pinched, 12 ¾ In.		25
Vase, Blue Enamel Flowers, Gilt Border, Oriental Pheasant, Paper Label, 17 In., Pair		472
Vase, Clambroth, Wavy Blue Rim, 9 ¾ In.		30
Vase, Fire Glow, Painted, Cream, Gold Flowers, 11 In., Pair		89
Vase, Pink Enamel Designs, Blue Ground, Bottle Shape, 10 In., Pair		150
Vase, Pink Enamel Flowers, Green Ground, Bottle Shape, 10 In.		261
Vase, White, White & Yellow Daisies, Blue Flowers, Pink Furled Rim, 11 In.		143

BRITANNIA, *see Pewter category*

BRONZE is an alloy of copper, tin, and other metals. It is used to make figurines, lamps, and other decorative objects. Bronze lamps are listed in the Lamp category. Pieces listed here date from the eighteenth, nineteenth, and twentieth centuries.

Ashtray, Cigar, Matchbox Holder, Bird Design, Incised F. Gornik, c.1930, 4 x 7 In.		344
Ashtray, Osmond, Maurice, Lily Pad Shape, Reclining Nude, Signed, Art Deco, 8 ¾ In.		308
Bowl, Loop Handles, Compressed Body, Foot Rim, Ming, 6-Character Seal Mark, 9 ½ In.		900
Bowl, Squat, Bulbous, Ring Foot, Saigas, Flowers, Tibet, 1800s, 4 In. Diam.		237
Box, Medieval Style, Figural Relief, Bracket Feet, Hinged Lid, 3 ½ x 8 ¼ In.		196
Bust, Abraham Lincoln, Gorham, c.1920, 18 In.		5938
Bust, Apollo, Sideward Glancing, Drape, Pedestal Base, 17 x 10 In.		923
Bust, Ball, T., Woman, Eyes Downcast, La Petite Pensee, 1871, 16 In.		1440
Bust, Barbedienne, George Washington, c.1800, 3 ¾ In.		320
Bust, Bergman, Franz, Bedouin, Man, Woman, Marble Base, c.1910, 5 In., Pair		800
Bust, Boy, Pan Flute, Art Deco Style, Marble Base, 15 x 21 In.		1000
Bust, Bush, H.K., U.S. Grant, Brown, Socle, 1885, 7 ⅜ In.		1250
Bust, Dante, Capped Head, Marble Base, c.1850, 12 ¾ In.		365
Bust, Diana, Profile, Hair Crescent, Marble Base, c.1950, 17 ¾ In.		531
Bust, Diana, Waisted Pedestal, Square Base, 19th Century, 24 In.		1200
Bust, Epstein, Sir J., M.S. Myers, Man, Wearing Suit, c.1945, 17 In.		600
Bust, George Washington, Profile, Cloak, Sash, White Marble Pedestal, 19 ¾ In.		3438
Bust, Gutierrez, G., Maiden, Hat, Collar, Marble Base, 19 In.	*illus*	625
Bust, Henry-Bonnard, George Washington, 1898, 19 In.		948
Bust, Hercules, Armor, Lion Head Helmet, Stepped Round Socle, c.1900, 18 ½ In.		1476
Bust, Indian, Braids, Feather Necklace, 1902, 14 x 8 In.		2629
Bust, Jeanne D'Arc, Amour, France, c.1890, 12 In.		649
Bust, Lady Liberty, Crown, Ormolu Bars, Eagle Support, Continental, 10 In.	*illus*	1673
Bust, Moeller, J. Howling Dog, Snout Facing Upward, Round Wood Base, c.1950, 9 In.		413
Bust, Muller, Longfellow, Socle Base, Signed, 11 In.		356
Bust, Napoleon, Marble Base, c.1950, 31 x 17 In.		805
Bust, Napoleon, Sideways Glancing, Hat, Marble Stepped Base, 15 x 11 In.		1230
Bust, Oscar Meyer, Mustache, Marble Base, 1900s, 20 In.		588
Bust, Tembach, Joseph, William Rush, Long Hair, 1971, 20 In.		243
Bust, Van Der Straeten, Georges, Young Woman, Tricorn Hat, 13 ¾ x 7 In.		288
Bust, Victorian Woman, Hat, 16 In.		294
Cannon, 50 Cal. Barrel, Inscriptions, Wood, Japan, c.1850, 6 ¾ x 10 In.	*illus*	593

Cassolette, Campagna Shape, Pedestal, Interior Candle Socket, 1800s, 10 In., Pair	418
Censer, 3 Animal-Head Feet, Handles, Pierced Dome Lid, Buffalos, c.1900, 17 ½ In.	9560
Censer, Archaic Style, Cicada Design, Inscription, Chinese, 1800s, 4 ¾ In. ....*illus*	122
Censer, Bell Shape, Animal Form Handles, Scrolling Flowers, 1700s, 3 x 3 ⅝ In.	3259
Censer, Footed, Upturned Handles, Squat, Chinese, c.1800, 8 x 8 ½ In.	369
Censer, Lid, Diapered, Open Ring Handles, Round Foot, Finial, Chinese, 1800s, 23 In.	590
Censer, Phoenix Shape, Folded Wings, Hanging, c.1900, 6 ½ x 8 ¼ In.	153
Censer, Pierced Lid, Head Twisted Back, Foo Dog, c.1850, 12 In.	4780
Censer, Squat, Dragon Upright Handles, Tripod, Tapered Feet, c.1900, 4 ¾ x 8 In.	767
Censer, Squat, Ring Foot, Mythological Beast, Lug Handles, Marked, 3 x 7 ½ In.	2820
Censer, Squat, Saucer Foot, Foo Dog Lug Handles, Gilt, 6 In.	6325
Censer, Tripod, Bulbous, Waisted Neck, Marked, Chinese, 1800s, 5 In.	1080
Centerpiece, Empire Style, Figural, 3-Part Base, Caryatids, Pierced Bowl, c.1900, 24 In.	2952
Centerpiece, Green Glass Insert, Dore Swags, Mounts, France, c.1900, 7 ½ x 19 In.	938
Centerpiece, Hinged, Woman, Putto Climbing Rim, Dish Base, France, c.1890, 12 In.	281
Chalice, Gothic Style, Dore, Royalty Porcelain Plaques, Pierced Lid, c.1890, 11 ½ In., Pair	1416
Container, Ice, Jian, Lion Head Handles, Incised Mark, Chinese, 1900s, 10 In. ....*illus*	29520
Cup, Figural Dragon Support, Japan, 6 x 8 In.	330
Desk Set, Art Nouveau, Celtic Knot, Gilt, Marshall Field, 20th Century, 15 Piece	1722
Dish, Dragon & Pearl Design, Scalloped, Water & Sky, Chinese, c.1900, 9 In. Diam.	295
Drapery Ring, Neoclassical, Engine Turned, Gilt, 1800s, 4 ½ x 9 In.	122
Ewer, Bell Foot, Animal Spout, Loop Handle, Lid Chained To Handle, 1700s, 7 x 6 In.	492
Ewer, Cupid, Standing On Turtle, Shell Shape Jug, Renaissance Style, c.1900, 19 In. ......*illus*	1045
Fountain, Figural, Venus Maritima, Seminude, Round Base, 1800s, 16 x 7 In.	1220
Frame, Oak Leaves, Acorns, Rustic Bezel & Foot, Easel, 14 ¼ x 10 In.	369
Garniture, Goddess, Nude, Seated, Wings, Black Seat, c.1820, 7 x 14 In., Pair	1416
Globe, Celestial, Islamic Inscriptions, Middle East, 6 ¾ In. Diam.	1045
Hook, Clothes, Wall Mount, Flower, Grape Designs, 6 In., Pair	130
Incense Burner, Figural, Chinese, c.1800, 2 In.	362
Inkstand, Gilt Bronze, Scrolled Cartouche Crest, Candleholders, Mask, 9 x 17 In.	837
Jardiniere, Gilt, Classical Scenes, Branches, Handles, Paw Feet, c.1885, 12 x 25 In.	5228
Letter Opener, Hound Head, Monogram, Austria, 13 In.	780
Medallion, Loudray, C., Lute Player, Face, Round, 2 ¾ In. Diam.	240
Medallion, Queen Victoria, 60 Years Of Reign, 2 ³⁄₁₆ In.	78
Mirror, Banded Knob, Writhing Dragons, 5 ¼ In. Diam.	615
Mortar & Pestle, Engraved Bands, 6 ⅞ In.	300
Paperweight, Lion's Head, Curly Mane, 2 ¾ In.	59
Pedestal, Embossed Leaf Base, 48 In.	652
Plant Stand, Gilt, Iron, Scroll Legs, Ram's Heads, France, 1900s, 12 In.	590
Planter, Elephant Handles, Chinese, 8 x 24 x 16 In. ....*illus*	575
Planter, Elephants, Japan, Late 19th Century, 16 x 21 In. ....*illus*	9200
Planter, Square, Lobed Corners, Bracket Feet, 1800s, 6 ½ x 16 ½ In.	1080
Plaque, Aphrodite Riding In Shell, Multicolor, Embossed, 27 x 15 ½ In.	325
Plaque, Barbedienne, F., Men, Boys, Looking At Book, France, 11 x 7 In.	452
Plaque, Battle Of Amazons, Marked, 26 In. Diam.	812
Plaque, Boy, Playing Horn, Reclining Girl, 6 ½ x 19 ½ In.	406
Plaque, Hercules & Cerberus, Cast Relief, Oval, 15 x 11 ¼ In.	242
Plaque, Men, Doublet Attire, Flagstaffs, Swords, c.1900, 25 x 10 In., Pair	113
Plaque, Neoclassical, Kneeling Nymph, Lamp, Round Walnut Frame, 1800s, 11 In.	299
Plaque, Warner, O.L., Man & Woman In Profile, Round, 1880, 10 In.	1375
Rain Drum, Pinched Waist, Handle, Burma, 11 x 23 In.	944
Sconce, Goat Shape, Eating Leaves, Art Glass Shade, Electric, 1900s, 17 x 13 In.	2125
Sculpture, 2 Dancers, Male Figure Holding Female In Air, Marble Base, 1918, 38 In.	1416
Sculpture, 2 Sea Turtles, Swimming, Round Base, Harmony, 28 ½ In.	590
Sculpture, 2 Whippets, Marble Base, Paris, 1875, 7 x 10 In.	413
Sculpture, 3 Birds, On Branch, Cold Paint, c.1885, 3 ¾ x 6 ½ In.	243
Sculpture, 3 Figures, Struggling, Nude, Round Marble Base, 1900s, 32 ¼ In.	777
Sculpture, 3 Muses, Standing, Embracing, Marble Base, France, c.1900, 23 ½ In.	2242
Sculpture, African Warrior, Crawling, Curved Blade, Austria, c.1900, 6 In.	360
Sculpture, Aitken, R., Orpheus, Playing Lute, Green Patina, 24 x 21 In.	1416
Sculpture, Alligator, Alert Pose, Original Patina, 44 In.	1342
Sculpture, American Bison, Stone Base, Inscribed Milo, 8 ¼ x 11 In.	570
Sculpture, Angelfish, Gilded Fins, Slate Base, Incised, Siberia, c.1950, 15 ⅜ In.	1680
Sculpture, Apollo Belvedere, Standing, Nude, Drape, Round Base, c.1800, 24 In.	3585
Sculpture, Arab, Running, Rifle, Cold Paint, Marked, Geschutzt, c.1900, 10 In.	2133
Sculpture, Arab, Shield, Sword, Palm Tree, Cold Paint, Geschutzt, c.1900, 8 x 3 In. ....*illus*	1215

Bronze, Sculpture, Cannon, Military, Wood Wagon, 30 x 14 x 10 In.
$570

The Stein Auction Co.

Bronze, Sculpture, Carrier-Belleuse, Albert, Diana, Greyhound, Signed, 28 ½ In.
$3,500

Rago Arts & Auction Center

Bronze, Sculpture, Chiparus, D.H., Nude, Seated, Stamped, c.1925, 17 ½ x 19 In.
$492

Skinner Auctioneers & Appraisers

TIP
Never oil a basket. It will attract dirt.

Bronze, Sculpture, Chiparus, Demetre, Friends Forever, Ivory, Marble, c.1910, 25 In.
$60,000

Cowan's Auctions

Bronze, Sculpture, Chiparus, Demetre, Nubian Dancer, Ivory, Marble Base, 1925, 16 In.
$46,740

New Orleans Auction Galleries, Inc.

Bronze, Sculpture, Clark, Allan, Charmion, Nude Woman, Falcon, Marble Base, Signed, 14 ¾ In.
$12,000

Skinner Auctioneers & Appraisers

Sculpture, Archer, Black Marble Base, Signed, c.1900, 12 ½ x 3 ½ In.	359
Sculpture, Archer, Holding Crossbow, Marble Base, Germany, c.1900, 8 ⅛ In.	600
Sculpture, Arhat Pindola Bharadaja, Gilt, Tibet, 18th Century, 3 ¾ In.	19280
Sculpture, Aronson, David, Choir Director, Holding Paper, Arms Out, c.1950, 11 In.	438
Sculpture, Art Nouveau, Coiled Cobra, France, 15 x 6 ½ In.	439
Sculpture, Ballerina, Dancing, Toe Pointed, Revolving Round Base, France, c.1900, 16 In.	575
Sculpture, Barbedienne, Narcissus, Cast, Brown Patina, 25 ½ In.	978
Sculpture, Barrias, Louis Ernest, Nature Revealing Herself To Science, Silvered, c.1900, 21 In.	10000
Sculpture, Barthelemy, Loie Fuller, Standing, Raised Arms, Ivory, Marble Base, c.1925, 16 In.	3600
Sculpture, Barye, Antoine Louis, Lion, Stamped, 1800s, 9 x 15 ½ In. *illus*	2875
Sculpture, Basket, Woven, Twig Handles & Feet, Native Boy, Seated, Book, 7 In. Diam.	1320
Sculpture, Bearded Man, Holding Spear, Eagle On Back, Pedestal Base, c.1890, 13 In.	1625
Sculpture, Berge, Edward, Frog Baby, Verdigris Patina, Marked, 7 ¾ In.	1680
Sculpture, Bergman, Arab, Cold Paint, Standing, Arms Outstretched, Base, Austria, c.1900, 13 In.	1400
Sculpture, Bergman, Arab, Sable Antelope Head, 1838-94, 5 x 5 ½ In. *illus*	2015
Sculpture, Bergman, Child, Standing Outside Thatched Tent, Cold Paint, c.1890, 5 In.	2100
Sculpture, Bergman, Dancer, Erotic, Holding Skirt, Namgreb, Austria, 1900s, 7 x 6 In.	711
Sculpture, Bergman, Egyptian Figure, Nude Woman Inside, Erotic, Namgreb, 5 In.	3000
Sculpture, Bergman, Man, Praying, On Rug, Shoes Off, Cold Paint, c.1910, 5 ⅝ In.	1020
Sculpture, Bergman, Moor, Running, Holding Stick, Multicolor Enamel, c.1900, 9 ¼ In.	1353
Sculpture, Bergman, Peddler, At Table, Cold Paint, 5 ½ In.	1380
Sculpture, Bergman, Tray, Arab, Riding Camel, Onyx, Cold Paint, Namgreb, 5 ⅛ x 6 ⅜ In.	1200
Sculpture, Bergman, Water Boy, Seated Next To Jug, Cold Paint, c.1910, 4 ½ In.	1500
Sculpture, Bird, Golden Pheasant, Cold Paint, Austria, 20th Century, 5 ¼ In.	270
Sculpture, Bissel, G.E., Abraham Lincoln, Bust, Brown, Green Patina, 1898, 6 ¾ In.	688
Sculpture, Blacksmith, Resting, Carved Base, France, c.1920, 15 ¾ In.	120
Sculpture, Bodhisattva, Seated, Lotus Base, Flaming Mandorla, 11 ⅛ In.	976
Sculpture, Bodhisattva, Seated, Lotus Stalk, Nepal, c.1800s, 7 ¼ In. *illus*	2520
Sculpture, Bonegar, M.A., Woman, Peasant, Horse, Wolfhound, Oval Base, Russia, c.1910, 11 In.	8260
Sculpture, Bonheur, Isidore-Jules, Jockey Sur Son Cheval, Signed, c.1880, 24 x 28 In.	1740
Sculpture, Borghese Gladiator, c.1885, 12 In.	418
Sculpture, Boucher, A., La Terre, Nude Man, Digging, 20 x 22 In.	2057
Sculpture, Boulton, J., Cougar, Impressed J. Boulton, c.1950, 8 ½ x 9 ½ In.	230
Sculpture, Bouret, E., Boy Standing On Turtle, Late 1800s, 9 ½ In. *illus*	748
Sculpture, Boy, Holding 2 Baskets, Marble Base, 10 ½ In.	181
Sculpture, Bucking Bronco, Marble Base, 1900s, 22 x 12 In.	554
Sculpture, Buddha Head, Cone Headpiece, Long Earlobes, Thailand, 1800s, 7 x 11 In.	236
Sculpture, Buddha Head, Elongated Earlobes, Curled Hair, Wood Pedestal, 1800s, 9 In.	1020
Sculpture, Buddha, Raised Right Hand, Plastic Base, 19th Century, 12 In.	9560
Sculpture, Buddha, Seated, Full Lotus Pose, Meditating, Gilded, 8 x 6 ½ In.	9360
Sculpture, Buddha, Seated, Lotus Throne, Gilt, Paint, 1900s, 8 x 5 ½ In.	236
Sculpture, Buddha, Seated, Lotus Tiered Pedestal, Arch, Thailand, c.1800, 9 x 6 In.	11800
Sculpture, Buddha, Standing, Jeweled Tunic, Gilt, Stepped Base, Thailand, 1800s, 21 In.	472
Sculpture, Buddha, Waisted Lotus Pedestal Base, 24 In.	1830
Sculpture, Bull, Striding, Patina, c.1900, 45 x 62 In.	3690
Sculpture, Cannon, Military, Wood Wagon, 30 x 14 x 10 In. *illus*	570
Sculpture, Captain Nathan Hale, Standing, Uniform, Stepped Base, 1773, 7 In.	538
Sculpture, Capy, H., Putto, On A Globe, First Raised, France, c.1860, 6 ¾ x 3 In.	188
Sculpture, Carrier-Belleuse, Albert, Diana, Greyhound, Signed, 28 ½ In. *illus*	3500
Sculpture, Carrier-Belleuse, Albert-Ernest Gypsy, Orpheus, Patina, Marble Base, 13 x 15 In.	265
Sculpture, Carrington, L., Crocodile Dreams, Boat, Passengers, Marble Base, 1990s, 17 x 17 In.	3250
Sculpture, Cat Figure, Egyptian Style, Faux Patina, 20 x 8 ¼ x 9 ¾ In.	276
Sculpture, Cemin, Man With Fish, On Back, Signed, Brazil, 1991, 23 x 13 In.	9375
Sculpture, Cheetah, Standing, Striding, Paint, 38 ½ x 12 In., Pair	3585
Sculpture, Cheyenne, Native American Warrior, Horse, Charging, Marble Base, 22 x 24 In.	688
Sculpture, Chiparus, D.H., Nude, Seated, Stamped, c.1925, 17 ½ x 19 In. *illus*	492
Sculpture, Chiparus, Demetre, Egyptian Dancer, Patina, Cold Paint, 1920s, 29 x 10 In.	10625
Sculpture, Chiparus, Demetre, Friends Forever, Ivory, Marble, c.1910, 25 In. *illus*	60000
Sculpture, Chiparus, Demetre, Nubian Dancer, Ivory, Marble Base, 1925, 16 In. *illus*	46740
Sculpture, Chrysalis, Nude Woman, Crouched, Long Hair, 1900s, 24 x 13 In.	3198
Sculpture, Clam Hunters, Barefoot Woman, Girl, Searching For Shellfish, c.1890, 41 In.	1230
Sculpture, Clark, Allan, Charmion, Nude Woman, Falcon, Marble Base, Signed, 14 ¾ In. *illus*	12000
Sculpture, Classical Figure, Holding Vessel On Shoulder, c.1850, 28 In.	345
Sculpture, Clesinger, Jean-Baptiste, Sappho, Seminude Woman, Rock, Lyre, 1800s, 14 In.	1845
Sculpture, Clodion, Michel Claude, Bacchante, Figure On Base, Brown Patina, c.1800, 36 In.	1438
Sculpture, Cobra, Coiled, Silvered, Antiqued, Mounted, Black Slate Base, 4 x 3 In.	955

Sculpture, Coinchon, J.A., Theodore, Pan, c.1880, 17 ¼ In.		688
Sculpture, Coming Through The Rye, 4 Cowboys, Galloping, Rifles, 28 x 33 In.		1416
Sculpture, Crane, Perched On Rock, Plants, Deer, Lotus, Flower, Japan, 53 In.		1320
Sculpture, Cupid, Seated On Log, Bow & Quiver, Doves, c.1900, 6 ¼ In.		240
Sculpture, Dalou, Aime-Jules, Peasant, France, 4 ¼ In.		854
Sculpture, Dalou, Woman, Carrying Pitcher, 4 ¾ In.		563
Sculpture, Dancer, Castanets, Raised Leg, Flowing Dress, Ivory, c.1900, 13 In.		4800
Sculpture, Dancer, Exotic, Seated, Curule Chair, Chin Resting On Hand, c.1900, 11 In.		8610
Sculpture, Dancing Boy, Engraved, Japan, c.1900, 10 In.		338
Sculpture, Dancing Monkey, Band Leader, Cold Paint, Austria, 3 ½ x 2 In.	*illus*	360
Sculpture, Dashwood, Lapwing, Standing, Signed, c.1950, 9 ¾ x 10 ¾ In.		1718
Sculpture, D'Aste, Joseph, Dutch Boy, Wood Clogs, Hat, Ivory, Hardstone Base, 8 ½ In.		650
Sculpture, Deity, Multiple Arms, Seated Lotus Throne, Java, 9th Century, 11 In.		6628
Sculpture, Diana, Standing, Draped Gown, Hair Up, Square Base, 32 In.		2032
Sculpture, Dog Band, Musical Instruments, Cold Paint, Vienna, c.1890, 1 ⅝ In., 11 Piece		1722
Sculpture, Dog, RCA Nipper, Seated, Head Cocked, Floppy Ears, 1900s, 14 x 14 In.		531
Sculpture, Dog, Striding, Black Marble Base, c.1960, 12 In.		295
Sculpture, Donoghue, John Talbott, Sophocles, Nude, Singing Praises To The Gods, 44 ½ In.		6396
Sculpture, Draped Woman, Standing, Holding Tambourine, Putto, France, 32 ½ In.		3250
Sculpture, Drappier, E., Farmer, Backing Horse, Signed, Paris, 13 x 19 In.		4248
Sculpture, Dumaige, Henri-Etienne, Calliope, Holding Stylus & Scroll, 21 In.	*illus*	1722
Sculpture, Dying Bull, Round Onyx Base, c.1900, 8 ½ x 10 In.		418
Sculpture, Eagle, Spread Wings, Cold Paint, Signed, Austria, 1900s, 4 ½ x 8 ½ In.		1007
Sculpture, Education Of Achilles By Centaur Chiron, Archery Lesson, c.1875, 17 x 18 In.		5313
Sculpture, Elephant, Ivory Tusks Up, Foot On Balls, Japan, 16 x 19 In.		1920
Sculpture, Elephant, Ivory Tusks, Natural Root Base, Signed, Japan, 12 x 12 In.	*illus*	920
Sculpture, Elephant, On Ball, Trunk Raised, Round Base, 13 In.		230
Sculpture, Elwell, Robert F., ndian In A Canoe, c.1930, 36 x 12 In.		1625
Sculpture, English Bulldog, Seated, Studded Collar, 1900s, 19 In.		480
Sculpture, Faun Of Pompeii, Nude, Dancing, Arms Up, Square Base, 33 ¼ In.		1375
Sculpture, Faun, Pan Playing Pipes, Round Base, Italy, c.1850, 9 ¼ In.		384
Sculpture, Foo Dog, Silvered, Seated, Collar, Chinese, 5 x 4 ½ In., Pair		600
Sculpture, Foundry Men, Miquel Blay Y Fabrega, 38 In.		5490
Sculpture, Fremiet, Emmanuel, Credo, Medieval Knight, Banner, 16 ¼ In.	*illus*	4800
Sculpture, Fugere, Dancer, With Castanets, Ivory, Gilt, Multicolor Cold Paint, 12 ¾ In.		2100
Sculpture, Ganesh, Standing On Lotus Base, 7 In.		104
Sculpture, Gaudez, A., Gypsy Maiden, Cast, Multicolor Dress, Holding Tray, Oval Base, 31 In.		1800
Sculpture, Gaudez, Adrien Etienne, Forgeron, Man, Hammer, Anvil, 17 In.		584
Sculpture, Gazing Jockey, On Horse, 13 In.		500
Sculpture, Girl, Baizeman, Saul, c.1940, 3 ½ In.		243
Sculpture, Girl, Holding Duck, 5 In.		51
Sculpture, Girl, Holding Watering Can, Hat, Round Base, U.S.A., 50 In.		1875
Sculpture, Girl, Nude, Standing, Reading, Continental, c.1800, 6 ¾ In.		438
Sculpture, Gladiator, Square Base, 22 In.		938
Sculpture, Gory, A., Nude Acrobat, Ivory Ball, Kneeling, Arm Raised, Art Deco, 22 In.		3500
Sculpture, Greek Warrior, Medusa Shield, Spear, Marble Base, 6 In.		308
Sculpture, Gross, C., Dance, Mother & Daughter, Wood Base, Signed, c.1925, 17 In.		4182
Sculpture, Gross, C., Woman, Nude, Reclining, Kicking Feet, Black Base, c.1980, 14 x 19 In.		885
Sculpture, Guandi, Seated On Bench, Armor, Robes, Dragon Roundels, Cap, 1900s, 9 In.		2880
Sculpture, Guanyin, Lacquered, Seated, Barefoot, Lotus Throne, Openwork, 1900s, 16 In.		1200
Sculpture, Guanyin, Seated, Buddhist Figures, Chinese, 6 ¼ x 4 ½ In.		123
Sculpture, Guanyin, Seated, Gilt, Robes, Round Pedestal, Chinese, 14 x 7 In.		1680
Sculpture, Guanyin, Silver Inlay, Seated, Barefoot, Chignon, Necklace, 1900s, 13 In.		2040
Sculpture, Hagenauer, Woman, Kneeling, Jug On Head, Nickel Base, Stamped WHW, 7 x 8 In.		625
Sculpture, Hercules, Antaeus, Wrestling, Stepped Base, c.1915, 22 In.		1464
Sculpture, Horse & Rider, Nude Man, Holding Lance, Oval Base, 16 x 21 In.		1680
Sculpture, Horse, Standing, Head Down, c.1860, 12 x 16 In.		1560
Sculpture, Hound Dog, Cast, Verdigris Finish, 8 x 12 In.		236
Sculpture, Houser, Allan Capron, Indian Figure, Seated, Blanket Enveloped, 1990, 5 In.		2250
Sculpture, Icarus, Standing On Precipice, Wings Attached To Arms, c.1900, 28 In.		4200
Sculpture, Indian Chief, On Horseback, Extended Arms, Square Base, 19 x 16 ½ In.		590
Sculpture, Iris, Dragonfly, Scroll Feet, Leaves, Japan, c.1935, 25 x 7 In., Pair		738
Sculpture, Kalish, Max, Fatigue, Man, Hand To Head, Meroni Radice, Poland, c.1900, 16 In.		30500
Sculpture, Kauba, C., Sleeping Dragon, Erotic Group, Nude Woman Inside, c.1910, 6 ⅜ In.		4250
Sculpture, Kearney, J., Lady Godiva, On Warthog, c.1980, 6 ½ x 7 In.		325
Sculpture, King, Paul, Fox, Curled Up Sleeping, 4 ¾ In.		266

Bronze, Sculpture, Dancing Monkey, Band Leader, Cold Paint, Austria, 3 ½ x 2 In.
$360

DuMouchelles Art Gallery

Bronze, Sculpture, Dumaige, Henri-Etienne, Calliope, Holding Stylus & Scroll, 21 In.
$1,722

New Orleans Auction Galleries, Inc.

Bronze, Sculpture, Elephant, Ivory Tusks, Natural Root Base, Signed, Japan, 12 x 12 In.
$920

Cottone Auctions

Bronze, Sculpture, Fremiet, Emmanuel, Credo, Medieval Knight, Banner, 16 ¼ In. $4,800

Cowan's Auctions

Bronze, Sculpture, Mongolian Warrior, Spear, c.1900, 18 x 9 In. $356

James D. Julia Auctioneers

Bronze, Sculpture, Moreau, Mathurin, Apollo, 1870, 20 x 11 x 9 In. $3,000

Rago Arts & Auction Center

Sculpture, King, William, My Ex, Angular Woman, 1966, 29 x 8 In.	2813
Sculpture, Kley, L., Woman, Partially Clad, Holding Tambourine Over Head, c.1900, 14 In.	460
Sculpture, Korschann, C., Woman, On Flower Draped Bowl, Green Patina, c.1900, 12 x 10 In.	1534
Sculpture, Korschann, C.H., Woman, Flowers, Art Nouveau, Flower Bouquets, Signed, 13 In.	1900
Sculpture, Krupka, J., Woman, Nude, Shielding Eyes With Arm, Signed, 1916, 7 x 3 In.	688
Sculpture, Lanceray, E., Bear, Sweeping, Russia, c.1865, 5 In.	767
Sculpture, Lantaka, Cannon, Mounted On Elephant, Malaysia, c.1800, 36 x 49 In.	1534
Sculpture, Lawn, Crane, Upturned Head, Looking Down, 57 ¼ In., Pair	885
Sculpture, Lecornet, Nicolas, Boy, With Coins, Polished, Cobblestone Base, Signed, 11 In.	615
Sculpture, Leonard, A., Biking Warrior, Brown Patina, Marble Base, France, 18 In.	480
Sculpture, LeVerrier, Max, Archer, Bow Drawn, Kneeling, Marble Base, c.1955, 30 x 33 In.	1875
Sculpture, Lion, Resting, Marble Base, 14 In.	237
Sculpture, Lion, Standing, Growling, Curled Tail, c.1980, 50 x 62 In., Pair	4920
Sculpture, Louis-Philippe, Standing, Holding Hat, Opens, Napoleon, c.1850, 3 ¼ In.	1220
Sculpture, Maiden, Nude, Seated, Eyes Closed, Arm Over Head, Austria, c.1900 In.	1080
Sculpture, Maiden, Playing Violin, Flowing Robe, Wreath On Head, c.1900, 21 In.	308
Sculpture, Male River God, Nude, Reclining, Headless, c.1850, 15 x 31 In.	3107
Sculpture, Man, Nude, Standing, Crossed Feet, Arms Behind, c.1900, 18 In.	1076
Sculpture, Man, Seminude, Reclining Cat, Cat Toy, Marble Base, 18 ½ In.	522
Sculpture, Man, Sower, Knee Britches, Vest, c.1910, 17 In.	469
Sculpture, Man, Standing, Dock Worker, Hands On Hips, c.1900, 18 ¼ In.	1250
Sculpture, McVey, Old Grizzley, Cast, Brown Patina, Oak Platform, 1900s, 7 x 12 x 7 In.	1639
Sculpture, Mene, Pierre Jules, Whippet, Brown Patina, Oval Base, Inscribed, 6 In.	660
Sculpture, Mercury Attaching Sandals, After Jean-Baptiste Pigalle, France, 1700s, 24 x 14 In.	1800
Sculpture, Mercury In Flight, Round Base, Italy, c.1900, 31 ½ In.	625
Sculpture, Mercury, Black Marble Stepped Base, Italy, 1800s, 19 ½ x 6 In.	430
Sculpture, Mercury, Seated, Nude, Square Marble Base, 7 ⅝ In.	239
Sculpture, Mercury, Stepped Base, Brown Patina, 19th Century, 32 In.	780
Sculpture, Miller, Carol, Cougar, Crouching, Green Patina, c.1965, 15 x 46 In.	1125
Sculpture, Mogi, Rudolf, Woman Nude Torso, Flat Back, Hanger, Initials, 11 ½ In.	240
Sculpture, Moigniez, Jules, Dog, Hunting, Pheasant, Signed, 19th Century, 6 ½ In.	625
Sculpture, Moigniez, Jules, Lion, Resting, France, c.1880, 4 x 10 In.	425
Sculpture, Mongolian Warrior, Spear, c.1900, 18 x 9 In. ....*illus*	356
Sculpture, Monkey, Carrying Basket, 1900s, 15 x 14 In.	657
Sculpture, Monkey, Seated, Dressed, Book, Oval Base, Japan, c.1890, 9 In.	1875
Sculpture, Monkey, Seated, Dressed, Holding Object, Japan, 6 In.	2813
Sculpture, Moose, Walking Upstream, Naturalistic Shape Base, 1973, 21 In.	1250
Sculpture, Moreau, Auguste, Boy Holding Branch, 2 Birds, Patina, c.1900, 29 x 30 ¾ In.	1250
Sculpture, Moreau, Auguste, Putto & Goose, c.1900, 5 x 7 In.	657
Sculpture, Moreau, Mathurin, Apollo, 1870, 20 x 11 x 9 In. ....*illus*	3000
Sculpture, Moses, Seated, Brown Patina, 11 ½ In.	625
Sculpture, Mother & Child, Seated, Draped Dress, Square Base, 17 ½ In.	1298
Sculpture, Muller, H., Metal Worker, Apron, Hammer Raised, Signed, c.1920, 22 In.	595
Sculpture, Musician, Ivory, Flute, Lute, Sheet Music, Shaped Base, c.1890, 16 In., Pair	5700
Sculpture, Napoleon, Standing, Pensive Pose, St. Helene, Square Marble Base, c.1900, 10 In.	720
Sculpture, Nude, Holding 2 Baskets, Green Marble Base, 11 ¼ In.	517
Sculpture, Official, Seated, Voluminous Robes, Cap, Holding Tablet, c.1640, 8 In.	7380
Sculpture, Omerth, Exotic Dancer, Ivory, Turban, Harem Pants, Vest, Raised Arms, 11 ½ In.	2500
Sculpture, Owl, Enameled Detail, Impressed Austria, c.1890, 2 ½ In.	150
Sculpture, Pandiani, Antonia, Gentleman Of Fashion, 1800s Attire, Italy, c.1900, 34 In.	3750
Sculpture, Paris, Roland, Pierrot Playing Mandolin, Art Deco, Cold Paint, c.1900, 12 ½ In.	3000
Sculpture, Parrot, Red Glass Eyes, Austria, 9 In.	1800
Sculpture, Pattison, Abbott, Weather Machine, Braised, Welded, 1960, 11 x 15 In.	813
Sculpture, Perseus, Holding Head Of Medusa, Nude, Italy, 1900s, 27 x 19 In.	793
Sculpture, Peter Pan, Standing, Hand On Hip, Marble Base, 50 In.	1500
Sculpture, Peynot, Emile E., La Bonne Aventure, France, c.1900, 28 In.	2875
Sculpture, Pheasant, Brown Patina, Naturalistic Ground, Oval Base, 8 ¼ In.	200
Sculpture, Pheasant, Gilt, Standing, Leaves, Rocky Base, France, c.1885, 9 ½ x 6 ½ In.	984
Sculpture, Picault, P., Ave Caesar Victor Salvet, Hail Victorious Caesar, Black Base, 24 In.	1936
Sculpture, Piccirilli, Furio, Duckling, Signed, c.1925, 12 ½ x 7 ¼ In.	3776
Sculpture, Pina, Alfredo, Head Of A Woman, Incised, c.1950, 19 x 12 In.	2340
Sculpture, Pina, Alfredo, Mother, Child, Incised, c.1945, 17 x 16 In.	936
Sculpture, Popliteo, Bing Cherries, Red, Green Paint, Black Marble Base, 14 ½ In.	2884
Sculpture, Preiss, Ferdinand, Archer, Ivory, Onyx Base, Marked, 1900s, 10 In. ....*illus*	15600
Sculpture, Prelude, Putto, Playing Mandolin, Marble Base, c.1960, 18 In.	1000
Sculpture, Reusch, F., Miner, Uniform, Marble Base, 24 In.	908

Sculpture, Rhinoceros, Cast, Verdigris Patina, 5 ¾ x 11 In.	196
Sculpture, Risque, C., Child With Fish, Signed, 1921, 20 ¾ In.	2000
Sculpture, Sand Crab, 6 ¼ In.	58
Sculpture, Sardeau, Singer, 10½ In.	1000
Sculpture, Satyr, Seated, Nymph In Lap, Seminude, France, 31 In.	7670
Sculpture, Schmidt-Hofer, Otto, Norse Warrior, Standing, Sword, Shield, Marble Base, 16 In.	1107
Sculpture, Scottish Deerhounds, Brown Patina, Green Marble Base, Art Deco, 6 x 12 In.	118
Sculpture, Seated Official, Robes, Holding Blade, Calligraphy, Headpiece, 1900s, 11 In.............	354
Sculpture, Shorebird, Worm In Beak, Reeds, 1800s, 9 ½ In.	600
Sculpture, Sievers, Frederick William, 3 Pointers, Naturalistic Base, Signed, 1909, 7 x 16 In.	2242
Sculpture, Silvestre, Paul, Nude, Leaping Goat, Marble Base, Signed, 1900s, 7 x 16 x 4 In.	1000
Sculpture, Slim Pickens, Partners, Wood Base, 1972, 14 x 13 In.	1180
Sculpture, Soldier, Prussian, On Horse, Gun, Sword, c.1890, 18 ¾ In........	2280
Sculpture, Spanish Dancer, Flower Scarf Over Head, Layered Dress, Fan, c.1900, 10 In.	540
Sculpture, Stallions, Fighting, On Hind Legs, Shaped Round Base, c.1980, 17 x 16 In.	354
Sculpture, Stotz, P., Boy, Hands In Pocket, Brown Patina, Black Round Base, c.1870, 13 ¾ In.......	413
Sculpture, Strasser, A., Nubian Musician, String Instrument, Smoking Pipe, c.1900, 24 In......	2360
Sculpture, Tantric Divinity, Multi-Armed, Yab Yum, Standing, Oval Base, c.1900, 10 In.	711
Sculpture, Tereszczuk, P., Satyr, Faun, Ivory, Naturalistic Base, AR Foundry Mark, 9 In.	1200
Sculpture, Thiebaut, Vor, Man, Jumping Rope, Nude, Vor, France, c.1860, 13 ⅞ In.	2596
Sculpture, Tiger, Striding, Tail Up, Roaring Head, c.1900, 6 ½ x 11 In......	246
Sculpture, Timber Man, Raised Hammer, Stepping Position, Rocks, 26 In.	1875
Sculpture, Triton, Sea Creature, Seated, Tail, Green Patina, 28 x 28 In........	1968
Sculpture, Troika, Triple Horse Drawn Sleigh, Oval Marble Base, c.1935, 37 x 18 In.	6150
Sculpture, Turtles, Entwined, Climbing On Each Other, Japan, c.1900, 4 ½ x 11 In..............	1315
Sculpture, Ulrich, J., Dancer, Nude, Cloth Over Head, Art Deco, Ivory, Onyx Pedestal, 8 ⅝ In......	2700
Sculpture, Vendome Column, Thermometer En Verso, Marble Base, 1800s, 11 ⅛ In........	615
Sculpture, Vienna, Elephant, Trunk Upraised, Cold Paint, Early 20th Century, 4 ¼ In.	308
Sculpture, Vienna, Lady, Leaning On Bicycle, Cold Paint, c.1900, 6 In......	2400
Sculpture, Vienna, Man, Arab, Seated, On Rug, Smoking Pipe, Black Round Base, 5 ¾ In.........	432
Sculpture, Vienna, Man, Arabian, Seated, On Rug, Smoking Pipe, 5 ¼ In.....	432
Sculpture, Vienna, Man, Bearded, Arms Crossed, White Robe, Cold Paint, 7 In.	3480
Sculpture, Vienna, Man, Bearded, Standing, Holding Food Bowls, Cold Paint, 7 In...................	930
Sculpture, Vienna, Man, Camel Rider, Cold Paint, 8 ½ In.	1050
Sculpture, Vienna, Man, Peddler, At Table, Cold Paint, 5 ½ In.	1380
Sculpture, Vienna, Man, Seated, Crossed Legs, Rifle, Cold Paint, 3 ¼ In.....	1200
Sculpture, Virgin Mary, Bronze, Ebonized Wood Plinth, c.1875, 13 ½ In.	325
Sculpture, Warrior, Demons, Japan, 12 In.	1033
Sculpture, Warrior, On Horseback, Spear, Tommaso Campaiola, Italy, 1900s, 25 In.	826
Sculpture, Warrior, Walking, Holding Sword, Helmet, Seminude, Square Base, 69 In.................	4183
Sculpture, Watchin' For The Roan, Cowboy, Lasso, 1991, 22 In.	1375
Sculpture, Water Nymph, Green Patination, Inscribed, Green Marble Base, 1900s, 9 ½ In.........	615
Sculpture, Wegener, Knight, Full Armor, On Horseback, Marble Base, c.1900, 12 In.	1845
Sculpture, Weschler, A., Head, Man, Signed, 17 In...............................	238
Sculpture, Wheeler, H., Pep, Horse, Standing, Signed, Gorham Co., c.1950, 9 x 8 In.	1250
Sculpture, Whippet, Dead Rabbit, Seated, Paw Up, Oval Base, France, c.1900, 8 x 8 ½ In.........	472
Sculpture, Wildman Of The Woods, Bearded Man, Loincloth, Holding Club, 1800s, 17 ½ In.......	600
Sculpture, Winged Figure, Standing On Sphere, Arm Out, Pedestal Base, c.1900, 8 ½ In.	657
Sculpture, Winged Man, Icarus, Black Patina, Stepped Marble Base, Art Deco, 15 x 20 In.	748
Sculpture, Winged Putto, Seminude, Hands To Lips, Round Marble Base, c.1915, 18 In............	430
Sculpture, Winged Victory, Brown Patina, Floral Wreath, Outstretched Arms, 1800s, 23 In........	700
Sculpture, Wolf, Capitaline, Standing, Stepped Marble Base, 6 ½ x 9 In......	177
Sculpture, Woman, Bread Loaves On Head, Marble Base, 19 In................	1121
Sculpture, Woman, Crouched Down, Picking Flowers, Draped Gown, 15 ½ In......	1500
Sculpture, Woman, Fashionable, Holding Bonnet, Seated Alabaster Bench, c.1900, 12 In...........	431
Sculpture, Woman, Flower, 1900, 20 In.	750
Sculpture, Woman, Half Clothed, Holding, Leaves, Green Marble Base, c.1855, 28 In..................	2375
Sculpture, Woman, On Horse, Stag Hunter, Dogs, France, c.1800, 15 ½ x 13 ½ In..................	2223
Sculpture, Woman, Partly Nude Kneeling, Egyptian Headdress, 13 ½ In.	188
Sculpture, Woman, Seminude, At Well, Filling Ewer, France, 34 In.	5250
Sculpture, Woman, Standing, Arms Reaching Up, Seminude, Marble Base, 1912, 21 In.	1170
Sculpture, Woman, Striding, Reading Book, Carrying Briefcase, Germany, c.1900, 27 In.	875
Sculpture, Women, Standing, Raised Arm, Round Base, 6 ¼ In., Pair...........	420
Sculpture, Yama Dharmaraja, Gilt, Silvered, Tibet, c.1890, 4 ¾ In.	331
Seal, Wax, Fox In Trap, Grapes, Spring Trap Terminal, Intaglio Carved, Austria, 1800s, 4 In.	270
Stirrups, Dragon Heads, Gilt, Chinese, 1900s, 4 ¾ In., Pair ....*illus*	1304

Bronze, Sculpture, Preiss, Ferdinand, Archer, Ivory, Onyx Base, Marked, 1900s, 10 In.
$15,600

Cowan's Auctions

Bronze, Stirrups, Dragon Heads, Gilt, Chinese, 1900s, 4 ¾ In., Pair
$1,304

James D. Julia Auctioneers

Bronze, Urn, Neoclassical, Figures, Mask Handles, Pedestal Base, 1800s, 19 x 7 ¼ In., Pair
$1,195

Neal Auction Co.

B

Bronze, Wine Vessel, Ceremonial, Relief Band, Handle, Tripod Feet, Chinese, 8 In. $12,600

Garth's Auctioneers & Appraisers

Brownies, Candlestick, Policeman, Badge, Billy Club, Glazed, Majolica, c.1890, 9 In. $158

Hake's Americana & Collectibles

Tazza, Gilt Bronze, Medallion, Music, Swan Handles, Reticulated Base, 1800s, 12 In.	244
Tazza, Gilt, Leaf Cartouche, Mask Handles, Molded Base, c.1850, 5 x 8 In.	299
Tazza, Neoclassical, Twisted Vine Handles, Marble Pedestal, Continental, 1800s, 11 In., Pair	860
Tray, Spider Web Design, Patina, Signed E.T. Hurley, 3 ½ In., Pair	563
Umbrella Stand, Dog Shape, On Hind Legs, Baton, Drip Pan Base, 34 x 23 In.	2952
Urn, Baluster, Cloisonne, Flange Handles, Banding, 11 ½ In.	108
Urn, Baluster, Pegasus Cartouche, Masks, Reeded Handles, Gilt, Glass, 19 In., Pair	2091
Urn, Entwined Grapevine Handles, Bearded Heads, Lion Masks Embossed, c.1850, 18 x 23 In.	1770
Urn, Lid, Belle Epoque, Flower Swags, Bowknots, Stone Base, c.1900, 23 In., Pair	1353
Urn, Lid, Stork Shape Knop, Molded Rococo Ornament, c.1885, 6 ½ x 8 In., Pair	492
Urn, Mythical Creature, Pedestal Foot, Flared Flat Rim, Japan, 14 In., Pair	660
Urn, Neoclassical, Figures, Mask Handles, Pedestal Base, 1800s, 19 x 7 ¼ In., Pair *illus*	1195
Urn, Ribbed, Acanthus Rim, Lamb's Tongue Foot, Square Plinth, Continental, 1800s, 11 In.	418
Urn, Stand, Champleve, Flowers, Leaves, Multicolor, D'Ore, France, c.1900, 7 In.	360
Urn, Waisted Neck, Twist Handles, Reeded, 36 In., Pair	3075
Vase, Apotheosis Of Homer, Achilles, Odysseus, Dore, Swags, France, 1800s, 5 In.	800
Vase, Applied Silver Dragonfly, Thistle, Impressed Silver Crest, 3 ½ x 10 ½ In.	175
Vase, Art Nouveau, Applied Fisherman, Pulling In Net, Wavy Rim, 9 ¾ In.	203
Vase, Birds On Branches, Shouldered, Tapered, Ring Foot, Japan, 1900s, 10 x 4 In., Pair	531
Vase, Birds, Branches, Dragon Handles, Japan, 19 In., Pair	1250
Vase, Bulbous Body, Trumpet Neck, Lug Handles, Saucer Foot, Banded, 1700s, 12 In.	819
Vase, Dragon Handles, Relief, 3 Friends Of Winter, Phoenix, Parrots, Chinese, 1700s, 13 In.	2214
Vase, Erte, Oriental Mystery, Applied Dancer, Marked Seven Arts, 1990, 9 x 12 In.	750
Vase, Horses, In Relief, c.1950, 10 ½ In.	444
Vase, Mother-Of-Pearl Inlay, Tapered, Swollen Shoulder, Flowers, Stems, c.1900, 10 In.	150
Watch Holder, Cobra Form, Head Raised, Pocket Watch In Open Mouth, Victorian, 7 In.	492
Wine Vessel, Ceremonial, Relief Band, Handle, Tripod Feet, Chinese, 8 In. *illus*	12600

BROWNIES were first drawn in 1883 by Palmer Cox. They are characterized by large round eyes, downturned mouths, and skinny legs. Toys, books, dinnerware, and other objects were made with the Brownies as part of the design.

Bank, Figural, Pottery, Goldenrod, 5 ½ In.	125
Book, Adventures Of A Brownie, Black & White Illustrations, 1898	49
Candlestick, Figural, Policeman, Night Stick, Palmer Cox, Continental, 9 ¼ In.	272
Candlestick, Policeman, Badge, Billy Club, Glazed, Majolica, c.1890, 9 In. *illus*	158
Candlestick, Uncle Sam, Majolica, 8 In.	495
Charm, Sterling Silver, c.1910, 1 ⅛ In.	75
Doll, Cloth, Stuffed, Red Vest, Palmer Cox, 1893, 7 ¼ In.	110
Doll, Elf, Embroidered, Side-Glancing Eyes, c.1900, 8 In.	45
Doll, Felt, Drummer, Brass Buttons, Cardboard Tag, Box, 8 ½ In.	425
Game, Horseshoes, M.H. Miller Co., Box, c.1900	135
Humidor, Sailor, Face Is Body, Hat Lid, Glazed Ceramic, c.1890, 6 ½ In.	173
Ornament, Papier-Mache, Peg Jointed, Black Jacket, 4 ⅞ In.	295
Plate, 3 Brownies, Pink Ruffled Rim, 6 In.	80
Thermometer Holder, Figural, Flower Design, 4 ½ x 7 In.	173
Tool Box, Turnbuckles, Wood, 6 x 8 x 2 In.	40
Toothpick Holder, Under Umbrella, Silver Plate, Marked, Pairpoint Mfg., c.1890, 3 In.	431
Tray, Ice Cream, Brownies Eating Ice Cream Mound, 1920s, 13 x 10 In.	84 to 115
Tray, Large Bowl Of Ice Cream, Brownies With Musical Instruments, Tin Lithograph, 13 In.	454

BRUSH-MCCOY, *see Brush category and related pieces in McCoy category.*

BRUSH POTTERY was started in 1925. George Brush first worked in 1901 in Zanesville, Ohio. He started his own pottery in 1907, but it burned to the ground soon after. In 1909 he became manager of the J.W. McCoy Pottery. In 1911, Brush and J.W. McCoy formed the Brush-McCoy Pottery Co. After a series of name changes, the company became the Brush Pottery in 1925. It closed in 1982. Old Brush was marked with impressed letters or a palette-shaped mark. Reproduction pieces are being made. They are marked in raised letters or with a raised mark. Collectors favor the figural cookie jars made by this company. Because there was a company named Brush-McCoy, there is great confusion between Brush and Nelson McCoy pieces. Most collectors today refer to Brush pottery as Brush-McCoy. See McCoy category for more information.

Candlestick, Rockcraft, Brush-McCoy, 5 In., Pair	115
Cookie Jar, Elephant, Pink, Monkey Finial, Marked *illus*	1020
Cookie Jar, Hillbilly Frog, Marked, c.1969 *illus*	108

Cookie Jar, Humpty Dumpty, Yellow Beanie, Winton, Marked, 1956-61 ....*illus*	108
Cookie Jar, Pig, Green Coat, Winton Design, Marked, W7 USA ....*illus*	84
Cookie Jar, Squirrel On Log, Hitting Acorn, 1965, 10 x 10 In................	165
Vase, Jetwood, Conifer Tree Landscape, Hills, At Dusk, Blue, Brown, White, Orange, 10 In............	767
Vase, Onyx, Blue, 3 ¼ In...................................	5
Vase, Zuni, Indian Designs, Symbols, Earth Tones, 4 In.....................	142
Wall Pocket, Owl, Cream, Brown, 8 In.	64

BUCK ROGERS was the first American science fiction comic strip. It started in 1929 and continued until 1967. Buck has also appeared in comic books, movies, and, in the 1980s, a television series. Any memorabilia connected with the character Buck Rogers is collectible.

Binoculars, Official Space Glasses, Plastic, Box, 4 ½ x 5 ¼ In.........................	285
Button, Expo, I Saw Buck Rogers, Did You?, Rocket Pistol, 1934, 1 ⅛ In.	190
Button, Movie Serial, Strange World Adventures Club, Blue, Silver, 1939, 1 ¼ In...................	1150
Cut Out Adventure Book, Lead Figure, Cocomalt Premium, Folder, 1933, 6 ½ x 13 In........	380
Pencil Box, Buck & Wilma, Scooters, Clouds, Planets, Cardboard, 1936, 8 x 5 In............	125
Pencil Box, Buck Rogers In 25th Century, Black Lithograph, Brick, 1938, 8 x 3 In.	65
Ring, Initial, Birthstone, Cocomalt Premium, Brass Ring, Adjustable, 1934...............................	230
Ring, Ruby Color Stone, Solar Scouts, Cream Of Wheat, 1936.............................	999
Storybook, In The 25th Century, Kellogg's Premium, Breakfast Of The World, 1933, 32 Pages...	167
Sweater Emblem, Solar Scouts, Cream Of Wheat Premium, Felt, 1936, 3 In. ....*illus*	1150
Toy, Flash Blast Attack Ship, Tootsietoy, Painted, Box, 4 ½ In.........................	276
Toy, Gun, Sonic Ray, Plastic, Battery Operated, Folder, Box, 1952, 6 x 8 In................	474
Toy, Pistol, Disintegrator, Metal, XZ-38, Daisy Mfg. Co., 1935, 10 In.	221 to 270
Toy, Rocket Police Patrol, Tin, Marx, Windup, Box, 12 x 4 In.........................	1080
Toy, Rocket Ship, Battlecruiser, No. 1031, Tootsietoy, Box, 1930s, 5 In.......................	192
Toy, Rocket Ship, Tin Lithograph, Windup, Marx, c.1934, 12 In. ....*illus*	720
Toy, Rocket Ship, Venus Duo Destroyer, No. 1032, Tootsietoy, Box, 1930s, 5 In..............	192
Toy, Rubber Band Gun, Stiff Paper Punch-Out, Onward School Supplies, 1940, 5 x 10 In...........	115
Toy, Ship Set, Tootsietoy, Cast Metal, Cardboard Box, 1937, 5 In.	949
Toy, Spaceship, Tin Lithograph, Key Windup, Wings, Multicolor, 1927, 12 In........................	1195

BUFFALO POTTERY was made in Buffalo, New York, after 1902. The company was established by the Larkin Company, famous manufacturers of soap. The wares are marked with a picture of a buffalo and the date of manufacture. Deldare ware is the most famous pottery made at the factory. It has either a khaki-colored or green background with hand-painted transfer designs.

BUFFALO POTTERY

Bowl, Oriental Garden, Flow Blue, Flared Rim, 1910, 7 x 8 ½ In........................	47
Chamber Pot, Rose, Cup, c.1910, 5 ⅝ x 11 In.	60
Cup & Saucer, Willow, Marked, 1911	45
Pitcher & Basin, Chrysanthemum, Teal, White Ground	35
Pitcher, Cinderella, Carriage, Trying On Slipper, 6 ¼ In.	312
Pitcher, Flow Blue, Flowers, Stems, Gold Trim, Shaped Rim, 1896, 8 ¼ In. ....*illus*	108
Pitcher, Geraniums, Leaves, Cobalt Blue, White, 5 ¼ x 6 ½ In....................	325
Pitcher, Roosevelt Bears, 8 x 4 ½ In......................*illus*	277
Plate, Advertising, Christmas Carol, 1957..................	18
Plate, Advertising, J.P. Alley's Hambone, Cigars, 5 Cents, 1930s, 10 ½ In.	120
Plate, Advertising, Woodman Head Camp, Green, 1911, 7 ½ In.	80
Plate, Dinner, Lune 612, Blue & White, c.1950, 10 In., 5 Piece	95
Plate, Wildlife, c.1900, 9 ¼ In., 6 Piece...............	159
Platter, Willow, 1909, 14 x 11 In.	195
Sugar, Lid, Lune 612, Blue, White, c.1940...........	35

BUFFALO POTTERY DELDARE

Bowl, Ale, On Stand, Emerald, Marked, 1911, 10 In. & 12 ¾ In. ....*illus*	726
Bowl, Death, Fallowfield Hunt, 1908, 9 In.........................	850
Bowl, Plateau, Flowers, Butterflies, 12 ¾ x 10 ½ In.	708
Bowl, Ye Village Tavern, Marked, c.1924, 9 x 3 ¾ In.	495
Cake Plate, Ye Village Gossips, Cutout Handles, 1908, 11 ¼ In..........	550
Card Tray, Ye Lion Inn, 2 Men, 1 Holding Mug, 2 Tab Handles, 7 In.	52
Cup & Saucer, Ye Olden Days, 1909...................	170
Humidor, Lid, Ye Lion Inn, Men At Table, 8-Sided, Tapered, 7 In.	277
Humidor, Sailor, Sitting, There Was An Old Sailor & He Had A Wooden Leg, 6 In.	308
Mug, Ye Lion Inn, 2 Men, Bulbous, 4 ½ In.........................	46
Plate, Death, Fallowfield Hunt, The Start, Hunting Scene, 1909, 9 ½ In.	469

Brush, Cookie Jar, Elephant, Pink, Monkey Finial, Marked
$1,020

Brush, Cookie Jar, Hillbilly Frog, Marked, c.1969
$108

Brush, Cookie Jar, Humpty Dumpty, Yellow Beanie, Winton, Marked, 1956-61
$108

Brush, Cookie Jar, Pig, Green Coat, Winton Design, Marked, W7 USA
$84

Victorian Casino Antiques

Buck Rogers, Sweater Emblem, Solar Scouts, Cream Of Wheat Premium, Felt, 1936, 3 In.
$1,150

Hake's Americana & Collectibles

Buck Rogers, Toy, Rocket Ship, Tin Lithograph, Windup, Marx, c.1934, 12 In.
$720

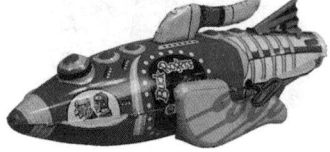

Victorian Casino Antiques

Plate, Dr. Syntax, Garden Trio, 3 Musicians, Round, 9 ½ In.	305
Plate, Fallowfield Hunt, Breakfast At The 3 Pigeons, 12 In.	52
Plate, Ye Lion Inn, 1908, 6 ⅞ In.	52 to 125
Plate, Ye Town Crier, 2 Men, Woman, Houses Around Border, 8 ½ In.	48 to 225
Plate, Ye Village Street, 1908, 7 ¼ In.	125
Serving Bowl, Ye Village Tavern, 9 x 3 In.	450
Tankard, Great Controversy, Marked, 12 ¾ In. ....*illus*	236
Tea Tile, Breaking Cover, Signed, 1908, 6 ½ In.	150
Vase, Art Nouveau, Daisies, Marked, 6 ¾ In. ....*illus*	472

BUNNYKINS, *see Royal Doulton category.*

BURMESE GLASS was developed by Frederick Shirley at the Mt. Washington Glass Works in New Bedford, Massachusetts, in 1885. It is a two-toned glass, shading from peach to yellow. Some pieces have a pattern mold design. A few Burmese pieces were decorated with pictures or applied glass flowers of colored Burmese glass. Other factories made similar glass also called Burmese. Related items may be listed in the Fenton category, the Gundersen category, and under Webb Burmese.

Bowl, Hexagonal, 6 Applied Acanthus Leaves, Mt. Washington, 9 In.	2415
Cruet, Daisy Clusters, Ribbed Pillar, Stopper, Mt. Washington, 6 ½ In. ....*illus*	1840
Cup & Saucer, Demitasse, Flowers, Medallion, Mt. Washington, 2 ½ In.	748
Cup & Saucer, Peach To Yellow, 2 ¼ x 4 In.	138
Cup & Saucer, Yellow To Pale Peach, 2 ¼ x 2 ¾ In.	207
Epergne, Optic Ribbed, 2 Arms, Bronze Standard, Libbey, 9 In. ....*illus*	2300
Ewer, Shaded Pink To Yellow, Applied Handle, 2 Black Dragons, Flowers, Scrolls, 9 ½ In.	3674
Fairy Lamp, Pyramid, Domed Shade, Footed Holder, 4 ½ In.	356
Pitcher, Owls, Verse, Painted, Handle, 5 ½ In. ....*illus*	2875
Pitcher, Peach Satin, Vaseline, Thomas Hood Verse, Mt. Washington, 1885, 4 ⅜ In. ....*illus*	767
Rose Bowl, Glossy Glaze, Rigaree Collar, Mt. Washington, 4 In.	403
Sugar & Creamer, Glossy, Footed, Applied Handle, 3 ¾ In.	460
Sugar & Creamer, Oval, Quadrafold Rim, Applied Feet, Satin Finish, 3 In.	58
Sugar & Creamer, Wishbone Feet, Mt. Washington, 4 ½ In.	1610
Toothpick Holder, Tricorner Rim, Flowers, Yellow, Mt. Washington Glass Co., c.1886, 2 In.	207
Vase, Applied Scroll Handles, Enameled Ibis, Pyramids, Gold Palm Trees, Label, 11 In.	593
Vase, Bulbous, Elongated Neck, Flowers, Stems, Verse, Mt. Washington, 12 In. ....*illus*	3437
Vase, Epergne, Satin Glass, Yellow To Peach, Silver Base, Flared Wavy Rim, c.1880, 11 In.	110
Vase, Folded, Flared Rim, Peach, To Yellow, 4 ½ x 2 ¾ In.	104
Vase, Urn Shape, Egyptian Design, Gold Flowers, Raised Gilt Outlines, Handles, 12 In.	6383

BUSTER BROWN, the comic strip, first appeared in color in 1902. Buster and his dog, Tige, remained a popular comic and soon became even more famous as the emblem for a shoe company, a textile firm, and other companies. The strip was discontinued in 1920. Buster Brown sponsored a radio show from 1943 to 1955 and a TV show from 1950 to 1956. The Buster Brown characters are still used by Brown Shoe Company, Buster Brown Apparel, Inc., and Gateway Hosiery.

Bag, Buster & Tige, Vinyl, Drawstring, Blue Ground, 1960s	62
Bank, Buster & Tige, Cast Iron, A.C. Williams, c.1910, 5 x 3 In.	125
Bank, Horse, Standing, Horseshoe, Buster & Tige, Arcade, c.1908, 7 In.	395
Book, Buster Brown Goes Swimming, Cupples & Leon, N.Y., 21 Pages, 1907, 6 x 7 In.	90
Book, Comic Strip, Busy Body, Cardboard, Red Cloth Spine, 1909, 11 x 16 In.	150
Book, Comic Strip, Tige, Jolly Times, Cardboard Covers, 1905, 11 x 16 In.	150
Button, Buster & Tige, Brownbilt Club, Celluloid, ¾ In.	32
Button, Buster Holding Suspenders, Celluloid, ⅞ In.	36
Can, Buster Brown Cigar, Seated Man, Tige, Buster, Lid, Paper Label, 5 x 5 In.	719
Canister, Black Pepper, Buster Brown, Tige, Cardboard, Cylindrical, 5 ⅜ x 3 In. ....*illus*	150
Chair, Rocking, Health Shoes For Boys & Girls, Store Use, Wood, 21 In.	90
Charm, Tige, Brass, Embossed, 1 ⅛ In.	28
Coloring Set, Buster, Painting Tige, Milton Bradley, c.1900, 10 x 6 In.	95
Display, Buster & Tige, Figural, Plastic, 25 x 8 x 34 In. ....*illus*	240
Display, Mannequin Leg, Figural, Tige Pulling Sock, 15 ½ In.	65
Doll, Buster & Tige, c.1900, 14 In.	75
Doll, Buster & Tige, Stuffed, 1974, 11 In.	34
Figurine, Standing, Hands On Hips, Pink Clothes, Hat, Bisque, c.1900, 6 In.	173
Game, School's Out Target Toss, 3 Figures, Heads Bend, Paper On Wood, Litho, 24 In.	295
Kite, Buster & Tige, Cloth, Tail & Sticks, 36 ½ x 34 ½ In.	81
Lantern, Buster's Head, Glazed Composition, Bail Handle, 3 ½ In.	944
Mirror, Shoe Co. Makers, Buster & Tige, Celluloid, Round, 2 ¼ In. Diam.	288

Paint Set, Embossed Cards, Buster Painting, Milton Bradley, Box, c.1900, 10 x 6 In.	95
Pin, Card, Smilin' Ed McConnel's Buster Brown, Gang, 2 x 3 ½ In.	139
Pin, Vote For Buster Brown, Tug Of War With Tige, 1 ¼ In.	21
Sign, Buster Brown Shoes, Fiberboard, Silkscreen, Buster, Tige, 1950s, 14 x 13 In.	139
Sign, Dancing Elephant, Dressed, Red, Yellow, Cutout, Plywood, Frame, c.1935, 36 x 23 In.	108
Spoon, Sterling Silver, Flower Handle, Bust & Tige In Bowl, 3 ¼ In.	155
Watch, Buster & Tige, Red Leather, Manual Wind	175

BUTTER CHIPS, or butter pats, were small individual dishes for butter. They were the height of fashion from 1880 to 1910. Earlier as well as later examples are known.

Bird, In Flight, Grass, Fan Shape, Holdcroft	90
Blackberry, Woven, Majolica	30
Blue Flowers, Scalloped Rim, Embossed, Delft	15
Brown Flowers, Hotel Metrepole, Script	40
Chrysanthemum, Hawkes, 3 In.	100
Diamond, Flowers, 6-Sided, 3 ¼ In.	110
Flow Blue, Gold Trim, Scalloped Edge, c.1910, 3 ⅜ In. ....*illus*	25
Golden State, Oranges, Chicago Rock Island & Pacific Railroad, c.1910, 3 In. ....*illus*	225
Green Trim, Ritz Villahermosa	40
Green, Hotel Brunswick, Ship Mark, Dunn Bennett's Medal Hotel Ware, England	45
Leaf On Brown Ground, Majolica	35
Medley Of Fruit, Bone China, Royal Vale	15
Pink & Blue Flowers, Gold Trim, Haviland	15
Strawberry Diamond	25
White, Haviland, 1890	10
White, Ironstone, Pie Crust Rim, Royal Ironstone China, Charles Meakin	10

BUTTER MOLDS *are listed in the Kitchen category under Mold, Butter.*

BUTTON collecting has been popular since the nineteenth century. Buttons have been used on clothing throughout the centuries, and there are millions of styles. Gold, silver, or precious stones were used for the best buttons, but most were made of natural materials, like bone or shell, or from inexpensive metals. Only a few types favored by collectors are listed for comparison.

Brass, Art Glass, Green, Filigree, Czechoslovakia, 1920s, 1 ⅜ In.	10
Brass, Castle With Turrets, Silvered Finish, Round, 1880s, ⅞ In.	14
Brass, Dragon, On Warrior's Shield, c.1880, 1 1/16 In.	31
Brass, St. Andrew's Golf, Crossed Clubs, Crown, Thistle, 2 Golf Balls, 7/16 In., 3 Piece	10
Caramel Glass, Goddess Minerva, Cameo Style, Heart Border, c.1890, 1 1/16 In.	15
Celluloid, Cream, Wafer Shape, Rhinestone Center, 1 1/16 In.	2
Celluloid, Flowers, Rope Twist Stems, Ball Buds, Mother, Daughter, 1930s, 1 & ¾ In.	20
Celluloid, Purple, Fluted Demilunes On Half, Round, 1 ⅜ In.	3
Celluloid, Woven, Green, 1940s, 1 ⅜ In., Pair	10
Ceramic, Woman Dancing, Raised Arm, Multicolor Costume, 1 ½ In.	24
Enamel, Cut Steel, Paisley Shapes, Red, Victorian, 15/16 In., 4 Piece	150
Enamel, Green, 6 Silver Feather Foil Leaves, Brass Back, France, ⅞ In.	45
Enamel, Rosebuds, Gilt Brass, Domed, Victorian, c.1895, ⅞ In.	52
Glass, Barbell Style, Flower Openwork, Goldtone Metal, Blue, Green, 1 ⅜ x ½ In.	26
Glass, Flower Shape, 18 Petals, Coralene, Iridescent, 2 In.	10
Glass, Paperweight, Lime Green Swirl, Gold Mica Flecks, 1860s, 11/16 In.	17
Glass, Paperweight, Millefiori Center, White Cane Surround, Loop Shank, ½ In.	19
Glass, Paperweight, Pink Rose, Goldstone Swirl, Black Ground, 1920s, ⅜ In.	24
Glass, Ruby, Gold Luster, Paisley Design, Bar Shape, Faceted, 1890s, ¾ In.	8
Glass, Scarab, Turquoise, Oval Brass Mount, 1 In.	53
Glass, White, Multicolored Overlay, Goldstone Swirl, Rosette Shank, 9/16 In.	22
Goldtone, Chanel, Round, Impressed Logo, Chanel, ½ In., 3 Piece	18
Horn, Daisy, Lattice Ground, 1 In.	8
Horn, Leafy Scrolls, Pierced Brass Medallion Center, 1 ¼ In.	47
Horn, Silver & Abalone Inlay, c.1890, ⅝ In.	8
Jet, Carved, Mother-Of-Pearl Inlay, Curling Border, 1 ½ In.	50
Metal Under Glass, High Cut Faceted, Tinted, Gold Rim, Lilac Gray, 1 ¼ In.	25
Metal, Flared Stylized Petals, Central Rhinestones, Multicolor, 2 In.	41
Micro Mosaic, Glass, Building, Brass Back, ⅜ In.	14
Pottery, Satsuma, Geisha, Self Shank, c.1775, 1 ½ x ½ In.	167
Shell, Abalone, Owl Face, c.1900, ⅝ In.	12
Stud, Mother-Of-Pearl, Flower, Carved, ¾ In.	15

Buffalo Pottery, Pitcher, Flow Blue, Flowers, Stems, Gold Trim, Shaped Rim, 1896, 8 ¼ In.
$108

Stanon Auctions

Buffalo Pottery, Pitcher, Roosevelt Bears, 8 x 4 ½ In.
$277

Roland Antiques

Buffalo Pottery Deldare, Bowl, Ale, On Stand, Emerald, Marked, 1911, 10 In. & 12 ¾ In.
$726

Humler & Nolan

TIP

If you move glass in cold weather, be sure to let it sit at room temperature for several hours before you try unpacking it. The glass will break more easily if there is an abrupt temperature change.

Buffalo Pottery Deldare, Tankard, Great Controversy, Marked, 12 ¾ In. $236

Humler & Nolan

Buffalo Pottery Deldare, Vase, Art Nouveau, Daisies, Marked, 6 ¾ In. $472

Humler & Nolan

Burmese, Cruet, Daisy Clusters, Ribbed Pillar, Stopper, Mt. Washington, 6 ½ In. $1,840

Early Auction Co.

BUTTONHOOKS have been a popular collectible in England for many years and are now gaining the attention of American collectors. The buttonhooks were made to help fasten the many buttons of the old-fashioned high-button shoes and other items of apparel.

Celluloid, Metal, D. Buchanan Leeds, 3 ¾ In.	30
Silvertone, Art Nouveau Handle, 5 ¼ In.	10
Sterling Silver, Baroque Style, c.1890, 6 In.	25
Sterling Silver, Repousse Flowers, Victorian, 3 In.	35
Sterling Silver, Repousse Rose Design, Scrolls, Swirls, 2 ½ In.	27
Sterling Silver, Roses, 4 ½ In.	79
Sterling Silver, Woman's Face, Flowing Hair With Flowers, 7 ¾ In.	75

CALENDARS made to hang on the wall or to be displayed on a desk top have been popular since the last quarter of the nineteenth century. Many were printed with advertising as part of the artwork and were given away as premiums. Calendars with guns, gunpowder, or Coca-Cola advertising are most prized.

1897, Aetna Insurance Co., Stage Coach Scene, Paper, Frame, 29 x 22 In.	1020
1897, Antikamnia, Skeletons, Family Scenes, Partial, 4 Of 6 Pages	254
1899, United States Fidelity & Guaranty, Tricorner Hat, Boy, Flags, Frame, 28 x 20 In.	960
1900, Excelsior Bottling, Victorian Fashionable Woman, 17 x 23 In.	889
1903, Peters Cartridge Co., Dawn Of A New Era, Dec. Page, 16 x 24 ¾ In. ....*illus*	5400
1904, Landes, Livery, Stables, Feed & Exchange, Va., Girl, Flowers, Frame, 16 x 9 In.	518
1904, S.S. Patterson Beer, Dillon, Mont., Woman, Formal, Feet Up, Jan., Frame, 30 x 22 In.	1020
1905, DeLaval Cream Separators, Farm Girl, Full Pad, Frame, 15 x 10 In. ....*illus*	242
1907, Jos. L. Barth & Co., Outfitters, Woman, Green Hat, Flowers, Frame, 21 x 13 In.	345
1911, Warren's Store, Couple, Embossed, Frame, 30 x 21 In. ....*illus*	120
1912, Wm. Scott Co., Fine Teas & Coffees, Partial Pad, 19 ½ x 8 In. ....*illus*	115
1914, Old Hundred Year Cigars, January, Boy, Girl, Flag, Patriotic Attire, Frame, 14 x 11 In.	360
1915, DeLaval Cream Separators, Boy, Feeding Cow, Frame, 28 x 16 In.	570
1915, S.S. Redifer & Co., Hiawatha Wedding, Full Pad, Frame, 16 x 27 In. ....*illus*	450
1917, Winchester Guns & Cartridges, Elk Hunters, Calming Horse, W.R. Leigh, 15 x 30 In.	3259
1926, Winchester, Game Hunter, Grizzly Bear, Philip R. Goodwin, 14 ⅝ x 26 ½ In. ....*illus*	6518
1935, Hercules Powder Co., New Trails, Daniel Boone & Scout, Frame, 28 x 12 In.	243
1942, Maas & Steffen Co., Receivers Of Fine Furs, Otter's Playground, E. Eire, Pad, 14 x 26 In.	798
1947, 7Up, Girl With Blond Hair & Blue Bow, Frame, 23 x 13 In.	120
1947, A. Johnson Trucking, Pinup, Elvgren, Frame, 27 x 15 In.	360
1949, Scranton Beverage Co., Woman In Bikini On Boat, Full Pad, Frame, 39 x 20 In.	210
1951, Pinup, Nude Woman, The Dancer, March, Earl Moran, 33 x 16 In.	120
1954, Great Northern Railway, Aged Indian Warrior, 33 ½ x 16 In.	173
1955, Alexander's Grocery, Marilyn Monroe Pinup, Full Pad, 10 x 16 In. ....*illus*	115

CALENDAR PLATES were popular in the United States as advertising giveaways from 1906 to 1929. Since then, a few plates have been made every year. A calendar and the name of a store, a picture of flowers, a girl, or a scene were featured on the plate.

1909, Roses, Violets, Carnation, McNicol, 9 In.	55
1910, Monk Drinking, Changing Seasons Border, Steubenville, 9 ¼ In.	15
1911, Flatbush Trust Co., Brooklyn, N.Y., 22K Gold Designs, 8 ½ In.	70
1912, Horned Owl, Open Book, C.H. & D.P. Johnson, General Merchandise, 7 In.	22
1912, Martyred Presidents, Flags, Log Cabin Foods, 8 ½ In.	150
1914, Swiss Boy, Alps, Compliments Of Faggard Grocery, Crown China, 8 In.	50
1956, Gilt Flowers, Scrolls, Windmill, Ship, Taylor, Smith & Taylor, 10 In.	30
1961, Cottage, Stream, Bridge, Zodiac Signs, Mulberry, Staffordshire, 9 In.	10
1975, Farmhouse, Scalloped, Red Transferware, Alfred Meakin, 9 In.	16
1976, Eagle, Flag, 200th Anniversary, Red, White, Blue, 9 ⅛ In.	28
1978, Samurai Warriors, Wedgwood, 10 In.	24
1980, Blue & White, Currier & Ives, 10 In.	13

CAMARK POTTERY started out as Camden Art Tile and Pottery Company in Camden, Arkansas. Jack Carnes founded the firm in 1926 in association with John Lessell, Stephen Sebaugh, and the Camden Chamber of Commerce. Many types of glazes and wares were made. The company was bought by Mary Daniel in the early 1960s. Production ended in 1983.

Ashtray, Egyptian King, Green, Paper Label, 8 In, Diam.	66
Base, Drip Glaze, Yellow, Oval, 6 ½ x 4 ¼ In.	125

Basket, Mustard, Woven, Handle, Footed, Tag, 6 ½ In.	45
Bowl, Blue, Paper Label, c.1940, 4 x 5 ¼ In.	150
Candleholder, Ruffled Rim, Turquoise Matte Glaze, 4 x 2 ¾ In., Pair	36
Ewer, Coral, Ribbed, Elongated Handle, Footed, 11 ½ In.	48
Jug, Pure Corn Whiskey, Gold Glaze, Cork Stopper, 5 In.	48
Pitcher, White, Ribbed Mouth, Footed, Foil Label, 4 ¾ In.	34
Rose Bowl, Lavender Matte Glaze, Melon, Ribbed, 1930s	31
Salt & Pepper, S & P Letter Shape, Pink, Cork, 1 ½ In.	25
Sign, Arkansas Shape, Green Matte Glaze, 6 ⅛ In.	413
Teapot, Green, Swirled, Paper Label, Curled Finial, 5 In.	25
Vase, Arts & Crafts, Green Over Mustard, Footed, Paper Label, 7 ½ In.	425
Vase, Palm Trees, Beach, Luster Glaze, Gold, Green, Black, Red, Swollen, Lessel, 13 In.	484
Vase, Scenic, Luster, Rose Ground, Oval, 8 ¼ In.	649

CAMBRIDGE GLASS COMPANY was founded in 1901 in Cambridge, Ohio. The company closed in 1954, reopened briefly, and closed again in 1958. The firm made all types of glass. Its early wares included heavy pressed glass with the mark *Near Cut*. Later wares included Crown Tuscan, etched stemware, and clear and colored glass. The firm used a *C* in a triangle mark after 1920.

Aero Optic, Tumbler, Green, Footed, 6 Oz., 3 ¾ In.	12
Amber, Decanter, Cut Flute, Golf Ball Stopper, 20 Oz.	50
Apple Blossom, Candelabrum, 3-Light, Keyhole	40
Ardsley, Goblet, Water, 6 ½ In.	16
Ardsley, Tumbler, Juice, 4 ⅝ In.	15
Arlington, Plate, Dessert, 8 In.	10
Arlington, Sherbet, 5 ⅜ In.	8
Arlington, Wine, 5 ⅝ In.	17
Aurora, Cordial, Amber, 3 ⅜ In.	37
Aurora, Cordial, Green, 3 ⅜ In.	28
Aurora, Tumbler, Amber, 4 ⅜ In.	19
Aurora, Tumbler, Green, 4 ⅜ In.	18
Aurora, Wine, Amber, 4 ¾ In.	30
Aurora, Wine, Green, 4 ¾ In.	27
Autumn, Tumbler, Juice, 4 ⅜ In.	19
Azurite, Candlestick, Gold Trim, 10 In., Pair	75
Azurite, Compote, Gold Trim, 10 ½ In.	125
Bexley, Cordial, 4 ⅜ In.	29
Bexley, Goblet, Water, 6 ½ In.	21
Bexley, Plate, Salad, 7 ½ In.	4
Bexley, Tumbler, Juice, 4 ¼ In.	23
Bexley, Wine, 5 ⅝ In.	37
Blossom Time, Ice Bucket, Handle	62
Cadet, Cordial, 4 ⅝ In.	34
Cadet, Goblet, Water, 6 ½ In.	17
Cadet, Plate, Dessert, 8 In.	7
Cadet, Sherbet, 5 ⅜ In.	7
Cadet, Wine, 5 ¾ In.	12
Caprice, Bowl, 2 Handles, Oval, 4-Footed, 11 In.	36
Caprice, Bowl, Moonlight Blue, Crimped, 4-Footed, 11 ½ In.	95
Caprice, Bowl, Oval, Handle, 11 In.	23
Caprice, Cordial, 4 ⅜ In.	31
Caprice, Creamer, Footed, 3 ¼ In.	15
Caprice, Cup & Saucer	8
Caprice, Goblet, Water, 9 Oz., 7 ⅝ In.	23
Caprice, Plate, Bread & Butter, Moonlight Blue, 6 In.	24
Caprice, Plate, Luncheon, 8 ½ In.	12
Caprice, Plate, Salad, 8 In.	12
Caprice, Sherbet, 6 Oz., 5 ¾ In.	9
Caprice, Tray, Round, Swirl Ribbed, Gold Flowers, Rim, Footed, 1 ¾ x 14 In.	28
Caprice, Tumbler, Juice, 4 ⅛ In.	11
Caprice, Wine, 2 ½ Oz., 5 ⅝ In.	14
Cascade, Cocktail, 5 In.	10
Cascade, Goblet, Water, 6 ½ In.	8
Cascade, Goblet, Water, 8 Oz., 5 ½ In.	15
Castleton, Tumbler, Juice, 4 ¾ In.	11

Burmese, Epergne, Optic Ribbed, 2 Arms, Bronze Standard, Libbey, 9 In.
$2,300

Early Auction Co.

Burmese, Pitcher, Owls, Verse, Painted, Handle, 5 ½ In.
$2,875

Early Auction Co.

Burmese, Pitcher, Peach Satin, Vaseline, Thomas Hood Verse, Mt. Washington, 1885, 4 ⅜ In.
$767

Conestoga Auction Co., Inc.

Burmese, Vase, Bulbous, Elongated Neck, Flowers, Stems, Verse, Mt. Washington, 12 In.
$3,437

James D. Julia Auctioneers

Buster Brown, Canister, Black Pepper, Buster Brown, Tige, Cardboard, Cylindrical, 5 ⅜ x 3 In.
$150

Wm Morford Auctions

Buster Brown, Display, Buster & Tige, Figural, Plastic, 25 x 8 x 34 In.
$240

Victorian Casino Antiques

Castleton, Wine, 5 ¾ In.	7
Century, Cordial, 3 ⅞ In.	33
Century, Sherbet, 5 ¼ In.	8
Century, Wine, 5 ½ In.	20
Chantilly, Cordial, 4 ⅜ In.	49
Chantilly, Goblet, Water, 7 ¾ In.	27
Charleston, Compote, 4 ½ In.	9
Charleston, Cordial, 4 ⅜ In.	30
Charleston, Goblet, Water, 6 ½ In.	6
Chintz, Compote, Rose, 7 ⅛ In.	48
Chrysanthemum, Tumbler, Amber, 12 Oz., 5 ⅛ In.	20
Cleo, Candlestick, Moonlight Blue, 3 ¾ In., Pair	150
Cleo, Candy Dish, Lid Only, Pink, For Footed Bottom	35
Cleo, Ice Bucket, Blue, Handle, Signed	79
Cleo, Ice Tub, Wavy Rim, Signed	51
Colonial, Wine, 5 ⅛ In.	12
Cordelia, Goblet, Water, 7 ½ In.	31
Cordelia, Plate, Salad, 7 ⅜ In.	19
Cordelia, Sherbet, 5 ⅝ In.	8
Cordelia, Tumbler, Juice, 4 ⅛ In.	25
Corsage, Plate, Luncheon, 8 In.	11
Corsage, Sherbet, 5 In.	8
Corsage, Tumbler, Iced Tea, 7 ⅝ In.	7
Cranston, Ice Bucket, 4 ½ In.	159
Crown, Tumbler, Iced Tea, 5 ¾ In.	18
Decagon, Creamer, Pink	12
Decagon, Ice Bucket, Carmen Red, Wavy Rim, Handle, Signed	68
Decagon, Ice Bucket, Ritz Blue, Handle, Signed	50
Decagon, Server, Ebony, Etched	75
Decagon, Sugar & Creamer, Green, Lightning Bolt Handles	32
Decagon, Sugar & Creamer, Tray, Green, Lightning Bolt Handles	45
Decagon, Sugar, Pink, Lightning Bolt Handles	16
Diane, Goblet, Water, 11 Oz., 7 ¼ In.	32
Diane, Ice Bucket, Green, Handle, Signed	158
Diane, Sherbet, Low, 7 Oz., 4 ¼ In.	22
Diane, Sherbet, Tall, 7 Oz., 6 ⅜ In.	25
Dover, Cordial, 4 ¼ In.	47
Dover, Finger Bowl, 4 ⅜ In.	33
Dover, Goblet, Water, 7 ½ In.	21
Dover, Plate, Salad, 7 ½ In.	14
Dover, Sherbet, 4 ⅜ In.	10
Dover, Wine, 5 ⅝ In.	30
Empire, Sherbet, 4 ⅝ In.	13
Everglade, Plate, Amber, Leaf Line, 8 ½ In.	50
Everglade, Plate, Cattail & Swan, 16 In.	65
Festoon, Bell	26
Festoon, Juice, 4 ⅜ In.	17
Festoon, Tumbler, Goblet, Water, 6 In.	13
Festoon, Tumbler, Iced Tea, 5 ¾ In.	14
Firenze, Jug, 20 Oz., 4 ¾ In.	33
Flame, Ice Bucket, Gold Accents	90
Flame, Wine, 5 ¼ In.	9
Fuchsia, Bowl, Footed, 11 ½ In.	79
Fuchsia, Goblet, Water, 6 ⅝ In.	31
Fuchsia, Sherbet, 4 ⅛ In.	15
Fuchsia, Wine, 5 ¼ In.	23
Glendale, Cordial, 4 ⅜ In.	41
Glendale, Plate, Salad, 7 In.	14
Glendale, Sherbet, 5 ⅝ In.	6
Glendale, Tumbler, Iced Tea, 6 In.	17
Glendale, Wine, 5 ¾ In.	26
Gloria, Bowl, Pink, 4-Toed, 12 In.	80
Gloria, Cup & Saucer	31
Gloria, Ice Bucket, Pink, Gold, Handle, Signed	260
Gloria, Plate, Bread & Butter, 6 ⅜ In.	21

Gloria, Tumbler, Yellow, Footed, 10 Oz., 6 3/8 In. 50
Gold Bands, Tumbler, Iced Tea, 7 3/8 In. 8
Golden Wheat, Sherbet, 6 Oz., 5 3/4 In. 16
Hanover, Cordial, 4 3/8 In. 38
Hanover, Goblet, Water, 6 1/2 In. 27
Hanover, Wine, 5 5/8 In. 29
Imperial Hunt Scene, Sherbet, 3 3/4 In. 34
Jefferson, Sherbet, Blue, 4 7/8 In. 7
Jefferson, Tumbler, Footed, Blue, 5 Oz., 4 In. 7
Jefferson, Tumbler, Juice, Blue, 4 7/8 In. 8
Juliana, Cordial, 4 1/2 In. 35
Juliana, Goblet, Water, 6 5/8 In. 17
Juliana, Tumbler, Iced Tea, 6 1/4 In. 13
Juliana, Tumbler, Juice, 4 3/4 In. 23
Lotus, Sugar, Footed, 4 In. 38
Lynbrook, Creamer, 2 1/4 In. 23
Lynbrook, Goblet, Water, 5 7/8 In. 15
Lynbrook, Plate, Salad, 7 In. 14
Lynbrook, Tumbler, Iced Tea, 5 5/8 In. 8
Lynbrook, Wine, 4 1/2 In. 34
Majestic, Bowl, Mayonnaise, Moonlight Blue, Ladle 75
Manor, Creamer, 3 1/2 In. 21
Manor, Plate, Salad, 7 1/2 In. 17
Manor, Sherbet, 3 1/2 In. 11
Manor, Tumbler, 5 5/8 In. 28
Manor, Tumbler, Juice, 4 5/8 In. 28
Marlene, Sherbet, 4 In. 28
Marlene, Wine, 3 Oz., 4 In. 26
Martha, Plate, Salad, 7 1/2 In. 12
Maytime, Iced Tea, 6 In. 5
Maytime, Sherbet, 6 In. 6
Maytime, Tumbler, Goblet, Water, 6 5/8 In. 15
Montrose, Goblet, Water, 6 1/2 In. 23
Montrose, Plate, Salad, 7 1/2 In. 12
Montrose, Tumbler, Juice, 4 5/8 In. 18
Montrose, Wine, 5 7/8 In. 23
Mt. Vernon, Creamer, Carmen Red 20
Nautilus, Oil Bottle, Stopper, Individual 25
No. 1066, Goblet, Amethyst, 11 Oz., 6 1/4 In. 30
No. 3077, Tumbler, Regal Blue, Footed, 5 Oz., 3 5/8 In. 15
No. 3126, Goblet, Mulberry, Amethyst, 9 Oz., 7 7/8 In. 35
No. 3400, Pitcher, Royal Blue, 80 Oz. 135
No. 5062, Compote, Green, Farber Bros, Chrome Holder, High 35
Old English, Sherbet, 4 7/8 In. 5
Old English, Tumbler, Juice, 4 In. 21
Plaza, Goblet, Water, 6 1/2 In. 15
Plaza, Tumbler 20
Plaza, Tumbler, Iced Tea, 6 1/2 In. 8
Plaza, Tumbler, Juice, 4 3/4 In. 16
Plaza, Wine, 5 3/4 In. 16
Plymouth, Sherbet, 4 5/8 In. 31
Portia, Candlestick, Green, Keyhole, 5 In., Pair 200
Pristine, Candy Dish, Lid, Red Rose Finial, 3-Legged, 6 In. 75
Ravenna, Sherbet, 5 5/8 In. 11
Rosalie, Flower Holder, Pink, 3-In. Frog 95
Rosalie, Ice Tub, Amber, Signed 23
Rose Point, Celery Dish, 3 Sections, Tab Handles, c.1940, 11 In. 50
Rose Point, Ice Bucket, Gold Accents, Handle 226
Roselyn, Basket, Handles, 6 In. 14
Roselyn, Cordial, 4 3/8 In. 58
Roselyn, Goblet, Water, 7 3/4 In. 34
Roselyn, Tumbler, Iced Tea, 6 1/2 In. 23
Roselyn, Wine, 5 3/4 In. 42
Rubina, Bowl, Flared, 11 In. 124
Rubina, Compote, Rolled Rim, Footed, 9 1/2 In. 85

C

TIP
Glue broken china with an invisible mending cement that is waterproof.

Butter Chip, Flow Blue, Gold Trim, Scalloped Edge, c.1910, 3 3/8 In.
$25

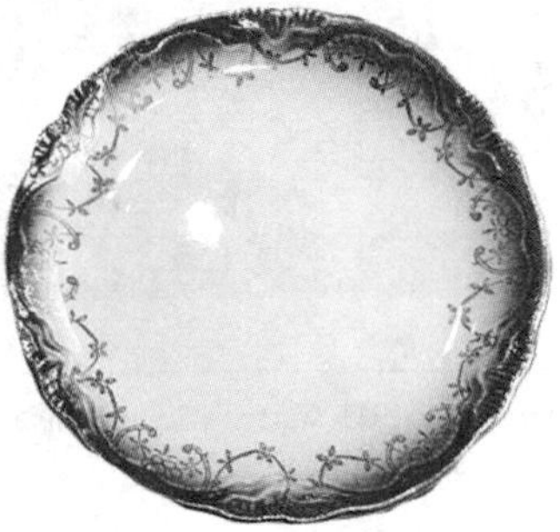

Ruby Lane, Inc.

Butter Chip, Golden State, Oranges, Chicago Rock Island & Pacific Railroad, c.1910, 3 In.
$225

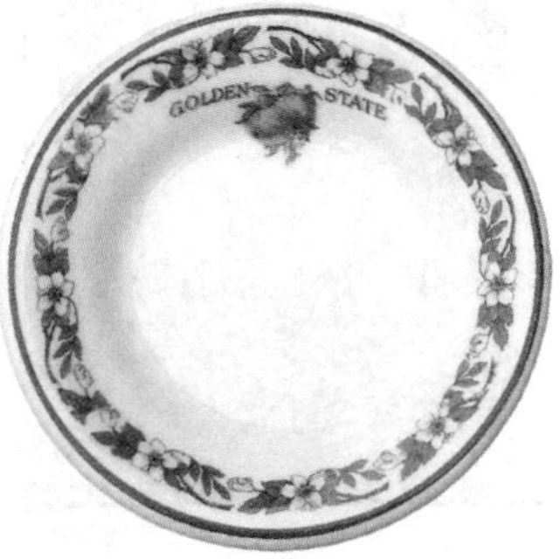

Ruby Lane, Inc.

Calendar, 1903, Peters Cartridge Co., Dawn Of A New Era, Dec. Page, 16 x 24 3/4 In.
$5,400

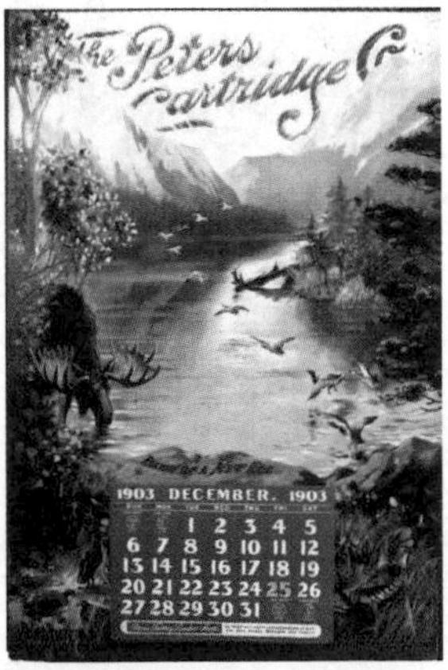

Showtime Auction Services

Calendar, 1905, DeLaval Cream Separators, Farm Girl, Full Pad, Frame, 15 x 10 In.
$242

Wm Morford Auctions

Calendar, 1911, Warren's Store, Couple, Embossed, Frame, 30 x 21 In.
$120

Morphy Auctions

Calendar, 1912, Wm. Scott Co., Fine Teas & Coffees, Partial Pad, 19 ½ x 8 In.
$115

Wm Morford Auctions

Rubina, Pitcher, Bulbous	396
Sonora, Goblet, Water, 8 ¼ In.	23
Sonora, Relish, 5 Sections, 12 ⅜ In.	43
Strathmore, Goblet, Water, 6 ½ In.	13
Strathmore, Tumbler, Juice, 4 ⅝ In.	18
Strathmore, Wine, 5 ½ In.	26
Sunnybrook, Sherbet, 6 ⅝ In.	8
Sunnybrook, Tumbler, Iced Tea, 7 In.	9
Swirl, Sherbet, 5 In.	4
Tally-Ho, Bowl, Salad Dressing, Royal Blue, 2 Compartment, 6 In.	45
Tally-Ho, Finger Bowl, Amber, Cupped, 4 ½ x 3 In.	16
Tally-Ho, Ice Bucket, Chromium Plated Handle, Frosted Inner Surface	65
Tally-Ho, Ice Bucket, Crown Tuscan, Handle	317
Tally-Ho, Ice Bucket, Farber, Purple	96
Tally-Ho, Shaker, Emerald Green	35
Tally-Ho, Tumbler, Carmen Red, 9 Oz., 3 ⅞ In.	25
Tempo, Cordial, 4 ½ In.	14
Tempo, Goblet, Water, 6 ½ In.	22
Tempo, Plate, Salad, 7 ½ In.	9
Tempo, Sherbet, 4 ⅝ In.	7
Tempo, Tumbler, Juice, 4 ⅝ In.	14
Vintage, Finger Bowl, 4 ⅝ In.	26
Vintage, Goblet, Water, 6 ⅝ In.	24
Wedding Rose, Juice, 4 ⅛ In.	28
Wedding Rose, Sherbet, 4 ½ In.	13
Wildflower, Compote, Footed, 10 In.	72
Wildflower, Cordial, 1 Oz., 5 ¼ In.	44
Wildflower, Goblet, Water, 10 Oz., 8 ¼ In.	39
Wildflower, Plate, Salad, 8 ¼ In.	16
Wildflower, Tumbler, Iced Tea, 12 Oz., 7 ⅝ In.	32
Wildflower, Tumbler, Juice, 5 Oz., 5 ⅝ In.	23
Wildflower, Wine, 3 ½ Oz., 6 ⅜ In.	93

CAMBRIDGE POTTERY was made in Cambridge, Ohio, from about 1895 until World War I. The factory made brown glazed decorated artwares with a variety of marks, including an acorn, the name *Cambridge*, the name *Oakwood*, and the name *Terrhea*.

Bowl, Emerald Green Matte, Ribbed Design, ¾ In.	58
Ewer, Wild Roses, Glazed, Bulbous, Cinched Neck, Ruffled Edge, 9 x 7 In.	145
Pitcher, Flowers, Leaves, Vines, Standard Glaze, c.1900, 5 ½ In.	145
Vase, Celadon Glaze, Bulbous, Flared Neck, 6 ¾ x 5 In.	36
Vase, Cucumber Green Glaze, Squat, 3 x 6 ½ In.	177
Vase, Green & Red Fronds, Black Glaze, Double Gourd Shape, Marked, 6 ½ In.	46
Vase, Orange Rose, Thorny Stem, Glazed, Bulbous, Tapered, 4 In.	45

CAMEO GLASS was made in much the same manner as a cameo in jewelry. Parts of the top layer of glass were cut away to reveal a different colored glass beneath. The most famous cameo glass was made during the nineteenth century. Signed cameo glass pieces are listed under the glasswork's name, such as Daum, Galle, Legras, Mt. Joye, Webb, and others.

Bell, White Flower Sprays, Red Ground, c.1900, 6 ½ In.	984
Biscuit Jar, Blue, White Scalloped Border, Ferns, Inverted Baluster, Silver Plate Rim, 5 ¾ In.	300
Perfume Bottle, Flat Sides, Flowers, Leaves, Insect, Sterling Lid, England, 4 In. .... *illus*	5175
Shaker, Spherical, Silver Plate Lid, White Bands, Leaf Lattice, Red Ground, c.1900, 3 ½ In.	180
Vase, Abstract Flower Design, Signed, D'Argyl, France, 1900s, 12 x 6 In., Pair .... *illus*	1875
Vase, Amber, White Flowers, Tapered, Cameo, c.1915, 5 ¼ In.	92
Vase, Azuerettes, Blue, Tapered, Le Verre Francais, c.1930, 8 In.	649
Vase, Blue Ground, Carved Poppies, Leaves, Bulbous Shape, Feathering At Rim, 10 ½ In.	1896
Vase, Blue, White Fruit Cuttings, Leafy Branches, Bird, Insect, Stylized Bands, 8 ½ In.	4313
Vase, Bud, Vines, Orange Ground, Richard, Paris, c.1910, 7 x 3 ½ In.	281
Vase, Bulbous Smokestack Shape, Blue, Stemmed Flowers, Sawtooth Rim, 2 ½ In.	891
Vase, Cameo, Bulbous Stick Shape, Stemmed Flowers, Arrow Point Border Rim, 6 ½ In.	805
Vase, Classic Shape, Red, Fan Palms, Blossoming Leaves, Butterfly, Woodall, 21 In.	4600
Vase, Cobalt Blue, Green, Ribbon Pattern, Bun Foot, Le Verre, 13 In.	345
Vase, Double Gourd, Long Stem Leafy Poppy, Butterfly, England, 5 In.	460

Vase, Florentine, Red Frosted, Perched Bird, Blossoming Cherry Branch, 8 In.	58
Vase, Lemon Yellow Over Cased White, Red Honeysuckle, Arrow Points, England, 4 ½ In.	690
Vase, Mottled Pink, Silver Inclusions, Flared, Lobed, Iron Casing, Delatte, France, 8 x 10 In.	976
Vase, Orange Berries, Leaves, Yellow & Cream Mottled Ground, Signed L. Bours, 5 In.	178
Vase, Purple, Game Birds, Red, Cream Landscape, P. Nicholas, France, c.1930, 8 ¾ In.	2375
Vase, Red & White Wheel Carved Flowers, Stems, Leaves, 6 In.	711
Vase, Stylized Japanese Lanterns, Fire Polished, Signed, Charder, c.1910, 9 ½ In. ....*illus*	748
Vase, Wooded Landscape, Footpath, Lamartine, c.1910, 6 ½ In. ....*illus*	1062

CAMPAIGN *memorabilia are listed in the Political category.*

CAMPBELL KIDS were first used as part of an advertisement for the Campbell Soup Company in 1904. The kids were created by Grace Drayton, a popular illustrator of the day. The kids were used in magazine and newspaper ads until about 1951. They were presented again in 1966; and in 1983, they were redesigned with a slimmer, more contemporary appearance.

Doll, Campbell Soup Girl, Plastic, Original Checked Dress & Apron, 10 In.	18
Doll, Centennial Costume, Composition, Hong Kong, Box, c.1972, 10 In., Pair	38
Hankie, Chuck Wagon, Boots, Spurs, Amsco, 1950s, 13 x 14 In.	32
Mug, Kids, 43 Seasons, 15 Oz., 3 ¼ In., Pair	12
Mug, Kids, Playing Outside, Houston Harvest, 15 Oz., 3 ¼ In.	7
Mugs, Kids Eating Sandwich, M'm M'm Good, Westwood, 15 Oz., 3 ½ In.	6
Print, Kids, Blackboard, Tomato Is A Fruit, Textured Paper, 1970s, 8 x 10 In.	14
Spoon, Kids, Female, Marked	10

CANDELABRUM refers to a candleholder with more than one arm to hold many candles; a candlestick is designed to hold one candle. The eccentricity of the English language makes the plural of candelabrum into candelabra.

2-Light, Brass, Swirled Acanthus Leaf Arms, Continental, 8 x 7 In., Pair	180
2-Light, Bronze Dore, Figural, Marble Base, Ball Feet, c.1900, 11 ½ x 8 In., Pair	1800
2-Light, Bronze, Egyptian Revival, Winged Sphinx, Snakes, Sun, Marble Base, 18 In., Pair	2813
2-Light, Bronze, Empire, Gilt, Classical Maiden, Amphora, c.1815, 20 In., Pair	2270
2-Light, Cut Glass, Bobeches, Suspended Prisms, Swags, Moon Finial, 19 In., Pair	2174
2-Light, Gilt Bronze, Classical Figure, Amphora, Wreath, c.1815, 9 ¾ In.	2214
2-Light, Glass, Pale Blue, Venice, 12 In., Pair	1560
2-Light, Glass, Pale Green, Gold Inclusions, Dolphin, 9 ½ In., Pair	840
2-Light, Porcelain, Gilt Bronze, Baluster, Leaf Arms, Festoons, 11 ½ In.	313
2-Light, Porcelain, Seated Maiden, Flower Branches, Singing, Flute, 8 In., Pair	250
2-Light, Silver, Scrolled Arms, Hammered, Berry Finial, G. Jensen, c.1948, 8 ¾ In.	7500
2-Light, Silver, Tapered Column, U-Shape, Soren, G. Jensen, c.1963, 7 In.	3750
2-Light, Wrought Iron, Tripod Bases, Penny Feet, Adjustable Cross Bars, 1800s, 23 In., Pair	1020
3-Light, Brass, Copper, Scrolled Arms, Etched Glass Shades, c.1840, 26 ¼ In.	593
3-Light, Bronze, Empire, Figure Standing, Scroll Arms, Gilt, c.1815, 18 ½ In., Pair	4920
3-Light, Bronze, Porcelain, Cobalt Blue Vase Shape, Stem Arms, 19 In., Pair	472
3-Light, Empire Style, Gilt, Bronze, Woman, Basket, Stepped Base, 21 In., Pair	875
3-Light, Empire, Woman, Holding Cornucopia, Gilt Bronze, Marble Base, 17 ½ In., Pair	660
3-Light, Gilt Bronze, Agate, Urn Shape, Rose Cups, Square Base, 10 In., Pair	4000
3-Light, Gilt Bronze, Art Nouveau, Relief, Wahlstrom, Bergman, c.1910, 11 In. ....*illus*	738
3-Light, Gilt Bronze, Cut Glass, Oval, Flowers, Hoof Shaped Legs, Base, 13 In., Pair	1000
3-Light, Gilt Bronze, Ebonized, Obelisk, Flower Shape Arms, 1800s, 17 In., Pair	492
3-Light, Gilt Bronze, Figural, Columnar, Stepped Base, 1800s, 24 In., Pair	6100
3-Light, Gilt Bronze, Marble, Flowers & Leaf Arms, 1900s, 14 ¼ In., Pair	649
3-Light, Gilt Bronze, Marble, Urn Shape, Ram Mask, Festoon, 12 In., Pair	594
3-Light, Gilt Bronze, Putto, Cornucopia Shaped Arms, France, 19 In., Pair	2750
3-Light, Gilt, Baluster, Square Base, Figural, Scroll Arms, c.1840, 19 In., Pair	861
3-Light, Inlaid Wood, Cross, Half-Moon Shape, Round Base, Syria, 14 In., Pair	72
3-Light, Molded Glass, Prisms, Twisted Standard, 22 In., Pair	531
3-Light, Porcelain, Dore Bronze, Turquoise Rooster, Scroll Arms, 1800s, 21 In., Pair	1920
3-Light, Silver Plate, Gadrooned, Entwined, M. Boulton & Co., England, c.1810, 22 In., Pair	4800
3-Light, Silver Plate, Reeded Arms, 3-Legged Post, c.1850, 24 x 17 ¼ In., Pair	3068
3-Light, Silver Plate, Reeded Twisting Arms, Gadrooned, 20 In., Pair	1434
3-Light, Silver Plate, Reeded Twisting Arms, Trumpet Shaft, c.1810, 18 In., Pair	2689
3-Light, Silver Plate, Scrolls, Flowers, Victorian, 14 In.	73
3-Light, Silver, Acanthus Detail, Whiting Mfg., 15 ¼ x 13 In.	190
3-Light, Silver, Convertible, 4 Parts, Scroll Arms, 15 x 15 In., Pair	799

Calendar, 1915, S.S. Redifer & Co., Hiawatha Wedding, Full Pad, Frame 16 x 27 In.
$450

Morphy Auctions

Calendar, 1926, Winchester, Game Hunter, Grizzly Bear, Philip R. Goodwin, 14 ⅝ x 26 ½ In.
$6,518

James D. Julia Auctioneers

Calendar, 1955, Alexander's Grocery, Marilyn Monroe Pinup, Full Pad, 10 x 16 In.
$115

Hake's Americana & Collectibles

Cameo Glass, Perfume Bottle, Flat Sides, Flowers, Leaves, Insect, Sterling Lid, England, 4 In.
$5,175

Early Auction Co.

Cameo Glass, Vase, Abstract Flower Design, Signed, D'Argyl, France, 1900s, 12 x 6 In., Pair
$1,875

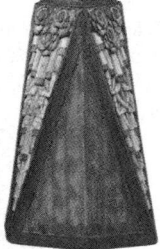

Rago Arts & Auction Center

Cameo Glass, Vase, Stylized Japanese Lanterns, Fire Polished, Signed, Charder, c.1910, 9 ½ In.
$748

Cottone Auctions

TIP

To easily remove wax that has dripped on a candlestick, put the candlestick in the freezer for about an hour. The wax will flake off.

3-Light, Silver, Rope Twist Design, Spread Foot, Towle, 1900s, 14 x 13 In., Pair	300
3-Light, Silver, Scroll Arms, Tapered, Round Foot, 1918, 19 x 17 In., Pair	1888
3-Light, Silver, Scrolled Arms, Footed, Chased Knop, Mexico, c.1950, 11 ½ In., Pair	5000
3-Light, Silver, Swirl Branch Arms, English Rose, 1900s, 12 x 13 In., Pair	590
3-Light, Wrought Iron, Flower Shape Candle Cups, Footed, 64 In.	600
4-Light, Bronze, William IV, Flame Finial, 26 x 9 In., Pair	584
4-Light, Copper, Tapered Cylindrical Support, Art Deco, c.1940, 13 In., Pair	207
4-Light, Gilt Bronze, Angel, Raised Arms, Scrolling, France, 1800s, 22 In., Pair	1888
4-Light, Gilt Bronze, Crane Finial, Vase Shape, Handles, Cherub, 28 In., Pair	2706
4-Light, Gilt Bronze, Oval Back, Top Shape, Cupola, Flowers, Openwork Arms, 21 In.	438
4-Light, Gilt Metal, Cherub Standard, Flower, Gilt Metal, Marble, Continental, 20 In., Pair	432
4-Light, Gilt, Paint, Blackamoor Figure, Scrolling Branches, 1900s, 39 In., Pair	431
4-Light, Neoclassical, Leaf, Flower Arms, Fluted Column, Tripod Base, Birds, 20 In., Pair	950
4-Light, Silver, Figural, Tree Shape Supports, Scroll Arms, Germany, 1900s, 21 In., Pair	236
4-Light, Silver, Scroll Tube Arms, U.S.A., 1900s, 6 x 16 In., Pair	177
4-Light, Victorian, Gilt Bronze, Grapevine, Leaf Shape Feet, Pierced Bases, c.1850, 12 x 12 In.	861
5-Light, Bisque, Gilt, Urn Shape, Scroll Arms, Hanging Prisms, 1800s, 28 In., Pair	2706
5-Light, Brass, Leaves, Hanging Prisms, Faux Candles, c.1900, 23 x 11 In., Pair	354
5-Light, Bronze, Champleve, Leaf Arms, Plaque, Birds, Lion Mask Feet, 18 In., Pair	2750
5-Light, Bronze, Figural, Pedestal Base, 1800s, 25 In., Pair	6000
5-Light, Gilt Bronze, Figural, Goddess, Cornucopia, Scroll, Swags, c.1850, 26 In., Pair	2151
5-Light, Gilt Bronze, Leaf Scroll Arms, Rococo, c.1850, 18 x 14 In.	717
5-Light, Gilt Bronze, Louis XV Style, Leaves, Branches, c.1910, 23 In., Pair	2125
5-Light, Gilt Bronze, Maiden, Wreath, Scroll Arms, 23 In., Pair	2000
5-Light, Gilt Metal, Leafy Arms, Mask, Urn, Fluted Columnar Stem, 20 In., Pair	500
5-Light, Gilt, Patinated Spelter, Victory Figure, Holding Torch, Scrolls, 32 In., Pair	1500
5-Light, Giltwood, Flower, Swag Carved, Italy, 29 In.	3025
5-Light, Porcelain, Gilt Bronze, Urn Shape, Plaque, Scroll Arms, 1800s, 18 In., Pair	185
5-Light, Rope Twist Branches, Prisms, Baccarat, c.1965, 23 x 15 In.	938
5-Light, Silver Plate, 2 Parts, Bead Border, Round Base, 18 x 17 In., Pair	179
5-Light, Silver Plate, Leaves, Scroll Arms, Reeded Stem, Paw Feet, 1800s, 28 In.	615
5-Light, Silver Plate, Rococo Style, Baluster Stem, Iris Banding, c.1950, 13 x 19 In.	492
5-Light, Silver Plate, Scroll Arms, Baluster Standard, Flowers, Leaves, 19 In., Pair	448
5-Light, Silver, Leaf, Laurel Footed Base, Italy, c.1955, 19 In., Pair	4000
5-Light, Silver, Leafy Branch Shape Stem, S-Scroll Arms, Girl & Boy, 21 In., Pair	1500
5-Light, Silver, Maiden's Heads, Palmettes & Lotus, c.1815, 23 ½ In.	2318
5-Light, Silver, Over Copper, Convertible, Beaded, Scrolled, Epee, England, 14 In., Pair	826
6-Light, Bronze, Art Nouveau Style, Figural, Woman With Mirror, 1900s, 25 In., Pair	270
6-Light, Bronze, Maiden, Urn On Shoulders, Winged Feet, c.1885, 31 x 13 In., Pair	652
6-Light, Bronze, Reeded Columnar Stem, Scroll Arms, Square Base, 31 ½ In., Pair	956
6-Light, Gilt Bronze, Columnar, Incurvate Triangular Base, Paw Feet, 26 In., Pair	1554
6-Light, Gilt Bronze, Marble, Quiver Standard, Scroll Arms, 26 ½ In., Pair	1063
6-Light, Gilt Bronze, Shaped Arms, Flower Shaped Cups, Prisms, 22 In., Pair	813
6-Light, Gilt Bronze, Winged Victory, Figure, Globe, Column, 30 In., Pair	2390
6-Light, Silver, Ormolu, Scroll & Leaf Design Arms, Columnar Stem, 1800s, 28 In., Pair	720
6-Light, Silver, Scroll Arms, Baluster Stem, Cabochons, c.1850, 29 x 15 In., Pair	8365
7-Light, Bronze Dore, Louis XV Style, 2 Putti, Gilt Standard, 37 In.	443
7-Light, Bronze, 2 Tiers, Scroll Arms, Columnar, Flowers, c.1850, 19 x 22 In., Pair	1434
7-Light, Bronze, 6 Branches, Tiffany Studios, 14 In.	2125
7-Light, Bronze, Glass, Flowering Tree, Tripod Base, 1800s, 39 In.	270
7-Light, Bronze, Ormolu, Spelter, Figure, Holding Onto Stem, France, 19 In., Pair	600
7-Light, Bronze, Slate, Gilt, Pierced Scroll Arms, Columnar Stem, 1800s, 33 In., Pair	1800
7-Light, Bronze, Tripartite, Fluted Column, Scroll Branches, c.1835, 28 In., Pair	615
7-Light, Gilt Brass, Avika, Scrolls, Lars Holmstrom, Svenskt Tenn Co., 1940s, 4 x 8 In.	875
7-Light, Gilt Brass, Leaf Arms, Openwork Stem, Scroll Base, c.1850, 30 In., Pair	1098
7-Light, Gilt Bronze, Leaf Arms, Urn, Wreath, Marble, 20 In.	2500
7-Light, Gilt Bronze, Seated Child, Flowering Branches, Leaves, France, 22 ½ In.	688
7-Light, Patinated Bronze, Gilt, Tapered Column, Stepped Base, 29 In., Pair	1625
7-Light, Silver Plate, Acanthus, Blossoms, Mason & Co., 1800s, 26 ½ x 21 In.	813
7-Light, Silver Plate, Scrolled, Repousse, Gorham, 23 In., Pair	668
7-Light, Silver, Knopped Stem, Scrolls, Rocaille, Continental, c.1905, 24 ½ In., Pair	5000
7-Light, Silver, Urn Shape, Festoons, Scroll Arms, Tripartite Base, 23 In., Pair	3500
8-Light, Gilt Bronze, Reeded Stem, Scroll Arms, Tripartite Base, 46 In., Pair	2750
9-Light, Gilt Bronze, Flower & Scroll Arms, Tiered, Reeded Stem, 29 In., Pair	6875
9-Light, Gilt Bronze, Urn, Leaves, Scroll Arms, Paw Feet, Trophee, 32 In., Pair	3294

C

11-Light, Gilt Bronze, Woman Holding Cornucopia, Leafy Arms, 44 In., Pair		5975
13-Light, Bronze, Jugendstil Cast, Bruno Paul, 1901, 117 x 28 In.		6000
24-Light, Gilt Bronze, Brass, Louis XIV Style, Stepped Stem, 2 Tiers, Scroll, 44 x 45 In.		7072

CANDLESTICKS were made of brass, pewter, glass, sterling silver, plated silver, and all types of pottery and porcelain. The earliest candlesticks, dating from the sixteenth century, held the candle on a pricket (sharp pointed spike). These lost favor because in times of strife the large church candlesticks with prickets became formidable weapons, so the socket was mandated. Candlesticks changed in style through the centuries, and designs range from Classical to Rococo to Art Nouveau to Art Deco.

Brass, Acorn Knob, Mid Dished Drip Tray, Domed Round Base, c.1660, 9 In.	900
Brass, Black Figure, Holding Cup, Marble Base, 10 In., Pair	192
Brass, Capstan, Threaded Base, Urn Shape Socket, Extractor Holes, c.1660, 5 In.	331
Brass, Columnar, Narrow Sconce, Fluted Stem, Stepped Base, c.1790, 8 ½ In., Pair	240
Brass, Cross, Openwork, Cupid Finial, 26 x 16 In.	120
Brass, Figural, Woman, Sinewy Stem, Spread Lily Base, Art Nouveau, 10 In., Pair	147
Brass, Gallery Rim, Square Base, Threaded Stem, Spain, c.1700, 5 In., Pair	323
Brass, Griffin, 6 x 6 ½ In., Pair	105
Brass, Hexagonal Base, Baluster, Leaf Border, Swelled Knop, 10 ¾ In.	1440
Brass, Louis XV, Knopped Standard, c.1785, 10 In., Pair	480
Brass, Neoclassical, Marble Base, Faux Candle, 16 ½ x 4 In., Pair	338
Brass, Petal Base, Shaped Stem, Flat Rim, 1700s, 7 In., Pair	470
Brass, Pierced Bowl Drip Tray, Serpent Handle, Embossed Flowers, 12 ½ In.	165
Brass, Push-Up, England, c.1860, 19 ¾ In., Pair	711
Brass, Quatrefoil Base, Inverted Shaft, Sausage Turnings, c.1750, 8 In., Pair	338
Brass, Queen Anne, Octagonal Base, Baluster, England, c.1710, 8 ⅛ In., Pair	369
Brass, Queen Anne, Petal Base, England, c.1760, 9 In.	830
Brass, Queen Anne, Petal Base, Ring-Turned Stem, 1700s, 8 ¼ In., Pair	300
Brass, Queen Of Diamonds, c.1900, 11 ½ In., Pair	360
Brass, Reeded, Louis Philippe Style, Patinated Metal Cup, Base, 10 In., Pair	438
Brass, Ribbed Stem, Inverted Baluster Knob, Round Foot, 1700s, 7 ¼ In.	840
Brass, Shape Stem, Square Base, Reeded Border, Flared Rim, 10 ½ In., Pair	350
Bronze, Bell Foot, Center Bowl, Rolled Rim, Chinese, 1800s, 11 x 5 In., Pair	180
Bronze, Cylindrical Standard, Wide Base, Epsilon Shape, Jarvie, 6 x 6 In.	5300
Bronze, Dragon Shape Feet, Baluster Stem, Petal Rim, c.1600, 10 ½ In., Pair	307
Bronze, Figural, Bearded Man, Footed, 12 In.	180
Bronze, Figural, Vestal Virgin, Holding Flame, Tapered Pedestal, 1900s, 14 In., Pair	1220
Bronze, Gilt, Rosettes, Cut Glass, c.1825, 8 ½ In., Pair	1107
Bronze, Pharaoh, Headdress, Stepped Round Base, 8 ½ In., Pair	1063
Bronze, Sea Turtles, Dolphins, Relief, Round Base, 9 In., Pair	210
Bronze, Seahorse, Signed, E.T. Hurley, 13 x 5 In., Pair	1000
Burl, Turned Cup Shape, 1800s, 2 ½ In.	554
Copper, Arts & Crafts, Twisted Stems, Tooled Designs, Patina, c.1925, 4 x 8 In., Pair	397
Cut Glass, Hanging Prisms, 2 Tiers, Sawtooth Bobeches, c.1850, 10 x 4 In., Pair	610
Flint Enamel, Bennington, c.1850, 9 In., Pair	668
Gilt Brass, Ship's Gimbal, Spring Loaded, Baker Arnold & Co., c.1875, 10 ½ In.	215
Gilt Bronze, Empire Style, Leaf Stem, Tripartite Base, Swans, 12 In., Pair	2000
Gilt Bronze, Figural, Eagle, Serpent In Beak, Bronze, Marble, c.1815, 7 ¼ In., Pair	1098
Gilt Bronze, Figural, Leaf Cup, Round Marble Base, 10 In., Pair	938
Gilt Bronze, Marble, Figural, Woman, Columnar Pedestal, Glass Shade, 17 In., Pair	984
Gilt Bronze, Marble, Winged Cherub, Round Footed Base, 1800s, 7 ¾ In., Pair	657
Gilt Bronze, Oriental Figure, Hanging Prisms, Marble Base, 13 ½ In., Pair	1375
Giltwood, Altar, Tapered, Leaves, Fluting, Pricket, Paw Feet, c.1815, 34 In., Pair	1599
Giltwood, Baluster, Carved, Leaf & Swag Design, Italy, 52 ¼ In., Pair	1750
Giltwood, Pricket, Carved, Leaf Stem, Triangular Base, Hoof Feet, c.1800, 22 In., Pair	777
Glass, Egyptian Figure, Lacquered Brass Nozzle, France, c.1900, 17 In.	984
Glass, Spiral Stem, Footed, Applied Designs, c.1970, 50 In.	250
Glass, Starburst, Swarovski, 4 In., Diam., Pair	120
Iron, Hog Scraper, Brass Faucet Wedding Band, Flared Drip Tray, Push-Up, 8 ½ In., Pair	443
Iron, Hog Scraper, Brass, Dome Base, Brass Medial Band, c.1800, 7 ½ x 4 In.	403
Iron, Spiral Screw, Triple Shell Drip Pan, 1800s, 7 ½ In.	575
Ivory, Biedermeier, Turned & Reeded, Baluster, Flare Cup, c.1835, 6 x 3 In., Pair	738
Marble, Palm Tree, Splayed Leaves, Architectural Base, Black Marble, 15 In., Pair	161
Patinated Bronze, Arts & Crafts Style, Green, Black Webbing, 18 ¼ In., Pair	861

Cameo Glass, Vase, Wooded Landscape, Footpath, Lamartine, c.1910, 6 ½ In.
$1,062

Brunk Auctions

Candelabrum, 3-Light, Gilt Bronze, Art Nouveau, Relief, Wahlstrom, Bergman, c.1910, 11 In.
$738

Skinner Auctioneers & Appraisers

Candlestick, Silver, George III, Tapered, Urn & Bellflower, Sheffield, 1776, 11 ¼ In., Pair
$1,067

James D. Julia Auctioneers

Candlestick, Silver, Regency, John Roberts & Co., Hallmark, c.1810, 12 ½ In., Pair
$2,706

New Orleans Auction Galleries, Inc.

Candy Container, Belsnickle, Red Robe, Composition, Rabbit Fur Beard, Feather Tree, 22 In.
$3,540

Bertoia Auctions

Candy Container, Elephant, Vegetable Body, Potato, Melons, Turnip, Corn Stalk Trunk, 7 In.
$3,245

Bertoia Auctions

Pewter, Openwork Column, Flower Base, A. Knox, Liberty & Company, 6 x 10 In., Pair	2500
Porcleain, Diving Fish Standard, Scalloped Gilt Cup, Cream Glaze, 10 In., Pair	98
Silver Plate, Gothic Revival, Bulbous Nozzle, Column Standard, Molded Base, 8 In., Pair	875
Silver Plate, Repousse Flowers, Roswell, Gleason & Sons, Mass., Pair	130
Silver Plate, Shaped Stem & Foot, Scroll Embossed, c.1900, 19 ¼ In., Pair	488
Silver Plate, Tapered Standard, Sheffield, c.1800, 1 ½ In.	240
Silver, Column Shape, Durgin Co., 11 In.	325
Silver, Corinthian Column, Stepped Base, Gadroon, England, 1892, 11 In., Pair	413
Silver, Cylindrical, Rolled Rim, Round Base, Greek Key Border, 6 ¾ In., Pair	330
Silver, Egyptian Revival, Snake Shape, Lotus Cup, Gorham, c.1880, 9 In., Pair	28125
Silver, Etched Glass Shade, Inserts, Monogram, 12 ⅜ In., Pair	300
Silver, Fluted Column, Square Base, Mappin Bros., 1899, 5 In., 4 Piece	1170
Silver, George II, Baluster, Square Foot, John Cafe, London, c.1750, 9 In., Pair	2813
Silver, George III, Tapered, Urn & Bellflower, Sheffield, 1776, 11 ¼ In., Pair *illus*	1067
Silver, Hammered Borders, Tapered, c.1915, 9 ½ In., Pair	472
Silver, Iris Repousse, Monogram, Geo. W. Shielbler, 4 ½ x 11 ½ In.	938
Silver, James Dixon & Sons, Victorian, c.1900, 7 ¾ In., Pair	540
Silver, Paneled Baluster, Shaped Base, England, 1853, 7 In., Pair	590
Silver, Petal Shape Bobeche, Knopped Baluster, 1742, 8 ¼ In., Pair	6000
Silver, Portrait Medallion, Swags, Repousse, Round Base, England, c.1810, 5 x 6 In., Pair	1150
Silver, Regency, John Roberts & Co., Hallmark, c.1810, 12 ½ In., Pair *illus*	2706
Silver, Removable Bobeche, Balustrade Stem, Round Foot, 10 In., Pair	900
Silver, Repousse, Flower Band, Rim, Weighted Bases, S. Kirk & Son, 3 ½ In., Pair	132
Silver, Rococo Designs, John Watson, Sheffield, 1820, 11 In., Pair	2160
Silver, Tapered, Thomas Bradbury & Sons, 1908, 4 ½ In., Pair	600
Silver, Tapering, Reeded, Flower Medallion, c.1900, 8 ¼ In., Pair	826
Tin, Hog Scraper, 15 ¾ In., Pair	972
Vaseline Glass, Dolphin, Hexagon Bases, 7 & 7 ½ In., Pair	413
Wrought Iron, Spiral Standard, Drip Pan, Penny Feet, c.1800, 11 In.	304

CANDLEWICK *items may be listed in the Imperial Glass and Pressed Glass categories.*

CANDY CONTAINERS have been popular since the late Victorian era. Collectors have long favored the glass containers, but now all types, including tin and papier-mache, are collected. Probably the earliest glass container sold commercially was the Liberty Bell made in 1876 for sale at the Centennial Exposition. Thousands of designs were made until the cost became too high in the 1960s. By the late 1970s, reproductions were being made and sold without the candy. Containers listed here are glass unless otherwise described. A Belsnickle is a nineteenth-century figure of Father Christmas. Some candy containers may be listed in Toy or in other categories.

Belsnickle, On Snowball, Green Robe, Composition, Germany, 6 ½ In.	885
Belsnickle, Red Robe, Composition, Rabbit Fur Beard, Feather Tree, 22 In. *illus*	3540
Clown, Riding Rocking Horse, Glass, Metal Closure, 4 ¼ In.	210
Egg Shape, Papier-Mache, Multicolor Flowers, Up To 7 In., 8 Piece	114
Elephant, Vegetable Body, Potato, Melons, Turnip, Corn Stalk Trunk, 7 In. *illus*	3245
Father Christmas, Composition, Silver Fox Fur Coat, Germany, 16 In.	4130
Father Christmas, Composition, White Fur, Dresden Lantern, 18 In.	4720
George Washington, Stands On Rock, Great Shield, Composition, Germany, 9 In.	2655
Girl On Goat, Bisque Head, Fur Covered Goat, Felt Dresden Collar, Bell, 13 In.	2360
Goat, Standing, Blue Suit Top, White Base, Composition, Round Base, 8 ¼ In.	577
Halloween, Boar's Head, Composition, Multicolor, Germany, 3 ½ In.	384
Halloween, Hunched Cat, Black, Cloth, 7 ½ In.	480
Halloween, Jack-O'-Lantern, Candle Shape, Pressed Paper, Cloth Wick, 7 In.	2006
Halloween, Jack-O'-Lantern, Crepe Drawstring, Dresden Trim, Germany, 4 In. *illus*	708
Halloween, Jack-O'-Lantern, Orange, Plaster, 2 In.	90
Halloween, Pumpkin Head Girl, Multicolor, Germany, 4 ½ In.	330
Halloween, Pumpkin Head Man, Pumpkin Bowl, Papier-Mache, Germany, 3 ¾ In.	240
Halloween, Pumpkin Head, Smiling Chauffer, Blue Suit, 3 ¾ In.	450
Halloween, Skeleton, Papier-Mache Head, Cloth Body, 6 In.	210
Halloween, Tennis Player, Pumpkin Head, Multicolor Paint, 4 ½ In.	90
Halloween, The Lucky Box, Spinner, Witch, Cat, Round, Black, Orange, Tin, 5 ½ In.	540
Halloween, Veggie People, Cats, Devils, Box, Lid, Cardboard, String Handle, 1½ In.	649
Halloween, Witch, Cardboard, Wood, Papier-Mache Head, Germany, c.1930, 15 In. *illus*	2552
Halloween, Witch, On Black Cat, Composition, Crepe, Mohair, Germany, 8 In.	885
Halloween, Witch, On Goose, Side Saddle, Spun Cotton, Wood, Cloth, 7 In.	384

Halloween, Witch, Standing, Broom, Composition, Wood, Paper, 16 In.	3245
Halloween, Witch, Standing, Human Hair, Satin Cape, Beaded, Twig Broom, 12 In.	3245
Happifat, On Drum, Glass, Coin Slot, Geo. Borgfelt License, 4 ½ In. ....*illus*	295
Happy Hooligan, Movable Arms, Round Base, 5 ½ In.	180
Hen On Egg, Yellow, Green, Tin, 4 x 4 In.	89
Jonah & Whale, Papier-Mache, Composition, Painted, Glass Eyes, Jaw Opens, 12 In.	1422
Kaleidoscope, Moving Pictures, Cylindrical, Metal, West Bros., Box, 7 ½ In.	7200
Little Bo Peep, Bisque Head, Sitting On Wooly Sheep, Leather Ears, Bell, 11 In.	2950
Mama Katzenjammer, Holding Kids Under Arms, Removable Head, Composition, 6 ½ In.	1080
Milkmaid On Cow, Bisque Head, Felt Cow, Leather Belt Collar, Bell, 12 In.	944
Moon Face, Smiling Moon Man, Dresden, 4 In.	266
Mushroom Man, Opens At Base, Dresden, 3 ½ In. ....*illus*	236
Old Woman In Shoe, Papier-Mache, Cloth, Nodding Head, Germany, 6 ½ x 5 In. ....*illus*	770
Pail, Lovell & Covel Co., Rabbits, Verse, Tin Lithograph, Bail Handle, 3 In.	150
PEZ, Psychedelic Eye In Hand, Go Go PEZ, Front & Back, Late 1960s, 4 ¼ In. ......*illus*	158
Rabbit Feeder, Carrot To Mouth, Mechanical, Germany, 6 ¾ In.	1680
Rooster, Red, Silk Bag, Dresden, Germany, 3 In. ....*illus*	1180
Santa Claus, Composition, Felt Robe, Rabbit Fur Beard, Germany, 17 In.	4425
Santa Claus, Folded Hands, Glass, 5 ⅜ x 2 ⅛ In.	546
Santa Claus, On Polar Bear, Mohair, Composition, Red Felt, Fur, 11 In.	3835
Santa Claus, On Reindeer, Felt, Metal Antlers, Rabbit Fur Beard, 11 In.	3540
Santa Claus, Pilot In Wicker Airplane, Feather Tree Sprig, 15 In.	4720
Santa Claus, Roly Poly, Composition, Red Felt Robe, Fur Beard, 7 In.	531
St. Patrick's Day, Man, Standing, Red Hair, Top Hat, Pipe, Suit, Cane, Composition, 10 In.	948
Tree Trunk, With Face, Pressed Paper, Twig Arms, Germany, 4 In.	413
Turtle, Copper Luster, Dresden, Germany, 3 ¼ In.	472
Veggie Man, Standing, Composition, Germany, 4 In. ....*illus*	295
Victrola, Glass, Tin Enclosure & Horn, Red Paint ....*illus*	177
Watermelon, Smiling Face, Oval, Cardboard, 3 ¾ In.	150

CANES and walking sticks were used by every well-dressed man in the nineteenth century, but by World War I the style had changed. Today canes are used by few but the infirm. Collectors prize old canes made with special features, like hidden swords, whiskey flasks, or risqué pictures seen through peepholes. Examples with solid gold heads or made from exotic materials are among the higher-priced canes. See also Scrimshaw.

2 Snakes, Winding Around Shaft, Multicolor, 34 ½ In., Pair	780
7 Pines Battlefield, Inscription, Red Painted Shaft, Henrico County, Va., c.1900, 33 ½ In.	173
Amethyst Quartz, Tapered, Vermeil Wire, Pear Shape Citrines, Rosewood Shaft, 37 In.	690
Aventurine, Green, Knob, Flattened, Tapered Neck, Snakewood Shaft, Art Deco, 35 In.	460
Baleen, 8-Sided, Inlaid Compass Rose, Abalone Points, Barley Twist Shaft, c.1850, 36 In.	1725
Ball In Cage, Clinging Man, Winding Snake, Alligatored Surface, Wood, 1800s, 36 In.	660
Bone, Dog Head Grip, Bone Ferrule, c.1780	295
Brass Handle, Ferrule, Entwined Animals, Painted, J.F. W. To F. Wright, c.1900, 35 x 5 In.	2500
Cloisonne, Flowers, Red, Yellow, Blue, Tan, Gold, Crook Handle, Wood Shaft, c.1900, 35 In.	863
Cobra, Wood, Carved, Painted, Entwined Shaft, Red Jewel Eyes, Brass End Cap, 35 In.	201
Damascene, Black Steel, Gold Design, Crook Handle, Ebony Shaft, 36 In.	978
Dog Head Handle, Brass Ferrule, Root, Attr., Schtockschnitzler Simmons, c.1900, 37 x 5 In.	1150 to 4375
Dog Head Handle, Entwined Animal Shaft, Metal Ferrule, Rubber Tip, Pa., 33 x 5 In.	4063
Dogwood, Horse Head, Bridle Handle, Brass Ferrule, c.1905, 36 x 53 In.	5000
Eagle, Wood, Snake, Lizard Shaft, Incised Shaft, c.1905, 37 x 6 In.	2813
Elephant Ivory Handle, Fist, Holding Snake, c.1850, 3 ½ In.	413
Fruitwood, Silver Mount, c.1920, 36 In.	94
Glass, Blue Aqua, Opalescent Spiral Bands, Tapered, Knob End, 33 ¼ In.	69
Glass, Goldstone, Ball, In Silver 5-Finger Cradle & Collar, Ebony Shaft, Faux Thorns, 36 In.	345
Glass, Red, White & Blue Spiral Bands, Tapered, Curled End, 47 ½ In.	115
Green Guilloche, Turned Pattern, Entwined Silver Panther, Snakewood Shaft, 37 In.	8050
Hickory, Hearts, Snake, Engraved, Camp, Chase, Prison, c.1862, 34 In.	1528
Hickory, Ship Captain Terminal, Carved, New England, c.1850, 33 x 2 ¼ In.	34375
Horn, Embossed Silver Mount, c.1890, 36 In.	212
Horn, Horse's Hoof, Applied Silver Metal Shoe, c.1900, 36 In.	1093
Ivory & Ebony, Spanish Woman, Black Mantilla, Coral Accents, Ebony Shaft, 35 In.	5463
Ivory Handle, Carved, Bacchanalian, Burl, Gilt Metal Collar, Brass Ferrule, 33 ½ In. ....*illus*	840
Ivory Handle, Carved, Flowers, Acanthus, Late 19th Century, Japan, Signed, 4 In.	270
Ivory Handle, Dog Head, Carved, Glass Beaded Eyes, Bamboo Stem, 5 ¾ x 3 ¼ In.	502

Candy Container, Halloween, Jack-O'-Lantern, Crepe Drawstring, Dresden Trim, Germany, 4 In,
$708

Bertoia Auctions

Candy Container, Halloween, Witch, Cardboard, Wood, Papier-Mache Head, Germany, c.1930, 15 In.
$2,552

James D. Julia Auctioneers

Candy Container, Happifat, On Drum, Glass, Coin Slot, Geo. Borgfelt License, 4 ½ In.
$295

Bertoia Auctions

This is an edited listing of current prices. Visit Kovels.com to check thousands of prices from previous years and sign up for free information on trends, tips, reproductions, marks, and more.

Candy Container, Mushroom Man, Opens At Base, Dresden, 3 ½ In. $236

Bertoia Auctions

Candy Container, Old Woman In Shoe, Papier-Mache, Cloth, Nodding Head, Germany, 6 ½ x 5 In. $770

James D. Julia Auctioneers

Candy Container, PEZ, Psychedelic Eye In Hand, Go Go PEZ, Front & Back, Late 1960s, 4 ¼ In. $158

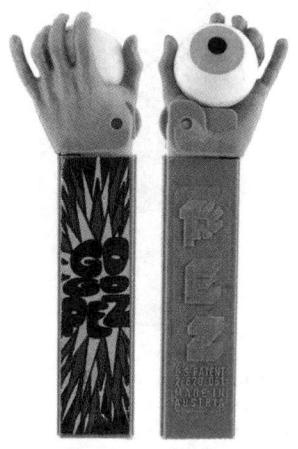

Front   **Back**

Hake's Americana & Collectibles

Ivory Handle, Smiling Child's Head, Elephant Tusk, 2 In.	266
Ivory, Art Nouveau Flower, Tangled Vine, Bud, Ebony Shaft, c.1900, 36 ½ In.	1380
Ivory, Bust, Spanish Matador, Ebony Shaft, Metal Ferrule, c.1915, 37 ¼ In.	1725
Ivory, Carved Pig Handle, Silver Ferrule, c.1905, 36 In.	750
Ivory, Cluster Of Rats, Curled Into Ball, Black Jet Eyes, Snakewood Shaft, Japan, 36 In.	1093
Ivory, Dog Head, Greyhound, Amber Glass Eyes, Mouth Open, Chestnut Shaft, 34 In.	920
Ivory, Elephants, Lions, Whales, Ships, Ebony, Mother-Of-Pearl, Silver, c.1845, 32 x 2 In.	46875
Ivory, Horse Shape Handle, Gold Fill Collar, Wood Shaft, 34 ½ In.	625
Ivory, Hound's Head Handle, Glass Eyes, Brass Collar, Cocobolo Shaft, c.1875, 26 In.	469
Ivory, Monk, Carousing, Holding Wine Glass & Playing Cards, Mahogany Shaft, 34 In.	1495
Ivory, Rabbit Head, Yellow Glass Eyes, Ears Back, Silver Collar, Wood Shaft, 1892, 36 In.	2760
Ivory, Seasick Sailor, Frock Coat, Silver Wire, Malacca Shaft, England, c.1885, 34 In.	2875
Ivory, Talon Gripping Walnut, Gold Fill Collar, Ebonized Shaft, 37 ⅛ In.	500
Jade, Dog's Head Handle, Glass Eyes, Sterling Collar, Ebonized Shaft, c.1915, 31 In.	875
Maple, Eagle Head Handle, Carved, Feathers, Ball, Spiral Shaft, Stain, c.1900, 35 ½ In.	480
Olivewood, Horse's Head, Leather Bridle, L Handle, Metal Ferrule, Greece, c.1895, 37 In.	690
Poplar, Entwined Snake, Paint, c.1900, 33 ½ x 2 In.	1000
Porcelain, Boy's Head, 2 Faces, Happy, Sad, Brass Collar, Ebony Shaft, c.1890, 38 In.	690
Porcelain, Chinoiserie, Figures, Meissen, Silver Acanthus Collar, Malacca, c.1725, 39 In.	4313
Porcelain, Courting Couples In Garden, Gold Trim, Tau Handle, Ebony Shaft, c.1860, 37 In.	575
Rock Crystal, Greek Key Band, Frosted Cut To Clear, Enamel, Rosewood, Art Deco, 38 In.	1955
Rose Quartz, Silver Festoons, 2 Sapphires, Guilloche, Silver Buds, Wood Shaft, 37 In.	2530
Silver Plate On Bronze, Horse Head & Jockey Handle, Wood, Rubber Ferrule, c.1875, 37 In.	485
Silver, Bird's Head Handle, Long Beak, Garnet Eyes, Crook, Reed Shaft, c.1885, 35 In.	750
Silver, Book, Hinged C-Scroll Lid, Pillbox, Ebonized Shaft, c.1900, 36 In.	1495
Silver, Duck Head, Glass Eye, Malacca Shaft, Continental, c.1910, 35 In.	660
Silver, Eagle Head, Curved Beak, L Handle, Blackened Hardwood Shaft, 36 In.	748
Silver, Golf Putter, Inscribed To Mrs. Wm. Wilson, 1905, Partridgewood Shaft, 32 ½ In.	978
Silver, Hammered, Brass Gecko & Fly, Tau Handle, Malacca Shaft, c.1895, 34 In.	345
Silver, Ivory Handle, Engraved Scrolls, Wood Shaft, Continental, c.1900, 34 ¾ In.	570
Silver, Lighter, Hinged Lid, Acanthus Band, Malacca Shaft, Dunhill, 1930s, 36 In.	4313
Silver, Polar Bear, L Handle, Snakewood Shaft, Tiffany & Co., c.1895, 36 In.	11500
Sword, Cane Wood, Woven Baleen, Triangular Blade, Gold Inlay, 1800s, 37 In.	837
Telescope, Wood, Brass, c.1910, 35 In.	469
Tiger's-Eye, Sphere Shape, Faux Rosewood Shaft, 36 In.	236
Walking Stick, Black Boot Handle, Carved Wood, Metal Cuff, Birds, Plants, 34 In.	179
Walking Stick, Carved, 5 Skeletons On Shaft, Asia, c.1950, 35 ½ In.	154
Walking Stick, Ebony, Gold Plated Handle, Monogram, C.M. Burton, 35 ½ In.	300
Walking Stick, Horse Head, Carved Wood, Incised, Folk Art, 34 ¾ In.	179
Walking Stick, Kaleidoscope, Carved Wood Handle, Male Bust, Bead Eyes, 39 ⅛ In.	179
Walking Stick, Maple, Metal Ferrule, Acorn, Alligator, Bird, Leaves, A.P., c.1905, 32 In.	431
Walking Stick, Presentation, Branches, Fraternal Symbols, F.L.T., Heart-In-Hand, c.1890, 34 In.	646
Walking Stick, Rosewood, Yellow Gold Handle, Scrolling, U.S.A., c.1900, 33 ½ In.	354
Walking Stick, Silver, Ivory, Skull Shape Handle, Ebonized Shaft, 1922, 33 ½ In.	813
Walking Stick, Snake, Wood, Spiral Carved, Painted Black, Glass Eyes, Brass Tip, 38 In.	300
Walking Stick, Sterling & Ebony, Monkey's Fist Knot, Roper Wrapping, 1900s, 35 ½ In.	570
Walking Stick, Wood, Entwined Dragons, Chasing Comet, c.1900, 38 In.	687
Whale Ivory, Bird Handle, Bone, Ink Inscribed Ring, 200 WET, c.1860, 39 ¾ x 4 ¾ In.	18750
Whale Ivory, Turk's Head Knot, Whalebone & Ebony Checkerboard Band, c.1860, 38 In.	2300
Whalebone, Knotted Rope Handle, 3 Twisted Snake Shaft, c.1860, 34 x 1 In.	9375
Wood, Alligator, 2 Boots In Mouth Handle, c.1900, 34 In.	94
Wood, Bird Grip, Carved, Painted, Schtockschnitzler Simmons, c.1900, 32 In.	652
Wood, Black Child Handle, Hat, Bisque, c.1900, 33 ½ In.	325
Wood, Bull Head, Coin Holder, Brown Glass Eyes, 2 Horn Horns, c.1920, 36 In.	460
Wood, Carved Dog Head Handle, Alligator, Fish, Snake, Red Paint, c.1900, 39 In.	259
Wood, Dog Head, French Bulldog, Brown Glass Eyes, Mouth Opens, Ears Swing, 37 In.	1093
Wood, Dog Head, Hound, Silver Features, Crook Handle, Brass Ferrule, Denmark, c.1915, 34 In.	403
Wood, Dog, Rooster, Ink, Varnish, July 1896, 34 ¼ x 4 ½ In.	5625
Wood, Ebonized, Man Bust Handle, Twist Carved Shaft, c.1905, 36 ½ In.	236
Wood, Entwined Snake, Carved, Black Paint, c.1890, 35 In.	148
Wood, Fish, Alligator, Spotted Body, Carved Name Gordon, Dump Truck, 37 ½ In.	920
Wood, Fox Chasing Man, Grasping Man's Beard, Carved, L-Shape Handle, c.1890, 36 ½ In.	115
Wood, Fraternity, Indian Handle, Dartmouth, Names, Signed F.S. Whitcomb, 1911, 36 In.	144
Wood, Hand Pointing, Raised Heart, Tapered Shaft, Letters P & J, 1800s, 34 In.	3075
Wood, Horse Head Hand, Animal, Vines, Paint, c.1905, 30 x 4 ½ In.	4063

C

C

Wood, Horse Hoof, Figural Decorations, Red Brown, Eagle, Wheat Sheaf, Monkey, 34 In.	29
Wood, Incised Shaft, The Timed, 39 x 1 In.	6250
Wood, Ivory Skull Handle, 36 In.	960
Wood, Men, Animals, Entwined Snakes, Folk Art, Carved, Painted, c.1900, 41 ½ In.	122
Wood, Nesting Bird, Entwined Snake, Metal Ferrule, Wood, Paint, N.Y., c.1900, 38 x 2 In.	5313
Wood, Olive, Snake, Fist Handle, Ivory, Brass, Incised R, c.1890, 34 ½ x 2 In.	4063
Wood, Root Handle, Lizard, Eagle, Snake Carved, c.1910, 35 ½ In.	118
Wood, Seated Man Holding Chalice Grip, Folk Art, Carved, c.1890, 38 In.	356
Wood, Shoe Carved Handle, Exposed Toes, c.1865, 34 ½ In.	472
Wood, Snake, Carved, Painted Maroon, Black, Snake Moves On Shaft, 34 ½ In.	115

CANTON CHINA is blue-and-white ware made near the city of Canton, in China, from about 1795 to the early 1900s. It is hand decorated with a landscape, building, bridge, and trees. There is never a person on the bridge. The "rain and cloud" border was used. It is similar to Nanking ware, which is listed in this book in its own category.

Basin, Famille Rose, Court Figures, Scenes, c.1825, 18 In.	2160
Basin, Wood Stand, Casters, Landscape, 1800s, 17 x 26 In.	4500
Basket, Chestnut, Reticulated Sides, Oval, 11 x 10 In.	236
Bowl, Salad, Scalloped Rim, c.1860, 9 ⅝ x 9 ⅝ In.	510
Cedar Jug, Lid, 1800s, 11 ½ In.	840
Chamber Pot, Lid, Houses, Trees, Boats At Sea, Handle, c.1850, 8 In.	1422
Pitcher, Basin, Elongated Oval Shape, Molded Bamboo Handle, c.1860, 15 x 16 In.	1625
Pitcher, Water, Small Spout, 1800s, 10 In., Pair	1188
Plate, Landscape Scenes, c.1860, 9 In., 11 Piece	354
Platter, 16 x 19 In.	492
Platter, Cut Corner, Oval, 17 In.	266
Platter, Rectangular, Canted Corners, 17 x 14 In.	413
Platter, Rectangular, Canted Corners, Houses, Pagodas, Sea, c.1890, 18 ½ In.	360
Platter, Well & Tree, Deep Chamfered, Dome Lid, c.1885, 11 ⅜ x 14 In.	600
Teapot, Outdoor Vignettes, Blue & White, Swollen, Twisted & Shaped Handle, 7 ½ In.	218
Tureen, Lid, Sea Scene, Houses, Leaf Finial, Handles, c.1855, 9 x 13 In.	547
Tureen, Lid, Underplate, Boar's Head Handles, 13 ½ In.	960
Tureen, Soup, Dome Lid, Knob Finial, Boar's Head Handles, c.1850, 7 x 13 In.	325
Tureen, Soup, Lid, Boar's Head Handles, 1880, 12 In.	480
Tureen, Undertray, Aquatic Landscape, Boar's Head Handles, c.1825, 8 x 13 In. *illus*	547
Vase, Bottle Shape, 1800s, 14 ½ In.	1200
Warming Dish, Painted Landscape Lid, Floral Sprays, 16 ½ In.	288

CAPO-DI-MONTE porcelain was first made in Naples, Italy, from 1743 to 1759. The factory moved near Madrid, Spain, and operated there from 1771 until 1821. The Ginori factory of Doccia, Italy, acquired the molds and began using the crown and *N* mark. It eventually became the modern-day firm known as Richard Ginori, often referred to as Ginori or Capo-di-Monte. This company also used the crown and *N* mark. Richard Ginori went into bankruptcy in 2013.

Bowl, Lid, Women, Oval, Raised Classical Designs, Brass Handles, Finial, 7 In.	354
Chest, Raised Classical Figures, Hinged Roof Lid, Brass Mounts, c.1885, 14 x 7 In.	1955
Ewer, Neoclassical Style, Embossed Bacchanalian Infant, Harvest Scenes, c.1890, 8 ¼ In.	96
Goblet, Raised Design, Putti Dancing, Gilt, Marked, Inscribed, 1900s, 7 In., 4 Piece	123
Group, Chariot, 2 Horses, 2 Figures, 30 x 21 In.	124
Mug, Bacchus, Golden Horns, Interior Green Frog, c.1900, 4 ¾ In.	94
Pitcher, Man On Mountain Handle, Painted Cherubs, 16 In.	210
Plate, Molded Landscape Scenes, Shield Center, 9 ¼ In., 12 Piece	406
Tankard, Figures, Multicolor, Triangular Handle, Lid, Finial, 16 x 9 In.	90
Urn, Classical, Winged Male Figural Handles, Diana, Endymion, Multicolor, 24 x 18 In.	1920
Urn, Pedestal, Handles, Embossed, Bacchanalian Scenes, Painted, 23 ½ & 40 In.	150
Wine Cooler, Neoclassical Style, Bacchanalian Figures, c.1900, 7 In.	72

CAPTAIN MARVEL was introduced in February 1940 in Whiz comic books. An orphan named Billy Batson met the wizard, Shazam, and whenever he said the magic word he was transformed into a superhero. A movie serial was released in 1940. The comic was discontinued in 1954. A second Captain Marvel appeared in 1966, a third in 1967. Only the original was transformed by shouting "Shazam."

Button, Captain Marvel Club, Shazam, Red, White, Blue, c.1941, ⅞ In.	18
Figure, Cutout, Ski Jumping, Premium, Reed & Assoc., Box, 1944, 10 x 7 In.	30

Candy Container, Rooster, Red, Silk Bag, Dresden, Germany, 3 In.
$1,180

Bertoia Auctions

Candy Container, Veggie Man, Standing, Composition, Germany, 4 In.
$295

Bertoia Auctions

Candy Container, Victrola, Glass, Tin Enclosure & Horn, Red Paint
$177

Bertoia Auctions

TIP
Door hinges should never be on the outside of an entrance door. The pins can easily be removed.

Cane, Ivory Handle, Carved, Bacchanalian, Burl, Gilt Metal Collar, Brass Ferrule, 33 ½ In.
$840

Cowan's Auctions

Canton, Tureen, Undertray, Aquatic Landscape, Boar's Head Handles, c.1825, 8 x 13 In.
$547

James D. Julia Auctioneers

Carnival Glass, Buzz Saw, Pitcher, Water, Marigold
$55

Seeck Auctions

Carnival Glass, Diamonds, Pitcher, Water, Amethyst, Millersburg, c.1915, 7 ⅜ In.
$156

Jeffrey S. Evans & Assoc.

Jigsaw Puzzle, One Against Many, Captain Marvel Flying, 1944, 10 x 7 In.	35
Painting, Full Figure, On Mountaintop, D. Newton, Signed, Frame, 17 x 21 In.	1455
Patch, Glow In The Dark, Canada, c.1945, 3 x 4 ¾ In.	550
Picture, Captain Marvel, Arms Crossed, Glow In Dark, Cardboard, 1946, 8 x10 In.	278
Racer, Tin Lithograph, Numbered, Windup, Automatic Toy Co., 1947, 2 In., 4 Piece	411
Watch, Chromed Metal Case, Red Vinyl Band, Box, 1 ¼ x 1 ½ In.	204
Watch, Chromed Metal Case, Red Vinyl Band, Fighter Jet, Box, 1948	221

CAPTAIN MIDNIGHT began as a network radio show in September 1940. The first comic book appeared in July 1941. Captain Midnight was really the aviator Captain Albright, who was to defeat the Nazis. A movie serial was made in 1942 and a comic strip was published for a short time. The comic book version of Captain Midnight ended his career in 1948. Radio premiums are the prized collector memorabilia today.

Badge, Cereal Premium, Pinback, 1940s, 1 ¾ x 3 ⅛ In.	70
Badge, Ovaltine Premium, Code-O-Graph, Case, 1941, 1 ½ x 2 ⅛ In.	50
Badge, Wings, Mysto Magic Weather Forecasting, Skelly Gas, 1930s	42
Book, Joyce Secret Squadron, Hardcover, Whitman Publishing, 1942	8
Decoder, Secret Squadron, Photo-Matic, Brass Badge, Flag, Photo, 1942, 2 ⅛ In.	159
Decoder, SQ, Plastic, Silver Luster, Jet Plane, c.1957, 2 ⅛ In.	115
Poster, Movie, Mistaken Identity, Chapter 4, 1942, 27 x 41 In.	230
Ring, Flight Commander, Eagle & Shield, Ovaltine, 1941	230
Ring, Mystic Sun God, Brass Bands, Aztec Design, Red Plastic Stone, 1946	460
Tumbler, Captain Midnight Face, Ovaltine, Plastic, Red, Wander Co., 3 In.	20

CARAMEL SLAG, *see Imperial Glass category.*

CARDS listed here include advertising cards (often called trade cards), playing cards, baseball cards, and others. Color photographs were rare in the nineteenth century, so companies gave away colorful cards with pictures of children, flowers, products, or related scenes that promoted the company name. These were often collected and stored in albums. Baseball cards also date from the nineteenth century, when they were used by tobacco companies as giveaways. Gum cards were started in 1933, but it was not until after World War II that the bubble gum cards favored today were produced. Today over 1,000 cards are issued each year by the gum companies. Related items may be found in the Christmas, Halloween, Movie, Paper, and Postcard categories.

Baseball, Al Kaline, No. 130, Topps, 1965	50
Baseball, Babe Ruth, No. 32, U.S. Caramel, 1932	2251
Baseball, Brooks Robinson, No. 439, Topps, 1959	40
Baseball, Duke Snider, No. 150, Topps, 1956	65
Baseball, Early Winn, No. 260, Topps, 1959	30
Baseball, Joe DiMaggio, No. 1, Leaf, 1948	2133
Baseball, Lou Gehrig, No. 160, Goude, 1933	1540
Baseball, Mantle & Boyer, No. 160, Topps, 1960	75
Baseball, New York Yankees, No. 513, Topps, 1965	40
Baseball, Pete Rose, No. 207, Topps, 1965	300
Baseball, Roger Maris, No. 155, Topps, 1965	75
Baseball, Ted Williams, No. 76, Leaf, 1948-49	2962
Baseball, Tom Seaver, No. 45, Topps, 1968	125
Baseball, Tris Speaker, No. 89, Goudey, 1933	3259
Baseball, Willie Mays, No. 564, Topps, 1960	40
Baseball, Willie Mays, No. 261, Topps, 1952	1540
Baseball, Willie McCovey, No. 440, Topps, 1969	35
Baseball, Willie McCovey, No. 517, Topps, 1961	30
Baseball, Yogi Berra, No. 121, Bowman, Color, 1953	1896
Boxing, Jem Mace, Tom King, 1862, 3 x 2 In.	45
Football, O.J. Simpson, Rookie, No. 90, Topps, 1970	25
Greeting, Valentine, Cutout, 4 Joined Paper Hearts, Blue Woven Hearts, Virginia, c.1885, 5 In.	81
Greeting, Valentine, Doll, Woman, Flowers, Flax Threads, Silk Flowers, Round, c.1810, 9 In.	1904
Greeting, Valentine, Heart, Hand Love Tokens, Watercolor, Cut Gilt Paper, c.1820, 9 x 14 In.	34375
Greeting, Valentine, Lovebird Token, Watercolor, Cut Paper, Johnson, Pa., c.1810, 16 x 16 In.	37500
Greeting, Valentine, Man On Horseback, Puffy Threads, Silk Flowers, Round, c.1810, 11 In.	1904
Greeting, Valentine, Puzzle Purse Love Token, Ink, Poem, Hearts, c.1800, 12 ½ x 12 ¼ In.	6250
Greeting, Valentine, String Work, Flowers, Mahogany Frame, Victorian, c.1890, 9 x 9 In.	182
Greeting, Valentine, Watercolor, Ink, Paper, Verse, Flowers, Urns, Hearts, Frame, 1860, 15 x 20 In.	500
Greeting, Valentine, Watercolor, Scherenschnitte, Red, Black Frame, Pa., 1825, 13 x 14 In.	889

Penny Arcade, Cowboy, James Drury, Gray, White, 1950s, 3 x 5 In.		8
Penny Arcade, Cowboy, Rufus Davis, Gray, White, 1940s, 3 x 5 In.		7
Playing, Cats, Congress Playing Cards, 1970s, 52 Piece		25
Playing, Rook, Parker Brothers Inc., 1943		17
Playing, W.C. Fields, 52 Cards, 2 Jokers, Box, 1971		15
Trading, Acme Soap, Lautz Bros. & Co., Girl, Smiling, Clasped Hands, c.1890		5
Trading, Dunham's Cocoanut, Concentrated, Monkeys, In Trees, 2 ¾ x 4 ½ In.		10
Trading, Great China & Pacific Tea Co., Doves, Basket Of Flowers, c.1900, 7 x 5 In.		15
Trading, Haddock's Cards, Crabapples, 4 x 2 ¾ In.		5
Trading, Soapine, Girl, Hands On Lap, 4 ¼ x 3 In.		7
Trading, Supreme Brand Leaf Lard, Pigs, Playing Baseball, 1890s, 5 ¾ x 3 ½ In.		15

CARDER, *see Aurene and Steuben categories.*

CARLTON WARE was made at the Carlton Works of Stoke-on-Trent, England, beginning about 1890. The firm traded as Wiltshaw & Robinson until 1957. It was renamed Carlton Ware Ltd. in 1958. The company went bankrupt in 1995, but the name is still in use.

Basket, Foxglove Design, Leaf Shaped, Twig Handle, Green, c.1930, 6 x 10 In.		185
Bowl, Fruit, Chinaland Design, Pagoda, Pedestal Foot, c.1925, 12 x 7 In.		249
Bowl, Spider Web, Rouge Royale, Gilded, Luster, Marked, c.1938, 8 x 10 In.		225
Creamer, Apple Blossom, Twig Handle, Ruffle Rim, Saucer Foot, c.1940, 3 ½ In.		95
Dish, Rose & Curlicue Shell, Gilt, c.1915, 9 x 9 In.		199
Pitcher, Flower Bouquets, Cobalt Blue & Gold Drape At Shoulder, c.1880, 7 In.		145
Plate, Baby, Seesaw, Lipped		19
Plate, Red Lobster, White Ground, Embossed Seaweed, 9 ¼ In., 6 Piece		75
Teapot, Tumbling Clowns, Figural, Black & White, 1970s, 9 x 9 In.		599
Vase, Fantasia, Exotic Birds, Fantasy Garden, Cobalt Blue, Gold, 7 In.		300

CARNIVAL GLASS was an inexpensive, iridescent pressed glass made from about 1907 to about 1925. More than 1,000 different patterns are known. Carnival glass is currently being reproduced.

Acorn Burrs, Butter, Cover, Amethyst, Northwood, c.1910, 6 x 7 ⅞ In.		288
Acorn Burrs, Butter, Cover, Amethyst, Northwood, c.1918, 6 x 7 ⅞ In.		388
Acorn Burrs, Punch Bowl, Cup, Green, Jagged Rim, Footed, Northwood		290
Acorn Burrs, Punch Set, Bowl, Cups, Green, Northwood, c.1925, 10 ⅝ In. & 2 ⅜ In.		1035
Acorn Burrs, Water Set, Pitcher, Tumbler, Marigold, Northwood, c.1915, 8 ⅞ In., 5 Piece		161
Acorn Burrs, Water Set, Purple, 7 Piece		575
Acorn, Bowl, Red, Ruffled Edge		300
Apple Tree, Water Set, White, 7 Piece		800
April Showers, Vase, Blue, 11 In.		30
April Showers, Vase, Green, 12 In.		30
Basketweave, Basket, Blue, Open Edge, Ruffled Edge		15
Beaded Cable, Rose Bowl, Aqua Opal, Butterscotch		150
Beaded Cable, Rose Bowl, White		80
Beaded Shell, Mug, Purple		20
Blackberry, Basket, Red, Open Edge, 2 Sides Up		200
Bo Peep, Mug, Marigold		60
Bulls-Eye & Leaves, Bowl, Green, Ruffled Edge		15
Bushel Basket, Bowl, Aqua Opalescent, Handles, 4-Footed, Northwood, c.1918, 4 ¾ x 4 ½ In.		374
Butterflies, Bonbon, Amethyst		20
Butterfly & Berry, Berry Set, Marigold, 5 Piece		35
Butterfly & Berry, Bowl, Master, Blue		70
Butterfly & Fern, Water Set, Pitcher, Tumbler, Fenton, c.1910, 10 In., 4 In., 7 Piece		150
Butterfly & Tulip, Bowl, Purple, Scalloped Rim, 4 Ball Feet, c.1918, 4 x 13 In.		2185
Buzz Saw, Pitcher, Water, Marigold	*illus*	55
Captive Rose, Bowl, Blue, 3-In-1 Edge		65
Captive Rose, Plate, Blue, 9 In.		105
Captive Rose, Plate, Green, 9 In.		300
Captive Rose, Plate, Marigold, 9 In.		375
Chatelaine, Tumbler, Purple		150
Cherry & Cable, Tumbler, Marigold		50
Cherry Chain, Plate, Marigold, 6 In.		65
Chrysanthemum, Bowl, Blue, Scalloped Rim, 3 Ball Feet, Fenton, c.1915, 4 ⅛ In.		127
Chrysanthemum, Bowl, Ice Cream, Green, Footed		35

Carnival Glass, Good Luck, Bowl, 3-In-1 Edge, Ribbed, Blue, Northwood, c.1915, 2 x 8 ¾ In.
$240

Jeffrey S. Evans & Assoc.

Carnival Glass, Grape & Cable, Humidor, Lid, Green, Fenton, 1900s, 7 x 6 In.
$108

Jeffrey S. Evans & Assoc.

Carnival Glass, Heirloom Sunset, Pitcher, Water, Red, Indiana Glass
$25

Seeck Auctions

Carnival Glass, Hobnail Swirl, Rose Bowl, Marigold, Millersburg, c.1915, 3 ⅝ In.
$168

Jeffrey S. Evans & Assoc.

Carnival Glass, Inverted Strawberry,
Punch Set, Red, Miniature, 7 Piece
$55

Seeck Auctions

Carnival Glass, Many Fruits, Sherbet,
8-Sided, Pedestal, Amethyst, Millersburg,
3 ¼ x 4 In.
$360

Jeffrey S. Evans & Assoc.

Carnival Glass, Marilyn, Pitcher, Water,
Amethyst, Millersburg, c.1915, 8 In.
$330

Jeffrey S. Evans & Assoc.

Carnival Glass, Nesting Swan, Bowl,
Ruffled Rim, Green, Millersburg, c.1915,
2 ⅞ x 10 In.
$144

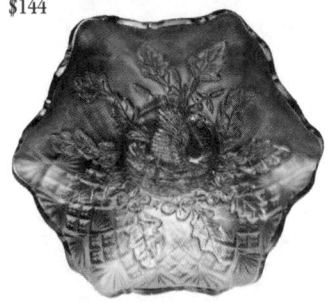

Jeffrey S. Evans & Assoc.

Coin Dot, Bowl, Green, 3-In-1 Edge, 9 In.	40
Coin Spot, Compote, Marigold, Ruffled Edge	5
Concord, Bowl, Marigold, Ruffled Edge	140
Corn, Vase, Stalk Base, Ice Green	175 to 200
Corn, Vase, Stalk Base, Marigold	1100
Corn, Vase, Stalk Base, Purple	400
Corn, Vase, Stalk Base, White	190 to 250
Corn, Vase, White, Footed, Northwood, 6 ½ In.	139
Cosmos & Cane, Tumbler, Honey Amber	10
Cosmos, Bowl, Marigold, Ruffled Edge, 10 In.	35
Crab Claw, Water Set, Marigold, 7 Piece	40
Daisy Cut, Bell, Marigold	200
Dandelion, Tumbler, Lime Green, Ribbed Interior, Northwood	45
Diamond & Rib, Vase, Amethyst, 11 In.	15
Diamond & Rib, Vase, Amethyst, 12 In.	20
Diamond & Rib, Vase, Green, Squat, 8 In.	30
Diamond Lace, Tumbler, Purple	20
Diamond Point, Vase, Green, 10 ½ In.	35
Diamonds, Pitcher, Water, Amethyst, Millersburg, c.1915, 7 ⅜ In. ....*illus*	156
Double Dutch, Bowl, Marigold, Round, Footed	5
Double Scroll, Candlestick, Smoke, Pair	105
Dragon & Lotus, Bowl, Blue, 3-In-1 Edge	30
Dragon & Lotus, Bowl, Ice Cream, Blue, Silver Iridescence	40
Drapery, Rose Bowl, Aqua Opal, Butterscotch	120
Embroidered Mums, Bowl, Ice Blue, Ruffled Edge, Ribbed Back	400
Fanciful, Bowl, Peach Opal, 3-In-1 Edge	45
Fanciful, Plate, Peach Opal, 9 In.	275
Fashion, Punch Set, Marigold, 10 Piece	125
Feather & Heart, Tumbler, Amethyst, Millersburg	70
Feathered Serpent, Bowl, 3-In-1 Edge, Amethyst, Silver, Gold Iridescence	25
Feathered Serpent, Sauce Bowl, Green, Round	10
File & Fan, Bowl, Peach Opal, Ruffled Edge	30
Fine Cut & Roses, Rose Bowl, Ice Blue	20
Fine Cut & Roses, Rose Bowl, Ice Blue, Scalloped Rim, 3 Ball Feet, Northwood, c.1918, 4 In.	316
Fine Cut & Roses, Rose Bowl, Purple	20
Fishscale & Beads, Bowl, Marigold, Ruffled Edge, 7 In.	15
Floral & Grape, Pitcher, Water, Amethyst	65
Floral & Grape, Water Set, Marigold, 7 Piece	40
Flowers, Rose Bowl, Amethyst, Fenton	55
Flowers, Rose Bowl, White, Fenton	30 to 35
Flute, Toothpick Holder, Purple	25
Four Flowers, Plate, Peach Opal, 6 In.	50
Four Flowers, Sauce Bowl, Peach Opal, Ruffled Edge	15
Four Pillars, Vase, Aqua Opal, 10 ½ In.	60
Four Seventy Four, Pitcher, Milk, Green	105
Four Seventy Four, Tumbler, Aqua	55
Four Seventy Four, Tumbler, Lime Green	25
Four Seventy Four, Tumbler, Marigold	15
Fruits & Flowers, Sauce Bowl, Purple, Ruffled Edge	15
Garden Path Variant, Bowl, White, Ruffled Edge, 11 In.	80
Garland, Rose Bowl, Blue	25 to 35
Good Luck, Bowl, Basketweave Back, Purple, Ruffled Edge	120
Good Luck, Bowl, Blue, Ruffled Rim, Northwood, c.1920, 2 ⅛ x 9 In.	230
Good Luck, Bowl, Cobalt Blue, Scalloped Sawtooth Rim, Northwood, 9 In.	220
Good Luck, Bowl, 3-In-1 Edge, Ribbed, Blue, Northwood, c.1915, 2 x 8 ¾ In. ....*illus*	240
Good Luck, Bowl, Purple, Northwood, 8 ½ In.	350
Good Luck, Bowl, Purple, Ribbed Back, Ruffled Edge	100
Good Luck, Bowl, Stippled, Marigold, Ruffled Edge, Ribbed Back	50
Good Luck, Plate, Green, Ribbed Back, 9 In.	1050
Good Luck, Plate, Marigold, Basketweave Back, 9 In.	240
Good Luck, Plate, Purple, Basketweave Back, 9 In.	325
Grape & Cable Variant, Plate, Stippled, Green, Ribbed Back, 9 In.	95
Grape & Cable, Bowl, 3-In-1 Edge, Green, Basketweave Back	45
Grape & Cable, Bowl, Amethyst, 3-Footed, 6 ½ x 11 In.	250
Grape & Cable, Bowl, Centerpiece, Purple, Turned In, Footed	25

Grape & Cable, Bowl, Marigold, Pink & Yellow Iridescent, Ruffled Edge, 9 In.	225
Grape & Cable, Butter, Purple	35
Grape & Cable, Dish, Sweetmeat, Lid, Pedestal, 8 ½ In.	175
Grape & Cable, Hatpin Holder, Green	190
Grape & Cable, Hatpin Holder, Marigold	105
Grape & Cable, Hatpin Holder, Purple	130
Grape & Cable, Humidor, Lid, Green, Fenton, 1900s, 7 x 6 In. ....illus	108
Grape & Cable, Water Set, Pitcher, Tumbler, Amethyst, Northwood, c.1920, 8 In., 4 In., 7 Piece	316
Grape, Plate, Amethyst, Sawtooth Rim, Northwood, 9 In.	93
Greek Key, Plate, Purple, Basketweave Back, 9 In.	350
Hattie, Bowl, Marigold, Round	10 to 15
Heart & Vine, Bowl, Blue, 3-In-1 Edge	60
Hearts & Flowers, Bowl, Ice Blue, Ruffled Edge, Ribbed Back	190
Hearts & Flowers, Bowl, Ice Green, 3-In-1 Edge, Ribbed Back	650
Hearts & Flowers, Bowl, White, Ruffled Edge	140
Hearts & Flowers, Compote, Aqua Opal, Butterscotch, Ruffled Edge	110
Hearts & Flowers, Compote, Marigold, Ruffled Edge	50
Hearts & Flowers, Compote, White, Ruffled Edge	45
Heavy Grape, Bowl, Green, Ruffled Edge, 10 In.	10
Heirloom Sunset, Pitcher, Water, Red, Indiana Glass ....illus	25
Hobnail Swirl, Rose Bowl, Marigold, Millersburg, c.1915, 3 ⅝ In. ....illus	168
Holly, Bowl, Blue, 3-In-1 Edge	35
Holly, Bowl, Blue, Ruffled Edge	25
Holly, Bowl, Ice Cream, Amethyst	45
Holly, Bowl, Ice Cream, Marigold	25
Holly, Compote, Red, Ruffled Edge	240
Holly, Dish, Blue, Square Hat Shape, Crimped Edge	30
Holly, Hat Shape, Marigold, Ruffled Edge	10
Holly, Plate, Amethyst, 9 In.	140
Holly, Plate, Green, 9 In.	200
Honeycomb, Rose Bowl, Peach Opal	45
Imperial Grape, Basket, Marigold, Handle	30
Imperial Grape, Punch Bowl, Base, Amber	275
Inverted Strawberry, Punch Set, Red, Miniature, 7 Piece ....illus	55
Inverted Strawberry, Tumbler, Blue, Signed Near Cut	15
Knotted Beads, Vase, Blue, Crimped Top, 9 In.	25
Lattice & Grape, Pitcher, Water, Tankard Shape, 2 Tumblers, Marigold	45
Leaf & Beads, Bowl, Green, Ruffled Edge, Dome Foot, 9 In.	15
Leaf & Beads, Rose Bowl, Aqua Opal, Butterscotch	120
Leaf Chain, Plate, Blue, 9 In.	450
Leaf Chain, Plate, Marigold, 9 In.	275
Leaf Chain, Plate, White, 9 In.	120
Leaf Columns, Vase, Purple, 10 In.	35
Little Flowers, Sauce Bowl, Blue, Round	30
Lotus & Grape, Plate, Green, 9 In.	400
Luster Rose, Bowl, Centerpiece, Marigold, Footed	20
Many Fruits, Sherbet, 8-Sided, Pedestal, Amethyst, Millersburg, 3 ¼ x 4 In. ....illus	360
Marilyn, Pitcher, Water, Amethyst, Millersburg, c.1915, 8 In. ....illus	330
Mikado, Compote, Purple, Pedestal Foot, Fenton, c.1915, 7 ⅛ x 10 In.	518
Mitered Ovals, Vase, Amethyst, Millersburg	9000
Morning Glory, Tumbler, Amethyst, Millersburg	130
Near Cut, Tumbler, Marigold, Northwood	450
Nesting Swan, Bowl, Ruffled Rim, Green, Millersburg, c.1915, 2 ⅞ x 10 In. ....illus	144
Ohio Star, Vase, Amethyst, Millersburg Glass Co., c.1915, 10 ¼ In. ....illus	960
Omnibus, Tumbler, Marigold	45
Open Rose, Plate, Amber, 9 In.	160
Open Rose, Plate, Purple, 9 In.	325
Orange Tree, Bowl, Fruit, 3-Footed, Marigold, Fenton, c.1915, 5 ⅜ x 10 In. ....illus	144
Orange Tree, Bowl, Scalloped Rim, 3 Ball Feet, Fenton, c.1920, 5 ½ x 10 ¼ In.	230
Orange Tree, Hatpin Holder, Blue, Crimped Rim, Fenton, c.1920, 6 ¾ x 3 ¾ In.	288
Orange Tree, Plate, Marigold, 9 In.	105
Orange Tree, Punch Set, Blue, Ruffled Edge, 8 Piece	300
Orange Tree, Punch Set, Marigold, Round, 10 Piece	135
Oriental Poppy, Water Set, Tankard, Green, 7 Piece	600
Paneled Dandelion, Pitcher, Water, Tankard, Green	85
Paneled Dandelion, Tumbler, Green	10 to 60
Paneled Dandelion, Tumbler, Marigold	15

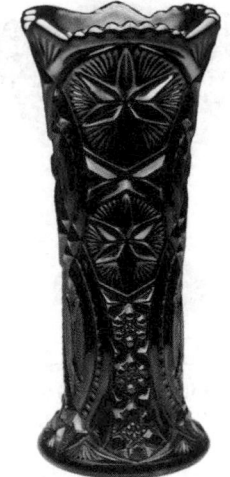

Carnival Glass, Ohio Star, Vase, Amethyst, Millersburg Glass Co., c.1915, 10 ¼ In.
$960

Jeffrey S. Evans & Assoc.

Carnival Glass, Orange Tree, Bowl, Fruit, 3-Footed, Marigold, Fenton, c.1915, 5 ⅜ x 10 In.
$144

Jeffrey S. Evans & Assoc.

Carnival Glass, Peacock & Urn, Bowl, Blue, Ruffled Rim, Northwood, c.1915, 2 x 8 ¾ In.
$180

Jeffrey S. Evans & Assoc.

TIP
To clean carnival glass, try using a mixture of ½ cup ammonia and ⅛ cup white vinegar.

Carnival Glass, Poppy, Compote, Scalloped Rim, Green, Millersburg, c.1915, 6 ¾ x 7 ½ In.
$84

Jeffrey S. Evans & Assoc.

Carnival Glass, Primrose, Bowl, Scalloped Rim, Marigold, Millersburg, c.1915, 2 ⅜ x 9 In.
$96

Jeffrey S. Evans & Assoc.

Carnival Glass, Strawberry Wreath, Compote, Green, Millersburg, c.1915, 3 ½ x 6 ¾ In.
$168

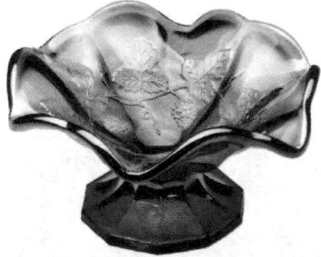

Jeffrey S. Evans & Assoc.

Pansy, Bowl, Green, Ruffled Edge	35
Peacock & Grape, Bowl, Ice Cream, Green, Footed	40
Peacock & Urn, Bowl, Blue, Ruffled Rim, Northwood, c.1915, 2 x 8 ¾ In. *illus*	180
Peacock & Urn, Compote, Blue, Ruffled Edge	40
Peacock & Urn, Plate, Marigold, 9 In.	150
Peacock At The Fountain, Bowl, Fruit, Blue	450
Peacock At The Fountain, Pitcher, Blue, c.1920, 8 In.	345
Peacock Tail, Bowl, Ice Cream, Green, 7 In.	40
Peacocks, Blue, Stippled, Ribbed Back, 9 In.	500
Peacocks, Bowl, Marigold, Ruffled Edge, Ribbed Back	110
Peacocks, Plate, Amethyst, Ribbed Back, 9 In.	900
Peacocks, Plate, Blue, Ribbed Back, 9 In.	700
Peacocks, Plate, Cobalt Blue, Sawtooth Rim, Northwood, 9 In.	435
Peacocks, Plate, Ice Green, Ribbed Back, 9 In.	90 to 325
Persian Garden, Bowl, Ice Cream, White, 11 In.	80
Persian Garden, Sauce, Ice Cream, White	25
Persian Medallion, Bonbon, Lime Green	70
Persian Medallion, Bonbon, Red	450
Persian Medallion, Sauce Bowl, Ice Cream, Blue	20
Persian Medallion, Sauce Bowl, Powder Blue, Marigold Overlay, Ruffled Edge	35
Pillow & Sunburst, Bowl, Amethyst, Ruffled Edge	10
Pinecone, Bowl, Ice Cream, Blue, 7 In.	20
Poppy Show, Bowl, Marigold, Ruffled Edge	300
Poppy, Compote, Scalloped Rim, Green, Millersburg, c.1915, 6 ¾ x 7 ½ In. *illus*	84
Primrose, Bowl, Scalloped Rim, Marigold, Millersburg, c.1915, 2 ⅜ x 9 In. *illus*	96
Pulled Loop, Vase, Peach Opal, 13 In.	25
Raindrops, Bowl, Peach Opal, Deep Ruffled Edge, Footed	35
Raspberry, Pitcher, Milk, Marigold	100
Raspberry, Pitcher, Milk, Purple	90
Ribbon Tie, Bowl, Blue, 3-In-1 Edge	30
Ripple, Vase, Marigold, 8 ½ In.	10
Ripple, Vase, Purple, 9 ½ In.	50
Rose Show, Bowl, Aqua Opalescent, Wavy Rim, Northwood, 9 In.	551
Rose Show, Bowl, Green, Ruffled Edge	950
Rose Show, Plate, Amethyst, 9 In.	800
Rose Show, Plate, Amethyst, Scalloped Rim, Northwood, c.1925, 1 ⅞ x 9 ½ In.	748
Rose Show, Plate, Marigold, 9 In.	450
Round Up, Bowl, White, Ruffled Edge	65
Round Up, Plate, Blue, 9 In.	180
Round Up, Plate, Peach Opal, 9 In.	100
Rustic, Vase, Blue, Crimped Top, 10 In.	25
Rustic, Vase, Marigold, 11 In.	20
Singing Birds, Mug, Ice Blue	425
Singing Birds, Mug, Purple	25
Single Flower, Basket, Peach Opal, Whimsy Handle	30
Single Flower, Bowl, Peach Opal, 3-In-1 Edge	25
Six Petals, Bowl, Peach Opal, Tricornered	15
Ski Star, Sauce Bowl, Purple, Ruffled Edge	55
Stag & Holly, Bowl, Blue, Ruffled Edge	80
Stag & Holly, Bowl, Blue, Scalloped Rim, 3 Ball Feet, Fenton, c.1915, 4 ½ x 10 ½ In.	127
Stag & Holly, Bowl, Marigold	50
Stag & Holly, Bowl, Orange, Blue, Scalloped Rim, Fenton, c.1920, 4 ⅞ x 9 In.	138
Star Of David & Bows, Bowl, Amethyst, Ruffled Edge, Dome Footed	20
Stippled Rays, Bowl, Amethyst, Crimped Ruffled Edge, Fenton, 9 In.	15
Stippled Rays, Bowl, Amethyst, Dome Footed, 11 In.	20
Stippled Rays, Sugar, Blue	10
Stippled Singing Birds, Mug, Marigold	35
Stippled Three Fruits, Plate, Aqua Opal, Ribbed Back, 9 In.	1950
Stippled Three Fruits, Plate, Purple, Ribbed Back, 9 In.	110
Strawberry Wreath, Compote, Green, Millersburg, c.1915, 3 ½ x 6 ¾ In. *illus*	168
Strawberry, Plate, Green, 9 In.	50
Stream Of Hearts, Compote, Marigold, Ruffled Edge	20
Target, Vase, Peach Opal, 11 In.	55
Thistle, Bowl, Amethyst, Crimped Ruffled Edge	45
Thistle, Bowl, Ice Cream, Amethyst	30
Three Fruits, Plate, Amethyst, Jagged Rim, Northwood, 8 ½ In.	104

Three Fruits, Plate, Marigold, Basketweave Back, 9 In.	15
Three Fruits, Plate, Purple, Basketweave Back, 9 In.	40 to 60
Tornado, Vase, Green	400
Town Pump, Green	1800
Town Pump, Purple	1050
Tree Trunk, Vase, Green, 10 In.	25
Tree Trunk, Vase, Green, Squat, 7 ½ In.	45
Two Flowers, Bowl, Blue, Ruffled Edge, Footed	50
Two Flowers, Sauce Bowl, Marigold, Ruffled Edge	20
Vintage, Bowl, Blue, Silver Iridescence, Crimped Ruffled Edge	35
Vintage, Bowl, Green, 3-In-1 Edge, 9 In.	50
Vintage, Bowl, Red, Ruffled	700
Vintage, Fernery, Blue	25
Vintage, Fernery, Green	10
Vintage, Fernery, Marigold	15
Vintage, Plate, Blue, 7 In.	75
Vintage, Powder Jar, Marigold	80
Vintage, Rose Bowl, Purple	30
Water Lily, Sauce Bowl, Blue, Ruffled Edge, Footed	25
Wild Rose, Dish, Green, Open Edge, Footed	30
Wild Strawberry, Berry Set, Purple, Ruffled Edge, 7 Piece	130
Windmill, Bowl, Smoke, 3-In-1 Edge	20
Wishbone & Spades, Plate, Purple, 6 In.	425
Wishbone, Bowl, Purple, Ruffled Edge, Footed	55
Wreath Of Roses, Compote, Blue, Ruffled Edge	20
Wreathed Cherry, Sauce Bowl, Peach Opal, Banana Boat Shape, Dugan	50
Zippered Heart, Sauce Dish, Purple, Ruffled Edge	45

CAROUSEL or merry-go-round figures were first carved in the United States in 1867 by Gustav Dentzel. Collectors discovered the charm of the hand-carved figures in the 1970s, and they were soon classed as folk art. Most desirable are the figures other than horses, such as pigs, camels, lions, or dogs. A jumper is a figure that was made to move up and down on a pole; a stander was placed in a stationary position.

Cat, Running, Carved, Painted, Brass Label, Limonaire Freres Paris, c.1910, 30 x 39 In.	3792
Chariot, Winged Cherubs, Winged Tigers, Landscape On Back, Upholstery, Dentzel, 80 x 49 In.	41218
Donkey, Running, Carved, Open Mouth, Glass Eyes, Bells, Tassels, c.1905, 59 In.	3105
Elephant Saddle, Wood, Iron, Carved Horse, Painted, 18 x 22 In.	428
Giraffe, Basswood, Glass Eyes, Leather Reins, Carved, Painted, W. Dentzel, c.1900, 70 x 52 In.	22500
Horse Head, Wood, Carved, Metal Stand, c.1885, 23 x 36 In.	2880
Horse, Jumper, Armor Under Saddle, Carved, Painted, Stein & Goldstein, 69 x 64 In. ....*illus*	5428
Horse, Jumper, Carved, Armor Blanket, Glass Eyes, Pole, Coney Island, 63 In. ....*illus*	1888
Horse, Jumper, Dapple Gray, Enamel Paint, Cast Iron, Stirrups, c.1910, 78 x 49 In.	823
Horse, Jumper, Inside Row, Pole, Coney Island Style, M.C. Illions, c.1909, 48 x 48 In.	5310
Horse, Jumper, Outside, Eagle Saddle, Jewels, Carved, Painted, Looff, c.1890, 64 x 51 In.	4063
Horse, Jumper, Pierced Mane, Brass Pole, Carved, Painted, Looff, c.1912, 61 x 50 In.	53125
Horse, Jumper, Wood, Carved, Leather Reins, Metal Stirrups, Painted, Germany, 66 x 58 In. *illus*	7840
Horse, Prancer, Carved, Painted Black, Red Saddle, c.1900, 48 In.	4029
Horse, Prancer, Pine, Stripped Paint, X-Shape Base, c.1900, 51 In.	240
Horse, Prancer, Pole, Carved, Blue, Black Painted, c.1900, 38 x 53 In.	1126
Horse, Prancer, Wood, White, Multicolor Saddle, Reins, 58 In.	1800
Horse, Stander, Head Up, Outside Row, Carved, Painted, Charles Carmel, c.1891, 55 x 56 In.	11250
Horse, Stander, Inside Row, Pine, Carved, Painted, Looff, Brooklyn, c.1900, 58 x 54 In.	5040
Horse, Walker, Composition, Painted, 57 x 53 In.	152
Horse, Yellow Paint, Brass Pole, 62 In.	210
Rabbit, Basswood, Carved, Painted, William Dentzel, c.1905, 61 x 50 In.	22500
Rooster, Wood, Carved, Painted, 24 x 30 In.	4800
Zebra, Stander, Basswood, Middle Row, Painted, Carved, Joy Morris, c.1900, 55 x 58 In.	18750

CARRIAGE means several things, so this category lists baby carriages, buggies for adults, horse-drawn sleighs, and even strollers. Doll-sized carriages are listed in the Toy category.

Baby Buggy, Rattan, Oak, Springs, Upholstery, Whitney Carriage Co., c.1900, 36 x 35 x 20 In.	836
Baby Buggy, Wicker, White Paint, Wood Wheels, 44 x 45 In.	28
Child's, Wicker, Iron Frame Wheels, Scrolls, Monumental Carriage Factory, c.1890, 35 In.	144
Pull Cart, Wood, Iron, Painted Red, Yellow, Decorated, c.1890, Child's, 48 In.	120
Sleigh, Open, Lull Carriage Co., Kalamazoo, Mich., 61 x 44 In.	1026

Carousel, Horse, Jumper, Armor Under Saddle, Carved, Painted, Stein & Goldstein, 69 x 64 In.
$5,428

Brunk Auctions

Carousel, Horse, Jumper, Carved, Armor Blanket, Glass Eyes, Pole, Coney Island, 63 In.
$1,888

Bertoia Auctions

Carousel, Horse, Jumper, Wood, Carved, Leather Reins, Metal Stirrups, Painted, Germany, 66 x 58 In.
$7,840

Theriault's

CARRIAGE

Cash Register, National, Barber Shop, Brass, 17 x 11 ½ In.
$480

Morphy Auctions

Cash Register, National, Model 226, 2 In 1, Fleur-De-Lis, Oak
$428

Showtime Auction Services

Cash Register, National, Model 312, Candy Store, Drink Coca-Cola On Back Of Top Sign
$720

Victorian Casino Antiques

Sleigh, Utility, Painted, Red Runners, Green Bed, Release Lever, Child's, 58 x 15 In...................... 89
Sleigh, Victorian, Curved Seat Back, Runners, Wood, Blue, Red Paint, 46 x 80 In........................ 741

CASH REGISTERS were invented in 1884 because an eye on the cash was a necessity in stores of the nineteenth century, too. John and James Ritty invented a large model that resembled a clock and kept a record of the dollars and cents exchanged in the store. John Patterson improved the cash register with a paper roll to record the money. By the early 1900s, elaborate brass registers were made. More modern types were made after 1920.

Manifold Autographic Machine, Egry Register Co., Nickel Plated Iron, 7 x 6 x 13 In.	171
McCaskey, Receipt, Tin Trays, Instruction Manual, 23 x 27 In.	257
National Receipt, Manifold Autographic Machine, Receipts Included, 7 ¼ x 10 x 16 In............	146
National, Barber Shop, Brass, 17 x 11 ½ In. ....*illus*	480
National, Model 5 ½, Original Paperwork, Breast Plate, Keys...................................	1995
National, Model 6, Oak Base, Barber Shop Model...	2850
National, Model 30 Receipt	855
National, Model 36, Marble Shelf, Oak Plinth Base, 17 x 19 x 16 In.	275
National, Model 216, Keys	1053
National, Model 226, 2 In 1, Fleur-De-Lis, Oak ....*illus*	428
National, Model 311, Copper Oxidized, Keys	1026
National, Model 312, Brass, Topper Sign, 20 ½ In.	840
National, Model 312, Candy Store, Drink Coca-Cola On Back Of Top Sign ....*illus*	720
National, Model 313, Brass, 21 ½ In.	770
National, Model 313, Candy Store, Brass, Marble Coin Shelf, 1921, 9 ¾ x 15 x 17 In.	598
National, Model 317, Candy Store...	900
National, Model 327, Extended Marble 3-Sided Base, Printer Cover, Breast Plate	1920
National, Model 333, Brass, Enjoy Pepsi-Cola, Hit The Spot	1020
National, Model 356-G, Oak Base, Marble Top, Receipt Cage, Marquee	510
National, Model 416, Bronze, Empire Pattern, Marquee, Oak Base...............................	593
National, Model 442, Receipt Slip Printer, Mahogany Base, Top Sign, Keys.....................	1521
National, Model 442-E-L, Gooseneck Lights, Keys	6600
National, Model 452, Relief Patterns, Oak Base, Pennsylvania, c.1890, 22 x 25 In.	240
National, Model 547-2-E, Class 500, Illuminated Electric Top Sign, Keys.....................	1053
National, Model 720, Metal Case, Painted Wood Grain, Single Drawer, c.1940	69
Osborn, Imperial, Patent 1891, Embossed Tin, Key, 19 x 22 In................................	1020

CASTOR JARS for pickles are glass jars about six inches in height, held in special metal holders. They became a popular dinner table accessory about 1890. Each jar had a top that was usually silver or silver plate. The frame, also of a silver metal, had a handle that arched above the jar and a hook that held a pair of tongs. By 1900, the pickle castor was out of fashion. Many examples found today have reproduced glass jars in old holders. Additional pickle castors may be found in the various Glass categories.

Pickle, Clear Glass, Metal Handles, Spoon, 12 In.	79
Pickle, Cranberry Glass, Melon Rib, Plated, Tongs, Queen City Silver Co., 10 In.	443
Pickle, Cranberry Opalescent, Crisscross, James Rufts Silver Plated Holder, 7 In...........	316
Pickle, Cranberry, Coin Spot, Coralline Flowers, Branches, Rockford Silver Plated Caddy, 8 In. ..	345
Pickle, Cranberry, Double, Lobed Optic Diamond Jars, Pictorial Medallions, 12 In...........	460
Pickle, Cranberry, Opalescent Snowflake, Embossed Frame, 11 In.............................	259
Pickle, Crimson Cameo Glass, Gilt Highlights, Marked Benedict, 11 In.	374
Pickle, Dogwood Blossoms, Peachblow, Rogers Holder, 10 In. ....*illus*	1035
Pickle, Eastlake Victorian Caddy, Pink, Mother-Of-Pearl, Diamond Quilted, 11 In............	316
Pickle, Inverted Thumbprint, Cranberry, Multicolor, Metal Frame, Lid, c.1875, 13 x 4 In. ...	805
Pickle, Satin Glass, Egg Shape, Painted Flowers, James Tufts Caddy, 10 In. ....*illus*	719
Pickle, Satin Glass, Mother-Of-Pearl, Raindrop, Reed & Barton Holder, 10 In. ....*illus*	345
Pickle, Spot Optic, Cranberry, Flower, Bird, Metal, Leaves, Pickle Frame, c.1880, 9 x 5 In.	690
Pickle, White Opalescent, Swirled, Coin Spot, 9 ½ In..	144

CASTOR SETS holding just salt and pepper castors were used in the seventeenth century. The sugar castor, mustard pot, spice dredger (shaker), bottles for vinegar and oil, and other spice holders became popular by the eighteenth century. These sets were usually made of sterling silver. The American Victorian castor set, the type most collected today, was made of silver plated Britannia metal. Colored glass bottles were introduced after the Civil War. The sets were out of fashion by World War I. Be careful when buying sets with colored bottles; many are reproductions. Other castor sets may be listed in various porcelain and glass categories in this book.

1 Bottle, 2 Shakers, Silver Plate, Ring Handle, Ribbed Pillar, Burmese, Faceted Stopper, 6 ½ In.	460
3 Bottles, Burmese, Salt, Pepper, Vinegar, Wilcox Caddy, Mt. Washington, 8 In.....................*illus*	345

CATALOGS *are listed in the Paper category.*

CAUGHLEY porcelain was made in England from 1772 to 1814. Caughley porcelains are very similar in appearance to those made at the Worcester factory. See the Salopian category for related items.

Custard Pot, Lid, Blue, White, Triple Flowers, Scroll Handle, Flower Knop, c.1780, 4 In.	550
Dish, Blue Transfer Chinoiserie Figure Scene, Cushion Shape, Gold Rim, c.1785, 7 ⅝ In.	161
Mustard, Lid, Blue, White, Flowers, Scroll Handle, 18th Century, 4 In.	995
Plate, Fisherman, Blue, White, 9 In.	395
Plate, Fluted, Cobalt Blue Stripes, Gilt Leaves, c.1790, 8 ½ In.	225
Tea Bowl & Saucer, Mother & Child, Blue, White, c.1785	695

CELADON is the name of a velvet-textured green-gray glaze used by Chinese, Japanese, Korean, and other factories. The name refers both to the glaze and to pieces covered with the glaze. It is still being made. Only celadon-colored ceramics are listed here.

Bottle, Gourd Shape, Ribbed, Flowers, Glazed, Korea, 12 In. *illus*	540
Bowl, Alms, Crackled, Foot Ring, Korea, 9 In.	523
Bowl, Blossom, Wide Rim, Bernard Leach, c.1970, 7 ¾ In. Diam.	1968
Bowl, Cone Shape, Molded, Upright Leaves, Foot Ring, 6 ¼ In. Diam.	478
Bowl, Footed, Beaded Rim, Squat, Bulbous, Stephen Sheppard, 3 ¾ x 12 ½ In.	8190
Bowl, Incised Leaves, Scrolls, Flared, Japan, 1800s, 4 ¾ x 9 In.	575
Bowl, Ruyi Mushrooms, Cranes, Clouds, Double & Triple Rings, Crackled, 7 ⅜ In.	677
Bowl, Wavy Rim, Flower Carved Interior, 3 x 8 ½ In.	300
Box, Lid, Chrysanthemum In Square, Lightning, Incised, Round, 2 ⅞ In.	1845
Brush Rest, Table Style, Outswept Scrolled Feet, C-Scrolls, c.1900, 6 x 1 ¼ In.	615
Censer, Cylindrical, Tapering, Carved Horizontal Ribs, 4 ¼ In. Diam.	427
Censer, Molded Lotus Flowers, Leaves, Wavy Neck, Crackled, Tripod, 10 ½ In.	246
Charger, Wavy Rim, Incised, Chinese, 16 In. Diam.	1200
Dish, Carved Lotus Petals, Inward Rolled Rim, Chinese, 6 ½ In.	540
Dish, Chrysanthemum Petal Shape, Scalloped, 7 In. Diam.	976
Dish, Famille Rose, Leaf Shape, Footed, Chinese, 10 ¼ x 8 In.	81
Figurine, Fisherman, Chinese, 2 ¾ In.	388
Figurine, Monk, Loose Robes, Standing On Lotus, Stoneware, Unglazed Head, 9 In.	1320
Garden Seat, Famille Rose, Round, Barrel Shape, Chinese, 18 ¼ In.	3840
Jar, Flower Scrolls & Lines, Bulbous, Waisted Foot, Stand-Up Rim, Chinese, 6 ¼ In.	984
Jar, Lid, Flowers, Blue & White, Emblems Of 8 Immortals, Oval, Wood Stand, 9 In.	185
Jardiniere, Crackle Glaze, Incised Archaic Designs, Gilt Bronze, Rim, Handles, 1900s, 15 In.	108
Tea Bowl, Purple, Crackle Glaze, Narrow Foot, Wide Rim, c.1900, 2 ½ x 5 In.	1298
Tea Bowl, Recessed Base, Chinese, 13th Century, 5 ½ In.	1680
Vase, Body Scrollwork, Ruyi Border To Waist, c.1800s, 11 In.	6785
Vase, Dome Lid, Upright Flange Handles, Loose Rings, Mask, 10 x 6 In.	461
Vase, Loop Handles, Ribbed, Metal Rim, 1900s, 12 In.	185
Vase, Pear Shape, Loop Handles, Moss Green Glaze, 3 ¼ In.	478
Vase, Peonies, Cloud & Thunder Border On Rim, Cylindrical, 6 ½ In.	96
Vase, Relief Carved, Flowers, Crackle Glaze, Late 1800s, 24 In. *illus*	690
Vase, Ribbed, Pear Shape, Flared, Lobed Rim, Animal Head Ring Handles, Footed, 10 In.	780
Vase, Square Shape, Dragons, Plantain Leaves, 1900s, 13 In.	837
Vase, Trumpet, Deer, Crane, Butterflies, Flowers, Famille Rose, 13 ½ In.	615

CELLULOID is a trademark for a plastic developed in 1868 by John W. Hyatt. Celluloid Manufacturing Company, the Celluloid Novelty Company, Celluloid Fancy Goods Company, and American Xylonite Company all used celluloid to make jewelry, games, sewing equipment, false teeth, and piano keys. The name *celluloid* was often used to identify any similar plastic. Celluloid toys are listed under Toy.

Alligator, Japan, c.1925, 7 ½ In.	17
Barrette, Rudolph The Red Nose Reindeer, 1940s, 2 ½ x 1 ¾ In.	30
Box, Flowers, Oval, Hinged, c.1892, 8 x 6 x 4 In.	131
Clock, Table, Footed, Arched, c.1920, 4 ½ x 4 x 1 ½ In.	75
Crucifix, Ottawa, Canada, 6 ⅞ In.	18
Cuff Links, Woman's, Amber, Facet Cut, Rectangular, 1950s, 1 ¼ x ¾ In.	40
Eyeglasses, Cat's-Eye Lorgnette, Rhinestones, Folding, Black, 1950s, 4 ⅝ In.	60
Figure, Little Bopeep, Holding Lamb, Japan, 1920s, 3 ½ In.	30
Mug, Santa Face, Handle, 1950s, 1 ½ x 2 ½ In.	6
Pin, Holy Name Society, Whitehead & Hoag Co., c.1900, 2 ⅞ x 1 ⅜ In.	39
Ring Box, Hinged, Ribbed, Magenta Velvet, High Dome, 2 x 2 x 1 In.	65

Castor, Pickle, Dogwood Blossoms, Peachblow, Rogers Holder, 10 In. $1,035

Early Auction Co.

Castor, Pickle, Satin Glass, Egg Shape, Painted Flowers, James Tufts Caddy, 10 In. $719

Early Auction Co.

Castor, Pickle, Satin Glass, Mother-Of-Pearl, Raindrop, Reed & Barton Holder, 10 In. $345

Early Auction Co.

Castor Set, 3 Bottles, Burmese, Salt, Pepper, Vinegar, Wilcox Caddy, Mt. Washington, 8 In.
$345

Early Auction Co.

Celadon, Bottle, Gourd Shape, Ribbed, Flowers, Glazed, Korea, 12 In.
$540

Skinner Auctioneers & Appraisers

Celadon, Vase, Relief Carved, Flowers, Crackle Glaze, Late 1800s, 24 In.
$690

Cottone Auctions

Shoehorn, c.1940, 6 In.	8
Tape Measure, Monkey Head, Japan, 1900s, 2 In.	63
Tray, Vanity, Marbleized Yellow, Oval, Glass Insert, Handles, 11 x 7 In.	35

CELS *are listed in this book in the Animation Art category.*

CERAMIC ART COMPANY of Trenton, New Jersey, was established in 1889 by Jonathan Coxon and Walter Scott and was an early producer of American belleek porcelain. It became Lenox, Inc. in 1906. Do not confuse this ware with the pottery made by the Ceramic Arts Studio of Madison, Wisconsin.

Jug, Berry Design, Brown, c.1900, 5 ½ In.	148
Pitcher, Flowers, Berries, Vines, Dotted Handle, 5 ½ In.	225
Tankard, Abstract Flowers Pods, Leaves, 5 ¾ In.	135
Tankard, Berries, Quince, Pastels, Left Handed, Gilt Rim & Handle, 5 ¾ In.	175
Tankard, Grapes, Leaves, Sponged Ground, Green, Purple, Gilt Scrolling, 14 In.	320
Vase, Blue Iris, Gold Trim, Green Palette, 10 ⅞ In. ....*illus*	413
Vase, Bulbous, Stick Neck, Geraniums, Peach, Green, Marked, 12 In.	400
Vase, Globular, Roses, Yellow, c.1900, 6 ½ In.	395
Vase, Pansies, Purple, White, Shouldered, Gilt Foot, 13 In.	845
Vase, Pink, White & Yellow Roses, Raised Gilt, 13 In.	325
Vase, Roses, Pink, Cherub Handles, Globular, c.1890, 12 x 10 In.	1720

CERAMIC ARTS STUDIO was founded about 1940 in Madison, Wisconsin, by Lawrence Rabbett and Ruben Sand. Their most popular products were molded figurines. The pottery closed in 1955. Do not confuse these products with those of the Ceramic Art Co. of Trenton, New Jersey.

Figurine, Dog, Pomeranian, Sitting, Brown, 2 In.	36
Figurine, Little Bo Peep, Yellow Dress, 5 ¼ In.	49
Figurine, Little Boy Blue, Reclining, Hat, Horn, 5 x 2 In.	49
Figurine, Pixie Girl, Waving, c.1945, 2 In.	26
Figurine, Shelf Sitter, Budgie, Blue, 1940s, 6 In.	75
Figurine, Shelf Sitter, Maurice & Michele, Green, 6 In., Pair	350
Head Vase, Becky, Braids, Hat, Striped Collar, c.1950, 5 ½ In.	75
Plaque, Jack & The Beanstalk, Brown Hair, Blue Jacket, 7 In.	150
Salt & Pepper, Chinese Boy & Girl, Yellow, 3 ¼ In.	65
Salt & Pepper, Dutch Boy & Girl, Folk Costume, 3 In.	40
Salt & Pepper, Mouse & Cheese, 2 In.	38

CHALKWARE is really plaster of Paris decorated with watercolors. One type was molded from Staffordshire and other porcelain models and painted and sold as inexpensive decorations in the nineteenth century. This type is very valuable today. Figures of plaster, made from about 1910 to 1940 for use as prizes at carnivals, are also known as chalkware. Kewpie dolls made of chalkware will be found in their own category.

Bank, Black Girl, Holding Bowl, For Our Missions, Nodder, c.1910, 13 ½ In.	510
Bust, Girl, Crossed Arms, Paint, Pa., c.1850, 11 ¾ In.	474
Bust, Henry Wadsworth Longfellow, Painted, Wooden Pedestal, c.1890, 69 In. ....*illus*	240
Figurine, Angel, Kneeling, Hollow, Red, Yellow, Green Highlights, Pedestal, 1800s, 8 In.	59
Figurine, Bird, Preening, Yellow Paint, Multicolor Feathers, Pa., c.1850, 5 ¾ In.	3081
Figurine, Boy, Seated, With Schoolbook, Yellow Hat, White, Pa., 1800s, 17 In.	1896
Figurine, Cat, Brown, Gray, c.1845, 13 In.	1126
Figurine, Cat, Seated, Brown, Tan, c.1960, 13 In.	720
Figurine, Cat, Seated, Hollow Cast, Red, Green, Black Highlights, 1800s, 5 ¾ In.	885
Figurine, Cat, Seated, Painted Black & White, c.1900, 7 ½ In.	210
Figurine, Cat, Seated, Painted, Late 19th Century, 5 In.	1845
Figurine, Cat, Seated, White, Red Collar, Daniel Guilmet, 15 ½ In.	213
Figurine, Cat, Seated, Yellow, Black Paint, Guilmet, 15 ½ In.	92
Figurine, Cat, Yellow, Red Paint, c.1865, Pa., 9 ½ In.	2607
Figurine, Deer, Reclining, Green Paint, c.1900, 10 ½ In., Pair	1140
Figurine, Deer, Resting, Painted, 1800s, 10 x 8 ½ In. ....*illus*	472
Figurine, Dog, Pug, Standing, Painted Face, Collar, c.1885, 8 ½ x 6 ¾ In.	35
Figurine, Dog, Seated, Basket In Mouth, Brown, Tan Paint, c.1860, 10 In.	2252
Figurine, Dog, Spaniel, Standing, Multicolor Paint, 1800s, 8 In.	504
Figurine, Dog, Spaniel, Standing, Multicolor Paint, c.1850, 7 In., Pair	330
Figurine, Doves, Brown, White, Branch, Leaf White Base, Pa., c.1860, 10 ¾ In., Pair	385

Figurine, Fireman, Holding Yellow Trumpet, Black Suit, Painted, Pa., 1800s, 14 In.	3792
Figurine, Girl, Praying, Kneeling, White, Pa., c.1850, 15 In., Pair	237
Figurine, Girl, Riding Horse, Multicolor Paint, Pa., c.1850, 7 ¼ In.	444
Figurine, Goat, Standing, Brown, Tan Paint, Pa., c.1865, 7 ¾ In.	356
Figurine, Pelican In Piety, 19th Century, 5 ¾ In.	3081
Figurine, Rabbit, Seated, Multicolor Paint, 9 ½ In.	2133
Figurine, Ram, Reclining, Yellow, Red Spotted, 1800s, 3 ½ In.	415
Figurine, Rooster, Multicolor Paint, Pa., c.1850, 7 In.	326
Figurine, Rooster, Standing, Green, Red, Yellow Paint, 1800s, 7 In.	531
Figurine, Sheep, Lamb, Reclining, Hollow Cast, Multicolor Paint, Pa., 1800s, 6 ½ x 9 In.	767
Figurine, Squirrel, Eating Nut, Paint, Pa., c.1820, 6 ¼ In.	563
Figurine, Stag, Lying Down, Red, Brown Trim, Pa., c.1850, 5 ¾ In.	972
Figurine, Stag, Seated, Reddish Brown, c.1850, 9 In., Pair	425
Garniture, Bowl Of Fruit, Multicolor Paint, Pa., c.1870, 12 ¾ In.	770
Garniture, Fruit, Mustard Yellow, Brown Paint, White Base, c.1850, 10 In.	1067
Garniture, Fruit, Painted, 13 In., Pair	486
Garniture, Lovebirds, Kissing, Green Mustard Paint, Pa., c.1865, 11 ½ In.	711
Statue, Dog, Coonhound, Redbone, Sitting, Glass Eyes, Droopy Ears, 26 x 21 In.	356

CHARLIE CHAPLIN, the famous comedian, actor, and filmmaker, lived from 1889 to 1977. He made his first movie in 1913. He did the movie *The Tramp* in 1915. The character of the Tramp has remained famous, and in the 1980s appeared in a series of television commercials for computers. Dolls, candy containers, and all sorts of memorabilia with the image of Charlie's Tramp are collected. Pieces are being made even today.

Chocolate Mold, Figural, Tramp, Hat, Cane, 1920s, 7 ½ In.	415
Photograph, Black & White, Signed In Magenta Ink, 1920s, 5 x 7 In.	250
Pipe, Figural, Charlie Standing Next To Bowl, Bisque Clay, 1920s, 6 In.	325
Postcard, New Year, Pig, Pulling Charlie, Germany, 1920	35
Print, Woodblock, Black & White, Signed, Lavy Lee, 10 x 13 In.	125
Purse, Mesh, Black, White, Chain Strap, Whiting, Davis, 6 x 4 In.	1150
Toy, Dancing Figure, Tin Lithograph, Hinged Limbs, Germany, c.1915, 7 In.	590
Toy, Figure, Windup, Key, Paint, Holding Cane, Tin, c.1920, 8 ½ In.	768
Toy, Top Hat, Cane, Wheeled Base, Paint, Cast Iron, Bell Toy, Watrous, 6 ¾ In.	152
Toy, Tramp Character, Die Cut, Mechanical, Tin Lithograph, 4 x 1 ¾ In.	184
Window Card, Gold Rush, Chaplin, Snow, Cardboard, 1925, 13 ½ x 17 In. *illus*	8070

CHARLIE MCCARTHY was the ventriloquist's dummy used by Edgar Bergen from the 1930s. He was famous for his work in radio, movies, and television. The act was retired in the 1970s.

Alarm Clock, Painted Metal, Charlie's Head, Windup, 4 x 6 ¼ In.	230
Book, Charlie McCarthy Meets Snow White, 24 Pages, Whitman Pub., 1938, 9 x 11 In.	110
Charm, Sterling Silver, Charlie Sitting, Movable Head, ⅞ x ¼ In.	36
Doll, Composition Head, Painted Hair, Eyes, Muslin Body, Effanbee, c.1937, 19 In.	392
Doll, Composition, Cloth, Tuxedo, Hat, 20 In.	153
Doll, Composition, Moveable Jaw, 12 ½ In.	47
Drummer, Parade Dress, Top Hat, Rolling Bass Drum, Tin Litho, Clockwork, 9 In.	443
Fur Clip, Enamel, Pat. 2038343, 1936, 1 ¼ x ¾ In.	235
Fur Clip, Movable Mouth, Monocle, c.1930, 1 ½ In.	235
Game, Radio Party Game, Premium, Chase & Sanborn, Envelope, 1938	50
Marionette, 12 In.	250
Paper Doll, Accessories, Clothes, 1930s, 15 In., 4 Piece	200
Pencil Sharpener, Bakelite, Yellow, 1 In. Diam.	45
Pin, Figural, Portrait, Celluloid, c.1938, 1 ⅛ x ¾ In.	25
Pin, Portrait, Plastic, C-Clasp, 1 ¼ In.	8
Punchboard, Charlie McCarthy Radio Prize, Majestic, 1938, 9 ½ x 10 In.	115
Radio, Edgar Bergen, Brown Bakelite, Almond, Tube, Painted, Die Cast, 7 In.	668
Spoon, Dutchess Silver Plate, 1950s, 4 In.	11
Spoon, Silver Plate, Duchess Silver Plate, 1950s, 6 In.	10
Toy, Benzine Buggy, Red, White Wheel, Spins, Tin Lithograph, Marx, 7 In.	375 to 560
Toy, Car, Charlie & Mortimer Snerd, We'll Mow You Down, Tin Litho, Marx, 16 In.	1062
Toy, Drummer Boy, Charlie Pushing Bass Drum, Tin Lithograph, Marx, Box, 9 In.	1121
Toy, Mortimer Snerd Private Car, Tin Lithograph, Marx, 16 ½ x 6 In.	767
Toy, Mortimer Snerd, Walker, Tin, Windup, Hat Flaps, Marx, 1950s, 8 In.	225 to 531
Toy, Private Car, With Mortimer Snerd, Tin Litho, Multicolor, Windup, c.1939, 16 In.	1221
Toy, Walker, Tin Lithograph, Clockwork, Marx, 8 In.	160 to 236
Toy, Walker, Tin, Windup, Louis Marx, c.1940, 8 ½ In.	185

Ceramic Art Co., Vase, Blue Iris, Gold Trim, Green Palette, 10 ⅞ In.
$413

Humler & Nolan

Chalkware, Bust, Henry Wadsworth Longfellow, Painted, Wooden Pedestal, c.1890, 69 In.
$240

Garth's Auctioneers & Appraisers

Chalkware, Figurine, Deer, Resting, Painted, 1800s, 10 x 8 ½ In.
$472

Brunk Auctions

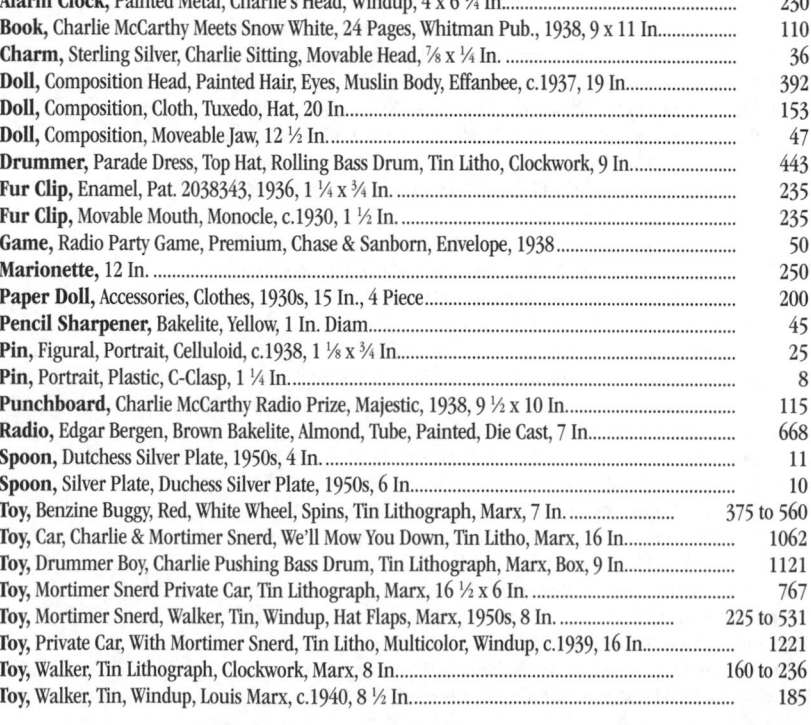

Charlie Chaplin, Window Card, Gold Rush, Chaplin, Snow, Cardboard, 1925, 13 ½ x 17 In.
$8,070

Hake's Americana & Collectibles

Chinese Export, Dish, Scenic Center, Figures, Blue & White, 1800s, 6 ¼ In.
$215

Cowan's Auctions

Chinese Export, Figurine, Old Chinese Man, Export Seal, Label, 1900s, 16 ¼ In.
$708

Brunk Auctions

Toy, Walker, Top Hat, Tin Lithograph, Marx, 8 In.	325
Toy, Windup, Cane, Celluloid, Jaw Flaps, 7 In.	310

CHELSEA porcelain was made in the Chelsea area of London from about 1745 to 1769. Some pieces made from 1770 to 1784 are called Chelsea Derby and may include the letter *D* for *Derby* in the mark. Ceramic designs were borrowed from the Meissen models of the day. Pieces were made of soft paste. The gold anchor was used as the mark, but it has been copied by many other factories. Recent copies of Chelsea have been made from the original molds. Do not confuse Chelsea porcelain with Chelsea Grape, a white pottery with luster grape decoration. Chelsea Keramic is listed in the Dedham category.

Dish, Painted, Grapes, Leaves, Fruit, Insects, Brown Ruffled Edge, Oval, c.1760, 6 ¾ x 8 In.	984
Figurine, Cherub, Hanging Basket Of Fruit, Goat, 3 In.	165
Figurine, Courting Couple, 7 ½ In., Pair	125
Plate, Flowers, Multicolor, Scalloped, Shaped Rim, c.1775, 9 In., 6 Piece	345
Plate, Fruits, Nuts, Multicolor, Scalloped, Ribbed, c.1775, 9 In., Pair	345

CHELSEA GRAPE pattern was made before 1840. A small bunch of grapes in a raised design, colored with purple or blue luster, is on the border of the white plate. Most of the pieces are unmarked. The pattern is sometimes called Aynsley or Grandmother. Chelsea Sprig is similar but has a sprig of flowers instead of the bunch of grapes. Chelsea Thistle has a raised thistle pattern. Do not confuse these Chelsea patterns with Chelsea Keramic Art Works, which can be found in the Dedham category, or with Chelsea porcelain, the preceding category.

Cup & Saucer, Copper Luster, c.1850	30
Cup & Saucer, Flared, Paneled	10
Cup & Saucer, Purple Luster, Footed	50
Plate, Copper Luster, c.1840, 7 In.	16
Plate, Luncheon, Purple Luster, 8 ⅜ In.	24
Sugar & Creamer, Blue Luster	45
Teapot, Blue Luster, Finial, Footed, c.1890, 9 ½ In.	69

CHELSEA SPRIG
Bowl, Lavender, c.1875, 3 ½ x 6 In.	100

CHINESE EXPORT porcelain comprises the many kinds of porcelain made in China for export to America and Europe in the eighteenth, nineteenth, and twentieth centuries. Other pieces may be listed in this book under Canton, Celadon, Nanking, Rose Canton, Rose Mandarin, and Rose Medallion.

Bottle, Apothecary, Teardrop Form, Blue Landscape, Twist Cap, 10 In.	263
Bough Pot, Lid, Famille Rose, Courtesans, Butterflies, Gilt Handles, c.1850, 8 ¾ In., Pair	2252
Bowl, Central Garden Scene, Flower Clusters Banding, 1700s, 9 In., 8 Piece	1195
Bowl, Famille Rose, Bell Shape, Winged Dragons, Flowers, Waves, 7 In.	1968
Bowl, Famille Rose, Daoguang Mark, Chinese, 2 ¼ x 4 ¼ In.	646
Bowl, Famille Rose, Dragon, Phoenix, U-Shape, Foot Ring, c.1900, 10 In.	1220
Bowl, Famille Rose, Emperor & Harem, Landscape, Marked, 1900s, 4 x 22 In.	767
Bowl, Famille Rose, Flared Rim, Raised Foot, Flowers, Gilt, c.1900, 7 In.	1200
Bowl, Famille Rose, Gilt, Scalloped Edge, Flowering Branches, 1800s, 2 x 5 In.	415
Bowl, Famille Rose, Iron Red, 4 ¼ In.	179
Bowl, Famille Rose, Iron Red, Birds, Flowers, Blue Lotus Interior, 1900s, 7 In.	369
Bowl, Monteith, Armorial, Blue & White, Lakes, Pagodas, c.1800, 5 x 10 In., Pair	4977
Bowl, Vegetable, Lid, Fitzhugh, Rectangular, 9 ⅜ In., Pair	240
Brushpot, Famille Rose, Cylindrical, Yellow Ground, Flowers, 6 In.	531
Butter Tub, Cover, Stand, Famille Rose, Scroll Grounds, Peonies, 2 ½ x 6 In., Pair	1599
Charger, Armorial, Arms Of D'Hane Steenhuyse, Flowers, c.1730, 12 In.	1020
Charger, Canton Famille Rose, Horses, Flutes, Flowers, Celadon Ground, 16 In.	660
Charger, Famille Rose, Medallion, Dragons, Butterflies, c.1900, 14 In., Diam.	2196
Chocolate Pot, Famille Rose, Lighthouse Shape, Prunus Blossoms, 1700s, 7 In.	554
Chocolate Pot, Lid, Famille Verte, Pear Shape, Waves, Sea Life, c.1700, 7 In.	2390
Cider Jug, Famille Rose, Sacred Bird, Butterfly, Twisted Handle, c.1850, 9 In.	415
Cider Jug, Lid, Famille Rose, Mandarin, Women, Butterfly, Foo Dog Finial, c.1850, 11 In.	4266
Dish, Blue & White, Floral, Leaves, Octagonal, 14 ½ In.	240
Dish, Famille Verte, Flowering Branch, Perched Bird, Trellis, c.1900, 9 In.	2760
Dish, Scenic Center, Figures, Blue & White, 1800s, 6 ¼ In. .... *illus*	215
Figurine, Cockerels, Famille Rose, Jun Sheng Sheng Mark, 12 In., Pair	120
Figurine, Mandarin, Seated, Flowering Branch, Multicolor, 11 In.	1722
Figurine, Mystical Beast, Famille Rose, Head Turned, c.1890, 10 ¼ In., Pair	7500

Figurine, Old Chinese Man, Export Seal, Label, 1900s, 16 ¼ In.................................*illus*	708
Fishbowl, Bird, Famille Rose, Flower, Blue Scroll Ground, Stand, 1900s, 20 In........................	1793
Fishbowl, Famille Verte, Yellow Ground, 18 x 21 In., Pair...	1188
Flask, Moon, Famille Rose, Figures, Gilt, Marked, Chinese, c.1900s, 6 ¼ In.................*illus*	2400
Flowerpot, Undertray, Famille Rose, 6-Sided, Multicolor, c.1890, 5 x 6 In.........................	1580
Ginger Jar, Figures, Text, Crackle Glaze, 1800s, 13 ½ In...*illus*	360
Jar, Famille Noir, Oval, Long Tailed Birds, Prunus Flowers, 1900s, 10 In...........................	154
Jar, Famille Rose, Flared Rim, Flowers, Pink Ground, c.1900, 10 In.................................	1920
Jar, Famille Rose, Oval, Children Playing, c.1890, 12 In...	338
Jar, Famille Verte, Lid, Buddha, Women, Blue Seal, Chinese, 20th Century, 9 ½ In., Pair............	264
Jar, Famille Verte, Villagers, Deer Shape Handles, Marked, c.1800, 14 In............................	2337
Jar, Lid, Buddhist Emblems, Stand, 1900s, 8 ½ In..*illus*	123
Jar, Lid, Famille Rose, 17 In., Pair..	2125
Jar, Lid, Famille Rose, Mille Fleur, Marked, 10 In..	210
Jardiniere, Famille Rose, Tapered, Ribbon Handles, Fluted, Birds, 23 ½ In., Pair....................	1708
Jardiniere, Tray, Famille Rose, Yellow Ground, 1800s, 7 ¾ In..	3438
Lamp Base, Porcelain, Underglaze Blue, Baluster Shape, Dragons, Trees, 1800s, 10 In., Pair.....	720
Planter, Famille Rose, Fishbowl Shape, Figures, Flowers, 17 In. Diam................................	180
Plate, Dinner, Blue Fitzhugh, c.1845, 9 ¾ In., 7 Piece..	480
Plate, Famille Rose, Buddha, Lotus Throne, Clouds, 9 ½ In...	885
Plate, Famille Rose, Flowers, Butterfly, 9 ¼ In...	1195
Plate, Koi Fish Design, Multicolor, c.1800, 9 In..	180
Plate, Soup, Famille Rose, Tiered, Figures, Birds, Flowers, 9 ⅞ In. Diam., 8 piece..................	615
Platter, Famille Rose, Courtyard Scenes, Round, c.1865, 15 ¾ x 18 ¾ In.............................	1067
Platter, Famille Rose, Yellow Ground, Flowers, Characters, Oval, 18 In.............................	900
Platter, Orange, Bird & Butterfly Design, c.1800, 9 ½ x 12 ½ In....................................	799
Punch Bowl, Cobalt Blue, Red, Gold Enamel, Diaper, Spear Border, Shields, 1800s, 12 x 5 In. ...	780
Punch Bowl, Famille Rose, Figures, Flowers, Wide Rim, 1800s, 5 ¾ x 14 ¾ In.........................	472
Punch Bowl, Famille Rose, Panels, Domestic Scenes, 1700s, 15 In. Diam..............................	1107
Punch Bowl, Famille Rose, Pierced Stand, 1900s, 10 x 16 In...	461
Punch Bowl, Famille Verte, Horsemen, Pavilion, Dignitaries, 15 ¾ In. Diam..........................	671
Punch Bowl, Rooster Armorial, Flowers, c.1800, 14 In...	472
Saucer, Famille Verte, Plants, Insects, c.1900, 6 ½ In..	1708
Shrimp Dish, Shell Shape, Butterflies, Peonies, 1800s, 9 x 10 In...................................	276
Teapot, Dome Lid, Famille Rose, Turquoise Ground, Pink, Bulbous, 1900s, 7 In.......................	236
Teapot, Famille Rose, Globular, Loop Handle, Scroll Spout, Flowers, 1700s, 4 In....................	896
Teapot, Famille Rose, Globular, Songbird, Flowers, 1900s, 3 ½ x 6 ½ In.............................	677
Teapot, Lid, Bulbous, Couple, Children, Landscape, Flowers, Gilt, c.1785, 5 In.....................	480
Teapot, Lid, Famille Rose, Gilt Mouse, Climbing Up Vine, c.1750, 4 ⅝ In............................	900
Teapot, Lid, Famille Rose, Pear Shape, Loop Handle, Flowers, Bamboo, 1700s, 5 In...................	299
Teapot, Lid, Paneled Flowers, Field, c.1785, 5 ¼ In..	450
Tile, Round, Famille Rose, Scholars, Garden Landscape, c.1900, 16 In. Diam.........................	3198
Tray, River Landscape, Well, Deer, Women, Gold Highlights, Oval, 9 ½ x 12 In.......................	330
Tureen, Cow Head Shape, 2 Parts, Lid, c.1900, 13 x 15 In...	1320
Tureen, Famille Rose, Underplate, Flowers, Boar's Head Handles, 1800s, 13 x 10 In.............*illus*	2988
Tureen, Lid, Blue & White, Footed, Dog Finial, Flowers, c.1865, 9 x 13 In..........................	600
Tureen, Lid, Famille Rose, Figures, Flowers, Gold Finial, Handles, c.1865, 11 x 15 In..............	770
Urn, Lid, Famille Rose, Dragon Handles, Gilt, Lion Finial, 1700s, 11 ½ In....................*illus*	1200
Urn, Lid, Famille Verte, c.1865, 14 ½ In., Pair..	3645
Vase, Birds, Flowers, Square, Famille Rose, 1800s, 5 x 10 In...................................*illus*	365
Vase, Bottle Shape, Symbols, Flowers, Blue, Red, 17 ½ In..	354
Vase, Double Gourd, Animal Head Ring Handles, Yellow Ground, 9 ¼ In................................	531
Vase, Famille Noir, Bottle Shape, Wrapped Dragon At Neck, 1800s, 15 ½ In...........................	840
Vase, Famille Rose, Bottle Shape, Figures, Landscape, Net Pattern, 1800s, 13 In....................	427
Vase, Famille Rose, Bulbous, Long Neck, Flare Rim, Flowers, Lotus, 1900s, 14 In....................	1230
Vase, Famille Rose, Downturned Rim, Gardens, Marked, 19 In., Pair..................................	7073
Vase, Famille Rose, Elephant Head Handles, Flowers, c.1800, 14 In..................................	1599
Vase, Famille Rose, Elephant Head Handles, Flowers, c.1885, 19 In..................................	330
Vase, Famille Rose, Figures, Flowers, Butterflies, 1800s, 30 In....................................	3321
Vase, Famille Rose, Figures, Interior Scenes, 18 In..	448
Vase, Famille Rose, Flared Rim, Flared Bottom, Flowers, 1900s, 9 In., Pair.........................	3075
Vase, Famille Rose, Flowers, Butterflies, Bottle Shape, 6 Character Mark, c.1900, 15 In............	270
Vase, Famille Rose, Horse, Mountain Landscape, Signed Rouleau, c.1930, 13 ¼ In.....................	360
Vase, Famille Rose, Moon Flask, Round, Dragon Handles, c.1920, 9 In................................	246
Vase, Famille Rose, Pheasants, Parakeets, Deer Head Handles, Marked, 1800s, 13 In..................	1708
Vase, Famille Rose, Scenes, Gilt, c.1785, 13 ¾ In., Pair...	2813

Chinese Export, Flask, Moon, Famille Rose, Figures, Gilt, Marked, Chinese, c.1900s, 6 ¼ In.
$2,400

Skinner Auctioneers & Appraisers

Chinese Export, Ginger Jar, Figures, Text, Crackle Glaze, 1800s, 13 ½ In.
$360

Garth's Auctioneers & Appraisers

Chinese Export, Jar, Lid, Buddhist Emblems, Stand, 1900s, 8 ½ In.
$123

Skinner Auctioneers & Appraisers

Chinese Export, Tureen, Famille Rose, Underplate, Flowers, Boar's Head Handles, 1800s, 13 x 10 In. $2,988

Neal Auction Co.

Chinese Export, Urn, Lid, Famille Rose, Dragon Handles, Gilt, Lion Finial, 1700s, 11 ½ In. $1,200

Cowan's Auctions

Chinese Export, Vase, Birds, Flowers, Square, Famille Rose, 1800s, 5 x 10 In. $365

James D. Julia Auctioneers

Vase, Famille Verte, Fan, Garden Reserves, Blue Ground, c.1720, 6 In., Pair		2520
Vase, Famille Verte, Flowering Branches, Red, Green, White, 22 In.		150
Vase, Famille Verte, Hexagonal, Gourd & Stem Handles, c.1900, 23 x 9 In.		1534
Vase, Famille Verte, Landscape, Yellow Ground, 12 In.		1452
Vase, Famille Verte, Noblemen, Military, Garden, 23 ¾ In.		2562
Vase, Famille Verte, Trumpet, Ears, Immortals, Animals, 1900s, 30 In.		3600
Vase, Peonies, Peacocks, Gilt Metal Base, Mounted, 18 x 9 In.		1107
Water Bottle, Famille Rose, Stick Neck, Bulbous Base, c.1860, 13 In.		944
Water Bottle, Squat, Stick Neck, Famille Rose, Gilt, 1800s, 13 In.		522
Water Dropper, Peony Shape, Enameled Pink Shaded To Rose, Green Stem Handle, 8 In.		900
Wedding Lamp, Pierced, Reticulated, Painted Flowers, 8-Sided, c.1860, 12 ½ In., Pair		1320
Wine Pot, Lid, Famille Verte, Barrel Shape, Lion, Flowers, c.1700, 4 x 7 In.		2032

CHINTZ is the name of a group of china patterns featuring an overall design of flowers and leaves. The design became popular with English makers about 1928. A few pieces are still being made. The best known are designs by Royal Winton, James Kent Ltd., Crown Ducal, and Shelley. Crown Ducal and Shelley are listed in their own sections.

Anemone, Dish, Sweetmeat, Blue Ground, Royal Winton, 4 ⅞ In.	56
Anemone, Teapot, Lid, Blue Ground, Royal Winton, 4 ¾ In., 4 Cup	458
Apple Blossom, Creamer, Scalloped, Pink, James Kent, 2 ½ In.	104
Apple Blossom, Cup, Footed, James Kent	56
Apple Blossom, Plate, Salad, Scalloped, Pink, James Kent, 7 In.	53
Balmoral, Cup & Saucer, Black Ground, Footed, Royal Winton	76
Balmoral, Plate, Dinner, Royal Winton, 10 In.	183
Black Beauty, Pitcher, Bulbous, Lord Nelson, 4 ¼ In.	395
Blue Anemone, Tray, Royal Winton, 10 x 6 In.	125
Blue Pansy, Cup & Saucer, Royal Albert	28
Chelsea, Bowl, Vegetable, Black Ground, Lid, Round, Royal Winton, 9 ½ In.	566
Chelsea, Mug, Black Ground, Royal Winton 3 In.	96
Dorset, Bowl, Cereal, Gold Trim, Royal Winton 6 ⅜ In.	37
Dorset, Cup & Saucer, Gold Trim, Royal Winton	74
Dorset, Plate, Dinner, Gold Trim, Royal Winton 10 In.	83
DuBarry, Bowl, Dessert, James Kent, 5 ¾ In.	74
DuBarry, Bowl, Vegetable, Round, James Kent, 8 In.	159
DuBarry, Plate, Bread & Butter, James Kent, 6 ½ In.	56
DuBarry, Plate, Dinner, James Kent, 9 ⅞ In.	108
DuBarry, Platter, James Kent, Oval, 10 In.	197
DuBarry, Sugar, Lid, James Kent	146
English Rose, Cup & Saucer, Yellow Ground, Royal Winton	54
Floral Feast, Chop Plate, Ivory Ground, Royal Winton, 11 ½ In.	228
Floral Feast, Cup & Saucer, Ivory Ground, Royal Winton	69
Floral Feast, Plate, Dinner, Ivory Ground, Royal Winton, 10 In.	136
Florita, Bowl, Fruit, James Kent, 6 ¼ In.	48
Florita, Bowl, Nut, Footed, James Kent	57
Hazel, Bonbon, Black Ground, Footed, Royal Winton, 6 ½ In.	219
Hazel, Cup & Saucer, Black Ground, Royal Winton	94
Hazel, Plate, Dinner, Black Ground, Square, Royal Winton, 9 ¾ In.	198
Hazel, Relish, Black Ground, 3 Sections, Royal Winton, 8 ½ In.	267
Julia, Breakfast Set, Royal Winton, Teapot, Sugar, Creamer, Large Cup, Tray	102
June Roses, Butter, Cover, Royal Stafford	159
June Roses, Cup & Saucer, Scalloped, Gold Trim, Footed, Royal Stafford	36
June Roses, Plate, Bread & Butter, Scalloped, Gold Trim, Royal Stafford, 6 ½ In.	13
June Roses, Relish, Royal Stafford, 9 ¼ In.	38
Lilac Time, Vase, Cylindrical, Gilt Trim, Footed, Empire, 4 In.	295
Lydia, Gravy Boat, Underplate, Black Ground, James Kent	79
Marguerite, Bonbon, Divided, Royal Winton, 5 ½ x 9 ¼ In.	78
Marguerite, Eggcup, Double, Royal Winton	94
Marguerite, Plate, Gilt Trim, Royal Winton, 6 x 6 In.	125
Old Cottage, Cup & Saucer, Royal Winton	34
Old Cottage, Relish, Oval, Handles, Royal Winton, 7 x 11 In.	65
Old Cottage, Sugar & Creamer, Royal Winton, 5 In.	89
Old English, Plate, Luncheon, Scalloped, Johnson Brothers, 9 In.	23
Orient, Cake Plate, Black Ground, Royal Winton, 12 In.	177
Orient, Salt & Pepper, Black Ground, Royal Winton	98
Paisley, Pitcher, Green, Bulbous, Royal Winton, 5 ½ x 7 In.	250

Pink Surprise, Cup & Saucer, Gilt Trim, Royal Albert.........................	95
Queen Anne, Butter, Cover, Tan Check Ground, Royal Winton, 6 ½ In.........	192
Queen Anne, Cup & Saucer, Royal Winton	48
Queen Anne, Cup & Saucer, Tan Check Ground, Footed, Royal Winton	69
Queen Anne, Gravy Boat, Tan Check Ground, Royal Winton	196
Queen Anne, Plate, Bread & Butter, Tan Check Ground, Royal Winton, 6 In. ...	25
Queen Anne, Platter, Tan Check Ground, Oval, Royal Winton, 12 In............	163
Rosa, Teapot, Lid, James Kent, 4 In.	37
Rosalynde, Creamer, James Kent	129
Rosalynde, Cup & Saucer, Footed, James Kent	54
Rosalynde, Plate, Dinner, James Kent, 9 ¾ In.....................	139
Royal Brocade, Plate, Burgundy, Cream Flowers, Octagonal, 6 ½ In.	115
Royalty, Plate, Tab Handles, Royal Winton, 9 ½ x 5 ¾ In..............	125
Sunshine, Cake Plate, Handles, Gold Trim, Royal Winton, 10 ¾ In.	149
Sunshine, Creamer, Scalloped, Gold Trim, Royal Winton, 3 ¼ In.	119
Sunshine, Cup & Saucer, Scalloped, Gold Trim, Royal Winton..............	63
Sunshine, Pitcher, Footed, Royal Winton, 4 ½ In.	125
Victorian, Plate, Bread & Butter, Royal Winton, 6 ⅛ In.	29
Victorian, Relish, Royal Winton, 8 ⅛ In....................	89

CHOCOLATE GLASS, sometimes mistakenly called caramel slag, was made by the Indiana Tumbler and Goblet Company of Greentown, Indiana, from 1900 to 1903. It was also made at other National Glass Company factories. Fenton Art Glass Co. made chocolate glass from about 1907 to 1915. More recent pieces have been made by Imperial and others.

Austrian, Creamer, Greentown, 4 ¾ In.	46
Beaded Oval, Toothpick Holder, 2 ¾ In.	24
Cactus, Compote, Greentown, c.1903, 5 ½ In.	85
Cactus, Cruet, 6-Sided, Greentown, 5 In.	85
Cactus, Tumbler, Greentown, 4 In.	20
Compote, Greentown, 8 In.	40
Dish, Hen On Nest Lid, Diamond, Basket Weave Base, Greentown, c.1905, 4 x 4 In.	431
Leaf Bracket, Nappy, 3-Sided, Handle, c.1900, 6 x 3 In..................	50
Serenade, Plate, Scalloped Rim, McKee, 1900s, 6 ¼ In.............	35
Wild Rose & Bowknot, Tumbler, McKee, c.1902, 4 In.	50

CHRISTMAS PLATES *that are limited edition are listed in the correct factory listing.*

CHRISTMAS collectibles include not only Christmas trees and ornaments listed below, but also Santa Claus figures, special dishes, and even games and wrapping paper. A Belsnickle is a nineteenth-century figure of Father Christmas. A kugel is an early, heavy ornament made of thick blown glass, lined with zinc or lead, and often covered with colored wax. Christmas cards are listed in this section under Greeting Card. Christmas collectibles may also be listed in the Candy Container category. Christmas trees are listed in the section that follows.

Belsnickle, Blue Robe, Mica, Tree Stump, Germany, 11 In...................*illus*	1062
Belsnickle, Chalkware, Black Suit, Painted, Pa., 1800s, 14 In................	1185
Belsnickle, Composition, Crushed Mica, Feather Tree, Germany, 12 In............*illus*	1003
Belsnickle, Composition, White Coat, Blue Trim, Feather Tree Sprig, Germany, 13 In...........	649
Belsnickle, Holding Fir Tree, Gold Coat, Painted Face, Papier-Mache, 13 ¼ In.	1121
Belsnickle, Mica Flake Coat, Red Beard, Tree In Arm, Composition, 28 In.	5214
Belsnickle, Putz Animals, American Flag, House Shape Shadowbox, Germany, 21 x 11 In.........	1541
Book, Night Before Christmas, A Visit From St. Nicholas, McLoughlin, 1888, 12 x 10 In............	60
Book, Night Before Christmas, Linen, McLoughlin, 1910, 12 x 9 ¾ In.	60
Button, Bricker's Bread, Fabric Santa Claus, Holding Toy Pack, 1 ¼ In.	86
Button, Santa Claus, Kresge Department Store, Newark, Bastian Paper, 1 ½ In...............*illus*	475
Button, Santa Claus, Portrait, Store, Meet Me At People's Outfitting Co., 1 ½ In....	1075
Button, Santa Claus, Riding In Sleigh, Boston Store, c.1910, 1 ¼ In.	380
Cake Mold, Santa Claus, Embossed, Hello Kiddies, Cast Iron, Griswold, Erie, Pa., 12 In............	354
Candy Containers are listed in the Candy Container category.	
Display, Santa Claus, Teem, Drinking Bottle, Green, White Suit, Composition, Cloth, 56 In.	300
Doll, Coca-Cola Santa Claus, 1950s, 18 In..................	72
Doll, Santa Claus, Composition, Jointed, 19 In..................	283
Doorstop, Poinsettia, Red, Green Paint, Cast Iron, 8 ½ In.........	130
Father Christmas, Holding Twigs, Basket, Composition, Cloth, Germany, c.1890, 25 In.	3750
Greeting Card, Wood Cut, Nativity Scene, Asian Figures, Japan, 3 x 5 In.	75
Lamp, Fluid, Figural, Santa Claus, Painted, Thumbwheel Mark, Pat. 1887, 9 ¾ In..............*illus*	3068

Christmas, Belsnickle, Blue Robe, Mica, Tree Stump, Germany, 11 In.
$1,062

Bertoia Auctions

Christmas, Belsnickle, Composition, Crushed Mica, Feather Tree, Germany, 12 In.
$1,003

Bertoia Auctions

Christmas, Button, Santa Claus, Kresge Department Store, Newark, Bastian Paper, 1 ½ In.
$475

Hake's Americana & Collectibles

Christmas, Lamp, Fluid, Figural, Santa Claus, Painted, Thumbwheel Mark, Pat. 1887, 9 ¾ In.
$3,068

Conestoga Auction Co., Inc.

Christmas, Lantern, Santa Claus Head, Composition, Paper, Bail Handle, Germany, 10 In.
$2,006

Bertoia Auctions

Christmas, Poster, Santa Claus, Xmas Joys, Nabisco Biscuit Co., Uneeda Bakers, 28 x 36 In.
$798

Showtime Auction Services

Christmas, Print, Cloth, Santa Claus, Thomas Nast, Night Before Christmas, Frame, 26 In.
$472

Bertoia Auctions

Christmas, Santa Claus, Toy Sack, Pressed Cotton, Crepe Paper, Fur Beard, Germany, 7 In.
$177

Bertoia Auctions

Christmas, Stocking, Fabric, Ready Cut & Sew, 14 x 27 In.
$468

Showtime Auction Services

Christmas, Toy, Santa Claus, Driving Car, Tin Lithograph, Windup, CK, Japan, 7 In.
$37,760

Bertoia Auctions

Christmas, Toy, Santa Claus, Sleigh, 2 Reindeer, Cast Iron, Painted, Gold Highlights, Hubley, 14 In.
$708

Bertoia Auctions

Christmas Tree, Feather, Wood Base, Germany, 38 In.
$83

Conestoga Auction Co., Inc.

Christmas Tree, Ornament, Baby Face, Pouting, Pink Night Cap, Glass, 2 ¾ In.
$826

Bertoia Auctions

Lantern, Krampus, Bad Christmas Spirit, Devil Face, Tongue Out, Composition, 4 In.	2655
Lantern, Santa Claus Head, Composition, Paper, Bail Handle, Germany, 10 In. .....*illus*	2006
Light, Belsnickle, Standing On Church, Red, Tan, Yellow, Green, Chalkware, c.1870, 19 In.	2370
Nativity Set, Stable, 10 Figures, Goebel 1965, 18 x 12 In.	71
Nodder, Santa Claus, On Donkey, Feather Tree, Donkey Nods, Felt, Glass, Fur, Windup, 22 In.	5900
Nodder, Santa Riding Elephant, Tree Sprig, Basket, Composition, Felt, Rabbit Fur, 13 In.	1534
Pail, Peanut Butter, Merry Christmas, Sledding Scene, Red, Bail Handle, c.1890, 3 In.	450
Poster, Santa Claus, Xmas Joys, Nabisco Biscuit Co., Uneeda Bakers, 28 x 36 In. .....*illus*	798
Print, Cloth, Santa Claus, Thomas Nast, Night Before Christmas, Frame, 26 In. .....*illus*	472
Santa Claus & Sleigh, 2 Reindeer, Paper On Wood, Lithograph, R. Bliss, c.1890, 17 In.	2950
Santa Claus, Coca-Cola, Toys, Sleeping Boy, Bottle, Cutout, Cardboard, 1950s, 49 x 32 In.	120
Santa Claus, Drum, Bell, Walking, Battery, Japan, 10 ½ In.	75
Santa Claus, Face, Plaster, Chalk, Red Hat, White Beard, 3-D, 13 x 24 In.	142
Santa Claus, Hands In Sleeves, Gray, Cream Paint, Carved, White Base, c.1890, 23 x 12 In.	87500
Santa Claus, In Twig Sleigh, Red Robe, Rabbit Fur Beard, Holds Flag, Toys, 12 In.	649
Santa Claus, Papier-Mache, Red, White Long Robe, Holding Toys, Russia, 17 In.	48 to 60
Santa Claus, Papier-Mache, White Long Robe, Holding Basket, Fir Tree, Russia, 15 In.	84
Santa Claus, Primitive, Painted, On Printer's Tray, A. Glazier, Pennsylvania, 32 x 16 In.	360
Santa Claus, Sack On Back, Red, White, Pressed Cardboard, 57 ½ In.	356
Santa Claus, Sitting On Log With Toy Sack, Composition, Cardboard, Blue Coat, 8 In.	3540
Santa Claus, Standing, Carved, Red, White, Samuel A. Robb, New York, 1923, 39 x 16 In.	875000
Santa Claus, Toy Sack, Pressed Cotton, Crepe Paper, Fur Beard, Germany, 7 In. .....*illus*	177
Santa Claus, With Walking Stick, Holds Feather Tree With Electric Candles, Germany, 10 In.	1298
Stocking, Fabric, Ready Cut & Sew, 14 x 27 In. .....*illus*	468
Toy, Santa Claus Jack-In-The-Box, Santa & Deer Pop Up, Wood, Paper, Composition, 5 In.	885
Toy, Santa Claus Jack-In-The-Box, Santa Holds Feather Tree, Wood, Paper, Composition, 7 In.	325
Toy, Santa Claus, Driving Car, Tin Lithograph, Windup, CK, Japan, 7 In. .....*illus*	37760
Toy, Santa Claus, Reindeer, Sleigh, Celluloid, Windup, Japan, 1920s, 6 x 2 In.	60
Toy, Santa Claus, Sleigh, 2 Reindeer, Cast Iron, Painted, Gold Highlights, Hubley, 14 In. .....*illus*	708
Toy, Santa Claus, Sleigh, Cast Iron, 2 Reindeer, Cast Gold Antlers, Hubley, 15 In.	826
Toy, Santa Claus, Sleigh, Tin Litho, Mechanical, Key Wind, Ferdinand Strauss, c.1923, 11 In.	450
Toy, Santa Claus, Walker, Lead Head, Felt Clothes, Backpack, Clockwork, Ives, 10 In.	2963

CHRISTMAS TREES made of feathers and Christmas tree decorations of all types are popular with collectors. The first decorated Christmas tree in America is claimed by many states, including Pennsylvania (1747), Massachusetts (1832), Illinois (1833), Ohio (1838), and Iowa (1845). The first glass ornaments were imported from Germany about 1860. Paper and tinsel ornaments were made in Dresden, Germany, from about 1880 to 1940. Manufacturers in the United States were making ornaments in the early 1870s. Electric lights were first used on a Christmas tree in 1882. Character light bulbs became popular in the 1920s, bubble lights in the 1940s, twinkle bulbs in the 1950s, plastic bulbs by 1955. In this book a Christmas light is a holder for a candle used on the tree. Other forms of lighting include light bulbs. Other Christmas collectibles are listed in the preceding section.

Feather, Goose, Green, Red Berries, Round Red Bucket Base, Gold Band, 20 In.	207
Feather, Wood Base, Germany, 38 In. .....*illus*	83
Kugel, Grape Cluster, Cobalt Blue, Germany, c.1875, 4 In.	523
Ornament, Angel, Golden Hair, Holding Trumpet, Hinged Wings, Composition, 6 In.	384
Ornament, Arab On Camel, Holding Shield, Dresden, 3 ½ In.	708
Ornament, Baby Face, Pouting, Pink Night Cap, Glass, 2 ¾ In. .....*illus*	826
Ornament, Bottle Of Champagne, In Ice Bucket, Candy Container, Dresden, 3 In.	708
Ornament, Buffalo, No Horns, Dresden, 3-D, 3 ¾ In.	240
Ornament, Chimney Sweep, Bisque Face, Pressed Cotton, Golden Dresden Ladder, 5 In.	472
Ornament, Collie, Brown, Dresden, 3-D, 3 ¾ In.	120
Ornament, Elephant, Silver Howdah, Dresden, 3 ¼ In.	1003
Ornament, Girl On Sled, Pressed Cotton, Bisque Head, Wood Sled, Germany, 3 In.	443
Ornament, Greyhound, Gray, Dresden, 3-D, 3 ¾ In.	150
Ornament, Horned Owl, Glass Eyes, Dresden, 3 ½ In.	590
Ornament, Indian Bust, Blown Glass, 4 In. .....*illus*	354
Ornament, Indian Warrior, Horse, Full Headdress, Tomahawk, Dresden, Germany, 4 In. .....*illus*	2950
Ornament, Lizard, Green, Gold, Red Eye, Dresden, 4 In. .....*illus*	2124
Ornament, Maine Lobster, Red, Dresden, 4 In. .....*illus*	443
Ornament, North Atlantic Swordfish, Dresden, 6 In.	649
Ornament, Pink Flamingo, Pink Beak, Dresden, 4 In.	826
Ornament, Ram Pulling Beer Barrel, Silver Cart, Spoke Wheels, Dresden, 5 In.	1534
Ornament, Santa Claus, Side-Glancing Eyes, Glass, 4 In. .....*illus*	384
Ornament, Speckled Carp, Multicolor, Dresden, 6 ¼ In.	354

Christmas Tree, Ornament, Indian Bust, Blown Glass, 4 In.
$354

Bertoia Auctions

Christmas Tree, Ornament, Indian Warrior, Horse, Full Headdress, Tomahawk, Dresden, Germany, 4 In.
$2,950

Bertoia Auctions

Christmas Tree, Ornament, Lizard, Green, Gold, Red Eye, Dresden, 4 In.
$2,124

Bertoia Auctions

This is an edited listing of current prices. Visit Kovels.com to check thousands of prices from previous years and sign up for free information on trends, tips, reproductions, marks, and more.

Ornament, Stable, 2 Horses, Wagon, Dresden, 2 In.	1888
Ornament, Steamboat, Movable Paddle Wheels, Silver, Dresden, 3 ¾ In.	1180
Ornament, Tree Topper, Angel Holding Trumpet, Sunburst, Oak Leaves, Dresden, 8 In.	826
Pine, Tin, 13 Candleholder Prickets, Paint, Stand, c.1925, 77 ½ x 36 ¼ In.	720
Stand, Musical, Nickeled Tin, Wood Base, Round, 14 In.	148
Stand, Musical, Revolves, Lador, Switzerland	189
Stand, Rotating, Musical, Embossed Ladgy Swiss, Wood Base, Aluminum, Iron, 14 x 9 In.	456
Stand, Santa Claus, Red Robe, Angel Thumbscrews, Cast Iron, Germany, 12 In. *illus*	1003
Whimsy, In Bottle, Glittered, Faux Tinsel Stockings, Dolls, Balls, Stopper, 10 In.	201

CHROME items in the Art Deco style became popular in the 1930s. Collectors are most interested in high-style pieces made by the Connecticut firms of Chase Brass & Copper Co., Manning-Bowman & Co., and others.

Cocktail Shaker, Chase Brass & Copper Co.	75
Figure, Ostriches, Plated, Stamped, Karl Hagenauer, 2 ¾ In.	151
Goblet, Cocktail, Blue Moon, Cobalt Blue, Metal Serving Tray, 9 Piece	120
Wall Sculpture, Raindrops, Patinated, Signed, C. Jere, Dated 1975, 30 x 60 In.	2750

CIGAR STORE FIGURES of carved wood or cast iron were used as advertisements in front of the Victorian cigar store. The carved figures are now collected as folk art. They range in size from counter type, about three feet, to over eight feet high.

Indian Princess, Wood, Carved, Painted, c.1900, 39 In.	570
Indian, Full Bodied, Headdress, Necklace, c.1870, 15 x 7 ½ In. *illus*	9480
Indian, Maiden, Hands Up, Carved, Painted, Log Base, c.1865, 75 In.	10270
Indian, Maiden, Headdress, Arm Up Holding Tomahawk, Cigars, 1800s, 68 x 25 In. *illus*	42550
Indian, Reclining, Full Regalia, Display, Countertop, Red Indian Cut Plug, 26 x 11 In.	4740
Indian, Standing, Shawl, Necklace, Headdress, Painted, c.1890, 52 ½ In.	4888
Indian, Woman, Arm Out, Feather Headdress, Multicolor Paint, 1900, 78 In.	19200
Naval Officer, Pine, Carved, Painted, 28 In.	577
Punch, Holding Tray, Embossed, Wooden, Wheels, 62 In. *illus*	3300
Uncle Sam, Red, White Stripe Paint, Blue Coat, & Top Hat, 48 In.	1610
Warrior, Holding Container, Multicolor Paint, Black Stand, c.1900, 63 ½ In.	5520

CINNABAR is a vermilion or red lacquer. Pieces are made with tens to hundreds of thicknesses of the lacquer that is later carved. Most cinnabar was made in the Orient.

Box, Carved Design, Rounded Rectangular, c.1900, 4 x 8 In.	90
Box, Chinese, 19th Century, 1 ¼ x 3 In.	121
Box, Lid, Carved, Pouncing Dragon, Leaf Scroll, Chinese, 3 ½ x 8 In.	2360
Box, Lid, Tiered, Carved, Sages, Attendants, Rocky Garden, Flowers, c.1820, 5 x 12 In.	1107
Dish, Black Carved To Red, Flowering Peonies, 1800s, 6 ¼ In.	365
Panel, 4 Seasons, Lattice, Lotus, Scrolls, Metal Crest, Chinese, 70 x 20 In., 4 Piece	37440
Vase, Carved Figural Landscape, Brass Dragon Handles, Wood Stand, Chinese, c.1910, 15 In.	3660
Vase, Carved, Immortals, Mountains, Drilled As A Lamp, c.1910, 16 In.	300

CIVIL WAR mementos are important collectors' items. Most of the pieces are military items used from 1861 to 1865. Be sure to avoid any explosive munitions.

Badge, Regimental Corp, 1st Lt., Mass., Hooker's Division Ribbon, Fob, c.1860, 3 ¾ In.	3540
Belt Buckle Tongue, Cast Brass, Confederate, 2 ⅛ x 1 ¾ In.	316
Belt Buckle, Brass, Silver Wreath, 2 x 3 ¼ In.	210
Box, Wood, Slide Top, Confederate Soldier's, Engraved Memorium, 1862, 2 x 2 In.	28
Cannon Ball, Marked, 12 Lb.	275
Canteen, Drum, Cedar, Round, Incised S.H. Hendrix, S.J. Kirkpatrick, c.1863, 7 ½ In.	2750
Canteen, Target, Metal, Painted, Inscribed Comp., E 128, Rect., O.V.I.	142
Chair, Folding, Carpet Seat, Gilt Paint, F.C. Roberts, Confederate Captain, 31 In. *illus*	705
Diary, Nurse's, Levi Capp, Leather Cover, Pocket, 1863, 5 x 3 ¼ In.	690
Dice, Cheater, Bone, Chip, Pip Off Center, ⁷/₁₆ In. Square	85
Drawing, Pen, Ft. Ellsworth, Va., Cannons, Troops, 2nd Lt., Ira Gensel, 1861, 10 x 15 In.	652
Drawing, Pen, Ink, Watercolor, Arlington Hts. Encampment, 13 x 31 In.	2370
Drum, Regimental, Eagle, Inscribed Regt. U.S. Infantry, A. Rogers, Painted, 14 x 17 In.	4029
Flag, Fragment, Crossed Blue Bands, Stars, Red Ground, Confederate, Frame, 24 x 28 In.	4500
Flask, Gunstock, Dixon, Marked, Jan. 7, 1854, 8 In.	330
Kepi, Confederate, Cadet Gray, Satinet Band, U.S. Marine Buttons, Lined *illus*	2400
Knife, Bowie, D-Handle, Confederate, 19 In.	275

c

Christmas Tree, Ornament, Maine Lobster, Red, Dresden, 4 In. $443

Bertoia Auctions

Christmas Tree, Ornament, Santa Claus, Side-Glancing Eyes, Glass, 4 In. $384

Bertoia Auctions

Christmas Tree, Stand, Santa Claus, Red Robe, Angel Thumbscrews, Cast Iron, Germany, 12 In. $1,003

Bertoia Auctions

Map, Pen & Ink, Manuscript, No. Vir. Attr. Confederate Jedediah Hotchkiss, 21 x 15 In.	6960
Pike, Wood Haft, Double-Edge Steel, Ferrule, Georgia, Confederate, c.1862, 97 In.	1080
Soldier Service Memorial Certificate, Volunteers, Jacob Haldeman, Paper, 1862, 33 x 27 In. .	130
Sword, U.S. Light Artillery, Ames, Marked A.D.K., 1863, 34 ½ In.	120
Travel Case, Ebonized, Brass Inlay, Silk Lined, Hinged Lid, Engraved, 1800s, 6 x 14 In.	413
Trunk, Ironbound, Flag Uniform, Documents, Awards, Lt. Col. Daniel Kent Cross, c.1862	22800
Uniform, Coat, Pants, Suspenders, Shirt, Wool, Confederate Reenactment	35
Uniform, Union Reenactment, Coat, Pants, Suspenders, Vest, Shirt, Hat	33

CKAW, *see Dedham category.*

CLARICE CLIFF was a designer who worked in several English factories, including A.J. Wilkinson Ltd., Wilkinson's Royal Staffordshire Pottery, Newport Pottery, and Foley Pottery after the 1920s. She is best known for her brightly colored Art Deco designs, including the Bizarre line. She died in 1972. Reproductions have been made by Wedgwood.

Beehive, Fantasque, Honey Pot, Multicolor Enamel, Applied Bee, Mark, c.1930, 3 ⅝ In.	300
Blue Autumn, Ashtray, Wilkinson	213
Blue Chintz, Dish, Grapefruit, Blue, Green, Pink, White, Shaped Flared-Out Rim	155
Bramble, Jug, Leaves & Berries, Horizontal Ribs, Newport, 7 ⅞ In.	232
Butterfly, Fantasque, Teapot, Lid, Cone Shape, Multicolor Enamel, c.1930, 5 In.	1080
Castellated Circle, Bizarre, Bachelor Teapot, Lid, Globe Shape, Multicolor, c.1930, 4 In.	900
Character Jug, Churchill, Seated, Holding Ship, Union Jack, Bulldog, c.1941, 12 In.	1680
Coronet, Bizarre, Jug, Black Tree, Multicolor Circles, Wilkinson, 7 In.	446
Crocus, Plate, 3 Crocus Sprays, Yellow & Green Border, Newport, 8 In.	87
Delecia Citrus, Plate, Stylized Oranges & Lemons, Round, Newport, 9 In.	209
Delecia Poppy, Jug, Lotus, Green, Yellow Ground, Horizontal Ribs, 12 In.	1123
Fantasque Bizarre, Vase, Lotus, House, Landscape, Handles, c.1930, 11 ⅜ In. ....*illus*	431
Forest Glen, Jug, Multicolor Enamel, Cottage, Tree Landscape, c.1936, 8 ¾ In.	420
Gayday, Bizarre, Cup & Saucer, Coffee Can, Dish Saucer	75
Harvest Brown, Plate, Flowers, Swirled Rim, Wilkinson, Ltd., 8 In.	13
Hydrangea, Bizarre, Jam Jar, Lid, Yellow Bands, Globular	128
Indian Summer, Vase, Yellow, Orange, Blue, Black, Green, Swollen, Flared, 8 In.	99
Latona, Bizarre, Plate, Stylized Drippy Tree, 6 ½ In.	209
Melon, Bizarre, Plate, Stylized Fruit, Orange, Yellow, Blue, Green, 9 In.	348
Moonlit, Fantasque Bizarre, Iris Jug, Multicolor Enamel, Tree Landscape, c.1933, 9 ½ In.	1230
My Garden, Bizarre, Vase, Blue, Orange & Yellow Flowers, Yellow Glaze, Tapered, 8 In.	218
Red Autumn, Fantasque, Vase, Multicolor Enamel, Tree Landscape, c.1930, 8 In.	861
Red Broth, Fantasque, Lotus Jug, c.1930, 11 ½ In.	923
Secrets, Sugar Shaker, 5 ½ In.	667
Swirls, Bizarre, Athens Jug, Multicolor Enamel, Stylized, Octagonal, c.1930, 7 In.	510
Taormina, Sugar Shaker, Inverted Cone Shape, Poppies, Tree, Water, Wilkinson, 6 In.	252
Tonquin, Bone Dish, Crescent Shape, Black, Royal Staffordshire, 6 ½ In.	10
Tonquin, Gravy Boat, Black, Landscape, Royal Staffordshire	26
Water Lily, Strainer, Underplate, 5 Holes, Wavy Water Border, Newport, 2 Piece	136

CLEWELL was made in limited quantities by Charles Walter Clewell of Canton, Ohio, from 1902 to 1955. Pottery was covered with a thin coating of bronze, then treated to make the bronze turn different colors. Pieces covered with copper, brass, or silver were also made. Mr. Clewell's secret formula for blue patinated bronze was burned when he died in 1965.

Bowl, Lid, Copper Clad, 7 x 4 In.	63
Cider Set, Copper Clad, Pitcher 10 In., Mug 5 In., 7 Piece	813
Vase, Bronze, Classical Shape, 2 Handles, 5 x 9 In.	732
Vase, Bronze, Green Verdigris, Rolled Rim, 4 ⅝ In.	161
Vase, Bronze, Verdigris Patina, Cylinder, 4 ¾ In.	104
Vase, Copper Clad, Black, Mottled, Green, Baluster, Signed, 5 x 13 ½ In.	610
Vase, Copper Clad, Brown, Green Drip, Shouldered, 6 x 12 In.	938
Vase, Copper Clad, Bulbous Base, 7 x 15 ½ In.	688
Vase, Copper Clad, Footed, Blue, Rust Patina, Tapered, Marked, 4 x 8 ½ In.	281
Vase, Copper Clad, Green Rust Patina, Footed, 5 x 9 In.	688
Vase, Copper Clad, Long Neck, Bottle Shape, 5 x 10 ½ In.	458
Vase, Copper Clad, On Ceramic, Bottle Shape, Signed, 5 x 10 ½ In.	458
Vase, Copper Clad, Shouldered, Tapered, 7 x 15 In.	875
Vase, Copper Clad, Swirled Designs, 7 ½ In.	272
Vase, Copper Clad, Tapered Cylinder, Rolled Rim, 8 x 11 In.	976
Vase, Copper Clad, Verdigris Patina, Shouldered, Tapered, 7 In.	219

Cigar Store Figure, Indian, Full Bodied, Headdress, Necklace, c.1870, 15 x 7 ½ In. $9,480

James D. Julia Auctioneers

Cigar Store Figure, Indian, Maiden, Headdress, Arm Up Holding Tomahawk, Cigars, 1800s, 68 x 25 In. $42,550

Cottone Auctions

Cigar Store Figure, Punch, Holding Tray, Embossed, Wooden, Wheels, 62 In. $3,300

Victorian Casino Antiques

C

Civil War, Chair, Folding, Carpet Seat, Gilt Paint, F.C., Roberts, Confederate Captain, 31 In.
$705

Cowan's Auctions

Civil War, Kepi, Confederate, Cadet Gray, Satinet Band, U.S. Marine Buttons, Lined
$2,400

Skinner Auctioneers & Appraisers

Clarice Cliff, Fantasque Bizarre, Vase, Lotus, House, Landscape, Handles, c.1930, 11 ⅜ In.
$431

Skinner Auctioneers & Appraisers

Vase, Copper Clad, Verdigris Patina, Tapered, Footed, Signed, 11 In.	92
Vase, Copper, Turquoise Drip, Footed, Marked, 8 x 15 In.	813
Vase, Dark Green, Bulbous, Tapered, Small Mouth, 5 ¼ In.	115
Vase, Green Matte Glaze, Tapered, Handles, 5 x 9 In.	732
Vase, Green, Mottled, Weller Hudson Mold, 9 In.	150

CLIFTON POTTERY was founded by William Long in Newark, New Jersey, in 1905. He worked there until 1909 making lines that included Crystal Patina and Clifton Indian Ware. Clifton Pottery made art pottery until 1911 and then concentrated on wall and floor tile. By 1914, the name had been changed to Clifton Porcelain and Tile Company.
Another firm, Chesapeake Pottery, sold majolica marked *Clifton Ware.*

Bowl, Indian Ware, Black, Red Band, Umbrella Shape, 8 In.	58
Cup, Handle, Indian Ware, Stylized Designs, Black, Red, 4 In.	29
Humidor, Lid, Indian Ware, Red, Black Design Band, 5 ½ In.	23
Pot, Indian Ware, Signed Clifton, Marked 241 Florida, c.1950, 10 In.	300
Teapot, Indian Ware, Low Lines, 2 ⅞ x 8 ½ In.	23
Vase, Brown Matte Glaze, Nasturtiums, Leaves, Impressed Mark, 11 ¼ In.	200
Vase, Squat, Indian Ware, Brown, Black, Marked, 5 ½ x 3 In.	35 to 69

CLOCKS of all types have always been popular with collectors. The eighteenth-century tall case, or grandfather's, clock was designed to house a works with a long pendulum. The name on the clock is usually the maker but sometimes it is a merchant or other craftsman. In 1816, Eli Terry patented a new, smaller works for a clock, and the case became smaller. The clock could be kept on a shelf instead of on the floor. By 1840, coiled springs were used and even smaller clocks were made. Battery-powered electric clocks were made in the 1870s. A garniture set can include a clock and other objects displayed on a mantel.

Advertising, 7Up, Get Real Action, Metal, Glass, Plastic, Light-Up, 1950s, 16 x 16 In.	161
Advertising, Borden's Ice Cream, Elsie, Metal & Glass, Red, Yellow, Light-Up, 15 x 3 In.	719
Advertising, Canada Dry, Light-Up, Pam, c.1960, 15 In.	210
Advertising, Champion Spark Plugs, Lighted, Plastic, Electric, 16 x 16 In.	207
Advertising, Diamond Black Leather Oil, Globe Oil Co., Baird, c.1900, 31 In. ....*illus*	1680
Advertising, Electric, Gruen Watch Time, Octagonal, Metal, Glass, 1940s, 15 ½ In.	36
Advertising, Genuine Chevrolet, Round, Bubble, Yellow, Red, Light-Up, 16 In.	300
Advertising, Hastings Piston Rings, Man In Striped Shirt, Glass, Metal, Round, 15 In.	738
Advertising, Iroquois Beer, Indian Chief Profile, Light-Up, Bubble, Glass, 16 In. Diam.	489
Advertising, Maremont Springs & Mufflers, Art Deco, Light-Up, Electric, 21 x 14 In.	640
Advertising, Mishler's Herb Bitters, Baird, Wood, Papier-Mache, 1890s, 30 In. ....*illus*	3163
Advertising, Moxie, Baird, 30 ½ In. ....*illus*	5100
Advertising, Packard, Neon, Painted, Blue, Red, Yellow, White Face, 20 ½ In.	855
Advertising, Packard, Neon, Round, Electric, 1960s, 19 ½ In.	1017
Advertising, Phillips 66 Tires, Batteries, Double Bubble Pam, Red, Black, Round, Electric, 15 In.	590
Advertising, Pontiac, Full Feather Indian, Light-Up, Round, Electric, 18 In.	2360
Advertising, Prestone, Raised Numbers, Sheet Metal, c.1915, 10 In. Diam.	98
Advertising, Purina Chows Sanitation Products, Light-Up, Convex Glass, 15 In.	485
Advertising, Socony, Is Standard, Seth Thomas, Electric, 14 x 14 In.	295
Advertising, Tetley Tea Time, Tin, Embossed, Waterbury Electric Maker, 14 x 20 In.	600
Advertising, Time For Sunshine Milk, Yellow Metal, Round, Open Hands, Neon Light, 21 In.	518
Advertising, Time For Yuengling Ice Cream, Light-Up, Art Deco Style, 1940s, 13 x 17 In.	840
Advertising, Toledo Steel Products, Octagonal, Neon, Green, Red, White, 18 x 18 In.	420
Advertising, Whistle Soda, Die Cut, Phelps Mfg. Co., Indiana, 24 x 24 In. ....*illus*	1320
Advertising, Wilno Kosher Products, Double Bubble, Round, Electric, 1950s, 15 In.	562
Animated, Early Bird, Jointed Robin, Paper, Painted Metal, Alarm, Canada, 4 ½ In. ....*illus*	115
Ansonia, Calendar, Mahogany, Reverse Painted, Star, Flower Panel, Round, 26 In.	2366
Ansonia, Gloria, Swinging Ball, Winged Figure, Lyre, Ball Pendulum, 28 In.	3120
Ansonia, Huntress, Spelter Figure, Bronze Ball, 25 In.	1200
Ansonia, Huntress, Spelter Figure, Pierced Hands, 25 In.	1599
Ansonia, Huntress, Spelter, Swinging Ball, Brass Sphere, Iron Base, c.1900, 25 In.	2583
Ansonia, Ornate Embossed, Porcelain Dial, Escapement, 17 In.	283
Ansonia, Ossipee, Porcelain, Painted, Rococo Case, Enameled Dial, c.1900, 11 x 12 ½ In.	270
Ansonia, Peer, Regulator Cast Frame, Beveled Glass, 8-Day, Pendulum, 12 In.	400
Ansonia, Shelf, Black Cast Iron, Lion Head Accents, Applied Feet, 16 x 11 In.	96
Ansonia, Wall, Arts & Crafts, Oak, Horizontal & Vertical Lines, Brass Numerals, 36 In.	138
Ansonia, Wall, Baghdad, Mahogany, Plume Top, Glazed Door, Porcelain Dial, 50 In.	1020
Ansonia, Wall, Queen Elizabeth, Oak, Columns, Glazed Door, 38 In.	180
Ansonia, Woman Seated, Brass, Porcelain, Pendulum, Key, 17 In.	390

Clock, Advertising, Diamond Black Leather Oil, Globe Oil Co., Baird, c.1900, 31 In. $1,680

Clock, Advertising, Mishler's Herb Bitters, Baird, Wood, Papier-Mache, 1890s, 30 In. $3,163

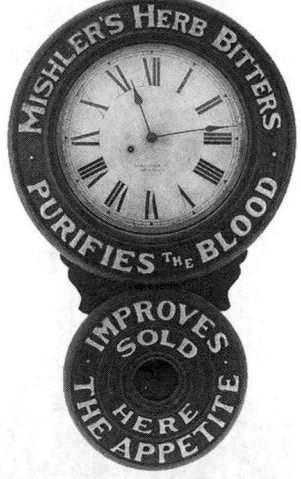

Clock, Advertising, Moxie, Baird, 30 ½ In. $5,100

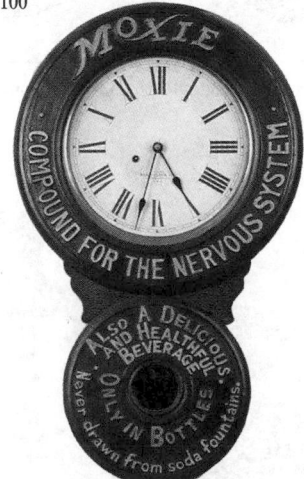

Clock, Advertising, Whistle Soda, Die Cut, Phelps Mfg. Co., Indiana, 24 x 24 In. $1,320

Clock, Animated, Early Bird, Jointed Robin, Paper, Painted Metal, Alarm, Canada, 4 ½ In. $115

Clock, Banjo, Federal, Mahogany, Gilt Gesso, Martin Kingsbury Dial, 8-Day, c.1820, 33 In. $4,800

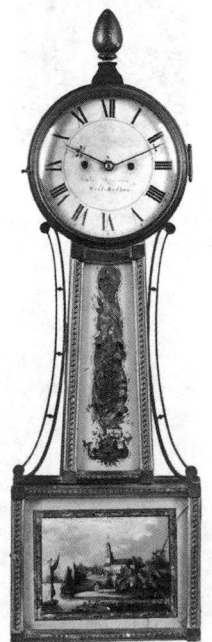

Clock, Banjo, Presentation, Mahogany, Eagle, Gilded Glass, Weight Driven, 1800s, 35 In. $1,422

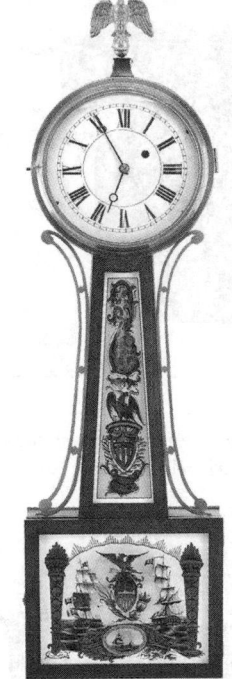

Clock, Bordes A Bordeaux, Wall, Rosewood, Inlay, Reverse Painted, 8-Day, c.1840, 23 In. $480

Clock, Burry, John, Lantern, Brass, Engraved, 30-Hour, Weight, Berry, London, c.1700, 9 In. $6,600

Clock, Carriage, Bovet Fleurier, Engraved, 8-Day, Key, Travel Box, Signed, c.1860, 5 ¾ In.
$1,599

Cowan's Auctions

Clock, Carriage, Brass, Sonnerie, Beveled Glass, Porcelain Dial, 8-Day, c.1900, 7 ½ In.
$960

Skinner Auctioneers & Appraisers

Clock, Carriage, Brass, Tourbillion Triple, Calendar, Alarm, Swiss, c.1990, 7 ¼ In.
$1,968

Skinner Auctioneers & Appraisers

Clock, Concord W. Co., Travel, Enamel, Silver Case, 8-Day, Swiss, 1 ¾ In.
$1,020

Skinner Auctioneers & Appraisers

Clock, Desk, Art Deco, Gray Marble, Cloissone Enamel, France, 1930s, 14 ¼ In.
$1,722

Cowan's Auctions

Clock, Figural, Man Holding Whiskey Flask, Instrument, Eyes Move, 9 ½ x 4 In.
$518

Wm Morford Auctions

Clock, Figural, Mars, Roman God Of War, Bronze, Suspension, c.1835, 24 x 11 In.
$4,182

New Orleans Auction Galleries, Inc.

Clock, French, Neo-Grec, Bronze, Napoleon III, Roman Emperor Septimius Severus, c.1875, 22 x 13 In.
$922

New Orleans Auction Galleries, Inc.

Clock, Guyerdet, Shelf, Charles X, Bronze, Nymph, Silk Thread, c.1830, 24 x 18 In.
$2,510

Neal Auction Co.

Clock, Heiko, Figural, Elephant, Pendulum, 10 In.
$314

Showtime Auction Services

Ansonia, Zenith, Regulator, Brass, Scrolled Frame, Glass Panels, c.1914, 15 In.	219
Astrolabe, Brass, Round, Scalloped Top, Embossed Persian Decoration, c.1900, 5 ½ In.	480
Banjo, A. Willard, Mahogany, Rope Twist, Reverse Painted Glass, Ships, Iron Dial, 41 In.	2040
Banjo, F. Campos, Tiger Maple, Ebony Inlay, Brass, Painted Naval Battle On Glass, 34 In.	3690
Banjo, Federal, Mahogany, Gilt Gesso, Martin Kingsbury Dial, 8-Day, 33 In. ....*illus*	4800
Banjo, Federal, Mahogany, Giltwood, Acorn Finial, Green Enamel, 33 x 10 In.	594
Banjo, Foster Campos, Sea Battle Panels, Gilt Eagle Finial, c.1865, 41 In.	1320
Banjo, Mahogany Veneer, Eagle Finial, Roman Numerals, Tablets, c.1835, 34 In.	570
Banjo, Mahogany, Carved, Brass Movement, Painted Tin Face, c.1820, 40 x 11 ½ In.	1811
Banjo, Presentation, Mahogany, Eagle, Gilded Glass, Weight Driven, 1800s, 35 In.........*illus*	1422
Banjo, S. Edgerly, Mahogany, Reverse Painted, Eagle, Wreath, Iron Dial, 8-Day, 32 In.	2880
Banjo, Waltham, Mahogany, Inlaid, Reverse Painted, Boston State House, 1930, 42 In.	1722
Banjo, Waltham, Mahogany, Rope Front, Reverse Painted Panels, Eagle Finial, 8-Day, 40 In.	615
Banjo, Willard's Patent, Federal, Eglomise Neck, Naval Battle Panel, c.1815, 30 In.	1304
Berthoud, F., Travel, Ormolu, Porcelain Dial, Pierced Hands, Wreath Handle, Case, 10 In.	1920
Bigelow & Kennard, Mahogany, Portico, 2 Columns, Ormolu Decoration, Gilt Bob, 18 In.	510
Birge & Fuller, Shelf, Steeple, Mahogany, Painted Tablets, Fruit, Wagon Spring, 27 In.	1845
Black Forest, Cuckoo, Nesting Birds, Leaves, Roman Numerals, Pinecone Weights, 25 In.	180
Black Forest, Cuckoo, Quail, Pitched Pediment, Grape Leaves, Crow, Black Paint, 27 In.	308
Black Forest, Renaissance Style, Brass, Rococo Scrolling, Mask, Dolphins, c.1890, 21 In.	300
Black Forest, Stag's Head, Crossed Guns, Oak Leaves, Rabbit, Bird, Horn, Pouch, 43 In.	787
Bordes A Bordeaux, Wall, Rosewood, Inlay, Reverse Painted, 8-Day, c.1840, 23 In.............*illus*	480
Bracket, Ormolu, 8-Day, 19th Century, 21 In.	406
Bracket, Rosewood, Mother-Of-Pearl Inlay, Glazed Sliding Door, 8-Day, c.1860, 21 In.	2400
Bracket, Taylor, John, George III, Ebonized, Brass & Steel Dial, 1700s, 13 In.	1645
Bracket, Walnut, Carved, Paneled, Enamel Dial, France, c.1890, 19 x 12 In.	390
Bradley & Hubbard, Figural, Soldier, Round Belly Case, Cast Iron, Painted, c.1850, 16 In.	1659
Bretby, Art Nouveau Style, Spread Base, Japonesque Panel, Bird, Cherry Blossoms, 20 In.	938
Burry, John, Lantern, Brass, Engraved, 30-Hour, Weight, Berry, London, c.1700, 9 In. ....*illus*	6600
Caldwell, Edward F., Desk, Brass, Beveled Glass, Beaded Dial Surround, 15 Jewel, 7 ½ In.	450
Carriage, Belle Epoque, Gilt Bronze, Porcelain, Balustrade, France, 6 ½ x 3 In.	338
Carriage, Bovet Fleurier, Engraved, 8-Day, Key, Travel Box, Signed, c.1860, 5 ¾ In. ....*illus*	1599
Carriage, Brass, Glass Panels, Shaped Handle, Key, Tiffany & Co., 5 x 4 In.	411
Carriage, Brass, Painted Porcelain Panels, Woman Playing Lute, Trees, 8-Day, 7 ½ In.	984
Carriage, Brass, Repeater, Flowers, Birds, Beveled Glass Sides, France, c.1880, 6 In.	600
Carriage, Brass, Sonnerie, Beveled Glass, Porcelain Dial, 8-Day, c.1900, 7 ½ In. ....*illus*	960
Carriage, Brass, Tourbillion Triple, Calendar, Alarm, Swiss, c.1990, 7 ¼ In. ....*illus*	1968
Carriage, Bronze, Grand Sonnerie, Guilloche Enamel, Strike & Repeat, 7 x 3 In.	2990
Carriage, Fruitwood, Gilt Bronze, Leaf Corners, Beveled Glass, Enamel, c.1900, 5 x 3 x 3 In.	861
Carriage, Tortoiseshell, Hour Repeater, Silver, Filigree Mounts, Tiffany, c.1900, 5 x 3 x 2 In.	2500
Cartel, Gilt Bronze, Leaves, Putto, Chariot, Doves, Clouds, 25 ½ In.	750
Cartier, Agate, Citrine Corners, Ribbed Bezel, Roman & Baton Numerals, 1940s, 3 x 3 In.	7200
Cartier, Desk, Brass, Faux Red Stone Enamel Sides, Battery, 6 ½ x 4 ¼ In.	96
Cartier, Desk, Quartz, Date, Oval Face, Roman Numerals, Faux Burl, Signed, 5 x 3 In.	564
Cartier, Shelf, Silvered, Enamel Lines, Arched Top, Roman Numerals, Swiss, 3 ⅛ In.	840
Chelsea, Carriage, Eagle Series, Brass, Beveled Glass, Faux Tortoiseshell, 8-Day, c.1980, 10 In.	510
Cincinnati Time Recorder Co., Oak Cabinet, 19 x 45 In.	960
Cincinnati Time Recorder Co., Oak, Card Holder, Property Defense Plant Corp., 14 x 30 In.	798
Concord W. Co., Travel, Enamel, Silver Case, 8-Day, Swiss, 1 ¾ In. ....*illus*	1020
Crowley, John, Shelf, Federal, Mahogany, Arched Glass Door, Brass Bail, Phila., c.1805, 18 In.	4688
D. Evans, Wall, Papier-Mache, Scrolls, Mother-Of-Pearl Inlay, 8-Day, Fusee, Wales, 21 In.	780
Daggett, Thomas, Blue, Gold Eglomise Panel, c.1825, 32 ¾ x 9 ¾ In.	3125
Deniere, Shelf, Ormolu, 2 Cupids, Porcelain, Beaded Bezel, Marble Base, Paris, 12 x 15 In.	1230
Desk, Art Deco, Gray Marble, Cloissone Enamel, France, 1930s, 14 ¼ In. ....*illus*	1722
Desk, Brass, Putto, Satyr Heads, Porcelain Dial, Pierced Hands, Marble Base, c.1910, 10 In.	660
Desk, Silver, Turquoise Enameled Case, Ribbed Pagoda Top, Flower Basket, 15 Jewel, 2 ¼ In.	960
Dixie Boy, Green Hat, Orange Necktie, Lux, 1930s, 9 In.	281
Dubey, Paul, Shelf, Bronze, Marble Base, c.1850, 28 In.	420
Elgin, Shelf, Blue Russian Lapis, Silver Crown, Gilt, Ruby, Diamonds, 8-Day, 7 x 5 In.	4688
Elliot, J.C., Skeleton, Gothic Style, Brass, Glass, Marble, Silvered Roman Numeral Dial, 21 In.	3360
Farcot, Swinging Cherub, Gilt Rococo Stand, Ebonized Base, Glass Dome, Paris, 1890, 11 In.	450
Figural, Clock Seller, Tole, 14 In.	438
Figural, Eagle, Bronze, Clear Ball Clock In Beak, 8-Day, Marble Base, 1800s, 13 In.	2250
Figural, Man Holding Whiskey Flask, Instrument, Eyes Move, 9 ½ x 4 In. ....*illus*	518
Figural, Mars, Roman God Of War, Bronze, Suspension, c.1835, 24 x 11 In. ....*illus*	4182
Figural, Woman, Louis XV Style, Gilt, Cherub, Garland, Urn, c.1890, 26 x 16 In.	590

Clock, Howard Miller, Chess Piece, G. Nelson, 1950s, 19 x 8 ½ In. $1,750

Rago Arts & Auction Center

Clock, Howard Miller, Diamond Markers, No. 2267, George Nelson, 1959, 13 In. $5,000

Los Angeles Modern Auctions (LAMA)

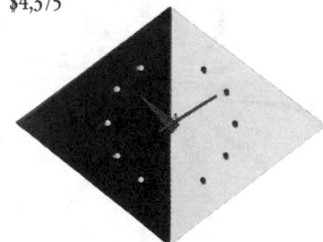

Clock, Howard Miller, Kite, Enameled Metal, No. 2201, G. Nelson, 1950s, 16 ½ x 22 In. $4,375

Los Angeles Modern Auctions (LAMA)

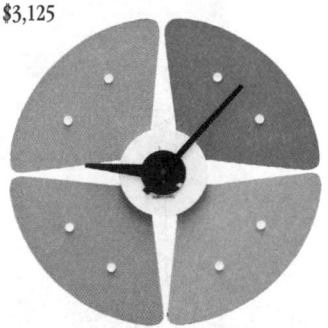

Clock, Howard Miller, Petal, No. 7513, George Nelson, 1957, 18 In. $3,125

Los Angeles Modern Auctions (LAMA)

Clock, Howard Miller, Popsicle, No. 2257-A, George Nelson, 1957, 14 In.
$4,375

Los Angeles Modern Auctions (LAMA)

Clock, Howard Miller, Pretzel, No. 4775, George Nelson, 1952, 17 In.
$5,938

Los Angeles Modern Auctions (LAMA)

Clock, Howard Miller, Spike, No. 2202-D, George Nelson, 1952, 18 ½ In.
$2,000

Los Angeles Modern Auctions (LAMA)

Clock, Howard Miller, Triangle, No. 2225-G, George Nelson, 1955, 20 In.
$2,375

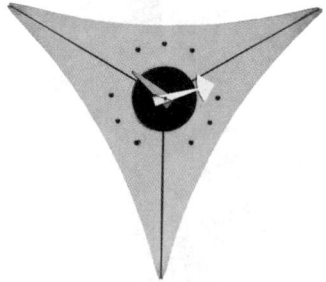

Los Angeles Modern Auctions (LAMA)

French, Neo-Grec, Bronze, Napoleon III, Roman Emperor Septimius Severus, c.1875, 22 x 13 In. *illus*	922
G. Rohde, World's Fair, Burl Veneer, 3 Chromed Stripes, Rectangular, H. Miller, 13 In.	1500
General Electric, Fused Glass, Red Hands, Michael Frances Higgins, 8 ¼ x 8 ¾ In.	610
Gilbert Clock Co., Shelf, Wood, Metal, Time & Strike, Key, Pendulum, 19 ¾ In.	840
Guyerdet, Shelf, Charles X, Bronze, Nymph, Silk Thread, c.1830, 24 x 18 In. *illus*	2510
Hamilton Watch Co., Chronometer, Lancaster, Pa., Model 22, Wood Box, 6 x 6 x 6 In.	984
Hampton, Regulator, Crystal, Gilt Bronze, Hour Strike, c.1910, 11 In.	150
Heiko, Figural, Elephant, Pendulum, 10 In. *illus*	314
Herman Miller, Wall, Wood, Starburst, c.1960, 18 In. Diam.	330
Howard Miller, Asterisk, Black Enamel, White Enamel Hands, Round, 10 In.	313
Howard Miller, Asterisk, Enameled Wood, Metal, G. Nelson, 1950s, 10 x 10 In.	375
Howard Miller, Chess Piece, G. Nelson, 1950s, 19 x 8 ½ In. *illus*	1750
Howard Miller, Diamond Markers, No. 2267, George Nelson, 1959, 13 In. *illus*	5000
Howard Miller, Kite, Enameled Metal, No. 2201, G. Nelson, 1950s, 16 ½ x 22 In. *illus*	4375
Howard Miller, Petal, No. 7513, George Nelson, 1957, 18 In. *illus*	3125
Howard Miller, Popsicle, No. 2257-A, George Nelson, 1957, 14 In. *illus*	4375
Howard Miller, Pretzel, No. 4775, George Nelson, 1952, 17 In. *illus*	5938
Howard Miller, Round, Orange Balls, Aluminum, Brass, Wood, G. Nelson, 1940s, 13 In.	344
Howard Miller, Spike, No. 2202-D, George Nelson, 1952, 18 ½ In. *illus*	2000
Howard Miller, Stoneware, Round, Yellow, Orange, G. Nelson, 1960s, 14 In.	594
Howard Miller, Triangle, No. 2225-G, George Nelson, 1955, 20 In. *illus*	2375
Industrial, Round, Painted, Distressed Patina, Parcel Gilt, Roman Numerals, 48 In.	246
Ingraham & Co., Servant's Call, Oak, Carved, 15 Position Box, c.1890, 33 x 15 In.	380
Ingraham, Regulator, Calendar, Oak, Carved Pediment, 37 In.	267
Ingraham, Shelf, Grecian, Rosewood Veneer, Paper Dial, Roman Numerals, c.1880, 15 In.	123
Ithaca Calendar Clock, Box Skeleton, Cased, 20 ½ x 11 x 8 ½ In.	9900
Ithaca, Wall, Parlor, No. 3 ½, Walnut, Ebony, Columns, 2 Dials, Greek God, Swags, 37 In.	4500
Ives, Joseph, Shelf, Mahogany, Wagon Spring, Eglomise House, Tree, c.1830, 28 x 16 In.	34375
J. Wilson & Faire, Wall, Masonic, Mother-Of-Pearl, Rosewood Inlay, 1800s, 32 In. *illus*	531
Jaccard, Shelf, Brass, Beveled Glass, Porcelain Panels, Wine Cellar Scene, c.1890, 13 In.	960
Japy Freres, Shelf, Figural, Young Couple, Porcelain, Putti, Garlands, Breguet Hands, 17 In.	900
Japy Freres, Wall, Tole, Flowers, 8-Sided, Enamel Dial, Brass Bezel, Glass Door, 17 In.	338
Jerome & Co., Wall, Walnut, Heron, Day Of Week Calendar, Printed Paper Dial, 8-Day, 31 In.	1200
LeCoultre, Atmos, Brass & Glass Case, Engraved Presentation Plaque, c.1966, 9 ½ In.	480
LeCoultre, Atmos, Brass, Glass Panels, Cut Corner Base, c.1962, 9 In.	460
LeCoultre, Atmos, Brass, Glass, Roman & Baton Numerals	322
LeCoultre, Atmos, Gilt Brass, Glass, Swiss, c.1990, 9 x 7 ½ In.	406
Liberty & Co., Carriage, Cymric, Sterling Silver, Turquoise, A. Knox, c.1904, 4 x 3 In. *illus*	12500
Lighthouse, Rotating Windmill, Dials, Tole, Marked, c.1890, 24 x 13 In. *illus*	1968
Lux, Dixie Boy, Black Face, Smiling, Tie Pendulum, 1930s, 9 In. *illus*	281
Lyre, Mahogany, Brass, Gilt, Reverse Painted, Goddess Of Music, 8-Day, 40 In. *illus*	1722
Lyre, Maxant, E., Ormolu, Swags, Sun King, Beaded, Porcelain, Marble Base, Paris, 23 In.	4200
Lyre, Mystery, Rosewood, Musical Marquetry, Moon Hands, France, c.1870, 23 In.	1020
Lyre, Shelf, Alabaster, Gilt Bronze Ormolu, Beaded Edge, Enameled Face, France, 23 In.	726
Lyre, Shelf, Rosewood, Marquetry Inlay, Dore Bronze Mounts, c.1950, 23 In.	1500
Lyre, Stennes, Mahogany, Carved Scrolls, Painted Glass, Woman With Harp, 40 In.	2160
Mahogany, Carved, Brass Face, Flags, Bats, Vines, Enameled, Chinese, 1800s, 20 x 12 In.	4820
Mahogany, Convex Dial Glass, Roman Numerals, 8-Day Fusee Movement, 29 In.	720
Marble, Mourning Woman, Draped Urn, Jeweled Face, France, 29 ½ In.	1140
Marble, Square, Stepped Base, Roman Numerals, Spade Hands, Tiffany & Co., 6 In.	369
Marc, H., Shelf, Brass, Gothic Style, Arched, Porcelain Panels, Rural & Urban Scenes, 22 In.	1722
Marc, Henry, Figural, Lighthouse, 4 Dials, Faux Brick, Stepped Base, 15 In.	420
Marti Et Cie, Regulator, Brass, Beveled Glass, c.1900, 5 ½ In.	600
Marti, Shelf, Beaux Arts Style, Scrolled Feet, Caryatids, Enamel Panel, 13 x 8 In.	399
McCabe, J., Dark Mahogany, Round, Enamel Dial, Roman Numerals, London, 14 In.	702
Metz, Wall, Serpentine Case, Inlaid Boulle, Marble, Porcelain, France, c.1860, 33 In. *illus*	720
Mystery, Diana, Cast Metal, Ebonized Wood Base, Spring Powered, Time Only, c.1900, 12 In.	360
Mystery, Thais, Woman, Swinging Blue Ball, Pierced Hands, Marble Base, France, 42 In.	4500
New Haven, Shelf, Regulator, Calendar, Reverse Painted, Victorian, 28 In.	360
Newman, A.G., Servant's Call, Wood Cabinet, Carved Turrets, Shells, Victorian	1968
Novelty, John Bull, Blinking Eye, Cast Iron, Painted, 16 In.	593
Pei, I.M., Anodized Aluminum, Black & White, Rectangular Base, 20 x 13 ¾ In. *illus*	1560
Petit, Jacob, Shelf, Boy, Girl, Flowers, Porcelain c.1850, 20 x 14 In. *illus*	1476
Ralls, Henry, Shelf, Walnut, Brass Leafy Mounts, Finial Top, Twickenham, England, 16 In.	461
Regina, Arts & Crafts, Oak, Style 81, Chimes, Plays Music	3540
Regulator, Champleve Dome & Panels, 6-Sided, 4 Glass Panels, Spool Feet, France, 16 In.	11070

Clock, J. Wilson & Faire, Wall, Masonic,
Mother-Of-Pearl, Rosewood Inlay, 1800s, 32 In.
$531

Brunk Auctions

Clock, Liberty & Co., Carriage, Cymric, Sterling
Silver, Turquoise, A. Knox, c.1904, 4 x 3 In.
$12,500

Rago Arts & Auction Center

Clock, Lighthouse, Rotating Windmill, Dials,
Tole, Marked, c.1890, 24 x 13 In.
$1,968

Neal Auction Co.

Clock, Lux, Dixie Boy, Black Face, Smiling, Tie
Pendulum, 1930s, 9 In.
$281

Jackson's Int'l Auctioneers and Appraisers

Clock, Lyre, Mahogany, Brass, Gilt, Reverse
Painted, Goddess Of Music, 8-Day, 40 In.
$1,722

Skinner Auctioneers & Appraisers

Clock, Metz, Wall, Serpentine Case, Inlaid
Boulle, Marble, Porcelain, France, c.1860,
33 In.
$720

Skinner Auctioneers & Appraisers

Clock, Pei, I.M., Anodized Aluminum, Black &
White, Rectangular Base, 20 x 13 ¾ In.
$1,560

Skinner Auctioneers & Appraisers

Clock, Petit, Jacob, Shelf, Boy, Girl, Flowers,
Porcelain c.1850, 20 x 14 In.
$1,476

New Orleans Auction Galleries, Inc.

Clock, Shelf, Classical Figure, Seated, Bronze
Dore, Silk Thread, France, c.1810, 16 ½ In.
$1,625

Rago Arts & Auction Center

Clock, Shelf, Goddess Aurora, Gilt Bronze, Columns, France, c.1835, 24 x 12 In.
$6,150

New Orleans Auction Galleries, Inc.

Clock, Shelf, Marble, Architectural, From New York Bank, c.1940, 35 ½ x 77 In.
$8,125

Rago Arts & Auction Center

Clock, T.S. Sperry Mfg. Co., Shelf, Metal, Painted, Mother-Of-Pearl, 12 x 18 ¾ In.
$171

Showtime Auction Services

TIP
To make a clock run faster, raise the pendulum; to slow it, lower the pendulum.

Regulator, Crystal, Brass, Champleve, Columns, Tiffany & Co., c.1890, 17 In.	3444
Regulator, French, Brass, Champleve Decoration, Glass Panels, Shreve, Crump & Low, 11 In.	3075
Regulator, Pub, Walnut, Inlay, England, 19th Century	240
Regulator, Victorian, Walnut, Carved, Brass, Pin Escapement, 82 x 20 In.	4029
Regulator, Vienna, Walnut, Broken Arch, 3 Finials, Turned Columns, 46 In.	633
Sessions, Figural, Airplane, 2 Propellers, 3 Wheels, Metal, Dial Center Front, 21 In.	78
Sessions, Shelf, Arts & Crafts, Oak, Shaped Pediment, Cutouts, Brass Numerals, 18 In.	98
Seth Thomas, Federal, Mahogany, Pillar & Scroll, Painted Dial, Enamel Panel, c.1815, 30 In.	1541
Seth Thomas, Federal, Pillar & Scroll, Flower Basket, 2 Buildings, 31 In.	800
Seth Thomas, Gallery, Mahogany, Round, 24 In.	1063
Seth Thomas, Regulator No. 3 Variant, Mahogany, 6-Sided, Painted Zinc Dial, c.1885, 47 In.	6150
Seth Thomas, Regulator No. 4, Rosewood, Veneered, Glazed Door, Molded, c.1880, 47 In.	9600
Seth Thomas, Regulator, Empire, No. 4, Bronze, Beveled Glass, Porcelain Dial, 11 In.	431
Seth Thomas, Regulator, No. 1, Mahogany, Black & Gold Reverse Painted, 34 In.	3600
Seth Thomas, Restauration, Rosewood Veneer, Calendar, Double Dial, c.1877, 27 x 14 In.	307
Seth Thomas, School, Oak, c.1830, 37 In.	384
Seth Thomas, Shelf, Mahogany, Pillar & Scroll, Reverse Painted House, c.1825, 28 x 17 In.	4063
Seth Thomas, Shelf, Rosewood Adamantine Case, Brass Bezel, Sonora Chime, c.1920, 10 In.	324
Seth Thomas, Shelf, Rosewood, Calendar, Double Dials, c.1876, 26 ¾ In.	489
Seth Thomas, Shelf, Wood, Marbleized, Black Pillars, Lion Handles, 17 x 12 In.	107
Seth Thomas, Wall, Mahogany, Jupiter, Pagoda Top, Zinc Dial, Moon's Age, 2 Weights, 59 In.	9600
Seth Thomas, Wall, Office Calendar No. 3, Peanut Form, Rosewood Veneer, 2 Dials, 23 In.	3120
Shelf, Alabaster, Gilt Bronze, Swags, Garlands, Birds, Urn Finial, Musical, France, 18 In.	3335
Shelf, American Indian, Bronze, Steel Dial, Copper Plinth, France, 1800s, 17 x 13 In.	590
Shelf, Art Deco, Mahogany Tambour, Silver Pierced Hands, Germany, 9 In.	120
Shelf, Art Deco, Rose Quartz, Pillars, Nephrite Bands, Dogs, Swiss, c.1920, 3 ⅞ x 4 ½ In.	9375
Shelf, Belle Epoque, Marble, Gilt Metal, Scrolling, Draped Woman, c.1900, 26 x 13 In.	276
Shelf, Brass, Columns, Champleve Panel, Flowers, France, c.1890, 13 In.	2400
Shelf, Brass, Porcelain, Gardens, Lovers, Putti, Roman Numerals, France, c.1890, 12 In.	960
Shelf, Bronze Dore, Cherubs, Scroll Feet, Rotterdam, 1800s, 16 x 19 In.	1440
Shelf, Bronze Dore, Cupid, Urns, Wheat Sheaves, Porcelain, France, c.1845, 16 x 12 In.	938
Shelf, Cabrier, C., Mahogany, Pagoda, Moon Dial, Musical, 14 Bells, London, 23 In.	16800
Shelf, Classical Figure, Seated, Alabaster, Gilt, France, 15 x 16 In.	375
Shelf, Classical Figure, Seated, Bronze Dore, Silk Thread, France, c.1810, 16 ½ In. ....*illus*	1625
Shelf, Cylinder, White Marble, 2 Children, Enameled, Urn Base, France, 1800s, 15 In.	236
Shelf, Ebonized Case, Ormolu, Gilt Brass Pendulum, Handles, 8-Day, c.1890, 27 In.	4500
Shelf, Empire Style, Tower Shape, Gilt, Patinated Bronze, Lion Head, Block Feet, 19 In.	1625
Shelf, Empire, Gilt Bronze, Classical Woman, Seated, Harp, Bun Feet, c.1825, 15 In.	1375
Shelf, Federal, Mahogany, Eglomise, Eagle Finial, Round Face, Square Base, c.1805, 35 In.	984
Shelf, Figural, Terra-Cotta, Gilt Metal, Girl, Birds, Nest, Enamel Dial, 11 In.	375
Shelf, Figural, Traveler, Spelter, Porcelain, Marble, Scroll Feet, c.1890, 21 In.	308
Shelf, French Aesthetic Style, Figural, Ormolu, Diana The Huntress, Ormolu, c.1890, 12 In.	150
Shelf, Gilt Brass, Portico, 4 Columns, 8-Day, Strike, Pendulum, c.1840, 17 In.	900
Shelf, Gilt Bronze, Cut Glass, Columns, Capitals, Stepped Base, Bun Feet, 1800s, 18 In.	406
Shelf, Gilt Bronze, Flowers, Bow, Quiver, Enamel Dial, Footed, Paris, 12 ¾ In.	625
Shelf, Goddess Aurora, Gilt Bronze, Columns, France, c.1835, 24 x 12 In. ....*illus*	6150
Shelf, Louis XV Style, Bronze, Tortoiseshell, Brass Movement, Tiffany & Co., 34 x 19 x 7 In.	5904
Shelf, Mahogany, Scrolling Brackets, Stepped Base, Tiffany & Co., 12 x 21 In.	470
Shelf, Marble, Architectural, From New York Bank, c.1940, 35 ½ x 77 In. ....*illus*	8125
Shelf, Moorish Revival, Domes, Columns, Metal, Marble Case, Painted, c.1890, 32 In.	5120
Shelf, Napoleon III, Cathedral, Gilt Bronze, Silk Suspension, Striking Bell, c.1860, 16 x 6 In.	2091
Shelf, Oak, Carved Dolphins, Rope, Pennants, Sailboat Dial, 12 x 23 In.	119
Shelf, Ormolu, Crossed Torch & Arrows, Scrolled Leaves, Gray Marble Base, French, 17 In.	1200
Shelf, Pillar & Scroll, Urn Finials, Shaped Skirt, Peg Feet, c.1825, 30 ½ In.	369
Shelf, Porcelain, Painted, Gilt, Columns, Domed, Footed, c.1900, 20 x 9 In.	1770
Shelf, Rosewood, Gilt Brass, Scroll, Acanthus Leaf, Footed, 8-Day, c.1860, 29 In.	2091
Shelf, Vincenti Et Cie, Spelter, Man, Feathered Cap, Seated On Clock Face, Black, 24 x 22 In.	533
Skeleton, Brass Plinths, Silvered Roman Numeral Chapter Ring, 8-Bell, Glass Dome, 17 In.	12000
Smith, William, Shelf, Georgian, Wood, Engraved Backplate, Silvered, London, c.1800, 15 In.	4503
Starr, T.B., Carriage, Brass, Champleve Decoration, 8-Day, Shaped Handle, 1880, 4 ½ In.	2483
Stennes, Coffin, Pine, Iron Dial, Rocking Ship, Brass Eagle Finial, 8-Day, 50 In.	1440
Stennes, Girandole, Mahogany, Gilt, Brass Bezel, Painted Glass, Aurora, Iron Dial, 44 In.	4500
T.S. Sperry Mfg. Co., Shelf, Metal, Painted, Mother-Of-Pearl, 12 x 18 ¾ In. ....*illus*	171
Tall Case, A. Castillion, Baroque, Gilt, Enamel, France, c.1800, 92 x 17 In. ....*illus*	885
Tall Case, A. Fromanteel, Ebonized, Peaked Pediment, Gilt Brass Swag, Paneled Door, 75 In.	7800
Tall Case, A. Kirkwood, Pine, Swan's Neck, Painted Schooner, Paisley, Scotland, 88 In.	677

Clock, Tall Case, A. Castillion, Baroque, Gilt, Enamel, France, c.1800, 92 x 17 In.
$885

Clock, Tall Case, Aaron Willard, Federal, Mahogany, Painted Arch, Calendar, c.1785, 92 In.
$14,760

Clock, Tall Case, Baroque, Japanned, Parcel Gilt, Chinoiserie Scenes, Swiss, 1800s, 84 In.
$2,124

Clock, Tall Case, Colonial Mfg. Co., Mahogany, 8-Day Time & Strike, Brass, c.1950, 98 In.
$1,080

Clock, Tall Case, Colonial Style, Oak, Brass, c.1910, 84 x 27 In.
$4,375

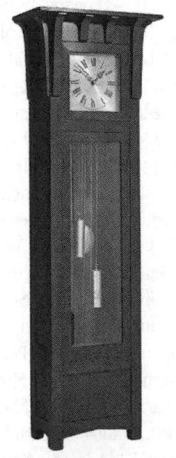

Clock, Tall Case, Enamel Dial, Stamped Brass Surround, Flowers, France, 1800s, 92 In.
$1,440

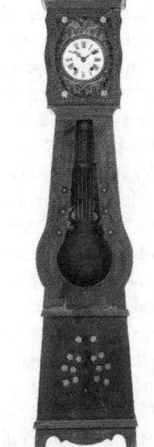

Clock, Tall Case, George III, Mahogany, 2-Weight, Time & Strike, c.1815, 88 In.
$1,168

Clock, Tall Case, Herschede, Mahogany, Carved, Pendulum, Chimes, c.1928, 72 In.
$615

Clock, Tall Case, Howard Miller, Walnut, Brass, Velvet, George Nelson, 1958, 71 x 14 In.
$2,500

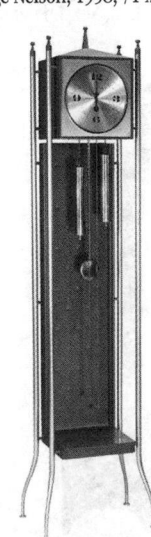

Clock, Tall Case, Oak, Carved, Inlay, Broken Arch, Brass Finial, Columns, 1800s, 91 In.
$1,722

Neal Auction Co.

Clock, Tall Case, Riley Whiting, Pine, Grain Painted, 30-Hour, c.1825, 81 In.
$720

Garth's Auctioneers & Appraisers

Clock, Tall Case, Silas Hoadley, Federal, Birch, Pine, 30-Hour, New England, c.1820, 98 In.
$960

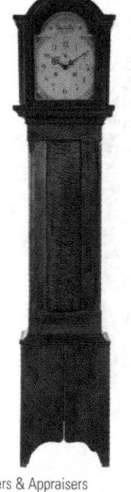

Garth's Auctioneers & Appraisers

Tall Case, A. Miller, Regency, Mahogany, Round Dial, Waisted Case, Columns, Scotland, 81 In. ..	3000
Tall Case, Aaron Willard, Federal, Mahogany, Painted Arch, Calendar, c.1785, 92 In.............*illus*	14760
Tall Case, Baroque, Japanned, Parcel Gilt, Chinoiserie Scenes, Swiss, 1800s, 84 In................*illus*	2124
Tall Case, Bisset, St. Andrews, Mahogany, Shell Inlay, Swan's Neck Pediment, Columns, 86 In.....	2520
Tall Case, Cherry, Pagoda, Fretwork, Iron Numerals, Moon's Age, Connecticut, 1790, 91 In........	3900
Tall Case, Chippendale, Mahogany, Carved, Broken Pediment, c.1765, 97 x 19 In......................	5900
Tall Case, Chippendale, Poplar, Broken Swan Crest, 3 Finials, Flower Face, Pa., 116 In.	889
Tall Case, Colonial Mfg. Co., Mahogany, 8-Day Time & Strike, Brass, c.1950, 98 In.............*illus*	1080
Tall Case, Colonial Style, Oak, Brass, c.1910, 84 x 27 In...*illus*	4375
Tall Case, D. Rittenhouse, Chippendale, Walnut, Stepped Cornice, 34-Hour, c.1765, 81 In...........	4480
Tall Case, D. Rose, Chippendale, Walnut, Maple Inlay, Arched Door, Moon Phase, Pa., 96 In.........	10530
Tall Case, D. Weatherby, Burl Mahogany, Walnut, Painted Metal Dial, Philadelphia, 98 In..........	5463
Tall Case, De Saintican, Art Deco, Burl Walnut, Shaped Crest, Paris, c.1930, 84 In...................	720
Tall Case, Donne & Son, Mahogany, Carved, Brass Columns, Tubular Bells, London, 99 In.........	12000
Tall Case, E. Taber, Mahogany, Arched, Fretwork, Moon's Age, Inlaid, 8-Day, c.1810, 95 In........	5000
Tall Case, Eliazer Warren, Mahogany, Carved, Lion Mask, Bonnet, Dublin, c.1790, 98 In.	5938
Tall Case, Elliot, Oak, Arched Hood, Egg & Dart Molding, Carved Columns, 8-Day, 94 In.	5100
Tall Case, Enamel Dial, Stamped Brass Surround, Flowers, France, 1800s, 92 In.................*illus*	1440
Tall Case, Ephraim Willard, Federal, Cherry, 8-Day, Painted Face, Mass., c.1810, 97 In...........	2066
Tall Case, Federal, Cherry, Curly Maple, 8-Day Movement, Painted Face, Pa., c.1820, 92 In........	2673
Tall Case, Federal, Cherry, Inlay, Urn Finials, Flower Painted Wood Face, c.1820, 94 x 18 In.......	875
Tall Case, Federal, Mahogany, Fretwork, 3 Finials, Roxbury School, Mass., 1800, 95 In...........	6875
Tall Case, Federal, Mahogany, Swan's Neck Pediment, Philadelphia, c.1800, 96 In.	3198
Tall Case, Federal, Walnut, Broken Arch Bonnet, Painted Face, 8-Day, Pa., c.1810, 91 ½ In.	1304
Tall Case, G. Breneisen, Federal, Maple, Urn Finial, Painted Dial, Pa., c.1805, 88 x 20 In.	1375
Tall Case, George III, Mahogany, 2-Weight, Time & Strike, c.1815, 88 In. ....*illus*	1168
Tall Case, George III, Mahogany, Arched Pediment, Inlay, Reeded Columns, 1700s, 86 In..........	1375
Tall Case, George III, Mahogany, Scrolled Pediment, Finial, Scotland, c.1790, 87 x 21 In...........	1000
Tall Case, George Levely, Federal, Mahogany, Inlay, Baltimore, c.1810, 95 In.......................	4375
Tall Case, Georgian, Oak, Arched Painted Dial, Broken Pediment, Finial, 1800s, 80 x 20 In........	1062
Tall Case, Herschede, Mahogany, Carved, Pendulum, Chimes, c.1928, 72 In.........................*illus*	615
Tall Case, Howard Miller, Walnut, 9 Tubes, c.1960, 87 x 24 x 16 In......................................	450
Tall Case, Howard Miller, Walnut, Brass, Velvet, George Nelson, 1958, 71 x 14 In. ....*illus*	2500
Tall Case, J. Doll, Swan's Neck Bonnet, Inlaid Eagle, Vines, 8-Day, Moon Phase Dial, 86 In.	1170
Tall Case, J. Wilder, Federal, 3 Turned Finials, Fret Carving, 30-Hour, c.1810, 61 In.	2750
Tall Case, John Keim, Chippendale, Cherry, Painted Metal Dial, Pa., c.1800, 91 In...................	3555
Tall Case, John Watt Irvine, Mahogany Inlay, Painted Lunette, 8-Day Time & Strike, 83 In.........	639
Tall Case, Joseph Fix, Soap Hollow Style Painted, Broken Arch Pediment, c.1820, 92 In..........	5900
Tall Case, L. Hutchins, Federal, Cherry, Pierced Fret, 3 Brass Finials, Bird Face, c.1835, 48 In.....	14080
Tall Case, Mahogany, Broken Arch Pediment, Brass Movement, Sun Moon Dial, c.1840, 106 In.	1763
Tall Case, Mahogany, Inlaid, Brass Finials, Broken Arch, Reeded Stiles, c.1790, 94 In................	3050
Tall Case, Mahogany, Pagoda Top, Blind Fret, Columns, Scallop Skirt, c.1785, 92 In................	5843
Tall Case, N. Brown, Mahogany, Scroll Top, Brass Dial, Dials, 8-Day, 108 In.	923
Tall Case, Napoleon III Style, Gilt, Brass, Tortoiseshell, Ebonized Frame, 1900s, 93 x 29 In........	3125
Tall Case, Oak, Arched, Rope Twist, Beaded, Glass Panel, Bim Bam Strike, Germany, 75 In.........	805
Tall Case, Oak, Carved, Inlay, Broken Arch, Brass Finial, Columns, 1800s, 91 In..................*illus*	1722
Tall Case, Oak, Convex Glass Door, Brass Dial, Westminster Chime, Germany, 1890, 82 In..........	570
Tall Case, Oak, Stained, Shell Carved Crest, Painted Door, Columns, 108 x 29 In.	1722
Tall Case, Peter Miller, Chippendale, Poplar, Stained, Carved Rosettes, Finials, 87 In..................	2430
Tall Case, Pine, Grain Paint, Gilt Dial, Flowers, Village, Shaped Skirt, c.1825, 83 ½ In.	5100
Tall Case, Pine, Grain Painted, Swan's Neck Crest, Tombstone Opening, c.1810, 89 In.	21600
Tall Case, R. Dickinson, Mahogany, Broken Arch Bonnet, Painted Dial, England, c.1840, 93 In..	1287
Tall Case, Renaissance Revival, Walnut, Sphinx Mask, Pinwheel Regulator, c.1875, 106 In.	7072
Tall Case, Riley Whiting, Pine, Grain Painted, 30-Hour, c.1825, 81 In.................................*illus*	720
Tall Case, S. Hoadley, Pine, Carved Pediment, Plymouth, 80 In..	474
Tall Case, S. Taber, Mahogany, Fretwork, String & Fan Inlay, Ship In Arch, 8-Day, 95 In.	7800
Tall Case, S. Willard, Mahogany, Marquetry, Fretwork, Columns, 88 In..................................	5400
Tall Case, S. Willard, Mahogany, Rocking Ship, Fret Top, Brass, Columns, c.1810, 91 In.	31200
Tall Case, Sheraton, Cherry, 8-Day Movement, Painted Face, Moon Phase, Pa., c.1825, 98 In.....	2015
Tall Case, Silas Hoadley, Federal, Birch, Pine, 30-Hour, New England, c.1820, 98 In.............*illus*	960
Tall Case, Spalding, Cherry, Fretwork Bonnet, 3 Finials, Gilt, Fan Carved Case, c.1790, 95 In........	16520
Tall Case, Swedish Baroque, Painted Dial, Sarcophagus Top, Appliques, 1700s, 92 x 11 In........	2016
Tall Case, T. Harland, Federal, Mahogany, Crest, Pinwheel Inlay, Columns, c.1800, 90 In............	2560
Tall Case, Vander Cloese, Marquetry, Gilt Brass, Steel, Moon, Dutch, c.1710, 98 In...............*illus*	4063
Tall Case, W. Durfee, Mahogany, Scroll Top, Gilt, Tubular Bells, Providence, 102 In....................	14400
Tall Case, W. Durfee, Mahogany, Westminster & Whittington Chimes, c.1890, 97 In....................	17835

Tall Case, Waltham, Quartersawn Oak, Horner Movement, Tiffany & Co., 112 In.................*illus*		84000
Tall Case, Weatherstone, Arched Hood, 2 Ball Finials, Chinoiserie, England, c.1750, 93 In..........		1875
Tall Case, William & Mary, Chinoisserie, Arched Brass Dial, Finials, 1700s, 104 x 21 In.		2124
Tall Case, Wm. Huston, Chippendale, Walnut, Finials, Rosettes, Painted Face, c.1780, 106 In.		10000
Tall Case, Wood, Carved Acanthus Leaves, Gilt, Bulbous, Sweden, c.1750, 88 x 25 In.		10455
Taylor, John, Shelf, Ebonized, Acorn Finials, Bell Handles, Bracket Feet, London, 19 In.		2250
Terry, Eli, Mahogany Veneer, Pillar & Scroll, Brass, Reverse Painted, c.1825, 32 In. ....*illus*		510
Terry, Eli, Shelf, Federal, Mahogany, c.1825, 27 ¾ In.		851

Tiffany clocks that are part of desk sets made by Louis Comfort Tiffany are listed in the Tiffany category. Clocks sold by the store Tiffany & Co. are listed here.

Travel Alarm, Gold Plate, 8-Day Swiss Movement, Leather Case, Tiffany, 2 x 1 In.		460
Vincenti & Cie, Shelf, Flowers, Bronze Dore, Porcelain, Stamped, 1855, 12 x 7 In. ....*illus*		885
Vincenti & Cie, Shelf, Spelter, Man, Feathered Cap, Seated On Clock Face, 24 x 22 In.................		533
Wag-On-Wall, Alabaster, Gilt Bronze, Weighted Pendulum, France, c.1840, 49 In.		420
Wag-On-Wall, Floral Painted Wood Dial, Brass Movement, Germany, 1800s, 16 ¼ In.		120
Wag-On-Wall, Wood Frame, Painted Metal Crest, Trumpeting Angels, Urn, Friesland, 27 In.......		540
Waterbury, Portico, Cherry, Marble Columns, Ormolu, Glass Dome, 1800s, 21 In...................		360
Waterbury, Regulator, Rococo Gilt Bronze Case, Beveled Crystal Panels, c.1900, 11 In................		240
Waterbury, Shelf, Oak, Carved Backsplash, c.1900, 22 In.		150
Waterbury, Shelf, Walnut, 8-Day Movement, Perpetual Calendar, Victorian, 24 In.		180
Webb, D., Desk, Sunburst Frame, 18K Gold, Cabochon Sapphires, Diamond Numerals, 3 In.		10800
Welch, Wall, No. 4, Rosewood, Round Head, Painted Zinc Dial, Lower Calendar Dial, 32 In.		780
Willard, Simon, Regulator, Mahogany, Painted Dial, Reverse Painted, 8-Day, c.1815, 57 In.		9600

CLOISONNE enamel was developed during the tenth century. A glass enamel was applied between small ribbons of metal on a metal base. Most cloisonne is Chinese or Japanese. Pieces marked *China* are twentieth-century examples.

Basin, Footed, Peach Branches, Bats, Clouds, Turquoise Ground, Insert, 1900s, 8 In..................		2133
Bowl, Rounded Steep Sides, Flat Rim, Stylized Lotus Roundel, Scrolling, 1900s, 8 In...............		210
Box, Egg Shape, Silver, Scrolling Leaves, Applied Images, Russia, 4 ⅛ In..............................		1875
Box, Lid, Fan Shape, Turquoise Ground, Symbols, Brass Feet, c.1900, 4 ½ x 15 In.		593
Box, Rounded Pentagon Shape, Flower Scrolling, Dragons, 1900s, 3 ½ x 1 ½ In.		1778
Casket, Jewelry, Bamboo Frame, Gilt Scroll Feet, Flowers, Leaves, 1800s, 3 x 9 In.		649
Censer, Bronze, Handles, 3-Footed, Chinese, 4 ½ In...*illus*		17250
Censer, Lid, Leaves, Flowers, Blue, Upswept Handles, Footed, 1900s, 10 x 9 In........................		295
Censer, Multicolor, Animal Finial, Shaped Handles, Footed, c.1900, 50 x 25 In.....................*illus*		1845
Charger, Flowers, Stems, Multicolor, Scalloped Rim, 1800s, 23 ½ In. Diam.		600
Charger, Storks, Roses, Blue, Pink, Gilt, Japan, c.1900, 2 x 19 In.		354
Cigarette Case, Medallion, Arabesques, Champleve, Silver, Ovchinnikov, 1884, 4 x 3 In............		2500
Cigarette Case, Rounded Square, Fans, Flowers, Figures, Gilt Tracery, 3 ½ x 3 In.		118
Cigarette Case, Swans, Flowers, Silver, P. Ovchinnikov, Russia, c.1915, 4 x 3 In.		896
Cricket Cage, Flowers, Silver, Hanging Hook, Chinese, 6 x 3 ½ In..		480
Cup & Saucer, Gilded Silver, Flowers, Leaves, Shaded, Russia, c.1917, 4 ⅝ x 3 ⅜ In.		5000
Ewer, Bulbous, Sculpted Dragon Handle, Lotus Scrolls, Multicolor, 1800s, 10 In.		5333
Figurine, Hound, Dalmatian, Seated On Haunches, Spots, 1900s, 29 x 19 In., Pair.....................		1952
Figurine, Ram, Standing, Foursquare, 12 x 13 ¾ In.		595
Figurine, Rat, Bronze, Reclining, Wearing Cape & Halter, 1800s, 5 ½ x 9 In.		2196
Figurine, Tree, Swaying Branches, Birds, Rounded Square Base, Flower Border, 6 In..................		84
Incense Burner, Duck Shape, Head Raised, Stand, c.1880, 13 x 23 In., Pair		550
Jar, Dome Lid, High Shoulder, Blues, Green, Black, Red, Green Reserves, Phoenix, 7 In.		69
Jardiniere, Footed Bowl, Loop Handles, Stylized Masks, Shields, 12 ¾ In. Diam.		657
Jardiniere, Ming Style, Bronze, Mythical Beasts, Oval Reserves, 1800s, 12 In.		360
Jewelry Box, Brass, Cobalt Blue, Roundel, Ball Feet, c.1935, 4 ¼ x 9 ¼ In.		676
Kovsh, Exotic Flowers, Bicolor Blue, Beaded Rim, Roped Edge Handle, 5 ¾ In.		10005
Kovsh, Green Flower Heads, Vines, Russian Silver, 5 ¾ In.		3450
Kovsh, Scrolled Flowers, Beaded, Hook Handle, Russia, c.1900, 5 ⅞ In.................................*illus*		9000
Mirror, Hand, Round, Silver, Blue, Ivory Handle, Eda Lord Dixon, c.1915, 9 x 5 In.		25000
Planter, Flowering Trees, Butterflies, Lotus Scroll Border, Saucer Foot, c.1800, 20 In.		2214
Reliquary, Silver Gilt, Dome Top, Footed, Russia, c.1908, 25 In.		11250
Scent Bottle, Prancing Elephant, Flattened Oval, Sterling Silver, India, 4 x 2 In.		81
Table, Round, Flower Medallion, Dragons, Turned, Splay Legs, c.1900, 24 x 29 In.		2214
Tazza, 100 Butterfly, Gilt Bronze, Flared Rim, Shallow Bowl, c.1920, 12 In.		480
Tea Strainer, Russian Silver, Gold Wash, Tab Handle, Flowers, Scrolling Leaves		747
Teapot, Lapis Lazuli, Ribbed, Lobed, Flower Shape, Ox Head, Flowers, 1900s, 7 ½ In.		5400
Teapot, Phoenix Birds, Globe Shape, Knob Feet, Japan, 1900s, 3 ½ In.		330

Clock, Tall Case, Vander Cloese, Marquetry, Gilt Brass, Steel, Moon, Dutch, c.1710, 98 In.
$4,063

Neal Auction Co.

Clock, Tall Case, Waltham, Quartersawn Oak, Horner Movement, Tiffany & Co., 112 In.
$84,000

Skinner Auctioneers & Appraisers

Clock, Terry, Eli, Mahogany Veneer, Pillar & Scroll, Brass, Reverse Painted, c.1825, 32 In.
$510

Garth's Auctioneers & Appraisers

Clock, Vincenti & Cie, Shelf, Flowers, Bronze Dore, Porcelain, Stamped, 1855, 12 x 7 In.
$885

Brunk Auctions

Cloisonne, Censer, Bronze, Handles, 3-Footed, Chinese, 4 ½ In.
$17,250

Cottone Auctions

Cloisonne, Censer, Multicolor, Animal Finial, Shaped Handles, Footed, c.1900, 50 x 25 In.
$1,845

Gray's Auctioneers LLC

Cloisonne, Kovsh, Scrolled Flowers, Beaded, Hook Handle, Russia, c.1900, 5 ⅞ In.
$9,000

Skinner Auctioneers & Appraisers

Tray, Gallery, Flower Sprays, Scholars, 8 x 11 In.	584
Vase, Birds, Pink Chrysanthemums, Blue Ground, Shouldered, c.1860, 14 x 7 In.	184
Vase, Cylindrical, Rolled Rim, Stylized Serpent Handles, Multicolor, c.1815, 18 In.	1150
Vase, Double Lobed Shape, Peonies, Poppies, Lotus Flowers, 1900s, 15 ½ x 6 ¾ In.	307
Vase, Gilt Bronze, Tapered, Shouldered, Dragons, Flames, Clouds, c.1850, 14 In.	6274
Vase, Millefleur, Black Ground, Japan, 17 ¾ In.	288
Vase, Moonflask, Dragon-Like Heads, Scrolls, Marked, Chinese, 14 ¼ In., Pair ....*illus*	18450
Vase, Palm, Rose, Pink, Green, Metallic Red, Dimpled, Ginbari Jippo, 3 x 4 In.	100
Vase, Rounded Square, Shouldered, Multicolor, Flowers, Leaves, 12 In., Pair	330
Vase, Scrolling Stylized Dragons, Green Ground, Wood Stand, 10 In., Pair	84
Vase, Shouldered, Roses, Yellow Ground, Metal Trim, 1900s, 12 In.	300
Vase, Shouldered, Tapered, Pinched Neck, Rolled Rim, Black, Flowers, 1800s, 7 In.	120
Vase, Tapered, Pink Ground, White Egrets, Marked, c.1900, 24 In.	677
Vase, Tapered, Shouldered, Flared Rim, Dragons, Butterflies, Flowers, 19 x 8 In.	644
Vase, Trumpet Neck, Flowering Plants, Bands, Wood Base, c.1850, 16 In.	2706
Water Coupe, Dipper, Globular, Footed, Bats, Double Fish, Lotus, Gilt, 1900s, 3 ¼ In.	593
Wine Cup, Dragons, Turquoise Ground, Gilt, Wide Rim, Pedestal Foot, c.1900, 3 In.	122
Wine Pot, Bell Shape, Waisted Neck, Scroll Spout, Loop Handle, Lotus, Bats, 5 ½ In.	244

CLOTHING of all types is listed in this category. Dresses, hats, shoes, underwear, and more are found here. Other textiles are to be found in the Coverlet, Movie, Quilt, Textile, and World War I and II categories.

Apron, Flower, Rockwork Embroidery, Silk, Chinese, Shadowbox, 50 x 25 In.	615
Belt, A.B.D. Jeffries, Brown Belt, End Snaps, 49 x 1 ¼ In.	63
Belt, Art Nouveau, Silver, Double Chain, Buckle, Back Ornament, Tassels, 24 x 8 In.	196
Belt, Concha, Sand Cast Silver Flowers, Open Work, Turquoise Center, Leather Strap, 37 In.	702
Belt, Metallic Threadwork, Glass, Metalwork, Double Rosette, Middle East, c.1890, 10 In.	333
Belt, Rhinestone, Scalloped, 1960s, 3 ¼ x 25 In.	48
Belt, Silver, Reticulated Links, Stamped, Chinese, 32 In.	242
Blouse, Gold, Silk, Hermes, 1980s, Size 42	269
Blouse, Green, Gold, Snakeskin Silk, Yves St. Laurent, c.1992, Size 38	84
Blouse, Green, Linen, Long Sleeves, Valentino Boutique, 1970s, Size 12	36
Blouse, Silk, Silver Gray, Buttons, Long Sleeves, c.1988	120
Bodice & Skirt, Cream, Lace, Silk, Day Wear, Edwardian, c.1900	227
Bodice & Skirt, Cream, Pink, Silk, Moore, New York, Edwardian, c.1900	120
Body Suit, Black, Alaia, Paris, 1980s, Size Medium	179
Bonnet, Calash, Blue, Accordion Pleat, Bow, Silk Lining, c.1800	600
Boots, Embroidered, Red Orange Ground, Blue Satin Stitch Peonies, Chinese, Child's, 8 In.	89
Boots, Heels, High Button, Green, Woman's, 1890s, Size 10	600
Boots, Leather, Black, Castello, Chloe, Size, 38/8B	120
Boots, Louis Heel, High Lace, Red, c.1900, Size 9	3000
Breastplate, Engraved Scrollwork, Soldier Medallion, Italy, c.1625, 19 x 14 In.	1750
Breeches, Wool, White, Fall Front, Self-Covered Buttons, c.1818	1560
Cap, Baseball, White, NASA Logo, Signed, Neil Armstrong, 1969	1150
Cap, Uniform, Atlantic Greyhound Lines Badge, c.1930s Style Bus, 9 x 11 In. ....*illus*	431
Cap, Velvet, Silver Overlay, 4 Saint Plaques, Domed, Russia, c.1890, 9 In.	2000
Cape, Opera, Black, Purple Velvet Lining, Cocoon Style, Ruched Collar, c.1915, 46 In.	840
Cape, Opera, Velvet, Red, White Asktrakhan Collar, Deco Roses, Chiffon Lining, 48 In.	570
Chaps, Fringed Shotgun, Slotted Conchas, Basket Stamped Belt, Nickel Studs, 37 In.	1416
Chaps, Wool, Canvas Lining, Leather Back, White, Basket Stamp Belt, c.1925, 42 In.	2655
Coat, Coyote, Fox Trim, LJM Monogram, No Label, ¾ Length.	240
Coat, Evening, Cream, Silk Brocade, Fur Trim, Franklin Simon & Co., c.1918	155
Coat, Evening, Olive, Cerise Red Reversible, Satin, 1950s	108
Coat, Fur, Lamb, Black, Petra's Custom Furs, Iowa, Medium, 40 In.	100
Coat, Fur, Mink, Black, Full-Length, Baaca Furs, Medium, 48 In.	406
Coat, Fur, Raccoon, Floor Length, Shawl Collar, Medium.	472
Coat, Mink Lined, Green Nylon Shell, Yves Saint Laurent, 1980s, Medium	885
Coat, Mink, Black, Full-Length, JHL Monogram, c.1985, 49 x 17 In.	454
Coat, Mink, Brown, Black Silk Lining, ¾ Length, Size 6	649
Coat, Mink, Chocolate Brown, Swing, Shawl Collar, ¾ Bias Sleeves, Size 8, 42 In.	1968
Coat, N.Y. Militia, National Guard, Swallowtail, Civil War Epaulets, 1870s	192
Coat, Red Cashmere, Silk Lining, Gold Tone CC Logo Buttons, Chanel Boutique, Size 36	590
Coat, Silk, Black, Flowers, Slash Pockets, Gold Lining, Knot Frog Closures, c.1960, Size M	215
Coat, Spring, Sea Green, Wool, Adi Fashions, 1960	48
Coat, Stroller, Alternating Silver Mink, Taupe Suede, Notch Collar, Pockets, Size 6, 32 In.	922

Coat, Swing, Brown Taffeta, Mink Notched Collar, Cuffs & Trim, Koslow's, Size 6, 50 In...............	1045
Coat, Vinyl, Black & White Stripes, Woman's, 1960s, 42 In..............	390
Coat, Wool, Cotton, Leather Trim, Ribbed Pattern, Yves Saint Laurent, c.1980, Size 42	325
Coat, Wool, Mink Trim, Brown, Pellicceria R.C. Carnesecchi, Paris, Size 44	72
Corset, Sateen, Linen, Lacing, Brown, Adjustable, c.1845, Man's....................	768
Dress, Black, Lace, Silk, Edwardian, c.1905..............................	84
Dress, Cocktail, Black Lace, Givenchy Nouvelle Boutique, 1970s, Size 40	478
Dress, Cocktail, Black, Knee Length, Sleeveless, Nina Ricci, 1950s	568
Dress, Cocktail, Black, Sleeveless, Adele Simpson, c.1958...........................	108
Dress, Cocktail, Navy, Satin, Larry Aldrich, c.1960, Size 12	60
Dress, Cocktail, Peach, Lace, Prima, Woodward & Lothrop, 1955, Size 16	60
Dress, Cocktail, Satin, Velvet, Blue, Black, Oleg Cassini, c.1955, Small.............	472
Dress, Cocktail, Sequins, Black, White, Belt, Bill Blass, 1970s, Size 10	191
Dress, Cocktail, Silk, Navy, Bow Detail, Joseph Halpert & Co., 1953, Small.........	502
Dress, Cocktail, White, Silk, Cashmere, Sleeveless, Barbara Tfank, Size 8..........	227
Dress, Cotton, Square Collar, Blow, Snaps, Cotton, c.1950, Infant's, 12 In...........	10
Dress, Day, Bronze Brown, Crochet, 1960s, Size 40	36
Dress, Day, Green Shot Silk, Pleated Bodice, Teal Fringe, Pleated, Lined, c.1840	384
Dress, Dinner, Black, Purple, Maxi, Emilio Pucci, Saks Fifth Ave., 1960s, Size 12	568
Dress, Evening, Black, Silk, Thurn, New York, Edwardian, c.1912.................	120
Dress, Evening, Blue, Gold, Silk Brocade, Simcox, N.Y., c.1915..................	203
Dress, Evening, Blue, Silk, Carolina Herrera, Neiman Marcus, Size 12	269
Dress, Evening, Celadon Green, Long, 1930s..............................	155
Dress, Evening, Iridescent Blue, Silk, Cream Lace Collar, c.1912...................	299
Dress, Evening, Pink, Silk, Lace, Long, c.1925..............................	329
Dress, Evening, Turquoise, Embellished, Strapless, Robert David Morton, 1970s.........	120
Dress, Front Buttons, Blue, Green, Purple, Emilio Pucci, c.1975, Size 12............	388
Dress, Halter, Green, Orange Flower Print, Robert David Morton, 1970s	120
Dress, Maxi, Long Sleeves, Geometric, Jersey, 1980s........................	96
Dress, Party, Emilio Pucci, Navy, Silk, Lord & Taylor, c.1964, Size 14	269
Dress, Peasant, Mollie Parnis, 1970s, Size 6	120
Dress, Purple, Red Striped, Silk, Missoni, 1980s, Medium	60
Dress, Sheath, Sleeveless, Wool, Angora, Cobalt Blue, Studded Details, Akris Punto, Size 6	282
Dress, Sheath, Zebra Silk, Black & White, Cap Sleeves, Dolce & Gabbana, Size 8	121
Dress, Silk, C Logo, Red, Long Sleeves, Lion Plastic Buttons, Chanel, 1970s, Size 8-10	118
Dress, Sleeveless, Peach, Red Flowers, Emilio Pucci, 1960s, Size 12...............	299
Dress, Wool, Black, Tan, Keyhole Insert, Notched Cap Sleeves, Pierre Cardin, 1970s, Bust 34	1680
Dress, Wrap Style, Navy, Crepe, Marie Valerie, 1950s.......................	60
Evening Gown, Crepe, Beading, Black, Long, Sleeves To Elbow, 1930s, Size 4.............	89
Hair Clip, Net Bow, Pearls, Gem Center, Back Comb, Yves Saint Laurent	60
Hard Hat, D. Slayton, NASA, Yellow, Made By Hard Boiled, c.1959..............	500
Hat, Mink, Mahogany, Roll Brim, Kidskin Bolo, Adolfo II, 22 ½ In.	276
Hat, Snakeskin, Lazy Stitch, Beaded Band & Brim, c.1975, Size Large, 5 In. Tall ....*illus*	600
Hat, Taxi, Yellow Cab, Driver's Uniform Cap, 5 x 11 x 9 ½ In. ....*illus*	173
Hat, Top, Silk, Grosgrain Band, Cavanaugh, Park Avenue, NYC, Byer-Rolnick, Box, Strap	104
High Hat, Beaver, Cream, Silk Band, Bow, Paper Label, Tweedy & Smith Buffalo, 1840s...........	2040
Jacket, Black Reptile Pattern, Flared Waist, Faux Fur Collar, Armani Collezioni, Size 6	259
Jacket, Chinese, Embroidered Silk, Ambassador Goodwin Cooke, Syracuse, N.Y., 39 In.	460
Jacket, Chinese, Embroidered Silk, Butterflies, Flowers, Figures, Sleeve Borders, 36 In..................	1955
Jacket, Collage, Koos Van Den Akker, 1980s, Size 4	120
Jacket, Denim, Barbie Beverly Hills, Faded Blue, Glitter, Pins, Adult Size ....*illus*	114
Jacket, Feather, Marabou, Green Silk, Yves Saint Laurent, 1970s, Size 6-12..............	708
Jacket, Mink, White, Cropped	42
Jacket, Navy, Wool & Silk Blend, Double Breasted, Hermes, 1970s, Size 42	143
Jacket, Purple Plaid, Wool, Silk Lining, Goldtone Logo Buttons, France, Woman's	119
Jacket, Purple, Boucle, Automne 1997, Chanel, Size 36........................	478
Jacket, Safari-Style, Cloth, Orange, Belt, Carolina Herrera, Size 6	60
Jacket, Slouch, Hooded, Jasmine Mink, White Fox, Velvet & Satin Lining, Zipper, Size 8..............	1476
Jacket, Waiter's, Black, Cotton, Yves St. Laurent Rive Gauche, 1980s, Size 36	84
Jacket, White, Woven, Tattersall Pattern, Double Breasted, 1920s, Size 38	330
Jacket, Wrap, Black, Wool, Herve Leger, 1990s, Size 38/6........................	84
Kimono, Wedding, Ivory, Embroidered, Flowers, Birds, Leaves, Japan	210
Necktie, Blue & Cream, Chain Design, Silk, Hermes, Box..........................	96
Necktie, Burgundy, Gold, Silk, Logo, Chanel, Box	48
Necktie, Red, Navy, Silk, Hermes, Box	120
Pantsuit, Zigzag Pattern, Crochet, Missoni, 1980s............................	227

Cloisonne, Vase, Moonflask, Dragon-Like Heads, Scrolls, Marked, Chinese, 14 ¼ In., Pair
$18,450

Skinner Auctioneers & Appraisers

Clothing, Cap, Uniform, Atlantic Greyhound Lines Badge, c.1930s Style Bus, 9 x 11 In.
$431

Wm Morford Auctions

Clothing, Hat, Snakeskin, Lazy Stitch, Beaded Band & Brim, c.1975, Size Large, 5 In. Tall
$600

Allard Auctions

Clothing, Hat, Taxi, Yellow Cab, Driver's Uniform Cap, 5 x 11 x 9 ½ In.
$173

Wm Morford Auctions

Clothing, Jacket, Denim, Barbie Beverly Hills, Faded Blue, Glitter, Pins, Adult Size
$114

Theriault's

Clothing, Robe, Court, Baskets, Flowers, Li Shui Borders, Chinese, 1800s, 57 In.
$10,665

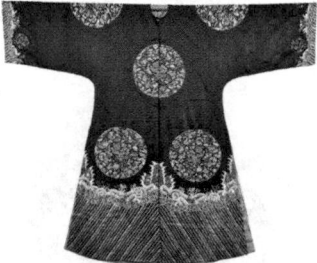

James D. Julia Auctioneers

Clothing, Robe, Embroidered, Figures, Gardens, Gold Fret, Silk, Frame, c.1800s, 47 x 63 In.
$13,200

Skinner Auctioneers & Appraisers

Clothing, Robe, Silk, Embroidered, Flowers, Butterflies, Chinese, c.1900, Woman's, 48 In.
$1,920

Skinner Auctioneers & Appraisers

Robe, Blue, Embroidered, Butterflies, Scattered Flowers, Satin Stitch, Woman's, 38 In.	893
Robe, Court, Baskets, Flowers, Li Shui Borders, Chinese, 1800s, 57 In. ....*illus*	10665
Robe, Embroidered, Figures, Gardens, Gold Fret, Silk, Frame, c.1800s, 47 x 63 In. ....*illus*	13200
Robe, Embroidery, Silk, Chinese, Below The Knee, c.1880	359
Robe, Linen Gauze, Dragon Designs, Imperial Symbols, Plum Color, c.1900, 53 In.	1003
Robe, Silk, Embroidered, Flowers, Butterflies, Chinese, c.1900, Woman's, 48 In. ....*illus*	1920
Robe, Silk, Gold Embroidery, Multicolor, Asian Scenes, Chinese, 39 x 63 In.	11700
Robe, Silk, Yellow, Embroidered Bands, Collar, Cuffs, Damask Lining, Chinese, Early 1900s	118
Robe, Wedding, Manchu, Satin, Embroidered, Butterflies, Flowers, Chinese, 1900s	1722
Scarf, Clic Clac, Brown, Tan, Black, Silk, Julia Abadie, Hermes, 35 x 34 In.	657
Scarf, Fleur De L'Opera, Blue Flower, Multicolor Surround, Silk, Hermes, c.1990, 35 x 35 In.	325
Scarf, Gold Chain Necklace Design On Black Ground, Chanel, 1980s, 35 x 35 In.	443
Scarf, Grande Tenue, Blue, Green, Yellow, Silk, H. Dorigny, Hermes, c.1900, 35 x 35 In.	354
Scarf, La Promenade De Longchamps, Carriages, Pink, Silk, P. Ledoux, Hermes, 35 x 35 In.	266
Scarf, Linen, Burgundy Print, Emanuel Ungarlo, 55 x 54 In.	60
Scarf, L'Opera, 2 Art Deco Women, Opera Box Seats, Silk, Erte, Frame, 32 x 32 In.	132
Scarf, Qu'Importe Le Flacon, Silk, Perfume Bottles, Catherine Baschet, Hermes, 36 x 36 In.	259
Scarf, Silk, Black Rays In Circle, Pink Ground, Club 21, Ray Strauss, c.1955, 31 x 32 In.	131
Scarf, Silk, Chains, Logos, Black Ground, Chanel, Paris, 35 x 34 In.	215
Scarf, Silk, Multicolor Camillias, Chanel, 34 x 34 In.	143
Scarf, Silk, Nile, Metal Frame, Erte, 36 x 35 In. ....*illus*	413
Scarf, Silk, Twill, Washington Carriage, Signed Caty, Hermes, 72 x 12 In.	155
Scarf, Vent Portant, Silk, Y. Manier, Hermes, 36 x 36 In.	143
Scarf, Vue De Carrosse, Red, White, Black, Silk, H. Grygkar, Hermes, c.1980, 35 x 35 In.	325
Shawl, Black & White Silk, Wool Paisley Design, Fringe, c.1870, 65 x 141 In.	420
Shawl, Jamawar Type, Leaves, Tendrils, Scrolls, Quilted, Kashmir, 1800s, 72 x 44 In. ....*illus*	1200
Shawl, Kashmir Paisley, Fringe, c.1910, 62 x 62 In.	150
Shawl, Paisley, Kashmiri, Wool, Cream Ground, c.1850, 54 x 120 In.	1180
Shawl, Paisley, Red, Cream, Black, Wool, Victorian, c.1890, 130 x 63 In.	418
Shirt, Linen, White, V Front, Ruffles, Fold Down Collar, Pleated Bib, Man's, c.1800	1320
Shirt, Western, Woman's, Made In California, Size 8	114
Shoes, Mules, Faux Shagreen, Animal Print, 4-In. Heel, Bamus Razza, Manolo Blahnik, Size 8 .	63
Shoes, Patent Leather, Pink, 4-In. Stiletto Heel, Box, Dust Bag, Manolo Blahnik, Size 8 ½	207
Shoes, Pumps, Leather, Brown, Bordeaux, Gucci, 38AA	24
Shoes, Python, Black & White, Leather Sole, GG Tab, 4-In. Heel, Gucci Roccia, Size 7 ½	242
Shoes, Sandals, Metallic Purple, Bow, Size 8	24
Shoes, Sandals, Silk Shantung, Gold Leather, Pistachio, Prada, Size 38	24
Shoes, Slingback, Leather, Peacock Feather, Green, Carolyne, Monolo Blahnik, Size 8 ½	230
Skirt, Circle, Green, Blue Stripe, Cotton, Nelley De Grab, 1950s	131
Skirt, Cream Linen, Hermes, 1980s, Size 42	227
Skirt, Midnight Blue, Embroidery, Tan Wide Belt, Chinese, c.1890	388
Skirt, Silk Satin, Orange, Pleated, Yves Saint Laurent, Rive Gauche, c.1992, Size 38	48
Skirt, Silk, Black, Gianfranco Ferre, Size 42	84
Skirt, Top Ensemble, Sea Green, Silver Thread, Wool, Bargello, 1970s, Size 9	36
Skirt, Umbrella, Flowers, Pink, Purple, Green, Silk, Satin, Victorian, c.1890	60
Skirt, Wool, Black, Mid-Calf Length, Chanel Boutique, Size 36	42
Sleep Cap, Linen, Monogram, 1700s, Man's, 11 x 7 ½ In.	115
Sombrero, Felt, Gold, Braided Band, Double Tassels, Mexico, 8 x 6 ½ In.	590
Stockings, Patriotic, Stars & Stripes, Silver Metal Frame, c.1900, 33 x 14 In.	720
Stole, Cashmere, Silk, Blue, Eyelash Fringe Trim, Loro Piana, 79 x 27 ½ In.	288
Stole, Mink, Sheared Cream, c.1950s, 18 x 33 In.	54
Suit, Cotton, Norfolk Jacket, Pockets, Cuffed Pants, White, Palm Beach, 1940s, Size 44	120
Suit, Evening, Black Jacket, Gold Lace Overlay, Pencil Skirt, Black Velvet, Bill Blass, Size 6	72
Suit, Tweed, Brown, Double Breasted, Oscar De La Renta, Size 14	84
Tailcoat, Broadcloth, Black, Double Notched Collar, Double Breasted, Man's, c.1815	6600
Tailcoat, Hunting, Red, Wool, Brushed Brass Domed Buttons, Silk Lining, 1800s, 37 Chest	3300
Top Hat, Beaver Skin, Leather Case, Brush, Balch, Price & Co., c.1890, 6 In.	230
Top Hat, Beaver, Leather Travel Case, By Knox, Patton Brothers, Mason City, Iowa, Size 6 ½	150
Vest, Cashmere, Black, Theory, Size Small	42
Vest, Graphic, Books, Shelves, Fornasetti, Italy ....*illus*	180
Vest, Lynx, White Fox Trim, Fitted, Slash Pockets, Satin Lining, Size 6, 24 In.	1353
Vest, Silk, Embroidered, Linen Lining, Flower Borders, Metallic Threads, 1790s, Man's	246
Waistcoat, Cream, Silk Satin, Green Flower Embroidery, Double Breasted, c.1790, Man's	768
Wig, Barrister's, Ravenscroft Wig & Robe Makers, London, 10-In. Black Tole Case	1020
Wrap, Mink, Brown, Black Silk, Rhinestones, Sonia Rykiel, 55 In.	266

CLUTHRA glass is a two-layered glass with small bubbles and powdered glass trapped between the layers. The Steuben Glass Works of Corning, New York, first made it in 1920. Victor Durand of Kimball Glass Company in Vineland, New Jersey, made a similar glass from about 1925. Durand's pieces are listed in the Durand category. Related items are listed in the Steuben category.

Vase, Art Deco Handles, Wheel Carved, Signed, Charles Schneider, 13 x 6 In.	4375
Vase, Tinted Textured Green, Metallic Inclusions, Square Rim, Bulbous Foot, c.1890, 3 x 4 In.	275
Vase, Tinted, Textured Green, Red, White Inclusions, Cylindrical, c.1890, 2 ½ x 3 In.	250
Vase, Yellow Over Orange, Shouldered, Flared Rim, Marked, 6 ¾ In.	295

COALBROOKDALE was made by the Coalport porcelain factory of England during the Victorian period. Pieces are decorated with floral encrustations.

Dresser Jar, Flowers, Butterflies, Handles, Footed, c.1800, 5 ¼ In.	595
Platter, Flowers, Gilt Scrolls, Rococo Scalloped Rim, Lobed, Footed, c.1825, 8 ½ In.	80
Potpourri Vase, Flowers, Vine Twisted Handles, c.1850, 17 ½ In., Pair	5500
Teapot, Scallop Shell, Leaves, Lid, Marked, c.1830, 6 In.	625

COALPORT ware was made by the Coalport Porcelain Works of England beginning about 1795. Early pieces were unmarked. About 1810–25 the pieces were marked with the name *Coalport* in various forms. Later pieces also had the name *John Rose* in the mark. The crown mark was used with variations beginning in 1881. The date 1750 is printed in some marks, but it is not the date the factory started. Coalport was bought by Wedgwood in 1967. Coalport porcelain is no longer being produced. Some pieces are listed in Indian Tree.

Box, Lid, Screw Top, Flower Bouquet, Gilt Banded, c.1825, 3 ¼ In.	115
Cigarette Holder, Revelry, Blue Panels, Cupids, 2 ½ x 2 ⅝ In.	7
Coaster, Scalloped, Central Roses, 5 In.	15
Cup & Saucer, Blue Panels, Cupids, Revelry	15
Cup & Saucer, Jays, Yellow, Gold Garland, Silver Holder, 1930, 3 Piece	420
Eggcup, Double, Raised Scroll Pattern, Blue On White, Insects, Birds, 3 ⅞ In.	29
Figurine, Elephant, White, Rose Bouquet, 3 In.	35
Figurine, Moll Flanders, Cream, Brown, Hair Ringlets, 8 ¾ In.	69
Mug, Ironbridge, Shropshire View, Gilt Rim, Puce, c.1845, 4 In.	104
Plate, Dessert, Green, Red, Cobalt Blue Flowers, Scalloped Rim, c.1825, 9 ¾ In., 11 Piece	690
Plate, Dinner, Flowers, Red, Cobalt Blue, Wavy Gilt Rim, c.1835, 10 ½ In., 12 Piece	403
Plate, Painted Fruit, Signed Richard Budd, 10 ½ In.	118
Plate, Plate, Flowers, Open Tab Handles, 10 ¼ In.	65
Sugar & Creamer, Flower Bouquets, White	56
Teapot, Flowers, Insects, Birds, Blue On White, Gilt Trim, 3 ⅝ In.	140
Teapot, Lid, Flowers, Waisted, Gadrooned Collar, Scrolled Spout, Round, Gilt, 1820s, 7 ½ In.	127

COBALT BLUE glass was made using oxide of cobalt. The characteristic bright dark blue identifies it for the collector. Most cobalt glass found today was made after the Civil War. There was renewed interest in the dark blue glass in the late 1930s and dinnerware were made.

Ashtray, Top Hat Shape, Lowell, c.1950, 2 ½ x 3 In.	28
Charger, Basket Weave Trim, Reticulated, 8 ½ In.	49
Decanter, Napoleon's Column, Clear Napoleon Finial, France, 17 ⅜ In.	281
Dish, Leaf Shape, Gold Trim, 5 ½ x 4 In.	12
Glass, Wine, Grape Bunches, Vines, 7 In., Pair	125
Pitcher, Straight-Sided, Royal Lace, Hazel Atlas, 48 Oz., 7 ¾ In.	50
Saltshaker, Cylindrical, Sterling Silver Cap, c.1890, 2 ⅝ In.	48
Vase, Diamond Design, Crimped Rim, Hong Kong, 2 ½ In.	17
Vase, Square, 1970s, 10 x 3 x 3 In.	35

COCA-COLA was first served in 1886 in Atlanta, Georgia. It was advertised through signs, newspaper ads, coupons, bottles, trays, calendars, and even lamps and clocks. Collectors want anything with the word *Coca-Cola*, including a few rare products, like gum wrappers and cigar bands. The famous trademark was patented in 1893, the *Coke* mark in 1945. Many modern items and reproductions are being made.

Bank, Bottle Vending Machine Shape, Plastic, Red, White, Box, 5 ½ In.	230
Bank, Cooler, Drink Coca-Cola, Tin, 4 ¾ x 5 In.	450
Bookmark, Celluloid, Heart Shape, Girl Center, 1899, 5 ¾ x 3 ½ In. ....*illus*	1320
Bookmark, Die Cut, Frame, 1903 & 1904, 2 x 6 In., 2 Piece	533
Bottle Carrier, Enjoy Coke, Aluminum, Tin Inserts, 6 Holes, 1950s, 8 In.	83
Bottle Case, 12 Bottles, c.1905, 13 x 11 In.	270

Clothing, Scarf, Silk, Nile, Metal Frame, Erte, 36 x 35 In.
$413

Brunk Auctions

Clothing, Shawl, Jamawar Type, Leaves, Tendrils, Scrolls, Quilted, Kashmir, 1800s, 72 x 44 In.
$1,200

Skinner Auctioneers & Appraisers

Clothing, Vest, Graphic, Books, Shelves, Fornasetti, Italy
$180

Palm Beach Modern Auctions

Coca-Cola, Bookmark, Celluloid, Heart Shape, Girl Center, 1899, 5 ¾ x 3 ½ In.
$1,320

Morphy Auctions

Coca-Cola, Calendar, 1919, Girl With Knitting Bag, Full Pad, Frame, 41 ½ x 22 ½ In.
$600

Morphy Auctions

Coca-Cola, Clock, Dome, Contessa, Plastic Base, 1950s, 6 In.
$120

Morphy Auctions

Coca-Cola, Display, Bottle, Christmas, Glass, 20 In.
$660

Showtime Auction Services

Coca-Cola, Display, Girl, Wicker Chair, Die Cut, Easel Back, Floor Standing, Frame, 1920s, 25 x 35 In.
$11,850

James D. Julia Auctioneers

Coca-Cola, Plate, Vienna Art, Gesso Frame, Shadowbox, 16 x 16 In.
$840

Morphy Auctions

Coca-Cola, Sign, Coca-Cola Chewing Gum, Hilda Clark, Cardboard, Embossed, 1903, 20 x 16 In.
$45,000

Morphy Auctions

Coca-Cola, Sign, Coca-Cola Gum, Girl, Cardboard, Oak Frame, 1916, 45 ½ x 27 In.
$16,200

Morphy Auctions

Coca-Cola, Sign, Coca-Cola Gum, Suits Me By Gum, Boy, Wooden Shoes, 1914-16, 29 x 22 In.
$55,200

Morphy Auctions

Bottle, Letters, Green Glass, Straight-Sided, Seattle, 8 ¼ In.	36
Bowl, Pretzel, 3 Bottle Supports, Silvered, 1930s, 9 In.	96
Box, Syrup Jug, Tan, Red, Wood, c.1930, 13 x 8 In.	72
Calendar, 1916, Girl With Basket Of Flowers, Frame, 40 x 21 In.	7200
Calendar, 1918, June Caparice Holding Glass, Allison's News Stand, Okla., Frame, 14 In.	207
Calendar, 1919, Girl With Knitting Bag, Full Pad, Frame, 41 ½ x 22 ½ In. ...illus	600
Calendar, 1938, Girl At Shade, 25 x 12 In.	210
Carrier, 6 Bottle Indents, Red Handle, Aluminum, 1950s, 7 In.	108
Carrier, 6 Bottle Indents, Red Handle, Yellow Ground, Wood, 1941, 8 In.	330
Carrier, 6 Dividers, Cutout Handle, Yellow Ground, Wood, 1940s, 9 In.	150
Carrier, 6-Pack, Red, Yellow, Black, Cardboard, 1930s, 8 x 7 In.	2400
Carton, 6-Pack, Red, Tan, 1920s, 14 ¾ In.	72
Clock, Button Style, Metal, Red & White, Round, 15 ½ In. Diam.	374
Clock, Dome, Contessa, Plastic Base, 1950s, 6 In. ...illus	120
Clock, Drink Coca-Cola In Bottles, Electric, Wood Frame, Selectoclock, 1939, 16 x 16 In.	127
Clock, Drink Coca-Cola In Bottles, Tin, Wood, 16 x 16 In.	266
Clock, Electric, Plastic, Rectangular, Light-Up, 1960s, 20 x 12 In.	36
Clock, Ice Cold Coca-Cola, Silhouette, 8-Sided, Light-Up, Neon Products, Lima, Oh., 18 In.	4720
Clock, Red, White, Black Frame, Round, Electric, 1940s, 15 In.	480
Cooler, Airline Style, Red, Handle, Spigot, 1950s, 19 In.	270
Cooler, Picnic, Igloo, Fitted Interior, Red, 1970s, 19 ½ In.	36
Cooler, Radio, 5 Tubes, Knobs, 12 In.	270
Cutout, Uncle Remus, Children, Frame, 1930s, 21 x 16 In.	210
Decal, Window, Blue Ground, Frame, 1940s, 18 x 12 In.	48
Dispenser, Mutiplex, 5 Cent, Hexagonal, Metal, 1930s, 27 In.	1560
Display, Bottle, Christmas, Glass, 20 In. ...illus	660
Display, Come On In Coke, Blond Athletic Girl, 1960s, 67 In.	360
Display, Girl, Wicker Chair, Die Cut, Easel Back, Floor Standing, Frame, 1920s, 25 x 35 In. ...illus	11850
Display, Shopping Girl, Green Check Suit, Feather In Hat, Cutout, 1950s, 68 In.	1560
Display, Sprite Boy, Holding 6-Pack, Cutout Cardboard, 19 x 17 In.	1560
Display, Stock Up Now Take Some Home, Bottle, Buffet Tray, Cardboard, 1954, 34 x 36 In.	720
Doll, Delivery, Plastic, Striped Uniform, Patch, Drink Coca-Cola, Buddy Lee, 14 In.	602
Door Push, Thanks, Call Again For A Coca-Cola, 14 x 4 In.	207
Fan, Hand Holding Bottle, Quality Carries On, Paper, Wood, c.1950, 11 In.	35
Game, Target Board, Cork & Wood, Painted Details, Baseball, Darts, 1940s, 18 x 18 In.	150
Golf Bag, Red Leather, Enjoy Coca-Cola In White, Straps, Rain Cover, Keychain, TR 9-99	180
Hat, Driver's, Blue Brim, White, Red, c.1955, 11 In.	240
Jacket, Soda Fountain Attendant's, White Ground, Red Collar, 1930s, Size Small	150
License Plate Frame, Metal, 1930s, 14 In.	180
Menu Board, Fishtail Logo, Chalkboard, Tin Litho, c.1960, 28 x 19 ¾ In.	127
Menu Board, Plywood, 1930s, 25 x 14 In.	570
Menu Board, Wood, Drink Coca-Cola, Hanging Chain, 1940s, 13 x 24 x 5 In.	419
Napkin, Rice Paper, Woman, Seated, Drinking Coke, Frame, c.1912, 18 x 18 In.	36
Opener, Bottle, 50th Anniversary In Bottles, 3 ¾ In.	84
Pin, Ask Me, Logo, Western Hemisphere, Red, Cream, 1939, 2 ½ In.	240
Plate, Sandwich, Bottle, Glass, Cream Ground, 1930s, 7 ¼ In.	90
Plate, Vienna Art, Gesso Frame, Shadowbox, 16 x 16 In. ...illus	840
Policeman, Blue Suit, Hand Up, Slow School Zone, Iron Base, 1950, 64 In.	4800
Pull Handle, White, Black, 1930s, 11 ¾ In.	480
Radio, Red, Logo, Cooler Shape, 1950s, 12 In.	150
Radio, Transistor, Red, White, Bottle Machine Shape, Box, 1960s, 7 x 10 In.	120
Radio, Vendo Slant Shelf Cooler Shape, Portable, Transistor, Box, c.1966, 7 x 10 In.	190
Sheet Music, Rum & Coca-Cola, Andrews Sisters, 1940s, 12 x 9 In.	12
Sidewalk Marker, Round, Brass, 3 ¾ In.	60
Sign, 12-Pack Carton With Bottles, Tin, Cutout, 1954, 14 x 20 In.	2160
Sign, Arrow, Drive-In, 2-Sided, Green, Red, Yellow, Tin, Black Stand, 1960s, 78 In.	1200
Sign, Blue Hatted Flapper, Eyeing Bottle, Frame, 24 x 16 In.	510
Sign, Bottle Shape, Porcelain, 1950s, 12 ⅜ x 4 In.	189
Sign, Bottle, Christmas, Tin, Embossed, American Artworks, Coshocton, Oh., 1932, 39 In.	1298
Sign, Bottle, Cutout, Aluminum, 1951, 17 In.	108
Sign, Bottle, Tin, Frame, 34 In.	267
Sign, Button, Bottle, Logo, Red, Porcelain, Round, 1950s, 24 In.	420
Sign, Coca-Cola Chewing Gum, Hilda Clark, Cardboard, Embossed, 1903, 20 x 16 In. ...illus	45000
Sign, Coca-Cola Gum, Girl, Cardboard, Oak Frame, 1916, 45 ½ x 27 In. ...illus	16200
Sign, Coca-Cola Gum, Green Gold, Red Letters, Reverse Glass, c.1920, 7 x 15 In.	1200
Sign, Coca-Cola Gum, Suits Me By Gum, Boy, Wooden Shoes, 1914-16, 29 x 22 In. ...illus	55200

Coffee Mill, American Duplex Electric Coffee Cutter, Coffeepot Shape, Restored
$1,265

Victorian Casino Antiques

Coffee Mill, Enterprise, 2 Wheels, No. 2, Cast Iron, Grip Handle, Decals, Drawer, 12 ½ In.
$649

Conestoga Auction Co., Inc.

Coffee Mill, Enterprise, 2 Wheels, No. 5, Decals, Drawer, 13 x 20 In.
$741

Showtime Auction Services

Coffee Mill, John C. Dell, Hopper, Bucket, Painted, 57 ¼ In.
$1,440

Morphy Auctions

A Lot of Flour
Washburn-Crosby Company opened in 1877, then merged with other millers in 1928 to create General Mills, Inc. At one time it was the largest flour miller in the world.

Sign, Coca-Cola, Yes, Swimmer Eyeing Bottle, Kay Frame, 1945, 26 x 42 In.	1140
Sign, Coke Bottle, Red & White, Round, Celluloid, Cardboard, c.1950s, 9 In. Diam.	489
Sign, Drink Coca-Cola Large Size, Red, White, Embossed Plastic, 1960s, 15 ¾ In.	108
Sign, Drink Coca-Cola Work Refreshed, 2-Sided, Round, Cardboard, Canada, 1943, 11 In.	450
Sign, Drink Coca-Cola, Couple Sharing Bottle, Tin, 1941, 18 x 54 In.	272
Sign, Drink Coca-Cola, Girl In Yellow Dress, Man, Tin, 1942, 19 x 27 In.	1140
Sign, Drink Coca-Cola, Ice Cold, Dispenser, 2-Sided, c.1950, 28 ¼ x 27 ¼ In.	2415
Sign, Drink Coca-Cola, Porcelain, Red, Round, 24 In.	201
Sign, Drink Coca-Cola, Tin Flange, 13 x 20 In.	420
Sign, Drink Coca-Cola, Tin, 1927, 32 x 12 In.	147
Sign, Drugstore, Cap Flange, 18 x 23 In.	2160
Sign, Fountain Service, Drink Coca-Cola, Porcelain, 2-Sided, Shaped, c.1938, 25 x 23 In.	2832
Sign, Fountain Service, Drink Coca-Cola, Red, Green, Porcelain, c.1950, 12 x 30 In.	460
Sign, Frame, Farm Boy, Clown, 1930, 43 x 26 In.	420
Sign, Girl Aviator, Frame, 1940, 21 x 37 In.	6000
Sign, Girl Drinking Coke, By Cooler, Frame, 1941, 27 x 16 In.	1440
Sign, Girl, Drinking, Red Ice Chest, Refreshment Right Out Of The Bottle, 33 In.	720
Sign, Girl, Red Jacket, Dog, Sundblom, Frame, 1939, 56 x 38 In.	360
Sign, Glass, Sprite Boy, Bottle, Logo, Reverse Painted, Round, Hanging, Germany, 10 In.	1180
Sign, Great Serve, Tennis Couple, Cardboard, 1957, 66 x 33 In.	158
Sign, Green Ground, Tin Flange, 1961, 15 x 18 In.	330
Sign, Hanging, Drink Coca-Cola Fountain Service, Red & Green, Metal Mount, 23 x 25 In.	633
Sign, Have A Coke, Sprite Boy, Spinner, Rounded, Light-Up, 1948, 18 ½ In.	8400
Sign, Ice Cold Coca-Cola Sold Here, Embossed Tin, Frame, 1927, 20 x 28 In.	3000
Sign, Lunch With Us, Waterfall, Light-Up, 1950s, 19 ½ In.	900
Sign, Navy Service Girl, Die Cut, Easel Back, Lithograph, Snyde & Black, c.1944, 7 x 17 In.	240
Sign, Refreshment Ahead, Nautical Couple Clowning, Kay Frame, 1952, 57 x 35 In.	600
Sign, Rotating, Light-Up, Sprite Boy, Have A Coke, 18 ½ x 18 ½ In.	6000
Sign, Santa Holding Bottle, Dog, Tree, Gifts, Cardboard, Die Cut, 1960s, 24 In.	106
Sign, School Zone Crossing, 20, White, Yellow, Red Paint, Plywood, 1960s, 49 In.	360
Sign, Serve Coke At Home, 3-Sided Carton, 6 Bottles, Pilaster, Button Top, 1940s, 54 In.	1180
Sign, Sign Of Good Taste, Fishtail Flange, Red, White, Green, Steel, c.1960, 1 x 18 In.	288
Sign, Snowman Display, Folding, Cardboard, 1960s, 22 In.	180
Sign, Spinner, Vending Machine, 4 Rubber Suction Feet, 1950s, 12 ½ In.	2074
Sign, Take Home A Carton, 6-Pack, Tin Lithograph, Wood Frame, 1930s, 27 x 19 In.	855
Sign, The Drink They All Expect, Couple At Party Table, Frame, 1942, 28 x 57 In.	960
Sign, Things Go Better With Coke, 1960s, 24 x 24 In.	180
Sign, Welcome Friend Have A Coke, Embossed Cutout, Cardboard, 14 x 30 In.	1140
Sign, Willie Hope, Suited Pool Player, Cardboard, 1947, 13 x 15 In.	51
Stadium Vendor, Red, Basket Shape, Handle, 1950s, 12 ½ In.	120
Stamp Holder, Victorian Lady, Holding Glass, Red, Black, 1902, 2 ½ x 1 ½ In.	1140
Stringholder, Take Home Coca-Cola In Cartons, Tin, 15 ¾ In.	270
Syrup Dispenser, Countertop, Insulated Lid, Painted Red, 20 In.	415
Table Set, Round Top, Base, Red Leather Chairs, Enjoy Coca-Cola Logo, 36 x 30 In., 5 Piece	840
Tape Measure, Drink Coca-Cola In Bottles, Yellow, 1 ½ In. Diam.	35
Teapot, Betty Boop, Pup, Restaurant Counter, Geometric Handle, Coca-Cola Co., 2000, 8 In.	127
Thermometer, Bottle Shape, Embossed Tin, 1929, 14 ½ In.	180
Thermometer, Bottle Shape, Embossed Tin, 1950s, 16 ½ In.	60
Thermometer, Bottle Shape, Embossed, Tin Lithograph, Christmas, 1920s, 16 x 5 In.	242
Thermometer, Bottle Shape, Red Ground, Tin, 1937, 16 In.	150
Thermometer, Bottle, Logo, Masonite, 17 In.	210
Thermometer, Dial, Round, 1950s, 12 In.	330
Thermometer, Drink Coca-Cola In Bottles, Round, Glass Lens, 1950s, 12 In.	325
Thermometer, Porcelain, Red, Yellow, Green, Silhouette, 18 x 5 ½ In.	748
Thermometer, Red Ground, Metal Rim, Round, 12 In.	120
Thermometer, Things Go Better With Coke, Round, 1960s, 24 x 68 In.	360
Thermometer, White, Wood, 21 In.	180
Tip Tray, Exhibition Girl, Nighttime Fair Scene, Tin Lithograph, Oval, 1909, 6 ¼ x 4 ½ In.	230
Tip Tray, Golfer Girl, Yellow Dress, Cream Hat, Tin, Oval, 1920, 6 ¼ x 4 ½ In.	450
Tip Tray, Relieves Fatigue, 1907, Girl, White Dress, 6 ¼ x 4 ½ In.	84
Toaster, Sandwich, Script Logo Grilled Into Sandwich, Round, Metal, Electric, 8 In.	237
Toy, 3-D Glasses, Verigraph, Red & Green Lenses, 1914, 5 In.	840
Toy, Paint, Pressed Steel, Rubber Tires, Metal Craft, c.1945, 11 In.	184
Toy, Truck, Delivery, Pressed Steel, White Brand, 10 Glass Bottles, Metalcraft, 1930s, 11 In.	296
Toy, Truck, Pressed Steel, 10 Original Bottles, Metalcraft, 11 In.	413
Toy, Truck, Pressed Steel, Red, Yellow Bottle Carrier, 10 Bottles, Metalcraft, 11 In.	576

Toy, Truck, Yellow, Metal, Lithographed Cases On Sides, Marx, 17 x 6 ¾ In.	531
Toy, Van, Tin, Friction, Japan, Box, 1950s, 9 In.	225
Tray, 1905-07, Topless Girl, Woman, Seated, Vienna Art, Shadowbox Frame, 16 x 16 In.	2400
Tray, 1909, Exhibition Girl, Holding Glass, Oval, 13 x 10 ¾ In.	270
Tray, 1914, Betty, Girl In Bonnet, Pink Bow, Ribbon, Rectangular, 13 x 10 ½ In.	180
Tray, 1916, Elaine, Girl With Basket Of Flowers, Rectangular, 19 x 8 ½ In.	72
Tray, 1920, Golfer Girl, Yellow Dress, Holding Glass, Rectangular, 13 ¼ x 10 ½ In.	360 to 420
Tray, 1921, Autumn Girl, Holding Glass, Rectangular, 13 ¼ x 10 ½ In.	210
Tray, 1923, Flapper Girl, Holding Glass, Rectangular, 13 ¼ x 10 ½ In.	72
Tray, 1925, Party Girl, Holding Glass, Fox Stone, Rectangular, 13 ¼ x 10 ½ In.	60
Tray, 1926, Golfing Couple, American Art Works, Rectangular, 13 ¼ x 10 ½ In.	48
Tray, 1929, Girl In Swimsuit, American Art Works, 13 ¼ x 10 ½ In.	72
Tray, 1930, Bathing Beauty, White Swimsuit, 1930, 13 ¼ x 10 ½ In.	84
Tray, 1931, Barefoot Boy, Norman Rockwell, American Art Works, 13 x 10 ½ In.	108
Tray, 1932, Girl In Yellow Bathing Suit, Bottle, American Art Works, 13 ¼ x 10 ½ In.	180
Tray, 1933, Frances Dee, Seated On Wall, American Art Works, 13 ¼ x 10 ½ In.	900
Tray, 1934, Maureen O'Sullivan, Johnny Weismuller, American Art Works, 10 ½ x 13 In.	240 to 328
Tray, 1935, Madge Evans, American Art Works, 13 ¼ x 10 ½ In.	150
Tray, 1936, Hostess, White Gown, Reclining In Chair, 13 ¼ x 10 ½ In.	240
Tray, 1942, 2 Girls At Car, American Art Works, 13 ¼ x 10 ½ In.	108
Umbrella, Fabric, Canvas, 1930s, 37 In.	330
Vending Machine, Red, White, Cavalier, 72, 58 In.	3300

COFFEE MILLS are also called coffee grinders, although there is a difference in the way each grinds the coffee. Large floor-standing or counter-model coffee mills were used in the nineteenth-century country store. Small home mills were first made about 1894. They lost favor by the 1930s. The renewed interest in fresh-ground coffee has produced many modern electric mills and hand mills and grinders. Reproductions of the old styles are being made.

American Duplex Electric Coffee Cutter, Coffeepot Shape, Restored ....*illus*	1265
Chas. Parker, No. 5000, 2 Wheels, Stenciling, 12 ½-In. Wheels	900
Cherry, Pewter Hopper, Dovetailed Case, Iron Crank Handle, Signed D.W., 10 In.	142
Elgin National, 2 Wheels, Cast Iron, Eagle Finial, Woodruff & Edwards Co., 29 In.	420
Elgin National, 2 Wheels, Cast Iron, Green, Gold, Wood Base, Woodruff & Edwards	1200
Elgin National, 2 Wheels, No. 33, Nickel Plate Hopper, Eagle Finial, 28-In. Wheel	513
Elgin National, 2 Wheels, Painted Red, Nickel Plated Hopper, 17-In. Wheel	570
Elgin National, Floor Standing, Cast Iron, 69 In.	652
Elgin National, No. 42, Cast Iron, Red, Woodruff & Edwards Co., Elgin, Ill., 25 In.	365
Enterprise, 2 Wheels, Brass, Cast Iron, Drawer, Eagle Finial, Red, Black Paint, 1800s, 16 In.	900
Enterprise, 2 Wheels, Cast Iron, Drawer, Finial, 1873, 23 In.	390
Enterprise, 2 Wheels, Cast Iron, Drawers, Red Paint, 14 ½ In.	330
Enterprise, 2 Wheels, Cast Iron, Paint, Red, Drawer, 12 ½ In.	510
Enterprise, 2 Wheels, Model 12, Counter, 25-In. Wheel.	1026
Enterprise, 2 Wheels, No. 2, Cast Iron, Grip Handle, Decals, Drawer, 12 ½ In. ....*illus*	649
Enterprise, 2 Wheels, No. 2, Cast Iron, Painted Red, Blue, Patent 1873, 10 In.	443
Enterprise, 2 Wheels, No. 5, Decals, Drawer, 13 x 20 In. ....*illus*	741
Enterprise, No. 5, Red Paint, c.1865, 16 In.	711
Enterprise, Single Wheel, Cast Iron, Yellow Letters, Black, Red, 12 ½ x 12 ¾ In.	304
Hoffmann's, Old Time Brand, Wood, Handle, 13 x 8 In.	776
John C. Dell, Hopper, Bucket, Painted, 57 ¼ In. ....*illus*	1440
Persepolis, Cast Iron, Chrome, Black, Crank Handle, 12 In.	1722
Standard Computing Scale Co., Electric, Nickel Plated Brass Hopper, Bucket	200
Star Mill, Red Paint, Cast Iron, Commercial, 32 x 19 ¾ In.	344

COIN SPOT is a glass pattern that was named by collectors for the spots resembling coins, which are part of the glass. Colored, clear, and opalescent glass was made with the spots. Many companies used the design in the 1870–90 period. It is so popular that reproductions are still being made.

Dish, Jelly, Amber, Scalloped Rim, 3 ¾ In.	69
Lamp, Finger, Oil, Opalescent, c.1900, 13 In.	195
Lamp, Stand, Twisted Stem, Ribbed Base, Crimped Chimney, Blue, 1800s, 14 In.	465
Pitcher, Red To Clear, Reeded Handle, Footed, c.1900, 8 ¾ In.	111
Sugar Shaker, Cranberry, Paneled, c.1875, 4 ½ In.	366
Sugar, Nine Panel, Green Opalescent, 1800s, 4 ¾ In.	325
Syrup, Applied Handle, Blue Opalescent, Metal, c.1890, 5 ½ In.	100

Coin-Operated Machine, Arcade, Billiards Table, Ball Racks, Cue Sticks, Home Billiardette, 46 In.
$1,020

Morphy Auctions

Coin-Operated Machine, Arcade, Crane Digger, Be A Sidewalk Engineer, Williams, Floor Model, c.1955
$1,020

Victorian Casino Antiques

Coin-Operated Machine, Arcade, Pinball, Pretty Baby, 2 Player, William, 1965, 68 In.
$330

Morphy Auctions

Coin-Operated Machine, Arcade, Pinball, Tropicana, Flipperless, Bumper Caps, United, 1948, 63 In. $1,440

Morphy Auctions

Coin-Operated Machine, Fortune Teller, Mlle. Zita, 1 Cent, Roovers, 73 In. $21,600

Morphy Auctions

COIN-OPERATED MACHINES of all types are collected. The vending machine is an ancient invention dating back to 200 B.C., when holy water was dispensed in a coin-operated vase. Smokers in seventeenth-century England could buy tobacco from a coin-operated box. It was not until after the Civil War that the technology made modern coin-operated games and vending machines plentiful. Slot machines, arcade games, and dispensers are all collected.

Ad-Lee Co., Vending, Gum, Cast Iron, Glass Globe, Umpire Decal, Ad-Lee Co., 24 x 8 In.	1154
Arcade, Billiards Table, Ball Racks, Cue Sticks, Home Billiardette, 46 In. ....*illus*	1020
Arcade, Cail-O-Scope, San Francisco Earthquake, Quartersawn Oak, Nickel Plate, 1906, 71 In..	3300
Arcade, Climbing Fireman, 1st To Top Gets Coin Back, 1920s, 72 x 25 In.	4444
Arcade, Clown, Tin Lithograph, Oak Case, Saxony, c.1900, 24 x 18 In.	770
Arcade, Crane Digger, Be A Sidewalk Engineer, Williams, Floor Model, c.1955 ....*illus*	1020
Arcade, Electricity Is Life, Mills Novelty Co., Key, 9 x 12 x 7 In.	1368
Arcade, Lung Tester Recreation, Caille, 1 Cent, Mike Gorski, 72 In.	3600
Arcade, Lung Tester, Caille, Little Wonder, Iron Marquee, Tin Container, 26 x 14 In.	2734
Arcade, Pinball, Dragonette, Double Award, Gottlieb, 1954, 66 In.	1800
Arcade, Pinball, Five Star Final, 1 Cent, c.1932, 34 In.	300
Arcade, Pinball, King Cole, Fairy Tale Series, 1948, 67 In.	420
Arcade, Pinball, Lights, Camera, Action, Gottlieb, 1989, 75 In.	1440
Arcade, Pinball, Pretty Baby, 2 Player, William, 1965, 68 In. ....*illus*	330
Arcade, Pinball, Tropicana, Flipperless, Bumper Caps, United, 1948, 63 In. ....*illus*	1440
Arcade, Rock-Ola, Horse Race, Official Sweepstakes, Aluminum, Wood, c.1925, 12 x 15 In.	2489
Arcade, Shocker, Mills, Electricity Cures Many Ills, Lion's Head, 12 In.	1200
Arcade, Supply 6 Shooter, Dale Exhibit, Arcade, c.1950, 76 In.	720
Automaton, 2 Birds In Cage, Wire, Giltwood, Flowers, c.1920, 22 ¼ In.	1080
Fortune Teller, Mlle. Zita, 1 Cent, Roovers, 73 In. ....*illus*	21600
Fortune Teller, Puss & Boots, 1 Cent, Oak, Iron Legs, Roovers, 76 x 16 In. .... 15405 to 21000	
Fortune Teller, Wizard, 1 Cent, Key, Mills, c.1926, Countertop ....*illus*	1560
Fortune, Whom You Should Marry, Oak, Iron Legs, Exhibit Supply, 72 x 24 In.	2403
Gambling, The Clown, c.1915, 25 x 19 In.	748
Gum, Kola-Pepsin, 5 Cent, Porcelain Over Metal, Pulver, 24 In. ....*illus*	2700
Gumball, 1 Cent, Metal, Glass, Key, Master, 16 In. ....*illus*	480
Gumball, Elvis Marquee, 25 Cent, Plastic, Gas Pump Shape, 89 In.	210
Movie Card Viewing, Regent, 25 Cent, Oak, Iron Legs, Ball Feet, Rosenfield, 71 In.	2006
Music Box, Polyphon, Style 104, Walnut, Double Comb, Plays, 19 ⅝-In. Disc	2950
Music Box, Polyphon, Upright, Double Disc, Oak, Glazed Door, Penny Drop, 38 In.	3878
Mutoscope Reel, Cohens & Kellys In Paris, Wood Crate	780
Mutoscope Reel, Good Vs. Evil, American Mutoscope & Biographic Co.	1200
Mutoscope, Indian Design, Cast Iron	8400
Mutoscope, Multiscope, 4 Fisheye Lenses, Control Knobs, Quartersawn Oak, 65 x 31 In.	34020
Mutoscope, Original Marquee, Aviation Reel, 5 Cent, 74 In.	1080
Mutoscope, Peep Show, 10 Cent, Eyeholes, Flipping Cards, Wood, Table Top Model	322
Mutoscope, Proposal, Oak, Table Top, 9 x 18 ½ x 20 In.	5400
Phonograph, Hexaphone, No. 104, Oak, Regina, 49 x 24 In.	6518
Pianist, Googly Eyes Roll, Fingers Move, Sheet Music Backdrop, 1930s, 69 In.	2126
Pinball, Baffle Ball, Walnut Case, Vending Machine Co., 12 x 16 In.	330
Pinball, Buffalo Bill, Wood Rail, Gottlieb, c.1950, 65 In.	2040
Pinball, Contact Master, Pacific Amusement, 5 Cent, 40 In.	660
Pinball, Hang Glider, 25 Cent, Bally, c.1976 ....*illus*	144
Pinball, Subway 1 Cent, 38 x 17 ¼ In.	570
Pinball, Twin Win, Racing Car, Logos, Flag Girl, Bally, 1974	826
Pinball, Williams Yanks, Baseball Theme, Wood Rail, 1948 ....*illus*	840
Skill, Caille Arcade, Wood, Red Paint, Iron Feet, Nude Woman Plaque, 37 x 16 In.	1481
Skill, Shooting Gallery, Silver Dollar Saloon, Tall Metal Legs, 15 x 28 In.	283
Skill, Try-Skill, Penny, Deposit Coin Balance It Home To Success, 12 ½ In. ....*illus*	570
Slot, Bally, Gold Rush, 25 Cent, 3-Coin, 42 In.	360
Slot, Bally, Money Honey Special, Model 742, 25 Cent, Single Coin, 33 In.	420
Slot, Bally, Reel Dice, 5 Cent, 6-Coin, 43 In.	390
Slot, Caille, Bull Frog, Wood, Metal, 5 Cent	19200
Slot, Caille, Puck Upright, 5 Cent, Music, c.1880, 63 In.	19800
Slot, Caille, Sphinx, 5 Cent, Geometric Designs, 3-Reel, 24 In.	1320
Slot, Columbia, 3-Reel, Painted Steel, Table Top, 5 Cent, Groetchen Mfg., 19 x 14 In.	450
Slot, Groetchen, Twenty One, Black Jack, 3-Reel, 1937	440
Slot, Jennings, 4-Star, 5 Cent, 28 In.	2400
Slot, Jennings, Baseball, 5 Cent, Field, Players, 26 In.	5100
Slot, Jennings, Dixie Bell, 25 Cents, Red, 28 In.	2700

C

Coin-Operated Machine, Fortune Teller, Wizard, 1 Cent, Key, Mills, c.1926, Countertop
$1,560

Victorian Casino Antiques

Coin-Operated Machine, Gum, Kola-Pepsin, 5 Cent, Porcelain Over Metal, Pulver, 24 In.
$2,700

Morphy Auctions

Coin-Operated Machine, Gumball, 1 Cent, Metal, Glass, Key, Master, 16 In.
$480

Morphy Auctions

Coin-Operated Machine, Pinball, Hang Glider, 25 Cent, Bally, c.1976
$144

Victorian Casino Antiques

Coin-Operated Machine, Pinball, Williams Yanks, Baseball Theme, Wood Rail, 1948
$840

Morphy Auctions

Coin-Operated Machine, Skill, Try-Skill, Penny, Deposit Coin Balance It Home To Success, 12 ½ In.
$570

Morphy Auctions

Coin-Operated Machine, Slot, Jennings, Little Duke, 1 Cent, 3-Wheel, c.1932
$1,725

Victorian Casino Antiques

Coin-Operated Machine, Slot, Mills, Dewey Musical, Upright, 5 Cent, Nickel Finish, Oak, 69 In.
$21,600

Morphy Auctions

COIN-OPERATED MACHINE

Coin-Operated Machine, Slot, Watling Rol-A-Top, 5 Cent, Bird Of Paradise, Restored, Key, 14 x 18 In.
$3,876

Showtime Auction Services

Coin-Operated, Strength Tester, Grip Or Blow, Oak Cabinet, Iron, Caille, 32 x 12 In.
$4,740

James D. Julia Auctioneers

Coin-Operated Machine, Trade Stimulator, Gumball, E-Z, 5 Cent, Ad-Lee Novelty Co., 18 ½ In.
$3,000

Morphy Auctions

Coin-Operated Machine, Trade Stimulator, Poker Card Game, Free Cigars, Iron, Leo Canada, Floor Model
$3,300

Morphy Auctions

Coin-Operated Machine, Trade Stimulator, Whiz Ball, 1 Cent, Keys, Pace Mfg., Countertop, c.1931
$420

Victorian Casino Antiques

Coin-Operated Machine, Vending, Cigar, W.L. Kline, Penny, Countertop, 1897
$1,120

Victorian Casino Antiques

Coin-Operated Machine, Vending, Condom, Spanish Fly, 25 Cents, Topless Woman, Cash Box, Lock, 31 In.
$450

Morphy Auctions

Slot, Jennings, Little Duke, 1 Cent, 3-Wheel, c.1932 ....*illus*	1725
Slot, Jennings, Nevada Club, 1 Dollar, Light-Up, 28 ½ In..	2700
Slot, Mills Novelty, Elk Special, Lock & Key, 19 In..	5100
Slot, Mills, 7-7-7, 10 Cent, Special Award, High Top, Gold, Aqua, Wood, 27 x 16 In.	1337
Slot, Mills, Brownie, 5 Cent, Oak Case, Coppered Metal, Marbleized Stand, 65 In.	7800
Slot, Mills, Castle Front, 5 Cent, Side Arm, Key, 26 In.	1200
Slot, Mills, Cowboy, Gun In Hand, Figural, 5 Cent, Red & Black Paint, Frank Polk, 70 In............	16800
Slot, Mills, Dewey Musical, Upright, 5 Cent, Nickel Finish, Oak, 69 In.........................*illus*	21600
Slot, Mills, High Top Deuces Wild, Blue, Red, 25 Cent, 26 ½ In.	1440
Slot, Mills, High Top Special Award, 7-7-7 Jackpot, Red, Black, Chrome, 27 x 16 In.	649
Slot, Mills, High Top Token Bell, 5 Cent, Green, 26 ½ In...	1200
Slot, Mills, High Top, 25 Cent, Red, Black, 25 ½ In..	1320
Slot, Mills, Poinsettia, Gooseneck, 25 Cent, 24 In...	1200
Slot, Mills, Sweetheart, 5 Cent, 3-Reel Slot, 12 x 19 x 13 In.	1026
Slot, Mills, War Eagle, 26 In.	1560
Slot, Mills, War Eagle, 5 Cent, 3-Reel, Wood, Aluminum Casting, 1930s, 26 x 16 In.	1304
Slot, Mills, Wise Cracker, 5 Cent, 25 In.	2280
Slot, Trade, Silver Cup, Mills, Keys, 20 x 26 x 12 In.	5700
Slot, Watling Rol-A-Top, 5 Cent, Bird Of Paradise, Restored, Key, 14 x 18 In. ....*illus*	3876
Slot, Watling, Baby Lincoln, Lincoln Penny, 5 Cent, 24 In.	1680
Slot, Watling, Jefferson, 1 Wheel, Nickel Play, Wood Base, 20 In....................................	4800
Slot, Watling, Rol-A-Top, 5 Cent, Coin Front, Eagle, Scrolls, 26 In.	2400
Slot, Watling, Rol-A-Top, Cherry Front, 5 Cent, Twin Jackpot, 3-Reel, 26 In.	4800
Slot, Watling, Treasury 1 Cent, Wood Sides, Yellow, 24 In. .... 1800 to 3600
Slot, Watling, Twin Jackpot, 1 Cent, Gum, 23 x 16 In.	1770
Strength Tester, Grip Or Blow, Oak Cabinet, Iron, Caille, 32 x 12 In................................*illus*	4740
Strength Tester, National Novelty Co., Key, Minneapolis, 71 In.	2520
Trade Simulator, Poison The Rat, 1941, 24 In..	10800
Trade Stimulator, 1 Cent, Upright, Mills, 20 ½ In.	3300
Trade Stimulator, Cigarette Reels, Token Payout, Columbia, 10 Cent, 1930s, 19 In.	330
Trade Stimulator, Gumball, E-Z, 5 Cent, Ad-Lee Novelty Co., 18 ½ In. ....*illus*	3000
Trade Stimulator, Kicker Catcher, Red, 1 Cent, Frantz Manufacturing Co., 25 In.....................	510
Trade Stimulator, Official Sweepstakes, Horse Race, Wood Case, 11 ½ In.	668
Trade Stimulator, Poker Card Game, Free Cigars, Iron, Leo Canada, Floor Model ....*illus*	3300
Trade Stimulator, Pok-O-Reel, 5 Playing Card Reels, 12 ½ In.	420
Trade Stimulator, Puritan, Baby Bell, Key, Lion Mfg., Chicago, c.1935, 11 x 9 x 7 In................	550
Trade Stimulator, Whiz Ball, 1 Cent, Keys, Pace Mfg., Countertop, c.1931 ....*illus*	420
Trade Stimulator, Whoopee Ball, Ball Flip, 5 Shots, 1 Cent, Spiral Track, 17 In.	1020
Vending, Adams Chewing Gum, 1 Cent, 22 ½ In.	330
Vending, Beech-Nut Gum, 5 Cent, Tin Lithograph, Brass, Glass, Decals, 11 x 15 x 6 In.	1560
Vending, Chewing Gum, Pulver, 1 Cent Delivers Tasty Chew, Happy Hooligan, 24 In....................	6000
Vending, Cigar, W.L. Kline, Penny, Countertop, 1897 ....*illus*	1120
Vending, Cigarettes, Little Merchant, O.D. Jennings, 11 ¾ In.......................................	720
Vending, Collar Buttons, Zeno, Marquee, Drop 10 Cent In Slot, 6 Columns, 11 In.	1140
Vending, Condom, Spanish Fly, 25 Cents, Topless Woman, Cash Box, Lock, 31 In.................*illus*	450
Vending, Gold Changer, Garrett's Bijou, Cast Iron, Dispensing Tray, England, 11 In.................	450
Vending, Gum & Confections, Klinkerts, 1 Cent, 5 Column, Wood, c.1910, 35 ½ In.	7200
Vending, Gumball, Pike's Peak, 1 Cent Slot, Groetchen, c.1939, 15 In.	660
Vending, Gum, 4 Columns, 5 Cent, Superior Mfg., 19 x 11 x 7 In.	153
Vending, Gum, Baker Boy, Indian, Drop Penny, Turn Crank, Clockwork, Manikin, 16 In.............	3209
Vending, Gum, Drop, Zeno, 1 Cent Here, Yellow Porcelain, 17 In.	1080
Vending, Gum, Four Aces, Flip Game, Rock-Ola, Nickel, 17 In.......................................	1800
Vending, Gum, Happy Jap, Orange, Black, 10 x 13 ½ x 10 ½ In..	1080
Vending, Gum, Kola-Pepsin, 1 Cent, Clown Inside, Pulver's, c.1900, 24 In. ....*illus*	7800
Vending, Gum, Short's, 1 Cent, Iron Base, Steel Case, Padlock, Key, 8 ¼ x 29 In.	513
Vending, Gumball, 1 Cent, Glass Globe, Maroon Base, Columbus, Model A, 17 In......................	720
Vending, Gumball, Ace Vendor, Aluminum, Glass, Paneled, c.1935, 14 In.	1093
Vending, Gumball, Alball, Copper Flashed Base & Lid, Glass, 14 x 8 In.............................	2300
Vending, Gumball, Barnyard Golf, 1 Cent, 17 ¼ In..*illus*	1020
Vending, Gumball, D.D. Lewis, Cast Iron, Glass, 11 ¼ x 5 In.	380
Vending, Gumball, Digesto, Copper Flashed, Glass, Blue Ridge Gum Co., 10 In.	3910
Vending, Gumball, Glass Globe, Red Metal Base, Advance Machine Co., 12 In.	120
Vending, Gumball, Lincoln, Ohio Vending, Cast Iron, Glass Dome, 14 x 7 In.	1495
Vending, Gumball, Little Twin, Type C, Cast Iron, 2 Globes, 10 x 14 In.	3680
Vending, Gumball, Shooting Gallery, 1 Cent, A.B.T. Challenger, 1939, 16 In.........................	715
Vending, Gumball, Y & S, Glass Dome, Red Base, Alball Co., c.1912, 10 In...........................	1668

Coin-Operated Machine, Vending, Gum, Kola-Pepsin, 1 Cent, Clown Inside, Pulver's, c.1900, 24 In.
$7,800

Morphy Auctions

Coin-Operated Machine, Vending, Gumball, Barnyard Golf, 1 Cent, 17 ¼ In.
$1,020

Morphy Auctions

Coin-Operated Machine, Vending, Link Collar Button, 25 Cent, Metal, Plastic, 13 In. Without Sign
$1,560

Morphy Auctions

Coin-Operated Machine, Vending, Marbles, Baby Grand, 1 Cent, Oak, Keys, Victor Vending, Chicago, 1950s
$390

Victorian Casino Antiques

Comic Art, Cover Art, Swamp Thing, No. 102, Simon Bisley, DC Comic, 1990, 18 x 22 In.
$11,500

Hake's Americana & Collectibles

Comic Art, Strip, Peanuts, Snoopy As Joe Cool, Schulz, 9-22, 1971, 7 ½ x 28 In.
$19,102

Hake's Americana & Collectibles

Vending, Jergens Lotion, 1 Cent, Wall Mount, Black, 16 ½ In.	450
Vending, Jergens Lotion, Art Deco, Wall Mount, Salesman's Sample, Case, 1937, 20 In.	711
Vending, Lighter Fluid, 1 Cent, Gas Pump Shape, Red, Countertop, 20 x 7 ⅝ In.	863
Vending, Link Collar Button, 25 Cent, Metal, Plastic, 13 In. Without Sign *illus*	1560
Vending, Man-Lite Lighter Fluid, 19 In.	443
Vending, Marbles, Baby Grand, 1 Cent, Oak, Keys, Victor Vending, Chicago, 1950s *illus*	390
Vending, Match Dispenser, 1 Cent, Copper Flashed, Cast Iron, 5 ¾ x 13 In.	600
Vending, Match Dispenser, Round Up Hotel, Cast Iron, Montana, 5 ¾ x 13 ½ In.	780
Vending, Mr. Peanut, Roaster, Papier-Mache, Wood, Copper, Planters Peanut, 1920, 50 x 45 In.	16800
Vending, Name Plate, Rover, 5 Cent, Punches Nametags On Aluminum Strip, 56 In.	900
Vending, Nuts, Nut House, Rates, 1 Cent, Figural, Aluminum, Cast Iron, 8 x 7 In.	2415
Vending, Peanut, Smilin' Sam From Alabam', 1 Cent, Red Man's Head, 14 In.	2160
Vending, Roll Mints, Puritan, Chicago Mint Co., 3-Reel, Silver Metal, 10 ½ In.	780
Vending, Stoner Fresh Candy, 7 Selections, 65 In.	450
Vending, Toilet Seat Cover, Protect Yourself, Pressed Steel, Label, c.1926, 9 In.	138
Vending, Watling, 5 Cent, Rol-A-Top, Yellow, White, 27 In.	3600

COMIC ART, or cartoon art, is a relatively new field of collecting. Original art for comic strips, magazine covers, and even printed strips are collected. The first daily comic strip was printed in 1907. The paintings on celluloid used for movie cartoons are listed in this book under Animation Art.

Book Page, Savage Tales, No. 2, 8 Panels, Dark Tomorrow, Gray Morrow, 1973, 15 x 20 In.	278
Cartoon Pages, Harper's Weekly, T. Nast, 10 ¾ x 15 ¾ In.	348
Cover Art, Swamp Thing, No. 102, Simon Bisley, DC Comic, 1990, 18 x 22 In. *illus*	11500
Illustration, Smuggler, Santa In Airplane, Booze, Charles A. Hughes, 1919, 23 In.	180
Strip, Batman, Featuring Batgirl, Al Plastino, Ink, Screen Tone Shading, 1969, 6 x 21 In.	975
Strip, Donald Duck, Asking Uncle Scrooge For A Raise, 4 Panels, 1966, 5 x 18 In.	342
Strip, Donald Duck, Sculpting Daisy Duck, Okay Now Smile, 4 Panels, King, 1957, 5 x 19 In.	506
Strip, Hughes Hippo, Judge Magazine, 4 Panels, Charles A. Hughes, 1922, 10 x 25 In.	84
Strip, Moon Mullins, World's Fair, Art Board, 1933, 4 ⅞ x 20 ¾ In.	329
Strip, Mutt & Jeff, Run For President, 1923, 11 x 30 In.	392
Strip, Peanuts, Snoopy As Joe Cool, Schulz, 9-22, 1971, 7 ½ x 28 In. *illus*	19102
Strip, Popeye, Goons, Enough Rope For Hanging, 6 Panels, Ink, Wash, Segar, 1937, 5 x 22 In.	4617
Sunday Krazy Kat, April 30, 1916, G. Herriman, Frame, 28 ½ x 31 In. *illus*	26565
Sunday, Bungle Family, Sunday, Art Board, 1926, 23 x 29 In.	115
Wonder Woman, Art Board, Pen & Ink, Jose Delbo, 10 ½ x 15 ½ In.	152

COMMEMORATIVE items have been made to honor members of royalty and those of great national fame. World's Fairs and important historical events are also remembered with commemorative pieces. Related collectibles are listed in the Coronation and World's Fair categories.

Medal, 300 Years House Of Romanov, Nicholas II, Metal, c.1913, 1 ⅛ In.	100
Medal, Challenger, One Minute Of Eternity, Sterling Silver, 1986	400
Model, Dyna-Soar, Signed, Crews & Knight, 1960s, 6 x 11 In.	375
Patch, Apollo 10, Crew, Grumman, 1969, 4 In.	260
Patch, Gemini 12, Lovell, Aldrin, Black, Yellow, 1966, 3 In. Diam.	280
Photo, Apollo 10, Astronauts, 1969, 8 ½ x 11 In.	130
Pitcher, Admiral Dewey, Ship, Transfer, Eagle Spout, Rope Handle, Ironstone, 1899, 6 In.	150
Pitcher, King William IV, Queen Adelaide, Scalloped Rim, Purple Transfer, 1830s, 8 In.	104
Pitcher, Lafayette, Cornwallis, Ribbed Neck, Red, Copper, Staffordshire, c.1825, 4 In.	288
Plate, Titanic, Fated Trip Details, White, Scalloped Edge, Carlton China, 6 ¾ In.	400
Tin, Queen Victoria, Portrait, Multicolor, South Africa, New Year Gift, 1900	40
Watch, Dive, Mercury Astronaut, Gordon Cooper, Celsius 9, 1970s	170

COMPACTS hold face powder. A woman did not powder her face in public until after World War I. By 1920, the beauty parlor, permanent waves, and cosmetics had become acceptable. A few companies sold cake face powder in a box with a mirror and a pad or puff. Soon the compact was designed by jewelers and made of gold, silver, and precious materials. Cosmetic companies began to sell powder in attractive compacts of less valuable metal or plastic. Collectors today search for Art Deco designs, commemorative compacts from World's Fairs or political events, and unusual examples. Many were made with companion lipsticks and other fittings.

14K Gold, Diamond Pattern, Monogram, Mirror, Finger Ring, Chain, 1 ¾ x 1 ¼	316
14K Tricolor Gold, Geometric Design, Diamond Clasp, Fold-Out Mirror, Art Deco, 2 In.	1560
Amami, Silvertone, Geometric Design, Hinged Mirror, Round, 1926, 2 In.	29
Bakelite, Mirror In Lid, Powder Puff, Corded Handle, Tassel, 3 ½ x 4 ¼ In. *illus*	230

Cartier, 14K Gold, Line Engraving, Sapphire Thumbpiece, Mirror Inside, 2 ½ In.	2280
Cartier, Ribbed 18K Gold, Platinum, Ruby, Diamond, c.1945, 3 x 5 In.	12500
Cartier, Silver, Brushed Finish, Lapis Lazuli, Signed, 3 ½ In.	472
Celluloid, Carved Elephant Scene, Round, 2 ¾ In.	29
Elgin, Enamel, Black, Silvertone, Hinged, Fitted Interior, Arrowhead Shape, 4 ½ x 2 In.	104
Elgin, Guilloche, White Enamel, Pink Rose, 14K Gold, 3 ¼ x 2 ¼ In.	40
Enamel, Blue Champleve, Chased Silvertone, 2 Women, Dove, Puff, 3 In.	92
Enamel, Blue Guilloche, Silver, Oval, Courtyard Scene, Germany, 2 x 4 In.	575
Enamel, Blue, White, Lipstick Fob, Enamel Finger Ring, 4 ¼- In. Chain	1150
Enamel, Champleve, Red, Black, Bolster Shape, Attached Cord, 3 ½ x 1 ½ In.	184
Enamel, Courting Scene, Chased Scalloped Frame, Marked Oros, Italy, 2 ¾ x 3 ¾ In.	403
Enamel, Flower, Silvertone Frame, Round, Italy, 3 In.	52
Enamel, Green Champleve, Silver, 2 ¼ In.	115
Enamel, Guilloche, Courting Scene, Teal Blue Band, Octagonal, Austria, 2 ¼ In.	207
Enamel, Orange Champleve, Silver Flower Overlay, Oval Scene, Italy, 2 ½ x 3 In.	161
Enamel, Red, White, Jade Carved Top, Mirror Lid, Powder Wells, 3 x 2 ¼ In.	184
Enamel, Viking Ship, Stepped, Chain Handle, Finger Ring, Fitted Interior, 2 ½ x 2 In.	489
Goldtone, Filigree, Leaves, Blue Stone, Black Fabric, Fitted Interior, Round, 2 ½ In.	46
Goldtone, Filigree, Red Jewels, Over Red Satin Ground, Round, 2 In.	58
Goldtone, Vine, Flowers, Red Enamel, Lipstick Holder, Fitted Interior, 2 x 3 ½ In.	58
Guilloche, Goldtone, Silver Bands, Painted Courting Scene, Round, Austria, 2 In.	150
Guilloche, White, Painted Rose, Leaves, Gold Plated, Elgin, 2 x 2 In.	52
Guilloche, Yellow, Heart Shape Flowers, Rouge Well, Chain Handle, 2 ¾ x 2 ¼ In.	81
Henriette, Silvertone, Red, Green Enamel Berry Branch, Fan Shape, 1938, 4 ¾ x 3 ¼ In.	69
Lambert Bros., Silver, 14K Gold, Ruby, Engraved Line, Arched Clasp, 2 ¾ In.	295
Mondaine, Black Enamel, Flowers, 2 x 3 In.	35
Paul Flato, Stars, Paste Centers, Goldtone Metal, 1950s, 2 x 2 In.	300
Silver, Brushed, Purse Shape, Ruby Stones Border, Round Puff, Italy, 2 x 3 ½ In.	127
Silver, Chased Asian Scene, 4 ½ x 4 ½ In.	316
Silver, Chased Flowers, Mirror Lid, Powder Well, 8-Sided, 3 ¼ x 3 ¼ In.	115
Silver, Chased Peacock, Flowers, Fitted Interior, 3 x 3 In.	207
Silver, Chased, Enamel Courting Scene, Multicolor, Mirror, 2 x 2 ¼ In.	207
Silver, Chased, Flower Shape, 3 ½ x 3 ½ In.	127
Silver, Chased, Lavender Stones, Woman's Portrait, Yellow Dress, Square, 3 x 3 In.	173
Silver, Enamel, Yellow, Green, White, Black Abstract Design, 2 ½ In.	207
Silver, Filigree Overlay, Egyptian Etchings, Round, 3 In.	58
Silver, Stylized Flower, Mesh Sifter, Puff, R. Blackinton, 3 In.	69
Stratton, Enamel Flowers, Multicolor, Goldtone Frame, Round, Box, 3 In.	29
Udall & Ballou, Enamel Troubadour Scene, 14K Gold, Diamond Clasp, Round, 2 x 1 ½ In.	2243
Vanity Case, Tortoiseshell, Mirror In Lid, Corded Handle, Tassels, 4 ½ x 17 In. *illus*	161
Yardley, Goldtone, Black, White Enamel, Hinged, Fitted Interior, 1931, 2 ½ x 2 In.	40

CONSOLIDATED LAMP AND GLASS COMPANY of Coraopolis, Pennsylvania, was founded in 1894. The company made lamps, tablewares, and art glass. Collectors are particularly interested in the wares made after 1925, including black satin glass, Cosmos (listed in its own category in this book), Martele (which resembled Lalique), Ruba Rombic (1928–32 Art Deco line), and colored glasswares. Some Consolidated pieces are very similar to those made by the Phoenix Glass Company. The colors are sometimes different. Consolidated made Martele glass in blue, crystal, green, pink, white, or custard glass with added fired-on color or a satin finish. The company closed for the final time in 1967.

Ashtray, Santa Maria, Green Wash	300
Bowl, Catalonian, Green, 8 ½ In.	40
Bowl, Martele, Parakeets, Molded, Sky Blue Tint, 6 In. *illus*	561
Bowl, Mayonnaise, Iris, Green Wash, 5 ¾ x 3 In.	55
Butter, Cover, Florette, Clear Base, Finial, c.1890, 5 ½ x 7 ¾ In.	104
Candlestick, Catalonian, Green	35
Compote, Tropical Fish, Green Wash, 6 In.	85
Lamp, Dogwood, Satin Custard, Tricolor Highlighting	195
Plate, Fruit, Green Wash, 8 In.	25
Sugar & Creamer, Ruba Rombic, Jungle Green	700
Vase, Catalonian, Green, Flared, 5 ½ In.	45
Vase, Catalonian, Reuben Blue, Ruffled Top, 12 In.	450
Vase, Ruba Rombic, Green Glass, Reuben Haley, c.1928, 9 ½ In.	6875
Water Set, Guttate, Pink, Pressed Fan, c.1890, 9 ½ In., 3 ¾ In., 5 Piece	196

Comic Art, Sunday Krazy Kat, April 30, 1916, G. Herriman, Frame, 28 ½ x 31 In. $26,565

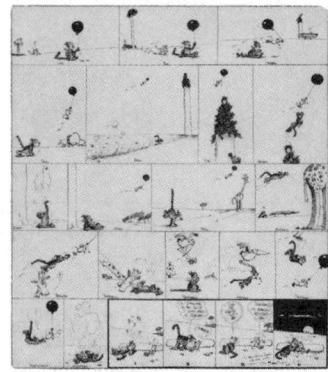

Hake's Americana & Collectibles

Compact, Bakelite, Mirror In Lid, Powder Puff, Corded Handle, Tassel, 3 ½ x 4 ¼ In. $230

Dirk Soulis Auctions

Compact, Vanity Case, Tortoiseshell, Mirror In Lid, Corded Handle, Tassels, 4 ½ x 17 In. $161

Dirk Soulis Auctions

COOKBOOK

Consolidated Lamp and Glass Company, Bowl, Martele, Parakeets, Molded, Sky Blue Tint, 6 In.
$561

Humler & Nolan

Cookbook, Jell-O, Genesee Pure Food Co., Lithograph, 6 ¼ x 3 ½ In.
$35

Conestoga Auction Co., Inc.

Cookbook, Prudential Cookbook, Prudential Insurance, Lithograph, c.1910, 5 ¾ x 3 ⅞ In.
$12

Conestoga Auction Co., Inc.

CONTEMPORARY GLASS, *see Glass-Contemporary.*

COOKBOOKS are collected for various reasons. Some are wanted for the recipes, some for investment, and some as examples of advertising. Cookbooks and recipe pamphlets are included in this category.

Betty Crocker, Dinner In A Dash, Spiral Bound, 1960s, 156 Pages, 10 x 8 In.	65
Betty Crocker, Ways With Hamburger, Golden Press, 1969, 28 Pages, 6 x 5 In.	14
Bisquick, Betty Crocker, Spiral Bound, 112 Pages, 1964	22
Book Of Valuable Recipes, Arm & Hammer, Church & Co.'s Soda, c.1897, 6 x 3 In.	12
Borden's Eagle Brand, Condensed Milk, Woman Cooking, Lithograph, 4 ½ x 6 In.	24
Campbell, Cooking With Soup, Hardcover, Spiral, 1950s, 199 Pages, 8 x 5 In.	28
Cream Of Wheat, 50 Ways Of Serving Cream Of Wheat, Chef On Banner, c.1924, 7 x 4 In.	11
Edith Bunker's All In The Family Cookbook, June Roth, 1971	26
Food For Tho't, Mary Taylor, Spiral Bound, 1967, 233 Pages	40
Foods From Sunny Lands, Hills Bros. Co., Lithograph, c.1925, 8 x 5 ¾ In.	35
General Foods, Hardcover, 600 Recipes, 1932, 370 Pages, 8 ½ x 5 ¾ In.	29
Good Housekeeping Illustrated Cookbook, Hardcover, 1980, 512 Pages	39
Greens Cookbook, 396 Pages, 10 ¼ x 7 ¼ In.	22
Heinz Book Of Salads, Lithograph, Lobster, Fruit, Vegetables, c.1925, 7 ½ x 4 ½ In.	11
Jell-O Ice Cream Powder, Lithograph, Child Eating Ice Cream, c.1906, 6 x 4 ¼ In.	11
Jell-O, Genesee Pure Food Co., Lithograph, 6 ¼ x 3 ½ In. ....*illus*	35
Mike Roy Cookbook, No. 2, 1969, 147 Pages	12
Mike Roy, Hardcover, c.1969, 135 Pages	10
New Pillsbury Family Cookbook, Hardcover, 1973, 408 Pages, 10 x 7 In.	75
Old Sleepy Eye Milling Co., Indian Cover, 96 Pages, 4 ½ x 4 ¾ In.	200
Pi Beta Phi, Settlement School Committee, Gatlinburg, Tenn., Spiral Bound, 1963, 128 Pages..	18
Presto Cooker, Model 60, 1946, 128 Pages	12
Prudential Cookbook, Prudential Insurance, Lithograph, c.1910, 5 ¾ x 3 ⅞ In. ....*illus*	12
Royal Baker & Pastry Cook, Royal Baking Powder, Lithograph, 1898, 8 x 5 In. ....*illus*	35
Rumford Cookbook, Rumford Chemical Works, Lithograph, 1898, 6 ½ x 4 ⅛ In.	47
Ruth Wakefield's Toll House Recipes, Little, Brown & Co., 1952, 376 Pages, 8 x 6 In.	32
Someone's In The Kitchen With Dinah, J.P. Tarcher, 1971, 179 Pages	49
War-Time Cook & Health Book, 1917, 32 Pages, 7 x 4 ½ In.	46

COOKIE JARS with brightly painted designs or amusing figural shapes became popular in the mid-1930s. Many companies made them and collectors search for cookie jars either by design or by maker's name. Listed here are examples by the less common makers. Major factories are listed under their own names in other categories of the book, such as Abingdon, Brush, Hull, McCoy, Metlox, Red Wing, and Shawnee. See also the Disneyana category.

Amish Couple, Fruit Cart, Brown, Pennsbury Pottery, 7 ½ x 7 ¼ In.	110
Apple, Red, Maurice Of California, 1960s, 11 x 9 In.	33
Baby Huey, Black Hair, Bisque, USA	1020
Ball Shape, Wild Poppies, c.1935, 8 In.	73
Black Mammy, Hand On Hips, Yellow Scarf, White Apron, Brayton Laguna, c.1950, 13 In.	281
Black Mammy, Red Dress, Zigzag Design On Apron, Brayton Laguna ....*illus*	58
Black Mammy, Yellow Dress, Mosaic Tile, 13 ¼ In.	175
Champ Kangaroo, Yellow Sweater, Winton Design, DeForest ....*illus*	780
Chef, White, Hands At Side, American Bisque, 9 x 5 ½ In.	46
Chick, Hat, Yellow, Red, Blue, American Bisque	95
Chick, Pink Vest, Pompom Hat, American Bisque, c.1955, 11 ⅞ In.	110
Clown, Rotund Belly, Derby Hat, Red, White, Blue, American Bisque, 11 ¼ In.	49
Crock Style, Pottery, Brown, Tan, Cookie, 1950s, 8 ½ x 6 ½ In.	45
Dinosaur, Reclining, Green, Sinclair Oil, 1943	1800
Face Jug, 2-Color Swirl, Pointed Hat Lid, Stamped, Walter Fleming, 10 In.	150
Flintstones, Fred & Dino, American Bisque ....*illus*	115
Herman & Katnip, American Bisque Co., Paper Label, Bisque	1560
Herman & Katnip, Harvey Cartoons, American Bisque Co., c.1962, 10 x 11 In.	1392
Keystone Cop, Mustache, Hat, Brown, 11 ½ In.	35
Keystone Cop, Star, Belt, Club, Brown, Black, USA, 11 In.	35
Leprechaun Face As Lid, Smiling, Gold, Doranne Of California, 13 In.	95
Matilda, Yellow Bonnet & Ribbon, Brayton Laguna ....*illus*	30
Native American, McCoy, 11 In.	200
Panda, Sad Face, Black, White, Red Hat, Eating Cookie	48
Peek-A-Boo, White, Red, Regal China, c.1950, 11 In.	138
Smokey Bear, Prevent Forest Fires, Norcrest ....*illus*	60

C

Strawberry, Red, Green, American Bisque Co., 1940s, 9 In.	100
Strawberry, Red, Sears Exclusive, 1940s, 9 x 9 In.	100
Trolley, Cookie Face Figures, Cookie Trolley, Treasure Craft, USA, 9 x 11 x 5 In.	48
Water Works, Arched, Sun, Hose, Cloud Handle, P. Warashina, 1970, 10 x 10 In.	2640

COORS ware was made by the Coors Porcelain Company of Golden, Colorado, a company founded with the help of the Coors Brewing Company. Its founder, John Herold, started the Herold China and Pottery Company in 1910. The company name was changed in 1920, when Herold left. Dishes were made from the turn of the century. Coors stopped making nonessential wares at the start of World War II. After the war, the pottery made ovenware, teapots, vases, and a general line of pottery, but no dinnerware—except for special orders. The company is still in business making industrial porcelain. For more prices, go to kovels.com.

COORS
U.S.A.

Ashtray, Burgundy, Marked, 1940s, 5 In, Diam.	29
Cake Plate, Rosebud Pattern, Green, 11 In.	35
Custard Cup, Rosebud, Blue, 2 ½ x 3 ¾ In.	18
Jar, Rosebud Pattern, Green, Twisted Handles, 1930s, 4 ½ x 6 In.	49
Mortar & Pestle, White, Marked, 1920s	25
Pitcher, Swollen Body, Footed, White, 5 In.	18
Plate, Dessert, Rosebud, 7 ⅛ In.	12
Plate, Luncheon, Rosebud, Blue, 9 ¼ In.	32
Plate, Luncheon, Rosebud, Orange, 9 ¼ In.	30
Plate, Luncheon, Rosebud, Yellow, 9 ¼ In.	32
Salt & Pepper, Wheat Stalk, Gilt Trim, Oval, 4 ⅝ In.	30
Vase, Ball, Twisted Rope Handles, Green, c.1940, 10 In.	134
Vase, Blue, Handles, Footed, c.1930, 10 In.	135

COPELAND pieces listed here are those that have a mark including the word *Copeland* used between 1847 and 1976. Marks include *Copeland Spode* and *Copeland & Garrett*. See also Copeland Spode, Royal Worcester, and Spode.

Figurine, Beatrice, Star On Forehead, Robe, Roses, Sprigs, Sandals, c.1870, 22 In.	1150
Figurine, Man, Standing, Hand On Hip, Period Attire, Chelsea Derby, Richard Quinn, 9 In.	58
Figurine, Rebekah, Holding Amphora, Parian, c.1851, 20 x 7 ½ In. *illus*	2868
Figurine, Temperance The Water Pourer, Woman, Robe, Vessel, Parian, c.1865, 20 In.	230
Group, Emily & The White Doe, White, Parian, c.1878, 17 ¾ In.	633
Pitcher, Panels, Gilt Lotus, Handle, Majolica, Marked, c.1890, 10 ½ x 8 In. *illus*	885
Plate Set, Hunting Scene, Gilt Rim, L. Edwards, Sloane & Smith, c.1930, 10 In., 12 Piece	4063
Platter, Blue, Orange, White, Chinoiserie Scene, Canted Corners, 18 ½ In.	200
Punch Bowl, Gone Away, Fox Hunting Scenes, L. Edwards, Footed, 9 ½ x 16 ½ In.	266
Vase, Brown Ground, Flowers, Flared Rim, Majolica, 11 In.	54
Woman, Seated, Nuzzling Deer, Parian, Signed F.M. Miller, 18 ½ In.	334

COPELAND SPODE appears on some pieces of nineteenth-century English porcelain. Josiah Spode established a pottery at Stoke-on-Trent, England, in 1770. In 1833, the firm was purchased by William Copeland and Thomas Garrett and the mark was changed. In 1847, Copeland became the sole owner and the mark changed again. W.T. Copeland & Sons continued until a 1976 merger when it became Royal Worcester Spode. The company was bought by the Portmeirion Group in 2009. Pieces are listed in this book under the name that appears in the mark. Copeland, Royal Worcester, and Spode have separate listings.

COPELAND
SPODE
ENGLAND

Mug, Seated Drinker, White Relief, Pale Green Ground, 6 x 5 In., 8 Piece	79
Plate, Center Flowers, Basket, Wide Blue Branch, Bird Border, c.1920, 9 In., 12 Piece	81
Plate, Cottage Center, Red, White Flower, Scalloped Fern Border, c.1950, 11 In., 10 Piece	92
Platter, Oriental Landscape, River, Bridge, Trees, Pink Transfer, Fluted Rim, 21 In.	259

COPPER has been used to make utilitarian items, such as teakettles and cooking pans, since the days of the early American colonists. Copper became a popular metal with the Arts & Crafts makers of the early 1900s, and decorative pieces, like desk sets, were made. Other pieces of copper may be found in Arts & Crafts, Bradley & Hubbard, Kitchen, Roycroft, and other categories.

Ale Measure, Riveted Handles, Bell Shape, Spout, Flat Ring Foot, 19 In.	246
Ash Bucket, Brass, Embossed Lid, Spiral Lobed Pattern, Loop Handles, 1800s, 11 ¼ In.	480
Bed Warmer, Pierced Bird Design, Long Wood Handle, c.1865, 43 In.	178
Box, Art Deco, Bulbous, Hammered, Enamel On Lid, Boston School, c.1910, 5 x 4 ½ In.	813
Box, Hammered, Repousse, Enameled Fruit, England, Arts & Crafts, 4 ½ x 3 In.	563

Cookbook, Royal Baker & Pastry Cook, Royal Baking Powder, Lithograph, 1898, 8 x 5 In.
$35

Conestoga Auction Co., Inc.

Cookie Jar, Black Mammy, Red Dress, Zigzag Design On Apron, Brayton Laguna
$58

Victorian Casino Antiques

Cookie Jar, Champ Kangaroo, Yellow Sweater, Winton Design, DeForest
$780

Victorian Casino Antiques

Cookie Jar, Flintstones, Fred & Dino, American Bisque
$115

Victorian Casino Antiques

Cookie Jar, Matilda, Yellow Bonnet & Ribbon, Brayton Laguna
$30

Victorian Casino Antiques

Cookie Jar, Smokey Bear, Prevent Forest Fires, Norcrest
$60

Victorian Casino Antiques

Box, Lid, Hammered, Red, Black Enamel Geometric Design, Round, c.1905, 10 x 4 In.	732
Chafing Dish, Silver Plate, Rabbit Supports, Joseph Heinrich, c.1890, 10 x 13 In.............*illus*	2375
Charger, Hammered, Oval Ring Handles, Signed, G. Stickley, 20 In.	563
Charger, Tulip Design, c.1950, 10 ¾ In., 16 Piece	250
Chocolate Pot, Hammered, Brass, Horn Handle, Theodore Pond, c.1905, 6 x 9 In.............*illus*	8125
Cigar Cutter, Silver Riveted Edge, Marked Joseph Heinrich, 5 In.	1875
Cigarette Case, Hammered, Cedar, Harry Dixon, San Francisco, 1923, 2 ½ x 2 ½ In.	1750
Coffeepot, Hinged Top, Ball Finial, Wood Handle, 12 In., Pair	338
Coffeepot, Wrigglework, Pa., c.1920, 11 In.	1422
Finial, Eagle, On Sphere, Green Marble Base, c.1900, 21 In.	780
Funnel, Riveted, c.1860, 13 In.	123
Humidor, Art Nouveau, Handles, c.1900, 4 x 9 x 7 In.	875
Ice Bucket, Lid, Repousse Flowers, Enamel Inserts, Footed, Arts & Crafts, Eng., 15 x 15 In.	2000
Jardiniere, Art Nouveau, Bacchanalian Scenes, Raised Petals, Footed Base, France, 19 x 16 In.	443
Jug, Hammered, Riveted Brass Nails, Signed WMF, 5 ½ x 4 ½ In.	344
Kettle, Apple Butter, Handle, 1800s, 20 x 28 In.	780
Kettle, Apple Butter, Riveted, Iron Bail, c.1865, 28 In.	633
Kettle, Hammered, Riveted, 15 x 19 In.	210
Kettle, Hot Water, Dovetailed, 13 ½ x 12 In.	554
Kettle, Lid, Swing Handle, Impressed C. Raborg, Baltimore, c.1800, 11 ¾ In.	593
Kettle, Lid, Swing Handle, Impressed G. Tryon, Philadelphia, c.1860, 12 In.	456
Kettle, Lid, Swing Handle, Impressed W. Heyser, Pa., c.1865, 10 ¾ In.	668
Kettle, Punched Monogram Handle, Pa., c.1810, 13 In.	296
Kettle, Rolled Rim, Bail Handle, 16 x 24 In.	330
Kettle, Round Tapered Shape, Riveted Band, 14 x 19 In.	179
Kettle, Swing Handle, c.1850, 22 x 13 ½ In.	117
Kettle, Tin Lined, Wicker Handle, Eagle Finial, Bird Spout, Burner Base, c.1770, 11 In.	325
Lavabo, Pressed Lyre Design, Oval Basin, Ring Handles, Finial, 16 In.	359
Mailbox, Repousse Designs, Newspaper Holder, c.1920, 7 ½ x 16 In.	366
Mask, Repousse, Earrings, Hat, c.1900, 23 x 20 In.	4183
Measure, Haystack Shape, London, c.1860, 4 Gal., 18 In.	211
Measure, Pitcher Shape, Handle, 1800s, 11 x 9 ½ In.	58
Molds are listed in the Kitchen category.	
Pan, Sauce, Dovetailed, Long Handle, c.1850, 5 x 17 ½ In.	29
Panel, Mask, Face, Radiating Headdress, Verdigris, c.1900, 30 x 44 In.	2880
Pitcher, Arts & Crafts, Jester Mask, Silver Plate, Joseph Heinrichs, c.1907, 8 ¼ In.	891
Pitcher, General Jackson, Canary Yellow Luster, Portrait, Loop Handle, Ribbed, 5 In.	867
Pitcher, Hammered, Handle With Fish Terminus, Stickley Brothers, 10 ½ x 10 In.	732
Pitcher, Hammered, Rabbit Handle, Joseph Heinrich, 10 x 10 In.	2000
Plaque, Hammered, Spade Design, Repousse, Round, Benedict Studios, 15 ½ In.	1625
Plaque, Kabarett, Fledermaus, Bat, Man's Face, Enamel, Wiener Werkstatte, c.1912, 3 In.	8125
Pot, Black Iron Handles, Rounded Bottom, Rolled Rim, 25 In. Diam.	338
Pot, Jam, Lid, Abstract Design, Ceramic Liner, Tan Glaze, Arts & Crafts, Eng., c.1910, 6 x 5 In.	427
Puzzle Box, Turquoise Cabochons, Harry St. John Dixon, c.1920, 2 ¾ x 5 ¾ In.............*illus*	6250
Samovar, Brass Garland, Saucer Foot, Plume Finial, Ram's Head Handle, 1800s, 24 In.	519
Sculpture, Insect, Waterstrider, Melissa Strawser, c.1960, 18 ½ x 45 In.	652
Sculpture, Lobster Okimono, Movable, Japan, c.1900, 3 ½ In.	708
Sculpture, Sonambient, Harry Bertoia, Beryllium Copper, Brass, 1970s, 36 In.	21250
Sculpture, Tree, Signed C. Jere, 34 x 58 In.	375
Teakettle, Brass, Gooseneck Spout, Stationary Handle, 19th Century, 11 ½ In.	59
Teakettle, Gooseneck Spout, Stationary Handle, Brass Stepped Mushroom Finial, 13 In.	118
Teakettle, Gooseneck Spout, Swing Handle, c.1820, 6 Qt., 13 x 10 In.	259
Teakettle, Impressed C. Raborg Pratt Street Baltimore, c.1800, 7 In.	972
Teakettle, Impressed J. Gable, Lancaster, Pa., c.1830, 14 In.	948
Teakettle, Lid, Impressed J. Geddes, Baltimore, 7 In.	1215
Teakettle, Lid, Impressed W. Bailey, c.1800, 6 In.	3081
Teapot, Applied, Brass Sunflowers, Vines, Geo. Robbins & Co., 13 x 13 In.	324
Teapot, Impressed F. Steinman, Lancaster, Pa., c.1805, 6 ½ In.	1778
Tray, Enameled Berries, Leaves Border, Buffalo Arts & Crafts Shop, c.1905	813
Tray, Enameled Green, Red, White Scalloped Edges, Buffalo Art Crafts Shop, c.1905, 11 x 8 In.	938
Tray, Indented Border, Well Center, Rounded, Patina, Gustav Stickley, 6 In.	344
Tray, Octagon Shape, Scrolled Handles, G Monogram, 12 x 15 In.	59
Tray, Oval, Handles, G. Stickley, 23 x 11 In.	375
Tray, Smoking, Hammered, Dall Sheep Horns, Silver Accents, Joseph Heinrich, 8 x 30 In.	5625
Urn, Hot Water, Deer Head Handles, White Porcelain Grip, 17 x 16 In.	180

Vase, Hammered, Gold Plated, Marie Zimmerman, Stamped, 1930s, 9 ¾ x 10 In.............*illus*	1875
Vase, Hammered, Repousse, Keswick School, 2 ½ x 5 In..	750
Vase, Hammered, Signed Marco Martinez, c.1960, 16 In...	375
Vase, Hammered, Vertical Lines, Rounded, Tapered, Kalo, 6 x 5 In..........................	406
Vase, Repousse Poppy Design, 3 Wrought Iron Handles, Arts & Crafts, Eng., c.1900, 7 x 15 In.....	793
Wall Sconce, Repousse Design, Arrow Shape, Arts & Crafts, Scotland, 1900, 5 x 16 ¼ In............	250
Watering Can, Angled Spout, England, 15 In.	51
Wine Cooler, Hammered, Wrought, Handles, c.1910, 12 ½ x 11 ½ In. ....*illus*	1250
Wine Ladle, Curved Bamboo Shape Handle, Gilt, Silver, 1800s, 5 ¾ In.	2370

COPPER LUSTER *items are listed in the Luster category.*

CORALENE glass was made by firing many small colored beads on the outside of glassware. It was made in many patterns in the United States and Europe in the 1880s. Reproductions are made today. Coralene-decorated Japanese pottery is listed in the Japanese Coralene category.

Biscuit Barrel, Apricot Mother-Of-Pearl Glass, Beaded Branches, Silver Plated Lid, 7 x 5 In.......	92
Biscuit Barrel, Cranberry Glass, Beige Net Overlay, Metal Lid, Victorian, 8 ½ x 6 In..............	299
Biscuit Barrel, Metal Lid, Handle, Cranberry, Gold Bead Overlay, Tapered, Victorian, 9 x 7 In.....	300
Cheese Dish, Dome Lid, Gold Flowers & Rim, 8 In. Diam..	295
Figurine, Pheasant, Rock Base, Multicolor, Double Crossed Arrows Mark, c.1890, 16 x 19 In......	183
Vase, Amber, Daisies, Blue, Yellow, Pink, Hourglass Shape, 8 In.	59
Vase, Blue To White Satin Glass, 5 In.	135
Vase, Blue, Gold Wavy Beading, Shouldered, c.1900, 7 In....................................	118
Vase, Pink Satin Glass, Gold Branch Overlay, c.1900, 5 In..................................	89
Vase, Pink To White, Gold Designs, Bulbous, c.1890, 4 ½ In.................................	40

CORKSCREWS have been needed since the first bottle was sealed with a cork, probably in the seventeenth century. Today collectors search for the early, unusual patented examples or the figural corkscrews of recent years.

Barrel Shape, Sterling Silver, Banding, Marked, S. Pemberton, c.1790, 3 ⅝ In...............	625
Bartender Handle, Carved Wood, Paint, Holding Towel & Bottle, 1960s, 8 In.	50
Brass, Whalebone, c.1865, 7 In.	502
Dog Head Handle, Boston Terrier, Wood Composition, 3 ½ In.	95
Dog, Inlaid Eyes, Bone, Carved, 5 ¼ In..	130
Dusting Brush, Bone, Royal Coat Of Arms, English Thomason, 10 In.	875
Fish, Silver, Textured Scales, JBD & S. Birmingham, 1973...................................	170
Flamingo Head Handle, Brass & Carved Wood, 8 In..	185
Grape Clusters, Metal, Carved, c.1930, 4 ½ x 3 In.	150
Hootch Owl, Cast Brass, Eye Hinges, Wings Are Bottle Openers, 2-Sided, 6 In.	1815
Jolly Chappy, Figural, Victorian, Pocket, 5 In.	285
Lady's Leg, Silvered Metal, Celluloid, Germany, 1900s, 2 ⅝ In.........................*illus*	380
Monkey Head Handle, Carved Tropical Nut, Metal Eyes, Red Hat, 4 ¼ In.	36
Stag Head, Bone, Carved, 7 ¾ In..	154
Walrus Tusk, Carved Vine & Flowers, Sterling Cap, 1913, 6 ¼ In............................	675
Wood Handle, Walnut, Chrome, Bar & BBQ Products, Japan, c.1960, 5 ¼ In.....................	8

CORONATION souvenirs have been made since the 1800s. Pottery, glass, tin, silver, and paper objects with a picture of the monarchs and date have been sold at many coronations. The pieces that mention King Edward VIII, the king who was never crowned, are not rare; collectors should be sure to check values before buying. Related pieces are found in the Commemorative category.

Beaker, King George V & Queen Mary, Blue, White, Copeland Spode, 1910, 6 In.	93
Beaker, Saucer, Tsar Alexander III, Glass, Frosted, Entwined Initials AA, c.1883, 3 ½ In............	2500
Biscuit Tin, Queen Elizabeth II, Prince Philip, Portraits, Blue, Gilt Trim, 1953, 5 x 5 x 4 In.	35
Butter Knife, Queen Elizabeth, Profile, Crown, Electroplated, Cook & Clark, 1953, 4 In.	12
Cup & Saucer, King Edward VIII, Portrait, Blue Trim, 1937	55
Cup & Saucer, King George VI, Queen Elizabeth, Portraits, Kensington Pottery, 1937	32
Cup, King George V, Queen Mary, Long May They Reign, Flag, Crown, 1911, 3 In.	70
Dish, Trinket, Queen Elizabeth II, Initials, Crown, Gilt, Crown Staffordshire, 1953, 3 x 2 In........	25
Figurine, Queen Elizabeth II, Regalia, Holding Scepter & Orb, Royal Doulton, 8 In...............	699
Handkerchief, King Edward, Silk, ER VIII & Crown Border, 1937, 12 x 12 In.	40
Invitation Ticket, Tsar Alexander III, Empress Maria Feodorovna, Russia, 1881, 3 ¾ x 7 In.	950
Medal, Nicholas II, Portrait, Inscription, Silver, Purple Ribbon, 1896, 1 ⅛ In.	125
Pin, King George VI & Queen Elizabeth, Portrait, Ribbon, Red, 3 ¾ In.	50

Copeland, Figurine, Rebekah, Holding Amphora, Parian, c.1851, 20 x 7 ½ In. $2,868

Neal Auction Co.

Copeland, Pitcher, Panels, Gilt Lotus, Handle, Majolica, Marked, c.1890, 10 ½ x 8 In. $885

Brunk Auctions

Copper, Chafing Dish, Silver Plate, Rabbit Supports, Joseph Heinrichs, c.1890, 10 x 13 In. $2,375

Rago Arts & Auction Center

TIP

Don't display copper on bare wooden shelves. The wood should be sealed with varnish to avoid allowing the acids in the wood and the acid vapors to attack the copper.

Copper, Chocolate Pot, Hammered, Brass, Horn Handle, Theodore Pond, c.1905, 6 x 9 In.
$8,125

Rago Arts & Auction Center

Copper, Puzzle Box, Turquoise Cabochons, Harry St. John Dixon, c.1920, 2 ¾ x 5 ¾ In.
$6,250

Los Angeles Modern Auctions (LAMA)

Copper, Vase, Hammered, Gold Plated, Marie Zimmerman, Stamped, 1930s, 9 ¾ x 10 In.
$1,875

Rago Arts & Auction Center

Copper, Wine Cooler, Hammered, Wrought, Handles, c.1910, 12 ½ x 11 ½ In.
$1,250

Rago Arts & Auction Center

Plate, King Edward VIII, Portrait, Blue & Gilt Trim, Sutherland China, 1937, 6 x 6 In.	40
Plate, King George VI & Queen Elizabeth, Scalloped, Blue Trim, Handle, 1937, 8 In.	85
Proclamation, Tsar Nicholas II & Empress Alexandra, Chromolitho, Gilt, 15 x 11 In.	1600
Scuttle Cup, King George VI & Queen Elizabeth, Crown, Flags, 1937	124
Tankard, King George VI, Pewter, Hammered, Portrait, 1937, 2 ¾ In.	89
Teapot, Edward VII & Alexandra, Portrait, Rule Brittania, Red, Lid, 1902, 6 In.	195
Tin, King George V, Queen Mary, Portraits, Scenes, Rowntree & Co., 1911, 6 x 3 In.	125

COSMOS is a pressed milk glass pattern with colored flowers made from 1894 to 1915 by the Consolidated Lamp and Glass Company. Tablewares and lamps were made in this pattern. A few pieces were also made of clear glass with painted decorations. Other glass patterns are listed under Consolidated Lamp and also in various glass categories. In later years, Cosmos was also made by the Westmoreland Glass Company.

Butter, Cover, White, Flowers, Pink, Yellow, Blue, Round, 5 ¾ In.	125
Condiment Set, Pink & Yellow Flowers, Salt, Pepper, Mustard, Stand, 7 x 5 ½ In.	118
Pitcher, White, Pink Neck, Daisies, Multicolor, Footed, 9 In.	260
Syrup, White, Multicolor Flowers, Applied Handle, 5 In.	195
Tumbler, White, Netted Ground, Daisies, Pin, Yellow, Blue, 3 ¼ In.	55

COVERLETS were made of linen or wool during the nineteenth century. Most of the coverlets date from 1800 to the 1880s. There was a revival of hand weaving in the 1920s and new coverlets, especially geometric patterns, were made. The earliest coverlets were made on narrow looms, so two woven strips were joined together and a seam can be found. The weave structures of coverlets can include summer and winter, double weave, overshot, and others. Jacquard coverlets have elaborate pictorial patterns that are made on a special loom or with the use of a special attachment. Quilts are listed in this book in their own category.

Double Weave, Capital In Washington 1846, Wool, Cotton, Inscription, 78 x 88 In. ....*illus*	1560
Double Weave, Star & Heart Design, Inscription, Wool, Cotton, 1845, 88 x 83 In..................*illus*	1200
Jacquard, 4 Rose Field, Bird, Rose Bush Borders, Daniel L. Myhers, 1845, 74 x 94 In.	210
Jacquard, Birds, Stars, Flowers, Red, Blue, Cream, Andre Kump, 1839, 88 x 88 In.	234
Jacquard, Black, Red, Blue, Emanuel Ettinger, Aaronsburg, Pa., 1836, 91 x 77 In.	711
Jacquard, Blocked Flower Center, Rose, Bush Borders, Wool, Cotton, Fringe, 1845, 90 x 98 In.	300
Jacquard, Blue & White, c.1850, 84 x 65 In.	207
Jacquard, Blue, Red, Green, Inscribed Louisa Renoll, c.1840, 90 x 77 In.	152
Jacquard, Blue, Red, John Amelton Jackson, Northumberland, Pa., 1838, 98 x 86 In.	119
Jacquard, Blue, Red, John Brosy Manheim, Lancaster, 1835, 84 x 96 In.	237
Jacquard, Double Weave, Red, Green, Blue, Bird Border, J. Witmer, Pa., c.1837, 92 x 82 In.	115
Jacquard, Double Weave, Stars, Red, Blue, Green, John S. Goodman, c.1850, 96 x 84 In.	144
Jacquard, Double Weave, Stylized Flower Field, Borders, c.1860, 76 x 85 In.	215
Jacquard, Eagle, Arrows, Red, White, Blue, c.1840, 77 x 76 In.	182
Jacquard, Floral Wreath, Leaves, Borders, Wool, Cotton, Caroline Helt, 1843, 72 x 90 In.	180
Jacquard, Flowering Urns, Red, White, Signed Sarah, c.1960, 87 x 79 In.	58
Jacquard, Flowers, Bird, Rose Bush, Cotton, Wool, Fringe, 1839, 73 x 90 In.	720
Jacquard, Flowers, Birds, Trees Border, Red, Green, J. Heilbronn, Ohio, 73 x 88 In.	720
Jacquard, Flowers, Blue, Green, Red, Wm. Ney Meyerstown, Lebanon Co., Pa., 83 x 83 In.	210
Jacquard, Flowers, Building Borders, Center Seam, Signed C. Boden, Ohio, 1843	852
Jacquard, Flowers, Leaves, Borders, Wool, Cotton, J. Kaufman, Pa., 1838, 76 x 89 In. ....*illus*	215
Jacquard, Flowers, Leaves, Corner Block Star, 4 Colors, 2 Parts, 82 x 90 In..........................*illus*	142
Jacquard, Flowers, Leaves, Red, Blue, Inscribed, Henry Oberly, Pa., c.1945, 93 x 82 In.	577
Jacquard, Flowers, Stars, Eagle Border, Blue, Green, Red, Martin Hoke, 1835, 100 x 82 In.	540
Jacquard, Grapevine, Eagle & Rose Border, Leaf Corners, Cotton, Wool, 1842, 72 x 87 In.	480
Jacquard, Green, Red, Cream, Navy, E. Miller, Pa., 1847, 95 x 86 In.	178
Jacquard, Memorial Hall, Eagles, Centennial 1876, Red, White, 82 x 84 In.	273
Jacquard, Peacock, Turkey, Blue, Cream, Red, c.1840, 85 x 79 In.	444
Jacquard, Red, Cream, Navy, Inscribed Peter Leisey, Lancaster Co., c.1840, 97 x 74 In.	296
Jacquard, Red, White, Cream, C. Wiand, Allentown, 1844, 88 x 74 In.	154
Jacquard, Rose, Medallion Field, Eagle, Tree Border, Multicolor, A. Kump, 1836, 95 x 91 In.	375
Jacquard, Snowflake, Double-Lily Panels, Rebecca Spengler, Pa., 1845, 84 x 96 In.	374
Jacquard, Stars, Birds, Flowers, Red, Green, Blue, Inscribed R. Wilmer, c.1840, 85 x 92 In.	207
Jacquard, Urn, Pitcher, Blue, White, M.A. Moore, Ohio, c.1845, 84 x 80 In.	1067
Overshot, Fox's Chase, Variant, Red, White, Shenandoah Valley, Vir., c.1850, 73 x 87 In.	184
Woven, Chariot Wheels, Green, Purple, White Ground, c.1870, 93 x 66 In.	29
Woven, Wool, Cotton, Corner Block, C. Wiand, Allentown, 1856, 110 x 98 In........................*illus*	3444

COWAN POTTERY made art pottery and wares for florists. Guy Cowan made pottery in Rocky River, Ohio, a suburb of Cleveland, from 1913 to 1931. A stylized mark with the word *Cowan* was used on most pieces. A commercial, mass-produced line was marked *Lakeware*. Collectors today search for the Art Deco pieces by Guy Cowan, Viktor Schreckengost, Waylande Gregory, or Thelma Frazier Winter.

Ashtray, Ram, Egyptian Blue Glaze, E. Eckhardt, 5 In.	345
Ashtray, Unicorn, Metal Stand, Feu Rouge Glaze, W. Gregory, 5 ½ In.	80
Bookends, Bucking Horse, Egyptian Blue Glaze, Waylande Gregory, 9 In.	570
Bookends, Elephant, Copper Glazed Luster, 5 x 5 ¾ In. ....*illus*	308
Bookends, Pouter Pigeon, October Glaze, G. Cowan, 4 ½ In.	575
Bookends, Pouter Pigeon, Puffed-Out Chest, October Glaze, E. Novotny, c.1929, 4 x 4 In.	420
Bookends, Scottie Dog, Shadow White Glaze, Waylande Gregory, 1931, 8 In. ....*illus*	1298
Bookends, Stylized Elephant, Metallic Bronze Glaze, c.1928, 5 x 3 ⅝ In.	660
Bowl, Flower, Carved Stylized Flowers, Azure, Matrix Glaze, R. Josset, 2 Handles, 4 x 17 In.	156
Bowl, Octagonal, Fir Green Glaze, G. Cowan, 9 ½ x 3 ½ In.	115
Bowl, Pink Luster, Flared Rim, c.1922, 3 x 9 In.	40
Bowl, Pterodactyl Handles, Oval, Footed, Green, October Glaze, A. Blazys, 15 x 6 In.	92
Bowl, Teal, Orange & Tan, Scalloped, Marked, 9 ⅛ x 9 ⅝ In.	95
Bowl, Wave, Antique Green, Caramel Glaze Interior, W. Gregory, 6 In.	81
Box, Lid, Impressed, April Green Glaze, Handles, Martin, 6 x 4 In.	138
Candelabra, Swirl Dancer, 2 Cups, Ivory Glaze, G. Cowan, 9 ¾ x 7 In.	230
Candleholder, Ivory, Octagonal Base, 4 In., Pair	60
Candlestick, Leaf, Cocoa Glaze, W. Gregory, 6 ¼ In., Pair	69
Candlestick, Stepped Scalloped Base, Marigold Luster, c.1924, 3 In., Pair	40
Candlestick, Wildwood Gazelle, Caramel Glaze, W. Gregory, 5 ¾ In., Pair	196
Compote, Curled Wave Base, Scalloped Dish, Oval, Green, Ivory, c.1928, 6 ½ In., Pair	175
Decanter, Figural, King, Crown Stopper, Ivory, Waylande Gregory, 10 In.	750
Dish, Lid, Fruit Finial, Impressed Rim, Egyptian Blue Glaze, Martin, 6 x 5 In.	242
Figurine, Accordion Player, Alexander Blazys, Impressed Mark, 1927, 8 ¼ In. ....*illus*	189
Figurine, Awakening Woman, Ivory Glaze, G. Cowan, 9 In.	460
Figurine, Aztec Man, Rays, Rising Sun, Antique Green Glaze, W. Gregory, c.1929, 13 In.	480
Figurine, Bird, Cardinal, Oriental Red Glaze, Speckled, Walter Sinz, 13 ¾ In.	204
Figurine, Burlesque Dancer, Modernist, Shadow White Glaze, W. Gregory, c.1930, 17 In.	4800
Figurine, Bust, Female, Plaster, Walter A. Sinz, 7 ¾ In. ....*illus*	295
Figurine, Dancer, Spanish, Ivory Glaze, Elizabeth Anderson, 8 ¾ In.	242
Figurine, Mother & Child, Walter A. Sinz, 8 In. ....*illus*	590
Figurine, Navajo Maiden, Kneeling With Pot, Green, Ivory, Luis Mora, c.1930, 9 x 6 In.	510
Figurine, Pierette, Dancer, Tan Glaze, G. Cowan, 8 In.	345
Figurine, Pierette, Ivory Glaze, Impressed Mark, 8 In.	195
Figurine, Russian Peasant Dancer, Arm Over Head, Ivory, A. Blazys, 10 ¾ In.	546
Figurine, Russian Tambourine Player, Seated, Ivory Glaze, A. Blazys, 9 In.	518
Figurine, Spanish Dancer, Man, Woman, Dancing, Glazed, E. Anderson, c.1929, 9 In., Pair	390
Figurine, Stylized Peacock, Egyptian Blue Glaze, Scroll Plumes, Lobed Base, c.1920, 14 In.	276
Figurine, Woman, Bent Winged, Ivory Glaze, G. Cowan, 8 In.	460
Figurine, Woman, Draped, Looking Up, Ivory Gloss Glaze, c.1926, 6 In.	325
Flower Figure, Laurel, Woman Gazing Down, Ivory Glaze, G. Cowan, 9 ⅞ In.	253
Flower Figure, Repose, Woman Leaning Back, Ivory, G. Cowan, 6 ½ In.	138
Flower Frog, Blue, Marked, 1920s, 8 x 3 In.	90
Flower Frog, Diver, Ivory Glaze, G. Cowan, 8 In.	489
Flower Frog, Grace, Bent Woman, Ivory Glaze, G. Cowan, 6 ½ In.	345
Flower Frog, Heavenward, Woman Gazing Up, Ivory Glaze, G. Cowan, 8 In.	230
Flower Frog, Loveliness, Woman, Hand Over Head, Ivory Glaze,	242
Flower Frog, Nude, Female, Kneeling, Looking Up, Ivory Glaze, Walter Sinz, 6 In.	489
Flower Frog, Nude, Female, Standing, Arms On Shoulders, Ivory Glaze, 9 In.	230
Flower Frog, Pan, On Toadstool, Ivory Glaze, W. Gregory, 9 In.	288
Flower Frog, Toad Stool Shape, Cream, c.1925, 4 ¾ x 5 ¼ In.	250
Lamp, Electric, Waylande Gregory, White Queen, Marked, 1930, 8 ⅜ In. ....*illus*	413
Lamp, Lorelei Figure, April Green Glaze, Waylande Gregory, c.1930, 16 ¾ In.	660
Lamp, Stylized Cat, Modernist Style, White, Clear Crackle, W. Gregory, c.1928, 9 ½ In.	660
Match Holder, Seahorse, Ivory Gloss, 3 In.	45
Paperweight, Elephant, Black Matte Glaze, Impressed, Margaret Postgate, 3 ⅝ In.	472
Paperweight, Elephant, Head Down, Black Glaze, M. Postgate, 4 ⅝ In.	316
Plaque, Golf, Stylized Golfer, Clubs, Round, V. Schreckengost, c.1931, 11 ½ In.	510
Plaque, The Hunt, Horse & Rider Jumping Fence, V. Schreckengost, c.1931, 11 ⅜ In.	840

Corkscrew, Lady's Leg, Silvered Metal, Celluloid, Germany, 1900s, 2 ⅝ In.
$380

Coverlet, Double Weave, Capital In Washington 1846, Wool, Cotton, Inscription, 78 x 88 In.
$1,560

Coverlet, Double Weave, Star & Heart Design, Inscription, Wool, Cotton, 1845, 88 x 83 In.
$1,200

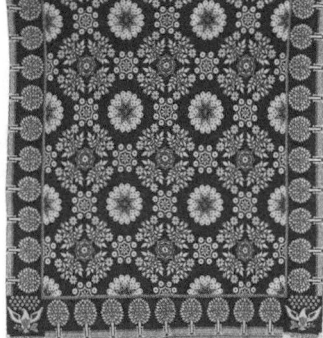

TIP

Textiles need to "breathe." Don't put them in high stacks or hang them in tight groups. Leave room for air to circulate.

Coverlet, Jacquard, Flowers, Leaves, Borders, Wool, Cotton, J. Kaufman, Pa., 1838, 76 x 89 In.
$215

Garth's Auctioneers & Appraisers

Coverlet, Jacquard, Flowers, Leaves, Corner Block Star, 4 Colors, 2 Parts, 82 x 90 In.
$142

Conestoga Auction Co., Inc.

Coverlet, Woven, Wool, Cotton, Corner Block, C. Wiand, Allentown, 1856, 110 x 98 In.
$3,444

Skinner Auctioneers & Appraisers

Plaque, Woman's Head, Gunmetal Glaze, A. Drexler Jacobson, 5 In. ....*illus*	443
Plate, Couple Dancing To Jazz Music, Viktor Schreckengost, 1931, 11 ¼ In. ....*illus*	17110
Plate, Hunting Scene, Viktor Schreckengost, c.1930, 11 In.	1450
Plate, Orange Flower, Black Loop Rim, 11 In.	230
Plate, Sea Design, Blue, Green Mother-Of-Pearl Glaze, T. Frazier, 11 ½ In.	173
Strawberry Jar, Saucer, 5 Openings, Oriental Red, c.1930, 7 ½ In.	195
Vase, Arabian Nights Glaze, Marked, 6 ½ In.	23
Vase, Artichoke, Egyptian Blue Glossy Glaze, Stylized Vines, Flared, Oval, 12 x 8 In.	196
Vase, Bud, Copper Luster, Flared Feet, c.1921, 7 In.	75
Vase, Bud, Paneled, Silver, Black, c.1929, 6 ½ In.	150
Vase, Bud, Seahorse Stem, Footed, Ribbed, April Green, c.1926, 7 ¼ In.	85
Vase, Chalice Shape, Footed Base, Antique Green Glaze, c.1928, 7 In.	95
Vase, Chinese Bird Design, Flared, Pink Glaze, 11 ⅜ In.	219
Vase, Cylindrical, Tan Glaze, Loop Handles, Viktor Schreckengost, 6 In.	175
Vase, Fish, Bubbles, Waves, Blue Over Black Glaze, V. Schreckengost, c.1931, 6 x 2 In.	4000
Vase, Flambe Glaze, Matte & Glossy, Delphinium, Baluster Shape, Lakewood Ware, 13 In.	480
Vase, Flambe Glaze, Plum & April Green, Bulbous, 5 ¼ x 3 ½ In.	120
Vase, Flared Rim, Squat, Blue Green Luster, c.1923, 4 ¾ In.	125
Vase, Flared, Feu Rouge Glaze, G. Cowan, 8 In.	219
Vase, Flowers, Brown Glaze, Clear Crackle, Flared, Thelma Frazier, c.1930, 6 x 7 In.	360
Vase, Globular, Handles, Tan Glaze, Black Glass Base, V. Schreckengost, 6 In.	173
Vase, Green, Yellow Scroll Band, Clear Crackle, Ball Shape, Raised Rim, Curled Handles, 4 In.	360
Vase, Hummingbirds, Daffodil Yellow Glaze, Rectangular, Flattened, 10 In.	84
Vase, Leaf & Berry Band, Egyptian Blue, Bulbous, Paul Bogatay, c.1930, 8 x 5 ½ In.	132
Vase, Lemon Tree, Multicolor, Signed, Thelma Frazier, 1930, 9 ½ x 6 In. ....*illus*	625
Vase, Lemon Trees, Gray Ground, Bulbous, Thelma Frazier, c.1930, 9 ¼ x 4 In.	660
Vase, Logan, Leaf Glaze, Handles, G. Cowan, 8 In.	230
Vase, Maple Leaf Glaze, W. Gregory, 10 ⅝ In.	173
Vase, Modernist, Black, Silver Glaze, Flared, Footed, G. Cowan, 8 In.	460
Vase, Round, Handles, Egyptian Blue Glaze, Black Base, V. Schreckengost, 6 In.	311
Vase, Turquoise Glaze, Maroon Mottled, Marked, c.1929, 7 ¼ In.	121
Vase, Urn Shape, Flared Embossed Rim, Upswept Handles, Blue, Lakeware, c.1930, 5 In.	75

CRACKER JACK, the molasses-flavored popcorn mixture, was first made in 1896 in Chicago, Illinois. A prize was added to each box in 1912. Collectors search for the old boxes, toys, and advertising materials. Many of the toys are unmarked.

Belt Buckle, Enamel On Metal, Jack Saluting, Red, Blue, 2 ½ x 2 ¼ In.	35
Bookmark, Tin, Cocker Spaniel, Cracker Jack, 1930s, 2 ⅝ In.	12
Cup & Saucer, Pot Metal, Painted, Silver, Scroll Pattern, 1920s	10
Pendant, Indian Chief, Celluloid, Painted, 1930s, 1 In.	23
Postcard, Bears, No. 13, Box Flying Over Building, c.1909	32
Stock Certificate, 1940	45
Toy, Baseball Player, Throwing Ball, Pot Metal, Collar Stud, 1920s, ⅞ In.	35
Toy, Encyclopedia Of Birds, Volume 1, 1970s	10 to 13
Toy, Encyclopedia Of Insects, Volume 9, 1970s	6 to 7
Toy, Encyclopedia Of Musical Instruments, Volume 11, 1970s	7
Toy, Penguin, Black, White, Celluloid, c.1925	15
Toy, Pitcher, Metal, Celluloid Insert, c.1910, 1 In.	35
Toy, Table, Pot Metal, Gold Finish, Checkerboard Top, Pedestal, 1920s, ½ In.	28
Toy, Top, Wood, Metal, Always On Top, White Blue, 1 ½ In.	50

CRANBERRY GLASS is an almost transparent yellow-red glass. It resembles the color of cranberry juice. The glass has been made in Europe and America since the Civil War. It is still being made, and reproductions can fool the unwary. Related glass items may be listed in other categories, such as Rubina Verde.

Bowl, Hobnail, c.1880, 8 ¾ In.	93
Centerpiece, Gilt, Leaf Handle, Bowl, Tripartite Base, Putti, 16 ¼ In.	2000
Epergne, 4 Vases, Crimped, Ruffled, c.1890, 20 x 9 In.	431
Epergne, Opalescent Trim, Scalloped, Applied Rigaree, 3 Levels, 7 Conical Cups, 21 x 11 In.	1243
Jar, Apothecary, Inverted Thumbprint, Lid, Late 19th Century, 11 x 5 ¼ In., Pair............	300
Light, Hanging, Round Metal Mount, 3 Chains, c.1850, 32 x 9 In.	138
Pitcher, Threaded, Clear Handle, Victorian, 8 ¾ x 6 ¾ In.	52
Pitcher, Vaseline Hobnail, Yellow To Red, 8 ½ x 7 In.	124

Powder Box, Lid, White Flowers, Vines, Enameled, Gilt Metal Rim, Victorian, 3 x 5 In.	127
Punch Bowl, Barrel Shape, Reeded Bands, Gilt, Dome Lid, 1800s, 14 x 9 In.	1315
Salt, Double, Brass Sand, Filigree Holders, Handle, c.1910, 5 x 5 ¾ In.	127
Sugar Shaker, White Opalescent Lattice, Vertical Ribs, Metal Lid, 4 ¾ In.	243
Tantalus Set, Baluster, Fluted, 4 Decanters, Stoppers & Cordials, 12 Piece	600
Tumble-Up, Cane Pattern, Cut To Clear, 7 In.	767
Vase, Bud, Cornucopia Shape, Bronze Hand Holder, Marble Base, 8 In., Pair	106
Vase, Pink Clover, Leaves, Gold Rim, Cylindrical, 15 x 4 In., Pair	283

CREAMWARE, or queensware, was developed by Josiah Wedgwood about 1765. It is a cream-colored earthenware that has been copied by many factories. Similar wares may be listed under Pearlware and Wedgwood.

Basket, Pierced, Oval, Handles, England, c.1810, 4 ⅞ In.	138
Creamer, Barrel Shape, American Ship, Flag, Coastal Town, c.1815, 10 ½ In.	7800
Jug, 3 Nozzle Collar, Pierced Neck Row, Staffordshire, c.1790, 7 In.	258
Jug, John Adams, Ship, American Eagle, Black Transfer, Paint, 10 ¾ In.	3360
Jug, Perry, Pike, Black Transfer Printed, Purple Luster Banded, c.1820, 7 In.	240
Jug, Putting Off, American Ships, Eagle, Black Transfer, c.1800, 11 In.	1680
Jug, Ship Orphelia, Black Transfer Print, England, c.1790, 9 In.	780
Jug, Soldier, Horse, Canopy, Landscape, Cross, Black Transfer, c.1800, 5 In.	480
Jug, Thomas Jefferson, American Eagle, Gilt, Black Transfer, c.1809, 12 ½ In.	4500
Jug, Transfer Design, Brig, Bust Of Washington, States, c.1815, 10 In.	840
Jug, Washington Map, Ship, Eagle, Black Transfer, Paint, Staffordshire, c.1805, 8 In.	4080
Jug, Washington's Apotheosis, American Ship, Eagle, Gilt, Black Transfer, c.1810, 11 In.	3120
Jug, Wasp Boarding Frolic, Black Transfer, Purple Luster Band, Staffordshire, c.1818, 5 ⅝ In.	2040
Mug, Enameled Chinoiserie, Painted, Red, Green, Yellow, Scholar & Student, c.1785, 4 ½ In.	540
Mug, George Washington, Flowers, 5 In.	1438
Plaque, George Washington, Black, White Transfer, Oval Frame, 4 ⅞ x 4 In.	1320
Plaque, Relief Molded, Winged Mask, Bacchanalian Procession, Putti, Cart, c.1800, 5 ¼ In.	240
Plate, Green, Ocher Sponged, 8-Sided, England, c.1770, 8 ½ In.	431
Plate, Reticulated Rim, Molded Minerva Heads, c.1800, 10 In.	240
Platter, Admiral Horatio Lord Nelson, Liverpool, Herculaneum Pottery, c.1805, 13 In.	600
Sardine Box, Lid, Underplate, Branches, Blue Rim, Powell & Bishop, c.1880, 4 x 9 In.	104
Sauceboat, Reticulated Lids, Flower Knob, Ladle, Urns, Flowers, c.1800, 7 In., Pair	480
Teapot, Basket, Grapes, Vines, S-Spout, Loop Handle, c.1770, 4 ¾ In.	4484
Teapot, Staffordshire, Tortoiseshell Glaze, Spherical, Crabstock Handle, c.1765, 4 In.	270
Toby Jug, Sharp Faced, Staffordshire, Brown Hair, Tricorn, Buckled Shoes, c.1790, 10 ½ In.	2040

CREIL, France, had a faience factory as early as 1794. The company merged with a factory in Montereau in 1819. It made stoneware, mocha ware, and soft paste porcelain. The name *Creil* appears as part of the mark on many pieces. The Creil factory closed in 1895.

Jug, French Character, Hands On Belly, Toothy Grin, Blue, Montereau, 1800s, 7 ½ In.	145
Plate, Harvester, Scythe, Couple, Haystack, Green, White Diamond Border, c.1880, 8 In.	120
Plate, No. 3 Escune, 2 Fencers, Onlookers, Blue Leaf Border, Les Sport, 6 ⅝ In.	65
Plate, No. 10, Automobile, Women In Car, 2 Men, Blue Leaf Border, Les Sport, 6 ⅝ In.	45

CROWN DERBY is the name given to porcelain made in Derby, England, from the 1770s to 1935. Andrew Planche and William Duesbury established Crown Derby as the first china-making factory in Derby. Pieces are marked with a crown and the letter *D* or the word *Derby*. The earliest pieces were made by the original Derby factory, while later pieces were made by the King Street Partnerships (1848–1935) or the Derby Crown Porcelain Co. (1876–90). Derby Crown Porcelain Co. became Royal Crown Derby Co. Ltd. in 1890. It is now part of Royal Doulton Tableware Ltd.

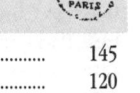

Bowl, Footed, Imari, 10 ½ x 3 ¼ In.	195
Candlestick, Red Aves, Gold Detail, 11 In., Pair	1200
Compote, Gold Aves, Raised Dolphins, Gilt, Bronzed Pedestal, 5 ½ x 10 ½ In.	950
Cup & Saucer, Chatsworth, Flowers, White Ground, Gilt Edges	35
Cup & Saucer, Imari, Gold Trim, 6 x 2 ¾ In.	60
Dinner Set, Red Aves, Cup & Saucer, Plate, 4 ½ & 6 ¼ & 10 ½ In., 12 Piece	218
Dresser Jar, Lid, Blue, Iron Red, Gold, Scalloped Edge, Shaped Knop, 2 ¾ x 4 In.	20
Pin Dish, Imari, 1975, 4 ⅛ In.	50
Plate, Serving, Pink Peonies, Purple, Pink Iris, Narcissus, Gold Trim, Shell Shape	150
Vase, Raised Roses, Scrolls, Red, Lobed Melon Shape, Pedestal Foot, c.1909, 9 ½ In.	998

Cowan, Bookends, Elephant, Copper Glazed Luster, 5 x 5 ¾ In.
$308

Cowan's Auctions

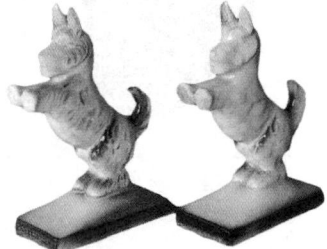

Cowan, Bookends, Scottie Dog, Shadow White Glaze, Waylande Gregory, 1931, 8 In.
$1,298

Rachel Davis Fine Arts

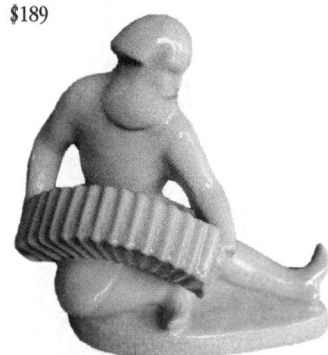

Cowan, Figurine, Accordion Player, Alexander Blazys, Impressed Mark, 1927, 8 ¼ In.
$189

Rachel Davis Fine Arts

Cowan, Figurine, Bust, Female, Plaster, Walter A. Sinz, 7 ¾ In.
$295

Rachel Davis Fine Arts

Cowan, Figurine, Mother & Child, Walter A. Sinz, 8 In.
$590

Rachel Davis Fine Arts

Cowan, Lamp, Electric, Waylande Gregory, White Queen, Marked, 1930, 8 ⅜ In.
$413

Rachel Davis Fine Arts

Cowan, Plaque, Woman's Head, Gun Metal Glaze, A. Drexler Jacobson, 5 In.
$443

Rachel Davis Fine Arts

CROWN DUCAL is the name used on some pieces of porcelain made by A.G. Richardson and Co., Ltd., of Tunstall and Cobridge, England. The name has been used since 1916. Crown Ducal is a well-known maker of chintz pattern dishes. The company was bought by Wedgwood in 1974.

Berry Strainer, Footed, Underplate, Yellow, Orange Border, Flowers, Scalloped, 9 In.	68
Bowl, Carnation, White Ground, Multicolor, Charlotte Rhead, 10 In.	98
Bowl, Center, Chintz, Bird Of Paradise, Footed, Blue, c.1930, 9 x 5 In.	249
Bowl, Rounded Shell Shape, Ridged, Roses, 8 x 9 x 4 In.	57
Dish, Clover Shape, 3 Sections, Flowers, Blue Rim, Hole Handle, 8 In.	59
Plate, Birthplace Of Washington, Flower Border, Mulberry, Square, 8 In.	40
Plate, Colonial Times, Purple Transfer, Scalloped Rim, c.1960, 10 ½ In., 12 Piece	88
Plate, Landing Of Pilgrims, 10 In.	22
Plate, Men In Pub, Gold Trim, 8 In.	30
Plate, Purple, Octagonal, Yellow Border, c.1935, 8 ½ In.	80
Plate, Scenes Of Old New Orleans, Mulberry, 10 In.	36
Plate, Tulips, Wildflowers, Square, 8 ¼ In.	45
Vase, Bird Of Paradise, Butterfly, Bulbous, Yellow Ground, 5 ¼ In.	48
Vase, Birds, Flowers, Grapes, Butterflies, Shouldered, 5 ¾ In.	119
Vase, Flowers, Black Ground, Cylindrical, Orange Interior, 6 In.	46
Vase, Hydrangea, Red, Purple, Green, Charlotte Rhead, 6 In.	138
Vase, Persian, Blue, Green, Orange, Yellow, Charlotte Rhead, 9 In.	148
Vase, Tudor Rose, Charlotte Rhead, 6 ¼ In.	167

CROWN MILANO glass was made by the Mt. Washington Glass Works about 1890. It was a plain biscuit color with a satin finish decorated with flowers and often had large gold scrolls. Not all pieces are marked.

Berry Bowl Set, Flowers, Gold Highlights, Pairpoint Silver Plated Stand, 20 In. ....*illus*	3738
Biscuit Jar, Cream, Gold Scrolls, Embossed Metal Lid, Handle, 6 ½ x 5 ½ In.	173
Bride's Bowl, Painted Flowers, Mauve Ground, Rectangular Cut Top, 9 In.	173
Creamer, Flowers, Applied Handle, Marked, c.1875, 3 ⅞ In.	312
Cruet, Opal, Orange Flowers, Gilt Leaves, Stopper, 7 In. ....*illus*	1150
Cup & Saucer, Violet Sprays, Gilt Trim, 2 ¼ x 3 In.	403
Dish, Sweetmeat, Melon Ribbed, White, Cream Panels, Flowers, Lattice, Silver Plated Lid, Bail, 4 In.	413
Ewer, Lid, Shadow Eagle, Jeweled Flower Clusters, Berries, 17 ½ In. ....*illus*	16100
Jar, Lid, Spider Web, 7 In.	4658
Jug, Thistle, Opal, Wide Mouth, Applied Handle, 12 In.	1840
Lamp, Bulbous, Stick, Mottled Orange, Gilt Flowers, 15 In.	480
Rose Bowl, Queens's Pattern, Stylized Flowers, 4 ⅝ In.	460
Sugar & Creamer, Floral Swags, Silver Plate, 3 & 4 In.	230
Syrup, Enameled Flowers, Silver Mounts, 4 ½ In.	232
Vase, 4 Cartouches, Flowers, Cherub On Dragon, Sun, Scrollwork, Bulbous, 6 x 6 In.	513
Vase, Cut, Carved Top, Snow Geese, Gold Scrolling, Thorn Handles, Signed, 15 ½ In.	403
Vase, Ducks, Flying, Swirled, Signed, 7 ½ In. ....*illus*	2070
Vase, Opal Body, Enameled Flowers, Gold Scrolling, Bird Mouth Top, 13 ¼ In.	1150
Vase, Quadrafold Rim, Gold, Green Fern, Globe Shape, 5 In.	230
Vase, Spider Web Gold Iris, Multicolor, Cutouts, c.1894, 15 In.	1495
Vase, Stick, English Ivy, Fall Colors, Gold Outlines, 7 ⅜ In. ....*illus*	201
Vase, Stylized Flowers, Scroll, 11 ½ In. ....*illus*	1035
Vase, Thistles, Raised Gilt, Spider Webs, Ruffled Edge, Marked, c.1885, 14 In. ....*illus*	2091

CROWN TUSCAN *pattern is included in the Cambridge glass category.*

CRUETS of glass or porcelain were made to hold vinegar, oil, and other condiments. They were especially popular during Victorian times and have been made in a variety of styles since the eighteenth century. Additional cruets may be found in the Castor Set category and also in various glass categories.

American Pattern, Fostoria, c.1940, 6 In.	45
Bull's-Eye & Daisy, Polished Pontil, U.S. Glass, c.1909, 6 In.	18
Cameo, Flowers, Chantilly Pattern, Footed, Cambridge Glass, 1940s, 7 In.	195
Coral Pink, Fortune Symbols, Elongated Spout, Chinese, 1970s, 4 ¾ In.	32
Cut Glass, Diamond Pattern, Notched Applied Handle, Faceted Stopper, 8 In.	95
Cut Glass, Starburst, Cross Hatching, Scalloped Spout, 6 In.	36
Feather Pattern, Pontil, McKee Brothers, c.1896, 5 ½ In.	45
Flute Pattern, Pressed Glass, Shouldered, 6 ½ In.	18

C

Glass, Silver Lid, Frame, Handle, 4 Bottles, Emes & Barnard, London, c.1818, 8 x 6 In.	384
Green, Hollow Stopper, Bulbous, Trefoil Rim, Applied Handle, Pontil, 6 In.	35
Inverted Thumbprint, Amberina, Faceted Stopper, Applied Handle, 4 ¼ In.	290
Milk Glass, Grape Pattern, Paneled, Relief, 4 ¾ In.	28
Opal Cut To Cranberry, Flowers, Crisscross Panels, 7 In.	546
Pink Slag Glass, Inverted Fan & Feather, Dugan, 7 In.	403
Purple, Bulbous, Flower Scrolling, 8 ½ In.	201
Swirl Center, Inverted Goblet Body, Ribbed Neck, Tricorn Spout, Crisscross Band, 1950s, 7 In.	35
Yellow, Etched Flowers, Rope Twist Handle, 7 In.	144

CT GERMANY was first part of a mark used by a company in Altwasser, Germany (now part of Walbrzych, Poland), in 1845. The initials stand for C. Tielsch, a partner in the firm. The Hutschenreuther firm took over the company in 1918 and continued to use the *CT*.

C.T.

Bowl, Blossoms, Crimson, Pink, Yellow, Reticulated Border, c.1900, 12 In. Diam.	80
Bowl, Centerpiece, Roses, Blue & Green Leaves, Pierced Handles, c.1900, 13 x 8 In.	125
Bowl, Peach Blossoms, Maroon Border, Scalloped, c.1900, 14 x 6 ¼ In.	90
Cup & Saucer, Yellow Roses, Leaves, Gilt Rim, Marked, c.1900	75
Dish, Contoured, Curved Handle, Pink & White Flowers, c.1910, 8 x 10 x 2 In.	55
Trivet, Pink Blossom Border, Ivory Ground, 1890s, 5 ¾ In.	45

CUP PLATES are small glass or china plates that held the cup while a diner of the mid-nineteenth century drank coffee or tea from the saucer. The most famous cup plates were made of glass at the Boston and Sandwich factory located in Sandwich, Massachusetts. There have been many new glass cup plates made in recent years for sale to gift shops or collectors of limited editions. These are similar to the old plates but can be recognized as new.

Clear, 4 Central Hearts, Scalloped Edge, 3 ¼ In.	15
Clear, Eagle, Scalloped, 3 ⅛ In.	27
Clear, Maid Of The Mist, 3 ⁷⁄₁₆ In.	38
Clear, Rope Scalloped Rim, Scalloped, 3 ⅝ In.	65
Glass, Purple, Flower, Embossed, Scalloped, 3 ⅝ In.	30
Pearlware, Flowers, Vases, Blue Staffordshire, c.1830, 3 ¾ In.	165
Pearlware, Multicolor, Flowers, Prattware, c.1815, 4 In.	250
Pearlware, Roses, Leaves, Medium Blue, c.1825, 4 In.	225
Porcelain, Black Transfer, Wild Animals, William Hackwood, c.1835, 5 In.	115
Porcelain, English Luster, Girl Holding Basket, Garden, c.1820, 3 ¾ In.	95
Porcelain, Figures In Boat, Staffordshire, Podmore, Walker & Co., 1875, 4 In.	100
Porcelain, Luster, Girl, Sitting, Holding Basket, c.1820, 3 ¾ In.	95

CURRIER & IVES made the famous American lithographs marked with their name from 1857 to 1907. The mark used on the print included the street address in New York City, and it is possible to date the year of the original issue from this information. Earlier prints were made by N. Currier and use that name from 1835 to 1847. Many reprints of the Currier or Currier & Ives prints have been made. Some collectors buy the insurance calendars that were based on the old prints. The words *large, small,* or *medium folio* refer to size. The original print sizes were very small (up to about 7 x 9 in.), small (8.8 x 12.8 in.), medium (9 x 14 in. to 14 x 20 in.), large (larger than 14 x 20 in.). Other sizes are probably later copies. Other prints by Currier & Ives may be listed in the Card category under Advertising and in the Sheet Music category. Currier & Ives dinnerware patterns may be found in the Adams or Dinnerware categories.

Ambuscade, Frame, Medium Folio	960
American Country Life, Pleasures Of Winter, Frame, 1855, Large Folio	960
American Express Train, Frame, 1864, 17 ¼ x 27 In. *illus*	2706
American Farm Scenes, No. 1 Spring, Frame, 1853, Large Folio	1020
American Field Sports, A Chance For Both Barrels, Frame, 1857, Large Folio	2040
American Fireman, Always Ready, Frame, 1858, Medium Folio	780
American Fireman, Prompt To The Rescue, Frame, 1858, Medium Folio	1080
American Forest Scene, 1856, Large Folio	1080
American Hunting Scenes, An Early Start, Men On Shore, Canoe, Frame, 29 x 35 In.	3997
Camping Out, Some Of The Right Sort, Frame, 1856, Large Folio	1800
City Of Boston, Mahogany Frame, 1873, 33 ½ x 45 ½ In. *illus*	6518
Cod Fishing Off Newfoundland, Frame, 1872, Small Folio	1080
Declaration Committee, Frame, 1876, Small Folio	1560
Express Train, Frame, Small Folio	1920
Farm-Yard In Winter, Frame, 1861, Large Folio	3120
Floating Down To Market, 1870, Small Folio	780

Cowan, Plate, Couple Dancing To Jazz Music, Viktor Schreckengost, 1931, 11 ¼ In.
$17,110

Humler & Nolan

Cowan, Vase, Lemon Tree, Multicolor, Signed, Thelma Frazier, 1930, 9 ½ x 6 In.
$625

Rago Arts & Auction Center

Crown Milano, Berry Bowl Set, Flowers, Gold Highlights, Pairpoint Silver Plated Stand, 20 In.
$3,738

Early Auction Co.

Crown Milano, Cruet, Opal, Orange Flowers, Gilt Leaves, Stopper, 7 In. $1,150

Early Auction Co.

Crown Milano, Ewer, Lid, Shadow Eagle, Jeweled Flower Clusters, Berries, 17 ½ In. $16,100

Early Auction Co.

Crown Milano, Vase, Ducks, Flying, Swirled, Signed, 7 ½ In. $2,070

Early Auction Co.

Futurity Race At Sheepshead, Frame, 1889, Large Folio	720
Good Chance, Fishing In Canoe, Frame, 29 x 35 In.	3075
Got The Drop On Him & Tumbled To It, 1881, Small Folio	1440
Great Fire At St. John, N.B., June 20th 1877, Small Folio	510
Hudson From West Point, Grounds Of U.S. Military Academy, 1862, Frame, Medium Folio	1800
Hudson Highlands, Near Newberg, Frame, 1853, Small Folio	270
Hung Up With The Starch Out, Frame, 1878, Small Folio	450
Judge Fullerton, Color Lithograph, c.1900, 16 ½ x 24 In.	215
Life Of A Fireman, The Race, Jump Her Boys, Jump Her, Frame, 1854, Large Folio	1200
Midnight Race On The Mississippi, Frame, 1860, Large Folio	6240
Narrows, New York Bay, Frame, Small Folio	360
Night Express, The Start, Frame, Small Folio	5280
Old Plantation Home, 1872, Small Folio	600
Prairie Fires Of The Great West, Steam Locomotive, Lithograph, Frame, 16 ½ x 19 ½ In.	840
Rabbit Catching, The Trap Sprung, Frame, c.1845, Small Folio	780
Road, Winter, Frame, 1853, Large Folio	24000
Robinson Crusoe & His Pets, 1874, Small Folio	570
Sinking Of The Cumberland, Frame, 1800s, 17 x 21 In.	60
Sleigh Race, Frame, 1859, Small Folio	5280
Some Of The Right Sort, Camping Out, Frame, 25 x 33 In.	1020
Sperm Whale In A Flurry, Frame, 1852, Small Folio	960
Time Is Precious, Hand Colored, Frame, 1872, Small Folio	240
Trotting Cracks At Home, Frame, 1868, Large Folio	2760
View Of New York From Brooklyn Heights, Frame, 1849, Medium Folio	30
View Of The Park Fountain & City Hall, Frame, 1846, Small Folio	330
View On The Potomac, Near Harper's Ferry, Frame, 1866, Large Folio	1560
Welcome, Frame, 1873, Small Folio	390
Whale Fishery, Attacking A Right Whale, Frame, Small Folio	1140
Winter Morning, Feeding The Chickens, Frame, 1863, Large Folio	2520
Young Blood In An Old Body, Frame, 1874, Small Folio	480

CUSTARD GLASS is a slightly yellow opaque glass. It was made in England in the 1880s and was first made in the United States in the 1890s. It has been reproduced. Additional pieces may be found in the Cambridge, Fenton, and Heisey categories. Custard glass is called *Ivorina Verde* by Heisey and other companies.

Bead Swag, Pickle Dish, Rectangular	17
Bowl, Roses, Piecrust Edge, 7 ¾ x 4 ¼ In.	114
Bowl, Scalloped Edge, Pink & Red Roses, 8 In.	108
Compote, Daisies, Flat Rim, Gilt, 8 In.	169
Everglades, Cruet, Northwood, 1902, 7 In.	767
Finger Lamp, Oil, Paneled, c.1890, 14 In.	235
Geneva, Salt & Pepper, Flower Garland, Metal Lid	46
Georgia Gem, Celery Vase, Flowers, Footed	58
Georgia Gem, Spooner, Green, Gilt Trim, Footed	12
Grape, Berry Bowl, Master, Tan, White, Footed, Deeply Scalloped Rim	17
Harvard, Toothpick Holder, Souvenir, Markesan, Wis., Green	50
Lamp Shade, Bleeding Heart Design, Bell Shape, Green, 3 ¼ In., 4 Piece	50
Lamp, Finger, Kerosene, Yellow, Queen Anne, Burner, c.1890, 14 In.	235
Little Gem, see Georgia Gem pattern in this category.	
Maize is its own category in this book.	
Toothpick Holder, Sawtooth Rim, Beaded Panels, Souvenir, Russell, N.Y., 2 In.	40
Trailing Vine, Spooner, Scalloped, Flared Rim	12
Wildflowers, Biscuit Jar, Gold To White, Silver Plated Lid	250
Winged Scroll, Bowl, Whimsy, Gilt Scalloped Rim, 5 In.	12
Winged Scroll, Butter, Dome Cover, Flowers	29

CUT GLASS has been made since ancient times, but the large majority of the pieces now for sale date from the American Brilliant period of glass design, 1875 to 1915. These pieces have elaborate geometric designs with a deep miter cut. Modern cut glass with a similar appearance is being made in England, Ireland, Poland, and the Czech and Slovak republics. Chips and scratches are often difficult to notice but lower the value dramatically. A signature on the glass adds significantly to the value. Other cut glass pieces are listed under factory names, like Hawkes, Libbey, and Sinclaire.

Banana Boat, Modified Flash Hobstar, Hobstar, Strawberry Diamond, Block & Fan, 4 x 10 In.	150
Basket, Florence Star, Hobstar Base, Meriden, 10 x 8 In.	275

Basket, Hobstar, Nailhead & Strawberry Diamond, Notched Fan, Handle, 8 x 8 In.	125
Basket, Hobstar, Strawberry Diamond & Fan, Oval, Embossed Silver Rim, 2 ½ x 6 In.	150
Berry Bowl, Hobstars, Palmettes, Notched, Hoare, 4 x 8 In.	123
Bowl, 5-Point Star Center, Hobstar, Cane, Vesica, Wreath, Anderson, 2 x 8 In.	148
Bowl, Branch & Leaf, Engraved, Sinclaire, 8 ¾ In.	50
Bowl, Carolyn, Signed J. Hoare, 2 x 8 ½ In.	150
Bowl, Cluster Brilliant, Sawtooth Scalloped Rim, Egginton, c.1920, 4 x 9 In.	219
Bowl, Finger, Underplate, Russian, Star Cut Buttons, Signed Hawkes	40
Bowl, Fruit, 3 Medallions, Stars, Double Line Lattice, Notched, Brilliant Period, 3 x 10 In.	174
Bowl, Harvard Cut, 4 x 9 In.	30
Bowl, Hobstar, Nailhead Diamond, Prism, 8-Sided, 3 ¾ x 11 ¾ In.	125
Bowl, Hobstar, Star & Fan, Sterling Silver Rim, 3 ½ x 8 ¼ In.	100
Bowl, Hobstar, Strawberry Diamond, Interlocking Vesica, 4 x 11 In.	500
Bowl, Hobstar, Vesica, Nailhead Diamond, Beaded, 4 ¼ x 9 In.	125
Bowl, Imperial, Straus, 5 x 11 ¼ In.	350
Bowl, Lyndale, Blackmer, 2 x 8 In.	50
Bowl, Newport, Signed J. Hoare, 3 ½ x 8 In.	75
Bowl, Royal, Hobstar & Lattice Center, 4 x 8 ¾ In.	25
Bowl, Royal, Hunt, 8-Sided, 3 ½ x 9 In.	148
Bowl, Russian Center, 8-Framed Hobstar Border, 3 ¾ x 8 In.	250
Bowl, Salad, Underplate, Russian, Star Cut Buttons, Oval, 4 ½ x 12 ½ In.	300
Bowl, Sherwood, Unger Brothers, 3 ½ x 8 ¾ In.	150
Bowl, Signed J. Hoare, 7 In.	90
Bowl, Square Blocks, Cane, Strawberry Diamond, Lattice, 5 x 10 In.	50
Bowl, Starburst & Geometric Design, c.1900, 4 x 10 In.	418
Bowl, Starburst & Geometric Design, Scalloped Sawtooth Rim, 9 In. Diam.	149
Bowl, Thistle Design, Silver Collar, c.1915, 5 x 12 In.	944
Bowl, Wavy Sawtooth Rim, Etched, c.1900, 9 In. Diam.	180
Box, Lid, Hobstar, Strawberry Diamond, Nail Head Diamond, 4 ¾ x 5 ½ In.	200
Butter, Cover, Hobstar, Nailhead Vesica, Prism & Fan, Clear Blank, 7 ½ x 9 In.	250
Butter, Cover, Monarch, J. Hoare, 7 x 9 In.	236
Candleholder, Crystal, Suspended Prisms, Footed, 7 ¼ In.	368
Carafe Set, 6 Tumblers, Monarch, J. Hoare, 8 In.	250
Carafe, Hobstar, Flashed Hobstar, Strawberry Diamond Band Neck, 7 In.	60
Celery Dish, Hiawatha, Sinclaire, Hobstars, Prism Cutting, Folded, 11 ¾ In.	83
Celery Dish, Hobstar, Strawberry Diamond & Fan, Leaf Shape, Dorflinger, 16 In.	350
Celery Dish, Persian Pattern, Canoe Shape, Fry, 11 ½ In.	125
Celery Vase, Fan & Diamond, Flared, Turned Foot, 19th Century, 8 x 5 ⅜ In.	246
Celery Vase, Florence Star, Hobstar Foot, Meriden, 9 ½ In.	750
Celery Vase, Horn Of Plenty, Cut Diaper Design, 1800s, 9 ¼ In.	2196
Centerpiece, Inverted Pear Shape, Square Base, 10 ½ x 10 ½ In.	240
Centerpiece, Pedestal, Hobstar, Crosscut Diamond & Fan, Facet Cut Stem, 9 ¾ x 10 In.	177
Cologne Bottle, Emerald Green Cut To Clear, Swirled Pillar, 6 In.	350
Cologne Bottle, Engraved Wild Rose, Engraved Sterling Stopper, 5 In.	200
Cologne Bottle, Rock Crystal, Engraved Flowers, Pattern Cut Stopper, 6 ½ In.	25
Compote, 6 Stars, Fine Cut Panel Dividers, Air Bubble Stem, Notched, Sunburst Base, 9 In.	58
Compote, 8 Panels, Stars, Crosscut Stars, Sunburst, Flared, Scalloped Foot, 9 x 9 In.	290
Compote, Drape, Straus, 8 x 9 In.	150
Compote, Fan & Diamond, Star Cut Foot, 19th Century, 6 ⅛ In.	369
Compote, Footed, Square Base, Boat Shape, Basket Weave, 8 x 12 In.	108
Compote, Hobstar, Vesica, Cane & Star, Notched Teardrop Stem, Scalloped Foot, 12 In.	100
Compote, Notched Rim, Palmettes, Punty, Scallops, Star Cut Base, 10 ½ In. Diam.	360
Compote, Spread Foot, Wide Scalloped Rim, c.1900, 8 In. Diam.	72
Cordial, Pattern No. 17, Elmira, Double Teardrop Stem, Hobstar, 3 ½ In.	125
Cordial, Rock Crystal, Engraved Flowers, Rococo Cut Base, 4 In.	25
Cordial, Rock Crystal, Engraved, Flowers, Cut Stem, Base, Signed Hawkes, 3 ¾ In.	70
Decanter, 5 Hobstars, Cane Band, Fan Highlights, Stopper, Handle, 13 In.	550
Decanter, Faceted, Diaper Design, Footed, Hollow Blown Stopper, 1800s, 11 ¼ In.	777
Decanter, Hobstar, Strawberry Diamond & Fan, 11 In.	200
Decanter, Sterling Grape Shape Mount, Tear Shape Stopper, c.1900, 11 In., 6 Piece	500
Dish, Hobstars, Russian Panels, Notched Scalloped Rim, J. Hoare & Co., 9 ½ In.	184
Dish, Ice Cream, Russian, Star Cut Buttons, 6 In.	250
Dish, Strawberry Diamond, Geometric, 4 ½ x 5 In.	40
Dish, Sweetmeat, Fan Edge, Stars, Silver Dolphins, Continental, 1800s, 5 x 6 In., Pair *illus*	850
Dresser Jar, Whirling Hobstars, Fine Cut, Star & Sunburst Panels, Sunburst Lid, 4 In.	46

Crown Milano, Vase, Stick, English Ivy, Fall Colors, Gold Outlines, 7 ⅜ In.
$201

Humler & Nolan

Crown Milano, Vase, Stylized Flowers, Scroll, 11 ½ In.
$1,035

Early Auction Co.

Crown Milano, Vase, Thistles, Raised Gilt, Spider Webs, Ruffled Edge, Marked, c.1885, 14 In.
$2,091

New Orleans Auction Galleries, Inc.

Currier & Ives, American Express Train, Frame, 1864, 17 ¼ x 27 In. $2,706

Neal Auction Co.

Currier & Ives, City Of Boston, Mahogany Frame, 1873, 33 ½ x 45 ½ In. $6,518

James D. Julia Auctioneers

Cut Glass, Dish, Sweetmeat, Fan Edge, Stars, Silver Dolphins, Continental, 1800s, 5 x 6 In., Pair $850

James D. Julia Auctioneers

Cut Glass, Pitcher, Lemonade, Sterling Silver Cap, Wayne Silver Co., 12 In. $522

New Orleans Auction Galleries, Inc.

Flower Center, Harvard, Step Cut Neck, Hobstar Base, 8 ½ x 10 In.	450
Flower Center, Richmond, Step Cut Neck, Hobstar Base, Straus, 6 x 8 In.	270
Fork & Spoon, Hobstar, Geometric Star, Silver Collars, 12 In., Pair	100
Girandole, 5-Light, George III, Urn, Scroll Arms, Beads, Pendants, c.1800, 22 In., Pair	1952
Goblet, Wine, Bright Yellow Cut To Clear, Strawberry Diamond, Button & Fan, 5 In., 4 Piece	550
Goblet, Wine, Cranberry Cut To Clear, Engraved Floral Swirl, Pattern Cut Base, 5 ¼ In.	502
Goblet, Wine, Cranberry To Clear, Hob Button, Long Thumbprint, 5 In., 4 Piece	250
Goblet, Wine, Green Cut To Clear, Diamond Cut Stem, 4 ¾ In.	450
Ice Cream Tray, Hobstar, Cane, Strawberry Diamond, Star & Fan, 17 x 10 In.	354
Ice Cream Tray, Stretched Star Base, Fans, Ruffled, Notched, 14 x 8 In.	261
Knife Rest, Prism & Geometric, 5 In.	225
Knife Rest, Prism Cut, 4 ¼ In.	47
Lamp, Kerosene, Hobstar, Punty & Star, Victor Burner, P & A Mfg., 7 In.	944
Pitcher, Bengal, Hobstar Foot, Triple Notched Handle, Signed Sinclaire, 11 ½ In.	750
Pitcher, Champagne, Whirling Hobstars, Diamond Sunbursts, Faceted Handle, 11 In.	46
Pitcher, Crosshatched Bottom, Ball Shape, Cylindrical Neck, 10 x 5 In.	307
Pitcher, Federal, Brilliant, Clear, Serrated Rim, Notched Handle, J.D, Bergen, c.1905, 9 In.	127
Pitcher, Lemonade, Sterling Silver Cap, Wayne Silver Co., 12 In. ....*illus*	522
Pitcher, Pedestal, Hobstar, Vesica, Strawberry Diamond, Prism, Fan, 14 ¼ In.	450
Pitcher, Sunburst, Strawberry Diamond, Prism, Hobstar Base, Double Notch Handle, 11 In.	225
Pitcher, Water, Hob Diamond, New England, 7 ¾ In.	125
Plate, Alhambra, Wafer Base, Scalloped, 10 In.	650
Plate, Hobstar, Strawberry Diamond, Vesica, Prism, Star & Fan, 8 In.	47
Plate, Nassau, Signed J. Hoare, 7 In.	100
Punch Bowl, 4 Whirling Hobstars, Star, Button & Fine Cut Panel Dividers, 10 x 11 In.	203
Punch Bowl, Argo Pattern, Wavy Rim, Footed, Flared Base, Empire Glass Co., 14 x 14 In.	424
Punch Bowl, Clear, Strawberry Diamond, Round, c.1900, 9 x 11 In.	316
Punch Bowl, Pinwheel & Diamond Design, Pedestal Foot, Scallop Rim, c.1900, 8 In.	826
Punch Bowl, Stand, Fan-Cut Scalloped Rim, Diamond-Cut Panels, c.1890, 14 In. ....*illus*	5400
Punch Bowl, Stand, Pinwheels, Hobstars, Scalloped Border, c.1900, 12 x 13 ½ In.	1107
Relish, Hobstar, Cane, Strawberry Diamond & Fan, Signed Fry, 7 ½ In.	50
Rose Bowl, Greek Key, Engraved Flowers, 3 ½ In.	25
Rose Bowl, Monarch, Hobstar Base, 4 ½ In.	59
Rose Bowl, Sultana, Dorflinger, 6 x 6 In.	275
Salt, Bull's Eye, Oval Bowl, Scallop Rim, Scroll Stem, Oval Foot, 3 x 3 ¾ In.	184
Salt, Lid, Lily-Of-The-Valley, Flower Finial, Pedestal Base, c.1895, 4 x 2 ⅜ In.	288
Salt, Lid, Prism, Point Rim, Rayed Foot, c.1895, 4 x 2 ¾ In.	92
Salt, Lid, Ribbed Ivy, Beaded Rim, Rayed Foot, c.1880, 4 ½ x 2 ⅞ In.	127
Salt, Lid, Thumbprint, Hexagonal Finial, Clear, c.1895, 3 ¾ x 2 ½ In.	150
Sandwich Plate, Starburst & Geometric Design, Wafer Base, Signed, Taylor Brothers, 10 In.	25
Server, Alhambra, Sterling Rim, Meriden, 3 x 10 In.	650
Server, Hobstar, Nailhead Diamond, Strawberry Diamond Star, Flowers, Silver Rim, 3 x 10 In.	75
Shot Glass, Russian, Persian, Signed Hawkes, 2 ¾ In.	150
Shot Glass, Russian, Star Cut Buttons, 2 ¾ In.	125
Sugar & Creamer, Plymouth, Pitkin & Brooks	177
Sugar, Lid, Blue Opalescent, Buckeye Glass Co., c.1890, 5 In.	12
Sugar, Lid, Blue, Ribbed Opal Lattice, c.1888, 4 ½ x 2 ⅜ In.	115
Tankard, Brilliant, Daisy Flowers, Stopper, Bowling Pin Shape, c.1900, 15 ¾ In.	184
Tray, Hobstar, Vesica, Nailhead Diamond, Strawberry Diamond, 9 In.	75
Tray, Ice Cream, Wallace, Quaker City, 14 x 7 In.	100
Tray, Pansy Pattern, Kelly & Steinmann, 9 ¾ x 7 In.	100
Tray, Tab Handle, Russian, Star Cut Buttons, 14 ½ In.	800
Tumbler, Kalana Poppy & Crosscut Diamond Arches, Dorflinger, 3 ¾ In.	236
Tumbler, Lemonade, Handle, No. 20, Dorflinger, 3 In.	150
Tumbler, Russian, Star Cut Buttons, 3 ¾ In.	200
Urn, Lid, Fan & Strawberry, Square Base, Knop Handle, c.1830, 11 x 6 In., Pair	1195
Vase, Brunswick, Corset Shape, Hawkes, 13 ¾ In., Pair	250
Vase, Cornucopia Shape, Flared Rim, Controlled Bubble Paperweight Base, c.1910, 12 In.	96
Vase, Emerald Green Cut To Clear, Fan Shape, Crosscut Diamond & Fan, 5 ½ In.	266
Vase, Etched, Cylindrical, Rounded Bottom, c.1950, 10 x 5 ½ In.	84
Vase, Hobstar, Strawberry Diamonds, Pinched, c.1900, 14 x 7 In.	1380
Vase, Paneled, Fine Cut Stars & Bars, Ovals, Feathered Cane Top, Tapered, Pinched, 10 In.	93
Vase, Primrose, Corset Shape, Dorflinger, 8 In.	350
Vase, Roosevelt, Bulbous, Hobstar, Pinwheel, Strawberry Diamond, Vesica, Fern, Fan, 9 ½ In.	450
Vase, Ruby, Clear Spiral, Torch Shape, Gilt Putto Standard, Stepped Base, 23 In.	1875

Vase, Trumpet Shape Neck, Green Cut To Clear, Flowers, Leaves, c.1890, 11 ⅞ In. ....*illus*	720
Vase, Trumpet Shape, Round Foot, Wavy Rim, c.1900, 11 x 10 In..........	240
Water Carafe, Hobstar & Fan, 8 In..........	35
Water Set, Basket Weave, Blue, Pitcher, 6 Goblets, c.1890, 8 ⅝ x 5 ⅝ In., 7 Piece	81

CYBIS porcelain is a twentieth-century product. Boleslaw Cybis came to the United States from Poland in 1939. He started making porcelains in Long Island, New York, in 1940. He moved to Trenton, New Jersey, in 1942 as one of the founders of Cordey China Co. and started his own company, Cybis Porcelains, about 1950. The firm is still working.

CYBIS

Box, Heart Shape, Red & White Heart, Flowers, 1987	225
Bust, Young Boy, Wood Block, Signed, 9 In.	500
Figurine, Baby Owl, On Branch, 1957, 4 ½ In.	75
Figurine, First Flight, Court Jester, Signed, Numbered, 1978, 15 ½ In..........	1400
Figurine, Girl, Kneeling, Holding Bird, Wood Base, 1966-73, 3 In.	195
Figurine, Goldilocks & Panda, 1973-75, 6 In.	310
Figurine, Little Jamie, Sitting, Basket Of Chicks, 1966-73, 6 In.	195
Figurine, Little Red Riding Hood, 1973-75, 6 ¾ In.	225
Figurine, Madonna With Bird, 1956, 11 ½ In.	700
Figurine, Melissa, Woman, Wearing Cape, Holding Rabbit, 1976, 10 In.	325
Figurine, Panda Bears, 1973-75, 3 ½ In..........	250
Figurine, Turtle Doves, Doves Of Peace, Wood Base, 1957-70, 8 In.	1900
Figurine, Unicorn, Signed, Numbered, c.1969-74, 10 x 13 In..........	1600

CZECHOSLOVAKIA is a popular term with collectors. The name, first used as a mark after the country was formed in 1918, appears on glass and porcelain and other decorative items. Although Czechoslovakia split into Slovakia and the Czech Republic on January 1, 1993, the name continues to be used in some trademarks.

CZECHOSLOVAKIA GLASS

Atomizer, Frosted Ground, Embossed Flowers, Multicolor Highlights, Yellow, 7 ½ In.	118
Atomizer, Yellow, Orange, Blue Mottled, 7 In..........	59
Vase, Iridescent Green, Purple, Applied Metallic Sunflower Design, Tapered, 6 x 10 In.	250
Vase, Squat, Flat Cobalt Blue Neck, Hlava, 5 x 6 ½ In.	420
Vase, Trumpet, Orange, Amethyst Stripes, Rim & Knop, 11 x 7 ½ In..........	186

CZECHOSLOVAKIA POTTERY

Bowl, Pinwheels, Blue & Black, White Ground, 1930s, 2 x 5 In.	95
Candlestick, Pinwheel, Black & Blue, White Ground, 1930s, 6 x 4 In.	150
Figurine, Dog, Scottie, Sitting, Black, White, 1930s, 7 ¼ In.	295
Pitcher, Poinsettia, Gourd Shape, Scroll Handle, Yellow, 1930s, 7 In..........	95

DANIEL BOONE, a pre–Revolutionary War folk hero, was a surveyor, trapper, and frontiersman. A television series, which ran from 1964 to 1970, was based on his life and starred Fess Parker. All types of Daniel Boone memorabilia are collected.

Comic Book, No. 96, Classics Illustrated, 1969, 10 x 7 In..........	5
Doll, Plastic, Jointed, Swivel Head, Sleep Eyes, Fur Cap & Coat, 1940s, 8 In.	35
Match Safe, Brass, 29th Natl. Encpt., Louisville, c.1895, 2 ⅞ In.	950
Plate, Image, Flag & Eagle Border, Daniel Boone Hotel, Lamberton Scammel, 11 In.	30
Spoon, Sterling Silver, Log Cabin, Our Kentucky Home, 5 ⅝ In.	49

D'ARGENTAL is a mark used in France by the Compagnie des Cristalleries de St. Louis. The firm made multilayered, acid-cut cameo glass in the late nineteenth and twentieth centuries. D'Argental is the French name for the city of Munzthal, home of the glassworks. Later the company made enameled etched glass.

D'argental

Atomizer, Pear Shape, Berries, Flowers, Vines, Cameo, 8 In..........	224
Goblet, Hills, Trees, Ruins, Vines, Frosted, Raspberry, Flared Rim, c.1900, 7 In.	375
Toothpick Holder, Cameo, Side Rim Dips, Scenic, Red, Sienna, 2 ½ In.	237
Vase, Boats, Shore, Purple, Yellow, Orange, Crimped Rim, Flattened Oval, 6 In..........	1063
Vase, Cameo, Bulbous, Chateau, Leaves, Trees, Green, Brown, Signed, 10 In.	1304
Vase, Tree, Lake, Sea Gulls, Shouldered, 7 ¾ In.	442

DAUM, a glassworks in Nancy, France, was started by Jean Daum in 1875. The company, now called *Cristalleries de Nancy*, is still working. The *Daum Nancy* mark has been used in many variations. The name of the city and the artist are usually both included. The term *martele* is used to describe applied decorations that are carved or etched in the cameo process.

DAUM NANCY

Bowl, Mottled Pink, Orange, Ruffled Rim, Squat, c.1900, 2 ⅜ x 4 ⅞ In..........	413

Cut Glass, Punch Bowl, Stand, Fan-Cut Scalloped Rim, Diamond-Cut Panels, c.1890, 14 In, $5,400

Skinner Auctioneers & Appraisers

D

Cut Glass, Vase, Trumpet Shape Neck, Green Cut To Clear, Flowers, Leaves, c.1890, 11 ⅞ In, $720

Skinner Auctioneers & Appraisers

Daum, Cruet, Bellflower, Gilt Highlights, Textured, Cameo, Stopper, Signed, 7 ¼ In. $2,185

Early Auction Co.

DAUM

Daum, Cruet, Dutch Winter Scene, Church, Mottled, Cameo, Bird Stopper, Signed, 4 In.
$4,025

Early Auction Co.

Daum, Figurine, Car, Coupe Riviera, 1930s Model, Label, 15 ¼ In.
$240

Garth's Auctioneers & Appraisers

Daum, Vase, Lake Scene, Trees, Shoreline, Signed, Cameo, 9 In.
$1,035

Early Auction Co.

Daum, Vase, Lakeside Landscape, Sunset, Signed, Cameo, c.1910, 7 x 11 In.
$2,124

Brunk Auctions

Bowl, Squat, Cylindrical, Mottled Yellow & Brown, Leaves, Nuts, Branch, c.1910, 3 x 9 In.	960
Cruet, Bellflower, Gilt Highlights, Textured, Cameo, Stopper, Signed, 7 ¼ In. ....*illus*	2185
Cruet, Dutch Winter Scene, Church, Mottled, Cameo, Bird Stopper, Signed, 4 In. ....*illus*	4025
Dresser Box, Lid, Harbor, Sailboats, Ring Foot, Amber, Signed, 4 ½ x 6 In.	2457
Ewer, Flowers, Leaves, Gold Green Cameo Glass, Applied Handle, Footed, 13 In.	10000
Ewer, Iris, Green, Beige, Flared Foot, Square Handle, Upturned Spout, Signed, 17 In.	6372
Figurine, Car, Coupe Riviera, 1930s Model, Label, 15 ¼ In. ....*illus*	240
Figurine, Christmas Tree, Clear, Signed, 23 In.	330
Figurine, Reclining Torso, Cast Glass, Mottled Purple To Blue, 1900s, 4 x 7 In.	708
Inkwell, Applied Glass, Multicolor Oak Leaves, Applied Acorns, Cameo 4 x 4 ½ In.	3555
Jar, Lid, Applied Glass, Green Cabochon, Insect, Applied Leaf, Etched Maple Leaves, 4 ½ In.	2844
Lamp, Art Deco, Stylized Flowers, Peach, Chartreuse, Frosted, Mushroom Shade, 9 x 4 In.	5333
Lamp, Domed Shade, Earth Tones, Grapevines, Yellow Mottled, Peach Ground, 15 x 24 In.	5333
Lamp, Pendant, Ceiling, Cameo, Flowers, Leaves, Glass, Iron, Signed, 16 x 31 In.	6250
Paperweight, Woman, Nude, Reclining On Leaf, Pate-De-Verre, 7 x 2 In.	610
Perfume Bottle, Flowers, Green, Gilt, Perfume De Vertus Band, c.1900, 4 ⅜ In.	1750
Perfume Bottle, Leaves, Vines, Pink, Green, Smokestack, Ring Foot, Ball Stopper, 7 x 5 In.	1652
Powder Box, Lid, Art Nouveau, Flowers, Stems, Green Mottled, Blue, Cameo, 2 x 4 In.	237
Rose Bowl, Winter Scene, Trefoil Shape, Snow Tipped Trees, Fiery, 2 ¾ In.	2963
Salt, Master Bucket, Thistle Flowers, Red, Gold Enamel, Leaves, Cameo, Rim, Handles, 3 In.	948
Toothpick Holder, Mottled Rose, Etched Flowers, Leaves, Gilt, c.1915, 2 In.	184
Tray, Grape Leaves, Vines, Yellow, Orange, Mottled, Vitrified Cameo, 5 x 5 In.	1126
Tray, Vitrified Glass, Multicolor Grapes, Leaves, Cameo, Scalloped Border, 8 ¼ In.	948
Tumbler, Green Trees, Distant Pond Shoreline, Shaded Orange, Yellow, Cameo, Signed, 5 In.	1481
Vase, Autumn Leaves, Frosted, Cameo, c.1905, 5 ½ x 5 In.	750
Vase, Black, Green Forest Interior, Mottled Yellow, Red, Tapered, Signed, 5 ½ x 17 ½ In.	9150
Vase, Blooming Clematis, Purple, Tapered, Cylindrical Neck, Handles, c.1900, 8 In.	1888
Vase, Blue, Green Flowers, Vines, Over Frosted, Squared Cylinder, 6 ½ In.	360
Vase, Blue, Green Lake Scene, Frosted, Cylinder, Cameo, c.1905, 5 ½ In.	813
Vase, Branches, Leaves, Mottled Frosted Green Blue, Purple, Cameo, Tapered, 9 x 26 In.	3600
Vase, Bud, Lilies, Maroon, Green Leaves, Square, c.1900, 4 ¾ In.	1188
Vase, Cameo, Aesop Fable, Fox & Crow, Black, Frosted, Green, Gold, Cameo, 8 In.	1659
Vase, Cameo, Mottled Ground, Blue To Green, Cameo, Signed, 17 ¾ In.	5036
Vase, Cream, Orange, Branches, Leaves, Bulbous, Loop Handles, Cameo, c.1900, 6 x 8 In.	2006
Vase, Daffodil, Pate-De-Verre, Signed, 9 ½ x 7 ¾ In.	3600
Vase, Flowers & Clover, Pink, Blue, Beaker Shape, Signed, c.1915, 13 ½ In.	6490
Vase, Flowers & Leaves, Amber, Burnt Orange, Yellow, Oval, Flat Rim, 1900s, 10 In.	8968
Vase, Flowers, Cylindrical, Silver Scroll Handles, Spread Foot, Cameo, 6 ¼ In.	1170
Vase, Flowers, Leaves, Blue, Green, Mottled Yellow, Frosted, Cameo, Footed, Signed, 4 x 9 In.	610
Vase, Flowers, Pink, Amber, Shouldered, Tapered, c.1915, 13 ½ In.	2832
Vase, Flowers, Translucent Yellow, Pinched Triangle Shape, c.1905, 4 x 3 In.	1250
Vase, Flowers, Yellow Ground, Metal Top, Tapered Cylinder, Cameo, 4 ½ In.	1750
Vase, Flowers, Yellow, White Etched, 7 x 4 In.	944
Vase, Frosted Yellow, Violet, Blossoms, Cylindrical, c.1910, 4 ⅞ In.	1440
Vase, Green Glass, Textured, Footed, Signed, 7 x 6 ¾ In.	878
Vase, Iris, Black, Fuchsia, Bottle Shape, Smokestack Bottom, Signed, c.1900, 9 ½ In.	7316
Vase, Iris, Violets, Leaves, White Mottled, Cameo, Pinched Oval, Cross Of Lorraine, 7 x 6 In.	2473
Vase, Lake Scene, Trees, Shoreline, Signed, Cameo, 9 In. ....*illus*	1035
Vase, Lakeside Landscape, Sunset, Signed, Cameo, c.1910, 7 x 11 In. ....*illus*	2124
Vase, Leaves, Green, Gilt, Bottle Shape, Signed, c.1900, 6 ¼ In.	1625
Vase, Mottled Blue, Green, Yellow, Oblong, Signed, 7 x 4 ½ In.	250
Vase, Mottled Cobalt Blue, Green, Tapered, c.1920, 10 In.	500
Vase, Mottled Orange, Yellow, c.1910, 4 ½ x 7 In.	156
Vase, Mottled Plum, Pink, Flared Rim, Globular, Angled Handles, c.1930, 10 In.	1125
Vase, Mottled White To Clear, Autumn Landscape, Lake, Beaker Shape, c.1900, 14 In.	6490
Vase, Orange Flowers, Green Leaves, Purple Stem, Yellow, Cameo, c.1905, 3 In.	1062
Vase, Pear Shape, Etched Design, Amber Color, Rolled Rim, 13 x 8 ½ In.	1170
Vase, Pillow, Winter Village Scene, 4 ¾ x 2 ¼ In.	3776
Vase, Purple Flowers, Silver Mounts, A. Burgun, Schverer, 6 ⅞ In.	3250
Vase, Purple Iris, Amber, Signed, 10 ½ In.	207
Vase, Purple, Black Flower, Over Orange, Green, Tapered, c.1910, 9 ¾ In.	960
Vase, Raspberry Clusters, Branches, Cameo, Signed, 13 In. ....*illus*	3163
Vase, Red & Orange Mottled, Frosted, Bottle Shape, Thin Neck, Signed, 21 ¼ In.	400
Vase, Red, Yellow, Gourd Shape, Green & Yellow Tulips, Cameo, Signed, 4 ½ In.	1668
Vase, Saffron, Cut Leaves, Flowers, Cameo, Long Cylindrical Neck 14 ½ In.	1770
Vase, Stylized Owl, Enamel, Etched, Cabochon Eyes, Marked, c.1902, 7 In. ....*illus*	1200

Vase, Sweetgum, Blue, Gold Leaves, Lobe Shape, Pinched, Gilt Rim, 4 x 5 In.		1652
Vase, Thistle, Carved, Enameled, Textured, Long Neck, Cameo, 9 In.		443
Vase, Trees, Plant Life, Smoky Green, Cylindrical, Ring Foot, Flat Rim, 1900s, 11 x 10 In.		1003
Vase, Violets, Gilt Outlines, 3 Applied Loop Feet, Cameo, Engraved, 4 x 4 ⅝ In.	*illus*	9480
Vase, Violets, Green Leaves, Gilt Highlights, Frosted, Cameo, 3 ¼ In.		1121
Vase, Winter Landscape, Yellow, Black, Cameo, Signed, 3 ½ In.		1309
Vase, Winter Scene, Enameled, Orange, Brown, Oval, Cross Of Lorraine, c.1900, 2 In.		450
Vase, Winter Scene, Trees, Shouldered, Cameo, Etched, 1900s, 11 x 4 ½ In.		5938
Vase, Woodland, Snow, Panoramic, Orange Sky, Cameo, 7 ¼ In.		3304
Vase, Yellow & Brown Mottled, Pillow Shape, Engraved Daum Nancy, 7 In.		115

DAVENPORT pottery and porcelain were made at the Davenport factory in Longport, Staffordshire, England, from 1793 to 1887. Earthenwares, creamwares, porcelains, ironstone, and other ceramics were made. Most of the pieces are marked with a form of the word *Davenport*.

Bowl, Vegetable, Lid, Macao, Flow Blue Transfer, 7 In.	*illus*	142
Pitcher, Flowers, Blue, Orange, Green Serpent Handle, 7 ¾ In.		23
Platter, Blue Printed Transfer, Impressed Mark, c.1865, 19 In.		90
Platter, English Countryside, Flower Border, Transfer Blue, c.1850, 21 In.		94

DAVY CROCKETT, the American frontiersman, was born in 1786 and died in 1836. The historical character gained new fame in 1954 when the Walt Disney television show ran a series of episodes featuring Fess Parker as Davy Crockett. Coonskin caps and buckskins became popular and hundreds of different Davy Crockett items were made.

Alarm Clock, Metal Case, Davy Seated Holding Rifle, Bayard, c.1955, 2 x 7 x 5 In.	230
Button, King Of Wild Frontier, Portrait, Yellow, Black, 1 ¼ In.	15
Cap Gun, Buck N' Bronc, Die Cast, G. Schmidt, 1955, 11 In.	345
Comic Book, Cover, Indian Fighter, F. Parker, Signed, 1955, 11 x 14 In.	115
Cookie Jar, Figural, Holding Rifle, Name On Base, 1950s, 11 In.	172
Flashlight, Display, Box, Davy Holding Rifle, 1955, 8 ⅝ x 12 In.	309
Game, Coin, Davy's Shoot The B'ar, Wood, Cast Metal, c.1955, 8 x 14 x 6 In.	386
Holster Set, Cap, Marbled Grip, Double Barrel, Leather, Fringe, Carnell Mfg., 1955	172
Lunch Box, Indian Fighting, Bear, Thermos, American Thermos Bottle Co., 1955	115
Mug, Figural, Davy Holding Rifle, Coonskin Hat, Brush Pottery, 1950s, 4 In.	49
Puppet, Push Button, Paper Label, Box, c.1955, 6 ¼ In.	127
Rifle, Plastic, Box, Handle, Ideal, c.1955, 38 In.	316
Store Display, 12 Davy Crockett Toys, On Horse, Centaur Productions, 1950s, Box, 11 x 8 In.	390
Store Display, Davy Crockett, Holding Gun, Flashlights, Boxed, Usalite, 12 x 8 ¾ In.	360
Store Display, Davy Crockett, Indian, 27 Toy Rings, Adjustable, 24K Gold Plate, 12 x 8 In.	660
Toy, Gun & Holster Set, Black Stag Grip, Leather Belt, Box, 1950s, 7 In.	127
Watch, 2-Tone Chrome, Crossed Pistols, Engraved, Pocket, Box, c.1955	1724
Watch, Powder Horn Stand, Leather, Box	253

DE VEZ was a signature used on cameo glass after 1910. E. S. Monot founded the glass company near Paris in 1851. The company changed names many times. Mt. Joye, another glass by this factory, is listed in its own category.

Vase, Bleeding Heart Flowers, Etched, Cristallerie De Pantin, Signed, c.1920, 5 x 6 In.		281
Vase, Cameo, Blue, Green Medieval Castle, Lake, Cylindrical, Signed 5 ¼ In.		460
Vase, Cameo, Ships In Harbor, Mountains, Clouds, Pineapples, Signed, 5 ½ In.		474
Vase, Lake Scene, Sailing Ships, Green & Blue, Cone Shape, Signed, 7 In.		230
Vase, Mountain Scene, Birds, Blue, Yellow Ground, Cameo, Signed, 5 In.	*illus*	575
Vase, Mountain Scene, Crown Point Rim, Cameo, 10 ¼ In.	*illus*	518
Vase, Nautical, Blue Cameo Trees, Shoreline, Boat On River, Yellow River, Signed, 14 In.		1007

DECORATED TUMBLERS *may be by maker or design or in Advertising, Coca-Cola, Pepsi-Cola, Sports, and other categories.*

DECOYS are carved or turned wooden copies of birds, fish, or animals. The decoy was placed in the water or propped on the shore to lure flying birds to the pond for hunters. Some decoys are handmade; some are commercial products. Today there is a group of artists making modern decoys for display, not for use in a pond. Many sell for high prices.

Black Bellied Plover, Paint, New York, Rocky Mount, 9 In.	1659
Black Duck, Hollow Body, Glass Eyes, Thomas Fitzpatrick, c.1940, 15 In.	575
Black Duck, Relief Wings, Carved, Painted, c.1955, 15 ¼ In.	60

Daum, Vase, Raspberry Clusters, Branches, Cameo, Signed, 13 In.
$3,163
Early Auction Co.

Daum, Vase, Stylized Owl, Enamel, Etched, Cabochon Eyes, Marked, c.1902, 7 In.
$1,200
Skinner Auctioneers & Appraisers

Daum, Vase, Violets, Gilt Outlines, 3 Applied Loop Feet, Cameo, Engraved, 4 x 4 ⅝ In.
$9,480
James D. Julia Auctioneers

Davenport, Bowl, Vegetable, Lid, Macao, Flow Blue Transfer, 7 In.
$142

Conestoga Auction Co., Inc.

De Vez, Vase, Mountain Scene, Birds, Blue, Yellow Ground, Cameo, Signed, 5 In.
$575

Early Auction Co.

De Vez, Vase, Mountain Scene, Crown Point Rim, Cameo, 10 ¼ In.
$518

Early Auction Co.

Black Duck, Turned Head, Lifted Tail, Paint, Ward Brothers, Maryland, 1933, 18 In.	47150
Black Duck, Wood, Hen, Carved Feathers, Glass Eyes, Branded, 1900s, 19 In.	147
Bluebill Drake, Painted, Herters, 1930s	36
Bluebill Hen, Carved, Painted, New York, c.1910, 14 ½ In.	330
Bluebill Hen, Wood, Paint, Marked, Clarence Krieser, 1920, 11 In.	230
Bluebill, Carved, Painted, Male, Female, A.E. Crowell, 3 & 2 ¾ In., Pair	1169
Bluebill, Stamped, C. Lowe, Havre De Grace, Md., 14 In. ....*illus*	177
Blue-Winged Teal Hen, Turned Head, Glass Eyes, c.1950, 7 ¼ x 16 ¼ In.	360
Brant, Carved, Painted, New Jersey, c.1910, 18 In.	123
Brant, Cobb Island Style, Carved, Painted, Signed M.S. McNair, c.1950, 24 In.	660
Brant, Hollow Body, Carved, Glass Eyes, Painted, c.1930, 14 ¾ In.	115
Brant, Swimming, Carved, Painted, Stamped Colburn C. Wood Jr., c.1950, 27 In.	240
Broadbill, Glass Eyes, 14 In.	242
Bufflehead Duck, Painted, Platform Base, Signed Jeff Jester, Chincoteague, 1983, 15 In.	47
Canada Goose, Canvas, Over Wood Frame, Painted, c.1930, 34 In.	353
Canada Goose, Cobb Island Style, Carved, Painted, Signed M. S. McNair, c.1950, 28 In.	2880
Canada Goose, Pine, Painted, 20th Century, 25 In.	176
Canada Goose, Swollen Body, Removable Head, Weight, 13 ½ x 21 In. ....*illus*	711
Canvasback Drake, Painted, Dog Bone Weight, Havre De Grace, Md., c.1910, 14 ¾ In.	144
Canvasback Drake, Painted, Natural Driftwood Base, Jeff Jester, 1984, 14 ½ In. ....*illus*	71
Canvasback Drake, Signed Gene Travis, 14 In.	354
Canvasback Drake, Stylized Humpback, Glass Eyes, Susquehanna River Region, 16 In.	173
Canvasback Hen, Fluted Tail, Hollow Carved, Stylized Paint, c.1890	25878
Canvasback, Gray, Black, White Paint, Carved, Donald Wheatcraft, Del., 1983	106
Canvasback, Painted Eyes, 16 ½ In.	138
Canvasback, Painted, Inscribed Willie Parsons, Fruitwood, Md., 1940, 16 In.	270
Duck, Sink Box, Cast Iron, 8 ½ x 15 ½ In.	652
Field Mouse, Ice Fishing, Wood, Metal Legs, Brass Tack Eyes, Inset Weights, c.1910, 7 In.	711
Fish, Bass, Metal Fins, Painted, Carved Gills, 7 ½ In. ....*illus*	120
Fish, Brook Trout, Sheet Metal Fins, Brass Tack Eyes, Lead Weights, c.1910, 9 In. ....*illus*	189
Fish, Carved, Painted, Black, Tan, Mounted, c.1950, 30 In.	1680
Frog, Ice Fishing, Wood, Carved, Painted, Metal Legs, Inset Lead Weight, c.1910, 6 In.	165
Goldeneye Drake, Paint, Mason Decoy Co.	169
Goose, Feeding, Wood, Carved, Upswept Tail, Extended Neck, c.1920, 26 ½ In.	201
Goose, Swimming, Carved, Painted, c.1910, 35 In.	296
Green-Winged Teal Hen, Turned Head, Paint, L.T. Ward & Bro., 15 In.	43125
Green-Winged Teal, Carved Wing Edges, Etched Feathers, Flat Bottom, Quebec, 12 ½ In.	384
Green-Winged Teal, Painted, A. Elmer Crowell, Mass., c.1935, 3 ¾ In., Pair	960
Louisiana Mallard Drake, Wood, Carved, Painted, 15 In.	330
Mallard Drake, Carved, Black, Green, Gray Painted, Donald Wheatcraft, Del., 1982	83
Mallard Drake, Painted, Skippy Barto	333
Mallard Drake, Wood, Painted, Stamped JHM, 17 In., Pair	114
Mallard Hen, Carved Bottom, 16 In. ....*illus*	384
Mallard Hen, Mound Base, Paint, c.1900, 2 ⅞ In.	480
Merganser Drake, Red Breast, Carved Eyes, Virginia, c.1910	236
Merganser, Carved, Painted, New England, c.1905, 19 ½ In.	510
Michigan Canvasback Drake, Tobin Meldrum, c.1910, 15 In.	1020
Owl, Stuffed Cloth Figure, Yellow Glass Eyes, Wood Beak, Branch Mounted, c.1905, 19 In.	813
Owl, Wood, Black Glass Eyes, Movable Wings, Carved, Painted, Stand, c.1910, 12 In.	625
Pintail Hen, Paint, Mason, 8 In.	145
Plover, Distressed Paint, Glass Inset Eyes, c.1960, 9 ½ In.	206
Plover, Painted, Carved, Driftwood Mount, Mass., c.1890, 8 In., Pair	1185
Red-Breasted Merganser, Painted, A. Elmer Crowell, Mass., c.1930, 5 ½ In., Pair	4320
Redhead, Hollow Body, Carved, Painted, c.1850, 14 ½ In., Pair	660
Redhead, Painted, Male, Female, A. E. Crowell, Miniature, 3 & 2 ¾ In., Pair	1169
Ruddy Duck, Paint, Alvirah Wright, Duck, North Carolina, c.1910, 14 In.	29900
Sea Coot, Canvas Over Wood, Clarence Bailey, Mass., c.1930, 21 In.	3840
Sea Gull, Carved, Painted, Gus Wilson, c.1940, 31 In.	960
Shorebird, Carved, Painted, c.1915, 11 ½ In.	593
Shorebird, Carved, Painted, Marked S. McNair, Stand, c.1960, 14 ¾ In.	900
Shorebird, Carved, Painted, William Gibian, Virginia, Stand, 12 ½ In.	600
Shorebird, Jack Curlew, Painted, A.E. Crowell, 3 ¼ x 5 In.	191
Swan, Carved, Painted, Hollow Body, Flattened Tail, Glass Eyes, R.W. Schaap, 1900s, 21 In.	259
Swan, Carved, White Paint, 1900s, 35 In.	1020
Swan, Head Turned Back, Wood, 17 In.	173
Swan, Preening, Carved, Painted, 1900s, 28 In.	450

Swan, Wood, Carved, Canvas, White, Black Paint, c.1910............................		420
Wood Duck, Carved, Painted, A.E. Crowell, Miniature, 3 x 4 ½ In. ....*illus*		1560
Wood Duck, Green, White, Brown, Purple Paint, Carved, Donald Wheatcraft, Del., 1983............		59
Yellowlegs Shorebird, Carved, Painted, Massachusetts, c.1900, 9 ½ In............................		780
Yellowlegs, Calling Position, Glass Eyes, Clamshell Base, Elmer Crowell, c.1910, 10 In. .....*illus*		10200
Yellowlegs, Carved, Painted, New Jersey, c.1880, 9 ½ In............................		972
Yellowlegs, Relief Carved Wings, New York, c.1890, 9 ½ In...........................		1422

DEDHAM POTTERY was started in 1895. Chelsea Keramic Art Works was established in 1872 in Chelsea, Massachusetts, by members of the Robertson family. The factory closed in 1889 and was reorganized as the Chelsea Pottery U.S. in 1891. The firm used the marks *CKAW* and *CPUS*. It became the Dedham Pottery of Dedham, Massachusetts. The factory closed in 1943. It was famous for its crackleware dishes, which picture blue outlines of animals, flowers, and other natural motifs. Pottery by Chelsea Keramic Art Works and Dedham Pottery is listed here.

Azalea, Plate, Rabbit, 8 In..................................		155
Elephant, Bowl, Marked, 5 ¾ In. ....*illus*		118
Flower Frog, Rabbit On Dome Holder, Mass., c.1930, 6 ½ In...............		246
Lobster, Plate, Blue, Gray Glaze, 9 ¾ In................................		319
Moth, Plate, Blue & White, Impressed Rabbit Mark, 8 ⅜ In..............*illus*		230
Night & Morning, Pitcher, Blue & White, Relief Roosters, Owl, Blue Mark, 5 In........................		369
Pitcher, Olive Green Glaze, Greek Key Borders, Chelsea Keramic, c.1878, 7 ⅞ In. ....*illus*		420
Pond Lily, Plate, Dinner, Blue & White, c.1900		85
Rabbit, Creamer, Blue, White, Handle, 3 ⅓ In..............................		130
Rabbit, Dish, 5-Sided, Marked, 7 ¼ In..............................		118
Snow Tree, Plate, Dinner, Blue, White, c.1900, 8 ½ In...........................		245
Swan, Plate, 8 ¼ In..		76
Turkey, Plate, Blue & White, Maude Davenport, 10 In. ....*illus*		173
Turkey, Plate, Gray, Blue Border, c.1900, 8 ½ In............................		180
Vase, Bottle, Oxblood Glaze, Stoneware, Hugh Robertson, 1880s, 7 ½ x 3 ½ In.		625
Vase, Brown, Green & Lapis Drip Glaze, Bulbous, Swollen, Hugh Robertson, 9 ¾ In.....................		1875
Vase, Gray, Cream & Brown Drip Glaze, Hugh Robertson, 10 x 5 In.		1125
Vase, Luster Glaze, Oxblood, Incised, Hugh Robertson, c.1900, 8 ¼ x 3 ¼ In. ....*illus*		600
Vase, Mottled Glossy Green Glaze, Hugh Robertson, c.1910, 8 ½ In. ....*illus*		5100
Vase, Oxblood Drip Glaze, Squat, Swollen, Signed, H.C. Robertson, 2 ½ x 3 In.		2375
Vase, Oxblood, Orange Peel, Hugh Robertson, CKAW, 1880s, 4 ¼ x 4 ½ In. ....*illus*		2125
Vase, Pigeon Feather Glaze, Baluster, Flared Rim, Spread Foot, CKAW, 11 ½ In.		750
Vase, Stick, Mums, Yellow, Blue & Green Ground, B.R. Guila, 8 In.........................		384
Vase, Stoneware, Oxblood Mottled Iridescent, Green, Blue Glazes, H.C. Robertson, 9 In................		2625
Vase, Stoneware, Volcanic Glaze, Baluster Shape, H.C. Robertson, CKAW, 7 x 3 In........................		1500

DEGUE is a signature acid-etched on pieces of French glass made by the Cristalleries de Compiegne in the early 1900s. Cameo, mold blown, and smooth glass with contrasting colored rims are the types most often found.

Vase, Lime, Cobalt Blue, Gourd Lobes, Iron Mounts, c.1930, 16 In.		4063

DELDARE, *see Buffalo Pottery Deldare.*

DELFT is a special type of tin-glazed pottery. Early delft was made in Holland and England during the seventeenth century. It was usually decorated with blue on a white surface, but some was polychrome, decorated with green, yellow, and other colors. Most delftware pieces were dishes needed for everyday living. Figures were made from about 1750 to 1800, and are rare. Although the soft tin-glazed pottery was well-known, it was not named delft until after 1840, when it was named for the city in Holland where much of it was made. Porcelain became more popular because it was more durable and Holland gradually stopped making the old delft. In 1876 De Porceleyne Fles factory in Delft introduced a porcelain ware that was decorated with blue and white scenes of Holland that reminded many of old delft. It became popular with the Dutch and tourists. By 1990 all of the blue and white porcelain with Dutch scenes was made in Asia, although it was marked *Delft*. Only one Dutch company remains that makes the traditional old-style delft with blue on white or with colored decorations. Most of the pieces sold today were made after 1891, and the name *Holland* usually appears with the Delft factory marks. The word *Delft* appears alone on some inexpensive twentieth- and twenty-first-century pottery from Asia and Germany that is also listed here.

Bidet Insert, Multicolor Scrolls, Lobed Shape, 22 In............................		406
Bowl, Barber, Bleeding, Blue & White, Panels Of Flowers, Medallions, c.1750, 10 ⅛ In................		1080
Bowl, Fazackerly, Multicolor, Squirrel, England, c.1760, 12 In.		558

Decoy, Bluebill, Stamped, C. Lowe, Havre De Grace, Md., 14 In.
$177

Conestoga Auction Co., Inc.

Decoy, Canada Goose, Swollen Body, Removable Head, Weight, 13 ½ x 21 In.
$711

James D. Julia Auctioneers

Decoy, Canvasback Drake, Painted, Natural Driftwood Base, Jeff Jester, 1984, 14 ½ In.
$71

Conestoga Auction Co., Inc.

Decoy, Fish, Bass, Metal Fins, Painted, Carved Gills, 7 ½ In.
$120

Los Angeles Modern Auctions (LAMA)

This is an edited listing of current prices. Visit Kovels.com to check thousands of prices from previous years and sign up for free information on trends, tips, reproductions, marks, and more.

Decoy, Fish, Brook Trout, Sheet Metal Fins, Brass Tack Eyes, Lead Weights, c.1910, 9 In.
$189

Conestoga Auction Co., Inc.

Decoy, Mallard Hen, Carved Bottom, 16 In.
$384

Conestoga Auction Co., Inc.

Decoy, Wood Duck, Carved, Painted, A.E. Crowell, Miniature, 3 x 4 ½ In.
$1,560

Cowan's Auctions

Decoy, Yellowlegs, Calling Position, Glass Eyes, Clamshell Base, Elmer Crowell, c.1910, 10 In.
$10,200

Skinner Auctioneers & Appraisers

Bowl, Flowers, Butterfly, Leaves, Footed, Marked, Dutch, c.1700, 6 x 10 In.	588
Bowl, Square, Notched Corners, Blue, White, Bird, Garden Scene, c.1745, 9 ½ In.	1200
Charger, Blue & White, Dutch River Scene, Cottage, Children, c.1945, 15 ½ In.	83
Charger, Blue, White, Vase, Bouquet, 12 ½ In.	259
Charger, Center Flower Head, Heart Shape Cartouches, Trees, Multicolor, c.1725, 13 In.	738
Charger, Chinoiserie Style, Pointed Arch Panels In Flowers, Justus De Berg, c.1759, 15 ½ In.	615
Charger, Oriental Figures, Courtyard, Marked, c.1750, 15 ¾ In. ....*illus*	1800
Charger, Painted, Rooster, Birds, Multicolor, 13 In. Diam.	25875
Charger, Round, Tin Glazed, Geometric Design, Purple, Red, 1700s, 13 ½ In. Diam.	308
Charger, Tin Glaze, Blue Asian Theme Flower, Buds, 18th Century, 13 ¼ In.	241
Charger, Trees, River Scene, Shaped Flower Border, Cobalt Blue & White, 16 In. Diam.	120
Cheese Box, Lid, Round, Ear Shape Strap Handles, Quatrefoil Medallions, c.1760, 5 ½ In.	246
Cheese Pot, Lid, Stylized Flower Bands, Blue, White, c.1750, 4 ½ x 5 In.	480
Dish, Bird & Insect, Tree, Multicolor, Marked, 1700s, 16 ¾ In. ....*illus*	1121
Dish, Lobed, Manganese, Yellow, Oriental Figures, Scalloped Rim, c.1690, 11 ¾ In. Diam.	960
Figurine, Lion, Seated, Paw On Shield, Tin Glaze, Blue, White, c.1865, 10 x 9 ½ In., Pair	1770
Flowerpot, Cylindrical, Shell Shape Handles, Blue & White, Flowers, 7 ¾ In. Diam.	584
Ginger Jar, Lid, Blue & White, Chinoiserie Scenes, Figure, c.1750, 12 In., Pair	2912
Inkstand, Faience, Blue & White Sailing Scenes, 2 Wells, 1700s, 3 ½ x 4 ½ In.	413
Jar, Blue & White, Man Playing Instrument, 8 ¾ In., Pair	177
Jar, Wet Drug, Blue & White, Inscribed S De Hisopo, Cartouche, Birds, Swags, c.1730, 7 ¾ In.	1200
Mug, Blue, White, Flowers, Heraldic Crest, Cylindrical, c.1800, 5 ½ In.	266
Plaque, Shaped Pastoral Scene, Mask Crest, Blue, White, 18 In., Pair	580
Plaque, Town Scene, Multicolor, Shaped Oval, 23 ½ In.	1440
Plate, Blue & White, Chinese Man, Holding Pole, Island, London, c.1770, 9 In., Pair	480
Plate, Building, Rock, Flowers, Diaper Panels, Blue & White, Dutch, c.1790, 10 In.	390
Plate, Leaves, Flowers, Asian Figure, Tin Glaze, Eng., c.1790, 9 In., Pair	690
Plate, Marriage, Blue & White, Richard & Mary Stoneham, 1744, 12 In.	660
Plate, Portrait, General Chasse, Marked, Dutch, Early 19th Century, 9 ½ In.	151
Plate, Seated Figure, Table, Flowers, Multicolor Glaze, APK Monogram, c.1865, 9 ½ In.	330
Plate, Vase, Flowers, Diaperwork Border, England, c.1770, 14 In.	537
Porringer, Round Bowl, Pierced Handles, Blue, Fruit Basket Design, c.1690, 9 ⅜ In.	480
Posset Pot, Blue & White, Bulbous, Scroll Handles, c.1690, 6 x 9 In.	2006
Punch Bowl, Blue Flower Sprays, Diapering, Scroll Band Border, Footed, 12 In. Diam.	1800
Punch Bowl, Piecrust Edge, Blue & White, Leafy Sprig, 1700s, 10 ½ In.	708
Tobacco Jar, Brass Dome Lid, Indians Smoking Pipe, Rappe De Duinkerque, Oval, c.1780, 12 In.	1353
Tobacco Jar, Brass Lid, Blue & White Leaves, Indian, Marked BP, c.1850, 14 ½ In., Pair	2125
Tobacco Jar, Brass Lid, Blue & White, Flowers, Vine Cartouche, Tonka, c.1750, 10 In.	738
Urn, Blue & White, Chinoiserie Landscapes, Figures, Animals, c.1725, 12 ½ x 11 In.	2464
Urn, Lid, Blue & White, Baluster Shape, 17 In., Pair	767
Vase, Fish, Crackle Ground, Marked, Porceleyne Fles, 4 ¼ In. ....*illus*	236
Vase, Garniture, Blue, White, Vase Of Flowers, Mounted As Lamp, Dutch, 12 In.	540
Vase, Garniture, Lid, Multicolor, Flowers, Leaves, Bird Finial, De Pauw Mark, 15 In., Pair	1140
Vase, Garniture, Stag, Landscape, Blue & White, Dutch, c.1790, 10 ½ In.	660
Water Bottle, Rolled Rim, Ring Foot, Blue & White, Landscape, England, c.1750, 9 ½ In.	510

DENTAL cabinets, chairs, equipment, and other related items are listed here. Other objects may be found in the Medical category.

Cabinet, Cherry, 26 Drawers, American, c.1900, 38 x 27 In.	881
Cabinet, Mahogany, 3 Upper Doors, Porcelain Top, Graduated Drawers, 40 x 63 In.	367
Cabinet, Mahogany, 20 Drawers, 3 Frosted Glass Over 3 Paneled Doors, Sterilizer, 66 In.	1638
Cabinet, Victorian, Mirror, Tambour Door, Pull-Out Surface, Revolving Holder, 72 x 29 In.	1770
Chair, Reclining, Rack & Pinion Gear, Adjusting Wheels, Salesman's Sample, 12 x 7 In.	2489
Drill, Cast Iron, Pedal-Operated Flywheel, Tripod Base, 56 x 21 x 12 In.	176
Light, Dentiscope, Pittsburgh Electric Supply Co., Swivel Mount	480
Sign, Tooth, Figural, Wood, Carved, Attached Hanger, 1800s, 9 x 23 ½ In. ....*illus*	5710
Tray, Custard Glass, Scalloped, 1920s, 14 In. Diam.	75

DENVER is part of the mark on an American art pottery. William Long of Steubenville, Ohio, founded the Lonhuda Pottery Company in 1892. In 1900 he moved to Denver, Colorado, and organized the Denver China and Pottery Company. This pottery, which used the mark *Denver*, worked until 1905, when Long moved to New Jersey and founded the Clifton Pottery. Long also worked for Weller Pottery, Roseville Pottery, and American Encaustic Tiling Company. Do not confuse this pottery with the Denver White Pottery, which worked from 1894 to 1955 in Denver.

DENVER
C T &
P | Co

Vase, Parrot Tulips, Green, Marked, Denaura, c.1903, 8 ½ x 5 ¾ In. ....*illus*	2500

DEPRESSION GLASS is an inexpensive glass that was manufactured in large quantities during the 1920s and early 1930s. It was made in many colors and patterns by dozens of factories in the United States. Most patterns were also made in clear glass, which the factories called *crystal*. If no color is listed here, it is clear. The name *Depression glass* is a modern one and also refers to machine-made glass of the 1940s through 1970s. For more prices, go to kovels.com. Sets missing a few pieces can be completed through the help of one of the many matching services listed on our website.

Adam, Bowl, Dessert, Pink, 4 ¾ In.	25
Adam, Bowl, Lid, Pink, 9 In.	80
Adam, Bowl, Pink, 8 In.	40
Adam, Bowl, Vegetable, Lid, Pink	65
Adam, Butter, Cover, Pink	60 to 95
Adam, Candy Dish, Lid, Green	125
Adam, Coaster	25
Adam, Creamer, Pink	22
Adam, Grill Plate, Green, 9 In.	28
Adam, Pitcher, Pink, 32 Oz., 8 In.	55
Adam, Plate, 6 In.	10
Adam, Plate, Dinner, Pink, Square Rim, Scalloped Edge, 4 Piece	30
Adam, Plate, Luncheon, Green, 7 ¾ In., 4 Piece	30
Adam, Sugar, Lid, Pink	35
Adam, Tumbler, Iced Tea, Pink, 5 ½ In. ....*illus*	40
Adam, Vase, Green, 7 ½ In.	150
Adam, Vase, Green, 7 ¾ In.	225
Adam, Vase, Pink, 7 ¾ In.	250
Adam's Rib, Compote, Pink, Oval, 8 In.	18
Adam's Rib, Cup & Saucer, Green	9
Alice, Cup & Saucer, Fire-King, Jade-Ite	14
American Pioneer, Plate, Luncheon, Pink, 8 In.	12
American Sweetheart, Berry Bowl, Pink, 8 ½ In.	65
American Sweetheart, Creamer, Monax	11
American Sweetheart, Cup, Pink	15
American Sweetheart, Plate, Bread, Pink, 5 ¾ In., 12 Piece	45
American Sweetheart, Plate, Dinner, Monax, 10 In.	28
American Sweetheart, Plate, Dinner, Pink, 9 ¾ In.	40
American Sweetheart, Plate, Luncheon, Monax, 9 In.	12
American Sweetheart, Plate, Salad, Pink, 8 In.	15
American Sweetheart, Salver, Monax, 12 In.	25
American Sweetheart, Saucer, Monax	3
American Sweetheart, Sherbet, Pink, Footed, 4 ¼ In.	22
American Sweetheart, Soup, Cream, Monax, 4 ¾ In.	100
American Sweetheart, Sugar, Monax	8
American Sweetheart, Sugar, Pink	22
Apple Blossom pattern is listed here as Dogwood.	
Aramis, Tumbler, Cobalt Blue, 12 Oz., 5 In.	20
Artura, Server, Yellow, Center Handle	50
Aunt Polly, Berry Bowl, Blue, 4 In.	12
Aunt Polly, Bowl, Pickle, Blue, Handle, 7 ¼ In.	45
Aunt Polly, Bowl, Pickle, Green, 2 Handles, Oval, 7 ¼ In.	20
Aunt Polly, Serving Bowl, Blue, 8 In.	40
Aurora, Bowl, Cereal, Pink, 5 ⅜ In.	10
Aurora, Tumbler, Ritz Blue, 4 ¾ In.	20
Autumn, Bowl, Seville Yellow, Oval, Footed, 5 ½ x 3 ¾ In.	30
Autumn, Console, Black, 2 Handles, Oval, Footed, 9 In.	45
Autumn, Console, Jadite, 2 Handles, Oval, Footed, 9 In.	125
Avocado, Bowl, 2 Handles, Oval, 8 In.	11
Ballerina pattern is listed here as Cameo.	
Baltimore Pear, Water Set, Pitcher, Goblet, Jeanette, c.1890, 9 In., 6 In., 6 Piece	518
Bamboo Optic, Console, Pink, Rolled Edge, 13 ½ In.	95
Bamboo Optic, Creamer, Green	10
Bamboo Optic, Plate, Luncheon, Pink, Round, 8 In.	8
Bamboo Optic, Plate, Salad, Pink, Octagonal, 7 In.	6
Banded Rib pattern is listed here as Coronation.	
Banded Ring, Ice Tub, Handles	18
Banded Ring, Plate, Luncheon, Colored Rings, 8 ¼ In.	8

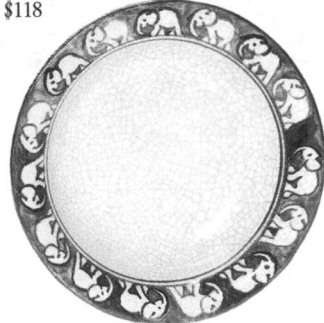

Dedham, Elephant, Bowl, Marked, 5 ¾ In.
$118

Humler & Nolan

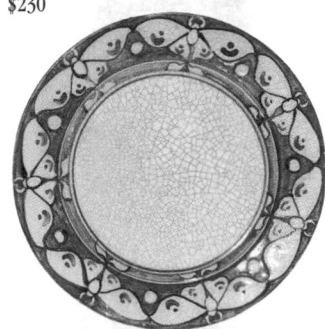

Dedham, Moth, Plate, Blue & White, Impressed Rabbit Mark, 8 ⅜ In.
$230

Humler & Nolan

Dedham, Pitcher, Olive Green Glaze, Greek Key Borders, Chelsea Keramic, c.1878, 7 ⅞ In.
$420

Skinner Auctioneers & Appraisers

Dedham, Turkey, Plate, Blue & White, Maude Davenport, 10 In.
$173

Humler & Nolan

Dedham, Vase, Luster Glaze, Oxblood, Incised, Hugh Robertson, c.1900, 8 ¼ x 3 ¼ In.
$600

Skinner Auctioneers & Appraisers

Dedham, Vase, Mottled Glossy Green Glaze, Hugh Robertson, c.1910, 8 ½ In.
$5,100

Skinner Auctioneers & Appraisers

Banded Ring, Plate, Sherbet, Colored Rings, 6 ⅜ In.	3
Banded Ring, Tumbler, Juice, Royal Ruby, 3 ¾ x 5 Oz.	40
Banded Ring, Tumbler, Water, Colored Rings, 9 Oz., 4 ⅛ In.	8
Banded Ring, Tumbler, Water, Colored Rings, Footed, 10 Oz., 5 ½ In.	8
Basket pattern is listed here as No. 615.	
Beaded Block, Bowl, Round, 7 In.	20
Beaded Block, Creamer	12
Beaded Block, Dish, Jelly, Pink, 2 Handles, 4 ¾ In.	30
Black Forest, Candlestick, Pink, Mushroom Style, 2 ¾ In., Pair	175
Black Forest, Plate, Salad, Green, Van Deman & Son, 7 ⅜ In.	25
Blanche, Server, Pink, Center Handle, Lace Edge, Standard Glass Co., 11 ¾ In.	45
Block pattern is listed here as Block Optic.	
Block Optic, Berry Bowl, Green, 8 In.	36
Block Optic, Bowl, Cereal, Green, 5 ½ In.	12
Block Optic, Butter, Cover Only	80
Block Optic, Cup, Pink, Fancy Handle	9
Block Optic, Goblet, Water, 9 Oz., 5 ¾ In.	15
Block Optic, Pitcher, Green, 54 Oz. 8 ½ In.	65
Block Optic, Plate, Luncheon, Pink, 8 In.	8
Block Optic, Plate, Salad, Green, 8 In.	7
Block Optic, Plate, Sandwich, 10 ¼ In.	12
Block Optic, Plate, Sherbet, Green, 6 In.	4
Block Optic, Plate, Sherbet, Pink, 5 In.	3
Block Optic, Saucer, Cup Ring, Green	9
Block Optic, Sherbet, Footed, 5 ½ Oz., 3 ½ In.	8
Block Optic, Sherbet, Footed, 6 Oz., 4 ¾ In.	10
Block Optic, Sugar & Creamer, Footed, Tall	28
Block Panel, Berry Bowl, Pink, 4 ½ In.	12
Bouquet & Lattice pattern is listed here as Normandie.	
Bowknot, Cup, Green	10
Bubble, Bowl, Cereal, Forest Green, Anchor Hocking, 5 ¼ In.	8
Bubble, Bowl, Fruit, Anchor Hocking, 4 ¼ In.	4
Bubble, Plate, Dinner, Anchor Hocking, 10 In.	10
Bullseye pattern is listed here as Bubble.	
Burple, Berry Bowl, Forest Green, 3-Footed, Anchor Hocking, 4 ⅝ In.	15
Burple, Bowl, Dessert, Forest Green, Anchor Hocking, 4 ⅝ In.	9
Burple, Bowl, Dessert, Green, Anchor Hocking, 8 ½ In.	18
Cabbage Rose pattern is listed here as Sharon.	
Cameo, Bowl, Dessert, 4 ½ In.	7
Cameo, Bowl, Vegetable, Green, Oval, 10 In.	30
Cameo, Cake Plate, Green, 3-Footed, 10 In.	40
Cameo, Candlestick, Green, Pair	95
Cameo, Compote, Mayonnaise, Green, 5 In.	45
Cameo, Cookie Jar, Lid, Green	60
Cameo, Cup, Green, Fancy Handle	7
Cameo, Decanter, Stopper, Green, 10 In.	175
Cameo, Plate, Dinner, 9 In.	25
Cameo, Plate, Dinner, Yellow, 9 ⅛ In.	15
Cameo, Plate, Luncheon, Green, 8 In.	14
Cameo, Plate, Salad, 7 In.	5
Cameo, Plate, Sherbet, Green, 6 In.	6
Cameo, Relish, Green, 3 Sections, 3-Footed, 7 ½ In.	30
Cameo, Shaker, Green, Footed	40
Cameo, Sherbet, Green, 3 ¼ In.	15
Cameo, Sugar, Green, 3 ¼ In.	22
Cameo, Vase, Green, 8 In.	65
Cameo, Water Bottle, Dark Green, White House Vinegar	25
Candlewick pattern is listed in the Imperial Glass category.	
Caprice pattern is included in the Cambridge Glass category.	
Charm, Cup & Saucer, Forest Green, Anchor Hocking	6
Charm, Plate, Forest Green, Anchor Hocking, 8 ⅜ In.	12
Charm, Saucer, Fire-King, Jade-Ite	5
Cherry Blossom, Bowl, Delphite, 2 Handles, 9 ½ In.	25
Cherry Blossom, Cup, Delphite	18
Cherry Blossom, Pitcher, Green, Scalloped Base, 6 ¾ In.	75
Cherry Blossom, Saucer, Pink, Child's, 4 ½ In.	5

Cherry Blossom, Sugar & Creamer, Lid, Pink	60
Cherryberry, Plate, Sherbet, Green, 6 In.	10
Cherryberry, Sherbet, Green	10
Chevron, Pitcher, Milk, Blue, 4 ¼ In.	24
Chinex Classic, Plate, Castle Decoration, 9 ¾ In.	25
Cloverleaf, Plate, Luncheon, Pink, 8 In.	10
Cloverleaf, Salt & Pepper, Black, 3 ¾ In.	45
Colonial Block, Creamer, Pink	15
Colonial Block, Sherbet, Footed, Green, 3 x 3 ¼ In., 4 Piece *illus*	35
Colonial Block, Sugar, Green	15
Colonial Block, Sugar, Lid, Pink	25
Colonial Block, Sugar, Lid, White	15
Colonial Fluted, Bowl, Cereal, Green, 6 In.	18
Colonial Fluted, Cup & Saucer, Green	10
Colonial, Berry Bowl, Green, 4 ½ In.	20
Colonial, Cruet, Pink, Westmoreland, 1920s, 5 ¼ In. *illus*	28
Colony, Water Set, Green, Hazel-Atlas, 7 Piece	116
Colored Spirals, Pitcher, Blue, Ice Lip, Hazel-Atlas, 82 Oz.	65
Colored Spirals, Tumbler, Blue, Hazel-Atlas, 9 Oz., 4 In.	16
Columbia, Bowl, Cereal, 5 In.	18
Columbia, Plate, Bread & Butter, 6 In.	3
Coronation, Berry Bowl, 4 ½ In.	8
Coronation, Berry Bowl, 8 In.	20
Cremax, Cup & Saucer, Bluebell	12
Cremax, Sugar, Bluebell	10
Cube pattern is listed here as Cubist.	
Cubist, Bowl, Dessert, Pink, Toothed Edge, 4 ½ In.	10
Cubist, Bowl, Salad, Green, Toothed Edge, 8 In.	24
Cubist, Bowl, Underplate, Gold Trim, 4 ½ & 6 In.	8
Cubist, Butter, Cover, Pink	85
Cubist, Candy Jar, Green	15
Cubist, Candy Jar, Lid, Pink	38
Cubist, Cup, Green	12
Cubist, Plate, Luncheon, Green, 8 In.	12
Cubist, Plate, Pink, 6 In.	4
Cubist, Salt & Pepper, Green	45
Cubist, Saucer, Green	3
Cubist, Saucer, Pink	3
Cubist, Sugar & Creamer	10
Cubist, Sugar, Small	6
Dancing Girl pattern is listed here as Cameo.	
Deerwood, Server, Pink, Center Handle, U.S. Glass	85
Della Robbia, Bowl, Red Flashed, Belled, Footed, 12 In.	125
Diamond pattern is listed here as Miss America.	
Diamond Arches, Berry Set, Ritz Blue, Ruffled, Hazel-Atlas, 8 ½ x 4 ½ In., 7 Piece	80
Diamond Arches, Bowl, Green, Plain, Hazel-Atlas, 4 ¼ In.	8
Diamond Arches, Bowl, Green, Ruffled, Hazel-Atlas, 8 ½ In.	16
Diamond Arches, Bowl, Ritz Blue, Ruffled, Hazel-Atlas, 4 ½ In.	10
Diamond Block, Bowl, Green, Oval, 2 Handles, 6 ½ In.	20
Diamond Block, Bowl, Lily, Pink, 5 In.	18
Diamond Block, Bowl, Pink, Oval, 2 Handles, 6 ½ In.	20
Diamond Block, Creamer, Green	15
Diamond Block, Jug, 16 Oz.	20
Diamond Block, Nappy, Green, Handle, 4 ½ In.	16
Diamond Line, Pitcher, Pink, 60 Oz.	48
Diamond Line, Tumbler, Pink, 9 Oz., 4 In.	12
Diamond Quilted, Bowl, Black, Crimped Edge, 7 In.	20
Diamond Quilted, Bowl, Pink, Straight Edge, 7 In.	20
Diamond Quilted, Candlestick, Black, Flat	18
Diamond Quilted, Candlestick, Blue, Flat	18
Diamond Quilted, Candlestick, Green, Domed	25
Diamond Quilted, Candlestick, Green, Flat	15
Diamond Quilted, Candlestick, Pink, Flat, Pair	30
Diamond Quilted, Candy Dish, Lid, Pink, 6 ½ x 5 ½ In. *illus*	75
Diamond Quilted, Creamer, Black	15
Diamond Quilted, Creamer, Pink	12

Dedham, Vase, Oxblood, Orange Peel, Hugh Robertson, CKAW, 1880s, 4 ¼ x 4 ½ In.
$2,125

Rago Arts & Auction Center

Delft, Charger, Oriental Figures, Courtyard, Marked, c.1750, 15 ¾ In.
$1,800

Skinner Auctioneers & Appraisers

Delft, Dish, Bird & Insect, Tree, Multicolor, Marked, 1700s, 16 ¾ In.
$1,121

Brunk Auctions

TIP

When you open your windows in warm weather, watch out for blowing curtains. They may hit glass or china displayed nearby and cause damage.

Delft, Vase, Fish, Crackle Ground, Marked, Porceleyne Fles, 4 ¼ In. $236

Humler & Nolan

Dental, Sign, Tooth, Figural, Wood, Carved, Attached Hanger, 1800s, 9 x 23 ½ In. $5,710

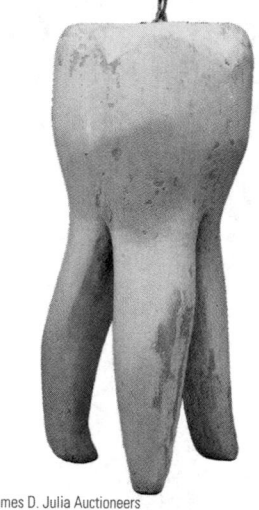

James D. Julia Auctioneers

Denver, Vase, Parrot Tulips, Green, Marked, Denaura, c.1903, 8 ½ x 5 ¾ In. $2,500

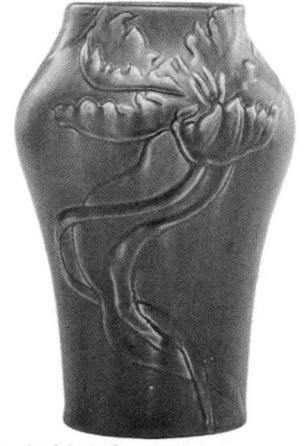

Rago Arts & Auction Center

Diamond Quilted, Cup, Black	17
Diamond Quilted, Cup, Pink *illus*	12
Diamond Quilted, Nappy, Black, Handle, 5 ½ In.	18
Diamond Quilted, Nappy, Pink, Handle, 5 ½ In.	15
Diamond Quilted, Plate, Luncheon, Blue, 8 In.	12
Diamond Quilted, Plate, Luncheon, Green, 8 In.	12
Diamond Quilted, Plate, Luncheon, Pink, 8 In.	12
Diamond Quilted, Punch Bowl, Base, Green	195
Diamond Quilted, Saucer, Black	6
Diamond Quilted, Soup, Cream, Black, 4 ¾ In.	25
Diamond Quilted, Sugar & Creamer, Green	22
Diamond Quilted, Sugar & Creamer, Pink *illus*	35
Diamond Quilted, Sugar, Black	15
Diamond Quilted, Sugar, Pink	10
Diana, Console, Flared, Scalloped, 12 In.	16
Diana, Creamer, Amber	12
Diana, Cup & Saucer, Demitasse	12
Diana, Sherbet, Amber, Footed Cone	12
Dish, Ice Cream, Birds & Leaves, Heart Shape, Heart Shape Foot, 3 ½ In.	303
Dogwood, Berry Bowl, Pink, 8 ½ In.	50
Dogwood, Cup & Saucer, Pink, Thin	18
Dogwood, Cup, Pink, Thick	15
Dogwood, Grill Plate, Pink, Border Design, 10 ½ In.	25
Dogwood, Saucer, Pink, Thick	7
Dogwood, Saucer, Pink, Thin	7
Dogwood, Sugar, Pink, Thick, 3 ¼ In.	18
Dogwood, Tumbler, Pink, Molded Band, 10 Oz., 4 ¾ In.	25
Doric & Pansy, Plate, Sherbet, Pink, 6 In.	8
Doric, Berry Bowl, Pink, 4 ½ In.	12
Doric, Cup, Pink	12
Doric, Plate, Dinner, Pink, 9 In.	18
Doric, Plate, Sherbet, Green, 6 In.	8
Doric, Saucer, Pink	4
Doric, Shaker, Pink	22
Doric, Sugar, Lid Only, Green	30
Doric, Tray, Pink, 8 x 8 In.	40
Doric, Tumbler, Pink, Flat, 9 Oz., 4 ¼ In.	75
Double Shield pattern is listed here as Mt. Pleasant.	
Dutch Rose pattern is listed here as Rosemary.	
English Hobnail, Bonbon, Handle, Hexagonal, 6 In.	15
English Hobnail, Candlestick, Green, Square, 5 ¾ In.	35
English Hobnail, Coaster	8
English Hobnail, Cologne Bottle, Stopper, Green	50
English Hobnail, Console, Amber, Rolled, 11 In.	30
English Hobnail, Cordial, Stem, 1 Oz., 3 ¼ In.	15
English Hobnail, Creamer, Green, Square Footed	55
English Hobnail, Nappy, Amber, Square, 6 In.	11
English Hobnail, Plate, Amber, 8 In.	15
English Hobnail, Plate, Amber, Round, 10 ½ In.	18
English Hobnail, Plate, Round, 8 In.	10
English Hobnail, Plate, Sherbet, 6 ½ In.	6
English Hobnail, Sugar, Footed, Hexagonal	10
English Hobnail, Toilet Bottle, Stopper, Ice Blue, Wide Mouth	100
English Hobnail, Tumbler, Pink, Barrel, 8 Oz., 3 ⅜ In.	20
English Hobnail, Tumbler, Round Footed, 5 Oz.	9
English Hobnail, Tumbler, Square Footed, 11 Oz.	12
English Hobnail, Vanity Jar, Lid, Green, 5 x 2 In. *illus*	45
English Hobnail, Wine, 2 Oz., 4 ½ In.	9
Fine Rib pattern is listed here as Homespun.	
Fire-King, Bowl, Chili, Jade-Ite, 5 In.	22
Fire-King, Bowl, Maple Leaf Shape, Tab Handle, Jade-Ite, 6 ½ In.	25
Fire-King, Cup & Saucer, St. Denis, Jade-Ite	18
Fire-King, Grease Jar, Tulip Lid, Jade-Ite	85
Fire-King, Mixing Bowl, Beaded Edge, Jade-Ite, 7 ⅛ In.	40
Fire-King, Saucer, St. Denis, Jade-Ite	5
Fire-King, Vase, Art Deco, Jade-Ite, 6 In.	20

Floradora, Sherbet, Amber, Footed, 6 Oz., 3 ¼ In.	6
Floradora, Tumbler, Cordial, Amber, Footed, 1 Oz., 1 ⅝ In.	8
Floral & Diamond Band, Berry Bowl, 8 In.	20
Floral & Diamond Band, Butter, Cover Only, Green	75
Floral & Diamond Band, Butter, Cover Only, Pink	75
Floral & Diamond Band, Sherbet, Green	8
Floral & Diamond Band, Sugar, Green, 5 ¼ In.	20
Floral & Diamond Band, Tumbler, Water, Green, 4 In.	25
Floral, Bowl, Vegetable, Lid, Pink, 8 In.	55
Floral, Butter, Dome Cover, Pink, 6 ½ In. ....illus	59
Floral, Butter, Pink	25
Floral, Coaster, Pink, 3 ¼ In.	12
Floral, Coaster, Pink, Jeannette Glass, 3 In. ....illus	10
Floral, Cup, Green	15
Floral, Cup, Pink	14
Floral, Goblet, 7 ¾ x 3 ½ In., 3 Piece	60
Floral, Plate, Dinner, Pink, 9 In.	12
Floral, Plate, Sherbet, Pink, 6 In.	8
Floral, Platter, Pink, Oval, 10 ¾ In.	25
Floral, Shaker, Green, Footed	25
Floral, Sherbet, Green	12
Florentine No. 1, Creamer, Green	10
Florentine No. 1, Cup, Green	10
Florentine No. 1, Pitcher, Yellow, Footed, 6 ½ In.	50
Florentine No. 2, Butter, Yellow	68
Florentine No. 2, Cup, Green	8
Florentine No. 2, Cup, Yellow	10
Florentine No. 2, Plate, Salad, Yellow, 8 ¼ In.	10
Florentine No. 2, Relish, Pink, Oval, 3 Sections, 10 In.	30
Florentine No. 2, Tumbler, Green, Flat, 5 Oz., 3 ⅜ In.	12
Florentine No. 2, Tumbler, Green, Footed, 5 Oz., 3 ¼ In.	14
Flower & Leaf Band pattern is listed here as Indiana Custard.	
Forest Green, Ashtray, Hocking Glass Co., 4 ⅝ In.	8
Forest Green, Bowl, Dessert, Seashell, Hocking Glass Co., 7 In.	10
Forest Green, Bowl, Metal Stand, 3 Wood Ball Feet, 3 ¼ x 6 In.	20
Forest Green, Bowl, Scalloped, Hocking Glass Co., 6 ½ In.	10
Forest Green, Candy Dish, Swedish Modern, Hocking Glass Co., 7 x 3 ½ In.	35
Forest Green, Pitcher, Polka Dots, Ice Lip, Hocking Glass Co., 86 Oz.	45
Forest Green, Plate, Dinner, Provincial, Anchor Hocking, 9 ⅜ In.	14
Forest Green, Punch Cup	2
Forest Green, Salt & Pepper, Bullet, Owens-Illinois, 3 In.	18
Forest Green, Shaker, Banded, Owens-Illinois, 4 ⅛ In.	8
Forest Green, Shaker, Paneled, Owens-Illinois, 4 ⅜ In.	8
Forest Green, Shaker, Skyscraper, Owens-Illinois, 4 ⅛ In.	8
Forest Green, Shaker, Stacked, Owens-Illinois, 4 ¼ In.	8
Forest Green, Sugar & Creamer, Provincial, Anchor-Hocking	20
Forest Green, Sugar Shaker, Forest Green, Owens-Illinois, 4 ½ In.	15
Forest Green, Tumbler, Gay Nineties Series, Surrey With Fringe On Top	8
Forest Green, Tumbler, Lily Of The Valley, 12 Oz., 5 ¼ In.	10
Forest Green, Tumbler, Radio Star Series	8
Fortune, Candy Dish, Lid, Pink	30
Fortune, Plate, Sherbet, Pink, 4 Piece	28
Fruits, Cup, Pink	12
Georgian Rib, Tumbler, Burgundy, Hazel-Atlas, 9 Oz., 4 In.	12
Georgian Rib, Tumbler, Hazel-Atlas, 9 Oz., 4 In.	6
Georgian Rib, Tumbler, Ritz Blue, Hazel-Atlas, 9 Oz., 4 In.	12
Georgian, Berry Bowl, Green, 4 ½ In.	10
Georgian, Butter, Green	45
Georgian, Candy Dish, Lid, Ruby, Viking, 6 In.	45
Georgian, Creamer, Green, Footed, 4 In.	18
Georgian, Plate, Luncheon, Green, 8 ½ In.	12
Georgian, Tumbler, Green, Federal Glass Co., c.1933, 5 ¼ In., 6 Piece	230
Grape, Vase, Hanging, Green, Copper Hanger, 5 ½ x 4 ¼ In.	48
Hairpin pattern is listed here as Newport.	
Hex Optic pattern is listed here as Hexagon Optic.	
Hexagon Optic, Mixing Bowl, Green, Ruffled, 6 ½ In.	20

Depression Glass, Adam, Tumbler, Iced Tea, Pink, 5 ½ In.
$40

Ruby Lane, Inc.

Depression Glass, Colonial Block, Sherbet, Footed, Green, 3 x 3 ¼ In., 4 Piece
$35

Ruby Lane, Inc.

Depression Glass, Colonial, Cruet, Pink, Westmoreland, 1920s, 5 ¼ In.
$28

Ruby Lane, Inc.

Depression Glass, Diamond Quilted, Candy Dish, Lid, Pink, 6 ½ x 5 ½ In.
$75

Ruby Lane, Inc.

Depression Glass, Diamond Quilted,
Cup, Pink
$12

Ruby Lane, Inc.

Depression Glass, Diamond Quilted,
Sugar & Creamer, Pink
$35

Ruby Lane, Inc.

Depression Glass, English Hobnail,
Vanity Jar, Lid, Green, 5 x 2 In.
$45

Ruby Lane, Inc.

Depression Glass, Floral, Butter, Dome
Cover, Pink, 6 ½ In.
$59

Ruby Lane, Inc.

Hexagon Optic, Mixing Bowl, Green, Ruffled, 7 ½ In.	25
Hexagon Optic, Tumbler, Juice, Iridescent Marigold, 6 Oz., 3 ¾ In.	3
Hexagon Optic, Tumbler, Pink, Flared Top, 11 Oz., 5 In.	10
Hexagon Optic, Tumbler, Pink, Tapered, 11 Oz., 5 In.	10
Homespun, Berry Set, Pink, 7 Piece	120
Homespun, Cup & Saucer, Pink	30
Homespun, Pitcher, Ritz Blue, Tilted Ball, 80 Oz.	125
Homespun, Platter, Pink, Oval	20
Homespun, Tumbler, Juice, Ritz Blue, 5 Oz., 3 ¼ In.	12
Homespun, Tumbler, Pink, Flat, 9 Oz., 4 ¼ In.	25
Homestead, Snack Tray, Snack Cup, Boxed, 4 Sets	40
Honeycomb pattern is listed here as Hexagon Optic.	
Horizontal Ribbed pattern is listed here as Manhattan.	
Horseshoe pattern is listed here as No. 612.	
Indiana Custard, Berry Bowl, French Ivory, 5 ½ In.	15
Indiana Custard, Bowl, Cereal, French Ivory, 6 ½ In.	24
Indiana Custard, Plate, Dinner, French Ivory, 9 ¾ In.	36
Indiana Custard, Saucer, French Ivory	10
Iris & Herringbone pattern is listed here as Iris.	
Iris, Butter, Cover Only	35
Iris, Candleholder, 2-Light	25
Iris, Cup	16
Iris, Pitcher, Footed, 9 ½ In.	40
Iris, Plate, Luncheon, Frosted, 8 In.	35
Iris, Plate, Sandwich, Frosted, 11 ¾ In.	20
Iris, Sauce Bowl, Ruffled, 5 In.	10
Iris, Sherbet, Marigold, 2 ³⁄₁₆ x 2 ¼ In., Pair	10
Iris, Tumbler, Iced Tea, Iridescent Marigold, Footed, 6 In.	12
Jadite, Bowl, Breakfast, Red Ivy Trim, 16 Oz., 5 In.	170
Jadite, Bowl, Horizontal Rib, Jeannette, 12 In.	100
Jadite, Canister, Ginger, Jeannette	195
Jadite, Eggcup	35
Jadite, Pitcher, Milk, 20 Oz.	80
Jadite, Plate, Dinner, 9 ⅛ In.	25
Jadite, Shaker, Cinnamon, Jeannette	50
Jadite, Shaker, Cloves, Jeannette	45
Jadite, Shaker, Flour, Square, Jeannette	85
Jadite, Shaker, Jeannette	30
Jadite, Shaker, Pepper, Jeannette	45
Jane Ray, Bowl, Dessert, Fire-King, Jade-Ite, 4 ⅞ In.	12
Jane Ray, Bowl, Oatmeal, Fire-King, Jade-Ite, 5 ⅞ In.	25
Jane Ray, Creamer, Fire-King, Jade-Ite	20
Jane Ray, Cup, Fire-King, Jade-Ite	7
Jane Ray, Plate, Dinner, Fire-King, Jade-Ite, 9 In.	16
Jane Ray, Plate, Salad, Fire-King, Jade-Ite, 7 ¾ In.	12
Jane Ray, Sugar & Creamer, Lid, Fire-King, Jade-Ite	60
Knife & Fork pattern is listed here as Colonial.	
Lace Edge pattern is listed here as Old Colony. There is also a pattern called Lace Edge listed in the Imperial Glass category.	
Laurel, Berry Bowl, Ivory, 4 ¾ In.	8
Laurel, Bowl, Cereal, Jade Green, 6 In.	28
Laurel, Candlestick, Ivory	24
Laurel, Cup & Saucer, Ivory	10
Laurel, Sugar, Ivory	12
Laurel, Sugar, Jade Green	35
Lorain pattern is listed here as No. 615.	
Lovebirds pattern is listed here as Georgian.	
Madrid, Bowl, Salad, 8 In.	14
Madrid, Candlestick, Amber, 2 ½ In.	12
Madrid, Candlestick, Iridescent, 2 ½ In.	12
Madrid, Cookie Jar, Lid, Pink	45
Madrid, Creamer, Amber, Footed	12
Madrid, Cup & Saucer, Amber	15
Madrid, Grill Plate, Green, 10 ½ In.	18
Madrid, Pitcher, Amber	35
Madrid, Plate, Dinner, Amber, 10 ½ In.	50

Madrid, Platter, Amber, 11 ½ In.	18
Madrid, Tumbler, Amber, Footed, 10 Oz.	34
Madrid, Tumbler, Iced Tea, Amber, Flat, 12 Oz., 5 ½ In.	25
Manhattan, Bowl, Pink, 2 Handles, 5 ¼ In.	25
Manhattan, Candleholder, 4 ½ In., Pair	15
Manhattan, Creamer, Pink, Oval	15
Manhattan, Shaker, Pink	25
Mayfair Open Rose, Bowl, Blue, Low, Flat, 11 ½ In.	95
Mayfair Open Rose, Bowl, Green, Low, Flat, 11 ¾ In.	45
Mayfair Open Rose, Cookie Jar, Lid, Pink	50
Mayfair Open Rose, Cup & Saucer, Blue	70
Mayfair Open Rose, Cup, Blue	45
Mayfair Open Rose, Grill Plate, Blue, 9 ½ In.	60
Mayfair Open Rose, Pitcher, Pink, 80 Oz., 8 ½ In.	95
Mayfair Open Rose, Server, Green, Center Handle	35
Mayfair Open Rose, Sugar, Pink	30
Melba, Plate, Pink, Pebbled Rim, Octagonal, L.E. Smith, 8 In.	8
Miss America, Berry Bowl, Anchor Hocking, 6 ¼ In.	9
Miss America, Bowl, Cereal, Pink, 6 ¼ In.	30
Miss America, Bowl, Vegetable, Pink, Oval, 10 In.	52
Miss America, Celery Dish, Anchor Hocking, 10 ¾ In.	11
Miss America, Compote	14
Miss America, Compote, Pink, 5 In.	28
Miss America, Creamer	10
Miss America, Cup & Saucer, Anchor Hocking	7
Miss America, Cup & Saucer, Pink	30
Miss America, Plate, Bread & Butter, Anchor Hocking, 5 ¾ In.	6
Miss America, Plate, Dinner, Pink, 10 ¼ In.	45
Miss America, Platter, Oval, 12 ¼ In.	18
Miss America, Platter, Pink, Oval, 12 ¼ In.	42
Miss America, Sherbet, Pink, 3 ½ In. ....*illus*	20
Miss America, Sugar & Creamer, Anchor Hocking	20
Miss America, Sugar & Creamer, Pink	55
Miss America, Tumbler, Pink, 10 Oz., 4 ½ In. ....*illus*	80
Miss America, Tumbler, Water, 10 Oz., 4 ½ In.	18
Moderntone, Berry Bowl, Blue, 8 ¾ In.	55
Moderntone, Cup & Saucer, Green, Hazel-Atlas ....*illus*	9
Moderntone, Cup, Amethyst	12
Moderntone, Cup, Blue	10
Moderntone, Plate, Blue, Chrome Lid, Red Bakelite Knob, 8 In.	40
Moderntone, Plate, Dinner, Amethyst, 9 ⅛ In.	15
Moderntone, Plate, Sherbet, Amethyst, 5 ¾ In.	7
Moderntone, Platter, Cobalt Blue, Oval, 11 x 8 In.	20
Moderntone, Salt & Pepper, Blue	42
Moderntone, Soup, Cream, Amethyst, 2 Handles, 4 ¾ In.	20
Moderntone, Soup, Cream, Blue, 2 Handles, 4 ¾ In.	23
Moderntone, Soup, Cream, Blue, Ruffled, 5 In.	65
Moderntone, Sugar & Creamer, Metal Lid, Blue	65
Moderntone, Tumbler, Juice, Green, 5 Oz., 3 ¾ In.	6
Moderntone, Tumbler, Water, Green, 9 Oz., 4 In.	8
Moondrops pattern is listed in the New Martinsville category.	
Mt. Pleasant, Bowl, Mayonnaise, Black, 3-Footed, 5 ½ In.	28
Mt. Pleasant, Candlestick, Black, 2-Light, Pair	48
Mt. Pleasant, Cup, Black	12
Mt. Pleasant, Cup, Blue	12
Mt. Vernon pattern is included in the Cambridge Glass category.	
New Century, Salt & Pepper, Green	35
Newport, Berry Bowl, Amethyst, 4 ¼ In.	20
Newport, Bowl, Cereal, Amethyst, 5 ¼ In.	35
Newport, Cup & Saucer, Amethyst	17
Newport, Plate, Luncheon, Amethyst, 8 ⅜ In.	15
Newport, Plate, Luncheon, Fired-On Green, 8 ½ In.	8
Newport, Plate, Luncheon, Fired-On Yellow, 8 ½ In.	8
Newport, Platter, Amethyst, Oval, 11 ¾ In.	25
Newport, Shaker, White, Footed	15

No. 601 pattern is listed here as Avocado.

Depression Glass, Floral, Coaster, Pink, Jeannette Glass, 3 In.
$10

Depression Glass, Miss America, Sherbet, Pink, 3 ½ In.
$20

Depression Glass, Miss America, Tumbler, Pink, 10 Oz., 4 ½ In.
$80

Depression Glass, Moderntone, Cup & Saucer, Green, Hazel-Atlas
$9

Depression Glass, Old Colony, Vase, Amber, 4 ¼ x 4 ⅜ In. $15

Ruby Lane, Inc.

Depression Glass, Rest Well, Mixing Bowl, Green, Hazel-Atlas, 5 ½ In. $15

Ruby Lane, Inc.

Depression Glass, Royal Lace, Pitcher, Ice Lip, Cobalt Blue, 96 Oz., 9 ¾ In. $450

Ruby Lane, Inc.

Depression Glass, Strawberry, Plate, Pink, 7 ½ In. $15

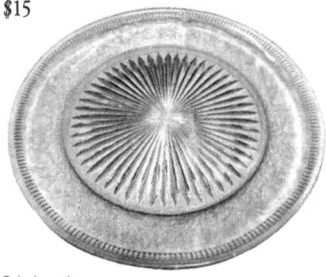

Ruby Lane, Inc.

No. 612, Bowl, Cereal, Yellow, 6 In.	25
No. 612, Cup & Saucer, Green	18
No. 615, Plate, Salad, Yellow, 7 ¾ In.	15
No. 615, Relish, Yellow, Square, 4 Sections	40
No. 615, Sugar	18
No. 618, Bowl, Vegetable, Amber, Oval, 10 In.	18
No. 618, Luncheon Set, Amber, 15 Piece	120
Normandie, Bowl, Iridescent Pink, 7 In.	6
Normandie, Creamer, Amber	8
Normandie, Creamer, Iridescent Pink	8
Normandie, Cup & Saucer, Pink	9
Normandie, Cup, Amber	6
Normandie, Grill Plate, Iridescent Pink, 11 In.	8
Normandie, Shaker, Amber	20
Old Cafe, Berry Bowl, Pink, Tab Handles, 3 ¾ In.	14
Old Cafe, Bowl, Cereal, Royal Ruby, 5 ½ In.	30
Old Cafe, Candy Dish, 2 Handles, 8 In.	8
Old Cafe, Candy Jar, Royal Ruby Lid, Open Handles	25
Old Cafe, Cup & Saucer, Royal Ruby	18
Old Cafe, Nappy, Pink, Loop Handle, 5 In.	15
Old Cafe, Relish Insert	15
Old Cafe, Relish, Clear, Royal Ruby Insert	150
Old Cafe, Sherbet, Pink, 3 ¾ In.	16
Old Cafe, Tumbler, Juice, Royal Ruby, 3 In.	22
Old Cafe, Tumbler, Water, Pink, 9 Oz., 4 In.	22
Old Cafe, Vase, 7 ¼ In.	10
Old Colony, Bowl, Plain, Pink, 9 ½ In.	25
Old Colony, Butter, Cover, Pink	55
Old Colony, Candlestick, Frosted Pink	40
Old Colony, Grill Plate, Pink, 10 ½ In.	20
Old Colony, Plate, Dinner, Pink, 10 ½ In.	20
Old Colony, Platter, Pink, Lace Edge, 12 ⅝ In.	15
Old Colony, Vase, Amber, 4 ¼ x 4 ⅜ In. ....*illus*	15
Old English, Tumbler, Amber, Footed, 4 ½ In.	18
Old English, Water Set, Fired-On Orange Crystal, 7 Piece	150
Old Florentine pattern is listed here as Florentine No. 1.	
Open Lace pattern is listed here as Old Colony.	
Open Rose pattern is listed here as Mayfair Open Rose.	
Optic Design pattern is listed here as Raindrops.	
Ovide, Bowl, Cereal, 15 Oz., 5 ½ In.	9
Ovide, Creamer	9
Ovide, Cup & Saucer	9
Ovide, Plate, Bread & Butter, 6 In.	5
Ovide, Plate, Dinner, 9 In.	12
Oyster & Pearl, Relish, Pink, 10 ¼ In.	20
Panelled Aster pattern is listed here as Primo.	
Park Avenue, Ashtray, Round, Anchor Hocking	10
Park Avenue, Cup, Anchor Hocking	5
Parrot pattern is listed here as Sylvan.	
Patrician, Berry Bowl, Amber, 8 ½ In.	35
Patrician, Bowl, Cereal, Amber, 6 In.	20
Patrician, Bowl, Vegetable, Oval, 10 In.	18
Patrician, Creamer, Green	12
Patrician, Cup, Green	10
Patrician, Shaker, Amber	20
Patrician, Tumbler, Water, Amber, 9 Oz., 4 ⅜ In.	20
Peacock & Wild Rose pattern is listed in the Paden City category.	
Petal Swirl pattern is listed here as Swirl.	
Petalware, Berry Bowl, Pink, 8 ½ In.	24
Petalware, Cup & Saucer, Cremax, Regency Gold Trim	12
Petalware, Cup & Saucer, Florette	12
Petalware, Cup & Saucer, Monax	9
Petalware, Lampshade, Monax, 6 ⅜ In.	20
Petalware, Mustard, Ritz Blue, Metal Cover, Bakelite Knob	15
Petalware, Plate, Dinner, Monax, 9 In.	15
Petalware, Plate, Fruits, Cherries, 8 In.	15

Petalware, Plate, Fruits, Lemons, 8 In.	15
Petalware, Plate, Pink, 8 ½ In.	10
Petalware, Plate, Salad, Cremax, 8 In.	9
Petalware, Plate, Salad, Cremax, Regency Gold Trim, 8 In.	10
Petalware, Salver, 11 In.	15 to 25
Petalware, Salver, Pink, 11 In.	18
Petalware, Saucer, Cremax	2
Petalware, Sugar & Creamer, Cremax, Gold Trim	14
Petalware, Sugar, Monax	6
Pillar Optic, Bowl, Plate, Pink, 11 ½ & 13 ½ In.	75
Pillar Optic, Cup & Saucer, Green	18
Pillar Optic, Plate, Luncheon, Green, 8 In.	15
Pillar Optic, Plate, Sherbet, Green, 6 ½ In.	15
Pillar Optic, Refrigerator Dish Set, Green, 3 Piece	140
Pillar Optic, Saltshaker, Green, Round, Embossed Diamond Crystal Salt	45
Pillar Optic, Tumbler, Water, Green, 9 Oz., 4 In.	20
Pillar Optic, Water Set, Pink, 60 Oz., 7 Piece	149
Pineapple & Floral pattern is listed here as No. 618.	
Pinwheel pattern is listed here as Sierra.	
Poinsettia pattern is listed here as Floral.	
Poppy No. 1 pattern is listed here as Florentine No. 1.	
Poppy No. 2 pattern is listed here as Florentine No. 2.	
Pretty Polly Party Dishes, see the related pattern Doric & Pansy.	
Primo, Cup, Green	12
Primo, Plate, Green, 7 ½ In.	15
Princess, Bowl, Vegetable, Oval, 9 ½ In.	24
Princess, Butter, Cover, Green	75
Princess, Butter, Pink	35
Princess, Pitcher, Juice, Green, 6 In.	70
Princess, Plate, Dinner, Green, 9 In., Pair	25
Princess, Plate, Green, 9 In., Pair	25
Princess, Sherbet, Green, Footed, 3 ½ x 3 ⅜ In., 3 Piece	45
Princess, Vase, Green, 8 In.	45
Princess, Vase, Pink, 8 In.	55
Prismatic Line pattern is listed here as Queen Mary.	
Provincial pattern is listed here as Bubble.	
Queen Mary, Plate, 12 In.	14
Quilted Diamond, Pitcher, Ritz Blue, Ice Lip, Hazel-Atlas, 48 Oz., 8 In.	60
Quilted Diamond, Tumbler, Green, Hazel-Atlas, 5 Oz., 3 In.	9
Quilted Diamond, Tumbler, Iced Tea, Green, Hazel-Atlas, 11 Oz., 5 ⅛ In.	14
Quilted Diamond, Tumbler, Water, Ritz Blue, Hazel-Atlas, 9 Oz., 4 In.	15
Radiance pattern is listed in the New Martinsville category.	
Raindrops, Cup & Saucer, Green, 8 Piece	65
Rest Well, Mixing Bowl, Green, Hazel-Atlas, 5 ½ In. .....illus	15
Restaurant Ware, Bowl, Jade-Ite, 15 Oz., 5 ⅝ In.	28
Restaurant Ware, Plate, Salad, Jade-Ite, 6 ¾ In.	14
Restaurant Ware, Saucer, Jade-Ite, 6 In.	7
Romanesque, Bowl, Black, Footed, 10 In.	65
Romanesque, Plate, Octagonal, Amber, 8 In.	10
Rose Cameo, Berry Bowl, Green, 4 ½ In.	14
Rose Cameo, Plate, Green, 7 In.	15
Rose Cameo, Sherbet, Green, Footed	15
Rose Cameo, Tumbler, Green, Cupped Rim, Footed, 5 In.	25
Rosemary, Bowl, Fruit, Federal Glass, 5 In.	4
Royal Lace, Pitcher, Ice Lip, Cobalt Blue, 96 Oz., 9 ¾ In. .....illus	450
Royal Lace, Plate, Dinner, Green, 9 ⅞ In.	35
Royal Lace, Plate, Dinner, Pink, 9 ⅞ In.	24
Royal Lace, Soup, Cream, Green, 4 ¾ In.	32
Royal Lace, Water Set, Pink, 7 Piece	275
S Pattern, Grill Plate, Platinum Trim, 10 ⅜ In.	9
Sailboat pattern is listed here as Sportsman Series.	
Sandwich, Candlesticks, 8 In., Pair	22
Saxon pattern is listed here as Coronation.	
Sharon, Butter, Cover Only, Pink	25
Sharon, Tumbler, Amber, Thin, 4 ⅛ In., 9 Oz.	24
Shell, Bowl, Cereal, Jade-Ite, 6 ⅜ In.	28

DEPRESSION GLASS

Depression Glass, Waterford, Cup & Saucer
$11

Ruby Lane, Inc.

Dinnerware, Willow, Plate, Luncheon, Blue, Royal China
$10

Ruby Lane, Inc.

> **TIP**
> Don't put celluloid in the sun. It is highly flammable and may burn.

Dionne Quintuplets, Dolls, Composition, Madame Alexander, Scooter, c.1935, 8 In., 6 Piece
$952

Theriault's

Dirk Van Erp, Bookends, Copper, California Faience Tile, 3-Masted Ship, 1920s, 4 x 4 In.
$5,000

Rago Arts & Auction Center

DEPRESSION GLASS

Dirk Van Erp, Lamp, Copper, Hammered, Paneled Mica Shade, Rivets, Signed, 16 In.
$8,295

James D. Julia Auctioneers

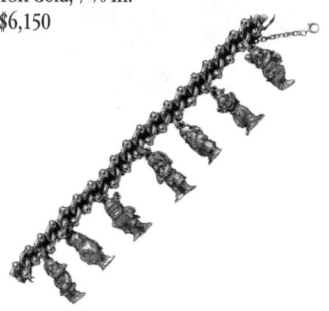

Disneyana, Bracelet, Charm, Figural, Seven Dwarfs, Colored Gem Stones, 18K Gold, 7 ⅞ In.
$6,150

Skinner Auctioneers & Appraisers

Disneyana, Charm, Mickey Mouse, Enamel, 14K Gold, 2-Sided, 1930s, ¹³⁄₁₆ In.
$2,935

Hake's Americana & Collectibles

Disneyana, Cookie Jar, Mickey Mouse, Leather Ears, Walt Disney, Enesco Label
$52

Victorian Casino Antiques

Shell, Cup & Saucer, Jade-Ite	25
Sierra, Butter, Cover Only, Pink	50
Sierra, Plate, Dinner, Green	25
Soreno, Butter, Cover, Green, Anchor Hocking	10
Spiral Flutes pattern is listed in the Duncan & Miller category as Swirl.	
Spiral, Cup & Saucer, Green	8
Spiral, Plate, Bread & Butter, Green, 6 ⅛ In., 4 Piece	15
Spiral, Plate, Green, 6 ¼ In., 6 Piece	25
Spiral, Tumbler, Footed, Green, 5 ⅝ x 2 ⅝ In.	10
Spoke pattern is listed here as Patrician.	
Sportsman Series, Tumbler, Water, Ritz Blue, Red Ship, 4 ⅝ In.	25
Spun, Pitcher, Stiegel Green, Ice Lip, Crystal Applied Handle, 8 In.	95
Spun, Tumbler, Iced Tea, Cobalt Blue, 15 Oz.	24
Spun, Vase, Bud, Stiegel Green, 6 In.	35
Stippled Rose Band pattern is listed here as S Pattern.	
Strawberry, Plate, Pink, 7 ½ In. ....*illus*	15
Sunflower, Cake Plate, Green, 3 Shaped Feet, 10 In., Pair	35
Sunflower, Cup, Pink	15
Sunflower, Pitcher, Green, 5 In., 32 Oz.	45
Sunflower, Plate, Dinner, Pink, 9 In.	24
Swirl, Cake Plate, Crystal, 3-Footed, 11 ¼ In.	20
Swirl, Mixing Bowl Set, Fire-King, Jade-Ite, 6, 7, 8, 9 In., 4 Piece	180
Swirl, Sherbet, Pink	12
Sylvan, Berry Bowl, Green, 5 In.	35
Tea Room, Bowl, Green, 2 Handles, 8 ½ In.	95
Tea Room, Plate, Pink, 2 Handles, 10 ½ In.	60
Tea Room, Sugar & Creamer, Pink	58
Tea Room, Sugar, Pink, 4 ½ In.	35
Tea Room, Tumbler, Green, Footed, 8 Oz., 5 ¼ In.	35
Threading pattern is listed here as Old English.	
Trojan, Goblet, Water, Topaz, 8 ¼ In.	35
Trojan, Plate, Salad, Topaz, 7 ⅜ In.	7
Trojan, Platter, Topaz, 12 In.	95
Trojan, Sherbet, Topaz, Fluted Stem, 6 In.	15
Tulip, Ice Tub, Green, 4 ⅞ x 3 In.	50
Tulip, Plate, Bread & Butter, Amethyst, 6 In.	10
Vertical Ribbed pattern is listed here as Queen Mary.	
Waffle pattern is listed here as Waterford.	
Waterford, Creamer, Oval	5
Waterford, Cup & Saucer ....*illus*	11
Waterford, Plate, Salad, Pink, 7 ⅛ In.	15
Waterford, Plate, Sandwich, Forest Green, 13 ¾ In.	45
Whirly-Twirly, Tumbler, Forest Green, Anchor Hocking, 18 Oz., 6 ½ In.	20
White Ship pattern is listed here as Sportsman Series.	
Wig-Wam, Console Set, Ritz Blue, 3 Piece	225
Wild Rose pattern is listed here as Dogwood.	
Windmill pattern is listed here as Sportsman Series.	
Windsor, Bowl, Cereal, Pink, 20 Oz., 5 ½ In.	30 to 35
Windsor, Bowl, Green, 20 Oz., 5 ½ x 2 ⅝ In.	30
Windsor, Bowl, Green, Boat Shape, 11 ¾ In.	45
Windsor, Bowl, Pink, Boat Shape, 11 ¾ In.	45
Windsor, Butter, Cover, Pink	65
Windsor, Cup & Saucer	6
Windsor, Plate, Dinner, Pink, 9 In.	15
Windsor, Platter, 11 ½ In.	8
Windsor, Sugar, Lid, Jeannette Glass, 4 ¾ x 4 In.	15
Windsor, Tumbler, Green, 9 Oz., 4 In.	25
Zig-Zag, Tumbler, Pink, Footed, 7 Oz., 4 ¾ In.	20

DERBY has been marked on porcelain made in the city of Derby, England, since about 1748. The original Derby factory closed in 1848, but others opened there and continued to produce quality porcelain. The Crown Derby mark began appearing on Derby wares in the 1770s.

Basket, Handles, Pierced Sides, Applied Flowers, Rope Twist Handles, 9 x 7 In.	345
Candlestick, Floral Bocage, Sheep, Scrolls, Flower Head Thumb Rest, c.1770, 9 ½ In., Pair	360
Centerpiece, Bourbon Sprig Pattern, Green, Purple, Basket Shape, Handles, c.1820, 4 x 12 In.	69

Cup & Saucer, Demitasse, Spiral Fluted, Cobalt Blue, Gilt, 2 ½ x 5 ¼ In.	58
Figurine, Farmer Gentleman, Gentlewoman, Fishing Net, England, 1800s, 7 In., Pair	354
Figurine, Man, Riding Coat, Period Attire, 5 ½ In.	196
Sugar, Lid, Roses, Leaves, Squat, Handles, c.1810, 4 x 7 In.	46
Vase, Lid, Cobalt Blue, Pierced, Scrolled Floral Leaf Handles, Bottle Shape, c.1880, 11 ½ In.	600

DICK TRACY, the comic strip, started in 1931. Tracy was also the hero of movies from 1937 to 1947 and again in 1990, and starred in a radio series in the 1940s and a television series in the 1950s. Memorabilia from all these activities are collected.

Badge, Sergeant, Secret Service Patrol, Premium, Quaker Oats, 1938, 2 ¾ In.	50
Belt Badge, Brass, Detective Club, Portrait, Leather Clip, Shield Shape, 1937, 3 x 2 In.	35
Book, Better Little Book, Bicycle Gang, No. 1424, 1948, 3 x 4 ½ In.	45
Book, Big Little Book, Dick Tracy Returns, No. 1495, 1939	30
Book, Big Little Book, The Adventures Of Dick Tracy Detective, 1932	2435
Game, Public Enemy No. 1, Tin Lithograph, Target, 15 x 15 x 5 In.	90
Lamp, Shade, Plaster, Figure Bust, Gun, Plastic, Buyer Paints, 1951, 4 ½ x 9 In.	575
Lunch Box, Police, Bank Robbers, Metal, Thermos, Aladdin, c.1967	115
Playing Card Game, Lithograph, 1930s, 6 ½ x 5 x 1 In.	95
Puzzle, Jigsaw, Police Car, Crime Lab, 1938, 7 x 10 In., Set Of 2	417
Ring, Monogram, Brass, Adjustable, Geometric Designs, Silver Luster, AM, Quaker, 1938	173
Ring, Portrait, Horseshoe, Clover, Sunburst, Brass, Premium, 1938, Adjustable	75
Sign, Power-Jet Squad Gun, Mattel Official, Glossy, 1962, 10 x 16 In.	538
Target, Bursting Through Target Graphic, Multicolor, Box, c.1930, 17 ½ x 17 ½ In.	151
Toy, B.O. Plenty, Walker, Baby, Gift, Tin Lithograph, Clockwork, Marx, 9 In.	207
Toy, Squad Car No. 1, Pedal, Pressed Steel, Green, Yellow, 15 x 35 x 20 In.	778

DICKENS WARE *pieces are listed in the Royal Doulton and Weller categories.*

DINNERWARE used in the United States from the 1930s through the 1950s is listed here. Most was made in potteries in southern Ohio, West Virginia, and California. A few patterns were made in Japan, England, and other countries. Dishes were sold in gift shops and department stores, or were given away as premiums. Many of these patterns are listed in this book in their own categories, such as Autumn Leaf, Azalea, Coors, Fiesta, Franciscan, Hall, Harker, Harlequin, Red Wing, Riviera, Russel Wright, Vernon Kilns, Watt, and Willow. For more prices, go to kovels.com. Sets missing a few pieces can be completed through the help of one of the many matching services listed on our website, www.kovels.com.

Acapulco, Chop Plate, Tab Handles, Salem China, 13 ¼ In.	45
Acapulco, Salt & Pepper, Salem China	28
Admiral, Bowl, Dessert, Homer Laughlin, 5 ¼ In.	6
Admiral, Gravy Boat, Underplate, Homer Laughlin	34
Admiral, Relish, Homer Laughlin	31
Allegro, Bowl, Vegetable, Round, Homer Laughlin, 8 ¾ In.	14
Allegro, Plate, Bread & Butter, Homer Laughlin, 6 In.	5
Allegro, Platter, Oval, Homer Laughlin, 11 In.	18
Allegro, Saucer, Homer Laughlin	4
Antoinette, Creamer, Salem China	18
Antoinette, Cup & Saucer, Salem China	12
Apple Blossom, Sugar, Lid, Edwin Knowles	28
Autumn, Bowl, Vegetable, Edwin Knowles, 9 In.	18
Autumn, Cup & Saucer, Edwin Knowles	12
Autumn, Plate, Dinner, Edwin Knowles, 9 ⅝ In.	12
Autumn, Platter, Edwin Knowles, 14 In.	25
Autumn, Salt & Pepper, Edwin Knowles	18
Autumn, Sugar, Lid, Bavaria	45
Avalon, Bowl, Vegetable, Round, Homer Laughlin, 9 In.	37
Barclay, Cup & Saucer	9
Barclay, Plate, Dessert, Homer Laughlin, 7 ¼ In.	6
Barclay, Platter, Oval, Homer Laughlin, 13 In.	28
Bittersweet, Gravy Boat, Underplate, Crooksville	48
Blue Rose, Bowl, Cereal, Crooksville	12
Blue Rose, Plate, Bread & Butter, Crooksville, 6 In.	8
Bridal White, Soup, Dish, Iroquois, 7 ¼ In.	15
Bristol, Bowl, Fruit, Castleton, 5 ⅝ In.	22
Bristol, Cup & Saucer, Castleton	35
Bristol, Plate, Bread & Butter, Castleton, 6 ⅜ In.	14

Disneyana, Dish, Figural, Mickey Mouse Head, Lid, Japan, 1930s, 3 ¼ x 3 ½ In.
$115

Hake's Americana & Collectibles

Disneyana, Display, Post Cereal Bowls, Mickey Mouse, Donald Duck, 12 Bowls, 10 x 15 In.
$1,012

Hake's Americana & Collectibles

Disneyana, Marionette, Jiminy Cricket, Wood, Plaque, Bob Baker, Box, 12 In.
$1,035

Victorian Casino Antiques

Disneyana, Purse, Mickey & Minnie Mouse, Pluto, Brass, Cohn & Rosenberger, 1930s, 2 ¼ In.
$1,035

Hake's Americana & Collectibles

Disneyana, Standee, Mickey, Donald, Pepsodent, Paste & Powder, Cardboard, 1937, 15 x 31 In., Pair
$863

Hake's Americana & Collectibles

Disneyana, Toy, Donald Duck, Fireman, Tin Lithograph, Linemar, Japan, 12 In.
$265

Bertoia Auctions

Buttercup, Plate, Bread & Butter, Edwin Knowles, 6 In.	8
California Farmhouse, Coffeepot, Brock, 10 Cup	64
California Farmhouse, Plate, Bread & Butter, Brock, 6 ½ In.	5
California Farmhouse, Plate, Salad, Brock, 9 In.	14
Carrousel, Gravy Boat, Brock	35
Carrousel, Plate, Dinner, Brock, 9 ¾ In.	24
Chelsea, Cup, Adderley	17
Chelsea, Soup, Dish, Adderley, 9 In.	45
Chusan, Cup & Saucer, Adams	17
Chusan, Plate, Bread & Butter, Adams, 6 ¼ In.	8
Chusan, Plate, Dinner, Adams, 10 ¼ In.	25
Country Sage, Bowl, Cereal, Homer Laughlin, 6 ¼ In.	5
Country Sage, Butter, Cover, Homer Laughlin	18
Country Sage, Cup & Saucer, Homer Laughlin	6
Country Sage, Mug, Homer Laughlin	7
Country Sage, Plate, Salad, Homer Laughlin, 7 ¼ In.	6
Dinner Rose, Bowl, Vegetable, Round, Tab Handles, Crooksville, 9 ½ In.	38
Dinner Rose, Creamer, Crooksville	26
Dinner Rose, Cup & Saucer, Crooksville	12
Dinner Rose, Plate, Bread & Butter, Crooksville, 6 ⅛ In.	6
Dinner Rose, Platter, Tab Handles, Crooksville, 13 ½ In.	45
Dinner Rose, Sugar, Lid, Crooksville	35
Dixie Dogwood, Bowl, Fruit, Joni China, 5 ¼ In.	5
Dixie Dogwood, Bowl, Vegetable, Joni China, 9 In.	21
Dixie Dogwood, Cup & Saucer, Joni China	8
Dixie Dogwood, Cup, Joni China	7
Dixie Dogwood, Plate, Bread & Butter, Joni China, 6 ¼ In.	4
Dixie Dogwood, Platter, Oval, Joni China, 11 ¾ In.	18
Dogwood, Cup & Saucer, Salem China	12
Dogwood, Plate, Salad, Salem China, 7 In.	8
Dorset, Bowl, Vegetable, Lid, Harmony House	89
Dorset, Cup & Saucer, Harmony House	18
Dorset, Gravy Boat, Underplate, Harmony House	48
Eggshell Georgian, Platter, Homer Laughlin, 13 ½ In.	25
Eternal Love, Cup & Saucer, Ashley	15
Eternal Love, Plate, Dinner, Ashley, 10 In.	12
Eternal Love, Soup, Dish, Ashley, 8 ⅛ In.	8
Fairfax, Berry Bowl, Harmony House, 5 ¼ In.	8
Fairfax, Plate, Salad, Harmony House, 7 ⅜ In.	8
Fairfax, Soup, Dish, Harmony House, 7 ¾ In.	12
Fantasy, Bowl, Vegetable, Round, Edwin Knowles	35
Fantasy, Cup & Saucer, Edwin Knowles	12
Fantasy, Plate, Dinner, Edwin Knowles, 10 ¼ In.	12
Flair, Cup & Saucer, Castleton	25
Flower Chain, Bowl, Vegetable, Lid, Edwin Knowles	79
Forever Yours, Cup, Brock	15
Forever Yours, Mug, Brock, 3 ⅜ In.	15
Forever Yours, Salt & Pepper, Brock	24
Gala, Bowl, Vegetable, Edwin Knowles, 8 ¾ In.	38
Gala, Cup & Saucer, Edwin Knowles	15
Gala, Plate, Bread & Butter, Edwin Knowles, 6 In.	6
Gala, Platter, Edwin Knowles, 13 ¾ x 10 ¼ In.	45
Gloria, Creamer, Castleton, 8 Oz.	55
Gloria, Cup & Saucer, Castleton	21
Gloria, Plate, Bread & Butter, Castleton, 6 ⅜ In.	10
Gloria, Plate, Dinner, Castleton, 10 ⅝ In.	28
Golden Wheat, Bowl, Fruit, Edwin Knowles	6
Golden Wheat, Bowl, Fruit, Homer Laughlin, 5 ½ In.	4
Golden Wheat, Cup & Saucer, Edwin Knowles	12
Golden Wheat, Cup, Homer Laughlin	3
Golden Wheat, Plate, Bread & Butter, Homer Laughlin, 6 In.	4
Golden Wheat, Plate, Dinner, Edwin Knowles, 10 In.	12
Golden Wheat, Soup, Dish, Homer Laughlin, 7 ½ In.	5
Grapevine, Berry Bowl, Edwin Knowles, 5 ⅝ In.	8
Grapevine, Cup & Saucer, Edwin Knowles	12
Grapevine, Plate, Dinner, Edwin Knowles, 10 ¼ In.	12

D

Grapevine, Platter, Edwin Knowles, 12 ⅝ In.	28
Green Arbor, Creamer, Continental Kilns	12
Green Arbor, Gravy Boat, Continental Kilns	35
Green Arbor, Platter, Continental Kilns, 13 ½ In.	50
Green Plaid, Bowl, Vegetable, Oval, Blue Ridge, 9 ½ In.	45
Green Plaid, Cup & Saucer, Blue Ridge	15
Green Plaid, Plate, Dinner, Blue Ridge, 10 ½ In.	18
Green Plaid, Platter, Oval, Blue Ridge, 13 ¾ In.	45
Harvest Time, Plate, Dinner, Iroquois, 10 ¼ In.	18
Harvest, Gravy Boat, Salem China	35
King Edward, Soup, Cream, Underplate, Castleton	41
Leaf Dance, Plate, Bread & Butter, Edwin Knowles, 6 In.	8
Lowesoft, Cup & Saucer, Adams	28
Mexicana, Baking Dish, Homer Laughlin, 9 ½ In.	42
Milano, Cup & Saucer, Edwin Knowles	12
Milano, Plate, Bread & Butter, Edwin Knowles, 6 In.	8
Milano, Plate, Dinner, Edwin Knowles, 10 In.	12
Penthouse, Chop Plate, Edwin Knowles	45
Pink Dogwood, Plate, Bread & Butter, Edwin Knowles, 6 In.	8
Pink Dogwood, Plate, Dinner, Edwin Knowles, 10 In.	12
Pink N' Charcoal, Bowl, Fruit, Marcrest, 5 ¼ In.	9
Pink N' Charcoal, Plate, Bread & Butter, Marcrest, 6 ¼ In.	6
Pink N' Charcoal, Saucer, Marcrest	5
Shell Pink, Cup, Castleton	28
Soreno, Chip & Dip, Green, Metal Holder, Anchor Hocking, 1970s, 8 ½ In.	25
South Pacific, Plate, Dinner, Brock, 10 ⅞ In.	21
South Pacific, Plate, Salad, Brock, 8 ⅞ In.	16
Southern Dogwood, Bowl, Fruit, Blue Ridge, 5 In.	12
Southern Dogwood, Bowl, Vegetable, Divided, Round, Blue Ridge, 8 ½ In.	40
Southern Dogwood, Cup & Saucer, Blue Ridge	18
Southern Dogwood, Plate, Dinner, Blue Ridge, 10 ½ In.	24
Splatter Blue, Bowl, Cereal, Homer Laughlin, 7 ¼ In.	12
Splatter Blue, Bowl, Vegetable, 9 ¼ In.	35
Splatter Blue, Creamer, Homer Laughlin	25
Splatter Blue, Plate, Dinner, Homer Laughlin, 10 ⅝ In.	21
Splatter Blue, Sugar, Homer Laughlin	24
Sunlight, Cup & Saucer, Edwin Knowles	14
Sunlight, Plate, Bread & Butter, Edwin Knowles, 6 In.	6
Sunlight, Plate, Dinner, Edwin Knowles, 10 In.	12
Tahiti Flower, Gravy Boat, Underplate, Edwin Knowles	48
Tahiti Flower, Plate, Bread & Butter, Edwin Knowles	8
Tahiti Flower, Platter, Edwin Knowles, 12 In.	28
Tahiti Flower, Platter, Edwin Knowles, 15 ½ In.	55
Tea Rose, Soup, Dish, Edwin Knowles, 7 ¾ In.	12
Terrace, Plate, Dinner, Marcrest, 9 ¾ In.	14
Terrace, Soup, Dish, Marcrest, 7 ¾ In.	9
Trotter, Plate, Dinner, Crooksville, 10 In.	22
Trousseau, Cup, Castleton	30
Weather Vane, Platter, Edwin Knowles, 13 ¾ In.	32
Whipped Cream, Bowl, Cereal, Epoch, 6 ½ In.	10
Whipped Cream, Chop Plate, Epoch, 11 ½ In.	21
Whipped Cream, Creamer, Epoch	11
Willow, Plate, Luncheon, Blue, Royal China ....*illus*	10
Yellow Nocturne, Cup & Saucer, Blue Ridge	24
Yellow Nocturne, Plate, Bread & Butter, Blue Ridge, 6 ¼ In.	10
Yellow Nocturne, Plate, Dinner, Blue Ridge, 10 ¼ In.	22
Yellow Nocturne, Platter, Blue Ridge, 13 ⅜ In.	48

Disneyana, Toy, Mickey Mouse Express, Tin, Louis Marx, 10 In.
$240

Showtime Auction Services

D

Disneyana, Toy, Mickey Mouse, Car, Celluloid, Roly Poly, Pull Toy, Japan, 1930s, 5 x 10 In.
$950

Hake's Americana & Collectibles

Disneyana, Toy, Mickey Mouse, Roller Skater, Tin Lithograph, Clockwork, Linemar, 6 ¼ In.
$1,003

Bertoia Auctions

Disneyana, Toy, Mickey Mouse, Umbrella, Celluloid, Windup, Occupied Japan, 1940s, 5 ⅜ In.
$288

Hake's Americana & Collectibles

DIONNE QUINTUPLETS were born in Canada on May 28, 1934. The publicity about their birth and their special status as wards of the Canadian government made them famous throughout the world. Visitors could watch the girls play; reporters interviewed the girls and the staff. Thousands of special dolls and souvenirs were made picturing the quints at different ages. Emilie died in 1954, Marie in 1970, Yvonne in 2001. Annette and Cecile still live in Canada.

Bowl, Silver Finish, Impressed In Center, Names On Border, 1934, 6 In.	100
Doll, Dr. Dafoe, Composition, Mohair Wig, Madame Alexander, 14 In.	198
Doll, Yvonne, Molded Hair, Pink Dress, Necklace	70

Disneyana, Toy, Mickey Mouse, Walker, Tin Lithograph, Windup, Built-In Key, Distler, c.1930, 8 In.
$2,875

Hake's Americana & Collectibles

Disneyana, Toy, Minnie Mouse, Knitter, Rocking Chair, Tin Lithograph, Linemar, Japan, 6 ½ In.
$590

Bertoia Auctions

Disneyana, Toy, Pinocchio, Walker, Tin Lithograph, Windup, Marx, Box, c.1939, 8 In.
$450

Victorian Casino Antiques

Dolls, 5 Babies, Plastic, Madame Alexander, Box, 5 In., 5 Piece	192
Dolls, Composition, Madame Alexander, Scooter, c.1935, 8 In., 6 Piece ....*illus*	952
Dolls, Composition, Madame Alexander, Toddler, Human Hair, Dress, 12 In., 5 Piece	900
Fan, Sepia Tone Photo, In Highchairs, The Family Circle, 1934, 8 x 8 In.	49
Handkerchief, Linen, Embroidered, 5 Quints Pictures, 10 x 10 In.	24
Magazine, Life, Quints Turn 3, May 17, 1937, 10 ½ x 14 In.	20
Paper Dolls, 5 Dolls, Uncut, Colgate-Palmolive-Peet Co., 1937	75
Platter, Girls In Highchairs, Scalloped, Tab Handles, 12 In.	125
Portrait, Print, Girls On Stomachs, Frame, 12 x 8 In.	32
Postcard, Girls Sitting On Suitcase, Callander, Ontario, 1938	9
Spoon, Emilie, Silver Plate, Carlton Silverplate Co., c.1935, 6 In.	25
Spoon, Marie, Silver Plate, Carlton Silverplate Co., c.1935, 6 In.	25
Spoon, Yvonne, Silver Plate, Carlton Silverplate Co., c.1935, 6 In.	25

DIRK VAN ERP was born in 1860 and died in 1933. He opened his own studio in 1908 in Oakland, California. He moved his studio to San Francisco in 1909 and the studio remained under the direction of his son until 1977. Van Erp made hammered copper accessories, including vases, desk sets, bookends, candlesticks, jardinieres, and trays, but he is best known for his lamps. The hammered copper lamps often had shades with mica panels.

Bookends, Copper, California Faience Tile, 3-Masted Ship, 1920s, 4 x 4 In. ....*illus*	5000
Bowl, Copper, Hammered, Impressed, 12 x 2 ½ In.	1000
Jardiniere, Copper, Hammered, Rolled Rim, 13 x 8 ½ In.	2600
Jardiniere, Hammered Copper, Rolled Rim, Van Erp, Signed GAW, 11 x 7 In.	5490
Lamp, Bean Pot, Copper, Hammered, 11 x 11 ½ In.	6100
Lamp, Bean Pot, Copper, Hammered, Mica Shade, 11 x 12 ½ In.	10000
Lamp, Cobra Arm, Trapezoid Shade, Hammered Copper, Mica, 8 x 18 In.	18750
Lamp, Copper, Hammered, 3-Panel Mica Shade, 18 ½ x 22 In.	11250
Lamp, Copper, Hammered, Paneled Mica Shade, Rivets, Signed, 16 In. ....*illus*	8295
Lamp, Copper, Hammered, Trumpet Base, Conical Mica Shade, 14 x 17 ½ In.	9375
Lamp, Flat Top, Copper, Hammered, Flower Cutouts, Mica Inserts, 18 x 21 In.	15000
Lamp, Mica Shade, Hammered Copper Base, 22 x 25 ½ In.	36600
Vase, Copper, Hammered, 6 ½ x 10 In.	4270
Vase, Copper, Hammered, Tapered, 3 x 6 In.	813
Vase, Red Glaze, Warty, Shouldered, 6 x 7 ½ In.	4500

DISNEYANA is a collectors' term. Walt Disney and his company introduced many comic characters to the world. Collectors search for examples of the work of the Disney Studios and the many commercial products modeled after his characters, including Mickey Mouse and Donald Duck, and recent films, like *Beauty and the Beast* and *The Little Mermaid*.

Alarm Clock, Snow White, 7 Dwarfs, Round, Bayard, Box, 1964, 4 ¾ In.	115
Ashtray, Minnie Mouse, German Metal, Round Tray, Figure, c.1915, 5 In.	2461
Baby Rattle, Mickey Mouse, Squeaker, Celluloid, 1930s, 6 In.	115
Badge, Mickey Mouse, Police Dept., Brass, Red & Black Paint, c.1935, 1 ½ In.	144
Biscuit Tin, Mickey Mouse, Minnie Mouse, Round, Lid, 1930s, 5 ¼ x 8 ¼ In.	268
Book, Big Little Book, Mickey, The Great Big Midget Book, 1934	575
Book, Donald Duck, Donald Duck Is Here Again, File Copy, 1944	353
Bowl, Mickey Mouse, Alphabet, Mickey On Train, Bavaria, c.1932, 7 In.	172
Box, Pencil, Mickey Mouse, Cardboard, Drawers, Mickey Shape, 1930s, 8 x 5 In.	196
Box, Pencil, Mickey Mouse, Cardboard, Slide-Out Tray, 1930s, 6 x 8 ½ In.	127
Bracelet, Charm, Figural, Seven Dwarfs, Colored Gem Stones, 18K Gold, 7 ⅞ In. ....*illus*	6150
Cel, see Animation Art category.	
Charm, Mickey Mouse, Enamel, 14K Gold, 2-Sided, 1930s, ¹³⁄₁₆ In. ....*illus*	2935
Comic Book, Mickey Mouse, Hebrew, Deidat & Sons, Tel Aviv, 1947, 8 Pages	375
Cookie Jar, Mickey Mouse, Leather Ears, Walt Disney, Enesco Label ....*illus*	52
Costume, 20,000 Leagues Under The Sea, Nautilus Crew, Denim, c.1954, Size 40	977
Dish, Figural, Mickey Mouse Head, Lid, Japan, 1930s, 3 ¼ x 3 ½ In. ....*illus*	115
Display, Mickey Mouse, Mechanical, Old King Cole, c.1935, 30 x 42 In.	6734
Display, Post Cereal Bowls, Mickey Mouse, Donald Duck, 12 Bowls, 10 x 15 In. ....*illus*	1012
Doll, Donald Duck, Velvet, Oilcloth, Walt Disney's Silly Symphony, 15 In.	450
Doll, Dopey, Glazed Muslin, Painted Face, Stuffed Mohair Body, Prewar, 13 In.	119
Doll, Jiminy Cricket, Wood, Fabric, Jointed, Ideal, 1940s, 8 ½ In.	297
Doll, Mickey & Minnie, Stuffed, Felt, Flower, Lars, c.1960, 20 In., Pair	506
Doll, Mickey Mouse, Pie Eyes, 4 Fingers, Felt Shoes, Steiff, 9 In.	472
Doll, Mickey Mouse, Stuffed, Felt, Oilcloth Eyes, Pearl Buttons, Steiff, 1930s, 7 In.	1113
Doorstop, Donald Duck, Walking Stick, Blue, White, Orange Paint, Cast Iron, c.1925, 9 In.	236

Doorstop, Mickey Mouse, Full-Figured, Hands On Hips, Cast Iron, Unpainted, 8 In.	1298
Drawing, Mickey Mouse, Apron, Holding Syringe, Pencil, 1937, 10 x 12 In.	173
Drawing, Mickey Mouse, Cry In The Night, Mickey Plays Papa, Pencil, c.1934, 6 x 6 In.	368
Drawing, Mickey Mouse, Riding Broom, Pencil, c.1929, 9 ½ x 12 In.	288
Drawing, Snow White, 7 Dwarfs, Pickaxes, 1937, 10 x 12 In., Pair	727
Drawing, Snow White, Haunted Forest, F. Horvath, c.1936, 9 ½ x 12 In.	2657
Figurine Set, 3 Little Pigs, Bisque, Painted, Box, Geo. Borgfeldt, 3 ¾ In.	266
Figurine Set, Snow White & 7 Dwarfs, Bisque, Painted, Box, Geo. Borgfeldt, 3 In.	177
Figurine, 3 Little Pigs, Big Bad Wolf, Tin, House Boxes, Brick Graphics, 4 Piece	1416
Figurine, Mickey Mouse, Sorcerer's Apprentice, Fantasia, Composite, Painted, 21 In.	1400
Figurine, Minnie Mouse, Black & White, Top Hat, Shy Face, Rosenthal, c.1932, 3 In.	575
Fountain Pen, Mickey Mouse Ink-D-Cator, Black, Decals, Box, Inkograph, 6 ¼ In.	1320
Game, Ferdinand The Bull In The Arena, 26 Marbles, Board With Holes, Box, 1938	90
Lithograph, Uncle Scrooge, Till Death Do Us Part, C. Barks, Signed, 1983, 20 x 24 In.	230
Marionette, Jiminy Cricket, Wood, Plaque, Bob Baker, Box, 12 In. ....*illus*	1035
Pencil Sharpener, Donald Duck, Figural, Plastic, 1930s, 1 ¾ In.	86
Pencil Sharpener, Mickey Mouse, Celluloid, Black, Red, Japan, 1940s, 2 ¾ In.	150
Pencil Sharpener, Mickey Mouse, Figural, Celluloid, 1930s, 3 In.	115
Perfume Bottle, Mickey Mouse, Figural, Glass, 1930s, 5 ½ In.	173
Pill Box, Mickey Mouse With Gun, Enameled, Metal, Round, c.1931, 1 ⅜ x ⅝ In.	1075
Pin, Donald Duck, Brass, Rhinestone, Paint, 1950s, 2 ¾ In.	114
Pin, Mickey Mouse, Mechanical, Tin Lithographic, Die Cut, 5 Fingers, c.1932, 1 ½ x 2 ¼ In.	463
Pin, Minnie Mouse, Parasol, Glossy Black, 1930s, 1 In.	759
Pin, Wolf, Who's Afraid Of The Big Bad Wolf, 1934, 1 ¼ In.	86
Playset, Zorro, Figures, 500 Piece, Box, c.1958, 15 x 24 x 4 In.	491
Poster, Donald Duck, Dude Duck, Frame, 1951, 39 x 25 In.	1320
Poster, Little Mermaid, Frame, 1989, 38 x 24 In.	360
Poster, Pluto, RPM Motor Oil, Doggone It's Tops!, Paper, 28 x 41 In.	1162
Potty, Child's, Mickey & Minnie, Pluto, Porcelain, Handle, Rolled Rim, 1930s, 7 In.	345
Purse, Mickey & Minnie Mouse, Pluto, Brass, Cohn & Rosenberger, 1930s, 2 ¼ In. ....*illus*	1035
Push Puppet, Donald Duck, Plastic, Kohner Brothers, 1960, 2 ½ In.	22
Radio, Mickey Mouse, Playing Bass, Lacquer, Wood, Emerson, 1930s, 6 x 7 In.	974
Record, Mickey Mouse, Yankee Doodle Mickey, 14 Patriotic Songs, 78 RPM, 1980	8
Rug, Mickey Mouse, Conductor Of Train, Disney Characters, Hooked, Wool	59
Rug, Mickey Mouse, Donald Duck, Pluto, Velveteen Fringe, Italy, 1930s, 22 x 44 In.	463
Sign, Mickey Mouse, Calso Gasoline, Cardboard, Alpine Skier, 1939, 14 x 17 In.	778
Sign, Parking Lot, Pinocchio, Metal, Paint, 61 x 24 In.	288
Spare Tire Cover, Donald Duck, Standard Gasoline, Unsurpassed, 1939, 30 In. Diam.	942
Standee, Mickey, Donald, Pepsodent, Paste & Powder, Cardboard, 1937, 15 x 31 In., Pair ...*illus*	863
Telephone, Candlestick, Snow White & Dopey, Pressed Steel, Hill Brass Co., c.1937, 7 In.	230
Tin, Mickey Mouse, Mickey, Minnie, Donald Duck, Round, Multicolor, 2 x 6 In.	161
Toothbrush Holder, Donald Duck, Hand On Head, Porcelain, Japan, 5 ¼ In.	49
Toothbrush Holder, Mickey Mouse, Standing, Hands On Hips, 1930s, 4 In.	190
Toothbrush Holder, Pig, Playing Flute, Pink Copyright, 4 In.	125
Toy, Begging Pluto, Rolls Over, Felt Covered Tin, Windup, Linemar, 6 ½ In.	384
Toy, Carousel, Mickey Mouse, Goofy & Donald Duck, Tin Lithograph, Celluloid, 7 In.	295
Toy, Donald Duck, Dipsy Car, Head Nods, Tin Litho, Clockwork, Marx, Box, 5 ¼ In.	325
Toy, Donald Duck, Drummer, Tin Lithograph, Clockwork, Linemar, 5 ½ In.	125 to 236
Toy, Donald Duck, Drummer, Tin, Windup, Linemar, Japan, 5 In.	285
Toy, Donald Duck, Fireman, Tin Lithograph, Linemar, Japan, 12 In. ....*illus*	265
Toy, Donald Duck, Handcar, Pluto In Doghouse, Composition, Tin Litho, Lionel, 10 In.	300
Toy, Donald Duck, Huey, Tin, Windup, Linemar, Box, 1950s, 5 In.	850
Toy, Donald Duck, Mickey's Delivery, Donald Duck, Trike, Cart, Tin, Friction, Linemar, 6 In.	182
Toy, Donald Duck, Stuffed, Leather Face, Felt Feet, Arms, 13 In.	171
Toy, Donald Duck, Tricycle, Tin Lithograph, Bell, Clockwork, Celluloid Figure, Linemar, 4 In.	443
Toy, Donald Duck, Walker, Tin, Plastic Feet, Arms & Beak, Waddles, Schuco, Box, 6 In.	384
Toy, Dumbo, Seated, Jumps & Flips Over, Tin Lithograph, Marx, Box, 4 ½ In.	443
Toy, Ferris Wheel, Mickey Mouse, Hercules, Tin, Windup, J. Chein, 16 In.	148 to 216
Toy, Fire Engine, Mickey Mouse, Pluto, Nephews, Tin, Friction, Box, Disneyland, Linemar, 21 In.	3300
Toy, Goofy Riding Unicycle, Tin Lithograph, Clockwork, Cloth Pants, Linemar, 5 In.	354
Toy, Guitar, Mickey Mouse, Mousegetar, Mattel, Box, 23 In.	85
Toy, Jetliner, Disney Characters, 4 Propellers, Tin Lithograph, Friction, Linemar, 7 ½ In.	413
Toy, Mickey & Minnie Riding Motorcycle, Tin Lithograph, Tipp & Co., Germany, 1930s, 9 In.	56050
Toy, Mickey Mouse Express, Tin, Louis Marx, 10 In. ....*illus*	240
Toy, Mickey Mouse Whirligig, Celluloid, Marked, Made In Occupied Japan, 7 In.	150
Toy, Mickey Mouse, Car, Celluloid, Roly Poly, Pull Toy, Japan, 1930s, 5 x 10 In. ....*illus*	950

Doll, A.M., 231, Fanny, Gentleman, Bisque Head, Composition, Wood, Ball-Jointed, 12 In.
$3,42)

Theriault's

Doll, Advertising, Radiotron, Composition, Wood, Cameo, Parrish, c.1926, 15 In.
$1,904

Theriault's

Doll, Automaton, Tea Party, 3 Dolls At Table, Bisque Head, Germany, c.1898, 12 x 11 In.
$6,765

Cowan's Auctions

Doll, Bahr & Proschild, Tommy Tucker, Bisque, Composition, Wood, c.1915, 17 In. $1,026

Theriault's

Doll, Band Leader, Composition, Wood, Jointed, Maxfield Parrish, c.1930, 19 In. $1,232

Theriault's

Doll, Chad Valley, Felt, Googly, Painted, Muslin Body, Velvet-Jointed, 1930s, 12 In. $336

Theriault's

Toy, Mickey Mouse, Drummer, Drum, Tail Stand, Tin Lithograph, Germany, 7 In.	300
Toy, Mickey Mouse, Drummer, Pull, Black-Line, Fisher-Price	145
Toy, Mickey Mouse, Jazz Drummer, Red Drum Head, Tin Lithograph, Chein, c.1935, 7 In.	1416
Toy, Mickey Mouse, Magician, On Stage, Magic Hat, Chick, Batteries, Linemar, 10 In.	531
Toy, Mickey Mouse, Musical Top, Tin Litho, Red, Lackawanna Mfg. Co., 1930s, 8 x 10 In.	337
Toy, Mickey Mouse, Racer, Mickey Mouse Driver, Tin, Windup, 1936, 4 In.	219
Toy, Mickey Mouse, Rambler, Celluloid, Windup, Box, 1930s, 8 In.	2370
Toy, Mickey Mouse, Rocking On Pluto, Windup, Linemar, Box, c.1960, 7 In.	1837
Toy, Mickey Mouse, Roller Skater, Tin Lithograph, Clockwork, Linemar, 6 ¼ In. ....*illus*	1003
Toy, Mickey Mouse, Umbrella, Celluloid, Windup, Occupied Japan, 1940s, 5 ⅜ In. ....*illus*	288
Toy, Mickey Mouse, Walker, Tin Lithograph, Windup, Built-In Key, Distler, c.1930, 8 In. ......*illus*	2875
Toy, Mickey Mouse, Xylophone Player, Tin Lithograph, Clockwork, Linemar, 6 In.	295
Toy, Minnie Mouse, Knitter, Rocking Chair, Tin Lithograph, Linemar, Japan, 6 ½ In. ....*illus*	590
Toy, Monorail Set, Jetrail Express, 3 Cars, Schuco For Walt Disney, Germany, 1950s	180
Toy, Pinocchio, Acrobat, Monstro The Whale Base, Tin Litho, Windup, Marx, 17 x 12 In.	295
Toy, Pinocchio, Pushing Delivery Cart, Tin Lithograph, Windup, Marx, 9 In.	237
Toy, Pinocchio, Walker, Tin Lithograph, Windup, Marx, Box, c.1939, 8 In. ....*illus*	450
Toy, Pluto, Drum Major, Bell In Hand, Tin Lithograph, Clockwork, Linemar, 6 In.	236
Toy, Pluto, On Tricycle, Tin Litho, Windup, Bell, Celluloid Figure, Linemar, Box, 3 ¾ In.	177
Toy, Pluto, Walking, Tail Wags, Felt-Covered Tin, Clockwork, Linemar, Box, 6 In.	236
Toy, Professor Von Drake, Tin, Windup, Linemar, 8 In.	475
Toy, Sand Pail, Donald Duck, Nephews, Swimming, Diving, Multicolor, 3 ¼ In.	758
Toy, Train Set, Lionel, No. 6-8311 Engine, 10 Boxcars, Caboose, Disney Characters	300
Watch, Mickey Mouse, Hands As Dials, Silvered Metal, 1934, Pocket, 2 In.	226
Wristwatch, Mickey Mouse, Birthday Series, Luminous Dial, U.S. Time, Box, c.1948	502
Wristwatch, Mickey Mouse, Leather Wristband, Marked Walt Disney, Bradley, Swiss, 8 ½ In.	60
Wristwatch, Mickey Mouse, Rectangular, Dial Arms, Red Vinyl Band, Ingersoll, Box, 1948	443

DOCTOR, *see Dental and Medical categories.*

DOLL entries are listed by marks printed or incised on the doll, if possible. If there are no marks, the doll is listed by the name of the subject or country or maker. Notice that Barbie is listed under Mattel. Eskimo dolls are listed in the Eskimo section and Indian dolls are listed in the Indian section. Doll clothes and accessories are listed at the end of this section. The twentieth-century clothes listed here are in mint condition.

A.M., 231, Fanny, Gentleman, Bisque Head, Composition, Wood, Ball-Jointed, 12 In. ....*illus*	3420
A.M., 243, Composition, Googly, Navy Suit, Straw Hat, 9 In.	396
A.M., 252, Impish Face, Googly Intaglio Eyes, Molded Hair, Composition, Baby, 12 In.	960
A.M., 253, Bisque Head, Googly, Wide Mouth, Brown Mohair Wig, Composition, 7 In.	678
A.M., 323, Toddler Boy, Bisque Head, Googly, Blond Mohair Wig, Bob, Lederhosen, 12 In.	2160
A.M., 351, Bisque Head, Sleep Eyes, Composition, Baby, 18 In.	170
A.M., 390, Bisque Brown Head, Set Eyes, Jointed, Composition, Child, 11 In.	254
A.M., 390, Bisque Head, 4 Teeth, Human Brown Wig, Composition, 28 In.	200
A.M., 390, Bisque Socket Head, Set Eyes, Blond Braid Wig, Navy Coat, Hat, 7 In.	113
A.M., 390N, Bisque Head, Sleep Eyes, Mohair Wig, 25 In.	141
A.M., 393, Bisque, Sleep Eyes, Brown Human Wig, Composition, 9 In.	452
A.M., 401, Bisque Socket Head, Brown Mohair, Slender Jointed Body, Satin Dress, 14 In.	1560
A.M., 560A, Bisque Socket Head, Sleep Eyes, Jointed, Human Hair Wig, Dress, 19 In.	452
A.M., 1894, Bisque Head, Blond Wig, Brown Sleep Eyes, White Cape, 18 In.	70
A.M., Baby, Bisque Head, Open Mouth, Mohair Wig, Composition, 25 In.	311
A.M., Betty, Bisque Head, Mohair Wig, Sleep Eyes, Jointed, Composition, Dress, Cap, 13 In.	254
A.M., Bisque Socket Head, Topknot, Googly, Closed Mouth, Composition, c.1920, 8 In.	560
A.M., Bisque, Mohair Blond Wig, Bent Limb Composition, Baby, 25 In.	311
Advertising, Buddy Lee, Cowboy, Plastic, Original Shirt & Jeans, Felt Hat, 14 In.	207
Advertising, Buddy Lee, Plastic, Molded Hair, Googly Eyes, Lee Jeans, Red Shirt, 12 In.	150
Advertising, Buddy Lee, Plastic, Striped Denim, Cap, Overalls, Tag, 13 In.	367
Advertising, Buddy Lee, Standard Oil Of Indiana, Composite, Googly Eyes, Uniform, 13 In.	260
Advertising, Buddy Lee, Train Engineer, Plastic, Striped Denim Overalls, C & O Hat, 14 In.	472
Advertising, Radiotron, Composition, Wood, Cameo, Parrish, c.1926, 15 In. ....*illus*	1904
Alexander dolls are listed in this category under Madame Alexander.	
Alt, Beck & Gottschalk, 1362, Bisque Head, Sleep Eyes, Teeth, Jointed, Composition, 21 In.	170
Alt, Beck & Gottschalk, Bisque, Blue Sleep Eyes, Painted Teeth, 5 ½ In.	102
American Character, Sweet Sue, Hard Plastic, Walker, Hat, Pale Blue Gown, Box, 21 In.	254
American Character, Toni, Vinyl, Plastic, Blond Hair, Wardrobe, Trunk, 10 ½ In.	180
Andreas Voit, Papier-Mache Shoulder Head, Leather Body, Wood Arms, Box, 16 In.	4029

D

Armand Marseille dolls are listed in this category under A.M.	
Arranbee, Nancy Lee, Hard Plastic, Blond Wig, Braid, Blue Dress, Box, 17 In.	170
Arranbee, Nanette, Plastic, Walker, Blond Wig, Purple Dress, Box, 15 In.	68
Automaton, 2 Black Dancers, Mahogany Box Platform, Clockwork, Ives, 1880, 11 In.	1154
Automaton, Bisque Girl, Crying, With Polichinelle, Musical, Lambert, 19 In.	6720
Automaton, Bisque, 2 Dancing Dolls, Platform, Hand Crank..	880
Automaton, Girl Playing Mandolin, On Wood Box, 17th-Century Style, 13 ½ x 8 In.	322
Automaton, Tea Party, 3 Dolls At Table, Bisque Head, Germany, c.1898, 12 x 11 In. ....*illus*	6765
Automaton, Training The Dancing Dog, Musical, Roullet & Decamps, c.1890, 18 In.	6720
Automaton, Walking, Bisque Head, Brass Boots, Clockwork, Martin & Runyon, 1862, 10 In.......	767
Automaton, Waltzing, Celluloid Face & Hands, Tin Frame, Clockwork, Lehmann, Box, 9 In.......	1416
Bahr & Proschild, Bisque, 2 Faces, Crying, Painted Eyes, Smiling, Glass Eyes, Gown, 12 In.......	390
Bahr & Proschild, Tommy Tucker, Bisque, Composition, Wood, c.1915, 17 In. ....*illus*	1026
Band Leader, Composition, Wood, Jointed, Maxfield Parrish, c.1930, 19 In. ....*illus*	1232
Barbie dolls are listed in this category under Mattel.	
Bergmann dolls are in this category under Simon & Halbig.	
Bisque Head, Lady, Sculpted Hair, Bodice, Snood, Painted Face, Muslin Body, c.1870, 20 In.	616
Bisque Shoulder Head, Lady, Sculpted Hair, Muslin Body, c.1880, 25 In..........................	672
Bisque Shoulder Head, Lady, Sculpted Hair, Painted Face, Stitch-Jointed Body, c.1880, 20 In. ..	784
Bisque Shoulder Head, Painted Brown Hair, Face, Muslin Stitch-Jointed Body, c.1875, 16 In.....	616
Bisque Shoulder Head, Sculpted Hair, Glass Eyes, Stitch-Jointed Body, c.1870, 16 In.................	1232
Bisque Swivel Head, Paperweight Eyes, Lambswool Wig, Kid Body, Jointed, c.1882, 15 In.........	1904
Bisque, Boy, Swivel Head, Glass Eyes, Mohair, Peg-Jointed, Birdcage, Guitar, c.1900, 4 In...........	448
Bisque, Dome Socket Head, Character Baby, Glass Eyes, Composition, Nippon, c.1915, 14 In......	1232
Bisque, Guard, Painted Face & Hair, Red, Black Outfit, Hat, Spats, Whip, 7 In.	1413
Bisque, Physician, Painted Face, Molded Mustache, Black Suit, Chamber Pot, 8 In......................	226
Bisque, Sculpted Lavender Ruffled Coif, Glass Eyes, Stitch-Jointed Body, c.1880, 20 In.	5040
Bisque, Toddler, Showing Muscles, Papier-Mache Dog, Front Wheels, c.1915, 4 ½ In.	504
Bisque, Woman, Dresden Ruffled Snood, Sculpted Hair, Bodice, Germany, c.1870, 19 In.............	1344
Black dolls are also included in the Black category.	
Bru Jne, Bebe, Bisque Shoulder Head, Blond Wig, Amber Eyes, Kid & Bisque Limbs, 23 In.	4253
Bru Jne, Bebe, Bisque Socket Head & Limbs, Dark Paperweight Eyes, Mohair, Chunky, 23 In......	18000
Bru Jne, Fashion, Bisque Head, Painted Face, Mohair Wig, Kid Body, c.1873, 16 In...................	6440
Bru Jne, Fashion, Bisque Swivel Head, Glass Eyes, Mohair Wig, c.1867, 17 In............................	2800
Bruckner, Red Riding Hood, Pressed Cloth Mask Face, Cloth Body, 13 In........................ 365 to 396	
Bye-Lo, Bisque Head, Blue Sleep Eyes, Cloth Body, 10 In...	141
Bye-Lo, Bisque Head, Blue Sleep Eyes, Cloth Body, White Bonnet, Dress, 13 In........................	79
Bye-Lo, Bisque Head, Brown Sleep Eyes, Closed Mouth, Cloth Body, 13 In...............................	113
Bye-Lo, Bisque Head, Brown Sleep Eyes, Cloth Body, 10 In..	170
Bye-Lo, Bisque Head, Painted Hair, Cloth Body, Celluloid Hands, Silk Dress, Bonnet, 20 In........	510
Bye-Lo, Bisque Head, Sleep Eyes, Jointed, Wicker Basket, Layette, Grace Putnam, 5 In.............	600
Cabbage Patch, Cloth, Stitched Features, Baby, 26 In..	36
Chad Valley, Felt, Googly, Painted, Muslin Body, Velvet-Jointed, 1930s, 12 In. ....*illus*	336
Chad Valley, Princess Margaret, Cloth, Glass Eyes, Mohair Wig, 16 In....................................	1535
Chase, Hospital Baby, Stockinet, Oil-Painted, Blond Hair, Cotton Dress, 22 In............................	210
Cloth, Izannah Walker, Painted Features, Single Piece Head & Torso, c.1860, 29 In.	14220
Cloth, Oil-Painted, Human Hair Wig, Muslin Stitch-Jointed Body, c.1890, 27 In........................	952
Cloth, Painted Face, Blue Dress, Bonnet, Shenandoah Valley, c.1920, 20 ½ In.	633
Cloth, Pressed Face, Painted, Human Hair, Pinafore, Gertude Rollinson, c.1920, 21 In..............	3024
Cloth, Primitive, Embroidered Flat Face, Jointed, Mitten Hands, Dress, Bonnet, 30 In...............	720
Cloth, Tubby, Little Lulu, Stuffed, Linen Faces, Vinyl Handbag, 1944, 14 ½ In., Pair	230
Clown, Bisque Head, Painted Smile, Sleep Eyes, Mohair, Wood Body, Hands Clap, 12 In.............	550
Dewees Cochran, Cindy, Latex, Brown Human Hair Wig, Painted Face, Velvet Dress, 15 In.	254
Dewees Cochran, Cindy, Latex, Human Hair Wig, Painted Face, Wool Skirt, Jacket, 15 In.	452
Dewees Cochran, Tiny Tim, Latex, Human Hair Wig, Painted Face, Scarf, Crutch, 11 ½ In........	735
Doleac, Fashion, Bisque Swivel Head, Mohair Wig, Kid Body, Jointed, Paris, c.1867, 17 In.	4480
Door Of Hope, Amah & Baby, Wood, Cloth, Black Bun, Tunic, Baby In Cloth Carrier, 11 In.......	1560
Door Of Hope, Amah & Baby, Wood, Swivel Head, Carved, Painted, Baby On Back, 11 In..........	1185
Door Of Hope, Boy, Wood Head & Hands, Cloth Body, Silk Robe, Vest, Shoes, 6 ½ In.	1920
Door Of Hope, Bride & Groom, Wood Head, Arms, Carved, Painted, 11 ½ & 11 In., Pair 900 to 1000	
Door Of Hope, Wood Head & Hands, Black Bob, Cloth Body, Silk Tunic & Pants, 8 ½ In.	600
Door Of Hope, Wood Head & Hands, Cloth Body, Silk Jacket & Pants, 7 In.	900
Door Of Hope, Wood, Carved, Socket Head, Painted Face, Cloth Body, Tunic, c.1920, 7 In.	392
Door Of Hope, Worker, Wood, Painted Eyes, Hair, c.1925, 12 In. ....*illus*	784
Dressel, Admiral Dewey, Bisque, Molded Gray Hair, Papier-Mache Body, Uniform, 8 In..............	660
Dressel, Bisque Socket Head, Glass Sleep Eyes, Mohair Wig, Jointed, c.1915, 14 In....................	1680

Doll, Door Of Hope, Worker, Wood, Painted Eyes, Hair, c.1925, 12 In.
$78

Theriault's

Doll, Effanbee, Anne Of Green Gables, Composition, Mohair Wig, Box, c.1934, 13 In.
$448

Theriault's

Doll, Effanbee, Pat-O-Pat, Cloth, Mask Face, Googly, Yarn Hair, Stitch-Jointed, 1930s, 15 In.
$280

Theriault's

This is an edited listing of current prices. Visit **Kovels.com** to check thousands of prices from previous years and sign up for free information on trends, tips, reproductions, marks, and more.

Doll, Effanbee, Patsy Joan, Composition, Mohair, Sleep Eyes, 5-Piece Body, c.1935, 16 In.
$560

Theriault's

Doll, Effanbee, Patsy Jr., Composition, Sculpted Hair, Painted, 5-Piece Body, c.1935, 11 In.
$220

Theriault's

Doll, Effanbee, Patsy, Socket Head, Sculpted Hair Under Mohair Wig, c.1930, 14 In.
$560

Theriault's

Earthenware, Neopolitan Village Woman, Shoulder Head, Painted Face, Chignon, 13 In.	1904
Effanbee, Anne Of Green Gables, Composition, Mohair Wig, Box, c.1934, 13 In. ....*illus*	448
Effanbee, Anne Shirley, Composition, Dotted Swiss Dress, 21 In.	141
Effanbee, Anne Shirley, Composition, Mohair, Sleep Eyes, Marked, 1940s, 18 In.	325
Effanbee, Anne Shirley, Composition, Sleep Eyes, Human Hair Braids, Pinafore, 21 In.	90
Effanbee, Boy, Composition, Painted Eyes, Human Hair, Wool Suit, Dewees Cochran, 17 In.	840
Effanbee, Development Of Culture, Composition, White High Wig, Blue 1750 Dress, 16 In.	254
Effanbee, Girl, Cochran American Children Series, Composition, Blond, Plaid Dress, 20 In.	504
Effanbee, Grumpykins, Policeman, Composition Head, Painted, Muslin Body, 1930s, 11 In.	560
Effanbee, Honey, Plastic, Brunette Wig, Dress, Straw Hat, Flowers, Heart Tag, 18 In.	300
Effanbee, Kippy, Composition, Molded Hair, Painted Eyes, 14 In.	84
Effanbee, Pat-O-Pat, Cloth, Mask Face, Googly, Yarn Hair, Stitch-Jointed, 1930s, 15 In. ......*illus*	280
Effanbee, Patsy Joan, Composition, Mohair, Sleep Eyes, 5-Piece Body, c.1935, 16 In. ....*illus*	560
Effanbee, Patsy Jr., Composition, Sculpted Hair, Painted, 5-Piece Body, c.1935, 11 In. ....*illus*	220
Effanbee, Patsy Jr., Composition, Socket Head, Sculpted Hair, Painted Face, 1930s, 11 In.	224
Effanbee, Patsy Mae, Composition, Sleep Eyes, Human Hair, Muslin, Box, 1935, 27 In.	1568
Effanbee, Patsy, Socket Head, Sculpted Hair Under Mohair Wig, c.1930, 14 In. ....*illus*	560
Effanbee, Patsyette, Brown Complexion, Socket Head, Painted Hair, Eyes, 1930s, 9 In.	224
Effanbee, Patsyette, Composition, Socket Head, Sculpted Hair, Travel Case, c.1931, 9 In.	784
Effanbee, Patsyette, Composition, Socket Head, Sleep Eyes, Paper Label, c.1945, 9 In.	448
Effanbee, Patsykins, Composition, Socket Head, Sculpted Hair, Painted, Box, c.1930, 11 In.	504
Effanbee, Rosemary, Composition, Sleep Eyes, Human Hair, Cloth, Heart Necklace, 17 In.	180
Effanbee, Woman's Suffrage Movement, Composition, Painted Eyes, 1908 Fashion, 16 In.	113
Fashion, Bisque, Enamel Eyes, Painted, Kid Body, Nun's Habit, France, c.1860, 18 In. ....*illus*	3472
Fashion, Normandy Nanny, Bisque, Swivel Head, Glass Eyes, Human Hair Wig, c.1880, 15 In.	2800
Fashion, Papier-Mache, Glass Eyes, Shoulder Head, Painted Hair, Sateen Body, c.1845, 19 In.	2912
Fashion, Porcelain Shoulder Head, Sculpted Chignon, Muslin, Stitch-Jointed, c.1870, 18 In.	448
French, Bebe, Paperweight Eyes, Jointed Wood & Composition, Human Hair Wig, 34 In.	830
French, Boy, Composition, Glass Eyes, Blond Mohair Wig, Marquis Costume, 12 In.	660
French, Fashion, Bisque Swivel Head, Mohair Wig, Kid Body, Jointed, c.1867, 17 In. ....*illus*	9690
French, Mignonette, Bisque, Swivel Neck, Mohair Braids, Jointed, Silk, Lace, c.1877, 5 ½ In.	4200
French, S & H, Ondine, Swimmer, Bisque, Cork, Mechanical, Elie Martin, 1876, 16 In. ....*illus*	2576
French, Wax, Yarn Wig, Cloth Wrapped Legs, Silk Period Costume, Hat, Stand, 16 In.	600
Freundlich, Baby Sandy, Composition, Socket Head, Sculpted Hair, Box, 1930s, 16 In.	392
Gaultier, Fashion, Bisque Socket Head, Glass Eyes, Mohair Wig, Leather Body, 19 In.	896
Gebruder Heubach dolls may also be listed in this category under Heubach.	
Gebruder Heubach, 5636, Bisque Socket Head, Sleep Eyes, Mohair Wig, c.1915, 13 In.	806
Gebruder Heubach, Bisque Socket Head, Painted, Mohair Wig, Dutch Shoes, c.1915, 9 In.	280
Gerbruder Kuhnlenz, 44, Bisque Socket Head, Set Eyes, Composition, 6 ½ In.	141
German, Asian Child, Bisque Head, Painted, Mohair Wig, Papier-Mache, 9 ½ In. ....*illus*	830
German, Baby, Bisque Head, Sleep Eyes, Teeth, Mohair Wig, Composition, 12 In.	170
German, Bisque Head, Painted Hair, Face, Composition, Boy, 8 In.	198
German, Bisque Head, Paperweight Eyes, Gusseted Kid Body, Bisque Arms, Gown, 17 In.	780
German, Bisque Shoulder Head, Glass Eyes, Muslin Body, c.1870, 22 In. ....*illus*	896
German, Bisque Shoulder Head, Sculpted Hair, Printed Face, Muslin Body, c.1875, 18 In.	672
German, Bisque Shoulder Head, Sculpted Helmet, Goatee, Uniform, c.1870, 11 In.	728
German, Bisque Socket Head, Painted Eyes, Human Hair Wig, 14 In.	424
German, Bisque, Bathing Beauty, Painted, Auburn Mohair With Flowers, 6 ½ In.	510
German, Bisque, Glass Eyes, Red Wig, Jointed, Pink Outfit, 6 In.	57
German, Bisque, Sculpted Hair, Blue Ruffled Snood, Muslin Body, Silk Dress, c.1870, 11 In.	784
German, Bisque, Set Eyes, Blond Mohair Wig, Composition, Regional Dress, 7 In.	113
German, Chubby, Googly, Sculptured Brown Hair, Painted Face, 7 In.	392
German, Cloth, Oil-Painted, Center Seam Face, Closed Mouth, Muslin Body, c.1910, 14 In.	392
German, Lady, Bisque Shoulder Head, Painted Face, Mohair Wig, Muslin, c.1860, 19 In.	616
German, Lady, Bisque, Glass Eyes, Painted Face, Stitch-Jointed, c.1880, 26 In.	1064
German, Lady, Porcelain, Sculpted Hair, Snood, Painted Face, Stitch-Jointed, c.1870, 14 In.	840
German, Mother Goose, Papier-Mache, Composition, Muslin Body, Cape, Peaked Hat, 16 In.	780
German, Muslin, Papier-Mache, Human Hair Wig, Wood, Jointed, c.1850, 15 In. ....*illus*	6440
German, Nun, Wood, Painted, Dowel-Jointed, Grodner, c.1850, 8 ½ In.	616
German, Parian Head, Lead Base, Pull String, Doll Revolves & Step Dances, 10 In.	668
German, Porcelain Shoulder Head, Black Sculpted Hair, Finger Curls, c.1870, 23 In.	1064
German, Porcelain Shoulder Head, Painted Face, Brown Hair, Muslin, Stitch-Jointed, c.1870, 27 In.	448
German, Porcelain Shoulder Head, Sculpted Chignon, Looped Braids, c.1855, 28 In.	1680
German, Porcelain Shoulder Head, Sculpted Hair, Muslin Body, c.1865, 29 In. ....*illus*	672
German, Porcelain Shoulder Head, Sculpted, Ringlets, Muslin Body, c.1875, 24 In.	952
German, Queen Victoria, Porcelain Shoulder Head, Sculpted Chignon, Painted Face, c.1850, 15 In.	1344

Doll, Fashion, Bisque, Enamel Eyes, Painted, Kid Body, Nun's Habit, France, c.1860, 18 In.
$3,472

Theriault's

Doll, French, Fashion, Bisque Swivel Head, Mohair Wig, Kid Body, Jointed, c.1867, 17 In.
$9,690

Theriault's

What Are Composition Dolls Made Of?

Composition dolls, introduced in the early 1900s, are made of a combination of materials like sawdust, wood pulp, and glue that is molded into the heads and bodies of the dolls.

Doll, French, S & H, Ondine, Swimmer, Bisque, Cork, Mechanical, Elie Martin, 1876, 16 In.
$2,576

Theriault's

Doll, German, Asian Child, Bisque Head, Painted, Mohair Wig, Papier-Mache, 9 ½ In.
$830

James D. Julia Auctioneers

Doll, German, Bisque Shoulder Head, Glass Eyes, Muslin Body, c.1870, 22 In.
$896

Theriault's

Doll, German, Muslin, Papier-Mache, Human Hair Wig, Wood, Jointed, c.1850, 15 In.
$6,440

Theriault's

Doll, German, Porcelain Shoulder Head, Sculpted Hair, Muslin Body, c.1865, 29 In.
$672

Theriault's

Doll, German, Welsh Peddler, Papier-Mache, Kid Body, Wood Legs, c.1850, 11 In.

$4,480

Doll, Heubach, 8050, Bisque, Sculpted Hair, Painted Eyes, Composition, c.1910, 17 In.

$5,130

Doll, Jumeau, Bebe, Bisque Head, Paperweight Eyes, Composition, Jointed, 23 ½ In.

$2,963

German, Welsh Peddler, Papier-Mache, Kid Body, Wood Legs, c.1850, 11 In. ....*illus*	4480
German, Wood, Yellow Tuck Comb, Black Painted Hair, Jointed, Grodner, c.1830, 18 In.	6720
Half Dolls are listed in the Pincushion Doll category.	
Handwerck, 69, Bisque, Sleep Eyes, Pierced Ears, Mohair Wig, Jointed, Hat, 24 In.	226
Handwerck, 109, Nun, Bisque Head, Sleep Eyes, Teeth, Composition, Jointed, 17 In.	311
Handwerck, 110, Bisque Head, Glass Eyes, Teeth, Mohair Wig, Composition, Jointed, 20 In.	198
Handwerck, 1159, Nurse, Bisque, Mohair Curls, Red Striped Uniform, Headdress, 24 In.	2280
Handwerck, Child, Bisque Head, Sleep Eyes, Blond Human Hair, Composition, 18 In.	390
Happifats, Bisque, Painted, Brown Curl, Chubby, Boy, Girl, Germany, 3 ½ In., Pair	90
Hertel Schwab, 141, Bisque Head, Blue Intaglio Eyes, Mohair, Composition, Jointed, 20 In.	4200
Heubach, see also Gebruder Heubach.	
Heubach, 6970, Bisque, Human Hair Braids, Closed Mouth, Festival Outfit, 19 In.	1440
Heubach, 7247, Boy, Bisque Head, Sleep Eyes, Mohair Wig, Jointed, Composition, 17 ½ In.	1243
Heubach, 7602, Bisque Dome Head, Painted, Composition, 15 In.	254
Heubach, 7602, Pouty, Bisque Head, Googly Eyes, Closed Mouth, Composition, 8 ½ In.	113
Heubach, 7850, Coquette, Bisque Shoulder Head, Painted, Composition, 14 In.	339
Heubach, 7977, Bisque, Dome Head, Painted, Composition, 8 In.	565
Heubach, 8050, Bisque, Sculpted Hair, Painted Eyes, Composition, c.1910, 17 In. ....*illus*	5130
Heubach, Bisque Dome Head, Painted, Face, Flocked Hair, 6 In.	113
Heubach, Bisque Socket Head, Molded Bob, Pouty, Wood, Composition, 10 In.	360
Heubach, Bisque Socket Head, Sculpted Hair, Googly, Composition Body, c.1915, 8 In.	336
Heubach, Boy & Girl, Bisque Shoulder Head, Sculpted, Muslin Body, c.1912, 13 In., Pair	560
Heubach, Boy, Bisque Head, Molded Hair, Kid Body, Cloth Arms, Silk Blouse, 14 ½ In.	226
Heubach, Coquette, Bisque Head, Painted Hair, Bow, Googly, Jointed, Composition, 12 In.	283
Horsman, Baby Dimples, Composition, Sleep Eyes, Rosy Cheeks, Cloth, 21 In.	120
Ideal, Deanna Durbin, Brown Wig, Lace Gown, 21 In.	198
Ideal, Deanna Durbin, Composition, Human Hair Wig, Pale Blue Gown, 21 In.	45
Ideal, Mary Hartline, Hard Plastic, Blond, Uniform, Batons, Hair Curlers, Box, 16 In.	452
Ideal, Miss Revlon, Vinyl Head, Green Velvet Dress, White Stole, 18 In.	141
Ideal, Patti Playpal, Plastic, Original Tan Dress, Green Rickrack, White Shoes, 36 In.	35
Ideal, Scarecrow, Wizard Of Oz, Cloth, Original Tag, 18 In.	1748
Ideal, Toni, Plastic, Brown Hair, Lashed Sleep Eyes, Plaid Jumper, 19 In.	120
Ideal, Toni, Plastic, Jointed, Blond Wig, Red Bow, Yellow, Green Dress, 14 In.	141
Ideal, Toni, Plastic, Sleep Eyes, Blond Wig, Plaid Jumper, Wrist Tag, Box, 14 In.	210
Indian dolls are listed in the Indian category.	
J.D.K. dolls are listed in this category under Kestner.	
Jackie Robinson, Composition, Painted Hair, Face, Original Costume, Box, c.1950, 13 In.	1456
Jumeau, Bebe Triste, Bisque Socket Head, Paperweight Eyes, Mohair, Cutwork Dress, 28 In.	16240
Jumeau, Bebe, Bisque Head, Paperweight Eyes, Closed Mouth, Blond Mohair, Dress, 16 In.	4200
Jumeau, Bebe, Bisque Head, Paperweight Eyes, Composition, Jointed, 23 ½ In. ....*illus*	2963
Jumeau, Bebe, Bisque Head, Paperweight Eyes, Mohair, Composition, Lace Dress, 24 In.	904
Jumeau, Bebe, Bisque Head, Set Eyes, Teeth, Human Hair Wig, Wood, Composition, 26 ½ In.	1130
Jumeau, Bebe, Bisque Socket Head, Brown Complexion, Wood, Jointed, c.1884, 16 In.	588
Jumeau, Bebe, Bisque Socket Head, Human Hair, Composition, Wood, 27 In.	4480
Jumeau, Bebe, Socket Head, Human Hair, Paperweight Eyes, Composition, Wood, 23 In.	830
Jumeau, Bisque Head, Fixed Eyes, Open Mouth, Jointed Composition, 1907, 30 ½ In.	504
Jumeau, Bisque Head, Glass Eyes, Human Hair, Wood, Composition, 1907, 22 ½ In.	1126
Jumeau, Bisque Head, Paperweight Eyes, Mohair Wig, Composition, Jointed 9 ½ In.	2712
Jumeau, Bisque Head, Paperweight Eyes, Mohair Wig, Composition, Jointed, 10 ½ In.	3620
Jumeau, Bisque, Paperweight Eyes, Pierced Ears, Blond Wig, 20 In.	678
Jumeau, Bleuette, Bisque Head, Mohair, Composition, Jointed, Straw Hat, Linen Dress, 11 In.	1808
Jumeau, Fashion, Bisque Swivel Head, Paperweight Eyes, Wig, c.1884, 16 In.	5880
Jumeau, Fashion, Pressed Bisque Swivel Head, Glass Eyes, Mohair, c.1875, 5 ½ In.	2352
Jumeau, Fashion, Pressed Bisque, Blue Eyes, Blond Wig, Gusseted, 19 In.	6125
Jumeau, Paris Bebe, Bisque Socket Head, Human Hair, Composition, Jointed, 32 In.	4032
K * R, 101, Boy, Bisque Head, Painted Eyes, Closed Mouth, Composition, Jointed, 13 ½ In.	1185
K * R, 101, Marie, Bisque Socket Head, Brown Wig, Brown Eyes, Dress, Pinafore, c.1910, 12 In...	1680
K * R, 107, Karl, Bisque Head, Painted Face, Mohair, Composition, Wood, 21 In. ....*illus*	47040
K * R, 114, Bisque Head, Pouty Face, Glass Eyes, Mohair Curls, Jointed Composition, 21 In.	9000
K * R, 114, Bisque Head, Pouty Mouth, Painted Eyes, Composition, Jointed, 10 In.	1304
K * R, 115/a, Bisque Head, Sleep Eyes, Mohair Wig, Composition, Baby, 15 In.	1413
K * R, 117, Mein Liebling, Bisque Socket Head, Sleep Eyes, Mohair, Wood, c.1912, 23 In.	4480
K * R, 192, Bisque Head, Sleep Eyes, Composition, Sailor Dress, 7 In.	226
K * R, 546, Bisque Head, Sleep Eyes, Chubby Cheeks, Composition, Jointed, 17 In.	3300
K * R, 1221, Bisque Head, Sleep Eyes, Teeth, Composition, 14 In.	254
K * R, Bisque Socket Head, Sleep Eyes, Blond Mohair Wig, Composition, 6 In.	170

Kamkins, Cloth Pressed, Socket Head, Oil-Painted Face, Human Hair Wig, c.1920, 18 In.	2016
Kathe Kruse, Boy, Cloth, Painted, Brown Eyes, Brown Human Hair, Lederhosen, 20 In.	1080
Kathe Kruse, Character, Cloth, Painted Face, Disc-Jointed, Germany, c.1940, 18 In. *illus*	1904
Kathe Kruse, Cloth, Painted Face, Downcast Eyes, Closed Mouth, Human Hair Wig, c.1950, 14 In.	448
Kathe Kruse, Girl, Cloth, Painted Features, Mohair Bun, Blue Dress, Scarf, Clogs, Box, 12 In.	240
Kathe Kruse, Girl, Cloth, Painted Pouty Face, Blond Human Hair, Jointed, Blue Dress, 18 In.	1200
Kathe Kruse, Hempelschen, Cloth, Painted, Pointed, Blue & White Suit, 1931, 16 In.	2700
Kathe Kruse, Schlenkerchen, Type II, Stockinet Head, Painted, Brown Eyes, c.1910, 13 In.	7200
Kathe Kruse, Series I, Cloth, Oil Painted, Closed Mouth, Disc Joints, c.1915, 17 In.	2688
Kathe Kruse, Plastic Head, Painted, Human Wig, Cloth, U.S. Zone, Germany, 15 In.	565
Kestner, 146, Bisque Head, Sleep Eyes, Jointed, Human Hair Wig, Dress, Hat, 29 In.	396
Kestner, 150, Bisque, Sleep Eyes, Jointed, 5 ½ In.	113
Kestner, 152, Bisque Socket Head, Sleep Eyes, Mohair Wig, Jointed, 19 In.	537
Kestner, 156, Bisque Head, Sleep Eyes, Jointed, Blond Mohair Wig, 24 In.	735
Kestner, 171, Bisque Head, Blond Human Hair Wig, Composition, Jointed, 31 In.	231
Kestner, 171, Bisque Head, Sleep Eyes, Mohair Wig, Composition, 31 In.	537
Kestner, 172, Gibson Girl, Bisque Head, Sleep Eyes, Mohair Wig, Kid, Lace Dress, 19 In.	961
Kestner, 172, Gibson Girl, Bisque Shoulder Head, Mohair Wig, Kid, 20 In.	904
Kestner, 172, Gibson Girl, Bisque Shoulder Head, Sleep Eyes, Kid, 10 In.	480
Kestner, 211, Bisque Socket Head, Blond Human Hair, Composition, Baby, 16 In.	141
Kestner, 243, Asian Baby, Bisque Socket Head, Sleep Eyes, Composition, Bent Limbs, 13 In.	2689
Kestner, 245, Bisque Head, Sleep Eyes, Composition, Baby, 24 In.	678
Kestner, 245, Hilda, Bisque Head, 2 Teeth, Brown Wig, Composition, 24 In.	378
Kestner, 245, Hilda, Bisque Head, Sleep Eyes, Composition, Lace Baby Bonnet, 16 In.	791
Kestner, 245, Hilda, Child, Sleep Eyes, Wood, Composition, Jointed, Mohair, 1914, 16 In.	1778
Kestner, 257, Bisque Head, Sleep Eyes, Open Mouth, Mohair, Composition, Baby, 13 In.	420
Kestner, 257, Bisque, Open Mouth, Composition, Mohair Wig, Baby, 23 In.	311
Kestner, 282, Mama, Bisque Shoulder Head, Sleep Eyes, Human Hair, Composition, 24 In.	450
Kestner, Bisque Dome Head, Open Mouth, Sleep Eyes, Baby, 24 In.	311
Kestner, Bisque Head, Sleep Eyes, Skin Wig, Composition, Baby, 20 In.	226
Kestner, Bisque Socket Head, Sleep Eyes, Brown Wig, Composition, Jointed, 14 In.	226
Kestner, Bisque Socket Head, Sleep Eyes, Mohair, Composition, Ball-Jointed, c.1900, 36 In.	2352
Kestner, Bisque, Brown Complexion, Swivel Head, Inset Eyes, Closed Mouth, c.1885, 6 In.	1568
Kestner, Bisque, Multi-Head, Glass Sleep Eyes, Teeth, Mohair Wig, c.1910, 15 In.	7280
Kestner, Century Baby, Bisque Head, Sleep Eyes, Molded Hair, Cloth, Composition, 14 In.	180
Kestner, Gibson Girl, Bisque Head & Limbs, Blond Mohair Up-Do, Cloth Body, Dress, 10 In.	780
Kestner, Max & Moritz, Bisque, Swivel Head, Googly Eyes, Jointed, c.1915, 6 In., Pair *illus*	5040
Kewpie dolls are listed in the Kewpie category.	
Kling, 223, Bisque Shoulder Head, Molded Hair, Set Eyes, Cloth Body, 15 In.	509
Kling, Boy, Bisque, Sculpted Bonnet, Glass Eyes, Painted, Kid, Gusset-Jointed, c.1875, 13 In.	1680
Lanternier, Bisque Socket Head, Paperweight Eyes, Mohair Wig, 18 In.	198
Lanternier, Cherie, Bisque Head, Set Eyes, Mohair Wig, Jointed Composition, 17 ½ In.	170
Lenci, 300, Molded, Painted Face, Googly, Mohair Wig, Felt Body, Plaid Skirt, 17 ½ In.	848
Lenci, 300, Pouty Boy, Felt, Closed Mouth, Jointed, Shorts, Knitted Sweater & Socks, 16 In.	720
Lenci, Alma, Felt Swivel Head, Googly, Mohair Wig, Jointed, Italy, c.1935, 17 In. *illus*	560
Lenci, Aristocrat, Felt Head, Pressed, Painted Face, Wide Coat, Tea Cozy, 1920s, 18 In.	1680
Lenci, Boy, Swivel Head, Painted Face, Googly, Mohair Wig, Jointed, 1930s, 9 In.	280
Lenci, Girl, Felt Swivel Head, Googly, Blond Curls, Polka Dot Bow, Pink Bloomers, 14 In.	180
Lenci, Girl, Felt, Painted Eyes, Blond Mohair Wig, Blue Felt Dress, Cape & Shoes, 13 In.	780
Lenci, Girl, Felt, Painted Face, Mohair Wig, Red Costume, 10 ½ In.	254
Lenci, Girl, Felt, Socket Head, Pressed, Painted Face, Mohair Wig, c.1933, 22 In.	2016
Lenci, Girl, Felt, Swivel Head, Painted Face, Red, White Dress, c.1935, 25 In.	1008
Lenci, Opium Smoker, Felt, Swivel Head, Closed Eyes, Pipe, Chinese Outfit, c.1921, 11 In.	1232
Lenci, Pouty, Felt, Painted, Googly, Mohair Wig, 19 In.	434
Lenci, Sonja, Felt Swivel Head, Painted, Mohair Wig, Muslin Torso, 27 In. *illus*	1232
Madame Alexander, Alexander-Kins, Hard Plastic, Straight Leg, Organdy Dress, 8 In.	283
Madame Alexander, Alexander-Kins, June Wedding, 1956, 8 In.	226
Madame Alexander, Alexander-Kins, Quiz-Kin, Plastic, Brown Hair, Organdy Dress, Box, 8 In.	420
Madame Alexander, Alexander-Kins, Straight Walker, Dress, 8 In.	226
Madame Alexander, Alexander-Kins, Tosca, Plastic, Red Hair, Dress, Straw Hat, 8 In.	300
Madame Alexander, Alexander-Kins, Walker, Blue Romper, 8 In.	141
Madame Alexander, Alexander-Kins, Wendy, Bent Walker, 8 In.	79
Madame Alexander, Baby Genius, Blond Wig, Sleep Eyes, Romper, Hat, Booties, c.1957, 8 In.	168
Madame Alexander, Baby Genius, Plastic, Cloth, Composition, Christening Gown, 17 In.	90
Madame Alexander, Ballerina, Plastic, Blond Wig, Pink Satin Tulle Dress, 22 In.	367

Doll, K * R, 107, Karl, Bisque Head, Painted Face, Mohair, Composition, Wood, 21 In.
$47,040

Theriault's

Doll, Kathe Kruse, Character, Cloth, Painted Face, Disc-Jointed, Germany, c.1940, 18 In.
$1,904

Theriault's

Doll, Kestner, Max & Moritz, Bisque, Swivel Head, Googly Eyes, Jointed, c.1915, 6 In., Pair
$5,040

Theriault's

Doll, Lenci, Alma, Felt Swivel Head, Googly, Mohair Wig, Jointed, Italy, c.1935, 17 In.
$560

Theriault's

Doll, Lenci, Sonja, Felt Swivel Head, Painted, Mohair Wig, Muslin Torso, 27 In.
$1,232

Theriault's

Doll, Madame Alexander, Bridesmaid, Composition, Mohair Wig, c.1948, 17 In.
$616

Theriault's

Madame Alexander, Bride, Plastic, Blond Mohair Curls, White Tiered Dress, Veil, 19 In.	360
Madame Alexander, Bridesmaid, Composition, Mohair Wig, c.1948, 17 In. *illus*	616
Madame Alexander, Cissette, Lavender Dress, c.1957, 10 In.	367
Madame Alexander, Cissette, Tagged Dress, Hat, c.1960, 10 In.	57
Madame Alexander, Cissy, 2143, Lavender Dress, Hat, c.1957, 20 In.	1187
Madame Alexander, Cissy, 2283, Plastic, Pink Camelia, c.1958, 20 In.	1017
Madame Alexander, Cissy, Bride, Plastic, Brunette Hair, Curly Bangs, Satin Gown, 20 In.	360
Madame Alexander, Cissy, Hard Plastic, Jointed, Blond Wig, Print Cotton Dress, 20 In.	565
Madame Alexander, Cissy, Plastic, Blond Wig, Black Velvet Gown, White Stole, c.1957, 20 In.	1413
Madame Alexander, Cissy, Plastic, Blond Wig, Red Cotton Jumper, High Heel Feet, 21 In.	210
Madame Alexander, Cissy, Plastic, Brown Wig, Black Velvet Gown, Fur Cape & Hat, 21 In.	480
Madame Alexander, Cissy, Plastic, Tagged Skirt Outfit, 20 In.	565
Madame Alexander, Cissy, Tagged, Yellow Dress, Coat, c.1956, 20 In.	367
Madame Alexander, Elise, Bride White Organdy Dress, 16 ½ In.	254
Madame Alexander, Elsie, Plastic, Blond Wig, Jointed, Taffeta Dress, Fur Hat, Box, 16 In.	252
Madame Alexander, Fairy Queen, Composition, Blond Hair, Tulle Gown, Wings, 14 In.	280
Madame Alexander, Godey Lady, Tosca Hair, Velvet Gown, c.1950, 14 In. *illus*	798
Madame Alexander, Guardian Angel, Hard Plastic, Straight Leg, Harp, Shoes, Halo, 8 In.	424
Madame Alexander, Jacqueline, Plastic, Brown Wig, Yellow Sheath, Coat, Hat, c.1962, 10 In.	565
Madame Alexander, Little Shaver, Cloth, Painted, Googly, Tagged Dress, 17 In.	210
Madame Alexander, Little Women, Beth, Plastic, Tagged Dress, 14 In.	102
Madame Alexander, Little Women, Jo, Plastic, Plaid Outfit, 14 In.	170
Madame Alexander, Little Women, Meg, Blond Wig, White Apron, Checked Dress, 14 In.	170
Madame Alexander, Little Women, Meg, Composition, Mohair Wig, 7 In.	57
Madame Alexander, Little Women, Meg, Plastic, Tagged Dress, 14 In.	254
Madame Alexander, Madelaine De Baine, Blond, Pantaloons, White Dress, Red Trim, 15 In.	198
Madame Alexander, Maggie Face, Hard Plastic, Blond Wig, Violet Taffeta Dress, 14 In.	90
Madame Alexander, Maggie Mixup, Plastic, Straight Red Hair, Pants, Sweater, Hat, Box, 16 In.	240
Madame Alexander, Maggie, Hard Plastic, Dark Wig, Walker, Orange Dress, 18 In.	141
Madame Alexander, Maggie, Plastic, Skirt, Blouse, Roller Skates, 17 In.	424
Madame Alexander, Margaret O'Brien, Composition, Mohair Braids, Tagged Dress, 20 In.	270
Madame Alexander, Margaret O'Brien, Mohair Braids, Composition, Green Dress, Hat, 14 In.	311
Madame Alexander, Margaret O'Brien, Tagged Pink Dress, 20 In.	396
Madame Alexander, McGuffey Ana, Composition, Blond Human Hair, Pinafore, Coat, 15 In.	90
Madame Alexander, Princess Elizabeth, Composition, Formal Gown, 13 In.	90
Madame Alexander, Scarlett O'Hara, Sleep Eyes, Composition, Green Dress, Hat, 18 In.	283
Madame Alexander, Sonja Henie, Composition, Human Hair, Swivel Waist, Skirt, Hat, 13 In.	113
Madame Alexander, Sonja Henie, Composition, Skating Outfit, 15 In.	254
Madame Alexander, Sonja Henie, Composition, Sleep Eyes, Yellow Dress, Skates, 20 In.	180
Madame Alexander, Victorian Bride, Plastic, 5-Piece Body, Satin Gown, 1951, 21 In. *illus*	7840
Madame Alexander, Wendy Bride, Plastic, Walker, White Gown, Garter, Veil, Box, 18 In.	226
Madame Alexander, Wendy-Kins, Plastic, Organdy Dress, Box, 1965, 8 In.	360
Madame Alexander, Wendy-Kins, Tosca Wig, Blue Dress, Trunk, Costumes, c.1957, 8 In.	784
Madame Hendren, Dolly Reckord, Composition, Cloth, Phonograph In Torso, 26 In.	510
Mannequin, Artist's, Wood, Bald Head, Swivel Neck, Dowel-Jointed, 38 In.	3920
Marotte, Bisque Head, Set Eyes, Blond Wig, Whistle Base, 113 In.	226
Marseille, 241, Bisque Socket Head, Googly, Painted Hair, Face, Papier-Mache, c.1920, 6 In.	336
Marseille, Just Me, Bisque Socket Head, Sleep Eyes, Mohair, Composition, c.1925, 9 ½ In.	1456
Mary Hoyer, Bride, Composition, Ballet Dress, Veil, Original Box, 1940s, 14 In.	180
Mary Hoyer, Composition, Sleep Eyes, Mohair Wig, Jointed, Green Crocheted Suit, Box, 14 In.	360
Mattel, Barbie, American Girl, Blond, Gilbert Honey West, Mink Jacket, Shoes	226
Mattel, Barbie, American Girl, Brunette, Music Center Matinee, c.1966	464
Mattel, Barbie, Blond Bubble Cut, Bendable Leg, Box	261
Mattel, Barbie, Blond Bubble Cut, Sophisticated Lady Ensemble, 1961, 11 In. *illus*	228
Mattel, Barbie, Blond Ponytail, Wedding Day Set, White Dress, Necklace, Veil, Box	5650
Mattel, Barbie, Blond Ponytail, White Dress	128
Mattel, Barbie, Blond Swirl Ponytail, Original Box	197
Mattel, Barbie, Brunette Bubble Cut, Side Part Titian, Red Swimsuit	377
Mattel, Barbie, Fashion Queen Set, 3 Wigs, Striped Headdress, Bathing Suit, Box	424
Mattel, Barbie, No. 1, Blond Ponytail, No. 961, Evening Spendour Dress, Display, Box, c.1960	4300
Mattel, Barbie, No. 1, Blond Ponytail, Striped Swimsuit, Heels, Sunglasses	2900
Mattel, Barbie, No. 1, Blond Ponytail, Swimsuit, Accessories, Box	2700
Mattel, Barbie, No. 1, Brunette, Top Knot Ponytail, Swimsuit, Sunglasses, Box, Gimbels Tag	2599
Mattel, Barbie, No. 2, Blond Ponytail, Black Striped Swimsuit, Sunglasses, Box	1921
Mattel, Barbie, No. 2, Blond Ponytail, Swimsuit, Hoop Earrings, Stand, Box, 11 In.	3300

Mattel, Barbie, No. 3, Blond Ponytail, Box..	522
Mattel, Barbie, No. 3, Blond Ponytail, Striped Swimsuit...............................	197
Mattel, Barbie, No. 3, Blond Ponytail, Striped Swimsuit, Shoes.....................	396
Mattel, Barbie, No. 3, Blond Ponytail, Wearing Picnic Set Outfit...................	116
Mattel, Barbie, No. 3, Brunette Ponytail, Black & White Striped Dress, Ensemble..........	452
Mattel, Barbie, No. 3, Brunette Ponytail, Striped Swimsuit.........................	435 to 493
Mattel, Barbie, No. 4, Blond Ponytail, Swimsuit, Accessories, Box	330
Mattel, Barbie, No. 4, Brunette Ponytail, Bride's Dream, White Gown, Veil	113
Mattel, Barbie, No. 4, Brunette Ponytail, Wearing Suburban Shopper, No. 969, c.1960	162
Mattel, Barbie, No. 5, Blond Ponytail, American Airlines Outfit, Bag, 1961............	120
Mattel, Barbie, No. 5, Blond Ponytail, Busy Gal Ensemble, Accessories, 1961, 11 In. ....*illus*	228
Mattel, Barbie, No. 5, Blond Ponytail, Ski Queen Outfit, Box, 1961	240
Mattel, Barbie, No. 967, Blond Swirl Ponytail, Wearing Picnic Set..................	209
Mattel, Barbie, No. 993, American Girl, Sophisticated, Tiara, Necklace, Pink Gown, c.1964........	261
Mattel, Barbie, No. 1817, Brunette Ponytail, , Red Fantastic, 1967	232
Mattel, Barbie, No. 3461, 1st Black, Peach Flush, Jointed, c.1972..................	696
Mattel, Barbie, Titian American Girl, Saturday Matinee Outfit, 1965...............	348
Mattel, Casey, Twist 'n Turn, Original Box..	186
Mattel, Christie, Live Action, Yellow Coat, Fur Collar, Sleeves.....................	128
Mattel, Francie, Growin' Pretty Hair, Blond, Brown Eyes, Bendable Legs, Box, 1970, 11 In.	168
Mattel, Francie, Twist 'n Turn, Brunette, Played-With Condition	162
Mattel, Ken, Blond Painted Hair, Bendable Legs, Swimsuit, Box, 1964, 12 In. ....*illus*	456
Mattel, Midge, Blond Flip, 2-Piece Blue Swimsuit, Box..............................	141
Mattel, Midge, Plastic, Blond Hair, Bendable Legs, Wrist Tag, Box	300
Mattel, Mrs. Beasley, Glasses, Blond Wig, Blue Polka Dot Dress, 20 In............	47
Mattel, Skipper, Bendable Leg, Brass Headband, Wearing Town Togs, No. 1922, Box	139
Mattel, Skipper, Pose 'n Play, 1973, 9 In.	83
Mollye, Sabu, Thief Of Bagdad Series, Composition, Swivel Neck, Painted, 1950s, 15 ½ In.	79
Monica, Composition, Painted Face, Brunette Human Hair, Gown, 1941-52, 14 In.	672
Moravian, Polly Heckewelder, Cloth, Painted, Original Dress, Underwear & Shoes, 18 In............	3000
Nancy Ann Storybook, Bisque, Star Hands, Baby, Dress, Bonnet, Slip, Diaper, Box, 3 ½ In.	150
Nancy Ann Storybook, Hush-A-Bye Series, Bisque, Star Hands, Dress, Bonnet, Box, 4 In.	90
Nancy Ann Storybook, Muffie, Platinum Blond Wig, Taffeta Party Dress, Shoes, Box, 8 In........	390
Nancy Ann Storybook, Style Show, Auburn Wig, Hard Plastic, High Bun, Ball Gown, 18 In.......	339
Nancy Ann Storybook, Style Show, Hard Plastic, Belle Gown, Hat, Velvet Roses, 18 In................	735
Nancy Ann Storybook, Style Show, Hard Plastic, Blond Wig, Ponytail, Peach Gown, 18 In.......	141
Nancy Ann Storybook, Style Show, Lawn Party, Brown Wig, Pink Print, Hat, Box, 18 In.	565
Nancy Ann Storybook, Style Show, Summer Resort, Pink Organdy Dress, Hoop, Box, 18 In......	622
Nancy Ann, Storybook, Muffie, Auburn Wig, Box, Pamphlets, 8 In.	283
Nockler & Tittel, Bisque, Molded Blond Bob, Googly, Jointed, 12 In.	1080
Norah Welling, Boy, Fabric, Painted, Blond Mohair Wig, Jointed, Black Suit, 17 In.	113
Old Cottage, Tweedledee & Tweedledum, Painted Features, Mohair Wig, 1950s, 10 In., Pair........	1008
Orsini, Bisque, Sleep Eyes, Smile, Upper Teeth, Mohair Bob, Jointed, Dress, Hat, 5 In..................	780
Paper dolls are listed in their own category.	
Papier-Mache, Molded, Painted, Apollo Knot Hair, Cloth Body, Gown, Germany, 13 In................	660
Parian Shoulder Head, Molded Blond Braids Cornet, Cloth Body, Bisque Arms, 15 In.	480
Parian Shoulder Head, Molded Blond Hair, Painted Features, Kid Body, 22 In..........................	207
Pincushion dolls are listed in their own category.	
Porcelain Shoulder Head, Pink Tint, Kid Body, Silk Gown, c.1850, 17 In.	2240
Raggedy Ann & Andy, Button Eyes, Muslin, Georgene Novelties, c.1938, 18 In., Pair	840
Raggedy Ann, Cloth, Sewn Wig, Long Nose, Dress, Georgene, 18 In.................	68
Raggedy Ann, Cloth, Sewn Wig, Shoebutton Eyes, Georgene, 18 In.	113
Revalo, Bisque Head, Sleep Eyes, Teeth, Human Hair Wig, Jointed, Composition, 21 In.	198
Ruth Gibbs, Godey's Little Lady, Bride, China, Cloth, Caracul Wig, Box, 1940s, 10 In..................	450
S & H dolls are also listed here as Simon & Halbig.	
S.F.B.J., 60, Bebe, Bisque, Blue Eyes, Blond Human Wig, Composition, Wood, 11 In.	960
S.F.B.J., 229, Bisque Socket Head, Glass Eyes, Mohair Wig, Jointed, c.1912, 18 In...........	3360
S.F.B.J., 301, Bisque Head, Sleep Eyes, Mohair Wig, Pierced Ears, Composition, 16 In.	198
S.F.B.J., 301, Bisque Head, Sleep Eyes, Teeth, Composition, Wood, Outfit, 20 In.........................	678
Sasha, Blond, Painted Eyes, Sailing Suit, Box, Red Tam, 1960s.......................	141
Sasha, Gregor, Vinyl, Platinum Hair, Blue Eyes, Jeans, Shirt, Sandals, Box, 16 In.	180
Sasha, Plastic, Blond Hair, Wispy Bangs, Blue Eyes, Corduroy Dress, Wrist Tag, Gotz, 16 In........	480
Sasha, Plastic, Brown Eyes & Hair, Bangs, Kilt Outfit, Wardrobe, Trunk, 16 In......	540
Sasha, Plastic, Brown Hair & Eyes, Pink Dress, Red Felt Coat, Germany, 16 In..........................	450
Sasha, Ruth, Painted Eyes, Red Wig, Short Plaid Skirt, Plane Ticket, Tube Box, Gotz.................	311

Doll, Madame Alexander, Godey Lady, Tosca Hair, Velvet Gown, c.1950, 14 In.
$798

Theriault's

Doll, Madame Alexander, Victorian Bride, Plastic, 5-Piece Body, Satin Gown, 1951, 21 In.
$7,840

Theriault's

Doll, Mattel, Barbie, Blond Bubble Cut, Sophisticated Lady Ensemble, 1961, 11 In.
$228

Theriault's

Doll, Mattel, Barbie, No. 5, Blond Ponytail, Busy Gal Ensemble, Accessories, 1961, 11 In.
$228

Theriault's

Doll, Mattel, Ken, Blond Painted Hair, Bendable Legs, Swimsuit, Box, 1964, 12 In.
$456

Theriault's

Doll, Simon & Halbig, 1199, Bisque Socket Head, Mohair, Composition, Child, 17 In.
$1,778

James D. Julia Auctioneers

Sasha, Yamka Gypsy, Painted Eyes, Black Wig, Beads, Pink Dress, Tube Box, Gotz	537
Schoenhut, 308, Intaglio Eyes, Tacked Wig, Wood, Jointed, 16 In.	170
Schoenhut, Boy, Dolly Face, Painted, Wood, Jointed, 16 In.	198
Schoenhut, Boy, Tacked Wig, Wood, Jointed, Union Suit, 17 In.	141
Schoenhut, Carved Socket Head, Painted Face, Wig, Wood, Spring-Jointed, c.1915, 14 In.	1456
Schoenhut, Felix The Cat, Wood, Jointed, Leather, Pat Sullivan Copyright 1922, 1924, 8 In.	143
Schoenhut, Girl, Painted Features, Intaglio Eyes, Carved Hair, Sailor Dress, 14 In.	480
Schoenhut, Miss Dolly, Wood, Blue Painted Eyes, Closed Mouth, Blond Curls, Box, 15 In.	1200
Schoenhut, Molded Hair, Painted Face, Arms & Legs, Dress, Knit Leggings, 15 In.	330
Schoenhut, Pouty Mouth, Brown Intaglio Eyes, Mohair Bob, Wool Dress, 18 In.	600
Schoenhut, Rolly-Dolly, Dutch Girl, Papier-Mache, Sculpted Cap, Round Base, c.1910, 15 In.	728
Schoenhut, Toddler, Painted Face, Bobbed Mohair Wig, Jointed Body, 11 In.	210
Schoneau & Hoffmeister, Bisque Socket Head, Sleep Eyes, Painted Face, c.1915, 13 In.	504
Shirley Temple dolls are included in the Shirley Temple category.	
Simon & Halbig, 7, Bisque Head, 4 Teeth, Jointed, Brown Wig, White Dress, 32 In.	339
Simon & Halbig, 19, Bisque Head, Mohair Wig, Jointed, Composition, Child, 24 In.	283
Simon & Halbig, 127, Bisque Dome Head, Molded Hair, Composition, Baby, 17 In.	424
Simon & Halbig, 550, Bisque Socket Head, Mohair Wig, Jointed, Dress, Cap, 20 In.	283
Simon & Halbig, 1009, Bisque Head, Composition, Jointed, Long Lace Gown, 28 In.	108
Simon & Halbig, 1010, Bisque Shoulder Head, Kid Body, Mohair Wig, 13 In.	452
Simon & Halbig, 1079, Bisque Head, Sleep Eyes, Blond Wig, Composition, 25 In.	311
Simon & Halbig, 1159, Bisque Head, Sleep Eyes, Composition, Jointed, Body, Hat, 18 In.	851
Simon & Halbig, 1159, Bisque Socket Head, Sleep Eyes, Brown, Mohair Wig, 13 In.	848
Simon & Halbig, 1199, Bisque Socket Head, Mohair, Composition, Child, 17 In. ....*illus*	1778
Simon & Halbig, 1279, Bisque Socket Head, Sleep Eyes, Composition, Jointed, c.1900, 16 In.	1064
Simon & Halbig, Baby Blanche, Bisque Head, Human Hair, Composition, Jointed, 23 In.	270
Simon & Halbig, Bisque Head, Brown Sleep Eyes, Composition Body, White Gown, 24 In.	207
Simon & Halbig, Bisque Socket Head, Blond Mohair Wig, Jointed, 13 In.	226
Simon & Halbig, Bisque Socket Head, Brown Sleep Eyes, Ball-Jointed, c.1900, 20 In.	7840
Simon & Halbig, Bisque Socket Head, Mohair Wig, Composition, 6 In.	254
Simon & Halbig, Bisque Socket Head, Sleep Eyes, Mohair Wig, Jointed, 16 In.	622
Simon & Halbig, Globe Baby, Bisque, Almond Sleep Eyes, Teeth, Human Hair, 8 In.	240
Sonneberg, Bisque Dome Head, Paperweight Eyes, Wood, Composition, Dress, 18 In.	509
Sonneberg, Bisque Head, Set Eyes, Pierced Ears, Human Hair Wig, Composition, Jointed, 13 In.	537
Sonneberg, Princess, Bisque Head, Paperweight Eyes, Wood, Composition, Dress, 11 ½ In.	283
Steiff, Young Hero Michel, Felt, Painted Hair, Jointed, c.1918, 8 In.	565
Steiner, Bebe, Bisque Head, Composition, Lace Dress, Hat, Marked BeBe Le Parisian, 8 ¼ In.	1582
Steiner, Clown, Bisque Head, White Painted Face, Composition Body, Painted Shoes, 7 In.	141
Steiner, Phenix, 96, Bebe, Bisque Socket Head, Blue Eyes, Brown Human Hair, 25 In.	5400
Terri Lee, Brownie Outfit, Platinum Hair, Girl Scout Label, 1950s, 16 In. ....*illus*	399
Terri Lee, Brunette Curly Hair, Brown Eyes, Yellow Taffeta Dress, Black Lace, 1950s, 16 In.	224
Terri Lee, Plastic, Blue Dress, Straw Hat, 16 In.	83
Topsyturvy, Cloth, Painted Faces, 1 End Black Girl, Other White Parlor Maid, 16 In.	336
Topsyturvy, Cloth, Painted Mask Faces, Original Dress & Apron, 11 In.	84
Vogue, Ginnette, Vinyl, Molded Hair, Baby Outfit, Bottle, Box.	113
Vogue, Ginny, Blond Wig, Painted Lashes, Black & White Dress, Straw Hat, Box, 1952, 8 In.	339
Vogue, Ginny, Brown Wig, Painted Lashes, Skirt, Plaid Tam, 1952, 8 In.	283
Vogue, Ginny, Crib Crowd Baby, Plastic, Platinum Caracul Wig, Organdy Dress, Shoes, 7 In.	480
Vogue, Ginny, Mistress Mary, Plastic, Non-Walker, 8 In.	226
Vogue, Ginny, Plastic, Blond Braids, Pink Tutu, Box, 8 In.	120
Vogue, Ginny, Plastic, Blond Hair, 7 Outfits, Shoes, Hats, Trunk, 8 In.	240
Vogue, Ginny, Plastic, Blond Hair, Lacy Dress, Shoes, Hat, Curlers, Zipper Series, 1953, 8 In.	420
Vogue, Ginny, Plastic, Blond Pigtails, 6 Outfits, Trunk, 1950s, 8 In.	390
Vogue, Ginny, Queen Elizabeth, Plastic, Beaded Gown, Cape, Crown, Scepter, Trunk, 8 In.	660
Vogue, Ginny, Red Hair, Painted Lashes, Silver Tag, No. 81, Box, 1952, 8 In. ....*illus*	627
Vogue, Ginny, Roller Skater, Brunette, Red & White Costume, Sport Series, 1950, 8 In.	280
Vogue, Jill, Plastic, Blond Hair, Heart-Shaped Earrings, 5 Outfits, 11 ½ In.	150
Vogue, Jill, Plastic, Sleep Eyes, Blond Wig, Black Bathing Suit & Heels, Box, 1957, 10 In.	150
Vogue, Prince Charming, Satin Cushion, Plastic, Mohair Wig, 8 In.	48
Wax, Aristocrat, Beard, Silk, Brocade Costume, Embossed Gold Leaf, c.1790, 11 In.	1008
Wax, Over Papier-Mache, Sleep Eyes, Wire Lever, Human Hair, Muslin, c.1850, 26 In. .....*illus*	912
Wax, Shoulder Head, Boy, Muslin Body, Scottish Costume, c.1855, 30 In.	5880
Wood, Mandrake The Magician & His Assistant, Tuxedo, Evening Gown, 41 In., Pair	830
Wood, Shoulder Head, Carved, Painted Black Curls, Top Knot, Jointed, c.1830, 11 In.	3584

DOLL CLOTHES

Barbie & Midge, Fashion Luncheon, Pink Sheath, Jacket, Hat, Shoes, No. 1656, Box	735
Barbie Ensemble, After 5, Black Dress, Organdy Trim, Matching Hat, Shoes, No. 934	226
Barbie Ensemble, Red Riding Hood & Wolf, Box, No. 0880	367
Barbie, All Aboard Ship, Dress, Jacket, No. 1631	396
Barbie, Busy Morning, Pink-Striped Dress, Hat, Basket, Fruit, Phone, Box, No. 956	424
Barbie, Cheerleader, Pompom, Sweater, Skirt, Shoes, Red, White, Box, No. 0876	254
Barbie, Coat, Red Wool, Fur Trim, Box	113
Barbie, Commuter Set, T.M. Mark, c.1960	174
Barbie, Everything For Babysitter, Baby, Pretzel, Phone, Bottles, Apron, Box, No. 953	283
Barbie, Lovely Lingerie Pack, Pink, c.1962	198
Barbie, Pajama Party, Blue Pajamas, Alarm Clock, Box	141
Barbie, Saturday Matinee, Black Knit Suit, Fur Trim, No. 1610, Box	254
Barbie, Senior Prom, Green Blue Gown, Shoes, Box, No. 951, c.1963	283
Barbie, Ski Queen, Pants, Parka, Gloves, Skis, Poles, No. 948, Box	226
Barbie, Skipper, Pink Poodle Skirt, Top, Box	305
Barbie, Student Teacher, Red Checked Dress, Shoes, Globe, Pencil, Book, Box, No. 1622	339
Barbie, Wedding Day, White Gown, Shoes, Veil, Necklace, No. 972	434
Bleuette, Jeannette, Navy Blue Skirt, Top, Cape, Felt Hat, 1937	170
Bleuette, Red Cross Costume, White Dress, Apron, Blue Veil, Blue Wool Cape, 1940	226
Bleuette, Red Plaid Skirt, Blouse, Coat, Hat, Chardon D'Ecosse, 1956	198
Madame Alexander, Cissy, Blue Coat, Straw Hat, For 20-In. Doll	102
Modes Des Nouveautes, Millinery Arts, Hats, Ribbons, Flowers, Wood Box, c.1910, 17 ½ In.	1064

DONALD DUCK *items are included in the Disneyana category.*

DOORSTOPS have been made in all types of designs. The vast majority of the doorstops sold today are cast iron and were made from about 1890 to 1930. Most of them are shaped like people, animals, flowers, or ships. Reproductions and newly designed examples are sold in gift shops.

Anne Radcliffe, On Plinth, 1st Woman Donor To Harvard, Cast Iron, c.1900, 14 x 7 ½ In.	420
Aunt Jemima, Hands On Hips, Red Bandanna, Iron, Littco, c.1920, 13 In. ....*illus*	948
Barney Google & Sparkplug, Barney Riding Sparkplug, Cast Iron, 5 In.	3540
Baseball Player, Batting Stance, Iron, Marked O.C.F. 1912, 17 In. ....*illus*	2489
Basket Of Jonquils & Tulips, Embossed Woven Basket, Cast Iron, 11 ½ In.	266
Basket Of Roses, Cast Iron, Multicolor, A.M. Greenblat Studios, c.1926, 10 In.	450
Basket, Cast Iron, Multicolor Paint, Hubley, 11 In.	58
Bathing Beauties, Cast Iron, Anne Fish, Hubley, 8 ⅜ In.	330
Bathing Beauties, Under Umbrella, Cast Iron, Painted, Marked Fish, 11 In.	230 to 1778
Bellhop, Black, Red Suit, Gold Trim, Holding Valise, Cast Iron, Creations Co., 7 ½ In.	1180
Black Boy Sitting On Upside-Down Basket, Holding Pipe & Leg, Pot Metal, 7 ½ In.	1770
Black Man Sitting On Bale Of Cotton, Striking Match, Cast Iron, 10 In.	4130
Boston State House, Cast Iron, Wood, U.S.A., c.1900, 14 x 8 In.	660
Bowl Of Daisies, Cast Iron, Blue, White, Yellow, Hubley, 7 ¼ In.	108
Boy, Asian Costume, Solid Casting, Full Figure, Cast Iron, 7 ¾ In.	84
Butler, Blue Uniform, Black Bowtie, Checkered Floor Base, Marked, B & H, 11 In.	1003
Cape Cod Cottage, Climbing Flowers, Trees, Cast Iron, Hubley, 5 ½ In.	207
Cat On Chimney, Black Cat, Wedge Back, Cast Iron, Judd Mfg. Co., 6 ½ In.	1180
Cat, Art Deco, Black, Hubley, 10 ½ In. ....*illus*	1888
Cat, Black, Yellow Eyes, Painted, Cast Iron, 12 ¾ In.	216
Cat, Fat Cat, Sitting, Googly Eyes, Cast Iron, Judd, 7 In.	96
Cat, Fireside, Painted Black, Green Eyes, Cast Iron, Hubley, 5 ½ x 10 In.	69
Cat, Lying Down, White, Gray, Cast Iron, Hubley, 10 ½ In.	120
Cat, Reclining, White Paint, Cast Iron, Hubley, 10 ½ In.	94
Cat, Red, 7 x 9 ¼ In.	795
Cat, Sitting, Cast Iron, Creations Company, 8 ½ In.	96
Cat, Tail Raised, Black, White, Green Eyes, Cast Iron, Hubley, 10 ¾ In.	356
Charleston Dancers, Intertwined Dancers, Cast Iron, Hubley, 8 ¾ In.	2360
Church, Bell Tower, Stained Glass Windows, Cast Iron, 7 ½ In.	72
Clipper Ship, Painted, Cast Iron, A.M. Greenblatt Studios, 1925, 9 ¾ x 12 In.	354
Cockatoo In Ring, 2-Sided, Cast Iron, Bradley & Hubbard, 13 ¾ In.	240
Cockatoo, Green, Yellow Paint, Cast Iron, c.1910, 14 In.	120
Colonial Man, With 2 Bouquets, Blue Coat, Multicolor Flowers, Cast Iron, 9 ½ In.	413
Conestoga Wagon, Oxen, Cast Iron, Hubley, 1930s, 7 ¼ x 14 In.	125
Cottage, Painted, Cast Iron, 5 ¾ x 7 ½ In.	71
Cottage, Painted, Cast Iron, Richardson, Quincy, Mass., 4 ½ In.	94

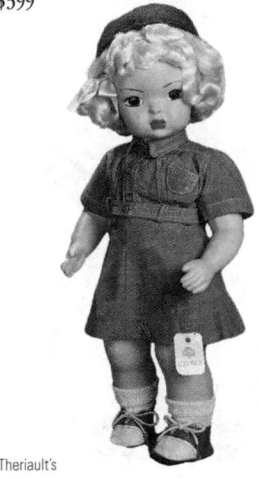

Doll, Terri Lee, Brownie Outfit, Platinum Hair, Girl Scout Label, 1950s, 16 In.
$399

Theriault's

Doll, Vogue, Ginny, Red Hair, Painted Lashes, Silver Tag, No. 81, Box, 1952, 8 In.
$627

Theriault's

Doll, Wax, Over Papier-Mache, Sleep Eyes, Wire Lever, Human Hair, Muslin, c.1850, 26 In.
$912

Theriault's

Doorstop, Aunt Jemima, Hands On Hips, Red Bandanna, Iron, Littco, c.1920, 13 In. $948

James D. Julia Auctioneers

Doorstop, Baseball Player, Batting Stance, Iron, Marked O.C.F. 1912, 17 In. $2,489

James D. Julia Auctioneers

Doorstop, Cat, Art Deco, Black, Hubley, 10 ½ In. $1,888

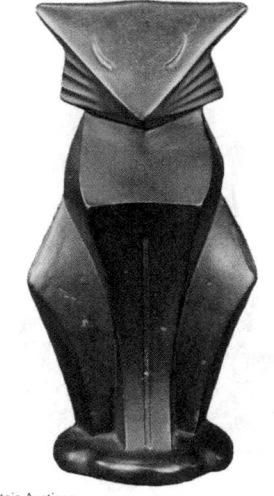

Bertoia Auctions

Cottage, With Red Roof, Trees, Greenery, Wedge Back, Cast Iron, 7 In.	59
Dapper Dan, Whimsical Man, Tails, Derby Hat, Cane, Wedge, Cast Iron, Judd Co., 7 In.	767
Dog, Airedale, Brown Paint, Cast Iron, Hubley, 8 x 8 ½ In.	92
Dog, Boston Terrier, Brown Paint, Cast Iron, 9 x 9 ½ In.	115
Dog, Boston Terrier, Facing Right, Brown Paint, Cast Iron, Hubley, 10 In.	120 to 144
Dog, Boxer, Standing, Brown Paint, Cast Iron, Hubley, 8 ¾ In.	300
Dog, Bulldog, Seated, Black Paint, Cast Iron, France, 8 ¼ x 7 In.	138
Dog, Cocker Spaniel, Standing, Tail Out, Tan, Full Figure, Cast Iron, Hubley, 7 In.	472
Dog, Dachshund, Cast Iron, Hubley, 6 In.	720
Dog, Dachshund, Standing, Full Figure, Cast Iron, Bradley & Hubbard, 6 ½ In.	1298
Dog, English Setter, Painted, Cast Iron, Hubley, 14 x 8 ¾ In.	173
Dog, Fox Terrier, Cream, Brown Paint, Cast Iron, Hubley, 8 ½ In.	300
Dog, Fox Terrier, Standing, Cast Iron, Hubley, 10 In.	300
Dog, French Bulldog, Cast Iron, Hubley, 8 In.	96
Dog, German Shepherd, Brown Paint, Cast Iron, 9 ½ In.	240
Dog, German Shepherd, Standing, Cast Bronze, 13 In.	106
Dog, Pekinese, Full Figure, Cast Iron, Hubley, 9 In.	1560
Dog, Russian Wolfhound, White Paint, Cast Iron, 15 ½ In.	148
Dog, Scottie, Cast Iron, 11 In.	79
Dog, Scottish Terrier, Black Paint, Cast Iron, 10 In.	130
Dog, Scottish Terrier, Collar, Black Paint, Cast Iron, 10 x 8 ½ In.	546
Dog, Seated, Leash, Collar, Brown Mottled, Stoneware, Albany Slip Glaze, c.1890, 9 ½ In.	431
Dog, Setter, Black & White, Pointing, Full Figure, Cast Iron, Hubley, 5 ½ In.	177
Dog, Setter, Black, White, Cast Iron, 15 In.	148
Dog, Setter, Standing, Tail Pointing, Black, White, Cast Iron, c.1910, 6 x 2 ¼ In.	115
Dog, Spaniel, Lying Down, Cast Iron, 2 In.	12
Dog, Terrier, Ears Up, Black & Tan, Cast Iron, 10 x 10 In.	150
Dog, Terrier, Standing, Black Paint, Cast Iron, 10 In.	106
Dogs, Bulldog Puppies In Basket, 3 Puppies, Cast Iron, Steacy & Wilton, 1932, 6 ½ In.	1298
Dolly, Girl Holding Doll, Grace Drayton, Marked, Hubley, 10 ½ In. *illus*	1003
Dolphin, Bronze, Signed, Hurley, E.T., 1925, 17 x 8 x 4 ½ In.	2750
Double Footman, Red, Black Paint, Cast Iron, Marked Fish, Hubley, 8 x 12 In.	345
Duck, Walking, Wearing Pants & Top Hat, 2-Sided, Cast Iron, 8 ½ In.	240
Duck, Whimsical, Walking, Cast Iron, 7 ½ In. *illus*	4130
Ducks, 2, White, Brown, Orange, Cast Iron, F. Everett, Hubley, 8 In.	180
Dutch Girl, Apple, Painted, Blue Bonnet, Red Apron, Green Dress, Cast Iron, 6 ½ In.	59
Dutch Girl, Cast Iron, Littco, 12 ½ In.	84
Dutch Girl, Painted Cast Iron, Hubley, 9 ¾ In.	58
Elephant, Standing, Painted, Cast Iron, c.1900, 10 x 11 ½ In.	900
Flower Basket, Apple Blossom, Cast Iron, Hubley, c.1930, 7 x 5 In.	100
Flower Basket, Cast Iron, Hubley, 1920s, 9 ¼ x 7 ⅝ In.	125
Flower Basket, French, Cast Iron, Hubley, 1930s, 10 x 6 In.	110
Flower Basket, Painted, Cast Iron, 6 ¾ In.	18
Flower Basket, Petunias, Asters, Cast Iron, Hubley, c.1930, 9 x 6 In.	150
Flowers In Urn, Painted Marble Style Base, Cast Iron, Marked B & H, 10 In.	384
Flowers, Modernistic, Stylized Daisies, Cast Iron, 6 ½ In.	266
Flowers, Poinsettia In Pot, Cast Iron, Judd Co., 9 ¾ In.	120
Flowers, Poppies, Cornflowers, Basket, Cast Iron, Hubley, c.1930, 7 x 6 In.	125
Flowers, Urn, Cast Iron, 1920s, 6 In.	50
Flowers, Urn, Multicolor, Stepped Blue Base, Marked Hubley, 7 x 6 In.	52
Flowers, Vase, Black Paint, Cast Iron, 10 ½ x 6 In.	40
Fox, Curled Up, Sleeping, Cast Iron, Wilton, 1 ¾ In.	36
Fox's Head, Cast Brass, England, 16 In., Pair	384
Frontier Soldier, Cast Iron, 12 In.	68
Fruit Basket, Wicker Style, Cast Iron, 11 ½ In. *illus*	885
Giraffe, Standing On Grass, Cast Iron, Wedge Back, 14 ¼ In.	1003
Girls Reading, Sitting Back To Back, Bonnets, Cast Iron, 4 ¾ In.	1652
Gladiolas, Urn, Multicolor Paint, Cast Iron, Hubley, 10 ¼ In.	180
Golf Caddy, Boy Holding Bag Of Clubs, Orange Jacket & Pants, Cast Iron, 8 In.	1652
Golfer, Putting, Red, Brown, Green Paint, Cast Iron, Hubley, 8 ½ In.	210 to 270
Golfer, Swinging Club, Knickers, Red Jacket, Cast Iron, Hubley, 8 ½ In.	360
Harlequin, Pompom Buttons, Looking At Owl On Fence, Grassy Base, Cast Iron, 11 In.	2242
Horse, Chestnut Brown Paint, Cast Iron, Hubley, 8 In.	90
Horse, Prancing, Cast Pewter, England, 11 In.	360
Horse, Standing, Cast Iron, Painted, Hubley, 12 x 10 ½ In.	201

Horse, Thoroughbred, Standing, Brown Paint, Cast Iron, Hubley, 7 ¾ In.		120
Kittens, Twins, Side-Glancing Eyes, Drayton, 7 ½ In.		502
Lighthouse, Cape Cod, Cottages, Highland Light, Painted Cast Iron, c.1900, 8 x 9 In.		708 to 1920
Lighthouse, Cape Hatteras, Window Walk Fence, Cast Iron, c.1920, 21 x 9 In.		2074
Lighthouse, On Sea Rocks, White Brick, Crashing Waves, Cast Iron, 10 In.		472
Lilies Of The Valley, Cream Basket, Blue Bow, Cast Iron, Hubley, 11 In.		207
Little Black Sambo, Holding Green Umbrella, Cast Iron, Blodgett Studios, 8 In.		4130
Mammy, Hands On Hips, White Apron, Red Kerchief, Cast Iron, Hubley, 12 In.		144 to 165
Man & Horse Plowing, Multicolor Paint, Iron, Signed Burns, c.1925, 5 ¾ x 10 ¾ In.		259
Man, Black Pants, White Jacket, Fez, Cast Iron, Full Figure, 10 In.		360
Minuet Girl, Yellow Gown, Cast Iron, Judd Co., 8 ¾ In.		60
Monkey & Organ Grinder, 2-Sided, Cast Iron, 10 In.		180
Monkey, Seated, Painted, Cast Iron, c.1910, 9 In.		450
Monkey, Sitting, Cast Iron, 8 ⅞ In.		150
Nude, Dolphin, Shell Base, Gilt, Bradley & Hubbard, 6 x 4 x 2 In.		395
Old Salt, Fisherman In Yellow Raincoat & Hat, Cast Iron, Eastern Specialty Co., 6 ¾ In.		384
Old Salt, Sailor, Black Face, Yellow Slicker, Knife, Paint, Cast Iron, 14 In.		1652
Oriental Girl, Cast Iron, Painted, Hubley, 8 In.		104
Owl, Brown, Wedge, Cast Iron, 11 In.		330
Parrot On Stump, Multicolor, Cast Iron, Judd Co., 7 ¾ In.		150
Parrot, Multicolor Paint, Albany Foundry, Cast Iron, c.1910, 12 ½ In.		266
Penguin, Full Figure, Cast Iron, Littco Products, 10 ½ In.		720
Pilgrim Boy, Arm Out, Brown & White Suit, Cast Iron, Judd Co., 9 ½ In.		236
Poppies, Urn, Orange, Green, White Paint, Cast Iron, Hubley, 11 In.		120
Punch, Figural, Holding Letter & Pen, Stack Of Books, Cast Iron, c.1885, 12 x 9 In.		923
Quail, 2, Sitting On Branch In Tall Grass, Fred Everett, 7 In.		826
Quail, Cast Iron, Fred Everett, Hubley, 7 ½ In.		243 to 270
Rabbit, Begging, White Cast, Iron, 11 In.		420
Rabbit, On Hind Legs, Cast Iron, Embossed Base, Marked, B&H 7800, 15 In.	*illus*	2950
Rabbit, White Paint, Cast Iron, c.1900, 12 In.		147
Revolutionary War Soldier, Rifle, Little Heiskel, Painted, Cast Iron, Hagerstown, 1789, 9 In.		144
Rooster, Crowing, Cast Iron, 7 In.		84
Sailor, Ship's Wheel, Painted, Cast Iron, 6 ½ In.		384
Soldier, Civil War, Union, Painted, Cast Iron, 7 ½ In.		81
Southern Belle, Holding Hat, Cast Iron, Painted, c.1900, 11 In.		165
Spanish Girl, Painted, Cast Iron, Hubley, 9 In.		104
Squirrel, Eating Nut, Bradley & Hubbard, 11 ½ In.		240
Stained Glass Window, Arched, Painted, Wedge, Cast Iron, 8 ½ In.		36
Sunbonnet Girl, Blue Dress, Orange & White Bonnet, Cast Iron, 9 ¼ In.		120 to 1003
Teddy Roosevelt, On Horseback, Cast Metal, 8 x 10 In.		169
Topsy, Paint, Cast Iron, 6 In.		94
Turkey, Cast Iron, Bradley & Hubbard, 12 ¼ In.		150
Whale, Cast Iron, c.1910, 12 ½ In.		1058
Windmill, Door Partly Open, Painted, Cast Iron, Marked, N152, 8 ¼ In.	*illus*	118
Woman, Art Deco, Holding Gown Out At Sides, Painted Black, Cast Iron, 9 ¼ x 7 ½ In.		155
Woman, Blue Coat, White Fur Muff, Cast Iron, Albany Foundry, 9 ½ In.		472
Woman, Entering House, Yellow, Purple Wisteria, Picket Fence, Eastern Specialty, 6 In.		354
Woman, Senorita With Fruit Basket, Yellow Dress, Teal Scarf, Cast Iron, 11 In.		325
Ye Cheshire Cat, Brass, c.1890, 10 x 8 ¾ In.	*illus*	115

DOULTON pottery and porcelain were made by Doulton and Co. of Burslem, England, after 1882. The name *Royal Doulton* appeared on the company's wares after 1902. Other pottery by Doulton is listed under Royal Doulton.

Biscuit Barrel, Flow Blue, Fruit, Parcel Gilt Ground, Tracery, 1879, 7 ¾ In.		184
Bisquit Jar, Iris, Yellow & Purple, Lobed, Shaped Shoulder, Silver Plated Lid, Burslem		116
Centerpiece, Shell Bowl, Woman, Gold, Pink, Petals By Face, c.1890, 21 ½ x 21 ½ In.		203
Ewer, Cattle, Geese, High Loop Handle, Lambeth, 1882, 14 ½ In.		780
Ewer, Stoneware, Silver Plated Lid, Masked Spout, Loop Handle, Ring Foot, c.1885, 9 In.		177
Pitcher, Mottled Blue, Flower Vine, Impressed Geometric, Bands, Lambeth, 1890s, 8 ½ In.		80
Urn, Lid, Countess Gowe Portrait Reserve, Handles, Signed Sutton, c.1890, 13 In.		2500
Vase, Blue Flowers, Tan Wicker Ground, Tapered, Signed Lambeth, 9 In.		270
Vase, Daffodils, Shouldered, 14 ½ In.		47
Vase, Rouge Flambe, Man, Plowing, Horses, 8 ½ In.		390
Vase, Stoneware, Glazed, Incised Stylized Leaves, Arthur B. Barlow, 1875, 11 ¼ In., Pair		270

Doorstop, Dolly, Girl Holding Doll, Grace Drayton, Marked, Hubley, 10 ½ In.
$1,003

Bertoia Auctions

Doorstop, Duck, Whimsical, Walking, Cast Iron, 7 ½ In.
$4,130

Bertoia Auctions

Doorstop, Fruit Basket, Wicker Style, Cast Iron, 11 ½ In.
$885

Bertoia Auctions

TIP
The less you handle an antique or collectible the better. Always pick it up with two hands.

Doorstop, Rabbit, On Hind Legs, Cast Iron, Embossed Base, Marked, B&H 7800, 15 In.
$2,950

Bertoia Auctions

Doorstop, Windmill, Door Partly Open, Painted, Cast Iron, Marked, N152, 8 ¼ In.
$118

Bertoia Auctions

Doorstop, Ye Cheshire Cat, Brass, c.1890, 10 x 8 ¾ In.
$115

Locati Auctions

DRESDEN china is any china made in the town of Dresden, Germany. The most famous factory in Dresden is the Meissen factory. Figurines of eighteenth-century ladies and gentlemen, animal groups, or cherubs and other mythological subjects were popular. One special type of figurine was made with skirts of porcelain-dipped lace. Do not make the mistake of thinking that all pieces marked *Dresden* are from the Meissen factory. The Meissen pieces usually have crossed swords marks, and are listed under Meissen. Some recent porcelain from Ireland, called *Irish Dresden,* is not included in this book.

Bowl, Birds, Trees, Painted, Oval, Scalloped Rim, Reticulated, Gilt, c.1960, 11 x 9 In.	92
Bowl, Lid, Painted, Landscapes, Swags, Spherical, Knop, Helena Wolfsohn, c.1880, 7 In.	180
Bowl, Oval, Footed, Outswept Acanthus Handles, Flower Garlands, c.1900, 5 ½ x 20 In.	177
Candelabrum, 3 Scrolled Arms, Applied Flowers, Cherubs, Schierholz, 20 ¾ In., Pair	180
Chocolate Pot, Painted Woman, Child Scene Oval, Cobalt Blue, Gilt Trim, c.1880, 8 ½ In.	443
Compote, Figural, Woman Feed Dove, Applied Leaves, Flowers, c.1910, 19 ¾ In.	72
Compote, Round Pedestal Foot, Wavy Rim, Flowers, 4 ½ x 7 ½ In.	120
Cup & Saucer, Flowers, Gilt Trim, c.1869	95
Dish, Basket Shape, Reticulated, Branch Shape Handles, Flowers, 9 In. Diam.	200
Figurine, Woman, Blue Blouse, Print Skirt, c.1865, 5 ½ In.	130
Group, Man Courting Woman, Angel On Shoulder, 7 x 8 In.	480
Jug, Liquor, Royal Vienna Style, Monk, Drinking Wine, Hand Painted, Handle, c.1900, 10 In. *illus*	1476
Mirror, Scrolled Frame, Putto, Shelf, Basket, Bird, Flowers, 33 x 15 In., Pair	1107
Plaque, Plaque, Oval, Portrait, Seated Woman, Holding Lamp, Gilt Frame, c.1900, 7 In.	330
Plate, Reticulated, Courting Scenes At Cavetto, 8 ¾ In., 13 Piece	330
Plate, White, Green, Pink Flowers, Gilt, Scalloped Rim, Center Design, 11 In. Diam., 9 Piece	240
Plate, White, Pink Flowers, Leaves, Scalloped Rim, Gilt, 9 In. Diam., 13 Piece	360
Urn, Bulbous, Long Bottle Neck, Double Branched Filigree Handles, 22 In., Pair	2006
Urn, Portrait Oval, Gold, White Ground, Handles, Lid, 16 In., Pair	537
Vase, Flowers, Hand Painted, Gold Square Handles, 13 In.	226
Vase, Fruit, Green, Rose Paint, Gourd Shape, Waist Handles, 15 In.	34
Vase, Portrait, Maiden, Gilt, Marked, c.1910, 8 ⅜ In. *illus*	531
Vase, Rococo Style, Relief Carved Flowers, Gilt, 13 In., Pair	324

DUNCAN & MILLER is a term used by collectors when referring to glass made by the George A. Duncan and Sons Company or the Duncan and Miller Glass Company. These companies worked from 1893 to 1955, when the use of the name *Duncan* was discontinued and the firm became part of the United States Glass Company. Early patterns may be listed under Pressed Glass.

American Way, Candleholder, c.1945, 4 ½ In., Pair	43
Canterbury, Bowl, Flared, Ruffled, Silver Roses	42
Canterbury, Bowl, Scalloped, 5 x 3 In.	29
Canterbury, Candy Dish, Lid, Chartreuse, 3 Sections	75
Canterbury, Cigarette Box, 4 ¾ x 3 ¾ x 1 ¾ In.	24
Canterbury, Plate, Footed, 7 x 5 ¼ In.	22
Canterbury, Relish, Divided, Scalloped, Triple Tab Handles, 8 In.	14
Chanticleer, Cocktail Shaker, Amber, c.1935, 6 In.	125
Colonial, Salt Dip, Scalloped, 6 Panels, Pedestal Base, 2 In., Pair	10
First Love, Bowl, Flared, 11 In.	68
First Love, Goblet, Water, 1937, 6 ½ In.	34
First Love, Nappy, Crimped, 6 x 1 ¾ In.	22
First Love, Sugar & Creamer, Stackable	75
Georgian, Plate, Honeycomb, 6 In.	25
Hobnail, Bowl, Blue Opalescent, Low Console, 11 ½ In.	85
Indian Tree, Bowl, Crimped, 11 In.	60
Ladder With Diamonds, Bonbon, Upturned Edge, Gilt Trim, c.1915, 5 ¾ x 4 In.	50
Mardi Gras, Compote, 4 ¾ x 6 In.	40
Pharaoh, Bowl, Green, Art Deco, 12 ½ In.	75
Pharaoh, Bowl, Pink, Art Deco, Foot Style Variation, 12 ½ In.	125
Punty Band, Cruet, Stopper, 6 ½ In.	35
Ruby Red, Goblet, Water, c.1950, 5 ⅝ In., 8 Piece	165
Sandwich, Basket, Clear, c.1950, 9 x 14 ½ In.	127
Sanibel, Relish, 3 Sections, Swirl, 13 x 9 In.	23
Sylvan, Bowl, Swan Shape, 9 ¾ x 12 x 7 In.	55
Teardrop, Ashtray, Individual, 3 In.	9
Teardrop, Bonbon, Square, 4 Handles, 6 In.	15
Teardrop, Bowl, 5 ¼ In.	8
Teardrop, Butter, Cover, Tab Handles, Silver Plate, Rogers Bros., 7 ¼ In.	34
Teardrop, Butter, Silver Cover	28

Teardrop, Candlestick, Ball Loop Center, c.1945, 6 ½ x 4 In., Pair		48
Teardrop, Coaster		7
Teardrop, Cup & Saucer		8
Teardrop, Goblet, Water, Footed, 4 ½ In., 9 Oz.		10
Teardrop, Mint Tray, Heart Handle, c.1940, 6 In. Diam.		15
Teardrop, Nut Dish, Divided, c.1940, 6 In. Diam.		12
Teardrop, Plate, Luncheon, 8 ½ In.		8
Teardrop, Plate, Salad, 7 ½ In.		5
Teardrop, Plate, Sherbet, 6 ½ In.		5
Teardrop, Relish, 3 Sections, Tab Handles, 8 In.		18
Teardrop, Sugar & Creamer		14
Teardrop, Tumbler, Iced Tea, Footed, 6 In., 14 Oz.		18
Terrace, Bowl, Dessert, 4 ⅝ In.		20
Terrace, Centerpiece, Cogwheel Foot, c.1945, 11 x 3 In.		50

DURAND art glass was made from 1924 to 1931. The Vineland Flint Glass Works was established by Victor Durand and Victor Durand Jr. in 1897. In 1924 Martin Bach Jr. and other artisans from the Quezal glassworks joined them at the Vineland, New Jersey, plant to make Durand art glass. They called their gold iridescent glass Gold Luster.

Bowl, Amber, Blue, White Pulled Feather, Rose Cut Center, Turned Out Rolled Rim, 16 In.		978
Plate, White Pulled Feather, Pink Outline, Cranberry Ground, 10 In.		152
Shade, White, Green, Leaf Design, Gold Threading, 4 x 4 In., Pair		188
Vase, Blue Iridescent, Genie Bottle Shape, Narrow Neck, Flattened Rim, Signed, 15 In.		575
Vase, Blue Iridescent, Purple Highlights, Base, Flared Neck, Signed, 1920s, 6 x 8 In.		920
Vase, Blue Iridescent, Tapered, Signed, 8 In.		415
Vase, Blue, Gold Threaded Design, Iridescent, Signed, 7 ¾ In.		531
Vase, Blue, Green, Pulled, Swirled, Iridescent, Long Neck, Wide Base, c.1910, 9 ½ In.		649
Vase, Blue, Wide Mouth Rim, Tapered, c.1950, 7 In.		420
Vase, Cranberry, White Opalescent Pulled Feather, Gorham Sterling Foot, 11 x 8 In.		590
Vase, Gold Luster, Amber, Tapered, Flared Mouth, c.1930, 8 In.		406
Vase, Green Coil, Blue, Silver Highlights, Signed, 6 In.		780
Vase, King Tut, Bulbous Bottom, Elongated Neck, Flared Rim, Green, 18 In.		2430
Vase, King Tut, Gold Luster, Pinched Waist, Cylindrical, Signed, 9 ½ In.		1035
Vase, King Tut, Gold Metallic, Shouldered, Tapered, c.1915, 8 In.		720
Vase, King Tut, Iridescent Pulled Design, Orange, Yellow Glass, Shouldered, 4 x 7 In.		425
Vase, King Tut, Pulled Design, Cream, Blue, Gold Luster, Footed, 8 ½ In.		1180
Vase, King Tut, Squat Bottle Shape, Gold Interior, White Cased, Blue, Gold Swirls, 6 ¾ In.		677
Vase, Pinched Waist, Ruffled Rim, Blue Luster, 4 ½ In.		590
Vase, Pulled Feather, Magenta & Blue Highlights, 9 ⅜ In.		472
Vase, Red Crystal Crackle, Flared, 9 ½ In.		480
Vase, Shoulder, Cobalt Blue, White & Blue Pulled Feather, 6 ¾ x 6 ¾ In.		652
Vase, Trumpet Shape, Green Vines, Marigold Ground, Spooled Base, 12 In.		708
Vase, White Pulled Feather, Cut Rose Design, Flared Cranberry Glass Top, Footed, 6 In.		197

ELVIS PRESLEY, the well-known singer, lived from 1935 to 1977. He became famous by 1956. Elvis appeared on television, starred in twenty-seven movies, and performed in Las Vegas. Memorabilia from any of the Presley shows, his records, and even memorials made after his death are collected.

Bracelet, Charm, Records, Gold, Metal Link, Plastic, 1956		171
Figurine, Plastic, Hollow, Copper Colored, Playing Guitar, 1956, 7 ⅝ In.		896
Lighter, From Elvis & The Colonel, Gilt Metal, 1969, 1 ½ x 2 In.		687
Poster, Red Shirt, June Kelly Painting, 1957, 20 x 16 In.		25
Record, Double Dynamite, 2 Record Set, Camden RCA, 33 ⅓, 1975		10
Record, Elvis, White Jumpsuit, Legendary Concert Performances, LP, 2 Record Set, 1978		30

ENAMELS listed here are made of glass particles and other materials heated and fused to metal. In the eighteenth and nineteenth centuries, workmen from Russia, France, England, and other countries made small boxes and table pieces of enamel on metal. One form of English enamel is called *Battersea* and is listed under that name. There was a revival of interest in enameling in the 1930s and a new style evolved. There is now renewed interest in the artistic enameled plaques, vases, ashtrays, and jewelry. Enamels made since the 1930s are usually on copper or steel, although silver was often used for jewelry. Graniteware is a separate category, and enameled metal kitchen pieces may be included in the Kitchen category. Cloisonne is special type of enamel and is listed in its own category.

Basin, Octagonal, Figural Scenes, 8 Symbols, 10 x 7 In.		649
Bowl, Flared Rim, Straight Foot, 8 Immortals, Pines, Clouds, 1800s, 6 In. Diam.		2520

Dresden, Jug, Liquor, Royal Vienna Style, Monk, Drinking Wine, Hand Painted, Handle, c.1900, 10 In.
$1,476

New Orleans Auction Galleries, Inc.

Dresden, Vase, Portrait, Maiden, Gilt, Marked, c.1910, 8 ⅜ In.
$531

Brunk Auctions

Enamel, Bowl, Hammered, Marcello Pantoni, 12 In.
$120

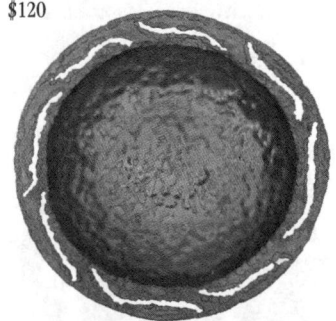

Palm Beach Modern Auctions

Enamel, Bowl, On Stand, Silver Ground, Raised Figures, Chinese, Bowl 5 x 5 In. $430

New Orleans Auction Galleries, Inc.

Enamel, Charger, Orange Picker, Copper, Signed, Thelma Winter, 11 ½ In. $153

Rachel Davis Fine Arts

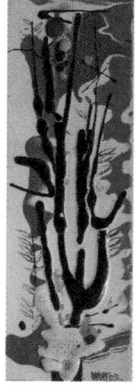

Enamel, Plaque, Black Tree, Copper, Signed, Edward Winter, 12 x 4 In. $153

Rachel Davis Fine Arts

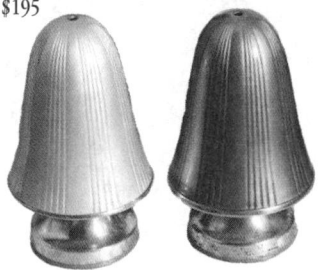

Enamel, Salt & Pepper, Mushroom, Sterling, Guilloche, David Anderson, 1960s, 2 ½ In. $195

Ruby Lane, Inc.

Bowl, Hammered, Marcello Pantoni, 12 In.	*illus*	120
Bowl, On Stand, Silver Ground, Raised Figures, Chinese, Bowl 5 x 5 In.	*illus*	430
Box, Egyptian Style, Sphinx Finial, Mother-Of-Pearl, Silver Hallmarks, 1800s, 1 ½ In.		470
Box, Flowers, Turquoise, Bronze Frame, France, c.1880, 3 x 6 In.		375
Case, Open Scroll Design, Multicolor, Gilt, Silver, Hinged Lid, Russia, 1900s, 3 x 2 ¾ In.		413
Case, Ribbed, Gold, Black, Cartier, 1930s, 3 ⅜ x 2 ¼ In.		4248
Censer, Lid, Rectangular, Lotus Flowers, Pierced Symbols, Foo Dog Finial, 1900s, 12 In.		3600
Charger, Orange Picker, Copper, Signed, Thelma Winter, 11 ½ In.	*illus*	153
Cigarette Case, Guilloche, Cobalt Blue, Gilt Wash, Art Deco Decoration, Lapis Catch, 3 In.		296
Cigarette Case, Scrolls, Flowers, Turquoise Bead Border, Silver Gilt, Moscow, c.1910, 4 In.		1875
Coin Purse, Silver, Rectangular, Scrolling, Flowers, Gilt, Russia, c.1900, 3 ¾ x 2 ¼ In.		944
Figure, Peacock, Standing, Flaring Tail, Japan, c.1900, 10 x 13 ½ In.		1003
Goblet, Plique-A-Jour Irises, Silver Overlay, Swollen Stem, Multicolor, 7 x 4 In.		4095
Jar, Blue, Figures, Rocks, Banana Trees, Rings At Shoulder, Openwork Lid, 1700s, 7 In.		4500
Jardiniere, Cranes, Pines, Stalks Cloisonne, Round, Squat, Bronze Bands, c.1910, 14 In.		563
Jewelry Box, Domed Cupola, Cupid Finial, Columns, Bracket Feet, Doors, 10 ½ In.		3750
Jewelry Box, Gilt, Oval, Medallions, Courting Scenes, 1 ½ x 3 In.		590
Pill Box, Round, Silver Gilt, Flowers, Scrolls, Beaded Border, Lid, 1 ¾ In.		355
Plaque, Art Nouveau, 2 Women In Gowns Standing On Shore, Frame, 9 ¼ x 13 ¼ In.		5036
Plaque, Black Tree, Copper, Signed, Edward Winter, 12 x 4 In.	*illus*	153
Salt & Pepper, Mushroom, Sterling, Guilloche, David Anderson, 1960s, 2 ½ In.	*illus*	195
Spoon, Silver Gilt, Multicolor Flowers, Geometrics, Fan Shape Handle, Moscow, c.1915, 7 In.		938
Sugar Service, Silver, Champleve, Pavel Ovchinnikov, Russia, 3 ⅛ & 5 ¾ In.		1000
Tea Strainer, Champleve, Silver, Stippled Gilt Ground, Moscow, c.1900, 6 In.		1375
Teapot, Dome Lid, Flowers, Leaves, Gold Accents, Knop, 3 ⅜ In.		4800
Teapot, On Copper, Flower Reserves, Tall Loop Handle, 7 x 5 x 3 ½ In.		799
Tray, Champleve, Brass, Leaf Handles, Continental, c.1890, 21 x 11 ¾ In.	*illus*	1076
Trinket Box, Gilt Silver, Round, Phoenix, Flowers, Beaded, Lid, 1892, 2 ¼ x 3 In.		1298
Trinket Box, Round, Birds, Flowers, Vines, Ovchinnikov, 1884, 1 x 3 In.		4720
Vase, Waisted Neck, Flanged Mouth, Animal Heads, 4-Sided, 1900s, 24 In.		1560
Wedding Cup, Woman, Brass Body, Scenes, 6 In.	*illus*	5640
Whistle, Guilloche, Silver Gilt, Green Enamel, F. Afanassiev, Russia, c.1915, 2 ½ In.		875

ERICKSON glass was made in Bremen, Ohio, from 1943 to 1961. Carl and Steven Erickson designed and made free-blown and mold-blown glass. Best known are pieces with heavy ball bases filled with controlled bubbles.

Decanter, Stopper, Clear, Amethyst Flame, c.1955, 13 In.	316
Decanter, Stopper, Clear, Green Flame, c.1955, 11 In.	158
Decanter, Stopper, Clear, Smoke Flame, c.1950, 10 ½ In.	136
Vase, Clear, Amethyst Flame, Cylinder, c.1950, 11 In.	120
Vase, Clear, Green Flame, Applied Accents, Rounded Cylinder, c.1955, 7 In.	147
Vase, Clear, Green Flame, Square Base, c.1955, 15 ½ In.	124

ES GERMANY porcelain was made at the factory of Erdmann Schlegelmilch from 1861 to 1937 in Suhl, Germany. The porcelain, marked *ES Germany* or *ES Suhl*, was sold decorated or undecorated. Other pieces were made at a factory in Saxony, Prussia, and are marked *ES Prussia.* Reinhold Schlegelmilch made the famous wares marked *RS Germany.*

Creamer, Three Graces, Transfer, Gilt Trim, 2 ¾ In.	29
Gravy Boat, Underplate, Pink Flowers, Leaves, c.1902	45
Nappy, Primroses, Twining Leaves, Gold Rim & Handle, c.1900, 6 In.	28
Sugar, European Bullfinch, On Branch, Handles, Lid, c.1900, 5 x 3 In.	15

ESKIMO artifacts of all types are collected. Carvings of whale or walrus teeth are listed under Scrimshaw. Baskets are in the Basket category. All other types of Eskimo art are listed here. In Canada and some other areas, the term *Inuit* is used instead of Eskimo.

Basket, Storage, Lid, Fine Weave, Painted Design, c.1910, 12 ½ x 12 In.	*illus*	184
Bust, Family, Caribou Fur, Fringes, Chalkware, c.1925, 13 x 11 In.		165
Carving, Stone, Men Fighting Bear, Inuit, 6 In.		283
Doll, Plastic, Sleep Eyes, Faux Leather Jacket, 1960s, 7 ½ In.		25
Doll, Suede, Cloth, Fur Parka, c. 1950, 15 In.		295
Figurine, Bird, Feeding Babies, Inuit, Caribou Horn, c.1970, 6 In.		140
Figurine, Hunter, Bag, Inuit, Soapstone, 1950s, 10 In.		950
Figurine, Water Buffalo, Child, Soapstone, Signed, 7 x 6 In.		1200
Mask, Bone, Carved, Stand, c.1960, 6 ¾ In.		480

Mask, Chalkware, 1968, 6 ½ In.	40
Mask, Face, White, Black Face, Hoop Suspending Hands, Legs, Feather, c.1935, 10 In.	1298
Mask, Wood, Carved, Painted, Stylized Face, Bird Head Chin, Pegs, c.1890, 6 ¾ In.	14400
Mask, Wood, Carved, Smiling, Point Hope, c.1875, 10 x 6 ¼ In. ....*illus*	1800
Moccasins, Muskrat, Coyote Trim, Inuit, Size 10	89
Pipe, Opium, Inuit, Kayak Ivory, Whale Hunters In Canoe, c.1905, 11 ½ In.	1875
Postcard, Little Eskimo Beauty, Girl, Igloo, 1908	12
Scraper, Bone, Arched Handle, Standing Bear Figure, Inuit, 1900s, 3 ¼ x 7 ¾ In.	649
Vest, Felted Wool, Braided Trim, Rosettes, Loop Closure, Horn Buttons, 45 x 27 In.	49

FABERGE was a firm of jewelers and goldsmiths founded in St. Petersburg, Russia, in 1842, by Gustav Faberge. Peter Carl Faberge, his son, was jeweler to the Russian Imperial Court from about 1870 to 1917. The rare Imperial Easter eggs, jewelry, and decorative items are very expensive today. ФАБЕРЖЕ КФ

Box, Bird, Flowers, Etched Crystal, Gilt Metal Frame, Hinged Lid, For Neiman Marcus, 7 In.	660
Cane Handle, Chased Leaves, Scrolls, Tau Shape, c.1890, 4 ⅞ In.	4012
Charm, Egg, 18K Gold, Green Enamel, 6 Diamonds, Hinged Bail, 1 ¼ In.	480
Figurine, Silver, Winged Lion Body, Woman's Head, Hairpiece, Green Jade Platform, 4 ¼ In.	1126
Frame, Jade, Rose Cut Diamonds, Gold, Mikhail Perchim, 3 ⅞ x 2 ¼ In. ....*illus*	6490
Goblet, Odessa, Multicolor, 8 ¾ In., 12 Piece	717
Napkin Ring, Gilded Silver, Pan-Slavic Enamel, Feodor Ruckert, Box, c.1910, 1 ⅜ In., Pair	13000
Plate, Dessert, Neiman Marcus, 7 ¾ In., 12 Piece	538
Trinket Box, Jade, Gold, Silver, Ruby, Round, Bow & Swag Design, 1 x 1 ½ In.	2832

FAIENCE refers to tin-glazed earthenware, especially the wares made in France, Germany, and Scandinavia. It is also correct to say that faience is the same as majolica or Delft, although usually the term refers only to the tin-glazed pottery of the three regions mentioned.

Charger, Battle Scene, Armored Soldiers, Horses, Multicolor, Continental, 11 ¼ In.	1063
Charger, Landscape Center, Flower, Geometric Wide Band, Swiss, c.1865, 16 In.	69
Charger, Leaping Yellow Stag, Blue, Red Flowers, Designs, c.1800, 13 ¾ In., Pair	1250
Ewer, Barrel Shape, Figures, Animals, Leaves, Iron Strapwork, Tripod Base, 23 In.	2500
Ewer, Bulbous, Trumpet Neck, Loop Handle, Hinged Lid, Blue, White, Figure, c.1690, 9 In.	215
Flask, Moon, France, Fleur-De-Lis, Blue, Gray, Yellow, Vive LeRoy, France, 1757, 8 ½ In.	213
Jardiniere, Nautilus Shell, Rocky Base, Burmantofts, c.1900, 20 x 19 ½ In. ....*illus*	1135
Platter, Applied Fish, Mussels, Scallops, Hippolyte Boulenger, France, c.1900, 11 ¾ In.	360
Platter, Fish Shape, Armorial Medallion, Le Roi, 21 ¾ In.	344
Stein, 2 Soldiers, Rifles, Pewter Lid, Germany, 1700s, 10 ½ In.	593
Tankard, Pewter Lid, Blue, Yellow, Green Farmer, Strap Handle, c.1800, 10 ¾ In.	173
Tureen, Lid, Bowl, Handles, Flowers, Scrolling Feet, Marked, 13 ¼ In.	375
Vase, Earthenware, Glazed, Berkeley, Signed California Faience, 10 ½ x 7 ½ In.	1625

FAIRINGS are small souvenir boxes and figurines that were sold at country fairs during the nineteenth century. Most were made in Germany. Reproductions of fairings are being made, especially of the famous *Twelve Months after Marriage* series.

Box, Basin, On Table, Curtain, Conta Boehme Co., c.1880, 3 ¼ x 2 In.	68
Box, Boy, Rocking Horse, Conta Boehme, c.1890, 4 ½ In.	72
Box, Cherries, Leaves, Curved Handle, Gilt, 4 x 2 ¼ x 2 ½ In.	65
Box, Child, On Dresser, Staffordshire, 19th Century, c.1860, 4 In.	55
Box, Clock, On Dresser, Staffordshire, c.1850, 3 x 2 ½ In.	119
Box, Cradle, Baby, Quilt, 5 x 3 x 3 In.	350
Figurine, Bear, Drinking Out Of Barrel, Germany, c.1900, 5 x 3 In.	89
Figurine, Boy, Playing Lute, Tricornered Hat, 2 ½ x 1 ⅞ x 1 ¼ In.	45
Figurine, Couple, Canopy Bed, Candle On Table, 19th Century, 3 ¼ x 3 ½ In.	143
Figurine, Dog, Biting Boy, Germany, c.1925, 3 ½ x 2 ½ In.	69
Figurine, Last In Bed To Put Out The Light, c.1875, 4 x 3 In.	150
Figurine, Man, Woman, Playing Lute, Germany, 6 x 5 In.	68
Figurine, Puppy, In Basket, Googly Eyes, Ear Sticking Up, c.1900, 3 ½ x 2 In.	54
Figurine, Sailor, Hands In Pocket, Germany, 19th Century, 4 In.	44
Toothpick Holder, Pink Pigs, Top Hat, c.1880, 2 x 3 In.	49
Trinket Box, Dog, On Sofa, Staffordshire, 2 ¼ x 1 x 2 In., Pair	95
Vase, Spill, Tree Trunk, Momma Bear, Baby Bear, Germany, c.1880, 4 ¼ x 4 ¾ In.	95

FAIRYLAND LUSTER *pieces are included in the Wedgwood category.*

FAMILLE ROSE, *see Chinese Export category.*

Enamel, Tray, Champleve, Brass, Leaf Handles, Continental, c.1890, 21 x 11 ¾ In.
$1,076

Neal Auction Co.

Enamel, Wedding Cup, Woman, Brass Body, Scenes, 6 In.
$5,640

The Stein Auction Co.

F

TIP

Always walk to your hotel room or across a parking lot to your car holding your key in your fist like a weapon. Have the head of the key inside your curled hand, the key blade protruding from between your two top fingers. If grabbed by an assailant, hit him in the face with the blade and your fist, yell "help," and run to find other people.

Eskimo, Basket, Storage, Lid, Fine Weave, Painted Design, c.1910, 12 ½ x 12 In.
$184

Allard Auctions

Eskimo, Mask, Wood, Carved, Smiling, Point Hope, c.1875, 10 x 6 ¼ In.
$1,800

Cowan's Auctions

Faberge, Frame, Jade, Rose Cut Diamonds, Gold, Mikhail Perchim, 3 ⅞ x 2 ¼ In.
$6,490

Brunk Auctions

FANS have been used for cooling since the days of the ancients. By the eighteenth century, the fan was an accessory for the lady of fashion and very elaborate and expensive fans were made. Sticks were made of ivory or wood, set with jewels or carved. The fans were made of painted silk or paper. Inexpensive paper fans printed with advertising were giveaways in the late nineteenth and early twentieth centuries. Electric fans were introduced in 1882.

Advertising, Moxie, Smiling Children, Clown Attire, Hand Held, 1890s, 11 ½ In.	660
Advertising, Neurene, Woman, Large Hat, Drinking Glass, Hand Held, 1915, 14 ¾ In.	48
Bone, Chiffon, Lace, Painted Flowers, Vines, Blue Birds, Blossoms, c.1865, 14 In.	130
Classical Scene, Painted, 9 x 15 In.	58
Electric, Diehl Manufacturing, Oscillating, 4 Blades, Wire Cage, Pat. Aug. 13, 1895, 20 In.	180
Electric, General Electric, Model No. 272917-1, 16 ½ In.	59
Electric, General Electric, Whiz, c.1920	92
Electric, Robbins & Meyers, Oscillating, Tabletop, Cast Iron, 3-Speed, Blue, 18 In.	84
Electric, Westinghouse, Brass, 6 Blades, Oscillating, 1920s *illus*	300
Ivory, Brise, Woman's, Holding Doves, Oval Cartouche, c.1800, 10 In.	768
Ivory, Embroidered, Carved Handles, Reticulated, Lacquer Box, Canton, c.1910, 12 ¼ In.	1560
Ivory, Genre Reserves, Box, c.1900, 19 x 10 ½ In.	344
Ivory, Silver, Paper, Figures, Landscape, Hand Painted, Gilt, Box, France, c.1700s, 11 In.	422
Mother-Of-Pearl, Lace, Continental, Signed, Frame, 22 x 15 In.	312
Mother-Of-Pearl, Leaf Hand Rococo Scene, J. Donzellot, Shadowbox, France, 29 x 17 In.	480
Painted Figures, Court Scenes, Mother-Of-Pearl Faces, Fan-Shape Frame, 1800s, 14 x 22 In.	590
Paper, Wood, Flowers, Red, Blue, Cream, Japan, 14 x 8 ½ In.	18
Pierced Ivory Blades, Couples Panels, Arched Painted Frame, c.1880, 16 x 25 In.	1188
Propeller, 5 Blades, Brass, c.1905, 21 In.	130
Silk & Ivory, Figures In Palace Scene, Lacquered Stays, Box, Chinese, 1800s, 11 In. *illus*	740
Silk, Inset Medallion Scene, Faux Tortoise, 16 Blades, Filigree Fretwork, Gilt, c.1850, 7 In. *illus*	224
Tortoiseshell, Painted Grand Tour Scene, Acrylic, c.1860, 11 In.	1625
Wood Frame, Hand Painted, Ink & Watercolor Landscape, Chinese, 20th Century, 19 ½ In.	331

FAST FOOD COLLECTIBLES *may be included in several categories, such as Advertising, Coca-Cola, Toy, etc.*

FEDERZEICHNUNG, *see Loetz category.*

FENTON ART GLASS COMPANY was founded in 1905 in Martins Ferry, Ohio, by Frank L. Fenton and his brother, John W. Fenton. They painted decorations on glass blanks made by other manufacturers. In 1907 they opened a factory in Williamstown, West Virginia, and began making glass. The company stopped making art glass in 2011 and assets were sold. A new division of the company makes handcrafted glass beads and other jewelry. Copies are being made from leased original Fenton molds by an unrelated company, Fenton's Collectibles. The copies are marked with the Fenton mark and Fenton's Collectibles mark. Fenton is noted for early carnival glass produced between 1907 and 1920. Some of these pieces are listed in the Carnival Glass category. Many other types of glass were also made. Spanish Lace in this section refers to the pattern made by Fenton.

Aqua Crest, Compote, Flared, 4 ½ In.	16
Aqua Crest, Top Hat, Crimped, 5 In.	34
Aqua Crest, Vase, Fan, 8 ½ In.	42
Aqua Crest, Vase, Triangular, Crimped, 5 In.	80
Basket Weave, Basket, Green, Open Edge, 7 In.	40
Basket Weave, Box, Rooster Lid, Black, 4 ¾ In.	57
Blue Moon & Stars, Basket, Split Handle, Scalloped, Paper Label, 5 x 4 In.	34
Burmese, Ewer	142
Butterfly & Berry, Pitcher, 7 In.	537
Cameo Opalescent, Candleholder, Pair	45
Cameo, Bowl, Gold Ruby, Over French Opalescent, Reynolds, Delaney, 1994, 15 In.	104
Coin Dot, Basket, Pink To Cranberry Opalescent, Crimped Edge, Clear Handle, 10 x 10 In.	58
Coin Dot, Candy Dish, Lid, Blue Opalescent, Bulbous, 6 In.	58
Coin Dot, Cruet, Cobalt Blue, Reeded Handle, 7 In.	95
Coin Dot, Lampshade, Cranberry, 6 ½ x 7 In.	89
Coin Dot, Pitcher, Blue Opalescent, Swollen, Clear Crimped Handle, 5 In.	29
Coin Dot, Tumbler, Honeysuckle, 5 ¾ In.	132
Cookie Jar, Big Cookies, Macaroon, Ebony, Handle, c.1933, 7 In.	125
Daisy & Button, Boot, Amberina, 1970s	22
Daisy & Button, Top Hat, White, Milk Glass, 3 ¼ x 4 ¾ In.	18
Daisy & Fern, Pitcher, Cranberry Opal, Round, Ruffled Ice Lip, Clear Ribbed Handle, 9 In.	128
Diamond Optic, Ivy Ball, Green Opalescent, Stand, 4 ¾ In.	46
Diamond Optic, Vase, Green Opalescent, 1930s, 7 x 5 ¾ In.	688

Dolphin, Bonbon, Pink, Swirl Handles, 6 ½ In.	31
Dolphin, Bowl, Aqua Blue, Rolled Edge, 8 In.	35
Dolphin, Bowl, Floral Intaglio, Crimped, 9 In.	19
Dolphin, Candy Jar, Lid, Amethyst	35
Dot Optic, Syrup, Blue Opalescent, Neck Ring, Blue Ribbed Handle, Metal Lid, 7 In.	151
Dot Optic, Vase, Topaz Opalescent, Squat Base, Narrow Neck, Ruffled Rim, 7 ⅜ In.	35
Dusty Rose, Candleholder, 4 ¼ In.	15
Elizabeth, Jug, Jade Green, 48 Oz., 6 ⅜ In.	125
Elizabeth, Plate, Black, 8 In.	26
Elizabeth, Saucer, Black	9
Elizabeth, Sherbet, Ruby Red, 5 Oz., 3 ¼ In.	20
Elizabeth, Tumbler, Footed, Ruby Red, 9 Oz., 5 ⅜ In.	24
Emerald Crest, Plate, 10 ⅜ In.	80
Figurine, Donkey, White	62
Figurine, Elephant, Ruby, 3 ½ In.	350
Figurine, Fawn, Pink Blossoms, 3 ⅝ In.	46
Figurine, Rooster, White, Multicolor Feathers, 5 ⅜ In.	76
Florentine, Vase, Fan, 5 In.	54
Flowerform, Ashtray, Black, 3-Legged	18
Flowerform, Bowl, Jade Green, Closed Flowers, 6 In.	60
Flowerform, Candleholder, Jade Green, 3-Legged, Pair	60
Flowerform, Candleholder, Ruby, 3-Legged, Pair	45
Flute, Vase, Amethyst, 10 In.	20
Georgian, Bell, Black, 4 In.	34
Georgian, Cocktail Shaker, Aristocrat, Red, Chrome Top	55
Georgian, Creamer, Ruby, 3 ⅜ In.	23
Georgian, Cup & Saucer, Ruby	21
Georgian, Finger Bowl, Cobalt Blue, 4 In.	21
Georgian, Sugar, Ruby, 3 ¼ In.	19
Grape & Cable, Bowl, Amethyst, Scroll Feet, 11 x 5 In.	125
Hanging Hearts, Cruet, Custard Glass, 1976, 7 ¼ In.	81
Hanging Hearts, Vase, Blue Custard, Straight Sided, 7 ¼ In.	104
Hobnail, Basket, Blue Marble, 6 In.	42
Hobnail, Basket, Ruffled Rim, Blue Opalescent, 8 In.	48
Hobnail, Basket, Ruffled, Twisted Handle, Blue, Green, 6 In.	32
Hobnail, Candleholder, Milk Glass, Ruffled, Pedestal, 2 ¾ In.	40
Hobnail, Creamer, Blue Opalescent, 1 ⅞ In.	15
Hobnail, Cruet, Opal, Topaz	66
Hobnail, Cruet, Opalescent, Blue Handle, 4 ¾ In.	12
Hobnail, Jug, Milk Glass, 8 In.	68
Hobnail, Jug, Ruffled Rim, Blue Opalescent, 80 Oz., 7 ¼ In.	258
Hobnail, Slipper, Amber, 6 In.	9
Hobnail, Toothpick Holder, Amber, Footed, 2 ⅞ In.	23
Hobnail, Vase, Honey Amber, White Cased Inside, Footed, Ruffled Rim, 8 In.	46
Hobnail, Water Set, Pitcher, 8 Tumblers, Cranberry Opalescent, Crimped, c.1965	196
Jade Green, Bowl, Flower Form, Closed Flower, 6 In.	60
Jade Green, Candy Jar, Lid, ½ Lb., 9 ½ In.	74
Jade Green, Ice Bucket, 2 Knob Handles	75
Lacy Edge, Compote, Milk Glass, 7 In.	23
Milk Glass, Plate, Bicentennial, Figures, Congress, 8 ¼ In.	42
Moonstone, Creamer, Footed, Lilac	25
Mother & Child, Bell, Red	15
Optic Swirl, Vase, Cranberry Opalescent, Narrow Neck, Pulled Crimped Rim, 6 ½ In.	46
Orange Tree, Bowl, Marigold, Scalloped Rim, 3 Ball Feet, No. 921, c.1917, 5 ½ x 10 ¼ In.	67
Panther, Bowl, Amethyst, Sawtooth, Scalloped Edge, Claw & Ball Feet, 9 ½ In.	400
Peach Crest, Basket, Clear Handle, 7 In.	41
Peach Crest, Bowl, Crimped, 6 In.	34
Peach Crest, Vase, Bulbous, Ribbed, Crimped, 5 In.	27
Peach Crest, Vase, Cylindrical, Ruffled Rim, 6 In.	40
Peking Blue, Bowl, Float, Stand, Cupped, 8 ½ In.	45
Persian Medallion, Bowl, Blue, Crimped, 6 In.	47
Pink Blossoms, Globe, Fairy Lamp	18
Plymouth, Tumbler, Red, 8 Oz., 5 In.	25
Polka Dot, Muffineer, Red Opalescent, Squat, Metal Lid, 4 ¾ In.	70
Polka Dot, Pitcher, Cranberry Opalescent, 7 In.	159
Poppy, Vase, Custard Satin, Ruffled Rim, 5 ½ In.	28
Priscilla, Creamer, Green, 2 ⅞ In.	23

Faience, Jardiniere, Nautilus Shell, Rocky Base, Burmantofts, c.1900, 20 x 19 ½ In.
$1,135

Neal Auction Co.

Fan, Electric, Westinghouse, Brass, 6 Blades, Oscillating, 1920s
$300

Victorian Casino Antiques

Fan, Silk & Ivory, Figures In Palace Scene, Lacquered Stays, Box, Chinese, 1800s, 11 In.
$740

James D. Julia Auctioneers

Fan, Silk, Inset Medallion Scene, Faux Tortoise, 16 Blades, Filigree Fretwork, Gilt, c.1850, 7 In.
$224

Theriault's

Fenton, Silver Crest, Dish, Mayonnaise, Underplate, Milk Glass, 3 x 4 ½ & 6 ¼ In. $60

Ruby Lane, Inc.

Fenton, Silver Crest, Vase, Blue Roses, Buds, Green Leaves, Ruffled Rim, Signed, 5 x 4 ¼ In. $32

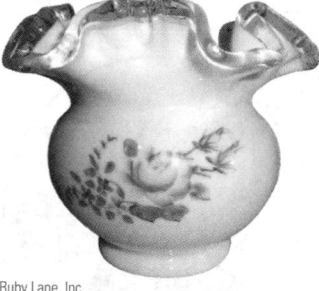

Ruby Lane, Inc.

Fiesta, Turquoise, Compote, 1936-46, 5 ½ In. $65

Ruby Lane, Inc.

Fiesta, Yellow, Pitcher, Disk, 30 Oz., 5 ¾ In. $32

Ruby Lane, Inc.

Priscilla, Sugar, Green, 2 In.	22
Red Iridescent, Bowl, Gold Highlights, Rounded Rim, 1 ¾ x 10 ½ In.	90
Rib Optic, Sugar & Creamer, Cranberry Opalescent, 1953, 4 ¼-In. Creamer	58
Rosalene, Compote, Cover, Pink, Water Lilies, 1970s, 7 ½ In.	45
Rose Bowl, Spiral Optic, Blue Ridge Opalescent, Disc Shape, Wide, Flattened, 3 ½ x 7 In.	46
Rose Crest, Epergne	98
Rose Crest, Vase, Double Crimped, 4 ½ In.	21
Rose Overlay, Bowl, Ruffled, 7 In.	22
Rose Overlay, Jug, Handle, Ribbed, 5 In.	30
Rose, Compote, Colonial Pink, 7 ⅝ In.	21
Silver Crest, Ashtray, 7 In. Diam.	24
Silver Crest, Cake Stand, Scalloped Edge, 13 In.	97
Silver Crest, Compote, Ruffled, 8 In.	40
Silver Crest, Dish, Mayonnaise, Underplate, Milk Glass, 3 x 4 ½ & 6 ¼ In. *illus*	60
Silver Crest, Dish, Mayonnaise, Underplate, White, Crimped Rim, 3 x 4 ½ In.	60
Silver Crest, Jug, 70 Oz., 8 ¼ In.	400
Silver Crest, Vase, Blue Roses, Buds, Green Leaves, Ruffled Rim, Signed, 5 x 4 ¼ In. *illus*	32
Silver Rose, Basket, Clear Handle, 7 ⅛ In.	63
Silver Turquoise, Bowl, Square, Footed, 9 x 8 ¼ In.	100
Silver Turquoise, Relish, Heart Shape, Crystal Loop Handle, 7 In.	45
Snow Crest, Bowl, Ruby, Crimped, 10 In.	98
Spiral Optic, Vase, Caramel Opalescent, Bulbous, Pinched Neck, Ruffled Rim, 6 ¾ In.	35
Stag & Holly, Bowl, Blue, Scalloped Rim, 3 Ball Feet, c.1917, 4 ½ x 10 ½ In.	127
Stretch Glass, Candy Jar, Lid, Florentine Green, ½ Lb.	48
Stretch Glass, Jug, Nightstand, Green, 7 In.	95
Swirled Feather, Fairy Light, Rose Satin, Opalescent Swirls, Ruffled Dish Base, 5 ½ In.	174
Swirled Feather, Pitcher, Cranberry Opalescent, Clear Handle, Ruffled Ice Lip, 8 ⅜ In.	104
Vasa Murrhina, Vase, Blue, Green & White Spatter, 12 Ribs, Ruffled Rim, 11 In.	35
Vasa Murrhina, Vase, Rose Mist, Melon Ribbed, Straight Neck, Ruffled Rim, 7 ¾ In.	46
Vase, Bud, Pink, Swung, 13 ½ In.	49
Vase, Green Transparent, Etched, Cut, 12 In.	85
Vase, Pink Transparent, Etched, Cut, 12 In.	65
Vase, Ruby Red Transparent, Etched, Cut, 12 In.	95
Water Lily, Bowl, Marigold, 9 ½ In.	76
Wisteria, Candlestick, 6-Sided Base, 8 ¾ In., Pair	1199
Zig-Zag, Water Set, Blue, Flowers, c.1925, 10 In., 3 ⅞ In., 7 Piece	575

FIESTA, the colorful dinnerware, was introduced in 1936 by the Homer Laughlin China Co., redesigned in 1969, and withdrawn in 1973. It was reissued again in 1986 in different colors and is still being made. New colors, including some that are similar to old colors, are introduced regularly. The simple design was characterized by a band of concentric circles beginning at the rim. Cups had full-circle handles until 1969, when partial-circle handles were made. Harlequin and Riviera were related wares. For more prices, go to kovels.com.

Apricot, Gravy Boat	35
Apricot, Plate, Dinner, 10 ½ In.	15
Black, Bowl, Cereal	5
Black, Creamer, Disk, 3 ¼ In.	25
Black, Plate, 8 ¼ In.	37
Chartreuse, Cup & Saucer	26
Chartreuse, Eggcup	128
Chartreuse, Pitcher, Disk	325
Chartreuse, Pitcher, Disk, Water, 6 ¼ In.	178
Chartreuse, Plate, Salad, 7 ½ In.	17
Cobalt Blue, Bowl, Cereal, 6 ⅞ In.	5
Cobalt Blue, Bowl, Cereal, 7 ¼ In.	32
Cobalt Blue, Chop Plate, 14 In.	82
Cobalt Blue, Creamer, Ring Handle, 6 Oz., 3 In.	32
Cobalt Blue, Mixing Bowl, No. 5, 8 ¾ In.	148
Cobalt Blue, Mixing Bowl, No. 6, 9 ⅞ In.	292
Cobalt Blue, Pitcher, Lid, 10 In.	250
Cobalt Blue, Pitcher, Lip, 6 ¼ In.	110
Cobalt Blue, Plate, Dinner, 10 ½ In.	41 to 45
Cobalt Blue, Plate, Salad, 7 ¼ In.	5
Cobalt Blue, Platter, Oval, 12 In.	48
Cobalt Blue, Salt & Pepper	9
Cobalt Blue, Syrup	395

Forest Green, Bowl, Fruit, 5 ½ In.	35
Forest Green, Cup & Saucer	32
Forest Green, Eggcup, 3 In.	132
Forest Green, Grill Plate, 10 ½ In.	73
Forest Green, Plate, Bread & Butter, 6 ½ In.	14
Forest Green, Plate, Dinner, 10 ⅜ In.	62
Gray, Bowl, Fruit, 5 ¼ In.	21
Gray, Cup & Saucer	21
Gray, Pitcher, Water, Disk, 7 ½ In.	395
Gray, Pitcher, Water, Disk, 2 Qt., 4 ¼ In.	218
Gray, Plate, Salad, 7 ⅜ In.	14
Gray, Salt & Pepper, Ball Shape	38
Gray, Teapot, Lid, 6 ⅜ In.	245
Green, Casserole, Lid, 8 ½ In.	49
Green, Mixing Bowl, No. 2	80
Green, Platter, 12 In.	45
Ivory, Chop Plate, 15 In.	60
Ivory, Pitcher, Disk, 7 ¹/₂ In.	165
Light Green, Mixing Bowl, No. 2	100
Light Green, Mixing Bowl, No. 4	120
Light Green, Nappy, c.1940, 8 ½ In.	49
Red, Bowl, 9 ½ In.	50
Red, Bowl, Fruit, 5 ½ In.	40
Red, Chop Plate, 13 In.	85
Red, Coffeepot, Lid, 8 ½ In.	171
Red, Mixing Bowl, No. 5	285
Red, Pitcher, Lip, 6 ⅜ In.	165
Red, Pitcher, Water, Disk, 7 ½ In.	225
Red, Plate, Bread & Butter, 6 ⅜ In.	13
Red, Salt & Pepper, Ball Shape	37
Red, Tumbler, 3 ½ In.	65
Rose, Casserole, Lid, 1950s	295
Rose, Creamer, 6 Oz., 3 In.	30
Rose, Cup & Saucer	21
Rose, Eggcup	33
Rose, Eggcup, 3 In.	132
Rose, Pitcher, Disk, 2 Qt.	95
Rose, Plate, Bread & Butter, 6 ½ In.	9
Rose, Platter, Oval, 12 In.	42
Turquoise, Compote, 1936-46, 5 ½ In. .....*illus*	65
Turquoise, Mixing Bowl, No. 2, c.1936	120
Turquoise, Mixing Bowl, No. 4, 7 ¾ In.	99
Turquoise, Mixing Bowl, No. 4, c.1936	104
Turquoise, Mixing Bowl, No. 6, 9 In.	254
Turquoise, Pitcher, Water, Disk, 2 Qt., 6 ¼ In.	89
White, Chop Plate, 11 ¾ In.	20
White, Salt & Pepper, 2 ½ In.	15
Yellow, Chop Plate, 1930s, 13 In.	40
Yellow, Mixing Bowl, No. 5	98
Yellow, Mixing Bowl, No. 6	230
Yellow, Mug	22
Yellow, Pitcher, Disk, 30 Oz., 5 ¾ In. .....*illus*	32
Yellow, Plate, Bread & Butter, 6 ⅜ In.	8
Yellow, Plate, Dinner, 10 ½ In.	18
Yellow, Soup, Dish, 8 ½ In.	22
Yellow, Sugar, Lid	12 to 179

FINCH, *see Kay Finch category.*

FINDLAY ONYX AND FLORADINE are two similar types of glass made by Dalzell, Gilmore and Leighton Co. of Findlay, Ohio, about 1889. Onyx is a patented yellowish white opaque glass with raised silver daisy decorations. A few rare pieces were made of rose, amber, orange, or purple glass. Floradine is made of cranberry-colored glass with an opalescent white raised floral pattern and a satin finish. The same molds were used for both types of glass.

Butter, Cover, Floradine, Red Satin, White Inclusions, 6 In.	2013
Celery Vase, Onyx, Platinum Flowers, Mottled, Dalzell, Gilmore & Leighton, c.1889, 6 In.	173

Findlay, Spooner, Floradine, Satin Red, White Flowers, 4 ½ In.
$575

Early Auction Co.

Findlay, Toothpick Holder, Onyx, Raspberry, Opaline, Flowers, 2 ½ In.
$2,415

Early Auction Co.

Dating the Symbols
The symbol © was first used on dishes in 1914. The symbol ® wasn't used until 1949.

Firefighting, Bucket, Leather, Painted Medallion, No. 2, G. Manent, F.F.S. 1789, 13 ¾ In.
$1,440

Garth's Auctioneers & Appraisers

Firefighting, Bucket, Leather, Stylized Flowers, Handle, Eben, Francis, A.F.S., 1810, 12 ½ In.
$6,150

Skinner Auctioneers & Appraisers

Fireplace, Andirons, Brass, Ball & Claw Top, 10 ½ In.
$118

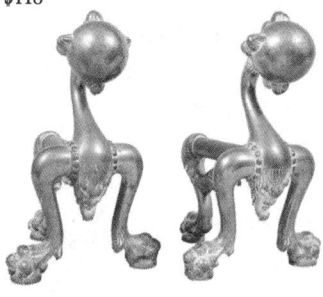

Conestoga Auction Co., Inc.

Fireplace, Andirons, Brass, Federal, Lemon Top, Acorn Finial, c.1810, 19 x 21 In.
$1,195

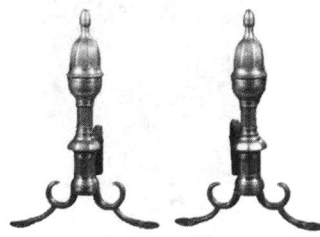

Neal Auction Co.

Creamer, Onyx, Ivory Pattern, Platinum Flowers, c.1889, 4 ½ x 2 ⅝ In.	92
Muffineer, Onyx, Opalescent, Gold Flowers, Fluted Neck, 5 In.	162
Spooner, Floradine, Satin Red, White Flowers, 4 ½ In. ....*illus*	575
Spooner, Onyx, Ivory Pattern, Platinum Flowers, c.1889, 4 ¼ x 2 ½ In.	127
Syrup, Onyx, Opal Glass, Silver Flowers, 7 In.	259 to 489
Toothpick Holder, Floradine, Red Satin, White Inclusions, 2 ½ In.	1093
Toothpick Holder, Ivory Onyx, Platinum Flowers, Dalzell, Gilmore & Leighton Co., c.1889	58
Toothpick Holder, Onyx, Raspberry, Opaline, Flowers, 2 ½ In. ....*illus*	2415
Tumbler, Onyx, Ivory Pattern, Platinum Flowers, Barrel Shape, c.1889, 3 ½ x 2 In.	173
Tumbler, Onyx, Opal, Amber To Silver Inclusions, Barrel Shape, 3 ¾ In.	489

FIREFIGHTING equipment of all types is wanted, from fire marks to uniforms to toy fire trucks. It is said that every little boy wanted to be a fireman or a train engineer 75 years ago and the collectors today reflect this interest.

Alarm Box, Gamewell Alarm, Gamewell Co., Newton, Mass., 13 x 18 In.	173
Alarm Box, Gamewell, 53 City Cables, 86 In.	228
Alarm Box, Outdoor, Flashing Top Light, Base, 120 In.	840
Alarm Box, Outdoor, General Enterprises, No. 41, Key, 12 ¼ x 17 In.	171
Alarm Box, Outdoor, Pedestal, Cast Iron, Key, Gamewell, 70 In.	270
Alarm Box, Pedestal, Red, Blue Base, 2-Sided, Gamewell, 81 In.	1440
Alarm, Telephone, Utica Fire Alarm Co.	395
Alarm, Wood Case, Alarm Box Number Indicator, Gamewell Fire Alarm Co., N.Y., 27 In.	2400
Ax, Fire, Polished Steel, Red Handle, c.1850, 36 In.	356
Ax, Parade, Viking Style, 35 ½ In.	300
Ax, Parade, Viking, Steel Head, Painted Handle, Red, White, Blue, 17 ½ In.	300
Bell Box, Cast Iron, Floor Model, No. 239, Red, Lamp, Fort Dodge Fire Dept., 78 In.	6000
Bell, Brass, Fall River, Seagrave Plaque, 1900s, 10 x 12 ½ In.	600
Bell, Fire, Wall Mount, J. Redding & Co., Boston, Patented Feb. 19, 1884	720
Bell, Gong, Oak, Brass Tag, Gamewell Fire Alarm Telegraph Co., 21 In.	480
Bell, Gong, Oak, Brass, Gamewell, Beveled Glass Front Door, 18 x 27 x 7 In.	1824
Bucket, Fire, Leather, Paint, c.1850, 13 In.	182
Bucket, Leather, Cherub, Banner, Handle, Black Paint, Gilt, c.1885, 13 ¼ In.	277
Bucket, Leather, Dark Green Paint, Inscribed J.B. Kirkham, c.1845, 12 In., Pair	1500
Bucket, Leather, Gilt, Paint, Scrolling Leaves, Banner, Handle, c.1833, 19 In.	615
Bucket, Leather, Green, Red, Yellow, Ned Richardson Prompt In Danger, 11 In.	118
Bucket, Leather, Holmes No. 1, Green, Paint, Handle, 11 ½ In.	240
Bucket, Leather, Inscribed G. Critson Union, Yellow Paint, Handle, c.1805, 12 In.	770
Bucket, Leather, No. 1, Wm. Rodman, 1787, 12 ½ In.	590
Bucket, Leather, No. 2, Painted Green, Gold Stenciling, 1803, 12 In.	420
Bucket, Leather, Painted Medallion, No. 2, G. Manent, F.F.S. 1789, 13 ¾ In. ....*illus*	1440
Bucket, Leather, Painted, Eagle & Banner, Franklin Fire Society, 1830, 13 In., Pair	823
Bucket, Leather, Painted, Eagle, Yellow, Red Ground, 1793, 17 In.	911
Bucket, Leather, Painted, Inscribed No. 1 M. Langdon 1792, H.G. Tanton 1881, 11 In.	356
Bucket, Leather, Painted, Red Yellow, Black, No. 1, c.1870, 13 In.	472
Bucket, Leather, Painted, Scroll Leaves, J. Young, Handle, Iron Rings, c.1815, 19 In.	1244
Bucket, Leather, Red, Crest, England, 14 ½ In.	188
Bucket, Leather, Scrolled Piece Holder, Neptune Hose T.J.N., c.1850	326
Bucket, Leather, Shield, Lion, Unicorn, Painted, Handle, 9 In.	360
Bucket, Leather, Stylized Flowers, Handle, Eben, Francis, A.F.S., 1810, 12 ½ In. ....*illus*	6150
Bucket, Painted Blue, Gilt, Red, Medallion, S.S.P., Hose, 12 ½ In.	840
Bucket, Rubber, Marked Home Hose 7, 11 ½ In.	270
Bucket, Wooden, Paint, Oval, Turned, Blue Shield, Gilt 5, 1800s, 6 In.	900
Extinguisher, Harden No. 1, Copper, 21 ½ In.	114
Extinguisher, Phoenix, Over Flames, 22 In.	240
Extinguisher, Pioneer, Frontiersman Label, 22 In.	240
Extinguisher, Statue Of Liberty Label, Gold Seal, 22 In.	300
Extinguisher, Stop Fire, Brass, Embossed Eagle, 13 In.	270
Extinguisher, Tip-Top, Brass, Peter Pirsch & Sons, Kenosha, Wis., 2 ½ Gal.	270
Extinguisher, Tube, Fire Paralyzer, Paper Tube, Label, 1920s, 14 In.	660
Extinguisher, Woman Entering Room Label, Quick Out, 22 In.	210
Extinguishing Kit, 6 Extinguishers, Metal Case, Black Handle, Shur-Stop, 12 In.	270
Fire Mark, Barrel, Coiling Hose, Fireman's Association, Cast Iron, c.1860, 11 ½ In.	207
Fire Mark, Clasped Hands, Cast Iron, Equitable Insurance Co., 1794, 11 x 10 In.	300
Fire Mark, Clasped Hands, Wood Mount, Philadelphia Contributorship, 8 ¼ x 9 In.	143
Fire Mark, United Fireman's Insurance Co. Of Philadelphia, Oval, Cast Iron, c.1850, 11 In.	240

F

Fire Mark, United Fireman's Insurance, Philadelphia, Embossed, Cast Iron, 1800s, 12 In.	316
Fire Wagon, Chemical, Instant Fyr-Fyter, French & Hacht Inc., Springfield, 35 x 42 In.	257
Fireman's Cap, Dress, Wool, Leather Bill, M.F.D., James M. Hirsch & Co., c.1900	143
Grenade, C. & N-W. Ry., Tube, Clear, Blue Contents, Tooled Mouth, 17 x 2 In.	269
Grenade, Harden's Hand, Sapphire Blue, Quilted, 4 Flat Panels, Footed, 4 ¾ In.	439
Grenade, Harden's Hand, Star, Blue, Diamond Diaper, 4 Flat Panels, 4 Sled Feet, 6 In.	152
Grenade, Hazelton's High Pressure Chemical Fire Keg, Orange Amber, Barrel, 11 In.	345
Grenade, Perfection, Horseshoe, Pat'd By A. Jones, 1885, Amber, Fish Scales, 7 ½ In.	2645
Hat, Parade, Inscribed Independence Hose Co., Gilt Banners, Black, Painted, 1800s, 7 In.	2673
Hat, Parade, Inscribed Never Sink Fire Company No. 3, Gilt, Green, c.1850, 6 ¾ In.	4503
Hat, Parade, Stovepipe, Tin, Red Paint, c.1950, 5 In., Pair	356
Helmet, Aluminum, High Eagle, Metal Front Shield, Ladder 1, Lieutenant, c.1897, Cairns	314
Helmet, Aluminum, Lion Front Holder, Painted, Portland Hose 2, Anderson & Jones, Pat. 1889	570
Helmet, Black Leather, Clover Embossing, Eagle Front Holder, Wool Liner, John Olson Co.	428
Helmet, Black Leather, Eagle Front Holder, Elmhurst 5, Cairns	270
Helmet, Black Leather, Eagle Front Holder, Goodwill Hose 25 CNB	399
Helmet, Brass Front Piece Holder, Shiffer Hose W.C., Philadelphia, 1800s	444
Helmet, Crown Comb, Carl Henkel, Bielefeld, Continental	120
Helmet, Derby Style, Leather, Brass Eagle Front Holder, Cairns & Brother, c.1900	356
Helmet, Eveready Smoke & Ammonia, No. 1018, Brass, Steel, Mica Goggles, 18 In.	2400
Helmet, Leather, Black, Red, Highland Hose Co., No. 1	115
Helmet, Leather, Brass Dog Front Piece Holder, Inscribed Fire Patrol, c.1900	593
Helmet, Leather, Brass Eagle Front Holder, Beach Pirates, Cairns & Brother, c.1865	504
Helmet, Leather, Brass Eagle Front Holder, Painted, Pioneer H & L.W.F.D., c.1920	365
Helmet, Leather, High Eagle, Poughkeepsie Exempt, Cairns, 1886	540
Helmet, Leather, Jockey Style, Eagle Front Holder, Friendship No. 1, Anderson & Jones	1083
Helmet, Leather, Painted Water Witch 5, J.S., Shield, 1833	668
Helmet, Red Leather, High Eagle, 2 Hanover, Pa., Cairns	456
Helmet, White Leather, Lion Front Holder, Hose 1 PFD	900
Hose Nozzle, Brass, 11 In.	30
Hydrant, Red, Cast Iron, Rensselaer Valve Co., Troy, N.Y., 1951, 29 In.	230
Lamp, Engine, Roxy No. 6, Electrified, Stand, New England, 36 In.	6600
Lamp, Fire Truck, Devoursney Bro's, Cobalt, Ruby Etched Glass Panels, Silver Plate, NYC, 20 In.	855
Lantern, American LaFrance Fire Co., Copper Fuel Tank, Dietz King, 15 In.	150
Lantern, Fire Station, Red, Green Lenses, Chicago, 21 In., Pair	510
Lantern, Nickel Plated, Kerosene, Dietz King, Fire Dept., 1907	395
Lantern, Wrist, Brass, Aetna Hose & Hook & Ladder Co., Wilmington, Del., 13 ½ In.	5100
Nozzle, Brass, Leather Handles, Shutoff, Rubberized Shaft, Stamped H.F.D., 35 ½ In.	200
Nozzle, Brass, Stamped Chicago, Manufacturer Stamp, c.1900, 29 ½ In.	90
Nozzle, Playpipe, Brass, Nickel Plated, Handles, Larkin, McEwen Hose Co. No. 4, 19 In.	200
Nozzle, Playpipe, Brass, Twine Wrap, Leather Handles, Shutoff, Elkhart, 1917, 16 ½ In.	120
Nozzle, Playpipe, Brass, Twine Wrapped Handle, W.D. Allen Underwriters, 30 In.	143
Nozzle, Playpipe, Leather Wrap, Handle, Buckeye, Marked Friendship Hose, 25 ¼ In.	270
Sign, Fire Exit, Hand Pointing, Red, White, 2-Sided Porcelain, 9 x 18 In.	177
Torch, Parade, Silver Plated, Gimbaled, Engraved, Turned Wood Handle, 29 In.	480
Truck, Ariel Ladder, La France, Automatic, Tandem Driver, Net, 1917, 94 x 105 x 562 In.	57000
Trumpet, Brass, 6 ½ x 17 ¼ In.	228
Trumpet, Brass, Yellow Tassels, 7 x 19 In.	330
Trumpet, Presentation, Engraved Flowers, Fire Designs, Fluted Bell, 9 ½ x 20 ½ In.	855
Trumpet, Speaking, Silver, Presentation, Boston, 1848, 20 In.	3000

FIREPLACES were used to cook food and to heat the American home in past centuries. Many types of tools and equipment were used. Andirons held the logs in place, firebacks reflected the heat into the room, and tongs were used to move either fuel or food. Many types of spits and roasting jacks were made and may be listed in the Kitchen category.

Andirons, Acorn Shape Finials, Tapered, Trefoil, Greek Key Legs, c.1850, 32 In.	120
Andirons, Arts & Crafts, Sphere Finial, Rope Twist Swing Handles, Scroll Feet, 14 x 23 In.	275
Andirons, Black Metal, Cat, Pointed Ears, Slanted Eyes, 16 x 10 x 14 In.	240
Andirons, Brass, Anchor Shape, 18 x 17 ½ In.	660
Andirons, Brass, Ball & Claw Top, 10 ½ In.	118	*illus*
Andirons, Brass, Bearded Man, Urn, Ram's-Head Handles, Claw Feet, c.1865, 42 In.	2963
Andirons, Brass, Cannonball Finials, c.1970, 19 ¾ x 10 ½ In.	88
Andirons, Brass, Cast Iron, Elongated Cat, Seated, Chrome Plate Co., 1960s, 20 x 16 ½ In.	750
Andirons, Brass, Cast Iron, Music Notes, Nashville, 1960s, 17 ½ x 14 ¼ In.	938
Andirons, Brass, Chippendale, Urn Finial, Column Stem, Cabriole Legs, 26 ¾ In.	688

Fireplace, Andirons, Cast Iron, Gothic Revival, Savery & Co., Marked, c.1850, 18 x 9 In.
$1,195

Neal Auction Co.

Fireplace, Andirons, Cast Iron, Hessian, Painted, 19 ½ In.
$325

Conestoga Auction Co., Inc.

Fireplace, Bellows, Leather, Brass Tip, Painted Face, c.1890
$2,565

Showtime Auction Services

Fireplace, Chenets, Andirons, Bronze, Putti Reclining, Garlands, c.1900, 21 ½ x 22 ½ In.
$922

New Orleans Auction Galleries, Inc.

Fireplace, Footman, Brass, Iron, Cut Out Skirt, Heart, Cabriole Legs, 1800s, 14 x 18 In.
$236

Conestoga Auction Co., Inc.

Fireplace, Screen, Brass, Fan, Articulated, 1900s, 29 ½ x 44 In.
$250

Rago Arts & Auction Center

Fireplace, Screen, Copper, Hammered, Repousse Panel, c.1910, 20 x 16 ¾ In.
$708

Brunk Auctions

Andirons, Brass, Chippendale, Wrought Iron, Twist Standard, N.Y., c.1770, 22 x 13 In.	5938
Andirons, Brass, Federal, Ball & Spire Top, Stamped R. Whittingham, 23 x 19 In.	1020
Andirons, Brass, Federal, Ball Top, Boston, c.1825, 17 x 26 In.	420
Andirons, Brass, Federal, Lemon Finial, c.1815, 19 ¾ In.	207
Andirons, Brass, Federal, Lemon On Urn Finial, Tapered Shaft, c.1800, 28 In.	704
Andirons, Brass, Federal, Lemon Top, Acorn Finial, c.1810, 19 x 21 In. ....*illus*	1195
Andirons, Brass, Federal, Marked R. Whittingham, New York, c.1795, 22 In.	1659
Andirons, Brass, Federal, Urn Finials, Pennyfeet, c.1810, 18 ½ In.	356
Andirons, Brass, Fluted Knops, Spheres, Scroll Base, Mask, 1800s, 28 x 13 In.	431
Andirons, Brass, George III, Scrolled Legs, 21 In., Pair	96
Andirons, Brass, Georgian, Faceted Finial, 20 x 22 In.	443
Andirons, Brass, Grate, Applied Stylized Faced, 20th Century, 27 In.	235
Andirons, Brass, Iron, Faceted, Belted, Lemon Top, Tools, c.1785, 20 x 12 In.	1920
Andirons, Brass, Iron, Knife Blade, Urn Finials, Shield, Curved Legs, c.1785, 20 x 9 In.	270
Andirons, Brass, Iron, Punch Design, Flame Finials, Cabriole Legs, 1700s, 21 x 12 In.	900
Andirons, Brass, Iron, Ring & Baluster, Ball Finials, 1800s, 14 x 24 In.	295
Andirons, Brass, Iron, Steeple Top, Faceted, Pedestal, Scroll Legs, c.1815, 25 x 24 In.	177
Andirons, Brass, Iron, Urn Top, Column Shafts, Spurred Legs, c.1815, 21 x 20 In.	400
Andirons, Brass, Lemon Tops, Spurred Legs, Ball Feet, c.1815, 21 x 22 In.	413
Andirons, Brass, Lighthouse Shape, England, 1900s, 18 x 20 ¼ In.	3600
Andirons, Brass, Queen Anne, Ball Finial, 13 In.	861
Andirons, Brass, Ribbed Ball Finial, Downswept Supports, England, 8 x 7 In.	147
Andirons, Brass, Scroll Base Legs, c.1850, 18 ½ In.	89
Andirons, Brass, Square Towers, Arched Panels, Scroll Leaves, c.1865, 31 x 30 In.	2015
Andirons, Brass, Tapered, Fluted, Masks, Garlands, Flame Finial, Scroll Feet, France, 36 In.	819
Andirons, Brass, Turned, Federal, c.1860, 22 In.	123
Andirons, Brass, Turned, Hexagonal Mounts, Cabriole Legs, 20 x 19 In.	153
Andirons, Bronze, Blown Glass, Controlled Bubbles, Baluster Shape, c.1919, 23x 19 In.	201
Andirons, Bronze, Hercules, Diana, On Winged Sphinx, Baroque, Patina, 33 In., Pair	3125
Andirons, Bronze, Iron, Figural, Seated Lion, England, 15 In.	813
Andirons, Bronze, Neoclassical, Hercules, Lion Cloak, Claw Foot, Dolphin Tails, 43 In., Pair	270
Andirons, Bronze, Standing Woman Figure, Caryatids, Masks, 39 In.	6875
Andirons, Cast Iron, Brownie, Black & White Paint, Stamped Freihofer, 15 ½ In.	308
Andirons, Cast Iron, Cat, Glass Eyes, 16 In.	288
Andirons, Cast Iron, Dachshund, Black, Red Paint, 1930s, 7 x 6 In.	219
Andirons, Cast Iron, Dachshund, Elongated Bodies, 1800s, 8 x 22 In.	210
Andirons, Cast Iron, Dog, Cat, Howes, 17 In.	178
Andirons, Cast Iron, Engraved Lines, Circles, c.1800, 14 In.	120
Andirons, Cast Iron, George Washington, Standing, c.1850, 15 ¾ In.	240
Andirons, Cast Iron, Gothic Revival, Savery & Co., Marked, c.1850, 18 x 9 In. ....*illus*	1195
Andirons, Cast Iron, Hessian Soldier, Painted, 19 ½ In. ....*illus*	325
Andirons, Cast Iron, Hessian Soldier, Striding, c.1860, 17 In.	152 to 185
Andirons, Cast Iron, Horse, Rearing, 15 x 19 In.	293
Andirons, Cast Iron, Hound Dog, Seated, c.1900, 18 x 17 In.	660
Andirons, Cast Iron, Owl, Amber Eyes, Branch Base, 14 In.	94
Andirons, Cast Iron, Owl, c.1850, 15 In.	770
Andirons, Cast Iron, Owl, Standing On Branch, Inset Glass Eyes, Howes, Boston, 15 In.	115
Andirons, Cast Iron, Painted, George Washington, c.1900, 20 ¼ In.	531
Andirons, Cast Iron, Pedestal Base, Round Chrome Finial, c.1970, 12 x 6 In.	75
Andirons, Cast Iron, Soldiers, Rifle, France, 9 ½ In.	1000
Andirons, Cast Iron, Whippet, 27 In.	3438
Andirons, Fire Deer, Stylized Deer, Cast Iron, Circus Series, Russel Wright, c.1930, 15 x 21 In.	8288
Andirons, Horse, Bridled, Chain Joined, Iron, Bronze, 17 In.	1375
Andirons, Iron, Curled Designs, Grooved Finials, c.1915, 35 ½ In.	660
Andirons, Iron, Gothic Revival, Arched Crocketed Shape, Savery & Co., c.1850, 17 x 14 In.	861
Andirons, Tool Set, Aluminum, Steel, Tubular, Textured Handles, E. Saarinen, 5 Piece	2125
Andirons, Tool Set, Enameled Iron, Brass, Flattened Shapes, Donald Desky, 5 Piece	2125
Andirons, Wrought Iron, Brass, Knife Blade Design, 25 In.	360
Andirons, Wrought Iron, Brass, Knife Blade Shaft, Brass Finial, c.1900, 21 x 10 In.	184
Andirons, Wrought Iron, Brass, Urn Finial, 1700s, 21 In.	210
Andirons, Wrought Iron, Brass, Urn Shape, c.1920, 21 x 15 In.	173
Andirons, Wrought Iron, Flower Shape, Ring Handles, 1985s, 27 x 22 In.	472
Andirons, Wrought Iron, Gooseneck, Faceted Heads, Flattened Feet, Black, 15 x 16 ¼ In.	29
Andirons, Wrought Iron, Rustic Style, Twist, 29 In.	48
Andirons, Wrought Iron, Scrolled Top & Base, Ring Handle, c.1900, 31 x 25 In.	472

Bellows, Carved, Green Man Face, Leaves, Brass	115
Bellows, Flowers, Yellow Ground, Painted, 17 ½ In.	30
Bellows, Fruit, Designs, Red Ground, Painted, c.1835, 18 In.	510
Bellows, Leather, Brass Tip, Painted Face, c.1890 ....*illus*	2565
Bellows, Pine, Leather, Red, Yellow, Black Painted, Conrad Kistler, Pa., 1847, 18 x 8 In.	7500
Bellows, Scalloped Borders, Scalloped Demilune, New York, 20 In.	1000
Bellows, Wood, Leather, Brass Tacks, Scene, Painted, New England, c.1830, 18 x 7 In.	5313
Box, Brass, Repousse, 22 x 21 In.	104
Box, Copper, Hammered, Ceramic Cabochon, England, c.1910, 22 x 22 In.	1625
Chenets, Andirons, Bronze, Gilt, Figural, Putto Seated, Scrolled Leaves, c.1850, 27 x 12 In.	1912
Chenets, Andirons, Bronze, Lions, c.1905, 19 x 16 In.	1750
Chenets, Andirons, Bronze, Louis XVI Style, Winged Woman, Hoof Feet, c.1910, 31 ¾ In.	2500
Chenets, Andirons, Bronze, Putti Reclining, Garlands, c.1900, 21 ½ x 22 ½ In. ....*illus*	922
Chenets, Andirons, Cast Iron, Middle Eastern Man, Seated, Bearded, 15 In.	1063
Chenets, Andirons, Garland Draped Urn, Fluted Pedestal, Flower Band, 13 x 14 In.	984
Chenets, Andirons, Gilt Bronze, Cupid, Arrows, Draped Table, c.1890, 15 x 17 In.	2813
Chenets, Andirons, Gilt Bronze, Leafy Scrolls, Swags, Urns, France, 12 ½ In.	1125
Chenets, Andirons, Gilt Bronze, Napoleon III, Putti, Warming Hands, c.1885, 11 x 13 In.	3198
Chenets, Andirons, Gilt Bronze, Napoleon III, Putti, Playing Pan Pipes, c.1865, 14 x 10 In.	676
Chenets, Andirons, Gilt Bronze, Plumed Mask, Paw Foot, Urn, Swag, 17 x 12 In.	1195
Chenets, Andirons, Gilt Bronze, Putti, Playing Pan Pipes, Urn Finials, c.1875, 20 x 52 In.	1722
Chenets, Andirons, Gilt Bronze, Regency Style, Cupid, Riding Lion, Scrolls, 16 x 12 In.	594
Chenets, Andirons, Gilt Bronze, Urn Shape, Ram's Heads, France, c.1900, 16 x 12 In.	236
Chenets, Andirons, Silvered Bronze, Louis XV Style, 13 In.	750
Coal Scoop, Agate Ware, Gray, 2 Handles, 21 In.	148
Coal Scuttle, Black, Tin, Princess Handles, Victorian, 12 x 27 In.	62
Coal Scuttle, Brass, Embossed Medallions, Handle, Continental, c.1865, 20 x 18 In.	1590
Coal Scuttle, Brass, Hammered Dragons, Crusaders, Flowers, Ring Handles, Eng., 21 In.	625
Coal Scuttle, Copper, Painted, Handle, Upturned Spout, Ring Foot, 26 x 14 In.	180
Coal Scuttle, Mahogany, Tole Painted White Dog, England, c.1890, 18 x 12 In.	1476
Crane, Owl Finial, Arts & Crafts, Iron, c.1910, 4 ½ In.	60
Crane, Wrought Iron, Scroll & Twist Design, 1800s, 49 In.	118
Cricket, Oak, Brass, Pierced Leaf Panels, Square, Handle, England, c.1800, 7 x 9 In.	1000
Fender Bench, Cast Iron, Curved, Pierced, Brass Base, Sailing Ship, Lions, 61 x 19 In.	1392
Fender, Aesthetic Movement, Brass, Flower Repousse, Eng., c.1890, 11 x 58 In., Pair	94
Fender, Brass, Edwardian, Reticulated Flowers, 36 In.	72
Fender, Brass, Openwork Gallery, Flowers, Dolphins, Stepped Base, 1900s, 9 x 59 In.	594
Fender, Brass, Pierced, Fans, Leaves, Scrollwork, c.1900, 10 ½ x 51 ½ In.	246
Fender, Brass, Pierced, Flower Medallion Border, Paw Feet, 1800s, 8 x 45 In.	185
Fender, Brass, Steel, Pierced Sides, Lion's Head Ring Pulls, Paw Feet, c.1815, 14 x 67 In.	399
Fender, Brass, Wire, Scrolls, 12 x 47 In.	360
Fender, Brass, Wirework, C-Shape, 1800s, 6 ½ x 35 In.	598
Fender, Brass, Wirework, D-Shape Rail, Vertical Wires, Swag Border, c.1810, 21 x 38 In.	900
Fender, Brass, Wirework, Federal, Faceted Finials, Molded Feet, c.1815, 15 x 48 In.	1195
Fender, Brass, Wirework, Serpentine, Scroll, c.1815, 12 x 51 In.	767
Fender, Brass, Wirework, Swags, Diamond & Lozenge Design, c.1800, 28 x 50 In.	492
Fender, Brass, Wrought Iron, Scrolling Flowers, 60 In.	688
Fender, Bronze, Vented, c.1865, 60 x 24 In.	104
Fender, Copper, Steel, Fan Shape, Pierced Flowers, Paw Feet, c.1885, 31 x 40 In.	1353
Fender, Tile Work, 10 Ball Finials, Balustrade, Blue Leaves, 11 ½ x 10 ¾ In.	600
Fender, Wire, Brass Swags, Federal, Bowfront, 12 x 42 In.	443
Fender, Wrought Iron, Scrolled Panel Elements, 1900s, 26 x 28 In.	201
Fire Screen, Arts & Crafts, Oak Frame, Crewelwork, Trestle Base, Bun Feet, 31 x 26 In.	115
Fire Screen, Brass, Hammered, Repousse Birds, Rocks, Waves, Fish, Newlyn, 26 x 37 In.	1830
Fire Screen, Louis XV Style, Fruitwood, Needlework, Carved Shield Frame, 40 In.	984
Fire Screen, Louis XV Style, Shaped Brass Scrolls, Urns, Mesh Insert, 1900s, 30 x 27 In.	1500
Fire Screen, Rosewood, Needlepoint Panel, Carved, Turned Frame, c.1890, 51 x 27 In.	178
Fire Screen, Tin, Punched Flower Pot, Table, Paint, Curved, c.1920, 24 x 20 In.	420
Fire Tongs, Brass, Federal, Eagle, Gripping Banner Ends, 36 In.	480
Fire Tool Set, Scraper, Poker, Brush, Tongs, Stand, Ebonized Metal, c.1980, 26 ½ In.	1375
Fireback Panels, Wrought Iron, Lockwood De Forest, c.1900, 15 x 32 In., Pair	1250
Fireback, Cast Iron, Arched, Crowns, Plumes, Fleur-De-Lis, England, 1800s, 19 In.	90
Fireboard, Wood, Louvered, Paint, Oval, New England, 31 x 46 In.	1440
Footman Trivet, Brass, Front Cabriole Legs, England, 10 ½ x 20 In.	330
Footman, Brass, Iron, Cut Out Skirt, Heart, Cabriole Legs, 1800s, 14 x 18 In. ....*illus*	236

Fireplace, Tool Set, Chromed Steel, Jean Paul Creations, 1970s, 24 x 9 ½ x 4 ¼ In., 4 Piece
$1,500

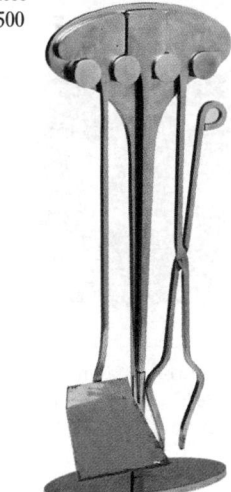

Rago Arts & Auction Center

Fireplace, Trammel, Brass, Figural, Ratchet, Man Wearing Hat, Lion, 1763, 35 ½ In.
$1,800

Garth's Auctioneers & Appraisers

This is an edited listing of current prices. Visit **Kovels.com** to check thousands of prices from previous years and sign up for free information on trends, tips, reproductions, marks, and more.

Fishing, Creel, Rattan, Metal Latch,
14 x 9 x 7 In.
$29

Showtime Auction Services

Fishing, Lure, Oscar The Frog, Raised
Eye, Wood Body, Metal Legs, Auclaire &
Associates, Detroit, c.1940
$242

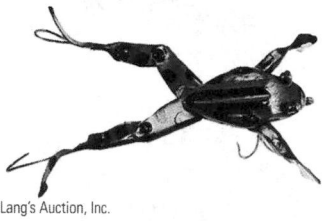

Lang's Auction, Inc.

Fishing, Lure, Surface Bait, Winter's
Weedless, Wood Body, Celluloid Wings,
1 ⅞ In.
$424

Lang's Auction, Inc.

Fishing, Net, Lyle Dickerson, Trout,
Egg Shape Basket, Marked,
21 ¼ x 9 ¼ x 13 ¾ In.
$1,694

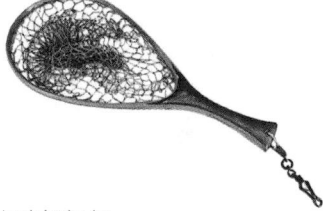

Lang's Auction, Inc.

Appraising Lures
There are websites that will
appraise antique fishing lures
from a posted picture.

Footman, Brass, Pierced Top, Sides, England, 19th Century, 14 ¼ In.	96
Grate, Wrought Iron, Arts & Crafts, Dragons, Open Mouths, 40 x 22 In.	2750
Log Basket, Chromed Steel, Leather, Allessandro Albrizzi, Italy, 1960s, 12 x 16 In.	531
Log Holder, Arts & Crafts, Wrought Iron, Open U-Shape, Stylized Serpent, 23 x 15 In.	610
Mantel is listed in the Architectural category.	
Screens are also listed in the Architectural and Furniture categories.	
Screen, Brass, 3-Panel, Flower Band, c.1900, 30 x 53 In.	125
Screen, Brass, Fan, Articulated, 1900s, 29 ½ x 44 In. ....*illus*	250
Screen, Brass, Victorian, c.1890, 16 x 50 In.	178
Screen, Brass, Wire, Federal, Scrolls, 24 x 57 In.	1440
Screen, Brass, Wirework, Folding, Swags, Scrolls, U.S.A., c.1815, 24 x 37 In., Pair	3120
Screen, Brass, Wirework, Serpentine, Scrolls, c.1800, 10 x 48 In.	600
Screen, Brass, Wirework, Swags & Scrolls, c.1800, 24 ½ x 42 ½ In.	720
Screen, Bronze, Beveled Glass, Crest, Flame Finials, 1900s, 40 x 27 In.	984
Screen, Bronze, Brass, Pierced, Scrolled Crests, 3 Panels, c.1910, 78 x 13 In.	360
Screen, Bronze, Flowers, Ribboned, Fluted Standards, Swags, Hoof Feet, 1800s, 27 In.	478
Screen, Bronze, Mesh, Retractable, Pierced, Scrolled, 37 x 36 In.	1353
Screen, Bronze, Stylized Plate, Pierced, Art Nouveau Style, 28 x 24 In.	1121
Screen, Copper, Hammered, Raised Flowers, Iron Tripod Stand, c.1910, 31 x 18 In.	188
Screen, Copper, Hammered, Repousse Panel, c.1910, 20 x 16 ¾ In. ....*illus*	708
Screen, Gilt Bronze, Fan Shape, Pierced Figures, Flame Pot, France, 30 x 47 In.	615
Screen, Gilt Bronze, Louis XV Style, Pierced Rocaille, Tool Hooks, c.1885, 16 x 45 In.	399
Screen, Gilt Bronze, Napoleon III, Folding, Brevette S.G.D.G., 1800s, 40 x 29 In.	738
Screen, Mahogany, Gothic, Steeple Pilasters, Needlepoint, Gentleman, c.1850, 51 x 35 In.	1845
Screen, Mesh, Metal, Black Paint, 44 x 37 In.	58
Screen, Pole, Federal, Mahogany, Hinged, Shelf, Cabriole Snake Legs, New Eng., c.1800, 54 In.	1250
Screen, Pole, Georgian, Walnut, 8-Sided, Flower Needlework, Black Ground, c.1845, 55 In.	270
Screen, Pole, Mahogany, Brass, Octagonal Hudson River Scene, Oil On Canvas, c.1825, 39 In.	2625
Screen, Pole, Queen Anne, Hardwood, Needlepoint Flower, Tree Canvas, Tripod Base, 36 In.	295
Screen, Pole, Queen Anne, Mahogany, Needlepoint Flowers, Spiral Stand, 58 x 20 In.	360
Screen, Round Panel, Papier-Mache, Mother-Of-Pearl, Volcano, c.1850, 59 x 16 In., Pair	6875
Screen, Wire, Brass, Empire, 1800s, 21 x 41 In.	239
Seat, Leather, Elephant Trumpeting, Gray, 17 x 36 In.	780
Stand, Wrought Iron, 2 Candleholders, Crucifix, Trestle Feet, 22 x 32 In.	1200
Tool Set, Brass, Steel, Tongs, Shovel, Poker, Flowers, 1700s, 26 In., 3 Piece	3300
Tool Set, Chrome, c.1950, 26 ½ In., 4 Piece	708
Tool Set, Chrome, Tubular, Flat Curled Hangers, Square, M. Taylor, 1970s, 31 In., 5 Piece	1875
Tool Set, Chromed Steel, Jean Paul Creations, 1970s, 24 x 9 ½ x 4 ¼ In., 4 Piece ....*illus*	1500
Tool Set, Iron, Nickel, Poker, Shovel, Broom, c.1945, 28 ¼ In.	100
Tool Set, Shovel, Tongs, Ball Top, Brass, 34 In.	1020
Tool Set, Wrought Iron, Adirondack Style, Deer Antler, 31 In.	738
Tool Set, Wrought Iron, Scrolled Stand, Shovel, 2 Pokers, Tongs, 28 To 49 ½ In., 5 Piece	784
Tool, Log Fork, Cast Iron, Brass Wall Mount, 47 In.	165
Trammel, Brass, Figural, Ratchet, Man Wearing Hat, Lion, 1763, 35 ½ In. ....*illus*	1800
Trammel, Wrought Iron, Adjustable Sawtooth Edge, Rooster Finial, c.1900, 12 ½ In.	236
Trammel, Wrought Iron, Scrolls, Sawtooth Edge, Flattened Handle, 34 x 10 In.	211

FISCHER porcelain was made in Herend, Hungary, by Moritz Fischer. The factory was founded in 1839 and is still in business. The wares are sometimes referred to as Herend porcelain.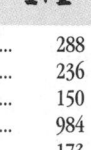

Bowl, Lid, Flowers, Lemon Slices, Lemon Finial, Green Branch Handles, 9 ½ In.	288
Bowl, Square, Rothschild Bird, Scalloped Rim, Bird Scene, 4 x 10 In.	236
Bowl, Vegetable, Rothschild Bird, Scalloped, 4 x 7 In.	150
Cachepot, Birds On Branch, Fishnet Dolphin Shape Handles, Painted, 9 ½ x 8 ½ In.	984
Figurine, Bald Eagle, Wings Out, Painted, 2000, 6 ½ In.	173
Figurine, Cat, White, Reclining, Head Raised, 4 ½ x 9 ½ In.	119
Figurine, Draped Nude, Kneeling, Looking In Mirror, 9 In.	208
Figurine, Elephant On Ball, Pink, 2 ½ In.	95
Figurine, Elephant, Trunk Up, White, Black Spots, 4 In.	192
Figurine, Lion & Lioness, Black, Gray, Gilt, Logo, 7 x 8 ½ x 4 In.	633
Figurine, Parrot, Perched, Rust Fishnet, Multicolor Wings, Gold Trim, 7 In.	293
Figurine, Peasant Madonna & Child, Multicolor, Plinth Base, 13 ¾ In.	104
Figurine, Rabbit, Seated, White, 1900s, 5 ½ In.	177
Figurine, Rooster, Green Fishnet, Multicolor Wings, Gold Accents, 9 In.	380
Figurine, Tiger, Stalking, Mouth Open, Teeth, Rust Fishnet, Gold Trim, 6 x 15 In.	1053
Perfume Bottle, Queen Victoria, Butterfly Finial, 5 ½ In.	300

F

Plate, Butterfly, Flowers, Multicolor, 11 In.	158
Plate, Red Butterfly & Flower, Square, 11 In.	96
Plate, Rothschild Bird, Trees, Bugs, Butterflies, 10 ⅞ In., 12 Piece	1770
Salt & Pepper, Chinese Bouquet, Yellow, Egg Shape, White Ground, 1 ¼ In.	68
Teapot, Rothschild Bird, Marked Herend, c.1965, 8 ½ x 5 In.	375
Tureen, Lid, Rothschild Bird, Finial, Green Handles, Herend, 9 ½ x 15 In.	1003
Tureen, Lid, Underplate, Rothschild Bird, Lemon Finial, 15 ¾-In. Tray	403
Tureen, Rothschild Bird, Finial, Marked Herend, c.1960, 9 x 12 In.	688
Tureen, Underplate, Bouquet, Green, Scalloped, Basket Weave, Lemon Knop, 15 & 16 In.	799
Tureen, Underplate, Lid, Rothschild Bird, 11 x 15-In. Tureen, 16-In. Platter	1652
Tureen, Underplate, Rothschild Bird, Twig Handles, Lemon Knop, 12 ¾ x 16 & 12 x 17 ¾ In.	1722
Vase, Butterfly, Purple, Yellow, Green, 6 ½ In.	90
Vase, Fruit, Branch, Flared, 8 In.	60

FISHING reels of brass or nickel were made in the United States by 1810. Bamboo fly rods were sold by 1860, often marked with the maker's name. Lures made of metal, or metal and wood, were made in the nineteenth century. Plastic lures were made by the 1930s. All fishing material is collected today and even equipment of the past thirty years is of interest if in good condition with original box.

Bag, Brady-Halesowen, Canvas, Leather Trim, Mesh Front, Strap, 20 In.	109
Case, Rod, Leather Strap, Handle, 41 In.	242
Creel, Rattan Weave, Leather, Canvas Shoulder Strap, 11 ½ x 8 ½ In.	86
Creel, Rattan, Metal Latch, 14 x 9 x 7 In. *illus*	29
Creel, Tooled Leather Trim, Front Zip Leather Pouch, A.E. Nelson, 15 x 9 ½ In.	513
Creel, Wicker, Wood, Measuring Ruler, 16 x 7 x 7 In.	29
Dipper, Splint Oak, Iron Band, Used With Extension Pole, 1800s, 20 In.	59
Fly, Edward Hewitt, Dry, Silver Badger Pattern, Catskill, c.1935	73
Fly, Herman Christian, Wet, Dark Cahill Pattern, c.1925	48
Fly, Lee Wulff, Salmon, c.1965	48
Fly, Ray Bergman, Trout, Gray Hackle Dry, 12 Hook, c.1950	36
Gaff, Spring, Jaw Points, 1889 Patent, 71 ½ In.	333
Grabber, Spring, Serrated Jaws, Sweden, 56 ½ In.	73
Harpoon, Iron, Diamond Shape Point, Wood Shaft, 1800s, 76 In.	201
Hook Display, Mustad & Son, Folding, Various Sizes, Norway, 69 ½ In.	194
Hook, G.A. Stanton Gaff, Leverage, 2 Hooks, 12 In., Wood Handle 24 In.	908
Line Dryer, Wood, Crank, 17 In.	114
Lure, Oscar The Frog, Raised Eye, Wood Body, Metal Legs, Auclaire & Associates, Detroit, c.1940 *illus*	242
Lure, Surface Bait, Winter's Weedless, Wood Body, Celluloid Wings, 1 ⅞ In. *illus*	424
Net, Charles Orvis, Landing, Burlwood, Cork Handle, c.1945, 43 In.	236
Net, Lyle Dickerson, Trout, Egg Shape Basket, Marked, 21 ¼ x 9 ¼ x 13 ¾ In. *illus*	1694
Oyster Bucket, Painted Red, Stave Construction, Wire Bound, Swing Handle, N.C., 12 In.	502
Reel, Billy Pate, Trout, Left Hand Wind, 8 Weight Line, 3 ½ x ¾ In.	454
Reel, Fly, Salmon, Brass, Check & Serpentine Crank, 4 ¼ x 1 ½ In.	169
Reel, J.F. & B.F. Meek, Casting, Brass, Inscription, Theo. Steele 1850, No. 3 Size *illus*	3146
Reel, Pflueger Norka, No. 1335, Box, Fabric Pouch	171
Reel, St. George, Hardy Bros. Ltd. England, Size 3 ⅜	1260
Rod Case, Pine, Brass Mounts, 3 Compartments, 4-Footed, Wood Drawer Pulls, 63 x 5 In.	472
Rod, Dickerson, Chrome Snake Guides, Western Style Grip, 2/2, 8 In.	2904
Rod, Fly, E.F. Payne, Brown Wraps, Purple Tip, Nickel Reel Seat, Bag, Tube, 3/2, 9 ½ In.	514
Rod, Fly, Orvis Impregnated Deluxe, 6 Ft. 6 In., 2 Piece	533
Rod, Passport, Abercrombie & Fitch, Red Enameled, 10 Piece, Collapsible, 6 ½ Ft.	420
Rod, Thomas & Thomas, Paradigm, Trout, Yellow Orange Varnish, 2/2, 7 In.	968
Spear, Eel, 6 Prongs, P.S. Rent, Ma., 14 In.	83
Tackle Box, Abercrombie & Fitch, Mahogany, Brass, Lift Lid, 2 Drawers, c.1950, 9 x 20 In.	443
Tip Up, Ice Fishing, Spring Movement Tin Flag, Reel, Green Paint	85

FLAGS *are included in the Textile category.*

FLASH GORDON appeared in the Sunday comics in 1934. The daily strip started in 1940. The hero was also in comic books from 1930 to 1970, in books from 1936, in movies from 1938, on the radio in the 1930s and 1940s, and on television from 1953 to 1954. All sorts of memorabilia are collected, but the ray guns and rocket ships are the most popular.

Action Figure Sets, 4-In. Figures, Illustrated Box, Mattel, 1979, 4 x 5 ½ In., 8 Piece	388
Cel, Animation, Hand Painted, Saving Woman, Cliff's Edge, 1979, 18 x 14 In.	195
Clicker Gun, Wallet, Radio Repeater, Tin Litho, Embossed Leatherette, c.1937, 10 In.	301

Fishing, Reel, J.F. & B.F. Meek, Casting, Brass, Inscription, Theo. Steele 1850, No. 3 Size
$3,146

Lang's Auction, Inc.

F

Flow Blue, Platter, Bluebell & Fern, Ironstone, 15 ½ In.
$295

Conestoga Auction Co., Inc.

Flow Blue, Platter, Cockfighting, Flared Rim, Marked Spanish Festivities 1798, 1800s, 14 x 11 In.
$236

Brunk Auctions

TIP

To remove a dried cork that has fallen inside a bottle, try this: Pour some household ammonia in the bottle. Let it sit for a few days. Most of the cork should dissolve and can easily be removed.

F

Folk Art, Bird, Cockatiel, Gesso, Painted, c.1900, 9 x 5 In.
$780

Cowan's Auctions

Folk Art, Birdhouse, Schoolhouse, Mixed Materials, Tree Trunk Stand, Vermont, c.1925, 28 In.
$1,080

Garth's Auctioneers & Appraisers

Folk Art, Cannon, Turned Wood Barrel, Iron Carriage, Iron-Rimmed Wheels, c.1900, 48 In.
$330

Garth's Auctioneers & Appraisers

Figure, Wood, Painted, Multi Products, Disc Base, 1944, 4 ¾ In.	338
Game, Die Cut Hawkmen Playing Pieces, Cards, Spinner, Box, 1965, 9 ½ x 18 ½ In.	173
Greeting Card, Christmas, Flash & Dale Arden, Bulbs, 1934, 6 x 5 In.	40
Photograph, Flash Gordon Conquers The Universe, Signed Buster Grabbe, Frame, 20 x 28 In.	86
Poster, Flash Running, Multicolor, Lithograph, R. Lichtenstein, Pop Art Portraits, 52 x 32 In.	295
Toy, Rocket Fighter Ship, Shoots Sparks, Windup, Tin Lithograph, 1939, 12 In.	468
Toy, Rocket Fighter Ship, Tin Lithograph, Windup, Marx, Box, 12 x 5 In.	720
Toy, Rocket Ship, Fighter, Tin Lithograph, Windup, c.1935, 12 In.	489
Toy, Siren Space Gun, Decal, Red, Green, Silver, Metal, 7 In.	570
Toy, Star Ship, Green, Wheels, Tootsietoy, 1970s	25
Watch, Blue Vinyl-Covered Leather Band, Round Dial, Box, 1971, 4 ¾ x 9 ½ In.	617
Whistle Knife, Spaceship Shape, Red, Yellow, 1950s	65

FLOW BLUE was made in England and other countries about 1830 to 1900. The dishes were printed with designs using a cobalt blue coloring. The color flowed from the design to the white body so that the finished piece has a smeared blue design. The dishes were usually made of ironstone china. More Flow Blue may be found under the name of the manufacturer.

Bowl, Oval, Footed, 8 x 12 In.	102
Bowl, Vegetable, Waldorf, Blue Transfer, New Wharf Pottery, 9 In., 2 Piece	71
Clock, Shelf, Key, Pendulum, Pink Flowers, Blue & Gilt Shaped Border, 12 ½ In.	210
Ewer, Basin, Coburg, Ironstone, John Edwards & Co., Staffordshire, c.1845, 12 In., 2 Piece	431
Jar, Lid, Adderley Lily, Gold Handles, England, 12 In.	68
Jardiniere, Leaves, Flowers, Gilt Accents, Shaped Standard, c.1850, 42 In.	178
Pitcher, Milk, Coburg, 6 In.	87
Plate, Gold Shell, Square, 8 ½ In.	40
Platter, Bluebell & Fern, Ironstone, 15 ½ In. ....*illus*	295
Platter, Brush Stroke, Stick Spatter, Wild Asters, Oval, Baker & Co., 12 ½ In.	118
Platter, Clover, Grindley, 14 In.	64
Platter, Cockfighting, Flared Rim, Marked Spanish Festivities 1798, 1800s, 14 x 11 In. ....*illus*	236
Platter, Ironstone, Leaf & Swag, Brush Stroke, 15 ½ In.	177
Platter, Keele, 14 In.	64
Platter, Oval, Kirkee, 16 ½ In.	128
Platter, Scinde, Canted Corners, Rectangular, Asian Scene, J. & A. Alcock, Eng., 16 In.	138
Platter, Temple, Canted Corners, Rectangle, 16 In.	162
Teapot, Footed, 8 In.	104
Tray, Grace Pattern On Border, Flowers, Shaped Scrolled Rim, Grindley, 13 In.	46
Tureen, Lid, Underplate, Chapoo, Oblong, Footed, c.1850, 7 x 13 In.	259
Vase, Urn, Flowers, Oval, Footed, Gilt Scroll Handles & Rim, Art Nouveau, Adderly, 12 In.	215

FLYING PHOENIX, *see Phoenix Bird category.*

FOLK ART is also listed in many categories of this book under the actual name of the object. See categories such as Box, Cigar Store Figure, Paper, Weather Vane, Wooden, etc.

Bank, Bank Building, Wood, Incised Brickwork, Windows & Doors, 11 x 11 In.	885
Basket, Bottle Cap, Multicolor, Handle, Oval, 9 In.	144
Bat, Vampire, Spread Wings, Sharp Teeth, Wood, Copper Ears, Hanging, 1890s, 19 x 47 In.	230
Belt, Wood, Carved, Dog Buckle, c.1900, 14 ¼ In.	150
Bird Tree, Wood, Painted, Multicolor, Walter & June Gottshall, Pa., c.1975, 18 ¾ In.	470
Bird, Cockatiel, Gesso, Painted, c.1900, 9 x 5 In. ....*illus*	780
Birdhouse, Building, Spire, Porch, Carved, Paint, Signed Allen Miller, c.1900, 20 x 14 In.	215
Birdhouse, Schoolhouse, Mixed Materials, Tree Trunk Stand, Vermont, c.1925, 28 In. ......*illus*	1080
Bookplate, Watercolor On Paper, Bird, Flowering Branch, Frame, 1976, 5 ½ x 5 In.	3525
Box, Log Cabin, Wood, Fabric Lined, 10 x 7 In.	146
Bugler, Blue Cap, Red Coat, Yellow Bugle To Lips, Wood, Paint, 1930s, 31 ½ In.	575
Bust, Man, Hardwood, Bald, Tenn., c.1900, 5 In.	288
Cane, Ball In Chamber, Conifer Wood, Old Red Paint, Cutouts, Floating Ball, 36 In.	374
Cannon, Turned Wood Barrel, Iron Carriage, Iron-Rimmed Wheels, c.1900, 48 In. ....*illus*	330
Circus Wagon Seat, Plank, Paint, Cats, Red, Orange, Yellow, Green, c.1885, 41 x 11 In.	148
Coach, 2 Horses, Wood, Hinged Doors, Full Tack, Multicolor Paint, c.1920, 24 x 5 In.	316
Crow, Carved, Painted Wood, Square Base, U.S.A., c.1900, 12 In.	523
Dart Board, Wood, Paint, Flower Stencil Design, 3 Darts, Metal, c.1900, 42 x 36 In.	3304
Diorama, Croatian Farmer, Sculptural Group, Landscape, Applied Seeds, Nuts, 1900s, 10 In.	840
Diorama, Ferris Wheel, Made From Toothpicks, Ohio State Prison, 1940s, Case, 20 In.	1620
Dog, Spaniel, Standing, Wood, Carved, Painted, W. Schimmel, Pa., c.1880, 4 ½ x 6 ¾ In.	9113
Dog, Spaniel, Wood, Cumberland Valley, Wilhelm Schimmel, 1800s, 15 x 24 In. ....*illus*	7965

Folk Art, Dog, Spaniel, Wood, Cumberland Valley, Wilhelm Schimmel, 1800s, 15 x 24 In.
$7,965

Conestoga Auction Co., Inc.

Dog's Head, Wood, Fur-Like Carving, c.1900, 13 x 8 ½ In. 288
Dove, Preening, Carved, Painted Wood, Wire Legs, Base, c.1915, 7 x 13 In. 420
Eagle, Giltwood, Carved, Head To Right, Rock Base, 14 In. 1920
Eagle, Giltwood, Carved, Outstretched Wings, Plinth, 32 x 36 In. 2813
Eagle, Sheet Metal, Spread Wings, Gilt, Dome Base, Handmade, 18 x 35 In. 960
Eagle, Spread Wings, Arrows Shield Talons, Giltwood, Paint, c.1950, 22 x 76 In. 2242
Eagle, Spread Wings, Carved, Brown, Cream Paint, 16 x 23 In. 345
Eagle, Spread Wings, Pine, Carved, Painted, Wilhelm Schimmel, Pa., c.1870, 8 x 14 In. 11250
Eagle, Spread Wings, Wood, Carved, Black, Orange, Brown, W. Schimmel, c.1870, 9 x 17 In. 2252
Eagle, Spread Wings, Wood, Carved, Painted, Wilhelm Schimmel, 6 ¾ In. 22525
Eagle, Wood, Spread Wings, Carved, Paint, 32 x 14 In. 575
Ferris Wheel, Wood, 1930s, 27 x 30 In. 403
Fish, Trout, Carved, Green, Black, Orange Paint, Shadowbox Frame, 15 ½ In. 2160
Fisherman, White Beard, Holding Pole, 2 Fish, Wood Carved, Painted, Stand, c.1965, 20 In. 296
Funeral In A Box, Outsider, Found Panel, Painted, Purvis Yound, 32 x 32 In. 540
G. Washington, Ye Hero Of '76, Holds Flag, Carved, Wood, Hinged Limbs, Box, 10 In. 1837
Horse, Standing, Reclining Dog, Carved, Painted, U.S.A., 7 ¾ x 2 ½ In. 450
Houseboat, Carved Wood, Painted White, Turned Detail, 23 x 22 In. 348
Humidor, Figural, Painted Green, Red, Speckled Bird Finial, Stump Base, 19 x 15 In. 2640
Indian, Headdress, Hand Raised To Eyes, Multicolor Paint, Plaster, c.1945, 38 ½ In. 150
Ink Blotter, Figural, Rocker, Oak, Man's Head Handle, Lizards, c.1890, 5 ¾ x 7 In. 720
Man, Acrobat With Ball, Movable Arms, Paint, Carved, Wood, c.1915, 23 In. 470
Man, Dancing, Wooden, Carved, Articulated Legs, U.S.A., c.1850, 8 ½ In. 206
Man, Standing, Bowler Hat, Carved, Buttons, Alligatored White, Black, c.1910, 17 In. 720
Man, Top Hat, Sword, American Flag, Wood, Paint, Chas. F. Chidsey, Jr., 1894, 12 In. 5120
Mirror, Steeple Top, Carved, Blue, Brown, Gold Painted, Canada, 43 x 24 In. 780
Model, Steam Yacht, Shell Rim Oval Base, Painted, Carved, 19 x 25 In. 1020
Napoleon, Gouache & Ink On Woven Paper, Rearing Horse, Frame, 1800s, 11 x 13 In. 300
Owl, Brown, Carved, Painted, c.1900, 19 ½ In. 652
Owl, Carved, Painted, Tin Wings, Long Legs, Spread Base, c.1870, 10 ¼ In. 2252
Owl, Tin Wings, Branch, 1900s, 13 In. 264
Parrot, Carved & Painted, Perched On Branch, c.1900, 15 x 12 In. 1080
Penguin, Carved, White, Black, Orange Paint, c.1910, 24 In. 900
Pig, Carved, Painted Pink, c.1950, 25 In. 308
Plant Stand, Cake, Mixed Woods, Octagonal, Thread Spool Design, c.1900, 12 x 12 In. 176
Plaque, Eagle, Liberty Shield, Gold, Red, White, Blue Paint, Cast Metal, c.1960, 21 x 19 In. 118
Punch, Multicolor Paint, Wood, Carved, Incised, C.H. Henkel, Vt., 1870, 25 x 9 In. 209000
Puppet, Alligator, Carved Wood, Reflector Eyes, Cloth Sleeve, 1900s, 4 x 27 In. 149
Rooster, Pine, Yellow, Black Paint, Carved, G.R. Lawton, c.1845, 3 x 3 In., Pair 5938
Sand Bottle, Flag, 36 Stars, Eagle, 1886, Verso, Minnie, Flowers, Clemens, 5 ¼ In. *illus* 24282
Sign, Officer, Keep Off, Wood, Painted, 19 In. *illus* 246
Spirit House, Stand, Red Removable Roof, Gold Painted House, Baskets, c.1910, 51 x 26 In. 236
Sprinkler, Man, Overalls, Wood, Paint, 33 x 10 In. 205
Stag, Leaping, Doc Wininger, Indiana, Base, 48 x 52 In. 690
Stag, Leaping, Sheet Tin, 39 ½ x 44 ½ In. 461
Table, Tree Branch Legs, Splayed, 25 x 16 ½ In. 259
Wastebasket, Mermaid, Holding Shell, Paint, Metal, Martha Farham Cahoon, c.1985, 14 In. 325
Whale, Orca, Open Mouth, Conical Teeth, Carved, Glass Eye, 1900s, 35 ½ x 13 In. 711
Whirligig, 2 Pecking Chickens, Pine, Multicolor Paint, Early 1900s, 28 In. 1058
Whirligig, Airplane, Wood, Painted Multicolor, Round Newell Post Base, 1916, 16 x 24 In. 1265
Whirligig, Black Man, Paddle Arms, Carved Wood, Metal, Top Hat, c.1885, 23 x 14 In. 3600
Whirligig, Boxer, Carved, Painted, Tin Arms, Turned Base, Rotates, 1900s, 16 x 8 In. 1200
Whirligig, Carved Wood, Tin, Figure, Cap, Glass Eyes, Paddle Arms, c.1890, 25 In. 2460
Whirligig, Dewey Boy, Wood, Carved, Painted, Sailor, Holding Paddles, c.1911, 22 x 36 In. 431
Whirligig, Duck, Flying, Tin, Paint, Base, 13 ½ x 15 ½ In. 150
Whirligig, Jockey Atop Fox, Paint, Sheet Metal, U.S.A., c.1925, 9 ½ x 22 ½ In. 240
Whirligig, Lighthouse, Wood, Metal, White, Red, Black Paint, 19 ½ x 46 In. 660
Whirligig, Man, Cutting Wood, Painted, Metal Support, Wood Base, 10 x 14 In. 65
Whirligig, Man, Green Jacket, Metal Rod, Paint, Wood, c.1905, 18 In. 250
Whirligig, Man, Sharpening Ax On Wheel, Stove Top Hat, Pipe, Iron, c.1910, 36 ½ In. 4320
Whirligig, Man, Top Hat, Hooked Nose, Curled Toe Shoes, Pine, Paint, c.1890, 14 In. 2040
Whirligig, Pedal Boat, Driver, Patriotic Painted, 39 ½ x 39 In. 960
Whirligig, Penny Farthings Bicycle, Rider, Metal, Wood, c.1970, 16 x 14 In. 1380
Whirligig, Pine, Star Shape, Red, White, Blue Paint, c.1920, 52 In. 900
Whirligig, Plane, Wood Latticework, Waffleboard, Painted, c.1910, 29 x 28 In. 441
Whirligig, Sailor, Carved, Painted, Tin Flags, Eng., 16 ½ In. 1140

Folk Art, Sand Bottle, Flag, 36 Stars, Eagle, 1886, Verso, Minnie, Flowers, Clemens, 5 ¼ In.
$24,282

Cowan's Auctions

Folk Art, Sign, Officer, Keep Off, Wood, Painted, 19 In.
$246

Cowan's Auctions

TIP

Sculptures should be dusted with a clean, dry paintbrush. Never use water.

Foot Warmer, Punched Tin, Mortised, Pegged, Hinged Door, Wire Latch, Pennsylvania, 6 x 9 In.
$83

Conestoga Auction Co., Inc.

Franciscan, Apple, Plate, Bread & Butter, 6 ⅜ In.
$25

Ruby Lane, Inc.

Franciscan, Apple, Platter, Oval, 14 x 10 In.
$40

Ruby Lane, Inc.

Franciscan, Desert Rose, Berry Bowl, 1940s, 5 ¼ In., 6 Piece
$50

Ruby Lane, Inc.

Whirligig, Wood, Airplane, Prop, Stand, 22 x 12 In.	173
Whistle, Parrot Shape, Redware, Pa., 1800s, 3 ½ In.	176
Woodpecker, Rocking, On Stick, Bird Perched Above, Carved, Painted, c.1920, 16 ½ In.	711

FOOT WARMERS solved the problem of cold feet in past generations. Some warmers held charcoal, others held hot water. Pottery, tin, and soapstone were the favored materials to conduct the heat. The warmer was kept under the feet, then the legs and feet were tucked into a blanket, providing welcome warmth in a cold carriage or church.

Chip Carved, Handle, Engraved JS, 1851, Square	360
Flint Enamel, Rooster Shape, Yellow Brown, c.1870, 12 x 10 In.	177
Punched Tin, Mortised, Pegged, Hinged Door, Wire Latch, Pennsylvania, 6 x 9 In. ....*illus*	83

FOOTBALL *collectibles may be found in the Card and the Sports categories.*

FOSTORIA glass was made in Fostoria, Ohio, from 1887 to 1891. The factory was moved to Moundsville, West Virginia, and most of the glass seen in shops today is a twentieth-century product. The company was sold in 1983; new items will be easily identifiable, according to the new owner, Lancaster Colony Corporation. Additional Fostoria items may be listed in the Milk Glass category.

American, Bottle, Oil, Stopper, 5 Oz.	54
American, Bowl, 2 Handles, Footed, 8 ½ In.	60
American, Bowl, Cupped, 8 x 4 ½ In.	50
American, Bowl, Fruit, Folded, Curved Feet, 10 x 4 In.	49
American, Butter, Cover, Round, Dome Cover, 7 ½ In.	120
American, Cup & Saucer	18
American, Goblet, Hexagonal Foot, 7 In.	18
American, Pitcher, Ice Lip, Footed, 3 Pt., 6 ½ In.	60
American, Plate, Dessert, 8 In.	8
American, Shaker, Glass Top, 3 In.	10
American, Tray, 12 In. Diam.	125
American, Tray, 4 Sections, 9 x 6 In.	53
American, Vase, Footed, Flared, Bud, 9 In.	28
American, Vase, Hat Shape, 4 In.	45
Artichoke, Cake Stand, Clear, Frosted, Up & Down Rim, c.1891, 5 ⅝ x 9 ½ In.	184
Baroque, Bowl, Azure, Handles, 4-Footed, 10 ½ In.	75
Baroque, Bowl, Winged, Azure, Blue, 10 x 9 x 2 In.	250
Baroque, Candleholder, 3-Light, Curves, 5 x 8 In., Pair	73
Baroque, Plate, Azure, 6 In.	9
Baroque, Tidbit, Blue, 3-Toed, 8 In.	38
Betsy Ross, Basket, Peach, 11 ½ In.	54
Betsy Ross, Candlestick, Milk Glass, Paper Label, 3 In., Pair	25
Bouquet, Relish, 3 Sections, 8 In.	53
Century, Bonbon, Footed, 7 ¼ In.	15
Chintz, Bowl, Flared, 12 In.	55
Chintz, Creamer, Footed, 3 ¼ In.	14
Coin Glass, Ashtray, Blue, 4 Coins, Round, 7 ½ In.	35
Coin Glass, Ashtray, Red, 1 Coin, Round, 5 In.	24
Coin Glass, Wedding Bowl, Lid, Amber	60
Coin, Bowl, Ruby, Footed, 8 x 3 In.	28
Coin, Dish, Amber, Lid, Footed, 8 In.	62
Coin, Sugar & Creamer, Ruby Red	75
Colonial Dame, Goblet, Empire Green, 11 Oz., 6 ⅜ In.	16
Colonial Dame, Sherbet, Empire Green Bowl, 4 ⅝ x 6 ½ In.	20
Colony, Bowl, Pickle, Oval, 9 ½ In.	25
Colony, Sugar & Creamer, Individual	25
Colony, Torte Plate, 13 In.	57
Coronet, Bowl, Flared, Etching, Willomere, 12 In.	65
Coronet, Sugar & Creamer, Etching, Willomere	20
Fairfax, Creamer, Footed, Pink, 3 In.	8
Fairfax, Ice Bowl, Tumbler Liner, Green	32
Fairfax, Saucer, Pink	4
Fairfax, Sugar & Creamer, Blue	24
Fairfax, Sugar & Creamer, Topaz, Footed	22
Fascination, Sherbet, Lilac Bowl, 7 Oz., 4 ¾ In.	15
Figurine, Rooster, Chanticleer, 10 In., Pair	294

Florentine, Candlestick, Single Light, 5 ½ In.	45
Grape Brocade, Console, Green, 12 ¾ In.	110
Grape Brocade, Ice Bucket, Green	95
Grape Brocade, Vase, Green, 8 In.	95
Grape Brocade, Vase, Orchid, Bulbous, 4 In.	65
Heather, Tumbler, Footed, 5 Oz., 4 ⅞ In.	18
Heirloom, Bowl, Pink Opalescent, Crimped, 11 In.	40
Heirloom, Bowl, Red, Crimped, 11 In.	65
Heirloom, Bowl, Red, Oblong, 8 In.	30
Heirloom, Candleholder, Bittersweet, 3 ½ In., Pair	50
Heirloom, Console, Slopes, Angles, Spike Rim, Pink Opalescent, 14 x 4 x 4 In.	89
Heirloom, Vase, Blue Opalescent, 9 ½ In.	50
Heirloom, Vase, Pitcher Shape, Red	110
Heritage, Epergne, Lily, Green Opalescent, 5 x 14 In.	250
Hermitage, Tumbler, Cocktail, Blue, 4 Oz., 3 In.	18
Holly, Sherbet, 5 ¾ In., 6 Piece	65
Jamestown, Goblet, Blue, 6 In.	10
Jamestown, Tumbler, Blue, Footed, 11 Oz., 6 In.	18
Jamestown, Tumbler, Pink, Footed, 5 ¾ In.	15
Jenny Lind, Decanter, Milk Glass, 11 ½ In.	57
Lafayette, Cup & Saucer, Wisteria	40
Lafayette, Plate, Wisteria, 7 ½ In.	22
Lafayette, Sugar & Creamer, Regal Blue	55
Lampshade, Flower Shape, Green & Gold Pulled Feather, 4 x 5 In., Pair	188
Layfayette, Sherbet, Wisteria, 5 Oz., 4 ¾ In.	18
Lido, Sherbet, Scepter Stem, 5 ½ In., 5 Piece	50
Line No. 2298, Candlestick, Amber, 3 ½ In., Pair	45
Line No. 2373, Vase, Window, Flower Frog Lid, Green Transparent, Large	95
Line No. 2443, Ice Tub, Pink	55
Line No. 5097, Goblet, Water, Pink, Crystal Twist Stem, 9 Oz., 7 ¼ In.	24
Line No. 6007, Goblet, Wisteria, Loop Optic Bowl, 10 Oz., 7 ½ In.	60
Line No. 6007, Sherbet, Wisteria, Tall, 5 ½ Oz., 5 ⅜ In.	40
Line No. 6007, Whiskey, Wisteria, Loop Optic Bowl	45
Manor, Bonbon, Topaz, Mayfair, 6 ½ In.	32
Manor, Vase, Green, Etched, 9 In.	400
Mayfair, Plate, Topaz, 7 In.	10
Mayfair, Soup, Cream, Green, Etched Minuet	45
Mayfair, Sugar & Creamer, Empire Green	69
Meadow Rose, Sugar & Creamer	35
Mesa, Goblet, Ruby Bowl, Footed, 13 Oz.	18
Mt. Vernon, Creamer, Cobalt Blue, 5 In.	12
Navarre, Plate, Luncheon, 8 In.	12
Navarre, Sugar & Creamer	55
Palm Leaf Brocade, Candlestick, Rose Pink, 3-Toed	70
Priscilla, Bouillon, Blue	18
Priscilla, Creamer, Amber	10
Priscilla, Creamer, Blue	15
Priscilla, Custard Cup, Green, Handles, Footed, 6 Oz., 4 In.	30
Priscilla, Jug, Green, Footed, 9 ¾ In.	90
Rambler, Nut Dish, Handles, 2 Section, 8 ¼ x 1 ½ In.	32
Romance, Tray, Handle, 11 ½ In.	50
Royal, Plate, Soup, Blue, Etching, 8 ½ In.	50
Spool, Ashtray, 5, 4 & 3 In., 3 Piece	18
Strawholder, Zipper Glass, Scalloped Rim & Foot, Arched Lid, Fan Finial, 11 ½ In.	272
Sunglow, Sherbet, Gilt Trim, 5 ¼ In.	12
Trojan, Bowl, Topaz, Scroll Handle, 10 In.	235
Trojan, Candlestick, Topaz, 3-Legged, 2 In.	35
Trojan, Creamer, Topaz	22
Trojan, Ice Bucket, Topaz, Handle	125
Trojan, Plate, Canape, Rose, 6 ¼ In.	20
Trojan, Plate, Topaz, 2 Handles, 7 In.	25
Trojan, Platter, 12 In.	95
Trojan, Sugar & Creamer, Topaz	115
Verona, Candlestick, Amber, Scroll, 5 In., Pair	75
Victorian, Goblet, Cordial, Regal Blue, 1 Oz., 3 ⅛ In.	55
Victorian, Goblet, Water, Empire Green, 10 Oz., 5 ¾ In.	35

Franciscan, Desert Rose, Plate, Salad, 1940s, 8 In.
$14

Ruby Lane, Inc.

Franciscan, Desert Rose, Teapot, Lid, 4 ½ In., 4 Cup
$90

Ruby Lane, Inc.

Franciscan, Duet, Cruet Set, Oil & Vinegar, Stoppers, 7 ¾ In., 2 Piece
$52

Ruby Lane, Inc.

Franciscan, Forget-Me-Not, Platter, Oval, 11 ½ In.
$32

Ruby Lane, Inc.

Franciscan, Ivy, Salt & Pepper, 2 ½ In.
$24

Ruby Lane, Inc.

Franciscan, Mariposa, Platter, Oval,
12 ½ In.
$96

Ruby Lane, Inc.

Franciscan, Maytime, Gravy Boat,
Attached Underplate, c.1965
$16

Ruby Lane, Inc.

Victorian, Plate, Luncheon, Empire Green, 8 ⅝ In.	12
Victorian, Tumbler, Iced Tea, Empire Green, 12 Oz., 5 ½ In.	35
Virginia, Candy Dish, Lid, Footed, Finial, 5 x 4 In.	63
Wedding Bells, Toothpick Holder	16
Willowmere, Bowl, Flared Coronet, 12 In.	65
Wisteria, Candlestick, 2-Light, Alexandrite, 7 x 5 In., Pair	100

FOVAL, *see Fry category.*

FRAMES *are included in the Furniture category under Frame.*

FRANCISCAN is a trademark that appears on pottery. Gladding, McBean and Company started in 1875. The company grew and acquired other potteries. It made sewer pipes, floor tiles, dinnerware, and art pottery with a variety of trademarks. It began using the trade name *Franciscan* in 1934. In 1936, dinnerware and art pottery were sold under the name *Franciscan Ware.* The company made china and cream-colored, decorated earthenware. Desert Rose, Apple, El Patio, and Coronado were best sellers. The company became Interpace Corporation and in 1979 was purchased by Josiah Wedgwood & Sons. The plant was closed in 1984, but a few of the patterns are still being made. For more prices, go to kovels.com.

Acacia, Chop Plate, 13 ⅜ In.	69
Acacia, Cup & Saucer, Footed	6 to 9
Acacia, Plate, Bread & Butter, 6 ⅜ In.	8 to 9
Acacia, Plate, Salad, 8 ⅜ In.	7
Acacia, Teapot, Lid, 4 Cup, 5 ⅞ In.	128
Alpine Meadow, Cup & Saucer	8
Alpine Meadow, Plate, Dinner, 10 In.	9
Apple, Plate, Bread & Butter, 6 ⅜ In. *illus*	25
Apple, Platter, 14 ½ In.	30
Apple, Platter, Oval, 14 x 10 In. *illus*	40
Apple, Server, 3 Tiers, 1950s, 14 ½ In.	125
Appleton, Plate, Bread & Butter, 6 ⅜ In.	12
Appleton, Platter, Oval, 12 In.	68
Applique, Cup & Saucer	11
Applique, Plate, Bread & Butter, 6 ¼ In.	9
Arden, Bowl, Vegetable, Oval, 9 In.	58
Arden, Chop Plate, 13 In.	83
Arden, Cup & Saucer, Footed	34
Arden, Gravy Boat, Underplate	59 to 63
Arden, Plate, Dinner, 10 ⅝ In.	14
Ariel, Cup & Saucer, Footed	12
Ariel, Plate, Bead & Butter, 6 ¼ In.	7
Autumn, Platter, Oval, 16 ½ x 12 ½ In.	48
Blue Fancy, Plate, Dinner, 10 ¼ In.	11
Brentwood, Creamer, 8 Oz., 2 ½ In.	14
Brentwood, Cup & Saucer	8
Canton, Chop Plate, 13 In.	85
Canton, Coffeepot, Lid, 5 Cup, 7 ⅜ In.	142
Canton, Cup & Saucer	13
Canton, Gravy Boat, 3 ¼ In.	59
Canton, Plate, Dessert, 8 ¼ In.	9
Canton, Plate, Dinner, 10 ½ In.	41
Canton, Platter, Oval, 16 In.	129 to 138
Capri, Cup & Saucer	8
Capri, Gravy Boat	48
Capri, Plate, Dinner, 10 ⅜ In.	11
Capri, Platter, Oval, 15 In.	58
Claremont, Bowl, Dessert, 6 ¼ In.	23
Claremont, Bowl, Vegetable, Oval, 9 In.	104
Claremont, Chop Plate, 13 In.	138
Claremont, Cup & Saucer, Footed	7 to 8
Claremont, Plate, Dinner, 10 ⅝ In.	21
Claremont, Platter, Oval, 16 In.	118
Corinthian, Creamer, 10 Oz., 4 In.	47
Corinthian, Plate, Bread & Butter, 6 ⅛ In.	14
Corinthian, Plate, Dinner, 10 ¾ In.	33

Desert Rose, Berry Bowl, 1940s, 5 ¼ In., 6 Piece	*illus*	50
Desert Rose, Cup & Saucer		9 to 15
Desert Rose, Grill Plate, 10 ¾ In.		30
Desert Rose, Plate, Dinner, 10 ⅝ In.		18
Desert Rose, Plate, Salad, 1940s, 8 In.	*illus*	14
Desert Rose, Serving Bowl, 2 Sections, 10 ½ x 7 In.		39
Desert Rose, Sugar & Creamer		32
Desert Rose, Syrup, 6 ¼ In.		40
Desert Rose, Teapot, Lid, 4 ½ In., 4 Cup	*illus*	90
Duet, Butter, Cover		22
Duet, Cruet Set, Oil & Vinegar, Stoppers, 7 ¾ In., 2 Piece	*illus*	52
Echo, Ashtray, 4 ¾ In.		4
Echo, Bowl, Vegetable, Divided, Oval, 13 In.		17
Echo, Casserole, Lid, Individual, c.1950, Pair		25
Echo, Pitcher, 28 Oz., 8 ¼ In.		16
Echo, Relish, 12 In.		12
El Patio, Gravy Boat, Underplate, Attached, Aqua, 1950s		40
Forget-Me-Not, Cup & Saucer		10
Forget-Me-Not, Plate, Bread & Butter, 6 ½ In.		23
Forget-Me-Not, Plate, Dinner, 10 ⅝ In.		48
Forget-Me-Not, Platter, Oval, 11 ½ In.	*illus*	32
Glenfield, Bowl, Dessert, 4 ⅝ In.		9
Glenfield, Cup & Saucer		8
Glenfield, Relish, 3 Sections, Metal Stand		36
Glenfield, Sugar & Creamer		24
Granada, Cup & Saucer, Footed		13
Granada, Plate, Bread & Butter, 6 ⅜ In.		8
Granada, Plate, Dinner, 10 ⅝ In.		17
Hacienda Gold, Pitcher, 1970s, 9 In.		14
Heritage, Plate, Dinner, 10 ⅜ In.		14
Heritage, Sugar, Lid		21
Homeland, Plate, Bread & Butter, 6 ⅞ In.		8
Homeland, Plate, Dinner, 10 In.		25
Ivy, Butter, Cover, ¼ Lb.		22
Ivy, Cup & Saucer		30
Ivy, Gravy Boat, Underplate, Attached, 9 x 6 In.		29
Ivy, Salt & Pepper, 2 ½ In.	*illus*	24
Malaya, Bowl, Vegetable, Oval, 9 In.		23
Malaya, Creamer		18
Malaya, Cup & Saucer, Footed		7
Malaya, Gravy Boat		30
Malaya, Plate, Bread & Butter, 6 ⅜ In.		6
Malaya, Plate, Salad, 8 ⅛ In.		7
Malaya, Platter, Oval, 12 In.		29
Mandarin, Soup, Dish, 6 ⅜ In.		10
Mariposa, Platter, Oval, 12 ½ In.	*illus*	96
Maytime, Gravy Boat, Attached Underplate, c.1965	*illus*	16
Montego, Bowl, Vegetable, Round, 9 In.		35
Montego, Casserole, Lid, 3 Qt., 9 ¾ In.		98
Montego, Creamer, 12 Oz.		15
Montego, Platter, Oval, 13 In.		22 to 23
Montego, Soup, Dish, 7 In.		7
Moon Glow, Sugar & Creamer		45
Newport, Cup & Saucer, Footed		8
Newport, Plate, Bread & Butter, 6 ⅜ In.		7
Newport, Plate, Dinner, 10 ⅜ In.		15
October, Gravy Boat, Attached Underplate, 6 x 4 In.		42
October, Platter, 14 In.		48
Petalpoint, Cup & Saucer, Footed		15
Pickwick, Bowl, Vegetable, Divided, Oval, 11 In.		25 to 26
Pickwick, Creamer, 10 Oz.		10
Pickwick, Plate, Bread & Butter, 6 In.		4
Pickwick, Plate, Dinner, 10 ⅜ In.		11
Pickwick, Platter, Oval, 13 In.		12
Pickwick, Platter, Oval, 15 In.		23
Poppy, Chop Plate, 12 In.		67

F

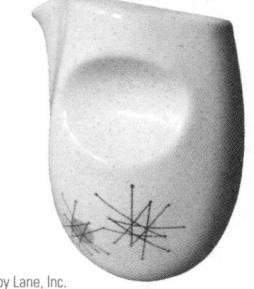

Franciscan, Starburst, Creamer, 4 In.
$23

Ruby Lane, Inc.

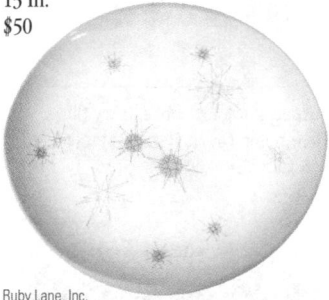

Franciscan, Starburst, Platter, Oval, 13 In.
$50

Ruby Lane, Inc.

Fraternal, Kiwanis, Pin, Past Vice President, 14K Gold, Enamel, Screwback, Marked, Lapel
$45

Ruby Lane, Inc.

Fraternal, Knights Of Pythias, Belt Buckle, Slide Sword Hanger, Nickel, c.1900, 2 ¼ x 1 ¼ In., Pair
$48

Fraternal, Masonic, Watch Fob, Presentation, 14K Gold, Hinged, 1 ¼ x ¾ In.
$1,763

Fulper, Bowl, Artichoke, Ivory Glaze, Flemington Green Flambe, Marked, 5 ½ x 8 ½ In.
$826

Vasekraft

The Fulper Pottery began making its Vasekraft art ware line in 1909. This pottery had classical and new glazes: best-known were Mirror Glaze, a high-gloss, crystalline glaze; Mission Matte, a brown-black glaze with shaded greens; and the expensive rose shades.

Radiance, Casserole, Lid, Round, 1 ½ Qt., 7 In.		78
Regency, Bowl, Salad, 6 ⅛ In.		16
Regency, Platter, Oval, 12 In.		37
Rose Trellis, Bowl, Vegetable, Divided, Oval, 9 In.		33
Rose Trellis, Creamer, 3 ½ In.		15
Rose Trellis, Cup & Saucer, Footed		13
Rose Trellis, Plate, Bread & Butter, 6 ½ In.		3
Rose Trellis, Platter, Oval, 16 In.		47
Rose Trellis, Sugar, Lid, 3 In.		20
Shasta, Chop Plate, 13 In.		98
Shasta, Cup & Saucer		14
Shasta, Plate, Bread & Butter, 6 ⅜ In.		11
Shasta, Plate, Dinner, 10 ½ In.		39
Shasta, Platter, Oval, 16 In.		127
Silver Mist, Bowl, Vegetable, Oval, 9 In.		33
Silver Mist, Cup & Saucer		7
Silver Mist, Gravy Boat, Attached Underplate		49
Silver Mist, Plate, Dinner, 10 ½ In.		10
Silver Mist, Relish, 3 Sections		47
Snow Pine, Cup & Saucer		16
Snow Pine, Gravy Boat, Underplate		69
Snow Pine, Platter, Oval, 12 In.		45
Starburst, Creamer, 4 In.	*illus*	23
Starburst, Cup & Saucer, c.1955		19
Starburst, Platter, Oval, 13 In.	*illus*	50
Tahoe, Plate, Bread & Butter, 6 ⅜ In.		6
Tara, Cup & Saucer, Footed		12
Tara, Sugar, Lid		18
Teak, Bowl, Dessert, 4 ⅞ In.		94
Teak, Bowl, Vegetable, Oval, 8 In.		37
Teak, Cup & Saucer		9
Teak, Platter, Oval, 16 In.		138
Teak, Relish, 3 Sections		118
Tiempo, Teapot, Square, Olive Green, 5 ½ In.		45
Topaz, Butter, Cover, ¼ Lb.		21
Topaz, Coffeepot, Lid, 5 Cup		28
Topaz, Creamer, 2 ½ In.		10
Topaz, Plate, Dinner, 10 ⅜ In.		10
Waterfall, Cup & Saucer, Footed		12
Westwood, Bowl, Vegetable, Oval, Footed, 9 In.		78
Westwood, Coffeepot, Lid, 3 Cup, 6 ½ In.		55
Westwood, Creamer, 2 ⅝ In.		14
Westwood, Cup & Saucer		9 to 11
Westwood, Plate, Bread & Butter, 6 ⅜ In.		8
Westwood, Plate, Dinner, 10 ½ In.		26
Westwood, Plate, Salad, 8 ⅜ In.		18
Westwood, Salt & Pepper		47
Wildflower, Ashtray, 3 ⅞ In.		108
Wildflower, Bowl, Vegetable, Round, 9 In.		209
Wildflower, Casserole, Lid, 10 ¼ x 5 ¾ In.		679
Wildflower, Cup & Saucer		74
Wildflower, Pitcher, 64 Oz., 8 ½ In.		679
Wildflower, Plate, Bread & Butter, 6 ⅜ In.		27
Wildflower, Plate, Dinner, 10 ⅝ In.		104
Wildflower, Relish, 12 ¼ In.		178
Wildflower, Teapot, Lid, 5 Cup, 4 ¾ In.		869
Woodside, Teapot, Lid, 5 In.		142

FRANKART INC., New York, New York, mass-produced nude "dancing lady" lamps, ashtrays, and other decorative Art Deco items in the 1920s and 1930s. They were made of white lead composition and spray-painted. *Frankart Inc.* and the patent number and year were stamped on the base.

Bookends, Nude On Book, Spelter, Painted, 10 In.		750
Bookends, Nudes, Kneeling In Circle Of Leaves, Cast Iron, Ivory, Painted, 5 x 6 In.		200
Candleholder, Nude, On Base, Holding Knees, Looking Up, Green Metal, 4 In., Pair		550

Centerpiece, 2 Nude Women, Kneeling, Inset Fulper Bowl, Green Glaze, 6 ½ x 14 In.	1062
Figurine, Nude, Bucket On Shoulder, 1922, 12 In.	525
Lamp, Art Deco, Base Metal Nude Woman, On Slag Green Panel, Metal Base, Signed, 10 In.	590
Lamp, Nude, Kneeling, Holding Tray, Marked, 1934, 16 In.	425
Nude Nymph, Brass, Holding Bowl, 8 ½ In.	275
Nude Woman, Black, Holding Globe, 1922, 10 In.	249

FRANKOMA POTTERY was originally known as The Frank Potteries when John F. Frank opened shop in 1933. The factory is now working in Sapulpa, Oklahoma. Early wares were made from a light cream-colored clay from Ada, Oklahoma, but in 1956 the company switched to a red clay from Sapulpa. The firm made dinnerware, utilitarian and decorative kitchenwares, figurines, flowerpots, and limited edition and commemorative pieces. John Frank died in 1973 and his daughter, Joniece, inherited the business. Frankoma went bankrupt in 1990. The pottery operated under various owners for a few years and was bought by Joe Ragosta in 2008. It closed in 2010. The buildings, assets, name, and molds were sold at an auction in 2011.

Bean Pot, Lazy Bones, 2 Qt.	30
Bowl, Cereal, Oklahoma Plainsman, Brown Satin, 5 ⅝ In.	7
Bowl, Cereal, Oklahoma Plainsman, Woodland Moss, 5 ¾ In.	12
Bowl, Cereal, Wagon Wheel, Green, 5 ¼ In.	12
Bowl, Fruit, Wagon Wheel, Desert Gold	4
Bowl, Vegetable, Wagon Wheel, Desert Gold, 2 Sections, 13 ½ In.	35
Cup, Wagon Wheel, Green	6
Dish, Vegetable, Wagon Wheel, Desert Gold, Divided, 13 ½ In.	35
Figurine, Fan Dancer, Green Glaze Over Caramel, 8 ¼ x 13 ¼ In.	431
Honey Pot, Lazy Bones, 5 ⅝ In.	15
Mug, Oklahoma Plainsman, Brown	22
Platter, Oklahoma Plainsman, Desert Gold, 11 ¼ In.	28
Salt & Pepper, Oklahoma Plainsman, Brown Satin	21

FRATERNAL objects that are related to the many different fraternal organizations in the United States are listed in this category. The Elks, Masons, Odd Fellows, and others are included. Also included are service organizations, like the American Legion, Kiwanis, and Lions Club. Furniture is listed in the Furniture category. Shaving mugs decorated with fraternal crests are included in the Shaving Mug category.

Eagles, Parade Hat, 4th Of July, Fabric, Sequins, Feathers, Mixed Media, 22 x 36 In.	150
Elks, Keno Goose, Wire Cage, Wood Base, Sandpoint, Id., c.1940, 12 x 5 x 12 In.	30
Foresters Of America, Ax, Wood, Painted, Multicolor, Court Quaboag 172, 1900, 29 In.	780
International Brotherhood Of Magicians, Button, Blue, Orange, Symbols, 1930s, 2 ¼ In.	86
Junior Order Of United American Machinists, Shaving Mug, Flags, H.C. Heck, Gilt, 4 In.	60
Kiwanis, Pin, Past Vice President, 14K Gold, Enamel, Screwback, Marked, Lapel ....*illus*	45
Knights Of Pythias, Belt Buckle, Slide Sword Hanger, Nickel, c.1900, 2 ¼ x 1 ¼ In., Pair ..*illus*	48
Masonic, Apron, Collar, Star, Moon, Sun, Embroidery, Silk, c.1800, 15 ½ x 14 In.	4063
Masonic, Apron, Symbols, Painted, Kidskin, Gen. P. Muhlenbergs, c.1870, 17 x 22 In.	4688
Masonic, Bowl, Science Scenes, Chinese, 11 ⅝ In. Diam.	938
Masonic, Fire Bucket, Leather, Hands Clasped, Friendship In Adversity, J. Beach, No. 2, 12 In.	2252
Masonic, Jug, Bees, Eagle Transfer Symbols, Lobed, White Porcelain, Gilt, c.1845, 7 ½ In.	938
Masonic, Jug, Stoneware, Coggle Wheel Circle, Emblems, Handle, J.F. Brower, Gal., 12 In.	472
Masonic, Pendant, Compass & Protractor, Silver, Engraved, Gilt Brass, Jeweled, 5 ¼ In.	840
Masonic, Pendant, Silver Gilt, Engraved, Jeweled, Swampscott Chapter, c.1927, 6 In.	1080
Masonic, Pin, Plaque, Suspended Head, Bearded, Horns, Wreath, Gold, Enamel, 1937, 3 In.	720
Masonic, Pin, Tin, Annual Meeting Of Aleppo Temple 1909, Man In Hat, 3 In.	540
Masonic, Pitcher, Symbols, Black Transfer, Cream Ground, Liverpool, c.1850, 10 ¾ In.	960
Masonic, Presentation Piece, Behold How Good & Pleasant, 1800s, 27 x 24 In.	448
Masonic, Ribbon, C. & J. Of Am, Labor Day, Local No. 1070, Black, White, 5 In.	15
Masonic, Sign, Love, Purity, Fidelity, Triangular, Painted, 14 x 16 In.	840
Masonic, Watch Fob, Presentation, 14K Gold, Hinged, 1 ¼ x ¾ In. ....*illus*	1763
Odd Fellows, Apron, 3-Link Chain, Bible, Branch, Leather, Henry Kelly, c.1860, 16 x 16 In.	316
Odd Fellows, Ax, Wood, Carved, Calumet Lodge, No. 279, 1800s, 34 In.	330
Odd Fellows, Bedspread, Presentation, Quilted, Names, Embroidered, c.1902, 81 x 69 In.	86
Odd Fellows, Covenant Ark, Gold, Red Paint, Cutout Gallery, c.1900, 15 x 58 In.	450
Odd Fellows, Lodge Sign, Oval, Chamfered, 3-Link Chain, Gold FLT Letters, 21 x 37 In.	780
Odd Fellows, Match Safe, Symbols, Metal, Hendrick Hudson Hotel, N.Y.	117
Odd Fellows, Paddle, Initiation, The Pettibone, Wood, 26 In.	59
Odd Fellows, Pedestal, Triangular, c.1900, 31 x 27 In.	173
Odd Fellows, Staff, Owl Terminal, Carved, c.1830, 71 ½ In.	652

F

Fulper, Doorstop, Dog, French Bulldog, Bum, Glazed, 1910s, 8 x 9 ½ In.
$1,375

Rago Arts & Auction Center

Fulper, Flower Frog, Woman In Canoe, Green Matte Glaze, Marked, 3 ¾ x 7 ½ In.
$83

Humler & Nolan

Fulper, Jar, Pedestal, Cucumber Green Crystalline Glaze, Racetrack Mark, c.1920, 11 x 10 In.
$4,063

Rago Arts & Auction Center

Fulper, Lamp, Mushroom Shade, Leaded Glass, Cat's-Eye Flambe, Vasekraft, c.1908, 17 x 14 In.
$9,375

Rago Arts & Auction Center

Furniture, Armoire, Aesthetic Revival, Maple, Faux Bamboo, Mirror, Drawer, c.1880, 96 In.
$717

Neal Auction Co.

Furniture, Armoire, Arts & Crafts, English Oak, Mirror, Smee & Cobay, c.1900, 73 x 49 In.
$3,690

Skinner Auctioneers & Appraisers

Shriners, Cup, Glass, Gilt Lettering, Al Koran Temple, Cleveland, Ohio, 1913, 4 ½ In.	12
Shriners, Pin, Scimitar With Crescent, 14K White Gold, Pave Diamonds, 3 In.	2106

FRY GLASS was made by the H.C. Fry Glass Company of Rochester, Pennsylvania. The company, founded in 1901, first made cut glass and other types of fine glasswares. In 1922 it patented a heat-resistant glass called Pearl Ovenglass. For two years, 1926–1927, the company made Fry Foval, an opal ware decorated with colored trim. Reproductions of this glass have been made. Depression glass patterns made by Fry may be listed in the Depression Glass category. Some pieces of cut glass may also be included in the Cut Glass category.

FRY GLASS

Bowl, Petal Footed, Swirl Connector, Green, Flair Rim, 10 x 5 In.	295
Bowl, Poppy, Banana Boat, Pointed Rim, 11 ½ x 5 ½ x 6 ½ In.	75
Dish, Diamond Points & Fans, Maple Leaf Shape, Star Center, Marked, 9 In.	81
Glass, Tumbler, Black Amethyst, Petal Foot, 4 Oz., 8 Piece	35
Goblet, Wide Optic, Cobalt Blue, Crystal Threaded Spiral Stem, Foot, 10 Oz., 7 ⅝ In.	30
Platter, Pearl Opalescent, Flower Border, Engraved, 1920s, 12 x 17 In.	65
Reamer, Opalescent, Tab Handle, 7 x 7 x 2 In.	100
Tumbler, Black Petal Foot, 5 Oz., 3 In.	5
Vase, Bubbles, Gold Threading, Cylindrical, 10 In.	90
Vase, Stemmed Flowers, Veins, Dental Cut Rim, Cylindrical, 10 In.	118

FRY FOVAL

Atomizer, Engraved, Diamond, Jade Green Foot, 1920s, 8 In.	299
Casserole, Lid, Opalescent, Ovenglass, Oval, Metal Holder, 11 x 3 In.	75
Cup & Saucer, Jade Trim	125
Grill Plate, Opalescent, Ovenglass, 3 Sections, c.1925, 10 In.	50
Pitcher, Lid, Jade Handle, Finial, c.1925, 9 ½ In.	395
Sherbet, Underplate, Jade Green Stem, 3 ⅝ In.	149

FULPER POTTERY COMPANY was incorporated in 1899 in Flemington, New Jersey. It made art pottery from 1909 to 1929. The firm had been making bottles, jugs, and housewares from 1805. Doll heads were made about 1928. The firm became Stangl Pottery in 1929. Stangl Pottery is listed in its own category in this book.

Basket, Leaves Lid, Green Glaze Bowl, Relief Flowers, Handle, 1920s, 9 In.	69
Basket, Lid, Handle, Multicolor, 9 In.	76
Bookends, Garland, Woman, Seated, Full Pale Blue Skirt, Holding Garland, 1920s, 7 In., Pair	92
Bowl, Artichoke, Ivory Glaze, Flemington Green Flambe, Marked, 5 ½ x 8 ½ In. *illus*	826
Bowl, Blue Flambe Interior, Brown Matte Exterior, 3 x 6 ¾ In.	175
Bowl, Blue Flambe, Footed, 4 ½ x 9 ¾ In.	175
Bowl, Chinese Blue Flambe, Flared, 9 ¾ In.	150
Bowl, Fish, Green & Ivory Glaze, Stamped, Flemington, N.J., 2 ¾ x 11 In.	1063
Bowl, Flared, Blue Matte Glaze, 6 ¾ x 2 ¾ In.	69
Bowl, Lid, Peaked Hump, Multicolor Molded Flowers, Leaves, Green Ground, 1920s, 6 ¾ In.	34
Bowl, Triangular, Cat's-Eye Flambe, Marked, 1 ¾ x 4 ½ In.	165
Candleholder, Rounded, c.1935, 10 ¾ In.	395
Candy Jar, Lid, Woman, Kneeling, Orange Slip, Brown Hair, Black, 1920s, 8 In.	207
Compote, Aztec Blue, 3 Figural Supports, 10 ¾ x 7 ½ In.	424
Doorstop, Chinese Sleeping Cat, Flambe, Marked, 5 ⅛ x 9 ¾ In.	1380
Doorstop, Dog, French Bulldog, Bum, Glazed, 1910s, 8 x 9 ½ In. *illus*	1375
Flower Frog, Lotus Shape, Blue-Green Glaze, Signed, 4 x 4 In.	68
Flower Frog, Woman In Canoe, Green Matte Glaze, Marked, 3 ¾ x 7 ½ In. *illus*	83
Jar, Lid, Butterscotch Flambe, 7 ½ x 5 ¼ In.	245
Jar, Pedestal, Cucumber Green Crystalline Glaze, Racetrack Mark, c.1920, 11 x 10 In. *illus*	4063
Jar, Temple, Flemington Blue Flambe Glaze, Racetrack Mark, 1916-22, 11 ¾ x 8 ½ In.	813
Jug, Flower, Copper Dust Crystalline Glaze, Incised Racetrack Mark, 1916-1922, 12 x 8 In.	1500
Lamp, 2-Light, Vasekraft, Cafe Au Lait, Cucumber Glaze, Leaded Glass, c.1908, 23 x 16 In.	11250
Lamp, Dancing Dutch Girl, Purple White Stripe Bodice, Holding Purple Skirt, 1920s, 8 In.	127
Lamp, Mushroom Shade, Leaded Glass, Cat's-Eye Flambe, Vasekraft, c.1908, 17 x 14 In. *illus*	9375
Lamp, Perfume, Ballerina, Deep Bow, Blue Tutu, 1920s, 6 In., Pair	230
Lamp, Perfume, Ballerina, Deep Bow, Orange Tutu, Black Hair, 1920s, 4 In.	127
Lamp, Perfume, Cardinal, Red Feathers, Pink Rock Perch, 1920s, 8 ¼ In.	230
Lamp, Perfume, Parrot, Red, Yellow Plumage, Round Black Perch, 1920s, 12 ½ In.	184 to 230
Lamp, Perfume, Woman, Cytherea, Yellow, Purple Dress, Gold Hair Accent, 1920s, 11 In.	374
Lamp, Perfume, Woman, Nude, White Bisque, 2 Parts, 1920s, 10 ¾ In.	288
Lamp, Powder Jar, Mademoiselle, Woman, Seated, Holding Fan, Pink Skirt, 1920s, 7 In., Pair	230
Lamp, Woman, 1800s Curled Upswept Hair, Orange Dress, Bisque Body, 1920s, 12 In.	127

F

Lamp, Woman, Antebellum, Demure, Blue, White, c.1925, 12 In.	115 to 207
Lamp, Woman, Seated, Hands To Crossed Knees, Orange Hat, Black Hair, 1920s, 6 ⅜ In., Pair....	345
Lamp, Woman, The Mask, Harlequin, Flapper, Mask, Green Dress, 1920s, 13 In.	173
Lamp, Woman, The Mask, Harlequin, Flapper, Mask, Orange Dress, 1920s, 13 In.	288
Lamp, Woman, The Mask, Harlequin, Flapper, Mask, Yellow Dress, 1920s, 13 In.	207
Pitcher, Blue Matte Glaze, 4 In.	12
Sugar & Creamer, Green Flambe Glaze, c.1915, 3 In.	188
Urn, Blue Crystalline Glaze, Knobby Handles, Incised Racetrack Mark, 12 x 8 ½ In.	2000
Urn, Cafe Au Lait Glaze, 4-Footed, Racetrack Stamp, 1916-22, 16 ½ x 5 ¾ In.	563
Urn, Cat's-Eye Flambe Glaze, Flared Rim, Pedestal, 6 In.	245
Urn, Cat's-Eye Glaze, Hammered, Handles, c.1920, 12 x 8 In.	688
Urn, Green Crystalline Glaze, Stamped, Flemington, N.J., c.1915, 12 x 8 ½ In.	1000
Urn, Leopard Skin Glaze, Crystalline Glaze, Hammered, Green, c.1918, 13 x 14 ½ In.	594
Urn, Royal Blue, Famille Rose Glaze, 4 Handles, c.1920, 13 x 12 In.	813
Vase, Bell Pepper Shape, Blue Green Matte Glaze, 4 ¼ In.	402
Vase, Blue Crystalline Glaze, Flared Rim, Tapered Bulbous Base, Marked, c.1926, 12 x 18 In.	688
Vase, Blue, Crystalline, Tapered, Mark, 7 x 4 ½ In.	180
Vase, Blue Matte Glaze, Copperdust Crystalline Flambe Drip, Narrow Neck, 8 In.	142
Vase, Blue, Marked Rafco, 3 ¾ In.	46
Vase, Brown Crystalline Glaze, 2 Handles, Stamped Signature, 9 ¼ In.	1003
Vase, Brown, Blue, Pink Flambe Glaze, 8 x 7 ½ In.	625
Vase, Bulbous, Textured, Green Matte Glaze, Marked, 7 x 8 In.	400
Vase, Bullet, Green Flambe, Over Rose Glaze, Marked, 6 ¾ In.	81
Vase, Cat's-Eye Flambe Glaze, Ink Racetrack Stamp, 14 x 6 ½ In.	1875
Vase, Chinese Blue Flambe Glaze, Incised, Flemington, N.J., c.1922, 1 ½ x 8 ½ In.	1750
Vase, Chinese Blue Flambe, Shouldered, 6 ¾ x 7 ¾ In.	138
Vase, Crystalline Green, Prang Marked, 4 ⅜ In.	109
Vase, Faceted, Mottled Green, Flemington, c.1918, 9 ¾ In.	330
Vase, Flemington Green Glaze, Bulbous Base, 15 In.	345
Vase, Floor, Green Crystalline Glaze, Shouldered, 12 x 33 In.	3625
Vase, Frothy Chinese Blue Flambe Glaze, Squat, Ink Stamp, c.1910, 8 x 10 In.	938
Vase, Green Flambe, Bottle Neck, 8 ½ In.	2006
Vase, Green, Blue, High Brown Handles, 7 ½ x 10 In.	104
Vase, Green, Blue, Red Flambe, Handles, Signed, 7 x 8 In.	688
Vase, Handles, Turquoise, 7 ¾ x 11 In.	185
Vase, Leopard Skin Crystalline Glaze, Handles, Racetrack Stamp, 6 ¼ In.	177
Vase, Light Purple Flambe, Shouldered, Tapered, 7 ⅜ In.	58
Vase, Mirrored Black Glaze, Incised Racetrack Mark, 1916-22, 17 x 7 In.	2875
Vase, Moss To Rose, Stepped Squat Shape, 3 ⅞ x 6 ½ In.	138
Vase, Mottled Blue & Green Shaded To Pink, Round, Cylindrical Neck, c.1920, 10 In.	460
Vase, Oval, Speckled Brown, Green, 12 x 7 In.	232
Vase, Tapered, Blue Luster, Amphora, 11 ¾ In.	184
Vase, Trophy Shape, Cat's-Eye Flambe, Handles, 8 ¼ x 7 In.	215
Vase, Turquoise, Rolled Rim, Round, Tapered, 5 ¼ In.	92
Vase, Venetian Blue Glaze, Raised Racetrack Mark, c.1916-22, 17 x 9 In.	688
Vase, Violet Glaze, Ball Shape, Raised Rim, 3 Loop Handles, 6 ½ In.	259
Vase, Wisteria Glaze, Shaded Lavender, Tapered, Marked, 6 ¾ In.	36
Vase, Wisteria Purple, Round, 3 Handles, Marked, 6 ½ x 8 ½ In.	75

FURNITURE of all types is listed in this category. Examples dating from the seventeenth century to the 1970s are included. Prices for furniture vary in different parts of the country. Oak furniture is most expensive in the West; large pieces over eight feet high are sold for the most money in the South, where high ceilings are found in the old homes. Condition is very important when determining prices. These are NOT average prices but rather reports of unique sales. If the description includes the word *style*, the piece resembles the old furniture style but was made at a later time. It is not a period piece. Small chests that sat on a table or dresser are also included here. Garden furniture is listed in the Garden Furnishings category. Related items may be found in the Architectural, Brass, and Store categories.

Armchairs are listed under Chair in this category.

Armoire, Aesthetic Revival, Maple, Faux Bamboo, Mirror, Drawer, c.1880, 96 In. ....*illus*	717
Armoire, Arts & Crafts, English Oak, Mirror, Smee & Cobay, c.1900, 73 x 49 In. ....*illus*	3690
Armoire, Arts & Crafts, Oak, Copper, Overhang, Mirrored Door, P.E. Gane, 85 x 47 In.	3000
Armoire, Biedermeier, Mahogany, Side Columns, 2 Graduated Panel Doors, 87 x 45 In.	625
Armoire, Biedermeier, Walnut, Burl Recess Panel Door, 68 x 41 In., Pair.	1500
Armoire, Edwardian, Walnut, Molded Cornice, Arch Mirror Door, c.1890, 80 x 49 In.	369

Furniture, Armoire, Neoclassical, Inlay, Doors, Dentil Cornice, 113 x 95 In. $1,625

Leslie Hindman Auctioneers

Furniture, Armoire, Provincial Louis XV Style, Cherry, Panels, c.1835, 97 x 61 In. $1,230

New Orleans Auction Galleries, Inc.

Furniture, Bar Cart, Terrestrial Globe, Hinged Lid, Fitted Interior, c.1980, 39 x 28 In. $390

Garth's Auctioneers & Appraisers

Furniture, Bed, Dog's, French Provincial, Canopy, Low Posts, Carved, c.1800, 29 x 25 In.
$1,722

New Orleans Auction Galleries, Inc.

Furniture, Bed, Hired-Man's, Hewn & Carved Posts, Later Webbing, 1800s, 27 ½ x 74 In.
$240

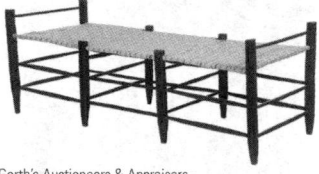

Garth's Auctioneers & Appraisers

Furniture, Bench, G. Nakashima, Black Walnut, Hickory, Signed, 1983, 32 x 90 x 33 In.
$35,000

Rago Arts & Auction Center

Furniture, Bookstand, Display, Oak, Hinged Rack, Pierced Crest, 1700s, 14 In.
$1,320

Garth's Auctioneers & Appraisers

Armoire, French Provincial, Fruitwood, Dome Cornice, Leaves, c.1815, 105 x 65 In.	2952
Armoire, French Provincial, Fruitwood, Molded Cornice, Leaves, c.1800, 85 In.	1599
Armoire, French Provincial, Painted, Dome Cornice, Grill Panels, c.1900, 94 x 63 In.	1722
Armoire, Fruitwood, Carved Surround, France, c.1850, 88 x 52 In.	1230
Armoire, Louis XV Style, Fruitwood, Molded, Wreath, 3-Panel Doors, 102 x 63 In.	5166
Armoire, Louis XV Style, Gris Peinte, Carved, Arch Doors, Scroll Apron, 77 x 54 In.	1098
Armoire, Mahogany, Satinwood Inlay, Door Mirror, 2 Mirror Panels, c.1880, 87 x 51 In.	360
Armoire, Neoclassical, Inlay, Doors, Dentil Cornice, 113 x 95 In. ....*illus*	1625
Armoire, Provincial Louis XV Style, Cherry, Panels, c.1835, 97 x 61 In. ....*illus*	1230
Armoire, Renaissance Revival, Burl Walnut, Carved Crest, Paneled Doors, 92 x 64 In.	1080
Armoire, Rococo Revival, Rosewood, 1 Door, Fitted Interior, c.1870, 105 x 46 In.	3198
Armoire, Rosewood, Pierced Crest, Leaf Scrolls, Mirrored Doors, c.1850, 118 x 67 In.	5904
Armoire, Yew, Fruitwood, Door, 2 Drawers, Continental, c.1840, 79 x 53 In.	1337
Bar Cart, Terrestrial Globe, Hinged Lid, Fitted Interior, c.1980, 39 x 28 In. ....*illus*	390
Bar, Faux Malachite, Folding Doors, Fitted Interior, Mirror, Drawers, Shelf, 80 x 48 In.	1416
Barstool, Wood Slat Seat, Backrest, Tubular Frame, A. Umanoff, 1950s, 42 x 28 In., 6 Piece	259
Bed Steps, Chestnut, Carved Legs, Sides, 2 Treads, Pennsylvania, c.1800, 17 x 14 In.	246
Bed Steps, Mahogany, Leather Treads, Shaped Rail, Turned Uprights, c.1815, 23 In.	2629
Bed Steps, Mahogany, Leather Treads, Tapered Turned Legs, 1800s, 14 x 18 In.	418
Bed Steps, William IV, Mahogany, Leather Treads, Turned Legs, c.1850, 25 x 28 In.	923
Bed, Dog's, French Provincial, Canopy, Low Posts, Carved, c.1800, 29 x 25 In. ....*illus*	1722
Bed, Edwardian, Satinwood, Head & Footboard, Tapered Legs, 40 ½ In., Pair	1875
Bed, Four-Poster, Empire, Mahogany, Acorn Finials, Va., c.1825, 86 x 60 In.	460
Bed, Four-Poster, Federal, Birch, Shaped Head, Footboard, Acorn Finials, 74 x 82 In.	600
Bed, Four-Poster, Neoclassical, Mahogany, Scrolling, 6-Sided Columns, c.1840, 88 x 66 In.	543
Bed, Four-Poster, Pencil Posts, Wood, Faceted Posts, Green Paint, 1900s, 80 x 81 In.	705
Bed, Four-Poster, Sheraton Style, Canopy, Maple, Scroll Headboard, 94 x 76 In.	646
Bed, Four-Poster, Sheraton, Cherry, Acorn Finials, c.1830, 90 x 81 In.	2844
Bed, G. Stickley, Oak, Paneled Head, Footboard, Full Size, c.1910, 45 x 58 x 79 In.	2125
Bed, Headboard, Maple, Cherry, Tall Post, Urn Finial, c.1810, 65 x 60 In.	500
Bed, Hired-Man's, Hewn & Carved Posts, Later Webbing, 1800s, 27 ½ x 74 In. ....*illus*	240
Bed, Louis XVI Style, Fruitwood, Upholstered Headboard, c.1910, 76 x 30 In.	584
Bed, Low Posts, Mahogany, Head, Footboards, Carved, c.1850	118
Bed, Maple, Turned Rails, Shaped Headboards, Single, c.1850, Pair	530
Bed, Rococo Revival, Rosewood, Carved, Paneled, Mitchell & Rammelsberg, 90 x 93 In.	660
Bed, Rococo Revival, Rosewood, Sleigh Shape, Belter, 62 x 86 In.	3936
Bed, Rococo Revival, Veneer, Ormolu, Crested Headboard, Footboard, Rails, 61 x 72 In.	489
Bed, Sheraton, Maple, Turned Posts, Shaped Headboard, 86 In.	1200
Bed, Turned Posts, Pine, Blue Paint, Peaked Headboard, Rope, c.1810, 34 x 75 In.	780
Bedroom Set, Arts & Crafts, Oak, Armoire, 4-Drawer Chest, Mirror, 2-Door Chest, 7 Piece	270
Bedroom Set, Split Log, Stirrup Handles, Timberline, Colorado Woodcraft, 1950s, 4 Piece	259
Bench & Chairs, English Oak, Cane Seat, Open Paneled Back, 1800s, 41 x 95 In., 3 Piece	240
Bench Table, Painted, 3-Board Top, Plank Seat, Cutout Feet, Pa., 1800s, 36 x 22 In.	2242
Bench, Ali Baba, Split Log Top, Low Stretcher, Roycroft, 42 x 12 In.	6250
Bench, Baroque, Walnut, Turned Stretcher, Continental, 16 x 33 In.	1680
Bench, Billy Baldwin, Upholstered, 1960s, 20 x 22 In., Pair	313
Bench, Bootjack, Gray Paint, c.1860, 45 In.	150
Bench, Bootjack, Green Paint, c.1860, 70 In.	230
Bench, Bootjack, Green Paint, Cutout Legs, 1800s, 78 In.	92
Bench, Bucket, 2 Shelves, Scalloped Ends, Blue Paint, 34 x 44 In.	3480
Bench, Bucket, Blue Paint, Arched Apron, Cutout Slab Ends, New York, 1800s, 23 x 44 In.	813
Bench, Bucket, Pine, 2 Shelves, Red Paint, c.1850, 36 ½ x 36 ½ In.	770
Bench, Bucket, Pine, Blue Paint, 2 Tiers, 38 x 43 ½ In.	4740
Bench, Bucket, Pine, Green Paint, c.1905, 31 x 22 In.	237
Bench, Bucket, Pine, Red Paint, 2 Shelves, Pa., c.1860, 34 In.	2015
Bench, Bucket, Pine, Red Paint, c.1820, 55 x 55 In.	474
Bench, Bucket, Pine, Red Stain, 2 Tiers, c.1865, 45 ½ x 62 In.	889
Bench, Bucket, Pine, Shaped Ends, 3 Graduated Shelves, Painted, 1800s, 46 x 52 In.	1116
Bench, Bucket, Softwood, Green, Orange, Punched Tin Paneled Doors, Peacock, 41 x 29 In.	590
Bench, Bucket, Softwood, Red Paint, Cutout Supports, Pa., 1800s, 48 x 38 In.	1298
Bench, Butterfly, Painted, Gilt, Human Foot Feet, Pedro Friedeberg, 18 x 39 In.	7072
Bench, Carved, Curved Arms, Scroll Feet, Upholstered, 24 x 16 In.	288
Bench, Cassone, Oak, Carved Front Panels, c.1750, 25 x 72 In.	1750
Bench, Cat-Shape Supports, Black, White Paint, Stephen Huneck, 1994, 34 x 25 In.	585
Bench, Chippendale Style, Mahogany, Damask Upholstery, Elephant Knees, c.1900, 43 In.	499

Bench, Deacon's, 3-Part Back, Arms, Cutout Slats, c.1840	213
Bench, Deacon's, Maple, Brown Stain, 5 Segments, Arms, 1950, 95 In........	142
Bench, Deacon's, Spindle Back & Arms, Stenciled, Painted, 8 Legs, c.1860, 33 x 79 In. ...	688
Bench, Deacon's, Stickley, Cherry, Horizontal Top Frame, Tulip Splats, c.1920, 32 x 80 In..........	540
Bench, Florence Knoll, Chrome Base, Black Vinyl Upholstery, 3 Sections, 108 x 17 In................	2250
Bench, G. Nakashima, Black Walnut, Hickory, Signed, 1983, 32 x 90 x 33 In. ....*illus*	35000
Bench, G. Nakashima, Walnut, Grass Woven Seat, New Hope, Pa., 1960s, 13 x 18 In.	2375
Bench, George III Style, Mahogany, Cabriole Legs, Ball & Claw Feet, 19 x 31 In.	369
Bench, George III, Mahogany, Scroll Arms, Green Upholstery, c.1780	1375
Bench, Hall, Renaissance Style, Walnut, Scroll Back, Lift Seat, Trestle, 1800s, 45 x 68 In........	3120
Bench, Hardwood, Carved Dragon, Clouds, Flowers, Downswept Arms, c.1890, 39 x 50 In.	338
Bench, Jacobean Style, Oak, Carved Apron, Turned Legs, Square Stretchers, 16 x 12 In.	293
Bench, Lift Seat, Pine, Shaped Arms, Brown Paint, Pennsylvania, 29 x 63 In.	1080
Bench, Louis Sognot, Beech, Nylon Wrapped Cord, France, 1950s, 15 x 18 In., Pair	6250
Bench, Louis XVI Style, Giltwood, Cane, Carved Frame, Stretchers, 6 Legs, Oval, 37 x 15 In........	299
Bench, Louis XVI Style, Giltwood, Rolled, Upholstered, Backless, Arms, Curved, 32 In.	530
Bench, Low Shelf, Mortised, Gray Paint, Pa., c.1850, 24 x 38 In.	830
Bench, Mahogany, Masque-Carved Cabriole Legs, Hairy Paw Feet, Ireland, 21 x 27 In........	1195
Bench, Mahogany, Scroll Ends, Slip Seat, Saber Legs, New York, c.1845, 40 In.	2813
Bench, Mahogany, Upholstered, Scroll Arms, Hairy Paw Feet, Carved, c.1835, 61 In.	3840
Bench, Maison Jansen Style, Steel Base, Yellow Upholstery, 1960s, 23 x 20 In., Pair	1063
Bench, Mixed Wood, Mortised Construction, Green Over Black Paint, 1800s, 18 x 78 In.	392
Bench, Monastery, Rustic, Oak, Mortised, Trestle Base, 86 x 7 In........................	196
Bench, Mortised, Blue Gray Paint, Pa., c.1870, 24 x 38 In.	830
Bench, Mortised, Blue Paint, c.1865, 18 x 52 In.	148
Bench, Oak, Carved Flowers, Pierced Splat Back, Saddle Seat, c.1890, 43 In.	480
Bench, Oak, Elm, 91 x 19 In..	605
Bench, Oak, Paneled, Lift Top, Carved Rims, England, c.1780, 48 x 40 In.	2829
Bench, Oak, Plank Top, Curved Apron, Splayed Legs, 43 x 29 In.	184
Bench, Piano, Chippendale Style, Mahogany, Lift Top, Claw Feet, 18 x 40 In.............	154
Bench, Piano, G. Stickley, V-Apron, Flared Feet, 36 x 16 In..........................	13750
Bench, Pine, Green, Red Paint, Pa., 19 x 69 In.....................................	148
Bench, Pine, Mortised, Carved Ends, Fascia, Paint Traces, 1800s, 42 x 15 x 16 In......	115
Bench, Pine, Painted, c.1845, 17 x 51 In.	119
Bench, Pine, Scalloped Skirt, Gray Paint, 19th Century, 27 x 16 In....................	1058
Bench, Pine, Scroll Cut Back & Skirt, Lower Shelf, 1800s, 30 x 44 In.................	264
Bench, Pine, Shaped Ends, Red & Gray Paint, 1800s, 19 x 78 In.	180
Bench, Pine, Splayed Legs, Red Wash, c.1830, 16 ½ x 53 In..........................	354
Bench, Pine, Trestle Base, Lancaster Co., c.1850, 19 x 72 In.	889
Bench, Queen Anne, Upholstered, Carved Legs, Shaped Stretcher, c.1920, 21 x 19 In.	102
Bench, Renaissance Revival, Carved Splats, Base, Open Arms, Hinged Seat, c.1890	250
Bench, Risom, Walnut, Tapered Legs, Upholstered Cushion, c.1946, 54 x 21 In.	452
Bench, Robsjohn-Gibbings, Mahogany, Vinyl, Tapered, Flared Legs, Widdicomb, 35 x 16 In........	2000
Bench, Rocker, Windsor, Arrow Back, Painted Rail, 36 In., Child's	1320
Bench, Rodback, Arms, Black Paint, c.1845, 32 x 44 In............................	474
Bench, Rounded Ends, Mortise & Tenon Construction, Maryland, 1800s, 74 In., Pair...............	144
Bench, Roycroft, Ali Baba, Oak, Chestnut, Carved Orb & Cross Mark, c.1907, 19 x 42 In............	5625
Bench, Rush Seat, Wood, Black Paint, Italy, 1950s, 18 x 18 In., Pair....................	500
Bench, Shaker, Pine, Red Stain, Arched Braces, Bootjack Ends, c.1830, 15 x 35 In......	1180
Bench, Stenciled, Painted, Flower, Leaf, Green, Scroll Arms, c.1840, 35 x 78 In.	3000
Bench, Storage, Pine, Blue Paint, Paneled Chest, Spindle Back, c.1815, 31 x 54 In.	705
Bench, Vanity, Empire Style, Metal Sling Seat, Iron X-Frame, Cast Bronze, 21 x 22 In.......	132
Bench, Victorian, Mahogany, Padded Seat, Cabriole Legs, 1800s, 22 x 29 In.	2000
Bench, Wagon, Pine, Shaped Apron, Stretcher, 21 x 34 In............................	35
Bench, Waiting Room, Depot, Oak, 5 Leather Padded Seats, Back, Arms, 121 x 56 In.	3000
Bench, Walnut, Plank Top, Carved Shaped Supports, Stretcher, c.1800, 19 x 70 In...........	1016
Bench, Windsor, Rodback, Leather Writing Arm, Low Drawer, Grain Paint, c.1810................	770
Book Rest, Pine, Painted, c.1790, 11 ½ In.	900
Bookcase, Arts & Crafts, Oak, 2 Glazed Doors, Leaded Glass Detail, 1880-1900, 57 x 42 In.........	1920
Bookcase, Barrister, Arts & Crafts, Oak, Leaded Glass, 6 Sections, c.1910, 49 x 51 In.........	1750
Bookcase, Barrister, Oak, 3 Shelves, Leaded Glass Doors, Drawer, c.1900, 35 x 34 In........	708
Bookcase, Cabinet, Georgian Style, Mahogany, Glass Doors, Shelves, 1800s, 86 x 53 In.........	492
Bookcase, Cherry, 2 Parts, Glazed Doors, Round Design, Doors, c.1840, 107 x 54 In.........	11045
Bookcase, Cherry, Hardwood, Arched Pediment, Doors, Brass Mesh, 1800s, 94 x 35 In.	840
Bookcase, Chippendale Style, Mahogany, 2 Parts, Broken Crest, 1800s, 88 x 40 In................	4700

Furniture, Breakfront, George III, Figured Mahogany, Drawers, Doors, c.1790, 89 x 68 In.
$5,664

Brunk Auctions

Furniture, Bureau, Neoclassical, Mahogany, Carved, Mirror, Drawers, c.1830, 72 x 37 In.
$615

Neal Auction Co.

Furniture, Cabinet, Baroque, Hardwoods, Ebonized, Doors, Shelves, Dutch, c.1700, 88 x 95 In.
$4,012

Brunk Auctions

F

Furniture, Cabinet, Baroque, Walnut, Inlaid Case, Drawers, Continental, 1700s, 15 x 18 ½ In.
$767

Brunk Auctions

Furniture, Cabinet, Corner, Biedermeier, Cherry Veneer, Bowed, Isolde Munzer, c.1850, 69 In.
$738

Skinner Auctioneers & Appraisers

Furniture, Cabinet, Corner, Chippendale, Tiger Maple, Door, Shelf, c.1775, 28 x 25 In.
$1,067

James D. Julia Auctioneers

Bookcase, Chippendale, Mahogany, 2 Glass Doors, 2 Panel Doors, 86 x 37 In.	1320
Bookcase, Chippendale, Mahogany, 2 Glass Doors, 4 Drawers, England, 79 x 55 In.	2400
Bookcase, Empire Style, Mahogany, Gilt Bronze, Open Shelves, 62 x 49 In.	938
Bookcase, Federal, Mahogany, Inlay, Urn Finials, Glass Doors, 5 Drawers, 65 x 40 In.	1000
Bookcase, G. Stickley, 2 Doors, Cathedral Arches, Eastwood, N.Y., c.1901, 54 x 75 In.	25000
Bookcase, G. Stickley, Harvey Ellis, Doors, Label, Eastwood, N.Y., c.1906, 58 x 43 In.	6520
Bookcase, G. Stickley, Oak, Doors, Mullions, Pull Rings, Gallery Top, c.1902, 55 x 35 In.	6600
Bookcase, George III Style, Mahogany, 4 Glass Doors, 4 Panel Doors, 1800s, 90 x 100 In.	4063
Bookcase, George III, Mahogany, 4 Graduated Shelves, Drawer, c.1815, 46 x 31 In.	1195
Bookcase, George III, Mahogany, Glass & Panel Doors, Block Feet, c.1800, 99 x 55 In.	4063
Bookcase, George III, Mahogany, Slant Front, Carved, Doors, 4 Drawers, 1800s, 90 x 45 In.	1250
Bookcase, George IV, Rosewood, 2 Shelves, Grillwork Doors, c.1820, 62 x 28 In.	2000
Bookcase, Georgian, Mahogany, Glazed Panel Doors, Curved Bracket Feet, 65 x 60 In.	2106
Bookcase, Hale, Oak, Stacking, 4 Sections, Early 1900s, 59 x 34 In.	270
Bookcase, L. & J.G. Stickley, Oak, Metal, Doors, 12 Panes, Gallery, Pinned, 57 & 52 In.	2400
Bookcase, Mahogany, Carved Figures, Paw Feet, c.1900, 59 x 77 In.	1580
Bookcase, Mahogany, Ebonized, Doors, Drawers, Columns, Eagle Head, c.1845, 80 x 46 In.	1500
Bookcase, Maple, 2 Parts, Desk, 4-Pane Door, Turned Feet, c.1835, 85 x 55 In.	3408
Bookcase, Neoclassical, Mahogany, Veneer, Doors, Panels, Scrolls, c.1830, 75 x 42 In.	923
Bookcase, Oak, Broken Arch Crest, Cabochon & Vines, 2 Glazed Doors, 1800s, 108 In.	800
Bookcase, Oak, Glass Door, Shelves, 55 x 28 In.	1346
Bookcase, Regency, Rosewood, Shelves, Columns, 1800s, 42 x 60 In.	1554
Bookcase, Renaissance Revival, Walnut, Glass Doors, Panel Doors, c.1870, 102 x 53 In., Pair	5313
Bookcase, Revolving, Mahogany, Gadrooned Top, Tiered, Slats, c.1900, 45 x 20 In.	1076
Bookcase, Victorian, Walnut, 2 Glass Doors, Drawer, c.1860, 62 x 50 In.	530
Bookshelf, Russel Wright, 2 Upright Planks, 3 Plank Shelves, Conant Ball, 39 x 31 In.	277
Bookstand, Dictionary, Oak, Turned, Distressed, 20th Century, 49 In.	60
Bookstand, Display, Oak, Hinged Rack, Pierced Crest, 1700s, 14 In. ....*illus*	1320
Bookstand, Hymnal, Shaker, Walnut, Angled Shelf, Trestle, Stretcher, c.1850, 32 x 38 In.	1180
Bookstand, Mahogany, Brass Inlay, Round Top, 2 Tiers, Triangle Plinth, 1800s, 34 x 22 In.	3125
Bookstand, Mahogany, Flower Basket, Baluster Stem, Cabriole Legs, 33 x 22 In.	530
Bookstand, Regency Style, Mahogany, Tripod, Scroll Feet, c.1885, 26 x 26 In.	1353
Bookstand, Regency, Mahogany, Inlaid, Serpentine, 3 Conforming Drawers, 33 x 24 In.	575
Bookstand, Roycroft Little Journeys, Arched Ends, Clover Cutouts, 24 ½ x 7 In., Pair	500
Bookstand, Walnut, Carved Leaves, Acorns, Jabbar Kahn & Son, c.1900, 14 x 11 In.	207
Bottle Case, Stand, Chippendale, Walnut, Hinged Lid, Cabriole Legs, Feet, c.1770, 29 x 23 In.	6325
Breakfront, Chippendale Style, Lighted Upper Section, Pediment, Panel Doors, 91 x 71 In.	1175
Breakfront, Federal, Walnut, 2 Glass Doors, 4 Panel Doors, Drawer, c.1820, 97 x 72 In.	2370
Breakfront, George III Style, Mahogany, 2 Parts, Mullioned Doors, 91 x 97 In.	2460
Breakfront, George III, Figured Mahogany, Drawers, Doors, c.1790, 89 x 68 In. ....*illus*	5664
Breakfront, George III, Mahogany, Glass Doors, Drawers, Low Doors, c.1770, 99 x 69 In.	2607
Breakfront, Regency Style, Mahogany, Astragal Glazed Doors, Doors, Plinth, 93 x 94 In.	4920
Buffet, French Provincial, Oak, Leaf Border, Splayed Feet, c.1850, 42 x 58 In.	1168
Buffet, Louis XV Style, Elm, Molded Cornice, Shaped Doors, Flowers, 97 x 56 In.	2952
Buffet, Louis XV, Fruitwood, Fluted Drawers, Basket Carved, c.1790, 44 x 55 In.	1968
Buffet, Pine, 2 Paneled Cupboard Doors, Shaped Feet, c.1860, 41 x 64 In.	1599
Bureau, Belter, Rococo Revival, Rosewood, Marble Top, 94 x 56 In.	5904
Bureau, Mahogany, Mirror, Carved, Drawers, Figured Legs, c.1825, 68 x 43 In.	2360
Bureau, Neoclassical, Mahogany, Carved, Mirror, Drawers, c.1830, 72 x 37 In. ....*illus*	615
Bureau, Neoclassical, Mahogany, Marble, Roll Top, Square Legs, c.1850, 48 x 49 In.	2337
Bureau, Pine, Red Paint, Thumb-Molded Overhang Top, 4 Drawers, 13 x 15 In.	600
Bureau, Sheraton, Mahogany, Bowfront, 4 Drawers, Beaded, Columns, c.1810, 44 x 41 In.	1416
Bureau, Slant Front, Walnut, Banded, Leather Surface, c.1815, 43 x 45 In.	1845
Butcher's Rack, Pine, Iron, 3 Rails, Wrought Hooks, Cast Steer, Red Paint, c.1890, 54 x 94 In.	1293
Cabinet, 4 Doors, 2 Drawers, Carved Panels, Green Paint, Sweden, c.1800, 78 x 47 In.	5000
Cabinet, 4 Doors, Molded Cornice, 2 Drawers, Shaped Apron, c.1850, 78 x 46 In.	938
Cabinet, Aesthetic Revival, Inlay, Demilune, Glove Box Top, Columns, c.1890, 47 x 41 In.	1150
Cabinet, Anglo-Indian, Hardwood, Inlay, Pediment, Doors, Drawers, 12 Cubbies, 16 x 13 In.	430
Cabinet, Art Deco, Black Lacquer, Parchment, Mirror Handles, 36 x 63 In.	4095
Cabinet, Art Deco, Macassar Ebony, Shageeen, 2 Doors, Staggered Handles, 60 x 47 In.	4095
Cabinet, Art Deco, Maple Burl Veneer, Wine Rack, Liquor Storage, France, 53 x 40 x 20 In.	385
Cabinet, Art Deco, Rosewood, Chrome, Glass, 2 Doors, Fitted Interior, c.1930, 59 x 47 In.	1188
Cabinet, Art Nouveau, Mahogany, Mother-of-Pearl Inlay, Glass Doors, Shelves, c.1900, 52 x 40 In.	1250
Cabinet, Baker Furniture, Georgian Style, Mahogany, Drawer, Doors, 1900s, 29 x 22 In.	176
Cabinet, Baroque, Hardwoods, Ebonized, Doors, Shelves, Dutch, c.1700, 88 x 95 In. ....*illus*	4012

Cabinet, Baroque, Inlay, Carved, Panel Door, Turned Columns, c.1700, 53 x 44 In.	1534
Cabinet, Baroque, Walnut, Bone Inlay, Center Compartment, 1600s, 15 x 25 In.	1673
Cabinet, Baroque, Walnut, Carved, Italy, 36 x 29 In.	4320
Cabinet, Baroque, Walnut, Inlaid Case, Drawers, Continental, 1700s, 15 x 18 ½ In. ....*illus*	767
Cabinet, Black Lacquer, Trees, Pagodas, Boats, Doors, Stand, Gilt, Chinese, c.1860, 56 x 40 In.	1500
Cabinet, Chinese Chippendale Style, Pagoda Top, Gallery, Glass Door, Shelves, 82 x 42 In.	900
Cabinet, Console, Italian Style, Green Paint, Neoclassical Designs, Marble Top, 63 x 20 ½ In.	518
Cabinet, Corner, Beech, Cherry, 4 Panel Doors, Fluted Stiles, Black Feet, 93 In. x 51 In.	1375
Cabinet, Corner, Biedermeier, Cherry Veneer, Bowed, Isolde Munzer, c.1850, 69 In. ....*illus*	738
Cabinet, Corner, Cherry, Canted Corners, 4 Raised Panel Doors, 81 x 51 In.	995
Cabinet, Corner, Chippendale, Tiger Maple, Door, Shelf, c.1775, 28 x 25 In. ....*illus*	1067
Cabinet, Corner, Hepplewhite, Mahogany, Inlay, Glass Door, 43 x 29 In.	840
Cabinet, Corner, Mahogany, Flared Crown, 2 Glazed Panels Over 2 Paneled Doors, 82 In.	1520
Cabinet, Corner, Mixed Wood, Door, Banded, England, c.1850, 46 x 32 In.	565
Cabinet, Corner, Walnut, Serpentine Front, Brass, Glass Doors, France, c.1910, 64 x 58 In.	2625
Cabinet, Curio, Wall, Mirror, 1900s, 27 x 22 In.	180
Cabinet, Danish Modern, Teak, 4 Drawers, 2 Sliding Doors, c.1950, 26 x 61 In.	2125
Cabinet, Danish Modern, Teak, 5 Drawers, Splayed Legs, Signed H.G., c.1960, 28 x 37 In.	400
Cabinet, Display, 2 Glass Shelves, Gilt Brass Mounts, France, c.1920, 56 ½ In.	633
Cabinet, Display, Louis XV Style, Inlay, M. & Cia, Buenos Aires, c.1900, 57 x 31 In. ....*illus*	2040
Cabinet, Display, Mahogany, Inlay, Stringing, Glass Doors, Mullions, Drawers, 46 x 72 In.	1524
Cabinet, Display, Mahogany, Satinwood Inlay, 3 Interior Glass Shelves, c.1900, 69 x 31 In.	660
Cabinet, Display, Painted, Glass Shelf, Mirror Back, Italy, Mid 20th Century, 71 x 32 In.	72
Cabinet, Display, Rosewood, Hinged Top, Shelves, Drop Front, Casters, c.1890, 37 x 33 In.	750
Cabinet, Drawer, Door, Painted Figural Scenes, Chinese, 24 x 22 In., Pair	750
Cabinet, Dutch Colonial, Hardwood, Brass Bound, Door, Drawer, 24 x 19 In.	780
Cabinet, E.A. Taylor, Mirrored, 2 Doors, Paris, c.1940	885
Cabinet, Eames, Birch Plywood, Steel, Masonite, Laminate, ESU 270-C, c.1950, 33 x 24 In.	9600
Cabinet, Ebonized, Inlaid Panels, Gilt Bronze Mounts, Porcelain Medallion, 1870, 55 x 48 In. *illus*	4025
Cabinet, Edwardian, Mahogany, Glazed Door, Mirrored Back, c.1900, 78 x 36 In.	1353
Cabinet, Edwardian, Satinwood, 2 Doors, Inlay Edging, Oval Cloth Recess, 34 x 42 In.	2250
Cabinet, Elm, Bronze Mounts, 2 Doors, Chinese, 1800s, 73 x 43 In.	250
Cabinet, Elm, Red Lacquer, Gilt Scenes, Fitted Interior, Chinese, 1800s, 82 x 50 In. ....*illus*	1599
Cabinet, Empire Style, Mahogany Veneer, Shaped Front, Drawer, 2 Doors, 42 x 15 In.	150
Cabinet, Empire Style, Mahogany, Marble Top, Tamboor Doors, 27 x 24 In.	688
Cabinet, Federal, Mahogany, Dome Top, 2 Glass Doors, 3 Drawers, Reeded Legs, 95 x 47 In.	16800
Cabinet, Filing, Oak, Tambour Door, 24 Drawers, 3 Columns, Amberg's Peerless, 43 x 44 In.	542
Cabinet, Florence Knoll, Rosewood, Drawers, Bookmatched Grain, Steel Frame, 75 x 25 In.	3500
Cabinet, Florence Knoll, Walnut, 2 Cane Sliding Doors, Fitted Interior, 72 x 31 In.	3125
Cabinet, Florence Knoll, Walnut, Marble Top, Steel Frame, 5 Drawers, c.1965, 26 x 38 In.	3125
Cabinet, Folk Painted, Reverse Painted Mirror, Doors, Flowers, Birds, 1800s, 35 x 19 In.	960
Cabinet, French Style, 3 Drawers, Scrolling Legs, Black Marble Top, 25 x 17 In., Pair	518
Cabinet, Fruitwood, Mother-of-Pearl Inlay, Ivory, Japan, c.1910, 80 x 53 In. ....*illus*	3750
Cabinet, G. Nakashima, Elm, Walnut, Laurel, Widdicomb, 1950s, 32 x 74 x 22 In. ....*illus*	6250
Cabinet, G. Nakashima, Hanging, Cherry, Freeform Top, Sliding Doors, c.1966, 15 x 72 In.	8850
Cabinet, G. Nakashima, Walnut, 3 Sliding Doors, Fitted Interior, 1982, 32 x 100 In.	10000
Cabinet, G. Nakashima, Walnut, Pandanus Cloth, Sliding Door, c.1970, 32 x 60 In.	9375
Cabinet, G. Nelson, Thin Edge, Rosewood, Aluminum, Herman Miller, c.1960, 32 x 68 In.	3750
Cabinet, G. Stickley, Glass Pane Doors, Iron Hardware, Red Decal, 40 x 65 In.	11875
Cabinet, George III, Mahogany, 2 Figured Paneled Doors, Drawer, c.1790, 32 x 33 In.	2214
Cabinet, George III, Mahogany, Bowfront, Cupboard Door, c.1815, 28 x 24 In.	354
Cabinet, George III, Mahogany, Vase, Flower Inlay, Drawer, 2 Doors, 34 ½ x 54 In.	530
Cabinet, Gothic Revival, Oak, 3 Linenfold Panels, Iron Bound Door, c.1900, 72 x 65 In.	720
Cabinet, Gun Display, Chippendale Style, Glass Doors, 1900s, 77 x 46 In.	960
Cabinet, Hanging, Cherry Frame, Tiger Maple Half Columns, Red, Pa., c.1830, 15 x 18 In.	1458
Cabinet, Hanging, Georgian, Mahogany, Molded Cornice, Doors, c.1815, 43 x 28 In.	657
Cabinet, Hanging, Wood, Urn, Bird, Flower Carved, 10 ½ x 28 ½ In.	360
Cabinet, Hardwood, Spindled Panel Doors, Stepped Cornice, 1900s, 65 x 40 In.	236
Cabinet, Italian Renaissance Revival Style, Carved, Cherub Frieze, Painted, 72 x 42 In.	4025
Cabinet, Jacobean Style, Oak, Paneled, Demilune, Portrait Roundels, c.1900, 60 x 33 In.	360
Cabinet, Loewy, DF 2000, Steel, Acrylic, Rosewood, France, 1970s, 50 x 22 In. ....*illus*	6875
Cabinet, Louis XVI Style, Mahogany, Door, Urn, Putti, Flowers, 1900s, 37 x 44 In.	4674
Cabinet, Louis XVI Style, Mahogany, Marble Top, Tambour Door, c.1935, 40 x 43 In.	1599
Cabinet, Mahogany, 2 Doors, Square Knobs, c.1950, 22 x 24 In.	1063
Cabinet, Mahogany, 2 Panel Doors, Carved, Gilt Painted, c.1960, 64 x 87 In.	2125

Furniture, Cabinet, Display, Louis XV Style, Inlay, M. & Cia, Buenos Aires, c.1900, 57 x 31 In.
$2,040

Skinner Auctioneers & Appraisers

Furniture, Cabinet, Ebonized, Inlaid Panels, Gilt Bronze Mounts, Porcelain Medallion, 1870, 55 x 48 In.
$4,025

Cottone Auctions

Furniture, Cabinet, Elm, Red Lacquer, Gilt Scenes, Fitted Interior, Chinese, 1800s, 82 x 50 In.
$1,599

Garth's Auctioneers & Appraisers

Furniture, Cabinet, Fruitwood, Mother-of-Pearl Inlay, Ivory, Japan, c.1910, 80 x 53 In.
$3,750

Rago Arts & Auction Center

Furniture, Cabinet, G. Nakashima, Elm, Walnut, Laurel, Widdicomb, 1950s, 32 x 74 x 22 In.
$6,250

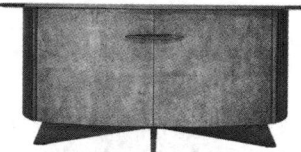

Rago Arts & Auction Center

Furniture, Cabinet, Loewy, DF 2000, Steel, Acrylic, Rosewood, France, 1970s, 50 x 22 In.
$6,875

Rago Arts & Auction Center

Furniture, Cabinet, Napoleon III, Ebonized, Gilt Bronze, KPM Plaques, 1800s, 64 x 84 In.
$33,350

Cottone Auctions

Cabinet, Mahogany, 2 Parts, Dentil Cornice, Paneled Doors, Bracket Feet, 73 x 23 In., Pair	558
Cabinet, Mahogany, Marquetry, Shaped Cornice, 2 Doors, Stretcher, 87 x 65 In.	3690
Cabinet, Maple, Tiger Maple, Shaped Crest, Panel Door, Over 2 Drawers, 24 x 20 In.	118
Cabinet, McCobb, Planner Group, Maple, Brass, Drawers, Sliding Doors, c.1950, 34 x 72 In.	826
Cabinet, Mixed Wood, 2 Doors, Moon Brasses, Carved Apron, Foo Lions, c.1890, 36 x 35 In.	723
Cabinet, Music, Mahogany, Side Columns, 1920s, 23 x 48 In.	158
Cabinet, Music, Rohlfs, Lift Top, Carved Front, Hinged Handles, Green Interior, 36 x 11 In.	9375
Cabinet, Napoleon III, Ebonized, Gilt Bronze, KPM Plaques, 1800s, 64 x 84 In. *illus*	33350
Cabinet, Napoleon III, Ebonized, Marble Top, Turreted, Doors, c.1865, 44 x 50 In.	5412
Cabinet, Neoclassical, Mahogany, Hinged Top, Drawers, Doors, Dutch, 1800s, 40 x 51 In.	2813
Cabinet, P. Evans, Copper, Bronze, Pewter, Patchwork, 4 Doors, 2 Drawers, c.1970, 72 x 25 In.	18750
Cabinet, P. Evans, Cylinders, Steel, Lacquered Acrylic, Brass, 1980s, 31 x 81 In. *illus*	26250
Cabinet, P. Evans, Steel, Lacquered Wood, Laminate, Directional, 1970s, 32 x 94 In.	6875
Cabinet, P. Hvidt, Teak, Shelves, Door, Drop Front, Drawers, Denmark, 66 x 53 In.	2457
Cabinet, Parzinger, Lacquered Wood, Studded, Nickeled Brass, 1950s, 21 x 31 In. *illus*	6875
Cabinet, Pine, 11 Drawers, White Porcelain Pulls, c.1925, 37 x 28 In.	590
Cabinet, Pine, Red Paint, 2 Plank Doors, 12 Drawers, American, 1800s, 28 x 20 In.	940
Cabinet, Potty, Curly Maple, Door In Front, Lid Top, 4-Footed, c.1840, 18 x 19 In.	29
Cabinet, Printer's, Oak, 20 Drawers, Cast-Iron Pulls, Hamilton Mfg. Co., 43 x 32 In.	382
Cabinet, Regency Style, Cherry Finish, Butler Specialty Co., c.1910, 38 In.	108
Cabinet, Regency, Rosewood, Drawers, Grillwork Doors, Gilt Frieze Designs, 36 x 46 In.	1626
Cabinet, Regency, Rosewood, Gilt, Gallery Shelves, Drawer, Wirework Door, 53 x 24 In.	1920
Cabinet, Renaissance Revival, Ebonized, Dentil Cornice, Figural Doors, 1800s, 88 x 38 In.	3444
Cabinet, Renaissance Revival, Walnut, Doors, Drawers, Radiant Flower Carvings, 66 x 37 In.	1875
Cabinet, Renaissance Revival, Walnut, Frieze Drawers, Mask Pulls, Italy, 44 x 53 In.	4956
Cabinet, Renaissance Revival, Walnut, Gilt, Inlay, Moore, York, Howell, c.1870, 56 x 50 In.	2500
Cabinet, Robsjohn-Gibbings, Mahogany, 6 Drawers, Cane Handles, Widdicomb, 68 x 32 In.	2125
Cabinet, Robsjohn-Gibbings, Walnut, Wicker, Brass, Widdicomb, 1950s, 32 x 67 In. *illus*	1500
Cabinet, Satinwood, Amboyna, Marble Top, Leaves, Cupboards, c.1900, 46 x 53 In.	2952
Cabinet, Specimen, Pine, 6 Drawers, Glazed Drawer Tops, 19th Century, 17 x 15 In.	210
Cabinet, Spice, Curly Maple, 14 Graduated Drawers, c.1890, 33 ½ x 39 In.	2242
Cabinet, Spice, Hepplewhite, Inlay, Escutcheon, Crossbanding, Handle, c.1800, 19 x 16 x 8 In.	1168
Cabinet, Tea, Red Lacquer, 2 Doors, Drawers, Chinese, c.1900, 10 x 40 In.	177
Cabinet, Teak, Brass, Rattan, 2 Solid, 2 Woven Doors, Fitted Interior, c.1950, 32 x 83 In.	590
Cabinet, Victorian, Oak, Scalloped Backsplash, Flowers, Shelves, Claw Feet, 64 x 30 In.	240
Cabinet, Wall, Glass Front, Scalloped Door, Shaped Crest, Painted, Shelf, 26 x 12 In.	98
Cabinet, Walnut, Maple Burl, Aluminum, White Furniture Co., 1960s, 32 x 76 In.	438
Cabinet, Wig, Empire, Mahogany, Dresser Top, Compartments, Molded Drawer, 26 x 20 In.	108
Cabinet, Wood, Brass Bound, 2 Drawers, 2 Doors, Korea, 58 x 42 In.	2000
Candlestand, Bird's-Eye Maple, Tilt Top, Turned Standard, 28 x 20 In.	570
Candlestand, Cherry, Round, Faceted, Leg-Shaped Base, 1835, 29 x 21 In.	529
Candlestand, Chippendale, Birch, Turned Stem, Snake Feet, c.1790, 27 x 15 In.	2952
Candlestand, Chippendale, Cherry, Porringer Top, Baluster Shaft, c.1775, 25 In.	2040
Candlestand, Chippendale, Cherry, Turned Stem, Snake Feet, c.1790, 28 x 16 In.	1076
Candlestand, Chippendale, Mahogany, Ash, Tilt Dish Top, Baluster, c.1790, 29 x 22 In.	235
Candlestand, Chippendale, Mahogany, Dish Top, Snake Feet, c.1790, 29 x 18 In.	235
Candlestand, Chippendale, Mahogany, Round Top, Ball & Claw Feet, c.1770, 27 x 24 In.	1185
Candlestand, Double-Arm, Adjustable, Screw Pedestal, New England, 43 In.	277
Candlestand, Empire Style, Mahogany, Fluted Column, Scroll Legs, c.1910, 28 x 18 In.	96
Candlestand, Federal, Birch, 3 Legs, Turned Standard, New England, c.1820, 28 x 15 In.	385
Candlestand, Federal, Birch, Round Top, 3 Legs, New England, 27 x 15 In.	207
Candlestand, Federal, Birch, Tilt Top, Cabriole Legs, 28 x 29 In.	420
Candlestand, Federal, Cherry, Inlaid, Drawer, Turned Post, c.1815, 27 x 16 In.	2400
Candlestand, Federal, Cherry, Octagonal Top, Red Stain, Splayed Legs, c.1790, 28 x 17 In.	1185
Candlestand, Federal, Cherry, Oval Top, Baluster Shaft, Snake Feet, c.1815, 27 x 19 In.	330
Candlestand, Federal, Cherry, Painted Flowers, Arcs, Round Top, c.1790, 27 x 18 In.	1659
Candlestand, Federal, Cherry, Round Top, 3 Legs, New England, c.1800, 29 x 15 In.	415
Candlestand, Federal, Cherry, Serpentine Top, Vase Shape, Snake Feet, c.1790, 26 In.	717
Candlestand, Federal, Cherry, String Inlay, Turned Post, Cabriole Legs, c.1800, 27 x 15 In.	1680
Candlestand, Federal, Cherry, Tilt Top, Reeded Post, c.1820, 28 x 20 In.	4500
Candlestand, Federal, Cherry, Urn Inlay, Banding, Tilt Top, New England, 28 x 17 ½ In.	119
Candlestand, Federal, Curly Maple, Octagonal Top, Ring & Urn Shaft, c.1800, 27 x 17 In.	266
Candlestand, Federal, Mahogany Veneer, Inlaid Banding, Mass., c.1800, 15 x 21 In. *illus*	677
Candlestand, Federal, Mahogany, Clover Shape, Tilt Top, Vase Stem, c.1815, 29 In.	359
Candlestand, Federal, Mahogany, Octagonal, Crossbanded, Lunettes, Tilt Top, c.1790, 28 In.	3960

Candlestand, Federal, Mahogany, Octagonal, Star, Tilt Top, c.1800, 9 x 10 In. 1107
Candlestand, Federal, Mahogany, Oval, Tilt Top, Spider Legs, c.1815, 29 x 23 In. 860
Candlestand, Federal, Mahogany, Round, Tripod Base, Pa., c.1790, 28 ½ x 19 In. 652
Candlestand, Federal, Mahogany, Scalloped, Tilt Top, New England, c.1820, 30 x 21 In. 237
Candlestand, Federal, Mahogany, Shaped Tilt Top, Downswept Legs, 29 x 27 In. 280
Candlestand, Federal, Mahogany, Square, Tilt Top, Ring & Urn Standard, 29 x 22 In. 560
Candlestand, Federal, Maple, Octagonal, Crossbanded, Tilt Top, Vase Stem, 1800s, 29 In. 600
Candlestand, Federal, Octagonal, Tilt Top, Green, 14 ½ x 18 In. 330
Candlestand, Federal, Painted Design, Square Top, Swelled Post, c.1815, 27 x 16 In. 240
Candlestand, Federal, Pine, Cherry, c.1810, 30 x 22 In. 267
Candlestand, Federal, Red Paint, Oval Top, 28 x 21 In. 480
Candlestand, Federal, Wood, Inlay, Round Checkerboard Top, Drawer, 27 ½ x 17 In. 360
Candlestand, George II Style, Green Japanned, Tilt Top, Tripod Base, 27 x 30 In. 375
Candlestand, George II, Mahogany, Round Piecrust, Tilt Top, Tripod Base, 25 x 18 In. 1188
Candlestand, George II, Oak, Tilt Top, Round, c.1770, 28 x 21 In. 148
Candlestand, George III Style, Walnut, Carved, Fluted Pedestal, Claw Tripod Base, 43 In. 120
Candlestand, George III, Mahogany, c.1770, 28 x 17 In. 910
Candlestand, George III, Walnut, Raised Rim, Round, Cabriole Legs, c.1845, 25 x 17 In. 150
Candlestand, Hepplewhite, Curly Maple, Turned Pedestal, Octagonal Top, 28 x 20 ½ In. 212
Candlestand, Hepplewhite, Mahogany, Round, Tilt Top, Spider Legs, New England 480
Candlestand, Hepplewhite, Maple, Drawer, Tapered Legs, 30 x 18 In. 266
Candlestand, Hepplewhite, Satinwood, Inlay, Octagonal, Tilt Top, New England, 31 x 20 In. 900
Candlestand, Louis XIV Style, Mahogany, Boulle, Ebonized, 21 x 12 In., Pair 1875
Candlestand, Mahogany, Birdcage & Urn Standard, Philadelphia, c.1790, 26 ½ x 21 In. 1126
Candlestand, Mahogany, Dish Top, Birdcage, Ball Standard, Cabriole Legs, 27 In. 13035
Candlestand, Mixed Wood, Painted, Round Dish Top, Tripod, 2 Adjustable Arms, c.1815 2115
Candlestand, Mixed Wood, Round Top, England, c.1750, 25 x 20 In. 415
Candlestand, Pine, Octagonal Top, Turned Shaft, Brown Paint, c.1700, 23 In. .... *illus* 2337
Candlestand, Pine, Octagonal Top, X-Stretcher, Red Paint, c.1750, 25 x 13 In. 1422
Candlestand, Pine, Round Top, Gray Paint, c.1820, 26 x 18 In. 652
Candlestand, Queen Anne, Birch, Painted, Round Top, Tripod, Cabriole Legs, c.1775, 27 In. 240
Candlestand, Queen Anne, Cherry, Round Top, Drawer, Cabriole Legs, New England, 27 In. 270
Candlestand, Queen Anne, Cherry, Round, Tilt Top, c.1850, 29 x 18 In. 563
Candlestand, Queen Anne, Mahogany, Birch, Round, 3-Footed, c.1785, 25 x 25 In. 122
Candlestand, Queen Anne, Mahogany, Handkerchief, Triangle Corners, Tilt Top, 26 x 19 In. 944
Candlestand, Queen Anne, Mahogany, Round, Tilt Dish Top, 28 x 23 In. 480
Candlestand, Queen Anne, Mahogany, Tilt Dish Top, Ball Standard, c.1770, 28 x 22 In. 13035
Candlestand, Queen Anne, Mahogany, Tilt Top, Ball Standard, Pa., c.1770, 28 x 26 In. 2607
Candlestand, Queen Anne, Mahogany, Tilt Top, Tripod Base, New England, 28 x 17 In. 1200
Candlestand, Queen Anne, Square, Tilt Top, Turned Standard, England, 27 x 22 In. 960
Candlestand, Queen Anne, Walnut, Dish Top, Birdcage Support, Pa., c.1780, 28 x 23 In. 1422
Candlestand, Queen Anne, Walnut, Dish Top, Turned Post, Tripod Base, 26 x 18 In. 420
Candlestand, Queen Anne, Walnut, Round, Tilt Top, Birdcage Standard, 28 ½ x 22 In. 652
Candlestand, Queen Anne, Walnut, Round, Turned Pedestal, Snake Feet, 1700s, 28 x 17 In. 360
Candlestand, Red Paint, Oval Top, Turned Post, T-Base, England, c.1715, 25 x 18 In. 3480
Candlestand, Satinwood, Octagonal, Gallery, Shell Inlay, Continental, c.1800, 25 x 11 In. 1230
Candlestand, Shaker, Cherry, Beveled Top, Turned Shaft, Mt. Lebanon, 26 In. .... *illus* 2832
Candlestand, Shaker, Cherry, Beveled, Turned Shaft, 1950s, 26 x 14 In. 2832
Candlestand, Shaker, Tiger Maple, Round Top, Turned Shaft, Tripod Legs, c.1825 7965
Candlestand, Shaker, Walnut, Square Top, Beaded Edge, Tripod, c.1850, 29 x 19 In. 1998
Candlestand, Square Top, Blue Paint, Spider Leg Base, 29 x 17 In. 2880
Candlestand, Tiger Maple, c.1850, 27 x 21 In. 625
Candlestand, Victorian, Shaped Top, Painted Scrolls, Flowers, 22 x 11 ½ In. 30
Candlestand, Walnut, Checkerboard Top, Turned Post, c.1830, 27 x 17 In. 3600
Candlestand, Walnut, Pa., c.1790, 27 x 18 In. 504
Candlestand, Walnut, Painted, Scrubbed Top, Curved Legs, Turned Post, c.1860, 28 x 16 In. 1446
Candlestand, Walnut, Parquetry, Round Top, Tripod Base, Germany, c.1850, 27 x 19 In. 2813
Candlestand, Walnut, Tripod Base, Pa., c.1820, 27 x 19 In. 356
Canterbury, Bamboo, 2 Compartments, Carrying Handle, c.1915, 24 x 22 In. 120
Canterbury, George III, Mahogany, Drawer, 19 x 18 In. 900
Canterbury, George III, Rosewood, Inlay, Drawer, 2 Sections, c.1810, 19 x 14 In. .... *illus* 1075
Canterbury, George IV, Mahogany, Turned Finials, Drawer, c.1815, 19 x 19 In. 418
Canterbury, Georgian, Mahogany, Tiers, Openwork, Columns, c.1850, 36 x 24 In. 1003
Canterbury, Regency, Mahogany, c.1825, 20 x 19 ½ In. 385
Canterbury, Regency, Mahogany, Dovetailed Drawer, 1800s, 38 x 31 In. .... *illus* 1298

Furniture, Cabinet, P. Evans, Cylinders, Steel, Lacquered Acrylic, Brass, 1980s, 31 x 81 In.
$26,250

Rago Arts & Auction Center

Furniture, Cabinet, Parzinger, Lacquered Wood, Studded, Nickeled Brass, 1950s, 21 x 31 In.
$6,875

Rago Arts & Auction Center

Furniture, Cabinet, Robsjohn-Gibbings, Walnut, Wicker, Brass, Widdicomb, 1950s, 32 x 67 In.
$1,500

Rago Arts & Auction Center

Furniture, Candlestand, Federal, Mahogany Veneer, Inlaid Banding, Mass., c.1800, 15 x 21 In.
$677

Skinner Auctioneers & Appraisers

Furniture, Candlestand, Pine, Octagonal Top, Turned Shaft, Brown Paint, c.1700, 23 In.
$2,337

Garth's Auctioneers & Appraisers

Furniture, Candlestand, Shaker, Cherry, Beveled Top, Turned Shaft, Mt. Lebanon, 26 In.
$2,832

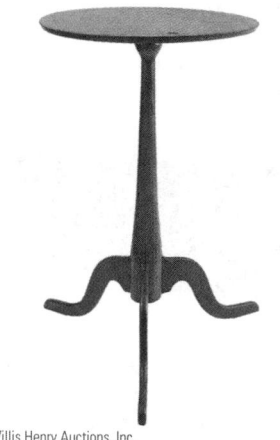

Willis Henry Auctions, Inc.

Furniture, Canterbury, George III, Rosewood, Inlay, Drawer, 2 Sections, c.1810, 19 x 14 In.
$1,075

Neal Auction Co.

Canterbury, Regency, Mahogany, Drawer, Open Shelf, England, 20 x 17 In.	660
Canterbury, Rosewood, Reticulated Scrollwork, Drawer, Turned Feet, 1800s, 19 x 21 In.	538
Canterbury, Sheraton, Mahogany, Inlay, 20 x 20 In.	1080
Canterbury, Victorian, Burl, Serpentine, Carved, Drawer, Casters, c.1870, 21 x 17 In.	219
Canterbury, Victorian, Parcel Gilt, Harps, Swags, Columns, White Paint, c.1865, 22 x 22 In.	750
Canterbury, Walnut, Reticulated Sides, Drawer, Casters, c.1850, 20 x 22 In. *illus*	598
Canterbury, William IV, Rosewood, Slatted, Bulbous Legs, c.1850, 23 x 23 In.	1107
Canterbury, William IV, Walnut, Drawer, Bulbous Turned Feet, c.1835, 20 x 24 In.	657
Cart, Rolling, Oak, Dark Stain, F. Chaleyssin, France, c.1930, 28 x 35 In.	625
Cassone, Walnut, Hairy Paw, Italy, 22 x 51 In.	960
Cassone, Walnut, Hinged Top, Paneled, Shield Carving, Paw Feet, 1800s, 22 x 62 In.	338
Cellarette, Chippendale, Mahogany, Inlay, Door, Brass Handles, England, 18 x 18 In.	360
Cellarette, Federal, Cherry, Hinged Case, Drawer, Tapered Legs, c.1800, 38 x 21 In.	3105
Cellarette, Federal, Cherry, Hinged Lid, Fitted Interior, Virginia, c.1800, 26 x 18 In.	1265
Cellarette, George III, Mahogany, Brass Bound, Oval, Square Legs, Handles, 23 In.	563
Cellarette, George III, Mahogany, c.1790, 24 x 19 In.	948
Cellarette, Georgian Style, Mahogany, Hinged Top, Molded, Disc Feet, 22 x 26 In.	1250
Cellarette, Georgian, Mahogany, Coffered Lid, 28 x 21 In.	1210
Cellarette, Mahogany, Inlay, Brass, Octagonal, Raised Legs, 26 x 18 In.	1500
Cellarette, Mixed Wood, Divided, Hinged Lid, Tapered Legs, 39 x 18 In.	1287
Chair Set, Adirondack, Splint Woven Back, Seat, Carved Stiles, Legs, c.1910, 6	1046
Chair Set, Arne Jacobsen, Molded Veneer, Chrome Legs, Series 7, F. Hansen, 1900s, 30 In., 6	542
Chair Set, Art Nouveau, Mahogany, Arm & Side, S. Karpen Bros., 42 & 40 In., 2 *illus*	3680
Chair Set, Biedermeier, Walnut, Curved Back, Pad Seat, Tapered Legs, c.1845, 6	1500
Chair Set, Chippendale Style, Mahogany, Upholstered Seat, 2 Armchairs, 38 In., 8	1495
Chair Set, Chippendale, Pierced Ribbon Splat, Ball & Claw Feet, 40 In., 4	2223
Chair Set, Country Empire, Cherry, Shaped Splat, Caned Seat, Stretchers, Jacob Fisher, 8	4446
Chair Set, Eames, Management, Leather Upholstery, Aluminum, Casters, Herman Miller, 4	2468
Chair Set, Eames, Plastic, Metal, Naugahyde, Red, DAX, Herman Miller, 1971, 32 x 25 In., 7	1298
Chair Set, Eames, Walnut, Enameled Steel, Rubber, Herman Miller, 1950s, 30 x 20 In., 6	2250
Chair Set, Empire, Burl, Needlepoint Seat, Saber Leg, c.1890, 8	334
Chair Set, Frank Lloyd Wright, Fruitwood, Barrel Shape, Slats, Arms, Cassina, c.1990, 6	11250
Chair Set, French Style, Rush Seat, Shaped Rail, Slat Splat, Marked Habersham, 42 In., 6	546
Chair Set, G Nakashima, Cherry, Spindle Back, Carved Triangular Seat, 1966, 27 x 17 In., 6	4248
Chair Set, G. Nakashima, Curved Rail, Rod Back, Florence Knoll, 1950s, 31 x 22 In., 3	1750
Chair Set, G. Stickley, Harvey Ellis, 3 Vertical Splats, Padded Seat, Red Decal, 39 In., 9	5313
Chair Set, G. Stickley, Ladder Back, Rush Seat, Eastwood, N.Y., Red Decal, c.1905, 36 In., 6	2750
Chair Set, Gehry, High Sticking, Maple, Laminated, Florence Knoll, 1994, 43 In., 3 *illus*	3000
Chair Set, George III, Mahogany, Arch Crest Rail, Pierced Splats, Slip Seats, 1700s, 6	2032
Chair Set, H. Bertoia, Yellow Fiberglass Shell, Black Powder-Coated Steel, Knoll, 12	1416
Chair Set, H. Bertoia, Yellow Fiberglass, Steel, Knoll, c.1965, 31 x 21 In., 12	1829
Chair Set, Hvidt & Molgaard-Nielsen, Teak, Upholstered, Shaped Backrest, 31 In., 10	3600
Chair Set, Louis XVI Style, Multicolor, Domed Back, Padded, Molded Frame, 37 In., 6	1968
Chair Set, Mahogany, Shield Back, Pierced Splat, Leather Seat, Carved, c.1910, 38 In., 6	572
Chair Set, Mario Bellini, Red Leather Zipper, c.1978, 32 x 19 In., 4	4248
Chair Set, Neoclassical Style, Walnut Veneer, Curved Rail, Penwork, Cushion Seat, 36 In., 5	960
Chair Set, Pedro Friedeberg Style, Hand Shape, Carved, c.1970, 17 x 39 In., 3	2625
Chair Set, Regency Style, Mahogany, Upholstered, Medallion Cuffs, 1900s, 37 In., 4	470
Chair Set, Regency, Rosewood, Ivory Inlay, Curved Backrest, Pad Seat, c.1820, 6	2500
Chair Set, Regency, Rosewood, Scroll Brackets, Cane Seat, 2 Armchairs, c.1820, 8	3883
Chair Set, Robert Venturi, Plywood, Sheraton, Screenprint, Knoll, c.1985, 34 In., 4 *illus*	9600
Chair Set, Rococo Revival, Oak, Entwined Branch Back, Upholstered, Dutch, c.1850, 36 In., 8	4375
Chair Set, Shaker, Birch, Ladder Back, 1 Rush & 5 Cane Seats, c.1840, 41 In., 6 *illus*	8850
Chair Set, Spanish Colonial Style, Ladder Back, Painted, Large Crest, Rush Seat, 50 In., 4	127
Chair Set, Stencil Painted Back, Rush Seat, Jennersville, Pa., 6	270
Chair Set, Thonet, Bentwood, Curved Back, Arms, 29 x 16 In., 4	702
Chair Set, Victorian, Balloon Back, Carved Grape Cluster Crest, 35 In., 3	60
Chair Set, Victorian, Balloon Back, Molded Carved Frames, Hip Rests, Upholstered, 36 In., 4	210
Chair Set, Wegner, Woven Seat, Denmark, 20th Century, 30 In., 6	1845
Chair Set, Windsor, Bow Back, 7 Turned Spindles, c.1800, 35 In., 6	688
Chair Set, Windsor, Bow Back, 9-Spindle Back, Virginia, c.1810, 37 x 37 In., 6	5463
Chair Set, Windsor, Bow Back, Pierced Splat, Spindle Back, Arms, 42 x 22 In., 6	3540
Chair Set, Windsor, Rodback, Plank Seat, c.1850, 16 x 35 In., 4	345
Chair Set, Windsor, Shaped Crest, Black Paint, Lausch, 4	770
Chair Set, Windsor, Square Back, Bamboo Rod Back, Splayed Legs, 1800s, 34 In., 4	246

Chair, Adirondack, Green Paint, Rush Seat, Back, Arms, Stretchers, c.1900, 38 In.	92
Chair, Adrian Pearsall, Lounge, Birch, Wilkes-Barre, Pa., 1960s, 31 x 33 In. ....*illus*	531
Chair, Aesthetic Revival, Mother-Of-Pearl, Mahogany, Brass Inlay, Garland, Herts Bros., 36 In....	1599
Chair, Aesthetic Revival, Rosewood, Brass, Openwork Carved, Inlaid, c.1880, 35 In.	384
Chair, Arata Isozaki, Monroe, Ebonized Beech, Leather Seat, 55 ½ In.	184
Chair, Arata Isozaki, Monroe, Ebonized Beech, Leather Seat, 55 ½ In., Pair	472
Chair, Arata Isozaki, Monroe, Ebonized Beech, Leather, 1980s, 60 In.	587
Chair, Arched Back, Turned Legs, Needlework Seat, Continental, c.1710, 37 In. ....*illus*	1320
Chair, Arne Jacobsen, Grand Prix, Teak, Beech, Foil Labels, Fritz Hansen, c.1960, 31 In., 6.........	3250
Chair, Art Deco, Rosewood, Bone Inlay, Slope Back, Print Upholstery, 39 x 20 In., Pair	7605
Chair, Art Nouveau, Carved, Curvilinear Grooved Frame, Upholstered Seat, Back, 40 In.	863
Chair, Art Nouveau, Oak, Leather Seat, Splat, Brass, Inlaid Landscapes, Curved Arms, 51 In.	1800
Chair, Arts & Crafts, Back Slats, Leather Seat, Arched Rails, Arms, 25 ½ x 38 In.	1000
Chair, Arts & Crafts, High Slat Back, Sides, Leather Cushion, Arched Seat Rail, 29 x 45 In.	469
Chair, Arts & Crafts, Mahogany, Fruitwood Inlay, Arms, J.S. Henry, c.1895, 42 In. ....*illus*	1125
Chair, Arts & Crafts, Oak, Ladder Back, Rush Seat, c.1910, 37 x 15 In., Pair	266
Chair, Austrian Secession, Vernacular, Josef Zotti, Arms, Rush Seat, c.1911, 39 In.	118
Chair, B. Mathsson, Eva, Woven Canvas, Beech Frame, Sweden, c.1970, 1935, 33 x 28 In., Pair ..	875
Chair, Ballroom, Louis XVI Style, Antiqued Gilt, Shaped Back, Upholstered, 36 In., Pair	587
Chair, Banister Back, Carved Cutout Crest Rail, Arms, New England, c.1750	652
Chair, Banister Back, Maple, Heart, Finials, Rush Seat, Sausage Legs, Arms, 1700s, 46 In.	295
Chair, Banister Back, Rush Seat, c.1770, 49 x 19 In., Pair	1625
Chair, Banister Back, Tulip Cutout Crest, Black Paint, New England, c.1765	4740
Chair, Barcelona, Black Leather, Tufted, Chrome Steel, Pair	2000
Chair, Baroque, Carved Apron, Putti, Beaded Open Arms, c.1900, 57 In., Pair	922
Chair, Baroque, Mahogany, Oak, Openwork Back, Scroll, Mask Carved, Pair	875
Chair, Baroque, Walnut, Barley-Twist Splat & Legs, Curved, 1800s, 27 x 28 In.	1120
Chair, Baroque, Walnut, Carved, Burl Panel, Plank Seat, Arms, Italy ....*illus*	246
Chair, Baroque, Walnut, Carved, Pierced Stretcher, Arms, c.1700, 53 x 25 In. ....*illus*	354
Chair, Barrel, Art Deco, Mahogany, Ebonized, Brass Lion Head Terminals, Leather, Pair	3630
Chair, Beech, Upholstered, Shaped Skirt & Arms, c.1790, 27 In.	354
Chair, Belter, Rococo Revival, Rosewood, Rosalie Without Grapes, c.1865, 43 In. ....*illus*	1476
Chair, Belter, Rococo, Rosewood, Carved Crest, Balloon Back, Upholstered, 38 x 19 In., Pair.......	2714
Chair, Belter, Slipper, Rococo Revival, Laminated Rosewood, Pierced Carved, 45 In.	3444
Chair, Bentwood, Carved Rod Back, Shaped Crest Rail, Cane Seat, Stretchers, Pair	180
Chair, Bergere, Louis XV Style, Beech, Molded, Closed Padded Arms	1220
Chair, Bergere, Louis XV Style, Parcel Gilt, Curved Back, Upholstered, Closed Arms, c.1800	875
Chair, Bergere, Louis XVI Style, Carved, Upholstered, Closed Arms, Pair	3125
Chair, Bergere, Louis XVI Style, Fruitwood, Dome Back, Closed Arms, c.1885, 38 In.	790
Chair, Bergere, Louis XVI, Brown Leather, Carved Painted Frame, Closed Arms	2880
Chair, Bergere, Mahogany, Barrel Shape, Ball & Claw Feet, Closed Arms, c.1900, 36 In.	125
Chair, Biedermeier, Burl, Concave Back, Scroll Arms, Cream Upholstery, 37 In., Pair	944
Chair, Biedermeier, Fruitwood, Ebonized Triangle Back, Upholstered Seat	938
Chair, Biedermeier, Fruitwood, Ebonized, Open Arms, Upholstered, Pair	750
Chair, Black Forest Style, Carved Bears, Arched Back, Arms, c.1960, 40 x 29 In.	210
Chair, Bone, Brass Inlay, Bust Finials, Stretcher Shelf, Italy, c.1895, 47 x 18 In., Pair	2125
Chair, Brewster Style, Tiger Maple, Rush Seat, Spindle Arms, Legs, Stretchers	960
Chair, C. Pollock, Lounge, No. 657, Leather, Arms, Cast Aluminum, Knoll, 29 In., Pair	705
Chair, Camp, Rustic, Carved, Branch Frame, Cloth Seat, Back, Folding, c.1890, 30 x 17 In.	406
Chair, Campeche, Scroll Arms, Brown Leather, Brass Nailheads, 33 x 25 In., Pair	1416
Chair, Captain's, Oak, Carved Spindles, England, Pair	180
Chair, Carved Crest, Banister Back, Open Arms, Rush Seat, c.1720	1200
Chair, Charles II Style, Walnut, Scroll Arms, H-stretcher, Flower Heads, 1900s, 46 In.	150
Chair, Charles II, Cane Back, Pierced Crest, Arms, Cushion, Black Paint, Scroll Feet	720
Chair, Cherry, Pierced Splat, Slip Seat, Cabriole Legs, Connecticut	840
Chair, Chippendale Style, Mahogany, Carved, Upholstered Seat, c.1900, 53 In. ....*illus*	219
Chair, Chippendale Style, Mahogany, Carved, Upholstered, Arms, 1800s, 44 ½ In. ....*illus*	1188
Chair, Chippendale Style, Mahogany, Open Splat, Carved, Knees, Scroll Feet, c.1910, 40 In.	206
Chair, Chippendale Style, Mahogany, Upholstered, Cabriole Legs, c.1800, 43 In.	529
Chair, Chippendale Style, Mahogany, Upholstered, Fluted Arms & Legs, 34 In.	472
Chair, Chippendale Style, Pierced Slats, Slip Seat, Cabriole Legs, c.1955, 32 In., Pair	443
Chair, Chippendale Style, Revolving, Arms, Shell Carved, Leather Seat, England	2880
Chair, Chippendale Style, Walnut, Carved Back, Slip Seat, Pair	750
Chair, Chippendale, Mahogany, Carved Crest, Plank Seat, Arms, Pair	840
Chair, Chippendale, Mahogany, Carved Crest, Splat, Philadelphia, c.1765	1778

Furniture, Canterbury, Regency, Mahogany, Dovetailed Drawer, 1800s, 38 x 31 In.
$1,298

Brunk Auctions

Furniture, Canterbury, Walnut, Reticulated Sides, Drawer, Casters, c.1850, 20 x 22 In.
$598

Neal Auction Co.

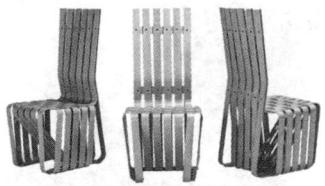

Furniture, Chair Set, Art Nouveau, Mahogany, Arm & Side, S. Karpen Bros., 42 & 40 In., 2
$3,680

Cottone Auctions

Furniture, Chair Set, Gehry, High Sticking, Maple, Laminated, Florence Knoll, 1994, 43 In., 3
$3,000

Rago Arts & Auction Center

This is an edited listing of current prices. Visit **Kovels.com** to check thousands of prices from previous years and sign up for free information on trends, tips, reproductions, marks, and more.

F

Furniture, Chair Set, Robert Venturi, Plywood, Sheraton, Screenprint, Knoll, c.1985, 34 In., 4
$9,600

Skinner Auctioneers & Appraisers

Furniture, Chair Set, Shaker, Birch, Ladder Back, 1 Rush & 5 Cane Seats, c.1840, 41 In., 6
$8,850

Willis Henry Auctions, Inc.

Furniture, Chair, Adrian Pearsall, Lounge, Birch, Wilkes-Barre, Pa., 1960s, 31 x 33 In.
$531

Rago Arts & Auction Center

Chair, Chippendale, Mahogany, Carved Splat, Stretchers, c.1800, 20 ½ In., Child's		122
Chair, Chippendale, Mahogany, Carved, Owl's-Eye Splat, c.1780, 37 In. ....*illus*		1320
Chair, Chippendale, Mahogany, Crest, Openwork Carved Back, Slip Seat, c.1850, 39 x 22 In.		272
Chair, Chippendale, Mahogany, Flared Openwork Back, Philadelphia, c.1790, Pair		1304
Chair, Chippendale, Mahogany, Pierced Gothic Splat, Slip Seat, Pa., c.1770, Pair		3080
Chair, Chippendale, Mahogany, Pierced Horizontal Slats, Slip Seat, Philadelphia		600
Chair, Chippendale, Mahogany, Pierced, Scrolled Splat, Slip Seat, c.1795, 36 x 17 In.		150
Chair, Chippendale, Mahogany, Ribbonback, Slip Seat, Straight Legs, c.1800, 38 x 20 In.		69
Chair, Chippendale, Mahogany, Tassel Back, Leaf Carved, Pad Seat, Arms, c.1760, 38 In.		4688
Chair, Chippendale, Shaped, Pierced Splat, Slip Seat, Williamsburg, Repro, 37 x 17 In.		2990
Chair, Chippendale, Walnut, Carved Crest, Shell Apron, Ball & Claw Feet, Phil., c.1770		2607
Chair, Chippendale, Walnut, Curved, Pierced Keyhole Splats, Arms, Va., c.1780, 21 In.		35000
Chair, Chippendale, Walnut, Gothic Splat, Cabriole Legs, Pennsylvania, c.1770		1944
Chair, Chippendale, Walnut, Oak, Upholstered, Scroll Crest, Open Arms		720
Chair, Chippendale, Walnut, Poplar, Serpentine Crest Rail, Outscrolled Arms, 41 In.		1920
Chair, Chippendale, Walnut, Serpentine Crest, Skirt, Ball & Claw Feet, 1700s, 43 x 29 In.		530
Chair, Chippendale, Walnut, Serpentine Leaf Carved Rail, Slip Seat, Pa., c.1780, 37 In.		1875
Chair, Chippenndale, Mahogany, Arched Crest, Pierced Splat, c.1785, 38 x 20 In.		472
Chair, Clear Round Back, Lucite, Brass, Hide, Chromed Steel, c.1980, 36 x 24 In.		5535
Chair, Club, Art Deco, Burl Maple, Black Leather, France, 1920, 31 x 33 In., Pair		1062
Chair, Club, Rolled Arms, Back, Brown Leather, France, 39 x 32 In.		1625
Chair, Club, Upholstered, Stretcher, Carved Feet, c.1905, 33 x 33 In.		270
Chair, Corner, Abalone, Bone, Ebony, Inlay, Trellis Work, Arms, c.1930, 28 In. ....*illus*		1033
Chair, Corner, Chippendale Style, Mahogany, Carved, Upholstered Seat, 32 In., Pair		300
Chair, Corner, Chippendale, Elm, Continuous Rail, Pierced Slats, England, c.1750, 30 x 27 In.		502
Chair, Corner, Chippendale, Mahogany, Outscrolled Hands, New England, c.1800, 31 In.		625
Chair, Corner, Chippendale, Mahogany, Pine, Double Splat, Slip Seat, Arms, 31 x 31 In.		944
Chair, Corner, Chippendale, Mahogany, Slip Seat, Pierced Slats, c.1790, 32 x 29 In.		944
Chair, Corner, Country Sheraton, Horizontal Splats, Rush Seat, Stretchers, 1800s, 29 In.		96
Chair, Corner, George II Style, Mahogany, 2 Shaped Slats, Upholstered Seat, Miniature		188
Chair, Corner, George III, Curved Crest Rail, Pierced Splats, Pad Seat, c.1850		875
Chair, Corner, George III, Walnut, Curved Backrest, Pierced Splats, Slip Seat, Cabriole Legs		530
Chair, Corner, Georgian, Concave Back, Pierced Splats, Scroll Arms, Padded, 32 x 17 In.		497
Chair, Corner, Queen Anne, Flat Arms, Shaped Back, Pierced, Commode Seat, c.1790, 33 In.		2250
Chair, Corner, Queen Anne, Mahogany, 3 Turned Supports, 2 Pierced Slats, Square Seat		406
Chair, Corner, Queen Anne, Mahogany, Shaped Skirt, Cabriole Legs, 1760, 34 In.		1763
Chair, Corner, Queen Anne, Maple, Rush Seat, New England, c.1760		92
Chair, Corner, Queen Anne, Maple, Turned Spindles, Rush Seat, 1700s, 29 ½ In. ....*illus*		240
Chair, Corner, Queen Anne, Tiger Maple, Birch, Mixed Wood, 1700s, 32 x 21 In. ....*illus*		767
Chair, Corner, Queen Anne, Walnut, Shaped Slats, Apron, Cabriole Legs, Pennsylvania, c.1765		1896
Chair, Corner, Regency Style, Chinoiserie Frame, Spindle Back, Slip Seat, Pair		750
Chair, Corner, Smoking, Chippendale, Mixed Wood, Pierced Slats, Scroll Arms, c.1790, 35 In.		489
Chair, Corner, Walnut, 8 Turned Stretchers, Rush Seat, c.1750		530
Chair, Cowboy, Wood, Wagon Wheel Sides, Faux Leather, Embossed Horse Head, c.1950 .....*illus*		300
Chair, Deacon's, Victorian, Architectural Pediment, Turned Legs, Upholstered, 55 In.		184
Chair, Desk, Brown Leather Triangular Back, Contoured Arms, Chrome, Frame, Swivel		203
Chair, Dining, Queen Anne Style, Walnut, Cutout Back, Slip Seat, c.1970, Pair		210
Chair, E. Franzolini, Teak, Metal, Open Arms, Florence Knoll, c.1955, 31 ½ In.		316
Chair, Eames, DAX, Red Paint, Gray Fiberglass, Herman Miller, 31 x 24 In.		177
Chair, Eames, DCW, Birch Plywood, Stamped, Herman Miller, 1950s, 20 x 29 In.		313
Chair, Eames, Fiberglass, Naugahyde, Chrome, Shaped Back, Arms, Herman Miller, 32 x 22 In.		439
Chair, Eames, LCW, Birch, Herman Miller, 22 x 27 In.		1375
Chair, Eames, Lounge, Walnut, Enameled Aluminum, Herman Miller, 1960s, 32 x 34 In.		625
Chair, Eames, Plastic, Yellow Fiberglass, Enameled Steel, Herman Miller, 1940s, 32 x 25 In.		625
Chair, Eames, Shell, Green Fiberglass, Zinc Legs, Herman Miller, 18 x 32 In., Pair		375
Chair, Eames, Shell, Stacking, Yellow, Fiberglass, Zinc Base, Herman Miller, 19 x 32 In., Pair		313
Chair, Eames, Soft Pad, Leather, Aluminum Frame, Casters, Herman Miller, 1900s, 33 In.		999
Chair, Edwardian, Mahogany, Padded Ear Back, Outscrolled Arms, c.1900, 42 In.		1230
Chair, Eero Saarinen, Womb, Chrome Frame, Gold Velour Upholstery, 36 x 34 In.		819
Chair, Egyptian Revival, Black & Gold Paint, Animal Terminal Arms		530
Chair, Elm, Slanted Slat Back, Open Arms, Plank Seat		1440
Chair, English Style, Oak, Square Back, Turned Legs, Arm Supports, Upholstered, 44 In.		127
Chair, Esherick, Maple, Oak, Leather, Incised WE XXXII, 1932, 38 x 18 In. ....*illus*		17500
Chair, Ettore Sottsass, Lounge, Leather, Steel, Plastic, Knoll, 1980s, 33 ½ In., Pair ....*illus*		3125
Chair, Fauteuil, Charles X, Mahogany, Carved, Open Upholstered Arms, c.1835, Pair		4270

Chair, Fauteuil, Directoire Style, Multicolor, Carved Crest, Padded Back, Seat, Arms, 36 In.........	922
Chair, Fauteuil, Empire Style, Mahogany, Ormolu, Upholstered, Arms, c.1850, 38 In.	1107
Chair, Fauteuil, Louis Philippe, Mahogany, Upholstered, Flat Back, Arms, c.1850, 43 x 28 In., Pair	375
Chair, Fauteuil, Louis XV, Beech, Flat Back, Upholstered, Arms, P. Gourdin, c.1750......................	3125
Chair, Fauteuil, Louis XV, Beech, Rounded, Cabriole Legs, Upholstered, Arms, c.1770, Pair	2500
Chair, Fauteuil, Louis XV, Upholstered, Flat Back, Arms, X-Stretcher, c.1790, 39 x 27 In..............	1003
Chair, Fauteuil, Louis XVI Style, Upholstered, Painted, Carved, Arms, c.1810, 34 x 22 In., Pair....	600
Chair, Fauteuil, Louis XVI, Arched Back, Cabriole Legs, Upholstered, Flat Back, Arms, c.1800	4063
Chair, Fauteuil, Louis XVI, Beech, Oval Flat Back, Upholstered, Arms, Pair..................................	1188
Chair, Fauteuil, Neoclassical Style, Beech, Upholstered, Flat Back, Arms, Pair............................	530
Chair, Federal, Mahogany Inlay, Shield Back, Upholstered, Splayed Feet, c.1800, 38 In., Pair......	14160
Chair, Federal, Mahogany, 3 Tobacco Leaf Splats, Slip Seat, c.1820, 36 x 21 In., Pair	590
Chair, Federal, Mahogany, Brass, 3 Splats, c.1810, 36 In.	750
Chair, Federal, Mahogany, Carved, Reeded, Cushion, c.1808-15, 33 In. ....*illus*	10200
Chair, Federal, Mahogany, Splat Back, Drapery, Urn Pierced, Pad Seat, Phila., c.1800, 36 In.	1408
Chair, Federal, Mahogany, Upholstered, Carved Swags, Tassel Crest Rail, Arms, c.1800, 33 In.	5938
Chair, Finn Juhl, Lounge, Teak, Upholstered, Baker Furniture, 1950s, 33 In., Pair ....*illus*	9375
Chair, Flared Sides, Back, Pink Upholstery, Tapered Legs, 1950s, 29 x 31 In.	125
Chair, Frankl, D Lounge, Black Lacquer, Cushions, Johnson Furniture Co., c.1930, 27 x 25 In....	272
Chair, French Style, Carved Wood Frame, Cane Back, Seat, 26 In., Child's..................................	184
Chair, Frits Henningsen, Lounge, Mahogany, Leather, Denmark, 1940s, 31 x 28 In. ....*illus*	1875
Chair, G. De Carlo, Flared Arms, Black Tube Frame, Green Silk, Arflex, 1950s, 35 x 35 In.	1250
Chair, G. Fleishman, Lumberest, Zigzags, Black Laminated Birch Plywood, 1985, 42 In., Pair	316
Chair, G. Nakashima, New Chair, Walnut, Hickory, Slat Back, c.1970, 36 x 19 In., Pair...............	3125
Chair, G. Nakashima, Walnut, Hickory, Upholstered, 1989, 34 x 35 In., Pair	20000
Chair, G. Stickley, 3 Horizontal Splats, Leather Seat, Red Decal, 27 x 38 In.	375
Chair, G. Stickley, Morris, Bow Arm, Eastwood, Red Decal, c.1901, 38 x 32 In. ....*illus*	10000
Chair, G. Stickley, Thornden, 2 Horizontal Slats, Leather Seat, 18 x 36 In.	670
Chair, Gehry, Wiggle, Laminated Cardboard, Masonite, Vitra, 1990s, 32 x 13 In.........................	1625
Chair, George I, Oak Wainscot, Arms, Cushion, c.1740	4029
Chair, George I, Oak, Wainscot, Carved Back, Scroll Arms, Plank Seat, c.1700	2133
Chair, George II Style, Mahogany, Arched Pad Back, Seat, Carved Legs, Paw Feet, 1800s...........	750
Chair, George II Style, Mahogany, Pierced Splat, Scrollwork, Flowers, Arms, 25 In.	584
Chair, George II Style, Mahogany, Shaped Solid Back, Open Arms, Upholstered, Carved Legs	344
Chair, George II, Walnut, Pierced Splat, Pad Seat, Open Arms, c.1770	530
Chair, George II, Walnut, Shaped Back, Upholstered, Open Arms, c.1765	1250
Chair, George II, Walnut, Upholstered, Cabriole Legs, c.1790, Pair	2250
Chair, George III Style, Flower Crest & Splat, Open Arms, Cabriole Legs, 40 In., Pair...................	738
Chair, George III Style, Gilt Limewood, Leaf-Carved Frame, Arms, Cabriole Legs, 1800s, Pair......	4375
Chair, George III Style, Mahogany, Eared Crest, Pierced Splat, Arms, c.1885, 39 In., Pair	492
Chair, George III Style, Mahogany, Padded Back, Leaf-Carved Arms, Legs, c.1850	1500
Chair, George III, Arched Back, Upholstered, Open Arms, Carved	360
Chair, George III, Mahogany, Oval Back, Seat, Open Arms, Upholstered, 1700s, Pair...................	3125
Chair, George III, Mahogany, Rounded Padded Back, Seat, Fluted Legs, Arms, c.1750, Pair.........	1375
Chair, George III, Mahogany, Shield Back, c.1800, Pair	480
Chair, George III, Pierced Back, Pad Seat, Open Arms, Painted, c.1780, Pair.............................	1625
Chair, George III, Walnut, Cartouche Shape Back, Upholstered, Open Arms, c.1800...................	15000
Chair, Georgian, Walnut, Shell-Carved Back, Pierced Splat Slip Seat, Cabriole Legs, c.1750	189
Chair, Gothic Revival, Carved, Trefoils, Quatrefoils, Crockets, Spires, Stiles, 46 In., Pair.............	492
Chair, Gothic Revival, Mahogany, Arched Crest, Finial Stiles, Square Legs, c.1830......................	854
Chair, Gothic Revival, Rosewood, Carved, Crocketed Cathedral Back, Square Legs, c.1850, Pair .	976
Chair, Gothic Revival, Rosewood, Crest, Pierced Quatrefoil, Arms, Turned Legs, 1800s...............	366
Chair, Gothic Revival, Walnut, Arch Carved Back, Upholstered Seat, Phila., c.1845, 37 In.	313
Chair, Gothic Revival, Walnut, Carved, Ogee Arch, Tracery, Pinnacles, 1800s ....*illus*	717
Chair, Great, Ash, Spindles, Turned Finials, Ring Turned Horizontal Rails, 45 x 19 In.	5100
Chair, Hall, Gothic Revival, Walnut, Arched Back, Pierced Quatrefoil, Tapered Legs, c.1850	246
Chair, Hardwood, Yoke Back, Dragon-Carved Splat, Woven Seat, c.1900, 40 In., Pair..................	590
Chair, Henrik Thor-Larsen, Ovalia, Fiberglass, Aluminum, Upholstered, 1968, 51 x 36 In.	2250
Chair, Hepplewhite Style, Shield Back, Plumes, Flowers, c.1815, 36 In.	460
Chair, Hepplewhite, Cherry, Strapwork Splat, Tapered Legs, c.1800, 40 In.	185
Chair, Hepplewhite, Mahogany, Pierced Back, Open Arms, Upholstered, England........................	780
Chair, Hepplewhite, Mahogany, Shield Back, Carved Urn Splat, c.1790, 38 In.	3105
Chair, Hepplewhite, Openwork Shield Back, Upholstered Seat, c.1750, 19 x 41 In., Pair..............	230
Chair, High Back, 3 Horizontal Slats, Spindles, Arms, Stenciled Flowers, Green Paint	212
Chair, High, Mixed Wood, Ladder Back, Rush Seat, 18th Century, 35 ½ In.	330
Chair, High, Windsor, Grain Paint, Flowers, 30 In..	120

Furniture, Chair, Arched Back, Turned Legs, Needlework Seat, Continental, c.1710, 37 In.
$1,320

Skinner Auctioneers & Appraisers

Furniture, Chair, Arts & Crafts, Mahogany, Fruitwood Inlay, Arms, J.S. Henry, c.1895, 42 In.
$1,125

Los Angeles Modern Auctions (LAMA)

Furniture, Chair, Baroque, Walnut, Carved, Burl Panel, Plank Seat, Arms, Italy
$246

Neal Auction Co.

Furniture, Chair, Baroque, Walnut, Carved, Pierced Stretcher, Arms, c.1700, 53 x 25 In.
$354

Brunk Auctions

Furniture, Chair, Belter, Rococo Revival, Rosewood, Rosalie Without Grapes, c.1865, 43 In.
$1,476

New Orleans Auction Galleries, Inc.

Furniture, Chair, Chippendale Style, Mahogany, Carved, Upholstered Seat, c.1900, 53 In.
$219

Rago Arts & Auction Center

Chair, Horn, Cattle-Hide Seat, Glass Ball Feet, Arms, Texas, c.1889	5904
Chair, Horn, Faux Leopard Seat, Arms, c.1890, 32 ½ x 22 In. ....*illus*	510
Chair, J. Hoffmann, Alleegass, Channel Back, Barrel Shape, Upholstered, c.1940, 29 x 24 In., Pair	2250
Chair, J. Hoffmann, Oak, Brass, Upholstered, Arms, Austria, c.1900, 41 x 26 In.	3438
Chair, Jacobean Style, Carved, Acanthus, Scrolls, Openwork Back, Twisted Columns, 52 In.	72
Chair, Jacobean, Walnut, Carved Back, Stiles, Frame, Spiral Turned Legs, Upholstered, Pair	3375
Chair, James Mont, Silver Finish, Upholstered, 40 In. ....*illus*	489
Chair, Jean-Michel Frank Style, Leather, Mahogany, 3-Pillow Back, France, 1930s, 39 x 19 In. ...	3250
Chair, Joe Colombo, Elda, Coiled Brown Leather, White Fiberglass, c.1975, 37 x 38 In.	2250
Chair, Joseph Ricchio, Stiletto, Wood, Black Paint, Arms, Stendig, Midcentury, Pair	80
Chair, Katavolos Littell & Kelley, Lounge, Leather Sling, Chrome, Enameled Steel, 23 x 26 In.	625
Chair, Knoll, Gothic Revival, Maple, Laminated, Dyed, R. Venturi, 1980s, 41 In., Pair ....*illus*	10625
Chair, Ladder Back, 4 Slats, Ocher Grain Paint, Pa., c.1780	1304
Chair, Ladder Back, Curly Maple, Arched Slats, Rush Seat, Pa., c.1780, 46 In.	294
Chair, Ladder Back, Maple, Oak, 5 Arch Slats, Splint Seat, Arms, New England, 49 In.	127
Chair, Ladder Back, Shaped Slats, Rush Seat, c.1800, 17 In.	480
Chair, Ladder Back, Turned Stile, Arch Slats, Arms, Black Paint, Woven Seat, N.J., c.1850	889
Chair, Laminated Teak, Bentwood, Open Arms, Norman Cherner, 31 x 25 In.	760
Chair, Laverne International, Acrylic, Upholstered, 1960s, 37 x 33 x 30 In. ....*illus*	3250
Chair, Le Corbusier, Basculant, Leather, Chrome Steel, 1960s, 26 x 25 In., Pair	1250
Chair, Library Steps, Gothic, Oak, Carved, Leather Steps, England, c.1890, 36 In. ....*illus*	1075
Chair, Limbert, 3 Vertical Slats, Leather Seat, Open Arms, 28 x 25 In.	344
Chair, Lolling, Chippendale, Mahogany, Arched Crest, Shaped Arms, Stretchers, c.1790	5378
Chair, Lolling, Federal, Mahogany, Inlay, Serpentine Crest, Shaped Arms, 46 x 17 In.	7380
Chair, Lolling, Kittinger, Line Inlaid Arms, Legs, Red Leather, c.1975, 48 x 26 In., Pair	920
Chair, Lolling, Mahogany, Serpentine Crest, Open Arms, Peach Upholstery	2520
Chair, Lolling, Sheraton, Mahogany, Open Arms, Turned Legs, c.1810, 47 In.	922
Chair, Lolling, Sheraton, Mahogany, Silk Upholstery, Open Arms, New England, c.1815	1896
Chair, Louis XV Style, Beech, Open Arms, Cabriole Legs, c.1900, 33 In., Pair	295
Chair, Louis XV Style, Painted, Carved, Upholstered, Shaped Crest, Open Arms, 41 In., Pair	708
Chair, Louis XV Style, Upholstered, Leaves & Shells, Open Arms, 1900s, 44 In.	649
Chair, Louis XV Style, Walnut, Carved, Open Arm, Upholstered, 39 x 27 In., Pair	720
Chair, Louis XV, Flower Carved, Round Back, Upholstered, Painted	540
Chair, Louis XVI Style, Giltwood, Carved, Crossed Stretcher, Arms, Upholstered, Casters, 50 In. ...	495
Chair, Louis XVI Style, Stained, Carved, Upholstered, Open Arms, 39 In., Pair	708
Chair, Louis XVI Style, Upholstered, Arched Back, Shaped Apron, c.1895, 38 In., Pair	885
Chair, Lounge, Art Deco, Split Reed, Wood, Upholstered, c.1930, 33 x 34 In.	1230
Chair, Lounge, Bentwood, Open Arms, Upholstered, Martin Craig, c.1935, 35 x 35 In.	1875
Chair, Lounge, Ottoman, Eames, Rosewood, Leather, Herman Miller, 1950s, 35 In. ....*illus*	3250
Chair, Lounge, Plantation, Cane, Teak, Curled Arms, Indonesia, c.1970, 36 x 25 In., Pair	688
Chair, M. Nakashima, Walnut, Hickory, 7-Slat Back, Round Seat, c.1953, 28 x 19 In.	1250
Chair, Mahogany, Carved Crest, Splat, Cabriole Legs, Octagonal Pad Feet, 1700s, 38 In.	120
Chair, Mahogany, Curved Rail, Carved, Pierced Splat, Reeded, Pad Seat, c.1815, 33 In.	313
Chair, Mahogany, High Back, Tapestry Upholstery, Open Arms, c.1910, 25 x 52 In.	192
Chair, Mahogany, Rose-Carved Back, Saber Legs, Rose Needlepoint Seat	57
Chair, Maple, Carved, Banister Back, Rush Seat, Turned Stretcher, 1720s, 52 x 19 In.	1080
Chair, Maple, Pierced Splat, Rush Seat, c.1759	118
Chair, Marcel Wanders, Open Weave, Knotted, Cappellini, 29 x 27 In.	439
Chair, Masonic, Gothic, Pierced Splat, Cushion, Padded Arms, Shekromeko Lodge, 55 In.	316
Chair, Matte Chrome Steel, Black Upholstery, Italy, 1950s, 28 x 22 In., Pair	1000
Chair, McCobb, Calvin, Mahogany, Upholstered, 1950s, 43 x 31 In.	1625
Chair, McCobb, Captain, Spindles, Round Back, Winchendon, 30 x 22 In., Pair	384
Chair, Metal, Curved Back, Egg-Shape Arms, Upholstered, France, 1950s, 32 x 36 In., Pair	2500
Chair, Mies Van Der Rohe, Lounge, MR, Tubular Steel, Leather, Knoll, c.1972, 33 In. ....*illus*	799
Chair, Milo Baughman Style, Lounge, Chrome Frame, Upholstered, c.1970, 29 x 30 In., Pair	1722
Chair, Milo Baughman, Chrome Frame, Orange Upholstery, Thayer-Coggin, 25 x 31 In., Pair....	813
Chair, Milo Baughman, Lounge, Chrome Frame, Nubby Upholstery, 30 x 28 In., Pair	1375
Chair, Milo Baughman, Lounge, Chrome Steel Frame, Upholstered, 30 x 27 In., Pair	938
Chair, Milo Baughman, Lounge, Chromed Steel, Thayer-Coggin, 1970s, 26 In., Pair ....*illus*	3250
Chair, Milo Baughman, Swivel, Walnut, Ebonized, Upholstered, T. Coggin, 1960s, 26 x 29 In.	500
Chair, Milo Baughman, Upholstered, Chrome Steel, Thayer-Coggin, 1970s, 28 x 30 In., Pair	1750
Chair, Molded Green Plastic, Fiberglass, Enameled Steel, Arms, L. Peabody, 32 x 25 In.	88
Chair, Morris, Mahogany, 3 Slats, Rose Valley, Pa., 1901-06, 48 x 34 In. ....*illus*	7500
Chair, Morris, Stickley Bros., Oak, Adjustable Back, Cushions, 37 In.	1880
Chair, Neoclassical Style, Fruitwood, Carved Plumes, Scroll Arms, c.1950, 39 In., Pair	2952

Chair, Neoclassical Style, Mahogany, Marquetry, Open, Scroll Arms, Upholstered, 36 x 28 In.	219
Chair, Neoclassical, Mahogany, Carved, Tablet Crest, Reeded, Arms, Slip Seat, c.1810	7768
Chair, Neoclassical, Wood, Latticework Back, Tapered Legs, Italy, Pair..........................	840
Chair, Neo-Renaissance, Mahogany, Portrait Medallion, Pierced Crest, Arms, 46 In.	738
Chair, Nursing, George III, Mahogany, Husk Carved, Serpentine Crest, Pierced	369
Chair, Oak, Carved, Owl, Folding, V Inside Rose, Signature, 1905, 33 x 28 In.	5625
Chair, Oak, Leather, Arm, Robert Mouseman Thompson, c.1950, 40 x 32 In., Pair	1875
Chair, Oak, Paneled Back, Carved, Turned Legs, Box Stretcher, 17th Century, 48 In.	4583
Chair, Oak, Red Paint, Carved Crest Apron, Flowers, Berry Design, Arms, England, c.1790	944
Chair, Oak, Shaped Top Rail, Turned Stiles, Knob Finial, Single Paneled Seat, c.1800, 36 In.	550
Chair, Oak, Wainscot, Tulip-Carved Back, Arms, England, c.1740	830
Chair, Odelberg Olson, Birch, Adjustable, Steel Base, Sweden, 1940s, 18 x 19 In.	500
Chair, Old Hickory, Cane Seat, Back, Stretchers, 39 ½ In., Pair..................................	104
Chair, Ottoman, Eames, Cherry, Leather, Herman Miller, 1960s, Chair 33 In., Ottoman 17 In.....	2875
Chair, Ottoman, Eero Saarinen, Womb, Chromed Steel, Knoll, c.1950, 39 In. ....*illus*	1920
Chair, Ottoman, Leaf Shape, Green Enameled Steel, Stamped Cricket Forge, 1990s, 54 x 39 In...	1625
Chair, Oxbow Back, Carved Skirt, Square Legs, Stretcher, Chinese, 43 x 21 In..................	350
Chair, Pedro Friedeberg, Hand, Mahogany, Laminated, Mexico, 1960s, 35 x 22 In. ....*illus*	11875
Chair, Philippe Starck, Costes, Ebonized Wood, Steel, Leather, 3 Legs, c.1985, 35 In., Pair	308
Chair, Pierre Folie Charpentier, Lounge, Stainless Steel, France, 1970s, 28 x 24 In.	1000
Chair, Plywood, Green Paint, Nathan Lerner, Polar Home, 1940s, 16 x 30 In.	688
Chair, Porter's, Georgian Style, Barrel Back, Mahogany, Tufted Leather, Storage, 68 In. ......*illus*	1315
Chair, Poul Kjaerholm, PK22, Brushed Nickel-Plated Steel, Leather Seat, c.1950, 29 In., 2..........	2160
Chair, Queen Anne Style, Maple, Yolk Crest, Solid Splat, Pad Feet, c.1900, 43 In.	118
Chair, Queen Anne, Cherry, Shaped Crest & Splat, Slip Seat, Cabriole Legs, c.1765	1250
Chair, Queen Anne, Cherry, Vase Shape Splat, Slip Seat, c.1740-60, 39 ½ In. ....*illus*	3600
Chair, Queen Anne, Compass Seat, Scroll Crest, Vase Shape Splat, Drop-In Seat, 1700s, 40 In.....	350
Chair, Queen Anne, Dutch Style, Carved, Shaped Padded Seat, Ball & Claw Feet, 45 In., Pair	1162
Chair, Queen Anne, Mahogany, Serpentine Crest, Cabriole Legs, c.1750, 43 In............................	14400
Chair, Queen Anne, Mahogany, Shaped Splat, Spoon Back, Slip Seat, H-Stretcher, c.1760...........	1120
Chair, Queen Anne, Mahogany, Turned Stretchers, Cabriole Legs, 1800s, 39 In............................	235
Chair, Queen Anne, Maple, Shaped Splat, Rush Seat, Bulbous Stretcher, Pair	72
Chair, Queen Anne, Maple, Spoon Scroll Crest, Turned Legs, c.1730, 42 In................................	960
Chair, Queen Anne, Maple, Vase Shape Splat, Painted, Gold Trim, c.1700s, 40 ½ In. ....*illus*	570
Chair, Queen Anne, Mixed Wood, 6 Spindles, Yoke Crest, Rush Seat, 1900s, 40 In. ....*illus*	800
Chair, Queen Anne, Rush Seat, Arms, c.1790, 18 x 49 In..................................	345
Chair, Queen Anne, Rush Seat, New England, c.1750, Pair	213
Chair, Queen Anne, Tiger Maple, Carved Crest, Pad Seat, New England, c.1750	2252
Chair, Queen Anne, Walnut, Carved Frame, Slip Seat, England, Pair	1200
Chair, Queen Anne, Walnut, Scroll Crest, Scalloped Frame, Arms, Delaware Valley, c.1760	9480
Chair, Queen Anne, Walnut, Shaped Crest, Vase Splat, Balloon Seat, Stretcher, Pad Feet	6000
Chair, Queen Anne, Walnut, Shell-Carved Crest, Slip Seat, Pennsylvania, c.1760........................	2300
Chair, Regence Style, Walnut, Upholstered, Shaped Padded Back, Carved Arms, 1700s, 37 In......	540
Chair, Regency Style, Fruitwood, Shaped, Cane Seat & Back, Reeded Arms, 38 In........................	676
Chair, Regency, Mahogany, Rectangle Back, Painted Armorial Crest, Plank Seat, c.1820, Pair	4063
Chair, Regency, Mahogany, Slat Back, Saddle Seat, Square Front Legs, Arms, c.1810, 31 In., Pair	7200
Chair, Regency, Mahogany, Tablet Crest, Rosettes, Cane Seat, Scroll Arms, c.1810	3050
Chair, Renaissance Revival, Carved Crest, Upholstered, Turned Legs, Casters, 38 x 19 In., Pair ...	438
Chair, Renaissance Revival, Ebonized Cherry, Upholstered, Arms..	6250
Chair, Renaissance Revival, Incised, Inlaid, Openwork Carved Back, Pad Seat, c.1875, 43 In......	150
Chair, Renaissance Revival, Walnut, Carved Crest, Velvet Upholstery, c.1870, 37 x 17 In..........	344
Chair, Risom, Lounge, Maple, Cotton, Woven Seat, Back, Florence Knoll, 1941, 30 In., Pair........	660
Chair, Risom, Lounge, Vostra, Beech, Canvas Woven, 29 x 29 In.	585
Chair, Risom, Lounge, Webbed, 30 ½ x 20 In. ....*illus*	360
Chair, Rocker, is listed under Rocker in this category.	
Chair, Rococo Revival, Carved Crest, Upholstered Seat, Back, 1800s, 42 In., Pair........................	720
Chair, Rococo Revival, Cast Iron, Spring, Thomas Warren, American Chair Co., c.1850 ......*illus*	1075
Chair, Rococo Revival, Rosewood, Rose, Scroll Openwork Back, Cabriole Legs, Pair....................	1375
Chair, Rococo, Carved, Painted, Gilt, Ram's Head, Hoof Feet, Italy, c.1890, Pair ....*illus*	2684
Chair, Rohlfs, High Carved Pierced Back, Slab Seat, 1901, 18 x 55 In.	7500
Chair, Roycroft, Carved Edward, Orb & Cross Mark, East Aurora, N.Y., c.1905, Child's................	625
Chair, Russel Wright, Maple, Arms, Continuous Seat & Back, Conant & Ball, 29 In., Pair............	976
Chair, Rustic Branch Back, Arms, Legs, c.1850, 33 x 26 In., Pair....................................	3750
Chair, Savonarola, Walnut, Carved, Arms, Beast Terminals, Italy, 54 In. ....*illus*	1625
Chair, Savonarola, Walnut, Winged Lion, Female Figure, Slat Seat, Paw Feet, c.1775, 39 In.	2460

F

Furniture, Chair, Chippendale Style, Mahogany, Carved, Upholstered, Arms, 1800s, 44 ½ In.
$1,188

Leslie Hindman Auctioneers

Furniture, Chair, Chippendale, Mahogany, Carved, Owl's-Eye Splat, c.1780, 37 In.
$1,320

Garth's Auctioneers & Appraisers

Furniture, Chair, Corner, Abalone, Bone, Ebony, Inlay, Trellis Work, Arms, c.1930, 28 In.
$1,033

James D. Julia Auctioneers

Furniture, Chair, Corner, Queen Anne, Maple, Turned Spindles, Rush Seat, 1700s, 29 ½ In.
$240

Garth's Auctioneers & Appraisers

Furniture, Chair, Corner, Queen Anne, Tiger Maple, Birch, Mixed Wood, 1700s, 32 x 21 In.
$767

Brunk Auctions

Furniture, Chair, Cowboy, Wood, Wagon Wheel Sides, Faux Leather, Embossed Horse Head, c.1950
$300

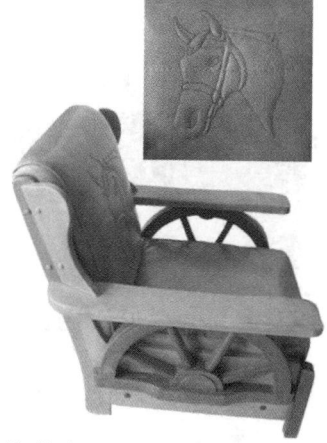

Allard Auctions

Chair, Savronola, Wood, Carved Acanthus, Leather, Folding Style, c.1900, 34 ½ In.	72
Chair, Sculptural Seat, Vinyl Upholstery, Tapered Legs, Singer & Sons, 19 x 17 In., Pair	813
Chair, Sedan, Louis XVI Style, Chinoiserie, Painted, Upholstered, 1800s, 66 x 29 In. ....*illus*	4481
Chair, Sewing, Bamboo-Turned Spindles, Painted Flowers, Maroon Ground, 34 x 17 In.	2520
Chair, Shaker Style, Ladder Back, 2 Slats, Woven Splint Seat, Finials, 1800s, 24 In., Child's	60
Chair, Shaker, Ladder Back, Maple, Birch, Leather Over Woven Splint Seat, 39 In. ....*illus*	708
Chair, Shaker, Ladder Back, Maple, Splint Seat, New Lebanon, c.1835 ....*illus*	531
Chair, Shaker, Ladder Back, Painted, Rush Seat, Union Village, 1800s, 39 In. ....*illus*	1920
Chair, Shaker, Tilter, Red Paint, 3 Arched Slats, Tape Seat, 1800s, 38 x 14 In.	780
Chair, Sheraton, Mahogany, Pine, Pierced Plume Back, Carved Legs, Slip Seat, c.1810, Pair	1298
Chair, Sheraton, Painted, Tablet Back, Stenciled, Cane Seat, Turned Legs, 31 In.	492
Chair, Slat Back, Ring-Turned Stiles, Top Finials, Mushroom Handholds, 42 x 17 In.	1046
Chair, Spanish Style, Iron, Leather, Sling Back, Seat, Finials, Crossover Base, 34 In., Pair	738
Chair, Spindle Back, Stained, c.1850, 17 x 34 In., Pair	80
Chair, Splint Back, Seat, Base Stretcher, Pair	150
Chair, Splint Seat, Woven, c.1850, 34 x 15 ½ In.	173
Chair, Square Back, Arms, Scallop Upholstery, Casters, 1960s, 27 In., Pair	360
Chair, Stepped Back, Trelliswork, Inlay, Ivory, Bone, Ebony, Middle East, c.1930, 48 In. ......*illus*	593
Chair, Swedish Modern, Bentwood, Walnut, Black Leather Back, Seat, c.1950, 40 x 26 In.	1089
Chair, Swivel, Curved Back, Painted Wood, Brass, Upholstered, Kroehler, 1950s, 26 x 28 In.	1000
Chair, Swivel, Molded Fiberglass, Vinyl Upholstery, Grid Metal Back, Herman Miller, 31 In.	176
Chair, Tall Back, Linen Upholstery, White Paint, c.1950, 43 x 16 In., Pair	1404
Chair, Teak, Carved Panel, Pierced Apron, Arms, Stretcher, Chinese, c.1900, 39 x 25 In., Pair	8125
Chair, Teak, Metal Frame, Borge Mogensen, 20 x 29 In., Pair	875
Chair, Tete-A-Tete, Spindles, S-Curve Arm Rail, Basket Weave Seat & Back, 63 In.	184
Chair, Thayer-Coggin, Lounge, Chromed Steel, Vinyl Cushions, Mid-Century, 26 x 28 In., Pair	1622
Chair, Thomas Lamb, Steamer, Canadian Maple, Bent Slats, Folds Flat, 1979, 34 x 24 In.	531
Chair, Throne, Gothic Revival, Oak, Stiles, Square Arms, Molded Feet, c.1900, 46 In., Pair	1107
Chair, Tiger Maple, Low, 2 Slats, Turned Lemon Finials, Wovan Splint Seat, c.1850, 28 x 12 In.	80
Chair, Tribal, Carved, Woven Fiber, Iron Mounts, Africa, c.1900, 32 x 25 In., Pair	236
Chair, Tub, Biedermeier, Maple, Upholstered, Pair	1375
Chair, V. Kagan, Lounge, Ottoman, Walnut, Chenille, 1950s, 36 x 30 & 15 x 20 In.	11250
Chair, V. Kagan, Lounge, Walnut, Adjustable, Stainless Steel, 1950s, 33 x 27 x 61 In. ....*illus*	6875
Chair, V. Kagan, Wing, Ottoman, Aluminum, Upholstered, 41 In., 18 x 28 In. ....*illus*	2640
Chair, Victorian Style, Steer Horn, Leather Upholstery, 1900s, 42 x 31 x 22 In. ....*illus*	1188
Chair, Victorian, Walnut, Finger Mold Carved Frame, Arms, Upholstered, 41 In.	108
Chair, Victorian, Walnut, Heart-Shape Back, Flower-Carved Crest, 1800s	420
Chair, Victorian, Walnut, Hoop Back, Rose-Carved Crest, Pair	57
Chair, Victorian, Walnut, Open Arms, Upholstered, Carved, c.1890	89
Chair, Vignelli, Handkerchief, Fiberglass, Steel Legs, Florence Knoll, 1980s, 23 x 29 In., Pair	500
Chair, W. Castle, Molar, Gel-Coated Fiberglass, Tooth Shape, 1960s, 26 x 32 In.	1375
Chair, W. McArthur, Tubular, Metal Slats, Green Paint, Label, c.1930, 34 ½ In., Pair............*illus*	3555
Chair, W. Platner, Bronze Wire Back, Base, Red Upholstery, Knoll, 1976, 27 x 30 In.	1375
Chair, W. Platner, Nickel Plated Steel Frame, Upholstered, Arms, c.1966, Knoll, 27 x 29 In.	587
Chair, W. Platner, Steel Base, Frame, Upholstered, Knoll, 1950s, 31 x 36 In., Pair	2500
Chair, Walnut, Bone Inlay, Vase Shape Splat, Arms, Italy, c.1850, 38 In. ....*illus*	300
Chair, Walnut, Upholstered Back, Seat, Fluted Apron, Carved, Scroll Arms, Dutch	180
Chair, Walter Lamb, Copper Frame, Patina, Plastic Rope Back, Seat, Brown Jordan, 21 x 33 In. .	1000
Chair, Walter Lamb, Lounge, Copper Frame, Plastic Rope, Woven, Brown Jordan, 29 x 66 In.	3000
Chair, Wassily, Chromed Steel, Leather, M. Breuer, Italy, 1960s, 28 x 31 In., Pair	469
Chair, Wegner, Danish Modern, Folding, Black Painted Frame, Rush Back, Seat, 31 In.	118
Chair, Wegner, Mama Bear, Wool, Hardwood, Teak, Marked, 1950s, 42 In.	7380
Chair, Wegner, Peacock, Ash, Teak, Paper Cord Seat, Johannes Hansen, c.1960, 42 In. ....*illus*	2280
Chair, Wegner, Teak, Leather, Denmark, 20th Century, 30 In., Pair	2335
Chair, Wegner, Valet, Teak, Pine, Brass, Johannes Hansen, 1960s, 37 In. ....*illus*	8750
Chair, William & Mary, Banister Back, Arched Crest, Acorn Finials, Rush Seat, c.1800, 44 In.	500
Chair, William & Mary, Ladder Back, Mushroom Cap Handrests, Red Paint, c.1740	1778
Chair, William IV, Mahogany, Curved Back, Arms, Carved Legs, Tufted Upholstery, c.1835	750
Chair, Windsor Style, Oak, Turned Spools, Pierced Splat, Arms, 58 x 35 In.	184
Chair, Windsor, Arms, Branded D. Putnam, c.1800, Youth Size	237
Chair, Windsor, Back Brace, 8 Spindles, E.B. Tracy, c.1800, 35 In.	3625
Chair, Windsor, Bamboo-Turned Spindles, Stiles, Writing Arm, Painted, 38 x 19 In.	1440
Chair, Windsor, Birdcage, c.1820, Pair	185
Chair, Windsor, Birdcage, Mixed Wood, Bamboo Turning, Mass., c.1805, 35 In., Pair	353
Chair, Windsor, Black Paint, Arms, New England, c.1790	830

F

Chair, Windsor, Bow Back, 9 Spindle Back, Arms, J. Brown, Virginia, c.1805, 37 In.	2185
Chair, Windsor, Bow Back, Black Paint, Splayed Legs	210
Chair, Windsor, Bow Back, Elm, Plank Seat, Turned Legs, Arms	150
Chair, Windsor, Bow Back, Red Paint, Swelled Spindles, c.1785, 16 ½ In.	1046
Chair, Windsor, Bow Back, Shaped Arms, New England	420
Chair, Windsor, Bow Back, X-Stretcher, Black Paint, New England, c.1810	593
Chair, Windsor, Brace Back, 7 Spindles, Mid-Atlantic, c.1810, 17 In.	104
Chair, Windsor, Cage Back, Arms, c.1810	130
Chair, Windsor, Comb Back, 7 Spindles, Shaped Crest, Arms, 1800s, 40 In. ....*illus*	720
Chair, Windsor, Comb Back, Arms, c.1815	444
Chair, Windsor, Comb Back, Black Paint, Arms, Michie Tavern Group, Va., 1936, 45 x 18 In., Pair	489
Chair, Windsor, Comb Back, Black Paint, New England, c.1775	770
Chair, Windsor, Comb Back, Continuous Arm, Nichols & Stone, 25 x 45 In., Pair	270
Chair, Windsor, Comb Back, Mixed Wood, Volute-Carved Ears, Outswept Arms, 43 In.	2169
Chair, Windsor, Comb Back, Scroll Ears, Splayed Legs, Arms, Painted, Phila., c.1780	7703
Chair, Windsor, Fanback, Green Paint, Yellow Pinstripes, Pennsylvania, c.1790	710
Chair, Windsor, Fanback, Mixed Wood, Volute-Carved Ears, Baluster Legs, c.1790, 35 In.	1175
Chair, Windsor, Fanback, Red, Green Paint, Pennsylvania, c.1790	296
Chair, Windsor, Hoop Back, Black Paint, Stamped Tyson, Pennsylvania, c.1800, Pair	415
Chair, Windsor, Low Rod Back, Exaggerated Triangular Seat, Brown Paint, c.1790	3068
Chair, Windsor, Maple, Ash, Pine, Arched Continuous Arm & Back	560
Chair, Windsor, Mixed Wood, Volute-Carved Crest, Baluster Arms, c.1900, 48 In.	1140
Chair, Windsor, Rhode Island Style, Brace Back, 12 Spindles, c.1790	354
Chair, Windsor, Rod Back, Shaped Seat, New England, c.1820, 35 In.	69
Chair, Windsor, Sack Back, 7 Spindles, Black Paint, H-Stretcher, c.1820, 36 In., Pair	660
Chair, Windsor, Sack Back, Birdcage Writing Arm, Drawer, Pennsylvania, c.1789	4266
Chair, Windsor, Sack Back, Mixed Wood, Bamboo Turnings, c.1790, 39 In.	422
Chair, Windsor, Scroll Ears, Knuckle Arms, Splayed Baluster-Turned Legs, Painted, c.1780	7703
Chair, Windsor, Spindle Back, Arms, England, 17 ½ x 46 In., Pair	316
Chair, Windsor, Step-Down, Black Paint	330
Chair, Windsor, Umber Paint, Continuous Arm, New England, c.1790	770
Chair, Windsor, Walnut, Ash, Tall Slated Back, Arms, M. Brown, 47 x 28 In.	1062
Chair, Windsor, Writing Arm, Painted, c.1950	474
Chair, Windsor, Yew, Pierced Splats, Turned Legs, Arms, England, c.1890, 34 ½ In. ......*illus*	120
Chair, Windsor, Yew, Slatted Back, Arms, England, c.1860, 17 x 33 In.	196
Chair, Wing, Chippendale Style, Mahogany, Outscrolled Arms, Bellflower, Claw Feet	984
Chair, Wing, Early American Style, Mahogany Legs, Velour Upholstery, c.1950, 48 In.	36
Chair, Wing, Federal Style, Carved Arms, Upholstered, c.1860, 17 x 46 ½ In.	316
Chair, Wing, Federal, Mahogany, Arched Back, Wings, Upholstered, Phila., c.1810, 43 In.	2750
Chair, Wing, Federal, Mahogany, Wavy Back, Sides, Upholstered, c.1800	1125
Chair, Wing, George I, Walnut Frame, Upholstered, Downswept Arms, c.1730	1944
Chair, Wing, George III Style, Mahogany, Eagle, Cabriole Legs, c.1900, 49 In.	2460
Chair, Wing, Jacobean Style, Oak, Scroll-Carved Frame, Upholstered, c.1860, 50 x 31 In.	1534
Chair, Wing, Notch-Carved Round Frame, Upholstered, c.1920, 39 x 29 In., Pair	1652
Chair, Wing, Ottoman, Tufted, Leather Upholstery, 40 x 28 In.	600
Chair, Wing, Queen Anne, Walnut, Scroll Arms, Upholstered, England	1440
Chair, Wood Frame, Arms, Tufted Upholstery, Rene Prou, France, 1930s, 26 x 30 In., Pair	3125
Chair, Wood, Horseshoe Back, Mythical Beast, Rope Seat, Folding, Chinese, 45 x 29 In.	374
Chair, Wormley, Green Leather, Tufted, Dunbar, 28 x 35 In.	1500
Chair, Wormley, Slipper, Wood, Upholstered, 32 x 24 In., Pair	1968
Chair, Woven Rush Seat, Painted Flowers, Turned Supports, Shaped Stretchers, Slats, 17 In.	47
Chair, Yellow, Painted Flowers, Plank Seat, George Turner Label, Philadelphia, c.1830, Pair	948
Chair-Table, Maple, Round, Seat, Panel Supports, 27 x 41 In.	625
Chair-Table, Pine, 2-Board Top, Bench Seat, Lidded Compartment, Painted, 29 x 53 In.	2938
Chair-Table, Pine, Ash, Shoe Feet, New England, c.1775, 27 x 45 In. ....*illus*	2952
Chair-Table, Pine, Maple, Round Top, Chamfered Legs, 30 x 48 In.	443
Chair-Table, Pine, New England, c.1810, 30 x 48 In.	729
Chair-Table, Pine, Red Paint, 3-Board, Hinged Seating, Turned Feet, 1800s, 27 x 41 In.	1410
Chair-Table, Pine, Red, Blue Paint, Adjustable, New England, c.1800, 31 x 48 In.	3159
Chair-Table, Removable, c.1890, 48 x 45 In.	2070
Chair-Table, Round Top, Red Paint, 28 x 55 In.	3840
Chair-Table, Tilt Top, Red Paint, Shoe Feet, Overhanging Top, 27 x 51 In.	16800
Chaise Longue, Campaign, Mahogany, Cane, Folding, Turned Legs, c.1860	1320
Chaise Longue, Daybed Shape, Blond Legs, Caramel Striped Upholstery, 1950s, 80 x 30 In.	147
Chaise Longue, Heywood-Wakefield, Wicker, Scroll Arm, Hinged Seat, Brown, 75 In.	480

Furniture, Chair, Esherick, Maple, Oak, Leather, Incised WE XXXII, 1932, 38 x 18 In.
$17,500

Rago Arts & Auction Center

Furniture, Chair, Ettore Sottsass, Lounge, Leather, Steel, Plastic, Knoll, 1980s, 33 ½ In., Pair
$3,125

Rago Arts & Auction Center

Furniture, Chair, Federal, Mahogany, Carved, Reeded, Cushion, c.1808-15, 33 In.
$10,200

Skinner Auctioneers & Appraisers

Furniture, Chair, Finn Juhl, Lounge, Teak, Upholstered, Baker Furniture, 1950s, 33 In., Pair
$9,375

Rago Arts & Auction Center

Furniture, Chair, Frits Henningsen, Lounge, Mahogany, Leather, Denmark, 1940s, 31 x 28 In.
$1,875

Rago Arts & Auction Center

Furniture, Chair, G. Stickley, Morris, Bow Arm, Eastwood, Red Decal, c.1901, 38 x 32 In.
$10,000

Rago Arts & Auction Center

Furniture, Chair, Gothic Revival, Walnut, Carved, Ogee Arch, Tracery, Pinnacles, 1800s
$717

Neal Auction Co.

Furniture, Chair, Horn, Faux Leopard Seat, Arms, c.1890, 32 ½ x 22 In.
$510

Garth's Auctioneers & Appraisers

Furniture, Chair, James Mont, Silver Finish, Upholstered, 40 In.
$489

Cottone Auctions

Furniture, Chair, Knoll, Gothic Revival, Maple, Laminated, Dyed, R. Venturi, 1980s, 41 In., Pair
$10,625

Rago Arts & Auction Center

Furniture, Chair, Laverne International, Acrylic, Upholstered, 1960s, 37 x 33 x 30 In.
$3,250

Rago Arts & Auction Center

Furniture, Chair, Library Steps, Gothic, Oak, Carved, Leather Steps, England, c.1890, 36 In.
$1,075

Neal Auction Co.

Furniture, Chair, Lounge, Ottoman, Eames, Rosewood, Leather, Herman Miller, 1950s, 35 In.
$3,250

Rago Arts & Auction Center

Chaise Longue, Lucite, c.1960, 35 x 63 In.	472
Chaise Longue, Marcel Breuer, Beech Plywood Frame, Upholstered, Knoll, 54 x 32 In.	1375
Chaise Longue, Mies Van Der Rohe, Leather Chrome Metal, Palazzetti, c.1997, 39 x 41 In.	875
Chaise Longue, Robsjohn-Gibbings, Painted Walnut, Upholstered, Widdicomb, 35 x 59 In.	5938
Chamberstand, Rosewood, Grain Paint, Pierced, Drawer, c.1810, 32 x 16 In. ....*illus*	1230
Chest, 2 Drawers, Marble Top, France, c.1850, 10 x 11 In.	474
Chest, 4 Drawers, Blue Paint, 36 x 38 In.	720
Chest, 4 Drawers, Red Paint, Scroll Feet, 47 x 43 In.	420
Chest, 4 Graduated Drawers, Glass Knobs, Shaped Skirt, c.1830, 44 x 41 In.	575
Chest, 5 Graduated Drawers, Red Paint, Bracket Feet, New England, c.1820, 45 x 38 In.	1540
Chest, 6 Drawers, Blue Paint, 32 x 51 In.	4080
Chest, Anglo Colonial, Camphorwood, Brass Bound, 7 Drawers, c.1810, 41 x 41 In.	3304
Chest, Bachelor's, Burl Walnut Veneer, Inlay, 4 Drawers, Pullout, 1800s, 31 x 32 In.	554
Chest, Bachelor's, Chippendale, Mahogany, Slide, 4 Drawers, Bracket Feet, 35 x 34 In.	1560
Chest, Bachelor's, Federal, Mahogany, 4 Drawers, 32 x 30 In.	329
Chest, Bachelor's, Georgian Style, Mahogany, 4 Graduated Drawers, 30 x 26 In.	250
Chest, Bachelor's, Mahogany, 4 Drawers, Bracket Feet, c.1800, 31 x 35 In.	2000
Chest, Bachelor's, Mahogany, 4 Drawers, Bracket Feet, c.1860, 32 x 35 In.	1000
Chest, Baroque, Fruitwood, Bombe, Marquetry Inlaid, Flowers, 12 x 18 In.	1353
Chest, Baroque, Walnut, Inlay, 3 Drawers, Pilasters, Bracket Feet, Italy, c.1690, 42 x 45 In.	1875
Chest, Beech, Pine, Notch Edges, 6 Drawers, 12 In.	230
Chest, Biedermeier, Birch Veneer, Marble, Frieze Drawer, 1800s, 35 x 51 In. ....*illus*	480
Chest, Biedermeier, Birch Veneer, Projecting Upper Section, 3 Drawers, c.1835, 33 x 41 In.	1320
Chest, Biedermeier, Curly Maple, Molded, Ebonized Columns, 36 x 35 In.	3172
Chest, Biedermeier, Fruitwood, Marble Top, 3 Drawers, Brass Lion Mask Rings, Paw Feet	478
Chest, Biedermeier, Mahogany, 3 Graduated Drawers, Shaped Top, 34 ½ x 29 In.	375
Chest, Biedermeier, Maple, 4 Drawers, Canted Corners, 27 x 29 ½ In.	633
Chest, Biedermeier, Rosewood, 6 Drawers, 48 x 24 In.	1063
Chest, Black Paint, Dentil Detail, Brass Escutcheons, Tapered Legs, c.1810, 36 x 29 In.	4400
Chest, Blanket, 2 Drawers, Blue Paint, 40 x 45 In.	3840
Chest, Blanket, 2 Drawers, Vinegar Paint Designs, Pennsylvania, 45 x 44 In.	960
Chest, Blanket, Arched Ends, Blue Paint, 22 x 41 In.	900
Chest, Blanket, Basswood, Schoolhouse, Shell Painted, New England, c.1850, 15 x 13 In.	1540
Chest, Blanket, Bootjack Base, Red Paint, c.1850, 50 x 21 In.	242
Chest, Blanket, Brown, New England, c.1740, 20 x 46 In.	1659
Chest, Blanket, Cherry, Dovetailed Case, Turned Ball Feet, 1800s, 25 x 38 In.	510
Chest, Blanket, Chippendale, Cherry, Butternut, 2 Drawers, Bracket Feet, c.1810, 29 x 48 In.	646
Chest, Blanket, Chippendale, Maple, Pine, Painted, New England, c.1790, 21 x 40 In. ....*illus*	360
Chest, Blanket, Chippendale, Pine, Blue Paint, c.1790, 25 x 50 In.	1880
Chest, Blanket, Chippendale, Pine, Blue Paint, Ogee Feet, c.1790, 23 x 20 In.	2300
Chest, Blanket, Chippendale, Pine, Reeded, Lift Top, Shaped Feet, c.1800, 15 x 26 In.	472
Chest, Blanket, Chippendale, Walnut, 2 Drawers, Strap Hinges, Footed, Pa., c.1800, 29 x 54 In.	530
Chest, Blanket, Chippendale, Walnut, Inlay, Low Drawer, c.1800, 24 x 38 In.	2300
Chest, Blanket, Chippendale, Walnut, Lift Top, 2 Drawers, Pa., c.1800, 28 x 45 In.	652
Chest, Blanket, Chippendale, Walnut, Pine, Dovetailed, Drawers, c.1790, 29 x 49 In.	1560
Chest, Blanket, Chippendale, Walnut, Stars, 2 Drawers, Shenandoah Valley, c.1810, 30 x 52 In.	2070
Chest, Blanket, Chippendale, Wood, 2 Drawers, Strap Hinges, Footed, Pa., c.1800, 29 x 52 In.	500
Chest, Blanket, Chippendale, Yellow Pine, Dovetailed Case, Drawer, Ogee Feet, 29 x 49 In.	270
Chest, Blanket, Cutout Feet, White Paint, New England, 23 x 37 In.	360
Chest, Blanket, Drawer, Blue Green Paint, 35 x 47 In.	1200
Chest, Blanket, Drawer, Blue Paint, c.1820, 39 x 33 In.	1035
Chest, Blanket, Drawer, Bootjack Base, c.1850, 48 x 18 In.	265
Chest, Blanket, Drawer, Snipe Hinges, Blue Green Paint, 35 x 39 In.	1140
Chest, Blanket, Federal, Walnut, Inlay, Hinged Lid, Flared Feet, c.1825, 26 x 49 In.	1093
Chest, Blanket, Federal, Walnut, Reeded Edges, Divided Interior, Virginia, 8 x 14 In.	489
Chest, Blanket, Fitted Interior, Yellow, Brown Grain Paint, Bootjack Legs, c.1850, 22 x 37 In.	406
Chest, Blanket, French Provincial, Oak, Curved Panel, Wrought Iron Hardware, 49 x 24 In.	460
Chest, Blanket, George III, Oak, c.1800, 31 ½ x 20 ½ In.	710
Chest, Blanket, Georgian, Mahogany, Lift Top, Open Interior, Drawer, c.1800, 24 x 31 In.	840
Chest, Blanket, Grain Painted, Dovetailed, Hinged Lid, Bracket Feet, 25 x 44 In.	760
Chest, Blanket, Grain Painted, Molded Lid, Till, Split Dovetailed Case, Pa., 1868, 25 x 40 In.	325
Chest, Blanket, Grain Painted, Pennsylvania, c.1845, 23 x 42 In.	213
Chest, Blanket, Grain Painted, Raised Turned Legs, 22 x 36 In.	594
Chest, Blanket, Hinged Top, Drawer, Cutout Apron, 1800s, 10 x 15 In.	418
Chest, Blanket, Hinged Top, Tulip Panels, Grain Painted, Pennsylvania, c.1800, 24 x 51 In.	5625

Furniture, Chair, Mies Van Der Rohe, Lounge, MR, Tubular Steel, Leather, Knoll, c.1972, 33 In.
$799

New Orleans Auction Galleries, Inc.

Furniture, Chair, Milo Baughman, Lounge, Chromed Steel, Thayer-Coggin, 1970s, 26 In., Pair
$3,250

Rago Arts & Auction Center

Furniture, Chair, Morris, Mahogany, 3 Slats, Rose Valley, Pa., 1901-06, 48 x 34 In.
$7,500

Rago Arts & Auction Center

Furniture, Chair, Ottoman, Eero Saarinen, Womb, Chromed Steel, Knoll, c.1950, 39 In.
$1,920

Skinner Auctioneers & Appraisers

FURNITURE

Furniture, Chair, Pedro Friedeberg, Hand, Mahogany, Laminated, Mexico, 1960s, 35 x 22 In.
$11,875

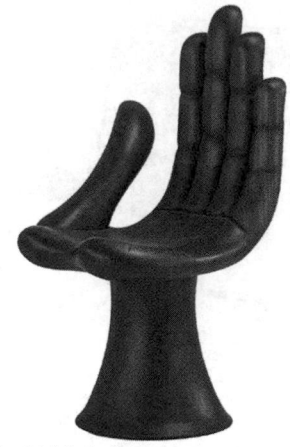

Rago Arts & Auction Center

Furniture, Chair, Porter's, Georgian Style, Barrel Back, Mahogany, Tufted Leather, Storage, 68 In.
$1,315

Neal Auction Co.

Furniture, Chair, Queen Anne, Cherry, Vase Shape Splat, Slip Seat, c.1740-60, 39 ½ In.
$3,600

Skinner Auctioneers & Appraisers

Chest, Blanket, J. Lehn, Decoupage Flowers, Umber Ground, c.1870, 8 x 14 In.	2133
Chest, Blanket, J. Lehn, Softwood, Painted, Portraits, Hinged Lid, Turned Feet, 6 x 8 ½ In.	5900
Chest, Blanket, Lift Top, 2 Drawers, Hinged, Elifabeth Sawyer, 1802, 40 x 18 In.	288
Chest, Blanket, Lift, Blue Green Paint, Iron Straps, Bracket Base, Mass., c.1820, 29 x 50 In.	649
Chest, Blanket, Maple, c.1850, 22 x 41 In.	1000
Chest, Blanket, Mixed Wood, Lift Top, c.1850, 12 x 19 In.	178
Chest, Blanket, Oak, Drawer, 2 Doors, Carved, England, 25 x 39 In.	720
Chest, Blanket, Oak, Drawer, Salmon Color, Flowers, Leaves, Curls, Table, c.1690, 34 x 46 In.	9600
Chest, Blanket, Oak, Lift Top, Paneled, Block Legs, 1600s, 28 x 51 In.	1534
Chest, Blanket, Painted, Applied Edge Opening, Interior Till, Bracket Feet, 26 ½ x 41 In.	780
Chest, Blanket, Painted, Applied Molded Edge, Interior Till, 19 x 49 In.	1560
Chest, Blanket, Painted, Blue, Cream & Red Panels, Flowers, 2 Drawers, 1791, 29 x 49 In.	2106
Chest, Blanket, Painted, Blue, Red, 3 Arched Recessed Panels, Bun Feet, 1846, 24 x 52 In.	585
Chest, Blanket, Painted, Lift Top, Faux Drawers & 2 Working, c.1710, 40 x 36 In. *illus*	1920
Chest, Blanket, Painted, Lift Top, Strap Hinges, Drawer, Bracket Feet, c.1815, 34 x 46 In.	478
Chest, Blanket, Painted, Tombstone Panels, Till, Iron Jaw Lock, Iron Strap, 24 x 52 In.	2124
Chest, Blanket, Paneled, Pilasters, Square Feet, Painted, 1800s, 24 x 39 In.	512
Chest, Blanket, Pegged Lid, Compass-Point Design, Block Feet, Continental, 26 x 50 In.	358
Chest, Blanket, Pine, 3 Low Drawers, Painted, Pennsylvania, c.1830, 29 x 48 In.	415
Chest, Blanket, Pine, Black, Yellow Sponge Paint, New York, c.1840, 22 x 43 In.	444
Chest, Blanket, Pine, Breadboard Lid, Strap Hinges, Drawer, Fruitwood Pulls, 28 x 42 In.	15340
Chest, Blanket, Pine, Ditty Box, Iron Handles, Salmon Red Paint, c.1850, 17 x 40 In.	236
Chest, Blanket, Pine, Dovetailed, Shoe Feet, Painted, Hudson River Valley, c.1815, 16 x 43 In.	1020
Chest, Blanket, Pine, Dovetailed, Orange Paint, Hearts, Crescents, c.1840, 26 x 78 In.	4406
Chest, Blanket, Pine, Fitted Interior, Green Paint, Bail Handles, 18 x 50 In.	106
Chest, Blanket, Pine, Green Paint, Molding, Iron Handles, Strap Hinges, 1800s, 18 x 39 In.	470
Chest, Blanket, Pine, Green, Gold Paint, c.1895, 15 x 21 In.	593
Chest, Blanket, Pine, Hinge Lid, Drawers, Painted Designs, Footed, Pa., c.1820, 29 x 46 In.	288
Chest, Blanket, Pine, Lift Top, Bracket Feet, Pennsylvania, c.1800, 24 x 48 In.	420
Chest, Blanket, Pine, Lift Top, Drawer, c.1840, 38 x 39 In.	236
Chest, Blanket, Pine, Lift Top, Drawer, Red Paint, c.1860, 41 x 28 In.	288
Chest, Blanket, Pine, Lift Top, Grain Painted, Iron Handles, S. Phillipson, c.1840, 22 x 35 In.	295
Chest, Blanket, Pine, Nails, Grain Painted, c.1850, 22 x 44 In.	235
Chest, Blanket, Pine, Painted Hearts, Tulips, Signed D. Ellinger, 1957, 20 x 32 In.	4029
Chest, Blanket, Pine, Painted, Dovetailed, Shaped Skirt, Tulips, c.1840, 29 x 51 In.	2233
Chest, Blanket, Pine, Painted, Flower Design, Dovetailed, 1800s, 24 x 53 In.	210
Chest, Blanket, Pine, Painted, Lift Top, Lower Drawer, Cutout Ends, c.1790, 36 x 39 In.	600
Chest, Blanket, Pine, Painted, Lift Top, Urn, Roses, Multicolor, c.1820, 21 x 47 In.	11070
Chest, Blanket, Pine, Painted, New England, c.1820, 22 x 37 In.	533
Chest, Blanket, Pine, Painted, Stile Feet, Applied Molding, c.1810, 24 x 39 In.	660
Chest, Blanket, Pine, Painted, Turned Feet, Flower & Star Design, c.1850, 16 x 23 In.	2233
Chest, Blanket, Pine, Pennsylvania, c.1820, 24 ½ x 41 In.	1007
Chest, Blanket, Pine, Poplar, 3 Low Drawers, Pennsylvania, c.1820, 30 ½ x 47 In.	237
Chest, Blanket, Pine, Poplar, Grain, Turned Feet, Interior Till, 20 x 37 In.	823
Chest, Blanket, Pine, Red & Black Paint, Dovetailed, Turned Feet, 24 x 38 In.	440
Chest, Blanket, Pine, Red Stain, Pa., Miniature, c.1850, 13 ½ x 20 In.	729
Chest, Blanket, Pine, Red Stain, Pennsylvania, Miniature, c.1850, 13 ½ x 20 In.	729
Chest, Blanket, Pine, Red Wash, Hinged Lid, Ball Feet, c.1830, 24 x 46 In.	144
Chest, Blanket, Pine, Red, Black Paint, Swirl Decoration, 1800s, 11 x 21 In.	189
Chest, Blanket, Pine, Red, Yellow Grain Paint, Pennsylvania, c.1830, 24 x 41 ½ In.	710
Chest, Blanket, Pine, Red, Yellow Sponge Paint, Pennsylvania, 23 x 40 In.	563
Chest, Blanket, Pine, Shaped Base, Gray Paint, Multicolor Flowers, 1800s, 24 x 50 In.	264
Chest, Blanket, Pine, Sunken-Panel Case, Flame Grain Paint, c.1820, 28 x 48 In.	326
Chest, Blanket, Pine, Tulips, Flowers, Hearts, Painted, Signed David Ellinger, 1957, 20 x 32 In.	4029
Chest, Blanket, Pine, Walnut, Raised Feet, c.1860, 22 x 28 In., Child's	267
Chest, Blanket, Pine, Yellow Paint, Combed Tree, 4 Ball Feet, Molded Edge Lid, 38 x 19 In.	173
Chest, Blanket, Pine, Yellow, Brown Grain Painted, New England, 1826, 23 x 48 In.	385
Chest, Blanket, Poplar, Applied Molding, Bracket Feet, Blue Paint, Pa., c.1845, 21 x 42 In.	345
Chest, Blanket, Poplar, Blue Paint, Lift Top, Cutout Bracket Base, c.1785, 23 x 45 In.	1320
Chest, Blanket, Poplar, Brown, Ocher Sponge, Blue Tombstone Panels, Pa., c.1830, 25 x 48 In.	4503
Chest, Blanket, Poplar, Dovetailed, Hinged Lid, Breadboard Ends, Bracket Feet, 22 x 41 In.	322
Chest, Blanket, Poplar, Hinged Lid, Heart Incised Front, Red Paint, Pa., c.1820, 23 x 51 In.	633
Chest, Blanket, Poplar, Iron Hinges, Turned Feet, Mid-Atlantic, c.1850, 7 x 12 In.	403
Chest, Blanket, Poplar, Ocher Sponge Designs, Scalloped Apron, 1800s, 19 x 34 In.	2133
Chest, Blanket, Poplar, Red, Black Sponge Paint, Pennsylvania, c.1865, 24 x 48 In.	563

Chest, Blanket, Poplar, Red, Yellow Grain Paint, Pennsylvania, c.1820, 23 ½ x 42 In.	770
Chest, Blanket, Poplar, Stained, Pennsylvania, c.1805, 7 x 11 In.	710
Chest, Blanket, Poplar, Tulips, Urns, Panels, Iron Hinges, Bracket Feet, 1802, 25 x 50 In.	34500
Chest, Blanket, Poplar, Umber, Yellow Paint, Pennsylvania, c.1830, 26 x 48 In.	563
Chest, Blanket, Red Paint, Pa., 27 x 52 In.	240
Chest, Blanket, Salmon Paint, Pennsylvania, 12 x 18 In.	660
Chest, Blanket, Schwenkfelder, Grain Painted, Drawers, Rosina Schultz 1810, 29 x 52 In.	9375
Chest, Blanket, Shaker, Drawer, Blue Paint, Lift Top, Cutout Base, 41 x 39 In.	10200
Chest, Blanket, Shaker, Pine, Breadboard Lid, Strap Hinges, 29 x 43 In. ....*illus*	15340
Chest, Blanket, Shaker, Pine, Green Paint, 6-board, Dovetailed, c.1850, 16 x 43 In.	353
Chest, Blanket, Shaker, Pine, Single-Board Top, Dovetailed, c.1845, 32 x 42 In. ......*illus*	3304
Chest, Blanket, Shaker, Pine, Strap Hinges, Dovetailed, c.1810, 41 x 40 In. ....*illus*	18880
Chest, Blanket, Shaker, Walnut, 6-Board, Bracket Feet, c.1835, 23 x 38 In.	1416
Chest, Blanket, Sheraton, 2 Drawers, Cat's-Eye Painted, 32 x 41 In.	1200
Chest, Blanket, Sheraton, Softwood, Painted, Mahantongo Valley Style, Till, D. Ellinger, 21 x 32 In.	4130
Chest, Blanket, Softwood, Grain Painted, Tulip, Paneled Lid, Cutout Skirt, 30 x 55 In.	189
Chest, Blanket, Spanish Colonial, Carved Cartouche, Scrolls, Painted, Hinged, 22 x 36 In.	184
Chest, Blanket, Walnut, Carved Apron, Pennsylvania, c.1800, 20 x 36 In.	1337
Chest, Blanket, Walnut, Lift Top, Bracket Feet, Pennsylvania, c.1790, 21 x 46 In.	420
Chest, Blanket, Walnut, Pennsylvania, c.1780, 14 ½ x 25 In.	3318
Chest, Blanket, Walnut, Wallpaper Interior, Pennsylvania, c.1790, 11 x 19 In.	14220
Chest, Blanket, William & Mary, 4 Drawers, Snipe Hinges, 44 x 41 In.	2880
Chest, Blanket, William & Mary, Lift Top, 2 Drawers, Blue Paint, 39 x 42 In.	1500
Chest, Blanket, William & Mary, Pine, Lid, 5 Drawers, Red, Black Paint, c.1740, 47 x 40 In.	7703
Chest, Blanket, William & Mary, Tilled Interior, Red Paint, Side Handles, 21 x 53 In.	240
Chest, Blanket, Yellow & Red Grain Painted, Black Ball Feet, c.1860, 50 x 27 In.	173
Chest, Blue Paint, 5 Drawers, New England, 52 x 29 In.	1200
Chest, Blue Paint, Side Handles, c.1860, 42 x 17 In.	260
Chest, Butler's, Hinged Drawer, 3 Lower Drawers, Turned Pilasters, Pa., c.1825, 46 x 44 In.	530
Chest, Butler's, Sheraton, Mahogany, Fitted Maple Interior, 3 Low Shelves, Pa., 43 x 41 In.	830
Chest, Butternut, Lift Top, Chip Carved, Reeded, Dovetailed, 1700s, 12 ½ x 19 In.	1755
Chest, Campaign, Mahogany, Brass Corners, 5 Drawers, Turned Feet, 1800s, 47 x 42 In.	717
Chest, Campaign, Mahogany, Side Handles, England, c.1850, 19 x 32 In.	243
Chest, Campaign, Mahogany, Walnut, 5 Drawers, c.1850, 44 x 42 In.	1534
Chest, Campaign, Victorian, Brass Corners, 4 Drawers, Bun Feet, c.1890, 36 x 42 In.	1476
Chest, Camphorwood, Carved Scenes, Etched Brass Latch, 22 x 41 x 24 In. ....*illus*	230
Chest, Carved Flowers, Leaves, Columns, 6 Drawers, White Paint, Mass., c.1830, 45 x 41 In.	1560
Chest, Cherry, 4 Drawers, Reeded Columns, c.1810, 17 x 18 In. ....*illus*	1320
Chest, Cherry, 5 Flat Drawers, Fan-Carved Drawer, 37 x 19 In.	776
Chest, Cherry, 6 Curly Maple Drawers, Southern Ohio, 1800s, 49 x 41 In. ....*illus*	2280
Chest, Cherry, Fan Carved, 9 Drawers, c.1775, 36 x 58 In.	1150
Chest, Cherry, Grain Painted, 6 Drawers, New England, c.1780, 56 x 38 In.	2252
Chest, Cherry, Walnut, Inlay, Cutout Apron, Inscribed, c.1850, 10 x 13 In.	374
Chest, Chippendale, 4 Drawers, Bracket Feet, Pennsylvania, c.1770, 40 x 39 In.	1020
Chest, Chippendale, Cherry, 3 Drawers, 40 x 36 In.	396
Chest, Chippendale, Cherry, 4 Drawers, Columns, Ogee Feet, Pennsylvania, c.1780, 34 x 39 In.	2370
Chest, Chippendale, Cherry, 4 Drawers, New England, c.1780, 36 x 39 In.	1126
Chest, Chippendale, Cherry, 4 Drawers, Ogee Feet, Connecticut, c.1770, 33 x 43 In.	2252
Chest, Chippendale, Cherry, 4 Graduated Drawers, Columns, c.1785, 33 x 40 In.	2125
Chest, Chippendale, Cherry, 4 Graduated Drawers, Ogee Bracket Feet, c.1780, 35 x 40 In.	1188
Chest, Chippendale, Cherry, 5 Drawers, c.1780, 40 x 38 In.	1580
Chest, Chippendale, Cherry, 5 Drawers, Molded Top, Bracket Feet, Pa., 42 x 37 In.	2160
Chest, Chippendale, Cherry, 5 Drawers, Ogee Bracket Feet, Pennsylvania, c.1780, 36 x 38 In.	948
Chest, Chippendale, Cherry, 8 Drawers, Fluted Columns, Ogee Bracket Feet, Pa., c.1780	2252
Chest, Chippendale, Cherry, 8 Drawers, Fluted Corners, Ball, New York, c.1770, 83 x 47 In.	3080
Chest, Chippendale, Cherry, 8 Drawers, Pennsylvania, c.1790, 66 x 36 In.	1896
Chest, Chippendale, Cherry, Line Inlay, Oxbow Front, 4 Drawers, New England, 40 x 21 In.	2040
Chest, Chippendale, Cherry, Poplar, 7 Drawers, Bracket Feet, c.1790, 54 x 38 In.	1645
Chest, Chippendale, Fruitwood, Molded Frame, 5 Drawers, Bracket Feet, 34 x 35 In.	2280
Chest, Chippendale, Grain Painted, 5 Drawers, Shaped Base, 41 x 36 In.	960
Chest, Chippendale, Grain Painted, Turned Feet, Pennsylvania, 22 x 35 In.	330
Chest, Chippendale, Mahogany, 4 Beaded Drawers, Bracket Feet, c.1790, 37 x 42 In.	5000
Chest, Chippendale, Mahogany, 4 Drawers, Columns, Philadelphia, c.1770, 34 x 30 In.	17775
Chest, Chippendale, Mahogany, 4 Drawers, Fluted Columns, Philadelphia, 35 x 38 In.	3318
Chest, Chippendale, Mahogany, 5 Drawers, Molded Rim, England, 39 x 39 In.	1320

Furniture, Chair, Queen Anne, Maple, Vase Shape Splat, Painted, Gold Trim, c.1700s, 40 ½ In.
$570

Garth's Auctioneers & Appraisers

Furniture, Chair, Queen Anne, Mixed Wood, 6 Spindles, Yoke Crest, Rush Seat, 1900s, 40 In.
$800

Garth's Auctioneers & Appraisers

Furniture, Chair, Risom, Lounge, Webbed, 30 ½ x 20 In.
$360

Palm Beach Modern Auctions

F

Furniture, Chair, Rococo Revival, Cast Iron, Spring, Thomas Warren, American Chair Co., c.1850
$1,075

Neal Auction Co.

Furniture, Chair, Rococo, Carved, Painted, Gilt, Ram's Head, Hoof Feet, Italy, c.1890, Pair
$2,684

Neal Auction Co.

Furniture, Chair, Savonarola, Walnut, Carved, Arms, Beast Terminals, Italy, 54 In.
$1,625

Leslie Hindman Auctioneers

Chest, Chippendale, Mahogany, Bowfront, Ogee Feet, Handles, c.1770, 38 x 43 In.	499
Chest, Chippendale, Mahogany, Inlay, 5 Drawers, Chester Co., Pa., c.1790, 35 x 36 In.	1016
Chest, Chippendale, Mahogany, Reverse Serpentine, c.1785, 32 x 32 In.	16800
Chest, Chippendale, Maple, 11 Drawers, Fan Carved, New Hampshire, c.1790, 80 x 40 In.	7500
Chest, Chippendale, Maple, 6 Drawers, Bracket Base, c.1750, 42 x 55 In.	1265
Chest, Chippendale, Maple, 6 Drawers, Bracket Feet, c.1790, 52 x 40 In.	2813
Chest, Chippendale, Maple, 8 Drawers, Bracket Feet, New England, c.1780, 72 x 38 In.	3080
Chest, Chippendale, Mixed Wood, 4 Beaded Drawers, Reeded Columns, Pa., c.1795, 29 x 18 In.	1840
Chest, Chippendale, Oak, 4 Drawers, 31 x 23 In.	1020
Chest, Chippendale, Oak, 4 Drawers, Bracket Feet, England, 37 x 20 In.	900
Chest, Chippendale, Pine, 4 Drawers, c.1790, 34 x 33 In.	456
Chest, Chippendale, Swan Neck Crest, 9 Drawers, Fan Carved, Bracket Feet, 87 x 40 In.	3600
Chest, Chippendale, Tiger Maple, Finials, Shell Carved, 9 Drawers, c.1770, 84 x 39 ½ In.	3555
Chest, Chippendale, Walnut, 4 Drawers, Bracket Feet, Pennsylvania, c.1790, 33 x 34 In.	1800
Chest, Chippendale, Walnut, 4 Drawers, c.1780, 34 x 40 In.	2250
Chest, Chippendale, Walnut, 4 Graduated Beaded Drawers, Phila., c.1790, 35 x 39 In.	4160
Chest, Chippendale, Walnut, 4 Graduated Drawers, Bracket Feet, Lancaster, c.1790, 36 x 39 In.	5938
Chest, Chippendale, Walnut, 8 Drawers, Cove-Molded Cornice, Pa., c.1790, 55 x 41 In.	1250
Chest, Chippendale, Walnut, 8 Drawers, Ogee Bracket Feet, Pennsylvania, c.1810, 66 x 42 In.	2176
Chest, Chippendale, Walnut, 8 Drawers, Side Columns, Bracket Feet, Pennsylvania, 62 x 42 In.	3555
Chest, Chippendale, Walnut, 9 Drawers, Tall Ogee Feet, Pennsylvania, c.1780, 58 x 40 In.	3080
Chest, Chippendale, Walnut, Dovetailed Drawers, Fluted Columns, c.1780, 37 x 39 In. ......*illus*	826
Chest, Chippendale, Walnut, Graduated Drawers, Bracket Feet, c.1780, 40 x 22 In. ....*illus*	472
Chest, Chippendale, Walnut, Ogee Feet, Pennsylvania, c.1790, 62 ½ x 35 In.	1659
Chest, Chippendale, Walnut, Pennsylvania, c.1800, 51 ½ x 38 In.	1185
Chest, Chippendale, Walnut, Reeded Columns, Ball & Claw Feet, Pa., c.1785, 71 x 40 In.	4977
Chest, Chippendale, Yellow Paint, 4 Drawers, Shaped Apron, Feet, Maine	863
Chest, Commode, Louis XV, Cherry, Serpentine, 3 Drawers, Scroll Feet, c.1750, 36 x 49 In.	9375
Chest, Commodini, Rococo, Serpentine, Drawer, Door, Cabriole Legs, Walnut, Italy, 32 x 20 In.	1000
Chest, Curly Maple, 4 Drawers, Straight Legs, Zoar, Ohio, c.1890, 37 x 34 In.	2169
Chest, Dome Top, Painted, Carved Name, Iron Handles, Till, Secret Drawers, 1869, 31 x 16 In.	115
Chest, Dower, Flower Medallions, Blue Paint, Inscribed Catrina Schins 1752, Pa., 24 x 50 In.	710
Chest, Dower, Oak, 3 Carved Front Panels, 4-Panel Lid, Pegged Mortise & Tenon	460
Chest, Dower, Painted Scenes, Flowers, 2 Drawers, Pennsylvania, c.1845, 51 x 25 In.	546
Chest, Dower, Painted Tulip Reserves, Painted, c.1841, 23 x 43 In.	326
Chest, Dower, Painted, Pennsylvania, c.1790, 23 x 48 In.	178
Chest, Dower, Pine, Painted, Dated 1828, 21 x 48 In.	444
Chest, Dower, Pine, Vibrant Flower Panels, Grained Ground, Pa., c.1790, 21 x 48 In.	1185
Chest, Dower, Poplar, 3 Painted Panels, Red Sponged Ground, Pa., c.1795, 22 x 49 In.	2015
Chest, Dower, Poplar, Grain Painted, c.1820, Pa., 24 x 48 In.	152
Chest, Dower, Poplar, Paneled, Painted, Pennsylvania, Inscribed 1767, 19 x 37 In.	400
Chest, Empire Style, Mahogany, Marble Top, 3 Drawers, 37 x 44 In.	375
Chest, Empire Style, Side Columns, 2 Drawers, Ball Feet, 15 x 10 In.	334
Chest, Empire, Curly Tiger Maple, 4 Drawers, Rope-Turned Pilasters, 43 x 46 In.	367
Chest, Empire, Drawers, Grain Painted, Scrolled, Footed, John Rupp, c.1840, 46 x 42 In.	266
Chest, Empire, Mahogany Veneer, Scroll Pilasters, c.1850, 19 In.	510
Chest, Empire, Mahogany, 5 Drawers, Scroll Rails, Rolled Front Feet, 1800s, 43 x 48 In.	288
Chest, Federal, Blond Cherry, Bowfront, 4 Drawers, Scalloped Skirt, French Feet, 36 x 43 In.	959
Chest, Federal, Bowfront, Figured, Sphinx Head Handles, c.1815, 36 x 42 In.	2596
Chest, Federal, Cherry, 4 Graduated Drawers, Beaded, c.1805, 38 x 21 In.	563
Chest, Federal, Cherry, 4 Graduated Drawers, Bracket Base, c.1800, 39 x 40 In.	1063
Chest, Federal, Cherry, 4 Graduated Drawers, Scalloped Skirt, Virginia, c.1820, 42 x 41 In.	1265
Chest, Federal, Cherry, 4 Graduated Drawers, Shenandoah Valley, c.1810, 37 x 38 In.	8050
Chest, Federal, Cherry, 8 Drawers, Signed W.B. Heister, Pennsylvania, c.1818, 69 x 45 In.	2125
Chest, Federal, Cherry, 9 Drawers, Pennsylania, c.1810, 62 x 40 In.	1185
Chest, Federal, Cherry, Inlay, 3 Drawers, Splayed Feet, c.1850, 13 x 8 In.	1610
Chest, Federal, Cherry, Inlay, 4 Drawers, Bracket Feet, c.1800, 39 x 36 In.	2625
Chest, Federal, Cherry, Inlay, 4 Drawers, Reeded Corners, Bracket Feet, c.1830, 36 x 40 In.	938
Chest, Federal, Cherry, Walnut, Inlay, 4 Drawers, Flared Feet, Virginia, c.1820, 42 x 42 In.	3450
Chest, Federal, Fruitwood, 4 Graduated Drawers, c.1820, 37 x 40 In.	1500
Chest, Federal, Inlay, 4 Drawers, Shaped Apron, Splayed Legs, c.1840, 42 x 43 In.	1063
Chest, Federal, Inlay, Banding, 4 Graduated Drawers, 35 x 36 In.	563
Chest, Federal, Mahogany, 4 Drawers, Bracket Feet, Pa., c.1800, 35 x 38 In.	1046
Chest, Federal, Mahogany, 5 Drawers, Pennsylvania, c.1805, 37 x 44 In.	356
Chest, Federal, Mahogany, Banded, 4 Drawers, Splayed Feet, c.1805, 38 x 39 In.	1063

Chest, Federal, Mahogany, Banded, 4 Graduated Drawers, Virginia, c.1800, 39 x 41 In.	16100
Chest, Federal, Mahogany, Bird's-Eye Maple, 4 Drawers, Cutout Apron, c.1820, 41 x 42 In.	7500
Chest, Federal, Mahogany, Cherry, 3 Drawers, Shaped Apron, c.1820, 12 x 9 In.	326
Chest, Federal, Mahogany, Inlay, 5 Drawers, 41 x 40 In.	1062
Chest, Federal, Mahogany, Inlay, Biscuit Corners, Turned Legs, c.1815, 39 x 43 In.	1003
Chest, Federal, Mahogany, Inlay, Bowfront, 4 Drawers, Scalloped Apron, c.1800, 40 In.	813
Chest, Federal, Mahogany, Serpentine, 4 Graduated Drawers, Virginia, c.1800, 43 x 49 In.	3840
Chest, Federal, Maple, 4 Drawers, New England, c.1790, 34 x 40 In.	2000
Chest, Federal, Maple, Inlay, New England, 36 x 41 In.	1560
Chest, Federal, Mixed Wood, 5 Drawers, Spur Legs, c.1820, 45 x 40 In.	1003
Chest, Federal, Mixed Wood, Inlay, 5 Beaded Drawers, Tenn., c.1810, 42 x 42 In.	1725
Chest, Federal, Painted, Bowfront, Chamfered Top, Brass Handles, c.1800, 36 x 37 In.	3900
Chest, Federal, Pine, 4 Drawers, New England, c.1830, 44 x 40 In.	608
Chest, Federal, Tiger Maple, Bowfront, Dart, Inlay, Drawers, New Eng., c.1810, 39 x 43 In.	3080
Chest, Federal, Tiger Maple, Drawers, Reeded Corners, Apron, New Eng., c.1820, 43 x 44 In.	2375
Chest, Federal, Tiger Maple, Molded Cornice, Drawers, Flared French Feet, c.1810, 70 x 38 In.	5100
Chest, Federal, Walnut, 4 Drawers, Applied Moldings, Cutout Apron, Va., c.1810, Child's	24150
Chest, Federal, Walnut, 5 Drawers, c.1820, 38 x 37 In.	547
Chest, Federal, Walnut, 5 Graduated Drawers, Cutout Skirt, Virginia, c.1810, 49 x 39 In.	805
Chest, Federal, Walnut, Brass Handles, Reeded Edge, Bracket Feet, c.1800, 42 x 35 In.	5192
Chest, Federal, Walnut, Inlay, 4 Beaded Drawers, Apron, Flared Feet, Va., c.1810, 42 x 40 In.	1380
Chest, Federal, Walnut, Inlay, 4 Drawers, Scalloped Skirt, c.1810, 42 x 43 In.	690
Chest, Federal, Walnut, Line, Shell Inlay, 9 Drawers, Flared Feet, Pa.	6000
Chest, Federal, Yellow Pine, Dovetailed, Jac Stirewalt, N.C., c.1820, 39 x 37 In. ....*illus*	5664
Chest, Federal-to-Empire, Mahogany, Carved, Notched, Claw Feet, c.1830, 44 x 43 In.	1195
Chest, Frank Lloyd Wright, 4 Drawers, Squared Base, Heritage Henredon, 33 x 34 In.	1888
Chest, French Style, Mahogany, Carved, Serpentine Front, 3 Drawers, c.1930, 29 x 30 In.	470
Chest, George I, Burl Veneer Frame, 7 Drawers, Ball Feet, c.1730, 44 x 41 In.	1422
Chest, George I, Walnut, 5 Drawers, Bracket Base, 39 x 38 In.	1560
Chest, George I, Walnut, 5 Drawers, Bun Feet, 39 x 38 In.	960
Chest, George II, Burl Walnut, 5 Drawers, Bracket Feet, c.1790, 39 x 40 In.	1326
Chest, George II, Mixed Wood, Burl, Banding, 5 Drawers, c.1790, 35 x 37 In.	1770
Chest, George II, Mixed Wood, Burl, Inlay, 5 Drawers, c.1750, 36 x 38 In.	2242
Chest, George III Style, Mahogany, 4 Drawers, Bracket Feet, 33 x 35 In.	1000
Chest, George III Style, Mahogany, 5 Drawers, Panel Sides, 40 x 38 In.	688
Chest, George III, Chippendale, Mahogany, 8 Drawers, Beaded, 75 x 47 In.	1416
Chest, George III, Mahogany, 2 Parts, 8 Drawers, Splayed Bracket Feet, 1800s, 75 x 42 In.	4375
Chest, George III, Mahogany, 4 Drawers, Banded, Escutcheons, 1800s, 33 x 22 In.	860
Chest, George III, Mahogany, 5 Drawers, c.1770, 33 ½ In.	395
Chest, George III, Mahogany, 5 Drawers, French Feet, 37 x 43 In.	1063
Chest, George III, Mahogany, 5 Drawers, Splayed Legs, c.1790, 39 x 39 In.	119
Chest, George III, Mahogany, 8 Drawers, Bracket Feet, 69 x 40 In.	948
Chest, George III, Mahogany, 9 Beaded Drawers, Bracket Base, c.1800, 70 x 40 In.	1652
Chest, George III, Mahogany, Banded, Drawers, Splayed Feet, c.1885, 35 x 35 In.	1107
Chest, George III, Mahogany, Bowfront, 5 Drawers, c.1790, 38 x 43 In.	770
Chest, George III, Mahogany, Bowfront, 5 Drawers, c.1790, 43 x 46 In.	267
Chest, George III, Mahogany, Bowfront, Shaped Apron, French Feet, c.1790, 41 In.	598
Chest, George III, Mahogany, Fir, Banded, Bowfront, 6 Drawers, c.1800, 42 x 48 In.	1888
Chest, George III, Mahogany, Pine, 5 Drawers, Bracket Feet, c.1780, 40 x 43 In.	1416
Chest, George III, Mahogany, Serpentine, Carved Edge, 4 Drawers, Footed, 33 x 37 In.	5313
Chest, George III, Walnut, 5 Drawers, Bracket Feet, 36 x 38 In.	1755
Chest, George III, Walnut, Drawers, Columns, c.1760, 34 x 38 In.	3080
Chest, Georgian Style, Burl, 3 Drawers, 28 x 24 In.	1063
Chest, Georgian Style, Mahogany, 5 Drawers, 42 x 48 ½ In.	500
Chest, Georgian Style, Mahogany, Shaped Top, 4 Drawers, 36 x 38 In.	250
Chest, Georgian, Mahogany Veneer, Bowfront, 4 Graduated Drawers, Bracket Feet, 41 x 41 In.	400
Chest, Georgian, Mahogany, 4 Drawers, Raised Flared Feet, c.1810, 38 x 49 In.	316
Chest, Georgian, Mahogany, Line Inlay, 7 Drawers, c.1800, 72 x 39 In.	1353
Chest, Georgian, Mahogany, Pine, Banded, 5 Beaded Drawers, c.1790, 42 x 45 In.	1298
Chest, Georgian, Mahogany, String Inlay, Bowfront, 5 Drawers, c.1820, 43 x 37 In.	546
Chest, Georgian, Oak, 5 Graduated Drawers, Bracket Feet, c.1790, 35 x 38 In.	316
Chest, Hanging, 21 Drawers, Painted, c.1890, 31 x 21 In.	630
Chest, Hepplewhite Style, Mahogany, Banding, 4 Drawers, c.1910, Miniature, 11 x 11 In.	944
Chest, Hepplewhite Style, Tiger Maple, 4 Drawers, 39 x 37 In.	3068
Chest, Hepplewhite, 4 Drawers, Bracket Feet, 40 x 40 In.	900

F

Furniture, Chair, Sedan, Louis XVI Style, Chinoiserie, Painted, Upholstered, 1800s, 66 x 29 In.
$4,481

Neal Auction Co.

Furniture, Chair, Shaker, Ladder Back, Maple, Birch, Leather Over Woven Splint Seat, 39 In.
$708

Willis Henry Auctions, Inc.

Furniture, Chair, Shaker, Ladder Back, Maple, Splint Seat, New Lebanon, c.1835
$531

Willis Henry Auctions, Inc.

Furniture, Chair, Shaker, Ladder Back, Painted, Rush Seat, Union Village, 1800s, 39 In.
$1,920

Cowan's Auctions

Furniture, Chair, Stepped Back, Trelliswork, Inlay, Ivory, Bone, Ebony, Middle East, c.1930, 48 In.
$593

James D. Julia Auctioneers

Furniture, Chair, V. Kagan, Lounge, Walnut, Adjustable, Stainless Steel, 1950s, 33 x 27 x 61 In.
$6,875

Rago Arts & Auction Center

Chest, Hepplewhite, 4 Drawers, Shaped Apron, New Hampshire, 38 x 41 In.	1200
Chest, Hepplewhite, Birch, String Inlay, Shaped Skirt, French Feet, c.1815, 43 x 43 In.	499
Chest, Hepplewhite, Bowfront, 4 Drawers, Shaped Apron, New England, c.1800, 42 x 21 In.	590
Chest, Hepplewhite, Curly Maple, Pine, Original Brasses, c.1810, 42 x 42 In. ....*illus*	2706
Chest, Hepplewhite, Curly Walnut, String Inlay, French Feet, c.1800, 42 x 36 In.	1410
Chest, Hepplewhite, Inlay, Scalloped Apron, 4 Drawers, 38 x 41 In.	1320
Chest, Hepplewhite, Mahogany, 3 Drawers, England, c.1800, 33 x 33 In.	385
Chest, Hepplewhite, Mahogany, 4 Drawers, Splayed Legs, c.1810, 42 x 38 In.	474
Chest, Hepplewhite, Mahogany, 6 Drawers, c.1800, 37 x 43 In.	590
Chest, Hepplewhite, Mahogany, Inlay, 4 Drawers, Serpentine Apron, 38 x 39 In.	960
Chest, Hepplewhite, Mahogany, Inlay, Drop Front, 3 Lower Drawers, 47 x 46 In.	1020
Chest, Hepplewhite, Mahogany, Pole Inlay, 4 Drawers, 42 x 35 In.	4029
Chest, Hepplewhite, Mahogany, Tiger Maple, Banded, 4 Drawers, c.1800, 34 x 42 In.	787
Chest, Hepplewhite, Rosewood, 5 Drawers, Flared Feet, England, 41 x 42 In.	600
Chest, Hepplewhite, Satinwood, Bowfront, 5 Drawers, England, 18 x 18 In.	2400
Chest, Hepplewhite, Walnut, 5 Drawers, French Feet, c.1815, 45 x 39 In.	940
Chest, Hepplewhite, Walnut, Cock Beaded, String Inlay, French Feet, c.1805, 47 x 38 In.	1998
Chest, Jacobean Style, Oak, Carved Panels, c.1850, 24 x 48 In.	266
Chest, John Stuart, Janus Collection, Mahogany, 3 Drawers, c.1960, 25 x 26 In., Pair	1188
Chest, Louis XV, Walnut, Hinged Top, False Drawer, Cabriole Legs, c.1800, 12 x 17 In.	625
Chest, Louis XVI Style, Mahogany, Drawers, Canted Corners, c.1910, 58 x 18 In. ....*illus*	1230
Chest, M. Headley, Mahogany, 14 Drawers, Bonnet Top, Virginia, c.1980, 39 x 16 In.	4740
Chest, Mahogany Veneer, Pine, Bowfront, 5 Drawers, Thistle Hardware, 41 x 20 In.	776
Chest, Mahogany, 3 Drawers, Bracket Feet, Brass Hardware, 11 ½ x 16 ½ In.	150
Chest, Mahogany, 5 Drawers, Bone Inlaid Keyhole, Oval Mount, Bail Handle, 36 x 36 In.	350
Chest, Mahogany, 5 Drawers, Bracket Feet, 1800s, 9 x 8 In.	240
Chest, Mahogany, 5 Drawers, Turned Feet, Brass, Virgin Islands, c.1815, 43 x 43 In.	353
Chest, Mahogany, 5 Graduated Drawers, Beaded, Shaped Skirt, Flared Feet, 43 x 41 In.	1888
Chest, Mahogany, 8 Graduated Drawers, 80 x 42 In.	750
Chest, Mahogany, Beveled Mirror, 2 Doors, 4 Drawers, c.1910, 24 x 67 In.	424
Chest, Mahogany, Bowfront, 6 Drawers, Carved Supports, Turned Feet, 55 x 51 In.	452
Chest, Mahogany, Bowfront, 6 Drawers, Carved, 54 x 46 In.	1120
Chest, Mahogany, Bowfront, Reeded Columns, Ball Feet, c.1815, 46 x 48 In.	3585
Chest, Mahogany, Brass Bound, 5 Drawers, 40 x 36 In.	3900
Chest, Mahogany, Carved, Reeded Pilasters, 4 Drawers, c.1820, 48 x 23 In.	688
Chest, Mahogany, Inlay, Serpentine, 4 Drawers, Mid-Atlantic, c.1820, 36 x 42 In.	1495
Chest, Mahogany, Mixed Wood, String Inlay, 5 Drawers, c.1800, 8 x 12 In.	875
Chest, Mahogany, String Inlay, 5 Drawers, Shaped Skirt, Splayed Feet, 43 In.	1520
Chest, Maple, 7 Drawers, Scroll-Carved Apron, Cabriole Legs, New Hampshire, 59 x 39 In.	1680
Chest, Maple, Cut Steel Inlay, Casket Shape, Hinged Lid, Handles, Ball Feet, 11 x 20 In.	360
Chest, Maple, Red Stain, 6 Drawers, New England, 1802, 56 x 36 In.	3080
Chest, Marquetry, Star Inlay, Banding, 3 Drawers, Tapered Legs, Italy, 31 x 22 In.	1920
Chest, McCobb, Drawers, 4 Metal Legs, Planner Group, 33 x 24 In. ....*illus*	480
Chest, Mixed Wood, Painted, 15 Drawers, American, 1800s, 23 x 21 In.	2233
Chest, Mule, Chippendale, Painted, Well, Drawers, Bracket Feet, c.1800, 37 x 19 In.	4200
Chest, Mule, Lower Drawer, Painted, Shaped Apron, c.1820	3500
Chest, Mule, Mixed Wood, Red Grain Paint, Bootjack Ends, 1800s, 42 x 42 In.	646
Chest, Mule, Pine, 2 Low Drawers, New England, c.1750, 36 x 43 In.	356
Chest, Mule, Pine, 4 Drawers, Painted, New England, c.1850, 39 x 39 In.	390
Chest, Mule, Pine, Brown Paint, 5 Drawers, Brass Pulls, Hinges, c.1850, 45 x 39 In.	793
Chest, Mule, Pine, c.1845, 30 x 39 In.	152
Chest, Mule, Pine, Dark Stain, Dovetailed, Drawer, 3 Faux Drawers, c.1925, 36 x 36 In.	558
Chest, Mule, Pine, Drawer, 2 Doors, Yellow Brown Graining, 1800s, 38 x 47 In.	1024
Chest, Mule, Pine, Lift Top, Hinged Lid, Dovetailed, c.1800, 34 x 40 In.	590
Chest, Mule, Pine, New England, 1700s, 38 ½ x 36 In.	486
Chest, Mule, Pine, Painted, 6 Graduated Drawers, New England, c.1790, 53 x 36 In.	710
Chest, Mule, Queen Anne, Pine, Spanish Brown Paint, 2 Drawers, Cutout Feet, 47 x 39 In.	1763
Chest, Mule, Softwood, Lid Top, Molded Drawer, New England, c.1845, 32 x 40 In.	316
Chest, Neoclassical Style, Walnut, 2 Drawers, 31 x 33 In.	530
Chest, Neoclassical, Faux Painted Books, Papers, 2 Drawers, c.1950, 17 ½ x 18 In.	660
Chest, Oak, 6 Drawers, c.1910, 30 x 48 In.	288
Chest, Oak, Domed, Carved Panels, Painted, Strap Hinges, England, c.1765, 23 x 48 In.	488
Chest, Oak, Green Tinted Varnish, 4 Drawers, 4 Curved Feet, c.1910, 37 x 18 In.	96
Chest, Ole Wanscher, Rosewood, Brass, Double, 5 Drawers Per Side, Denmark, 31 x 36 In.	4063
Chest, Painted Flower, White Ground, 2 Drawers, 29 ½ x 24 In., Pair	1063

Chest, Painted Shell Top, Yellow Ground, Carved Splash, 4 Drawers, New England, 34 x 30 In.....	840
Chest, Philippe Starck, Wood, Laminated, Metal, Leather, 29 x 21 In., Pair..................................	585
Chest, Pine, 3 Drawers, c.1840, 12 x 9 In...	326
Chest, Pine, 3 Graduated Drawers, Cutout Feet, New England, c.1780, 23 x 19 In., Child's...........	748
Chest, Pine, 4 Drawers, c.1850, 38 x 34 In..	288
Chest, Pine, 4 Drawers, c.1850, 45 ½ x 41 ½ In..	504
Chest, Pine, 4 Drawers, c.1860, 39 x 35 In..	288
Chest, Pine, 4 Drawers, c.1890, 39 x 35 In..	374
Chest, Pine, Empire, 2 Drawers, Over Drop Drawer, 2 Doors, 48 x 43 In....................................	295
Chest, Pine, Hinged Top, Double Arch Case, c.1715, 41 x 37 In...	1353
Chest, Pine, Painted, 4 Drawers, New England, c.1820, 38 x 42 In.	385
Chest, Pine, Painted, c.1815, 31 x 48 In..	486
Chest, Pine, Painted, Graduated Drawers, Shaped Skirt, Trees, c.1805, 38 x 37 In.	2938
Chest, Pine, Red & Black Grain Painted, New England, c.1810, 39 x 43 In.	840
Chest, Pine, Red Stain, 3 Drawers, Pennsylvania, c.1820, 35 x 36 In.......................................	420
Chest, Pine, Red Wash, Pennsylvania, c.1820, 21 x 40 In.	237
Chest, Poplar, Tabletop, Drawer, Painted, Pennsylvania, c.1850, 14 x 14 In.............................	456
Chest, Quartersawn Oak, Scrolled, Molded Gallery, 6 Drawers, Paw Feet, 62 x 40 In..................	325
Chest, Queen Anne, Cherry, 7 Drawers, Scalloped Apron, New England, c.1770, 51 x 36 In........	1304
Chest, Queen Anne, Cherry, Pine, Escutcheons, Massachusetts, c.1740, 67 x 38 In. ....*illus*	5100
Chest, Queen Anne, Mahogany, 12 Drawers, Carved Legs, Philadelphia, c.1765, 75 x 40 In.	8888
Chest, Queen Anne, Maple, 11 Molded Drawers, Fan Carved, Cabriole Legs, Mass., c.1760	10625
Chest, Queen Anne, Maple, 3 Faux Drawers, 6 Drawers, Fan Carved, N.H., c.1790, 60 x 43 In.....	1875
Chest, Queen Anne, Maple, 7 Drawers, 2 Parts, New England, c.1765, 68 x 38 In.........................	2370
Chest, Queen Anne, Maple, Carved Apron, Drop Finials, 5 Drawers, 1700s, 31 x 37 In...............	708
Chest, Queen Anne, Maple, Carved, 6 Drawers, New England, c.1770, 65 x 37 In.......................	1896
Chest, Queen Anne, Maple, Pine, 2 Sections, Drawers, 1700s, 67 x 40 In. ....*illus*	2760
Chest, Queen Anne, Tiger Maple, 8 Drawers, New England, c.1760, 65 x 37 In..........................	9480
Chest, Queen Anne, Walnut, 2 Parts, 8 Drawers, Raised Cabriole Legs, 72 x 37 In......................	1375
Chest, Queen Anne, Walnut, 2 Parts, 9 Drawers, Shaped Apron, 71 x 38 In...............................	1625
Chest, Queen Anne, Walnut, 9 Drawers, Scalloped Apron, Pa., c.1770, 66 x 36 In......................	1680
Chest, Queen Anne, Walnut, Flat Cove Top, 7 Drawers, Cabriole Legs, c.1750, 65 x 41 In.	5313
Chest, Queen Anne, Walnut, Herringbone Inlay, 9 Drawers, Bracket Feet, c.1760, 58 x 39 In.	11850
Chest, Queen Anne, Walnut, Pennsylvania, c.1770, 64 x 38 In..	2015
Chest, Red Paint, 4 Graduated Drawers, Scalloped Base, 1800s, 41 x 35 In................................	173
Chest, Regency Style, Mahogany, Bowed Top, 4 Drawers, Banding, 35 x 42 In., Pair....................	1845
Chest, Regency, Mahogany, Rosewood, Inlay, 5 Drawers, Carved Apron, c.1810, 44 x 36 In.........	826
Chest, Renaissance Revival, Walnut, Marble Top, 3 Drawers, Carved, c.1870, 34 x 46 In.............	1063
Chest, Rococo, Walnut, Serpentine, 2 Drawers, Cabriole Legs, 34 x 44 In.	2250
Chest, Sendai Tansu, Drawers, Door, Japan, 35 x 35 In..	1625
Chest, Shaker, Pine, Drawers, Dovetailed, 2 Sections, Label, c.1835, 48 x 56 In. ....*illus*	21240
Chest, Sheraton, Birch, Bird's-Eye Maple, Carved, Red Stain, 4 Drawers, c.1820, 51 x 44 In.	1540
Chest, Sheraton, Bird's-Eye & Tiger Maple, 4 Drawers, Pennsylvania, c.1830, 42 x 40 ½ In........	2252
Chest, Sheraton, Bird's-Eye Maple, Bowfront, 4 Drawers, Raised Legs, 40 x 42 In.......................	1020
Chest, Sheraton, Cherry, 4 Drawers, Sandwich Glass Knobs, Carved Apron, Backsplash, 46 In.....	1320
Chest, Sheraton, Cherry, 4 Drawers, Wood Pulls, 43 x 47 In..	452
Chest, Sheraton, Cherry, 8 Beaded Drawers, Turned Feet, Pennsylvania, c.1845, 64 x 44 In.........	748
Chest, Sheraton, Cherry, Bird's-Eye Maple, 4 Drawers, Turned Legs, c.1810, 38 x 41 In..............	1287
Chest, Sheraton, Cherry, Half Columns, Turned Feet, Brass Pulls, c.1820, 65 x 46 In..................	1058
Chest, Sheraton, Cherry, Mahogany, 4 Drawers, Pennsylvania, c.1830, 45 x 44 In.	326
Chest, Sheraton, Cherry, Mahogany, Bowfront, 4 Drawers, c.1815, 17 x 18 In.	593
Chest, Sheraton, Cherry, Overhanging Top, 4 Scratch-Beaded Drawers, 42 x 40 In.....................	936
Chest, Sheraton, Cherry, Poplar, Reeded Stiles, Shaped Skirt, c.1835, 49 x 40 In.......................	588
Chest, Sheraton, Figured Mahogany, Drawers, New England, c.1810, 53 x 40 In. ....*illus*	1062
Chest, Sheraton, Green Paint, Panel Ends, 4 Drawers, 43 x 43 In...	2400
Chest, Sheraton, Mahogany, Bowfront, 4 Drawers, c.1815, 40 x 40 In......................................	444
Chest, Sheraton, Mahogany, Bowfront, 4 Drawers, Massachusetts, c.1815, 40 x 40 In.	710
Chest, Sheraton, Mahogany, Shaped Backsplash, 4 Drawers, Carved Sides, Wilder, 44 x 41 In.....	960
Chest, Sheraton, Maple, Cherry, 4 Drawers, Turned Legs, c.1820, 39 x 39 In.............................	1567
Chest, Sheraton, Maple, Cock-Beaded, Glass Pulls, Turned Feet, c.1830, 41 x 41 In.	529
Chest, Sheraton, Pine, Grain Painted, Ribbed, Carved Pilaster, 5 Drawers, c.1850, 44 x 38 In......	480
Chest, Sheraton, Tiger Maple, 4 Drawers, George Christine, Pa., c.1825, 42 x 40 In.....................	1080
Chest, Sheraton, Tiger Maple, 6 Drawers, Half Columns, Pennsylvania, c.1840, 54 x 41 In..........	1778
Chest, Sheraton, Tiger Maple, Bowfront, 4 Drawers, 42 x 42 In.	1200
Chest, Sheraton, Walnut, 4 Graduated Drawers, Mid-Atlantic, c.1835, 47 x 37 In.	489

F

Furniture, Chair, V. Kagan, Wing, Ottoman, Aluminum, Upholstered, 41 In., 18 x 28 In.
$2,640

Palm Beach Modern Auctions

Furniture, Chair, Victorian Style, Steer Horn, Leather Upholstery, 1900s, 42 x 31 x 22 In.
$1,188

Rago Arts & Auction Center

Furniture, Chair, W. McArthur, Tubular, Metal Slats, Green Paint, Label, c.1930, 34 ½ In.. Pair
$3,555

James D. Julia Auctioneers

Furniture, Chair, Walnut, Bone Inlay, Vase Shape Splat, Arms, Italy, c.1850, 38 In.
$300

Skinner Auctioneers & Appraisers

FURNITURE

Furniture, Chair, Wegner, Peacock, Ash, Teak, Paper Cord Seat, Johannes Hansen, c.1960, 42 In.
$2,280

Furniture, Chair, Wegner, Valet, Teak, Pine, Brass, Johannes Hansen, 1960s, 37 In.
$8,750

Furniture, Chair, Windsor, Comb Back, 7 Spindles, Shaped Crest, Arms, 1800s, 40 In.
$720

Furniture, Chair, Windsor, Yew, Pierced Splats, Turned Legs, Arms, England, c.1890, 34 ½ In.
$120

Furniture, Chair-Table, Pine, Ash, Shoe Feet, New England, c.1775, 27 x 45 In.
$2,952

Furniture, Chamberstand, Rosewood, Grain Paint, Pierced, Drawer, c.1810, 32 x 16 In.
$1,230

Furniture, Chest, Biedermeier, Birch Veneer, Marble, Frieze Drawer, 1800s, 35 x 51 In.
$480

Furniture, Chest, Blanket, Chippendale, Maple, Pine, Painted, New England, c.1790, 21 x 40 In.
$360

Furniture, Chest, Blanket, Painted, Lift Top, Faux Drawers & 2 Working, c.1710, 40 x 36 In.
$1,920

Furniture, Chest, Blanket, Shaker, Pine, Breadboard Lid, Strap Hinges, 29 x 43 In.
$15,340

Chest, Sheraton, Walnut, 4 Incised Drawers, Ebonized Columns, c.1830, 21 x 19 In.	608
Chest, Softwood, Blue Sponged Paint, Drawers, Till, Wrought-Iron Strap Hinges, 30 x 52 In.	649
Chest, Softwood, Feather Grain Paint, Molded Lid, Till, Hinged, 28 x 44 In.	590
Chest, Spice, Chippendale Style, Tiger Maple, Fan-Carved Opening, 11 Drawers, 17 x 14 In.	1140
Chest, Storage, Elm, Dovetailed, Handles, Brass Hardware, Korea, 26 x 32 In. ....*illus*	119
Chest, Sugar, Cherry, Hinged Opening, Panel Front, 2 Drawers, Kentucky, c.1830, 37 x 42 In.	2300
Chest, Sugar, Cherry, Hinged Top, Turned Legs, Removable Box, Drawers	8658
Chest, Sugar, Cherry, Single-Board Lift Top, Drawer, Turned Feet, 1800s, 34 x 29 In.	1770
Chest, Sugar, Federal Style, Cherry, Hinged Lid, Stand, Square Legs, 32 x 19 In.	598
Chest, Sugar, Sheraton, Low Drawer, c.1835, 33 x 36 In.	1896
Chest, Teak, Brass, 10 Graduated Drawers, Arcadia Glen, 1950s, 51 x 22 In.	1875
Chest, Treasure, Wood, Painted, Tigers, Leaves, Hinged Lid, Handles, 1900s, 8 x 13 In.	1020
Chest, Victorian, Mahogany, 10 Drawers, Wellington, 60 x 37 In.	1250
Chest, Walnut, 3 Drawers, c.1890, 11 ½ In., Child's	177
Chest, Walnut, 3 Drawers, String Inlay, Bracket Feet, c.1850, 19 x 18 In.	1265
Chest, Walnut, 4 Drawers, Carved Bracket, New England, 37 x 43 In.	1440
Chest, Walnut, Burl, Plank Top, 4 Drawers, Serpentine Skirt, 1800s, 16 x 13 In.	212
Chest, Walnut, Column Carved, 4 Over 2 Drawers, Tennessee, 46 x 44 ½ In.	9594
Chest, Walnut, Line & Berry Inlay, 5 Drawers, Ball Feet, c.1740, 42 x 40 In.	23700
Chest, Walnut, Marble Top, 3 Drawers, Carved, 46 x 33 In.	136
Chest, Walnut, Poplar, 4 Drawers, North Carolina, c.1820, 21 x 17 In., Child's	748
Chest, Walnut, Seaweed Marquetry, 4 Drawers, England, c.1800, 34 x 29 In.	1750
Chest, Walnut, Voluted Case, 4 Drawers, Stepped Base, c.1850, 40 x 51 In.	3125
Chest, William & Mary Style, Walnut, Inlay, 4 Graduated Drawers, Bun Feet, 1800s, 29 x 37 In.	1440
Chest, William & Mary Style, Walnut, Top-Banded Conforming Case, 38 x 42 In.	2952
Chest, William & Mary, Burl Veneer, 8 Drawers, England, 63 ½ x 41 In.	1700
Chest, William & Mary, Pine, 3 Drawers, Applied Molding, c.1740, 55 In.	813
Chest, William & Mary, Pine, Brown Stain, 4 Drawers, Ball Feet, c.1750, 36 x 36 In.	1875
Chest, William & Mary, Walnut, Banding, 9 Beaded Drawers, Apron, Ball Feet, 64 x 43 In.	1434
Chest, William & Mary, Walnut, Line Inlay, 4 Drawers, Bracket Feet, 31 x 36 In.	1125
Chest, Wormley, Janus, Walnut, Brass, Inset Natzler Tiles, Dunbar, 1956, 33 x 34 In. ....*illus*	2250
Chest-On-Chest, Chippendale, Applewood, Fluted Columns, Footed, c.1780, 73 x 40 In.	3792
Chest-On-Chest, Chippendale, Mahogany, Lamb's Tongue Corners, c.1750, 73 x 40 In. ......*illus*	20060
Chest-on-Chest, Chippendale, Walnut, 5 Drawers, Ogee Bracket Feet, 66 x 42 In.	4200
Chest-On-Chest, George III, Burl Walnut, 2 Sections, 9 Drawers, 70 x 42 In.	2300
Chest-On-Chest, Georgian, Elm, Breakfront Cornice, Bracket Feet, 1700s, 67 x 41 In.	1968
Chest-On-Frame, Mahogany, 6 Drawers, England, 20 x 37 In.	500
Chest-On-Frame, William & Mary, Walnut Veneer, Spiral-Turned Legs, 63 x 39 In. ....*illus*	1476
Chiffonier, Regency, Rosewood, Gilt Bronze Gallery, Egypt Masks, 2 Doors, c.1810, 43 x 42 In.	1375
China Press, Federal, Cherry, Inlay, Projecting Cornice, Drawer, Fluted Legs, 35 x 42 In.	615
China Press, Mixed Wood, Glass Doors, Panel Doors, Painted, New Eng., c.1780, 101 x 47 In.	4248
Clothes Press, Black Lacquer, Painted Landscapes, Doors, Brass Pulls, Chinese, 80 x 44 In.	558
Coat Rack, Baroque, Gilt, Carved, Wrought-Iron Hook, Hat Shelf, 11 x 31 In.	399
Coat Rack, Carved, Entwined Tree Shape, Wood, 1990s, 75 x 29 In.	938
Coat Rack, Hanging, Wood, Carved, Hook, Shaped Back, Painted, 11 x 32 In.	230
Coat Rack, Wood, Carved, 5 Hooks, American, 11 x 53 In.	323
Coffer, Baroque, Oak, Carved, Paneled, Iron Lock, c.1700, 26 x 53 In.	590
Coffer, Hardwood, Bone Inlay, Flowers, Lift Top, c.1885, 29 x 41 In.	430
Coffer, Oak, Carved, Diamond Panels, Flowers, Till, Initials, England, 1700s, 28 x 48 In.	440
Coffer, Renaissance Style, Gilt, Hinged Lid, Scroll Leaves, Carved, 1700s, 15 x 27 In.	1476
Commode, 4 Drawers, Italy, 36 x 41 In.	1320
Commode, Baroque, Serpentine, Painted, Gilt Highlights, Swiss, 1700s, 31 x 36 In. ....*illus*	2006
Commode, Bombe, 4 Graduated Drawers, Leaf-Carved Apron, Claw Feet, 32 x 34 In.	1169
Commode, Bombe, Painted, Serpentine Top, Drawers, Venetian, 48 x 22 In. ....*illus*	2375
Commode, Burl Veneer, Marble Top, 3 Drawers, France, c.1920, 37 x 56 In.	474
Commode, Chippendale Style, Mahogany, Inlay, Gallery Top, c.1900, 36 x 38 In.	590
Commode, Empire, Walnut, Gilt Bronze, Marble Top, 3 Drawers, Columns, c.1850, 35 x 45 In.	2250
Commode, French Style, Satinwood, Marble Top, Serpentine Front, 2 Drawers, 33 x 43 In.	540
Commode, Fruitwood, 2 Drawers, 30 x 32 In.	250
Commode, Fruitwood, Marquetry, Inlay, Shipping Scene Top, 4 Drawers, 37 x 48 In.	3600
Commode, Georgian, Mahogany, Crossbanded Top, Doors, Bracket Feet, c.1815, 31 In.	800
Commode, Georgian, Mahogany, Tray Top, Cutout Handles, Drawer, 1700s, 31 x 22 In.	984
Commode, Louis XIV Style, Black Lacquer, Ebonized, 4 Drawers, 31 x 40 In.	4688
Commode, Louis XV Style, Drawers, Marquetry, Marble, France, c.1925, 16 x 11 In.	442
Commode, Louis XV Style, Kingwood, Bombe, Marble Top, 1900s, 36 x 47 In.	615

Furniture, Chest, Blanket, Shaker, Pine, Single-Board Top, Dovetailed, c.1845, 32 x 42 In.
$3,304

Willis Henry Auctions, Inc.

Furniture, Chest, Blanket, Shaker, Pine, Strap Hinges, Dovetailed, c.1810, 41 x 40 In.
$18,880

Willis Henry Auctions, Inc.

Furniture, Chest, Camphorwood, Carved Scenes, Etched Brass Latch, 22 x 41 x 24 In.
$230

Victorian Casino Antiques

Furniture, Chest, Cherry, 4 Drawers, Reeded Columns, c.1810, 17 x 18 In.
$1,320

Skinner Auctioneers & Appraisers

TIP

Liquid household cleaner on a paper towel is a good way to clean gilding.

Furniture, Chest, Cherry, 6 Curly Maple Drawers, Southern Ohio, 1800s, 49 x 41 In.
$2,280

Cowan's Auctions

Furniture, Chest, Chippendale, Walnut, Dovetailed Drawers, Fluted Columns, c.1780, 37 x 39 In.
$826

Conestoga Auction Co., Inc.

Furniture, Chest, Chippendale, Walnut, Graduated Drawers, Bracket Feet, c.1780, 40 x 22 In.
$472

Conestoga Auction Co., Inc.

Commode, Louis XV Style, Kingwood, Marble Top, Sabots, c.1885, 33 x 45 In.	3444
Commode, Louis XV Style, Marble Top, Drawers, Shaped Skirt, c.1890, 34 x 46 In.	3075
Commode, Louis XV Style, Marble Top, Drawers, Shaped Skirt, c.1980, 35 x 51 In.	177
Commode, Louis XV Style, Tulipwood, Marble Top, Gilt, France, c.1920, 34 x 23 In.	715
Commode, Louis XV Style, Walnut, 2 Drawers, Applied Scroll Molding, 27 x 37 In.	250
Commode, Louis XV, 3 Serpentine Drawers, Painted, 49 x 39 In.	4500
Commode, Louis XV, Black Marble Top, 3 Drawers, Painted Flowers, 41 x 55 In.	2813
Commode, Louis XV, Cherry, Bombe, 3 Drawers, Carved, Peg Toes, c.1750, 33 x 52 In.	5000
Commode, Louis XV, Fruitwood, 3 Drawers, 33 ½ x 45 In.	2640
Commode, Louis XV, Fruitwood, Inlay, 2 Drawers, Cabriole Legs, c.1780, 35 x 50 In.	2360
Commode, Louis XV, Kingwood, Marble Top, Shaped Apron, 1700s, 34 x 47 In.	4428
Commode, Louis XV, Walnut, Cherry, Bombe, 3 Drawers, c.1750, 35 x 53 In.	3750
Commode, Louis XV, Walnut, Marble, Serpentine, 3 Drawers, c.1775, 39 x 50 In.	2000
Commode, Louis XV, Walnut, Serpentine Top, Cartouches, Scallop Apron, 31 x 37 In.	2214
Commode, Louis XVI Style, 3 Drawers, Green, Orange, White Paint, 32 x 48 In.	4375
Commode, Louis XVI Style, Fruitwood, Vernis Martin, Marble Top, 36 x 46 In. ....*illus*	478
Commode, Louis XVI, Cherry, Gray Marble Top, 3 Graduated Drawers, c.1800, 34 x 50 In.	5625
Commode, Louis XVI, Parquetry, Marble Top, Shaped Skirt, c.1800, 35 x 51 In.	2360
Commode, Mahogany Veneer, 3 Drawers, Serpentine, Crossbanded, Germany, c.1790, 33 x 40 In.	1600
Commode, Mahogany, Inlay, 2 Blind Maple Drawers, Reeded, Raised Legs, c.1815, 29 x 25 In.	875
Commode, Mahogany, Marble Top, Bronze, 3 Drawers, c.1905, 35 x 50 In.	6875
Commode, Mahogany, Marble Top, Drawers, Brass Bail Pulls, c.1900, 38 x 51 In.	3444
Commode, Maple, Faux Bamboo, Marble Top, Turned Feet, c.1890, 33 x 19 In.	239
Commode, Neoclassical Style, Walnut, Carved, Paneled Top, Drawers, Columns, 35 x 50 In.	1230
Commode, Neoclassical, Allegorical, Inlaid Top Door, Banded Drawer, c.1865, 25 x 16 In.	847
Commode, Neoclassical, Banded Top, Drawers, Tapered Square Legs, c.1875, 32 x 50 In.	1623
Commode, Neoclassical, Burl, Parquetry, 3 Drawers, c.1815, 37 x 48 In.	3304
Commode, Neoclassical, Mahogany, Banding, Scroll Inlay, c.1850, 35 x 42 In.	2952
Commode, Neoclassical, Mahogany, Marble Top, Drawers, Cabriole Legs, 1800s, 29 x 33 In.	500
Commode, Neoclassical, Maple, Wood Pulls, 1800s, 23 ½ x 19 In. ....*illus*	1476
Commode, Neoclassical, Marble Top, 3 Drawers, Painted, Sweden, c.1800, 32 x 38 In.	2500
Commode, Neoclassical, Veneer, Inlay, Drawer, Animals, Tapered Legs, 1800s, 31 x 24 In.	826
Commode, Neoclassical, Walnut, 4 Drawers, Tapered Legs, c.1800, 37 x 46 In.	2360
Commode, Oak, Marble Top, Shaped Skirt, Shell, Cabriole Legs, 35 x 45 In.	896
Commode, Painted, 5 Drawers, Decoupage, Bulbous Feet, c.1900, 32 x 45 In.	1353
Commode, Regency Style, Fruitwood, Bombe, Banded Top, 1700s, 35 x 48 In.	4674
Commode, Regency Style, Fruitwood, Parquetry, Marble Top, 4 Drawers, Ormolu, 63 x 40 In.	5445
Commode, Regency Style, Kingwood, Gilt, Serpentine Marble Top, 51 In.	1434
Commode, Regency Style, Mahogany, Rounded Sides, 3 Drawers, Metal Mounts, 34 x 60 In.	500
Commode, Regency, Cherry, Banded, Bowed, Scroll Toes, 1700s, 37 x 50 In.	5904
Commode, Rococo Style, Fruitwood, Gilt Bronze Mounts, Marble Top, 5 Drawers, 35 x 47 In.	625
Commode, Rococo Style, Red, Green Flowers, Yellow Ground, Painted, 2 Drawers, 35 x 52 In.	3438
Commode, Rococo, Mahogany, Serpentine Marble Top, Beading, 32 x 20 In.	777
Commode, Rococo, Walnut, Rosewood, Serpentine, Drawers, Apron, Italy, c.1770, 83 x 49 In.	3438
Commode, Rosewood, Marble Top, Cupboard Door, Bracket Feet, c.1885, 30 In.	1793
Commode, Veneer, 3 Drawers, Chamfered Corners, Strapwork, Footed, c.1800, 34 x 25 In., Pair	3250
Commode, Walnut, Inlay, Serpentine Front, 3 Drawers, Italy, 31 x 24 In.	1920
Cradle, Cherry, Cutout Design, Dovetailed, 20 x 40 In.	118
Cradle, Curly Maple, Hanging Frame, Slats, Wrought Iron, 1800s, 32 x 45 In.	440
Cradle, Federal, Mahogany, Shell Inlay, c.1820	90
Cradle, Hooded, Tree Of Life, Black, Red Paint, c.1790, 33 x 39	454
Cradle, Pine, Dovetailed, Heart Cutout, Painted, New England, 1800s, 20 x 41 In. ....*illus*	185
Cradle, Pine, Picket Sides, Green Paint, c.1910, 17 In.	60
Cradle, Tiger Maple, Carved Head & Footboards, c.1860, 32 x 27 In.	188
Cradle, Walnut, Platform, Spindles, Carved Shaped Head & Footboards, Victorian	260
Cradle, Wood, Bentwood Slats, Wood Frame, Iron Wheels, 47 In.	58
Cradle, Wood, Grain Painted, Hood, Dovetailed, Late 19th Century, 27 x 34 In.	65
Credenza, Adrian Pearsall, Silvered Composite, Laminate, 1970s, 26 ½ x 69 In. ....*illus*	3375
Credenza, Baroque, Walnut, Cabinet Doors, Dovetailed, Paw Feet, 41 x 48 In.	9440
Credenza, Burl, String Inlay, 2 Doors, Arabesque, Glass Demilune Doors, 42 x 71 In.	450
Credenza, Rosewood Veneer, Drawers, Cabinet, Marble Top, c.1900, 43 x 71 x 18 In.	400
Credenza, Walnut, 1960s, 30 x 67 In.	1500
Credenza-Desk, Risom, 3 Drawers, Danish-American, c.1946, 20 x 75 & 28 x 75 In.	1646
Crib, Curly Maple, Acorn Finials, American, c.1835, 40 x 47 In.	764
Crib, Maple, Spindle Sides, Finial Ends, c.1865, 53 x 31 In.	188

Cupboard, 2 Doors, Blue Paint, c.1850, 49 x 49 ½ In.	490
Cupboard, 2 Doors, Bootjack Base, Blue Paint, c.1855, 37 x 18 ½ In.	545
Cupboard, 2 Doors, Geometric Panels, Painted, Red Ground, 41 x 43 In.	2640
Cupboard, 2 Doors, Paneled, Green Paint, c.1850, 35 x 61 In.	575
Cupboard, 2 Drawers, 2 Doors, Carved Spiral Designs, Canada, 38 x 44 In.	1320
Cupboard, 2 Glass Doors, 2 Drawers, 2 Panel Doors, Painted, Soap Hollow, 1800s, 85 x 64 In.	12500
Cupboard, 2 Panel Doors, Blue Paint, New York, 79 x 53 In.	1440
Cupboard, 3 Doors, Blue Paint, c.1860, 43 ½ x 19 In.	575
Cupboard, 4 Drawers, 2 Panel Doors, Grain Painted, White Knobs, c.1830, 51 x 44 In.	720
Cupboard, Baker's, Dry Sink, Tin, 3 Glass Doors, 2 Doors, 3 Drawers, c.1900, 60 x 69 In.	430
Cupboard, Blue Paint, Step Back, 2 Open Shelves, Drawer, Door, 45 x 21 In.	1495
Cupboard, Butternut, 2 Paneled Doors, Interior Shelves, Red Paint Trace, 70 x 50 In.	499
Cupboard, Charles II, Court, Oak, Carved, Doors, Drawer, Shelf, 1600s, 50 x 53 In. ......*illus*	8365
Cupboard, Cherry, 2 Glass Doors, 2 Drawers, 2 Panel Doors, c.1840, 88 x 48 In.	608
Cupboard, Cherry, Panel Door, Raised Base, Virginia, c.1800, 47 x 32 In.	1495
Cupboard, Cherry, Reeded & Canted Corners, 4 Paneled Doors, 1800s, 80 x 44 In.	734
Cupboard, Cherry, Walnut, Dovetailed, 2 Diamond-Paneled Doors, c.1850, 30 x 37 In.	558
Cupboard, Chimney, Long Panel Door, Grain Painted, c.1850, 68 In.	1020
Cupboard, Chimney, Pine, 2 Doors, Paneled, 82 x 29 In.	960
Cupboard, Chimney, Pine, 3 Interior Shelves, Yellow Paint, 1800s, 51 x 18 In.	844
Cupboard, Chimney, Pine, Brown Paint, c.1820, 79 x 26 In.	2252
Cupboard, Chimney, Pine, Door, Brown Paint, New England, 78 x 27 In.	840
Cupboard, Chippendale, Walnut, Step Back, Glass, Panel Doors, Drawers, c.1780, 86 x 53 In.	1495
Cupboard, Corner, Barrel Back, 2 Tombstone Doors, Flat Door, c.1790, 47 x 93 In.	3450
Cupboard, Corner, Cherry, 2 Glass Doors, 2 Panel Doors, 91 x 58 In.	2420
Cupboard, Corner, Cherry, 2 Glass Doors, 2 Panel Doors, c.1845, 85 x 50 In.	750
Cupboard, Corner, Cherry, 2 Glass Doors, 2 Panel Doors, Drawers, Pa., c.1815, 87 x 51 In.	948
Cupboard, Corner, Cherry, 2 Glass Doors, 2 Panel Doors, Mid-Atlantic, c.1830, 85 x 52 In.	889
Cupboard, Corner, Cherry, 2 Glass Doors, 2 Panel Doors, Scalloped Apron, 48 x 72 In.	1017
Cupboard, Corner, Cherry, 12 Glass Doors, 3 Shelves, c.1850, 78 In.	1610
Cupboard, Corner, Cherry, 8-Pane Glass Doors, Drawer, Panel Doors, c.1850	13455
Cupboard, Corner, Cherry, Bowfront, 2 Sections, Dentil Cornice, c.1800, 98 x 51 In.	3819
Cupboard, Corner, Cherry, Cornice, Glass Doors, Drawers, Panel Doors, 1800s, 84 x 53 In.	1107
Cupboard, Corner, Cherry, Cornice, Paneled Doors, Shelves, Drawers, 1700s, 85 x 45 In.	2520
Cupboard, Corner, Cherry, Glass Doors, Panel Doors, Drawers, Pa., c.1830, 84 x 48 In.	2133
Cupboard, Corner, Cherry, Molding, Panel Doors, Shelves, Drawers, 1700s, 85 x 45 In.	2520
Cupboard, Corner, Chippendale, Gumwood, Glass & Panel Doors, c.1780, 71 x 50 In.	1778
Cupboard, Corner, Chippendale, Mahogany, Panel Doors, Ogee Bracket Feet, 102 x 24 In.	530
Cupboard, Corner, Chippendale, Pine, Doors, Drawer, Painted, c.1790, 102 x 56 In.	5900
Cupboard, Corner, Chippendale, Walnut, Arched & Square Doors, Pa., c.1770, 99 x 51 In.	1422
Cupboard, Corner, Chippendale, Walnut, Glass Door, Panel Door, Pa., 1850, 77 x 40 In.	237
Cupboard, Corner, Federal, Cherry, Arched Glass Doors, Drawer, c.1905, 93 x 44 In.	3318
Cupboard, Corner, Federal, Cherry, Inlay, 2 Doors, 2 Drawers, 87 ½ x 47 In.	2813
Cupboard, Corner, Federal, Cornice, Glass & Panel Doors, Painted, Pa., 83 x 43 In.	2280
Cupboard, Corner, Federal, Maple, Glass, Panel Doors, Carved, Columns, c.1820, 81 x 48 In.	3750
Cupboard, Corner, Federal, Shelves, Drawers, Doors, Fluted Columns, 78 x 38 In.	1320
Cupboard, Corner, Federal, Walnut, 4 Paneled Doors, Southern, c.1790, 88 x 47 In.	4025
Cupboard, Corner, Federal, Walnut, Cock-Beaded, French Feet, c.1800, 73 In.	2160
Cupboard, Corner, Glass Door, Drawers, 2 Doors, Grain Painted, Rupp, 1800s, 87 x 48 In.	5925
Cupboard, Corner, Hanging, Georgian Style, Mahogany, Glass Door, c.1900, 28 x 19 In.	430
Cupboard, Corner, Hanging, Mahogany, Panel Glass, England, 25 x 21 In.	295
Cupboard, Corner, Hanging, Mahogany, Pine, Glass Door, Mullions, England, 44 x 31 In.	502
Cupboard, Corner, Hanging, Mahogany, Pine, Inlaid, Curved Mullions, 43 x 29 In.	353
Cupboard, Corner, Hanging, Oak, Carved Door, Shaped Shelves, 26 x 35 In.	299
Cupboard, Corner, Hanging, Oak, Inlay, 3 Base Drawers, England, c.1790, 37 x 32 In.	590
Cupboard, Corner, Hanging, Oak, Ornate Carved Doors, England, 40 x 30 In.	296
Cupboard, Corner, Hanging, Oak, Panel Door, England, c.1800, 42 ½ x 28 In.	243
Cupboard, Corner, Hanging, Pine, 1855, 25 x 28 In.	593
Cupboard, Corner, Hanging, Pine, Bird Panels, Stippled Paint, Continental, c.1790, 42 x 23 In.	830
Cupboard, Corner, Hanging, Pine, Door, Base Shelf, Pennsylvania, c.1770, 61 x 37 In.	710
Cupboard, Corner, Hanging, Pine, Door, Drawer, Shelf, Red Paint, Pa., c.1790, 50 x 33 In.	2607
Cupboard, Corner, Hanging, Pine, Scalloped Sides, New England, c.1810, 56 x 26 In.	3318
Cupboard, Corner, Hanging, Tiger Maple, Door, 26 x 25 In.	1185
Cupboard, Corner, Hanging, Yellow Pine, Glass Door Pane, c.1860, 25 x 20 In.	353
Cupboard, Corner, Hepplewhite, Cherry, Door, England, 40 x 27 In.	450

Furniture, Chest, Federal, Yellow Pine, Dovetailed, Jac Stirewalt, N.C., c.1820, 39 x 37 In.
$5,664

Brunk Auctions

Furniture, Chest, Hepplewhite, Curly Maple, Pine, Original Brasses, c.1810, 42 x 42 In.
$2,706

Cowan's Auctions

Furniture, Chest, Louis XVI Style, Mahogany, Drawers, Canted Corners, c.1910, 58 x 18 In.
$1,230

New Orleans Auction Galleries, Inc.

Furniture, Chest, McCobb, Drawers, 4 Metal Legs, Planner Group, 33 x 24 In. $480

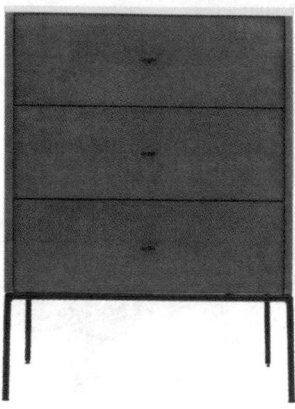

Palm Beach Modern Auctions

Furniture, Chest, Queen Anne, Cherry, Pine, Escutcheons, Massachusetts, c.1740, 67 x 38 In. $5,100

Skinner Auctioneers & Appraisers

Furniture, Chest, Queen Anne, Maple, Pine, 2 Sections, Drawers, 1700s, 67 x 40 In. $2,760

Garth's Auctioneers & Appraisers

Cupboard, Corner, Jelly, Pine, White Paint, Pennsylvania, c.1850, 64 x 51 In.	2880
Cupboard, Corner, Pine, 3 Open Shelves, 2 Panel Doors, Painted, Va., c.1820, 88 x 43 In.	863
Cupboard, Corner, Pine, Doors, Greek Key, Salmon Stain, New Eng., c.1790, 91 x 57 In.	830
Cupboard, Corner, Pine, Glass Door, 2 Panel Doors, c.1820, 75 x 30 In.	354
Cupboard, Corner, Pine, Glass Door, Divided Panel Door, Pa., c.1830, 83 x 41 In.	2133
Cupboard, Corner, Pine, Red Wash, Doors, Shelves, 2 Sections, c.1835, 84 In. *illus*	1067
Cupboard, Corner, Pine, Yellow Paint, Pink 5-Shelf Interior, c.1830, 79 x 44 In.	948
Cupboard, Corner, Poplar, 12-Light Door, 2 Panel Doors, Drawer, Shelves, c.1850, 78 In.	403
Cupboard, Corner, Poplar, Blue Paint, 4 Panel Doors, Cutout Base, c.1835, 82 x 53 In.	3290
Cupboard, Corner, Poplar, Drawers, 2 Sections, Faux Graining, c.1830, 87 In. *illus*	4200
Cupboard, Corner, Poplar, Faux Maple Paint, 4 Paneled Doors, c.1830, 85 x 46 In.	2703
Cupboard, Corner, Poplar, Painted, Glass Door, Panel Doors, Pa., c.1830, 85 x 39 In.	3555
Cupboard, Corner, Poplar, Red Paint, 2 Doors, Shaped Skirt, c.1850, 80 x 43 In.	3055
Cupboard, Corner, Softwood, Red, Green Paint, Molded Stiles, Paneled Doors, 78 x 46 In.	649
Cupboard, Corner, Tiger Maple, Glass & Panel Doors, Drawers, Pa., c.1820, 83 x 44 In.	14220
Cupboard, Corner, Walnut, 2 Glass Doors, 2 Panel Doors, Virginia, c.1850, 89 x 50 In.	1495
Cupboard, Corner, Walnut, 2 Glass Doors, Over 2 Panel Doors, Va., c.1800, 85 x 39 In.	4600
Cupboard, Corner, Walnut, Glass Door, 2 Panel Doors, Henkel-Harris, c.1985, 75 x 36 In.	633
Cupboard, Corner, Walnut, Glass Door, 2 Panel Doors, Pennsylvania, c.1800, 82 x 41 In.	652
Cupboard, Corner, William & Mary, Walnut, Glass Doors, Panel Doors, Pa., 89 x 47 In.	1320
Cupboard, Curly Maple, Step Back, 8-Pane Doors, Drawers, Panel Doors, c.1890, 87 x 60 In.	3760
Cupboard, Dry Sink, Pine, Raised-Panel Doors, Drawers, Well, Painted, 80 x 81 In.	5640
Cupboard, Dutch, 4 Doors, 3 Drawers, Red Grain Paint, c.1865, 82 x 51 In.	3080
Cupboard, Dutch, Pine, 2 Glass Doors, 2 Drawers, 2 Panel Doors, Pa., c.1800, 84 x 56 In.	1700
Cupboard, Dutch, Pine, Glass Doors, Drawers, Panel Doors, Painted, Pa., c.1800, 79 x 51 In.	3318
Cupboard, Dutch, Sheraton, Cherry, Doors, Step Back, Drawers, Pa., c.1835, 84 x 56 In.	1659
Cupboard, Elizabethan Gothic Style, Oak, Doors, Alcove, Drawers, Shelf, c.1910, 62 x 47 In.	723
Cupboard, Federal, Cherry, Step Back, Glazed Doors, 1800s, 80 x 53 In.	3304
Cupboard, Georgian, Oak, Crossbanded Mahogany Veneer, Doors, c.1810, 86 In.	1920
Cupboard, Georgian, Pine, Sienna Paint, Blue Shelves, Arched Panels, 1800s, 85 x 48 In.	270
Cupboard, Grain Painted, 4 Doors, 2 Drawers, Pennsylvania, c.1820, 84 x 56 In.	2133
Cupboard, Green Paint, Step Back, 2 Open Shelves, 2 Doors	776
Cupboard, Hanging, Blue Paint, Raised Panel Door, Fitted Interior, c.1850, 28 x 24 In.	500
Cupboard, Hanging, Bowfront, Softwood, 4 Shelves, Shaped Crest, Blue Paint, 52 x 35 In.	676
Cupboard, Hanging, Chippendale, Pine, Door, Drawer, Scalloped, Pa., c.1780, 35 x 22 In.	4977
Cupboard, Hanging, Inlaid, Lower Shelf, Tulip, Scrollwork Inlay, 1700s, 33 x 26 In.	529
Cupboard, Hanging, Mahogany, Raised Panel Door, 1700s, 38 x 27 In.	1000
Cupboard, Hanging, Pine, Arched Cornice, Door, Virgin Islands, c.1790, 27 x 22 In.	723
Cupboard, Hanging, Pine, Backsplash, Open Shelves, Painted, c.1810, 27 x 13 In.	277
Cupboard, Hanging, Pine, Brown Paint, Pennsylvania, 21 x 17 In.	593
Cupboard, Hanging, Pine, Door, Shaped Base, Pennsylvania, c.1820, 43 x 31 ½ In.	326
Cupboard, Hanging, Pine, Grain Paint, Pennsylvania, c.1840, 29 x 32 In.	369
Cupboard, Hanging, Pine, Painted, Dovetailed, Plank Doors, 1800s, 29 x 29 In.	499
Cupboard, Hanging, Pine, Poplar, Mauve Paint, Single-Board Door, Breadboard Ends, 1800s	410
Cupboard, Hanging, Poplar, Brown Paint, Door, c.1870, 18 x 12 In.	288
Cupboard, Hanging, Poplar, Door, Open Shelf, Ephrats Cloister, 31 x 18 In.	3792
Cupboard, Hanging, Poplar, Panel Door, Molded Cornice, Pa., c.1800, 37 x 28 In.	1003
Cupboard, Hanging, Walnut, Molded Cornice, Panel Door, Pa., c.1780, 30 x 25 In.	563
Cupboard, Hanging, Walnut, Pine, Panel Door, Virginia, c.1785, 50 x 38 In.	345
Cupboard, Heart Pine, Step Back, Glazed & Raised Panel Doors, S. Carolina, 80 In.	1638
Cupboard, House Facade, Painted Yellow, Door Open, Iron Handles, c.1860, 38 x 30 In.	3600
Cupboard, Jacobean, Oak, Tulip, Thistle, Flower Carvings, c.1650, 59 x 54 In.	1422
Cupboard, Jelly, 2 Glass Doors, 2 Low Panel Doors, 1800s, 67 x 34 In.	837
Cupboard, Jelly, Backsplash, Raised Panel Doors, Shelf, Bun Feet, 58 x 46 In.	295
Cupboard, Jelly, Green Paint, Splash Back, Split Drawers, Paneled Doors, 55 x 21 In.	944
Cupboard, Jelly, Painted, Backsplash, 2 Drawers, 2 Doors, Pa., c.1850, 57 x 42 In.	563
Cupboard, Jelly, Pine, 2 Doors, Painted, 2 Drawers, Backsplash, c.1850, 50 x 47 In.	215
Cupboard, Jelly, Pine, 2 Drawers, 2 Doors, c.1850, 47 x 20 In.	288
Cupboard, Jelly, Pine, Backsplash, 2 Drawers, 2 Doors, Pennsylvania, c.1860, 50 x 43 In.	593
Cupboard, Jelly, Pine, Door, c.1890, 45 x 36 In.	295
Cupboard, Jelly, Pine, Poplar, Red Paint, Drawer, Panel Doors, Cutout Feet, 62 x 40 In.	1880
Cupboard, Jelly, Pine, Red Paint, Shaped Gallery, Drawer, Doors, 1800s, 52 x 39 In.	1058
Cupboard, Jelly, Pine, Yellow Paint, Gallery, 2 Drawers, 2 Doors, Pa., 48 ½ x 42 In.	1896
Cupboard, Jelly, Pine, Yellow Paint, Scalloped Back, Drawers, Doors, c.1850, 57 x 49 In.	948
Cupboard, Jelly, Red Paint, 2 Doors, 43 x 40 In.	294

Cupboard, Jelly, Softwood, Red Paint, Backsplash, Drawer, Paneled Doors, 57 x 40 In..............	1652
Cupboard, Jelly, Walnut, Pine, Backsplash, Doors, Pendleton Co., c.1870, 47 x 42 In.............	920
Cupboard, Jelly, Walnut, Shaped Gallery, Drawer Over 2 Paneled Doors, 47 x 43 In.............	382
Cupboard, Kas, Gumwood, Panel Doors, Drawers, Red, Hudson Valley, c.1780, 78 x 60 In.	10665
Cupboard, Kas, Gumwood, Raised Panels, New Jersey, 78 x 56 In.	6075
Cupboard, Maple, Red Paint, Hinged Door, Panels, Cutout Base, c.1800, 78 x 36 In.	1200
Cupboard, Milk, Softwood, Arched Backsplash, Panel Door, Cutout Feet, 50 x 28 In.	1003
Cupboard, Mustard Paint, Panel Doors, 79 x 44 In.	5760
Cupboard, Oak, Door, Stretcher Base, Turned Legs, England, 32 x 36 In...........................	1920
Cupboard, Oak, Molded Cornice, 2 Panel Doors, Shoe Feet, England, 45 x 57 In...................	460
Cupboard, Open Top, Pine, Beaded Doors, Painted, 1800-50, 63 x 36 x 17 In.	4200
Cupboard, Painted, Step Back, Glass Door, Drawer, Panel Doors, 1861, 78 x 32 In.	21250
Cupboard, Pennsylvania Dutch, Cherry, Step Back, Glazed, Panel Doors, c.1840, 88 In.	995
Cupboard, Pewter, Pine, 3 Open Shelves, 2 Panel Doors, c.1820, 79 x 52 In.......................	1540
Cupboard, Pine, 2 Panel Doors, Red Paint, New Hampshire, c.1790, 84 x 41 In.	12000
Cupboard, Pine, 4 Doors, 2 Drawers, Step Back, c.1890, 32 x 16 In.	119
Cupboard, Pine, 4 Panel Doors, 3 Drawers, 73 In.	780
Cupboard, Pine, 9-Pane Door Over Double Panels, 18th Century, 79 x 35 x 13 In.	4800
Cupboard, Pine, Beaded Doors, Open Top, Painted, 1800-50, 63 x 36 x 17 In.	4200
Cupboard, Pine, Brown Paint, Drawer, Chimney Shape, Southern, c.1890, 33 x 15 In.............	127
Cupboard, Pine, Bucket Bench, Paneled Doors, Shelves, Red Paint, 1800s, 84 x 71 In.	5405
Cupboard, Pine, Carved Crest Sides, Open Shelves, 2 Doors, England, c.1800, 76 x 58 In.	972
Cupboard, Pine, Flat Doors, Pennsylvania, c.1820, 48 x 50 In.	326
Cupboard, Pine, Glass Doors, Drawers, Step Back, Panel Doors, Bracket Feet, 86 x 69 In.	3792
Cupboard, Pine, Glass Doors, Recessed Panel Doors, Mid-Atlantic, c.1810, 68 x 38 In.	2607
Cupboard, Pine, Grain Painted Panels, Yellow Moldings, Canada, c.1830, 46 x 58 In.	2015
Cupboard, Pine, Grain Painted, 2 Panel Doors, Pennsylvania, c.1845, 60 x 42 In.	770
Cupboard, Pine, Green & White Paint, Open Shelves, Doors, 1800s, 75 x 57 In.	764
Cupboard, Pine, Green Paint, Drawers, Paneled Doors, Shelves, 1800s, 68 x 54 In. ....*illus*	2880
Cupboard, Pine, Painted, 2 Sections, 9-Pane Door, Paneled Door, c.1850, 83 x 44 In.............	3290
Cupboard, Pine, Painted, Raised Panel Doors, Lower Tins, Flower Urn, c.1850, 76 x 52 In.........	734
Cupboard, Pine, Poplar, Faux Oak Graining, Shelves, 3-Panel Door, 1800s, 58 x 37 In.	1687
Cupboard, Pine, Red & Blue Paint, Glass Panes Door, Drawer, American, 1900s, 37 x 26 In.	410
Cupboard, Pine, Red Paint, 2 Drawers, 2 Angled Supports, Pa., c.1850, 26 x 62 In...............	600
Cupboard, Pine, Red Paint, Door, Pennsylvania, c.1820, 66 x 35 In.	948
Cupboard, Pine, Red Stain, Panel Door, Drawer, Pennsylvania, c.1860, 29 x 25 In.	277
Cupboard, Pine, Red Wash, 4 Panel Doors, Pennsylvania, c.1850, 80 x 57 In.	729
Cupboard, Pine, Step Back, 4 Doors, Iron Handles, 77 x 49 In.	240
Cupboard, Pine, Step Back, Open Top, Paneled Doors, 1800s, 77 x 50 In.	646
Cupboard, Pine, Step Back, Pierced, Shelves, Drawers, Doors, Canada, c.1865, 90 x 54 In.	1304
Cupboard, Pine, Step Back, Plate Rails, Paneled Door, Cutout Feet, 1700s, 80 x 46 In.	529
Cupboard, Pine, Tan Paint, Step Back, 2 Sections, Blind Doors, 3 Drawers, 89 x 50 In.	1998
Cupboard, Pine, White Paint, Door, 21 In...	118
Cupboard, Pine, Yellow Red Paint, Star, Monogram D.L., 25 x 13 In.	13035
Cupboard, Poplar, Gray Paint, Board & Batten Door, Shelves, Cutout Feet, 77 x 44 In.	880
Cupboard, Poplar, Green Paint, Paneled Door, Cutout Feet, 67 x 33 In.	4230
Cupboard, Poplar, Open Shelves, Doors, Drawers, New England, 1800s, 76 ½ In. ....*illus*	2760
Cupboard, Poplar, Red Paint, Pennsylvania, c.1840, 76 ½ x 35 In..................................	5214
Cupboard, Red Stain, Step Back, Glass Doors, Panel Doors, Drawers, c.1820, 79 x 58 In.	2500
Cupboard, Schrank, Chippendale, Walnut, Inlaid Initials, Doors, Drawers, 1785, 81 x 79 In.	1500
Cupboard, Shaker Style, Pine, White Paint, 2 Panel Doors, 6 Drawers, c.1870, 80 x 38 ½ In.......	1200
Cupboard, Shaker, 2 Doors, Drawer, Mt. Lebanon, N.Y., 46 ½ x 81 In.	690
Cupboard, Shaker, Cherry, Dovetailed, 2 Paneled Doors, c.1850, 42 x 37 In.	999
Cupboard, Shaker, Walnut, Single-Board Top, Panel Doors, Skirt, 1800s, 29 x 32 In.	823
Cupboard, Sheraton, Walnut, 2 Glass Doors, Base Panel Door, c.1860, 48 x 26 In., Child's	504
Cupboard, Softwood, Painted, Step Back, Scroll-Cut Cornice, Paneled Doors, 86 x 76 In.	5288
Cupboard, Softwood, Step Back, Blind Door Cupboard, Paneled Picture, 1800s, 82 x 57 In.	1770
Cupboard, Step Back, 2 Sections, Drawers, Doors, c.1830-40, 89 x 53 In. ....*illus*	923
Cupboard, Step Back, 4 Shelves, 2 Panel Doors, c.1810, 81 x 46 In................................	1750
Cupboard, Step Back, Yellow, Glass Doors, Panel Doors, Bracket Feet, 73 x 55 In.	3120
Cupboard, Victorian, Mahogany, 3 Drawers Over 2 Doors, 3-Mirror Back, Shelves, 63 x 49 In....	180
Cupboard, Walnut, 4-Panel Doors, Drop Front, Virginia, c.1825, 82 x 45 In.	1725
Cupboard, Walnut, Drawer Over Divided Panel Door, Turned Feet, Pa., 65 ½ x 38 In.	2607
Cupboard, Walnut, Panel Door, Base Shelf, Scalloped Sides, Apron, Iron, c.1770, 37 x 24 In.	18960
Cupboard, Walnut, Pine, 4 Pane Door, Ashland County, Ohio, Tabletop, 1800s, 34 x 31 In..........	499

Furniture, Chest, Shaker, Pine, Drawers, Dovetailed, 2 Sections, Label, c.1835, 48 x 56 In.
$21,240

Willis Henry Auctions, Inc.

Furniture, Chest, Sheraton, Figured Mahogany, Drawers, New England, c.1810, 53 x 40 In.
$1,062

Brunk Auctions

Furniture, Chest, Storage, Elm, Dovetailed, Handles, Brass Hardware, Korea, 26 x 32 In.
$119

James D. Julia Auctioneers

This is an edited listing of current prices. Visit Kovels.com to check thousands of prices from previous years and sign up for free information on trends, tips, reproductions, marks, and more.

Furniture, Chest, Wormley, Janus, Walnut, Brass, Inset Natzler Tiles, Dunbar, 1956, 33 x 34 In.
$2,250

Los Angeles Modern Auctions (LAMA)

Furniture, Chest-On-Chest, Chippendale, Mahogany, Lamb's Tongue Corners, c.1750, 73 x 40 In.
$20,060

Brunk Auctions

Furniture, Chest-On-Frame, William & Mary, Walnut Veneer, Spiral-Turned Legs, 63 x 39 In.
$1,476

Skinner Auctioneers & Appraisers

Cupboard, Walnut, Poplar, 4-Pane Glass Door, Virginia, Tabletop, c.1820, 29 x 32 In.		518
Cupboard, Walnut, Raised Panel Door, Pennsylvania, c.1800, 61 ½ In.		2133
Cupboard, Walnut, Step Back, 2 3-Pane Doors Over 2 Drawers Over 2 Paneled Doors, 86 In.		940
Cupboard, Walnut, Step Back, 4 Panel Doors, Drawer, c.1860, 79 x 49 In.		418
Cupboard, Welsh, Pine, Architectural Top, Plate Racks, Open Shelf, 1800s, 73 x 64 In.		235
Cupboard, William & Mary, Mahogany, Gumwood, 2 Panel Doors, 2 Drawers, 81 x 68 In.		2160
Cupboard, William & Mary, Oak, Mother-of-Pearl, Bone Inlay, c.1700, 50 x 46 In.		5900
Cupboard, Wood, White Paint, 40 x 33 In.		200
Daybed, Art Deco, Lacquered Mahogany, Velvet Upholstery, France, 1940s, 24 x 76 In.		2125
Daybed, G. Stickley, Slanted Headrest, Cushions, 29 ½ x 77 In.		650
Daybed, Limbert, Angled Headrest, Upholstered, Branded Mark, c.1908, 23 x 74 In.		1063
Daybed, Louis XV Style, Multicolor, Cushion Seat, Outscrolled Ends, c.1860, 38 x 76 In.		2214
Daybed, Neoclassical, Openwork Sides, Italy, 33 x 75 In.		1680
Daybed, Oak, Upholstered, c.1905, 27 x 72 In.		190
Daybed, William & Mary, Maple, Baluster & Turned Legs, Spanish Feet, 37 x 65 In.		860
Desk, Accountant's, Sheraton, Cherry, Swirl Paint, Slant Front, Doors, c.1841, 51 x 46 In.		18880
Desk, Adam Style, Marquetry Inlay, Doors, Drawers, Stretcher, 43 x 33 In.		530
Desk, Aesthetic Revival, Walnut, Burl Walnut, Carved, Drawers, Anglo-Japanese, 29 x 52 In.		860
Desk, Aesthetic Revival, Walnut, Roll Top, Writing Slide, Casters, 1800s, 56 x 43 In. ....*illus*		900
Desk, Arts & Crafts, Drawer, Bookshelves, Slats, c.1910, 44 x 28 In. ....*illus*		549
Desk, Baker Furniture, Georgian Style, Mahogany, Kneehole, 76 x 36 In. ....*illus*		780
Desk, Baroque, Walnut, Inlay, 3 Drawers, 2 Doors, Pedestal Base, 31 x 55 In.		6000
Desk, Biedermeier, Burl Elm, Inset Leather, Drawers, Ormolu, Turret Feet, c.1850, 30 x 55 In.		5953
Desk, Biedermeier, Fruitwood, Leather, Fans, Scroll Feet, c.1900, 30 x 41 In.		1722
Desk, Biedermeier, Mappa Burl, 2 Drawers, Turned Stretcher Base, 52 x 31 In.		158
Desk, Biedermeier, Slant Front, Crossbanded Veneer, Interior Drawers, c.1810, 39 x 36 In.		750
Desk, Burl Walnut, Maple, Doors, Wooton Desk Co., 72 x 40 In. ....*illus*		9430
Desk, Carlton House, George III Style, Brass Gallery, 40 x 48 In.		2250
Desk, Carlton House, George III Style, Mahogany, Inlay, Backsplash, 5 Drawers, 41 x 55 In.		750
Desk, Chalet, Arts & Crafts, Key & Tenon, Shaped Top, Lower Shelf, 46 x 21 ½ In.		1112
Desk, Chalet, G. Stickley, Paneled Drop Front, Key & Tenon, Letter Rack, 46 x 25 In.		3050
Desk, Cherry, Maple, Drop Front, Fitted Interior, 4 Drawers, c.1770, 43 x 36 In.		1750
Desk, Chippendale Style, Mahogany, Carved, 4 Drawers, Cabriole Legs, 30 x 48 In.		474
Desk, Chippendale, Birch, Slant Front, 4 Drawers, New England, c.1800, 41 x 35 In.		385
Desk, Chippendale, Cherry, Drop Front, Fitted Interior, Fan Carved, c.1790, 42 x 36 In.		8888
Desk, Chippendale, Cherry, Inlay, Slant Front, Fitted Interior, 4 Drawers, c.1820, 45 x 39 In.		500
Desk, Chippendale, Cherry, Panel Doors, Slant Front, Fitted Interior, 5 Drawers, 85 x 38 In.		3120
Desk, Chippendale, Cherry, Slant Front, Fitted Interior, 5 Drawers, c.1790, 43 x 40 In.		1000
Desk, Chippendale, Mahogany, Slant Front, Fitted Interior, Drawers, Carved, 41 x 36 In.		480
Desk, Chippendale, Mahogany, Slant Front, Fitted Interior, Drawers, Mass., 43 x 43 In.		960
Desk, Chippendale, Mahogany, Slant Front, Green Tooled Leather		345
Desk, Chippendale, Mahogany, Slant Front, Quarter Columns, Cubbyholes, Drawers		863
Desk, Chippendale, Maple, Chestnut, Pine, Slant Front, 4 Graduated Drawers, 41 x 36 In.		844
Desk, Chippendale, Maple, Drop Front, Fitted Interior, 4 Drawers, 40 x 31 In.		875
Desk, Chippendale, Maple, Slant Front, Fitted Interior, 4 Drawers, 45 x 37 In.		16800
Desk, Chippendale, Maple, Walnut, Slant Front, Fitted Interior, 4 Drawers, Mass., 42 x 37 In.		2640
Desk, Chippendale, Mixed Wood, Drop Front, Fitted Interior, Drawers, Va., c.1800, 42 x 36 In.		7475
Desk, Chippendale, Tiger Maple, Slant Front, Fitted Interior, 4 Drawers, c.1780, 42 x 36 In.		17775
Desk, Chippendale, Walnut, Slant Front, 4 Graduated Drawers, Pa., c.1770, 44 x 39 In.		1304
Desk, Chippendale, Walnut, Slant Front, Fitted Interior, 5 Drawers, c.1780, 40 x 38 In.		1067
Desk, Chippendale, Walnut, Slant Front, Pennsylvania, c.1770, 41 x 38 In.		1659
Desk, Clerk's, Neoclassical, Mahogany, Walnut, Drawers, Doors, Cubbies, c.1830, 43 x 51 In.		345
Desk, Davenport, Victorian, Walnut, Slant Front, 4 Side Drawers, 32 x 21 In., Child's		615
Desk, Davenport, Walnut, Fitted Interior, Faux Drawers, England, c.1840, 33 x 24 In.		826
Desk, Donald Deskey, Walnut, Single Pedestal, 3 Drawers, 1920s, 28 x 48 In.		1375
Desk, Drop Front, Fitted Interior, 3 Drawers, Serpentine Front, 41 x 22 In.		960
Desk, Drop Front, Rosewood, Fitted Interior, 5 Drawers, Chinese, 41 x 41 In.		508
Desk, Eastlake, Drop Front, Drawers, Pigeonholes, Compartments, 60 x 48 x 25 In.		108
Desk, Edwardian, Adam Style, Satinwood, Drawers, Leather, c.1900, 40 x 28 In. ....*illus*		3690
Desk, English Style, Oak, Leather Top, 5 Drawers, Reeded Legs, Brass Casters, 31 x 58 In.		660
Desk, Faux Bamboo, Maple, Rail Backsplash, Drop Front, Drawer, Shelf, c.1880, 44 x 27 In.		1000
Desk, Federal Style, Mahogany Inlay, Kneehole, 5 Drawers, c.1915, 30 x 71 In.		577
Desk, Federal Style, Mahogany, Inlay, Kneehole, 4 Drawers, 31 x 36 In.		1560
Desk, Federal Style, Mixed Woods, Inlay, Tambour, Fitted Top, Foldover, Drawers, 45 x 37 In.		390
Desk, Federal, Cherry, Slant Front, Fitted Interior, 4 Drawers, New England, c.1800, 44 x 39 In.		530

Desk, Federal, Mahogany, Flower, Oval Inlay, Roll Top, 4 Drawers, c.1795, 43 x 41 In.	8750
Desk, Federal, Mahogany, Roll Top, Fitted Interior, Drawers, G. Hendree, c.1800, 48 x 49 In.	875
Desk, Federal, Mahogany, Tambour, Flat Doors, 2 Drawers, 43 x 37 In.	375
Desk, Federal, Maple, Slant Front, Fitted Interior, 4 Drawers, Apron, c.1805, 44 x 45 In.	6250
Desk, Florence Knoll, Walnut Frame, Laminate Top, 6 Drawers, Paper Label, 29 x 30 In.	59
Desk, French Provincial, Fruitwood, Banded, Frieze Drawer, Cabriole Legs, 30 x 73 In.	3444
Desk, G. Nakashima, Free-Edge Top, Drawers, Cross Legs, New Hope, Pa., 1973, 29 x 62 In.	20000
Desk, G. Nelson, Wood, Ebonized, Chrome Legs, Handles	224
Desk, G. Stickley, Drop Front, Facets Knobs, Letter Rack, 47 x 26 In.	2074
Desk, G. Stickley, Oak, Drop Front, Drawers, Fitted Interior, c.1912, 45 x 36 In. ....*illus*	2583
Desk, G. Stickley, Postcard, Letter Boxes, Drawers, Shelf, Red Decal, c.1903, 36 x 40 In.	1875
Desk, G. Stickley, Woman's, Paneled Drop Front, Iron Hinges, Decal, 44 x 30 In.	3294
Desk, George II, Yew, Slant Front, Fitted Interior, 5 Drawers, 43 x 34 In.	840
Desk, George III Style, Slant Front, Fitted Interior, 4 Drawers, Columns, 40 x 30 In.	334
Desk, George III, Mahogany, Drop Front, Fitted Interior, 4 Drawers, 41 x 20 In.	750
Desk, George III, Mahogany, Leather Top, 3 Drawers, c.1810, 30 x 56 In.	530
Desk, George III, Mahogany, Slant Front, 4 Drawers, Shaped Apron, c.1800, 44 x 37 In.	649
Desk, Gothic Revival Style, Mahogany, Bird's-Eye Maple, Leather, Drawers, 1900s, 29 x 34 In.	150
Desk, Gothic Revival, Cupboard, Glass Doors, Incised, Lower Shelf, c.1865, 56 x 49 In.	570
Desk, Kem Weber, Tubular Chrome, Maple, Formica, Drawers, Heywood-Wakefield, 30 x 60 In.	450
Desk, L. & J.G. Stickley, Oak, Blind Center Drawers, Bookshelves, Slats, 29 x 44 x 28 In. ......*illus*	793
Desk, Lady's, Federal, Mahogany, Tambour Door, New England, c.1810, 43 x 41 In. ....*illus*	826
Desk, Limbert, Drawers, Kneehole, Stretcher, Branded, 31 x 48 x 30 In. ....*illus*	976
Desk, Limbert, Drop Down, Cutout, Grand Rapids, Mich., c.1905, 51 x 22 In.	3750
Desk, Louis XV, Fruitwood, Drawer, Brass Mounts, Folding Chair, c.1910, 29 x 37 In.	150
Desk, Louis XVI Style, Mahogany, Leather Top, 2 Drawers, 30 x 43 In.	1375
Desk, Louis XVI, Fruitwood, Mahogany, Inlay, Roll Top, Drawers, Metal Mounts, 41 x 28 In.	250
Desk, Mahogany, On Stand, Fitted Interior, Inscribed Plaque, Dr. Carmont, 1882, 21 x 20 In.	215
Desk, Mahogany, Side Galleries, Drawers, Turned Legs, Brass Feet, 1900s, 36 x 72 In.	4994
Desk, Mahogany, Slant Front, Fitted Interior, 4 Drawers, Shell Carving, 42 In.	2880
Desk, Maple, Spindled Gallery, Lattice Doors, Hinged, Turned Legs, c.1880, 54 x 32 In.	717
Desk, Master's, Poplar, Slant Front, Square Tapered Legs, 48 x 27 In.	210
Desk, Neoclassical Style, Fruitwood, Compass Star, Bombe, 1800s, 30 x 44 In.	2090
Desk, Neoclassical, Walnut, Carved, Kneehole, Lyre Trestle, Stretcher, Italy, c.1810, 31 x 41 In.	860
Desk, Oriental Style, Drawer, Lion-Mask Ring Handles, Lobed Legs, Splayed Feet, 35 x 18 In.	1737
Desk, Partners, Georgian, Double Pedestal, Leather Inset, 9 Drawers, 36 x 72 In.	1500
Desk, Pine, Scrubbed Top, Hanging Drawer, Shoefoot Trestle, c.1800, 31 x 62 In.	1800
Desk, Pine, Slant Front, Fitted Interior, 4 Drawers, Bracket Base, 42 x 38 In.	502
Desk, Plantation, Empire, Curly Oak, Fitted Case, Slant Shelf, Drawers, Eng., 60 x 54 In.	299
Desk, Plantation, Grain Painted, Panel Doors, Fitted Interior, 2 Drawers, Va., 78 x 43 In.	1920
Desk, Plantation, Mahogany, Hinged Panel Door, Turned Legs, 1800s, 38 x 21 In.	1315
Desk, Plantation, Rosewood Grain Painted, Panel Doors, Drawers, Yellow Springs, 81 x 36 In.	1140
Desk, Poplar, Slant Front, 2 Drawers, Dovetailed, American, Tabletop, c.1855, 14 x 21 In.	118
Desk, Queen Anne Style, Burl, Walnut, Kneehold, Banded, Shaped Skirt, 4 Drawers, 47 In.	1989
Desk, Queen Anne, Cherry, Slant Front, 4 Graduated Drawers, c.1750, 39 x 35 In.	1250
Desk, Queen Anne, Tiger Maple, Slant Front, Compartments, c.1710, 37 x 35 In. ....*illus*	3000
Desk, Regency, Mahogany, 5 Small Drawers, Tall Legs, c.1830, 38 x 54 In.	2673
Desk, Renaissance Style, Mahogany, Drawers, Scroll, Runner Feet, c.1900, 30 x 72 In.	676
Desk, Risom, Executive, 6 Drawers, Midcentury, Label, 80 ½ x 36 In.	1955
Desk, Risom, Walnut, Chromed Steel, 4 Drawers, 1960s, 30 x 66 In.	625
Desk, Rococo Revival, Serpentine Fold-Out Lid, Flowers, c.1865, 42 x 34 In.	1722
Desk, Rosewood, Floating Top, 6 Drawers, Denmark, 55 x 47 In.	625
Desk, Roycroft, Writing, Drop Front, Copper, Mackmurdo Foot, 44 x 38 x 19 In.	4575
Desk, Ruhlmann, Art Deco, Mahogany, Burl, Ebony, Slant Front, Geometric, 46 x 38 In.	1320
Desk, Salmon Paint, Slant Front, Fitted Interior, 37 x 24 In.	150
Desk, School, Walnut, Lift Top, Trestle Feet, Lancaster County, c.1760, 28 x 46 In.	652
Desk, School, Wood Seat & Back, Hinged, Iron Scroll Frame, Salesman's Sample, 8 In.	1200
Desk, Schoolmaster's, Lift Top Compartment, Box Stretcher, 1800s, 17 x 19 x 36 In.	115
Desk, Schoolmaster's, Pine, Blue Paint, Slant Front, Drawers, Pigeonholes, 49 x 38 In.	3860
Desk, Schoolmaster's, Pine, Painted, Lift Top, Pa., 49 x 31 In.	889
Desk, Schoolmaster's, Poplar, Carved Backsplash, Red Paint, Pa., c.1830, 36 x 29 In.	178
Desk, Schoolmaster's, Poplar, Slant Front, Concealed Drawers, c.1865, 39 x 37 In. ....*illus*	330
Desk, Schoolmaster's, Sheraton, Cherry, Lift Top, Turned Legs, c.1830, 38 x 24 In.	296
Desk, Schoolmaster's, Slant Front, Fitted Interior, Drawer, Turned Legs, c.1830, 40 x 35 In.	248
Desk, Schoolmaster's, Walnut, Poplar, Slant Front, Drawer, Turned Legs, 1800s, 34 x 31 In.	294

F

Furniture, Commode, Baroque, Serpentine, Painted, Gilt Highlights, Swiss, 1700s, 31 x 36 In.
$2,006

Brunk Auctions

Furniture, Commode, Bombe, Painted, Serpentine Top, Drawers, Venetian, 48 x 22 In.
$2,375

Leslie Hindman Auctioneers

Furniture, Commode, Louis XVI Style, Fruitwood, Vernis Martin, Marble Top, 36 x 46 In.
$478

Neal Auction Co.

Furniture, Commode, Neoclassical, Maple, Wood Pulls, 1800s, 23 ½ x 19 In.
$1,476

Cowan's Auctions

Furniture, Cradle, Pine, Dovetailed, Heart Cutout, Painted, New England, 1800s, 20 x 41 In.
$185

Garth's Auctioneers & Appraisers

Furniture, Credenza, Adrian Pearsall, Silvered Composite, Laminate, 1970s, 26 ½ x 69 In.
$3,375

Rago Arts & Auction Center

Furniture, Cupboard, Charles II, Court, Oak, Carved, Doors, Drawer, Shelf, 1600s, 50 x 53 In.
$8,365

Neal Auction Co.

Furniture, Cupboard, Corner, Pine, Red Wash, Doors, Shelves, 2 Sections, c.1835, 84 In.
$1,067

James D. Julia Auctioneers

Desk, Shaker, Trustee's, Pine, Drop Front, 2 Paneled Doors, Drawers, 62 x 37 In. ....*illus*	7375
Desk, Shaped Top, Shelves, Carved, Pierced Dragon, Scroll Feet, 52 In.	2700
Desk, Sheraton, Cherry, Slant Front, 4 Graduated Drawers, c.1830, 51 x 39 In.	948
Desk, Sheraton, Mahogany, Drop Front, Urn Finial, Figured Veneer, 1800s, 68 x 35 In.	885
Desk, Sheraton, Pine, Drop Front, Drawer, Turned Legs, Pa., c.1850, 38 x 31 In.	178
Desk, Sheraton, Tiger Maple, Slant Front, Fitted Interior, c.1840, 45 x 36 In.	2607
Desk, Slant Front, Grained Tiger Maple, Graduated Drawers, Cubbyhole, Fan Carved, 32 In.	385
Desk, Spanish Baroque, Walnut, Drawers, Arched Stretcher, Carved, 37 x 39 In.	1560
Desk, Spinet, Mahogany, Burl Trim, Fold Top, 3 Drawers, Carved, 1920s, 42 x 20 In.	125
Desk, Victorian, Walnut, Carved, Drawer, Shelf Stretcher, Carved Feet, c.1890, 29 x 35 In.	304
Desk, Walnut Sides, Black Enamel Drawers, Chrome Legs, 1950s, 49 x 29 In.	406
Desk, Walnut, Bone Inlay, Figural Scene, Pedestals, Drawers, Italy, c.1850, 32 x 50 In.	1800
Desk, Walnut, Lift Top, 2 Drawers, Ball Feet, Pennsylvania, 17 x 18 In.	5214
Desk, Walnut, Lift Top, England, Tabletop, c.1850, 17 x 30 In.	385
Desk, Walnut, Stepped Top, Trestle Base, Italy, c.1900, 35 x 41 In.	1003
Desk, William & Mary, Blue, Fitted Interior, Drawers, Bootjack Supports, c.1750, 37 x 32 In.	938
Desk, William & Mary, Walnut, Slant Front, Fitted Interior, Tabletop, c.1750, 18 x 23 In.	2844
Desk, Yellow Pine, Slant Front, Fitted Interior, Drawer, H Stretcher, 1800s, 33 x 35 In.	180
Desk-Bookcase, Chippendale, Curly Maple, 6-Pane Doors, Drawers, 1700s, 80 x 36 In.	3408
Dining Set, Arts & Crafts, Oak, Pedestal, 2 Leaves, 4 Chairs, 30 x 48 & 39 In.	1058
Dining Set, Baker Furniture, Neoclassical, Mahogany, 8 Chairs, 1940s, 120 x 44 In., 9 Piece	830
Dining Set, Butternut, Trestle Table, Ribbonback Chairs, Rush Seats, 1800s, 106 In., 11 Piece	6169
Dining Set, Federal Style, Mahogany, 3 Pedestals, Leaves, 1950s, 108 x 41 In., 8 Piece	2520
Dining Set, Jacobean Style, Oak, Carved, 5 Chairs, Armchair, China Cabinet, c.1920, 8 Piece	540
Dining Set, Robsjohn-Gibbings, Walnut, Upholstered, Widdicomb, 1950s, 5 Piece	3690
Dining Set, RomWeber, Danish Modern, H. Schwartz, Oak Inlay, Sideboard, 8 Chairs, 9 Piece	1205
Dough Trough, French Provincial, Fruitwood, Lift Top, Flowers, c.1850, 36 x 39 In.	3198
Dresser, 5 Drawers, Adjustable Mirror, Copper Strap Hardware, 48 x 66 In.	11875
Dresser, Bamboo, Maple, Mirror, 3 Drawers, Fretwork Frame, c.1885, 35 x 49 In.	1770
Dresser, Contemporary, Wood Case, Painted Drawers, Ron Fisher, 36 x 48 In.	115
Dresser, Empire, Cherry, Serpentine Top, 4 Drawers, Beaded Edge, Scroll Feet, 44 x 43 In.	237
Dresser, Faux Bamboo, Fruitwood, Mirror, 4 Drawers, Long Drawer, c.1890, 79 x 57 In.	438
Dresser, Federal, Mahogany, Bowfront, 4 Drawers, c.1810, 38 x 42 In.	948
Dresser, Federal, Mahogany, Marble, Mirror, Fish Supports, Doors, c.1820, 68 x 45 In.	1652
Dresser, Florence Knoll, Triple, Laminate, Matte-Chromed Steel, Marble, 1950s, 29 x 110 In. 1230 to	5000
Dresser, G. Nelson, Thin Edge, Rosewood, Aluminum, Herman Miller, 1950s, 33 x 67 In. ...*illus*	7500
Dresser, G. Stickley, Green Paint, 6 Drawers, Backsplash, c.1912, 48 x 41 In.	4688
Dresser, James Mont, 3 Drawers, Cerused Oak, Bronze, Upholstered, 1950s, 32 x 46 In., Pair	5312
Dresser, Maple, 8 Drawers, Brass Pulls, Tapered Legs, Murray, 1950s, 36 x 45 In.	625
Dresser, McCobb, Planner Group, 3 Drawers, 18 x 30 In.	295
Dresser, Mixed Wood, Swivel Mirror, 2 Glove Drawers, 4 Drawers, c.1900, 39 x 40 In.	138
Dresser, Oak, 2 Parts, Molded Cornice, Drop Front, Marlboro Legs, 1700s, 81 x 55 In.	960
Dresser, Oak, Molded Crest, Pierced Frieze, Shelves, Bracket Feet, 1800s, 81 x 62 In.	3198
Dresser, Painted, 4 Drawers, Tan, Flower, Huntsman, Deer, R.E. Cahoon, c.1970, 42 x 26 In.	1003
Dresser, Pine, 4 Drawers, Painted Lovebirds, c.1845, 10 x 9 In.	1700
Dresser, Renzo Rutili, Cherry, 8 Drawers, Splayed Legs, Johnson Furniture, 68 x 32 In.	1250
Dresser, Renzo Rutili, Maple, 6 Drawers, Johnson Furniture, 40 x 45 In.	375
Dresser, Shaker, Pine, Dovetailed, 6 Drawers, Stenciled H.N. Morse, 48 x 35 In. ....*illus*	4012
Dresser, Sheraton, Mahogany, Bird's-Eye Maple, Mirror, Scrolls, 7 Drawers, c.1815, 75 x 37 In.	23600
Dresser, Sheraton, Mahogany, Shaped Backsplash, 5 Drawers, c.1860, 41 x 45 In.	489
Dresser, Walnut, Tiger Maple, 4 Drawers, 1874, 16 x 17 In.	830
Dresser, Welsh, Georgian, Oak, Plate Racks, Drawers, Apron, Stretcher Shelf, 58 x 76 In.	1573
Dresser, Welsh, Oak, Carved, Shelves, Jas. Schoolbred & Co., c.1890, 82 x 72 In. ....*illus*	1015
Dresser, Welsh, Oak, Cock-Beaded, 2 Parts, Shelves, Drawers, Doors, 85 In. ....*illus*	4000
Dresser, Welsh, Oak, Open Back, 2 Shelves, 2 Beaded Drawers, England, c.1790, 80 x 55 In.	2478
Dresser, Welsh, Walnut, Step Back, Carved Open Shelves, 2 Doors, 4 Drawers, 1800s, 86 x 96 In.	3125
Dresser, Wormley, Wood, 5 Graduated Drawers, Drexel, c.1960, 48 x 33 In.	288
Dressing Table, 3 Stacked Drawers, Backsplash, c.1850, 36 x 37 In.	316
Dressing Table, George II, Burl, Lift Top, Cabriole Legs, c.1750, 28 x 31 In.	1067
Dressing Table, William & Mary, Painted, 3 Drawers, Carved Apron, Legs, 29 x 31 In.	1007
Dry Sink, Chestnut, Poplar, Drawers, 2 Doors, 34 x 66 In.	783
Dry Sink, Copper Lining, Spigot, Pennsylvania, c.1850, 31 x 36 In.	360
Dry Sink, Corn Grain Painted, Lift Top, Door, 2 Drawers, Maine, 32 x 37 In.	13200
Dry Sink, Hooded, Softwood, Open Sink, Backsplash, 3 Drawers, Doors, Shelf, 51 x 40 In.	590
Dry Sink, Mustard Paint, Work Slide, Tapered Legs, 34 x 41 In.	720

Dry Sink, Pine, 2 Recessed Panel Doors, c.1890, 36 x 50 In.........................	600
Dry Sink, Pine, Blue Gray Paint, Black Dots, c.1855, 32 x 44 In.....................	3318
Dry Sink, Pine, Blue Paint, Beaded Boards, Door, New England, 1800s, 31 x 33 In. ....*illus*	780
Dry Sink, Pine, Copper Lining, 2 Lower Panel Doors, Bracket Feet, c.1845, 46 x 44 In......	210
Dry Sink, Pine, Poplar, Spotted Salmon Paint, Pennsylvania, c.1890, 32 x 44 In.	2370
Dry Sink, Pine, Raised Sides Over 2 Paneled Doors, Hudson Valley, N.Y., 36 x 36 In.	430
Dry Sink, Pine, Yellow Paint, Paneled Doors, 19th Century, 71 x 21 In........................	3055
Dry Sink, Poplar, Gray Paint, High Back, Panel Doors, Shaped Skirt, 1800s, 41 x 50 In.	705
Dry Sink, Sheraton, Double, Yellow Paint, Deep Gallery, Low Shelf, 44 x 57 In..........................	1200
Dry Sink, Softwood, Green Paint, 2 Lower Sunken-Panel Doors, Cutout Feet, 33 x 49 In...........	708
Dry Sink, Softwood, Red Paint, Drawer, Double Sink, Half Copper Lined, Doors, 33 x 59 In........	354
Dry Sink, Softwood, Shelf, 2 Drawers Over Setback, 2 Panel Doors, Pa., c.1850, 50 x 49 In.	430
Dumbwaiter, 3 Tiers, Pierced Brass Galleries, Tripod Base, 16 In.	240
Dumbwaiter, Georgian, Mahogany, 3 Tiers, Cabriole Legs, c.1780, 44 In.	240
Dumbwaiter, Georgian, Mahogany, 3 Tiers, Round Shelves, Carved, c.1850, 41 In.	480
Dumbwaiter, Georgian, Mahogany, Carved, Dish Top, 3 Tiers, Pad Feet, 43 x 25 In..............	780
Dumbwaiter, Mahogany, 3 Graduated Tiers, Piecrust Edge, Revolving, 43 x 24 In...............	263
Easel, Carved Wood, Acanthus, Scallop Medallion, Cabriole Legs, Spain, 72 In...........................	300
Easel, Eastlake, Walnut, Adjustable Shelves, Tripod Supports, c.1875, 78 x 32 In.	358
Easel, Renaissance Revival, Incised Walnut, Ebonized, Gilt, Inlaid, 1800s, 76 x 37 In. ....*illus*	3585
Easel, Victorian, Gilt Walnut, Portfolio, Ebonized, Inlay, 1800s, 82 In..............................	6440
Easel, Victorian, Pine, Carved, 66 ½ In.	89
Etagere, Chrome Steel, Glass, John Stuart, 1960s, 79 x 37 In.	280
Etagere, Chrome, Brass, 4 Shelves, 1970s, 31 x 15 x 74 In.	80
Etagere, Corner, Regency Style, Black, Chinoiserie, 5 Tiers, 61 x 27 In.	875
Etagere, English Walnut, Ebonized, Shelves, Burl, Drawer, Turned Feet, c.1890, 27 x 20 In........	492
Etagere, Federal, Mahogany, Shelves, Baluster-Turned Supports, c.1815, 57 x 19 In.	1793
Etagere, Federal, Mahogany, Tiered Shelves, Ring Turnings, 1800s, 52 x 20 In. ....*illus*	2390
Etagere, Mahogany, 3 Shelves, Turned Corner Columns, Finials, England, c.1910, 42 x 47 In. ...	362
Etagere, Mahogany, Carved Flower Corners, 6 Tiers, c.1900, 43 x 24 In.	3125
Etagere, Mahogany, Carved, Shaped Mirrors, Glass Door, Shelves, c.1885, 81 x 52 In.	474
Etagere, Regency Style, Metal, Painted, 3 Tiers, 32 x 25 In.	469
Etagere, Rococo Style, Gilt Metal, Onyx, Shelves, Mirror Back, c.1900, 64 x 26 In. ....*illus*	1188
Etagere, Sheraton, Mahogany, 4 Tiers, Drawer, England, 56 x 18 In.	900
Etagere, Victorian, Walnut, Mirror, Marble Top, Shelves, Drawer, 70 x 96 In.	1356
Etagere, Victorian, Walnut, Scroll-Cut Backsplash, Turned Supports, 5 Shelves, 55 x 31 In........	48
Folio Stand, Mahogany, Sheaf, Leaf Carved, c.1910, 45 x 33 In.	1659
Footstool, Brass, Cutout Design, Shaped Crest, Square Legs, c.1800, 16 x 14 In..........................	330
Footstool, Cast Iron, Pierced Leaves, Porcelain Casters, Bargello Needlepoint, 15 x 15 In.............	127
Footstool, Faux Mahogany, Grain Painted, Turned Legs, c.1840, 18 x 14 In...........................	115
Footstool, French Style, Needlepoint Top, Nailhead Detail..........................	35
Footstool, Giltwood, Scroll Legs, Shaped, Carved, Upholstered, 17 x 18 In.	98
Footstool, Louis XV Style, Gilt, Needlepoint, Carved Cabriole Legs, 1800s, 9 x 15 In.	475
Footstool, Neoclassical, Mahogany, Needlepoint, Scroll Supports, 1810, 13 x 17 In...................	854
Footstool, Painted Bird, Shaped Cutout Skirt, Mortised Legs, Feet, 7 x 14 In.	47
Footstool, Painted, Horse, Tulips, Mortised Legs, Arch Cutout Feet, 6 In.	83
Footstool, Queen Anne Style, Mahogany, Shaped Skirt, Cabriole Legs, 1900s, 17 In.	88
Footstool, Queen Anne Style, Mahogany, Slip Seat, Scalloped Apron, c.1900, 14 x 20 In.	354
Footstool, Rococo Revival, Iron, Serpentine Top, Reticulated Frame, Scroll Feet, 1800s	1098
Footstool, Shaker, Pine, 2-Step, Column Legs, Button Feet, 17 x 15 In.	2596
Footstool, Softwood, Painted, Shaped Skirt, Cutout Feet, 9 In.	24
Footstool, Walnut, Carved Skirt, Heart Cutout, Mortise Construction, Pa., 1800s ....*illus*	1440
Footstool, Wood, Carved, Upholstered, Cabriole Legs, 16 x 12 In..........................	75
Footstool, Wood, Ormolu Mythical Creatures, Upholstered, France, c.1900, 18 x 20 In............	1540
Frame, Eagle Crest, Green, Red, Painted, 37 x 26 In.	460
Frame, Gesso, Gilt, Carved, 19th Century, 20 x 16 ½ In.	30
Frame, Heart, Carved Punch Design, Inscribed Rosi Wood, c.1890, 12 x 10 In..........................	173
Frame, Leaf, Duck Carved, Painted, Shenandoah Valley, c.1900, 15 x 9 In.	4600
Frame, Plasterwork, Carved Floral Corners, Gilt, 19th Century, 37 x 36 ½ In.........................	23
Frame, Stanford White, Giltwood, 33 x 37 In.	3080
Frame, Wood, Stenciled Designs, Black, Gilt Paint, 1800s, 15 x 17 In.................	480
Hall Seat, Byrdcliffe Style, Poplar, Carved Designs, c.1905, 65 x 44 In.	1500
Hall Seat, G. Stickley, Cutout Panel Back, Slab Seat, Label, 48 x 24 In.	3000
Hall Stand, Arts & Crafts, Diamond-Shape Mirror, Brass Hooks, Umbrella Stand, 19 x 72 In......	500
Hall Stand, Victorian, Walnut, Mirror, Carved Crest, c.1850, 90 x 46 In.	275

F

Furniture, Cupboard, Corner, Poplar, Drawers, 2 Sections, Faux Graining, c.1830, 87 In.
$4,200

Garth's Auctioneers & Appraisers

Furniture, Cupboard, Pine, Green Paint, Drawers, Paneled Doors, Shelves, 1800s, 68 x 54 In.
$2,880

Cowan's Auctions

Furniture, Cupboard, Poplar, Open Shelves, Doors, Drawers, New England, 1800s, 76 ½ In.
$2,760

Skinner Auctioneers & Appraisers

Furniture, Cupboard, Step Back,
2 Sections, Drawers, Doors, c.1830-40,
89 x 53 In.
$923

Skinner Auctioneers & Appraisers

Furniture, Desk, Aesthetic Revival,
Walnut, Roll Top, Writing Slide, Casters,
1800s, 56 x 43 In.
$900

Cowan's Auctions

Furniture, Desk, Arts & Crafts, Drawer,
Bookshelves, Slats, c.1910, 44 x 28 In.
$549

Treadway Toomey Galleries

Hall Tree, Arts & Crafts, Oak, Splayed Rails, Hooks, Light Engineering Div., 1930s, 74 In.	357
Hall Tree, Rococo, Cast Iron, Scroll Back, Hooks, Shell, Umbrella Holder, c.1850, 79 In.	1255
Headboard, G. Nakashima, Walnut, Queen Size, Widdicomb, 1960s, 43 x 85 In.	1500
Headboard, M. Nakashima, Walnut, Free-Form, Signed, 1998, 47 x 91 In.	1215
Highboy, Chippendale, Maple, Bonnet Top, Flame Finials, Shell Carving	690
Highboy, Chippendale, Walnut, Shell, Leaf Carved, Drawers, Phila., c.1770, 36 x 44 In.	3555
Highboy, Queen Anne Style, Curly Maple, 5 Drawers, Cabriole Legs, c.1870, 69 x 38 In.	1534
Highboy, Queen Anne, Birch, 10 Drawers, Shaped Apron, Cabriole Legs, 1770, 77 x 40 In.	5400
Highboy, Queen Anne, Maple, 9 Drawers, Shaped Apron, Cabriole Legs, Conn., 71 x 39 In.	7200
Highboy, Queen Anne, Maple, Arched Bonnet Top, Fan Carved, 10 Drawers, 82 x 39 In.	3120
Highboy, Queen Anne, Maple, Japanned, 9 Drawers, Shell Carving, Mass., 71 x 40 In.	9600
Highboy, Queen Anne, Mixed Wood, 4 Drawers, Cabriole Legs, c.1780, 36 x 39 In.	266
Highboy, Queen Anne, Tiger Maple, 12 Drawers, Fan-Carved, 31 x 75 In.	2373
Highboy, Queen Anne, Tiger Maple, Flat Top, Fan, Cabriole Legs, 1700s, 70 x 39 In.	2337
Highboy, Queen Anne, Walnut, 5 Drawers, Over 4 Drawers, Mass., c.1770, 71 x 39 In.	7500
Highboy, William & Mary, Burl Walnut, 9 Drawers, Low Stretcher, Carved, Mass., 67 x 40 In.	5400
Highboy, William & Mary, Walnut, 8 Drawers, Trumpet-Turned Legs, Stretcher, 57 x 35 In.	2880
Highchair, Arthur Espenet Carpenter, Walnut, Signed, 1958, 37 x 13 x 20 In. *illus*	11875
Highchair, Black Paint, Pennsylvania, c.1830	119
Highchair, Black, Red Paint, Bulbous Terminals, Woven Seat, c.1845, 37 In.	444
Highchair, Maple, Ladder Back, Oak Splint Seat, Acorn Finials, 1800s, 39 In. *illus*	607
Highchair, Mixed Wood, Spindle Back, Arms, Woven Seat, Painted, c.1845, 31 x 20 In.	1150
Highchair, Windsor, Black Paint, Pennsylvania, c.1845	1540
Hook, Eames, Hang-It-All, Maple, Painted Steel, Multicolor Balls, 1953, 15 x 20 In., 2 Piece	1107
Humidor, Mahogany, Carved, Marble Top, Porcelain Interior, 1930s, 16 x 32 In.	120
Huntboard, Federal, Cherry, 3 Drawers, Reeded, Square Legs, c.1815, 41 x 54 In.	3776
Huntboard, Federal, Walnut, Pine, Carved Apron, Tapered Legs, 1800s, 49 x 43 In.	1180
Huntboard, Fruitwood, Brass Hardware, 3 Drawers, 35 x 69 In.	1076
Huntboard, Hepplewhite, Walnut, Inlay, 2 Drawers, Door, Virginia, 43 x 53 In.	5040
Huntboard, Pine, 2 Drawers, Square Beaded Legs, c.1900, 40 x 48 In.	288
Huntboard, Pine, 3 Drawers, Raised Square Legs, Southern, c.1845, 32 x 53 In.	374
Huntboard, Victorian, Walnut, Marble Top, Carved Fruit, Grape Clusters, 36 x 51 In.	360
Huntboard, Welsh, Pine, 3 Drawers, Scalloped Apron, 74 x 33 In.	1120
Huntboard, Yellow Pine, Slab Top, 2 Drawers, Tapered Legs, c.1800, 43 x 48 In.	7670
Hutch, Oak, Beaded, 2 Glass Doors, Drawer, 2 Panel Doors, c.1890, 49 x 22 In., Child's	207
Hutch, Pine, Rectangular Top, Bench Seat, Painted, Shoe Feet, 1800-50, 44 x 34 In. *illus*	450
Hutch-Table, Flip Lid Base, c.1860, 42 ½ In.	834
Lap Desk, Boulle, Burl Walnut, Scrolling Brass Inlay, Leather Top, 20 x 10 In.	575
Lap Desk, Cherry, Brass Trim, 12 x 9 In.	85
Lap Desk, Rosewood, Brass Bound, c.1845, 7 x 19 ¾ In.	22
Lap Desk, Rosewood, Brass Bound, Camphorwood Base, 1835, 7 x 16 ½ In.	480
Lap Desk, Rosewood, Brass Inlay, Leather, Stand, Sea Captain's, England, c.1810, 25 x 20 In.	2090
Lap Desk, Rosewood, Brass Mounts, England, 6 x 17 In.	236
Lap Desk, Victorian, Inlaid Burl, Folding, Fitted Compartments, Inkwell, c.1850, 16 In.	150
Lectern, Gothic Revival, Oak, Figural, Eagle, Spread Wings, Tracery Design, 68 In.	4750
Lectern, Gothic Revival, Walnut, Document Stand, Fluted Columns, c.1850, 42 x 37 In.	1722
Lectern, Mahogany, Hinged, Brass Candle Arms, Turned Standard, Ball Feet, c.1890, 32 x 17 In.	999
Lectern, Oak, Carved Eagle, Leaves, American, c.1890, 90 In. *illus*	5625
Library Steps, Mahogany, Paneled Side Door & Drawer, 4 Reeded Legs, 27 x 29 In.	995
Library Steps, Regency Style, Mahogany, 35 x 24 In.	1230
Library Steps, Regency Style, Mahogany, Scrolls, 34 In.	1053
Library Steps, Regency, Mahogany, Leather Inset, 3 Risers, Footed, 27 x 28 In.	1250
Library Steps, Regency, Mahogany, Leather, 4 Treads, Adjustable, 28 x 27 In.	3320
Linen Press, Cherry, Inlay, Cupboard Top, 3 Shelves, 4 Drawers, c.1810, 81 x 44 In.	2583
Linen Press, Chippendale, Gumwood, 2 Panel Doors, 3 Drawers, N.J., c.1790, 79 x 46 In.	2916
Linen Press, Chippendale, Mahogany, 2 Doors, 3 Drawers, Pa., c.1790, 79 x 48 In.	2370
Linen Press, Federal, Walnut, Cove-Molded Cornice, Paneled Doors, Drawers, 81 x 48 In.	3540
Linen Press, Federal, Walnut, Pine, 2 Panel Doors, Drawer, c.1850, 73 x 49 In.	1840
Linen Press, George III Style, Mahogany, Dentil Cornice, Serpentine, 1800s, 80 x 50 In.	1180
Linen Press, George III Style, Mahogany, Molded Cornice, Crossbanded Doors, 66 In.	430
Linen Press, George III, Mahogany, Panel Doors, Drawers, Bracket Feet, c.1820, 82 x 49 In.	1875
Linen Press, Mahogany, Maple, Mirrors, 2 Doors, c.1890, 81 x 48 In.	1020
Linen Press, Yew, Pocket Doors, Inlaid Fans, 4 Drawers, 85 x 46 In.	878
Love Seat, George II, Walnut, Upholstered, c.1730, 35 x 45 ½ In.	3080
Love Seat, Louis XVI Style, Gilt Frame, Loose Cushion, c.1890, 34 x 50 In.	625

Lowboy, Cherry, Carved Shell, 4 Drawers, Scalloped Apron, 33 x 24 In.	15000
Lowboy, Chippendale Style, Mahogany, 3 Drawers, Carved Apron, Philadelphia, 30 x 28 In.	540
Lowboy, Chippendale Style, Mahogany, 4 Drawers, Carved, Cutout Apron, c.1950, 30 x 33 In.	1080
Lowboy, Chippendale Style, Mahogany, Carved Ball & Claw Feet, c.1950, 31 x 36 In.	120
Lowboy, Chippendale Style, Tiger Maple, Cabriole Legs, Ball & Claw Feet, 16 x 18 In.	676
Lowboy, Chippendale, Cherry, 4 Drawers, Carved Apron, Fluted Columns, 36 x 20 In.	4500
Lowboy, Queen Anne Style, Mahogany, 3 Drawers, Colonial Manufacturing Co., 30 x 35 In.	710
Lowboy, Queen Anne, Mahogany, 4 Drawers, Shell Carved, Cabriole Legs, 30 x 36 In.	6000
Mirror, Aesthetic Revival, Fruitwood, Part Ebonized, Incised Designs, c.1890, 34 x 28 In.	813
Mirror, Art Deco, Brass, Oval, Footed, Tabletop, 39 x 7 In.	380
Mirror, Art Deco, Cast Aluminum, Hammered, Wrought-Iron Leaf Surround, 20 x 35 In.	380
Mirror, Arts & Crafts, Silver, Oval, Turquoise, Glass, Wood, England, c.1900, 16 x 12 In.	500
Mirror, Baroque, Faux Tortoiseshell, Shaped Crest, Griffins, Shield, 38 x 24 In.	598
Mirror, Baroque, Walnut, Stepped Carved Frame, Flemish, c.1790, 51 x 42 In.	7500
Mirror, Biedermeier, Cherry Veneer, Part Ebonized, Pediment, Germany, c.1850, 41 x 28 In.	308
Mirror, Blue & Red Paint, Reverse Painted, Sweden, 1800s, 42 x 19 In.	588
Mirror, Bronze, Articulating Candlesticks, Oval, c.1900, 24 x 20 In.	280
Mirror, Bull's-Eye, Regency, Giltwood, 8 In.	1320
Mirror, Burl Veneer Frame, Sawtooth Shape, Italy, c.1980, 35 x 35 In.	469
Mirror, C. Mollino, Venus De Milo, Zanotta, 30 x 18 In.	325
Mirror, Cartouche, Shield Shape, Silver Putti, Grotesques, Rocaille Scrollwork, 17 ¼ In.	450
Mirror, Cast Brass, Eagle Crest, Flower-Carved Frame, 12 ½ x 9 ½ In., Pair	472
Mirror, Cheval, Empire, Mahogany, Ormolu Trim, Eagle Finials, c.1825, 75 x 44 In. ....*illus*	3125
Mirror, Cheval, Mahogany, Brass Inlay, c.1870, 82 x 38 In.	598
Mirror, Cheval, Mahogany, Marquetry, c.1920, 31 x 75 In.	622
Mirror, Cheval, Mahogany, Turned Supports, Ball Finials, Arched Legs, c.1815, 63 In.	1434
Mirror, Cheval, William IV, Mahogany, Casters, c.1835, 71 x 35 In. ....*illus*	1185
Mirror, Chippendale Style, Giltwood, 3 Parts, Eagle Crest, c.1865, 47 x 59 In.	2460
Mirror, Chippendale Style, Giltwood, Pagoda Crest, Openwork Leaves, 52 x 34 In.	1195
Mirror, Chippendale Style, Giltwood, Pierced Scrollwork, Eagle Crest, 64 x 32 In.	1476
Mirror, Chippendale Style, Mahogany, Gilt Gesso Urn, Finial, Garlands, Swags, 35 x 18 In.	530
Mirror, Chippendale Style, Mahogany, Giltwood, Plumage, Scrolled, c.1760, 44 x 21 In.	800
Mirror, Chippendale Style, Pine, Curly Maple, c.1950, 35 x 19 In.	118
Mirror, Chippendale Style, Walnut, Parcel Gilt, Rosettes, Figured, c.1900, 52 x 29 In.	1180
Mirror, Chippendale, Carved, Stylized Sheaf Of Wheat Crest, 18th Century, 30 x 17 In.	173
Mirror, Chippendale, Giltwood, Mahogany, Carved, Scrolls, Eagles, 63 x 27 In.	3240
Mirror, Chippendale, Giltwood, Walnut, Broken Arch, Phoenix, Scalloped Base, c.1750, 58 In.	4540
Mirror, Chippendale, Mahogany, c.1800, 33 In.	123
Mirror, Chippendale, Mahogany, Carved Crest, c.1790, 42 In.	148
Mirror, Chippendale, Mahogany, Carved, 37 x 22 In.	540
Mirror, Chippendale, Mahogany, Cutout Crest, Frame Base, Philadelphia, 49 In.	1337
Mirror, Chippendale, Mahogany, Inlay, Carved, c.1800, 37 In.	889
Mirror, Chippendale, Mahogany, Openwork Shell Crest, Giltwood, England, 1700s, 40 x 22 In.	499
Mirror, Chippendale, Tiger Maple, Carved Crest, c.1800, 33 x 18 In.	237
Mirror, Chrome, Brass Banding, Rounded Corners, 1983, 28 x 28 In., Pair	1107
Mirror, Convex, Federal Style, Giltwood, Eagle Crest, 36 x 26 In.	2252
Mirror, Convex, Giltwood, c.1920, 27 In.	395
Mirror, Convex, Giltwood, Carved Eagle, Oak Leaves, Carved, c.1845, 52 x 31 In.	5938
Mirror, Convex, Giltwood, Eagle Finial, Candle Supports, Leaf Apron, 1800s	1875
Mirror, Convex, Giltwood, Eagle, Shield Crest, c.1876, 39 x 28 In.	354
Mirror, Convex, Giltwood, Leaf Crest, Carved, c.1800, 23 In.	304
Mirror, Convex, Giltwood, Spread Eagle Crest, c.1950, 47 x 24 In.	138
Mirror, Convex, Giltwood, Spread Eagle, 28 x 17 In.	1063
Mirror, Convex, Mahogany Frame, Swivel, 18 x 15 ½ In.	677
Mirror, Convex, Regency Style, Giltwood, Entwined Serpent & Arrow Frame, 1800s, 36 x 23 In.	8750
Mirror, Convex, Regency, Giltwood, Eagle, Leaf, Carved, c.1825, 33 x 18 In.	2813
Mirror, Convex, Regency, Girandole, Giltwood, Eagle, Candle Arms, c.1820, 38 x 27 In.	2813
Mirror, Convex, Round, Gesso, Carved, Gold Paint, Scotland, 51 x 29 In.	780
Mirror, Copper, Wood, Repousse Leaf, Berries & Vines, John Pearson, c.1900, 37 x 30 In.	2760
Mirror, Cosmopolitan, Incised Mosaic, Giltwood, 47 x 34 In.	48
Mirror, Courting, Faux Marble Paint, Flower Crest, c.1820, 17 x 12 In.	153
Mirror, Courting, Gentleman, Servant, Black Paint, 1700s, 16 x 10 In. ....*illus*	480
Mirror, Courting, Molded Wood, Reverse Painted, Striated Borders, 18 x 13 In.	1800
Mirror, Courting, Queen Anne, Walnut Veneer, Reverse Painted Panel, c.1730, 18 x 12 In.	1422
Mirror, Dresser, Anglo-Indian, Teak, Carved, Dragon, Peacock, Reticulated, 1800s, 38 In.	240

Furniture, Desk, Baker Furniture, Georgian Style, Mahogany, Kneehole, 76 x 36 In.
$780

Gray's Auctioneers LLC

Furniture, Desk, Burl Walnut, Maple, Doors, Wooton Desk Co., 72 x 40 In.
$9,430

Cottone Auctions

Furniture, Desk, Edwardian, Adam Style, Satinwood, Drawers, Leather, c.1900, 40 x 28 In.
$3,690

Neal Auction Co.

Mollino Furniture
Carlo Mollino, the famous Italian artist who made unique curvy furniture from 1936 to 1973, was an eccentric prodigy. He not only designed "out of the box" pieces, but he could also draw the objects with both hands at the same time.

Furniture, Desk, G. Stickley, Oak, Drop Front, Drawers, Fitted Interior, c.1912, 45 x 36 In.
$2,583

Skinner Auctioneers & Appraisers

Furniture, Desk, L. & J.G. Stickley, Oak, Blind Center Drawers, Bookshelves, Slats, 29 x 44 x 28 In.
$793

Treadway Toomey Galleries

Furniture, Desk, Lady's, Federal, Mahogany, Tambour Door, New England, c.1810, 43 x 41 In.
$826

Brunk Auctions

Furniture, Desk, Limbert, Drawers, Kneehole, Stretcher, Branded, 31 x 48 x 30 In.
$976

Treadway Toomey Galleries

Mirror, Dresser, Tiger Maple, Parcel Gilt, Curved Supports, Drawer, 23 x 24 In.	266
Mirror, Dressing, Art Nouveau, Giltwood, Carved Flowers, Leaves, Pulled Shape, 23 x 20 In.	1000
Mirror, Dressing, Carved, Flower Painted, Tilting Column Uprights, Drawer, 24 x 18 In.	960
Mirror, Dressing, Chinoiserie, Black, Oval, Scroll Legs, c.1875, 23 x 16 In.	984
Mirror, Dressing, George III, Mahogany, 3 Drawers, 25 x 19 In.	375
Mirror, Dressing, George III, Satinwood, Mahogany, Swivel, 3 Drawers, c.1820, 14 x 18 In.	430
Mirror, Dressing, Giltwood, 3 Parts, Molded, Curved Side Panels, c.1815, 76 x 75 In.	1107
Mirror, Dressing, Silver Plate, Oval, Columnar Supports, Candlearms, c.1885, 26 x 28 In.	1793
Mirror, Empire, Giltwood, Columns, Applied Rosettes, c.1810, 34 x 18 & 37 x 25 In., 2 Piece	180
Mirror, Empire, Giltwood, Reverse Painted, Fruit Basket, Corner Medallions, 40 x 20 In.	86
Mirror, Empire, Mahogany, Molded, American Homestead Summer Litho, c.1840, 22 x 42 In.	480
Mirror, Empire, Mahogany, Painted, Split Balusters, Black, Giltwood, 23 x 17 In.	200
Mirror, Enameled, Oval Plate, Rectangular Frame, Scroll Crest, Italy, 43 x 30 In.	5000
Mirror, Federal Style, Giltwood, Applied Ball, 2 Side Candelabrum, c.1900s, 39 x 28 In.	403
Mirror, Federal Style, Giltwood, Bull's Eye, Eagle Crest, Acanthus Leaf Surround, 35 x 18 In.	150
Mirror, Federal Style, Giltwood, Eagle, Liberty, Shield Crest Carved, 42 x 31 In.	295
Mirror, Federal Style, Giltwood, Girandole, Scroll Candlearms, Eagle, Round, 37 x 18 In.	777
Mirror, Federal Style, Giltwood, Grape Clusters, Leaves, Turned Columns, 36 x 17 In.	188
Mirror, Federal, Divided, Turned Columns, Acanthus, Lyre, Overhang Top, 21 x 36 In.	580
Mirror, Federal, Giltwood Frame, Woman, Curtains, Reverse Painted, c.1820, 39 x 18 In.	770
Mirror, Federal, Giltwood, Carved, Cornice, Spherules, Lion Heads, Columns, 38 x 22 In.	703
Mirror, Federal, Giltwood, Convex, Carved Eagle, Leaf Crest, 39 x 25 In.	1020
Mirror, Federal, Giltwood, Painted Family Panel, c.1845, 23 x 47 In.	316
Mirror, Federal, Giltwood, Reverse Painted, Panel, House, Lake, Trees, 36 x 20 In.	344
Mirror, Federal, Giltwood, Scroll Candle Arms, Leaf & Dragon Crest, c.1850, 35 In.	823
Mirror, Federal, Giltwood, Split Pane, 33 ½ x 19 In.	345
Mirror, Federal, Girandole, Convex, Giltwood, Eagle Finial, c.1865, 33 x 18 In.	1500
Mirror, Federal, Girandole, Giltwood, Eagle Crest, Laurel, 2 Candle Arms, c.1820, 33 x 23 In.	2808
Mirror, Federal, Girandole, Giltwood, Eagle, Cornucopia, Orbs, Leaves, 36 x 26 In.	8400
Mirror, Federal, Houses, Reverse Painted Panel, 32 ½ x 14 In.	948
Mirror, Federal, Mahogany, Carved Corners, c.1815, 48 x 24 In.	30
Mirror, Federal, Mahogany, Leaf Cutouts, Parcel Gilt Swags, Eagle, c.1815, 37 x 20 In.	1625
Mirror, Federal, Mahogany, String Inlay, Giltwood Eagle Crest, 67 ½ In.	5310
Mirror, Federal, Reverse Painted, Stone Bridge, Cottage Scene, Giltwood, 27 x 15 In., Pair	120
Mirror, Federal, Tiger Maple, Couple At Lake, Reverse Painted Panel, 35 x 17 ½ In.	889
Mirror, Forest, Arts & Crafts, Gilt Gesso, Tree Pattern, c.1940, 25 x 16 In.	1968
Mirror, Fornasetti, Giltwood, Radiating Sun Rays, Italy, 20 x 20 In.	1416 to 2583
Mirror, French Empire, Mahogany, Bronze, Poseidon, Columns, 1800s, 67 x 36 In.	1434
Mirror, G. Stickley, Chamfered Board Back, Red Decal, 36 x 27 In.	1500
Mirror, George II Style, Giltwood, Shell-Carved Finial, Scroll Pediment, 55 x 32 In.	938
Mirror, George II Style, Giltwood, Tombstone Top, Leaves, Stippled, c.1900, 52 x 25 In.	676
Mirror, George III Style, Gold Paint, Carved Urns, Leaves, 2 Candleholders, 36 x 20 In., Pair	406
Mirror, George III, Giltwood, Scroll, Oval Plate, c.1800, 28 x 14 In., Pair	2500
Mirror, George III, Mahogany, Giltwood, Scroll Pediment, Swags, Eagle Carved, 56 x 24 In.	2160
Mirror, George III, Mahogany, Giltwood, Shaped, Feather, Fruit, Leaves, c.1810, 44 In.	644
Mirror, George III, Walnut, Parcel Gilt, Plume Crest, Scalloped Frame, c.1760, 35 In.	5688
Mirror, Georgian Style, Giltwood, Pagoda Crest, Ornately Carved, c.1960, 57 x 30 In.	375
Mirror, Georgian, Giltwood, Carved, 1800s, 37 x 20 In.	295
Mirror, Giltwood, 3 Parts, Projecting Cornice, Twist Columns, c.1885, 32 x 59 In.	922
Mirror, Giltwood, Carved Leaves, c.1880, 46 x 36 In.	299
Mirror, Giltwood, Carved Leaves, Scrolls, Rectangular Plate, Italy, c.1765, 66 x 45 In.	6875
Mirror, Giltwood, Carved Openwork, Leaf Crest, Italy, 27 x 19 In.	280
Mirror, Giltwood, Carved, 49 x 28 In.	300
Mirror, Giltwood, Carved, 54 ½ x 48 In.	365
Mirror, Giltwood, Carved, Egg & Dart, Beaded Border, c.1810, 34 x 23 In., Pair	330
Mirror, Giltwood, Carved, Stepped Leaves, Berry Molding, 1800s, 45 x 36 In.	478
Mirror, Giltwood, Cherubs, Gathering Corn Panel, Reverse Painted, c.1800, 59 x 30 In.	3750
Mirror, Giltwood, Copper, Repousse, Scrolled Leaves, Raised Borders, Octagonal, 13 x 11 In.	540
Mirror, Giltwood, Dentil Edging, Oval, c.1975, 41 x 33 In., Pair	625
Mirror, Giltwood, Ebonized, Shadowbox Frame, Flowers, Scrolls, c.1885, 59 x 72 In.	472
Mirror, Giltwood, Flower Clusters, Oval, 36 x 28 In.	180
Mirror, Giltwood, Gadrooned, Arched Top, Pierced Shell Scrolls, c.1900, 89 x 54 In.	5658
Mirror, Giltwood, Gesso, Carved Flower Basket Crest, 22 x 20 In.	900
Mirror, Giltwood, Inset Leopard Suede Panel, 30 x 42 In.	530
Mirror, Giltwood, Leaf, Scroll Crest, 1700s, 36 x 18 In.	1000

Furniture, Desk, Queen Anne, Tiger Maple, Slant Front, Compartments, c.1710, 37 x 35 In.
$3,000

Skinner Auctioneers & Appraisers

Furniture, Desk, Schoolmaster's, Poplar, Slant Front, Concealed Drawers, c.1865, 39 x 37 In.
$330

Garth's Auctioneers & Appraisers

Furniture, Desk, Shaker, Trustee's, Pine, Drop Front, 2 Paneled Doors, Drawers, 62 x 37 In.
$7,375

Willis Henry Auctions, Inc.

Furniture, Dresser, G. Nelson, Thin Edge, Rosewood, Aluminum, Herman Miller, 1950s, 33 x 67 In.
$7,500

Rago Arts & Auction Center

Furniture, Dresser, Shaker, Pine, Dovetailed, 6 Drawers, Stenciled H.N. Morse, 48 x 35 In.
$4,012

Willis Henry Auctions, Inc.

Furniture, Dresser, Welsh, Oak, Carved, Shelves, Jas. Schoolbred & Co., c.1890, 82 x 72 In.
$1,015

Neal Auction Co.

Furniture, Dresser, Welsh, Oak, Cock-Beaded, 2 Parts, Shelves, Drawers, Doors, 85 In.
$4,000

Leslie Hindman Auctioneers

Furniture, Dry Sink, Pine, Blue Paint, Beaded Boards, Door, New England, 1800s, 31 x 33 In.
$780

Garth's Auctioneers & Appraisers

Furniture, Easel, Renaissance Revival, Incised Walnut, Ebonized, Gilt, Inlaid, 1800s, 76 x 37 In.
$3,585

Neal Auction Co.

Furniture, Etagere, Federal, Mahogany, Tiered Shelves, Ring Turnings, 1800s, 52 x 20 In.
$2,390

Neal Auction Co.

Furniture, Etagere, Rococo Style, Gilt Metal, Onyx, Shelves, Mirror Back, c.1900, 64 x 26 In.
$1,188

Rago Arts & Auction Center

Furniture, Footstool, Walnut, Carved Skirt, Heart Cutout, Mortise Construction, Pa., 1800s
$1,440

Garth's Auctioneers & Appraisers

Mirror, Giltwood, Molded & Beaded Frame, Carved, 46 x 38 In.	1550
Mirror, Giltwood, Molded, Leaf Carved, Beveled Plate, 1800s, 41 x 35 In.	239
Mirror, Giltwood, Openwork Crest, Lyre, Wreath, Bellflowers, c.1885, 63 x 30 In.	2706
Mirror, Giltwood, Openwork Leaf & Flower Crest, Round, 28 In.	162
Mirror, Giltwood, Oval, Carved Birds At Crest, Flowers, Leaves, 1800s, 39 x 26 In.	936
Mirror, Giltwood, Pediment, Garlands, Urn, Italy, c.1800, 83 x 29 In., Pair	3438
Mirror, Giltwood, Reverse Painted Tablet, Mt. Vernon, c.1825, 38 x 26 In.	780
Mirror, Giltwood, Reverse Painted, Divided Panes, Eagle, Flags, 50 x 29 In.	406
Mirror, Giltwood, Reverse Painted, Landscape Scene, 42 x 25 In.	500
Mirror, Giltwood, Scrolling Leaf Crest, Shell, Beaded Border, c.1815, 53 x 40 In.	1195
Mirror, Giltwood, Spiral Reeded Columns, Leaves & Rosettes, c.1825, 61 x 26 In.	369
Mirror, Giltwood, Split Columns, Carved Flowers, 38 x 27 In.	150
Mirror, Giltwood, Sunburst, Flower Head Rays, Flower Center, 21 In. Diam.	460
Mirror, Giltwood, Sunburst, Oval, Bellflower Rays, 34 x 30 In.	799
Mirror, Giltwood, Three Entwined Triangles, 51 x 62 In.	1125
Mirror, Girandole, Giltwood, Candle Arms, Scrolled Leaf Frame, Eagle, 1815, 39 In.	1500
Mirror, Girandole, Giltwood, Eagle Crest, c.1950, 56 In.	504
Mirror, Girandole, Giltwood, Spread Eagle, Leaf Crest, c.1925, 50 In.	3500
Mirror, Hand, Glass, Blue, Gold Gilt Overlay, Pressed Flower, c.1910, 11 ¼ In. *illus*	185
Mirror, Hepplewhite Style, Mahogany, Metal Acanthus Leaf & Urn Finial, c.1940, 48 x 26 In.	136
Mirror, Italianate, Mahogany, Chinese Style, Giltwood, Carved, Openwork, c.1910, 61 x 39 In.	780
Mirror, Lacquer, Painted, Bronze Relief, Front & Back, c.1900, 15 x 10 ½ In. *illus*	259
Mirror, Louis-Philippe Style, Giltwood, Oval, Carved Crest, France, c.1900, 41 x 24 In.	413
Mirror, Louis XV Style, Giltwood, Molded Shell & Scroll, c.1885, 24 x 20 In.	530
Mirror, Louis XV Style, Giltwood, Oval, Scrollwork, Cabochons, Pierced, 38 x 25 In.	460
Mirror, Louis XV Style, Giltwood, Serpentine Crest, Flowers, France, c.1885, 72 x 55 In.	4182
Mirror, Louis XV Style, Silver Plate, Cartouche Plate, O. Prevost, France, 26 x 43 In.	12100
Mirror, Louis XV, Giltwood, Leaf & Scroll Carved, Arched Plate, 1750, 69 x 37 In.	2250
Mirror, Louis XVI Style, Giltwood, Beaded, Trophy Crest, c.1900, 59 x 41 In.	584
Mirror, Louis XVI Style, Giltwood, Carved, 67 x 44 In.	2813
Mirror, Louis XVI Style, Giltwood, Divided Pane, Carved Crest, 57 x 34 In.	1063
Mirror, Louis XVI Style, Giltwood, Domed Top, Crest, Guilloche, c.1900, 73 x 46 In.	2337
Mirror, Louis XVI Style, Giltwood, Domed, Beveled, Shield Crest, c.1875, 75 x 47 In.	2952
Mirror, Louis XVI Style, Giltwood, Plaster Medallion, Putti, c.1890, 60 x 31 In. *illus*	1230
Mirror, Louis XVI Style, Giltwood, Torch & Arrow Crest, Beveled Plate, 63 x 42 In.	2750
Mirror, Louis XVI, Giltwood, Openwork Crest, Trophy, Ball Feet, c.1785, 34 x 22 In.	717
Mirror, Mahogany Veneer, 2 Sections, Beveled Edges, Cut Designs, England, 1700s, 38 x 20 In.	558
Mirror, Mahogany, 2 Parts, Half Turnings, Acorn Drops, Roundels, c.1835, 42 x 23 In.	118
Mirror, Mahogany, Beveled Frame, Square, England, 18 ½ x 14 In.	179
Mirror, Mahogany, Giltwood, Pediment, Reverse Painted Panel, 54 x 23 In.	1416
Mirror, Mahogany, Giltwood, Swags, Swan's Neck Pediment, Eagle Finial, 54 x 25 In.	1045
Mirror, Mahogany, Ogee, c.1850, 22 x 32 In.	115
Mirror, Marriage, Giltwood, Ribbon-Tied Trophy Crest, France, 25 x 15 In.	563
Mirror, Napoleon III, Giltwood, Arched Crest, Beaded Border, c.1850, 57 x 35 In.	860
Mirror, Neoclassical Style, Giltwood, Beaded & Carved Frame, Urn Crest, 43 x 22 In.	799
Mirror, Neoclassical Style, Giltwood, Carved Crest, c.1860, 68 x 25 In., Pair	5378
Mirror, Neoclassical Style, Giltwood, Dentil Edges, Divided Panes, 39 x 28 In.	750
Mirror, Neoclassical Style, Giltwood, Leaf Scroll Crest, Oval, 51 x 34 In.	5563
Mirror, Neoclassical Style, Giltwood, Leaf Tip, Beaded Frame, c.1900, 36 x 31 In.	180
Mirror, Neoclassical Style, Giltwood, Painted, Arched Panels, Maidens, c.1900, 33 x 53 In.	420
Mirror, Neoclassical Style, Giltwood, Pierced, Flower Urn Crest, 81 x 33 In., Pair	7687
Mirror, Neoclassical Style, Giltwood, Round, Carved Flower Base, 32 x 36 In.	530
Mirror, Neoclassical Style, Giltwood, Scroll, Vine Crest, 72 x 52 In.	406
Mirror, Neoclassical, Fruitwood, Fluted, Basket Crest, Instruments, c.1785, 38 x 21 In.	922
Mirror, Neoclassical, Giltwood, Berries, Medallion, Shell Crest, c.1815, 63 x 26 In.	799
Mirror, Neoclassical, Giltwood, Carved Leaves, Flowers, Crest, Sweden, 49 x 27 In.	1000
Mirror, Neoclassical, Giltwood, Carved, Urn, Flower Crest, Italy, 1700s, 42 x 27 In.	2150
Mirror, Neoclassical, Giltwood, Cornucopia Crest, Leaves, 1800s, 42 x 32 In. *illus*	3286
Mirror, Neoclassical, Giltwood, Faux Paint, Square, Shell & Flowers, 1900s, 49 x 31 In.	472
Mirror, Neoclassical, Giltwood, Floral Drop, Scroll Leaf Surround, c.1810, 53 x 50 In.	1770
Mirror, Neoclassical, Mahogany, Ebonized, Stencil, Half Baluster, Painted, c.1830, 27 x 14 In.	1560
Mirror, Neoclassical, Parcel Gilt, Fluted Pilaster, Corinthian Capitals, Italy, c.1800, 40 x 36 In.	1375
Mirror, Neoclassical, Segmented, Gesso, Painted, Leaf Corners, Italy, 1800s, 20 x 17 In.	1599
Mirror, Oak, Carved Birds Crest, Grapevines, Square Shape, c.1890, 50 x 33 In.	590
Mirror, Parcel Wood, Cartouche, Painted, Venice, 38 x 74 In.	1150

Mirror, Pier, Federal, Giltwood, Reverse Painted Ship Panel, c.1815, 47 x 34 In.	10200
Mirror, Pier, Federal, Giltwood, Swag & Acorn Pediment, c.1865, 62 x 29 In.	593
Mirror, Pier, Giltwood, Block Front, Eagle, Flower Swag, Reeded Columns, 52 In.	375
Mirror, Pier, Giltwood, Molded, Scroll Leaf Band, Rosette Blocks, 1800s, 94 x 34 In.	1464
Mirror, Pier, Giltwood, Roundel, Courting Couple, 66 x 49 In.	500
Mirror, Pier, Giltwood, Spiral Columns, Arch Crest, Angels, c.1885, 80 x 30 In.	1599
Mirror, Pier, Louis XVI Style, Flower Crest, Family, Landscape, Gilt, c.1800, 62 x 31 In.	1968
Mirror, Pier, Mahogany, Turned Columns, Divided Pane, 47 x 24 In.	469
Mirror, Pier, Renaissance Revival, Giltwood, Shells, c.1885, 104 x 34 In.	1168
Mirror, Pier, Victorian, Walnut, Carved Crest, Marble Top Base, Drawer, 38 x 105 In.	678
Mirror, Pier, Victorian, Walnut, Raised Burl Panels, 83 In.	96
Mirror, Pine, Applied Half Turnings, Gilding, Painted, c.1840, 13 x 11 In.	264
Mirror, Plateau, Silver Plate, Round, Wide Frame, 3-Footed, c.1890, 15 ½ In.	259
Mirror, Queen Anne, Divided Pane, 43 x 20 In.	720
Mirror, Queen Anne, Mahogany, Carved Giltwood Crest, c.1760, 39 x 22 In.	770
Mirror, Queen Anne, Mahogany, Scroll Crest, c.1760, 18 ½ x 11 In.	504
Mirror, Queen Anne, Mahogany, Shaped Frame, 2 Brass Candle Arms, c.1800, 33 In.	750
Mirror, Queen Anne, Walnut Veneer, Carved Crest, c.1740, 16 x 9 In.	178
Mirror, Queen Anne, Walnut, Carved, Shaped Crest, Divided Pane, 42 x 16 In.	2160
Mirror, Queen Anne, Walnut, Giltwood, Gesso, Scroll Crest, Shell, c.1750, 47 In.	523
Mirror, Queen Anne, Walnut, Scroll Cornice, Molded, c.1750, 32 x 13 In.	308
Mirror, Regency, Girandole, Giltwood, Round Plate, Eagle & Dolphin Pediment, 38 x 22 In.	3393
Mirror, Renaissance Revival Style, Giltwood, Gesso, Cherubs, Scrolls, c.1900, 49 x 35 In.	210
Mirror, Renaissance Revival, Giltwood, Leaves, Scroll Finials, c.1865, 88 x 68 In.	2460
Mirror, Reverse Glass Panel, Woman, Drapery, Stencil Border, Turnings, c.1840, 30 x 5 In.	440
Mirror, Rococo Style, Giltwood, Carved Flowers & Scrolls, 1800s, 38 x 49 In.	295
Mirror, Rococo Style, Giltwood, Carved Flowers, Scalloped Crest, 1800s, 31 In.	360
Mirror, Rococo Style, Giltwood, Carved, c.1950, 39 x 25 In.	313
Mirror, Rococo Style, Giltwood, Leaves, Flowers, Scrolls, Italy, c.1965, 50 x 27 In., Pair	575
Mirror, Rococo Style, Giltwood, Openwork, Carved, 51 x 35 In.	938
Mirror, Rococo Style, Giltwood, Openwork, Carved, 54 x 28 In., Pair	1000
Mirror, Rococo Style, Giltwood, Openwork, Shell-Carved Frame, c.1880, 66 x 42 In.	1250
Mirror, Rococo Style, Giltwood, Scroll Crest, Divided Pane, Italy, 45 x 28 In.	875
Mirror, Rococo Style, Giltwood, Scroll Leaves, Openwork Crest, 1800s, 60 x 30 In.	3466
Mirror, Rococo Style, Giltwood, Shield Crest, Pierced Scrolling Leaves, c.1875, 33 x 28 In.	215
Mirror, Rococo, Giltwood, Cartouche, c.1750, 29 x 13 In.	1000
Mirror, Rococo, Silver Angels, Oval, Dutch, 19th Century, 37 x 24 In.	8125
Mirror, Santa Fe, Walnut, Beveled Glass, 40 x 34 In.	390
Mirror, Shaving, Edwardian, Mahogany, Carved, Inlay, Lamp Stands, Drawer, 37 x 35 In.	425
Mirror, Shaving, Federal, Mahogany, Line Inlay, 5 Drawers, 30 x 26 In.	154
Mirror, Shaving, George III, Mahogany, c.1810, 19 x 17 ½ In.	89
Mirror, Shaving, Neoclassical, Lyre Supports, Drawer, 1800s, 21 x 23 In.	230
Mirror, Shaving, Wood, Shaped Frame, Easel Back, 9 x 14 In.	185
Mirror, Sheraton, Giltwood, Fruit, Basket, Reverse Painted Panel, Turned, c.1830, 34 x 16 In.	415
Mirror, Silver Plate, Medallion Crest, Oval, 27 x 19 In.	509
Mirror, Silvered Metal Hayrack, Spiral Shape, c.1920, 63 ½ In.	1872
Mirror, Spanish Colonial, Cutout, Women's Portraits, Green Paint, c.1769, 21 x 19 In.	563
Mirror, Steel, Painted Glass Blocks, 36 ½ x 36 ½ In., Pair	563
Mirror, Tiger Maple, Ogee, c.1850, 25 x 17 In.	474
Mirror, Venetian Style, Giltwood, Ogee Frame, Scrollwork Crest, c.1910, 25 x 18 In.	799
Mirror, Venetian Style, Oval, Ribbon & Bowknot, Engraved Flowers, 28 x 21 In.	460
Mirror, Venetian Style, Scroll Crest, Etched Leaves, Silvered Wood, c.1910, 50 x 48 In.	1000
Mirror, Venini, Brass, Illuminated, 1940s, 28 x 27 ½ In. ....*illus*	5625
Mirror, Victorian, Giltwood, Carved, 42 x 36 In.	80
Mirror, Victorian, Green Paint, Hall, Planter Base, 36 x 97 In.	460
Mirror, Walnut, Carved Eagle Crest, Leafy Urn, Rosette Blocks, 1800s, 52 x 24 In.	732
Mirror, Walnut, Giltwood, Incising, Pierced Crest, Candleholders, c.1885, 73 x 58 In., Pair	3198
Mirror, Walnut, Reverse Painted Tablet, Landscape, Side Columns, c.1845, 28 x 14 In.	115
Mirror, William & Mary, Walnut, Cushion, England, c.1715, 21 x 18 In., Pair	590
Mirror, Wood, Carved, Split Column, Fruit Baskets, Rope Turnings, 41 x 23 In.	840
Mirror, Wood, Painted, Columns, Pediment, Heart, Flowers, Oval, 32 x 42 In.	650
Ottoman, Frank Lloyd Wright, Hexagonal, Upholstered, Heritage Henredon, 16 x 31 In.	1120
Ottoman, Louis XV Style, Serpentine, Cabriole Legs, Shaped Apron, 17 x 79 In.	1107
Overmantel mirror, see Architectural category.	
Pantry, Pine, 2 Panel Doors, Punched Tin Panels, Virginia, c.1860, 69 x 42 In.	1840

Furniture, Highchair, Arthur Espenet Carpenter, Walnut, Signed, 1958, 37 x 13 x 20 In.
$11,875

Rago Arts & Auction Center

Furniture, Highchair, Maple, Ladder Back, Oak Splint Seat, Acorn Finials, 1800s, 39 In.
$607

Cowan's Auctions

Furniture, Hutch, Pine, Rectangular Top, Bench Seat, Painted, Shoe Feet, 1800-50, 44 x 34 In.
$450

Garth's Auctioneers & Appraisers

Furniture, Lectern, Oak, Carved Eagle, Leaves, American, c.1890, 90 In. $5,625

Rago Arts & Auction Center

Furniture, Mirror, Cheval, Empire, Mahogany, Ormolu Trim, Eagle Finials, c.1825, 75 x 44 In. $3,125

Rago Arts & Auction Center

TIP
Trying to remove old glue from a furniture repair? Use vinegar in a squeeze bottle and force some of the vinegar into the glue. The glue will slowly dissolve.

Parlor Set, Settee, 2 Armchairs, Mahogany, Pierced Backs, Upholstered, 41 x 47 & 39 In.	294
Pedestal, Brass, Marble, Ivory, Rose, Square Base & Top, 1900s, 44 x 12 In., Pair	885
Pedestal, Cappellini, French Empire Revival, Gilt Burl, Marble Top, Italy, 44 In.	420
Pedestal, Edwardian, Mixed Wood, Carved, Inlay, Concave Top, c.1900, 42 x 12 In.	885
Pedestal, Empire, Mahogany, Bronze, Scroll Capital, Wreath, Plinth, c.1900, 47 x 11 In.	1434
Pedestal, Hardwood, Round Top, Dragon Border, Pierced Base, c.1900, 10 x 37 In.	922
Pedestal, John-Richard, French Empire Style, Giltwood, Ebonized, 54 In., Pair	390
Pedestal, Louis XVI Style, Rosewood, Burr Amboyna, Ebonized, Gilt, c.1890, 40 In. ....*illus*	3998
Pedestal, Mahogany, Carved, Griffins, Brass Lion's Head Masks, c.1890, 39 In. .....*illus*	2832
Pedestal, Mahogany, Shaped Top, Twisted Rope Stem, Round Base, c.1900, 41 x 14 In.	644
Pedestal, Oak, Carved, Caryatid Shape, Hands Raised, Extending Feet, 50 x 11 In.	900
Pedestal, Olive Green Glaze, Molded Flowers, Marked, 1800s, 30 ¼ In.	64
Pedestal, Onyx, Ormolu Mount, Square Top, Column Stem, Brass Brackets, 41 x 11 In.	475
Pedestal, Pine, Faux Marble Paint, c.1845, 39 x 15 In.	652
Pedestal, Renaissance Revival, Walnut, Round Top, Carved, c.1870, 48 In., Pair	2360
Pedestal, Stone, Black, Round Top, Metal Frame, Tripod, Splayed Legs, 40 x 17 In.	527
Pedestal, Walnut, Carved Dragons, Asian, c.1900, 42 x 14 In.	313
Pedestal, Walnut, Ebonized, Incised Gilt, Marble Top, Flags, c.1885, 34 x 16 In.	1912
Pedestal, White Marble, Ormolu, Octagonal Top, 44 x 11 In.	480
Pie Safe, Blue Paint, Punched Tin Panels, 2 Doors, Shenandoah Valley, 55 x 52 In.	1680
Pie Safe, Cherry, Tin, Green, Red, 4 Interior Shelves, Drawer, c.1850, 55 x 39 In.	1320
Pie Safe, Georgia Federal, Yellow Pine, Punched Tin Panels, 1800s, 57 x 48 In. ......*illus*	4956
Pie Safe, Hanging, Door, Spiral-Punched Tin Panels, c.1850, 34 x 30 In.	720
Pie Safe, Maple, Punched Tin Panels, Drawer, Doors, c.1850, 44 x 40 In.	910
Pie Safe, Pine, 6 Panels, Circle Tins, Punched Heart, 2 Doors, Southern, c.1820, 50 x 40 In.	847
Pie Safe, Pine, Flower, Pinwheel Punched Tin Panels, Virginia, 65 x 47 In.	3159
Pie Safe, Pine, Painted Tin, Pierced Stars, Hinged Door, c.1885, 31 x 30 In.	9225
Pie Safe, Pine, Punched Tin Panels, Door, Green Paint, Pennsylvania, c.1845, 58 x 21 In.	1020
Pie Safe, Pine, Punched Tin Panels, Scrubbed Blue Paint, c.1859, 63 x 39 In.	1215
Pie Safe, Pine, Star Punched Tin Panels, Sides, Black Paint, c.1850, 42 x 43 In.	705
Pie Safe, Poplar, 2 Doors, Punched Tin Panels, Geometric Design, Drawer, 58 x 31 In.	470
Pie Safe, Poplar, Drawers, Doors, Punched Tin Panels, Bittersweet Red, c.1870, 55 x 45 In.	1175
Pie Safe, Poplar, Urn, Punched Tin Panels, Drawers, Doors, Painted, c.1865, 47 x 55 In.	2645
Pie Safe, Punched Tin Panels, Star In Circle, Shelves, Drawer, Painted, 1800s, 55 x 39 In.	885
Pie Safe, Sheraton, Softwood, Punched Panels, Jelly Cupboard, Grain Painted, Pa., c.1840	767
Pie Safe, Softwood, Grain Painted, Molded, Screen Door, Sides, Va., c.1890, 54 x 30 In.	472
Pie Safe, Tin Door, Quatrefoil Pierced, Scalloped Backsplash, Green Paint, c.1880, 36 x 12 In.	259
Pie Safe, Walnut, 3 Tin Flower Punched Panels, 2 Drawers, 2 Doors, c.1875, 57 x 41 In.	1150
Pie Safe, Walnut, Chestnut, Gallery, Tin Doors, Hinges, Shaped Base, c.1850, 69 x 65 In.	173
Pie Safe, Walnut, Pine, Punched Tin Panels, 2 Doors, 64 x 58 In.	2015
Pie Safe, Walnut, Punched Tin Panels, Doors, Frame Legs, 1800s, 19 x 16 In.	2714
Pie Safe, Wood, Star Punched Tin Panel, 18 Panels, 58 x 37 In.	480
Pipe Rack, Hanging, George III, Oak, Slant Front, Drawer, c.1789, 28 x 14 In.	240
Planter, Brass, Patchwork Squares, Black Painted Interior, 15 x 15 In.	313
Prie-Dieu, Mahogany, Upholstered Crest, Pierced Scrolls, Cross, 1800s	418
Rack, Baking, Iron, Nickel Plate, Brass, 3 Shelves, Scrollwork, c.1900, 93 x 80 In.	1599
Rack, Baking, Napoleon III Style, Wrought Iron, Brass, 3 Tiers, 92 x 21 In.	799
Rack, Baking, Napoleon III Style, Wrought Iron, Brass, Scrollwork, 91 x 75 In.	922
Rack, Baking, Wrought Iron, Scrolled Brackets, 3 Tiers, Brass Detail, France, 96 x 68 In.	1062
Rack, Cane, Wood, England, 25 x 48 In.	104
Rack, Drying, Folding, Shaped Feet, 26 x 29 In.	480
Rack, Factory, Metal, Wood, 7 Shelves, c.1900, 51 x 55 In.	173
Rack, Game, Blue, Salmon Paint, Serpentine, Carved Pinwheels, 11 Hooks, 1800s, 9 x 36 In.	325
Rack, Magazine, Art Deco, Iron, Silvered, Applied Jumping Hound, Leaf Ring, 14 x 13 In.	502
Rack, Magazine, Iron, Silvered, Applied Jumping Hound, Leaf Ring, Art Deco, 13 ¾ x 13 In.	502
Rack, Magazine, Midcentury Modern, Teak, Jens Harald Quistgaard, 19 x 18 In.	35
Rack, Quilt, Folding, Painted, Mortise & Tenon Construction, Brown Paint, c.1875, 55 x 42 In.	29
Rack, Spoon, Hanging, Pine, 2 Shelves, Red Paint, Carved Sides, c.1850, 15 ½ x 12 ½ In.	830
Rack, Spoon, Softwood, Shaped Back, 19 ½ In.	130
Recamier, Neoclassical, Mahogany, Carved, Rolled Arms, Legs, c.1830, 32 x 72 In.	1375
Recamier, Regency Style, Mahogany, Shaped Padded Back, Outscrolled, c.1870, 36 x 71 In.	1230
Recamier, Rosewood, Upholstered, c.1840, 35 x 94 In.	2133
Recamier, Scroll Ends, Shaped Back, Cane Seat, Ball Feet, Philadelphia, c.1815, 29 x 80 In.	688
Recliner, Adjustable, Metal Mesh, White, Russell Woodard, 1950s, 16 x 41 In.	1150
Rocker, Arts & Crafts, Oak, Cutout Splat, London Furniture Mfg., Ontario, Canada, 39 In.	259

Rocker, Arts & Crafts, Oak, Mortise & Tenon, Pegged, Upholstered Seat, 40 In. ....*illus*	354
Rocker, Arts & Crafts, Oak, Upholstered Seat, 3-Slat Back, Arms, 35 In..........................	59
Rocker, Barrister, Turned Spindles, Arms, Woven Seat, 16 x 40 In..................................	173
Rocker, Brown, Wicker, Woven Seat, 25 x 33 In.	73
Rocker, Eames, Plastic, Fiberglass, Enameled Metal, Birch, Herman Miller, 1950s, 27 x 25 In. ...	750
Rocker, Eames, RAR, Orange Fiberglass, Wire Struts, Label, Herman Miller, 25 x 26 In.............	1000
Rocker, Eames, RAR, Yellow, Molded, 26 x 25 In. ....*illus*	600
Rocker, G. Stickley, 3 Horizontal Slats, Leather Seat, 18 x 20 In.................................	225
Rocker, G. Stickley, Tall Back, Cushion Seat, Branded Mark, c.1912, 43 x 27 In....................	1063
Rocker, Goose, Wood, Cutouts, Green Paint, c.1910, 21 In..	210
Rocker, Horizontal Slat Back, Leather Seat, Open Arms, 25 x 32 In.................................	500
Rocker, Mahogany, Lion Carvings, Back Inlay, c.1910, 24 x 37 In...................................	215
Rocker, Mahogany, Paper Lithograph, Scholarly Man, Bliss, England, 1890, 13 In., Child's *illus*	608
Rocker, Milo Baughman, Chrome Tube Frame, Brown Velvet, 28 x 39 In................................	1063
Rocker, Mixed Wood, 2-Slat Back, Woven Seat, Scroll Arms, Virginia, c.1870, 21 In., Child's.......	460
Rocker, Nanny's, Windsor Style, Red & Black Grain, Flowers, Leaves, New York, 30 In...............	354
Rocker, Pine, Flower Painted, c.1850, Child's..	237
Rocker, Poplar, Turned Stiles, White Oak Splint Seat, c.1845, 21 x 9 In., Child's.................	58
Rocker, Shaker, Arched Rungs, Rolled-Out Arm Knuckles, Woven Seat, N.Y., c.1910, 47 In..........	250
Rocker, Shaker, Ladder Back, Maple, Cane Seat, Shag Rug Seat, Union Village, 44 In. ....*illus*	67260
Rocker, Shaker, Ladder Back, Woven Seat, Ebonized, Stamped Mt. Lebanon, N.Y., 35 x 21 In.	388
Rocker, Shaker, Maple, 4-Slat Back, Tape Seat, Stamped 4, c.1830, 46 In. ....*illus*	2832
Rocker, Shaker, Maple, Black Paint, Acorn Finials, Shaped Slats, 29 In............................	708
Rocker, Shaker, Maple, Tape Seat & Back, Mt. Lebanon, N.Y., c.1880, 43 In. ....*illus*	472
Rocker, Shaker, No. 7, 4-Slat Back, Open Arms, Woven Seat, c.1870, 16 x 40 In....................	546
Rocker, Warren Fenzi, Exeter III, Lacewood, 4 Back Spindles, Half Arms, 1997, 25 x 45 In.........	2063
Rocker, Wicker, Chrome Yellow Paint, Continuous Arm, 14 ½ x 31 ½ In...............................	115
Rocker, Windsor, Bent Rod Back, Painted Fruit, Yellow, Stamped N. Rollins, Dearborn..............	60
Rocker, Windsor, Comb Back, Arms, Painted, c.1850, 42 x 16 In....................................	259
Rocker, Windsor, Maple, Ash, Shaped Comb, Bamboo Turnings, Arms, c.1810, 39 x 16 In..........	240
Rocker, Windsor, Mixed Wood, Bamboo Turnings, Black Paint, c.1815, 40 In.........................	240
Room Divider, Erik Hoglund, Zodiac Medallions, Sweden, 1960s, 40-In. Strands, 10 Piece........	2000
Screens are also listed in the Architectural and Fireplace categories.	
Screen, 2-Panel, Bamboo, Folding, Chrysanthemum, Birds, Japan, 1695, 68 x 38 In..................	1800
Screen, 3-Panel, Arts & Crafts, Brown Leather, Brass Tacks, 60 x 62 In...........................	2250
Screen, 3-Panel, Leaves, Scrolls, Flowers, Painted, 74 In..	1000
Screen, 3-Panel, Musician, Exotic Landscape, France, c.1890, 66 In...............................	1416
Screen, 3-Panel, Oak, Textile, Mauve & Brown On Cream, 61 x 66 In................................	360
Screen, 3-Panel, Wallpaper, Painted, France, 1800s, 63 x 24 In...................................	1000
Screen, 3-Panel, Wood, Church Scene, c.1890, 30 x 30 In..	118
Screen, 4-Panel, Brown Lacquer, Applied Ivory Figures, Horses, Chinese, 72 x 18 In..............	3300
Screen, 4-Panel, Figures, River Trade, Chinese, 84 x 70 In.......................................	2880
Screen, 4-Panel, Flowers, Gilt Ground, 80 x 71 In..	3950
Screen, 4-Panel, Higgins, Wood, Painted, Bubble Rondelay Glass Inserts, c.1960, 84 x 64 In.	3690
Screen, 4-Panel, Needlepoint, Shaped Beveled Tops, c.1855, 64 x 82 In............................	500
Screen, 4-Panel, Rosewood, Carved, Dragons, Lattice, Chinese, c.1900, 76 x 21 In.................	3444
Screen, 4-Panel, Teak, High Relief Carved Panels, Fruit, Allegorical Scenes, 72 In...............	230
Screen, 4-Panel, Wallpaper, French Peasant Scenes, Flowers, Folding, 65 x 72 In..................	510
Screen, 6-Panel, Women, Courtyard Scene, Black Lacquer Ground, Chinese, 86 x 111 In.	1125
Screen, 6-Panel, Women, Landscape, Abalone Shell, Black Lacquer, 96 x 72 In......................	649
Screen, 8-Panel, Coromandel, Folding, Chinese, c.1900, 97 x 137 In...............................	830
Screen, 9-Panel, Plastic, Kartell, 1960s, 60 x 72 In...	500
Screen, Gothic Revival, Rosewood, Upholstered Panel, Crested Frame, c.1850, 55 In................	430
Screen, Hardwood, Carved, Silk Needlework, Chinese, 1800s, 71 x 44 In. ....*illus*	13225
Screen, Leaded & Stained Glass, Walnut, Carved Flowers, Owl, Branch, 47 x 25 In..................	406
Screen, Mahogany, Brass, Tapestry, Rooster, Shaped Crest, Splayed, c.1850, 33 x 23 In............	246
Screen, Oak, Shell Carved Frame, Bather, Ribbon, Hoof Feet, England, 53 ½ In.....................	813
Screen, Queen Anne Style, Mahogany, Needlework, Flowers, Vase, c.1900, 51 x 25 In................	875
Screen, Rosewood, Needlepoint, United States Seal, 19th Century, 70 x 24 x 20 In.................	625
Screen, Sheet Tin, Steel Hinges, Indians, Campfire, Thomas Molesworth, 30 x 49 In................	47500
Screen, Victorian, Carved, Ebonized, Printed, Embroidery Panel, 43 x 25 In.......................	533
Screen, Walnut, Carved Flowers, Owl, Branch, Leaded & Stained Glass, 47 x 25 In..................	406
Seat Table, Risom, Tandem, Upholstered Chairs, Teak Table, 1900s, 32 x 79 In....................	723
Seat, Wagon, Maple, Turned Stretchers, Splint Seat, Mid 1800s, 30 x 36 In.......................	470
Secretary, Arne Vodder, Teak, Flip-Top Vanity, Mirror, Denmark, 1960s, 42 ½ x 34 In.............	1250

Furniture, Mirror, Cheval, William IV, Mahogany, Casters, c.1835, 71 x 35 In.
$1,185

James D. Julia Auctioneers

Furniture, Mirror, Courting, Gentleman, Servant, Black Paint, 1700s, 16 x 10 In.
$480

Garth's Auctioneers & Appraisers

Furniture, Mirror, Hand, Glass, Blue, Gold Gilt Overlay, Pressed Flower, c.1910, 11 ¼ In.
$185

DuMouchelles Art Gallery

Furniture, Mirror, Lacquer, Painted, Bronze Relief, Front & Back, c.1900, 15 x 10 ½ In.
$259

Cottone Auctions

Furniture, Mirror, Louis XVI Style, Giltwood, Plaster Medallion, Putti, c.1890, 60 x 31 In.
$1,230

New Orleans Auction Galleries, Inc.

Furniture, Mirror, Neoclassical, Giltwood, Cornucopia Crest, Leaves, 1800s, 42 x 32 In.
$3,286

Neal Auction Co.

Furniture, Mirror, Venini, Brass, Illuminated, 1940s, 28 x 27 ½ In.
$5,625

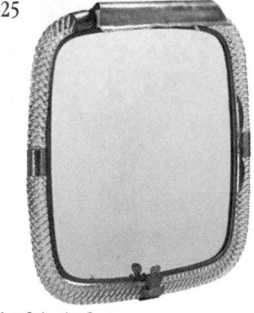

Rago Arts & Auction Center

Secretary, Birch, Drop Front, Drawers, Copper, A. Sornay, France, c.1940, 57 x 33 In.	1750
Secretary, Borge Mogensen, Teak, Drop Front, Fitted Interior, Drawers, c.1965, 49 x 39 In.	780
Secretary, Butler's, Federal, Mahogany, Glass Shelves, 4 Drawers, Salem, 92 x 44 In.	1200
Secretary, Butler's, George III, Mahogany, Inlay, 2 Glass Doors, Flat Doors, 90 x 43 In.	2000
Secretary, Chippendale, Cherry, Finials, Panel Doors, Scrolls, Drawers, c.1765, 40 x 39 In.	37920
Secretary, Chippendale, Cherry, Slant Front, 2 Doors, 4 Drawers, New England, 81 x 42 In.	2640
Secretary, Chippendale, Mahogany, Drop Front, 2 Panel Doors, Bowed, 4 Drawers, 92 x 41 In.	2280
Secretary, Chippendale, Mahogany, Drop Front, Fitted Interior, 1700s, 88 x 42 In. ....*illus*	18880
Secretary, Chippendale, Slant Front, Mahogany, Drawers, New England, 89 x 41 In.	533
Secretary, Chippendale, Walnut, c.1770, 88 x 39 In.	1304
Secretary, Empire, Mahogany, Drop Front, 2 Doors, Ball Feet, Boston, 53 x 39 In.	900
Secretary, Empire, Mahogany, Gilt Bronze, Drop Front, 4 Drawers, 56 x 38 In.	750
Secretary, Empire, Mahogany, Glass & Carved Doors, Drawers, N.Y., c.1840, 93 x 44 In.	147
Secretary, Federal, Mahogany, 2 Glass Doors, 5 Drawers, Boston, c.1810, 74 x 42 In.	1625
Secretary, Federal, Mahogany, 3 Doors, Fitted Interior, 4 Drawers, c.1860, 53 x 42 In.	1063
Secretary, Federal, Mahogany, Glass Doors, Drawers, Compartments, c.1810, 70 x 40 In.	3884
Secretary, Federal, Mahogany, Pierced Scrolls, Glass Doors, 5 Drawers, c.1820, 98 In.	7500
Secretary, Federal, Mixed Wood, 2 Glass Mullion Doors, 5 Drawers, c.1800, 92 x 43 In.	5192
Secretary, Federal, Reeded Doors, 2 Tambour Doors, Drawers, c.1805, 75 x 36 In.	1375
Secretary, George III, Mahogany, 2 Glass Doors, 5 Drawers, 90 x 55 In.	1250
Secretary, Georgian, Mahogany, Drop Front, Fretwork, Glass Doors, c.1800, 90 x 38 In.	2500
Secretary, Hepplewhite, Mahogany Veneer, String & Bellflower Inlay, Tambour Door.	715
Secretary, Louis XV Style, Mahogany, Scroll Cornice, 3-Panel Doors, 100 x 49 In.	4674
Secretary, Mahogany, 3-Panel Doors, Cubbies, Concave Stretcher, c.1900, 51 x 28 In.	738
Secretary, Mahogany, Bombe, Drop Front, 2 Glass Doors, 3 Drawers, 1800s, 38 x 24 In., Child's	1046
Secretary, Mixed Wood, Carved, Drop Front, Panel Doors, Drawers, N.C., c.1845, 89 x 39 In.	3776
Secretary, Mixed Wood, Dutch Marquetry, Drop Front, Fitted Interior, Doors, 58 x 36 In.	1375
Secretary, Neoclassical, Mahogany, Fold-Out Desk, Arched Doors, 101 x 52 In.	3444
Secretary, Queen Anne Style, Cheminais Stinkwood, Slant Front, Doors, c.1930, 43 x 30 In.	450
Secretary, Queen Anne, Tiger Maple, Drop Front, 2 Doors, 3 Drawers, c.1760, 81 x 37 In.	5925
Secretary, Rosewood, Drop Front, Fitted Interior, 2 Doors, c.1875, 64 x 42 In.	938
Secretary, Sheraton, Mahogany, 2 Glass Doors, 3 Drawers, Pennsylvania, c.1820, 76 x 36 In.	504
Secretary, Sheraton, Tiger Maple, Tambour Doors, 8 Drawers, 54 x 45 In.	3840
Secretary, Walnut, Maple, Slant Front, 2 Panel Doors, Drawer, c.1860, 62 x 32 In.	729
Secretary, Walnut, Marquetry, Drop Front, 2 Drawers, Inlaid Figures, 1800s, 65 x 45 In.	3125
Secretary, Walnut, Rounded, Drop Front, Arched Open Cupboard, c.1835, 64 x 45 In.	1722
Semainier, Bowfront, Concave Base, 61 x 16 In.	2270
Semanier, Empire Style, Mahogany Veneer, Plinth Base, c.1850, 54 x 28 In.	460
Server, Arts & Crafts, Oak, Drawer, Carved Panels, 2 Doors, c.1910, 42 x 45 In.	440
Server, Directoire, Walnut, 2 Drawers, 2 Doors, c.1810, 37 x 49 In.	2125
Server, Federal, Mahogany, Bowfront, Turned Reeded Legs, c.1815, 38 x 40 In.	3304
Server, Fruitwood, Carved Sunburst Panels, Italy, 33 x 53 ½ In.	516
Server, George III, Mahogany, Serpentine, Fluted Frieze, Drawer, c.1790, 34 x 78 In.	3750
Server, Georgian, Mahogany, Satinwood, Shell Inlay, 3 Drawers, 31 x 28 In.	575
Server, Hepplewhite, Mahogany, 3 Drawers, Bowfront, Arched Apron, England, 31 x 37 In.	1080
Server, Mahogany, Drawers, Scalloped Stretcher Shelf, Turned Legs, c.1815, 36 x 30 In.	478
Server, Mahogany, Shaped Gallery, Shelves, Doors, Bun Feet, c.1815, 55 x 41 In.	2032
Server, Ormolu, Marble Top, Mirror, 2 Drawers, Doors, France, c.1900, 44 x 59 In.	489
Server, Pine, Mahogany, Grain Painted, Gallery, Drawer, Paneled Doors, Footed, 53 x 45 In.	764
Server, Sheraton, Backsplash, Grain Painted, 3 Drawers, Turned Legs, c.1810, 34 x 32 In.	390
Server, Victorian, Oak, 2 Drawers, 2 Doors, Columns, Paw Feet, c.1900, 35 x 41 In.	543
Server, Walnut, 2 Drawers, Carved Column Supports, Italy, c.1945, 37 x 55 In.	207
Server, William IV, Mahogany, Drawers, Doors, Thin Columns, Ball Feet, c.1800, 35 x 41 In.	676
Serving Cart, McCobb, Bleached Mahogany, Marble, Shelf, Calvin, Tag, 29 x 36 x 19 In.	2440
Serving Cart, Poul Hundevad, Teak, Denmark, 23 x 29 x 20 In.	275
Settee, Art Deco, Veneer, Satinwood Inlay, Continental, c.1910, 82 In. ....*illus*	1534
Settee, Bentwood, Cane Seat, 11 x 15 In.	47
Settee, Chippendale Style, Mahogany, Strapwork Splats, Chairback, Arms, 40 x 51 In.	523
Settee, Ebonized, 3-Part Back, Spindles, Stenciled Gilt Designs, Arms, c.1835	3792
Settee, Empire Style, Mahogany, Parcel Gilt Mounts, Upholstered, Open Arms, 43 In.	1063
Settee, Empire Style, Mahogany, Parcel Gilt, Upholstered, Open Arms, 54 In.	469
Settee, Federal Style, Mahogany, Panel Crest Rail, Outscrolled Arms, Upholstered, 79 In.	1188
Settee, Fruitwood, Shaped Crest, Cane, Scroll Legs, 1800s, 41 x 57 In.	369
Settee, Georgian Style, Walnut, Double Back, Splats, Slip Seat, Open Arms, c.1890, 37 x 50 In.	805
Settee, Georgian, Mahogany, Double Pierced Fan Back, Upholstered, c.1800, 38 x 41 In.	688

Furniture, Pedestal, Louis XVI Style, Rosewood, Burr Amboyna, Ebonized, Gilt, c.1890, 40 In.
$3,998

Neal Auction Co.

Furniture, Pedestal, Mahogany, Carved, Griffins, Brass Lion's Head Masks, c.1890, 39 In.
$2,832

Conestoga Auction Co., Inc.

Furniture, Pie Safe, Georgia Federal, Yellow Pine, Punched Tin Panels, 1800s, 57 x 48 In.
$4,956

Brunk Auctions

Furniture, Rocker, Arts & Crafts, Oak, Mortise & Tenon, Pegged, Upholstered Seat, 40 In.
$354

Conestoga Auction Co., Inc.

Furniture, Rocker, Eames, RAR, Yellow, Molded, 26 x 25 In.
$600

Palm Beach Modern Auctions

Furniture, Rocker, Mahogany, Paper Lithograph, Scholarly Man, Bliss, England, 1890, 13 In., Child's
$608

James D. Julia Auctioneers

Furniture, Rocker, Shaker, Ladder Back, Maple, Cane Seat, Shag Rug Seat, Union Village, 44 In.
$67,260

Willis Henry Auctions, Inc.

Furniture, Rocker, Shaker, Maple, 4-Slat Back, Tape Seat, Stamped 4, c.1830, 46 In.
$2,832

Willis Henry Auctions, Inc.

Furniture, Rocker, Shaker, Maple, Tape Seat & Back, Mt. Lebanon, N.Y., c.1880, 43 In.
$472

Willis Henry Auctions, Inc.

FURNITURE

Furniture, Screen, Hardwood, Carved, Silk Needlework, Chinese, 1800s, 71 x 44 In.
$13,225

Cottone Auctions

Furniture, Secretary, Chippendale, Mahogany, Drop Front, Fitted Interior, 1700s, 88 x 42 In.
$18,880

Brunk Auctions

Furniture, Settee, Art Deco, Veneer, Satinwood Inlay, Continental, c.1910, 82 In.
$1,534

Brunk Auctions

Furniture, Settee, Gilt Trim, Stenciled, Shaped Back, Arms, New York, c.1830, 31 x 19 In.
$2,875

Cottone Auctions

Furniture, Settee, Windsor, Corner, Mixed Wood, Stenciled Fruit, Arms, c.1835, 32 In.
$900

Garth's Auctioneers & Appraisers

Furniture, Settle, L. & J.G. Stickley, Oak, Slat Back, Cushions, c.1907, 37 x 77 In.
$3,500

Rago Arts & Auction Center

Settee, Georgian, Walnut, Carved, Double Back, Upholstered Seat, 6 Legs, 51 In.	9000
Settee, Gilt Trim, Stenciled, Shaped Back, Arms, New York, c.1830, 31 x 19 In. .... *illus*	2875
Settee, Hardwood, Wooden Seat, Carved Rails, Arms, Cabriole Legs, France, 1900s, 40 x 52 In....	572
Settee, Hepplewhite, Triangular, Sloped, Black Paint, Upholstered, 63 In.	1800
Settee, Jacobean, Oak, Carved Crest Rail, 5 Panels, Open Arms, c.1790, 42 x 18 In.	373
Settee, Louis XV Style, Carved Crest, Upholstered, 75 In.	530
Settee, Louis XV Style, Mahogany, Upholstered, Carved Crest, Arms, c.1960, 47 In.	625
Settee, Louis XVI Style, Giltwood, Carved, Crossed Stretchers, Upholstered, 72 x 25 In.	890
Settee, Louis XVI Style, Walnut, Carved, Ribbon Crest, Upholstered, Arms, 37 x 48 In.	180
Settee, Louis XVI, Beech, Leather Upholstery, Arms, Canape, c.1750, 56 ½ In.	1625
Settee, Mahogany, Marquetry, Flowers, Serpentine Back, Scroll Armrests, 29 x 48 In.	120
Settee, Mahogany, Padded Back, Downswept Arms, Bulbous Legs, c.1850, 37 x 69 In.	2460
Settee, Mahogany, Rope Twist, Leaf-Carved Crest, Arms, Upholstered, c.1824, 37 x 83 In.	9375
Settee, Neoclassical Style, Fruitwood, Plume Splat, Outswept Arms, c.1850, 37 x 60 In.	492
Settee, Neoclassical Style, Pendant Swags, Apron, Reeded & Tapered Legs, 1800s, 35 x 53 In.	369
Settee, Oak, Low Paneled Back, Finials, Planked Seat, 34 x 71 In.	1230
Settee, Pine, Arrow Back, Stenciled, Painted, 35 x 80 In.	593
Settee, Rococo Revival, Carved Crest, Black Upholstery, Arms, c.1860, 40 x 68 In.	469
Settee, Sheraton, Double Back, Rush Seat, Gilt Flower Stencils, Black Ground, 31 x 38 In.	3318
Settee, Sheraton, Mahogany, Carved, Arched Back, Upholstered, Massachusetts, 57 In.	1320
Settee, Sheraton, Scroll Crest, Arms, Flower Painted Rail, Red Ground, 51 x 18 In.	6000
Settee, Sheraton, Triple Back, Carved, Painted, Cane Seat, L. Barnes, New Hampshire	8400
Settee, Triple Bootjack Back, Plank Seat, Scroll Arms, Brown Paint, Flowers, 1800s, 73 In.	224
Settee, Victorian, Walnut, Carved, Finger Molded, Medallion Back, Upholstered, 55 x 36 In.	60
Settee, W. Platner, Nickel Plated Steel, Upholstered, Knoll International, c.1966, 68 x 33 In.	2473
Settee, William & Mary Style, High Back, Turned Legs, Stretchers, Upholstered, 50 x 48 In.	470
Settee, Windsor, Bamboo-Turned Spindles, Black Paint, c.1890, 60 In.	875
Settee, Windsor, Corner, Mixed Wood, Stenciled Fruit, Arms, c.1835, 32 In. .... *illus*	900
Settee, Windsor, Molded Crest Rail, Spindle Back, Green Paint, W. Va., c.1820, 30 In.	1093
Settee, Windsor, Pine, Hickory, Curved Ends, Spindles, Turned Posts, c.1810, 34 x 76 In.	1408
Settee, Windsor, Rodback, Pennsylvania, c.1850, 77 In.	668
Settee, Windsor, Spindle Back, Continuous Arm, Scroll Knuckles, Bulbous Stretchers, 74 In.	236
Settee, Wood, Double Balloon Back, Upholstered, 34 x 16 In.	150
Settee, Wood, Spindles, Carved Back, Painted Fruit, Birds, Pennsylvania, 32 x 72 In.	178
Settle, Arts & Crafts, Vertical Splats, Armrests, Leather Cushion, 66 x 24 In.	438
Settle, Elm, High Plank Back, Scroll Arms, Board Seat, Reeded Legs, England, 57 x 64 In.	590
Settle, Even-Arm Back, Arms, Leather Cushion, 74 x 37 In.	3125
Settle, Fruitwood, Paneled Back, Upswept Arms, c.1800, 33 x 28 In., Child's	593
Settle, Half Moon Cutouts On Ends, 18th Century, 14 x 69 In.	940
Settle, Jacobean, Oak, Arched Raised Panels, Curved Arms, Cabriole Legs, c.1750, 73 x 45 In.	2950
Settle, L. & J.G. Stickley, Crib, Slatted Sides, Back, Leather Cushion, c.1915, 39 x 76 In.	4063
Settle, L. & J.G. Stickley, Oak, Slat Back, Cushions, c.1907, 37 x 77 In. .... *illus*	3500
Settle, Pine, c.1820, 32 ½ x 71 In.	770
Settle, Pine, Carved Panels, Fold-Out Bed, England, c.1780, 49 x 73 In.	533
Settle, Pine, High Back, Scalloped Sides, Lift Seat, Red Stain, New England, c.1760, 56 x 60 In.	4029
Settle, Pine, Paneled, Open Arms, c.1820, 61 x 59 ½ In.	830
Settle, Pine, Shaped Arms, Plank Seat, High Curved Back, 77 In.	4500
Settle, Softwood, Pegged Construction, 4-Panel Back, Lift-Out Seat, Arms, 51 x 61 In.	530
Settle, Windsor, Bow Back, Pine, Conforming Seat, England, 64 x 51 In.	900
Settle, Windsor, Poplar, Bamboo Turnings, Plank Seat, 19th Century, 36 x 73 In.	764
Settle, Wood, Painted, Turned Legs, c.1820, 74 x 24 In.	1017
Shelf Support, Art Deco, Nude Woman, Playing Horn, Scrolls, Metal, Gilt, 16 In., Pair	153
Shelf, Black Forest, Wood, Carved, 12 x 9 In., Pair	334
Shelf, Bowfront, Pine, Arched, Double Half Moon Ends, Paint, 1800s, 47 x 21 In.	1620
Shelf, Corner, Hanging, Multicolor, Ivory Ground, Flowers, Heart, Signed P.H., c.1940, 13 In.	59
Shelf, Curly Maple, Poplar, Shaped Sides, 8 Shelves, Jim Johnston, 20th Century, 73 x 33 In.	542
Shelf, Hanging, Black Forest, Carved Deer, c.1845, 11 x 9 In.	113
Shelf, Hanging, G. Nakashima, Black Walnut, Abstract Shape, c.1960, 93 In.	6250
Shelf, Hanging, Italianate, Carved, Blackamoor, Multicolor, Gilt, 22 ½ In., Pair	1020
Shelf, Hanging, Oak, Carved, Graduated Shelves, Continental, c.1810, 27 x 41 In. ...... *illus*	118
Shelf, Hanging, Painted, Scroll Frame, 4 Shelves, 55 x 21 In.	570
Shelf, Hanging, Pine, c.1850, 51 x 60 In.	326
Shelf, Hanging, Pine, Carved Sides & Top, 3 Shelves, 34 x 32 In.	625
Shelf, Hanging, Pine, Green Paint, c.1850, 34 x 41 In.	415
Shelf, Hanging, Pine, Overhung Top, 4 Shelves, Blue Paint, c.1900, 31 x 31 In.	316

Furniture, Shelf, Hanging, Oak, Carved, Graduated Shelves, Continental, c.1810, 27 x 41 In.
$118

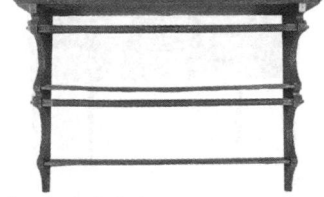

Conestoga Auction Co., Inc.

Furniture, Sideboard, Arts & Crafts, Oak, Mirror, James Phillip & Son, c.1910, 75 x 66 In.
$2,040

Skinner Auctioneers & Appraisers

Furniture, Sideboard, Burl Walnut, Carved, Marble Top, Mirror, Shelf, c.1870, 96 x 83 In.
$7,080

Brunk Auctions

TIP

Mother-of-pearl for inlays can be found at a guitar factory. You may have to sand the back to make the inlay thinner.

Furniture, Sideboard, Federal, Mahogany Veneer, Inlay, Drawers, Doors, c.1810, 42 x 68 In.
$5,100

Skinner Auctioneers & Appraisers

Furniture, Sideboard, Federal, Mahogany, Pine, Inlay, Curved Doors, 1800s, 41 x 62 In.
$885

Brunk Auctions

Furniture, Sideboard, Regency, Mahogany, Carved, Drawers, Panel Doors, c.1800s, 48 x 74 In.
$1,708

Neal Auction Co.

Furniture, Sofa, Adrian Pearsall, Walnut, Cotton Velvet, Craft Associates, Pa., 1960s, 32 x 85 In.
$1,125

Rago Arts & Auction Center

TIP

Veneered furniture should not be placed near steam radiators, open windows, or groups of potted plants. The veneer will eventually "bubble" from the moisture.

Shelf, Hanging, Plate, Oak, Scalloped Top, Open Shelves, England, 38 x 51 In.	1020
Shelf, Hanging, Softwood, Brown Paint, Scroll Sides, American, 1800s, 29 x 28 In.	588
Shelf, Hanging, Spice, Pine, 5 Apothecary Drawers, 2 Long Drawers, 4 Shelves, c.1900, 43 In.	345
Shelf, Hanging, Walnut, Carved Sides, 3 Tiers, c.1850, 32 x 30 In.	210
Shelf, Hanging, Walnut, Pointed Cornice, Drawer, Roll Lid, 1800s, 20 x 14 In.	180
Shelf, Hanging, Wood, Painted, Scalloped Border, Wavy Crest, c.1800, 20 x 12 In.	7020
Shelf, Oak, 2 Tiers, Fretwork, Carved Leaves, Stag, Openwork, c.1865, 17 ½ x 18 In.	254
Shelf, Pine, Bow Front, Arched, Double Half Moon Ends, Painted, 1800s, 47 x 21 In.	1620
Shelf, Plate, French Provincial, Fruitwood, Leaves, c.1805, 71 x 44 In.	922
Shelf, Regency Style, Mahogany, Scroll-Cut Sides, Shelves, Drawers, c.1970, 38 x 24 In.	120
Shelf, Wall, Carved Deer, Black Forest, c.1845, 11 x 9 In.	113
Shelf, Walnut, Lobed Design, Stepped, Porcelain Knob, American, 1800s, 13 x 16 In.	764
Shelf, White Paint, 6 Tiers, Cutout Base, New England, 68 x 49 In.	6000
Sideboard, Arts & Crafts, Oak, 2 Doors, Drawers, Display Shelves, Beveled Mirror, 60 x 73 In.	288
Sideboard, Arts & Crafts, Oak, Mirror, James Phillip & Son, c.1910, 75 x 66 In. *illus*	2040
Sideboard, Biorge Mogensen, Teak, 2 Banks Of Drawers, c.1965, 34 x 59 In.	1200
Sideboard, Burl Walnut, Carved, Marble Top, Mirror, Shelf, c.1870, 96 x 83 In. *illus*	7080
Sideboard, Danish Modern, Teak, Sliding Doors, Drawers, Shelves, H. Kjaern, 43 x 79 In.	615
Sideboard, Danish Modern, Teak, Sliding Doors, Recessed Pulls, Fitted, c.1960, 34 x 59 In.	615
Sideboard, Empire, Mahogany, Carved, 2 Drawers, 2 Doors, c.1840, 53 x 54 In.	296
Sideboard, Empire, Mahogany, Hidden Drawer, End Slides, c.1845, 44 x 76 x 24 In.	3500
Sideboard, Federal Style, Mahogany, Drawer, Doors, Square Tapered Legs, 40 x 48 In.	1063
Sideboard, Federal Style, Mahogany, Inlay, 3 Drawers, 6 Doors, 39 x 73 In.	590
Sideboard, Federal Style, Mahogany, Inlay, 4 Drawers, 4 Doors, 41 x 67 In.	5313
Sideboard, Federal, Cherry, 3 Drawers, 4 Doors, Square Legs, c.1810, 40 x 62 In.	1063
Sideboard, Federal, Cherry, Mahogany, Drawers, Doors, Tapered Legs, c.1810, 40 x 47 In.	5925
Sideboard, Federal, Inlay, Shaped Top, Doors, Tapered Legs, c.1815, 40 x 70 In.	4012
Sideboard, Federal, Mahogany Veneer, Inlay, Drawers, Doors, c.1810, 42 x 68 In. *illus*	5100
Sideboard, Federal, Mahogany, 3 Drawers, 4 Doors, Bowed, Reeded, c.1810, 43 x 73 In.	750
Sideboard, Federal, Mahogany, 9 Drawers, 2 Bottle Drawers, Va., c.1814, 43 x 74 In.	748
Sideboard, Federal, Mahogany, Inlay, 4 Doors, 3 Drawers, c.1815, 41 x 72 In.	4688
Sideboard, Federal, Mahogany, Inlay, Drawers, Doors, c.1790, 38 x 74 In.	3080
Sideboard, Federal, Mahogany, Inlay, Drawers, Doors, Square Legs, c.1820, 40 x 77 In.	1625
Sideboard, Federal, Mahogany, Line & Flower Inlay, Baltimore, 40 x 76 In.	10665
Sideboard, Federal, Mahogany, Pine, Inlay, Curved Doors, 1800s, 41 x 62 In. *illus*	885
Sideboard, Federal, Mahogany, Recessed Doors, Tapered Legs, c.1800, 41 x 67 In.	1230
Sideboard, Federal, Mahogany, Serpentine Inlay, Drawers, Doors, Phila., c.1805, 41 x 57 In.	8750
Sideboard, Federal, Walnut, Inlay, Drawers, Doors, Tapered Legs, c.1815, 39 x 62 In.	4484
Sideboard, Fruitwood, 2 Doors, Drawer, France, c.1860, 40 x 54 In.	469
Sideboard, G. Nakashima, Cherry, 2 Sliding Cloth Doors, Fitted Interior, c.1966, 32 x 60 In.	11800
Sideboard, G. Nelson, Walnut, 4 Drawers, Door, Herman Miller, 56 x 57 In., Pair	3510
Sideboard, George III Style, Mahogany, 3 Drawers, 60 x 22 In.	500
Sideboard, George III Style, Mahogany, Bowed Top, Tapered Legs, c.1885, 36 x 44 In.	676
Sideboard, George III Style, Mahogany, Bowed, Banded, Square Legs, 37 x 68 In.	5904
Sideboard, George III, Mahogany, Banded, Serpentine, Spade Feet, c.1785	3050
Sideboard, George III, Mahogany, Bowfront, 4 Drawers, Tapered Legs, 35 x 60 In.	2125
Sideboard, George III, Mahogany, Drawer, 2 Bottle Doors, 35 x 54 In.	5330
Sideboard, George III, Mahogany, Inlay, Bowfront, 6 Drawers, Door, c.1850, 38 x 96 ½ In.	1625
Sideboard, George IV, Mahogany, Shaped Gallery, Rope-Twist Legs, c.1825, 42 In.	2629
Sideboard, Hepplewhite Style, Mahogany, Inlay, Tambour Door, 1900s, 39 x 72 In.	708
Sideboard, Hepplewhite, Mahogany, Drawers, Doors, Serpentine Front, Mass., 40 x 75 In.	7800
Sideboard, Hepplewhite, Mahogany, Inlay, 2 Doors, 2 Cellarette Drawers, c.1890, 38 x 66 In.	418
Sideboard, Hepplewhite, Mahogany, Inlay, 3 Drawers, England, c.1790, 34 x 55 In.	474
Sideboard, Hepplewhite, Mahogany, Inlay, 5 Drawers, 37 x 52 In.	622
Sideboard, Hepplewhite, Mahogany, Inlay, 5 Drawers, Tapered Legs, England, 37 x 73 In.	6900
Sideboard, Hepplewhite, Mahogany, Inlay, Bowed, 3 Drawers, 4 Doors, c.1805, 42 x 67 In.	4800
Sideboard, Hepplewhite, Mahogany, Inlay, Serpentine Front, 4 Drawers, 2 Doors, 41 x 68 In.	2640
Sideboard, Hepplewhite, Mahogany, Serpentine, Urn Inlay, 52 x 19 In.	706
Sideboard, Hepplewhite, Mahogany, String Inlay, 5 Drawers, 3 Doors, c.1790, 41 x 73 In.	15340
Sideboard, Karl Springer, Green, Textured, 4 Flush Drawers, Flat Backboard, 36 x 72 In.	354
Sideboard, Kittinger Furniture Co., Federal Style, Mahogany, Drawer, Doors, 53 x 23 In.	780
Sideboard, Mahogany, 2 Drawers, Carved Legs, c.1865, 36 x 34 In.	280
Sideboard, Mahogany, 3 Beaded Drawers, 2 Recessed Drawers, 4 Doors, c.1835, 42 x 69 In.	625
Sideboard, Mahogany, 3 Drawers, 4 Doors, Rope-Twist Columns, c.1840, 44 x 71 In.	353
Sideboard, Mahogany, Bird's-Eye Maple Inlay, Step Back Doors, Baltimore, 44 x 68 In.	1053

Sideboard, Mahogany, Flower Inlay, Drawers, Bottle Doors, England, 36 x 82 In.	530
Sideboard, Mahogany, Marble Top, Scroll Sides, Doors, Drawers, Phila., c.1835, 41 x 60 In.	3125
Sideboard, Mahogany, Marble, Backsplash, 3 Drawers, 3 Doors, Columns, c.1835, 67 x 58 In.	560
Sideboard, Mahogany, Turned Gallery, 5 Drawers, Paw Feet, c.1830, 54 x 55 In.	3760
Sideboard, Neoclassical Style, Mahogany, Inlay, Round Ends, 9 Drawers, 34 ½ x 70 In.	1125
Sideboard, Oak, Carved Leaves, Dolphins, Shaped Skirt, Cabriole Legs, 34 x 79 In.	2000
Sideboard, Pedestal Base, Mahogany, 3 Drawers, 2 Doors, Shaped Backsplash, 46 x 73 In.	2400
Sideboard, Queen Anne, Oak, 3 Drawers, Scalloped Skirt, England, c.1790, 34 x 79 In.	6490
Sideboard, Regency, Mahogany, Bowed Top, Doors, Tapered Legs, c.1815, 36 x 66 In.	2706
Sideboard, Regency, Mahogany, Carved, Drawers, Panel Doors, c.1800s, 48 x 74 In. ....*illus*	1708
Sideboard, Risom, Walnut, 4 Drawers, Door, Raised Legs, c.1960, 32 x 54 In.	594
Sideboard, Sheraton, Mahogany, Concave Center, Doors, Drawers, Reeded, Mass., 42 x 68 In.	7200
Sideboard, Sheraton, Tiger Maple, Mahogany Inlay, Raised Legs, 43 x 72 In.	4200
Sideboard, Victorian, Mahogany, Marble Top, Carved Mirror, Doors, England, 60 x 47 In.	310
Sideboard, Victorian, Rosewood, Marble Top, Mirror, Side Shelves, Wood Carvings, 55 x 49 In.	385
Sideboard, Walnut, 3 Parts, Arches, Reeded Legs, Italy, c.1835, 39 x 71 In.	922
Silver Chest, Federal Style, Mahogany, Inlay, Drawers, Potthast Label, c.1950, 13 x 19 In.	660
Sofa & Chair, Danish Modern, Straight Upholstered Back, Seat, Tapered Legs, 1900s, 30 In.	588
Sofa Set, Risom, Upholstered Back & Seat, Square Table.	382
Sofa, Adrian Pearsall Style, Open Wood Base, Upholstered, Midcentury, 103 x 32 x 26 In.	978
Sofa, Adrian Pearsall, Walnut, Cotton Velvet, Craft Associates, Pa., 1960s, 32 x 85 In. ....*illus*	1125
Sofa, Art Deco, Burl, Ebonized, U-Shape Frame, Leather Upholstery, France, 82 In.	1770
Sofa, Bastiano, Rosewood, Brown Leather, 3 Cushions, Knoll, 83 x 30 In.	1187
Sofa, Chesterfield, Leather, Oak, Brass Studs, 1950s, 28 x 76 In.	1875
Sofa, Chippendale Style, Camelback, Hickory Chair Furniture Co., 35 x 80 In. ....*illus*	420
Sofa, Chippendale Style, Camelback, Mahogany, Shaped Arms, 1900s, 38 x 78 In.	330
Sofa, Chippendale Style, Camelback, Mahogany, Square Legs, American, 37 x 80 In.	353
Sofa, Chippendale Style, Camelback, Upholstered, Hairy Paw Feet, c.1850, 80 x 37 In.	678
Sofa, Chippendale Style, Camelback, Walnut, Curved Front, Stretcher, Upholstered, 80 In.	823
Sofa, Chippendale, Mahogany, Carved Back, Curled Arms, Spade Feet, c.1785, 36 x 90 In.	7703
Sofa, Eames, Enameled Steel, Chrome, Angled Back, Seat, Upholstered, 1960s, 34 x 73 In.	1000
Sofa, Empire, Mahogany, Shaped Rail, Ram's-Horns, S-Shape Arms, c.1830, 35 x 86 In.	1320
Sofa, Federal Style, Mahogany, Yellow Upholstery, 35 x 82 In.	830
Sofa, Federal, Carved Back Terminals, Upholstered, Arms, Paw Feet, c.1820, 72 x 35 In.	546
Sofa, Federal, Straight Crest, Scroll Arms, Upholstered, Spiral Feet, New York, 72 In.	1638
Sofa, Fiberglass, White, 3 Yellow Vinyl Cushions, 1960s, 79 x 27 In.	500
Sofa, Frank Lloyd Wright, Oak, 3 Leather Cushions, Copel and Furniture, 31 x 79 In.	546
Sofa, G. Nelson, Marshmallow, Chrome Plated, Enamel, Herman Miller, 1954, 51 In. ....*illus*	10000
Sofa, George III Style, Mahogany, Shaped Back, Curled Arms, Upholstered, 40 x 74 In.	334
Sofa, George IV, Mahogany, Shaped Crest, Dolphins, Scroll Arms, c.1815, 37 x 83 In.	1230
Sofa, Hepplewhite, Mahogany, Carved, Serpentine, Rolled Arms, Eng., c.1800, 76 In.	3540
Sofa, Hepplewhite, Mahogany, Yellow Upholstery, 79 In.	480
Sofa, Herter Bros., Renaissance Revival, Rosewood, Scroll Stiles, Steel Arms, 79 In.	11992
Sofa, Leather, Aluminum, 4-Cushion Back, Rolf Benz, Germany, 31 x 75 In.	938
Sofa, Louis XV Style, Beech, Carved, Open Arms, Cabriole Legs, 37 x 76 In. ....*illus*	2390
Sofa, Mahogany, Molded Crest, Swags, Scroll Arms, Paw Feet, c.1815, 35 In.	1793
Sofa, Mahogany, Rolled Out Arms, Upholstered, Eagle, Carved Legs, c.1830, 38 x 92 In.	365
Sofa, McCobb, 3 Back Cushions, Tan Upholstery, Directional, 87 x 31 In.	1875
Sofa, Milo Baughman, Chrome Frame, Brown Cushion, 98 x 27 In.	1000
Sofa, Milo Baughman, Metal Frame, 3 Seats, Upholstered, Thayer-Coggin, 1970s, 27 x 82 In.	1500
Sofa, Milo Baughman, Serpentine, Tan Velour Upholstery, Thayer-Coggin, 141 x 107 In.	1500
Sofa, Neoclassical, Mahogany, Carved Crest, Arms, Legs, Upholstered, 81 ½ In.	2040
Sofa, Neoclassical, Mahogany, Carved, Scroll Crest, Scroll Arms, c.1810, 92 In. ....*illus*	1169
Sofa, Neoclassical, Mahogany, Carved, Veneer, Turned Rail, Scroll Arms, c.1830, 93 In.	1722
Sofa, Neoclassical, Mahogany, Eagle's Heads, Scroll Arms, c.1815, 35 x 79 In. ....*illus*	492
Sofa, Neoclassical, Mahogany, Scroll Arms & Legs, Brass Caps, c.1810, 79 x 37 In.	3286
Sofa, Queen Anne, Walnut, Scroll Arms, Back, Carved Legs, Upholstered, England, 64 In.	3120
Sofa, Regency, Mahogany, Padded Back, Splayed Legs, Brass Feet, c.1825, 83 In.	1230
Sofa, Rosewood, Wool Upholstery, Hans Olsen, Vatne Mobler, Norway, 1960s, 76 In.	625
Sofa, Serpentine, Brown Vinyl, Tufted Seat & Back, Casters, 1900s, 73 In. ....*illus*	900
Sofa, Sheraton, Mahogany, Carved, Inlay, Arched Back, Slope Arms, Upholstered, 72 In.	1800
Sofa, Sheraton, Mahogany, Leaf Carved, Rolled Back, Shaped Arms, Upholstered, 76 In.	1920
Sofa, Sheraton, Mahogany, Scroll Arms, Reeded Legs, Upholstered, Massachusetts, 78 In.	1080
Sofa, Sheraton, Mahogany, Striped Upholstery, Carved Arms, 8 Turned Legs, 78 In.	266
Sofa, Walnut, Serpentine Back, Scroll Arms, Splayed Legs, c.1850, 15 x 34 In.	1998

Furniture, Sofa, Chippendale Style, Camelback, Hickory Chair Furniture Co., 35 x 80 In.
$420

Gray's Auctioneers LLC

Furniture, Sofa, G. Nelson, Marshmallow, Chrome Plated, Enamel, Herman Miller, 1954, 51 In.
$10,000

Los Angeles Modern Auctions (LAMA)

Furniture, Sofa, Louis XV Style, Beech, Carved, Open Arms, Cabriole Legs, 37 x 76 In.
$2,390

Neal Auction Co.

Furniture, Sofa, Neoclassical, Mahogany, Carved, Scroll Crest, Scroll Arms, c.1810, 92 In.
$1,169

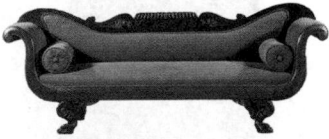

Neal Auction Co.

Furniture, Sofa, Neoclassical, Mahogany, Eagle's Heads, Scroll Arms, c.1815, 35 x 79 In.
$492

Cowan's Auctions

Furniture, Sofa, Serpentine, Brown Vinyl, Tufted Seat & Back, Casters, 1900s, 73 In.
$900

Garth's Auctioneers & Appraisers

Furniture, Stand, Corner, Marble Top, Foo Dogs, Ball & Claw Feet, Chinese, 1800s, 32 x 26 In.
$2,760

Cottone Auctions

Furniture, Stand, Magazine, Limbert, 4 Shelves, Cutouts, Branded Mark, c.1910, 37 x 20 In.
$1,500

Rago Arts & Auction Center

Sofa, Walnut, Silk Upholstery, 3 Seats, Shaped Stretcher, 1920, 34 x 78 In.	240
Sofa, Wegner, Shell, Teak Plywood, Beech, c.1948, 28 x 48 In.	5535
Sofa, William & Mary, Serpentine Back, Upholstered, Open Arms, Stretcher, c.1850, 38 x 72 In.	1408
Sofa, Wormley, Angled, Tufted Back, Cushion, White Wool Upholstery, Dunbar, 103 x 31 In.	6875
Sofa, Wormley, Mahogany, Sculpted, Upholstered, Dunbar, 1950s, 28 x 90 In.	3250
Stand, Agate Top, Openwork Brass Detail, Early 20th Century, 32 x 16 In.	410
Stand, Art Deco, Burl Walnut, 2 Drawers, 25 x 16 In.	263
Stand, Basin, Corner, Sheraton, Mahogany, Bowfront, Backsplash, S. Myer, c.1826, 38 x 24 In.	266
Stand, Basin, Federal, Mahogany, Hinged Top, Column Supports, Shelf, c.1815, 33 In.	492
Stand, Biedermeier, Mahogany, 3 Scroll Legs, Shaped Plinth, Fluted Ball Feet, c.1900, 31 In.	450
Stand, Black Forest, Carved, Opalescent Trumpet-Vase Insert, Ruffled Rim, 15 x 4 ½ In.	460
Stand, Brass, Longwy Inset Standard, Snakes, Wings, Scarabs, Pierced Border, 31 x 13 In.	2337
Stand, Carved Flowers, Vines, Marble Top, Round, c.1910, 36 x 35 ½ In., Pair.	533
Stand, Carved Wood, Marble Inset Top, Fretwork Apron, Shelf, 1800s, 32 x 17 In.	132
Stand, Cherry, Brown Paint, Drawer, Turned Legs, Pennsylvania, 1800s, 29 x 21 In.	210
Stand, Cherry, Maple, Overhung Top, Drawer, c.1810, 26 x 19 In.	237
Stand, Cherry, Pine, 2 Drawers, Turnings, Carved Turned Legs, Ohio, c.1835, 29 x 21 In.	300
Stand, Chippendale, Mahogany, Octagonal, Tripod Base, 30 x 24 In.	1188
Stand, Chippendale, Pine, Drawer, c.1800, 27 x 28 In.	296
Stand, Corner, Marble Top, Foo Dogs, Ball & Claw Feet, Chinese, 1800s, 32 x 26 In. ....*illus*	2760
Stand, Cream Laminate, 2 Drawers, 25 x 20 In., Pair.	497
Stand, Crock, Pine, Low Gallery, 2 Plank Doors, Yellow Paint, Michigan, 1900s, 32 x 49 In.	429
Stand, Crock, Softwood, Demilune, 3 Tiers, Green Paint, c.1900, 37 x 44 In.	323
Stand, Drink, G. Stickley, Oak, Copper, c.1910, 22 x 18 In.	1125
Stand, Drying, Wood, Painted, Swiveling Arms, X-Stretcher, Pedestal Base, c.1900, 14 x 48 In.	325
Stand, Empire Style, Burl, Round Marble Top, c.1920, 35 ½ In.	122
Stand, Federal, Cherry, Inlay, Drawer, Pennsylvania, 28 ½ x 19 ½ In.	533
Stand, Federal, Cherry, Maple, Drawer, Scroll Legs, 28 x 19 In.	180
Stand, Federal, Cherry, Tray Top, Drawer, c.1810, 26 x 17 In.	385
Stand, Federal, Mahogany Veneer, Leaf-Carved Base, 2 Drawers, 3 Legs, 28 x 18 In.	266
Stand, Federal, Mahogany, Shaped Top, Tripod Base, 23 x 27 In.	594
Stand, Federal, Tiger Maple, 2 Drawers, Pennsylvania, c.1815, 29 x 20 In.	1659
Stand, Fern, Chippendale Style, Mahogany, Marble Top, Reticulated Skirt, 1900s, 33 In.	120
Stand, Fern, Sheraton, Mahogany, Baluster Stem, Tripod Base, Tin-Lined Planter, 48 In.	207
Stand, Fern, Wood, Rouge Marble, Waisted Top, Prunus Branch Frieze, Hoof Feet, 35 In.	359
Stand, Folio, Cyma-Scroll Crest, Lattice Dividers, Scroll Feet, 1800s, 42 x 25 In.	2510
Stand, French Style, Painted, Faux Tortoiseshell, Shelf, Cabriole Legs, c.1925, 23 x 15 In.	270
Stand, Grain Painted, Acorn Drop Corners, 2 Drawers, Scroll Feet, c.1830, 19 x 29 In.	115
Stand, Hall, Black Forest, Carved, 2 Bears, Climbing Trees, Umbrella Ring, c.1885, 78 In.	4375
Stand, Hardwood, Marble Top, Carved Openwork, Shelf, Square Legs, 32 x 16 In.	468
Stand, Hardwood, Square Marble Top, Openwork Skirt, Chinese, 18 ½ x 16 ½ In.	468
Stand, Hepplewhite, Cherry, Blue Paint, Tapered Legs, c.1835, 29 x 24 In.	646
Stand, Hepplewhite, Cherry, Inlaid Pinwheel, Drawer, Tapered Legs, c.1800, 28 x 16 x 16 In.	984
Stand, Hepplewhite, Cherry, Square Top, Drawer, Splayed Legs, c.1800, 28 x 18 In.	123
Stand, Hepplewhite, Cherry, Walnut, Drawer, Tapered Legs, c.1815, 27 x 22 In.	323
Stand, Hepplewhite, Maple, Tiger Maple Drawer, Tapered Legs, c.1800, 29 x 19 In.	354
Stand, Hepplewhite, Mixed Wood, Drawer, England, c.1800, 28 x 30 In.	560
Stand, Hepplewhite, Walnut, Curly Walnut Top, Beaded Edge, c.1810, 28 x 18 In.	264
Stand, Incense, Elm, Round, 6 Legs, Red Lacquer, Carved Apron, Chinese, 1800s, 23 x 23 In.	150
Stand, Incense, Wood, Lacquer, Shaped Top, Pierced, Flowers, c.1850, 15 x 12 In.	1464
Stand, Louis XV, Walnut, Carved, Marble Top, 3 Drawers, 31 x 20 In., Pair.	625
Stand, Magazine, G. Stickley, Harvey Ellis, Red Decal, Paper Label, c.1905, 41 x 22 In.	1625
Stand, Magazine, G. Stickley, V-Trough, Shelf, Cutout Handles, c.1902, 31 x 33 In.	1625
Stand, Magazine, G. Stickley, Wood, 3 Open Shelves, 16 x 16 In.	1464
Stand, Magazine, Limbert, 4 Shelves, Cutouts, Branded Mark, c.1910, 37 x 20 In. ....*illus*	1500
Stand, Map, Carved, Pierced, Curved Legs, Apron, 30 x 23 In.	943
Stand, Marble, Tray Top, Flame Finial, Stretcher, Pedestal Base, 27 In.	142
Stand, Mixed Wood, 3 Drawers, Italy, c.1850, 29 x 24 In.	530
Stand, Mixed Wood, Blue Paint, Scrubbed Top, Drawer, Tapered Legs, 28 x 20 In.	470
Stand, Music, Bubinga, Walnut, Curved Base, L. Hendricks, 43 x 20 In.	1625
Stand, Music, Chippendale Style, Mahogany, c.1910, 41 x 27 In.	122
Stand, Music, Duet, Cherub Holding Shaft, Carved Leaves, Incised, Tripod Legs, 54 x 17 In.	989
Stand, Music, Forged Iron, Scrollwork, Arched Legs, Curled Feet, 59 In.	189
Stand, Music, George III, Mahogany, Blind Fretwork, Tabletop, c.1760, 14 x 22 In.	830
Stand, Music, Metal Base, Adjustable Wood Column, Painted, Lyres, Electric Light, 42 x 27 In.	242

Furniture, Stand, Portfolio, Renaissance Revival, Walnut, Adjustable, c.1890, 44 x 24 In.
$836

Neal Auction Co.

Furniture, Stand, Smoking, Butler's, Cast Iron, Painted, Match Holder, Matchbox Holder, Ashtray
$150

Victorian Casino Antiques

Furniture, Stand, Walnut, Carved, Hercules Kneeling, Rotating Top, Italy, 1800s, 22 x 13 In.
$1,434

Neal Auction Co.

Furniture, Stand, Work, Shaker, Mixed Wood, Drawer, T-Head Nails, c.1825, 27 In.
$1,062

Willis Henry Auctions, Inc.

Furniture, Stool, Grotto, Walnut, Mermaid, Parcel Gilt, Masques, Italy, c.1900, 25 x 17 In.
$738

New Orleans Auction Galleries, Inc.

Furniture, Stool, McCobb, Steel, Vinyl, Directional Mfg. Co., 1956, 16 ½ x 20 ½ In.
$625

Los Angeles Modern Auctions (LAMA)

Furniture, Stool, Piano, Italian Grotto Style, Walnut, Carved, Shell-Shape Seat, 1800s, 25 x 17 ½ In.
$1,673

Neal Auction Co.

Furniture, Stool, Piano, Mahogany, Bronze, Leather Seat & Laces, Boot-Shape Legs, 22 In.
$2,510

Neal Auction Co.

Furniture, Stool, Rococo Revival, Rosewood, Carved, Upholstered, c.1840, 17 ½ x 31 In.
$1,107

Neal Auction Co.

Furniture, Stool, Sori Yanagi, Butterfly, Rosewood, Brass, 16 x 16 ½ In.
$540

Skinner Auctioneers & Appraisers

Furniture, Storage Unit, Finn Juhl, Rosewood, Laminated, Steel, Denmark, 1960s, 82 x 105 In.
$3,500

Rago Arts & Auction Center

Furniture, Table & Stools, Frank Lloyd Wright, Henredon, c.1955, 15 x 22 In., 4 Piece
$2,125

Los Angeles Modern Auctions (LAMA)

Furniture, Table, Carved Trestle Base, Marble Top, c.1910, 23 x 27 In.
$375

Rago Arts & Auction Center

Stand, Music, Regency, Mahogany, Carved, Candle Arms, Columnar, c.1800, 47 In.	1046
Stand, Music, Victorian Style, Mahogany, Carved, Adjustable, Tripod Base, 72 x 24 In.	600
Stand, Music, Victorian, Walnut, Lyre Sides, Paw Feet, c.1880, 40 x 28 In.	486
Stand, Music, W. Esherick, Cherry, 3 Splayed Legs, Middle Triangle Shelf, 1962, 44 x 18 In.	25000
Stand, Neoclassical Style, Mahogany, Granite, Column Legs, France, c.1920, 24 x 16 In., Pair	475
Stand, Neoclassical, Mahogany, Marble Top, Ormolu Mounted, 20 In.	83
Stand, Parquetry, Star Designs, 2 Drawers, Turned Legs, c.1850, 29 x 27 In.	243
Stand, Pine, Brown Paint, Single Board, Drawer, Turned & Splayed Legs, c.1850, 31 x 23 In.	323
Stand, Plant, 4 Tiers, c.1900, 32 x 48 In.	360
Stand, Plant, Brooks, Cutout, Lower Shelf, Square Top, Rounded Corners, c.1912, 28 x 18 In.	1375
Stand, Plant, Carlo Bugatti, Painted, Inlay, Medial Shelf, Italy, 45 ½ In.	9102
Stand, Plant, French Baker Style, Scrolled, Iron, 3 Brass Pot Holders, 39 ½ In.	584
Stand, Plant, George III Style, Mahogany, Inlay, Molded Top, Square Legs, 38 x 12 In.	277
Stand, Plant, Iron, Wire, White Paint, 41 x 18 In.	594
Stand, Plant, Judy Kensley McKie, Standing Birds, Painted Wood, Glass, 1981, 34 x 18 In.	13750
Stand, Plant, Pine, 5 Tiers, New England, c.1850, 31 x 18 In.	390
Stand, Plant, Rusted Metal, Leaves, Vines, Flowers, Tripod Base, 37 x 14 In.	390
Stand, Plant, Wrought Flowers, Leaves, Snake, Tripod Base, Hoof Feet, Iron, S. Yellin, 37 In.	1287
Stand, Portfolio, Renaissance Revival, Walnut, Adjustable, c.1890, 44 x 24 In. ....*illus*	836
Stand, Queen Anne, Mahogany, Dish Top, Tripod Legs, 25 x 23 In.	250
Stand, Red Paint, Drawer, Splayed Legs, Pennsylvania, c.1845, 28 x 19 In.	237
Stand, Rohlfs, Oak, Black, Pierced, Rounded Triangle, Fitted Interior, 1902, 32 x 23 In.	5445
Stand, Rosewood, Chromed Metal Base, Cube Shape, c.1950, 21 x 18 In., Pair	875
Stand, Rosewood, Marble, Drawers, Door, Ribbon Molding, 30 x 18 In.	553
Stand, Rosewood, Octagonal Marble Top, Pierced Apron, Dragons, Hoof Feet, 36 In.	180
Stand, Shaker, Cherry, Pine, Single-Board Top, 2 Drawers, Turned Legs, 1800s, 29 x 19 In.	1528
Stand, Shaker, Maple, Tripod Base, c.1850, 25 x 24 In.	250
Stand, Shaving, Empire Style, Mahogany, Burl Veneer, 5 Drawers, 1900s, 25 x 24 In.	96
Stand, Shaving, Sheraton, Mahogany, Inlay, Swing Mirror, 5 Drawers, c.1820, 27 x 26 In.	189
Stand, Sheraton Style, Drop Leaf, Plaid Paint, Checkerboard Top, Skirt Drawer, 28 x 16 In.	295
Stand, Sheraton, Cherry, 2 Drawers, c.1830, 29 x 20 In.	395
Stand, Sheraton, Curly Maple, Cock-Beaded Drawer, Turned Legs, c.1840, 30 x 23 In.	588
Stand, Sheraton, Curly Maple, Drop Leaf, Turned Legs, c.1835, 29 x 16 In.	1028
Stand, Sheraton, Curly Maple, Turned Legs, Drawers, Shaped Backsplash, c.1870, 31 x 17 In.	1175
Stand, Sheraton, Grain Painted, Pennsylvania, c.1830, 30 x 21 In.	456
Stand, Sheraton, Mahogany, Drop Leaf, 2 Drawers, c.1830, 29 x 42 In.	326
Stand, Sheraton, Mahogany, Drop Leaf, 2 Drawers, Ring-Turned Legs, 29 x 18 In.	264
Stand, Sheraton, Pine, Drawer, Turned Legs, Red Wash, 1820-50, 30 x 20 In.	235
Stand, Sheraton, Poplar, Drawer, Ocher Grain, Pennsylvania, c.1835, 29 x 20 In.	326
Stand, Sheraton, Tiger Maple, 2 Drawers, Pennsylvania, c.1820, 28 ½ x 19 ½ In.	1067
Stand, Sheraton, Tiger Maple, Pine, Drawer, Turned Legs, New England, 28 x 18 In.	472
Stand, Sheraton, Walnut, Overhung Top, Drawer, 30 x 23 In.	119
Stand, Sheraton, Walnut, Splayed Legs, c.1850, 28 x 20 In.	188
Stand, Sheraton, White Paint, Drawer, 28 x 20 In.	360
Stand, Smoking, Butler's, Cast Iron, Painted, Match Holder, Matchbox Holder, Ashtray ......*illus*	150
Stand, Smoking, G. Stickley, Door, Fitted Interior, Signed Decal, 17 x 27 In.	6875
Stand, Urn, George III, Mahogany, Rectangular, Curved Supports, Carved Feet, 29 x 14 In.	2000
Stand, Victorian, Gilt Brass, Onyx Top, Leaf Molded, 2 Tiers, 32 In.	690
Stand, Victorian, Marble Top, Round, Hound, Stag Carved, Tripod Base, 36 In.	425
Stand, Walnut, Carved, Hercules Kneeling, Rotating Top, Italy, 1800s, 22 x 13 In. ......*illus*	1434
Stand, Walnut, Pine, Square Top, Rounded, Drawer, Splayed Legs, c.1840, 27 x 19 In.	705
Stand, Wine, George III, Mahogany, Tray Top, Candle Slide, c.1790, 26 x 13 ½ In.	1007
Stand, Wood, Painted, Serpentine Top, Figural Base, Turbaned Child, c.1900, 30 In.	1168
Stand, Wood, Serpentine Molded Top, Bacchante Support, 1800s, 37 In.	492
Stand, Work, Federal, Cherry, Red Stain, Drawer, Turned Legs, c.1815, 29 x 20 In.	266
Stand, Work, Hepplewhite, Brown Paint, Square Top, Drawer, Beaded Skirt, 30 x 16 In.	236
Stand, Work, Mahogany, Column Base, Drawer, Drop Leaves, 14 x 29 In.	150
Stand, Work, Shaker, Mixed Wood, Drawer, T-Head Nails, c.1825, 27 In. ......*illus*	1062
Stand, Work, Sheraton, Cherry, 2 Drawers, Turned Legs, Virginia, c.1850, 29 x 24 In.	374
Stand, Work, Sheraton, Walnut, 2 Drawers, Turned Legs, c.1850, 30 x 24 In.	150
Stand, Work, Softwood, Grain Painted, Plank Top, Deep Skirt, Tapered Legs, 29 x 22 In.	165
Stand, Work, Walnut, Overhung Top, Drawer, Turned Legs, c.1905, 29 x 24 In.	104
Stool Set, Bar, H. Bertoia, Steel Frame, Brown Leather Seat, 41 x 22 In., 4 Piece	1770
Stool Set, Eames, Round, Turned Standard, Herman Miller, c.1960, 15 x 13 ½ In., 3	2703

Stool, Art Deco, Wood, Inlay, Upholstered, Master Craftsmen, W. & J. Sloane, 18 x 20 In.	1287
Stool, Baroque, Oak, Carved Frieze, Column Legs, Cushion, 21 x 20 In., Pair	1000
Stool, Birch Top, Round, 3 Iron Legs, c.1950, 12 x 18 In., Pair	750
Stool, Enameled Steel, Oak, Adjustable, Toledo Metal Furniture, 1940s, 41 x 18 In.	313
Stool, Frank Gehry, Wiggle, Cardboard, Fiberboard, Signed, Easy Edges Collection, 16 x 15 In.	813
Stool, G. Nakashima, Cherry, Woven Grass Seat, 12 x 20 In.	1888
Stool, G. Stickley, Oak, Pegged, Leather, Tacks, Square Legs, 16 x 20 In.	584
Stool, George III Style, Padded Square Seat, Frieze, Cabriole Legs, Pad Feet, 17 In.	270
Stool, Grotto, Walnut, Mermaid, Parcel Gilt, Masques, Italy, c.1900, 25 x 17 In. ....*illus*	738
Stool, Jacobean Style, Oak, Elm, Hinged Top, Block & Ring Turnings, 1600s, 17 x 14 In.	1920
Stool, Joint, Spanish Brown Over Blue Paint, c.1790, 18 ½ x 12 In.	2844
Stool, Louis XIV Style, Gilt, Bulbous Legs, H-Stretcher, Leaf Feet, 18 x 19 In., Pair	1230
Stool, Mahogany, Sarcophagus Shape, Base Molding, Block Feet, c.1835, 17 x 35 In.	984
Stool, McCobb, Steel, Vinyl, Directional Mfg. Co., 1956, 16 ½ x 20 ½ In. ....*illus*	625
Stool, Mixed Wood, Tree & Snake Carved Legs, 22 ½ In.	720
Stool, Neoclassical, Figural, Shaped Cushion, Ogee Bracket Feet, c.1825, 16 x 20 x 15 In., Pair	1107
Stool, Oak Seat, Round, Tapered Cast-Iron Base, Adjustable, Victor, 30 In.	430
Stool, Oak, England, 21 x 18 ½ In.	1440
Stool, Oak, Joint, Shaped Seat, Turned Splayed Legs, Bun Feet, 1600s, 20 x 16 In.	717
Stool, Oak, Splint Seat, Green Paint, Turned Legs, c.1865, 18 x 15 In.	345
Stool, Oak, Walnut, Heart-Shape Seat, 3 Legs, 1800s, 11 x 13 In.	127
Stool, Piano, Italian Grotto Style, Walnut, Carved, Shell-Shape Seat, 1800s, 25 x 17 ½ In. ..*illus*	1673
Stool, Piano, Mahogany, Bronze, Leather Seat & Laces, Boot-Shape Legs, 22 In. ....*illus*	2510
Stool, Piano, Rococo Revival, Rosewood, Serpentine Upholstered Seat, 20 x 16 In.	375
Stool, Piano, Walnut, Carved Legs, c.1870, 9 ½ In., Child's	60
Stool, Pine, Painted, c.1855, 9 ½ x 14 In.	119
Stool, Pine, Red, Black Grain Paint, Pennsylvania, c.1845, 6 x 12 In.	178
Stool, Poplar, Painted Flowers, Splayed Legs, Green Paint, Pennsylvania, c.1865, 8 ½ x 10 In.	182
Stool, Queen Anne, Mahogany, Stretcher, Cabriole Legs, Pad Feet, c.1750, 18 x 20 In.	3240
Stool, Rattan, Round, Franco Albin, Italy, 24 x 15 In., Pair	750
Stool, Red Paint, Hinged Top, Bootjack Ends, 1800s, 17 x 15 In.	288
Stool, Rococo Revival, Rosewood, Carved, Upholstered, c.1840, 17 ½ x 31 In. ....*illus*	1107
Stool, Shoeshine, Victorian, Oak, Hinged Lift Top, c.1910, 16 x 14 ½ In.	58
Stool, Sori Yanagi, Butterfly, Rosewood, Brass, 16 x 16 ½ In. ....*illus*	540
Stool, Thomas Moser, Fruitwood, Spindle Back, Pair	938
Stool, Weaver's, Poplar, Hickory, Splint Seat, North Carolina, c.1845, 24 x 19 In.	104
Stool, Windsor, Brown Paint, 3 Splayed Legs, c.1810, 16 ½ x 13 ½ In.	547
Stool, Wood, Carved, Drum Shape, 5 Pierced Curved Legs, Fret Border, 18 In.	1020
Storage Unit, Eames, Birch, Steel, Enameled Wood, Red & Blue Panels, 1990s, 33 x 47 In.	875
Storage Unit, Finn Juhl, Rosewood, Laminated, Steel, Denmark, 1960s, 82 x 105 In. ....*illus*	3500
Storage Unit, Wormley, Mahogany, 2 Shelves, Suspended Shelf, Drexel, 1956, 40 x 52 In.	1625
Sugar Chest, Mahogany, Lift Top, Brass Side Handles, 23 x 17 In.	1298
Table & Stools, Frank Lloyd Wright, Henredon, c.1955, 15 x 22 In., 4 Piece ....*illus*	2125
Table, A. Pearsall, Walnut, Glass, Craft Associates, Wilkes Barre, Pa., 1960s, 14 x 45 ½ In.	530
Table, Altar, Elm, Blue Sponging, 3 Drawers, Chinese, 1900s, 31 x 15 In.	240
Table, Altar, Elm, Shaped Frieze, Pierced Ends, Carved Feet, Chinese, 36 x 65 In.	676
Table, Altar, Hardwood, Carved, Flared Top, Pierced Supports, c.1960, 35 x 59 In.	313
Table, Altar, Hardwood, Panel Top, Pierced Vines Frieze, Trestle, c.1815, 35 x 82 In.	4780
Table, Altar, Hardwood, Scalloped Sides, Tray Top, Square Legs, 1900s, 73 x 40 In.	590
Table, Altar, Mixed Wood, Burl Top, Carved Apron, Chinese, c.1910, 33 x 47 In.	22500
Table, Altar, Pierced Ends, Bats, Scrolling Leaves, Square Legs, Flowers, 35 x 18 In.	7380
Table, Altar, Rosewood, Banded Top, Pierced, Plank Legs, Peg Feet, c.1900, 33 x 50 In.	4428
Table, Altar, Rosewood, Mother-of-Pearl, Pierced, Flowers, 1800s, 54 x 109 In.	5904
Table, Altar, Softwood, Lacquer, Gilt, Pierced & Carved Apron, Legs, Chinese, 1700s, 44 x 65 In.	422
Table, Amboyna Wood, 2 Drawers, France, 1920s, 36 x 63 In.	1840
Table, Anglo-Indian, Rosewood, Geometric Bone Inlay, Bird-Carved Legs, 18 x 24 In.	938
Table, Art Deco, Burl, 8-Sided Top, Asymmetrical Shelves, 28 x 24 In.	188
Table, Art Deco, Ebonized, Shelf, Demilune Support, Rectangular, 1920s, 22 x 25 In., Pair	1188
Table, Art Deco, Rosewood, Ebonized, Round Medial Shelf, 1920s, 24 x 26 In.	330
Table, Art Deco, Walnut, 2 Shelves, Sloped Corners, 26 x 17 In.	88
Table, Arts & Crafts, Oak, Paneled Base, Dentil Border Top, c.1920, 33 x 34 In.	1750
Table, Baker Furniture, Mahogany, Double Pedestal, Inlay, 3 Leaves, c.1970, 46 x 126 In.	1495
Table, Baroque, Gilt, Scroll Column Pedestal, Beaded, Flowers, 39 x 23 In.	1353
Table, Baroque, Oak, Drawer, Ring-Turned Legs, Box Stretcher, c.1800, 31 x 38 In.	369
Table, Baroque, Rosewood, Ivory, Flowers, Birds, Twist Legs, X-Stretcher, 32 x 48 In.	2242

Furniture, Table, Center, Inlaid Top, Porcelain Plaques, Ormolu, c.1865, 29 x 55 In.
$3,444

New Orleans Auction Galleries, Inc.

Furniture, Table, Center, Neoclassical, Mahogany, Tilt Top, Stencil, c.1825, 31 x 42 In.
$1,599

New Orleans Auction Galleries, Inc.

Furniture, Table, Cherry, Poplar, Carved, Drawer, 2 Parts, c.1825, 48 x 95 In.
$1,046

Garth's Auctioneers & Appraisers

Furniture, Table, Coffee, LaVerne, Chinoiserie Scenes, Relief, Pedestal, 1900s, 17 x 42 In.
$4,248

Brunk Auctions

Furniture, Table, Coffee, P. Evans, Cityscape, Bird's-Eye Maple, Glass, Directional, 1970s, 48 In.
$2,625

Rago Arts & Auction Center

Furniture, Table, Console, Bob Trotman, Figural, Woman, Painted Wood, Carved, 24 x 31 In.
$10,000

Rago Arts & Auction Center

Furniture, Table, Console, Kaizo Oto, Memphis, 27 ½ x 48 In.
$1,320

Palm Beach Modern Auctions

Furniture, Table, Console, Oak, Carved, Drawer, Box Stretcher, American, c.1890, 78 x 21 In.
$2,160

Cowan's Auctions

> **TIP**
> *Don't store dining table leaves on end. They may warp. Flat under the bed is an ideal storage location.*

Table, Baroque, Walnut, Beadboard Top, Base Stretcher, Drawer, 25 x 25 ½ In.	1320
Table, Baroque, Walnut, Carved Frieze, Lyre Supports, Paw Feet, 31x 63 In.	2813
Table, Baroque, Walnut, Drawer, Carved Apron, Stretcher Base, 31 x 54 In.	1320
Table, Baroque, Walnut, Drawer, Turned Legs, 28 x 29 In.	2640
Table, Baroque, Walnut, Overhung Top, Base Stretcher, Drawer, 24 x 35 In.	3600
Table, Baroque, Walnut, Trestle Base, Drawer, Ornate Carving, Italy, 22 x 30 In.	1920
Table, Baroque, Walnut, Turned Legs, Stretcher Base, 30 x 30 In.	840
Table, Baroque, Walnut, Urn Supports, Base Stretcher, 32 x 67 In.	2813
Table, Bench, Pine, 2 Tiers, c.1860, 29 x 60 In.	406
Table, Bench, Pine, c.1845, 30 x 83 In.	889
Table, Bench, Pine, Red Wash, Pennsylvania, 29 x 65 In.	326
Table, Bentwood, Marble Top, Loop Stretcher, c.1900, 30 x 38 In.	456
Table, Biedermeier, Fruitwood, Drop Leaves, 2 Frieze Drawers, Swag, Urn Inlay, 43 x 30 In.	2178
Table, Biedermeier, Maple, Drop Leaves, Cylindrical Standard, 30 x 39 In.	750
Table, Biedermeier, Walnut, Lyre Supports, 32 x 50 In.	1500
Table, Birch, Drop Leaf, New England, c.1820, 27 x 46 ½ In.	504
Table, Black Lacquer, Elm, Stretcher Base, Demilune, Chinese, c.1900, 32 x 50 In., Pair	118
Table, Blue Green Paint, Tapered Legs, 30 x 36 In.	480
Table, Blue Paint, Drawer, Turned Legs, 28 x 32 In.	480
Table, Blue Paint, Overhung Top, Drawer, 29 x 31 In.	600
Table, Bouillotte, Mahogany, Marble Top, Brass Gallery, Drawer, Round, 28 x 28 In., Pair	500
Table, Brass, Pierced Leaf Gallery, Round Top, Triangular Base, c.1815, 28 In.	598
Table, Burl Top, Scalloped Edge, 1930s, 27 x 18 In.	45
Table, Burl Veneer, 3 Drawers, France, c.1920, 30 ½ In.	593
Table, Burl, Inlay, Drawer, Cabriole Legs, Continental, c.1860, 28 x 34 In.	863
Table, Butterfly, Maple, Drawers, Splayed, 29 x 34 In.	550
Table, Calligraphy, Teak, Early 20th Century, Chinese, 12 x 16 In.	150
Table, Card, Chippendale, Mahogany, Flip Top, Drawer, Gadrooned Apron, c.1780, 30 x 34 In.	4740
Table, Card, Chippendale, Mahogany, Overhung Top, Cabriole Legs, Rhode Island, 29 x 34 In.	9600
Table, Card, Curly & Bird's-Eye Maple, 3 Drawers, Scalloped Apron, Towel Bar, 30 x 28 In.	180
Table, Card, Federal, Mahogany, Banded, Inlay, Turned Legs, Paw Feet, 29 x 36 In.	3744
Table, Card, Federal, Mahogany, Inlaid Ovals, Foldover Top, c.1800, 28 x 18 In.	2250
Table, Card, Federal, Mahogany, Inlay, Foldover Top, 29 x 35 In.	1625
Table, Card, Federal, Mahogany, Inlay, Hinged Top, Swivel Leg, c.1820, 29 x 36 In.	805
Table, Card, Federal, Mahogany, Inlay, Shaped Foldover Top, Turned Legs, c.1810, 29 x 35 In.	750
Table, Card, Federal, Walnut, Line & Ball Inlay, c.1800, 30 x 40 In.	652
Table, Card, Federal, Wood, Inlay, Foldover Top, c.1820, 35 x 29 In.	242
Table, Card, George III Style, Mahogany, Foldover Top, Drawer, 28 x 36 In., Pair	1000
Table, Card, Hepplewhite, England, c.1790, 29 x 38 ½ In.	326
Table, Card, Hepplewhite, Mahogany, Foldover Top, Casters, c.1790, 30 x 35 In.	207
Table, Card, Hepplewhite, Mahogany, Inlay, Foldover Top, 31 x 36 In.	1020
Table, Card, Hepplewhite, Mahogany, Inlay, Foldover Top, Tapered Legs, 30 x 15 In.	1140
Table, Card, Hepplewhite, Mahogany, Oval Inlay, Foldover Top, 30 x 35 In.	1200
Table, Card, Mahogany, Demilune, Flip Top, Tapered Legs, Spade Feet, c.1810, 29 x 42 In.	235
Table, Card, Mahogany, Foldover Top, c.1835, 29 x 335 In.	260
Table, Card, Mahogany, Poplar, Shaped Top, Veneered Frieze, Reeded Legs, 1800s, 29 x 36 In.	210
Table, Card, Mahogany, Rounded, Carved, Scroll Skirt, Massachusetts, c.1830, 27 x 36 In.	1320
Table, Card, Queen Anne, Walnut, Carved, Hinged Top, 2 Drawers, Demilune, 29 x 42 In.	2040
Table, Card, Restauration, Mahogany, Foldover Top, Molded Apron, Scroll Feet, 30 x 36 In.	125
Table, Card, Sheraton, Mahogany, Bird's-Eye Maple Inlay, Foldover Top, Boston, 30 x 37 In.	660
Table, Card, Sheraton, Mahogany, Flip Top, Pennsylvania, c.1810, 30 x 36 In.	213
Table, Card, Sheraton, Mahogany, Foldover Top, Turned Legs, c.1850, 30 x 38 In.	83
Table, Card, Sheraton, Mahogany, Line Inlay, Reeded Legs, Massachusetts, c.1810, 28 x 37 In.	668
Table, Card, Sheraton, Mahogany, Shaped Foldover Top, Philadelphia, c.1825, 29 x 36 In.	390
Table, Card, Victorian, Walnut, Pullout Back Legs, Shelf, Demilune, 36 x 36 In.	158
Table, Carved Galley, Drawer, Medial Shelf, White Paint, 38 x 21 In.	720
Table, Carved Trestle Base, Marble Top, c.1910, 23 x 27 In. ....*illus*	375
Table, Carved, Marble Inset Top, Pierced Apron, Pedestal, Cabriole Legs, 37 x 18 In.	817
Table, Center, Biedermeier, Walnut Veneer, Round Matchbook Top, 3 Columns, 31 x 44 In.	3320
Table, Center, Edwardian, Satinwood, Flowers, Shaped Stretcher, c.1900, 27 In.	1195
Table, Center, Empire Style, Giltwood, Marble, Medallions, Ram's Heads, c.1900, 31 x 31 In.	7102
Table, Center, Empire Style, Mahogany, Gilt, Parquetry Top, Winged Face, 30 x 40 In.	1912
Table, Center, Empire Style, Mahogany, Sunburst Veneer, Frieze, Winged Lions, 40 x 32 In.	3198
Table, Center, French Provincial, Fruitwood, Round Corners, Scalloped Frieze, 27 x 39 In.	1168
Table, Center, French Provincial, Fruitwood, Scalloped Apron, c.1890, 30 x 52 In.	676

F

Table, Center, Fruitwood, Banded Top, Lyre Supports, Stretcher, 30 x 59 In.	553
Table, Center, Hardwood, Marble Top, Pierced Skirt, Paw Feet, Chinese, 33 x 51 In.	9775
Table, Center, Inlaid Top, Porcelain Plaques, Ormolu, c.1865, 29 x 55 In. *illus*	3444
Table, Center, Louis-Philippe, Mahogany, Reeded Urn, Paw Feet, c.1815, 39 In.	1673
Table, Center, Mahogany, Ormolu, Round Top, Star Inlay, Tapered Legs, 31 x 43 In.	1353
Table, Center, Mahogany, Round, Bulbous Chamfered Stem, Scroll Legs, c.1815, 35 In.	717
Table, Center, Napoleon III, Boulle, Ebonized, Turtle-Shape Top, Cabriole Legs, 30 x 52 In.	1722
Table, Center, Neoclassical, Mahogany, Tilt Top, Stencil, c.1825, 31 x 42 In. *illus*	1599
Table, Center, Oak, Marble Top, Scalloped Frieze, Leaves, Pad Feet, c.1815, 30 x 33 In.	1168
Table, Center, Octagonal, Needlework, Mask, Leaves, Tilt Top, Runner Feet, 1800s, 28 In.	460
Table, Center, P. Evans, Chromed Steel, Brass, Glass, Signed, 1970s, 25 x 48 x 48 In.	2250
Table, Center, Regency Style, Mahogany, Round, Starburst, Tilt Top, Splay Legs, 60 In.	3444
Table, Center, Rococo Revival, Walnut, Marble Top, Scalloped, Scrolls, c.1865, 34 In.	799
Table, Center, Rosewood, Marble Top, Ripple Frieze, Scroll Support, c.1840, 29 x 38 In.	2090
Table, Center, Rosewood, Serpentine Marble Top, Stretcher, c.1835, 28 x 44 In.	1968
Table, Center, Walnut, Oval Marble Top, Paw Feet, 30 x 41 In.	938
Table, Center, Walnut, Scroll Trestle Base, Stretchers, 1700s, 33 x 59 In.	1560
Table, Center, White Marble, Turtle Top, c.1865, 30 x 41 In.	1350
Table, Center, William IV, Rosewood, Tilt Top, Leaf Stem, c.1835, 29 x 54 In.	3107
Table, Cherry, 3-Board Overhung Top, 2 Drawers, Box Stretchers, c.1790, 30 x 32 In.	374
Table, Cherry, Extension Top, Leaves, Turned Legs, c.1900, 29 x 41 In.	150
Table, Cherry, Poplar, Carved, Drawer, 2 Parts, c.1825, 48 x 95 In. *illus*	1046
Table, Chippendale Style, Walnut, Round Piecrust Top, Cabriole Legs, 28 x 27 In.	400
Table, Chippendale, Birch, Scalloped Drop Leaves, New England, c.1780, 27 x 14 In.	385
Table, Chippendale, Cherry, Cutout Ends, Swing Legs, Drop Leaf, Virginia, c.1790, 28 x 42 In.	1035
Table, Chippendale, Cherry, Drawer, Skirt, Cabriole Legs, N. Carolina, c.1790, 29 x 44 In.	3450
Table, Chippendale, Mahogany, Demilune Cutout Skirt, c.1765, 29 x 17 In.	948
Table, Chippendale, Mahogany, Drop Leaf, Carved Skirt, Cabriole Legs, c.1780, 28 x 42 In.	944
Table, Chippendale, Mahogany, Openwork Leg Brackets, c.1750, 31 x 48 In.	1625
Table, Chippendale, Mixed Wood, Overhung, Drawer, Splayed Legs, 25 x 29 In.	130
Table, Chippendale, Walnut, Pine, Drawer, H-Stretcher, c.1780, 28 x 31 In.	207
Table, Chrome, Glass, Round, Adjustable, Half-Circle Base, Eileen Gray, 25 x 20 In., Pair	1125
Table, Chrome, Glass, Tray Top, Adjustable, Eileen Grey, c.1960, 28 x 20 In.	590
Table, Cini Boeri, Glass Top, Off-Center Steel Base, Round, Knoll, 59 In.	1000
Table, Coffee, Art Deco, Curved Wood Sides, Painted Tray Top, Leather Trim, 36 x 17 In.	94
Table, Coffee, Baker Furniture, Chinoiserie Base, Wood Top, 15 x 22 x 42 In.	240
Table, Coffee, Bamboo, Roger Capron Red Tile, Wood, Audoux-Minuet, 1960, 19 x 40 In.	430
Table, Coffee, Finn Juhl, Walnut, Asymmetrical Top, Baker Furniture, 64 x 22 In.	1188
Table, Coffee, G. Nakashima, Mingueren II, Walnut, Rosewood, 1989, 16 x 58 In.	16250
Table, Coffee, George III Style, Scalloped Top, Gilt Designs, Chinoiserie, Red Paint, 24 x 39 In.	594
Table, Coffee, Glass Top, Enameled Metal Frame, P. Piva, Italy, 1960s, 11 x 48 In.	2000
Table, Coffee, Glass Top, Marble, Chrome, R. Schmidt, Germany, 1970s, 16 x 48 In.	313
Table, Coffee, Glass Top, Oval, Aluminum Cylinder Base, Habitat, 48 x 15 In.	250
Table, Coffee, I. Noguchi, Triangular, Tinted Green Glass, Walnut Curved Arms, 16 In.	940
Table, Coffee, Karl Springer, Illuminated, Black, Textured, New York, 47 x 16 In.	1250
Table, Coffee, L. Mercer, Cantilevered, Angled Marble Column, Glass Top, Knoll, 18 x 39 In.	649
Table, Coffee, Lacquer, Goatskin, 2 Tiers, Adjustable, c.1980, 14 x 48 In.	1599
Table, Coffee, LaVerne, Chan, Round, Bronze, Pewter, Signed, Acid Etch, 1960s, 18 x 48 In.	2688 to 5300
Table, Coffee, LaVerne, Chinoiserie Scenes, Relief, Pedestal, 1900s, 17 x 42 In. *illus*	4248
Table, Coffee, Louis XVI Style, Mahogany, Marble Top, Brass Gallery, c.1900, 21 x 36 In.	1476
Table, Coffee, Louis XVI Style, Mahogany, Marble Top, Gallery, c.1900, 18 x 43 In.	922
Table, Coffee, Maple, Round Top, Tapered & Splayed Legs, 15 x 36 In.	295
Table, Coffee, McCobb, Brass Frame, Glass Top, 32 x 32 In.	1250
Table, Coffee, Mies Van Der Rohe, Barcelona, Chrome, Glass, 20th Century, 16 x 36 In.	443
Table, Coffee, Milo Baughman, Burl, Bookmatched, Thayer-Coggin, 48 x 11 In.	530
Table, Coffee, Milo Baughman, Chrome Base, Round, Inset Glass Top, 17 x 43 In.	236
Table, Coffee, Muller & Barringer, Lotus, Wood, Gilt, Lacquered, Round, Fretwork, 15 x 42 In.	308
Table, Coffee, Neoclassical Style, Mahogany, Inset Glass, Marble Border, 19 x 59 In.	430
Table, Coffee, P. Evans, Chrome, Brass Patchwork Base, Glass Top, Directional, 42 x 42 In.	1000
Table, Coffee, P. Evans, Cityscape, Bird's-Eye Maple, Glass, Directional, 1970s, 48 In. *illus*	2625
Table, Coffee, P. Evans, Skyline, Polychromed Steel, Bronze, Glass, 1966, 16 x 30 In.	20000
Table, Coffee, Roger Sprunger, Smoke Glass Top, Flared Bronze Base, Dunbar, 45 x 19 In.	1063
Table, Coffee, Round Wood Top, Cast-Iron Pineapple Base, Black Paint, c.1960, 24 x 32 In.	117
Table, Coffee, Teak, Round, J.O. Carlsson, Sweden, 1960s, 20 x 39 ½ In.	313
Table, Coffee, W. Platner, Nickel-Plated Steel, Beveled Glass Top, Knoll, c.1966, 36 In.	518

Furniture, Table, Dining, Adrian Pearsall Style, Composite, Walnut, 27 x 42 In.
$188

Rago Arts & Auction Center

F

Furniture, Table, Dining, Federal, Mahogany, Extension Mechanism, Extended 121 In.
$4,200

Skinner Auctioneers & Appraisers

Furniture, Table, Dining, Gio Ponti, Sycamore, Leaf, Italy, c.1938, 31 x 47 x 42 In.
$3,125

Rago Arts & Auction Center

Furniture, Table, Dining, P. Evans, Steel, Bronze, Glass, Directional, Signed, 1968, 82 x 43 In.
$5,625

Rago Arts & Auction Center

Furniture, Table, Dining, Richard Schultz, Redwood, Enameled Iron, Knoll, 1950s, 28 x 42 In.
$1,500

Rago Arts & Auction Center

Furniture, Table, Dining, Wormley, Rosewood, Ebonized, 2 Leaves, Dunbar, c.1960, 52 In.
$600

Skinner Auctioneers & Appraisers

Furniture, Table, Drafting, Adam Style, Mahogany, Leather Top, Drawer, Adjustable, 37 x 24 In.
$5,000

Leslie Hindman Auctioneers

Furniture, Table, Drafting, George III, Mahogany, Ratchet Mechanism, Slides, c.1790, 36 x 24 In.
$2,337

Neal Auction Co.

Table, Coffee, Widdicomb, Mahogany, Painted Bouquets, Swags, Fluted Legs, c.1940, 30 In.	270
Table, Coffee, Wood, 2-Tone, Round, 3 Brass Legs, S.J. Campbell, 1950s, 54 x 15 In.	1000
Table, Coffee, Wormley, Mahogany, Laminate Top, Shelves, Brass Stretcher, Dunbar, 48 In.	344
Table, Coffee, Wormley, Mahogany, Signed, Dunbar, 32 x 17 In.	250
Table, Coffee, Wormley, Olive Burl, Barrel Base, Round Glass Top, Dunbar, 42 x 17 In.	1125
Table, Colonial Style, Maple, Overhang, Breadboard Ends, Turned Legs, c.1960, 30 x 54 In.	530
Table, Conservatory, Empire Style, Gilt, Iron, Lyre Supports, Swan Heads, 28 x 54 In.	1315
Table, Conservatory, Marble, Gilt Metal, 3-Footed, 2 Tiers, France, c.1950, 28 x 24 In.	502
Table, Console, Art Deco, Flip Top, Walnut, Lacquer, Curved Support, 1920s, 31 x 54 In.	313
Table, Console, Art Deco, Maple, Ebonized, Brass, 3 Curved Supports, 1920, 30 x 41 In., Pair	1188
Table, Console, Baroque Carved, Mermaid Support, Faux Marble Top, Painted, 41 x 35 In.	908
Table, Console, Baroque, Parcel Gilt, Marble, Carved, Pierced, Continental, 37 x 48 In.	3750
Table, Console, Bob Trotman, Figural, Woman, Painted Wood, Carved, 24 x 31 In. ....*illus*	10000
Table, Console, Empire, Marble Top, Gilt Bronze Mounts, Stretcher Base, 33 x 34 In.	1125
Table, Console, George II, Mahogany, Shell Carved, Scroll Apron, Ireland, c.1790, 29 x 42 In.	9375
Table, Console, George III Style, Mahogany, Parquetry Inlay, Square Legs, 32 x 54 In.	598
Table, Console, George III Style, Tulipwood, Mahogany, Inlay, Reeded Legs, 30 x 38 In.	750
Table, Console, George III, Mahogany, Inlay, Demilune, c.1800, 33 x 27 In., Pair	2242
Table, Console, George IV, Ebonized, Gilt, Brass Inlay, Carved Columns, Mirror, 38 x 39 In.	2500
Table, Console, Georgian Style, Gilt, Satinwood, Demilune, 33 ½ x 63 In.	2000
Table, Console, Georgian Style, Mahogany, Inset Top, Carved, 32 x 65 In.	972
Table, Console, Georgian, Mahogany, Chippendale, Serpentine Front, c.1760, 33 x 62 In.	4200
Table, Console, Hardwood, Pierced Leaves, Cutout Scrolling Vines, 1800s, 45 x 47 In.	2749
Table, Console, Kaizo Oto, Memphis, 27 ½ x 48 In. ....*illus*	1320
Table, Console, Karl Springer, Lacquered Parchment, 1980s, 35 x 20 In.	4375
Table, Console, Louis XV Style, Walnut, Leaf Carved Frieze, Cabriole Legs, 37 x 49 In.	750
Table, Console, Louis XVI Style, Gilt, White Marble Top, Carved, K-Stretcher, 38 x 45 In.	594
Table, Console, Louis XVI, Giltwood, Marble, Pierced Frieze, Demilune, c.1800, 35 x 39 In.	1750
Table, Console, Louis XVI, Tulipwood, Parquetry, Marble, Bronze, Demilune, c.1780, 34 x 32 In.	3750
Table, Console, Neoclassical Style, Brass Gallery, Lacquer, Inverted Legs, 31 x 30 In., Pair	688
Table, Console, Oak, Carved, Drawer, Box Stretcher, American, c.1890, 78 x 21 In. ......*illus*	2160
Table, Console, Oak, Metal Grillwork, Brown Marble Top, Gilt, Floral Carving, 34 x 44 In.	604
Table, Console, Painted, Blackamoor Stem, Holding Basket, Rock Base, 34 In., Pair	2270
Table, Console, Regency, Burl, Red, Gold, Black Paint, 33 x 50 In.	375
Table, Console, Walnut, Plank Top, Drawers, Spiral Legs, H-Stretcher, Bun Feet, 51 In.	1046
Table, Console, Wormley, Mahogany, 2 Tiers, Dunbar, 28 x 48 In.	2457
Table, Console, Wrought Iron, Travertine Top, Molded Edge, Scroll Base, 34 x 48 x 19 In.	158
Table, Contemporary, Scalloped Top, Open Shelf, 1900s, 24 x 22 In., Pair	118
Table, Corner, Chippendale, Mahogany, Single Drop Leaf, Scalloped Apron, 27 x 36 In.	1200
Table, Country, Sheraton, Red Paint, c.1840, 27 x 27 In.	173
Table, Dessert, Louis XVI, Mahogany, Demilune, Marble Top, Shelf, 34 x 37 In.	2000
Table, Dinette, Piet Hein & B. Mathsson, Laminate, Metal Legs, Fritz Hansen, 40 x 29 In.	259
Table, Dining, 2 Column Pedestals, Single-Board Top, Paw Feet, c.1830, 30 x 90 In.	1845
Table, Dining, Adrian Pearsall Style, Composite, Walnut, 27 x 42 In. ....*illus*	188
Table, Dining, Black Lacquer, Drop Leaf, Round Ends, c.1950, 30 x 48 In.	875
Table, Dining, Cherry, Painted, Overhung, Square Legs, c.1800, 27 x 40 In.	1800
Table, Dining, Chippendale, Mahogany, Wavy Tilt Top, 6 Molded Round Panels, 28 x 20 In.	1560
Table, Dining, Danish Modern, Rosewood, Drop Leaf, Gateleg, c.1960, 58 x 35 In.	480
Table, Dining, Drop Leaf, Federal, Mahogany, Oval, Massachusetts, c.1780, 48 In.	1035
Table, Dining, Eames, Laminate Top, Round, Nylon Base, Herman Miller, 48 x 28 In.	188
Table, Dining, Eero Saarinen, Marble, Aluminum, Round, Pedestal Base, c.1960, 28 x 42 In.	938
Table, Dining, Eldred Wheeler, Maple, Double Pedestal, 6 Arch-Carved Legs, 30 x 42 In.	2006
Table, Dining, Federal Style, Mahogany, 30 x 67 In.	326
Table, Dining, Federal Style, Mahogany, Drop Leaf, 30 x 42 In.	444
Table, Dining, Federal, Mahogany, Drop Leaf, Turned Legs, c.1820, 31 x 48 In.	3125
Table, Dining, Federal, Mahogany, Extension Mechanism, Extended 121 In. ....*illus*	4200
Table, Dining, Frank Lloyd Wright, Allen, Fruitwood, Cassina, c.1990, 98 x 28 In.	1375
Table, Dining, Frankl, Mahogany, Cork Top, Brass, Extension, 72 x 42 In.	3042
Table, Dining, G. Nakashima, Walnut, Rosewood, 1976, 28 x 102 In.	40000
Table, Dining, G. Stickley, Split Pedestal, 4 Leaves, Red Decal, c.1907, 29 x 48 In.	2000
Table, Dining, George II Style, Mahogany, Round, Carved Legs, 3 Leaves, 30 x 96 In.	500
Table, Dining, George III, Hepplewhite, Mahogany, Tapered Legs, c.1790, 48 x 66 In.	922
Table, Dining, George III, Mahogany, Banded, Double Pedestal, 2 Leaves, 30 x 78 In.	1063
Table, Dining, George III, Mahogany, Drop Leaf, Ball & Claw Feet, c.1770, 28 x 42 In.	356
Table, Dining, Gio Ponti, Sycamore, Leaf, Italy, c.1938, 31 x 47 x 42 In. ....*illus*	3125

Table, Dining, Gran Basilisco, Wood, Radiating, Wavy Top, E. Testa, Italy, 1980s, 29 x 71 In........	11875
Table, Dining, Hepplewhite Style, Mahogany, Inlay, 30 x 40 In.	652
Table, Dining, Kittinger, Georgian Style, Mahogany, Triple Pedestal, 88 x 48 In..........................	3360
Table, Dining, Kittinger, Mahogany, Double Pedestal, Leaves, 44 x 100 In.	735
Table, Dining, L. & J.G. Stickley, Drop Legs, 5 Leaves, Branded, c.1917, 29 x 54 In.	1500
Table, Dining, L. Majorelle, Art Nouveau, Walnut, Carved Corners, 6 Leaves, c.1906, 15 Ft..........	5938
Table, Dining, Louis XVI Style, Mahogany, Pierced Ormolu, Shaped Feet, c.1900, 45 x 95 In.	2090
Table, Dining, Milo Baughman, Olive Ash Burl, 2 Leaves, Thayer-Coggin, 39 x 29 In.	1000
Table, Dining, N. Koefoed, Rosewood, V-Shape Base, Gateleg, 79 x 51 In..	2500
Table, Dining, Napoleon III, Mahogany, Gilt Bronze Rosettes, c.1900, 28 x 48 In.........................	48
Table, Dining, Oak, Tapered Square Legs, 31 x 77 In.	3198
Table, Dining, Oval Glass Top, Vertical Brass Supports, Mastercraft, 1980s, 30 x 84 In.	938
Table, Dining, P. Evans, Cityscape, Walnut, Maple Burl, Brass, Directional, 1970s, 30 x 79..........	7500
Table, Dining, P. Evans, Patchwork, Copper, Bronze, Glass, Directional, 1960s, 30 x 86 In.	9375
Table, Dining, P. Evans, Steel, Bronze, Glass, Directional, Signed, 1968, 82 x 43 In. ....*illus*	5625
Table, Dining, Parzinger, Mahogany, Line Inlay, 4 Leaves, c.1950, 94 x 41 In.	1250
Table, Dining, Pine, Black & Red Paint, Drop Leaf, Turned Legs, 1800s, 30 x 42 In.	176
Table, Dining, Queen Anne, Mahogany, Drop Leaf, c.1760, 28 x 45 In..	365
Table, Dining, Queen Anne, Mahogany, Drop Leaf, England, 28 x 48 In.	900
Table, Dining, Queen Anne, Round Top, Black Paint, 27 x 41 In.	2400
Table, Dining, Queen Anne, Walnut, Drop Leaf, Drawer, c.1750, 29 x 48 In.	1416
Table, Dining, Renaissance Style, Oak, Molded Top, Drum, Rosettes, Paw Feet, 1800s.................	1230
Table, Dining, Richard Schultz, Redwood, Enameled Iron, Knoll, 1950s, 28 x 42 In. ....*illus*	1500
Table, Dining, Shaker Style, Pine, 4-Board Top, Square Legs, Trestle Feet, 29 x 96 In...................	944
Table, Dining, Stickley Bros., Round Top, 5 Legs, 3 Leaves, c.1910, 29 x 54 In...........................	1063
Table, Dining, W. Platner, Carrara Marble, Bronze Plated Steel, Knoll, 1960, 28 x 53 In..............	400
Table, Dining, Walnut, Drop Leaf, Stretcher Base, Pennsylvania, c.1770, 29 x 72 In.....................	5214
Table, Dining, Walnut, Round, Chamfered Stem, Bracket Base, c.1850, 30 x 58 In.	2689
Table, Dining, Wormley, Rosewood, Ebonized, 2 Leaves, Dunbar, c.1960, 52 In. ....*illus*	600
Table, Dish Top, Baluster Standard, 3 Splayed Legs, New England, 1700s, 20 x 31 In.	1035
Table, Dough, Sheraton, Pine, Overhung Top, c.1855, 29 x 47 In...	178
Table, Drafting, Adam Style, Mahogany, Leather Top, Drawer, Adjustable, 37 x 24 In. ....*illus*	5000
Table, Drafting, Adjustable, Fitted Leather Drawer, England, c.1820, 28 x 38 In...........................	1888
Table, Drafting, Arts & Crafts, Oak, Steel, Leather, Adjustable, 2 Drawers, 30 x 46 In.	563
Table, Drafting, George III, Mahogany, c.1790, 30 x 36 In.	2066
Table, Drafting, George III, Mahogany, Double Folding, Drawer, c.1750, 30 x 35 In.	5938
Table, Drafting, George III, Mahogany, Ratchet Mechanism, Slides, c.1790, 36 x 24 In. ......*illus*	2337
Table, Dressing, Baroque, Oak, Turned Legs & Stretcher, Ball Feet, c.1685, 30 x 34 In.................	885
Table, Dressing, Chippendale, Mixed Wood, 2 Side Drawers, Curved Skirt, c.1790, 28 x 37 In......	7475
Table, Dressing, Chippendale, Oak, Inlaid, Shaped Skirt, Square Legs, c.1790, 28 x 31 In...........	767
Table, Dressing, Chippendale, Walnut, Drawers, Columns, Carved Legs, c.1770, 29 x 33 In.	10665
Table, Dressing, George I, Pine, Scalloped Skirt, Turned Legs, X-Stretcher, c.1725, 27 x 31 In.	4029
Table, Dressing, George III, Mahogany, Arched Apron, Chamfered Legs, 1700s, 28 In..................	359
Table, Dressing, George III, Mahogany, Mirror Drawer, 4 Drawers, 2 Doors, 30 x 37 In.	750
Table, Dressing, George III, Satinwood, Hinged, Divided Top, 8 Drawers, Kneehole, 33 x 29 In....	2000
Table, Dressing, Mahogany, 2 Drawers, Flower Mount, Mirror, Column Legs, 31 x 27 In.	5900
Table, Dressing, Mahogany, Curule Base, Paw Feet, Stretcher, c.1820, 35 x 40 In.........................	5412
Table, Dressing, Mahogany, Mirror, Drawer, Shelf, Paw Feet, Carved, N.Y., c.1860, 29 x 20 In.	1200
Table, Dressing, Marquetry Inlay, c.1820, 30 x 24 In.	182
Table, Dressing, Neoclassical, Mahogany, Drawers, Mirror, Scroll Supports, c.1830, 61 x 35 In. ..	600
Table, Dressing, Neoclassical, Walnut, Swan Supports, c.1850, 76 x 38 In.	1560
Table, Dressing, Pine, Painted, 2 Drawers, Setback Shelf, New England, c.1830, 39 x 41 In.	1800
Table, Dressing, Pine, Yellow Paint, Fruit, Shaped Backsplash, c.1830, 37 x 36 In.	499
Table, Dressing, Queen Anne Style, Walnut, Inlay, Shaped Skirt, 33 x 37 In................................	354
Table, Dressing, Queen Anne, Mahogany, Brass Pulls, 1700s, 33 x 20 In. ....*illus*	20060
Table, Dressing, Queen Anne, Oak, 3 Drawers, Kneehole, 29 x 30 In.	1125
Table, Dressing, Queen Anne, Oak, 3 Drawers, Shaped Apron, England, 28 x 33 In......................	1020
Table, Dressing, Queen Anne, Walnut, 4 Drawers, Spanish Feet, Phila., c.1750, 31 x 34 In..........	7110
Table, Dressing, Rococo, Rosewood, Cartouche Mirror, Marble Top, c.1850, 61 In......................	1315
Table, Dressing, Sheraton, Pine, Drawers, Backsplash, Stencil, Painted, c.1825, 38 x 30 In..........	1007
Table, Dressing, Sheraton, Yellow Paint, Carved, Backsplash, 3 Drawers, c.1830, 38 x 33 In.........	710
Table, Dressing, William & Mary Style, Marble Inset, Ball Turned Legs, c.1885, 29 In..................	1003
Table, Dressing, William & Mary, Oak, Turned Legs, Box Stretcher, 1700s, 28 x 30 In....................	1003
Table, Dressing, Wood, Carved, 3-Part Mirror, Drawers, Cabriole Legs, 55 x 43 In........................	600
Table, Dressing, Yellow, Fruit Stencil, Scroll Backsplash, Drawer, Maine, c.1830, 34 x 31 In.	499

Furniture, Table, Dressing, Queen Anne, Mahogany, Brass Pulls, 1700s, 33 x 20 In.
$20,060

Brunk Auctions

Furniture, Table, Drop Leaf, George IV, Mahogany, Rosewood, c.1825, 29 x 47 In.
$1,845

Neal Auction Co.

Furniture, Table, Drum, Regency, Mahogany, Tooled Leather, Splayed Legs, 1800s, 31 x 41 In.
$3,900

Skinner Auctioneers & Appraisers

Furniture, Table, Frank Lloyd Wright, Usonian, Douglas Fir Plywood, 1940s, 29 x 36 In.
$4,062

Rago Arts & Auction Center

Furniture, Table, Game, Federal, Mahogany, Flip Top, Rope-Turned Legs, c.1810, 29 ½ x 38 In.
$1,554

Neal Auction Co.

Furniture, Table, Game, George III, Mahogany, Inlay, Hinged, Leather, Drawer, c.1810, 20 x 20 In.
$2,500

Leslie Hindman Auctioneers

Furniture, Table, Library, Lifetime, Drawer, Stretcher, Paine Furniture, 29 x 36 x 24 In.
$670

Treadway Toomey Galleries

Furniture, Table, Library, Regency Style, Mahogany, Hickory Chair Furniture Co., 27 x 30 In.
$420

Gray's Auctioneers LLC

Table, Drink, Stickley Bros., Copper Top, Round, Arched Apron, Tapered Legs, 18 x 28 In.	1375
Table, Drop Leaf, 2 Drawers, Turned Legs, c.1845, 29 x 21 In.	153
Table, Drop Leaf, Chippendale, Mahogany, Apron, Cabriole Legs, Mass., c.1760, 42 x 15 In.	3120
Table, Drop Leaf, Chippendale, Mahogany, Philadelphia, c.1780, 28 x 56 In.	1375
Table, Drop Leaf, Chippendale, Mahogany, Shaped Apron, Cabriole Legs, 28 x 44 In.	469
Table, Drop Leaf, Chippendale, Mahogany, Square Sides, c.1780, 28 x 36 In.	178
Table, Drop Leaf, Chippendale, Square Legs, c.1780, 28 x 43 x 46 In.	147
Table, Drop Leaf, Chippendale, Walnut, Ball & Claw Feet, Pa., c.1775, 28 x 47 In.	474
Table, Drop Leaf, Chippendale, Walnut, Cabriole Legs, 28 x 48 In.	1140
Table, Drop Leaf, Duncan Phyfe, Mahogany, Drawer, 29 x 25 In.	1298
Table, Drop Leaf, Empire, Mahogany, Scroll Feet, 1800s, 39 x 20 In.	144
Table, Drop Leaf, Federal, Mahogany, Drawer, Saber Legs, c.1800, 29 x 44 x 22 In.	1314
Table, Drop Leaf, Federal, Mahogany, Pine, Drawer, Spiral-Carved Legs, 29 x 25 In.	472
Table, Drop Leaf, Federal, Maple, Bird's-Eye Maple, Reeded Legs, c.1830, 29 x 42 In.	764
Table, Drop Leaf, Gateleg, Turned, 12-In. Leaves, 1700s, 11 x 22 x 28 In.	374
Table, Drop Leaf, George II, Mahogany, Gateleg, Rounded Leaves, c.1765, 28 x 34 In.	406
Table, Drop Leaf, George II, Mahogany, Oval, c.1769, 28 x 13 In.	948
Table, Drop Leaf, George II, Mixed Wood, Tapered Legs, c.1790, 29 x 48 In.	767
Table, Drop Leaf, George III Style, Mahogany, Round, 28 ½ x 47 In.	1500
Table, Drop Leaf, George III, Mahogany, Gateleg, Rectangular Leaves, 28 x 32 In.	375
Table, Drop Leaf, George IV, Mahogany, Rosewood, c.1825, 29 x 47 In. ....*illus*	1845
Table, Drop Leaf, Handkerchief, Queen Anne, Fruitwood, Pad Feet, England, 28 x 26 In.	720
Table, Drop Leaf, Harvest, Pine, Maple, Turned Legs, Casters, c.1815, 29 x 72 In.	4500
Table, Drop Leaf, Hepplewhite Style, Mahogany, 3 Parts, Swing Leg, c.1935, 30 x 72 In.	922
Table, Drop Leaf, Hepplewhite Style, Mahogany, Inlay, Drawer, 27 x 15 In., Pair	770
Table, Drop Leaf, Hepplewhite Style, Mahogany, Satinwood Banding, Drawer, 28 x 26 In.	130
Table, Drop Leaf, Hepplewhite, Blue Paint, New England, 27 x 36 In.	840
Table, Drop Leaf, Hepplewhite, Cherry, Shaped Leaves, Tapered Legs, c.1805, 40 x 35 In.	264
Table, Drop Leaf, Hepplewhite, Walnut, Leaves, 6 Tapered Legs, 1800s, 30 x 53 In.	180
Table, Drop Leaf, Hunt, Mahogany, Demilune, Square Legs, Ireland, 29 x 82 In.	1800
Table, Drop Leaf, Mahogany, Carved, Brass, 2 Drawers, New York, c.1865, 18 x 17 In.	540
Table, Drop Leaf, Mahogany, Turned Leaf-Carved Legs, c.1835, 28 x 80 In.	1845
Table, Drop Leaf, Mahogany, Turned Legs, Brass Casters, c.1800, 29 x 47 In.	153
Table, Drop Leaf, Maple, Frieze Drawer, Splayed Legs, c.1860, 30 x 20 In.	2125
Table, Drop Leaf, Maple, Scrubbed Top, 27 x 44 In.	210
Table, Drop Leaf, Oak, Gateleg, Oval Leaves, Ring-Turned Legs, Box Stretcher, 29 x 72 In.	3444
Table, Drop Leaf, Oval Leaves, Drawer, Splayed Reeded Legs, c.1865, 30 x 24 In.	344
Table, Drop Leaf, Oval Leaves, Gateleg, England, c.1850, 26 x 41 In.	438
Table, Drop Leaf, Pine, Red Paint, New England, c.1820, 30 x 65 In.	1375
Table, Drop Leaf, Pine, Turned Leg, c.1845, 5 x 23 In.	115
Table, Drop Leaf, Queen Anne Style, Gateleg, Pad Feet, 1800s, 28 x 36 In.	300
Table, Drop Leaf, Queen Anne Style, Mahogany, Demilune Leaves, Tapered Legs, 1800s, 29 In.	360
Table, Drop Leaf, Queen Anne, Curly Maple, Pine, Cabriole Legs, Pad Feet, 1700s, 27 x 39 In.	588
Table, Drop Leaf, Queen Anne, Fruitwood, 6 Square Legs, 30 x 30 In.	570
Table, Drop Leaf, Queen Anne, Mahogany, 6 Legs, Round Ends, Pad Feet, 28 x 48 In.	472
Table, Drop Leaf, Queen Anne, Mahogany, Drawer, England, 28 x 27 In.	1200
Table, Drop Leaf, Queen Anne, Mahogany, Figured Top, Paw Feet, 1700s, 28 x 19 In.	649
Table, Drop Leaf, Queen Anne, Mahogany, Leaves, Turned Legs, Pad Feet, 1700s, 28 x 19 In.	176
Table, Drop Leaf, Queen Anne, Mahogany, Pad Feet, England, 28 x 48 In.	660
Table, Drop Leaf, Queen Anne, Mahogany, Shaped Ends, Pad Feet, 1700s, 28 x 43 In.	944
Table, Drop Leaf, Queen Anne, Maple, New England, c.1760, 28 x 42 In.	1778
Table, Drop Leaf, Queen Anne, Maple, Oval Leaves, c.1770, 27 x 44 In.	326
Table, Drop Leaf, Queen Anne, Maple, Rolled Apron, Cabriole Legs, c.1750, 24 x 43 x 41 In.	960
Table, Drop Leaf, Queen Anne, Maple, Scalloped Apron, Raised Cabriole Legs, 27 x 45 In.	375
Table, Drop Leaf, Queen Anne, Oak, Gateleg, Oval, England, 29 x 45 In.	649
Table, Drop Leaf, Queen Anne, Walnut, c.1760, 27 x 44 In.	360
Table, Drop Leaf, Queen Anne, Walnut, Cabriole Legs, Pennsylvania, 43 In.	960
Table, Drop Leaf, Queen Anne, Walnut, Scalloped, New England, c.1770, 27 x 15 In.	474
Table, Drop Leaf, Regency Style, Mahogany, Burl, 3 Drawers, Trestle Legs, 31 x 59 In.	875
Table, Drop Leaf, Regency, Mahogany, 2 Drawers, 28 x 34 In.	900
Table, Drop Leaf, Regency, Mahogany, Trestle Base, 2 Drawers, England, 30 x 37 In.	480
Table, Drop Leaf, Regency, Mahogany, Trestle, Outswept Legs, c.1815, 29 x 35 In.	1793
Table, Drop Leaf, Sheraton, 2 Drawers, Rope-Turned Legs, 28 ½ In.	384
Table, Drop Leaf, Sheraton, Cherry, 2 Drawers, c.1840, 21 x 39 In.	385
Table, Drop Leaf, Sheraton, Cherry, Drawer, Pennsylvania, 29 x 21 In.	59

Table, Drop Leaf, Sheraton, Cherry, Turned Legs, 42 x 21 In.	120
Table, Drop Leaf, Sheraton, Curly Maple, 2 Drawers, Pennsylvania, c.1830, 29 x 26 In.	593
Table, Drop Leaf, Sheraton, Gateleg, Turned Legs, Casters, 29 x 61 In.	288
Table, Drop Leaf, Sheraton, Mahogany, 2 Drawers, Turned Carved Legs, c.1815, 26 x 19 In.	325
Table, Drop Leaf, Sheraton, Mahogany, Turned Legs, 29 x 48 In.	118
Table, Drop Leaf, Sheraton, Robin's-Egg Blue Paint, 29 x 42 In.	600
Table, Drop Leaf, Sheraton, Walnut, 6 Turned Legs, 1800s, 31 x 44 In.	118 to 136
Table, Drop Leaf, Victorian, Walnut, Carved Stretcher, Sides, c.1890, 29 x 30 In.	207
Table, Drop Leaf, Victorian, Walnut, D-Shape Ends, Drawer, Fluted Legs, 29 x 41 In.	108
Table, Drop Leaf, Walnut, Drawer, Cabriole Legs, 19 x 28 In.	57
Table, Drop Leaf, Walnut, Drawer, Spiral Fluted Legs, 29 x 40 In.	180
Table, Drop Leaf, William & Mary, Elm, Gateleg, Drawer, 28 x 41 In.	1080
Table, Drop Leaf, William & Mary, Oak, Drawer, Gateleg, England, 29 x 35 In.	1140
Table, Drop Leaf, William & Mary, Walnut, Drawer, Spanish Feet, 28 x 42 In.	780
Table, Drop Leaf, William & Mary, Walnut, Oval Ends, Drawer, Gateleg, 28 x 48 In.	13200
Table, Drum, Regency, Mahogany, Tooled Leather, Splayed Legs, 1800s, 31 x 41 In. ....*illus*	3900
Table, Drum, Wood, Painted, Glass Top, Tin, Rope, Royal Arms Of Great Britain, 16 x 30 In.	338
Table, Dunbar, Dining, Burl Olive Wood Veneer, Triangular Legs, 66 x 42 In.	719
Table, Elm, Black Lacquer, Chinese, 16 x 37 x 65 In.	120
Table, Empire Style, Mahogany, Gilt Mask Mounts, Round Top, Medial Shelf, 20 x 15 In., Pair...	438
Table, Empire Style, Mahogany, Gilt Metal Mounts, Round, 3-Part Base, 19 x 33 In.	1000
Table, Empire Style, Mahogany, Gilt, Round Marble Top, Column Legs, 28 x 24 In.	418
Table, Empire Style, Mahogany, Round Marble Top, Ormolu Maidens, c.1900, 28 x 24 In.	1722
Table, Empire Style, Mahogany, Round, Carved, 3 Paw Feet, 29 x 29 In.	259
Table, Empire, Kingwood, Fruitwood, Round Malachite Top, 3-Part Base, 16 In., Pair	1107
Table, Empire, Mahogany, Carved Apron, Reeded Legs, Lion's Head & Scroll Feet, 32 x 24 In.	294
Table, Empire, Mahogany, Scroll Carved Standard, Drawer, Paw Feet, 40 x 26 ½ In.	249
Table, Enameled Metal, Round Reverse-Painted Glass Top, Chrome, Howell, 1930s, 18 x 13 In...	250
Table, Federal Style, Mahogany, Scalloped Top, Tripod Base, 26 x 20 In.	813
Table, Federal Style, Tiger Maple, Oval Top, Square Legs, 1700s, 29 x 37 In.	472
Table, Federal, Mahogany, 2 Drawers, Leaf-Carved Tapered & Reeded Legs, c.1820, 28 x 19 In....	938
Table, Federal, Mahogany, 2 Parts, Round Corners, Tapered Legs, Ball Feet, c.1800, 28 x 82 In...	1830
Table, Federal, Mahogany, Barber Pole Inlay, Demilune, c.1800, 29 x 32 In., Pair	395
Table, Federal, Mahogany, Demilune, String & Flower Inlay, Foldover Top, 29 x 36 In.	3438
Table, Federal, Mahogany, Inlay, Foldover Top, Reeded Legs, 28 x 36 In.	530
Table, Federal, Mahogany, Maple, Demilune, Inlay, Foldover, Square Legs, c.1890, 29 x 33 In.....	1875
Table, Federal, Maple, Pine, Rectangular, Tapered Legs, H-Stretcher, c.1815, 27 x 37 In.	440
Table, Federal, Walnut, 2-Board Top, Drawer, Virginia, c.1820, 30 x 27 In.	575
Table, Federal, Walnut, Tapered Legs, North Carolina, c.1800, 30 x 30 In.	259
Table, Flame Mahogany, Cylindrical Pedestal, c.1830, 25 x 36 In.	1375
Table, Fornasetti, Cubo, Metal, Painted Faux Malachite, Glass Top, 1950s, 20 x 20 In.	8550
Table, Frank Lloyd Wright, Usonian, Douglas Fir Plywood, 1940s, 29 x 36 In. ....*illus*	4062
Table, Free-Form Glass Top, Ebonized Wood Base, 16 x 50 In.	293
Table, French Style, Veneer Inlay, Brass Gallery, Kidney Shape, Shelf, Drawer, 31 x 25 In.	247
Table, Fruitwood, Glazed Ceramic Base, Round Top, c.1950, 22 x 24 In.	563
Table, Fruitwood, Scroll Frieze, Cabriole Legs, Hoof Feet, c.1815, 30 x 78 In.	1722
Table, G. Nakashima, Minguren II, Walnut, Rosewood, Rough Hewn Design, 1987, 21 x 25 In..	15000
Table, G. Nakashima, Walnut, Florence Knoll, 22 x 32 In.	1875
Table, G. Stickley, Cut Corner, Drop Leaf, Gateleg, 40 x 42 In.	8125
Table, G. Stickley, Leather Top, Trumpeted X-Stretcher, 37 x 29 In.	1625
Table, G. Stickley, Oak, Trestle, Shelf, Branded Mark, Paper Label, c.1912, 38 x 29 In.	1625
Table, G. Stickley, Round X-Stretcher, Signed, 24 x 22 In.	4375
Table, Galle, Marquetry Inlay, Landscape, Wisteria, Top, 2 Tiers, c.1900, 31 In.	2250
Table, Game, Chippendale, Mahogany, Flip Top, Leaf Carved, England, 29 x 37 In.	1020
Table, Game, Federal, Inlay, Foldover, Demilune, Flower Frieze Ovals, c.1800, 29 x 38 In.	563
Table, Game, Federal, Mahogany, Birch, Inlay, Flip Top, 29 x 37 In.	938
Table, Game, Federal, Mahogany, Flip Top, Reeded Edge & Legs, c.1815, 30 x 36 In.	793
Table, Game, Federal, Mahogany, Flip Top, Reeded, Button Feet, c.1815, 30 x 36 In.	670
Table, Game, Federal, Mahogany, Flip Top, Rope-Turned Legs, c.1810, 29 ½ x 38 In. ....*illus*	1554
Table, Game, Federal, Mahogany, Inlay, Serpentine Flip Top, c.1810, 29 x 36 In.	1265
Table, Game, Federal, Mahogany, Maple, Flip Top, Brass Edge, c.1815, 29 x 36 In.	2187
Table, Game, Federal, Mahogany, Shaped Top, Reeded Legs, c.1815, 29 x 36 In.	657
Table, Game, Federal, Mahogany, Shaped Top, Reeded, Rope-Twist Legs, c.1815, 30 In.	837
Table, Game, Federal, Mahogany, Shaped Top, Reeded, Turned Legs, c.1810, 29 x 35 In.	885
Table, Game, George I, Walnut, Demilune, Foldover Top, Turned Legs, 1700s, 29 x 32 In.	860

TIP

To remove the musty smell from old furniture drawers, fill a small plastic container with white vinegar, seal the container with its lid, then punch a few holes in the lid. Leave the container in the closed drawer overnight or longer to absorb odors.

F

Furniture, Table, Neoclassical Style, Iron, Marble, Carved, Animals, Italy, c.1890, 27 In.
$600

Skinner Auctioneers & Appraisers

Furniture, Table, P. Evans, Mixed Metals, Nailheads, Slate Top, Casters, 21 x 29 ½ In.
$7,800

Palm Beach Modern Auctions

Furniture, Table, P. Evans, Polychrome, Gilt Steel, Wood, Slate, 1962, 18 ½ x 30 In.
$10,000

Rago Arts & Auction Center

FURNITURE

Furniture, Table, Pembroke, Neoclassical, Mahogany, Bird's-Eye Maple, c.1840, 29 x 42 In.
$1,464

Neal Auction Co.

Furniture, Table, Pier, Neoclassical, Mahogany, Marble Top, Mirror, 1815-20, 43 x 20 In.
$9,600

Skinner Auctioneers & Appraisers

Furniture, Table, Pier, Neoclassical, Mahogany, Marble Top, Mirrored Back, c.1810, 36 x 40 In.
$1,586

Neal Auction Co.

Furniture, Table, Pier, Queen Anne Style, Mahogany, Marble, Drawer, England, 1800s, 31 x 50 In.
$4,012

Brunk Auctions

Furniture, Table, Regency Style, Pedestal, Leather Top, Chamfered, c.1910, 28 x 24 In.
$250

Rago Arts & Auction Center

Furniture, Table, Sewing, Federal, Maple, Mahogany Inlay, Bag Drawer, c.1810, 28 x 18 In.
$3,900

Skinner Auctioneers & Appraisers

Furniture, Table, Sewing, Shaker, Sisters, Walnut, Inset Maple Yardstick, c.1870, 26 x 39 In.
$1,239

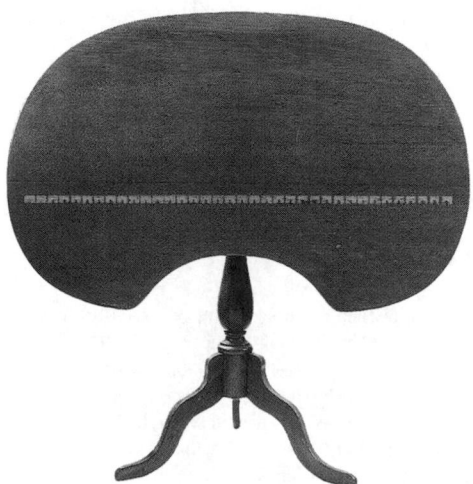

Willis Henry Auctions, Inc.

Table, Game, George II Style, Flip Top, 28 x 32 In.	500
Table, Game, George II, Mahogany, Drawer, Scroll Legs, 30 x 31 In.	1440
Table, Game, George II, Walnut, Flip Top, Shell-Carved Cabriole Legs, 1700s, 29 x 33 In.	2500
Table, Game, George III, Flip Top, Fluted Legs, 29 x 35 ½ In.	237
Table, Game, George III, Mahogany, Drawer, Chamfered Tapered Legs, c.1800, 29 x 35 In.	799
Table, Game, George III, Mahogany, Hinged, Fan Inlay, Square Legs, 29 ½ x 36 In.	708
Table, Game, George III, Mahogany, Inlay, Hinged, Leather, Drawer, c.1810, 20 x 20 In. .....*illus*	2500
Table, Game, George III, Rosewood, Inlaid, Banded, Demilune, Square Legs, 30 In.	1076
Table, Game, Hepplewhite, Mahogany, Demilune, Flip Top, England, c.1820, 28 x 36 In.	1416
Table, Game, Hepplewhite, Mahogany, Flip Top, 36 x 29 In., Pair	1029
Table, Game, Hepplewhite, Mahogany, Inlay, Swivel Top, 34 x 17 In.	170
Table, Game, LaVerne, Etruscan, Wood, Etched Bronze, Round, 48 x 24 In.	9075
Table, Game, Mahogany, Bronze, Flip Swivel Top, Columnar, c.1815, 30 x 36 In.	3346
Table, Game, Mahogany, Demilune, Flip Top, Square Legs, 1800s, 30 x 43 In.	2196
Table, Game, Mahogany, Flip Top, Leaf-Carved Supports, New York, c.1805, 30 x 36 In.	5000
Table, Game, Mahogany, Inlaid, Serpentine, Flip Top, Eagles, Flowers, 30 x 36 In.	1098
Table, Game, Mahogany, Round, Gilt, Marble Top, Gameboard, Hexagonal Stem, 29 x 36 In.	4780
Table, Game, Neoclassical, Satinwood, Inlaid, Bowfront, Flowers, 1700s, 28 x 35 In.	600
Table, Game, Queen Anne, Mahogany, Triple Top, 30 x 33 In.	1800
Table, Game, Regency, Mahogany, Flip Top, Vase Stem, c.1815, 29 x 35 In.	598
Table, Game, Serpentine Flip Top, Spiral Reeded Legs, c.1815, 29 x 35 In.	2629
Table, Game, Sheraton, Mahogany, Flip Top, Philadelphia, c.1815, 30 x 36 In.	356
Table, Game, Square Top, Inlaid Checkerboard, Backgammon, X-Stretcher, 29 x 34 In.	240
Table, George II, Oak, 3 Drawers, Arched Apron, Raised Cabriole Legs, 27 x 32 In.	938
Table, George II, Walnut, Drawer, Carved Legs, 27 x 29 In.	2125
Table, George III Style, Mahogany, 3 Drawers, 30 x 36 In.	500
Table, George III Style, Mahogany, Banding, Vase Pedestal, c.1890, 28 x 54 In.	418
Table, George III Style, Mahogany, Blind Fret-Carved Frieze, Square Legs, 33 x 72 In.	2000
Table, George III Style, Mahogany, Drawer, Fitted Backsplash, Writing Surface, 36 x 43 In.	563
Table, George III Style, Mahogany, Gallery, Slide-Out Tray, 28 x 29 In.	344
Table, George III, Mahogany, 2 Drawers, Square Legs, c.1790, 29 x 30 In.	1750
Table, George III, Mahogany, Banded, 28 ½ x 54 In.	530
Table, George III, Mahogany, Bowed Front, Fluted Tapered Legs, c.1800, 21 x 33 In.	300
Table, George III, Mahogany, c.1800, 30 ½ x 35 ½ In.	215
Table, George III, Mahogany, Drawer, Bracket Legs, 30 x 33 In.	530
Table, George III, Mahogany, Pierced Lattice Gallery, Frieze, Legs, c.1780, 29 x 29 In.	5000
Table, George III, Mahogany, Round, 2 Leaves, Triple Pedestal, 29 x 80 In.	2813
Table, George III, Mahogany, Round, Baluster Pedestal, 27 x 39 In.	702
Table, George III, Satinwood, Mahogany Bands, 8-Sided, 4 Drawers, Square Legs, 29 x 43 In.	1750
Table, George III, Satinwood, Painted Cherubs, Garlands, Drawer, Square Legs, 28 x 33 In.	4375
Table, Giltwood, White Marble Top, Round, 1960s, 20 x 42 In.	313
Table, Glass Top, Round, Lucite Base, Signed Mikhail Laznikou, 1990, 17 ½ x 4 In.	1112
Table, Glass, Chrome, 2 Tiers, Shaped Legs, Curved Stretcher, Ball Feet, Chapman, 18 x 41 In.	350
Table, Gothic Revival Style, Box Base, Carved, c.1965, 16 ½ x 60 In.	826
Table, Gothic Revival, Rosewood, Marble Top, Ripple Molded, Cluster Columns, c.1845, 29 In.	5975
Table, Grain Paint, Stenciled, Scroll Back, 2 Drawers, New England, c.1825, 35 x 34 In.	750
Table, Grain Painted, 2 Tiers, Spool-Carved Legs, New England, 31 x 42 In.	1080
Table, Grain Painted, c.1850, 29 x 36 In.	425
Table, Gueridon, Gothic Revival, Mixed Wood, 8-Sided, Acorn, Flower, Leaf Carved, 27 x 19 In.	1375
Table, Hall, Victorian, Oak, Round Tapered Legs, 32 x 99 In.	2000
Table, Hardwood, Banded Top, Fret Pierced, Square Legs, Carved Feet, 14 x 42 In.	799
Table, Hardwood, Burl Panel Inset, Fretwork, Spiraling Feet, 1900s, 15 x 29 In.	553
Table, Hardwood, Carved, Apron, Pierced Brackets, Vines, Shelf, Chinese, 32 x 16 In.	75
Table, Hardwood, Carved, Scroll Openwork Skirt, Chinese, 1800s, 11 x 31 In.	530
Table, Harvest, Cherry, Plank Top, Square Skirt, Tapered Legs, c.1860, 39 x 37 In.	497
Table, Harvest, French Provincial, Cherry, Hinge Top, Shaped Legs, c.1850, 30 x 64 In.	2214
Table, Harvest, Oak, c.1850, 29 x 71 In.	510
Table, Harvest, Pine, Breadboard Ends, Drawer, Carved Maple Legs, c.1865, 29 x 83 In.	826
Table, Harvest, Pine, Scrubbed Top, Red Paint, Drawer, Pennsylvania, 1800, 30 x 52 In.	450
Table, Hepplewhite, Cherry, Drawer, c.1815, 29 x 20 In.	165
Table, Hepplewhite, Cherry, Eagle Inlay, Drawer, Tapered Legs, c.1800, 28 x 18 In.	354
Table, Hepplewhite, Drawer, Red Paint, 30 x 24 In.	210
Table, Hepplewhite, Drawer, Red Paint, Tapered Legs, 29 x 31 In.	450
Table, Hepplewhite, Mahogany, England, c.1800, 28 ½ x 29 In.	533
Table, Hepplewhite, Mahogany, Flame Bird Inlay, Bowfront, New Hampshire, 29 x 35 In.	360

Furniture, Table, Side, Ebonized, Marble Top, Pietra Dura, Gilt, Carvings, Italy, 34 x 47 In.
$1,968

New Orleans Auction Galleries, Inc.

Furniture, Table, Side, Figural, Bronze Monkey, Tooled Leather Books, Gilt, 28 x 17 In.
$1,342

Neal Auction Co.

Furniture, Table, Side, Peter Shire, Glass Top, 4-Sided Abstract Base, 1984, 26 x 22 x 19 In.
$3,750

Los Angeles Modern Auctions (LAMA)

TIP
American 18th-century furniture can lose as much as 80 percent of its value if it has been refinished. European furniture that has been refinished or even restored does not lose much value as long as the work is done well.

Furniture, Table, Side, Phil Powell, Walnut, Triangular, New Hope, Pa., 1960s, 21 x 27 In.
$3,750

Rago Arts & Auction Center

Furniture, Table, Tavern, Maple, Pine, Breadboard Ends, Painted, c.1750, 46 x 30 In.
$5,040

Skinner Auctioneers & Appraisers

Furniture, Table, Tavern, Walnut, Dovetailed Drawer, Turned Legs, 1800s, 41 x 28 In.
$960

Cowan's Auctions

Furniture, Table, Tea, Tilt Top, Queen Anne, Mahogany, Cabriole Legs, 1700s, 28 x 27 In.
$300

Cowan's Auctions

Table, Hepplewhite, Mahogany, Inlay, Demilune, Foldover Top, 29 x 36 In.	1080
Table, Hepplewhite, Mahogany, Oval Leaves, Drawer, England, 28 x 32 In.	510
Table, Hepplewhite, Overhung Beadboard Ends, Drawer, Blue Paint, 29 x 28 In.	960
Table, Hepplewhite, Scalloped Apron, Blue Paint, 29 x 37 In.	3480
Table, Hunt, George II, Yew, c.1800, 29 x 16 ½ In.	334
Table, Hunt, Georgian Style, Mahogany, Tray Top, Wavy Gallery, 1900s, 27 x 31 In.	345
Table, Inlaid Designs, Barley-Twist Legs, X-Stretchers, Finial, Octagonal, Ferguson, 22 x 24 In.	316
Table, Inlaid, Serpentine, Flip Top, c.1850, 36 ½ x 17 In.	518
Table, Iron, Round, White Paint, 31 x 38 In.	313
Table, J. Adnet, Rosewood, Round Mirror Top, c.1930, 22 x 28 In.	813
Table, Jacobean, Oak, Carved Apron, Legs, Stretcher Base, England, c.1759, 27 x 30 In.	406
Table, Karl Springer, Racetrack, Laminated Linen, Spherical, Roller Feet, 21 x 46 In.	4795
Table, L. & J.G. Stickley, Round Top, X-Stretcher Base, 24 x 29 In.	688
Table, Lacquered, Brown, Silver, 2 Tiers, Pavilions, Pines, Birds, c.1900, 9 x 21 In.	989
Table, Library, George III, Mahogany, Inlay, Leather, Drawers, Pedestal, c.1800, 30 x 36 In.	956
Table, Library, Herter Bros., Aesthetic Revival, Mahogany, Leather Inset, Drawers, 30 x 38 In.	676
Table, Library, Lifetime, Drawer, Stretcher, Paine Furniture, 29 x 36 x 24 In. ....*illus*	670
Table, Library, Limbert, 3 Drawers, Medial Shelf, c.1908, 29 x 59 In.	2625
Table, Library, Mahogany, Drop Leaf, Columnar Stem, 1800s, 28 x 48 In.	369
Table, Library, Mahogany, Trestle Style, Fluted Edge Design, Turned Legs, c.1920, 29 x 68 In.	450
Table, Library, Regency Style, Mahogany, Hickory Chair Furniture Co., 27 x 30 In. ....*illus*	420
Table, Library, Regency Style, Rosewood, Burl, Leaves, Square Legs, 32 x 75 In.	5412
Table, Lilac Glass, Round, 1980s, 15 x 26 In.	1625
Table, Louis XV Style, Cherry, Drawer, Gallery Top, 26 ½ x 13 In.	594
Table, Louis XV Style, Ebonized, Leather-Lined Top, Brass, c.1900, 30 x 55 In.	1770
Table, Louis XV Style, Fruitwood, Drawers, 26 x 33 In.	2160
Table, Louis XV Style, Fruitwood, Scalloped Apron, Cabriole Legs, c.1800, 26 x 33 In.	1107
Table, Louis XV Style, Kingwood, Drawers, Ormolu, Shield, Plume, c.1900, 33 x 69 In.	1230
Table, Louis XV Style, Marble Top, Marquetry Inlay, Round, 1900s, 20 x 30 In.	1003
Table, Louis XV Style, Oak, Banded, Shaped Frieze, Shaped Legs, 1800s, 29 x 30 In.	1045
Table, Louis XV Style, Parcel Gilt, Black Paint, Drawer, Cabriole Legs, c.1850, 30 x 33 In.	1125
Table, Louis XV, Veneer, Drawers, Tooled Leather Top, Brass Mounts, Carved Legs, 35 x 68 In.	4025
Table, Louis XVI Style, Gilt, Marble Top, Scroll, Shells, Rosettes, 33 x 43 In.	1793
Table, Louis XVI Style, Mahogany, Gilt Metal, 30 x 26 ½ In.	188
Table, Louis XVI Style, Mixed Wood, Musical Symbols, 2 Drawers, 30 x 25 In.	500
Table, Louis XVI Style, Wood, Brown Stain, Leather Top, 2 Drawers, 29 x 51 In.	1125
Table, Louis-Philippe, Mahogany, Marble Top, Urn Standard, Tripod Base, 1800s, 29 x 39 In.	2125
Table, Louis-Philippe, Mahogany, Round, Triangle Standard, Bun Feet, c.1845, 30 x 40 In.	2000
Table, Low, Elm, Zitan, Paneled Sides, Cutouts, Chinese, c.1890, 33 x 18 In.	530
Table, Lucite, 2 Tiers, Block Shape, 22 x 16 In., Pair	176
Table, Mahogany, Birdcage Standard, Scalloped Top, Round, c.1920, 27 x 27 In.	283
Table, Mahogany, Drawer Lid, Mirror Fitted Interior, Tambour Door, New York, 29 x 26 In.	6000
Table, Mahogany, Drum Shape, Bookmatch Top, Carved Legs, Paw Feet, 1822, 28 In.	2440
Table, Mahogany, Gimbal Yacht, Flower Carved Trestle Base, c.1880	1800
Table, Mahogany, Octagonal Top, Fitted Interior, Drawers, c.1850, 24 x 20 In.	875
Table, Mahogany, Reeded Edge, 2 Frieze Drawers, Stretcher, Boston, c.1845, 29 x 27 In.	1188
Table, Mahogany, Ring & Spiral Turned Legs, c.1825, 29 x 25 In.	610
Table, Mahogany, Round Top, Banded Standard, 4 Splayed Legs, 28 x 35 In.	344
Table, Mahogany, Round Top, Fluted Pedestal, Concave Base, c.1850, 30 x 48 In.	615
Table, Mahogany, Round Top, Square Standard, c.1890, 30 x 54 In.	1500
Table, Mahogany, Round, Carved Standard, c.1835, 30 x 40 In.	122
Table, Mahogany, Scalloped Gallery, 2 Round Tiers, Turned Legs, c.1940, 28 x 18 x 27 In.	180
Table, Mahogany, Shaped Standard, Domed Arched Legs, c.1890, 27 x 26 In., Pair	90
Table, Mahogany, Swivel Double Pedestal, Paw Feet, Adjusts To 2 Tables, c.1845, 29 x 98 In.	1045
Table, Mahogany, Tilt Top, Serpentine, Turned Pedestal, c.1775, 29 x 32 In.	236
Table, Maple, Brown Paint, Drawer, Shelf, Scalloped Gallery, c.1850, 27 x 26 In.	382
Table, Maple, Cherry, 2 Drawers, Turned Legs, 1845, 29 x 21 In.	750
Table, Maple, Overhung Porringer Top, New England, 27 x 33 In.	2160
Table, Maple, Overhung Top, 2 Drawers, Pennsylvania, c.1810, 30 x 58 ½ In.	296
Table, Maple, Tiger Maple, 2 Drawers, Brass Pulls, Turned Legs, 27 x 22 In.	443
Table, Marble, Leather Inlay, Stretcher Shelf, Round, France, 36 x 31 In.	4235
Table, Marble, Round Top, Concave 3-Part Stem, Base Molding, 30 x 42 In.	2337
Table, Marquetry Top, Round, Turned Column Support, Tripod Base, 30 x 30 In.	180
Table, Marquetry, Ormolu Mounts, France, c.1915, 30 x 30 In.	356
Table, McCobb, Mahogany, Cane Lower Shelf, 2 Drawers, Calvin, 24 x 19 In.	313

Table, Metal, Marble, Reverse Painted Glass, Cantilevered, 1990s, 22 x 28 In., Pair	313
Table, Milliner's, Pine, Scalloped Edge, Salmon Paint, 1800s, 31 x 66 In.	1067
Table, Napoleon III, Ebonized, Gilt Metal, Round, Painted Couples Panels, 32 x 20 In.	375
Table, Neoclassical Style, Iron, Marble, Carved, Animals, Italy, c.1890, 27 In. ....*illus*	600
Table, Neoclassical Style, Multicolor Paint, Parcel Gilt, Drawer, 9 Legs, Stretchers, 29 x 33 In.	1440
Table, Neoclassical Style, Round, Carved Standard, Painted, Italy, 30 x 36 In.	500
Table, Neoclassical, Birch, Dentil Frieze, Ebonized Paw Feet, c.1850, 30 x 56 In.	1845
Table, Neoclassical, Mahogany, Caryatid Supports, Shelf, Urn, Swans, c.1800, 39 x 46 x 24 In.	4920
Table, Neoclassical, Mahogany, Line Inlay, Leaf-Carved Legs, Claw Feet, c.1810, 29 x 36 In.	2125
Table, Nesting, Mahogany, Tooled Leather Top, Henredon, 24 x 22 In., 3 Piece	180
Table, Oak, 2 Drawers, Scalloped Apron, Low Stretcher, 29 x 70 In.	11400
Table, Oak, Carved, Barley Twist Legs, Incised, X-Shape Stretchers, Finial, 12 x 18 In., Pair	213
Table, Oak, Drawer, Barley Twist Supports, Rectangular Base Stretcher, 1698, 26 x 31 In.	2500
Table, Oak, Octagonal, Carved Frieze, Tapered Legs, Thomas Robertson, c.1860, 27 x 25 In.	363
Table, Oak, Plank Top, Drawer, Turned Legs, Box Stretcher, c.1690, 26 x 33 In.	956
Table, Oak, Round, Tripod Base, England, 28 x 21 In.	563
Table, Oak, Stretcher Shelf, Twist-Carved Legs, Glass & Iron Ball & Claw Feet, 48 x 28 ½ In.	537
Table, P. Evans, Mixed Metals, Nailheads, Slate Top, Casters, 21 x 29 ½ In. ....*illus*	7800
Table, P. Evans, Polychrome, Gilt Steel, Wood, Slate, 1962, 18 ½ x 30 In. ....*illus*	10000
Table, Painted, 15 Manganese Delft Tile Insets, Flower Vases, Reeded Legs, 25 x 31 In.	550
Table, Painted, Geometric Designs, Octagonal, Turned Legs, X-Shape Base, 16 x 16 In.	230
Table, Painted, Overhung Top, Stretcher Base, c.1860, 42 x 32 In.	460
Table, Painted, Tray Top, Scalloped Skirt, Cabriole Legs, American, 1800s, 29 x 36 In.	1003
Table, Parquetry, 8-Sided, Stretcher Shelf, Bowed Legs, Morocco, 1912, 31 x 19 In.	395
Table, Pembroke, Applewood, Square Leaves, c.1805, 29 x 20 In.	123
Table, Pembroke, Cherry, Oval, Drawer, X-Stretcher, c.1900, 28 x 32 In.	556
Table, Pembroke, Chippendale, Cherry, Drawer, Shaped Stretcher, c.1785, 41 x 21 In.	944
Table, Pembroke, Chippendale, Mahogany, Carved X-Stretcher, England, 20 x 19 ½ In.	2040
Table, Pembroke, Chippendale, Mahogany, Drawer, c.1790, 29 x 30 In.	1200
Table, Pembroke, Chippendale, Mahogany, Drawer, Wavy Leaves, Phila., c.1790, 29 x 21 In.	8125
Table, Pembroke, Chippendale, Mahogany, Flower-Carved Rim, Drawer, England, 27 x 26 In.	1680
Table, Pembroke, Chippendale, Mahogany, Scallop Top, New England, c.1790, 28 x 20 In.	2133
Table, Pembroke, Chippendale, Mahogany, X-Stretcher, Philadelphia, c.1785, 28 x 22 In.	415
Table, Pembroke, Federal Style, Mahogany, Rounded Leaves, c.1915, 28 x 20 In.	267
Table, Pembroke, Federal, Mahogany, Carved, Drawer, Ring-Turned Legs, 1800s, 29 In.	2150
Table, Pembroke, Federal, Mahogany, Frieze Drawer, Twist-Carved Legs, c.1820, 30 x 27 In.	750
Table, Pembroke, Federal, Mahogany, Inlay, Oval Leaves, c.1820, 28 x 21 In.	1188
Table, Pembroke, Federal, Mahogany, Inlay, Square Legs, c.1850, 29 x 22 In.	594
Table, Pembroke, Federal, Mahogany, Oval Leaves, 2 Drawers, c.1855, 29 x 23 In.	938
Table, Pembroke, Federal, Mahogany, Round Leaves, 28 x 35 In.	420
Table, Pembroke, Federal, Mahogany, Shaped Leaves, New England, c.1855, 29 x 22 In.	594
Table, Pembroke, Federal, Mahogany, Shaped Leaves, Reeded Legs, c.1810, 29 x 22 In.	235
Table, Pembroke, George III Style, Mahogany, 28 x 20 In.	280
Table, Pembroke, George III Style, Mahogany, Oval Ends, Square Legs, 29 x 20 In.	1125
Table, Pembroke, George III, Mahogany, Beaded Inlay, Spade Feet, c.1790, 28 x 30 In.	819
Table, Pembroke, George III, Mahogany, Drawer, Oblong, Medial Shelf, 29 x 39 In.	720
Table, Pembroke, George III, Mahogany, Drawers, Rounded Leaves, 28 x 33 In.	625
Table, Pembroke, George III, Mahogany, Oak, Tapered Legs, c.1800, 28 x 28 In.	118
Table, Pembroke, George III, Mahogany, Oval Leaves, c.1790, 42 x 25 In.	598
Table, Pembroke, Georgian, Mahogany, Demilune Leaves, Drawer, 29 x 29 In.	1200
Table, Pembroke, Georgian, Mahogany, Ebony Inlay, Tapered Legs, c.1820, 29 x 38 In.	374
Table, Pembroke, Hepplewhite, Mahogany, Flower Inlay, Demilune, c.1790, 29 x 18 In.	8888
Table, Pembroke, Hepplewhite, Mahogany, Rounded Leaves, Square Legs, c.1800, 30 x 20 In.	189
Table, Pembroke, Mahogany, Drawers, Square Legs, New England, 29 x 34 In.	150
Table, Pembroke, Neoclassical, Mahogany, Bird's-Eye Maple, c.1840, 29 x 42 In. ....*illus*	1464
Table, Pembroke, Regency, Mahogany, Cock-Beaded, c.1815, 28 x 18 In.	600
Table, Pembroke, Sheraton, Mahogany, Drawer, Rope-Carved Legs, 36 In.	300
Table, Pembroke, Sheraton, Mahogany, Pennsylvania, c.1820, 28 ½ x 20 ½ In.	267
Table, Pembroke, Sheraton, Mahogany, Scalloped, Turned Legs, Pa., c.1815, 29 x 23 In.	296
Table, Pembroke, Sheraton, Tiger Maple, c.1830, 28 x 22 ½ In.	770
Table, Pembroke, Sheraton, Tiger Maple, Shaped Leaves, Drawer, 36 In.	1080
Table, Pembroke, Sheraton, Walnut, Drawer, c.1850, 11 ½ x 10 In.	243
Table, Pier, Burl Ash, Mahogany, Marble Top, Concave Shelf, c.1825, 38 x 40 In.	1968
Table, Pier, Empire, Mahogany, Marble Top, Scrolls, Paw Feet, c.1815, 35 x 53 In.	956
Table, Pier, Federal, Mahogany, Demilune, Reeded, Carved, Haines-Connelly, Pa., 36 x 42 In.	26250

Furniture, Table, Tea, Victorian, Silver Plate, Ringed Ram's Mask, Casters, c.1885, 31 x 30 In.
$3,198

New Orleans Auction Galleries, Inc.

Furniture, Table, Tilt Top, Lacquer, Black & Gilt, Chinese Export, 32 x 33 In.
$1,912

Neal Auction Co.

Furniture, Table, Tray, George III, Papier-Mache, Gilt, Black, Metal Stand, c.1820, 31 x 24 In.
$531

Leslie Hindman Auctioneers

TIP
Don't use window cleaner to wipe off picture frames and mirror frames. It may remove the gliding.

Brushed Aluminum, c.1929, 18 x 13 In.
$2,250

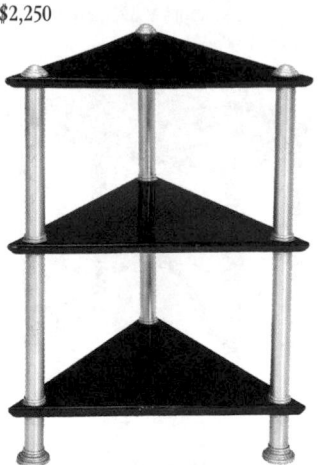

Los Angeles Modern Auctions (LAMA)

Furniture, Table, Wendell Castle, Mushroom, Walnut, Initialed WC, 1972, 31 x 46 x 44 In.
$42,000

Cottone Auctions

Furniture, Table, Wine, Tilt Top, Chippendale Style, Mahogany, England, Centennial, 27 x 30 In.
$400

Cowan's Auctions

Table, Pier, Mahogany, Gilt, Columnar Supports, Pilasters, Paw Feet, 37 x 39 In.	777
Table, Pier, Mahogany, Marble Top, Columns, Mirror, Ormolu Mounts, c.1820, 37 x 42 In.	8295
Table, Pier, Mahogany, Marble Top, Mirror Back, Scrolls, c.1815, 39 x 43 In.	1230
Table, Pier, Mahogany, Marble Top, Mirror, Column Sides, Boston, 33 x 45 In.	1200
Table, Pier, Mahogany, Marble Top, Rounded, 2 Drawers, Scroll Legs, c.1840, 48 x 19 In.	1625
Table, Pier, Mahogany, Marble Top, S-Scroll Supports, Mirror Back, c.1835, 38 In.	1434
Table, Pier, Mahogany, Star, Fan Inlay, Mirror, 7 ½ x 9 In.	267
Table, Pier, Mahogany, White Marble Top, c.1845, 35 x 19 x 31 In.	2500
Table, Pier, Neoclassical, Giltwood, Mahogany, Marble Top, Stenciled, c.1825, 37 x 42 In.	1230
Table, Pier, Neoclassical, Mahogany, Marble Top, Mirror, 1815-20, 43 x 20 In. ....*illus*	9600
Table, Pier, Neoclassical, Mahogany, Marble Top, Mirrored Back, c.1810, 36 x 40 In. ....*illus*	1586
Table, Pier, Neoclassical, Mahogany, Stenciled, Marble Top, c.1810, 36 x 37 In.	1150
Table, Pier, Neoclassical, Painted, Shaped Top, Carved Shell, Lion Mask, 1900s, 35 x 47 In.	530
Table, Pier, Queen Anne Style, Mahogany, Marble, Drawer, England, 1800s, 31 x 50 In. ......*illus*	4012
Table, Pier, Regency Style, Mahogany, Marble, Lion's Head, Pilasters, 40 x 58 In.	1845
Table, Pier, Victorian, Walnut, Rolled Scroll Sides, Mirror, Drawer, 35 ½ x 28 ½ In.	237
Table, Piet Hein, Rosewood Veneer, Aluminum Pedestal, 5-Point Base, 1900s, 27 x 46 In., Pair...	603
Table, Pietra Dura Marble Top, Round, Shell-Carved Base, 36 x 22 In.	805
Table, Pine, 3 Drawers, England, c.1845, 30 x 131 In.	1126
Table, Pine, 3 Drawers, Turned Legs, France, c.1850, 32 x 71 In.	430
Table, Pine, 3 Drawers, Turned Legs, Paint, Pa., c.1850, 31 x 77 In.	2880
Table, Pine, Blue Paint, Drawer, Splayed Legs, 29 x 18 In.	2607
Table, Pine, Blue Paint, Southern, 29 x 33 In.	2040
Table, Pine, Brown Paint, Tapered Legs, 29 x 23 In.	295
Table, Pine, Cream Paint, 3 Drawers, Turned Legs, c.1900, 63 x 29 In.	523
Table, Pine, Drawer, Turned Legs, c.1850, 16 x 33 In.	173
Table, Pine, Drawers, Sawtooth Stretcher Shelf, New England, c.1810, 29 x 18 In.	207
Table, Pine, Gray Paint, Drawer, Tapered Legs, 29 x 41 In.	780
Table, Pine, Oval Top, Stretcher Base, New England, 26 x 33 In.	1007
Table, Pine, Overhung Top, Drawer, Pennsylvania, 29 x 40 In.	267
Table, Pine, Overhung Top, Stretcher Base, Drawer, Pennsylvania, 27 x 39 In.	770
Table, Pine, Overhung Top, Stretcher Base, Virginia, c.1795, 28 x 51 In.	345
Table, Pine, Painted, Overhung Top, Stretcher Base, Pennsylvania, c.1820, 26 x 36 In.	7890
Table, Pine, Pin Top, 2 Drawers, 29 x 47 ½ In.	267
Table, Pine, Pin Top, 2 Drawers, Beaded Skirt, Virginia, c.1775, 32 x 56 In.	575
Table, Pine, Poplar, Painted, Stretcher Base, Pennsylvania, 1700s, 28 x 19 In.	237
Table, Pine, Red & Yellow Paint, Overhung Top, Drawer, Pennsylvania, c.1800, 24 x 34 In.	213
Table, Pine, Red Paint, Turned Legs, c.1890, 16 x 20 In., Child's	30
Table, Pine, Round Top, Red Paint, New England, c.1760, 26 x 43 In.	8888
Table, Pine, Spanish Brown Paint, c.1820, 31 x 69 In.	593
Table, Pine, Turned Legs, 29 x 84 In.	280
Table, Pine, X-Stretcher, New England, c.1800, 28 x 45 ½ In.	385
Table, Plank, Hardwood, Beaded Ends, Square Legs, England, 29 x 60 In.	960
Table, Polished Steel Frame, Round Glass Top, Nico Zographos, 24 x 19 In, Pair	1063
Table, Poplar, Overhung Top, Drawer, Red Paint, Pennsylvania, c.1790, 29 x 37 In.	3792
Table, Queen Anne Style, Cherry, 4 Drawers, Carved Sunburst, 29 x 23 In.	1250
Table, Queen Anne Style, Walnut, Satinwood, c.1930, 30 x 20 x 15 In.	180
Table, Queen Anne, Cherry, 5 Drawers, Carved Sunburst, New England, c.1880, 29 x 33 In.	1375
Table, Queen Anne, Cherry, Birdcage Standard, 27 x 24 In.	360
Table, Queen Anne, Cherry, Porringer Top, Scalloped Apron, Cabriole Legs, 26 x 35 In.	1080
Table, Queen Anne, Cherry, Shaped Square Tilt Top, Cabriole Legs, Connecticut	360
Table, Queen Anne, Maple, Turned Legs, Pad Feet, New England, c.1760, 28 x 35 In.	2252
Table, Queen Anne, Mixed Wood, Walnut, Drawers, Shaped Corners, Feet, 1700s, 27 x 30 In.	558
Table, Queen Anne, Pine, Green Paint, Overhung, Tapered Legs, Southern, c.1765, 28 x 25 In.	748
Table, Queen Anne, Round Tilt Top, 28 x 29 In.	420
Table, Queen Anne, Tiger Maple, Turret Corners, Pad Feet, 1765, 27 x 32 In.	26070
Table, Queen Anne, Walnut, 3 Drawers, 1700s, 28 x 34 In.	600
Table, Queen Anne, Walnut, 3 Drawers, Banded Border, Pendant Drops, Mass., 29 x 28 In.	3900
Table, Queen Anne, Walnut, 4 Drawers, Scroll Apron, Pennsylvania, c.1760, 31 x 35 In.	5625
Table, Queen Anne, Walnut, Drawer, Scalloped Skirt, c.1765, 29 x 36 In.	30810
Table, Queen Anne, Walnut, Overhung, 3 Drawers, Cabriole Legs, Pa., c.1765, 29 x 33 In.	4503
Table, Queen Anne, Walnut, Pine, Pennsylvania, c.1790, 30 x 75 In.	3318
Table, Queen Anne, Walnut, Tray Top, Shell-Carved Knees, Ribbed Feet, 28 x 29 In.	3000
Table, Red Stain, Turned Splayed Legs, c.1865, 29 x 20 In.	219
Table, Refectory, Baroque, Walnut, Plank Top, Carved, Block Legs, 1600s, 31 x 61 In.	3690

Table, Refectory, Chestnut, Plank Top, Drawers, Trestle, Iron Stretcher, 32 x 77 In......	1673
Table, Refectory, Fruitwood, Walnut, Reeded Rim, Plank Stretcher, 1900s, 29 x 14 In.....	7670
Table, Refectory, Oak, Paneled End Supports, Stretcher, 1800s, 33 x 84 In.	1599
Table, Refectory, Oak, Shaped Supports, Stretcher, Runner Feet, 30 x 79 In.	1968
Table, Refectory, Walnut, Plank Top, Baluster Legs, Stretcher, Italy, c.1700, 31 x 68 In.....	5975
Table, Refectory, Walnut, Rope Edge, Turned Legs, Box Stretcher, Ball Feet, 34 x 54 In......	3998
Table, Regency Style, Gilt, Marble Top, Mask, Shell-Carved Apron, Legs, 30 x 37 In......	2500
Table, Regency Style, Mahogany, Banded, Double Pedestal, Splayed Legs, 29 x 80 In.	750
Table, Regency Style, Mahogany, Fruitwood, Middle Shelf, 32 x 38 In......................	188
Table, Regency Style, Mahogany, Pierced Brass Gallery, Drawer, 30 x 36 In................	438
Table, Regency Style, Pedestal, Leather Top, Chamfered, c.1910, 28 x 24 In. ....*illus*	250
Table, Regency, Drawers, Supports, Casters, 28 x 37 In....................................	2500
Table, Regency, Mahogany, 2 Drawers, Trestle Supports, 28 x 41 In.	438
Table, Regency, Mixed Wood, Leather Top, 2 Drawers, Downswept Legs, c.1820, 28 x 42 In.....	3422
Table, Regency, Rosewood, Brass Inlay, 4 Drawers, Shaped Stretcher, c.1810, 29 x 37 In.....	2370
Table, Regency, Rosewood, Brass, Inlay, Round Top, Tapered Stem, 29 x 48 In............	2813
Table, Renaissance Revival, Walnut, Marble Top, Carved Frieze, c.1870, 30 x 28 In........	530
Table, Renaissance Revival, Walnut, Marble Top, Carved Support, c.1870, 29 x 20 In.	250
Table, Renaissance Revival, Walnut, Marble Top, Oval, Carved Supports, c.1870, 30 x 33 In.	594
Table, Renaissance Style, Walnut, Cutout Trestle Supports, 32 x 45 In....................	2813
Table, Risom, Walnut, Flip Top, 1950s, 30 x 60 In..	1188
Table, Risom, Walnut, Shelf Over Drop Front Compartment, 25 x 23 x 15 In...............	353
Table, Robsjohn-Gibbings, Mahogany, Drawer, Cane Handle, 20 x 24 In.	1000
Table, Rococo Revival, Walnut, Round, Fruit, Leaf-Carved Pedestal, c.1865, 30 x 56 In.	4428
Table, Rococo Style, Walnut, Drawer, Continental, 28 x 30 ½ In...........................	156
Table, Rosewood, Enameled Steel, Round, Jorge Zalszupin, Brazil, 1960s, 28 x 21 In.....	1063
Table, Rosewood, Mahogany, Drawers, Trestle Supports, Carved Feet, c.1845, 28 x 49 In.....	938
Table, Salterini, Glass Top, Iron Frame, c.1950, 29 x 48 In.	230
Table, Sawbuck, Green Paint, Pine, Overhang Top, Drawer, Pa., c.1800, 29 x 76 In.	4977
Table, Sawbuck, Maple, Brown Paint, c.1895, 23 x 36 In.................................	153
Table, Sawbuck, Mixed Wood, 3-Board Top, 1800s, 29 x 37 In...........................	4406
Table, Sawbuck, Pine, c.1750, 27 ½ x 48 In..	237
Table, Sawbuck, Pine, Green Paint, Underhung Drawer, Pennsylvania, c.1800, 29 x 76 In.	4717
Table, Sawbuck, Pine, Painted, Overhung, 2-Board Top, X-Supports, c.1815, 29 x 59 In.	2400
Table, Sawbuck, Pine, Painted, Pennsylvania, c.1865, 29 x 72 In.......................	1304
Table, Sawbuck, Pine, Red Paint, Pennsylvania, c.1810, 27 x 49 In.....................	450
Table, Sawbuck, Pine, Underhung Drawer, Pennsylvania, c.1805, 28 x 76 In.............	1778
Table, Sawbuck, Pine, Yellow Grain Paint, Pennsylvania, c.1820, 28 ½ x 48 In.........	1304
Table, Serving, Mahogany, Scroll Backsplash, Turned Legs, c.1815, 58 x 42 In.	4780
Table, Serving, Walnut, Cypress, Drawers, Vase Shape Turned Legs, 1800s, 29 x 35 In.....	1673
Table, Sewing, Federal Style, Mahogany, Drop Leaf, Baluster, 1800s, 34 x 19 In.	344
Table, Sewing, Federal Style, Mahogany, Inlay, Drawers, Compartments, c.1910, 29 x 29 In........	127
Table, Sewing, Federal, Mahogany, 2 Drawers, Square Legs, c.1800, 27 x 18 In...........	360
Table, Sewing, Federal, Mahogany, Basket Slide, Turned, Reeded Legs, c.1815, 30 In.....	1434
Table, Sewing, Federal, Mahogany, Drawers, Bag, Fluted, Reeded Legs, c.1802, 29 x 22 In.	4375
Table, Sewing, Federal, Mahogany, Drawers, Shelf, Rope-Twist Legs, c.1815, 28 x 21 In.....	1315
Table, Sewing, Federal, Mahogany, Rope Twist, Reeded Legs, c.1815, 30 x 22 In.	1180
Table, Sewing, Federal, Mahogany, Twist Columns, Finial, Outswept Legs, 30 x 22 In.....	1062
Table, Sewing, Federal, Maple, Mahogany Inlay, Bag Drawer, c.1810, 28 x 18 In. ....*illus*	3900
Table, Sewing, French Empire, Mahogany, Brass, Stretcher, Paw Feet, c.1800, 30 In.....	585
Table, Sewing, Georgian, Mahogany, Inlay, Drawer, 30 x 23 In..........................	2160
Table, Sewing, Lift Top, Pine, Brown Paint, Compartments, Drawer, 1800s, 30 x 24 In.....	1998
Table, Sewing, Mahogany, Drop Leaf, Cove-Molded Pedestal, Scroll Feet, c.1835, 29 In.....	492
Table, Sewing, Mahogany, Drop Leaf, Drawers, Basket, Turned Legs, c.1815, 28 x 18 In.....	717
Table, Sewing, Mahogany, Drop Leaf, Octagonal Pedestal, c.1815, 27 x 21 In.............	554
Table, Sewing, Mahogany, Molded Drawers, Slide, Shelf, c.1815, 29 x 21 In.	1220
Table, Sewing, Mahogany, Pendant, Bulbous Stem, Outswept Legs, c.1815, 30 In.	956
Table, Sewing, Mahogany, Poplar, Figured, Drawers, Carved Legs, c.1835, 31 x 24 In.....	1293
Table, Sewing, Mahogany, Sarcophagus Top, Basket, Stretcher, 1840, 32 x 21 In.........	244
Table, Sewing, Neoclassical, Mahogany, Pullout Basket, Drawers, c.1810, 29 x 19 In.....	1554
Table, Sewing, Neoclassical, Rosewood, Ebonized, Ormolu, Drawers, c.1815, 30 x 21 x 17 In.	43750
Table, Sewing, Pine, Painted, Drawer, Overhung, Turned Legs, c.1750, 25 x 28 In........	1200
Table, Sewing, Poplar, Pine, Mustard Paint, Drawer, Pennsylvania, 30 x 39 In............	450
Table, Sewing, Queen Anne, Pine, Red Paint, Drawer, Turned Legs, 1700s, 26 x 36 In.....	1175
Table, Sewing, Red Paint, Single-Board Top, Drawer, Tapered Legs, c.1810, 28 x 38 In.....	617

Furniture, Table, Work, Neoclassical, Mahogany, Drawers, Writing Desk, c.1810, 23 x 17 In.
$1,912

Neal Auction Co.

Furniture, Table, Work, Neoclassical, Mahogany, Turreted Corners, Lyre Base, c.1825, 31 x 21 In.
$860

Neal Auction Co.

Furniture, Table, Work, Shaker, Maple, Drawers Front & Side, Pullout Slide, 38 x 32 In.
$31,860

Willis Henry Auctions, Inc.

Furniture, Table, Writing, Bonheur Du Jour, Regency Style, England, c.1875, 43 x 27 In.
$2,460

Skinner Auctioneers & Appraisers

Furniture, Tabouret, Carved, Marble Top, Cabriole Legs, Pierced, Chinese, c.1890, 36 In.
$711

James D. Julia Auctioneers

Furniture, Tea Cart, Aalto, Birch, Wicker Basket, Tile Top, c.1975, 23 x 36 x 25 In.
$295

Brunk Auctions

Table, Sewing, Regency Style, Black Paint, Round, Lift Top, Gilt, c.1900, 30 x 13 In.	177
Table, Sewing, Regency, Mahogany, Drop Leaf, 2 Drawers, Green Bag, Trestle Base, 28 x 19 In.	1140
Table, Sewing, Regency, Rosewood, Turned Legs, Casters, England, c.1815, 29 x 22 In.	300
Table, Sewing, Rococo Revival, Rosewood, Walnut, Lift Top, Trestle, c.1865, 29 x 28 In.	460
Table, Sewing, Rosewood, Double Lift Lid, 2 Drawers, Carved, Cabriole Legs, 33 x 21 In.	588
Table, Sewing, Rosewood, Drop Leaf, Arabesque Marquetry, 2 Drawers, 28 x 29 In.	325
Table, Sewing, Rosewood, Mahogany, 2 Drawers, Turned Legs, c.1800, 29 x 23 In.	708
Table, Sewing, Shaker, Cherry, Shelf, Tapered Legs, Round Knobs, c.1810, 38 x 40 In.	2106
Table, Sewing, Shaker, Sisters, Walnut, Inset Maple Yardstick, c.1870, 26 x 39 In. ....*illus*	1239
Table, Sewing, Sheraton, 2 Drawers, Ring-Turned Legs, 29 x 20 In.	3120
Table, Sewing, Sheraton, Cherry, Beaded Drawer, Turned Legs, Southern, c.1845, 29 x 21 In.	1495
Table, Sewing, Sheraton, Mahogany, Beaded Edges, Drawer, Fitted Interior, c.1805, 28 x 24 In.	236
Table, Sewing, Soap Hollow, Flowers, Yellow Ground, Paint, LW, 1873, 15 x 8 In.	948
Table, Sewing, Softwood, Blue Gray Paint, Dome Pincushion Top, Leaves, Beaded, 17 In.	189
Table, Sewing, William IV, Rosewood, Basket, Trestle, Rosettes, c.1835	366
Table, Shaker, Seed Sorting, Oval, Bentwood Gallery, Green, Union Shaker Village, 33 x 26 In.	1687
Table, Shaker, Seed Sorting, Oval, Gallery, Painted, South Union Village, 33 x 26 In.	1687
Table, Shaped Top, Painted Flowers, Lines, Green, Orange, White, 28 x 21 In.	4375
Table, Sheraton Style, Mahogany, 3 Drawers, Bowfront, England, 35 x 66 In.	3300
Table, Sheraton Style, Tiger Maple, Octagonal Top, 2 Drawers, Reeded Legs, 29 x 16 In.	1652
Table, Sheraton, Bird's-Eye Maple, Drawer, Canted Corners, c.1805, 28 x 18 In.	900
Table, Sheraton, Cherry, Drawer, 21 x 21 In.	136
Table, Sheraton, Curly Maple, Drawer, Turned Legs, c.1820, 27 x 18 In.	830
Table, Sheraton, Drawer, Turned Legs, c.1840, 28 x 20 In.	150
Table, Sheraton, Mahogany, Backsplash, Medial Shelf, Drawer, Pa., c.1830, 36 x 34 In.	516
Table, Sheraton, Mahogany, Drawer, Turned Legs, New England, c.1820, 30 x 16 In.	395
Table, Sheraton, Mahogany, Reeded, 2 Leaves, England, 31 x 49 In.	708
Table, Sheraton, Mahogany, Rosette Corners, Drawers, Spiral-Carved Legs, 1820s, 30 x 21 In.	590
Table, Sheraton, Mahogany, Tray Top, Beaded Drawer, England, c.1810, 29 x 20 In.	384
Table, Sheraton, Red Paint, Scrubbed Top, Turned Legs, 31 x 72 In.	2280
Table, Sheraton, Rosewood, Line Inlay, Medial Shelf, Drawer, 33 ½ x 31 In.	480
Table, Sheraton, Walnut, Beaded Drawer, Turned Legs, Drawer, Virginia, c.1835, 30 x 24 In.	316
Table, Sheraton, Walnut, Drawer, Turned Legs, Virginia, c.1850, 29 x 18 In.	184
Table, Sheraton, Walnut, Pine, Drawer, Turned Legs, c.1860, 30 x 20 In.	196
Table, Sheraton, Walnut, Pine, Poplar, Drawer, Mid-Atlantic, c.1860, 30 x 32 In.	288
Table, Side, Carved Wood, Square Top, Flower Fretwork Apron, 1800s, 27 x 15 In.	149
Table, Side, Cypress, Painted, Overhung, Square Tapered Legs, 1800s, 27 x 21 In.	598
Table, Side, Ebonized, Marble Top, Pietra Dura, Gilt, Carvings, Italy, 34 x 47 In. ....*illus*	1968
Table, Side, Figural, Bronze Monkey, Tooled Leather Books, Gilt, 28 x 17 In. ....*illus*	1342
Table, Side, French Provincial, Oak, Shaped Frieze, Peg Feet, c.1890, 30 x 57 In.	3690
Table, Side, French Provincial, Scalloped Apron, Cabriole Legs, c.1890, 32 x 68 In.	3690
Table, Side, Georgian, Oak, Molded Top, Chamfered Square Legs, 1700s, 29 x 38 In.	610
Table, Side, Hardwood, Bone Inlay, Carved Apron, Pendant Drawer, c.1885, 29 x 43 In.	1168
Table, Side, Hardwood, Molded Apron, Pierced Coin Design, Round Legs, 35 x 52 In.	6000
Table, Side, Louis XV Style, Kingwood, Shaped, Banded, Flowers, c.1900, 30 x 39 In.	922
Table, Side, Louis XVI Style, Painted, Marble Top, Bowed, Fluted Legs, 34 x 52 In.	2337
Table, Side, Louis XVI, Fruitwood, Gilt, Shaped Top, Crossbanded, Sabots, 30 In.	1125
Table, Side, Mahogany, Demilune, Bowed Top, Reeded Legs, c.1900, 45 x 19 In.	1476
Table, Side, P. Evans, Bronze, Composite, Slate, Gilt, Signed, 1970, 16 x 24 In.	5000
Table, Side, Parcel Gilt, Painted, Round, Columnar, Leaves, Melon Feet, c.1815, 28 In.	738
Table, Side, Peter Shire, Glass Top, 4-Sided Abstract Base, 1984, 26 x 22 x 19 In. ....*illus*	3750
Table, Side, Phil Powell, Walnut, Triangular, New Hope, Pa., 1960s, 21 x 27 In. ....*illus*	3750
Table, Side, Pine, Blue Paint, Overhung, Square Legs, Pegged, 1800s, 27 x 26 In.	354
Table, Side, Pine, Mixed Wood, Round, Triangular Base, Square Legs, c.1815, 28 In.	708
Table, Side, Round Glass Top, Chrome Support, Spiral Standard, Italy, 1900s, 19 x 14 In.	176
Table, Side, Round, Scrolling Flowers, Elephant Legs, Glass Eyes, c.1900, 23 x 23 In.	415
Table, Side, William & Mary, Walnut, Inlay, Twist Legs, Stretcher, Bun Feet, 27 x 35 In.	1793
Table, Side, Wrought Iron, Pietra Dura, Round, Bird, Flowers, Tripod, 1800s, 30 x 30 In.	1560
Table, Spanish Colonial, Walnut, Chip-Carved Front Drawer, Apron, Turned Legs, 27 x 32 In.	1680
Table, Stickley Bros., 2 Drawers, Copper Pulls, Low Stretcher, 60 x 30 In.	2625
Table, Stickley Bros., Oak, Round, X-Stretcher Base, 29 x 41 In.	1003
Table, Stone, Tessellated Fossil, Brass, Maitland Smith, 56 x 28 In.	375
Table, Tavern, Chippendale, Pine, Plank Top, Drawers, American, 1700s, 30 x 62 In.	3540
Table, Tavern, Federal, Red Paint, Drawer, Overhung Top, c.1815, 29 x 44 In.	1800
Table, Tavern, George I, Walnut, Beaded Drawer, Box Stretcher, 27 x 30 In.	1126

Table, Tavern, Hepplewhite, Cherry, Drawer, Pennsylvania, c.1830, 30 x 36 In.	215
Table, Tavern, Maple, Overhung Top, Drawer, Red Stain, New England, c.1750, 27 x 42 In.	3555
Table, Tavern, Maple, Pine, Breadboard Ends, Painted, c.1750, 46 x 30 In. *illus*	5040
Table, Tavern, Nutting, Mixed Wood, Ball-Carved Stretcher, Legs, Stamped, c.1910, 27 x 35 In.	400
Table, Tavern, Overhung Top, Drawer, Stretcher Base, c.1830, 36 x 24 In.	489
Table, Tavern, Pine, Ash, Breadboard Ends, Square Stretchers, 1700s, 26 x 29 In.	570
Table, Tavern, Pine, Brown Strain, Stretcher Base, 29 x 38 In.	94
Table, Tavern, Pine, Drawer, Stretcher Base, 25 x 38 In.	384
Table, Tavern, Pine, Drawer, Stretcher Base, 26 x 29 In.	189
Table, Tavern, Pine, Maple, Carved Apron, Splayed Legs, New England, c.1750, 25 x 29 In.	5214
Table, Tavern, Pine, Maple, Grain Paint, Drawer, Overhung Top, New Eng., c.1770, 28 x 42 In.	1823
Table, Tavern, Pine, Maple, New England, c.1800, 28 x 37 In.	504
Table, Tavern, Pine, Maple, Red Stain, Drawer, Stretcher, New England, c.1770, 27 x 36 In.	474
Table, Tavern, Queen Anne, Maple, Red Wash, Turned Legs, Pad Feet, 1700s, 27 x 37 In.	588
Table, Tavern, Queen Anne, Pine, Single-Board Top, Box Stretcher, 1700s, 25 x 28 In.	1120
Table, Tavern, Queen Anne, Walnut, Poplar, Overhung, Drawer, c.1800, 29 x 47 In.	472
Table, Tavern, Queen Anne, Walnut, Scalloped Apron, New England, 25 x 37 In.	504
Table, Tavern, Revolving Center Server, Round Top, 1800s, 30 ½ x 60 In.	764
Table, Tavern, Round, Medial Shelf, 3 Legs, c.1850, 25 x 30 In.	345
Table, Tavern, Walnut, c.1790, 27 x 33 ½ In.	300
Table, Tavern, Walnut, Dovetailed Drawer, Turned Legs, 1800s, 41 x 28 In. *illus*	960
Table, Tavern, William & Mary Style, Maple, Oval Top, Turned Legs, 1900s, 27 x 36 In.	440
Table, Tavern, William & Mary Style, Oak, Pegged, 1800s, 29 x 34 In.	676
Table, Tea, Cherry, Tray Top, Shaped Apron, Cabriole Legs, c.1750, 26 x 24 x 17 In.	1200
Table, Tea, Edwardian, Satinwood, Inlay, Square Legs, X-Stretcher, c.1900, 30 x 27 In.	480
Table, Tea, Eldred Wheeler Label, Shaped Skirt, Pad Feet, 19 x 25 In.	316
Table, Tea, George II, Mahogany, 8-Sided Tilt Top, Pierced Galley, Trifold Base, 29 x 29 In.	486
Table, Tea, George III Style, Mahogany, Shaped Top, Spindle Galley, 30 x 25 In.	406
Table, Tea, Georgian, Mahogany, Round Top, c.1750, 29 x 33 In.	237
Table, Tea, Heywood Bros., Wicker, Shaped Top, Scrolls, Orbs, White Paint, 29 x 28 In.	720
Table, Tea, Kittinger Furniture Co., Chippendale Style, Mahogany, Tilt Top, 28 In. Diam.	450
Table, Tea, Mahogany, 8-Sided, 3 Splayed-Leg Base, 20 x 30 In., Pair	1452
Table, Tea, Maple, Pine, Painted, Square Overhung Top, Splayed Legs, c.1815, 25 x 34 In.	2400
Table, Tea, Queen Anne, Birch, Shaped Skirt, Turned Legs, Pad Feet, 1700s, 28 x 36 In.	603
Table, Tea, Queen Anne, Carved Apron, New England, 29 x 20 In.	15600
Table, Tea, Queen Anne, Mahogany, Piecrust Top, Carved Support, Tripod Feet, 27 x 25 In.	6960
Table, Tea, Queen Anne, Mahogany, Porringer Top, Turned Legs, c.1750, 27 x 31 In.	3819
Table, Tea, Queen Anne, Maple, Pine, Painted, Turned Legs, Stretchers, 1700s, 24 x 28 In.	1085
Table, Tea, Queen Anne, Maple, Porringer Top, 27 x 35 In.	8400
Table, Tea, Queen Anne, Tiger Maple, Cutout Apron, c.1765, 25 x 34 x 26 In.	45000
Table, Tea, Queen Anne, Walnut, Tripod Base, Pennsylvania, c.1770, 28 ½ x 32 In.	948
Table, Tea, Tilt Top, Chippendale, Leaf Carved, Square, Cabriole Legs, Mass., 29 x 29 In.	1800
Table, Tea, Tilt Top, Chippendale, Mahogany, Ball & Claw Feet, Phila., c.1770, 29 x 35 In.	1778
Table, Tea, Tilt Top, Chippendale, Mahogany, Piecrust Top, Acanthus Legs, c.1790, 28 In.	1434
Table, Tea, Tilt Top, Chippendale, Maple, Red Wash, Round, Snake Feet, 27 x 30 In.	823
Table, Tea, Tilt Top, Chippendale, Santo Domingo Mahogany, Egg & Claw Feet	275
Table, Tea, Tilt Top, George II, Mahogany, Piecrust, Birdcage Stem, c.1750, 28 x 30 In.	413
Table, Tea, Tilt Top, George III Style, Mahogany, Leaf-Shape Dish Top, Tripod, 28 In.	375
Table, Tea, Tilt Top, Georgian, Round, Tripod Support, Baluster Stem, 3 Pad Feet, 29 x 47 In.	300
Table, Tea, Tilt Top, Queen Anne, Mahogany, Cabriole Legs, 1700s, 28 x 27 In. *illus*	300
Table, Tea, Tilt Top, Queen Anne, Mahogany, Dish Top, Ring Turned Stem, c.1790, 28 In.	1800
Table, Tea, Tilt Top, Queen Anne, Mahogany, Dish, Birdcage, Pedestal, 1700s, 27 x 27 In.	270
Table, Tea, Tilt Top, Queen Anne, Walnut, Round, Pennsylvania, c.1780, 27 x 30 In.	770
Table, Tea, Victorian, Silver Plate, Ringed Ram's Mask, Casters, c.1885, 31 x 30 In. *illus*	3198
Table, Tiger Maple, Turned Legs, c.1850, 20 x 30 In.	345
Table, Tile Top, Mosaic, Blue, Green, Round, Splayed Wood Legs, Signed Hohenberg, 1956	1652
Table, Tilt Top, Chippendale, Cherry, Round, Tripod, Shenandoah Valley, c.1795, 28 x 36 In.	805
Table, Tilt Top, Chippendale, Cuban Mahogany, Tripod Base, Boston, 28 x 32 In.	120
Table, Tilt Top, Chippendale, Mahogany, Dish Top, Ball & Claw Feet, c.1775, 29 x 31 In.	1920
Table, Tilt Top, Chippendale, Mahogany, Leaf-Carved Cabriole Legs, 28 x 33 In.	2375
Table, Tilt Top, Chippendale, Mahogany, Piecrust Rim, Cabriole Legs, 23 x 21 In.	1200
Table, Tilt Top, Chippendale, Mahogany, Piecrust, Tripod Base, 1700s, 27 ½ x 31 In.	413
Table, Tilt Top, Chippendale, Mahogany, Rectangular, Scalloped Rim, England, 28 x 27 In.	780
Table, Tilt Top, Chippendale, Mahogany, Round Top, Cabriole Legs, New York, 27 x 22 In.	1000
Table, Tilt Top, Chippendale, Mahogany, Round Top, Tripod Base, c.1775, 29 x 35 In.	345

Furniture, Tea Cart, Brass, Wood, 3 Glass Shelves, Casters, Stamped, Italy, 1950s, 29 x 17 x 31 In.
$1,061

Treadway Toomey Galleries

Furniture, Tea Cart, Cesare Lacca, Walnut Frame, Glass Top, Casters, Italy, 28 x 34 x 17 In.
$1,037

Treadway Toomey Galleries

Furniture, Tea Cart, Wormley, Mahogany, Glass, Removable Trays, Dunbar, c.1950, 33 x 39 In.
$510

Skinner Auctioneers & Appraisers

Gateleg Table

The gateleg table was a seventeenth-century form. Usually the more legs on a gateleg table, the more expensive the table.

Furniture, Umbrella Stand, Renaissance Revival, Walnut, Carved, Brass Handle, 45 x 14 In.
$1,554

Neal Auction Co.

Furniture, Vitrine, Aesthetic Revival, Brass, Mirror, Hinged Top, Door, c.1890, 60 In.
$1,195

Neal Auction Co.

TIP

If you have museum-quality wooden furniture, do not use modern furniture-spray polish. Use wax and apply it about once a year. Just dust it regularly.

Table, Tilt Top, Empire Style, Mahogany, String Inlay, Paw Feet, 1800s, 59 x 42 In.	660
Table, Tilt Top, Federal, Maple, Round, Baluster Standard, Cabriole Legs, c.1790, 28 x 35 In.	313
Table, Tilt Top, George II Style, Mahogany, Round, Carved Edge, Turned Standard, 29 x 29 In.	250
Table, Tilt Top, George II, Mahogany, Piecrust Top, Reeded Column, Ball & Claw, 28 x 20 In.	2000
Table, Tilt Top, George II, Mahogany, Round Piecrust, Carved Standard, Legs, 29 x 28 In.	438
Table, Tilt Top, George II, Walnut, Round, Tripod Base, 26 x 26 In.	1000
Table, Tilt Top, George III Style, Mahogany, Carved, 27 x 33 In.	500
Table, Tilt Top, George III Style, Mahogany, Piecrust, Spiral Stem, Tripod, c.1900, 33 In.	553
Table, Tilt Top, George III Style, Mahogany, Tripod Legs, 1800s, 28 x 24 In.	625
Table, Tilt Top, George III, Mahogany, Banded, Turned Stem, Arched Legs, 29 x 43 In.	717
Table, Tilt Top, George III, Mahogany, Carved, Pierced Gallery, Blind Fret, Tripod, 28 x 27 In.	2500
Table, Tilt Top, George III, Mahogany, Round, c.1820, 28 x 49 In.	1067
Table, Tilt Top, George III, Mahogany, Scalloped Trim, 27 x 19 In.	406
Table, Tilt Top, George III, Mahogany, Wavy Edge, Turned Support, Tripod, 30 In.	2500
Table, Tilt Top, Georgian Style, Mahogany, Round Top, 3 Splayed Feet, 27 x 27 In.	563
Table, Tilt Top, Lacquer, Black & Gilt, Chinese Export, 32 x 33 In. *illus*	1912
Table, Tilt Top, Maple, Turned Pedestal Base, Spider Legs, 30 x 21 In.	384
Table, Tilt Top, Maple, Turned Pedestal, 3 Slipper Feet, 26 x 23 In.	142
Table, Tilt Top, Papier-Mache, Flowers, Scroll Feet, 27 x 20 In.	1140
Table, Tilt Top, Queen Anne, Mahogany, Round Top, Carved Pedestal, 1700s, 28 x 34 In.	480
Table, Tilt Top, Queen Anne, Round Top, Grain Painted, 28 x 36 In.	600
Table, Tilt Top, Queen Anne, Walnut, Dish Top, Turned Pedestal, Tripod Base, 29 x 21 In.	443
Table, Tilt Top, Queen Anne, Walnut, Round, Birdcage, 3 Cabriole Legs, c.1790, 28 x 33 In.	938
Table, Tilt Top, Queen Anne, Walnut, Round, Cabriole Legs, c.1810, 28 x 30 In.	2125
Table, Tilt Top, Queen Anne, Walnut, Splayed Legs, 26 ½ x 31 In.	359
Table, Tilt Top, Regency, Mahogany, 4 Reeded Downswept Legs, c.1845, 27 x 57 In.	403
Table, Tilt Top, Regency, Mahogany, Crossbanded Edge, Reeded Legs, c.1815, 29 x 52 In.	652
Table, Tilt Top, Regency, Mixed Wood, Canted Corners, Tripod, England, c.1810, 29 x 27 In.	295
Table, Tilt Top, Round, Smoke Designs, Painted, Tripod Base, 30 x 29 In.	1200
Table, Tilt Top, Tripod Base, c.1845, 28 ½ In.	259
Table, Tilt Top, Victorian, Mahogany, Round, Carved Pedestal Base, 48 x 29 In.	518
Table, Tom Corbin, Bronze, Round Top, Abstract Standard, c.1990, 20 x 18 In.	4000
Table, Tray, Butler's, Mahogany, Gallery, Handle, Stand, Folding, c.1900, 32 ½ x 27 In.	173
Table, Tray, George III, Papier-Mache, Gilt, Black, Metal Stand, c.1820, 31 x 24 In. *illus*	531
Table, Tray, Hepplewhite, Mahogany, Inlay, Kidney Shape, Conforming Stand, 19 x 23 In.	360
Table, Tray, Lyre Ends, Low Shelf, England, 24 x 30 In.	374
Table, Tray, Papier-Mache Top, Faux Bamboo Stand, England, 19 ½ x 30 x 22 In.	720
Table, Tray, Wood, Carved, Faux Bamboo, Leaves, Stretcher, c.1900, 24 x 30 In.	179
Table, Trestle, Cherry, Hinged Compartment, Blue Paint, C. Coombs, 1994, 29 x 39 In.	333
Table, Trestle, Henry II Style, Walnut, Plank Top, Baluster Supports, c.1900, 39 x 97 In.	1722
Table, Trestle, Pine, Vase Shape Trestles, Shoe Feet, 30 x 105 x 33 In.	5400
Table, Trestle, Shaker, Cherry, Maple, Pine, Mount Lebanon, c.1830, 38 x 98 In.	10000
Table, Trestle, Walnut, Urn Supports, Curled Iron Stretcher, Spain, 52 x 27 In.	1452
Table, Trivet, Wood, Oval Top, Faux Bamboo Base, Porcelain Draining Platter, 18 ½ x 17 In.	299
Table, Tuckaway, Oak, Round Top, Turned Legs, England, 24 x 32 In.	60
Table, Tulip, Eero Saarinen, Wood, Aluminum Powder Base, Florence Knoll, 15 x 18 In.	382
Table, Turned Legs, Yellow Mustard Paint, 27 x 18 In.	480
Table, Victorian, Burl Walnut, Round, Carved, Splayed Legs, 54 x 29 In.	1150
Table, Victorian, Cast Iron Base, Blue Paint, Vase & Ring Shape Post, 1800s, 30 x 39 In.	540
Table, Victorian, Drafting, Mahogany, Adjustable, Turned Stretcher, Casters, 35 x 23 In.	815
Table, Victorian, Iron, Marble Top, 2 Scroll Legs, Leaf Apron Designs, 29 x 37 In.	1896
Table, Victorian, Mahogany, Carved, White Marble, Turtle Top, 30 x 37 In.	1185
Table, Victorian, Mahogany, Round, Turned Standard, 30 x 42 In.	406
Table, Victorian, Shellwork, Octagonal Top, 29 x 29 In.	1080
Table, Victorian, Walnut, Inlay, Checkerboard Top, Carved Standard, 30 x 19 In.	780
Table, Victorian, Walnut, Square White Marble Top, c.1880, 30 x 30 In.	184
Table, Victorian, Walnut, White Marble, Turtle Shape, Carved Frame, c.1880, 29 x 31 In.	345
Table, W. McArthur, Enamel, Brushed Aluminum, c.1929, 18 x 13 In. *illus*	2250
Table, W. Platner, Glass, Round Top, Chrome Plated Steel, c.1970, 15 x 43 In.	1125
Table, Wake, Chippendale Style, Mahogany, Molded Legs, Round Leaves, c.1910, 60 x 89 In.	844
Table, Wake, Drop Leaf, Georgian Style, Mahogany, Open, 84 x 72 In.	438
Table, Walnut, 2 Drawers, 30 x 49 In.	530
Table, Walnut, 2 Drawers, Pin Top, Pad Feet, Pennsylvania, 30 x 58 In.	420
Table, Walnut, 2 Drawers, Stretcher Shelf, 40 x 26 In.	124
Table, Walnut, 2 Drawers, Turned Legs, c.1880, 33 x 21 In.	2875

Table, Walnut, 8-Sided, Pierced Apron, Carvings, Stepped Pedestal, New York, 32 x 61 In.	1800
Table, Walnut, Bentwood, Round, 3 Scroll Supports, c.1890, 30 x 26 In.	2125
Table, Walnut, Drawer, Overhang Top, Tapered Legs, Checkerboard, 1800s, 28 x 36 In.	708
Table, Walnut, Lift Top, 2 Drawers, Inlaid Apron, Turned Legs, 30 x 48 In.	1185
Table, Walnut, Marble Top, Trestle Base, Carved Cherub Head, c.1920, 20 x 26 In.	180
Table, Walnut, Notched Corners, Overhang, Tapered Legs, Pa., 29 x 36 In.	1896
Table, Walnut, Overhang, 2 Drawers, Stretcher Base, c.1770, 31 x 55 In.	780
Table, Walnut, Overhang, Drawer, Stretcher Base, c.1780, 31 x 43 In.	502
Table, Walnut, Pine Overhang Top, Drawer, Turned Legs, Pa., c.1790, 28 x 43 In.	518
Table, Walnut, Pine Overhang, Pa., c.1800, 28 x 54 In.	593
Table, Walnut, Pine Top, Drawer, Turned Legs, Stretcher Base, c.1800, 31 x 55 In.	2596
Table, Walnut, Round Molded Top, Musical Trophy, Saber Legs, Hoof Feet, c.1865, 31 In.	2150
Table, Walnut, Round, Splay Legs, Pa., c.1800, 24 x 19 ½ In.	356
Table, Walnut, Trestle, 2-Board Top, Rosettes, Splayed Block Legs, c.1900, 31 x 48 In.	418
Table, Wendell Castle, Mushroom, Walnut, Initialed WC, 1972, 31 x 46 x 44 In. ....*illus*	42000
Table, Widdicomb, Teak, Fruitwood, Multi-Tier, c.1970, 24 x 25 In., Pair	1375
Table, William & Mary, Maple, 8-Sided Top, Lip Molded, Turned Feet, c.1745, 26 x 30 In.	4375
Table, William & Mary, Oak, Drawer, Galley, Turned Legs, X-Stretcher, 29 x 31 In.	900
Table, William & Mary, Oval Top, Turned Legs, Base Stretcher, Painted, c.1750, 26 x 33 In.	6875
Table, William & Mary, Pine, Red Paint, Drawer, Stretcher Base, c.1750, 26 x 42 In.	780
Table, William IV, Rosewood, Round, Parcel Gilt Edge, Tripod Base, c.1845, 30 x 48 In.	2000
Table, Winchendon, Birch, 10 x 60 In.	344
Table, Wine Tasting, Flip Top, Pine, Oval, Trestle Base, Leaf Support, 1800s, 31 x 55 In.	1062
Table, Wine Tasting, Tilt Top, Hardwood, Round, Iron Latch, France, 28 x 51 In.	960
Table, Wine, Rosewood, Openwork Apron, Spiral Legs & Stretcher, c.1885, 27 x 22 In.	3540
Table, Wine, Tilt Top, Chippendale Style, Mahogany, England, Centennial, 27 x 30 In. ....*illus*	400
Table, Wine, Walnut, Shaped Legs, Stretcher, Apron, Mortised & Tenon, Chinese, 35 x 38 In.	210
Table, With Marble Turtle Top, Drop Down Finials, Splayed Feet, 36 x 29 In.	295
Table, Wood, Painted, Dragons, Clouds, Pierced, Foldover, Tibet, c.1900, 9 x 23 In.	360
Table, Wood, Panel Top, Reticulated Frieze, Cylindrical Legs, Stretcher, 32 x 46 In.	3107
Table, Wood, Portable, Molded Border, Lotus Flowers, Drawer, Tibet, 1700s, 17 x 25 In.	900
Table, Wood, Turned Legs, White Paint, c.1865, 30 x 90 In.	3120
Table, Work, Biedermeier, Maple Burl, Drawer, 22 x 28 In.	147
Table, Work, Bird's-Eye Maple, Overhung Top, Drawer, Turned Legs, c.1805, 30 x 19 In.	1000
Table, Work, Charles X, Rosewood, Inlay, Hinged Top, Fitted Interior, Shelf, c.1810, 29 x 19 In. ..	717
Table, Work, Drop Leaf, American Empire, Mahogany, Drawers, Square Pedestal, 29 x 33 In.	270
Table, Work, Federal, Mahogany, c.1815, 30 x 20 In.	273
Table, Work, Federal, Mahogany, Hinged Ends, 2 Drawers, Oval, c.1820, 29 x 24 In.	1250
Table, Work, Flame Mahogany, 2 Drawers, Pressed Glass Pulls, Turned Legs, 1820s, 28 x 19 In...	240
Table, Work, Lacquer, Hinged Lift Top, Stretcher, Chinoiserie Design, 27 x 26 In.	500
Table, Work, Mahogany, Maple, 2 Drawers, Stretcher Shelf, N.Y., c.1816, 31 x 22 In.	296
Table, Work, Mahogany, Tambour Opening, Adjustable Mirror, Splayed Legs, 28 x 26 In.	3360
Table, Work, Mahogany, Tambour Sides, Drawers, Brass Feet, New York, 28 x 26 In.	1440
Table, Work, Maple, Mahogany, 2 Drawers, Inlay, Barry School, c.1800, 29 x 18 In.	5000
Table, Work, Neoclassical, Cherry, Draw Leaf, 1800s, 28 x 27 ½ In.	188
Table, Work, Neoclassical, Mahogany, Drawers, Writing Desk, c.1810, 23 x 17 In. ....*illus*	1912
Table, Work, Neoclassical, Mahogany, Marble, Drawers, Spiral Acanthus Legs, c.1800, 30 x 21 In.	1912
Table, Work, Neoclassical, Mahogany, Turreted Corners, Lyre Base, c.1825, 31 x 21 In. ....*illus*	860
Table, Work, Neoclassical, Maple, Mahogany, Poplar, 2 Drawers, Columns, 30 x 22 In.	482
Table, Work, Pine, Green Paint, Drawer, Turned Legs, 19th Century, 28 x 32 In.	323
Table, Work, Queen Anne, Maple, Pine, Painted, Breadboard Top, Drawer, 1700s, 27 x 42 In.......	1528
Table, Work, Queen Anne, Walnut, Pine, Drawer, Turned Legs, Stretcher, 20 x 52 In.	1175
Table, Work, Shaker, Maple, Drawers Front & Side, Pullout Slide, 38 x 32 In. ....*illus*	31860
Table, Work, Walnut, Drawer, Casters, Pa., c.1845, 30 x 50 In.	633
Table, Work, Walnut, Turned Legs, Pa., c.1780, 43 ½ x 30 In.	1007
Table, Wormley, Burl Elm, Surfboard Shape, Brass Stretcher, Legs, Dunbar, 15 x 72 In.	2925
Table, Writing, Bonheur Du Jour, Regency Style, England, c.1875, 43 x 27 In. ....*illus*	2460
Table, Writing, Charles X, Mahogany, Veneer, Inlay, Gallery, Drawers, c.1840, 33 x 51 In.	2090
Table, Writing, Neoclassical, Fruitwood, Paneled Top, Tapered Legs, 1800s, 28 x 46 In...............	1080
Table, Writing, Regency Style, Mahogany, Drawer, Turned Legs, c.1885, 31 x 42 In.	236
Table, Writing, Satinwood, Inlay, Scrolling Leaves, Square Legs, c.1800, 30 x 30 In.	1554
Table, Writing, William IV, Mahogany, Leather Top, Turned Legs, c.1835, 29 x 36 In.	1076
Table, Wrought Iron, Round Marble Top, Curving Base, Legs, 26 x 18 In.	80
Table, Wrought Iron, Wood Top, Gilt Scrolled Crown, Round, 30 ½ x 48 In.	300
Tabouret, Carved, Marble Top, Cabriole Legs, Pierced, Chinese, c.1890, 36 In. ....*illus*	711

Furniture, Vitrine, Louis XV Style, Carved, Glass Door, Gilt, France, c.1900, 66 x 46 In.
$649

Brunk Auctions

Furniture, Vitrine, Vernis Martin, Glazed Door, Cabriole Legs, c.1900, 55 x 26 In.
$750

Rago Arts & Auction Center

This is an edited listing of current prices. Visit **Kovels.com** to check thousands of prices from previous years and sign up for free information on trends, tips, reproductions, marks, and more.

Furniture, Washstand, Shaker, Pine, 2-Board Top, Dovetailed, Casters, 28 x 48 In.
$4,425

Willis Henry Auctions, Inc.

Furniture, Washstand, Tole Painted, Marble Top, Decoupage Scenes, 50 x 21 In.
$1,298

Brunk Auctions

TIP

If a marble tabletop is damaged, a good repair is preferred to a new top. If there is a lot of damage, an old top from another piece is the best replacement.

Furniture, Window Seat, Neoclassical, Mahogany, Swan's Neck, Casters, Boston, 59 In.
$4,541

Neal Auction Co.

Tabouret, L. & J.G. Stickley, Clip Corners, Stretchers, Decal, c.1912, 20 x 18 In.	1250
Tabouret, Rosewood, Red Marble Top, Carved, Pierced Skirt, Stretcher, c.1900, 20 In.	474
Tansu, Rustic, Wood, Bracket Feet, Brass Mounts, Hinged Door, Japan, 25 x 22 In.	288
Tea Cart, Aalto, Birch, Wicker Basket, Tile Top, c.1975, 23 x 36 x 25 In. ....*illus*	295
Tea Cart, Brass, Wood, 3 Glass Shelves, Casters, Stamped, Italy, 1950s, 29 x 17 x 31 In. ......*illus*	1061
Tea Cart, Brass, Wood, 3 Shelves, Tapered, Italy, 1950s, 17 x 30 In.	1750
Tea Cart, Cesare Lacca, Walnut Frame, Glass Top, Casters, Italy, 28 x 34 x 17 In. ....*illus*	1037
Tea Cart, Edwardian, Mahogany, Round Galleried Caddies, Shelf, 29 x 42 In., Pair	922
Tea Cart, Iron, Glass Top, Scrolls, Leaves, Black Paint, 33 x 29 In.	153
Tea Cart, Regency, Tole, Shakespearian Play Scene, Oval, c.1800, 30 x 23 In.	1045
Tea Cart, Wormley, Mahogany, Glass, Removable Trays, Dunbar, c.1950, 33 x 39 In. ....*illus*	510
Teapoy, William IV, Rosewood, Lion Masks, Casket Shape, Splayed Saber Legs, 31 x 19 In.	826
Tete-A-Tete, French Style, Wood Frame, Carved, Gilt, Tufted Upholstery, Casters, 47 x 22 In.	529
Umbrella Stand, Arts & Crafts, Oak, Tapered, c.1915, 30 x 15 In.	563
Umbrella Stand, Black Forest, Figural, Bear, Glass Eyes, Drip Pan, 1800s, 40 x 16 In.	3320
Umbrella Stand, Lacquered Brass Repousse, Fruit Basket, Scrolls, Mask, 1900s, 29 In.	120
Umbrella Stand, Renaissance Revival, Walnut, Carved, Brass Handle, 45 x 14 In. ....*illus*	1554
Umbrella Stand, Walnut, Umbrella Shape, Brass Hoof Handle, Bun Feet, 46 In.	3294
Umbrella Stand, Whippet Dog Shape, Seated, Riding Crop, Cast Metal, 35 x 27 In.	2714
Valet, Golfer's, Putting Station, Ball Return, Club Holders, Maitland-Smith, 39 In.	48
Vitrine, Aesthetic Revival, Brass, Mirror, Hinged Top, Door, c.1890, 60 In. ....*illus*	1195
Vitrine, Edwardian, Fruitwood, Inlay, Hinge Top, Tapered Legs, c.1910, 30 x 24 In.	316
Vitrine, Edwardian, Mahogany, Hinged, Glazed, Shelf Stretcher, c.1900, 30 x 30 In.	922
Vitrine, George III Style, Mahogany, Square Top, Square Legs, c.1900, 29 x 16 In.	676
Vitrine, Georgian Style, Mahogany, Carved, Doors, Shelves, Drawers, 1900s, 88 x 57 In.	1075
Vitrine, Giltwood, Mirrors, Carved Pediment, France, c.1900, 60 ½ x 38 In.	1304
Vitrine, Hanging, Stick Style, Oak, c.1900, 21 x 9 In., Pair	1375
Vitrine, Louis XV Style, Carved, Glass Door, Gilt, France, c.1900, 66 x 46 In. ....*illus*	649
Vitrine, Louis XV Style, Mahogany, Burl, Glaze Door, Shelves, Sabots, 59 x 24 In.	799
Vitrine, Louis XV Style, Mahogany, Marble Top, Glass Doors, c.1865, 67 x 45 In.	4674
Vitrine, Louis XV Style, Walnut, Flowers, Arched Panel Door, 1800s, 75 x 32 In.	2952
Vitrine, Louis XVI Style, Kingwood, Glass Top, Door, Cabriole Legs, c.1890, 36 x 26 In.	7688
Vitrine, Mahogany, Banded Inlay, Beveled Glass Top & Sides, 1900s, 36 x 32 x 17 In.	937
Vitrine, Napoleon III, Kingwood, Octagonal, Sunburst Inlaid Lid, c.1865, 45 x 29 In.	1045
Vitrine, Rococo, Mahogany, Pewter Inlay, c.1925, 60 x 25 x 13 In.	562
Vitrine, Vernis Martin, Glazed Door, Cabriole Legs, c.1900, 55 x 26 In. ....*illus*	750
Wardrobe, Ash, Eastlake, Murphy Bed Convertible, Salesman Sample, 30 x 12 In.	374
Wardrobe, Faux Grain Paint, Pine, Paneled Doors, Interior Shelves, c.1910, 74 x 54 In.	3525
Wardrobe, Georgian, Veneer, Figured Mahogany Ovals, Doors, Bowfront, 76 x 85 In.	1035
Wardrobe, Grain Painted, Door, Drawer, Pa., c.1855, 78 x 44 In.	1067
Wardrobe, Grain Painted, Poplar, Divided Panel Door, Turned Feet, Pa., c.1850, 68 x 42 In.	1896
Wardrobe, Mixed Wood, 2 Doors, Recessed Carvings, Thomas Day, c.1850, 80 x 51 In.	2950
Wardrobe, Oak, Beveled Cornice, Doors, Carved, Shelves, Belgium, 1900s, 76 x 74 In.	390
Wardrobe, Red Stain, Drawer, 2 Panel Doors, c.1850, 65 x 23 In.	834
Wardrobe, Softwood, Red Finish, Sunken-Panel Doors, Wall Pegs, Pa., c.1860, 80 x 49 In.	2006
Wardrobe, Spanish Colonial, Mahogany, Leaves, Doors, Paw Feet, c.1885, 75 x 57 In.	553
Washstand, Corner, Federal, Mahogany, Basin Cutout, Shelf, Drawer, c.1820, 32 x 26 In.	46
Washstand, Corner, Sheraton, 2 Shelves, Pa., c.1815, 39 ½ x 22 ½ In.	296
Washstand, Double, Marble Top, Scroll Sides, Reeded Legs, Serpentine, c.1850, 40 x 49 In.	4063
Washstand, Faux Bamboo Detail Legs, White Marble Top, Gallery, Drawers, 39 x 43 In.	200
Washstand, Federal, Blue Paint, Softwood, Skirt Drawer, Turned Legs, c.1840, 30 x 22 In.	413
Washstand, French Provincial, Wood, Marble Top, Cupboard Doors, 42 x 32 In.	270
Washstand, George III, Mahogany, c.1790, 43 x 19 In.	148
Washstand, Grain Painted, Scalloped Gallery, Drawer, Shelf, New England, 33 x 23 In.	360
Washstand, Green Paint, Carved Backsplash, Low Shelf, New England, c.1820, 35 x 25 In.	652
Washstand, Mahogany Veneer, 3 Turned Legs, Marble Shelf, Stoneware Bowl, 31 x 17 In.	184
Washstand, Mahogany, Backsplash, Bookmatch, Drawer, Shelf, c.1835, 37 x 25 In.	210
Washstand, Mahogany, Shaped Gallery, Serpentine & Lower Shelf, 2 Drawers, 35 In.	206
Washstand, Mahogany, Sheraton, Carved Love Birds, Drawer, 34 x 21 In.	360
Washstand, Mixed Wood, Painted, 2 Tiers, Shelves, Turned Legs, 1800s, 37 x 18 In.	118
Washstand, Pine, Drawer, Painted, Backsplash, New England, c.1820, 32 x 33 In.	365
Washstand, Pine, Green Paint, Set Back Shelf, Stretcher Shelf, c.1830, 37 x 22 In.	615
Washstand, Pine, Red Paint, High Backsplash, c.1850	235
Washstand, Shaker, Pine, 2-Board Top, Dovetailed, Casters, 28 x 48 In. ....*illus*	4425
Washstand, Shaker, Pine, Yellow Stain, Cherry Pulls, Dovetailed, 38 x 28 x 18 In.	44250

F

Washstand, Sheraton, Applied Gallery Top, Shelf, Turned Feet, Va., c.1835, 32 x 29 In.	196
Washstand, Sheraton, Cherry, Shaped Backsplash, 3 Drawers, 38 x 33 In.	158
Washstand, Sheraton, Faux Rosewood Stain, Stretcher Drawer, Stencils, c.1825, 38 x 18 In.	889
Washstand, Sheraton, Walnut, Shaped Backsplash, 3 Drawers, 38 x 34 In.	180
Washstand, Tole Painted, Marble Top, Decoupage Scenes, 50 x 21 In. *illus*	1298
Washstand, Victorian, Oak, Towel Rack, Drawer, 2 Doors, c.1920, 28 ½ x 30 In.	138
Washstand, Victorian, Walnut, Burl Walnut, Tilt Mirror, Drawers, Base Molding, 75 x 33 In.	266
Washstand, Walnut, Backsplash, Towel Bars, Drawer, Lower Shelf, 30 x 17 In.	79
Washstand, Walnut, Marble Top, Drawer, Doors, Ogee Bracket Feet, c.1890, 34 x 36 In.	717
Washstand, Walnut, Poplar, Grain Painted, Top & Gallery, Base Shelf, c.1865, 31 x 27 In.	374
Window Seat, Carved Wood, Painted, Lift Top, Arched Sides, Ball Feet, c.1900, 27 x 36 In.	236
Window Seat, Neoclassical, Birch, Painted, Scroll Ends, Footed, Upholstered, c.1845, 23 x 49 In., Pair	8750
Window Seat, Neoclassical, Mahogany, Swan's Neck, Casters, Boston, 59 In. *illus*	4541
Wine Cooler, George III, Mahogany, Domed, Pineapple Finial, Mask Handles, 25 In.	4720
Wine Cooler, Mahogany, Brassbound, Flared Legs, England, 31 x 18 In.	1020
Wine Cooler, Regency Style, Mahogany, Spiral Pedestal Base, Copper Liner, 30 x 30 In.	495
Wine Stand, George III, Mahogany, Round, Dish Top, Cabriole Legs, 21 x 9 In.	2400
Wine Stand, Mahogany, Dish Top, Round, Cabriole Legs, Pad Feet, 21 x 10 In.	480
Work Stand, Pine, Splayed Legs, Blue Paint, c.1810, 30 x 33 In.	710
Work Stand, Regency, Mahogany, Fitted Drawer, c.1820, 29 x 14 In.	237
Work Stand, Sheraton, Mahogany, 2 Drawers, Carved, Reeded Legs, 29 x 22 In.	3080

FURSTENBERG PORCELAIN WORKS was started in Furstenberg, Germany, in 1747. It is still working and is still using the *F* with crown mark. Many of the modern products are made in the old molds.

Urn, Lid, Ram's Head, Handles, Flowers, Footed, Gilt, 15 In.	240

G. ARGY-ROUSSEAU is the impressed mark used on a variety of glass objects in the Art Deco style. Gabriel Argy-Rousseau, born in 1885, was a French glass artist. In 1921, he formed a partnership that made pate-de-verre and other glass. The partnership ended in 1931 and he opened his own studio. He worked until 1952 and died in 1953.

G-ARGY-ROUSSEAU

Diffuser, Top Only, Purple Petals, Fan Shape, Pare-De-Verre, 7 ⅝ In.	10625
Jar, Lid, Bachelor Button Flowers, Mottled, Frosted, Signed, 2 ½ In. *illus*	2963
Paperweight, Pate-De-Verre, 2 Molded Moths, Amber Mottled, Signed, 2 ¾ In.	2500
Pendant, Ballerina, Pate-De-Verre, Silk Cord, Tassle, Signed, 1920s, 2 In. *illus*	1875
Pendant, Cicada, Rose, Blue, Black, Oval, c.1910, 2 ½ In.	923
Pendant, Pate-De-Verre, Purple Moth, Black, Blue, Pink Ground, 18 x 2 ½ In.	547
Vase, Butterfly, Tan, Amber, Wide Rim, Tapered, c.1915, 3 In.	7670
Vase, Pate-De-Verre, Prunus, Bulbous Top, Purple, Opalescent, Signed, 5 ½ In.	5333
Vase, Poppy, Amber, Coral, Wide Mouth, Tapered, 7 ½ In.	7670
Vase, Woman, Picking Fruit, Pate-De-Verre, 1920s, 9 ½ x 6 In.	8750

GALLE was a designer who made glass, pottery, furniture, and other Art Nouveau items. Emile Galle founded his factory in France in 1874. After Galle's death in 1904, the firm continued to make glass and furniture until 1931. The *Galle* signature was used as a mark, but it was often hidden in the design of the object. Galle glass is listed here. Pottery is in the next section. His furniture is listed in the Furniture category.

Galle

Bowl, Pink Hydrangeas, White Ground, Elongated Oval, Rolled Pinched Rim, 11 ⅝ In.	2125
Ewer, Enameled Glass, Flowers, Crowned Phoenix Handle, Flat Baluster, Footed, 12 ½ In.	8125
Lamp, Boudoir, Plants, Flowers, Cameo, Signed, 14 In. *illus*	7703
Lamp, Domed Shade, Flowers, Leaves, Cranberry, Cream, Cameo, c.1905, 13 In.	385
Perfume Atomizer, Orange Flowers, Yellow Ground, Cameo, Gilt, France, c.1890, 6 x 4 In.	344
Pitcher, Flowers, Butterflies, Orange Ground, Double Handles, 4 ¾ x 4 ¾ In.	700
Powder Box, Lid, Green Leaves, White, Pink Ground, Signed Cameo, 5 In.	1188
Scent Bottle, Wheel Carved, Red Flowers, Red & Crystal Ground, Stopper, 5 In.	7898
Shade, Dome, Violets, Cherries, Cameo Glass, France, 5 x 9 In.	1053
Tray, Rose Red, Berries, Leaves, Organic Shape, Signed, c.1900, 8 ½ In.	338
Vase, Black Dragonfly, Orange Ground, Cylindrical, Cameo, 8 ¼ In.	319
Vase, Bleeding Heart, Blue Acid Cutback, Pink, Green, Cameo, Signed, 13 In.	7110
Vase, Bleeding Heart, Frosted Yellow Ground, Cameo, Signed, 6 In. *illus*	3673
Vase, Blue Morning Glories, Green, Pinched Rim, Long Ribbed Neck, Cameo, Signed, 5 x 11 In.	2500
Vase, Brown Iris, Yellow, White Mottled Ground, Marquetry, Tapered, Footed, Cameo, 7 ¼ In.	12500
Vase, Bud, Orange Flowers, White Frosted Ground, Tapered, Cameo, 6 x 3 In.	234
Vase, Bud, Plum Flowers, Amber, Clear, Long Neck, Globe Base, c.1900, 6 In.	688
Vase, Bud, Plums, Stems, Green, Purple, Frosted, Oval, Mottled Amber, Cameo, c.1900, 8 In.	1250
Vase, Bud, Purple, Green Wisteria, Silver, White Leaves, Signed Cameo, 8 ⅜ In.	938

G. Argy-Rousseau, Jar, Lid, Bachelor Button Flowers, Mottled, Frosted, Signed, 2 ½ In.
$2,963

James D. Julia Auctioneers

G. Argy-Rousseau, Pendant, Ballerina, Pate-De-Verre, Silk Cord, Tassle, Signed, 1920s, 2 In.
$1,875

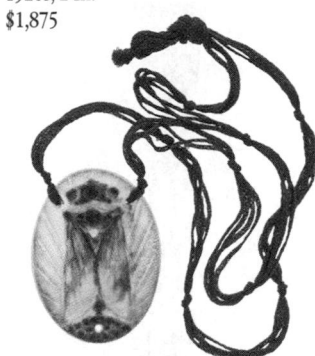

Rago Arts & Auction Center

Galle, Lamp, Boudoir, Plants, Flowers, Cameo, Signed, 14 In.
$7,703

James D. Julia Auctioneers

Galle, Vase, Bleeding Heart, Frosted Yellow Ground, Cameo, Signed, 6 In. $3,673

James D. Julia Auctioneers

Galle, Vase, Dragonfly, Lily Pads, Amber, Frosted, Cameo, Signed, 22 ½ In. $10,665

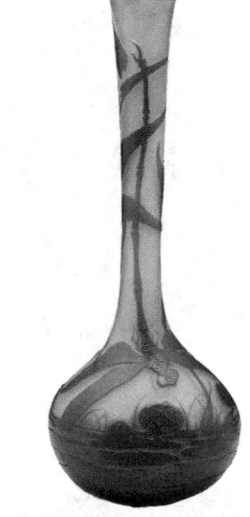

James D. Julia Auctioneers

Galle, Vase, Trees, Pond, Olive Green, Cameo, Signed, 8 In. $2,133

James D. Julia Auctioneers

Vase, Bulbous, Thistle, Cameo, Signed, Sticker, c.1875, 4 In.		469
Vase, Clear To Red Frosted, Cameo, Glass, Cylindrical Neck, Spherical Body, c.1910, 9 ¾ In.		900
Vase, Clematis, Mold Blown, Brown Leaves, Stems, Red Flowers, Yellow Frosted, 6 ¾ In.		7110
Vase, Daisies In Windowpane, Cameo, Acid Etched, Signed, 1900s, 6 ½ x 8 In.		2750
Vase, Dragonflies, Scrolls, Martele Finish, Footed, Cameo, 6 ¼ In.		16250
Vase, Dragonfly, Lily Pads, Amber, Frosted, Cameo, Signed, 22 ½ In.	*illus*	10665
Vase, Dragonfly, Pond, Green, Orange, Blue, Long Neck, Cameo, c.1900, 23 In.		10000
Vase, Enameled Glass, Middle East Design, Brown, Tan, Yellow, Handles, Marked, 6 In.		11875
Vase, Fire Polished Finish, Cameo, Cut, Irises, Plum, Amber To Lavender, 10 ¼ In.		2300
Vase, Flowers & Leaves, Purple, Tapered, Round Bottom, c.1915, 10 ½ In.		1121
Vase, Flowers, Cameo, Acid Etched, Signed, 1900s, 10 x 4 ½ In.		2125
Vase, Flowers, Leaves, Gold, Dark Purple, Tapered Mouth & Base, Cameo, c.1820, 5 x 6 In.		1750
Vase, Flowers, Leaves, Pink, Yellow Ground, Rolled Rim, 10 In.		911
Vase, Gilt, Enamel Flowers, 6 Ring Handles, Tan, Brown, Yellow, E. Cross, G. Depose, 8 ¾ In.		15000
Vase, Green Fuchsia Flowers, Pink, Frosted, Bulbous, 3 x 2 ¼ In.		250
Vase, Green Leaves, Amber, Yellow, Frosted, Elongated Oval, Rolled Rim, 1900s, 13 In.		1652
Vase, Green Leaves, Cream Ground, Tapered, Cameo, 5 ¾ In.		356
Vase, Green Pasture Landscape, Pink Frosted Ground, Tapered, Footed, c.1910, 6 In.		750
Vase, Green, Amber, Landscape, Frosted, Clear, Oval, Acid Etched Cameo, c.1900, 25 In.		7500
Vase, Green, Brown Leaves, Tomatoes, Tapered Cylinder, Footed, Signed Cameo, 11 ¼ In.		15000
Vase, Iris, Marquetry, Purple, Yellow, Red, Yellow & White Mottled Ground, Signed, 8 In.		21330
Vase, Lake, Landscape, Green, Rose, Yellow, Flattened Oval, Shouldered, 6 In.		1000
Vase, Lakeside Scene, Pink Frosted Ground, Cameo, Squat, Tapered, c.1910, 5 In.		563
Vase, Lakeside Scene, Yellow, Blue, Black, Tapered, Cameo, 15 ½ In.		3300
Vase, Landscape, Lime & Olive Green, Orange Neck, Oval, Cameo, c.1900, 12 In.		2500
Vase, Landscape, Trees, Purple To Blue, Bulbous, Pedestal Foot, Rolled Rim, c.1915, 8 In.		3304
Vase, Lavender Leaves, Yellow Ground, Squat, Wide Mouth, Cameo, 2 ¾ x 4 In.		608
Vase, Lavender Stylized Flowers, Green, White Ground, Tapered, Cameo, 4 ¾ In.		356
Vase, Lavender, Green Flowers, Peach Ground, Tapered Bulbous, Signed, Cameo, 2 ½ In.		502
Vase, Leaf & Berry, Vines, Red, Black, Tapered, Flat Rim, c.1900, 5 x 4 ⅛ In.		3540
Vase, Leaves, Flowering Branches, Green, Brown, White, Tapered Cylinder, 15 ½ In.		2375
Vase, Orange, Green Flowers, Yellow Ground, Cameo Cut, Signed, 4 ½ x 9 ½ In.		1875
Vase, Peach Frosted, Elongated Leaf Stemmed Flowers, Cameo, Cylindrical, Signed, 13 ¼ In.		805
Vase, Pink Frosted, Green, Blue Hydrangea, Squat Bottle Shape, Signed, 8 ½ In.		863
Vase, Pink, Blue Butterflies, Blue Ground, Cylindrical, Cameo, 9 ½ In.		406
Vase, Purple Flowers, Leaves, Yellow Ground, Inverted Funnel Shape, Marked, c.1810, 6 x 5 In.		688
Vase, Purple Flowers, Leaves, Yellow, Amber, Ground, Cameo, Cylinder, 17 ½ In.		3025
Vase, Purple Flowers, Yellow, Opaque Ground, Flared Cylinder, 25 In.		4840
Vase, Purple Hydrangea, Yellow White Ground, Tapered Cylinder, Signed Cameo, 10 ⅜ In.		2125
Vase, Purple Iris, White, Yellow Ground, Elongated Oval, Cameo Signed, 9 ¾ In.		3750
Vase, Purple, Vines, Tapered Cylinder, c.1900, 15 ½ In.		1500
Vase, Red Flowers, Green Ground, Cameo, 5 In.		911
Vase, Red Flowers, Leaves, Yellow Frosted Ground Shaded To Cream, Cameo, Signed, 4 ¾ In.		2133
Vase, Red Leaves Cut To Yellow Ground, Cameo, Mark, c.1910, 24 In.		1800
Vase, Red Leaves, Frosted Ground, Bulbous, Handles, Cameo, 11 ½ In.		2430
Vase, Red, Green Rhododendron, Branches, Mold Blown, Globe Shape, Cameo, 10 In.		25000
Vase, Scenic, Trees, Bridge, Castle, Lake Scene, Yellow, Green Ground, Cameo, 14 In.		5333
Vase, Squat, Tapered, Swollen Shoulder, Flat Rim, Sunflower, Amber, Orange, 6 ½ In.		5382
Vase, Stylized Flowers, Relief, Cameo, Tapered, Signed, c.1875, 5 In.		375
Vase, Swollen, Pinched Waist, Round Base, Spread Foot, Cameo, Flower, 1800s, 11 In.		8658
Vase, Tiger Lilies, Green, Long Neck, Squat Base, Cameo Glass, France, c.1910, 5 x 4 In.		531
Vase, Translucent Amber, Thistles, Cross Of Lorraine, Flat Globular, Footed, c.1900, 6 In.		1625
Vase, Trees, Pond, Olive Green, Cameo, Signed, 8 In.	*illus*	2133
Vase, Water Lilies, Pads, Carved, Purple, Blue, Yellow Ground, Cameo, Signed, 6 In.		790
Vase, White, Blue, Yellow Crocus, Marquetry Glass, Tapered, Flattened Cylinder, 13 ½ In.		30000
Vase, Winter Landscape, Sparrows, Tapered Cylinder, Signed Cameo, 14 In.		22500
Vase, Yellow, Cascading Crimson Wisteria, Cameo, Banjo Shape, Signed, 6 ½ In.		489
Vase, Yellow, Flowers, Leaves, Amber Grapes, Stems, Leaves, Cameo, Signed, 5 x 6 In., Pair		911

GALLE POTTERY was made by Emile Galle, the famous French designer, after 1874. The pieces were marked with the initials *E. G.* impressed, *Em. Galle Faiencerie de Nancy,* or a version of his signature. Galle is best known for his glass, listed above.

Bowl, Praying Mantis, Flowers, Blue, Red, Brown, Smoky Ground, Triangular, 4 ½ x 7 In.		790
Centerpiece, Tray, Pigeon, Ruffled Feathers, Japonisme Faience, Marked, c.1885, 11 In.		316
Figurine, Cat, Seated, Yellow Glaze, Blue Spots, 11 x 13 In.		2420
Figurine, Cat, Yellow, Blue Hearts, Dots, Faience, Nancy, c.1885, 14 In.	*illus*	492
Figurine, Owl, Green Majolica Glaze, Glass Eyes, France, 1890s, 12 ¾ x 5 In.		938

G

GAME collectors like all types of games. Of special interest are any board games or card games. Transogram and other company names are included in the description when known. Other games may be found listed under Card, Toy, or the name of the character or celebrity featured in the game.

American Football Game, Cards, Complete, 1930s, 15 ½ x 18 ½ In.	58
American Football, Cards, American New Co., c.1935, 18 x 18 In.	35
Bean Bag Toss, Clown, Open Mouth, Painted, 27 In.	144
Board, Backgammon, Pine, Yellow, Red, Black, Blue, Early 20th Century, 22 x 19 In.	1650
Board, Billiard, Oak, Round, Hand Painted Numbers, England, c.1850, 10 ¾ In., Pair	1180
Board, Chinese Checkers, Oak, Drilled Holes, Painted, c.1885, 13 ½ x 13 ½ In. ....*illus*	711
Board, Horse Race, Pinball, Arched Tablet Shape, Green, Raised Nail Hole Guards, 29 x 15 In.	660
Board, Parcheesi & Checkers, Incised, Painted, Collage, Applied Decals, 20 x 20 In.	649
Board, Parcheesi & Checkers, Multicolor, Applied Edge, c.1900, 18 x 19 In.	540
Board, Parcheesi & Checkers, Painted Sheet Iron, Faux Marble Border, 18 x 18 In. ....*illus*	3900
Board, Parcheesi, Hinged, Basswood, Signed, New England, c.1875, 18 x 19 In. ....*illus*	2370
Board, Parcheesi, Inlaid Stars, Dots, c.1890, 20 ½ x 20 ¾ In.	456
Board, Parcheesi, Pine, Multicolor, Breadboard Ends, c.1900s, 10 x 20 ½ In.	482
Board, Parcheesi, Pine, Paint, 1800s, 19 x 18 In.	3645
Board, Parcheesi, Square Panel, Green, Red, Orange, Black Paint, c.1885, 17 x 17 In.	8400
Board, Parcheesi, Stenciled, Molding, Stags, Rosette, Multicolor, c.1930, 16 x 16 In.	840
Board, Parcheesi, Wood, Painted, Geometric Pattern, U.S.A., c.1885, 17 x 17 In.	4800
Board, Parquetry, 2-Sided, Inlay, Gallery, U.S.A., c.1890, 13 x 13 ½ In.	588
Board, Reverse Mother-Of-Pearl, Paint, Black & White, 1900s, 11 ½ x 11 ½ In.	49
Board, Walnut, Red, Black Paint, Battens On Back, c.1890, 16 ½ x 23 ½ In.	570
Board, Wood, Black, Red, Paint, 1900s, 28 x 24 In.	146
Buddy L Golf, Green Table, Stand-Up Golfer, Flag, Score Sheets, Box, 1944, 7 x 22 In.	7080
Checkerboard, 2-Sided, Yellow & Orange Paint, c.1900, 16 ½ x 16 ½ In.	392
Checkerboard, 144 Squares, Painted Scroll Ends, Red, Gray, Raised Edge, Canada, 20 x 28 In.	720
Checkerboard, Applied Gallery, Mid 1900s, 14 ½ x 21 ½ In.	154
Checkerboard, Cream & Black, Applied Raised Edges, Inscribed, Susan Wooley, 14 x 14 In.	540
Checkerboard, Mixed Woods, Folding, Game Pieces, Scotland, Victorian, 17 x 15 In.	480
Checkerboard, Painted, Cream & Black, Molded Edge, c.1900, 17 ½ x 17 ½ In.	588
Checkerboard, Painted, Tan, Black, New England, Miniature, 8 x 8 In.	2400
Checkerboard, Pine, Scrubbed Surface, Applied Gallery, Red, Ivory Paint, c.1900, 14 x 14 In.	441
Checkerboard, Poplar, Painted Black, Mustard, Applied Edge, c.1910, 16 x 16 In.	180
Checkerboard, Poplar, Painted Yellow, Black, Applied Edge, 14 ½ x 14 ½ In.	1200
Checkerboard, Red, Black Paint, c.1920, 16 ½ x 28 In.	230
Checkerboard, Red, Orange, Black, Stenciled, Sewing Pattern, c.1910, 17 ½ x 18 ¾ In.	180
Checkerboard, Red, Yellow, Applied Edge, c.1910, 14 ¾ x 16 ¾ In.	431
Checkerboard, Reverse Painted Glass, Boston Advertising Border, Victorian, 22 In.	240
Checkerboard, Slate, Paint, c.1900, 15 x 10 ½ In.	122
Checkerboard, Soft Wood, Applied Gallery, Red, White, Blue Paint, c.1900, 12 ½ x 12 ½ In.	512
Checkerboard, Storage Drawer, Red, Black Paint, 16 x 16 In.	240
Checkerboard, Walnut, Gray, Black & Red Border, Green & Black Squares, c.1900, 23 x 23 In.	384
Checkerboard, Walnut, Red, Black Paint, Pa., c.1890, 14 ¾ x 14 ½ In.	533
Checkerboard, Wood, Black & White, Red End Galleries, 1900s, 15 ½ x 24 ½ In.	353
Checkerboard, Wood, Carved, Massachusetts Institute Of Technology Seal, 1908, 22 x 16 In.	270
Checkerboard, Yellow & Black Painted Checks, Side Panels, c.1885, 27 x 16 In.	338
Chess Set, Chased, Repousse Silver, Carved Ivory Faces, Jewels, 7 ½ In., 32 Piece	12800
Chess Set, Mahogany Marquetry Case, Lion's Paw Feet, Sterling Pieces, 5 x 20 In.	3444
Chiromagica, Wizard, Astronomer Tools, McLoughlin Bros., Box, c.1900	368
Coin Toss, Carnival, Wood Frame, Frog, Cast Iron, 22 ½ x 34 ½ In.	316
Cribbage, Sliding Top, Bone Dominoes, Prisoner Of War, Board, c.1810, 5 ½ In.	212
Croquet Set, Mallets, Balls, Wickets, Case, Wood, Child's	59
Dominoes, Set Of 28, Ebony, Bone, Box, c.1850, 7 ¾ In.	266
Dominoes, Set Of 28, Leather Case, France, c.1890 ....*illus*	86
Faro, Bucking The Tiger, Wood, Carved, Plank Base, c.1880, 43 x 23 In.	5310
Game Of Voyage Round The World, Milton Bradley, Board, 1930s, 16 x 12 In.	106
Horse Race, Wood, 8 Lanes, Tin Litho Horses, Betting Discs, Electric Motor, Vibrates, 43 In.	237
Jigsaw Puzzle, Custer's Last Stand, 905 Pieces, Frame, 1934, 32 x 40 In.	360
Landing Of Columbus, Flag, Figure, Paper On Wood, Litho, Reed, Marbles, Board, 10 In.	885
Life Boat Game, Adventure Series, Parker Brothers, Board, 20 ¾ x 10 ½ In.	150
Magic Wheel, Wood, Paint, Round, 11 In.	144
Magnetic Fish Pond, Tank, Children, McLoughlin Bros., Board, 1891, 14 ½ In.	148
Mahjong Set, 136 Bone & Bamboo Tiles, 3 Die, Wood Case, 6 ½ x 10 ¼ In.	34
Mahjong Set, Bone, Bamboo Tiles, Pamphlet, Cased Lacquer Box, c.1910	130

Galle Pottery, Figurine, Cat, Yellow, Blue Hearts, Dots, Faience, Nancy, c.1885, 14 In.
$492

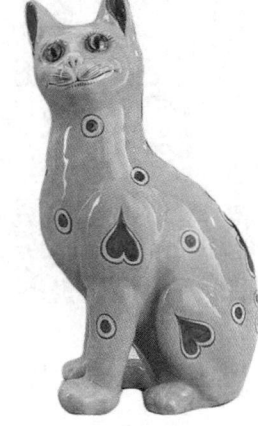

New Orleans Auction Galleries, Inc.

Game, Board, Chinese Checkers, Oak, Drilled Holes, Painted, c.1885, 13 ½ x 13 ½ In.
$711

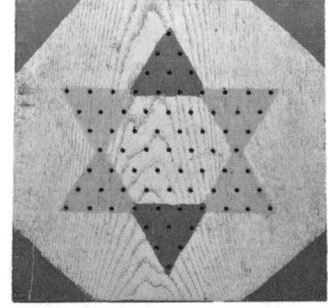

James D. Julia Auctioneers

Game, Board, Parcheesi & Checkers, Painted Sheet Iron, Faux Marble Border, 18 x 18 In.
$3,900

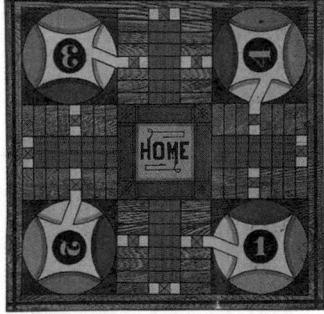

Cowan's Auctions

Game, Board, Parcheesi, Hinged, Basswood, Signed, New England, c.1875, 18 x 19 In.
$2,370

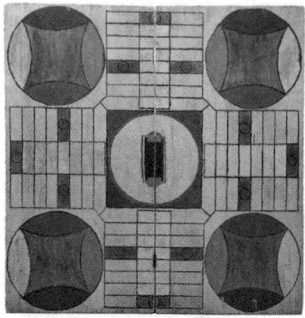

James D. Julia Auctioneers

Game, Dominoes, Set Of 28, Leather Case, France, c.1890
$86

Potter & Potter Auctions, Inc.

Game, Poker, Chip Caddy, Lever Pull Dispenses Chips, 280 Bakelite Chips, 2 Card Decks
$540

Victorian Casino Antiques

Game, Poker, Chip Rack, 120 Bakelite Chips, Leatherette Case, c.1930, 4 ¼ x 3 In.
$369

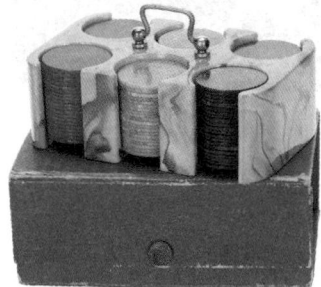

Potter & Potter Auctions, Inc.

Marble Bingo, Tin Lithograph, Shoots Marbles, 16 ½ In.	12
Marble, Extended Clown Launcher, Iron, Painted, Round, 14 Marble Wells, Arcade, 10 In.	236
Military Ten-Pins, 10 Captain Figures, Wood, Paper Litho, Wood Balls, Box, Ives, 10-In. Pins	649
Poker, Chip Caddy, Lever Pull Dispenses Chips, 280 Bakelite Chips, 2 Card Decks........*illus*	540
Poker, Chip Rack, 120 Bakelite Chips, Leatherette Case, c.1930, 4 ¼ x 3 In.........*illus*	369
Puzzle, Enameline Stove Polish, Black, Man, Child, Woman Cleaning Stove, 1912, 9 x 12 In.	390
Puzzle, Game Of The Globe, 3-Dimensional, 40 Pieces, Paper On Wood, Pedestal Base, 11 In.	608
Puzzle, Singer Sewing Machine, Indians, Horse, Tepee, Frame, c.1930, 14 x 11 In.	108
Roulette Table, Saloon, Wheel, Spinner, Oilcloth Cover, Geo. Mason & Co., c.1890, 94 x 46 In.	3540
Roulette Wheel, Orange, Wood Mounting Bracket, Brass Axis, Spokes, c.1910, 24 x 20 In.	2200
Shooting Gallery Target, Ram, Iron, Pitted, 13 ½ x 11 ½ In.	115
Shooting Target, Bull's-Eye, Round, Steel, Bell Sound, Lifts Bird, 17 x 12 In.	810
Shooting Target, Squirrel, Iron, c.1910, 8 In.	173
Skittles, Kittens In A Basket, 9 Composition Kittens, Wicker Basket, 7-In. Cats	1534
Skittles, Turkey Base, Full Figure, Composition, Pull String, 16 In. ....*illus*	2241
Sphere On Stand, Ivory, String, Openwork Carving, Tapered, 5 In.	72
Table, Carnival, Wheel, Spokes, Pine, Pedestal Base, Paint, c.1915, 31 x 20 In.	300
Table, Checkerboard, Pine, Paint, Folding, c.1920, 36 x 20 In.	390
Table, Horse Racing, Felt Track, Horses, Jockeys, Crank, France, c.1900, 33 x 28 In. ....*illus*	4200
Table, Roulette Wheel, Walnut, Felt Top, Trestle Base, Claw Feet, Foot Bar, B.C. Wills, 35 x 72 x 96 In.	5400
Target, 2 Roosters, Iron, c.1912, 10 In.	152
Target, 8 Ethnic Men Targets, Paper Litho On Wood, Case, 7 x 17 ½ In. ....*illus*	180
Target, Boar, Stepped Base, Iron, 11 x 6 ¾ In.	23
Target, Carnival, Leaping Deer Figure, Silver Paint, Cast Iron, U.S.A., c.1900, 22 x 24 In.	2640
Target, Incline, Cast Iron Lever, Wood Frame, Triangular, 29 In.	61
Walker's Tour Through Ireland, Geographical Pastimes, William Darton, 1812, 20 x 31 In.	342
Wheel, Gambling, Carnival, Wood, Names, Numbers, Metal Spokes, 1930s, 45 In.........*illus*	150
Wheel, Gambling, Painted Wood, Tabletop, Platform Base, Dominoes On Wheel, c.1910, 35 In.	236
Wheel, Gambling, Wood, 2-Sided, Vase Shape Splats, Multicolor Paint, c.1900, 36 ½ In.	1528
Wheel, Gambling, Wood, Green, Red Paint, 49 ½ In.	374
Wheel, Gambling, Wood, Paint, Numbers, c.1920, 24 In.	201

GAME PLATES are plates of any make decorated with pictures of birds, animals, or fish. The game plates usually came in sets consisting of twelve dishes and a serving platter. These sets were most popular during the 1880s.

Birds, Scalloped & Beaded Rim, Limoges, 9 ½ In., 11 Piece	2699
Fish, Gilded Grillwork, Spode, c.1875, 8 ¾ In., 8 Piece	1800
Fish, Green Rim, Wave Relief Rim, Wheeling Pottery, 8 In., 9 Piece	420
Fish, Scalloped Edge, Blakeman & Henderson, c.1900, 8 In., 7 Piece	925
Grebes, Sandy Beach, Plants, Gold Trim, Pitkins & Brooks, 8 ¾ In., 7 Piece	899
Mallard Duck, In Flight, Marshland, Limoges, c.1890, 8 ½ In.	129
Marsh & Prairie Scenes, Gold Rococo Rim, T & V Tressemann & Vogt, 8 In., 3 Piece	180
Pheasant, Platter, Scalloped, Gold Trim, Flower Border, Bavaria, 12 ½ In.	45
Pheasants, Green Gilt Border, Bavaria, Germany, 10 ⅜ In., 2 Piece	55

GARDEN FURNISHINGS have been popular for centuries. The stone or metal statues, urns and fountains, sundials, small figurines, and wire, iron, or rustic furniture are included in this category. Many of the metal pieces have been made continuously for years.

Arch, Lattice, Shield Crest, Painted, Wood, 121 x 74 In.	3840
Basin, Lion Mask Crest, Lobed Urn, Pedestal Base, Cast Iron, 1900s, 48 x 26 In.	944
Basin, Shell Shape, Stone, England, 15 x 30 In.	2520
Bench, Birds, Flowers, Finials, Cast Iron, c.1950, 42 x 72 x 26 In.	1149
Bench, Fern Fronds, Dished Pierced Seat, Cast Iron, c.1875, 34 x 57 x 20 In.	1894
Bench, Flowers, Double Chairback, Bird Head Arms, Iron, c.1900, 30 x 40 x 21 In.	2091
Bench, Gothic Revival, Quatrefoils, Arches, Openwork, Scroll, Cast Iron, 34 x 56 In., Pair	2952
Bench, Iron, Wire, Paint, 47 ½ In.	406
Bench, Leaves, Pierced, Cast Iron, Stamped James W. Carr, Richmond, Virginia, 30 x 45 In.	1920
Bench, Molded Flowers, Lyre Shaped Supports, Cement, c.1950, 18 x 39 In.	177
Bench, Neoclassical Style, Siena Marble, Acanthus Leaf Carved Supports, 18 x 72 In.	1875
Bench, Opposing Plank Backs & Seats, Blue Paint, Carved Wood, Cast Iron, 35 x 62 In.	1230
Bench, Roman Column Pedestal Base, Marble, 19 x 19 x 36 In.	403
Bench, Strapwork, Wrought Iron, c.1935, 33 x 72 In.	799
Bench, Terra-Cotta, Griffin Supports, 19 x 47 In.	813
Bench, William IV, Coiled Serpent, Cast Iron, Wood, 32 x 60 ½ x 23 In.	1284
Birdbath, Bird, Fauna Support, Cast Metal, 37 x 32 In.	575
Birdbath, Cast Iron, 28 ¾ In.	82

Boot Scraper, Horse Shape, Cast Iron, 15 x 15 x 9 In.	741
Chair, Arched Crest, Scrolled, Pierced, Cast Iron, Robert Wood Foundry, c.1810, 35 In.	500
Chair, Patio, Male, Female Face Back, Wrought Iron, c.1950, 39 In., Pair	750
Cornucopia, Composition, c.1920, 20 ½ In., Pair	480
Figure, Alligator, Cast Iron, 5 ½ x 27 x 15 In., Pair	478
Figure, David, After Michelangelo, Cast Cement, 48 In.	276
Figure, Egyptian Sphinx, Rectangular Base, Cast Stone, Pair	2460
Figure, Lion, Reclining, Cast Stone, Rectangular Base, 25 x 46 ½ In., Pair	3444
Figure, Lion, Reclining, Terra-Cotta, Glazed, Molded Platform, c.1800, 15 x 30 In. ....*illus*	354
Figure, Lion, Standing, Holding Shield, Stepped Base, Cast Iron, 1900s, 15 x 27 In., Pair	1652
Figure, Putti, Cast Cement, 1800s, 50 ½ x 28 In. ....*illus*	1920
Figure, Rabbit, Resting, Stone, 16 x 22 In.	2000
Figure, Snake, Coiled, Leafy Base, Cast Stone, 24 x 10 x 20 In.	354
Figure, Woman, Classical Roman, Marble, Patina, 1800s, 42 In. ....*illus*	2625
Figure, Woman, Classical, Standing, Hand On Horse Head, Marble, 51 In.	1000
Figure, Woman, Dolphin, Cast Stone, 48 In.	1125
Figure, Woman, Nude, Holding Urn, Bronze, C.S. Paolo, c.1945, 43 In.	4248
Finial, Hitching Post, Horse Head, Ring In Mouth, Iron, Tan, Black Paint, c.1860, 13 ½ In.	2015
Font, Empire Style, Bowl, 3 Women Supports, Round Plinth, Marble, c.1890, 45 x 29 In.	10000
Fountain, Baby Triton, Bronze, Helen Journeay, c.1930, 25 In.	2714
Fountain, Bear, Catching Fish, Lead, 25 3 ¾ In.	600
Fountain, Cast Stone, Grotto Shape, 17th Century Style, Bronze, 78 x 58 x 30 In.	4674
Fountain, Cherub, Frog, Turtle, In Shell, Swan Pedestal, Bronze, Electric, 48 x 30 In.	1200
Fountain, Classical, Goddess Of Youth, Bronze, 89 In.	3444
Fountain, Figural, Jumping Frog, Cast Iron, Shaped Base, c.1925, 28 In.	584
Fountain, Figure, Boy, Standing, Blowing 2 Pipes, Metal, 32 In.	468
Fountain, Infant & Frog, Lead Shell, 1900s, 17 x 14 ½ In. ....*illus*	531
Fountain, Lead, Putto, Pouring Water From Jar, 19 In.	813
Fountain, Lion's Head, Pedestal, Women, Quatrefoil Base, Bronze, 90 In.	6573
Fountain, Putto, Holding Shell Over Head, Basin, Terra-Cotta, Painted, Barent, 43 x 15 In.	308
Fountain, Seated Frog, Porcelain, Green, Yellow Paint, 13 ½ x 14 ½ In.	669
Fountain, Shell Shape Pan, Dolphin, Tail Up, 1900s, Bronze, 33 x 29 In.	1599
Fountain, Tortoise, Cast Iron, Verdigris, 9 ½ x 19 x 24 In.	1045
Fountain, Woman, Carrying Vase, Pitcher, Bronze, c.1945, 41 In.	563
Garden Seat, Octagonal, Paneled, Blue Underglaze, Landscape, Flowers, 14 x 11 In., Pair	5664
Gnome, Holding Basket, Multicolor Paint, Pottery, 18 ½ In.	60
Hitching Post, Eagle Head, Ring, Iron, Black Paint, 75 In.	1800
Hitching Post, Figural, Jockey, Iron, Green, White, c.1900, 47 In.	455
Hitching Post, Horse Head, Fluted Column, Cast Iron, 45 x 8 In.	861
Hitching Post, Horse Head, Iron, Black Paint, 31 ½ In., Pair	900
Hitching Post, Horse Head, Nose Ring, Iron, Black Paint, 14 In.	115
Hitching Post, Horse Head, Ribbed, Iron, c.1875, 45 In.	947
Hitching Post, Jockey, Black, Arm Extended, Cap On Head, Iron, c.1900, 22 In.	119
Hitching Post, Jockey, Black, Cast Iron, Blue, Green, White Paint, 38 In.	625
Hitching Post, Jockey, Black, Cast Metal, Red, Cream Paint, c.1910, 35 ¾ In.	75
Hitching Post, Jockey, Black, Painted, Cast Iron, c.1890, 45 In.	523
Hitching Post, Jockey, Black, Ring, Stand Base, Black, White, Red Paint, Iron, c.1920, 12 In.	175
Hitching Post, Jockey, Black, Vest, Cast Iron, 1800s, 36 x 10 In.	1554
Hitching Post, Jockey, Multicolor Paint, Cast Iron, 47 In.	1320
Hitching Post, Tree Trunk Shape, White Paint, Cast Iron, c.1890, 49 In.	270
House Shape, White Paint, Openwork, Wrought Iron, 36 x 28 In.	431
Jardiniere, 4 Neoclassical Tiles, Art Deco, Multicolor, Cast Metal, c.1900, 10 In.	127
Jardiniere, George III, Lion Mask Ring Handles, Tapered Legs, Mahogany, 19 x 11 In.	563
Jardiniere, Lion Mask, Ring In Mouth, Iron, Wood, Tin Liner, 24 x 16 In., Pair	750
Jardiniere, Terra-Cotta, Bacchus, Standing, Hand Raised Holding Bowl, 70 In.	2500
Jardiniere, Turbaned Couple, Bust Shape, Ceramic, M. Morales, c.1990, 12 In., Pair	875
Lion, Reclining, Stone, 17 x 10 In., Pair	230
Pagoda, Cast Aggregate, 20 x 30 In.	334
Pedestal, Urn, Scroll Handles, Columns, Stepped Base, Marble, c.1915, 36 x 16 In., Pair	799
Plant Stand, see Furniture, Stand, Plant	
Planter, Barrel Shape, Panels, Cast Lead, 18 x 19 In., Pair	1003
Planter, Bowl, Tripart Flared Base, Stone, 1930s, 40 In.	259
Planter, Elephant, Leaves, Lava Stone, Cylindrical, Southeast Asia, 1900s, 40 x 26 In.	649
Planter, Embossed Flowers, Leaves, Scalloped, Footed, Cast Iron, 20 x 12 In.	104
Planter, Famille Verte, Slanted Square Shape, Peaches, Magpies, Porcelain, 9 x 11 In., Pair	7200
Planter, Flowers, Empress Dowager Ware, Porcelain, Ta Ya Chai, c.1910, 12 In. ....*illus*	1304
Planter, Foldover Rim, Scroll Pierced Handles, Pedestal, Cast Iron, c.1885, 53 x 52 In.	2360

Game, Skittles, Turkey Base, Full Figure, Composition, Pull String, 16 In.
$2,241

Bertoia Auctions

Game, Table, Horse Racing, Felt Track, Horses, Jockeys, Crank, France, c.1900, 33 x 28 In.
$4,200

Garth's Auctioneers & Appraisers

Game, Target, 8 Ethnic Men Targets, Paper Litho On Wood, Case, 7 x 17 ½ In.
$180

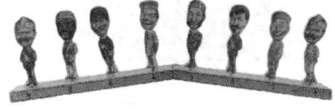

Morphy Auctions

Game, Wheel, Gambling, Carnival, Wood, Names, Numbers, Metal Spokes, 1930s, 45 In.
$150

Victorian Casino Antiques

TIP

Dust frequently if you live near the seashore. Salt air causes problems.

Garden, Figure, Lion, Reclining, Terra-Cotta, Glazed, Molded Platform, c.1800, 15 x 30 In.
$354

Brunk Auctions

Garden, Figure, Putti, Cast Cement, 1800s, 50 ½ x 28 In.
$1,920

Skinner Auctioneers & Appraisers

Garden, Figure, Woman, Classical Roman, Marble, Patina, 1800s, 42 In.
$2,625

Rago Arts & Auction Center

Planter, Pierced, Fans, Scrolls, Wood, White Paint, Footed, 21 x 38 In.	3075
Planter, Putti, Animals, Carved, Marble, Raffaello Romanelli, c.1910, 53 x 21 In., Pair.......*illus*	21240
Planter, Scroll Base, Wire, Metal Tray Insert, 27 x 38 In.	69
Planter, Trough Shape, Relief Cherubs, Aggregate, Fitted Metal Liner, 14 x 44 x 12 In.	380
Sculpture, Bacchus, On Barrel, Holding Grapes, Cast Stone, c.1900, 37 In.	502
Sculpture, Cherub, Playing Lute, Composition, Paint, 34 In., Pair	438
Sculpture, Figures, Standing, 4 Seasons, Pedestal Base, Cast Iron, 4 Piece	7170
Sculpture, Mobile, Kinetic, Stone Base, Metal Stem, Seagull, Fish Balance, 53 x 41 In.	219
Sculpture, Putti, Holding Urn, Black Paint, Cast Iron, Durenne, France, 58 In., Pair	3125
Sculpture, Putti, Pulling At Cloth, Lead, c.1890, 16 ½ In., Pair	2091
Sculpture, Rooster, Cast Iron, Black Paint, c.1970, 36 In.	560
Seat, Barrel Shaped, Pierced, Court Figures, Diamond Diaper, 1800s, 19 In.	2400
Seat, Blue & White, Barrel Shape, Painted Flowers, 19th Century, 19 x 14 In., Pair	3360
Seat, Blue & White, Fitzhugh, Barrel Shape, Pierced Caches, Raised Bands, c.1810, 19 In.	2160
Seat, Blue, Plum Blossoms, Birds, Pierced, Chinese, 14 ½ x 13 ½ In.	1045
Seat, Carved, 2 Parts, Round Cushion Seat, Waisted Base, Beasts, Stone, 19 In., Pair	1845
Seat, Celadon Ground, Fish, Lotus Plants, Chinese Export Porcelain, 26 x 21 x 16 In.........*illus*	522
Seat, Celadon, Painted, Warriors On Horseback, Porcelain, 20th Century, 17 x 11 In., Pair	922
Seat, Elephant, Trunk Down, Brown, Multicolor Blanket, Terra-Cotta, 17 In., Pair	360
Seat, Famille Rose, 6-Sided, Chinese Export Porcelain, c.1850, 18 ½ In.	6300
Seat, Famille Rose, Figures, Courtyard Scenes, Chinese, c.1825, 18 ¾ In., Pair	4080
Seat, Famille Rose, Multicolor Tables, Seats, White Ground, Chinese, 19 In., Pair	6250
Seat, Famille Rose, Women, Landscape, Flowers, Chinese Porcelain, c.1870, 18 ½ In.	4660
Seat, Famille Verte, Drum Shape, Fish, Aquatic Plants, 1900s, 26 In.	369
Seat, Flowers, Blue & White, Drum Shape, c.1850, 18 ½ In.	237
Seat, Flowers, Urn, Turquoise, Yellow, Chinese, 17 ½ In.	911
Seat, Green Glaze, Pierced Decorations, Pottery, Chinese, 1800s, 18 x 15 In., Pair	1175
Seat, Hexagon, Blue & White, Openwork, Double Coin Design, c.1900, 19 In.	240
Seat, Hexagon, Emperor & Attendants, Flowers, Battle Scene, c.1900, 20 x 13 In.	649
Seat, Rose Mandarin, Barrel Shape, Pierced, c.1900, 19 x 13 In.	584
Seat, Rose Mandarin, Hexagonal Drum, Pierced Symbols, 19 x 15 In.	2952
Seat, Round Top, Drum Shape, Openwork Scroll, Hardwood, 1900s, 18 x 16 In., Pair	354
Seat, Scallop Top, Children, Flower Shape Stretcher, Lacquer, Parcel Gilt, Chinese, 18 In.	295
Seat, Stacked Pillow Shape, Terra-Cotta, Tin Glazed, 13 ½ x 15 In.	461
Seat, Tree Stump Shape, Vines, Majolica, 20th Century, 19 ½ In., Pair	646
Seat, White, Yellow Irises, Barrel Shape, Porcelain, England, 18 In.	84
Sprinkler, Alligator, Holding Water Release In Mouth, Green, Cast Iron, c.1910, 10 ½ In.	188
Sprinkler, Black Man, Holding Red Hose, Carved, Painted, Metal Base, c.1935, 51 In.	184
Sprinkler, Duck, Seated, Painted, Cast Iron, c.1915, 13 ½ In.	313
Sprinkler, Duck, Standing, Painted, Cast Iron, c.1910, 12 ¼ In.	469
Sprinkler, Frog, On Ball, Painted, Cast Iron, c.1910, 13 ½ In.	688
Squirrel, White Paint, Cast Iron, 11 In., Pair	345
Stool, Liberty, Celtic Knots, Terra-Cotta, Knox, Stamped, c.1900, 15 x 14 In., Pair	3750
Sundial, Horizontal, Brass Plate, Sliding Gnomon, Engelbrecht, Dutch, 1700s, 5 ¼ x 6 In.	3000
Sundial, Inscribed, I Also Am Under Authority, Calendar, Bronze, c.1900, 37 x 24 In.	472
Sundial, Noon Cannon, Brass Base, Bird Shape Gnomon, 1800s, 2 ¼ x 3 In.	1230
Sundial, Octagonal, Inscription, Lead, 1800s, 13 In.	118
Sundial, Pewter, Signed Goldsmith Chandlee, Va., c.1800, 3 x 5 In.	9200
Sundial, Pocket, Johan Schrettegger, Brass, Hour Ring, Latitude Scale, Level, c.1750, 2 ½ In.	984
Sundial, Roman Numerals, Compass Points, Cast Metal, Aggregate Base, 27 In.	466
Sundial, Signal Gun, Lens, Fires At Noon, Marble Base, Brass Mounts	4200
Table, Alabaster Top, Round, Molded Standard, Black Paint, Cast Iron, 30 x 36 In.	780
Table, Bird & Flower Border, Pierced Post, Cast Iron, Casters, Victorian, 28 ½ In.......*illus*	711
Table, Blackamoor, Seated, Round Top, Glazed Terra-Cotta, Yellow, Black, 20 x 21 In.	1188
Table, Pierced Round Top, Cabriole Legs, X-Stretcher, Cast Iron, c.1850, 26 x 39 In.	531
Tree Tub, Mandarin Figures, Garden, Pierced Stand, 8 ½ x 21 In.	676
Trolley, Green Paint, 4 Handles, Wood, 22 x 69 In.	1200
Urn, 3 Swans, Leaves, Shell Molded, Ribbed, Cast Iron, c.1900, 37 x 20 In.	984
Urn, Campana Shape, Leaf Body, Mask Handles, Pedestal, Wreaths, 44 In., Pair	837
Urn, Cast Iron, Rococo Style, Flowers, Handles, Pedestal, Kramer Bros., c.1890, 43 In.	1375
Urn, Cherub Face Mask, Embossed, Black Paint, Cast Iron, 21 In., Pair	295
Urn, Cloaked, Drapery Swags, Carved Limestone, c.1900, 26 In., Pair	922
Urn, Directoire, Faux Marble, Painted, Campana Shape, Bronze Handle, Iron, 20 In., Pair	2813
Urn, Egret Base, Cast Iron, c.1890, 43 x 32 In.	1580
Urn, Flared Rim, Grapevines, Figures, Square Base, Cast Stone, 38 x 25 In.	1793
Urn, Flared Rim, Square Base, Cast Iron, c.1890, 17 x 26 In., Pair	1180
Urn, Fluted Body, Pedestal, Cast Iron, 1900s, 26 ½ x 22 In.......*illus*	177

G

Urn, Iron, Art Deco Style, Black Paint, Open Handles, Stand, 1900-30, 26 In.....................*illus*	780
Urn, Iron, Campagna Shape, Flared, Lobed Body, Square Foot, Red Paint, 19 x 15 In., Pair	598
Urn, Iron, Leaf Flared Rim, Green Paint, 14 x 21 In., Pair	610
Urn, Iron, Trophy Pattern, Kramer Bros., Dayton, Oh., 40 ½ x 29 In., Pair..................................	2164
Urn, Lava Stone, Carved Flowers, Cylindrical, Rounded Shoulder, Asia, 1900s, 23 In....................	236
Urn, Lion Mask, Rings, Handles, Pedestal, Iron, White Paint, 24 ½ In., Pair..................................	469
Urn, Ribbed, Molded Rim, Black Paint, Cast Iron, Victorian, 24 In., Pair.......................................	472
Urn, Scroll Handles, Pierced Pedestal, Iron, White Paint, J. Carr, c.1910, 49 In.	2478
Urn, Tree Root & Deer Head, Iron, 1800s, 45 x 19 In..*illus*	2300
Urn, Victorian, Green Paint, Cast Iron, Molded Rim, Handles, 20 In., Pair....................................	708
Windmill, Lighthouse Shape, Carved, Painted, c.1915, 47 In.	510
Window Box, Openwork, Leaves, Green Paint, Pine, c.1910, 6 ¾ x 23 ¾ In., Pair	213

GAUDY DUTCH pottery was made in England for the American market from about 1810 to 1820. It is a white earthenware with Imari-style decorations of red, blue, green, yellow, and black. Only sixteen patterns of Gaudy Dutch were made: Butterfly, Carnation, Dahlia, Double Rose, Dove, Grape, Leaf, Oyster, Primrose, Single Rose, Strawflower, Sunflower, Urn, War Bonnet, Zinnia, and No Name. Other similar wares are called Gaudy Ironstone and Gaudy Welsh.

Bowl, Single Rose, 5 ½ x 3 In...	92
Coffeepot, Dome Lid, Oyster, c.1825, 11 ½ In..	390
Cup & Saucer, Single Rose, Handleless, c.1850	180
Cup Plate, Double Rose, c.1820, 3 ½ In...	296
Mug, Child's, Grape, c.1830, 2 In...	61
Pitcher, Grape, 6 ¼ In..	265
Plate, Butterfly, 7 ½ In...	975
Plate, Carnation, 8 ⅜ In.	875
Plate, Carnation, Cobalt Blue, Double Border, 10 In...	325
Plate, Grape, Orange, Blue, Green, White, c.1850, 10 In..	142
Plate, Oyster, c.1820, 8 In., 4 Piece..	395
Plate, Oyster, Paneled, Leaf Border, Center Design, 10 In.	413
Plate, Soup, Double Rose, Cobalt Blue Border, Full Body Design, 10 In..	224
Plate, Urn, Paneled, 7 ½ In...	139
Sugar, Lid, Single Rose, Gilt Handles, Knop, 8 In.	58
Teapot, Dove, c.1865, 6 In...	729
Teapot, Oyster, Squat, Goose-Neck Spout, Loop Handle, Spurs, 5 ¾ In..	649

GAUDY WELSH is an Imari-decorated earthenware with red, blue, green, and gold decorations. Most Gaudy Welsh was made in England for the American market. It was made from 1820 to about 1860.

Coffeepot, Morning Glory, Angular Handle, 8 ¾ In.	59
Cup & Saucer, Handleless, Flow Blue, Copper Lusterware, c.1830	60
Cup & Saucer, Handleless, Paneled, Flow Blue, Orange..	195
Pitcher, Angle Handle, 8 In..	93
Pitcher, Milk, Flow Blue, Flowers, Buds, Bulbous, C-Scroll Handle, Embossed, 7 In.....................	106
Pitcher, Octagonal Base, Dragon Handle, Orange, Blue, 5 x 5 In.	320
Pitcher, Washbowl, Flowers, Serpent Handle, Stamped, 10 ½ & 4 ½ x 13 In.	240
Plate, Baskets, Scalloped, Blue, Red, Green, 9 In...	90
Punch Bowl, Flow Blue, Stick Pattern Designs, Cobalt Blue Flowers, Scrolls, c.1850, 7 x 14 In....	316
Tea Set, Teapot, Creamer, Sugar, Cups, Saucers, Bowls, c.1850, 35 Piece	444

GEISHA GIRL porcelain was made for export in the late nineteenth century in Japan. It was an inexpensive porcelain often sold in dime stores or used as free premiums. Pieces are sometimes marked with the name of a store. Japanese ladies in kimonos are pictured on the dishes. There are over 125 recorded patterns. Borders of red, blue, green, gold, brown, or several of these colors were used. Modern reproductions are being made.

Bowl, Geisha, Mountains, Flowers, Rust Border, Scalloped, Japan, c.1920, 7 In............................	50
Bowl, Portrait, Holding Fan, Purple Robe, Flowers, Blue Ground, Gilt, c.1900, 3 x 10 In.............	150
Creamer, Geisha, Lanterns, Gold Trim, B & Co., Limoges, c.1920, 5 In.	69
Cup & Saucer, 3 Geisha, Mountain, Birds, Butterflies, Green Border..	25
Cup & Saucer, Geisha, Trees, Umbrellas, Transfer, Red Trim, c.1935..	25
Eggcup, Geisha, Village, Red Foot, 2 ½ In...	19
Plate, Geisha, Man, Boat, Village, Garden, Pierced Handles, 9 In..	69
Plate, Geishas, Playing Instruments, Garden, Red, Japan, c.1920, 8 ¾ In......................................	34
Tray, Geisha, Cherry Blossoms, Gilt Trim, D & C, France, 13 In..	165
Vase, Geisha, Kneeling, Garden, Bulbous, Green Border, 2 In...	24

G

Garden, Fountain, Infant & Frog, Lead Shell, 1900s, 17 x 14 ½ In.
$531

Rago Arts & Auction Center

Garden, Planter, Flowers, Empress Dowager Ware, Porcelain, Ta Ya Chai, c.1910, 12 In.
$1,304

James D. Julia Auctioneers

Garden, Planter, Putti, Animals, Carved, Marble, Raffaello Romanelli, c.1910, 53 x 21 In., Pair
$21,240

Brunk Auctions

TIP

Outdoor stonework and statues, even if made of granite, can be damaged by acid rain, frost, and plants like ivy. Put garden statues on stands to keep the moisture from the grass away from the statue. Wash with a hose and a soft brush.

289

Garden, Seat, Celadon Ground, Fish, Lotus Plants, Chinese Export Porcelain, 26 x 21 x 16 In.
$522

New Orleans Auction Galleries, Inc.

Garden, Table, Bird & Flower Border, Pierced Post, Cast Iron, Casters, Victorian, 28 ½ In.
$711

James D. Julia Auctioneers

Garden, Urn, Fluted Body, Pedestal, Cast Iron, 1900s, 26 ½ x 22 In.
$177

Brunk Auctions

TIP

Set your sundial at noon, June 15. Place it so the shadow falls on the 12.

GENE AUTRY was born in 1907. He began his career as the "Singing Cowboy" in 1928. His first movie appearance was in 1934, his last in 1958. His likeness and that of the Wonder Horse, Champion, were used on toys, books, lunch boxes, and advertisements.

Badge, Flying A Ranch Sheriff's Posse, Brass, Serial No. 27332, Star Shape, 2 ⅝ In.	209
Big Little Book, Red Bandit's Ghost, No. 1461, 1949	45
Button, Boston Rodeo, I Saw Gene Autry, Nov. 1-11, Tin Lithograph, Multicolor, 1 ⅛ In.	86
Cap Gun, Black Leather Holster, Horse Head Grips, Star, 1950s	125
Cap Gun, Repeating, Junior Model, Plastic, Orange, Box, 1940s	345
Cap Gun, Repeating, Metal, Shell-Like Grip, Box With Graphics, 8 ½ In.	108
Cutout Book, Cowboy, Bandits, Champion, Single-Sided, 1941, 13 x 13 In., 5 Pages	126
Cutout Book, Ranch, Figures, Single-Sided, Merrill Publishing, 1940, 10 x 15 In., 6 Pages	172
Pin, Portrait, Tin, Red Ground, 1 ¼ In.	18
Postcard, Gene Autry's Home, North Hollywood, Calif., 1950s, 5 x 3 In.	10
Standee, Gene & Champion, Cardboard, World's Greatest Cowboy, 1940s, 31 x 58 In.	581
Toy, Drum Set, Gene Autry On Champion On Bass Drum, 1950s, 19 ½ In.	180
Toy, Guitar, Cowboys Scenes, Emenee, 1950s, Box, 33 In.	150 to 225
Watch, Gene In Champion Horseshoe, Faux Alligator Bands, Silver Luster Case, 5 x 5 In.	711

GIBSON GIRL black-and-blue decorated plates were made in the early 1900s. Twenty-four different 10 ½-inch plates were made by the Royal Doulton pottery at Lambeth, England. These pictured scenes from the book *A Widow and Her Friends* by Charles Dana Gibson. Another set of twelve 9-inch plates featuring pictures of the heads of Gibson Girls had all-blue decoration. Many other items also pictured the famous Gibson Girl.

Illustration, Portrait, Low-Cut Dress, Bow In Hair, 1906, 10 x 13 In.	250
Plate, Message From The Outside World, 10 ½ In.	90
Plate, Miss Babbles, The Authoress, Calls & Reads Aloud, 10 ½ In.	85
Plate, Quiet Dinner With Dr. Bottles, 10 ½ In.	102
Plate, She Contemplates The Cloister, 10 ½ In.	95
Plate, She Decides To Die In Spite Of Dr. Bottles, 10 ½ In.	85
Plate, She Goes Into Colors, 10 ½ In.	90
Plate, She Goes To The Fancy Dress Ball As Juliet, 10 ½ In.	70
Plate, She Is Disturbed By A Vision, 10 ½ In.	75
Plate, She Looks For Relief Among The Old Ones, 10 ½ In.	95 to 138
Plate, They Go Fishing, 10 ½ In.	120
Plate, They Take A Morning Run, 10 ½ In.	105
Postcard, Girl, Sipping Wine, Feathers In Hat, Hearts	15
Print, Virginia Girl, Cheerleader, Holding Flag, Blue Dress, 10 x 14 In.	65

GILLINDER pressed glass was first made by William T. Gillinder pf Philadelphia in 1863. The company had a working factory on the grounds at the Centennial and made small, marked pieces of glass for sale as souvenirs. They made a variety of decorative glass pieces and tablewares.

Commemorative, Plate, Children, Seesaw, Dogs, Scalloped Edge, 1880s, 10 In.	55
Liberty Bell, Salt, Oval, Walled, Open, Etched, 1876, 2 ¼ In.	75
Man On Horse, Plate, Spearing Lion, Scalloped Points, Intaglio, 11 In.	100

GIRL SCOUT collectors search for anything pertaining to the Girl Scouts, including uniforms, publications, and old cookie boxes. The Girl Scout movement started in 1912, two years after the Boy Scouts. It began under Juliette Gordon Low of Savannah, Georgia. The first Girl Scout cookies were sold in 1928.

Barrette, Daisy & Girl Scout Designs, Gold Tone Metal, c.1949, 2 ⅛ x ½ In.	30
Cup, Insignia, Eagle, Collapsible, Aluminum, 1950s, 2 ¼ In.	20
First Aid Kit, Tin, Green, White, Red, Johnson & Johnson, 1950s, 6 x 3 x 2 In.	23
Handbook, Intermediate Program, Green, Gold, 527 Pages, 1952, 6 ½ x 4 In.	18
Ring, Faceted Emerald Green Stone, Raised Trefoils, 10K Gold Filled, 1970s	40
Socks, Knee High, Green, Emblem On Cuff, c.1935, Size 9 ½	32

GLASS-ART. Art glass means any of the many forms of glassware made during the late nineteenth or early twentieth century. These wares were expensive when they were first made and production was limited. Art glass is not the typical commercial glass that was made in large quantities, and most of the art glass was produced by hand methods. Later twentieth-century glass is listed under Glass-Contemporary, Glass-Midcentury, or Glass-Venetian. Even more art glass may be found in categories such as Burmese, Cameo Glass, Tiffany, and other factory names.

Ashtray, Chartreuse, Brown, Geometric Shapes, Ground Base, 1950s, 7 x 6 x 2 In.	13
Basket, Mica Flakes, Brown, Pink & Gold, White Cased, Crimped Form, Clear Handle, 6 In.	70

Biscuit Jar, Clear Overshot Ground, Flowers, Silver Plate Lid, Handle, 7 ½ In.		148
Bowl, 3 Black Metal Bats, Orange Enamel Paint, Verrerie D'Art Lorraine, c.1927, 4 x 5 In.		2813
Bowl, Green, Iridescent Blue, Threaded, Quadrafold Rim, Oval, 7 In.		58
Bowl, Lemon Yellow, Cranberry Lip Wrap, Ruffled Rim, Hobbs, Brockunier, 8 In.		75
Bowl, Pate-De-Cristal, Classical Mask, Francois-Emile Decorchemont, c.1920, 4 x 8 ¾ In.		6250
Bowl, Stylized Flowers, Orange, Plum, Etched Cameo, Footed, Charder, c.1930, 8 In.		813
Compote, Lid, Clear, Frosted Dog Finial, Pedestal Base, c.1885, 13 x 8 In.		575
Dish, Lid, Round, Molded, Butterflies, Signed, c.1940, 6 ¾ In. Diam.		209
Epergne, 6 Flower Shape Vases, Rigaree, Opalescent Amber, Pink, Wavy Base, c.1880, 16 In.		938
Epergne, Cranberry, 3 Tiers, 4 Vases, Flower-Form, Clear Rigaree, Ruffled Dish Base, 21 In.		215
Figurine, Isadora, Raised Arms, 8 In.		240
Goblet, Gold Iridescent, Amber, Trumpet Rim, Spread Foot, 8 ¾ In., Pair		300
Goblet, Gold Iridescent, Threaded Design, Circle Designs, 8 ½ In., Pair		390
Goblet, King Tut, Iridescent, Blue Swirling Pattern, Flared Lip, Footed, Pair		2223
Jewelry Box, Cobalt Blue, Silver Leaves, 4 ½ x 6 In.		148
Perfume Bottle, Green, Clear Stopper, 9 In.		170
Pickle Castor, Blue, Coinspot, White Enamel Flowers, Ball Feet, 10 ½ In.		3750
Pitcher, Pink Cased In White, Fish Scale Cameo, 4 ½ In.		173
Punch Bowl Set, Red, White Lining, Cased, Continental, 10 x 16 In., 13 2 ¾-In. Cups		132
Rose Bowl, Enamel Flowers, Yellow Satin, 5 In.		35
Sculpture, Sea Foam, Signed Stephen Dee Edwards, 1885, 6 ½ x 11 In.		308
Sculpture, Yin Yang, Clear & Black, Round, Tapered, Swarovski, c.1988, 2 x 5 In.		480
Shade, Leaded, Stained, Conical, Hanging, 23 In.		240
Shade, Leaded, Stained, Square Design, Flowers, Hanging, Finial, Tulip Shape, 20 In.		240
Shade, Tulip Shape, Pulled Feather, Gold Iridescent, Purple, Ruffled Rim, 6 x 4 In., Pair		300
Sugar Shaker, Rose Opalescent, Swirled, Tapered, c.1910, 5 ⅜ In.		196
Vase, Alexandrite, Bulbous Shape, Amethyst Shaded To Topaz, 2 ½ In.		1126
Vase, Alexandrite, Trumpet Shape, Ribbed, Purple To Topaz, Flared Rim, Blue Foot, 5 In.		2104
Vase, Art Nouveau, Green, Crimson, Gilt, Frosted, Cylindrical, Honesdale, 15 ½ In.		1898
Vase, Art Nouveau, La Pierre Sterling Overlay, Monogram, 4 ¾ In.		920
Vase, Brown, Blue Crystalline Glaze, Stick Shape, Incised A. Renoleau, 5 ½ x 10 In.		156
Vase, Brown, Crystalline Glaze, Twisted Neck Shape, Pierrefonds, 7 x 12 In.		156
Vase, Bud, Blue Iridescent, Green, Tapered, Rolled Rim, Spread Foot, 6 In.		450
Vase, Florentine, Cameo, Blue Ground, White Enamel Flowers, 4 ¾ In.		148
Vase, Gold Iridescent, Fuchsia, Shouldered, Swollen Neck, Flared Rim, 5 ¼ In.		330
Vase, Green Iridescent, Lava Mold, c.1900, 5 In.		207
Vase, Green Iridescent, Loop Handle, 1900s, 9 x 7 ¼ In.		413
Vase, Green, Tulip Carved Overlay, Gilt, Pinched Sides, Honesdale, Pa., c.1900, 6 ¾ In.		207
Vase, Iridescent, Organic Shape, Green Free-Form Design, Austria, 7 In.		1304
Vase, Iridescent, Scalloped Rim, Ribbing, Draped Design, c.1935, 8 ¼ In.		461
Vase, Lily, Glossy Glaze, Trumpet Shape, Trifold Rim, New England, 10 In.		460
Vase, Malachite, Molded Nude Women, Swollen Collar, Round Foot, 5 x 3 In.		120
Vase, Sterling Overlay, Purple Iridescent, Stems, Flowers, Spread Foot, c.1900, 4 In.		360
Vase, Trumpet Shape, Spread Foot, Flower Shape, Ruffle Rim, Green Leaves, Pink, 12 In.		720
Vase, Trumpet, Opalescent Foot, Amber Shaded To Cranberry, Scalloped Rim, 12 In.		52
Vase, Tulip, Clear Ground, Yellow, Green, Swollen Cylinder, c.1900, 8 ½ In.		2006
Vase, Wide Rim, Tapered, Round Foot, Black, Multicolor Swirls, 8 ¾ x 10 In.		210

GLASS-BLOWN. Blown glass was formed by forcing air through a rod into molten glass. Early glass and some forms of art glass were hand blown. Other types of glass were molded or pressed.

Baton, Drum Major's, Aqua, Opalescent Spiral Bands, Ball End, 35 In.		115
Bowl, Aqua, Bulbous Bottom, Round, Outward Rolled Rim, Pontil, 5 ¾ x 6 In.		585
Bowl, Aqua, Round, Folded Rim, c.1810, 8 x 10 In.		360
Bowl, Cobalt Blue, Flared Sides, Outward Rolled Rim, 3 ⅞ x 7 ½ In.		431
Canister, Cylindrical, Cobalt Blue Rings, Lid, Conical Finial, c.1850, 12 In.		235
Charger, Double Pinwheel Design, L. Tagliapietra, D. Navarra, 1980, 18 In.	*illus*	2250
Compote, Clear, Ribs, Folded Rim, c.1850, 5 ¼ In.		411
Creamer, Lily Pad, Threading, Handle, Green Aqua, c.1850, 3 ½ x 2 ⅜ In.	*illus*	4680
Decanter Set, Frosted, Purple Iris, Green Leaves, Ruffled Rim, 8-In. Decanter, 5 Piece		35
Decanter, Pink, White, Lavender, Vertical Lines, Ball Stopper, 1900s, 8 ½ x 5 In.		236
Decanter, Yellow Amber, Bulbous, Elongated Neck, Pontil, c.1863, 10 ⅝ In.		489
Dish, Swirled Ribs, Flared, Cobalt Blue Rolled Rim, c.1840, 3 x 5 In.		271
Goblet, Martini Shape, Black Rooster Stem Interior, 5 ½ x 3 ¾ In.		104
Goblet, Wine, Engraved Ships, Masts, Success To The British Navy, 6 ¾ In.		1053
Linen Smoother, Green Aqua, Convex Disc, Sausage Turned Handle, 4 ⅜ x 4 In.		1170

Garden, Urn, Iron, Art Deco Style, Black Paint, Open Handles, Stand, 1900-30, 26 In.
$780

Garden, Urn, Tree Root & Deer Head, Iron, 1800s, 45 x 19 In.
$2,300

Glass-Blown, Charger, Double Pinwheel Design, L. Tagliapietra, D. Navarra, 1980, 18 In.
$2,250

GLASS-BLOWN

Glass-Blown, Creamer, Lily Pad, Threading, Handle, Green Aqua, c.1850, 3 ½ x 2 ⅜ In.
$4,680

Norman C. Heckler & Company

Glass-Bohemian, Vase, Sea Urchin, Silvery Blue, Textured, Highlights, Kralik, 20 In.
$805

Humler & Nolan

Glass-Bohemian, Vase, Sporadic Ribbon Bands, Tricorner Rim, Kralik, 5 ½ In.
$177

Humler & Nolan

Ornament, Orb, Swirl, Swans, Applied Textile, Beading, Gems, Metal Hanger, 4 ¾ In., Pair	17
Pitcher, Amber, Bulbous, Squat, Flared Rim, Strap Handle, Ball Cover, 9 ½ In.	995
Pitcher, Blue Green, Applied Threading At Neck, Bulbous, Footed, 5 ¼ In.	17550
Pitcher, Ship's Ear Handle, Disc Base, Elongated Spout, 9 In.	1020
Salt, Yellow Olive, Bulbous, Outward Rolled Rim, Footed, Pontil, c.1830, 2 ½ In.	2691
Salver, Clear, Hollow Ringed Stem, Domed Foot, Pedestal, c.1835, 7 ½ x 10 In.	206
Sculpture, Free-Form, Swirling Rose, Cobalt Blue, Pink, Stand, 1900s, 8 x 31 In.	1416
Shade, Hurricane, Frosted, Leaf Bands, Gilt Stenciled, c.1860, 21 In., Pair	1440
Sugar, Dome Lid, Cobalt Blue, 12 Vertical Ribs, Bulbous, Footed, 7 ½ In.	16415
Sugar, Dome Lid, Round, Cobalt Blue, Applied Foot, Pa., c.1835	460
Sugar, Lid, Cobalt Blue, Bulbous, Turned Knop, Round Foot, Finial, 6 ⅜ In.	1755
Sugar, Lid, Cobalt Blue, Engraved, A.G. 1780, Bulbous, Footed, Acorn Finial, 7 In.	2925
Sugar, Opaque White, Rose Loopings, Bulbous, Galleried Rim, Clear Foot, 4 ⅝ In.	269
Vase, Frosted, Swan's Head Handles, Round, Rolled Rim, c.1915, 15 x 14 ½ In.	295
Vase, Green, Etched Fence & Flowers, Bulbous, 2 Angular Handles, 10 In.	53
Vase, Pink Clematis Flowers, Swollen Shoulder, 1900s, 10 ¼ x 6 In.	767
Whimsy, Hat, Flip, Bowler Style, Yellow Olive, Pontil, c.1825, 2 ¼ x 4 In.	460
Witch's Ball, Sapphire Blue, Gray Blue Base, Footed, c.1860, 5 ½ In., Pair	353

GLASS-BOHEMIAN. Bohemian glass is an ornate overlay or flashed glass made during the Victorian era. It has been reproduced in Bohemia, which is now a part of the Czech Republic. Glass made from 1875 to 1900 is preferred by collectors.

Beaker, Enamel, Gilt Flowers, Tapered, Cylindrical, 4 ⅛ In., 8 Piece	260
Bowl, Green, Iridescent Blue, Metal Rim, Owl, Grape Swag Handles, c.1910, 5 In.	1920
Bowl, White, Blue Interior, Enameled Flowers, Shell Shape, 2 Feet, 8 x 10 In.	150
Box, Red To Clear, Rounded Square, Etched, City Views, Scrolls, 1800s, 4 x 5 In.	431
Cachepot, Everted Rim, Paneled Sides, Gilt, Multicolor Flowers, White Cased, 4 x 6 In.	92
Claret Jug, Ruby Color, Stags, Castles, Cartouches, Stopper, 16 x 4 In., Pair	584
Compote, Roses, Violets, Cranberry Overlay, Gilt Waist, Bell Shape Base, c.1910, 14 In.	1063
Cordial, Etched, Flower Shape Bowl, Emerald Green Stem, Meyersneffe, c.1900, 5 In.	108
Decanter Set, Ruby Flashed, Etched Medallion Stopper, 5 Cordials, 12 In.	52
Decanter, Stopper, Cranberry, 15 In.	34
Finger Bowl, Underplate, Ruby, Etched Stag, Landscape, 4 x 6 In., 12 Piece	1020
Girandole, Gilt, Flowers, Portraits, Hanging Prisms, 1800s, 11 In., Pair	3120
Girandole, White To Cranberry, Gilt, Scalloped Rim, Prism Pendants, 14 In., Pair	1800
Goblet, Lid, Green, Gilt, Flower Vertical Bands, 9 ½ In., Pair	313
Goblet, Orange Bowl, Black, Stand, Silver Overlay, Flowers, Geometrics, 4 x 6 In., 6 Piece	225
Goblet, Pink To Clear, Stag, Dog, c.1950, 4 In., 8 Piece	184
Jar, Lid, Burnt Orange, Waisted, Round Foot, Deer, Woods, 17 In., Pair	900
Pokal, Figure On Bicycle, Silvered Metal, c.1900, 13 ¾ In.	625
Punch Bowl, Stand, Amethyst, Cut To Clear, Fruit, Leaves, 9 ⅜ In.	90
Strawholder, Frosted, Multicolor Vertical Ribbons, Latticinio, Metal Lid, 12 In.	303
Strawholder, Millefiori, Vertical Paperweight Canes, Bulbous Lid & Finial, 9 In.	230
Urn, Portrait, Cranberry Glass, Gilding, Scroll Handles, Bell Base, 1800s, 16 In.	3198
Vase, Amethyst, Iridescent, Wavy Rim, Bulbous Base, Rindskopf, 7 x 14 In.	438
Vase, Arabic Style, Gilt, Flowers, Borders, Calligraphy, Iridescent, Fritz Heckert, c.1890, 8 In.	570
Vase, Blue On Orange Design, Iridescent, Double Gourd Shape, Wavy Rim, Kralik, 5 x 7 In.	344
Vase, Blue Wave Pattern, Gold Ground, Flared, Fritz Heckert, 8 x 6 In.	427
Vase, Blue, Enameled Birds, Butterflies, Flowers, Cylindrical, c.1885, 8 x 3 In.	150
Vase, Blue, Green, Brown, Agate Design, Ribbed Foot, Top, 14 In.	360
Vase, Cameo, Flower Shape, Footed, Trumpet Shape, Scalloped Rim, Red Flowers, 8 ½ In.	345
Vase, Clear Over Pink, Gilt Flowers, Cartouches, Flared Rim, c.1900, 18 In.	522
Vase, Cranberry, Gilded, Flowers, Bulbous, Stick Neck, 33 ⅝ In., Pair	1200
Vase, Cylindrical, Flowers, Leaves, Butterflies, Gilded Trim, 1800s, 17 In., Pair	300
Vase, Frosted Ground, Burgundy Pinstripes, Flared, Round Base, 1920s, 5 ½ x 6 In.	50
Vase, Goblet Shape, Scallop Rim, Cranberry To Gold, Portraits, 1800s, 13 In.	2040
Vase, Green, Feathered Top, Amethyst Applied Threaded Design, Pallme-Koenig, 9 In.	354
Vase, Green, Octagonal, Gilt, Leaves & Berries, 1800s, 20 In.	330
Vase, Oval, White Smokestack Rim, Flying Ducks, Gold Sun, Graf Harrach, 5 In.	7475
Vase, Overlay, Flowers, White Ground, c.1950, 10 ½ x 5 In., Pair	125
Vase, Papillion, Red Iridescent Crackle, Ruffled Top, Rindskopf, 9 ¾ In.	770
Vase, Portrait, Cranberry, Bottle Shape, Scrolled Leaves, 1800s, 8 In., Pair	677
Vase, Portrait, Gilt Leaves, Oval Medallions, Cranberry, 1800s, 12 ¼ In., Pair	2280
Vase, Portrait, Green, Gilt, Leaves, Medallions, 11 ⅛ In., Pair	960
Vase, Portrait, Green, Gold, Leaves, Shouldered, Round Foot, 1800s, 12 In., Pair	1800
Vase, Purple, Pulled Multicolor Swirls, Scalloped Rim, 7 ¼ In.	113

G

Vase, Ruby, Footed Trumpet, Engraved, c.1925, 9 ½ In..	69
Vase, Ruby, Stag Rondel, 10 ½ In., Pair	600
Vase, Sea Urchin, Silvery Blue, Textured, Highlights, Kralik, 20 In.................*illus*	805
Vase, Sporadic Ribbon Bands, Tricorner Rim, Kralik, 5 ½ In..........................*illus*	177
Vase, White Flower, Leaves Etched, Footed, 4 In..	107
Wedding Cup, Blue, White Enamel, Gold Border, F. Heckert, 10 ½ In. ....*illus*	1560

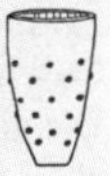

GLASS-CONTEMPORARY includes pieces by glass artists working after 1970. Many of these pieces are free-form, one-of-a-kind sculptures. Paperweights by contemporary artists are listed in the Paperweight category. Earlier studio glass may be found listed under Glass-Midcentury or Glass-Venetian.

Base, Lavender, Shaped Murrini, Tapered, R. Marquis, 1984, 9 x 6 In.	1750
Bowl, Clear, Red, Green Stripe, Flared, Signed Labino, 1970, 7 x 3 ½ In.	200
Bowl, Green, White, Spatter Design, 8 x 13 In.	180
Bowl, Incalmo, Turquoise, Emerald, Crystal, Amethyst, Sonja Blomdahl, 7 ½ x 15 ¼ In.	923
Bowl, Peach To White, Radiating Lines, Handle, Signed, Maurice Heaton, 2 ½ x 11 In................	88
Bowl, Sea Foam, White Wavy Lines, Lip Wrap, Chihuly, 1981, 5 x 14 In.	4688
Bowl, Sunrise, Lily Pond, Shouldered, Charles Lotton, 5 ¾ In...	805
Figure, Chili Pepper, Blown, Flora Mace, Joey Kirkpatrick, 10 x 27 In.......................*illus*	2124
Figure, Pumpkin, Orange, Twist Stem, Blown, Flora Mace, Joey Kirkpatrick, 17 x 14 In.	767
Sculpture, Emergence Flame, Veiled Candle, Dominick Labino, 1982, 10 ¾ In...................*illus*	4945
Sculpture, Emergence, Multicolor, Iridescent Veils, Blue, Signed, Labino, 7 In. ....*illus*	2950
Sculpture, Pink Seaform, White Wraps, Dale Chihuly, 1984, 18 x 14 In., 5 Piece ....*illus*	11250
Sculpture, Pink, Flower Shape, Scroll, Striped, Signed, Chihuly, 8 x 12 In.........................	4484
Teapot, White Specks Over Patchwork, Granular Murrine, R. Marquis, 6 In.	11875
Vase, Aventurine Peacock Eye, Oval, Green, Teal, Blue Pulled Feathers, Lotton, 7 In...............	633
Vase, Black, Figural Murrini, Guitar, Cat, Skull, Tapered, R. Marquis, 6 In.	1624
Vase, Branch, Oak Leaves, Acorns, Globular, Footed, Orient & Flume, 8 In.	345
Vase, Bulbous, Floating Leaf & Vine, Aventurine, Flared Rim, C. Lotton, 7 In.	546
Vase, Double Designs, White, Blue, Orient & Flume, c.1973, 7 ⅛ In..............................	230
Vase, Face, Mauve, Peach Rod, Tapered, Wm. Bernstein, 1982, 7 ½ In............................	472
Vase, Feather, Cased Opal, Charles Lotton, 1988, 7 In...................................*illus*	863
Vase, Fish, Plants, Oval, Clear, Orient & Flume, Paper Label, 7 In..............................	230
Vase, Flared Rim, Layered Pink, White Flowers, John Lotton, 1997, 11 x 27 In.	1792
Vase, Fused Multicolor Threads, Organic Shape, Signed, T. Zynsky, 5 x 10 In.	5040
Vase, Globular, Split Leaves, Curled Rim, Blue Aurene, C. Lotton, 6 ½ In.	632
Vase, Green, Blue Iridescent Swirls, Silver Threading, Lundberg, 1981, 5 ½ In.....................	240
Vase, Green, Undulating Tendrils, Bulbous, Signed Labino, 1969, 4 x 8 In.	250
Vase, Green, White, Bands, Marked, 9 In..	180
Vase, Iridescent, Pulled Waves, Stars, Clouds, Lundberg Studios, 1979, 3 In.	127
Vase, Lava, Cylindrical, Free-Form Cut Top, Purple, Iridescent Gold, Lotton, 7 In.	748
Vase, Nude Woman, Signed, Holmegaard, 4 ½ In..	24
Vase, Paperweight, Flower & Grass Stalks, Oval, M. Peiser, 1979, 8 In.	4688
Vase, Paperweight, Green, Oval Shape, Signed Labino, 1969, 5 ¾ In...............................	176
Vase, Paperweight, Green, Yellow, Gray, Signed Dominick Labino, 1972, 4 In........................	316
Vase, Pull Drape Pattern, Dominick Labino, 1975, 5 ⅝ In.................................*illus*	805
Vase, Pulled Green, Blue, Yellow, Signed, 1969, 8 ½ In...	368
Vase, Rainbow Mottled, Amber, White Hearts, Vines, Oval, Signed, Mary Angus, 5 ½ In.	75
Vase, Shouldered, Multicolor Feathers, Blue Threading, 7 In..	287
Vase, Stalks, Millefiori Flowers, Pulled Leaf Ground, Orient & Flume, 4 In.	230
Vase, Steuben Style, Blue Bulbous Shape, Green, Purple, Platinum Iridescent, 7 ¼ In.	326
Vase, Stick, Feathers, Coiled Tips, Gilt Threading, Orient & Flume, 10 In.........................	230
Vase, Swirled Silver, Blue, Yellow, Round, C. Lotton, 1987, 6 ½ In...............................	472
Vase, Wisteria, Bulbous, Signed, Charles Lotton, 1979, 9 ½ In. ....*illus*	748

GLASS-CUT, *see Cut Glass category.*

GLASS-DEPRESSION, *see Depression Glass category.*

GLASS-MIDCENTURY refers to art glass made from the 1940s to the early 1970s. Some glass factories, such as Baccarat or Orrefors, are listed under their own categories. Earlier glass may be listed in the Glass-Art and Glass-Contemporary categories. Italian glass may be found in Glass-Venetian.

Urn, Turned Wood Bowl, Gilt Base, 20th Century, 21 x 13 In., Pair..........................	176
Vase, Blue, Green Wavy Bands, F.M. Leerdam, Netherlands, c.1955, 6 x 5 In.	125
Vase, Cast, Pierced, Green, Incised, Round, Tapered Base, Charles Miner, c.1970, 16 x 27 In........	2500

Glass-Bohemian, Wedding Cup, Blue, White Enamel, Gold Border, F. Heckert, 10 ½ In.
$1,560

The Stein Auction Co.

Glass-Contemporary, Figure, Chili Pepper, Blown, Flora Mace, Joey Kirkpatrick, 10 x 27 In.
$2,124

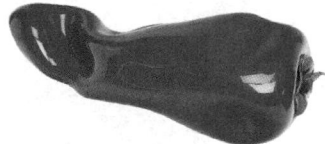

Brunk Auctions

Glass-Contemporary, Sculpture, Emergence Flame, Veiled Candle, Dominick Labino, 1982, 10 ¾ In.
$4,945

Humler & Nolan

Glass-Contemporary, Sculpture, Emergence, Multicolor, Iridescent Veils, Blue, Signed, Labino, 7 In.
$2,950

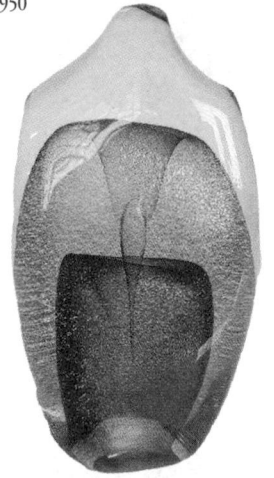

Rachel Davis Fine Arts

Glass-Contemporary, Sculpture, Pink Seaform, White Wraps, Dale Chihuly, 1984, 18 x 14 In., 5 Piece
$11,250

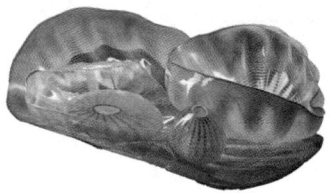

Rago Arts & Auction Center

Glass-Contemporary, Vase, Feather, Cased Opal, Charles Lotton, 1988, 7 In.
$863

Humler & Nolan

TIP

To remove stains from a glass vase, fill it with a mixture of ammonia and water and let it stand for a few hours.

Vase, Pulegoso Fasce, Red, Green, Yellow Bands, Squat, Cenedese, Italy, 7 ½ x 8 In.		923
Vase, Smoky Frosted, Raised Deer, Winter Moonlit Forest, H. Jager, Germany, c.1940, 9 x 6 In.		59

GLASS-PRESSED, *see Pressed Glass category.*

GLASS-VENETIAN. Venetian glass has been made near Venice, Italy, since the thirteenth century. Thin, colored glass with applied decoration is favored, although many other types have been made. Collectors have recently become interested in the Art Deco and fifties designs. Glass was made on the Venetian island of Murano from 1291. The output dwindled in the late seventeenth century but began to flourish again in the 1850s. Some of the old techniques of glassmaking were revived, and firms today make traditional designs and original modern glass. Since 1981, the name *Murano* may be used only on glass made on Murano Island. Other pieces of Italian glass may be found in the Glass-Contemporary and Glass-Midcentury categories of this book.

Ashtray, Clear, Red Interior, Gold Speckled Inner Layer, Murano, 3 x 6 In.		35
Bowl, Aubergine Filigrina, Leaf, Shape, Venini, 1938, 2 x 8 ¾ In.		600
Bowl, Blue, Green Striped, P. Venini, c.1954, 4 x 8 ½ In.		720
Bowl, Centerpiece, Globular, Vertical Ribbing, Brown, Tan, 6 x 8 ½ In.		480
Bowl, Clear, Blue Footed, Venini, 1954, 3 x 4 In., 4 Piece		300
Bowl, Clear, Green Blown Cane, Venini, 5 ½ x 7 In.		3200
Bowl, Clear, Yellow, Green Center, Barbini Battuto, Murano, 6 x 5 ½ In.		150
Bowl, Green, Clear Stripe, Orange Medallion, Black Ladybug, 6 x 8 ¾ In.		960
Bowl, Handkerchief, Pulled Eye Millefiori, 3 Pulled-Up Corners, Murano, 4 In.		35
Bowl, Losanghe, Checkerboard, Red, Ruffled, Seguso, Murano, 1950s, 4 x 7 In.		875
Bowl, Millefiori, Cut Canes, Red, Blue, Green, Yellow, Clear, Footed, Murano, 2 x 4 In.		58
Bowl, Zanfirico, Clear, Frosted Zigzag Rows, Venini, 1950, 3 ½ x 9 ½ In.		1560
Candelabrum, 5-Light, Clear, Gold Flecks, Murano, 26 In.		1265
Candlestick, 2-Light, U-Shape Scroll, Foot, Frosted, Murano, 1900s, 8 x 9 In., Pair		119
Console, Latticino, Clear, White Canes, Stripes, Lattice, Undulating Rim, 4 x 17 In.		443
Decanter, A Canne, Vertical Canes, Alternating Green, White, Fratelli Toso, 17 x 4 In.		886
Decanter, Blue, Green Spiral Stripes, Barovier & Toso, Italy, c.1960, 10 x 4 In.		523
Decanter, Sommerso, Clear Over Red, Tapered, Elongated Neck, Cenedese, 19 In.		923
Figurine, Black Horses, Rearing, Fornace & Bomeda, Signed, c.1980, 25 x 17 ½ In., Pair		1800
Figurine, Man, Woman, Carrying Baskets, Fruit, Flowers, 1900s, 14 x 8 In., Pair		413
Figurine, Octopus, Blue, Green, Inscribed Murano, Italy, 9 ¾ In.		240
Figurine, Parrot, Amethyst, Blue, Yellow, 16 In.		96
Figurine, Peacock, Head Down, Tail Up, Round Foot, Murano, c.1950, 13 In., Pair		84
Figurine, Pheasant, Gold Foil Inclusions, Murano, c.1945, 12 In., Pair		1500
Figurine, Rooster, Round Dome Foot, Red, White, Blue, c.1950, 10 ½ x 7 ½ In.		270
Figurine, Rooster, White & Lutz, Controlled Bubbles, Lobed Foot, Murano, 16 In.		70
Figurine, Woman, Tricorner Hat, Transparent Skirt, Domed Base, Opalescent, Murano, 7 ¾ In.		178
Goblet, Aubergine Filigrana, Clear Stem, Base, Venini, 1972, 4 In.		300
Hourglass, Clessidre, Blown, Paolo Venini, 10 x 4 ½ In.	*illus*	1200
Obelisk, Turquoise Blue, Paolo Venini, c.1960, 18 x 3 ½ In.	*illus*	5000
Pitcher, Vertical Ribbons, Blue, Pink, Green, Yellow, Gold Flecks, 7 In.		81
Sculpture, Aquarium Block, 2 Fish, Seaweed Suspended, Cenedese, 1960s, 6 ¾ x 9 In.		438
Sculpture, Aquarium Block, Fish, Seaweed, 1960s, 4 ¾ x 6 ½ In.		625
Sculpture, Fish, Clear, Bubbles, Dome Shape Vase, c.1960, 17 ¾ In.		369
Sculpture, Fish, Sommerso, Clear Over Green Over Red, Cenedese, Murano, 15 In.		461
Sculpture, Head & Hand, Cobalt Blue, Green, Murano, 20 ½ x 14 In.	*illus*	677
Sculpture, Nude, Pedestal, Signed Walter Furlan, Murano, 1998, 28 x 6 In.		688
Teapot, Mezza Filigrana, Clear, Yellow Lines, L. Tagliapietra, 1980, 10 ½ In.		9375
Vase, 3 Tiered Cones, Black, Black Spiral, Red, Vistosi, Murano, 1980s, 17 In.		813
Vase, Alternating Colored Quilted Design, Blue, Red, Green, Yellow, Murano, 9 In.		1062
Vase, Angelin, Spiral Ribbing, Twisting Canes, Tagliapietra, Murano, 1984, 8 ½ In.	*illus*	6765
Vase, Applied Broad Green Leaf, Barovier, Murano, 13 ¾ In.	*illus*	173
Vase, Applied Gold Grape Handles, Opalescent, Boat Shape, Barovier, 1930s, 7 x 9 In.		219
Vase, Bandiere, Multicolor Band, Frosted, Wavy Rim, Attr. Anzolo Fuga, c.1975, 19 x 9 In.		5000
Vase, Black Filigrana, Round, C. Scarpa, Venini, c.1970, 5 ½ In.		2640
Vase, Black, Red & Blue Swirling Canes Inside, Swollen, Murano, 1982, 12 In.		3250
Vase, Bottle, Tessuto, Vertical Stripes, Yellow & White, Yellow & Black, Scarpa, 14 In.		1771
Vase, Calabash, Black, Red & Green, Tapered, Ribbed, Carpenter, Venini, 1981, 12 In.		1375
Vase, Cane, Multicolor, Gio Ponti, Venini, Murano, 6 ½ x 5 ¼ In.	*illus*	2375
Vase, Cobalt Blue, 6 Orange Tulips, Floating Flowers, Yellow Stripes, Murano, 6 In.		29
Vase, Cordonato D'Oro, Blue, Gold Leaf, Ribbed Fan Shape, Murano, c.1960, 12 In.		750
Vase, Cylindrical, Multicolor Twisted Canes, Red Ground, c.1950, 11 ¾ In.		185
Vase, Elisse, Blue, Broken Lines, Signed, Giampaolo Seguso, Murano, 13 ¾ x 8 In.	*illus*	1800
Vase, Fazzoletto, Multicolor, Romano Dona, Murano, 14 ½ x 11 ½ In.	*illus*	1080

G

Glass-Contemporary, Vase, Pull Drape Pattern, Dominick Labino, 1975, 5 ⅝ In.
$805

Humler & Nolan

Glass-Contemporary, Vase, Wisteria, Bulbous, Signed, Charles Lotton, 1979, 9 ½ In.
$748

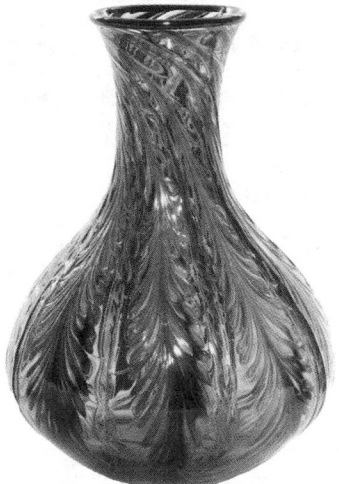

Early Auction Co.

Glass-Venetian, Hourglass, Clessidre, Blown, Paolo Venini, 10 x 4 ½ In.
$1,200

Palm Beach Modern Auctions

Glass-Venetian, Obelisk, Turquoise Blue, Paolo Venini, c.1960, 18 x 3 ½ In.
$5,000

Los Angeles Modern Auctions (LAMA)

Glass-Venetian, Sculpture, Head & Hand, Cobalt Blue, Green, Murano, 20 ½ x 14 In.
$677

Neal Auction Co.

Glass-Venetian, Vase, Angelin, Spiral Ribbing, Twisting Canes, Tagliapietra, Murano, 1984, 8 ½ In.
$6,765

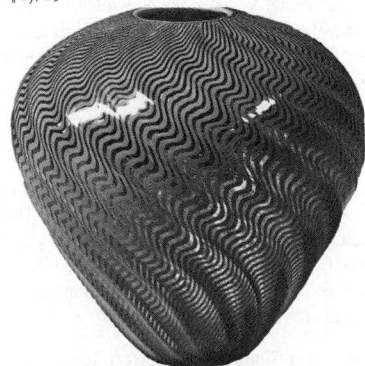

Skinner Auctioneers & Appraisers

Glass-Venetian, Vase, Applied Broad Green Leaf, Barovier, Murano, 13 ¾ In.
$173

Humler & Nolan

Glass-Venetian, Vase, Cane, Multicolor, Gio Ponti, Venini, Murano, 6 ½ x 5 ¼ In.
$2,375

Los Angeles Modern Auctions (LAMA)

Glass-Venetian, Vase, Elisse, Blue, Broken Lines, Signed, Giampaolo Seguso, Murano, 13 ¾ x 8 In.
$1,800

Palm Beach Modern Auctions

G

Glass-Venetian, Vase, Fazzoletto, Multicolor, Romano Dona, Murano, 14 ½ x 11 ½ In.
$1,080

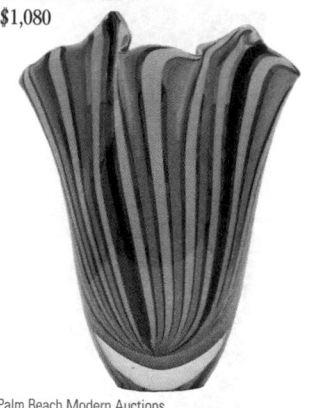

Palm Beach Modern Auctions

Glass-Venetian, Vase, Inciso, Alfredo Barbini, 1960s, 10 x 9 x 4 In.
$10,000

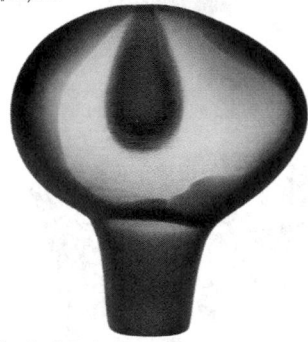

Rago Arts & Auction Center

Glass-Venetian, Vase, Latticinio Handkerchief, Venini, Italy, 10 ¾ x 12 In.
$1,560

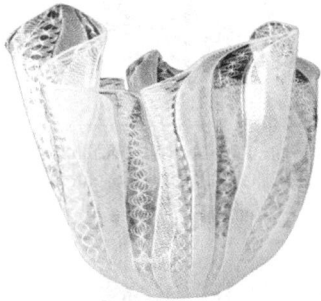

Palm Beach Modern Auctions

TIP
Keep your collection of glassware away from the speakers of your sound system. Heavy bass and high-pitched sounds can crack the glass.

Vase, Green, Black, Metallic Inclusions, Pitcher Shape, G. Radi, Italy, c.1980, 11 x 5 In.	3000
Vase, Green, Gold Inclusions, Ring Loop Handles, 9 ¾ In., Pair	1080
Vase, Green, Gold Leaf, Applied Bubble Lobes, Barovier, Murano, 1960s, 10 x 6 In.	250
Vase, Green, Textured, Rimmed, Cenedese Scavo, 1987, 8 x 10 In.	275
Vase, Handkerchief, Cobalt Blue, Folded, Venini, 9 x 9 In.	590
Vase, Handkerchief, Latticino, Clear, White Spiral Twist Canes, Venini, 11 x 12 In.	1599
Vase, Hourglass Shape, Red, Air Bubbles, 8 In.	210
Vase, Iceberg, Brown, Orange Swirls, Waisted, Murano, Attr. A. Fuga, c.1985, 20 x 6 In.	5938
Vase, Incalmo, Murrhina Stripe, Frosted, Dark Purple Band, R. Licata, 1950s, 7 ½ In.	3600
Vase, Inciso, Alfredo Barbini, 1960s, 10 x 9 x 4 In. ....*illus*	10000
Vase, Klee, Patchwork Rectangles, Green, Tan, Brown, DeSantillana, Venini, 10 In.	984
Vase, Latticinio Handkerchief, Venini, Italy, 10 ¾ x 12 In. ....*illus*	1560
Vase, Losanghe, Checkerboard, Beige, Flared, Folded, Seguso, Murano, 1950s, 8 In.	1000
Vase, Merletto, Lace, White, Pulled Threads, Round, Cenedese, Murano, 9 x 10 In.	1250
Vase, Mezza Filigrana, Horizontal Lines, Spherical, c. Scarpa, Murano, 12 In.	6250
Vase, Millefiori, Blown, Gold Inclusions, Oval, Murano, 9 ¾ In.	483
Vase, Millefiori, Cobalt, Scrambled Cut Canes, Multicolor, Flared, 5 ½in.	23
Vase, Paolo Venini, Incised, Etched 3-Line Mark, Italy, c.1960, 6 ½ x 11 ¾ In.	750
Vase, Pezzato, Patchwork, White & Clear, Air Bubbles, Barovier, 1956, 8 x 6 In.	1375
Vase, Pitcher, Ambrato, Handle, Red, Orange, Green Swirl, Barovier & Toso, 1950s, 6 x 10 In.	140
Vase, Pulegoso, Clear To Orange, Multicolor Border, Attr. Anzolo Fuga, c.1980, 18 x 7 In.	4375
Vase, Red & Clear, Trumpet Rim, Spread Foot, Flower, Wreath, Murano, 11 x 5 In.	210
Vase, White, Scavo, Domed Foot, Murano, Karl Springer, 1970s, 24 x 14 In., Pair	3625
Vase, Zanfirico Merletto, White, P. Venini, 10 ½ In.	1440

GLASSES for the eyes, or spectacles, were mentioned in a manuscript in 1289 and have been used ever since. The first eyeglasses with rigid side pieces were made in London in 1727. Bifocals were invented by Benjamin Franklin in 1785. Lorgnettes were popular in late Victorian times. Opera Glasses are listed in the Opera Glass category.

Glasses, Over Nose Style, Silver Repousse Case, c.1850	218
Lorgnette, Silver Chain, Platinum & Diamond Openwork Handle, c.1910, 30 In.	5625

GLIDDEN POTTERY worked in Alfred, New York, from 1940 to 1957. The pottery made stoneware, dinnerware, and art objects.

Casserole, Brown, Black, Tab Handles, Lid, 8 x 5 In.	196
Gravy Boat, Speckled Turquoise	28
Plate, Poodle, Gray, Black, Bow In Hair, Speckled Blue Border, 5 x 5 In.	45
Relish, 5 Sections, Speckled Turquoise Glaze, 14 x 11 In.	55
Vase, Black & Gray Speckled, Turquoise Interior, 4 x 4 x 3 In.	28
Vase, Foldover Scalloped Rim, Pink, Square, 4 x 4 In.	30
Vase, Mottled Turquoise Glaze, Undulating Ribbing, 7 ½ In.	40
Vase, Pillow, Speckled Turquoise Glaze, 5 x 9 In.	50

GOEBEL is the mark used by W. Goebel Porzellanfabrik of Oeslau, Germany, now Rodental, Germany. The company was founded by Franz Detleff Goebel and his son, William Goebel, in 1871. It was known as F&W Goebel. Slates, slate pencils, and marbles were made. Soon the company began making porcelain tableware and figurines. Hummel figurines were first made by Goebel in 1935 and are now being made by another company. Goebel is still in business. Old pieces marked *Goebel Hummel* are listed under Hummel in this book.

Figurine, Cat, Licking Paw, Gray, Brown, Black, c.1955, 10 In.	35
Figurine, Huedak, Woman, Yellow, White Dress, Hat, 8 In.	17
Figurine, Madonna, Jesus, Flower, Bird, 12 In.	35
Powder Box, Woman, On Lid, Riding Habit, Incised Mark, c.1920, 8 In. ....*illus*	513
Salt & Pepper, Mallard Duck, Green, Yellow, Brown, 1 ⅞ In.	35
Sugar & Creamer, Figures, Googly Eyes, Black Forehead Curl, Round Orange Body, 1920s	72

GOLDSCHEIDER was founded by Friedrich Goldscheider in Vienna in 1885. The family left Vienna in 1938 and the factory was taken over by the Germans. Goldscheider started factories in England and in Trenton, New Jersey. The New Jersey factory started in 1940 as Goldscheider–U.S.A. In 1941 it became Goldscheider-Everlast Corporation. From 1947 to 1953 it was Goldcrest Ceramics Corporation. In 1950 the Vienna plant was returned to Mr. Goldscheider and the company continues in business. The Trenton, New Jersey, business, called Goldscheider of Vienna, imports all of the pieces.

Bust, Moroccan Woman, Man, Scarves, Terra-Cotta, 22 In., Pair	6000
Figurine, Girl, Folded Hands, Closed Eyes, Marble Base, Marked, 9 In.	1330

Figurine, Man In Red Robe, Head Covering, Standing, Marked, Numbered, 18 ¾ In.	24
Figurine, Woman, Lace Dress, Holding Mask, Marked, 14 ¾ In.	885
Figurine, Woman, Nude, Resting, Terra-Cotta, c.1910, 27 In.	450
Mask, Woman's Head, Long Brown Hair, Terra-Cotta, A. Larroux, Austria, 12 In.	450

GOLF, *see Sports category.*

GOOFUS GLASS was made from about 1900 to 1920 by many American factories. It was originally painted gold, red, green, bronze, pink, purple, or other bright colors. Many pieces are found today with flaking paint, and this lowers the value.

Bowl, Crimped, Ruffled, Red & Gold, Opalescent, Footed, 8 In.	50
Bowl, Gold, Red Grapes, Panels, Scalloped, 7 In.	32
Bowl, Gold, Red Grapes, Scalloped Rim, 7 In.	38
Bowl, Grapes & Leaves, Footed, Dugan, 10 In.	34
Bowl, Roses, Lattice, Red, Gold, c.1900, 9 In.	22
Console, Strawberries, Vines, Gold, Red, 9 ¾ In.	42
Console, Vines, Strawberries, Gold & Red, Scalloped Edge, 9 ¾ In.	38
Plate, Apples, On Branch, Wide Rim, Thistles, Scrolls, 8 ⅜ In.	30
Plate, Long Stem Roses, Sawtooth Edge, Red, Gold, Footed, c.1900, 11 In.	76
Plate, Red & Gold, Long Stem Roses, Panels, Scalloped, Sawtooth Edge, Footed, 11 In.	40
Rose Bowl, Roses, Paneled, Woven, Red & Gold, 2 ¾ In.	24
Syrup, Red & Gold, Embossed, 6 ¾ In.	90
Syrup, Roses, Stems, Leaves, Red, Gold, c.1900, 6 ¾ In.	90
Vase, Peacock, Gold, Black, Red, Oval, 10 ½ In.	50
Vase, Puffy Poppies, Red & Gold, Oval, 7 In.	40
Vase, Raised Flowers, Basket Weave Ground, Pinched Neck, 9 ½ In.	35

GOUDA, Holland, has been a pottery center since the seventeenth century. Two firms, the Zenith pottery, established in the eighteenth century, and the Zuid-Hollandsche pottery, made the brightly colored art pottery marked *Gouda* from 1898 to about 1964. Other factories followed. Many pieces featured Art Nouveau or Art Deco designs.

Ashtray, Windmill Shape, Rosario Pattern, Marked, 4 ¼ In.	153
Bowl, Royal Blue Ground Gold Swirl, Black Matte Interior, 8 In.	237
Charger, Abstract Flowers, Matte Glaze, Marked, 1926, 19 ⅛ In. ......*illus*	960
Charger, Art Nouveau, Lilies, Swirl, Glazed, Signed, Zuid Holland, c.1900, 16 In. ......*illus*	813
Charger, Flowers, Impressed, 13 ½ In.	58
Ewer, Free-Form Triangular Panels, Green, Amber, Blue, White Swirls, 6 ¼ In.	59
Sign, Rosario Pattern, Regina Gould Platell, Red, Blue, 3 ⅞ x 6 ⅛ In.	165
Vase, Blue, Red Flowers, Light Brown Ground, Round, Tapered, 8 ½ x 8 ½ In.	182
Vase, Broad Shouldered, Tapered To Foot, Narrow Neck, Tulips, Marked, c.1900, 7 In.	330
Vase, Exotic Bird, Flowers, Marked, Zuid Holland, Incised, Mat Bloemen, 10 ⅝ In. ......*illus*	325
Vase, Gourd Shape, Tapered Neck, Ring Foot, Yellow, Blue, Rust, Marked, c.1928, 13 In.	300
Vase, Purple Flowers, Green Ground, 4 Handles, Zuid Mark, 9 ¼ In.	325
Vase, Ring Foot, Rolled Rim, Multicolor, Matte Glaze, Marked, c.1928, 11 ⅛ In.	510
Vase, Rolled Rim, City Gate, Tan, Brown, Rust, Marked, c.1900, 17 In.	1320
Vase, Stylized Flowers, Multicolor, Shouldered, Tapered, 13 x 11 In.	464

GRANITEWARE is enameled tin or iron used to make kitchenware since the 1870s. Earlier graniteware was green or turquoise blue, with white spatters. The later ware was gray with white spatters. Reproductions are being made in all colors. There is a second definition of the word *graniteware* meaning a blue speckled pottery. Only the metal graniteware is listed here.

Baking Dish, Blue & White, 1930s, 11 x 8 x 2 In.	25
Berry Bucket, Gray Swirl, Tin Lid, Wire Bail Handle, 5 x 7 In.	60
Coffeepot, Blue & White Swirl, Hinged Lid, 7 ½ In.	45
Coffeepot, Gray Speckled, Tin Lid, Bail Handle, Wood Grip, 13 In.	80
Cream Can, Blue, White Swirl, Lid, Handle, 9 ½ x 4 ½ In.	40
Cream Can, Blue Speckled, Bail & Strap Handle, 9 ¼ x 6 ¼ In.	15
Lunch Pail, Blue & White, Metal Bail Handle, Wood Grip, c.1915, 9 ½ In.	125
Milk Can, Blue & White, Confetti Style, Bail & Strap Handle, 9 ¼ x 6 ¼ In.	145
Mold, Turk's Head, Robin Egg Blue, c.1890, 4 x 9 ¾ In.	36
Pail, Blue & White Swirl, Wire & Wood Bail Handle, 9 x 11 In.	125
Pitcher, Measure, Gray, Cylindrical, Loop Handle, Flat Rim Spout, 10 x 9 In.	85
Pot, Blue Speckled, Bail Handle, Lid, c.1950, 10 In.	25
Teapot, Gray, Wavy, Mottled, Iron Handle, Porcelain Knob, 9 ¾ In.	165

Goebel, Powder Box, Woman, On Lid, Riding Habit, Incised Mark, c.1920, 8 In.
$513

Theriault's

G

TIP
Put a rubber collar on the faucet spout over the sink. This may save you from breaking a piece of glass or china you are washing.

Gouda, Charger, Abstract Flowers, Matte Glaze, Marked, 1926, 19 ⅛ In.
$960

Skinner Auctioneers & Appraisers

Gouda, Charger, Art Nouveau, Lilies, Swirl, Glazed, Signed, Zuid Holland, c.1900, 16 In.
$813

Rago Arts & Auction Center

Gouda, Vase, Exotic Bird, Flowers, Marked, Zuid Holland, Incised, Mat Bloemen, 10 ⅝ In.
$325

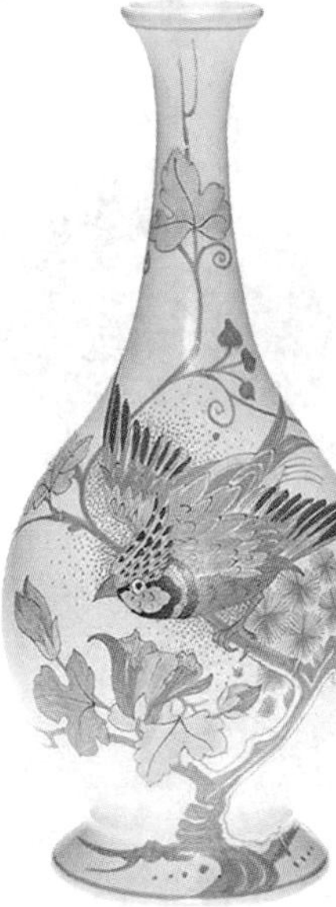

Humler & Nolan

Grueby, Tile, Yellow Tulip, Initials, Square, c.1905, 6 In.
$2,125

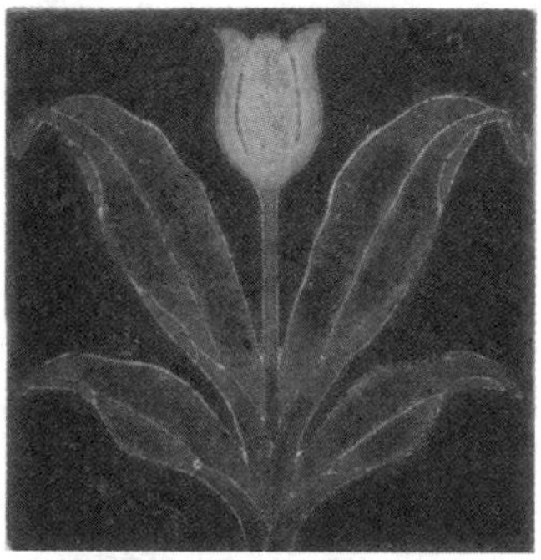

Rago Arts & Auction Center

Grueby, Vase, Green Curdled Glaze, Long Leaves, Buds, Lobed Rim, Faience, c.1900, 7 x 4 In.
$1,063

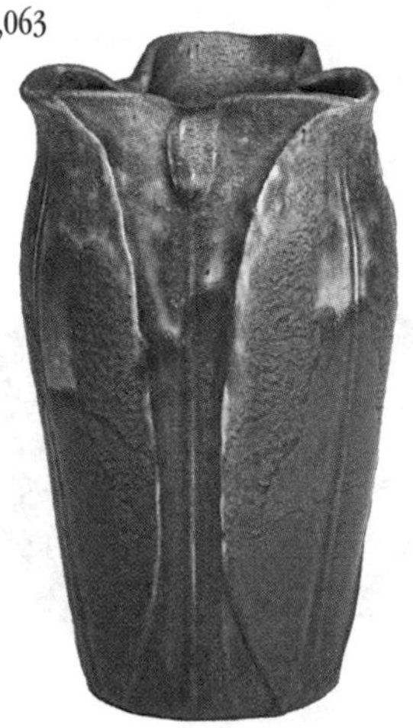

Rago Arts & Auction Center

GREENTOWN glass was made by the Indiana Tumbler and Goblet Company of Greentown, Indiana, from 1894 to 1903. In 1899, the factory became part of National Glass Company. A variety of pressed glass was made. Additional pieces may be found in other categories, such as Chocolate Glass, Holly Amber, Milk Glass, and Pressed Glass.

Cactus, Compote, Streaks, Swirls, Scalloped Rim, 5 ½ In. 77
Cactus, Tumbler, Panels, Vertical Lines, 4 In. 26
Cord Drapery, Pitcher, Scalloped Foot & Rim, 5 In. 30
Dewey, Butter, Cover, Flat Footed, Daisy Ruffled Edge, Green, Round, 7 In. 45
Wildrose & Bowknot, Tumbler, Frosted, Greentown, c.1892, 3 ¾ In. 55

GRUEBY FAIENCE COMPANY of Boston, Massachusetts, was founded in 1894 by William H. Grueby. Grueby Pottery Company was incorporated in 1907. In 1909, Grueby Faience went bankrupt. Then William Grueby founded the Grueby Faience and Tile Company. Grueby Pottery closed about 1911. The tile company worked until 1920. Garden statuary, art pottery, and architectural tiles were made until 1920. The company developed a green matte glaze that was so popular it was copied by many other factories making a less expensive type of pottery. This eventually led to the financial problems of the pottery. Cuerda seca and cuenca are techniques explained in the Tile category. The company name was often used as the mark, and slight changes in the form help date a piece.

Bowl, Carved Leaves, Blue Matte Glaze, 2 x 6 In. 885
Bowl, Green, Carved Stylized Leaves, Round Stamp, c.1905, 2 x 6 In. 875
Bowl, Leaves, Carved, Green Matte Glaze, Square, Shaped Rim, 4 x 10 In. 1625
Coupe, Green, Carved Leaves, Round Pottery Stamp, Artist's Cipher, c.1905, 8 x 4 ½ In. 2750
Lamp, Domed Glass Tile Shade, Leaf Embossed Base, Green Matte, Signed ER, 15 x 18 In. 4375
Sculpture, Scarab, Green Matte Glaze, 2 x 3 In. 281
Sculpture, Scarab, Green Matte Glaze, 3 x 4 In. 750
Tile, Alice In Wonderland, Dodo, Griffin, Crab, Rabbit, Parrot, Mad Hatter, 4 x 4 In., 6 Piece 5625
Tile, Boat, Moonlit Water, Octagonal Frame, c.1900, 9 ½ In. 1200
Tile, Center Flower Medallion, Blue Ground, Yellow Border, 12 In. 275
Tile, Cuenca Turtle, Leaf Garland, Brown, Green Glaze, White Body, 6 In. 1920
Tile, Cupid, Kneeling, Bow, Green, Blue Glaze, Frame, 10 ½ x 10 ½ In. 330
Tile, Sailboat, In Wind, Oak Frame, Art Nouveau, 14 x 14 In. 5300
Tile, Trivet, Lion Scene, Bronze Mounted, DC, 5 x 5 In. 3500
Tile, Tulip, Green, Yellow, Artist Initials, c.1907, 6 x 6 In. 2375
Tile, Yellow Border, Center Floral Medallion, Blue Ground, 12 x 12 In. 275
Tile, Yellow Tulip, Initials, Square, c.1905, 6 In. .... *illus* 2125
Vase, Brown Matte Glaze, Vertical Ribs, Flared Rim, Oval, 5 x 3 In. 1750
Vase, Carved, Applied Leaves, Buds, Blue Matte Glaze, 8 x 6 ½ In. 9760
Vase, Curdled Blue Glaze, Stamped, 1905, 5 x 3 ½ In. 531
Vase, Green Curdled Glaze, Leaves, Buds, c.1900, 26 x 11 ½ In. 6875
Vase, Green Curdled Glaze, Long Leaves, Buds, Lobed Rim, Faience, c.1900, 7 x 4 In. .... *illus* 1063
Vase, Green Matte Glaze, Buds, Tapered, c.1900, 4 x 3 ½ In. 188
Vase, Green Matte Glaze, Impressed Leaves, Bottle Shape, c.1900, 21 ¾ In. 1875
Vase, Green Matte Glaze, Incised Geometric Designs, 10 x 9 In. 1464
Vase, Green Matte Glaze, Irises, Buds, Leaves, Bulbous, Stamped, c.1905, 14 x 8 In. 8125
Vase, Green Matte Glaze, Stacked Leaves, Pear Shape, Stamped, c.1905, 9 x 5 In. 2750
Vase, Green Matte Glaze, Stepped High Waist Band, Incised Stylized Leaves, 8 x 12 In. 2440
Vase, Green Matte Glaze, Vertically Overlapping Leaves, Cylindrical, 4 x 8 ½ In. 3250
Vase, Green, Buds, Leaves, Triangle Stamp, c.1905, 7 x 4 ½ In. 2125
Vase, Green, Bulbous, Leaves, Round Pottery Stamped, Artist's Cipher, c.1905, 7 x 8 In. 813
Vase, Green, Leaves, Buds, c.1900, Round Faience Stamp, 23 x 9 In. 21250
Vase, Indigo Curdled Glaze, Gourd Base, Cylindrical Neck, 15 ¾ x 9 ¼ In. 3750
Vase, Leaves, Buds, Mauve Matte Glaze, Faience Stamp, c.1900, 7 ¼ x 5 In. .... *illus* 1875
Vase, Leaves, Carved, Brown Curdled Over Green Glaze, Oval, Rolled Rim, c.1905, 14 x 9 In. 12500
Vase, Leaves, Carved, Green Matte Glaze, Barrel Shape, c.1905, 12 x 8 In. 4375
Vase, Leaves, Green Matte Glaze, Wilhelmine Post, Impressed, 7 ¾ In. .... *illus* 2832
Vase, Overlapping Leaves, Bulbous Base, c.1905, 13 x 8 In. 4375
Vase, Pinched Rim, Leaves, Buds, 8 x 4 In. 3600
Vase, Ribbed, Green Matte Glaze, Bulbous Shape, 5 x 7 ½ In. 1250
Vase, Tooled & Applied Leaves, Green Matte Glaze, Marked, 7 ⅞ In. 2714
Vase, Tooled Buttresses, Green Matte Glaze, Bulbous, 7 In. 1652
Vase, Yellow Matte Glaze, Carved Leaves, Buds, Tapered, Flared, 4 ½ x 7 ½ In. 3250

GUN, *see Toy*

GUSTAVSBERG ceramics factory was founded in 1827 near Stockholm, Sweden. It is best known to collectors for its twentieth-century artwares, especially Argenta, a green stoneware with silver inlay. The company was sold in the 1990s.

Gustafsberg

Bowl, Argenta, Footed, Cloverleaves, Dotted Rim, Art Deco, 1 ½ x 3 ⅞ In.		149
Candleholder, Square Base, Pillar Column, Bulbous Top, Marked, 5 In., Pair		159
Compote, Green Bowl, Bulrushes, Lily Pads, Triple Stork Support, Majolica, 13 x 12 ½ In.		545
Creamer, White, Gra Rander Pattern, Ball Shape, Swooping Handle, Kage, 2 ¼ In.		70
Lamp, Vertical Lines, Stig Lindberg, c.1963, 31 ½ x 14 ¼ In.	*illus*	2000
Tray, Argenta, Art Deco, Flower Inlay, 5 ⅜ In. Diam.		100
Tray, Mottled Jade Green, Overlay Cloverleaves & Trim, Scalloped Rim, 4 In. Diam.		65
Vase, Argenta, Flower & Leaf Overlay, Shouldered, Marked, 4 ¼ In.		134
Vase, Blue, Green Flowers, Blue Ground, Bulbous, Straight-Sided Neck, 1911, 4 ½ In.		130
Vase, Blue, Horizontal Lines, Vertical Lines, Wilhelm Kage, c.1955, 7 ½ x 2 ½ In.	*illus*	1875
Vase, Purple Shamrocks, White Ground, Bulbous At Top, 1903, 6 ¼ In.		384
Vase, Spade Shape, Footed, W. Kage, Farsta, Stoneware, 1960s, 7 x 4 ½ In.	*illus*	938

HAEGER POTTERIES, INC., Dundee, Illinois, started making commercial artwares in 1914. Early pieces were marked with the name *Haeger* written over an *H*. About 1938, the mark *Royal Haeger* was used in honor of Royal Hickman, a designer at the factory. The firm is still making florist wares and lamp bases. See also the Royal Hickman category.

Haeger

Ashtray, Round, Orange, Earth Wrap, Royal Haeger, 1 ½ x 8 ¼ In.		50
Bowl, Ringed Neck, Impressed Letters, Rustic Glaze, Royal Haeger, 5 x 8 ¼ In.		35
Candleholder, Fish, Long Tail, Aqua Glaze, 1940s, 7 ½ In., Pair		50
Figurine, Cat, Seated, Elongated, Glass Eye, Pink, Blue Highlights, c.1950, 20 In.		92
Jardiniere, Basket Weave, Green, 5 ¼ x 7 In.		40
Vase, Beehive, Purple To Red, c.1938, 8 In.		125
Vase, Blue Lava, Bulbous, Stretch Neck, Footed, Royal Haeger, 14 ½ In.		50
Vase, Gold Lava, Handles, Shouldered, Scalloped Rim, 16 x 9 ½ In.		85
Vase, Orange Flowers, Black Matte Glaze, Royal Haeger, 16 ¾ In.		92
Vase, Orange, Blue Green Design, Black Matte Glaze, Bottle Shape, 15 In.		29
Vase, Yellow Orange, Green Drip, Black Matte Glaze, Marked Royal Haeger, 16 ¾ In.		109

HALF-DOLL, *see Pincushion Doll category.*

HALL CHINA COMPANY started in East Liverpool, Ohio, in 1903. The firm made many types of wares. Collectors search for the Hall teapots made from the 1920s to the 1950s. The dinnerware of the same period, especially Autumn Leaf pattern, is also popular. The Hall China Company merged with Homer Laughlin China Company in 2010. Autumn Leaf pattern dishes are listed in their own category in this book.

HALL'S
SUPERIOR
QUALITY
KITCHENWARE

Blue Blossom, Bean Pot, Lid, Leaves, Iris-Like Flowers, c.1939, 6 ¼ In.		175
Blue Bouquet, Casserole, Lid, Thick Rim, Silver Trim, 5 ½ x 8 In.		45
McCormick, Teapot, Maroon, Lid, 6 In.		75
Red Poppy, Bowl, Platinum Trim, 9 In.		12
Red Poppy, Sugar & Creamer, Daniel, c.1940		27
Refrigerator Ware, Casserole, Lid, General Electric, Gray, Yellow, Tab Handles, 9 x 3 In.		46
Refrigerator Ware, Dish, Lid, Westinghouse, Blue, 6 x 4 x 3 In.		29
Refrigerator Ware, Pitcher, Water, Westinghouse, Light Blue, Ribbed Bottom, Disc, 7 In.		39
Refrigerator Ware, Pitcher, Westinghouse, Cobalt Blue, Built-In Handle, 1930s, 8 In.		95
Tavern, Coffeepot, Figures, High Back Chairs, Black Decal, Silver Trim, 1930s, 9 In.		90
Wildfire, Tidbit Tray, 3 Tiers, Gold Trim, c.1945, 10 ¼ In.		55
Windshield, Teapot, Ivory, Gold Dots, Lid, 1940s, 6 Cup		89
Windshield, Teapot, Mustard, Flower Band, 1960s, 6 Cup		90

HALLOWEEN is an ancient holiday that has changed in the last 200 years. The jack-o'-lantern, witches on broomsticks, and orange decorations seem to be twentieth-century creations. Collectors started to become serious about collecting Halloween-related items in the late 1970s. The papier-mache decorations, now replaced by plastic, and old costumes are in demand.

Box, Chocolate, Johnston's, Woman, Black Hat, Pumpkin Shape, c.1930, 9 x 8 ½ In.		47
Cat, Black, Paint, Papier-Mache, 9 In.		106
Cat, Hollow, Pressed Paper, Black, Orange Paint, Wire Handle, 5 In.		188
Cat's Meow Sparkler Ranger, Tin, Cat Face, Orange, Black, Ranger Products, 6 x 3 ½ In.		83
Game, Cat & Witch, Pin Tail On The Witch, Whitman Pub. Co., 21 x 18 ½ In.		35
Horn, Pickle, Painted Smiley Face, Wooden Horn Piece, Papier-Mache, 8 In.	*illus*	119
Jack-In-The-Box, Skeleton, Japan, 5 ½ In.		150

H

Grueby, Vase, Leaves, Buds, Mauve Matte Glaze, Faience Stamp, c.1900, 7 ¼ x 5 In. $1,875

Rago Arts & Auction Center

Grueby, Vase, Leaves, Green Matte Glaze, Wilhelmine Post, Impressed, 7 ¾ In. $2,832

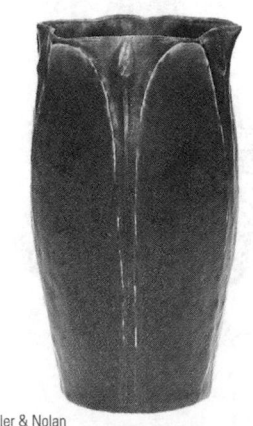

Humler & Nolan

Gustavsberg, Lamp, Vertical Lines, Stig Lindberg, c.1963, 31 ½ x 14 ¼ In. $2,000

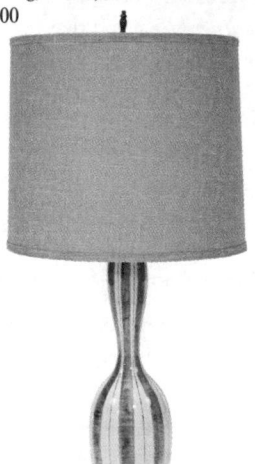

Los Angeles Modern Auctions (LAMA)

Gustavsberg, Vase, Blue, Horizontal Lines, Vertical Lines, Wilhelm Kage, c.1955, 7 ½ x 2 ½ In. $1,875

Los Angeles Modern Auctions (LAMA)

Gustavsberg, Vase, Spade Shape, Footed, W. Kage, Farsta, Stoneware, 1960s, 7 x 4 ½ In. $938

Rago Arts & Auction Center

Jack-O'-Lantern, Black Cat, Yellow Eyes, Cardboard, Germany, 3 ½ In.	240
Jack-O'-Lantern, Black, Ears, Handle, Cardboard, 4 ¼ In.	30
Jack-O'-Lantern, Clown, Composition, Multicolor, G.A. Schwarz Toys, 5 In. *illus*	2655
Jack-O'-Lantern, Devil Head, Orange, Black Horns, Wire Handle, Composition, 6 ½ In.	180
Jack-O'-Lantern, Devil, Standing, Bat Wings, Red, Black, Paper, 12 In.	3600
Jack-O'-Lantern, Handle, Orange, Papier-Mache, 4 ¾ In.	59
Jack-O'-Lantern, Monkey Head, 5 ½ In.	90
Jack-O'-Lantern, Orange, Blue Eyes, Paper Inserts, Handle, Composition, Germany, 7 In.	420
Jack-O'-Lantern, Orange, Handle, Papier-Mache, 5 ½ In.	330
Jack-O'-Lantern, Orange, Yellow Eyes, Cardboard, Paper, 6 ½ In.	120
Jack-O'-Lantern, Owl, Orange, Green Eyes, Cardboard, Paper, 5 In.	120
Jack-O'-Lantern, Plaster, Wire Handle, 4 In. *illus*	330
Jack-O'-Lantern, Plaster, Yellow, 4 In.	390
Jack-O'-Lantern, Pulp Devil, Open Mouth, Orange, Tan, Handle, Paper, 6 ½ In.	420
Jack-O'-Lantern, Pumpkin, Orange, Black Base, Pulp, 5 In.	150
Jack-O'-Lantern, Pumpkin, Orange, Paper, 7 In.	120
Jack-O'-Lantern, Skull Head, Bail Handle, Candleholder, Germany, 4 ½ In.	708
Jack-O'-Lantern, Tin, Half Spheres, Wood Knob, Candleholder, c.1900, 9 x 9 In., Pair	3600
Jack-O'-Lantern, Witch, Wire Candle, Paper, Plaster, Handle, 5 In.	2400
Jester, Jack-O'-Lantern Head, Jointed Arms & Legs, Cardboard, 28 In.	30
Lantern, Crazy Pear, Composition, Pear Shape, Ghoulish Face, Germany, 3 ½ In.	1298
Lantern, Devil's Head, Composition, Bail Handle, Germany, 2 In.	325
Lantern, Devil's Head, Composition, Glass Eyes, Teeth, Handle, Germany, 3 ½ In. *illus*	590
Lantern, Devil's Sitting On Smiling Skull, Composition, Germany, 4 In.	266
Lantern, Foxy Grandpa, Composition, Painted, Glazed, Germany, 3 ½ In. *illus*	443
Lantern, Pumpkin, Orange Papier-Mache, White Teeth, Round, Wire Hanger, 6 In.	92
Lantern, Standing Pumpkin, Boy Body, Composition, Crepe Clothing, Leaf Collar, 6 In.	1180
Lantern, Tree Trunk, Face, Composition, Glazed Tree Knots, Handle, 2 ¾ In. *illus*	826
Lantern, Watermelon, Scary Face, Composition, Bail Handle, 6 In.	1121
Lantern, Witch, Devil, Owl, Pumpkin, Cat, Paper, Cardboard, Germany, 12 In.	180
Man, Egg Head, Cloth Jacket, White Pants, Plaster Body, 5 ¾ In.	150
Mask, Man, Wrinkles, Spectacles, Top Hat, Composition, 14 In.	148
Moonman, Holds Owl, 2 Black Cats At Feet, Checkered Pants, Celluloid, 3 In.	649
Noisemaker, Clacker, Ghoulish Face, Big Features, Composition, Wood, 6 In.	89
Ornament, Jack-O'-Lantern, Blown Glass, Green, White, Germany, c.1900, 2 ⅜ x 3 In.	165
Rattle, Black Cat, Standing, Wide Mouth, Bow, Celluloid, 4 In.	120
Roly Poly, 2 Owls In Tree, Man In Moon Sky, Celluloid, Oval, 3 In.	443
Roly Poly, Scarecrow, Glasses, Green Coat, Pumpkin Bottom, Celluloid, 3 In.	443
Scarecrow, Pulling Ghoul In Car, Celluloid, 3 In.	295
Sparkler, Cat Flint, Black, White, Red Paint, Tin, Pull String, Archie Ronson, 1923, 9 In.	106
Spin Sparkler, Archie, Tin, Wood Box, Ronson, USA, c.1923 *illus*	63
Tin, Candy, The Lucky Box, Witch, Caldron, 5 ½ In. *illus*	540
Tin, Lantern, Face, Clown Comic, Handle, 7 In., Pair	35
Witch, Eyes Move, Composition, Horse Hair Wig, Corn Husk Broom, Clockwork, 35 In.	2655
Witch, On Motorcycle, Plastic, Orange, Green Wheels, Jack-O'-Lantern On Back, 7 In.	180

HAMPSHIRE pottery was made in Keene, New Hampshire, between 1871 and 1923. Hampshire developed a line of colored glazed wares as early as 1883, including a Royal Worcester–type pink, olive green, blue, and mahogany. Pieces are marked with the printed mark or the impressed name *Hampshire Pottery* or *J.S.T. & Co., Keene, N.H.* Many pieces were marked with city names and sold as souvenirs.

Bowl, Green Matte Glaze, Water Lilies, Stamped, c.1910, 3 x 10 In.	344
Bowl, Lotus, Brown Matte Glaze, 2 x 5 ¾ In.	265
Compote, Green Matte Glaze, Twig Handles, Molded Leaves, 5 ½ In.	149
Lamp, Bulbous, Green Glaze, Mosaic Shade, Panes, Tulips, Electric, c.1900, 17 In.	861
Pitcher, Green Matte Glaze, Mottled, Entwined Handle, 8 ¼ In.	35
Tankard, Green Matte Glaze, Leaf Handle, 11 ⅜ In.	259
Umbrella Stand, Bamboo, Ivy, Green Matte Glaze, Cylindrical, c.1910, 17 ½ x 8 In.	600
Vase, Blue Glaze, Leaf & Bud, 7 In.	450
Vase, Blue Matte Glaze, Impressed Geometric, Design, 4 x 7 ½ In.	438
Vase, Blue Matte Glaze, Mottled, Marked, 6 ⅝ In. *illus*	325
Vase, Bud, Brown Glaze, Asymmetrical Handles, c.1900, 6 x 3 In.	88
Vase, Green Feather Glaze, Raised Flowers, Split Handle, Marked, 8 ½ In.	600
Vase, Green Matte Glaze, Cinched Neck, 11 In.	184
Vase, Green Matte Glaze, Embossed Lower Body, Marked, 8 x 7 In.	450

Vase, Green Matte Glaze, Incised Designs, Cinched Waist, 6 ¾ In..............	115
Vase, Green Matte Glaze, Raised Corn Design, Bulbous, 5 ½ x 6 In...............	350
Vase, Green Matte Glaze, Ruffled Rim, Pinched Neck, 11 ¼ In....................	450
Vase, Green Matte Glaze, Shouldered Cylinder, 5 Panels, Marked, 7 ½ In......	420
Vase, Molded Leaf, Rose Over Green Matte Glaze, Emoretta Symbol, 9 In.	472
Vase, Naturalistic Design, Green Matte Glaze, Handles, 7 ⅝ In..................	443

HANDEL glass was made by Philip Handel working in Meriden, Connecticut, from 1885 and in New York City from 1893 to 1933. The firm made art glass and other types of lamps. Handel shades were made not only of leaded glass in a style reminiscent of Tiffany but also of reverse painted glass. Handel also made vases and other glass objects.

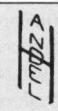

Lamp Base, 3-Light, 2 Acorn Pulls, Metal Bronze Patina, Signed, 23 x 9 In...........	604
Lamp, Chipped Glass Shade, Bronze, 3 Sockets, Marked, 1910s, 24 x 15 In. ....*illus*	3125
Lamp, Desk, Hexagonal Slag Shade, Palm Tree Overlay, Signed, c.1900, 14 ¼ In..........	1062
Lamp, Domed Reverse Painted Chipped Ice Shade, Landscape, Bronzed Base, 15 x 21 In.	2400
Lamp, Domed Shade, Reverse Painted, Flowers, Metal, Label, 1910s, 14 ½ x 7 In...............*illus*	875
Lamp, Green Chipped Ice Shade, Metal Tree Overlay, Bronze Trunk Base, 18 x 24 In.	5625
Lamp, Hawaiian Sunset, 9 Bent Panels, Overlay, Green Border, Elephant Foot Base, 24 x 27 In...	4740
Lamp, Leaded Glass Shade, Overlapping Leaves, Gooseneck Sockets, 30 In. ....*illus*	4740
Lamp, Leaded Panel Overlay, Acorn Pulls, Patina, Signed, 23 x 18 In. ....*illus*	2300
Lamp, Piano, Leaded Glass Shade, Green, Red Tile Flowers, Bronze Base, Signed, 7 x 5 In.	550
Lamp, Piano, Yellow Slag Glass, Patinated Lattice, Curled Arm, Round Base, 8 x 16 In................	1625
Lamp, Reverse Painted Chipped Ice Shade, Daffodil Design, Bronze Base, 14 x 20 In....................	2074
Lamp, Reverse Painted Domed Shade, Bird, Flower Border, Metal Base, c.1919, 17 x 23 In..........	6655
Lamp, Reverse Painted Shade, Green Mottled, Dropped Leaves, Bronze Lotus Base, 23 In............	11875
Lamp, Reverse Painted Shade, Landscape Design, Tapered Bronze Base, 19 x 25 In.	1375
Lamp, Reverse Painted Shade, Wildflowers, Butterflies, Mottled Sky, Spread Base, 14 In.	2125
Lamp, Slag Glass, Tulip Shade, Cast Bronze Base, Marked, c.1910, 24 ¼ In..........................*illus*	1599
Lamp, Student, Mosserine Shade, Celtic Knot Pattern, Patinated Metal Base, 13 ½ In................	2500
Lamp, Woodland Scene, Reverse Painted, Metal Cap, 23 In..	3000
Vase, Red, Green Trees, Flared Rim, Cinched Waist, Teroma, Signed Broggi, c.1910, 4 In............	438

HARDWARE, *see Architectural category.*

HARKER POTTERY COMPANY was incorporated in 1890 in East Liverpool, Ohio. The Harker family had been making pottery in the area since 1840. The company made many types of pottery but by the Civil War was making quantities of yellowware from native clays. It also made Rockingham-type brown-glazed pottery and whiteware. The plant was moved to Chester, West Virginia, in 1931. Dinnerware was made and sold nationally. In 1971 the company was sold to Jeannette Glass Company, and all operations ceased in 1972. For more prices, go to kovels.com.

Amy, Bean Pot	10
Amy, Bowl, Vegetable, Round, 8 In.	21
Amy, Custard Cup...	10
Amy, Soup, Dish, Lugged, 7 ⅛ In...	12
Amy, Sugar	21
Bakerite, Bowl, Vegetable, Round, 8 In..	25
Blue Mist, Bowl, Cereal, 6 ⅝ In.	10
Blue Mist, Creamer, 3 In.	9
Blue Mist, Cup & Saucer..	8
Blue Mist, Plate, Bread & Butter, 5 ⅞ In..	6
Blue Mist, Plate, Dinner, 10 In.	12
Blue Mist, Platter, 13 In...	45
Cock O'Morn, Soup, Dish, 7 ¾ In.	9
Corinthian, Plate, Dinner, 10 ⅜ In.	21
Coronet, Platter, Oval, 13 In..	41
Everglades, Plate, Dinner, 10 ¼ In.	18
Everglades, Platter, 13 In..	45
Everglades, Soup, Dish...	12
Everglades, Sugar & Creamer..	30
Golden Dawn, Bowl, Fruit, 5 ¼ In.	5
Golden Dawn, Bowl, Vegetable, 8 ½ In...	12
Golden Dawn, Cup & Saucer	8
Lemon Tree, Creamer..	21
Lemon Tree, Plate, Dinner, 10 In.	12
Pate Sur Pate, Gravy, Underplate, Chartreuse, 8 ¾ In..........................	12

Halloween, Horn, Pickle, Painted Smiley Face, Wooden Horn Piece, Papier-Mache, 8 In.
$119

James D. Julia Auctioneers

Halloween, Jack-O'-Lantern, Clown, Composition, Multicolor, G.A. Schwarz Toys, 5 In.
$2,655

Bertoia Auctions

Halloween, Jack-O'-Lantern, Plaster, Wire Handle, 4 In.
$330

Morphy Auctions

Halloween, Lantern, Devil's Head, Composition, Glass Eyes, Teeth, Handle, Germany, 3 ½ In.
$590

Bertoia Auctions

Halloween, Lantern, Foxy Grandpa, Composition, Painted, Glazed, Germany, 3 ½ In.
$443

Bertoia Auctions

Halloween, Lantern, Tree Trunk, Face, Composition, Glazed Tree Knots, Handle, 2 ¾ In.
$826

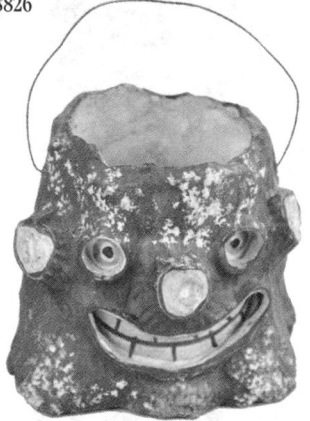

Bertoia Auctions

Halloween, Spin Sparkler, Archie, Tin, Wood Box, Ronson, USA, c.1923
$63

Victorian Casino Antiques

Pate Sur Pate, Green, Plate, Dinner, 10 In.	13
Pate Sur Pate, Platter, Oval, Chartreuse, 11 In.	15
Pate Sur Pate, Platter, Round, Chartreuse, 10 In.	21
Peacock Alley, Bowl, Vegetable, Divided, Oval, 10 ⅛ In.	48
Peacock Alley, Cup & Saucer	15
Peacock Alley, Plate, Bread & Butter, 5 ⅞ In.	6
Peacock Alley, Plate, Dinner, 10 In.	14
Quaker Maid, Creamer, 3 In.	15
Seafare, Bowl, Cereal, 6 ⅝ In.	10
Seafare, Plate, Bread & Butter, 5 ¾ In.	8
Seafare, Plate, Dinner, 10 In.	18
Shell Pink, Casserole, Lid, Round, 12 ½ In.	150
Shell Pink, Cup & Saucer	8
Shell Pink, Plate, Bread & Butter, 5 ⅞ In.	4
Shell Pink, Plate, Dinner, 10 In.	14
Shell Pink, Platter, Round, 13 In.	45
White Cap, Bowl, Fruit, 5 ¼ In.	8
White Cap, Bowl, Vegetable, 6 ⅞ In.	18
White Cap, Bowl, Vegetable, Divided, Oval, 10 ¼ In.	45
White Cap, Cup & Saucer	12
White Cap, Plate, Bread & Butter, 5 ⅞ In.	4
White Clover, Plate, Dinner, Coral Sand, 10 In.	21
White Daisy, Plate, Dinner, 10 In.	16

HARLEQUIN dinnerware was produced by the Homer Laughlin Company from 1938 to 1964, and sold without trademark by the F. W. Woolworth Co. It has a concentric ring design like Fiesta, but the rings are separated from the rim by a plain margin. Cup handles are triangular in shape. Seven different novelty animal figurines were introduced in 1939. For more prices, go to kovels.com.

Chartreuse, Cup & Saucer	17
Forest Green, Cup & Saucer	14
Gray, Bowl, 6 ⅜ In.	22
Mauve Blue, Casserole, Lid, 9 In.	30
Mauve Blue, Creamer	21
Mauve Blue, Gravy Boat	19
Medium Green, Nut Dish	48
Medium Green, Plate, Luncheon, 9 In.	46
Red, Nut Dish, Basket Weave, 3 In.	17
Rose, Plate, Bread & Butter, 6 ¼ In.	6
Rose, Teapot, Lid, 3 Cup, 4 ⅞ In.	138
Spruce Green, Plate, Luncheon, 7 In.	15
Spruce Green, Saucer, 6 In.	10
Turquoise, Creamer, 2 ⅝ In.	16
Turquoise, Pitcher, Tankard, 24 Oz., 4 ⅞ In.	118
Yellow, Creamer	30
Yellow, Gravy Boat	30
Yellow, Plate, Dinner, 9 In.	25
Yellow, Serving Bowl, 9 In.	65
Yellow, Sugar, Lid, 4 x 5 In.	50

HATPIN collectors search for pins popular from 1860 to 1920. The long pin, often over four inches, was used to hold the hat in place on the hair. The tops of the pins were made of all materials, from solid gold and real gemstones to ceramics and glass. Be careful to buy original hatpins and not recent pieces made by altering old buttons.

Bakelite, Bronze, Yellow, 9 In.	85
Beads, Black, Brass Headpin, c.1925, 5 In., Pair	62
Blown Glass, Teardrop Shape, Red, Metallic Gold Leaf, 6 In.	68
Brass, Sphere Shape, Twisted Wire Circles, 1800s, 9 In.	88
Copper, Reticulated Filigree, Flowers, 9 ¾ In.	79
Coral, Teardrop Shape, Diamond, Platinum Over Gold Stem, Edwardian, Tiffany & Co.	861
Ebony, 5 Holes Around Center Pole, Base, 6 In.	55
Faceted Amethyst Glass, Enamel, Scrolled, Flowered Center, c.1860, 7 ½ In.	375
Faux Pearls, Cluster, 1920s, 4 ⅞ In.	38
Glass, Bead, Faceted, c.1900, 9 In.	28
Glass, Rooster, Cobalt Blue, 9 In.	125

Glass, Tortoiseshell Like, Rhinestones, 6 In.	57
Gunmetal, Mourning, Egg Shape, 19th Century, 11 In.	125
Porcelain, Button Top, George Washington Portrait, 10 In., Pair	25
Silver, Art Nouveau, Victorian, c.1890, 8 In.	98
Silver, Golf Club Shape, Birmingham, 1908, 10 In.	195

HATPIN HOLDERS were needed when hatpins were fashionable from 1860 to 1920. The large, heavy hat required special long-shanked pins to hold it in place. The hatpin holder resembles a large saltshaker, but it often has no opening at the bottom as a shaker does. Hatpin holders were made of all types of ceramics and metal. Look for other pieces under the names of specific manufacturers.

Bronze, Art Nouveau, Blue Glass Stones, Prongs, 4 x 4 In.	295
Bronze, Figural, Asian Girl, Holding Umbrella, Marble Base, 6 ¾ In.	225
Cut Glass, Thistle Shape, Fleur-De-Lis Bronze Feet, 5 In.	100
Elfinware, 3 Sections, Flowers, Germany, c.1900, 4 In.	125
Limoges, Tray, Roses, Leaves, Scalloped, End Holes, c.1895, 10 x 3 In.	125
Porcelain, Child, Pierrot Costume, Dog, Germany, c.1920, 7 In.	480
Porcelain, Finch, On Pinecone, Stump, Germany, 4 ¼ In.	40
Porcelain, Man & Woman Caryatids, Art Nouveau, Incised Yuszkovits, 5 ¼ x 3 ¼ In.	3000
Porcelain, Vase Shape, Bouquet, Violets, Bavaria, c.1900, 5 ¼ In.	66
Porcelain, Vase Shape, Silver Overlay, Flowers, Pink, c.1900, 4 In.	155
Porcelain, Vase Shape, Twisted, Roses, Leaves, Cobalt Blue Rim, Nippon, c.1900, 8 In.	55
Porcelain, Violets, Shaded Yellow Ground, Gold Trim, Corseted, 7 ¼ In.	81

HAVILAND china has been made in Limoges, France, since 1842. The factory was started by the Haviland Brothers of New York City. Pieces are marked *H & Co., Haviland & Co.,* or *Theodore Haviland.* It is possible to match existing sets of dishes through dealers who specialize in Haviland china. Other factories worked in the town of Limoges making a similar chinaware. These porcelains are listed in this book under Limoges.   **HAVILAND & CO.**

Bowl, Footed, Pink Flowers, Leaves, Scallop Rim, 5 In. Diam.	50
Bowl, Lettuce, Green Tree, Flower Bands, White Ground, Gilt Rim, 4 x 10 In.	106
Bowl, Roses, Leaves, Ruffled Rim, Gold Trim, c.1900, 9 x 11 In.	200
Bowl, Vegetable, Belfort Pattern, Gilt, Round, Handles, Lid, c.1900, 4 x 10 ½ In.	250
Butter, Cover, Handle, Yellow Flowers, Branches, Marked Theodore Haviland, c.1900, 8 x 7 In.	44
Cake Plate, Flowers, Blue, Swirled Lip, c.1900, 9 ¾ In.	35
Charger, Roses, Leaves, Stem, Scallop Rim, Ella Hezeta, 13 In.	895
Chocolate Pot, Flowers, Leaves, Gilt Swirls, Ruffle Rim & Foot, Lid, c.1890, 9 x 6 In.	189
Chocolate Pot, Lid, Tulips, Stems, Gilt, Loop Handle, c.1905, 8 x 7 ½ In.	850
Creamer, Violets, Gold Trim, Ruffled Rim, Scroll Handle, c.1895, 5 ½ x 2 ½ In.	75
Cup & Saucer, White & Yellow Flowers, Leaves, Stems, Scalloped, 2 ½ x 2 ½ In.	65
Jardiniere, Applied Flowers, Stems, Footed, Multicolor, c.1880, 16 x 8 x 9 In.	6800
Mustache Cup, Pink Roses, Gilt Trim, Marked, 2 x 4 ½ In.	35
Oyster Plate, Cobalt Blue, Gilt Trim, 5 Wells, Wave Design, c.1895, 8 ½ In.	425
Pitcher, Flowers, Flared Spout, High Strap Handle, Gilt, c.1845, 8 ½ In.	80
Pitcher, Flowers, High Arch Handle, Gilt Rims, c.1850, 4 ⅝ In.	35
Pitcher, Pink Flowers, Gilt, Lobed, Scallop Rim & Foot, Loop Handle, c.1900, 6 x 5 In.	119
Plate, Bagatelle, Pink Rose, White Ground, Gilt Rim, Limoges, 10 In., 12 Piece	183
Plate, Blackberries, Green, Gold Leaves, Gilt Trim, 9 In.	226
Plate, Soup, Lobed Flow Blue Rim, Gold Flowers, Bands, c.1890, 9 In., 12 Piece	150
Platter, Pink Flower, White Ground, Round, Shaped Rim, 12 ½ In.	35
Powder Box, Lid, Flowers, Scalloped Base, c.1900, 4 x 3 ½ In.	100

HAWKES cut glass was made by T. G. Hawkes & Company of Corning, New York, founded in 1880. The firm cut glass blanks made at other glassworks until 1962. Many pieces are marked with the trademark, a trefoil ring enclosing a fleur-de-lis and two hawks. Cut glass by other manufacturers is listed under either the factory name or in the general Cut Glass category.

Basket, Geometric Cut Center, Hobstar Border, Triple Notched Handle, 6 ½ x 7 ½ In.	71
Berry Bowl, Starlight, Kohinoor Design, Engraved Leaf Vine, Border, 5 In.	50
Bowl, 5-Point Star, Engraved Flowers, Thumbprint Border, American Brilliant, 3 ½ x 8 In.	10
Bowl, Devonshire, American Brilliant, 2 ¾ x 9 ¾ In.	50
Bowl, Holland, 6-Sided, Signed, 3 ½ x 9 ½ In.	177
Bowl, Iridescent, Engraved Flower, Bead Swags, Acid Stamp, 8 x 2 ½ In.	58
Butter Pat, Hobstar & Fan, Club Shape, Signed, 3 ¼ In., 6 Piece	47
Candlestick, Sheridan, Signed, 8 ¾ In.	175
Candlestick, Swirled Geometric, Rayed Base, Signed, 9 In.	150

Halloween, Tin, Candy, The Lucky Box, Witch, Caldron, 5 ½ In.
$540

Morphy Auctions

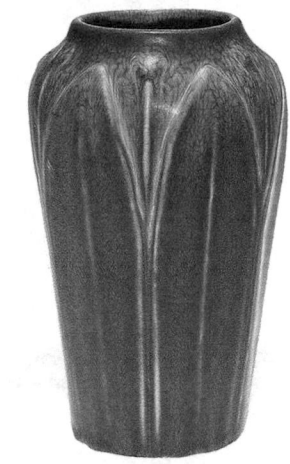

Hampshire, Vase, Blue Matte Glaze, Mottled, Marked, 6 ⅝ In.
$325

Humler & Nolan

Handel, Lamp, Chipped Glass Shade, Bronze, 3 Sockets, Marked, 1910s, 24 x 15 In.
$3,125

Rago Arts & Auction Center

Handel, Lamp, Domed Shade, Reverse Painted, Flowers, Metal, Label, 1910s, 14 ½ x 7 In.
$875

Rago Arts & Auction Center

Handel, Lamp, Leaded Glass Shade, Overlapping Leaves, Gooseneck Sockets, 30 In.
$4,740

James D. Julia Auctioneers

Handel, Lamp, Leaded Panel Overlay, Acorn Pulls, Patina, Signed, 23 x 18 In.
$2,300

Cottone Auctions

Ice Bucket, Lorraine, Sterling Rim & Handle, Signed, 4 x 6 In.	800
Pitcher, Water, Jubilee, Signed, 8 ½ In.	106
Punch Bowl, Chrysanthemum, Cut Glass, Scalloped, Notched Rim, c.1900, 14 ¼ In.	1320
Punch Bowl, Hobstar Center, 20 Chained Hobstars, Split Window, Signed, 6 x 11 ¾ In.	2006
Rose Bowl, Brazilian, 4 In.	225
Vase, London Pattern, Hobstar Foot, Trumpet Shape, Signed, 14 In.	177
Vase, Navarre, Trumpet Shape, Signed, 16 In.	118

HEAD VASES, generally showing a woman from the shoulders up, were used by florists primarily in the 1950s and 1960s. Made in a variety of sizes and often decorated with imitation jewelry and other lifelike accessories, the vases were manufactured in Japan and the U.S.A. Less elaborate examples were made as early as the 1930s. Religious themes, babies, and animals are also common subjects. Other head vases are listed under manufacturers' names and can be located through the index in the back of this book.

Baby, Boy, Blue Bonnet, Side-Glancing Eyes, Foil Sticker, Artmark, 1950s, 5 In.	45
Cameo Girl, Eve, Flapper, Curly Blond Hair, Earrings, Necklace, 6 ¼ In.	139
Cat, White, Blue Eyes, Paper Label, 5 ½ In.	45
Clown, Green Hat, Finger Over Lips, Napcoware, Japan, 6 In.	15
Clown, Red Hair, Polka Dot Shirt, 1950s, 6 In.	35
Fortune Teller, Blue Scarf, Snow Globe, Red Lips, Box, 6 In.	55
Girl, Blond Hair, Scarf, Long Lashes, Velco, 5 ½ In.	155
Girl, Blond Hair, Side Curl, Winking, Daisy Hat, 1950s, 5 In.	48
Girl, Bonnet, Pink Bow, 2 Hearts, Velco, 5 In.	185
Glamour Girl, Blond, Eyes Closed, Blue Dress, Red Heart Pendant, 5 ½ In.	65
Graduate, Girl, Blond, Cap & Gown, Diploma, Napco, 1959, 6 In.	139
Humpty Dumpty, Red, Black, Ivory, Hands, Feet, 1900s, 3 ¾ In.	34
Santa Claus, Japan, 6 In.	40
Woman, Blond Hair, Orange Dress, White Collar, 7 ½ In.	68
Woman, Blond Hair, Pearl Earring, Necklace, Green Bow, 8 In.	85
Woman, Blond Hair, White Hat, Dress, Rhinestone Bracelet, Gold Accents, 5 ½ In.	34
Woman, Blond Hair, White Hat, Green, Pink Rose, Beaded Earrings, 5 In.	136
Woman, Brown Hair, Upswept, Flower Dress, Pearl Necklace, 7 In.	79
Woman, Long Blond Hair, Yellow Dress, White Collar, 8 ½ In.	102

HEDI SCHOOP Art Creations, North Hollywood, California, started about 1945 and was working until 1954. Schoop made ceramic figurines, lamps, planters, and tablewares.

Box, Lid, Comedy Mask, Speckled Gold, 7 x 5 x 6 In.	225
Candlestick, Abstract, Gray, Black, 11 ⅝ In.	75
Figurine, Chinese Couple, Holding Fan & Basket, 11 In.	225
Figurine, Dutch Couple, 12 In.	75
Figurine, Oriental Woman With Flowers, 12 ½ In.	85
Figurine, Woman, Carrying 2 Vases, Hat, Flowers On Dress, 12 ¼ In.	124

HEINTZ ART METAL SHOP used the letters *HAMS* in a diamond as a mark. In 1902, Otto Heintz designed and manufactured copper items with colored enamel decorations under the name Art Crafts Shop. He took over the Arts & Crafts Company in Buffalo, New York, in 1903. By 1906 it had become the Heintz Art Metal Shop. It remained in business until 1930. The company made ashtrays, bookends, boxes, bowls, desk sets, vases, trophies, and smoking sets. The best-known pieces are made of copper, brass, and bronze with silver overlay. Similar pieces were made by Smith Metal Arts and were marked *Silver Crest.* Some pieces by both companies are unmarked.

Candlestick, Sterling On Bronze, Flower Cup, Garland Design, Impressed Mark, 6 x 15 In.	450
Humidor, Copper, Silver Overlay, Wood Liner, 9 x 4 In.	275
Inkwell, Sterling On Bronze, Flowers, Stones, Squat, Rolled Rim, 1900s, 3 x 4 In.	118
Lamp, Basket Weave Mica Shape, Silver Leaf Overlay, Sterling On Copper, 16 x 20 In.	3965
Lamp, Domed Shade, Sterling On Bronze, Geometric Border, Acorn Pull Chain, 8 x 10 In.	100
Lamp, Drum Shade, Sterling On Bronze, 6 ¾ x 9 ¾ In.	875
Lamp, Electric, Leaf Design Mica Shade, Triangular, Sterling On Copper, 8 ½ x 10 In.	1100
Lamp, Electric, Sterling On Bronze, Green Finish, 2 Curved Arms, Bell Shape Shade, 12 In.	443
Lamp, Geometric Designs, Sterling On Bronze, Pull Chain, 8 x 10 In.	1037
Lamp, Lilies, Sterling On Bronze, Red Silk Shade, c.1920, 12 x 10 ½ In.	875
Lamp, Sterling On Bronze, Gothic Overlay, Domed Shade, Electric, 1910s, 14 ¼ x 9 In.	1000
Lamp, Witch Hat, Conical Mica Shade, Sterling On Bronze, 9 ½ x 14 ½ In.	2600
Vase, Applied Flowers, Sterling On Bronze, 1912, 7 ½ x 4 In.	59
Vase, Daffodil, Sterling On Bronze, Cylindrical, 3 ½ x 8 In.	375 to 413

Vase, Flowers, Green, Sterling On Bronze, 4 ½ x 12 ½ In.	406
Vase, Flowers, Sterling On Bronze, Cylindrical, Impressed Mark, 4 ¾ x 11 In.	250
Vase, Flowers, Sterling On Bronze, Tapered, c.1905, 8 ¾ In.	156
Vase, Iris, Sterling On Bronze, Buffalo, c.1915, 12 x 5 In.	125
Vase, Pinecones, Needles, Silver On Bronze, Flared, Impressed, 5 x 10 ½ In.	406
Vase, Stick, Mistletoe, Sterling On Bronze, Trumpet Foot, Green Patina, Signed, 11 ¾ In.	236
Vase, Stick, Sterling On Bronze, Leaf & Branch Design, No. 3684, Marked, 11 ½ In.	153

HEISEY glass was made from 1896 to 1957 in Newark, Ohio, by A. H. Heisey and Co., Inc. The Imperial Glass Company of Bellaire, Ohio, bought some of the molds and the rights to the trademark. Some Heisey patterns have been made by Imperial since 1960. After 1968, they stopped using the *H* trademark. Heisey used romantic names for colors, such as Sahara. Do not confuse color and pattern names. The Custard Glass and Ruby Glass categories may also include some Heisey pieces.

Animal, Asiatic Pheasant	155
Animal, Chick	135
Animal, Colt, Rearing	325
Animal, Colt, Standing	145
Animal, Dog, Airedale	310
Animal, Dog, Scottie	90
Animal, Donkey	120
Animal, Duckling, Floating	375
Animal, Duckling, Standing	350
Animal, Hen	1200
Animal, Pouter Pigeon	475
Animal, Ringneck Pheasant	95
Animal, Rooster, Fighting	105 to 195
Animal, Swan	425
Animal, Tropical Fish	2500
Aristocrat, Candlestick, 11 In., Pair	160
Athena, Sugar & Creamer	17
Banded Picket, Basket, 7 In.	55
Beaded Swag, Cruet, 6 Oz.	25
Charter Oak, Pitcher, Flamingo	90
Coarse Rib, Celery Dish, 12 In.	15
Continental, Butter, Cover, Footed	150
Continental, Toothpick Holder	30
Criss Cross, Nappy, Crimped, Gilt, 5 In.	15
Crystolite, Candle Blocks, Swirl, Pair	20
Crystolite, Candlestick, 3-Light, Pair	30
Crystolite, Cup & Saucer	20
Crystolite, Relish, 3 Sections, Oval, 12 In.	15
Crystolite, Relish, Round, 5 Sections, 10 In.	40
Crystolite, Torte Plate, 11 In.	35
Empress, Ashtray, Alexandrite	100
Empress, Ashtray, Moongleam	65
Empress, Bowl, Etched Camellia, 3 Dolphin Feet, 11 In.	110
Empress, Bowl, Etched Minuet, 3 Dolphin Feet, 11 In.	110
Fancy Loop, Toothpick Holder, Emerald	65
Fandango, Rose Bowl, 4 In.	55
Fandango, Toothpick Holder	25
Greek Key, Fruit Jar, Crushed, 2 Qt.	315
Greek Key, Plate, Buffet, 21 In.	900
Grid & Square, Tankard, ½ Gal.	175
Groove & Slash, Plate, 6 In.	12
Hairpin, Basket, 9 In.	100
Lariat, Bowl, Flowers, Crimped, 12 In.	35
Lariat, Plate, Buffet, 21 In.	25
Lariat, Plate, Dinner, 10 ½ In.	25
Lariat, Relish, 3 Sections, Round, 10 In.	30
Lariat, Sugar & Creamer	15 to 35
Lariat, Torte Plate, 14 In.	45
Lariat, Vase, Etched Orchid, 7 In.	35
Locket On Chain, Butter, Cover	35
Locket On Chain, Compote, 8 In.	30
Minuet, Bowl, Empress 3 Dolphin Feet, 11 In.	110

Handel, Lamp, Slag Glass, Tulip Shade, Cast Bronze Base, Marked, c.1910, 24 ¼ In. $1,599

Cowan's Auctions

Heubach, Figurine, Curtsey & Bow, Boy, Girl, Sculpted, Bisque, c.1910, 15 In., Pair $1,456

Theriault's

This is an edited listing of current prices. Visit **Kovels.com** to check thousands of prices from previous years and sign up for free information on trends, tips, reproductions, marks, and more.

Heubach, Figurine, Girl, Comforting Baby Bird, Sculpted Hair, Bisque, c.1900, 9 ½ In.
$280

Theriault's

Hopalong Cassidy, Button, Hopalong Cassidy's Saving Rodeo Foreman, Lithograph, Metal, 2 ¼ In.
$115

Hake's Americana & Collectibles

Hopalong Cassidy, Night-Light, Pistol & Holster, Milk Glass, 10 In.
$342

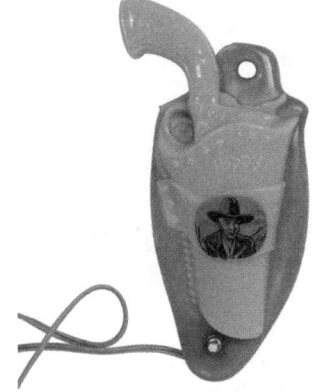

Showtime Auction Services

Narrow Flute, Banana Split, Footed, 9 In.	25
New Era, Plate, 9 In.	20
Oakleaf, Coaster, Flamingo	15
Old Sandwich, Jug, Ice Lip, ½ Gal.	55
Old Sandwich, Mug, 12 Oz.	30
Old Sandwich, Mug, 18 Oz.	110
Old Sandwich, Mug, Cobalt Blue, 18 Oz.	250
Old Williamsburg, Epergnette, 5 ½ In.	70
Panel & Sunburst, Plate, Beaded, 8 In.	25
Peerless, Punch Bowl, Stand, Clear, Marked, c.1901, 12 ½ x 15 In.	138
Peerless, Sherbet, Footed, 6 Oz.	15
Peerless, Toothpick Holder	10
Pineapple & Fan, Bowl, Oval, 12 In.	40
Pineapple & Fan, Vase, 6 In.	30
Pineapple & Fan, Vase, 10 In.	45
Pinwheel & Fan, Basket, 7 In.	120
Pinwheel & Fan, Nappy, 8 In.	20
Plantation, Bowl, Flowers, Crimped, 12 In.	70
Plantation, Candy, Footed, Lid, 8 In.	225
Plantation, Cheese, Footed, Lid, 6 In.	195
Plantation, Salt & Pepper	20
Plantation, Vase, 6 In.	150
Prince Of Wales Plumes, Water Set, Pitcher, Tumblers, Gilt, c.1920, 9 In., 4 In., 5 Piece	115
Priscilla, Jug, Qt.	45
Priscilla, Toothpick Holder	12
Punty & Diamond Point, Nappy, 8 In.	25
Punty & Diamond Point, Sugar & Creamer	130
Punty & Diamond Point, Sugar Sifter	100
Puritan, Butter, Cover	45
Puritan, Butter, Cover, Footed	75 to 95
Puritan, Celery Dish, Oval, 10 In.	17
Puritan, Compote, 4 ½ In.	10
Puritan, Jug, Pt.	100
Queen Anne, Toothpick Holder, Clear, Marked.c.1906, 2 ¼ In.	288
Ridgeleigh, Cup & Saucer	25
Ridgeleigh, Jelly, 3-Corner	25
Ridgeleigh, Nappy, 4 ½ In.	14
Rococo, Nappy, 4 In.	15
Star & Zipper, Nappy, Emerald, 8 In.	450
Strawholder, Clear, Log Form, 6 Vertical Panels, Shaped Cutout Center, 10 In.	333
Sunburst, Compote, 9 In.	75
Sunburst, Eggcup	95
Sunburst, Pitcher, Qt.	80
Sunburst, Sugar & Creamer, Beaded Panel	95
Sunburst, Toothpick Holder	80
Swan, Candlestick, Moongleam, Green, 6 ½ x 4 ¾ In.	250
Tudor, Nappy, 4 ½ In.	15
Tudor, Tankard, Footed, 3 Pt.	65
Twist, Celery Dish, 12 In.	10
Victorian, Celery Dish, 12 In.	5
Victorian, Tumbler, Footed, 12 Oz.	20
Waldorf Astoria, Toothpick Holder	60
Waverly, Compote, Light Amber, Oval, 7 In.	325
Waverly, Dish, Mayonnaise, Etched Orchid	28
Whirlpool, Bowl, Flared, 12 In.	20
Whirlpool, Nappy, 9 In.	55
Whirlpool, Sugar & Creamer	65
Wide Flat Panel, Horseradish Jar, 11 Oz.	65
Winged Scroll, Toothpick Holder, Gold Custard	95
Winged Scroll, Toothpick Holder, Green, Gold	110
Yeoman, Compote, Moongleam Stem, Footed, 6 In.	15
Yeoman, Plate, Amber, 7 ½ In.	30
Zodiac, Salt & Pepper	25

HEREND, *see Fischer category.*

HEUBACH is the collector's name for Gebruder Heubach, a firm working in Lichten, Germany, from 1840 to 1925. It is best known for bisque dolls and doll heads, the principal products. The company also manufactured bisque figurines, including piano babies, beginning in the 1880s, and glazed figurines in the 1900s. Piano Babies are listed in their own category. Dolls are included in the Doll category under Gebruder Heubach and Heubach. Another factory, Ernst Heubach, working in Koppelsdorf, Germany, also made porcelain and dolls. These will also be found in the Doll category under Heubach Koppelsdorf.

Figurine, Baby In High Chair, Bonnet, Gown, Pulling Sock, c.1900, 5 In.	135
Figurine, Bisque, Baby In Papa's Worn-Out Shoe, Sculpted Hair, Smock, c.1912, 12 x 11 In.	1008
Figurine, Bisque, Boy, Girl, As Musicians, Traditional Costume, Germany, c.1900, 13 In., Pair	560
Figurine, Boy, Fighting Roosters, 12 ½ In.	359
Figurine, Boy, Girl, Dutch, Sitting, Holding Knees, 3 In., Pair	145
Figurine, Boy, Sitting Backward On Chair, Glasses, Holding Cigar, c.1900, 6 ¼ In.	295
Figurine, Curtsey & Bow, Boy, Girl, Sculpted, Bisque, c.1910, 15 In., Pair *illus*	1456
Figurine, Dancing Girl, Pleated Skirt, Turquoise, c.1900, 6 ¼ In.	250
Figurine, Dancing Girl, Turquoise, Dancing Skirt, Blond, c.1900, 6 In.	250
Figurine, Dog, Affenpincher, Sitting, Begging, White, c.1900, 8 In.	195
Figurine, Dog, Dachshund, Gray, 6 ½ x 3 ⅛ In.	225
Figurine, Fox, Crawling, White, 11 ½ In.	151
Figurine, Girl, Comforting Baby Bird, Sculpted Hair, Bisque, c.1900, 9 ½ In. *illus*	280
Figurine, Girl, Holding Fish & Creel, Flowered Dress, Hat, c.1880, 9 ½ In.	85
Figurine, Listening For Ocean Waves, Children Playing At Seaside, c.1910, 12 In., Pair	392
Figurine, Surprise, It's Me, Toddler, Bunny Costume, Egg, Sculpted Face, c.1910, 9 In.	1344
Figurine, Tossing Snowballs, Boy, Standing, Holding Snowballs, c.1910, 13 In.	336
Match Holder, Dutch Boy, Sitting, Basket On Back, 4 In.	149

HISTORIC BLUE, *see factory names, such as Adams, Ridgway, and Staffordshire.*

HOBNAIL glass is a style of glass with bumps all over. Dozens of hobnail patterns and variants have been made. Clear, colored, and opalescent hobnail have been made and are being reproduced. Other pieces of hobnail may also be listed in the Duncan & Miller and Fenton categories.

Basket, Crimped, Fluted, Applied Handle, 12 x 10 x 10 In.	36
Basket, Green, White, Swirl, Ruffled, Applied Handle, 1950s, 6 x 5 ¾ In.	55
Compote, Flared Rim, Columbia Glass Co., c.1875, 9 ¼ x 7 In.	175
Creamer, Thumbprint Handle, Footed, Notched Rim, Blue, 4 ¼ In.	65
Dresser Jar, Metal Lid, Bakelite Knob Handle, 5 x 2 In.	28
Lamp, Hand, Applied Handle, 3 ¼ In. Diam.	95
Nappy, Opalescent, Moonstone, Heart Shape, Anchor Hocking, c.1940, 6 x 6 ¼ In.	25
Pitcher, Printed, c.1890, 7 ¼ In.	55
Plate, Luncheon, Pink, 8 ½ In.	9
Relish, 2 Sections, Iridescent Moonstone, Crimped Edge, c.1943, 7 In.	15
Salt & Pepper, Plum Opalescent, 3 In.	95
Sherbet, Pink	6
Toothpick Holder, Opalescent, Scalloped Rim, 3-Footed, c.1889, 2 ¾ In.	35
Tumbler, Blue, 3 ½ x 3 In.	40

HOLT-HOWARD was an importer that started working in New York City in 1949 and moved to Stamford, Connecticut, in 1955. The company sold many types of table accessories, such as condiment jars, decanters, spoon holders, and saltshakers. Its figural pieces have a cartoon-like quality. The company was bought out by General Housewares Corporation in 1969. Holt-Howard pieces are often marked with the name and the year or *HH* and the year stamped in black. The *HH* mark was used until 1974. The company also used a black and silver paper label. Holt-Howard production ceased in 1990. Similar pieces are being made today by Grant Holt, one of the founders, and are marked *GHA*.

Candle Climber, Snowman, Winking, Scarf, Hat, 3 ½ In.	12 to 15
Cookie Jar, Santa Claus, Red, White, 3 Parts, 1964, 8 ½ In.	48
Creamer, Rooster, Indented Sides, 1961, 2 ¾ In.	15
Cruet, French Dressing, Frenchman, Winking, Mustache, 1959, 6 In.	105
Dish, Cottage Cheese, 2 Kittens Kissing, Round, Lid, 1959	68
Incense Burner, Cozy Cat, Green Eyes, Pink Bow, 4 ½ In.	50
Mug, 3 Dollar Bill, Nixon's Face, 1972, 3 ½ In.	60
Mug, Rooster, Red, Marked, 1964, 10 Oz., 3 ½ In., Pair	22
Pencil Holder, Daisy Dorable, Smelling Daisy, Rectangular, c.1959, 4 x 4 In.	125

Horn, Pokal, Drinking Cup, Lid, Brass Mounts, Griffins, 18 x 19 ½ In.
$690

The Stein Auction Co.

Howdy Doody, Cookie Jar, Howdy Doody's Head, Purinton Pottery
$92

Victorian Casino Antiques

Hull, Little Red Riding Hood, Cookie Jar, Poppy, Gold Trim, Regal China Co.
$62

Victorian Casino Antiques

Hummel, Figurine, No. 3/II, Bookworm, Crown Mark, 8 In.
$720

The Stein Auction Co.

Hummel, Figurine, No. 123, Max & Moritz, Missing Bee, 5 ¼ In.
$185

Phoebus Auction Gallery

Icon, Reliquary, Dormition Of The Virgin, Tempera On Panel, Russia, 1700s, 11 x 16 In.
$11,800

Brunk Auctions

Plate, Butter, Holly Leaves, Berries, Ruffled Rim, Foil Label, 1959, 2 ½ In., 4 Piece	25
Stringholder, Cat, Kitten Head, Plaid Bow, 1950s	85
Trivet, Cast Iron, Ceramic Tile, Wacky Bird, Multicolor, c.1968, 4 x 4 In.	24

HOPALONG CASSIDY was a character in a series of twenty-eight books written by Clarence E. Milford, first published in 1907. Movies and television shows were made based on the character. The best-known actor playing Hopalong Cassidy was William Lawrence Boyd. His first movie appearance was in 1919, but the first Hopalong Cassidy film was not made until 1934. Sixty-six films were made. In 1948, William Boyd purchased the television rights to the movies, then later made fifty-two new programs. In the 1950s, Hopalong Cassidy and his horse, named Topper, were seen in comics, records, toys, and other products. Boyd died in 1972.

Barrette, Portrait, c.1950, 2 In.		35
Button, Hopalong Cassidy's Saving Rodeo Foreman, Lithograph, Metal, 2 ¼ In.	*illus*	115
Clock, Alarm, Hopalong & Topper, Box, 1950s, 5 ¼ x 5 ¾ In.		380
Clock, Hopalong On Horse, Cactus, Metal, Plastic, Electric, Sunbeam, 1950s, 9 In.		295
Lamp, Milk Glass Base, Hoppy Decal, Aladdin, 1950s, 4 ¼ x 10 In.		127
Lamp, White Glass, Tapered Paper Shade, Hopalong On Horse, Aladdin, 17 In.		443
Lunch Box, Thermos, Metal, Decal, 1950		351
Mug, Hoppy, Holding Guns, Signature, Milk Glass, Blue, Hazel Atlas, 1950s		52
Night-Light, Pistol & Holster, Milk Glass, 10 In.	*illus*	342
Plate, Ceramic, Hopalong On Horse, Marked, 1950s, 9 In.		35
Pogo Stick, Horse Head Top, Cassidy Image, Hi Pardner, Rubber, Metal, c.1950, 49 In.		120
Radio, Arvin, Model 441T, 5 ¼ x 8 In.		259
Ring, Compass, Removable Hat, Brass Base, HC, Post Cereal Premium, 1952		190
Rug, Split Rail Fence Border, Cowboy Boots, Pistol, 9 x 12 In.		278
Sign, Hoppy's Favorite, Bond Bread, Cardboard, c.1950, 21 x 27 In.		225
Toy, Range Rider, Lasso, Rocker, Tin, Windup, Box, 1950s, 11 x 10 In.		411
Toy, Range Rifle, Decal, Canvas Strap, Tin, 1950s, 30 ½ In.		336
Toy, Shooting Gallery, Mechanical, Tin Lithograph, Box, Automatic Toy Co., 1950s		120
Tumbler, Milk Glass, Hopalong Twirling Lasso, Hazel Atlas, 1950s, 4 In.		36
Wristwatch, Hopalong, Tooled Leather Band, 4-In. Saddle-Shape Box		150
Wristwatch, Hoppy Smiling, Stainless Steel, Display, Saddle Shape, 1950s		325
Wristwatch, Leather Straps, Saddle Display Box, Cardboard Box, 1950s		287

HORN was used to make many types of boxes, furniture inlays, jewelry, and whimsies.

Cup, Libation, Carved, Tree, Flowers, Chinese, 4 x 6 In.		1800
Knife, Dinner, Antler Handle, Fitted Leather Case, Early 20th Century, 12 Piece		207
Mull, Polished, Silver Rim Band, Monogram Inset, Engraved, Scotland, 3 x 2 ½ In.		173
Ornament, Art Nouveau, Carved, Woman's Head, Flower Crown, Ram's Heads, 2 x 3 In.		207
Pitcher Set, Pitcher, 2 Cups, Metal, 11 ½ In.		834
Pokal, Drinking Cup, Lid, Brass Mounts, Griffins, 18 x 19 ½ In.	*illus*	690

HOWDY DOODY and Buffalo Bob were the main characters in a children's series televised from 1947 to 1960. Howdy was a redheaded puppet. The series became popular with college students in the late 1970s when Buffalo Bob began to lecture on campuses.

Bicycle, Horn, Rubber Bulb, Plastic Nozzle, Ton-Air, 1950s, 4 ⅜ In.		201
Container, Kid-O-Modeling Compound, Cardboard Tube, 1950s, 10 In.		115
Cookie Jar, Howdy Doody's Head, Purinton Pottery	*illus*	92
Doll, Composition, Flanged Neck, Sculpted Red Hair, Sleep Eyes, Effanbee, c.1948, 19 In.		1904
Doll, Princess Summerfall Winterspring, Yarn Hair, Box, 1950s, 17 In.		310
Doll, Talking, Bandanna, Ribbon, Composition Head, Fabric Body, Ideal, 1950s, 20 ½ In.		324
Figure, Jointed, Wood, Composition Face, Art Quality, c.1950, 12 ½ In.		156
Musical Doodle Ball, Hard Plastic, Low Relief Image, Jolly Blinker, Box, 1950s, 4 ¾ In.		115
Plastic Figure Set, Movable Mouths, Box, Cellophane Window, 1950s, 5 x 12 In., 5 Piece		173
Toy, Figure, Howdy Doody, Wood, Jointed Limbs, Decal On Chest, Ideal, 13 In.		150
Toy, Howdy Doody & Bob Smith, Piano, Tin Lithograph, Unique Art, 5 In.		826 to 1652
Toy, Marionette, Clarabell, Original Clothing, 1950s, 15 In.		48
Toy, Marionette, Flub-A-Dub, Original Clothing, 1950s, 13 ½ In.		180
Toy, Marionette, Howdy Doody, Movable Mouth, Original Clothing, 1950s, 17 In.		48
Toy, Marionette, Princess Summerfall Winterspring, Box, 1950s, 14 In.		48
Toy, Phono Doodle, Wood, Cardboard, Laughing Circus Record, Shura-Tone, 12 In.		180
Toy, Puppet Show, 5 Plastic Figures, Movable Mouths, Original Card, 11 x 7 In.		48
Toy, Put-In-Head, 4 Heads, Costumes, Box, 1950s, 9 x 14 In.		144

Toy, Swing, Composition Figure, Tin Litho Base, Push Plunger, Arnold, Germany, 15 In.	36
Toy, Trace'N'Erase Kit, School Bag, Cardboard Handle, 1950s, 9 ½ x 11 ½ In.	115
Trading Cards, Uncut, Cardboard, Premium, Burry's Cookies, 1951, 14 x 21 In.	348

HULL pottery was made in Crooksville, Ohio, from 1905. Addis E. Hull bought the Acme Pottery Company and started making ceramic wares. In 1917, A. E. Hull Pottery began making art pottery as well as the commercial wares. For a short time, 1921 to 1929, the firm also sold pottery imported from Europe. The dinnerware of the 1940s (including the Little Red Riding Hood line), the matte wares of the 1940s, and the high gloss artwares of the 1950s are all popular with collectors. The firm officially closed in March 1986.

Bank, Corky Pig, Blue, Pink, 4 ½ x 3 x 3 In.	155
Bank, Corky Pig, Mauve, Pink Trim, Ring In Snout, Stopper, 7 In.	28 to 52
Bank, Corky Pig, Seated, Brown, Blue Trim, 6 ½ In.	52
Bank, Corky Pig, Yellow, Blue, 1957, 7 In.	30
Bank, Razorback Pig, Brown, Blue Trim, 10 In.	17
Blossom Flite, Basket, 9 In.	30
Blossom Flite, Console Set, Bowl, 2 Candleholders, 17-In. Bowl, 3 Piece	35
Blossom Flite, Console, Hoop Handles, c.1955, 16 ½ x 6 ¾ In.	125
Blossom Flite, Cornucopia, Pink Spout, Gray, 10 ¾ In.	46
Blossom Flite, Creamer, c.1955, 8 Oz.	24
Blossom Flite, Pitcher, Pink, Yellow, Marked, 13 ¾ In.	35
Blossom Flite, Vase, Pink, Black, Green, Asymmetrical Handles, 10 ½ In.	35
Bow Knot, Basket, Blue Scalloped Rim, Handle, 11 ¾ In.	460
Bow Knot, Basket, Pink & Blue, 11 ¾ In.	450
Bow Knot, Basket, Pink, Blue, Cream Shading, Marked, 11 ¾ In.	518
Bow Knot, Candlestick, Blue & Turquoise, 4 In., Pair	40
Bow Knot, Pitcher, Blue & Turquoise, 6 In.	40
Bow Knot, Pitcher, Pink To Blue Shading, 5 ¾ x 6 In.	46
Bow Knot, Vase, Blue, Turquoise, Flowers, Double Loop Handles, Marked, 10 ¾ In.	98
Bow Knot, Vase, Cinched Neck, Flowers, Blue Ground, 6 ⅝ In.	52
Bow Knot, Vase, Cornucopia, Blue & Turquoise, 6 ⅞ In.	45
Bow Knot, Vase, Flared Rim, Pink, Blue, 6 In.	55
Bow Knot, Vase, Pastels, 6 In.	55
Bow Knot, Vase, Pink, Blue, Flowers, Side Loop Handles, 8 ¾ In.	63
Bow Knot, Vase, Pink, Turquoise, Handles, c.1949, 10 ½ In.	387
Bow Knot, Wall Pocket, Whisk Broom Shape, Peach, 8 In.	23
Brown Drip, Ashtray, Deer, 8 In.	12
Brown Drip, Creamer, 4 ¼ In.	8
Brown Drip, Dish, Hen On Nest Lid, 8 ⅜ In.	60
Brown Drip, Salt & Pepper, Mushroom Shape, 3 ¾ In.	21
Butterfly, Basket, White, Teal Blue Interior, 3-Part Handle, 1956, 10 In.	19
Butterfly, Ewer, Pink, Turquoise, 1950s, 6 In.	45
Butterscotch, Mug, Soup, 4 ⅞ In.	9
Calla Lily, Cornucopia, Pink Base, 7 ⅞ In., Pair	23
Calla Lily, Vase, Green Ground, Angled Handles, 10 In.	40
Clock, Bluebird, Red Roof Case, 10 In.	160
Clock, Bluebird, Wall, Sessions Movement, 10 ¾ In.	75
Continental, Compote, Lid, 2-Tone Green, Chalice Shape, Footed, 8 ¼ In.	11
Corky Pig, Figure, Ring In Nose, Brown, Turquoise, 1957, 7 In.	12
Corky Pig, Figure, Ring In Nose, Yellow, Blue, 1957, 7 In.	35
Cornucopia, Twisted Ribbing, Pink, Blue, 10 x 5 x 4 In.	27
Ebb Tide, Ashtray, Mermaid, On Shell, Green, Marked, 9 In.	25 to 29
Ebb Tide, Basket, Green, Scaled, Lobbed, Triangular, Handle, 17 In.	21 to 58
Ebb Tide, Bowl, Snail, Gold Trim, 15 ¾ In.	50 to 58
Ebb Tide, Pitcher, 13 ¾ In.	45
Ebb Tide, Pitcher, Fish Shape, Green, Mauve, 8 ⅜ In.	46
Ebb Tide, Pitcher, Fish, Open Shell, Yellow, Brown, Orange, Marked, 13 ¾ In.	52
Ebb Tide, Planter, Mermaid On Shell Shape, Green, Mustard, Red, 8 ¾ In.	50 to 58
Ebb Tide, Tea Set, 6 ¼-In. Teapot, 3 Piece	85
Ebb Tide, Tea Set, Teapot, Lid, Sugar, Creamer, Green, Salmon Pink, 3 ½ To 6 In.	98
Ebb Tide, Vase, Fish Shape, Green, Red, Shaded, 7 In., Pair	46
Ebb Tide, Vase, Shell, Fish Base, Pink, Turquoise, 1955, 7 In.	125
Gingerbread Man, Cookie Jar, Brown, Marked Crooksville Ohio, Ovenproof, 11 In.	52
Hippo, Planter, Green, 8 ½ In.	70 to 81
Iris, Basket, Wavy Rim, Flowers, Handles, Footed, 7 In.	23
Iris, Vase, Bud, Pink, Scalloped Rim, Handles, 7 ⅞ In.	18

Imari, Charger, Landscape, Stylized Figure, Japan, Marked, c.1890, 18 In.
$357

Brunk Auctions

Imari, Charger, Panels, Flowers, Signed, Japan, 19th Century, 21 ½ In.
$575

Cottone Auctions

Imari, Jar, Lid, 6-Sided, Vases Of Flowers, 19 In.
$307

New Orleans Auction Galleries, Inc.

TIP
The material used to make repairs is warmer to the touch than the porcelain. Feel the surface of a figurine to see if there are unseen repairs

Imperial, Paneled Flower, Bowl, Carnival, Footed, Blue, Marked $25

Seeck Auctions

Indian, Bag, Apache, Hide, Beaded, Fringe, Drawstring Closure, c.1890, 12 In. $300

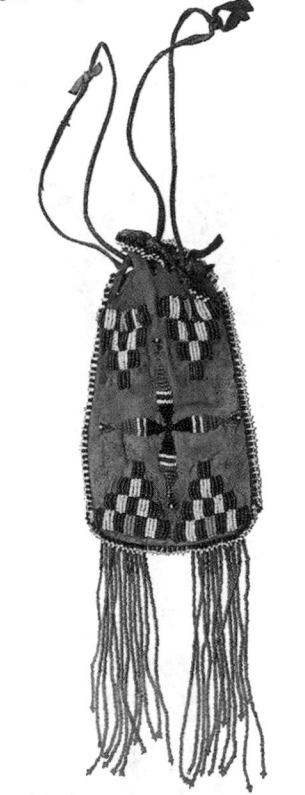

Cowan's Auctions

Indian, Bag, Plateau, Flat, Beaded Cloth, 2 Horses, Flowers, c.1900, 14 x 12 ¾ In. $2,091

Skinner Auctioneers & Appraisers

Jardiniere, Green, Purple, Green Panels, 2 ⅝ In.	11
Little Red Riding Hood, Bank, Painted, Floral Decal, 6 ¾ In.	142
Little Red Riding Hood, Cookie Jar, Basket, Flowers, Red, White, Gold Stars, 12 ¾ In.	92
Little Red Riding Hood, Cookie Jar, Poppy, Gold Trim, Regal China Co. ....*illus*	62
Little Red Riding Hood, Cookie Jar, Star Apron, 13 In.	209
Little Red Riding Hood, Creamer, 4 ½ In., 6 Oz.	449
Little Red Riding Hood, Grease Jar, Rose, Green, Flowers, Bow, 2 Parts, 1930s, 9 In.	92
Little Red Riding Hood, Pitcher, Poppy Up, 32 Oz., 8 In.	249
Little Red Riding Hood, Salt & Pepper, 3 ⅛ In.	24
Little Red Riding Hood, Salt & Pepper, 5 In.	30 to 35
Little Red Riding Hood, Salt & Pepper, Flower Decals, 5 ¼ In.	50
Little Red Riding Hood, Salt, White, Gold Trim, 5 ¼ In.	8
Little Red Riding Hood, Sugar, Crawling, 3 In.	50
Little Red Riding Hood, Teapot, Lid, Marked, 8 In.	40 to 46
Little Red Riding Hood, Wall Pocket, Painted, Floral Decal, 9 In.	142
Magnolia Glossy, Pitcher, Pink Flowers, Peach Ground, 8 ½ In.	40
Magnolia Matte, Vase, Yellow Ground, Brown Base Handles, 15 ½ In.	150
Magnolia, Candleholder, Pink Flowers, 4 ¼ In., Pair	30
Magnolia, Creamer, Glossy, 2 ¾ In.	48
Magnolia, Ewer, Footed, 8 ½ In.	55
Magnolia, Ewer, Glossy, 13 ½ In.	450
Magnolia, Vase, Cornucopia, Dusty Rose, 8 ¾ In.	21
Magnolia, Vase, Flowers, Yellow To Rose, Handles, 8 In.	35
Magnolia, Vase, Footed, Handles, c.1946, 8 ½ In.	80
Magnolia, Vase, Tassel Drop, Round Handles, Pink, c.1946, 8 ½ In.	86
Mirror Brown, Pitcher, 7 In.	17
Open Rose, Jardiniere, Ram's Head Handles, Scalloped Blue Rim, 9 In.	12
Open Rose, Wall Pocket, Marked, 9 ¼ In.	40
Orchid, Vase, Pink, Blue, Handles, 4 ⅞ In.	12
Parchment & Pine, Bowl, 15 ¾ In.	19
Parchment & Pine, Bowl, Green, Apricot, 15 ¾ In.	23
Parchment & Pine, Console Set, 11-In. Bowl, 3 Piece	30
Parchment & Pine, Pitcher, Green, Long Spout, Loop Handle, 14 In.	40
Parchment & Pine, Vase, Cornucopia, 7 ¾ In.	18
Parchment & Pine, Vase, Flared Cone Shape, Cream, Green, 10 ¾ In.	12
Parrot, Vase, Pulling Cart, Pink, Green, 1950s, 9 ½ x 6 In.	54
Pitcher, Pinecones, Carved, Stars, Butterfly, Green, Burgundy, Loop Handle, 8 ¾ In.	546
Planter, Dachshund, Red Brown Glaze, 14 ¼ In.	46
Poppy, Vase, Handles, 6 ¾ In.	12
Rosella, Ewer, Coral, White Flowers, 7 In., Pair	200
Serenade, Ewer, Pastel Flowers, Yellow Ground, Slanted Spout, 8 ⅝ In.	16
Serenade, Pitcher, Flowers, Pale Blue, Flared To Base, 6 ⅝ In.	12
Siamese Cat, Planter, White, Kitten, Resting, Green Paws Base, 12 In.	46
Tangerine, Pitcher, c.1965, 32 Oz., 6 ⅝ In.	27
Tokay, Basket, White, Green Leaves, Round, 10 ½ In.	16
Tokay, Bowl, Leaf Shape, Grapes, c.1958, 14 x 10 In.	36
Tokay, Comport, Lid, Flowers, Pink, Green, White, 8 ¼ In.	35
Tokay, Dish, Leaf Shape, White, c.1958, 12 In.	53
Tokay, Plate, Leaf Shape, White, Green, 13 In.	7
Tropicana, Basket, Black Man Dancing, Bird On Hand, Marked, 12 ½ In.	21 to 23
Tulip, Ewer, Pink, Blue, Double Handle, c.1940, 8 In.	92 to 137
Vase, Green, Rose, Blue Wide Stripes.7 ⅞ In.	13
Vase, Parchment & Pine, Angled Rim, Footed, Tan, Green, 10 ½ In.	24
Vase, Royal, Pink, Loop Brown Handles, 7 In.	12
Vase, Wildflower, Flowers, Pink, Yellow, Loop Handles, 10 ¾ In.	30
Water Lily, Ewer, Dusty Rose, Gold Trim, 5 ¾ In.	6
Water Lily, Teapot, Yellow To Rose, Yellow Flower, Green Leaves, 18 x 6 In.	58
Water Lily, Vase, Green To Pink, Scalloped Rim, Marked, 6 ½ In.	13
Water Lily, Vase, Pin, Green, Base Handles, Marked, 8 ¾ In.	35
Wild Flower, Basket, Tan, Pink, Marked, 10 ¾ In.	75
Wild Flower, Bowl, Dusty Rose, 12 ⅝ In.	14
Wild Flower, Candlestick, Dusty Rose, 2 ¾ In.	5
Wild Flower, Cornucopia, Pink & Blue, 6 ⅜ In.	38
Wild Flower, Cornucopia, Vase, 8 ½ In.	28
Wild Flower, Ewer, Flowers, Swirled Top, Pink To Green, 13 ⅜ In.	127
Wild Flower, Vase, 2 Handles, 9 In., Pair	89
Wild Flower, Vase, Dusty Rose, Handles, Marked, 5 ⅝ In.	15 to 17

Wild Flower, Vase, Flowers, Yellow Ground, Handles To Base, Marked, 9 ¾ In.	46
Wild Flower, Vase, Handles, Pink, Blue, Footed, Flared Rim, 7 ½ In.	77
Woodland, Basket, Hanging, Pastel, c.1949, 5 ¾ x 6 In.	45
Woodland, Basket, Peach, Pink, Glossy, Twig Handle, Footed, c.1950	72
Woodland, Basket, Twig Handle, Blue, Green, Glossy, 10 In.	149
Woodland, Console Set, Glossy, 14 ½-In. Bowl, 3 Piece	35
Woodland, Cornucopia, Yellow & Pink, Glossy, c.1950, 5 ½ In.	46
Woodland, Creamer, Peach, Pink, Glossy, c.1950, 6 Oz., 2 ⅞ In.	72
Woodland, Double Cornucopia, Yellow, Pink, Glossy, Marked, 9 In.	28
Woodland, Double Vase, Glossy, c.1953, 8 ½ In.	175
Woodland, Ewer, Double Twig Handle, Footed, Glossy, 13 In.	178
Woodland, Ewer, Glossy, 14 ¼ In.	40
Woodland, Ewer, Green, Yellow, Matte Glaze, 5 In.	65
Woodland, Ewer, Pink, Raised Foot, 6 In.	15
Woodland, Jardiniere, Peach, Pink, Glossy, Handles, c.1950, 5 In.	114
Woodland, Pitcher, Glossy, 6 ½ In.	12
Woodland, Pitcher, Yellow, Pink Base, Glossy, 6 ¾ In.	12
Woodland, Tea Set, Glossy, 6 ½-In. Teapot, 3 Piece	60
Woodland, Vase, Cornucopia, Yellow, Pink Matte, c.1950, 5 ½ In.	90
Woodland, Vase, Double, Flowers, 15 x 8 ½ In.	29
Woodland, Vase, Green, Pink, Handles, Footed, 11 In.	17
Woodland, Wall Pocket, Pink, Green, 7 ¾ In.	20
Woodland, Wall Pocket, Pink, Green, c.1950, 8 x 6 In.	80
Woodland, Yellow, Pink, Glossy, Basket, 9 In.	21

HUMMEL figurines, based on the drawings of the nun M.I. Hummel (Berta Hummel), were made by the W. Goebel Porzellanfabrik of Oeslau, Germany, now Rodental, Germany. They were first made in 1935. The *Crown* mark was used from 1935 to 1949. The company added the *bee* marks in 1950. The *full bee* with variations, was used from 1950 to 1959; *stylized bee,* 1957 to 1972; *three line mark,* 1964 to 1972; *last bee,* sometimes called *vee over gee,* 1972 to 1979. In 1979 the V bee symbol was removed from the mark. *U.S. Zone* was part of the mark from 1946 to 1948; *W. Germany* was part of the mark from 1960 to 1990. The Goebel *W. Germany* mark, called the *missing bee* mark, was used from 1979 to 1990; *Goebel, Germany,* with the crown and *WG*, originally called the *new mark,* was used from 1991 through part of 1999. A new version of the bee mark with the word *Goebel* was used from 1999 to 2008. A special *Year 2000* backstamp was also introduced. Porcelain figures inspired by Berta Hummel's drawings were introduced in 1997. These are marked *BH* followed by a number. They were made in the Far East, not Germany. Goebel discontinued making Hummel figurines in 2008 and Manufaktur Rodental took over the factory in Germany and began making new Hummel figurines. Hummel figurines made by Rodental are marked with a yellow and black bee on the edge of an oval line surrounding the words *Original M.I. Hummel Germany.* The words *Manufaktur Rodental* are printed beneath the oval. Manufaktur Rodental was sold in 2013 and new owners have taken over. Hummel Manufaktur GmbH is the new company. Other decorative items and plates that feature Hummel drawings have been made by Schmid Brothers, Inc., since 1971.

Ashtray, Joyful, Full Bee, 4 x 6 In.	35
Creamer, Friar Tuck, Full Bee, Paper Label, 2 ½ In.	20
Figurine, No. 3/II, Bookworm, Crown Mark, 8 In. ....*illus*	720
Figurine, No. 7/II, Merry Wanderer, Stylized Bee, 10 In.	378
Figurine, No. 49, To Market, 5 ½ In.	136
Figurine, No. 53, Banjo Betty, Full Bee, 3 ½ In.	35
Figurine, No. 70, Holy Child, Full Bee, 6 ¾ In.	850
Figurine, No. 81/0, School Girl, Stylized Bee, 5 In.	60
Figurine, No. 82/0, School Boy, Stylized Bee, 5 In.	50
Figurine, No. 112/1, Just Resting, Full Bee, 5 In.	68
Figurine, No. 112/3/0, Just Resting, Bee In V, 3 ⅞ In.	125
Figurine, No. 118, Little Thrifty Bank, 5 In.	45
Figurine, No. 123, Max & Moritz, Missing Bee, 5 ¼ In. ....*illus*	185
Figurine, No. 124/0, Hello, Missing Bee, 5 ¾ In.	35
Figurine, No. 130, Duet, c.1975, 2 ¾ In.	50
Figurine, No. 141/1, Apple Tree Girl, Crown Mark, 6 In.	65
Figurine, No. 142 3/0, Apple Tree Boy, Stylized Bee, 4 In.	65
Figurine, No. 174, She Loves Me, She Loves Me Not, Stylized Bee, 4 ½ In.	74
Figurine, No. 182, Good Friends, Stylized Bee, 4 In.	100
Figurine, No. 257/0, For Mother, Missing Bee, 5 ¼ In.	30
Figurine, No. 317, Not For You, Boy & Dog, 5 ½ In.	35
Figurine, No. 331, Crossroads, Missing Bee, 6 ¾ In.	317
Figurine, No. 340, Letter To Santa Claus, 7 ¼ In.	57

Indian, Basket, Hopi, Wicker, Woven, Bands, Vegetable Dyed, 1950s, 6 ½ x 11 ½ In.
$192

Allard Auctions

Indian, Basket, Klickitat, Cedar Root, Rim Loop Handles, c.1935, 7 ¾ x 7 In.
$570

Allard Auctions

Indian, Basket, Pima, Figural, 4 Spread Winged Eagles, 12 Dogs, c.1910, 4 x 18 In.
$923

Cowan's Auctions

Indian, Basket, Yokuts, 2-Tone Bands, Pedestal Base, c.1900, 5 ¾ In.
$720

Cowan's Auctions

H

Indian, Basket, Yokuts, Rattlesnake, Diamonds, Bands, c.1910, 3 ¾ x 6 ½ In. $677

Cowan's Auctions

Indian, Belt, Navajo, 8 Conchas, Silver, Turquoise, c.1970, 40 In. $1,140

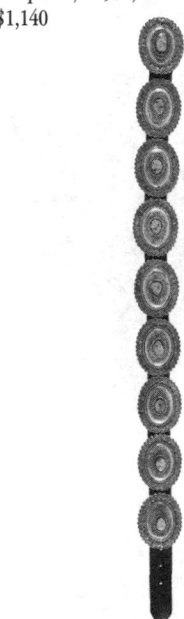

Cowan's Auctions

Indian, Belt, Navajo, Concha, Leather Backed, First Phase Revival, c.1950, 39 In. $2,400

Cowan's Auctions

Figurine, No. 348, Ring Around The Rosie, Stylized Bee, 6 ½ In.	1170
Figurine, No. 441, Call To Worship, Clock, Missing Bee, 11 ½ In.	324
Plaque, No. 92, Merry Wanderer, 5 x 5 ¼ In.	45
Plaque, No. 126, Retreat To Safety, Full Bee, 5 x 5 In.	45
Plate, Christmas, No. 268, Ride Into Christmas, Boy On Sled, 1975, 7 ½ In.	35
Salt & Pepper, Friar Tuck, Full Bee, 2 ¾ In.	35

HUTSCHENREUTHER PORCELAIN FACTORY was founded by Carolus Magnus in Hohenburg, Bavaria, in 1814. A second factory was established in Selb, Germany, in 1857. The company made fine quality porcelain dinnerware and figurines. The mark changed through the years, but the name and the lion insignia appear in most versions. Hutschenreuther became part of the Rosenthal division of the Waterford Wedgwood Group in 2000. Rosenthal was bought by Sambonet Paderno Industries, headquartered in Orfento, Novaro, Italy, in 2009.

LORENZ HUTSCHEN REUTER
GERMANY

Bonbon, Lid, Blue Onion, Bud Finial, 2 ½ In.	48
Cup & Saucer, Red, Gilt Design	16
Figurine, Cardinal, On Branch, Paper Label, 6 ⅝ In.	195
Figurine, Dancers, 2 Nude Women, Holding Sphere, 12 In.	660
Figurine, Dog, Doberman Pinscher, Dark Brown, 6 ¾ x 5 In.	195
Figurine, Elephant, Cream, Base, 3 x 3 In.	65
Figurine, Elephant, Trunk Up, Gray Glossy Glaze, 12 In.	104
Figurine, Man, Carrying Flowers, Green Vest, 5 ¼ In.	495
Figurine, Nude, Feeding Fawn, c.1940, 13 x 10 x 4 In.	615
Figurine, Nude, Raised Arms, On Sphere, Marked, 8 ½ In.	189
Figurine, Sparrow, Feeding Babies, 5 x 8 In.	375
Plate, Fortress Marienberg, Rhine River, c.1970, 7 ¾ In.	50
Plate, Swan, Water Lily, 22K Gold Border, 10 ½ In.	168
Plate, Wide Gold Rim, Raised Flowers, Geometrics, 22K Gold, c.1945, 10 ¾ In.	219
Sugar & Creamer, Gold, Chintz Pattern	18

ICONS, special, revered pictures of Jesus, Mary, or a saint, are usually Russian or Byzantine. The small icons collected today are made of wood and tin or precious metals. Many modern copies have been made in the old style and are being sold to tourists in Russia and Europe and at shops in the United States. Rare, old icons have sold for over $50,000. The riza is the metal cover protecting the icon. It is often made of silver or gold.

Archangel Michael, Armor, Sword, Gilt, Multicolor Enamel, Russia, c.1950, 10 x 12 In.	2952
Archangel Michael, Silver, Oklad, Russia, 12 x 10 In.	1800
Biblical Scene, Painted, Carved Giltwood Frame, Greece, c.1800, 26 x 18 In.	8125
Bishop, Carved Giltwood, Standing, Robes, Wood Stand, Italy, 1600s, 7 ½ In.	885
Christ Pantocrator, Kovcheg Panel, Applied Gold Leaf, c.1800, 21 x 17 In.	900
Christ Pantocrator, Oil On Panel, Russia, 1800s, 8 ¾ x 7 In.	3776
Cross, Pectoral, Applied Relief Crucifix, Gold, Leather & Silk Box, Russia, c.1918, 4 In.	4200
Crucifix, Brass, Enameled Design, Russia, 15 x 7 ½ In.	420
Crucifix, Carved Hardwood, Christ On Cross, 1700s, 24 x 9 In.	492
Crucifix, Wood, Carved Ivory, Coiled Serpent, c.1800, 27 x 12 In.	1230
Madonna & Child, Carved Wood, Gesso, Italy, 1800s, 20 x 6 In.	390
Madonna & Child, Gesturing, Saints, Angel Border, Orange Ground, c.1915, 21 x 18 In.	6000
Madonna & Child, Gilt Metal, Faux Jewel Design, Arch Top, Portable, Russia, 4 ½ In.	450
Madonna & Child, In Cloud, Kneeling Worshiper, Oil On Panel, Germany, 1748, 8 x 6 In.	120
Madonna & Child, Plaque, Ceramic, Arched, Mary Kneeling, Blue, White, 1900s, 28 In.	1440
Madonna & Child, Plaque, Porcelain, Gilt Frame, Germany, 1800s, 11 x 9 In.	1298
Madonna & Child, Seated, Throne, Carved Wood, Italy, 43 ½ In.	3540
Madonna & Child, Silver, Enameled, Hammered, Halos, Script, Russia, c.1890, 13 x 10 In.	1541
Madonna & Child, Silver, Jewels, Russia, 1837, 13 ½ x 10 ½ In.	3159
Madonna Enthroned, Infant Jesus Holding Dove, Saints, Angels, Sienese School, 11 x 6 In.	891
Mary, Christ, Baroque Carved, Billowing Robes, Jesus Holding Orb, Base, 1700s, 22 In.	738
Mary, Presented In Temple By Parents, Painted, c.1900, 12 x 10 In.	5230
Nicholas The Wonderworker, Plaque, Brass, Enameled, Frame, c.1890, 14 x 12 In.	264
Our Lady Of Kazan, Gilded Silver, Enameled Oklad, Halo, Pendant Collar, c.1838, 12 x 10 In.	13000
Our Lady Of The Sign, Houli, Gilt Ground, Border, Russia, 11 x 8 In.	550
Plaque, Jeanne D'Arc, Brass, 36 x 12 In.	600
Plaque, Madonna & Child, Wood, Carved, Frame, 13 x 17 In.	720
Reliquary, Dormition Of The Virgin, Tempera On Panel, Russia, 1700s, 11 x 16 In. ....*illus*	11800
Resurrection, Christ Outside Tomb, Gilded Border, Russia, c.1900, 10 ½ x 8 ⅝ In.	5500
Saint, Carved, Painted, Giltwood Frame, 20th Century, 28 x 19 ¾ In.	2280
St. George Slaying Dragon, Flowers, Silver Riza, Impressed Mark, c.1892, 5 ¾ x 7 In.	3250
St. Harlampy, Plaque, Gilt, Hand Raised, Blessing, Scripture, Russia, 1800s, 12 x 11 In.	240

H

St. Joseph, Christ Child, Asleep On Shoulder, Carved, Paint, 37 In.	1353
St. Nicholas, Oklad, Russia, 8 ½ x 7 In.	540
St. Nicholas, Wonderworker, Protecting The City, Russia, 1800s, 21 x 17 ½ In.	3000
St. Peter, Keys, St. Paul, Gospels, Gilt Arch Border, Incised, Painted, c.1915, 28 x 22 ½ In.	8750
St. Sergius Of Radonezh, Parents' Tomb, Incised, Faux Enamel, Russia, 1890, 11 x 10 In.	2040
The Cardinals, Watercolor On Paper, Multicolor, Frame, c.1902, 15 ½ x 12 ½ In.	598
Theotokos, With Christ, Xenia Pokrovsky, Kovcheg Panel, Gold Leaf, c.1900, 20 x 16 In.	250
Tile, Mary, Our Lady Of Bethlehem, Christ, Wood Frame, Portugal, 1600s, 20 x 17 In.	1180
Traveling, Brass, 5 Registers, Cyrillic Inscriptions, Arched Top, Russia, 4-Fold, 6 x 4 In.	150
Virgin, Holy Spirit, Disciples, Giltwood Frame, Russia, c.1800, 12 x 12 In.	5000

IMARI porcelain was made in Japan and China beginning in the seventeenth century. In the eighteenth century and later, it was copied by porcelain factories in Germany, France, England, and the United States. It was especially popular in the nineteenth century and is still being made. Imari is characteristically decorated with stylized bamboo, floral, and geometric designs in orange, red, green, and blue. The name comes from the Japanese port of Imari, which exported the ware made nearby in a factory at Arita. Imari is now a general term for any pattern of this type.

Bowl, Black Ship, Figure Reserves, 4 x 11 ½ In.	395
Bowl, Bleeding, Chrysanthemums, Peonies, Flower Reserves, Blue Ground, Gilt, 10 In., Pair	330
Bowl, Chrysanthemum Shape, Ribbed, Petal Lobed Rim, Medallion, 1900s, 11 In.	359
Bowl, Flower Basket, Phoenixes, Flowers, Red, Blue, c.1875, 7 ½ x 16 In.	461
Bowl, Flowers, Dragons, Mountains, Flared Rim, Gilt Band, Japan, c.1850, 4 ½ x 9 ½ In.	115
Bowl, Flowers, Pomegranates, Chrysanthemums, Cobalt Blue, Red, White, c.1800, 10 In.	359
Bowl, Panels, 3 Friends Of Winter, Birds, Turtles, Cranes, Butterflies, Blue & White, 7 In.	2460
Bowl, Wood Stand, 12 x 12 In.	396
Charger, Bugaku Dancers Design, Flowering Branches, Multicolor, c.1900, 18 In., Pair	553
Charger, Cranes, Plums, Pines, Alternating With Flowers, Japan, 18 In.	738
Charger, Fans, Books, Brocade Cloth, c.1880, 22 ¾ In.	861
Charger, Flower Basket, Foo Dog Panels, Peonies, 1800s, 24 ½ In. Diam.	861
Charger, Flower Reserves, Center Bamboo Roundel, Barbed Rim, 8-Sided, Japan, 18 In.	4200
Charger, Flowers, Hawks, Dragons, Winged Horses, Prunus, 15 In. Diam., Pair	388
Charger, Flowers, Scalloped Rim, Multicolor, c.1820, 18 In. Diam.	390
Charger, Landscape, Stylized Figure, Japan, Marked, c.1890, 18 In. ....*illus*	357
Charger, Paneled, c.1875, 18 In.	144
Charger, Panels, Flowers, Signed, Japan, 19th Century, 21 ½ In. ....*illus*	575
Charger, Panels, Women, Landscape, Round, c.1875, 21 In.	621
Charger, Transfer, Ducks On Stream Bank, Leaves, 1800s, 14 In.	59
Dish, Central Pine Band, Reserve Panels, Rectangular, 7 ½ x 8 ½ In., Pair	90
Dish, Fish Shape, Hawk, Pheasant, Red Flower Ground, c.1900, 15 ¾ In.	244
Dish, Reticulated, Scroll & Flower Design, Pierced Openwork Border, c.1900, 8 In., Pair	209
Ginger Jar, Lobed, Pierced Scroll Base, c.1885, 24 x 5 In., Pair	861
Jar, Dome Lid, Cylindrical, c.1875, 9 ¾ x 7 In.	153
Jar, Dome Lid, Flower Baskets, Peony Panels, Shi Shi Finial, c.1900, 25 In.	1076
Jar, Dome Lid, Foo Dog Finial, c.1875, 14 ½ In.	266
Jar, Lid, 6-Sided, Vases Of Flowers, 19 In. ....*illus*	307
Plate Set, Painted Flowers, Vines, Gilt Scalloped Border, 7 ⅝ In., 12 Piece	336
Punch Bowl, Fluted, Multicolor, c.1915, 9 ½ In. Diam.	276
Tankard, Flowers, Phoenix Birds, 1800s, 10 In.	359
Tankard, Lid, Peonies, Mums, Red, Gold, Chinese, c.1725, 6 ½ In.	1200
Tea Set, Orange, Blue, White Ground, Japan, 20th Century, 15 Piece	246
Tureen, Lid, Gilt Loop Handles, Finial, 12 x 9 ½ In.	161
Umbrella Stand, Samurai, Figures In Reserves, Flower & Leaf Ground, Cylindrical, 24 In.	120
Vase, Landscape, Flowers, Brocade, Multicolor, c.1900, 10 ¼ In., Pair	861
Vase, Quatrefoil, Flowers, Dragon & Phoenix Panels, c.1900, 12 ¼ In.	209
Vase, Ribbed Body, Garden Scenes, Panels, Flowers, 15 ¾ In.	359
Vase, Trumpet Mouth, Blue, Red, Orange, Flowers, Leaves, 1900s, 14 In., Pair	120
Vase, Trumpet Shape, Figures, Scrolling, Multicolor, Metal Base, 15 In.	210

IMPERIAL GLASS CORPORATION was founded in Bellaire, Ohio, in 1901. It became a subsidiary of Lenox, Inc., in 1973 and was sold to Arthur R. Lorch in 1981. It was sold again in 1982, and went bankrupt in 1984. In 1985, the molds and some assets were sold. The Imperial glass preferred by the collector is freehand art glass, carnival glass, slag glass, stretch glass, and other top-quality tablewares. Tablewares and animals are listed here. The others may be found in the appropriate sections.

Animal, Flying Mare, Wisteria, 9 In.	173
Beaded Block, Pitcher, 1930s, 6 In.	30

Indian, Belt, Navajo, Concha, Silver, Turquoise, Butterfly Spacers, Spider Buckle, 1960s, 42 In.
$360

Allard Auctions

Indian, Blanket, Multicolor Bands, Beaver State, Pendleton, c.1950, 81 x 64 In.
$184

Allard Auctions

Indian, Bow, Hupa, Hourglass Shape, Sinew Backing, Hide Grip, Painted, 1800s, 36 ½ In.
$1,200

Cowan's Auctions

Indian, Bowl, Pacific Northwest, Beaver, Holding Stick, Kwakwaka'wakw, c.1890, 15 ¼ In.
$3,480

Cowan's Auctions

Indian, Bowl, San Ildefonso, Blackware, Maria & Santana Martinez, Signed, c.1950, 3 x 8 ½ In.
$1,560

Cowan's Auctions

Indian, Box, Plains, Parfleche, Rawhide, Mineral Painted, Geometrics, c.1900, 7 x 14 x 9 In.
$720

Allard Auctions

Indian, Bracelet, Navajo, Cuff, Silver, Flower, Leaf, Turquoise, Coral, D.K. Lister, 5 x 3 In.
$330

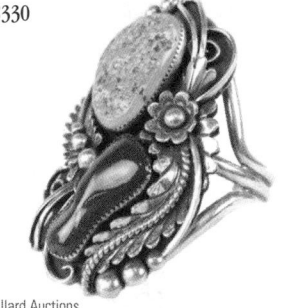

Allard Auctions

Bel-Aire, Tray, Rose Pink, Handles, 11 In.	45
Candlewick, Bowl, Belled, 10 In.	95
Candlewick, Bowl, Viennese Blue, Handles, 8 ½ In.	120
Candlewick, Compote, 5 ¼ In.	18
Candlewick, Nut Cup	8
Candlewick, Plate, Dinner, 10 ½ In.	45
Candlewick, Relish, Divided, Paper Label, 6 ¼ In.	80
Candlewick, Tumbler, 12 Oz., 5 ½ In.	22
Diamond Block, Bowl, Blue, Honey Dish, Square, 5 ½ In.	16
Diamond Block, Bowl, Green, Oval, Handles, 6 ½ In.	20
Diamond Block, Bowl, Pink, Handles, Oval, 6 ½ In.	20
Diamond Block, Nappy, Green, Handle, 4 ½ In.	16
Diamond Quilted, Bowl, Black, Crimped Edge, 7 In.	20
Diamond Quilted, Bowl, Pink, Straight Edge, 7 In.	20
Diamond Quilted, Candlestick, Pink, Flat, 4 ½ In.	15
Diamond Quilted, Compote, Green, Lid, Footed, 11 ½ In.	140
Diamond Quilted, Creamer, Pink	12
Diamond Quilted, Cup, Black	17
Diamond Quilted, Nappy, Black, Handle, 5 ½ In.	18
Diamond Quilted, Plate, Luncheon, Pink, 8 In.	12
Diamond Quilted, Punch Base, Green	250
Diamond Quilted, Saucer, Black	6
Fashion, Water Set, Pitcher, Tumbler, Smoke, Carnival, c.1945, 8 x 4 In., 7 Piece	518
Line 320, Console Set, Rose Pink, 3 Piece	95
Mayflower, Pitcher, Marigold, 9 In.	30
Newbound, Bowl, Fruit, Stiegel Green, Footed, 10 In.	55
Newbound, Candleholder, Green	15
Newbound, Candleholder, Pink	15
Newbound, Candleholder, Red	20
Newbound, Candleholder, Stiegel Green	20
Paneled Flower, Bowl, Carnival, Footed, Blue, Marked ....*illus*	25
Platter, Flow Blue, Landscape Scene, Steers, 17 x 13 In.	210
Provincial, Goblet, Turquoise, 12 Oz., 6 ½ In.	18
Reeded, Pitcher, Stiegel Green, Ice Lip, Crystal Applied Handle, 8 In.	65
Reeded, Tumbler, Iced Tea, Cobalt Blue, 15 Oz.	24
Reeded, Vase, Bud, Stiegel Green, 6 In.	35
Ripple, Vase, Amber, c.1900, 10 In.	65
Scroll Fluted, Sugar & Creamer, Blue Opalescent	55
Shaeffer, Rose Bowl, Stiegel Green, 6 In.	75
Square, Server, Black Amethyst, Center Handle, 10 ½ In.	45
Square, Sugar & Creamer, Red	45
Twisted Optic, Bowl, Pink, 10-Sided, Handles, 9 In.	35
Twisted Optic, Candy Dish, Lid, Green, 9 In.	35
Twisted Optic, Plate, Luncheon, Blue, 8 In.	12
Twisted Optic, Plate, Luncheon, Canary Yellow, 8 In.	12
Twisted Optic, Plate, Sherbet, Canary Yellow, 6 In.	8
Twisted Optic, Sherbet, Canary Yellow	15
Vase, Cylindrical, Marbleized Blue, White, Dark Blue Iridescent Interior, 9 In.	201
Vase, Iridescent Cobalt Blue, Pulled Opal Drapes, Flared Rim & Base, c.1925, 8 ½ In.	288
Vase, Iridescent Orange, Free Hand Pulled Loop, Corset Shape, 10 In.	148
Vase, Urn Shape, Squat, Orange, Blue Heart & Vine, Blue Lip Wrap, Paper Label, 6 ½ In.	403
Windmill, Water Set, Pitcher, Tumblers, Rubigold, Frosted, c.1950, 8 ½ x 4 In., 9 Piece	115

INDIAN art from North and South America has attracted the collector for many years. Each tribe has its own distinctive designs and techniques. Baskets, jewelry, pottery, and leatherwork are of greatest collector interest. Eskimo art is listed under Eskimo in this book.

Anklet, Quill Work, Red, White, Purple, Velvet Bands, Tine, Cone Danglers, 6 ½ In., Pair	384
Bag, Apache, Hide, Beaded, Fringe, Drawstring Closure, c.1890, 12 In. ....*illus*	300
Bag, Plateau, Flat, Beaded Cloth, 2 Horses, Flowers, c.1900, 14 x 12 ¾ In. ....*illus*	2091
Bag, Sioux, Beaded, Hide, Envelope Shape, Flap, Tassels, Feathers, c.1900, 11 x 15 In.	788
Bandolier, Chippewa, Beaded, Flowers, Bag Style, 38 x 13 In.	1035
Basket, Acorn, Hupa, Fine Weave, Multicolor, Stacked Triangles, c.1910, 5 x 7 ½ In.	173
Basket, Apache, 3 Geometric Bands, Red Cloth, Hide Straps, c.1945, 11 x 12 In.	1150
Basket, Apache, Coiled, Geometric, c.1910, 6 ¾ x 22 In.	2214
Basket, Apache, Lid, Closed Coil, Diamond Design, Oval, Willow, 6 x 8 In.	944
Basket, Apache, Star Design, 10 In.	649

Indian, Buffalo Skull, Carved, Inked, Eagle, Feathers, Symbols, Two Hawks, 1990s
$480

Allard Auctions

Indian, Canoe, Passamaquoddy, Model, Birch Bark, Animals, Tipi, Canoes, F. Tomah, 19 In.
$840

Skinner Auctioneers & Appraisers

Indian, Cradleboard, Ute, Hide, Beaded, Moccasins, Gauntlets, Lizard, c.1930s, 33 x 14 In.
$1,845

Cowan's Auctions

Indian, Dance Wrap, Osage, Beaded, Eagle Rosette & Flowers, Wool, 1970s, 36 x 104 In.
$420

Allard Auctions

Indian, Doll, Northern Plains, Beaded, Hide, Pigtails, Fringe, c.1890, 12 ½ In.
$800

Cowan's Auctions

Indian, Fetish, Sioux, Lizard Shape, Umbilical, Beaded Hide, c.1900, 7 ¼ In.
$780

Cowan's Auctions

Indian, Figurine, Cochiti, Mineral Paint, Pit Fired, c.1940s, 5 ¾ x 4 ½ In.
$270

Allard Auctions

Indian, Hat, Top, Osage, Beaver, Feather Plume, Beaded Band, France, c.1910, 21 x 6 In.
$345

Allard Auctions

Indian, Hide, Buckskin, War, Dance, Hunting Scenes, Painted, 60 x 50 In.
$16,675

Cottone Auctions

I

Indian, Jar, Acoma, Stylized Birds, Wings, Butterflies, c.1920, 8 ¼ x 10 ½ In. $1,200

Cowan's Auctions

Indian, Jar, Blackware, Symbols, Signed, Maria & Santana Martinez, 1943-54, 5 ½ x 7 In. $1,560

Cowan's Auctions

Indian, Jar, Seed, Hopi, Insect, Cross, Deanna Lomas Hu, c.1950, 4 x 5 ¼ In. $173

Allard Auctions

Indian, Jar, Zuni, 3 Molded & Applied Frogs, Cream, Brown, Slip Design, c.1910, 6 In. $2,880

Garth's Auctioneers & Appraisers

Basket, Burden, Apache, Cone Shape, Buckskin, Tin Cones, Fringe, 11 ½ x 14 ½ In.	196
Basket, Burden, Pomo, Twined, Cone Shape, Wrapped Rim, Geometric Bands, 17 x 22 In.	4200
Basket, Burden, Shasta, Cone Shape, c.1910, 15 ½ x 20 In.	1750
Basket, Hopi, Wicker, Woven, Bands, Vegetable Dyed, 1950s, 6 ½ x 11 ½ In. _illus_	192
Basket, Klickitat, Cedar Root, Rim Loop Handles, c.1935, 7 ¾ x 7 In. _illus_	570
Basket, Navajo, Geometrics, Round, 16 ½ In.	177
Basket, Pima, Figural, 4 Spread Winged Eagles, 12 Dogs, c.1910, 4 x 18 In. _illus_	923
Basket, Pomo, Maidu, California, c.1910, 5 x 11 In.	406
Basket, Pomo, Red Brown Geometric, Oval, 7 In.	266
Basket, Puma, Coiled, Lid, Red, Black, Natural Geometric, 1920s, 10 ½ x 5 In.	81
Basket, Puma, Storage, Coiled, Grass, 2 Color Geometric, 16 x 10 In.	288
Basket, Southwestern, Round, Coiled Geometric Panels, c.1945, 5 x 18 In.	1840
Basket, Storage, Pitt River, California, c.1920, 8 ½ x 12 In.	594
Basket, Taconic, Handles, Oval, c.1960, 33 x 23 x 14 In.	176
Basket, Washo, Sweet Grass, Red, Black Geometrics, 5 ¾ In.	177
Basket, Yokuts, 2 Tone Bands, Pedestal Base, c.1900, 5 ¾ In. _illus_	720
Basket, Yokuts, Rattlesnake, Diamonds, Bands, c.1910, 3 ¾ x 6 ½ In. _illus_	677
Belt, Navajo, 8 Conchas, Silver, Turquoise, c.1970, 40 In. _illus_	1140
Belt, Navajo, Concha, Leather Backed, First Phase Revival, c.1950, 39 In. _illus_	2400
Belt, Navajo, Concha, Silver, Turquoise, Butterfly Spacers, Spider Buckle, 1960s, 42 In. _illus_	360
Belt, Southwest, Concha, Sterling Silver, Turquoise, Man's, c.1980, Size 32-34	594
Blanket, Hopi, Red, Black, Yellow, White Stripes, 44 x 52 In.	649
Blanket, Multicolor Bands, Beaver State, Pendleton, c.1950, 81 x 64 In. _illus_	184
Blanket, Navajo, Red, Serrated Diamonds, Orange, Gray, Black, White, c.1900, 112 x 54 In.	1063
Bolo Tie, Zuni, Bird, Silver, Mother Of Pearl, Turquoise & Enamel Inlay	35
Bow, Blackfoot, Sheep Horn, Carved, Sinew Wrapped Handle, Tips, c.1920, 38 In.	1495
Bow, Hupa, Hourglass Shape, Sinew Backing, Hide Grip, Painted, 1800s, 36 ½ In. _illus_	1200
Bowl, Acoma, Geometric Design, Brown, Red, Shouldered, c.1900, 10 x 11 In.	531
Bowl, Hopi, Round, Animal, Nature Shapes, Tan, Brown, c.1940, 4 x 9 In.	118
Bowl, Mush, Hat Creek, c.1910, 6 ½ x 9 ½ In.	406
Bowl, Pacific Northwest, Beaver, Holding Stick, Kwakwaka'wakw, c.1890, 15 ¼ In. _illus_	3480
Bowl, San Ildefonso, Blackware, Awanyu, Water Guardian, M. & S. Martinez, 1960, 8 ½ In.	1888
Bowl, San Ildefonso, Blackware, Maria & Santana Martinez, Signed, c.1950, 3 x 8 ½ In. _illus_	1560
Box, Plains, Parfleche, Rawhide, Mineral Painted, Geometrics, c.1900, 7 x 14 x 9 In. _illus_	720
Bracelet, Navajo, Cuff, Silver, Flower, Leaf, Turquoise, Coral, D.K. Lister, 5 x 3 In. _illus_	330
Bracelet, Navajo, Cuff, Twist, Turquoise Hearts, Silver, 2 x 3 In.	2250
Bracelet, Navajo, Silver, 3 Bands, 5 Oxblood Red Coral Stones, 5 ¼ In.	150
Breastplate, Sioux, Woman's, Hair Pipe Bone, Beads, Fringe, North Dakota, c.1950, 46 In.	384
Breechcloth, Osage, Black, Tradecloth, Dance Panels, Flowers, Stars, c.1945, 63 x 22 In.	690
Buffalo Skull, Carved, Inked, Eagle, Feathers, Symbols, Two Hawks, 1990s _illus_	480
Canoe, Micmac, Birch Bark, Model, Porcupine Quill Design, Cedar Frame, 42 In.	944
Canoe, Pacific Northwest, Birch Bark, Model, Wood Frame, Gunwales, c.1900, 23 In.	443
Canoe, Passamaquoddy, Model, Birch Bark, Animals, Tipi, Canoes, F. Tomah, 19 In. _illus_	840
Cigar Case, Micmac, Flowers, Quilled, Birch Bark, c.1850, 5 ½ x 3 In.	354
Cradle Cover, Cheyenne, Figural, Quilled Hide, Sinew Sewn, Stars, Butterflies, Birds, 31 In.	4800
Cradleboard, Ute, Hide, Beaded, Moccasins, Gauntlets, Lizard, c.1930s, 33 x 14 In. _illus_	1845
Dance Wrap, Osage, Beaded, Eagle Rosette & Flowers, Wool, 1970s, 36 x 104 In. _illus_	420
Doll, Cheyenne, Beaded, Buckskin Clothing, Lazy Stitch Beadwork, 13 x 7 In.	374
Doll, Northern Plains, Beaded, Hide, Pigtails, Fringe, c.1890, 12 ½ In. _illus_	800
Doll, Skookum, Chief, Papoose, Squaw, Headdress, Beads, 36 In., 3 Piece	2442
Dress, Apache, Sunrise Ceremony, Buckskin, Fringe, Beaded, Jingles, c.1945, Size 12-14	403
Dress, Lakota, Blue Yoke, Multicolor Geometrics, Beads, Buckskin, c.1920, 51 x 67 In.	7680
Drum, Northwest Coast, Rawhide, 2-Sided, Painted Figure, 1970s, 4 ¾ x 23 In.	127
Fetish, Hopi, Stone Frog, 1 ¼ x 1 ½ In.	28
Fetish, Plains, Lizard, Beaded	99
Fetish, Plains, Turtle, Beaded	440
Fetish, Sioux, Lizard Shape, Umbilical, Beaded Hide, c.1900, 7 ¼ In. _illus_	780
Figure, Tlingit, Transformation, Wood, Carved, Animalistic, Painted, c.1890, 14 ¼ x 5 In.	1800
Figurine, Cochiti, Mineral Paint, Pit Fired, c.1940s, 5 ¾ x 4 ½ In. _illus_	270
Gauntlets, Gloves, Cree, Beaded Flowers, Fringe, Box, c.1890, 12 In.	173
Gauntlets, Nez Pierce, Beaded, Sky Blue Ground Flowers, Tanned Hide	798
Gauntlets, Plateau, Beaded, Pink Ground, Flowers, Tanned Hid	1020
Gauntlets, Plateau, Beaded, White Ground, Flowers, Tanned Hide	900
Gauntlets, Santee Sioux, Multicolor Beadwork, Black Ground, Early 1900s	207
Gauntlets, Yakama, Tanned Hide, Fringe, Beads, Flowers, Blue, Yellow, Black, 15 x 10 In.	708
Hair Band, Navajo Style, Sterling, Impressed Designs, 13 In.	69
Hair Roach, Prairie, Porcupine, Dyed, c.1900, 12 In.	840

Indian, Katsina, Hopi, Tuskiapaya, c.1930, 8 ¼ In.
$492

Indian, Mask, Iroquois, False Face, Carved, 1900s, 10 ½ x 6 ½ In.
$960

Indian, Moccasins, Sioux, Hide, Beaded, Stripes, c.1910, 10 ½ In.
$660

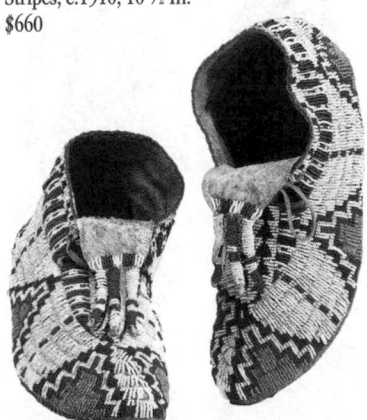

Indian, Necklace, Assiniboine, Buffalo Tooth, Blue Beads, c.1910, 34 In.
$403

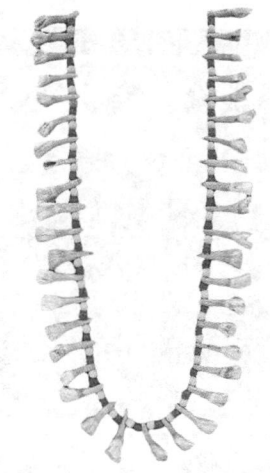

Indian, Necklace, Navajo, Squash Blossom, Silver & Turquoise, c.1975, 28 In.
$600

Indian, Necklace, Navajo, Squash, Naja Tufa Cast, 1940s Silver Half Dollars, c.1946, 27 In.
$360

Indian, Necklace, Navajo, Turquoise, Silver Pendant, Leonard & Marion Nez, c.1980, 17 In.
$1,035

Indian, Necklace, Pueblo, Crosses, Silver, Beads, Hand Wrought, c.1875, 25 In.
$660

Indian, Necklace, Zuni, Animals, Carved, Pipestone, Turquoise, Olive Heishi, c.1975, 28 In.
$480

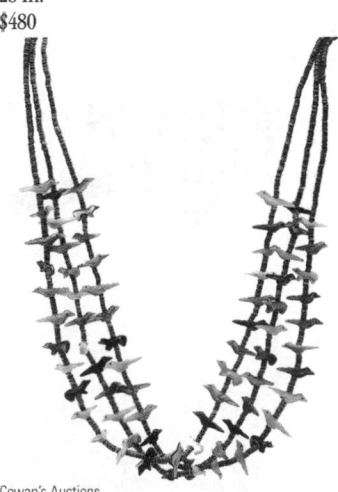

Indian, Olla, Apache, Dogs, Humans With Hands Up, Headdress, c.1915, 14 x 12 In.
$2,214

Cowan's Auctions

Indian, Rattle, Makah, Bird, Carved Wood, Metal, c.1890, 12 In.
$9,000

Skinner Auctioneers & Appraisers

Indian, Rattle, Northwest Coast, Shaman's, Bird, Creature, Painted, R. LaValle, c.1950, 13 In.
$840

Allard Auctions

Indian, Rug, Navajo, Ganado, Optical Valero Star, Homespun Wool, 1960s, 62 x 38 In.
$288

Allard Auctions

Indian, Rug, Navajo, Valero Star, Stepped Star, Fine Weave, Wool, c.1960, 48 x 26 In.
$138

Allard Auctions

Indian, Rug, Navajo, Yei Figures, Woven, c.1980s, 39 x 61 In.
$360

Allard Auctions

Indian, Rug, Runner, Navajo, Klagetoh, c.1935, 97 ½ x 49 In.
$1,169

Cowan's Auctions

Indian, Shirt, Blackfoot, Hide, Beaded, Open Sides, Painted, c.1920s, 37 In.
$1,476

Skinner Auctioneers & Appraisers

Indian, Snowshoes, Athabascan, Bentwood, Rawhide Lace, c.1910, 42 ½ x 15 ½ In.
$180

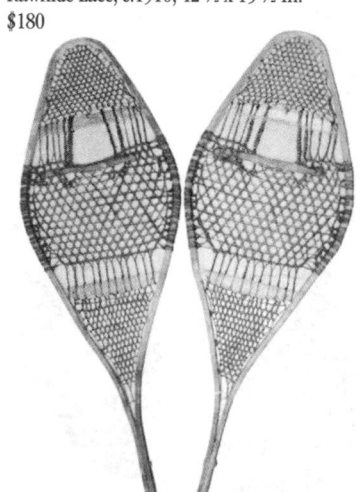

Allard Auctions

Hat, Top, Osage, Beaver, Feather Plume, Beaded Band, France, c.1910, 21 x 6 In. .... *illus* 345
Hide, Buckskin, War, Dance, Hunting Scenes, Painted, 60 x 50 In. .... *illus* 16675
Jar, Acoma, Black On White, Fineline & Bold, c.1940, 4 ¼ x 6 ¼ In. 35
Jar, Acoma, Stylized Birds, Wings, Butterflies, c.1920, 8 ¼ x 10 ½ In. .... *illus* 1200
Jar, Blackware, Symbols, Signed, Maria & Santana Martinez, 1943-54, 5 ½ x 7 In. .... *illus* 1560
Jar, Pueblo, Zia Bird Design, Orange, Dark Brown, Tan Ground, Squat, Swollen, 8 ½ In. 1495
Jar, San Ildefonso, Blackware, Feathers, Tapered Base, M. Popovi, c.1950, 6 x 7 ½ In. 3800
Jar, Santo Domingo, Multicolor Birds, Flowers, Lacing Holes, c.1920, 11 x 12 In. 575
Jar, Seed, Hopi, Insect, Cross, Deanna Lomas Hu, c.1950, 4 x 5 ¼ In. .... *illus* 173
Jar, Wyandot, Round, Tapered, Swollen Shoulder, Geometric Design, 13 ½ In. 4200
Jar, Zia, Pottery, 3 Stylized Birds, Leaves, Multicolor, c.1890, 6 ¾ x 9 In. 2400
Jar, Zuni, 3 Molded & Applied Frogs, Cream, Brown, Slip Design, c.1910, 6 In. .... *illus* 2880
Katsina, Hopi, Carved, Wolf Or Bear Dancer, Bow, Knife, Painted, 15 x 7 In. 58
Katsina, Hopi, Feather, Hands Together, Carved, Painted, 1800s, 7 In. 6400
Katsina, Hopi, Ho-O-Te, Rattle, Staff, Carved Wood, Multicolor Paint, 10 In. 584
Katsina, Hopi, Tuskiapaya, c.1930, 8 ¼ In. .... *illus* 492
Knife Sheath, Cree, Beaded, Flower Vine, Crosses, Multicolor, Fringe, c.1865, 10 ½ In. 948
Knife Sheath, Plains Cree, Beaded Buffalo Hide, Geometric, Multicolor, c.1870, 9 ¼ In. 4800
Ladle, Great Lakes, Carved, Wide Scoop, Beveled, Tapering Handle, c.1900, 9 ½ In. 450
Ladle, Iroquois, Effigy, c.1820, 7 x 5 In. 1422
Ladle, Iroquois, Elm, Openwork Crescent Cutout, c.1850, 9 ¾ In. 474
Leggings, Arapaho, Beaded Hide, Yellow Pigment On Hide, c.1900, 23 ½ In. 2091
Leggings, Sioux, Buckskin, Beads, White, Red, Blue Geometrics, 14 In., Pair 626
Leggings, Sioux, White Beads, Blue Wool, Bells, Fort Yates, c.1910, 53 In., Pair 1125
Mask, Iroquois, False Face, Carved, 1900s, 10 ½ x 6 ½ In. .... *illus* 960
Mat, Saskatchewan, Grass Woven, Beads, Lane Stitch Strap, Edge, Round, c.1890, 9 ½ In. 352
Moccasins, Cheyenne, Beaded, Leather Soles, c.1950 257
Moccasins, Cheyenne, Beaded, Teepee Design, Multicolor, Sinew Sewn, 10 ½ In. 1534
Moccasins, Hide, Blue White Flowers, Beads, Embroidery, Montana, c.1935, 10 ½ In. 448
Moccasins, Lakota, Beaded Hide, Stepped Triangles, Blue Ground, c.1890, 10 In. 492
Moccasins, Prairie, Beaded Flowers, White Outline, Hide, Woman's, c.1945, 11 ½ In. 250
Moccasins, Santee, Sinew, Hard Sole, Buckskin, Multicolor Flowers, c.1890, 10 ½ In. 748
Moccasins, Sioux, Beaded, Rawhide Soles, c.1920 420
Moccasins, Sioux, Hide, Beaded, Stripes, c.1910, 10 ½ In. .... *illus* 660
Moccasins, Sioux, High Top, Tanned Hide, Canvas Uppers, Geometrics, c.1890 1475
Moccasins, Sioux, Tanned Hide, Hard Soles, Yellow, Red, Blue, 10 ½ In. 1062
Mola, Kuna, Applique, Red, Multicolor, Birds, Animals, San Blas, c.1940, 21 x 17 In. 104
Necklace, Assiniboine, Buffalo Tooth, Blue Beads, c.1910, 34 In. .... *illus* 403
Necklace, Navajo, Squash Blossom, Silver & Turquoise, c.1975, 28 In. .... *illus* 600
Necklace, Navajo, Squash, Naja Tufa Cast, 1940s Silver Half Dollars, c.1946, 27 In. .... *illus* 360
Necklace, Navajo, Turquoise, Silver Pendant, Leonard & Marion Nez, c.1980, 17 In. .... *illus* 1035
Necklace, Pueblo, Crosses, Silver, Beads, Hand Wrought, c.1875, 25 In. .... *illus* 660
Necklace, Pueblo, Green Turquoise Roundels, Sterling Cones, Chain, 23 In. 127
Necklace, Zuni, Animals, Carved, Pipestone, Turquoise, Olive Heishi, c.1975, 28 In. .... *illus* 480
Olla, Acoma, Geometric Design, c.1920, 10 ½ x 12 In. 1710
Olla, Acoma, Geometric Design, c.1920, 7 ½ In. 540
Olla, Apache, Dogs, Humans With Hands Up, Headdress, c.1915, 14 x 12 In. .... *illus* 2214
Olla, Birds, Flowers, c.1910, 11 In. 1532
Olla, San Ildefanso Pueblo, Organic Design, c.1910, 8 ¼ x 9 ½ In. 1560
Pestle, Iroquois, Oak, Double Ended, c.1850, 53 In. 59
Pipe Bag, Sioux, Beaded, Sinew Sewn, Cow Hide, c.1890, 7 x 33 In. 2700
Pipe, Plains, Tack Decorated, 24 In. 88
Pipe, Stem, Plains, Black Stone Bowl, Carved, Brass Tacks, c.1920, 4 x 3 x 22 In. 207
Plate, San Ildefonso, Feather Design, Black, Burnished, c.1950, 14 ½ In. Diam. 3600
Pot, Effigy, Shipibo, Multicolor, Human Face, Glaze Finish, 7 x 8 In. 150
Pouch, Apache, Beaded Buffalo Hide, Maltese Cross, Tin Cones, Pigment, c.1870, 5 In. 1560
Rattle, Makah, Bird, Carved Wood, Metal, c.1890, 12 In. .... *illus* 9000
Rattle, Northwest Coast, Raven Shape, Mother-Of-Pearl Inlay, Red, Green, Black, 8 ½ In. 590
Rattle, Northwest Coast, Shaman's, Bird, Creature, Painted, R. LaValle, c.1950, 13 In. .... *illus* 840
Rattle, Northwest Coast, Shaman's, Transformation, Bird Shape, Multicolor, c.1950, 14 In. 1610
Rattle, Northwest, Coastal, Raven Shape, Frog Carving, Red, Black Paint, 11 3/34 In. 502
Ring, Zuni, Coiled Snakes, Silver, Turquoise Eyes & Stones, Effie Calavaza, Man's, Size 11 58
Rug, Navajo, Double Diamond Eye Dazzler, Red, Black, Cream, 40 x 59 In. 316
Rug, Navajo, Double Diamond, Orange, Black, 16 x 47 In. 215
Rug, Navajo, Ganado, Optical Valero Star, Homespun Wool, 1960s, 62 x 38 In. .... *illus* 288
Rug, Navajo, Red Mesa, Geometric, Red, Black, Gray, Ivory, 1940s, 40 x 69 In. 546
Rug, Navajo, Teec Nos Pos, Geometric Designs, Multicolor, 67 x 42 In. 10625

Indian, Spoon, Northwest Coast, Wood, Carved, Totem Pole Handle, 2 Figures, c.1950, 17 In.
$240

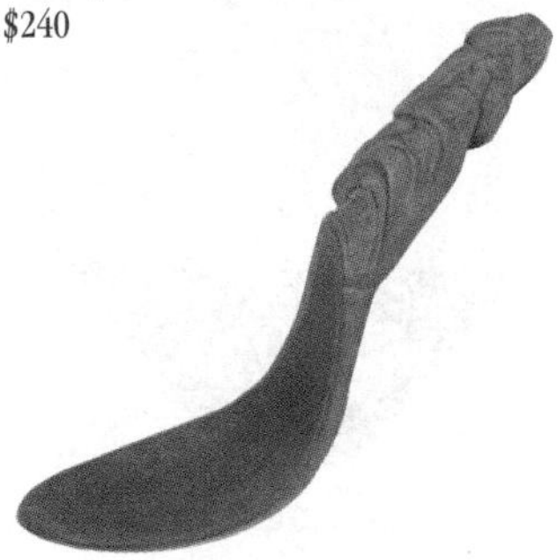

Allard Auctions

Indian, Totem Pole, Pacific Northwest, Painted, Charlie James, Kwakwaka'wakw, c.1920, 14 In.
$1,107

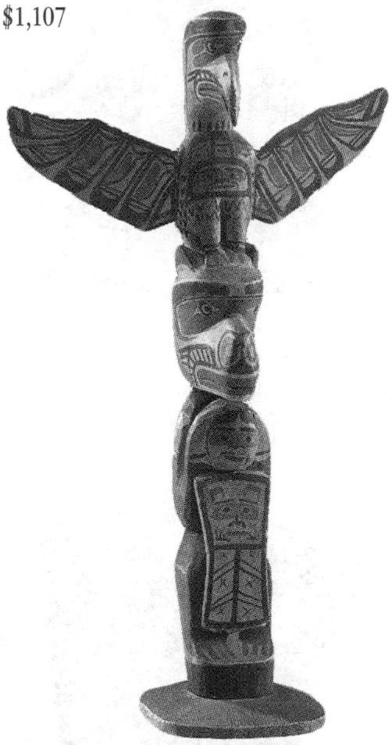

Cowan's Auctions

Indian, Toy, Toucan Bird, Navajo, Made From Pendleton Wool Blanket, 1980s, 16 x 11 In.
$115

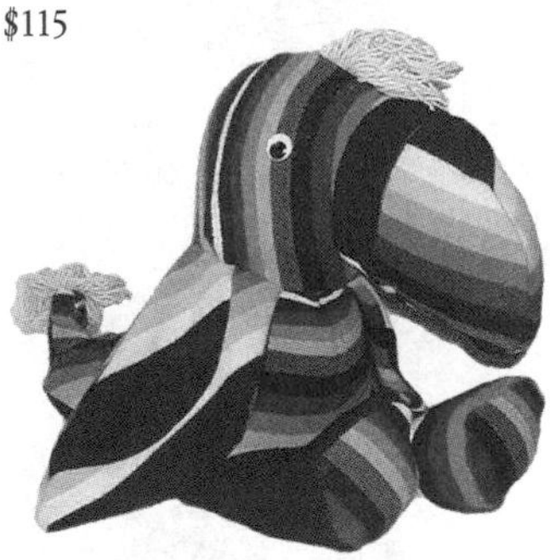

Allard Auctions

I

Indian, Vase, Shipibo, Face, Peru, c.1950, 32 x 33 In.
$472

Brunk Auctions

Indian, Vest, Lakota, Hide, Cloth, Horse Road, Beaded On Back, c.1885, 21 x 18 In.
$2,091

Skinner Auctioneers & Appraisers

Indian, War Bonnet, Blackfoot, Feathers, Canvas Cap, Beaded Band, c.1890, 16 In. High
$3,300

Allard Auctions

Indian, Whimsy, Iroquois, Boot Shape, Beadwork, c.1900, 11 x 9 In.
$81

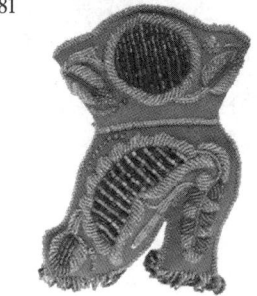

Allard Auctions

Rug, Navajo, Valero Star, Stepped Star, Fine Weave, Wool, c.1960, 48 x 26 In. ....*illus*	138
Rug, Navajo, Yei Figures, Woven, c.1980s, 39 x 61 In. ....*illus*	360
Rug, Navajo, Yei, Figures, Black, Blue, Red, White, 30 x 38 In.	367
Rug, Runner, Navajo, Klagetoh, c.1935, 97 ½ x 49 In. ....*illus*	1169
Saddle Bags, Arapaho, Beads, Hide, Fringe, Geometric Design, Blue, White, 75 x 16 In.	6490
Saddle Blanket, Sioux, Beaded, 1890	4446
Saddle Blanket, Sioux, Hide, Beads, Geometrics, Bells, Yellow Fringe, 74 x 26 In.	4720
Scoop, Burl, Carved Bird Terminal, 9 ½ In.	1722
Scoop, Iroquois, Elm, 9 ⅜ x 6 ¾ In.	326
Seed Jar, Hopi, Wing, Tail Feather Design, c.1900, 5 ¼ x 9 ½ In.	900
Sheath, Cheyenne, Beaded Hide, Sinew, Multicolor, Tin Cones, Horsehair, c.1875, 23 In.	3600
Shirt, Blackfoot, Hide, Beaded, Open Sides, Painted, c.1920s, 37 In. ....*illus*	1476
Shirt, Navajo, Red Velvet, 192 Silver Buttons, Cross Design, c.1920	354
Snow Snake, Iroquois, Pewter Tip, Carved, 55 ½ In.	770
Snowshoes, Athabascan, Bentwood, Rawhide Lace, c.1910, 42 ½ x 15 ½ In. ....*illus*	180
Spoon, Northwest Coast, Wood, Carved, Totem Pole Handle, 2 Figures, c.1950, 17 In. ....*illus*	240
Tomahawk, Plain, Brass Head, Steel Blade, Beaded Wood Handle, c.1945, 18 In.	431
Totem Pole, Northwest Coast, 4 Levels, Carved, Painted, c.1920, 18 ½ In.	1250
Totem Pole, Northwest Coast, Cedar, Carved, Hollow, Green, Black, Red, c.1910, 24 In.	3480
Totem Pole, Northwest Coast, Yellow Cedar, Paint, Spread Wings, R. Williams, c.1975, 11 In.	184
Totem Pole, Pacific Northwest, Painted, Charlie James, Kwakwaka'wakw, c.1920, 14 In. ....*illus*	1107
Toy, Toucan Bird, Navajo, Made From Pendleton Wool Blanket, 1980s, 16 x 11 In. ....*illus*	115
Vase, Acoma, Brown, White, Geometrics, Double Strap Handle, 8 In.	266
Vase, Shipibo, Face, Peru, c.1950, 32 x 33 In. ....*illus*	472
Vest, Beaded, Sinew Sewn, Teepee Design, Multicolor, Child's, c.1900, 14 ½ x 14 In.	2006
Vest, Lakota, Hide, Cloth, Horse Road, Beaded On Back, c.1885, 21 x 18 In. ....*illus*	2091
War Bonnet, Blackfoot, Feathers, Canvas Cap, Beaded Band, c.1890, 16 In. High ....*illus*	3300
War Shirt, Leggings, Sioux, Presented To Dr. Sebring, Deer Hide, Buffalo Tendon, 1949	12540
War Shirt, Plateau, Hide, Beaded, Wrapped Ermine Tails, Fringe, c.1920, Man's, 25 x 46 In.	1845
Weaving, Navajo, Chief's Design, Stripes, Diamond Shapes, c.1900, 5 x 6 Ft.	2223
Weaving, Navajo, Chief's Style, 3rd Phase Design, Yarn, Red, Black, White, 62 x 52 In.	2880
Weaving, Navajo, Yei, Woven, Ella Thomas, c.1950, 59 x 35 In.	369
Wedding Hat, Wasco-Wishram, Beaded, Blue Cloth, Multicolor, Rawhide, c.1890, 14 In.	2829
Whimsy, Iroquois, Boot Shape, Beadwork, c.1900, 11 x 9 In. ....*illus*	81

INDIAN TREE is a china pattern that was popular during the last half of the nineteenth century. It was copied from earlier Indian textile patterns that were very similar. The pattern includes the crooked branch of a tree and a partial landscape with exotic flowers and leaves. Green, blue, pink, and orange were the favored colors used in the design. Coalport, Spode, Johnson Brothers, and other firms made this pottery.

Bowl, Cereal, Coalport, 6 In.	18
Bowl, Cereal, Johnson Brothers, 6 In.	14
Bowl, Vegetable, Oval, Coalport, 8 In.	99
Bowl, Vegetable, Oval, Minton, 9 In.	145
Bowl, Vegetable, Oval, Spode, 10 In.	118
Bowl, Vegetable, Round, Aynsley, 8 In.	35
Butter Chip, Spode, 3 ½ In.	32
Creamer, Johnson Brothers, 3 ¼ In.	26
Creamer, Spode, 3 ¼ In.	50
Cup & Saucer, Demitasse, Spode	30
Cup & Saucer, Footed, Aynsley	14
Cup & Saucer, Footed, Coalport	28
Cup & Saucer, Footed, Spode	45
Cup & Saucer, Johnson Brothers	18
Cup & Saucer, Minton	37
Eggcup, Spode, 2 ¼ In.	46
Gravy Boat, Coalport	115
Gravy Boat, Underplate, Spode	223
Mug, Spode, 3 ¼ In.	114
Pitcher, Coalport, 16 Oz., 5 ¼ In.	123
Pitcher, Johnson Brothers, 32 Oz.	74
Plate, Bread & Butter, Minton, 5 ¾ In.	32
Plate, Bread & Butter, Salem, 6 ½ In.	9
Plate, Bread & Butter, Spode, 6 In.	16
Plate, Dinner, Coalport, 10 ⅝ In.	53

I

Plate, Dinner, Johnson Brothers, 10 ⅜ In.	38
Plate, Dinner, Minton, 9 ¾ In.	77
Plate, Salad, Aynsley, 8 In.	11
Plate, Salad, Coalport, 7 ⅞ In.	13
Platter, Oval, Coalport, 11 In.	66
Platter, Oval, Minton, 15 In.	217
Platter, Oval, Spode, 14 In.	176
Soup, Dish, Salem, 8 ⅜ In.	8
Soup, Dish, Spode, 9 ⅜ In.	43
Teapot, Lid, Coalport, 4 Cup, 5 ⅛ In.	318
Tureen, Lid, Indian Tree Pattern, Shaped Foot, Open Tab Handles, Johnson Bros., 10 In.	58

INKSTANDS were made to be placed on a desk. They held some type of container for ink, and possibly a sander, a pen tray, a pen, a holder for pounce, and even a candle to melt the sealing wax. Inkstands date to the eighteenth century and have been made of silver, copper, ceramics, and glass. Additional inkstands may be found in these and other related categories.

Bergman, Bedouin, On Camel, Ancient Ruins, Bronze, Enameled, Cold Paint, 8 ¾ In.	2100
Brass, 2 Figural Sphinx, Square Well, Hinged Lid, Roman Designs, Oval Tray, Footed, 9 In.	161
Brass, Standish, Tripartite Stand, 3 Canisters, Servant's Bell, 7 x 7 In.	492
Bronze, Louis XVI Style, Crossed Arrow, Quiver, Torch, Garland Swag, 4 x 12 In.	430
Bronze, Marble, Boy Lounging In Chair, Serpentine Base, 2 Pots, 1880, 15 ¾ x 21 In.	2091
Gilt Bronze, Mirrored Base, Cut Glass Pots, France, c.1900, 7 ½ x 12 ½ In.	307
Majolica, 3 Wells, Lion Mask, Painted Leaved, Triangular, Italy, 5 ½ In.	660
Oak, Victorian, Glass Wells, Footed, Arch Handle, c.1885, 7 x 14 In.	180
Redware, Stepped, Incised Bird, Flowers, Presentation, D. Wardell's, 1831, 5 x 4 In. ....*illus*	2530
Silver, Jade Birds, Ivory Pulls, Drawer, 2 Glass Wells, J.E. Caldwell & Co., 5 x 9 In.	1250

INKWELLS, of course, held ink. Ready-made ink was first made about 1836 and was sold in bottles. The desk inkwell had a narrow hole so the pen would not slip inside. Inkwells were made of many materials, such as pottery, glass, pewter, and silver. Look in these categories for more listings of inkwells.

Black Man's Head, Red Cap, Wood, Carved, Glass Eyes, c.1980	360
Blue Opaline Glass, Silver Flip Top, 2 ¾ In.	59
Brass, Pen Tray, Art Nouveau, Hinged Top, 3 ¼ x 8 x 5 ¾ In. ....*illus*	47
Bronze, Art Nouveau, Pen Tray, Woman's Face, Flowing Hair, Glass Insert, 10 In. ....*illus*	259
Bronze, Camel, Kneeling, 6 ⅗ In.	840
Bronze, Dude Figure, Glass Insert, Marked, 19th Century, 9 ½ In., Diam.	437
Bronze, Figural, Girl, Dog On Leash, Chasing A Duck, c.1890, 5 x 7 In.	316
Bronze, Horse Head, 5 In.	207
Bronze, Lily Pad Shape, Bulbous Inkwell, Dolphin Handles, c.1900, 5 x 9 x 7 In.	100
Bronze, Relief Heads, Garland, Onyx Block Feet, c.1875, 5 x 13 In.	200
Bust, Queen Victoria, Silver Plated, Hinged Crown, Square Base, Holder, c.1897, 7 x 6 In.	354
Cut Glass, Silver Lid, Cube, Wood Base, Odessa, Russia, c.1910, 5 ½ In.	3000
Dore Bronze, Champleve Enamel, Marble, Hinged Lid, 3-Footed, Bell Shape, c.1915, 3 x 4 In.	127
Gilt Bronze Wells, Napoleon III, Trim, Marble Base, 11 x 7 ⅜ In.	650
Glass Millefiori Base, Stopper, White Friars, c.1820, 5 ½ x 3 ½ In.	252
Glass, Cloisonne, Silver, Square Twist, Spiral Cap, Blue, White, A. Kuzmichiev, c.1875, 5 In.	4063
Glass, Cobalt Blue, Lid, Diamond Shape, 19th Century, 1 ¾ In.	85
Glass, Iridescent Green, Engraved, Hinged Bronze Lid, Austria, c.1900, 4 ¾ x 4 ¾ In.	230
Glass, Iridescent, Brass Lid, Pallme Konig, 2 ¼ x 5 In.	219
Iron, Regimental, Ulan Helmet, 4 In.	168
Metal, Figural, Indian Head, Chief, Painted, Glass Inside, 4 x 3 ¾ In. ....*illus*	661
Metal, Gold Wash, Woman In Boat, Rowing, 1915, 9 ½ In.	330
Metal, Man's Shoe Shape, Hinged Lid, Lace Up, 2 ¼ x 4 ½ In.	58
Mixed Metal, Figural, American Indian, Holding Spear Cold Painted, Full Body	94
Onyx, Ormolu, Square, Gilt Scrolling Leaves, Top Shape Feet, 4 Pen Rests, 1800s, 9 In.	240
Pewter, Round, Molded Rim, 5 Quill Holes, Center Receptacle Holder, 1800s, 3 ½ In.	12
Pottery, Figural, Grandmother & Child, Alphabet Book, Staffordshire Style, 5 ¼ In.	81
Rosewood, 2 Parts, Painted, Gilt Stenciled Eagles, Banners, S. Sillman & Co., 3 ½ x 5 In.	438
Silver, Cylindrical, Sand Dollar Shape Lid, Hammered, Over Copper, Roycroft, 3 x 3 In.	52
Silver, Figural, Cobra, Ruby Eyes, Glass Interior, Onyx, Inscribed, 1869, 7 ¼ In. ....*illus*	3000
Silver, Figural, Dolphins, Repousse, Relief Work, Footed, 8 x 13 x 9 ½ In.	2530
Staffordshire, Bird, 2 Chicks, Snake, Mother Bird, Multicolor Coleslaw Finish, 2 ¾ In.	71
Standish Pewter, Lid, Drawer, Fitted Interior, England, c.1790, 2 ½ x 7 In.	325
Stoneware, Raised Horizontal Bands, Coggled Decoration, R.L. Lasher, 2 ⅝ x 6 In.	633
Stopper, Base Concentric Millefiori, White Friars, 1948, 6 In.	144

Inkstand, Redware, Stepped, Incised Bird, Flowers, Presentation, D. Wardell's, 1831, 5 x 4 In.
$2,530

Crocker Farm, Inc.

Inkwell, Brass, Pen Tray, Art Nouveau, Hinged Top, 3 ¼ x 8 x 5 ¾ In.
$47

Conestoga Auction Co., Inc.

Inkwell, Bronze, Art Nouveau, Pen Tray, Woman's Face, Flowing Hair, Glass Insert, 10 In.
$259

Early Auction Co.

Inkwell, Metal, Figural, Indian Head, Chief, Painted, Glass Inside, 4 x 3 ¾ In.
$661

Wm Morford Auctions

Inkwell, Silver, Figural, Cobra, Ruby Eyes, Glass Interior, Onyx, Inscribed, 1869, 7 ¼ In.
$3,000

Rago Arts & Auction Center

Insulator, Patent, Willington Glass Works, Mold Blown, 8-Sided, Olive Green, 5 ½ In.
$644

Norman C. Heckler & Company

Iron, Aquarium, Wrought, Green Glass Bowl, c.1910, 60 In.
$805

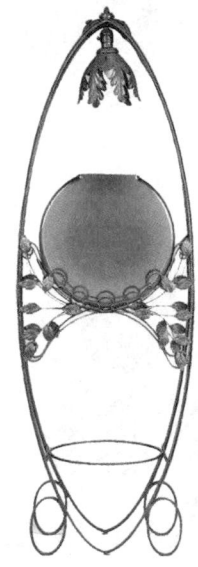

Cottone Auctions

Wood, Furry Dog Shape, Carved, Hinged Head, Glass Inset, Log, c.1900, 4 In.	960
Wood, Seal Head, Carved, Glass Eyes, Smoking Cigar, 4 x 3 In.	127

INSULATORS of glass or pottery have been made for use on telegraph or telephone poles since 1844. Thousands of styles of insulators have been made. Most common are those of clear or aqua glass; most desirable are the threadless types made from 1850 to 1870.

Am. Tel. & Tel. Co., Amethyst	67
Am. Tel. & Tel. Co., Green, Embossed, 3 ¾ In.	39
B.G.M. Co., Amethyst, Baltimore Glass Co.	39
Brookfield, Dark Aqua	134
Brookfield, Light Aqua, Embossing	3
Brookfield, Light Aqua, Wire Groove	5
Canadian North West Telegraph Co., Pale Aqua Green	15
Canadian Pacific Railway, Porcelain, Dome, Pittsburgh High Voltage Insulator Co., 4 In.	29
Canadian Pacific RY Co., Dark Royal Purple	112
Ceramic, Mottled Brown, Double Skirt Haystack, 4 ⅛ In.	20
CEW, Aqua Blue, c.1880	90
Diamond, No. 1, Dark Yellow Green	9
Diamond, No. 6, Dark Yellow Green	10
E.C. & M. Co. S.F., Bright Aqua, H, Old, 4 ¼ In.	246
E.C. & M. Co. S.F., Cobalt Blue, Rounded Dome, Flared Skirt, c.1875, 4 ⅜ In.	1792
Hemingray, Aqua, Double Groove, c.1915, 3 ¾ In.	49
Hemingray, Blue, Mouse Ears	43
Hemingray, No. 9, Patent May 2, 1893, Streaked Amethyst	146
Hemingray, No. 16, Dark Olive, Amber Tones, Toll Style	28
Hemingray, No. 19, Olive Green	100
Lapp Co., LeRoy, N.Y., Porcelain, Brown, Glossy, 1929, 3 ¾ In.	12
Lapp, Pottery, Mottled Pumpkin Brown, Split Ear Top, 1930, 3 ¾ In.	25
Maydwell, Milk Glass, Open Bubble On Dome	10
McLaughlin, No. 16, Yellow Green	34
Patent, Willington Glass Works, Mold Blown, 8-Sided, Olive Green, 5 ½ In. *illus*	644
Pyrex, Clear, Single Skirt, Metal Sleeve Lining, 4 In.	15
Star, Blob Top, Light Yellow Green	50
Threadless, Porcelain, Egg Shape, Parr's Pottery	336
U.P.R.R., Dark Blue, Threadless, Mulford & Biddle	1008
VTS Industrial Co., Number 8, Ruby Red, c.1970	101
W. Brookfield, Aqua To Clear, Embossed, Cauvet's Pat., 1870s	45
W. Brookfield, N.Y., Light Gray, Pony Style	90
W. Brookfield, N.Y., Pat. April 28, 1885, Aqua	700
Whitall, Aqua, Crackle Glass, Telegraph, 4 In.	30

IRISH BELLEEK, *see Belleek category.*

IRON is a metal that has been used by man since prehistoric times. It is a popular metal for tools and decorative items like doorstops that need as much weight as possible. Items are listed here or under other appropriate headings, such as Bookends, Doorstop, Kitchen, Match Holder, or Tool. The tool that is used for ironing clothes, an iron, is listed in the Kitchen category under Iron and Sadiron.

Aquarium, Wrought, Green Glass Bowl, c.1910, 60 In. *illus*	805
Bathtub, Claw Foot, Painted Sides, 15 x 22 In.	533
Birdhouse, Gabled House With 2 Porches, Green Paint, 1868, 11 ½ x 15 In.	2607
Book Press, Signed Mon Cabany Fend, c.1925, 12 x 14 In.	304
Boot Scraper, 2 Horses, Flanking Brushes, Black Paint, c.1920, 14 x 20 In.	547
Boot Scraper, Cat, Prancing, 9 x 9 ½ In.	35
Boot Scraper, Cat, Upswept Tail, Blue Paint, c.1900, 9 ¾ x 15 In. *illus*	1540
Boot Scraper, Cocker Spaniel Ends, 16 x 7 In.	144
Boot Scraper, Curlicue, Ends, 1870, 12 ½ x 12 ½ In.	210
Boot Scraper, Curved Leaf Shape, Iron Base, 18 x 9 ½ In.	70
Boot Scraper, Duck, Black Paint, 14 ½ x 5 ½ In.	316
Boot Scraper, Forged, Ram's-Horn Scrolled Sides, Granite Block, c.1800, 16 x 16 In. *illus*	270
Boot Scraper, Limestone Block, Lyre Shape, Tennessee, c.1840, 11 x 16 In.	288
Boot Scraper, Lyre Shape, Scrolls, Leaves, White Paint, c.1855, 8 x 7 In.	69
Boot Scraper, Rococo Revival, Lyre Shape, Stone Block, Openwork, c.1850, 10 ½ In.	118
Boot Scraper, Squirrel On Wood, Eating Nut, 7 x 8 In.	1062
Bootjack, Naughty Nellie, Painted, 10 ½ In.	35
Box, Clown Head, Hat Lid, Paint, 5 ¾ In.	122

Casket, Intertwining Fleurs-De-Lis, Hinged Lid, Claw Feet, Wrought, 1900, 6 x 11 In.		369
Eagle, Closed Wings, c.1850, 7 In.		161
Eagle, Gold Paint, Cast Iron, 5 ¾ x 10 ½ In., Pair		266
Eagle, Spread Wings, c.1850, 15 x 7 In.		115
Eagle, Spread Wings, Cast, 1900s, 31 x 10 In.	*illus*	259
Elevator Floor Indicator, Beaded Triangles, Numbers 1 Through 5, Samuel Yellin, 22 In.		660
Figure, Horse, Standing, Brown Paint, Black Mane & Tail, White Blaze, c.1900, 6 ½ x 7 In.		270
Figure, Mermaid, Seated, Hands Behind Head, 15 ½ In., Pair		553
Figure, Pig, Standing, Articulated Features, c.1900, 8 ½ x 16 ½ In.		767
Fish Gig, Fishing, Forged, 7 Tines, Shaping, 12 ¾ In.		47
Floor Safe, Gothic Revival, Ebonized, Stenciled, Door, 3 Combination Dials, 51 x 24 In.		1107
Forge Blower, Tscheulins, Baltimore, 65 ¼ In.		395
Hall Tree, Art Deco, Scroll & Leaf Openwork, Glass Shelf, Mirror, c.1925, 70 x 22 In.		840
Handcuffs, 10 In., Pair		900
Hasp, Trefoil Spade Terminal, Pa., c.1800, 17 In.		1422
Hasp, Tulip Terminal, Pa, c.1800, 14 In.		1541
Hook, Stylized Wreath, Finial Over Hook, 1800s, 7 x 11 In.		127
Horse Hitch, 5-Point Star Shape, Horse's Head In Horseshoe, Attached Ring, 9 In.		70
Jardiniere, Paneled Fence Shape, Strapwork, Shaped Feet, Finials, 1800s, 16 x 12 In., Pair		984
Letter Opener, Bradley & Hubbard, 9 In.		115
Lock Box, Stagecoach, c.1890, 6 ½ x 13 In.		182
Mailbox, Figural, Cast Iron, Griswold No. 3.		75
Meat Rack Marquee, Buffalo Bill, Painted Gold, 13 x 12 In.		285
Plaque, Man, Cooking Pig, Wagon, Cottage, Embossed Sheets, c.1890, 29 In., Pair		600
Rack, Wall, 4 Hearts, 4 Hooks, Arched, 11 ½ In.		201
Running Horse, Black, Red & White Paint, Stand, Folk Art, 28 x 51 In.		295
Safe, Combination Lock, Copper Flash, Ideal Security, 3 x 4 x 5 In.	*illus*	201
Safe, Lighthouse Design, G.A. Barrable, 11 x 16 ½ x 14 In.		257
Safe, Painted Flowers, Key Lock, Geo. Zech, York, Pa., Salesman's Sample, c.1907, 8 In.		4200
Safe, Painted Lattice, Flowers, Hummingbird, Combination Lock, 4-Footed, 1867, 12 x 9 In.		413
Safe, Rectangular, Roller Feet, Paint Design, Combination Lock, c.1890, 32 x 21 In.		1410
Safe, Ship Scene, E.K. Talcott, Combination & Key, 23 x 34 In.	*illus*	200
Sculpture, Dog, German Sheppard, Seated, Rectangular Base, Victorian, c.1885, 22 x 14 In.		1107
Sculpture, Dog, Seated, Snipe, Collar At Feet, Rounded Base, 37 x 37 In., Pair		2952
Sculpture, Horseback Rider, Wood Base, Caballero Arnau, Barcelona, 1967, 21 x 25 In.		375
Sculpture, Lion, Seated, Gold Paint, Victorian, Back Support, England, 13 x 26 In.		590
Sculpture, Pig, Standing, Pink, Black Paint, 19 In.		92
Sculpture, Wart Hog, Iron Chain Links, Wrought, Signed Fred Jones 1968, 13 In.		236
Shoeshine Stand, Camel Shape, 7 ½ In.		80
Shoeshine Stand, Smith's Ottoman, Excelsior Blacking, 8-Sided, Cloth Cover, 1889, 11 In.		308
Sign, No Parking, Paint, 50 In.		207
Spurs, Iron, 8 ½ In., Pair		120
State Seal, New York, Round Medallion, Latin Motto, 1664, Stand, 18 In.		330
Stringholder, High Button Shoe Shape, Black, White, Iron, 10 In.		180
Stringholder, Pilgrim Boy, Judd Co., 8 ¼ In.		72
Stringholder, Woman At Mirror, Yellow Flowered Gown, Blond Hair, Judd Co., No. 1463, 8 In.		177
Table, Pub, Mahogany, Bacchus Masks, Painted, Stretcher Shelf, 1800s, 27 x 21 In.	*illus*	478
Tieback, Flower Bouquet, Multicolor, Waverly Studios, 3 ¾ In., 8 Piece		207
Tree Marker, Fruit Tree, Oval, Paint, Cast Iron, 10 ¾ In.		90
Trivet, Dated 1846, Punched Monogram, 3-Boot Feet, Pa., 10 ¾ In.		1896
Umbrella Stand, Edwardian, Seated Dog, Dog-Headed Canes, c.1900, 24 In.		307
Umbrella Stand, Man, Standing Over Begging Dog, Red Coat, Black Helmet, 26 x 18 In.		563
Umbrella Stand, Man, Top Hat, Standing, Holding Shillelagh, Ireland, c.1865, 29 x 16 In.		2091
Utensil Holder, Ship In Full Mast, Enameled, 13 ½ In.		84
Valet, Enameled, Stitched Leather, Tapered, Stretcher Base, Jacques Adnet, 1960s, 45 x 19 In.		2500
Vase, Lid, Footed, Hanging Ring Handles, Finial, Carved, Chinese, 9 x 8 In.		3600
Washboard, Embossed Moon, Stars, c.1890, 22 In.		125
Water Sprinkler, Figural, Frog, c.1900, 8 ¾ In.		237
Windmill Weight, Bull, Fairbury, Nebraska, c.1900, 18 x 25 In.		425
Windmill Weight, Crescent Moon, Fairbanks & Morse, c.1900, 10 ½ In.		152
Windmill Weight, Eclipse, 12 In.		115
Windmill Weight, Horse, Blue Paint, 17 ½ x 16 ½ In.		345
Windmill Weight, Horse, Bobtail, Dempster, c.1900, 16 ½ x 17 In.		356
Windmill Weight, Horse, Dempster Mill Manufacturing, c.1900, 16 ½ x 17 In.		415
Windmill Weight, Horse, Long Tail, Dempster, c.1900, 18 ½ x 18 In.		2133
Windmill Weight, Horse, Standing, White Paint, 16 ½ x 18 In.		480
Windmill Weight, Rooster, Elgin Woodmanse, c.1900, 15 ¾ x 16 ¾ In.		948

Iron, Boot Scraper, Cat, Upswept Tail, Blue Paint, c.1900, 9 ¾ x 15 In.
$1,540

James D. Julia Auctioneers

Iron, Boot Scraper, Forged, Ram's-Horn Scrolled Sides, Granite Block, c.1800, 16 x 16 In.
$270

Cowan's Auctions

Iron, Eagle, Spread Wings, Cast, 1900s, 31 x 10 In.
$259

Victorian Casino Antiques

Iron, Safe, Combination Lock, Copper Flash, Ideal Security, 3 x 4 x 5 In.
$201

Victorian Casino Antiques

This is an edited listing of current prices. Visit Kovels.com to check thousands of prices from previous years and sign up for free information on trends, tips, reproductions, marks, and more.

Iron, Safe, Ship Scene, E.K. Talcott, Combination & Key, 23 x 34 In. $200

Showtime Auction Services

Iron, Table, Pub, Mahogany, Bacchus Masks, Painted, Stretcher Shelf, 1800s, 27 x 21 In. $478

Neal Auction Co.

Iron, Windmill Weight, Squirrel, Sitting Up, 13 ½ x 17 x 13 In. $2,850

Showtime Auction Services

Windmill Weight, Rooster, Figural, Paint, Square Base, U.S.A., c.1900, 22 x 20 In.		2596
Windmill Weight, Rooster, Painted, Elgin, c.1900, 16 x 16 In.		805
Windmill Weight, Rooster, Painted, Embossed Hummer, c.1900, 17 ½ x 17 In.		1067
Windmill Weight, Rooster, Rainbow Tail, Elgin Power & Pump Co., c.1910, 18 In.		1998
Windmill Weight, Squirrel, Elgin, c.1900, 14 ¾ In.		889
Windmill Weight, Squirrel, Sitting Up, 13 ½ x 17 x 13 In.	*illus*	2850
Windmill Weight, Star, c.1900, 15 x 15 In.		889

IRONSTONE china was first made in 1813. It gained its greatest popularity during the mid-nineteenth century. The heavy, durable, off-white pottery was made in white or was decorated with any of hundreds of patterns. Much flow blue pottery was made of ironstone. Some of the decorations were raised. Many pieces of ironstone are unmarked, but some English and American factories included the word *Ironstone* in their marks. Additional pieces may be listed in other categories, such as Chelsea Grape, Chelsea Sprig, Flow Blue, Gaudy Ironstone, Mason's Ironstone, Moss Rose, Staffordshire, and Tea Leaf Ironstone.

Barrel, Rum, Green, White, Spigot, England, 13 In.		360
Bowl, Vegetable, Lid, Wheat & Cable, White, Elsmore & Forster, Ceres Shape, 7 In.		94
Coffeepot, Mulberry Brush Stroke, Strawberry, Paneled, 9 ½ In.		212
Coffeepot, Prairie Shape, White, 4 Inverted Arched Panels, Embossed Poppies, Wheat, 10 In.		59
Coffeepot, Purple Holly, Cut Sponge, Turnip Finial, Bulbous Body, C-Scroll Handle, 9 In.		35
Coffeepot, Wheat & Cable, Elsmore & Forster, 10 In.	*illus*	83
Creamer, Laurel Wreath, George Washington, Black Transfer, 6 ¼ In.	*illus*	165
Ewer, Tea Leaf With Berry, Copper Luster, England, c.1892, 11 ½ In.		173
Footbath, White, Scrolled Handles, c.1890, 19 In.		594
Pitcher, Basin, Grosvenor Pattern, c.1860, 9 x 5 ½ In., 2 Piece		161
Pitcher, Basin, Wide Spout, Loop Handle, Flowers, c.1890, 10 x 16 In.		150
Pitcher, Red & Blue Flowers, Vines, Trees, Octagonal, 10 In.		85
Pitcher, Serpent Handle, Red, Blue Flowers, White Ground, England, 8 ½ In.		57
Pitcher, Water, Laurel Wreath, White, Elsmore & Forster, 10 In.		201
Pitcher, White, Col. Elmer Ellsworth Shooting, Civil War Commemorative, 8 In.		533
Plate, Blue Spatter, Rose, Paneled, Red, Green, 8 ½ In.		94
Plate, Camellia, Vermilion Flowers, Cut Sponge, 9 ¼ In.	*illus*	83
Plate, Laurel Wreath, Elsmore & Forster, 6 ¾ In., 6 Piece		47
Plate, Ship, The Huguenot, Wavy Gilt Rim, Handles, 9 ¼ In.		330
Plate, Soup, Cut Sponge, Red Flower Border, Blue, Brown Flowers, Leaves, 11 In., 2 Piece		71
Platter Set, Camellia, Cut Sponge, Red Flowers, Green Leaves, 12 ¼ x 13 ½ In., 3 Piece		472
Platter, Lacaonia, Blue Transfer, Barker & Till, 16 In.	*illus*	47
Platter, Mulberry Brush Stroke, Tulip & Fern, Octagonal, 13 ¼ In.		106
Tureen, Soup, Lid, Ladle, Gilt, Scroll Handles, Pedestal Foot, c.1815, 11 ½ x 14 In.		649

ISPANKY figurines were designed by Laszlo Ispanky, who began his American career as a designer for Cybis Porcelains. In 1966, he established his own studio in Pennington, New Jersey; since 1976, he has worked for Goebel of North America. He works in stone, wood, or metal, as well as porcelain. The first limited edition figurines were issued in 1966.

Figurine, Amazon, Nude Woman Fighter, Arms Over Pole, Bronze, Signed, c.1970, 29 x 27 In.		938
Figurine, Ballerina, Green Dress With Flowers, Raised Arms, 15 In.		375
Figurine, Boy, Wearing Coveralls, Painting, 10 In.		250
Figurine, Girl, Holding Hat & Basket, 9 In.		250
Figurine, Girl, In Recliner, Flowers, 8 In.		150
Figurine, Girl, On Stool, Draped Cloth, 11 In.		575
Figurine, Guinevere, Blond, Braided Hair, c.1969, 11 ½ In.		1250
Figurine, Moses, Holding 10 Commandments, Raised Arm, 12 ½ In.		895
Figurine, Nude With Child, 10 ¼ In.		300
Figurine, Owl, Brown, On Branch, Ladybug, c.1960, 9 ¼ In.		75
Figurine, Young Girl, Seated On Tree Stump, Wrapped Arms, 12 In.		295
Sculpture, Bronze, Nadia, Nude, Balancing On Log Base, 1980, Signed, 20 x 12 In.		594
Vase, Seminude, Flower Panels, Square, 1950s, 11 In.		200

IVORY from the tusk of an elephant is thought by many to be the only true ivory. To most collectors, the term *ivory* also includes such natural materials as walrus, hippopotamus, or whale teeth or tusks, and some of the vegetable materials that are of similar texture and density. Other ivory items may be found in the Scrimshaw and Netsuke categories. Collectors should be aware of the recent laws limiting the buying and selling of elephant ivory and scrimshaw.

Ball, Cue, Engraved Globe, Ships, Mermaids, Whales, Elephant Ivory, c.1910, 2 ¼ In.		1003
Blotter, Ink, Elephant, Whale Ivory, 3 x 5 ½ In.		200

Ironstone, Coffeepot, Wheat & Cable, Elsmore & Forster, 10 In.
$83

Ironstone, Creamer, Laurel Wreath, George Washington, Black Transfer, 6 ¼ In.
$165

Ironstone, Plate, Camellia, Vermilion Flowers, Cut Sponge, 9 ¼ In.
$83

Ironstone, Platter, Lacaonia, Blue Transfer, Barker & Till, 16 In.
$47

Ivory, Box, Quillwork, Pincushion, Mirror, Compartments, Anglo-Indian, 1831, 8 In.
$7,200

Ivory, Figurine, Dragons, Clouds, Birds, Flowers, Wood Stand, Chinese, 1800s, 11 ⅝ In.
$7,200

Ivory, Figurine, Man, Wooden Leg, Cane, Continental, 1800s, 6 In.
$688

Ivory, Figurine, Rat Catcher, Japanese, 1800s, 2 x 1 ½ In.
$1,045

Ivory, Figurine, Sennin, Immortal Person, On Horse, Incised, Japan, c.1900, 8 ⅜ In.
$540

Ivory, Figurine, Virgin Of The Immaculate Conception, 1700, 7 ½ x 2 ¼ In.
$2,091

Ivory, Group, Hoi Tei, Children, Signed Tamakazu, Japan, 1800s, 5 ½ In.
$830

James D. Julia Auctioneers

Ivory, Tusk, Carved, 8 Chinese Figures, Cranes, Pine Trees, Wood Stand, Chinese, 20 ½ In.
$554

Skinner Auctioneers & Appraisers

Ivory, Tusk, Narwhal, Mounted, Burl Stand, 59 In.
$10,935

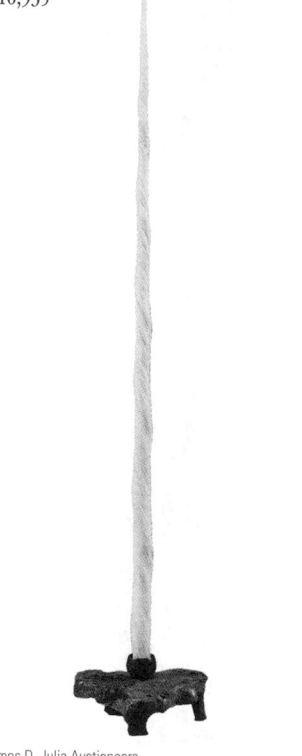

James D. Julia Auctioneers

Box, Carved, Chinese Scenes, Rectangular, Flip Lid, 3 ¼ x 8 ½ In.	3627
Box, Jewelry, Fruitwood Marquetry, Footed, Leaves, Duvinage, France, c.1875, 4 x 8 In.	6600
Box, Quillwork, Pincushion, Mirror, Compartments, Anglo-Indian, 1831, 8 In. ......*illus*	7200
Brushpot, Landscape Carved, Rectangular, Chinese, 1800s, 5 In.	5400
Bust, African Woman, Hood, Necklace, c.1952, 7 ⅞ In.	258
Bust, Child, Carved Flowers In Hair, Square Marble Base, 8 ⅛ In.	338
Candlestick, Carved, Turned & Reeded, 4 In., Pair	60
Cane, Walking Stick, Ivory, Dragon, Open Mouth, Scaled Neck, 1800s, 8 ½ In.	1244
Carving, Woman, Standing, Holding Flower, Carved Wood Base, Japan, c.1900, 10 In.	590
Censer, Lid, Pedestal, Oval, Openwork, Flowers, Leaves, Handles, 1800s, 7 x 8 ½ In., Pair	7200
Centerpiece, Elephant, Crystal Ball On Back, Draped, Hematite, Glass, c.1890, 5 x 4 In.	3198
Figurine, Adam & Eve, Carved, Netherlands, 1700s, 3 In.	120
Figurine, Apsara, Celestial Woman, In Flight, Bottle, Elixer, Bangles, Beads, 1900s, 14 In.	1920
Figurine, Ballet Dancer, Acrobatic Pose, Outstretched Arms, On Point, 8 In.	2640
Figurine, Buddhist Goddess, Jeweled Robe, Holding Flaming Pearl, 11 In.	738
Figurine, Cabbage, Grasshopper On Leaf, Light Green Stain, Chinese, 7 In.	1920
Figurine, Cabbage, Grasshopper, Perched Insect, Blossom, Chinese, c.1900, 9 ¼ In.	960
Figurine, Child, Reclining, Multicolor Robe, Chinese, 2 In.	120
Figurine, Dragon, Coiled, Carved, Round Geometric Design Base, Signed, 2 In.	120
Figurine, Dragons, Clouds, Birds, Flowers, Wood Stand, Chinese, 1800s, 11 ⅝ In. ......*illus*	7200
Figurine, Elephant, Walking, Trunk Down, Incised Details, Chinese, 5 ½ x 6 ¾ In.	277
Figurine, Elephant, Walking, Trunk Up, Incised, 9 In.	338
Figurine, Father, Carrying 2 Children, Signed, Asian, c.1800s, 9 ½ x 4 x 3 In.	1875
Figurine, Fisherman, Standing, Holding Spear & Fish, Long Robes, Signed, c.1950, 13 In.	480
Figurine, Fortune Teller, Lantern, Shelves, Round Base, Signed, Chikakumi, c.1900, 7 ½ In.	875
Figurine, Geisha, Standing, Holding Lantern, Round Base, 4 In.	90
Figurine, Girl, Holding Shovel, Broom Over Shoulder, 5 ½ In.	984
Figurine, Guanyin, Clouds, Chinese, 8 In.	480
Figurine, Guanyin, Praying Hands, Seated, Lotus Flower Base, Chinese, 4 In.	150
Figurine, Guanyin, Standing, Lotus Pedestal, Robe, Hair Up, Holding Bottle, 1900s, 12 In.	2040
Figurine, Imperial Couple, On Throne, 3-Panel Screen, Openwork Dragons, 16 In., Pair	2091
Figurine, Jesus, On Donkey, Palm Sunday, Continental, 18th Century, 14 ½ In.	5937
Figurine, Knight, Horseback, Sword, Wood Base, 1800s, 3 ⅝ In.	240
Figurine, Longboat, Figures Rowing, Fishing, Wave Stand, China, 13 In.	1440
Figurine, Madonna, Halo, Standing, Praying Hands, Germany, c.1920, 8 In.	330
Figurine, Maiden, Standing, Seminude, Holding Shell, Round Base, 1800s, 8 ⅝ In.	1169
Figurine, Maitreya, Multi Armed, Seated, Lotus Throne, Crown, Chinese, 1800s, 8 x 5 In.	2706
Figurine, Man, Holding Fan, Long Robe, Beard, Headpiece, Chinese, 3 ¾ In.	180
Figurine, Man, Standing, Long Robe, Hands Behind Back, Round Base, Japan, Signed, 6 In.	180
Figurine, Man, Woman, 1800 Period Attire, Round Socle, c.1900, 6 In., Pair	269
Figurine, Man, Wooden Leg, Cane, Continental, 1800s, 6 In. ......*illus*	688
Figurine, Monk, Holding Staff & Rosary, Brown & White Stain, 7 ¼ In.	570
Figurine, Okimono, Basket Weaver, Sitting On 1 Leg, Japan, c.1890, 2 ½ In.	461
Figurine, Openwork Sphere, Elephant Supports, Tiered, Round Base, 6 ½ In.	270
Figurine, Pied Piper, Black Marble Plinth, 10 ½ In.	1000
Figurine, Rat Catcher, Japanese, 1800s, 2 x 1 ½ In. ......*illus*	1045
Figurine, Samurai, Holding Arrow, Bow On Back, Incised Flowers, Brown Stain, 7 ¼ In.	1020
Figurine, Scholar, Standing, Holding Scroll, Long Robes, Signed, 5 In.	351
Figurine, Scholar, Standing, Sword, Carved Robe, Footed Round Stand, 1900s, 12 In.	472
Figurine, Sennin, Immortal Person, On Horse, Incised, Japan, c.1900, 8 ⅜ In. ......*illus*	540
Figurine, Ship On Sea, Morphs Into Chicken, 7 Applied Figures, Waves, Fish, 10 In.	461
Figurine, Street Vendor, Man Carrying Pots, Brooms, Drums, Masks, 8 ½ In.	787
Figurine, Sumo Wrestlers, Carved, Signed Ishi Kawa, Japan, c.1890, 4 In.	940
Figurine, Virgin Of The Immaculate Conception, 1700, 7 ½ x 2 ¼ In. ......*illus*	2091
Figurine, Warrior, General, Armor, Sword, Hat, Carved Lotus, Pedestal, c.1900, 10 In.	584
Figurine, Warrior, Holding Sword, Chinese, 2 ½ In.	72
Figurine, Warrior, Standing, Headdress, Helmet, Armor, Ring Tassel, Stand, c.1900, 9 In.	359
Figurine, Woman, Holding Flowers, Long Robes, Hat, Wood Stand, 9 ½ In.	450
Figurine, Woman, Seated At Game Table, Hanging Lantern, Chinese, c.1910, 10 In.	353
Figurine, Woman, Standing, Holding Plum Blossom Branch, Black Stained Hair, 9 In.	720
Figurine, Woman, Standing, Holding Staff, Kimono, Wood Stand, Chinese, 10 In., Pair	900
Frame, Carved, Songbirds, Easel Back, Signed, Asia, c.1900, 5 In., Pair	844
Globe, World Map, Hinged At Equator, Opens To Sundial, Brass Gnomon, Socle Base, 3 In.	840
Group, Goddess, On Foo Dog, Surrounding Attendants, Chinese, c.1910, 10 In.	588
Group, Hoi Tei, Children, Signed Tamakazu, Japan, 1800s, 5 ½ In. ......*illus*	830
Incense Burner, Carved, Out Scrolled Handles, Openwork, Rings, Footed, 12 x 12 In.	1500

I

PRICE IT RIGHT

How to Set Prices to Sell Your Things

"My mother-in-law died and left us with around 125 Hummels, including some made for military personnel only, all sizes, and 100-125 collector plates, most from the 1970s and '80s."

"I need to sell numerous items as part of a divorce situation."

"I'm downsizing and I don't know how set prices on my furnishings and collections."

Kovels' Antiques & Collectibles Price Guide 2015 lists prices of antiques and collectibles sold this year—more prices than in any other book. But thousands of other antiques are not listed and need to be priced. Even an exact duplicate may not sell for the same price at two different sales. Price is determined by location, condition, rarity, history (did it belong to someone well known?), and sometimes the weather. A seller at an auction may get more money than expected because two buyers get into a bidding war. Or the seller is lucky enough to be selling exactly what a buyer needs. We once paid too much for a dozen Royal Worcester dinner plates because they matched a luncheon set that we inherited.

When trying to sell your antiques or collectibles, there is one firm rule: THE MORE YOU KNOW ABOUT THE PIECE THE MORE ACCURATE THE SELLING PRICE WILL BE. Dealers, auctioneers, and even eBay sellers are successful because they know what makes a piece valuable. It is not age, beauty, or family stories. It is knowledge of what is *currently* selling where you are trying to sell. Some things, like dining room tables and tablecloths, can sell based on "use" value. But higher-priced items are usually bought by collectors who will pay extra for a signature or proof of a known artist or maker. Little differences can make a big price difference. The color of a bottle may make it rare, and a baseball card in mint condition can be worth so much more than the same card in very good condition. But do not forget that fads, current events, and styles can change a price very quickly. Today the "hottest" antiques are ancient Chinese ceramics, large pieces of studio pottery and glass made over the past fifty years, modernist silver jewelry by now-famous artists, very expensive vintage purses like Hermès or Chanel, hard-to-find toys, and rare bottles. Ten or twenty years ago that list might have included Hummel figurines and Royal Doulton character mugs, both now at the bottom of the price scale. And both ordinary eighteenth-century Chippendale furniture and elaborate Victorian Rococo Revival furniture have dropped in price.

> **BEWARE**
>
> The newest problem for sellers are the endangered species laws that forbid most sales of elephant ivory and rhinoceros horns. Other legal restrictions forbid most sales of furs and taxidermy mounts, antiquities and stolen art from past wars, used mattresses, human parts, guns or ammunition without the proper license, clay jars made with uranium that could be radioactive, or even dishes with lead glaze.
>
> Do not sell poison or old food, even in a can or bottle. And it is considered bad taste to sell a fifty-star American flag. It should be given away.

THE BEGINNING

How do you get the right price for something you want to sell? It takes research. Sometimes it's as simple as asking a relative for information. But it usually involves checking websites, marks, books, collector clubs, dealers, and experts who collect or buy what you want to sell.

DON'T THROW ANYTHING AWAY

Remember: "One man's trash is another man's treasure." Don't discard anything until you have tried to find where it can sell and how much you can ask for it. People collect almost anything: banana stickers (no value), flower frogs (iron animal shapes retail for $60 to $2,500), tattoo designs, medical models, iron water-main covers with raised designs (big in England), gas pump globes, sewing patterns, road maps from gas stations, and expensive maps from the eighteenth century. You never know who will want to buy what you are selling.

This Santa Barbara vase made by Frederick Hurten Rhead sold for $516,000 in spite of a few hairline cracks.

Some old magazines, especially comic books, nudist magazines, TV Guides, historic documents and autographs, worn old teddy bears and toys, store displays and ads, and even old tools will sell. Broken items, if unusual, will find a buyer.

DECIDE IF YOU WANT TO HIRE HELP

If you haven't the time or inclination to sell your own things, you can sell to an antiques dealer, hire someone to sell your things online or run a house sale, or consign pieces to an auction. All of these methods can sell some or all of the contents of a house in a few months, but you will have to pay a 25 percent to 50 percent commission or even more for the help.

That is not what most people want to hear when they need money, move, downsize, or settle an estate, but selling antiques and collectibles is a business. There are many costs to the dealers—so they can't pay the retail price you see on shows like "Antiques Roadshow." Prices listed in books and online as well as many auction results are retail prices. The money you will receive is the retail price minus the commissions, charges, and profit for the dealer or auction house.

STEP ONE: THE HUNT

The first step in selling an item is determining how to price it. The many sections in *Kovels' Antiques & Collectibles Price List 2015,* plus added information you need to know—where to look, what clues add value, and possible groups or places to sell to that you might not know about—are here.

If the dishes aren't a full set or the glass is cracked or the toys have missing parts, they probably won't sell for a high price, if at all. Great condition is important. Put broken things aside. It may not seem worthwhile to spend a lot of time trying to sell them unless you are having a yard or house sale.

The easiest way to price a collectible is to learn what it's called or to learn the name of the maker. Look for any signature, mark, paper label, or other identifying feature. It could be raised, incised (cut in), etched, painted, or even written in pencil or chalk. Sometimes the metal handles on a piece will have a stamped mark on the back, so they have to be examined carefully. Take a close-up, in-focus photograph with a camera or cellphone.

In this book, to find a current price, look up information by alphabetic category or use the index at the end. You can search older prices online for free at **Kovels.com**. Notice that the prices are dated so you can see how they have gone up or down in past years. Next try an online search for named pieces. No computer? Search in the indexes of likely books. Many are listed in this report. Look at Google Images and Pinterest or other sites and see if a similar piece is shown with a clue to where it came from—usually a sale or exhibit. Ask a collector friend who goes to shows and might have seen a similar piece. You can search for books by author or title or sometimes subject on Amazon.com.

TIP
Put a flat dish on the glass surface of a photocopy machine. You may have to cover the dish and the exposed glass with a towel to cut out all light. The photocopy should give you a clear image of any marks on the bottom of the dish.

Take Photographs

If you can't find the name of a maker or what it is made of or clues to what it was used for, you might try taking a clear color picture of the piece, full front view and bottom view, and details like a close-up of a special decoration or the carving on a leg. Include that with the mark picture or description and any other information you have, along with accurate measurements of the piece. If you have a small item, you could pose it next to a nickel to show the size. All of this will be needed if you advertise your piece for sale or if you contact an auction gallery.

STEP TWO: HISTORY

Write the history of the piece. Don't say, "Mother got it when she got married." Instead say "…when she got married in 1946." If you have a letter or picture from the past that shows the piece, a room view with the lamp on a table, or a formal picture of someone wearing the jewelry at a birthday party, copy it or describe it to prove that your history is accurate. But remember, family memories are often inaccurate, with years added to the age of a piece. You can give all of this information to interested buyers and dealers at a show. It's not a good idea to take objects to a show, but you can make an appointment with a dealer or auctioneer to meet you at their store or your home.

When you decide on the price, you must pick the best way to sell. You can do it yourself online on eBay or Amazon or some other website. You can hire a local person to sell it online. You can sell or consign to a dealer or send it to an auction. Don't forget to include the cost of shipping, packing, expenses, and your time if you decide to try selling your own belongings online or in a sale.

STEP THREE: PRICING EXPENSIVE THINGS

Pricing expensive pieces requires more research. Some museum and public libraries will help if you have enough information—they will look up sold prices in expensive subscription databases for paintings, sculptures, and other art. They also have copies of useful books that help identify a painting:

Dictionary of American Sculptors, 18th Century to the Present by Glenn B. Opitz, ed.

The Dictionary of British Artists, 1880–1940 by J. Johnson and A. Greutzner

This 1934-35 pin is marked "Eisenberg Original" on the back.

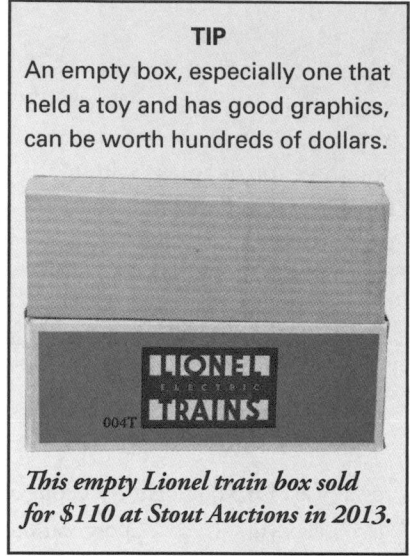
Dictionnaire des Peintres, Sculpteurs, Dessinateurs et Graveurs. 10 vols., by E. Bénézit

Mallett's Index of Artists: International—Biographical by Daniel Trowbridge Mallett

Supplement to Mallett's Index of Artists: International—Biographical by Daniel Trowbridge Mallett

Mantle Fielding's Dictionary of American Painters, Sculptors and Engravers by Glenn B. Opitz, ed.

Try checking prices at some specialized auctions, like RSL Auction Co. (toys and mechanical banks), James Julia and Cowan (guns), Showtime and Morphy (advertising), Neal and New Orleans (southern), Rago and Treadway Toomey (art pottery), Humler & Nolan (pottery and glass), Theriault's (dolls), Allard's (American Indian), Sotheby's and Christie's (anything worth more than $5,000). (See the list of auction houses at the end of this book beginning on page 647.)

If you think your piece will sell for more than $500, you might try writing to one of the antiques columns or online sites that answer questions from readers. This will be frustrating. It is like winning the lottery. Many people enter, only a few win. The letters columnists answer have to be of interest to their readers, and most columns answer fewer than ten questions a week. If you email an appraisal service online and pay a fee, you will get an answer but the price will probably be retail and may not reflect buying habits in your town. An auction or dealer or house-sale price can seem low. For a dealer to pay expenses like rent, overhead, travel, taxes, advertising, and much more and make a profit, the dealer can only pay you one-third to one-half of the retail price.

Sometimes an auction gets an amazing price. There is a list of this year's record prices in the front of this book beginning on page vii.

Be sure you write down what you find, who you talked to, etc., with the names, phone numbers, email addresses, websites, and book titles. Store the information with your antiques. Record everything in an order you will understand, like all the things in the living room or all the pottery and porcelain you are selling. Some of this information could "up" the prices.

- *Advertising sign for Grape-Nuts*
- *Well-known tin picture of girl and St. Bernard*
- *Rubbed spots on self frame*
- *Our first purchase, paid $25*
- *Seen in 2013 in online sales for $1,599 to $4,000 (different condition)*
- *There is a known fake, but it is smaller and I know mine is old*

UNEXPECTED THINGS TO
LOOK OUT FOR WHEN SETTING A PRICE

For low-priced household items and clothing, it is often a better decision to give some things to charity. (You can deduct the value of gifts to non-profits from your taxes as charitable contributions. Ask your income tax advisor to explain this, any limits, and the paperwork required.) Lists of prices are available from:

Goodwill: **Goodwill.org/wp-content/uploads/2010/12/Donation_Valuation_Guide.pdf**

Salvation Army: **SATruck.org/donation-value-guide**

Volunteers of America: **VOAGo.org/Give-a-Gift/Donate-Your-Used-Goods/Donation-Value-Guide**

If you want to donate part of your collection or higher priced items, be aware that written appraisals may be necessary.

The prices of your collectibles and antiques have gone up with inflation each year, and although some types of collectibles sell for lower prices today, most will sell for more dollars than you paid. You have owned and used furnishings and collections that added to the interest and comfort of your home and now those things pay you back in cash.

While you are examining your collections and discovering their value in dollars, also think about any belongings you want to list in your will. Find out if your family, friends, or local museums want anything. Then make out a list of any objects to be given away after you're gone. A serious collector should get legal advice. We know of a will that left the house and furnishings to one relative and the antiques to another. Most of the furnishings were less than 100 years old, so almost everything went with the house.

APPRAISALS

Sometimes you can get a free appraisal from auction houses, jewelry stores, carpet sellers, or antiquarian book dealers. Check locally for special appraisal-day fundraisers. You can also hire an appraiser to suggest prices. There are three national appraisal associations. They will email you names of appraisers in your neighborhood. Some appraisers offer online appraisals for a fee. You email the information about your piece, including pictures, and they send back a suggested retail price and the features and history that give your piece value.

Appraisers

American Society of Appraisers
11107 Sunset Hills Rd, Suite 310
Reston, VA 20190
800-ASA-VALU (800-272-8258) or 703-478-2228
Appraisers.org

International Society of Appraisers
225 West Wacker Drive, Suite 650
Chicago, Illinois 60606
312-981-6778
ISA-Appraisers.org

Appraisers Association of America, Inc.
212 West 35th Street
11th Floor South
New York, NY 1000
212-889-5404 Ext. 10
AppraisersAssociation.org

RESOURCES

Below are books, websites, and clubs with publications that share information or take ads for priced sales of their favorite collectibles.

Books – Specialties

Books are still important research sources. Some, like *American Bottles & Flasks and Their Ancestry* by Helen McKearin and Kenneth M. Wilson and *Collector's Encyclopedia of Dolls*, 2 vols., by Dorothy S., Elizabeth A., and Evelyn J. Coleman, list hundreds of items with dates and descriptions. Other useful books are:

1000 Chairs by Charlotte and Peter Fiell

1000 Lights, 2 vols., by Charlotte and Peter Fiell

Abage Encyclopedia: Bronzes, Sculptors and Founders, 4 vols., by Harold Berman

The Collector's Guide to Old Fruit Jars by Douglas M. Leybourne

**The Label Made Me Buy It: From Aunt Jemima to Zonkers—The Best-Dressed Boxes, Bottles, and Cans
from the Past** by Ralph and Terry Kovel

Pewter in America: Its Makers and Their Marks, 3 vols., by Ledlie Irwin Laughlin

Watchmakers and Clockmakers of the World: Complete 21st Century Edition by G.H. Baillie, et al.

Prices – Books

Kovels' Antiques & Collectibles Price Guide by Terry Kovel and Kim Kovel

Warman's Antiques & Collectibles 2015 Price Guide by Noah Fleisher, Editor

Prices – Online

You can find prices for antiques and collectibles online, but sometimes it takes time, effort, and a little luck. Some sites require you to register in order to get information, but registration is often free. Be sure to look for "sold" prices, not asking prices. The best place to look is **Kovels.com**. It's free and lists prices from auctions, shops, and online sources.

Sources for items that sold at auction are included on sites like LiveAuctioneers.com or Proxibid.com. Prices for china, glass, and silver can be found at sites like Replacements.com, which provides pictures of most of the patterns listed and also offers a pattern identification service. Asking prices for a variety of items can be found on online "malls," sites that include listings from several shops. Some of these are RubyLane.com, icollect247.com, Tias.com, and Trocadero.com.

A list of items for sale can be found on eBay. Sold prices are included for a short time. Other online sources that charge for price information are Artnet, ArtPrice, HammerTap, Invaluable, and Terapeak.

There are also many sites that specialize in one type of collectible. Some are VintageJewelryOnline.com (jewelry), JustArtPottery.com (art pottery), and SPGlass.com (Depression-era glass).

Books on Marks

Books on marks can help identify your pottery or porcelain. They may be available at your local library or bookstore. You can buy them from an online source like Amazon.com.

Encyclopaedia of British Pottery and Porcelain Marks by Geoffrey A. Godden

Keramik-Marken Lexikon: Porzellan und Keramik Report, 1885–1935 by Dieter Zühlsdorff. (written in German)

Kovels' American Art Pottery: The Collector's Guide to Makers, Marks, and Factory Histories by Ralph and Terry Kovel

Kovels' Dictionary of Marks—Pottery & Porcelain, 1650 to 1850 by Ralph and Terry Kovel

Kovels' New Dictionary of Marks—Pottery and Porcelain, 1850 to the Present by Ralph and Terry Kovel

Lehner's Encyclopedia of U.S. Marks on Pottery, Porcelain & Clay by Lois Lehner

Marks on German, Bohemian and Austrian Porcelain: 1700 to the Present by Robert E. Röntgen

Marks – Online

Kovels.com Premium Subscription includes access to marks on pottery and porcelain and on silver and other metals, as well as other identification help.

925-1000.com (silver marks)

PorcelainMarksAndMore.com (porcelain marks)

ThePotteries.org (information and marks for potteries in Stoke-on-Trent, England)

SilverCollection.it/hallmarks.html (silver marks)

F
COLUMBIA
LUDWIG WESSEL
Bonn, Rhineland, Germany (W. Germany)
Earthenware
ca.1905+ (1825–present)
(Wessel Ceramic Works AG)

G
FUNNY DESIGN
PAUL RAUSCHERT KG
Steinwiesen, Bavaria, Germany (W. Germany)
Porcelain
1971–1981 + (1965–present)
(acquired firm of Porcelain Factory Edward Haerter)

O
N
SOCIETÀ CERAMICA RICHARD
Milan, Italy
Porcelain (see page 271)
1850–present (1735–present)
(Richard-Ginori)

P
N
ERNST BOHNE SONS
Rudolstadt, Thuringia, Germany (E. Germany)
Porcelain, figurines. Blue underglaze, overglaze
1901–ca.1920 (1854–ca.1920)

Sample marks from Kovels' New Dictionary of Marks

CLUBS

Clubs have meetings, shows, sales, publications, and conventions devoted to their interest. This is a list of a few. Look for a club devoted to your interests.

American Art Pottery Association
907 Maurer St.
Wilton, IA 52778
AAPA.info

American Ceramic Society
735 Ceramic Place, Suite 100
Westerville, OH 43081
866-721-3322
Ceramics.org

American Cut Glass Association
Kathy Emmerson, Executive Secretary
P.O. Box 482
Ramona, CA 92065-0482
CutGlass.org
ACGA Pattern ID committee will try to identify the members' unknown patterns free of charge.

American Lock Collectors Association
13115 Millersburg Road SW
Massillon, OH 44647-9773
ALCA.name

American Political Items Collectors
APIC Membership Services
P.O. Box 55
Avon, NY 14414
APIC.us

Antique Advertising Association of America
1002 SW 2nd St., #2
Washington, IN 47501
Pastimes.org

$219,750 was bid for this Paul Evans cabinet at a 2014 Rago auction. It was made in 1969.

Antique Bottle & Glass Collector
P.O. Box 180
East Greenville, PA 18041
Glswrk-Auction.com

Antique Glass Salt & Sugar Shaker Club
Jim Beverage, Membership Chair
29 Autumn River Lane
Ogunquit, ME 03907
AntiqueSaltshakers.com

Antique Toy World
Antiquetoyworld.com

Association of Game & Puzzle Collectors
AGPC.org

Beckett sports magazines
15850 Dallas Parkway
Dallas, TX 75248
972-991-6657
Beckett.com

Griswold & Cast Iron Cookware Association
210 Kralltown Road
Dillsburg, PA 17019
315-783-3185
GCICA.org

National Association Breweriana Advertising
1585 W. Tiffany Woods Drive
LaPorte, IN 46350-7599
NABA.WildApricot.org

National Association of Watch and Clock Collectors
514 Poplar St.
Columbia, PA 17512
717-684-8261
NAWCC.org

National Insulator Association
Vickie McConnachie
NIA Membership Director, Dept. WWW
P.O. Box 1466
Corrales, NM 87048
NIA.org

Royal Doulton Collector's Club
Northern California
4011 Ravensworth Place
Roseville, CA 95747
916-899-5034

United Federation of Doll Clubs
10900 N. Pomona Ave.
Kansas City, MO. 64153
816-891-7040
UFDC.org

Upside Down World of an O.J. Collector (newsletter)
Facebook.com/theoccupiedjapancollectors

Libation Cup, Antelope Shape, 19th Century, 3 ½ x 7 ½ In.	2750
Mallet, Turned Handle, Walrus, Faceted Head, Wild Cat Mask, c.1915, 8 In.	119
Mallet, Walrus Tusk, Turned Handle, c.1890, 9 In.	354
Okimono, Elderly Bearded Scholar, Holding Basket, Cane, Marked, c.1900, 7 ½ In.	1440
Okimono, Fisherman, Child, Seagull On Leash, Basket Of Fish, Signed, c.1900, 6 ⅛ In.	308
Okimono, Fukurokuju, Crane, God Of Wisdom, Staff, Paper Roll, Signed, c.1900, 6 ⅛ In.	738
Okimono, Man With Grapes, Ram Jumping, Signed, c.1900, 8 ⅛ In.	510
Okimono, Silk Weavers, Silkworms, Stove, Spinning Wheel, Baskets, 1800s, 6 x 5 In.	1200
Page Turner, Art Nouveau, Openwork Irises, Silver Mounted, Mark, France, c.1900, 13 In.	240
Patch Box, Carved, Amorous Neoclassical Couple, Fitted, France, c.1810, 21 In.	180
Plaque, Dragon, Phoenix, Tea Stain, Chinese, c.1930, 7 In.	121
Puzzle Ball, Stand, Carved, 3 Monkeys, Pierced Flowers, Geometric Design, c.1900, 9 In.	246
Riding Whip, Silver Tip, 1780s, 34 ½ In.	99
Seal, Lion, 6 Characters, Incised, Openwork, Black Stain, 2 ⅜ In.	600
Seal, Wax, Israel Whelen, c.1810, 3 ¾ In.	188
Tankard, Hinged Lid, Silver Gilt, Engraved Mythical Scenes, Germany, c.1860, 11 In.	13125
Temple, Pagoda Style, Carved, 4 Tiers, Seated Figure, 4 Legs, Claw Footed, 39 x 22 In.	3850
Toothpick Holder, Sailor's, Naked Woman, Dagger, c.1800, 3 ¼ In.	207
Trinket Box, Engraved, Reeded, Painted Border, Buteh, Lock, 6 x 26 x 10 In.	3690
Trinket Box, Gilt, Paint, Figures, Landscape, Garland Surround, Lid, France, 1800s, 1 ⅛ In.	179
Triptych, Napoleonic Battle Scene, Carved, Domed, 8 ⅞ In.	1125
Tusk, 2 Dragons, Clouds Carved, Wood Stand, Chinese, 24 In.	1309
Tusk, Carved, 8 Chinese Figures, Cranes, Pine Trees, Wood Stand, Chinese, 20 ½ In. ....*illus*	554
Tusk, Carved, Birds, Fish, Crocodile, Human Hand, Leaves, 26 In., Pair	2375
Tusk, Cigar Cutter, Bear Head, Silver, 19th Century, 24 In.	17500
Tusk, Narwhal, Mounted, Burl Stand, 59 In. ....*illus*	10935
Tusk, Village, Figures Fishing, Pine Trees, Samurai, Japan, 1900s, 16 In.	1920
Vase, Cover, Town Scene, Relief Figures, Scroll Neck, Elephant Ring Handles, 10 In., Pair	2880
Watch Holder, Carved Armorial, c.1865, 3 ⅜ x 2 ½ In.	480
Wrist Rest, Relief Carved, Elephant Tusk, Fisherman, Fish In Hand, Pole, 1900s, 8 In.	1320

JACK-IN-THE-PULPIT vases, shaped like trumpets, resemble the wildflower named jack-in-the-pulpit. The design originated in the late Victorian years. Vases in the jack-in-the-pulpit shape were made of ceramic or glass.

Vase, Blue Opalescent, Hexagonal Base, Dugan, c.1908, 6 In.	125
Vase, Blue, Twisted Stem, Rounded Foot, Platinum, Purple Iridescent, 11 In.	948
Vase, Clear To Amber, Footed, Narrow Waist, 12 ½ In.	55
Vase, Clear, Enameled Flowers, Ruffled, Ribbed, 10 In.	84
Vase, Gold Iridescent, 12 In.	89
Vase, Gold Iridescent, Pulled Dark Petals, 8 ¾ In.	69
Vase, Gold Luster, Hearts, Lundberg Studios, 10 In.	210
Vase, Lavender Streaked, Swollen Base, Footed, 8 ¼ In.	15
Vase, Trumpet Shape, Silver Base, 5 ½ In.	210
Vase, Yellow, Pulled Feather Design, Metallic, 16 ½ In.	3000
Vase, Yellow Over White, Speckled, Flared Base, 13 ½ In.	95

JADE is the name for two different minerals, nephrite and jadeite. Nephrite is the mineral used for most early Oriental carvings. Jade is a very tough stone that is found in many colors from dark green to pale lavender. Jade carvings are still being made in the old styles, so collectors must be careful not to be fooled by recent pieces. Jade jewelry is found in this book under Jewelry.

Archer's Ring, Enameled Peaches, Celadon Green Color, Chinese, 1 ⅛ x 1 ½ In.	492
Bowl, Diaper Design, Green & White, Square Handles, Chinese, 1800s, 5 x 3 In.	2006
Bowl, Incised Birds, Flowers, Gold Inlay, Mottled Green, c.1780, 11 ⅜ In.	2714
Bowl, Spinach Jade, Chinese, 6 ¾ In., Pair	500
Box, Fish, White, Carved, Chinese, c.1800, 1 ¾ x 2 ¼ In.	9400
Box, Gold Mounts, Circle & Swag Inset Stones, Russia, c.1960, 3 ⅜ In.	8125
Box, Lid, Lavender, Apple Green, Carved, Leaf Shape, Silk Worm Feet, c.1900, 2 ½ x 5 In.	2337
Box, Lid, Quatrefoil, Lychee Branches, Cream & Brown Color, Carved, Chinese, 1 x 4 In.	6000
Brush Rest, Low Table Shape, Pierced Apron, Archaic Scrolls, Leaves, 2 ⅞ In.	5700
Brush Washer, Peach Shape, Carved, Serpentine, Chinese, c.1900, 4 ¼ In.	71
Carving, Mountains, Scholar, Boy, Bridge, Trees, Rocks, White, Green, Stand, 1900s, 15 In.	2706
Case, Cigarette, Gold Mounts, Nicholas II Jade Set Monogram, 3 ½ In.	5000
Cup, Carved, Lion-Like Handles, Ring Foot, White, 2 x 5 In.	3304
Dragon Seal, Green, Chinese, Late 20th Century, 3 ¾ In.	1293

Jade, Plaque, Aquatic Birds, Plants, Butterflies, Rosewood Stand, 1800s, 12 In., Pair
$13,035

James D. Julia Auctioneers

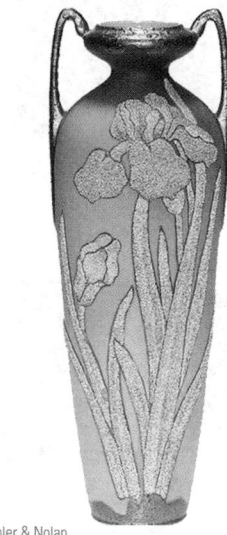

Japanese Coralene, Vase, Irises, Buds, Leaves, Handles, Marked, 12 ½ In.
$1,770

Humler & Nolan

Jasperware, Lamp Base, Blue, Raised Chariot Scenes, Gilt, Lion's Mask Handles, 16 ½ In.
$531

Brunk Auctions

J

Jewelry, Belt Buckle, Bucking Bronco, 14K Gold, Ruby, Bohlin, Alaska, c.2000, 2 ½ x 3 ¾ In.
$2,950

Brian Lebel's Old West Show & Auction

Jewelry, Belt Buckle, Bulldogger, Silver, Inscribed, Bohlin, c.2000, 2 x 3 ¼ In.
$944

Brian Lebel's Old West Show & Auction

Jewelry, Belt Buckle, Longhorn, Silver, 14K Gold, Bohlin, Alaska, c.2000, 2 x 3 In.
$2,655

Brian Lebel's Old West Show & Auction

Jewelry, Belt Buckle, Patriotic Symbols, 14K Gold, California Jewelry Co., 1868, 1 ⅝ x 2 ½ In.
$823

Cowan's Auctions

TIP

*Quick test for pearls:
Real pearls should feel
cold. Fakes will feel
room temperature.*

Ewer, Celadon, Lotus Pond Design, Lobed Cartouches, Handle, c.1900, 10 ½ x 7 In.	5669
Figurine, Buddha Hand, Brown, White, Chinese, c.1800, 3 In.	14100
Figurine, Buddha, Seated, Carved, Chinese, 1 ½ In.	60
Figurine, Cicada, Gray Green Color, Flat, Carved, Chinese, 1900s, 2 ¼ In.	304
Figurine, Crane, Carved, Standing, Square Base, 10 In., Pair	1680
Figurine, Crane, Ming Tree, Wood Root-Like Base, 9 ¾ In.	230
Figurine, Dragon, Urn, Carved, Celadon Color, Footed Stand, 1900s, 5 x 5 In.	767
Figurine, Farm Girl, Cabbages, Grasshopper, Wood Base, 7 ⅝ In.	345
Figurine, Foo Dog, Sitting, 4 x 3 x 3 In.	3000
Figurine, Guanyin, Elongated, Flowing Robes, Holding Scroll, Green, White, 8 In.	12000
Figurine, Horse Head, Black & Green, Tang Style, Wood Stand, 1900s, 9 ¾ x 11 ¼ In.	2390
Figurine, Horse, Serpentine, Running, Teakwood Stand, 5 x 6 In.	210
Figurine, Ox, Reclining, 7 In.	480
Figurine, Salamander, Carved, Chinese, 20th Century, 3 ½ In.	1205
Figurine, Sea Urchins, Base, 7 x 6 ½ In.	960
Figurine, Woman, Flowers, Flowing Gown, Chinese, 1900s, 7 In.	236
Fortune Wheel, Carved Ball, Shaped, 3 In. Diam.	840
Frame, Reticulated, Carved Flowers & Vines, White, Scalloped, c.1900, 11 ½ x 10 In.	472
Garment Hook, Celadon Green, Curved Shaft, Dragon, Crawling, 6 ⅜ In.	492
Group, Polar Bear, Cubs, 3 ½ x 2 ½ x 2 ⅛ In.	295
Plaque, Aquatic Birds, Plants, Butterflies, Rosewood Stand, 1800s, 12 In., Pair ....*illus*	13035
Plaque, Carved, Openwork, Huan, Chinese, c.1800, 2 ¼ In.	1410
Plaque, Celadon, Oval, Reticulated, Phoenix & Flowers, Chinese, 1800s, 2 ½ x 3 In.	885
Plaque, Figures, Pine Tree, Poem, Carved, Celadon Stone, Chinese, 2 ⅞ In.	1320
Plaque, White, Inscribed, Chinese, c.1800, 3 ½ In.	13255
Plaque, White, Openwork Carved, 2 ¼ x 2 ¾ In.	847
Teapot, Monkeys, Finial, Carved, Chinese, 20th Century, 3 ¾ In.	16870
Tray, Sugar Crystal Design, White, Flat Rim, Poem, Chinese, c.1800	8260
Urn, Lid, Openwork Design, Scroll Handles, Rings, White & Green Mottled, 6 x 4 In.	270
Vase, Figural, Carved, Archaic Beast, 2 Elephant Head Handles, Chinese, Late 1800s, 7 In.	15665
Vase, Lotus, Scrolling, Splayed Feet, Domed Lid, Handles, Wood Stand, 12 ½ In.	3860
Vase, Teardrop Finial, Cylindrical Handles, Footed, 9 ½ In.	23500
Wine Pot, Carved Lotus Petals, Bulbous, Ring Foot, Loop Handle, Lid, 1900s, 8 x 6 In.	356

JAPANESE CORALENE is a ceramic decorated with small raised beads and dots. It was first made in the nineteenth century. Later wares made to imitate coralene had dots of enamel. There is also another type of coralene that is made with small glass beads on glass containers.

Ewer, Mauve, Gold, 1909, 12 In.	1295
Vase, Irises, Buds, Leaves, Handles, Marked, 12 ½ In. ....*illus*	1770

JAPANESE WOODBLOCK PRINTS are listed in this book in the Print category under Japanese.

JASPERWARE can be made in different ways. Some pieces are made from a solid-colored clay with applied raised designs of a contrasting colored clay. Other pieces are made entirely of one color clay with raised decorations that are glazed with a contrasting color. Additional pieces of jasperware may also be listed in the Wedgwood category or under various art potteries.

Biscuit Jar, Horses, Hunters, Dogs, Blue, White, Silver Plate Handle, c.1890, 6 In.	117
Hair Receiver, Blue, White, Kissing Fairies, c.1900, 3 ¾ In. Diam.	48
Jam Pot, Blue, White, Hunt Scene, Silver Bail Handle, c.1890, 3 x 4 In.	85
Jardiniere, Blue, Leaf Band, England, 7 x 7 In., Pair	600
Lamp Base, Blue, Raised Chariot Scenes, Gilt, Lion's Mask Handles, 16 ½ In. ....*illus*	531
Mug, Green, Monks, Drinking, Cherubs, Card Sharks, 5 ⅛ In.	375
Plaque, Cameo, Pink, White, Portrait, Medusa, c.1914, 3 In. Diam.	125
Teapot, Green, White, Children, Trees, 1906, 8 ½ In.	100

JEWELRY, whether made from gold and precious gems or plastic and colored glass, is popular with collectors. Values are determined by the intrinsic value of the stones and metal and by the skill of the craftsmen and designers. Victorian and older jewelry has been collected since the 1950s. More recent interests are Art Deco and Edwardian styles, Mexican and Danish silver jewelry, and beads of all kinds. Copies of almost all styles are being made. American Indian jewelry is listed in the Indian category. Tiffany jewelry is listed here.

Belt Buckle, Bucking Bronco, 14K Gold, Ruby, Bohlin, Alaska, c.2000, 2 ½ x 3 ¾ In. ....*illus*	2950
Belt Buckle, Bulldogger, Silver, Inscribed, Bohlin, c.2000, 2 x 3 ¼ In. ....*illus*	944
Belt Buckle, Jugendstil, Needles, Silver, Enamel, F. Boeres, T. Fahrner, c.1905, 2 x 4 In.	2375

Belt Buckle, Longhorn, Silver, 14K Gold, Bohlin, Alaska, c.2000, 2 x 3 In.	*illus*	2655
Belt Buckle, Mermaid, Pierced Bone Plaque, Rectangular, Silver, Kalo, 2 ¾ x 2 In.		183
Belt Buckle, Patriotic Symbols, 14K Gold, California Jewelry Co., 1868, 1 ⅝ x 2 ½ In.	*illus*	823
Belt Buckle, Silver, 9 Turquoise Stones, Beaded Detail Between Bezels, 4 x 3 In.		219
Belt Buckle, Silver, Beaded Edge, Rectangular, Stamped, Revere, 18th Century, 6 In.		60
Bracelet & Earrings, Pink Beads, Flower, Clip-On, Signed, Miriam Haskell	*illus*	150
Bracelet, 5 Circus Animals, In Cages, Sterling, Gilt, Art Deco, 6 ¾ In.		180
Bracelet, 6 Plaques, Reverse Painted Glass, Golfers, 14K Gold Mounts, 7 ½ In.		1440
Bracelet, 10 Links, Openwork, Sapphire, Diamonds, Black, Starr & Frost, Edwardian, 7 In.		3600
Bracelet, Abstract Links, Citrines, Pink Quartz, 18K Gold, Ed Wiener, 6 ¾ In.	*illus*	7380
Bracelet, Ankle, Link, Tubular, Flexible, 18K Gold, Indo-Persian, c.1900, 9 ½ In.	*illus*	4063
Bracelet, Bakelite, Bangle, Carved, Tan & Red, 2 ½ x ⅝ In.	*illus*	23
Bracelet, Bakelite, Bangle, Red, Carved, 2 ½ x 1 ⅝ In.	*illus*	128
Bracelet, Bakelite, Mahjong Tiles, Green Glass Bead Spacers, 1 ¼ x ⅞ In.	*illus*	93
Bracelet, Balls, Vertical Dividers, Silver, Kalo, 6 In.		600
Bracelet, Bands, 4 Woven, 14K Gold, Pinched, Diamonds, Rows, Platinum, c.1950, 7 In.		3393
Bracelet, Bangle, 18K Gold, Bone Panels, Marked, Tiffany & Co., c.1970, 6 ½ In.		1500
Bracelet, Bangle, Baroque Pearl Cluster, Diamonds, Emeralds, 14K White Gold, c.1890		1404
Bracelet, Bangle, Cable, 18K Gold, Diamond Melee X, D. Yurman, 6 ¾ In.		1560
Bracelet, Bangle, Diamonds, Brilliant Cut, Baguettes, 18K White Gold, Birks, 2 ⅓ In.		4025
Bracelet, Bangle, Double Rope Twist, 14K Gold, Cartier, 7 ¾ In.		1320
Bracelet, Bangle, Gold, Flowers, Stylized Trefoil Edge, c.1870, 5 ¾ In., Pair		1500
Bracelet, Bangle, Hinged, 2 Cage Charms, Carnelian Beads, 18K Gold, Garrard, 6 ¼ In.		1968
Bracelet, Bangle, Hinged, Etoile, Diamond Melee, 18K Gold, Tiffany & Co., 6 ¾ In.		2520
Bracelet, Bangle, Hinged, Garnet, Rectangular, Faceted, Silver, Gold Shoulder, Cartier, 7 In.		660
Bracelet, Bangle, Hinged, Leaves, Green Rhinestones, Antonia Pineda, c.1920, 2 ⅜ In.		118
Bracelet, Bangle, Hinged, Silver, 2 Fish, Jet Eyes, Mexico, c.1950, 3 ½ In.		500
Bracelet, Bangle, Jadeite, 2 ¼ In.	*illus*	2666
Bracelet, Bangle, Link, 18K Gold, Yellow Enamel, Sapphires, Bands, Tiffany & Co., 6 In.		21250
Bracelet, Bangle, Love, 18K White Gold, Bypass, Screw Closure, Cartier, 2 ¼ In.		3220
Bracelet, Bangle, Pearl, Citrine, Green Garnet, 18K Gold, Marked, Stevens, 6 In.		4063
Bracelet, Bangle, Reindeer, Enamel, Red, White, Blue, Black, Gold Mount, Hermes, 8 In.		720
Bracelet, Belt Shape, Woven, 18K Gold, France, 1900s, 9 In.		2415
Bracelet, Cameo, Hope, Garland, Wirework, Latin Motto, 18K Gold, 6 ½ In.	*illus*	5100
Bracelet, Cameo, Lava, Literary Figures, Titles On Reverse, Rose Gold	*illus*	1230
Bracelet, Cameo, Shell, Bearded Man, Rope Twist Frame, Cylindrical Links, Guiliano, 7 In.		5400
Bracelet, Cameo, Shell, Gods & Goddesses, 7 Plaques, 14K Gold Shaped Links, 7 In.		800
Bracelet, Charm, Key, St. Christopher, Diamond, Ruby, Platinum, 14K Gold, 7 ¼ In.	*illus*	1200
Bracelet, Charm, Triple Links, 7 Charms, 14K Gold, c.1960, 7 ¼ In.	*illus*	3375
Bracelet, Cuff, Abstract, 18K Gold, Granulated, Brown Diamonds, A. King, 6 ½ In.		11070
Bracelet, Cuff, Faux Pearl, Goldtone Metal, Chanel, 1980s, 2 ¼ In.		956
Bracelet, Cuff, Flowers, Engraved, 18K Gold, 1900s, 1 ⅞ x 2 ¼ In.		978
Bracelet, Cuff, Gold, Rope Twist, c.1880, 6 ½ In.		1750
Bracelet, Cuff, Grapevine, Coral Grapes, Textured Gold Leaves, M. Buccellati, 6 ⅜ In.		10200
Bracelet, Cuff, Leaf, Textured 18K Gold, M. Buccellati, 6 ¾ In.		5400
Bracelet, Cuff, Link, Interlocking, 4 Rows, 18K Gold, Midcentury Modern, Italy, 7 ¾ In.		2223
Bracelet, Cuff, Mixed Metals, Circles Design, Marked, Tiffany & Co., 6 ⅜ In.	*illus*	3998
Bracelet, Cuff, Silver, Interwoven Fronds, Buds, Tapered, Georg Jensen, 1 ½ In.		585
Bracelet, Cuff, Silver, Molded Glass Disc, Modernist Style, J. Hill, Denmark		330
Bracelet, Cuff, Silver, Turquoise, Cluster, 2 ½ x 3 ⅜ In.		107
Bracelet, Cuff, Tapered, 14K Textured Gold, Stylized Hand Ends, C. Loloma, 1 ¼ In.		2420
Bracelet, Diamond, 2 Rows, Platinum, Gold, c.1905, 6 ½ In.		6875
Bracelet, Diamond, Emerald, Square Cut, Platinum, c.1920, 7 In.		5313
Bracelet, Diamond, Sapphire, Panel Set, 18K Gold, Art Deco, 6 In.		1770
Bracelet, Diamonds, European Cut, Platinum, Engraved Scrolls, Art Deco, 6 ¾ In.		2875
Bracelet, Garland Of Leaves, Platinum, Diamond Melee, Tiffany & Co., c.1999, 7 In.		5400
Bracelet, Garnet, Emerald Cut, Amethysts, Pearls, 14K Gold, Renaissance Revival, 6 In.		891
Bracelet, Gold, Painted, Engraved Birds, Flowers, 6 In., Pair		1599
Bracelet, Hardstone, Green, Sterling Bird Inlay, Marked, Los Castillo, 8 x 1 ⅓ In.		115
Bracelet, Ivory, Carved Flower Blossoms, Asia, c.1910		118
Bracelet, Leather, Purple, Palladium & Silver Plated Hardware, Hermes 14 ½ x ½ In.		196
Bracelet, Link, 6 Moonstone Cabochons, Intertwined Links, 18K Gold, G. Jensen, 7 In.		2640
Bracelet, Link, 6 Oval, Miniature Scenic Paintings, Famous Sites, Ribbed Frames, 8 In.		1560
Bracelet, Link, Anchor, Silver, Hermes, Box, 9 ½ In.		1020
Bracelet, Link, Art Deco, Gold, Black Onyx, Diamond, Red Enamel, c.1930, 7 In.		4375
Bracelet, Link, Buds, Silver, Moonstone Spacers, G. Jensen, 7 ¾ In.		540

Jewelry, Bracelet & Earrings, Pink Beads, Flower, Clip-On, Signed, Miriam Haskell
$150

Leslie Hindman Auctioneers

Jewelry, Bracelet, Abstract Links, Citrines, Pink Quartz, 18K Gold, Ed Wiener, 6 ¾ In.
$7,380

Skinner Auctioneers & Appraisers

Jewelry, Bracelet, Ankle, Link, Tubular, Flexible, 18K Gold, Indo-Persian, c.1900, 9 ½ In.
$4,063

Rago Arts & Auction Center

Jewelry, Bracelet, Bakelite, Bangle, Carved, Tan & Red, 2 ½ x ⅝ In.
$23

Martin Auction Co.

Jewelry, Bracelet, Bakelite, Bangle, Red, Carved, 2 ½ x 1 ⅝ In.
$128

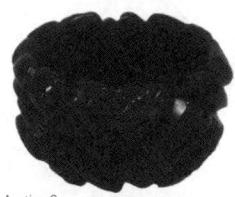

Martin Auction Co.

Jewelry, Bracelet, Bakelite, Mahjong Tiles, Green Glass Bead Spacers, 1 ¼ x ⅞ In.
$93

Martin Auction Co.

Jewelry, Bracelet, Bangle, Jadeite, 2 ¼ In.
$2,666

James D. Julia Auctioneers

Jewelry, Bracelet, Cameo, Hope, Garland, Wirework, Latin Motto, 18K Gold, 6 ½ In.
$5,100

Skinner Auctioneers & Appraisers

Men's Jewelry
Kanye West started the craze for men to wear four or five bangle bracelets. The masculine bracelets are usually made of rope, leather, beads, or heavy silver links.

Bracelet, Link, Double Chain, 14K Gold, 1900s, 8 ½ In.	1495
Bracelet, Link, Micro Mosaic, 7 Architectural Scenes, Brass Bezels, Victorian, 7 ¾ In.	661
Bracelet, Link, Oval, 6 Sugarloaf Onyx Cabochons, 18K Gold, Marzo, Paris, 7 ¾ In.	840
Bracelet, Link, Round, 2 Rows, Gold, Sapphire & Diamond Accents, Aletto Bros, 7 In.	5645
Bracelet, Link, Scalloped, Platinum, Diamond, Emerald Bow Clasp, c.1920, 6 ⅜ In.	31250
Bracelet, Link, Silver, 3 Panels, Marked, Arthur King, 6 ½ x 1 ¼ In. ....*illus*	354
Bracelet, Link, Silver, Buckle Clasp, Hermes, 7 ½ In.	2500
Bracelet, Link, Tire Track, Gold, R.L. Morris, 8 In.	420
Bracelet, Locket, Hinged, Hair, 10K Gold, c.1880, 7 ⅝ In.	374
Bracelet, Love, 18K Gold, Inset Screws, Screwdriver, Cartier, 7 ¾ In.	3900
Bracelet, Mosaic, Silver, Gold, Enamel, Gemstones, Earl Pardon, 7 ½ In. ....*illus*	5313
Bracelet, Painted Rural Scene, 10K Gold, Hair, Garnet Set Frame, c.1880, 6 In.	546
Bracelet, Sapphire, Diamond, 18K Gold Links, c.1960, 6 ½ In.	1062
Bracelet, Sapphire, Diamond, Gold, Rope Twist, Figure 8 Knot, c.1960, 7 In.	5625
Bracelet, Silver, 18K Gold Accents, Marked, David Yurman, Man's, 7 In.	403
Bracelet, Silver, Antonio Pineda, Taxco, Mexico, 1940s, 3 ½ In. ....*illus*	1500
Bracelet, Silver, Braided Crescent Links, Onyx, Box Clasp, Antonio Pineda, 7 In.	1121
Bracelet, Silver, Flowers, 3 Green Stones, Kalo, 6 In.	813
Bracelet, Silver, Geometric Cutouts, Kalo, 7 In.	438
Bracelet, Silver, Link, Abstract Geometric, Mexico, c.1950, 6 ½ In.	502
Bracelet, Silver, Overlapping Scrolls, William Spratling, 7 ½ In.	483
Bracelet, Sodalite Tablet, Battling Beasts, Flowers, 18K Gold, Lalaounis, 6 ¾ In. ......*illus*	3198
Bracelet, Strap, Enamel, Plique-A-Jour, Pastes, Arches, Art Deco, 7 ⅛ In.	570
Buckle, Carved Jade, Brass, Chinese, 1 ½ x 4 In.	180
Buckle, Fairy, Flowing, Gilt Silver, Plique-A-Jour Wings, Art Nouveau, J. Quercia, 3 In.	4200
Buckle, Peacock Feather, Shaped Blue Glass, Gilt Metal, Art Nouveau, Piel Freres, 4 In.	960
Buckle, Stylized Feather, Silver, Oval Mother-Of-Pearl, Onyx Plaques, Circle Fine Art, 5 In.	360
Buckle, Turquoise, Bezel Set, Rectangular Granulated Gold Mount, C. Loloma, 2 ½ In.	6900
Charm, Lovebirds, On Branch, Sun, Rays, 2 Sapphires, Diamonds, 18K Gold, 1 ⅜ In.	7800
Charm, Rocking Horse, 18K Gold, Openwork, Diamond Eye, Rubies, Van Cleef & Arpels, 1 In.	3480
Chatelaine, Gold, Embossed, Cases For Scissors, Needles, Thimble, Silk, c.1810, 7 In. ....*illus*	5415
Chatelaine, Porcelain, Gold, Guiloche Enamel, Cabbage Roses ....*illus*	173
Chatelaine, Silver, Bright Cut, Mackay & Chisholm, 19th Century, 6 ½ x 3 ¾ In.	83
Chatelaine, Silver, Engraved, Mesh Purse, Match Safe, Compact, Dance Card, 8 ½ In.	356
Cigarette Box, 18K Gold, White Enamel Stripes, Sapphire Edge, Diamond Clasp, Cartier, 3 In.	7200
Cigarette Case, 18K Gold, Basket Weave, Marked Mario Buccellati, 3 ¼ x 4 In.	8750
Cigarette Case, 18K Gold, Textured, Sapphire Monogram, N, Buccellati, Italy, 4 x 6 In.	5625
Cigarette Case, Mt. Fuji, Silver, Mixed Metals, Steel & Copper Inlay, Japan, 6 ¼ In.	184
Cigarette Holder, Silver, 14K Gold, Rose Gold Stripe, Elgin Am. Mfg., 4 x 3 In.	115
Clip, Butterfly, 18K Textured Gold, Ruby Eyes, Flexible Wings, M. Buccellati, 1 ¾ In.	4200
Clip, Dress, Shield Shape, Diamonds, Platinum, Beaded, Art Deco, 2 ¼ In., Pair	3600
Clip, Stacked Ribbed Ovals, 14K Bicolor Gold, Marked, Cartier, c.1940, 1 ⅜ x 3 In.	2375
Comb, Bakelite, Yellow, Green Overlay, Swirl, 8 ½ x 6 In.	155
Cuff Links, 18K Gold, Blue Enamel Bands, Marked, Deakin & Francis	667
Cuff Links, Abstract Dome, 18K Granulated Gold, Arthur King	1320
Cuff Links, Acorns, 18K Gold, Toggles, Potter & Mellen	546
Cuff Links, Balls, Green Enamel, 18K Gold Wrap, Tiffany & Co.	1476
Cuff Links, Bombe, 18K Gold, Diamonds, ⅝ x 5/16 In.	6250
Cuff Links, Bull's Head, Onyx, Ruby Eyes, 14K Gold Hoof Links, Tiffany & Co.	4200
Cuff Links, Cicada, Hardstone, Ruby Eyes, Diamond Melee Collar, 18K Gold, 1 In.	1800
Cuff Links, Citrine, 2 Rondels, Faceted, Bezel Set Ruby, 18K Gold Mount	780
Cuff Links, Concave, Stylized Flowers, Sterling, Marked, Georg Jensen, 1 In.	196
Cuff Links, Double Link, Oval, Scroll Borders, 14K Gold, Art Nouveau	480
Cuff Links, Double Link, Round, Side Ribbing, 14K Bicolor Gold, Retro, Larter & Sons	330
Cuff Links, Double Link, Scrollwork Border, 18K Gold, Art Nouveau	1080
Cuff Links, Fish, 18K Gold, Blue & Red Enamel Body, Diamond Eyes	1169
Cuff Links, Griffin-In-Shield, Silver, Kalo, 1 In., Pair	406
Cuff Links, Hammered Sterling, Poppy, Signed, Peer Smed, c.1909, 2 x 2 ¼ x 1 ¾ In.	1250
Cuff Links, Hematite, Oval Cabochon, Enamel Frame, 18K Gold Mount, Tiffany & Co.	1046
Cuff Links, Horse's Head In Profile, 18K Gold, Enamel, Oval Links	1800
Cuff Links, Lapis Beads, 18K Gold Leafy Mount, 1 ¼ In.	510
Cuff Links, Link, Flower, Gemstone Cabochons, 18K Gold	360
Cuff Links, Lozenge Shape, 14K Gold, Round Diamonds, Art Nouveau	253
Cuff Links, Mineral Plaque, Textured 14K Gold Mount, Bjorn Weckstrom, Lapponia	660
Cuff Links, Minuteman Holding Gun, 14K Gold, Rectangular, Rounded, Cartier, 1 In.	3900
Cuff Links, Nut & Bolt, 18K Gold, Verdura, Pouch	3998

Jewelry, Bracelet, Cameo, Lava, Literary Figures, Titles On Reverse, Rose Gold
$1,230

Skinner Auctioneers & Appraisers

Jewelry, Bracelet, Charm, Key, St. Christopher, Diamond, Ruby, Platinum, 14K Gold, 7 ¼ In.
$1,200

Skinner Auctioneers & Appraisers

Jewelry, Bracelet, Charm, Triple Links, 7 Charms, 14K Gold, c.1960, 7 ¼ In.
$3,375

Rago Arts & Auction Center

Jewelry, Bracelet, Cuff, Mixed Metals, Circles Design, Marked, Tiffany & Co., 6 ⅜ In.
$3,998

Skinner Auctioneers & Appraisers

Jewelry, Bracelet, Link, Silver, 3 Panels, Marked, Arthur King, 6 ½ x 1 ¼ In.
$354

Michann's Auctions

Trading Jewelry

If you're getting rid of unwanted jewelry, sell it to an antiques dealer or to a jeweler who will give you its gold or silver meltdown value. Never trade with a dealer for another piece of jewelry. You can't judge the true value of the stones and workmanship in your piece, let alone the dealer's piece. At best you will trade your piece for the wholesale value but get a dealer's piece priced at retail.

Jewelry, Bracelet, Mosaic, Silver, Gold, Enamel, Gemstones, Earl Pardon, 7 ½ In.
$5,313

Rago Arts & Auction Center

Jewelry, Bracelet, Silver, Antonio Pineda, Taxco, Mexico, 1940s, 3 ½ In.
$1,500

Rago Arts & Auction Center

Jewelry, Bracelet, Sodalite Tablet, Battling Beasts, Flowers, 18K Gold, Lalaounis, 6 ¾ In.
$3,198

Skinner Auctioneers & Appraisers

Jewelry, Chatelaine, Gold, Embossed, Cases For Scissors, Needles, Thimble, Silk, c.1810, 7 In.
$5,415

Theriault's

Jewelry, Chatelaine, Porcelain, Gold, Guiloche Enamel, Cabbage Roses
$173

Victorian Casino Antiques

Jewelry, Earrings, Hessonite Garnet, 18K Gold, Clip-On, Elizabeth Gage, 1 ¼ In.
$5,535

Skinner Auctioneers & Appraisers

Jewelry, Earrings, Jasper Disc, 18K Gold Mount, Sugarloaf Center, Clip-On, ⅞ In.
$1,080

Skinner Auctioneers & Appraisers

Jewelry, Earrings, Pendant, Girandole, Seed Pearls, Rubies, Gold, c.1760, 3 ⅝ In.
$18,000

Skinner Auctioneers & Appraisers

Jewelry, Earrings, Silver, Modernist, Otto R. Bade, Marked, Orb Sterling, 2 ½ In.
$83

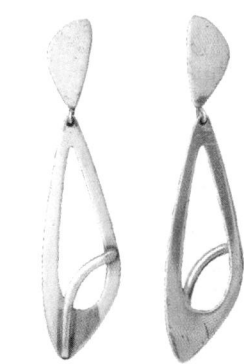

Michann's Auctions

Jewelry, Locket, Turquoise, Diamonds, Opens, Double Compartment, 18K Gold, France, 2 In.
$3,900

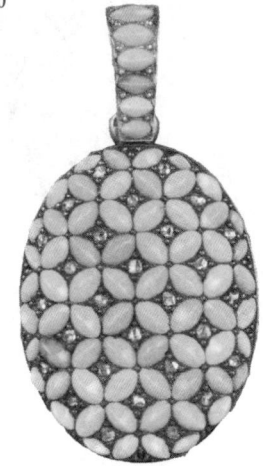

Skinner Auctioneers & Appraisers

Jewelry, Necessaire, Lipstick Holder, Enamel, Silver, Gilt, Compartments, Germany, c.1920, 3 ¼ In.
$813

Rago Arts & Auction Center

Jewelry, Necessaire, Purse, Velvet, Brass, Bronze, Beveled Mirror, France, c.1870, 6 In.
$342

Theriault's

Cuff Links, Nut & Bolt, Silver, Tiffany & Co.	554
Cuff Links, Scarab, Hardstone, Carved, 14K Gold Oval Mount, Lotus, Egyptian Revival	2340
Cuff Links, Square, 18K Bicolor Gold, Marked, Cartier, c.1940, ½ In., Pair	4375
Cuff Links, Stylized Leaves, Bone Berry, 18K Gold	360
Cuff Links, Stylized M, 18K Gold, Zolotas	450
Cuff Links, Sunburst, 14K Gold, Enamel, J.V. Aarne, Faberge, Russia, c.1915, 1 In., Pair	2625
Cuff Links, Sunburst, Lapis Cabochon, Fluted Bezel, 18K Gold, Tiffany & Co., 1 In.	1320
Cuff Links, Tablet, Garnets, 14K Gold, Florentine Finish, Lucien Picard	510
Dress Set, Man's, Moonstone, Oval Cabochons, 18K Gold, Carrington & Co., 5 Piece	523
Dress Set, Man's, Tablet, 18K Gold, Inlaid Black Jade & Opal, A. Cummings, 5 Piece	1800
Earrings, 3 Aquamarines, Cushion Cut, Sapphires, Diamonds, White Gold, J. Mavec, 1 In.	1440
Earrings, 3 Stones, Coral Cabochons, Diamonds, 18K Gold, Verdura, ¾ In.	6000
Earrings, 18K Gold, Inlaid, Mother-Of-Pearl, Onyx, Coral, Lapis, Malachite, Grossbardt, 1 In.	1200
Earrings, Alligator, 18K Gold, Diamond Eyes, Kieselstein Cord, Clip-On, 1 ¼ In.	1140
Earrings, Animal Face, Open Mouth, Chocolate Diamond, 14K Gold, Studs, 1900s	161
Earrings, Aquamarine, Marquis Cut, 14K Gold, Tiffany & Co., ⅞ In.	414
Earrings, Bell, Scalloped, 14K Bicolor Gold, Faceted Pink Stone Clapper, Retro, 1 ⅜ In.	600
Earrings, Bow, Rope Twist, 18K Gold, Tiffany & Co., ½ In.	570
Earrings, Briolette, Drop, Aquamarines, Engraved Cap, Chain, Day, Clark & Co., 1 ⅝ In.	840
Earrings, Burst, 18K Gold, Diamond Accents, Clip-On, G. Jensen & Wendel, 1 In.	2460
Earrings, Chalcedony, 2 Shaped Cabochons, 4- & 8-Sided, 14K Gold, R. Lewis, 1 ½ In.	1200
Earrings, Citrine, Oval, Carved, 18K Gold, Burle Marx, ⅝ In.	2091
Earrings, Cluster, Wire Loops, Rope Twist, 18K Gold, Tiffany & Co., 1 In.	1920
Earrings, Coils, Rope Twist, 18K Gold, Clip-On, Tiffany & Co., ¾ In.	1560
Earrings, Cushion, Sapphire, Diamonds, Multicolor, Clip-On, Marked, Piranesi, 1 x 1 In.	6875
Earrings, Diamond, Abstract Flowers, c.1950, 1 ⅛ In.	1888
Earrings, Dome, Ribbed Gold, Clip-On, Leather Pouch, Charles Garnier, 1 In.	550
Earrings, Faux Pearl, Goldtone, V. DeCastellane, Chanel	155
Earrings, Flower, Diamond, Emerald, Platinum, Van Cleef & Arpels	23750
Earrings, Flower, Rubies, Diamonds, Marked, Alexis, Post & Clip-On, 1 In.	7500
Earrings, Hessonite Garnet, 18K Gold, Clip-On, Elizabeth Gage, 1 ¼ In. ....*illus*	5535
Earrings, Hoop, 18K Gold, Fluted Swirls, Clip-On, Marked, Boucheron, 1 x ⅜ In.	3750
Earrings, Hoop, Atlas, 18K Gold, Diamond, Marked, Tiffany & Co., 1995	3125
Earrings, Hoop, Braided, 18K Gold, Clip-On, Marked, Cartier, 1993, 1 ¼ x ½ In.	2500
Earrings, Hoop, Conch Shell, Tricolor 18K Gold Grid Support, Van Cleef & Arpels, ⅝ In.	5100
Earrings, Hoop, Ribbed, 18K Gold, Van Cleef & Arpels, ¾ In.	2280
Earrings, Jasper Disc, 18K Gold Mount, Sugarloaf Center, Clip-On, ⅞ In. ....*illus*	1080
Earrings, Knot, 18K Gold, Black Enamel, Hinged Back, Tiffany & Co., 1 In.	1323
Earrings, Knot, Crepe De Chine, Rope Twist, 18K Gold, Buccellati, ⅞ In.	2040
Earrings, Lapis, Oval, Citrine & Peridot Drops, 18K Gold, Clip-On, J. Vendome, 2 In.	4375
Earrings, Leaf, Gold Over Aluminum, Clip-On, JAR, Paris, 2 x 2 In.	9375
Earrings, Opal, Oval, Over 2 Round Small Opals, 14K Gold, Clip-On, Marked, Kalo, 1 In.	2806
Earrings, Pearl, Stud, 18K Gold, Mikimoto	380
Earrings, Pendant, Girandole, Seed Pearls, Rubies, Gold, c.1760, 3 ⅝ In. ....*illus*	18000
Earrings, Pendant, Tiered, Gold, Diamonds, Ruby, Jaipur Enamel, India, 3 x 1 In.	3125
Earrings, Pink Tourmalines, Oval, Pear Shaped, Blue Topaz, Onyx, 18K Gold, Marina, France	4063
Earrings, Rose Quartz, Faceted, Bezel Set, 18K Gold, Pomellato, 1 In.	1476
Earrings, Shell, Nephrite Jade, Amethyst & Ruby Ends, Gold Rope Twist Trim, Verdura, 1 In.	7800
Earrings, Silver, Gold Bands, Emerald Center, Etta Goldstein	70
Earrings, Silver, Modernist, Otto R. Bade, Marked, Orb Sterling, 2 ½ In. ....*illus*	83
Earrings, Spiral Shell Shape, Shell, Turquoise, Pearls, 18K Gold, Clip-On, Trianon, ¾ In.	1845
Earrings, Spirals, Stepped, 18K Gold, Clip-On, Signed, Cartier, 1 ¼ x 1 In.	2500
Earrings, Sputnik, Pearl, Turquoise & Diamond Ball Ends, Retro, 1 In.	1020
Earrings, Starfish, Diamond, Platinum, ⅞ In.	1500
Earrings, Stylized Blossom, Amber, Diamonds, 18K White Gold, Aletto Brothers, 1 ½ In.	4800
Earrings, Stylized Butterfly, Puffy, 18K Gold, Bulgari, 1 In.	1920
Earrings, Stylized Feather, 14K Gold, Retro, Tiffany & Co., 1 ⅝ In.	840
Earrings, Stylized Flower, 14K Gold, Marked, Yard, c.1950, ⅞ In.	625
Earrings, Stylized Screw, Silver, Modernist Style, Clip-On, P. Von Musulin, 1 ½ In.	780
Earrings, Turquoise Swirled Round, Diamond, Accent, 18K Gold, Signed Lagos, Clip Back	1135
Flask, 14K Bicolor Gold, Hammered Square, Monogram, Pouch, Raymond Yard, 4 In.	4212
Flower, Jade, Pierced, Fluted Diamond, Oval, c.1915, ¼ x ½ In.	4375
Hair Comb, Tortoiseshell, Overlapping Coral Branches, 4 ¼ In.	510
Hatpins are listed in this book in the Hatpin category.	
Jabot, Rock Crystal & Aquamarine Ends, Oval, Diamonds, Platinum, Art Deco, 3 In.	2829
Kilt Pin, Silver, Griffins, Marked Scotland, 3 ½ In.	118

Jewelry, Necklace & Earrings, Dart, Verdigris, Robert Lee Morris, 17 ¾ In. & 2 In.
$1,080

Skinner Auctioneers & Appraisers

Jewelry, Necklace, Blue Enamel, Cultured Pearls, Link Chain, 18K Gold, 40 ½ In.
$2,040

Skinner Auctioneers & Appraisers

Jewelry, Necklace, Choker, Heart, Blue Crystals, Stamped, Made In France
$625

Leslie Hindman Auctioneers

JEWELRY

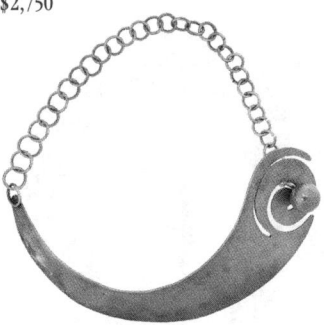

Jewelry, Necklace, Collar, Silver, Art Smith, New York, 6 In.
$2,750

Rago Arts & Auction Center

Jewelry, Necklace, Necktie, Silver, Hammered, Adjustable Neck Ring, Noma Copley, 15 ½ In.
$3,960

Skinner Auctioneers & Appraisers

Jewelry, Necklace, Pearls, Cultured, Silvertone, 18K Gold, Tambetti, 15 ½ In.
$2,337

Skinner Auctioneers & Appraisers

Lavaliere, Amethyst, Freshwater Pearl Drops, Trace Link Swags, Art Nouveau, 16 In.	510
Lavaliere, Scarab, Brass Garland Mount, 1 ¾-In. Lavaliere, 3 ¾-In. Chain	540
Locket, 14K Gold, Oval, Bale, Marked, Tiffany & Co., 1 x 1 In.	334
Locket, Heart, Incised Grid, Diamonds, 18K Gold, Charles Green, 1 ¼ In.	720
Locket, Sardonyx Tablet, Diamond Flower, Pearls, Gold, Ropework, Portrait Inside, 2 In.	960
Locket, Scrolls, Diamond, 14K Gold, Raised, Victorian, 1 In.	426
Locket, Turquoise, Diamonds, Opens, Double Compartment, 18K Gold, France, 2 In. ....*illus*	3900
Lorgnette, Diamonds, Pave Set, Platinum, Paperclip Link Chain, Art Deco, 22 In.	7200
Minaudiere, Onyx, 18K Gold, Platinum, Flowers, Semiprecious Stones, Art Deco, 3 x 2 ¼ In.	27658
Necessaire, Lipstick Holder, Enamel, Silver, Gilt, Compartments, Germany, c.1920, 3 ¼ In. *illus*	813
Necessaire, Purse, Velvet, Brass, Bronze, Beveled Mirror, France, c.1870, 6 In. ....*illus*	342
Necklace & Bracelet, Leaf & Bud Plaques, Silver, Malachite Accents, G. Jensen	2640
Necklace & Earrings, Crystal Bead, Rhinestones, Hattie Carnegie, 16 In.	181
Necklace & Earrings, Dart, Verdigris, Robert Lee Morris, 17 ¾ In. & 2 In. ....*illus*	1080
Necklace & Earrings, Lily Pad & Damselfly, Nephrite, 18K Gold, G. Kiss, 18-In. Necklace	3960
Necklace & Earrings, Link, Anchor, 18K Gold, Clip-On, Hermes, 17 In. & ¾ In.	20400
Necklace & Earrings, Pearl, Single Strand, Gold Clasp, Mikimoto, 17-In. Necklace	369
Necklace, 2 Braided Strands, Gold, Figure-8 Knots, 10 Oval Garnets, c.1880, 15 In.	6250
Necklace, 18K White Gold, Florentine Finish, Signed, Gianmaria Buccellati	984
Necklace, Bead, Coral, 6 Graduating Strands, 18K Gold Clasp, Verdura, 16 ½ In.	6150
Necklace, Bead, Oxidized Copper, Gold-Plated Brass, R.L. Morris, 20 In.	1080
Necklace, Beads, Lapis, 3 Strands, Faceted Carnelian, Silver Accents, Alice Kuo, 18 In.	210
Necklace, Blue Enamel, Cultured Pearls, Link Chain, 18K Gold, 40 ½ In. ....*illus*	2040
Necklace, Branch, Cultured Pearls, 18K Gold, Arthur King, 15 ¼ In.	5000
Necklace, Cameo, Woman's Profile, Rose In Hair, Gold Beads, Etruscan Revival, 14 In.	1200
Necklace, Chain, Antique Gold, Ribbed Rectanglar, Oval Links, c.1875, 20 In.	2375
Necklace, Chain, Link, 14K Gold, 1900s, 16 ¾ In.	1840
Necklace, Chain, Omega, 14K Gold, Sliding Diamond Accents, Jabel, 16 In.	2070
Necklace, Chain, Rope Twist, 18K Gold, Van Cleef & Arpels, 31 In.	5400
Necklace, Charm, 14K Gold, 1900s, 23 In.	2300
Necklace, Choker, Belle Epoque, Pearl, Diamond, Platinum, Openwork, France, c.1910, 12 In.	9375
Necklace, Choker, Heart, Blue Crystals, Stamped, Made In France ....*illus*	625
Necklace, Collar, 2 Leaves, Braided Chain, 18K Textured Gold, Buccellati, 16 ¾ In.	7800
Necklace, Collar, Silver, Art Smith, New York, 6 In. ....*illus*	2750
Necklace, Festoon, Turquoise Cabochons & Teardrops, 14K Gold, Art Nouveau, 15 In.	1845
Necklace, Fringe, Dart Shape, Braided Strap, 18K Gold, Edwardian, 14 In.	1560
Necklace, Gripoix Glass, Coco Chanel, c.1928, 20 ½ In.	508
Necklace, Gripoix Glass, Coco Chanel, c.1928, 32 In.	657
Necklace, Leaves, Jadeite, Bicolor Gold, Diamonds, Link Chain, Art Deco, Krementz, 15 In.	4305
Necklace, Link, 14K Gold, Hammered, Alternate Polished Beads, c.1950, 18 In.	1755
Necklace, Link, 14K Gold, Lapis, Rectangular c.1970, 35 In.	1652
Necklace, Link, Alternating, Navette & Trace, Diamonds, Pearls, Platinum, Art Deco, 31 In.	3000
Necklace, Link, Gold, Fringe, Leaf Pendants, c.1880, 16 In.	3750
Necklace, Link, Openwork & Bar, Gold, Pierced Pendant, Tiffany & Co., 2 ⅜ In.	28125
Necklace, Link, Silver, Acorn, Oak Leaves, Kalo, 14 In.	594
Necklace, Link, Silver, Geometric Shapes, Kalo, 14 In.	500
Necklace, Link, Silver, Leaves, Marked, Kalo, 14 In.	875
Necklace, Link, Tubular, 18K Gold, 2 Strands, 7 Diamond Ribbon Panels, c.1950, 15 In.	15000
Necklace, Link, Tubular, Gold, Platinum & Diamond Ribbon, Cartier, c.1950, 13 ⅞ In.	22500
Necklace, Maple Leaves, Graduated, 18K Gold, A. Cummings, Tiffany & Co., 1981, 16 In.	10200
Necklace, Naja, Silver, Turquoise Cabochon, Mercury Dimes, Liberty Half Dollars, 1945	450
Necklace, Necktie, Silver, Hammered, Adjustable Neck Ring, Noma Copley, 15 ½ In. ....*illus*	3960
Necklace, Onyx & Pearl Chain, Diamonds,Jade Watch, Pendant, Art Deco, c.1920, 22 In.	7500
Necklace, Opal, Scrolling 14K Gold Mount, Opal Drop, Chain, Art Nouveau, Durand, 15 In.	4200
Necklace, Pearl, Graduated, 14K White Gold Bow Clasp, Mikimoto, Matinee Length, 21 In.	600
Necklace, Pearls, 2 Strands, Emerald, 14K Gold Clasp, Mikimoto, 14 ½ In.	2006
Necklace, Pearls, 14 Strands, Twisted, Rhinestone Clasp, Blue Glass Cabochon, Ciner, 17 In.	123
Necklace, Pearls, Barrel Clasp, c.1900, 17 In.	5100
Necklace, Pearls, Cultured, 18K White Gold Clasp, Diamond, Mikimoto, 18 ½ In.	1722
Necklace, Pearls, Cultured, Silvertone, 18K Gold, Tambetti, 15 ½ In. ....*illus*	2337
Necklace, Pearls, Freshwater, 5 Strands, 18K Gold Clasp, Tiffany & Co., 17 In.	738
Necklace, Pendant, Multicolor Opalescent Stone, Chain, Link, Art Nouveau, 10 In.	438
Necklace, Pendant, Nantucket Basket, 14K Gold, Scrimshaw, Rope Twist Chain, G.E. Robbins	1440
Necklace, Pendant, Openwork, Diamond, Ruby, Gold, Pearl Chain, c.1910, 16 In.	7500
Necklace, Pendant, Puissance Neuf, Concentric Spirals 18K Gold, Agam, 1970, 16 ½ In.	8125
Necklace, Pendant, Silver Pearl, Openwork, Link Chain, Toggle Clasp, Georg Jensen, 20 In.	584

Jewelry, Necklace, Pendant, Turquoise, Silver, Kalo, c.1910, 1 ½-In. Pendant, 17-In. Chain
$1,375

Rago Arts & Auction Center

Jewelry, Necklace, Red Beaded Strands, Twin Bypass Snakehead Clasp, Signed, Kenneth Lane
$563

Leslie Hindman Auctioneers

Jewelry, Necklace, Sautoir, Red Crystal Chiclet, Signed, Chanel, 1981
$1,375

Leslie Hindman Auctioneers

Jewelry, Necklace, Serpents, Entwined, Opals, Garnets, 18K Gold, Art Nouveau, RD, 16 In.
$44,280

Skinner Auctioneers & Appraisers

Jewelry, Necklace, Silver, Leaves, Buds, Silver Pearl, Georg Jensen, 14 ¾ In.
$1,140

Skinner Auctioneers & Appraisers

Jewelry, Necklace, Slide, Round, Woven, Chain, Capped Tassel, Seed Pearls, Victorian, 45 In.
$1,722

Garth's Auctioneers & Appraisers

Jewelry, Necklace, Snake, Enamel Head, Seed Pearls, Scale Links, 14K Gold, France, 16 In.
$4,080

Skinner Auctioneers & Appraisers

Jewelry, Necklace, Tassels, Split Pearl, 14K Gold Link Chain, Victorian, 16 ¾ In.
$2,400

Skinner Auctioneers & Appraisers

Jewelry, Parure, Necklace, Earrings, Ring, Bees, Honeycomb, Citrines, Diamond, 14K Gold, C. Adell, 17 ½ In.
$3,567

Skinner Auctioneers & Appraisers

Jewelry, Pendant, Abstract, Acrylic Drop, Silver, Chain, Bjorn Weckstrom, 3 ¼ In.
$960

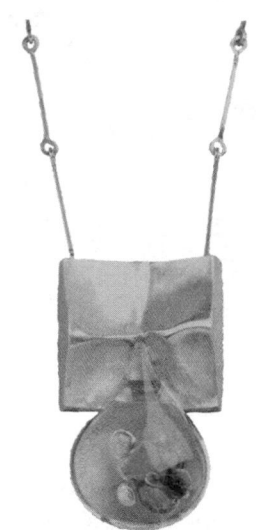

Skinner Auctioneers & Appraisers

Jewelry, Pendant, Circles, Sterling Silver, T. Wirkkala, N. Westerback, 1970s, 4 In.
$2,583

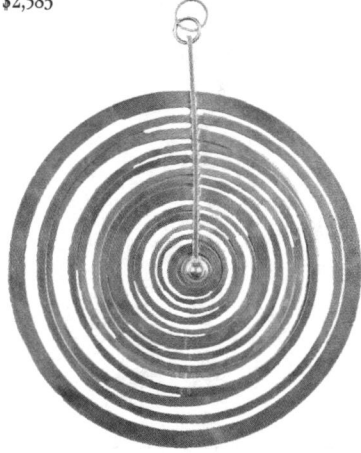

Skinner Auctioneers & Appraisers

Jewelry, Pendant, Coin, U.S. 1847 Ten Dollar, 14K Gold Frame, 5 Diamonds, 5 Sapphires, 1 ¾ In.
$2,214

New Orleans Auction Galleries, Inc.

Jewelry, Pendant, Cross, Diamonds, Black Onyx, 14K Gold, 2 ¼ x 1 ½ In.
$1,107

New Orleans Auction Galleries, Inc.

Jewelry, Pendant, Hardstone, 18K Gold, Marked, Bulgari, Italy, 3 In.
$4,800

Skinner Auctioneers & Appraisers

Jewelry, Pendant, Key, Carnelian, Cultured Pearls, 18K Gold, Angela Cummings, 2 ¾ In.
$1,560

Skinner Auctioneers & Appraisers

Jewelry, Pendant, Mourning, Ivory, Scene, Applied Hair, Inscribed, c.1790, 2 x 1 ½ In.
$1,140

Skinner Auctioneers & Appraisers

Jewelry, Pendant, Peacock Enamel, Silver, Pearl, Guild Of Handicraft, c.1890, 3 ¼ In.
$3,690

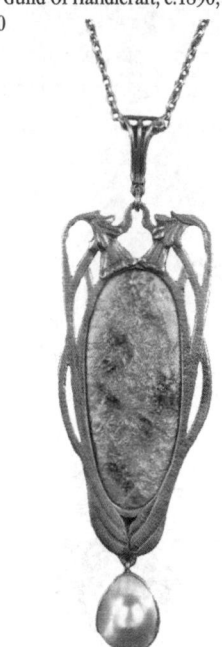

Skinner Auctioneers & Appraisers

Jewelry, Pendant, Pin, Butterfly, Precious Stones, Pearls, Gold, Silver, Victorian, 1 ¾ In.
$1,416

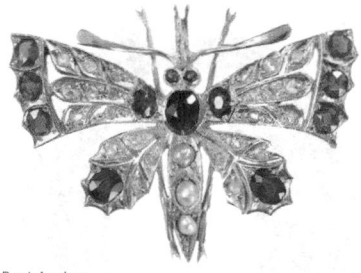

Brunk Auctions

Jewelry, Pendant, Silver, Enamel, Coral, Turquoise, T. Fahrner, c.1925, 1 ¾ x 3 In.
$1,875

Rago Arts & Auction Center

Necklace, Pendant, Smoky Citrine, 18K Gold, Woven, Silver Chain, J. Hardy, 16 In.	403
Necklace, Pendant, Stylized Bud, Moonstones, Silver, Paperclip Chain, G. Jensen, 17 In.	1080
Necklace, Pendant, Tiger's Eye, Mother-Of-Pearl, Inlaid, Rotating Insert, Bulgari, 24 In.	10200
Necklace, Pendant, Turquoise, Silver, Kalo, c.1910, 1 ½-In. Pendant, 17-In. Chain............*illus*	1375
Necklace, Pin & Ring, Fringe, Pearls, Suspended Teardrop Amethyst, Arts & Crafts, 16 In.	2640
Necklace, Red Beaded Strands, Twin Bypass Snakehead Clasp, Signed, Kenneth Lane ....*illus*	563
Necklace, Rope Twist, Graduated, 14K Gold, 15 ½ In.	1534
Necklace, Sautoir, Red Crystal Chiclet, Signed, Chanel, 1981 ....*illus*	1375
Necklace, Serpents, Entwined, Opals, Garnets, 18K Gold, Art Nouveau, RD, 16 In. ....*illus*	44280
Necklace, Silver, Leaves, Buds, Silver Pearl, Georg Jensen, 14 ¾ In. ....*illus*	1140
Necklace, Slide, Round, Woven, Chain, Capped Tassel, Seed Pearls, Victorian, 45 In. ....*illus*	1722
Necklace, Snake, Enamel Head, Seed Pearls, Scale Links, 14K Gold, France, 16 In. ....*illus*	4080
Necklace, Sophistication, Pendant, Silver, 14K Gold, Sapphires, Diamond, Erte, 4 In.	4248
Necklace, Tassels, Split Pearl, 14K Gold Link Chain, Victorian, 16 ¾ In. ....*illus*	2400
Necklace, Torque, 18K Gold, Michael Good, 15 In.	2640
Parure, Citrines, Flowers, Gold Filigree Leaf Mounts, Tiara, Earrings, c.1830, 6 Piece	21600
Parure, Necklace, Earrings, Ring, Bees, Honeycomb, Citrines, Diamond, 14K Gold, C. Adell, 17 ½ In. *illus*	3567
Pendant, Abstract, Acrylic Drop, Silver, Chain, Bjorn Weckstrom, 3 ¼ In. ....*illus*	960
Pendant, Aquamarine, Faceted, Teardrop, Diamond Bail, Edwardian, 2 ½ In.	11100
Pendant, Aquamarine, Silver, Herman Schmidt-Straub, 1930s, 1 In.	413
Pendant, Bird, Flowering Sprig, Scrolling Leaves, Jade, Carved & Pierced, White, 1 ½ In.	540
Pendant, Boy, Holding Peach, Jade, Pale Green, Carved & Pierced, 2 ⅜ x 1 ½ In.	492
Pendant, Buddha's Hand, Jade, Leafy Vine, Citron Finger, Curling Tendrils, 1800s, 3 In.	2337
Pendant, Bulla, Lapis, 18K Gold Bead & Ropework Mount, Hinged, Etruscan Revival, 2 In.	2040
Pendant, Circles, Sterling Silver, T. Wirkkala, N. Westerback, 1970s, 4 In. ....*illus*	2583
Pendant, Coin, U.S. 1847 Ten Dollar, 14K Gold Frame, 5 Diamonds, 5 Sapphires, 1 ¾ In. ..*illus*	2214
Pendant, Cornucopia, Gem Stones, Textured 18K Gold Disc, c.1950, 1 ½ In.	385
Pendant, Cross, 18K Bicolor, Gold, Rose Cut Diamonds, Chain, 2 ¼ x 20 In.	2706
Pendant, Cross, Diamonds, Black Onyx, 14K Gold, 2 ¼ x 1 ½ In. ....*illus*	1107
Pendant, Dog's Head, Basset Hound, Reverse Painted Glass, Gold & Diamond Bail, 1 In.	523
Pendant, Dragonfly, Green, Brown, Orange, Red Gem Eyes, Tiffany Studios, 10 x 6 In.	3835
Pendant, Dragons, Boy, Lotus, Firecrackers, Jade, Pale Green, Round Plaque, 2 ⅛ x 1 ½ In.	359
Pendant, Fish, Bubbles, Silver, Copper, Onyx, Estela Popowski, Mexico, 1950s, 2 In.	130
Pendant, Floating Heart, 18K Gold, Chain, Elsa Peretti, Tiffany & Co., 18 In.	776
Pendant, Flower, Peach, Silver, Ivory, Art Nouveau, A.T.M., 2 ¼ In.	325
Pendant, Hardstone, 18K Gold, Marked, Bulgari, Italy, 3 In. ....*illus*	4800
Pendant, Jadeite, Leaves & Berries, Carved, Pierced, Diamond Slide, Cartier, 2 In.	9225
Pendant, Key, Carnelian, Cultured Pearls, 18K Gold, Angela Cummings, 2 ¾ In. ....*illus*	1560
Pendant, Kissing Koi Fish, Jade, Asia, 20th Century, 2 ¾ In.	118
Pendant, Landscape, Jade, White, Carved, Inscription, Chinese, c.1800, 2 ¼ In.	21150
Pendant, Locket, Ship's Anchor, Coiled Rope, 14K Gold, Oval, Hinged, Victorian, 1 In.	144
Pendant, Loop, 18K Gold, Rhodonite Disk, Aldo Cipullo, 1972, 2 In.	1524
Pendant, LOVE, Stacked Block Letters, 18K Bicolor Gold, A. Cipullo, Cartier, 1972, 2 In.	2520
Pendant, Mourning, Ivory, Scene, Applied Hair, Inscribed, c.1790, 2 x 1 ½ In. ....*illus*	1140
Pendant, Mourning, Sepia On Ivory, Painted, 14K Gold, Inscription, c.1796, 2 In.	900
Pendant, Mourning, Woman By Grave, Watercolor On Ivory, Oval, c.1820, 2 ¾ x 2 ¼ In.	649
Pendant, Panier De Fruit, Fruit Basket, Cord, Knotted Fringe, Marked, Lalique, c.1910, 2 In.	813
Pendant, Peacock Enamel, Silver, Pearl, Guild Of Handicraft, c.1890, 3 ¼ In. ....*illus*	3690
Pendant, Perfume, Silver, Walnut Shape, Hinged, Glass Bottle Inside, 1 ½ In.	474
Pendant, Pin, Butterfly, Precious Stones, Pearls, Gold, Silver, Victorian, 1 ¾ In. ....*illus*	1416
Pendant, Queen Bee, 18K Gold, Granulated, Diamond Eyes, Pearl Drop, M. Neimanis, 2 In.	2280
Pendant, Reliquary, Panagia, Mother & Child, Gold, Enamel, Diamonds, Poland, c.1925, 4 In.	7200
Pendant, Rock Crystal, Silver Leaf Cap, Blue Stones, Chain, Arts & Crafts, S. Dunlop, 32 In.	300
Pendant, Scarab, Lapis Body, Turquoise Eyes, Plique-A-Jour Wing Tips, 18K Gold, 2 In.	923
Pendant, Silver, Enamel, Coral, Turquoise, T. Fahrner, c.1925, 1 ¾ x 3 In. ....*illus*	1875
Pendant, Sodalite, Pear Shape Tablet, 18K Gold, Bulgari, 2 In.	4800
Pendant, Stylized Fish, Diamonds, 18K White Gold, Frank Gehry For Tiffany, 1 In.	660
Pendant, Stylized Leaves, Amber Oval, Silver Frame, Georg Jensen, 2 x 1 ¼ In.	874
Pendant, Sun, Face, Silver, Pablo Picasso, 2 ¹⁵⁄₁₆ In. ....*illus*	141000
Pendant, Turquoise, Pear & Oval Shapes, White Gold, Diamond Rim, Zydo, Italy, 2 ½ In.	2160
Pendant, Watch, 18K Gold, Chased, Arabic Numerals, Ornate Hands, Patek Philippe	1476
Pendant, Watch, Green Guilloche Enamel, Diamond, Hinged Case, 18K Gold, Edwardian	1800
Pin & Earrings, Amethyst, Rock Crystal, Diamonds, 18K White Gold, Austria, 3 ½ In. ....*illus*	960
Pin & Earrings, Blue Green Stones, Round, Hattie Carnegie	47
Pin & Earrings, Cameo, Hardstone, Dancing Bacchante, Pearl Accents & Drops, 3 In.	3000
Pin & Earrings, Cameo, Hardstone, Maiden, Upswept Hair, Gold, Pearl Accent & Drop	1920

Jewelry, Pendant, Sun, Face, Silver, Pablo Picasso, 2 ¹⁵⁄₁₆ In.
$141, 000

Jewelry, Pin & Earrings, Amethyst, Rock Crystal, Diamonds, 18K White Gold, Austria, 3 ½ In.
$960

Jewelry, Pin & Earrings, Dancer, Silver, Ed Wiener, c.1947, 3 x 2 In.
$1,750

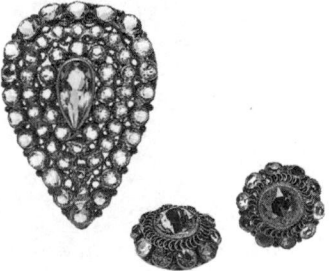

Jewelry, Pin & Earrings, Faux Amber & Rhinestones, Signed, Hobe
$63

J

Leslie Hindman Auctioneers

Brunk Auctions

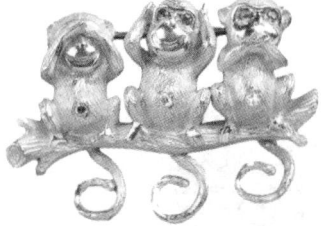

Skinner Auctioneers & Appraisers

Men's Wedding Rings
Wedding rings for men were not very popular until World War II. Only women wore a wedding ring before that.

Pin & Earrings, Dancer, Silver, Ed Wiener, c.1947, 3 x 2 In. ....*illus*	1750
Pin & Earrings, Faux Amber & Rhinestones, Signed, Hobe ....*illus*	63
Pin & Earrings, Rhinestones, Bouquet, Green & Clear, Clip-On, Eisenberg Ice ....*illus*	150
Pin, 2 Bows, Diamonds, Safety Chain, Marked, Depose, France, Art Deco, 2 ½ In.	7080
Pin, 2 Flowers, Aquamarine Petals, Sapphire Centers, 14K Gold Leaves, Tiffany, 2 ½ In.	660
Pin, 2 Leaves, Green Enamel, Rhinestone Edge, Goldtone Metal, Hattie Carnegie	47
Pin, 2 Parrots, 48 Diamonds, Ruby Eyes, Gold, 1 ¾ In. ....*illus*	1534
Pin, 2 Pinecones, 18K Gold, Diamond Accent, Hammerman Bros., 2 In.	720
Pin, 3 Stylized, Flowers, Square, Hammered 18K Gold, Polished Centers, Tiffany, 2 In.	1140
Pin, 3 Wise Monkeys, Diamonds, Sapphire & Ruby Eyes, 18K Gold, 1 ¾ In. ....*illus*	1680
Pin, Abstract Buds, Silver, Rafael Melendez, c.1930, 1 ⅞ x 1 ⅝ In.	148
Pin, Abstract Spray, Ball Ends, Center Knot, 18K Textured Gold, Tiffany & Co., 2 ½ In. ...	2280
Pin, Abstract, 18K Gold, Textured, 2 Amethysts, Burle Marx, 2 In.	1722
Pin, Abstract, Lapis, Bezel Set, 14K Gold, 2 ⅝ In. ....*illus*	600
Pin, Allegorical Scene, Relief, Framed By Figures, 14K Gold, E. DeKolb, 2 ½ In.	3120
Pin, Aquamarine, Oval, Diamonds, Leaf & Scroll Openwork Mount, Art Deco, 2 In.	1800
Pin, Bakelite, Butterscotch, Carved, 2 ⅞ x 1 ¼ In. ....*illus*	23
Pin, Bakelite, Doghouse, 3 Dog Charms, Glass Inset Eyes, 2 ½ In. ....*illus*	325
Pin, Bakelite, Horse's Head, Butterscotch, Carved, Dangling Charms, 2 ½ In. ....*illus*	110
Pin, Bar, 6 Opals, Diamonds, Platinum Over Gold Mount, Black, Starr & Frost, 1 ¾ In. ...	984
Pin, Bar, Platinum, Emerald, Diamonds, Rectangular, Shaped Ends, Art Deco, 2 In.	2880
Pin, Bar, Platinum, Filigree, Old European Cut Diamonds, Art Deco, 2 ⅞ In.	1560
Pin, Bee, Pearls, Ruby Eyes, Gold Mount, June Birthstone, Rosenthal, 1 In.	240
Pin, Beetle, Enamel, Diamonds, Ruby, Emeralds, 14K Gold, Victorian, 2 ¼ x 1 ¼ In. ....*illus*	3198
Pin, Bird Of Paradise, Brushed, 18K Gold, France, c.1960, 3 ½ In.	590
Pin, Bird On Branch, 18K Gold, Rubies On Tail, Turquoise Cabochons, Mauboussin, 2 In.	3600
Pin, Bird, 18K Gold, Diamonds, Jewel Eyes, Yellow, Green Enamel, 1900s, 2 In.	1495
Pin, Bird's Nest, 18K Gold, Branch Coral, Turquoise Egg, Diamonds, A. King, 2 In.	4305
Pin, Black Opal, Oval, Diamonds, Platinum Over Gold Openwork Mount, Edwardian, 1 In.	1920
Pin, Blackamoor, Diamonds, Sapphires, 18K Gold, G. Nardi, 1 ½ In. ....*illus*	4500
Pin, Bow, 14K Gold, 5 Loops, Emerald-Cut Citrine Center, Retro, 4 In.	2400
Pin, Bow, 18K Gold, 1905, 1 ⅛ In.	374
Pin, Bow, 4 Loops, Diamonds, Platinum Over Gold, Edwardian, James Robinson, 2 In.	2400
Pin, Bow, European & Single Cut Diamonds, Beaded Platinum Mount, Art Deco, 3 In.	1800
Pin, Bow, Rock Crystal, Platinum, Beaded, Diamond Melee Edge, Art Deco, 2 ¾ In.	3900
Pin, Brass, Copper, Shaped & Hammered Wire, Art Smith, c.1960, 2 ½ In.	660
Pin, Butterfly, 18K Gold, Blue Enamel, Diamonds, Emeralds, Marked, Tiffany, 2 ⅜ x 1 2/8 In.	8125
Pin, Butterfly, 18K Gold, Ruby Wings, Diamond Body, Marked, Alexis, 2 x 2 1/16 In.	8750
Pin, Butterfly, Agate, 14K Gold, 2 ⅝ In. ....*illus*	1020
Pin, Butterfly, Bellflowers, Reverse Painted Glass, 18K Gold, Blue Enamel, 1 ⅜ In.	1599
Pin, Butterfly, Diamond Melee Body, Blue Plique-A-Jour, Mosaic Wings, Cartier, 2 In.	4800
Pin, Butterfly, Sapphire & Garnet Body, Blue Enamel Wings, Silver, Art Nouveau, 2 ⅜ In.	1920
Pin, Butterfly, Trembler, 126 Old European-Cut Diamonds, 1 ½ x 2 ¼ In. ....*illus*	22420
Pin, Camellia Flower, White, Silk, Chanel, Box, 1980s, 4 In.	266
Pin, Cameo, Bakelite, Child's Face, 10K Gold, 1 ¾ x 1 ¼ In. ....*illus*	92
Pin, Cameo, Hardstone, Vestal Virgin, 14K Gold Frame, Split Pearl Border, 2 In.	1200
Pin, Cameo, Onyx, Angel, Diamonds, 18K Gold, Tiffany & Co. ....*illus*	3884
Pin, Cameo, Shell, Woman's Profile, Gold Frame, Open Scroll, Victorian, 2 x 1 In.	167
Pin, Cat & Mouse, 18K Gold, Diamond Eyes On Cat, Ruby Eyes On Mouse, Retro, 1 ¼ In.	480
Pin, Cat, Black Onyx, Emerald Eye, 18K Gold, Van Cleef & Arpels, 1 ½ x ¾ In. ....*illus*	2706
Pin, Cat, Turquoise, Pearl, 18K Gold, c.1960, 2 ½ In.	649
Pin, Cat, Winking, 18K Gold, Hardstone Belly, Sapphire Eye, Van Cleef & Arpels, 2 In.	5280
Pin, Circle, Diamonds, Old European, Shaped Ends, Beaded, Sapphires, Art Deco, 2 In.	2760
Pin, Circle, Leaves, Green, White Enamel, Edwardian, 1 In.	98
Pin, Circle, Platinum, Diamond, 14K Gold Stem, Edwardian, 1 ½ In.	4484
Pin, Circle, Platinum, Diamonds, Brilliant & Marquis Cut, Round Emeralds, Retro, 1 ¼ In.	2300
Pin, Citrine, Oval, Faceted, Seed Pearls, 14K Gold, Scallop Border, Edwardian, 1 x 1 In.	115
Pin, Cluster, Peridot, Topaz, Tourmaline, Citrine, 14K Gold, Potter & Mellen, 1 x 1 In.	265
Pin, Coil, Brass, Alexander Calder, 1939, 3 ½ x 2 ¾ In. ....*illus*	111000
Pin, Constellation, 18K Gold, Diamonds, Colored Stones, O. Heyman & Bros., 2 ¼ In.	1440
Pin, Cornucopia, Flowers, Rubies, Sapphires, Emeralds, 18K Gold, Tiffany & Co., 2 ½ In.	840
Pin, Crescent Moon & Stars, Blue Enamel Ground, Diamond Frame, 1 ¼ In.	2520
Pin, Crescent, Suspended Disc, Wire Coils, Ruby Accents, Pearl Ends, T. Fahrner, 1 ¼ In.	600
Pin, Cross, Maltese, Gripoix Glass, Green, Red, Purple, Chanel, 1994, 2 ¼ In.	1121
Pin, Crown, Diamonds, Platinum Over Gold Mount, Edwardian, 2 ½ In.	4200

Jewelry, Pin, Abstract, Lapis, Bezel Set, 14K Gold, 2 ⅝ In.
$600

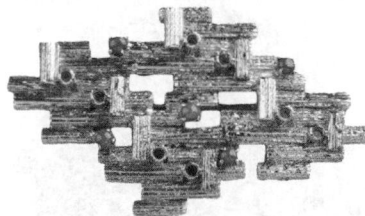

Skinner Auctioneers & Appraisers

Jewelry, Pin, Bakelite, Butterscotch, Carved, 2 ⅞ x 1 ¼ In.
$23

Martin Auction Co.

Jewelry, Pin, Bakelite, Doghouse, 3 Dog Charms, Glass Inset Eyes, 2 ½ In.
$325

Leland Little Auction

Jewelry, Pin, Bakelite, Horse's Head, Butterscotch, Carved, Dangling Charms, 2 ½ In.
$110

Leighton Galleries

Jewelry, Pin, Beetle, Enamel, Diamonds, Ruby, Emeralds, 14K Gold, Victorian, 2 ¼ x 1 ¼ In.
$3,198

New Orleans Auction Galleries, Inc.

Jewelry, Pin, Blackamoor, Diamonds, Sapphires, 18K Gold, G. Nardi, 1 ½ In.
$4,500

Skinner Auctioneers & Appraisers

Jewelry, Pin, Butterfly, Agate, 14K Gold, 2 ⅝ In.
$1,020

Skinner Auctioneers & Appraisers

Jewelry, Pin, Butterfly, Trembler, 126 Old European-Cut Diamonds, 1 ½ x 2 ¼ In.
$22,420

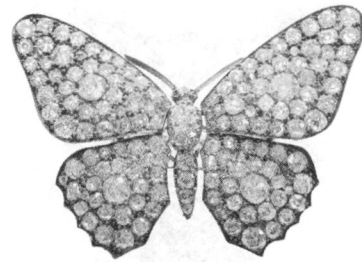

Brunk Auctions

Jewelry, Pin, Cameo, Bakelite, Child's Face, 10K Gold, 1 ¾ x 1 ¼ In.
$92

Clars Auction Gallery

Jewelry, Pin, Cameo, Onyx, Angel, Diamonds, 18K Gold, Tiffany & Co.
$3,884

Neal Auction Co.

Jewelry, Pin, Cat, Black Onyx, Emerald Eye, 18K Gold, Van Cleef & Arpels, 1 ½ x ¾ In.
$2,706

New Orleans Auction Galleries, Inc.

Jewelry, Pin, Coil, Brass, Alexander Calder, 1939, 3 ½ x 2 ¾ In.
$111,000

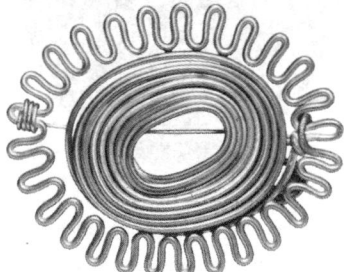

Skinner Auctioneers & Appraisers

Jewelry, Pin, Day & Night Flower, Open & Closing Mechanism, Signed, Les Bernard
$188

Closed

Open

Leslie Hindman Auctioneers

Jewelry, Pin, Doves Of Pliny, Micro Mosaic, Engraved 10K Gold Mount, Italy, c.1890, 3 In.
$5,192

Brunk Auctions

Jewelry, Pin, Dragonfly, Plique-A-Jour Enamel, Opal, Diamonds, Silver, 18K Gold, 2 ⅝ In.
$3,198

Skinner Auctioneers & Appraisers

Jewelry, Pin, Female Face, Modernist, Silver, Agate, Marked 925, 1 x 1 ¾ x 2 ½ In.
$94

Michann's Auctions

Jewelry, Pin, Fish, Jelly Belly, Rhinestones, Signed, Trifari, 1996
$100

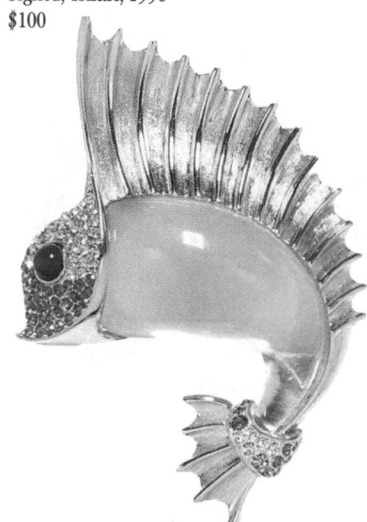

Leslie Hindman Auctioneers

Jewelry, Pin, Flower Basket, Gemstones, Hardstones, 18K Gold, 3 In.
$3,240

Skinner Auctioneers & Appraisers

Jewelry, Pin, Flower, Black Enamel, Signed, Valentino
$63

Leslie Hindman Auctioneers

Jewelry, Pin, Flower, Enamel Petals, Cultured Pearls, 18K Gold, Bucherer, 2 ⅜ In.
$1,169

Skinner Auctioneers & Appraisers

Pin, Dart, Brass, Graduated Rows Of Stylized Darts, R.L. Morris, 3 ¼ In.	338
Pin, Day & Night Flower, Open & Closing Mechanism, Signed, Les Bernard ....*illus*	188
Pin, Diamond, Pearl, C Clasp, Victorian, 1 ¾ In.	236
Pin, Diamond, Sapphire, 18K Gold Lobed Mount, Tiffany, 2 In.	1180
Pin, Diamonds, Pearls, Silver Filigree, Victorian, 2 ½ In.	2700
Pin, Diamonds, Platinum, Filigree, Oval, Art Deco, c.1920, 1 x 2 In.	761
Pin, Dog, Dachshund, 14K Gold, Tiffany & Co., 2 In.	1440
Pin, Dog, Terrier, 14K Gold, Split Pearls, Enamel Collar, Sloan & Co., 1 In.	450
Pin, Dog's Head, Afghan Hound, Shaded Brown, Kay Finch, California Pottery, 2 ¾ In.	153
Pin, Doves Of Pliny, Micro Mosaic, Engraved 10K Gold Mount, Italy, c.1890, 3 In. ....*illus*	5192
Pin, Dragonfly, Coral Head & Wings, 18K Gold, Diamond Melee Tail, Wander, 3 In.	3000
Pin, Dragonfly, Plique-A-Jour Enamel, Opal, Diamonds, Silver, 18K Gold, 2 ⅝ In. ....*illus*	3198
Pin, Earrings, Silver, Star Shape, Paloma Picasso, Tiffany, 4 ½ x 1 ⅜ In.	460
Pin, Female Face, Modernist, Silver, Agate, Marked 925, 1 x 1 ¾ x 2 ½ In. ....*illus*	94
Pin, Fish, Jelly Belly, Rhinestones, Signed, Trifari, 1996 ....*illus*	100
Pin, Flower Basket, Gemstones, Hardstones, 18K Gold, 3 In. ....*illus*	3240
Pin, Flower, 6 Petals, Red & Topaz Cabochons, Marked, Miriam Haskell, 2 In.	165
Pin, Flower, Black Enamel, Signed, Valentino ....*illus*	63
Pin, Flower, Enamel Petals, Cultured Pearls, 18K Gold, Bucherer, 2 ⅜ In. ....*illus*	1169
Pin, Flower, Rose Gold Petals, White Gold Stem, 3 Gold Leaves, M. Buccellati, 3 ½ In.	3422
Pin, Flower, Ruffled Petals, 18K Gold, Diamond Melee Center, McTeigue, 1 ⅜ In.	1020
Pin, Flower, Seed Pearl, Tourmaline, Peridot, 14K Gold, Edwardian, 2 x 1 ½ In.	1770
Pin, Flowering Branch, 14K Gold, Ruby, Tiffany, 1 ¾ In.	708
Pin, Foo Dog, Resin, Carved, Reclining On Rose Quartz, Diamond Eyes, Ruby, 2 ¾ In.	1020
Pin, Frog, Swarovski Crystals, Marked, Chr. Dior, 2 In.	118
Pin, Glass, Reverse Painted, Horse & Rider, Jumping Hedge, Riding Crop Mount, 1 ⅜ In.	480
Pin, Glass, Reverse Painted, Sailing Ship, Gold & Enamel Frame, Enos Richardson, 2 In.	3000
Pin, Grand Canyon, Abstract View, 18K Gold, Swiss, c.1970, 1 ½ x 1 ¼ In.	1121
Pin, Grecian Woman's Head, 18K White Gold, Diamond, Mother-Of-Pearl, Victorian, 1 ⅜ In.	8888
Pin, Heart, Quartz, Faceted, Diamond & Ruby Crown, Chased Scroll, c.1950, 2 In. ....*illus*	875
Pin, Hummingbird, 14K Gold, Freshwater Pearl Wings, Sapphire Eye, Ruser, 2 In.	615
Pin, Hummingbird, 18K Gold, Ruby Eye, H.W. Beattie & Sons, 1 x 1 In.	414
Pin, Insect, 18K Gold, Diamond Wings, Emerald Eyes, D. Claflin, Tiffany, 1 ½ In.	4500
Pin, Insect, Coral, Textured 18K Gold Legs, Diamonds, 2 In.	1140
Pin, Iris, 18K Gold, Satin, Marked, Depose, France, c.1960, 2 ¾ In.	826
Pin, Iris, Silver, Multicolored Guilloche Enamel, Art Nouveau, 2 x 1 In.	127
Pin, Jabot, Arrow, 18K Gold, Diamond Melee Accent, 3 ½ In.	523
Pin, Jabot, Arrow, Diamonds, Sapphires, Platinum, Beaded, Art Deco, 4 ½ In.	3000
Pin, Koala Bears, On Branch, 18K Textured Gold, Ruby Eyes, Clip, Cartier, 1 ¾ x 1 ⅜ In.	4375
Pin, Ladybug, Amber Glass Stone, Pearl Head & Wings, Gold Metal, H. Carnegie, 1 In.	180
Pin, Ladybird, Coral Wings, Diamonds, Black Lacquer, 18K Gold, Cartier, 1 In.	18000
Pin, Lamassu, Human Head, Bull Body, Eagle Wings, 15K Gold, Assyrian Revival, 1 ½ In.	900
Pin, Leaf Branch, 18K Gold, Blue Sapphires, Tiffany & Co., 1 ½ x 1 ⅛ In.	529
Pin, Leaf, 18K Gold, Openwork, 5 Diamonds, Cartier, 1 ½ In.	1230
Pin, Leaf, Berries, Silver, Openwork, G. Jensen, 2 ½ In.	397
Pin, Leaf, Pressed, Navette Case, 18K Gold, Crimped Border, Tiffany & Co., 3 In.	965
Pin, Leaves, Overlapping, 7 Diamond Accents, 18K Textured Gold, M. Buccellati, 3 In.	3000
Pin, Lion, Roaring, Enamel, 18K Gold, Ruby Eyes, c.1960, 1 ½ x 1 ⅝ In.	472
Pin, Lizard, Green & Clear Pastes, Jean Cocteau, 4 ½ In. ....*illus*	800
Pin, Lover's Eye, Enamel, Woven Hair, Gold Mount, Elliptical, Beaded Edge, Victorian, 2 In.	2904
Pin, Married Man, Silver, 14K Gold, Ebony, Enamel, Jade, Gemstone, T. Pardon, 3 ¾ In. ......*illus*	1750
Pin, Micro Mosaic, Coliseum, Oval Gold Ropework Mount, Beaded Border, 1 In.	1046
Pin, Moonstone, Cabochon, Diamond Surround, Sapphires, 14K Gold, Tiffany, c.1940, 3 In.	1440
Pin, Moonstone, Intaglio, Venus, Sea Chariot, Dolphins, Gold & Diamond Frame, 1 In.	6600
Pin, Mosaic, Silver, Gold, Enamel, Ebony, Earl Pardon, 1 ¼ x 2 ½ In. ....*illus*	2500
Pin, Mourning, Urn, Enamel Ground, Split Pearl Frame, Gold Mount, 1 In.	150
Pin, Mushroom, Enamel, Diamonds, 18K Gold, 1 ¾ In. ....*illus*	1320
Pin, Nymph, Plique-A-Jour Wings, Sapphire & Diamond Accents, 18K Gold, Masriera, 2 In.	3240
Pin, Octopus, Ruby Melee Eyes, 18K Gold, 1 ¾ In. ....*illus*	510
Pin, Opal, 76 Diamond Surround, Squat Scroll Frame, Opal Drop, Marcus & Co., 4 In.	22800
Pin, Owl, Lapis, Turquoise, 18K Gold, c.1970, 1 ½ x 1 ¼ In.	1298
Pin, Owl, Silver, Amethyst Eyes, William Spratling, 2 ⅜ In. ....*illus*	2520
Pin, Pansy, Enamel, Diamond Center, Split Pearl Rim, Retractable Bail, Art Nouveau, 1 In.	1476
Pin, Pansy, Enamel, Pearl, 14K Gold, Marked, Wm. Barthman, 1 ¼ In.	531
Pin, Pendant, Cameo, Diamond, Filigree Flower Frame, 14K Gold ....*illus*	189

Jewelry, Pin, Heart, Quartz, Faceted, Diamond & Ruby Crown, Chased Scroll, c.1950, 2 In.
$875

Jewelry, Pin, Lizard, Green & Clear Pastes, Jean Cocteau, 4 ½ In.
$800

Jewelry, Pin, Married Man, Silver, 14K Gold, Ebony, Enamel, Jade, Gemstone, T. Pardon, 3 ¾ In.
$1,750

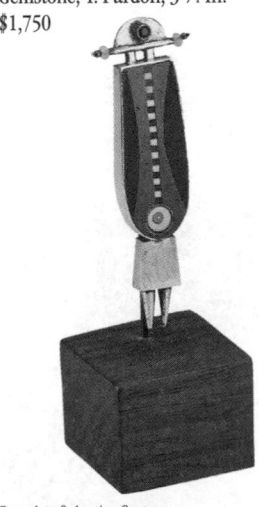

JEWELRY

Jewelry, Pin, Mosaic, Silver, Gold, Enamel, Ebony, Earl Pardon, 1 ¼ x 2 ½ In.
$2,500

Rago Arts & Auction Center

Jewelry, Pin, Mushroom, Enamel, Diamonds, 18K Gold, 1 ¾ In.
$1,320

Skinner Auctioneers & Appraisers

Jewelry, Pin, Octopus, Ruby Melee Eyes, 18K Gold, 1 ¾ In.
$510

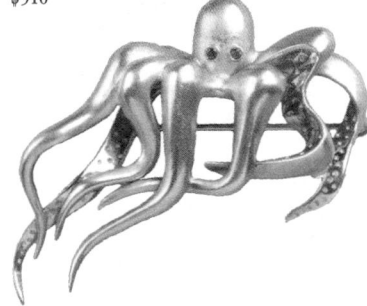

Skinner Auctioneers & Appraisers

Jewelry, Pin, Owl, Silver, Amethyst Eyes, William Spratling, 2 ⅜ In.
$2,520

Skinner Auctioneers & Appraisers

Jewelry, Pin, Pendant, Cameo, Diamond, Filigree Flower Frame, 14K Gold
$189

Conestoga Auction Co., Inc.

Jewelry, Pin, Pendant, Modern Head, Enamel, Benday Dots, Roy Lichtenstein, c.1968, 3 In.
$4,500

Skinner Auctioneers & Appraisers

Jewelry, Pin, Penguin, Bakelite, Moveable Flipper Swings Basket, c.1910, 3 ½ In.
$185

Skinner Auctioneers & Appraisers

Jewelry, Pin, Reflection, Sapphires, Diamonds, Platinum, 14K, Mauboussin, c.1940, 2 ½ In.
$2,000

Rago Arts & Auction Center

Jewelry, Pin, Sailfish, Cobalt Blue & White Enamel, Diamond Eye, 14K Gold, 2 x 2 In.
$590

Brunk Auctions

Jewelry, Pin, Silver & Stone, Open Incised, Modernist Design, Marked 925, 2 In.
$47

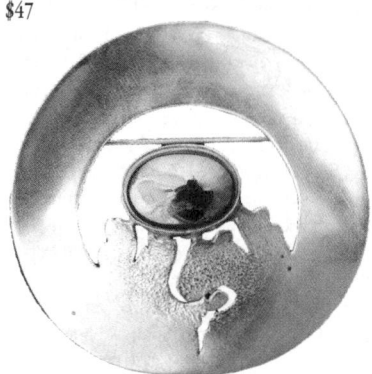

Michann's Auctions

Pin, Pendant, Modern Head, Enamel, Benday Dots, Roy Lichtenstein, c.1968, 3 In. ....*illus* 4500
Pin, Pendant, Watch, Moonstones, 18K Gold Scroll Mount, Diamonds, Gallopin, 2 In.................. 1320
Pin, Penguin, Bakelite, Moveable Flipper Swings Basket, c.1910, 3 ½ In. ....*illus* 185
Pin, Platinum, Diamonds, Black Onyx, Oval, France, Art Deco, c.1920, ¹³⁄₁₆ x 3 ¼ In.................... 8125
Pin, Portrait, Joan Of Arc, Gold Breastplate, Diamond Bow, Drop, Platinum, Edwardian, 2 In..... 1440
Pin, Portrait, White Terrier, Gold Rope Twist Frame, Dog Bone Shape, Flowers, Tiffany, 3 In. 9600
Pin, Reflection, Sapphires, Diamonds, Platinum, 14K, Mauboussin, c.1940, 2 ½ In. ....*illus* 2000
Pin, Ribbon, Diamonds, 14K Gold, Silver Wash, Victorian, 2 In. 878
Pin, Sailfish, Cobalt Blue & White Enamel, Diamond Eye, 14K Gold, 2 x 2 In. ....*illus* 590
Pin, Sapphire, Oval, Diamonds, 18K White Gold Filigree, 6-Sided, Art Deco, 1 ¾ In.................. 585
Pin, Sash, Art Nouveau Maiden, Sinewy Hair, Gold Over Silver, Unger Bros., 3 x 4 In............... 875
Pin, Scarab, Red Stone, Blue, Green & Red Enamel, Goldtone Metal, Hattie Carnegie, 2 In......... 738
Pin, Sea Monster, Emerald Eye, Ruby Accents, 18K Gold, Chaumet, 2 In........................... 984
Pin, Silver & Stone, Open Incised, Modernist Design, Marked 925, 2 In. ....*illus* 47
Pin, Silver, Amber Cabochon, 4 Chrysoprase Cabochons, G. Jensen, 1 ½ In. 1080
Pin, Silver, Buds, Leaves, Blue Hardstone, Suspended Drop, Skonvirke, 5 ½ In. ....*illus* 2829
Pin, Silver, Cultured Pearl, Beach Pebbles, Margaret De Patta, c.1959, ¾ x 2 ¾ In. ....*illus* 8750
Pin, Silver, Geometric Cutouts, Aqua Stone, Marked, Kalo, 1 ½ In. 344
Pin, Silver, Leaf & Berry, Kalo, 2 ½ In. 219
Pin, Silver, Lily Of The Valley, Openwork, Round, Kalo, 2 ½ In. 281
Pin, Silver, Round, 6 Applied Balls, Kalo, 1 ¼ In. 125
Pin, Silver, Scroll Design, Spratling, 2 In. 130
Pin, Spider, Diamonds, Demantoid Garnets, Platinum Over Gold, Edwardian, 1 ⅝ In............... 2280
Pin, St. George Slaying Dragon, Carved, Round, Gold, Openwork, Frame, Victorian, 3 In. 885
Pin, Star Of David, Mother-Of-Pearl, c.1955, 2 x 2 In... 39
Pin, Starburst, Diamond, European Cut, Seed Pearls, 14K Gold, Victorian, 1 In................... 345
Pin, Starburst, Garnet, Vermeil, Bohemian, 1 In.. 92
Pin, Stradivarius Violin, Enamel, Diamonds, 18K Gold, Box, 2 ⅞ In. ....*illus* 1476
Pin, Straw Hat, Bow, Gold, Chanel, 2 In. 300
Pin, Stylized Feather, 14K Gold, Retro, 3 ¾ In. 1200
Pin, Stylized Feather, Silver, Gilt Accents, Blue Enamel, Line Vautrin, 1960s, 2 In. 625
Pin, Stylized Flower, Cobalt Blue & White Enamel, Silver, J. Youngerman, 3 In. 390
Pin, Stylized Pea Pod, Haricot, Diamonds, 18K Gold, Van Cleef & Arpels, 2 ½ In., Pair 8400
Pin, Swan, Cat's-Eye Moonstones, Diamonds, 18K Gold, 3 In. ....*illus* 2760
Pin, Think Too Much, Silver, Copper, Bruce Metcalf, 1986, 3 x 3 ½ In. ....*illus* 2000
Pin, Thistle, Textured 18K Gold Leaves, Silver Wire Thistles, Buccellati, 3 In..................... 4200
Pin, Toad, Green Enamel, Coral Cabochon Belly, Ruby Eyes, Diamonds, 18K Gold, 2 In............ 1680
Pin, Toucan, Lucite, Onyx, Coral, Ivory, Rhinestones, Garnet Eyes, Hattie Carnegie.............. 225
Pin, Toucan, On Branch, 18K Gold, Multicolor Enamel, Bulgari, 2 ⅜ In. 2214
Pin, Trefoil, Platinum, Sapphire, Diamond, Calligaris-Querio, Paris, c.1915, 2 ⅝ In.................. 3750
Pin, Triangles, Fluted, 4 Sapphires, 18K Gold, Tiffany, 2 x 1 In. ....*illus* 767
Pin, Turtle, Chrysoprase, Diamond Accents, 18K Gold Mount, Emis, 1 ½ In. 1320
Pin, Turtle, Enamel, 18K Gold, Diamond Accents, 1900s, 1 ½ In. 633
Pin, Turtle, Enamel, Diamond, 18K Gold, 1950s, 2 x 1 ½ In...................................... 1320
Pin, Turtle, Jade Tablet, Pierced, Ruby Eyes, 14K Gold Mount, Seaman Schepps, 2 In.............. 900
Pin, Umbrella, 18K Gold, Tiffany & Co., 1 ⅝ In. ....*illus* 1020
Pin, Venus & Cupid, Enamel, 14K Gold Frame, Ruby & Diamond Border, Tiffany, 1 In............... 4059
Pin, Watch, 18K Gold, Griffin Crest, Pierced, Peso Coin, P. Flato, c.1980, 1 ½ In................... 7500
Pin, Whale, Silver, Garnet, Brass, Sam Kramer, 1940s-50s, 2 ¾ x 4 ½ In. ....*illus* 4688
Pin, Woman's Head In Profile, Flowing Hair, Scroll Surround, Silver, Art Nouveau, 2 In. 173
Pin, Zebra, Goldtone Metal, Black Enamel Stripes, Rhinestones, Hattie Carnegie 214
Ring, 2 Opals, Tumbled, Abstract Form, Textured 18K Gold Mount, Marcus & Co., Size 6 1200
Ring, 6 Diamond Cluster, Half-Round Gold Band, Art Carved, c.1990, Size 7 600
Ring, 23 Diamonds, Navette Mount, 14K Gold, Size 5 ¾ ....*illus* 1888
Ring, Amethyst, Emerald Cut, Gilt Flower, 14K Gold, Diamond, Seed Pearls, Victorian, Size 7 253
Ring, Amethyst, Intaglio, Classical Scene, Gold Garland Shank, Sapphires, M. Zimmerman 5400
Ring, Arrow, Wrapped, Diamond Point & End, Platinum, Gucci, Size 5 ½ 1320
Ring, Band, 18K Gold Rope Twist, Platinum, Diamond Xs, Marked, Tiffany & Co., Size 5 ¼ 2375
Ring, Band, 18K White Gold, Inset Diamond & Sapphires, Chanel, Size 6 ½ 1920
Ring, Band, Diamond, French Cut, Platinum, Art Deco, Tiffany, c.1925, Size 6 ½ 3776
Ring, Band, Eternity, Diamond, Platinum, Cartier, Size 7 ¼ 1440
Ring, Band, Script Logo, 18K Rose Gold, Chopard, Size 5 ½ In.................................... 510
Ring, Black Onyx Tablet, Diamond, Synthetic Rubies, 14K Gold, Art Deco, Size 5 ¾ 345
Ring, Buckle, 18K Gold, Ruby, Diamonds, Brickwork Strap, Van Cleef & Arpels, 1936.............. 2091
Ring, Candy Box, Hinged, 18K Bicolor Gold, N. Copley, Size 6 1920

Jewelry, Pin, Silver, Buds, Leaves, Blue Hardstone, Suspended Drop, Skonvirke, 5 ½ In.
$2,829

Skinner Auctioneers & Appraisers

Jewelry, Pin, Silver, Cultured Pearl, Beach Pebbles, Margaret De Patta, c.1959, ¾ x 2 ¾ In.
$8,750

Rago Arts & Auction Center

Jewelry, Pin, Stradivarius Violin, Enamel, Diamonds, 18K Gold, Box, 2 ⅞ In.
$1,476

Skinner Auctioneers & Appraisers

TIP

If your old ivory-beaded necklace is becoming yellow, do not clean it. Yellowing is just a sign of age.

JEWELRY

Jewelry, Pin, Swan, Cat's-Eye Moonstones, Diamonds, 18K Gold, 3 In.
$2,760

Skinner Auctioneers & Appraisers

Jewelry, Pin, Think Too Much, Silver, Copper, Bruce Metcalf, 1986, 3 x 3 ½ In.
$2,000

Rago Arts & Auction Center

Jewelry, Pin, Triangles, Fluted, 4 Sapphires, 18K Gold, Tiffany, 2 x 1 In.
$767

Brunk Auctions

Jewelry, Pin, Umbrella, 18K Gold, Tiffany & Co., 1 ⅝ In.
$1,020

Skinner Auctioneers & Appraisers

Jewelry, Pin, Whale, Silver, Garnet, Brass, Sam Kramer, 1940s-50s, 2 ¾ x 4 ½ In.
$4,688

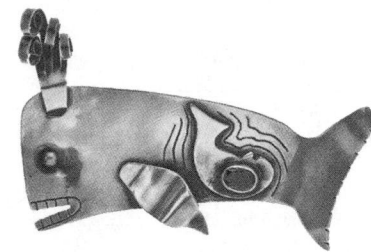

Rago Arts & Auction Center

Jewelry, Ring, 23 Diamonds, Navette Mount, 14K Gold, Size 5 ¾
$1,888

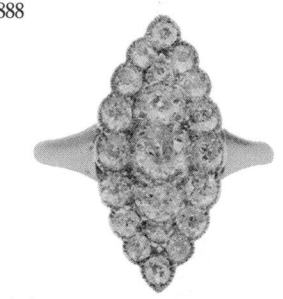

Brunk Auctions

Jewelry, Ring, Diamonds, Black Onyx Inlay, 18K White Gold, Cartier, Size 10
$2,832

Brunk Auctions

Jewelry, Ring, Opal, 18K White Gold, Diamond Frame
$2,706

Neal Auction Co.

Jewelry, Ring, Opal, Pear Shape, Diamonds, Platinum, Gold, Scrolls, Size 5 ½
$4,680

Skinner Auctioneers & Appraisers

Jewelry, Ring, Pearl, Baroque, Claw Set, 18K Gold, Size 6
$1,770

Brunk Auctions

Jewelry, Tussie-Mussie, Mother-Of-Pearl, Gilt, Oak Leaves, Acorns, 1800s, 5 In.
$741

Theriault's

Ring, Carnelian, Intaglio, Classical Maiden, Enamel Bezel, Palm Leaves, M. Zimmerman	6150
Ring, Cat's-Eye Chrysoberyl, Diamonds, Platinum, F & F Felger, Size 9 ½	4920
Ring, Citrine, Cut Corners, Step Cut, 10 Rubies, Retro Gold, c.1940, Size 7	4063
Ring, Citrine, Oval, Gold, Scrolled Wire Ribbons, Diamonds, Platinum, c.1940, Size 8	1875
Ring, Citrines, Shield Shape, 14K White Gold, Art Deco, Size 6	236
Ring, Cocktail, Rubies, Flower Cluster, 18K Gold, Italy, c.1960, Size 6 ¼	472
Ring, Coin, 1928 Indian Head, 2 Half Dollars, Pebble Textured Gold Mount, Size 9 ½	360
Ring, Coral, Oval, Pearl Surround, 14K Gold, 1900s, Size 7	345
Ring, Diamond, 14K Gold, Diamond Wrap, 1900s, Size 6 ½	1093
Ring, Diamond, Black Onyx Stone & Diamond Surround, Platinum, 8-Sided, Art Deco	7200
Ring, Diamond, Oval Cut, Rubies, 18K Gold, C. Krypell, Size 7	20300
Ring, Diamond, Pierced & Beaded Band, 14K Rose Gold, c.1910, Size 5 ¾	533
Ring, Diamonds, Black Onyx Inlay, 18K White Gold, Cartier, Size 10 ....*illus*	2832
Ring, Diamonds, Citrines, Gold Mount, Curved Dome Shape, JCR, Size 6 ¼	826
Ring, Diamonds, Round, Platinum Filigree, Art Deco	690
Ring, Diamonds, Sapphires, 18K Gold, Rectangular Filigree Mount, Art Deco, Size 7	334
Ring, Dinner, Diamond, Pierced & Beaded Band, 14K Rose Gold, c.1910, Size 5 ¾	533
Ring, Dome, 18K Bicolor Gold, Pave Set Diamonds, Gold Bead Sawtooth Mount, c.1960, Size 6..	3438
Ring, Dome, 18K Textured Gold, Diamonds, David Webb, Size 5	1968
Ring, Emerald, Diamond Rows, Cabochon, Platinum, c.1950	767
Ring, Emerald, Old Cut Diamonds, Gold Mount, Art Nouveau, Marcus & Co., Size 7 ¾	10200
Ring, Garnet, Hessonite, Cushion Shape, Platinum, c.1910, Size 5 ¼	2500
Ring, Happy Diamond, Bezel Set Diamond Melee, 18K Gold, Chopard, Size 5 ¾	1320
Ring, Jadeite, Oval Cabochon, Old Single Cut Diamond Melee Accents, Art Deco, Size 7	2520
Ring, Kinetic, Round, Flexible Rods, 18K Gold, Pol Bury, Size 7 ¼	7380
Ring, Leaves, Plique-A-Jour Enamel, Diamonds, Openwork, 18K Gold, Masriera, Size 6 ½	1750
Ring, LOVE, 18K Gold, Inset Screws, Cartier, Size 4 ¾	540
Ring, Man's, Cat's-Eye Chrysoberyl, 2 Tapered Baguette Diamonds, Art Deco, Size 8 ½	2460
Ring, Onyx Tablet, Oval, Diamond, 14K Gold, Scrolls, Art Deco	426
Ring, Opal, 18K White Gold, Diamond Frame ....*illus*	2706
Ring, Opal, Pear Shape, Diamond, Gold, 1900s, Size 7	575
Ring, Opal, Pear Shape, Diamonds, Platinum, Gold, Scrolls, Size 5 ½ ....*illus*	4680
Ring, Pearl, 12-Diamond Surround, Platinum Over Gold Mount, Edwardian, Size 4	1680
Ring, Pearl, Baroque, Claw Set, 18K Gold, Size 6 ....*illus*	1770
Ring, Pearl, Diamonds, 18K Gold, 6 Petal Surround, Marked, Buccino, Size 6 ½	896
Ring, Pearl, South Sea, Pave Diamond Shoulders, 18K Gold, Gump's, Size 6	1200
Ring, Peridot, Oval, 2 Rubellite Surrounds, 18K Gold, Platinum, Size 8 ¼	4375
Ring, Pink Hardstone, Cushion Shape, 4 18K Gold Rings At Corners, Gucci, Size 6	1680
Ring, Platinum, Geometric, Diamonds, Art Deco, Size 7 ¼	1553
Ring, Regard, Diamond, Multicolored Stones, Foil Back, Gold Mount, 1835, Size 8	461
Ring, Rose Cut Diamonds, Turquoise Oval, 18K Gold, Pierced, Buccellati, Size 7 ¼	5313
Ring, Sapphire, Cabochon, Diamonds, 18K Gold, David Webb, Size 5 ¾	2006
Ring, Sapphire, Diamond, 14K Gold, c.1920, Size 5 ½	242
Ring, Sapphire, Intaglio, Armored Knight, Oval, 14K Gold Bezel Mount, Size 10	600
Ring, Sapphire, Oval, Diamond Surround, Platinum, David Webb, Size 6 ¼	6250
Ring, Seal, Hunting Dog Among Reeds, 18K Gold, Van Cleef & Arpels	10200
Ring, Shell, Rock Crystal, Frosted, 14K Gold Lobed Band, Lalounis, 6 ¾ In.	1320
Ring, Silver Cabochon, Marked, Georg Jensen, Size 5	130
Ring, Snake, 18K Gold, Green Enamel, Diamond Melee Nose & Tail, D. Webb, Size 6 ¾	4500
Ring, Stylized Owl, 18K Gold, Chrysoberyl Cat's Eye Cabochons, Potter & Mellen, Size 12	604
Ring, Turquoise, Marquis Mount, Tapered, 14K Gold, Victorian, Size 7 ½	127
Ring, Turquoise, Pharaoh Shoulders, 18K Gold, Egyptian Revival, Size 8	374
Ring, Walrus Head, 18K Gold, Sapphire Eyes, Size 7 ¾	3120
Stickpin, Black Opal, 14K Gold Scrolling Leaf Mount, Art Nouveau, Walton & Co.	1140
Stickpin, Black Opal, Oval, Bezel Set	7200
Stickpin, Bulldog's Head, Diamonds, Ruby Eyes, Platinum Over Gold, Edwardian	1200
Stickpin, Bust, Bearded Man, Middle Eastern Dress, Agate, Carved	369
Stickpin, Coral, Entwined Snake, Blue Enamel, Diamond Head, 18K Gold Mount, France	523
Stickpin, Hound's Head, Pate-De-Verre, Gold & Enamel Collar, Suspended Horn, 3 In.	1476
Stickpin, Trout, Reverse Painted Glass, 18K Gold, Tiffany & Co., 3 ¼ In.	492
Tie Bar, Horse, Reverse Painted Glass, 14K Riding Crop Mount, 2 ¼ In.	360
Tussie-Mussie, Mother-Of-Pearl, Gilt, Oak Leaves, Acorns, 1800s, 5 In. ....*illus*	741

Watches are listed in their own category.

Wristwatches are listed in their own category.

John Rogers, Group, Council Of War, President Lincoln, Grant, Stanton, 38 In. $1,250

Leslie Hindman Auctioneers

Judaica, Etrog Container, Hinged Lid, Silver, Scrollwork, Leaves, Germany, 1900s, 5 ¾ In. $584

Skinner Auctioneers & Appraisers

Judaica, Hanukkah Menorah, Silver, Lions, Marked, Pogorzelski, Warsaw, 9 In. $2,460

Skinner Auctioneers & Appraisers

J

This is an edited listing of current prices. Visit **Kovels.com** to check thousands of prices from previous years and sign up for free information on trends, tips, reproductions, marks, and more.

Judaica, Magillah Scroll, Silver Case, Scrollwork, Crown, Sephardic Lettering, 16 ¾ In.
$3,360

Skinner Auctioneers & Appraisers

Judaica, Spice Box, Fish, Hinged Head, Articulated, Glass Eyes, Silver, c.1910, 14 ¾ In.
$2,400

Skinner Auctioneers & Appraisers

Judaica, Spice Box, Lid, Filigree, Blessing, Bezalel, c.1910, 4 ½ In.
$2,160

Skinner Auctioneers & Appraisers

JOHN ROGERS statues were made from 1859 to 1892. The originals were bronze, but the thousands of copies made by the Rogers factory were of painted plaster. Eighty different figures were created. Similar painted plaster figures were produced by some other factories. Rights to the figures were sold in 1893, and the figures were manufactured for several more years by the Rogers Statuette Co. Never repaint a Rogers figure because this lowers the value to collectors.

Group, Coming To The Parson, Man, Woman, Sitting Parson, 22 In.	290
Group, Council Of War, President Lincoln, Grant, Stanton, 38 In. ....*illus*	1250
Group, Courtship In Sleepy Hollow, 16 ½ x 15 In.	261
Group, Favored Scholar, 1880s, 23 In.	550
Group, Favored Scholar, Teacher, 2 Students, Signed, April 1, 1873, 20 x 16 x 12 In.	400
Group, Fetching The Doctor, Man & Boy On Horse, 16 x 18 In.	360
Group, Frolic At The Old Homestead, c.1887, 22 ½ In.	675
Group, Is It So Nominated In The Bond, 1880, 23 In.	895
Group, Parting Promise, 22 x 9 ½ In.	360
Group, Rip Van Winkle On The Mountain, 21 In.	319
Group, School Days, c.1800s, 21 ½ In.	500
Group, The Peddler At The Fair, 24 In.	600
Group, Weighing The Baby, 21 In.	218

JOSEF ORIGINALS ceramics were designed by Muriel Joseph George. The first pieces were made in California from 1945 to 1962. They were then manufactured in Japan. The company was sold to George Good in 1982 and he continued to make Josef Originals until 1985. The company was then sold to Southland Corporation. The name is now owned by Applause, and the Birthday Girl series is still being made.

Creamer, Holly, Pinecones, Label, 1950s, 4 Oz., 2 ¾ In.	10
Figurine, Birthday Girl, February, Purple Dress & Flower, Foil Label, 5 In.	35
Figurine, Birthstone Girl, July, Lavender Dress, Bouquet, Marked	8
Figurine, Days Of The Week, Sunday, Girl With Wings, Holding Hymnal, 5 In.	85
Figurine, Days Of The Week, Wednesday, Girl Crying, Holding Baby Doll, 5 In.	85
Figurine, Fairy, Pixie Sprite, Wings, Holding Roses, 5 In.	95
Figurine, Garden Party, Lady, Lilac Dress & Hat, 5 ½ In.	49
Figurine, Girl, Valentine Birthday, Purple Gown, Hat, Flowers, 4 In.	55
Figurine, Little Internationals, Greece, Woman, Apron, Pink Flowers, Shawl	46
Figurine, Little Internationals, Hawaii, Green Swirling Skirt, 3 ½ x 3 ½ In.	48
Figurine, Mama, Blue Dress, Apron, Holding Bottle, 7 In.	49
Figurine, Mama, Holding Ointment, Apron, Blue Dress, 7 ½ In.	49
Figurine, Mouse, Flocked, Brown, Black, Japan, 1 ¾ In.	15
Figurine, Sandman, Japanese, Red Lips, Wings, 4 In.	58
Figurine, Secret Pal, Pixie, Wings, Crescent Moon, Roses, 5 In.	95
Figurine, Wee Folks, Boy, Clock, Megaphone, 3 In.	12
Figurine, Woman, Holding Heart Necklace, Green Dress, Butterflies, c.1950, 9 In.	99
Figurine, Woman, Seated At Table, Looking At Ballerina Figurine, 5 ¾ In.	40
Head Vase, Woman, Long Hair & Eyelashes, Green Dress, Pink Roses, 5 In.	89
Lipstick Holder, Woman, Skirt Forms Holders, 4 Tubes, 3 ½ x 4 In.	59
Music Box, Girl Playing Piano, 1950s, 7 In.	45
School Bell, Belle Carrying Apple, School Books, Yellow Gown, Hat, 3 ½ In.	55
Vase, Bud, Girl, Shawl, Hat, Roses On Dress, Blue, Pink, Tree Trunk, 7 In.	48

JUDAICA is any memorabilia that refers to the Jews or the Jewish religion. Interests range from newspaper clippings that mention eighteenth- and nineteenth-century Jewish Americans to religious objects, such as menorahs or spice boxes. Age, condition, and the intrinsic value of the material, as well as the historic and artistic importance, determine the value.

Belt Buckle, Yom Kippur, Silver, Gilt, Jonah, Whale, Paste Stones, 1800s, 8 In.	3240
Bookends, Entry To Hebrew Union College, Wine Madder Glaze, Rookwood, 1948, 5 x 7 In.	1250
Candlestick, Havdalah, Roe Blossom, Spreading Leaves, Spices, Snuffer, 3 ½ In.	720
Etrog Container, Hinged Lid, Silver, Fruit Finial, Cabriole Feet, Austria-Hungary, c.1900, 5 x 7 In.	461
Etrog Container, Hinged Lid, Silver, Scrollwork, Leaves, Germany, 1900s, 5 ¾ In. ....*illus*	584
Flag, Chaplain's, U.S. Army, 2 Tablets, Star Of David, Blue Ground, 4 ½ x 5 ½ In.	417
Hanukkah Menorah, Lions Flanking Crown Back, Cast Iron, Poland, c.1945, 5 In.	750
Hanukkah Menorah, Silver, Lions, Marked, Pogorzelski, Warsaw, 9 In. ....*illus*	2460
Honey Pot, Glass, Silver Base, Lid, Embossed Hebrew Text, c.1980, 3 ¾ In.	225
Inkwell, Silver, Star Of David, Lion On Top, Shield Shape, 4-Footed, Russia, 1880s, 3 ½ In.	774
Kiddush Cup, Venetian Glass, Cobalt, Enamel, Gilt, Vignettes, Moses, c.1900, 7 In.	450
Kosher Stamp, Bronze, Wood Handle, Hebrew Word Carved, Eastern European, 1900s, 3 In.	375

J

Lamp, Sabbath, Hanging, Bronze, Star Shape Oil Container, Germany, 1800s, 10 In.	1875
Magillah, Silver Cased, Chased Leaves, Ink On Vellum Scroll, c.1900, 4 x 8 In.	1560
Magillah Scroll, Silver Case, Scrollwork, Crown, Sephardic Lettering, 16 ¾ In. ....*illus*	3360
Marriage Plate, Pewter, Chased, Marriage Scene, Text Border, 9 In.	625
Menorah, 7 Twisted Arms, Scrolled Base, Wrought Iron, c.1820, 34 x 28 In.	800
Menorah, Lion, Brass, Wood, Folk Art Carved, c.1950, 15 x 29 In.	375
Menorah, Silver, Shaped, Chased, Wm. Weinranck, Germany, c.1900, 7 ¼ In.	1375
Menorah, Sterling Silver, Fauxberzhe, Painted, 1896, Marked, 5 x 7 In.	950
Menorah, Train Shape, Silver Plate, Flowers, Brass Candleholders, 10 In.	144
Mezuzah, Miniature Scroll, Silver Filigree, Enamel Script, c.1900, 3 In.	270
Plaque, Mizrach, Cut Paper, Lions, Decalogue, Columns, Blossoms, Frame, c.1900, 19 x 25 In.	3600
Platter, Sabbath, Silver, Oval, Lobed, Hebrew Border Text, 23 ½ In.	1500
Ring, 18K Gold, Interlocking Hands, Compartment, Mazel Tov, 20th Century	2400
Ring, Marriage, Gold, Applied Round Designs, Hebrew Text, Continental, 1600s, Size 8	8125
Sconce, Synagogue, Brass, Copper, Star Of David Top, c.1920, 25 x 7 In., Pair	1000
Scroll Case, Esther, Flower Engraved, Snake Shape Thumbpiece, Silver, Austria, 1852, 5 In.	5000
Spice Box, Fish, Hinged Head, Articulated, Glass Eyes, Silver, c.1910, 14 ¾ In. ....*illus*	2400
Spice Box, Lid, Filigree, Blessing, Bezalel, c.1910, 4 ½ In. ....*illus*	2160
Spice Box, Silver, Cello Shape, c.1950, 7 In.	250
Spice Box, Silver, Fish, Hinged Head, Scales, Paste Eyes, B. Havdala, 5 ½ In.	1625
Torah Mantle, Crown, Text, Velvet, Embroidery, Green, c.1880, 32 x 54 In.	937
Torah Mantle, Velvet, Blue, Silver Embroidery, Hungary, c.1880, 31 x 19 In.	1875
Torah Mantle, Velvet, Gilt Embroidery, Hebrew Text, Lions, Flowers, 19 x 32 In.	1250
Torah Pointer, Ivory, Spiraled Shaft, Hand With Pointed Finger, Chain, 19th Century, 13 In.	2640
Torah Pointer, Pewter Figural Hand, Wood Shaft, 1800s, 23 ½ In. ....*illus*	342
Torah Pointer, Silver, Lions, 1878, 6 In.	1200
Tzedakah Box, Hinged Lid, Star Of David, Wertheimisegat, 84, Polish, 6 ¾ In. ....*illus*	2280
Wall Hanging, Hebrew, English Commandments, Silk Embroidery, c.1920, 24 x 34 In.	625
Wine Cup Set, Sterling, Stem, Applied Leaves, Star Of David, 4 In., 6 Piece	132

JUGTOWN POTTERY refers to pottery made in North Carolina as far back as the 1750s. In 1915, Juliana and Jacques Busbee set up a training and sales organization for what they named Jugtown Pottery. In 1921, they built a shop at Jugtown, North Carolina, and hired Ben Owen as a potter in 1923. The Busbees moved the village store where the pottery was sold to New York City. Juliana Busbee sold the New York store in 1926 and moved into a log cabin near the Jugtown Pottery. The pottery closed in 1959. It reopened in 1960 and is still working near Seagrove, North Carolina.

Bowl, Turquoise Mottled Glaze, Footed, 4 ½ In.	46
Creamer, Flared Mouth, Incised Lines & Waves, 3 ¼ In.	35
Honey Pot, Lid, Brown Salt Glaze, Wildflowers, Marked, 5 In.	25
Jar, Oil, Black Mirror Glaze, Tapered Bulbous, Ridged, Handles, 8 ⅝ In.	649
Pie Plate, Orange, Scalloped Rim, 9 ¾ In.	18
Pitcher, Brown Mottled Glaze, Incised, 10 In.	375
Vase, Blue Glaze, Red Highlights, Marked, 5 ½ In. ....*illus*	472
Vase, Blue, Red Highlights, Shouldered, Tapered, c.1930, 6 ¼ x 6 In.	649
Vase, Blue, Red, Concentric Ridges, Shouldered, Marked, 8 ½ In.	501
Vase, Blue, Red, Mottled, Strap Ear Handles, Marked, 10 ⅛ In. ....*illus*	4945
Vase, Gray Mottled Glaze, 4 Pinched Ribbons On Shoulder, 6 ¼ In.	165
Vase, Han, Chinese Blue Glaze, Oxblood Red, Ben Owen, Stamped, 1930s, 10 ¼ In.	1540
Vase, Oval, Blue Green Glaze, Marked, 4 ⅛ In.	395
Vase, Turquoise Mottled Glaze, Red Veining, Handles, Marked, 8 ¾ In.	885

JUKEBOXES play records. The first coin-operated phonograph was demonstrated in 1889. In 1906 the Automatic Entertainer appeared, the first coin-operated phonograph to offer several different selections of music. The first electrically powered jukebox was introduced in 1927. Collectors search for jukeboxes of all ages, especially those with flashing lights and unusual design and graphics.

AMI Top Flight, Chrome, 1936, 50 x 34 x 25 In.	9500
Rock-Ola, CM-39, Tabletop, Red, Green, c.1939, 25 In.	1560
Rock-Ola, Model No. 1422, Rounded Sides, 57 In.	1140
Rock-Ola, Rocket Model 1434, 78 Records, Plays Both Sides, 58 In.	2700
Seeburg, Colonel, Yellow, Green, 1940s, 58 x 37 x 27 In.	8000
Seeburg, Elect-O-Matic, Model No. KD 200, 58 In.	1440
Seeburg, Model D, Art Deco, Veneer, Walnut, Blond Maple, 1937	7500
Wurlitzer, Model 71, Tabletop, 23 x 22 In.	5832

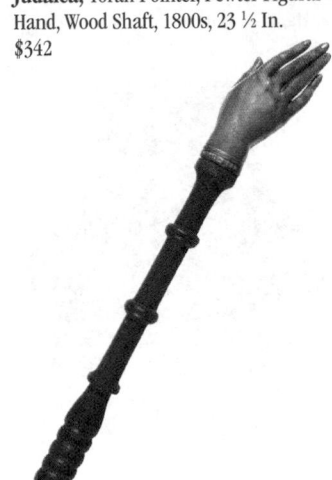

Judaica, Torah Pointer, Pewter Figural Hand, Wood Shaft, 1800s, 23 ½ In.
$342

The Stein Auction Co.

Judaica, Tzedakah Box, Hinged Lid, Star Of David, Wertheimisegat, 84, Polish, 6 ¾ In.
$2,280

Skinner Auctioneers & Appraisers

Jugtown, Vase, Blue Glaze, Red Highlights, Marked, 5 ½ In.
$472

Humler & Nolan

J

347

Jugtown, Vase, Blue, Red, Mottled, Strap Ear Handles, Marked, 10 ⅛ In. $4,945

Humler & Nolan

Kew Blas, Vase, Iridescent Gold, Scalloped Rim, Green Accents, Etched Mark, 3 ⅝ In. $480

Skinner Auctioneers & Appraisers

Kew Blas, Vase, Iridescent, Gold, Purple, Platinum, Flower Shape, Signed, 12 In. $304

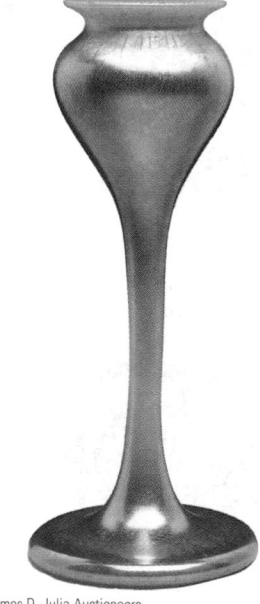

James D. Julia Auctioneers

Wurlitzer, Model 700, Multi-Selector, Laminated Wood, Plastic, Chrome, 56 x 33 In.	3042
Wurlitzer, Model 780E, Wagon Wheel, c.1941	1600
Wurlitzer, Model 850, Peacock, Key, c.1942	16200
Wurlitzer, Model 1015, Multi-Selector Phonograph, Bubbler, 24 Selection, 5 To 25 Cents	3300

KATE GREENAWAY, who was a famous illustrator of children's books, drew pictures of children in high-waisted Empire dresses. She lived from 1846 to 1901. Her designs appear on china, glass, napkin rings, and other pieces.

Toothpick Holder, Square Mouth, Tufts Caddy, Boy, New England Agate, 3 ½ In.	403
Toothpick Holder, Venetian Diamond Optic, Amberina, Silver, c.1880, 4 In.	316

KAY FINCH CERAMICS were made in Corona Del Mar, California, from 1935 to 1963. The hand-decorated pieces often depicted whimsical animals and people. Pastel colors were used. *Kay Finch* CALIFORNIA

Figurine, Angel, Blue Wings, Hands Up, Blond, 4 ¼ In.	48
Figurine, Camel, 5 x 5 In.	77
Figurine, Cherub's Bust, Wings, Black Hair, Pink Cheeks, 2 ¼ x 4 ¾ In.	20
Figurine, Couple, Godey, Pink, Cape, Muff, Hat, 9 ½ In.	120
Figurine, Dog, Shih Tzu, 13 x 10 In.	150
Figurine, Dog, Yorkshire Terrier, Gold Leaf, Marked, 7 x 11 In., Pair	76
Figurine, Elephant, Peanut, Pink, Flowers On Ears, 8 x 6 x 5 In.	325
Figurine, Elephant, Peanuts, Trunk Up, Flowered Ears, Pink, Purple, 8 ¼ x 6 ½ In.	80
Figurine, Elephant, Pink, Green Blanket, Flowered Ears, Marked, 14 x 17 In.	154
Figurine, Girl, Cape, Hands In Muff, Purple Flowers, 7 In.	48
Figurine, Owl, Ma Ma Tootie, Brown, Tan, 5 ¾ In.	45
Figurine, Owl, Tootsie, White, Brown Eyes, 3 ¾ In.	15
Figurine, Pekingese, Lying Down, Soft Pink, 13 In.	450
Figurine, Poodle, Gold Bow, 4 ½ In.	225
Planter, Ikebana, Celadon Green Glaze, Offset Opening, 5 x 11 In.	85
Powder Box, Cover, White, Pink & Blue Stylized Flowers, Round, 2 x 3 ½ In.	41

KAYSERZINN, *see Pewter category.*

KELVA glassware was made by the C. F. Monroe Company of Meriden, Connecticut, about 1904. It is a pale, pastel-painted glass decorated with flowers, designs, or scenes. Kelva resembles Nakara and Wave Crest, two other glasswares made by the same company. **KELVA**

Box, Green Mottled Ground, Pink Flowers, Gilt Metal Rim, 2 ½ x 6 ½ In.	177
Dresser Box, Bishop Hat Shape, Flower Heads, Green Marbled Ground, 4 ½ x 6 ½ In.	354
Dresser Box, Pink Roses, Green Mottled Ground, Marked, 3 ½ x 8 In.	383
Humidor, Blue Mottled Ground, Pink Flowers, Gilt Cigar, 5 ¾ In.	550
Pin Holder, Flowers, Leaves, Pierced Handles, c.1890, 1 ¼ x 4 ¼ In.	100
Vase, Gray Mottled Background, Pink Flowers, Gilt Metal Feet, Signed, 8 ½ In.	472

KENTON HILLS POTTERY in Erlanger, Kentucky, made artwares, including vases and figurines that resembled Rookwood, probably because so many of the original artists and workmen had worked at the Rookwood plant. Kenton Hills opened in 1939 and closed during World War II.

Bowl, English Ivy, Blue, Ivory Ground, R. Dickman, Square, Footed, 5 ½ In.	220 to 264
Bust, Sigrid, Woman's Head, David Seyler, Dusty Pink Glaze, Tulip Mark, 6 ½ In.	66
Jar, Peaked Lid, Green, Brazilian Cat's-Eye Glaze, 6 ¾ In.	96
Vase, Antelope, Crosshatching, Persian Blue, Tapered, W. Hentschel, c.1940, 6 ½ In.	204
Vase, Danish Blue, Spanish Red, Mandarin Yellow Top, Bulbous, Flared, 7 In.	252
Vase, Dusty Pink, Black Horizontal Lines, Beads, Bulbous, Tapered, 6 ½ In.	144
Vase, Jungle Black, Band Of Crosshatched Lines, Cylindrical, W. Hentschel, 12 In.	720
Vase, Lamp Base, Iris, Standard Glaze, Swollen Shape, W. Hentschel, 12 ½ In.	264

KEW BLAS is the name used by the Union Glass Company of Somerville, Massachusetts. The name refers to an iridescent golden glass made from the 1890s to 1924. The iridescent glass was reminiscent of the Tiffany glass of the period. *KEW-BLAS*

Vase, Gold Iridescent, Green Accents, Pulled Rope Design, Signed, 1900, 8 x 4 In.	472
Vase, Iridescent Gold, Scalloped Rim, Green Accents, Etched Mark, 3 ⅝ In. .....*illus*	480
Vase, Iridescent, Gold, Purple, Platinum, Flower Shape, Signed, 12 In. .....*illus*	304
Vase, Jack-In-The-Pulpit, Gold Iridescent, Spreading Stretch Border Face, 11 ¾ In.	3738
Vase, Pulled Feather, Gold, Scalloped Rim, Footed, Signed, 12 ¼ In. .....*illus*	1955

KEWPIES, designed by Rose O'Neill, were first pictured in the *Ladies' Home Journal*. The figures, which are similar to pixies, were a success, and Kewpie dolls and figurines started appearing in 1911. Kewpie pictures and other items soon followed. Collectors search for all items that picture the little winged people.

Bisque, Black Cat, Cameo Doll Products, 3 In.	424
Bisque, Boy, Standing, Pigeon Toed, Orange Shorts & Bow, Japan, c.1925, 4 In.	65
Bisque, Bride & Groom, Side-Glancing Eyes, Jointed Arms, 5 ½ In., Pair................*illus*	840
Bisque, Composition, Kestner Toddler Body, Jointed, Germany, c.1912, 11 In. ....*illus*	5600
Bisque, Head Peeking From Basket, Flowers, Rose O'Neill, c.1915, 3 ½ In. ....*illus*	840
Bisque, Huggers, Starfish Hands, Rose O'Neill, c.1920, 4 In.	115
Bisque, Jointed Shoulders, Heart Label, Box With Poem, Germany, 5 In.	270
Bisque, On Belly, Winking, Lefton, 5 In.	25
Bisque, Playing Guitar, Blue Wings, 4 In.	395
Bisque, Seated, Hands Under Chin, Arms Propped On Knees, Kestner, 1913, 6 ½ In.	152
Bowl, Kewpies Playing, Gilt Trim, Germany, 1912, 8 In.	335
Cake Topper, Bisque, Hugger, Bouquet, Japan, 3 ¼ x 3 ½ In.	95
Cake Topper, Bride, Groom, Hugging, Bisque, Paper Outfits, 4 In.	254
Chocolate Mold, Black Metal, 11 In.	94
Chocolate Mold, Metal, Holding Belly, Tree Stump, 1913, 6 In.	295
Composition, Elbows On Knees, Smiling, Wings, Rose O'Neill, 3 ½ In.	32
Composition, Yellow Sundress, Flowers, Side-Glancing, 1930s, 12 In.	225
Mug, Farmer, Flag, Lithopone Base, Handle, Cameo Design, Germany, c.1915, 3 In.	173
Paper Dolls, Uncut, Saalfield Artcraft, Box, 1963	35
Pin, Silver Plate, Hat, Holding Rake, 1 In.	85
Plate, Action, 3 Kewpies, Holding Bouquets, Rose O'Neill, 1973, 8 In.	32
Plate, Being Loved, Kewpie In Flower, Rosie O'Neill, Japan, 1973, 8 In.	20
Plate, Kewpie Baby In Rose Petal, Rosie O'Neill, Cameo Products, 1973, 8 In.	20
Quilt, Embroidered, Cotton, Dancing Kewpies, Pink, 1930s, 29 x 38 In.	95
Salt & Pepper, Kewpie Dolls, Sterling Silver, Sheffield, 2 ⅞ In.	195
Salt & Pepper, Sterling Silver, Footed, Sheffield, 2 ⅞ In.	195
Teapot, Couple, Ruffled Rim, Embossed Beaded Foot, Pink Highlights, Germany, 5 In.	115
Tobacco Rug, Holding Cranberry Rake & Bowl, Multicolor, Rose O'Neill, 1914, 5 x 6 In.	34
Tray, Castles Ice Cream, Kewpies, Strawberry, Rose O'Neill, 13 ⅜ In. ....*illus*	288
Vase, Brush, Placecard Holder, Incised Rose O'Neill, 2 ½ In.	480

KING'S ROSE*, see Soft Paste category.*

KITCHEN utensils of all types, from eggbeaters to bowls, are collected today. Handmade wooden and metal items, like ladles and apple peelers, were made in the early nineteenth century. Mass-produced pieces, like iron apple peelers and graniteware, were made in the nineteenth century. Also included in this category are utensils used for other household chores, such as laundry and cleaning. Other kitchen wares are listed under manufacturers' names or under Advertising, Iron, Tool, or Wooden.

Ashtray, Matchbook Holder, Griswold No. 770, Square	18
Barrel, Vinegar, Oak, 4 Iron Bands, Round, Tapered, Brass Spigot, c.1900, 13 x 16 In.	148
Bin, Grain, Pine, Red Paint, Divided Interior, Turned Feet, 1800, 26 x 62 In.	529
Bird Spit, Heart Cutouts, Penny Feet, Adjustable, Wrought Iron, c.1765, 34 In.	1659
Bird Spit, Wrought Iron, Tulip Finial, Penny Feet, c.1770, 26 ¾ In.	415
Bowl, Burl, 19th Century, 6 x 14 ½ In.	1928
Bowl, Burl, Dark Patina, 1800s, 4 x 14 In.	1880
Bowl, Maple Burl, Turned, Semi-Squared Rim Molding, Figuring, 3 ¾ x 12 ⅜ In.	374
Bread Slicer, Cast Iron, Wood, c.1920, 9 x 15 In.	81
Broiler, Iron, Rotating, 25 ½ In.	115
Broiler, Iron, Tripod Base, 26 ½ In.	403
Broiler, Scotch, Hand Wrought, Iron, 12 In.	104
Broiler, Wrought Iron, Double Handle Heart Cutouts, Scrolled Feet, 32 In.	948
Broiler, Wrought Iron, Rotating, Ram's Horn Handle, 1800s, 28 In.	180
Broiler, Wrought Iron, Star, Heart Cutouts, c.1890, 25 In.	1304
Butcher Block, Maple, Turned Wood Legs, Metal Wheels, Hooks, Cleavers, Metal Basket	489
Butter Cutter, Porcelain Base, Elgin, Patent 1901, 8 x 9 x 4 ½ In.	257
Butter Mold, look under Mold, Butter in this category.	
Butter Paddle, Acorn, Birds, Star, Flowers, Initials, Early 1800s, 12 ¼ In.	518
Butter Paddle, Curly Maple, 19th Century, 9 In.	120
Butter Paddle, Curly Maple, Carved Handle, U.S.A., 1800s, 9 In.	3408
Butter Stamp, Tulip, Bird, c.1865, 4 In.	663

Kew Blas, Vase, Pulled Feather, Gold, Scalloped Rim, Footed, Signed, 12 ¼ In.
$1,955

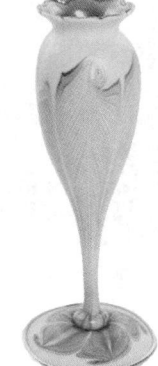

Early Auction Co.

Kewpie, Bisque, Bride & Groom, Side-Glancing Eyes, Jointed Arms, 5 ½ In., Pair
$840

Theriault's

Kewpie, Bisque, Composition, Kestner Toddler Body, Jointed, Germany, c.1912, 11 In.
$5,600

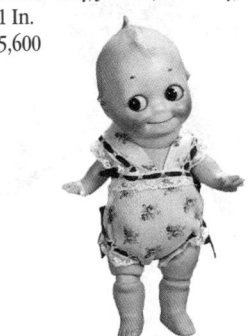

Theriault's

Kewpie, Bisque, Head Peeking From Basket, Flowers, Rose O'Neill, c.1915, 3 ½ In.
$840

Theriault's

K

Kewpie, Tray, Castles Ice Cream, Kewpies, Strawberry, Rose O'Neill, 13 ⅜ In. $288

Wm Morford Auctions

Kitchen, Casserole, Lid, Friendship Pattern, Divided, 13 x 9 In. $34

Ruby Lane, Inc.

Kitchen, Churn, Pine, Stave Construction, A-Frame Stand, Blue Paint, c.1875, 31 In. $120

Garth's Auctioneers & Appraisers

Kitchen, Measuring Cup, Green, 3 Spouts, Embossed Kellogg's, Hazel-Atlas, 3 ½ In. $45

Ruby Lane, Inc.

Butter Stamp, Tulip, Stylized Starflowers, Wood Handle, c.1850, 5 In.	270
Butter Stamp, Wood, Tulip, Geometric Designs, 2-Sided, 1800s, 4 ½ x 2 In.	1955
Cake Board, Mahogany, Fireman, Pumper, Reverse Side Figures, Rooster, 1800s, 9 x 13 In.	948
Casserole, Lid, Friendship Pattern, Divided, 13 x 9 In. *illus*	34
Cheese Strainer, Round, Hole In Center, Burled, c.1810, 4 x 10 In.	2370
Churn, Oak, Piggin Table Top, Staved, Handle, New England, c.1800, 16 x 7 ¼ In.	150
Churn, Paint, c.1850, 41 ½ In.	178
Churn, Pine, Poplar, R.B. Dunning, No. 4, Yellow Paint, c.1890, 32 x 20 In.	411
Churn, Pine, Stave Construction, A-Frame Stand, Blue Paint, c.1875, 31 In. *illus*	120
Churn, Pine, Tapered, Blue Green Paint, Pennsylvania, c.1850, 43 ½ In.	492
Churn, Wood Band, 3 Metal Bands, Blue Milk Paint, Stencil, Lury & Berc, 1800s, 21 ½ In.	259
Churn, Wood, Red Paint, Marked J.U. Fiesters, Patent Feb 26, 1856, 58 In.	259
Coffee Bin, Glass Panel, Tin, Brass, 42 ¼ x 15 In.	119
Coffee Grinders are listed in the Coffee Mill category.	
Coffee Mills are listed in their own category.	
Cookie Board, Springerle, Horse-Drawn Vehicle, Man, Plough, Carriage, Sulky, 26 x 4 ½ In.	86
Cookie Board, Springerle, Pig, Feeding Trough, 11 ¼ x 7 ⅜ In.	29
Cookie Board, Springerle, Seated Cat, Horseman, 2-Sided, 12 x 7 In.	230
Cookie Cutter, Tin, Amish Man, Tipping Hat, Full Bodied Silhouette, 1800s, 8 ½ x 4 In.	295
Corn Husk Cutter, Cast Iron, Wheel, 4 Legs, Wood Board Top, Salesman's Sample, 12 In.	369
Corn Sheller, Cast Iron, Painted, Middleton, Eagle Head Terminal, Wall Mounted, c.1870	295
Dough Box Base, Wood, Painted, Pa., c.1850, 27 x 35 In.	415
Dough Box, Cleated, Canted Box, Splayed Legs, Red Paint, c.1820, 29 x 50 In.	750
Dough Box, Kneader, Pine Trough, Crank, 3 Square Legs, French Provincial, 34 x 33 In.	178
Dough Box, Lid, William & Mary, Red Paint, Cantered, c.1750, 29 x 42 In.	450
Dough Box, Painted Red, Lid, Arched Handle, Handle, 1800s, 28 x 17 In.	115
Dough Box, Pine, 1800s, Pa., 27 x 48 In.	830
Dough Box, Pine, Maple Top, Breadboard Ends, c.1890, 29 x 50 x 23 In.	529
Dough Box, Poplar, Red Paint, Square Legs, Lift Top, 1800s, 31 x 32 In.	147
Dough Box, Poplar, Red Stain, Pa., 12 x 33 In.	356
Dough Box, Stand, Grain Paint, Pennsylvania, c.1850, 30 x 36 In.	185
Dough Box, Walnut, Turned Legs, Pa., 29 ½ x 40 ½ In.	593
Dough Scraper, Iron, Brass, Peter Deer, Impressed, Pa., 1856, 4 In.	770
Dough Scraper, Wrought Iron, Triangular Face, Punched Rosette, c.1755, 3 ½ x 4 In.	345
Dough Scraper, Wrought Iron, Twist Handle, 5 ½ In.	123
Dry Measure, Copper, Brass Banding, Oval, Impressed Ohio, 7 ½ x 16 In.	356
Drying Rack, Wood, Horizontal Slats, c.1845, 30 x 40 ½ In.	173
Dutch Oven, Tite-Top, Griswold No. 9, Lid	140
Feather Duster, Peacock Feathers, Turned Wooden Handle, 19th Century, 39 In.	59
Fish Mold, Redware, Pennsylvania, c.1850, 13 ½ In.	150
Flour Sifter, Handle, Wood, Pat. 1861, 13 x 11 In.	184
Food Chopper, Clamps, Cast Iron, Nickel Plated, Arcade, c.1902, 3 ½ In.	150
French Fry Cutter, King, Oak, Brass Bucket, Iron Handle, Wall Mount, Strite Anderson	300
Grater, Drawer, Yellow Pine, c.1890, 5 x 13 In.	81
Grater, Nutmeg, Wood, Brass Fittings, Hand Crank, c.1865, 7 ½ In.	177
Grater, Wood, Miniature, 1800s, 7 ½ x 5 In.	52
Griddle, Griswold No. 8, Oval, Slant Logo, Erie	85
Griddle, Griswold No. 9.	20
Griddle, Griswold No. 12, Bail	30
Griddle, Griswold No. 12, Bail, Diamond Logo	80
Gridiron, Iron, Snake Grids, Curled End, 4 Feet, Black Paint, c.1805, 4 x 12 ½ In.	138
Hoosier Cabinet, Wood, 2 Doors, 5 Drawers, Blue, White Paint, 48 x 35 In.	184
Icebox, Oak, Brass, Paneled, Carved Flowers, Baldwin, Vermont, 41 x 28 In.	264
Ice Chest, Victorian, Walnut, Carved Crest, Door, c.1870, 79 x 33 In.	911
Ice Cream Cone Oven, Double Oven, Cast Iron, Wooden Handles, Parisian, 8 ½ x 16 In.	847
Ice Cream Freezer, Crank, Wood, Metal, Dana, Salesman's Sample, c.1915, 7 In.	360
Ice Cream Freezer, Fitchburg, Mass., Wood, Metal, Instant Freezer, 1891, 15 x 19 In.	666
Ice Cream Freezer, Glass, Cylindrical, Horizontal Ribs, Wire Closure, Consolidated, 11 In.	109
Ice Cream Freezer, Hand Crank, White Mountain, 16 In.	59
Ice Cream Freezer, White Metal, Hinged Lid, Side Crank, Mi Rapid Freezer, 12 In.	216
Ice Cream Freezer, Wood & Metal Bucket, Shepard's Lightning, Crank, Child's, 7 In.	303
Ice Cream Freezer, Yellow Metal Canister, Side Crank, Instant Freeze, Decal, 12 In.	272
Ice Cream Server, Gun Type, Metal, Trigger, Prince Castle Mfg., 6 In.	145
Ice Cube Maker, Du-More Ice Cuber, Chrome Plated, Martocello & Co., Box, 9 In.	97
Iron, Smoothing Board, Painted, Horse Handle, Continental, c.1890, 27 ½ In.	118
Jar, Apple Butter, Green Mottled Glaze, Redware, c.1855, 5 ¼ In.	147

K

Kettle Stand, George III, Mahogany, Piecrust Top, 4 Columns, Tripod Base, 21 x 12 In.	1250
Kettle Stand, Iron, Spear Point Terminals, Turned Wood Handle, Tripod Base, 1800s. 12 ½ In.	593
Kettle Stand, Serpentine Reticulated Gallery, Pierced Legs, c.1730 x 13 In., Pair	2390
Kettle, Griswold No. 8, Erie	40
Kettle, Hearth, Iron, Brass, Domed Lid, Swing Handle, Hook, 3 Gal., 1800s, 19 In.	210
Kettle, Sugar, Iron, Plantation, c.1860, 24 x 40 In.	2337
Ladle, Wrought Iron, Tapered, Twisted Handle, Shenandoah, Vir., c.1820, 7 ½ In.	115
Lazy Susan, Mahogany, 2 Tier, c.1890, 8 ½ x 27 ½ In.	395
Match Holders can be found in their own category.	
Match Safes can be found in their own category.	
Measuring Cup, Green, 3 Spouts, Embossed Kellogg's, Hazel-Atlas, 3 ½ In. ....*illus*	45
Meat Fork, Heart Shape Flattened Handle, Iron, Stamped D. Rohrer, c.1843, 17 ¾ In.	748
Meat Fork, Iron, Brass, Copper Bands, Engraved, Rattail Terminal, Pa., 1843, 16 ½ In.	978
Meat Spit, Hearth Dangle, Cage Shape, Swivel Hooks, 1800s, 21 x 11 In.	196
Mixer, Milk Shake, Cast Iron, Hand Crank, Fly Wheel, 2 Containers, Philadelphia, 23 In.	2057
Mixer, Milk Shake, Hamilton Beach, Square Brass Shaft & Ball, Marble Base, Electric, 17 In.	157
Mixer, Milk Shake, Kar Lac Hot & Cold, Brass, Porcelain, Cup, Electric, Richardson, 18 In.	194
Mixer, Milk Shake, Kwikmix, Metal, Hand Crank, Shaped Wood Base, 10 ½ In.	157
Mixer, Milk Shake, Meyer's Bullet, Tan, Red Porcelain Base, Metal Cup, Electric, 19 In.	272
Molds may also be found in the Pewter and Tinware categories.	
Mold, Butter, Carved Swan Stamp, c.1865, 6 x 4 ½ In.	40
Mold, Butter, Wood, Cow Impressed, c.1865, 7 ½ x 4 ½ In.	81
Mold, Butter, Wood, Rose Stamp, Carved, Pat. 1866, 6 ½ x 4 ½ In.	40
Mold, Cake, French Kugelhopf, Copper, Round, Center Tube, c.1930, 4 x 11 ½ In.	73
Mold, Cake, Heart Shape, Tin, 15 x 14 In.	460
Mold, Cake, Rabbit, Sitting, Griswold No. 862-863	180
Mold, Candle, see Tinware category.	
Mold, Cheese, Heart Shape, Tin, Punched, Applied Handle, Angled Feet, 4 In. ....*illus*	189
Mold, Cheese, Heart Shape, Tin, Punched, Tamper, Tubular Feet, Hanging Ring, 3 ½ In.	384
Mold, Chocolate, Rabbit, Driving Car, Hinged, Metal, 7 ¼ x 7 ¼ In., 3 Piece ....*illus*	150
Mold, Chocolate, Rabbit, Standing, Basket On Back, 18 In.	354
Mold, Food, Lamb Shape, Griswold, No. 866, 12 x 7 In.	48
Mold, Ice Cream, Santa, Holding Bag, Lead, Hinged, 11 In.	454
Mold, Ice Cream, see also Pewter category.	
Mold, Jelly Or Cake, Pig, Lying Down, Tin, 10 ¾ x 12 ¾ In., 2 Piece	360
Mold, Redware, Swirl, Orange & Brown Glaze, Scalloped Rim, 1800s, 3 x 8 ⅛ In. ....*illus*	177
Mold, Redware, Turk's Head, Scalloped Coggled Rim, Ribbed Post, Orange, Green, 3 x 9 In.	59
Mold, Redware, Turk's Head, Scalloped Edge, Ribbed Post, Manganese, Brown Glaze, 3 x 7 In.	24
Mold, Redware, Turk's Head, Scalloped, Manganese Sponged Rim, Red Orange Glaze, 2 x 7 In.	1180
Mold, Sugar, Maple, 1800s, 11 x 3 In.	52
Mold, Vienna Bread Roll, Griswold, No. 26	70
Mold, Wheat & Corn Stick, Griswold No. 27	130
Mortar & Pestle, Blue Paint, Oval, c.1820, 12 In.	1304
Mortar & Pestle, Burl, Turned, Flared Rim, 6 ½ In.	120
Mortar & Pestle, Wood, Turned Base, Lingnum Vitae, c.1900	59
Mortar & Pestle, Wood, Turned, Yellow Paint, c.1860, 8 ¼ In.	1410
Mortar, Burl, Carved, Mellow Patina, c.1759, 6 ¾ In.	1337
Muffin Stand, Mahogany, Satinwood Inlay, 3 Tiers, Hinged, Trestle Leg, 35 In.	48
Muffineer, Mahogany, 3 Tiers, 35 ½ In.	148
Pan, Daubiere, Lid, Copper Clad, Oval, Brass Handles, 10 x 20 x 8 ¾ In.	356
Pan, Fish Poaching, Cover, Copper, Oval, 2 Brass Raised Handles, 7 x 27 In.	237
Pantry Box, 1 Finger, Bentwood, Blue Paint, Oval, Copper Tacks, U.S.A., c.1865, 1 ½ x 4 In.	294
Pantry Box, Bentwood, Oval, Finger Lap Joint, Blue Paint, 7 x 17 In.	1599
Pantry Box, Bentwood, Round, Paint, Lapped Seams, Copper Tacks, U.S.A., c.1860, 6 x 12 In.	264
Pantry Box, Bentwood, Vinegar Graining, Round, Lid, c.1885, 5 x 8 In.	235
Pantry Box, BFH Monogram, Blue Green Paint, Lid, 1800s, 2 ½ x 6 In.	840
Pantry Box, Painted, Swing Bail Handle, Lid, New England, c.1850, 6 ½ x 11 ¼ In. ....*illus*	2666
Pantry Box, Round, Handle, White Paint, c.1860, 15 ½ x 9 In.	34
Pantry Box, Round, Maple & Pine, Painted, Swinging Bail Handle, Lid, 5 x 9 In.	711
Peel, Wrought Iron, Ram's Horn Finial, Flattened End, Rounded Shaft, c.1800, 47 ¼ In.	29
Peeler, Apple, Crank Action, Tabletop, Painted Red, 29 In.	24
Peeler, Apple, Mechanical, Wood, Carved, c.1850, 12 ¾ x 26 ½ In.	196
Pie Crimper, Bone, 6 Wheels, Heart Cutouts, Star, Pierced Handle, c.1800, 7 ½ In.	2040
Pie Crimper, Brass, Flattened Handle, Wriggle Work, Lollipop Terminal, 1800s, 7 ¾ In.	189
Pie Crimper, Iron, 1794 Large Cent Make-Do Wheel, Whale Tail Handle, Notched, 5 ½ In.	345
Pie Crimper, Iron, Rooster Terminal, Southeastern Pennsylvania, c.1800, 2 ⅜ x 8 ¼ In.	11875

Kitchen, Mold, Cheese, Heart Shape, Tin, Punched, Applied Handle, Angled Feet, 4 In.
$189

Conestoga Auction Co., Inc.

Kitchen, Mold, Chocolate, Rabbit, Driving Car, Hinged, Metal, 7 ¼ x 7 ¼ In., 3 Piece
$150

Wm Morford Auctions

Kitchen, Mold, Redware, Swirl, Orange & Brown Glaze, Scalloped Rim, 1800s, 3 x 8 ⅛ In.
$177

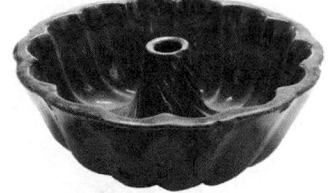

Brunk Auctions

Kitchen, Pantry Box, Painted, Swing Bail Handle, Lid, New England, c.1850, 6 ½ x 11 ¼ In.
$2,666

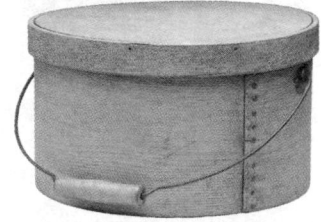

James D. Julia Auctioneers

K

Kitchen, Vacuum Cleaner, Regina Pneumatic, Model A, Double Acting, c.1910, 41 ¾ In.
$75

Aspire Auctions

Kitchen, Washing Machine, Metal Tub, Cast Iron, Salesman's Sample, Continental, 7 x 6 In.
$1,067

James D. Julia Auctioneers

Knife, Pocket, Pirelli Tires, Superflex, Figural Tire, 2 Blades, 3 ⅛ x 1 In.
$690

Wm Morford Auctions

TIP

Store a clean iron pot or pan in a dry place with a clean piece of paper towel inside.

Pie Crimper, Rabbit Shape, Pewter, 5 ¾ In.	224
Pie Crimper, Wrought Iron, Pierced 1838 Penny Wheel, 7 In.	770
Poacher, 7 Hole, Griswold No. 32	30
Popover, Griswold No. 10	40
Press, Fruit, Oak, Turned Supports, Feet, Iron Screw, France, 19th Century, 18 x 11 In.	296
Rack, Broiling, Iron, Horseshoe Shape, Cross Bars, C-Hooks, Easel Back, 13 x 12 In.	384
Rack, Oak, 4 Open Rung Shelves, c.1850, 52 x 45 In.	180
Rack, Utensil, Iron, Bird Finials, Scrolls, 1800s, 22 x 25 ¾ In.	360
Reamers are listed in their own category.	
Refrigerator, G.E., Monitor Top, Art Deco, Black, Gold Designs, Wire Shelves, 29 x 50 In.	546
Rolling Pin, Springerle, Maple, Carved Grid, Animals, Plants, Figures, 16 In.	147
Salt & Pepper Shakers are listed in their own category.	
Salt Box, Wood, Hanging, Barrel Shape, New England, c.1860, 10 ½ x 5 In.	115
Sausage Stuffer Press, Cast Iron, Hibbard, Spencer, Bartlett & Co., Chicago, c.1897, 24 In.	120
Scoop, Ice Cream Sandwich, Dan-Dee Dipper Press, Dipper Co., September, 1920, 12 In.	605
Scoop, Ice Cream Sandwich, Polished Brass, Set Screw, Wood Handle, Maryland, 10 ½ In.	484
Scoop, Ice Cream Sandwich, Polished Metal, Turned Wood, Mayer Mfg. Corp., 12 In.	85
Scoop, Ice Cream, Banana Split, Elliptical Bowl, Fisher Wood Handle, Gilchrist, 10 ½ In.	121
Scoop, Ice Cream, Banana Split, No. 34, Wood Handle, Gilchrist, 11 In.	333
Scoop, Ice Cream, Brass, Polished, Wood Handle, Flat Paddle, Mosteller, No. 78, 10 In.	48
Scoop, Ice Cream, Brass, Polished, Wood Handle, Gem Spoon Co., 1905, 10 In.	18
Scoop, Ice Cream, Clave Pie Ala Mode, Triangle, Bakelite Handle & Knob, 12 ½ In.	2662
Scoop, Ice Cream, Cold Dog Type, Brass Cylinder & Hinge, Wood Handle, 7 ½ In.	1331
Scoop, Ice Cream, Cone Shape, Looped Thumbscrew, Sheet Metal, 7 ½ In.	12
Scoop, Ice Cream, Dimpler, Cone Shape, Quick & Easy, Erie Specialty, 11 In.	108
Scoop, Ice Cream, Dover Slicer, Brass, Double Mechanism, Lever, Wood Handle, 11 In.	303
Scoop, Ice Cream, Flip Bowl, Wood Handle, Mosteller, July, 1906, 10 ½ In.	109 to 393
Scoop, Ice Cream, Kingery, Victor, Cast Metal, Open Handle, Pat. Oct. 1908, 11 In.	61
Scoop, Ice Cream, Metal, Split Bowl, Squeeze Handle, Bohlig, No. 20, 9 ½ In.	169
Scoop, Ice Cream, Sundae Top With Thumbscrew, Sheet Metal, Open Handle, 7 In.	84
Scoop, Tiger Maple, Handle Impressed Morlan, c.1810, 10 In.	119
Scotch Bowl, Bail Handle, Tipping Ring, Griswold No. 4, Erie	30
Scouring Box, Pine, Poplar, Open, Angled Center Block, c.1850, 1 ½ x 9 ¾ x 16 In.	81
Sifter, Chrome Metal, Plastic Handle, 3 Screens, Label, Ohio, 6 ½ x 5 ½ In.	10
Skillet, Cast Iron, Elongated Handle, Cutout End, 43 In.	76
Skillet, Double, Griswold No. 8	180
Skillet, Fry, Griswold No. 3, Square	35
Skillet, Griswold No. 4	35
Skillet, Griswold No. 4, Slant Logo, Heat Ring	65
Skillet, Griswold No. 5	25
Skillet, Griswold No. 8	20
Skillet, Griswold No. 9	100
Skillet, Griswold No. 10, Slant Logo, Heat Ring	140
Skillet, Griswold No. 14, Block Logo, Heat Ring	210
Skillet, Posnet, Bell Metal, Signed Ino Taylor Richmond, Vir., c.1785, 7 x 18 In.	3081
Slaw Board, Cherry, Lollipop End, Single Blade, Oak Strips, 16 ½ In.	35
Slicer, Swing, Spring Loaded, Cast Iron, Ash Wood, 1800s, 14 x 17 ½ In.	161
Slicer, Turnip, Ash Wood, Blade, Keeper Spikes, New England, c.1850, 13 ½ x 18 In.	115
Spatula, Heart Cutout Plate & Handle, Wrought Iron, 18 In.	180
Spice Box, Wall, Walnut, Cherry, Slant Lid, Fitted Interior, Drawer, Pa., c.1845, 17 x 11 In.	633
Spoon Rack, Carved Wood, 2 Slotted Tiers, Arch Crest, Heart, Flowers, 1767, 23 x 9 In.	3600
Spoon Rack, Tin, Punched, Tiered, Scrolls, Lovebirds, Applied Brass Rosettes, 7 ¾ In.	840
Sugar Cutters, Iron, Wooden Handle, Shaped Terminals, Brass Support, 6 ½ x 14 In.	384
Sugar Nips, Wrought Iron, Monogram M.K., Scrolls, c.1800, 17 In.	304
Teapot, Lid, Iron, Red Raised Dots, Black Handle, Diffuser, Tetsubin, Japan, c.1980, 4 ½ In.	46
Toaster, Hearth, Rotary, Wrought Iron, Brass, Twisted, Rack Bars, Maple Handle, 25 x 14 In.	360
Toaster, Long Handle, 28 In.	35
Toaster, Wrought Iron, Twisted Arch Braces, Ram Horn Details, c.1800, 18 ½ x 12 In.	86
Tray, Knife, Pine, Cutout Heart Handle, Green Paint, c.1850, 8 x 12 In.	2370
Tray, Knife, Wood, Double Fish Handle	1080
Trencher, Ash, Painted Green, Scrubbed Interior, Oblong, New England, 1800s, 13 x 21 In.	1440
Trencher, Walnut, Rectangular, Flared Sides, Shendandoah Valley, c.1845, 11 x 26 In.	230
Trencher, Wood, Continental, 1800s 9 ½ x 39 In.	123
Trencher, Wood, Green Painted Exterior, Mid 19th Century, 4 x 20 In.	470
Trencher, Wood, Wide Border, Rectangular, Black Paint, c.1860, 25 In.	118
Trivet, see Trivet category.	

Vacuum Cleaner, Regina Pneumatic, Model A, Double Acting, c.1910, 41 ¾ In. ....*illus*	75
Wafer Iron, Domino Style, Wrought & Cast Iron, Scissor Handles, c.1825, 28 In.	104
Waffle Iron, Griswold No. 8-885	65
Waffle Iron, Griswold No.18, Heart & Star...	115
Waffle Iron, Wrought, Cast Iron, Scissors Handles, Locking Hook, Chatham, c.1830, 29 In.	35
Washing Machine, Metal Tub, Cast Iron, Salesman's Sample, Continental, 7 x 6 In. ....*illus*	1067
Washing Machine, Pine Frame, Nickeled Tub & Cone Agitator, Treadle, Crank, Case, 15 In.	2607
Washtub Wringer, American Wringer, N.Y., Salesman's Sample, 7 ½ In..	154
Wine Corking Tool, Cast Iron, Wood Handle, 4-Footed, La Meilleure, 19th Century, 38 In.	711

KNIFE collectors usually specialize in a single type. In the 1960s, the United States government passed a law that required knife manufacturers to mark their knives with the country of origin. This seemed to encourage the collectors, and knife collecting became an interest of a large group of people. All types of knives are collected, from top-quality twentieth-century examples to old bone- or pearl-handled knives in excellent condition.

Bowie, Bone Handle, S.C. Wraggs & Co., Sheath, c.1845, 13 ¾ In..	16
Bowie, Horse Head Pommel, Checkered Bone Handle, Sheffield, 16 In.	467
Bowie, Walrus Tusk, 14 ¾ In.	220
Buffalo Skinner, Carved Bone Handle, Sheath, R.E. Wappen Solingen, Germany, Pair..............	142
Cheese, Round Iron Plate, Steel Blade, Increment Measure, Enterprise, 19 x 26 In......................	510
Crooked, Coffin & Gem Tintype Inlay, Chip Carved, Brass Wire Hardware, 1800s, 10 In.	1722
Dagger, Gilt Brass, Reeded Wood Grip, 1850, 18 In.	161
Dagger, Parrying, Sword Breaker Type, 18th Century, 28 In.	937
Dagger, Phurba, Steel, Figure Shape Handle, Crown, Chinese, 5 In...	210
Dagger, Sumatra, Bone Inlays, Sheath, 19th Century, 16 ½ In...	55
Hunting, Stag Handle, Etched Blade, Leather Scabbard, 21 ½ In.	354
Kard, Wootz Steel, Silver Bird's Beak Hilt, Sheath, Embroidered, Indo Persian, 1700s, 8 In.	540
Katar, Damascus 2-Edge Blade, Gold Damascene Hilt, Prince Size, Sheath, India, 1700s, 8 In....	3600
Khanja, Damascus, Parrot Head Pommel, Glass Eye, Sheath, Persia, 1700s, 9 ½ In....................	3000
Kris, Wavy Meteor Iron Blade, Mahogany Hilt, Brass Clad Sheath, Indonesia, 1800s, 12 In........	900
Pocket, Pirelli Tires, Superflex, Figural Tire, 2 Blades, 3 ⅛ x 1 In. ....*illus*	690

KNOWLES, *Taylor & Knowles items may be found in the KTK and Lotus Ware categories.*

KOREAN WARE, *see Sumida.*

KOSTA, the oldest Swedish glass factory, was founded in 1742. During the 1920s through the 1950s, many pieces of original design were made at the factory. Kosta and Boda merged with Afors in 1964 and created the Afors Group in 1971. In 1976, the name Kosta Boda was adopted. The company merged with Orrefors in 1990 and is still working.

KOSTA

Bowl, Cameo, Pears, Pink, Green, 1960s, 6 ½ In. Diam...	495
Bowl, Whimsical Tree, Pink, Signed, 3 x 3 ½ In.	150
Sculpture, Fish, Marked, 1958, 8 ½ In.	495
Sculpture, Kangaroo, Joey In Pouch, Paul Hoff, 7 ½ In..	60
Vase, 2 Stylized Face To Face Silhouettes, Snake In Center, Black, White, Oval, 13 In..................	230
Vase, Blue & Green Swirls, Goran Warff, 2 ¾ x 3 In.	168
Vase, Clear, Fan Shape, Signed, 4 ¼ x 3 ½ In..	95
Vase, Orchid, Free-Form, V. Lindstrand, c.1955, 9 ¾ In...	700
Vase, Thread Pattern, Multicolor, 11 x 3 ¾ In.	575
Vase, Trees In Fog, Tapered, Vicke Lindstrand, c.1954, 13 In. ....*illus*	2583

KPM refers to Berlin porcelain, but the same initials were used alone and in combination with other symbols by several German porcelain makers. They include the Konigliche Porzellan Manufaktur of Berlin, initials used in mark, 1823–1847; Meissen, 1723–1724 only; Krister Porzellan Manufaktur in Waldenburg, after 1831; Kranichfelder Porzellan Manufaktur in Kranichfeld, after 1903; and the Krister Porzellan Manufaktur in Scheibe, after 1838.

K.P.M

Cup & Saucer, Birds, Butterfly Reserves, Green Ground, Gilt Interior..	116
Fairy Lamp, Owl Face, Yellow Eyes, Cat Face, Green Eyes, Dog Face, Amber Eyes, 4 In................	649
Figurine, Monkey, Seated, Porcelain, Anton Puchegger, 12 In...	1750
Flagon, Brown Glaze, Side Grapevines, Center Flower, Pewter Mount, c.1910, 14 In.	104
Jardiniere, Ladies, Putti, Flowers, Quatrefoil Shape, Raised Feet, Gilt Handles, 14 ½ In.	2750
Lampshade, 5 Panel, Women, Children, Black, White, Lithophane, c.1890, 6 ½ In......................	354
Lithophane, see also Lithophane category.	
Perfume Bottle, Orange Flowers, Cherub Reverse, Brass, Cork Stopper, 5 ½ In.	266

Kosta, Vase, Trees In Fog, Tapered, Vicke Lindstrand, c.1954, 13 In.
$2,583

Skinner Auctioneers & Appraisers

KPM, Plaque, Maiden, Lounging, Reading Book, Frame, Marked, 23 ⅜ x 19 ⅜ In.
$4,859

James D. Julia Auctioneers

K

KPM, Plaque, Man, Smoking Pipe, Frame, Marked, 10 ½ x 13 ¾ In.
$1,620

The Stein Auction Co.

TIP
Pictures look best if hung on a light-colored wall.

KPM, Plaque, Woodcutter Defforge, Boy, Axes, Woman, 3 Men, Frame, 18 x 14 ¾ In. $5,074

Humler & Nolan

Kutani, Vase, Birds & Flowers, Panels, c.1900, 29 ½ In. $688

Rago Arts & Auction Center

Lacquer, Box, Scene, Hinged Lid, Russia, c.1950, 4 x 3 ½ x 1 ¼ In. $150

DuMouchelles Art Gallery

Plaque, Ayesta, Portrait, Woman, Long Hair, Giltwood Frame, 6 ½ x 4 ¾ In.		1000
Plaque, Barbele, Portrait, Germany, Frame, c.1900, 9 ⅝ x 7 ⅜ In.		1230
Plaque, Beggar Boys Eating Grapes & Melons, Stamped, c.1650, 9 ½ x 7 ½ In.		1230
Plaque, Children, Seated On Floor, Reading Book, Gilded Frame, Marked, c.1890, 10 In.		2400
Plaque, Coblenz, Lithophane, Leaded Glass Frame, 5 ½ x 7 ½ In.		127
Plaque, Coliseum, Gladiator, Lions, Woman, Shell, Vine Border, 1800s, 16 x 20 In.		29900
Plaque, Girl, Reaching Into Fountain, Column, Marked, Gilt Frame, c.1890, 6 x 9 In.		2425
Plaque, Hansel & Gretel, Children, Forest, Gilt Frame, c.1910, 8 x 6 In.		1188
Plaque, Maiden, Lounging, Reading Book, Frame, Marked, 23 ⅜ x 19 ⅜ In.	*illus*	4859
Plaque, Man, Smoking Pipe, Frame, Marked, 10 ½ x 13 ¾ In.	*illus*	1620
Plaque, Ruth, Wheat Sheaf, Signed Meinelt, Berlin, c.1890, 31 x 27 In.		4750
Plaque, Saint Jerome, Head Resting On Hand, Reading Book, Marked, c.1890, 7 x 6 In.		960
Plaque, Sea Views, 2 Girls, Seashore, Boat, Frame, c.1900, 6 ¼ x 9 ¼ In.		354
Plaque, St. Agnes, Palm, Lamb, J. Kuhn, Frame, c.1890, 27 x 20 In.		9375
Plaque, Woman, Classical, Leaning On Wall, Carved Bronze Frame, c.1900, 12 ¾ x 8 In.		4688
Plaque, Woman, Profile, Semi-Nude, Frame, Signed Wagner, Royal Berlin, 5 ½ x 4 In.		1936
Plaque, Woman, Water Carrier, Palm Trees, Gilt Frame, Purposely Distressed, 9 x 6 In.		5938
Plaque, Woodcutter Defforge, Boy, Axes, Woman, 3 Men, Frame, 18 x 14 ¾ In.	*illus*	5074
Plaque, Young Man, Blue Cravat, Signed H. Meisel, Frame, Gilt Liner, 11 ¼ x 8 ¾ In.		949
Plate, Dessert, Gold Scroll Bands, c.1850, 7 ½ In.		35
Plate, Enameled Purple Flowers, Cobalt Blue Border, Gilt, Royal Berlin, 9 ¾ In., 12 Piece		5150
Punch Bowl, Undertray, Lid, Round, Finial, Greek Key Banding, c.1890, 11 x 12 In.		120
Tazza, Molded Rim, Vase Shape Standard, Flared Base, Gilt, c.1847, 6 ⅜ x 10 In.		179
Teapot, Flowers, White Ground, Gilt Accents, 4 ⅝ In.		500
Tureen, Lid, Kneeling Boy Finial, Rococo Style, Flowers, Gilt, Lobed, Handles, 1870		489
Tureen, Lid, White, Multicolor Flowers, Gilt Highlights, Cherub Knop, Marked, 1900s, 8 In.		360
Tureen, Underplate, Lid, Putto Finial, Flowers, 16 ½ In.		1125
Urn, White, Gold, Swan Handles, Footed, 16 ½ In.		85
Vase, Bulbous, Stick Neck, Tassels, Blue, White Ground, 11 In., Pair		600
Vase, Lid, Cobalt Blue, Gold Trim, Handles, Oval, Pedestal Foot, c.1901, 19 ¾ In.		1200
Vase, Woman's Profile, Flower In Hair, Iridescent, Tapered, 3 Gilt Handles, A. Berlin, 10 In.		813
Woman's Head, Black Hat, Draped With Blue Flowered Scarf, Wood Shaft, 35 In.		633

KTK are the initials of the Knowles, Taylor & Knowles Company of East Liverpool, Ohio, founded by Isaac W. Knowles in 1853. The company made many types of utilitarian wares, hotel china, and dinnerware. It made the fine bone china known as Lotus Ware from 1891 to 1896. The company merged with American Ceramic Corporation in 1928. It closed in 1934. Lotus Ware is listed in its own category in this book.

K.T.&K. CHINA

Bowl, Vegetable, Lid, Gold & Pink Rose Trim, Handles, 1920s, 11 ½ x 8 x 3 In.	48
Chop Plate, Central Bouquet, Gold Swag Border, c. 1905	19
Planter, Art Deco, Green, Tan, 5 ½ x 5 In.	50
Platter, Pink, Red Flowers, Transfer, 15 x 12 In.	100

KU KLUX KLAN items are now collected because of their historic importance. Literature, robes, and memorabilia are seen at shows and auctions. Laws passed in 1870 and 1871 caused the decline of the Klan. A second group calling itself the Ku Klux Klan emerged in 1915. There are still local groups using the name.

Booklet, Ku Klux Klan In Prophecy, Bishop Alma White, A.M., Graphic Cover, 1925	61
Knife, Bowie, KA-Bar, Knight Of Ku Klux Klan, September 23, 1923, 14 In.	128
Magazine, Look, Cover Story, May 3, 1966, 10 ¼ x 13 In.	17
Money Clip, Raised Design, Man In Robes, Flag, Crosses, Brass	34
Padlock, Key, Member KKK In Good Standing, Iron	95
Sheet Music, Bright Fiery Cross, Our Song, Alvia O. DeRee, 1913, 9 x 12 In.	75
Sheet Music, Mystic City, Knights Of Ku Klux Klan, J. Nelson, N. Tillery, 1922, 9 x 12 In.	250

KUTANI porcelain was made in Japan after the mid-seventeenth century. Most of the pieces found today are nineteenth-century. Collectors often use the term *Kutani* to refer to just the later, colorful pieces decorated with red, gold, and black pictures of warriors, animals, and birds.

Bottle, Bulbous, Phoenix, Lotus, Reds, Browns, Stopper, c.1875, 13 In.	593
Bottle, Panels, Garden, Pheasants, Trees, Multicolor, c.1880, 6 In.	200
Bowl, Flower Reserves, 3 Friends Of Winter Interior, Blue Underglaze, 8 ½ In.	246
Figurine, Foo Dogs, Playing, Blue, White, 19th Century, 6 x 6 In.	399
Figurine, Rabbit, Belly On Ground, Head Looking Left, Aubergine Glaze, 5 x 11 In.	338
Incense Burner, Foo Dog, Bird, On Branch, 5 x 2 x 2 In.	125

K

Patch Box, Peach Shape, Symbols, Red, Orange, Signed, 2 ½ In.	165
Pitcher, Birds, Flowers, Red, Yellow, 6 In.	271
Plate, Chrysanthemum Blossoms, Leaves, Sprays, Red, Gilt, 7 ½ In.	100
Poem Jar, Figures, Brocaded Robes, Cylindrical, c.1875, 3 In.	435
Relish, Figures, Flowers, Pines, Deer At Center, 7 Fitted Shaped Sections, Ribbed, 14 In.	123
Vase, Birds & Flowers, Panels, c.1900, 29 ½ In. *illus*	688
Vase, Figures In Reserves, Birds On Neck, Bottle Shape, 9 In.	3900
Vase, Rounded Square, Trumpet Neck, Scalloped Rim, Multicolor, c.1850, 35 In., Pair	210

L.G. WRIGHT Glass Company of New Martinsville, West Virginia, started selling glassware in 1937. Founder "Si" Wright contracted with Ohio and West Virginia glass factories to reproduce popular pressed glass patterns like Rose & Snow, Baltimore Pear, and Three Face, and opalescent patterns like Daisy & Fern and Swirl. Collectors can tell the difference between the original glasswares and L.G. Wright reproductions because of colors and differences in production techniques. Some L.G. Wright items are marked with an underlined *W* in a circle. Items that were made from old Northwood molds have an altered Northwood mark—an angled line was added to the *N* to make it look like a *W*. Collectors refer to this mark as "the wobbly W." The L.G. Wright factory was closed and the existing molds sold in 1999.

Daisy & Button, Console, Apple Green, 4-Footed, 1960s, 10 In.	65
Eyewinker, Goblet, Wine, Red, 4 ½ In.	10
Magnet & Grape, Goblet, Ruby, 6 ⅜ In.	25
Moon & Stars, Compote, Yellow, 9 ¾ In.	66
Moon & Stars, Goblet, Water, Blue	8
Moon & Stars, Pitcher, Amber, Scalloped, 32 Oz.	26
Moon & Stars, Salt & Pepper	14
Stippled Star, Goblet, Wine, Ruby, 3 Oz.	17
Wildrose, Goblet, Green, 12 Oz.	11
Wildrose, Goblet, Red, 12 Oz.	11

LACQUER is a type of varnish. Collectors are most interested in the Chinese and Japanese lacquer wares made from the Japanese varnish tree. Lacquer wares are made from wood with many coats of lacquer. Sometimes the piece is carved or decorated with ivory or metal inlay.

Bowl, Lotus Flower Shape, Ruffled Rim, Green & Red, Carved, 11 ¼ In.	948
Box, Cover, Daoist Immortal Riding On Carp, Allover Flowers, Scrolls, Red, Round, 11 In.	738
Box, Document, Black, Mother-Of-Pearl Inlay, Dragons, Pearl, Lotus, Phoenix, 16 In.	300
Box, Dutchess Yusupova Portrait, Fedoskino, 6 x 5 In.	177
Box, Lid, Round, Sand Grain Surface, Abalone Inlay, Japan, 20th Century, 6 x 14 In.	411
Box, Prince Sigfried, Odette, Swan Lake Maidens, Kurnikova, Russia, 4 In.	189
Box, Scene, Hinged Lid, Russia, c.1950, 4 x 3 ½ x 1 ¼ In. *illus*	150
Box, Woman Holding Easter Egg, Oval, Krasnov, Russia, 4 In.	177
Box, Writing, Red, Inset Panel, Dragon, Scroll, Ink Sticks, Lid, Inkstone, 2 x 9 In.	246
Document Box, Sprinkled Lacquer Birds, Flowers, Gold, Black, Silver, Japan, 4 ½ x 16 In. *illus*	1230
Glove Box, Gilt, Serpentine, Sarcophagus Shape, Garden Setting, c.1800, 4 x 12 In.	538
Humidor, Crackle, Rosewood, Cedar, Wendell Castle, Signed, 1996, 7 x 19 x 12 In. *illus*	4063
Panel, Les Vendanges, Men, Oxen, Colors, Gold Leaf On Wood, J. Dunand, c.1935, 10 x 24 In.	75000
Pedestal, Square, Black, Figures, Trees, Archway, 36 x 11 In.	270
Tray, Black, Gold Chrysanthemums, Asia, c.1890, 11 x 15 In.	235
Tray, Rectangular, Scroll Design, Brown Red, Shaped Corners, c.1800, 16 x 11 In.	1944
Trinket Box, Figural Design, Band Of Animals, Oval, Lid, 13 In.	1000
Trinket Box, Gilt, Rectangular, Canted Corners, Figures, Courtyard, 1800s, 4 ½ x 15 In.	896
Vase, Dragon Design, Trumpet Neck, Flared Base, 1800s, 15 ¼ In.	826

LADY HEAD VASE, *see Head Vase.*

LALIQUE glass and jewelry were made by Rene Lalique (1860–1945) in Paris, France, between the 1890s and his death in 1945. Beginning in 1921 he had a manufacturing plant in Alsace. The glass was molded, pressed, and engraved in Art Nouveau and Art Deco styles. Most pieces were marked with the signature *R. Lalique*. Lalique glass is still being made. Most pieces made after 1945 bear the mark *Lalique*. After 1980 the registry mark was added and the mark became *Lalique ® France*. In the prices listed here, this is indicated by Lalique (R) France. Some pieces that are advertised as ring dishes or pin dishes were listed as ashtrays in the Lalique factory catalog and are listed as ashtrays here. Jewelry made by Rene Lalique is listed in the Jewelry category.

R.LALIQUE

Ashtray, Reclining Tiger Edge, Clear Crystal, Box, 4 ½ x 8 ½ In.	584
Bowl, Antilles, Clusters Of Grapes, Clear & Frosted, Etched Lalique, 7 In.	288
Bowl, Chicoree, Leaves, Blue, c.1920, 9 In.	420

Lacquer, Document Box, Sprinkled Lacquer Birds, Flowers, Gold, Black, Silver, Japan, 4 ½ x 16 In.
$1,230

New Orleans Auction Galleries, Inc.

Lacquer, Humidor, Crackle, Rosewood, Cedar, Wendell Castle, Signed, 1996, 7 x 19 x 12 In.
$4,063

Rago Arts & Auction Center

Lalique, Figurine, Liberte, Eagle, Clear, Frosted, Etched Lalique, France, c.1980, 9 ¼ In.
$984

Neal Auction Co.

Iris by Lalique

The Iris vase first made by Rene Lalique in 1934 is being made again by the company. It was also made in 1937, 1947, and 1951. Price for the new vase: $2,600.

Lalique, Perfume Burner, Sirenes, Mermaids, Opalescent, Blue, R. Lalique, c.1920, 7 In.
$3,125

Rago Arts & Auction Center

Lalique, Vase, Avallon, Birds, Cherries, Branches, Opalescent, Engraved, R. Lalique, 5 ¾ In.
$1,725

Humler & Nolan

Lalique, Vase, Bacchantes, Nudes, Frosted, Signed, 9 In.
$854

Neal Auction Co.

Bowl, Frosted Bottom, Scrolling Flowers On Rim, 9 In.	1800
Bowl, Luxembourg, Cherubs, Frosted, Signed, 8 ¼ In.	2252
Bowl, Mesanges, Birds, Frosted Relief Band, Faceted, Engraved, 10 In.	299
Bowl, Nonnettes, Lovebirds, 3 Pairs, Marked, 2 ¼ x 8 ½ In.	489
Bowl, Oblong, Frosted Leaf Border, Signed, 3 ¾ x 7 ¾ In.	220
Bowl, Perruches, Parrots Hanging From Branches, Clear, Blue, 1900s, 4 x 10 In.	5664
Bowl, Pinsons, Finches, Nesting, Ferns, Frosted, Engraved, 9 ¼ In.	242
Buckle, Amethyst Glass Panel, Stag, Curling Fern Bows, Box, Marked, 4 ¼ In.	8888
Candelabrum, 2-Light, Auriac, Clear & Frosted, Etched Lalique, c.1944, 3 x 9 In.	307
Carafe, Clear, Head & Swirls Finial, Amber Patina, Tapered, R. Lalique, 1924, 11 In.	1000
Charger, Calypso, Opalescent, M 413, 1950s, 2 x 14 ½ In.	3250
Charger, Roscoff, Fish Border, 14 In.	265
Compote, Moineau, Sparrow, Bird & Leaf, Signed In Script, 5 ¼ x 5 ¼ In.	207
Door Push, 2 Overlapping Leaves, Clear & Frosted	336
Figurine, Bamara, Seated Lion, Frosted, Paris, c.1955, 7 ¾ x 3 In.	438
Figurine, Chat, Couche, Cat, Crouching, Signed, 9 In., Pair	799
Figurine, Chrysis, Nude, Kneeling, Flowing Hair, 5 In.	125
Figurine, Cockatoo, Wings Spread, Head Turned, Plume, Signed, 12 x 10 In.	1045
Figurine, Elephant, Curled Trunk, Base, 6 x 6 In.	360
Figurine, Liberte, Eagle, Clear, Frosted, Etched Lalique, France, c.1980, 9 ¼ In. ....*illus*	984
Figurine, Madonna & Child, Frosted, Black Base, 14 ½ In.	242 to 402
Figurine, Reindeer, Semi-Reclining, Clear & Frosted, 10 ¼ In.	161
Figurine, Toad, Crystal, Signed, 3 x 4 In.	180
Goblet, Anges, Angels, Clear, Frosted, 8 In., 12 Piece	1007
Group, Enfants, Circle Of Children, 8 x 6 ½ In.	480
Inkwell, Serpents, Clear, Frosted, Lid, Engraved R. Lalique, c.1910, 6 In.	2556
Perfume Bottle, 4-Petal Flowers, Frosted, 4 Arched Panels, Flower Finial, 4 In.	1680
Perfume Bottle, D'Orsay, Leurs Ames, Their Souls, 2 Nudes Hanging From Tree, 5 In.	9375
Perfume Bottle, Forvil, Mushroom Stopper, Spirals, Clear, c.1924, 8 In.	500
Perfume Burner, Sirenes, Mermaids, Opalescent, Blue, R. Lalique, c.1920, 7 In. ....*illus*	3125
Perfume Flask, Les Sirenes, Molded Cire Perdue Glass, Jeweled Metal Lid, c.1905, 4 In.	284800
Pin, Deux Figurines Dos A Dos, 2 Figures Back To Back, Foil, Gilt Metal, 1913, 2 x 1 In.	2000
Pin, Quatre Cabochons Bleuets, 4 Blueberry Cabochons, Silver Foil, Gilt Metal, c.1900, 3 x 1 In.	3500
Sculpture, Deux Poissons, 2 Fish, Clear, 11 ¼ In.	1452
Shot Glass, Enfants, Children, Amber, Signed, 1 ¾ In., 5 Piece	580
Statue, Madonna, Standing, Praying Hands, Long Robe, 8 ½ In.	240
Tray, Carnations Border, Light Green, Rectangular, Stamped, 9 ¾ x 15 ⅝ In.	649
Vase, Aigrettes, Egrets, Flying, Branches, Frosted, Clear, Cylindrical, c.1935, 10 In.	2813
Vase, Aras, Macaws, Berries, Thorns, Frosted, Green Patina, Clear, Sqaut, Round, c.1935, 9 In.	3125
Vase, Archers, Amber, White Patina, Round, Stand Up Rim, Etched R. Lalique, 1921, 10 In.	11250
Vase, Avallon, Birds, Branches, Clear, Frosted Glass, Engraved, c.1905, 5 ¾ In.	1625
Vase, Avallon, Birds, Cherries, Branches, Opalescent, Engraved, R. Lalique, 5 ¾ In. ....*illus*	1725
Vase, Avallon, Birds, Grapes, Clear, Frosted, c.1935, 5 ¾ In.	2125
Vase, Bacchantes, Nudes, Frosted, Signed, 9 In. ....*illus*	854
Vase, Bagatelle, Birds Nesting, Relief, Cased, Matte Finish, Engraved, 6 ¾ x 4 ¼ In.	357 to 780
Vase, Ceylan, Lovebirds, Clear, Frosted, Birds Relief, Footed, Etched, 4 ¾ x 4 ½ In.	265
Vase, Chamarande, Wild Roses, Topaz, 2 Rose Handles, Raised Thorns, 1926, 8 x 9 In.	2375
Vase, Chardons, Thistle Leaves, Frosted, Melon Shape, 1900s, 7 ½ x 7 ¼ In.	885
Vase, Danaides, Nude Water Carriers, Women, Pale Blue, Cylindrical, 1900s, 7 In.	5900
Vase, Deauville, Clear, Frosted, Signed, 8 x 4 In.	780
Vase, Deauville, Square, Flared Rim, Ring Foot, Flowers, 5 ¾ x 3 ¾ In.	330
Vase, Domremy, Thistles, Dark Green, Signed, R. Lalique, c.1926, 8 ¾ In. ....*illus*	3540
Vase, Domremy, Thistles, Leaves, Frosted, Sepia Accents, Tapered, c.1940, 8 In.	1063
Vase, Druids, Opalescent Berries, Impressed Stems, Signed, 7 In.	1422
Vase, Escargot, Snail Shell, Opalescent, 8 ¼ In.	2300
Vase, Escargot, Snail, Clear, Frosted, Blue Patina, R. Lalique, 1920, 8 ¼ x 7 ½ In. ....*illus*	3750
Vase, Esterel, Laurel Leaves, Blue Netted Design, White Ground, Tapered, 1900s, 6 In.	938
Vase, Formose, Swirling Carp, Gray Cased, Ball Shape, Molded R. Lalique, 1924, 7 In.	8125
Vase, Graines, Seeds, Frosted, Brown Patina On Bottom, Flared, Stamped R. Lalique, 7 ¾ In.	1320
Vase, Grenade, Dark Amber, Ball Shape, Signed, R. Lalique, 5 In.	940
Vase, Grenade, Pomegranate, Black, White Enamel, Round, 1930, 4 ½ x 5 In.	2750
Vase, Ispahan, Roses, Molded, Signed, 9 ¼ x 7 ½ In. ....*illus*	799
Vase, Jack-In-The-Pulpit, Favrile, Signed L.C.T., 1906, 18 ¾ In.	6250
Vase, Malesherbes, Loquat Leaves, Amber, White Patina, Tapered, Etched R. Lalique, 9 In.	5625
Vase, Malines, Pointed Leaves, Pulled Feathers, White Ground, Stamped, c.1905, 5 In.	500
Vase, Marisa, Fish, Sphere Shape, Clear, Satin, M 1002, 1927, 9 In.	1800

Vase, Marisa, Opalescent, Signed, M 1002, 9 x 9 In.	3500
Vase, Martinets, Clear, Frosted, Migrating Swifts, Marked, 9 ¾ In.	1075
Vase, Monnaie Du Pape, Money Plant, Amber, Frosted, Bulbous, Footed, 1914, 9 x 6 In.	3750
Vase, Nefliers, Blue Flowers, Frosted Ground, Tapered, c.1905, 5 ½ In.	750
Vase, Ondines, Nude Women Bathers, Waves, Frosted, Clear, Tapered, 9 In.	1063
Vase, Ondines, Water Nymphs, Frosted, Rippled Crystal, 1900s, 9 ½ x 7 ½ In.	1135
Vase, Orchidee, Orchids, Opalescent Flowers, Handles, Signed, 6 ½ x 8 ½ In.	1020
Vase, Orleans, Flowers, Frosted, Blue Accents, Waisted Cylinder, c.1935, 8 In.	875
Vase, Osumi, Leaves, Frosted, Signed, 7 In.	210
Vase, Palissy, Snail Shells, Frosted, Signed, R. Lalique, 7 In.	702
Vase, Perruches, Parakeets, Opalescent, Tapered, Rolled Rim, Signed, c.1930, 9 ½ x 5 ¼ In.	4012
Vase, Piriac, Clear & Frosted, Blue Patina, Etched, R. Lalique France, 1930, 7 x 8 In. ....*illus*	1750
Vase, Poissons, Scrolling Fish, Opalescent, Design, Bulbous, Flare Rim, 1900s, 9 x 9 In.	4012
Vase, Poissons, Swimming Fish, Blue, Signed, 9 In. ....*illus*	1460
Vase, Poivre, Pepper Berries, Frosted, Gray, Tapered, c.1935, 9 ½ In.	3125
Vase, Poseidon, Turquoise, Opalescent, Signed, Box, 11 ¾ x 14 ½ In. ....*illus*	7995
Vase, Prunes, Molded Berries, Leaves, Gray Glass, Stamped R. Lalique, c.1955, 7 In.	2000
Vase, Rampillons, Flower Etched, Blue, Clear, Frosted Glass, Tapered, c.1905, 5 In.	813
Vase, Rosine, 2 Birds, Clear & Frosted, Footed, Flared Rim, 5 In.	173
Vase, Saint Francois, Frosted, Opalescent, Green Patina, c.1930, M 1055, 7 x 6 ½ In.	1875
Vase, Satyr, Dancing Figures, Ivy, Frosted, Etched R. Lalique, c.1940, 7 x 6 In.	944
Vase, Sophora, Leaves, Amber, Ball Shape, Flared Rim, Etched R. Lalique, 10 x 10 In.	6250
Vase, Sylvie, 2 Birds, 8 ½ x 6 ¾ In.	480
Vase, Tournesols, Sunflowers, Electric Blue, Protrusions, Bulbous, Etched R. Lalique, 4 In.	3125
Vase, Tulipes, Relief Tulips, Opalescent, Flared Rim, Turquoise Accents, c.1940, 8 In.	3125
Vase, Yasna, Frosted, Square, Carved Furrows, Gilt Rim, 8 In.	316

LAMPS of every type, from the early oil-burning Betty and Phoebe lamps to the recent electric lamps with glass or beaded shades, interest collectors. Fuels used in lamps changed through the years; whale oil (1800–40), camphene (1828), Argand (1830), lard (1833–63), turpentine and alcohol (1840s), gas (1850–79), kerosene (1860), and electricity (1879) are the most common. Other lamps are listed by manufacturer or type of material.

Advertising, G & W, Backbar, Light-Up, Gooderham & Works Ltd., 11 ½ In.	480
Advertising, Gossard, Frosted Glass, Figural Shade, Armless Woman In Corset, Art Deco, 28 In.	1085
Aladdin, Electric, G-257, Alacite, Oak Leaf, Scrolled Feet, Wreath Finial, 20 In.	80
Aladdin, Electric, G-338, Alacite, Precision Finial, 2-Tier Shade, 30 In.	148
Aladdin, Kerosene, B-52, Amber, Nu Type B Burner, White Shade.	289
Aladdin, Kerosene, B-53, Washington Drape, Clear Stem, V Foot Base, 9 In.	59
Aladdin, Kerosene, B-75, Tall Lincoln Drape, Alacite, Shade, Chimney, 1940s, 26 In.	144 to 250
Aladdin, Kerosene, B-75, Tall Lincoln Drape, Nu Type Burner, Alacite, 24 In.	96
Aladdin, Kerosene, B-104, Corinthian, Black & Clear Base, 501 Shade, c.1936, 23 In.	145
Aladdin, Kerosene, G-23, Short Lincoln Drape, Amber, Ribbed, 8 ¾ In.	70
Aladdin, Washington Drape, Plain Stem	65
Alcohol & Lard, Iron, Cone Shape, Saucer Base, Tripod, J.K. Leedy Pat. Jan. 24 1860, 9 x 7 In.	1380
Arc, Brass, Enclosed, Fluted, Westinghouse Electric Mfg., No. 36000, Victorian, 30 In.	1200
Arc, Chromed Steel, Brushed Aluminum, Marble, Enameled Steel, Floor, 65 x 40 In.	250
Arc, Focus, Chrome Frame, Plastic Shade, Round, Fabio Lenci, Floor, c.1972, 89 x 99 In.	313
Arc, Hanging, Metal, Glass Globe, Central Scientific Co., 13 In.	1080
Argand, Bronze, Double Arm, Prisms, Etched Glass, H.N. Hooper & Co., c.1830, 20 In., Pair	1673
Argand, Gilt Bronze, Bearded Man, Snake, Standard, Glass Shade, c.1840, 21 In., Pair	938
Arredoluce, Chromed, Enameled Metal, Leather, Adjustable Arm, Marble, 1960s, 57 In.	3125
Astral, The Bailey's, New England School Furnishing Co., Boston, Square, 16 In.	3000
Bradley & Hubbard lamps are included in the Bradley & Hubbard category.	
Brass, Enameled Metal, George Kovacs, Floor, c.1970, 45 ½ x 25 In., Pair	430
Burl Fir, Mica & Leather Shade, Beaded Fir Pulls, Thomas Molesworth, 28 In.	30000
Chandelier, 3-Light, Sockets, Scrolled Arms, Wrought Iron, Floral Shaft, Hook, 28 In.	443
Chandelier, 4-Light, Amber Glass, Twisted Scrolls, Drops, Tapered Urn, Leaves, Venetian, 25 In.	296
Chandelier, 4-Light, Amber Glass, Twisted Scrolls, Drops, Tapered Urn, Leaves, Venetian, 25 In.	296
Chandelier, 4-Light, Bronze, Porcelain, Ribbon Corona, Jar Standard, Leaves, c.1900, 17 In.	1830
Chandelier, 4-Light, Orange, White Shades, Prisms, Brass, Jewels, Electrified, 33 x 30 In.	3250
Chandelier, 4-Light, Sonneman, Chrome, Enamel, 3 Shaped-Flute Tiers, 1970s, 28 In.	2625
Chandelier, 4-Light, Wrought Iron, Ruffled Glass Shades, Scroll, c.1900, 23 x 26 In.	1107
Chandelier, 5-Light, Gilt Metal, Urn Shape Stem, Tassel Pendant, Bellowers, Leaves, 21 In.	875
Chandelier, 5-Light, Glass, Brass, Twisted Arms, Crystal Drops, 1800s, 31 x 37 In.	826
Chandelier, 5-Light, Glass, Cranberry Color, Flowers, Gilt, Beaded Swags, c.1885, 30 In.	590

Lalique, Vase, Domremy, Thistles, Dark Green, Signed, R. Lalique, c.1926, 8 ¾ In. $3,540

Brunk Auctions

Lalique, Vase, Escargot, Snail, Clear, Frosted, Blue Patina, R. Lalique, 1920, 8 ¼ x 7 ½ In. $3,750

Rago Arts & Auction Center

Lalique, Vase, Ispahan, Roses, Molded, Signed, 9 ¼ x 7 ½ In. $799

New Orleans Auction Galleries, Inc.

L

TIP

Think about the signature. Acid etched marks can be added. So can signatures. Be sure the mark seems appropriate.

Lalique, Vase, Piriac, Clear & Frosted, Blue Patina, Etched, R. Lalique France, 1930, 7 x 8 In.
$1,750

Rago Arts & Auction Center

Lalique, Vase, Poissons, Swimming Fish, Blue, Signed, 9 In.
$1,460

James D. Julia Auctioneers

Lalique, Vase, Poseidon, Turquoise, Opalescent, Signed, Box, 11 ¾ x 14 ½ In.
$7,995

New Orleans Auction Galleries, Inc.

Hood Ornaments

Rene Lalique designed and made 27 different car mascots (hood ornaments) from 1920 to 1931. Others were made for special events. One was made for Prince George (later George VI), and a limited edition of 200 for Rolls-Royce executives. A few were mounted on square glass bases to be used as bookends.

Chandelier, 6-Light, Alabaster, Bronze, Leaf Corona, Rope Design, Scroll Arms, 22 In.	1750
Chandelier, 6-Light, Blown Glass, Clear, Amber, Flower Drops, Murano, c.1900, 42 x 28 In.	1770
Chandelier, 6-Light, Brass, Dutch, c.1750, 21 x 24 In.	1422
Chandelier, 6-Light, Empire Style, Cut Glass, Bronze, Basket Shape, Angels, 23 x 19 In.	2706
Chandelier, 6-Light, Gilt Bronze, Cut Glass, Torch, Hanging Prisms, Beads, c.1900, 40 In.	5676
Chandelier, 6-Light, Gilt Bronze, Flowers, Berries, Leaves, 3 Chains, 27 x 19 In.	531
Chandelier, 6-Light, Gilt Bronze, Molded Leaf Corona, Scrolling Standard, 31 x 18 In.	2390
Chandelier, 6-Light, Louis XIV Style, Gilt, Spiral Fluted, Scroll Arms, 31 x 32 ½ In.	1476
Chandelier, 6-Light, Louis XV Style, Gilt Metal, Clear Pendants, Curved Arms, 44 x 22 In.	1625
Chandelier, 6-Light, Louis XV, Silvered Metal, c.1900, 21 In.	2813
Chandelier, 6-Light, Louis XVI Style, Bronze, Gilt, Urn, Scroll Arms, 1800s, 36 In., Pair	2440
Chandelier, 6-Light, Metal Flower Cups, Prisms, 1920s, 31 x 36 In.	311
Chandelier, 6-Light, Murano Glass, Clear, Gold Threads, Molded Flowers, 35 x 24 In.	3690
Chandelier, 6-Light, Pink Quartz, Cabochon & Faceted Hanging Prisms, 1800s, 28 In.	837
Chandelier, 6-Light, Venetian Glass, Multicolor Flowers, Leaves, Scroll Arms, 1900s, 31 In.	590
Chandelier, 6-Light, Venetian Glass, Twisted Arms, Pressed Glass, 36 x 31 In. *illus*	1673
Chandelier, 6-Light, Wrought Iron, Cage Shape, Glass Spike, 4 Tiers, Prisms, Pears, 27 In.	531
Chandelier, 7-Light, Belle Epoque, Gilt Bronze, Blue Glass, Bronze Frame, c.1900, 38 x 16 In.	1599
Chandelier, 8-Light, Brass, Cut Glass, Bell Shape, Prisms, c.1900, 32 x 33 In.	2032
Chandelier, 8-Light, Bronze, Crystal Drops, Rosettes, Scrolled Arms, c.1890, 27 x 23 In.	767
Chandelier, 8-Light, Bronze, Louis XIV Style, Hanging Prisms, c.1915, 35 x 18 In.	1845
Chandelier, 8-Light, Crystal, Brass, Hanging Pendants, Scroll Frame, c.1900, 32 x 24 In.	885
Chandelier, 8-Light, Cut Crystal, Star Shape Cups, Hanging Prisms, c.1935, 42 In.	7080
Chandelier, 8-Light, Elk Antlers, 30 x 60 x 24 In.	738
Chandelier, 8-Light, Empire Style, Gilt, Bronze, Eagle Branches, 1870, 31 x 22 In.	2988
Chandelier, 8-Light, Gilt, 2 Tiers, Scroll Arms, Pierced, Vase Shape Canopy, 36 x 29 In.	738
Chandelier, 8-Light, Louis XVI Style, Gilt Bronze, Festoons, Pendants, c.1900, 52 In.	6100
Chandelier, 8-Light, Murano Glass, 2 Tiers, Clear Stems, Multicolor Flower Ends, 36 In.	1968
Chandelier, 8-Light, Patinated Metal, Scroll Arms, Faux Candles, c.1900, 36 x 30 In.	1353
Chandelier, 8-Light, Turned Standard, Orb Pendant, Scroll Arms, Ratchet Hanger, 36 x 24 In.	840
Chandelier, 9-Light, Gilt, Tole, Corona, Eros, Torch, Swan Branches, 1800s, 40 x 23 In.	3383
Chandelier, 9-Light, Prisms, Gilt Metal, France, 33 x 20 In.	938
Chandelier, 9-Light, Tole, Gilt Metal, Faceted Crystal Swags, Curved Arms, 42 x 33 In.	3346
Chandelier, 10-Light, Louis XV Style, Gilt Metal, Glass Prisms, c.1855, 36 x 28 In.	1500
Chandelier, 12-Light, Baluster, C-Scroll Arms, Prisms, Swags, Purple Glass, 24 In.	625
Chandelier, 12-Light, Bronze Dore, Faceted Stem, Caryatids, Scroll Arms, 32 x 18 In.	1195
Chandelier, 12-Light, Cut Glass, Basketwork, Urn, Fluted Arms, Chain Beads, 1800s, 45 In.	4481
Chandelier, 12-Light, Delft Style, Brass Central Column, Blue, White, Pottery Balls, 25 x 26 In.	59
Chandelier, 12-Light, Gilt Bronze, Lilies, Pierced Canopy, France, c.1885, 34 x 27 In.	2214
Chandelier, 12-Light, Louis XV Style, Gilt Bronze, Cut Glass, Prisms, 1900s, 30 In.	1464
Chandelier, 15-Light, Hans-Agne Jakobsson, Brass, Glass, 1960s, 31 x 26 In. *illus*	2875
Chandelier, 18-Light, Brass, Central Baluster, Dutch, 41 x 43 In.	8400
Chandelier, 18-Light, Gilt, Clear Glass Pendants, 2-Tier Candle Arms, 54 x 34 In.	1500
Chandelier, 24-Light, Glass Scroll Arms, Hanging Prisms, Beaded Swags, 32 x 33 In.	875
Chandelier, 25-Light, Renaissance, Gold Details, Swarovski Crystals, Schonbek, 52 x 45 In.	6200
Chandelier, 42-Light, Chromed Steel, Faceted Glass Squares, 11 Tiers, Ott, 1970s, 44 x 36 In.	2500
Chandelier, 60-Light, Baroque Style, Gilt Metal, Crystal, Scroll Leaf Branches, 96 x 69 In.	10455
Chandelier, Art Deco, 6-Sided Shade, Geometric, Iron Frame, Glass Shades, 24 x 32 In.	1076
Chandelier, Art Deco, Metal, Geometric Fret Work, Signed Lincoln, 24 x 21 In.	108
Chandelier, Artichoke, Henningsen, Tiered, Enameled Aluminum, Steel, Plastic, 54 In.	4688
Chandelier, Gilt Metal, Cut Glass, Round Cage, Prism Swags, 51 x 28 In.	1250
Chandelier, Hunting Lodge, Antlers, Wolves' Heads, 26 In.	2400
Chandelier, Leaf Shape Glass, Matte Steel, Camer, Italy, 1960s, 17 In.	2250
Chandelier, PH Artichoke, Copper, P. Henningsen, c.1960, 33 x 33 In.	6875
Chandelier, Stacked Disc Design, Frosted Glass, Aluminum, c.1975, 37 x 19 In.	1125
Chandelier, Triangular Prisms, Clear, Smoky, Venini, 14 x 21 In.	2478
Chandelier, Waterford Cut Crystal, Elongated Pendants, 20th Century, 20 In.	150
Chrome, White Fabric Shade, George Kovacs, Floor, c.1970, 58 In., Pair	246
Desk, Hartman, Counterbalance, Chrome, 3-Sided Shade, Round Base, 1990s, 14 x 23 In.	2000
Electric, 2 Cone Shades, Adjustable, Enameled, Chrome, Fiberglass, Brass, 1950s, 56 x 36 In.	344
Electric, 2-Light, Caramel Slag Glass Panels, Metal Frame, Pull Chains, Bronze Finish, 25 In.	201
Electric, 2-Light, Majolica, Vase Shape, Handles, Ruffled Rim, Multicolor Glaze, 23 x 8 In.	121
Electric, 3 Aluminum Tubes, Varying Heights, Black Matte Interior, USA, 48 In., Pair	976
Electric, 3 Candle Sockets, Adjustable, Tole Painted, Weighted Base, c.1850, 25 In. *illus*	780
Electric, 3 Shaped Supports, Bronze Base, Paw Feet, Colored Leaded Glass Shade, 44 x 19 In.	1200
Electric, 3-Arm Spray, Chromed Steel, Marble Base, Floor, Italy, 1970s, 81 ½ x 61 In.	344

Lamp, Chandelier, 6-Light, Venetian Glass, Twisted Arms, Pressed Glass, 36 x 31 In.
$1,673

Neal Auction Co.

Lamp, Chandelier, 15-Light, Hans-Agne Jakobsson, Brass, Glass, 1960s, 31 x 26 In.
$2,875

Rago Arts & Auction Center

Lamp, Electric, 3 Candle Sockets, Adjustable, Tole Painted, Weighted Base, c.1850, 25 In.
$780

Garth's Auctioneers & Appraisers

Lamp, Electric, Arredoluce, Triennale, Enameled Metal, Brass, Marble, Italy, 1950s, 75 In.
$3,750

Rago Arts & Auction Center

Lamp, Electric, Art Deco, Polar Bears, Icebergs, Bronze, T. Cartier, c.1925, 12 x 13 In., Pair
$800

Neal Auction Co.

Lamp, Electric, Art Nouveau, Jeweled, Bronze, Austria, c.1910, 19 In.
$1,750

Rago Arts & Auction Center

Lamp, Electric, Blown Glass, Cactus, Poliarte Style, Murano, Italy, Floor, 53 x 16 ½ In.
$1,140

Palm Beach Modern Auctions

Lamp, Electric, Brass Column, Mica Shade, Dolphin Finial, c.1910, 62 In.
$1,375

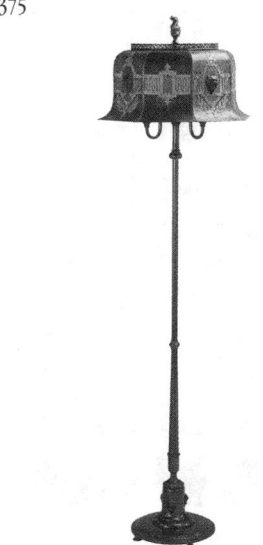

Rago Arts & Auction Center

Lamp, Electric, Brass, Scroll & Flower Design, Fluted Glass Panels, Austria, 24 In.
$1,422

James D. Julia Auctioneers

Lamp, Electric, Bruno Munari, Falkland, Metal, Collapsible Shade, Danese, Italy, 73 In.
$336

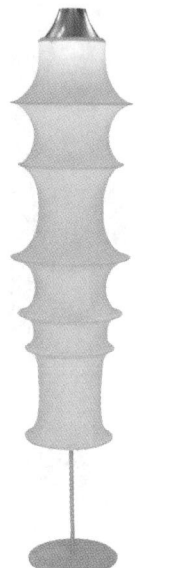

Treadway Toomey Galleries

Lamp, Electric, C. Jere, Looped, Chromed Steel, Ebonized Wood, Labels, 34 x 10 In., Pair
$1,875

Rago Arts & Auction Center

Lamp, Electric, Duffner & Kimberly, Mosaic Glass, 4 Sockets, Bronze Base, c.1910, 23 x 19 In.
$18,000

Skinner Auctioneers & Appraisers

Lamp, Electric, Figural, Frog, Grotesque, Brass, Copper, Glass, Austria, c.1900, 19 x 16 In.
$3,750

Rago Arts & Auction Center

Lamp, Electric, Fruit, Blue Porcelain Stand, Metalwork, Czechoslovakia, 13 x 18 In.
$237

James D. Julia Auctioneers

Lamp, Electric, G. Hansen, Crystal, Chrome, Stamped, Hansen Lamps, New York, 57 ½ In.
$1,830

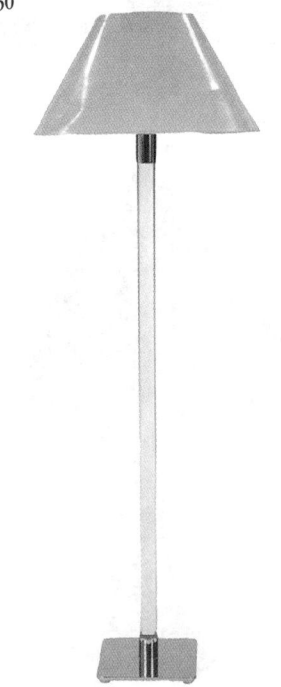

Treadway Toomey Galleries

Lamp, Electric, Ingo Maurer, Thomas Alva Edison Light, Stamped, Design M, 1979, 14 x 8 In.
$6,875

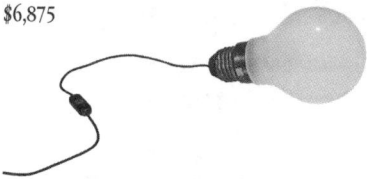

Los Angeles Modern Auctions (LAMA)

Lamp, Electric, Lamp Base, Guido Gambone, Earthenware, Glazed, Abstract, c.1950, 19 x 9 In.
$3,375

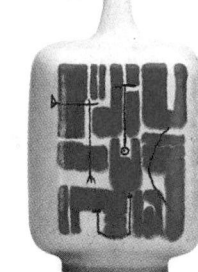

Rago Arts & Auction Center

Lamp, Electric, Leaded Glass, Flowers, 3-Socket Base, Signed, Joseph Porcelli, 26 In.
$11,850

James D. Julia Auctioneers

Lamp, Electric, Leaded Slag Glass, Lilies, Maiden Base, Metal, Suess, 1900s, 25 x 22 In.
$4,688

Rago Arts & Auction Center

Electric, 3-Light, Brass, Pierced Domed Shade, East Indian, 74 In.	472
Electric, 3-Light, Cone Shade, Adjustable, Brass, Steel, Aluminum, Marble, Italy, c.1950, 70 In.	3125
Electric, 12 Lily Shades, Gold Iridescent, Bronze Base, c.1970, 20 ½ In.	5750
Electric, Abalone Shell Shade, Green Copper Lily Pad Base, Elizabeth Burton, 12 x 12 In.	5300
Electric, Alabaster, Dome Top, Shade, Spiral Finial, Stepped Acanthus Base, 70 In.	1700
Electric, Arredoluce, Triennale, Enameled Metal, Brass, Marble, Italy, 1950s, 75 In. *illus*	3750
Electric, Art Deco, Cast Metal, Copper Gilt Finish, Piecework, Fan Shape, 13 ¾ In., Pair	299
Electric, Art Deco, Polar Bears, Icebergs, Bronze, T. Cartier, c.1925, 12 x 13 In., Pair *illus*	800
Electric, Art Nouveau, Caramel Slag Glass Shade, Floral Frame, c.1910, 23 x 20 In.	330
Electric, Art Nouveau, Green Glass, Textured, Mica Shade, Multicolor, 25 x 5 In.	351
Electric, Art Nouveau, Jeweled, Bronze, Austria, c.1910, 19 In. *illus*	1750
Electric, Art Nouveau, La Fortune Par Rousseau, Woman, 3 Flower Vine Sockets, 26 In.	189
Electric, Arteluce, G. Sarfatti, Chrome Plated, Enameled Steel, Aluminum, 1950s, 78 In., Pair	3000
Electric, Billiard, Double, Green Silk, Hanging, c.1920	193
Electric, Blown Glass, Cactus, Poliarte Style, Murano, Italy, Floor, 53 x 16 ½ In. *illus*	1140
Electric, Blue, Slag Glass, Spelter Frame, c.1911, 24 ½ In.	516
Electric, Boudoir, Alacite, 2 Arms, Urn Shape, Square Base	55
Electric, Boudoir, Alacite, Fired-On Coral Base, Silk Shade, 17 In.	75
Electric, Bradley & Hubbard, Globe Shade, White Iris, Scroll Feet, c.1900, 27 In.	570
Electric, Brass Base, Frame, Glass Inset Domed Shade, c.1900, 21 In.	875
Electric, Brass Column, Mica Shade, Dolphin Finial, c.1910, 62 In. *illus*	1375
Electric, Brass, Chrome Meta Geometric Base, Linen Shade, 25 x 14 In., Pair	1625
Electric, Brass, Classical Style, Drapery, 20th Century, 31 In., Pair	470
Electric, Brass, Scroll & Flower Design, Fluted Glass Panels, Austria, 24 In. *illus*	1422
Electric, Bronze, Blackamoor Figures, Holding Stem, 72 In., Pair	1469
Electric, Bronze, Female Figures, Cherub Masks, Baroque Revival Style, c.1910, 32 x 51 In.	660
Electric, Bruno Munari, Falkland, Metal, Collapsible Shade, Danese, Italy, 73 In. *illus*	336
Electric, C. Jere, Looped, Chromed Steel, Ebonized Wood, Labels, 34 x 10 In., Pair *illus*	1875
Electric, Caramel Slag Glass, Brass Frame, Pedestal Base, Paw Feet, Arts & Crafts, 21 In.	118
Electric, Carriage, Silver Plate, 2 Gothic Arches, Glass Panels, Electrified, 1800s, 42 In.	295
Electric, Casella, Chrome, Tubular Shade, Adjustable, Label, 36 x 23 x 6 In.	244
Electric, Cat Shape, Lit Eyes, Chrome, Italy, Signed Torino, 14 x 10 In.	450
Electric, Cedric Hartman, Adjustable Chrome Shade, Lucite Switch, Tubular Chrome Arms, 1900s, Pair	1687
Electric, Chrome Arm & Shade, Plastic Trim, Attributed To Robert Sonneman, 56 x 19 In.	183
Electric, Chrome, Arched Top, Adjustable Arm, Donneman, Floor, 62 x 40 In.	500
Electric, Classical Style, Woman's Figure, Branches, Flower Lights, Spelter, Bruchon, 34 In.	300
Electric, Copper, Aluminum, Glass, Kurt Versen, c.1960, 14 x 12 In.	3776
Electric, Curtis Jere, Chromed Metal, Wood, Artisan House, Floor, 1970, 61 x 9 In.	738
Electric, Cut Glass, Mushroom Shade, Dome Foot, Spear Prisms All Around, 20 In.	922
Electric, Desk, Adjustable, Chrome Metal, Clamp Base, 1900s, 22 In.	375
Electric, Desk, Green Shade, French Bellova, c.1905, 9 In.	456
Electric, Desk, Millefiori, Mushroom Shape, Blue, White, Yellow, Orange, 15 In.	148
Electric, Desk, Patinated Bronze, Cobra Shape, Norman B. Geddes, 1930s, 11 x 12 In.	625
Electric, Desk, Tole, Black, Painted Flowers, 2 Candle Standard Lights, 1800s, 11 In.	85
Electric, Dirk Van Erp, Copper, Hammered, Trumpet Shape, Mica, c.1915, 19 x 16 In.	10625
Electric, Duffner & Kimberly, Leaded, Geometric Panels, Green Glass, Art Nouveau, 19 x 22 In.	4740
Electric, Duffner & Kimberly, Mosaic Glass, 4 Sockets, Bronze Base, c.1910, 23 x 19 In. *illus*	18000
Electric, Duffner & Kimberly, Slag Glass Shade, Patinated Bronze Base, 23 In.	7703
Electric, Ear Of Corn, Gilt, Nickeled Brass, Paper, Maison Charles, 1950s, 34 In., Pair	3750
Electric, Enrico Franzolini, Baby Gilda, Collapsible Base, Linen Shade, Italy, 60 x 16 In.	305
Electric, Figural, Frog, Grotesque, Brass, Copper, Glass, Austria, c.1900, 19 x 16 In. *illus*	3750
Electric, Figural, Horse Head, Bronzed, Vellum Shade, 26 In.	72
Electric, Frosted Glass Shade, Mushroom Shape, Chrome Base, 1960s, 17 x 12 In., Pair	469
Electric, Fruit, Blue Porcelain Stand, Metalwork, Czechoslovakia, 13 x 18 In. *illus*	237
Electric, G. Crespi, Obelisk Form, Brass Base, Acrylic Shade, 1970s, 24 ¾ x 6 In., Pair	3250
Electric, G. Hansen, Crystal, Chrome, Stamped, Hansen Lamps, New York, 57 ½ In. *illus*	1830
Electric, G. Nelson, H. Miller, Bubble, Saucer Shape, Fiberglass, Wire, Bracket, 1950s, 18 In.	469
Electric, Gilt Metal, Urn, 3 Supports Stand, Square Base, Green Moire Shade, 24 In., Pair	1125
Electric, Glass, Opaque White Swirls, Cone Shape, Cylindrical Base, Murano, 26 In., Pair	176
Electric, Glass, White Cased, Red Tip, Cone Shape, Enameled Metal, 1960s, 18 x 14 In.	1188
Electric, Gun Metal, Lucite, Karl Springer, Floor, 71 x 18 In.	644
Electric, Hanging, Arts & Crafts, Iron, Green Stain Glass, Owl Shape, Chain, 42 In.	2832
Electric, Hanging, Chrome, Starburst Shape, 15 x 23 In.	118
Electric, Hanging, Cleopatra, Frosted Glass, Metal, Petitot, France, 1930s, 31 In.	1500
Electric, Hanging, Copper, Hammered, Riveted, Mica Shade, Aurora Studios, 27 x 32 In.	3660
Electric, Hanging, Gilt Bronze, Glass, Ram's Head Medallions, France, c.1890, 32 x 17 In.	2214

Lamp, Electric, Milk Glass, Painted Inside, Indian, Metal, Pittsburgh, c.1915, 21 x 16 In.
$5,938

Rago Arts & Auction Center

Lamp, Electric, Moe Bridges, Reverse Painted Shade, Birch Trees, Shore, Metal Base, 23 In.
$2,725

James D. Julia Auctioneers

Lamp, Electric, P. Henningsen, Bronze, Bakelite, Reverse Painted Glass, 1936, 8 x 9 In.
$7,620

Wright Auction House

L

Lamp, Electric, Pittsburgh Lamp Co., Reverse Painted, 2 Indians, Chipped Ice, 22 ½ In.
$9,145

Humler & Nolan

Lamp, Electric, Shell, Nude Female, Silvered Metal, Lily Pad Base, Art Nouveau, c.1910, 12 In.
$2,040

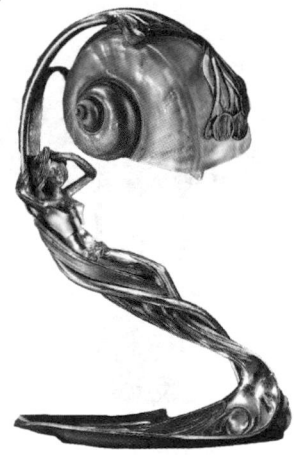

Skinner Auctioneers & Appraisers

Lamp, Electric, Snake, Coiled, Jeweled Inserts, Bronze Base, c.1910, 25 In.
$6,875

Rago Arts & Auction Center

Lamp, Electric, Von Nessen, Metal, Glass, Tiered Tower, Miller Lamp Co., 14 ½ x 5 ½ In.
$2,875

Rago Arts & Auction Center

Lamp, Fairy, Pink Satin, Brass Framed Jewels, Ruffled Shade & Base, 4 ¾ In., 2 Piece
$213

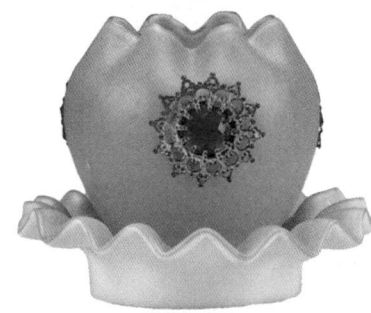

James D. Julia Auctioneersg

Lamp, Fairy, Webb Burmese, Domed Shade, Ruffled, Leaves, Clarkes Cricklite, 6 In.
$1,035

Early Auction Co.

Lamp, Gasolier, 2-Light, Brass, Bronze Patina, Gilt, Glass Shades, 1800s, 42 x 27 In.
$2,032

Neal Auction Co.

Lamp, Gasolier, 6-Light, Rococo, Gilt Bronze, Art, Science, Industry, Electrified, c.1850, 50 In.
$6,274

Neal Auction Co.

Lamp, Grease, Betty, Tidy, Tin, Hinged Lid, Hanging Hook, Saucer Base, Handle, 11 ½ In.
$236

Conestoga Auction Co., Inc.

Electric, Hanging, Milk Glass Globe, Brass Frame, Crystal Prisms, 27 x 15 In............................ 150
Electric, Hanging, Opalescent Glass, Egg Form, Silvered Cast Iron Acanthus Mount, 23 In. 1320
Electric, Henningsen, Snowball, Enameled, Polished Aluminum, 9 Round Tiers, 1960s, 16 In. .. 3625
Electric, Henry G. Cleaveland, Copper, Paper, Enameled, Metal, 2 Sockets, c.1910, 20 x 15 In..... 1000
Electric, Honeycomb Pattern Shade, Leaded Slag Glass, 2 Sockets, 1920s, 24 x 19 In................... 1063
Electric, Howard Miller, Bubble, Cigar Shape, Metal Splayed Legs, 13 x 36 In............................... 732
Electric, Hurricane, Glass Cylinder, Silver Plate Base, 21 In., Pair 1500
Electric, Industrial, Metal, Adjustable, Tripod, 89 In. x 24 In., Pair.. 1170
Electric, Ingo Maurer, Thomas Alva Edison Light, Stamped, Design M, 1979, 14 x 8 In. .....*illus* 6875
Electric, J. Adnet, Bamboo, Brass, Alternating Segments, Tripod, Paper Shade, 1960s, 64 In. 3750
Electric, J. Adnet, Stitched Segmented Leather, Brass Rings, Tripod Base, 1950s, 61 In................. 4375
Electric, J. Mont, Wood, Open Twist Support, 4 Turned Segments, Round Base, 31 x 7 In. 308
Electric, Jean Royere, Wrought Iron, Linen Shade, Adjustable, France, 1950s, 70 x 20 In. 2250
Electric, K. Springer, Parchment, Nickeled Brass, Cylindrical, Spread Foot, Paper Shade, 1980s, 63 In. ... 5625
Electric, Kneeling Maiden, Flowers, Ruby Glass Globe, Spelter, La Belle Specialty Co., 21 In. 173
Electric, La Gloire Couronnant Le Genie, Newel Post, Bronze, Aurene Shades, c.1890, 23 In....... 570
Electric, Lamp Base, Guido Gambone, Earthenware, Glazed, Abstract, c.1950, 19 x 9 In. .....*illus* 3375
Electric, Leaded Glass, Flowers, 3-Socket Base, Signed, Joseph Porcelli, 26 In. ....*illus* 11850
Electric, Leaded Pansy Shade, Spelter Tree, John Morgan & Sons, c.1905, 23 x 18 In.................... 15000
Electric, Leaded Slag Glass, Lilies, Maiden Base, Metal, Suess, 1900s, 25 x 22 In. ....*illus* 4688
Electric, Leaded, Poinsettia, Irregular Border Shade, Green, 3-Socket Base, 20 x 22 In.................. 7110
Electric, Lucite, Figural Base, Male, Female, White, Gold Costume, Moss, 24 x 24 In., Pair.......... 295
Electric, M. Bill, Enameled Metal, Spread Base, 9 Frosted Balloon Shades, 1960s, 62 x 19 In. 2500
Electric, Mantel, Iridescent, Ribbed, Flared Shades, Iridescent, Blue, Green, 9 ¾ In., Pair........... 237
Electric, Max Ingrand, 5-Light, Cased Glass, Metal, Fontana Arte, 1960s, 32 x 19 In., Pair........... 5625
Electric, Mercury Glass, Urn Shape, Ribs, Applied Handles, 1900s, 30 In., Pair........................... 294
Electric, Midcentury, Globe, Frank Ligteljin, Holland, 1960s, 28 In... 259
Electric, Milk Glass, Painted Inside, Indian, Metal, Pittsburgh, c.1915, 21 x 16 In. ....*illus* 5938
Electric, Moe Bridges, Domed Shade, Reverse Painted Landscape, 21 In................................... 425
Electric, Moe Bridges, Reverse Painted Shade, Birch Trees, Shore, Metal Base, 23 In. ....*illus* 2725
Electric, Moon Crest, Brushed Aluminum, Domed Shade, Smith Metal Arts, 16 In...................... 161
Electric, Mosaic, Leaded, Floral Glass Shade, 3-Light Tree Shape Base, 1900s, 24 x 18 In........... 1722
Electric, Murano Glass, Gold, Red Swirls, Cylindrical, Round Base, 10 x 23 In., Pair 1375
Electric, Nautilus, Bronze, Nymph, Lily Pad, Iridescent Shade, Art Nouveau, c.1900, 13 In. 1140
Electric, Nessen, Swing Arm, Adjustable, Round Base, Chrome, Shade, 1900s, 17 ½ In................ 147
Electric, P. Henningsen, Bronze, Bakelite, Reverse Painted Glass, 1936, 8 x 9 In. ....*illus* 7620
Electric, Parrot, On Perch, Suspended Socket, Glass Beaded Shade, Iron, Glass Ball, 15 In. 546
Electric, Pendant, Venini, 2 Blue Case Glass Shades, Adjustable, c.1960, 14 x 36 In. 708
Electric, Pierre Guariche, 2-Light, Counterbalance, Enameled Steel, Brass, 1950s, 69 x 54 In. ... 3000
Electric, Pittsburgh Lamp Co., Reverse Painted, 2 Indians, Chipped Ice, 22 ½ In. ....*illus* 9145
Electric, Pittsburgh, Reverse Painted Landscape Shade, Red, Blue, Bronze Base, 22 x 15 In........ 1000
Electric, Pole, Atomic, 4-Light, Brass, Adjustable, Crown Finial, Ball Foot, c.1960, 55 In. 266
Electric, Pool Table, White, Pink Flowers, Painted, Harpo Productions Label, 11 x 72 In.............. 615
Electric, Poppy, Yellow Shade, Multicolor, Fluted Base, Wilkinson, 27 x 20 In.............................. 5228
Electric, Porcelain, Painted, Ships, Dutch Landscape, Cream, Gilt Bands, Minton, 17 In.............. 720
Electric, Primitive Man, Openwork Design, Green, Roger Capron, France, c.1950, 22 x 13 In..... 1000
Electric, Radio, Multicolor, Reticulated Floral Embossed Detail, Flared Base, c.1930, 14 In. 120
Electric, Raymor, Metal, Paper Label, 43 ½ x 13 x 7 ½ In... 122
Electric, Reverse Painted Shape, Lakeside Scene, Metal Base, 19 x 16 In................................... 330
Electric, Roycroft, Copper, Mesh Lined Shade, Riveted Straps, Column Base, 10 x 14 In............. 2100
Electric, Sandwich Cut Overlay, Pressed Base, White To Ruby Quatrefoil, c.1870, 21 ½ In........... 338
Electric, Sandwich Cut Overlay, Pyriform Font, Blue Glass Shafts, Gilt Metal, 17 In., Pair........... 431
Electric, Sconce, Roycroft, Copper, Hammered, Mica Panels, Orb Signed, 10 x 13 In. 5300
Electric, Shell, Nude Female, Silvered Metal, Lily Pad Base, Art Nouveau, c.1910, 12 In. ......*illus* 2040
Electric, Slag Glass Shade, Green Tile, Bronze, Standard, Arts & Crafts, 1905, 20 x 16 In. 826
Electric, Snake, Coiled, Jeweled Inserts, Bronze Base, c.1910, 25 In. ....*illus* 6875
Electric, Street, Aluminum Housing, Concrete Post, Wood Base, Salesman's Sample, 29 In......... 365
Electric, Street, Eagle Finial, Silver, Gold Paint, Cast Iron, 11 ½ In., Pair.................................... 504
Electric, Street, Iron, Cooper, William Edgar & Son, 36 ½ x 17 In., Pair...................................... 1580
Electric, Student, Brass, Double, Cased Emerald Green Glass Ribbed Shades, 28 In.................... 480
Electric, Student, Electric, Brass, Double Arm, Clear, Green Glass Shade, 20 In............................ 240
Electric, T. H. Rodsjohn-Gibbings, Marble, Brass Fittings, String Shade, 1960s, 23 In., Pair 3500
Electric, Teak, Plastic Saturn, Modeline, A. Pearsall, Kroft Assoc., Floor, c.1950, 49 x 12 In......... 59
Electric, Tommi Parzinger, 4-Light, Iron, Floor, c.1960, 61 x 11 In... 1169
Electric, Tulip Shape, White, Acrylic, Metal, Rougier, c.1975, 34 x 15 In...................................... 984
Electric, Twist Standard, Fruitwood, Chrome Metal, c.1970, 26 In., Pair.................................... 313
Electric, Vetri Murano, Glass, Pyramid Shape, Black, White Stripes, c.1970, 26 ½ x 10 In. 594

Lamp, Oil, Gilt Bronze, Porcelain, Glass Shade, France, 29 ¾ In.
$813

Leslie Hindman Auctioneers

Lamp, Sconce, 1-Light, Tin, Mirrored Back, Round, c.1810, 11 ½ In., Pair
$1,107

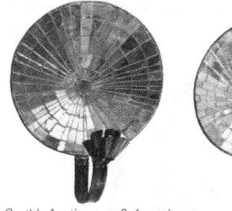

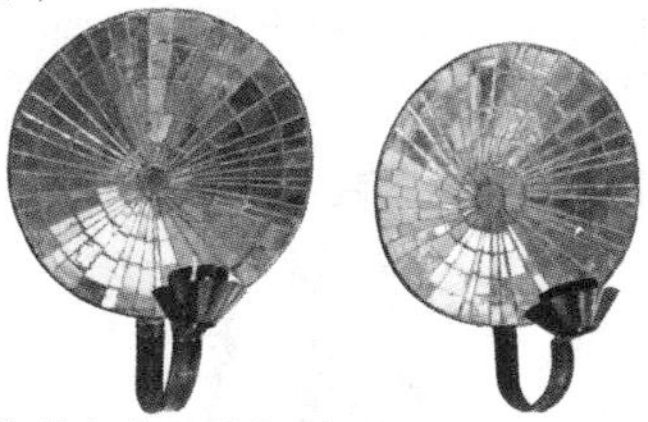

Garth's Auctioneers & Appraisers

Lamp, Sinumbra, Bronze, Copper, Brass, Column, Griffins, Etched Glass, c.1850, 30 In.
$956

Neal Auction Co.

L

Lamp, Solar, Brass, Bronze, Gilt, Lacquered, Cut Glass, Chimney, Dietz Brother & Co., 34 In.
$4,302

Neal Auction Co.

Lantern, Brass, Moorish, Bombe Shape, Metalwork Inset, Blue Glass, 1900, 34 x 13 In.
$793

Neal Auction Co.

TIP
Hold glass shades carefully when you remove a lightbulb from an old lamp. The Tiffany lily-shaped shade and others like are held in place by the screwed-in bulb.

Electric, Von Nessen, Metal, Glass, Tiered Tower, Miller Lamp Co., 14 ½ x 5 ½ In. ....*illus*	2875
Electric, Walnut, Tripod, Ribbed Plastic Ball Shade, Rispal, 1950s, 52 x 15 In.............................	3625
Electric, Wilkinson, Water Lily, Glass Shade, Turquoise Water, Peach, 4 Pad Feet, 28 x 21 In.......	6600
Electric, Wood, G. Jouve, Lacquer, Gilt, Blue Glaze Ceramic Face, Linen Shade, 1950s, 78 In.......	5000
Fairy, Epergne, Crystal Inverted Saucer, Vining Stem, 2 Bud Vases, Rigaree, Silk Shade, 17 In. ...	1126
Fairy, Figural, Court Page, Translucent Globe, Continental, 17 ½ In.	780
Fairy, Pedestal, Pressed Square Base, Conical Lithopone Shade, Victorian, 11 In., Pair	243
Fairy, Pink Satin, Brass Framed Jewels, Ruffled Shade & Base, 4 ¾ In., 2 Piece ....*illus*	213
Fairy, Webb Burmese, Domed Shade, Ruffled, Leaves, Clarkes Cricklite, 6 In. ....*illus*	1035
Fluid, Blown Glass, Onion Font, Swirled Pedestal, c.1885, 10 In..	325
Fluid, Burner, Pewter, Brass Double Tubes, Acorn Font, John Newell, c.1850, 9 x 4 ¾ In.	230
Fluid, Neoclassical, Cut Glass Shade, Column, Classical Designs, Onyx Base, 1800s, 22 In.	270
Fluid, Peg, Art Glass, Brass Stand, Green Font, Flowers, 13 In.	207
Fluid, Peg, Threaded, Brass Stand, Electric, Pallne-Konig, 13 In...	354
Gasolier, 2-Light, Brass, Bronze Patina, Gilt, Glass Shades, 1800s, 42 x 27 In. ....*illus*	2032
Gasolier, 6-Light, Rococo, Gilt Bronze, Art, Science, Industry, Electrified, c.1850, 50 In. .....*illus*	6274
Grease, 4 Spouts, Sheet Iron, Round, Sliding Cone Cover, Ring Finial, 1800s, 15 x 6 In............	138
Grease, Betty, Combination, Candle Socket, Round Shaft, Iron, Brass Rosettes, Adjustable, 16 In.	354
Grease, Betty, Copper, Iron, Hinged Lid, Chain, Hook, Peter Derr, 1835, 6 x 4 In.	2875
Grease, Betty, Tidy, Tin, Hinged Lid, Hanging Hook, Saucer Base, Handle, 11 ½ In. ....*illus*	236
Grease, Betty, Wrought Iron, Shaped Reservoir, Wick Holder, Hinged Lid, Hook, 4 ½ In.	106
Handel Lamps are included in the Handel category.	
Kerosene, Banquet, Burgundy Glass Shade, Gold Dragon, Brass & Onyx Base, Electrified, 28 In.	590
Kerosene, Banquet, Peach Satin, Fan Mold Font, Etched Shade, Embossed Brass Base, 25 ½ In.	354
Kerosene, Brass, Oak Leaf Font, Stepped Marble Base, Frosted Shade, Coffin Prisms, 19 In.........	153
Kerosene, Magic Lantern, Tin, Reflector, Arched Chimney, Burner, c.1870, 16 In.	390
Kerosene, Marble, Brass Overlay, Fluted Base, Blue Font, White Cased, Ball Shade, 24 x 6 In......	584
Kerosene, Piano, Metal, Patina, Putti, Curved Leaves, Scrolling, Ball Shade, 36 x 23 In.............	1107
Mariano Fortuny, Moda, Black, White, Linen Shade, Umbrella Shape, Tripod, c.1940, 77 x 34 In.	2242
Nessen, Swing Arm, Adjustable Height, Chrome, Shade, Floor, c.1970, 52 In., Pair........................	301
Oil To Electric, G. Stickley, Twisted Iron Handles, Copper Base, Hammered, Basket Shade, 18 x 25 In.	2700
Oil, Banquet, Consolidated Glass, Painted Shade Font, Pedestal, Gilt Base, Electrified, 23 In.	72
Oil, Brass, Cranberry Glass, Diamond Quilted, Oval, Veritas Lamp Works, Germany, 17 In..........	147
Oil, Gilt Bronze, Porcelain, Glass Shade, France, 29 ¾ In. ....*illus*	813
Oil, Glass Font, Amethyst Cut To Clear, Washington Cutting, Metal & Marble Base, 11 In.............	497
Oil, Glass Font, Quatrefoil & Oval, Cranberry Cut To Clear, Reeded Brass, Marble, 10 In.............	439
Oil, Glass Font, Quatrefoil, Thumbprint, Cranberry Cut To Clear, Reeded Brass, Marble, 11 In....	380
Oil, Glass Font, Thumbprint, Teal Cut To Clear, Reeded Brass & Marble Base, 13 In.	468
Oil, Gone With The Wind, Painted Tulips, Shaded Green & Yellow, 4 Leafy Feet, 24 In.	232
Oil, Miner's, Iron, Brass Rooster Finial, 1800s, 8 In..	246
Oil, Pegged Font, Quatrefoil & Punty, Green Cut To Clear, Etched Frosted Ball Shade, 18 In.	556
Oil, Pendant, 3-Light, Gilt Metal, Art Glass Opalescent Smoke Bell, Electrified, 18 x 9 In............	58
Oil, Pewter Stem & Font, Thumb Lift, Tapered, Dish Base, Glass Teardrop Shade, c.1830, 13 In. .	390
Oil, Pittsburgh, Hanging, Scrolled Harp, Embossed Burner, Flared Shade, 33 In..........................	120
Oil, Pressed Glass, Baroque Base, Cobalt Blue, Cut To Clear Font, 6-Petal Flowers, 10 In............	293
Oil, Whale, Pewter, Bull's-Eye Lens, Cylinder Font, Double Tube Burner, c.1845, 9 x 4 In.........	518
Pairpoint lamps are in the Pairpoint category.	
Perfume, Globe, Camel, Rider, Palm Trees, Flowers, Black Amethyst, Illidela, c.1925, 5 x 4 In......	219
Perfume, Orange, Black Painted, Silhouette Style, Gilt Brass, Devilbiss, c.1925, 7 ¾ In.	403
Rush, Combination, Candle Socket, Twisted Stem, Triangular Base, 3 Legs, Flattened Feet, 9 In.	236
Rush, Combination, Candle Socket, Wrought Iron, Scissors Style, Wood Base, 11 In.	224
Rush, Oak Notched Post, Wrought Iron Pincer Like Holder, 1800s, 31 In...	360
Rush, Wrought Iron, Scissor Type, Hinged, Scrolled Arm, Curled Terminal, Curled Feet, 8 In......	295
Rush, Wrought Iron, Turned Stepped Terminal Counter Weight, 9 ¼ In...	295
Sconce, 1-Light, Brass, Candle, Greek Revival, c.1815, 5 x 7 In., Pair	180
Sconce, 1-Light, Mirror Back, Tole, Starburst Design, c.1815, 12 ½ x 10 In................................	1180
Sconce, 1-Light, Tin, Mirrored Back, Round, c.1810, 11 ½ In., Pair ....*illus*	1107
Sconce, 1-Light, Wrought Iron, Impressed Rooster Design, 14 In..	288
Sconce, 2-Light, Brass, Embossed, Holland, 19th Century, 24 x 13 In., Pair	1560
Sconce, 2-Light, Brass, Shield Shape, Trophee Branches, Sea Serpents, c.1885, 12 In., Pair	615
Sconce, 2-Light, Bronze, U-Shape, Leaves, Woman's Head, Long Hair, c.1900, 27 In., Pair	4444
Sconce, 2-Light, Cut Glass, Mirror Back, Venetian Style, 1900s, 13 x 7 In., Pair........................	478
Sconce, 2-Light, French Empire Style, Bronze, Egyptian Heads, c.1915, 23 In., Pair....................	738
Sconce, 2-Light, Gilt Bronze, Louis XIV Style, Cherubs, France, c.1885, 22 x 9 In., Pair	2337
Sconce, 2-Light, Gilt Bronze, Scrolling Arms, Seated Figure, Leaves, 13 In., Pair........................	1554
Sconce, 2-Light, Gilt Bronze, Urn Shape, Satyr, Festoon, Scroll Arms, 21 In., Pair......................	1125

Sconce, 2-Light, Giltwood, Mirrored, Shaped, Cut Flowers & Shells, 28 x 11 In., 4 Piece 1793
Sconce, 2-Light, Green Man's Face, Scroll Arms, Glass Tulip Shades, 16 x 16 In., Pair 300
Sconce, 2-Light, Rock Crystal, Urn Shape, Opposing Birds, Leaves, 27 x 19 In., Pair 3050
Sconce, 2-Light, Tin, Embossed, Pierced Arch, Crimped Edges, Reeded Border, 15 x 10 In. 1722
Sconce, 2-Light, Venetian Glass, Mirrored, Garden Landscape, c.1800, 24 x 8 In., Pair 1298
Sconce, 3-Light, Brass & Crystal, Scroll Arms, Hanging Prisms, c.1885, 18 x 11 In 354
Sconce, 3-Light, Brass, Copper, Urn, Scroll Arms, c.1900, 16 ½ x 12 In. 369
Sconce, 3-Light, Bronze, Gilt, Goddess, Lion Masks, Leaves, Scroll Arms, 13 x 14 In., Pair 837
Sconce, 3-Light, Flowers, Metal, Porcelain, Glass, Plastic, c.1965, 30 In., Pair 313
Sconce, 3-Light, Gilt Bronze, Flaming Urn Finial, Ram Mask, Scroll Arms, 20 ½ In., Pair.......... 1063
Sconce, 3-Light, Gilt Bronze, Scroll Arms, Leaves, 1800s, 15 x 13 In., Pair 978
Sconce, 3-Light, Gilt Bronze, Shell & Scroll, Acorns, Stippled, France, 25 x 17 In., Pair 922
Sconce, 3-Light, Gilt Bronze, Torch Bearing Putti, Turned Sockets, 11 x 11 In., Pair 430
Sconce, 3-Light, Gilt Metal, Cut Glass, Neoclassical Style, Leaves, Prisms, 25 x 17 In., Pair 2091
Sconce, 3-Light, Gilt, Bronze, Scroll Arms, Ball Standard, Leaves, c.1815, 7 In., Set Of 4 2091
Sconce, 3-Light, Gilt, Mirror, Reticulated, Angel, Griffins, Masks, c.1885, 30 x 20 In., Pair 657
Sconce, 3-Light, Giltwood, Torch Shape Stem, Carved Leaves, Scroll Arms, 30 In., Pair 875
Sconce, 3-Light, Mirror, Shield Shape, Scroll Arms, Crystal Pendants, c.1900, 21 In., Pair 1434
Sconce, 3-Light, Napoleon III, Gilt Bronze, Lacquer, Porcelain, Blue Inserts, 13 x 10 In., Pair.... 492
Sconce, 3-Light, Paint, Carved, Loop Arms, Scalloped Cups, Italy, c.1985, 25 x 15 In., Pair 295
Sconce, 3-Light, Rock Crystal, Metal, Flowering Urn, Perched Birds, 32 x 23 In., Pair 3884
Sconce, 3-Light, Rock Crystal, Vase Shape, Birds, Leaves, Pendant Drops, 31 In., Pair 1673
Sconce, 4-Light, Bows, Ribbons, Shield, Shell, Masks, Leaf Arms, 1800s, 44 x 19 In., Pair 2829
Sconce, 4-Light, Gilt Bronze, Putti, Rope Twist Swing, France, 1900s, 32 x 17 In., Pair 1180
Sconce, 4-Light, Gilt Bronze, Scrolling Leaf Arms, Putto, Flowers, c.1890, 15 x 15 In., Pair........ 1080
Sconce, 4-Light, Gilt Bronze, White Glass Lily Shades, 1800s, 25 x 18 In., Pair 1150
Sconce, 4-Light, Tole, Giltwood, Leaf Backplate, Mirror, Leaf Arms, 1800s, 24 x 18 In., Pair 717
Sconce, 5-Light, Gilt Bronze, Painted Glass, Chinoiserie, Leaves, 1800s, 25 x 13 In., Pair 2562
Sconce, 5-Light, Gilt Bronze, Scrolling Leaves, Fluted Stem, 1800s, 15 x 12 In., Pair 2460
Sconce, 5-Light, Gilt Bronze, Shaped Backplate, Scroll Arms, Flame Finial, 19 x 14 In. 717
Sconce, 5-Light, Louis XV Style, Scroll Arms, Tassels, Masks, France, 1800s, 31 x 21 In. 767
Sconce, 6-Light, Figural, Putti, Cornucopia, Gilt Bronze, France, 1900s, 27 x 18 In., Pair 1062
Sconce, Art Deco, Metal, Painted Plate Rim, Signed Lincoln, 19 ½ x 9 In., 2 Pairs 210
Sconce, Art Deco, Radiating Rods, Metal, Brass, Glass Balls, c.1935, 15 x 11 ½ In., Pair 2500
Sconce, Brass, Hurricane, Blown Glass Shade, Regency Style, 29 x 8 In., Pair 861
Sconce, Bronze, Cartouche Backplate, Fluted Torch, Flame Shade, c.1900, 18 x 8 In., Pair......... 922
Sconce, Bronze, Silvered, Escutcheon Shape, Baluster Arm, Urn Socket, 1900s, 11 In., Pair........ 738
Sconce, Candle, Mirrored, Mosaic Design, Tin Frame, Crimped Candle Cup, 9 x 8 In., Pair......... 649
Sconce, Candle, Sheet Iron, Flower Top, Fluted Back, Punched, Cutout, c.1800, 19 In., Pair 948
Sconce, Candle, Tin, Crimped Edge, Mirrored, U.S.A., c.1815, 6 ⅝ In., Pair 1680
Sconce, Copper, Shield Backplate, Painted Chalice, Host, Cherubim, 1800s, 10 x 6 In., Pair........ 1792
Sconce, F. Agostini, 2-Light, Stylized Branch, Gilt Brass, Linen Shades, 1960s, 19 x 12 In., Pair .. 3500
Sconce, Felix Agostini, 2-Light, Brass, Linen Shades, France, 1960s, 19 x 13 In., Pair 9375
Sconce, Giltwood, 5 Step-Shape Shelves, Scrolling, Italy, c.1900, 28 x 19 In., Pair................... 531
Sconce, Girandole, 3-Light, Gilt Brass, Leaves, Grapes, Prisms, Boston, c.1855, 14 In., Pair 720
Sconce, Patinated Metal Tripod Legs, Drum Shade, c.1950, 10 x 7 In., Pair 1500
Sconce, Tin, Polished, Painted Flowers, 19th Century, 15 ½ In., Pair................................... 660
Sinumbra, Bronze, Copper, Brass, Column, Griffins, Etched Glass, c.1850, 30 In. ....*illus* 956
Sinumbra, Empire Revival, Bronze, Marble, Double Stepped Base, Cut Shade, 31 x 11 In. 984
Sinumbra, Renaissance Revival, Gilt Brass, White Glass, Blue Border, Fluted, Tapered, 22 In. 270
Solar, Brass, Bronze, Gilt, Lacquered, Cut Glass, Chimney, Dietz Brother & Co., 34 In. ....*illus* 4302
Solar, Brass, Marble, Double Stepped Base, Blown Cut & Frosted Glass Shade, 24 x 10 In. 522
Solar, Gilt Brass Column, Fluted, Tapered, Marble Base, Etched Frosted Glass Shade, 23 In......... 184
Solar, Rococo Revival, Brass, Tripartite Standard, Shell Feet, Dietz Bros., 25 x 9 In., Pair 922
Tiffany Lamps are listed in the Tiffany category.
Torchere, 6-Light, Scrolling Arms, Fluted Supports, Quadripartite Base, 98 x 38 In., Pair........... 6765
Torchere, 10-Light, Cast Metal, Leaf Arms, 2 Tiers, Fluted Stem, Ram Masks, 76 In. 813
Torchere, Art Deco, Chrome Steel, Walnut, Milk Glass, 1920s, 76 x 16 In................................ 313
Torchere, Bronze, Gilt, Figure, Egyptian Dress, Holding Candelabrum, 99 x 30 In., Pair 4780
Torchere, Marble, Bronze, Bowl, Iron Tripod Stand, Ram's Head, Paw Feet, 1900s, 38 In. 1800
Torchere, Neoclassical Style, Parcel Gilt, Leaves, Hexagonal Stem, Arch Legs, 60 In., Pair 1912
Torchere, Renaissance Style, Bronze, Putti, Masks, Urns, Medallions, c.1900, 58 In., Pair........... 5100
Torchere, Wrought Iron, Baroque Style, Leaf Basket, Twist Standard, c.1915, 72 In. 676
Wall Lantern, Candle, Wood Frame, Painted, 3 Glass Panes, Crest, Hanging Holes, 10 ½ In. 660
Whale Oil Burner, Chamber, Pewter, Roswell Gleason, 4 ¼ In.. 270
Whale Oil, Pressed Glass, Circle & Ellipse, Cobalt Blue, Hexagonal Pedestal, c.1870, 8 In. 1404
Whale Oil, Silver Plate, 2-Tube Burner, Baluster Stem, Rope Edge Base, c.1830, 11 x 6 In. 138

Lantern, Candle, Tin, Pierced, Geometric Design, Cone Top, Hanging Ring, Hinged Door, 17 In.
$94

Conestoga Auction Co., Inc.

Lantern, Carriage, Brass, Glass, Festoons, Iron Hooks, Olimpio Bertoni, Italy, 43 In., Pair
$5,500

Leslie Hindman Auctioneers

This is an edited listing of current prices. Visit **Kovels.com** to check thousands of prices from previous years and sign up for free information on trends, tips, reproductions, marks, and more.

L

Lantern, Pewter, Candle, 4 Glass Sides, Drip Pan Pick, Chinese, 1900s, 20 x 6 In., Pair
$369

Skinner Auctioneers & Appraisers

Lantern, Skater's, Brass, Blue Glass Globe, Marked W.B.G. Corp., Waterbury, 7 ¼ In.
$325

Conestoga Auction Co., Inc.

Le Verre Francais, Vase, Flowers, Leaves, Orange, Blue, Acid Cut, Cameo, 4 ½ In.
$533

James D. Julia Auctioneers

LAMPSHADE

Aladdin No. 501, 1930s, 10 In.	139
Aladdin, No. 401, Bellflower, Glass, Satin Frosted, c.1920, 7 ⅝ x 8 ¾ In.	124
Aladdin, White Milk Glass, Swirled, Ribbed, 10 In.	60
Ceiling Light, Pink Satin Glass, Zig-Zag, Dotted Vertical, Flower Bands, 10 x 9 ½ In., Pair	86

LANTERNS are a special type of lighting device. They have a light source, usually a candle, totally hidden inside the walls of the lantern. Light is seen through holes or glass sections.

Anglo-Indian, Green Blown Glass, Hanging, Smoke Bell, Gilt Metal Mounts, 16 In.	660
Barn, Mortised Pine Frame, Slate Blue Paint, Glass Panes, Tin Candle Socket, 13 In.	588
Barn, Wood, Pinned Construction, Snipe-Hinge Door, Wire Handle, Scalloped Opening, 11 In.	345
Brass, Hexagonal, Stylized Flowers, 30 In.	90
Brass, Moorish, Bombe Shape, Metalwork Inset, Blue Glass, 1900, 34 x 13 In. ....*illus*	793
Brass, Vented Onion Dome Top, Bail Handle, Embossed Door, Octagonal, Holland, 14 In.	1080
Bronze, Hexagonal, 6 Supports, Openwork Panels, Hinged Door, Corner Bells, Japan, 10 In.	476
Candle, Delft, Faience, Pewter Hanging Ring, Pyramid Shape Pierced Chimney, 9 ¾ In.	390
Candle, Iron, Pierced, Strap Handle, Circles, Bars, Cone Top, Hinged Door, 1800s, 16 x 5 In.	219
Candle, Sheet Iron, Pierced, Square, Cone Top, Ring Handle, 1800s, 8 x 3 In.	138
Candle, Tin, 2 Glass Panes, Sliding Panel, 19th Century, 18 x 15 In.	512
Candle, Tin, Dove Flying Punched, Cylindrical, Cone Cap, Hinged Door, c.1845, 12 x 5 In.	288
Candle, Tin, Glass, Pierced, Ring Handle, Chimney, Door, Handle, c.1815, 19 x 12 In.	1599
Candle, Tin, Pierced, Geometric Design, Cone Top, Hanging Ring, Hinged Door, 17 In. ......*illus*	94
Candle, Tin, Punched, Round Articulated Iron Handle, Conical Top, Hinged Door, Hasp, 15 In.	153
Carriage, Brass, Glass, Festoons, Iron Hooks, Olimpio Bertoni, Italy, 43 In., Pair ....*illus*	5500
Carriage, Copper, Paint, 6-Sided, Beveled Glass, c.1885, 27 x 8 In., Pair	837
Dietz King, Brass, Embossed Water Shield, Seagrave Co., Patent August 27, 1907	371
Dietz Queen, Cobalt Blue Globe, Nickel, Patent Date '06	600
Etched Glass Panel, 21 In., Pair	180
Hall, 3-Light, Blown Glass, Etched Grapes & Willow, Chains, Smoke Bell, c.1800, 22 In.	956
Hall, 3-Light, Bronze, Crystal, Panel Cut, Chain, Smoke Bell, Regency Style, 26 x 14 In.	1045
Hall, 3-Light, Silver Plate, Hexagonal, Rope Twist Glass, Prisms, c.1935, 30 x 16 In.	1722
Hall, Copper, Round, Tapered, Textured Glass, Iron Grid Cage, Arts & Crafts, 24 In.	1140
Hall, Glass, Blown, Cut, Etched, Bulbous Bell Shape, Grapes, Leaves, 26 x 12 In.	1586
Hall, Tole, Eglomise, Hexagonal, Leaf & Compass Star Design, 1800s, 24 x 9 ½ In.	492
Hanging, Gilt Metal, Glass, Dome Top, Angels, Bulbous Base, c.1915, 52 x 18 In.	1168
Hanging, Metal, Glass, Black Paint, Neoclassical Style, 30 x 22 In.	625
Hanging, Tin, Blown Glass, Elongated Globe, Oil Burner, c.1850, 18 In.	323
Hanging, Tole, Black Paint, Pagoda Shape, 22 x 14 In.	813
Keene, Fixed Globe, Wristlet, Etched Keene 1	855
Miner's Safety Lamp, Brass, Tin, Plaque, Protector Lamp & Lighting Co., 9 ½ In.	236
Pewter, Candle, 4 Glass Sides, Drip Pan Pick, Chinese, 1900s, 20 x 6 In., Pair ....*illus*	369
Pine, Clear Glass Sides, Wide Metal Handle, c.1850, 9 In.	300
Pine, Triangular, Loop Handle, Continental, c.1850, 16 ½ In.	600
Skater's, Brass, Amber Bulbous Shade, Bail Swing Handle, Stepped Molded Font, 7 In.	2950
Skater's, Brass, Blue Glass Globe, Marked W.B.G. Corp., Waterbury, 7 ¼ In. ....*illus*	325
Skater's, Brass, Clear Bulbous Shade, Chain Hanging Handle, Molded Font, 4 ½ In.	826
Skater's, Brass, Clear Tapered Shade, Hanging Chain Handle, Smoke Bell, Stepped Font, 9 In.	177
Skater's, Brass, Cobalt Blue, Bulbous Shade, Bail Swing Handle, Stepped Molded Font, 7 In.	177
Tin, Glass, Fluted Smoke Bell, Wire Twisted Hanging Ring, Hinged Door, 4 ½ In.	165
Tin, Hexagonal, Glass Panels, Painted, Gilt Frame, Electrified, c.1890, 26 In.	723
Tin, Japanned, Star & Diamond Pierced Dome Top, Ring Handle, Oval Globe, Oil Font, 17 In.	153
Tin, Paneled Glass, Tin, Candle Sockets, New England, c.1840, 12 In., Pair	180
Tin, Punched, Gothic Style, Spires, Loop Handle, c.1850, 20 ½ In.	840
Tin, Pyramid Shape, 2 Glass Panels, Wire Guards, Hinged Rectangular Font, Burner, 9 In.	165
Wood, Loop Handle, Panels, Tin, Cover, 12 In.	2216
Wrought Iron, 2-Light, Curled Accents, U.S.A., 28 x 12 In.	369

LE VERRE FRANCAIS is one of the many types of cameo glass made by the Schneider Glassworks in France. The glass was made by the C. Schneider factory in Epinay-sur-Seine from 1918 to 1933. It is a mottled glass, usually decorated with floral designs, and bears the incised signature *Le Verre Francais*.

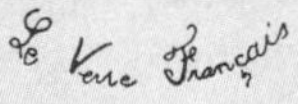

Vase, Bud, Etched Flower, Plum, Flared Rim, Footed, 8 In.	750
Vase, Cameo, Frenes, Orange, Yellow, Signed, Charles Schneider, c.1930, 14 x 5 In.	1875
Vase, Coprins, Stylized Cameo Flowers, Yellow, Green Mottled Ground, 6 ¼ In.	889

L

Vase, Eglantines, Stylized Flowers, Mauve Mottled, Thorned Stem, Orange, 18 In............. 2370
Vase, Flowers, Leaves, Orange, Blue, Acid Cut, Cameo, 4 ½ In. ....*illus* 533
Vase, Mottled Pink, Red, Foxgloves, Elongated Oval, Spread Foot, 1900s, 14 In. 944
Vase, Purple, Over Red, Round, Tapered To Foot, 6 In............................... 104
Vase, Tapered, Swollen Shoulder, Pedestal Foot, Blue, Orange, 13 ⅓ In.................. 1755

LEATHER is tanned animal hide and has been used to make decorative and useful objects for centuries. Leather objects must be carefully preserved with proper humidity and oiling or the leather will deteriorate and crack. This damage cannot be repaired.

Basket, Key, Crescent Moon, Diamond Designs, Oval, c.1890, 7 x 8 ½ In. 805
Basket, Key, Embossed Surface, Handle, Virginia, c.1860, 3 ½ x 7 In. 1067
Basket, Key, Red Stain, Handle, Applied Heart, Stamped J.R. McK, c.1840, 7 ⅜ x 7 ⅜ In............. 34375
Basket, Stitched Key, Hearts, Stars, Diamonds, Cutout Handle Guards, c.1850, 8 x 4 In. 5750
Boots, Tan, White Butterfly, Montie Montana, c.1950, 14 In. 1180
Bucket, Powder, American Navy Yard, Stamped, 14 In. 1560
Chaps, Fringed, Pockets, Dark Patina, 1880s, 37 In... 275
Cup, Embossed, Hunting Designs, HLK, c.1850, 3 ½ In... 30
Footrest, Rhinoceros Shape, 30 ½ In. 456
Rug, Cowhide, Black, White, 20th Century, 104 x 43 In. 185
Saddle, Parade, Dickson, Silver, Diamonds, Engraved, E.H. Bohlin, 1940s 32450
Saddle, Roper, Light Brown, c.1950 826
Saddle, Stitched Designs, c.1880, 27 In.. 46
Sculpture, Turtle, Glass Eyes, Dimitri Omersa, Abercrombie & Fitch, Eng., 1960s, 9 x 14 In. 1375
Stage Coach Seat, Tufted, Black, Wood Base, 38 x 44 In., Pair............................... 474
Tray, Trophy, Embossed Horse, Jockey, 1927, 17 x 19 ½ In.................................... 150

LEEDS pottery was made at Leeds, Yorkshire, England, from 1774 to 1878. Most Leeds ware was not marked. Early Leeds pieces had distinctive twisted handles with a greenish glaze on part of the creamy ware. Later ware often had blue borders on the creamy pottery. A Chicago company named Leeds made many Disney-inspired figurines. They are listed in the Disneyana category.

LEEDS POTTERY

Creamer, George Washington, Federal Eagle, c.1820, 6 In...................................... 354
Cup & Saucer, Peafowl, Miniature, c.1850... 360
Pitcher, Water, Flowers, Leaves, Multicolor, Bulbous, Trailing Vines & Buds, 7 In. 71
Plate, Blue Feather Edge, Arms Of The United States, c.1850, 7 ⅝ In. 851
Plate, Blue Feather Edge, Captain Joyce Of The Macedonian, c.1845, 10 In.................. 593
Plate, Blue Feather Edge, Eagle, Shield Design, 3 ⅝ In... 780
Platter, Green Feathered Rim, Oval, c.1835, 15 In.. 81
Tankard, Lid, Cylindrical, Fluted Sides, Cream Ground, Green Striping, c.1775, 5 In........ 720
Teapot, House & Trees, White, Yellow, Blue, Green, Lid, Acorn Finial, c.1845, 7 ½ In. 176
Teapot, Lid, Creamware, Fluted, Stripes, Underglaze Green, Pierced Gallery, c.1780, 5 ½ In......... 1800
Tureen, Dome Lid, Creamware, Pierced, Finial, Twisted Reed Handles, 9 ¾ x 10 In........ 68

LEFTON is a mark found on pottery, porcelain, glass, and other wares imported by the Geo. Zoltan Lefton Company. The company began in 1941. George Lefton died in 1996 and the company was sold in 2001. The company mark has changed through the years, but because marks have been used for long periods of time, they are of little help in dating an object.

Ashtray, Hat, Pipe, Brown, Red Sticker, 1950s, 5 x 6 In. 35
Bank, Lion, Brown, Yellow, Red Sticker, 6 ¼ In. 17
Basket, Tree Trunk, Leaves, Mushrooms, Handle, Stamped, Japan, 1970, 5 x 3 ¾ In. ....*illus* 11
Bell, Cardinal, Tree Shape, Wreath Handle, White, Red, Green, 3 ½ In. 10
Coffeepot, Lid, White, Black Trim, Roses, 8 ¾ In. 40
Cookie Jar, Basket Weave, Daisies, c.1950, 9 ¾ In. 32
Cookie Jar, Miss Dainty, c.1957, 7 ½ In. 72
Cup & Saucer, Flowers, Leaves, Purple, Green, Marked, 1960s................................. 22
Figurine, Angel, Harp, Bird, Red Sticker, 1960s, 3 ½ In. 15
Figurine, Angel, Holding Rabbit, Marked, 3 ¾ In. 15
Figurine, Artist, Red & Gold Foil Label, 6 ½ In. 60
Figurine, Birthday Girl, Number 6, 4 In. 12
Figurine, Couple, Courting, Multicolor, Bisque, 7 ½ In. 29
Figurine, Duck, Head Down, Yellow, Paper Label, c.1960-70s, 4 x 2 ¾ In. ....*illus* 10
Figurine, Madonna, Bust, Crown, Pastels, 5 ¾ In. 20
Holy Water Font, Statue Of Mary, Rose Arch, 6 In. 30
Nut Dish, Double Leaf Shape, 2 Sections, Violets, Roses, Gold Trim, Porcelain, 7 x 4 In. ......*illus* 12
Planter, Hat, Pipe, White, Black, Brown, 1963, 9 x 4 In.. 12

Lefton, Basket, Tree Trunk, Leaves, Mushrooms, Handle, Stamped, Japan, 1970, 5 x 3 ¾ In.
$11

Ruby Lane, Inc.

Lefton, Figurine, Duck, Head Down, Yellow, Paper Label, c.1960-70s, 4 x 2 ¾ In.
$10

Ruby Lane, Inc.

Lefton, Nut Dish, Double Leaf Shape, 2 Sections, Violets, Roses, Gold Trim, Porcelain, 7 x 4 In.
$12

Ruby Lane, Inc.

Lenox, Tyg, Iris, Wetlands Scene, Hoyt, Belleek, 7 ½ x 8 In.
$118

Humler & Nolan

Letter Opener, Sterling Silver, Grotesque Mask, Marked, Buccellati, Italy, 1900s, 11 In.
$660

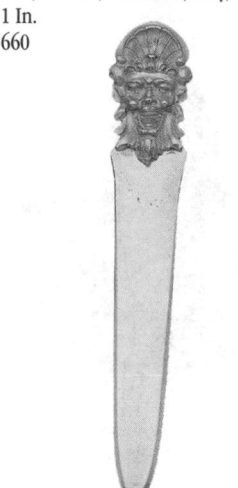

Cowan's Auctions

Lighter, Cigar, Figural, Swashbuckler, 18 In.
$330

Showtime Auction Services

Lighter, Dunhill, Bakelite Cigarette Box, Lid, Silent Flame, England, 5 ¼ In.
$35

Martin Auction Co.

Planter, Owl, 6 ½ x 7 In.	25
Salt & Pepper, Owls, Rhinestone Eyes, Graduate, 1956, 3 ½ In.	15
Salt & Pepper, Poinsettias, Red, Green	20

LEGRAS was founded in 1864 by Auguste Legras at St. Denis, France. It is best known for cameo glass and enamel-decorated glass with Art Nouveau designs. Legras merged with Pantin in 1920 and became the Verreries et Cristalleries de St. Denis et de Pantin Reunies.

Biscuit Jar, Enamel Swan, Silver Plate Lid, Bail, 7 ½ In.	207
Lamp, Desk, Art Glass, Metal Base, 12 In.	531
Vase, Cameo, Flat Sided, Cut Forest Scene, Green, Pond, Ships, 7 ½ In.	460
Vase, Hawthorne Branch, Flowering, Water Fall, Cameo, Burgundy, White, 8 In.	236
Vase, Landscape, Orange Sky, Cabinet, Cameo, Signed, c.1905, 4 x 6 In.	375
Vase, Oval, Winter, Trees, Pond, Cameo, Signed, 4 In.	708
Vase, Red, Yellow, Leaves, Vine, Opaque Ground, Tapered, Cameo, 16 In.	1089
Vase, Tortoise Shell Ground, Enamel Flowers, Signed, 6 ½ In.	413
Vase, Tortoise Shell Ground, Enamel Flowers, Signed, 7 ¾ In.	531
Vase, Trumpet, Lake, Boats, Trees, Signed, 8 In.	106
Vase, Woodland Scene, Dark Green, Over Yellow Orange, Cameo, 6 ¼ In.	288

LENOX porcelain is well-known in the United States. Walter Scott Lenox and Jonathan Coxon founded the Ceramic Art Company in Trenton, New Jersey, in 1889. In 1896 Lenox bought out Coxon's interest, and in 1906 the company was renamed Lenox, Inc. The company makes porcelain that is similar to Irish Belleek. In 2009, after a series of mergers, Lenox became part of Clarion Capital Partners. The marks used by the firm have changed through the years, so collectors can date the ceramics. Related pieces may also be listed in the Ceramic Art Co. category.

Cake Plate, Footed, Flower Bouquet Border, c.1920, 8 ⅞ x 4 ½ In.	75
Candlestick, Dutchman, Ships On Pier, Gold Trim, 8 ¼ In., Pair	125
Coffee Set, Coffeepot, Creamer, Sugar, Brown, Silver Flower Overlay, Coffeepot 8 In., 3 Piece	336
Coffee Set, Coffeepot, Creamer, Sugar, White, Silver Iris Overlay, Coffeepot 7 In., 3 Piece	219
Cup & Saucer, Festival, Blue, Yellow, Green, Demitasse	25
Dish, Fan Shape, Pink, Ribbed, Gold Trim, 10 ½ x 6 ¼ x 2 In.	85
Dish, Swan Shape, 120th Anniversary, Box, 1989, 5 x 3 In.	30
Figurine, Pintail Duck, Open Wings, Water Lilies, 4 ¾ In.	50
Figurine, Scarlet Tanager, On Branch, White Roses, 4 ¼ In.	55
Lamp, Pierced, Cylindrical, Brass Base & Cap, 14 In.	125
Nut Bowl, Sylvan Pattern, Scalloped & Gold Rim, 4 ½ In.	55
Plate, Barclay, Cream Ground, Black Gilt Flower Border, 10 ½ In., 12 Piece	173
Plate, Coral Border, Raised White Flowers, c.1940, 10 ½ In., 12 Piece	63
Salt & Pepper, Bulbous, Ribbed, Footed	30
Serving Bowl, Lid, Laurel Wreath Border, Handles, 9 In.	165
Stein, Rugby, Blue, Ceramic Art Co., 7 In.	1250
Tankard, Monk, Wine Barrel, Sterling Handle & Rim, 7 ¼ In.	850
Tea Set, Teapot, Creamer, Sugar, Cobalt, Silver Flower Overlay, Teapot 8 x 5 In., 3 Piece	200
Tea Set, Teapot, Creamer, Sugar, Cobalt, Silver Horizontal Bands, Teapot 9 x 6 In., 3 Piece	313
Tray, Center Handle, Chateau, 24K Gold Trim, 12 In.	75
Tyg, Iris, Wetlands Scene, Hoyt, Belleek, 7 ½ x 8 In. .... *illus*	118
Vase, Bud, Acanthus Leaf, Raised, Footed, 10 In.	30
Vase, Bulbous, Stick Neck, Rose, 24K Gold Trim, 1970s, 8 In.	60
Vase, Cylindrical, Woman, Standing With Arms In Air, Pink Flowers, c.1910, 11 ½ In.	240

LETTER OPENERS have been used since the eighteenth century. Ivory and silver were favored by the well-to-do. In the late nineteenth century, the letter opener was popular as an advertising giveaway and many were made of metal or celluloid. Brass openers with figural handles were also popular.

Brass, Harlequin Clown, Birds, Flowers, 8 ¾ In.	175
Brass, Mosaic, Tesserae, Flowers, Clover Leaf, 19th Century, 9 In.	360
Brass, Winchester College, Trusty Servant, c.1910, 9 In.	95
Enamel, Guilloche, Applied Eagles, Gold Wash, Box, Russia, 9 ¾ In.	1600
Metal, Shield, University Of Illinois, 4 ⅞ In.	28
Mother-Of-Pearl, Ribbed Handle, c.1900, 7 ⅝ In.	65
Scrimshaw, Whale Baleen, Whaling Scene, 12 In.	150
Silver Plate, Horn Handle, Light Brown, Scroll, 8 In.	25
Silver Plate, Kookaburra, c.1945, 7 In.	160
Soapstone, Fish Handle, c.1930, 7 In.	35

Sterling Silver, Grotesque Mask, Marked, Buccellati, Italy, 1900s, 11 In. ....*illus*	660
Sterling Silver, Owl, Figural, Gorham, 6 ½ In.	100
Sterling Silver, Ring End, Inscribed, Paul Revere Pattern, Tiffany, 1958	285
Sterling Silver, Rose Point, Wallace, c.1934, 7 ⅝ In.	85
Tortoiseshell, c.1885, 9 In.	195
Wood, Man, Profile, Open Mouth, Carved, Painted, 1940s, 7 ½ In.	26

LIBBEY Glass Company has made many types of glass since 1888, including the cut glass and tablewares that are collected today. The stemwares of the 1930s and 1940s are once again in style. The Toledo, Ohio, firm was purchased by Owens-Illinois in 1935 and is still working under the name Libbey Inc. Maize is listed in its own category.

Libbey

Bowl, Cut Glass, Cherry Blossom, Clear, c.1920, 3 ⅞ x 8 In.	150
Bowl, Finger, Imperial, Cut, Signed, 4 ½ In.	125
Bowl, Glenda, Cut, Signed, 8 In.	47
Bowl, Handgrip, Fleur-De-Lis, 3 x 9 ¾ In.	50
Bowl, Nash, Pulled Pink & White Pulled Feather, Crystal Foot, 11 ½ In.	1020
Bowl, Puritana, Wood Polished, Signed, 3 ½ x 9 In.	266
Bowl, Salad, Poppy, Engraved, Cut, 6 x 9 ½ In.	350
Bowl, Stars & Starbursts, Staggered Ray Base, Notched Edge, Cut Glass, 7 x 7 In.	70
Bowl, Underplate, Amberina, Scalloped Rim, Signed, 9 In.	230
Carafe, Water, Ellsmere, Cut, 9 In.	350
Carafe, Water, Imperial, Cut, 8 In.	250
Compote, Amberina, Scalloped Rim, Balled Standard, Trumpet Shape, Footed, 10 In.	1668
Compote, Clear, Cut, Hobstar, Diamond, Flared Stem, Rim, c.1910, 10 x 7 In.	207
Decanter, Ellsmere, Double Spout, Cut, Signed, 13 In.	275
Epergne, Engraved Flowers, Cut, Signed, 10 ½ x 7 ¾ In.	118
Plate, Kemberly, 7 In.	100
Sherbet, Eagle, 7 Oz., 5 ½ In.	15
Toothpick Holder, Maize, Custard, Green, Brown, c.1889, 2 ¼ In.	150
Tray, Colonna, Round, Cut, 11 ¾ In.	225
Tray, Colonna, Round, Signed, Cut, 12 In.	266
Tumbler, Old Crow, Stem, 4 ½ Oz., 5 ⅝ In.	20
Vase, Amberina, Amber Rigaree Collar, Pinched Sides, 7 In.	518
Vase, Amberina, Bulbous Stick Shape, Jack-In-The-Pulpit Rim, Acid Stamp, 16 In.	345
Vase, Amberina, Flower Shape, Bulging Tulip Bulb Top, Signed, 11 ½ In.	1093
Vase, Amberina, Pinched Sided, Rigaree Collar, Optic Diamond, 5 In.	259
Vase, Corinthian, Hobstar Base, Trumpet Shape, Signed, 8 ¾ In.	75

LIGHTERS for cigarettes and cigars are collectible. Cigarettes became popular in the late nineteenth century, and with the cigarette came matches and cigarette lighters. All types of lighters are collected, from solid gold to the first of the recent disposable lighters. Most examples found were made after 1940. Some lighters may be found in the Jewelry category in this book.

Cigar, Aladdin Lamp, Clam Shell Snuffer, Bronze, 7 x 5 ¼ In.	150
Cigar, Cutter, Oak, Brass, Excelentes, 10 Cent, Klein Cigar Co., 7 ½ x 7 ½ In.	1140
Cigar, Dolphin Head, Horn, Sterling Silver, 13 ½ In.	4560
Cigar, Figural, Swashbuckler, 18 In. ....*illus*	330
Cigar, Jump Spark, Midland, 2 Montana Sport Cigar Boxes, Label, 7 ¼ x 7 ¼ x 15 In. ...	500
Cigar, Midland, Jump Spark, Model L, Davenport Mfg. Co., Pat. 1909-1920	900
Dunhill, 14K Gold, Clock Insert, Square Dial, Rounded Case, Art Deco, 1 ¾ x 1 ⅜ In. ...	1625
Dunhill, Bakelite Cigarette Box, Lid, Silent Flame, England, 5 ¼ In. ....*illus*	35
Dunhill, Bumper, Tankard Shape, Polished Chromium, Inscribed, c.1950, 3 ½ In.	24
Flintlock Tinder, Continental, Iron, 7 In.	360
Royal Doulton, Beefeater, 4 In.	45
Table, Micronex Tread Mike, Rubber Tire Shape, Binney & Smith Co., 1930s, 6 ½ In.	115
Tinder, Iron, 3 Legs, Continental, c.1800, 8 In.	780

LIGHTNING RODS AND LIGHTNING ROD BALLS are collected. The glass balls were at the center of the rod that was attached to the roof of a house or barn to avoid lightning damage. The balls were made in many colors and many patterns.

LIGHTNING ROD

Bronze, 5 Rods Off Of Central Ball, c.1875, 9 ½ x 8 ½ In.	147
Cast Iron, Arrow, Ruby Glass Tail, 23 In.	125

LIGHTNING ROD BALL

Milk Glass, Lavender, 1800s, 5 x 5 In.	35
Milk Glass, White, 3 ¼ x 3 ¾ In.	35

Limoges, Fish Set, Fish, Plants, Gold Enamel, Impressed L S & S, Platter 22 In., 12 Plates
$711

James D. Julia Auctioneers

Limoges, Plate, Fluted Shape, Allover Gilt, 8 ⅜ In.
$75

Ruby Lane, Inc.

Loetz, Bowl, Metal Stand, Swirled Design, Green Iridescent, Rippled Rim, 9 ¼ In.
$518

Early Auction Co.

Loetz, Conch Shell, Neptune, Blue Matte, Wave Base, 3 ½ x 5 ⅞ In.
$575

Humler & Nolan

Loetz, Cornucopia, Mimosa, Yellow,
Confetti Threads, 4 ⅝ In.
$575

Humler & Nolan

Loetz, Jar, Lid, Blue Green Iridescent,
Silver Overlay, Vines, Flowers, 2 ¾ x 4 In.
$1,481

James D. Julia Auctioneers

Loetz, Vase, Cytisus, Iris, Silver Overlay,
Iridescent, Blue To Beige, Oil Spots, 6 In.
$4,740

James D. Julia Auctioneers

Milk Glass, White, Hobnail, Pear Shape, 1930s, 4 ¼ In.	80
Milk Glass, White, Stepped, 4 x 4 In.	49

LIMOGES porcelain has been made in Limoges, France, since the mid-nineteenth century. Fine porcelains were made by many factories, including Haviland, Ahrenfeldt, Guerin, Pouyat, Elite, and others. Modern porcelains are being made at Limoges, and the word *Limoges* as part of the mark is not an indication of age. Haviland, one of the Limoges factories, is listed as a separate category in this book.

Bowl, Vegetable, Dome, Lid, Perforated, Double Loop Handle, Roses, Haviland, c.1945, 9 In.	23
Charger, Painted, Garden Scene, Seated Woman, Kneeling Man, Bird Nest, Gold Rim, 13 In.	325
Charger, Portrait, Broken Arm, Ogallala Chief, Painted, J. Pouyat, c.1915, 16 In.	375
Fish Set, Fish, Plants, Gold Enamel, Impressed L S & S, Platter 22 In., 12 Plates..............*illus*	711
Ice Cream Service, Platter, Bowls, Storks, Standing In Marsh, 4-Lobe, c.1900, 10 In., 13 Piece .	138
Pitcher, Flowers, Cobalt, Gilt, Hexagon Panels, Flared Spout, Strap Handle, c.1845, 8 In.	80
Planter, Stand, Painted Poppies, Green Ground, Round, Footed Base, c.1910, 8 ½ In.	92
Plaque, Paint & Gilt, Jewel Accents, Procession Of The Magi, 1800s, 11 x 7 In.	2760
Plaque, Saint Petrus, Octagonal, c.1690, 7 ½ In.	500
Plate Set, Dinner, Flower Transfer, Reserves, Gilt, Wm. Guerin & Co., 11 In., 12 Piece	196
Plate, Blue Lapis, Gilt Band, Wm. Guerin & Co., 11 In., 10 Piece	875
Plate, Fluted Shape, Allover Gilt, 8 ⅜ In. ....*illus*	75
Plate, Napoleonic Scene, Gilt, Flower Border, J.E. Caldwell & Co., 9 ¼ In., Pair	50
Plate, Portrait, Woman, Long Curly Hair, Gilt Rim, Hand Painted, 10 In.	83
Plate, Service, Floral Bouquet Center, Gilt Border, Shoulder, c.1890, 11 In., 12 Piece	480
Punch Bowl, Raised Gold Leaves, Fruiting Grapevines, Marked, c.1900, 14 In. Diam.	215
Tea Set, Gilt Stripes, Teapot, Sugar, Creamer, Lid, 6 Cups & Saucers, c.1950, 9 In.	531
Tea Set, Teapot, Sugar, Creamer, Tray, Plate, Cup, Saucer, Service For 12, Plate 7 ½ In.	151
Vase, Garniture, Royal Scene Reserves, Gilt Grape Leaf Handles, c.1865, 28 In., Pair	1092
Vase, Rose Trellis, Hand Painted, Signed, 1923, 12 In.	96
Vase, Tapered, Square, Ormolu Mounts, Marked, 7 x 3 In., Pair	338

LINDBERGH was a national hero. In 1927, Charles Lindbergh, the aviator, became the first man to make a nonstop solo flight across the Atlantic Ocean. In 1932, his son was kidnapped and murdered, and Lindbergh was again the center of public interest. He died in 1974. All types of Lindbergh memorabilia are collected.

Bookends, Bust, Aviator Cap & Glasses, Cast Iron, Copper Patina, 5 x 4 In.	128
Doll, Our Lindy, Composition, Molded Hair, Cloth Body, Regal Doll Co., 1928, 30 In.	495
Figure, Charles Lindbergh, Bronze, Aviator Attire, Head Up, A. Ladd Mold, Boston, 22 In.	1125
Painting, Oil On Board, Plane, Bill Paxton, Frame, 10 x 7 In.	80
Paperweight, Bust, Cast Iron, Painted, 3 ¾ x 1 ¼ In.	140
Tapestry, Lindbergh, Plane, Statue Of Liberty, Paris Skyline, France, c.1927, 18 x 54 In.	220
Toy, Airplane, Lindy Across Wing, Blue Paint, Cast Iron, Hubley, 10 In.	1180
Toy, Airplane, Lindy, Spirit Of St. Louis, Cast Iron, Gray, Red, Hubley, Pull Cord, 13 In.	2360
Toy, Lindy, Airplane, Glider, Orange, Blue Paint, Cast Iron, Hubley, 6 In.	119
Toy, Airplane, Lindy, Sirius, Red Paint, Cast Iron, Hubley, 10 ½ In.	1580

LITHOPHANES are porcelain pictures made by casting clay in layers of various thicknesses. When a piece is held to the light, a picture of light and shadow is seen through it. Most lithophanes date from the 1825–75 period. A few are still being made. Many lithophanes sold today were originally panels for lampshades.

Candle Screen, Boy Painting, Teacher, Pot Of Brushes, 1800s, 8 x 6 In.	495
Lamp, 5 Panels, Children Scenes, PPM, 19 In.	775
Plaque, Boy, Dog, Leash In Mouth, 3 ⅝ x 2 ⅜ In.	125
Plaque, Boy, On Fence, Playing Flute, Dog, 4 x 5 In.	195
Plaque, Boy, Sleeping In Field, Chickens, 4 ⅜ x 5 ¼ In.	195
Plaque, Girl, Praying, German Phrase, c.1875, 5 x 4 In.	259
Plaque, Woman, Tree, Fall Scene, Metal Frame, c.1850, 5 x 4 In.	175

LIVERPOOL, England, has been the site of many pottery and porcelain factories since the eighteenth century. Color-decorated porcelains, transfer-printed earthenware, stoneware, basalt, figurines, and other wares were made. Sadler and Green made print-decorated wares starting in 1756. Many of the pieces were made for the American market and feature patriotic emblems, such as eagles and flags. Liverpool pitchers are called Liverpool jugs by collectors.

Coffeepot, Lid, Cobalt Blue Asian Scene, Flower Thumb Rest, J. Pennington, c.1775, 9 In.	207
Coffeepot, Lid, Multicolor Flowers, Knob Finial, Rococo Strap Handle, c.1780, 9 ½ In.	489

L

Jug, Ship, Alert, Flying U.S. Flag, Black Transfer, c.1800, 8 In.	7200
Jug, Ships, Compass Rose, Handle, c.1850, 9 ½ In.	236
Mug, Creamware, Flowers, George Washington, Handle, c.1815, 2 ¼ x 3 In.	1438
Pitcher, Inscribed Jenna Rogers, Gretna Green, Interior Drinking Scene, 1798, 8 ¾ In.	1200
Pitcher, Masonic Arch, Ship, Grape Clusters, De Jounge Neeltje, Transfer, c.1800, 9 In.	584
Plate, Blue Flowers, Cell & Diaper Pattern, Octagonal, J. Pennington, c.1765, 8 ½ In.	258
Teapot, Lid, Red Transfer Tea Party, Loop Handle, Richard Chaffers, c.1765, 5 ⅞ In.	460

LLADRO is a Spanish porcelain. Juan, Jose, and Vicente Lladro opened a ceramics workshop in Almacera in 1951. They soon began making figurines in a distinctive, elongated style. In 1958 the factory moved to Tabernes Blanques, Spain. The company makes stoneware and porcelain figurines and vases in limited and unlimited editions. Dates given are first and last years of production.

LLADRÓ®

Figurine, Child's Play, Girl With Doll, Tea Cup, Teapot, No. 1280, 1974-83, 7 ¾ In.	180
Figurine, Dalmatian, No. 1260, 1974-81, 2 In.	475
Figurine, Following Her Cats, No. 1309, 1974-2005, Box, 10 In.	138
Figurine, Gazelle, Leaping, Marked, No. 5271, 1985-88, 13 x 8 ½ In.	147
Figurine, Girl On Carousel Horse, No. 1469, 1985-2000, 15 ½ In.	540
Figurine, Girl Sitting On Tuffet, Trying On Hat, No. 1147, 1971-85, 9 In.	60
Figurine, Goddess With Unicorn, No. 6007, 1993-2004, 10 x 13 In.	600
Figurine, Golfer, No. 4824, 1972-92, 10 ¾ In.	71
Figurine, Jester Sad Face, Hands On Cheeks, No. 5129, 1982-2001, 12 ½ In.	156
Figurine, Little Traveler, Hobo Clown, Sack, No. 7602, 1986, 9 In.	90
Figurine, Nippon Lady, Seated Japanese Woman, With Fan, No. 5327, 9 In.	480
Figurine, Oriental Beauty, No. 6232, 1995-2000, 7 ½ In.	71
Figurine, Purr-Fect, Cat & Kittens In Basket, No. 1444, 1984-2005, Box, 5 ¼ In.	236
Figurine, Romeo & Juliet, No. 4750, 1971-92, 17 ¾ x 13 In.	432
Figurine, Roving Photographer, No. 5194, 1984-85, 11 ½ In.	179
Figurine, Sheriff Puppet, No. 4969, 1977-85, 10 ½ In.	150
Figurine, Songbird, No. 6093, 1993-2001, 9 In.	198
Figurine, Star Struck, No. 5610, 1989-98, 8 In.	209
Figurine, Student Flute Player, No. 4837, 1973-83, 8 In.	60
Figurine, Swan, Spread Wings, No. 5231, 5 In.	90
Figurine, The Debutante, No. 1431, 1982-98, 13 ¾ In.	130
Figurine, Two Nuns, No. 4611, 1970-2005, 13 In.	89
Group, Horses, Playing, White, No. 1022, 1969-2005, 17 ½ x 15 ½ In.	767

LOETZ glass was made in many varieties. Johann Loetz bought a glassworks in Klostermuhle, Bohemia (now Klastersky Mlyn, Czech Republic), in 1840. He died in 1848 and his widow ran the company; then in 1879, his grandson took over. Most collectors recognize the iridescent gold glass similar to Tiffany, but many other types were made. The firm closed during World War II.

Loetz Austria

Basket, Mother-Of-Pearl, Purple, Gold, Twist Handle, Blue, White Hearts, Footed, 10 In.	4255
Bowl, Ausfuhrung, Rosa, Silver Highlights, Black Rim, Marked, 12 x 3 ½ In.	875
Bowl, Gold Iridescent, Melon Shape, 3 x 12 ½ In.	236
Bowl, Green Iridescent Oil Spot, 3 ½ x 7 In.	94
Bowl, Green Leaves, Feathered, Silver Overlay, Marked, c.1910, 5 ¼ In.	813
Bowl, Metal Stand, Swirled Design, Green Iridescent, Rippled Rim, 9 ¼ In. ......*illus*	518
Conch Shell, Candia Papillon, Wave Base, Ribbed, Wave Base, Blue Highlights, 11 ⅞ In.	546
Conch Shell, Neptune, Blue Matte, Wave Base, 3 ½ x 5 ⅞ In. ......*illus*	575
Cornucopia, Mimosa, Yellow, Confetti Threads, 4 ⅝ In. ......*illus*	575
Creamer, Melon Ribbed, Gold Iridescent Oil Spot, Amethyst Threaded Highlights, 4 ½ In.	236
Inkwell, Gold Iridescent, Ball Shape, Brass Flip Top, Glass Insert, 3 In.	266
Jar, Lid, Blue Green Iridescent, Silver Overlay, Vines, Flowers, 2 ¾ x 4 In. ......*illus*	1481
Pitcher, Wine, Oil Spots, Silver Overlay, Grapes, Stopper, Henckel & Co., 1910s, 6 x 6 ½ In.	1500
Powder Box, Iridescent Gold Glass, Applied Silver Flowers, Lid, Round, 4 x 4 In.	800
Vase, Ausfuhrung Aventurine, Brown Glass, Gold Inclusions, Silver Overlay, Bulbous, 4 x 6 In.	1098
Vase, Blue Green Iridescent, Organic Tree Trunk Shape, 4 x 9 In.	366
Vase, Blue Iridescent, Footed Base, Pin, Flared Bowl, 6 ¾ x 8 In.	678
Vase, Blue Iridescent, Gold Cascading Feather, Cylindrical, Signed, 3 ¾ In.	805
Vase, Blue Leaves, Branches, Red Berries, Gold Iridescent, Cinched Waist, 6 ½ In.	290
Vase, Bronce Glatt, Iridescent, Ribbed, Flat, Flared Top, c.1900, 4 In.	240
Vase, Bud, Blue Glass, Pulled Blue, Gold Feathers, Double Gourd Shape, c.1900, 8 In.	1750
Vase, Bud, Red Translucent Glass, Blue Oil Spots, Double Gourd Shape, c.1900, 8 ⅝ In.	531
Vase, Bulbous, Shouldered, Flared Rim, Blue, Purple, Platinum Wave Pattern, Signed, 7 In.	2552
Vase, Candia Papillon, Scalloped Rim, 3 Ball Feet, 5 ¼ In.	230
Vase, Candia Silberiris, Diaspora Pattern, Scalloped Star Rim, Dimpled Shoulder, 4 ½ In.	259

Loetz, Vase, Federzeichnung, Mother-Of-Pearl, Orange, Gold Tracery, Signed, 5 ½ In.
$2,300

Early Auction Co.

Loetz, Vase, Federzeichnung, Octopus, Gold, Painted Flowers, Signed, 11 ½ In.
$5,333

James D. Julia Auctioneersa

Loetz, Vase, Pear Shape, Pearled Glaze, Red, Black, c.1908, 7 ¾ x 4 In.
$12,500

Rago Arts & Auction Center

L

Loetz, Vase, Phanomen, Onion Shape, Iridescent, Green Combed Feather, c.1898, 10 In.
$780

Skinner Auctioneers & Appraisers

Lone Ranger, Badge, Shield, Portrait, Die Cut, Round-Up Products, c.1948, 1 ⁹⁄₁₆ In.
$246

Hake's Americana & Collectibles

Longwy, Vase, Bird In Panel, Flowers, Enamel, 4-Sided, Stamped, c.1885, 25 ½ x 11 In.
$4,375

Rago Arts & Auction Center

Vase, Creta Papillon, Silver Overlay, Flower Shape Rim, 4 ½ x 7 In.	600
Vase, Creta Rusticana, Green High Shouldered, Flared, 1900, 10 ¾ In.	420
Vase, Cytisus, Iris, Silver Overlay, Iridescent, Blue To Beige, Oil Spots, 6 In. .....*illus*	4740
Vase, Cytisus, Silver Overlay, Blue Iridescent, Shaded To Yellow, Oil Spot, 4 ½ In.	2607
Vase, Deco, Candia Silberiris, Mushroom Shape, Rolled Rim, 1920s, 7 In.	720
Vase, Diaspora, Cornucopia Shape, Candia Glass, 7 x 6 In.	875
Vase, Diaspora, Rosa, Iridescent, Flared, Marked, 5 ½ x 8 ½ In.	1125
Vase, Federzeichnung, Mother-Of-Pearl, Air Trap Design, Gold Tracery, Jardiniere Shape, 8 In.	86
Vase, Federzeichnung, Mother-Of-Pearl, Orange, Gold Tracery, Signed, 5 ½ In. .....*illus*	2300
Vase, Federzeichnung, Octopus, Gold, Painted Flowers, Signed, 11 ½ In. .....*illus*	5333
Vase, Glatt, Green Creta Glass, Tendril Silver Overlay, Bulbous, Signed, 3 ½ x 5 In.	1625
Vase, Gold Iridescent Tile Design, Organic Shape, 6 ½ In.	928
Vase, Gold Iridescent, Astartig Glass, Pulled Beads, 2 Twisted Spouts, Tapered, c.1904, 11 In.	960
Vase, Gold Iridescent, Green Applied Handles, Signed, 4 ½ In.	115
Vase, Green Iridescent, Applied Gold Ormolu Rim, 4 In.	94
Vase, Green Iridescent, Gold Threading, Bulbous, Narrow Shaft, Swollen Neck, 5 x 3 In.	92
Vase, Green Iridescent, Pinched, Gold Snake Around Neck, Engraved Loetz, 9 x 3 In.	150
Vase, Green Iridescent, Swirl, 4 In.	89
Vase, Green, Yellow, Lily Silver Overlay, Bulbous, 3 x 4 ½ In.	488
Vase, Honey Amber, Astraa Pattern, Ruffled Rim, Dimpled, 7 ¼ In.	575
Vase, Honey Amber, Oceanik Pattern, Pinched Neck, 7 In.	575
Vase, Medici, Purple Iridescent, Applied Silver Flower Overlay, Corseted Waist, 4 ½ x 12 In.	5300
Vase, Medici, Purple Iridescent, Applied Swirled Ribbon, Flower Shape, Ruffled Rim, 5 x 11 In.	1700
Vase, Medici, Purple Iridescent, Lily Shape, Gold, Wavy Rim, Applied Leaves, Footed, 7 x 16 In. ..	1875
Vase, Medici, Purple, Blue Iridescent, Indented, Creta Glass, 4 ½ x 7 In.	1063
Vase, Mimosa, Shell Shape, Rosa, Gold Highlights, Footed, 6 x 12 In.	800
Vase, Oil Spots, Silver Overlay, Tulips, Austria, c.1900, 18 ½ x 8 In.	1875
Vase, Papillon, Art Deco, Cobalt Blue, Candia Glass Handles, Iridescent, 6 ½ x 7 In.	1250
Vase, Papillon, Cobalt Blue Iridescent Glass, Double Gourd, 6 x 10 In.	813
Vase, Papillon, Gold Iridescent, Smokestack Shape, 3 x 3 ½ In.	219
Vase, Papillon, Mottled Cream, Wildflower Silver Overlay, Gooseneck Shape, 4 x 9 In.	2684
Vase, Pear Shape, Pearled Glaze, Red, Black, c.1908, 7 ¾ x 4 In. .....*illus*	12500
Vase, Persimmon Color Roses, Vines, Cameo, Cut To Translucent Yellow, c.1910, 13 In.	575
Vase, Phanomen, Blue Iridescent, Waisted, Label, c.1900, 9 ½ x 7 In.	2250
Vase, Phanomen, Blue, Applied Silver Flower, Overlay, Bulbous, 3 ½ x 4 ½ In.	875
Vase, Phanomen, Green Stripe, Cylindrical, c.1900, 10 ½ In.	660
Vase, Phanomen, Indented, Shape, Amber, Pulled Waves, Signed, 5 x 5 In.	1063
Vase, Phanomen, Onion Shape, Iridescent, Green Combed Feather, c.1898, 10 In. .....*illus*	780
Vase, Ruffled Rim, Pinched Body, Blue Green Iridescent, Signed, c.1900, 9 In.	2400
Vase, Schneeflecken, Clear, Cut, Amber Paddle Handles, Fan Shape, 13 In.	1140
Vase, Silberiris Blue, Wavy Rim, Candia Glass, Creta Feet, 6 x 5 ½ In.	500
Vase, Silberiris, Cobalt Blue Iridescent, Double Thumb Design, c.1900, 9 ½ In., Pair	1440
Vase, Silberiris, Iris Silver Overlay, Mottled Green Ground, Ruffled Rim, 3 ½ x 5 ½ In.	1000
Vase, Silver Overlay, Blue Ground, Flared Rim, Long Neck, 11 In.	1380
Vase, Soft Gold Iridescent, Crocodile Embossed, Squat, Cinched Neck, Ruffled Rim, 6 In.	173
Vase, Spherical, Purple, Folded & Pinched Rim, Pontil, c.1900, 5 In.	72
Vase, Titania, Art Nouveau, Silver Overlay, Inverted Trumpet Shape, Flared Rim, 4 ½ In.	1422
Vase, Titania, Blue, Green, Silver Overlay, c.1900, 5 In.	1080
Vase, Titania, Orange Glass, Green, Platinum Inclusions, Austria, c.1910, 4 x 8 ½ In.	3416
Vase, Titania, Shouldered, Green Iridescent Ribbed, Silver Overtones, 5 ¼ In.	230
Vase, Titania, Silver Poppy Overlay, Blue, Green, Platinum Inclusions, Ruffled Rim, 6 x 13 In.	3000
Water Sprinkler, Phanomen Genre, Gold, Pulled Silver Designs, 4 ½ x 9 In.	3750

LONE RANGER, a fictional character, was introduced on the radio in 1932. Over three thousand shows were produced before the series ended in 1954. In 1938, the first Lone Ranger movie was made. The latest movie was made in 2013. Television shows were started in 1949 and are still seen on some stations. The Lone Ranger appears on many products and was even the name of a restaurant chain for several years.

Badge, Serial Republic, Star Shape, Brass, 1938, 1 ¼ In.	86
Badge, Shield, Portrait, Die Cut, Round-Up Products, c.1948, 1 ⁹⁄₁₆ In. .....*illus*	246
Badge, Supplee Club, Brass, Die Cut Star, Center Picture, Radio Station WFIL, 1938, 1 ⅜ In.	127
Bracelet, Premium, Ice Cream Cones, Enameled, Silvered Metal, 1939, 2 ¼ In.	288
Bullet, Toy, For 45 Gun	590
Button, Riding Silver, Galloping, Yellow, Black, c.1940, 1 ¾ In.	86
Costume, Lone Ranger, Shirt, Pants, Necktie, Wool, Blue, Embroidery, Tailoring, 44 Long	2655
Doll Set, Ranger & Tonto, Composition Head, Fabric Body, 1938, 16 In.	190

Doll, Composition Head, Flanged Neck, Painted Hair, Face, Muslin Body, c.1937, 15 In.............	1792
Doll, Lone Ranger, Horse Silver, Saddle, Mask, Hat, Guns, Hartland, Box, 8 In.	180
Flashlight, Lone Ranger Riding Silver, Tin Lithograph, Plastic, Box, 1950s, 6 ¾ In.	234
Lapel Watch, Die Cut Insert, Cast Metal Gun Holster Fob, Box, 3 ¼ x 3 ¾ In.............................	822
Movie Poster, Agent Of Treachery, 5 Masked Rangers, Tonto, 1938, 27 x 41 In........................	1393
Movie Poster, Serial, Silver, 15 Episodes, Blue, Yellow, Orange, 1938, 27 x 41 In.	2973
Painting, Oil On Board, Tonto, Cover Of Comic, No. 18, Signed, Feb.-Apr. 1955, 16 ½ x 12 In.	3540
Ring, Atomic Bomb, Kix, Mailing Box, 2 ½ In.	316
Ring, Marine Insignia, Brass, Photos, Kix Premium, Secret Compartment, 1942......................	230
Toy, Binocular, 3 Powered, Plastic, Hi-Yo Silver, Cardboard Box, 1950s, 5 x 6 In...................	291
Toy, Gun & Holster, Leather Belt, Running Horse, Medallions, 29 ½ In.	773

LONGWY WORKSHOP of Longwy, France, first made ceramic wares in 1798. The workshop is still in business. Most of the ceramic pieces found today are glazed with many colors to resemble cloisonne or other enameled metal. Many pieces were made with stylized figures and Art Deco designs. The factory used a variety of marks.

Candleholder, Griffin Shape Base, Metal, Blue Faience Standard In Mouth, c.1905, 8 x 6 In......	50
Charger, Faience, 2 Birds, Blooming Trees, Flowers, Multicolor, 14 In....................................	187
Match Striker, Flowers, Multicolor, Cylindrical, 1 ½ In..	100
Plate, Flowers, Leaves, 8-Sided, Brown Rim, Faience, 7 ½ x 7 ½ In.......................................	160
Plate, Holly Leave, Berries, Flower Border, Faience, 7 x 6 In...	211
Plate, Shaped Rim, Bird, On Rock, Water, Branches, Flowers, Blue Ground, c.1910, 10 In..........	75
Plate, Sunset Medallion, Flower Border, 8 In...	275
Stand, Enameled Bird, Blossoming Branch Reserve, Flowers, Blue Ground, 10 x 10 In..............	56
Tray, Flowers, Cerulean Ground, Stylized Geometric Border, Blue Handles, c.1910, 15 x 7 In.	250
Trivet, Flowers, Multicolor, c.1900, 5 In..	125
Vase, Art Deco, Flowers, Trees, Leaves, Craquelure Glaze, Signed, c.1930, 15 x 6 ½ In.............	1353
Vase, Bird In Panel, Flowers, Enamel, 4-Sided, Stamped, c.1885, 25 ½ x 11 In. ....*illus*	4375
Vase, Birds, Flowers, Blue Ground, Cylindrical, c.1910, 7 x 3 In..	213
Vase, Blue Dragon, Multicolor Flowers, Yellow Ground, Cylindrical, 10 In., Pair......................	800
Vase, Cylindrical, Stemmed Flowers, Red, Yellow, 5 ½ In.	340

LONHUDA POTTERY COMPANY of Steubenville, Ohio, was organized in 1892 by William Long, W. H. Hunter, and Alfred Day. Brown underglaze slip-decorated pottery was made. The firm closed in 1896. The company used many marks; the earliest included the letters *LPCO*.

Pitcher, Violent Sea, Fish Shape Handle, Faience, Marked, 10 ⅜ In. ....*illus*	767
Vase, Cavalier, Standard Glaze, Cinched Waist, 7 ¼ In..	236
Vase, Dark Brown To Green, Golden Wheat, Shouldered, Handles, c.1895, 8 In........................	335
Vase, Gold Trumpet Lily, Green Leaves, Dark Ground, Oval, Ruffled Rim, 2 Handles, 8 x 9 In......	149
Vase, Orange, Brown Yellow, Leaves, Standard Glaze, c.1900, 6 In....................................	1400
Vase, Painted Violets, Squat, Footed, Signed, 2 ½ x 1 ½ In..	250
Vase, Thistles, Orange, Green, Standard Glaze, Swollen Cylinder, 7 ⅝ In.	363
Vase, Yellow Wispy Flowers, Standard Glaze, Round, 7 ½ x 10 In..	148

LOSANTI was made by Mary Louise McLaughlin in Cincinnati, Ohio, about 1899. It was a hard paste decorative porcelain. She stopped making it in 1906.

Vase, Tulips, Carved, Oxblood, Celadon Glaze, Bulbous, Lobed, M.L. McLaughlin, 6 In...............	21250

LOTUS WARE was made by the Knowles, Taylor & Knowles Company of East Liverpool, Ohio, from 1890 to 1900. Lotus Ware, a thin porcelain that resembles Belleek, was sometimes decorated outside the factory. Other types of ceramics that were made by the Knowles, Taylor & Knowles Company are listed under KTK.

Butterfly Etch, Bowl, Amber, Ruffled, 11 ½ In...	65
Call Of The Wild, Bowl, Mayonnaise, Jade Green, Underplate, Silver Etched Sylvania................	145
La-Furiste, Ice Tub, Rose Pink, 2 Handles, 6 x 4 In.	135

LOW art tiles were made by the J. and J. G. Low Art Tile Works of Chelsea, Massachusetts, from 1877 to 1902. A variety of art and other tiles were made. Some of the tiles were made by a process called "natural," some were hand-modeled, and some were made mechanically.

Tile, Art Nouveau, Turquoise, Summer, Autumn, Winter, Spring, c.1885, 4 x 6 In., 4 Piece	600
Tile, Flower, Green, 1880s, 3 x 3 In..	32
Tile, Man, Profile, Bearded, Green, c.1883, 4 x 4 In...	175
Tile, Man, Woman, Facing Each Other, Green Glaze, Frame, c.1881, 6 x 12 In...........................	225

Lonhuda, Pitcher, Violent Sea, Fish Shape Handle, Faience, Marked, 10 ⅜ In. $767

Humler & Nolan

Lunch Box, Underdog, Simon Bar Sinister, Metal, Universal, 1974 $288

Hake's Americana & Collectibles

Majolica Mark

The word *majolica* was never used on any French majolica except Sarreguemines pieces. The Sarreguemines mark includes the company's name and the word *majolica*.

Majolica, Basket, Draped Grapevines, Minton, c.1890, 6 x 8 In.
$1,003

Brunk Auctions

Majolica, Jardiniere, Lily-Of-The-Valley, Ferns, Minton Mark, 13 x 19 In.
$1,875

Rago Arts & Auction Center

Majolica, Jug, Flowers, Basketweave Ground, Blue Interior, George Jones, c.1890, 7 ¼ In.
$826

Brunk Auctions

TIP

The value of lustres with hanging prisms is not changed if a few of the prisms have been replaced.

LOY-NEL-ART, *see McCoy category.*

LUNCH BOXES and lunch pails have been used to carry lunches to school or work since the nineteenth century. Today, most collectors want either early tobacco advertising boxes or children's lunch boxes made since the 1930s. These boxes are made of metal or plastic. Boxes listed here include the original Thermos bottle inside the box unless otherwise indicated. Movie, television, and cartoon characters may be found in their own categories. Tobacco tin pails and lunch boxes are listed in the Advertising category.

Children At Carnival, Multicolor, Metal, Universal, 1959	230
Flying Nun, Sister Bertrille Flying, Children, Metal, Aladdin, 1968	328
Indian Warrior, Cowboy On Horse, Metal, Universal, 1959	172
Jetsons, Dome, Characters, Metal, Aladdin Industries, 1963	421
Little House On The Prairie, Ingalls Family, Metal, King-Seeley Thermos Co., 1978	207
Lone Ranger, Thermos, With Tonto & Horses, Metal, Plastic, Aladdin, Tag, 1980	139
Peanuts, Charlie Brown, Snoopy, Lucy, Baseball Game, Flying Red Kite, Vinyl, 1965	78
Scenes From Israel, Map, Blue Ground, Oval, Handles, Tin, c.1960, 11 x 8 In.	350
Soupy Sales, Portrait, Blue, Vinyl, King-Seeley Thermos Co., 1966	144
Superman, Vs. The Robot, Metal, Universal, 1954	480
Thermos, Roy Rogers, Dale Evans, Double R Bar Ranch, Metal, American Thermos, 1950s	120
Underdog, Simon Bar Sinister, Metal, Universal, 1974 *illus*	288
USS Sea Wolf Submarine, Thermos, 1960	70
Wood, Carved 3-Tiers, Shaped Handle, Nesting Trays, Chinese, c.1900, 11 x 15 In.	354

LUNCH BOX THERMOS

Hogan's Heroes, Dome, Bing Crosby Productions, Aladdin, 1966	176

LUNEVILLE, a French faience factory, was established about 1730 by Jacques Chambrette. It is best known for its fine biscuit figurines and groups and for large faience dogs and lions. The early pieces were unmarked. The firm was acquired by Keller and Guerin and is still working.

Bowl, Flowers, Teal, White, Enamel, Footed, c.1900, 5 ½ x 3 In.	60
Candlestick, Rooster Shape, Multicolor, c.1900, 9 In., Pair	1100
Charger, Rose, Flowers, Multicolor, Scalloped Edge, Old Strasbourg Rose, Marked, 13 In.	79
Dish, Leaf Shape, Integrated Handle, Bouquet, Black, White, 6 x 7 In.	30
Jardiniere, Flowers, Leaves, Winged Griffin Handles, 16 x 9 x 6 In.	750
Jardiniere, Water Lilies, Brown, Tan, Black Flecks, Cylindrical, Tapered Neck, 9 x 13 In.	2250
Plate, Pierrots, Shadow Man, Gray, Green, c.1910, 10 In.	188

LUSTER glaze was meant to resemble copper, silver, or gold. The term *luster* includes any piece with some luster trim. It has been used since the sixteenth century. Some of the luster found today was made during the nineteenth century. The metallic glazes are applied on pottery. The finished color depends on the combination of the clay color and the glaze. Blue, orange, gold, and pearlized luster decorations were used by Japanese and German firms in the early 1900s. Fairyland Luster was made by Wedgwood in the 1900s. Tea Leaf pieces have their own category.

Copper, Mug, New York View, 3 ¾ In.	420
Copper, Pitcher, LaFayette, Bust, Black Transfer, Yellow Medial Band, Bulbous, 7 ⅜ In.	177
Copper, Pitcher, Little Jockey Transfer, Riding Dog, c.1850, 6 In., Pair	130
Copper, Pitcher, Pink Dog, Obverse Side Ram, Handle, Footed, 9 ½ In.	40
Fairyland luster is included in the Wedgwood category.	
Sunderland luster pieces are in the Sunderland category.	

LUSTRE ART GLASS Company was founded in Long Island, New York, in 1920 by Conrad Vahlsing and Paul Frank. The company made lampshades and globes that are almost indistinguishable from those made by Quezal. Most of the shades made by the company were unmarked.

Shade, Bell Shape, Marigold & Calcite, Wavy Lines, 5 ¼ In., Pair	500
Shade, Gold Iridescent, Pulled Feather, Marked, c.1925, 5 ¼ In.	200

LUSTRES are mantel decorations or pedestal vases with many hanging glass prisms. The name really refers to the prisms, and it is proper to refer to a single glass prism as a lustre. Either spelling, luster or lustre, is correct.

Amber Glass, Gilt & Grisaille Figures, Landscapes, Scalloped Rim, Clear Prisms, 12 In., Pair	281
Blue Opaline, Flowers, Parcel Gilt Detail, Victorian, c.1880, 11 ¾ In., Pair	300
Blue, Enameled Flowers, Ruffled Rim, Clear Faceted Prisms, Bristol, 1 ¼ In., Pair	180

L

Bohemian Glass, Brass Base, 16 Prisms, Electrified, c.1880, 14 ½ x 6 In., Pair	599
Bohemian Glass, Bull's-Eyes, Gilt Trim, Spear Point Prisms, 10 In., Pair	615
Bohemian Glass, Cased, White Cut To Ruby, Prism Drops, c.1890, 9 ¾ In., Pair	300
Bohemian Glass, Clear Cut, Pedestal Shape, Gilt, White Designs, 9 Prisms, c.1900, 17 In., Pair.	420
Bohemian Glass, Cranberry, Clear, Gilt, Hanging Prisms, Ruffle Rim, c.1885, 10 In., Pair	944
Bohemian Glass, Enameled Cased Glass, Gilt Trim Opaline, Prisms, c.1875, 11 x 5 In., Pair	1476
Bohemian Glass, Green, Gilt Base, Flowers, Clear Prisms, 11 ½ In., Pair	895
Bohemian Glass, Ruby Cut To Clear, Quatrefoil Rim, Double Prisms, 10 ¼ In., Pair	201
Bohemian Glass, Victorian, Pink Scalloped Rim, Flowers, Stepped Base, 14 x 6 In., Pair	367
Bohemian Glass, White, Gold Painted Flowers, Trim, Electrified, c.1900, 11 ½ In., Pair	165
Cased Glass, White, Roses, Ruffled Edge, 2 Prism Tiers, 12 ¼ In., Pair	600
Cased, Painted Roses, Gold Trim, 2 Tiers Prisms, Victorian, 12 ¼ In., Pair	600
Clear, Cut Glass, Chalice Form, Flowers, Notched Base, Spear Prisms, 14 In., Pair	184
Cobalt Blue, Gold Filigree, White Interior, Prisms, 12 x 5 ½ In., Pair	325
Cobalt Blue, Painted Accents, Crystal Prisms, Bristol, Victorian, 11 In., Pair	360
Cranberry Cased Glass, Painted Flowers, Pink, Orange, Yellow, Blue, Prisms, 12 x 6 In., Pair	625
Cut Glass, Candleholder, White Enameled Flowers, Hobnail, 21 In., Pair	420
Gilt Opaline, Flowers, Leaves, Double Cut Prisms, 10 In.	175
Green Opaline, Flowers, Ruffled Edge, 12 In., Pair	395
Green Opaline, Sawtooth Gilt Rim, Flower Garlands, 14 x 6 ¾ In.	102
Green, White Opaline Glass, Gilt, Trumpet Shape, Ball Shape Prisms, c.1844, 11 x 6 In.	1295
Millefiori, Yellow Ground, Gold Base, Ribbed, Prisms, 1920s, 12 x 6 In., Pair	1495
Pink Cased, Painted Flowers, Enameled, Beading, Prisms, 11 x 4 ¾ In., Pair	650
Pink, Opal, Flowers, Heavy Prisms, Cased Glass, c.1895, 14 In., Pair	460
Prisms, White Painted Flowers, Enameled, Gilt Accents, Bristol, 14 x 6 ¾ In., Pair	127
Red Double Cased, Cut Back Base, Gilt Veining, c.1870, 11 x 6 ⅜ In.	399
Ruby Cut To Clear, Cross Pattern, Long Prisms, 11 In., Pair	344
White, Painted Flowers, Designs, Blue, Green, Gilt, Electrified, 1800s, 14 In., Pair	425

MACINTYRE, *see Moorcroft category.*

MAIZE glass was made by W.L. Libbey & Son Company of Toledo, Ohio, after 1889. The glass resembled an ear of corn. The leaves were usually green, but some pieces were made with blue or red leaves. The kernels of corn were light yellow, white, or light green.

Muffineer, Yellow Leaves, c.1890s, 5 ¾ In.	325
Tumbler, Brown & Green Leaves, 4 In.	131
Vase, Ear Of Corn, Blue Leaves, c.1900, 6 ½ In.	149
Vase, Green Leaves, 1880s, 6 ½ x 4 In., Pair	195

MAJOLICA is a general term for any pottery glazed with an opaque tin enamel that conceals the color of the clay body. It has been made since the fourteenth century. Today's collector is most likely to find Victorian majolica. The heavy, colorful ware is rarely marked. Some famous makers include Minton; Griffen, Smith and Hill (marked *Etruscan*); and Chesapeake Pottery (marked *Avalon* or *Clifton*). Majolica made by Wedgwood is listed in the Wedgwood category.

Asparagus Cradle, Handles, Shaped Rim, Green & Tan, 1800s, 4 x 8 ½ In.	270
Basket, Draped Grapevines, Minton, c.1890, 6 x 8 In. ....*illus*	1003
Basket, Water Lily, Lavender Ground, Wicker-Like Rim, Handle, 9 x 7 In.	296
Bowl, 2 Tiers, Shell Shape, Turquoise, Brown, 5 x 15 ½ In.	344
Bowl, Base Punch Figure Support, Holly Trim, George Jones, c.1890, 8 ½ x 11 In.	5925
Bowl, Chestnut, Shell Shape Bowl, Scallop Edge, Chestnuts & Leaves, c.1870, 11 In.	180
Bowl, Scallop Shell, Conch Shell Feet, Cobalt, Turquoise, Holdcroft, Eng., 1800s, 5 x 10 In.	325
Bust, Man, Period Attire, Multicolor, Attributed To Holdcoft, 7 ½ In.	272
Butter, Cover, Yellow Flower Finial, Cobalt Blue Ground, Underplate, 7 ½ In.	91
Cachepot, Yellow Flowers, Green Leaves, Cobalt Blue Ground, 6 ½ In.	194
Centerpiece, 3 Cranes, Supporting Lily Pad, Shaped Base, c.1875, 14 x 13 In.	938
Centerpiece, Art Nouveau, 2 Girls, Watery Pool Bowl, Lilies, Leaves, Art Nouveau, 24 x 16 In.	575
Centerpiece, Flower Shape, Boy Seated On Petal, Footed, 10 ¾ In.	438
Centerpiece, Rustic Carved Leaves, Vines, Wood Fruits & Vegetables On Top, c.1890, 11 In.	500
Charger, Figures, Oval, Wavy Rim, Italy, 1800s, 30 x 21 In.	510
Charger, Mythological Scene, Blue, Gold Grotesque Border, c.1900, 18 In.	855
Charger, Pastoral Center Scene, Gold, Blue Fantastical Creature Border, 17 ¾ In.	850
Charger, Rape Of Sabines Scene, 25 x 22 In.	865
Charger, Relief, Dogs Attacking Fox, Fleur-De-Lis, Brown, Turquoise, c.1890, 14 In.	154
Cheese Keeper, Cylindrical, Bamboo Sides, Wheat Finial, W. & J.A. Bailey Alloa, c.1880, 11 In.	460

Majolica, Jug, Tavern, Figures Dancing, Drinking, Minton, c.1890, 10 x 8 ½ In.
$1,062

Brunk Auctions

Majolica, Pedestal, Tapered, Paw Feet, Women's Heads, Rorftrano, Sweden, 1800s, 45 In.
$1,323

Cottone Auctions

Malachite, Obelisk, Neoclassical, Boulle Style Pedestals, 19 x 4 In., Pair
$2,440

Neal Auction Co.

M

Map, Canada, Great Lakes Region, Bellin, Jacques Nicolas, 1755, 18 x 22 In. $4,113

Cowan's Auctions

Map, Globe, Celestial, Brass Meridian, Turned Legs, Kirkwood, Scotland, 1800s, 6 x 9 In. $1,200

Skinner Auctioneers & Appraisers

Map, Globe, Library, Regency, Mahogany, Marked, J. Addison & Co. London, 41 ½ x 24 In. $10,620

Brunk Auctions

Cheese Keeper, Dome Lid, Cover, Pineapple Knop, Berries, Green, Brown, c.1890, 11 x 8 In.	138
Cheese Keeper, Dome Lid, Underplate, Green, Ribbed, Yellow Finial, Brownfield, 12 x 10 In.	413
Cheese Keeper, Stand, Lotus Blossoms, Cattails, Dragonflies, Finial, G. Jones, c.1880, 11 In.	1375
Cheese Keeper, Swimming Green Fish, Blue Ground, England, c.1850, 9 x 11 In.	814
Compote, Birds, Tree, Green Ground, Footed, 8 ¾ In.	91
Ewer, Brown Ground, Winding Tendrils, Leaves, Blue, Green, c.1875, 14 In., Pair	625
Ewer, Frog & Basket Shape, Green, Gray Snake, 19 In.	750
Figurine, Clown Fox, Green Cap, Continental, 5 In.	97
Figurine, Dog, Greyhound, Seated, White, Glass Eyes, Italy, 36 x 14 In.	837
Figurine, Dog, Whippet, Seated, Yellow Coat, 27 In.	1375
Figurine, Duck, Yellow, Brown, Black, Orange, 14 ½ In., Pair	138
Figurine, Monkey, Climbing Pose, Stamped, Impressed, c.1900, 15 ½ In.	813
Figurine, Parrot, On Bamboo Branch, Signed Delphin Massier, c.1925, 14 In.	500
Garden Seat, Drum Shape, Mottled Green, Fretwork Borders, c.1885, 18 x 16 In.	269
Garden Seat, Monkey, Seated, Coconuts, Pillow On Head, England, c.1860, 18 ½ In.	6875
Garden Seat, Reeded Shape, Bowknot, Pale Green, Brown, c.1885, 19 x 14 In.	246
Garden Seat, Victorian, Signed, 19 x 13 In.	1230
Humidor, Cat, Fish, Bandage On Head, 6 ¾ In.	109
Humidor, Elephant, Red Jacket, Smoking Pipe, Continental, 7 In.	67
Humidor, Frog, Red Smoking Jacket, Smoking Pipe, 6 ½ In.	157
Jardiniere, Flower Garland, Brown, Blue, Lady Head Handles, Footed, Holdcroft, 9 x 13 In.	303
Jardiniere, Flowers, Ferns, Leaves, Brown, Green, Oblong, c.1890, 12 ½ In.	2000
Jardiniere, Lily Pads, White Blossom Handles, Round, 6 ½ x 8 In., Pair	563
Jardiniere, Lily-Of-The-Valley, Ferns, Minton Mark, 13 x 19 In. ....*illus*	1875
Jardiniere, Stand, Molded Flowers, Scroll Feet, Shaped Rim, Handles, c.1885, 60 In.	1680
Jardiniere, Storks, Morning Glory Flowers, Cobalt Blue Trim, Cylindrical, 8 ½ x 9 In.	145
Jug, Flowers, Basketweave Ground, Blue Interior, George Jones, c.1890, 7 ¼ In. ....*illus*	826
Jug, Frogs, Brown, Branch Handle, Turquoise Interior, George Jones, 1800s, 8 ¼ In.	885
Jug, Tavern, Figures Dancing, Drinking, Minton, c.1890, 10 x 8 ½ In. ....*illus*	1062
Nut Dish, Squirrel, Impress, Mark, George Jones, c.1875, 10 In., Diam.	472
Pedestal, Brown Glaze, Square Top, Lion Mask, Flared Standard, Paw Feet, c.1900, 34 x 14 In.	875
Pedestal, Square Top, Eagle, Mottled, Brown, Green, Tapered, Footed, c.1910, 39 x 12 In.	594
Pedestal, Tapered Standard, Scroll Feet, Flowers, Blue & White, c.1885, 42 x 13 In.	1845
Pedestal, Tapered, Paw Feet, Women's Heads, Rorftrano, Sweden, 1800s, 45 In. ....*illus*	1323
Pedestal, Tapered, Round Foot, Flared Rim, Applied Roses, c.1900, 36 In., Pair	1553
Pitcher, 4 Panels, Impressed Ground, Pewter Lid, Brown, Turquoise, Copeland, 1877, 10 In.	885
Pitcher, Art Nouveau Flowers, Leaves, Burgundy, Green, Turquoise, Tan, F. Onnaing, 8 In.	69
Pitcher, Blackberry, Multicolor, Victorian, 8 In.	120
Pitcher, Bull Dog Shape, Seated On Haunches, Brown, Red Glaze, Pink Mouth, c.1890, 8 In.	58
Pitcher, Etruscan Shell & Seaweed, Scalloped Rim, Square Handle, Marked, c.1885, 7 In.	196
Pitcher, Fish Shape, Green, Cobalt Blue, Fish Handle, 8 In.	218
Pitcher, Pink Flowers, Yellow, Dragon Handles, 10 In.	102
Pitcher, Shell Shape, Berries, Yellow Ground, Blue Handle, 8 ½ In.	133
Pitcher, Stork In Flight, Lavender Top, 5 ¾ In.	206
Pitcher, Yellow Kernels, Green Leaves, Handle, Corn Shape, 6 ½ In.	145
Plaque, Crab, Mollusks, Seaweed, Palissy Style, France, 23 In.	461
Plaque, Crab, Sand, Shells, Seaweed, Alvaro Jose, Portugal, 22 ½ In.	676
Plate Set, Rabbit, Various Scenes, Enamel Glazed, Higgins & Seiter, c.1900, 8 ¾ In., 9 Piece	1920
Plate, Yellow Pears, Apples, Burgundy Ground, Shaped Round, 8 In.	109
Platter, Bird, Fan Design, Blue, Purple, Green, Yellow, Diamond Shape, 16 In.	145
Platter, Fish, Palissy Ware, France, c.1910, 18 x 12 ½ In.	500
Platter, Oval, Fecundity, Venus, Putti, Fruit, France, 1500s, 20 x 16 In.	5900
Sardine Box, Fish Lid, Basket Weave Base, Victorian Pottery Co., Eng., c.1890, 3 x 8 In.	75
Sardine Box, Lid, Fish Finial, Cobalt Blue, Yellow Trim, 7 ½ In.	194
Server, Begonia Leaf, 2 Parts, Stork Handle, 11 ½ x 6 ½ In.	157
Sugar, Lid, Cauliflower, 5 In.	57
Teapot, Figural, Fish, Swallowing Fish, Dark Green Scales, Adam & Bromley, 11 ½ In.	145
Teapot, Figural, Monkey, Creil, 9 In.	95
Tobacco Jar, Lid, Elephant Shape, Sitting, Cigar In Mouth, Pink Jacket, c.1925, 7 ¼ In.	58
Tureen, Lid, Fish Shape, Glass Eyes, Scale Pattern, Brown, Blue, Yellow, c.1890, 18 In.	861
Tureen, Lid, Gourd Shape, Ribs, Alternating Green, Yellow Stripes, Stem Handle, 12 In.	660
Tureen, Lid, Quail, Chicks, Nest, George Jones, c.1890, 8 x 14 ¾ In.	9720
Umbrella Stand, Art Nouveau, Grapes, Brown Ground, 23 In.	121
Umbrella Stand, Cherub, Leaves, Cobalt Blue, Green, Yellow, c.1860, 21 In.	1353
Umbrella Stand, Green, Birds, Leaves, Rolled Rim, 21 x 9 In.	150
Vase, Applied Animals, Flowers, Green, 16 In., Pair	124

Vase, Applied Eagle, George Jones, 9 ½ In.	303
Vase, Castle, Scrolling, Blue, Yellow, Bulbous, Cylindrical Neck, 1600s, 11 ½ In.	649
Vase, Parrots, Butterflies, Moon Flask Shape, Mounted As Lamp, 20 In., Pair	3000
Vase, Renaissance Style, Painted, Angel, Satyr Mask Handles, Italy, 17 ½ In.	96
Vase, Rococo Style, Handle, Painted, Schiller, Embossed WS&S, Austria, 16 In.	120
Vase, Rooster, Corn Stalk, Signed Delphin Massier, c.1910, 13 ½ In.	531
Vase, Ship, Dolphin, River, Painted, Square, Italy, 14 ½ In.	780
Vase, Shouldered, 2 Swan-Head Handles, Wings, Round Foot, c.1900, 5 ½ x 10 In.	472
Vase, Spill, Tulip Shape, Girl, Holding Fruit Basket, 11 ½ In.	188

MALACHITE is a green stone with unusual layers or rings of darker green shades. It is often polished and used for decorative objects. Most malachite comes from Siberia or Australia.

Bowl, Vide Poche, Gilt Bronze Resting Bear, Russia, 11 In.	1188
Figurine, Balanese Buddha, In Meditation, 8 x 6 In.	153
Figurine, Duck, Carved, Chinese, 19th Century, 2 ¾ In.	206
Jardiniere, Round, Gilt Base, Handles, 13 ½ x 11 In., Pair	3300
Obelisk, Neoclassical, Boulle Style Pedestals, 19 x 4 In., Pair *illus*	2440
Perfume Bottle, Square Open Stopper, Draped Nude Woman, c.1920, 8 In.	625
Snuff Bottle, Candle Shape, Teak Wood Stand, Dragon Design, Red Flame Spoon, 7 In.	30
Vinaigrette, Silver, Waisted Flower Shape, Inset Panels, Gold Washed, c.1878, 1 ¼ In.	300

MAPS of all types have been collected for centuries. The earliest known printed maps were made in 1478. The first printed street map showed London in 1559. The first road maps for use by drivers of automobiles were made in 1901. Collectors buy maps that were pages of old books, as well as the multifolded road maps popular in this century.

Africa, Hand Colored, Gilt, Gold Leaf, Jan Jansson, Amsterdam, c.1680, 15 x 19 In.	501
Alexander The Great's Expedition In Middle East, Engraved, Fold Line, c.1810, 11 x 15 In.	88
America, Port St. Louis, Plymouth Colony, Samuel De Champlain, Paris, 1613, 6 x 6 In.	4720
Americas, Passage Around Cape Horn, Willem Blaeu, Amsterdam, 1617-33, 16 x 22 In.	2950
Britannia, England, Scotland, Wales, Blaeu Family, Amsterdam, Color, Gilt, 1672, 16 x 21 In.	2124
Canada, Great Lakes Region, Bellin, Jacques Nicolas, 1755, 18 x 22 In. *illus*	4113
Cape Cod, Color, Frame, Paul Paige, East Brewster, Mass., 26 x 35 In.	708
China, Provinces, Copper Engraved, London, 1790, 14 ¼ x 18 ¾ In.	178
Cleveland Park, Lithograph, Hand Colored, Sarony, Major & Knapp, 1859, 18 x 23 ¼ In.	118
Europe, Needlework, Silk On Cotton, Flower Border, Signed, Gilt Frame, 1824, 19 x 21 In.	570
Europe, Northern Africa, Holy Land, Greenland, Joan & Cornelius Blaeu, 1636, 16 x 22 In.	2714
France, Alexis Hubert Jaillot, Published In Amsterdam, 1720, 19 x 24 In.	590
Globe, Celestial, Brass Meridian, Turned Legs, Kirkwood, Scotland, 1800s, 6 x 9 In. *illus*	1200
Globe, Celestrial, Cary's New, Zodiac, Calendar Prints, Mahogany Frame, c.1850, 24 In.	2875
Globe, Celestrial, Terrestrial, Wood Frame, James Wilson & Sons, 1831, 18 x 17 In., Pair	5000
Globe, Frame, Brass, Gilt, Pietra Dura, Mother-Of-Pearl, U.S.A., 33 x 18 ½ In.	236
Globe, Library, Mahogany Frame, Stand, c.1950, 16 In.	400
Globe, Library, Paper, Mahogany Stand, c.1960, 16 In.	400
Globe, Library, Regency, Mahogany, Marked, J. Addison & Co. London, 41 ½ x 24 In. *illus*	10620
Globe, On Stand, Bronze, Replogle Globe, 1960s, 34 x 14 In.	443
Globe, Terrestrial, A.H. Andrews & Co., Chicago, Tapered Turned Wood Base, c.1900, 8 In.	1230
Globe, Terrestrial, Art Deco, Stepped Aluminum Stand, Airplane, France, c.1935, 14 x 23 In.	1375
Globe, Terrestrial, Celestial Medial Stand, Kittinger, c.1910, 35 In. *illus*	356
Globe, Terrestrial, Circumnavigators' Tracks, G. Joslin, Boston, Mahogany Stand, 21 In.	1920
Globe, Terrestrial, Color, Iron Ball, Stand, 3-Claw Feet Stand, 12-In. Globe, Weber Costello Co., 21 In.	720
Globe, Terrestrial, H.B. Nims, Troy, N.Y., Wood Base, 4 Turned Legs, 10 In.	3000
Globe, Terrestrial, Library Globe, Stand, G. Brueckman, Replogle Globes, c.1965, 50 x 32 In.	3125
Globe, Terrestrial, Mahogany Stand, c.1910, 19 ½ x 16 In.	708
Globe, Terrestrial, Rand McNally, 12 x 21 In.	456
Globe, Terrestrial, Smith's, c.1880, 15 ½ In.	1440
Globe, Terrestrial, Standing, W. & A.K. Johnston, 18 x 45 In.	711
Globe, Terrestrial, Table Top, George Cram, 10 ½ In.	334
Globe, Terrestrial, Table, Joslin's, Boston, Wood Stand, 3 Turned Legs, 1816, 6 In. Diam.	2767
Louisiana, Mississippi River, Engraved, Hand Colored, John Senex, London, 1721, 19 x 23 In.	1080
Maryland, Delaware Counties, Scrolling, Trees, Water Landmarks, 1756, Frame, 13 x 11 In.	345
New York, New England, Indians, Villages, Huts, Animals, West At Top, c.1677, 16 x 20 In.	2040
North America, Caribbean, Johann Baptist Homann, Engraved, c.1712, 20 x 23 In. *illus*	1195
North America, General Survey By John Russell, London, H.D. Symonds, 1794, 15 x 19 In.	446
North America, Hand Colored, Engraved, John Senex, London, 1710, 28 ¾ x 26 ¾ In.	1200
North Carolina, Copperplate Engraving, Benjamin Tanner, American Atlas, 1796, 16 x 20 In.	649

Map, Globe, Terrestrial, Celestial Medial Stand, Kittinger, c.1910, 35 In.
$356

James D. Julia Auctioneers

Map, North America, Caribbean, Johann Baptist Homann, Engraved, c.1712, 20 x 23 In.
$1,195

Neal Auction Co.

M

Marble Carving, Bust, Girl, Signed, Richard Hamilton Park, c.1875, 20 ½ In.
$1,075

Neal Auction Co.

Marble Carving, Bust, Woman, Bronze Bonnet & Bodice, Stepped Base, A. Gory, Paris, 14 In.
$2,460

Skinner Auctioneers & Appraisers

Marble Carving, Obelisk, Monument, Pedestal Base, Continental, 27 ½ In., Pair
$2,375

Leslie Hindman Auctioneers

Marblehead, Vase, Roses, Painted, Marked, 1920s, 3 ¾ x 3 ½ In.
$1,188

Rago Arts & Auction Center

Northern Germany, Brandenburg, Laid Paper, Frederick De Wit, 1688, 21 x 26 In.	242
Northern United States, Colored, Engraving, Laid Paper, Frame, c.1798, 14 x 20 In.	510
Pennsylvania, Hand Colored, Engraved, Fielding Lucas, Jr., Matted, c.1819, 8 ½ x 10 ½ In.	24
Planetarium, Globe, Painted Moon Ball On Wire Arm, Ideal, Vetter Co., Kansas City, 20 In.	861
Poland, Central, Copperplate Engraved, Chain Lined Paper, Antonio Zatta, c.1781, 15 x 21 In.	98
Poland, Topographical, Copperplate Engraving, Color, Chain Lined Paper, c.1783, 15 x 20 In.	103
Road, California & Arizona, General Gasoline, 1928	106
Road, Iowa, Mobilgas, 1934	41
Road, Northeastern United States, Freedom Gas, 1933	24
Road, Ohio & West Virginia, Freedom Gas, 1938	89
Rome, Campagna Di Roma Olim Latinum, Hand Colored, Blaeu, Amsterdam, c.1640, 20 x 24 In.	235
Russia, James Wyld, Engraving, Hand Colored, Laid Paper, John Thomson, 1824, 14 x 10 In.	92
Sclavonia, Croatia, Bosnia, Armorial Shields, Copperplate Engraving, c.1663, 20 x 24 In.	104
Spain, Portugal, Copper Engraving, Laid Paper, Wein, 1834, 13 ½ x 17 ½ In.	92
Sphere, Armillary, Brass Ellipses, Fluted & Scrolled Cast Iron Tripod Base, 12 In.	7800
State Of Ohio, Hand Colored, Engraving, Wove Paper, Matted, Frame, 1853, 21 x 18 In.	180
United States, Canada, Texas, Mexico, Olney's Geography, Sherman & Smith, 1844, 11 x 19 In.	325
United States, Watercolor & Ink On Paper, Frame, 1824, 21 x 25 In.	2640
World, Double Hemisphere, Australia, Antarctica Merged, Henricus Hondius, 1630, 15 x 21 In.	5605

MARBLE collectors pay highest prices for glass and sulphide marbles. The game of marbles has been popular since the days of the ancient Romans. American children were able to buy marbles by the mid-eighteenth century. Dutch glazed clay marbles were least expensive. Glazed pottery marbles, attributed to the Bennington potteries in Vermont, were of a better quality. Marbles made of pink marble were also available by the 1830s. Glass marbles seem to have been made later. By 1880, Samuel C. Dyke of South Akron, Ohio, was making clay marbles and The National Onyx Marble Company was making marbles of onyx. The Navarre Glass Marble Company of Navarre, Ohio, and M. B. Mishler of Ravenna, Ohio, made the glass marbles. Ohio remained the center of the marble industry, and the Akron-made Akro Agate brand became nationally known. Other pieces made by Akro Agate are listed in this book in the Akro Agate category. Sulphides are glass marbles with frosted white figures in the center.

Agate, Banded, Chevron, Shades Of Brown, White, ¾ In.	10
Agate, Slag, Electric Green, White Stripes, Christensen, 1 In.	80
Agate, Striped Opaque, Brown, Yellow & Gray Stripes, Turquoise Base, Christensen, ⁹/₁₆ In.	60
Agate, Striped Opaque, Yellow, Pink & Black Stripes, Green Base, Christensen, ⅝ In.	90
Agate, Swirl, Flame, Brown & Brick Red, Opaque Blue Base, Christensen, ⅝ In.	60
Agate, Swirl, Flame, Orange & Yellow Ribbons, Blue Base, Christensen, ¾ In.	425
Agate, Swirl, Flame, Salmon & Yellow, Black Base, Christensen, ¾ In.	650
Akro Agate, Corkscrew, Orange, Yellow Accents, Brown & Green Ribbons, ⅝ In.	50
Akro Agate, Corkscrew, Oxblood Ribbon, Amber Base, ⅝ In.	40
Akro Agate, Corkscrew, Purple Pop Eye, Yellow Ribbon, Wispy White, Clear, ¾ In.	80
Akro Agate, Corkscrew, Red, Yellow, Blue, Black, 1920s, ¹³/₁₆ In.	55
Akro Agate, Egg Yolk Green Patch, White, Yellow & Oxblood Veins, 1 In.	80
Akro Agate, Limeade, Oxblood Swirl, ²¹/₃₂ In.	60
Akro Agate, Milky Oxblood, Swirl, Black, White, Burgundy, c.1920, ⅝ In.	35
Akro Agate, Oxblood, Chocolate, Cherry, Honey, Egg Yolk, ⅝ In.	250
Akro Agate, Royal Patch, Yellow & Red, Black & Red Aventurine, ¹¹/₁₆ In.	110
Akro Agate, Silver Oxblood, Patch, c.1930, ⁹/₁₆ In.	29
Akro Agate, Sparkler, Multicolor, ⅝ In.	110
Akro Agate, Swirl, Blue & Oxblood Veins, Translucent Silver Moonie Base, ¹³/₁₆ In.	80
Akro Agate, Swirl, Carnelian Ribbons, Oxblood Veins, Silver Moonie Base, ¹³/₁₆ In.	30
Barnett's, Translucent White, Black Block Letters, Akro Agate, ⅝ In.	20
Bennington, Salt Glaze, Cobalt Blue Splotches Over Green & Brown Speckles, 1 In.	70
Bennington, Salt Glaze, Green, Blue, Brown & White, 1 In.	40
Cat's-Eye, Light Green, Rust, Yellow, ½ In.	13
Chalcedony Agate, Dark Brown & White Stripes, Medium Brown Base, ¹⁵/₁₆ In.	30
Chalcedony Agate, Dyed Blue, Many Rings, Translucent Green Pole, ⅝ In.	40
China, Banded, Overlapping Pink & Green Lines, Unglazed, ¹³/₁₆ In.	40
Clambroth, Blue, Pink & Green Stripes, ¹¹/₁₆ In.	170
End Of Day, Blue, Green, Pink, Germany, c.1890, ¾ In.	96
Indian, 360 Degree, Green, Yellow, Brown & Orange Bands, Black Base, ¹¹/₁₆ In.	450
Joseph's Coat, Blue, Green, Red, Yellow, Orange, White, Speckled, ⅞ In.	60
King Bengal Tiger, Purple, Gray Accents, Yellow Tracing, Orange Base, 1 In.	80
Lutz, 3 Bands, White & Blue Borders, Black Base, ⅝ In.	1100
Lutz, Green Mist, Cased Clear Over Green Base, ¹³/₁₆ In.	210
Lutz, Thick Band, Red Ribbon, ²⁵/₃₂ In.	475

Mica, Green, Emerald Green Base, ¹³⁄₁₆ In.		30
Onionskin, 6 Panels, Pink & White, Orange & Yellow, Blue & White, Clear, ¹⁵⁄₁₆ In.		120
Onionskin, Green Mist, Yellow Accent, ¹³⁄₁₆ In.		40
Onionskin, Lutz Bands, White & Green Ribbons, ¹³⁄₁₆ In.		240
Onionskin, Paneled, Pink, Blue & White Streaky Spiral, ³¹⁄₃₂ In.		70
Onionskin, Sunburst, Blues, Master Marble Co.		20
Peltier, Bumblebee, Black Ribbons, Aventurine, Opaque Yellow Base, ¹¹⁄₁₆ In.		50
Peltier, Ketchup & Mustard, Alternating Red & Yellow Swirled Ribbons, ³⁄₄ In.		30
Peltier, Miller Swirl, Rebel, Red & Black Ribbons, White Base, ³⁄₄ In.		80
Peltier, Superman, Red & Yellow Ribbons, Turquoise Base, ⁷⁄₈ In.		275
Peltier, Tiger, Rainbow, 4 Black Ribbons, Orange Base, ³⁄₄ In.		30
Peltier, Wasp, 4 Black Ribbons, Black Aventurine, Red Base, ¹¹⁄₁₆ In.		40
Shooter, White, Red & Orange Speckles, Mexico, 1 ¼ In.		16
Sulphide, Clear, Standing Elephant, c.1900, 2 ¼ In.		374
Swirl, Brown & White Slag, 1 ¼ In.		60
Swirl, Divided Core, 2 Multicolor Ribbons, Clear Base, ¹⁵⁄₁₆ In.		40
Swirl, Indian, Banded, Green & Yellow, Blue & White, Opaque Black Base, ¹¹⁄₁₆ In.		140
Swirl, Indian, Submarine, 2 Multicolor Bands, Translucent Blue Base, ²¹⁄₃₂ In.		300
Swirl, Indian, Yellow, Red, Orange, Blue & Green Bands, Jet Black Base, ²⁵⁄₃₂ In.		70
Swirl, Latticino Core, Orange Core, Blue & Yellow Bands, Clear Base, ¹³⁄₁₆ In.		20
Swirl, Orange, Black, White, Wood Stand, Venini, 4 In.		3600
Swirl, Peppermint, Red, White, Blue, ¹¹⁄₁₆ In.		100
Swirl, Solid Core, Black, White, Red, Green & Blue Stripes, Clear Base, ¹³⁄₁₆ In.		30

MARBLE CARVINGS, such as large or small figurines, groups of people or animals, and architectural decorations, have been a special art form since the time of the ancient Greeks. Reproductions, especially of large Victorian groups, are being made of a mixture using marble dust. These are very difficult to detect and collectors should be careful. Other carvings are listed under Alabaster.

Bust, Apollo, Signed Antonio Frilli, 18 In.		2440
Bust, Athena, Helmet, A. Frilli, c.1900, 23 ½ In.		3750
Bust, Art Nouveau, Woman, Lilies, White Socle Base, 22 ½ x 15 ¼ In.		1783
Bust, Child, With Hat, c.1900, 8 ½ x 5 In.		330
Bust, Classical Woman, Bare Shoulders, Styled Hair, Marble Socle, 1800s, 14 In.		1035
Bust, Girl, Signed, Richard Hamilton Park, c.1875, 20 ½ In.	*illus*	1075
Bust, Gypsy Maiden, Medallions, Winged Oroboros, Signed E. Del Santa, 22 In.		3250
Bust, Hermes, Hand Of Dionysus On Shoulder, Turned Socle Base, 24 x 19 In.		1912
Bust, Roman Statesman, Curly Hair, 3 Colors, White, Rouge, Honey, 1900s, 35 In.		840
Bust, Soldier, Roman, Variegated Tunic, 1800s, 26 In.		3438
Bust, Woman, Bronze Bonnet & Bodice, Stepped Base, A. Gory, Paris, 14 In.	*illus*	2460
Bust, Woman, Short Wavy Hair, Smiling, Signed Prof. V. Pochini, c.1900, 21 In.		1180
Bust, Woman, Sideward Down Glancing, Braid, Pedestal Base, 1886, 30 In.		2530
Bust, Woman, With Lyre, Italy, 19th Century, 22 ¾ In.		420
Group, Psyche Revived By Cupid's Kiss, Embracing, c.1800, 36 In.		3500
Head, Buddha, Unpolished, Clear Lucite Block Pedestal, 5 ½ x 4 In.		138
Head, Saint, Black Base, Italy, 6 In.		3438
Obelisk, Monument, Pedestal Base, Continental, 27 ½ In., Pair	*illus*	2375
Pedestal, Black On White, Columnar, c.1900, 40 x 11 x 11 In.		1020
Pedestal, Brown Mottled, Columnar, Octagonal Base, Square Top, Canted Corners, 44 In.		1420
Pedestal, Green, Rectangular Top, Octagonal Base, Columnar, 44 x 18 In.		1200
Pedestal, Green, Round Top, Twist Column, Octagonal Base, 34 x 11 In.		1320
Pedestal, Pink, Column Form, c.1960, 42 x 13 In.		594
Pedestal, Round Top, Stepped Base, 3 Pieces, c.1900, 33 x 11 In.		489
Pedestal, Square Top, Canted Corners, Turned Column, Stepped Base, 40 x 12 In.		354
Pedestal, Twisted Standard, 42 In.		136
Pedestal, White, Cylindrical, Stepped Base, c.1900, 42 x 11 ½ In.		354
Sphinx, Woman's Head, Crouched, White, Oval Base, 6 x 9 ¼ In., Pair		1063
Statue, Bee, Signed Daniel Dallacqua, Base, c.1870, 10 In.		652
Statue, Boy Playing Flute, Leaning On Tree Stump, Leafy Branch, Signed A. Gori, 27 In.		2500
Statue, Boy, With Dogs, 22 In.		1440
Statue, Child, Holding Rabbit, White, 13 x 4 ¼ In.		158
Statue, Child's Pose Figure, Mujer, Signed, Victor Hugo Casteneda, 1981, 13 x 7 In.		2500
Statue, Dying Gaul, Man, Resting On Leg, Green, 10 x 20 In.		469
Statue, Goddess Of War, Metal Helmet & Breastplate, Wooden Spear, c.1900, 30 In.		1476
Statue, Hooded Figure, Standing, Black, c.1932 In.		489
Statue, Kneeling Nude, Oval Base, After Lorenzo Bartolini, 20 ½ In.		1800

Mardi Gras, Invitation, Ball, Knights Of Momus, Feb. 17, 1885
$533

Crescent City Auction Gallery

Mardi Gras, Mask, Chubby Face, Papier-Mache, Painted, 1950s, 26 In.
$425

Ruby Lane, Inc.

M

Mardi Gras, Mask, Gold Tone, Open Eyes, Crystals, Filigree, Joseff Of Hollywood, 1940s, 2 ⅝ In.
$495

Ruby Lane, Inc.

TIP

Wear rubber gloves when handling bleaching materials, strong solvents, or other harsh chemicals.

Mardi Gras, Pin, Favor, Krewe Of Proteus, Romances Of Wales, Feb. 22, 1909
$750

Neal Auction Co.

Mardi Gras, Pin, Mask, Gold Tone Metal, Open Eyes, C-Clasp, 1970s, 2 ½ x 1 ½ In.
$22

Ruby Lane, Inc.

Mardi Gras, Pin, Queen's Crown, Tricolor Banner, Rex Krewe, 14K Gold, Tiffany, 1 ½ In.
$1,185

Crescent City Auction Gallery

Martin Brothers, Jug, Face, 2-Sided, Glazed Stoneware, Handle, Signature, 1889, 8 ½ x 7 ½ In.
$9,375

Rago Arts & Auction Center

Statue, Maiden, Seminude, Robe Tied At Waist, Braiding Hair, Signed, Italy, 1866, 32 In.	1320
Statue, Putti, Seated, Inverted Volute Bracket, Grapes, Scarf, White, 22 x 18 In., Pair	1434
Statue, Woman, Classical, Standing, Conti, 33 ½ In.	1413
Statue, Woman, Nude, Knee Bent, Reaching Down, Signed S.R. Mackeller, c.1900, 23 In.	748
Statue, Woman, Seminude, Holding Rose Garland, 1800s, 39 In.	3565
Statue, Woman, Standing, Arms Crossed, Flower Bouquet, Bird, Signed, c.1900, 47 In.	2400
Statue, Woman, White Wavy Cropped Hair, Black Base, 14 In.	181
Tazza, Neoclassical Style, Gilt Bronze Edge, Round, Footed, 7 x 16 In.	2500
Urn, Dome Lid, Fruit Finial, Swag, Mask Gilt Bronze, c.1915, 20 In., Pair	2000
Urn, Neoclassical Style, Flowers, Satyr Band, Curved, 20 In.	313
Urn, Neoclassical Style, Gilt Metal, 13 ¾ In., Pair	531
Urn, Neoclassical, Ram's Head Masks, Fruit, Flowers, 15 ¾ In.	281

MARBLEHEAD POTTERY was founded in 1905 by Dr. J. Hall as a rehabilitative program for the patients of a Marblehead, Massachusetts, sanitarium. Two years later it was separated from the sanitarium and it continued operations until 1936. Many of the pieces were decorated with marine motifs.

Bowl, Blue, Multicolor Berries & Leaves, Marked, 2 2/3 x 5 ½ In.	1695
Bowl, Flower Frog, Flared Rim, Blue Matte, Impressed Mark, 9 ¾ In.	138
Humidor, Jugendstil, Blue, Cone Shape, Incised, Arthur Baggs, 1910s, 6 x 6 In.	3000
Tile, Fish, Orange, Blue, Green Matte Glaze, Frame, 6 ½ x 6 ½ In.	2900
Tile, Landscape, House, Stamped Mark MP, 1910s, 6 x 6 In.	2750
Tile, Tree Silhouettes, Green, Matte Glaze Ground, Frame, 6 ½ x 6 ½ In.	7320
Vase, Blue Matte Glaze, Tapered, 7 In.	115
Vase, Bud, Stylized Blossoms, Green, Brown, Spread Base, A. Hennessey, 5 In.	2500
Vase, Bud, Stylized Trees, Green, Brown, Cylindrical, Spread Base, Hennessey, Tutt, 5 In.	3750
Vase, Cranes, Arthur Hennessey, Sarah Tutt, Stamped Mark, 1910s, 5 ¾ x 5 In.	1063
Vase, Curdled Blue Glaze, Bulbous, 11 ½ x 11 ½ In.	8125
Vase, Dark Blue Matte Glaze, Cylindrical, 3 ⅝ In.	184
Vase, Dark Blue Matte Glaze, Rolled Rim, Squat, 3 ⅜ In.	219
Vase, Dark Blue Matte Glaze, Round, 3 x 5 In.	230
Vase, Geometric Design, Arthur Baggs, Stamped Mark, 1910s, 5 ¾ x 3 ½ In.	11250
Vase, Gray Matte Glaze, Tapered, 4 x 7 In.	313
Vase, Gray, Cylindrical, 9 In.	127
Vase, Holly Boughs, Blue Ground, Stamped Mark, 1920s, 4 x 5 In.	1500
Vase, Light Blue, Over Purple, Squat, 3 ¾ x 5 ½ In.	207
Vase, Parrot, Painted, Berried Vine, Blue, Green, Brown, Gray Ground, c.1920, 11 ½ In.	3600
Vase, Parrots, Branches, Leaves, Tan Ground, A. Baggs, Ship Mark, c.1905, 7 x 5 In.	4063
Vase, Pinecones On Branch, Green Matte Glaze, A. Baggs, S. Tutt, 12 x 4 ½ In.	16250
Vase, Roses, Painted, Marked, 1920s, 3 ¾ x 3 ½ In.	1188
Vase, Stylized Blossoms, Green Ground, Tapered, Sarah Tutt, Mark, 1920s, 3 ½ x 4 ¼ In.	875
Vase, Stylized Flowering Branches, Arthur Hennessey, Sarah Tutt, Stamped, 4 ½ x 3 ½ In.	1750
Vase, Stylized Trees, Green Ground, S. Tutt, M. Milner, Ship Mark, 1910s, 11 In.	3375
Vase, Stylized Trees, Stoneware, 3 x 5 In.	938
Vase, Stylized Trees, Tan Ground, Hennessey, Tutt, Ship Mark, 4 ¾ x 4 In.	3250
Vase, Tan Matte Glaze, Tree Of Life Design, Bulbous, Tapered, Signed Hanna Tutt, 5 x 6 In.	4000
Wall Pocket, Brown Matte Glaze, Ribbed, 5 ½ x 4 ¼ In.	195

MARDI GRAS, French for "Fat Tuesday," was first celebrated in seventeenth century Europe. The first celebration in America was held in Mobile, Alabama, in 1703. The first krewe, a parading or social club, was founded in 1856. Dozens have been formed since. The Mardi Gras Act, which made Fat Tuesday a legal holiday, was passed in Louisiana in 1875. Mardi Gras balls, carnivals, parties, and parades are held from January 6 until the Tuesday before the beginning of Lent. The most famous carnival and parades take place in New Orleans. Parades feature floats, elaborate costumes, masks, and "throws" of strings of beads, cups, doubloons, or small toys. Purple, green, and gold are traditional Mardi Gras colors. Mardi Gras memorabilia ranges from cheap plastic beads to expensive souvenirs from early celebrations.

Badge, Ducal, Rex, Tricolor Ribbon, Arabian Nights Tales Ball, 1881, 4 ¾ x 3 ½ In.	5925
Invitation, Admit Card, Rex Organization, Pursuit Of Pleasure Theme, Feb. 21, 1882	830
Invitation, Ball, February 17, 1885, King, Moon, Cherubs, Momus Krewe, Paper	474
Invitation, Ball, Knights Of Momus, Feb. 17, 1885 *illus*	533
Invitation, Ball, March 1, 1881, Comus, Myths Of Northland, Urn, Peacock, Die Cut	1304
Invitation, Ball, March 2, 1897, Dragon Boat, Rex Krewe, Die Cut Paper	492
Invitation, Ball, March 9, 1886, Visions Of Other Worlds, Proteus Krewe, Paper	267
Invitation, Ball, Mistick Krewe Of Comus, Josephus Theme, Envelope, Feb. 14, 1899	533
Locket, Silver, Blue Enamel, Kidney Shape, 12th Night Revelers Krewe Favor, 1905, 1 In.	296
Mask, Chubby Face, Papier-Mache, Painted, 1950s, 26 In. *illus*	425

M

Mask, Gold Tone, Open Eyes, Crystals, Filigree, Joseff Of Hollywood, 1940s, 2 ⅝ In. ....*illus* 495
Mask, Minstrel, Papier-Mache, France, 16 ½ In. 2629
Parade Bulletin, Rex, In Utopia, Feb. 27, 1906, 28 In. 1778
Parade Bulletin, Rex, Reveries Of Rex, Feb. 14, 1899, 28 In. 154
Pin, Favor, Krewe Of Proteus, Romances Of Wales, Feb. 22, 1909 ....*illus* 750
Pin, Lily Of The Valley, Scalloped Edge, Enamel, Proteus Krewe Favor, 1902, 1 In. 652
Pin, Mask, Gold Tone Metal, Open Eyes, C-Clasp, 1970s, 2 ½ x 1 ½ In. ....*illus* 22
Pin, Music Staff, Notes, Minstrels Of The Olden Time, Silver, Krewe Favor, 1898, 2 In. 1185
Pin, Queen's Crown, Tricolor Banner, Rex Krewe, 14K Gold, Tiffany, 1 ½ In. ....*illus* 1185
Pin, Sunrise Over Water, Mountains, Rainbow, Amphictyons Krewe Favor, 1904, 1 In. 119
Pin, Wind Woman, Scrolls, Goldtone Metal, Atlanteans Krewe Favor, 1904, 1 In. 178
Pin, Winged Woman, Wolves, Enamel, Silver, Oval, Mithras Krewe Favor, 1907, 1 In. 652
Scepter, Queen's, Silver, Faux Diamonds, Comus Krewe Favor, 1917, 19 In. 1540
Stickpin, Arrow, Rome, SPQR, Silver, Enamel, Momus Krewe Favor, c.1896, 3 In. 1185

MARTIN BROTHERS of Middlesex, England, made Martinware, a salt-glazed stoneware, *Martin Bro* between 1873 and 1915. Many figural jugs and vases were made by the three brothers. Of *London* special interest are the fanciful birds, usually made with removable heads. Most pieces have the incised name of the artists plus other information on the bottom.

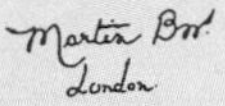

Candlestick, Taupe, Blue, Molded Geometric Designs, Eng., c.1875, 2 ³⁄₁₆ In. 92
Chess Piece, Bust, Samuel Pickwick, G.C.N.P.C., Signed, 1906, 4 ¼ In. 8125
Clock, Stoneware, Fish, Green, Blue, Textured, Arched, Spread Base, 1909, 13 In. 6250
Jug, Face, 2-Sided, Glazed Stoneware, Handle, Signature, 1889, 8 ½ x 7 ½ In. ......*illus* 9375
Jug, Face, Barrister, 2-Sided, Frothy Glaze Wig, Signed, 5 In. 1875
Jug, Face, Grotesque, Side-Glancing Eyes, Bulbous, Pinched Neck, 6 ¾ In. 11875
Jug, Face, Incised, Barrister, My Learned Friend, Bulbous, Signed, 1909, 6 ½ In. 5938
Spoon Warmer, Dog, Grotesque, Head Up, Open Mouth, Tail Handle, 10 In. 26250
Tobacco Jar, Bird, Glazed Stoneware, Signed, 1898, 11 x 6 In. ....*illus* 59375
Tobacco Jar, Bird, Long Bill, Glazed Stoneware, Signed, c.1886, 12 ½ x 6 In. 43750
Tobacco Jar, Frog, Sitting, Mottled Green, Turned Head Lid, Wood Base, 11 In. 87500
Vase, Armadillo, Stoneware, Glazed, Signed, Robert, 1890, 4 x 8 ½ x 3 ½ In. .....*illus* 43750
Vase, Birds, Relief Carved, Tan Glaze, Bulbous, Tapered, 1901, 9 x 5 In. 5938
Vase, Grotesque Fish, 4-Sided, Incised, 5 ⅛ In. ....*illus* 2242
Vase, Underwater Scene, 6-Sided, Incised, Signed, c.1900, 10 ¾ In. ....*illus* 7703

MARY GREGORY is the name used for a type of glass that is easily identified. White figures were painted on clear or colored glass as the decoration. The figures chosen were usually children at play. The first glass known as Mary Gregory was made in about 1870. Similar glass is made even today. The traditional story has been that the glass was made at the Boston & Sandwich Glass Company in Sandwich, Massachusetts, by a woman named Mary Gregory. Recent research has shown that none was made at Sandwich. In fact, all early Mary Gregory glass was made in Bohemia. Beginning in 1957, the Westmoreland Glass Co. made the first Mary Gregory–type decorations on American glassware. These pieces had simpler designs, less enamel paint, and more modern shapes. France, Italy, Germany, Switzerland, and England, as well as Bohemia, made this glassware. Children standing, not playing, were pictured after the 1950s.

Bottle, Dresser, Boy & Girl Playing, Stopper, 8 x 3 ¼ In., Pair ....*illus* 300
Box, Girl, Garden, Casket Shape, Cranberry, 2 Handles, c.1880, 4 x 2 x 2 In. 595
Bride's Basket, Children, Blue, Leaf & Berry Frame, Middletown Plate Co., 10 x 10 In. 714
Cruet, Ball Stopper, Amber, Clear Handle, Child, Flowers, 19th Century, 7 In. 150
Dresser Box, Amethyst, Lake Scene, Boy Painting Picture, 5 In. 345
Goblet, Prussian Blue, Amber Foot, Painted Gnome, 6 ¾ In. 86
Hyacinth Bulb Vase, Boy & Girl, Catching Butterflies, Amber, c.1900, 8 In., Pair 250
Jar, Lid, Couple Dancing, Cobalt Blue, Footed, c.1900, 9 In. 125
Mug, Boy, Standing, White Formal Suit, Blue Sash, Coin Spotted Cranberry Glass, 5 In. 35
Pitcher, Boy, Butterflies, Green, Gilt Trim, Footed, 11 In. 195
Powder Box, Boy, Green, Gilt Finial, Round, 4 x 3 ¾ In. 110
Strawholder, Blue Glass, White Decoration, Double Ribbed Fluted Collars, 7 In. 169
Sugar Shaker, Girl, Holding Bowl, Mountains, c.1940, 4 In. 300
Trinket Box, Holding Basket, Cranberry, Hinged, 4 ½ x 3 ½ In. 295
Tumbler, Girl, Dog, Amber, 2 ½ x 3 ¾ In. 25
Vase, Bohemian Glass, Electric Blue, Girl, c.1900, 10 ½ In. 108
Vase, Girl, Trees, Yellow, 5 ¼ In. 114
Vase, Woman, Brimmed Hat, Green, Ruffled Rim, 7 In. 115
Vase, Shouldered, Lime Green, Painted Children, 8 ½ In., Pair 75

MASONIC, *see Fraternal category.*

Martin Brothers, Tobacco Jar, Bird, Glazed Stoneware, Signed, 1898, 11 x 6 In.
$59,375

Rago Arts & Auction Center

Martin Brothers, Vase, Armadillo, Stoneware, Glazed, Signed, Robert, 1890, 4 x 8 ½ x 3 ½ In.
$43,750

Rago Arts & Auction Center

Martin Brothers, Vase, Grotesque Fish, 4-Sided, Incised, 5 ⅛ In.
$2,242

M

Humler & Nolan

Martin Brothers, Vase, Underwater Scene, 6-Sided, Incised, Signed, c.1900, 10 ¾ In.
$7,703

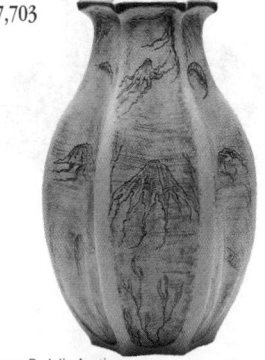

James D. Julia Auctioneers

Mary Gregory, Bottle, Dresser, Boy & Girl Playing, Stopper, 8 x 3 ¼ In., Pair
$300

DuMouchelles Art Gallery

Match Holder, Ceresota Flour, Boy, Tin, Side Panel Opening, 5 ½ In.
$150

Morphy Auctions

Match Holder, Detroit Stove Works, Woman's Boot, Crown Jewel Shoes, Embossed, 6 x 7 In.
$230

Wm Morford Auctions

MASON'S IRONSTONE was made by the English pottery of Charles J. Mason after 1813. Mason, of Lane Delph, was given a patent for this improved earthenware. He usually called it *Mason's Patent Ironstone China*. It resisted chipping and breaking, so it became popular for dinnerware and other table service dishes. Vases and other decorative pieces were also made. The ironstone was decorated with orange, blue, gold, and other colors, often in Japanese-inspired designs. The firm had financial difficulties but the molds and the name *Mason* were used by many owners through the years, including Francis Morley, Taylor Ashworth, George L. Ashworth, and John Shaw. Mason's joined the Wedgwood group in 1973 and the name is still found on dinnerware.

Pitcher, Asian Figures Cartouche, Green, Orange, Marked, 7 ⅝ In.	23
Pitcher, Basin Set, Japonesque Style, Dragon Handle, Multicolor Scenes, c.1890, 11 x 5 In.	177
Pitcher, Flowers, Green Serpent Handle, Marked, 8 In.	150
Pitcher, Imari Pattern, Blue, Pink, Orange, Cream Ground, c.1850, 10 ¾ In.	153
Plate, Dessert, Kakiemon, Birds, Flowers, Gilt, Orange Border, c.1820, 9 In.	316
Tureen, Soup, Lid, Underplate, Ladle, Vistas Pattern, Blue, White, 1800s, 14 x 15 In.	177
Urn, Lid, Bird, Flowers, Transfer, Octagonal, Applied Finial, Handle, 1800s, 20 In., Pair	225

MASSIER, a French art pottery, was made by brothers Jerome, Delphin, and Clement Massier in Vallauris and Golfe-Juan, France, in the late nineteenth and early twentieth centuries. It has an iridescent metallic luster glaze that resembles the Weller Sicardo pottery glaze. Most pieces are marked J. Massier. Massier may also be listed in the Majolica category.

Bowl, 2 Fawn Heads, Iridized, Tin Insert, Clement Massier, France, 1887, 11 In.	1800
Box, Scarab, Glazed, Iridescent, Signed, Clement, c.1900, 3 x 6 x 4 In.	3750
Candlestick, Majolica, Art Nouveau, Frogs, Yellow, Golf Juan, Clement, 8 ¾ In., Pair	73
Plaque, Raised Landscape, Green, Red Metallic Glaze, Signed Delphin Massier, 5 x 7 In.	406
Plaque, St. Cecilia, Glazed, Signed, Clement, c.1900, 20 x 14 In.	5625
Vase, Blue Iridescent, Lumpy Cylinder Shape, 10 In.	150
Vase, Entwined Woman In Relief, Painted Flowers, Flared Rim, Delphin, 10 x 25 In.	1200
Vase, Metallic Luster, Wide Square Collar, Long Neck, Signed, 6 x 10 In.	175
Vase, Pine Design, Metallic Glaze, Tapered, Signed Jerome Massier, 5 x 13 ½ In.	438

MATCH HOLDERS were made to hold the large wooden matches that were used in the nineteenth and twentieth centuries for a variety of purposes. The kitchen stove and the fireplace or furnace had to be lit regularly. One type of match holder was made to hang on the wall, another was designed to be kept on a tabletop. Of special interest today are match holders that have advertisements as part of the design.

Ashtray, Bird, Long Beak, Majolica, 10 In.	120
Black Girl, Standing, Finger To Chin, Painted, Majolica, Austria, c.1885, 6 ¼ In.	100
Boar's Head, Open Mouth, Brass, 7 In.	390
Boy, Leaning On Fence, Germany, 6 x 5 In.	192
Ceresota Flour, Boy, Tin, Side Panel Opening, 5 ½ In. *illus*	150
Child, Lamb, Germany, c.1875, 3 ¾ In.	85
Civil War Boot, Boot Jack Striker, Base, Cast Iron, 5 x 5 ¼ In.	279
DeLaval, Blue, Silver, Yellow, Tin, Die Cut, 6 ½ In.	960
Detroit Stove Works, Woman's Boot, Crown Jewel Shoes, Embossed, 6 x 7 In. *illus*	230
Dr. Shoop's, Health Coffee, Portrait, Tin Lithograph, 4 ⅞ x 3 ⅜ In.	207
E.O. Webber Lumber, Diamond Shape Back, Tin, 6 ½ x 6 ½ In.	546
Eclipse Co., Wall, Embossed, Cast Iron, c.1900, 11 x 8 ½ In.	60
Frog, Mouth Opens, Cast Iron, 4 x 2 In. *illus*	206
Frog, Playing Mandolin, Wearing Tricorner Hat, Majolica, 8 ½ In.	169
Goebel, Beer, Ashtray, Knight Holding Shield, Ceramic, 3 x 4 In.	46
Moxie, Match Box, Die Cut, Tin, Painted, 2 ½ x 7 In.	741
Nude Maidens, Flanking Bowl, Spread Base, Silver, Hardstone, Cartier, 3 ⅜ In.	2460
Osborne, Harvesting Machines, Tin Litho, Blue, 4 ⅞ x 3 ½ In.	489
Porcelain, Victorian Couple With Watering Cans, Hanging, Striker, Japan, 7 In.	35
Pottery, Copper, Lead, Manganese, Green Wash, Round Top, 3-Step Foot, c.1890, 3 x 2 ¾ In.	920
Skull On Book, Figural, Swinging Jaw, Bisque, 3 x 3 In.	81
Topsy Hosiery, Tin Lithograph, 3 ⅜ x 4 ¾ In.	1824
Topsy Hosiery, Woman Lying In Sand At Beach, Tin, c.1910, 5 In.	150

MATCH SAFES were designed to be carried in the pocket. Early matches were made with phosphorus and could ignite unexpectedly. The matches were safely stored in the tightly closed container. Match safes were made in sterling silver, plated silver, or other metals. The English call these "vesta boxes."

America's Leading Mill Builders, Flour, Eagle, Globe, Celluloid, 2 ⅜ x 1 ½ In.	403

M

Beach Wickham Grain Co., At Your Service, Horse Head, Celluloid, 2 ½ In.		345
Beautiful Woman, Red Hair Tie, Celluloid, 1 ½ x 2 ¾ In.		143
Black Cat Cigarettes, Book Style, Striker On Back, Celluloid, 2 ½ x 2 In.		330
Enamelware, Checkerboard Design, Red, White, Allumettes, 1930s, 7 x 3 x 6 In.		114
Fire Steamer, Home Insurance Co., Silver Plate, Embossed, 2 ¾ x 1 ½ In.		314
Fly Shape, Embossed Wings, No Flies On Davis Printing, Cast Iron, c.1890, 23 x 21 In.		403
Gilt Edge Brand Coffee, Cylindrical, Swirl Banding, Celluloid, 3 x 2 In.		150
Gold Medal, Flour, Yellow, Orange, Celluloid, 2 ⅜ x 1 ½ In.		104
Greens Lawn Mowers, Multicolor, Celluloid, 1 ½ x 2 ¾ In.		242
Harrison Bros., Child Holding Puppy, Celluloid, 2 ¾ x 1 ½ In.		184
Hunters, Game, Cast Iron, 10 ½ In.		94
Norwall Valves, Nude Woman On Rock, Water, Celluloid, 3 x 1 ½ In.		345
Oberon, Winged Nudes, Whitehead & Hoag Lithographers, Celluloid, 1 ½ x 2 ¾ In.		360
Owl, Figural, Brass, Head Pops Open, Striker Under Feet, c.1910, 2 ¼ In.	*illus*	209
Robert Mayer & Co., Inventor Of Lithography, Celluloid, 1 ½ x 2 ¾ In.		314
Rock Island Railroad Passenger Department, Celluloid, 1 ½ x 2 ¼ In.		300
Selig Bros. Wholesale Tailors, Nude With Bow & Arrow, Celluloid, 1 ½ x 2 ¾ In.		180
Stock Food, Molassine Veterinary, Reclining Nude Woman, Pig, 2 ¾ x 1 ½ In.		374
Tiffin Wagon Co., Ohio Gov. Edward Tiffin, Tiffin, Ohio, Celluloid, 1 ½ x 2 ⅝ In.		314
Tree Branch, High Relief, Sterling Silver, 1 ¼ x 2 ¾ In.		330
United Brewery Workmen, Union, Beer Barrel, Celluloid, 1 ½ x 2 ¾ In.		207
Woman, Seated Next To Barrel, Figural, Porcelain, c.1875, 7 ½ In.		90

MATT MORGAN, an English artist, was making pottery in Cincinnati, Ohio, by 1883. His pieces were decorated to resemble Moorish wares. Incised designs and colors were applied to raised panels on the pottery. Shiny or matte glazes were used. The company lasted less than two years.

Charger, Limoges-Style Painting, Luster Glaze, Incised, Stamped, 1882-84, 16 ¾ In.	*illus*	2000
Jug, Embossed, Corn, Nameplate, Chain, Blue, Yellow, c.1882, 6 ¾ In.		170
Vase, Birds, Grasses, Gold, Tan Ground, Swollen Body, 12 In.		450
Vase, Moorish, Ringed Foot & Rim, Indigo Glaze, Paper Label, c.1883, 10 x 8 x 6 In.		275
Vase, Moresque Form, Castle, Lake, Marked, 14 ⅞ In.		1300
Vase, Mouse, Grass, Full Moon, Oval, Flared Rim, c.1882, 12 In.		650
Vase, Swallows, Night Sky, Bamboo Trees, Clouds, Shouldered, c.1883, 12 In.		600

MCCOY pottery was made in Roseville, Ohio. Nelson McCoy and J.W. McCoy established the Nelson McCoy Sanitary and Stoneware Company in Roseville, Ohio, in 1910. The firm made art pottery after 1926. In 1933 it became the Nelson McCoy Pottery Company. Pieces marked McCoy were made by the Nelson McCoy Pottery Company. Cookie jars were made from about 1940 until December 1990, when the McCoy factory closed. Since 1991 pottery with the McCoy mark has been made by firms unrelated to the original company. Because there was a company named Brush-McCoy, there is great confusion between Brush and Nelson McCoy pieces. See Brush category for more information.

Apple, Yellow, Red Accents, Leaf Handle, 1950s, 8 x 7 In.		85
Cookie Jar, Basket, Leaves, Berries, Green Ground, 9 ½ In.		55
Cookie Jar, Double-Headed Duck Lid, Basketweave, 1950s, 10 ½ x 5 In.		75
Cookie Jar, Hot Air Balloon, Brown, Yellow, 9 In.		135
Cookie Jar, Leprechaun, Multicolor	*illus*	720
Cookie Jar, Oaken Bucket, c.1960, 9 x 7 In.		24
Jardiniere, Jewel, Enamel Triangles, Beadwork, 6 ¾ x 7 ½ In.	*illus*	259
Jardiniere, Quilted, Green, 10 ¼ In.		24
Planter, Bear On Log, 4 ¾ x 6 ½ In.		50
Planter, Doe, Fawn, Green, Brown, 7 ¼ In.		6
Vase, Calla Lily, Marked, 8 In., Pair		52
Vase, Mottled Green, 2 Handles, Flared Rim, 8 ¼ x 5 ¼ In.		75
Vase, White, Impressed Base, 8 In.		6

MCKEE is a name associated with various glass enterprises in the United States since 1836, including J. & F. McKee (1850), Bryce, McKee & Co. (1850 to 1854), McKee and Brothers (1865), and National Glass Co. (1899). In 1903, the McKee Glass Company was formed in Jeannette, Pennsylvania. It became McKee Division of the Thatcher Glass Co. in 1951 and was bought out by the Jeannette Corporation in 1961. Pressed glass, kitchenwares, and tablewares were produced. Jeannette Corporation closed in the early 1980s. Additional pieces may be included in the Custard Glass and Depression Glass categories.

Bowl, Bulb, Jade Green, 7 In.	65
Bowl, Colonial, Green Frosted	25

Match Holder, Frog, Mouth Opens, Cast Iron, 4 x 2 In.
$206

Bertoia Auctions

Match Safe, Owl, Figural, Brass, Head Pops Open, Striker Under Feet, c.1910, 2 ¼ In.
$209

Hake's Americana & Collectibles

M

Matt Morgan, Charger, Limoges-Style Painting, Luster Glaze, Incised, Stamped, 1882-84, 16 ¾ In.
$2,000

Rago Arts & Auction Center

Washington Photo a Fake
Think about the world your newly discovered antique lived in when you try to determine age. There are no photographs of George Washington. He died before the camera was invented.

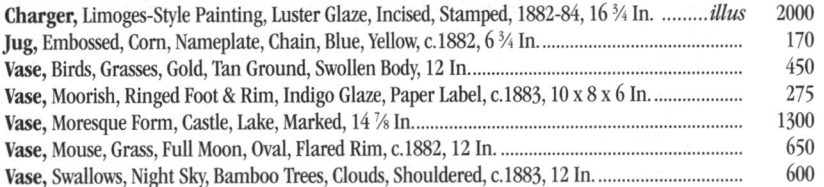

McCoy, Cookie Jar, Leprechaun, Multicolor
$720

Victorian Casino Antiques

McCoy, Jardiniere, Jewel, Enamel Triangles, Beadwork, 6 ¾ x 7 ½ In.
$259

Humler & Nolan

Medical, Cabinet, Apothecary, Walnut, Mahogany, Brass Handles, 1800s, 38 x 31 In.
$1,422

James D. Julia Auctioneers

Bowl, Flower, Black, Handles, Oval, 10 ½ In.	55
Bowl, Flower, Colonial, Caramel, Footed, 11 ½ In.	40
Bowl, Flower, Seville Yellow, Handles, Oval, 7 In.	35
Bowl, Fruit, Puritan, Seville Yellow, Flared, 3-Footed, 10 In.	65
Bowl, Innovation, Fruit, Pink, Snappy Cut, 10 In.	85
Cheese & Cracker Set, Rock Crystal, Amber, Indented Plate, With Comport	45
Planter, Lion Box, Window Sill, Jade Green	125
Salt & Pepper, Apron Lady, Custard Glass, White, Black Figures, Lid, 1930s, 5 x 2 ⅜ In.	175
Server, Rock Crystal, Green, Black Trim, Center Handle, 10 ¾ In.	35
Tom & Jerry Set, Black, 11 ½-In. Bowl, 12 Mugs	300
Toothpick Holder, Feather Doric, Green, Scalloped Rim, Footed, c.1896.2 ¾ In.	259

MECHANICAL BANKS *are listed in the Bank category.*

MEDICAL office furniture, operating tools, microscopes, thermometers, and other paraphernalia used by doctors are included in this category. Veterinary collectibles are also included here. Medicine bottles are listed in the Bottle category. There are related collectibles listed under Dental.

Amputation Kit, Surgeon's, Tools, Wood Fitted Box	480
Anesthesia Kit, McKesson, Model G, Toledo Technical Appliance Co., Case	300
Apothecary Kit, H.K. Mulford, Maker, Wood, Drop Front, Fitted Interior, Test Tubes	154
Bust, Pharmacy Display, Blackamoor, Turban, Open Mouth, Carved, Painted, 9 ½ In.	531
Cabinet, Apothecary, 24 Drawers, Green, Slant Front, Porcelain Knobs, c.1890, 36 x 18 In.	431
Cabinet, Apothecary, 24 Drawers, Painted, 33 x 36 In.	1200
Cabinet, Apothecary, Mahogany, 19th Century, 3 Hinged Sections, Drawer Base, 30 In.	600
Cabinet, Apothecary, Mahogany, Vaseline Knobs, Eglomise Panels, c.1850, 32 x 34 In., Pair	1896
Cabinet, Apothecary, Mixed Wood, 18 Small Over 4 Larger Drawers, Glass Pulls, 32 x 50 In.	527
Cabinet, Apothecary, Pine, 8 Drawers, Green Paint, White Stencil, 1800s, 12 x 55 In.	2133
Cabinet, Apothecary, Pine, 18 Drawers, Black Knobs, Continental, c.1900, 20 x 52 In.	885
Cabinet, Apothecary, Pine, 40 Graduated Drawers, c.1890, 54 ½ x 60 In.	3081
Cabinet, Apothecary, Poplar, 18 Drawers, White Knobs, Pennsylvania, c.1850, 27 x 29 In.	600
Cabinet, Apothecary, Walnut, 18 Drawers, Canted Top, 30 ½ x 16 In.	948
Cabinet, Apothecary, Walnut, Mahogany, Brass Handles, 1800s, 38 x 31 In. *illus*	1422
Cabinet, Apothecary, Wood, 12 Drawers, c.1900, 39 x 17 In.	288
Cabinet, Apothecary, Wood, Brass Mounts & Pulls, 19 Drawers, 1900s, 42 x 14 In.	354
Cabinet, First Aid, Johnson's, No. 10, Red Cross, Containing Articles For Emergency Use	60
Cabinet, Specimen, Mixed Woods, 12 Drawers, Pa., c.1890, 24 x 30 In.	385
Case, Optometrist, Oak, Lens Kit, c.1890, 19 x 23 ¾ In.	652
Chair, Padded Leather, Reclines To Table, Drawer, Tray, Case, Salesman Sample, 16 x 6 In.	4740
Chest, Apothecary, Bird's-Eye Maple, 8 Drawers, c.1860, 29 x 30 In.	2596
Chest, No. 2, Mahogany Box, Handles, Carpenter's, Drawer, Black Labels, c.1850, 11 x 13 In.	660
Coffin, Cooling, Wicker, Durfee Embalming Fluid Co., Clothed Rubber Corpse, 84 x 26 In.	719
Crutch, White Pine, 1800s, 50 In., Pair	94
Diatherapy Machine, Dynelectron, Model P, Liebel-Flarsheim Co., Cincinnati, 18 In.	980
Diathermy Machine, Fisher, Type Y, H.G. Fisher, Chicago, 23 In.	480
Doctor's Spoon, Sterling, Folding, 2 Bowls, Pierced Band, Currier & Roby, c.1900, 6 ¾ In.	155
Electro Therapy Machine, Wood, Dials, E.J. Rose Co., St. Louis, Serial No. 1114, 20 In.	492
Jar, Apothecary, Lid, Porcelain, Gilt, Caduceus, Oval Reserve, 1800s, 10 In., Pair *illus*	478
Jar, Leech, Blown Glass, Teardrop Shape, Wafer Base, Folded Foot Rim, 1800s, 8 In.	470
Massager, Electric, Victor, Chicago, Fitted Case, Quack Device, 11 ½ x 9 In.	615
Medicine Cabinet, Wood, Mirrored Door, Shelves, Open Shelf, 1900s, 20 x 28 In.	23
Model, Anatomical, Human Left Foot, Cross-Section, Inflexible Plastic, 1960s, 10 ½ In.	295
Model, Anatomical, Internal Body Cavity, Removable Organs, Papier-Mache, 53 In.	3600
Model, Anatomical, Male, Female, Folio Format, Pilz, Germany, 33 x 22 In., Pair	540
Model, Anatomical, Man, Torso, Removable Internal Organs, Composition, 39 In.	1046
Model, Anatomical, Woman, Front Opens, Composition, Clay-Adams Co., N.Y., 43 In.	2768
Nebulizer, Eureka, O.Q. Holman, Chicago, Ill., Quack Device, 70 In.	5228
Scale, Balance, Apothecary, Brass, Mahogany, Chains, c.1845, 23 ¼ x 20 In.	124
Surgeon's Kit, Instruments, Carl Reiner & Lieverknecht, Vienna, Fitted Oak Box	210
Surgeon's Kit, Instruments, Ebony, Nickeled Steel, Wood Case, Charriere, Paris, 17 In.	2100
Surgeon's Kit, Knives, Scissors, Bunsen Burner, Case, Mathieu, Paris, c.1870, 32 Piece	702
Walker, Child's, Turned Stretcher Base, Bentwood Attachments, c.1835, 21 In.	173
Wheelchair, Campaign, Mahogany, Cane Back, Leather Seat, England, c.1860	650
Wheelchair, Carved, Horseshoe Back, Splat, Woven Seat, Footrest, Arms, Chinese, 37 x 42 In.	1666

M

MEISSEN is a town in Germany where porcelain has been made since 1710. Any china made in the town can be called Meissen, although the famous Meissen factory made the finest porcelains of the area. The crossed swords mark of the great Meissen factory has been copied by many other firms in Germany and other parts of the world. Pieces of Meissen dinnerware in the Onion pattern are listed in their own category in this book.

Bowl, Blue, White Flowers, Pierced, Scalloped Border, 8 ¼ In.	84
Bowl, Reticulated, Flowers, 6 x 10 In.	59
Bowl, Sweetmeat, Figural, Colonial Man Holding, 8 ½ In.	124
Bowl, Undulating Rim, Gilt, Rosebuds, Blossom Center	46
Bust, Baby, Grape Leaves In Hair, On Shoulder, Gilt, Stamped, 10 x 5 ½ In.	817
Cake Stand, Blue Onion, Shaped Edge, Domed Foot, Crossed Swords, 12 ½ In.	345
Candelabrum, 4-Light, Putti, Leaves, Blue Onion Pattern, Marked, 9 ½ In., Pair	5000
Cane Handle, Woman, Gilt Accents, Blue Crossed Swords, c.1890, 4 ¾ In. ....illus	800
Centerpiece, Putto, Shaped, Pierced Bowl, Oval Reserves, Cabriole Legs, 16 x 26 In.	11500
Centerpiece, Schneeballen, Bottle Shape, Vines, Petals, Canaries, c.1910, 18 In.	3750
Centerpiece, Woman, Leaning Into Bowl, Applied Flowers, c.1920, 7 x 13 In.	938
Charger, Pate-Sur-Pate, Figures, Embracing Couple, Reticulated Rim, 8 ⅝ In. Diam.	3000
Chocolate Pot, Undertray, Flower Panels, Gilt Scrolls, Loop Handle, c.1900, 11 x 8 In.	799
Clock, Multicolor Applied Flowers, 4 Seasons Putti, Cartouche Shape, Enamel Dial, 12 x 19 In.	2420
Clock, Shelf, Porcelain, Applied Dresden Flowers, Brass, Maple Et Cie Clockworks, c.1860, 11 In. ...illus	2688
Compote, Grape & Leaf, Gilt, 1880s, 5 x 8 ¼ In.	795
Compote, Overlapping Leaves, Cobalt Blue & White, Gold Trim, Shaped Edge, 9 ½ In.	207
Cup, Centennial, Gilt Eagle, Profile Portraits, Presidents, Scroll Handle, c.1885, 5 x 5 In.	799
Cup, Stirrup, Fox Head Shape, c.1850, 3 ¼ In., Pair	1778
Figurine, 2 Girls, Draped In Green, Purple, Flowers, 4 ½ In.	406
Figurine, Boy, Seated, Eating Grapes, c.1910, 4 ½ In.	299
Figurine, Cherub, Holding Tasseled Pillow, Heart On Top, Marked, 1800s, 6 ½ In.	1534
Figurine, Dog, Tail Up, Bottger Steinzeug, 20th Century, 8 x 12 x 6 In.	150
Figurine, Eagle, On Stump, Naturalistic Style, Rockwork Base, Blue Crossed Swords, 24 In.	3042
Figurine, Girl, Hugging Cat, Seated, Wearing Bonnet, Konrad Hentschel, 5 In.	1320
Figurine, Good Housekeeper, Woman, Book, Table, Spinning Wheel, c.1900, 7 In.	375
Figurine, Lovers, Basket Of Flowers, Man Touches Woman's Face With Rose, 7 ¾ In.	1200
Figurine, Man, Child, Peering Into Blue Bowl, Jugendstil Devils, 5 ¼ In.	493
Figurine, Man, Woman, Holding Flower Garlands, Marked, 6 ½ In., Pair	885
Figurine, Monkey, Holding Flute, 2 Drums On Back, Multicolor, Marked, 5 ¼ In., Pair	767
Figurine, Putto, Holding Broken Arrow, Bow At Feet, Marbleized Socle Base, 7 ¼ In.	600
Figurine, Putto, Holding Eirath's Contract Scroll, Round Base, 11 In.	1815
Figurine, Tabby Cat, Crouching, Crossed Swords Mark, Underglaze Blue, c.1890, 5 ½ In.	420
Figurine, Woman Holding Basket, Man With Grapes On Back, c.1865, 5 In., Pair	649
Figurine, Woman, 1700s Attire, Dog, Lavender Bow On Neck, 7 x 3 ¾ In.	604
Figurine, Woman, Holding Basket, Pulling Skirt Up, Hat, c.1890, 8 In.	270
Figurine, Woman, Selling Flowers, Marked, 7 ½ In.	625
Fruit Cooler, Lid, Strawberry Finial, Applied Flowers, Birds, Green Handles, 11 x 8 In.	1452
Group, 3 Children Playing, Multicolor, Gilt, 3 ½ In.	261
Group, 4 Children, Collecting Flowers, 6 ½ x 6 In.	600
Group, 4 Children, Playing, On Pedestal, Marked, 6 ½ In.	1180
Group, Abduction Of Persephone By Pluto, Molded Base, 1800s, 8 In.	418
Group, Allegorical, 2 Women, 2 Children, 1 In Net, Mark, c.1900, 12 ½ In.	2280
Group, Boy Feeding Geese, Marked, 1800s, 5 ¼ In. ....illus	492
Group, Broken Bridge, Gilt, Multicolor Enamel, Crossed Swords Mark, 9 ½ In.	1900
Group, Children, Bird, On Cage, Flowers, Marked, 1800s, 5 ¾ In.	708
Group, Courtship, Gentleman, Woman, Bouquet, Blue Underglaze Mark, c.1910, 7 In. ......illus	492
Group, Cupid, Sharpening Arrows, Tree, Flowers, 1800s, 7 In.	531
Group, Gentleman, Helping Woman Up From Chair, Period Attire, 1800s, 6 In.	1888
Group, Man Holding Lamb, Woman, Spaniel, c.1800, 7 ½ In. ....illus	649
Group, Man, Woman Musicians, Period Attire, Dog, 9 ¼ In.	1375
Group, Mary, Hand Over Flame, Cherub, Crossed Swords Mark, 12 ½ In. ....illus	615
Group, Nymph Captured, Tritonefang, Incised, c.1910, 8 x 15 x 10 In.	920
Group, Putti, Holding Ledger, Kneeling, Book Stack, Scroll Base, 1800, 4 ½ x 4 ½ In.	418
Group, Satirical, 2 Putti, Lamb In Crib, Monkey, Crossed Swords Mark, 6 ¼ In.	360
Group, Woman, Painting, Putto, Crossed Swords Mark, 12 In. ....illus	1250
Jar, Lid, Gilt, Blue, Flowers, Baluster, Ring Foot, Finial, Marked, 1800s, 14 In.	295
Jewelry Box, Cartouche, Couple Seated At Table, Gilt Flowers, 8 x 6 In.	1020
Match Holder, Cherub, Standing In Fountain, Holding Bellows, Marked, 1800s, 7 ½ In.	1888
Plate, Dessert, Blue, Cream, Gilt, Basket Weave Border, Flowers Center, 8 In., 12 Piece	344

Medical, Jar, Apothecary, Lid, Porcelain, Gilt, Caduceus, Oval Reserve, 1800s, 10 In., Pair
$478

Neal Auction Co.

Meissen, Cane Handle, Woman, Gilt Accents, Blue Crossed Swords, c.1890, 4 ¾ In.
$800

Cowan's Auctions

M

Meissen, Clock, Shelf, Porcelain, Applied Dresden Flowers, Brass, Maple Et Cie Clockworks, c.1860, 11 In.
$2,688

Theriault's

Meissen, Group, Boy Feeding Geese, Marked, 1800s, 5 ¼ In.
$492

Cowan's Auctions

Meissen, Group, Courtship, Gentleman, Woman, Bouquet, Blue Underglaze Mark, c.1910, 7 In.
$492

Cowan's Auctions

Meissen, Group, Man Holding Lamb, Woman, Spaniel, c.1800, 7 ½ In.
$649

Conestoga Auction Co., Inc.

Meissen, Group, Mary, Hand Over Flame, Cherub, Crossed Swords Mark, 12 ½ In.
$615

Cowan's Auctions

Meissen, Group, Woman, Painting, Putto, Crossed Swords Mark, 12 In.
$1,250

Leslie Hindman Auctioneers

Merrimac, Vase, Red & Green Textured Glaze, c.1900, 12 ½ In.
$7,500

Skinner Auctioneers & Appraisers

Merrimac, Vase, Volcanic Glaze, Blue Matte Band, Marked, c.1900, 5 In.
$480

Skinner Auctioneers & Appraisers

Metlox, Cookie Jar, Raggedy Andy, Marked, Poppytrail, Calif. USA
$24

Victorian Casino Antiques

Platter, Red Dragon, Shaped Gilt Rim, Mark, 20th Century, 19 ¾ In.	180
Potpourri, Flowers, Reticulated Lid, Scroll Leaf Handles, Cherub, 1800s, 28 x 17 In.	5490
Salt, Double, Girl, Seated, 2 Basket Cellars, 5 ¾ In.	313
Salt, Master, Reclining Maid, Oval Bowl, 7 In.	563
Stein, Porcelain, Multicolor Flowers, Painted, Silver Lid & Foot Rings, c.1850, 1 Liter, 7 ½ In.	2520
Teapot, Flowers, White Ground, 9 In.	688
Tray, Writing, Painted & Applied Flowers, Gold Trim, Inkwell & Sander, 6 x 9 In., 3 Piece	230
Urn, Cobalt Blue, Gilt, Serpent Handles, Floral Sprays, Fluting, Trumpet Foot, c.1800s, 11 In.	984
Urn, Potpourri, Figures, Openwork Lid, Flowers, Scroll Handles, Cherub, 1800s, 28 In.	3660
Urn, Round Lift Lid, Putto Finial, Insects, Flowers, Fruit, Dolphin, Marked, 11 In., Pair	1625
Urn, White, Gilt, Entwined Snake Handles, 18 ½ In., Pair	1573
Vase, Art Nouveau, Pate-Sur-Pate, 3 Graces, c.1900, Crossed Sword, 9 x 3 ½ In.	16250

MERCURY GLASS, or silvered glass, was first made in the 1850s. It lost favor for a while but became popular again about 1910. It looks like a piece of silver.

Bottle Stopper, Mushroom Shape, 3 x 2 In., Pair	50
Bowl, Footed, 5 ½ x 1 ⅞ In.	85
Bowl, Leaves, Berries, Birds, 7 In.	120
Candlestick, Grape & Leaf Design, c.1880, 9 ¾ In.	135
Figure, Reindeer, Standing, 1920s, 5 x 4 In.	45
Garland, Green, Beads, ⅝ x 36 In.	20
Goblet, c.1870, 5 ¾ In.	95
Jar, Lid, Gold, Knob, 5 x 3 ½ In.	75
Ornament, Dutch Girl, Pink Scarf & Dress, 6 In.	69
Ornament, Santa Claus, Clip-On, c.1930, 4 In.	65
Ornament, Swan, 3 In.	49
Ornament, Swan, Tinsel Tail, Clip-On, 3 x 4 In.	30
Ornament, Zebra, Stripes, 1930s, 3 ½ In.	125
Vase, Diagonal Swirl, Rimmed Lip, 19th Century, 5 ½ x 5 ½ In.	200

MERRIMAC POTTERY Company was founded by Thomas Nickerson in Newburyport, Massachusetts, in 1902. The company made art pottery, garden pottery, and reproductions of Roman pottery. The pottery burned to the ground in 1908.

Vase, Leaves, Carved & Applied, Green Crystalline Glaze, Squat, c.1905, 5 x 5 In.	2875
Vase, Red & Green Textured Glaze, c.1900, 12 ½ In. *illus*	7500
Vase, Volcanic Glaze, Blue Matte Band, Marked, c.1900, 5 In. *illus*	480

METLOX POTTERIES was founded in 1927 in Manhattan Beach, California. Dinnerware was made beginning in 1931. Evan K. Shaw purchased the company in 1946 and expanded the number of patterns. Poppytrail (1946–89) and Vernonware (1958–80) were divisions of Metlox under E.K. Shaw's direction. The factory closed in 1989.

American Heritage, Cup & Saucer	8
American Heritage, Plate, Dinner, 10 ⅞ In.	9
Anytime, Creamer, 12 Oz., 4 In.	10
Aztec, Butter, Cover, Oval	129
Aztec, Celery Dish, 12 ¾ In.	41
Aztec, Cup & Saucer	9
Aztec, Gravy Boat	27
Aztec, Plate, Dinner, 10 ¼ In.	20
Aztec, Salt & Pepper	41
Beverly, Bowl, Vegetable, Oval, 9 In.	15
Beverly, Plate, Bread & Butter, 6 ½ In.	5
Blue Indigo, Cup & Saucer	7
Blue Indigo, Gravy Boat	19
California Apple, Bowl, Fruit, 5 ¼ In.	8
California Apple, Cup & Saucer	10
California Apple, Plate, Dinner, 10 ⅜ In.	21
California Apple, Platter, Oval, 13 In.	15
California Ivy, Bowl, Dessert, 5 ¼ In.	9
California Ivy, Cup & Saucer	11
California Ivy, Plate, Dinner, 10 ⅜ In.	19
California Rose, Bowl, Vegetable, Round, 9 In.	30
California Rose, Bowl, Vegetable, Round, Lid, Qt., 5 ¾ In.	59
California Rose, Creamer, 8 Oz., 3 ½ In.	12
California Rose, Platter, Oval, 13 In.	23

Mettlach, Figurine, No. 2157, Bartender, Keg, 10 In.
$575

Fox Auctions

Mettlach, Plaque, No. 126/1044 & 127/1044, Hunting Dog Scene, 16 ¼ In., Pair
$336

The Stein Auction Co.

M

Mettlach Was Famous
Mettlach steins were popular in America and won awards at the World's Fairs in the United States in 1876, 1893, and 1904.

Mettlach, Plaque, No. 2697, Gnome Eating, Mushrooms, H. Schlitt, 17 ½ In.
$4,200

The Stein Auction Co.

This is an edited listing of current prices. Visit **Kovels.com** to check thousands of prices from previous years and sign up for free information on trends, tips, reproductions, marks, and more.

Mettlach, Plaque, No. 2997, Woman Picking Fruit, Etched, 17 ½ In. $3,360

The Stein Auction Co.

Mettlach, Punch Bowl, No. 3360, Etched, Art Nouveau, 8 Liter $600

The Stein Auction Co.

M

Mettlach, Stein, No. 1949, Lovers, Flower Inlaid Lid, Etched, 2 Liter $484

Fox Auctions

How Bright the Light?
The light from one regular 60-watt lightbulb is equal to the light from twenty-five double-wick whale-oil lamps used in the nineteenth century.

Cape Cod, Bowl, Vegetable, Divided, Rectangular, 8 In.	21
Cape Cod, Cup & Saucer	8
Cape Cod, Plate, Dinner, 10 ½ In.	12
Cookie Jar, Bear, Sombrero, Fringed Serape, Grinning, 14 In.	75
Cookie Jar, Frosty The Penguin, Yellow Scarf & Cap, Smiling, 11 ¾ In.	95
Cookie Jar, Raggedy Andy, Marked, Poppytrail, Calif. USA ....*illus*	24
Del Rey, Chop Plate, 13 In.	37
Del Rey, Creamer, 8 Oz., 5 In.	12
Del Rey, Gravy Boat, Underplate	43
Del Rey, Platter, Oval, 11 In.	26
Desert Bloom, Bowl, Fruit, 6 In.	9
Desert Bloom, Casserole, Lid, Oval, Qt., 9 ½ In.	114
Desert Bloom, Plate, Bread & Butter, 6 ½ In.	7
Desert Bloom, Plate, Dinner, 10 In.	19
Desert Bloom, Platter, Oval, 16 In.	84
Dolores, Bowl, Vegetable, Oval, 9 In.	23
Dolores, Chop Plate, 12 In.	26
Dolores, Cup & Saucer	17
Dolores, Gravy Boat	29
Flower Basket, Bowl, Cereal, 6 ½ In.	7
Flower Basket, Coffeepot, Lid, 7 Cup, 9 ⅜ In.	23
Flower Basket, Cup & Saucer	8
Flower Basket, Plate, Dinner, 10 ⅝ In.	7
Flower Basket, Teapot, Lid, 5 Cup, 4 ⅜ In.	40
Fruitdale, Bowl, Vegetable, Round, 9 In.	38
Fruitdale, Chop Plate, 13 In.	43
Fruitdale, Cup & Saucer	9
Fruitdale, Salt & Pepper	31
Golden Fruit, Bowl, Cereal, 7 ¼ In.	9
Golden Fruit, Bowl, Dessert, 6 ¼ In.	6
Golden Fruit, Cup & Saucer	6
Golden Fruit, Plate, Dinner, 10 ⅝ In.	9
Golden Fruit, Platter, Oval, 16 In.	50
Harvest, Chop Plate, 12 In.	48
Heyday, Butter, Cover, ½ Lb.	21
Heyday, Cup & Saucer	7
Heyday, Pitcher, 16 Oz., 6 ⅛ In.	22
Homespun, Creamer, 10 Oz., 2 ⅝ In.	12
Homespun, Cup & Saucer	9
Homespun, Mug, 3 ½ In.	45
Homespun, Plate, Dinner, 10 ½ In.	45
Imperial, Coffeepot, 7 Cup, 9 ½ In.	89
Imperial, Cup & Saucer	8
Jamestown, Cup & Saucer	8
Jamestown, Pitcher, 32 Oz., 6 ⅞ In.	21
Jamestown, Plate, Bread & Butter, 6 ½ In.	7
Mardi Gras, Plate, Bread & Butter, 6 ⅜ In.	6
Marina, Casserole, Lid, Round, 6 In.	55
Marina, Cup & Saucer	5
Marina, Platter, Oval, 13 In.	17
Navajo, Bowl, Vegetable, Oval, 10 In.	17
Navajo, Cup & Saucer	6
Navajo, Relish, Divided, 15 In.	11
Palm Springs, Butter, Cover, ¼ Lb.	15
Palm Springs, Cup & Saucer	5
Palm Springs, Gravy Boat, Underplate	20
Provincial Flower, Bowl, Cereal, 7 In.	7
Provincial Flower, Bowl, Vegetable, Round, 10 In.	16
Provincial Flower, Cup & Saucer	7
Provincial Flower, Salt & Pepper	14
Shadow Leaf, Cup & Saucer	10
Shadow Leaf, Platter, Oval, 11 In.	30
Sierra Flower, Salt & Pepper	27
Trade Winds, Cup & Saucer	4
Trade Winds, Gravy Boat	23
Tropicana, Coffeepot, Lid, 7 Cup, 8 In.	36
Tropicana, Cup & Saucer	9

Woodland Gold, Bowl, Cereal, 5 ¾ In.	11
Woodland Gold, Bowl, Fruit, 5 ½ In.	7
Woodland Gold, Bowl, Vegetable, Lid, Round, Divided, Oval, 8 In.	23
Woodland Gold, Coffeepot, Lid, 8 Cup, 8 ⅝ In.	31
Woodland Gold, Creamer, 10 Oz., 3 ⅜ In.	6
Woodland Gold, Cup & Saucer	6
Woodland Gold, Gravy Boat, Underplate	17
Woodland Gold, Plate, Bread & Butter, 6 ⅜ In.	6
Woodland Gold, Plate, Dinner, 10 ⅜ In.	15
Young In Heart, Chop Plate, 12 In.	47
Young In Heart, Plate, Dinner, 10 In.	23
Young In Heart, Relish, 8 In.	17

METTLACH, Germany, is a city where the Villeroy and Boch factories worked. Steins from the firm are marked with the word *Mettlach* or the castle mark. They date from about 1842. *PUG* means painted under glaze. The steins can be dated from the marks on the bottom, which include a date-number code. Other pieces may be listed in the Villeroy & Boch category.

Ashtray, No. 2906, Art Nouveau, 4 In., Diam.	168
Charger, No. 2542, Maiden At Pond, R. Thevenin, 16 In.	847
Coaster, No. 1032, Drinking Dwarfs, PUG	60
Coaster, No. 2820, Cavalier Holds Stein, Etched, 4 ½ In.	96
Figurine, No. 2157, Bartender, Keg, 10 In. ....*illus*	575
Font, No. 47, Winged Angel, Earlyware, Platinum, 7 ½ In.	240
Jar, No. 1203, Mosaic, Silver Plate, Lid & Handle, Cylindrical, 7 In.	216
Jar, No. 1204, Mosaic, Silver Plate, Lid & Handle, 3 In.	228
Jar, No. 1347, Mosaic, Silver Plate, Lid & Handle, Barrel Shape, 7 In.	300
Jardiniere, No. 3041, Cameo, Women, 4 x 11 In.	84
Paperweight, Figural, Dwarf Lying In Grass, 6 x 3 ¼ In.	192
Pin Box, No. 7106, Phanolith, Lid, Round, 2 In.	336
Plaque, No. 126/1044 & 127/1044, Hunting Dog Scene, 16 ¼ In., Pair ....*illus*	336
Plaque, No. 128/1044, Hand Painted, Nurnberg Shloss, 12 In.	60
Plaque, No. 2549, Art Nouveau, Woman, Amid Lilies, Etched, 18 In.	480
Plaque, No. 2697, Gnome Eating, Mushrooms, H. Schlitt, 17 ½ In. ....*illus*	4200
Plaque, No. 2997, Woman Picking Fruit, Etched, 17 ½ In. ....*illus*	3360
Pokal, No. 1735, Etched, Couple, Raised Glass, Lid, 2 Liter, 19 In.	192
Pokal, No. 1785, Etched, Painted Figures, Helmeted Figure Heads, No Lid, 14 ¾ In.	636
Punch Bowl, Lid, No. 3037-1226, Bacharach In Rhein, PUG, 4 Liter	120
Punch Bowl, No. 3360, Etched, Art Nouveau, 8 Liter ....*illus*	600
Stein, Military, Wurttemberg, PUG, ½ Liter	1450
Stein, No. 376, Relief, Figural, Tree Trunk, Branch Handle, Inlaid Lid, Early Ware, 1 Liter	312
Stein, No. 1028, Domestic Scene, Porcelain, Pewter, c.1910, 13 x 6 ½ In.	88
Stein, No. 1949, Lovers, Flower Inlaid Lid, Etched, 2 Liter ....*illus*	484
Stein, No. 1995, Man, Drinking, Etched, Inlaid Lid, ½ Liter	264
Stein, No. 2191, ½ Liter, Roman Soldiers, Hiding Maiden, H. Schiltt, Pewter Lid, 9 ¼ In.	184
Stein, No. 2284, Relief, Pewter Lid, 4 In.	288
Stein, No. 2373, St. Augustine, Coat Of Arms, City Gate, Ft. Marion, Alligator Handle, 8 ½ In.	546
Stein, No. 2388, Pretzel, Inlaid Lid, ½ Liter	240
Stein, No. 2900, Etched, Inlaid Lid, 1906 Version, ½ Liter	216
Stein, No. 5192, Bulbous, Footed, Delft, Thumblift, 5 Liter	510
Tile, No. 1376, Portrait, Woman, Etched, Frame, 9 x 9 In. ....*illus*	216
Vase, No. 2416, Art Nouveau, Flowers, Daisies, Lilies, Etched, 6 Loop Handles, 16 In.	930
Vase, No. 2913, Etched, Art Nouveau, 13 ¾ In. ....*illus*	360
Vase, No. 3048, Art Deco, Handles, 12 In. ....*illus*	450

MILK GLASS was named for its milky white color. It was first made in England during the 1700s. The height of its popularity in the United States was from 1870 to 1880. It is now correct to refer to some colored glass as blue milk glass, black milk glass, etc. Reproductions of milk glass are being made and sold in many stores. Related pieces may be listed in the Cosmos, Vallerysthal, and Westmoreland categories.

Ashtray, Black, 3-Sided	20
Basket, Hobnail, Ruffled Rim, 12 ½ In.	30
Biscuit Jar, Painted White & Green Flowers, Oval, Silver Lid & Bail Handle, 8 In.	35
Bottle, Swirled Design, Stopper, Gilt, Victorian, 11 ½ In.	60
Bowl, Grapes, Scalloped Edge, 5 x 7 x 1 In., Pair	14
Bowl, Ruffled Rim, Molded Roses & Leaves, 8 In.	27

Mettlach, Tile, No. 1376, Portrait, Woman, Etched, Frame, 9 x 9 In.
$216

The Stein Auction Co.

Mettlach, Vase, No. 2913, Etched, Art Nouveau, 13 ¾ In.
$360

The Stein Auction Co.

Mettlach, Vase, No. 3048, Art Deco, Handles, 12 In.
$450

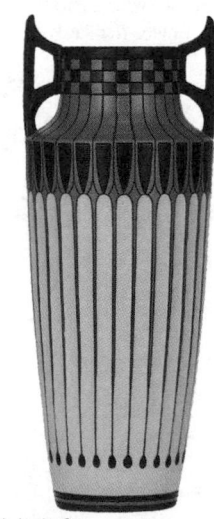

The Stein Auction Co.

M

Milk Glass, Ink Bottle, Cottage, S.I. Comp, Tooled Lip, Pennsylvania, 2 ⅝ In.
$345

Glass Works Auctions

Minton, Compote, Children, Enamel, Emile Lessore, Impressed Mark, c.1860, 10 ¾ In.
$660

Skinner Auctioneers & Appraisers

Minton, Pitcher, Wine, Henri Deux, Inlaid Clay, Dragon Handle, Footed, C. Toft, c.1875, 10 In.
$9,000

Skinner Auctioneers & Appraisers

Cake Stand, Constellation Pattern, Rum Well, Indiana Glass, 7 x 10 x 10 In.	110
Compote, Columbia, Figural Bust Stem, Fluted Sides, Scalloped Rim, 7 ½ x 8 ½ In.	30
Compote, Leaves, 1970s, 6 ½ In.	7
Compote, Raised Diamonds, Paneled Pedestal, Round Foot, Sawtooth Edge, 10 x 9 In.	36
Creamer, Colonial Man's Head, Federal Glass, 3 ½ In.	18
Cruet Set, Forget-Me-Not, Blue, Lobed, Cruet, Salt & Pepper, Tray, 4 Piece	58
Dish, Fox Lid, Lattice Edges, Atterbury Glass Co., c.1900, 8 x 6 ½ x 7 In.	100
Dish, Resting Cat Lid, Lattice Rim, Atterbury Glass, c.1889, 8 x 4 x 5 In.	125
Dish, Squirrel On Acorn Lid, Leaf Foot, Blue, 7 In.	64
Humidor, Hand Painted Pipe, Metal Lid, Art Nouveau	64
Ink Bottle, Cottage, S.I. Comp, Tooled Lip, Pennsylvania, 2 ⅝ In. ....*illus*	345
Inkwell, Opalescent, Strawberry Shape, Wavy Leaf Stand, 8 x 7 In.	50
Measuring Cup, Red Trim, Hazel Atlas, Qt.	98
Mug, Man, Flower, Enamel Design, Stiegel Type, c.1850, 6 In.	180
Plate, Eagles, Flags & Fleur-De-Lis Border, c.1903, 8 ¾ In.	55
Plate, Split Log Border, Abe Lincoln Portrait, 6 x 8 In.	225
Platter, Fish Shape, Glasbake, 17 ¾ x 8 ½ In.	18
Relish, 3 Sections, Double Scalloped Rim, Gilt, 10 In.	32
Rolling Pin, Imperial, Turned Wood Handles, Pat'd. 1921	17
Salt & Pepper, Apple Blossom, Lattice Ground, Painted, Bulbous, Metal Lids	29
Salt & Pepper, Apple Blossom, Pink, White Blossoms	29
Shade, Beehive, Art Deco, 8 x 6 ½ In.	50
Shaker, Figural, Man In Tuxedo & Hat, Atterbury, 6 ½ In.	125
Shaker, Grape & Leaf, Victorian, 3 ⅝ In.	40
Shoe, Hobnail, 6 x 2 In.	23
Strawholder, Ribbon Pattern, Metal Lid, 12 In.	450
Sugar & Creamer, Raised Flower Border, c.1935	38
Sugar Shaker, Lid, Netted Oak, Opaque, Gilt, Northwood, 4 x 3 In.	58
Syrup, Bellflower Vine, Vertical Flutes, Oval, Hinged Britannia Lid, 6 ½ In.	132
Syrup, Wedding Ring Band, Fiery Opalescent, Pear Shape, Footed, Metal Lid, 6 ⅜ In.	72
Table Set, Coreopsis, Painted, Pink Trim, Sugar, Creamer, Butter, Spooner, 4 Piece	148
Toby Jar, Owl Shape, Atterbury Glass, 6 ¾ In.	48
Tray, Shell Shape, Cherub, Wings, Avon, 1960s, 6 x 4 In.	10
Umbrella Vase, Thistles, Leaves, Raised, 18 In.	350
Vase, Embossed Birds & Branches, 4-Sided, Swollen Shape, 6 ½ In.	12
Water Set, Painted Purple Flowers, Gold Swag, 8 ½-In. Pitcher, 7 Piece	88

MINTON china has been made in the Staffordshire region of England from 1793 to the present. The firm became part of the Royal Doulton Tableware Group in 1968, but the wares continued to be marked *Minton*. In 2009 the brand was bought by KPS Capital Partners of New York and became part of WWRD Holdings. Many marks have been used. The word *England* was added in 1891. Minton majolica is listed in this book in the Majolica category.

Bread Plate, Encaustic, Waste Not Want Not, A.W.N. Pugin, Stamped, England, c.1850, 13 In.	2375
Compote, Children, Enamel, Emile Lessore, Impressed Mark, c.1860, 10 ¾ In. ....*illus*	660
Demitasse Cup & Saucer, Flowers, Leaves, 2-Tone Blue, Gilt Trim, Tiffany, 3 x 4 In.	396
Dish, Oval, Molded Wells, Quatrefoil, Angel & Devil Masks, 1873, 20 In.	240
Figurine, Babes In Woods, 2 Sleeping Children, White, Parian, England, c.1850, 6 x 12 In.	69
Figurine, Lady Of The Lake, Woman, Holding Oar, White, Parian, c.1870, 37 In.	963
Figurine, Reader, Classical Woman, Book, Leaning On Pillar, White, Blue, c.1875, 18 In.	546
Garden Seat, Yellow Flowers, Cobalt Blue, Gilt, c.1881, 18 x 13 In., Pair	625
Jardiniere, Blue Majolica, Medallion Bust, Band, Ring Handles, c.1890, 8 x 12 In., Pair	2000
Jardiniere, Underplate, Ram's Head Masks, Garland, Lobed, Tapered, 15 x 17 In., Pair	1875
Oyster Plate, 6 Wells, Cobalt Blue, White Shell & Seaweed Decoration, Majolica, Minton, 9 In.	1876
Pitcher, Wine, Henri Deux, Inlaid Clay, Dragon Handle, Footed, C. Toft, c.1875, 10 In. ....*illus*	9000
Plate, Blue Ground, Gilt Butterfly, Flowers, 9 ½ In., 5 Piece	73
Plate, York Pattern, Flowers, Leaves, 10 In., 12 Piece	180
Tea Set, Turquoise Cockatrice, Pink Bird, Teapot, Creamer, Sugar, Plates, Cups, Saucers, 19 Piece	180
Umbrella Stand, Art Nouveau, Stylized Flowers, Blue, Green, 19 In.	1089
Vase, Pate-Sur-Pate Flowers, White, Blue, Lid, Base, Aesthetic Movement, 11 In.	1250
Vase, Pomegranate Design, Blue Ground, Flared, Signed, 4 ¾ x 8 ¼ In.	313
Vase, Pomegranate, Elongated Neck, Tree Branch Handle, Leaves, Fruit, 1879, 21 In.	510
Vase, Red, Yellow Flowers, Green Leaves, Dark Ground, Cylindrical, Marked, 5 ½ x 13 In.	625
Vase, Yellow Bamboo Cylinder, Applied Playful Monkeys, Majolica, c.1872, 7 ⅜ In., Pair	4688

MIRRORS *are listed in the Furniture category under Mirror.*

MOCHA pottery is an English-made product that was sold in America during the early 1800s. It is a heavy pottery with pale coffee-and-cream coloring. Designs of blue, brown, green, orange, black, or white were added to the pottery and given fanciful names, such as Tree, Snail Trail, or Moss. Mocha designs are sometimes found on pearlware. A few pieces of mocha ware were made in France, the United States, and other countries.

Bowl, Earthworm, Bands, Green, Rust, Black, c.1810, 5 ¼ x 9 ⅞ In. ....*illus*	780
Creamer, Fury, Steam Engine Transfer, Blue Banding, c.1850, 3 ¾ In..	60
Creamer, Seaweed, c.1850, 7 ½ In..	1007
Jug, Mustard, Marbleized, Applied Loop Handle, 2 ¾ In...	295
Mug, Cat's-Eye, Applied Loop Handle, Leaf Ends, Straight Sides, 3 ¾ In................................	708
Mug, Earthworm, Looping, Applied Loop Handle, Leaf Ends, Straight-Sided, 3 ½ In....................	266
Mug, Frog Interior, Engine Turned, Banding, Leaves, c.1785, 4 ⅝ In.......................................	461
Mug, Seaweed, Black, Blue, Tan Band, Marked Quart, 6 In.	118
Mug, Strap Handle, Pale Green, Yellow, Orange, Brown, Banded, Tooled, c.1840, 6 In.	1725
Mug, Zigzag, Blue, Rust, Brown, White, Bands, c.1810, 4 ⅞ In. ....*illus*	369
Mustard Pot, Marbleized, Silver Mounted, Brown, Hinged Lid, c.1810, 3 ½ In.	180
Pitcher, Barrel Shape, Marbleized, Applied Loop Handle, 4 ½ In...	649
Pitcher, Blue, Black, White, Oval, Flared Foot, c.1840, 8 x 5 ½ In..	316
Pitcher, Blue, Brown Ribbed Bands, 7 In..	948
Pitcher, Cat's-Eye, Handle, Rust Banding, c.1815, 7 ⅛ In.	738
Pitcher, Cat's-Eye, Seaweed, Red, Green, Blue, c.1830, 7 ¾ In.	1215
Pitcher, Earthworm, Blue & White, Banded, Loop Handle, 1800s, 7 x 8 ½ In...........................	118
Pitcher, Earthworm, Zigzag, Barrel Shape, c.1815, 8 ½ In.	960
Pitcher, Marbleized, Full Body, Applied Loop Handle, Flower Ends, 4 In. ....*illus*	2124
Pitcher, Oval, Orange, White Bands, Engine Turned, 7 In..	1541
Pitcher, Seaweed, Olive, Blue, Rust, Bands, c.1810, 7 ⅜ In. ....*illus*	677
Pitcher, Strap Handle, Flowers, Brown, Orange, Banded, Tooled, England, c.1840, 7 ½ In.	3450
Porringer, Earthworm, Bands, Cream, Yellow, Brown, Handle, 1800s, 2 ½ In. ....*illus*	330
Wine Coaster, Earthworm, Blue Bands, Yellowware, c.1870, 2 ¾ x 4 In. ....*illus*	420

MONMOUTH POTTERY COMPANY started working in Monmouth, Illinois, in 1892. The pottery made a variety of utilitarian wares. It became part of Western Stoneware Company in 1906. The maple leaf mark was used until 1930. If *Co.* appears as part of the mark, the piece was made before 1906.

Ashtray, Brown, Maple Leaf Logo, 4 x 1 In.	66
Bowl, Brown Mirror, Marked, Maple Leaf, 10 In...	40
Crock, Maple Leaf, 2 Gal., 9 ¾ x 9 ¼ In...	35
Pitcher, Teal Green, Raised Deco Fan, 6 In..	25
Syrup, Lid, Ribbed, Stick Neck, Handle, Brown, 11 In...	85
Vase, Fern, Yellow, Footed, 1940s, 8 ½ x 11 x 4 In..	54
Vase, Gray Green, Ribbed, Handles, Raised Maple Leaf, 8 In..	70

MONT JOYE, *see Mt. Joye category.*

MOORCROFT pottery was first made in Burslem, England, in 1913. William Moorcroft had managed the art pottery department for James Macintyre & Company of England from 1898 to 1913. The Moorcroft pottery continues today, although William Moorcroft died in 1945. The earlier wares are similar to the modern ones, but color and marking will help indicate the age.

Bowl, Eventide, 2 Green Trees, Cobalt Blue Ground, 1 ¼ x 7 ½ In.	1500
Bowl, Florian, Green, Blue, Marked, 2 ⅜ x 7 ¾ In..	590
Bowl, Lid, Orchid Clusters, Green & Blue Ground, Tube Lined, 3 ½ x 6 In.	200
Compote, Wisteria Pattern, Dark Blue Ground, Footed, Marked, 6 ½ x 6 ½ In............................	188
Dish, Hibiscus, Blue Ground, Shallow, 1960s...	179
Ginger Jar, Lid, Magnolia, Cobalt Blue Ground, 8 In...	196
Jar, Lid, Painted Orchids, Spring Flowers, Green Ground, Bulbous, 5 x 6 In.............................	406
Jardiniere, Pomegranates, Burslem, Signed William Moorcroft, 1917, 11 ¾ In.	826
Lamp Base, Finch Pattern, Cobalt Blue Ground, 12 ¼ In...	288
Lamp Base, Finch Pattern, Cobalt Blue Ground, Squat, 8 ½ In...	316
Lamp Base, Red Anemone, Dark Ground, Foil Label, 6 ½ x 15 In..	125
Lamp Base, Yellow, Green, Bermuda Lily, Cream Ground, Signed, 6 x 13 In.	250
Lamp, Oil, Florian, Blue, Green, Rolled Foot, 8 ⅜ In..	2950
Sugar Shaker, Pomegranate, Ocher Ground, Signed, 1913, 6 ½ In..	952
Tankard, Stylized Flowers, Wavy Lines, White Ground, Angled Handle, 9 ½ In.	224
Teapot, Squat, Footed, Trees, Blue Glaze, Hammered Pewter Lid, 4 ½ In.	600
Tile, Cherry Blossom, Frame, 8 x 8 In.	198

Mocha, Bowl, Earthworm, Bands, Green, Rust, Black, c.1810, 5 ¼ x 9 ⅞ In.
$780

Skinner Auctioneers & Appraisers

Mocha, Mug, Zigzag, Blue, Rust, Brown, White, Bands, c.1810, 4 ⅞ In.
$369

Skinner Auctioneers & Appraisers

Mocha, Pitcher, Marbleized, Full Body, Applied Loop Handle, Flower Ends, 4 In.
$2,124

Conestoga Auction Co., Inc.

M

Mocha, Pitcher, Seaweed, Olive, Blue, Rust, Bands, c.1810, 7 ⅜ In.
$677

Skinner Auctioneers & Appraisers

M

Mocha, Porringer, Earthworm, Bands, Cream, Yellow, Brown, Handle, 1800s, 2 ½ In.
$330

Skinner Auctioneers & Appraisers

Mocha, Wine Coaster, Earthworm, Blue Bands, Yellowware, c.1870, 2 ¾ x 4 In.
$420

Skinner Auctioneers & Appraisers

Moorcroft, Vase, Chrysanthemum, Macintyre, 8 ⅝ In.
$3,186

Humler & Nolan

Vase, 3 Pandas, Red, Bamboo, Pinched Waist, S. Leeper, 9 ¼ In.		862
Vase, Anemone, Blue, 1950s, 3 In.		125
Vase, Anemones, Red, Blue, Dark Blue Ground, Flared Base, Signed, 10 x 8 In.		344
Vase, Chrysanthemum, Macintyre, 8 ⅝ In.	*illus*	3186
Vase, Claremont, Mottled Blue, Brown, Cream, Signed, Marked, Liberty & Co., 6 x 4 In.		2000
Vase, Claremont, Stylized Mushrooms, Green Glaze, Stick Neck, Squat Base, 10 In.		1188
Vase, Claremont, Toadstools, Marked, 6 In.	*illus*	2185
Vase, Clematis, Red, Green, Round, Signed, 9 x 9 In.		625
Vase, Cluny, Elongated Tree Trunks, Black, Pink, Green, Swollen, 10 ¼ In.		288
Vase, Eventide, Trees, Stamped, c.1935, 8 ¼ x 5 In.		2625
Vase, Fuchsia, Green Ground, Corseted, Flared, 12 In.		207
Vase, Grape, Leaf Design, Green Ground, Round, Marked, 6 x 6 In.		188
Vase, Landscape, Red Flambe Glaze, Turned Neck, 15 x 10 ½ In.		16250
Vase, Lid, King Lear, Cobalt Blue Ground, 6 ½ In.		196
Vase, Mamoura, Stylized Water, Rocks, Sky, Swollen Top, 12 ¼ In.		288
Vase, Moonlit Blue Landscape, Shouldered, Marked, 8 x 13 In.		5760
Vase, Moorish Floral, Cobalt Blue Ground, Swollen, 10 ½ In.		259
Vase, Morning Glory, Cobalt Blue Ground, Flared, Spread Foot, 9 In.		403
Vase, Multicolor Iridescent Glaze, Flared, Applied Metal Foot, 8 x 20 ½ In.		1188
Vase, Oberon, Dark Blue Ground, Double Gourd Shape, 11 ¼ In.		316
Vase, Orange Clematis, Blue Ground, Signed, 5 In.		207
Vase, Orange Poppies, Blue & Green Ground, 7 ½ In.		945
Vase, Orchid, Green Glaze, High Shoulder, 12 ½ In.		316
Vase, Owl, Oak Leaves, Night Sky, Crescent Moon, Blue, Green, Brown, 12 ½ In.		863
Vase, Poppies, Cobalt Blue Ground, Ovoid, 6 ¼ In.		360
Vase, Poppies, Handles, Florian Ware, Macintyre Stamp, 1902-13, 4 ½ x 2 In.		2750
Vase, Red Tulip Pattern, Burgundy, Beige, Black, Swollen Top, 12 ¼ In.		316
Vase, Simeon, Multicolor Flowers, Stamped, 5 ¼ In.		177
Vase, Waratah, Flower, Squeezebag Decoration, Signed, c.1932, 8 x 5 ½ In.	*illus*	8750
Vase, Water Lily, Bulrushes, Factory Marks, 8 ½ x 3 ½ In.		259
Vase, Wisteria, Dark Blue, White Ground, Flared, Signed, 4 ¼ x 8 ½ In.		250
Vase, Yellow, Red Wisteria, Dark Ground, Flared Base, Signed, 10 x 14 In.		469

MORGANTOWN GLASS WORKS operated in Morgantown, West Virginia, from 1900 to 1974. Some of their wares are marked with an adhesive label that says *Old Morgantown Glass*.

Bowl, Janice, Amethyst, Ribbed, Rolled & Folded Rim, Footed, 4 x 3 In.		200
Champagne, Empress, Ritz Blue, Stem, 12 Piece		345
Cocktail, Chanticleer, Spanish Red, Footed		29
Cocktail, El Patio, Stiegel Green, Foot, 3 ⅛ In.		25
Cocktail, Empire, Red, Clear Stem, 6 In.	*illus*	48
Cocktail, Mayfair, Footed		15
Cocktail, Stem, Monroe, Ruby Red, 1930s, 5 In.		15
Cordial, Pagoda, Topaz, 3 In.		55
Goblet, Brilliant, Spanish Red, Crystal Stem, 10 Oz.		55
Goblet, Juice, Golf Ball, Ritz Blue, 5 Oz., 4 ⅞ In.		35
Goblet, Water, Carlton, 7 In.		15
Juice, Golf Ball, Stiegel Green, 3 Oz.		40
Pitcher, Crinkle, Leaf Green, 50 Oz., 8 In.		40
Pitcher, Crinkle, Red, 50 Oz., 8 In.		165
Sherbet, Crinkle, Amber		9
Sherbet, Golf Ball, Stiegel Green, 6 Oz., 4 ⅜ In.		35
Tumbler, Crackle, Oxford, Honey, Handle, 5 In.		35
Tumbler, Crinkle, Amber, 10 Oz., 4 ¼ In.		9
Tumbler, Crinkle, Amethyst, 4 ¼ In., 10 Oz.		12
Tumbler, Crinkle, Blue, 4 ¼ In., 10 Oz.		12
Tumbler, Crinkle, Green, 4 ¼ In., 10 Oz.		12
Tumbler, Golf Ball, Ruby Red, Clear Stem, 6 ⅛ In.		28
Tumbler, Mayfair, Footed, 12 Oz., 5 ⅝ In.		22
Vase, Bud, Jade Green, Serenade, 10 In.		65
Wine, Summer Cornucopia, Stem, 6 In.		48

MORIAGE is a special type of raised decoration used on some Japanese pottery. Sometimes pieces of clay were shaped by hand and applied to the item; sometimes the clay was squeezed from a tube in the way we apply cake frosting. One type of moriage is called Dragonware by collectors.

Biscuit Jar, Lid, Green, Pink, Purple, Flowers, Handles, 19th Century, 5 x 8 In.	265
Bowl, Handles, Dragons, Orange Center, Gilt Border, Dragonware, Japan, 5 x 4 x 1 In.	18

Cup & Saucer, Pedestal, Roosters, Multicolor, Japan	27
Dresser Box, Lid, Swans, Sunset, Paneled, Blue, Purple, Orange, Japan, 1920s, 4 x 2 In.	25
Ewer, Long Neck, Flared, Yellow Ground, Nippon, 10 In.	192
Humidor, Brass Lid, Flowers, White Ground, Nippon, c.1900, 6 x 5 x 5 In.	110
Mug, Thistles, Pansies, Purple, Yellow, Art Nouveau Style, Nippon, 1900s, 5 ½ In.	195
Plate, Roses, Blue Ground, Green, Gold, Nippon, c.1891, 10 In., 3 Piece	135
Salt & Pepper, California, Gilt Top, Dragonware, 2 ¼ In.	20
Teapot, Lid, White, Gilt Daisies, Nippon, c.1915, 8 In.	220
Vase, 2 Swans Flying, Flowers, Ruffled Rim, Stylized Dragon Handles, 12 In.	116
Vase, Arts & Crafts Style, Pinecones, Pine Needles, Gold, Scroll Handles, Nippon, 8 In.	325
Vase, Copper, Hammered, Flowering Trees, Globular, c.1930, 7 x 9 In.	1475
Vase, Square Handles, Cylindrical, Crane, Leaves, Browns, Yellow, Japan, c.1920, 15 In.	379

MOSAIC TILE COMPANY of Zanesville, Ohio, was started by Karl Langerbeck and Herman Mueller in 1894. Many types of plain and ornamental tiles were made until 1959. The company closed in 1967. The company also made some ashtrays, bookends, and related giftwares. Most pieces are marked with the entwined MTC monogram.

Figurine, Bear, Black Matte Glaze, 8 x 9 ½ In.	120
Pen Tray, Nude, Reclining, Art Deco, 9 x 4 In.	125
Tile, Elephant, Standing On Ball, Blue, Black, c.1920, 6 x 6 In.	750
Tile, Man, Woman, Boat, River, 6 x 6 In.	95
Tile, Tableau, Rotund Monk, Grinning, Holding Mug, Burled Frame, 17 ¾ x 8 In.	500

MOSER glass is made by a Bohemian (Czech) glasshouse founded by Ludwig Moser in 1857. Art Nouveau–type glassware and iridescent glassware were made. The most famous Moser glass is decorated with heavy enameling in gold and bright colors. The firm, Moser Glassworks, is still working in Karlovy Vary, Czech Republic. Few pieces of Moser glass are marked.

Bowl, Amber Glass, Hobnail, Pink Ruffled Rim, Grape Leaves, Applied Grapes, 9 In.	474
Bowl, Amber, Banded Rim, 28 Elephants, Palm Trees, Marked Moser Karlsbad, 17 In.	633
Bowl, Gilt & Crystal, Oval, Faceted Banding, Everted Rim, c.1915, 4 x 9 In.	649
Bowl, Gold Color Classical Scenes, Red Etched Glass, Round, 4 ¾ x 8 ¾ In.	219
Bowl, Stylized Leaves, Berries, 4 Applied Gilded Leaf-Shape Feet, 9 x 4 ½ In.	4148
Card Vase, Cranberry, Overall Pink Scrolling, Leaves, 4 ½ In.	259
Cordial, Multicolor, Chalice Shape, 5 ½ In., 6 Piece	432
Creamer, Marquetry, Wheel Carved, Green & Blue Flower, Intaglio Cut, Signed, 3 ¾ In.	1067
Cruet, Cranberry, Oak Leaves, Jeweled Acorns, Stopper, Signed, Label, 8 In. ....*illus*	1553
Cruet, Donut, Green, Booted, Scrolling, Flowers, Flip Lid Stopper, 8 In.	104
Decanter, Amber, Gold, Silver Copper Figures, Hexagonal, Faceted Sides, Stopper, 4 ½ x 9 In.	63
Decanter, Soldier Profile, Green, Gilt Scroll Overlay, Long Neck, Stopper, 9 x 4 In.	196
Decanter, Spanish Market, Green, Enamel Birds, Flowers, Swan Finial, 13 ½ In.	89
Dresser Box, Hinged Lid, Metal Mounts, Ring Handles, Multicolor Enamel, 4 ¼ x 6 In.	104
Ewer, Bird, Ruby Glass, Oak Leaves, Gold Vines, Raised Acorn Jewels, 12 In. ....*illus*	7475
Ewer, Cranberry, Sculptured Bird, On Applied Grapevine, Jeweled, Copper Rim, 12 In.	1265
Ewer, Emerald Green, Multicolor Enameled Flowers, Leaves, Stopper, 11 ¾ In.	948
Ewer, Green, Enamel Flowers, Scrolls, Handle, 15 In.	413
Goblet, Amethyst, Gold Overlay Basket Design, Clear Stem, 5 ¾ In., 6 Piece	319
Goblet, Cranberry, Optic Bowl, Hollow Stem, Prunts, Gilt Accents, c.1900, 6 ½ In., 5 Piece	403
Jewelry Box, Cranberry Glass, Enameled Design, Brass Mounted, 3 ¾ In.	75
Perfume Bottle, Cranberry To Clear, Octagonal, Pyramid Shape, Triangular Stopper, 6 In.	325
Saltshaker, Blue, Molded Fish, Cattail, Multicolor Enameled Highlights, 4 In.	502
Toothpick Holder, Pedestal, Green, Enamel Flowers, 3 ½ In.	83
Urn, Lid, Amber, Painted Flowers, Green, Crimson Stems, Applied Cabochons, 13 In., Pair	690
Vase, Amber Crackle, 4 Pinched Sides, Pink Enameled Flowers, Green Stems, 10 In.	790
Vase, Amber, Enameled Birds, Leaves, Acorn Jewels, Scrolling Feet, Pillow Shape, 8 ½ In.	3450
Vase, Aqua, Enamel Daisies, Poppies, Signed, 11 In., Pair	413
Vase, Bird, Flowers, Leaves, Branches, Applied Rigaree, 11 ½ In. ....*illus*	1422
Vase, Blue, Enameled Flowers, Footed, 7 ¼ In.	104
Vase, Bud, Pink Opalescent, Oak Leaves, Jeweled Acorns, Footed, 6 ¼ In.	460
Vase, Carlsbad Amber Glass, Classical Figures Metal Band, Flared, Footed, 12 In.	625
Vase, Cornucopia, Cranberry, Gilded Flowers, Pedestal Foot, 12 ½ In. ....*illus*	1422
Vase, Cranberry, White Enameled Forest Scene, Flowers, Gold Centers, Footed, 10 In., Pair	1126
Vase, Emerald Green, Cut Ovals, 6-Sided, Leafy Scrolls, 10 ⅜ In.	236
Vase, Enameled Classical Figures Band, Green Ground, Tapered, Ribbed, 11 ½ x 4 In.	138
Vase, Fish & Seaweed Crackle Glass, Gold Iridescent, 4 ¾ In.	110
Vase, Pillow, Bird, Flat Sides, Applied Pleats, Gold Reeded Feet, 7 ¼ In. ....*illus*	575

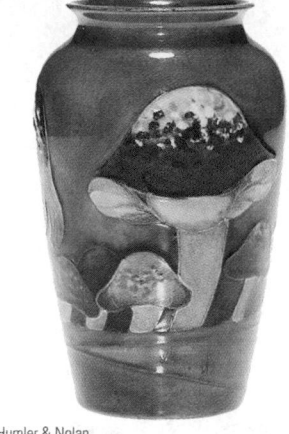

Moorcroft, Vase, Claremont, Toadstools, Marked, 6 In.

$2,185

Humler & Nolan

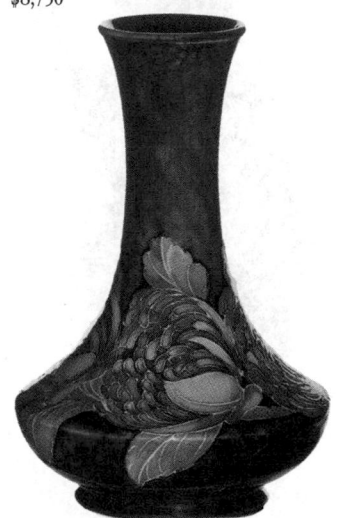

Moorcroft, Vase, Waratah, Flower, Squeezebag Decoration, Signed, c.1932, 8 x 5 ½ In.

$8,750

Rago Arts & Auction Center

Morgantown, Cocktail, Empire, Red, Clear Stem, 6 In.

$48

Ruby Lane, Inc.

M

Moser, Cruet, Cranberry, Oak Leaves, Jeweled Acorns, Stopper, Signed, Label, 8 In.
$1,553

Early Auction Co.

Collecting Is Healthy

Sometimes our collections turn out to be historically important or valuable. Most times they help keep us healthy and happy. As you age, doctors say, you should keep physically active (walk through a flea market), make new friends (join a club or go online to chat with other collectors), keep your mind active by learning something new (research prices, history, and marks for your collection), avoid obesity (at shows you get exercise—but terrible food), and stave off depression (those endorphins chase the blues).

Vase, Ruby To Clear, Flowers, Trumpet Shape, 15 ½ In.		118
Vase, Trumpet, Gilt Leaves, Flowers, Tapered, Lobed Stem, Footed, 16 In.		344
Vase, Trumpet, Paneled Design, Diamond Point Band, Gold Enamel Highlights, 10 ½ In.		472
Vase, Yellow, Engraved Deer, Oval, 5 ½ In.		136

MOTHER-OF-PEARL GLASS, or pearl satin glass, was first made in the 1850s in England and in Massachusetts. It was a special type of mold-blown satin glass with air bubbles in the glass, giving it a pearlized color. It has been reproduced. Mother-of-pearl shell objects are listed under Pearl.

Box, Hut Shape, Loose Lid, Brass Ring Handle, India, 1800s, 6 ½ x 4 ¾ In.		3000
Cruet, Pink, Melon Ribbed, Zipper Pattern, 6 In.	*illus*	2070
Dish, Shell Shape, Incised Sprigging, France, c.1865, 7 ¼ x 7 ¼ In.		553
Dresser Box, Lion & Unicorn Mark, Flower, 1 ¾ x 3 ¼ In.		189
Jar, Lid, Blue Satin, Diamond Quilted, 5 ½ In.		207
Magnifying Glass, Swing-Out Lens, Oval, Silver Plate Mounts, 3 ⅝ In.		125
Paper Knife, Tapered, Gilt Metal Napoleon End, 4 ½ In.		63
Rose Bowl, Rainbow, Alternating Frosted, Clear Stripe Bands, Diamond Quilted, 3 ½ In.		891
Rose Bowl, Squat, Green Shaded To Blue, Pinched Ruffled Rim, Zipper, Pink Inside, 5 In.		1323
Vase, Green Over Yellow, Diamond Quilted, Satin Finish, Bulbous, Flared Ruffled Rim, 13 In.		75
Vase, Pink & White Stripe, Ruffled Rim, Herringbone, Blue Flowers, Gold, 9 In.		1035
Vase, Satin Glass, Diamond Quilt, Shaded Blue, Ruffled Rim, Victorian, 10 ½ In., Pair		150
Vase, Shaded Rose Moire, Clear Rim, Jack-In-The-Pulpit Shape, 11 ¾ In.		127

MOTORCYCLES and motorcycle accessories of all types are being collected today. Examples can be found that date back to the early twentieth century. Toy motorcycles are listed in the Toy category.

Belt, Kidney, Buco, Braided Leather, Studded, Mounted, c.1950		350
Belt, Kidney, Harley-Davidson, 1940s		386
Brochure, Harley-Davidson, 4 Views, 1956, 8 x 10 In.		27
Brochure, Indian Motorcycles, 1931, 18 x 17 In.		106
Buckle, Easy Rider Style, Metal, 1970s, 3 x 2 ½ In.		18
Catalogue, Flying Merkel, Orange, Black Cover, New York		1125
Charm, Sterling Silver, ¾ In.		25
Cigarette Case, Engraved Motorcycle Racer, Silvertone, Tin, LCL Monogram, 1940s, 3 x 4 In.		250
Fuel Tank, Harley-Davidson Flat Head, Metallic Blue, 1940s, Pair		525
Gloves, Leather, Black, Men's, 13 In.		40
Jacket, Horsehide, Brown, Brent Sportsman, Men's Small, 1940s		224
License Plate, California, Black, Yellow, 1963		185
License Plate, New Jersey, Black On White, 1980, 3 x 8 In.		23
License Plate, Oklahoma, White, Red, 1967		45
Motorcycle, Harley-Davidson, 34B Single, Red, 1934		9200
Motorcycle, Henderson Four, No. 28267, Blue Frame, Black Seat, 1928		44850
Motorcycle, Honda, CL175, Blue Frame, Black Double Seat, 1972		1610
Motorcycle, Honda, S65 Frame, Engine, Blue, 1967		287
Motorcycle, Honda, Super Hawk, VTR1000, Black Seat, Red Frame, 1998		3200
Motorcycle, Indian Model, 402 Four Engine, No. EA340, Red Frame, Black Seat, 1929		73600
Motorcycle, Indian Pony Scout, Engine No. FC576, c.1938		14375
Motorcycle, Matchless, G80, Black, 1960		5750
Motorcycle, Tempo Cross, 175, Salmon Pink Frame, Orange Gas Tank, Silver, 1962		2300
Motorcycle, Triumph, Bonneville, T140, Red, White Frame, Black Seat, 1974		3565
Motorcycle, Yamaha, Bobber, XS650, Metallic Silver, 1980		4025
Painting, Santa Rosa Mile, Jim Rice Winning BSA, R. Carter, c.1970, 48 x 60 In.		2750
Pennant, Flying Merkel, Felt, Orange, Black, c.1910		1062
Photograph, Cleveland, Ohio, Police Officers, 2 Harley-Davidsons, 1930s, 8 x 10 In.		35
Plaque, 2 Racers, Garland Surround, Round, Cast Iron, c.1925, 7 In.		75
Saddlebag, Leather, Fringe, Applied Stud Design, Harley-Davidson, c.1950, Pair		275
Seat, Passenger, Handle, Denfield BMW R50S, Rubber, c.1960		275
Sign, Alcycon Bicyclettes, Motocyclettes, Riders, Going Up Hill, A. H. Rouit, 19 x 14 In.		400
Sign, BSA Moto-Cross National Poster, G. Ham, France, 1957, 23 x 15 In.		237
Sign, Dresch Stock Rechange, Man Silhouette, Red, Cream, c.1928		437
Sign, Favor Motorcycles, Bicycles, Riders, L. Mathry, France, Large, c.1930		687
Sign, Harley-Davidson Genuine Motor Oil, Porcelain, 11 In.	*illus*	575
Sign, Indian Motorcycle, Springfield, Mass., Yellow, Red Logo, Wood, Round, 24 In.		437
Sign, Le Moteurcycle, Man, Waving, Mountain, L, Rosengart, France, c.1925, 28 x 20 In.		525
Sign, Peugeot, La Grande Marque Nationale, Man, Motorcycle, Sea, G. Favre, 23 x 16 In.		312

M

Moser, Ewer, Bird, Ruby Glass, Oak Leaves, Gold Vines, Raised Acorn Jewels, 12 In.
$7,475

Early Auction Co.

Moser, Vase, Bird, Flowers, Leaves, Branches, Applied Rigaree, 11 ½ In.
$1,422

James D. Julia Auctioneers

Moser, Vase, Cornucopia, Cranberry, Gilded Flowers, Pedestal Foot, 12 ½ In.
$1,422

James D. Julia Auctioneers

Moser, Vase, Pillow, Bird, Flat Sides, Applied Pleats, Gold Reeded Feet, 7 ¼ In.
$575

Early Auction Co.

Mother-Of-Pearl, Cruet, Pink, Melon Ribbed, Zipper Pattern, 6 In.
$2,070

Early Auction Co.

Motorcycle, Sign, Harley-Davidson Genuine Motor Oil, Porcelain, 11 In.
$575

Victorian Casino Antiques

Movie, Poster, Ferdinand The Bull, Smelling Flower, R.K.O., Technicolor, 1938, 32 x 47 In.
$7,590

Hake's Americana & Collectibles

Music from the Movies
Watch out for reprints of old movie sheet music. Music before the 1960s was about 50 cents a copy. Now it is almost $3.00. The reprints are usually made to be sold in a store, not to fool the collector, so the price will be shown.

Movie, Poster, Forbidden Planet, Robby The Robot, MGM, 1956, 27 x 41 In.
$6,958

Hake's Americana & Collectibles

M

Mt.Joye, Vase, Pansies, Leaves, Shaded Clear To Opalescent, 13 ½ In. $948

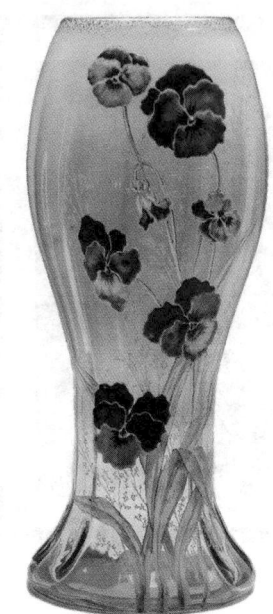

James D. Julia Auctioneers

Mt.Washington, Biscuit Jar, Napoli, Palmer Cox Brownies, Goose, Silver Plated Lid, Marked, 6 In. $5,750

Early Auction Co.

Mt.Washington, Bowl, Lava, Multicolor Shards, Folded Rim, 4 In. $1,610

Early Auction Co.

Sign, Triumph, McQueen, S McQueen Riding For USA Team, 1964, R. Carter, 36 x 56 In.	500
Skull Cap, White, Cotton, Goggle Snaps, Beck, c.1915	175

MOUNT WASHINGTON, *see Mt. Washington category.*

MOVIE memorabilia of all types are collected. Animation Art, Games, Sheet Music, Toys, and some celebrity items are listed in their own section. A lobby card is usually 11 by 14 inches, but other sizes were also made. A set of lobby cards includes seven scene cards and one title card. An American one sheet, the standard movie poster, is 27 by 41 inches. A three sheet is 40 by 81 inches. A half sheet is 22 by 28 inches. A window card, made of cardboard, is 14 by 22 inches. An insert is 14 by 36 inches. A herald is a promotional item handed out to patrons. Press books, sent to exhibitors to promote a movie, contain ads and lists of what is available for advertising, i.e., posters, lobby cards. Press kits, sent to the media, contain photos and details about the movie, i.e., stars' biographies and interviews.

Clothing, Hat, Stetson, Made For Tom Mix	2655
Costume Sketch, Cleopatra, Elizabeth Taylor, 20th Century Fox, 1963, 27 x 28 In.	4000
Insert, Barabbas, Anthony Quinn, 1962, 14 x 36 In.	20
Insert, Magic Sword, Basil Rathbone, United Artists, 1961, 14 x 36 In.	20 to 25
Insert, Voyage To The Bottom Of The Sea, 20th Century Fox, 1961, 14 x 36 In.	95
Lobby Card, Alligator Named Daisy, Diana Dors, VistaVision, 1955, 11 x 14 In., 8 Piece	80
Lobby Card, Little Women, Katharine Hepburn, 1933, 11 x 14 In.	65
Lobby Card, New Adventures Of Tarzan, Herman Brix, 1935, 11 x 14 In.	225
Lobby Card, Something For The Boys, Miranda, O'Shea, Blaine, 1944, 11 x 14 In., 6 Piece	75
Photograph, Gypsy, Natalie Wood, Shimmering Gown, Signed, 9 x 7 In.	525
Photograph, Hattie McDaniel, Wedding, Inscribed To Sister Etta, May, 1941	625
Poster, Batman Returns, Penguin's Campaign Rule Gotham, Warner Bros., Frame, 1992, 62 x 31 In.	600
Poster, Bronco Twister, Tom Mix, 1927, 22 x 28 In.	575
Poster, Children Of The Damned, Beware The Eyes That Paralyze, 1963, 27 x 41 In.	68
Poster, Clockwork Orange, Insert, Malcolm McDowell, Stanley Kubrick, 1972, 14 x 36 In.	173
Poster, Ferdinand The Bull, Smelling Flower, R.K.O., Technicolor, 1938, 32 x 47 In. ....*illus*	7590
Poster, Forbidden Planet, Robby The Robot, MGM, 1956, 27 x 41 In. ....*illus*	6958
Poster, Glass Houses, Viola Dana, 1922, 27 x 41 In.	375
Poster, Mother Wore Tights, Betty Grable, 20th Century Fox, 1947, 27 x 41 In.	85
Poster, My Gal Sal, Rita Hayworth, Victor Mature, 20th Century Fox, 1949, 41 x 27 In.	175
Poster, Ocean's 11, Frank Sinatra, Dean Martin, Warner Bros., 1960, 27 x 41 In.	1125
Poster, Psycho, Hitchcock, 1960, 27 x 41 In.	1200
Poster, Rebel Without A Cause, James Dean, Line Mounted, Nicholas Ray, 1955, 27 x 42 In.	569
Poster, Road To Morocco, Bing Crosby, Bob Hope, Dorothy Lamour, Linen Back, 27 x 41 In.	345
Poster, Souls At Sea, Gary Cooper, Paramount, 1937, 27 x 41 In.	1187
Poster, Sound Of Music, Julie Andrews, Christopher Plummer, 1965, 27 x 41 In.	1125
Poster, Stage Fright, Jane Wyman, Marlene Dietrich, Warner Bros., 1950, 40 x 30 In.	750
Poster, There's No Business Like Show Business, Merman, Monroe, O'Connor, 41 x 27 In.	234
Poster, Two-Faced Woman, Greta Garbo, Metro-Goldwyn-Mayer, 1941, 27 x 40 In.	750
Poster, You Only Live Twice, Sean Connery, United Artists, 1967, 27 x 41 In.	750
Press Kit, Artists & Models, Jack Benny, Ida Lupino, 1937, 12 x 15 In.	73
Press Kit, King Kong, Mighty Joe Young, 1956, RKO, 12 x 18 In.	75
Press Kit, Nothing Sacred, Carole Lombard, Frederic March, United Artists, 1937, 12 x 18 In.	55
Press Kit, Sky Parade, Jimmie Allen, William Gargan, Paramount, 1936, 11 x 17 In.	125
Ribbon, Coming Attractions, Diamonds Are Forever, James Bond, 1971, 4 x 8 In.	115
Screenplay, Don't Bother To Knock, Marilyn Monroe, 1951, 122 Pages	1125
Screenplay, Fedora, Billy Wilder, Annotated, 1977, 10 Pages	5000
Screenplay, Maltese Falcon, John Huston, c.1942, 8 ½ x 14 In.	2750
Title Card, Freaks, Scenes, Foamcore Mount, Tod Browning, 1949 Re-Release, 11 x 14 In.	230
Window Card, Connecticut Yankee, Will Rogers, H.C. Miner Litho Co., 1931, 14 x 22 In.	125
Window Card, Saludos Amigos, Donald Duck, Joe Carioca, RKO, 1942, 14 x 22 In.	175
Window Card, Thief Of Bagdad, Douglas Fairbanks, Ahmed On Pegasus, 1924, 11 x 22 In.	2419
Window Card, Untamed Frontier, Cotton, Winters, Brady, Universal, 1952, 14 x 22 In.	75

MT. JOYE is an enameled cameo glass made in the late nineteenth and twentieth centuries by Saint-Hilaire Touvier de Varraux and Co. of Pantin, France. This same company made De Vez glass. Pieces were usually decorated with enameling. Most pieces are not marked.

Biscuit Jar, Frosted Swirl Ground, Enamel Iris, Embossed Silver Plate Lid, Bail, 7 ¾ In.	207
Bowl, Cameo, Textured, Organic Shape, Applied Metal Flowers, Stems & Rim, 5 In.	230
Decanter, White Flower, Enameled, Gilt, Cranberry Glass, Stopper, 10 x 3 ¼ In.	242
Vase, Amethyst To Clear, Jack-In-The-Pulpit, Flowers, Gilt Rim, c.1900, 14 ¼ In.	400
Vase, Blue Cased Glass, Free-Form Rim, Gilt, Enamel Stargazer Lilies, 12 ½ x 5 In., Pair	354

Vase, Blue Translucent, Gilt Lip, Enameled Pansies, Stems, Leaves, 10 In.	593
Vase, Cameo, Textured, Gold, Cobalt Blue Stemmed Poppy, 10 In., Pair	259
Vase, Cameo, Trumpet Shape, Bulging Rim, Textured, Leafy Stem Thistle, France, 12 In.	288
Vase, Cobalt Blue, Enamel Poppies, 14 In., Pair	472
Vase, Enamel Sunflower, Gold Stencil Highlights, Cylindrical, 11 In.	148
Vase, Enamel Tulips, Transitional Amethyst To Clear, Cylindrical, 10 x 4 ½ In., Pair	350
Vase, Enameled White Flowers, Light Blue, Tapered Cylindrical, 10 In.	197
Vase, Green To Clear, Enamel Chrysanthemums, 16 In.	207
Vase, Pansies, Leaves, Shaded Clear To Opalescent, 13 ½ In. ....*illus*	948
Vase, Sapphire Blue, Enameled Pansies, Gold Stencil Highlights, 9 ½ In., Pair	384

MT. WASHINGTON Glass Works started in 1837 in South Boston, Massachusetts. In 1870 the company moved to New Bedford, Massachusetts. Many types of art glass were made there until 1894, when the company merged with Pairpoint Manufacturing Co. Amberina, Burmese, Crown Milano, Cut Glass, Peachblow, and Royal Flemish are each listed in their own category.

Biscuit Jar, Barrel Shape, Apple Blossom Branch, Silver Lid, Sea Shells, 6 In.	177
Biscuit Jar, Green, White, Pink Chrysanthemums, Silver Plate Lid, Bail, 5 ½ In.	148
Biscuit Jar, Napoli, Palmer Cox Brownies, Goose, Silver Plated Lid, Marked, 6 In. ....*illus*	5750
Bowl, Lava, Multicolor Shards, Folded Rim, 4 In. ....*illus*	1610
Bowl, Optic Diamond, Blue Daisies, Quad-Ra-Fold Rim, 3-Footed, 6 ½ In.	1495
Candlestick, Paneled Clambroth Base, Blue Petal Socket, c.1850, 8 In., Pair	123
Creamer, Satin, Double Spout, 2 Handles, 4 ½ In.	345
Cruet Set, Burmese Glass, 2 Cruets, 2 Shakers, Fluted, Pairpoint Silver Stand, 9 In.	1610
Egg Shaker, Cream Glass, Blue Berries, Colored Leaves, 4 ½ In.	115
Plate, Bristol Rose, American Brilliant, 7 In.	175
Salt & Pepper, Egg Shape, Enamel Flowers, Toronto Silver Plate Stand, 5 ½ In.	275
Salt & Pepper, Egg Shape, Flowers, Vines, Berries, 2 ½ In.	175
Saltshaker, Pillar, Ribbed, Blue Berries, Leaves, 3 ½ In.	72
Sugar & Creamer, Opal Glass, Purple, Blue Flowers, Leaves, Traceries, Ruffled, 3 ¾ & 4 In.	237
Sugar Shaker, Autumn Leaves, Acorns, Yellow Ground, Egg Shape, 4 ½ In.	297
Sugar Shaker, Egg Shape, Yellow To Orange, Raspberries, Branches, 4 ½ In.	150
Sugar Shaker, Ostrich Egg, Light Blue To Cream, Orchids, Label, 4 ¼ In.	189
Sugar Shaker, Pansies, Yellow Ground, Egg Shape, Metal Lid, 4 In.	270
Sugar Shaker, Red & White Flowers, Green Stems, 4 ½ In.	570
Toothpick Holder, Cream Color, Blue Berries, Colored Leaves, 2 ½ In.	235
Vase, Barrel, Black, Teal & Rose Shards, 7 ½ In.	1740
Vase, Cylindrical, Tapered, Spreading Flat Top, Applied Flowers, Signed, 13 ¾ In.	1500
Vase, Lava, Black Matte, Shards, 3 ½ In. ....*illus*	1067
Vase, Lava, Squatty Coupe, 2 Handles, Gilt Outlined Multicolor Shards, 3 ¾ In.	1495
Vase, Lava, Urn Shape, Colored Shards, 2 Handles, 3 ½ In.	1725
Vase, Rose Satin Glass, Diamond Quilted, Bulbous Body, Bulging Neck, 8 ¼ In.	474

MULBERRY ware was made in the Staffordshire district of England from about 1850 to 1860. The dishes were decorated with a reddish brown transfer design, now called mulberry. Many of the patterns are similar to those used for flow blue and other Staffordshire transfer wares.

Platter, Well & Tree, Gray & White, 21 In.	75
Tureen, Sauce Lid, Rose, Transferware, Blue, White, Gilt Handles	81

MULLER FRERES, French for Muller Brothers, made cameo and other glass from about 1895 to 1933. Their factory was first located in Luneville, then in nearby Croismare, France. Pieces were usually marked with the company name.

Chandelier, Wrought Iron, Art Glass, Tulip Shades, Orange, Blue, c.1900, 24 In.	1708
Lamp, 2-Light, 4-Arm Spider, Square Base, Domed Shade, Etched, c.1925, 12 In.	2280
Vase, Bats In Flight, Signed, Cameo, 6 ½ In. ....*illus*	2548
Vase, Birds, Waves, Martele Ground, White Drip, Irregular Baluster Shape, Cameo, 7 ¾ In.	10000
Vase, Brown Leaves, Orange Roses, Yellow, Oval, Rolled Rim, c.1915, 14 In.	590
Vase, Cameo, Geisha Girl, Looking At Lake, Green, Yellow, Earth Tones, Luneville, 8 ½ In.	356
Vase, Cameo, Peach, White Ground, Allover Trees, Signed, 2 In.	356
Vase, Cameo, Yellow Sunset, Dutch Scene, Sailing Ships, Windmills, Cylindrical, 7 ½ In.	546
Vase, Croismare, Berries, Leaves, Purple, Yellow, Jagged Rim, Flattened Oval, 12 ½ In.	4500
Vase, Dawn & Dusk, Double Gourd, Wheel Carved, Handle, c.1905, 8 ¼ In.	13750
Vase, Flower, Vines, Plum, Green, Peach, Long Neck, Squat Base, c.1900, 15 In.	750
Vase, Gold, Amber, Brown, Shouldered, Tapered, Luneville, 8 ½ In.	115
Vase, Painted Landscape, Dark Ground, Luneville, 6 In.	80

Mt. Washington, Vase, Lava, Black Matte, Shards, 3 ½ In.
$1,067

James D. Julia Auctioneers

Muller Freres, Vase, Bats In Flight, Signed, Cameo, 6 ½ In.
$2,548

James D. Julia Auctioneers

M

Muncie, Vase, Parakeet Pairs, Flowering Branches, Molded, R. Haley, 9 ½ x 11 In.
$1,840

Humler & Nolan

Muncie, Vase, Ruba Rombic, Green Over Rose, Matte Glaze, Marked, 8 In.
$1,003

Humler & Nolan

Music, Box, Regina, Mahogany, Double Comb, Crank, Disc, c.1900, 9 x 21 x 18 ½ In.
$2,280

Cowan's Auctions

Music, Box, Regina, Orchestral, Model 5, Mahogany, 2 Combs, 27-In. Discs, 77 ½ x 43 In.
$11,250

Leslie Hindman Auctioneers

Music, Box, Singing Bird, Bronze Filigree, Key Wind, Karl Griesbaum, 1920s, 2 ¾ x 4 In.
$3,623

Aspire Auctions

> **TIP**
> *The longer the cylinder on an old music box, the higher the price.*

Vase, Trees, Pond, Footed, Brown, Deep Red, Cameo, 7 In.	385
Vase, Yellow Cottage, Lake, Over Frost Ground, Low Waist Shape, Cameo, 6 In.	115

MUNCIE Clay Products Company was established by Charles Benham in Muncie, Indiana, in 1922. The company made pottery for the florist and giftshop trade. The company closed by 1939. Pieces are marked with the name *Muncie* or just with a system of numbers and letters, like *1A*.

Vase, Double Bud, Blue, White, 4 ¾ x 8 ½ In.	90
Vase, Floppy Hat, Green Matte Over Rose Glaze, 5 ½ In.	52
Vase, Green Matte Glaze, Over Rose, Marked, 6 ⅜ In.	30
Vase, Mottled Rust Red, Bottle Shape, 6 In.	85
Vase, Parakeet Pairs, Flowering Branches, Molded, R. Haley, 9 ½ x 11 In. ....*illus*	1840
Vase, Pillow, Handles, Red, Gray, 9 In.	135
Vase, Ruba Rombic, Green Over Rose, Matte Glaze, Marked, 8 In. ....*illus*	1003
Vase, Ruba Rombic, Multilinear, Pink & Green Matte Glaze, 4 In.	3339

MURANO, *see Glass-Venetian category.*

MUSIC boxes and musical instruments are listed here. Phonograph records, jukeboxes, phonographs, and sheet music are listed in other categories in this book.

Accordion, Metal, Cutout Design, Ivory Keys, Side Strap Handles, Alfred L. Fischer, Case	70
Accordion, Mother-Of-Pearl Inlays, George Riddle, Case, No. 4234, Italy	181
Amplifier, Gibson Lancer, Suitcase Shape, Handle, c.1965, 16 ½ x 20 In.	360
Aniphonal, Ink, On Vellum, 2-Sided, Decorative Letters, Frame, Continental, 32 x 22 In.	211
Banjo, Bacon Style, Tenor, Hard Shell Case, c.1927	177
Banjo, Bird's-Eye Maple, Mother-Of-Pearl Inlay, 30 In.	330
Banjo, Gibson Mastertone, 5-String, c.1966, 37 ½ In.	1500
Banjo, Gibson, 5-String, Hard Shell Case, RB-100, c.1965	1180
Banjo, Rover, 5-String, Model RB-20, No. 0500108, Soft Case, 37 ½ In.	79
Banjo, S.S. Stewart, Mother-Of-Pearl Inlays, 1894, 28 In.	720
Banjo, Weymann, No. 35990, 24 In.	120
Bass, Stand-Up, Maple Body, Varnished, 1800s, 77 ½ x 27 In.	448
Box Case, Regina, Style 6, Oak, Casket, Fold-Top, 27 In.	443
Box, Book-Operated, 10 Books, 100 Notes, Lohengrin, Germany, 22 x 28 x 11 In.	11500
Box, Bremond, Cylinder, Rosewood, Inlaid Scrolls, 11-In. Cylinder, 8 Tunes, 5 x 18 In.	474
Box, Carved, 13-In. Cylinder, Mandarin & Butterfly Strikers, Split Comb, 8 Tunes, 6 Bells,	1652
Box, Celestina, Wood, Paper Rolls, 14 x 15 In.	390
Box, Chest-On-Chest Shape, Enamel Mounted, Gilt, Austria, c.1900, 8 ⅜ In.	3198
Box, Concerta, Interchangeable Cylinder, Ideal, Burled Panel Inlay, 3 Cylinders, 31 x 16 In.	593
Box, Cylinder, 83-Tooth, Burl Wood Case, 9 Engraved Bells, 12 Tunes, Swiss, 10 x 28 x 12 In.	1208
Box, Cylinder, Bird's-Eye Maple, Rosewood, Drums, Bells, Organ, Castanets, c.1890, 37 In.	3000
Box, Cylinder, Black, Mandolin Style, Inlays, Key, 33 ¼ x 14 ½ In.	7800
Box, Cylinder, Burl Walnut Cabinet, 5 Bells, 18 x 11 ¾ In.	1560
Box, Cylinder, Chalet, Clock, 10 x 11 x 6 ¼ In.	553
Box, Cylinder, Mahogany, Inlaid, 13-In. Cylinder, Swiss	767
Box, Cylinder, Organ, Wood, Double Spring Barrel, Bird Window, Swiss, 33 x 17 In.	20400
Box, Cylinder, Picolo, Wood Case, 8 Tunes, 25 x 9 In.	2280
Box, Cylinder, Rosewood, Chinese Bell Ringer, Dancers, Flowers, Swiss, c.1850, 15 x 15 In.	5925
Box, Cylinder, Rosewood, Inlays, 13-In. Swiss, c.1850, 6 ½ x 24 ½ In.	948
Box, Cylinder, Walnut Burl Case, Combs, Fabrique De Geneve, 8 Tunes, 23 In.	1320
Box, Cylinder, Wood Case, 6-In. Cylinder, 3 Bells, 16 x 9 ¾ In.	1080
Box, Cylinder, Wood Case, Brass & Chrome, Label, U.S.A., 8 x 15 In.	590
Box, D. Allard & Co., Nickel, 13-In. Cylinder, Brass Bedplate, Dual Combs, Burl Walnut, 35 In.	3075
Box, G. Brendon, Cylinder, Wood, Organ, Handles, 24 x 13 In.	1800
Box, Imperial, Symphonion, No. 148, Double Offset Combs, Ratchet Wind, 6 Discs	413
Box, Kalliope, Style 50G, Inlaid Case, Single Comb, 6 Bells, 10 Discs	443
Box, Kalliope, Style 60G, Single Comb, 10 Bells, 12 13 ¼-In. Discs	1888
Box, L'Eppe, Cylinder, Ebony Case, Brass Inlay, 16 ½-In. Cylinder, 12 Tunes, 27 In.	889
Box, Mermod Freres, Cylinder, Gloria, Mahogany, Interchangeable, Zither, 33 x 12 In.	826
Box, Olympia, No. 10, Mahogany Cabinet, Carved, 20 ½-In. Disc	1534
Box, Organ, 11-In. Cylinder, 2 Pierced Soundboards, 6 Tunes, Walnut Veneer Case, 20 ½ In.	1920
Box, Paillard, Cylinder, Rosewood & Beryl, Inlaid, Mother-Of-Pearl, Zither, 12 Tunes, 36 In.	889
Box, Pallard, Interchangeable, 3 8-Tune 13-In. Cylinders, Burl Walnut, Rosewood Case, 37 In.	4920
Box, Polyphon, 4 Graduated Saucer Bells, Single Comb, Ratchet Wind, 2 8-In. Discs	472
Box, Polyphon, Walnut, Inlaid Flower & Leaves, Single Comb, 32 15 ½-In. Discs, 10 x 21 In.	770
Box, Regina, Mahogany, Double Comb, Crank, Disc, c.1900, 9 x 21 x 18 ½ In. ....*illus*	2280
Box, Regina, No. 22, Wood Case, Metal Discs, Combs, 7 ¾ x 12 ½ In.	840

Box, Regina, No. 62295, Mahogany, 15 Discs, Crank, c.1920, 11 x 17 In.	1265
Box, Regina, Orchestral, Model 5, Mahogany, 2 Combs, 27-In. Discs, 77 ½ x 43 In. *illus*	11250
Box, Regina, Reginaphone, Style 16, Duplex Comb, 12 Discs, Mahogany Cabinet	1485
Box, Regina, Style 22, Mahogany Case, Crank, Single Comb, 10 8-In. Discs	620
Box, Regina, Walnut Case, Double Comb, Crank, 12-In. Discs, c.1900, 11 x 16 ½ In.	4688
Box, S. Troll Et Fils, Cylinder, Rosewood, Inlaid, Bell, 10 Tunes, c.1880, 10 x 24 In.	497
Box, Seal, Box, Swivel Outer Panel, 7 Stacked Teeth, Micro Mosaic, 1805, 1 ¾ In.	3000
Box, Singing Bird, Bronze Filigree, Key Wind, Karl Griesbaum, 1920s, 2 ¾ x 4 In. *illus*	3623
Box, Singing Bird, Feathers, Gilt Metal, Brass Perch, c.1850, 11 In.	3080
Box, Singing Bird, In Brass Cage..	764
Box, Singing Bird, Peasant Scenes, Silver Gilt, Germany, c.1900, 3 ⅞ In. *illus*	3480
Box, Singing Bird, Swivels, Wings Move, Key Wind, Enameled Portrait, 3 ½ x 2 ¼ In.	22800
Box, Singing Birds, Perched On Tree, Metal Cage, 10 ½ x 6 In.	587
Box, Stella, Mahogany, Victorian Molding, Drawer, Double Combs, 34 Discs, 5 x 24 In.	4740
Box, Stella, Mira, Mahogany Cabinet, Single 15 ½-In. Comb, 10 Discs	1711
Box, Stella, Model 126, Mahogany, Carved Molding, Duplex Combs, 9 14-In. Discs	1180
Box, Sublime Harmonie, 22-Note Reed Violin Section, 8 Opera Arias, Marquetry, 1890, 22 In.	1100
Box, Swiss, Grained, Inlaid Case, 8 ¼-In. Cylinder, Victorian, 5 ¼ x 17 In.	120
Box, Swiss, Rosewood Case, 9-In. Cylinder, 5 Bells, Mahogany Stand, c.1900, 16 x 23 In.	1140
Box, Swiss, Rosewood Case, 13-In. Cylinder, 12 Tunes, 25 In.	570
Box, Wood, Inlay, Nicole Freres Overture, Piano Forte, Double Cones, 30 x 13 In.	31200
Bugle, Copper, Brass, 11 ½ In.	59
Bugle, Military, Silver, Holds Silk Armorial Banner, London, c.1920, 21 x 27 In.	1063
Calliope, Calliaphone, 41 Brass Pipes, Red Paint, Tangley Co., 1920, 63 x 31 In.	1375
Cello, After Stradivarius Label, Germany, c.1900, 48 ½ x 17 In.	392
Cornet, King Silvertone, Brass, Silver Bell, H.N. White, Cleveland, Ohio, c.1941	590
Drum, Bass, Inscribed Nick Bestor's Club Band, Red, Black, White Paint, Leedy	240
Drum, Military, Brass & Wood, Pencil Inscription, 1860s, 16 In. Diam.	497
Drum, Pine, Maple, Flowers, Painted, Deerskin, Brass, Rope, B. Brown, 1812, 11 x 13 In.	6250
Drum, Presentation, Union Veteran's, Eagle, Legs, Glass Top, Springfield, Mass, 1875, 31 In.	502
Drum, Snare, Military, Painted, Wood Hoops, Rope, Calfskin, c.1800, 15 x 14 In. *illus*	923
Drum, Wood, Rawhide, Painted Buffalo, Signed Guillermo Rosetti, New Mexico, 26 x 20 In.	235
French Horn, Brass, Engraved B.P.O.E. No. 34, Detroit, C.G. Conn, Fitted Case	600
Gong, Brass, Embossed, Oak Stand, Carved Mask, Round Frame, 43 x 25 In.	270
Guitar, Chet Atkins, Spruce Top, Stand, Amplification Pickup	1062
Guitar, Electric, Gretsch, Anniversary Model, Maple Archtop, Green, Ibanez Case, 1993	1298
Guitar, Fender, Jazz Bass, Strap, Stand	649
Guitar, Gibson, SG Melody Maker, Pelham Blue, Electric, Case, 1967	1534
Guitar, Mixed Woods, Hagstrom, Electric, c.1968	531
Harp, Child's, Clark, Ireland, c.1920, 39 ½ In.	450
Harp, Concert, Giltwood, Bird's-Eye Maple, 47 Strings, Erard, Paris, 1800s, 70 In.	2829
Harp, Gilt, Stenciled, 42 Strings, No. 784, Erard Freres, France, c.1890, 65 x 30 In.	1770
Harp, Maple, Spruce, Parcel Gilt, Carved Crown, 3 Greek Angels, Sebastian Erad, 66 ½ In.	1063
Harp, Regency, 8-Pedal, Rosewood, Parcel Gilt, Unstrung, Schwieso & Cos., 1800s, 67 In. *illus*	2829
Harp, Troubadour, 33-String, Ebonized Wood, Lyon & Healy, 64 In.	767
Hurdy-Gurdy, Wood, Painted, Vincente Llinares Favnetia Label, 2 Rolls, 49 x 33 In.	489
Mandolin, Bowlback, Antonio Gravso, Softshell Case, Italy, c.1900	94
Mandolin, Ibanez, 27 In.	57
Mandolin, Martin Style, Rosewood, 4-Bowl Back, Painted Flowers, Leather Case, c.1909	1121
Mandolin, No. 1318, Washburn Style 5983, Metal Mounts, Lyon & Healy, Case, c.1910, 25 In.	2125
Melodeon, Victorian, Walnut, Portable, Curved Folding Legs, 38 x 20 In.	124
Melodia, 1 Roll, Crank Winder, Bellows, Mechanical Organette Co., c.1900, 11 x 12 x 10 In.	518
Nickelodeon, Coinola, Oak, Slag Glass, Operators Piano Co., Chicago, 65 x 59 In. *illus*	9690
Organ, Autophone Roller, Walnut, Cutouts, Inlays, Drawer, Foot Pump, c.1860, 42 x 24 In.	1659
Organ, Barrel, 16 Pipes, 15-In. Barrel, Wooden Gear, Handle, Plays 6 Tunes, 1880s	440
Organ, Chautauqua, Roller, c.1900, 12 ½ x 17 In.	365
Organ, Reed, Table, Melodista, 14-Note Paper Roll, Stenciled Cabinet, G.H.W. Bates, 11 In.	660
Organ, Roller, Chestnut Case, 17-In. Rolls, Signed, Enrique Salva Mane, 25 x 23 In.	236
Organ, Roller, Gem Organetta, Style No. 1, Paper Roll, Massachusetts Organ Co.	443
Organ, Roller, Victorian, Walnut, 13 ½ In.	273
Organ, Street, Handles, Wood, Metal, Glass, Luis Casali, Spain, c.1900, 39 x 43 In.	460
Organette, Ariston, 5 Round Cardboard Discs	177
Piano Forte, Mahogany, Ivory Keys, John K. Scott, c.1820, 34 x 66 In.	443
Piano, Baby Grand, Kimball, Mahogany, 60 In.	1921
Piano, Baby Grand, Steinway, Model S, Ebony, c.1937	5150
Piano, Baby Grand, Steinway, Model S, Mahogany, c.1945, 67 In.	5000
Piano, Electric, Normophon Koestler, Case, 29 In.	57

Music, Box, Singing Bird, Peasant Scenes, Silver Gilt, Germany, c.1900, 3 ⅞ In.
$3,480

Skinner Auctioneers & Appraisers

Watch Your Head

Watch your head when you visit a restored house or village. There are two reasons for low doorways. People were shorter, and a low door helped keep heat in the room. (Remember, hot air rises.) Frank Lloyd Wright made low doorways, too, because he was about 5 foot 8 inches tall and designed for his own height. He didn't care if you bumped your head on the top of a doorway.

M

Music, Drum, Snare, Military, Painted, Wood Hoops, Rope, Calfskin, c.1800, 15 x 14 In.
$923

Skinner Auctioneers & Appraisers

TIP
You can remove stickers from most things by spraying them with a lubricant.

Music, Harp, Regency, 8-Pedal, Rosewood, Parcel Gilt, Unstrung, Schwieso & Cos., 1800s, 67 In. $2,829

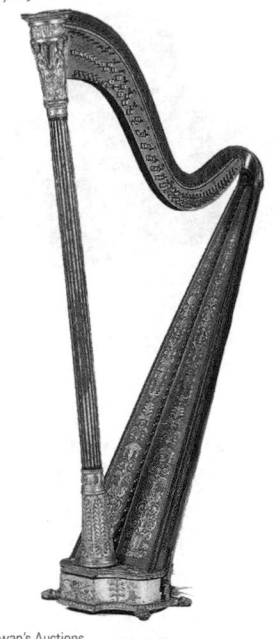

Cowan's Auctions

Music, Nickelodeon, Coinola, Oak, Slag Glass, Operators Piano Co., Chicago, 65 x 59 In. $9,690

Showtime Auction Services

Music, Piano, Gabriel Gaveau, Inlaid Rosewood, Maison Fondee, 1911, 38 x 55 In. $3,450

Cottone Auctions

Piano, Gabriel Gaveau, Inlaid Rosewood, Maison Fondee, 1911, 38 x 55 In. ....*illus*	3450
Piano, Grand, Hallet, Davis & Co., Mahogany, Bronze Columbian Exposition Medal, 84 In.........	1300
Piano, Grand, Starr, Walnut, 20th Century, 40 x 59 x 92 In.	1200
Piano, Grand, Steinway, Ebonized Case, Pierced, Scrolled Music Rest, 72 x 57 In.	7345
Piano, Grand, Steinway, Model M, Ebony, Bench, 1925, 66 x 56 In.	5310
Piano, Parlor Grand, Steinway, Model A, c.1918, 74 In.	10625
Piano, Player, Coin-Operated, Quartersawn Oak Cabinet, Glass, Chicago, 66 x 59 x 32 In.........	3000
Piano, Street, Cart, Interchangeable Wood Barrels, 6 Tunes, Painted, Spain, 32 x 20 x 48 In.	489
Piano, Upright, Andreas Christensen, Teak, Brass, Plastic, Signed, 1960s, 43 x 51 In. ....*illus*	2625
Piano, William E. Steinway, Centennial, Rosewood, Ornate Legs & Music Holder, 85 In.........	7020
Saxophone, Tenor, King Model, Bill Whittle, H.N. White Co., Bag Case.........	363
Stand, William IV, Mahogany, Giltwood, 49 In.........	344
Ukulele, Martin, Soprano Style, Mahogany Body, Neck, Rosewood Fingerboard, 8 ½ In.........	303
Viol Bow, Tiger Maple, Mahogany, Ivory, 1800s, 18 ½ In.........	29
Violin Case, Alligator, Key, Kantkrack G & S Company, 9 ¾ x 31 In.........	2800
Violin, Animal Carved Terminal & Hatch, c.1865, 14 ½ In.........	150
Violin, Bow, Lupot Label, Full Size, 14 In.........	1875
Violin, Jabobus Stainer, F.R. Hoyer Cello Bow, Wood Case, c.1900, 31 x 30 In.........	120
Violin, Maple Wood, Ebony, Theodore Heinrich Markneukirchen, Germany, 1921, 14 In.........	1236
Violin, Mother-Of-Pearl Inlay, 24 In.........	560
Violin, Scrimshaw Bridge, Fretboard, Tuning Pegs, Wood Case, 23 In.........	690
Violin, Watercolor, Pen, Ink, Painted Geometrics, New Eng., c.1830, 23 ½ x 8 In.........	12500
Xylophone, Multicolor, Painted Base, Mallet, 31 In.........	146
Zither, Wood, Carved, Scrolled End, Mother-Of-Pearl, William Tudbner, c.1890, 25 x 12 In.........	230

MUSTACHE CUPS were popular from 1850 to 1900 when the large, flowing mustache was in style. A ledge of china or silver held the hair out of the liquid in the cup. This kept the mustache tidy and also kept the mustache wax from melting. Left-handed mustache cups are rare but are being reproduced.

Cherry Blossoms, Scalloped, Rookwood, c.1889, 4 x 2 In.	450
Fishnet, Shells, Saucer, Majolica, Fielding	325
Garden Scene, Victorian Woman, Royal Bavarian, 3 In.	45
Gold Leaf, Mendelsohn Family, Ceramic, Germany, c.1860, 4 ½ In.	350
Hand, Playing Cards, Dice, Lucky Spots, Americana.........	300
Leaves, Bamboo Handle, Brownhills Pottery.........	32
Leaves, Earth Tones, Gold Accents, Saucer, Porcelain, 1880s ....*illus*	75
Painted Flowers, Narrowed Base, Scroll Handle, Multicolor.........	22
Pink & Blue Flowers, Gold Trim, Saucer, ...*illus*	48
Pink & White Flowers, Leaves, Gold Trim, Saucer ....*illus*	48
Shells, Coral, Fish Handle, Saucer, Majolica.........	90

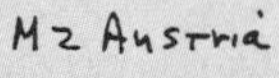

MZ AUSTRIA is the wording on a mark used by Moritz Zdekauer on porcelains made at his works in Altrolau, Austria, from 1884 to 1909. The mark was changed to MZ *Altrolau* in 1909, when the firm was purchased by C.M. Hutschenreuther. The firm operated under the name Altrolau Porcelain Factories from 1909 to 1945. It was nationalized after World War II. The pieces were decorated with lavish floral patterns and overglaze gold decoration. Full sets of dishes were made as well as vases, toilet sets, and other wares.

MZ Austria

Biscuit Jar, Flower Garland, Hearts, Greek Key Band, Ruffled Rim, Handles, 1890s, 9 x 4 In.......	75
Bonbon, Roses, Beading, Upward Handles, Marked, 7 x 2 In.	82
Bowl, Asymmetrical, Seafoam Border, Flowers, Ruffled Rim, c.1905, 12 x 2 x 5 In.	79
Bowl, Mums, Pink, White, Yellow, Gold Flared Feet, 1900s, 8 x 10 x 4 In.........	129
Chocolate Pot, Laurel Wreaths, Pink Roses, Gold Base & Rim, c.1875, 9 ¾ In.........	350
Plate Set, Dessert, Grapes, 7 ¾ In., 5 Piece.........	40
Plate, Flower & Vine Band, Purple, Green, c.1890, 8 ½ In.........	145
Salt & Pepper, Tea Roses, Pink, Bulbous, Gilt Tops, c.1900, 3 In.........	95

NAILSEA glass was made in the Bristol district in England from 1788 to 1873. The name also applies to glass made by many different factories, not just the Nailsea Glass House. Many pieces were made with loopings of either white or colored glass as decoration.

Bell, White Looping, Clear Handle, 9 ¾ In.........	149
Bowl, Shouldered, Cobalt Blue & Clear, c.1900, 7 ½ x 3 ¾ In.........	125
Fairy Lamp, Cranberry, Clear Bowl Holder, S. Clark, c.1880, 4 In.........	128
Fairy Lamp, Green, Square Ruffled Base, Crystal Clarke Insert, Green Shade, 7 ¼ In.........	295
Fairy Lamp, Ruffled Cranberry Base, White Pulled Feathers, c.1875, 7 x 8 In.........	495
Pipe, Whimsy, Blue Opalescent, Bulbous Bowl, c.1875, 16 ¾ In.........	405

M

Rolling Pin, Cobalt Blue, Knopped Ends, Flowers, c.1860, 13 ¾ In. 95
Rolling Pin, Pink & White Loopings, 17 In. 210
Vase, Bottle Shape, Blue & White, 9 In. 199
Vase, Cobalt Blue, White Looping, Club Shape, c.1930, 11 ¼ In. 265
Witch Ball, Cranberry, Cranberry Looping, Amethyst, 1800s, 4 In. 337

NAKARA

NAKARA is a trade name for a white glassware made about 1900 by the C. F. Monroe Company of Meriden, Connecticut. It was decorated in pastel colors. The glass was very similar to another glass, called Wave Crest, made by the company. The company closed in 1916. Boxes for use on a dressing table are the most commonly found Nakara pieces. The mark is not found on every piece.

Dresser Box, Cherubs, In Hay, Transfer, Blue, Enameling, Marked, 3 ¼ x 6 In. 324
Dresser Box, Hinged, Blue, Applied Blue Blossoms, 8-Sided, 4 ½ x 7 In. 443
Dresser Box, Pink, Bouquets, Scrollwork, 3 ¼ x 5 In. 195
Dresser Box, Wild Roses, Scrolls, Gibson Girl Portrait, Blue, 5 ½ x 8 In. 708
Ring Box, Pink Glass, White Daisies, Marked, 2 In. 489

NANKING is a type of blue-and-white porcelain made in China from the late 1700s to the early 1900s. It was shipped from the port of Nanking. It is similar to Canton wares listed in that category, but it is of better quality. The blue design was almost the same, a landscape, building, trees, and a bridge. But a person was sometimes on the bridge on a Nanking piece. The "spear and post" border was used, sometimes with gold added. Nanking sells for more than Canton.

Chestnut Basket, Landscape Center, Pierced Sides, Shell Handles, c.1860, 11 In., Pair 960
Cider Jug, Lid, House, Landscape, Flower Border, c.1860, 9 In. 1140
Dish, Vegetable, Blue, White, Oval, Applied Silver Handle, 5 ½ x 11 In. 325
Platter, Blue & White, Landscape, Boats, Pavilions, Lancelet Borders, c.1800s, 14 ⅝ In. .....*illus* 584
Platter, Landscape, Pagodas, Trees, Scrolled Border, c.1850, 14 x 18 In. 533
Platter, Oval, Riverfront Village Scene, 12 ¼ In., Pair 531
Platter, Ships On Water, Pagodas, Oval, Cantered Corners, c.1850, 17 x 20 In. 356
Punch Bowl, Houses, Trees, Seas, Blue & White, Flared, c.1865, 15 ¾ In. 3600
Tankard, Pagodas, Trees, Twisted Handle, c.1860, 8 In. 237
Tankard, Scalloped Rim, Twisted Handle, Pagodas, Trees, 6 In. 119
Tureen, Soup, Round, Interlacing Handles, Blue & White, Chinese, c.1800, 11 x 14 In. 615
Vase, Landscapes, Gilt Accents, Chinese, 19th Century, 7 ½ In. 241

NAPKIN RINGS were in fashion from 1869 to about 1900. They were made of silver, porcelain, wood, and other materials. They are still being made today. The most popular rings with collectors are the silver plated figural examples. Small, realistic figures were made to hold the ring. Good and poor reproductions of the more expensive rings are now being made and collectors must be very careful.

Bakelite, Chick, Art Deco, Amber, 2 ⅝ x 3 In. 75
Figural, Silver Plate, Boy & Girl, Victorian Clothes, Victorian, 3 In., Pair ....*illus* 130
Figural, Silver Plate, Boy, Crawling, Ring On Back, 2 ½ In. ....*illus* 30
Figural, Silver Plate, Cherubs, Barrel Shape, Rectangular Base, Rogers, 2 ⅞ x 2 ⅛ In. 275
Figural, Silver Plate, Double Rings, Wishbone, England, c.1910 160
Figural, Silver Plate, Elves, Holding Ring, Scrolled Pedestal, Reed & Barton, c.1875, 4 In. 850
Figural, Sterling Silver, Book Shape, Engraved, 1 ⅞ x 2 ⅛ x 1 In. 325
Sterling Silver, Art Nouveau, Shell & Scroll Border, 1 ¾ x 1 ½ In. 85
Sterling Silver, Enamel Flowers, Geometrics, Undulating Cylinder, Artel, c.1910, 1 ¾ In. 813
Sterling Silver, Fly On Rolled Leaf, George W. Shiebler, c.1885, 2 ¼ In. ....*illus* 2625
Sterling Silver, Hammered, Rectangular, 2 ¾ x 1 In. 69
Sterling Silver, Hand Wrought, Applied Monogram, Marked Kalo, 3 In., Pair 122
Sterling Silver, Leaf, Applied Metal Bug, Marked S ....*illus* 952
Sterling Silver, Medallion 1893, Tughra Of Sultan Abdulhamid II, Armenia, 2 In. ....*illus* 138
Sterling Silver, Raised Rose, Leaves, Whiting, 2 In. ....*illus* 135
Sterling Silver, Waisted, Flowers, Scallops, Cartouches, Minerva's Head, c.1915, 1 ½ In. 125
Tartanware, Green, Red, c.1880, 1 ½ x 1 In. 100

NASH

NASH glass was made in Corona, New York, from about 1928 to 1931. A. Douglas Nash bought the Corona glassworks from Louis C. Tiffany in 1928 and founded the A. Douglas Nash Corporation with support from his father, Arthur J. Nash. Arthur had worked at the Webb factory in England and for the Tiffany Glassworks in Corona.

Plate, Wavy Ribbons, Blue, Green, c.1930, 8 ¾ In. 395
Vase, Green Chintz, Shouldered, Striping, Applied Foot, 7 ½ x 8 In. 237
Vase, Paraboloid Shape, Paneled, Art Deco, 6 ¼ In. 250

Music, Piano, Upright, Andreas Christensen, Teak, Brass, Plastic, Signed, 1960s, 43 x 51 In.
$2,625

Rago Arts & Auction Center

Mustache Cup, Leaves, Earth Tones, Gold Accents, Saucer, Porcelain, 1880s
$75

Ruby Lane, Inc.

Mustache Cup, Pink & Blue Flowers, Gold Trim, Saucer
$48

Ruby Lane, Inc.

Mustache Cup, Pink & White Flowers, Leaves, Gold Trim, Saucer
$48

Ruby Lane, Inc.

Nanking, Platter, Blue & White, Landscape, Boats, Pavilions, Lancelet Borders, c.1800s, 14 ⅝ In.
$584

New Orleans Auction Galleries, Inc.

Napkin Ring, Figural, Silver Plate, Boy & Girl, Victorian Clothes, Victorian, 3 In., Pair
$130

Manor Auctions LLC

Napkin Ring, Figural, Silver Plate, Boy, Crawling, Ring On Back, 2 ½ In.
$30

Woody Auction

Napkin Ring, Sterling Silver, Fly On Rolled Leaf, George W. Shiebler, c.1885, 2 ¼ In.
$2,625

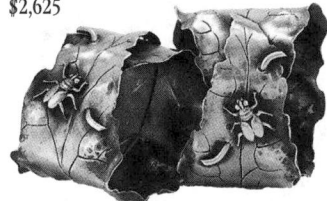

Rago Arts & Auction Center

NATZLER pottery was made by Gertrud Amon and Otto Natzler. They were born in Vienna, met in 1933, and established a studio in 1935. Gertrud threw thin-walled, simple, classical shapes on the wheel, while Otto developed glazes. A few months after Hitler's regime occupied Austria in 1938, they married and fled to the United States. The Natzlers set up a workshop in Los Angeles. After Gertrud's death in 1971, Otto continued creating pieces decorated with his distinctive glazes. Otto died in 2007.

Bottle, Green Crystalline Glaze, Teardrop Form, 1965, 5 In.	9375
Bottle, Tomato Red Glaze, Textured Clay, Cylindrical, 11 x 6 In.	11250
Bowl, Blue Mottled Glaze, Hemispherical, Otto & Gertrud Natzler, 1960, 2 ¼ x 5 ½ In.	1000
Bowl, Brown Mottled, Tan Glaze, Signed Gertrude & Otto Natzler, 6 x 3 ⅓ In.	1375
Bowl, Cone Shape, Chartreuse Glaze, Signed, 1967, 3 ¼ x 7 ¼ In. ....*illus*	3125
Bowl, Curvy Rim, Persimmon Glaze, Signed, c.1965, ½ x 1 ¼ x 1 ¼ In. ....*illus*	4688
Bowl, Gray, Plum Glaze, Flared, Signed, 2 x 6 ¾ In.	688
Bowl, Light Blue Glaze, Signed, 1957, 4 ¾ x 6 In.	5000
Bowl, Orange Red, Crater Glaze, Paper Label, Signed, 4 ½ x 6 In. ....*illus*	10625
Bowl, Peach Blossom Glaze, Signed, 1963, 2 ¾ x 5 ⅞ In. ....*illus*	5000
Bowl, Speckled Turquoise Glaze, Signed, Miniature, c.1965, ½ x ⅝ In. ....*illus*	3750
Bowl, Tiger Eye Reduction Glaze, Paper Label, Signed, 1963, 3 ¼ x 9 In. ....*illus*	6250
Bowl, Verdigris & Blue Pompeian Glaze, 4 x 6 In.	2375
Bowl, Yellow & Gray Volcanic Glaze, Otto & Gertrud Natzler, 1940s, 3 x 9 In.	5000
Bowl, Yellow Mottled, Brown Glaze, Gertrude & Otto Natzler, 5 ½ x 2 In.	1875
Vase, Apple Green Glaze, Pillow, Signed Natzler, 5 x 7 In.	2000
Vase, Bottle, Gunmetal Matte Glaze, Oval, 1958, 14 x 7 In.	17500
Vase, Brown, Tan, Mottled, Green Interior, Flared, Gertrude & Otto Natzler, 6 x 3 ¾ In.	3125
Vase, Cobalt Blue Glaze, Ikebana, Slab Shape, Signed, 1983, 9 ½ x 4 ½ In. ....*illus*	6875
Vase, Red, Brown, Tan Glaze, Small Foot, Gertrude & Otto Natzler, 4 ½ x 3 ½ In.	1375
Vase, Yellow Glaze, Flared, Pinched, Gertrude & Otto Natzler, 6 x 4 In.	2500

NAUTICAL antiques are listed in this category. Any of the many objects that were made or used by the seafaring trade, including ship parts, models, and tools, are included. Other pieces may be found listed under Scrimshaw.

Anchor, Brass, Double Hooks	98
Anchor, Double Fluke, Cast Iron, c.1915, 47 x 45 In.	325
Ax, Naval Boarding, Iron Head, Guard, 12 ½ In.	600
Beckets, Clasped Hands, Woven Rope, Seachest Handles, 10 In., Pair	2280
Bell, Ship's, Bronze Stand, Acorn Top, Wood Base, c.1855, 10 ¼ x 9 ¼ In.	660
Bell, Ship's, Bronze, Stand, Suspended, Stylized Dolphins, c.1940, 26 x 34 In.	770
Bell, Yacht, Brass, Marked Arcadia, 1953, 9 ½ x 9 ½ In.	443
Bell, Yacht, Brass, Mary Murray, Wood Base, Holder, 14 x 10 In.	325
Bench, Steamboat, Mahogany, Slat Back, Lift-Top Bench, c.1905, 37 x 95 In.	1003
Billet Head, Carved, Painted, Stand, 15 ½ x 18 In.	10200
Billet Head, Eagle, Carved, Open Beak, 1800s, 12 ½ x 24 In.	2360
Billet Head, Pine, Black, Gilt, Carved, Mahogany Stand, 23 ½ In.	3360
Billet Head, Pine, Carved, Gold, Black Paint, Schooner Dauntless, 10 In.	6240
Billet Head, Pine, Scrolls, Leaves, Gadrooned, New England, c.1845, 20 x 17 In.	518
Binnacle, Brass, Compass, 2 Oil Lights, 8 In.	1440
Binnacle, Brass, Gilt Metal, Griffin Support, Tripod Base, Maria Theresa Ship, 58 In.	6480
Binnacle, Brass, Oval Window, Compass, Iron Balls, John Lilley & Gillie, 54 In.	1298
Binnacle, Negus, Yacht, Brass, Glass Panes, Compass, Embossed, New York, c.1860, 31 In.	1534
Boat Motor, Johnson Seahorse 3 Hp.	300
Boat, Adirondack Guide, Pine, Mixed Woods, W. Hanmer, 1961, 14 Ft.	6875
Boat, Paddle Wheel, Dresden, Steam, Black, Red Hull, Rock & Graner, c.1890, 19 In.	8888
Bollard, Ship, Bronze, c.1850, 9 ½ x 21 In.	212
Buoy Light, Clear Lens, Brass, Steel, Copper Cap, c.1950, 48 In.	1770
Cannon, Yacht, Mahogany, Brass, Breech Loading, Conn., c.1890, 18 ½ x 37 ½ In.	26400
Canoe Seat, Oak, Slat Back, Fold Down, Old Town, 16 x 24 In.	97
Canoe, Bob Timberlake, Pine, Mahogany, Red Fiberglass, Corky Gray, Oar, 1990s, 164 x 33 In.	1888
Canoe, Wood, Ribs, Painted Exterior, 2 Seats, Old Town Canoe Co., 11 Ft. ....*illus*	855
Chair, Yacht, Teakwood, Leather Cushion, Slat Back, Steel Base, Cruikshank & Co.	1920
Chest, Sea Green, Paint, Rope Handles, c.1850, 17 ½ x 50 ½ In.	563
Chest, Sea, Camphorwood, Canted Front, Rope Handles, 17 ½ x 40 In.	960
Chest, Sea, Captain's, Wood, Painted, Boat, Ropes, Rope Handles, Ball Feet, 22 x 38 In.	176
Chest, Sea, Dovetailed, Painted, Eagle, Flags, Fitted Interior, c.1810, 17 x 36 In. ....*illus*	3240
Chest, Sea, Green Paint, Interior Lid Painted With Clipper, Handles, c.1860, 16 x 40 In.	590
Chest, Sea, Green, Black Paint, Cleated Ends, Rope Beckets, 1800s, 18 x 34 In.	500

Chest, Sea, Pine, Becket Handles, Green Paint, Painted Ship, 1800s, 15 x 40 In.	800
Chest, Sea, Pine, Blue, Compass Design, Lift Lid, Iron Handles, c.1815, 16 x 39 In.	780
Chest, Sea, Pine, Rope Beckets, c.1850, 16 ½ x 39 In.	165
Clock, Chelsea, Ship's Bell, Brass, Round, U.S. Shipping Board, Chelsea., Boston, c.1901, 8 In. ...	540
Clock, Chelsea, Ship's Bell, Brass, Silvered Dial, 8-Day, Mahogany Base, 6 ½ In.	300
Clock, Chelsea, Ship's Bell, Brass, Stepped Base, Boston, 9 x 10 In.	468
Clock, Chelsea, Ship's Bell, Nickel Plated, Silvered Dial, 8-Day, Barometer, 13 In.	360
Clock, Chelsea, Ship's Wheel Shape, Shreve, Crump & Low, 4 ¾ In.	157
Clock, Chelsea, Ship's Wheel, Mariner, Mahogany, Brass, Bronze, Silvered Dial, c.1940, 18 In.	1560
Clock, Chelsea, U.S. Navy Deck, No. 1, Brass, Screw Bezel, Black Dial, 8-Day, 11 In.	720
Clock, Ship's Bell, Mahogany, Chelsea Brass, 14 ½ In.	960
Clock, Ship's, Black Bakelite, Wall Mount, Chelsea Clock Co., 8 In. ....*illus*	186
Clock, Ship's, Seth Thomas, Exterior, Nickel Plated Case, Ship's Bell Strike, c.1890, 11 In.	360
Compass, Binnacle, Mahogany, Brass, Lantern, Louis Weule, c.1910, 7 x 8 In. ....*illus*	360
Compass, Boat, Brass, Illuminated, Marked Ontario Hughes Queens Cie, 1800s, 11 In.	224
Compass, Ship's, Brass, Gimbaled, Eggert & Son, New York, 7 In.	1320
Compass, Telltale, Brass, T.S. & J.G. Negus, 6 ¾ In.	189
Depth Gauge, Submarine, U.S., Bronze, Iron, Round, 3 x 18 In.	560
Diorama, In Bottle, Ships, Town, Zeppelin, Green Stopper, 8 ¾ In.	207
Diorama, Sailing Ship, 3 Masts, Hanni, Painted Waves, Sky, Shadowbox, c.1890, 11 x 7 In.	259
Diorama, Wood, Relief Carved, Painted, Signed L.R., c.1950, 13 x 16 In.	300
Ditty Bag, Canvas, Ropework Ties, c.1900, 17 ½ In.	142
Ditty Box, Baleen, Oval, Whaling Scenes, Sayings, Sailor Made, 1800s, 8 x 6 In.	944
Ditty Box, Mahogany, Rosewood, Whalebone, White House Views, Round, c.1845, 3 x 6 In.	13750
Diving Helmet, Mark V Type, Copper, Brass Trim, 12 Bolts, 19 ¼ x 19 ½ In. ....*illus*	1845
Diving Helmet, U.S. Navy, Brooklyn Navy Yard, Metal	2370
Document Box, Whaling Ship Magnolia, Yellow Grain Paint, c.1850, 10 x 20 In.	708
Eagle, Pilothouse, Wooden, Carved, Raised Wings, Painted, Brown, c.1890, 33 x 23 In.	1150
Fid, Whalebone, Turned Handles, c.1850, 15 ½ In.	590
Figurehead, Angel, Wood, Carved, Holding Gloria Banner, Brown Paint, 47 In.	3068
Figurehead, Maiden, Shawl, Carved, Painted, 1800s, 67 ½ In. ....*illus*	1250
Figurehead, Pine, Plumed Helmet, Curly Hair, France, 30 In.	3900
Figurehead, Schooner Mary Ann, High Bun, Rolled Sleeves, Paint, Carved, 1840, 41 x 19 In.	15600
Figurehead, Woman, Carved, Stained, Signed M. Ruault, Branded, 24 In.	1080
Figurehead, Woman, Draped In American Flag, Carved, Painted, c.1900, 21 In.	600
Figurehead, Woman, Ringlets, Ribbon, Wood, Carved, Varnished, c.1905, 38 In.	944
Foghorn, Brass, 1700s, 24 In.	472
Foghorn, Wood, Box Shape, Handle, 17 x 24 In.	266
Foghorn, Wood, Iron Base, Foot Powered, Seibe Gormana & Co. Ltd., 1800s, 24 In.	354
Lamp Filler, Brass, U.S. Lighthouse Service, c.1900, 13 ¾ In.	826
Lantern, Brass, Bull's-Eye Lens, Green, Red Panels, Handle, USLSS, Alton Bros., 10 ½ In.	83
Lantern, Copper, Cylindrical, Cone Shape Top, Electrified, 20 x 10 ½ In.	480
Lantern, Ship's, Brass, Copper, Tung Woo Embossed Label, Chinese, 1900s, 21 In.	36
Lantern, Ship's, Brass, USS Nieuw Amsterdam, Sherwoods Ltd., 20 In. ....*illus*	106
Lantern, Signal, Brass, Lever Swing Handle, c.1890, 16 In.	560
Lantern, Towing, Copper, Clear Lenses, Handle, W. Harvie & Co., c.1900, 26 In., Pair	1121
Model, Boat, Wood, Paint, Half-Hull, Portholes, Black, Red, c.1900, 11 x 50 In.	677
Model, Cabin Cruiser, Wood, Carved, 18 In.	540
Model, Friendship Sloop, Wood, Planked Deck & Hull, Stand, c.1900, 19 x 11 In.	531
Model, Sailboat, Flying Cloud, Copper, Walnut, c.1920, 29 x 40 In.	649
Model, Ship, Half-Hull, Mahogany, c.1900, 7 x 47 In.	2400
Model, Ship, Simonia, Wood, Carved, Painted, 21 ½ In.	600
Model, Sloop, Half Hull, Builder's, Oak, Carved, Mounted, c.1900, 8 ½ x 36 In.	2006
Model, Steamboat, Engine, Canopy, Painted Design Hull, Base, 1900s, 31 In.	390
Model, Tugboat Cora, Wood, Carved, Painted, 17 ¾ In.	1920
Net, Cargo, Heavy Rope, c.1940	767
Octant, Bronze Frame, Brass Scales, Wood Case, Triangular, c.1865	354
Octant, Mahogany, Boxwood, Bone Plaque, Capt. John Ashton, Keystone Box, c.1782, 19 In.	3900
Octant, Nantucket Scrimshander, Brass, Ivory Scale, Mahogany Case, 16 x 18 In.	2400
Pond Boat, Sailboat, Wood, Cloth Sails, Stand, 1900s, 42 x 42 In. ....*illus*	120
Pond Boat, Sloop, Wood, Cloth Sail, Stand, 1900s, 42 x 42 In.	210
Porthole, Brass, Black Paint, Glass, Oval, 9 ½ x 14 In., Pair	130
Porthole, Brass, Round, Single Dog Downs, Crittenden-Wilcox, 1900s, 12 x 12 In., Pair	150
Pot, Copper, Handles, Spigot, Stamped Cunard White Star, 18 x 18 In.	443
Quadrant, Brass, Glass Lens, Ebonized Frame, Case, Spencer, Barrett & Co., London, c.1860	413

Napkin Ring, Sterling Silver, Leaf, Applied Metal Bug, Marked S
$952

Hudson Valley Auctioneers

Napkin Ring, Sterling Silver, Medallion 1893, Tughra Of Sultan Abdulhamid II, Armenia, 2 In.
$138

Leslie Hindman Auctioneers

Napkin Ring, Sterling Silver, Raised Rose, Leaves, Whiting, 2 In.
$135

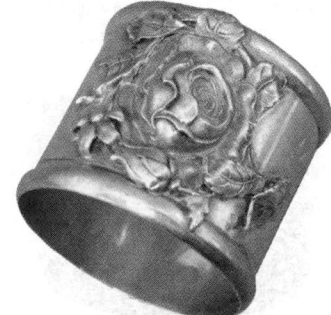

William H. Bunch Auctions

N

TIP
Don't mechanically buff silver. It will change the color and wear away bits of the silver.

Natzler, Bowl, Cone Shape, Chartreuse Glaze, Signed, 1967, 3 ¼ x 7 ¼ In. $3,125

Los Angeles Modern Auctions (LAMA)

Natzler, Bowl, Curvy Rim, Persimmon Glaze, Signed, c.1965, ½ x 1 ¼ x 1 ¼ In. $4,688

Los Angeles Modern Auctions (LAMA)

Natzler, Bowl, Orange Red, Crater Glaze, Paper Label, Signed, 4 ½ x 6 In. $10,625

Los Angeles Modern Auctions (LAMA)

Natzler, Bowl, Peach Blossom Glaze, Signed, 1963, 2 ¾ x 5 ⅞ In. $5,000

Los Angeles Modern Auctions (LAMA)

Sailor's Valentine, Octagonal, Shellwork, Inscribed Be Mine, Home Again, 2 Part, 9 In.	3125
Sailor's Valentine, Shells, Heart, Geometrics, Octagonal, B.A. Woodman, 1970s, 10 In.	2478
Sailor's Valentine, Shellwork, 2-Sided, Heart, Flowers, 1800s, 13 ½ x 3 In. ....*illus*	4385
Sailor's Valentine, Shellwork, Home Sweet Home, Heart, 1800s, 9 x 9 In.	1920
Sailor's Valentine, Shellwork, Inscription, Mahogany Stand, 1800s, 12 x 16 In. ....*illus*	4500
Seaman's Trunk, Camphorwood, Leather, Plaque, Brass Handles, c.1815, 13 x 31 In.	600
Sextant, Brass, Mahogany Case, Hughes Owens, 1930s, 5 x 10 x 9 ½ In.	180
Sextant, Brass, Marked Cary London, 8 In.	224
Sextant, Ebony Frame, Brass Mounts, Bone Measures, 1800s, 13 In.	384
Sextant, Ebony, Ivory, Wood Case, D. McGregor & Co., 1800s, 11 ¾ In.	316
Sextant, Husun, Henry Hughes & Son, Ltd., London, Fitted Box	270
Sextant, U.S. Navy, No. 777, Oak Case, 5 x 9 ½ x 9 ½ In.	215
Sextant, V. & M. Lepetit, Inlaid Steel Scale, Mahogany Box, c.1910	200
Ship Blocks, Wood, Spherical Glass Floaters, Netting, 2 Piece	180
Ship Model, see Nautical, Model.	
Ship's Control, Engine Room Telegraph, Brass, Miniature, 13 In.	252
Ship's Log, Slate, Incised Grids, Wood Case, Nautical Designs, 14 ½ x 10 In.	720
Ship's Wheel, Mahogany, Brass, Cast Iron, Baluster Spokes, U.S.A., c.1885, 59 In. Diam.	540
Ship's Wheel, Mahogany, c.1850, 45 In.	652
Ship's Wheel, Wood, Banded Inlay, c.1900, 42 In.	266
Ship's Wheel, Yacht, Brass, Wood, 8 Handles, c.1860, 24 In.	590
Ship's Wheel, Yacht, Oak, Brass Trim, 7-Spoke, c.1900, 33 ½ In.	236
Skiff, Bevin's, Spruce, Mixed Woods, Gray, Blue, Red Paint, 12 Ft. x 54 In.	590
Sounder & Core Sampler, Ocean Depth, Brass, Wood Sphere, 23 In.	590
Spear, Eel, Wrought Iron, c.1805, 24 In.	390
Sternboard Eagle, Banner, Gilded, Painted, Boston, c.1955, 22 x 82 In.	6000
Sternboard Section, Carved Serpent, Black Paint, 53 In.	1800
Sternboard, White Pine, Fruit Basket, Leaves, Carved, Gilt Paint, c.1850, 80 x 19 In.	12000
Sundial, Oak, 5 Paper Faces, Roman Numerals, Compass, Beringer, Germany, 1700s, 7 In.	1888
Telegraph, Brass, Charles Cory & Son, New York, 52 In.	652
Thermometer, Deep Sea, Adml. G.B. Macnaghi, c.1910, 14 ¾ In.	944
Traverse Board, Painted, 32 Compass Points, 8 Copper Pegs, Speed Recorder, 2 Parts, 17 In.	7200
Wall Pocket, Needlework, Naval, Silk, Velvet, Anchor, Eagle, 1800s, 7 ¾ x 4 In. ....*illus*	600
Wall Pocket, Sailor's, Canvas, Macrame, Painted Panels, Ships, Stars, c.1890, 30 x 23 In.	3998
Wheel Spoke, Ship's, Carved, Turned, Whalebone, c.1985, 7 In.	224
Whimsy, Wood, Carved, 4 Fish, Joined By Chains, 37 ½ In.	540
Whistle, Boatswain, Silver, c.1905, 5 ½ In.	130

NETSUKES are small ivory, wood, metal, or porcelain pieces used as toggles on the end of the cord that held a Japanese money pouch or inro. The earliest date from the sixteenth century. Many are miniature carved works of art. This category also includes the ojime, the slide or string fastener that was used on the inro cord.

Antler, Man, Standing, Round Glasses, Big Belly, Tapered Hat, 3 ½ In.	173
Bone, Dragon, Walking, Carved, 2 ¼ x 1 ¼ In. ....*illus*	97
Boxwood, Double Gourd Shape, Ivory Frog, Masatohi, c.1800, 2 ½ In.	536
Boxwood, Frog, On Nut, 1 ⅞ x 1 ⅜ x 1 ½ In.	72
Boxwood, Locust, On Gourd, 2 ¼ x 1 In.	125
Boxwood, Nautical Lady, On Spiral Shell, 1 ½ x 2 ½ In.	85
Boxwood, Snake In Palm Of Hand, 2 ½ x 1 ¼ In.	46
Copper, Elephant, c.1825, 1 ½ x 2 In.	225
Deer Antler, Human Skull, c.1900, 2 ¼ x 1 ½ In.	225
Ebony, Nude Okame Figure, 2 ¼ In.	100
Ivory, 2 Men, On Large Peach, Signed, Edo Period, 1800s, 1 ¾ In.	580
Ivory, 2 Rabbits, Prancing, c.1912, 3 ½ x 1 In.	451
Ivory, Bird, Signed, c.1900, 1 ½ x 2 In.	95
Ivory, Budai, Painted, Happy Buddha, Bamboo Fan, Sack, 2 x 2 In.	127
Ivory, Chinese Man, Fruit Peddler, Riding Bird, Multicolor, 2 ½ In.	64
Ivory, Chinese Man, Standing, White Beard, Staff, 1 ½ In.	35
Ivory, Daikoku, God Of Wealth, Carrying Mallet, Bag, Mounted On Rat, Masataka, 1 ¾ In.	180
Ivory, Face, Angry Man, Carved, Signed, 1940s, 1 ½ In. ....*illus*	255
Ivory, Farmer, Smiling, Bent Over Pig, Holding Tool, c.1890, 1 ½ x 1 ⅜ In.	615
Ivory, Flute Player, Seated On Reclining Elephant, Edo Period, 1800s, 1 ⅜ In.	324
Ivory, Horse, Head Bent Low, Brown Mane, Mitsohisa, 2 ⅜ In.	92
Ivory, Man, Seated, Holding Head In Hands, Signed, 1 ½ In.	180
Ivory, Man, Standing, Octopus Over Head, Holding Its Arm, Signed, 3 ¼ In.	900

Ivory, Man's Face, Smiling, Hat, c.1950, 2 x 1 ½ In.	95
Ivory, Mask, Roses, Teeth, c.1900, 2 x 1 In.	340
Ivory, Monkey, In Basket, Riding On Turtle, 1 ½ In.	58
Ivory, Mouse On Radish, Yuzon, 2 ½ In.	144
Ivory, Octopus, Reclining, Entwined Arms, Carved, 1800s, 2 In.	488
Ivory, Octopus, Snake, 1 ¾ x 1 ½ In.	350
Ivory, Panther, Reclining, Carved Fur, Edo Period, 1800s, 1 ¾ In.	2400
Ivory, Rat, On Corn, 19th Century, 2 ¼ x 1 ½ In.	400
Ivory, Sea Dragon, Head Turned Back, 2 In.	58
Ivory, Shishi, Seated, Ball, Flowers, Open Mouth, Amber Patina, 1700s, 1 ½ In.	356
Ivory, Shishi, Seated, With Ball, Sideward Glancing, Japan, c.1800, 1 ¼ In.	243
Ivory, Snail, Cut Bamboo, Manju, 2 In.	213
Ivory, Snake Squeezing Toad, Turquoise Eyes, 1 ½ In.	230
Ivory, Snake, Coiled, Fangs Out	180
Ivory, Snake, On Skull, Signed, 1 ¾ In.	225
Ivory, Toad, Baby Toad On Back, 1 ⅜ x 1 ⅛ In.	350
Ivory, Turtle, On Bag, Rope, Carved, Signed, 1 ½ x 1 In. ......illus	89
Ivory, Two Fish, Jumping Out Of Waves, 2 ¼ In.	64
Ivory, Woman, Crouching, Peering, Long Robe, 1 ½ In.	120
Mother-Of-Pearl, Hyotan, Double Gourd, c.1875, 2 ½ In.	850
Oxbone, Rats On Tortoise Back, Carved, Signed, 1 ⅝ x 1 In. ......illus	150
Oxbone, Rats, Tortoise, Marked, 1 ⅝ x 1 ⅝ In.	150
Shell, Conch, 19th Century, 2 x ¾ In.	275
Tortoiseshell, Water Buffalo, Recumbent, Flattened, 2 ⅜ In.	2300
Water Beetle, On Leaf, Inlaid Eyes, 2 ¾ In.	163
Wolf, Reclining, Head Turned Back Towards Tail, On Log, Stag Antler, 2 In.	688
Wood, Bearded Sage, Riding Fish, c.1925, 3 ½ In.	350
Wood, Daruma, Fluted, c.1875, 1 ½ In.	400
Wood, God Of Longevity, Smiling, Dancing, 1 ½ x 2 In.	310
Wood, Karako, Rolled Blanket On Shoulder, 19th Century, 2 ¼ x 1 In.	295
Wood, Mouse, 19th Century, 1 ¾ x 1 ½ In.	275
Wood, Mythological Animal, Barrel, 1 ¾ In.	23
Wood, Rabbit, Crouching Over Basket, Carved, Signed ......illus	125
Wood, Samurai, Seated Cross-Legged, 19th Century, 1 ½ x 1 In.	200

NEW MARTINSVILLE Glass Manufacturing Company was established in 1901 in New Martinsville, West Virginia. It was bought and renamed the Viking Glass Company in 1944. In 1987 Kenneth Dalzell, former president of Fostoria Glass Company, purchased the factory and renamed it Dalzell-Viking. Production ceased in 1998.

Addie, Cup & Saucer, Amethyst	14
Addie, Plate, Luncheon, Amethyst, 8 In.	12
Addie, Plate, Sandwich, Amber, 14 In.	28
Addie, Sugar & Creamer, Red, Footed	30
Addie, Sugar, Amber	10
Addie, Vase, Fan, Amber, 12 Points, 6 In.	22
Bookends, Horse, Rearing, 8 In., Pair	23
Candlestick, Jade Green, 2 ⅜ x 3 ¾ In., Pair	70
Canterbury, Bowl, Cupped, Curled Scalloped Rim, 11 x 3 In.	35
Carnation, Powder Jar, Lid, 1906, 4 ½ In.	34
Carnation, Powder Jar, Lid, Footed, c.1906, 3 In.	34
Cocktail Shaker, Chrome, Red Bakelite Handle, 6 Red Metal Base Stems	95
Crystal Eagle, Candelabrum, 2-Light, Amber, 6 x 7 ¼ In.	45
Decanter Set, Cobalt Blue, Crystal Fan Stopper, 9 Piece	350
Figurine, Hen, Head Down, 5 In.	125
Figurine, Police Dog, German Shepherd, Ruby, Sitting, Base, 5 In.	600
Figurine, Rooster, Crooked Tail, Crystal, 7 ½ In.	75
Figurine, Seal, Ball, Crystal, c.1938, 7 In.	75
Figurine, Woodsman, c.1940, 7 ⅜ In.	55
Flame, Candleholder, 6 ½ In.	22
Florentine Etch, Bowl, Console, Flared, 3-Toed, 12 In.	50
Florentine, Candleholder, 2-Light, Grape Leafs, Footed, c.1942, 5 In.	32
Florentine, Relish, 3 Sections, Handles, 10 x 8 In.	26
Hostmaster, Cup & Saucer, Cobalt Blue	18
Hostmaster, Cup & Saucer, Red	18
Hostmaster, Goblet, Cordial, Amber, Oz., 1 ⅞ In.	18
Hostmaster, Plate, Luncheon, Cobalt Blue, 8 In.	16

Natzler, Bowl, Speckled Turquoise Glaze, Signed, Miniature, c.1965, ½ x ⅝ In. $3,750

Los Angeles Modern Auctions (LAMA)

Natzler, Bowl, Tiger Eye Reduction Glaze, Paper Label, Signed, 1963, 3 ¼ x 9 In. $6,250

Los Angeles Modern Auctions (LAMA)

Natzler, Vase, Cobalt Blue Glaze, Ikebana, Slab Shape, Signed, 1983, 9 ½ x 4 ½ In. $6,875

Rago Arts & Auction Center

Nautical, Canoe, Wood, Ribs, Painted Exterior, 2 Seats, Old Town Canoe Co., 11 Ft. $855

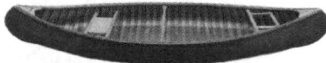

Showtime Auction Services

Book Sizes
The more books smaller than 18 inches in height that are on their sides on bookshelves, the less the owners read.

Nautical, Chest, Sea, Dovetailed, Painted, Eagle, Flags, Fitted Interior, c.1810, 17 x 36 In.
$3,240

Skinner Auctioneers & Appraisers

Nautical, Clock, Ship's, Black Bakelite, Wall Mount, Chelsea Clock Co., 8 In.
$186

Tom Harris Auctions

Nautical, Compass, Binnacle, Mahogany, Brass, Lantern, Louis Weule, c.1910, 7 x 8 In.
$360

Skinner Auctioneers & Appraisers

Hostmaster, Plate, Luncheon, Red, 8 In.	18
Hostmaster, Sugar & Creamer, Amber	22
Hostmaster, Tumbler, Iced Tea, Cobalt Blue, 14 Oz., 5 ¾ In.	25
Hostmaster, Whiskey Set, Amber, Amethyst, Cobalt Blue, Ruby Red, 4 Piece	48
Janice, Basket, Blue, Crystal Handle, 6 ½ x 9 In.	145
Janice, Bowl, Red, 3-Toed, 10 ¾ In.	75
Janice, Bowl, Swan, Cobalt Blue Neck, Head, 10 In.	50
Janice, Condiment Tray, Blue	20
Janice, Plate, Gold Scalloped Rim & Handles, c.1926, 7 In.	15
Meadow Wreath, Sugar, Handles, c.1938, 3 In.	12
Modernistic, Vase, Pink, Peony Etch, 3-Sided, 8 ½ In.	195
Moondrops, Bonbon, Tricorner, Ruby, 3-Toed, 8 x 3 In.	42
Moondrops, Bowl, Amethyst, Oval, 2 Handles, 8 ⅛ In.	50
Moondrops, Bowl, Console, Amber, Ruffled, Footed, 9 ½ In.	30
Moondrops, Bowl, Red, 3-Legged, 9 ¾ In.	65
Moondrops, Butter, Blue	40
Moondrops, Butter, Blue, Chrome Cover	45
Moondrops, Candlestick, Amber, Ruffled, Pair	36
Moondrops, Candlestick, Blue, Etched Lions, Footed, 4 ½ In.	45
Moondrops, Creamer, Amber, Regular, 3 ¾ In.	12
Moondrops, Cup & Saucer, Blue	25
Moondrops, Cup & Saucer, Green	14
Moondrops, Cup, Amethyst, Footed	10
Moondrops, Decanter, Rocket, Footed, Fan Stopper, Evergreen, c.1938, 12 In.	795
Moondrops, Sugar & Creamer, Red, Miniature	36
Moondrops, Sugar & Creamer, Ruby Red, Ribbed Foot, 1930s	45
Moondrops, Tumbler, Juice, Red, Footed, 3 ½ Oz., 3 ¼ In.	15
Moondrops, Vase, Rocket, Amethyst, Cupped, 3-Legged	60
Moondrops, Vase, Rocket, Pink, Cupped, 3-Legged	50
Moondrops, Whiskey, Amethyst, 2 ¾ x 2 In.	10
Moondrops, Whiskey, Red, 2 Oz., 2 ¾ In.	10
Notched Hexagon, Server, Pink, Center Handle	29
Oscar, Pitcher, Amethyst	75
Oscar, Tumbler, Amethyst	15
Oscar, Vase, Ruby, Vertical Ribbing, 9 In.	85
Oscar, Water Set, Cobalt Blue, 7 Piece	220
Prelude Etch, Bonbon, Cover, 5 ½ In.	25
Prelude Etch, Butter, Cover, Oval, 6 ½ In.	40
Prelude Etch, Cake Plate, Flowers, Scalloped Edge, 11 x 5 In.	52
Prelude Etch, Creamer, Ice Blue, Etched Meadow Wreath	45
Prelude Etch, Goblet, Cordial, Cobalt Blue	22
Prelude Etch, Plate, 2 Handles, 11 In.	40
Prelude Etch, Plate, Lemon, 3-Toed, 7 In.	24
Prelude Etch, Plate, Red, 11 In.	55
Prelude Etch, Relish, 3 Sections, Amber, Crimped, 9 In.	30
Prelude Etch, Salt & Pepper, Red	110
Prelude Etch, Server, Center Handle, 11 ½ In.	40
Prelude, Cake Plate, 14 In.	45
Queen Anne, Creamer, 1936, 6 In.	18
Radiance, Bonbon, Curved Edge, Meadow Wreath, Handles, 1930s, 6 In.	25
Radiance, Bowl, Meadow Wreath, Paneled, 12 ½ x 3 In.	65
Roberto Etch, Bowl, Red, Moondrops, 3-Legged, 9 ¾ In.	195
Roberto Etch, Sugar & Creamer, Amber, c.1934	60
Thumbprint, Mug, Beer, Cobalt Blue, 10 Oz., 3 ¼ In.	30
Thumbprint, Mug, Beer, Red, 10 Oz., 3 ¼ In.	25
Wine Set, Cobalt Blue, Crystal Fan Stopper, Decanter, Tray, 7 Stems, 9 Piece	350
Wine Set, Emerald Green, Acorn Stopper, Decanter, Tray, 6 Stems, 9 Piece	160
Wine Set, Red, Crystal Fan Stopper, Decanter, Tray, 6 Stems, 9 Piece	250

NEWCOMB POTTERY was founded at Sophie Newcomb College, New Orleans, Louisiana, in 1895. The work continued through the 1940s. Pieces of this art pottery are marked with the printed letters *NC* and often have the incised initials of the artist and potter as well. A date letter code was printed on pieces made from 1901 to 1941. Most pieces have a matte glaze and incised decoration.

Bowl, Blue Glaze, Painted Stylized Leaves, Ada Lonnegan, 1903, 7 ½ x 2 ½ In.	2440
Bowl, Japanese Plums, Footed, Sadie Irvine, 4 x 7 ½ In.	2095

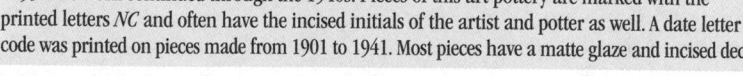

N

Bowl, Painted Flowers, Green, Apricot Flowers, Round, Anna Frances Simpson, 8 In.		1125
Bowl, White Flowers, Blue Ground, A.F. Simpson, 1924, 7 ½ x 2 ⅜ In.		1006
Bowl, Yellow Blossoms, Blue Green Underglaze, M. Williams Butler, 1908, 10 In.	*illus*	9560
Candlestick, Chamber, Narcissus, Marked, Henrietta Bailey, 1911, 6 ¼ In.	*illus*	1599
Candlestick, Impressed Abstract Design, Blue, Purple, Tapered Wide Cup, Simpson, 7 In.		1573
Candlestick, Trumpet Stick, 4-Sided Bobeche, Lavender, Blue, 1922, 7 ½ In.		330
Charger, Woman's Portrait, Dutch Hat, Daffodils, Harriet C. Joor, c.1902, 9 ¾ In.		6875
Chocolate Set, Spiderwort, Green, Blue, Pot, 5 Cups, S. Irvine, 1915, Pot 10 In., 6 Piece		10625
Inkwell, Lid, White Primrose, Bands, Blue High Glaze, Squat, M.T. Ryan, 1906, 4 In.		4538
Jardiniere, Incised Band, Persimmons, Blue Green, Joseph Meyer, 1909, 6 x 7 ½ In.		1912
Mug, Hop Band, Blue & Green Glossy Glaze, A.W. Lonnegan		2420
Mug, Trumpet Flower Band, Multicolor High Glaze, Bulbous, Tapered, Lonnegan, 1929		2299
Paperweight, Round, Church, Path, Pink, Purple, Tan, Incised New Orleans, c.1910, 4 In.		230
Pedestal, Blue Matte Glaze, Round, Footed, Signed Alma Mason, 4 In.		750
Pitcher, Daisies, Blue, Green, Yellow, Tapered Cylinder, Loop Handle, 1901, 8 In.		8963
Plaque, Satyrs, Playing Instruments, Frame, Leona Nicholson, 12 x 14 In.		2500
Plate, Chrysanthemum Border, Green Semimatte Glaze, Simpson, c.1913, 7 In.		2662
Plate, Maple Wing Design, Blue, Green, Yellow, Marked, 1909, 8 ¼ In. Diam.		1673
Pot, Blue Matte Glaze, Flared Rim, Joseph Meyer, c.1926, 3 ¾ x 8 In.		861
Pot, Blue Matte Glaze, Water Lilies, Joseph Meyer, c.1926, 3 x 4 ¾ In.		1168
Sugar, Lid, Stylized Leaves, Finial, Sadie Irvine, Aurelia Arbo, 1933, 4 In.	*illus*	1075
Tea Set, Teapot, Sugar, Creamer, Furled Flowers, Sabina Wells, Teapot 8 x 4 In., 3 Piece		5000
Trivet, Live Oaks, Spanish Moss, Round, A.F. Simpson, 1928, 5 ½ In.		3750
Tyg, Cotton Blossom Band, Green Glaze, 3 Handles, A.W. Lonnegan, c.1915, 5 In.		4235
Tyg, Hyacinth, Text, Blue, Cream, Cylindrical, Taper, Square Handles, 1903, 6 In.		2337
Vase, Blue & Green Glaze, Incised Design, Bulbous, Narrow Mouth, c.1910, 3 ½ In.		1800
Vase, Blue, White, Raised Trees, Dripping Spanish Moss, Squat		1035
Vase, Bud, Daffodil Band, Blue Ground, Tapered, Marie De Hoa LeBlanc, 1907, 7 In.		3933
Vase, Bud, Forsythia, Transitional, Henrietta Bailey, 1910, 4 ¾ x 2 ¾ In.		875
Vase, Bud, Glossy Copper Red Luster Glaze, 5 Incised Bands, Tapered, c.1932, 5 In.		605
Vase, Bulbous, Flat Rim, Daffodils, Blue, Green, Yellow, Matte Glaze, 1920, 5 ½ In.		3227
Vase, Bulbous, Swollen Collar, Blue, Green, Daffodils, Marked, 1918, 5 ⅛ In.		3585
Vase, Calla Lilies, Blue Underglaze, M. Williams Butler, 1902, 11 x 9 In.	*illus*	35850
Vase, Carved, Painted Flowers, Glaze, Marie De Hoa LeBlanc, 3 ½ x 9 ½ In.		7930
Vase, Cherokee Roses, Low Relief, Matte Glaze, Henrietta Bailey, 1921, 6 ⅜ In.	*illus*	5378
Vase, Copper Red, To Green Opaque Glaze, Tapered Cylinder, c.1900, 6 In.		875
Vase, Cylindrical, Flared Rim, Buds & Leaves, Green, Blue Matte Glaze, 1914, 6 In.		4183
Vase, Cypress Trees, Blue Gray, Tapered, Anna F. Simpson, 1915, 7 ½ x 16 In.		33750
Vase, Daffodils, White, Blue Green Ground, Round, Squat, 3 ½ x 6 In.		1125
Vase, Deep Blue Snowflakes, Light Blue, Carved, Tapered, A. Lonnegan, 8 x 10 In.		11250
Vase, Flowers, 4 Handles, Leaves, Flowers, Sadie Irvine, c.1912, 4 ½ x 5 ¾ In.		1195
Vase, Flowers, Blue, Green Squat, Tapered, S. Irvine, 1931, 2 x 3 In.		531
Vase, Flowers, Leaves, Blue, Green, La., 1929, 6 ¾ x 4 In.		1000
Vase, Freesia, Ivory, Yellow, Striated Blue Ground, Tapered, Mazie Ryan, 1911, 9 ½ In.		17500
Vase, Geraniums, Green, Ivory, Yellow, Signed, M.W. Butler, 1906, 6 x 8 ½ In.		10000
Vase, Gladiola, Squat, Sadie Irvine, 1925, 4 ½ x 5 In.	*illus*	1750
Vase, Green, Mauve, Drip Glaze, 3 ½ x 3 ½ In.		531
Vase, Horizontal Ribbed, Blue, Cream, c.1910, 6 ½ x 4 ¾ In.		469
Vase, Jonquils, Matte Glaze, Cynthia Pugh Littlejohn, 1916, 8 ½ In.		1298
Vase, Landscape, Moss-Laden Trees, Carved, Painted, A.F. Simpson, 3 ½ x 4 In.		3135
Vase, Live Oaks, Spanish Moss, Blue Ground, Anna Frances Simpson, 5 x 3 ½ In.		3375
Vase, Live Oaks, Spanish Moss, Blue, Green, Anna F. Simpson, c.1900, 6 ¼ x 6 ½ In.		5938
Vase, Live Oaks, Spanish Moss, Full Moon, Anna Frances Simpson, 8 ½ x 5 In.		6875
Vase, Live Oaks, Spanish Moss, Full Moon, Anna Frances Simpson, c.1900, 7 x 3 In.		3500
Vase, Live Oaks, Spanish Moss, Full Moon, Blue, Green, A.F. Simpson, 1927, 10 ¾ In.		12500
Vase, Live Oaks, Spanish Moss, Full Moon, Cabin, Oval, S. Irvine, 11 x 6 In.		5313
Vase, Live Oaks, Spanish Moss, Full Moon, Green To Blue Matte Glaze, c.1929, 5 ¾ In.		2380
Vase, Live Oaks, Spanish Moss, Moon, Blue, Green, Swollen Cylinder, A.F. Simpson, 8 In.		3750
Vase, Loblolly Pines, Vines, Blue, Striated Glaze, Cylindrical, L. Nicholson, 9 In.		2625
Vase, Magnolias, Harriet C. Joor, c.1902, 13 ¾ x 5 ½ In.		62500
Vase, Maple Leaves, Seed Pods, Henrietta Bailey, c.1922, 5 In.	*illus*	600
Vase, Mirrored Black Glaze, Oval, Marked, c.1910, 2 ¼ x 1 ¾ In.		350
Vase, Moon & Moss, Blue, Green Underglaze, Henrietta Davidson Bailey, 5 ½ x 4 In.		3198
Vase, Moon & Moss, Matte Glaze, Henrietta Davidson Bailey, 1933, 6 ¾ In.		5377
Vase, Moon & Moss, Trees, Blue Matte Glaze, Oval, Sadie Irvine, 1930, 5 x 3 In.		3555
Vase, Moon & Trees, Blue, Cylindrical, 7 ½ In.		4200

Nautical, Diving Helmet, Mark V Type, Copper, Brass Trim, 12 Bolts, 19 ¼ x 19 ½ In.
$1,845

New Orleans Auction Galleries, Inc.

Nautical, Figurehead, Maiden, Shawl, Carved, Painted, 1800s, 67 ½ In.
$1,250

Leslie Hindman Auctioneers

Nautical, Lantern, Ship's, Brass, USS Nieuw Amsterdam, Sherwoods Ltd., 20 In.
$106

Conestoga Auction Co., Inc.

N

Nautical, Pond Boat, Sailboat, Wood, Cloth Sails, Stand, 1900s, 42 x 42 In. $120

Garth's Auctioneers & Appraisers

Nautical, Sailor's Valentine, Shellwork, 2-Sided, Heart, Flowers, 1800s, 13 ½ x 3 In. $4,385

James D. Julia Auctioneers

Nautical, Sailor's Valentine, Shellwork, Inscription, Mahogany Stand, 1800s, 12 x 16 In. $4,500

Cowan's Auctions

Vase, Mustang Grapes & Leaves, Ada Wilt Lonnegan, Marked, 8 ½ x 8 ⅝ In.	5975
Vase, Narcissus, Rose, Bulbous, Sadie Irvine, 1922, 5 ⅞ In.	956
Vase, New Orleans Skyline, Windmill Palms, Crescent Moon, Bulbous, S. Irvine, 10 In.	15000
Vase, Nicotina, Blue Ground, Squat, Henrietta Bailey, 1926, 4 ¼ x 5 In.	1125
Vase, Painted Cypress Trees, Anna Frances, Simpson, 3 x 5 In.	700
Vase, Painted Landscape, Cypress Trees, Blue, Green, Carved, A. F. Simpson, 4 x 6 In.	3250
Vase, Painted Landscape, Moon, Mossy Trees, Carved, S. Irvine, 5 x 7 In.	8125
Vase, Panels, Shouldered, Blue, c.1924, 6 ½ x 2 ¾ In.	1495
Vase, Pine Trees, Underglaze, Marked, Sadie Irvine, 1913, 12 ½ In. .....*illus*	16730
Vase, Pinecones, Boughs, Shouldered, Blue, Footed, Bailey, c.1925, 4 x 6 ¼ In.	1900
Vase, Pink Irises, Green Leave, Blue Ground, S. Irvine, Label, 1928, 10 x 7 In.	4375
Vase, Red, Green, Cylindrical, Joseph Meyer, c.1900, 11 In.	1920
Vase, Spanish Moss, Pink Sky, Blue, Signed Anna Frances Simpson, 4 x 4 In.	2620
Vase, Spiderwort, Green Ground, Sadie Irvine, 1917, 2 ½ x 3 In.	1250
Vase, Stylized Flower Band, Yellow, Black Outline, Cylindrical, Guedry, 1901, 10 In.	1029
Vase, Stylized Flower Buds, Shades Of Blue, Round, 4 ¾ x 6 In.	2875
Vase, Swollen, Purple Matte, Pink, Flowers, Marked, 1919, 4 ¼ In.	2806
Vase, Transitional, Green, Flowers, Sadie Irvine, c.1915, 11 ½ x 4 ½ In.	5625

NILOAK POTTERY (*Kaolin* spelled backward) was made at the Hyten Brothers Pottery in Benton, Arkansas, between 1910 and 1947. Although the factory did make cast and molded wares, collectors are most interested in the marbleized art pottery line made of colored swirls of clay. It was called Mission Ware. By 1931 the company made castware, and many of these pieces were marked with the name *Hywood*.

Ashtray, Parts & Equipment, Crow-Burlingame, Oval	125
Candlestick, Applied Handle, Marbleized, Brown, Tan, 5 In.	265
Candlestick, Marbleized, c.1920, 8 In.	175
Ewer, Woman & Man Cameo, Ozark Blue, Marked, 10 x 4 ¼ In.	65
Flower Frog, Marbleized, Earth Tones, Marked, 1920s, 4 x 1 ½ In.	32
Pitcher, Ball, Blue, c.1930, 7 In.	35
Pitcher, Globular, Ozark Blue, 4 ¾ x 5 ¼ In.	45
Planter, Bulb, Tulip Bouquet Shape, Tan, 7 x 5 In.	47
Vase, Bulbous, Handles, Green Matte, 6 In.	35
Vase, Gray, Blue, 5 ½ In.	28
Vase, Gray, Blue, Marbleized, 8 ½ In.	11
Vase, Marbleized, Blue, Gray, Brown, Shouldered, Marked, 8 ½ In.	94
Vase, Marbleized, Blue, Red, White Swirl, Bulbous Shape, 6 x 12 ½ In.	214
Vase, Marbleized, Brown, Tan, Blue, Oval, Flared Rim, Marked, 8 In.	280
Vase, Marbleized, Brown, Tan, Green Swirl, Stamped, 9 ¾ In.	275
Vase, Marbleized, Cylindrical, Brown, Tan, Blue, c.1930, 6 In.	165
Vase, Marbleized, Green, Tan, Brown, Impressed, Paper Label, 6 In.	130
Vase, Squat, Brown, Grey, Cream, Marked, 3 ½ In.	325

NIPPON porcelain was made in Japan from 1891 to 1921. *Nippon* is the Japanese word for "Japan." A few firms continued to use the word *Nippon* on ceramics after 1921 as a part of the company name more than as an identification of the country of origin. More pieces marked *Nippon* will be found in the Dragonware, Moriage, and Noritake categories.

Chocolate Set, Lid, Enameled, Gilt Leaves, Cobalt Blue, 10-In. Pot, 3 x 4 ¾ In., 13 Piece	115
Humidor, Lid, Red Knob, Named Cottage, Swan, Scene, 7 In.	93
Humidor, Painted, Desert Man On Camel, 7 x 5 In.	570
Humidor, Painted, Gold & Black Flowers, 6 ½ x 4 ¼ In.	228
Plaque, Walking Geese, Water Landscape, Round, Gilt Band, c.1925, 11 In.	92
Tankard, Painted Roses, Gold Grapes, Handle, 12 In.	75
Teapot, Flowers, Lobed, Squat, Globular, Gilt, Japan, 5 ¾ In.	23
Urn, Arabian Scene, Painted, Gilt Square Handles, 17 ¾ In.	830
Vase, Bird Flower Scent, Gilt Handles, 7 In.	174
Vase, Blue, Gilt, Landscape Reserves, Tapered, High Squared Handles, c.1924, 13 In.	161
Vase, Daffodil Panel, Green Ground, Gilt Trim, Bulbous, 6 In., Pair	52
Vase, Landscape Scene, Square, Cylindrical Neck, Handles, Arched Feet, 6 ¾ In., Pair	210
Vase, Open Handles, Cobalt Blue, 4 Scenic Reserves, Squared Shape, Gilt Handles, c.1920, 10 In.	288
Vase, Painted Pink, White Roses, Handles, c.1925, 13 In.	431
Vase, Painted, Multicolor Flowers, Tapered, Hexagonal, Handles, 1900s, 12 In., Pair	177
Vase, Pink, White Roses, Leaves, Flared Rim, c.1925, 11 In.	316
Vase, Rose Reserve, Heavy Gilt Scrolls, Cylindrical, 15 In.	319
Vase, White Dogwood Reserves, Brown Bands, Footed, Handles, c.1910, 10 In., Pair	316

NODDERS, also called nodding figures or pagods, are figures with heads and hands that are attached to wires. Any slight movement causes the parts to move up and down. They were made in many countries during the eighteenth, nineteenth, and twentieth centuries. A few Art Deco designs are also known. Copies are being made. A more recent type of nodder is made of papier-mache or plastic. These often represent sports figures or comic characters. Most sports nodders are listed in the Sports category.

Black Porter, Luggage, Walker, Celluloid, Windup, Japan, 3 ½ In.	180
Dog, Barking, Pull Leash, Papier-Mache, 18 In. ....*illus*	1368
Donkey, Saddle, Basket, Wheeled Platform, Composition, Pull Toy, 8 In..........................	356
Hawaiian Hula Girl, Grass Skirt, c.1940, 5 ½ In.	78
Lion, Composition, Flocked Coat, Fur Mane, 13 x 18 In...	652
Pig, Papier-Mache, Nodding Head & Tail, Mohair Saddle, c.1920, 9 In. ....*illus*	474
Salt & Pepper Shakers are listed in the Salt & Pepper category.	
Sports Ways, Wally Waterlung, Scuba Equipment, 1960s, 6 ½ In...............................	158
Trade Stimulator, Black Child Holding Chicken, Composition, Wire, 20 In.	3540

NORITAKE porcelain was made in Japan after 1904 by Nippon Toki Kaisha. The best-known Noritake pieces are marked with the *M* in a wreath for the Morimura Brothers, a New York City distributing company. This mark was used until the early 1950s. There may be some helpful price information in the Nippon category, since prices are comparable. Noritake Azalea is listed in the Azalea category in this book.

Basket, Pink & Peach Buds, Leaves, Gilt Trim, c.1910, 8 x 4 In.	50
Bowl, Iris, Tulip, Blue Luster Border, Loop Handle, 1930s, 8 In............................	65
Bowl, Vegetable, Divided, Belinda, 10 ⅛ In.	37
Bowl, Vegetable, Divided, Round, Malibu, 10 ⅛ In..	38
Bowl, Vegetable, Havana, 10 In..	25
Bowl, Vegetable, Lid, Adrian, 10 In.	127
Bowl, Vegetable, Lid, Round, Belinda, 10 In.	112
Bowl, Vegetable, Lid, Round, Havana, 10 In.	39
Bowl, Vegetable, Oval, 10 In..	45
Bowl, Vegetable, Oval, Avalon, 10 In..	40
Bowl, Vegetable, Oval, Belinda, 10 In.	41
Bowl, Vegetable, Oval, Debell, 9 In...	36
Bowl, Vegetable, Oval, Dolores, 10 In.	48
Bowl, Vegetable, Round, Amy, 8 ¾ In.	43
Bowl, Yellow Roses, Leaves, Scroll Handles, Cabriole Feet, c.1918, 4 x 8 In.	95
Butter, Cover, ¼ Lb.	47
Cake Plate, Handles, Malibu, 9 ¾ In...	34
Cheese Dish, Tapered Lid, Cornucopia, Fruit, Multicolor, Green Border, c.1925, 7 x 5 In............	175
Chop Plate, Acton, 12 In...	72
Chop Plate, Harvard, 12 In.	38
Creamer, Aberdale...	14
Creamer, Adelpha..	15
Creamer, Always, 4 ¼ In.	13
Creamer, Amy, 4 In.	14
Creamer, Avalon, 4 In.	25
Creamer, Batista, 4 In.	14
Creamer, Belinda	18
Creamer, Belvoir	18
Creamer, Century	16
Creamer, Debell	23
Creamer, Elizabeth	15
Creamer, Esquire	15
Creamer, Floralee	15
Creamer, Havana	15
Creamer, Nolan	15
Cup & Saucer, Aberdale..	16
Cup & Saucer, Acton, Footed...	19
Cup & Saucer, Adrian..	14
Cup & Saucer, Alexis, Footed	34
Cup & Saucer, Always..	48
Cup & Saucer, Always, Footed	16
Cup & Saucer, Amy...	8
Cup & Saucer, Avalon, Footed..	23
Cup & Saucer, Batista, Footed...	7
Cup & Saucer, Beatrice, Demitasse...	11

Nautical, Wall Pocket, Needlework, Naval, Silk, Velvet, Anchor, Eagle, 1800s, 7 ¾ x 4 In.
$600

Skinner Auctioneers & Appraisers

Netsuke, Bone, Dragon, Walking, Carved, 2 ¼ x 1 ¼ In.
$97

Ruby Lane, Inc.

Netsuke, Ivory, Face, Angry Man, Carved, Signed, 1940s, 1 ½ In.
$255

Ruby Lane, Inc.

This is an edited listing of current prices. Visit **Kovels.com** to check thousands of prices from previous years and sign up for free information on trends, tips, reproductions, marks, and more.

N

Netsuke, Ivory, Turtle, On Bag, Rope, Carved, Signed, 1 ½ x 1 In. $89

Ruby Lane, Inc.

Netsuke, Oxbone, Rats On Tortoise Back, Carved, Signed, 1 ⅝ x 1 In. $150

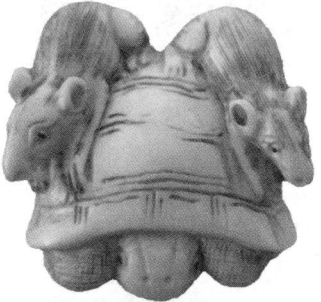

Ruby Lane, Inc.

Netsuke, Wood, Rabbit, Crouching Over Basket, Carved, Signed $125

Ruby Lane, Inc.

Newcomb, Bowl, Yellow Blossoms, Blue Green Underglaze, M. Williams Butler, 1908, 10 In. $9,560

Neal Auction Co.

Cup & Saucer, Cecily	7
Cup & Saucer, Debell, Footed	16
Cup & Saucer, Demitasse, Amy	15
Cup & Saucer, Demitasse, Capri	7
Cup & Saucer, Elizabeth, Footed	11
Cup & Saucer, Ensley, Footed	14
Cup & Saucer, Floralee	7
Cup & Saucer, Footed, Malibu	17
Cup & Saucer, Geneva, Footed	15
Cup & Saucer, Hacienda	16
Cup & Saucer, Havana	6
Dish, Parrot, Perch, Multicolor, Lusterware, 6 x 3 In.	60
Dish, Trinket, Tree, Meadow, Integral Handles, Scalloped, Yellow, Brown, c.1918, 6 x 4 In.	55
Dresser Box, Art Deco, Woman, Hand Mirror, Green M In Wreath Stamp, c.1925, 3 ¾ In.	210
Dresser Box, Lid, Flowers, Pink Trim, Gilt Feet, Round, c.1915, 3 ¾ In.	35
Gravy Boat, Attached Underplate, Acton	40
Gravy Boat, Attached Underplate, Always	47
Gravy Boat, Attached Underplate, Belinda	39
Gravy Boat, Attached Underplate, Capri	14
Gravy Boat, Underplate, Delta	53
Gravy Boat, Underplate, Gilda	36
Gravy Boat, Underplate, Malibu	31
Mustard Jar, Flowers, Leaf Border, Blue Luster Body, Ball Handles, c.1918, 3 x 3 In.	35
Plate, Bird, Tree, Blossoms, Cutout Handles, Blue Luster, 8 ¼ In.	95
Plate, Bread & Butter, 6 ¼ In.	7
Plate, Bread & Butter, Aberdale, 6 ⅜ In.	8
Plate, Bread & Butter, Cecily, 6 ⅜ In.	7
Plate, Bread & Butter, Debell, 6 ⅜ In.	6
Plate, Bread & Butter, Elizabeth, 6 ⅜ In.	5
Plate, Bread & Butter, Gala, 6 ½ In.	6
Plate, Bread & Butter, Hacienda, 7 ½ In.	6
Plate, Bread & Butter, Orleans, 6 ⅜ In.	7
Plate, Dinner, Acton, 10 In.	13
Plate, Dinner, Always, 10 ½ In.	25
Plate, Dinner, Amy, 10 ½ In.	26
Plate, Dinner, Avalon, 9 ⅞ In.	17
Plate, Dinner, Batista, 10 In.	11
Plate, Dinner, Belinda, 10 In.	23
Plate, Dinner, Debell, 10 ½ In.	13
Plate, Dinner, Ensley, 10 ¾ In.	13
Plate, Dinner, Floralee, 10 ⅝ In.	7
Plate, Dinner, Havana, 10 In.	24
Plate, Dinner, Malibu, 10 In.	11
Plate, Dinner, Orleans, 10 ½ In.	11
Plate, Gilt Scrolls, Flowers, 10 ½ In., 12 Piece	58
Plate, Plate, Bread & Butter, Acton, 6 ⅜ In.	7
Plate, Salad, Cecily, 8 ⅜ In.	8
Plate, Salad, Ensley, 8 ⅜ In.	7
Plate, Salad, Floralee, 8 ¼ In.	6
Plate, Salad, Havana, 7 ⅝ In.	8
Plate, Salad, Nolan, 7 ½ In.	7
Platter, Oval, Adrian, 13 In.	40
Platter, Oval, Avalon, 16 In.	48
Platter, Oval, Belinda, 16 In.	63
Platter, Oval, Carol, 13 In.	28
Platter, Oval, Century, 15 In.	53
Platter, Oval, Delta, 16 In.	46
Platter, Oval, Elizabeth, 16 In.	38
Platter, Oval, Ensley, 17 In.	41
Platter, Oval, Flora, 16 In.	73
Platter, Oval, Gilda, 16 In.	78
Platter, Oval, Harvard, 13 In.	37
Platter, Oval, Havana, 16 In.	43
Platter, Oval, Nolan, 16 In.	41
Relish, Alexis, 8 ½ In.	28
Saltshaker, 3 Holes, Always	14
Soup, Dish, Orleans, 7 ½ In.	8

N

Sugar, Lid, Acton	20
Sugar, Lid, Delta	16
Sugar, Lid, Malibu, 2 ⅝ In.	14
Tea Strainer, Pink Border, Black Scalloped Design, 1930s, 3 ⅝ In.	90
Vase, Nippon, Pansies, Wavy Rim, Gilt Overlay, Handles, Tapered, 10 ¾ x 6 ¾ In.	115
Vase, Painted, Cream, Tree Blossom, Peacock, Green M Wreath, 7 ¼ In.	118
Vase, Phoenix, Dragon, Wild Flowers, Multicolor, Square, Footed, 9 In.	495

NORSE POTTERY COMPANY started in Edgerton, Wisconsin, in 1903. In 1904 the company moved to Rockford, Illinois. The company made a black pottery, which resembled early bronze relics of the Scandinavian countries. The firm went out of business in 1913.

Candlestick, Black, Tapered, 11 ½ In., Pair	92
Candlestick, Black, Tapered, Footed, 6 ¾ In.	242
Jug, Shouldered, Handle, Stopper, 8 ¼ In.	403
Lamp Base, Green, Handles, 9 ¾ In.	345
Vase, Cylindrical, 9 In.	173
Vase, Ferns, Bronze & Verdigris Glaze, 4 Handles, Stamped, c.1900, 8 ¾ x 9 In. ....*illus*	1125

NORTH DAKOTA SCHOOL OF MINES was established in 1898 at the University of North Dakota. A ceramics course was included in the curriculum and pieces were made from the clays found in the region. Students at the university made pieces from 1909 to 1949. Although very early pieces were marked *U.N.D.*, most pieces were stamped with the full name of the university.

Bookends, Green Ivy Band, Blue Ground, Demilune Shape, Margaret Cable, 6 In.	661
Plaque, Oxen, Cart, Mottled Rust, 4 ¾ x 7 ¾ In.	590
Vase, Black To Gray To Red, Signed, 1926, 6 x 11 In.	125
Vase, Brown Glaze, Gear Shape Foot, 6 ¼ In.	23
Vase, Brown Matte Glaze, Over Green, Shouldered, Marked, 6 In.	58
Vase, Children Holding Hands, Matte Glaze, Marked, H. Klug, UND, 4 ¾ In. ....*illus*	748
Vase, Covered Wagon, Oxen, Tan, Bentonite Clay, Squat, Tapered, Huckfield, 3 x 5 In.	1750
Vase, Dark Blue, Over Plum, Julia Mattson, 5 ½ x 6 ½ In.	299
Vase, Deer, Stylized Trees, Carved, Blanche Anderson, 1948, 5 ⅞ In. ....*illus*	1062
Vase, Flickertail Wheat, Prairie Dogs, Brown, Bulbous, Tapered, 1943, 6 x 4 In.	1063
Vase, Flower Band, Blue, Purple, Tapered, Squat, Huckfield, 1935, 4 x 5 ¾ In.	438
Vase, Flowers, Carved, Green Matte Glaze, Blue Ink Stamp, Signed, 9 ½ x 5 In.	1250
Vase, Geometric Bands, J. Mattson, Elgin, 4 ⅝ x 6 ¼ In.	403
Vase, Giraffes, Relief, Marked, UND, 1948, 7 ⅞ In. ....*illus*	2875
Vase, Green, Brown Glaze, Incised, 1912, 4 ¾ x 7 In.	2375
Vase, Green, Brown Mottled Glaze, Tapered, Squat, J. Mattson, 2 ¾ In.	161
Vase, Green, Huck, Shouldered, Squat, Signed, Bridgeman, 4 x 5 ½ In.	115
Vase, Green, Tapered, Julia Mattson, 6 In.	58
Vase, Green, Wheat Stalks, Incised, Cabinet, Friedal Hammers, 1927, 6 x 3 In.	531
Vase, Incised Band, Squat Umbrella Shape, Brown, J. Mattson, 3 x 4 ½ In.	80
Vase, Incised Designs, Gunmetal Brown Glaze, 8 ½ In.	173
Vase, Lavender, Evans, Mattson, 5 x 3 ⅝ In.	150
Vase, Light To Dark Blue, Tapered, 7 ¾ In.	23
Vase, Orange, Tapered, Squat, 3 x 5 ¾ In.	150
Vase, Prairie Rose, Incised Green, Red Rim Band, Deep Apricot, M. Cable, 5 x 6 In.	374
Vase, Prairie Roses, Ivory, Cobalt Blue Ground, Bulbous, Squat, Jensen, 8 x 6 ¾ In.	2000
Vase, Purple, Over Indigo Blue, Rolled Rim, Shouldered, Tapered, Marked, 5 x 6 ⅜ In.	288
Vase, Speckled Green, Cylindrical, Signed R.W. Everson, 7 In.	322
Vase, Stylized Feathers, Yellow, Blue, Cylindrical, 1930, 6 ⅜ In.	604
Vase, Stylized Triangles, Ribbed Top Band, Squat, 4 In.	226

NORTHWOOD glass was made by one of the glassmaking companies operated by Harry C. Northwood. His first company, Northwood Glass Co., was founded in Martins Ferry, Ohio, in 1887 and moved to Ellwood City, Pennsylvania, in 1892. The company closed in 1896. Later that same year, Harry Northwood opened the Northwood Co. in Indiana, Pennsylvania. Some pieces made at the Northwood Co. are marked "Northwood" in script. The Northwood Co. became part of a consortium called the National Glass Co. in 1899. Harry left National in 1901 to found the H. Northwood Co. in Wheeling, West Virginia. At the Wheeling factory, Harry Northwood and his brother Carl manufactured pressed and blown tableware and novelties in many colors that are collected today as custard, opalescent, goofus, carnival, and stretch glass. Pieces made between 1905 and about 1915 may have an underlined *N* trademark. Harry Northwood died in 1919, and the plant closed in 1925.

Chrysanthemum, Cruet, Blue Custard, 5 ¼ In.	59
Coin Spot, Sugar Shaker, Lid, Chrysanthemum Swirl, Blue, 9-Panel, c.1900, 5 In.	207

Margaret Kelly Cable
Margaret Kelly Cable was the first trained potter who worked at the North Dakota School of Mines. She worked from 1910 to 1949.

Newcomb, Candlestick, Chamber, Narcissus, Marked, Henrietta Bailey, 1911, 6 ¼ In.
$1,599

Neal Auction Co.

Newcomb, Sugar, Lid, Stylized Leaves, Finial, Sadie Irvine, Aurelia Arbo, 1933, 4 In.
$1,075

Neal Auction Co.

Newcomb, Vase, Calla Lilies, Blue Underglaze, M. Williams Butler, 1902, 11 x 9 In.
$35,850

Neal Auction Co.

N

Newcomb, Vase, Cherokee Roses, Low Relief, Matte Glaze, Henrietta Bailey, 1921, 6 ⅜ In.
$5,378

Neal Auction Co.

Newcomb, Vase, Gladiola, Squat, Sadie Irvine, 1925, 4 ½ x 5 In.
$1,750

Rago Arts & Auction Center

Newcomb, Vase, Maple Leaves, Seed Pods, Henrietta Bailey, c.1922, 5 In.
$600

Skinner Auctioneers & Appraisers

TIP

Having trouble removing a ring that's too tight? Spray it with liquid window cleaner. It lubricates and cleans the ring at the same time.

Coin Spot, Sugar Shaker, Lid, Cranberry Opalescent, 9-Panel, c.1910, 4 ⅝ In.	288
Coin Spot, Sugar Shaker, Metal Lid, Green Opalescent, 9-Panel, c.1900, 4 ⅝ In.	259
Daffodils, Lemonade Set, Green, Pitcher, Applied Handle, 3 Tumblers, 9 & 4 In.	960
Inverted Thumbprint, Sugar Shaker, Lid, Cranberry, 9-Panel, c.1900, 4 ⅝ In.	161
Leaf Umbrella, Pitcher, Water, c.1880, 9 In.	173
Leaf Umbrella, Water Set, Frosted Blue, Feathers, c.1875, 9 In., 4 In., 5 Piece	575
Royal Ivy, Rose Bowl, Frosted Rubina, 4 In.	148
Royal Ivy, Water Set, Pitcher, Tumblers, ubina, c.1900, 8 ⅜ In., 4 In., 7 Piece	748

NU-ART *see Imperial category.*

NUTCRACKERS of many types have been used through the centuries. At first the nutcracker was probably strong teeth or a hammer. But by the nineteenth century, many elaborate and ingenious types were made. Levers, screws, and hammer adaptations were the most popular. Because nutcrackers are still useful, they are still being made, some in the old styles.

Alligator, Cast Iron, Kelly Green, Pat. 93675, 8 In.	85
Bear, Wood, Black Forest, c.1880, 6 In.	275
Legs, Knock Kneed, Boots, Brass, c.1790, 4 ¼ In.	575
Lion's Head, Wood, Flowing Mane, Glass Eyes, Black Forest, 7 ¾ In.	595
Man, Bavarian, Multicolor, Wood, Black Forest, 7 In.	195
Man, Night Cap, Smiling, Wood, Black Forest, 19th Century, 9 In.	350
Man, Painted Cap, Ruffled Collar, Carved Wood, c.1900, 11 In.	71
Mountain Goat, Horns, Wood, Black Forest, 1800s, 8 ¾ In.	240
Nickel Plate, Reversible, Ribbed, Charles Hull, England, c.1880, 5 In.	30
Seminude, Sarong, Wood, 13 ½ In.	54
Silver, Art Deco, 1940s, 5 ½ In.	64
Soldier, Wood, Black Helmet & Boots, Red Suit, 14 In.	79
Squirrel, Holding Nut, Cast Iron, Bronze Clad, 7 ¾ In.	68
Woman, Nude, Wood, 13 In.	94

NYMPHENBURG, *see Royal Nymphenburg.*

OCCUPIED JAPAN was printed on pottery, porcelain, toys, and other goods made during the American occupation of Japan after World War II, from 1947 to 1952. Collectors now search for these pieces. The items were made for export. Ceramic items are listed here. Toys are listed in the Toy category in this book.

Basket, Woven, Flower, Gilt Handle, 2 In.	10
Bowl, Berries, Leaves, Gilt Trim, Octagonal, 7 ½ x 1 ¾ In.	15
Bowl, Flowers, Pink, Reticulated Rim, Gilt, Oval, Bold China, 6 x 4 In.	16
Bust, Lady, Blond, Flower In Hair, Lace Collar, Base, 5 ¼ In.	45
Cachepot, Lid, Cut Out Flowers, Greens, Pastels, Central Flower, 6 In.	48
Creamer, Cow Head, Brown, 4 ¼ x 3 In.	65
Cup & Saucer, Demitasse, Rose Buds, Gilt Garland, Regal China	16
Cup & Saucer, Pagoda, Trees, Pond, Footed, Corona	75
Cup & Saucer, Rust & Blue, Pink Flowers, Scalloped Edges	10
Cup, Multicolor Flowers, Yamaka China, Demitasse	10
Dish, Trinket, Bouquet, Leaves, Blue, Purple, Gilt Handle, Scalloped, 5 x 5 In.	16
Dish, Vegetable, Aladdin, Fantasia, Gilt, 6 x 9 In.	52
Figurine, Bird, On Grapes, Multicolor, 4 In.	24
Figurine, Boy, Hand In Pocket, Ice Cream Cone, Black Cat, 3 ¾ In.	22
Figurine, Boy, Holding Basket, Feeding Pig, 2 ⅝ In.	21
Figurine, Clown, Holding Pig, Puppy, 5 In., Pair	12
Figurine, Colonial Couple, Dancing, 3 ¼ In.	16
Figurine, Colt, Brown, Running, Grass Base, 2 x 2 In.	12
Figurine, Elephant, Curved Trunk, Gray, 3 ¼ x 2 ¾ In.	25
Figurine, Flirty Girl, Ruffled Skirt, Hat, Blue Dress, 5 ½ In.	25
Figurine, Man, Puzzled Look, Hand On Chin, 6 ½ In.	38
Figurine, Pixie, Sitting On Rock, Ruffled Color, Green, 3 In.	35
Flower Frog, Polka Dots, Maruhon, 4 ½ x 1 ½ In.	26
Lemon Server, Flowers, Scalloped Corners, Gilt Trim, Handle, 5 x 5 In.	35
Match Holder, Colonial Couple, Bisque China, 7 x 4 In.	40
Plate, Panels, Flowers, Orange, Blue Border, Hohutosha, 5 ½ In.	55
Salt & Pepper, Ball Shape, Gilt Handle, Bouquet, 2 ½ In.	15
Salt Box, Weave Bottom, Flowers, Multicolor, Wood Flip Lid, 4 x 4 x 3 In.	45
Tea Set, Porcelain, Blue Transfer Print, Marked, 6-In. Teapot, 15 Piece	60

N

Teapot, Lid, Flowers, Scroll Handle, Lid, Sango China, 4 Cup, 8 In..................................	30
Vase, Bulbous, Reticulated, Handles, Flowers, Ucagco China, 6 In.....................................	20
Vase, Cherub, Sitting On Crescent Moon, Playing Horn, Yellow, 3 ½ In...............................	15

OFFICE TECHNOLOGY includes office equipment and related products, such as adding machines, calculators, and check-writing machines. Typewriters are in their own category in this book.

Calculator, Brunsviga-Midget, Brass, Grimme, Natalis & Co., c.1900, 12 In. ....*illus*	270
Check Printing Machine, Peerless Check Protecting Co., Rochester....................................	60
Desk Caddy, Inlaid Mahogany, Ebony, Cabinet Shape, Inkwells, c.1850, 20 x 14 In...............	243
Dictaphone Graphophone, Columbia, Metal, 12 ½ In.	108
Envelope Sealer, Footed, H.J. Reynolds & Co., Chicago, Patented Jan. 4, 1910.....................	215
Letter Press, Official, Cast Iron, 2 Rollers, Metal Arm, Golding, 18 In..............................	360
Pen Rest, Tiger Head, 2 Wells, Bronze, Continental, 7 x 4 ½ In......................................	288
Pen Wipe, Dog, Reclining, Cloth, Oval Rug, 9 In..	660
Pen Wipe, Dog, Standing, Cloth, Burgundy, Black Mat, Round, 5 In..................................	600
Pen Wipe, Rabbit, Cloth, Basket Weave Wings, Mat, 5 x 8 In.	960
Perforator, Cast Iron, Eagle & Flag Decoration, No. 2, Cummings, 1892, 9 In.....................	90
Seal Press, Eagle Shape, Cast Iron, Embossed, E Pluribus Unum, 7 In...............................	4200
Seal Press, Fist Shape, Cast Iron, Brass, Painted Pin Stripes, 8 In...................................	1722
Seal Press, Human Shape, Head Is Press, Cast Iron, Black Paint, R. Gordon	1046
Telegraph Register, Wood Base, L.S. Keeling	2214
Tickertape Machine, Glass, Brass, Steel, TA Edison Inc., 9214, c.1875, 13 ¾ x 7 In..............	8610
Tickertape Machine, Nickel, Glass, Spoked Wheel, Key, c.1875, 14 x 11 In.	240
Tickertape Machine, Textured Steel, Dow Jones Wall Street Journal, Floor Model, 48 In...........	410

OHR pottery was made in Biloxi, Mississippi, from 1883 to 1906 by George E. Ohr, a true eccentric. The pottery was made of very thin clay that was twisted, folded, and dented into odd, graceful shapes. Some pieces were lifelike models of hats, animal heads, or even a potato. Others were decorated with folded clay "snakes." Reproductions and reworked pieces are appearing on the market. These have been reglazed, or snakes and other embellishments have been added.

Ashtray, Green Speckled Glaze, Pipe Knocker Knob In Center, Signed, 2 ¼ x 4 ¾ In.	254
Bank, Pouch, Bisque, Unglazed, Stamped G.E. Ohr, c.1900, 2 ¾ x 3 In.	1063
Bowl, Crimped & Pinched Shape, Sgraffito Mark, c.1900, 2 ½ x 5 ½ In. ....*illus*	4661
Bowl, Green & Gunmetal Mottled Glaze, Exaggerated Outward Folded Rim, 2 x 5 ½ In..............	1250
Bowl, Green Speckled Glaze, Lobed & Folded-In Rim, 2 x 4 In..	1936
Bowl, In-Body Twist, Ocher, Brown Glaze, Stamped, c.1895, 2 ½ x 4 In.	1875
Bowl, Mixed Brown Glaze, Star At Center, Pinched & Crimped Rim, 2 ¼ x 4 ¼ In..................	484
Bowl, Squat, Round, Crimped, Folded Rim, Gunmetal Glaze, c.1900, 3 In...........................	1750
Bowl, Torn, Folded Rim, Green, Black, Gunmetal Speckled Glaze, c.1890, 3 ½ x 5 ¾ In...........	2875
Candleholder, Gunmetal Glaze, Jug Form, Tapered, Pinched, Signed, 5 ⅜ x 3 ¼ In.	605
Candlestick, Chamber, Raspberry, Purple, Sponged-On Glaze, 1898-1910, 4 In.	1750
Candlestick, Chamber, Twisted At Base, Pink, Teal Glaze, Incised, c.1900, 3 ¼ x 4 In.	1250
Creamer, Double Gourd Shape, Curved Handle, Unglazed Redware, Stamped Base, 4 In.	720
Inkwell, Artist's Pallet, Olive Paint Brush & 2 Tubes, Brown Glaze, 1 ⅝ x 6 x 5 In.................	3738
Inkwell, Mule Head, Corn, Green Mottled Glaze, c.1885, 2 x 6 In. ....*illus*	2070
Pitcher, Blue Glaze, Crimped, Cutout Handle, Signed, 4 x 5 ½ In.....................................	6250
Pitcher, Blue, Raspberry, Ocher Mottled Glaze, Handle, Stamped, 1897-1900, 7 ½ x 5 In.	1000
Pitcher, Burnt Baby, Folded, Pinched, Brown Glaze, Handle, Signed, 4 ½ x 2 ½ In...................	1625
Pitcher, Tree Trunk Pattern, Bisque Fired, Stamped, c.1900, 9 ½ x 11 ½ In.	1063
Puzzle Mug, Brown Glaze, Pierced, Spiral Twist Handle, Signed, 3 ¾ x 3 ½ In.	787
Tyg, Bisque, Cinched Waist, 3 Shaped Handles, Signed, 8 ½ x 8 ½ In.	2500
Vase, Bisque, Dimples, Ruffled Rim, Unglazed, Signed, c.1910, 5 ½ x 5 In..........................	1625
Vase, Bisque, In-Body Twist, Folded Rim, Signed, c.1900, 6 x 5 In.	2375
Vase, Bisque, Unglazed, Folded Rim, c.1896, 4 ¾ x 3 In...	2625
Vase, Blue Glaze, Mottled, Squat, Upright Handles, Narrow Rim, c.1900, 2 x 3 In.	2271
Vase, Boat Shape, Folded, Pinched Rim, Amber Orange, Gunmetal Glaze, 1895, 3 x 3 In...........	2500
Vase, Body Twist, Blistered Gunmetal Glaze, c.1900, 8 x 4 ½ In.....................................	5313
Vase, Bottle, Pink, Green, Purple & Gunmetal Glaze, Cylindrical, Stepped Flared Rim, 8 In........	3125
Vase, Brown Mottled, Gunmetal Glaze, Pinched, Folded Rim, c.1905, 3 ½ x 5 In.	2125
Vase, Brown, High Glaze, Round, Navette Rim, Pinched Ends, Footed, 3 x 4 In.	948
Vase, Brown, Speckled Black Glaze, Crimped Rim, Round, 5 x 4 ½ In................................	4688
Vase, Burnt Baby, Dimpled, Stamped, c.1894, 2 ½ x 3 In...	625
Vase, Coupe, Folded, Crimped, Crevices, Gunmetal Glaze, Stamped, 1900, 4 x 3 ½ In.............	3125
Vase, Crimped Rim, Bulbous, Signed, 5 x 4 ½ In..	1875

Newcomb, Vase, Pine Trees, Underglaze, Marked, Sadie Irvine, 1913, 12 ½ In.
$16,730

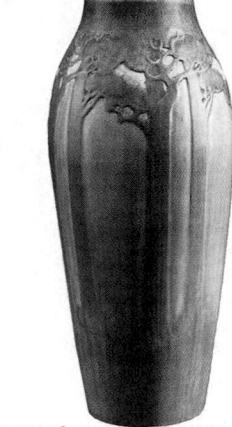

Neal Auction Co.

Nodder, Dog, Barking, Pull Leash, Papier-Mache, 18 In.
$1,368

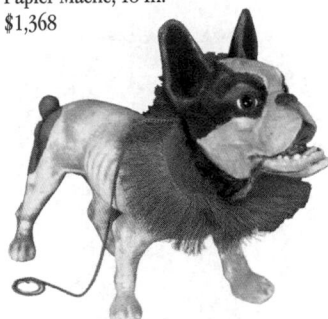

Showtime Auction Services

Nodder, Pig, Papier-Mache, Nodding Head & Tail, Mohair Saddle, c.1920, 9 In.
$474

James D. Julia Auctioneers

Norse, Vase, Ferns, Bronze & Verdigris Glaze, 4 Handles, Stamped, c.1900, 8 ¾ x 9 In.
$1,125

Rago Arts & Auction Center

O

North Dakota School Of Mines, Vase, Children Holding Hands, Matte Glaze, Marked, H. Klug, UND, 4 ¾ In.
$748

Humler & Nolan

North Dakota School Of Mines, Vase, Deer, Stylized Trees, Carved, Blanche Anderson, 1948, 5 ⅞ In.
$1,062

Humler & Nolan

North Dakota School Of Mines, Vase, Giraffes, Relief, Marked, UND, 1948, 7 ⅞ In.
$2,875

Humler & Nolan

Vase, Crimped Rim, Shaped, Unglazed Redware, 4 ½ In.	720
Vase, Dimpled, Folded Rim, Tricolor Glaze, Stamped, 1897-1900, 6 ¼ x 7 In.	7500
Vase, Flared, Green, Ocher, Gunmetal Sponged Glaze, c.1900, 6 x 5 In.	1750
Vase, Folded Rim, Brown, Green, Blue Sponged On Glaze, Stamped, c.1890, 4 x 5 In.	1625
Vase, Folded, Dimpled, Red Bisque Clay, Signature Mark, 1898-1910, 3 ½ x 5 In. *illus*	1125
Vase, Green & Yellow, Crimped, Hashed Neck, Gadroon Rim, c.1890, 4 ½ In.	1554
Vase, Green Speckled Glaze, Folded & Crimped Rim, Signed, 2 ½ x 4 ¼ In.	4375
Vase, Green, Yellow, Brown Speckled Glaze, Squat, Folded Rim, c.1900, 2 ½ x 5 In.	6875
Vase, Gunmetal & Green Glaze, Folded Rim, Signed, 5 ½ x 3 ½ In.	5000
Vase, Gunmetal Gray High Glaze, Bulbous, Folded Rim, 3 ½ x 4 In.	1541
Vase, In-Body Twist, Gunmetal, Green Glaze, Signed, c.1900, 6 ¾ x 4 ¼ In.	5000
Vase, In-Body Twist, Indigo & Green Glaze, Stamped, 3 ½ x 3 ½ In.	3125
Vase, Indigo Mottled, Sponged Multicolor Glazes, 2-Sided, Dimples, c.1900, 7 x 6 In.	26250
Vase, Mahogany, Ocher & Gunmetal Glaze, In-Body Twist, Dimples, Signed, 5 x 4 In.	6875
Vase, Maroon Over Black Dripped Glaze, Impressed, Tapered, 3 ½ In.	561
Vase, Mottled Glaze, Narrow Waist, Flared Neck, Footed, c.1890, 6 In.	2880
Vase, Ocher & Brown Glaze, G.E. Ohr, Biloxi, MS, c.1900, 9 ½ x 4 In.	1750
Vase, Ocher & Brown Speckled Glaze, Ruffled Rim, Stamped, 1897-1900, 6 x 4 In.	1750
Vase, Ocher & Mossy Green Speckled Glaze, Tapered, In-Body Fold At Neck, 4 x 4 In.	5625
Vase, Pinched, Raspberry Red, Multicolor Sponged Glaze, Stamped, 1895, 3 x 4 ½ In. *illus*	7500
Vase, Quatrefoil, Ocher, Brown Speckled Glaze, Stamped, c.1890, 7 ½ x 4 ¼ In.	8125
Vase, Raspberry, Indigo Sponge, Volcanic Glaze, Corseted, Ruffled Rim, c.1900, 5 x 2 In.	7500
Vase, Raspberry, Jade, Indigo Mottled Glaze, Folded Rim, 7 ¾ x 4 ¼ In.	15000
Vase, Red, Spider Web Glaze, Stamped G.E. Ohr, Biloxi, 2 ¾ x 3 ¾ In.	660
Vase, Twisted, Folded Rim, Mottled Blue, White, Sponged Glaze, Stamped, 5 x 4 ½ In. *illus*	25000
Vase, Yellow Glaze, Brown Spatter, Squat, Folded Waist, 3 x 4 In.	2726

OLD PARIS, *see Paris category.*

OLD SLEEPY EYE, *see Sleepy Eye category.*

ONION PATTERN, originally named bulb pattern, is a white ware decorated with cobalt blue or pink. Although it is commonly associated with Meissen, other companies made the pattern in the late nineteenth and the twentieth centuries. A rare type is called *red bud* because there are added red accents on the blue-and-white dishes.

Tureen, Lid, Blue & White, Handles, Meissen, 9 x 13 In.	600
Tureen, Lid, Twist Knob, Rococo, Oval, Handles, Dresden, c.1920, 9 ¾ In.	127

OPALESCENT GLASS is translucent glass that has the tones of the opal gemstone. It originated in England in the 1870s and is often found in pressed glassware made in Victorian times. Opalescent glass was first made in America in 1897 at the Northwood glassworks in Indiana, Pennsylvania. Some dealers use the terms *opaline* and *opalescent* for any of these translucent wares. More opalescent pieces may be listed in Hobnail, Pressed Glass, and other glass categories.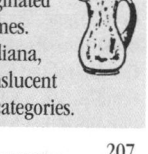

Cranberry, Sugar Shaker, Lid, Northwood, c.1900, 4 ¾ In.	207
Daisy & Fern, Pickle Castor, Lily Embossed Meriden Holder, Northwood, 9 In.	288
Daisy & Fern, Sugar Shaker, Lid, Cranberry, Northwood, c.1905, 4 ⅜ In.	161
Lattice, Strawholder, Blue, White, 3 Ribs, Top & Bottom Collars, 11 ½ In.	273
Swirl, Strawholder, Cranberry & White, Neck Rib, Bulbous Base, 9 ½ In.	454
Swirl, Water Set, Pitcher, Tumbler, Blue, Crimped Rim, c.1900, 9 In., 3 ¾ In., 7 Piece	173

OPALINE, or opal glass, was made in white, green, and other colors. The glass had a matte surface and a lack of transparency. It was often gilded or painted. It was a popular mid-nineteenth-century European glassware.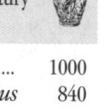

Bowl, Lid, Gilt Bronze Handles & Finial, Footed, France, 14 In.	1000
Bowl, Silver Overlay, Woman, Outstretched Arms, Vines, Whiting, c.1900, 8 In. *illus*	840
Cachepot, White, Aubergine & Gilt Striping, Fleur-De-Lis, 7 x 5 ¾ In., Pair	81
Cologne Bottle, Frosted Flower Stopper, Pink, Gilt Swags, Flecked Neck Snake, 17 ½ In.	92
Urn, Lid, Flowers, Gilt, White Paint, 24 ½ In., Pair	3125

OPERA GLASSES are needed because the stage is a long way from some of the seats at a play or an opera. Mother-of-pearl was a popular decoration on many French glasses.

Brass, Enamel Design, Case, Marked Chapman, 4 In.	161
Enameled, Flowers, Brass Frame, France, 4 ⅛ In.	313
Lorgnette, Sterling Silver, Marcasite, Chain, Victorian, c.1885	165

Mother-Of-Pearl, Brass, Lobed, France, c.1900, 4 x 3 ½ In.	129
Mother-Of-Pearl, Burgundy, Tasco, Leather Case, Japan, 2 ½ x 4 ½ In.	39
Mother-Of-Pearl, Leather Case, Audemair, Paris, 2 x 3 ¾ In.	65

ORPHAN ANNIE first appeared in the comics in 1924. The last strip ran in newspapers on June 13, 2010. The redheaded girl, her dog Sandy, and her friends were on the radio from 1930 to 1942. The first movie based on the strip was produced in 1932. A second movie was produced in 1938. A Broadway musical that opened in 1977, a movie based on the musical and produced in 1982, and a made-for-television movie based on the musical produced in 1999 made Annie popular again, and many toys, dishes, and other memorabilia have been made.

Ashtray, Annie & Sandy Sitting On Rim, Lusterware, Japan, 1930s, 4 x 3 x 3 In.	45
Bank, Dime Register, Tin Lithograph, Annie & Sandy, 1936, 3 x 5 In.	273
Book, Little Orphan Annie & The Pinch-Pennys, Wee Little Books, 1934, 6 x 9 In.	115
Doll, Composition, Jointed, Sandy, Cloth Dress, 1930s, 12 In.	348
Folder, Radio, Silver Star Members, 3 Panels, 1937, 6 ½ In.	320
Ring, Magnifying, Secret Guard, Quaker Cereals, 1941	863
Ring, March Birthstone, Faceted Stone, Ovaltine, 1936	173
Safety Guard Membership Kit, Captain Sparks, Glowbird Badge, Premium, 1942	173
Watch, Sport, Box, Hinged Lid, Annie & Sandy, 1935, 2 ¼ x 4 ½ In.	173

ORREFORS Glassworks, located in the Swedish province of Smaaland, was established in 1898. The company is still making glass for use on the table or as decorations. There is renewed interest in the glass made in the modern styles of the 1940s and 1950s. In 1990, the company merged with Kosta Boda. Most vases and decorative pieces are signed with the etched name *Orrefors*.

Orrefors

Bowl, Clear To Cranberry, Etched & Cut Design, 1982, 4 ¼ x 8 In.	295
Bowl, Clear, Frosted Dancing Nudes, Birds, Deer, Hexagonal, Signed, Bill Gates, c.1945, 8 x 9 In.	184
Bowl, Oak Leaves, Blue, Jans Johansson, 4 ½ x 8 ½ In.	1168
Bowl, Toprup Pattern, Signed, Sven Palmquist, 1960s, 7 x 2 ½ In.	150
Candlestick, Cobalt Blue Nozzle, Green Drip Pan, Column, Round Foot, 9 x 12 In., Pair	295
Candlestick, Crystal, Round Dome Foot, Wavy Rim, 12 In., Pair	60
Lamp Base, Textured, Cinched Waist, Nickeled Brass Fitting, Fagerlund, 1960s, 16 In., Pair	3625
Lamp, Hanging, Pressed Glass Plates, Brass Fittings, Bud Shape, C. Fagerlund, 9 ½ x 18 In.	531
Lamp, Pressed Glass Plates, Brass Fittings, Cylindrical, C. Fagerlund, 7 ½ x 20 In.	344
Sconce, Glass, Brass, Carl Fagerlund, Sweden, 1950s, 11 x 4 ¾ In., Pair	688
Sconce, Threaded & Textured, Brass Mount, C. Fagerlund, 1960s, 11 x 4 In., Pair	1250
Vase, Ariel, Woman, Dove, Burgundy Glass, Air Trap, Octagonal, Signed E. Ohrstrom, 4 x 7 In.	2074
Vase, Etched Diana, Crescent Moon, Lindstrand, 1930s, 6 x 5 In.	150
Vase, Fish Graal, Aquatic Plants, Thick Walls, Edvard Hald, 1900s, 7 In. ....*illus*	677
Vase, Girl & Dove, Ariel, Clear, Blue & Green Amoebic Swirls, E. Ohrstrom, 7 x 5 In.	4688
Vase, Woman Dancing, Engraved, 1951, 13 ½ In.	615

OVERBECK POTTERY was made by four sisters named Overbeck at a pottery in Cambridge City, Indiana. They started in 1911. They made all types of vases, each one-of-a-kind. Small, hand-modeled figurines are the most popular pieces with today's collectors. The factory continued until 1955, when the last of the four sisters died.

Figurine, Gentleman, Impressed Logo, 5 ¼ In. ....*illus*	83
Figurine, Southern Belle, Shovel Bonnet, Shawl, Hoop Dress, Polka Dot, Umbrella, 4 In.	425
Plate, Ducks, Glazed, Mary Frances, Incised OBK, F, c.1920, 7 In. ....*illus*	1875
Vase, Stylized Birds, Incised, Crackled Panels, Terra-Cotta Glaze, Bulbous, 3 x 4 In.	4063
Vase, Stylized Figures & Trees, Gray Glaze, Blue Inside, Chalice Shape, 7 x 5 In.	6875

OWENS POTTERY was made in Zanesville, Ohio, from 1891 to 1928. The first art pottery was made after 1896. Utopian Ware, Cyrano, Navarre, Feroza, and Henri Deux were made. Pieces were usually marked with a form of the name *Owens*. About 1907, the firm began to make tile and discontinued the art pottery wares.

Cider Jug, Opalescence, Inlaid Malachite, Painted Leaves, Flowers, Gold, 6 ¾ In.	212
Ewer, Utopian, Standard Glaze, Orange Flower, Footed, Cutout Handle, 6 In.	61
Jardiniere, Henri Deux, Woman, Blond Flowing Hair, Abstract Forest, Scalloped Rim, 8 In.	218
Jardiniere, Holland Scene, Woman Feeding Goose, Brick Wall, Delft Line, Bulbous, 9 In.	182
Jug, Liquid Bouillon, High Glass Brown, Ankers, 6 ¾ In.	75
Lamp, 2-Light, Utopian, Indian, Moon Flask Shape, 23 In.	1180
Mug, Utopian Glaze, Branch, Flowers, Leaves, Signed, Tot Steele, 4 ⅞ In.	23
Pitcher, Stork, Cream Shaded To Green Semigloss Glaze, Lotus Line, 8 ¼ In.	121
Pitcher, Utopian, Standard Brown Glaze, Orange Flower, 12 In.	79

Office Technology, Calculator, Brunsviga-Midget, Brass, Grimme, Natalis & Co., c.1900, 12 In. $270

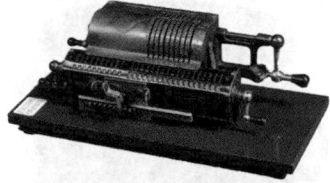

Skinner Auctioneers & Appraisers

Ohr, Bowl, Crimped & Pinched Shape, Sgraffito Mark, c.1900, 2 ½ x 5 ½ In. $4,661

Neal Auction Co.

Ohr, Inkwell, Mule Head, Corn, Green Mottled Glaze, c.1885, 2 x 6 In. $2,070

Glass Works Auctions

Ohr, Vase, Folded, Dimpled, Red Bisque Clay, Signature Mark, 1898-1910, 3 ½ x 5 In. $1,125

Rago Arts & Auction Center

O

Ohr, Vase, Pinched, Raspberry Red, Multicolor Sponged Glaze, Stamped, 1895, 3 x 4 ½ In.
$7,500

Rago Arts & Auction Center

Ohr, Vase, Twisted, Folded Rim, Mottled Blue, White, Sponged Glaze, Stamped, 5 x 4 ½ In.
$25,000

Rago Arts & Auction Center

Opaline, Bowl, Silver Overlay, Woman, Outstretched Arms, Vines, Whiting, c.1900, 8 In.
$840

Skinner Auctioneers & Appraisers

Orrefors, Vase, Fish Graal, Aquatic Plants, Thick Walls, Edvard Hald, 1900s, 7 In.
$677

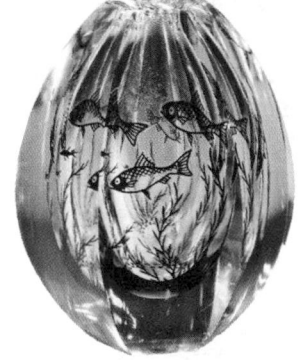

Skinner Auctioneers & Appraisers

Rose Bowl, Flowers, Green Glaze, 3-Footed, Round, 6 In.	35
Tile, Little Bo Peep, Nursery Rhyme, Square, 11 ⅝ In. ....*illus*	885
Vase, 2 Women, Stylized, Long Handles, Henri Deaux, 9 In.	240
Vase, Alpine, Flowers, Buff To Brown Ombre Slip, Bulbous, Tapered Neck, 15 In.	194
Vase, Autumn Leaves On Branch, Cream Shaded To Green Glossy Glaze, F. Ferrell, 12 In.	605
Vase, Brown Glaze, Yellow Flower, Applied Silver Stylized Overlay, Flared Rim, 3 x 3 In.	400
Vase, Bud, Gunmetal, Dimpled, Long Neck, Squat Base, 5 ¾ In.	52
Vase, Henri Deux, Nude Woman, Seated, Lotus Blossoms, 4 Color Glazes, Handles, 14 In.	708
Vase, Henri Deux, Poppies, Blue, Green, Gold, 6 ½ In.	130
Vase, Iguana, Carved, Mottled Green Matte Glaze, 3 Handles, 7 x 5 In.	250
Vase, Lotus, Grapevines, Grapes, Tan Shaded To Pink, Frank Ferrell, 16 ½ In.	1298
Vase, Painted Red, Gold Flower, Long Neck, Bulbous Base, White Frit Glaze, 2 ½ x 5 In.	188
Vase, Swirls & Lion Design, Brown High Gloss Glaze, Cylindrical, A. Haubrich, 15 In.	787
Vase, Twist, Matte Glaze, Raspberries, On Branch, Monogram, Cecil Excel, 13 ¾ In.	177
Vase, Utopian Standard Glaze, Orange Flowers, Green Leaves, Cylindrical, 14 In.	161
Vase, Utopian, Brown, Orange, Yellow, Standard Glaze, Cabinet, Marked J.B. Owens, 4 In.	69
Vase, Utopian, Kitten, Brown Glaze, Oval, Eberlein, 15 ½ In.	4000
Vase, Utopian, Standard Brown Glaze, Daffodils, 5 In.	85
Vase, Venetian, Gold Luster Finish, Rainbow Highlights, Handles, 10 ¼ In.	212
Vase, White Flowers, Gray Glaze, High Shouldered, 7 ¾ In.	127

OYSTER PLATES were popular from the 1880s. Each course at dinner was served in a special dish. The oyster plate had indentations shaped like oysters. Usually six oysters were held on a plate. There is no greater value to a plate with more oysters, although that myth continues to haunt antiques dealers. There are other plates for shellfish, including cockle plates and whelk plates. The appropriately shaped indentations are part of the design of these dishes.

4 Wells, Pink, Brown, Germany, 1880s, 8 ½ In.	85
5 Wells, Center Fish, Pink & White Flowers, Peach Ground, CT Germany, 9 In.	175
5 Wells, Crescent Shape, Yellow Palette, Pink Wells, 19th Century, 9 In.	45
5 Wells, Gold, Pearl White, C. Tielsch & Co., 9 In.	175
5 Wells, Majolica, Burgundy, Gold Trim, T.V. France, Limoges, 8 In.	97
5 Wells, Porcelain, Painted Ship & Sea Scenes, Blue & White, Gold Trim, 8 ¼ In.	133
5 Wells, Porcelain, Porcelain Shell Shape, Shell Decoration & Feet, Fielding, 10 In., 8 Piece	1107
5 Wells, Porcelain, Raised Gold Decoration, Ribbon, Shells, C. Tielsch, 9 In.	182
5 Wells, Porcelain, White, Pink Flower Dividers, Rope Twist Stems, 9 In.	79
5 Wells, Rock Rose, Cream Ground, Gilt Trim, Limoges, 8 ¾ In.	175
5 Wells, Sea Urchins, Enameled, Haviland, 8 ½ In.	185
5 Wells, Seaweed, Shells, Green, Red, Yellow, Wedgwood, c.1948, 8 In.	799
6 Wells, Center Dip Well, Quimper Style, Flowers, Peasant, Blue & White Trim, 11 In.	91
6 Wells, Figural, Cherub, Holding Plate, Copeland, c.1860, 12 In.	2750
6 Wells, Majolica, Black Shaded To Teal Shaded To Pink, Longchamp, 9 In.	97
6 Wells, Majolica, Fish Head, Majolica, Blue Scale Ground, Star Shape, Yellow Border, 10 In.	157
6 Wells, Majolica, Fish, Seaweed Ground, Italy, 12 In.	182
6 Wells, Majolica, Mottled & Iridescent Green, Long Cracker Well, Minton, 9 In.	454
6 Wells, Majolica, Pink, George Jones, 19th Century, 9 In.	536
6 Wells, Pink On White, Ribbed, Marked, 8 In.	80
6 Wells, Porcelain, Painted Roses, Green Leaves, White Ground, Austria, 8 ¾ In.	85
6 Wells, Porcelain, Seaweed Decoration, Gilt, Gray Shaped Border, Haviland, 9 ¼ In.	103
6 Wells, Porcelain, Sunflower, Center Blue Well, English Registry Mark, 1800s, 10 In.	177
6 Wells, Porcelain, White, Gilt Spiral Shell Dividers, 9 ¼ In.	169
6 Wells, Raised Starfish, Green Scalloped Border, c.1910, 9 In.	140
6 Wells, Rope Twist Border, Green, Red, Blue Black, Majolica, Round, c.1910, 9 In.	104
6 Wells, Roses, Gilt Shaped Rim, O. & E.G., Royal Austrian, c.1889, 8 ½ In.	54
6 Wells, Roses, Leaf Border, Martin & Duche, Limoges, c.1925, 10 In.	92
6 Wells, White, Bareuther Waldsassen, Germany, 9 ¼ In.	50
9 Wells, Turquoise, Shell Dividers, Majolica, Minton, 10 In.	303

PADEN CITY GLASS MANUFACTURING COMPANY was established in 1916 at Paden City, West Virginia. The company made over twenty different colors of glass. The firm closed in 1951. Paden City Pottery may be listed in Dinnerware.

Crow's Foot, Candleholder, 3-Light, Red, Irwin Etch	95
Crow's Foot, Candleholder, 3-Light, Wheel Cut	17
Crow's Foot, Candy Dish, Lid, Cobalt Blue, Pod Flower Silver Overlay, 3 Parts	295
Crow's Foot, Cheese & Cracker Set, Lattice Flower Overlay	65
Crow's Foot, Compote, Red, 3 ½ x 6 ¼ In.	30

Crow's Foot, Console, Cobalt Blue, Silver Overlay, 11 ½ In..............................	175
Crow's Foot, Creamer, Red, Footed	18
Crow's Foot, Cup & Saucer, Pink, Footed	12
Crow's Foot, Cup & Saucer, Red, Footed	24
Crow's Foot, Plate, Pink, Square, 8 ½ In...	8
Crow's Foot, Plate, Red, 2 Handles, 10 ½ In...	45
Crow's Foot, Soup, Cream, Red, 4 ½ In..	30
Crow's Foot, Sugar, Red..	18
Cupid, Bowl, Mayonnaise, Green	145
Cupid, Vase, Lavender, White Cased Glass, Silver Overlay, Germany, 10 In.	185
Eden Rose, Creamer, Green	45
Figurine, Chinese Pheasant, 13 x 16 In.	110
Gazebo, Candy Dish, Lid, Etched, Gold Trim, 3 Parts......................................	55
Gazebo, Sugar & Creamer	45
Glades, Compote, Ruby Red, 7 ½ x 5 ½ In...	75
Glades, Decanter, Ruby Red	75
Glades, Sugar, Red...	30
Glades, Tumbler, Red, 12 Oz., 5 In.	65
Largo, Bowl, Ice Blue, Footed, 10 x 6 ½ In...	45
Largo, Candlestick, Blue, 5 In.	45
Largo, Cup, Cobalt Blue	35
Largo, Sugar & Creamer, Ruby...	120
Maya, Bowl, Ice Blue, Rolled Edge, 12 In.	75
Maya, Plate, Dinner, Red, 9 In., 4 Piece	180
Maya, Tray, Red, 2 Handles, 11 ½ In..	125
Mr. B, Candy Dish, Lid, Heart Shape, Floral Cutting, 3 Parts, 7 ½ In.	35
Mrs. B, Vase, Black Amethyst, Silver Overlay, 9 In.	200
Partyline, Creamer, Green	12
Partyline, Cup, Green, 6 Oz.	9
Partyline, Cup, Pink	10
Partyline, Shaker, Amber	25
Partyline, Sugar, Pink	12
Peacock & Rose, Console, Rolled, 14 In.	55
Peacock & Rose, Plate, Cheese & Cracker, Pink, Indented, 10 ½ In...................	65
Peacock & Rose, Vase, Green, Elliptical, 8 ¼ In.	295
Penny, Cup, Red..	10
Penny, Finger Bowl, Red, 4 ⅜ x 2 ¼ In.	20
Penny, Plate, Luncheon, Blue, 8 In.	14
Penny, Saucer, Red	4
Penny, Tumbler, Iced Tea, Amber, 12 Oz., 5 ¼ In.	8
Penny, Tumbler, Iced Tea, Red, 12 Oz., 5 ¼ In.	15
Penny, Tumbler, Juice, Blue, 5 Oz., 3 ⅞ In...	15
Penny, Tumbler, Water, Red, 10 Oz., 4 ⅛ In.	12
Penny, Whiskey, Red, 3 Oz., 2 ¾ In.	10
Popeye & Olive, Saucer, Red..	15
Popeye & Olive, Sherbet, Red	18
Relish, Etched Dove, 4 Sections, Handles, 10 In.	48

PAINTINGS listed in this book are not works by major artists but rather decorative paintings on ivory, board, or glass that would be of interest to the average collector. Watercolors on paper are listed under Picture. To learn the value of an oil painting by a listed artist, you must contact an expert in that area.

Miniature, Oil On Board, Boy, Playing Croquet, Frame, 6 x 5 In........................	60
Miniature, Oil On Board, Woman, On Bench, Garden, Karin Schaefers, 4 x 5 In.	295
Miniature, Oil On Canvas, Desert Landscape, Frame, c.1950, 6 x 6 In................	90
Miniature, Oil On Ivory, Nude, Suitor, Cherubs, 3 ½ x 3 In.	399
Miniature, Oil On Ivory, Portrait Of Napoleon Bonaparte, 3 ½ x 2 ½ In.	599
Miniature, Oil On Ivory, Portrait Of Young Girl, Bonnet, Jean Guy, 1800s, 4 x 3 In.	425
Miniature, Oil On Ivory, Woman, Long Curly Hair, France, Frame, 1800s, 5 x 2 In.	985
Oil On Board, Allentown Street Scene, Walter Emerson Baum, c.1940, 10 x 11 In.	889
Oil On Board, Cape Cod House, Harold Matthews Brett, Frame, c.1940, 10 x 14 In.	531
Oil On Board, Fall Landscape, River, Walter Emerson Baum, c.1935, 11 x 14 In.	2607
Oil On Board, Fall Trees, Stream, Landscape, David Stirling, Frame, c.1950, 16 x 20 In.	875
Oil On Board, Gamecock, Strutting, England, Wood Frame, 15 x 22 In.	588
Oil On Board, Homecoming, Landscape, Birch Trees, Leo Blake, Frame, c.1965, 10 x 8 In.	106
Oil On Board, Interior Tavern Scene, Carved Giltwood Frame, c.1840, 13 x 11 In.	180

Overbeck, Figurine, Gentleman, Impressed Logo, 5 ¼ In.
$83

Humler & Nolan

Overbeck, Plate, Ducks, Glazed, Mary Frances, Incised OBK, F, c.1920, 7 In.
$1,875

Rago Arts & Auction Center

Owens, Tile, Little Bo Peep, Nursery Rhyme, Square, 11 ⅝ In.
$885

Humler & Nolan

Painting, Oil On Canvas, Cat, Seated, Painted Frame, Gilt Liner, 10 ¾ x 12 In. **$1,599**

Skinner Auctioneers & Appraisers

Painting, Oil On Ivory, Maidens, Pauper, Dutailty, Gilt Frame, 7 ½ In. **$375**

Leslie Hindman Auctioneers

Painting, Oil On Ivory, Portrait, Young Boy, Gilt Case, A. Costa, c.1900, 4 ½ x 3 ½ In. **$523**

Cowan's Auctions

TIP

The best place to store paintings is in a closet with no exterior walls. The temperature and humidity levels will be the best in your house.

Oil On Board, Landscape, Buildings, William Lathrop, c.1910, 15 ½ x 20 In.	3360
Oil On Board, Landscape, Harvested Farm Fields, Town, Frame, c.1860, 10 x 14 In.	540
Oil On Board, Montmartre, French Street, E. Maclet, 12 x 10 In.	2000
Oil On Board, Offshore Fishing Scene, Franklin D. Briscoe, Frame, c.1880, 10 x 14 In.	1298
Oil On Board, Pansies In Copper Pot, William Ewing III, Giltwood Frame, c.1950, 10 x 8 In.	246
Oil On Board, Shed, Trees, Untitled, Constance Mable Peters, Frame, c.1930, 9 ½ x 8 In.	500
Oil On Board, Sunset Landscape, Signed S.R. Gifford, Frame, 15 x 21 In.	2952
Oil On Board, Vermont Winter, Hilly Landscape, Andrew Thomas Schwartz, 9 x 12 In.	480
Oil On Board, Winter Landing At Minot's Light, 12 ¼ x 9 ½ In.	1560
Oil On Canvas, 3 Girls, Fall Colors, Frederic Menguy, Frame, c.1995, 24 x 24 In.	326
Oil On Canvas, Blacksmith Shop, Horse, Dog, Bird, E. Longley, Frame, 1800s, 30 x 26 In.	460
Oil On Canvas, Bouquet De Fleurs, c.1915, 32 x 25 ½ In.	2250
Oil On Canvas, Bull, Full Profile, Landscape, Frame, c.1860, 16 x 20 In.	810
Oil On Canvas, Cat, Seated, Painted Frame, Gilt Liner, 10 ¾ x 12 In. ....*illus*	1599
Oil On Canvas, Chinese Covered Jar, Teapot, Robert D. Hunter, Frame, c.1985, 20 x 34 In.	3540
Oil On Canvas, Compote, Fruit, Still Life, Giltwood Frame, c.1910, 13 x 20 In.	570
Oil On Canvas, Embarcadero, Dietz Edzard, c.1950, 18 x 15 In.	1200
Oil On Canvas, Flowers, Spilling From Basket, Gilt Frame, 1800s, 12 x 16 In.	649
Oil On Canvas, Frothy Waves, Rocks, Seascape, Leon Lundmark, c.1930, 26 x 30 In.	500
Oil On Canvas, Gentleman, Seated, c.1850, 30 x 25 In.	720
Oil On Canvas, Girl With Cat, Horacio, 1940s, 24 x 18 In.	590
Oil On Canvas, Girl, Portrait, Arm On Red Pillow, Frame, c.1860, 30 x 26 In.	1895
Oil On Canvas, Harbor Scene, Continental, Gold Frame, c.1810, 12 x 18 In.	431
Oil On Canvas, Harvest Scene, Workers Gathering Fruit, Nuts, Frame, 1800s, 14 x 20 In.	510
Oil On Canvas, Hunters, Dogs, Frame, Painting, E.A. Willis, c.1875, 17 x 13 In.	2015
Oil On Canvas, John Marshall, Court Justice, Signed Henrietta Duer, Frame 1935, 35 x 28 In.	215
Oil On Canvas, Lake, Trees, Mountains, Frame, c.1900, 16 x 24 In.	55
Oil On Canvas, Lakeside Scene, Fisherman, Cottage, H. Holstad, Frame, 1800s, 23 x 29 In.	181
Oil On Canvas, Landscape, Ducks, Signed, Calon, 1856, 19 x 23 In.	540
Oil On Canvas, Macara's Wharf, Provincetown, W.T. Robinson, Frame, c.1920, 16 x 24 In.	1121
Oil On Canvas, Man Playing Cello, Jack Koenig, 1950, 13 x 16 In.	2040
Oil On Canvas, Man, Seated, Black Coat, Red Chair, Frame, 1800s, 36 x 28 In.	354
Oil On Canvas, Mary Corcoran Wedding Portrait, James Reid Lambdin, Frame, 36 x 27 In.	2400
Oil On Canvas, Mother & Daughter, Sitting At Table, 21 x 27 In.	5175
Oil On Canvas, Mountain, Wildflowers, B. Champney, Frame, c.1900, 25 x 14 In.	3250
Oil On Canvas, Opportunist, Fox In Snowy Landscape, Jacob Pfeiffer, 1974, 38 x 16 ½ In.	600
Oil On Canvas, Portrait, Gentleman, c.1850, 21 x 16 ½ In.	180
Oil On Canvas, Portrait, Man, Beard, Frame, c.1890, 17 x 14 In.	215
Oil On Canvas, Portrait, Woman In Lace Cap, Signed, Oval, Frame, 1800s, 9 x 6 ½ In.	240
Oil On Canvas, Portrait, Woman, White Dress, Bouquet, Frame, c.1850, 32 x 25 ½ In.	300
Oil On Canvas, River Landscape, House, 2 Gentlemen Fishermen, 18 x 24 In.	308
Oil On Canvas, River, Waterfall, Artist, Easel, F. Richardt, Frame, c.1870, 25 x 17 In.	3600
Oil On Canvas, Seascape, C. Hamilton, Frame, c.1899, 24 x 30 In.	465
Oil On Canvas, Seascape, Sailing Ships, Frame, Signed, c.1910, 16 ½ x 20 In.	270
Oil On Canvas, Seascape, Steamship, A.C. Stuart, Frame, c.1870, 18 x 30 In.	1422
Oil On Canvas, Sheep, Cows, Farm Landscape, G. Higgins, Frame, c.1900, 14 x 22 In.	516
Oil On Canvas, Side Entrance, View Of Large Building, Signed, H.H. Travers, 1899, 22 x 18 In.	1500
Oil On Canvas, The Lesson, Man, Scolding Girl, Hearth, 1800s, 18 x 14 In.	500
Oil On Canvas, The Proposal, Man Putting Ring On Woman's Finger, 26 x 34 In.	6573
Oil On Canvas, Winter Skating Scene, Geo. Willoughby, 1863, 17 x 24 In.	1200
Oil On Canvas, Winter Sleigh Race, W.H. Look, Frame, 1898, 24 x 30 In.	1778
Oil On Canvas, Woman, Carrying Tray, c.1810, 36 x 25 In.	1067
Oil On Canvas, Woman, Nude, Back View, Frame, Wm. Meyerowitz, 35 x 23 In.	972
Oil On Canvas, Woman, Seated, Chinese, c.1850, 23 ½ x 17 ¾ In.	1560
Oil On Canvas, Woman, Seated, Gray Dress, Frame, c.1850, 17 x 14 In.	330
Oil On Canvas, Woman, Seated, Holding Reeds, Henry M. Carr, Frame, 1921, 24 x 18 In.	531
Oil On Canvas, Young Woman Holding Spool, F. Besson, 1847, 49 x 35 In.	1793
Oil On Ivory, Maidens, Pauper, Dutailty, Gilt Frame, 7 ½ In. ....*illus*	375
Oil On Ivory, Portrait, Young Boy, Gilt Case, A. Costa, c.1900, 4 ½ x 3 ½ In. ....*illus*	523
Oil On Masonite, Houses In The Winter, Alden L. Steck, Frame, 30 x 35 In.	960
Oil On Masonite, Landscape, Country Road, Will Hinds, c.1950, 14 x 18 In.	572
Oil On Masonite, Rainbow Fleet, Sailboats, Jerome Howes, Frame, c.1980, 10 x 36 In.	1062
Oil On Masonite, Rockport Fishing Wharf, Signed Bosa, c.1970, 12 x 15 ¾ In.	375
Oil On Masonite, Surrealist Kitchen, Gertrude Abercrombie, 1950, 5 x 7 In.	6500
Oil On Masonite, Windmill, Montmartre, Signed Quizer, c.1945, 11 x 16 In.	2500
Oil On Metal, Woman, Austrian Folk Costume, 19th Century, 5 x 5 In.	850
Oil On Panel, La Porte Du Grand Horloge A Rouen, Clock, Street, G. Madelian, 18 x 15 In.	688

Oil On Panel, Portrait, Young Woman, Basket, c.1830, 10 ½ x 8 In. 570
Oil On Panel, Woman In Garden, Signed Leon Duval-Gozlan, France, 6 x 8 ½ In. 625
Oil On Paper, Boat, Mountain Lake, American School, Frame, c.1890, 7 x 11 In. 236
Oil On Paper, Maharaja, Attendant, Basohli Style, Frame, c.1900, 14 ½ x 11 ½ In. .... *illus* 123
Oil On Tin, Alchemist, In Workshop, Frame, 1800s, 8 ½ x 9 ¾ In. 390
Oil On Tin, Sailing Ships At Sea, Frame, 12 ½ x 17 In. 300
Oil On Tin, Townscape, Steam Engine, Dollar Bay, Mich., Rhoda L. Pearce, c.1890, 10 x 21 In... 1353
Reverse On Glass, Basket Of Flowers, Multicolor, 19th Century, 13 ½ x 20 In. 1082
Reverse On Glass, Mother-Of-Pearl, Mt. Vernon, c.1875, 17 x 45 In. .... *illus* 360
Tinsel, Reverse On Glass, Vase, Flowers, Frame, c.1850, 28 x 22 In. .... *illus* 600

PAIRPOINT Manufacturing Company started in 1880 in New Bedford, Massachusetts. It soon joined with the glassworks nearby and made glass, silver-plated pieces, and lamps. Reverse-painted glass shades and molded shades known as "puffies" were part of the production until the 1930s. The company reorganized and changed its name several times but is still working today. Items listed here are glass or glass and metal. Silver-plated pieces are listed under Silver Plate.

Biscuit Jar, Pink, Cream, Pink Poppies, Embossed Silver Plate Lid, Bail, Marked, 6 In. 413
Bowl, Myrtle, Rolled Rim, Cut, 3 x 8 In. 150
Candlestick, Apple Green, Airtrap Knobs, 12 In. 212
Dresser Box, Cream, Flowers, 5 In. 86
Lamp, 2-Light, Seville Reverse Painted Shade, Verde Antico, Patinated Base, 23 x 16 In. 1476
Lamp, Flower & Butterfly Puffy Shade, Signed Base, 20th Century, 14 ½ In. 295
Lamp, Landscape Shade, Signed Hugo Fisher, 15 ½ x 23 In. 1243
Lamp, Peacock, Reverse Painted, Glass Shade, Flared Rim, Patinated Metal Base, 22 x 15 In. 2700
Lamp, Puffy Rose Bouquet, White, Rose, Burgundy, Blown Glass, Tree Trunk Base, 10 x 19 In.... 10935
Lamp, Puffy, Apple Tree, Trunk Base, Marked, 21 In. .... *illus* 23700
Lamp, Puffy, Frosted, Pink Glass Shade, Flowers, Landscape, Silver Lacquer Base, 9 x 15 In. 1875
Lamp, Puffy, Owl, Figural Metal Base, Signed, 20 ½ In. .... *illus* 77025
Lamp, Puffy, Rose, Closed Top, Base Signed, 15 x 10 In. .... *illus* 4600
Lamp, Reverse Painted Farm Scene Shade, Brass, Footed, Signed M. Ano, 20 x 15 In. 1888
Lamp, Reverse Painted Flared Shade, Landscape, Copper Base, Signed, 18 x 22 In. 1700
Lamp, Reverse Painted Shade, Bird, Flowers, Silver Plate Base, Signed, 18 x 22 In. 1586
Lamp, Reverse Painted Shade, Birds, Flowers, Multicolor, Signed Base, 18 x 22 In. 1823
Lamp, Reverse Painted Shade, Flowers, Leaves, Garlands, Patinated Metal, 1920s, 23 x 18 In. 1375
Lamp, Reverse Painted Shade, Silver Plate Base, Marked, c.1900, 22 In. 1875
Powder Box, Pale Green, Gilt Leaves, Flowers, Round, Signed, 1 ¾ x 5 In. 207
Vase, Carnation Design, Bulbous, Flared Rim, 14 In. 1500
Vase, Colonial, Cut, 15 In. 300
Vase, Henrietta, Cranberry Cut To Clear, Pinched Waist, Hobstar Cut Base, 9 In. 2000

PALMER COX, *Brownies, see Brownies category.*

PAPER collectibles, including almanacs, catalogs, children's books, some greeting cards, stock certificates, and other paper ephemera, are listed here. Paper calendars are listed separately in the Calendar category. Paper items may be found in many other sections, such as Christmas and Movie.

Birth Record, Ink, Watercolor, John Kilinger, Frame, 1824, 9 ½ x 7 ½ In. 570
Birth, Baptismal Certificate, Printed, Illuminated, Urn, Flowers, Pa., 1803, 13 x 16 In. 266
Book, Big Little, Mother Goose, Hardcover, 1934, 4 ¼ x 5 ¾ In. 1265
Book, Big Little, Paint Book Variant, Whitman, No. 1933, 3 ⅝ x 8 ½ In. 230
Book, Pop-Up, Little Black Sambo, Blue Ribbon Press, Hardcover, 1934, 60 Pages 475
Book, Pop-Up, Mickey Mouse, Blue Ribbon Books, 1933, 6 ¾ x 8 ¾ In., 28 Pages 247
Book, Pop-Up, Mother Goose, Blue Ribbon Press, 1934, 8 x 9 ¼ In., 20 Pages 153
Book, Pop-Up, Puss-In-Boots, Blue Ribbon Press, 1934, 8 x 9 ¼ In., 20 Pages 407
Bookplate, Armorial, Engraved, K.K., Van Rensselaer, 4 x 2 ¾ In. 960
Bookplate, Armorial, Loyal Au Mort, William Belcher, Savanah, 3 ¾ x 3 In. 420
Bookplate, Engraved, Library Of Congress, No. 2, 2 x 3 In. 300
Bookplate, Ink, Watercolor, Bird, Cutout, Inscribed Sarah Shaner, W.A. Faber, 1813, 6 x 3 In. 900
Bookplate, John Quincy Adams, Armorial, Engraved, 3 ¾ x 2 ¾ In. 1440
Bookplate, Minerva Allegory Engraved, New York Library, 1780, 6 ⅜ x 4 In. 360
Bookplate, Musical Instruments, Statue, Etching, Frame, F. Benson, c.1930, 6 ⅞ x 4 ⅞ In. 1320
Bookplate, Watercolor, Cutwork, Bird, Flowers, Blue, Orange, W. A. Faber, c.1800, 7 x 4 In. 4617
Bookplate, Watercolor, House, Bird, Tree, Sun, Frame, 4 ½ x 3 In. 2187
Bookplate, Watercolor, Ink, Flowering Tree, Frame, Pa., c.1810, 5 ¾ x 4 In. 267
Bookplate, Watercolor, Tulip Emerging From Heart, Inscribed Jacob Hefner 1793, 7 x 4 In. 356
Broadside, $300 Reward, Runaway Slave, Charles Co., Maryland, Frame, 1850s, 15 x 18 In. 2585

Invest in Collectibles
If you invest in collectibles, remember the rules. Buy the best you can, buy perfect items, and care for them so they remain perfect. Provenance (written history) adds to value, as does a signature. Try to spot the trends influenced by news events, such as the death of a celebrity.

Painting, Oil On Paper, Maharaja, Attendant, Basohli Style, Frame, c.1900, 14 ½ x 11 ½ In.
$123

Skinner Auctioneers & Appraisers

Painting, Reverse On Glass, Mother-Of-Pearl, Mt. Vernon, c.1875, 17 x 45 In.
$360

Garth's Auctioneers & Appraisers

Painting, Tinsel, Reverse On Glass, Vase, Flowers, Frame, c.1850, 28 x 22 In.
$600

Garth's Auctioneers & Appraisers

P

Pairpoint, Lamp, Puffy, Apple Tree, Trunk Base, Marked, 21 In.
$23,700

James D. Julia Auctioneers

Pairpoint, Lamp, Puffy, Owl, Figural Metal Base, Signed, 20 ½ In.
$77,025

James D. Julia Auctioneers

Pairpoint, Lamp, Puffy, Rose, Closed Top, Base Signed, 15 x 10 In.
$4,600

Cottone Auctions

Broadside, Chester Boot & Shoe Store, Selling Out At Cost, January 7th 1885, 21 x 12 In.	92
Broadside, Overland Mail Route To California, Stagecoach, Coated Stock, 1866, 16 x 19 In.	5288
Calling Card, Spencerian, Ink, Angels & Banner, John D. Burke, Frame, c.1850, 4 ½ x 6 In.	62
Coat-Of-Arms, Putnam Family, Watercolor On Paper, Frame, c.1806, 14 x 10 In.	2400
Coloring Book, Little Lulu, No. 1258, Whitman, 1955, 8 x 11 In., 64 Pages	1725
Comic Book, Iron Man, Number 1, Big Premier Issue, 1967	1337
Cutwork, 2 Birds, Blue & White, Branch, Gilt Frame, c.1900, 16 x 12 In.	58
Cutwork, Tree, Pot, Birds, Flowers, Children In Branches, Black, Frame, Pa., c.1835, 10 x 8 In.	474
Family Record, Silk On Linen, Hoadley Family, Augusta Hoadley, Conn., 1833, 17 x 17 In.	948
Fraktur, Baptism, Taufwunsch, Watercolor, Ink, c.1776, 6 x 8 In.	81250
Fraktur, Birth & Baptism, Watercolor & Ink, J. VanMinian, Frame, 1818, 10 x 8 In.	5625
Fraktur, Birth & Baptism, Watercolor, Catharina Eberhard, Pa., c.1780, 8 x 12 ¾ In.	149000
Fraktur, Birth Record, Color, Maria Magdelena Christman, 1791, Berks County Pa., 14 x 15 In.	510
Fraktur, Birth Record, Ink, Watercolor, Cecilia Keller Born 1855, D. Peterman, 13 x 11 In.	900
Fraktur, Birth Record, Watercolor, Ink, Ann Lippincott, New Jersey Artist, 1797, 8 x 10 In.	16250
Fraktur, Birth Record, Watercolor, Maria Cathrina, 1786, 8 x 12 In.	6250
Fraktur, Birth, Baptism, Watercolor, Checkerboard, Angels, Infant, 1823, 16 x 13 In.	826
Fraktur, Birth, Baptism, Watercolor, Ink, Rose, Star, John Fredrick Royer, Frame, 1867, 10 x 12 In.	266
Fraktur, Birth, Watercolor, Ink, E. Buck, 1827, 11 x 7 In.	18960
Fraktur, Birth, Watercolor, Ink, Isaac Broft, 2 Hearts, Birds, Children, 1806, 13 x 16 In.	296
Fraktur, Birth, Watercolor, Ink, Magdalina Wagener, Frame, 1797, 13 x 15 ½ In.	385
Fraktur, Birth, Watercolor, Ink, Samuel Moser, Heart, Birds, Flower, 1812, 12 x 15 In.	2607
Fraktur, Birth, Watercolor, Ink, Wilhelm Buger, Hearts, Tulips, Frame, 1769, 5 x 18 In.	2430
Fraktur, Bookplate, Ink, Watercolor, Rebecca Forrer, Landscape, 1843, 4 ¾ x 3 ½ In.	1020
Fraktur, Bookplate, Watercolor, Ink, Tulips, Vines, Script, Maria Hoffler, 1823, 7 x 4 ⅞ In.	1067
Fraktur, Bookplate, Watercolor, Pen & Ink, Tulips, Vine, Frame, 7 ½ x 4 ¾ In.	502
Fraktur, Bookplate, Watercolor, Red Bird, Tulip Tree, Striped Urn, 1800s, 4 ¾ x 3 In.	4977
Fraktur, Death Prayer, Watercolor, Ink, Jesse Laros, M. Miller, Frame, 1836, 5 x 7 ½ In.	770
Fraktur, Marriage Record, Ink, Watercolor, Frame, 1824, 10 x 8 In.	360
Fraktur, Paper, Birth, Baptism, Watercolor, Ink, Floral Wreath, Stars, C. Nies, Frame, 1853, 9 x 7 In.	1298
Fraktur, Schwenkfelder, Bookplate, Watercolor, Ink On Paper, Frame, 1823, 12 x 6 In.	1188
Fraktur, Vorschrift, Birth Record, Watercolor, Ink, German, Pa., c.1817, 9 ¾ x 7 ⅞ In.	53125
Fraktur, Vorschrift, Ink, Birds, German Text, Gottschall Family, Pa., 1834, 8 x 12 ¾ In.	25000
Fraktur, Watercolor, 6 Birds Perched In Tulip Branches, HR, Pennsylvania, 7 ½ x 5 In.	1320
Fraktur, Watercolor, Acrylic, Christmas Tree, Birds, V. Seagraves, c.1950, 16 x 17 In.	210
Fraktur, Watercolor, Bird Mirror Image, Tulips, Hearts, Signed D.Y. Ellinger, 12 x 15 In.	767
Fraktur, Watercolor, Bird, On Stone Perch, Frame, c.1850, 7 ¾ x 6 In.	425
Fraktur, Watercolor, Cross-Legged Angel, Birds, Flowers, Sun, Pa., Frame, 1811, 13 x 15 In.	2844
Fraktur, Watercolor, Ink, 2 Priests, German Text, c.1810, 8 ⅞ x 7 In.	15000
Fraktur, Watercolor, Ink, Compass, Signed M. Meldin, Frame, c.1850, 5 ½ x 5 ½ In.	304
Fraktur, Watercolor, Ink, Heart, Border, Birds, Tulips, Lydia Miller, Frame, 1810, 17 x 12 In.	345
Fraktur, Watercolor, Ink, Heart, Scalloped Border, Birds, Tulips, Lydia Miller, Frame, 1810, 17 x 12 In.	345
Fraktur, Watercolor, Ink, Inscribed Maria Meyer, Birds, Flowers, Pa., Frame, 6 ½ x 5 ½ In.	1007
Fraktur, Watercolor, Ink, Winged Angel Heads, Urns, Flowers, Eagles, 1752, 14 x 16 In.	296
Fraktur, Watercolor, Potted Tulips, Pennsylvania, Frame, c.1820, 9 ½ x 7 ½ In.	246
Journal, Whaling Voyage, Metacom Ship, Drawings, Text, 1842, 2 Vol., 36 Pages, 10 x 7 In.	1920
Ledger Page, Ink, Watercolor, Math Questions, Bird, Monkey In Tree, c.1850, 7 ¼ x 10 In.	264
Letter, Theodore Roosevelt Typed, Rough Rider Recruit, Navy Letterhead, N.Y., 1898	1016
Magazine, Playboy, Marilyn Monroe, 1st Issue, Cover, Interior, Dec. 1953	3896
Manuscript Leaf, Raja On Horseback, Pigment, Gold, India, c.1870, 13 ½ x 9 ¼ In.	767
Menu, Lithograph, Tahitian, Gauguin, c.1890, 8 ½ x 6 ¼ In.	639
N.Y. Tribune, Lincoln's Assassination, April 15, 1865, Vol. XXV, No. 7496, 15 x 21 In.	180
Pamphlet, Happy Hours, Magic Yeast, Litho, Mother Reading To Kids, c.1885, 5 ½ x 4 In.	24
Parade Flag, American, Crepe Paper, 42 Stars, 1890, 8 x 6 In.	94
Passport, Alejandro Oms, Cuban & Negro League Star, Signed, 1937, 2 ½ x 4 In.	2530
Passport, Minnie Minoso, Cuban, Major League Ballplayer, 1946, 4 x 5 ¾ In.	557
Program, The Who Concert, May 29, 1966, 12 Pages, Autographs, 11 x 8 ½ In.	1150
Religious Text, Watercolor, Ink, Heart Panel, Esther Meyer, Pa., 1820, 7 x 6 In.	8125
Stock Certificate, Standard Oil Trust, 50 Shares, July 25, 1882, Signed J.D. Rockefeller, 15 In.	1024
Ticket, Woodstock Concert, Aug. 15-17, 1969, 3 Perforated Stubs, Unused, No. 62700	104

PAPER DOLLS were probably inspired by the pantins, or jumping jacks, made in eighteenth-century Europe. By the 1880s, sheets of printed paper dolls and clothes were being made. The first paper doll books were made in the 1920s. Collectors prefer uncut sheets or books or boxed sets of paper dolls. Prices are about half as much if the pages have been cut.

Annette Funicello, Hawaii, Stand-Up Doll, Clothes, Folder, 1961, 10 x 13 In.	20
Bertie Bright, 4 Outfits, 4 Hats, Envelope, McLoughlin Brothers, 1860s	145

Betty & Billy, Black, Whitman, 1955, Uncut	48
Calendar, Girl, Standing, 10 Dresses, Months On Outfits, Hats, Swift Premium, 1917, Uncut	210
Comics Cutout Book, Popeye, Blondie, Dumb Dora, Just Kids, No. 2097, Saalfield Pub. Co.	413
Dottie Dimple, 4 Outfits, 4 Hats, Envelope, McLoughlin Brothers, 1860s	145
Elizabeth Taylor, 2 Dolls, 8 Pages, Outfits & Accessories, Whitman, 1952, Uncut	125
Flying Nun, 5 Dolls, Clothes, Box Set, 1969	38
Hildegarde Lives In Holland, 1924, Uncut	15
Jane Powell, 2 Dolls, Clothes & Accessories, Whitman, 1951	38
June Allyson, 2 Dolls, 8 Pages Clothes, Whitman, 1952, Uncut	125
Let's Play Eskimo, Alaskan Eskimo Village, 100 Pieces, 1950s, Uncut	48
Magic Princess, Record & Wand, 1964	38
Peg, Nan, Kay, Sue, Clothes, Whitman, 1966, Uncut	45
Polly Pratt, Little Country Cousin, 1920s, 8 x 11 ½ In., Uncut	15
Queen Holden, Hairdo Dolls, 3 Dolls, Outfits, Whitman, 1948	34
Susie Simple, 4 Outfits, 4 Hats, McLoughlin Brothers, 1860s	145
Snow White & The Seven Dwarfs, Whitman, No. 970, Unused, 1938, 11 ¾ x 17 In.	209

PAPERWEIGHTS must have first appeared along with paper in ancient Egypt. Today's collectors search for every type, from the very expensive French weights of the nineteenth century to the modern artist weights or advertising pieces. The glass tops of the paperweights sometimes have been nicked or scratched, and this type of damage can be removed by polishing. Some serious collectors think this type of repair is an alteration and will not buy a repolished weight; others think it is an acceptable technique of restoration that does not change the value. Baccarat paperweights are listed separately under Baccarat.

Advertising, Armour Auto Livery, Early Limousine, Glass, Rounded Corners, 2 x 4 In.	518
Advertising, Glass, Bourse Barber Shop, Seated Seminude Woman, 4 x 2 ½ In.	207
Advertising, None Such, Mince Meat, Glass, Woman Holding Pie, 4 x 2 ½ In.	115
Advertising, Ort & Co., Onion Dealer, Blown Glass, 2 ½ x 3 ¼ In.	345
Advertising, Parke-Davis Drug Co., Pewter, Figural, Baby In Uterus, 5 x 3 ¼ In.	80
Advertising, Trimble & Welcher, Coal Wagon, White Glass, 4 x 2 ⅝ In.	242
Advertising, Upjohn Pill & Granule Co., Milk Glass, Hand Crushing Pill, 4 x 3 In.	161
Ayotte, Bird, Scarlet Macaw, On Branch, Green Ground, 1983, 3 ¼ In.	840
Ayotte, Christmas Cactus, White Berries, Signed, 1988, 3 ½ In.	711
Ayotte, Hummingbird, Green & White, Flowers, Leaves, Signed, 3 ⅛ In. ....*illus*	533
Ayotte, Plum, White Flower, Signed, Inscribed, 3 ½ In.	889
Ayotte, Red, White Poinsettia, Signed, 3 ¾ In.	851
Banford, Bob, Blue Flower, Bee, 2 ½ In.	308
Banford, Bob, Rose, Pink, Faceted, 2 ½ In.	360
Banford, Purple Overlay Iris, Green, White Basket Base, 3 In.	1033
Banford, Ray, Pink Rose, Black Ground, 2 ½ In.	185
Banford, Red Rose, Clear Ground, Signed, 3 In.	365
Bohemian, Flat Cut Ruby Flash, Stag, Landscape, 3 ¾ In.	474
Bradford, 2 Orange Mums, Waffle Cut Base, 3 In.	334
Bradford, Pink Primrose, Cut Star Base, Clear Ground, Signed, 3 In.	444
Bronze, Duck, 4 ½ In.	45
Buzzini, Orange Flower, Bud, Signed, 1990, 3 In.	608
Buzzini, Red, Yellow Flower Bouquet, Clear Ground, Signed, 1987, 3 In.	668
Clichy, Cabbage Rose, Millefiori Canes, Multicolor, Clear Ground, 2 In.	300
Clichy, Cabbage Rose, White, Millefiori Canes, 3 Concentric Rings, Clear, 3 In.	510
Clichy, Millefiori, Open Concentric Canes, Multicolor, 3 x 2 ¼ In.	3081
Clichy, Mushroom, 6 Rose, White Staves, France, c.1850, 2 ½ In.	2640
Clichy, Scattered Millefiori, Clear Ground, 3 In.	1215
Clichy, Swirl, Millefiori Rainbow Cane, Amethyst & White Swirls, 3 x 2 ¼ In.	2133
Clichy, Trefoil Garland, Clear Ground, 2 ¾ In.	770
Cut Cane Center, Concentric Circles, Red, Blue, Yellow, Green, Round, 3 In.	58
Cut Canes, Red & Blue, Cut Daisies, Yellow & White, Dome Shape, 3 In.	58
Eickholt, King Tut Design, Yellow, Lines, Signed, 3 In.	115
Gaunt, Figural, Punch, Always On Top, Cast Brass, Silver Plate, 3 x 5 In.	336
Glass, Ball, Flowers, Russia, 3 ½ In.	120
Glass, Crown, Multicolor Swirl, 2 ¼ In.	326
Grubb, Yellow, White, Orange Flowers, Signed, 1986, 3 In.	425
Hacker, White, Purple Flowers, Snow Ground, 2 ¾ In.	237
Heilman-Roessler, Willow Tree, Frosted Ground, 1984, 3 ¾ In.	207
Interlacing Garland, Clear Ground, c.1900, 3 In.	204
Iron, Skater, Arm Raised, Paint, Hubley, 3 ¼ In.	60
Kaziun, Clematis, Green Leaves, Amethyst Ground, Faceted, Signed, 2 ½ In.	330

Paperweight, Ayotte, Hummingbird, Green & White, Flowers, Leaves, Signed, 3 ⅛ In.
$533

James D. Julia Auctioneers

Paperweight, New England Glass Co., Poinsettia, Leaves, Millefiori Center, Latticinio, 3 In.
$356

James D. Julia Auctioneers

Parian, Figurine, Dante, Standing, Molded Name Plate, c.1865, 20 x 7 ½ In.
$522

New Orleans Auction Galleries, Inc.

P

TIP
A matte glazed pottery piece can be rubbed with olive oil, then wiped clean.

Paris, Urn, People, Elizabethan, Winged Female Handles, Gilt, c.1815, 14 x 7 In., Pair
$799

New Orleans Auction Galleries, Inc.

Patent Model, Carousel, Clockwork, Hollow Tin, Bisque, Robert Steel, Jan. 4, 1876, 14 x 17 In.
$3,674

James D. Julia Auctioneers

Paul Revere, Bowl, Nasturtiums, Cuerda Seca, S.E.G., c.1910, 11 ¾ x 4 ¾ In.
$32,500

Rago Arts & Auction Center

Paul Revere, Bowl, Roosters, Cuerda Seca, Early To Bed, Early To Rise, R. Bacchini, 1909, 5 x 2 In.
$1,750

Rago Arts & Auction Center

Kaziun, Glass, Pedestal, Red Rose, Gold Bee, 3 Canes, c.1875, 1 ½ In.	330
Kaziun, Jr., Charles, Red Crimped Rose, 4 Green Leaves, Tilted, Crystal Pedestal Foot, 2 x 3 In.	830
Kaziun, Morning Glory, Yellow Rim, Bud, Lattice, Cobalt Ground, Gold Foil Bee, 2 In.	390
Labino, Serpent, Coiled, Light Green Ground, 1967, 2 ½ In.	60
Lewis, Close Packed Millefiori, Signed, 1999, 2 ¼ In.	504
Lotton, Charles, Glass, Yellow, White Flowers, Blue Ground, Signed, 1975, 1 ½ x 2 ¾ In.	127
Lotton, David, Purple Clematis, Leaves, 3 ¼ x 4 ¼ In.	126
Lundberg, Lily, Yellow Spotted Petals, Blue & Brown Stamens, Signed, 2 x 2 ¼ In.	326
Manson, Lizard, Green, Tan Scaly Ground, Signed, 1980, 2 ¾ In.	486
Millefiori, Green, Red, Blue Open Concentric Rows, Clear Ground, 1 ¾ In.	356
Millefiori, Pedestal, Blue, Yellow, White, Clear Ground, 1858, 3 ¾ In.	510
Millefiori, Stardust Carpet Ground, Multicolor Canes, France, 3 In.	8700
New England Glass Co., Blue Concentric Millefiori, White Latticinio Ground, 2 ½ In.	122
New England Glass Co., Pear, Red, Clear Base, 3 ⅓ In.	395
New England Glass Co., Poinsettia, Leaves, Millefiori Center, Latticinio, 3 In. ....*illus*	356
Parabelle, Close Packed Millefiori, Dark Ground, Paper Label, 2 ¾ In.	456
Parabelle, Concentric Roses, Pansies, 1996, 3 In.	1007
Parabelle, Spaced Millefiori, Red Ground, 2 ¾ In.	504
Perthshire, Blue & White Overlay, Central Bouquet, Clear Ground, Signed, 2 ¾ In.	356
Perthshire, Bouquet, Encased Double Overlay, 3 ¾ In.	547
Perthshire, Multicolor, Scotland, 2 ½ x 1 ½ In.	156
Perthshire, Sunflower, Orange & Yellow Millefiori Canes, 3 ¼ x 2 In.	652
Rondel Millefiori, Clear Ground, c.1900, 2 ½ In.	180
Rosenfeld, Sunflowers, Daffodils, Blue Ground, Inscribed, 1996, 2 ½ In.	213
Salazar, Angelfish, Iridescent Ground, Lundburg Studios, 1980, 2 ¾ In.	182
Sandwich, Glass, Weed Flower, Blue & White Striped Petal, Green Leaves, 2 ⅝ x 1 ⅝ In.	593
Smith, Red Orchid, Clear Ground, Initialed, 1984, 3 In.	365
Snow Globe, Ohio State Journal, Newspaper Boy Award, Plastic Base, c.1950, 3 ¾ In.	115
St. Louis, Flower, Red, Green Leaves, 5-Sided Black Ground, Clear Surround, 1970, 3 ¼ In.	360
St. Louis, Millefiori, Double Overlay Mushroom, 5 Light Green Sides, 1970, 3 In.	450
St. Louis, Scrambled, Pale Multicolor, 3 In.	326
St. Louis, White Flower, Orange Ground, Signed, 1973, 3 In.	243
Stankard, Cymbidium Orchid, Clear Ground, 1985, 3 In.	1541
Stankard, Flowers With Roots, Clear, Lamp Work, Rectangular, 1991, 4 ½ In.	4063
Stankard, Forget-Me-Nots, Roots, White Ground, Geometric Facets, 1972, 2 In.	570
Stankard, Japanese Anemone, Blackberries, Roses, Foxglove, 1979, 2 ¾ In.	1680
Stankard, Pond Lily, 3 Blossoms, White, Pink, Blue, Yellow, Aqua Ground, 3 x 2 In.	2370
Stankard, Rose Bouquet, Pink, Yellow, White, 7 Buds, Green Leaves, 3 In.	960
Stankard, Spider Orchid, Orange, Signed, 1975, 3 In.	790
Stankard, Yellow Cactus, Clear Ground, Signed, 1979, 3 In.	547
Tarsitano, Honeycomb With Wild Cherries, c.1981, 3 ¼ In.	660
Tarsitano, Red, Blue, Yellow Flowers, Signed, 2 ½ In.	486
Trabucco, Strawberry, White Flowers, Clear Ground, Signed, 1981, 2 ½ In.	243
Ward, Flower, Berry, Black Ground, Pedestal, Signed, 1998, 3 14 In.	456
Ward, Moon, Oak Tree, Black Ground, Signed, 2 ¾ In.	122
Whitefriars, Millefiori, Concentric Bands, 3 In.	360
Ysart, Flower, Purple, Blue Ground, Millefiori Border, 3 In.	420
Ysart, Green Millefiori Center, Yellow, Red Garland, Blue Ground, 3 x 2 ½ In.	711
Ysart, Pink Flowers, Green, White Ground, Domed, Box, 3 In.	375

PAPIER-MACHE is made from paper mixed with glue, chalk, and other ingredients, then molded and baked. It becomes very hard and can be painted. Boxes, trays, and furniture were made of papier-mache. Some of the nineteenth-century pieces were decorated with mother-of-pearl. Papier-mache is still being used to make small toys, figures, candy containers, boxes, and other giftwares. Furniture made of papier-mache is listed in the Furniture category.

Box, Figures Standing In Field, Rifle, Russia, c.1890, 4 x 5 ¾ In.	270
Box, Man, Peacocks, Ctemahob, Russia, 1 ½ x 6 In.	177
Carnival Head, Man, Painted, c.1900, 15 In.	295
Case, Eyeglass, Black, White Flowers, Oval, c.1850, 1 ¾ x 5 In.	46
Cherub Head, Wings, Veiled Prophet Parade Float Design, Painted, St. Louis, 10 ½ x 29 In.	236
Cow, Electric, Mechanical, Head & Mouth Move, Rings Bell Around Neck, 30 x 17 In.	2565
Figure, Lamb, Molded, Seated, White Paint, Removable Head, c.1900, 26 In.	764
Figure, Lion, Leaping, Spring On Hind Legs, France, c.1890, 15 x 19 In.	180
Hat Stand, Milliner's Head, Blue Eyes, Black, Cream Paint, c.1850, 15 In.	1067
Music Box, Cylinder, Kittens, Key, c.1900, 2 x 5 x 3 In.	100
Snuffbox, Portrait, James K. Polk, 1840s, 3 ¼ In. Diam.	940

Tray, Gilt Leaves, Ebonized, Bamboo Turned Stand, 25 x 31 In.	984
Tray, Oval, Impressed Flowers, Edge, Round, England, c.1860, 28 ½ In.	431
Tray, Regency, Ebonized, Scalloped, Raised Edge, Gilt Scrolling, c.1850, 21 x 31 x 25 In.	369
Tray, Stand, Victorian, Vine Border, Black Rectangle, Bamboo Stand, 1800s, 19 x 30 In.	531
Tray, Victorian, Painted Coastal Castle, Ships, Gilt Flowers, England, c.1810, 14 In.	72

PARASOL, *see Umbrella category.*

PARIAN is a fine-grained, hard-paste porcelain named for the marble it resembles. It was first made in England in 1846 and gained in favor in the United States about 1860. Figures, tea sets, vases, and other items were made of Parian at many English and American factories.

Bust, Apollo Belvedere, Dianna Chesseresse, Slip Cast, Fluted Column, 1900, 18 & 19 In., 2 Piece	560
Bust, Woman, Downward Glancing, Flowers In Hair, 7 ¼ In.	84
Figurine, Cherubs, Winged, Embracing, Round Base, 14 ½ In.	70
Figurine, Classical Woman, Leaning On Column, Oval Base, 16 x 7 In.	115
Figurine, Dante, Standing, Molded Name Plate, c.1865, 20 x 7 ½ In. ....*illus*	522
Figurine, Egeria, Roman Water Nymph, Seminude, Standing, Square Base, c.1850, 23 In.	1434
Figurine, Eros, Standing, Bow & Arrow, Seminude, Wings, Round Base, 1800s, 16 x 6 In.	1912
Figurine, Flora, Standing, Holding Flower Wreath, Draped Gown, Oval Base, 1800s, 22 In.	598
Figurine, Harvester, Mounted As Lamp, 16 ¾ In.	60
Figurine, Prometheus, Loosely Draped, Tree Stump, Flames, c.1861, 17 ¼ x 8 ¼ In.	2928
Figurine, Syrinx, Nymph, Seminude, Loose Drape, Round Base, Marked, 1800s, 14 ¼ In.	239
Group, Finding Moses, Seminudes, Baby In Basket, Kneeling Woman, c.1855, 21 x 16 In.	1434
Group, Isaac & Rebekah, Camel Reclining, c.1850, 20 x 13 ½ In.	1314
Group, Sacrifice Of Isaac, Abraham, Oval Base, 1800s, 8 ¾ x 5 ¾ In.	610
Pitcher, Gypsy Camp Scenes, Lavender Smear, Molded, White, Samuel Alcock, c.1850, 9 In.	92
Pitcher, Lady Liberty, Blue Glaze, Footed, 19th Century, 11 In.	46
Pitcher, Naomi & Daughters-In-Law, Lavender, Arch Handle, Pewter Lid, 1847, 10 In.	127
Plate, Water Lilies, Scalloped Rim, c.1850, 9 In.	325
Vase, Figural, Gilt, Enamel Trim, Globe Shape, 3 Cherub Supports, A. Carrier-Belleuse, 13 In.	1140
Vase, Handles, Footed, Grape Bunches, c.1870, 21 In., Pair	1200
Vase, Hummingbirds, Goldenrods, Bulrushes, Cylindrical, Molded Shell, c.1880, 10 In.	138

PARIS, Vieux Paris, or Old Paris, is porcelain ware that is known to have been made in Paris in the eighteenth or early nineteenth century. These porcelains have no identifying mark but can be recognized by the whiteness of the porcelain and the lines and decorations. Gold decoration is often used.

Basket, Corbeilles, Pierced, Flared, White, Gilt, 3 Paw Feet, c.1820, 4 x 9 In., Pair	489
Basket, Pierced, Kneeling Cupid Standard, Plinth, Paw Feet, White, Gilt, c.1820, 9 ⅞ In.	316
Basket, White, Pierced, Flared, Pedestal Base, c.1835, 7 ½ x 9 In.	104
Bowl, Diapered, Peach, Gilt Bands, Signed, 1800s, 5 x 10 In.	671
Cup, Gilt Lid, Handle, Flower Reserve, Pink Ground, Footed, c.1845, 4 In.	35
Dish, Shell Shape, Scalloped Rim, Gilt Band, Foot Rim, 4 x 11 In., Pair	478
Figurine, Court Dress, Offering Nosegays, 1800s, 16 ¼ In., Pair	615
Figurine, Shepherd, Shepherdess, Fanciful Period Attire, c.1870, 11 In., Pair	288
Mug, Italian Home, Rural Scene, Triangular Handle, Gilt Rim, c.1820, 2 In.	23
Perfume Bottle, Exotic Couple, Creme Des Barbados, c.1850, 12 In., Pair	600
Pitcher, Basin, Painted Flowers, Gilt Bands, 9 In., 13 In.	438
Pitcher, Woman, White Hair, Period Attire, Flowers, Baluster, Leaf Handle, 9 In.	188
Plate, Dessert, Fuchsia, Flower Reserves, Gilt Rim, c.1875, 9 In., 12 Piece	316
Plate, Fruit, Painted, Scrolled, Raised Gilt Border, Green, Monogram, 9 In., 11 Piece	425
Plate, Luncheon, Flower Center, Blue Rim, Floral Reserves, Gilt, 1800s, 9 In., 12 Piece	780
Tazza, Bronze, Rosette Center, Bulbous Stem, Flowers, Leaves, Round Foot, 1800s, 7 x 7 In.	120
Urn, People, Elizabethan, Winged Female Handles, Gilt, c.1815, 14 x 7 In., Pair ....*illus*	799
Vase, Courtyard Scene, Adults, Children, Shouldered, 2 Handles, c.1850, 18 In., Pair	2295
Vase, Palm Trees, Orange, Flowers, Scalloped Gilt Mouth, Triangle, Gilt, c.1860, 11 In., Pair	69
Vase, Pink Flowers, White Ground, Scalloped Rim, Gilt Metal Leaf Base, 16 In., Pair	249
Vase, Stand, Gilt, Flowers, Scrollwork, Handles, Scroll Feet, Ruffled Rim, c.1850, 11 In., Pair	2501
Vase, Women In Garden Reserves, Pink, Gold Accents, 16 ½ In.	226
Vase, Woods, Children Playing, Cylindrical, Flared Mouth, Footed, c.1860, 18 In., Pair	2495

PATE-DE-VERRE is an ancient technique in which glass is made by blending and refining powdered glass of different colors into molds. The process was revived by French glassmakers, especially Galle, around the end of the nineteenth century.

Bowl, Orchids, Purple, Signed, 5 ½ x 16 In.	1125

Paul Revere, Jar, Houses, Trees, Lake, Cuerda Seca, 6-Sided, Semimatte Glaze, S.E.G., 1912, 4 In.
$4,200

Skinner Auctioneers & Appraisers

Paul Revere, Paperweight, Ship, 8-Sided, Paper Label, 1 x 2 ⅝ In.
$201

Humler & Nolan

Peachblow, Cruet, Bulbous, Faceted Stopper, Hobbs, Brockunier, Wheeling, 6 ¾ In.
$489

Early Auction Co.

P

Peachblow, Cruet, Coral, Amber Handle, Faceted Stopper, Hobbs, Brockunier, 7 In. **$460**

Early Auction Co.

Peachblow, Cruet, Daisy Clusters, Ribbed Pillar, Stopper, Mt. Washington, 6 ½ In. **$5,750**

Early Auction Co.

Peachblow, Vase, Morgan, Amber Glass Holder, Hobbs, Brockunier, Wheeling, 10 In. **$1,150**

Early Auction Co.

Figurine, Rhino Samurai, Signed, c.1950, 12 ½ x 7 x 7 ½ In.	1875
Lamp, Iron, Yellow, Signed, 1920s, 8 ½ x 4 ¼ In.	3125
Paperweight, La Danse, Oval, Brown Nude, Cape, 10 ⅞ In.	500
Vase, Trout, Footed, Green, Signed, 17 ½ x 10 In.	2875

PATENT MODELS were required as part of a patent application for a United States patent until 1880. In 1926 the stored patent models were sold as a group by the U.S. Patent Office, and individual models are now appearing in the marketplace.

Animal Trap, Aug. 24, 1875, P.B. Gibbs, Wood, Wire, Clockwork Motor, No. 166927, 13 In.	425
Artificial Leg, Composition, Jointed, Kid Leather, S.G. Gregory, 1869, 12 In.	1304
Artificial Leg, Wood, Brass, Leather, Joseph O'Brien, Mi., 17 In.	851
Ballot Box, Wood Podium, Curved, Cutaway Back, Drawer, J. Welch, 1880, 11 x 11 In.	3437
Barometer, Wood, Beaded, Slender Glass Tube, Brass Accents, No. 24674, 41 In.	1481
Burglar Alarm, Wood Frame, Columns, Herschell Bauman & Locker, 1858, 14 x 11 In.	6518
Burial Casket, Walnut, Paneled, Viewing Window, Base, John Hornrighouse, 1878, 10 x 5 In.	2489
Cabinet Bed, Opens To Bed, L.C. Boyington, September 9, 1879, 9 x 5 x 8 In.	2133
Carousel, Clockwork, Hollow Tin, Bisque, Robert Steel, Jan. 4, 1876, 14 x 17 In. ....*illus*	3674
Carpet Sweeper, Bissell & Drew, Painted Flowers, Dust Pan, Iron Wheels, 1886, 14 x 9 In.	3851
Chair, Reclining, Curved Arms, Adjustable, Upholstered Seat, G.A. Doellenger, 1879, 20 x 9 In.	1422
Corpse Cooler, Preserver, Folding, Turned Legs, Lid, Viewing Window, 1874, 12 x 7 In.	3259
Corpse Preserver, Dry Ice Container, Viewing Window, J.J. Reichert, 1868, 12 x 7 In.	1778
Cracker Machine, Brass, Gears, Rollers, Conveyor Belt, W.R. Nivens, 1836, 10 x 8 In.	4556
Dishwasher, Tin Tub, Hinged, Revolving Wire Cage, Lever, Charles Palmleaf, 1894, 12 x 12 In.	356
Farm Vehicle, Wood, E.M. Dawson Smyrna, Del., Case Base, 5 x 12 In.	178
Harrower, Planet Junior, Curved Wood Handles, Wheel, 14 In.	4200
Harvester, August 18, 1868, G.W. Yost, Brass, 2 Spoke Wheels, No. 81241, 9 In.	3851
Invalid's Bed, February 2, 1858, G. Miller, Tiger Maple, Hinged, No. 19254, 12 In.	1778
Knitting Machine, Dec. 27, 1870, William Carter, Needham, Mass., No. 110479, 12 In.	450
Mower, Paint, Wood, Brass, Tin, 9 In.	2133
Pneumo-Electric Bath, Huffman & Huff, Patent Label, May 29, 1877	3300
Safe, Iron, Concrete Lining, Shelves, Key Lock, Brass Handles, O. Marland, 1854, 5 x 7 In.	2187
Scroll Saw, Pot Metal, C-Frame, Tripod Base, Offset Wheel, Belt, Foot Pedal, 1880, 9 x 11 In.	2489
Steam Boiler, Patented, Sept. 29, 1863, Tin, Metal, Perlins & Burnet, No. 40115, 7 x 10 In.	182
Steam Gauge, Brass Cylinder, 3 Wood Knobs, Open Glass Tube, C.H. Parshall, Detroit, 16 In.	593
Table, Collapsible, May 10, 1887, Oak, Hinged, 13 ½ x 6 In.	237
Velocipede, 3-Wheel, Hand Powered, Spokes, Tin Seat, W.H. Houff, 1881, 11 x 10 In.	7898
Washing Machine, Dec. 24th 1876, Wood, Tin, No. 188205, 8 In.	61
Washing Machine, Wood, Green, F. Hamblin, New York, January 20, 1880, 10 x 10 In.	316
Watchman's Time Detector, Shelf, Glass Door, Tin Face, George Shingleton, 1877, 8 x 12 In.	1422
Windmill, Wood, Iron, 17 In.	2700
Window, Weather Stripping, Wood Box, Hinged Door, Curved Roof, c.1890, 12 x 6 In.	59

PATE-SUR-PATE means paste on paste. The design was made by painting layers of slip on the ceramic piece until a relief decoration was formed. The method was developed at the Sevres factory in France about 1850. It became even more famous at the English Minton factory about 1870. It has since been used by many potters to make both pottery and porcelain wares.

Box, White, Blue Reserve, Cherubs, Lyre, Gilt Edged, Limoges, 2 x 3 In.	115
Dish, Center Green Medallion, White Slip, Woman, Cherubs, c.1850, 9 ½ In.	180
Plaque, Woman Kneeling, Cage, Cupid, White, Gray, Solon, c.1900, 5 x 6 In.	4063
Urn, Lid, Pierced, White Cupid, Gilt, Cobalt Blue, Feet, c.1905, 15 In.	13750
Vase, Olive Green, Putti, Morning Glory Wreaths, Gilt Rim, c.1895, 5 ½ In.	246
Vase, Pilgrim, Gilt, White Slip Flowers, Round, Square Feet, c.1880, 6 In.	1440
Vase, Red Medallion, Angel Kissing Woman, 2 Handles, 5 ¼ In.	29
Vase, White Bas Relief Woman, Cupids, Green Flat Globe, c.1900, 7 In.	1375

PAUL REVERE POTTERY was made at several locations in and around Boston, Massachusetts, between 1906 and 1942. The pottery was operated as a settlement house program for teenage girls. Many pieces were signed *S.E.G.* for Saturday Evening Girls. The artists concentrated on children's dishes and tiles. Decorations were outlined in black and filled with color.

Bowl, Cereal, Geese, Cuerda Seca, Rose Bacchini, S.E.G., 1910, 2 ¼ x 5 ¼ In.	1625
Bowl, Geese, Cuerda Seca, Ida Goldstein, S.E.G., 1911, 3 ¾ x 10 ¼ In.	3625
Bowl, Lily Border, Green, Blue, Yellow, Stamped, 8 ½ In.	236
Bowl, Nasturtiums, Cuerda Seca, S.E.G., c.1910, 11 ¾ x 4 ¾ In. ....*illus*	32500
Bowl, Painted Stylized Water Lily Design, Tan, Orange, Green, 8 ½ x 2 ½ In.	122
Bowl, Roosters, Cuerda Seca, Early To Bed, Early To Rise, R. Bacchini, 1909, 5 x 2 In. ....*illus*	1750

Bowl, Trees, Cuerda Seca, Fannie Levine, Marked, 1912, 2 ½ x 8 ½ In.	1250
Bowl, Tulips, Cuerda Seca, Edith Brown, S.E.G., 1926, 2 ½ x 9 In.	1500
Breakfast Set, Pink, Blue Band, Janice, Animals, S.E.G., 1940, 7 ½ In., 3 Piece	570
Calendar Holder, Incised Landscape, Monogram, A. Mangini, S.E.G., 1916, 3 x 3 In.	625
Fireplace Surround, Landscape, Cuerda Seca, c.1915, 38 x 52 & 21 x 60 In.	219750
Jar, Condiment, Lid, Green Matte Glaze, Signed P.R.P., 1936, 3 ⅜ In.	46
Jar, Houses, Trees, Lake, Cuerda Seca, 6-Sided, Semimatte Glaze, S.E.G., 1912, 4 In. .....*illus*	4200
Paperweight, Ship, 8-Sided, Paper Label, 1 x 2 ⅝ In. .....*illus*	201
Pitcher, Repeating Design, Blue, Gray, Initials Under Spout, Impressed, 4 ¼ In.	236
Pitcher, White Swan, Blue Sky, c.1924, 4 ⅜ In.	523
Tile, Geometric Border, Yellow, Ivory Ground, c.1916, 5 In.	150
Trivet, Lake, Trees, Cuerda Seca, Round, Signed, Fannie Levine, 1913, 5 ½ In.	1875
Vase, Baluster Shape, Green Mottled Glaze, Lili Shapiro, 1916, 11 In.	270
Vase, Baluster Shape, Slate Glaze, Teresa Molinari, 1917, 6 ½ In.	154
Vase, Blue Matte Glaze, Landscape Band, Tapered, 3 ½ x 6 ½ In.	800
Vase, Dark Blue, Cylindrical, Stamped, 6 ½ In.	29

PEACHBLOW glass was made by several factories beginning in the 1880s. New England peachblow is a one-layer glass shading from red to white. Mt. Washington peachblow shades from pink to bluish-white. Hobbs, Brockunier and Company of Wheeling, West Virginia, made Coral glass that it marketed as Peach Blow. It shades from yellow to peach and is lined with white glass. Reproductions of all types of peachblow have been made. Related pieces may be listed under Gundersen and Webb Peachblow.

Cruet, Bulbous, Faceted Stopper, Hobbs, Brockunier, Wheeling, 6 ¾ In. .....*illus*	489
Cruet, Coral, Amber Handle, Faceted Stopper, Hobbs, Brockunier, 7 In. .....*illus*	460
Cruet, Daisy Clusters, Ribbed Pillar, Stopper, Mt. Washington, 6 ½ In. .....*illus*	5750
Cruet, Stopper, Satin, Wheeling, 6 ½ In.	590
Cup & Saucer, Satin Glass, Blue Shaded To Pink, Mt. Washington, 4 ½ In.	978
Darner, Pear Shape, Shiny Pale Pink To Mauve, 4 ¾ x 2 ½ In.	69
Darner, Shiny Rose Ball, To Pink Handle, 5 ½ x 2 ½ In.	80
Fairy Lamp, Scalloped, Yellow Coralline, Wheat Shaft, Clarke Holder, 5 ½ In.	144
Figurine, Apple, Glossy Finish, Amber To Rose, Green Stem, Hobbs, Brockunier, 3 In.	1035
Figurine, Pear, Glossy, Satin Finish, New England, 5 In., 3 Piece	115
Jug, Pelican, Glossy, Hobbs, Brockunier, 6 ½ In.	2300
Pickle Castor, Gilt Holly, Bee, Oval, Rogers Bros. Pierced Holder, Thomas Webb, 12 In.	575
Pitcher, Folded Deep Pink Rim, Shiny Pale Pink Body, Round, Victorian, 3 x 3 In.	29
Pitcher, Glossy, Square Mouth, New England, 4 ¾ In.	215
Pitcher, Sugar & Creamer, Wild Rose, Reeded Shell Shape Handles, Squat, Scallop Rim, 6 In. ...	920
Rose Bowl, Trifold, Mt. Washington Art Glass Society Sticker, 3 ½ In.	374
Sugar & Creamer, Satin, Square Mouth, Globe Shape, Hobbs, Brockunier, 3 In.	1265
Tankard, Fuchsia Shaded To Amber, Applied Reeded Handle, White Interior, 10 ½ In.	4148
Toothpick Holder, 3-Corner Pinched Rim, Rose, New England Glass Co., c.1886, 2 ⅜ In.	207
Vase, Applied Fruit, Leaves, Ruffled Rim, Mt. Washington, 13 ½ In.	61
Vase, Bottle Shape, Diamond Quilt Pattern, White, Red To Gray, c.1890, 10 ½ In.	305
Vase, Bottle Shape, Diamond Quilt Pattern, Yellow, Gold, c.1890, 10 ½ In.	244
Vase, Bulbous, White, Red To Pink, Amber Glass Vine, c.1900, 9 x 6 In.	418
Vase, Double Gourd Shape, Wheeling, 7 In.	590
Vase, Gloss Finish, Shouldered, Hobbs, Brockunier, Wheeling, 13 In.	2588
Vase, Jack-In-The-Pulpit Rim, Pink To White, 9 x 4 ¼ In.	81
Vase, Lily Shape, Matte Finish, Tri-Con Top, Shaded Pink To Blue, 10 In.	948
Vase, Mauve To Pink, Crimped Rim, New Eng., 5 x 4 ½ In.	35
Vase, Morgan, Amber Glass Holder, Hobbs, Brockunier, Wheeling, 10 In. .....*illus*	1150
Vase, Morgan, Frosted Holder, 5-Footed, Hobbs, Brockunier, 10 In.	115
Vase, Pink To Mauve, Gold Enameled Flowers, Bug, 5 ½ x 2 ¾ In.	115
Vase, Red To Pink To Yellow, Rounded, Footed, Wheeling, 2 ¾ x 3 ½ In.	230
Vase, Satin, Optic Ribbed, Applied Collar & Bowtie, Mt. Washington, 4 ½ In. .....*illus*	3738
Vase, Satin, Quadrafold Rim, Pillow Shape, Mt. Washington Sticker, 5 ½ In.	5175
Vase, Satin, Ribbed, Red To White, Ruffled Rim, New England, c.1880, 8 ¼ In.	116
Vase, Stick, Hobbs, Brockunier, Wheeling, 8 ½ In. .....*illus*	489

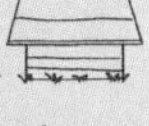

PEANUTS is the title of a comic strip created by cartoonist Charles M. Schulz (1922–2000). The strip, drawn by Schulz from 1950 to 2000, features a group of children, including Charlie Brown and his sister Sally, Lucy Van Pelt and her brother Linus, Peppermint Patty, and Pig Pen, and an imaginative and independent beagle named Snoopy. The Peanuts gang has also been featured in books, television shows, and a Broadway musical.

Badge, Snoopy For President, Weber's For Lunch, Red, White, Blue, 1968, 2 In.	20

Peachblow, Vase, Satin, Optic Ribbed, Applied Collar & Bowtie, Mt. Washington, 4 ½ In.
$3,738

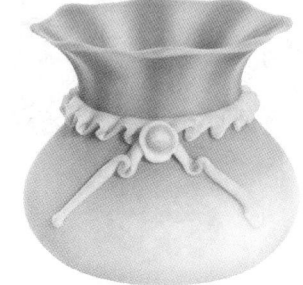

Early Auction Co.

Peachblow, Vase, Stick, Hobbs, Brockunier, Wheeling, 8 ½ In.
$489

Early Auction Co.

Peanuts, Comic Strip, Snoopy, Woodstock, Ink On Paper, Frame, Signed, 6 ¾ x 20 In.
$13,035

James D. Julia Auctioneers

Peanuts, Toy, Snoopy, Standing, Apollo Spacesuit, Mascot Of Apollo Program, 9 ½ In.
$107

Regency-Superior Auctions

P

Pearl, Etui, 4 Gold Plated Bottles Inside, France, c.1800, 8 In.
$2,070

Victorian Casino Antiques

Peking Glass, Bowl, Flared, Carved, Trees, Animals, Hardwood Stand, 1700s, 6 ½ x 4 In.
$2,133

James D. Julia Auctioneers

Peking Glass, Bowl, Green, 2-Tone, Carved, Stand, 1900s, 3 ¼ x 6 ⅞ In.
$236

Brunk Auctions

TIP
Modern bleach can damage eighteenth-century and some nineteenth-century dishes. To clean old dishes, try hydrogen peroxide or bicarbonate of soda. Each removes a different type of stain.

Bank, Belle, Snoopy's Sister, Foil Sticker, Korea, United Features Syndicate, c.1960, 4 In.	26
Book, Charlie Brown's All-Stars, World Publishing Co., 1966	32
Comic Strip, Snoopy, Woodstock, Ink On Paper, Frame, Signed, 6 ¾ x 20 In. *illus*	13035
Cookie Jar, Snoopy, Pottery, Holiday Designs, 1960, 12 In.	165
Figurine, Characters, Multicolor, 1972, Set Of 15	380
Lunch Box, Charlie Brown, Tree, Lucy, Linus, Snoopy, King Seeley Thermos Co., 8 x 9 In.	78
Mug, Snoopy, Charlie Brown, Christmas Tree, Merry Christmas 1977, 4 In.	24
Nodder, Lucy, Ceramic, 3 In.	40
Nodder, Lucy, Composition, 1952, 3 ½ In.	49
Ornament, Schroeder, Playing Piano, Ceramic, Yellow, Red, 1950s, 3 In.	29
PEZ Dispenser, Charlie Brown, Blue Cap, 1976, 4 In.	12
Pin, Snoopy, On Skis, Pompom Hat, Enamel, 1958, 1 ⅛ In.	26
Pocket Doll, Charlie Brown, Vinyl, Jointed, Hong Kong, 1960s, 5 In.	38
Toy, Chair, Sling Back, Snoopy, Red Vinyl, Japan, 1960s, 7 x 6 In.	20
Toy, Snoopy, Standing, Apollo Spacesuit, Mascot Of Apollo Program, 9 ½ In. *illus*	107
Toy, Snoopy, Walker, Joe Cool, Blue Shirt, Sun Glasses, Box, 1971, 3 In.	19
Wristwatch, Charlie Brown, Stretched Arms, Determined Productions, c.1971, 8 In.	68

PEARL items listed here are made of the natural mother-of-pearl from shells. Such natural pearl has been used to decorate furniture and small utilitarian objects for centuries. The glassware known as mother-of-pearl is listed by that name. Opera glasses made with natural pearl shell are listed under Opera Glasses.

Card Case, Bas Relief Flower Spray, Abalone Border, c.1875, 4 x 3 In.	338
Card Case, Bearded Man Profile, Flowers, Grapes, c.1890, 4 x 3 In.	266
Card Case, Sprigs, Lozenge Pattern, c.1875, 4 x 3 In.	246
Cruet, Diamond Quilted, Shaded Rose, Clear Thorn Handle, Stopper, c.1890, 6 In.	115
Etui, 4 Gold Plated Bottles Inside, France, c.1800, 8 In. *illus*	2070
Letter Opener, Applied Rose, Leaves, Opalescent White, 11 In.	41

PEARLWARE is an earthenware made by Josiah Wedgwood in 1779. It was copied by other potters in England. Pearlware is only slightly different in color from creamware and for many years collectors have confused the terms. Wedgwood pieces are listed in the Wedgwood category in this book. Most pearlware with mocha designs is listed under Mocha.

Pearl

Figurine, Apollo, Holding Lyre, Purple Robe, James Neale, c.1785, 5 ¾ In.	345
Figurine, Infant In Cradle, White & Blue Cap, Dress, Staffordshire, c.1800, 5 In.	240
Figurine, Jupiter, God Of Sky & Thunder, Bird, Crown, c.1815, 12 x 7 In.	2337
Figurine, Lion, Orange, Black Paint, Staffordshire, c.1780, 9 x 11 In., Pair	3120
Figurine, Sportsman & Dog, Tambourine Player, Neale & Co., c.1790, 8 In., 2 Piece	570
Figurine, Venus, Standing On Rock, Putto, Dolphin, Multicolor, Staffordshire, c.1780, 9 In.	258
Jug, Pierced, Reticulated Neck, 3 Nozzles, Strap Handle, Flowers, Wales, c.1800, 7 In.	978
Jug, Pierced, Reticulated Pierced Neck, 3 Nozzles, Blue Carnations, Wales, c.1805, 8 In.	489
Jug, Puzzle, Green, Brown Acanthus Leaf, Figural Handle, Winged Fame, Text Band, 8 ¾ In.	748
Jug, Strap Handle, Slip Sgraffito Tulips, 4 Nozzle Collar, Yellow Glaze, 1830, 12 In.	1725
Jug, Toby, Man Seated, Tricornered Hat, Neele & Co., 1794, 9 ¼ In.	3360
Mug, Beehive, Flowers, c.1845, 6 In.	2133
Pitcher, Blue Edge, Flowers, c.1850, 9 ½ In.	142
Pitcher, Flowers, Pink Luster Glaze, 8 ¾ x 11 In.	88
Pitcher, Pink Luster, Black Transfer, Success To The United States Of America, c.1810, 5 In.	649
Plate, Dessert, Rural Scenes, Impressed Dolphins, Gilt Rim, Wilson, c.1815, 9 In., 4 Piece	58
Platter, Chinoiserie, Blue Transfer Printed, Staffordshire, c.1850, 20 In.	210
Platter, Chinoiserie, Pagoda, Landscape, Brown Painted, Oval, c.1800, 18 ¾ In.	720
Platter, Flowers, Green Border, c.1820, 11 x 14 In.	1094
Platter, Green Feather Border, Enoch Wood & Sons, Staffordshire, c.1830, 14 ¾ x 18 ¾ In.	150
Soup, Dish, Stylized Strawberries, Vines, Scalloped Flattened Rim, c.1830, 9 In.	157
Tankard, Chinoiserie Designs, Blue, White, Gilt, England, c.1810, 6 In.	122
Teapot, Lid, Marbled, Copper Luster, Oval, Newcastle, 1820s, 6 ½ In.	270
Tureen, Lid, Hog At Bay, Shooting At Edge Of Jungle, Blue Transfer, c.1833, 14 In.	330
Vase, Quezal, Blue Feather Edge, c.1820, 8 In., Pair	563

PEKING GLASS is a Chinese cameo glass first made popular in the eighteenth century. The Chinese have continued to make this layered glass in the old manner, and many new pieces are now available that could confuse the average buyer.

Bowl, Amethyst Purple, Ring Foot, Wide Rollover Rim, Carved Flowers, 3 x 8 In.	1755
Bowl, Blue, Mica Flecks, Lotus Bud, Goldfish, Squat, 1900s, 4 ⅜ In.	474
Bowl, Flared, Carved, Trees, Animals, Hardwood Stand, 1700s, 6 ½ x 4 In. *illus*	2133
Bowl, Green, 2-Tone, Carved, Stand, 1900s, 3 ¼ x 6 ⅞ In. *illus*	236

P

Bowl, Lid, Yellow, Marked, Chinese, 4 In., Pair 542
Bowl, Red Overlay, Sloped Sides, Flared Rim, Roosters, c.1800, 6 ½ In. 1169
Bowl, Red, Carved Flowers & Birds, Square, Flared Rim, Footed, 7 x 4 ½ In. 277
Brushpot, Cylindrical, Orange Overlay, Butterflies, Peonies, c.1800, 5 ¼ In. 1440
Jar, Lid, Bulbous, Milky White, Green Overlay, 1900s, 6 ½ In. Diam. 600
Jar, Lid, Green Overlay, Cut To White, Flowers, Petals, Chinese, 7 ¼ In. 120
Snuff Bottle, Blue Green, Flat Oval, Carved Village Scene, Glass Top, Spoon, 3 ½ In. 325
Snuff Bottle, Blue, Snowflake, Round, Dome Glass Top, Spoon, c.1800, 3 ⅝ In. 826
Snuff Bottle, Snowflake, Oval, Cobalt Blue Cricket Overlay, Glass Top, Spoon, c.1800, 3 In. 177
Snuff Bottle, White, Red, Yellow, Green Dogs, Flattened, Lapis Dome Top, Spoon, 2 ½ In. 207
Urn, Lid, Green Leaves, White Ground, Tapered Baluster, c.1800, 5 ½ In., Pair 840
Vase, Blue To Silver, Turquoise Flecks, Birds, Flowers, 1900s, 9 In. 675
Vase, Cameo, Honeycomb, Aqua Over White, 8 In., Pair 236
Vase, Frosted Blue, Etched Immortals, Pear Shape, c.1960, 8 In. 83
Vase, Green Overlay, Lotus Flowers, Leaves, Flared Rim, c.1900, 8 ¼ In. 720
Vase, Orange Red Overlay, Bats, Flowers, 12 ¼ In. 472
Vase, Red Cut To Opaque White, Fruit Flower Branches, Double Gourd Shape, 9 In. 540
Vase, Stick Neck, Ringed Foot, Cobalt Blue, 12 ¼ In. 695
Vase, White & Green Overlay, Carved, Snowflake Ground, c.1800, 9 In. 600
Vase, Yellow, Garlic Shape, 8-Sided, Elongated Neck & Foot, 6 In. 720

PELOTON glass is a European glass with small threads of colored glass rolled onto the surface of clear or colored glass. It is sometimes called spaghetti, or shredded coconut, glass. Most pieces found today were made in the nineteenth century.

Pitcher, Square Shoulders, Flaring Neck Spout, Overshot Finish, Crystal Handle, 8 ½ In. 415

PENS replaced hand-cut quills as writing instruments in 1780, when the first steel pen point was made in England. But it was 100 years before the commercial pen was a common item. The fountain pen was invented in the 1830s but was not made in quantity until the 1880s. All types of old pens are collected. Float pens that feature small objects floating in a liquid as part of the handle are popular with collectors. Advertising pens are listed in the Advertising section of this book.

Black Face, Turban, Turquoise Bead, Brass Filigree, Italy, 1950s, 6 In. 88
Cartier, Ballpoint, Basket Weave, 14K Gold, 5 ½ In. 2200
Cartier, Fountain, Black Lacquer, Platinum Stripes, 18K Gold, Case, 7 ½ In. 281
Cartier, Fountain, Pasha, Gold, Ribbed, 1990, 5 ⅝ In. 875
Chilton, Fountain, No. 86S Clown, Celluloid, 1930s 1375
Conklin, Fountain, Crescent, Black, Gold Overlay, Monogram, Toledo, 5 ½ In. 212
Conway Stewart, Fountain, 14K Yellow Gold, c.1933, 5 In. 195
De La Rue, Fountain, 9K Gold, Etched Design, c.1919 812
Dip, Celluloid, Stanhope, St. Anne De Beaupre, 6 ⅞ In. 129
Dip, Glass, Red Liquid Stem, Germany, c.1875 80
Dip, Mother-Of-Pearl, Carved, Victorian, 7 ¾ In. 95
Dip, Scrimshaw, Carved Ivory, Asian Flowers, Pineapple End, Metal Nib, 9 In. 46
Dip, Tartan, Green, Red, c.1880, 7 ½ In. 225
Dunhill, Fountain, Gold, Engine Ground Design, Cap, 14K Gold Nib 192
Everlast, Fountain, Green, Onyx Celluloid, 1950s, 5 ¼ In. 40
Eversharp, Coronet, Gold Filled, c.1935 812
Eversharp, Fountain, Fifth Avenue, Brown, 14K Gold Top, Case, 5 ½ In. 104
Gucci, Enameled, Metallic Bronze, Marked, Velvet Box, 1970s, 5 ½ In. 159
Inkograph, Fountain, Chevron Clip, Ribbed Band, 1940s, 6 In. 45
Louis Vuitton, Fountain, Doc, Leather, Engine Turned, Silver, Box, 6 Refills 295
Louis Vuitton, Fountain, Red Leather, Gold Fittings, Cap, Engraved Lattice Design, 5 ½ In. 615
Montblanc, Fountain, Francois I, Tiger Eye, Black, Gold Bands, 18K Gold Nib, 5 ¾ In. 968
Montblanc, Fountain, Marbled Green Celluloid, Denmark, 1940s 375
Montblanc, Fountain, Meisterstuck Solitaire 146, Chevron, 18K Gold, Box 4375
Montblanc, Fountain, Meisterstuck Solitaire, Platinum, Box, Size 144 437
Montblanc, Fountain, Meisterstuck Solitaire, Silver, Barley Pattern, 14K Gold Nib, Box 615
Montblanc, Fountain, Meisterstuck, Black, Gold Fittings, Cap, Germany, 5 ⅝ In. 212
Montblanc, Fountain, Meisterstuck, Burgundy, Gold Nib, Black Case 154
Montblanc, Fountain, Monte Rosa, Gray, Box, 5 In. 154
Montblanc, Fountain, Oscar Wilde Limited Edition, 18K Gold Nib 1896
Nahiki, Fountain, Royal Rooster Maki-E Yukari Series, Medium No. 10, Japan 1375
Newton-Stoakes, Dip, Wood, Black Lacquered, c.1875, 6 ¾ In. 10
Parker, Fountain, Jotter 45, Chrome, Gold Tone, 7 In. 40
Parker, Fountain, MD Argent Massif, Silver, Engraved Rectangles, Gold Fittings, 5 In. 130
Parker, Fountain, Silver Overlay Over Black Rubber, Cap 225

Pepsi-Cola, Sign, Bottle, 5 Cents, 12 Ounces, Celluloid Over Tin, 1930s, 5 x 12 In.
$506

Hake's Americana & Collectibles

Pewabic, Vase, Baluster, Verdigris, Iridescent Gold Glaze, Stamped, 12 ¼ x 6 In.
$2,625

Rago Arts & Auction Center

Pewter, Coffeepot, Sugar, Lids, Rosewood, P. Evans, Sturbridge, 1950s, 13 x 5 x 3 In.
$4,063

Rago Arts & Auction Center

Pewter, Planter, Enameled Pewter, Mother-Of-Pearl Inlay, Dragonfly, 1900s, 4 ¾ In.
$180

Cowan's Auctions

Phoenix Glass, Lamp, Reverse Painted, Lake Scene, Patina, 1920s, 22 x 16 In.
$633

Cottone Auctions

Phoenix Glass, Vase, Flying Geese, Pillow Shape, Mother-Of-Pearl Luster, 9 ¼ x 12 In.
$118

Humler & Nolan

> ### TIP
> When buying old pens, look for a crack in the cap by putting a fingertip inside the cap and turning to feel any flaw.

Parker, Vacumatic, Golden Pearl Design, c.1936, 7 ⅜ In.	55
Pelikan, Fountain, 120, Green, Black	69
Sheaffer, Put-Able, Attaches To Metal, Plastic, Wood, Glass, Pamphlet, Box, c.1970, 7 In.	20
Sheaffer, Sterling Silver, Engine Turned Design, 14K Gold Nib, Box, 5 ¼ In.	209
Visconti, Ashford, Fountain, Red Celluloid, Silver, Decorative Clip, Box	104
Waterman's, Fountain, Edson, Sterling Silver	875
Waterman's, Fountain, Edson, Translucent Blue, 18K Gold Nib, Marked	366
Waterman's, Fountain, No. 0514S, Safety, Gold Filigree	272
Waterman's, Fountain, No. 58, Cardinal Red, Hard Rubber, c.1920	1750
Yard-O-Led, Fountain, Viceroy Sterling Silver, Barleycorn	375

PEN & PENCIL

Conklin, Mechanical 7, Fountain, Pyrolin, Black, Orange, Ring Top, 1930s	365
Kreisler, 14K Yellow Gold, Wood Box	210
Le Boeuf, Mechanical Pencil, Fountain Pen, No. 80, Black, Tan, Box, 1930s	937
Mabie Todd, Fountain Pen, Swan, 14K Gold Leverless, Mechanical Pencil, c.1925	687
Montblanc, Fountain Pen, Hard Rubber, 0 Size, Baby Mechanical Pencil, 1920s	562
Montblanc, Mechanical Pencil, Fountain Pen, Masterpiece, Gold, Green, Stripe, 1930s	350
Parker 51, Signet, Fountain Pen, Mechanical Pencil, Gold Filled, Box	177 to 182
Parker 75 Cisele, Ballpoint Pen, Mechanical Pencil, Sterling Silver, c.1965	62
Waterman's, Sterling Silver Overlay, Openwork, Box, 5 ½ In.	510

PENCILS were invented, so it is said, in 1565. The eraser was not added to the pencil until 1858. The automatic pencil was invented in 1863. Collectors today want advertising pencils or automatic pencils of unusual design. Boxes and sharpeners for pencils are also collected. Advertising pencils are listed in the Advertising category. Pencil boxes are listed in the Box category.

Chatelaine, Silver Plate, Virgin Mary, Repousse, Fleur-De-Lis, c.1905, 3 ⅜ In.	75
L & S, Propelling, British Sterling, 1908, 6 In.	120
Lead, Dixon, Red & Black, USA, 8 x ½ In.	5
Mechanical, Chatelaine, Enamel Flowers, Black Ribbon, c.1875, 2 ½ In.	60
Mechanical, Collapsible, 14K Gold, c.1900, 4 ½ In.	485
Mechanical, Green & Black Marbling, 4 In.	32
Mechanical, Marbleized, Yellow, 4 In.	24
Mechanical, Wood Grain, 1920s, 4 ¾ In.	35
Montblanc, Injector Style, Burgundy Matte, Germany, c.1980, 6 ⅝ In.	157
Montblanc, Mechanical, Meisterstuck Solitaire 165, Chevron, 18K Gold, Box	2750
Otis, Drafting, Sterling Silver, Expandable, 1897, 12 In. Open	425
Propelling, Faux Tortoiseshell, Brass Point, Dutch, c.1930	75
Propelling, Gold Filled, Green Cabochon Finial, c.1899, 3 ⅞ In.	175
Sheaffer, Marbled Celluloid, Black, Cream, Golf, c.1924, 2 ⅝ In.	49
Wahl-Eversharp, Sterling Silver, Foliate Scrolls, 3 ⅛ In.	175

PENCIL SHARPENER

Alarm Clock, Metal, Germany, 1 ½ x 1 In.	42
Bakelite, Red Swirling, 1 1/16 x 13/16 In.	25
Bingo Ball Spinner, Tin, Hong Kong, 2 ½ x 1 ½ In.	30
Car, Sedan, Cast Metal, Red, Germany, 1 ¾ In.	75
Dixon Enduro, No. 20, Red, Plastic, 4 ½ x 5 ⅞ x 2 ¾ In.	29
Dog Head, Black & White, Lead, Japan, 1930s, 1 ⅝ x 1 ⅝ In.	75
Donald Duck, Cowboy Hat, Scalloped Edge, Decal, Bakelite, Brown, Green, 1 In.	75
Elephant On Tub, Celluloid, Gray, Japan, c.1940, 1 ⅞ x 1 ⅞ In.	89
Globe, Base, Multicolor, Germany, 1920s, 3 ⅝ In.	155
Globe, Stand, Bronze, Tin, Hong Kong, 3 ¼ x 2 ½ In.	42
Hunting Dog Head, Gray, Black, Lead, Japan, c.1930, 1 ½ x 1 ½ In.	75
Joe Carioca, Bakelite, Round, 1 In.	45
Office, Self-Feeding, Drawer, Dome, Mottled Brown, Bakelite, 4 x 4 x 2 In.	185
Radio, Die Cast, 1970s, 2 ½ x 1 In.	15
Roadster, Lead, c.1935, 1 x 3 In.	100
Telephone, Hand Crank, Dovetail, Wood, Japan, 4 x 5 In.	16

PENNSBURY POTTERY worked in Morrisville, Pennsylvania, from 1950 to 1971. Full sets of dinnerware as well as many decorative items were made. Pieces are marked with the name of the factory.

Pennsbury Pottery

Amish, Cake Stand, Harvest, 11 ½ x 4 ½ In.	250
Amish, Cookie Jar, 7 ½ x 7 ¼ In.	110
Amish, Mug, Couple, Drinking, 3 ⅛ In.	35
Bookends, Eagle, Spread Wings, 6 ¾ x 5 ½ In.	200

Fish, Dish, Multicolor, 12 x 5 In., Pair	35
Fish, Platter, Multicolor, 17 x 9 ¾ x 1 In.	80
Hex, Plate, 10 ½ In.	12
Map, Plate, Rotary International, Delaware County, 8 In.	36
Red Rooster, Butter, Cover, 5 x 5 In.	16
Red Rooster, Pitcher, 2 Qt., 7 ½ In.	45

PEPSI-COLA, the drink and the name, was invented in 1898 but was not trademarked until 1903. The logo was changed from an elaborate script to the modern block letters in 1963. Several different logos have been used. Until 1951, the words *Pepsi* and *Cola* were separated by two dashes. These bottles are called "double dash." In 1951 the modern logo with a single hyphen was introduced. All types of advertising memorabilia are collected, and reproductions are being made.

Bottle, Glass, Thick, Embossed, Hutchinson, Escambia, Pensacola	600
Catalog, 39th Anniversary, 1939 Bottle, Draped Window Sill, 16 Pages, 10 ¾ x 8 ½ In.	600
Chair, Folding, Vinyl Seat, Oval Back, 32 In.	180
Display, Figural, Woman, Strapless Gown, Bottle, Sparkling Quality, 1940s, 11 In.	690
Door Handle, Enjoy, Bigger, Better, Tin, Shaped, 12 x 3 In.	177
Radio, Transistor, Dispenser Shape, Plastic, Multicolor, Industrial Contacts Inc.	330
Sign, Bottle Cap Shape, Drink Pepsi-Cola, 1950s, 18 In.	360
Sign, Bottle Cap Shape, Tin, Enameled, Stout Manufacturing Co., 1964, 28 In.	677
Sign, Bottle, 5 Cents, 12 Ounces, Celluloid Over Tin, 1930s, 5 x 12 In. *illus*	506
Sign, Buy Pepsi-Cola Today, 5 Cents, Police Officer, Die Cut, Hanging, 13 In.	118
Sign, Drink Pepsi-Cola Take Home A Carton, 6 Pack Graphics, 2-Sided, Masonite, 18 x 23 In.	118
Sign, Logo, Say Pepsi, Please, Tin, Embossed, 18 x 54 In.	330
Thermometer, Woman, Straw In Bottle, Tin, 1930s, 27 In.	339

PERFUME BOTTLES are made of cut glass, pressed glass, art glass, silver, metal, enamel, and even plastic or porcelain. Although the small bottle to hold perfume was first made before the time of ancient Egypt, it is the nineteenth- and twentieth-century examples that interest today's collector. DeVilbiss Company has made atomizers of all types since 1888 but no longer makes the perfume bottle tops so popular with collectors. These were made from 1920 to 1968. The glass bottle may be by any of many manufacturers even if the atomizer is marked *DeVilbiss*. The word *factice*, which often appears in ads, refers to store display bottles. Glass or porcelain examples may be found under the appropriate name such as Lalique, Czechoslovakia, Glass-Bohemian, etc.

Atomizer, Blue Opalescent Glass, Coin Dot, Loved Base, Fenton, 4 ¾ In.	93
Cherub With Bow & Arrow, Morning Glories, Bird's Nest Lid, Limoges, 2 ⅜ In.	461
Czech Art Glass, Reticulated Top, Cabochons, Reticulated Base, c.1915, 6 ½ In.	89
DeVilbiss Atomizer, Rose Overlay Glass, 8 Lobes With Clear Graduated Beads	46
Glass, Double Cut, Purple To Clear, Sterling Silver Cap, 3 In.	395
Glass, Swirled Body, Blue, 7 ¼ x 3 In.	79
Glass, Turquoise, Yellow & Gold Highlights, Hinged, Chain Stopper, c.1890, 2 In.	295
Guerlain Paris, Shalimar, Blue Fan Stopper, Label, c.1925, 3 x 2 In.	55
Le Golliwog, Glass, Black Feet & Collar, Face, Hair Stopper, Label, 1940s, 3 In.	275
Molinard Xmas Bells, Glass, Bell Shape, Label, c.1925, 3 x 2 In.	292
Rock Crystal, Cylindrical, Spiral Fluted, Silver & Gold Mount, Diamonds, 3 In.	2640
Teardrop, Glass, Gold Mount, Amethyst, Diamonds, Krementz, 3 ½ In.	1920
Urn, Flowers, Nude Baby, On Book, Mocco, Japan, 3 ⅛ In.	44

PETERS & REED POTTERY COMPANY of Zanesville, Ohio, was founded by John D. Peters and Adam Reed in 1897. Chromal, Landsun, Montene, Pereco, and Persian are some of the art lines that were made. The company, which became Zane Pottery in 1920 and Gonder Pottery in 1941, closed in 1957. Peters & Reed pottery was unmarked.

Ash Receiver, Frog Shape, Green, c.1920, 4 In.	100
Bowl, Dragonfly, Moss Aztec, 4 x 2 In.	56
Bowl, Marbleized, Blue, Arts & Crafts, 8 ½ x 2 ½ In.	55
Candlestick, Flower, Brown Glaze, Columnar, 8 In.	38
Flower Frog, Blue, 1920s, 5 In.	60
Flower Frog, Frog Shape, Green Matte Glaze, 4 ¾ x 3 In.	95
Jardiniere, Green, Blue, Brown Glaze, c.1915, 7 x 8 ½ In.	60
Mug, Grapes, Standard Brown Glaze, 5 x 3 In.	89
Vase, Copper Montese, Flared Rim, Ringed Base, 8 ¼ In.	52
Vase, Ivory, Relief Flowers, 15 In.	24
Vase, Landsun, Blue, Green, Tan, Lobed, 6 ¼ In.	46
Vase, Landsun, Fire Nozzle, Yellow, Blue, 7 ⅝ In.	142
Vase, Landsun, Runny Blue Over Speckled Tan, Marked, 7 ¾ In.	104

Phonograph, Victor, V, Oak Horn, Nickel Plated, Spring Motor, 6 Records, 16 x 20 In., Horn 22 In.
$4,503

James D. Julia Auctioneers

Photography, Ambrotype, Boy Seated In Dog-Drawn Cart, ½ Plate
$1,058

Cowan's Auctions

P

Photography, Cabinet Card, Paiute Medicine Man, Wovoka Or Jack Wilson
$646

Cowan's Auctions

Photography, Camera, Daguerreotype, Lewis-Type, Jamin/Darlot Lens, c.1856, ½ Plate
$10,575

Cowan's Auctions

Photography, Carte De Visite, Hospital Steward, Regular Army, Ink Signed
$764

Cowan's Auctions

Photography, Carte De Visite, Major Pauline Cushman, Union Spy & Scout
$529

Cowan's Auctions

Vase, Landsun, Tan, 8 In.	115
Vase, Marbleized, Black, Orange, Tan, Green, 8 ⅞ In.	35
Vase, Marbleized, Flared Rim & Base, 10 In.	75
Vase, Montene, Earth Tone Colors, Leaves, Glaze, 5 ½ In.	165
Vase, Montene, Mottled Green, Yellow, 6 ¼ In.	52
Vase, Moss Aztec, 6 ½ In.	16
Vase, Mountains, Waves, Cloud, Footed, Stick Neck, 10 ¾ In.	118
Vase, Shadow Ware, Black, Green, Stepped Neck, Cabinet, 2 ⅞ In.	30
Vase, Shadow Ware, Runny Tan, Over Blue, Cylindrical, Lobed, 9 In.	24
Wall Pocket, 5-Sided, Pink Glossy Glaze, 8 In.	40
Wall Pocket, Bouquet, Ribbed, Blue, 8 ½ In.	80
Wall Pocket, Flower, Brown Glaze, 1920s, 8 ¼ In.	40

PETRUS REGOUT, *see Maastricht category.*

PEWABIC POTTERY was founded by Mary Chase Perry Stratton in 1903 in Detroit, Michigan. The company made many types of art pottery, including pieces with matte green glaze and an iridescent crystalline glaze. The company continued working until the death of Mary Stratton in 1961. It was reactivated by Michigan State University in 1968.

Candleholder, Iridized Blue, Silver, Bowl Shape, 5 ½ In.	116
Plate, Geese, Flying, Blue, White Glaze, 10 In.	281
Tile, Horse Head Man, Queen, With Wings, Multicolor, Detroit, Frame, 1995, 14 x 16 In.	161
Vase, Baluster, Verdigris, Iridescent Gold Glaze, Stamped, 12 ¼ x 6 In. ....*illus*	2625
Vase, Black Matte Glaze, Blue, Gray Metallic Drip, Shouldered, 4 x 5 ½ In.	3416
Vase, Blue, Brown Metallic Glaze, High Shouldered, Ribbed, 5 ½ x 6 In.	1342
Vase, Brown, Tan Metallic Glaze Iridescent, Tapered, 4 x 5 ¾ In.	600
Vase, Cobalt Blue Glaze, Squat Base, Tapered Neck, 12 x 5 ½ In.	1375
Vase, Gray Metallic Glaze, Bulbous Shape, 2 x 2 In.	366
Vase, Green, Blue, Gray Metallic Glaze, 4 x 3 ½ In.	915
Vase, Green, Yellow Metallic Glaze, Shouldered, 5 x 5 In.	1342
Vase, Iridescent Lapis & Purple Glaze, Bulbous, Cinched Neck, Flared Rim, 9 x 8 In.	2125
Vase, Multicolor Metallic Glaze, Bulbous, 1 ¾ x 3 In.	875
Vase, Multicolor Metallic Glaze, Iridescent, Bulbous, Marked, 6 ½ x 5 In.	750
Vase, Multicolor Mottled Metallic Glaze, Iridescent, Shouldered, Marked, 2 ½ x 3 In.	2600
Vase, Multitoned Green Metallic Glaze, Shouldered, 5 ½ x 5 In.	4270
Vase, Purple & Gold Luster Glaze, Drippy, Vague Horizontal Ribs, Baluster, 14 x 9 In.	5000
Vase, Purple, Blue, Brown, Yellow Metallic Glaze, Iridescent, Footed, Marked, 5 x 9 ½ In.	5000
Vase, Purple, Blue, Gray Metallic Glaze, Ribbed, 5 ½ x 9 ½ In.	2684
Vase, Purple, Green, Gray Glaze, Hammered, Bulbous, 4 x 4 ½ In.	976
Vase, Red, Green Metallic Glaze, Bulbous, Shouldered, 3 ½ x 3 In.	3050
Vase, Tan, Red, Green, Metallic Glaze, Flared Base, 7 x 8 In.	2196
Vase, Textured Blue, Green, Gray Metallic Glaze, Bulbous, 5 ½ x 6 ½ In.	5785
Vase, Yellow Metallic Glaze, Green Matte Drip, 3 x 1 ½ In.	549
Vase, Yellow, Gold Metallic Glaze, Bulbous, Stepped Neck, 2 x 2 In.	1500

PEWTER is a metal alloy of tin and lead. Some of the pewter made after 1840 has a slightly different composition and is called Britannia metal. This later type of pewter was worked by machine; the earlier pieces were made by hand. In the 1920s pewter came back into fashion and pieces were often marked *Genuine Pewter.* Eighteenth-, nineteenth-, and twentieth-century examples are listed here.

Basin, Baptismal Bowl, Footed, Wide Rim, 4 ½ x 6 ¾ In.	499
Basin, Impressed Lovebirds, Philadelphia, c.1790, 12 ½ In.	1422
Bottle, Dram, Flattened, Round, Circle Decoration, 1775-1825, 5 In.	460
Bowl, Rice Serving, Lid, Cabriole Legs, Handles, Chinese Symbols, c.1950, 6 x 8 In.	360
Bowl, Scalloped, 3-Footed, c.1930, 10 ½ x 3 ¾ In.	45
Box, Lid, Oval, Inset Green Finial Stone, Liberty & Co., 3 ½ x 2 In.	313
Box, Repousse Flowers, Liberty & Co., 5 x 4 ½ In.	325
Bucket, Tapered, Flat Rim, Footed, Touchmark HAI, c.1810, 7 In.	97
Candlestick, Baluster Stem, Spread Foot, U.S.A., c.1900, 5 In., Pair	558
Candlestick, Double, Archibald Knox, Tudric, Liberty, England, c.1900, 11 x 9 In.	1750
Centerpiece, Art Nouveau, Women, Reaching, Round, 5 x 22 ½ In.	234
Charger, Alexander Cleeve, London, 23 ½ In.	708
Charger, Crossbow, Hunter's Horn, Zinnteller, 1700s, 12 In.	540
Charger, Gresham Jones, 13 In.	590
Charger, Hammered, Wide Flat Rim, England, 18th Century, 15 ¼ In. Diam.	264

Charger, Round, Flat Rim, U.S.A., c.1770, 13 In. Diam.	206
Charger, Stamped Richard, England, c.1800, 18 In.	180
Charger, Thomas Badger, Boston, c.1800, 12 In.	474
Charity Box, Handle, Padlock, Fence Posts, Carl Nordheim, Austria, c.1850, 8 x 5 In.	1534
Charity Box, Handled Compartment, Padlock, Domed Drawer, Fence Posts, 8 x 4 x 7 In.	1534
Coffee Urn, Brass & Ivory Spigot, Weighted, England, 1800s, 15 In.	88
Coffee Urn, Brass Spigot, Roswell Gleason, Mass., 1822-71, 16 ¾ In.	118
Coffeepot, Lighthouse Shape, Dome Lid, Wood Finial, Shield Designs, c.1830, 11 In.	431
Coffeepot, Sugar, Lids, Rosewood, P. Evans, Sturbridge, 1950s, 13 x 5 x 3 In. ....*illus*	4063
Figure, Mouse, Cheese, Signed, Italy, 2 x 2 ½ x 1 In.	150
Flagon, Baker, Pewter Lid, Cylindrical, Ball Feet, c.1870, 2 Liter, 14 In.	192
Flagon, Communion, Boardman & Co., c.1805, 12 In.	708
Flagon, Hoof Shape Feet, Winged Lion Finial, c.1865, 13 ¾ In.	156
Flagon, Lid, Applied Shield, Cherubs, 8-Sided, Germany, 1728, 18 In.	390
Flagon, Lion Finial, Flower Engraved, c.1890, 17 In.	443
Flagon, Zinnstitze, Hunter, 3-Footed, c.1880, 13 In.	252
Lamp, Fat, Cardan, Fixed Clear Pane, Ring Handle, c.1759, 14 x 7 In.	345
Lamp, Time, Spun, Blown Glass Ribbed Font, Handles, Saucer Base, 1800s, 14 ½ In.	236
Measure Set, Haystack Shape, Graduated, Austen & Con, Ireland, 3 To 7 ½ In., 5 Piece	176
Mirror, Fruits, Flowers, Oval, Arts & Crafts, 29 x 20 In.	976
Mold, Candle, 24 Tubes, Pa., c.1855, 18 x 22 In.	1007
Mold, Candle, 24 Tubes, Pine, Pa., 20 x 21 In.	652
Mold, Candle, 36 Tubes, Pine, Paint, Inscribed J.W. Bloomfield, c.1850, 11 x 14 In.	3888
Pitcher, Bell Shape, Loop Handle, Zinn Glockenkanne, c.1775, 11 In.	510
Pitcher, Shaped Handle, S-Spout, Hinged Lid, Finial, 1800s, 10 In.	206
Planter, Enameled Pewter, Mother-Of-Pearl Inlay, Dragonfly, 1900s, 4 ¾ In. ......*illus*	180
Plate, Gershom Jones, Providence, R.I., Touchmark, 1840, 8 ½ In.	382
Plate, Initials, Pennsylvania, c.1760, 9 ¼ In.	2400
Plate, Samuel Pierce, c.1790, 8 In.	106
Platter, Serpentine Trim, England, 15 ½ In.	83
Pokal, Tower, Landsknecht Finial, Pedestal, c.1875, 21 In.	738
Porringer, Openwork Flower Handle, c.1780, 5 ¼ In.	558
Porringer, Rhode Island, Marked SM, 5 In.	1541
Porringer, Samuel Danforth, Pierced Handle, c.1805, 4 ¼ In.	415
Porringer, Samuel Hamlin, Pierced Flower Handle, Marked, R.I., c.1800, 2 x 6 In.	259
Porringer, Scroll Crown Handle, Initials, c.1800, 5 ½ In.	271
Porringer, Tab Handle, Chester, c.1820, 5 ½ In.	770
Porringer, Tab Handle, Pa., c.1790, 5 ⅜ In.	385
Porringer, Tab Handle, Simon Pennock, Marked, Pa., c.1825, 5 ½ In.	1422
Porringer, William Calder, Pierced Handle, 5 In.	577
Pot, Scroll Spout, Shaped Handle, Finial, Saucer Foot, 1800s, 12 In.	206
Sugar, Cylindrical, Ring Foot, Dome Lid, Reeded Border, Eng., c.1815, 5 ½ In.	147
Sugar, Lid, Tapered, Footed, Philadelphia, c.1800, 4 ½ In.	3792
Tankard, Lid, Townsend & Compton, England, c.1790, 7 In.	600
Tankard, Rimmed Base, Curled Handle, New York, c.1770, 7 In.	4266
Teapot, A. Porter, Bulbous, Wood Handle, Marked, c.1830, 12 In.	130
Teapot, Dome Lid, Boardman & Hart No. 5, c.1850, 7 ½ In.	130
Teapot, Eben Smith, Mass., c.1830, 7 ¼ In.	267
Teapot, Lid, Red Pottery, Jade Handle, Spout, Finial, Ribs, Calligraphy, Chinese, c.1800, 5 In.	3450
Teapot, Lid, Reeded, Pedestal Foot, Exaggerated Spout, Shaped Handle, 1800s, 7 ½ In.	147
Teapot, Pear Shape, Paneled Spout, Scroll Handle, Finial, c.1835, 7 ½ In.	411
Teapot, Samuel Kilbourn, Lid, Footed, Marked Maryland, 8 ¾ In.	1541
Vase, Asymmetrical Handles, Flared Base, Liberty & Co., c.1905, 4 ½ x 7 ½ In., Pair	600
Vase, Pewter, Turned Handles, Liberty & Co., 4 ½ x 7 ½ In.	313
Vase, Rocket Shape, 3 Handles, Enamel Heart Accents, Archibald Knox, Liberty & Co., 4 x 7 In.	2250
Vase, Tudic, Tulip Shape, Twist Handle, Signed Liberty & Co., 7 x 10 In., Pair	1159

PHOENIX GLASS Company was founded in 1880 in Pennsylvania. The firm made commercial products, such as lampshades, bottles, and glassware. Collectors today are interested in the "Sculptured Artware" made by the company from the 1930s until the mid-1950s. Some pieces of Phoenix glass are very similar to those made by the Consolidated Lamp and Glass Company. Phoenix made Reuben Blue, lavender, and yellow pieces. These colors were not used by Consolidated. In 1970 Phoenix became a division of Anchor Hocking, which was sold to the Newell Group in 1987. The factory is still working.

Lamp, Reverse Painted, Lake Scene, Patina, 1920s, 22 x 16 In. ......*illus*	633
Perfume Bottle, Gold Iridescent, Millefiori, Paper Label, Signed Carl Radke, 6 In.	144

Photography, Daguerreotype, Fisherman Displaying Large Fish, Full Case, ⅙ Plate
$4,406

Cowan's Auctions

Photography, Graphotrope, Carte DeVisite Display Box, Walnut, William Walker & Co., 1866, 8 In.
$1,800

Skinner Auctioneers & Appraisers

Photography, Photograph, Living Uncle Sam, Camp Lee, Va., Mole & Thomas, 12 x 14 In.
$529

Cowan's Auctions

P

Photography, Photograph, Quniaka, Mohave, Platinum, Signed, Edward Curtis, 14 ¼ x 11 ¼ In.
$800

Cowan's Auctions

Photography, Tintype, Man, High Wheel Bicycle, Pressed Paper Case, ⅙ Plate
$360

Skinner Auctioneers & Appraisers

Photography, Tintype, Union Officer, 3 Infantry Senior NCOs, Frame, ¼ Plate
$1,410

Cowan's Auctions

TIP

Do not use photo albums with plastic or black paper pages. These will damage the photos in time.

Pitcher, Spatter, Spot Optic, Blue & Opal Flakes, Star Shape, Crimped, c.1890, 9 In.	92
Vase, Blown-Out Flowers, Brown, Cream, Tapered, Brass Handles, 13 In.	180
Vase, Consolidated Blue, White Leaves, 11 ½ In.	58
Vase, Flying Geese, Pillow Shape, Mother-Of-Pearl Luster, 9 ¼ x 12 In. ....*illus*	118
Vase, Yellow Flowers, Green Leaves, White Ground, 6 ½ In., Pair	35

PHONOGRAPHS, invented by Thomas Edison in 1877, have been made by many firms. This category also includes other items associated with the phonograph. Jukeboxes and Records are listed in their own categories.

Columbia, BGT, Cylinder, Mahogany, Rear-Mounted Horn, Lyre Reproducer, Crank	1062
Columbia, BH, Disc, Analyzing Reproducer, Black 8-Panel Horn, Crank	767
Columbia, BI, Disc, Morning Glory Horn, Oak, Nickeled Aluminum, c.1910, 29 x 21 In.	1063
Columbia, BI, Disc, Sterling, Analyzing Reproducer, Brass 9-Panel Horn, Crank	708
Columbia, BN, Reproducer, Crank, Rear-Mounted Nickel 9-Panel Horn	561
Columbia, DeLuxe, Mahogany, Lions' Heads, Record Storage, Floor Model	3565
Columbia, Grafonola, Ideal, Table Model, Disc, Reproducer, Ornamental Ring, Crank	118
Columbia, Graphophone, Horn, Wood Base, Drawer, Disc, 11 ¾ In.	1080
Columbia, Graphophone, Lyre-Type Reproducer, Brass Horn, 12 x 15 In.	360
Edison Standard, Wood Case, Domed Cover, Painted Banner, Brass Horn	738
Edison, Amberola 50, Cylinder, Mahogany Case, 15 ½ x 19 ¾ In.	300
Edison, Amberola 75, Cylinder, Mahogany Cabinet	83
Edison, Amberola 75, Cylinder, Oak Case, Reproducer, Crank, 25 Cylinder Records	413
Edison, Banner, Wood Case, Brass Horn, 18 x 15 ½ In.	540
Edison, Model A, Type SM, Cylinder, Mahogany Cabinet, Anodized Slide-In Reproducer	2655
Edison, Model C, Fireside, Cylinder, Reproducer, Crane, No. 10 Cygnet Horn, Crank, Cover	550
Edison, Model H, Triumph, Cylinder, Reproducer, Crank, Paneled Wood Case & Cover	495
Edison, Model S, Standard, Oak Case, Red Morning Glory Horn, 15 Rolls	522
Edison, Oak, Tin Morning Glory Horn, Stand, c.1900	504 to 711
Edison, Standard, Morning Glory Horn, Metal Bracket, Babson Bros., 35 In.	570
Edison, Triumph, Cygnet Horn, Oak Case, Domed Lid, Handle, Spring Driven, 18 x 13 x 39 In.	2750
Herzog, Mahogany Cabinet, Bifold Door, 4 Drawers, Papier-Mache Horn	900
Manophone, Oak Case, Universal Reproducer, Crank, Floor Model	59
Martenet, Oak Case, Floor Model, The Master Musician, Davenport, Iowa	35
Meteor, Mahogany, Disc, Star Of The Talking Machine World, Piqua, Ohio, Floor Model	3658
Mignophone, Pink, Blue Horn, Windup, 8 ½ In.	570
Pathe, Green Painted Morning Glory Horn, Wood Case, Center Start Disc, 15 x 15 In.	311
RCA, Victrola, Console, Mahogany, Records, 1930, 50 x 24 In.	2125
Standard, Style X, Disc, Front Mounted Morning Glory Horn	443
Talk-O-Phone, Beaded Case, Disc, Front Mounted Black Morning Glory Horn	413
Victor Victrola, VV-IX, Oak Case, Hand Crank, Disc, c.1911	219
Victor Victrola, XL, Oak Case, 44 In.	210
Victor, E, Disc, Exhibition Reproducer, Metal Tone Arm, 14-In. Brass Bell Horn	990
Victor, IV, Disc, Mahogany Spear Tip Horn	2750
Victor, IV, Wood Spear Tip Horn, Crank, 13 ¾ x 13 ¾ In.	1680
Victor, M Model, Rigid Arm, Disc, Concert Reproducer, Crank, Brass Bell, 20 In.	4400
Victor, Pre Dog, Brass Horn, 22 x 21 In.	660
Victor, Talking Machine, Type Vic. V, Oak Horn & Case, 31 x 27 In.	3510
Victor, V, Horn, Type R, No. 7528, 10 In.	1080
Victor, V, Oak Horn, Nickel Plated, Spring Motor, 6 Records, 16 x 20 In., Horn 22 In. .....*illus*	4503
Victor, VV-XIV, Mahogany, Victrola No. 2 Reproducer, Crank, Floor Model	266
Victor, Wood Horn, No. 39153, 14 In.	2400
Zon-O-Phone, Concert Grand, Disc, Morning Glory Horn, 11 Panels, Red, Pink	826

PHOTOGRAPHY items are listed here. The first photograph was a view from a window in France taken in 1826. The commercially successful photograph started with the daguerreotype introduced in 1839. Today all sorts of photographs and photographic equipment are collected. Albums were popular in Victorian times. Cartes de visite, popular after 1854, were mounted on 2 ½-by-4-inch cardboard. Cabinet cards were introduced in 1866. These were mounted on 4 ¼-by-6 ½-inch cards. Stereo views are listed under Stereo Card. Stereoscopes are listed in their own section.

Album, Black Forest Cover, Deer, Stags, Forest, Cylinder Music Box Inside	307
Album, Tintype, Children, Ebony, Firefighting Vignettes, 3 ¼ x 3 ¾ In.	257
Albumen Photograph, General, Rosecrans, Sitting, Tent, Mounted, 1863, 7 x 9 In.	1763
Albumen Photograph, Union Officers, Stone River Camp, Tenn., Mounted, 1863, 7 x 9 In.	881
Albumen Print Set, London, Holland, Francis Godolphin Osbourne Stuart, c.1890, 54 Prints	316
Albumen Print, Mossy Creek Mill, Child, Waterfall, Frame, c.1920, 11 x 14 In.	288

Ambrotype, Boy Seated In Dog-Drawn Cart, ½ Plate	*illus*	1058
Ambrotype, Gold Mining Scene, Water Wheel, Paper Case, 1850s, ½ Plate		7050
Ambrotype, Occupational, Barrel Maker, Hammer, Paper Case, ⅙ Plate		660
Ambrotype, Occupational, Man, Steam Piano, Paper Case, ⅙ Plate		3600
Ambrotype, Union Medical Corps Soldier, Tinted, Fireman's Duty Union Case, ⅙ Plate		185
Cabinet Card, D.F. Barry & Rain-In-The-Face, Holding Rifle		1080
Cabinet Card, Kiowa Warrior, Poor Buffalo, Headdress		558
Cabinet Card, Paiute Medicine Man, Wovoka Or Jack Wilson	*illus*	646
Cabinet Card, Pawnee Bill		270
Cabinet Card, Sitting Bull's Daughter, Standing Holy, c.1885		294
Cabinet Card, Sitting Bull's Son, Sitting, Headdress, Revolver		441
Camera Stand, Wood, Gray Cast Iron Mounts, Adjustable, Crank, 48 x 31 In.		527
Camera, Bell & Howell Co., Time Lapse, Eyemo, Chicago, 11 In.		330
Camera, Daguerreotype, Lewis-Type, Jamin/Darlot Lens, c.1856, ½ Plate	*illus*	10575
Camera, Dallmeyer, Sliding Box, Mahogany, Adjustable Stand, c.1900, 18 x 13 In.		1416
Camera, Eastman Kodak, Autographic Junior, No. 1, Leather Case, c.1917, 8 ½ x 5 ½ In.		60
Camera, Hasselblad, 500 Foot, 3 Lenses, Fitted Leather Case, Sweden.		1680
Camera, Kodak, No. 4, Folding, Model A, Black Case, Red Bellows, Travel Case, 8 x 11 In.		118
Camera, Korona, Bellows, Panoramic View, Gundlach Manhattan Optical, 20 In.		800
Camera, Leitz, Aerial, Handheld, Model KE-28A, Bayonet Filters, Case, c.1942, 11 x 12 In.		420
Camera, Movie, Bach Auricon, Model CM-74C, Hollywood, Calif.		615
Camera, News Reel, Western Electric, Model D89261		900
Camera, Press, Graflex Pacemaker, Speed Graphic, Negative Cases, Carrying Case, 1940s		190
Camera, Rolleiflex, 35 mm, Model SL-35, Zeiss 1/8 50 mm Lens, Cover, Strap, 1970s		61
Camera, Rolleiflex, Grey Baby, Twin Lens, Reflex, Xenar F 3/5 Filter, 1957-63		182
Camera, Studio, On Walnut Stand, Adjustable, Germany, c.1900, 31 x 62 In.		316
Carte De Visite, Hospital Steward, Regular Army, Ink Signed	*illus*	764
Carte De Visite, Major Pauline Cushman, Union Spy & Scout	*illus*	529
Carte De Visite, Tsar Nicholas II, Empress Alexandra, Grand Duchess Olga, c.1895		900
Daguerreotype, Erwin & Hunter Mill, Miami River, c.1875, ½ Plate		11163
Daguerreotype, Fisherman Displaying Large Fish, Full Case, ⅙ Plate	*illus*	4406
Daguerreotype, Infant, Postmortem, Holding Flower, Case, ⅙ Plate		323
Daguerreotype, Middle Age Couple, Case, J.P. Ball, ¼ Plate		264
Daguerreotype, Parker & Elder Storefront, Grass Valley, Calif., c.1850, ½ Plate		7050
Developer, Tintype, Emanuel W. Swiegard, c.1898, 15 x 8 In.		627
Graphotrope, Carte DeVisite Display Box, Walnut, William Walker & Co., 1866, 8 In.	*illus*	1800
Kinetoscope, Home, Thomas A. Edison, Inc., Orange, N.J., 2 Film Canisters, Tin Box		1560
Lens, Gorde, F/8, Marked Barrel, Paris, 1 ⅜ x 2 ½ In.		60
Lens, Jamin & Darlot, Cone, Brass Barrel, Rack & Pinion Focus, Paris, c.1860, 4 ½ In.		480
Lens, Wollensak Vesta, Portrait, Black Paint, Brass Aperture Ring, c.1910, 8 In.		360
Magic Lantern, A. Franks, Optician & Photographic Dealer, Manchester, 21 In.		1353
Magic Lantern, Brass, Tin, Wood, 21 In.		180
Magic Lantern, Drum Shape Slide Viewer, Stand, Leather, Paper, c.1850		431
Megalethoscope, Walnut, Turned Leg, 12 Slides, C. Ponti, c.1870, 23 x 35 In.		2673
Photograph, Boy On Sleigh, Russian Fur Hat, Winter Scene, c.1890, 2 ½ x 3 In.		90
Photograph, Drummer Boy, Union, Cased Frame, 6 x 5 In.		2250
Photograph, Elizabeth Taylor, Signed, 1970s, 8 x 10 In.		125
Photograph, Innocence, Nude Woman, Sitting On Floor, 7 ⅜ x 9 ⅜ In.		41
Photograph, Jayne Mansfield, Fur Wrap, Signed, 1960s, 9 x 9 ½ In.		446
Photograph, Johnny Cash, Signed, 1950s, 8 x 10 In.		125
Photograph, Living Uncle Sam, Camp Lee, Va., Mole & Thomas, 12 x 14 In.	*illus*	529
Photograph, Luna Park, Captive Balloon Ride, Coney Island, Frame, c.1910, 13 x 16 In.		300
Photograph, Man Sitting Dockside, Al Macy, 1950s, 4 ¾ x 6 ¾ In.		35
Photograph, Michael Jackson, 1991, Signed, 8 x 10 In.		190
Photograph, Ojibway Indian, Moose Call, Silver Gelatin, Roland Reed, 20 x 16 In.		861
Photograph, Quniaka, Mohave, Platinum, Signed, Edward Curtis, 14 ¼ x 11 ¼ In.	*illus*	800
Photograph, Vermont Camera Club, Al Macy, 1950s, 8 x 10 In.		12
Photograph, Vineyard Sound Lightship, Glass Plate, c.1900, 3 ¼ x 4 In.		118
Projector, Mahogany, Brass, Tin, A.H. Baird, Edinburgh, c.1870, 19 x 10 In.		660
Projector, Movie, Ernemann-Kinox, No. 797536, 15 ½ In.		240
Projector, Safety Cinema, Black Metal, Victor Animatograph Co., Davenport, Iowa		420
Reflector, Sound & Light, Mirrored Box, Hand Crank, Cast-Iron Base, 22 In.		923
Silver Print, Coyote, Howling, Charles J. Belden, c.1925, 11 x 16 In.		480
Silver Print, El Capitan, Ansel Adams, Signed, 18 ¼ x 14 In.		2460
Tintype, Man, High Wheel Bicycle, Pressed Paper Case, ⅙ Plate	*illus*	360
Tintype, Union Officer, 3 Infantry Senior NCOs, Frame, ¼ Plate	*illus*	1410

Picture, Drawing, Pencil, Lithograph, Woven Paper, M.C. Escher, Wood Frame, 20 x 17 In.
$17,700

Brunk Auctions

Picture, Embroidery, Memorial, Silk, Painted, 2 Women, Girl, Monument, c.1807, 16 x 20 In.
$1,260

Skinner Auctioneers & Appraisers

Picture, Engraving, Fashionable Women, La Mode Illustree Pages, Signed, Frame, 13 In., Pair
$171

Theriault's

Picture, Engraving, Snake, Recinoides Anguis, Mark Catesby, Frame, c.1700, 9 ¾ x 13 In.
$1,121

Brunk Auctions

P

Picture, Flint Points & Beads, Circular Designs, Sahara Desert, Frame, 30 x 36 In. $715

Old Barn Auction

Picture, Ink On Silk, Hawk, Garden Rock, Signed, Hsu Yang, Frame, 1800s, 40 x 23 In. $790

James D. Julia Auctioneers

Picture, Needlework, Children, Pets, Hannah Swire, December 25, 1846, Frame, 30 x 26 In. $969

Theriault's

Tintype, Union Soldier, John S. Kenyon, 18 Years Old, Lyre In Portal, c.1862, ¼ Plate	840
Tintype, Union Soldier, Seated, Armed, Hat Turned Up, Brown Union Case, ⅙ Plate	277

PIANO BABY is a collector's term. About 1880, the well-decorated home had a shawl on the piano. Bisque figures of babies were designed to help hold the shawl in place. They range in size from 6 to 18 inches. Most of the figures were made in Germany. Reproductions are being made. Other piano babies may be listed under manufacturers' names.

Baby, Crawling Out Of Basket, 4 In.	169
Baby, Crawling, Finger In Mouth, Intaglio Eyes, Heubach, 5 In.	150
Baby, Lying On Back, Hands, Legs Up, White Dress, 10 In.	110
Baby, Sitting, Fingers In Mouth, Hat With Feather, 6 In.	100
Boy, Holding Cup, Feeding Dog, Blue Outfit, 7 In.	225
Boy, Sitting, Holding Ankles, Open Mouth, Teeth, Germany, 3 ¾ In.	150
Boy, Sitting, Reading, Germany, 4 ½ In.	50
Girl, Dimples, Bow, Yellow, 6 In.	65
Girl, Nude, Crawling, Reaching Out, Blond Pigtails, 9 ½ In.	65
Girl, Pink Dress With Flowers, Bonnet, Germany, c.1900, 6 In.	135
Girl, Sitting, Arms Up, Red Hair, 7 ½ In.	55
Girl, Sitting, Jack-In-The-Box, Blanket On Head, Rudolstadt, 8 ½ In.	585
Girls, Sitting, 1 Holding Grapes, 1 Holding Apple, Yellow, Blue, Pink, 7 In., Pair	207

PICKARD China Company was started in 1893 by Wilder Pickard. Hand-painted designs were used on china purchased from other sources. In the 1930s, the company began to make its own china wares in Chicago, Illinois. The company now makes many types of porcelains, including a successful line of limited edition collector plates.

Ashtray, Floral Chintz, 3 ½ In.	14
Bowl, Cherries & Gold, Bunches Of Cherries, Gold Trim, Footed, 4 x 10 ¼ In.	259
Bowl, Dessert, Avena, 4 ½ In.	22
Bowl, Dessert, Floral Chintz, 5 ⅛ In.	21
Bowl, Dessert, Twilight, 5 ⅛ In.	15
Bowl, Fruit, Grapes, Peaches, Cherries, Plums, Gold & Blue Bands, Tab Handles, 2 x 10 In.	207
Bowl, Vegetable, Lid, Round, Pamela, 12 In.	239
Bowl, Vegetable, Oval, Festival, 9 In.	39
Bowl, Vegetable, Oval, Garland, 9 In.	69
Bowl, Vegetable, Oval, Laurel, 9 In.	89
Bowl, Vegetable, Oval, Savannah, 9 In.	47
Bowl, Vegetable, Round, Trailing Vine, 10 In.	129
Cake Stand, Pedestal, Verona	55
Charger, Palace, White, Gold Border, Flowers, 11 ⅝ In., 12 Piece	570
Coffeepot, Floral Chintz, 3 Cup, 6 In.	89
Coffeepot, Lid, Rose & Daisy, 3 Cup, 7 ½ In.	139
Creamer, Claridge	37
Creamer, Fantasy, 6 Oz., 3 ½ In.	20
Creamer, Pristine, 8 Oz., 3 ⅛ In.	37
Creamer, Regina	62
Creamer, Rose & Daisy, 8 Oz., 3 ½ In.	45
Creamer, Savannah, 5 Oz., 3 ½ In.	54
Creamer, Trailing Vine, 8 Oz., 3 In.	64
Cup & Saucer, Avena	9
Cup & Saucer, Claridge, Footed	27
Cup & Saucer, Empress, Footed	47
Cup & Saucer, Fantasy, Footed	13
Cup & Saucer, Festival, Footed	27
Cup & Saucer, Floral Chintz, Demitasse	20
Cup & Saucer, Floral Chintz, Footed	20
Cup & Saucer, Garland, Footed	20
Cup & Saucer, Laurel, Footed	13
Cup & Saucer, Laurel, Footed, Demitasse	21
Cup & Saucer, Marguerite, Footed	33
Cup & Saucer, Marilyn, Footed	33
Cup & Saucer, Pamela	39
Cup & Saucer, Pristine	9
Cup & Saucer, Rondelay, Footed	24
Cup & Saucer, Savannah, Footed	9
Cup & Saucer, Snowberry, Footed	12

Cup & Saucer, Twilight, Footed	14
Cup & Saucer, Verona, Footed	23
Cup & Saucer, Woodland Flower	16
Gravy Boat, Attached Underplate	79
Gravy Boat, Attached Underplate, Gossamer	139
Gravy Boat, Underplate, Marilyn	148
Gravy Boat, Underplate, Twilight	79
Jardiniere, Poinsettia, Gilt Trim, H. Tolley, 7 x 9 In.	559
Pitcher, Raspberries, White Flowers, Red, Orange & Cream Ground, Gold Trim, 7 In.	384
Plate, Bread & Butter, Marilyn, 6 ⅜ In.	14
Plate, Bread & Butter, Pristine, 6 ¼ In.	8
Plate, Bread & Butter, Woodland Flower, 6 ¼ In.	8
Plate, Dinner, Claridge, 10 ⅝ In.	9
Plate, Dinner, Empress, 10 ⅝ In.	78
Plate, Dinner, Fantasy, 10 ⅝ In.	12
Plate, Dinner, Festival, 10 ⅝ In.	17
Plate, Dinner, Floral Chintz, 10 ⅝ In.	8
Plate, Dinner, Garland, 10 ⅝ In.	27
Plate, Dinner, Verona, 10 ⅝ In.	27
Plate, Dinner, Woodland Flower, 10 ¼ In.	21
Plate, Salad, Rondelay, 8 ¼ In.	11
Platter, Landscape, Octagonal, Footed, Gilt Rectangular Handles, James, c.1915, 11 ½ In.	127
Platter, Oval, Festival, 15 In.	129
Platter, Oval, Laurel, 15 In.	69
Platter, Oval, Snowberry, 12 In.	47
Relish, 3 Sections, Marilyn	65
Relish, 3 Sections, Savannah	138
Relish, 3 Sections, Twilight	65
Relish, 4 Sections, Rose & Daisy, 8 ¾ In.	159
Sugar, Lid, Regina	89
Sugar, Lid, Snowberry, 3 In.	74
Sugar, Lid, Trailing Vine, 3 ⅛ In.	99
Tankard, Blackberries, Fired-On Gold Accents, Ribbon Handle, Ruffled Rim, 14 ½ In.	1936
Teapot, Lid, Rose & Daisy, 4 Cup, 6 In.	199
Vase, Garden, Roses, Stone Wall, Lake, Fountain, Marked, Cylindrical, 12 In.	590
Vase, Pink Flowers, Gilt Rim, Tapered, 9 ¼ x 4 In.	288
Vase, Pink Flowers, Green Leaves, Black Ground, Gold Leaves & Trim, 8 In.	413
Vase, Poinsettia Flowers, Fired-On Gold, Oval, 8 In.	303
Vase, Scenic, Garden, Pink Roses Over Brick Wall, Cylindrical, E. Challinor, 12 ⅝ In.	605
Vase, Scenic, Tropical, Palm Trees, Water, Tapered, E. Challinor, c.1915, 9 In.	424

PICTURES, silhouettes, and other small decorative objects framed to hang on the wall are listed here. Some other types of pictures are listed in the Print and Painting categories.

Charcoal & Red Chalk, Portrait Of Julie Harris, Rene R. Bouche, 1954, 23 x 18 ½ In.	500
Charcoal On Paper, Dusk, River, Snow, Medrard P. Klein, c.1960, 11 x 18 In.	150
Charcoal, Portrait, Woman, Lace Cap, Frame, c.1840, 18 ½ x 15 In.	210
Collage, Cutout, Watercolor, Seaside Cottage, Applied Seaweed, Frame, 1800s, 9 x 12 In.	1476
Cutout, Gouache On Paper, Noblemen, Attendants, Gold Foil, Mirror Back, 17 x 20 In.	120
Drawing, Colored Pencil, Ink, On Paperboard, Strawberry, Signed Andy Warhol, 7 x 5 In.	2559
Drawing, Pencil, Horse, Needlework Border, Lemon Gold Frame, 10 ¼ x 10 ¼ In.	720
Drawing, Pencil, Lithograph, Woven Paper, M.C. Escher, Wood Frame, 20 x 17 In. ......*illus*	17700
Embroidery, Memorial, Silk, Painted, 2 Women, Girl, Monument, c.1807, 16 x 20 In. ....*illus*	1260
Engraving, Fashionable Women, La Mode Illustree Pages, Signed, Frame, 13 In., Pair ......*illus*	171
Engraving, Snake, Recinoides Anguis, Mark Catesby, Frame, c.1700, 9 ¾ x 13 In. ....*illus*	1121
Feltwork, Bowl Of Strawberries, Black, Shadowbox Frame, 1800s, 13 ¾ x 10 ½ In.	1126
Flint Points & Beads, Circular Designs, Sahara Desert, Frame, 30 x 36 In. ....*illus*	715
Gouache On Paper, Old Mill Near Abingdon, Ray Hamaker, Frame, 1944, 20 x 24 In.	295
Hair Wreath, Memorial, Heart Shape, Braided Flowers, Box Fame, Victorian, 23 x 27 In.	425
Hairwork, Memorial, Mausoleum, Urn, Willow Tree, Curved Wood Frame, 1800s, 7 ¾ x 4 In.	230
Hairwork, River Landscape, Palm Tree, Painted, Paper, Glass, Shadowbox, c.1810, 10 x 8 In.	235
Ink On Paper, Ship, Providence, W. Gilkerson, Frame, c.1980, 12 x 14 In.	502
Ink On Silk, Hawk, Garden Rock, Signed, Hsu Yang, Frame, 1800s, 40 x 23 In. ....*illus*	790
Miniature, Gouache, Rustan & Sohrab, Delhi School, Persia, Frame, 1700s, 4 ¾ x 9 In.	420
Miniature, Watercolor, On Ivory, English Schoolgirl, Curly Hair, Acorn Frame, 2 ½ In.	144
Miniature, Watercolor, On Ivory, Man, Blue Coat, Yellow Striped Vest, Doyle, c.1814, 3 x 2 In.	420
Needlework, Children, Pets, Hannah Swire, December 25, 1846, Frame, 30 x 26 In. ....*illus*	969

Picture, Panel, Stained Glass, Sunflowers, Backlit, Framed Box, Robert Laessig, 67 ¾ x 37 In.
$210

Cowan's Auctions

Picture, Panel, Wood, Inlaid, Washington Crossing Delaware, Germany, 1917, 13 x 23 In.
$984

New Orleans Auction Galleries, Inc.

Picture, Thangka, Buddhist Image, Cloth, Gilt, Frame, Tibet, 1800s, 4 ¾ x 4 ¼ In.
$119

James D. Julia Auctioneers

P

Picture, Theorem, On Velvet,
Fruit In Glass Bowl, Giltwood Frame,
21 x 16 ¾ In.
$1,386

Skinner Auctioneers & Appraisers

Picture, Theorem, Watercolor, On Paper,
Vase, Flowers, Frame, J.W. Zook, 1864,
20 x 17 In.
$480

Garth's Auctioneers & Appraisers

Picture, Watercolor, Gouache, On Ivory,
Pendant, Woman, Miniature, Gold Case,
c.1810, 3 x 2 ⅜ In.
$1,845

Skinner Auctioneers & Appraisers

TIP
*Never wash, or even
wipe, a watercolor.*

Needlework, Coat-Of-Arms, Commonwealth Of Pa., Silk, Metallic Threads, Frame, 20 x 23 In...	1320
Needlework, Couple Looking At Bird's Nest, Watercolor & Ink, Silk, c.1800, 19 x 21 In.	470
Needlework, Family Memorial, Flowers, Vine Border, Silk On Linen, Frame, 20 x 21 In.	615
Needlework, Flower Urn, Silk, Chenille, Ivory Moire Silk Ground, c.1800, 16 ½ x 12 In............	330
Needlework, Flowers, Ribbon, Silk, Wool Ground, Susanna Stokes, Frame, c.1800, 9 x 7 In.	660
Needlework, Village, River, Boating, Buildings, Vine Border, Silk, c.1790, 17 x 20 In.	800
Needlework, Watercolor, On Silk, Shepherdess, Lambs, Flower Border, c.1800, 18 x 20 In..........	1020
Panel, Stained Glass, Sunflowers, Backlit, Framed Box, Robert Laessig, 67 ¾ x 37 In. ....*illus*	210
Panel, Wood, Inlaid, Washington Crossing Delaware, Germany, 1917, 13 x 23 In. ....*illus*	984
Pastel, On Paper, 2 Lions, Rocky Landscape, Sunset Sky, R. Wilson, c.1890, 15 x 22 In.	2214
Pastel, On Paper, Portrait, Boy, Seated, Frame, c.1940, 30 x 23 In...	531
Pastel, Trompe L'Oeil, 2 Ducks, Signed Morrow, Frame, c.1900, 28 x 15 ½ In........................	395
Pastel, Trompe L'Oeil, 2 Trout, Signed Morrow, Frame, c.1900, 28 x 15 ½ In.........................	395
Pencil, On Paper, Colored, Fish, Abstract, Signed, 12 x 18 In..	250
Petitpoint, Lamb, Book, Holding Religious Standard, Silk, Gold Thread, Frame, 1800s, 8 x 7 In.	270
Pinprick, Birds On Tulip Branch, Vuilliam E. Caphe, Frame, Germany, c.1885, 9 x 9 In.	296
Prometheotype, Henry Clay, Painted, Raised Image, Eagle Border, c.1850, 29 x 24 ½ In.	978
Silhouette, Child, Rattle, ¾ Portrait, Inked Details, Frame, 4 x 3 In.	540
Silhouette, Gentleman, Long Hair, Waistcoat, Oval, Frame, c.1850, 6 ¼ x 5 In.	35
Silhouette, Girl, Hat, Dress, Blue Paper, Oval Aperture, Frame, 1800s, 5 ½ x 3 ¾ In.	182
Silhouette, Man, Profile, Colonial Dress, Hollow Cut, Signed Williams, Frame, 5 x 4 ¼ In.	185
Silhouette, Older Woman, Seated, Chair, Inked, Pencil Notation, Frame, c.1810, 9 ¾ x 8 ¾ In...	240
Silhouette, Sperm Whale, Open Mouth, Spouting, Signed J.H., Frame, c.1870, 7 x 9 In.	767
Silhouette, Woman, High Tie Hat, Hollow Cut, Frame, 3 ½ x 3 In.	58
Silhouette, Woman, Portrait, Anna Mansfield, Hollow Cut, Frame, c.1830, 5 ¼ x 4 ¼ In.	62
Silhouette, Woman, Portrait, Hair Comb, Inked Dress, Hollow Cut, Frame, 5 ¼ x 4 ½ In............	960
Silhouette, Woman, White Bonnet, Collar, Frame, c.1850, 3 ¼ x 2 ½ In.	52
Sketch, Fred Gwynne, Herman Munster, Cardboard Sheet, Signed, 8 ½ x 11 In.	443
Thangka, Buddhist Image, Cloth, Gilt, Frame, Tibet, 1800s, 4 ¾ x 4 ¼ In. ....*illus*	119
Theorem, Basket Of Flowers, Giltwood Frame, 1800s, 9 ½ x 11 ¾ In.....................................	420
Theorem, Basket Of Fruit, Bird, Butterfly, Lemon Gilt Frame, 19th Century, 12 x 15 ½ In..........	1560
Theorem, Oil, On Velvet, Basket Of Fruit, Pigeon, Frame, Terrence Graham, 25 x 30 In.	940
Theorem, Oil, On Velvet, Bowl Of Fruit, 14 x 18 ½ In...	90
Theorem, Oil, On Velvet, Bowl Of Fruit, David Ellinger, Frame, c.1970, 16 x 20 In.	600
Theorem, Oil, On Velvet, Bowl, Strawberries, Signed D. Ellinger, Frame, c.1970, 13 ¾ x 17 In. ...	770
Theorem, Oil, On Velvet, Flower Basket, Rebecca Hanah, Uniontown, Pa., 1846, 16 x 28 In........	395
Theorem, Oil, On Velvet, Fruit, Bowl, William Rank, 21 ½ x 28 In.....................................	360
Theorem, Oil, On Velvet, Fruit Basket, Butterfly, Birds, D. Ellinger, Frame, c.1965, 24 x 29 In.	4977
Theorem, On Velvet, Cannon, For Willie Delancey, Sponge Painted Frame, c.1800, 16 x 13 In....	144
Theorem, On Velvet, Dog, Brown Shaggy Hair, Sitting On Lawn, Wm. Rank, 13 x 10 ½ In.	144
Theorem, On Velvet, Flower Basket, Eglomise Mat, Frame, 4 x 4 ½ In.	120
Theorem, On Velvet, Fruit In Glass Bowl, Giltwood Frame, 21 x 16 ¾ In. ....*illus*	1386
Theorem, On Velvet, Motto, God Bless Our Home, Photographs, Gilt Frame, c.1890, 9 x 22 In....	115
Theorem, Stoneware Jug, Bird, Grapes, Fruit, Leaves, Sponged Frame, 19 x 16 ½ In.................	384
Theorem, Watercolor, Fruit Basket, Frame, 4 x 5 ½ In...	360
Theorem, Watercolor, Ink, Potted Plants, Inscribed Catharine Holtzworth, c.1845, 12 x 7 In......	273
Theorem, Watercolor, On Paper, Vase, Flowers, Frame, J.W. Zook, 1864, 20 x 17 In. ....*illus*	480
Theorem, Watercolor, Urn, Flowers, Birds, Leaves, Big Valley, Frame, c.1845, 13 ½ x 11 In.	2370
Watercolor Stencil, Fruit, Names, J.W. Thompson Co., Frame, c.1870, 12 x 10 In., 8 Piece	353
Watercolor, Bullfrog, Bathrobe, Cigar, Martini, James Browning Wyeth, 6 x 4 In......................	3680
Watercolor, Chrysanthemum Bouquet, Gilt Molded Frame, Signed E.A.B. 1863, 7 ¾ x 6 In........	47
Watercolor, Coast Scene, Signed, George Howell Gay, 1919, 16 x 30 In.	300
Watercolor, Colorado & Southern Steam Engine, Mike Pearsall, Frame, 1986, 11 x 17 In.	688
Watercolor, Cutout, Eagle, Signed David Y. Ellinger, Frame, c.1970, 11 x 11 In........................	1304
Watercolor, Eagle, Spread Wings, Song Birds, Pennsylvania, Frame, c.1850, 10 x 8 In...............	450
Watercolor, English Ship, Smaller American Ship, Frame, 1800s, 14 x 21 In.............................	531
Watercolor, Gouache, On Ivory, Pendant, Woman, Miniature, Gold Case, c.1810, 3 x 2 ⅜ In. *illus*	1845
Watercolor, Gouache, On Paper, Retrieving Mallard, Signed, c.1900, 13 x 11 In.......................	4674
Watercolor, Gouache, Winter Landscape, Sleigh, H.K. Brunner, Frame, c.1976, 6 x 8 In.............	2370
Watercolor, Hudson River Valley Landscape, Frame, c.1890, 10 x 14 In.................................	246
Watercolor, Ink, Bird Tree, Tulips, Urn, Blue, Orange, Brown, Frame, 10 x 7 ½ In....................	106
Watercolor, Ink, Pen, Paper, Frame, 1873, 9 ½ x 7 ½ In...	4800
Watercolor, Man, Woman Folk Dancing, Frame, Pa., 1800s, 11 ½ x 8 In..............................	326
Watercolor, Oil On Paper, Bird, Branch, Blossom, Pot, Frame, c.1890, 9 ½ x 7 ½ In.................	510
Watercolor, On Ivory, Portrait, Woman, Pendant Case, Scotland, 1800s, 2 ¾ In. ....*illus*	4800
Watercolor, On Ivory, Woman, Seated, Yellow Windsor Chair, Frame, c.1825, 2 ¾ x 2 In.	1944

Watercolor, On Paper, 2 Children, Going To School, F. Eckersall, Frame, 1800s, 2 ¼ x 9 In.	588
Watercolor, On Paper, 2 Songbirds, William Mussill, Frame, c.1880, 6 x 9 In.	443
Watercolor, On Paper, Carriage With Horses, House, Frame, 1880s, 10 x 12 In.	500
Watercolor, On Paper, Cat, Tabby, Sleeping, Frame, 7 ½ x 9 ½ In.	615
Watercolor, On Paper, Distlefink, Bird, On Branch, Frame, 1819, 10 x 8 In.	720
Watercolor, On Paper, Farm Scene, Girl, Pigs, Frame, c.1860, 9 x 10 In.	540
Watercolor, On Paper, Figures Formal Dress, Woods, Signed, A. Fabre Paris, 1958, 37 x 24 In.	82
Watercolor, On Paper, Memorial, Graveyard, Woman Grieving, Frame, c.1818, 20 x 30 In.	2160
Watercolor, On Paper, Reading Time, Woman In Chair, Signed L. Ruiz Luna, 29 x 31 In.	1250
Watercolor, On Paper, Winter Landscape, Loring Coleman, Jr., Frame, c.1970, 20 x 27 In.	2360
Watercolor, On Paperboard, Rose Bush & Hummingbirds, Martha Balek, Frame, 15 x 14 In.	2706
Watercolor, Paper, River And Trees, John Francis Murphy, 12 ½ x 18 In.	225
Watercolor, Pencil, On Laid Paper, 2 Angels, Holding Wreath, Bird, Frame, c.1830, 7 x 6 In.	492
Watercolor, Rooster, D. Ellinger, Frame, c.1975, 3 ¾ x 4 In.	385
Watercolor, Sailboat, Shore Scene, Marblehead, Richard H. Lever, c.1930, 16 x 20 In.	1063
Watercolor, Silhouettes, Rev. & Mrs. T.B. Robinson, Hollow Cut, c.1830, 4 x 3 In., Pair	516
Watercolor, The Constitution & The Guerriere, John Benson, Frame, c.1820, 22 ½ x 27 In.	2760
Watercolor, Valentine Cake, Seth, Bethany, Tom, 3 Of My Children, Tasha Tudor, 8 x 7 In.	2844
Watercolor, Village By Stream, 19th Century, 7 x 1 In.	189
Watercolor, Woman, Infant, D.T. For Her Sister Sarah Smith, New Bedford, Frame, 6 x 5 In.	330
Wax, Portraits, Kaiser Franz, His Empress, Shadowbox Frame, Austria, c.1800, 3 x 2 ¼ In.	1200

PICTURE FRAMES *are listed in this book in the Furniture category under Frame.*

PIERCE, *see Howard Pierce category.*

PIGEON FORGE POTTERY was started in Pigeon Forge, Tennessee, in 1946. Red clay found near the pottery was used to make the pieces. Molded or thrown pottery with matte glaze and slip decoration was made. The pottery closed in 2000.

Bowl, Black & White, Salt Glaze, Marked, 1972, 8 ⅝ x 2 ¼ In.	75
Bowl, Dogwood, Beige, Blue Interior, 2 x 5 In.	40
Coaster, Slate Blue, Yellow, Animals, Birds, Flowers, 5 Piece	30
Creamer, Brown Textured Matte Glaze, Spotted Yellow Interior, c.1950, 2 ½ In.	15
Jug, Green, Black, Gray, 3 ½ In.	23
Vase, Brown Drips, Over Ocean Blue, Long Neck, 5 In.	23
Vase, Bulbous, Stick Neck, Brown, Crater Glaze, 6 In.	20
Vase, Cylindrical, Brown Speckled Glaze, c.1980, 9 x 3 In.	30
Vase, Oval, Brown, Yellow Interior, 1940s, 3 ½ x 3 ¼ In.	27
Vase, White Ground, Applied Slip Dogwood, Footed, 3 ⅝ In.	25

PILKINGTON TILE AND POTTERY COMPANY was established in 1892 in England. The company made small pottery wares, like buttons and hatpins, but soon started decorating vases purchased from other potteries. By 1903, the company had discovered an opalescent glaze that became popular on the Lancastrian pottery line. The manufacture of pottery ended in 1937. Pilkington's Tiles Ltd. has worked from 1938 to the present.

Charger, Berries, Flowers, Lapis Glaze, Royal Lancastrian, c.1928, 11 ½ In.	300
Tile, Art Nouveau, Flower, Vines, c.1900, 3 x 6 In.	64
Tile, Art Nouveau, Lily Pads, Water Lilies, Yellow, Blue, Green, c.1900, 6 x 6 In.	299
Tile, Pink Flowers, Leaves, c.1892, 6 x 6 In.	48
Tile, Stylized Flower, Yellow, Red, c.1900, 6 x 6 In.	55
Vase, Blue Green, Gourd Shape, Lancastrian, 10 In.	98
Vase, Goats, Leaves, Royal Lancastrian, Richard Joyce, Stamped, 1905-08, 8 x 7 In.	5625
Vase, Horned Deer, Lancastrian, Red, Gold, Oval, Richard Joyce, 8 In.	4500
Vase, Orange, Spongelike Glaze, Shouldered, c.1925, 8 ¼ In.	385
Vase, Stick Neck, Bronze Aventurine Glaze, Royal Lancastrian, c.1910, 6 In.	349
Vase, Swirling Grapevines, Yellow, Gold, Red, 6-Sided, Lancastrian, Luster, c.1911, 11 In.	832

PILLIN pottery was made by Polia (1909–1992) and William (1910–1985) Pillin, who set up a pottery in Los Angeles in 1948. William shaped, glazed, and fired the clay, and Polia painted the pieces, often with elongated figures of women, children, flowers, birds, fish, and other animals. Pieces are marked with a stylized Pillin signature.

Bowl, Shaded Green Ground, Abstract Horses, c.1950, 4 ½ x 9 ½ In.	492
Bowl, Women, Birds, Trees, Turquoise Face, Signed, c.1975, 4 ½ x 9 In.	375
Box, Lid, Pair Of Dancers, White, 3 x 5 ½ x 5 ½ In.	120
Plate, Woman, 2 Children, 1 Riding Horse, 1 With Bird, Multicolor, Square, 8 ¾ In.	726

Picture, Watercolor, On Ivory, Portrait, Woman, Pendant Case, Scotland, 1800s, 2 ¾ In.
$4,800

Cowan's Auctions

Pillin, Vase, Fish, Rainbow, Signed, Black Slip, 4 ½ In.
$316

Humler & Nolan

Pincushion Doll, Child, Dresden Flowers, N. Ernst Bohne Sohne, c.1910, 4 ½ In.
$1,482

Theriault's

P

Pincushion Doll, Woman, Bisque, Painted Face, Mohair Wig, Jointed Arms, Germany, c.1910, 4 ½ In.

$112

Theriault's

Pincushion Doll, Woman, Mistinguett, Hidden Candy Box, Dressel Kister, 1920s, 14 In.

$399

Theriault's

Pincushion Doll, Woman, Nude, Feathered Tiara, Gilt, Arms Out, Dressel Kister, c.1900, 5 In.

$228

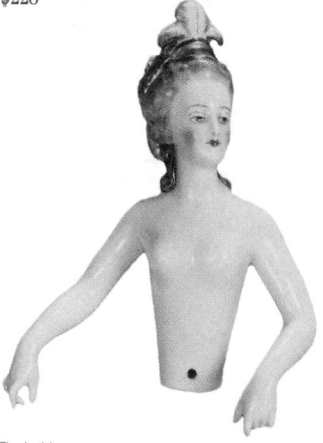

Theriault's

Vase, 2 Women, Birds, Tree, Bottle Shape, Short Neck, Pink, Lavender, Blue, 6 x 4 In.	1195
Vase, 3 Women, Brown Ground, Oval, Tapered, 8 ¼ x 4 In.	413
Vase, 3 Women, Pink Hair, Tree, Bulbous, Corseted Rim, Turquoise, Blue, Green, 9 ¼ In.	2295
Vase, Abstract Shapes, Lime Green Ground, Bulbous, Tapered, Squat, Signed, 4 ⅜ In.	475
Vase, Blue Green Glaze, Stick Neck, Round Base, 9 ½ In.	104
Vase, Dancer, Horses, Tree, Bird, Brown Ground & Interior, Cylindrical, 10 ½ x 8 In.	563
Vase, Dancers, Multicolor, Yellow, 8 ½ x 9 In.	3200
Vase, Fish, Rainbow, Signed, Black Slip, 4 ½ In. ....*illus*	316
Vase, Girl With Horse & Bird, Oval, Pink, Orange, Blue, Tapered, Flared Rim, Signed, 7 In.	424
Vase, Horses, Tree, Dancer, Woman Bird, Brown Ground, Cylindrical, 8 x 11 In.	450
Vase, Oval, Eight Fish, Blue, Green, Brown, 3 ⅞ In.	275
Vase, Rainbow Fish, Blue Green Ground, Bottle Shape, 4 ½ In.	333
Vase, Rooster, Square, 4 ¼ x 3 In.	800
Vase, Rose Bowl, Melon Green Over Blue Glaze, Round, W&P Pillin, 8 ⅜ x 14 ½ In.	726
Vase, Tricornered, 3 Scenes, Acrobats With Bird, Woman With Flowers, Horses, Pinched, 6 In.	1210
Vase, Woman, Blond, Holding Flower & Bird, Pinched Neck, 14 In.	1195
Vase, Woman, Dancing, Striated Yellow Ground, Orange Inside, Cylindrical, 6 ¾ x 4 In.	949
Vase, Woman, Holding Net Of Birds, Boy & Girl, Tree, 10 ½ In.	1295
Vase, Woman, Horse, Bulbous, Stick Neck, Blue, Teal, 15 In.	895
Vase, Woman, Playing Mandolin, Cup Like, Cylindrical, 3 x 2 ½ In.	495

PINCUSHION DOLLS are not really dolls and often were not even pincushions. Some collectors use the term "half-doll." The top half of each doll was made of porcelain. The edge of the half-doll was made with several small holes for thread, and the doll was stitched to a fabric body with a voluminous skirt. The finished figure was used to cover a hot pot of tea, powder box, pincushion, whiskbroom, or lamp. They were made in sizes from less than an inch to over 9 inches high. Most date from the early 1900s to the 1950s. Collectors often find just the porcelain doll without the fabric skirt.

Child, Dresden Flowers, N. Ernst Bohne Sohne, c.1910, 4 ½ In. ....*illus*	1482
Dance Hall Girl, Mistinguett, Saucer Tutu, Bra Top, France, 1920s, 9 ½ In.	1076
Flapper, Hands On Hip, Tulle Shirt, Marked, c.1925, 4 In.	395
Pierrot, Black Skullcap, Ruffled Collar, Germany, 1920s, 2 In.	175
Woman, Bisque, Painted Face, Mohair Wig, Jointed Arms, Germany, c.1910, 4 ½ In. ....*illus*	112
Woman, Cream Fishnet Gown, Green Sash, Blond Wig, Germany, 7 In.	716
Woman, Curly Hair, Yellow Taffeta, Lace, Germany, 3 ½ In.	185
Woman, Hands On Chest, Bronze Satin Dress, Germany, 8 In.	44
Woman, Holding Flowers, Blue Dress, Germany, 1 ¾ In.	22
Woman, Mistinguett, Hidden Candy Box, Dressel Kister, 1920s, 14 In. ....*illus*	399
Woman, Nude, Art Deco, Gold Earrings, Germany, 6 ½ x 6 In.	165
Woman, Nude, Feathered Tiara, Gilt, Arms Out, Dressel Kister, c.1900, 5 In. ....*illus*	228
Woman, Nude, Outstretched Arms, Roses & Feathers In Hair, Germany, c.1900, 5 In.	445
Woman, Tray, Serving Cocoa, Gebruder Heubach, c.1910, 4 ½ In. ....*illus*	513

PINK SLAG *pieces are listed in this book in the Slag Glass category.*

PIPES have been popular since tobacco was introduced to Europe by Sir Walter Raleigh. Carved wooden, porcelain, ivory, and glass pipes and accessories may be listed here.

Bamboo, Henry Clay, Portrait, c.1844, 3 x 21 In.	127
Burl Bowl, Carved, Bearded Head, Federal Shield, Sword, Civil War, 2 x 3 In. ....*illus*	240
Burl, Carved Creatures, Stippled, Stylized, Free-Form, U.S.A., 1800s, 13 In.	210
Burl, Carved Embracing Figures, U.S.A., 1800s, 4 ⅛ In.	210
Burl, Carved, Civil War, Union Forever, Eagle, Banner, c.1861, 3 ½ In.	3360
Meerschaum, Black Man, Wearing Hat, 3 ½ In.	200
Meerschaum, Coat Of Arms, Crown, Carved, 1800s, 4 x 4 ¾ In.	150
Meerschaum, Eagle Claws, Holding Bowl, Amber Stem, Case, 6 ½ In.	314
Meerschaum, Figural, Napoleon, 7 In.	75
Meerschaum, Nude Woman, Carved, 3 ⅝ x 7 In.	184
Meerschaum, Scene, Man, Arm In Sling, Crouching Man, Man With Sword, 1800s, 5 x 4 In.	210
Meerschaum, Woman In Loincloth, Amber Stem, Case, 6 ¼ In.	285
Porcelain, Barmaid, Holding Steins ....*illus*	230
Wood, Carved, Eagle, Arrows, Branch, Cumberland Mountains, Metal, c.1862, 3 ¼ In. ......*illus*	2400
Wood, Carved, Rope, Acorn Tassels, M. Kinell, Co. B, 94th O.V.I., c.1862, 3 ¾ In.	3240
Wood, Eagle, Banner, Liberty Or Death, c.1862, 3 ½ In.	9000
Wood, Man's Head, Beard, Military Cap, Bead Inset Almond Eyes, 1800s, 4 In.	3600
Wood, Rose, Carved, Knobby Natural Branch, Patina, 1800s, 4 In.	336

PIRKENHAMMER is a porcelain manufactory started in 1802 by Friedrich Holke and J. G. Lilst. It was located in Bohemia, now Brezova, Czechoslovakia. The company made tablewares usually decorated with views and flowers. Lithophanes were also made. The mark of the crossed hammers is easy to remember as the Pirkenhammer symbol.

Cup & Saucer, Birds & Butterflies, Blue, Brown, c.1880, Demitasse	155
Figurine, Clown, Red, Gold, Ruffled Collar, Hat, Looking Up, 6 In.	550
Figurine, Dog, English Setter, Black, White, Brown, 8 x 3 In.	350
Plate, Oriental Crane, Water, Butterflies, c.1880, 8 ⅞ In.	225
Vase, Tree Trunk, Dog, Rabbit, Bird, c.1850, 8 x 5 x 4 In.	475

PISGAH FOREST POTTERY was made in North Carolina beginning in 1926. The pottery was started by Walter B. Stephen, who had been making pottery in that location since 1914. The pottery continued in operation after his death in 1961. The most famous kinds of Pisgah Forest ware are the cameo type with designs made of raised glaze and the turquoise crackle glaze wares.

Coffeepot, Lid, Applied Stagecoach Scene, Green, White, 1952, 8 ¾ In.	295
Vase, Crystalline Glaze, Blue, Yellow, White, c.1941, 5 In.	354
Vase, Crystalline Glaze, Pink Interior, Flaring Rolled Rim, 4 ½ In.	177
Vase, Green, Marked, 6 ¼ In.	20
Vase, Light Green Gloss Glass, North Carolina, 1935, 4 ⅜ In.	24
Vase, Turquoise Glaze, Pink Interior, 1939, 3 In.	25
Vase, Turquoise, Over Plum, Shouldered, Tapered, 1941, 4 x 5 ¾ In.	69

PLANTERS PEANUTS memorabilia are collected. Planters Nut and Chocolate Company was started in Wilkes-Barre, Pennsylvania, in 1906. The Mr. Peanut figure was adopted as a trademark in 1916. National advertising for Planters Peanuts started in 1918. The company was acquired by Standard Brands, Inc., in 1961. Standard Brands merged with Nabisco in 1981. Some of the Mr. Peanut jars and other memorabilia have been reproduced and, of course, new items are being made.

Bank, Vendor, Mr. Peanut Head, Mechanical, Plastic, Box, 1950s, 7 x 5 x 5 In.	690
Box, Candy Bar, Crunchy, 10 Cents, Red, Blue, White, Canada, 5 ¼ x 10 In.	978
Box, Roasted Peanuts, Mr. Peanut, Cardboard, 3 Lb. Size, 10 x 6 x 6 In.	34
Can, Clean Crisp, Salted Peanuts, Tin Lithograph, Red, Green, Flowers, 4 x 4 In.	834
Candy Bars, Jumbo Block, 5 Cents, Mr. Peanut, Sealed, 2 ¼ x 4 ½ In., Pair	69
Costume, Mr. Peanut Promotional Suit, Top Hat, Monocle, Fiberglass, Painted, 50 In.	660
Costume, Mr. Peanut, Mask, Top Hat, Cardboard, 14 ½ x 13 In.	184
Display Rack, Countertop, Z Shape, Planters Peanut Specialties, 4 x 14 x 7 In.	891
Display, Jar, Clear, Tin Lid, 10 In.	72
Display, Planters Best Peanut, Tin, Die Cut, Multicolor, Counter, 12 In.	900
Figure, Mr. Peanut, Papier-Mache, Life Size, 75 In. ....*illus*	7800
Hand Puppet, Mr. Peanut, Rubber, 6 In.	489
Salesman's Case, Mr. Peanut, Fold-Out Staircase Style, Gold Print, 9 x 17 x 7 In.	345
Scale, Mr. Peanut, Iron, Hamilton Scale Co., Toledo, Ohio, 44 ½ In. ....*illus*	7200
Tin, Clean, Crisp, Luscious Golden-Meated, c.1918, 10 Lbs., 9 x 8 In.	241
Tin, High Grade Confections, Mr. Peanut, Cylindrical, 9 ⅝ x 8 ⅜ In.	2415
Tin, Salt-In-Shell, Mr. Peanut, Ocean Waves, White, Blue, 12 x 10 In.	834

PLASTIC objects of all types are being collected. Some pieces are listed in other categories; gutta-percha cases are listed in the Photography category. Celluloid is in its own category.

Cigarette Box, Bakelite, Black, Green Lid, Silver Feet, Fan Shape Finial, 1930s, 2 Piece	354
Salt & Pepper, Globular, Bakelite, Swirling, 1930s, 1 ⅜ In.	65
Tray, Melamine, Figural Designs, Black, P. Fornasetti, Italy, c.1985, 10 ½ x 8 In.	250
Vase, Clear Special, Resin, Fish Design Store, Gaetano Pesce, 14 x 12 In. ....*illus*	1140
Wall Organizer, Black, Attached Containers, D. Becker, I. Maurer, Germany, 1969, 34 x 26 In.	250

PLATED AMBERINA was patented June 15, 1886, by Joseph Locke and made by the New England Glass Company. It is similar in color to amberina, but is characterized by a cream colored or chartreuse lining (never white) and small ridges or ribs on the outside.

Bowl, Vertical Ribs, Ruffled Top, White Lining, 8 x 3 In. ....*illus*	2666
Lamp, Ruffled, Undulating Rim Shade, Gilt Metal Stylized Base, 20 ¼ In.	8050
Punch Cup, Ribbed, Applied Amber Handle, 2 ½ In. ....*illus*	2300
Tumbler, Amber Foot Shaded To Ruby Rim, New England, 3 ¾ In.	2185
Tumbler, Fuchsia Shaded To Amber, Vertical Ribbing, White Interior, 3 ¾ In.	2370
Tumbler, Vertical Ribs, White Lining, Ground Pontil, 3 ¾ In. ....*illus*	1067

Pincushion Doll, Woman, Tray, Serving Cocoa, Gebruder Heubach, c.1910, 4 ½ In. $513

Theriault's

TIP
Never clean plastic dishes with a harsh abrasive. It will scratch the dishes.

Pipe, Burl Bowl, Carved, Bearded Head, Federal Shield, Sword, Civil War, 2 x 3 In. $240

Skinner Auctioneers & Appraisers

Pipe, Porcelain, Barmaid, Holding Steins $230

Fox Auctions

Pipe, Wood, Carved, Eagle, Arrows, Branch, Cumberland Mountains, Metal, c.1862, 3 ¼ In.
$2,400

Cowan's Auctions

Planters Peanuts, Figure, Mr. Peanut, Papier-Mache, Life Size, 75 In.
$7,800

Morphy Auctions

Planters Peanuts, Scale, Mr. Peanut, Iron, Hamilton Scale Co., Toledo, Ohio, 44 ½ In.
$7,200

Morphy Auctions

Vase, Lily, Amber To Yellow, Trifold Fuchsia Rim, 8 In. ....*illus* 4313

PLIQUE-A-JOUR is an enameling process. The enamel is laid between thin raised metal lines and heated. The finished piece has transparent enamel held between the thin metal wires. It is different from cloisonne because it is translucent.

Bowl, Lid, Translucent Blue, Green, Yellow Flowers, Gilt, Wood Stand, Chinese, 5 In.	150
Bowl, Multicolor Flowers, Leaves, Translucent, Pierced Panels, Scalloped, Footed, 6 In.	90
Bowl, Translucent Blue, Pink, Yellow Flowers, Chinese, Green Band, 7 In.	90
Spoon, Silver, Flowers, Red, Green, Maker's Mark, Continental, c.1900, 5 ½ In.	390

POLITICAL memorabilia of all types, from buttons to banners, are collected. Items related to presidential candidates are the most popular, but collectors also search for material related to state and local offices. Memorabilia related to social causes, minor political parties, and protest movements are also included here. Many reproductions have been made. A jugate is a button with photographs of both the presidential and vice presidential candidates. In this list a button is round, usually with a straight pin or metal tab to secure it to a shirt. A pin is brass, often figural, sometimes attached to a ribbon.

Andirons, Washington, Standing On Draped Plinth, Cast Iron, Paint, c.1890, 21 In.	474
Ashtray, Lyndon Johnson, Stetson Hat Shape, Metal, 5 ½ x 3 ½ In.	217
Badge, Press, McKinley, Brass Spreadwing Eagle, Ribbon, 1896, 8 ½ In.	330
Bandanna, Garfield, Arthur, Portraits, Eagles, Red, 1880, 20 x 20 ½ In.	173
Bandanna, Major General Zachary Taylor, Red, White, Brown, Drums, Eagles, 1848, 25 x 29 In.	4406
Bandanna, Roosevelt, Hats, Cloth, National Kerchief Co., 1912, 19 x 19 In.	95
Bandanna, TR Brands, Rough Rider Hat, Cotton, c.1912, 19 x 19 In.	225
Bandanna, Win With Ike For President, Flags, Red, Cotton, c.1952, 27 x 27 In.	44
Banner, Flag, James K. Polk, George M. Dallas, 1844, 27 x 21 In.	1204
Banner, Roosevelt For President, Canvass, Red, White, Blue, Sweeney Litho Co., 58 x 39 In.	995
Booklet, Progressive Battle Hymns, Roosevelt, Johnson, Bull Moose Party, 64 Pg., 5 x 8 In.	50
Booklet, Your Social Security, Old Age & Survivors Insurance, 1955, 43 Pg., 4 x 5 ½ In.	10
Bootjack, McKinley, Goldbug, Cast Iron, High Relief, 4 ¼ x 11 ½ In.	299
Bootjack, Roosevelt In 32, Donkey's Head, Cast Iron, Cold Painted, 11 x 5 In.	581
Bowl, Remember The Maine, Paint, Wood, Embossed Composition, c.1900, 12 ¾ In.	75
Broadside, National Union Ticket, President, Lincoln, Johnson, King, Baird, 1864, 46 x 32 In.	32250
Bumper Sticker, Re-Elect Nelson A. Rockefeller, 1966, 4 x 14 In.	40
Bust, George Washington, Multicolor, Incised, E. Wood, Staffordshire, c.1810, 8 ½ In.	2750
Bust, George Washington, Pearlware, Inscribed, Enoch Wood, 8 ¾ In.	1560
Bust, John F. Kennedy, Chalkware, Bronze Finish, Marked Austin, 1964, 10 ½ In.	125
Button, Bryan, Miss Liberty, Sitting In Chair, Flag Outfit, Round, 1908, 1 ¾ In.	2910
Button, Calvin Coolidge, Portrait Within Keystone, 1924, ⅞ In.	85
Button, Civil Rights Symbol, Power To The People, Right On, White, Red, 1960s, 1 ¼ In.	25
Button, Dick & Pat Nixon, For President, First Lady, Red, White, Blue, 1960, 1 ¾ In.	19
Button, End The War In Viet Nam Now, Columbia Indep. Committee, 1 ½ In. ....*illus*	182
Button, Flag, Red, Communist Party Election, Work Award, Foster Signature, 1936, ⁹⁄₁₆ In.	144
Button, Ford, Dole, 76, America's Choice, Red, White, Blue, Elephant, 1976, 3 In.	144
Button, Get Out Of Vietnam, Oval, Blue, Black, 1966, 2 ¾ In.	134
Button, Hoffa For President, Portrait, Cream, Black, Celluloid, c.1958, 3 In.	86
Button, Hoo For Hoover, Poppy Flower, Portrait, ⅞ In.	1044
Button, I Am A Goldwater Delegate, Celluloid On Silk Rosette, 3 ½ In.	100
Button, I Am Against War, Pre-Pearl Harbor, World Globe, Blue, Red, Lithograph, ⅞ In.	127
Button, I Like Ike, Time For A Change, Baby, 1 In.	145
Button, I'm Extremely Fond Of Barry, Blue, Red, White Ground, Blue Rim, 1964, 1 ¼ In.	12
Button, Jugate, Roosevelt, Fairbanks, Lady Liberty, Bunting, W.F. Miller & Co., 1904, 1 ¼ In.	300
Button, Kennedy, Election Night Press, Green, Cardboard Back, 3 ½ In.	2211
Button, Kennedy, Ted Kennedy, Senatorial Race, Blue, White Lettering, 1 ½ In.	5
Button, Landon, Knox, Portraits, Flower Petal Border, Tin, Jugate, 2 ⅛ In.	3795
Button, Learn To Say President Willkie, ⅞ In.	10
Button, Lincoln, Round, Brass, Portrait, For President 1864, ¹⁵⁄₁₆ In.	380
Button, Louis Pontchartrain, Chancellor Of France, Portrait, Stick, c.1905, 2 In.	75
Button, LSD, Melts In Your Mind, Blue, Purple, Sugar Cube, 1960s, 1 ½ In.	115
Button, Malcolm X, Black Panther Party, Black Power, c.1968, 1 ¾ In.	86
Button, Mama Hippie, Bells & Beads, All Your Needs, Woman, 2 In.	86
Button, McCarthy, Flowers, Multicolor, Homemade, c.1968, 2 ¼ In.	86
Button, McGovern, Flying Peace Dove, Blue Ground, White, Red, 1972, 3 In.	127
Button, McKinley, Goldbug, Brass Shell Stars, Stripes, Portrait, 1 ¾ In.	190
Button, McKinley, Hobart, Goldbug, Portraits In Wings, Mechanical, 1896, 1 ¼ x 1 ½ In.	173

P

Button, McKinley, Riding Gold & Silver Bike, To The White House, 1896, 1 ¼ In.	767
Button, Mondale, Ferraro, Portrait, Jugate, 6 In.	12
Button, Nixon For Governor, Blue, White, Lithograph, 1962, ⅞ In.	13
Button, Nix-On War Now, Southeast Asia Countries, Peace Sign, Red, White, Blue, c.1971, 2 In.	506
Button, Obama, All You Need Is Love, The Beatles, Celluloid, 2012, 3 In. *illus*	32
Button, Our Next President, Wendell Lewis Willkie, 1 ¼ In.	13
Button, Owl Shape, Who?, Who?, Hoover, Enameled Brass, ⅜ x ⅝ In.	45
Button, Pro Bryan Anti-Trust Rebus, Ant, Eye, Trust, Pat'd-1-23-1900, W&H, ⅞ In. *illus*	254
Button, Remember Pearl Harbor, We Will Win F.D.R., Axis Leaders' Heads, 1 ¼ In. *illus*	448
Button, Robert Kennedy, Caricature, Black Drawing On White, Marked D. Levine 64, 6 In.	173
Button, Roosevelt, Babcock, Portraits, Round, Jugate, 1904, 1 ¼ In.	342
Button, Roosevelt, For President, Rose, Velt, Celluloid, 1 ¼ In. *illus*	175
Button, Royal Canadian Artillery, Quebec, Quadrille Club, Flags, c.1896, 1 ¼ In.	144
Button, Support Johnson & Civil Rights, Lithograph, Bar Pin, Red, White, Blue, 3 In.	980
Button, T. Roosevelt, Elephant, Donkey, Red, White, Blue Ribbon, 1905, 1 ½ x 3 In.	1689
Button, Taft, Trumpeter, Celluloid, 1 ¾ In.	560
Button, Teddy Roosevelt, Fairbanks, Portraits, Eyeglass Shape, Silvered Brass, Jugate, 1904	193
Button, The McGovern Spirit Lives, 1972, 1 ½ In.	13
Button, They're For You, Ike, Dick, Eisenhower, Nixon, Tin Lithograph, 1952, 1 ⅜ In.	35
Button, Time For A Change, I Like Ike, Baby In Diaper, 1 ¼ In.	173
Button, Truman, I'm Just Wild About Harry, White, Blue, Celluloid, 2 ⅛ In.	173
Button, Vietnam War Protest, Together For Peace, Princeton, White, Black, 1970, 1 ¾ In.	86
Button, Wallace For President, Stand Up For America, Red, White, Blue, 1968, 1 ½ In.	5
Button, William H. Harrison, Liberty On Horseback Crossing Stream, Sepia, Large Pinback	150
Button, Wilson, For Me & Mine, Celluloid, ⅝ In.	18
Cane, Abraham Lincoln, Bust, Gutta Percha, Malacca Shaft, c.1870, 33 In.	633
Cane, Campaign, FDR, Governor Of New York, Banner, 1920s	200
Cane, Committeeman, Agriculture Dept., Morrisville, N.Y., 4-Sided, Yard Stick, 1967	25
Cane, Grover Cleveland Bust, Pewter, Hardwood Shaft, 36 In.	148
Cane, Wm. H. Harrison, Root Handle, Cider Barrel, Eagle, Wood, 1840, 36 In.	460
Chin Tapper, FDR, Going To Run 3rd Term, Cast Aluminum, 1940, 2 ¾ x 3 x 1 ¾ In.	156
Cigar Box, Cleveland, Stevenson, Portraits, Stars, Bars, Flag, 1892, 5 ¼ x 8 In.	371
Clock, Prohibition Repeal, Bar, Woman, Martini, United Electric Clock, 1933, 13 x 10 In.	1007
Coffee Mill, Teddy Roosevelt, Rough Rider, Horseback, Flag, Bronson-Walton, 5 x 9 In.	316
Coin Purse, McKinley, Roosevelt, Portraits, Jugate, Cartoon, Round, 1 In.	1392
Coin Set, U.S. Mint Gold Presidential Dollar, Collector's Book, 2007-13, 28 Piece	59
Cup, Coffee With Kennedy, Red, White, Paper, 1960, 3 ¼ In.	19
Doll, Theodore Roosevelt, Rough Rider, Stuffed Cotton, Painted Face, c.1900, 11 In. *illus*	531
Donkey, Kennedy, Johnson, Stuffed, Yarn Mane & Tail, 1960, 2 ¼ x 7 ½ In.	509
Door Panel, Abraham Lincoln, Etched Glass, Ruby Glass, c.1860, 18 x 29 In. *illus*	1200
Elephant, Life Begins In '40, Plaster, Constitution In Trunk, 1939, 3 ½ x 12 In.	86
Elephant, Taft, GOP, Inset Photo, Cast Iron, Bronze, 1908, 6 ½ x 4 ½ In.	253
Figure, John Kennedy, Wood, Carved, John Erickson, 1960s, 8 ¼ In.	428
Flag, American, Harrison, Morton & Protection, Muslin, 5 Stars, 2 ¼ x 4 In. *illus*	460
Flag, Lincoln & Hamlin, Wide Awake, Cotton, Red, White, Blue, 13 Stars, 11 x 17 In.	44650
Game, The Kennedys, Cards, Play Money, Transco Adult Games Inc., 1962, 19 In. *illus*	86
Glass, Happy Days Are Here Again, Donkey, Red, Blue, c.1932, 3 In.	15
Handkerchief, Commemorative, Maine Well Remembered, Silk, c.1898, 19 x 19 In.	100
Hat, Poll Worker's, Reagan, Bush, Styrofoam, Red, White, Blue Band, N.H., 1980	48
Jug, T. Roosevelt, Elephant Head Handle, Lenox, Pat. Applied For, E. Penfield, 7 x 7 ½ In. *illus*	830
License Plate, Beer, Metal, Embossed, FDR Campaign, c.1932, 4 x 12 In. *illus*	316
License Plate, FDR, Rise With Roosevelt, 1932, 4 ½ x 11 ½ In.	139
License Plate, Re-Elect Roosevelt, Capital, Flags, Tin, Die Cut, 7 x 5 ½ In.	118
Match Safe, Harrison Profile, Figural, 2-Sided, Spring Lid, 1888, 2 ⅝ x ½ In.	173
Medal, George Washington, Centennial, Bronze, Philip Martiny, 4 ½ In.	356
Mirror, Coolidge, DuPont, Robinson, Woman Requested To Vote, Pocket, 2 ¼ In.	302
Mirror, Maj. Gen. Zachariah Taylor, Pewter Encased, Bracket, Round, 3 ⅛ In. Diam.	460
Mug, Abraham Lincoln Club, Ain't It Hell To Be Poor, Brooklyn, N.Y., 1908, 4 ½ In.	175
Mug, The New Deal, FDR Profile, Brown, Ceramic, c.1936	25
Mug, To Washington The Patriot Of America, White, Staffordshire, c.1830, 2 ½ In.	316
Necktie, Elephant, Horn Rimmed Glasses, c.1964	24
Necktie, I Like Ike, c.1952	34
Pamphlet, Citizen's Handbook, Great Depression, Prohibition, Sun Oil Co., 1932	24
Paper Dolls, First Family, Reagan, Nancy, Patti, Ronald Jr., Al Kilgore, Dell, 1981, 9 x 13 In.	90
Paperweight, Medallion, JFK Bust, Presidential Seal, Bronze, 3 In.	44
Pencil, Roosevelt, 14K, Tiffany & Co., Monogram, 2 ½ In.	690

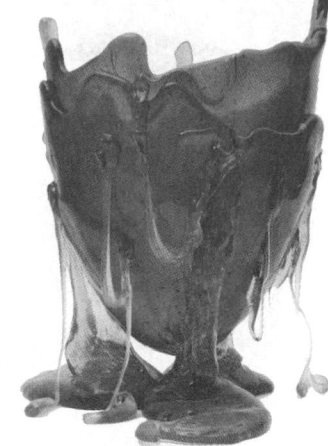

Plastic, Vase, Clear Special, Resin, Fish Design Store, Gaetano Pesce, 14 x 12 In. $1,140

Palm Beach Modern Auctions

Plated Amberina, Bowl, Vertical Ribs, Ruffled Top, White Lining, 8 x 3 In. $2,666

James D. Julia Auctioneers

Plated Amberina, Punch Cup, Ribbed, Applied Amber Handle, 2 ½ In. $2,300

Early Auction Co.

P

Plated Amberina, Tumbler, Vertical Ribs, White Lining, Ground Pontil, 3 ¾ In. $1,067

James D. Julia Auctioneers

Plated Amberina, Vase, Lily, Amber To Yellow, Trifold Fuchsia Rim, 8 In. $4,313

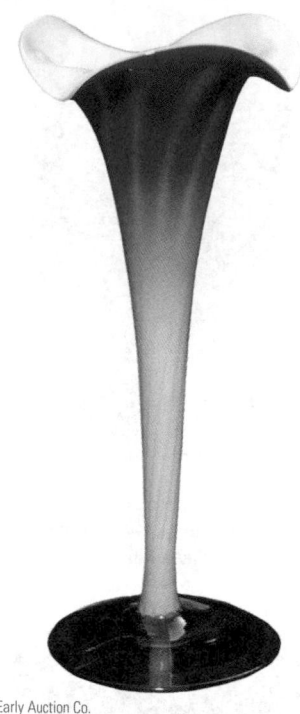

Early Auction Co.

Political, Button, End The War In Viet Nam Now, Columbia Indep. Committee, 1 ½ In. $182

Hake's Americana & Collectibles

Political, Button, Obama, All You Need Is Love, The Beatles, Celluloid, 2012, 3 In. $32

Anderson Americana

Pendant, Inaugural Ball, Johnson, Humphrey Heads, Sterling, Octagonal, 1965, 1 x 1 In.	50
Pennant, Taft, Felt, Red, White, c.1910, 17 ½ In.	55
Photograph, Abraham Lincoln, A. Hessler Photo, 1860, 7 x 9 In.	2700
Photograph, Andrew Jackson, By Mathew Brady Or Edward Anthony, 1845, 6 x 9 In.	425
Picture, Abraham Lincoln, Reverse Painted Glass, c.1870, 29 x 25 In.	633
Pillow Cover, Franklin D. Roosevelt, Campaign, Pink Rayon, Portrait, 1938, 11 x 11 In.	45
Pin, Garfield, Arthur, Cardboard Photo Jugates, Brass Shell, Brass Tab, 1 ⅛ In.	1392
Pin, Gold Bug, Jugate, McKinley, Hobart, Brass, Wings Move, 1896, 1 ¼ x 1 ½ In.	250
Pin, GOP Elephant, Figural, Black, Metal, ¾ x ½ In.	25
Pitcher, Andrew Jackson, Tapered, Yellow Paint, Copper Luster, Staffordshire, 1820s, 8 ½ In.	3738
Pitcher, Harrison, Reid, Blue Transfer, Jugate, 1892, 6 ½ In.	390
Pitcher, James Madison, Black Transfer, Text, Creamware, Eng., c.1810, 8 ¾ In.	4080
Plaque, Theodore Roosevelt, Profile, Text, Bronze, J.E. Fraser, 13 x 10 In.	750
Plate Topper, Franklin Roosevelt, Uncle Sam, Rubbery Composition, c.1936, 8 x 11 In. ....*illus*	207
Plate, Everyone For Elephants, Republican, Halco Corp., 1972, 10 ¾ In.	18
Plate, James Garfield, Embossed Glass, 1888	45
Plate, McKinley Profile, Pierced Rim, Milk Glass, 9 In.	30
Plate, William Howard Taft, James Sherman, Presidential Candidates Border, Tin, 1908, 9 In.	111
Postcard, Rutherford B. Hayes, Embossed Photo Lithograph, Flag, Eagle, 1906	7
Postcard, Taft, Standing, 3 ½ In. ....*illus*	57
Postcard, Teddy Roosevelt, Bull Moose, My Hat Is Still In The Ring, 1912, 5 ½ In.	36
Postcard, Washington Entering New York 1732, 1799, Depicts Crossing, Multicolor, 1910s	9
Poster, Anti-Air Pollution, Statue Of Liberty, Gas Mask, 1969, 12 x 17 In.	75
Poster, FDR, Portrait, Stars, 1944, 11 x 14 In.	40
Poster, Flag, Give It Your Best, Charles Coiner, 1942, 20 x 28 In.	720
Poster, Goldwater-Miller, For Better Government, Elect, Cardboard, 1964, 14 x 22 In.	40
Poster, Kennedy For President, Leadership For The 60s, 13 x 18 In.	69
Poster, Lyndon Johnson, Hippie, Turn Off, Tune Out, Drop In, 1967, 19 x 25 In. ....*illus*	115
Poster, RFK, Portrait, 12 x 19 In.	30
Poster, Ronald Reagan, Jelly Bean Kid, Make American Strong Again, Frame, 1981, 33 x 21 In.	47
Poster, Roosevelt Jugate, Metropolitan Printing Co., N.Y., Frame, 1900, 35 x 25 In.	1800
Poster, Teddy Roosevelt For President, Color, 12 ¾ x 17 ¾ In.	1995
Puzzle, Harrison, 8 Cabinet Members, Jewel Gasoline Stove, c. 1889, 7 x 7 In. ....*illus*	86
Puzzle, Puzzle Of Watergate, Army Bugs Crawling Out Of White House, 1975, 9 x 13 In.	30
Puzzle, Theodore Roosevelt, Rough Riders, McLoughlin, Box, 1898, 18 x 13 In., 73 Piece ..*illus*	1175
Rebus, Dewey, Donkey, White House, Get Your, Off The Grass, It's Dewey, 1 ¾ In.	863
Ribbon, Harrison, Jugate, Portraits, Blue Fringe, Flags, 1888, 8 ¼ In.	86
Ribbon, Inauguration Day, I Like Ike & Dick, Red, White, 1957, 3 ½ In.	110
Ribbon, Millard Fillmore, For President, Silk, Blue, North Or South Quote, 1856, 2 ¼ x 7 In.	535
Ribbon, Roosevelt, Fairbanks, Protection, Prosperity, 1904, 3 In.	773
Ring, McKinley, Hobart, Horseshoe Nail, Brass Luster, Incised Names, 1896, Size 9, 1 In.	115
Ring, Seal, Geo. Washington, Laurel Wreath, Silver, c.1800, Size 9 ½	826
Scarf, Hubert Humphrey, Presidential Candidate, H, Blue, White, Green, 1968, 20 x 20 In.	8
Screen, Commemorative, Lincoln, Relief Carved, Emancipation 1863, 74 x 36 In. ....*illus*	29625
Sign, Teddy Roosevelt, Cardboard, Frame, c.1905, 19 ½ x 12 In.	600
Snuffbox, Andrew Jackson, Papier-Mache, Civilian Dress, Round, 1829, 3 ¼ In.	2530
Snuffbox, Round, Jackson, Van Buren, Clay, Webster, 1832, 3 ⅝ In. Diam	1961
Songbook, Grant, Wilson Campaign, Portraits, Republican, Paper, 3 ¾ x 5 ¾ In.	144
Stickpin, Hughes, America First, Flag Shape, Celluloid, 1 ½ In.	450
Stickpin, McKinley, Hobart, Bicycle Shape, 1 ⅛ In.	74
Suspenders, Willkie For President, Red, White, Blue, c.1940	75
Table Runner, Theodore Roosevelt, Portrait, Life Scenes, Woven, Fringe, 16 ½ x 54 In.	148
Tieback, George Washington Bust, Transfer, Brass & Enamel Frame, c.1795, 2 In., Pair	2133
Tip Tray, Grand Old Party, Taft, Sherman, Portraits, 4 ¼ In.	120
Torch, Campaign, W.H. Harrison, Eagle, Brass, Oil Font, Burners Wings, 1840, 9 x 12 In. ...*illus*	1645
Toy, Bell Ringer, Harold Lloyd, Face Moves, Bell Goes To Ear, Tin Lithograph, 6 In.	148
Toy, Gladstone, Disraeli, Wrestling, Wood, Papier-Mache, Painted, Box, England, 8 ½ In.	180
Toy, J.F.K. Figure, Rocking Chair, Kamar, Box, 11 In.	380
Toy, Theodore Roosevelt, Rough Rider, On Horse, Mohair, Steiff, Germany, 1958, 37 In.	4375
Trivet, James A. Garfield, Portrait, Horseshoe, Cast Iron, Footed, 1880s, 5 x 4 In.	65
Watch Fob, Charles E. Hughes, Photo, Cello, Portrait, Round, 1 ¾ In.	115
Watch Fob, Taft, Arrow Head Shape, Gold Metal, Straight To White House, 1 In.	90
Watch Fob, Taft, Sherman, Jugate, Leather Strap, 1908	84
Watch Fob, Theodore Roosevelt, Celluloid, Mirror Back, 1 ¾ In.	250
Wristwatch, Spiro Agnew, Windup, Red & Blue Vinyl Band, Swiss, c.1972, 9 In.	35

P

Political, Button, Pro Bryan Anti-Trust Rebus, Ant, Eye, Trust, Pat'd-1-23-1900, W&H, ⅞ In.
$254

Political, Button, Remember Pearl Harbor, We Will Win F.D.R., Axis Leaders' Heads, 1 ¼ In.
$448

Political, Button, Roosevelt, For President, Rose, Velt, Celluloid, 1 ¼ In.
$175

White House Decorating
There were moose heads hanging in the White House during President Teddy Roosevelt's term.

Political, Doll, Theodore Roosevelt, Rough Rider, Stuffed Cotton, Painted Face, c.1900, 11 In.
$531

Political, Door Panel, Abraham Lincoln, Etched Glass, Ruby Glass, c.1860, 18 x 29 In.
$1,200

Political, Flag, American, Harrison, Morton & Protection, Muslin, 5 Stars, 2 ¼ x 4 In.
$460

Political, Game, The Kennedys, Cards, Play Money, Transco Adult Games Inc., 1962, 19 In.
$86

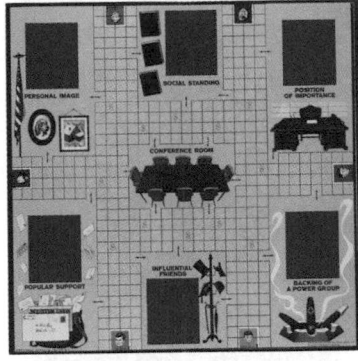

Political, Jug, T. Roosevelt, Elephant Head Handle, Lenox, Pat. Applied For, E. Penfield, 7 x 7 ½ In.
$830

Political, License Plate, Beer, Metal, Embossed, FDR Campaign, c.1932, 4 x 12 In.
$316

Political, Plate Topper, Franklin Roosevelt, Uncle Sam, Rubbery Composition, c.1936, 8 x 11 In.
$207

P

Political, Postcard, Taft, Standing, 3 ½ In.
$57

Anderson Americana

Political, Poster, Lyndon Johnson, Hippie,
Turn Off, Tune Out, Drop In, 1967, 19 x 25 In.
$115

Hake's Americana & Collectibles

Political, Puzzle, Harrison, 8 Cabinet Members,
Jewel Gasoline Stove, c. 1889, 7 x 7 In.
$86

Hake's Americana & Collectibles

Political, Puzzle, Theodore Roosevelt, Rough
Riders, McLoughlin, Box, 1898, 18 x 13 In.,
73 Piece
$1,175

Cowan's Auctions

Political, Screen, Commemorative, Lincoln,
Relief Carved, Emancipation 1863, 74 x 36 In.
$29,625

James D. Julia Auctioneers

Political, Torch, Campaign, W.H. Harrison,
Eagle, Brass, Oil Font, Burners Wings, 1840,
9 x 12 In.
$1,645

Cowan's Auctions

Popeye, Cookie Jar, Popeye Head, Real
Corncob Pipe, American Bisque
$173

Victorian Casino Antiques

Popeye, Toy, Olive Oyl, Ballet Dancer, Tin,
Linemar, Japan, c.1950s, 6 In.
$540

Victorian Casino Antiques

Popeye, Toy, Olive Oyl, Windup, Neck Stretches
Up & Down, Linemar, Box, c.1958, 5 ½ In.
$1,659

James D. Julia Auctioneers

P

POMONA glass is a clear glass with a soft amber border decorated with pale blue or rose-colored flowers and leaves. The colors are very, very pale. The background of the glass is covered with a network of fine lines. It was made from 1885 to 1888 by the New England Glass Company. First grind was made from April 1885 to June 1886. It was made by cutting a wax surface on the glass, then dipping it in acid. Second grind was a less expensive method of acid etching that was developed later.

Bowl, Daisies, Etched, Ruffled Top, Footed, Pontil, c.1885, 8 ¼ x 3 ¾ In.	595
Cruet, Frosted, Bulbous, Multicolor Stemmed Flowers, 6 ½ In.	86
Finger Bowl, Flowers, Leaves, Crimped Rim, c.1895, 2 ½ x 5 ½ In.	95
Sugar & Creamer, Ice Blue, Dot Optic, Squat, Amber Ruffled Rim & Handles, 1st Grind	177
Sugar, Cornflower, Inverted Thumbprint, Ruffled, Handles, c.1900, 2 ¾ x 5 In.	115
Toothpick Holder, Frosted, Cinched Waist, Clear Rigaree, Scalloped Edge, 2nd Grind, 3 In.	71
Tumbler, Diamond Optic, Amber Stain, 1st Grind, 3 ⅝ In.	300
Tumbler, Frosted, 3 ¾ In.	75
Vase, Fan, Clear, Dot Optic, Amber Ruffled Border & Petal Foot, 1st Grind, 3 In.	48
Vase, Frosted, Flowers, Oval, Clear Ruffled Rim & Petal Foot, 6 ½ In., Pair	71
Water Set, Cornflower, 2nd Grind, New England Glass Works, 7 In., 7 Piece	177
Water Set, Diamond Optic, Frosted, Amber Stained Band, 2nd Grind, 11-In. Pitcher, 6 Piece	144

PONTYPOOL, *see Tole category.*

POOLE POTTERY was founded by Jesse Carter in 1873 in Poole, England, and has operated under various names since then. The pottery operated as Carter & Co. for several years and established Carter, Stabler & Adams as a subsidiary in 1921. The company specialized in tiles, architectural ceramics, and garden ornaments. Tableware, bookends, candelabra, figures, vases, and other items have also been made. The name *Poole Pottery Ltd.* was taken in 1963. The company went bankrupt in 2003, but is in business today with new owners.

Bowl, Aegean Pattern, Yellow, Orange, Brown, 10 ½ In.	95
Dish, Trinket, Flower, Blue Gray, Brown, Cupped Edge, c.1955, 3 In.	25
Figurine, Cat, Siamese, Sitting, Regal Turquoise, 6 ½ In., Pair	140
Figurine, Dolphin, Waves, Art Deco, 1930s, 6 ½ x 4 ¾ In.	40
Lid, Casserole, Retro Design, Cornflower Blue, 1950s, 2 Qt., 8 In.	55
Pin Dish, Flowers, Dotted Edge, 4 In.	16
Plate, Delphis, Yellow, c.1974, 10 In.	120
Posy Bowl, Flowers, Red, Yellow, Blue, Green, 2 x 4 In.	103
Vase, Delphis, Red, Slab Sided, 1970s, 10 In.	65

POPEYE was introduced to the Thimble Theatre comic strip in 1929. The character became a favorite of readers. In 1932, an animated cartoon featuring Popeye was made by Paramount Studios. The cartoon series continued and became even more popular when it was shown on television starting in the 1950s. The full-length movie with Robin Williams as Popeye was made in 1980. KFS stands for King Features Syndicate, the distributor of the comic strip.

Bank, Coin Register, Daily Quarter, Popeye Holding Can Of Spinach, Tin, 4 ¾ In.	177
Button, The Sailor, Witley Juvenile Suits, Blue & White, Round, 1929, ¹⁵⁄₁₆ In.	95
Cookie Jar, Popeye Head, Real Corncob Pipe, American Bisque ....*illus*	173
Display, Popeye, Boson, Flashlights, Whistles, Paper Label, King Features, 15 x 10 In.	330
Doll, Jeep, Wood, Jointed, King Features Syndicate, 8 ½ In.	627
Doll, Popeye, Motorcycle Rider, Cast Iron, King Features, 1929, 5 In.	531
Doll, Popeye, Spinach Crate Tag, Stuffed Fabric, Wooden Pipe, Anchor Tattoos, 1935, 17 In.	253
Doorstop, Full Figure Of Popeye, Cast Iron, Hubley, No. 328, 1929, 9 In.	1770
Figure, Popeye, Celluloid, Painted, Clockwork, 8 ½ In.	384
Game, Pipe Toss, No. 17, Box, Rosebud Art Co.	150
Lamp Shade, Cardboard, Wire Bulb Clip, Wimpy & Duck, Popeye, Olive Oyl, 1935, 6 x 8 In.	506
Lantern, Popeye Figure, Tin Litho, Glass Mid-Section, Battery, Linemar, Box, 7 ½ In.	413
Paperweight, Popeye, Olive Oyl, Full Figures, Cast Iron, Painted, Hubley, 3 ¼ In., Pair	177
Pencil Sharpener, Bakelite, Yellow, Popeye Holding Pencil, Copyright, 1929, 1 ¾ x 1 In.	45
PEZ Dispenser, Popeye, Blue Base, 4 In.	47
Pin, Jeep, Brass, Enamel, Standing, Red Nose, 1930s, 1 ¼ In.	104
Statue, Cast Plaster, Pipe In Mouth, King Features Syndicate, 1933, 10 In.	126
Toy, Barnacle Bill, Walker, Tin Lithograph, Clockwork, Chein, 6 In.	148
Toy, Dippy Dumper, Dump Truck, Popeye At Wheel, Tin, Celluloid, Clockwork, Marx, 9 In.	443
Toy, Express Baggage Cart, Tin, Windup, Pop-Up Parrot, Marx, c.1935, 8 ½ In.	502
Toy, Olive Oyl, Ballet Dancer, Tin, Linemar, Japan, c.1950s, 6 In. ....*illus*	540
Toy, Olive Oyl, Windup, Neck Stretches Up & Down, Linemar, Box, c.1958, 5 ½ In. ....*illus*	1659
Toy, Popeye & Olive Oyl Tossing Ball, Tin, Ball On Wire Stand, Windup, Linemar, 19 In.	561

Popeye, Toy, Popeye, Olive Oyl, Dancing, Tin Litho, Windup, Marx, c.1930, 9 In. $900

Victorian Casino Antiques

Popeye, Toy, Popeye, Playing Basketball, Tin Litho, Continuous Action, Linemar, Japan, 9 In. $885

Bertoia Auctions

Popeye, Toy, Popeye, Smoking, Tin Lithograph, Battery, Japan, c.1950s, 8 ¾ In. $2,400

Victorian Casino Antiques

445

Porcelain, Group, Cats Climbing Ladder, Germany, 4 ½ In.
$230

Locati Auctions

Porcelain, Jardiniere, Sevres Style, Courting Couples, Flowers, Putti, 9 x 18 In.
$3,250

Leslie Hindman Auctioneers

Porcelain, Pedestal, Sevres Style, Painted, Putti, Brass & Onyx, 1800s, 46 x 12 In.
$3,150

Cottone Auctions

Toy, Popeye, Air-O-Plane, Tin Lithograph, Windup, Linemar, Japan, Box, 6 x 5 In.	11258
Toy, Popeye, Bag Puncher, Overhead Bag, Tin, Celluloid, Chein, 1930s, 9 In.	1652
Toy, Popeye, Barrel Walker, Tin Lithograph, Windup, 7 In.	371
Toy, Popeye, Bubble Blowing, Holds Spinach Can, Tin Litho, Battery, Linemar, Box, 12 In.	708
Toy, Popeye, Carrying Parrot Cages, Tin, Key Wind, Chein, Box, 8 In.	325
Toy, Popeye, Carrying Parrot Cages, Walker, Tin Lithograph, Marx, 8 In.	300
Toy, Popeye, Cyclist, High Wheel, Tin Lithograph, Windup, Linemar, Japan, Box, 6 ½ In.	1215
Toy, Popeye, Drummer, Spinach Come & Get It, Wood, Pull, King, 1928, 8 ½ In.	513
Toy, Popeye, Drumming, Tin Lithograph, Hinged Arms, Chein, 7 In.	620
Toy, Popeye, Floor Puncher, Tin Lithograph, Windup, 7 ½ In.	912
Toy, Popeye, Heavy Hitter, Key Wind, Tin Lithograph, Chein, 1932, 6 ½ In.	2166
Toy, Popeye, In Barrel, Walks, Tin Lithograph, Clockwork, 7 In.	531
Toy, Popeye, Jointed Arms, Vibrates, Celluloid, Windup, Japan, 1929, 8 ½ In.	729
Toy, Popeye, Olive Oyl, Dancing, Tin Litho, Windup, Marx, c.1930, 9 In. ....*illus*	900
Toy, Popeye, Playing Basketball, Tin Litho, Continuous Action, Linemar, Japan, 9 In. ....*illus*	885
Toy, Popeye, Riding Tricycle, Silk Pants, Tin, Bell, Linemar, 5 x 7 In.	885
Toy, Popeye, Riding Tricycle, Tin Lithograph, Celluloid Hands, Legs, Bell, Windup, 4 In.	371
Toy, Popeye, Roller Skater, Holding Platter, Tin Lithograph, Linemar, 6 ½ In. ....590 to 1026
Toy, Popeye, Rowboat, Tin Lithograph, Remote Control, Battery, Linemar, Box, 9 ½ In.	3584
Toy, Popeye, Shadow Boxer, Wearing Boxing Gloves, Tin Lithograph, Windup, 7 In.	1534
Toy, Popeye, Smoking, Tin Lithograph, Battery, Japan, c.1950s, 8 ¾ In. ....*illus*	2400
Toy, Popeye, Sparkling, Noisemaker, Chein, Box, 1959, 5 ¼ In.	228
Toy, Popeye, The Champ, Boxing Ring, Popeye & Brutus, Tin, Celluloid, Marx, Box, 7 In.	1770
Toy, Popeye, Tumbling, Muscular Forearms, Tin Lithograph, Windup, Box, Linemar, 4 ½ In.	729
Toy, Roof Dancer, Tin Lithograph, Windup, Marx, 9 ½ In.	300
Toy, Turnover Tank, Popeye Lifts, Tin Lithograph, Windup, Linemar, Box, 4 In.	649
Toy, Walker, Tin Lithograph, Windup, Chein, c.1932, 6 ¼ In.	266
Watch, Nickel Case, Popeye On Dial, Wimpy, Flying Hamburger, Pocket, 1935, 2 In.	689
Watch, Yam Always On Time, Character Profiles, New Haven Clock Co., Box, 1935	1207

PORCELAIN factories that are well known are listed in this book under the factory name. This category lists pieces made by the less well-known factories. Additional pieces of porcelain are listed in this book in the categories Porcelain-Contemporary, Porcelain-Midcentury, and under the factory name.

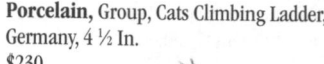

Basket, Woven Brass Center, Porcelain Plaque, Flowers, Ribbons, France, c.1890, 11 x 13 In.	120
Bowl, U-Shape, Liver Red Glaze, Foot Ring, Marked, 2 ⅜ x 5 ½ In.	96
Chocolate Set, Orange Poppies, Garden Gate, Germany, 8-In. Pot, 9 Piece	81
Coffeepot, Dome Foot, Scroll Handle, Spout, Lid, White, Gilt, Flowers, 10 In.	60
Compote, Couple Scene, Blue Border, Scrolled Handles, Bronze, c.1920, 7 x 9 In., Pair	2000
Cup & Saucer, Kuznetsov, Gilt, Blue Enamel Border, Russia, c.1880, 5 ½ In., 6 Piece	2800
Cup & Saucer, Popov, Gilt, Multicolor Enamel, Lattice Borders, Flowers, c.1885, 5 In., Pair	1800
Dish, Blue & White, Flowers, Leafy Scrolls, Flowers, Geometric Design, 13 In.	3000
Egg, Archangel Michael, Multicolor Enamel, Gilded, Ribbon, Russia, 1800s, 3 ½ In.	3000
Egg, Imperial, Gilt, Monogram For Tsarevich Alexei Nikolaevich, 1900s, 2 ½ In.	2100
Egg, Imperial, Photogravure, Empress Alexandra's Cipher, Cross, c.1914, 2 ½ In.	550
Figurine, 2 Pigs In A Purse, Pink, Green Latticework Purse, Germany, 4 In.	54
Figurine, Animal, Playing Musical Instrument, Round Base, Germany, 1700s, 5 In.	420
Figurine, Bird, Long Beak, Shells, Flowers, Scrolls, Gilt Bronze Mount, Continental, 10 In., Pair	1750
Figurine, Boy, Leaning On Tree Stump, Barefoot, Multicolor, c.1865, 6 ½ In.	196
Figurine, Clown, Pierrot, Arms Out, Holding Mask, Schwarzburger Werk, 15 In.	576
Figurine, Dancer, Nude Woman, Pink Scarf, Arms Up, German, 9 ½ In.	120
Figurine, Dancing Woman, Ruffled Gown, Lifting Dress, Pink, 9 ½ x 8 In.	180
Figurine, Frog, Open Mouth, Green, Black Dots, France, 5 In.	240
Figurine, Great Dane, Seated, Black & White, Crop Ears, Leather Collar, 31 In.	649
Figurine, Man, Feather Attire, Bow, Arrow, France, c.1850, 6 ½ In.	161
Figurine, Napoleon, Standing, Coronation Robes, Scheibe-Alsbach, Germany, c.1945, 14 In.	1000
Figurine, Ostyak Woman Peasant, Figures Of Russia, Gardner, Russia, c.1890, 10 In.	7188
Figurine, Peddler Peasant, Wares On Head, Gardner, Moscow, 1800s, 8 ¾ In.	4750
Figurine, Volleyball Player, Woman, White Uniform, Mark, Schaubach Kunst, c.1940, 9 In.	109
Figurine, Wino, On Street Corner, Smoking Cigar, Painted, Italy, 20th Century, 11 ½ In.	24
Figurine, Woman, Nude, 2 Birds, T. Galli, Italy, 1940s, 24 In.	420
Group, Cats Climbing Ladder, Germany, 4 ½ In. ....*illus*	230
Jar, Bulbous, Eared, Flared Mouth, Turquois Glaze, c.1900, 6 ¼ In.	600
Jar, Dome Lid, Bulbous, Splayed Foot, Round Shoulder, Flowers, Gilt Rim, 1900s, 8 In.	1476
Jardiniere, Bronze Mounts, Mask Handles, Tapered Pot, Reeded, c.1885, 13 x 11 In.	1722

P

Jardiniere, Sevres Style, Courting Couples, Flowers, Putti, 9 x 18 In. ....*illus*	3250
Jug, Painted Multicolor Flowers, White Ground, Tucker, c.1840, 9 In.	813
Pedestal, Sevres Style, Painted, Putti, Brass & Onyx, 1800s, 46 x 12 In. ....*illus*	3150
Pitcher, Basin, Flowers, Gilt Leaf Sprays, White, Tucker & Hemphill, Phila., c.1830, 12 x 14 In. .	2000
Pitcher, Multicolor Flowers, White Ground, Gilt Trim, Tucker, Philadelphia, c.1830, 9 In............	1304
Plaque, Woman, Standing On Stairs, Arm On Column, Germany, c.1900, 9 x 6 In.......................	590
Plate, Blue & White, Round Sides, Rocks, Grains, Flowers, Medallion, 1900s, 5 ½ In.	1353
Plate, CSA Lieutenant General James Longstreet, Gilt, Rudolph Lux, c.1850, 8 In. ....*illus*	956
Plate, Dessert, Imari, Aynsley, 8 In., 12 Piece	188
Plate, Dinner, Metallic, Transfer, Forks, Wine Openers, Fornasetti, 1956, 10 In., 8 Piece..............	875
Plate, Dinner, Sunnyvale, Castleton, 1950s, 10 ⅝ In.	33
Plate, Salad, Metallic, Transfer, Roman Coins, Fornasetti, c.1960, 8 In., 12 Piece	813
Plate, Yacht, 2-Headed Eagle, Purple, Green, Imperial Porcelain, Russia, c.1787, 13 In..............	15000
Platter, Oval, Leaf Rim, Cherubs, Garden, Gilt, Hungary, 17 ¼ x 12 In.	149
Powder Box, Woman, Seated, Flapper Style, Puff, Germany, c.1920, 8 In. ....*illus*	456
Powder Dish, Satyr & Asian Woman, Attached Puff, Germany, c.1920, 4 In. ....*illus*	855
Powder Jar, Lid, Figural, Woman, Hidden Perfume Bottle, Germany, c.1925, 7 In. ....*illus*	399
Powder Jar, Pierrot, Seated On Lid, Green Stamp, Henri Delcourt, France, c.1920 ....*illus*	285
Sculpture, Ball Shape, Brown, Tan, Blue, Toshiko Takaezu, c.1980, 5 ½ In. Diam...................	2280
Stirrup Cup, Hound's Head, Piercing Gaze, 1 Brown Ear, 1 Spotted, c.1820, 5 x 4 In.	1650
Teapot, Lid, Globular, Molded Pineapple, Green, Yellow, Brown, Derbyshire, c.1765, 8 x 5 In.	1920
Teapot, Lid, White Glaze, Globular, Faceted Spout, Scroll Handle, Festoons, c.1740, 5 In.	3900
Tray, Encrusted Lobster, Frog, Lizard, Palissy Style, England, c.1835, 14 x 7 In. ....*illus*	553
Tureen, Lid, Scroll Leaf Handles, Flower Garlands, Scroll Feet, c.1850, 11 x 15 In......................	837
Tureen, White, Gilt Trim, Lavender Bands, Fruit Finial, France, 10 In. Diam.............................	508
Urn, Lid, Finial, Pedestal Base, Figures, Gilt Accents, Czechoslovakia, 6 x 5 In.	120
Urn, Lid, Hand Painted Classical Scenes, Signed E. Deniere, France, c.1865, 22 In., Pair	2625
Urn, Lid, Landscape, Woman, Cupid, Enamel, Bronze, Pierced Handles, 20 In...........................	1500
Urn, Sevres Style, Painted Scenes, Gilt Bronze Mounts, 1800s, 35 ½ x 21 In. ....*illus*	2990
Vase, Birds, Flowers, Tree Branches, Pale Green Ground, 1900s, 24 ½ In...............................	677
Vase, Blue & Green Crackled Glaze, Adelaide Robineau, New York, 1920, 3 ½ x 4 In. ....*illus*	7500
Vase, Figural, Victorian Style, Boy & Dog, Girl & Dog, 1900s, 15 In., Pair	120
Vase, Flower Bouquet, Arched Handle, Flared Spout, Plinth, England, c.1820, 11 ½ In.	115
Vase, Globular, Waisted Neck, Flared Rim, Handles, Women, Child, Gilt, 1900s, 8 In.	1046
Vase, Irises, Leaves, Shaded Ground, Cylindrical, Lillian Baker, Austria, 1914, 14 In................	128
Vase, Lobed, Flowers, Butterflies, Turquoise Sgraffito Ground, 1900s, 15 ½ In., Pair	2460
Vase, Mourners, Tomb, Claret Color, Gilt Cartouche, c.1865, 16 In., Pair...........................	1476
Vase, Pink Classical Scene, Black Matte Ground, Gilt, Flared Mouth, France, c.1875, 13 In.........	142
Vase, Spill, Lion, Rocky Base, J. Liemann & Co., Germany, c.1875, 8 In.	92
Vase, Test, Crystalline Glaze, Incised M, c.1910, 2 x 1 ½ In..	2875
Vase, Winter, Summer Outdoor Scenes, Signed Deligny, c.1890, 15 In., Pair........................	474

PORCELAIN-ASIAN includes pieces made in China, Japan, Korea, and other Asian countries. Asian porcelain is also listed in Canton, Chinese Export, Imari, Japanese Coralene, Moriage, Nanking, Occupied Japan, Satsuma, Sumida, and other categories.

Basin, Blue & White, Scrolling Flowers, Wide Flat Rim, 11 ½ In. Diam.	120
Bowl, 6-Sided, Yellow Ground, Flowers, Turquoise Interior, Signed, 3 x 6 In.	575
Bowl, Bell Shape, Ring Foot, Yellow Glaze, Dragons, Cranes, c.1885, 5 ⅛ In., Pair......................	1195
Bowl, Blue & White, Flower, Swirl Design, 6 ½ In. Diam.	60
Bowl, Blue & White, Flowers, Branches, Bird, Chinese, 13 ¾ In. Diam...............................	660
Bowl, Blue & White, Flowers, Shapes, Border, c.1800, 14 In. Diam.	960
Bowl, Blue & White, Upturned Rim, Tree, Flowers, Vines, 14 In. Diam.	900
Bowl, Cobalt Blue, Green, Dragon, Pearls, Bell Shape, Ring Foot, 5 ¼ In...........................	4880
Bowl, Cone Shape, Foldover Rim, Yellow Glaze, Dragons, Clouds, 4 x 8 ½ In.	633
Bowl, Dragons & Pearls, Yellow, Green, Ring Foot, Flared Rim, 1800s, 6 x 4 In.......................	1185
Bowl, Enamel Design, Figures, Flowers, Flat Rim, c.1900, 4 ½ x 15 In..............................	960
Bowl, Enamel, Red, Green, Flowers, Symbols, c.1850, 13 x 9 ½ In.	450
Bowl, Footed, Squat, Round, 2 x 3 In.	270
Bowl, Green Dragons, Gold Ground, 8 ½ In.	267
Bowl, Juny Yao, Green, Lotus Shape, Footed, Chinese, 19th Century, 1 ¾ In.	3254
Bowl, Narcissus, Purple Jun Yao, Chinese, c.1890, 3 ½ x 9 ¾ In.	940
Bowl, Raised Rings, Bird & Flower, Gilt Rim, Chinese, 6 In.	480
Bowl, Ring Foot, Wide Rim, Plum Glaze, Flowers, 2 ½ x 5 ½ In.	497
Bowl, Scalloped, Flared Rim, Flowers, Vines, Blue & White, 1800s, 16 ¼ In........................	708
Bowl, Stand, Flowers, Blue & White, Wide Wavy Rim, c.1900, 3 ¼ x 16 In..........................	472

Porcelain, Plate, CSA Lieutenant General James Longstreet, Gilt, Rudolph Lux, c.1850, 8 In.
$956

Neal Auction Co.

Porcelain, Powder Box, Woman, Seated, Flapper Style, Puff, Germany, c.1920, 8 In.
$456

Theriault's

Porcelain, Powder Dish, Satyr & Asian Woman, Attached Puff, Germany, c.1920, 4 In.
$855

Theriault's

P

Porcelain, Powder Jar, Lid, Figural, Woman, Hidden Perfume Bottle, Germany, c.1925, 7 In.
$399

Theriault's

Porcelain, Powder Jar, Pierrot, Seated On Lid, Green Stamp, Henri Delcourt, France, c.1920
$285

Theriault's

Porcelain, Tray, Encrusted Lobster, Frog, Lizard, Palissy Style, England, c.1835, 14 x 7 In.
$553

New Orleans Auction Galleries, Inc.

Porcelain, Urn, Sevres Style, Painted Scenes, Gilt Bronze Mounts, 1800s, 35 ½ x 21 In.
$2,990

Cottone Auctions

Porcelain, Vase, Blue & Green Crackled Glaze, Adelaide Robineau, New York, 1920, 3 ½ x 4 In.
$7,500

Rago Arts & Auction Center

Porcelain-Asian, Figurine, Chinese Woman, Seated, 1800s, 9 ¼ In.
$2,074

James D. Julia Auctioneers

Porcelain-Asian, Figurine, God Of Longevity, Staff, Famille Rose, Chinese, 1900s, 23 ½ In.
$911

James D. Julia Auctioneers

Porcelain-Asian, Figurine, Liu Hai & His Frog, Famille Verte, c.1910, 6 x 4 In.
$122

James D. Julia Auctioneers

Porcelain-Asian, Jar, Lid, Butterflies, Guang Xu Mark, Chinese, c.1900, 16 In.
$5,900

Brunk Auctions

P

Bowl, Stylized Peacock, Birds & Flowers, Yellow Ground, 15 In. Diam. 173
Bowl, U-Shape, Ring Foot, Iron Red, Gilt, Bats, Flower Scrolls, c.1900, 6 In., Pair 1464
Box, Lid, Round, Saucer Shape, Turquoise, Pink, Lotus, Bats, c.1900, 5 In. Diam. 415
Brushpot, Blue & White Landscape, Chinese, 4 ¾ In. 362
Brushpot, Cylindrical, Blue & White, Dragon Design, 1900s, 6 x 6 ½ In. 295
Brushpot, Shou Character Banding, Lotus Petal Borders, c.1800, 6 x 8 ½ In. 492
Censer, Ball Shape, Reticulated Lid, Dragons, Spread Foot, c.1800, 3 x 4 In. 1003
Censer, Birds, Foo Dog Handles, Aubergine Glaze, c.1890, 4 x 6 ½ In. 492
Censer, Blue & White, Branches, Round, Footed, Outswept Handles, 7 In. 180
Charger, Bird, Flowering Branch, Basket, Yellow Border, Japan, 1900s, 16 In. 185
Charger, Blue & White, Banded Rim, Flowers, Branches, 15 ½ In. Diam. 450
Charger, Blue & White, Chrysanthemums, Plum Blossoms, Flowers, 14 In. 1800
Charger, Blue & White, Figures, Trees, 1800s, 15 ½ In. Diam. 450
Charger, Blue & White, Tree, Flowers, Branches, 1800s, 15 ½ In. 840
Charger, Scholars, Artists, Scrolls, Flower Border, c.1920, 21 In. 3120
Cup, Red, Gilt Inscription Design, Wood Base, Marked, 2 ½ x 3 ¼ In. 2006
Cup, White, Blue Flowers, Chen Hua Mark, Chinese 2169
Cup, Wine, Doucai, Yong Zhen Mark, Chinese, 1 ¾ x 2 ½ In. 1763
Dish, Blue & White, Deer, Landscape, 2 Flower Bands, 16 ⅝ In. Diam. 615
Dish, Blue & White, Dragon, Carp, Waves, Banding, c.1700, 10 ⅜ In. Diam. 2214
Dish, Blue & White, Flower Head Medallion, Leaves, c.1700, 15 In. Diam. 2196
Dish, Green Enamel, Dragons, Flaming Pearls, Clouds, Marked, 1800s, 8 In. 1200
Dish, Saucer Shape, Blue, White, Interlocking Scrolls, Ruyi, 1900s, 6 In. Diam. 671
Figurine, Buddha, Seated, Long Robes, Glazed, 14 x 9 In. 150
Figurine, Chinese Woman, Seated, 1800s, 9 ¼ In. ....*illus* 2074
Figurine, Crane, Standing, White, Black Glaze, 19 ¾ In., Pair 11250
Figurine, Foo Dog, Yellow Glaze, c.1880, 10 In., Pair 7500
Figurine, God Of Longevity, Staff, Famille Rose, Chinese, 1900s, 23 ½ In. ....*illus* 911
Figurine, Liu Hai & His Frog, Famille Verte, c.1910, 6 x 4 In. ....*illus* 122
Flask, Moon Shape, Blue & White, Flowers, Ring Handles, 11 x 10 In. 270
Food Stand, Dish Top, Fruit, Flowers, Handles, Blue, White, Chinese, c.1800, 11 x 11 In. 3120
Hat Stand, Cylindrical, Figural Landscape Design, c.1900, 11 ½ x 5 In. 531
Hibachi, Blue & White, Flowers, Overturned Rim, Chinese, 1800s, 11 x 14 In. 295
Jar, Baluster, Blue, White, Phoenix, Peonies, Fish Scale Ground, 1800s, 13 In. 1076
Jar, Dome Lid, Enameled, Cobalt Blue, Red, Flowers, Bulbous, c.1900, 10 In. 540
Jar, Globular, Lid, Blue & White, Prunus Blossoms, Cracked Ice, c.1700, 10 In. 4305
Jar, Lid, Blue & White, Blossoms, Branches, Baluster Shape, 1800s, 12 In. 191
Jar, Lid, Butterflies, Guang Xu Mark, Chinese, c.1900, 16 In. ....*illus* 5900
Jar, Lid, Wucai, Courtyard, Trees, Flowers, Chinese, 17th Century, 14 ½ In. ....*illus* 7200
Jar, Prunus, Cracked Ice, Reticulated Wood Cover, c.1690, 9 In. ....*illus* 3705
Jardiniere, Gilt, Bronze, Cobalt Blue, Lion Mask Handles, Branch Border, 1900s, 13 In. 717
Planter, Blue, White, Square, Stepped, Bracket Feet, Gardens, 1900s, 13 In., Pair 549
Planter, Canted, Pierced Base, Blue & White, Birds, Flowers, 12 In., Pair 2684
Planter, Green, Flowering Branches, Footed, 12 x 11 In. 150
Plaque, Blue & White, Landscape, Wangbu Mark, 14 ½ In. 627
Plaque, Chinese Landscape, Blue & White, Rame, 16 x 24 In. 1564
Plaque, Figures, Preparing For Festival, Flowering Trees, Frame, 27 x 21 In. 7380
Plaque, Waterside, Temple, Waterfall, Trees, Carved Wood Frame, 1900s, 26 x 20 In. 2400
Plate, Armorial, Octagonal, c.1755, 8 ½ In., 4 Piece 2375
Plate, Blue & White, Scalloped, Lotus Rim, Blue 6-Figure Mark, Japan, 9 In. 940
Plate, Blue & White, Copper Red, c.1850, 11 In. 972
Punch Bowl, Figures, Birds, Flowers, Blue Rim, Round, c.1790, 12 ¾ In. 1875
Punch Pot, Lid, Figural Panels, Gilt, Scroll Handle, Chinese, 1700s, 8 x 12 In. ....*illus* 861
Ruyi Scepter, Ink Box, Chinese, 20th Century, 14 & 3 In. 241
Tea Bowl, White, Cone Shape, Ring Foot, Medallion, Leaves, Banding, 4 In. 427
Tray, Lobated Shape, Brick Red Ground, Lotus Scrolling, 1900s, 6 x 4 In. 533
Urn, Lid, Incised Flowers, Vines, Blue Glaze, Chinese, 20th Century, 21 In. 121
Vase, Beaker Shape, Blue & White, Lotus, Scrolling Leaves, c.1800, 18 In. 1722
Vase, Beaker, Flared Rim, Flowers, Branches, Blue, White, c.1800, 18 In., Pair 1534
Vase, Biscuit, Dragons, Pearls, Glazed Black & White Ink, c.1845, 15 ½ In. 600
Vase, Blue & White Animals, Balls, Streamers, Chinese, c.1920, 18 In. 3840
Vase, Blue & White, Baluster, Trumpet Rim, Landscapes, 1800s, 18 In. 922
Vase, Blue & White, Bottle Shape, Globular, Splay Foot, Plum Blossoms, 16 In. 923
Vase, Blue & White, Bulbous, Figural Scenes, Leaf Mark, Chinese, 20th Century, 7 ½ In. 1058
Vase, Blue & White, Emperor & Attendants, Garden, Pavilion, 22 In. 738

Chinese Prices Drop

The wealthy Chinese have been paying high prices for many types of old Chinese art, paintings, scrolls, netsuke, jade, ivory, rhinoceros horn, wood carvings, and furniture —only the best-quality items. But the Chinese economy is having problems and Chinese collectors are not spending as much as they used to, so prices have dropped since 2011.

Porcelain-Asian, Jar, Lid, Wucai, Courtyard, Trees, Flowers, Chinese, 17th Century, 14 ½ In. $7,200

Skinner Auctioneers & Appraisers

Porcelain-Asian, Jar, Prunus, Cracked Ice, Reticulated Wood Cover, c.1690, 9 In. $3,705

Neal Auction Co.

P

This is an edited listing of current prices. Visit **Kovels.com** to check thousands of prices from previous years and sign up for free information on trends, tips, reproductions, marks, and more.

Porcelain-Asian, Punch Pot, Lid, Figural Panels, Gilt, Scroll Handle, Chinese, 1700s, 8 x 12 In.
$861

Neal Auction Co.

Porcelain-Asian, Vase, Double Gourd, Dragons, Cranes, Medallions, 1800s, 10 In.
$1,154

James D. Julia Auctioneers

Porcelain-Asian, Vase, Meiping, Birds, Rocks, Flowers, Drilled Base, 1644-1911, 16 ⅞ In.
$7,688

Neal Auction Co.

Vase, Blue & White, Flaring Neck, Trumpet, Boys, Garden, Chinese, 1900s, 18 In.	584
Vase, Blue & White, Historical Scene, Figures, Trees, Flowers, 1800s, 18 In.	492
Vase, Blue & White, Mallet Shape, Sages, Bamboo Grove, c.1700, 10 In.	13145
Vase, Blue & White, Scholars, Peasants, Mountains, 1800s, 11 In.	488
Vase, Blue & White, Scroll Design, Ball Shape, Pinched Lip, 3 x 3 In.	210
Vase, Blue & White, Tied Up Boats, Garden, 17 ¾ In.	3585
Vase, Blue & White, Yellow, Oval, Buddhist Lion Panels, Flowers, 1900s, 15 In.	246
Vase, Blue Glaze, Applied Dragon, Egg Shape, c.1900, 7 x 5 In.	2596
Vase, Blue Glaze, Gourd Shape, 6 Character Blue Mark, Chinese, c.1900, 6 ¼ In.	118
Vase, Blue, Bottle Shape, Ring Foot, Chinese, Signed, c.1800, 20 x 10 In.	1680
Vase, Blue, Dragon, 6 Character Blue Mark, Chinese, c.1900, 6 ¾ In.	271
Vase, Blue, Red, Flambe Glaze, Streaked, Bulbous, Trumpet Neck, c.1900, 18 In.	4180
Vase, Bottle, 9 Peaches, Flowering Branches, Iron Red, c.1900, 15 In., Pair	492
Vase, Bottle, Oval, Flared Neck, Peachbloom, Upright Petals, 1800s, 8 In.	431
Vase, Bulbous Waist, Scholars, Warriors, Court Figures, Blue, White, Chinese, c.1722, 17 In.	11400
Vase, Bulbous, Trumpet Neck, Blue & White, Flowers, c.1700, 6 In.	1554
Vase, Cobalt Blue Glaze, Genie Bottle, Trumpet Rim, Shaped Neck, 7 x 4 In.	150
Vase, Cong, Square Shape, Celadon Rectangles, 1800s, 11 In.	329
Vase, Copper Red Glaze, Green, Round Foot, Bulbous, Trumpet Rim, 1800s, 15 In.	354
Vase, Deer, Pines, Blue & White, Bulbous, c.1720, 13 ¾ In.	5700
Vase, Double Gourd, Blue & White, Lobed, Flowers, Horses, c.1600, 11 In.	3050
Vase, Double Gourd, Cobalt Blue Glaze, Gilt, Spheres, 12 In.	1045
Vase, Double Gourd, Dragons, Cranes, Medallions, 1800s, 10 In. ....*illus*	1154
Vase, Elongated Oval, Trumpet Neck, Ruffle Rim, Cranes, Flowers, 1800s, 44 In.	575
Vase, Enamel Design, Flowers, Birds, Baluster, Flared Rim, 24 ½ x 10 In.	270
Vase, Enamel Design, Pear Shape, Trumpet Neck, Pedestal Foot, 10 ¼ In., Pair	840
Vase, Faceted Hexagonal Shape, Molded Gourds, Red, c.1900, 10 ⅛ In.	1722
Vase, Famille Verte, Pear Shape, Peach Trees, Dragons, Pearls, c.1800, 7 In.	799
Vase, Flat Gourd Shape, Belt Handles, Flowers, Blue, White, c.1900, 10 x 7 In.	236
Vase, Genie Bottle, Garlic Mouth, Iron Red, Cream Color Asters, c.1900, 11 In.	3444
Vase, Gourd Shape, Stylized Flower Vines, Cutout Design, 1900s, 8 ½ x 5 In.	472
Vase, Guan Yao Shape, Glazed, Qianlong Mark, Chinese, 9 In.	1206
Vase, Lemon Yellow Glaze, White Interior, Squat, Wide Rim, 1 ¼ x 5 ½ In.	2196
Vase, Lid, Serpentine, Birds, Peonies, Wood Base, c.1900, 8 ⅜ In.	323
Vase, Meiping, Birds, Rocks, Flowers, Drilled Base, 1644-1911, 16 ⅞ In. ....*illus*	7688
Vase, Ming Style, Flowers, Blue, White, Qianlong Mark, Chinese, c.1900, 9 ½ In.	210
Vase, Molded, Lug Handles, Flambe, Chinese, c.1890, 11 ¾ In.	1076
Vase, Mottled Cobalt Blue Glaze, Stand, Pierced Lid, c.1700, 14 In., Pair	8963
Vase, Oxblood, Red Shading To White, Chinese, c.1910, 15 ⅞ In. ....*illus*	830
Vase, Pear Shape, Blue & White, Seated Figure, Fan, Bats, 1900s, 8 ½ In.	2440
Vase, Pear Shape, Teadust Glaze, Marked, 14 ½ In.	1180
Vase, Pear Shape, White Glaze, Cricket, Flowers, Bamboo, 1900s, 6 In.	584
Vase, Perch & Shrimp, Water Weeds, Signed, c.1930, 12 In., Pair	2988
Vase, Red Flowers, Rouge De Fer, Stick Neck, Bulbous Base, Chinese, c.1720, 17 In.	3600
Vase, Shouldered, Square Rim, Black Ground, Orange Fish, 14 x 6 In.	480
Vase, Shouldered, Trumpet Neck, Blanc E Chine, Trailing Flowers, 1800s, 18 In.	270
Vase, Square Paneled, Trumpet Neck, Cylinder Handles, Flowers, 22 x 11 In.	840
Vase, Tulip, Blue & White, Landscape, 5 Lobes, Artichoke Bulb Finial, c.1900, 9 In.	390
Vase, Yen Yen, Blue & White, Flowers, Swollen, Trumpet Rim, c.1850, 17 In.	2214
Wine Cup, Bell Shape, White, Blue, Lotus, Scrolling Leaves, c.1900, 3 ½ In.	615
Wine Cup, Birds, Fruiting Branches, 1900s, 3 ⅛ x 2 ⅝ In.	854
Wine Ewer, Lid, Lobed Oval Body, Waisted Neck, Strap Handle, Flowers, 10 In.	2460

PORCELAIN-CONTEMPORARY lists pieces made by artists working after 1975.

Bowl, Red, Rust Glaze, Footed, Laura Anderson, Calif., 1977, 4 x 11 In.	688
Charger, Abstract Design, Gray, Butterscotch Glaze, K. Weiser, c.1975, 20 ½ In.	2125
Figurine, Virgin Mary, Seated, Holding Jesus, Zaphir, Spain, 1982, 5 In.	60
Moonpot, Rattle, Glazed, Signed Toshiko Takaezu, 7 x 6 In.	3000
Moonpot, Rattle, Matte Glaze, Signed Toshiko Takaezu, 6 ½ x 4 ½ In.	2875
Sculpture, Joy, Woman, Seated, Chair, Eva Stettner, 1986, 46 x 37 In.	750
Vase, Closed Top, Glazed, Toshiko Takaezu, Signed, TT, 4 ½ x 5 ¼ In. ....*illus*	1875
Vase, Green, Blue Crystalline Glaze, Cylindrical, Footed, J. Foster, c.1970, 7 x 3 In.	1500
Vase, Multicolor Glaze Swirls, Suzanne Stephenson, Michigan, 1980s, 11 x 11 In.	531
Vase, Scene From Disputa, Tapered, Handles, C. Kolodziejski, Calif., 1990, 18 x 7 In.	219
Vase, Wooden Paddle Marks, Shouldered, Minnesota, 1970s, 12 ½ x 7 ½ In.	1250

P

PORCELAIN-MIDCENTURY includes pieces made from the 1940s to about 1975.

Bowl, Glass Center, Abstract Design, Signed W. Gregory, 6 ½ In.	75
Bowl, White, Gold Leaves, Brown Ground, 7 ½ x 5 ½ In., Pair.	250
Centerpiece, Blue Glaze, 3 Seahorse Standard, Signed C.A.S. Vietri, 1950s, 16 x 13 In.	313
Figurine, Cyrano De Bergerac, Standing, Gazing At Rose, Pattarino, c.1950, 32 x 12 In.	1140
Figurine, Pigeon, Fan-Tailed, Pink, White, Brown Glaze, Waylande Gregory, 10 x 8 In.	100
Planter, Free-Form, Burnt Orange, 1960s, 13 x 9 In.	25
Server, Gilt Handle, Orange Brown, Drip Glaze, Ruffled Edge, U.S.A., c.1950, 12 In.	34
Vase, Coral, Ribbed, Hyalyn Pottery, 1950s, 7 ½ In.	35
Vase, Cubist Figures, Flutes, White Ground, Blue Interior, Fantoni, 1950s, 11 x 5 In.	313
Vase, Gilt Fish, Mermaid, Teal Ground, Waylande Gregory, c.1965, 15 x 11 ½ In.	1770
Vase, Gold Crackleware, Marked, Ugo Zaccagnini, c.1945, 10 ½ x 6 In.	219
Vase, Lid, Crystalline Glaze, Ball Shape, Green, Brown, H. Sanders, c.1967, 7 ½ In.	600
Vase, Multicolor Abstract Designs, Sgraffito, Signed Fantoni, Italy, 1960s, 7 In.	188

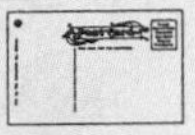

POSTCARDS were first legally permitted in Austria on October 1, 1869. The United States passed postal regulations allowing the card in 1872. Most of the picture postcards collected today date after 1910. The amount of postage can help to date a card. The rates are: 1872 (1 cent), 1917 (2 cents), 1919 (1 cent), 1925 (2 cents), 1928 (1 cent), 1952 (2 cents), 1958 (3 cents), 1963 (4 cents), 1968 (5 cents), 1971 (6 cents), 1973 (8 cents), 1975 (7 cents), 1976 (9 cents), 1978 (10 cents), March 1981 (12 cents), November 1981 (13 cents), 1985 (14 cents), 1988 (15 cents), 1991 (19 cents), 1995 (20 cents), 2001 (21 cents), 2002 (23 cents), 2006 (24 cents), 2007 (26 cents), 2008 (27 cents), 2009 (28 cents), 2011 (29 cents), 2012 (32 cents), 2013 (33 cents), 2014 (34 cents). While most postcards sell for low prices, a small number bring high prices. Some of these are listed here.

Cat, Louis Wain, Glass Of Water, Raphael Tuck, No. 8614	52
City Park Stadium, New Orleans, La., c.1940, 3 x 5 In.	3
Dancers, Louis Wain, Mascot, Raphael Tuck, No. 3551	50
Father Time, Happy New Year, Clock, c.1910	4
Flowers Of Japan, Louis Wain, Amateur Reciter, Raphael Tuck, No. 6084	65
Froheostern, Wiener Werkstatte, 4 x 5 ½ In.	281
Good Fortune On St. Patrick's Day, Boy, Shamrocks, Pig, 4 x 5 In.	12
Oscar Nelson Vs. Joe Gans, Boxing, Portraits, 1906, 3 ½ x 5 ½ In.	139
Public School Stadium, Sioux City, Iowa, c.1940	3
Puss In Boots, Louis Wain, Raphael Tuck, No. 6724	40
Railroad Station, Edwards Park, Lake Waubesa, Wisconsin, 1911, 3 x 5 In.	5
Route 66, Main Street Of America, H.S. Crocker Co., 1960s, 3 x 5 In.	3

POSTERS have informed the public about news and entertainment events since ancient times. Nineteenth-century advertising and theatrical posters and twentieth-century movie and war posters are of special interest today. The price is determined by the artist, the condition, and the rarity. Other posters may be listed under Movie, Political, and World War I and II.

Art Nouveau, Le Vivre De Magda Poesies Par Armand Silvestre, Woman, Garden, Berthon, 18 x 25 In.	717
Artists' Daze, Are Here Again, Grand Bal, Color Lithograph, Joseph Jicha, 1930s, 41 x 27 In.	949
Atlantic City, Hotel, Bathers, Ocean, c.1874, 19 x 24 In.	1168
Biscuits Lefevre-Utile, Lithograph, Mat, Frame, Signed, Alphonse Mucha, 1897, 23 ½ In. *illus*	7500
Book Of Posters, Promo, Peter Max, Quote, Art Education, 1970, 24 x 35 ½ In. ....*illus*	127
Canadian Pacific, St. Lawrence Route To Europe, Ship On Water, 1930s, 36 In.	679
Carpano, Knight, On Horseback, Armando Testa, Italy, Frame, 1952, 54 x 38 In.	826
Cathedrale De Reims Edite Par La Cie Des Chemins, Color Litho, 1919, 41 x 29 In.	270
Chocolat Menier, Color, Lithograph, Frame, F. Bouisset, 1893, 12 ¾ x 9 In.	250
Circus, Barnum & Bailey, Balloon Horse, Jupiter, Strobridge Litho Co., 1909, 30 x 40 In. ...	900
Circus, Barnum & Bailey, Elephant, 1945, 28 x 41 In.	225
Circus, Barnum & Bailey, Rhinoceros, c.1945, 28 x 41 In.	175
Circus, Barnum & Bailey, Tiger, 1945, 28 x 41 In.	175
Circus, Fioto Circus, Buffalo Bill's Wild West, Lithograph, c.1926, 35 x 22 In.	2537
Circus, Ringling Bros. & Barnum & Bailey, Greatest Show On Earth, Tiger, 42 x 28 In.	720
Circus, Ringling Bros. & Barnum & Bailey, Greatest Show, Tiger, Erie Lith. & Prtg., 27 x 41 In. ...	285
Cognac Monnet, Flapper Dancing, Lithograph, Leonetto Cappiello, 1927, 75 x 47 In.	2124
Concert, Buffalo Springfield, Apr. 28-30, 1967, Fillmore Auditorium, 21 x 14 In.	414
Concert, Byrds, April 7, 1967, San Jose, Ca., Psychedelic Images, Sparta Graphics, 22 In.	127
Concert, Doors, Fillmore Jan. 6-7, 1967, San Francisco, Pink Psychedelic Woman, 24 In.	437
Concert, Doors, July 25th, 8 PM, Cow Palace, Randy Tuten Artwork, 1969, 21 x 14 In.	207
Concert, Grateful Dead, Benefit, April 12, 1967, Fillmore, Psychedelic Design	173
Concert, Grateful Dead, Spring Tour 1988, Skull Image, Peter Max, Signed, 24 x 34 In. ....*illus*	419

Porcelain-Asian, Vase, Oxblood, Red Shading To White, Chinese, c.1910, 15 ⅞ In.

$830

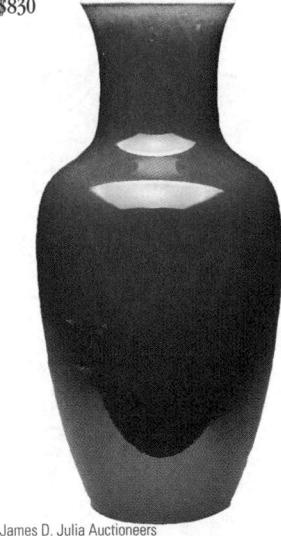

Porcelain-Contemporary, Vase, Closed Top, Glazed, Toshiko Takaezu, Signed, TT, 4 ½ x 5 ¼ In.

$1,875

Poster, Biscuits Lefevre-Utile, Lithograph, Mat, Frame, Signed, Alphonse Mucha, 1897, 23 ½ In.

$7,500

P

Poster, Book Of Posters, Promo, Peter Max, Quote, Art Education, 1970, 24 x 35 ½ In.
$127

Hake's Americana & Collectibles

Poster, Concert, Grateful Dead, Spring Tour 1988, Skull Image, Peter Max, Signed, 24 x 34 In.
$419

Hake's Americana & Collectibles

Poster, Exposition International D'Electricite, Marseille, David Dellepiane, 1908, 45 x 58 In.
$4,305

Cowan's Auctions

Poster, Fernand Leger, Exhibition, Abstract Woman, 1967, 33 x 23 ½ In.
$60

Palm Beach Modern Auctions

Poster, H. Wilkens & Co., Monumental City Tobacco Works, Baltimore, Frame, 25 x 30 In.
$600

Morphy Auctions

Poster, Little Eva's Temptation, Donaldson Lithographing, 1920s, 28 ½ x 20 In.
$344

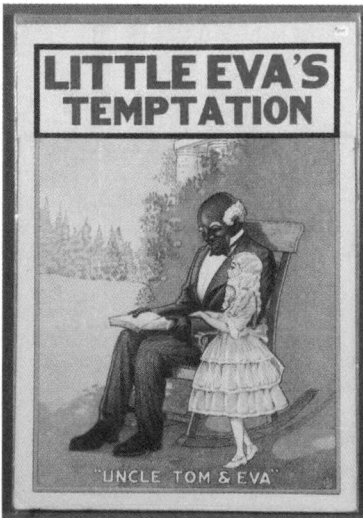

Jackson's Int'l Auctioneers and Appraisers

Poster, Marx Email, Streichfertige Lacke, Artur Berger, Vienna, 1912, 37 x 25 In.
$4,800

Swann Auction Galleries

Poster, Spirit Of America, Join, Red Cross, Nurse, Flag, Paper Lithograph, c.1919, 30 x 20 In.
$7,475

Wm Morford Auctions

Poster, Turmac, La Cigarette Turque, Adolphe Mouron Cassandre, 1925, 63 x 46 ¾ In.
$66,000

Swann Auction Galleries

P

Concert, Jimi Hendrix, Pinnacle Concert, John Van Hamerscheld, 1968, 19 x 27 In.	4750
Concert, Jimi Hendrix Experience, Psychedelic Summerthing, Boston, 1969, 14 x 21 In.	3416
Concert, Kinks, Taj Mahal, Sha-Na-Na, Fillmore West, Randy Tuten, 1969, 14 x 21 In.	127
Concert, Miller Blues Band, Jan. 10-15, 1967, San Francisco, Psychedelic, Neon Rose, 20 In.	288
Concert, Ravi Shankar, May 24, 1968, Fillmore East, David Byrd, 22 x 14 In.	81
Concert, Rolling Stones, Nov. 9, 1969, Oakland Coliseum, Second Show Same Night	230
Concert, Telluride Rock 'N' Roll Festival, July, 1982, Jesse Colin Young, New Riders, 22 In.	81
Concert, Woodstock, White Lake, N.Y., Bird On Guitar, 1969, 1st Print, 36 In.	920
Cordial Medoc, Clown, Bottle, Frame, 63 x 47 In.	210
Cycles De Dion-Bouton, Color Lithograph, Signed, Felix Fournery, Frame, 1925, 45 x 29 In.	938
Dracula, Life Size, Door, Glossy, Lowel Toy Co., 1960s, 26 x 69 In.	261
Exposition International D'Electricite, Marseille, David Dellepiane, 1908, 45 x 58 In. ...illus	4305
Fernand Leger, Exhibition, Abstract Woman, 1967, 33 x 23 ½ In. ....illus	60
H. Wilkens & Co., Monumental City Tobacco Works, Baltimore, Frame, 25 x 30 In. ......illus	600
Kokoon Arts Club, Bal Artistique, Seminude Woman Dancing, August Leysens, 1935, 21 x 14 In.	1794
Last Tragical Moment On Ocean Liner Titanic, Litho, H. Ginsberg, 1912, Frame, 22 x 28 In.	518
Little Eva's Temptation, Donaldson Lithographing, 1920s, 28 ½ x 20 In. ....illus	344
Marionette Show, Jules Cheret, France, 34 x 48 In.	2100
Marvelo The Magician, Man, Rabbit, Doves, Cards, Multicolor, Erie Litho, 20 x 28 In.	86
Marx Email, Streichfertige Lacke, Arthur Berger, Vienna, 1912, 37 x 25 In. ....illus	4800
Mistinguett, French Actress, Blue Dress, In Field, D. DeLosques, Paris, Frame, c.1910, 82 x 48 In.	2242
Montana Frank Wild West Show, Indian Warrior Charge, Lithograph, 3 Sheet, 80 x 41 In.	7670
Olympics, 1948, London, Discus Thrower, Big Ben, Litho, Herz, Frame, 20 x 30 In.	777
Pennsylvania Railroad, New Jersey Seashore, Boy, Playing, J. Collins, c.1950, 27 x 17 In.	3125
Pennsylvania Railroad, New York Always Exciting, Bridge, J. Collins, c.1950, 40 x 25 In.	6250
Picasso Exhibition, Galerie Beyler-Bale, Janvier-Mars 1967, 32 x 20 ¾ In.	207
Picasso, Festival De Lyons, Charbonnieres, Painting, Lithograph, 1953, 27 x 21 In.	701
Pink Floyd, The Wall, Head With Open Mouth, 1982, 41 x 27 In.	75
Sorrows Of Satan, Man In Devil Costume, Mask, On Clouds, Stafford & Co., 20 x 30 In.	240
Spirit Of America, Join, Red Cross, Nurse, Flag, Paper Lithograph, c.1919, 30 x 20 In. ...illus	7475
Summer Olympics XXII, Moscow 1980, Red Star, Stone Color Lithograph, 45 x 29 In.	238
Surfari, Man, Woman, Motorboat, Beach Names On Waves, Festoon, 1963, 22 x 14 In.	205
Target Lithograph, 6 Animals Within Circle, Germany, c.1890, 17 x 24 ½ In., Pair	58
Theatre National De L'Opera Comique, Man & Woman Embracing, City Lights, 32 x 24 In.	360
Travel, Paris, Emile Zola, Alexandre Steinen, Chromolitho, Charles Verneau, 1898, 77 x 54 In.	1880
Travel, Rochers De Naye, Switzerland, Johann Emil Mueller, Linen Mounted, c.1927, 41 x 29 In.	330
Travel, Skiing, Photographic, Plexiglas Sheet Frame, Italy, 1990, 35 x 34 In.	127
Travel, Visit Palestine, Land Of The Bible, Jerusalem, c.1947, 16 x 22 In.	375
Turmac, La Cigarette Turque, Adolphe Mouron Cassandre, 1925, 63 x 46 ¾ In. ....illus	66000
Viajes Agradables A Alemania, Hindenburg, Plane, Ship, Jupp Wiertz, c.1935, 40 x 25 In. illus	4080
War Savings Stamps, Uncle Sam, Children, Paper Lithograph, 30 x 20 In.	1150
West Virginia State Fair, Wheeling, Sept. 10-11-12-13-14, Frame, 1906, 44 x 30 In. ....illus	390
Where The Trails Meet, Addison Aulger, Ackermann-Quigley, 29 x 44 In. ....illus	1320

POTLIDS are just that, lids for pots. Transfer-printed potlids had their heyday from the 1840s to the early 1900s. The English Staffordshire potteries made ceramic containers with decorative lids for bear's grease, shrimp or meat paste, cold cream, and toothpaste. Printed advertising and pictures of historical events, portraits of famous people, or scenic views were designed in black and white or color. Reproductions have been made.

Caviar, Fortnum & Mason, Transfer, Black, c.1890, 3 ¼ In.	135
Cherry Toothpaste, Transferware, c.1880, 2 ½ x 2 ½ In.	140
Cries Of London, Fine Black Cherries, Couple, Dog, Prattware, c.1850, 5 ½ In.	125
Fish Mongers, Prattware, F & R Pratt & Co., c.1875, 4 ¼ In.	145
H.O. Mitchell Cold Cream, Otto Of Rose, Stoneware, 3 In.	95
Jules Hauel Perfumer, Red Transfer, White Glazed Pottery, c.1850, 3 ½ x ³⁄₁₆ In. ....illus	195
Perfumers H.P. & W.C. Taylor, Philadelphia, Washington Crossing The Delaware, 5 In.	3450
Potted Beef Paste, Black Transferware, Staffordshire, England, c.1885, 4 ¼ In.	113
Potted Game, English Coat Of Arms, Fortnum & Mason, London, c.1885, 4 ⅛ In.	125
Quack Medicine Rare Carbolic Tooth Paste, 3 x 1 ½ In.	126
Room In Which Shakespeare Was Born, Stratford On Avon, c.1880, 3 ½ In.	185
S. Maw & Son Carbolic Tooth Paste, Black & White, 2 ⅝ In.	35
Strasburg, Dock, Boats, Prattware, 19th Century, 4 ¾ In.	115
Taylor's Saponaceous Compound, Man Shaving, Mirror, c.1850, 3 ¾ In.	805
The Rivals, Gentlemen Competing Over Woman, Cat, Staffordshire, c.1850, 4 In.	110
Wolf & Lamb, Rowdy Boys, Lamb, Transfer, Prattware, c.1875, 4 ¼ In.	120

Poster, Viajes Agradables A Alemania, Hindenburg, Plane, Ship, Jupp Wiertz, c.1935, 40 x 25 In.
$4,080

Swann Auction Galleries

Poster, West Virginia State Fair, Wheeling, Sept. 10-11-12-13-14, Frame, 1906, 44 x 30 In.
$390

Morphy Auctions

Poster, Where The Trails Meet, Addison Aulger, Ackermann-Quigley, 29 x 44 In.
$1,320

Cowan's Auctions

P

TIP
When buying postcards, remember—usually the larger the city the lower the value of the card. The smaller the city the higher the value of the card because fewer cards were made.

Potlid, Jules Hauel Perfumer, Red Transfer, White Glazed Pottery, c.1850, 3 ½ x ³⁄₁₆ In.

$195

Glass Works Auctions

Pottery, Figurine, Lion & Cub, Resting, Yellow Clay, Ohio, c.1890, 7 x 11 ½ In.

$600

Garth's Auctioneers & Appraisers

Pottery, Jar, Squat, Stylized Tiger, Korea, c.1900

$984

Garth's Auctioneers & Appraisers

Pottery, Plate, Peaches & Blueberries, Crest, Quote, Edwin Bennett Pottery, 9 ½ In.

$118

Humler & Nolan

POTTERY and porcelain are different. Pottery is opaque; you can't see through it. Porcelain is translucent. If you hold a porcelain dish in front of a strong light, you will see the light through the dish. Porcelain is colder to the touch. Pottery is softer and easier to break and will stain more easily because it is porous. Porcelain is thinner, lighter, and more durable. Majolica, faience, and stoneware are all pottery. Additional pieces of pottery are listed in this book in the categories Pottery-Art, Pottery-Contemporary, Pottery-Midcentury, and under the factory name. For information about pottery makers and marks, see *Kovels' Dictionary of Marks—Pottery & Porcelain: 1650–1850* and *Kovels' New Dictionary of Marks—Pottery & Porcelain: 1850 to the Present*.

Basin, Shaped Rim, Dragon Handles, Tripod Foot, Wave Design, Green, Chinese, 5 x 8 In.	531
Bowl, Cone Shape, Petal Lobed Rim, Flower Sprays, 4 ⅝ In. Diam.	488
Bowl, Earthenware, Underglaze, Blue Flowers, Cream Ground, 3 ¼ x 11 In.	46
Bowl, Ruffled Spout At Rim, Transparent Multicolor Glaze, Shapes, Gold, 6 x 9 In.	1800
Dish, Footed, Bird Slip Design, Sariware, Persia, 1 ¼ x 7 ¾ In.	826
Dish, Tin Glazed, Flowers, Grasses, Rocks, 13 ½ In. Diam.	185
Figurine, Dog, Mastiff, Seated, Tan Sponging, Blue Accents, White, c.1900, 6 ½ In.	176
Figurine, Dog, Mastiff, Seated, White Clay, Blue Sponging, Brown Accents, c.1900, 6 ¾ In.	450
Figurine, Foo Dog, Seated, Growling, Green Glaze, Square Stepped Base, 23 In., Pair	1230
Figurine, Lion & Cub, Resting, Yellow Clay, Ohio, c.1890, 7 x 11 ½ In. ....*illus*	600
Figurine, Lion, Reclining, Glazed, Italy, c.1885, 6 x 12 In., Pair	615
Figurine, Lion, Reclining, Oval Stepped Base, White, 1906, 6 ½ In.	264
Figurine, Lion, Reclining, Tooled, White Clay, Facing, c.1890, 10 In., Pair	330
Figurine, Lion, Reclining, Yellow Clay, Scalloped Base, Ohio, c.1890, 10 In.	120
Figurine, Rooster, Molded, White, Brown Glaze, Ohio, c.1870, 8 ¼ In.	382
Figurine, Woman, Standing, Pregnant, Green Dress, Orange Cape, P. Ipsen Enke, 1920s, 8 In.	150
Flowerpot, Hanging, Raised Stylized Leaves, Blue Sponge Glaze, 6 ¾ x 8 In.	575
Herb Jar, Persian Blue & White, Shouldered, Rolled Rim, 1700s, 8 x 6 In.	366
Humidor, Dog Head, Pipe In Mouth, Blue Hat, 6 In.	780
Humidor, Woman's Head, Green Hat, 6 ¾ In.	1080
Jar, Blue & White, Flower Head Banding, Cloud Scroll, 3 ¾ In.	305
Jar, Olive, Oval, Rolled Rim, Yellow Glaze, French Provincial, 21 x 12 ½ In.	1230
Jar, Squat, Stylized Tiger, Korea, c.1900 ....*illus*	984
Jar, Storage, Lid, Green Glaze, Straw Roping, Chinese, 20th Century, 28 In., Pair	176
Jug, Face, Bug-Eyed, Albany Slip, B.B. Craig, 3 In.	649
Pitcher, Water, Salt Glaze, Octagonal Arch Panel Body, Mask, Scroll Handle, 1800s, 9 In.	418
Plate, Peaches & Blueberries, Crest, Quote, Edwin Bennett Pottery, 9 ½ In. ....*illus*	118
Platter, Turkey, Spread Feathers, Grass, Pond, c.1950, 16 x 12 In.	45
Teapot, Smoking Jack, Oval, Molded Dashes, White, P. Cornellius, c.1885, 7 ½ In.	92
Teapot, Terra-Cotta Color, Elongated Handle, YiXing, Gu JinZhou, Chinese	723
Teapot, Yi Hsing, Poem, Sprig Of Prunus, Chinese, 20th Century, 5 ½ In. ....*illus*	972
Teapot, YiXing, Gray Brown, 3-Footed, Artist Signed, c.1900, 3 In.	264
Trivet, Flowers, Leaves, Matte Glaze, California Faience Ink Stamp, 5 ⅜ In. ....*illus*	944
Trivet, Green Ivy, Blue Ground, Rookwood, 1916, 5 ⅝ In.	127
Tobacco Jar, Monk's Head, Painted, c.1900, 5 ¼ In.	201
Vase, 2 Figural Cats, Flowers, Leaves, Ernst Wahliss, Austria, 10 ⅜ In. ....*illus*	325
Vase, 2 Spouts, Leaf & Berry Design, Handles, Marked, Elton, Black Slip, 5 ⅜ In. ....*illus*	94
Vase, Cone Shape, Applied Handles, Drip Glaze, Sunset Mountain Pottery, 9 ½ In. ....*illus*	83
Vase, Cylindrical, Slight Bottom Flair, Flat Rim, Blue Streaky Glaze, 12 ½ In.	4720
Vase, Fish, Drip Glaze, Red Clay Body, Handles, William J. Walley, c.1905, 9 ½ In. ....*illus*	2760
Vase, Fish, Insect, Swirls, Green, Signed Freiwald, 14 In.	121
Vase, Flambe Glaze, Mottled Red, Green, Brown Glaze, 1900s, 7 In.	185
Vase, Globular, Long Neck, Tea Dust, Golden Yellow Glaze, c.1900, 13 ½ In.	488
Vase, Green & Purple Glaze, Bulbous, Squat, Wood Footed Stand, Chinese, 3 x 4 ½ In.	210
Vase, Green Crackle, Bottle Shape, Chinese, c.1800, 11 ½ In.	7670
Vase, Lake, Boat, Mountains, Applied Trees, Rocks, Handles, Odell & Booth, 13 In. ....*illus*	2714
Vase, Oval, Olive Color Glaze, Tea Dust Flecked, Yellow Mist, c.1900, 2 ¾ In.	519
Vase, Shouldered, Flat Rim, Turquoise, Black, Flowers, Shapes, Iran, 1800s, 9 x 7 In.	180

POTTERY-ART Art pottery was first made in America in Cincinnati, Ohio, during the 1870s. The pieces were hand thrown and hand decorated. The art pottery tradition continued until the 1930s when studio potters began making the more artistic wares. American, English, and Continental art pottery by less well-known makers is listed here. Most makers listed in *Kovels' American Art Pottery*, such as Arequipa, Ohr, Rookwood, Roseville, and Weller, are listed in their own categories in this book. More recent pottery is listed under the name of the maker or in another pottery category.

Bowl, Crocuses, Blue, Green Glaze, Mary L. Yancey, 1920s, 2 ½ x 6 ¾ In.	2125
Bowl, Crystalline Glaze, Signed, Charles F. Binns, 1925, 3 ½ x 9 In.	1500

P

Pottery, Teapot, Yi Hsing, Poem, Sprig Of Prunus, Chinese, 20th Century, 5 ½ In. $972

James D. Julia Auctioneers

Pottery, Trivet, Flowers, Leaves, Matte Glaze, California Faience Ink Stamp, 5 ⅜ In. $944

Humler & Nolan

Pottery, Vase, 2 Figural Cats, Flowers, Leaves, Ernst Wahliss, Austria, 10 ⅜ In. $325

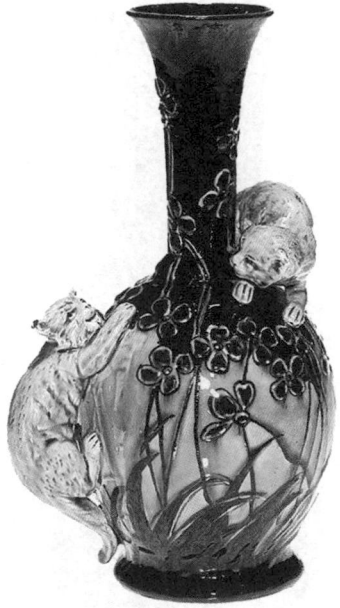

Humler & Nolan

Pottery, Vase, 2 Spouts, Leaf & Berry Design, Handles, Marked, Elton, Black Slip, 5 ⅜ In. $94

Humler & Nolan

Pottery, Vase, Cone Shape, Applied Handles, Drip Glaze, Sunset Mountain Pottery, 9 ½ In. $83

Conestoga Auction Co., Inc.

Pottery, Vase, Fish, Drip Glaze, Red Clay Body, Handles, William J. Walley, c.1905, 9 ½ In. $2,760

Skinner Auctioneers & Appraisers

Pottery, Vase, Lake, Boat, Mountains, Applied Trees, Rocks, Handles, Odell & Booth, 13 In. $2,714

Humler & Nolan

Pottery-Art, Figurine, Woman's Head, Lotte Calm, Wiener Werkstatte, 1920s, 9 x 6 In. $2,375

Rago Arts & Auction Center

Pottery-Art, Jardiniere, Leaves, 6 Handles, Jervis, Stamped, c.1908, 8 ½ x 11 In. $2,250

Rago Arts & Auction Center

P

POTTERY-ART

Pottery-Art, Pitcher, Iris, Green, Gray, Matte Glaze, William Jervis, 5 ⅛ In.
$863

Pottery-Art, Pitcher, Modeled Flowers, Birds, Green, N. Orleans Art Pottery Club, c.1890, 6 ½ In.
$598

Pottery-Art, Pitcher, Monkey, With Coconut, Majolica Glaze, Incised, Oakwood, 11 ¾ In.
$805

Pottery-Art, Vase, 2 Fish, Aquatic Plants, Wave Design, Incised, Baron Barnstable, 7 In.
$118

Pottery-Art, Vase, Blue Crystalline Glaze, Impressed, Pierrefonds, Logo, 7 In.
$224

Pottery-Art, Vase, Corset Shape, Green Matte Glaze, Copper Spots, Impressed Zark, 5 In.
$443

Pottery-Art, Vase, Flames, Middle Lane, Theophilus Brouwer, 1894, 4 ⅜ In.
$2,714

Pottery-Art, Vase, Jeweled, Loop Handles, Stamped, Bretby England, c.1900, 14 x 8 x 5 ½ In.
$625

Pottery-Art, Vase, Ribbed, Turquoise Blue, Red, Purple Glaze, Dalpayrat, France, c.1900, 2 ¾ In.
$277

P

Bowl, Green Enamel, Stylized Landscape, Frederick H. & Agnes Rhead, c.1911, 2 ½ x 7 ¾ In.	55000
Centerpiece, Shells, Seahorse Triangle, White Glaze, Pedestal Base, Italy, c.1900, 18 In.	243
Charger, Mermaids, Multicolor, J.W. Mijnlieff, Holland Utrecht, c.1895, 20 In.	5625
Charger, Red Abstract Flambe Glaze, Stoke-Upon-Trent, Bernard Moore, c.1900, 18 ½ In.	2250
Figurine, Girl, Lounging Outfit, Bobbed Hair, Art Deco, Wiener Werkstatte, 12 In.	127
Figurine, Woman's Head, Lotte Calm, Wiener Werkstatte, 1920s, 9 x 6 In. *illus*	2375
Jardiniere, Leaves, 6 Handles, Jervis, Stamped, c.1908, 8 ½ x 11 In. *illus*	2250
Jardiniere, Pedestal, Jeweled, Bulbous, Ruffled Rim, Round Foot, Bretby, 31 x 10 In.	1250
Jardiniere, Stylized Cattails, Tan, Multicolor Drip Glaze, A. Robineau, 10 x 14 In.	20000
Jug, Jugendstil, Ceramic, Organic Designs, Pewter Lid, Alfred W. Finch, 8 ¾ x 8 ½ In.	313
Pitcher, Branch Handle, Flared Collar, Clematis, Odell & Booth Brothers, c.1880, 8 In.	161
Pitcher, Green To Orange Glaze, W. Brouillard, Cleveland, 12 In.	46
Pitcher, Iris, Green, Gray, Matte Glaze, William Jervis, 5 ⅛ In. *illus*	863
Pitcher, Modeled Flowers, Birds, Green, N. Orleans Art Pottery Club, c.1890, 6 ½ In. *illus*	598
Pitcher, Monkey, With Coconut, Majolica Glaze, Incised, Oakwood, 11 ¾ In. *illus*	805
Planter, Overlapping Leaves, Glazed Earthenware, W.J. Walley, c.1900, 8 x 7 In.	3250
Plaque, Ceramic, Glazed, Art Deco Nude Woman, Signed, Waylande Gregory, 1930s, 17 x 17 In.	1250
Plaque, Grog, Crystalline Glaze, Alexandre Bigot, Pierre Roche, 1897, 9 ¾ In.	4688
Purple Clematis, Yellow Ground, Swollen Cylinder, Straight Neck, J. Bennett, 15 In.	23750
Urn, Squeezebag Shape, Vines, Cobalt Blue, Handles, Max Laeuger, 15 ¼ x 7 In.	875
Vase, 2 Fish, Aquatic Plants, Wave Design, Incised, Baron Barnstable, 7 In. *illus*	118
Vase, Art Deco, Flowers, Multicolor, Bulbous, L. Lourioux, c.1910, 11 ½ x 10 In.	750
Vase, Blue Crystalline Glaze, Impressed, Pierrefonds, Logo, 7 In. *illus*	224
Vase, Blue Ground, Green, Pink Blossoms, Shawsheen, Mason City, Ia., c.1910, 4 x 5 In.	3750
Vase, Blue, Brown Crystalline Glaze, Grasshopper Handles, Round, Pierrefonds, 7 x 7 ½ In.	188
Vase, Blue, Brown, Gray Crystalline Glaze, 3 Applied Lobsters, Denbac, 7 x 8 In.	488
Vase, Bottle, Curdled Green & Brown Glaze, W.J. Walley, 15 ½ x 7 In.	3125
Vase, Brown, Green Drip, Pinched Shoulder, Gilbert Metenier, France, c.1925, 4 In.	58
Vase, Burnished Clay, Frogs, Leaves, Redlands, c.1905, 3 x 3 ¼ In.	16250
Vase, Byrdcliffe Blue Matte Glaze, Eucalyptus Leaves, Ralph, Jane Whitehead, c.1920, 4 x 7 In.	2318
Vase, Corset Shape, Green Matte Glaze, Copper Spots, Impressed Zark, 5 In. *illus*	443
Vase, Double Gourd, Textured Brick Glaze, c.1900, 2 ⅝ In.	246
Vase, Flame Painted, Mottled Green & Brown, Oval, T. Brouwer, Middle Lane, 7 In.	1000
Vase, Flames, Middle Lane, Theophilus Brouwer, 1894, 4 ⅜ In. *illus*	2714
Vase, Flowers, Gourd Shape, J. Bennett, 1878, 11 x 5 In.	938
Vase, Glazed Earthenware, Squeezebag Shape, Pine Cones, Max Laeuger, 10 x 8 In.	938
Vase, Glazed Earthenware, Stylized Flowers, Distel, Amsterdam, c.1900, 7 ½ x 5 ¾ In.	1750
Vase, Glazed Stoneware, Crackleware Drips, Stamped Emile Lenoble, c.1910, 7 x 6 ½ In.	4688
Vase, Gourd Shape, Multicolor Crystalline Glaze, Stamp, Desveres, 1900s, 9 x 7 In.	406
Vase, Gres Flamme Glaze, Art Nouveau Shape Iron Mount, Stylized Leaves, Denbac, 5 x 13 In.	250
Vase, Incised Irises, Water, Orange, Purple, Blue, Round, Footed, Japan, c.1910, 9 In.	69
Vase, Iris, Water Lilies, Mahogany Glaze, Bulbous, Flared Neck, C. Dresser, 18 In.	1250
Vase, Jeweled, Loop Handles, Stamped, Bretby England, c.1900, 14 x 8 x 5 ½ In. *illus*	625
Vase, Lobed, Molded, Dark, Light Green, Blue, Handles, Gilbert Metenier, France, c.1925, 4 In.	46
Vase, Majolica, Albarello, Portraits, L'arte Della Ceramica, Galileo Chini, 10 ¾ x 5 In.	3750
Vase, Mocha, Gunmetal & Blue Hare's Fur Glaze, Baluster, C. Binns, 1924, 10 In.	8750
Vase, Mottled Blue Green Glaze, Bulbous, Galloway, 1920s, 10 x 10 In.	188
Vase, Mustard Yellow, Crystalline Glaze, Squat, Tapered, A. Robineau, 4 x 6 In.	12500
Vase, Peacock, Branches, Incised FHR, Agnes & Frederick Hurten Rhead, 1920, 17 ½ In.	596125
Vase, Red, Green Metallic Birds, Brown Matte, Bulbous, D. Zumbo, France, c.1885, 7 x 9 In.	976
Vase, Ribbed, Turquoise Blue, Red, Purple Glaze, Dalpayrat, France, c.1900, 2 ¾ In. *illus*	277
Vase, Round, Prunts, Multicolor, c.1900, 2 ¾ In.	308
Vase, Sailboats, Windmills, Yellow, Double Loop Handles, Stamped, Holland, c.1920, 20 x 14 In.	1063
Vase, Seed Pods, Matte Glaze, Red Clay, Handicraft Guild, Minneapolis, 6 ½ In. *illus*	633
Vase, Spaniel, Seated, Salamander Handles, Barbotine, Gien, 1880s, 16 x 11 In. *illus*	1750
Vase, Stoneware, Drip Glaze, Bulbous, Narrow Neck, Signed Jean Carries, c.1880, 6 x 4 In.	8750
Vase, Tapered Shape, Green & Brown Crystalline Glaze, Galloway, 10 x 16 ½ In.	976
Vase, Tulip & Leaf, Incised, Hy-Long, Muscle Shoals, Ala., 6 In. *illus*	826
Wall Pocket, Leaves, Sparrow, Mottled Green Glaze, Lobed, W. Jervis, Briarcliff, 8 In.	688

POTTERY-CONTEMPORARY lists pieces made by artists working about 1975 and later.

Basket, Stoneware, Organic, Crumpled, Cracked, P. Voulkos, 1965, 8 x 7 In.	6875
Bowl, Landscape Series, Raku Fired, Wayne Higby, Chop Mark, 1980s, 11 ½ x 20 In.	4063
Bowl, Landscape Series, Raku Fired, Wayne Higby, Chop Mark, 1987, 8 ½ x 13 In.	1750
Bowl, Manganese Lip, Glazed, Lucie Rie, c.1980, 3 ½ x 4 ¾ In. *illus*	3125
Bowl, Stoneware, Slip Painted, Carved, Glazed, Signed, Don Reitz, 6 ½ x 19 In.	1750

Pottery-Art, Vase, Seed Pods, Matte Glaze, Red Clay, Handicraft Guild, Minneapolis, 6 ½ In.
$633

Humler & Nolan

Pottery-Art, Vase, Spaniel, Seated, Salamander Handles, Barbotine, Gien, 1880s, 16 x 11 In.
$1,750

Rago Arts & Auction Center

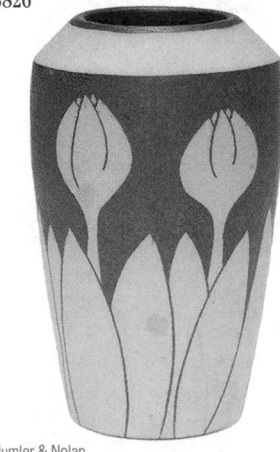

Pottery-Art, Vase, Tulip & Leaf, Incised, Hy-Long, Muscle Shoals, Ala., 6 In.
$826

Humler & Nolan

P

Pottery-Contemporary, Bowl, Manganese Lip, Glazed, Lucie Rie, c.1980, 3 ½ x 4 ¾ In.
$3,125

Rago Arts & Auction Center

Pottery-Contemporary, Charger, Fish, Yellow & Green, Black Rim, Pablo Picasso, 17 x 13 In.
$150

Palm Beach Modern Auctions

Pottery-Contemporary, Charger, Glazed, Stoneware, Peter Voulkos, Signed, 1987, 20 In.
$8,750

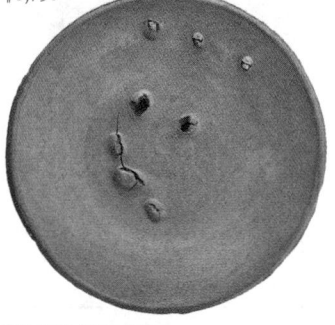

Rago Arts & Auction Center

Picture Displays

Modern houses with high ceilings need large paintings to fill the wall space. But big is expensive, so many wall displays are groupings of paintings, photos, prints, plates, or mountable collections. Overlapping picture frames that are not hung in even rows are popular, but they're hard to hang.

Bowl, Tea, Blue Abstract Design, Round, Footed, c.1975, 5 x 5 In.	344
Bowl, Verdigris Volcanic Glaze, Folded, B. Wood, Signed, Beato, 5 x 10 In.	4688
Box, Landscape Series, Lid, Wayne Higby, 1987, 6 ¾ x 11 In. & 6 x 12 In., 2 Piece	1750
Charger, Black, Green, Blue, House, Tree, Pablo Picasso, 1952, 16 ½ In. Diam.	5880
Charger, Fish, Yellow & Green, Black Rim, Pablo Picasso, 17 x 13 In. *illus*	150
Charger, Glazed, Stoneware, Peter Voulkos, Signed, 1987, 20 In. *illus*	8750
Charger, Roofscape, Blue Sky, Burnished, Lidya Buzio, 1988, 16 In. Diam.	369
Charger, Stoneware, Multicolor Glaze, Viola Frey, 1984, 6 x 26 In.	2625
Compote, Spread Saucer Foot, Figures, Tan, Gold Luster, B. Wood, 8 x 10 In.	5535
Cup, North Of El Prado, Red, Spots, Exaggerated Handle, K. Price, 1993, 3 In.	8125
Feelie, Malachite & Lapis Glaze, Rose & Erni Cabat, 7 ¾ x 5 ½ In. *illus*	5000
Figurine, Lion, Reclining, Brown, Ocher, Signed, Billy Ray Hussey, c.1987, 7 x 5 In.	300
Figurine, Stylized Nude Woman, Glazed, Raku Fired, E. Gronborg, 1970s, 10 In.	750
Garden Seat With Rattle, Stoneware, Brown & Green Glaze, T. Takaezu, 9 x 15 In.	2560
Jar, Acorn Shape, Lid, Reduction Glaze, V. Cushing, 1984, 23 ½ x 14 In. & 17 x 12 In.	1125
Jar, Rice, Stoneware, Iron Oxide Sgraffito Decoration, Bulbous, 1953, 17 In.	16250
Jar, Totemic, Stoneware, Glazed, Signed, Val Cushing, 34 x 9 ½ In.	1125
Jug, Devil Face, Yellow, Multicolor, Stamped, Carl Block, 9 In.	450
Moonpot, Rattle, Stoneware, Oxblood Glaze, T. Takaezu, 6 x 4 In.	2625
Salt & Pepper, Heads, Grotesque, Spots, Stripes, W. Anderegg, 1996, 6 In.	625
Sculpture, Cup, Saucer, Roy Lichtenstein, Ka-Kwong Hui, c.1990, 10 x 6 ½ In. *illus*	5000
Sculpture, Hear No, See No, Speak No Evil, Billy Ray Hussey, 12 x 6 In.	266
Sculpture, Heart Stone, Face, Bird Images, Hand Shape, Glazed, Gary Spinosa, 3 ½ In.	311
Sculpture, Honeycomb, White Stoneware, Copper Oxide Slip, William Parry, 15 x 27 In.	1500
Shot Glass, Self-Portrait, Face, Mustache & Beard, R. Arneson, c.1979, 2 ⅜ In.	4059
Teapot, Earthenware, Honey Glazed, Mark Pharis, c.1988, 6 x 10 ½ In.	780
Teapot, Earthenware, Multicolor Glazed, Signed, Peter Shire, 1982, 13 ¾ x 18 ½ In.	1250
Teapot, Hotel Porter, Walking, Gray, Black, Yellow, Swineside Ceramics, 1980s, 10 In.	259
Teapot, Lid, Iron Shape, Faux Rope Handle, Black, Orange, Purple, Saito, c.1985, 8 In.	230
Teapot, Lid, Mosques, Chairs, Buildings On Slant, Triangular, D. Dapkins, 1983, 6 In.	115
Teapot, Stoneware, Tenmoku Glaze & Slip, P. Voulkos, 1953, 7 In.	3750
Teapot, Well Knop, Jack & Jill Falling, Flared Shape, J. & G. Morten, 1986, 7 In.	69
Teapot, White Glaze, Silver Trim, Art Deco, P. Schreckengost, Oh., 12 x 7 In.	2300
Vase, Balche, Earthtones, Plastic Inlay, Claude Conover, 11 x 14 In. *illus*	4425
Vase, C. Conover, Stoneware, Cylindrical, Triangular Handle, Tapered, c.1966, 13 In.	1320
Vase, Chicken, Stoneware, Engobe Decoration, C. Conover, 22 x 16 In.	7500
Vase, Chocula, Plastic Inlay, Claude Conover, 11 x 13 In. *illus*	3186
Vase, Clear Special, Resin, Orange, Drippy, Fish Design, G. Pesce, 14 x 12 In.	1132
Vase, Closed Shape, Glazed, Signed, Tochiko Takaezu, 5 ½ x 5 ¾ In.	1625
Vase, Double Wall, Cutout, Blue, White, Flared Rim, N. Zager, 1970, 7 In.	69
Vase, Earth Tones, Lines Around Center, Toshiko Takaezu, 7 ¼ In. *illus*	1416
Vase, Engobe Decoration, Taham, Ohio, Claude Conover, 1970s, 21 In. *illus*	3750
Vase, First Snow, Stoneware, Carved, Sculpted, Iron Slips, Anne Goldman, 7 ½ x 9 In.	1375
Vase, Frothy White Glaze, Bulbous, Pinched, Flaring, Lucie Rie, 10 x 6 In.	13750
Vase, Hogzah, Cylinder Piercing Ball, Stoneware, Engobe, C. Conover, 26 x 16 In.	10000
Vase, Knobs, Iridescent Glaze, Beatrice Wood, 7 x 8 ½ In. *illus*	1750
Vase, Nuuc, Cross-Hatched, Striped Impressions, Claude Conover, 16 x 8 In.	3335
Vase, Oxblood Glaze, Squat, Signed Robert Turner, c.1985, 6 ½ x 7 ¾ In.	469
Vase, Paisley Pot, Whiteware, Howard Kottler, c.1970, 11 x 4 x 12 ½ In. *illus*	2520
Vase, Patolli, Cylinder Piercing Ellipse, Stoneware, Engobe, C. Conover, 11 x 15 In.	3500
Vase, Purple Glaze, Faceted, Tapered, Squat, O. & V. Heino, 7 x 11 In.	1500
Vase, Rows Of Incised Lines, Brown, Tan, Gourd Shape, Clyde Burt, 12 x 8 In.	2000
Vase, Sabac, Pottery, Glazed, Incised Lines, C. Conover, 1970s, 22 x 14 In.	6875
Vase, Stoneware, Barrel Shape, Glazed, Robert Turner, 1967, 21 x 14 x 11 ½ In.	3250
Vase, Stoneware, Glazed, Robert Turner, 8 ½ x 7 ½ In.	1625
Vase, Stoneware, Reduction Glaze, Robert Turner, 13 x 11 ½ In.	8125
Vase, Stoneware, Split Wing Sides, Narrow Rim, K. Karnes, 7 x 27 In.	3720
Vase, Stoneware, Textured Surface, Bronzed Glaze, Don Reitz, 1980s, 27 x 13 In.	8125
Vase, Stoneware, Untitled, Japanese Influence, Tom Marsh, 9 ½ x 13 ½ In.	480

POTTERY-MIDCENTURY includes pieces made from the 1940s to about 1975.

Bottle, Stoneware, Glazed, Flared Rim, P. Voulkos, 1950s, 9 x 4 ½ In.	1250
Bottle, Stopper, 3-Footed, Glazed Ceramic, Leza McVey, c.1965, 7 x 3 In. *illus*	1845
Bowl, 3-Footed, Gray Green Matte Glaze, Flattened Rim, T. Randall, c.1960, 3 ¾ x 6 In.	185
Bowl, Abstract Design, Signed, P. Voulkos, 1940s-50s, 9 ¼ x 12 In. *illus*	3250

Pottery-Contemporary, Feelie, Malachite & Lapis Glaze, Rose & Erni Cabat, 7 ¾ x 5 ½ In. $5,000

Rago Arts & Auction Center

Pottery-Contemporary, Sculpture, Cup, Saucer, Roy Lichtenstein, Ka-Kwong Hui, c.1990, 10 x 6 ½ In. $5,000

Rago Arts & Auction Center

Pottery-Contemporary, Vase, Balche, Earthtones, Plastic Inlay, Claude Conover, 11 x 14 In. $4,425

Rachel Davis Fine Arts

Pottery-Contemporary, Vase, Chocula, Plastic Inlay, Claude Conover, 11 x 13 In. $3,186

Rachel Davis Fine Arts

Pottery-Contemporary, Vase, Earth Tones, Lines Around Center, Toshiko Takaezu, 7 ¼ In. $1,416

Rachel Davis Fine Arts

Pottery-Contemporary, Vase, Engobe Decoration, Taham, Ohio, Claude Conover, 1970s, 21 In. $3,750

Rago Arts & Auction Center

Pottery-Contemporary, Vase, Knobs, Iridescent Glaze, Beatrice Wood, 7 x 8 ½ In. $1,750

Rago Arts & Auction Center

Pottery-Contemporary, Vase, Paisley Pot, Whiteware, Howard Kottler, c.1970, 11 x 4 x 12 ½ In. $2,520

Cowan's Auctions

Pottery-Midcentury, Bottle, Stopper, 3-Footed, Glazed Ceramic, Leza McVey, c.1965, 7 x 3 In. $1,845

Cowan's Auctions

P

Pottery-Midcentury, Bowl, Abstract Design, Signed, P. Voulkos, 1940s-50s, 9 ¼ x 12 In.
$3,250

Rago Arts & Auction Center

Pottery-Midcentury, Bowl, Folded, Blue Volcanic Glaze, Beatrice Wood, Signed Beato, 3 x 8 x 5 In.
$1,250

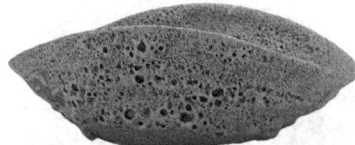

Rago Arts & Auction Center

Pottery-Midcentury, Charger, Lady Godiva, Signed, Viktor Schreckengost, 1936, 15 In.
$93,750

Rago Arts & Auction Center

Pottery-Midcentury, Figurine, Bird, Signed, Thelma Winter, 4 ¼ In.
$130

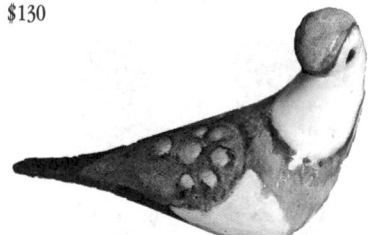

Rachel Davis Fine Arts

Pottery-Midcentury, Figurine, Cat, Signed, Leza McVey, 15 In.
$4,425

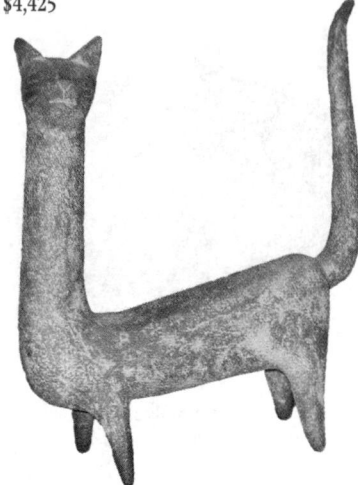

Rachel Davis Fine Arts

Pottery-Midcentury, Figurine, Nude Woman, Glazed, Waylande Gregory, 1930s, 6 ¼ x 11 ½ In.
$1,250

Rago Arts & Auction Center

Pottery-Midcentury, Figurine, Woman's Head, Glazed, Waylande Gregory, Signed, 1930s, 10 x 6 x 7 In.
$1,875

Rago Arts & Auction Center

Pottery-Midcentury, Flower Frog, Bulbs, Man's Head, Bjorn Wiinblad, 1962, 43 x 16 In.
$1,500

Rago Arts & Auction Center

Pottery-Midcentury, Plate, Face, No. III, Pablo Picasso, Madoura, Signed, 1963, 10 In.
$7,500

Los Angeles Modern Auctions (LAMA)

P

Bowl, Black Clay, Blue Matte Glaze, Signed James Lovera, 10 x 4 ½ In.	1000
Bowl, Crystalline, Green, Foldover Ruffled Rim, Flared, Rolled Rim, c.1950, 4 ¾ x 14 In.	117
Bowl, Folded, Blue Volcanic Glaze, Beatrice Wood, Signed Beato, 3 x 8 x 5 In. .... *illus*	1250
Bowl, Green, Ivory Matte Glaze, Glen Lukens, Footed, 13 x 5 In.	6250
Bowl, Leaf Incised Rim, Blue Green, 10 ½ In.	81
Bowl, Mottled Red, Black, Gray Rim, S Shapes, Textured, M. Fantoni, Raymor, 2 x 12 In.	123
Bowl, Pink Glaze, Brown Lines, Swirls, Laura Anderson, 1950, 2 ½ x 8 ½ In.	438
Bowl, Redware, Dappled Green Glaze, Flared, Signed E. Winter, 7 x 2 In.	127
Bowl, Redware, Dappled Green Glaze, Flared, Signed E. Winter, 7 x 2 In.	978
Bowl, Signed, John Gill, c.1975, 4 x 5 ½ In.	123
Bowl, Stoneware, Unglazed, Rice Straw Marking, Box, Fujiwara Kei, c.1962, 2 ¾ x 10 In.	492
Bowl, Swirls, Purple, Antonio Prieto, 3 x 13 In.	156
Bowl, Turquoise Crackled, Indigo Glaze, Signed Glen Lukens, 3 ½ x 11 ¼ In.	1250
Bowl, Yellow, Orange, Crackled Finish, Flared, G. Lukens, 1930s, 4 ¾ x 8 In.	281
Charger, 2 Modern Dancers, Man In Blue, Woman In Red, P. Bogatay, 1937, 15 In.	176
Charger, Jacqueline's Profile, Earthenware, Pablo Picasso, 1956, 15 ½ In.	6250
Charger, Lady Godiva, Signed, Viktor Schreckengost, 1936, 15 In. .... *illus*	93750
Charger, Stoneware, Tan Teardrops, Green & Brown Speckled Glaze, H. McIntosh, 13 In.	1000
Decanter, Glazed Geometrics, Blue Ground, G. Gambone, Italy, 1960s, 13 ½ x 4 In.	406
Face Jug, Mottled Green Alkaline Glaze, Oval, L. Meaders, Georgia, 10 In.	978
Figurine, Bird, Signed, Thelma Winter, 4 ¼ In. .... *illus*	130
Figurine, Bull, Standing, Head Down, Tan, Brown, Nicodemus, 8 In.	374
Figurine, Cat, Signed, Leza McVey, 15 In. .... *illus*	4425
Figurine, Nude Woman, Glazed, Waylande Gregory, 1930s, 6 ¼ x 11 ½ In. .... *illus*	1250
Figurine, Pelican, Nicodemus, 8 ½ In.	431
Figurine, Poodle, Seated, Nicodemus, 6 ¼ In.	184
Figurine, Woman's Head, Glazed, Waylande Gregory, Signed, 1930s, 10 x 6 x 7 In. .... *illus*	1875
Flower Frog, Bulbs, Man's Head, Bjorn Wiinblad, 1962, 43 x 16 In. .... *illus*	1500
Jug, Handle, Gambone, Italy, c.1960, 27 x 11 In.	1353
Plate, Face, No. III, Pablo Picasso, Madoura, Signed, 1963, 10 In. .... *illus*	7500
Plate, Le Profil De Taureau, Bull's Profile, P. Picasso, Madoura, 1956, 10 In.	4688
Platter, Visage Dans Etoile, Faience, Blue, Green, Red, White, Picasso, 1947, 12 x 15 In.	5750
Teapot, Art Deco, Paul Schreckengost, Gem Clay Forming Co., c.1940, 7 x 11 In. .... *illus*	2250
Vase, Black, Incised, Bulbous, A. Prieto, 1950s, 10 x 7 In.	438
Vase, Blue & Buff, Stoneware, Ken Price, c.1958, 10 ½ x 4 ¼ In. .... *illus*	2160
Vase, Blue & White, Marcello Fantoni, 13 x 7 In. .... *illus*	660
Vase, Blue Drip Over White Glazes, Teardrop, Marked, Fantoni, Italy, 13 In.	677
Vase, Blue Matte Glaze, Persian Bottle Shape, White Pines Pottery, Signed, 7 x 13 In.	915
Vase, Blue, Gray Drip Matte Glaze, Bulbous, Signed F. Carlton Ball, 7 x 8 ½ In.	438
Vase, Blue, Green, Brown, White, Bulbous, T. Takaezu, 7 x 9 In.	2875
Vase, Bottle Shape, Black, Cream Slip, Signed A. Prieto, Cal., 5 ½ x 4 ¾ In.	375
Vase, Brown Speckled Glaze, Oval, Maija Grotell, Michigan, c.1950, 8 ¾ In.	1063
Vase, Cobalt Blue, Abstract Trees, Maija Grotell, 1950s, 5 ½ In. .... *illus*	1063
Vase, Concentric Circles, Stoneware, White Glazed, Bulbous, A. Prieto, 13 In.	1063
Vase, Earth Tones, Animals, Narrow Mouth, Guido Gambone, 5 ½ x 4 In. .... *illus*	480
Vase, Floor, Brown, Black, White, Blue, Marguerite Wildemhain, 12 x 19 In.	1375
Vase, Glazed Faience, Il Putti Con La Serpe, Ginori, Gio Ponti, Italy, 9 ½ x 7 ½ In. .... *illus*	4375
Vase, Gray Slip, Over Red Brown, Baluster, 3 High Handles, M. Cardew, Eng., 10 ½ In.	633
Vase, Hand, Footed, Robert Turner, c.1960, 4 ½ x 3 ¾ In. .... *illus*	360
Vase, Horses, Plants, Glazed, Stoneware, A. Bohrod, F. Carlton Ball, 1950s, 14 In. .... *illus*	1250
Vase, Incised, Painted, Brown, Black Designs, Bulbous, Signed Clyde Burt, 8 x 10 In.	531
Vase, Jane Russell, Photographic Transfer, Black, Tan, Signed Robert Engle, 8 ½ x 11 In.	1375
Vase, Lid, Incised Design, Mottled Brown Glaze, Signed Claude Conover, 18 x 19 In.	5000
Vase, Line Textured, Yellow Glaze, Maija Grotell, c.1960, 11 ½ x 12 ½ In. .... *illus*	1800
Vase, Linear Design, Gray Matte Glaze, Bulbous Cylinder, Harrison McIntosh, 4 x 5 In.	500
Vase, Mottled Green, Black Design, Round, Signed L. Blazey, Oh., 4 In.	150
Vase, P. Voulkos, Rust, Brown Lines, Stoneware, Cylindrical, Ring Foot, c.1950, 10 In.	2400
Vase, Stoneware, Brown S Lines, Tan Glaze, Round, H. McIntosh, 1970s, 6 In.	1250
Vase, Stylized Animal Figures, Brown, Ochre, Ivory, G. Gambone, 6 x 4 In.	492
Vase, Stylized Birds, Gunmetal Glaze, Signed Antonia Prieto, 6 x 13 In.	1125
Vase, Tan Glaze, Slightly Cinched Cylinder, M. Fantoni, 13 x 4 ½ In.	338
Vase, Teardrop, Iridescent Glaze, Signed, Beatrice Wood, 7 x 5 ½ In. .... *illus*	3000
Vase, Volcanic Glaze, Bulbous, W. Wyman, c.1962, 7 x 5 ½ In.	738
Vase, White Matte, Ribbed, Oval, Flared Lip, K. Pleydell-Bouverie, Eng., c.1955, 4 ¾ In.	23
Vase, Yellow & Red, Cylindrical, Cinched Neck, G. Gambone, 1960s, 21 x 4 In.	5938

Pottery-Midcentury, Teapot, Art Deco, Paul Schreckengost, Gem Clay Forming Co., c.1940, 7 x 11 In. **$2,250**

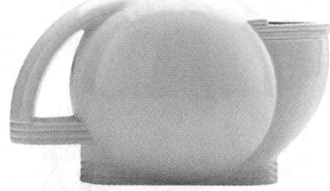

Rago Arts & Auction Center

Pottery-Midcentury, Vase, Blue & Buff, Stoneware, Ken Price, c.1958, 10 ½ x 4 ¼ In. **$2,160**

Cowan's Auctions

Pottery-Midcentury, Vase, Blue & White, Marcello Fantoni, 13 x 7 In. **$660**

Palm Beach Modern Auctions

Pottery-Midcentury, Vase, Cobalt Blue, Abstract Trees, Maija Grotell, 1950s, 5 ½ In. **$1,063**

Rago Arts & Auction Center

P

Pottery-Midcentury, Vase, Earth Tones, Animals, Narrow Mouth, Guido Gambone, 5 ½ x 4 In.
$480

Palm Beach Modern Auctions

Pottery-Midcentury, Vase, Glazed Faience, Il Putti Con La Serpe, Ginori, Gio Ponti, Italy, 9 ½ x 7 ½ In.
$4,375

Rago Arts & Auction Center

Pottery-Midcentury, Vase, Hand, Footed, Robert Turner, c.1960, 4 ½ x 3 ¾ In.
$360

Cowan's Auctions

POWDER FLASKS AND POWDER HORNS were made to hold the gunpowder used in antique firearms. The early examples were made of horn or wood; later ones were of copper or brass.

POWDER FLASK

Brass, Embossed Pheasant, Pear Shape, 6 In.	85
Brass, Embossed Running Rabbit Scene, 1800s, 7 In.	35
Brass, Embossed Shell Design, Rawhide Loop Handle, 7 ¾ In.	155
Brass, Embossed Shell, Leaf, Signed Am. Flask & Cap Co., 1800s, 8 ½ In.	24
Brass, Stamped Designs, Brass Spout, Measure, 4 Iron Loops, c.1860, 8 ½ In.	62
Copper, Pear Shape, Embossed Flowers & Leaves, G.W. Ingram, c.1850, 7 ½ In.	65
Copper, Woven, Oval, Italy, 9 ¼ In.	135
Leather, Brass Stopper, c.1850, 8 In.	115
Leather, Spring-Loaded Door, Embossed Dog, 1800s, 8 ½ x 3 ½ In.	110
Pewter, Tin, Jug Shape, c.1890, 4 ⅝ In.	30

POWDER HORN

7th Regiment Of Foot, Coat Of Arms, c.1776, 15 In.	3500
Bone Stopper, Engraved, Mihael Deck, Fort Mcintoth, 1778, 12 In.	1456
Bone, Black, Embossed, Leaves, Flowers, Tibet, 1900s, 9 In.	150
Carved, Buildings, Boats, Birds, Insects, Animals, Mermaid, Wood Plug, c.1830, 14 In.	1800
Curved Oval Shape, Spring Cot, Islamic-Persian, 18th Century, 6 ½ In.	850
Engraved Inn, Sailboat, Elijah Ely's, Maine, c.1800, 7 ½ In.	1320
Engraved Sailing Ship, Dedication, Made By Brad Carpenter Ford, c.1776, 13 ½ In.	7080
Engraved, J. Jones, Carved Rings, 1778, 15 ½ In.	1770
Engraved, Made 1827 Caleb P. Thurbers Horn, Carved Wooden Cap, 10 In. ....*illus*	3068
Horse, Initials M.R., Carved, 6 In.	180
Incised, William Henry Harrison Portrait, 8 Presidential Vignettes, 1841, 13 ½ In.	4212
Militia, Beehive & Crosshatch Banding, Ring-Carved Throat, 1780, 13 ¾ In.	708
New Orleans Cityscape, Snake, Anchor, Eagle, Marked Cunrath Neumeier, 1807, 17 In.	2880
Peleg Crabtree, Wood Plug, Fish, Deer, Birds, Stockade, British Flag, Soldier, c.1759, 15 In.	1920
Scrimshaw, Man, Wheat, Leaves, Dog, Flowers, John H. Ryphenburgh, c.1800, 7 ½ In., Pair	460
Staghorn, Fork Shape, Sun Symbols, Folk Style, Hungarian, c.1750, 10 x 7 In.	3200
Wood Cap, Brass Bail, 3-Ring Throat, c.1820, 16 In.	345

PRATT ware means two different things. It was an early Staffordshire pottery, cream-colored with colored decorations, made by Felix Pratt during the late eighteenth century. There was also Pratt ware made with transfer designs during the mid-nineteenth century in Fenton, England. Reproductions of the transfer-printed Pratt are being made.

PRATT FENTON

Pitcher, Cerberus, Duke Of Cumberland, Pearlware, c.1850, 7 ½ In.	240
Pitcher, Cream, Fox Head Spout, Swan Handle, c.1820, 5 In.	1440
Pitcher, Mischievous Sport, Children, In Blue Heart Panel, Pearlware, c.1850, 7 ½ In.	210
Pitcher, Mischievous Sport, Children, In White Heart Panel, Pearlware, c.1850, 8 ½ In.	180
Plaque, Woman, Striding, Staff, Dog, Organ, Blue, c.1850, 6 ¾ In.	300
Platter, Landscape Scene, Brown, Cream Scrolled Border, Oval, 19 In.	70
Watch Hutch, Pedestal, Classical Boy, Girl, c.1850, 10 In.	390

PRESSED GLASS, or pattern glass, was first made in the United States in the 1820s after the invention of glass pressing machines. Hundreds of patterns of pressed glass were made in complete table settings. Although the Boston and Sandwich Works was the most famous of the pressed glass factories, there were about sixteen other factories making pressed glass from 1830 to 1850, and still more from 1850 to 1900, when pressed glass reached its greatest popularity. It is now being widely reproduced. The pattern names used in this listing are based on the information in the book *Pressed Glass in America* by John and Elizabeth Welker. There may be pieces of pressed glass listed in this book in other categories, such as Lamp, Ruby Glass, Sandwich Glass, and Souvenir.

Actress, Relish, Love's Request Is Pickles, Oval, Beaded Rim, 9 ¼ In.	5
Atlas, Pitcher, 52 Oz., 12 In.	78
Atterbury, Cake Stand, Milk Glass	51
Aztec, Strawholder, Dome Lid, Knob Finial, Scalloped Foot, 12 In.	514
Ball & Swirl, Cake Stand, 9 ½ In.	96
Barberry, Bowl, 3 ¾ In.	10
Barberry, Plate, Dessert, 6 In.	15
Barley, Cake Stand, Pedestal, 9 ½ In.	64
Beautiful Lady, Compote, 4 ¼ In.	16
Beautiful Lady, Compote, 6 ⅜ In.	26
Bellflower, Compote, 5 x 8 In.	37

Bellflower, Pitcher, Elongated Spout, S-Handle, 8 In.	206
Bethlehem Star, Celery Dish, 10 In.	26
Bethlehem Star, Compote, 5 In.	30
Bethlehem Star, Creamer, 4 ⅜ In.	17
Block & Pleat, Cake Stand, 9 ¼ In.	30
Bull's-Eye With Diamond Point, Pitcher, Amber, Bryce, Higbee, c.1890, 9 x 4 ⅝ In.	173
Bull's-Eye With Diamond Point, Pitcher, Clear, Bryce, Higbee, c.1890, 8 ⅞ In.	127
Buttons & Arches, Creamer, Ruby, Gold Band, Mother, Loop Handle, 4 In.	35
Daisy & Button, Ashtray, Vaseline, 5 x 5 In.	8
Daisy & Button, Compote, Lid, Amber, 6 ½ In.	15
Daisy & Button, Strawholder, Trough Form, Shaped Feet, 8 In.	145
Daisy & Button, Toothpick Holder, Amber, 2 ½ In.	9
Daisy & Button, Tray, Fan Shape, Amber, 10 ½ In.	19
Deer & Dog, Compote, Lid, 7 ⅜ In.	204
Diamond Point, Bonbon, 3-Toed, 5 In.	6
Diamond Point, Butter, Cover, Ruby, 8 ⅞ In.	24
Diamond Point, Creamer, 6 Oz., 4 In.	5
Diamond Point, Creamer, Ruby, 3 ⅞ In.	10
Diamond Point, Decanter, Stopper, Ruby, 12 In.	45
Diamond Point, Dish, Mayonnaise, Ruby, 3 ⅜ In.	19
Diamond Point, Nappy, Ruffled Rim, Ruby, 5 In.	10
Diamond Point, Tumbler, Ruby, 4 ⅝ In.	14
Diamond Quilted, Pitcher, Bluerina, Shaded, Clear Twisted Handle, 8 In.	70
Dolphin, Candlestick, Canary Yellow, Flower Cup, Square Base, 10 ¾ In., Pair	553
Eyewinker, Marmalade, Green, 3 In.	13
Eyewinker, Toothpick Holder, 2 ⅜ In.	12
Fleur-De-Lis, Reamer, Vaseline, Red Slag, c.1935, 6 In.	69
Frosted Artichoke, Compote, Lid, 6 ½ In.	99
Garfield Drape, Creamer, 8 Oz., 5 ½ In.	60
Georgian, Goblet, Stem, Ruby Red, Viking Glass Co., 6 ¼ x 3 ½ In.	17
Gooseberry, Cake Stand, 10 In.	110
Hawaiian Lei, Creamer, 4 In.	15
Hawaiian Lei, Dish, Jelly, 5 ¼ In.	28
Holly, Cake Stand, 9 In.	144
Horn Of Plenty, Bowl, Fruit, 4 ½ In.	14
Horseshoe, Bowl, Oval, Lid, 7 In.	225
Horseshoe, Plate, Give Us This Day Our Daily Bread, Adams & Co., 13 x 9 In.	35
Illinois, Strawholder, Dome Lid, Green, Square, Spread Bottom, 12 In.	1694
Lion, Compote, Frosted, Gillinder, c.1870, 7 x 7 In.	75
Moon & Star, Ashtray, Ruby, 4 ½ In.	30
Moon & Star, Cake Stand, 10 In.	105
Moon & Star, Compote, Lid, Ruby, 8 In.	34
Moon & Star, Decanter, Stopper, Amber, 12 In.	74
Moon & Star, Goblet, Water, Ruby, 5 In.	37
Moon & Star, Salt, Ruby, 2 ¼ In.	19
Moon & Star, Sugar Shaker, Amber, 4 ½ In.	44
Moon & Star, Toothpick Holder, Amber, 2 ¼ In.	14
Nail, Cake Stand, 9 ½ In.	51
Palace, Creamer, 5 ¾ In.	48
Palace, Open Spooner, 5 ½ In.	40
Palm & Scroll, Cake Stand, Green, 8 ½ In.	87
Palmette, Salt, Master.	29
Paneled Grape, Bowl, Dessert, Ruby, 4 ¼ In.	24
Paneled Grape, Pitcher, Ruby, 28 Oz., 7 ¾ In.	58
Paneled Thistle, Goblet, Water, 5 ½ In.	14
Paneled Thistle, Sauce Bowl, 3 In.	11
Pitcher, Milk, Paneled, Log Feet, Gillinder, c.1885, Qt., 8 ¾ In.	280
Pressed Diamond, Compote, Amber, Lid, 7 ½ In.	103
Psyche & Cupid, Creamer, Footed, 7 In.	78
Roman Key, Sugar, Lid, Frosted.	136
Roman Rosette, Cake Stand, 10 ¼ In.	55
Shell & Tassel, Cake Stand, Clear, Duncan, c.1885, 7 ½ In.	259
Sheraton, Celery Vase.	19
Texas Star, Punch Bowl, 10 In.	305
Thistle, Butter, Round, 5 ⅜ In.	42
Thistle, Compote, 3 ⅜ In.	9

Pottery-Midcentury, Vase, Horses, Plants, Glazed, Stoneware, A. Bohrod, F. Carlton Ball, 1950s, 14 In.
$1,250

Rago Arts & Auction Center

Pottery-Midcentury, Vase, Line Textured, Yellow Glaze, Maija Grotell, c.1960, 11 ½ x 12 ½ In.
$1,800

Cowan's Auctions

Pottery-Midcentury, Vase, Teardrop, Iridescent Glaze, Signed, Beatrice Wood, 7 x 5 ½ In.
$3,000

Rago Arts & Auction Center

P

Powder Horn, Engraved, Made 1827
Caleb P. Thurbers Horn, Carved Wooden
Cap, 10 In.
$3,068

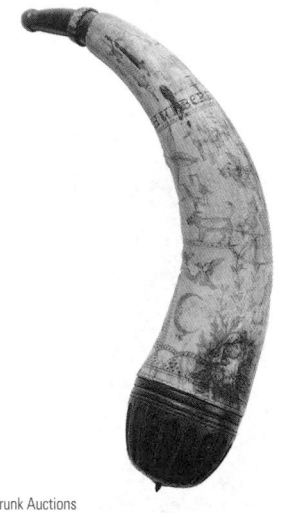

Brunk Auctions

Pressed Glass, Victoria, Compote, Lid,
10 In.
$30

Cowan's Auctions

Print, Calder, Alexander, Les Rubans,
Lithograph, Signed, 1971, 29 ½ x 21 ½ In.
$1,586

Neal Auction Co.

Thistle, Jar, Pickle, 8 ¼ In.	37
Thistle, Sugar, 4 ⅛ In.	22
Victoria, Compote, Lid, 10 In. ....*illus*	30
Viking, Vase, Flared, 8 In.	662
Wildflower, Cake Stand, 9 ¼ In.	64
Wildflower, Creamer, Amber, 4 ¾ In.	15
Wildflower, Goblet, Water, Amber, 5 ⅞ In.	14
Wildflower, Tumbler, Light Blue, 4 In.	15
Wildflower, Wine, Amber, 5 In.	9
Wyandotte, Cake Stand, Button Band, 9 ½ In.	132

PRINT, in this listing, means any of many printed images produced on paper by one of the more common methods, such as lithography. The prints listed here are of interest primarily to the antiques collector, not the fine arts collector. Many of these prints were originally part of books. Other prints will be found in the Advertising, Currier & Ives, Movie, and Poster categories.

Abbot, John, Pileated Woodpecker, Watercolor On Paper, Inscribed, 138, c.1800, 11 x 8 In.	7380

Audubon bird prints were originally issued as part of books printed from 1826 to 1854. They were issued in two sheet sizes, 26 ½ inches by 39 ½ inches and 11 inches by 7 inches. The height of a picture is listed before the width. The quadrupeds were issued in 28-by-22-inch prints. Later editions of the Audubon books were done in many sizes, and reprints of the books in the original sizes were also made. The words *After John James Audubon* appear on all of the prints, including the originals, because the pictures were made as copies of Audubon's original oil paintings. The bird pictures have been so popular they have been copied in myriad sizes using both old and new printing methods. This list includes originals and later copies because Audubon prints of all ages are sold in antiques shops.

Audubon, American Bison, Male, Imperial Folio, J.T. Bowen, 22 x 28 In.	15860
Audubon, American Robin, Plate, Engraving, Aquatint, Havell, 1832, 37 ½ x 24 ½ In.	11520
Audubon, Baltimore Oriole, Engraving, Robert Havell, 38 ½ x 26 ½ In.	39500
Audubon, Bay-Breasted Warbler, Havell, 1829, 26 ¼ x 16 ¾ In.	600
Audubon, Bemaculated Duck, Engraving, Laid On Board, 22 x 28 In.	3000
Audubon, California Vulture, Engraving, Havell, c.1836, 38 x 25 In.	6000
Audubon, Canvas Backed Duck, View Of Baltimore, Aquatint, Havell, 1836, 24 x 36 In.	600
Audubon, Columbia Jay, Engraving, Robert Havell, 38 x 25 In.	47800
Audubon, Great American Cock Male, Engraving, Lizards, 8 ⅝ x 25 ⅝ In.	35100
Audubon, Grey Fox, Imperial Folio, J.T. Bowen, 22 x 27 In.	25620
Audubon, Passenger Pigeon, Aquatint, Havell, 38 x 25 ½ In.	16250
Audubon, Red-Headed Duck, Engraving, Aquatint, 1836, 21 ¼ x 26 ¾ In.	1440
Audubon, Red-Shouldered Hawk, Engraving, Havell, c.1829, 38 x 25 In.	5400
Audubon, Rock Grouse, Engraving, Aquatint, Havell, 1837, 17 ¼ x 22 ½ In.	1440
Audubon, Ruffled Grouse, Engraving, Robert Havell, 26 x 38 In.	36600
Audubon, White Ibis, 22 x 26 In.	8190
Audubon, White Ibis, Engraving, Robert Havell, 25 ½ x 38 In.	21960
Audubon, White-Headed Eagle, Engraving, Hand Color, Robert Havell, 25 ½ x 38 In.	15860
Audubon, Whooping Crane, Florida, Sand Hills, Engraving, c.1835, 38 x 25 In.	14040
Audubon, Wild Turkey, Female, Poults, Engraving, Hand Color, 26 x 39 In.	73200
Audubon, Wild Turkey, Male, Aquatint, 39 x 26 ½ In.	91500
Benson, Frank Weston, Tal, Drypoint, On Paper, Signed, 1925, 8 x 10 ¾ In.	246
Benson, Frank, Bunch Of Bluebills, Drypoint Etching, Frame, 1931, 4 ⅜ x 6 ⅜ In.	300
Benson, Frank, Canoeman, Etching, Frame, 1919, 7 ⅞ x 5 ⅞ In.	1800
Benson, Frank, Chickadees, Drypoint Etching, Frame, 1919, 8 ¾ x 6 ¾ In.	840
Benson, Frank, Springing Teal, Drypoint Etching, Frame, 1930, 14 ¾ x 10 ½ In.	1080
Benson, Frank, Wild Geese, Etched, Frame, 1917, 7 ⅝ x 11 ½ In.	480
Calder, Alexander, Escargot, Lithograph, Pencil Signed, Frame, 26 x 38 In.	2070
Calder, Alexander, Les Rubans, Lithograph, Signed, 1971, 29 ½ x 21 ½ In. ....*illus*	1586
Catesby, Mark, Bastard Baltimore Bird, Plate 49, Mat, Frame, 1700s, 15 x 11 In. ......*illus*	671
Clarke, Sacred To The Memory Of The Illustrious G. Washington, 1801, 8 ½ x 8 ½ In.	357
Currier & Ives prints are listed in the Currier & Ives category.	
Erte, Aquarius, Color Lithograph, Mat, Frame, 20 x 14 In.	360
Erte, Birdcage, Lithograph, Color, Signed In Pencil, Mat, Frame, 27 x 20 In.	546
Erte, Temptress, Lithograph, Color, Signed In Pencil, Mat, Frame, 19 x 14 In.	403
Flower, Thornton, Dr. Robert John, Nodding Renealmia, Frame, c.1800, 21 x 16 In. ....*illus*	1195
Garden Of Allah, Frame, 21 ½ x 13 In.	165
Gerbault, Henry, Chocolat Carpentier, Cat, Dog, Baby, Cup, Chromolitho, c.1895, 27 x 23 In.	151
Homer, Winslow, Thanksgiving In Camp, Union Troops, Harper's, Frame, 1862, 21 x 17 In.	120

Icart prints were made by Louis Icart, who worked in Paris from 1907 as an employee of a postcard company. He then started printing magazines and fashion brochures. About 1910 he created a series of etchings of fashionably dressed women, and he continued to make similar etchings until he died in 1950. He is well known as a printmaker, painter, and illustrator. Original etchings are much more expensive than the later photographic copies.

Icart, Lady Holding Goldfish Bowl, Aquatint, Signed, Oval Frame, 18 x 12 In.	225
Icart, Minuet, Ballerina, Window, Drypoint Etching, Windmill Stamp, Signed, 22 x 14 In.	944
Icart, Miss America, Woman, Flag, Doves, Red, White, Blue, Signed, 1927, 28 x 22 In.	1476
Icart, Woman With French Doll, Aquatint, Signed, Oval Frame, 18 x 12 In.	225

Jacoulet prints were designed by Paul Jacoulet (1902–1960), a Frenchman who spent most of his life in Japan. He was a master of Japanese woodblock print technique. Subjects included life in Japan, the South Seas, Korea, and China. His prints were sold by subscription and issued in series. Each series had a distinctive seal, such as a sparrow or butterfly. Most Jacoulet prints are approximately 15 x 10 inches.

Jacoulet, Aux Lunettes, Mandchoukuo, Woodblock, Embossing, Signed, 15 ½ x 11 ¾ In.	584
Jacoulet, Chikabumi Hokkaido Japan, Man, Scarf, Green Jacket, Signed, c.1940, 18 x 14 In.	384
Jacoulet, Le Tresor Coree, Woman, Holding Small Child, Signed, c.1940, 19 x 14 In.	708
Jacoulet, L'Homme Accoupi Chinois, Man, Blue Coat, Squatting, Signed, 1947, 19 x 14 In.	472
Jacoulet, Longevite Coree Moppo, Man Standing, White Gown, Deer, c.1948, 18 x 14 In.	531
Jacoulet, Vendeur De Masques, Man Seated, Selling Masks, Signed, c.1940, 18 x 14 In.	472
Jacoulet, Woman, Wearing Blue & Tan Shawl, White Flowers, Frame, 15 x 12 In.	230

Japanese woodblock prints are listed as follows: Print, Japanese, name of artist, title or description, type, and size. Dealers use the following terms: Tate-e is a vertical composition. Yoko-e is a horizontal composition. The words Aiban (13 by 9 inches), Chuban (10 by 7 ½ inches), Hosoban (13 by 6 inches), Koban (7 by 4 inches), Nagaban (20 by 9 inches), Oban (15 by 10 inches), Shikishiban (8 by 9 inches), and Tanzaku (15 by 5 inches) denote approximate size. Modern versions of some of these prints have been made. Other woodblock prints that are not Japanese are listed under Print, Woodblock.

Japanese, 2 Women & Boy, Working Near Furnace In Room With Screen, Frame, 8 x 7 In.	123
Japanese, Ando, Hiroshige, Edo Meisho, Multicolor, 20th Century, 8 ½ x 13 ½ In.	35
Japanese, Hasui, Kawase, Shinso, Machi, Enshu, Calligraphy, Seal, c.1931, 15 x 10 In.	644
Japanese, Hasui, Kawase, Snow At Hinoeda Shrine, Seal, 14 x 9 In.	300
Japanese, Hasui, Kawase, Woman Holding Umbrella In Rain, 14 x 9 In. ....*illus*	270
Japanese, Hiroshi, Ohura Beach, Signed, Frame, 21 ½ x 16 In.	167
Japanese, Hiroshi, Sarusawa Pond, Signed, Frame, 15 ¾ x 10 ½ In.	269
Japanese, Hiroshige, Ichiryusai, Loyal Ones In Snow, c.1810, 14 x 9 ⅝ In. ....*illus*	767
Japanese, Hiroshige, View Of Basho's Hut On Camellia Hill, Aqueduct, 14 x 9 In.	584
Japanese, Kam Kamado, Kishiki City Scene, Signed, 16 x 24 In.	390
Japanese, Kataoka, 2 Women In Interior, 10 ½ x 9 In.	6
Japanese, Kiyonaga, Torii, Precious Children's Games, 5 Festivals, Oban, 15 x 10 In.	369
Japanese, Kunisada, Utagawa, Kabuki Actor, Color, 20th Century, 14 ½ x 8 ½ In.	47
Japanese, Masaji, Aoyama, Black Cat I, Signature, Seal, 1900s, 17 x 11 ¾ In.	119
Japanese, Saito, Kiyoshi, Summer In Aizu, Signed, 11 ½ x 17 In.	196
Japanese, Saito, Kiyoshi, Winter Scene, House, People Walking In Snow, 9 ¾ x 15 ¼ In.	277
Japanese, Sharaku, Ichikawa Komazo & Idhikawa Momosuke, 1794, 15 x 9 ¾ In., Pair	200
Japanese, Toyokuni, Triptych, Geisha, Dancing, Playing Shamisen, Oban, Frame, 22 x 38 In.	185
Japanese, Tsuchiya, Rakusan, Western Flower Path, Frame, 1931, 24 x 18 In., Pair	151
Japanese, Yoshida, Strolling Figures In Ueno Park, Pavilion, Signed, Frame, 14 x 10 In.	180
Japanese, Yoshida, White Plum In Farmyard, Frame, 1951, Oban, 15 x 10 In.	154
Japanese, Yoshitoschi, Shrunken Head Left Behind On Kikaishima, c.1886, 27 x 9 ¼ In.	800
Kellogg & Thayer, The Yankee Tar, Sailor Waving, Folk Art Chip Frame, 24 In.	1320
Lefcort, Allison, Marilyn Monroe, Giclee On Paper, Pink Background, Signed, 12 x 12 In.	633
Lithograph, Balloons, Stylized Design, Red, Blue, Yellow, Signed, A. Calder, 40 x 28 In.	1875
Max, Peter, Colossus, Serigraph, On Arches Paper, Signed, Frame, c.1973, 29 x 25 In.	264
Max, Peter, Figures Running, Lithograph, Signed, Mat, Frame, 1973, 3 ⅝ x 4 In.	253

Nutting prints are popular with collectors. Wallace Nutting is known for his pictures, furniture, and books. Collectors call his pictures Nutting prints although they are actually hand-colored photographs issued from 1900 to 1941. There are over 10,000 different titles. Wallace Nutting furniture is listed in the Furniture category.

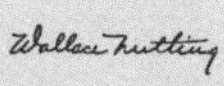

Nutting, Apple Tree Road, 11 ½ x 19 ½ In.	12
Nutting, Birch Bend, Colored, Signed, Mat, 7 ¼ x 9 ½ In.	53

Print, Catesby, Mark, Bastard Baltimore Bird, Plate 49, Mat, Frame, 1700s, 15 x 11 In.
$671

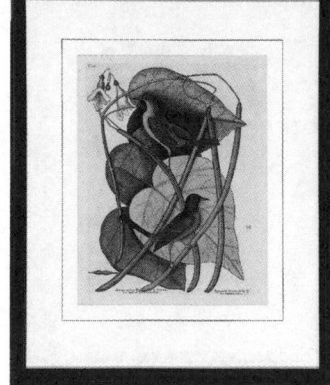

Neal Auction Co.

Print, Flower, Thornton, Dr. Robert John, Nodding Renealmia, Frame, c.1800, 21 x 16 In.
$1,195

Neal Auction Co.

Print, Japanese Woodblock, Hasui, Kawase, Woman Holding Umbrella In Rain, 14 x 9 In.
$270

Cowan's Auctions

Print, Japanese Woodblock, Hiroshige, Ichiryusai, Loyal Ones In Snow, c.1810, 14 x 9 ⅝ In.
$767

Brunk Auctions

Print, Parrish, 2 Women, Sunlit Canyon, 1933 Edison Mazda Calendar, Frame, 11 x 8 In.
$138

Wm Morford Auctions

Print, Parrish, Edison Mazda, Venetian Lamplighters, Cardboard, 1920s, 17 x 11 In.
$719

Wm Morford Auctions

Nutting, Colonial Woman Sewing, Signed, Frame, 7 ¾ x 10 In.	49
Nutting, Dell Dale Road, c.1910, 15 x 13 In.	500
Nutting, Maple Sugar Cupboard, Woman, By Hearth, Frame, c.1910, 15 x 19 In.	30
Nutting, Tall Trees, Road, Poem, Frame, c.1940, 8 x 2 ½ In.	79
Nutting, Tree, Falling Over River, Frame, c.1920, 18 x 21 In.	250
Nutting, Trees, Path, Lovers Lane, Signed, Frame, c.1900, 8 ¾ x 6 ¾ In.	89
Nutting, Woman, Sewing, Colonial Room, Signed, Frame, 18 x 12 In.	95

Parrish prints are wanted by collectors. Maxfield Frederick Parrish was an illustrator who lived from 1870 to 1966. He is best known as a designer of magazine covers, posters, calendars, and advertisements. His prints have been copied in recent years. Some Maxfield Parrish items may be listed in Advertising.

Parrish, 2 Women, Sunlit Canyon, 1933 Edison Mazda Calendar, Frame, 11 x 8 In. ....*illus*	138
Parrish, Air Castles, Frame, 1904, 12 x 16 In.	349
Parrish, An Odd Angle Of The Isle, Frame, Signed, 13 x 11 In.	185
Parrish, Buds Below The Roses, Frame, 1913, 20 x 13 In.	129
Parrish, Circes Palace, Frame, 1908, 11 x 13 In.	275
Parrish, Daybreak, Frame, 1923, 34 x 22 In.	1200
Parrish, Dinky Bird, Castle, Frame, 15 x 10 In.	86
Parrish, Edison Mazda, Venetian Lamplighters, Cardboard, 1920s, 17 x 11 In. ....*illus*	719
Parrish, Evening Shadows, Frame, 1953, 19 ¾ x 16 In.	196
Parrish, Florentine Fete, Frame, 1925, 13 x 15 In.	375
Parrish, King Presented With Tarts, 1925, 10 x 12 In.	95
Parrish, Life Magazine Cover, Masquerade, Oct. 19, 1922, 11 x 8 In.	127
Parrish, Morning, Frame, 1922, 16 x 13 In.	289
Parrish, Pandora, Frame, c.1909, 13 x 16 In.	375
Parrish, Prince Cocadad, Brothers, Princess Deryabar, Boat, Frame, 1907, 12 x 10 In.	135
Parrish, Rubaiyat, c.1917, 10 x 32 In.	776
Parrish, Shuffle, Old Man, Boy, Building Blocks, Paper Label, 1904, 7 x 5 In.	295
Parrish, Sing A Song Of Sixpence, Frame, c.1910, 11 ¾ x 23 ¾ In.	1035
Parrish, Stars, Nude Woman, Seated, Looking Up, Rocks, Sea, Frame, 33 x 22 In.	396
Parrish, The Characters, Knave Of Hearts, 10 x 12 In.	55
Parrish, Triptych, Florentine Fete, Call To Joy, Love's Pilgrimage, c.1915, 25 x 29 In.	1035
Parrish, Ursula Kneeling Before The King, 1925, 10 x 12 In.	95
Pennell, Joseph, Alcantara Bridge, Etching, On Paper, Mat, Frame, c.1900, 10 x 8 In.	92
Soda Fountain, Wood Frame, Marked, 128-Printed In Germany, 23 x 27 In. ....*illus*	56
Watercolor, Suffolk Tower, Signed L. Mayer, Frame, 9 ¾ x 14 In.	246

Woodblock prints that are not in the Japanese tradition are listed here. Most were made in England and the United States during the Arts and Crafts period. Japanese woodblock prints are listed under Print, Japanese.

Woodblock, Albee, Grace, Forgotten Things, Pencil Signed, 8 x 11 14 In.	307
Woodblock, Baumann, Gustave, Aspen Red River, Mat, Frame, Signed, 9 x 10 ½ In. ....*illus*	8750
Woodblock, Baumann, Gustave, Aspens, Color, Frame, 1920, 9 ½ x 11 In.	11250
Woodblock, Baumann, Gustave, Marigolds, Color, Signed, Frame, 1920, 21 ¾ x 17 ½ In.	4375
Woodblock, Baumann, Gustave, Pelican Rookery, Color, Frame, Mat, 9 ¼ x 11 In.	10000
Woodblock, Baumann, Gustave, Singing Trees, Color, Aluminum Leaf, Frame, 12 x 12 In.	20000
Woodblock, Frank, Hans, Butterfly No. 4, Pencil Signed, c.1924, 6 ⅛ x 4 ⅝ In.	142
Woodblock, Hopkins, Edna Boies, Cineria, Color, Signed, Frame, 1915-17, 9 x 8 In.	9375
Woodblock, Leighton, Clare, House Near Durham, 1900s, 6 ½ x 7 ½ In.	354
Woodblock, Pugh, Mabel, Flower, Hyacinth, Frame, 14 x 12 In.	295
Woodblock, Pugh, Mabel, House, Woods, Hillsboro, Frame, 15 x 17 In.	50
Woodblock, Rice, William, Eucalyptus, Northbrae, Pencil Signed, c.1900, 7 ¾ x 3 ½ In.	2000
Woodblock, Rice, William, Magnolia Grandiflora, Handmade Paper, Signed, 7 x 8 ½ In.	2750
Woodblock, Rice, William, Windy Summit, Handmade Paper, Signed, Frame, 9 x 12 In. ....*illus*	4375
Woodbury, Charles H., July Century, Lithograph, Les Maitres De L'Affiche, Mat, 1896, 15 x 11 In..	161
Woodcut, Aspen, Deer Among Trees In Winter, Toshi, Yoshida, Frame, 19 ¾ x 11 ¾ In.	184
Woodcut, Escher, M.C., Sky & Water, Birds Flying, Fish, Signed, Frame, 28 In. ....*illus*	8400

PURINTON POTTERY COMPANY was incorporated in Wellsville, Ohio, in 1936. The company moved to Shippenville, Pennsylvania, in 1941 and made a variety of hand-painted ceramic wares. By the 1950s Purinton was making dinnerware, souvenirs, cookie jars, and florist wares. The pottery closed in 1959.

Apple, Chop Plate, 11 ¾ In.	48
Apple, Salt & Pepper, 3 ¾ In.	25

Apple, Salt & Pepper, Loop Handle, 2 ½ In.	12
Fruit, Jug, 32 Oz., 5 ¾ In.	41
Fruit, Tumbler, 4 ¾ In., Pair	32
Ivy, Teapot, Lid, 6 In.	18
Normandy Plaid, Cruet, Oil & Vinegar, Square	45
Petals, Syrup, 6 ½ In.	15
Pitcher, Water, Angled Handle, 5 ½ In.	30
Shooting Star, Vase, Ginger Jar Shape, 5 ⅞ In.	45

PURSES have been recognizable since the eighteenth century, when leather and needlework purses were preferred. Beaded purses became popular in the nineteenth century, went out of style, but are again in use. Mesh purses date from the 1880s and are still being made. How to carry a handkerchief and lipstick is a problem today for every woman, including the Queen of England.

18K Gold, Clutch, Diamond Monogram, Basket Weave, Cartier, 7 x 4 In.	15350
31 Fevrier, Egg, Crystal Encrusted, Black Satin Loop Handle & Lining, 5 In.	799
Alligator, Black, Bellestone, Handle, c.1955, 7 x 9 In.	143
Alligator, Ocher, Satin Interior, Chain, Judith Leiber, 4 ¾ x 7 In.	717
Basket, Nantucket, Carved Ivory Whale On Lid, Stamped Boyer, 7 x 8 In.	1304
Basket, Nantucket, Whale Ivory Plaque, Knobs, Jose Formoso Reyes, c.1960, 7 x 10 In.	2242
Beaded, Brown, Black, Gold Rows, Chain, Mary Francis, 7 ½ In.	50
Beaded, Flowers, Silvertone Frame, 12 x 8 ¾ In.	52
Beaded, Home Scene, Deer, Silver Frame, Incised, Ring Handle, c.1810, 9 In. ....*illus*	798
Beaded, Metal, Flowers, Box Shape, Handles, Calem, Saks Fifth Avenue, 1947, 4 x 8 In.	54
Beaded, Steel, Flower Design, Satin Lined, Double Chain, 13 ¼ x 5 ¼ In.	127
Beaded, Steel, Knitted, Silvertone Frame, Pink Satin Lining, 13 x 5 ½ In.	92
Black Quilted, Lambskin, Chanel, 7 ½ x 3 ¾ In.	270
Black Satin, Clear Crystal, Judith Leiber, 5 ¼ x 8 ½ In.	191
Blue Jean Twill, Tote, Woven, Handles, Togo Leather Flap, Valparaiso, Hermes, 11 x 16 In.	713
Calfskin, Tote, Double Handles, Snap Closure, Borsa Cerniera, Prada Saffiano, 11 x 9 ½ In.	874
Canvas, Black, Red, Green Stripe, Handles, Speedy Bag, Wallet, Gucci, 1980s, 8 x 11 In.	649
Canvas, Brown, Tote, Monogram, Gucci, 1970s, 11 x 14 ¾ In.	120
Canvas, Caramel Leather Trim, Keepall 55, Monogram, Louis Vuitton, 1970s, 14 x 19 In.	560
Canvas, Envelope Shape, Irish Stitch, William B. Property, 1794, 4 ¾ x 8 In. ....*illus*	2040
Canvas, Leather Handles, Weekender PM, Monogram, Zipper, Louis Vuitton, 17 x 16 In.	767
Canvas, Leather Strap, Shoulder Style, Zipper Closure, Louis Vuitton, 12 ¾ x 12 In.	767
Canvas, Leather Strap, Zipper, Monogram, Trocadero 27, Louis Vuitton, c.1995, 7 x 11 In.	708
Canvas, Speedy, Monogram, Louis Vuitton, 1970s, 8 x 12 ½ In.	299
Canvaswork, Pocketbook, Double Folding, Zigzag Diamond, Multicolor, c.1790, 5 x 8 In.	420
Cloth, Print, Goldtone Chain, Pucci, 1960s, 5 x 7 ¾ In.	215
Clutch, Leather, Black Epi, Louis Vuitton, 5 x 9 ½ In.	131
Compact, Mesh, Art Deco, 14K Gold, Black Onyx Inlay, Enamel, 15 In. ....*illus*	3540
Crocodile, Black, Kelly, Luc Benoit, 7 ¾ x 10 ½ In.	359
Crocodile, Brown, Maltiparmi, Clutch, 12 x 8 In.	95
Crocodile, Brown, Separate Bottom Compartment, 16 x 22 In.	702
Crocodile, Kelly, Black, Silver Hardware, Shoulder Strap, Hermes, Dust Cover, 11 In.	8400
Crystal Encrusted, Amber To Clear Stripe, Leather Interior, Judith Leiber, 6 ¾ x 3 In.	1254
Epi Leather, Shoulder, Black Goldtone Hardware, Bag, Cluny, Louis Vuitton, 12 ½ x 10 In.	529
Epi, Leather, Black, Suede Interior, Zipper, Straps, Bucket PM, Louis Vuitton, 10 x 9 In.	1003
Faux Fur, Napa Antik & Eco Peliccia, Metallic Lambskin Flap, Chain, Prada, 6 x 8 In.	357
Fiera, Nylon, Quilted, Jungle Print Panels, Leather Strap, Bag, Ferragamo, 11 x 14 In.	322
Jeweled, Bulldog, Chain Strap, Mirror, Comb, Bag, Judith Leiber, 4 x 5 In. ....*illus*	4484
Jeweled, Cat Shape, Flowers, Gold Lame Interior, Dust Bag, Box, J. Leiber, 3 x 6 In.	1880
Knitted, Black Beads, Shaped Silver Clasp, Fringe, Lined, 9 x 5 In.	89
Lambskin, Navy Blue, Leather Handle, Mirror, Coin Purse, Goldtone Clasp, Hermes, 7 x 10 In.	604
Lambskin, Navy, Quilted, Shoulder Strap, Snap Closure, Gold Chain, Chanel, 9 x 12 In.	1353
Lambskin, White, Quilted, Flap, Tap Closure, Gold CC, Chain, Chanel, 6 x 10 In.	3444
Leather, Black, Braided, Bottega Veneta	235
Leather, Black, Handles, Miu Miu, 16 x 6 ½ In.	252
Leather, Black, Turquoise, Stripe Print, Signed, Emilo Pucci, 4 x 14 In.	179
Leather, Blue, Cloisonnne, Ferragamo, 7 x 8 In.	84
Leather, Brown, Slouchy, Shoulder Strap, Goldtone Hardware, Zipper, Hermes, 17 In.	1560
Leather, Brown, Valentino, 8 x 10 ½ In.	179
Leather, Bucket, Drawstring Closure, Salvatore Ferragamo, c.1995, 12 x 12 In.	560
Leather, Butterscotch, Top Stitching, Flap Pocket, Silvertone Clasp, Furla, 16 x 6 In.	92
Leather, Clutch, Blue, Frame, Gold Snake Link Chain, Judith Leiber, c.1980, 7 x 11 In.	861

Print, Soda Fountain, Wood Frame, Marked, 128-Printed In Germany, 23 x 27 In.
$56

Victorian Casino Antiques

Print, Woodblock, Baumann, Gustave, Aspen Red River, Mat, Frame, Signed, 9 x 10 ½ In.
$8,750

Rago Arts & Auction Center

Print, Woodblock, Rice, William, Windy Summit, Handmade Paper, Signed, Frame, 9 x 12 In.
$4,375

Rago Arts & Auction Center

Print, Woodcut, Escher, M.C., Sky & Water, Birds Flying, Fish, Signed, Frame, 28 In.
$8,400

Garth's Auctioneers & Appraisers

Purse, Beaded, Home Scene, Deer, Silver Frame, Incised, Ring Handle, c.1810, 9 In.
$798

Theriault's

Purse, Canvas, Envelope Shape, Irish Stitch, William B. Property, 1794, 4 ¾ x 8 In.
$2,040

Skinner Auctioneers & Appraisers

Purse, Compact, Mesh, Art Deco, 14K Gold, Black Onyx Inlay, Enamel, 15 In.
$3,540

Brunk Auctions

Purse, Jeweled, Bulldog, Chain Strap, Mirror, Comb, Bag, Judith Leiber, 4 x 5 In.
$4,484

Brunk Auctions

Purse, Mesh, Edwardian, 14K Gold, Diamonds, Sapphires, Platinum, Fringe, 6 ¼ In.
$3,900

Skinner Auctioneers & Appraisers

Purse, Mesh, Moxie, Farmer, Dog, Bag, Frame, Clasp, Whiting & Davis, 1915-25, 6 ½ In.
$4,800

Morphy Auctions

Purse, Minaudiere, Crystal Beads, Peacock, Leather Lining, Judith Leiber, 4 ¾ x 6 In.
$4,200

DuMouchelles Art Gallery

Purse, Minaudiere, Enamel, Snake, Leather, Chain Strap, Judith Leiber, 3 x 4 ½ In.
$1,560

DuMouchelles Art Gallery

Purse, Minaudiere, Ladybug, Leather Lining, Chain Strap, Judith Leiber, 5 x 4 ¼ In.
$3,600

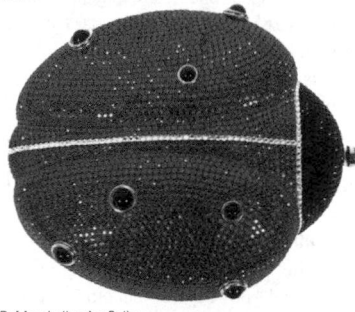

DuMouchelles Art Gallery

Purse, Minaudiere, Snowy Owl, Leather Lining, Chain Strap, Judith Leiber, 5 ¼ In.
$2,640

DuMouchelles Art Gallery

Leather, Kelly, Black, Gold Hardware, Hermes, Dust Bag, 12 ½ In.	984
Leather, Navy Blue, Gold H Clasp, Shoulder Strap, Hermes, 9 In.	2540
Leather, Pouch, Silver & Brass Mounts, Lotus & Flower Design, Strap, Tibet, 1900s, 5 In.	120
Leather, Quilted, Navy, Zipper, Braided Goldtone Handles, Chanel, 9 x 11 In.	1003
Leather, Red, Basket Weave Design, Zipper Closure, Bottega Veneta, Italy, 8 x 12 In.	584
Leather, Satchel, Red, Silver Plated Fittings, Key Tassel, Prada, 8 x 14 In.	253
Leather, Shoulder, Black, Goldtone Fittings, Chain Strap, Ferragamo, 8 x 9 ¾ In.	253
Leather, Shoulder, Woven, Camel, Magnetic Closure, Bottega Veneta, 8 ¼ x 11 In.	822
Leather, Tan Togo, Goldtone Hardware, Birkin, Hermes, Dust Cover, 14 In.	7995
Leather, Tan, Silver Hardware, Intertwined C Logo, Zippered, Chanel, 6 ½ x 11 ½ In.	1062
Leather, Vanilla, Quilted, Double Flap, Leather & Gold Chain Strap, Chanel, 6 x 9 In.	1287
Leather, Zebra Painted, Black Handle, Zipper Closure, Christian Louboutin, 4 x 10 In.	325
Lizard, Clutch, Brown, Ribbed, Arched Frame, Tiger Eye Clasp, Judith Leiber, 1980s, 7 x 9 In.	207
Lizard, Red, Foldover Closure, Handle, Corina, 1960s, 8 x 8 ¾ In.	60
Mesh, 14K Gold, Cabochon Sapphire Thumbpieces, Edwardian, Carter & Howe & Co.	3720
Mesh, 14K Gold, Engraved Leaves, Sapphire Thumbpiece, Tiffany & Co., Edwardian, 6 In.	4200
Mesh, Abstract Pastel, Scalloped Skirt, Goldtone Frame, Chain, Whiting & Davis, 8 x 4 In.	1014
Mesh, Armor, Enamel, Multicolor, Flap Closure, Goldtone Chain, 4 ¾ x 4 In.	196
Mesh, Blue, Pink, Silver, Red, Art Deco, Mandalian, 9 x 4 ½ In.	148
Mesh, Cream, Lavender, Green Flower, Art Deco, Mandalian, 6 ¼ x 3 ½ In.	177
Mesh, Edwardian, 14K Gold, Diamonds, Sapphires, Platinum, Fringe, 6 ¼ In. ....*illus*	3900
Mesh, Enameled, Brown, Cream, Silvertone Frame, Chain, 6 ¼ In.	62
Mesh, Goldtone, Chain Handle, 6 ½ x 6 ¼ In.	69
Mesh, Mandalian, Art Deco, Silvertone, Cream, Green, Brown, Chain, 7 In.	85
Mesh, Moxie, Farmer, Dog, Bag, Frame, Clasp, Whiting & Davis, 1915-25, 6 ½ In. ....*illus*	4800
Mesh, Pin, Green, Goldtone, Whiting & Davis, Chain, 8 ¼ In.	28
Mesh, Ring, Exterior Monogram Compact, Chain Handle, Clasp, 5 ¾ x 5 In.	150
Mesh, Scissor Neck Closure, Chain Fringe, Silvertone, Chain, 10 x 4 In.	58
Mesh, Silvertone Frame, Cream, Turquoise, Brown, Chain, Art Deco, Mandalian, 9 In.	203
Mesh, Silvertone, Link Pattern, Drop Bead Fringe, Rectangular, Nacco, 9 ½ In.	81
Mesh, White, Green, Brown, Metal Clasp, Lining, Art Deco, Mandalian, 8 ¼ x 4 ½ In.	307
Metal, Silver, Clutch, Saks Fifth Avenue, c.1955, 4 x 7 In.	36
Minaudiere, Beads, Eggplant, Pushbutton, Chain Strap, Judith Leiber, 6 ¾ x 2 ½ In.	1800
Minaudiere, Cabochon, Peacock, Leather Lining, Chain Strap, Judith Leiber, 4 x 6 In.	4200
Minaudiere, Crystal Beads, Asparagus, Push Button, Mirror, Comb, Judith Leiber, 6 x 3 In.	2400
Minaudiere, Crystal Beads, Peacock, Leather Lining, Judith Leiber, 4 ¾ x 6 In. ....*illus*	4200
Minaudiere, Enamel, Snake, Leather, Chain Strap, Judith Leiber, 3 x 4 ½ In. ....*illus*	1560
Minaudiere, Gold, Pencil Inserts, Cigarette Compartment, Money Clip, 3 ¾ x 2 ½ In.	196
Minaudiere, Ladybug, Leather Lining, Chain Strap, Judith Leiber, 5 x 4 ¼ In. ....*illus*	3600
Minaudiere, Satin, Crystals, Chatelaine, Rose Cabochon Closure, Judith Leiber, 1991, 4 ½ In.	649
Minaudiere, Silver, Chased Leaves, Flowers, Emerald, Ruby Stones, Comb, 5 x 4 In.	345
Minaudiere, Silver, Monogram, Hinged Powder Well, Chain, 3 ½ x 2 ½ In.	127
Minaudiere, Snowy Owl, Leather Lining, Chain Strap, Judith Leiber, 5 ¼ In. ....*illus*	2640
Minaudiere, Tomato, Leather Lining, Chain Strap, Coin Purse, Judith Leiber, 3 x 4 In.	2400
Needlepoint, Jade Ormolu Handle, Oval Locking Button, Continental, 10 ½ x 8 ½ In.	270
Ostrich Skin, Brown, Corbeau Curio, 1960s, 8 ½ x 12 In.	84
Ostrich Skin, Brown, Lanvin, Italy, 9 x 12 In.	269
Resin, Beads, Ruffled Trim, Black, Gray, Flower, Beaded Strap, Mary Francis, 7 In.	79
Rhinestones, Crystals, Metal Frame, Satin Ribbon, Lavender, Judith Leiber, 5 ½ x 3 In.	295
Satin, Black, Rhinestone Camillia, CC Logo, Snap Closure, Chanel, 5 x 5 ¼ In.	443
Silk, Brown, Satin, Pierre Cardin, 1960s, 6 x 5 ½ In.	42
Silver Plate, Compact, Coin Holder, Art Nouveau, Chain Handle, 1920s, 3 ½ x 2 ⅝ In. ....*illus*	60
Snakeskin, Black, Handle, Judith Leiber, 9 ½ x 11 In.	144
Snakeskin, Mottled Spots, Handle, Judith Leiber, 15 x 14 In.	329
Snakeskin, Teal Blue, Satin, Gold Frame, Chain, Clutch, Judith Leiber, 1980s, 5 x 9 In.	177
Snakeskin, White, Judith Leiber, 5 ¾ x 6 ¾ In.	120
Sterling Silver, Velvet, Cherubs, Flower, Berry Closure Band, Chain, Clutch Size, c.1910	281
Textile, Girly Rose Clair, White Trim, Flowers, Pearl, Crystals, Mini Recta, Dior, 4 x 9 In.	121
Tote, Canvas, Brown Leather, 2 Handles, Snap Closure, Haymarket, Burberry, 11 x 11 In.	767
Turtle, Beige, Saks Fifth Avenue, c.1955, 6 x 9 In.	131
Turtle, Turquoise, Dabal De Lis, Handle, c.1960, 6 ½ x 7 ¾ In.	203
Twaifaille, Brown, Faux Tortoise Frame, Kiss Clasp, Rosenfeld, c.1960, 8 x 8 x 2 In.	85
Velvet, Black, Silver Frame & Chain, c.1850, 6 ½ In. ....*illus*	456
Velveteen, Black, Petit Point Medallion, Goldtone Frame, Michel Swiss, France, 6 x 6 ½ In.	69
Wood, Acacia, Animal Print, Gold, Black, Round, Cord, Timmy Woods, Beverly Hills, 7 ½ In.	68
Wool, Linen, Red, Green, Silk Lining, Twill Binding, Richard Inksons, 1776, 8 In.	5000

Purse, Silver Plate, Compact, Coin Holder, Art Nouveau, Chain Handle, 1920s, 3 ½ x 2 ⅝ In.
$60

Ruby Lane, Inc.

Purse, Velvet, Black, Silver Frame & Chain, c.1850, 6 ½ In.
$456

Theriault's

Quilt, Amish, Crazy Anne, Spiraling Fern & Daisy, Cotton, Names, c.1935, 68 x 82 In.
$420

Garth's Auctioneers & Appraisers

P

TIP
"A stitch in time" is good advice. Always repair a torn quilt immediately to avoid further damage.

Quilt, Amish, Sunshine & Shadow, Lancaster County, Pa., 1930s, 87 x 87 In. $165

Conestoga Auction Co., Inc.

Quilt, Patchwork, 9 Wagon Wheel, Tulip Pattern, Flower Print Trim, 74 x 81 In. $59

Conestoga Auction Co., Inc.

Quilt, Patchwork, Appliqued, Cherry Baskets, Multicolor, Cotton, c.1890, 94 x 82 In. $960

Skinner Auctioneers & Appraisers

QUEZAL glass was made from 1901 to 1924 at the Queens, New York, company started by Martin Bach. Other glassware by other firms, such as Loetz, Steuben, and Tiffany, resembles this gold-colored iridescent glass. Martin Bach died in 1921. His son-in-law, Conrad Vahlsing Jr., went to work at the Lustre Art Company about 1920. Bach's son, Martin Bach Jr., worked at the Durand Art Glass division of the Vineland Flint Glass Works after 1924.

Quezal

Compote, Green, Gold Iridescent, Flower Shape, Twisted Leaf Stem, Ribbed Foot, 6 x 5 In.	2242
Cup & Saucer, Gold, Iridescent, 2 x 4 In.	259
Lamp, Hanging, Gold Pulled Feather, 1 Large, 4 Small Green Shades, Bronze, 9 x 10 In.	3050
Lampshade, Bronze, Vine & Leaf Shade, White Threading, Scalloped, 7 ¾ In., Pair	561
Lampshade, Brown, Green, White Feather, Threading, Flower Shape, 3 ½ x 5 In., Pair	275
Lampshade, Gold Iridescent, White Pulled Feathers, Bronze Finish Base, 4 ½ In.	177
Lampshade, Snakeskin Pattern, Iridescent Green, Gold, Pink, Blue, 4 ¼ In., 7 Piece	6600
Shade, Green Hooked Feather, Gold Trim, Opal Ground, Gold Iridescent Interior, 2 x 3 In.	415
Shade, Hooked Feather, Gold, Blue Iridescent, Cream, White Interior, 4 ¼ x 11 ¾ In.	1169
Sorbet Cup, Underplate, Chalice Shape, Gold Orange Iridescent, 3 ⅝ x 3 & 5 In.	127
Vase, Blue Iridescent, Bulbous, Flaring Rim, Signed, 6 In.	460
Vase, Gold Iridescent, Purple Iridescent Coil, Trifold Rim, Signed, 2 In.	3795
Vase, Gold, Green Draped Loops, Footed, Oval, Signed, 4 In.	518
Vase, Green & Gold Pulled Feathers, Flower Shape, Flared, Opal Rim, Signed, 6 In.	1208
Vase, Green Pulled Feather, Gold, Trumpet Shape, Stretched Ruffled Top, Signed, 7 In.	1541
Vase, Green, Platinum Hooked Feather, Gold Trim, Ivory Iridescent, Bulbous, Flared Lip, 6 In.	1541
Vase, Iridescent Pulled Feather, Opal, Bulbous Flower Shape, Scalloped Rim, 9 ½ In.	2415
Vase, Jack-In-The-Pulpit, Gold Iridescent, Green & Gold Pulled Feathers, 9 ¼ In.	3350
Vase, Jack-In-The-Pulpit, Gold Luster, Green Iridescent, Signed Base, 8 In.	1140
Vase, Lily, Green Iridescent, Yellow, Purple, Gold Interior, Signed, 11 In.	1580
Vase, Purple, Green Iridescent, Clover Silver Overlay, Shouldered, 7 x 11 In.	2000

QUILTS have been made since the seventeenth century. Early textiles were very precious and every scrap was saved to be reused. A quilt is a combination of fabrics joined to a filler and a backing by small stitched designs known as quilting. An appliqued quilt has pieces stitched to the top of a large piece of background fabric. A patchwork, or pieced, quilt is made of many small pieces stitched together. Embroidery can be added to either type.

Album, Applique, 25 Blocks, Floral Wreaths, Urn, Cotton, Pa., 1852, 81 x 78 In.	5405
Album, Appliqued, Flowers, Red, Green, Grapevine Border, Cotton, c.1860, 84 x 80 In.	1035
Amish, Baskets Pattern, Pieced, Green, Pink, Blue, Cotton, Sateen, 1933, 70 x 80 In.	646
Amish, Baskets, Blue Sashing, Black Border, LaGrange County, Ind., Crib, 57 x 64 In.	264
Amish, Crazy Anne, Spiraling Fern & Daisy, Cotton, Names, c.1935, 68 x 82 In. ....*illus*	420
Amish, Diamond In Square, Pink, Red, Green, Purple Borders, Pa., c.1900, 76 x 78 In.	5875
Amish, Diamond, Blue, Maroon, Green, Cotton, Wool, Lancaster County, c.1910, 75 x 77 In.	3408
Amish, Dresden Plate, Wreaths, Plumes, Hearts, Cotton Sateen, 1941, 70 x 80 In.	499
Amish, Flower Basket, Black, Multicolor, Pink Border, Muslin, 1983, 78 x 92 In.	211
Amish, Lightning Streak Design, Blue, Gray, Cotton, Chambray, 1940s, 48 x 69 In.	529
Amish, Patchwork, 16 Squares, 80 In.	1725
Amish, Patchwork, 9-Patch, Blue, Maroon, Quilted Plume Border, 80 x 81 In.	118
Amish, Patchwork, Bear Claw, Multicolor, c.1900, 66 x 79 In.	516
Amish, Patchwork, Diamond In Square, Red, Orange, Green, Quilted Hearts, Stars, 15 x 15 In.	649
Amish, Patchwork, Double Nine-Block, Blue, Red, Lancaster, Pa., c.1930, 84 x 68 In.	182
Amish, Patchwork, Irish Chain, Sawtooth Border, Blue, Lancaster, Pa., c.1930, 84 x 77 In.	273
Amish, Patchwork, Tumbling Blocks, c.1950, Crib Size, 46 x 36 In.	385
Amish, Sawtooth Diamond, Red & White, 1880s, 71 x 72 In.	165
Amish, String Stars, Cable, Diamond, Suiting Weight Wools, Indiana, c.1910, 80 x 87 In.	392
Amish, Sunshine & Shadow, Lancaster County, Pa., 1930s, 87 x 87 In. ....*illus*	165
Amish, Sunshine & Shadow, Multicolor, Plume Border, Lancaster County, 85 x 88 In.	443
Amish, Wool, Diamond In Square, Green, Red, Gray, Wool, c.1900, 71 x 74 In.	382
Applique, Red Bud, Green Stem Flowers, 9 Blocks, 90 x 94 In.	660
Appliqued, Bird, Cherry, c.1920, 89 x 77 In.	533
Appliqued, Birds, Central Star Inside Star, Red, Orange, White, c.1900, 81 x 84 In.	182
Appliqued, Birds, Pinwheel Flowers, Red, Green, Swag Border, N.Y., c.1850, 84 x 74 In.	4563
Appliqued, Cockscomb, Red, Tan, c.1895, 67 x 77 In.	119
Appliqued, Cockscomb, Red, Tan, Green, Bound, c.1895, 82 x 82 In.	152
Appliqued, Double Heart, Signed Richard Chapman, 1857, 91 x 96 In.	356
Appliqued, Eagles, Stars, Red, Green, Yellow, c.1890, 84 x 82 In.	2133
Appliqued, Floral, Red, Orange, Tan, Vining Oak Leaf Border, Cotton, c.1860, 76 x 83 In.	323
Appliqued, Flower & Star, Blue, White, Swag Border, 98 x 89 In.	444
Appliqued, Flower Wreaths, Orange, Red, Green, Cream, Pa., c.1865, 82 x 64 In.	385

Appliqued, Flower, Scroll Border, Chintz Birds, Trees, Baskets, c.1805, 114 x 113 In.	4063
Appliqued, Flowerpots, Flowers, Vine Border, Wreaths, Red & Green, c.1850, 85 x 86 In.	1058
Appliqued, Flowers, Orange, Red, Green Vines, Crib, c.1850, 41 x 43 In.	533
Appliqued, Flowers, Red, Green, Cream Ground, c.1920, 89 x 89 In.	575
Appliqued, Flowers, Red, Green, Yellow, Flowering Vine Borders, c.1870, 78 x 81 In.	392
Appliqued, Gold Eagle, On Shield, Stars, Red, Blue, White, c.1950, 91 x 76 In.	850
Appliqued, Irish Chain, Red, Green, Vine Border, Cotton, c.1885, 104 x 100 In.	1476
Appliqued, Mariner's Compass, Chintz, Cotton, Maryland, c.1830, 107 x 104 In.	1093
Appliqued, Oak Leaf, 9 Blocks, Blue & White, Blue Border, c.1860, 78 x 71 In.	230
Appliqued, Oak Leaves, Berries, Red, Green, Orange, Diamond Pattern, c.1900, 78 x 76 In.	510
Appliqued, Patchwork Star, Green, Pink, Rose, Cotton, Medallion, Fern, Cotton, 112 x 96 In.	316
Appliqued, Patchwork, Blue & White Cotton, Feathered Stars, Goose Border, U.S.A., 79 x 80 In.	646
Appliqued, Patchwork, Grapes, Green, Purple, Cotton, Tenn., c.1930, 87 x 71 In.	403
Appliqued, Patchwork, Healing Hands, Multicolor, Cotton, Sarah Mary Taylor, 72 x 78 In.	1440
Appliqued, Patchwork, Mariner's Compass, Red, Cream, Yellow, c.1890, 80 x 101 In.	356
Appliqued, Patchwork, Rosettes, White, Red, Blue Border, Cotton, c.1850, 84 x 80 In.	584
Appliqued, Patchwork, Sunflower, Green, Orange, Lattice, Cotton, c.1875, 77 x 77 In.	1035
Appliqued, Patchwork, Whig Rose, Green, Red, Yellow, Rose, Cotton, Ky., c.1855, 70 x 70 In.	2530
Appliqued, Potted Flowers, Yellow, Green, Red, c.1860, 76 x 76 In.	2607
Appliqued, Pride Of Iowa, Variation, Cranberry, Tan, c.1880, 74 x 77 In.	1067
Appliqued, Princess Feather, 2 Inner Borders, Fleur-De-Lis, c.1890, 80 x 82 In.	764
Appliqued, Princess Feather, Red, Blue Green, Sashing, Borders, Cotton, c.1870, 82 x 84 In.	206
Appliqued, Princess Feather, Red, Green, Pa., c.1870, 84 x 81 In.	1126
Appliqued, Roses, Leaves, Red, Pink, Green, Crib, c.1895, 48 x 47 In.	770
Appliqued, Roses, Pink, Green, c.1890, 78 x 78 In.	296
Appliqued, Sampler, Pig, Horse, Anchor, Woman, Sunflower, Signed Abbie, 1887, 79 x 79 In.	978
Appliqued, Tree Of Life, Chintz, c.1820, 101 x 95 In.	4029
Appliqued, Trees, Birds, Vine Border, Green, Black, Yellow, White, c.1910, 89 x 86 In.	5688
Appliqued, Tulips, Sawtooth Border, Red, Green, Yellow, Signed, 1861, 84 x 100 In.	663
Appliqued, Vines, Flowers, Multicolor, c.1874, 91 x 89 In.	431
Appliqued, Whig Rose, Flowers, Leaves, Red, Green, White, Cotton, c.1870, 85 x 80 In.	813
Appliqued, Whig Rose, Flowers, Vines, Red, Green, c.1870, 92 x 86 In.	219
Appliqued, Whig Rose, Running Grapevine Border, c.1860, 80 x 82 In.	840
Appliqued, Wreath, Vine, Leaf Border, Green, Black, White, 102 x 100 In.	360
Chintz, Cotton, Flowers, Red, Tied, Cotton, 1800s, 90 x 72 In.	240
Crazy, Birds, Animals, Embroidered, Wool, Flannel, Crepe, Silk, c.1900, 70 x 70 In.	259
Crazy, Flags, Flags, Flowers, Fans, Embroidered, Multicolor, c.1890, 56 x 46 In.	144
Crazy, Iowa Political Ribbons, Felt Backing, Scalloped Edges, Dubuque, c.1876, 77 x 66 In.	86
Crazy, Silk Neck Ties, Famous People, 10 Squares, Satin Back, c.1930, 81 x 71 In.	431
Mennonite, Stars, 110 Squares, Wool, Applied Felt Buttons, Crocheted, c.1900, 74 x 70 In.	403
Patchwork, 12 Flower Blocks, Embroidered, Yellow, Rosettes, Waves, Bars, 88 x 77 In.	75
Patchwork, 12 Flower Blocks, Peach Ground, c.1920, 92 x 72 In.	75
Patchwork, 4 Nested Stars, Orange, Yellow, Green, Apricot, Red Paisley Border, Penn., 82 In.	756
Patchwork, 42 Square Blocks, Checkered, Multicolor, c.1900, 79 x 91 In.	316
Patchwork, 72 Multicolor Square Blocks, Fan Shape, Blue Border, Va., c.1945, 68 x 84 In.	161
Patchwork, 9 Patch, Multicolor, Red Print Ground, Tied, c.1890, 81 ½ x 70 In.	270
Patchwork, 9 Patch, Print, Solid Blocks, Blue Ground, c.1945, 82 x 85 In.	92
Patchwork, 9 Wagon Wheel, Tulip Pattern, Flower Print Trim, 74 x 81 In. ....*illus*	59
Patchwork, Album Patch, Ink Signatures, Multicolor, Blue, Black Borders, c.1840, 84 x 82 In.	360
Patchwork, Album, Alabama, Georgia, Signed, 42 Blocks, Multicolor, c.1855, 74 x 98 In.	2160
Patchwork, Amish, Squares, Gray, Black, Blue, Green, 14 ½ x 22 In.	10
Patchwork, Appliqued, Cherry Baskets, Multicolor, Cotton, c.1890, 94 x 82 In. ....*illus*	960
Patchwork, Bars, Patterned Cotton, Checkerboard Border, c.1830, 115 x 97 In.	115
Patchwork, Basket, Blue, White Ground, Pennsylvania, 1890s, 64 x 74 In.	106
Patchwork, Bear Paw, Red, Rose, Brown, Red Sashing, Cotton, c.1860, 74 x 72 In.	144
Patchwork, Blazing Star, Triple Border, Print Backing, Cotton, 20th Century, 93 x 95 In.	331
Patchwork, Blazing Stars, Double Diamond Borders, Cotton, Frame, 1920-40, 68 x 83 In.	940
Patchwork, Bowtie, Blue Calico, Cream, Border, Blue Binding, 77 x 72 In.	270
Patchwork, Broken Star, 20 Blue & White Blocks, Diamond Stitching, c.1900, 71 x 91 In.	219
Patchwork, Carolina Lily, Red, Green, White, Plume, Sawtooth Border, 1846, 94 x 96 In.	2360
Patchwork, Chimney Sweep, Red, White, Double Sawtooth Border, Cotton, 1848, 95 x 94 In.	863
Patchwork, Compass Stars, Blue, Red, Maroon, Calico Border, Cotton, c.1880, 57 x 35 In.	345
Patchwork, Crazy, Log Cabin, Brown, Blue, Red, Green, Victorian, 68 x 80 In.	948
Patchwork, Diamond Design, Flower Petals, Print Bars, Cotton, 1843, 100 x 103 In.	1175
Patchwork, Double Irish Chain, White Ground, Blue, Cotton, c.1860, 92 x 81 In.	633
Patchwork, Double Irish Chain, White Ground, Pink, Green, 1800s, 86 x 86 In.	173

Quilt, Patchwork, Log Cabin, Barn Raising, Flower Print Back, Pa., 1870s, 91 x 92 In. **$708**

Conestoga Auction Co., Inc.

Radford, Vase, 2 Storks, Taking Flight, Impressed, Ruko, Albert Haubrich, 19 ¾ In. **$1,093**

Humler & Nolan

This is an edited listing of current prices. Visit **Kovels.com** to check thousands of prices from previous years and sign up for free information on trends, tips, reproductions, marks, and more.

Radio, Bluebird, Walter Dorwin Teague, Model 566, Disc, Decal, c.1934, 14 ½ x 6 In. $2,706

Skinner Auctioneers & Appraisers

Radio, Fada, Catalin, Model 53, Tubes, Bakelite, c.1938, 6 x 8 ½ In. $2,783

Cottone Auctions

Radio, Fada, Model F 55 AU, Tortoiseshell Type Grill, Art Deco, Bakelite, 5 ½ x 9 In. $1,936

Conestoga Auction Co., Inc.

Radio, Gloritone, Model 26, Cathedral, Oak, United States Radio & Television, c.1931 $120

Victorian Casino Antiques

Patchwork, Dresden Plate, Stars, Navy, Yellow, White, Rose, Calico, c.1880, 95 x 75 In.	489
Patchwork, Eagle Rows, Cranberry, Peach, 1800s, 68 x 73 In.	273
Patchwork, Feathered Star, Sawtooth Border, Cotton, Henrietta Copeland, c.1900, 86 x 67 In.	633
Patchwork, Flower Baskets, Embroidered, Blue Ground, c.1955, 79 x 77 In.	88
Patchwork, Flying Geese, Blue, White, Pa., c.1890, 78 x 80 In.	178
Patchwork, Flying Geese, Green, Orange, Reverse Bars, c.1890, 84 x 82 In.	207
Patchwork, Grandmother's Flower Garden, Blue Border, c.1945, 82 x 94 In.	533
Patchwork, Grandmother's Flower Garden, Multicolor Pastels, Cotton, c.1930, 96 x 86 In.	144
Patchwork, Hands All Around, Red, Cream, Lime Green, Ribbon Border, 82 x 82 In.	825
Patchwork, Hearts, Blue, Red, White Ground, Cotton, c.1925, 85 x 65 In.	201
Patchwork, Honeycomb, Gingham Red, Yellow, Blue, White, c.1930, 62 x 72 In.	356
Patchwork, Irish Chain, Blue & White, Blue Border, c.1900, Wood Frame, 40 x 40 In.	153
Patchwork, Irish Chain, Red, Green, Salmon, Cotton, c.1930, 77 x 88 In.	764
Patchwork, Jacob's Ladder, Indigo, Gray, Alternating Diamonds, Ohio, c.1890, 78 x 61 In.	86
Patchwork, Lemon Peel, Red & White, Hearts & Flower Quilting, 1890s, 80 x 82 In.	354
Patchwork, Log Cabin, Barn Raising, Flower Print Back, Pa., 1870s, 91 x 92 In. *illus*	708
Patchwork, Log Cabin, Blue, Black, Red, Tan, Gray, Green, c.1920, 76 x 71 In.	115
Patchwork, Log Cabin, Flag, Blue Bars, Floral Backing, A. K. Beitler, c.1920, 72 x 72 In.	5500
Patchwork, Log Cabin, Multicolor, Sawtooth Border, c.1880, 81 x 73 In.	259
Patchwork, Mariner's Compass, Blue, White, Pa., c.1890, 82 x 66 In.	395
Patchwork, Mariner's Compass, Stars, Swags, Green, Pink, Cream Ground, 82 x 100 In.	690
Patchwork, Ohio Star, Yellow, Orange, White, c.1900, 71 x 72 In.	122
Patchwork, Pinwheel, Blue Green, Red, White, c.1890, 90 x 94 In.	252
Patchwork, Red Calico Squares, White Cross, Zigzag Design, 1836, 104 x 82 In.	420
Patchwork, Robbing Peter To Pay Paul, Blue & Cream, c.1860, 86 x 86 In.	460
Patchwork, Sawtooth Diamond, In Square, Sawtooth Border, Cotton, 1800s, 68 x 69 In.	330
Patchwork, Schoolhouse, Blue & White, Signed Motelle Mullins, 78 x 88 In.	189
Patchwork, Schoolhouse, Navy, White, c.1875, 95 x 85 In.	805
Patchwork, Shoe Fly, Flower Printed Border, 1870s, 74 x 77 In.	236
Patchwork, Sister's Choice, Pink, White, Black, c.1920, 72 x 84 In.	119
Patchwork, Snail's Trail, Blue Tan, Multicolor, Calico, c.1945, 76 x 68 In.	243
Patchwork, Snowflake, Blue, White, c.1920, 83 x 73 In.	385
Patchwork, Star Of Bethlehem, 8 Multicolored Points, Green Ground, Zigzag Border, 80 In.	324
Patchwork, Star, Fans, Sawtooth Edge, Pumpkin, Green, Yellow, White, 80 x 82 In.	767
Patchwork, Star, Flowers, Red, Green, Cream, 80 x 84 In.	575
Patchwork, Star, Multicolor, Pa., c.1890, 82 x 80 In.	711
Patchwork, Starburst, Bird, Flower Applique Border, Sawtooth, Cotton, c.1875, 80 x 78 In.	546
Patchwork, Tree Of Life, Interlocking, Hand Stitch, c.1900, 80 x 81 In.	125
Patchwork, Trip Around The World, Multicolor, Pennsylvania, 1870s, 78 x 80 In.	324
Patchwork, Turkey Tracks, 18 Blocks, Green, Red, Gold, White, Cotton, c.1900, 83 x 76 In.	240
Patchwork, Turkey Tracks, Green, Magenta, Diamond Sashing, Stars, c.1860, 90 x 85 In.	316
Patchwork, Wild Goose Chase, Yellow, Red Sashing, Print Backing, Cotton, 37 x 38 In.	441

QUIMPER pottery has a long history. Tin-glazed, hand-painted pottery has been made in Quimper, France, since the late seventeenth century. The earliest firm was founded in 1708 by Pierre Bousquet. In 1782, Antoine de la Hubaudiere became the manager of the factory and the factory became known as the HB Factory (for Hubaudiere-Bousquet), de la Hubaudiere, or Grande Maison. Another firm, founded in 1772 by Francois Eloury, was known as Porquier. The third firm, founded by Guillaume Dumaine in 1778, was known as HR or Henriot Quimper. All three firms made similar pottery decorated with designs of Breton peasants and sea and flower motifs. The Eloury (Porquier) and Dumaine (Henriot) firms merged in 1913. Bousquet (HB) merged with the others in 1968. The group was sold to an American holding company in 1984. More changes followed, and in 2011 Jean-Pierre Le Goff became the owner and the name was changed to Henriot-Quimper.

HR. Quimper

Basket, Rosemary, Bleeding Heart, Blue Sponge Trim, Swan Head Handles, Henriot, 11 In.	58
Bell, Figural, Man, Bagpipes, Flowers, 3 ½ In.	65
Cruet Set, 2 Bottles, 3 Dishes, Stand, Breton Figures, Henriot, c.1960, 13 In., 6 Piece	92
Dish, Swan Shape, Cobalt Blue, Yellow, Green, Basket, Flowers, c.1920, 4 x 5 x 2 In.	399
Dish, Woman, Crocus, Crescent Shape, Scalloped, Blue Trim, 1920s, 9 x 7 In.	225
Eggcup, Man, Walking Stick, Woman, Holding Flower, 3 ¾ In., Pair	85
Figurine, Violin, Breton Couple, Blue, Yellow, Green, Orange, c.1925, 17 In.	225
Pitcher, Applied Frog, Red, Yellow, Blue, White, Shield, France, c.1885, 11 In.	230
Pitcher, Breton Woman, Yellow & Blue Bands, 5 ½ In.	125
Pitcher, Dog's Head Spout, Standing Breton Woman, Blue, Yellow, Oval, Henriot, 9 In.	80
Plate, Breton Woman, Tree, c.1900, 9 In.	40
Plate, Peasant Woman, Flower Border, c.1900, 7 ½ In.	70
Salt, Double, Peasant Man & Woman, Shoe Shape, Fence, Bush, c.1920	200

Serving Dish, Breton Couple, Blue Rim, Swan Head Handle, 3-Part, 1900s, 6 x 11 In.............. 80
Tea Set, Breton Figures, Tray Teapot, Lid, Sugar, Lid, Creamer, 1900s, Tray 14 x 9 In., 4 Piece 184
Tray, Fish, Red Sponge Rim, Crayfish Handles, Tentacles, Octagonal, Henriot, 25 x 10 In......... 69
Urn, Lid, Musicians, Bag Pipes, Oboe, Flower Border, 2 Handles, c.1900, 14 In............ 595
Vase, Breton Couple, Standing, Flowers, Blue Rim, Baluster, Henriot, 8 ½ In., Pair......... 92
Wall Pocket, Flowers, Man, Woman, Cone Shape, 8 In., Pair........................ 270

RADFORD pottery was made by Alfred Radford in Broadway, Virginia; Tiffin and Zanesville, Ohio; and Clarksburg, West Virginia, from 1891 until 1912. Jasperware, Ruko, Thera, Radura, and Velvety Art Ware were made. The jasperware resembles the famous Wedgwood ware of the same name. Another pottery named Radford worked in England and is not included here.

RADURA

Vase, 2 Storks, Taking Flight, Impressed, Ruko, Albert Haubrich, 19 ¾ In. ....*illus* 1093

RADIO broadcast receiving sets were first sold in New York City in 1910. They were used to pick up the experimental broadcasts of the day. The first commercial radios were made by Westinghouse Company for listeners of the experimental shows on KDKA Pittsburgh in 1920. Collectors today are interested in all early radios, especially those made of Bakelite plastic or decorated with blue mirrors. Figural advertising radios and transistor radios are also collected.

American Bosch, No. 305, 5 Tubes, Knobs, Ingraham Upper Clock, Round, 15 ½ In.................... 270
Atwater Kent, Breadboard, Brown Cans, Painted, 31 x 10 In. 780
Atwater Kent, Cathedral, No. 82, 7 Tubes, 19 ½ In. 450
Atwater Kent, Model 46, F-2 Speaker, Crosshatching, c.1928... 90
Atwater Kent, No. 84, 6 Tubes, Inlays, Superheterodyne, Tall Case Clock, Wood, 70 In. 780
Atwater Kent, No. 246, 6 Tubes, Knobs, Wood, Table, c.1933, 18 In. 360
Atwater Kiel Kent, No. 55C, Wood, Table, Turned Legs, 30 x 36 In. 360
Bluebird, Walter Dorwin Teague, Model 566, Disc, Decal, c.1934, 14 ½ x 6 In. ....*illus* 2706
Bulova, No. G8, 7 Tubes, Knobs, Wood, Tall Case Clock, Finials, 67 ½ In......................... 330
Champion Spark Plug, AM Radio, Gray, Cream, Spark Plug Shape 90
Detrola, No. 568, Tube, Chrome Front, Signed Paper Label, 1946, 12 x 8 In. 469
Detrola, No. 3281, Knobs, Upper Clock, Round, Wood Case, 12 In......................... 300
DeWald, No. A502, Knobs, Brown Marbled Catalin, 9 ¾ In......................... 1080
Emerson, AC/DC, 5 Tubes, Knobs, Wood, Table, 11 In......................... 120
Emerson, Aristocrat, Orange, Catalin, c.1940, 11 In......................... 540
Emerson, Ivory Tombstone Type, No. U-5A, Knobs, Round Dial, Plastic, c.1935, 10 In. 360
Fada, Bullet, No. 1000, Knobs, Yellow, Red Catalin, 10 ½ In......................... 660
Fada, Catalin, Model 53, Tubes, Bakelite, c.1938, 6 x 8 ½ In. ....*illus* 2783
Fada, Model F 55 AU, Tortoiseshell Type Grill, Art Deco, Bakelite, 5 ½ x 9 In. ....*illus* 1936
Federal, Type 59, 4 Tubes, Knobs, Headphones, 15 x 23 In......................... 900
Gloritone, Model 26, Cathedral, Oak, United States Radio & Television, c.1931 ....*illus* 120
Microphone, Electro-Voice, Ribbon, Art Deco, No. VI, 1950s 360
Microphone, RCA, Model 44, Series Ribbon, Electro Voice Stand, c.1935 1062
Microphone, Shure Bros., Model 2A, Round, Springs, Stand, Nickel, Brass, c.1930, 11 In. 461
Philco, Cathedral, No. 37-84, Wood Case, Arched, 14 ¾ In......................... 240
Philco, Cathedral, No. 118, 8 Tubes, Shadow Tuning, Knobs, 2-Tone Wood, 18 ¾ In............. 240
Philco, Model 90, Cathedral, Wood, Fluted, Arched, Cutout Speaker, 18 ½ In......................... 240
Philco, No. 70, 7 Tubes, Wood, Finials, Superheterodyne, Knobs, Tall Case Clock, 71 In.............. 270
Philco, No. 551, 5 Tubes, Knobs, Clock, Shelf, Federal, Wood, 22 In. 330
RCA, Radiola, No. 25, Tubes, Antenna, Knobs, c.1925, 28 In......................... 150
Royalist, 5 Tubes, Knobs, Wood Case, Tall Case Clock, 68 ½ In......................... 300
Spartan, No. 132, AC/DC, Woody Plastic, Demilune Dial, Knobs, c.1950, 13 In. 360
Sparton, Walter Dorwin Teague, Mirror Glass, Blue, Metal, Wood, 1936, 9 x 17 ½ In. ....*illus* 2500
Telefunken Super, Bayreuth 653 WLK, Bakelite, Speaker Fabric, 6 Valves, 1933 ....*illus* 311
Westinghouse, No. WR-15, 9 Tubes, Knobs, Wood, Tall Case Clock, 61 In. 300

RAILROAD enthusiasts collect any train memorabilia. Everything is wanted, from oilcans to whole train cars. The Chessie system has a store that sells many reproductions of its old dinnerware and uniforms.

Bowl, Fruit, Hiawatha, Chicago, Milwaukee, St. Paul & Pacific, Syracuse, c.1936, 4 In................ 299
Cup & Saucer, Hiawatha, Chicago, Milwaukee, St. Paul & Pacific, Syracuse, Demitasse.............. 805
Lantern, Flagman, Red Globe, 13 In.......................... 120
Lantern, Iron, Brass Plaque, Welch, London, 12 x 6 In., Pair........................ 189
Lantern, Kosmo Brenner, Steel, Oil Tank, Reflector, Brass Wick, 22 x 11 In.......................... 98
Lantern, Metal, Red, Blue Glass Lenses, Smoke Bell, Bail Handle, Adlake, 16 In.......................... 144
Lantern, Switching, Blue, Orange Bull's-Eye Glass, NYC Lines, 18 x 11 In.......................... 115

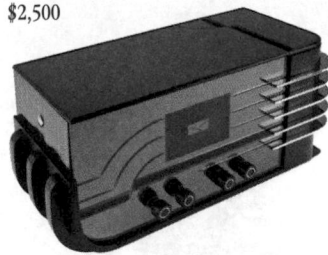

Radio, Sparton, Walter Dorwin Teague, Mirror Glass, Blue, Metal, Wood, 1936, 9 x 17 ½ In.
$2,500

Los Angeles Modern Auctions (LAMA)

Radio, Telefunken Super, Bayreuth 653 WLK, Bakelite, Speaker Fabric, 6 Valves, 1933
$311

Auction Team Breker

Red Wing, Random Harvest, Gravy Boat, Attached Underplate, Futura, 1950s, 4 x 7 x 5 In.
$24

Ruby Lane, Inc.

Red Wing, Random Harvest, Platter, Futura, 15 ¼ x 10 ½ In.
$30

Ruby Lane, Inc.

R

Redware, Figurine, Shoe, Arch Base, Mottled Glaze, Shenandoah Valley, 1800s, 4 In.
$767

Conestoga Auction Co., Inc.

Redware, Pitcher, Scene With Children, Arched Handle, Incised, S Bell, c.1850-80, 9 ¾ In.
$2,588

Crocker Farm, Inc.

Redware, Plate, Multicolor Slip, Sgraffito, Tulips, Leaves, 1818 In Heart, 4 ¼ In.
$6,038

Crocker Farm, Inc.

Rookwood, Bookends, Bear, Walking, Blue & Tan Matte Glaze, 1923, 4 ¼ In.
$1,534

Humler & Nolan

Lantern,	Yellow, Green, Red Lights & Frames, 19 ½ In.	230
Platter,	Hiawatha, Chicago, Milwaukee, St. Paul & Pacific, Syracuse, Oval, 10 In.	805
Sign,	Railroad Crossing, Black, White, Cross Shape, 40 x 40 In.	345
Sign,	Stop On Red, Jeweled, Pole Mounting Bracket, 26 x 23 In.	780
Stepstool,	Steel, Painted Blue, Rubber Footed Legs, Perforated Top, c.1920, 15 x 11 In.	173
Ticket Box,	New London Northern Railroad, Painted Red, Hinged, 1863, 13 x 20 In.	540
Train Bench,	Victorian, Mahogany, Tufted Padded Seat, Carved Arm Supports, 35 x 66 In.	2952
Uniform,	Milwaukee Road, Jacket, Vest, Pants, Cap, Carlson & Co., Man's 40 Regular, c.1950	180

RAZORS were used in ancient Egypt and subsequently wherever shaving was in fashion. The metal razor used in America until about 1870 was made in Sheffield, England. After 1870, machine-made hollow-ground razors were made in Germany or America. Plastic or bone handles were popular. The razor was often sold in a set of seven, one for each day of the week. The set was often kept by the barber who shaved the well-to-do man each day in the shop.

Bakelite,	Marbleized, Italy, 3 ⅛ In.	45
Evans,	Sterling Silver, Black Enamel, Marcasite, Blades, Case, 1930s, 2 x 1 In.	250
Ever-Ready,	Travel, Brass, Blades, Case, Hinged, 3 ½ x 2 ½ In.	68
Laurel,	Case, Woman's, England, 1 ½ In.	55
Ronson 260,	Electric, Leather & Plastic Case, c.1960, 4 ¼ x 3 ¾ In.	45
Straight,	Engraved, Germany, c.1930, 5 ¾ In.	40
Straight,	Molded Celluloid, Eagle, Stamped Maroon & Michael	1140
Straight,	Silver, Mother-Of-Pearl, Spike Point, Serrated Jimping, Germany, c.1900	215

REAMERS, or juice squeezers, have been known since 1767, although most of those collected today date from the twentieth century. Figural reamers are among the most prized.

Glass,	Amber, Measuring Cup, Tab Handle, 6 In.	50
Glass,	Amber, Ribbed, Open Loop Handle, Federal Glass Co., 5 x 2 In.	10
Glass,	Clear, Side Tab Handle, Orange Juice Extractor, 6 x 6 ¼ x 4 In.	24
Glass,	Cobalt Blue, Crisscross Pattern, Hazel Atlas	263
Glass,	Cobalt Blue, Swirls, 2 Spouts, 3 x 3 ¾ In.	18
Glass,	Crisscross Pattern, Clear, Hazel Atlas, 1938, 6 x 4 In.	14
Glass,	Green Uranium, Hocking, 5 x 2 ¼ In.	25
Glass,	Opalescent, Fry Glass Co., 7 ⅜ x 2 ½ In.	100
Glass,	Yellow Opalescent, Sunkist, McKee, 1940s	94
Ironstone,	Attachment, Hexagonal Mounting, 2 ¼ x 2 In.	9
Jadite,	Loop Handle, Jeanette, 7 x 5 ¼ In.	75
Milk Glass,	Sunkist, Embossed, c.1925, 8 ½ x 6 x 2 In.	21
Pitcher,	Ceramic, Jester, Topcoat, Polka Dots, 6 In.	65
Pitcher,	Toucan, Pearlescent Luster, 1930s, 5 ¾ x 2 ¾ In.	165
Porcelain,	Art Deco, Yellow, Vines, Roses, France, 2 Piece, 3 x 4 In.	325
Porcelain,	Clown, Pitcher, Multicolor, Japan, 2 Piece, 1920s, 6 x 5 ½ In.	75
Porcelain,	Flower Shape, Red, Green, Yellow, Japan, 1 ½ x 6 x 4 In.	20
Porcelain,	Lemon Juicer, Cup, With Spout, Painted Flowers, Gilt, Dresden, 1900s, 3 In.	570
Porcelain,	Pear Shape, Dimpled, Yellow Luster, Japan, 3 Piece, 1930s, 5 x 5 ½ In.	72
Vaseline Glass,	Green, Fluted, Handle, 5 ¼ x 2 ½ In.	15

RECORDS have changed size and shape through the years. The cylinder-shaped phonograph record for use with the early Edison models was made about 1889. Disc records were first made by 1894, the double-sided disc by 1904. High-fidelity records were first issued in 1944, the first vinyl disc in 1946, the first stereo record in 1958. The 78 RPM became the standard in 1926 but was discontinued in 1957. In 1932, the first 33 ⅓ RPM was made but was not sold commercially until 1948. In 1949, the 45 RPM was introduced. Compact discs became available in the U.S. in 1982 and many companies began phasing out the production of phonograph records.

Beach Boys,	Endless Summer, Faces In Leaves, Capitol Records, LP, 1974	12
Carl Perkins,	Blue Suede Shoes, Sun Records, LP, 1956	200
Cherry Hill Jerry,	Columbia, Box, 6 In.	130
Deep Purple,	Live, Concert, Yellow Harvest Label, 1970	20
Grease,	Soundtrack, Olivia Newton John, John Travolta, 33 LP, 1970s	30
Hair,	Musical, Red, Green, Faces, RCA Label, LP	20
I'm Going Right Back To Chicago,	Columbia, Box, 6 In.	94
Love Story,	Skating In The Park, 45 RPM, 1970s	10
Old Black Joe,	Box, Columbia, 6 In.	5
Somebody's Waiting For You,	Box, Columbia, 6 In.	106
Terri Lee,	Dolly's Lullaby, Story Of 3 Bears, 45 RPM	25

R

RED WING POTTERY of Red Wing, Minnesota, was a firm started in 1878. The company first made utilitarian pottery, including stoneware jugs and canning jars. In the 1920s art pottery was introduced. Many dinner sets and vases were made before the company closed in 1967. Rumrill pottery made by the Red Wing Pottery for George Rumrill is listed in its own category. For more prices, go to kovels.com.

Beige Fleck, Platter, Oval, 12 ½ In.	24
Beige Fleck, Platter, Round, 12 In.	21
Beige Fleck, Relish, 5 Sections, 12 ½ In.	32
Blue Shadows, Cup	6
Blue Shadows, Cup & Saucer	15
Blue Shadows, Plate, Dinner, 10 ⅜ In.	12
Blue Shadows, Plate, Salad, 7 ½ In.	9
Blue Shadows, Soup, Dish, 6 ⅜ In.	10
Bob White, Bowl, Cereal, 6 ¼ In.	21
Bob White, Bowl, Fruit, Lug Handle, 5 ¾ In.	21
Bob White, Bowl, Vegetable, 9 ½ In.	21
Bob White, Bowl, Vegetable, Divided, 14 In.	21
Bob White, Butter, Cover	81
Bob White, Carafe, Stopper, 70 Oz., 13 ½ In.	90
Bob White, Casserole, Handles, Qt.	50
Bob White, Casserole, Lid, Handles, 4 Qt.	100
Bob White, Creamer, 7 ¼ In.	20
Bob White, Gravy Boat, Handle, Lid.	50
Bob White, Plate, Bread & Butter, 6 ½ In.	8
Bob White, Plate, Dinner, 10 ⅞ In.	17
Bob White, Platter, 13 ⅝ In.	30
Bob White, Platter, Oval, 19 ½ In.	65
Bob White, Relish, 3 Sections.	30
Bob White, Salt & Pepper	35
Bowl, Bowl, Beige, Free Form, 12 In.	8
Brittany, Plate, Bread & Butter, 6 In.	9
Brittany, Plate, Salad, 7 ¼ In.	12
Brittany, Saucer	8
Capistrano, Bowl, Cereal, 6 ¾ In.	18
Capistrano, Bowl, Vegetable, 11 ½ In.	43
Capistrano, Creamer	25
Capistrano, Plate, Dinner, 11 In.	17
Capistrano, Salt & Pepper	35
Capistrano, Sugar, Lid.	35
Crock, Wing Logo, Cylindrical, 2 Gal., 9 x 9 ½ In.	40
Damask, Bowl, Fruit, 5 In.	7
Damask, Plate, Dinner, 10 ⅜ In.	10
Damask, Plate, Salad, 7 ½ In.	6
Geometric, Vase, Apple Green Interior, 9 ½ x 5 In.	31
Lute Song, Bowl, Cereal, 6 ¼ In.	25
Lute Song, Bowl, Vegetable, 8 ¼ In.	30
Lute Song, Butter, Cover	65
Lute Song, Cup & Saucer	9
Lute Song, Plate, Dinner, 10 ⅜ In.	14
Lute Song, Tray, Tidbit, 10 ⅜ In.	35
Merrileaf, Cup & Saucer.	12
Oomph, Casserole, Oval, Provincial, 12 In.	50
Oomph, Mug, Provincial, 4 ⅞ In.	25
Pepe, Bowl, Vegetable, 8 In.	30
Pepe, Creamer	12
Pepe, Gravy	35
Pepe, Gravy Boat.	35
Pepe, Plate, Dinner, 10 ¼ In.	12
Pitcher, Green, Double Handle, Marked, 8 ¾ In.	35
Random Harvest, Bowl, Fruit, 5 In.	6
Random Harvest, Butter, Cover	20
Random Harvest, Cup & Saucer.	8
Random Harvest, Gravy Boat	30
Random Harvest, Gravy Boat, Attached Underplate, Futura, 1950s, 4 x 7 x 5 In. ....*illus*	24
Random Harvest, Pitcher, Ball	35

Rookwood, Bookends, Double Reader, Purple Matte Glaze, Marked, 1922, 7 In.
$1,062

Humler & Nolan

Rookwood, Bookends, Dutch Girl & Boy, Multicolor High Glazes, Sallie Toohey, 1928, 6 In.
$502

Humler & Nolan

Rookwood, Bookends, Flower Basket, Multicolor High Glazes, Marked, 1929, 5 In.
$561

Humler & Nolan

R

Rookwood, Bookends, Owl, On Book, Green High Glaze, 1949, 5 ⅝ In.
$460

Humler & Nolan

Rookwood, Bowl, Yellow Flowers, Sara Sax, Marked, 1 ⅝ x 10 ½ In.
$1,610

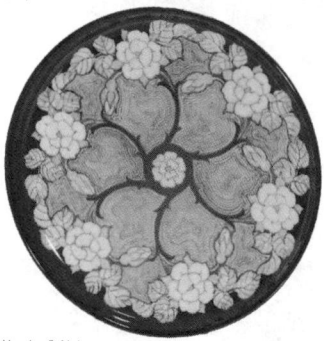

Humler & Nolan

Rookwood, Ewer, Fish, Gorham Silver Overlay, Albert Valentien, 1894, 12 ⅝ In.
$7,965

Humler & Nolan

Rookwood, Paperweight, Cat, Seated, Orange Matte Glaze, William Hentschel, 1928, 5 ⅜ In.
$295

Humler & Nolan

Random Harvest, Plate, Bread & Butter, 6 ⅞ In.	4
Random Harvest, Plate, Dinner, 10 ¾ In.	14
Random Harvest, Plate, Salad, 7 In.	12
Random Harvest, Platter, Futura, 15 ¼ x 10 ½ In. ....*illus*	30
Random Harvest, Platter, Round, 12 ¾ In.	30
Random Harvest, Relish, Divided, 13 In.	16
Random Harvest, Salt & Pepper	27
Random Harvest, Sugar, Lid	21
Tampico, Bowl, Vegetable, 9 In.	30
Tampico, Creamer	18
Tampico, Plate, Dinner, 10 ¾ In.	15
Tampico, Soup, Dish, 7 ¾ In.	22
Tip Toe, Bowl, Vegetable	24
Tip Toe, Gravy Boat	25
Tip Toe, Plate, Bread & Butter, 6 ½ In.	7
Tip Toe, Plate, Dinner, 11 In.	12
Turtle Dove, Plate, Bread & Butter, 6 In.	7
Turtle Dove, Plate, Dinner, Orange, 10 ⅜ In.	12
Turtle Dove, Plate, Dinner, Yellow, 10 ⅜ In.	12
Turtle Dove, Salt & Pepper	24
Vase, Nokomis, Brown, Tan, Green Matte Glaze, Incised, 10 ⅜ In.	266

REDWARE is a hard, red stoneware that originated in the late 1600s and continues to be made. The term is also used to describe any common clay pottery that is reddish in color.

Bank, Lion, Sitting, 8 In.	1920
Bank, Spaniel, Coleslaw Mane, Brown, Green Glaze, Pa., c.1860, 6 ¾ In.	2015
Barber Bowl, Yellow Slip Trailing, Green Splotches, Pierced Rim, c.1815, 3 x 9 In.	210
Basket, White Stripes, Manganese Streaks, Pinched, Scalloped Rim, Ribbed Handle, 3 ½ x 2 ½ In.	1035
Bean Pot, Lid, Squat, Ribbed Strap Handle, J. Eberly & Co., Strasburg, Va., 10 In.	288
Birdhouse, Inscribed To Rent For A Song, c.1850, 5 ¾ In.	1896
Bowl, Copper & Manganese Splotches, Incised Bands, Flared, A. Baecher, 4 x 7 In.	1955
Bowl, Cream & Brown Tabs, Round, Flared, Rolled Rim, Hagerstown, Md., 11 ½ In.	1610
Bowl, Flared Sides, Piecrust Rim, Fluted Molded Body, Round, 1800s, 4 x 9 In.	118
Bowl, Lid, Double Walled, Openwork, Rope Twist Handles, Dog Finial, c.1850, 7 x 7 In.	360
Bowl, Manganese Drip Glaze Interior, Tapered Sides, Applied Loop Handles, 5 ½ x 16 In.	24
Bowl, Manganese Interior, Tapered, Rounded Rim, Sponged, John W. Bell, c.1880, 10 ½ In.	316
Bowl, Manganese, Splotches, Handles, c.1850, 6 ½ x 16 ½ In.	138
Bowl, Orange Flecked Ground, Copper Spots, Tapered, Rounded Rim, Glazed Interior, 16 In.	230
Bowl, Pitcher, Green, Cream Glazes Over Slip, Scroll Handle, Va., c.1880, 7 x 11 ½ In.	9200
Bowl, Sgraffito, Daisies, Yellow Glaze, Green Detail, L. & B. Breininger, 4 x 12 ¾ In.	83
Bowl, Sgraffito, Eagle Design, Jacob Medinger, c.1900, 7 ⅞ In.	444
Bowl, Sponged Manganese Decoration, Coggled Shoulder, Rounded Rim, 7 ¾ In.	374
Bowl, Tea Mixing, Cylindrical, Flowerpots, Bird, Huntsman, c.1750, 4 x 4 In.	840
Bowl, Yellow, Brown Slip, France, 6 x 19 In.	207
Bust, Man, Grotesque, 19th Century, 6 In.	3792
Butter Chip, Sgraffito, Daisies, Yellow Glaze, Green, L. & B. Breininger, 1972, 4 In., 6 Piece	59
Charger, 2 Tulips, Dotted Border, Swag, Fern Rim, c.1800, 15 In.	65175
Charger, Slip Inscription, Break Away More Making, c.1865, 13 In.	415
Charger, Wavy Yellow Dot & Slip, Pa., 12 ½ In.	830
Churn, Running Lead Glaze, 2 Applied Handles, c.1850, 19 ½ In.	450
Coffeepot, Lid, Crabstock Handle, Rococo Spout, Acorn Finial, Flowers, c.1760, 7 In.	1560
Coffeepot, Lid, Engine Turned, Geometric Design, Elongated Pear, c.1770, 9 In.	720
Colander, Molded Rim, Tapered Body, Glazed Interior, Round, 1800s, 3 ½ x 9 ½ In.	443
Creamer, Bulbous Body, Coggle Wheel Band, Pinched Spout, Loop Handle, 4 In.	266
Creamer, Heart Shape Opening, Pa., c.1865, 2 ¼ In.	237
Creamer, Manganese Splash, c.1860, 3 ¾ In.	178
Creamer, Pitcher Shape, Green & Orange Glaze, Loop Handle, c.1860, 4 ½ In.	294
Crock, Green, Mottled, Brown, Tan Glaze, Impressed S. Bell Strasburg, Vir., c.1865, 6 In.	2370
Crock, Lid, Manganese Splash, Shiny Glaze, Handles, c.1860, 10 In.	210
Crock, Mottled, Wide Mouth, Shenandoah Valley, c.1865, 6 ½ x 5 In.	259
Crock, Storage, Bulbous, Manganese Splotch, Glazed, Applied Ear Handles, 9 ¼ In.	266
Crock, Yellow, Manganese Slip Squiggle, Handles, Bucks County, c.1860, 8 In.	2252
Cup, Splashed Manganese, Olive Mottled & Yellow Orange, A. Baecher, 3 In.	1840
Cuspidor, Round, Tapered, Incised Bands, Phila., c.1850, 5 In.	288
Cuspidor, Swags, Flared Base, Rounded Edge, Shenandoah Valley, c.1875	173
Dish, Deep, Sgraffito Roosters, Fish, Tulips, Green Copper, Brown Manganese, 1824, 12 In.	4600

R

Dish, Wedding, Sgraffito, Couple, Flowers, Jacob Medinger, c.1900, 11 In.		356
Egg, Sgraffito, Slip Flowers, Birds, L.B. Breininger, 1972, 13 Piece		295
Eggcup, Streaky Green & Brown Over Cream, J. Eberly, Strasburg, Va., c.1890		863
Ewer, Tin Glazed, Swirling Leaves & Flowers, Blue Trim, 10 ½ x 5 ½ In.		615
Figurine, Dog, Seated, Basket In Mouth, Pa., c.1860, 4 ½ In.		7110
Figurine, Dog, Spaniel, Sitting, Streaky Manganese, John Bell, c.1860, 9 ¼ In., Pair		42550
Figurine, Dog, Standing, Basket Of Fruit In Mouth, Pa., c.1865, 6 ½ In.		8295
Figurine, Dog, Whippet, Black, White & Red Eyes, Green Base, S. Bell, 1841, 9 ¾ In., Pair		115000
Figurine, Shoe, Arch Base, Mottled Glaze, Shenandoah Valley, 1800s, 4 In. ....*illus*		767
Flask, Donut Shape, Inscribed Joe Reinhardt Pottery, Vale, N.C., c.1975, 8 ½ In.		42
Flowerpot, Cream Mottled Glaze, Attached Saucer, c.1850, 3 ½ In.		30
Flowerpot, Green, Yellow Paint, Tapered, Shenandoah Valley, 1800s, 7 ¾ In.		480
Flowerpot, Manganese Designs, Impressed John Bell, Pa., c.1850, 5 ½ In.		593
Flowerpot, Streaky Yellow Over Olive, Double Crimped Rim, Attached Saucer, 4 ⅝ In.		3680
Jar, Apple Butter, Impressed C. Link, Berks Country, Pa., 1870s, 4 In.		180
Jar, Lid, Oval, Brown Speckles, Splotches & Streaks, c.1815, 7 ¾ In.		2040
Jar, Manganese Glaze, Ring Handles, Tapered Neck, Flared Rim, Hagerstown, c.1810, 11 In.		144
Jar, Manganese, Green Oxide Glaze, Pa., c.1820, 8 In.		1185
Jar, Olive Brown Glaze, Cylindrical, Flared Rounded Rim, John Bell, c.1860, 5 ⅜ In.		230
Jar, Oval, Flared Rim, Streaky Green Copper Glaze Over White Slip, Footed, 7 ½ In.		633
Jar, Oval, Reeded Band, Brown Manganese Splotches, Lug Handles, c.1815, 11 In.		210
Jar, Reeded Band, Brown Manganese Splotches, Lug Handles, Oval, c.1810, 11 In.		210
Jar, Storage, Cylindrical, Flared Rim, Manganese Detail, 19th Century, 12 In.		236
Jar, Storage, Cylindrical, Flared Rim, Manganese Splotch, Red Orange Glaze, 11 In.		236
Jar, Storage, Flared Mouth, Cylindrical Body, Incised Rings, Molded Base Rim, 6 x 4 ½ In.		236
Jug, Barrel Shape, Manganese Bands, Child Holding Doll, Figural Finial, c.1890, 9 In.		3888
Jug, Bulbous, Loop Handle, Green Glaze, Orange Daubs, c.1860, 7 In.		411
Jug, Grotesque, Applied Handle, Pottery Shard Teeth, Matthew Hewell, 12 In.		180
Jug, Grotesque, Applied Ring Encircled Handles, Stone Teeth, Joe Reinhardt, c.1993, 8 ¾ In.		300
Jug, Grotesque, Pottery Shard Teeth, Applied Handled, Incised, B.B. Craig, Vale, N.C., 8 ½ In.		210
Jug, Harvest, 2 Spouts, Applied Lizard Curls Around Body, 8 ¾ In.		403
Jug, Harvest, Red Brown Speckled Lead, Manganese Glaze, Oval, Handle, Spout, 10 ¼ In.		115
Jug, Manganese, Oxide Splotching, New England, c.1865, 3 ½ In.		237
Jug, Pear Shape, White Slip Rim, Strap Handle, Sprigging, Squirrel, Berries, c.1760, 5 In.		960
Jug, Presentation, Inscribed, J. Medinger, For Henry Titlow, 1931, 8 In.		3318
Jug, Ring, Streaky Lead Glaze Over Green Orange Spots, Spout, Galena, Ill., 9 ½ In.		86
Jug, Ring, Yellow & Brown Drip Over Orange, Lead Glaze, Spout, 8 ¾ In.		3738
Loaf Pan, 4 Bands Of Yellow Slip, Coggled Edge, 13 ¾ In.		403
Loaf Pan, Coggled Rim, Yellow Slip Decoration, Pa., c.1830, 3 x 16 In.		2040
Loaf Pan, Coggled Rim, Yellow Slip Feather, c.1850, 11 x 14 In.		1320
Loaf Pan, Oblong, Coggled Rim, Yellow Slip Line & Dot Borders, c.1815, 15 x 20 In.		690
Loaf Pan, Sgraffito, Eagle, Holding Shield, Arrows, Star Border, 1972, 14 In.		212
Loaf Pan, Wavy Yellow Slip Lines, Coggled Edge, 12 In.		518
Loaf Pan, Yellow Slip, Oval, 10 ¼ In.		1126
Match Holder, Dog, Reclining, Dead Game, Tree Stump, J. Weaber Maker, 1878, 3 x 6 In.		593
Mold, Candle, 12-Tube, Pine Frame, Medley & Co., 15 x 18 In.		1353
Mold, Turk's Cap, Green & Manganese Alternating Bands, Glazed, 1800s, 3 x 9 In.		106
Mug, Green & Brown Over Orange & Cream, Strasburg, Va., 4 ½ In.		978
Mug, Impressed Baecher Winchester, Vir., c.1850, 3 ⅞ In.		474
Pan, Lead Glaze, Yellow Slip Band, Tapered Sides, c.1890, 10 ¼ In.		144
Pie Plate, Yellow Slip Clef, Pa., c.1850, 8 In.		652
Pie Plate, Yellow Slip Lines & Swirls, Coggled Edge, 8 ¼ In.		324
Pie Plate, Yellow Slip, 1800s, 7 In.		593
Pie Plate, Yellow Slip, Coggled Rim, c.1845, 9 ¼ In.		711
Pie Plate, Yellow Slip, Pa., c.1850, 5 In.		516
Pie Plate, Yellow, Green Slip Grid, Green Crescent, c.1845, 9 In.		593
Pie Plate, Yellow, Green Slip, Impressed, Willoughby Smith, Pa., c.1900, 7 ⅞ In.		7703
Pie Plate, Yellow, Green Slip, Willoughby Smith, c.1880, 7 ⅜ In., Pair		4266
Pitcher, Applied Hearts, Scrolls, Pa., 1800s, 5 ¼ In.		593
Pitcher, Green Mottled Copper Glaze, Footed, Flared Collar, 7 In.		460
Pitcher, Grotesque, Pottery Shard Teeth, Applied Handle, Stamped Walter Fleming, 8 In.		210
Pitcher, Hunt Scene, Relief, Hounds, Deer, Boar, Tree, Grapevine, S. Bell, c.1890, 8 In.		3680
Pitcher, Lead, Copper, Manganese Glaze, Slip, Flared Rim, Strap Handle, c.1890, 10 x 5 In.		1495
Pitcher, Lead, Copper, Manganese, Green Slip, Hunt Scene, Wavy Rim, Va., c.1890, 8 x 5 In.		978
Pitcher, Oval Green Over Mottled Red, Footed, Ribbed Handle, 10 ½ In.		863
Pitcher, Oval, Green, Streaks, Reeded Strap Handle, Banded Neck, c.1815, 10 In.		3900

Rookwood, Perfume Jug, 3 Spiders, Webs, Painted, Applied Beads, Handle, 1883, 4 ¾ In.
$480

Cowan's Auctions

Rookwood, Perfume Jug, Butterfly, Grasses, Clouds, Limoges Style, 1884, 4 ⅝ In.
$265

Humler & Nolan

Rookwood, Pitcher, Flying Swallow, Grasses, Clouds, Handle, W. McDonald, 1882, 6 ½ In.
$345

Humler & Nolan

R

Rookwood, Pitcher, Toad Of Toad Hall, Silver Overlay, Bruce Horsfall, Gorham, 1893, 5 ¾ x 7 In.
$4,375

Rago Arts & Auction Center

Rookwood, Plaque, Birch Trees, Lake, Lenore Asbury, Frame, 1917, 9 ⅜ x 12 ⅜ In.
$4,366

Humler & Nolan

Rookwood, Vase, Black Cranes, Diving, Sea Green, Matt Daly, 1899, 13 In.
$27,140

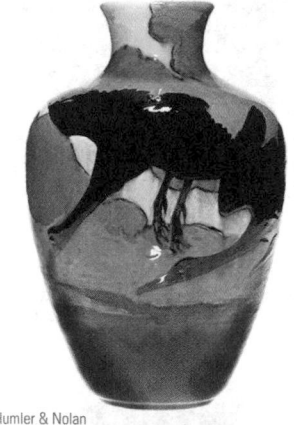

Humler & Nolan

Pitcher, Oval, Manganese, Marbled Glaze, Ribbed Strap Handle, A. Baecher, 8 In.	690
Pitcher, Pumpkin Ground, Blue, Black Slip, Signed Cesbron, France, c.1925, 6 In.	71
Pitcher, Scene With Children, Arched Handle, Incised, S Bell, c.1850-80, 9 ¾ In. ....*illus*	2588
Pitcher, Slip Marbled, Green, Cream, Brown, Red, Turned Band, Reeded Handle, 6 In.	360
Pitcher, Splashed Manganese, Octagonal, Bearded Man's Face Spout, 8 In.	115
Pitcher, Squat, Lead, Copper, Manganese, Handle, Va., c.1890, 11 x 5 In.	4313
Pitcher, Tankard Shape, Green Splash & Brown Over Cream Glaze, 9 ⅝ In.	1955
Planter, Hanging, Drip Glaze, Breininger, 1974, 4 ½ x 9 ¼ In.	71
Planter, Hanging, Flared, Molded, Manganese Detail, L.B., 1973, 4 ½ x 8 ¾ In.	47
Planter, Hanging, Molded, Wavy Striped Manganese Design, Breininger, 8 ½ x 8 ¼ In.	35
Plaque, Seated Angel, Relief, Dentil Molding Border, Initials SP IS, 6 x 5 ¼ In.	58
Plate, 3 Wavy Center Lines, Musical, Coggled Rim, 8 In.	189
Plate, Multicolor Slip, Sgraffito, Tulips, Leaves, 1818 In Heart, 4 ¼ In. ....*illus*	6038
Plate, Sgraffito, Bird, Flowers, Yellow Glaze, Green, Brown, Coggled Rim, Greg Shooner, 11 In.	130
Plate, Sgraffito, Bird, Tree, Jacob Medinger, c.1900, 8 ¾ In.	267
Plate, Sgraffito, Birds, Flowers, Yellow Glaze, Green Highlights, J. Seagraves, 10 ½ In.	94
Plate, Sgraffito, Peafowl, Flowers Branch, Yellow Glaze, Brown, Green, 12 ⅜ In.	94
Plate, Slip Alphabet, Green & Cream Slip Bull's Eye, Berks County, 1824, 9 ¾ In.	4888
Plate, Slip Inscription Cheap Dish, Coggled Rim, c.1850, 11 In.	1265
Plate, Slip Tulip, Leaves, 1747, Round, Coggled Rim, Greg Shooner, 19 ¾ In.	47
Plate, Slip, 3 Yellow, Green Fern Bands, Pa., c.1870, 11 ¼ In.	2015
Plate, Slip, Coggle Wheel Rim, 19th Century, 9 In.	236
Plate, Yellow Slip Tulip, Pa., 1800s, 10 In.	563
Puzzle Jug, Cut Out Flowers, Running Brown Glaze, Applied Frog, Handle, c.1820, 8 In.	154
Standish, Dog Finial, Incised Pinwheels, Inscribed John Mohr, Pa., 1856, 4 ½ x 8 ¼ In.	1185
Tankard, Manganese, Yellow Wavy Slip, Pa., c.1850, 6 ½ In.	1778
Tankard, Swelled Sides, Mouth, Flat Handle, Slip, Flowers, c.1850, 6 In.	119
Teapot, Lid, Squat, Globular, Lion Mask & Paw Feet, Berries, Leaves, c.1755, 4 ⅝ In.	960
Umbrella Stand, Tree Stump Shape, Leafy Vine & Berries, Rustic Style, 21 In.	316
Urn, Copper, Manganese Tulips, Lion Mask Handles, S. Bell, c.1865, 15 x 10 In., Pair	3105
Urn, Flower, Manganese Necklace, Handles, J. Eberly & Bro., c.1865, 15 In.	9200
Vase, Figures, Geometric Design, Handles, Oval, Pedestal, Pinched Neck, 18 x 7 In.	8850
Vase, Hat Shape, Scroddleware, Marbleized Glaze, Slip, 1895, 4 ¼ In.	142

RICHARD was the mark used on acid-etched cameo glass vases, bowls, night-lights, and lamps made by the Austrian company Loetz after 1918. The pieces were very similar to the French cameo glasswares made by Daum, Galle, and others.

Vase, Grapes, Leaves, Pinched Neck, Cameo, Signed, 9 ½ In.	1917
Vase, Yellow Ground, Mulberry Leaves, Stick, Cameo, Signed, 15 ¾ In.	2200

RIDGWAY pottery has been made in the Staffordshire district in England since 1808 by a series of companies with the name Ridgway. Ridgway became part of Royal Doulton in the 1960s. The transfer-design dinner sets are the most widely known product. Other pieces of Ridgway may be listed under Flow Blue.

Bowl, Scrolled Gilt Leaf Band, Old Paris Style, Hunting Scene Interior, c.1825, 14 In.	748
Cake Stand, Capitol Washington, Blue Transfer, Round, 2 ⅝ x 11 ⅝ In.	889
Pitcher, Blue, White, Cat, Obverse Bull, 9 ½ In.	116
Platter, Pennsylvania Hospital, Blue Transfer, 1800s, 14 x 19 In.	851
Soup, Dish, Octagon Church, Boston, Blue Transfer, 1800s, 9 ¾ In.	326
Strainer, Capital Washington, Blue Transfer, Oval, 1800s, 15 In.	3081
Tureen, Tray, Devonshire, Flowers, Birds, c.1890, 7 & 18 In.	84
Vase, Landscape Scene, Gilt Rim, Handles, Pedestal Base, c.1830, 4 ⅝ In., Pair	161

RIFLES *that are firearms made after 1900 are not listed in this book. BB guns and air rifles are listed in the Toy category.*

RIVIERA dinnerware was made by the Homer Laughlin Co. of Newell, West Virginia, from 1938 to 1950. The pattern was similar in coloring and in mood to Fiesta and Harlequin. The Riviera plates and cup handles were square. For more prices, go to kovels.com.

Green, Bowl, Vegetable, Lid, Rectangular	102
Green, Creamer	14
Green, Creamer, Footed, Rectangular, 1930s	15
Green, Plate, Luncheon, 8 ¾ In.	19
Ivory, Cup & Saucer, Footed	16
Ivory, Platter, Oval, 11 In.	36

Mauve Blue, Bowl, Vegetable, Lid, Rectangular	126
Mauve Blue, Plate, Dessert, 7 ¼ In.	28
Mauve Blue, Plate, Dinner, 9 ⅝ In.	128
Mauve Blue, Platter, Oval, 11 In.	44
Red, Creamer, 8 Oz., 2 ¾ In.	18
Red, Salt & Pepper, 7 Holes	42
Yellow, Bowl, Vegetable, Lid, Rectangular	160
Yellow, Cup, Footed	18

ROBLIN ART POTTERY was founded in 1898 by Alexander W. Robertson and Linna Irelan in San Francisco, California. The pottery closed in 1906. The firm made faience with green, tan, dull blue, or gray glazes. Decorations were usually animal shapes. Some red clay pieces were made.

Tile, Bluebell, Green, 3 In. Diam.	1250
Tile, Flower, Leaf, 2 ⅞ x 2 ⅞ In.	990
Vase, Green, Shoulder Band Design, Footed, c.1900, 2 In.	1102

ROCKINGHAM, in the United States, is a pottery with a brown glaze that resembles tortoiseshell. It was made from 1840 to 1900 by many American potteries. Mottled brown Rockingham wares were first made in England at the Rockingham factory. Other types of ceramics were also made by the English firm. Related pieces may be listed in the Bennington category.

Baking Dish, Molded, Rounded Rim, Yellow Brown Streaks, Summit Pottery, 13 x 10 In.	86
Candlestick, Mottled Green, Brown & Ivory Glaze, Square Stepped Base, 6 In., Pair	54
Compote, Pierced, Pinwheel Designs, Footed, c.1860, 5 x 10 ¼ In.	830
Cup & Saucer, Bouquet, Bird, Green Border	85
Figurine, Dog, Spaniel, Seated, c.1850, 10 ½ In.	150
Figurine, Lion, Paw On Globe, Vines, c.1850, 13 x 14 In.	750
Figurine, Ram, Lying Down, Curled Horns, Grassy Base, Brown, c.1850, 5 In.	115
Figurine, Spaniel, c.1890, 10 ¼ In., Pair	267
Flask, Book Shape, Blue Glaze, Jeffords Pottery, Philadelphia, c.1840, 5 In.	151
Flask, Book Shape, Flint, c.1815, 5 ½ In.	356
Flask, Fish Shape, Flattened Sides, Scale Detail, Brown Mottled Glaze, c.1890, 11 In.	201
Pitcher, Dog, Seated, Collar, Open Mouth Spout, c.1875, 8 ½ In.	316
Pitcher, Glazed, Embossed Horses, Figures, c.1850, 9 In.	35
Pitcher, Glazed, Embossed Hounds, c.1850, 9 ½ In.	115
Pitcher, Hunt Scene, Hound Handle, Harker & Taylor, 7 In.	588

ROGERS, see John Rogers category.

ROOKWOOD pottery was made in Cincinnati, Ohio, beginning in 1880. All of this art pottery is marked, most with the famous flame mark. The *R* is reversed and placed back to back with the letter *P*. Flames surround the letters. After 1900, a Roman numeral was added to the mark to indicate the year. The company went bankrupt in 1941. It was bought and sold several times after that. The name and some of the molds were bought by a collector in 1984. In 2004, investors bought the company and 3,700 original molds, the name, and trademark. Martin and Marilyn Wade bought the company in 2011. Today they make new items and remake some old items, architectural tile, art pottery, and special commissions. Pieces are marked with the *RP* mark and a Roman numeral for the four-digit date.

Ashtray, Devil Mask, Nubian Black Glaze, 1951, 3 ½ x 6 In.	126
Ashtray, Green Glaze, Ship Logo, 1957, 7 ¾ In.	46
Ashtray, Rook, Beige, 1954, 4 ¼ In.	259
Bookends, Angel, Clotilda Zanetta Design, White, Marked, 1945, 7 In.	649
Bookends, Bear, Walking, Blue & Tan Matte Glaze, 1923, 4 ¼ In. ....*illus*	1534
Bookends, Cornucopia, Green Matte Glaze, 1920, 4 ¾ In.	287
Bookends, Double Reader, Purple Matte Glaze, Marked, 1922, 7 In. ....*illus*	1062
Bookends, Dutch Girl & Boy, Multicolor High Glazes, Sallie Toohey, 1928, 6 In. ....*illus*	502
Bookends, Elephant, Trunk Down, Ivory Matte Glaze, 1919, 6 x 4 ½ In.	281
Bookends, Flower Basket, Multicolor High Glazes, Marked, 1929, 5 In. ....*illus*	561
Bookends, Nude Woman, Kneeling, White, Louise Abel, 1930, 7 In.	138
Bookends, Owl, On Book, Green High Glaze, 1949, 5 ⅝ In. ....*illus*	460
Bookends, Panther, Sitting, Brownish Orange Matte Glaze, 1935, 5 ½ In.	531
Bookends, Parrots, White, Pink, Flowers, Sallie Toohey, 1927, 5 ½ x 7 In.	1063
Bookends, Rook, Blue Over Tan Matte Glaze, 1925, 5 ⅜ In.	384
Bookends, Rook, Dark Blue Matte Glaze, Marked, 1926, 6 ¼ In.	1003
Bookends, Rooks, Tan Matte Glaze, William McDonald, 5 ½ x 5 ½ In.	344

Rookwood, Vase, Dandelions, Carrie Steinle, 1906, 4 In.
$330

Cowan's Auctions

Rookwood, Vase, Frogs, Octopi, Crab, Tug-Of-War, Dull Finish, M.L. Nichols, 1882, 10 x 7 In. Illus
$12,500

Rago Arts & Auction Center

Rookwood, Vase, Holly Branches, Berries, Iris Glaze, Sara Sax, 1904, 8 ½ In.
$1,534

Humler & Nolan

R

Rookwood, Vase, Monkeys, Seated In Tree, Bruce Horsfall, 1893, 8 ¾ In. $4,140

Humler & Nolan

Rookwood, Vase, Nudes, Flowers, Squeezebag, William Hentschel, 1927, 16 ⅝ In. $5,900

Humler & Nolan

Rookwood, Vase, Peacock Feather, Blue Matte Glaze, Production, 1919, 5 ⅜ In. $201

Humler & Nolan

Bowl, Flowers, Lorinda Epply, 1924, 13 x 3 In.	427
Bowl, Flowers, Vellum Glaze, Louise Abel, 1923, 4 ½ x 7 In.	875
Bowl, Ivory, Blue Interior, Petal Rim, 1918, 3 ¼ In.	35
Bowl, Vellum Glaze, Pink, Blue, Round, Footed, 1919, 4 ½ In.	107
Bowl, Yellow Flowers, Sara Sax, Marked, 1 ⅝ x 10 ½ In. ....*illus*	1610
Cup, Mustache, Cherry Blossom, Standard Glaze, Sallie Toohey, 1889, 4 ½ x 2 In.	563
Ewer, Autumn Leaves, Standard Glaze, C. Baker, 1897, 10 In.	184
Ewer, Cherry Blossoms, Silver Overlay, Standard Glaze, E. Foertmeyer, 1893, 7 x 10 In.	3500
Ewer, Fish, Gorham Silver Overlay, Albert Valentien, 1894, 12 ⅝ In. ....*illus*	7965
Ewer, Leaf, Berry, Silver Overlay, Standard Glaze, Handle, V. Demarest, 1901, 5 x 9 ½ In.	610
Ewer, Orange Blossom, Standard Glaze, Lobed Base, H. Strafer, 1893, 7 ½ In.	253
Figurine, Cat, Golden, 24K Gold Finish, Logo, 1989, 4 In.	106
Figurine, Dog, Chow, Smiling, Caramel Over White, High Glaze, 1936, 8 In.	1035
Flower Holder, Nude, Resting On Mushroom, Blue High Glaze, 1921, 6 ¼ In.	259
Jug, Corn, Standard Glaze, Silver Overlay Grapevine, Handle, Olga Reed, 1896, 6 x 8 In.	600
Jug, Portrait, After Champagne, Man With Mustache, Standard Glaze, G. Young, 1897, 5 In.	161
Mug, Hunting Scene, Dog, Man, Iris Glaze, Handle, Carl Schmidt, 1902, 5 x 5 In.	1186
Mug, Pinecones, Incised, Green, Tapered, L. Epply, 7 ⅜ In.	287
Paperweight, Cat, Seated, Orange Matte Glaze, William Hentschel, 1928, 5 ⅜ In. ....*illus*	295
Paperweight, Duck, Blue Matte Glaze, 1965, 2 ⅛ x 3 ¾ In.	230
Paperweight, Elephant, Green Matte Glaze, 1926, 3 ¼ In.	287
Paperweight, Fox, Reclining, Tan Matte Glaze, 1930, 2 ⅛ x 5 ½ In.	546
Paperweight, Ladybug, Green Matte Glaze, Red & Black High Glaze, 1936, 1 x 3 In.	4025
Paperweight, Lamb, Reclining, Ivory Matte Glaze, 1939, 2 ¾ In.	690
Paperweight, Lily, White Matte Glaze, c.1932, 4 In.	862
Paperweight, Rabbit, Yellow Glaze, 1940s, 3 ⅛ In.	460
Paperweight, Rooster, Multicolor, Square Base, 1946, 4 ⅞ In.	316
Perfume Jug, 3 Spiders, Webs, Painted, Applied Beads, Handle, 1883, 4 ¾ In. ....*illus*	480
Perfume Jug, Butterfly, Grasses, Clouds, Limoges Style, 1884, 4 ⅝ In. ....*illus*	265
Pitcher, Blue & White Flower, Cameo Glaze, Bulbous, A. Bookprinter, 1887, 6 ¼ In.	85
Pitcher, Cherry Blossoms, Brown Drip & Green Over Blue Glaze, Ball, Sax, 1925, 7 In.	968
Pitcher, Daisies, Handle, Albert Valentien, 6 x 9 ½ In.	375
Pitcher, Flower, Green Glaze, Logo, K.G., 1882, 4 ¾ In.	189
Pitcher, Flying Swallow, Grasses, Clouds, Handle, W. McDonald, 1882, 6 ½ In. ....*illus*	345
Pitcher, Toad Of Toad Hall, Silver Overlay, Bruce Horsfall, Gorham, 1893, 5 ¾ x 7 In. ....*illus*	4375
Plaque, Birch Trees, Lake, Lenore Asbury, Frame, 1917, 9 ⅜ x 12 ⅜ In. ....*illus*	4366
Plaque, Nudes Reclining, Blue, White, Round, Jensen, 1935, 16 In.	13750
Plaque, Scenic, Along The River, Vellum, Lorinda Epply, 1916, 8 ½ x 10 ½ In.	4720
Plaque, Scenic, River At Twilight, Vellum Glaze, C. Schmidt, Frame, c.1917, 9 x 11 In.	3480
Plaque, Scenic, Snow Cap, Vellum, Elizabeth McDermott, 1919, 9 x 14 ½ In.	3500
Plaque, Venetian Harbor Scene, Vellum Glaze, C. Schmidt, Frame, 1913, 16 x 14 ½ In.	5635
Plaque, Winter In The Woods, Ed Diers, 1914, 5 x 8 In.	3250
Tea Caddy, Lid, Dogwood Blossoms, Standard Glaze, Pinched, Laura Fry, 1885, 5 ¼ In.	666
Tile, Grapes, Vines, Pink, Green, Blue Ground, 1927, 5 ¾ x 5 ¾ In.	172
Tile, Ship Sailing, Frame, 12 In.	826
Tile, Swan, White & Blue Matte Glaze, 1924, 5 ¾ x 5 ¾ In.	259
Trivet, Pink Flowers, Green Leaves, Blue Ground, Star Shape, 1930, 6 In.	138
Trivet, Poppies, Multicolor Matte Glaze, 1931, 5 x 5 In.	172
Trivet, Purple Grapes, Green Leaves, Tan Ground, Star Shape, 1921, 6 In.	172
Trivet, Yellow Bird, Perched On Branch, Round, 6 In.	431
Vase, 3 Butterflies, Vellum Glaze, Lenore Asbury, 1905, 3 ½ x 4 ½ In.	1188
Vase, Abstract Purple Flowers, Aqua Matte Glaze, Bulbous, Z-Line, Matt Daly, 1902, 6 In.	182
Vase, Apple Blossoms, Branches, Vellum, Lenore Asbury, 1926, 9 ¾ In.	1800
Vase, Beech Tree Branches, Standard Glaze, Silver Overlay, E. Foertmeyer, 1892, 6 x 6 ½ In.	3500
Vase, Bird In Flight, Leaves, Yellow Ground, Standard Glaze, Bulbous, L. Fry, 1885, 11 In.	1694
Vase, Black Cranes, Diving, Sea Green, Matt Daly, 1899, 13 In. ....*illus*	27140
Vase, Blue Flowers, Tan Ground, Tapered, Jens Jensen, 1946, 12 In.	173
Vase, Blue Matte Glaze, Incised Neck Band, C.S. Todd, 1917, 9 ½ In.	604
Vase, Blue, 1921, 6 ½ In.	62
Vase, Blue, Green, Runny Matte Moderne Glaze, E. Barrett, 1927, 7 x 7 In.	688
Vase, Blue, Purple Landscape, Vellum Glaze, Tapered Cylinder, Fred Rothenbusch, 1918, 7 In.	1323
Vase, Blueberries On Branch, Vellum Glaze, Bulbous, Folded In Rim, E. Lincoln, 5 In.	484
Vase, Boats, Sea Green, Blue, Vellum Glaze, Baluster, Sallie Toohey, 1906, 17 ⅜ In.	1380
Vase, Bottle, Flowers, Leaves, Standard Glaze, Tapered, Shirayamadani, 1894, 12 In.	1089
Vase, Brown & Green Flowers, Yellow Ground, Black Inside, Flared, S. Sax, 1922, 6 In.	514
Vase, Brown Flowers, Raised, Yellow Ground, Green Band, Bulbous, E. Barrett, 7 In.	787

Vase, Brown, Abstract Gilding, Glossy Glaze, Pillow, 4 Feet, 1882, 8 In.	454
Vase, Cat, E.T. Hurley, 1902, 4 x 7 In.	6100
Vase, Charcoal Glaze, Round, 1884, 3 ½ x 2 ½ In.	344
Vase, Cherry Blossoms, Yellow Vellum, Lenore Asbury, 6 ½ In.	1265
Vase, Cherry Branches, Black Ground, Silver Overlay Neck, Bulbous, M. Perkins, 5 x 4 In.	976
Vase, Conifers, Blue, Orange Glaze, Cylindrical, S. Coyne, 1916, 9 x 3 ¼ In.	1063
Vase, Crocus, Black Opal Glaze, Handles, Sara Sax, 3 ½ x 8 In.	2250
Vase, Daffodil Spray, Standard Glaze, Lenore Asbury, 1903, 10 ¼ In.	1022
Vase, Daisies, Leaves, Cobalt & Green Standard Glaze, Swollen, Shirayamadani, 5 In.	1452
Vase, Dandelions, Carrie Steinle, 1906, 4 In. ....illus	330
Vase, Dogwood Flowers, Standard Glaze, Kidney Bean Shape, Pulled Rim, Valentien, 7 In.	266
Vase, Donkeys, At Fence, Standard Glaze, Tapered, Lobed, Bruce Horsfall, 1893, 5 x 7 In.	3750
Vase, Double Vellum Glaze, Blue Rim & Interior, Brown, Green Blossoms, 1930, 10 In.	1208
Vase, Ducks, Gray, Peach, Tapered, K. Shirayamadani, 1910,	2250
Vase, Flower, Carved Blue To Red, Matte Glaze, Beaker Shape, c.1913, 12 ¾ In.	1638
Vase, Flowers, Apricot, Forest Green, Vellum, F. Rothenbusch, 1919, 8 In.	316
Vase, Flowers, Blue Glaze, Shouldered, Squat, K. Shirayamadani, 1930, 5 In.	863
Vase, Flowers, Blue Ground, Vellum, Footed, Alice Craven, 1917, 9 ½ x 3 ½ In.	390
Vase, Flowers, Blue, Pink, Vellum, C. Schmidt, 1913, 6 x 3 In.	250
Vase, Flowers, Dark Blue Ground, Vellum Glaze, Tapered, K. Jones, 1923, 6 ⅞ In.	322
Vase, Flowers, Deep Blue Ground, Shouldered, Tapered, E.T. Hurley, 1924, 5 ½ x 13 In.	1952
Vase, Flowers, Green Ground, Vellum Glaze, Ed Diers, 1908, 8 ½ In.	489
Vase, Flowers, Incised, Pink, 1928, 6 In.	181
Vase, Flowers, Incised, Yellow Matte Glaze, 1926, 6 ¾ In.	138
Vase, Flowers, Lavender, Shouldered, Tapered, Katherine Jones, 1929, 7 x 4 ½ In.	600
Vase, Flowers, Leaves, Purple & Green, Matte Glaze, Shouldered, Rolled Rim, c.1925, 9 In.	1170
Vase, Flowers, Molded, Ivory Matte Glaze, Oval, Flared Rim, 12 In.	211
Vase, Flowers, Pink, Blue, White, Vellum Glaze, E. Diers, 1926, 7 x 4 In.	625
Vase, Flowers, Standard Glaze, 3 Handles Extend To Feet, Shirayamadani, 1888, 8 In.	968
Vase, Flowers, Standard Glaze, Handles, A. Willits, 1906, 5 In.	127
Vase, Flowers, Standard Glaze, Silver Overlay, Amelia Sprague, 1892, 5 x 10 In.	1250
Vase, Flowers, Turquoise Glaze, Globular, Sara Sax, 1924, 4 ¾ x 6 ¾ In.	196
Vase, Flowers, Vellum Glaze, M.H. McDonald, 1922, 8 ½ x 4 In.	938
Vase, Frogs, Octopi, Crab, Tug-Of-War, Dull Finish, M.L. Nichols, 1882, 10 x 7 In. ....illus	12500
Vase, Girl's Portrait, Standard Glaze, Pillow, Bruce Horsfall, 1894, 7 ¾ In.	1020
Vase, Golden Standard Glaze, Flared Rim, Bulbous, A. Valentien, 1886, 8 x 8 In.	600
Vase, Grapes, Leaves, Green Shaded To Blue, 8 In.	1320
Vase, Gray, Stick Neck, Bulbous Base, 10 In.	136
Vase, Greek Key, Incised, Pink, 1928, 6 In.	107
Vase, Green Glaze, Concave Shoulder, Bulbous Tapered, 1927, 7 In.	165
Vase, Green Matte Glaze, Incised Neck Band, 1904, 5 x 4 In.	600
Vase, Gunmetal Glaze, c.1948, 6 ¾ In.	120
Vase, Holly Berries, Purple Wax Matte Glaze, E.N. Lincoln, 1926, 9 x 5 In.	688
Vase, Holly Branches, Berries, Iris Glaze, Sara Sax, 1904, 8 ½ In. ....illus	1534
Vase, Hydrangea, Baluster, Iris Glaze, c.1898, 20 ½ In.	4740
Vase, Insects, Landscape, Textured Bands, Bulbous, Baluster Shape, 18 In.	1323
Vase, Iris Glaze, Gray Shaded To White, Irene Bishop, 1907, 6 x 4 In.	600
Vase, Iris Glaze, High Shouldered, Carl Schmidt, 1902, 6 x 17 In.	8750
Vase, Landscape, Cream Ground, Bulbous, Margaret McDonald, 1937, 5 x 6 In.	425
Vase, Landscape, Rural, Blue, Green, Cream Ground, Baluster, F. Rothenbusch, 1920, 5 In.	575
Vase, Landscape, Vellum Glaze, E.T. Hurley, 1919, 4 x 8 In.	2000
Vase, Landscape, Vellum Glaze, Gray, Pink, Yellow, Flared, L. Asbury, 1912, 4 ½ x 8 ¼ In.	800
Vase, Landscape, Vellum Glaze, Tapered, E.T. Hurley, 1948, 4 ½ x 7 ½ In.	1830
Vase, Lavender Iris Glaze, Shouldered, Carl Schmidt, 1901, 7 In.	334
Vase, Leaf, Standard Glaze, Sallie Coyne, 1899, 5 x 9 ½ In.	344
Vase, Lemon Tree, Wavy Rim, Standard Glaze, Matt Daly, 1889, 7 ½ x 25 In.	4700
Vase, Molded Squash, Pink, Green Matte Glaze, 1929, 6 x 14 In.	375
Vase, Monkeys, Seated In Tree, Bruce Horsfall, 1893, 8 ¾ In. ....illus	4140
Vase, Nudes, Flowers, Squeezebag, William Hentschel, 1927, 16 ⅝ In. ....illus	5900
Vase, Oak Leaves, Brown, Mottled Green, Painted Mat, Cylindrical, W. McDonald, 1901, 13 In.	1140
Vase, Oranges, Standard Glaze, Silver Overlay, Tapered, Handles, Harriet Wilcox, 8 x 9 In.	1750
Vase, Pansies, Standard Glaze, Ed Diers, 5 x 7 In.	350
Vase, Parrot & Leaves, Raised, Turquoise Glaze, Inward Folded Rim, Shirayamadani, 11 In.	460
Vase, Peace Lily, Wide Leaves, Pink Matte Glaze, 1919, 6 x 10 In.	406
Vase, Peacock Feather, Blue Matte Glaze, Production, 1919, 5 ⅜ In. ....illus	201
Vase, Pink & White Roses, Shirayamadani, 1925, 14 In. ....illus	3894

Rookwood, Vase, Pink & White Roses, Shirayamadani, 1925, 14 In.
$3,894

Humler & Nolan

Rookwood, Vase, Portrait, Native American, High Hawk, Sioux, Handles, Grace Young, 1900, 13 In.
$34,220

Humler & Nolan

Rookwood, Vase, Portrait, Old Man, Handles, Matt Daly, 1898, 13 ½ In.
$2,300

Humler & Nolan

R

Rookwood, Vase, Thistle, Iris Glaze, Tapered, Carl Schmidt, 1909, 10 ¾ In. $2,337

Skinner Auctioneers & Appraisers

Rookwood, Vase, Yellow Flowers, Gorham Silver Overlay, Sallie Coyne, 1893, 6 ¼ In. $1,265

Humler & Nolan

Rose Mandarin, Punch Bowl, Gilt Details, 1800s, 16 x 6 ½ In. $1,200

Garth's Auctioneers & Appraisers

Vase, Pink Blossom, Branch, Leaves, Vellum Glaze, Mary Nourse, 1905, 7 In.	360
Vase, Pink Flowers, Iris Glaze, Caroline Steinle, 1911, 3 ½ x 7 ½ In.	438
Vase, Poppies, Flared, Wax Matte Glaze, Elizabeth Lincoln, 1926, 8 x 15 In.	3000
Vase, Poppies, Red, Green, Matte Glaze, Tapered, Olga Reed, 1906, 4 ½ x 10 ½ In.	1625
Vase, Portrait, Native American, High Hawk, Sioux, Handles, Grace Young, 1900, 13 In. .....*illus*	34220
Vase, Portrait, Native American, Little Raven, Tapered, Grace Young, 1902, 5 x 11 In.	8750
Vase, Portrait, Old Man, Handles, Matt Daly, 1898, 13 ½ In. .....*illus*	2300
Vase, Purple Flowers, Blue Matte Glaze, Kataro Shirayamadani, 1926, 9 In.	1243
Vase, Red Flowers, Cream Matte Glaze, Black Rim, Oval, Ear Handles, C. Todd, 6 In.	454
Vase, Rooks, Molded Dark Blue Matte Glaze, Cylindrical, 6 ⅜ In.	196
Vase, Scenic, Banded, Lenore Asbury, c.1918, 7 x 4 ½ In.	1375
Vase, Scenic, Forest, Pink Shaded To Yellow Sky, Swollen, Shirayamadani, 9 In.	2541
Vase, Scenic, Landscape, Vellum Glaze, Swollen, Spread Foot, L. Asbury, 1913, 9 In.	1029
Vase, Stylized Flowers, Red, White, Blue, Vellum, Waisted, Asbury, 7 In.	1331
Vase, Stylized Tulips, Carved, Blue & Green Matte Glaze, Oval, C. Todd, 1917, 10 x 14 In.	1159
Vase, Sunrise, Lake, Pines, Tapered Cylinder, Elizabeth Lincoln, 5 ⅞ In.	413
Vase, Swollen, Stick Neck, Flowers, Footed, Pink, Violet, E. Barrett, 1946, 9 In.	461
Vase, Thistle, Iris Glaze, Tapered, Carl Schmidt, 1909, 10 ¾ In. .....*illus*	2337
Vase, Thistles, Green, Brown, Orange, Cream, Vellum, L. Epply, 1908, 6 x 4 In.	1000
Vase, Trees, Yellow, Green, Blue, Brown, Vellum Glaze, E.T. Hurley, 1909, 17 ½ In.	2530
Vase, Tulip, Green, Gray, White, Vellum Glaze, Sara Sax, 1905, 8 In.	661
Vase, Tulips, Black Opal Glaze, 11 ½ In.	242
Vase, Turquoise, Carved Neck, Rolled Rim, Baluster, c.1915, 14 In.	1287
Vase, Venetian Harbor Scene, Green Glaze, Carl Schmidt, 1923, 4 x 9 In.	4075
Vase, Vista Blue Glaze, Pinched Rim, 1959, 8 ½ x 8 In.	938
Vase, White Cat, Black Iris Glaze, E.T. Hurley, 1902, 4 x 9 In.	2375
Vase, White Dogwood, Iris Glaze, Edith Noonan, 1906, 5 In.	354
Vase, White Flower, Brown Stem, Yellow Ground, Round, M. Daly, 6 In.	575
Vase, White Flowers, Blue Shaded To Pink, Footed, E. T. Hurley, 1912, 8 x 4 In.	600
Vase, White Iris, Black Opal Glaze, Cylindrical, Swollen, Sara Sax, 1926, 16 In.	6655
Vase, White Swans, Iris Glaze, Tapered, K. Shirayamadani, 1898, 7 x 13 In.	10625
Vase, Wisteria, Wine Madder Glaze, 1955, 6 x 14 In.	406
Vase, Yellow Flower, Brown, Long Neck, F. Rothenbusch, 1900, 5 ¾ In.	98
Vase, Yellow Flowers, Gorham Silver Overlay, Sallie Coyne, 1893, 6 ¼ In. .....*illus*	1265
Vase, Yellow Flowers, Standard Glaze, Inverted Funnel Shape, Ruffled Rim, 1888, 7 ¾ In.	207
Vase, Yellow Flowers, Standard Glaze, Oval, Rolled Rim, Clara Lindeman, 1906, 5 In.	403
Vase, Yellow Iris, Standard Glaze, Wavy Rim, Anna Marie Valentien, 1898, 12 ½ In.	374
Wall Pocket, Blue Matte Glaze, Cone Shape, Panels, 1926, 7 In.	402
Wall Pocket, Gardenia, Brown, Fan Shape, Round Handles, 8 ¾ In.	748
Wall Pocket, Stylized Overlapping Leaves, Blue Gray Matte Glaze, 1920, 6 ¼ In.	288

RORSTRAND was established near Stockholm, Sweden, in 1726. By the nineteenth century Rorstrand was making English-style earthenware, bone china, porcelain, ironstone china, and majolica. The company is still working and is now owned by Fiskars Sweden. The three-crown mark has been used since 1884.

Rörstrand

Bowl, Brown, Cream, Marked, 7 In.	45
Bowl, Light Green, Red Center, 1950s, 20 In.	375
Bowl, Vegetable, Blue Fire, Oval, 1960s, 11 x 7 In.	80
Condiment Jar, Cobalt Blue, Ribbed, Ladle, 3 In.	45
Cup & Saucer, White, Blue, Flowers	53
Ewer, Glazed Stoneware, Flared Mouth, Gunnar Nylund, 1960s, 9 x 3 In.	500
Figurine, Hippopotamus, Glazed Stoneware, Gunnar Nylund, 1950s, 4 x 7 ½ In.	750
Jug, Houses, Trees, Loop Handle, 11 ¾ In.	375
Plate, Christmas, Shining Star, Birds, Seals, Flow Blue, 1978, 8 x 8 In.	20
Plate, Father's Day, Father & Son, Woodworking, 1972, 8 In.	10
Plate, Mother's Day, Woman Holding Child, Blue, 1972, 8 In.	10
Plate, Whimsical Figures, Flow Blue, Rounded Square, 1700s, 7 ¾ In.	99
Platter, Flora, Oval, c.1960, 14 x 8 In.	45
Stein, Satyr, Playing Music, Woman In Cart, Cupids, Birds, Man Handle, 13 In.	500
Sugar, Shaker, Blue Fire White, Pear Shape, c.1960, 3 ¾ In.	60
Vase, Flowers, White, Ice Blue, Crystalline Glaze, Squat, Stick Neck, Gilt Fittings, 8 In.	1500
Vase, Stylized Penguins, Tan, Black, Bulbous, Tapered, Signed, Nils Lundstrom, 6 x 11 In.	325
Vase, Wildflowers, Pillow, Flattened, Rectangular, Narrow Neck, 8 x 5 x 3 In.	85

ROSALINE, *see Steuben category.*

ROSE BOWLS were popular during the 1880s. Rose petals were kept in the open bowl to add fragrance to a room, a popular idea in a time of limited personal hygiene. The glass bowls were made with crimped tops, which kept the petals inside. Many types of Victorian art glass were made into rose bowls.

Cherry Blossoms, Spider Web, Drippy Feet, 4 x 5 In.	275
Cobalt Blue, White Honeycomb, 19th Century, 4 ½ x 3 ½ In.	80
Cranberry Pink, Mother-Of-Pearl, Herringbone, Victorian, c.1875, 3 x 3 In.	150
Flowers, Buds, Leaves, Paint, Enamel, Cream Ground, 4 x 5 In.	119
Grape Clusters, 6-Footed, Fluted Lip, Curled In, 4 x 4 In.	49
Green Satin Glass, Mother-Of-Pearl, Diamond Quilted, White Interior, 4 ¼ x 5 In.	237
Heart & Thumbprint, Gold Rim, c.1898, 2 ½ In.	40
Lavender Iridescent, Apricot Scrolls & Flowers, Victorian, 4 ½ In.	25
Lily Of The Valley, Painted, 2 ¾ x 3 In.	20
Rows Of Knobby Corn Kernels, Husks, Dusty Rose, Footed, 7 x 4 ¾ In.	170

ROSE CANTON china is similar to Rose Mandarin and Rose Medallion, except that no people or birds are pictured in the decoration. It was made in China during the nineteenth and twentieth centuries in greens, pinks, and other colors.

Cup & Saucer, Pink Roses, Stylized Symbols, Lithophane	150
Platter, Gold, Multicolor, 4 Panels, Roses, 13 In.	350
Platter, Peonies, Figures, Lobed, c.1850, 12 x 9 ¾ In.	288
Punch Bowl, Flower Medallions, White Ground, 13 x 5 In.	2950

ROSE MANDARIN china is similar to Rose Canton and Rose Medallion. If the panels in the design picture only people and not birds, it is Rose Mandarin.

Bowl, Bat Borders, Gilt, Orange Peel Glaze, Chinese, c.1850, 5 x 11 In.	176
Bowl, Pavilion Garden Scenes, Cut Corners, Chinese, c.1850, 5 x 9 ⅞ In.	1840
Bowl, People, Insects, Leaves, Cell & Diaper, Chinese, c.1780, 5 x 11 In.	3450
Bowl, People, Landscape, Orange Ground, Chinese, c.1820, 5 ½ x 13 In.	770
Cider Jug, Lid, People, Flowers, Barrel Shape, c.1850, 11 In.	1750
Garden Seat, Court Scenes, Barrel Shape, Chinese, c.1860, 19 x 13 In., Pair	8888
Punch Bowl, Gilt Details, 1800s, 16 x 6 ½ In. ....*illus*	1200
Punch Bowl, Multicolor, Courtyard Setting, People, Leaf Bands, 1800s, 14 ½ In.	750
Punch Bowl, Pink, Red Flowers, White Ground, Chinese, c.1850, 5 x 10 In.	273
Tankard, c.1850, 5 In.	385
Vase, Baluster, Gilded Foo Dogs & Dragons, Flowers, 1800s, 23 ½ In.	1230
Vase, Cartouches, Flower Ground, Lion Handles, Chinese, 18 In.	649
Vase, Lid, Painted Home Scenes, Blue Flowers, Scrolls, c.1800, 13 In., Pair	3840
Vase, Roses, Peonies, Scalloped Rim, Gilded Dragons, Footed, 8 In.	145
Washbowl, Round, Scene, c.1850, 16 In.	3444

ROSE MEDALLION china was made in China during the nineteenth and twentieth centuries. It is a distinctive design with four or more panels of decoration around a central medallion that includes a bird or a peony. The panels show birds and people. The background is a design of tree peonies and leaves. Pieces are colored in greens, pinks, and other colors. It is similar to Rose Canton and Rose Mandarin.

Bowl, Centerpiece, Gilt, Multicolor Figures, Flowers, c.1850, 6 ½ x 15 ¾ In.	2370
Bowl, People, Pavilions, Birds, c.1850, 5 x 11 In.	259
Candelabrum, 4-Light, Baluster Stem, Gilt Pierced Foot, c.1885, 22 x 9 In.	615
Charger, Courtyard Scenes, Multicolor, c.1850, 13 ¾ In.	153
Dish, Hot Water, Dome Lid, Handles, Scenes, c.1850, 7 x 14 In.	1045
Jardiniere, Birds, Butterflies, Goldfish Interior, 1900s, 14 x 15 ¾ In. ....*illus*	780
Platter, Oval, c.1865, 15 x 18 ¾ In.	889
Punch Bowl, Cylindrical, Wide Rim, 1900s, 9 ¼ x 18 In.	472
Punch Bowl, Dragon & Bat Border, Bronze Stand, Elephant Feet, 11 x 18 In.	1722
Punch Bowl, Gilt Bronze Pedestal Foot & Scroll Handles, c.1865, 15 x 18 In.	4920
Tray, Paneled, Oval, c.1900, 16 x 11 In.	240
Tureen, Underplate, Lid, People, Birds, Flowers, Gilt, Chinese, 13 x 14 In.	502
Umbrella Stand, Cylindrical, Carved Flowers, Birds, Chinese, 1800s, 30 ½ In.	360
Vase, Baluster, Lobed Sides, Gilt Metal Base, c.1885, 20 x 7 ½ In.	1353
Vase, Landscape, People, Birds, Gilt Dog Masks, Chinese, c.1850, 24 ½ In., Pair	1416
Vase, Palace, Applied Foo Dog Handles, Base Dragons, c.1865, 35 ½ In.	4029

ROSE O'NEILL, *see Kewpie category.*

Rose Medallion, Jardiniere, Birds, Butterflies, Goldfish Interior, 1900s, 14 x 15 ¾ In.
$780

Skinner Auctioneers & Appraisers

Rosenthal, Plate, Zeppelin III, Sammelteller Erinnerung Z.R. III, 1925, 8 ½ In.
$450

The Stein Auction Co.

Roseville, Baneda, Vase, Green, Leaves, Pumpkins, Handles, 6 In.
$225

Humler & Nolan

R

Roseville, Della Robbia, Vase, Daisies, Rozane, Initials, c.1905, 8 x 7 In.
$20,000

Roseville, Donatello, Jardiniere, Cherub, Landscape Band, Ribbed, 7 x 9 In.
$120

Roseville, Ferella, Vase, Tan, Green Accents, Squat, Openwork, 4 In.
$230

Roseville, Freesia, Cookie Jar, Blue, Handles, c.1940s
$144

ROSE TAPESTRY porcelain was made by the Royal Bayreuth factory of Tettau, Germany, during the late nineteenth century. The surface of the porcelain was pressed against a coarse fabric while it was still damp, and the impressions remained on the finished porcelain. It looks and feels like a textured cloth. Very skillful reproductions are being made that even include a variation of the Royal Bayreuth mark, so be careful when buying.

Creamer, Pink, White, Yellow Roses, Footed, Gilt Handle, 3 ½ x 4 In.	99
Tray, Dresser, White & Pink Roses, Gold Rim, 11 ½ x 8 In.	59
Vase, Flowers, Scalloped Rim, Handles, c.1875, 3 ¼ In.	100
Vase, Pink & White Roses, Bulbous, Stick Neck, 4 ¾ In.	78
Vase, Roses, Gold Trim, Oval, 5 ¼ x 3 ⅛ In.	115

ROSEMEADE POTTERY of Wahpeton, North Dakota, worked from 1940 to 1961. The pottery was operated by Laura A. Taylor and her husband, R.I. Hughes. The company was also known as the Wahpeton Pottery Company. Art pottery and commercial wares were made.

Figurine, Dog, Borzoi, Bronze Metallic, 7 x 9 In.	150
Flower Holder, Tulip Shape, Hole In Petals, Blue Matte Glaze, 3 In.	29
Salt & Pepper, Dog's Head, Chow, Red, Black	139
Salt & Pepper, Pelican, Pink, Green Base, 3 In.	125
Salt & Pepper, Pheasant, Male, Female, Tails Up, Brown, Tan, c.1950	45
Salt & Pepper, Skunk, Black & White, Tails Up, Paper Label, 2 ½ x 3 In.	65
Vase, Deer, Kneeling, Yellow Matte Glaze, 1950s, 3 ½ x 3 In.	36
Vase, Deer, Standing, Leafy Fronds, Yellow, Pink, 8 In.	55

ROSENTHAL porcelain was made at the factory established in Selb, Bavaria, in 1880. The factory is still making fine-quality tablewares and figurines. A series of Christmas plates was made from 1910. Other limited edition plates have been made since 1971. In 1998 Rosenthal was acquired by the Waterford Wedgwood Group. Rosenthal was bought by Sambonet Paderno Industries, headquartered in Orfento, Novaro, Italy, in 2009. Rosenthal china is still being produced in Bavaria.

Charger, Classical Profile, Gilt, Cobalt Blue Border, 12 In., Pair	344
Cruet, Milk Glass, Face, 3-Dimensional, Raised Features, 6 In.	125
Figurine, Child Riding Grasshopper, Stamped, c.1900, 3 ½ x 4 In.	563
Figurine, Dog, Borzoi, Black & White, M. Valentin, 15 In.	173
Figurine, Woman, Nude, Crouched, White, Marked, Fritz Klimsch, c.1955, 24 x 7 In.	469
Ginger Jar, Lid, Blue, White, Gilt Trim, 12 In.	42
Plate, Zeppelin III, Sammelteller Erinnerung Z.R. III, 1925, 8 ½ In. ....*illus*	450
Tea & Coffee Set, White On White, Rows Of Ovals, Bulbous, Domed Lids, 4 Piece	55
Vase, Bowl, Fantasy, Studio Line, Cobalt Blue Ground, Bjorn Wiinblad, 10 & 9 In.	300

ROSEVILLE POTTERY COMPANY was organized in Roseville, Ohio, in 1890. Another plant was opened in Zanesville, Ohio, in 1898. Many types of pottery were made until 1954. Early wares include Sgraffito, Olympic, and Rozane. Later lines were often made with molded decorations, especially flowers and fruit. Most pieces are marked *Roseville.* Many reproductions made in China have been offered for sale the past few years.

Apple Blossom, Basket, Hanging, Yellow, Green Ground, Tapered, 8 In.	115
Apple Blossom, Basket, Pink, Footed, Circle Handle, 8 ½ x 8 In.	150
Apple Blossom, Bowl, Blue, Handles, 3 ¾ x 18 In.	125 to 150
Apple Blossom, Candlestick, Blue, 2 x 3 ½ In., Pair	80
Apple Blossom, Ewer, Blue, Handle, 15 ½ In.	425
Apple Blossom, Rose Bowl, Bulbous, Blue, 6 x 9 ½ In.	150
Apple Blossom, Vase, Green, Asymmetrical Rim, Low Handles, 10 ¼ In.	98
Apple Blossom, Wall Pocket, Blue, Handle, 8 ½ x 6 In.	200
Apple Blossom, Wall Pocket, Green, Handle, 8 ½ x 6 In.	225
Apple Blossom, Wall Pocket, Pink, 8 ⅜ In.	173
Apple Blossom, Wall Pocket, Twig Handle, 8 ½ x 6 In.	225
Artcraft, Jardiniere, Black, 6 ¼ x 9 In.	215
Artcraft, Jardiniere, Blue, Green, Tan Matte Glaze, 12 x 8 In.	431
Artcraft, Jardiniere, Ivory, 5 ½ x 7 In.	185
Artcraft, Jardiniere, White Glaze, Buttresses, 5 ¼ x 7 In.	200
Aztec, Jardiniere, Pedestal, Blue, Artist's Cipher, c.1915, 35 ½ x 16 In.	1875
Aztec, Pitcher, Yellow Squeezebag Designs, Blue Ground, 5 x 7 In.	127
Azurean, Vase, Blue, Swimming Fish, Cylindrical, Shouldered, 13 In.	1195
Azurean, Vase, Bulbous, Blue, 5 ½ x 4 In.	225
Azurean, Vase, White Pansies, Blue Ground, Long Neck, Squat Base, 5 ¼ In.	127
Baneda, Bowl, Green, Globular, Tab Handles, Footed, 5 ¼ x 6 ¾ In.	450

Baneda, Candlestick, Pink, Octagonal Base, Foil Label, 5 In., Pair	625
Baneda, Jardiniere, Green, Blue, Round, Handles, 4 In.	207
Baneda, Vase, Green, Flowers, Leaves, Footed, Handles, 7 In.	127
Baneda, Vase, Green, Footed, Handles, 7 ¼ In.	265
Baneda, Vase, Green, Leaves, Pumpkins, Handles, 6 In. *illus*	225
Baneda, Vase, Green, Low Open Handles, c.1933, 12 ½ x 6 ½ In.	978
Baneda, Vase, Orange Flower Band, Green, Round, Blue Base, Handles, 6 x 7 In.	316
Baneda, Vase, Pink, Shouldered, Footed, Handles, 6 ½ x 6 ½ In.	325
Bittersweet, Basket, Hanging, White, Pink, Round Brown Handles, 8 In.	104
Bittersweet, Bookends, Gray, Marked, 5 ¼ x 4 ½ In.	165
Bittersweet, Bookends, Yellow, 5 ¼ x 4 ½ In.	160
Bittersweet, Cornucopia, Yellow, Base, 4 ½ x 6 In.	100
Bittersweet, Double Cornucopia, Gray, 4 ¼ x 8 ½ In.	95
Blackberry, Jardiniere, Green, Orange, Leaves, 5 In.	219
Blackberry, Vase, Green, Handles, 8 ¼ In.	242
Bleeding Heart, Cornucopia, Green, Footed, 6 x 7 ¼ In.	115
Bleeding Heart, Jardiniere, Pedestal, Blue Ground, 1940s, 32 x 18 In.	813
Bleeding Heart, Jardiniere, Pedestal, Blue, Base Handles, 25 ½ In.	546
Bleeding Heart, Rose Bowl, Pink, Round, Hexagonal Rim, Handles, 6 ¼ In.	63
Bushberry, Cornucopia, Blue, Marked, 8 ½ x 7 In.	120
Bushberry, Jar, Sand, Orange Berries, Green Ground, Handles, 14 x 13 In.	805
Bushberry, Vase, Cornucopia, Brown, Footed, 6 In.	85
Bushberry, Wall Pocket, Red Berries, Brown, Asymmetrical Handles, 8 In.	138
Capri, Ashtray, Green, Art Deco, Marked, 1 ¼ x 7 ½ In.	45
Capri, Bowl, Mottled Red, Art Deco, 2 ¾ x 9 ¼ In.	110
Carnelian I, Wall Pocket, Drip Glaze, Triangular Rim, Base, 8 ½ In.	98
Carnelian II, Flower Frog, Blue, 1 ½ x 3 ¾ In.	50
Carnelian II, Pitcher, Mottled Blue, 12 In.	138
Carnelian II, Vase, Green, Stepped Smokestack Shape, 16 In.	1208
Carnelian II, Vase, Red, Green Drip Glaze, Handles, 9 In.	316
Carnelian II, Wall Pocket, Green, 7 In.	28
Carnelian II, Wall Pocket, Handles, 8 In.	138
Clematis, Bowl, Green, Oval, Shaped Handles, 14 ½ In.	40
Clematis, Vase, Blue, Bulbous Base, Angular Handles, 7 ¼ In.	29
Clematis, Vase, White Flowers, Blue Ground, Shouldered Cylindrical, Handles, 6 In.	184
Columbine, Basket, Hanging, Pink, 8 ½ In.	81
Columbine, Basket, Hanging, Yellow Flowers, Green Leaves, Blue Ground, 8 ¾ In.	98
Columbine, Bookends, Pink, 5 ¼ x 5 In.	225
Cosmos, Planter, Green, Brown, Handles, 4 In.	34
Cosmos, Vase, Brown, Flared Rim, Low Handles, 6 In.	51
Cosmos, Vase, Tan, Bulbous Bottom, Cylindrical Neck, Handles, 6 ½ In.	58
Crystallis, Vase, Blue Snowflake Crystals, Tan Ground, Tapered To Waist, 10 In.	480
Dahlrose, Vase, Handles, Footed, Marked, 6 ¼ x 3 ½ In.	110
Dahlrose, Wall Pocket, Green, Squared, Handles, 10 In.	52
Dahlrose, Wall Pocket, Handles, 10 ¼ x 7 In.	295
Dawn, Vase, Green, Square Foot, Handles, 6 ¼ In.	135
Dawn, Vase, Pink, Bulbous, Footed, Handles, 6 x 5 ¼ In.	125
Della Robbia, Vase, Blue Flowers, Green Leaves, Vines, Tapered, 15 x 7 In.	10800
Della Robbia, Vase, Daisies, Rozane, Initials, c.1905, 8 x 7 In. *illus*	20000
Dogwood I, Vase, Bud, Green, Yellow, Flared Base, 8 ¾ In.	69
Dogwood I, Wall Pocket, White Flowers, Textured Green, 9 ⅜ In.	161
Donatello, Bowl, Brown, 2 ¼ x 7 ¼ In.	50
Donatello, Compote, Cherub Band, Green, Cream, Brown, Ribbed, Footed, 5 In.	57
Donatello, Jardiniere, Cherub, Landscape Band, Ribbed, 7 x 9 In. *illus*	120
Donatello, Jardiniere, Pedestal, Green, Brown Ribbed Bands, Scenes, c.1945, 28 In.	230
Donatello, Umbrella Stand, Green, Brown, 21 x 10 ¼ In.	325
Donatello, Vase, Brown, Green, Flared Rim, Handles, 6 ¼ x 3 ¾ In.	595
Donatello, Vase, Bud, Double, Green, Brown, Ribbed, 4 ¼ x 8 In.	65
Donatello, Vase, Shouldered, Elongated Handles, 10 ½ In.	1195
Donatello, Wall Pocket, Tan, Classical Band, 10 In.	69
Earlam, Bowl, Brown, Green, Loop Handles, 3 ¼ x 11 ½ In.	295
Earlam, Vase, Brown, Green, Globular, 2 Handles, 7 x 8 ¼ In.	995
Earlam, Vase, Brown, Squared Rim, 8 ¾ In.	316
Egypto, Vase, Green Matte Glaze, Bulbous, Stick Neck, 5 ½ In.	323
Falline, Candlestick, Tan, Green Accents, Handles, 4 ¼ In., Pair	165
Falline, Vase, Blue, Green, Orange, Bulbous, Handles, Foil Label, 6 ¼ x 8 ¼ In.	1195

Roseville, Freesia, Jardiniere, Pedestal, Stalks Of Flowers, Handles, Marked, 25 In.
$472

Humler & Nolan

Roseville, Futura, Vase, Cone, Telescoping Buttresses, Green, Tan, 8 ⅛ In.
$288

Humler & Nolan

Roseville, Imperial I, Vase, Textured, Leaves, 15 ½ In.
$374

Humler & Nolan

R

Roseville, Jonquil, Jardiniere, Pedestal, Handles, Marked, 28 In.
$1,298

Humler & Nolan

Roseville, Ming Tree, Vase, Stylized Tree, Branch Handles, 14 ½ In.
$288

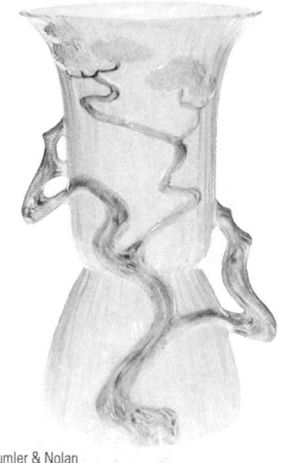

Humler & Nolan

Roseville, Rosecraft Panel, Vase, Nudes, Brown, Orange, Handles, 11 ½ In.
$830

James D. Julia Auctioneers

Falline, Vase, Blue, Large Handles, 6 ¾ In.	253
Falline, Vase, Orange, Green Demilune Inserts, Handles, 7 In.	104
Ferella, Vase, Flared Rim, Red, Footed, 8 ¼ In.	895
Ferella, Vase, Red, Handles, 6 In.	253
Ferella, Vase, Tan, Green Accents, Squat, Openwork, 4 In. *illus*	230
Ferella, Wall Pocket, Urn Shape, Brown, Green, 6 ¾ x 6 ½ In.	1025
Florane, Vase, Handles, 6 ⅛ In.	29
Florentine, Wall Pocket, Incised Rows, Brown, 7 In.	58
Foxglove, Basket, Hanging, Pink, Mauve, Handles, 10 In.	80
Foxglove, Bookends, Blue, 5 ¾ x 5 ½ In.	215
Foxglove, Bowl, Blue, Globular, Handles, 6 ½ x 9 In.	185
Foxglove, Cornucopia, Blue, Marked, 5 ¾ x 6 ¼ In.	75
Foxglove, Ewer, Blue, Squat, Handle, 6 ¾ x 7 ½ In.	135
Foxglove, Ewer, Green, Handle, 6 ¾ x 7 ½ In.	135
Foxglove, Ewer, Pink, Handle, Footed, 10 ½ x 6 In.	175
Foxglove, Vase, Blue, Bulbous, Handles, 6 ¼ In.	125
Foxglove, Vase, Pink, Cylindrical, Handles, Footed, 8 ¼ x 5 ¾ In.	145
Foxglove, Wall Pocket, Blue, Shaped Rim, 8 ⅜ In.	161
Freesia, Basket, Brown, 8 x 8 ½ In.	145
Freesia, Basket, Green, Triangular, Tapered, Handle, 7 In.	51
Freesia, Candlestick, Blue, Handles, 5 x 3 ¾ In., Pair	95
Freesia, Console, Blue, Handles, 3 ½ x 14 In.	95
Freesia, Cookie Jar, Blue, Handles, c.1940s *illus*	144
Freesia, Cookie Jar, Lid, Blue, 11 In.	208
Freesia, Ewer, Green, 15 ¾ In.	173
Freesia, Ewer, Yellow, Purple Flowers, Green Ground, Marked, 15 ½ In.	196
Freesia, Jardiniere, Pedestal, Blue Matte Glaze, 20th Century, 24 ½ In.	288
Freesia, Jardiniere, Pedestal, Stalks Of Flowers, Handles, Marked, 25 In. *illus*	472
Freesia, Tea Set, Green, 3 Piece	109
Freesia, Vase, Bud, Blue, Bulbous, Stick Neck, 7 ½ In.	135
Fuchsia, Bowl, Flower Frog, Brown, Mushroom Shape, 3 ¼ x 5 In.	100
Fuchsia, Jardiniere, Handles, Marked, 6 In.	69
Fuchsia, Pitcher, Brown, 8 x 9 In.	425
Fuchsia, Planter, Underplate, Green, Handles, 6 In.	90
Fuchsia, Vase, Blue, Handles, 9 ¼ In.	242
Fujiyama, Vase, Daffodils, Flared Bottom, 8 ½ In.	695
Futura, Beer Mug, Orange, Brown, Stepped Neck, Handles, 6 In.	81
Futura, Bowl, Applied Flowers, Leaves, Green, Caramel Glaze, Footed, 6 ½ x 5 In.	445
Futura, Jardiniere, Pedestal, Orange Ground, High Waisted, Handles, 28 In.	1830
Futura, Vase, Blue, Shooting Star, Stepped Base, 10 x 5 In.	570
Futura, Vase, Blue, Weeping Tulip, 12 ¾ In.	1840
Futura, Vase, Bottle, Stick Neck, Green, Pink, 8 In.	150
Futura, Vase, Cone, Telescoping Buttresses, Green, Tan, 8 ⅛ In. *illus*	288
Futura, Vase, Egg With Leaves, Brown, Tan, 8 In.	207
Futura, Vase, Fan, Chevrons, Blue, Brown, 9 x 6 In.	242
Futura, Vase, Green, Yellow, Twisted, 7 In.	242
Futura, Vase, Orange, Gray, Egg Shape, Footed, Square Base, 7 ½ In.	518
Futura, Vase, Orange, Green, 8 In.	390
Futura, Vase, Pink, Green, Twisted Hexagon, 8 In.	127
Futura, Vase, Shooting Star, 2-Tone, Green, Tapered, 10 In.	150
Futura, Vase, Telescope Neck, Green, Orange, Handles, 7 In.	104
Futura, Vase, Torch, Geometric, Flared, Stepped Top, Gray & Green Matte Glaze, 6 In.	363
Futura, Vase, Yellow To Green, Tapered, 12 x 4 ½ In.	780
Gardenia, Wall Pocket, Brown, Fan Shape, Round Handles, 8 ¾ In.	80
Gardenia, Wall Pocket, Gray, Fan Shape, 8 ½ In.	81
Imperial I, Vase, Textured, Leaves, 15 ½ In. *illus*	374
Imperial I, Wall Pocket, Green, Brown, Double Opening, 10 In.	115
Imperial II, Vase, Blue, Crystalline Glaze, Yellow Drip, 11 ½ x 7 In.	840
Imperial II, Vase, Blue, Green & Brown Drip, 7 In.	161
Imperial II, Vase, Brown, Burnt Orange, Tapered, Handles, 8 In.	253
Imperial II, Vase, Green, Blue Drip, Ribbed Bands, 5 In.	161
Imperial II, Vase, Green, Cutout Neck Band, Squat, 4 ½ x 6 In.	104
Imperial II, Vase, Green, Ribbed, Tapered, 4 ½ x 8 In.	115
Imperial II, Vase, Purple, Yellow Mottled, Tapered, 6 In.	184
Imperial II, Vase, Red, Ribbed Neck, 7 In.	207
Imperial II, Vase, Volcanic Glaze, Green Over Orange, Flared Rim, 6 x 6 ½ In.	390

Imperial II, Wall Pocket, Triple, 8 x 6 ½ In.	242
Iris, Jardiniere, Blue, Handles, 6 x 8 In.	175
Iris, Jardiniere, Brown, Globular, Squat, Handles, 5 In.	29
Iris, Jardiniere, Brown, Handles, Footed, 3 ½ x 5 ¼ In.	70
Iris, Vase, Cornucopia, Blue, 6 ¼ x 5 In.	145
Ivory II, Cornucopia, 9 ¼ x 8 ¾ In.	30
Jonquil, Bowl, Round, Handles, 4 In.	81
Jonquil, Jardiniere, Pedestal, Handles, Marked, 28 In. ....*illus*	1298
Juvenile, Creamer, Tan, Brown Band, 3 ½ In.	40
Laurel, Vase, Green Glaze, Handles, 7 In.	219
Laurel, Vase, Green, 7 ¼ In.	92
Laurel, Vase, Green, Orange, Stepped Neck, 9 In.	276
Lombardy, Wall Pocket, Lobed, Green, 8 In.	115
Luffa, Vase, Brown, Incised Wavy Green Lines, 6 In.	75
Magnolia, Ashtray, Blue, 7 ¼ In.	95
Magnolia, Ashtray, Brown, 7 ¼ In.	70
Magnolia, Cornucopia, Blue, 5 ¾ x 6 ½ In.	80
Magnolia, Creamer, Brown, 3 ¼ x 5 ½ In.	60
Magnolia, Jardiniere, Pedestal, Green, 30 In.	328
Matte Green, Jardiniere, Pedestal, Incised Bowl, Tripart Support, 13 x 30 In.	1063
Matte Green, Planter, 5 In.	161
Mayfair, Wall Pocket, Corner, Green, Yellow Interior, 8 In.	75
Ming Tree, Bookends, White, 5 x 5 ¼ In.	135
Ming Tree, Conch Shell, Blue, 5 ¼ x 8 ¼ In.	95
Ming Tree, Vase, Stylized Tree, Branch Handles, 14 ½ In. ....*illus*	288
Ming Tree, Wall Pocket, Brown Craggy Branch Handle, White, 8 ½ In.	150
Mock Orange, Basket, Hanging, Green, Round, 7 ½ In.	104
Monticello, Vase, Blue, Basket, 6 ½ In.	184
Monticello, Vase, Blue, Brown, Handles, 7 In.	127
Monticello, Vase, Blue, Handles, 4 In.	115
Monticello, Vase, Brown, Handles, 4 In.	150
Morning Glory, Vase, Green, Square Handles, 6 ¼ In.	265
Moss, Vase, Leaves, Orange, Tapered, Angular Handles, 12 ½ In.	161
Moss, Vase, Pillow, Orange Shaded To Green, Footed, Handles, 8 ½ In.	150
Mostique, Vase, Ecru, Yellow, Red, Green, Arts & Crafts Designs, 10 In.	130
Mostique, Wall Pocket, Stylized Flowers, Green Ground, 10 In.	104
Orian, Vase, Brown Glaze, Turquoise Interior, Low Handles, 9 ¼ In.	115
Pauleo, Vase, Purple, Gold, Shouldered, Tapered, 11 ¾ In.	184
Peony, Basket, Yellow, Spread Foot, 10 In.	104
Peony, Conch Shell, Yellow & Green, Footed, 6 ½ x 9 ½ In.	150
Peony, Cornucopia, Pink, 8 ¼ x 7 In.	85
Peony, Ewer, Yellow, 15 ¼ In.	75
Peony, Ewer, Yellow, Tapered Neck, Long Spout, 10 In.	46
Peony, Teapot, Pink, Footed, 8 ¼ x 9 ½ In.	150
Peony, Window Box, Yellow, 8 In.	18
Persian, Basket, Hanging, Creamware, Green & Yellow Lotus, Round, 7 In.	120
Persian, Jardiniere, Pedestal, Stylized Flowers, Creamware, c.1928, 32 x 15 In.	219
Pine Cone, Ashtray, Green, Round, 4 ¾ In.	29
Pine Cone, Bookends, Planter, Brown, 5 ¼ x 5 In.	500
Pine Cone, Bowl, Green, 11 In.	127
Pine Cone, Jardiniere, Blue, Bulbous, Tapered, Branch Handles, Footed, 8 ½ x 7 In.	330
Pine Cone, Pitcher, Ball Shape, Green, 7 ¾ x 8 ½ In.	395
Pine Cone, Vase, Brown, Flared, Round Foot, Marked, 6 ¼ In.	59
Pine Cone, Vase, Green, Bulbous, Gold Foil Label, 6 In.	118
Poppy, Vase, Pink, Blue, Bulbous, Footed, Handles, 9 In.	81
Primrose, Basket, Hanging, Yellow Flower, Pink, Round, Handles, 8 In.	80
Primrose, Vase, Peach Blossoms, Green Ground, Shouldered, Angular Handles, 6 In.	86
Rosecraft Panel, Vase, Nudes, Brown, Orange, Handles, 11 ½ In. ....*illus*	830
Rosecraft Panel, Vase, Nudes, Stamped, RV, 10 ¼ In. ....*illus*	575
Rozane Royal Dark, Pitcher, Scroll Handle, 15 ½ In.	120
Rozane Royal, Vase, Peach Tulip, Green Ground, Ball Shape, Footed, 4 x 5 ½ In.	161
Rozane Royal, Vase, Pink Flowers, Cream Ground, Flared, Signed, W. Myers, 8 ⅞ In.	127
Rozane, Tankard, Grapes, Leaves, Brown, 14 ½ x 6 ¼ In.	32
Rozane, Umbrella Stand, Scalloped Top, Cinched, Square, 22 ½ x 11 In.	825
Silhouette, Vase, Cornucopia, White, 8 In.	29
Silhouette, Vase, Green, Flared Rim, 9 In.	57
Silhouette, Wall Pocket, Rusty Red, Fanned Rim & Handles, 8 In.	75

Roseville, Rosecraft Panel, Vase, Nudes, Stamped, RV, 10 ¼ In.
$575

Humler & Nolan

Roseville, Vista, Vase, Basket, Trees, Oblong, 6 ¾ In.
$165

Humler & Nolan

Royal Bayreuth, Creamer, Embossed Gold Band, Flowers, Marked, After 1902
$50

Ruby Lane, Inc.

R

TIP

The best time to buy an antique is when you see it.

Royal Bayreuth, Creamer, Tomato, Leaf Spout, Stem Handle, 5 x 3 ¾ In.
$85

Ruby Lane, Inc.

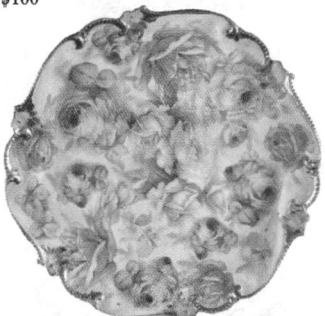

Royal Bayreuth, Plate, Rose Tapestry, Gold Trim, Blue Mark, 9 ½ In.
$100

Ruby Lane, Inc.

Royal Bayreuth, Plate, Shepherdess, Flock Of Goats, Pond, Gold Rim, 9 In.
$85

Ruby Lane, Inc.

Royal Bayreuth, Vase, Hunt Scene, Riders, Horses, Stylized Leaf Handles, Blue Mark, c.1900, 5 x 6 In.
$75

Ruby Lane, Inc.

Snowberry, Basket, Hanging Applied Yellow Berries, Green, Brown, 8 In.	69
Snowberry, Console Set, Blue, 10-In. Bowl, 4 ½-In. Candlesticks, 3 Piece	58
Snowberry, Cornucopia, Pink, Marked, 6 ¼ x 5 In.	70
Snowberry, Vase, Green, White Flowers, Handles, Footed, 18 ¾ In.	288
Sunflower, Basket, Hanging, Orange, Squat, 5 x 7 In.	390
Sunflower, Vase, Handles, 5 ⅛ In.	276
Sunflower, Vase, Handles, 8 In.	575
Sunflower, Vase, Jardiniere, 4 In.	316
Sunflower, Vase, No. 512-5, 5 ¼ In.	138
Sunflower, Vase, Yellow, Green, 8 In.	196
Sunflower, Wall Pocket, 7 ⅜ In.	690
Thorn Apple, Vase, Pink, Green, Bulbous, Flared Rim, Foil Label, 9 ½ In.	138
Thorn Apple, Wall Pocket, Brown, 9 In.	52
Tuscany, Flower Frog, Green, 1 ½ x 3 ¾ In.	40
Tuscany, Flower Frog, Pink, 1 ¾ x 3 ¾ In.	40
Velmoss, Jardiniere, Overlapping Green Leaves, 7 ⅞ In.	403
Velmoss, Vase, Green, Orange Leaves, Zanesville, Ohio, 11 ¾ x 8 In.	375
Vista, Basket, Hanging, Pink Flowers, Green, Blue Ground, Squat, 8 ¾ In.	92
Vista, Umbrella Stand, Green, 19 ¾ x 10 In.	1095
Vista, Vase, Basket, Green, Blue Flowers, Handle, 10 In.	403
Vista, Vase, Basket, Trees, Oblong, 6 ¾ In. ....*illus*	165
Vista, Vase, Yellow, Purple Flowers, Trees, Cylindrical, 14 ¾ In.	288 to 518
Vista, Wall Pocket, Flowers, Flowering Trees, Green Ground, 9 ½ In.	219
White Rose, Bookends, Pink & Green, 4 ½ x 5 ¼ In.	155
White Rose, Jardiniere, Pedestal, Blue Ground, 1940s, 15 x 12 In.	313
White Rose, Vase, Fan, Blue, 9 ¼ In.	58
Wincraft, Basket, Hanging, Ivy Vine, Yellow Ground, Round, 6 In.	69
Wincraft, Bookends, Orange, Art Deco, 6 ¼ x 5 In.	100
Wincraft, Ewer, Blue, 8 ¼ In.	52
Wincraft, Vase, Cornucopia, Chartreuse, Yellow, Green, c.1945, 5 x 9 In.	60
Wincraft, Vase, Flower, Cylindrical, Footed, 10 ¼ In.	46
Windsor, Vase, Ferns, Blue Ground, Loop Handles, 7 In.	138
Windsor, Vase, Impressed Ferns, Blue Matte Glaze, Handles, 7 ¼ In.	230
Wisteria, Vase, Brown, Squat, Handles, 6 ½ In.	127
Woodland, Vase, Incised Berries, Leaves, Tan, 6 ½ In.	230
Zephyr Lily, Vase, Green, Orange, Yellow Flowers, Handles, 11 In.	115

ROWLAND & MARSELLUS COMPANY is part of a mark that appears on historical Staffordshire dating from the late nineteenth and early twentieth centuries. *Rowland & Marsellus* is the mark used by an American importing company in New York City. The company worked from 1893 to about 1937. Some of the pieces may have been made by the British Anchor Pottery Co. of Longton, England, for export to a New York firm. Many American views were made. Of special interest to collectors are the plates with rolled edges, usually blue and white.

Bowl, St. Louis, Missouri, Blue & White, Rolled Edge, 10 In.	125
Cup & Saucer, Blue & White	50
Plate, Annapolis Basin, Nova Scotia, Canada, Flow Blue, 10 In.	95
Plate, Chicago, Illinois, Flow Blue, 10 In.	95
Plate, Great American Poets, Blue & White, 10 In.	175
Plate, Harrisburg, Pennsylvania, Blue & White, 10 In.	71
Plate, Hartford, Connecticut, Blue & White, c.1903, 10 ⅛ In.	125
Plate, Longfellow, Blue & White, Rolled Edge, 10 In.	100
Plate, Minneapolis, Minnesota, Cobalt Blue, 10 In.	85
Plate, New Post Office, Chicago, Brownish-Red Transfer, 1921, 6 In.	45
Plate, New York City, Dark Blue, c.1900, 10 In.	89
Plate, Niagara Falls, Canada, Flow Blue, c.1900, 10 In.	69
Plate, Zanesville, Ohio, Rolled Edge, Blue & White, 10 ½ In.	78
Platter, Turkey, Blue, c. 1920, 20 x 16 In.	275

ROY ROGERS was born in 1911 in Cincinnati, Ohio. In the 1930s, he made a living as a singer; in 1935, his group started work at a Los Angeles radio station. He appeared in his first movie in 1937. From 1952 to 1957, he made 101 television shows. The other stars in the show were his wife, Dale Evans, his horse, Trigger, and his dog, Bullet. Roy Rogers memorabilia, including items from the Roy Rogers restaurants, are collected.

Calendar, 1959, Nestle's Premium, 10 x 13 ⅞ In.	153
Cap Gun, Holster, Long Tom 6-Shooter, Plastic Grips, 10 In., Pair	1518

Cap Gun, Silver Metal, White Plastic Grip, Kilgore, 1950s	90
Display, Key Chain, Straight Shooter Puzzle, Red Plastic, 14 x 11 In.	420
Figurine, Roy Rogers On Trigger, Beswick, 1950s, 9 In.	1018
Guitar, Kawai, Acoustic 12-String, Painted Portraits, Signed, Plexiglas Case, 42 In.	443
Harmonica, Engraved Portrait, 1950s, 4 ¼ In.	35
Holster Set, King Of Cowboys, Roy, Trigger, Leather Belt, 2 Pockets, 27 In.	234
Holster Set, Official, Leather, Cast Metal Kilgore Cap Guns, Box, 9 ¼ x 9 ¼ In.	230
Holster Set, Roy Rearing Trigger, Leather, Box, 13 x 13 x 2 In.	1898
Lantern, Tin Litho, Horseshoe, Wire Handle, Battery, Box, Ohio Art Co., 1950s, 8 In.	190
Lunch Box, Thermos, Wood Grain Design, Roy With Gun Drawn, 1953, 8 ½ In.	173
Playset, Ranch Set, Cardboard Box, 1950s, 8 x 21 In.	297
Ring, Microscope, Initials RR, Trigger, Brass, Red Plastic, Mailer, Instructions, 1949, 5 ¼ x 7 In.	158
Toy, Pedal Car, Nellybelle, Steel, 1954 License Plate, 40 In.	1495

ROYAL BAYREUTH is the name of a factory that was founded in Tettau, Bavaria, in 1794. It has continued to modern times. The marks have changed through the years. A stylized crest, the name Royal Bayreuth, and the word *Bavaria* appear in slightly different forms from 1870 to about 1919. Later dishes may include the words *U.S. Zone*, the year of the issue, or the word *Germany* instead of *Bavaria*. Related pieces may be found listed in the Rose Tapestry, Sand Babies, Snow Babies, and Sunbonnet Babies categories.

Bowl, Pink, Yellow & White Roses, Gold Trim, Corner Shell Tab Handles, 10 ⅝ In.	163
Box, Lid, Boar's Head Handles At End, Shaded Gray, 5 ½ In.	944
Box, Rose Tapestry, Pink, Yellow, 5 ½ x 3 ¼ x 2 ¼ In.	175
Condiment Set, Red Lobster & Green Lettuce, 3 Piece	266
Creamer, Alligator, 4 ½ In.	125
Creamer, Alligator, Blue Eye, Brown, Tan Glaze, Tail Handle, 4 ¼ In.	116
Creamer, Apple, 3 ⅞ x 5 In.	215
Creamer, Apple, Red, Green, 4 In.	58
Creamer, Bear, Brown, 4 ¼ In.	400
Creamer, Butterfly, Multicolor, 4 In.	413
Creamer, Conch Shell, Green, Rust, c.1910, 2 ½ In.	125
Creamer, Dachshund, c.1900, 4 ½ In.	225
Creamer, Deck-Of-Cards, Red Devil Handle, 4 ½ In.	189
Creamer, Embossed Gold Band, Flowers, Marked, After 1902 ....*illus*	50
Creamer, Frog, Red, Angled Green Handle, 2 ½ In.	70
Creamer, Lamplighter, c.1902, 5 ½ In.	195
Creamer, Milkmaid, Red, White, 4 ¾ In.	104
Creamer, Monkey, Green, 4 In.	275
Creamer, Moose, Brown, Raised Antler Rim, Mouth Spout, 3 ¾ In.	531
Creamer, Mouse, Sitting, Gray, Curly Tail Handle, 4 ½ In.	649
Creamer, Penguin, 4 ¾ In.	300
Creamer, Pig, Gray, 4 In.	58
Creamer, Poppy, c.1900, 3 ¾ In.	165
Creamer, Tomato, Leaf Spout, Stem Handle, 5 x 3 ¾ In. ....*illus*	85
Creamer, Turtle, Green, Brown, Orange, Yellow, Mouth Spout, 2 In.	236
Dish, Club Shape, Farm, Horses, c.1900, 4 ½ x 4 ⅞ In.	35
Loving Cup, Woman, Feeding Chickens, 3 Handles, 4 ½ In.	79
Match Holder, Devil & Playing Cards, 4 ¾ In.	266
Mustard Pot, Poppy, c.1903, 3 ½ In.	145
Nursery Rhyme Set, Plates, Bowls, Creamer, Sugar, Mug, Candleholder, c.1900, 19 Piece	448
Pitcher, Alligator, Blue Eye, Brown, White Glaze, Tail Handle, 7 ½ In.	826 to 3364
Pitcher, Alligator, Brown, Green, Pink, Tail Handle, 5 ¼ In.	174
Pitcher, Beetle, Red, Green Leaf, 6 ½ In.	754
Pitcher, Beetle, Red, Green, Blue Mark, 6 In.	2478
Pitcher, Chick, Yellow, Green Angular Handle, 7 In.	551
Pitcher, Devil, Orange Red, Brown Accents, Head Spout, Shaped Handle, 4 In.	185
Pitcher, Frog, Green, Yellow, Angled Handle, 3 ¼ In.	162
Pitcher, Hunt Scene, Dogs, Green, Transfer, c.1900, 5 ¾ In.	140
Pitcher, Lemon, Leaf Handle, 6 ¾ In.	236
Pitcher, Leopard, Orange, Brown Spots, Mouth Spout, Tail Handle, 3 In.	4012
Pitcher, Mouse, Gray, Pink, 7 ½ In.	754
Pitcher, Poodle, Standing, Green, 5 ½ In.	377
Pitcher, Poppy, Peach, Gray, 6 ½ In.	128
Pitcher, Robin, Beak Spout, 7 In.	207
Pitcher, Rooster, Black, Red Comb, 7 ½ In.	232
Pitcher, Shell Shape, Seahorse Handle, Brown, Gray, Purple, 7 ½ In.	348
Pitcher, Shell, Pearlescent, Seahorse Handle, 7 ½ In.	275

Royal Copenhagen, Figurine, Boy With Dog, 7 ½ In.
$84

DuMouchelles Art Gallery

Royal Copenhagen, Figurine, Horned Owl, Mottled, Brown, Gray, Knud Kyhn, 1930, 22 ½ In.
$2,760

Skinner Auctioneers & Appraisers

R

This is an edited listing of current prices. Visit **Kovels.com** to check thousands of prices from previous years and sign up for free information on trends, tips, reproductions, marks, and more.

Royal Copenhagen, Group, Wave &
Rock, Entwined Lovers, Marked,
12 x 18 ½ In.
$900

DuMouchelles Art Gallery

Royal Crown Derby, Plate, Imari,
Cobalt Blue Ground, Stamped, 8 ¼ In.,
12 Piece
$1,652

Brunk Auctions

Royal Doulton, Animal, Tiger, Flambe,
Signed Noke, 14 In.
$480

Skinner Auctioneers & Appraisers

Pitcher, Snake, Coiled, Brown, Yellow, Mouth Spout, 6 ¼ In.	1298
Pitcher, Squirrel, Standing, Gray, Bushy Tail Handle, 8 In.	3540
Pitcher, St. Bernard, Black, Brown, 5 ½ In.	174
Pitcher, Tomato, Leaf Spout, 3 ¾ In.	68
Pitcher, White, Mottled, Satin Glaze, 4 ¾ In.	261
Plate, Rose Tapestry, Gold Trim, Blue Mark, 9 ½ In. ....*illus*	100
Plate, Shepherdess, Flock Of Goats, Pond, Gold Rim, 9 In. ....*illus*	85
Plate, Woman, Pond, Sheep, Apron Full Of Flowers, 9 In.	70
Spoon Holder, Lobster Shape, 5 ½ In.	23
Sugar & Creamer, Boy, Donkey, 5 ¼ x 3 ½ In. & 4 ¼ x 2 ¾ In.	85
Sugar & Creamer, Clown, Satin Pearlescent White, Green Trim, 4 x 4 ½ In.	354
Sugar, Tomato, Lid, 4 x 3 ¼ In.	65
Syrup, Grapes, Green, c.1910, 6 ½ In.	180
Toothpick Holder, Bell Ringer, 3 ½ In.	69
Toothpick Holder, Lamplighter Shape, Green Paint, c.1925, 3 ½ In.	150
Toothpick Holder, Little Boy Blue, Painted, 4 Flattened Handles, c.1915, 2 ⅝ In.	23
Toothpick Holder, Shell Shape, Footed, 3 In.	149
Vase, Girl With Muff, Tapestry, Beige Ground, Gold Trim, Oval, Tapered, 8 In.	118
Vase, Hunt Scene, Riders, Horses, Stylized Leaf Handles, Blue Mark, c.1900, 5 x 6 In. ....*illus*	75
Vase, Landscape, Cows, Textured, Gilt Handles, c.1900, 2 ¾ x 3 ⅛ In.	95
Vase, Polar Bears On Ice, Scenic Mountains, Bulbous, Tapered Neck, 8 ½ In.	2478
Vase, Yellow Roses, Shouldered, Narrow Neck, Flared Rim, 7 In.	129
Wall Pocket, Cottage & Waterfall Scene, Tapestry	11

ROYAL BONN is the nineteenth- and twentieth-century trade name used by Franz Anton Mehlem, who had a pottery in Bonn, Germany, from 1836 to 1931. Porcelain and earthenware were made. The factory was purchased by Villeroy & Boch in 1921 and closed in 1931. Many marks were used, most including the name Bonn, the initials FM, and a crown.

Bisquit Jar, Iris, Yellow, Pink, Purple, Silver Trim & Lid, Green Castle Mark, 8 In.	104
Charger, Green Ground, Poppies, Game Birds, Scenic, Signed A. Hoffmann, 12 ¾ In.	118
Clock, Ansonia, La Lavon, Flowers, Molded Crest, Feet, Scroll Handles, c.1900, 14 In.	575
Clock, Ansonia, La Nord, Pink Roses, Leaves, Blue & White Scroll Case, 12 x 14 In.	259
Jardiniere, 2-Part Pedestal, Roses, Scrolled Gilt Feet, Handles, F.A. Mehlem, c.1900, 50 In.	46000
Jardiniere, Glazed, Thistle, White, Green, Ochre, Franz Anton Mehlem, c.1900, 7 x 10 ½ In.	1250
Jug, Painted Flowers, Woodland, Tapestry Ware, Gilt Handle, c.1905, 9 ½ In.	69
Pitcher, Owl, Full Moon, Butterfly, Franz Anton Mehlem, 5 In.	63
Plaque, Molded, Shell, Scroll Borders, Pastoral Scenes, c.1880, 20 x 13 In., Pair	210
Plate, Portrait, In Archadia, 2 Women, Enamel, Gilt Border, Signed Richter, 9 ½ In.	1888
Umbrella Stand, Hollyhocks, Molded, Scalloped Rim, Cylinder, Mehlem, c.1900, 21 In.	173
Umbrella Stand, Iris, Peonies, Molded Scrolls, Flared, Cylindrical, Mehlem, c.1900, 17 In.	184
Urn, Domed Lid, Pineapple Finial, Rotates, Gilt Ground, Blue Flowers, 3 Sections, 28 In.	826
Vase, Bird, Flowers, Bulbous, Gilt Handle, Base, 12 ½ In.	93
Vase, Bud, Painted Flowers, Long Neck, Side Flanges, Square Rim, c.1900, 9 In.	92
Vase, Bulb, Red Top Cup, Yellow Flowers, Triangular Body, Mehlem, c.1900, 9 ⅝ In.	92
Vase, Daisies, Pinecones, Needles, Molded, Gilt Scalloped Rim, Handles, Mehlem, c.1900, 18 In.	161
Vase, Dome Lid, Flower Knop, Iris, Purple Ground, Gold, Bottle Shape, Mehlem, c.1900, 49 In.	1035
Vase, Flowers, Blue Ground, Baluster, Gilt Dolphin Handles, Feet, Mehlem, c.1900, 22 In.	115
Vase, Flowers, Multicolor, Gilt Foot, Flared Mouth, Gourd Shape, c.1910, 11 ½ In.	150
Vase, Flowers, Multicolor, Green, Blue Ground, Gilt Accents, Relief Masks, 50 x 12 In.	4025
Vase, Green, Pink, Yellow, Irises, Gold Highlights, Handles, 10 In.	148
Vase, Hollyhocks, Multicolor, Fence, Ivoryware, Long Neck, Low Waist, 23 In.	104
Vase, Lid, Button Knop, Flowers, Green Ground, Four Gilt Handles, c.1900, 9 ⅝ In.	138
Vase, Lid, Gilt Knop, Boy Picking Flowers, Tapestry, Mehlem, c.1910, 21 In.	173
Vase, Lid, Painted Courting Couple, Period Attire, Flowers, Gilt, Mehlem, c.1900, 16 In.	127
Vase, Musterschultz, Flowers, Mottled Ground, Pinched Rim, Gilt, Cylindrical Body, 6 In.	196
Vase, Old Dutch, Flowers, Moonflask Shape, Brown Handles, Footed, c.1905, 10 ½ In.	92
Vase, Pink Flowers, Tapered, Signed Rhenus VI, 8 In.	81
Vase, Poppies, Multicolor, Green Ground, Double Gourd, Draped Handles, c.1905, 8 ⅜ In.	69
Vase, Portrait Woman, Blond Hair, Narrow Neck, Swollen Body, Mehlem, c.1905, 8 ½ In.	138
Vase, Portrait, Peasant Woman, Water Landscape, Oval, C. Stirher, c.1905, 13 ½ In.	431
Vase, Portrait, Woman, Brunette, Flowers, Gilt, Wide Mouth, Flared, Ebertz, 6 ¼ In.	161
Vase, Portraits, Women, Green, Yellow, Signed P. Dingendorf, 10 ¼ In., Pair	413
Vase, Roses, Pastel Ground, Gold Accents, Oval, Footed, Mehlem, c.1900, 38 In.	374
Vase, Ruysdael, Textured, Red Body, Stylized Poppies, Tapered Cylinder, c.1890, 7 In.	150
Vase, Seminude Woman, Seated, Stream, Flowers, Gilt Foot, J. Bauer, c.1910, 14 In.	127
Vase, Tapestry, Flowers, Terrace, 7 ½ In.	148

Vase, Thistles, Gourd Shape, Green, White Ground, Germany, 7 ¾ In.	212
Vase, Woman, Flowers In Hair, Landscape, Applied Blackberry Handles, c.1920, 12 In.	374
Vase, Yellow Roses, 14 In., Pair	116
Vase, Yellow, Mottled, Orange Flowers, Flared Mouth, Gourd Shape, Mehlem, c.1900, 9 ½ In.	104
Vase, Yellow, Pink Hibiscus, Painted, Gourd Shape, c.1920, 12 ½ In.	127

ROYAL COPENHAGEN porcelain and pottery have been made in Denmark since 1775. The Christmas plate series started in 1908. The figurines with pale blue and gray glazes have remained popular in this century and are still being made. Many other old and new style porcelains are made today.

Bowl, Incised Line Exterior, Brown Interior, Axel Salto, Denmark, 10 x 4 ½ In.	2000
Cup & Saucer, Flora Danica, Printed Marks, Denmark	330
Dish, Vegetable, Lid, Flora Danica, Oval, Marked, 15 ½ x 12 ¼ In.	2688
Figurine, Amager Girls, Traditional Scandinavian Costume, Carl Martin-Hansen, 8 ½ In.	311
Figurine, Boy With Dog, 7 ½ In. ....*illus*	84
Figurine, Cat, Reclining, Marked, 4 ¾ x 10 ½ In.	748
Figurine, Girl, Holding Golden Horn, Kristin Svendsdatter, 1962, 8 ¾ In.	150
Figurine, Henrik & Elise, Couple Holding Hands, 1900s, 16 ¾ In.	375
Figurine, Horned Owl, Mottled, Brown, Gray, Knud Kyhn, 1930, 22 ½ In. ......*illus*	2760
Figurine, Man, Woman, Examining His Arm, 1900s, 18 ¾ In.	500
Figurine, Nathan The Wise, Painted, Printed Mark, Denmark, 14 In.	210
Figurine, Panther, Stalking, Stoneware, Speckled Glaze, K. Kyhn, 1950s, 6 x 16 In.	1000
Figurine, Pig, Head Down, Floppy Ears, 5 In.	90
Figurine, Polar Bear, Seated, Mouth Open, Growling, 13 In.	210
Figurine, Shepherd Boy, 2 Lambs, 8 ¼ In.	84
Figurine, Sleeping Cat, 3 ½ In.	142
Figurine, Tiger, Marked, 5 ½ x 3 ½ In.	388
Figurine, Woman, On Chimney, Cuddling Man In Black, Denmark	690
Figurine, Woman, Sewing, 5 ¾ In.	84
Group, Wave & Rock, Entwined Lovers, Marked, 12 x 18 ½ In. ......*illus*	900
Plaque, Leaping Deer, Faience, Knud Khyn, 12 ½ x 15 ¾ In.	590
Plate, Christmas, 1911, Danish Landscape, Snowy Fence, Wheat, Birds, 7 In.	30
Plate, Christmas, 1921, Market Place In Aabenraa, 7 In.	175
Plate, Christmas, 1951, Christmas Angel, Jul, 7 ¼ In.	94
Plate, Christmas, 1956, Rosenborg Castle, Copenhagen, 7 ¼ In.	180
Plate, Christmas, 1960, The Stag, 7 In.	25
Plate, Christmas, 1964, Fetching The Christmas Tree, 7 ¼ In.	65
Plate, Christmas, 1965, Little Skaters, 7 ¼ In.	55
Plate, Christmas, 1967, The Royal Oak, 7 ¼ In.	25
Plate, Christmas, 1968, The Last Umiak, 7 ¼ In.	35
Plate, Christmas, 1971, Hare In Winter, 7 ¼ In.	15
Plate, Christmas, 1973, Going Home For Christmas, 7 ¼ In.	15
Plate, Christmas, 1983, Merry Christmas, 7 ¼ In.	40
Plate, Flora Danica, 9 In., 12 Piece	2813
Plate, Flora Danica, Plant, Gilt, Pink Border, 7 ¾ In., 8 Piece	1000
Plate, Flora Danica, Sawtooth Edge, Gilt Dots, Leaves, c.1950, 8 ¾ In.	207
Tureen, Lid, Flora Danica, Botanical, Branch Handles, Applied Flowers, Oval, 13 In.	3450
Tureen, Lid, Underplate, Blue Flower Pattern, Tab Handles, 12-In. Tureen	184
Tureen, Underplate, Flora Danica, Branch Handles, Finial, Pierced Border, 13 In.	4688
Vase, Bud, Green, Black, Axel Salto, 1957, 10 ⅝ In.	12500
Vase, Coastal Scene, Thatched Cottage, c.1950, 8 In.	83
Vase, Gourd Shape, Crystalline Glaze, P. Proschowsky, 3 Wavy Lines, 7 In.	938
Vase, Great Crested Grebes, Signed, G. Heilmann, 3 Wavy Lines, 1890s, 14 In.	3250
Vase, Sailing Ship, Blue, Cream, Bulbous, 8 ½ In.	46

ROYAL CROWN DERBY COMPANY, LTD., is a name used on porcelain beginning in 1890. There is a complex family tree that includes the Derby, Crown Derby, and Royal Crown Derby porcelains. The Royal Crown Derby mark includes the name and a crown. The words *Made in England* were used after 1921. The company became part of Allied English Potteries Group in 1964. It was bought in 2000 and is now privately owned.

Cake Plate, Blue Mikado, Handles, 12 x 12 In.	110
Coffeepot, Black On White, Birds, Trees, 1930, 9 ½ In.	298
Creamer, Royal Blue, Rust, Gold, 1900s, 4 x 3 ½ In.	220
Cup, Stirrup, Fisher's Delight, Marked, c.1885, 4 ½ In.	750
Dish, Gilded Handles, Roses, Fruits, c.1899, 1 ¾ x 10 In.	122

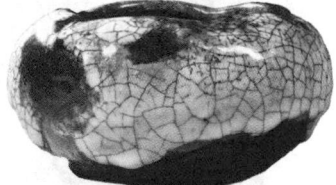

Royal Doulton, Bowl, Flambe, Crackled, Chang, Signed, Noke, c.1930, 6 ¼ In. $2,400

Skinner Auctioneers & Appraisers

Royal Doulton, Character Jug, Old Charley, D 5420, 6 In. $20

Rachel Davis Fine Arts

Royal Doulton, Character Jug, Old King Cole, D 6036, 6 In. $25

Rachel Davis Fine Arts

Royal Doulton, Character Jug, Robinson Crusoe, D 6532, 7 ½ In. $15

R

Rachel Davis Fine Arts

Royal Doulton, Figurine, Balloon Man, HN 1954, 7 ¼ In.
$30

Rachel Davis Fine Arts

Royal Doulton, Figurine, Celeste, HN 2237, 7 in.
$75

Woody Auction

Royal Doulton, Figurine, Teatime, HN 2255, 7 ½ In.
$10

Rachel Davis Fine Arts

R

Figurine, Royal Cats, Egyptian, Siamese, Abyssinian, 8 ½ To 9 In., 3 Piece	360
Goblet, Rust, Dark Blue, Green & Gold Trim, Imari, c.1901, 5 In.	125
Jar, Ball, Lid, Peacock Pattern, Blue, White, Gold Trim, Fluted Finial, 5 In., Pair	92
Paperweight, Anniversary Robin	49
Paperweight, Bird, Wye Blue Tit, Box	59
Paperweight, Country Mouse, Multicolor, 4 In.	100
Paperweight, Epsom Filly	348
Paperweight, Jacob's Sheep	78
Paperweight, Mother Cat, Box	98
Paperweight, Platinum Black Swan	194
Paperweight, Puffin, Multicolor, 4 In.	150
Paperweight, Red Dragon, Box	68
Paperweight, Starfish	136
Paperweight, Tortoiseshell Mother Cat	67
Pin Dish, Fan Shape, Cobalt Blue, White, Scalloped Edge, 5 x 3 In.	45
Plate, Central Flowers, Green Border, Gilt, c.1942, 10 In., 9 Piece	750
Plate, Gilt Scroll Border, 9 ⅝ In., 6 Piece	1500
Plate, Hunting Scene, Hounds, Green Border, 10 ⅜ In.	152
Plate, Imari, Cobalt Blue Ground, Stamped, 8 ¼ In., 12 Piece ....*illus*	1652
Plate, Peony Pattern, Red, White, Flowers, Leaves, Black Ground, 10 ½ In., 16 Piece	875
Plate, Salad, King's Pattern, Imari, Iron Red, Blue Rim, c.1910, 9 In., 12 Piece	431
Urn, Old Iman Pattern, Handles, 5 In., Pair	208
Vase, Bud, Squat Body, Narrow Neck, Painted, Printed Mark, 4 ¼ In.	240
Vase, Landscape Panels, Gilt, Black Designs, Base Handles, Plinth, 7 ½ In., Pair	660
Vase, Pink, Orange, Flat Round Body, Gilt Designs, Handles, 1887, 3 In.	127

ROYAL DOULTON is the name used on Doulton and Company pottery made from 1902 to the present. Doulton and Company of England was founded in 1853. Pieces made before 1902 are listed in this book under Doulton. Royal Doulton collectors search for the out-of-production figurines, character jugs, vases, and series wares. Some vases and animal figurines were made with a special red glaze called flambe. Sung and Chang glazed pieces are rare. The multicolored glaze is very thick and looks as if it were dropped on the clay. In 2005 Royal Doulton was acquired by the Waterford Wedgwood Group, which was bought by KPS Capital Partners of New York in 2009 and became part of WWRD Holdings.

Animal, Cat, Seated, Flambe Veined, Marked, 11 ½ In.	431
Animal, Pig, Brown, 6 ½ In.	73
Animal, Rhinoceros, Flambe, 15 In.	420
Animal, Tiger, Flambe, Signed Noke, 14 In. ....*illus*	480
Animal, Trout, Flambe, 12 ⅜ In.	240
Bowl, Flambe, Crackled, Chang, Signed, Noke, c.1930, 6 ¼ In. ....*illus*	2400

ROYAL DOULTON character jugs depict the head and shoulders of the subject. They are made in four sizes: large, 5 ¼ to 7 inches; small, 3 ¼ to 4 inches; miniature, 2 ¼ to 2 ½ inches; and tiny, 1 ¼ inches. Toby jugs portray a seated, full figure.

Character Jug, Aladdin's Genie, D 6971, 7 ½ In.	249
Character Jug, Albert Einstein, D 7023, S.J. Taylor, 1995, 7 In.	83
Character Jug, Bacchus, D 6499, 7 In.	397
Character Jug, Beefeater, D 6206, 6 ½ In.	45
Character Jug, Captain Hook, D 6601, 4 In.	79
Character Jug, Cavalier, D 6114, 7 In.	42
Character Jug, Charles Dickens, D 6939, 1993, 7 In.	149
Character Jug, Clown, D 6834, 6 ½ In.	73
Character Jug, Collector, D 6796, 7 In.	79
Character Jug, Davy Crockett, 2-Faced, Davy & Santa Ana, D 6729, 7 In.	115
Character Jug, Falstaff, D 6287, 6 In.	12
Character Jug, George Washington, D 6669, 7 ½ In.	45
Character Jug, Golfer, D 6623, 7 In.	54
Character Jug, Henry V, D 6671, 7 ¼ In.	40
Character Jug, Johnny Appleseed, D 6372, 6 In.	40
Character Jug, Jolly Toby, D 6109, 6 In.	12
Character Jug, King Arthur, Robert Tabbenor, 1996, 7 In.	149
Character Jug, Long John Silver, D 6386, 4 In.	23
Character Jug, Lord Nelson, D 6336, 7 In.	53
Character Jug, Mephistopheles, With Verse, D 5758, 4 In.	339
Character Jug, Merlin, Owl Handle, D 6529, 7 ¼ In.	66
Character Jug, Mr. Micawber, D. Biggs, 1996, 7 ½ In.	149

Character Jug, Mr. Pickwick, D 5839, 5 ½ In.	40
Character Jug, Old Charley, D 5420, 6 In. *illus*	20
Character Jug, Old King Cole, D 6036, 6 In. *illus*	25
Character Jug, Pearly Girl, 3 ¼ In.	793
Character Jug, Pharaoh, D 7028, 8 In.	237
Character Jug, Poacher, D 6464, 4 In.	60 to 72
Character Jug, Quaker Oats Limited, c.1985, 7 ½ In.	210
Character Jug, Robinson Crusoe, D 6532, 7 ½ In. *illus*	15
Character Jug, Romeo, D 6670, 7 In.	45
Character Jug, Santa Claus, Holly Wreath Handle, D 6794, 7 In.	277
Character Jug, Scaramouche, D 6558, Max Henk, 7 In.	325
Character Jug, Smuts, D 6198, 1946-48, 6 ½ In.	720
Character Jug, Snake Charmer, D 6912, 7 In.	107
Character Jug, Uncle Tom Cobbleigh, D 6337, 7 In.	28
Character Jug, Veteran Motorist, D 6633, 7 ½ In.	54
Character Jug, Winston Churchill, D 6172, 6 In.	40
Character Jug, Winston Churchill, D 6907, 7 In.	139
Figurine, Afternoon Tea, HN 1747, 5 x 7 In.	168 to 240
Figurine, All Aboard, HN 2940, 1981, 9 In.	60
Figurine, April, HN 3333, 5 ½ In.	51
Figurine, Autumn Breezes, HN 1934, 8 In.	68
Figurine, Bachelor, HN 2319	46
Figurine, Balloon Man, HN 1954, 7 ¼ In. *illus*	30
Figurine, Bell O' The Ball, HN 1997, 1946	132
Figurine, Bess, HN 2002, 7 In.	79
Figurine, Bunny, HN 2214	60
Figurine, Bunnykins, Jester, Black, Yellow, White, Green Backstamp	793
Figurine, Bunnykins, Jogger, DB 22, 3 ½ In.	11
Figurine, Bunnykins, Little Red Riding Hood, DB 230, Box, Certificate	49
Figurine, Bunnykins, Rainy Day, DB 147, Gold Special Edition, Green Backstamp	149
Figurine, Bunnykins, Ship Ahoy, DB 279, Box, Certificate	49
Figurine, Bunnykins, Witches Cauldron, DB 293, Box, Certificate	60
Figurine, Celeste, HN 2237, 7 In. *illus*	75
Figurine, Christopher Columbus, HN 3392	600
Figurine, Clockmaker, HN 2279, 7 In.	144
Figurine, Clown, HN 2890, 1978	90
Figurine, Country Maid, No. 3163	120
Figurine, Empress Dowager, Tzu-Hsi, HN 2391, 8 ½ In.	400
Figurine, February, HN 2703, 7 In.	57
Figurine, Guardsman, HN 2784	132
Figurine, Guy Fawkes, HN 98	991
Figurine, Helen Of Troy, HN 2387, 9 ½ In.	520
Figurine, Helena, CL 3994, Box, 11 In.	74
Figurine, Holly, HN 3647, 8 ½ In.	144
Figurine, Hornpipe, HN 2161, 1954	348
Figurine, Isadora, HN 2938, 8 ¼ In.	90
Figurine, Isobel, CL 3980, 11 In.	62
Figurine, January, HN 2697, 8 ¼ In.	57
Figurine, Jessica, HN 3497, 8 ½ In.	68
Figurine, Jester, HN 2016, 9 ½ In.	90
Figurine, Joker, HN 2252, 8 ½ In.	96
Figurine, Jolly Sailor, HN 2172, 1954	372
Figurine, Kirsty, HN 2381, 7 ½ In.	79
Figurine, Kurdish Dancer, HN 2867, 8 ½ In.	120
Figurine, Lady Charmian, HN 1948, 8 In.	90
Figurine, Margaret, HN 3496, Box, 8 In.	68
Figurine, Mary Had A Little Lamb, HN 2048, 3 ½ In.	28
Figurine, Maytime, HN 2113, 1952	84
Figurine, Nanny, HN 2221, 6 In.	107
Figurine, Natalie, HN 3498, Box, 8 ½ In.,	68
Figurine, Omar Khayyam, HN 2247, 6 ½ In.	46 to 138
Figurine, Paisley Shawl, HN 1988, 7 In.	68
Figurine, Princess Badoura, HN 3921, 22 In.	2280
Figurine, Prue, HN 1996, 1946	114
Figurine, Punch & Judy Man, HN 2765	118
Figurine, Puppet Maker, HN 2253	107
Figurine, Reverie, HN 2306, 1963	90

Royal Doulton, Vase, Chalice Shape, Crackle Glaze, Footed, Chang Ware, c.1925, 4 ½ x 5 In.
$2,875

Rago Arts & Auction Center

Royal Doulton, Vase, Flambe, Chang, Crackled, Chinese Design, Flambe, c.1930, 9 ¾ In.
$3,000

Skinner Auctioneers & Appraisers

Royal Doulton, Vase, Flambe, Marked, Charles Noke, Fred Moore, 10 ⅜ In.
$472

Humler & Nolan

R

Royal Doulton, Vase, Flambe, Sterling Silver Overlay, Gorham Hallmarks, 5 ¼ In.
$173

Humler & Nolan

Royal Doulton, Vase, Flambe, Veined, 1900s, 11 In.
$210

Skinner Auctioneers & Appraisers

Royal Doulton, Vase, Stylized Flowers, Glazed, Cobalt Blue Interior, 18 ½ In., Pair
$413

Rachel Davis Fine Arts

Figurine, Sea Sprite, HN 2191, 1957, 7 ½ In.	98
Figurine, Silks & Ribbons, HN 2017, 1948, 6 In.	12
Figurine, Slapdash, Clown, HN 2277, 10 In.	96
Figurine, Stitch In Time, HN 2352, 6 ½ In.	78
Figurine, Suitor, HN 2132, 1961	96
Figurine, Swimmer, Blue Swimsuit, Red Robe, HN 4246	118
Figurine, Teatime, HN 2255, 7½ In. *illus*	10
Figurine, Tip Toe, Clown, HN 3293, 9 ¼ In.	96
Figurine, Top O' The Hill, Green Dress, HN 1833, 7 ½ In.	68 to 84
Figurine, Top O' The Hill, Woman, Red Dress, HN 1834	25
Figurine, Tracy, HN 3291, 8 In.	45
Figurine, Tumbling, HN 3283, 1989	120
Figurine, Vanessa, Classiques, CL 3989, Marble Base	78
Figurine, Washington At Prayer, HN 2861, Signed L. Ispanky, 1974	1320
Figurine, Windflower, HN 2029, 7 ½ In.	130
Figurine, Yeoman Of The Guard, Seated, HN 2122	228
Jug, Lord Nelson, Mottos, Portrait Medallions, c.1910, 6 ½ In.	720
Pitcher, Brown Glaze, Stylized Designs, Yellow, Cream, Black, 7 In.	59
Pitcher, Peach Flowers, Gilt, Scroll Handle, c.1890, 15 x 9 In.	625
Pitcher, Polar Bear Band, Blue, Green, 8 ½ In.	62
Plaque, Sheep, Grazing, White, Tan Field Ground, Hannah Barlow, Frame, 4 x 7 In.	6250
Plate, Gilt Swags, Leaves, Raspberry Pink Ground, 9 In., 12 Piece	665
Toby Jug, Santa Claus, D 6675, 7 ½ In.	62
Vase, Chalice Shape, Crackle Glaze, Footed, Chang Ware, c.1925, 4 ½ x 5 In. *illus*	2875
Vase, Chang Ware, Flambe Glaze, Charles Noke, Harry Nixon, c.1925, 7 ¼ x 6 ½ In.	4375
Vase, Deer, Landscape, Cylindrical, Signed Hodkinson, 1805, 9 In.	390
Vase, Fern, Tree Band, Blue Ground, Yellow Interior, 7 In.	102
Vase, Flambe, Chang, Crackled, Chinese Design, Flambe, c.1930, 9 ¾ In. *illus*	3000
Vase, Flambe, Landscape, Globular, 1900s, 11 ¾ In.	300
Vase, Flambe, Lobed, Squat, Mark, c.1925, 6 ¾ In.	540
Vase, Flambe, Marked, Charles Noke, Fred Moore, 10 ⅜ In. *illus*	472
Vase, Flambe, Maroon, Cottage, Landscape, Tapered, Footed, 6 ½ x 4 ½ In.	62
Vase, Flambe, Red, Sailing Ships, Round, 3 In.	80
Vase, Flambe, Sterling Silver Overlay, Gorham Hallmarks, 5 ¼ In. *illus*	173
Vase, Flambe, Veined, 1900s, 11 In. *illus*	210
Vase, Flambe, Veined, 1900s, 15 ½ In.	246
Vase, Flambe, Veined, 1900s, 9 ⅝ In.	210
Vase, Flambe, Veined, c.1945, 6 x 2 ½ In., Pair	188
Vase, Flame, Mottled Red, Blue, Signed Sung, 8 ½ In.	540
Vase, Fuchsia, Rust, Blue & Green Glaze, Stoneware, Art Nouveau, Ada Tosen, 7 ¼ In.	138
Vase, Geometric, Stoneware Purple Enamel, B. Newberry, c.1930, 10 x 4 In., Pair	750
Vase, Green, Orange, White, Goats, Landscape, Tapered, Handles, W. Hodkinson, 7 In.	27
Vase, Spanish, Flowers, Gilt Rim, Stoneware, Footed, 8 In., Pair	138
Vase, Stylized Flowers, Glazed, Cobalt Blue Interior, 18 ½ In., Pair *illus*	413
Vase, Sung, Mottled Green, Red Drip Glaze, Tapered, Charles Noke, 6 ¾ In.	393
Vase, Titanian, 2-Tone Blue, Brown, Yellow, Owl, Moonlight, Harry Allen, 6 In.	1500

ROYAL DUX is the more common name for the Duxer Porzellanmanufaktur, which was founded by E. Eichler in Dux, Bohemia (now Duchov, Czech Republic), in 1860. By the turn of the twentieth century, the firm specialized in porcelain statuary and busts of Art Nouveau–style maidens, large porcelain figures, and ornate vases with three-dimensional figures climbing on the sides. The firm is still in business.

Centerpiece, 2 Tiers, Attached Woman, Cherub, Gold, 9 ½ x 10 ½ In.	48
Centerpiece, Woman, Standing On Wave, Fishnet, 2 Scalloped Shells, Green, Gilt, 14 In.	174
Console, Handles, Pink Roses, Leaves, Handles, Scalloped Edge, 1920s, 11 x 6 In.	115
Figurine, Cat, Sitting, Pink Nose, Dark Eyes, 16 In.	249
Figurine, Cockatoo, On Branch, Pastels, Marked, 16 In.	245
Figurine, Cockatoo, White, Pink Highlights, Perched On Branch, Leaves, 15 ¼ In., Pair	561
Figurine, Cockatoo, White, Pink, 16 In.	110
Figurine, Dolphin, In Water, Moving Up, Gray, White, 14 In.	40
Figurine, Farm Girl At The Well, Basket On Back, Green Long Dress, 15 In.	96
Figurine, Fisherman, Cobalt Blue, Gilt Accents, Marked, 21 In.	120
Figurine, Hunting Dog, Setter, Game Bird In Mouth, Brown, Ivory, 6 x 14 In.	70
Figurine, Mahatma Gandhi, White Shorts, Seated, Meditating, 10 In.	219
Figurine, Market Sellers, Woman, Basket, Man, Jug, Pink Triangle Mark, 19 & 19 ½ In., Pair	450
Figurine, Mother & Daughter, Dancing, Marked, 1896, 19 ¾ In.	2495

Figurine, Peasant Boy, Holding Cantaloupe, Basket, Vegetables, Marked, 11 In. ....*illus*	58
Figurine, Polar Bear, White, Seated, 14 In.	74
Figurine, Polar Bear, White, Standing, 12 In.	62
Figurine, Potter, Painting Urn, Green Toga, Bohemia, 7 ⅜ In.	210
Figurine, Woman Dancer, Flowing Skirt, Flowers, 22 In.	1395
Figurine, Woman, Gold Dress, 13 In.	60
Figurine, Woman, Standing, Tambourine In Hand, Pink Gown, Green Scarf, 12 In.	69
Group, 2 Women, Seminude, Green Drape, Divided Bowl, 16 ¼ In.	300
Group, Couple, Courting, Classical Attire, Green, Rose, 8 ½ In.	250
Urn, Lid, Cobalt Blue Ground, Gold Detail, Ram's Head Handles, 14 ½ In.	106
Vase, Blackberries, White Bisque, Lattice Handles, 19 In.	29
Vase, Flower Girl, Light Blue Blooms, Blue Ground, Gilt Handles, Octagonal Base, 11 In.	40
Vase, Flowers, Dangling, Repousse Rim, Green, Orange, 7 In.	450
Vase, Irises, Relief, Gilt Handles, Bulbous, 13 ½ In.	299
Vase, Mermaids, Merman, Sea Creatures, Bohemia, c.1900, 14 In.	1020
Vase, Nude, On Shell, 16 In.	181
Vase, Pedestal, Cobalt & Pale Blue, Gilt, Loop Handles, c.1910, 5 ½ In.	110

ROYAL FLEMISH glass was made during the late 1880s in New Bedford, Massachusetts, by the Mt. Washington Glass Works. It is a colored satin glass decorated with dark colors and raised gold designs. The glass was patented in 1894. It was supposed to resemble stained glass windows.

Biscuit Jar, Dragon Design, Metal Collar, Lid, Mt. Washington, 6 ¼ In.	1298
Ewer, Gold Cathedral Window Panels, Rose, Gray, Gold Mums, Red Ground, 11 ½ In.	1452
Ewer, Pillow, Griffin, Putti, Fish, Flowers, Twisted Rope Handle, 9 ¾ In. ....*illus*	7110
Lamp, Kerosene, Garden Of Allah, Camels, Arabs, Mt. Washington, 22 In. ....*illus*	12443
Mug, Flowers, Jeweled Centers, Circles, Rope Twist Handle, 7 In. ....*illus*	402
Sugar & Creamer, Medallion, 3 ½ In.	443
Vase, Gold Winged Mythological Creature, Raised Gilt Scrolling, Amethyst Ground, 14 In.	5229
Vase, Hedge Rose, Bull's-Eye, Cut Shape Mouth, 9 ¾ In.	1840
Vase, Mythical Creature, Gold Winged, Multicolor Panels, Amethyst Ground, 14 In.	4977
Vase, Raised Gold Chysanthemum, Scrolled Neck, 13 ½ In.	665

ROYAL HAEGER, *see Haeger category.*

ROYAL HICKMAN designed pottery, glass, silver, aluminum, furniture, lamps, and other items. From 1938 to 1944 and again from the 1950s to 1969, he worked for Haeger Potteries. Mr. Hickman operated his own pottery in Tampa, Florida, during the 1940s. He moved to California and worked for Vernon Potteries. During the last years of his life he lived in Guadalajara, Mexico, and continued designing for Royal Haeger. Pieces made in his pottery listed here are marked *Royal Hickman* or *Hickman*.

Bowl, Amoeba, Free-Form, Brown, Cream Drip Glaze, 1940s, 3 x 7 x 13 In.	50
Dish, Spiral Plume, c.1942, 7 x 1 In.	42
Lamp Base, Swan, Green, Gold, 15 In.	125
Vase, Double Shell, Mauve Agate Glaze, Marked, 6 ½ In.	48
Vase, Fish On Wave, Agate Green, c.1949, 10 In.	150
Vase, Free-Form, Coral Shapes, Aqua, 1940s, 8 In.	60
Vase, Gladiola, Brown, White Drip Glaze, Marked, c.1950, 11 x 10 In.	200
Vase, Gladiola, Ruffled, Bluish Green, Drip Glaze, c.1950, 11 x 9 In.	150
Vase, Swan, Green, Leaf Like Feathers, 11 In.	160

ROYAL NYMPHENBURG is the modern name for the Nymphenburg porcelain factory, which was established at Neudeck-ob-der-Au, Germany, in 1753 and moved to Nymphenburg in 1761. The company is still in existence. Marks include a checkered shield topped by a crown, a crowned *CT* with the year, and a contemporary shield mark on reproductions of eighteenth-century porcelain.

Bowl, Lid, Geese, Oval, Handles, Footed, 9 x 14 In.	210
Figurine, Bacchus, Ewer, Grapes, Blanc De Chine, 14 ¼ In.	32500
Figurine, Couple, Seated, Bird, Cage, Cream Glaze, 7 ½ In.	116
Figurine, Dog, Standing, Blanc De Chine, 6 In.	406
Figurine, Hippopotamus, Blanc De Chine, Mark, Terletski-Scherff, 9 ¾ In.	230
Tureen, Lid, Artichoke Knop, Flowers, White Ground, Handles, Gilt, c.1945, 9 ¾ In.	184
Vase, Burgundy, Green, Blue, 4 Recesses, White Busts, Bottle Shape, 9 In.	625

ROYAL RUDOLSTADT, *see Rudolstadt category.*

ROYAL VIENNA, *see Beehive category.*

Royal Dux, Figurine, Peasant Boy, Holding Cantaloupe, Basket, Vegetables, Marked, 11 In.
$58

Humler & Nolan

Royal Flemish, Ewer, Pillow, Griffin, Putti, Fish, Flowers, Twisted Rope Handle, 9 ¾ In.
$7,110

James D. Julia Auctioneers

Royal Flemish, Lamp, Kerosene, Garden Of Allah, Camels, Arabs, Mt. Washington, 22 In.
$12,443

R

James D. Julia Auctioneers

Royal Flemish, Mug, Flowers, Jeweled Centers, Circles, Rope Twist Handle, 7 In. $402

Early Auction Co.

Royal Worcester, Figurine, Scarlet Tanager, Branch, Dorothy Doughty, 13 In.
$210

DuMouchelles Art Gallery

Royal Worcester, Fruit Cooler, Lid, Dragon Pattern, Gilt, Tab Handles, Marked, Signed, 10 ½ x 7 ½ In., Pair
$1,168

New Orleans Auction Galleries, Inc.

ROYAL WORCESTER is a name used by collectors. Worcester porcelains were made in Worcester, England, from about 1751. The firm went through many different periods and name changes. It became the Worcester Royal Porcelain Company, Ltd., in 1862. Today collectors call the porcelains made after 1862 "Royal Worcester." In 1976, the firm merged with W.T. Copeland to become Royal Worcester Spode. The company was bought by the Portmeirion Group in 2009. Some early products of the factory are listed under Worcester. Related pieces may be listed under Copeland, Copeland Spode, and Spode.

Box, Pen, Lid, Knop, Blue, White, Gilt Ferns, Rectangular, 8 In.	75
Bust, Clytie, Woman, Emerging From Flower, Socle Base, Aqua, c.1865, 11 In.	431
Bust, Clytie, Woman, Emerging From Flower, Socle Base, White, c.1860, 11 In.	161
Candlestick, Pillar, Square Rim, Green Standard, Laurel Wreath, Swags, 1888, 8 ½ In.	92
Charger, Blue, White Swallows, Bamboo, Black Ground, James Bradley, 18 In.	266
Charger, Flowers, James Callowhill & Raby, c.1880, 16 In.	1125
Ewer, Recessed Shell Shape Flower Panels, Apricot Ground, Gilt Handle, 7 ¾ In.	70
Figurine, Baltimore Oriole, Among Leaves, Flowers, Square Base, Pair, 9 x 9 ⅜ In.	960
Figurine, Bather Surprised, Seminude, Woman, Branch, c.1895, 26 x 11 In.	984
Figurine, Beach Baby, Blond, Blue Dress, Ball In Hand, 5 In.	68
Figurine, Chaffinch, Dorothy Doughty, 7 In., Pair	390
Figurine, Edward VI, After Holbein, 8 ¼ In.	150
Figurine, Grandmother's Dress, 7 In.	28
Figurine, Horse, Royal Guard Rider, Rectangular Base, 7 x 9 In.	960
Figurine, January, Boy In Red Coat, Green Bow, Spats, F. Doughty, 6 x 4 In.	59
Figurine, Magnolia Warbler, Dendroica Magnolia, Dorothy Doughty, 15 & 16 In., Pair	4500
Figurine, Mockingbirds, Dorothy Doughty, 12 In., Pair	1560
Figurine, Oven Bird, Lady Slipper Orchid, Wood Stand, 11 In.	354
Figurine, Scarlet Tanager, Branch, Dorothy Doughty, 13 In. ....*illus*	210
Figurine, Shire Stallion, Prancing, Elongated Oval Base, 9 ¼ x 9 ½ In.	900
Figurine, Woman, Man, Turban, Carrying Water Jugs, J. Hadley, 1888, 21 In., Pair	863
Fruit Cooler, Lid, Dragon Pattern, Gilt, Tab Handles, Marked, Signed, 10 ½ x 7 ½ In., Pair *illus*	1168
Ice Jug, Antler Shape Handle, Swans In Flight, Gilt, c.1888, 9 In.	780
Match Holder, Figural, Colonial Boy, Green Suit, Tricorn Hat, Stump Holder, 7 In.	29
Oyster Plate, 6 Wells, White, Green Basket Weave Ground, 8 ½ In.	230
Pitcher, Cream Ground, Yellow Flowers, Gold Trim Highlights, Handle, 7 ¼ In.	118
Pitcher, Flowers, Cream Ground, Gilt Handle, Base, 10 ½ In.	87
Plate, Bird, Leafy Bough Center, 10 ½ In., 8 Piece	531
Plate, Daytona, 10 ½ In., 12 Piece	242
Plate, Dinner, Ivory, Green & Yellow Floral Border, Center, 10 In., 12 Piece	390
Plate, Fish, Ivory Borders, Gilt, Fish, England, c.1933, 9 In., 11 Piece	1107
Plate, Vase, Flowers, Blue Ground, 10 ½ In., 12 Piece	605
Scent Bottle, Bird, Flowers, Shield Shape, c.1880, 3 ⅝ In.	58
Sugar & Creamer, Lavinia, Gold Rim, c.1940, 2 ⅜ In. ....*illus*	90
Vase, Apple Green, Lid, Gilt Swags, Swirled Cream, Gold Overlay, c.1900, 3 x 4 ½ In.	219
Vase, Bird, Leaves, Multicolor, Long Neck, Bottle Shape, Loop Handles, 14 In.	104
Vase, Birds, Branch, Rolled Rim, Oval, Shouldered, Ring Foot, 4 ½ In.	108
Vase, Blue, Gilt Dragon, Green Ground, Bottle Shape, Footed, 6 ½ In.	197
Vase, Bud, Flowers, Butterfly, Stick Neck, Low Gilt Handles, 10 In.	99
Vase, Flowers, Ruffled Flared Rim, Footed, Wavy Gilt Handles, 16 ¾ In.	139

ROYCROFT products were made by the Roycrofter community of East Aurora, New York, in the late nineteenth and early twentieth centuries. The community was founded by Elbert Hubbard, famous philosopher, writer, and artist. The workshops owned by the community made furniture, metalware, leatherwork, embroidery, and jewelry. A printshop produced many signs, books, and the magazines that promoted the sayings of Elbert Hubbard. Furniture by the Roycroft community is listed in the Furniture category.

Ashtray, Floor, Wrought Iron, Twisted, Curled, Copper Bowl, Orb Signed, 16 x 32 In.	1500
Bookends, Copper, Hammered, Hanging Bail, c.1920, 5 x 4 In.	219
Bowl, Brass, Copper, 4 ½ x 12 In.	207
Bowl, Trillium, Copper, Hammered, Perforated Round Bands, Repousse Design, 9 x 2 In.	344
Box, Copper, Hammered, Wood Liner, 6 x 2 In.	344
Candlestick, Copper, Hammered, 3 Arm Buttresses, Marked, c.1900, 9 In., Pair	3042
Candlestick, Copper, Hammered, Double Cylinder, Square Base, 3 ½ x 7 ½ In., Pair	700
Candlestick, Strap Design, Patina, Orb Signature, 4 ½ x 4 ½ x 12 In.	3538
Plaque, Motto, Be Yourself, Oak, Carved, Orb & Cross Mark, c.1920, 5 x 19 ½ In.	1250
Tray, Copper, Hammered, Organic Designs, Oval, Handles, 10 x 23 In.	469
Vase, American Beauty, Copper, Hammered, 8 x 22 In.	1830

R

Vase, American Beauty, Copper, Hammered, Polished Patina, Marked, 8 x 19 In.	1375
Vase, Bud, Copper, Hammered, Nickel Silver, Karl Kipp, Orb Mark, 1906-10, 8 x 3 In. ....*illus*	4062
Vase, Copper, Hammered, American Beauty, Rivets, Patina, 8 x 21 ½ In.	7320
Vase, Copper, Hammered, Bulbous, Impressed Mark, 5 x 5 In.	313
Vase, Copper, Hammered, Leaf Design, Tooled, 4 x 3 ½ In.	1250
Vase, Copper, Hammered, Quatrefoil, Cylindrical, 1920s, 5 x 2 ½ In.	313
Vase, Copper, Hammered, Smokestack, Cylindrical Neck, Flared Rim, Ring Foot, 19 In.	1463
Vase, Copper, Hammered, Tapered, Alligatored Patina, 3 x 5 In.	875
Vase, Copper, Hammered, Tooled, Tree Of Life Rim, Cylindrical, Impressed, 2 ¾ x 7 In.	813

ROZANE, *see Roseville category.*

ROZENBURG worked at The Hague, Holland, from 1890 to 1914. The most important pieces were earthenware made in the early twentieth century with pale-colored Art Nouveau designs.

Clock, Flowers, Butterfly, Shaped, Green, Blue, Black, Burgundy, 14 x 8 ½ In.	4888
Ewer, Stylized Sunflowers, Tan, Green, Blue, Elongated Lip, 9 In.	523
Jar, Orange, Brown, Blue, Flowers, c.1900, 5 x 4 ½ In.	750
Plaque, Blue & White, Landscape, Windmills, Signed, c.1890, 15 x 18 In.	840
Plaque, Iris Blooms, Water, Grass, Colored Enamel, Samuel Schellink, c.1909, 9 In. ....*illus*	1140
Plate, Juliana Pattern, Red, Blue, Green, Marked, c.1914, 8 In.	300
Vase, Brown Lizard, Purple Poppies, Bulbous, Flared Rim, 5 x 4 ½ In.	813
Vase, Bulbous, Blue, Green, Orange, 10 ¼ In.	1850
Vase, Butterflies, Flowers, Paneled, Brown, Green, c.1897, 7 ⅛ In.	324
Vase, Candlestick, Purple Morning Glory Vines, Tan Brushed Glaze, Arts & Crafts, 6 In.	60
Vase, Painted Lizard, Poppy, Black, Gold, Bulbous, Signed, 4 ½ x 5 In.	793
Vase, Painted Scene, Lizard, Poppy, Bulbous, Signed, Marked, 4 ½ x 5 In.	793
Vase, Pansies, Eggshell Ground, Signed, c.1900, 5 x 2 In. ....*illus*	1500
Vase, Pansies, Eggshell Porcelain, 4-Sided, Swollen, Flared Rim, c.1900, 5 x 2 In.	1536
Vase, Stylized Butterflies & Flowers, High Glaze, 4-Sided, Swollen, c.1897, 7 In.	333
Vase, Zomerbloemen, Flowers, Black, Cream, Brown, High Glaze, Footed, 9 In., Pair	369

RRP, or RRP Roseville, is the mark used by the firm of Robinson-Ransbottom. It is not a mark of the more famous Roseville Pottery. The Ransbottom brothers started a pottery in 1900 in Ironspot, Ohio. In 1920, they merged with the Robinson Clay Product Company of Akron, Ohio, to become Robinson-Ransbottom. The factory closed in 2005.

Bean Pot, Lid, Handle, Brown, Rust Band, Cream, Marked, 7 In.	45
Cookie Jar, Hey Diddle Diddle, Yellow, Blue, Robinson Ransbottom Pottery ....*illus*	58
Cookie Jar, Sailor Girl, Blond, Red Lips, 1940s	595
Cuspidor, Flat Rim, Dark Brown, Scalloped, Ribbed, 4 ¾ x 8 In.	67
Jardiniere, Flowers, Raised, Brown Rim, Green Glaze, c.1940, 9 ½ x 7 ½ In.	55 to 75
Jardiniere, Sun & Stars, Brown, Green, 1970s, 6 In.	49
Pitcher, Brown, Tan, Drip Glaze, 7 ¼ In.	45
Vase, Cornflower Blue, Speckled, Double Looped Handles, Footed, Oval, c.1939, 8 ½ In.	95

RS GERMANY is part of the wording in marks used by the Tillowitz, Germany, factory of Reinhold Schlegelmilch from 1914 until about 1945. The porcelain was sold decorated and undecorated. The Schlegelmilch families made porcelains marked in many ways. See also ES Germany, RS Poland, RS Prussia, RS Silesia, RS Suhl, and RS Tillowitz.

Bowl, Pink Flowers, Green Leaves, Square Gilt Handles, Footed, c.1915, 7 In. Diam.	165
Bowl, White Roses, Green Iridescent, Lettuce Leaf Shaped, 1920s, 10 In.	119
Hatpin Holder, Pink Roses, Green Leaves, 19 Pin Holes, Footed Beaker Shaped	55
Hatpin Holder, Trailing Roses, Yellow Ground, Pinched Waist, Gold Trim, 5 In.	35
Hatpin Holder, White Clematis, White Shaded To Green Ground, Pinched Waist, 7 In.	35
Pitcher, Anemones, Pink, Cranberry, Pearl Finish, c.1910, 11 ½ In.	259
Powder Dish, Lid, White & Cream Roses, Round, Gold Trim, 1 ½ x 5 In.	45
Syrup, Lid, White Poppies, Green Leaves, Elongated Oval, Loop Handle, c.1900, 6 In.	125
Tray, Yellow Roses, Leaves, Elongated Oval, Cutout Handles, 1920s, 15 ⅜ In.	119
Vase, Islamic Design, Orange, Blue Iridescent, Oval, Flat Rim, c.1920, 7 x 4 ½ In.	165

RS POLAND (German) is a mark used by the Reinhold Schlegelmilch factory at Tillowitz from about 1946 to 1956. After 1956, the factory made porcelain marked *PT Poland*. This is one of many of the RS marks used. See also ES Germany, RS Germany, RS Prussia, RS Silesia, RS Suhl, and RS Tillowitz.

Bowl, Flowers, Footed, Scalloped Edge, c.1950, 8 x 4 In.	95

TIP

Put books in the freezer overnight to get rid of many types of insects.

Royal Worcester, Sugar & Creamer, Lavinia, Gold Rim, c.1940, 2 ⅜ In. $90

Ruby Lane, Inc.

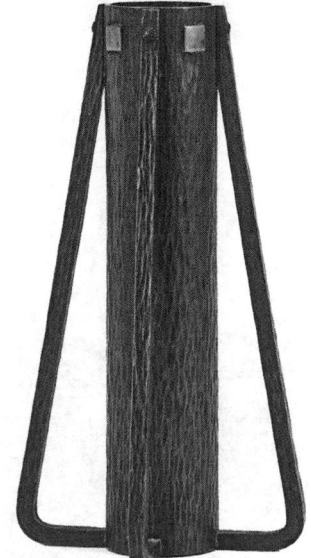

Roycroft, Vase, Bud, Copper, Hammered, Nickel Silver, Karl Kipp, Orb Mark, 1906-10, 8 x 3 In. $4,062

Rago Arts & Auction Center

R

Rozenburg, Plaque, Iris Blooms, Water, Grass, Colored Enamel, Samuel Schellink, c.1909, 9 In. $1,140

Skinner Auctioneers & Appraisers

Rozenburg, Vase, Pansies, Eggshell Ground, Signed, c.1900, 5 x 2 In. $1,500

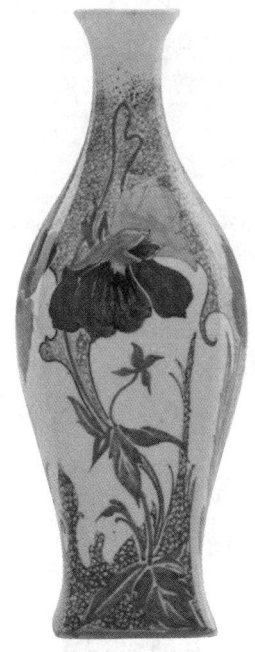

Rago Arts & Auction Center

RRP, Cookie Jar, Hey Diddle Diddle, Yellow, Blue, Robinson Ransbottom Pottery $58

Victorian Casino Antiques

Rug, Agra Serapi, 12 Ft. x 17 Ft. 9 In. $3,198

New Orleans Auction Galleries, Inc.

Hatpin Holder, Flowers, Ribbed, Scalloped Rim, Marked, 5 x 2 ½ In.	122
Plate, Pink Roses, Cutout Handles, Molded Edge, Marked, 10 In.	135

RS PRUSSIA appears in several marks used on porcelain before 1917. Reinhold Schlegelmilch started his porcelain works in Suhl, Germany, in 1869. See also ES Germany, RS Germany, RS Poland, RS Silesia, RS Prussia, and RS Tillowitz.

Biscuit Jar, Carnation Mold, Green & White, Magnolia Flowers, Handles, 5 x 9 In.	177
Bowl, Flowers, Scalloped Rim, Painted Flowers, Blue, Yellow, Pink, c.1890, 10 ½ In.	35
Bowl, Ostriches, Landscape, Scalloped Rim, c.1900, 9 ⅜ In.	920
Bowl, Roses, Iris, Scalloped Rim, Red Star Mark, 10 ½ In.	93
Bowl, Winter Season, Woman, Snowy Landscape, Lobed, Scalloped Rim, c.1900, 11 In.	575
Cake Plate, Icicle, Man In Sailboat, Cliff, Set-In Handles, c.1905, 10 In.	374
Cake Plate, Iris Mold, Pink, Cream & White, Poppies, Handles, 10 ¼ In.	89
Celery Tray, Lily Mold, Yellow, Green, Pink, Roses, 12 ¼ In.	71
Chocolate Pot, Hidden Image, Flower Bouquet, White Shaded To Peach Ground, 8 In.	70
Chocolate Pot, Roses, Cream Ground, Elongated Spout, Cupped Top, Marked, 8 ¼ In.	46
Chocolate Set, Pot, 6 Cups, Saucers, Yellow, Brown Flowers, c.1910, 11 In., 13 Piece	196
Hatpin Holder, Roses, Pink & White, Gold Trim, Attached Ring Tray, 4 ¾ In.	46
Pitcher, Flowers, Tankard Shape, c.1905, 11 In.	345
Pitcher, Iris, Pink, Blue, c.1905, 10 In.	184
Pitcher, Poppies, Pink, Cream, Blue, Tankard Shape, c.1905, 14 In.	288
Plate, Iris, Mill Scene, Satin Finish Border, 9 ½ In.	118
Relish, Ribbon & Jewel, Roses, Light Yellow, Green, Shaped, Open Handles, 12 In.	58
Salt & Pepper, Green, White Dogwood, Luster Finish, Pair	59
Toothpick Holder, Swan Woodland Scene, Flared Oval, Handles, c.1945, 2 In.	161
Vase, Man In The Mist, Sailing Ships, Swans, 2 Handles, Red Wreath Mark, 7 In.	316

RS SILESIA appears on porcelain made at the Reinhold Schlegelmilch factory in Tillowitz, Germany, from the 1920s to the 1940s. The Schlegelmilch families made porcelains marked in many ways. See also ES Germany, RS Germany, RS Poland, RS Prussia, RS Suhl, and RS Tillowitz.

Creamer, Pink Rose Band, Gold Handle, c.1920, 3 ¼ x 4 ⅝ In.	87
Nut Dish, Pink Flowers, Leaves, Footed, 6 In.	77
Plate, Flowers, Beige To Brown, c.1920, 8 ⅜ In.	150
Plate, Flowers, Green Edge, Marked, 6 ⅜ In.	112
Syrup, Lid, Underplate, Lilies, Lily Of The Valley, Green, 3 ½ In.	95

RS SUHL is a mark used by the Reinhold Schlegelmilch factory in Suhl, Germany, between 1900 and 1917. The Schlegelmilch families made porcelains in many places. See also ES Germany, RS Germany, RS Poland, RS Prussia, RS Silesia, and RS Tillowitz.

Bowl, Lavender Flowers, Leaves, Footed, Loop Handles, Marked, 9 ½ In. Diam.	115
Cake Plate, Flowers, Multicolor, Green, Open Handles, Crimped Edge, 10 In.	185
Cup & Saucer, Flower Border, Gold Trim, Handmaerei	40
Pitcher, Pink & Yellow Flowers, Pink To Blue Ground, 5 In.	69

RS TILLOWITZ was marked on porcelain by the Reinhold Schlegelmilch factory at Tillowitz from the 1920s to the 1940s. Table services and ornamental pieces were made. See also ES Germany, RS Germany, RS Poland, RS Prussia, RS Silesia, and RS Suhl.

Bowl, Mayonnaise, Flowers, Green, Bun Feet, Spoon, c.1920, 2 x 4 In.	45
Bowl, Orange Poppies, Cut In Handles, Yellow, Brown, Gold Trim, c.1920, 10 x 6 In.	85
Cheese Server, Pink Wild Roses, Gilt Trim, Marked, 6 In.	145
Creamer, White, c.1930, 3 ½ In.	37

RUBINA is a glassware that shades from red to clear. It was first made by George Duncan and Sons of Pittsburgh, Pennsylvania, in about 1885. This coloring was used on many types of glassware.

Butter, Cover, Honeycomb, 6 x 7 In.	100
Pitcher, Inverted Thumbprint, Enameled Daisies, Clear Ribbed Handle, 8 ½ In.	118
Pitcher, Red, To Clear, Faceted Pattern, Tapered, 8 ½ x 6 ½ In.	92
Powder Jar, Frosted Enameled Flowers, 7 ½ In.	118
Water Set, Pitcher, 6 Barrel-Shape Mugs, Enameled Decoration, Victorian, 9-In. Pitcher	1093

RUBINA VERDE is a Victorian glassware that was shaded from red to green. It was first made by Hobbs, Brockunier and Company of Wheeling, West Virginia, about 1890.

Pickle Castor, Swirl Diamond, Dog On Lid, Silver Frame, 11 In.	348

R

Pitcher, Inverted Thumbprint, Ribbed Handle, 7 ½ In.	89
Vase, Swirled Clear Rigaree, Cylindrical, 9 ¼ x 3 ¼ In.	180

RUBY GLASS is the dark red color of a ruby, the precious gemstone. It was a popular Victorian color that never went completely out of style. The glass was shaped by many different processes to make many different types of ruby glass. There was a revival of interest in the 1940s when modern-shaped ruby table glassware became fashionable. Sometimes the red color is added to clear glass by a process called flashing or staining. Flashed glass is clear glass dipped in a colored glass, then pressed or cut. Stained glass has color painted on a clear glass. Then it is refired so the stain fuses with the glass. Pieces of glass colored in this way are indicated by the word *stained* in the description. Related items may be found in other categories, such as Cranberry Glass, Pressed Glass, and Souvenir.

Bowl, Painted Flowers, Swirled, Quilted Base, Flared, 3 x 7 In.	46
Bowl, Thumbprints, 3 x 4 ½ In.	71
Cocktail, Clear Coin Dot, 3 In., 6 Piece	26
Compote, Hobnail, Ruffled Rim, 6 ½ In.	59
Compote, Thumbprint, Scalloped Rim, 3 ½ x 4 ½ In.	28
Decanter, Ball Shape, Tapered Neck, Clear Twisted Handle, Faceted Stopper, c.1880, 9 In.	60
Decanter, Pinched Sides, Ruffled Tricorn Rim, Clear Handle & Stopper, 1950s, 7 x 5 In.	32
Ewer, Reticulated Scrolled Leaf Frame, Austria, c.1890, 5 In.	330
Figurine, Cat, Sitting, Franklin Mint, 2 ⅞ In.	200
Finial, Ribbed, Square Top, Brass Base, 19th Century, 6 In.	395
Oil Lamp Shade, Quilt Design, Ruffled Top, 10 In.	150
Punch Bowl, Underplate, Paneled Sides & Lid, Cup Finial, 8 In.	250
Salt & Pepper, Omaha Exposition, 1898, 3 ½ In.	55
Scent Bottle, Sterling Lid, Repousse, Scrolls, 1 ½ In.	450
Shaker, Bulbous, Molded Leaves, Silver Metal Lid, 2 ⅝ In.	132
Tieback, Flower Shape, 1930s, 3 ¼ In., Pair	48
Tumbler, Juice, Cylindrical Ribbed Foot, 1950s, 3 ½ In., 8 Piece	23
Vase, Flowers, Blue, Enamel, Bulbous, Stick Neck, 10 ¾ In.	195
Vase, Intaglio Poppies, Vertical Flutes, Bulbous, Cinched, Notched Rim, 6 x 5 In.	360
Vase, Jack In The Pulpit, Vertical Ribs, Flared Out Rim, Bulbous Foot, 6 ½ In.	30
Vase, Piecrust Scalloped Rim, Shouldered, 1940s, 9 In.	75

RUDOLSTADT was a faience factory in the Thuringia region of Germany from 1720 to about 1791. In 1854, Ernst Bohne began working in the area. From about 1887 to 1918, the New York and Rudolstadt Pottery made decorated porcelain marked with the RW and crown familiar to collectors. This porcelain was imported by Lewis Straus and Sons of New York, which later became Nathan Straus and Sons. The word *Royal* was included in their import mark. Collectors often call it "Royal Rudolstadt." Most pieces found today were made in the late nineteenth or early twentieth century. Additional pieces may be listed in the Kewpie category.

Bust, Woman, Frilly Blouse, Hat, Bow, Lavender, Green, c.1915, 5 In.	395
Figurine, 19th Century Man & Woman, Man Seated, Woman Standing, c.1900, 14 In.	107
Figurine, Dancing Oriental Figure, Painted, White Pedestal, Germany, 5 ½ & 6 ¼ In., Pair	360
Figurine, Gentleman, Holding Water Jug, Floral Pantaloons, Gold Trim, Marked RW, 17 In.	35
Vase, Japanese Musician, Dancer, c.1900, 8 ½ In.	42

RUGS have been used in the American home since the seventeenth century. The oriental rug of that time was often used on a table, not on the floor. Rag rugs, hooked rugs, and braided rugs were made by housewives from scraps of material. American Indian rugs are listed in the Indian category.

Agra Serapi, 12 Ft. x 17 Ft. 9 In. ....*illus*	3198
Agra, Flowers, Red Ground, Green Border, c.1900, 12 Ft. 6 In. x 12 Ft. 11 In.	17775
Akstafa, Prayer, Multicolor Diagonal, Borders, Caucasus, c.1885, 5 Ft. 8 In. x 3 Ft. 2 In. .....*illus*	4200
Anatolian Sannah, Red, Orange, Turkey, c.1910, 1 Ft. 11 In. x 3 Ft. 6 In.	123
Aubusson, Blue Medallion, Saffron Field, Garland, Vines, France, c.1790, 16 Ft. x 14 Ft. 3 In.	6875
Aubusson, Multicolor, Rosettes, Brown Vine Border, France, c.1850, 9 Ft. 3 In. x 8 Ft. 4 In.	4063
Aubusson, Roses, c.1900, 18 Ft. 3 In. x 12 Ft. 6 In.	1458
Bakhtiari, Stylized Flowers, Blue, Tan, Persia, c.1935, Runner, 9 Ft. 8 In. x 3 Ft. 8 In.	1625
Balouch, Red, Yellow, Teal Structures, Geometric Borders, Fringe, 2 Ft. 8 In. x 4 Ft. 3 In.	75
Baluchi, Geometric, Orange, Red, Gray, Green, Black, Blue, Fringe, 2 Ft. 10 In. x 6 Ft.	414
Bibikabad, Diamond Medallion, Gray, Blue, Tan, Persia, c.1925, 11 Ft. 10 In. x 8 Ft. 8 In.	1875
Bidjar, Diamond Medallion, Blue, Palmette Border, c.1920, 18 Ft. 3 In. x 11 Ft. 6 In.	4063
Bidjar, Navy Blue Field, Central Medallion, c.1940, 3 Ft. x 5 Ft.	472
Boukara, Prayer, Panels, Medallions, Red, Blue, Key Border, 4 Ft. 2 In. x 4 Ft. 7 In.	590

Rug, Akstafa, Prayer, Multicolor Diagonal, Borders, Caucasus, c.1885, 5 Ft. 8 In. x 3 Ft. 2 In.
$4,200

Skinner Auctioneers & Appraisers

Rug, Ege Rya, Squares, Crosses, Red, Orange, Yellow, Denmark, c.1970, 7 Ft. 7 In. x 5 Ft. 4 In.
$3438

Los Angeles Modern Auctions (LAMA)

Rug, Half Circles, Wavy Lines, Edward Fields, Signed, 1971, 9 Ft. 2 In. x 8 Ft.
$3,750

Los Angeles Modern Auctions (LAMA)

R

Rug, Heriz, Geometric & Flower Medallions, Red Field, Borders, 3 Ft. 5 In. x 14 Ft. 5 In. $1,416

Brunk Auctions

Rug, Hooked, Cats, Seated, Birds, Flowers, Multicolor, c.1910, 22 ½ x 39 ½ In. $47

Conestoga Auction Co., Inc.

Rug, Hooked, Dog Sled Scene, Rayon, Silk, Burlap Back, Grenfell, c.1910, 26 x 40 In. $1,800

Skinner Auctioneers & Appraisers

Boukara, Salor, Flower Center, Geometrics, Red, Blue, Ivory, Yellow, 8 Ft. 2 In. x 20 Ft.	3800
Chinese, Blue Border, Ivory Ground, c.1940, 6 Ft. x 9 Ft. 4 In.	206
Chinese, Red, Medallions, Checkerboard, Beige Border, Wool, c.1950, 8 Ft. 6 In. x 11 Ft. 5 In.	540
Dergazine, Allover Flowers, Blue Ground, 3 Borders, Runner, 8 Ft. 8 In. x 2 Ft. 6 In.	300
Donnemara, Art Nouveau Flowers, Vining, Charles Voysey, Donegal, c.1905, 13 Ft. x 9 Ft. 8 In.	22500
Dushak, Stylized Flowers, Blue Tones, Hand Knotted, Wool, 10 Ft. 5 In. x 13 Ft. 9 In.	2625
Ege Rya, Squares, Crosses, Red, Orange, Yellow, Denmark, c.1970, 7 Ft. 7 In. x 5 Ft. 4 In. *illus*	3438
English, Red Field, Flowers, Mustard Palmette Border, c.1920, 17 Ft. 8 In. x 11 Ft. 2 In.	10625
Felt, Penny Design, Brown, Orange, Blue, Triangular, c.1910, 4 Ft. 3 In. x 2 Ft. 5 In.	420
Feraghan, Center Diamond, Rose, Blue, Ivory, Persia, 1920s, 9 Ft. 9 In. x 5 Ft. 1 In.	719
Feraghan, Center Medallion, Red Ground, Persia, 7 Ft. 8 In. x 11 Ft. 7 In.	1046
Geometric Shapes, Multicolor, Mid-Atlantic, Runner, c.1900, 2 Ft. 7 In. x 7 Ft. 5 In.	127
Greek, Figural, Birds & Animals, Crane Border, Earth Tones, 4 Ft. 10 In. x 5 Ft. 7 In.	600
Half Circles, Wavy Lines, Edward Fields, Signed, 1971, 9 Ft. 2 In. x 8 Ft. *illus*	3750
Hamadan, Center Medallion, Multicolor Arabesque Edge, Spandrels, 3 Ft. 6 In. x 4 Ft. 9 In.	224
Hamadan, Orange Border, Navy, Blue Accents, Medallion, 1930s, 9 Ft. 5 In. x 13 Ft. 3 In.	1476
Hamadan, Red Floral Medallion, Pendants, Blue Field, Flowering Vine, Spandrels, 2 x 3 Ft.	83
Hamadan, Stylized Flowers, Brick Red Ground, 3 Borders, Runner, 9 Ft. 8 In. x 2 Ft. 6 In.	600
Hearth, Basket Of Flowers, Wool Yarn Stitched, Stripe Border, 35 x 69 In.	660
Heriz, Gabled Medallion, Blue, Red, Vines, Flowers, Spandrels, c.1945, 9 Ft. 3 In. x 12 Ft.	531
Heriz, Gabled Medallion, Ivory, Red, Blue, Leaves, Blue Border, 6 Ft. 7 In. x 9 Ft. 8 In.	649
Heriz, Geometric & Flower Medallions, Red Field, Borders, 3 Ft. 5 In. x 14 Ft. 5 In. *illus*	1416
Heriz, Geometric Flowers, Garnet Ground, c.1970, 8 Ft. 6 In. x 11 Ft. 9 In.	1375
Heriz, Geometric Medallion, Spandrels, Palmette Border, c.1900, 11 Ft. 8 In. x 8 Ft. 10 In.	3750
Heriz, Geometric Medallions, Leaves, Red, Blue, Tan, c.1940, 15 Ft. 2 In. x 11 Ft. 8 In.	4063
Heriz, Geometric, Center Medallion, Red Ground, 1930s, 8 Ft. 8 In. x 9 Ft. 1 In.	1968
Heriz, Hexagonal Medallion, Ivory Ground, Rust, Blue, Tan Border, 13 x 9 Ft.	5938
Heriz, Ivory Spandrels, Red, Blue Palmette, Vine Border, c.1925, 12 Ft. 3 In. x 8 Ft. 8 In.	2000
Heriz, Medallion, Spandrels, Leaves, Red, Blue, Brown, Tan, 12 Ft. 7 In. x 9 Ft. 6 In.	6250
Heriz, Multicolor Gabled Medallion, Pendants, Flowering Branches, 8 Ft. 7 In. x 11 Ft. 9 In.	531
Heriz, Triangle Medallion, Red, White, Cotton, Wool, Persia, c.1960, 10 Ft. 7 In. x 14 Ft. 2 In.	2360
Hooked, 1900s House, Multicolor, Canted Roof, Chimneys, Frame, 1910s, 21 x 30 In.	236
Hooked, 2 Ducks, Acorn Corner Border, Shenandoah Valley, c.1920, 27 x 44 In.	403
Hooked, 2 Stags, Tulips, Brown, Blue, Red, Black, 33 x 44 In.	840
Hooked, 3 Bears, Walking, Holding Bowls, 17 x 29 In.	660
Hooked, 3 Ducks In Flight, Mountains, Silk, Cotton, Grenfell Labrador Ind., 38 x 40 In.	960
Hooked, Alternating Flowers, Zigzag Stripes, Wool, On Burlap, c.1900, 71 x 73 In.	211
Hooked, Bear Cubs, Tossing Orange Ball, Stretcher Mount, c.1930, 29 x 43 In.	420
Hooked, Bird, Flower Panels, Pennsylvania, c.1920, 58 x 38 In.	1140
Hooked, Black Cat, Brown, Tan Leaf, Clover Border, Wool Yarn, c.1905, 41 x 46 In.	2000
Hooked, Blue Snowflake, Green, Red, Cream Ground, c.1900, 36 x 26 In.	840
Hooked, Brick Wall, Green, Red, Tan, Brown, c.1950, 16 x 24 In.	150
Hooked, Cat, Standing, Tan, Brown, Double Border, c.1945, 25 x 36 In.	720
Hooked, Cats, Birds, Flower Border, c.1900, 22 x 39 In.	48
Hooked, Cats, Seated, Birds, Flowers, Multicolor, c.1910, 22 ½ x 39 ½ In. *illus*	47
Hooked, Concentric Circles, Multicolor, Oval, 26 x 37 In.	210
Hooked, Cowboy, Brown, Pants, Lasso, Wool, Round, c.1940, 59 x 35 In.	9375
Hooked, Diamond, Star, Circles, Brown, Tan, Red, c.1945, 24 x 40 In.	330
Hooked, Diamonds, Sawtooth Designs, Red, Blue, Tan, 37 x 23 In.	540
Hooked, Dog Sled Scene, Rayon, Silk, Burlap Back, Grenfell, c.1910, 26 x 40 In. *illus*	1800
Hooked, Dog, Boxer, Black, White, Flower Corners, c.1910, 32 x 20 In.	200
Hooked, Dog, Lying, Edward Frost Pattern, Geometric, Flower Border, Frame, 27 x 43 In.	85
Hooked, Dog, Red Collar, Wooden Frame, c.1900, 16 x 32 In.	145
Hooked, Dog, Resting, Black, Brown, Tan, Green Border, c.1920, 17 x 18 ½ In.	2645
Hooked, Dog, Welcome, Brown, Cream, c.1900, 36 x 19 In.	575
Hooked, Doves, Trees, Flowers, Brown, Tan, c.1900, 16 ½ x 50 In.	570
Hooked, Duck, Red, Blue, Gray, c.1890, 39 x 26 In.	385
Hooked, Dutch Hex Signs, Striped Border, Frame, 1949, 31 x 60 In.	24
Hooked, Elopement, Couple, On Horseback, Hutchinson, c.1920, 18 x 59 In.	2400
Hooked, Farm Scene, Horses, Cows, Chickens, Multicolor, Runner, c.1910, 18 x 67 In.	130
Hooked, Fisherman's House, Fish, Pond, Blue, Rose, White, Brown, c.1890, 144 x 108 In.	2040
Hooked, Floral Medallion, Abstract Corner Designs, c.1930, 14 x 14 In.	58
Hooked, Flower Center, Spandrel Border, Blue Ground, New England, 144 x 108 In.	2040
Hooked, Flowers, Leaves, Striped Border, c.1910, 32 x 40 ¼ In. *illus*	36
Hooked, Flowers, Multicolor, Black Ground, c.1930, 28 x 46 In.	60
Hooked, Flowers, Multicolor, Brown Scroll Border, c.1890, 79 x 38 In.	123

Hooked, Flowers, Stylized Vine, Red, Black, c.1920, 31 x 52 In.	345
Hooked, Flowers, Triple Band Border, Octagonal, c.1920, 34 x 55 In.	259
Hooked, Flowers, Wavy Lines, Leaf Border, c.1920, 87 x 110 In.	316
Hooked, Fox, Grapevine Border, Barbara Wheeler Marian, Wool, Frame, 19 x 26 In. ...	323
Hooked, Geese, Swag Border, 1900s, 28 x 50 In.	1440
Hooked, Geometric Shapes, Red, Gold, Green, Blue, Brown, c.1910, 29 x 30 In.	900
Hooked, Geometric, Striated, Striped, Black Border, Wool, On Burlap, c.1910, 75 x 92 In. ...	235
Hooked, Geometrics, Multicolor, c.1900, 32 x 53 In.	230
Hooked, Hearth, Liberty Cap, Sunburst, Stars, Black, Gold, Demilune, c.1895, 28 x 47 In. ...	3360
Hooked, Horse, Flowers, Tan & Gray Ground, c.1850, 37 x 39 In.	960
Hooked, Horse, Multicolor Geometric Border, Corner Medallions, 25 x 38 In.	331
Hooked, Horses, Galloping, Medallion, Flower Corners, Multicolor, c.1900, 23 x 42 In. ...	48
Hooked, Leopard, Lying Down, Green Herringbone Ground, 1943, 36 x 89 In.	4080
Hooked, M.A.D. Cats, Seated, Checkered Floor, Variegated Border, c.1885, 26 x 45 In.	3120
Hooked, Multicolor, Flowers, Tan, Brown Border, c.1900, 28 x 61 In.	720
Hooked, Parrot, In Tree, Flowers, Leaves, c.1945, 30 x 51 In.	150
Hooked, People, Dogs, Must I Always Cook For My Husband's Kin, Hutchinson, 34 x 51 In. ...	840
Hooked, Pick Of The Litter, Sow, Piglets, White, Blue Ground, 21 x 37 In.	2280
Hooked, Postage Stamp Design, Geometric, Multicolor, c.1910, 28 ½ x 50 In.	240
Hooked, Red Barns, Snow Scene, c.1910, 25 x 39 In.	120
Hooked, Red Flowers, Blue, Geometric Ground, c.1915, 41 x 21 In.	267
Hooked, Red Flowers, Green Ground, Oval, 22 x 36 In.	150
Hooked, Rooster, 4 Leaping Horses, Green Ground, 33 x 19 ½ In.	546
Hooked, Rooster, Strutting, Multicolor, Blue Ground, Sunflower Vine, c.1950, 32 x 46 In. ...	400
Hooked, Roosters, Tree, Variegated Ground, Tan Border, Wool, Cotton, c.1900, 23 x 37 In. ...	7200
Hooked, Rose Blossom, Wool, c.1910, 24 x 34 In.	89
Hooked, Rose, Leaves, Waves, Mounted, c.1900, 27 x 46 In.	360
Hooked, Scottish Terrier, Gray, Black, Red, Blue, Green, Borders, Wool, c.1950, 19 x 32 In. ...	300
Hooked, Tabby Cat, Gray, 1900s, 24 x 37 In.	600
Hooked, Tile Pattern, Flowers, Runner, c.1950, 108 x 24 In.	813
Hooked, Tree Of Life, Stylized, Flowers, c.1930, 33 x 16 ½ In.	29
Hooked, Two Eagles, Flowers, New York, c.1880, 38 x 43 In.	1920
Hooked, Variegated Wave, c.1950, 32 x 48 In.	480
Hooked, Vase Of Flowers, Wool, Cotton, Frame, c.1890, 55 x 54 In. ....*illus*	2400
Hooked, Welcome, Homestead Scene, Multicolor, Wooden Frame, c.1910, 28 x 20 In.	384
Hooked, Welcome, Homestead, Frame, c.1900, 28 x 19 In.	384
Hooked, White Horse, Yellow Border, c.1900, 25 x 42 In.	510
Hooked, Wood, Dog, Red Collar, c.1900, 16 x 32 In.	144
Indo Serapi, Beige, Flowers, Brackets, Medallion, Blue Borders, Wool, c.1900, 9 x 12 Ft.	780
Isfahan, Tree Of Life, Wildlife, Ivory Field, Persia, c.1925, 7 Ft. 9 In. x 4 Ft. 7 In. ...	1875
Karaja, 3 Geometric Medallions, Blue, Red, Persia, c.1925, 6 Ft. 2 In. x 4 Ft. 9 In. ...	2813
Karaja, Geometric Medallion, Rust, Ivory, Blue, Persia, c.1945, 12 Ft. 4 In. x 9 Ft. 9 In. ...	2813
Kashan, Allover Flowers, Blue Field, Red Guard Border, c.1940, 9 Ft. 4 In. x 11 Ft. 8 In. ...	1534
Kashan, Multicolor Pendant, Palms, Vine Border, Persia, c.1935, 6 Ft. 11 In. x 4 Ft. 7 In. ...	1250
Kashan, Pendant Medallion, Flowers, Vines, Red, Blue Flowers, Silk, 6 Ft. 8 In. x 4 Ft. 5 In. ...	3750
Kazak, Cloud Band, 3 Medallions, Red Field, c.1900, 7 Ft. 7 In. x 4 Ft. 4 In.	385
Kazak, Stylized Cross, Multiple Borders, Caucasus, c.1890, 7 Ft. x 5 Ft. 3 In. ....*illus*	10200
Kerman, Blue Ground, Flower Border, Medallion, Corner Brackets, Red, Blue, Beige, 4 x 6 Ft. ...	300
Kerman, Flower Border, Winged Figures, Trees, Birds, Green, Fringed, c.1900, 7 x 4 Ft. ...	12000
Kerman, Ivory, Green Flowers, Burgundy Palmette, Vine Border, c.1885, 6 Ft. 8 In. x 4 Ft. 5 In. ...	1125
Kerman, Medallion, Red, Blue Tree, Shrubs, Ivory Field, c.1880, 19 Ft. 7 In. x 14 Ft. 5 In. ...	10000
Kerman, Tree Of Life, Animals, Plants, Persia, 1920s, 4 Ft. 7 In. x 6 Ft. 10 In. ....*illus*	3900
Kerman, Turquoise Blue Ground, Ivory Border, Cotton Weft, 6 Ft. 2 In. x 3 Ft. 11 In. ...	121
Kilim, 7 Diamond Medallions, Yellow Field, Anatolia, Runner, c.1915, 11 Ft. x 2 Ft. 5 In. ...	688
Kirman, Salmon Ground, c.1910, 16 Ft. 7 In. x 11 Ft. 7 In.	2252
Knitted, Multicolor Concentric Circles, Round, Elvira C. Hulett, Wool, c.1890, 50 In. ...	161000
Lillihan, Flowers, Blue, Green, Gold, Ivory, Medallion, Red Field, 5 Ft. 2 In. x 6 Ft. 11 In. ...	325
Mahal, Red Field, Flowers, Vines Rosette Border, Persia, c.1900, 12 Ft. 4 In. x 8 Ft. 7 In. ...	750
Mahal, Red, Blue Medallions, Borders, c.1930, 14 Ft. 8 In. x 10 Ft. 4 In.	1896
Mahal, Red, Blue, Tan, Gray, Leaves, Medallion Center, Borders, Fringe, 5 Ft. x 7 Ft. 9 In. ...	230
Mamluk Style, Geometric, Pastel, Hand Knotted, Wool, 6 x 9 Ft.	938
Oriental, Flowers, Burgundy Ground, c.1930, 4 Ft. 2 In. x 6 Ft. 10 In.	301
Oushak Style, Geometric Floral, Blue, Gray, Hand Knotted, Wool, 9 Ft. 3 In. x 11 Ft. 6 In. ...	3375
Oushak Style, Geometric Flowers, Blue, Brown, Tan Ground, 10 Ft. 1 In. x 13 Ft. 9 In. ...	2375
Oushak, Multicolor Medallion, Tan Spandrels, Ivory Ground, c.1925, 12 Ft. 8 In. x 8 Ft. 8 In. ...	406
Penny, Diamond Pattern, Double Diagonal Grid, Multicolor, Wool, Cotton, c.1900, 49 x 32 In. ...	360

Rug, Hooked, Flowers, Leaves, Striped Border, c.1910, 32 x 40 ¼ In.
$36

Rug, Hooked, Vase Of Flowers, Wool, Cotton, Frame, c.1890, 55 x 54 In.
$2,400

Rug, Kazak, Stylized Cross, Multiple Borders, Caucasus, c.1890, 7 Ft. x 5 Ft. 3 In.
$10,200

R

Persian, Flower Rows, Spandrels, Red, Blue, Green Gray, Yellow, 4 Ft. 1 In. x 6 Ft. 2 In.	354
Pictorial, Blue Field, Flowers, Hunters Horse, Ivory Border, Romania, 11 Ft. 8 In. x 9 Ft.	480
Pictorial, Chinese Immortals, Multicolor, Black Ground, Wool, 4 Ft. x 2 Ft. 6 In.	127
Sarouk, Feraghan, Flowers, Vines, Leaves, Wine Border, c.1880, 16 Ft. 8 In. x 10 Ft. 2 In.	10625
Sarouk, Flowering Branches, Red Field, Blue, Green, Gold, Border, 7 Ft. 6 In. x 9 Ft. 11 In.	385
Sarouk, Flowering Quatrefoil, Red, Green, Gold, Blue, Wide Border, 9 Ft. 4 In. x 12 Ft. 5 In.	2360
Sarouk, Flowers, Deer, Spandrel, Blue, Orange, Tan, Persia, 10 Ft. 5 In. x 6 Ft. 1 In.	1125
Sarouk, Red Ground, Blue Border, Flowers, Spandrels, Wool, 12 Ft. 10 In. x 23 Ft. 6 In.	1789
Serab, Animals, Flowers, Red Ground, Persia, Runner, 3 Ft. 5 In. x 12 Ft. 7 In.	600
Serapi, Flowers, Tan Border, Red, Blue, Persia, c.1875, 10 Ft. 10 In. x 9 Ft. 6 In.	13530
Serapi, Gold Medallion, Blue Pendants, Red, Ivory Field, c.1990, 5 Ft. 10 In. x 8 Ft. 10 In.	708
Sevas, Gray Field, Flowers, Ivory, Green, Rosette Border, Red, c.1925, 5 Ft. 6 In. x 4 Ft.	344
Sultanabad, Red Flower, Blue Vine Border, Persia, c.1890, 14 Ft. 3 In. x 10 Ft. 7 In.	4375
Tabriz, Birds, Animals, Flowers, Palm, Vine Border, Iran, 13 Ft. 8 In. x 10 Ft. 2 In.	3750
Tabriz, Floral, Red Ground, Corner Ornaments, 9 Ft. 5 In. x 12 Ft. 8 In.	431
Tabriz, Flowers, Blue, Pendants, Red Field, Green, Blue Border, 8 Ft. 2 In. x 11 Ft. 7 In.	767
Tabriz, Lobed Medallion, Salmon Red, Cream Field, Flowers, Vines, 9 Ft. 11 In. x 13 Ft. 4 In.	2478
Tabriz, Pendant, Medallion, Ivory Field, Spandrels, Vines, c.1890, 13 Ft. 8 In x 10 Ft.	20000
William Morris Style, Allover Flowers, Green Ground, 12 Ft. x 14 Ft. 6 In.	3000
William Morris Style, Red Flowers, Teal Blue Field, 8 Ft. 9 In. x 11 Ft. 10 In.	3250
Yomoud, Eggplant Field, Blue, Red, Turkestan, c.1920, 10 Ft. 2 In. x 6 Ft. 8 In.	2375

RUMRILL POTTERY was designed by George Rumrill of Little Rock, Arkansas. From 1933 to 1938, it was produced by the Red Wing Pottery of Red Wing, Minnesota. In January 1938, production was transferred to the Shawnee Pottery in Zanesville, Ohio. It was moved again in December of 1938 to Florence Pottery Company in Mt. Gilead, Ohio, where Rumrill ware continued to be manufactured until the pottery burned in 1941. It was then produced by Gonder Ceramic Arts in South Zanesville until early 1943.

Console, Pink Matte Glaze, Looping Scroll Handles, c.1935, 6 x 11 In.	95
Vase, Bud, Blue Matte Glaze, Footed, Quatrefoil, Flaring Rim, c.1937, 6 ¼ In.	55
Vase, Ivory, Blue Interior, Swirl, Footed, Handles, 7 In.	55
Vase, Mottled Green, Flared Wavy Rim, Winding Flower Foot, 7 In.	6
Vase, Turtle Handles, Water Lilies, Roses, c.1940, 6 ½ In.	175

RUSKIN is a British art pottery of the twentieth century. The Ruskin Pottery was started by William Howson Taylor, and his name was used as the mark until about 1899. The factory, at West Smethwick, Birmingham, England, stopped making new pieces in 1933 but continued to glaze and sell the remaining wares until 1935. The art pottery is noted for its exceptional glazes.

Bowl, Cream, Green, Flame Glaze, 1932, 12 x 9 In.	115
Candlestick, Stick Neck, Flat Base, Flame, Mottled, Speckled, 1925, 10 In.	251
Ginger Jar, Purple Luster, Lid, 1921, 5 In.	575
Lamp, Hexagonal Column, Blue, Orange, Green, c.1930, 9 In.	298
Vase, Blue, Gray, Handles, 1930s, 10 ½ In.	288
Vase, Crystalline Flambe, Tan, Gray, Green, Marked, 5 In. ....*illus*	265
Vase, Globular, Shaped Rim, Brown & Red Luster Glaze, 1924, 3 ½ In.	995
Vase, Gourd Shape, Yellow Crystalline Glaze, c.1930, 9 In.	290
Vase, Sang De Boeuf, Flared Rim, Maroon Glaze, Marked, 1910, 12 ½ In.	2006
Vase, Shouldered, Stick Neck, Yellow, Lusterware, c.1900, 8 In.	350
Vase, Shouldered, White, Yellow Sponging, Marked, 1915, 10 In.	785
Vase, Trumpet, Green, Orange, Blue, Marked, 1930s, 9 In.	295

RUSSEL WRIGHT designed dinnerware in modern shapes for many companies. Iroquois China Company, Harker China Company, Steubenville Pottery, and Justin Tharaud and Sons made dishes marked *Russel Wright*. The Steubenville wares, first made in 1938, are the most common today. Wright was a designer of domestic and industrial wares, including furniture, aluminum, radios, interiors, and glassware. A new company, Bauer Pottery Company of Los Angeles, is making Russel Wright's American Modern dishes using molds made from original pieces. The pottery is made in Highland, California. Pieces are marked *Russel Wright by Bauer Pottery California USA*. Russel Wright Dinnerware and other original pieces by Wright are listed here. For more prices, go to kovels.com.

Aluminum, Cocktail Set, No. 326, Cork, Shaker, Cups, 1930, 11-In. Tray, 8 Piece	6350
Aluminum, Punch Bowl, Lid, Saturn, Tray, 12 Cups, Ladle, c.1935, Tray 12 In. ....*illus*	2280
American Modern, Celery Dish, Chartreuse, 13 x 4 In.	40
American Modern, Cup & Saucer, Coral, After Dinner	30
Chrome, Corn Set, Blue, Round, Butter Pitcher, Salt, Pepper, Chase, 6-In. Tray, 4 Piece	188

Rug, Kerman, Tree Of Life, Animals, Plants, Persia, 1920s, 4 Ft. 7 In. x 6 Ft. 10 In. $3,900

Cowan's Auctions

Ruskin, Vase, Crystalline Flambe, Tan, Gray, Green, Marked, 5 In. $265

Humler & Nolan

Russel Wright, Aluminum, Punch Bowl, Lid, Saturn, Tray, 12 Cups, Ladle, c.1935, Tray 12 In. $2,280

Skinner Auctioneers & Appraisers

Iroquois Casual, Bowl, Oval, Coral, 11 ⅝ In.	20
Iroquois Casual, Casserole, Lid, Divided, Pink, 10 ¼ In.	85
Iroquois Casual, Cup & Saucer, Parsley	15
Iroquois Casual, Pitcher, Nutmeg, 5 ¾ In.	100
Iroquois Casual, Pitcher, Water, Cantaloupe, 9 In. ....*illus*	949
Iroquois Casual, Platter, Oval, Blue, 14 In.	35
Lamp, Torchere, Aluminum, Flared Shade, Disc Base, 67 ½ In.	90
Lamp, Torchere, Maple Stem, Tapered, Aluminum Flared Shade, c.1930, 66 In.	127
Vase, Pottery, Speckled Tan Glaze, Cylindrical, Bauer, 10 ⅜ In.	225

SABINO glass was made in the 1920s and 1930s in Paris, France. Founded by Marius-Ernest Sabino (1878–1961), the firm was noted for Art Deco lamps, vases, figurines, and animals in clear, colored, and opalescent glass. Production stopped during World War II but resumed in the 1960s with the manufacture of nude figurines and small opalescent glass animals. Pieces made in recent years are a slightly different color and can be recognized. Only vintage pieces are listed here.

Sabino France

Bowl, Sea Urchins, Seaweed, Smoky Gray, c.1925, 14 In.	475
Bowl, Shells, 4 ¾ x 2 In.	135
Compote, Rearing Stallions, 8 x 9 ¼ In.	750
Figurine, Butterfly, Opalescent, 3 x 2 In.	70
Figurine, Cherub, Holding Roses, Foil Label, 2 In.	56
Figurine, Dragonfly, 6 In.	495
Figurine, Fish, Opalescent, Red & Gold Label, 4 ¼ In.	150
Figurine, Kingfish, Opalescent, c.1925, 4 ½ In.	146
Figurine, Mouse, 2 ¾ In.	90
Figurine, Swan, Open Wings, Signed, 1 ½ In.	45
Figurine, Woman, Lamb, 6 ¾ In.	490
Figurine, Woman, Seated, Crossed Legs, Nude, c.1925, 6 ½ In.	695
Figurine, Woman, Walking, Flowing Hair, 6 ¾ In.	490
Knife Rest, Opalescent, 2 Level, Geometric Designs, 3 ¼ x 1 In., Pair	125
Perfume Bottle, Gaite, Opalescent, Blown-Out Women, Oval, Lattice Stopper, Paris, 6 In.	115
Perfume Bottle, Nudes, Opalescent, Pinecone Stopper, 6 In.	99
Plate, Henri IV Bust, Flower & Leaf Border, c.1970, 8 In.	200
Plate, Swallows, Relief, 10 In.	250
Plate, Violets, Leaves, Footed, 4 ½ In.	89
Vase, Fiery Opalescent, Fluted, Flower Moldings, Frosted Ground, Signed, 1900s, 8 ¾ In.	561
Vase, Globular, Amber, Footed, Flowers, 6 In.	550
Vase, Manta Ray, Opalescent, Sticker, 8 ¼ In.	590

SALT AND PEPPER SHAKERS in matched sets were first used in the nineteenth century. Collectors are primarily interested in figural examples made after World War I. Huggers are pairs of shakers that appear to embrace each other. Many salt and pepper shakers are listed in other categories and can be located through the index at the back of this book.

Acorn, Silver, Scalloped Base, 2 In.	155
Beer Bottle, Schlitz, Amber Glass, Box, 1957, 4 In.	14
Bone, Contoured, Notched, c.1935, 1 ⅛ In.	123
Butterfly Pattern, Pyrex, 1960s, 3 ½ In.	10
Cactus, Potted, Green, Brown, Orange, Mexico, 2 ¾ In.	35
Chef & Mammy Heads, Chef Hat, Kerchief, c.1930, 2 ⅞ In.	85
Chef, Figural Holder, Plastic, Tremax, Chicago, 8 ½ x 6 ¾ In. ....*illus*	32
Chick, Duck Holder, Porcelain, 1 ¾ In.	18
Chicks, Cracked Shell Tray, Yellow, Green, Ceramic, 1960s, 2 ¾ x 5 x 2 ½ In.	24
Cow, Ceramic, Black Horns & Feet, 2 ½ In.	28
Duck, Lavender, Yellow, Lusterware, Japan, 1 ⅜ In.	15
Flowers, Porcelain, Blue & Pink, Gold Gilt Top, 2 ¾ In. ....*illus*	14
Man, Wearing Sombrero, Multicolor, Mexico, 2 ½ In.	35
Nipper, Radio Corp. Of America, Impressed, 3 ½ In.	49
Rabbit, Ceramic, Purple & Pink Flowers, Cork Stopper, 2 In.	17
Ribbed, Footed, Ultra Marine, Aluminum Top, Jeanette Glass Co., 4 ¼ In.	45
Rocket Ship, Plastic, Blue, White, c.1945, 4 ¼ In.	50
Rocketship, Plastic, Blue & White, L-W, 4 ¼ In. ....*illus*	50
Rooster, Wood, Cylindrical, Bench Holder, 1950s, 4 ½ In.	12
Shotgun Shell, 12 Gauge, Red, Green, Plastic, Brass, Pachmayr	38
Siamese Cat, Bristle Whiskers, Victoria Ceramics, Japan, 6 In.	20

Russel Wright, Iroquois Casual, Pitcher, Water, Cantaloupe, 9 In.
$949

Ruby Lane, Inc.

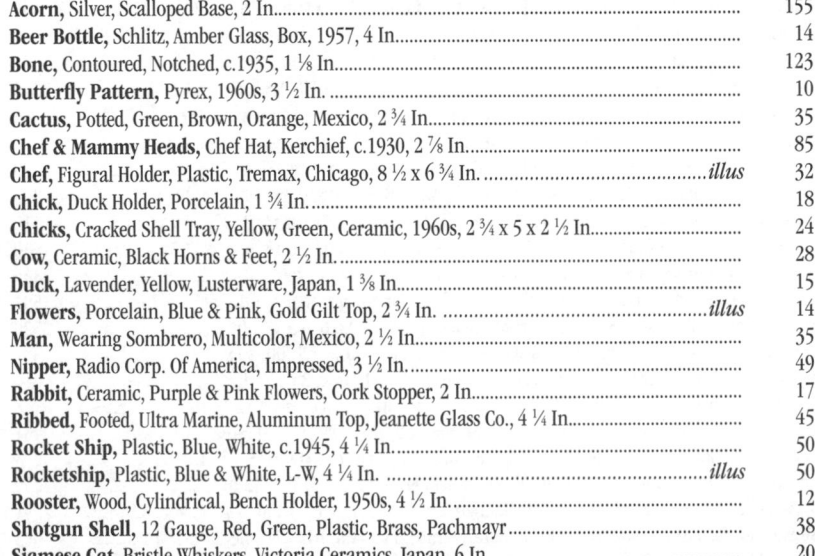

Salt & Pepper, Chef, Figural Holder, Plastic, Tremax, Chicago, 8 ½ x 6 ¾ In.
$32

Ruby Lane, Inc.

Salt & Pepper, Flowers, Porcelain, Blue & Pink, Gold Gilt Top, 2 ¾ In.
$14

Ruby Lane, Inc.

Salt & Pepper, Rocketship, Plastic, Blue & White, L-W, 4 ¼ In.
$50

S

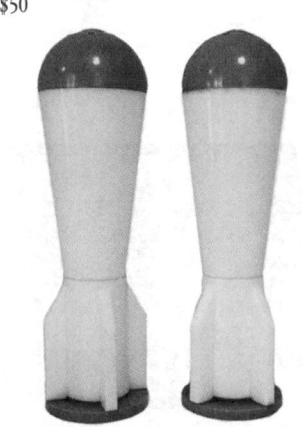

Ruby Lane, Inc.

Sampler, Alphabet, Flowers, Verse, Virtue's The Chief Beauty, c.1890, 13 x 10 In. $330

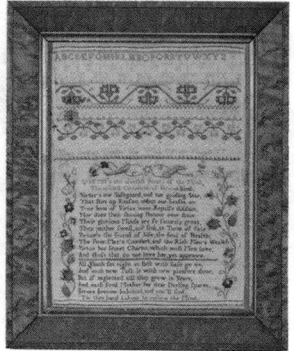

Cowan's Auctions

Sampler, Alphabet, House, Birds, Flowers, Silk On Linen, Sarah Esstle, 1824, 10 ½ x 7 ¾ In. $2,952

Pook & Pook, Inc.

Sampler, Alphabets, House, Trees, Silk, Linen, Elisabeth A. Stocker, 1836, Ohio, 8 ¾ x 17 In. $5,412

Pook & Pook, Inc.

Sampler, Alphabets, Numbers, Capital Letters & Script, 1849, 11 ½ x 14 In. $123

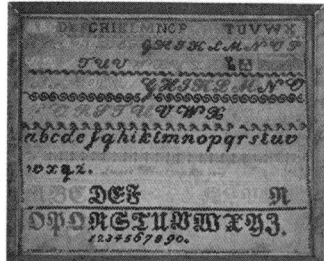

Pook & Pook, Inc.

SAMPLERS were made in America from the early 1700s. The best examples were made from 1790 to 1840. Long, narrow samplers are usually older than square ones. Early samplers just had stitching or alphabets. The later examples had numerals, borders, and pictorial decorations. Those with mottoes are mid-Victorian. A revival of interest in the 1930s produced simpler samplers, usually with mottoes.

AB CDE

Alphabet, Boxed Lines, Floral, Silk, Linen, Lydia W. McFarlin, Aged 11, 1814, 17 x 21 ½ In.	308
Alphabet, Castle, Birds, Deer, Ann Harstaff, Age 11, Early 1800s, 13 x 11 ½ In.	270
Alphabet, Cursive & Block Letters, Crosses, Birds, Aloisia Rosler, 1847, Frame, 20 x 17 In.	1200
Alphabet, Deer, Tree, Margaret Hicks, 1741, Silk On Linen, Frame, 13 ¾ x 8 ½ In.	770
Alphabet, Elizabeth Dawes, Weston School 1801, Pa., Red Frame, 12 x 15 In.	2707
Alphabet, Elizabeth Dawes, Weston School, Frame, 11 x 14 In.	2607
Alphabet, Figures, Flowers, Ann Amelia Matilda Border, Pa., 1839, 16 ½ x 16 In.	8750
Alphabet, Flower Basket, House, Hill, Lucy M. Bond, 12 Years, Cotton, Linen, 12 x 10 In.	480
Alphabet, Flowerpots, Stars, Silk On Linen, Signed, Frame, 18 In.	264
Alphabet, Flowers, Mary Ann Flory, 1857, Silk On Linen, Frame, 16 x 11 In.	288
Alphabet, Flowers, Signed Sarah Kennedy, 1803, Gilt Edged Frame, 14 x 12 ¾ In.	575
Alphabet, Flowers, Verse, Virtue's The Chief Beauty, c.1890, 13 x 10 In. ....*illus*	330
Alphabet, Fruit Basket, Bird, Frame, c.1820, 16 ½ x 13 ½ In.	243
Alphabet, House, Birds, Flowers, Silk On Linen, Sarah Esstle, 1824, 10 ½ x 7 ¾ In. ....*illus*	2952
Alphabet, House, Tree, Margaret Kingman, 1817, Scotland, Frame, 18 x 17 In.	1541
Alphabet, Inscribed Agnes Irwin, 1778, Pa., Silk On Linen, Frame, 15 ¾ x 12 ¾ In	4560
Alphabet, Landscape, Flower Vine Border, Silk On Linen, Frame, c.1805, 19 x 14 In.	588
Alphabet, Numbers, Cat, Dog, Flowers, Abstract, Mrs. H.S. Ficke, 1870, Frame, 29 x 21 In.	115
Alphabet, Numbers, Ship, Shepherd, Tree, Flowering Urns, Initials, 1799, Frame, 18 x 13 In.	345
Alphabet, Numbers, Sprays, House, Nancy Wason, Age 10, 1827, Silk On Linen, 16 x 19 In.	11400
Alphabet, Religious Verse, Landscape, Flower Border, Silk On Linen, 1831, 21 x 18 In.	598
Alphabet, Sawtooth Border, Mary Lowell 1830, Silk On Linen, Frame, 11 x 8 In.	127
Alphabet, Silk On Linen, Frame, c.1850, 19 x 12 In.	840
Alphabet, Stitches, Signed, Polly H. Oxford, Silk On Linen, 1788, Frame, 11 x 16 In.	323
Alphabet, Strawberry Vine, Betsy Swett's Sampler, 1818, Frame, 27 x 18 In.	529
Alphabet, Vase & Cartouche, Flower Border, Roxana McGee, 1839	7020
Alphabet, Verse, Couple, Crooks, Greek Key Border, Hannah Frances Formon, 1837, 19 x 21 In..	420
Alphabet, Verse, Flowers, Figures, Mary Coffin, 1801, Mass., Frame, 15 x 20 ½ In.	75000
Alphabet, Verse, Sawtooth Border, Wreath, Flowers, c.1805, 17 x 15 In.	2520
Alphabet, Verse, Strawberry Border, Catherine Ann Manning, Silk On Linen, 1830, 19 x 19 In. ..	330
Alphabets, House, Trees, Silk, Linen, Elisabeth A. Stocker, 1836, Ohio, 8 ¾ x 17 In. ....*illus*	5412
Alphabets, Numbers, Capital Letters & Script, 1849, 11 ½ x 14 In. ....*illus*	123
Alphabets, Numbers, Elizabeth Harris, 1836, Silk, Linen, Nova Scotia, 22 x 10 In. ....*illus*	984
Alphabets, Numbers, Johanna Pehmollex, Marked, 1860-61, 11 ½ x 12 In. ....*illus*	118
Alphabets, Numbers, Myra Lockwood, 1875, Stamford, Connecticut, 11 x 11 ½ In. ....*illus*	154
Alphabets, Numbers, Verse, Margaret Innerwick, Age 14, Silk, Linen, Frame, 1765, 17 x 10 In. ..	600
Alphabets, Verse, Anna LeFavour, Aged 11 Years 11 Months, Silk, Linen, Mass., 19 x 13 In.	840
Alphabets, Verse, Floral Basket, Butterfly, Flowers, Silk, Linen, 1821, 9 ½ x 17 ½ In.	2280
Alphabets, Verse, Flowers, Anna Norris, 1975, Silk On Linen, 17 x 8 In. ....*illus*	738
Alphabets, Verse, Strawberry Border, Elizabeth Williams, Silk On Linen, 1834, 22 x 22 In.	240
Band, Alphabet, S. Becker, Silk On Linen, Frame, c.1860, 17 ½ x 4 ¾ In.	119
Bird & Flower Band, Names, Initials, 1758, Silk On Wool, 8 ¾ x 6 In.	523
House, Gate, Fencing, Flowers, Animals, Eliza Gregory, Aged 7, 1836, Frame, 23 x 17 In.	2300
House, Red Brick, Black & White Dog, Ogee Frame, c.1860, 15 ¼ x 13 In.	1035
House, Trees, Flowers, Silk On Linen, Frame, c.1805, 20 x 20 ½ In.	150
House, Vines, Flowers, Sarah Ann Dodge, 1832, Silk On Linen, Frame, 18 x 15 In.	230
Pictorial, Adam & Eve, House, Trees, Shepherds, Mary Baxter, 1810, Frame, 15 x 12 In.	356
Pictorial, Adam & Eve, Tree, Prepare To Meet Thy God, Elizabeth Turner, 1822, 20 x 19 In.	1110
Pictorial, American Independence, Figures, Birds, Amelia Treadwell, 1826, 27 x 26 In.	1840
Solomon's Temple, Elizabeth Mellor, 1837, Wool, Silk, Frame, 23 x 22 In.	345
Trees, Blue, Green, Inscribed Elizabeth Licey, Silk On Linen, Frame, Pa., c.1815, 9 x 8 In.	504
Verse, Adam & Eve, Figures, Tree, Cherubs, Hearts, Birds, 1792, 6 ¼ x 4 ¼ In.	2520
Verse, Adam & Eve, Tree, Paradise, Birds, German Music, Frame, c.1800, 20 x 18 In.	331
Verse, Almighty Maker Of My Frame, School House, 1843, Frame, 24 x 24 In.	1016
Verse, Alphabet, Numbers, Vines, Hannah Clark, Aged 10, 1832, Frame, 19 x 19 In.	173
Verse, Alphabet, Quaker, Birds, Tree Of Life, Margaret Scarisbrick, 1789, Frame, 18 x 14 In.	431
Verse, Bird, House, M. Gardner, England, Silk On Linen, Frame, c.1890, 15 x 13 In.	273
Verse, Birds, Trees, Domed Building, Silk On Linen, Frame, c.1825, 37 x 32 In.	690
Verse, Center Basket, Borders, Caroline Bennett, Age 9, Silk, Linen, Frame, 1817, 19 x 18 In.	2091
Verse, Flower Baskets, Butterflies, Birds, Sarah Smith, 11 Years, 1818, Frame, 21 x 18 In.	603
Verse, Flower Garlands, Bows, Twisted Vines, 1830, Silk, Beads, Wool, 20 x 16 In.	1410

Verse, Flowers, Birds, Deer, Elizabeth MacCarry, Eng., c.1831, 16 x 12 In...	313
Verse, Flowers, Butterflies, 8-Point Stars, Trees, Riser, 1815, Silk On Linen, 16 x 12 In.................	600
Verse, Flowers, Martha Hiley, 1849, Wool On Linen, Frame, 24 x 25 ½ In.	296
Verse, Flowers, Sarah Rice, 1821, Silk On Linen, Frame, 16 x 16 In.	345
Verse, Flowers, Vines, Lizabeth Bruce, Silk On Linen, Frame, c.1820, 16 x 16 In.	196
Verse, House, Fence, Vines, Ellenor Linnahan 1807, Silk On Linen, 17 x 12 In.	1380
Verse, Houses, Trees, Birds, Elizabeth Edmonds, Aged 13, 1815, Frame, 25 x 20 In.	920
Verse, Letters, Numbers, Flowers, Urns, Silk, Cotton, Signed, Frame, 1841, 18 x 16 In.	1028
Verse, Lions, Figures, Inscribed Grace Swift, 1812, Silk On Linen, Frame, 25 x 22 In.	326
Verse, Oak Leaves, Flower Border, Sarah Hodden, Worth 1822, Silk, On Wool, 24 x 19 In..........	646
Verse, Pictorial, Building, Fenced Lawn, Flower Beds, Mary Iles, Aged 8, 1828, 17 ¼ x 21 In.	720
Verse, Psalm, Vignettes, Flowers, Vine Border, Ann Wattersley, Aged 15, 1848, 25 x 25 In............	761
Verse, Trees, Flowers, Urns, Catharine Robinson 1836, Silk On Linen, Frame, 27 x 24 In.	748
Verse, Woodman's Hut, Floral Border, Louisa Blake, Aged 10 Years, 1825, Linen, 17 x 12 In.	450

SAMSON and Company, a French firm specializing in the reproduction of collectible wares of many countries and periods, was founded in Paris in the early nineteenth century. Chelsea, Meissen, Famille Verte, and Chinese Export porcelain are some of the wares that have been reproduced by the company. The firm used a variety of marks on the reproductions. It closed in 1969.

Figurine, Flower Seller, Flowers, c.1850, 4 ¾ In...	46
Mug, Pink, Orange, Flower Sprigs, Plums, Double Strap Handle, c.1890, 4 ½ In............................	46
Punch Bowl, Armorial, Flowers, Multicolor, Gilt Trim, 4 ½ x 11 ¾ In.	148

SANDWICH GLASS is any of the myriad types of glass made by the Boston & Sandwich Glass Company of Sandwich, Massachusetts, between 1825 and 1888. It is often very difficult to be sure whether a piece was really made at the Sandwich factory because so many types were made there and similar pieces were made at other glass factories. Additional pieces may be listed under Pressed Glass and in other related categories.

Bottle, Smelling Salts, Amethyst, White & Opalescent Amber Striations, Waisted, 3 In.	281
Bottle, Smelling Salts, Marbleized Sea Green & Opaque White, 8-Sided, Waisted, 2 ½ In.	644
Bottle, Smelling Salts, Monument Form, Marbleized Blue Gray & White, Cap, 2 ½ In....................	468
Candlestick, Canary, Diamond Point Base, Hexagonal Socket, c.1830, 5 In.	60
Candlestick, Clambroth Stem, Hexagonal Base, c.1850, 7 ½ In., Pair..	241
Candlestick, Dolphin, Double Base, Clambroth, Cornflower Blue, c.1850, 9 In.	180
Candlestick, Dolphin, Stepped Base, 10 In., Pair...	325
Candlestick, Loop, Canary Yellow, 7 In., Pair..	502
Candlestick, Petal & Loop, Clambroth, 6 ½ In., Pair...	293
Cologne Bottle, 12-Sided, Cobalt Blue, Outward Rolled Lip, c.1850-70, 7 ⅜ In. ....*illus*	115
Cologne Bottle, Amethyst, 12-Sided, Tapered, Flared Mouth, 1840, 9 ¼ In.	556
Cologne Bottle, Amethyst, Paneled Hourglass Form, Flared Mouth, 4 ½ In...................................	351
Cologne Bottle, Canary Yellow, Tapered, Label, 12-Sided, c.1870, 7 ½ In. ....*illus*	4095
Cologne Bottle, Cobalt Blue, Bunker Hill Monument, Tapered, Flared Mouth, 8 In.	1170
Cologne Bottle, Shaded Amethyst, Paneled Hourglass Form, Flared Mouth, 6 In.........................	703
Decanter, Canary Yellow, Panel Cut Stopper, c.1850, 14 In., Pair..	266
Decanter, Horn Of Plenty Pattern, Faceted Stopper, 1800s, 11 ½ In.	59
Decanter, Scrolls, Teardrop Shoulder, Sapphire Blue, Bulbous, Tall Neck, Flared Rim, Qt.	1170
Fruit Basket, Openwork, Rayed Base, 16 Staves, Hexagonal Foot, Mass., 8 ½ x 8 In....................	1175
Hat, Blown, Cobalt Blue, Tooled Brim, Pontil, c.1830, 1 ¾ x 2 In. ....*illus*	7020
Inkwell, Cobalt Blue, Vertical Ribs, 1 ⅝ In.	316
Inkwell, Mild Glass, Vertical Ribs, 1 ⅝ In.	374
Lamp Base, Inverted Diamond & Thumbprint, 6-Sided Foot, 8 ¼ In.	78
Lamp, Fluid, Amethyst, Tulip Font, Brass Connector, Shaped Stepped Base, 12 ½ In.	403
Lamp, Fluid, Etched, Conical Font, Waterfall Base, Double Burner, c.1880, 13 In.	325
Lamp, Oil, Cornet Font, Baluster Column, 6-Sided Base, Gilt Trim, 10 In.	147
Lamp, Whale Oil, Teardrop Font, Engraved Grapevines, Square Base, 11 In.	118
Salt, Eagles, Roping, Shield, Clear, Basket Form, Looped Rope Rim, 4-Footed, 2 x 3 x 2 In.	468
Salt, Eagles, Trees, Clear, Rectangular, Footed Pillar Corners, Notched Rim, 1 ¾ x 3 In.	322
Vase, Hexagonal Base, Swirled Ribs Design, Ruffle Rim, c.1850, 10 ½ In., Pair.........................	705
Vase, Miter & Diamond Point, Clear, Blue, Clambroth, Scalloped Rim, c.1850, 8 ¾ In.	590

SARREGUEMINES is the name of a French town that is used as part of a china mark. Utzschneider and Company, a porcelain factory, made ceramics in Sarreguemines, Lorraine, France, from about 1775. Transfer-printed wares and majolica were made in the nineteenth century. The nineteenth-century pieces, most often found today, usually have colorful transfer-printed decorations showing peasants in local costumes.

Creamer, Tan Body, Strap Handle, Classical Figures, Hearts Band, c.1800, 2 ½ In.	80

Sampler, Alphabets, Numbers, Elizabeth Harris, 1836, Silk, Linen, Nova Scotia, 22 x 10 In.
$984

Pook & Pook, Inc.

Sampler, Alphabets, Numbers, Johanna Pehmollex, Marked, 1860-61, 11 ½ x 12 In.
$118

Copake Auction Inc.

Sampler, Alphabets, Numbers, Myra Lockwood, 1875, Stamford, Connecticut, 11 x 11 ½ In.
$154

Pook & Pook, Inc.

S

Sampler, Alphabets, Verse, Flowers, Anna Norris, 1975, Silk On Linen, 17 x 8 In. $738

Pook & Pook, Inc.

Sandwich Glass, Cologne Bottle, 12-Sided, Cobalt Blue, Outward Rolled Lip, c.1850-70, 7 ⅜ In. $115

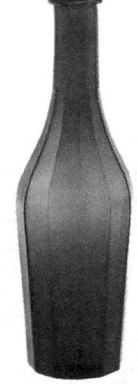

Glass Works Auctions

Sandwich Glass, Cologne Bottle, Canary Yellow, Tapered, Label, 12-Sided, c.1870, 7 ½ In. $4,095

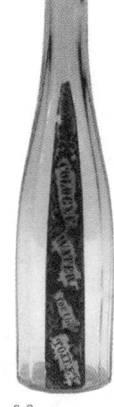

Norman C. Heckler & Company

Lavabo, Basin, Kingfisher Bird, Fish, Lobster, Bulrushes, Ferns, Cobalt Blue, Majolica, 18 In.	242
Lavabo, Turtle Shape, Green, Brown, Geometric Scale Pattern, Majolica, 19 In.	218
Pitcher, Green, French Crystalline, Angled Handle, 7 ½ In.	46
Plate, Portrait, Clement Armand Fallieres, 8 ½ In.	55
Plate, War Scene, Patrie, Gloire, Honneur, Green & Black Transfer, c.1870, 7 ¾ In.	25
Stein, Lid, 2 Deer, PUG, Pewter, 1 Liter ....*illus*	121
Toy, Washstand, Child's, Basin, Pitcher, Painted Wood Stand, 18 x 14 x 19 In.	720
Vase, Cobalt Blue, Draped Flowers, Flower Shape, Majolica, 17 ½ In.	157
Vase, Figural, Dolphin, Cattail, Turquoise Blue Ground, Majolica, 14 ½ In., Pair	1331

SASCHA BRASTOFF made decorative accessories, ceramics, enamels on copper, and plastics of his own design. He headed a factory, Sascha Brastoff of California, Inc., in West Los Angeles, from 1953 until about 1973. He died in 1993. Pieces signed with the signature *Sascha Brastoff* were his work and are the most expensive. Other pieces marked *Sascha B.* or with a stamped mark were made by others in his company. Pieces made by Matt Adams after he left the factory are listed here with his name.

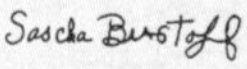

Sascha Brastoff

Ashtray, Prancing Horse, c.1950, 8 ¾ x 5 In.	49
Figurine, Seal, Resin, Green, Opalescent, 1960s, 10 In.	165
Planter, Footed, Pagodas, Signed, c.1955, 7 ½ x 5 In.	75
Plate, Feathery Design, Black & Gold, Signed, 1952, 10 ¼ In. Diam.	780
Plate, Mushrooms, Signed, 10 ¼ In. Diam.	375
Plate, Stylized Design, Brown, 10 ¼ In. Diam.	295
Vase, Gold Glaze, Symbols, Canoe Shape, Marked, 1966, 6 x 8 In.	799
Vase, Horse, Turquoise, Gold, Signed, 6 ¼ x 3 ⅛ In.	60

SATIN GLASS is a late nineteenth-century art glass. It has a dull finish that is caused by hydrofluoric acid vapor treatment. Satin glass was made in many colors and sometimes has applied decorations. Satin glass is also listed by factory name, such as Webb, or in the Mother-of-Pearl category in this book.

Candleholder, Blue, Lotus Shape, Westmoreland, 4 In., Pair	45
Compote, Blue, Paneled Grape, Ruffled, Milk Glass, Westmoreland, 4 x 6 ¼ In.	28
Compote, Shell & Tassel, Victorian Hand On Stem	23
Ewer, Cream Shaded To Orange, Blossoming Branch, Gilt, Ruffled, Clear Handle, 9 In.	12
Figurine, Owl, Blue, Blue Glass Eyes, Westmoreland, 5 ½ In.	38
Pitcher, Graniteware, Ruby Case, Opal Frit, Crimped Rim, Handle, Northwood, c.1890, 8 ½ In.	92
Plate, Rainbow, Raindrop Design, Raised Ruffled Rim, 6 ¼ In. ....*illus*	296
Rose Bowl, Blue, Embossed Shell, Coral, Enamel Flowers, 4 ¾ x 5 ¼ In.	59
Rose Bowl, Shaded Yellow, Alternating Orange Flowers & Beads, Ruffled, 5 In.	35
Tumbler, Blue Diamond-Quilted, Mother-Of-Pearl, 4 In.	60
Tumbler, Green Opaque, Gold Waves, Crackle Border, Mass., 3 ¾ In., 6 Piece	705
Vase, Black, White, Gold Flowers, Round, Ruffled Fan Rim, Raised Frosted Feet, 9 ½ In., Pair	375
Vase, Blue Flowers, Branches, Translucent Amber, Gilt, Oval, Bohemian, c.1895, 7 In.	1625
Vase, Blue, Enamel Flowers, Ruffled Top, 6 In., Pair	59
Vase, Blue, White Cased, Coin Dots, Bulbous, Ruffled Rim, Clear Rigaree, 6 In.	35
Vase, Clear Shaded To Ruby, Quilted, Bulbous, Stand Up Rim, 4 ¾ In.	58
Vase, Cobalt Blue, White, Yellow & Orange Spots, Elongated Ruffled Edge, 17 In.	41
Vase, Diamond Optic, Ruffled Edge, Turquoise Cased, 8 ¾ x 4 In.	300
Vase, Onion, Enameled, Green, Blue Flowers, Lobed, Gilt Rim, 3 x 3 In.	184
Vase, Peach Swirl, Mother-Of-Pearl, Vertical Ribbing, Pink To White, 4 Frosted Feet, 7 ¼ In.	478
Vase, Pink Shaded To Rose, Wave Pattern, Bulbous, Lady's Leg Neck, 6 In.	35
Vase, Pink Shaded To White, Enameled Flowers, Ruffled Top	60
Vase, Red Shaded To Orange, Quilted, Tapered Neck, 11 In.	212
Vase, Shaded Pink, Herringbone Pattern, Lobed, Cup Rim, Clear Handle, 5 In., Pair	30
Vase, Shaded Pink, Lattice Morphs To Dot Optic, Oval, Scalloped Edge, 8 x 6 In.	121
Vase, White Shaded To Pink, Orange & Blue Flowers, Baluster, Ruffled Rim, 7 In.	60
Vase, Yellow, Multicolor Enameled Fish, White Lining, Gold Rim, 4 ½ x 4 ½ In.	375
Vase, Zipper, Apricot To Blue, Vertical Ribbing, Creamy White Interior, Ruffled Rim, 5 In.	474

SATSUMA is a Japanese pottery with a distinctive creamy beige crackled glaze. Most of the pieces were decorated with blue, red, green, orange, or gold. Almost all Satsuma found today was made after 1860, especially during the Meiji Period, 1868–1912. During World War I, Americans could not buy undecorated European porcelains. Women who liked to make hand-painted porcelains at home began to decorate plain Satsuma. These pieces are known today as "American Satsuma."

Bottle, Children, Women, River Scene, Marked, 1800s, 9 ¾ x 6 ½ In. ....*illus*	369
Bowl, Kutani, Flowers, Gilt, Japan, c.1910, 3 ½ x 8 ½ In.	161

Box, Lid, Crackled Glaze, Temple, Scrolling Flowers, Dragon, Rectangular, 4 In.	390
Box, Lid, Domed, Rooster Knop, Figure Panels, Gilt Diaper Pattern, Bun Feet, 1800s, 6 In.	259
Censer, Domed Lid, Panels, Figures, Flowers, Marked, Kozan, c.1900, 3 ¾ x 4 In. ....*illus*	240
Censer, Lid, Figures In Butterfly Shape Panels, Flowered Ground, Gilt, Crackled, 3 In.	300
Censer, Lid, Gilt, Orange, Foo Dog Handles & Finial, Paw Feet, 19 x 12 In.	354
Censer, Oval, Crackled Glaze, Winter Scene, Gilt, 3 Panel Feet, 2 ⅝ In.	390
Censer, Oval, Enamel & Gilt, Crackled Glaze, Flowering Branches, Tripod Feet, 6 x 7 In.	330
Charger, Chrysanthemum, Peonies, Plum Blossoms, Daisies, Rust Rim, 14 ½ In.	369
Charger, Noble Woman In Formal Dress, 2 Attendants, 22 In.	240
Container, Buddhist Saints, In Relief, Painted, Gilt, Stoneware, Japan, 1800s, 14 In. ....*illus*	738
Flask, Imperial Moon, Figures, Geometrics, Gilt, Foo Dogs On Shoulders, 11 ½ In.	660
Incense Burner, Lid, Chrysanthemums, Iron Red, Leaves, Squat, Footed, c.1900, 5 In.	711
Jar, Koro, Figures In Garden, Lattice, Oval, Metal Lid, Openwork, Dragons, Clouds, 6 In.	1107
Jar, Lid, Animals, Figures, 20th Century, 6 x 5 In.	240
Jar, Lid, Palace Scene, Figures, Leaf Design, Finial, 1868-1912, 7 In. ....*illus*	720
Jar, Lid, Reticulated, Panels, Gold, Kinkozan Style, Marked, c.1900, 6 x 6 ½ In. ....*illus*	6875
Jardiniere, Figures, Butterflies, Bronze, Pierced, Japan, c.1885, 15 In. ....*illus*	676
Plate, Painted Deities, Earth Tones, Scalloped Rim, Japan, 20th Century, 6 In.	120
Teapot, Figures In Landscape, Gilt, Domed Cover, Flowers, Yellow Crackle Handle, 5 In.	120
Urn, Onion Dome Lid, Warriors, Women, Peonies, 23 x 12 In.	920
Vase, Bottle, Flowers, Birds, Enamel, Gold, Long Neck, Flared Mouth, 11 ¾ In.	523
Vase, Crane, Flying, Gray, White, Butterfly Handles, c.1925, 24 In.	142
Vase, Dragon, Phoenix, Chrysanthemums, Signed, Kinkozan, c.1900, 10 In. ....*illus*	2607
Vase, Figures, Gilt Design, 7-Sided, Pinched Neck, Rolled Rim, Signed, 1900s, 15 In.	708
Vase, Figures, Intricate Ground, Bulbous, Waisted Neck & Foot, Gilt Trim, 17 In.	450
Vase, Figures, Landscape, Multicolor, 18 x 9 In.	168
Vase, Flowers, Butterflies, Bamboo Style Handles, Signed, c.1910, 13 In., Pair ....*illus*	230
Vase, Flowers, Shouldered, Flared Rim, Tan, Orange, Marked, c.1900, 15 ½ x 8 In.	531
Vase, Gilt Figures, Landscape, Geometric, Flower Neck Rim, Flared, c.1895, 15 ½ In., Pair	384
Vase, Hanging Wisteria, Lavender, White, Cream Ground, Crackled, Oval, 5 In.	98
Vase, Long Neck, Bulbous, Ring Handles, Japan, c.1890, 15 In., Pair	502
Vase, Palace, Figures, Flowers, Figural Ring Handles, c.1900, 43 ¾ In. ....*illus*	5000
Vase, Peonies, Women & Children By Waterside, Iris, Oval, Flared, 12 In.	630
Vase, Samurai, Garden Scene, Crackled Glaze, Enameled, Shouldered, Gilt, 1800s, 5 In.	677
Vase, Samurai, Webbing, Gilt, Bulbous, Pinched Neck, 8 ½ In.	92
Vase, Women, Grouped In Pavilion, Applied Designs, Gold, Lacquer, 36 In.	450
Vase, Women, In Garden, Embossed Gold, Shouldered Cylinder, 36 In.	450
Vase, Women, Outdoor Scenes, Oval, Wood Stand, Japan, 22 In.	563

SATURDAY EVENING GIRLS, *see Paul Revere Pottery category.*

SCALES have been made to weigh everything from babies to gold. Collectors search for all types. Most popular are small gold dust scales and special grocery scales.

Balance, Brass Standard, Bull's Head, Casa Das, Brazil, c.1915, 60 In.	861
Balance, Brass, Dishes, Hardwood Base, Stamped Janodet & Amoud, 1800s, 59 In.	948
Balance, Brass, Iron, c.1900, 33 In.	29
Balance, Brass, Wrought Iron, Tray, Chain Supports, Arm, England, 32 In.	300
Balance, Detecto Gram, State Of California, Dept. Agriculture Sticker, 15 Lb., 1970	60
Balance, H. Troemner, Cast Iron, Brass, Painted, Weights, Philadelphia, 15 ½ In.	360
Balance, Howe, Cast Iron, 2 Beam, Weights, Decal	120
Balance, Iron, Chains, Turkey, 11 In.	216
Balance, J. Maxwell, Brass, Impressed, Albany, 19 ¼ In.	240
Balance, Onyx, Brass Plates, Marble Base, Column Standard, 23 In.	230
Balance, Porcelain, Dragons, Bats, Metal Mounts, Chinese, 1900s, 13 ½ In. ....*illus*	119
Balance, Snail Shape, Milk Glass Ink Jars, Rotating Arms, Metal, c.1860, 8 ¼ In.	861
Balance, Steelyard, Density, Cased, Brass Measure-On-Stand, Beaker, Thermometer, c.1890	53
Balance, Wrought Iron, Graduated Finials, 32 In.	207
Barrel, Cream Porcelain, Dayton, Patent 1901	570
Bathroom, Chatillon & Sons, Iron Base, Cream Paint, c.1850, 66 ¾ In.	240
Beam, Brass, Suspended Holding Ring, Incised, Shaped, 8 Weights, Continental, 17 ½ In.	119
Candy, Dayton Style, No. 166, Brass Scoop, 2 Lb. Capacity ....*illus*	351
Candy, National Store Specialty Co., Fan Shape, Round Glass Tray, Countertop, 14 ½ In.	384
Candy, Springless Angledile, Style 21G, Head Light, 10 ½ x 14 In.	960
Carnival, Fool The Mad Genius, Attached Chair, Wood Tripod, c.1915, 96 ½ x 72 In.	4720
Computing, Angledile Automatic, Mirror, Vitrolite Tray, Better Meats, 30 x 20 x 16 In.	1254

Sandwich Glass, Hat, Blown, Cobalt Blue, Tooled Brim, Pontil, c.1830, 1 ¾ x 2 In.
$7,020

Norman C. Heckler & Company

Sarreguemines, Stein, Lid, 2 Deer, PUG, Pewter, 1 Liter
$121

Fox Auctions

Satin Glass, Plate, Rainbow, Raindrop Design, Raised Ruffled Rim, 6 ¼ In.
$296

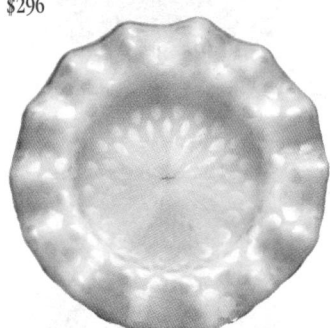

James D. Julia Auctioneers

S

Satsuma, Bottle, Children, Women, River Scene, Marked, 1800s, 9 ¾ x 6 ½ In. $369

New Orleans Auction Galleries, Inc.

Satsuma, Censer, Domed Lid, Panels, Figures, Flowers, Marked, Kozan, c.1900, 3 ¾ x 4 In. $240

Skinner Auctioneers & Appraisers

Satsuma, Container, Buddhist Saints, In Relief, Painted, Gilt, Stoneware, Japan, 1800s, 14 In. $738

New Orleans Auction Galleries, Inc.

Satsuma, Jar, Lid, Palace Scene, Figures, Leaf Design, Finial, 1868-1912, 7 In. $720

DuMouchelles Art Gallery

Computing, Barrel, Strubler, Style No. 140, Elkhart, Ind., 80 Lb. Capacity, 18 x 37 x 22 In.	840
Computing, Butcher, c.1895, 20 x 34 x 21 In.	960
Counter, Dayton Computing, Brass, 31 x 19 In.	121
Country Store, Wood, Nickeled Bevel, Reverse Glass Dial, Porcelain Pedestal, 69 In.	1121
Drugstore, Aristocrat, National Devices Corp., 60 In. x 20 In.	88
Grocery, John Chatillon & Sons, 2-Sided, Painted Porcelain Top, 35 Lb., 37 x 16 In.	58
Postage, Silver, Spread Wing Eagle, Gorham, 6 In.	300
Postal, Brass Weights, Platforms, Stepped Mahogany Base, c.1845, 6 x 9 In.	57
Postal, Inlaid Brass, Weights, India & Colonies, 1800s	224
Produce, Chatillon, Type 8200, Not For Other Foods, Hanging Tray Holder, Tray	1000
Produce, John Chantillon & Sons, Porcelain Shelf, N.Y., 35 In.	114
Spring Balance, Champion, Round Dial, Metal Wire Bracket, Platform Weigh Shelf, 1900s	58
Weighing, Coin-Operated, Mirror, Watling, 49 In.	356
Weighing, Coin-Operated, Pace, 1 Cent, Green Paint, 48 In.	360
Weighing, Food, 2-Sided Dial, Brass Hoop, Porcelain, Enterprise	240
Weighing, Lollipop, Penny, Iron, Porcelain Face, Claw Feet, Mills Novelty Co., 15 x 69 x 24 In.	4500
Weighing, Lollipop, Penny, Porcelain, Jennings, 70 In.	342
Weighing, Peerless Platform, Coin-Operated, 18 x 69 x 25 In.	1368
Weighing, Red Paint, Cast Iron, 29 x 25 In.	94
Weighing, Toledo Scale Co, Standing, Round, Square Pedestal, Brass Tag, 1918, 77 x 32 In.	708
Weighing, Toledo, No Springs, Honest Weight, Style 30, White Enamel, 20 ½ In.	60

SCHAFER & VATER, makers of small ceramic items, are best known for their amusing figurals. The factory was located in Volkstedt-Rudolstadt, Germany, from 1890 to 1962. Some pieces are marked with the crown and *R* mark, but many are unmarked.

Bottle, A Good Sip, Man In Top Hat, Kissing Woman In Glass, 5 In.	175
Bottle, Figural, Indian Woman, Headdress, Tray, Dog, A Little Scotch, 5 ½ In.	45
Bottle, Leg Stopper, Evil Clown, Carrying Off Drunken Woman, Blue, 5 x 4 ¾ In.	162
Bottle, Raised Eagle & Flag, Green, Oval, 4 ½ In.	95
Bottle, Stopper, Kiss Me, Blond Woman, Puckered Lips, Multicolor, 5 In.	116
Bottle, Stopper, Spirit Of Hollywood, Child, Movie Camera, Tripod, Blue, Orange, 4 ½ In.	150
Bottle, Stopper, Uncle Sam, Holding Glass, Your Health, Orange Thin, 7 ¾ In.	162
Bottle, Uncle Sam, Porcelain, 9 In. ....*illus*	300
Box, Lid, Woman's Head, Pink, Green, 4 ½ In.	118
Box, Lobster, Marked, 2 x 4 ½ In.	30
Creamer, Rooster, Multicolor, c.1900, 5 ¾ In.	245
Creamer, Witch, Kneeling, Blue, Flowers, Hat, c.1900, 3 ½ x 4 ½ In.	150
Creamer, Woman, Holding Goose, Braid As Handle, Orange Dress, 5 In.	325
Figurine, Woman Choir Singer, Wide Open Mouth, Teeth, Hymnal, Mauve, 4 ¾ In.	148
Hatpin Holder, Woman's Face, Lavender, Onion Dome Shape, 7 ¾ In.	155
Match Holder, Long Legged Scotsman, Seated, Kilt, Hat, Big Ears & Feet, 7 In.	185
Pin Tray, Ethnic Woman, Lifting Apron To Form Tray, Pointed Bonnet, 4 x 4 In.	98
Pitcher, Bull, Checkered Pants, Hat, Cow Bell, 1920s, 7 x 4 In.	95
Pitcher, Monkey, Blue, Coat, Hat, 5 ¾ In.	70
Plaque, Couple, Angel, Berry Border, Oval, 9 ½ x 7 In.	298
Teapot, Tall Hatted Man Handle, Coy Woman Lid, Dress Base, Pink Bisque, 9 x 8 In.	338
Tray, Monna, Figural, Girl Holding Dress Out At Arm's Length, 5 ½ x 5 ½ In.	89
Vase, Bisque, Kewpie, Paint, 4 In.	10735

SCHEIER POTTERY was made by Edwin Scheier (1910–2008) and his wife, Mary (1908–2007). They met while they both worked for the WPA, and married in 1937. In 1939, they established their studio, Hillcrock Pottery, in Glade Spring, Virginia. From 1940 to 1968, Edwin taught at the University of New Hampshire and Mary was artist-in-residence. They moved to Oaxaca, Mexico, in 1968 to study the arts and crafts of the Zapotec Indians. When the Scheiers moved to Green Valley, Arizona, in 1978, Ed returned to pottery, making some of his biggest and best-known pieces.

Bowl, Band Of Figures, Alternating Upside Down, Blue & Purple Glaze, 1992, 10 x 15 In.	1250
Bowl, Brown Semigloss Glaze, Signed, 7 ¾ In.	46
Bowl, Fish & Figures, Green & Tan Speckled Glaze, 1960s, 7 x 12 In.	5625
Bowl, Incised Band, Brown & Gray Glaze, Recessed Foot, Signed, c.1950, 5 ¾ In. ....*illus*	600
Bowl, Stylized Figures, Incised & Raised, Beaded Hands & Feet, Footed, 1985, 12 x 13 In.	5313
Bowl, Vase, Coupe, Figural Medallions, Manganese Volcanic Glaze, 1986, 10 x 9 In.	1500
Vase, Abstract Faces, Incised Signed, 1950s, 5 ½ x 3 ½ In.	688
Vase, Brown, Incised Faces, Black Matte Glaze, Signed, 1940s, 10 x 10 In.	5000
Vase, Coupe, Stylized Figures, Horizontal Lines, Sgraffito, Bulbous, Signed, 7 x 5 In.	2375
Vase, Faces, Magnetized Volcanic Glaze, Footed, Signed, 1988, 11 ½ In. ....*illus*	2625
Vase, Figures, Bronze & Turquoise, Volcanic Glaze, Signed, 1980s, 10 ½ x 8 ½ In. ....*illus*	3000

Vase, Figures, Peeking, Footed, Gunmetal Glaze, Signed, 13 x 9 In.	1625
Vase, Figures, Peeking, Gunmetal, Blue Glaze, 15 x 9 In.	625
Vase, Figures, Stylized, Black, Purple Glaze, Footed, Signed, 1990, 14 ½ x 12 In.	875
Vase, Figures, Volcanic Gunmetal, Purple Glaze, Signed, 1990, 7 x 7 In.	563
Vase, Green Glaze, Sgraffito Figures, Footed, c.1960, 15 x 10 In.	3321
Vase, Raised Figures, Faces, Footed, 1966, 22 ½ x 12 In.	21250
Vase, Sculpture, Mother, Child, Abstract Shape, Cutout, 28 x 20 In.	625

SCHNEIDER GLASSWORKS was founded in 1917 at Epinay-sur-Seine, France, by Charles and Ernest Schneider. Art glass was made between 1917 and 1930. The company still produces clear crystal glass. See also the Le Verre Francais category.

Bowl, Chardons, Cameo, Pedestal, Signed, c.1930, 9 ¼ x 8 In.	2000
Ewer, Art Deco, Yellow, Purple Powdered Glass, Strawberries, Leaves, Signed, 12 In.	4148
Goblet, Cobalt Blue Flared Cup, Peach To Pink Stem, Base, Marked, 13 x 5 In.	1208
Sphere, Clear, Bubble Clusters, Louis XVI Style Bronze Base, 7 In., Pair	750
Vase, Dahlias, Amethyst, Pedestal Base, Cameo, Signed, c.1930, 14 ½ x 7 In.	1000
Vase, Mottled Orange, Frosted, Round, Flared Rim, Le Verre France Charder, c.1920, 3 In.	1476
Vase, Mottled, Rose, Rust, Yellow, Le Verre Francais, Etched Signature, 14 ¾ In.	604
Vase, Necklace Pattern, Handles, Cameo, Signed, c.1928, 12 x 10 ½ In.	1875
Vase, Palmetto, Shaded Purple, Signed Charder, Marked Le Verre Francais, 1900s, 8 x 6 In.	750

SCIENTIFIC INSTRUMENTS of all kinds are included in this category. Other categories such as Barometer, Binoculars, Dental, Medical, Nautical, and Thermometer may also price scientific apparatus.

Ampere Meter, Edison System, Schenectady, Wood Frame, Etched Glass	2700
Astrolabe, Brass, Middle East, 14 x 11 ½ In.	708
Astrolabe, Brass, Middle East, 1700s, 7 ¾ x 4 ½ In.	502
Bell Tower Alarm, Gamewell, Electo-Mechanical, Brass, Iron, 28 x 28 In.	486
Binoculars, Marine Glass, Carl Zeiss Jena, 2 Turrets, 4 Eyepieces	1845
Boiler, G. Tagliabuf, High Temperature, Copper, Brass, Cylindrical, c.1862, 15 ½ In.	120
Calculator, Aktiebolaget Original, Metal, Crank, Sweden, 11 In.	338
Calculator, Marchant WL, Pinwheel, Raised Brass Label, 12 In.	300
Calculator, Millionaire, Hans W. Egli, Zurich, 1893-1935	3383
Calculator, Thatcher, Model 4012, Keuffel & Esser, New York, Wood Box	1200
Calculator, Thatcher, Oak Box, 1881 Patent, c.1900, 23 ½ In.	560
Chronometer, 2-Day, Mahogany, Silvered Dial, c.1845	7170
Chronometer, A. Johannsen & Co., 2-Day, Brass Gimbal, Mahogany Box, 7 ½ x 6 In.	1080
Chronometer, Graham & Parkes, Liverpool, 2-Day, Gimbaled Bowl, Inlaid Box	1680
Chronometer, T. Earnshaw, London, No. 2156, Chain Fusee, Mahogany Box	7800
Compass, Pocket, Dry Card, Paper Dial, Walnut Case, c.1805, 3 ½ x 4 In.	142
Compass, Sundial, Diptych, Fruitwood, Printed Paper Facings, Folding, c.1800, 2 ¾ In.	300
Compass, Surveyor's, B. Rittenhouse, Brass, Phila., c.1790, 14 x 7 In.	14580
Compass, Surveyor's, Camm Moore, Brass, 2 Hinged Posts, Case, N.C., c.1790, 9 x 3 In.	5428
Compass, Surveyor's, E. Duffield, Brass, Case, Phila., c.1790, 13 ½ In.	10625
Compass, Surveyor's, T. Wightman, Mahogany, Brass Vernier, Box, 14 In.	984
Compass, Surveyor's, T.F. Randolph, Wood Case, Buckle, 4 ½ x 17 In.	338
Compass, Surveyor's, Vernier, Andrew Meneely, Fleur-De-Lis North, c.1846, 7 ¾ In.	570
Electricity Gauge, Davidson & Conner, Rosewood Architectural Case, 19 In.	1800
Equinoctial Ring Dial, Brass, England, 1700s, 9 In.	10620
Generator, E.W. Shaw, Oak, Nickel, Hand Crank, Fitted Case, c.1900, 7 In.	215
Generator, Van De Graff, 33 In.	180
Graphometer, Brass, 1800s, 13 x 9 ¾ In.	502
Graphometer, Brass, Canivet, Round Wood Base, France, c.1765	885
Kaleidoscope, Brass, Wood Base, c.1830, 11 In.	267
Kaleidoscope, C.G. Bush & Co., Prov., R.I., 14 In.	677
Kaleidoscope, C.G. Bush, Baluster, Shaped Legs, c.1850, 13 x 11 In.	1200
Kaleidoscope, Composite Tube, Wood Eyepiece, Metal & Plastic Case, c.1915, 9 ½ In.	180
Lathe, Jeweler's & Watchmaker's, Precision, Brass, 14 In.	1140
Lens Cutting Machine, American Optical Co., Model M540-C, Cast Iron	240
Microscope, B. Pike's & Sons, 518 Broadway, N.Y., No. 92, 18 In.	840
Microscope, Bausch & Lomb, Brass, Cherry Case, 13 In.	237
Microscope, Bausch & Lomb, Fitted Oak Case, 13 x 7 x 8 In.	246
Microscope, Compound, Gimbaled Mirror, Accessories, Box, England, c.1850	360
Microscope, Culpeper Type, Pyramidal Mahogany Box, 10 ½ In.	1722
Microscope, Culpepper, Rack & Pinion Focus, Round Stage, Box, 12 ½ In.	861
Microscope, E. Leitz, Wetzlar, Germany, 14 In.	1320

Satsuma, Jar, Lid, Reticulated, Panels, Gold, Kinkozan Style, Marked, c.1900, 6 x 6 ½ In.
$6,875

Rago Arts & Auction Center

Satsuma, Jardiniere, Figures, Butterflies, Bronze, Pierced, Japan, c.1885, 15 In.
$676

New Orleans Auction Galleries, Inc.

Satsuma, Vase, Dragon, Phoenix, Chrysanthemums, Signed, Kinkozan, c.1900, 10 In.
$2,607

James D. Julia Auctioneers

S

Satsuma, Vase, Flowers, Butterflies, Bamboo Style Handles, Signed, c.1910, 13 In., Pair
$230

Cottone Auctions

Satsuma, Vase, Palace, Figures, Flowers, Figural Ring Handles, c.1900, 43 ¾ In.
$5,000

Rago Arts & Auction Center

Scale, Balance, Porcelain, Dragons, Bats, Metal Mounts, Chinese, 1900s, 13 ½ In.
$119

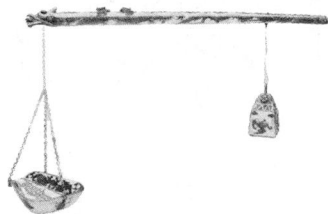

James D. Julia Auctioneers

Scale, Candy, Dayton Style, No. 166, Brass Scoop, 2 Lb. Capacity
$351

Victorian Casino Antiques

Microscope, F. & W. Grunow, New Haven, Ct., No. 101, 17 In.	1440
Microscope, Monocular, Rackwork Coarse Focus, Society Of Arts, c.1900, 12 ½ In.	180
Microscope, Pellin Colorimeter, Paris, France, 1868, 16 In.	240
Microscope, R. & J. Beck, Double Pillar, London, No. 5848, 22 In.	4613
Microscope, R. & J. Beck, London, No. 437, Brass, Mahogany Case, 12 In.	390
Microscope, Swift & Son, Military, Portable, Field, Leather Box	330
Milliamperes Meter, Jewell Electric Instrument Co., Chicago, 29 In.	300
Motor, Riker Electric Motor Co., Brooklyn, No. 1199, 10 In.	18000
Nocturnal, Boxwood, Carved, Heart Handle, Incised Both Bears, 1700s, 10 ¾ In.	5605
Pantograph, West, Brass, Lacquered, Calibrated Arms, Marked, London, c.1820, 33 In.	150
Pedometer, Spencer & Perkins, Brass Case, Strap, Porcelain Dial, 2 Subsidiary Dials, c.1800	960
Pressure Gauge, Ashton Valve Co., Boston, 12 ¼ In.	330
Spectroscope, Shore Instrument Co., Cast-Iron Tripod Stand, 1912	246
Static Machine, Brass, Wood, Glass Disc & Tubes, c.1825, 27 x 25 In.	4920
Stock Ticker, Western Union, Art Deco Style Pedestal, Glass Dome, 1920, 31 x 18 In.	15975
Stock Ticker, Western Union, Automatic Self-Winding, 1920s-40s, 13 In.	9480
Telescope, Bateman & Branches, Brass, Mahogany Stand, c.1885, 42 In.	944
Telescope, Brass, 2 Draw, Mahogany Case, 36 ½ In.	295
Telescope, Brass, 3 Draw, 1800s, 33 In.	130
Telescope, Brass, Leather, Day & Night, 1800s, 36 In.	142
Telescope, Brass, Wood Tripod, Marked U.S. Navy, c.1900, 57 x 40 In.	1298
Telescope, C.A. Spencer & Sons, Geneva, N.Y., Brass, Mahogany, 1876, 48 In.	4800
Telescope, Gilbert & Sons, London, Brass, Tripod Base, 40 In.	2400
Telescope, Hand, A.S. Aloe Co., St. Louis, Brass, 5-Pull, Leather Case	308
Telescope, J.H. Steward, Brass, 46 In.	813
Telescope, John Browning, Reflecting Mirror & Lens, 65 In.	1020
Telescope, John Bryne, Refracting, Rack Focus, Single Draw, 7 Eyepieces, c.1880, 60 In.	3900
Telescope, R.B. Tolles, Boston, No. 46, Brass, Tripod Stand	738
Telescope, Ross, England, Brass, Walnut, Tripod Base, c.1900, 47 In. ....*illus*	1125
Telescope, Surveyor's, Keuffel & Esser Co., New York, Fitted Box	270
Telescope, Tripod Stand, Brass, 1900s, 2 ½ x 24 In.	944
Telescope, Tripod, 2 Draw, Brass, Wood Casting, Marked, 1800s, 38 In.	767
Telescope, W. & S. Jones, England, Brass, Tripod Base, c.1850, 39 In.	502
Transit, Builder's, W. & L.E. Gurley, Enclosed Scale, Rack Focus, c.1900, 11 In.	390
Transit, Engineer's, W. & L.E. Gurley, Horizontal Scale, Rack Focusing, c.1900, 14 In.	492
Transit, Engineer's, W. & L.E. Gurley, Troy, N.Y., Fitted Box, 18 In.	270
Transit, Keuffel & Esser Co., N.J., Brass	178
Transit, Reconnaissance, W. & L.E. Gurley, Horizontal Scale, Wood Case, c.1895, 10 In.	780
Transit, Surveyor's, Brass, Inscribed D.D. Mendham, Case, c.1805, 13 In.	2252
Transit, Surveyor's, Compass, Heller & Brightley, Philadelphia, Brass, 12 In.	780
Transit, Surveyor's, W. & L.E. Gurley, Silvered Dial, Marked, c.1870, 5 ½ In. ....*illus*	461
Transit, Surveyor's, W. & L.E. Gurley, Spirit Level, Horizontal Scale, c.1858, 12 In.	615
Universal Ticker, Western Union Edison, Type 3-A, Brass, Twin Rolled, Tape Feed, 10 In.	5100
Vacuum Pump, Mahogany, Brass, Double Rack, Handle, 13-In. Glass Dome	780
Volt Meter, Calvin & James White, Electro Static, No. 645, Case, 1911, 18 In.	420
Wave Machine, Rayette Lectronic, Beige Bakelite, Round, 11 In.	330
Wye Level, W. & L.E. Gurley, 18-In. Telescope, Rack Focus, Spirit Level, Scale, c.1910	270
Wye Level, W. & L.E. Gurley, Troy, New York, Fitted Box	677

SCRIMSHAW is bone or ivory or whale's teeth carved by sailors and others for entertainment during the sailing-ship days. Some scrimshaw was carved as early as 1800. There are modern scrimshanders making pieces today on bone, ivory, or plastic. Other pieces may be found in the Ivory and Nautical categories.

Basket, Ivory, Carved Medallion, Pierced, Oval, 7 ⅝ In.	1320
Basket, Knitting, Ivory, Oval, Flared Spear Sticks, Nailed Band, 4 ⅝ x 6 In.	1800
Blackfish Jawbone, Ship, Land, Sea, c.1860, 19 In.	1534
Bodkin, Whale Ivory, Baleen Inlaid Bands, Pierced, Heart Shape Handle, 4 ½ In.	1020
Bow Saw, Carpenter's, Whalebone, Serrated Blade, c.1870, 9 ¾ x 11 ½ In.	840
Box, Cylindrical, Turned, Treaded Closure, Flowers, Red, 1800s, 1 ⅛ In.	600
Box, Mahogany, Hinged Lid, Abalone, Mother-Of-Pearl, Heart, 1800s, 5 x 11 In.	1680
Box, Sewing, Whalebone, Ivory, 6 ¾ x 7 In.	1560
Box, Whale's Tooth, Brass End, Ship, Landscape, 1841, 5 ¾ In.	590
Busk, Red & Green Wax, Eagle, Banner, Wreath, Flowers, 1800s, 14 x 1 ½ In.	3120
Busk, Whalebone, Carved Woman, Scrolls, Flowers, c.1850, 14 In.	1003
Cane, Whalebone Handle, Clenched Fist Shape, 31 ½ In.	767
Carpenter's Square, Whalebone, Pine, 2 Pins, Cove Molded Tip	480

Cribbage Board, Walrus Jawbone, Eagle's Head, Salmon, Ships, Whales, Flowers, 9 x 8 In.	6600
Cup, Handle, Animal Designs, Continental, 4 ⅝ In.	431
Desk, Mahogany, Whalebone Bound, Baleen Inlay, Fitted Interior, Stand, c.1850	1920
Dipper, Whalebone Handle, Coconut Wood Cup, 14 ¾ In.	600
Fid, Whalebone, Ivory, Clenched Fist, 6 ¾ In.	1080
Figurine, Sailor, Standing, Hands Clasped Behind Back, 1800s, 5 In.	480
Fishing Line Wheel, Whalebone, Diamond Head Terminal Handle, Reel Rotates, 12 ¾ In.	8640
Fist, Clenched, Whale Ivory, 3 In.	502
Horn, Cup, Surrender Of USS Chesapeake, 1813, Sailing Ship, Cannons, 1800s, 4 ½ In.	805
Mortar & Pestle, Whalebone, Burlwood, c.1870.	3360
Panbone, Ship At Anchor, c.1865, 8 x 8 In.	3600
Pie Crimper, Ivory, Ebony, Silver, Shell Inlay, c.1850, 6 In.	885
Pie Crimper, Walrus Ivory, Double Scroll Handle Terminal, Prong Stand, 6 ¾ In.	840
Rolling Pin, Ivory, Walnut, Sailor Made, 1800s, 17 ½ In.	711
Salad Fork & Spoon, Ivory, Captain & Wife, Ships, Nautical Symbols	237
Toilet Paper Holder, Oven Peel Shape, Whalebone, Brass, Wood, 1800s, 7 ¾ x 5 In.	1416
Walking Stick, Whalebone, Sailor Carved, Child's, 25 ⅞ In.	1080
Whale's Tooth, Bird, Mountains, c.1845, 7 In.	885
Whale's Tooth, Crucifixion, Obverse, Robed Woman, Angels, Vines, 5 In.	9600
Whale's Tooth, Engraved Ships, Leaf Borders, 5 ¾ In.	7800
Whale's Tooth, Engraved, Full-Rigged Ship, c.1880, 5 In.	1652
Whale's Tooth, Engraved, Sailor's Rights, Eagle & Anchor, Putto, Branch, 5 In.	2375
Whale's Tooth, Engraved, Ship, Lion, Crown Unicorn, Soldier, England, c.1850, 5 In.	1180
Whale's Tooth, Fist, Carved, c.1850, 1 ¾ In.	266
Whale's Tooth, Flag, Cannon, Drum, Shield, Red, White, Blue, A. White, 1959, 7 ½ In.	3304
Whale's Tooth, Flowering Plant, 1800s, 5 In.	266
Whale's Tooth, Island Woman, Flowers, Banner, Bird, c.1860, 6 In.	4425
Whale's Tooth, Lady Liberty, Standing Figure, U.S.A., 1900s, 5 x 1 ½ In.	1121
Whale's Tooth, Naval Battle, Eagle, Holding Flag, 1800s, 6 In.	288
Whale's Tooth, Neptune, Liberty, Inscribed, Liberty & Freedom, 1800s, 5 In., Pair ....*illus*	10200
Whale's Tooth, Rigged Ship, Arrows, Banners, Woman, 1830s Attire, 6 ½ In.	5400
Whale's Tooth, Sailing Ship, American Flag, Red, Blue, Black Ink, 5 ¾ In.	10800
Whale's Tooth, Seam Rubber, Carved Ship Scene, 1790, 6 In.	708
Whale's Tooth, Ship, American Flag, Flowers, Red, Green, Blue, 3 ⅜ x 6 ½ In.	2040
Whale's Tooth, Ship, American Flag, Palm Tree, Island Woman, Text, c.1850, 6 In.	3540
Whale's Tooth, Ship, Flag, Eagle, Sad Woman, Albert Garder's Memorial, c.1850, 5 ½ In.	2950
Whale's Tooth, Ship, House, Landscape, c.1850, 6 In.	1416
Whale's Tooth, Ship, Whaling Scene, c.1870, 4 ½ In.	885
Whale's Tooth, Sperm Whale, Ship Susan Of Nantucket, F. Myrick, 1829, 7 ½ x 3 In.	96000
Whale's Tooth, Spread Eagle, Shield, Flag, Red, White, Blue, c.1850, 6 ½ In.	64900
Whale's Tooth, Sun, Star, Phrase, Death To John Bull And Rebels, 1861, 4 ¾ In. ....*illus*	1185
Whale's Tooth, Woman, Bonnet, Fan, Flowers, Stars, c.1900, 7 ½ In.	1458
Whale's Tooth, Woman, Dress, Head Wreath, Red, White, Blue Shield, c.1855, 6 ½ In.	16520
Whale's Tooth, Woman, Dress, Hearts, Sperm Whale, Initials, c.1845, 7 ½ In.	2714
Whale's Tooth, Woman, Dress, Red Flowers In Hair, M.L. Monogram, 6 In.	944
Whale's Tooth, Woman, Victorian Dress, Eagle, Shield, Banners, c.1860, 4 ½ In.	295
Whistle, Whalebone, Wood, Carved, Sailor Made, c.1840, 2 ¾ In.	266

SEBASTIAN MINIATURES were first made by Prescott W. Baston in 1938 in Marblehead, Massachusetts. More than 400 different designs have been made, and collectors search for the out-of-production models. The mark may say *Copr. P.W. Baston U.S.A.*, or *P.W. Baston U.S.A.*, or *Prescott W. Baston*. Sometimes a paper label was used.

Colonial Watchman, P.W. Baston Corp., 1947, 4 ¼ In.	20
Little Nell & Her Grandfather, P.W. Baston, 2 ⅞ In.	20
Mother Dear, See Here!, See Here!, Jell-O, Black Sticker, P.W. Baston, 4 In.	220
Switching The Freight, Prescott W. Baston, 3 ¾ x 2 ¼ In.	25
Thomas Jefferson, Blue Label, Copr. 1949, P.W. Baston, 3 ½ In.	58

SEG, *see Paul Revere Pottery category.*

SEVRES porcelain has been made in Sevres, France, since 1769. Many copies of the famous ware have been made. The name originally referred to the works of the Royal Porcelain factory. The name now includes any of the wares made in the town of Sevres, France. The entwined lines with a center letter used as the mark is one of the most forged marks in antiques. Be very careful to identify Sevres by quality, not just by mark.

Bowl, Fluted, Round, Lobed Sides, Footed, Multicolor Flowers, Gilt Rim, 1757, 8 ½ In.	265

Schafer & Vater, Bottle, Uncle Sam, Porcelain, 9 In.
$300

The Stein Auction Co.

Scheier, Bowl, Incised Band, Brown & Gray Glaze, Recessed Foot, Signed, c.1950, 5 ¾ In.
$600

Skinner Auctioneers & Appraisers

Scheier, Vase, Faces, Magnetized Volcanic Glaze, Footed, Signed, 1988, 11 ½ In.
$2,625

Rago Arts & Auction Center

Scheier, Vase, Figures, Bronze & Turquoise, Volcanic Glaze, Signed, 1980s, 10 ½ x 8 ½ In.
$3,000

Rago Arts & Auction Center

S

Scientific Instrument, Telescope, Ross, England, Brass, Walnut, Tripod Base, c.1900, 47 In.
$1,125

James D. Julia Auctioneers

Scientific Instrument, Transit, Surveyor's, W. & L.E. Gurley, Silvered Dial, Marked, c.1870, 5 ½ In.
$461

Skinner Auctioneers & Appraisers

Scrimshaw, Whale's Tooth, Neptune, Liberty, Inscribed, Liberty & Freedom, 1800s, 5 In., Pair
$10,200

Skinner Auctioneers & Appraisers

Bowl, Man, Serenading A Woman, Gilt Bronze Base, Chateau De Tuileries, 1840	528
Bowl, Verriere, Blue, Flower Garlands, Scalloped Rim, Handles, 1800s, 5 x 11 In.	717
Box, Hand Painted, Ladies Sculpting, Painting, Octagonal, Signed Henry, 8 ½ In.	767
Box, Lid, Oval, Couple In Woods, Cobalt Blue, Gilt, 3 ¼ x 6 x 7 ½ In.	600
Centerpiece, Cartouches, Flowers, Cherubs, Sky, Flowers Inside, Bronze Mounts, 10 In.	750
Centerpiece, Pink, Dancing Couple, Garlands, Bronze Feet & Handles, 1872, 7 x 20 In.	1585
Centerpiece, Round, Footed, Cutout Handles, Painted, Signed, 15 x 10 In.	450
Compote, Bowl, Flowers, Couple, Scrolled Metal Feet & Handles, 10 In.	210
Compote, Painted, Cobalt Blue, Paneled Reserves, Silver Rim, France, 1800s, 6 x 7 ¾ In.	784
Cup & Saucer, Gilt, Enameled Jewel Design, Cobalt Blue Ground, 6-In. Saucer	4250
Cup & Saucer, Napoleonic, Variegated Blue Glaze, Gilt Interior, 1800s, 5 In., 12 Piece	720
Figurine, Monkey On Pedestal, Seated, Grasping Plum With Foot, c.1919, 25 x 9 In.	2706
Group, Napoleon, Josephine, Chair, Gilt Metal, Footed, Mark, 11 ¼ In.	813
Inkwell, Birds, Branches, Double Well, Black Trim, 19th Century, 3 x 8 ½ In.	120
Lamp, Oil, Porcelain, Ribbed, Blue, Gilt Base, Charles Ficquenet Sevres, c.1900, 14 In.	438
Plate, Central Flowers, Burgundy & Gilt Border, 8 ⅜ In., 12 Piece	1125
Plate, Roses, Berries, Cobalt Blue Border, Gilt Leaves, Marked, 9 ½ In.	1250
Urn, Lid, Classical Woman, Cherub Reserve, Blue, Signed E. Rozi, 29 In.	678
Urn, Lid, Landscape, Gilt Snake Handles, Metal Mounts, Signed Theobalis, c.1920, 21 In.	875
Urn, Lid, Rose Painted Reserve, Green, Ormolu Handles, Trim, 11 ½ In., Pair	237
Urn, Ram Handles, Festoons, Putti, Yellow, White, Pedestal Foot, 12 ½ In., Pair	1000
Vase, Abstract, Mottled Green & Blue, Oval, Cinched Neck, Taxile Doat, 1920s, 3 ½ In.	1000
Vase, Champleve, Putti, Flower Reserve, Cobalt Blue Ground, Gilt Scrolls, 8 ½ In.	208
Vase, Gourd Shape, Copper Red & Blue Glaze, Signed T. Doat, c.1900, 4 ¼ x 3 ½ In. ....*illus*	15000
Vase, Ivory Matte Glaze, Gourd Shape, Swollen Neck, Stylized Lattice, Taxile Doat, 4 In.	1000
Vide Poche, Stoneware, Cherubs, Crystalline Glaze, Stamped, 1898, 10 ½ x 8 ½ In.	6250

SEWER TILE figures were made by workers at the sewer tile and pipe factories in the Ohio area during the late nineteenth and early twentieth centuries. Figurines, small vases, and cemetery vases were favored. Often the finished vase was a piece of the original pipe with added decorations and markings. All types of sewer tile work are now considered folk art by collectors.

Bank, Goose, Walter Smith, Superior Clay Products Co., Lurichsville, c.1910, 10 x 16 In.	570
Bank, Yellow Kid Head, Inset Pottery Eyes, Teeth, Inscribed June, c.1910, 5 In.	211
Bread Container, Cylindrical Shape, 2 Handles, c.1900, 13 ½ x 16 ½ In.	450
Carriage Steps, Tree Trunk Shape, Textured, c.1900, 19 In. ....*illus*	554
Chimney Cap, Fluted Column, Shaped Rim, Decorative X Design, 29 In., Pair	390
Crock, Castle Wall, Storefront, Inscribed Drugs, 1800s, 6 ¼ In.	830
Doorstop, Cat, Seated, Incised Features, Red Brown Glaze, c.1900, 9 ½ In.	345
Downspout, Brick, Open Mouthed Lion, c.1900, 13 In.	294
Figure, 2 Owls & Eagle, On Stump, Inscribed EJE, c.1900, 10 ½ In.	510
Figure, Beaver, Glazed, Embossed Mark, Ohio, c.1900, 2 ½ In.	60
Figure, Dog & Frog, Seated Terrier, 1800s, 11 ½ x 2 ½ In.	150
Figure, Dog, Collie, Standing, Molded, Base, Inscribed, c.1900, 9 ½ In.	676
Figure, Dog, Green Paint, Molded, c.1915, 7 ½ In.	118
Figure, Dog, Seated Spaniel, Octagonal Base, U.S.A., 11 In.	241
Figure, Dog, Seated, Flathead, Ohio, c.1890, 11 In.	720
Figure, Dog, Sitting, On Round Tapered Base, c.1900, 4 In.	201
Figure, Dog, Spaniel, Incised Features, Speckled Gray Glaze, 1928, 10 ¼ In.	120
Figure, Dog, Spaniel, Ohio, c.1900, 10 ¼ In.	176
Figure, Dog, Spaniel, Seated, c.1910, 10 In.	210
Figure, Frog, Tooled Detail, Ohio, c.1910, 4 ½ x 8 In.	180
Figure, Lion, Crouching, Tree Stump Base, Signed Dick, c.1920, 16 In.	369
Figure, Lion, Reclining, Brown Glaze, 11 ½ x 7 In.	480
Figure, Lion, Reclining, Molded Ivy Base, Ohio, 9 In.	210
Figure, Lion, Stalking, Base, Ohio, Early 1900s, 13 ½ In.	570
Figure, Pig, Marked Dickey Clay, Kansas, Late 19th Century, 2 ½ In.	338
Figure, Pig, Seated, Long Eyelashes, Ohio, c.1950, 9 In.	270
Figure, Raccoon, Crouching, c.1940, 15 In.	240
Figure, Spaniel, Seated, c.1900, 7 x 8 ½ In., Pair	180
Figure, Squirrel, Nut In Mouth, Molded, c.1910, 11 In.	210
Figure, Squirrel, Seated, Seated, Unglazed Tail, Signed Walter Smith, c.1950, 6 In.	180
Paperweight, Maurice A. Knight Acid Proof Stoneware, Pomegranate, Lion, Frog, 5 ½ In.	154
Planter, Textured, Square, Round Feet, c.1900, 10 ½ x 10 ½ In., Pair	852
Planter, Tree Stump Shape, c.1900, 9 ½ In.	147
Planter, Tree Stump Shape, c.1900, 26 ½ In., Pair	705
Shoes, Square Toed, Punched, Pricked, 2 x 5 In., Pair	259

SEWING equipment of all types is collected, from sewing birds that held the cloth to tape measures, needle books, and old wooden spools. Sewing machines are included here. Needlework pictures are listed in the Picture category.

Bird, Brass, Clamp, Double Pincushions, Victorian, 4 ¾ In.	130
Bird, Cast Leaf, Flowers, Repousse Featherwork, Steel, Tin, Mid 1800s, 5 In.	59
Box, Bronze, Brass, Hive Shape, Jewel Bees, Linen Interior, Howell & James, London, 9 In.	1500
Box, Burl Walnut, Drawer, Thread Winder & Pincushion Top, Marked, Mama, 1880s, 7 In.	270
Box, Fish, 5 Sewing Tools, 3 ¾ In.	1140
Box, Lid, Lacquer, Footed, Cut Corner, Figures, 1800s, 6 x 14 In.	390
Box, Mahogany Veneer, Pincushion Top, Drawer, Iron Swing Out Clamp, 3 ½ x 5 ½ In.	142
Box, Mahogany, 2 Drawers, Lift Lid, 6 ½ x 18 ½ In.	236
Box, Mahogany, Fitted Interior, Inlays, c.1850, 6 x 14 In.	563
Box, Mahogany, Hinged Lid, Abalone, Mother-Of-Pearl Inlaid Bird, 1800s, 7 x 14 In.	2640
Box, Mahogany, Ivory, Baleen Inlays, Handles, c.1850, 6 x 13 ½ In.	34375
Box, Musical, Burl Walnut Case, Applied Ivory, Combs, Key, Implements, 1860, 7 x 5 In.	2400
Box, Pine, 3 Tiers, Cushion, Spool Pegs, Painted, Salmon Ground, 8 x 8 In.	593
Box, Pine, Drawer, Paint, Pincushion, Spool Holders, c.1850, 7 ¾ In.	148
Box, Spool Holder, Wood, Hinged, Molded Base, Medallion, Eve Schaeffer, 5 x 15 In.	443
Box, Walnut, Fitted Interior, 6 ¾ x 11 In.	504
Box, Walnut, Star, Leaf, Bird, Heart Abalone, Ebony Inlays, Drawer, Footed, 1800s, 4 x 7 In.	2060
Box, Wood, Carved Hunt Scene, Velvet Cushion Inset, Footed, 11 x 6 x 7 In.	450
Box, Wood, Painted, Drawers, Birds, Flowers, Urn, Bracket Feet, c.1830, 9 x 13 ½ In.	5100
Brooch Needle Holder, Flower Basket, Silver Plated	115
Cabinet, Spool, Walnut, 7 Glass-Front Drawers Over 3 Wood Drawers, c.1875, 31 x 23 In.	767
Cabinet, Spool, see also the Advertising category under Cabinet, Spool.	
Chest, Papier-Mache, Hinged Lid, Ferns, Gilding, Ivory Pulls, Bracket Feet, 1875, 9 ½ In.	660
Clamp, Pincushion, Needle Case, Carved Bone, Velvet, France, c.1850, 7 In. *illus*	684
Clamp, Pincushion, Sea Monster On Shell, Silver, Velvet, c.1850, 9 In. *illus*	1824
Darning Egg, Lacquer, Balalaika Player, Sterling Handle, Fedoskino, 1800s, 6 In.	180
Dress Form, Full Body, c.1900, 65 In.	4275
Dress Form, Pine Bottom, Composition, Wool Skirt, 18 In.	204
Dress Form, Shaped Wire Cage, France, 29 In., Pair	480
Etui, Mother-Of-Pearl, Carved, Brass, Hinged Lid, Engraved Scrolls, 1800s, 4 x 1 ½ In.	2070
Etui, Tool Case, Ivory, Gold Mounted, Gems, Oval, Marked Cartier, c.1850, 4 In.	3000
Jagging Wheel, Ivory, Crimping Fork, Star Shape Design, Carved, 6 ¾ In.	1121
Kit, Necessaire, Beehive Shape, Gilt Metal, Tools, Napoleon III, c.1860, 6 In. *illus*	4788
Kit, Necessaire, Bird Nest, Glass Egg, Gilt Metal, Enamel, Tools, c.1870, 7 In. *illus*	4332
Kit, Necessaire, Egg, Porcelain, 6 Scenes, Gilt, Gold Lined, Tools, c.1875, 3 ½ In. *illus*	6840
Kit, Necessaire, Fish, Ruby Eyes, Silver, Tools, c.1750, 6 In. *illus*	2622
Kit, Necessaire, White Leather, Brass Mounts, England, c.1750, 4 x ¾ In., 7 Piece	125
Knitting Needles, Cased Steel, Cylindrical Wood Case, Ivory Ball Ends, c.1880, 12 In.	150
Lacemaking Kit, Cylinder Container, Hinged, Oval, Bone, Cord Handles, 7 x 3 ½ In.	81
Lamp, Lacemaker's, Blown Glass, Applied Handle, c.1820, 9 ¼ In.	330
Loom, Tape, Heart Cutout, Carved, Blue Paint, 1829, 11 x 10 In.	1560
Loom, Tape, Walnut, Crank, c.1800, 14 x 7 ½ In.	770
Machine, Black Cast Iron, Painted Scrolls, Crank, Shaped Base, Paw Feet, c.1875, 12 In.	510
Machine, Clamp, Painted Flowers, Iron, Metal, Germany, Miniature, Box, 7 x 6 In.	212
Machine, Pony, Cast Iron, Black, Gold Decoration, Circular, Embossed Base, Crank, 7 In.	861
Machine, Singer, Cast Iron, Mother-Of-Pearl Inlay, Shaped Base, Crank, 15 In.	840
Machine, Singer, Wood Table, Lamp, 2 Drawers, Accessories, Thread, c.1900, 41 x 40 In.	30
Mannequin, Woman's Figure, Half Scale, Screw Base, Wolf Form Co., N.Y.C., 27 In.	480
Needle Box, Needles & Shuttles, Tin Lithograph, Arrow, Boye Brand, Sliding Door, 16 In.	123
Needle Case, Figural, Boy, Carved, Head Unscrews, Germany, c.1810, 3 ¼ In. *illus*	342
Needle Case, Figural, Boy, Hat, Silver, 2 ¼ In.	240
Needle Case, Figural, Chinese Man, Standing, Silver, c.1800, 2 ¾ In. *illus*	627
Needle Case, Figural, Lady, Dutch, Basket, Hat, Silver, c.1880, 2 ¼ In.	450
Needle Case, Hand Shape, Heart In Palm, Cloth, 4 ¾ x 2 ½ In.	1062
Needle Case, On Chain, 14K Yellow Gold, Tooled, Engraved, Carter Howe & Co., 2 In.	293
Needle Case, Painted, Columned Stone Mansion, Multicolor, Lid, 1800s, 4 x 12 In.	2074
Needle Case, Porcelain, Figural, Swaddled Baby, Germany, c.1850, 3 ½ In. *illus*	627
Needle Case, Revolving, Tin, Boye Needle Co., Chicago, 8 ½ x 18 In.	267
Pincushion Dolls are listed in their own category.	
Pincushion, Beaded, Birds, Flowers, Scalloped Edges, 7 x 9 ½ In.	59
Pincushion, Birds & Heart, Shaped Black Leather Panels, Flowers, Leaves, 9 x 7 In.	390
Pincushion, Figural, Aladdin, Porcelain, Germany, c.1925, 3 ½ In. *illus*	114
Pincushion, Lady's Shoe Shape, Silver, Scenes, England, c.1890, 6 In. *illus*	285

Scrimshaw, Whale's Tooth, Sun, Star, Phrase, Death To John Bull And Rebels, 1861, 4 ¾ In.
$1,185

James D. Julia Auctioneers

Sevres, Vase, Gourd Shape, Copper Red & Blue Glaze, Signed T. Doat, c.1900, 4 ¼ x 3 ½ In.
$15,000

Rago Arts & Auction Center

Sewer Tile, Carriage Steps, Tree Trunk Shape, Textured, c.1900, 19 In.
$554

Garth's Auctioneers & Appraisers

S

Sewing, Clamp, Pincushion, Needle Case, Carved Bone, Velvet, France, c.1850, 7 In.
$684

Theriault's

Sewing, Clamp, Pincushion, Sea Monster On Shell, Silver, Velvet, c.1850, 9 In.
$1,824

Theriault's

Sewing, Kit, Necessaire, Beehive Shape, Gilt Metal, Tools, Napoleon III, c.1860, 6 In.
$4,788

Theriault's

Sewing, Kit, Necessaire, Bird Nest, Glass Egg, Gilt Metal, Enamel, Tools, c.1870, 7 In.
$4,332

Theriault's

Sewing, Kit, Necessaire, Egg, Porcelain, 6 Scenes, Gilt, Gold Lined, Tools, c.1875, 3 ½ In.
$6,840

Theriault's

Sewing, Kit, Necessaire, Fish, Ruby Eyes, Silver, Tools, c.1750, 6 In.
$2,622

Theriault's

Sewing, Needle Case, Figural, Boy, Carved, Head Unscrews, Germany, c.1810, 3 ¼ In.
$342

Sewing, Needle Case, Figural, Chinese Man, Standing, Silver, c.1800, 2 ¾ In.
$627

Theriault's

Sewing, Needle Case, Porcelain, Figural, Swaddled Baby, Germany, c.1850, 3 ½ In.
$627

Theriault's

Sewing, Pincushion, Figural, Aladdin, Porcelain, Germany, c.1925, 3 ½ In.
$114

Theriault's

S

Pincushion, Leather, Cloth, 2 Lovebirds, Vase Shape, c.1845, 5 ¼ x 7 In.	1185
Pincushion, Leather, Cloth, Lovebird Shape, c.1845, 8 ½ x 6 In.	356
Pincushion, Leather, Lovebirds, Hearts, c.1850, 8 ¼ x 6 ¼ In.	2844
Pocket, Patchwork, Embroidered, Square, Heart, Lancaster, Pa., 1800s, 12 In.	563
Scissors, Embossed Handle, Cast White Metal, Italy..................................*illus*	115
Scissors, Sheath, Art Nouveau, Scrolls, Embossed, Germany, c.1900	230
Spool Cabinets are listed here or in the Advertising category under Cabinet, Spool.	
Spool Caddy, Shaker, Maple, Turned, Alligatored Finish, Pincushion, c.1865, 6 In.	558
Spool Caddy, Tiger Maple, Revolving, 4-Footed Base, Drawer, Pincushion, c.1830, 10 In.	546
Spool Holder, Pine, Revolving, Pincushion, Stars, Yellow, 2 Levels, 1800s, 12 In.	178
Spool Holder, Tiger Maple, Carved, Cutouts, Cast Iron, 7 ½ x 9 In.	119
Spool Holder, Walnut, c.1810, 20 x 2 ½ In.	35
Swift, Mixed Wood, Mounted On Tripod Base, Early 19th Century, 36 In.	294
Swift, Yarn Holder Cup, Whalebone, Ivory, Expandable, 1800s, 18 In.	5310
Tape Loom, Mahogany, Serpentine, Crest, Heart, Reel Holder, c.1800, 14 x 7 In. ....*illus*	767
Tape Measure, Bakelite, Bone Accents, France, c.1920, 5 In.	840
Tape Measure, Bald-Headed Man, Porcelain, Bug Extends Tape, c.1900, 1 ½ In. ....*illus*	1344
Tape Measure, Banjo Player, Black, Top Hat, Full Spring Tape, Celluloid, 4 ½ In.	240
Tape Measure, Barrel, Dark & Light Mother-Of-Pearl, France, 1 In.	392
Tape Measure, Birdcage, Mother-Of-Pearl, Gilt, Silk Tape, France, c.1830, ½ In. ....*illus*	280
Tape Measure, Charlie Chaplin, Full Body, Crossed Hands, Cream, Black, 5 ½ In.	300
Tape Measure, Charlie Chaplin, Mustache, Hat, Tape Extends, Celluloid, 2 In.	240
Tape Measure, Coronation Coach, Gilt Metal, Cherubs, Spoked Wheels, c.1890, 2 ½ In.	1456
Tape Measure, Devil Head, Winking, Orange, Porcelain, 1 ¾ In.	330
Tape Measure, Doll, Wood Face, Pink Curls, Pincushion Body, England, 3 ½ In.	45
Tape Measure, Figural, Apple, Plastic, Red, United Device Corp., 1950s, 2 ½ In.	14
Tape Measure, Figural, Dog, Poodle, Brass, Turn Tail To Rewind, c.1890, 2 ¼ In. ....*illus*	456
Tape Measure, Figural, Early Automobile, Brass, Winding Handle, 1 ¾ x 2 ½ In.	242
Tape Measure, Flapper Girl, On Cake, Ceramic, Germany, c.1925, 2 ¼ x 2 ¼ In.	125
Tape Measure, Fruit Basket, Celluloid, 1 ½ x 1 In.	125
Tape Measure, Horseshoe, 4-Leaf Clover, Red, Plastic, W. Germany, 1 ½ x 1 ¼ In.	45
Tape Measure, Pig, Silver Plate, c.1896, 2 ⅛ x 1 ½ In.	130
Tape Measure, Poodle, Cast Brass, England, c.1890, 2 ¼ In.	448
Tape Measure, Rabbit, Floppy Ears, Shamrock In Mouth, Windup, 3 ¼ In.	1320
Tape Measure, Sewing Machine, Gilt Tinplate, c.1880, 1 ½ In.	504
Tape Measure, Squirrel, Sitting, Eating Nut, Gilt Metal, Glass Eye, 2 ¼ In.	265
Tape Measure, Turtle, Brass, Cloth Tape, c.1875, 2 In.	336
Tape Measure, Vegetable & Bone Ivory, Carved, Pierced, c.1880, 1 ⅝ In.	75
Tape Measure, Water Mill, Porch, Stairwell, c.1880, 1 ½ In.	672
Thimble, Silver, Wood Case, Tortoiseshell Veneer, c.1800, 1 ½ In. ....*illus*	513
Thimble, Sterling Silver, Beaded Base, Germany, ¾ In.	35
Thread Holder, 5-Spool, Pincushion, Wood..................................*illus*	86
Thread Winder, Porcelain, Snowflake Shape, c.1810, 2 In. ....*illus*	399
Wall Pocket, Leather, C.M. Initials, Rings Encircle Pincushion, Va., c.1850, 8 x 3 In.	690
Winding Wheel, Wood, Painted Red, 19th Century, 19 x 32 In.	46
Yarn Reeler, Maple, Poplar, 6-Spoke Wheel, Green, Red, White Paint, 1821, 38 x 24 In.	31250
Yarn Winder, Mixed Wood, Turned Base, Acorn Finials, Red Paint, 1800s, 32 ½ In.	270

SHAKER items are characterized by simplicity, functionalism, and orderliness. There were many Shaker communities in America from the eighteenth century to the present day. The religious order made furniture, small wooden pieces, and packaged medicines, herbs, and jellies to sell to "outsiders." Other useful objects were made for use by members of the community. Shaker furniture is listed in this book in the Furniture category.

Basket, Oval, Handle, c.1890, 13 ½ x 5 ½ In.	448
Basket, Sisters, Oval, Wood Handle, c.1900, 6 ¼ x 6 In.	826
Basket, Splint, Black Ash, Woven, Handles, Copper Tacks, 3 ½ x 25 ½ In.	649
Box, 2-Finger, Oval, Grain Painted, 1800s, 2 x 5 ½ In.	384
Box, 2-Finger, Oval, Green Paint, Copper Tacks, 1800s, 1 ½ x 4 In.	295
Box, 3-Finger, Lid, Painted Green, Red, Copper Tacks, Oval, c.1890, 5 x 12 In.	450
Box, 3-Finger, Maple & Pine, Lid, Vines, Leaves, Flowers, Copper Tacks, 1 ¼ x 3 ½ In.	590
Box, 3-Finger, Oval, Lid, Pine, Maple, Yellow, Copper Tacks, c.1930-40, 4 x 11 ¼ In. ....*illus*	2950
Box, 3-Finger, Oval, Lid, Red Paint, Pine & Maple, Copper Tacks, 3 x 7 ½ In.	1180
Box, 3-Finger, Oval, Maple & Pine, Red Paint, Copper Tacks, 3 ⅛ x 8 ⅝ In.	2478
Box, 3-Finger, Oval, Maple & Pine, Yellow Paint, Cherry Lid, Copper Tacks, 2 x 6 In.	5310
Box, 4-Finger, Bentwood, Oval, Copper Tacks, Lid, c.1865, 5 x 12 In.	353

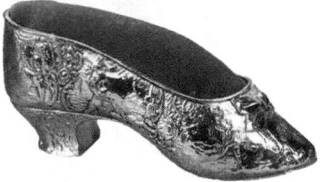

Sewing, Pincushion, Lady's Shoe Shape, Silver, Scenes, England, c.1890, 6 In. $285

Theriault's

Sewing, Scissors, Embossed Handle, Cast White Metal, Italy $115

Victorian Casino Antiques

Sewing, Tape Loom, Mahogany, Serpentine, Crest, Heart, Reel Holder, c.1800, 14 x 7 In. $767

Brunk Auctions

Sewing, Tape Measure, Bald-Headed Man, Porcelain, Bug Extends Tape, c.1900, 1 ½ In.
$1,344

Theriault's

Sewing, Tape Measure, Birdcage, Mother-Of-Pearl, Gilt, Silk Tape, France, c.1830, ½ In.
$280

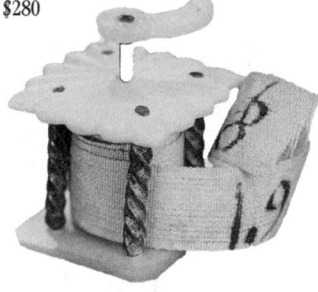

Theriault's

Sewing, Tape Measure, Figural, Dog, Poodle, Brass, Turn Tail To Rewind, c.1890, 2 ¼ In.
$456

Theriault's

Box, 4-Finger, Maple, Copper Tacks, Swing Handle, Silk Lined, c.1900, 11 In.	529
Box, 4-Finger, Oval, Pine & Maple, Red & Yellow Paint, Lid, c.1860, 4 x 10 In.	720
Box, 5-Finger, Oval, Lid, Maple, Pine, Copper Tacks & Points, 5 ½ x 14 ¼ In. ....*illus*	4130
Box, 5-Finger, Oval, Pine & Maple, Red Stain, Lid, Copper Tacks, c.1860, 5 x 13 ½ In.	1020
Box, 5-Finger, Round, Lid, Blue, M.S. Hemenway, Kentucky, c.1830, 14 x 7 In.	259
Box, Bentwood, Arched Fingers, Copper Tacks, Oval, Paint, c.1850, 3 x 8 In.	240
Box, Bentwood, Oval, Arched Fingers, Copper Tacks, Lid, c.1885, 4 x 10 ½ In.	235
Box, Berry, Bentwood, Swing Handle, Blue Paint, c.1970, 5 ½ x 5 ½ In.	948
Box, Kindling, Pine, Orange Stain, 6-Board, Molded Hinged Lid, 2 Sections, 25 x 25 In.	6490
Box, Kindling, Pine, Red Paint, Dovetailed, 2 Sections, Carved Feet, c.1840, 21 x 33 In.	1239
Box, Maple, Pine, Oval, Lid, Yellow Paint, Enfield, New Hampshire, 1836, 3 x 2 In.	59375
Box, Maple, Pine, Oval, Red Paint, Lid, c.1840, 4 ¾ x 3 In.	6875
Box, Maple, Pine, Round, Lid, Joseph Johnson, New Hampshire, c.1851, 1 ¾ x 3 In.	10000
Box, Pine, Maple, Mt. Lebanon, c.1850, 1 ¾ x 4 In.	375
Box, Sewing, Cardboard, 6 Turned Thread Spools, E.B. Thread, 3 x 5 ¼ In. ....*illus*	1416
Box, Sewing, Maple, Pine, Oval, Pincushion Top, Red Paint, Enfield, N.H., 2 x 4 In.	7500
Box, Sewing, Pine, Red Paint, Hinged Lid, Molding, 5 x 12 In.	2950
Box, Sewing, Round, Six Spools, Cardboard, Green, White, E.B. Thread, c.1840, 3 x 5 In.	1416
Box, Shakers' Garden Seed, Pine, Leather Hinge & Handle, Brass, 6 x 14 ¾ In. ....*illus*	2478
Box, Storage, Maple, Pine, Round, Lid, Copper Tacks, 2 ¼ x 4 In.	944
Box, Storage, Walnut, Diamond Escutcheon, 1-Board Hinged Lid, 17 x 42 In.	4484
Bucket, Black Bands, Iron Wire Bail, Stenciled W On Bottom, c.1840-50, 7 In. ....*illus*	2124
Bucket, Pine, Blue Paint, Steel Bail, Turned Wood Handle, c.1850, 13 In.	1239
Bucket, Pine, Lid, Yellow Paint, Wire Bail Handle, Copper Rivets, 6 x 10 In.	4012
Butter Churn, Lollipop Handle, Tapered Cylindrical Shape, Bands, c.1820, 25 x 9 In.	830
Buttonhole Chisel, Bone, Brass, Steel, Turned Rounded Top, Blade, 3 ¼ x ⅜ In.	826
Cabinet, Spice, Pine, Red Paint, 9 Drawers, Mushroom Shape Pulls, 1800s, 26 x 20 In.	3068
Candleholder, Wrought Iron, c.1850, 57 In., Pair	1200
Cheese Strainer, Pine, Blue Paint, Slope Sides, Pierced Finger Grips, c.1865, 10 x 24 In.	533
Dipper, Black Ash, Turned & Carved, Curved End Handle, Hanging, 6 ¼ x 4 ⅛ In.	1652
Doll, China Head, Painted Hair, Cloth Body, Underclothing, Bonnet, 21 In. ....*illus*	767
Mirror, Cherry, Square, Vertical Board, Hanger, Peg Hole, 16 x 12 In.	3776
Pail, Tin, Lid, Bail Handle, Canterbury, N.H., 8 x 8 ½ In.	60
Pincushion, Table Clamp, Maple, Red Stain, Turned Shaft, Red Velvet, 8 ½ x 4 In.	1003
Rack, 16 Pegs, Painted Oyster, 1800s, 127 In.	230
Spool Holder, Dry Measure, Cherry, Round, Turned Peg Handle, Copper Tacks, 3 x 5 In.	1770
Stockings, Shaker Sister's, Gray Wool, DR & 1807 In Red Thread, 18 ½ In. ....*illus*	354
Stove, Wood, Rectangular Fire Box, Hinged Door, Cast Iron, 26 x 13 ½ In. ....*illus*	4130
Yarn Winder, Maple, Birch, Red Stain, 6 Turned Spokes, Platform Base, 43 In.	3186

SHAVING MUGS were popular from 1860 to 1900. Many types were made, including occupational mugs featuring pictures of men's jobs. There were scuttle mugs, silver-plated mugs, glass-lined mugs, and others.

American Indian, Porcelain	171
Flags & Eagle, Scrolled Cartouche, W.J. Jackowski, 3 ½ In.	210
Frog, Legs Crossed Under Toadstool, Theo Jeffes, Jr., 3 ¾ In.	450
Gramophone, Piano, Music Box, Address, Gold Gilt, 3 ⅝ In. ....*illus*	360
Gunship, Spanish American War, Flag, P. Mangino, 3 ¾ In.	1440
Hunting Dogs, Geo W. Jones, Koken Barber Supply, Limoges, France, 4 In.	150
Lighthouse, Coast Scene, Wm. Beisner, W & G Co., Limoges, 3 ½ In.	420
Lighthouse, Red, White, W. Cole, Stamped D & C, 4 In.	3900
Maritime Scene, To My Father Banner, 4 In.	266
Occupational, 3 Men Bowling, John Monnet, 1913, 3 ½ In.	483
Occupational, Attorney, Court Scene, Gilt, Anchor Pottery, N.J., 1925, 3 ⅝ In. ....*illus*	2700
Occupational, Automobile, Early Lincoln, Semi-Porcelain, Anchor Pottery, 3 ⅝ In. ....*illus*	2400
Occupational, Baker, Horse Drawn Lorenz Bakery Truck, 3 ½ In.	420
Occupational, Baker, Man Making Rolls, G. Stallone, Green Wrap, Gilt, 3 ¾ In.	1920
Occupational, Baker, Putting Bread In Brick Oven, T&V, Limoges, France, 3 ⅝ In. ....*illus*	300
Occupational, Bar Scene, Bartender, 3 Customers, John R. Rogers, 3 ¾ In.	127
Occupational, Bar Scene, Nicola Cammarano, 1913, 3 ¾ In.	60
Occupational, Barber, 3 Barbers At Work, D.S. Ferguson, Gilt, Koken, 1893, 4 In.	1140
Occupational, Baseball Player, Ball, 2 Bats, 4 In.	330
Occupational, Billiards, 2 Men Playing Pool, A.J. Johnson, 3 ½ In.	334
Occupational, Blue Fish, F.W. Miller, Stamped Cincinnati, 3 ½ In.	360
Occupational, Boat Captain, Chas. Jarvis, 4 In.	1920

Occupational, Boat Captain, Early Steam Boat, Flag, Capt. G. Martin, 3 ¾ In.	2400
Occupational, Boat Skiff With 3 Men, Edmond T. Teirs, 3 ½ In.	920
Occupational, Boat, Paddlewheel, Side-Wheel, Frank Killdear, 3 ½ In.	1440
Occupational, Boater, Cabin Cruiser, Flag, Driver, Harry O'Bryan, T & V, Limoges, 3 ½ In.	1680
Occupational, Boater, Tugboat, Flags Flying, H.W. Hier, 3 ¾ In.	1800
Occupational, Bookkeeper, Man At Slant Front Desk, J.W. Tolle, 3 ¾ In.	236
Occupational, Bowler, Man, A.W. Kinzer, Gilt T&V, Limoges, 3 ½ In.	2160
Occupational, Brewer, King Gambrinus, Wood Keg, Happy Birthday, 1915, 4 In.	300
Occupational, Brewer, Patron Saint Of Brewing On Beer Barrel, H. Waldschmidt, 4 In.	510
Occupational, Brick Layer, With Trowel Laying Bricks, Fred Patzel, 3 ½ In.	109
Occupational, Building Contractor, House, J.A. Dries, Smith Barber Supply, 3 ½ In.	270
Occupational, Butcher Shop, W.G. & Co. France, 3 ⅝ In. ....illus	240
Occupational, Butcher, English, Bull Wearing Blanket, Geo. W. Killiam, 4 In.	295
Occupational, Butcher, Man At Counter, Hanging Meats, H. Buhrer, Gilt, 3 ¾ In.	300
Occupational, Captain, Sailing Schooner Boat, American Flag, Michael Pasco, 3 ¾ In.	1320
Occupational, Captain, Single Stack Steamer Ship, American Flag, Capt. J.S. Boyd, 3 ¾ In.	1920
Occupational, Carpenter, Tools, J.W. Ritter, 4 In.	109
Occupational, Carpenter's Workshop, Nick Vetrano, Felda China, Germany, 3 ½ In.	180
Occupational, Catamaran, Single Mast, A.P., 3 ½ In.	480
Occupational, Cattle Herder, Steer, Herbert Mowrey, Gilt, P. Eisenmann, Germany, 4 In.	840
Occupational, Church, Rev. S. Lightfoot, Blue Wrap, Gilt, Royal China, 3 ¾ In.	1560
Occupational, Cigar Roller, Man Rolling Cigar Leaves, T. Firestone, 3 ¾ In.	413
Occupational, Clerk, General Store, Customers, John Dix, KPM Germany, 3 ¾ In.	210
Occupational, Coal Cart Driver, Horse Drawn Wagon, V&D, Austria, 3 ¾ In.	236
Occupational, Cobbler, Fixing Shoe, John Bush, Gold Trim, Limoges, 3 ⅝ In.	472
Occupational, Commodities Trader, At Board, W.D. Carr, T&V, Limoges, 4 In.	17400
Occupational, Conductor, Electric Trolley, C.J. Wilson, Gilt, Limoges, c.1910, 3 ¾ In.	420
Occupational, Conductor, Electric Trolley, Samuel Nichol, Gilt, T&V, Limoges, 3 ⅝ In.	240
Occupational, Conductor, Trolley Car, Driver, Patrons, C.L. Underwood, Austria, 4 In.	1320
Occupational, Conductor, Trolley Car, No. 45, Men At Doorway, H.L. Seitz, 3 ¾ In.	510
Occupational, Cook, At Stove, Wearing Hat, Ch. Michaels, Royal International, 3 ¾ In.	780
Occupational, Cooper, Barrel Maker, Man, R.F. Cost, 3 In.	330
Occupational, Cooper, Barrel Maker, R.J. Edwards, Smith Barber Supplies, 3 ½ In.	120
Occupational, Cowboy, On Horse, Plains, Cattle, Castro, Germany, 4 In.	840
Occupational, Cowboy, Riding, Mike Hadmas, Dresden China, 3 ¾ In.	360
Occupational, Cowboy, Stephen Held, Stamped Koken Barber Supply, 3 ¾ In.	60
Occupational, Crossed Bats With Baseball, C. Bender, 3 ½ In.	920
Occupational, Delivery Man, Express Wagon, Horse Drawn, Frank Kroupa, Austria, 3 ½ In.	390
Occupational, Diver, Henry Evans, Diving Helmet, 3 ½ In.	6000
Occupational, Driver, Florist Truck, Ben Sheidon, Kern Barber Supply, 3 ¾ In.	529
Occupational, Driver, Potato Truck, Alfonzo Feo, Felda China, 1929, 3 ⅝ In.	3245
Occupational, Duck Hunter, Man Shooting, In Boat, Dog, James C. Platt, Gilt, 3 ¾ In.	600
Occupational, Early Automobile, Marked, Bavaria, 3 ⅞ x 3 ½ In. ....illus	863
Occupational, Engineer, C. Albright, J.B. Melville, Quincy, Ill.	150
Occupational, Farmer, Man, Horse Drawn Plow, John Schultz, 3 ½ In.	90
Occupational, Farmer, Tractor, Mark Weber, 3 ¾ In.	391
Occupational, Ferry Boat, Capt. M. Andravelt, Perth Amboy, 1913, 4 In.	1440
Occupational, Ferry Boat, J.J. Johnson, 3 ¾ In.	960
Occupational, Fire Pumper, Horse Drawn, D. Miller, T&V, Limoges, 3 ½ In.	780
Occupational, Fire Pumper, Horse Drawn, Steam, Koken Barber Supply, 4 In.	748
Occupational, Fireman, Steamer, Charles Bagley, By J.R. Voldan	360
Occupational, Fish Dealer, Blue Fish In Water, A. Citarella, Gilt, 1926, 3 ⅝ In.	660
Occupational, Fish Monger, Horse Drawn Fish Wagon, John W. Smith, 3 In.	300
Occupational, Fish Monger, Seafood Cart, Horse Drawn, John Southhard, 3 ½ In.	600
Occupational, Fish Vendor, Man Cleaning Fish, To Sell, Paul Reno, 3 ¾ In.	1680
Occupational, Fisherman, J. Crom, Catching A Trout, Currier & Ives Transfer, 3 ¾ In.	360
Occupational, Fisherman, Small Stream Fishing Boat, John F. Rea, 3 ½ In.	1440
Occupational, Fisherman, Trawler In Open Water, Chas. Campbell, 3 ¾ In.	2040
Occupational, Floor Tiler, Man Kneeling, Gold Gilt, 3 ⅝ In. ....illus	6490
Occupational, Gas Station, Floyd Severs, 4 In.	552
Occupational, Glass Grinder, F. Pavlovich, Gilt, W&G, Limoges, Koken, 4 In.	1560
Occupational, Golfer, Swinging, Al Thompson, 3 ½ In.	3450
Occupational, Grocery Store, Woman At Counter, Egidio Montano, Gilt, 3 ½ In.	960
Occupational, Grocery Store, Woman, J. Gallagher, T&V, Limoges, 3 ¾ In.	360
Occupational, Grocery, Fruit Display Stand, S. Isbell, 3 ½ In.	510
Occupational, Haberdasher, Clerk, Man's Clothing Store, Ed. Lewis, Gilt, Kern, 4 In.	270

Sewing, Thimble, Silver, Wood Case, Tortoiseshell Veneer, c.1800, 1 ½ In. $513

Theriault's

Sewing, Thread Holder, 5-Spool, Pincushion, Wood $86

Victorian Casino Antiques

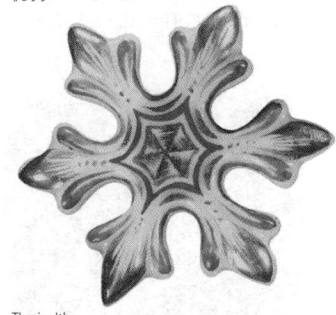

Sewing, Thread Winder, Porcelain, Snowflake Shape, c.1810, 2 In. $399

Theriault's

S

TIP

When freezing old clothes to kill any insects, watch out for pewter or painted glass or ceramic buttons. They may be damaged by the cold.

Shaker, Box, 3-Finger, Oval, Lid, Pine, Maple, Yellow, Copper Tacks, c.1930-40, 4 x 11 ¼ In.
$2,950

Willis Henry Auctions, Inc.

Shaker, Box, 5-Finger, Oval, Lid, Maple, Pine, Copper Tacks & Points, 5 ½ x 14 ¼ In.
$4,130

Willis Henry Auctions, Inc.

Shaker, Box, Sewing, Cardboard, 6 Turned Thread Spools, E.B. Thread, 3 x 5 ¼ In.
$1,416

Willis Henry Auctions, Inc.

Shaker, Box, Shakers' Garden Seed, Pine, Leather Hinge & Handle, Brass, 6 x 14 ¾ In.
$2,478

Willis Henry Auctions, Inc.

Shaker, Bucket, Black Bands, Iron Wire Bail, Stenciled W On Bottom, c.1840-50, 7 In.
$2,124

Willis Henry Auctions, Inc.

Shaker, Doll, China Head, Painted Hair, Cloth Body, Underclothing, Bonnet, 21 In.
$767

Willis Henry Auctions, Inc.

Shaker, Stockings, Shaker Sister's, Gray Wool, DR & 1807 In Red Thread, 18 ½ In.
$354

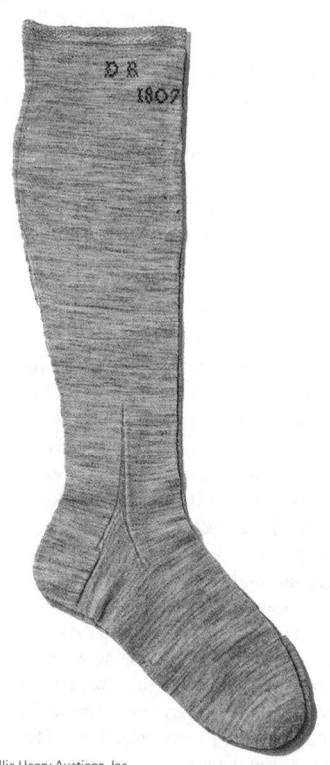

Willis Henry Auctions, Inc.

Occupational, Harness Maker, At Workbench, T. Grant, 3 ½ In.	109	
Occupational, House Painter, A.H. Godshall, Gilt, G.B.S. & Co., 3 ½ In.	420	
Occupational, House Painter, J.W. Roff, Stamped T&V, 4 In.	450	
Occupational, Hunter, Man Seated, Gun, Dog, J. Baum, 3 ½ In.	240	
Occupational, Hunter, Man, Birds, Dog, Joe Rummell, Royal Austria, 4 In..........	330	
Occupational, Hunter, Shooting, With Dog, P. Carbrey, Koken, St. Louis, 3 ¾ In. ...	86	
Occupational, Ice Salesman, Horse Drawn Wagon, Gilt Initials F.R., Limoges, 3 ⅝ In.	165	
Occupational, Ice Truck, Gold Gilt, Germany, 3 ⅝ In. ....*illus*	4130	
Occupational, Jeweler, Working On Clock, D.O. Brock, Gilt, Koken Barber Supply, 4 In..........	2040	
Occupational, Jockey, On Horseback, A.W. Goodnow, Limoges, 3 ½ In.	506	
Occupational, Kayaker, Black Kayak In Water, Oar, W.T. Straub, 3 ½ In.	1200	
Occupational, Landlord, Gentleman Collecting Rent, Woman, Gold Gilt, 4 In. ....*illus*	14160	
Occupational, Light Bulb Maker, In Factory, 3 ¾ In.	3000	
Occupational, Lunch Wagon, Man Exiting, N. Polchan, 3 ¾ In......................	4130	
Occupational, Machinist, Man Operating Machine, John A. Ludwig, Limoges, 3 ½ In. ...	230	
Occupational, Machinist, Man Working On Lathe, Gilt Name C.F. Williamson, 3 ⅝ In..........	212	
Occupational, Mail Wagon, Horse Drawn, Isaac Benson, 3 ½ In.	480	
Occupational, Mailman, Mail Cart, Horse Drawn, J.W. Herring, Germany, 3 ½ In. ...	60	
Occupational, Mailman, U.S. Mail Wagon, Horse Drawn, Victor, Stanton, 3 ½ In. ...	240	
Occupational, Merchant, Fabric Store, Woman Shopping, Charles Fester, 3 ½ In. ...	177	
Occupational, Military Warship, Louis Kalos, Homer Laughlin, 1922, 3 ½ In.	2040	
Occupational, Milk Truck, Pure Milk, T.T. Fallat, Felda China, 3 ⅝ In.	1888	
Occupational, Milkman, Dairy Cart, Albert Beyer, T&V, Limoges, 1919, 3 ½ In.	270	
Occupational, Paddlewheel Boat, Avalon, Photograph, Henry Breademeyer, 3 ½ In. ...	3300	
Occupational, Paddlewheel Boat, Rear Drive, J.C. Mitchell, 3 ¾ In.	450	
Occupational, Paddlewheel Steamboat, Geo. F. Stuart, 3 ½ In.	960	
Occupational, Paddlewheel Steamboat, J. Malloy, Gilt, 1910, 3 ¾ In.	3000	
Occupational, Pawn Broker, Symbol In Store Front, J.B. Baker, 3 ¾ In.	115	
Occupational, Photographer, Seated Lady In Gown, O.B. Tunison, Gilt, 3 ½ In.	1800	
Occupational, Photographer, William Lugis, Stamped C.B.G. 1912, 3 ¾ In.	90	
Occupational, Pilot, Early Airplane, Jerry Black, E. Berninghaus, Cincinnati, 3 ½ In. ...	1006	
Occupational, Plasterer, Chas. T. Hughes, 1910, Blue Wrap, Gilt, Footed, 3 ⅝ In..........	780	
Occupational, Plumber, Gilt Name Wm. Darecka, Man Repairing Pipe, Limoges, 3 ½ In.	201	
Occupational, Plumber, Toilet, Gold Gilt, 3 ½ In. ....*illus*	660	
Occupational, Printing Press, C.W. Hetzel, Gilt, H & C Company, 4 In................	570	
Occupational, Produce Wagon, Horse Drawn, Henry Alsheimer Jr., 3 ½ In.	180	
Occupational, Projectionist, Chas. Zingale, Germany, 3 ¾ In......................	4371	
Occupational, Race Car Driver, W. Thomas, 3 ½ In.	1150	
Occupational, Racing Boat, A.A. Newmark, St. Lawrence River, 3 ¾ In.	6000	
Occupational, Railroad, Caboose, Red, Gold, O.D. Dyer, 1875, 3 ½ In.	90	
Occupational, Ram, Knife, Sharpener, M.C. Hoeffner, Smith Barber Supply, 3 ¾ In. ...	420	
Occupational, Rowboat, Crossed Paddles, Thomas F. Arnes, 3 ½ In.	1208	
Occupational, Sailor, Ocean Liner, Choppy Sea, Oiler Jones, Carr China Co., 3 ¾ In. ...	1680	
Occupational, Sailor, Sailboat, Choppy Sea, R.S. Anderson, 3 ¾ In.	1200	
Occupational, Sailor, Sailing Ship, 2 Masts, Thom. Fox, 3 In......................	1080	
Occupational, Sailor, Single Mast Boat, American Flag, Jeno Christensen, Limoges, 3 ½ In.	1200	
Occupational, Sailor, Single Mast Skiff, U.S. Flag, S. Hoffman, Germany, 3 ½ In......	510	
Occupational, Sailor, Small Boat, Man Inside, R. Martin, 3 ½ In....................	2280	
Occupational, Sailor, Steam Freighter, On Open Sea, Oscar Boerner, 3 ½ In.	2400	
Occupational, Sailor, U.S. Battleship Maine, J.H. Culsen, Souvenir Spoon, 3 ¾ In. ...	2700	
Occupational, Saloon Keeper, Gilt Bands, Thomas Downs, c.1900, 3 ½ In.	138	
Occupational, Scottish Bagpiper, John Simpson, Stamped T&V, Limoges, 3 ½ In. ...	3300	
Occupational, Seafood Kitchen Store Front, T. Schizas, 3 ¾ In....................	575	
Occupational, Seafood Wagon, Gold Gilt, Royal China, 1917, 3 ½ In. ....*illus*	510	
Occupational, Seltzer Bottle, M. Goldberg, 1916, 3 ¾ In.	450	
Occupational, Ship Worker, Man Waving On Board, Wm. Benton, T&V, France, 3 ½ In.	1560	
Occupational, Shoe Salesman, Helping Woman Try On Shoes, W.J. Pinkney, 4 In. ...	120	
Occupational, Shoe Salesman, W.M. Watkins, Heckel Bros., 4 In...................	390	
Occupational, Shoe Store, Photograph, Gold Gilt Name, 3 ⅝ In. ....*illus*	2006	
Occupational, Shoemaker, Thomas Sanfilippo, T&V, Limoges, 3 ½ In.	90	
Occupational, Shoeshiner, Man Getting Shoes Shined, S. Cooper, 3 ½ In............	604	
Occupational, Sign Painter, Artist At Easel, Sign, Edw. C. Staples, 3 ⅝ In.	590	
Occupational, Storekeeper, Man Measuring Grain For Woman, F.W. Sundam, 3 ¾ In. ...	240	
Occupational, Surveyor, G. Wright, 3 ½ In.	334	
Occupational, Surveyor, M. Shaner Crisman, Limoges, France, 3 ½ In..............	2990	
Occupational, Surveyor, Stamped France, 3 ½ In................................	900	

Scuttle Mug
A scuttle mug is shaped like an old coal scuttle. There is an opening to hold the brush.

Shaker, Stove, Wood, Rectangular Fire Box, Hinged Door, Cast Iron, 26 x 13 ½ In. $4,130

Willis Henry Auctions, Inc.

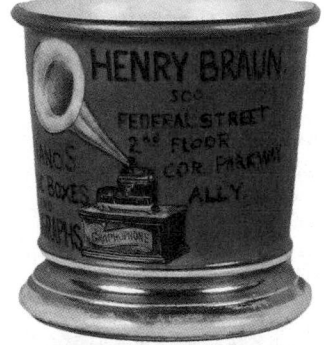

Shaving Mug, Gramophone, Piano, Music Box, Address, Gold Gilt, 3 ⅝ In. $360

Morphy Auctions

Shaving Mug, Occupational, Attorney, Court Scene, Gilt, Anchor Pottery, N.J., 1925, 3 ⅝ In. $2,700

Morphy Auctions

S

Shaving Mug, Occupational, Automobile, Early Lincoln, Semi-Porcelain, Anchor Pottery, 3 ⅝ In.
$2,400

Morphy Auctions

Shaving Mug, Occupational, Baker, Putting Bread In Brick Oven, T&V, Limoges, France, 3 ⅝ In.
$300

Morphy Auctions

Shaving Mug, Occupational, Butcher Shop, W.G. & Co. France, 3 ⅝ In.
$240

Morphy Auctions

Occupational, Tailor, Gold Gilt, Stamped, B.S.M., 3 ¾ In. ....*illus*	240
Occupational, Tailor, Man Cutting Out Clothing Pattern, 3 ¾ In.	60
Occupational, Telephone Lineman, On Telephone Pole, Insulators, E. Butler, 3 ⅝ In.	1416
Occupational, Tombstone Cutter, Thos. W. Shull, Limoges, 3 ¾ In.	920
Occupational, Tow Truck, C. Wiegand, Royal China, 3 ½ In.	10925
Occupational, Train, Red Caboose, G. Johnson, 3 ½ In.	115
Occupational, Upholsterer, Gold Gilt, 3 ½ In. ....*illus*	360
Occupational, Vendor, Tea & Coffee Wagon, Horse Drawn, Driver, 3 ¾ In.	360
Occupational, Windmill Salesman, W. Newman, 3 ½ In.	805
Occupational, Wine Bottler, Joseph Campers, Flowers, Gilt, 4 In.	900
Oyster, W. Collins, Stamped T&V, France, 3 ½ In.	570
Ship, Forget Me Not Banner, American Flag, France, c.1870, 4 In.	443
Stoneware, Salt Glaze, Attached Bowl At Rim, Ribbed Handle, c.1875, 4 ⅝ In.	173
Young Woman, Curly Blond Hair, Stephen Dzwonar, 3 ¾ In.	2280

SHAWNEE POTTERY was started in Zanesville, Ohio, in 1937. The company made vases, novelty ware, flowerpots, planters, lamps, and cookie jars. Three dinnerware lines were made: Corn, Lobster Ware, and Valencia (a solid color line). White Corn pattern utility pieces were made in 1945. Corn King was made from 1946 to 1954; Corn Queen, with darker green leaves and lighter colored corn, from 1954 to 1961. Shawnee produced pottery for George Rumrill during the late 1930s. The company closed in 1961.

Casserole, Corn King, Lid, c.1950, 11 In.	40
Cookie Jar, Smiley Pig, Eyes Closed, 11 ¼ In.	150
Cookie Jar, Winnie Pig, Red Collar & Feet, Blue Flower On Hat ....*illus*	144
Creamer, Elephant, Cream Color, 1940s, 4 ½ In.	55
Creamer, Elephant, White, 4 ¾ In.	75
Planter, Birds On Branch, 1950s, 7 x 8 x 5 In.	95
Planter, Donkey, White, Black Spots, 6 x 4 In.	38
Planter, Masks, White, 5 In.	50
Salt & Pepper, Milk Can, 3 ¼ In.	25
Teapot, Corn King, Marked, c.1950, 7 x 9 In.	80
Teapot, Granny Ann, Peach Apron, 8 In.	25
Teapot, Tom The Piper's Son, 7 In.	30
Vase, Bud, Ivory, Stipples, 10 In.	10
Vase, Pillow, Pink & Blue, Touche Pattern, 5 x 7 x 3 In.	19

SHEARWATER POTTERY is a family business started by Mr. and Mrs. G.W. Anderson Sr. and their three sons. The local Ocean Springs, Mississippi, clays were used to make the wares in the 1930s. The company was damaged by Hurricane Katrina in 2005 but was rebuilt and is still in business.

Bowl, Blended Blue Glaze, Footed, 10 ½ In.	92
Bowl, Cereal, Black & White Slip, Ducks, Stylized Waves, Squat, c.1955, 5 ⅝ In.	845
Bowl, Rooster, Black, White, Mulberry Geometric Design, 10 ¾ x 2 In.	1599
Figurine, Cat, Sitting, Blue, Yellow, Green, 5 ½ In.	1888
Figurine, Man, Horse, Green, Blue, Beige Glaze, Walter Anderson, Ink Stamp, 1930s, 11 In.	3585
Figurine, Seagull, Stylized, Antique Green Glaze, 50th Anniversary Mark, 5 x 9 ¾ In.	369
Jar, Flared, Figure & Animal Bands, Black Woman's Head Finial, 13 In.	354
Jardiniere, Stylized Scrolls, Blossoms, Roundels, White Slip, c.1940, 27 In. ....*illus*	17925
Mug, Dark Blue, White Slip, Ducks, Stylized Waves, Walter Anderson, 4 ½ In.	738
Pitcher, Beige Clay, Black & White Slip, Stylized Waves, Bulbous, c.1955, 5 In.	732
Pitcher, Brown & Cream Glaze, Ball Bottom, Upright Spout, c.1965, 11 ½ In.	366
Pitcher, Green, Marked, 5 In.	12
Spoon Holder, Girl, Flowers, Patricia Anderson Findeisen, 2002, 6 ¾ In. ....*illus*	325
Vase, Green Glaze, 2-Tone, Tapered, 6 In.	35
Vase, Green Glaze, Figure, Building House, Round, Rolled Rim, c.1940, 8 x 7 In.	5676
Vase, Multicolor, Patricia Anderson Findeisen, 6 ½ In.	374
Vase, Nude, Cat, Cylindrical, Flat Rim, Footed, 10 ¼ In.	826
Vase, Stylized Plants, Tapered, Dark Blue & Tan, 1930s-40s, 10 x 4 ½ In.	4688

SHEET MUSIC from the past centuries is now collected. The favorites are examples with covers featuring artistic or historic pictures. Early sheet music covers were lithographed, but by the 1900s photographic reproductions were used. The early music was larger than more recent sheets, and you must watch out for examples that were trimmed to fit in a twentieth-century piano bench.

Blushing Rose, Charles L. Johnson, c.1910, 10 x 14 In.	17

Shaving Mug, Occupational, Early Automobile, Marked, Bavaria, 3 ⅞ x 3 ½ In.
$863

Shaving Mug, Occupational, Floor Tiler, Man Kneeling, Gold Gilt, 3 ⅝ In.
$6,490

Shaving Mug, Occupational, Ice Truck, Gold Gilt, Germany, 3 ⅝ In.
$4,130

Shaving Mug, Occupational, Landlord, Gentleman Collecting Rent, Woman, Gold Gilt, 4 In.
$14,160

Shaving Mug, Occupational, Plumber, Toilet, Gold Gilt, 3 ½ In.
$660

Shaving Mug, Occupational, Seafood Wagon, Gold Gilt, Royal China, 1917, 3 ½ In.
$510

Shaving Mug, Occupational, Shoe Store, Photograph, Gold Gilt Name, 3 ⅝ In.
$2,006

Shaving Mug, Occupational, Tailor, Gold Gilt, Stamped, B.S.M., 3 ¾ In.
$240

Shaving Mug, Occupational, Upholsterer, Gold Gilt, 3 ½ In.
$360

S

Shawnee, Cookie Jar, Winnie Pig, Red Collar & Feet, Blue Flower On Hat
$144

Victorian Casino Antiques

Shearwater, Jardiniere, Stylized Scrolls, Blossoms, Roundels, White Slip, c.1940, 27 In.
$17,925

Neal Auction Co.

Shearwater, Spoon Holder, Girl, Flowers, Patricia Anderson Findeisen, 2002, 6 ¾ In.
$325

Humler & Nolan

522

Buttons & Bows, Paleface, Bob Hope, Jane Russell Signed, 1948, 9 x 12 In.	127
Funeral March, Abraham Lincoln, Lithograph Portrait, Oliver Ditson & Co., 11 x 14 In.	127
Home Run Gallop, F.W. Root, 4 Pages, 1867, 9 ¾ x 12 ¾ In.	948
Norwegian Concerto, Edvard Grieg, c.1945	10
One Song, Snow White & Seven Dwarfs, Disney, 1937, 9 x 12 In.	18
Twelfth Of Never, Donny Osmond, Frank Music Affiliates, 1973	10

SHEFFIELD *items are listed in the Silver Plate and Silver-English categories.*

SHELLEY first appeared on English ceramics about 1912. The Foley China Works started in England in 1860. Joseph Ball Shelley joined the company in 1862 and became a partner in 1872. Percy Shelley joined the firm in 1881. The company went through a series of name changes and in 1910 the then Foley China Company became Shelley China. In 1929 it became Shelley Potteries. The company was acquired in 1966 by Allied English Potteries, then merged with the Doulton group in 1971. The name Shelley was put into use again in 1980. A trio is the name for a cup, saucer, and cake plate set.

Coffeepot, German Chrysanthemum, Ripon, Blue Rims, c.1955, 9 In.	58
Cup & Saucer, Black Star, Black, White, c.1935, 2 ¼ In.	58
Cup & Saucer, Blue Plaid, Dainty, 1940s, 2 ⅜ In.	92
Cup & Saucer, Blue Rock, Canterbury, c.1955, 1 ⅝ In.	35
Cup & Saucer, Crackle, Cambridge, Lobed, Gilt Rim, c.1955, 2 ½ In.	104
Cup & Saucer, Dainty Pink, Canterbury, 1960s, 1 ⅝ In.	127
Cup & Saucer, Daisies, Pale Green Ground, c.1950	75
Cup & Saucer, Festoons & Fruits, Gainsborough, c.1915, 2 ⅝ In.	12
Cup & Saucer, Gold Star, Black, Gold, c.1930, 2 ¼ In.	92
Cup & Saucer, Green Plaid, Dainty, c.1945, 2 ½ In.	127
Cup & Saucer, Lyric, Westminster, Green Rim, c.1955, 1 ³⁄₁₆ In.	46
Cup & Saucer, Mauve, Dainty, 1960s, 2 ½ In.	46
Cup & Saucer, Maytime, Henley, Lobed, Gilt Rim, 1930, 2 ⅜ In.	23
Cup & Saucer, Rock Garden, Black Ground, Henley, Lobed, Gilt Rim, 1950, 2 ⅜ In.	23
Cup & Saucer, Rosebud, Canterbury, Pink Rim, c.1955, 1 ⅝ In.	35
Cup & Saucer, Star, Yellow, White, Dainty, c.1955, 2 ¼ In.	23
Hot Water Pot, Lid, Green, Dainty, 1960s, 6 ½ In.	460
Muffin Dish, Lid, Lily Of The Valley, Dainty, c.1960, 5 In.	46
Muffin Dish, Lid, Pink Star, Pink, Cream, Ridged, c.1930, 4 In.	58
Plate, Dessert, Chintz, Rounded Square, 7 In., 12 Piece	540
Plate, Dinner, Sheraton, 10 ¾ In., 12 Piece	266
Platter, Stylized Fruit, Queen Anne, 2 Handles, Gilt Rim, c.1935, 9 ½ In.	12
Serving Dish, 3 Shell Shape Sections, Fluted Rim, Blue, Green, Orange, c.1925, 8 ¼ In.	58
Sugar & Creamer, Maytime, Chintz	69
Sugar, Flowers, Black Ground, Peach Interior, Dainty, 1930s, 2 ½ In.	23
Sugar, Pink Star, Pink, Creamy White, Dainty, c.1935, 2 In.	23
Teapot, Lid, Blue, Dainty, c.1955, 5 ⁷⁄₁₆ In.	161
Teapot, Lid, Butcher's Rose Spray, Henley, c.1955, 6 ½ In.	69
Teapot, Lid, Pink Dog Roses, Regent, Tapered Cylinder, c.1930, 8 In.	161
Teapot, Melody Chintz, Green, Lid, 5 ½ x 8 ½ In.	476
Vase, Butterfly, Iridescent, 6-Sided, Signed Walter Slater, 7 In.	207

SHIRLEY TEMPLE, the famous movie star, was born in 1928. She made her first movie in 1932. She died in 2014. Thousands of items picturing Shirley have been and still are being made. Shirley Temple dolls were first made in 1934 by Ideal Toy Company. Millions of Shirley Temple cobalt blue glass dishes were made by Hazel Atlas Glass Company and U.S. Glass Company from 1934 to 1942. They were given away as premiums for Wheaties and Bisquick. A bowl, mug, and pitcher were made as a breakfast set. Some pieces were decorated with the picture of a very young Shirley, others used a picture of Shirley in her 1936 *Captain January* costume. Although collectors refer to a cobalt creamer, it is actually the 4 ½-inch-high milk pitcher from the breakfast set. Many of these items are being reproduced today.

Doll, Composition, Blond Ringlet Wig, Tagged Blue Dress, Headband, Ideal, 16 In.	170
Doll, Composition, Blond Wig, Brown Dress, Ideal, 16 In.	396
Doll, Composition, Cowboy Costume, Gun, Holster, Ideal, 12 In.	480
Doll, Composition, Flirty Eyes, Blond Curly Wig, Green Flower Dress, Ideal, 16 In.	311
Doll, Composition, Mohair Wig, Dress, Ideal, 15 In.	180
Doll, Composition, Sleep Eyes, Dimples, Blond Mohair Curls, Blue Dress, Ideal, 18 In.	240
Doll, Composition, Sleep Eyes, Mohair Curls, Bright Eyes Dress, Ideal, 16 In.	450
Doll, Composition, Sleep Eyes, Mohair Wig, Ideal, Box, c.1935, 17 In. ....*illus*	616

Doll, Composition, Sleep Eyes, Stand Up & Cheer Outfit, Ideal, 13 In.	300
Doll, Composition, Socket Head, Sleep Eyes, Mohair Wig, Ideal, c.1935, 20 In.	280
Doll, Composition, Yarn Wig, Painted Teeth, Eyes, Lei, Hawaiian, Skirt, Marama, 13 In.	141
Doll, Little Colonel, Composition, Tin Sleep Eyes, Mohair, Madame Alexander, 13 In.	254
Doll, Vinyl Outfits, TV-Like Box, 1960s, 12 In.	325
Doll, Vinyl, Blond Curls, Pink Nylon Dress, Stockings, Shoes, Ideal, 1950s, 36 In.	540
Movie Poster, Rebecca Of Sunnybrook Farm, 20th Century Fox, 1938, 27 x 41 In.	812
Paper Doll, 4 Pages Of Fashion, Whitman, 1976, Uncut	14
Paper Doll, Color, Edited By Grayce Pirmontesi, Uncut, 1962	25
Photograph, Captain January, Autograph, Temple & Ebsen, Black, White, c.1936, 11 x 14 In.	115
Photograph, Wedding, Gelatin Silver Print, September, Inscribed September 1945, 16 x 19 In.	350
Purse, Leatherette, Embroidery, 1700s Couple, Pyramid Co., Tag, 6 x 6 In.	115

SHRINER, *see Fraternal category.*

SILVER DEPOSIT glass was first made during the late nineteenth century. Solid sterling silver is applied to the glass by a chemical method so that a cutout design of silver metal appears against a clear or colored glass. It is sometimes called silver overlay.

Pitcher, Cranberry Glass, Grape Design, Spread Foot, Loop Handle, 12 ½ In.	2691
Vase, Cranberry Glass, Basket Weave Overlay, Swollen, Spread Foot, 1900s, 10 In.	767
Vase, Cranberry Glass, Engraved, Flowers, Lines, 3 Handles, c.1900, 9 ¾ In. ....*illus*	553
Vase, Globular, Gold Overlay, Bamboo, Birds, Flowers, 1900s, 20 In.	2160

SILVER FLATWARE includes many of the current and out-of-production silver and silver-plated flatware patterns made in the past eighty years. Other silver is listed under Silver-American, Silver-English, etc. Most silver flatware sets that are missing a few pieces can be completed through the help of one of the many silver matching services listed on our website, www.kovels.com.

SILVER FLATWARE PLATED

Adam, Ladle, Oneida Community, 1917, 5 ⅞ In.	17
Adam, Meat Fork, Oneida Community, 7 In.	20
Adam, Sugar Tongs, Oneida Community, 3 ⅝ In.	45
Alhambra, Cake Server, Rogers, 9 ½ In.	51
Antique Lily, Butter Knife, Towle, c.1880, 7 ¼ In.	10
Antique Lily, Fish Slice, Towle, c.1880, 11 ¼ In.	64
Antique Lily, Sardine Server, Towle, c.1880, 5 ⅞ In.	40
April, Jelly Spoon, Rogers & Brothers, 1950, 6 ¼ In.	13
April, Salad Fork, Rogers & Brothers, 1950, 6 ¾ In.	9
Camille, Salad Fork, International, 1971, 7 ⅛ In.	15
Cardinal, Dinner Fork, Wallace, c.1907, 7 ½ In.	14
Cardinal, Gravy Ladle, Wallace, c.1907, 7 In.	28
Cardinal, Meat Fork, Wallace, c.1907, 8 ½ In.	26
Daffodil, Cake Server, Rogers, 1950, 10 ¾ In.	43
Daffodil, Gravy Ladle, Rogers, 1950, 6 ¼ In.	40
Daffodil, Meat Fork, Rogers, 1950, 8 ⅞ In.	20
Daffodil, Sugar Spoon, Rogers, 1950, 6 In.	9
Daffodil, Tomato Server, Rogers, 7 ⅝ In.	36
First Love, Soup Ladle, Rogers Bros., 6 ¾ In.	150
Les Six Fleurs, Serving Spoon, Monogram G, Reed & Barton	354
Milady, Bonbon Spoon, Oneida Community, 4 ½ In.	10
Plymouth, Pie Server, Rogers, 10 ½ In.	91
Queen Bess, Meat Fork, Oneida Community, 1940s, 8 ⅜ In.	14

SILVER FLATWARE STERLING

Blackberry, Serving Spoon, Shell Bowl, Monogram, Tiffany & Co., c.1875, 8 ⅞ In.	406
Cactus, Lemon Fork, Georg Jensen, 4 ¼ In.	150
Chrysanthemum, Ladle Monogram, Stieff, 13 ½ In.	266
Chrysanthemum, Server, Pierced Bowl, Tiffany & Co., 9 In.	514
Chrysanthemum, Serving Pieces, Stieff, c.1904, 5 Piece	123
Chrysanthemum, Tablespoon, Tiffany, Engraved Crest, c.1880, 8 ¼ In., 22 Piece	2880
Crown Baroque, Cold Meat Fork, Gorham, Flannel Bag, 8 ½ In., 4 Piece	242
Crown Baroque, Gravy Ladle, Gorham, Flannel Bag, 7 ½ In., 4 Piece	265
Crown Baroque, Pie Slice, Stainless Steel Blade, Gorham, Flannel Bag, 12 In., 4 Piece	127
Crown Baroque, Sugar Spoon, Shell Shape Bowl, Gorham, 6 ¼ In., 4 Piece	104
Crown Baroque, Tablespoon, Gorham, Flannel Bag, 8 ¾ In., 7 Piece	518
Faneuil, Serving Spoon, Berry, Gold Washed Bowl, Tiffany & Co., 7 ½ In., 2 Piece	240

Shirley Temple, Doll, Composition, Sleep Eyes, Mohair Wig, Ideal, Box, c.1935, 17 In.
$616

Theriault's

Silver Deposit, Vase, Cranberry Glass, Engraved, Flowers, Lines, 3 Handles, c.1900, 9 ¾ In.
$553

New Orleans Auction Galleries, Inc.

Silver Flatware Sterling, Olympian, Ice Cream Slice, Edward C. Moore, Tiffany & Co., 1858, 11 ½ In.
$492

New Orleans Auction Galleries, Inc.

S

Silver Plate, Cake Basket, Handle, Fluted, Etched, Simpson Hall Miller & Co., c.1880, 9 x 3 ⅝ In.
$150

Ruby Lane, Inc.

Silver Plate, Centerpiece, Palm Trees, Plants, Ibis, August Adolphe Willms, c.1836, 9 x 8 ½ In.
$2,580

Ruby Lane, Inc.

Silver Plate, Cup, Knight's Face On Handle, Band Of Flowers, Flared Base, Marked, 4 ¾ x 3 ½ In.
$285

Ruby Lane, Inc.

Silver Plate, Tray, Pierced Gallery, Formica Center, Ball & Claw Feet, Sheffield, 10 ¾ x 2 ¾ In.
$49

Ruby Lane, Inc.

Francis I, Bouillon Spoon, Reed & Barton, 5 ⅜ In., 30 Piece	767
Francis I, Ice Cream Slice, Shaped, Reed & Barton, 11 In.	133
Francis I, Salad Set, Reed & Barton, 9 ⅜ In., 2 Piece	325
Golden Crown Baroque, Candlesnuffer, Gorham, Flannel Bag, 11 ½ In., Pair	184
Golden Crown Baroque, Iced Tea Spoon, Gorham, Flannel Bag, 7 ¾ In., 12 Piece	431
Grande Baroque, Ice Cream Slice, Shaped, Wallace, 13 In.	363
Isis, Preserve Spoon, Gorham, c.1880, 7 ½ In.	123
Labors Of Cupid, Serving Fork, Spoon, Dominick & Haff, Flannel Sleeve, 10 & 11 In.	431
Ladle, Hammered, Scrolled Leaves, Carl Poul Petersen, c.1966, 9 ¼ In.	120
Love Disarmed, Salad Servers, Cupid & Psyche, Scrolling, Reed & Barton, 10 ¾ In.	450
Old Colonial, Teaspoon, Leona Engraved On Back, Towle, 5 ⅞ In., 6 Piece	150
Olympian, Ice Cream Slice, Edward C. Moore, Tiffany & Co., 1858, 11 ½ In. ....*illus*	492
Persian, Dessert Knife, Tiffany & Co., 8 In., 10 Piece	1121
Persian, Fork Set, Monogram, Tiffany & Co., 1873-91, 7 ¼ In., 11 Piece	492
Princess Fuchsia, Salad Servers, Flowers, Frigast, Denmark, c.1960	163
Priscilla, Fork, Frank Smith, 20th Century, 12 Piece	375
Punch Ladle, Ebony Handle, Carved Bone, Leaf Rim, 22 In.	150
Renaissance, Punch Ladle, Dominick & Haff	502
Richelieu, Server, Kidney Shape Bowl, Tiffany & Co., c.1892, 9 ¼ In.	295
Salem, Sauce Ladle, Tiffany & Co.	212
Strawberries, Berry Spoon, Cast, Repousse, Pierced Handle	98
Strawberry, Serving Spoon, Square Terminal, Threading, Tiffany & Co., c.1930, 9 ⅜ In.	225
Watteau, Asparagus Server, Durgin	165
Winthrop, Tomato Server, Tiffany & Co., 7 ¾ In.	230

SILVER, *Sheffield, see Silver Plate; Silver-English categories.*

SILVER PLATE is not solid silver. It is a ware made of a metal, such as nickel or copper, that is covered with a thin coating of silver. The letters *EPNS* are often found on American and English silver-plated wares. *Sheffield* is a term with two meanings. Sometimes it refers to sterling silver made in the town of Sheffield, England. Sometimes it refers to an old form of plated silver.

Biscuit Barrel, Flower Swags, Chased, Hinged Lid, c.1900, 9 In.	150
Biscuit Barrel, Victorian, Gilt, Cylindrical, Hinged Lid, Apple Finial, 1870, 9 In.	1476
Biscuit Box, 3-Part, Coquiform, W. Adams, England, 1865, 10 In.	149
Biscuit Jar, Hinged Dome Lid, Cylindrical, Cartouches, Scroll Feet, c.1915, 8 x 9 In.	184
Bonbon, Baroque, Wallace, Heart Shape, c.1941, 4 ⅝ x 6 In.	32
Bowl, Montieth, Wavy Rim, Lion's Head & Ring Handles, Repousse, Lobed, c.1910, 11 In.	210
Box, Lid, Repousse Roses, Dog, Fowl Finial, T Monogram, Footed, 9 x 5 In.	240
Butter, Cover, Baroque, Octagonal Base, Wallace, c.1941, 7 ¼ x 3 ½ In.	71
Butter, Cover, First Love, Rogers, 7 ¼ In.	150
Butter, Cover, Turned Ivory Handle, Oval, Ferns, 1870, 4 ½ x 8 ½ In.	239
Cake Basket, Classical Figures, Swing Handle, Footed, Continental, 1800s, 9 x 12 In.	214
Cake Basket, Handle, Fluted, Etched, Simpson Hall Miller & Co., c.1880, 9 x 3 ⅝ In. ....*illus*	150
Cake Stand, Raised Base, Claw Feet, Embossed Detail, 1800s, 20 In.	118
Candlesnuffer, Baroque, Wallace, c.1941, 8 In.	24
Centerpiece, 2 Candle Cups, Women, Chased, Simpson, Hall Miller & Co., c.1880, 31 x 24 In.	2375
Centerpiece, Art Nouveau, Metal, Glass, 2 Tiers, Trumpet Vase, Openwork, c.1900, 10 In.	1440
Centerpiece, Candle Holder, Central Bowl, 4 Smaller Bowl Arms, Spread Base, 9 In.	216
Centerpiece, Crackle Glass Shell Shape, Plated Footed Stand, c.1900, 13 In.	236
Centerpiece, Figural, Etched Glass Bowl, Arbor, Putti, Scroll Feet, 23 x 25 In.	2829
Centerpiece, Gilt, Petal Fluted Dish, Knopped Standard, Dome Base, 1894, 15 In.	307
Centerpiece, Hammered, Handles, J. Hoffmann, Wiener Werkstatte, c.1930, 8 x 12 In.	16250
Centerpiece, Palm Trees, Plants, Ibis, August Adolphe Willms, c.1836, 9 x 8 ½ In. ....*illus*	2580
Centerpiece, Pedestal Foot, Wide Rim, Conical Lid, Openwork, Finial, 14 In.	390
Centerpiece, Round Pedestal Base, Dish, Woman, Standing, Trumpet Vase, 25 In.	478
Citrus Press, Curved Arm Support, Wood Mounted, Marble Base, 12 ½ x 9 ½ In.	738
Claret Jug, Art Nouveau, Pewter Overlay, Ribbed Glass, Flowers, Maidens, c.1900, 16 In.	1661
Claret Jug, Caryatid Handle, Beaded Masks, Strapwork, 9 In.	246
Claret Jug, Hinged Covered Spout, Loop Handle, Oval Body, Embossed, 13 In., Pair	492
Claret Jug, Hinged Lid, Melon Finial, Flowers, C-Scroll Handle, 12 ½ In.	359
Coaster, Scalloped Rim, Wood Base, Marked, Elkington, 1854, 2 ¼ x 8 In., Pair	177
Cocktail Set, Art Deco, Shaker, 7 Glasses, Bakelite, Folke Arastrom, 1930s, 8 ¾ In., 3 ½ In.	2125
Cocktail Shaker, Boston Lighthouse Shape, c.1985, 14 x 5 ¼ In.	1107
Cocktail Shaker, Lighthouse Shape, Pierced Strainer, Tapered, 14 In.	1159

Cocktail Shaker, Town Crier, Hand Bell Form, Mid-20th Century, 11 x 5 In.	338
Coffee Urn, Loop Handles, Stepped Spread Foot, Finial, Strainer, 1800s, 15 In.	472
Coffeepot, Christofle, Tapering Cylinder, Cone Shape Spout, Ebony Handle, 10 x 11 In.	430
Compote, Figure Holding Top Standard, Rotating Top, Ornate, c.1900, 11 In.	375
Compote, Victorian Style, Stag, Beneath Palm, Crystal Bowl, 1900s, 13 x 10 ¾ In.	108
Cup, Knight's Face On Handle, Band Of Flowers, Flared Base, Marked, 4 ¾ x 3 ½ In. ....*illus*	285
Decanter Stand, Trefoil Shape, Reticulated Gallery, Lion Mask Paw Feet, 14 x 10 In.	538
Decanter, Rooster Shape, Head, Tail, Handle, Base, Glass Body, Marked Etain, 11 x 13 In.	270
Dish, Entree, Stand, Lid, Gadroon Border, Scroll Feet, Handles, c.1820, 8 x 15 In., Pair	956
Dish, Lid, Oval Finial, Handles, Sheffield, 8 In., Pair	375
Epergne, Regency Style, 2 Tiers, Etched Glass Bowls, Scalloped, 10 ¾ In.	657
Ewer, Helmet Shape, Banding, Strapwork, Ogee Foot, Scroll Handle, c.1915, 11 In.	369
Figurine, Bird, Long Tail Feather, Standing, Italy, 9 ½ x 20 ½ In., Pair	210
Hot Water Server, Sculpted Flowers, Tilting, Christofle, France, c.1890, 14 ½ In.	450
Hot Water Urn, Applied Swags, Ring Side Handles, Sheffield, c.1865, 21 In.	533
Hot Water Urn, Lid, Oval, Handle, 4 Legs, Square Base, Ball Feet, c.1815, 17 x 12 In.	649
Hot Water Urn, Reeded, Lion Mask & Ring Handles, Bone Handle, c.1790, 20 In.	738
Hot Water Urn, Regency Style, Gadroon Border, Lion's Head Handles, Gorham, 17 In.	366
Meat Dish, Domed Lid, Gadroon, Shell, Reeded Handles, c.1815, 16 x 24 In.	3286
Meat Lid, Platter, Flower Banding, Turned Bone Handles, c.1835, 16 x 26 In.	2214
Meat Lid, Victorian, Banded, Gadroon Rim, Crest Handle, c.1865, 10 x 14 In.	522
Ornament, Pagoda, Bells At Roof Corners, 10 x 3 In.	184
Picture Frame, Oval, Ball Feet, Stamped Inman Sterling, 4 x 5 In.	24
Plateau, Mirrored, 3-Piece, Shaped, Cabriole Legs, 38 ½ In.	1250
Platter, Dome Lid, Oval, Scroll Feet, Beaded Border Handles, c.1885, 16 x 26 In.	568
Punch Bowl, 3 Cups, International Silver Co., 13 ½ In.	563
Punch Bowl, Chased, Fern, C-Scrolls, Garlands, Pedestal Base, Sheffield, 12 x 16 In.	127
Punch Bowl, Chased, Round, England, 12 In.	90
Punch Bowl, Gilt, Bucket Shape, Flower Scroll Band, Dome Foot, c.1965, 15 In.	369
Punch Bowl, Scalloped Rim, Twisted Raised, Stem, 18 ½ In., Pair	938
Salver, Chippendale Style, Piecrust Border, Shells, Flowers, c.1931, 20 In.	359
Salver, Feather Reticulated Edge, Rococo Scroll Rim, 4-Footed, Webser-Wilcox, 15 ¾ In.	246
Server, Pierced Hinged Double Lid, Shell Shape, Footed, Chased Handle, 11 In.	124
Spoon Warmer, Ornate, Chased, Boat Shape, 8 In.	107
Spoon, Souvenir, see Souvenir category.	
Table Set, Holder, Napkin Ring, Cut Glass Salt, Pepper, Butter Chip, Pairpoint, c.1894, 6 In.	593
Tea Set, Art Deco, Macassar Handles, Finials, Teapot, Coffeepot, Sugar, Pitcher, France	679
Tea Urn, George III, Sheffield, Spherical, Engraved Flower Band, Handles, c.1800, 16 In.	360
Tea Urn, Scroll Handles, Lid, Footed Pedestal Base, On Copper, 1800s, 15 ½ In.	150
Tray, Art Deco, Rigged Rim, Rounded Corners, Geometric Handles, 17 x 12 In.	257
Tray, Art Nouveau Style, Raised Repousse Border, Leaf, Flower, Masks, 22 ¾ In.	406
Tray, Chased, Acanthus Leaves, Swags, Greek Key, Handles, Johnson & Co., c.1890, 25 In.	300
Tray, Floral Border, Handles, Monogram, Reed & Barton, 22 x 32 In.	240
Tray, George V, Oval, Scalloped, Bellflowers, Rocaille Handles, c.1915, 30 x 20 In.	1845
Tray, Grapes, Acanthus Leaf Border, Engraved, Round, Handles, 20th Century, 16 In.	150
Tray, Oval, Footed, Scroll Handles, Embossed Border, Cherubs, Grapes, c.1852, 30 In.	431
Tray, Oval, Handles, Leaf Scrolling, Beaded Rim, Monogram, c.1885, 32 x 23 In.	554
Tray, Oval, Pierced Gallery, Arched Handles, Scroll Feet, c.1965, 24 x 16 In.	738
Tray, Oval, Scrollwork Handles, Chased Leafy Scroll, Gadroon Border, 31 ¼ In.	431
Tray, Pierced Gallery, Formica Center, Ball & Claw Feet, Sheffield, 10 ¾ x 2 ¾ In. ....*illus*	49
Tray, Pierced, Scalloped Sides, Faux Tortoiseshell Interior, Wood Handles, England, 6 x 26 In. ...	356
Tray, Presentation, Acanthus Rim & Handles, Medallions, Pendants, c.1925, 31 In.	338
Tray, Round, Lobed, Scrolling Leaf Border, Central Armorial, 1800s, 27 ¼ In.	149
Tray, Rounded, Beaded Rococo Scroll Rim, Stirrup Handles, c.1950, 24 x 13 In., Pair	276
Tray, Serpentine Border, Shells, Crest, Lion's, Scroll Feet, c.1815, 29 x 21 In.	2440
Tray, Serving, Open Lattice Design, England, 12 In., Pair	120
Trophy Cup, Repousse, Pedestal Base, Banding, Eagle, Shield, F & MN, Bavaria, 9 x 8 In.	63
Tureen, Dome Lid, Bulbous Oval, Gadroon, Handles, Paw Feet, c.1835, 11 x 17 In.	1353
Tureen, Lid, Hammered, Lobed, Pear Finial, Footed, Handles, 13 In.	300
Tureen, Lid, Navette Shape, Martin Hall & Co., England, 1800s, 11 ½ x 16 In.	149
Tureen, Lid, Oval, Gadroon Border, Scroll Finial, Handles, Footed, c.1885, 11 x 17 In.	354
Tureen, Lid, Repousse Flowers, Over Copper, Oval, Elkington, c.1890, 16 In.	72
Tureen, Lid, Revolving, Oval, Scroll Feet, England, 8 ½ x 13 ¼ In.	179
Tureen, Lid, Squat, Scroll Feet, Handles, Stag Finial, Greek Key, c.1884, 13 x 13 In.	257
Tureen, Navette Shape, Upswept, Reeded Handles, Dome Foot, c.1950, 11 x 15 In.	738
Tureen, Sauce, Oval, Gadroon Border, Leaf Handles, Scroll Feet, 1800s, 6 ½ x 9 In.	413

Silver Plate, Tussy Mussy, Rococo, Grape Leaves, Shells, Berries, Finger Ring, 1800s, 4 ½ In.
$395

Ruby Lane, Inc.

S

Silver Plate, Wine Coaster, Georgian, Matthew Boulton & Co., Sheffield, c.1810, 2 x 7 In.
$671

Neal Auction Co.

Silver-American, Basket, Reticulated Handle, Flared Rim, Kirk & Son, c.1915, 13 In.
$2,160

Skinner Auctioneers & Appraisers

Silver-American, Bowl, Art Nouveau, Applied Poppy, Pierced, Towle, c.1900, 14 ½ In.
$2,000

Rago Arts & Auction Center

Silver-American, Cake Basket, Pierced, Chased, Stylized Blossoms, Gorham, c.1900, 17 In.
$1,875

Rago Arts & Auction Center

Tureen, Soup, Urn Shape, Acanthus Handles, Pedestal Foot, 1900s, 11 x 19 In.	531
Tureen, Stand, Oval, Ram Mask Handles, Fluted Collar, Beaded, c.1835, 14 x 18 In.	1722
Tussy Mussy, Rococo, Grape Leaves, Shells, Berries, Finger Ring, 1800s, 4 ½ In. .....*illus*	395
Vase, Art Deco Style, Classical Woman, Applied To Handles, Swags, Footed, Liner, 20 In., Pair	313
Waiter, Oval, Handles, 4 Paw Feet, 25 In.	354
Waiter, Pierced Gallery Rim, Beaded, Handles, 23 ½ In.	472
Waiter, Pierced, Cutout Handles, Octagonal, 8-Footed, c.1900, 15 x 22 In.	184
Wine Bucket, Campagna Shape, Lobed, Gadroon Borders, c.1815, 10 In., Pair	2390
Wine Bucket, Ram's Head Mask Handles, Rings, Heidsieck & Cie, France, 8 x 8 In.	334
Wine Coaster, Flared, Scalloped, Beaded Rim, Flower Shape, c.1890, 7 In., Pair	150
Wine Coaster, Flared, Segmented, Lobed, Wood Bottoms, Sheffield, c.1815, 7 In.	598
Wine Coaster, Georgian, Matthew Boulton & Co., Sheffield, c.1810, 2 x 7 In. .....*illus*	671
Wine Cooler, Campagna Shape, Leaf Handles, Metal Liner, c.1950, 11 In., Pair	1250
Wine Cooler, Georgian Style, Armorial Crest, Campagna Shape, Liner, 11 In., Pair	1599
Wine Cooler, Regency Style, Pedestal Foot, Handles, Leaves, Scroll, 9 ½ In., Pair	2510
Wine Cooler, Regency, Urn Shape, Gadrooned, Cornucopia Handles, Old Sheffield, 8 x 12 In.	2460
Wine Cooler, Urn Shape, Scroll Handles & Rim, 1800s, 10 ½ In., Pair	2271
Wine Wagon, Victorian Style, 2 Coasters, Wheels, England, 17 ½ In.	330

SILVER-AMERICAN. American silver is listed here. Coin and sterling silver are included. Most of the sterling silver listed in this book is subdivided by country. There are also other pieces of silver and silver plate listed under special categories, such as Candelabrum, Napkin Ring, Silver Flatware, Silver Plate, Silver-Sterling, and Tiffany Silver. These prices are based on current silver values. For information about makers and marks, see *Kovels' American Silver Marks: 1650 to the Present.*

Ashtray Set, Scallop Shell, 3 Ball Feet, Cigarette Rest, Redlich & Co., 3 x 2 In., 18 Piece	265
Basket, Centerpiece, Round, Low Pedestal Base, Tall Handle, Reticulated, Towle, 10 x 9 In.	426
Basket, Flared, Cut, Repousse Flowers, Handle, J.E. Caldwell & Co., c.1890, 13 In.	1121
Basket, Fruit, Openwork Flowers, Scroll, Handle, Footed, F.M. Whiting, c.1915, 4 x 14 In.	938
Basket, Openwork Flower Shape, Reeded & Bead Handle, 1900s, 11 x 13 In.	472
Basket, Repousse Scrolls, Flowers, Rectangular, Footed, Handle, C. Bard & Son, c.1850, 12 In.	1500
Basket, Repousse, Oval, Handles, Scroll Feet, S. Kirk & Son, 14 In.	2125
Basket, Reticulated Handle, Flared Rim, Kirk & Son, c.1915, 13 In. .....*illus*	2160
Basket, Reticulated Lines & Ribbon, Shreve & Co., 11 ½ In.	783
Basket, Shaped Bowl, Rope Handle, Cattails, Footed, c.1850, 9 ½ x 10 ¼ In.	708
Beaker, Beaded Base, AFL Monogram, Coin, Churchill & Treadwell, c.1805, 3 In.	480
Beaker, Inverted Bell Shape, Cavetto Dome Foot, Meriden, 3 x 3 ⅜ In., 6 Piece	184
Belt Buckle, Art Nouveau Style, Woman's Face, Leaves, Cast, B. Kieselstein-Cord, 3 x 2 In.	150
Bowl, 6-Sided, Lobed, Flower Rim, Monogram, Graff, Washbourne & Dunn, c.1950, 3 x 11 In.	416
Bowl, Art Nouveau, Applied Poppy, Pierced, Towle, c.1900, 14 ½ In. .....*illus*	2000
Bowl, Art Nouveau, Shaped, Pierced Rim, Poppies, Redlich & Co., 13 In.	863
Bowl, Blossom Shape, Lobed Panels, Banded Rim, Gorham, c.1960, 2 ½ x 9 ¾ In.	281
Bowl, Boat Shape, Fixed Handle, Footed, Shiebler, 6 In.	118
Bowl, Chased Scrolls, Lobed Oval Body, Pierced Feet, Dominick & Haff, 1891, 11 In.	900
Bowl, Child's, Engraved Name, Date, Fairytale Figures, 2 Pair Fork & Spoon, Gorham, 5 In.	180
Bowl, Cinderella Pattern, Footed, Monogram, Gorham, 1926, 9 ⅞ In.	185
Bowl, Dot-Dash, Leaf Wave Rim, Simpson, Hall, Miller & Co., 10 ½ x 2 In.	230
Bowl, Elliptical Shape, Bulbous, Lobed, Footed, Flared Rim, 1902, 4 x 11 In.	7072
Bowl, Flared, Footed, Engraved Interior Swags, Whiting, c.1918, 12 x 5 ½ In.	726
Bowl, Footed, Chased Flower Border, Gorham, c.1930, 3 x 12 ½ In.	1375
Bowl, Footed, Lobed, Molded Scallop Rim, c.1840, 4 ⅝ x 6 ⅛ In.	3884
Bowl, Footed, Marked Gorham, c.1916, 4 ½ x 9 ¼ In.	359
Bowl, Footed, Square, Towle, 4 ¼ x 2 ½ In.	94
Bowl, Francis I, E. Meyers, Reed & Barton, c.1900, 5 x 11 In.	750
Bowl, Francis I, Shaped Rim, Flowers, Leaves, Reed & Barton, 3 x 12 In.	531
Bowl, Fruit, Lid, Rococo Revival, Repousse, Scrolls, Flowers, Shells, Coin, Va., c.1850, 11 In.	31050
Bowl, Fruit, Poppy Design, Wallace Silversmiths, c.1950, 10 In.	676
Bowl, Fruit, Round Foot, Figural Putto, Playing Fife, Gorham, 1868, 8 ½ x 10 In.	1625
Bowl, Hobstar & Fan Border, Crosshatching, Flared Rim, Flowers, c.1900, 4 x 12 In.	676
Bowl, Hollowware, Arthur Stone, 1940s, 2 ½ In.	1062
Bowl, Leaf Shape, Old Newbury Crafters, 12 ½ In.	325
Bowl, Lid, Apple Shape, Branch & Leaf Support, Monogram, 7 ¼ x 3 ¼ In.	237
Bowl, Monogram, Flared Rim, Round Foot, Frank Smith, c.1950, 9 In.	225
Bowl, Monogram, Kalo, 20 ½ In.	219
Bowl, Paul Revere Style, Ring Footed Base, International Silver Co.	813

Bowl, Pedestal, Reeded Rim, Monogram, Goodnow & Jenks, 5 ½ x 9 In.	413
Bowl, Pierced & Scrolled Rocaille Rim, Leaf Scrolls, Monogram, J.E. Caldwell, 18 ½ In.	2100
Bowl, Reeded Foot, Shaped Rim, Paul Revere, Reed & Barton, 4 x 8 In.	360
Bowl, Reeded Rim, Shaped Handles, Randahl, 6 In.	120
Bowl, Reeded, Rope Twist Rim, Gorham, 11 In.	360
Bowl, Repousse Flowers, Footed, S. Kirk & Son, 10 ½ In.	2460
Bowl, Repousse Flowers, Leaves, Ribbed Ring Foot, c.1910, 5 In.	360
Bowl, Repousse, Footed, A. E. Warner, c.1874, 7 ⅝ In.	900
Bowl, Repousse, Fruit, Fluted Enter, Engraved Flowers, 11 ½ In.	598
Bowl, Reticulated, Flared Rim, Raised Scrolling, Monogram, Frank M. Whiting, 8 x 3 In.	184
Bowl, Reticulated, Flared Rim, Round, Monogram, Footed, Redlich & Co., 9 x 3 ⅝ In.	242
Bowl, Revere, Richard M. Woods & Co., 5 ½ x 10 In.	738
Bowl, Round, Daffodils, Leaves, Monogram, Towle, J.E. Caldwell & Co., c.1965, 3 x 13 In.	500
Bowl, Rounded Sides, Undulating Rim, Repousse Flowers, Gorham, c.1890, 9 ¾ x 4 In.	1162
Bowl, Royal Danish, Reticulated Handles, Footed, Signed, International, 8 x 4 ½ In.	144
Bowl, Scalloped Rim, Reed & Barton, 1941, 9 ½ In.	359
Bowl, Shaped Sides, Gadroon Rim, Howard & Co., c.1900, 10 ¼ In.	480
Bowl, Sterling, Hand Hammered, Flared Rim, Round Foot, c.1930, 9 In.	600
Bowl, Sterling, Shells, C-Scrolls, Pierced Bowl, Monogram, Flared Foot, Durgin, 15 ½ In.	1600
Bowl, Sweetmeat, Wavy Rim, Flowers, Reeded Center, Whiting, 2 ¾ x 9 In.	450
Bowl, Swirling Flowers, Wavy Rim, Gilt Interior, Gorham, 1896, 3 x 9 In.	295
Bowl, Underplate, Lobed, Kalo, 5 x 2 In., 6 In.	580
Bowl, Vegetable, Chantilly-Duchess, Gorham, 1953, 2 ⅛ x 10 ¼ In.	307
Bowl, Vegetable, Lid, Oval, Shaped Leaf Relief Rim, Monogram, Gorham, 12 ½ x 10 ¼ In.	575
Bowl, Vegetable, Lid, Repousse Flowers, Kirk & Sons, c.1900, 11 ¾ In.	2160
Bowl, Vegetable, Shaped Rectangle, Banded Rim, Gorham, 1944, 2 x 11 In.	281
Bowl, Wavy Rim, Openwork Center, Grape Rim, C. Billings & Son, 7 x 12 In.	2250
Bowl, Wide Flower Repousse Border, Kirk & Sons, c.1930, 9 In.	179
Bowl, Yacht Race, Twisted Handles, Dolphins, 1800s, 10 x 17 x 9 In.	3750
Box, Lid, Round, Squat, Lapis Cabochons & Finial, Grogan & Co., 5 x 7 In.	3627
Bread Tray, Francis I, Oval, Reed & Barton, 11 ¾ In.	657
Bread Tray, Oval, Shaped Rim & Handles, Whiting, 11 In.	180
Brush, Oval, Flower Repousse Design, c.1885, 5 x 3 ¼ In., Pair.	118
Butter Knife, Flat Handle, Flowers, Leaves, Relief, Monogram, Stamped B.H. Stieff, 7 ¼ In.	138
Butter Pat, Repousse Pattern, S. Kirk & Son, 1900s, 3 ¼ In., 12 Piece.	438
Butter, Cover, Octagonal, Cartouches, Lions' Masks, Feet, Mazarine, Finial, c.1825, 6 x 5 In.	1107
Butter, Cover, Repousse, Monogram, Ball Black & Co., 8 ¾ In.	1062
Butter, Domed Cover, Chased Flowers, Doves, Inside Strainer, Kirk & Sons, c.1870, 6 In.	570
Butter, Domed Cover, Griffin & Acanthus Feet, Beading, c.1850, 5 x 7 In.	1121
Butter, Scalloped Edge, Repousse Roses, Marked J.S. MacDonald, 1900s, 7 In.	230
Cake Basket, Neoclassical Style, Reticulated Rim, Embossed, Medallions, 11 In.	338
Cake Basket, Pierced, Chased, Stylized Blossoms, Gorham, c.1900, 17 In. *illus*	1875
Cake Plate, Openwork Band, Foot Ring, G.A. Henckel & Co., c.1915, 12 In. *illus*	430
Cake Stand, Shaped Rim, Monogramed, Gorham, c.1950, 10 In.	420
Candelabra are listed in the Candelabrum category.	
Candlesticks are listed in their own category.	
Canister, Chased Flowers, Monogram, Black, Starr & Frost, 4 ½ In.	570
Cann, Cup, Baluster, Molded Spread Foot, Scroll Handle, c.1770, 4 In.	1554
Card Case, Washington's Tomb, Trees, Flowers, Scrolls, Coin, c.1865, 3 ½ x 2 ½ In.	413
Centerpiece, Grape Cluster Relief, Engraved Monogram, Marked, Davis & Galt, 14 In.	1121
Centerpiece, Viking Ship Model, Engraved 1911-1930, Gorham Mfg., c.1930, 14 In.	938
Chalice, Goblet Shape, Sunburst Engraving, Coin, c.1815, 8 In.	649
Charger, Louis XV, Towle, 11 In., 12 Piece	3565
Cheese Knife, Repousse, Acanthus Collar, Greenleaf & Crosby, Gorham, 8 ½ In., 5 Piece	587
Chocolate Pot, Art Deco, Curved Handle, Tapered, Lobed, Hammered, Reed & Barton, 8 In.	1001
Cigarette Box, Cedar Lined, Monogram L, Towle Mfg. Co., 8 x 3 In.	325
Cigarette Box, Etched Dogs, Cartier, 4 ¾ In.	875
Cigarette Box, Frog, Lily Pad Enamel Lid, Green, Yellow, Blue, Gorham, 6 x 4 In.	1500
Cigarette Case, Europe, U.S.A. Maps, C. Thomae Co., c.1970, 5 x 3 In.	625
Cigarette Case, Incised Lines, Monogram, Gorham, 3 x 5 ¼ In.	176
Citrus Spoon, Paris, Presentation Inscription, Gold Washed Bowl, Gorham, c.1900, 8 Piece	150
Cocktail Fork, Rose, Monogram, S. Kirk & Son, c.1937, 5 ¾ In., 6 Piece.	110
Cocktail Shaker, Lift-Off Lid, Spout Lid Attached By Chain, Reed & Barton, 1900s, 8 In.	492
Cocktail Shaker, Open Dome Lid, Tapered, Cylindrical, Yacht, Tiffany & Co., c.1900, 7 In.	1750
Coffee & Tea Set, Marie Antoinette, Dominick & Haff, 5 Piece.	1955
Coffeepot, Baluster Shape, Ebonized Wood Scroll Handle, R. Dimes c.1910	375

Silver-American, Cake Plate, Openwork Band, Foot Ring, G.A. Henckel & Co., c.1915, 12 In.
$430

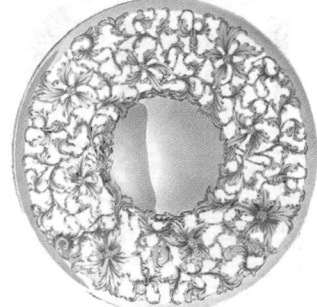

New Orleans Auction Galleries, Inc.

Silver-American, Coffeepot, Repousse, Ram's Head, Ivory Insulators, S. Kirk, c.1850, 11 ¾ In.
$2,520

Skinner Auctioneers & Appraisers

Silver-American, Coffeepot, Urn Shape, Coin, Gorham For J.E. Caldwell, c.1855, 12 ½ In.
$1,000

Rago Arts & Auction Center

Silver-American, Cup, Medallion, Chased, Handle, Coin, A.B. Griswold & Co., c.1868, 4 In.
$1,195

Neal Auction Co.

Silver-American, Cup, Presentation, Grape & Vine Repousse, Handle, Cann & Dunn, c.1850, 4 ½ In.
$246

Neal Auction Co.

Silver-American, Epergne, Francis I, Cornucopia, Fruit, Glass Liners, Reed & Barton, 1900s, 16 ½ In.
$14,160

Brunk Auctions

Coffeepot, Embossed, Footed, Coin, Marked Edward Kinsey, 1800s, 11 ½ In.	3081
Coffeepot, Engraved Leaves, Rope Twist Handle, Charters, Cann & Dunn, c.1850, 10 In.	608
Coffeepot, Flower Repousse, Oval, Flower Finial, Schofield, c.1900, 8 ⅜ In.	2700
Coffeepot, Neoclassical, Helmet Finial, Bead Border, Ball, Black & Co., c.1875, 10 In.	1200
Coffeepot, Octagonal Body, Engraved Flowers, Scrolls, Lows, Ball & Co., c.1845, 8 ¾ In.	823
Coffeepot, Puritan, Promotional, Gorham, c.1925, 32 In.	18750
Coffeepot, Repousse, Ram's Head, Ivory Insulators, S. Kirk, c.1850, 11 ¾ In. ......*illus*	2520
Coffeepot, Royal Danish, Baluster, Ivory Spacers, International Sterling, c.1975, 9 In.	313
Coffeepot, Tapered Cylinder, Hinged Lid, Wood Scroll Handle, Ensko, c.1950, 10 In.	813
Coffeepot, Turkish, Reeded Dome Lid, Long Neck & Spout, Gorham Mfg., 1884, 11 In.	1000
Coffeepot, Urn Shape, Coin, Gorham For J.E. Caldwell, c.1855, 12 ½ In. .....*illus*	1000
Coffeepot, Wood Handle, Gorham, 1946, 9 In.	329
Compote, Bowl, Pedestal, Paw Feet, Flat Rim, Flowers, c.1854, 5 x 8 In.	2510
Compote, Chased Flowers, Reticulated Rim, Footed, Towle, c.1910, 10 In.	281
Compote, Francis I, Ernest Meyer, Reed & Barton, 4 ¾ x 7 ¾ In.	522
Compote, Garland, Pedestal Foot, Wide Rim, Handles, Reed & Barton, 7 x 13 In.	690
Compote, Kylix Shape, Shallow Bowl, Handles, Monogram, Flared Foot, Robert Sturm, 6 In.	390
Compote, Maintenon, Footed, Round, Scrolling Acanthus Rim, Gorham, 1900s, 14 ½ In.	1169
Compote, Maintenon, Gorham, 4 x 9 ¼ In.	960
Compote, Repousse Floral Rim, Weighted Foot, Marked S. Kirk & Son, 4 ¾ x 7 ¼ In.	242
Compote, Repousse Flowers, Pedestal Base, Family Crest, Marked Warner, 8 ½ In.	403
Compote, Repousse Flowers, Pedestal, Shreve & Company, 9 In.	469
Cordial, Randahl, Chicago, 4 In., 12 Piece	212
Cream Ladle, Monogram, Coin, Richard Huntington, N.Y., c.1825, 6 ½ In.	89
Cream Pot, Engraved Flowers, Vine Border, Helmet Shape, George Aiken, c.1800, 6 In.	600
Creamer, Beaded Rim, Monogram, Coin, J. Lownes, 1790, 5 ½ In.	750
Creamer, Gadroon, Philadelphia, c.1790, 5 ¾ In.	243
Creamer, Helmet Shape, Beading, Wide Spout, Loop Handle, c.1800, 7 In.	3944
Creamer, Lid, Cylindrical, Swollen, Reeded Banding, Ball Finial, c.1820, 5 In.	3884
Creamer, Paneled, Engraved Designs, Bailey & Kitchen, Pa., Coin, c.1840, 6 ½ In.	345
Creamer, Tapered Octagon, Chased, Repousse, Lincoln & Reed, c.1847, 4 ¾ In.	331
Creamer, Urn, Pedestal, Scroll Handle, Banding, Wavy Spout, c.1830, 7 In.	3884
Cup, Gold Crown Baroque, Gorham, Child's, 2 ¼ In.	236
Cup, Inscribed Allen Park, Severance 1872, Handle, Coin, ¾ In.	325
Cup, Medallion, Chased, Handle, Coin, A.B. Griswold & Co., c.1868, 4 In. ......*illus*	1195
Cup, Presentation, Grape & Vine Repousse, Handle, Cann & Dunn, c.1850, 4 ½ In. ......*illus*	246
Cup, Presentation, Mountain Village, Beaded Rim, Scroll Handle, c.1900, 4 In.	308
Cup, Reeded, Engraved Text, Tapered, Lincoln & Reed, c.1840, Child's, 3 ½ x 4 In.	182
Dish, Arts & Crafts, Organic Leaf Handles, Round, Randahl, Stamped, 7 ⅞ In.	115
Dish, Entree, Lid, Handle, Gorham, 4 ½ x 9 ¾ In., Pair	972
Dish, Hammered, Scalloped Petal Shape, Galt & Bros., c.1965, 10 In.	416
Dish, Leaf Shape, Loop Handle, Reed & Barton, 1934, 9 x 9 In.	325
Dish, Lobed, Pierced Scrollwork Border, Engraved Leaves, Flowers, Gorham, c.1916, 13 In.	650
Dish, Oval, Pierced Flower Rim, Davis & Galt, c.1885, 14 In.	584
Dish, Reticulated Flower Border, Stamped Dominick & Haff Hallmark, 9 In.	190
Dish, Shell Shape, 2 Ball Feet, Gorham, 9 ⅛ x 9 ¼ In.	380
Dish, Wavy Rim, Pierced Handle, Richard Dimes, 1 ¼ x 7 In.	120
Dish, Windsor, Lobed Body, Reed & Barton, c.1940, 8 ½ In.	213
Egg Set, Sterling, Salt Cellars, Spoons, Gold Washed, Engraved, Ford & Tupper, 6 Sets	1100
Epergne, 4 Cut Crystal Bowls, Gorham, 17 x 10 In.	817
Epergne, Francis I, Cornucopia, Fruit, Glass Liners, Reed & Barton, 1900s, 16 ½ In. ......*illus*	14160
Ewer, 3 Gadroon Bands, Scroll Handle, Coin, Philemon Stacy, Jr., c.1820, 8 ¾ In.	1140
Ewer, Chased Flowers, Grapes, Scalloped Foot, Marked Wm. Gale, Coin, c.1855, 11 x 5 In.	748
Ewer, Pear Shape, Flowers, Branch Handle, Repousse, Gorham, c.1940, 5 Pt., 14 In.	2750
Ewer, Scroll Handle, Monogram, Marked J. Akin, Kentucky, Coin, c.1855, 15 x 5 In.	2760
Ewer, Scroll Handle, Stepped Foot, Marked E. Jaccard & Co., Mo., Coin, c.1860, 9 In.	633
Ewer, Vase Shape, Guilloche Borders, Scroll Handle, Flowers, c.1860, 12 In.	1315
Fish Knife, Chantilly, Monogram, Gorham, c.1920, 10 ⅛ In.	120
Fish Knife, Design Engraved Handle, Blade, Serrated, Bigelow	118
Fish Serving Set, Baltimore Style, Floral, Wave Scroll Edges, 8 ¼ & 10 ¼ In.	153
Flask, Cushion Shape, Crested Helmet, Crossed Sword, Rifled, Gorham, 4 x 4 In.	531
Flask, Flat Oval, Wind God, Profile, Sun, Clouds, Gorham, 5 ¾ In.	1250
Flask, Woven Sleeve, Plain Cap & Base, Over Glass, Flat Shape, Gorham, c.1900, 7 ¾ In.	813
Flower Basket, Pierced, Attached Handle, Whiting Mfg., 18 x 11 In.	1185
Flower, Leaf Engraved, Handle, Presentation, Henry Salisbury, 1853, 3 In.	325
Fork Set, Heraldic, Monogram, Whiting, c.1900, 7 ½ In., 12 Piece	570

Silver-American, Julep Cup, Applied Beading, J. Kitts, Engraved, Ky. S. Ag. Society, 1857, 4 In.
$1,440

Cowan's Auctions

Silver-American, Julep Cup, Applied Rim, Banded Foot, Marked, Poindexter, c.1850, 3 ½ In.
$840

Cowan's Auctions

Silver-American, Julep Cup, Tapered, Reeded Borders, Coin, Henry Hudson, c.1850, 4 In.
$708

Brunk Auctions

Silver-American, Ladle, Medallion, Bust, Woman, Gold Washed Bowl, Wood & Hughes, c.1875, 15 In.
$861

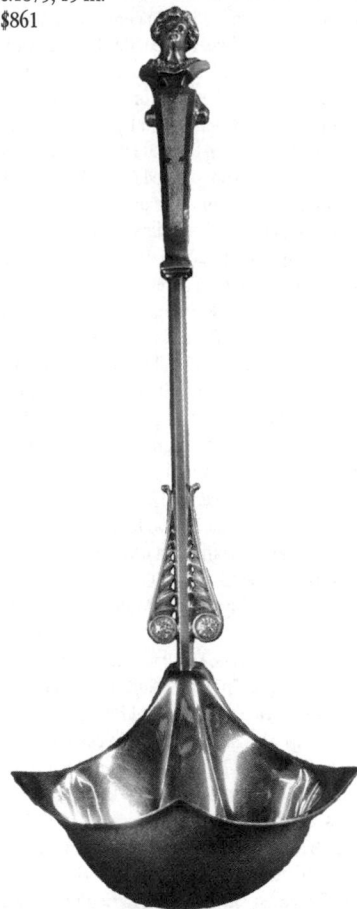

Skinner Auctioneers & Appraisers

Silver-American, Mug, Trophy, Agriculture, Scrolled Handle, Inscribed, J. Johnston, c.1850, 4 In.
$5,428

Brunk Auctions

Silver-American, Pitcher, Engraved, Georgia State Agricultural Soc., Coin, c.1870, 7 In.
$2,151

Neal Auction Co.

Silver-American, Pitcher, Ice Water, Tilting Stand, Presentation, Pairpoint Mfg., c.1890, 17 In.
$5,581

Cowan's Auctions

S

529

Silver-American, Pitcher, Pear Shape, Repousse Flowers, Coin, Hyde & Goodrich, c.1865, 13 In.
$3,444

New Orleans Auction Galleries, Inc.

Silver-American, Pitcher, Trophy, Engraved, Tobacco Leaf, Inscribed, Coin, c.1850, 11 ¾ In.
$12,980

Brunk Auctions

Silver-American, Pitcher, Water, Helmet Shape, Scroll Handle, Schofield, 8 x 9 ½ In.
$708

Brunk Auctions

Frame, Photo, Embossed, Frog & Goose Design, 1900s, 9 ½ x 7 ¼ In.	584
Goblet, Greek Key Bands At Rim & Foot, W.H. Calhoun Mark, c.1855	1404
Goblet, Presentation, Waisted Bowl, Banner, Shield, Flag, Laurel Wreath, Mauser, c.1904, 8 In.	600
Goblet, Repousse, Bell Shape, Tapered Stem, Grape Leaves, c.1850, 14 In., Pair	923
Gravy Boat, Underplate, Ribbed, Reed & Barton, 1948	238
Ice Bucket, Insulated Thermos Liner, Manchester Silver Co., c.1940, 9 ½ In.	777
Ice Cooler, Art Deco, Handles, Tong Hook, Glass Liner, Cartier, 8 ¾ In.	2813
Julep Cup, Applied Beading, J. Kitts, Engraved, Ky. S. Ag. Society, 1857, 4 In. *illus*	1440
Julep Cup, Applied Rim, Banded Foot, E. Garner, Kentucky, 1800s, 3 ½ In.	1200
Julep Cup, Applied Rim, Banded Foot, Marked, Poindexter, c.1850, 3 ½ In. *illus*	840
Julep Cup, Tapered Seamed Shape, Molded Rims, Engraved, c.1830, 3 ¼ In.	1076
Julep Cup, Tapered, Molded Rims, c.1850, 3 ¾ In.	1673
Julep Cup, Tapered, Reeded Borders, Coin, Henry Hudson, c.1850, 4 In. *illus*	708
Kettle, Hot Water, Stand, Flower Engraved, Wood Handle, Samuel Kirk & Sons, 12 ½ In.	708
Knife, Chased Leaves, Gorham, c.1900, 11 ⅝ In.	150
Ladle, Curved, Sheffield Touchmark, Atkin Brothers, c.1848, 12 In.	150
Ladle, Downturned Oval Handle, Oval Bowl, Engraved, c.1785, 13 ¼ In.	420
Ladle, Fiddle Handle, Flared Shoulders, c.1850, 13 In.	2032
Ladle, Fiddle Handle, Marked E. Outten, Kentucky, c.1820, 13 ½ In.	2091
Ladle, Medallion, Bust, Woman, Gold Washed Bowl, Wood & Hughes, c.1875, 15 In. *illus*	861
Ladle, Round Bowl, Engraved Handle, Rowland Parry, Pa., 1807	416
Ladle, Round Bowl, Tapered Handle, W. Ball, U.S.A., c.1815, 14 ¼ In.	708
Ladle, Spatulate Handle, Round Bowl, Monogram, c.1800, 12 ½ In.	922
Ladle, Tipped Fiddle Handle, Marked Harvey Lewis, Pa., Coin, c.1820, 12 ½ In.	207
Loving Cup, 3 Loop Handles, Spread Foot, Snake & Book, Gorham, 7 ¼ In.	1287
Macaroni Server, Plymouth, Monogram, Roger Williams, 9 ⅛ In.	153
Mug, Aesthetic, Sterling, Abstract Pattern, Gorham, 3 ½ In.	225
Mug, Engraved Flowers, Lily Pads, Geometric Banding, Gorham Mfg., 1868, 3 ½ In.	438
Mug, Flower, Name Engraved, Gorham, Child's, 3 ¾ In.	165
Mug, Trophy, Agriculture, Scrolled Handle, Inscribed, J. Johnston, c.1850, 4 In. *illus*	5428
Napkin Rings are listed in their own category.	
Nut Dish, 6 Different Repousse Flowers, Stamped, Reed & Barton, 1903, 3 In., 6 Piece	472
Nut Dish, Arts & Crafts, Scalloped, Hammered, Joel F. Hewes, c.1915, 4 ¾ & 5 In., 2 Piece	181
Nut Dish, Francis I, Repousse, Reed & Barton, 3 ½ In., 2 Piece	150
Nutmeg Grater, Nut Shape, Lobed, Gorham, 2 ⅛ In.	553
Pitcher, Bulbous, Flower Band, Curved Handle, Ring Foot, c.1955, 11 In., Pair	3050
Pitcher, Engraved, Georgia State Agricultural Soc., Coin, c.1870, 7 In. *illus*	2151
Pitcher, Helmet Shape, Scroll Handle, Stepped Ring Base, 1900s, 9 In.	885
Pitcher, Ice Water, Dominick & Half, Reed & Barton, 1932, 10 In.	960
Pitcher, Ice Water, Tilting Stand, Presentation, Pairpoint Mfg., c.1890, 17 In. *illus*	5581
Pitcher, Lobed Pear Shape, Flower Repousse, Scroll Feet, c.1840, 13 In.	1830
Pitcher, Modernist, Paneled, Angular, Tapered, Frank Lloyd Wright Design, 10 In.	7688
Pitcher, Paneled Bulbous Body, Pedestal, Scroll Arm, Gorham, 15 In.	1888
Pitcher, Paneled Cylinder Shape, Kalo Shop, 10 In.	3438
Pitcher, Pear Shape, Flower, Handle, Spout, Grosjean & Woodward, 9 In.	2714
Pitcher, Pear Shape, Repousse Flowers, Coin, Hyde & Goodrich, c.1865, 13 In. *illus*	3444
Pitcher, Reeded, Scroll Handle, Flared Rim, Marquand, 1800s, 4 x 6 In.	472
Pitcher, Repousse Scroll, Flowers, P. L. Krider, Pa., 1860, 13 In.	1152
Pitcher, Trophy, Engraved, Tobacco Leaf, Inscribed, Coin, c.1850, 11 ¾ In. *illus*	12980
Pitcher, Underplate, Grapevine Handle, c.1880, 9 x 10 ½ In.	2006
Pitcher, Urn Shape, Flowers, Stepped Foot, Wide Spout, 1900s, 12 In.	944
Pitcher, Urn Shape, Handle, Wide Spout, Flowers, c.1855, 12 ½ In.	2124
Pitcher, Urn Shape, Scroll Handle, Leaves, Beaded, c.1850, 11 x 6 In.	5900
Pitcher, Water, Acanthus, Scrolled Handle, Round Foot, Bennett & Caldwell, 13 In.	950
Pitcher, Water, Baluster, Applied Handle, Gorham, 7 ½ In.	531
Pitcher, Water, Berry & Vine Cartouche, Wavy Spout, Gorham, 1885, 7 x 7 In.	885
Pitcher, Water, Chased Leaf, Latticework, Engraved Scrolls, F. W. Smith, c.1920, 10 In.	1250
Pitcher, Water, George I, Tuttle, Boston, c.1929, 9 ½ In.	984
Pitcher, Water, Helmet Shape, Scroll Handle, Reeded Foot, 1900s, 10 In.	708
Pitcher, Water, Helmet Shape, Scroll Handle, Schofield, 8 x 9 ½ In. *illus*	708
Pitcher, Water, Holloware, Scrolled Handle, Pedestal Base, International Silver, 9 In.	483
Pitcher, Water, Leaf & Flower Repousse, Wood & Hughes, 9 ¼ In.	1586
Pitcher, Water, Lobed, C-Shape Handle, Wm. Durgin, 9 In.	1000
Pitcher, Water, Lotus, Monogram, Watson Co., 9 ½ In.	590
Pitcher, Water, Manchester Silver Co., c.1935, 9 In.	418
Pitcher, Water, Monogram, Lobed, Angled Handle, Gorham Mfg. Co., 1909	437

Pitcher, Water, Oblong, Flower Buttons, Reed & Barton, 1900s, 9 ¾ In. ....*illus*	1062
Pitcher, Water, Octagonal, Scrolls, Flowers, Flower Feet, Gorham, c.1903, 9 In............................	750
Pitcher, Water, Scroll Handle, Whiting Mfg. Co., 1906, 8 ½ In. ....*illus*	366
Pitcher, Water, Swags, Masks, Footed, T.B. Starr, 9 ½ In.	1625
Pitcher, Water, Urn Shape, Flowers, Fruit, Twisted Rope Borders, c.1885, 14 In.	4720
Pitcher, Water, Urn, Acanthus, Ribbons, Ear Handle, Coin, c.1849, 14 In.	937
Pitcher, Water, Victorian, Gorham, 1958, 10 ¼ In. ....*illus*	553
Pitcher, Water, Waisted, Wide Cylindrical Neck, Acanthus Foot, c.1883, 8 ½ In.	650
Pitcher, Water, Wide Mouth, Scrolled Handle, Flared Round Foot, Tuttle, c.1932, 9 In.	650
Plate, Bread & Butter, Gadroon Rim, Fisher Silversmiths, N.J., 6 In., 12 Piece............................	861
Plate, Bread & Butter, Monogram, Beaded Register To Edge, Gorham, 6 In., 12 Piece...................	720
Plate, Bread & Butter, Monogram, Wm. B. Durgin Co., c.1910, 12 Piece	750
Plate, Bread & Butter, Rose Pattern, Repousse, Stieff, 6 ⅛ In., 16 Piece	1409
Plate, Dinner, Engraved Flowers, Hammered, Reed & Barton, 1900s, 10 ¾ In., 12 Piece	4500
Plate, Dinner, Incised Border, Embossed Monogram, Dominick & Haff, 11 In., 12 Piece	5750
Plate, Repousse Flowers, Leaves, Beaded Rim, Coin, Marked David Rait & Co., c.1840, 8 In.	184
Plate, Reticulated Edge, Scrolls, Putti, Monogram, Bailey, Banks & Biddle, 10 In., Pair	500
Plate, Reticulated Rose Border, Engraved Rose & Scroll, Bailey, Banks & Biddle, 10 In., Pair	949
Plate, Reticulated, Flower Baskets, Rim Flowers, Footed, Frank Herschede Co., 8 ½ In...............	299
Plate, Round, Embossed Rim, Prelude, 10 In..	180
Plate, Round, Flat Rim, Embossed Design, Poole, 11 ½ In...	330
Platter Spoon, George W. Shiebler, Coffin Shape Handle, Acid Engraved, 12 ¾ In.	338
Platter, Francis I, Monogram, Reed & Barton, 18 x 13 ½ In...	2700
Platter, Meat, Oval, Shell, Scroll Rim, Well, Scrolled Feet, Dominick & Haff, 23 In......................	2100
Platter, Oval, Monogram, Reed & Barton, 1942, 18 x 13 In...	813
Platter, Presentation, Shaped Rim, Vines, Black, Starr & Frost, 14 ¼ In.....................................	650
Platter, Rounded Rectangular, Lobed, Reed & Barton, c.1931, 14 x 10 In.	430
Platter, Scalloped Rim, Molded, Dominick & Haff, 12 In.	500
Platter, Shaped Edge, Monogram, 1941, 14 In...	510
Platter, Well & Tree, Shaped Rim, Gorham, 23 x 17 In. .... 1625 to 2420
Porringer, Double Arch Keyhole, Samuel Vernon, c.1730, 5 In.	5400
Porringer, J. Hurd, Boston, c.1750, 8 In...	8125
Porringer, Keyhole Handle, B. Burt, c.1750, 8 ½ In...	4375
Porringer, Pierced Handle, Benjamin Burt, c.1760, 5 ½ In..	3402
Porringer, Pierced Lug Handle, Repousse, Flower Sprays, S. Kirk & Son, c.1910, 7 ¼ In...............	500
Pot, Rococo, Bulbous Body, Flared Scalloped Rim, Scroll Handle, Myer Myers, 4 ½ In.	12000
Punch Bowl, Rococo Cartouches, Flowers, Ring Lion's Head Handles, c.1925, 9 x 17 x 12 In.	2214
Punch Ladle, Bead & Cartouche Design, Marked Taylor & Lawrie, Pa., Coin, c.1860, 12 In.	196
Punch Ladle, Coin, Marked J. Meredith, Va., c.1810, 13 In.	690
Punch Ladle, Downturned Tip, Coin, Marked E.M.E., c.1840, 15 ½ In.	460
Punch Ladle, Lobed Cup, Mermaid Terminal, J.E. Caldwell, c.1890, 16 In................................	1500
Punch Ladle, Scalloped Bowl, Chased, Ball Black & Co., c.1875, 12 ¾ In.	125
Punch Ladle, Shell End Handle, Coin, Marked J.C. Farr, c.1845, 14 In.	259
Punch Ladle, Tipped Fiddle Handle, Monogram, W. Lawler, Cal., Coin, c.1850, 14 In.	219
Rattle, Coral Teether, Whistle, Rococo Repousse, Bells, Marked IR, c.1790 ....*illus*	1625
Salad Fork & Spoon, Stone & Assoc., 1940s...	283
Salad Servers, Lily, Fork & Spoon, Charles Osborne, Whiting, 11 ⅝ In. ....*illus*	553
Salt, Cobalt Blue Glass Liner, Gorham, 1 ¼ In., 8 Piece...	201
Salt & Pepper, Mushroom Shape, Guilloche Enamel, Cartier, c.1950, 1 ¾ In.............................	154
Salt & Pepper, Umbrella, Figural, Japan, 2 ¾ In. ....*illus*	165
Salver, Chippendale, Gorham, 1942, 12 In...	500
Salver, Flower, Leaf Rim, Round, Monogram, F. Marquand, c.1825, 11 In................................	1185
Sauceboat, Squat, Medial Ring, Coin, Lows, Ball & Co., c.1845, 3 ⅝ x 4 ¾ In............................	403
Serving Bowl, Oblong, Lobed, Scrolls, Flowers, Graff, Washbourne, Dunn, 4 x 13 In...................	875
Serving Spoon, Berry, Bird's-Nest Handle Terminal, Gorham Mfg., c.1865, 9 In........................	1500
Serving Spoon, Hammered, Scrolling, Leaf Vine, Rosebud, Marshall Field & Co., 10 ⅜ In..........	125
Shaker, Repousse, Flowers, Tapered, Footed, Stieff, 4 ½ In., Pair...	167
Shoe Buckle, Metal Latch Prongs, Oval, Faceted, John Meyers, Pa., 3 In., Pair	1188
Shoehorn, Repousse Flower Handle, Stamped Kirk & Son Co., 6 ½ x 1 ⅝ In.	144
Shovel Server, Engraved, Beaded, Twisted Handle, Gorham Mfg., c.1890	313
Soup Ladle, Monogram, Coin, Theodore Evans & Co., c.1860, 13 In.	266
Spoon Warmer, Shell Shape, Upturned Nautilus Shell, Hinged, Shell Handle, 5 In., Pair	250
Spur, Crockett Stainless, Engraved Mountings, Diamonds, E.H. Bohlin, Pair	1180
Straining Ladle, King Pattern, Coin, Marked Kirk, c.1824, 8 ½ In.	374
Sugar & Creamer, Georgian, Handles, Lion's Mask, Paw Legs, Poole, 3 ¼ x 2 ¼ In.....................	173
Sugar Basket, Repousse Castle, Flowers, Bale Handle, Kirk, c.1900, 6 In. ....*illus*	472

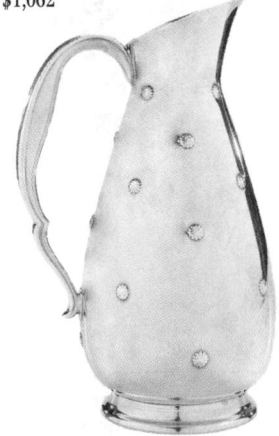

Silver-American, Pitcher, Water, Oblong, Flower Buttons, Reed & Barton, 1900s, 9 ¾ In.
$1,062

Brunk Auctions

Silver-American, Pitcher, Water, Scroll Handle, Whiting Mfg. Co., 1906, 8 ½ In.
$366

Neal Auction Co.

Silver-American, Pitcher, Water, Victorian, Gorham, 1958, 10 ¼ In.
$553

New Orleans Auction Galleries, Inc.

S

This is an edited listing of current prices. Visit **Kovels.com** to check thousands of prices from previous years and sign up for free information on trends, tips, reproductions, marks, and more.

Silver-American, Rattle, Coral Teether, Whistle, Rococo Repousse, Bells, Marked IR, c.1790
$1,625

Rago Arts & Auction Center

Silver-American, Salad Servers, Lily, Fork & Spoon, Charles Osborne, Whiting, 11 ⅝ In.
$553

New Orleans Auction Galleries, Inc.

S

Silver-American, Salt & Pepper, Umbrella, Figural, Sterling Silver, Japan, 2 ¾ In.
$165

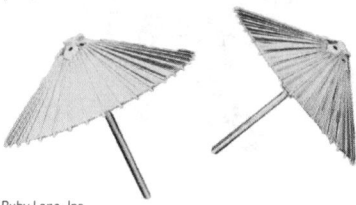

Ruby Lane, Inc.

TIP

Store silver, sterling or plated, away from high humidity. The ideal humidity is 40 to 45 percent. You can keep small pieces in a glassed-in cupboard with anti-tarnish paper or camphor balls (moth balls). Big pieces can be kept in tarnish-preventing bags that can be found at department and jewelry stores or online.

Silver-American, Sugar Basket, Repousse Castle, Flowers, Bale Handle, Kirk, c.1900, 6 In.
$472

Brunk Auctions

Silver-American, Sugar, Lid, Applied Shell & Rope Bands, Coin, James Black, c.1800, 7 ⅜ In.
$1,063

Rago Arts & Auction Center

Silver-American, Teapot, Leaves, Shells, Scrolls, Coin, Fletcher & Gardiner, c.1825, 10 ½ In.
$2,706

Skinner Auctioneers & Appraisers

Silver-American, Tureen, Lid, Tray, 1899 Pattern, Leaves, Engraved Flowers, Gorham, 17 In.
$3,998

Skinner Auctioneers & Appraisers

Silver-American, Urn, Classical Style, Leaves, Ring Handles, Medallions, Paw Feet, Gorham, 14 In.
$4,500

Cowan's Auctions

Sugar Basket, Scrolls, Repousse, Boat Shape, Handle, Coin, Marked E.M.E., c.1840, 6 x 4 In.	460
Sugar Tongs, Eagle & Shell Design, Script Monogram, c.1830, 6 ½ In.	369
Sugar Tongs, Engraved Monogram, Marked J. Shoemaker, Pa., Coin, c.1820, 6 In.	69
Sugar Tongs, Handles Ending In Shell, Coin, Cooke & Son, c.1835, 6 In.	196
Sugar Tongs, Lewis Heck, Lancaster, Pa., c.1790, 6 ½ In.	830
Sugar Tongs, Shell Wells, Monogram, Marked W. Mitchell, Coin, c.1840, 6 In.	127
Sugar, Lid, Applied Shell & Rope Bands, Coin, James Black, c.1800, 7 ⅜ In. .... *illus*	1063
Sugar, Lid, Urn, Stepped Pedestal, Scroll Handles, Leaf Collar, c.1850, 9 In.	2868
Sugar, Lid, Vase Shape, Beaded, Leaf Handles, Acorn Finial, c.1823, 9 In.	6274
Sugar, Monogram, Round, Flying Scroll Handles, Raised Round Foot, Gebelein, c.1930, 5 In.	350
Syrup, Urn Shape, Beaded, Greek Key Bands, Footed, J.E. Caldwell, 1800s, 9 In.	608
Tablespoon, Eagle To Handle, Monogram, Asa Blanchard	250
Tablespoon, Urn Back, Monogram, S. Williamson, c.1800, 10 In.	125
Tankard, Domed Lid, Cylindrical Body, Cartouche, Scrolled Handle, D. Rogers, c.1775, 6 In.	1680
Tankard, Tapered, Dome Base, Hinged Lid, Leaf Thumb Press, Gorham, 1 ½ Pt., 8 In.	1035
Tazza, Bail Handles, Beaded, Gadrooned, Marked Sutherland Period 1770, Gorham, 5 In.	900
Tazza, Neoclassical, Round, Monogram, Die Cast, Griffins, Ball, Black & Co., c.1875, 10 In.	4200
Tazza, Repousse Flowers, Tapered Stem, Spread Flower Foot, S. Kirk, 6 x 7 In.	362
Tazza, Stag Head Handles, Trumpet Stem, Coin, Gorham & Co., c.1865, 8 In.	1375
Tea Caddy, Architectural, Model Of Harvard Medical School, Laity & Miller, 12 x 15 In.	3240
Tea Set, Diamond Pattern, Wrapped Pot Handles, Reed & Barton, c.1950, 4 Piece..............	1085
Tea Set, Hampton Court, Melon Lobed, Squat, Reed & Barton, 5 Piece	1989
Tea Set, Maintenon, Teapot, Sugar, Creamer, Tray, Gorham	1705
Teapot, Coin, Marked Baldwin Gardiner, New York, c.1830, 10 ¼ In.	547
Teapot, Drum Shape, Angular Handle, S. Kirk & Sons, c.1830, 4 In.	832
Teapot, Leaves, Shells, Scrolls, Coin, Fletcher & Gardiner, c.1825, 10 ½ In. .... *illus*	2706
Teapot, Lobed, Grapevine Gadroon Borders, C. Burnett, c.1830, 10 In.	6300
Teapot, Oval, Hinged, Flower Gadroon, Bead Edge, Pineapple Finial, 10 ½ In.	2250
Teapot, Repousse Design, Bulbous, Scroll Handle, Dominick & Haff, 7 ¾ In.	2340
Teapot, Squat Urn Shape, Paneled Body, Finial, Ivory Heat Stops, Howard, c.1902, 8 ½ In.	400
Teaspoon, Coffin End, Script Engraved Monogram, Robert Evans Mark, 6 Piece	120
Teaspoon, Fiddle, Scrolling Monogram, John Tanguy, 6 In., 6 Piece.............................	81
Teaspoon, Tip Back Fiddle Handle, Marked G.O. Conrad, Coin, c.1860, 5 ⅝ In., Pair	161
Toddy Ladle, Scalloped, Navette Shape Bowl, Turned Wood Shaft, c.1750, 21 In.	307
Toddy Spoon, Twisted Handle, Drummer Terminal, L. Holland, c.1825, 8 In........................	90
Tongs, Embossed, Coin, c.1795, 6 In.	120
Tongs, Repousse Handle, Carved Leaf Shape End, S. Kirk & Son, 6 ¼ In., Pair....................	190
Tray, Chippendale, Round, Shaped Rim, Initials, Gorham, 13 In.	720
Tray, Elongated Oval, Repousse Flower Rim, Stieff, c.1900, 17 x 8 In.	531
Tray, Footed, Shaped, Cellini Craft, 1 ½ x 10 In...	300
Tray, Francis I, Round, Horn Of Plenty, Fruit, Floral Basket, Embossed, Reed & Barton, 8 In.......	540
Tray, Gadroon Rim, Monogram, Leaf Chased Rim, Round, Gorham, 14 In.	661
Tray, Oblong, Rounded Corners, Monogram, Leaf Relief Rim, Gorham, 15 x 11 In.	719
Tray, Oval, Allover Leaves, Flowers, Ball Feet, Gorham, c.1883, 14 In.	3438
Tray, Oval, Beaded Border, Ball & Claw Feet, Coin, 1800s, 10 x 8 In.	531
Tray, Oval, Openwork, Urn & Shield Gallery, Footed, 1900s, 16 x 5 In.	295
Tray, Rococo, Round, Flowers, Scrolls Openwork Border, Roger Williams Co., c.1900, 13 In.	1000
Tray, Round, Scroll, Shell Rim, Gorham, c.1950, 16 In.	938
Tray, Rounded Rectangular, Flower Border, Caldwell, c.1900, 14 x 11 In.	767
Tray, Scalloped Edges, Sides, Marked Reed & Barton, 8 ½ In.	253
Tray, Shaped, Rectangular, Handles, Ensko, 21 In.	2520
Trophy, Chalice Shape, Sterling, Handles, Grape Cluster, Swags, Crichton & Co., 7 In..............	357
Tureen, Lid, Tray, 1899 Pattern, Leaves, Engraved Flowers, Gorham, 17 In. .... *illus*	3998
Tureen, Repousse, Oval, Pedestal, Domed Lid, Boar Head Finial, c.1850, 14 In........................	3998
Urn, Classical Style, Leaves, Ring Handles, Medallions, Paw Feet, Gorham, 14 In. .... *illus*	4500
Vase, Bud, Cherub, Holding Trumpet, Shovel, Round Base, Gorham, 6 ½ x 2 ½ In......................	472
Vase, Bud, Mixed Metal Animals, Bugs, Flowers, Engraved, Dominick & Haff, 1979, 6 In.	1625
Vase, Crystal Insert, Reticulated, Scrolling, Reed & Barton, 8 x 7 ½ In..........................	180
Vase, Kneeling Egyptian Figures Standard, Applied Side Bees, Ball, Black & Co., 8 In., Pair	590
Vase, Trumpet, Beaded, Removable Liner, Dominick & Haff, 1898, 11 ⅝ In. .... *illus*	1195
Vase, Wavy Rim, Baluster Body, Raised Flowers, Leaves, Gorham, c.1905, 22 In.	3328
Waiter, Chippendale, Shaped Rim, Monogram, Poole, 11 ¼ In.	584
Waiter, Edwardian, Scroll Rim, Handles, Footed, Chased, Gorham, c.1910, 24 In.	3625
Waiter, Open Handles, Oval, Arthur Stone, 29 In.	7670
Wine Cooler, Grapevine, Globular, Branch Feet, Gorham, c.1900, 9 x 10 In.	3500

Silver-American, Vase, Trumpet, Beaded, Removable Liner, Dominick & Haff, 1898, 11 ⅝ In.
$1,195

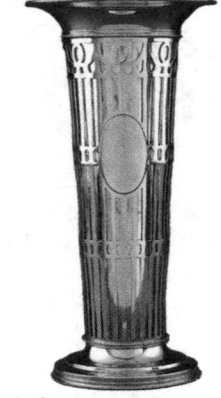

Neal Auction Co.

Silver-Anglo-Indian, Garniture, Elephant, Howdah Salt Cellar, Gilt, Hamilton & Co., c.1810, 7 In.
$8,066

Neal Auction Co.

Silver-Chinese, Dresser Box, Lid, Repousse, Sing Fat, Canton, Shanghai, 3 x 5 In.
$2,091

New Orleans Auction Galleries, Inc.

S

TIP
Don't have old Sheffield silver replated. You can replate wares that were originally electroplated.

Silver-Chinese, Teapot, Hinged Lid, Repousse Dragon, Marked, Zee Wo, c.1900, 5 ½ In.
$1,845

Skinner Auctioneers & Appraisers

Silver-Continental, Nef, Ship, Sail, 12 Sailors, Dragon Mast Head, c.1890, 12 x 8 ¾ In.
$2,125

Rago Arts & Auction Center

Silver-Continental, Tea Set, Repousse, Teapot, Wood Handle, Sugar & Creamer, 1800s, 6 x 10 In.
$575

Cottone Auctions

Wash Silver by Hand

Experts say you should never put silverware in a dishwasher for several reasons. Eventually the oxidation (black highlights) will disappear, hollow-handled knives are filled with a material that will melt, and if the silver touches stainless steel it will get black spots. Be safe. Wash silver by hand.

SILVER-ANGLO-INDIAN

Garniture, Elephant, Howdah Salt Cellar, Gilt, Hamilton & Co., c.1810, 7 In. .... *illus* 8066

SILVER-ARMENIAN

Belt, Carved Flowers Buckle, Coil Strap, Sliding Loops, Carved Bird, 33 ½ In. 860

SILVER-ASIAN

Incense Burner, Waisted, Lobed Container, Hinged, Pierced Lid, 3 Scrolled Feet, 9 In. 1169
Ladle, Raised Dancing Figures, Incised, Stippled, Silver Plate Terminal, 18 In. 150

SILVER-AUSTRIAN

Bowl, Scalloped, Lobed, Looped Rim, Footed, c.1920, 15 ½ In. 1250
Box, Peaceable Kingdom, Enamel, Garland, Chamfered Edge, Hinged, c.1900, 4 x 3 In. 3000
Chalice, Repousse Cherubs, Scrolls, Wide Foot, Marked, 1700s, 8 ½ In. 2000
Spade, Gilt, Scrolled Flowers, Leaves, 11 ½ In. 177
Tray, Art Nouveau, Rectangular, Pierced, Naturalistic Scrollwork, 14 ½ In. 250
Tray, Elongated Oval, Scalloped Rim, Stepped, 1900s, 22 x 12 In. 1003
Tray, Octagonal, Mahogany Plateau, Acanthus & Scroll Handles, c.1900, 28 x 18 In. 1187

SILVER-AUSTRO-HUNGARIAN

Platter, Fish, Oval, Molded Rim, 28 ½ In. 1125

SILVER-BOLIVIAN

Cup, Wine Taster's, Heart Shape, Engraved Flowers, Seahorse, Snake Chain, 1800s, 6 In. 384

SILVER-CANADIAN

Punch Bowl, Applied Grapevine, Turned Rim, Henry Birks & Sons, Montreal, 17 In. 6250
Sauceboat, Sterling, Round Foot, Hammered, Buds, Leaves, Carl Poul Petersen, 3 ¾ In. 450
Server, Etched Blade, Decorated Handle, Marked, Toronto Silver Plate, c.1890, 14 In. 84

SILVER-CHINESE

Bowl, Lobed, Bearded Dragon Handles, 7 ⅜ In. 2400
Box, Undulating Dragon, Chased, Repousse, Hinged Lid, Wang Hing & Co., c.1900, 6 In. 1800
Case, Repousse Figures, Pine, Cherry Trees, Luen Wo, c.1900, 4 x 3 In. 875
Cup, Dragon Handle, Chinese, 2 ½ In., Pair 663
Dresser Box, Lid, Repousse, Sing Fat, Canton, Shanghai, 3 x 5 In. .... *illus* 2091
Ewer, Urn Shape, Caryatid, Masks, Goats, Hinged, Gilt Spout, c.1871, 11 ½ In. 2500
Mug, Animals, Figures, Tapered Cylinder, Gilt Washed Interior, Canton, c.1845, 4 ⅞ In. 3375
Oval, Tapered, Lobed, Nobleman, Horse, Dragon Handles, 1899, 4 x 10 In. 4428
Pipe, Opium, Dragon, Clouds, Pheasant, 20 In. 3360
Tea Strainer, Box, 5 ½ In. 252
Teapot, Hinged Lid, Repousse Dragon, Marked, Zee Wo, c.1900, 5 ½ In. .... *illus* 1845
Tongs, Dragon, Hammered, Chased, Engraved Low Relief, c.1900, 6 In. 154
Whistle, Boson's, Dragon, Chased Engraved, Applied Flames 600

SILVER-CONTINENTAL

Bowl, Beaded Rim, Flowers, 2 x 11 In. 270
Bowl, Curled Handles, Etched, Footed, c.1850, 6 x 7 ¾ In. 444
Bowl, Oval, Wavy Rim, Ribbon, Swag, Trophy, Putti, 1900s, 3 x 12 ½ In. 590
Box, Enamel, Bulbous, Flower Banding, Venus, Cupid, Lid, c.1885, 5 x 4 In. 1168
Censer, Gold Overlay, Scroll, Leaves, Papal Tiara, Monogram, Pierced Lid, 6-Sided, 1800s 11500
Coffeepot, Raised, Chased Safari, Hunt Scenes, Staghorn Finial, Handle, 6 ½ In. 443
Cup, Chased Fruit, Scrolls, Footed, 3 ½ In. 118
Marriage Cup, Bride, Groom, Bell Shape, Scrolling, 13 In., Pair 5490
Nef, Ship, Sail, 12 Sailors, Dragon Mast Head, c.1890, 12 x 8 ¾ In. .... *illus* 2125
Page Slice, Eagle's Head Handle, Ivory Blade, c.1930, 16 ¾ In. 469
Punch Ladle, Nautilus Shape Bowl, Wood Twig Handle, c.1900, 16 ½ In. 531
Salad Servers, Ivory, Spoon, Fork, Stamped, 11 In. 288
Tea Set, Repousse, Teapot, Wood Handle, Sugar & Creamer, 1800s, 6 x 10 In. .... *illus* 575
Tumbler, Engraved Flowers, Marked Olpius, 1665, 3 ½ In. 649
Vase, Hammered, Reticulated, Trumpet Shape, c.1910, 9 In., 4 Piece 1500

SILVER-DANISH

Bell, Acorn Handle, Scrolls, Georg Jensen, 3 ¼ In. 360
Bell, Cactus Finial, Hammered, G. Jensen, 3 ¼ In. 502
Bell, Dinner, Ball Top, Figured Handle, G. Jensen, c.1932, 4 In. 330
Bowl, Applied Rim, Round, Ring Foot, G. Jensen, 8 ¾ In. 1625
Bowl, Domed Lid, Ball Finial, Grapes, Flared, Openwork Stem, Georg Jensen, 10 In. 3998
Bowl, Flared, Spot Hammered, Shallow, Ring Foot, G. Jensen, c.1925, 11 ½ In. 1375
Bowl, Hammered, Trumpet Shape, Fluted Stem, G. Jensen & Nils Wendell, c.1950, 4 ½ In. 813
Bowl, Louvre, Hammered, Leaf & Berry Openwork Pedestal, Footed, G. Jensen, 7 In. 2640

Bowl, Openwork Stem, Domed Foot, G. Albertus, G. Jensen, c.1933, 6 x 11 In.	6250
Bowl, Squat, Melon Ribbed, Bead Design, Rolled Rim, 1922, 4 ½ In.	180
Bowl, Stepped Foot, G. Jensen, 4 x 8 In.	448
Bowl, Wide Rim, Pedestal Base, Scroll Design Band, G. Jensen, 7 ¼ In.	1920
Box, Engraved Flower, Round, G. Jensen, 2 ½ In.	173
Compote, Flared, Grape S Applied To Twisted Stem, G. Jensen, c.1930, 7 x 7 In.	3438
Creamer, Round, Scalloped Rim, Straight Handle, G. Jensen, 7 ¼ In.	540
Dish, Blossom, Kidney Shape, Open Floral Edges, c.1930, 7 ½ x 5 ½ In., 2 Piece	3500
Gravy Boat, Blossom, Scroll Handle, Etched Band, Round Foot, G. Jensen, 8 In.	1320
Lobster Pick, Acorn, Georg Jensen, 1915, 7 ½ In., 14 Piece	2000
Marmalade Spoon, Peapod, Beaded Oval Mark, Georg Jensen, 5 ¼ In.	96
Pitcher, Cosmos, Upswept Handle, Georg Jensen, 9 In.	2880
Pitcher, Ebony Handle, Scrolls, Beads, Stepped Foot, c.1930, 10 ½ In.	3125
Pitcher, Stamped Kay Fisker, A. Michelsen, c.1950, 9 ½ x 6 In. ....illus	5000
Pitcher, Water, Sloped Mouth, Hammered, J. Rohde, Jensen, c.1930, 9 In.	3750
Pitcher, Wine, Sloped Rim, Ivory Handle, G. Jensen, c.1948, 10 ¾ In.	5000
Sauce Bowl, Cup Shape, Curved Handle, G. Jensen, c.1936, 8 In.	900
Sauce Ladle, Acorn Design, G. Jensen, c.1915, 8 In.	369
Sauce Ladle, Curled Handle, Beaded, Georg Jensen, c.1915, 5 In.	150
Sauce Ladle, Reeded Curled Handle, Wavy Rim, G. Jensen, 5 ½ In.	180
Sauceboat, Scrolled Blossom Handle, G. Jensen, c.1960, 5 In.	2250
Seafood Fork, Crown Shape Finial, Blue Enameling, Ela Denmark, Box, 5 In., 6 Piece	155
Serving Spoon, Hand Hammered, G. Jensen, 11 ½ In.	443
Spatula, Georg Jensen, 8 ¾ In.	267
Spur, Swan, Ruby Eyes, Copper Beak, Iron Rowels, Randy Butters, c.1980, Pair	1888
Sugar & Creamer, Bud Joint To Handle, Leafy Stem, Georg Jensen, c.1949	1845
Sugar Basket, Hammered, Stems, Blossoms, Georg Jensen, c.1948, 5 ¼ x 3 ¾ In. ....illus	1500
Tankard, Embossed Flowers, Jacob G. Fabritius, 8 ½ In.	956
Tankard, Ornate Flower Embossed, Carl Christiansen, c.1950, 8 In.	1154
Tankard, Repousse, Leaves, Fluted Bands, Hinged Lid, Lion Thumbpiece, 1954, 7 In.	1375
Tray, Oval, Reeded Rim, Beaded Banding, G. Jensen, 10 In.	900
Vase, Bud, Flared, Bifurcated Rim, Squat, Hans Bunde, c.1963, 7 In.	512

SILVER-DUTCH

Box, Marriage, Flower, Figural Design, Baluster Shape, Hinged Lid, c.1781, 2 ⅞ In.	354
Box, Marriage, Lobed, Gourd Shape, Crown Finial, c.1765, 2 ⅝ In.	177
Chalice, Diamond Set, Gilded Sterling, Adrian Hamers, 8 ⅜ In.	2100
Demitasse Spoon, Apostle Finial, Twist Handle, 6 Piece	63
Spoon, Strainer, Cockerel Finial, Reticulated, Lions, Coat Of Arms, Twist Handle, 9 x 4 In.	782
Tray, Applied Flower, Flower Handles, Oval, 13 In.	295

SILVER-EGYPTIAN

Dish, Pierced Border, Round, 3-Footed, Hallmarks, c.1946, 8 ¼ In.	120

SILVER-ENGLISH. English sterling silver is marked with a series of four or five small hallmarks. The standing lion mark is the most commonly seen sterling quality mark. The other marks indicate the city of origin, the maker, and the year of manufacture. These dates can be verified in many good books on silver. These prices are based on current silver values.

Barrel, Gold Washed Interior, Ribbed, Elizabeth Morley, 1812, 2 ½ In.	150
Basket, George III, Oval, Reticulated Border, Swing Handle, 13 In.	1063
Basket, George III, Oval, Reticulated, Beaded, Pierced, Swing Handle, W. Plummer, 4 x 14 In.	1888
Basket, Gilt, Oval, Blue Glass Insert, Ram's Head Handles, Engraved, 1834, 5 x 14 In.	2500
Basket, Oval, Flared Rim, Shells, Footed, Upright Handle, 1753, 10 x 13 In.	1416
Basket, Reticulated, Sections, Entwined Scroll Handle, Ring Foot, Rope Edge, 14 x 11 In.	750
Basting Spoon, George II, Richard Gosling, Elliptical Bowl, Initials, c.1743, 13 In.	720
Bottle Labels, Whiskey, Sherry, Bacchus Mask, Grapes, Birmingham, 2 ¼ x 2 ¼ In., Pair	132
Bowl, Chased, Fluted, Flowers, Ring Foot, William Fearn, c.1796, 5 x 2 ½ In.	207
Bowl, Edward VII, Double Scroll Handles, Walker & Hall, c.1900, 8 x 15 In.	1250
Bowl, Lion's Head Bail Handles, Garlands, Acanthus Leaves, Gold Washed Interior, 10 In.	800
Bowl, Paneled, Petal Rim, Engraved Lion, Footed, Crichton & Co., 5 x 10 In.	563
Bowl, Reeded Interior, Flat Rim, Beaded, Edward Barnard & Sons, c.1912, 7 In.	150
Bowl, Repousse, Pierced Bird, Flower Border, Gorham, 4 ½ x 15 In.	1337
Bowl, Vegetable, Lid, George III, Crest, Motto, Handles, Marked H. Chawner, 1792, 15 In.	1500
Bowl, Vegetable, Lid, Gourd Finial, Raised Plate Stand, Birmingham, c.1840, 13 ¾ In., Pair	3750
Bowls, Scroll & Shell Design, Reeded Border, Footed, P. Storr, 1813, 8 In., Pair	1062
Box, Edwardian, Etched Designs, Turquoise Inset, c.1907, 5 ½ In.	1029
Brandy Warmer, George I, Britannia, Flared Body, Turned Handle, Marked, c.1717, 8 In.	738

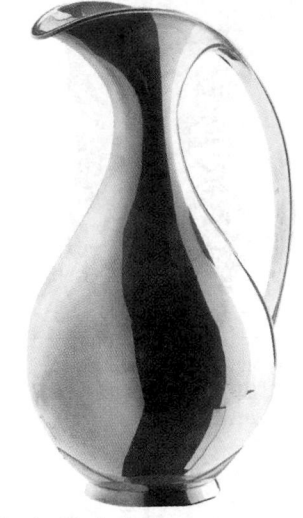

Silver-Danish, Pitcher, Stamped Kay Fisker, A. Michelsen, c.1950, 9 ½ x 6 In. $5,000

Rago Arts & Auction Center

Silver-Danish, Sugar Basket, Hammered, Stems, Blossoms, Georg Jensen, c.1948, 5 ¼ x 3 ¾ In. $1,500

Rago Arts & Auction Center

Silver-English, Cruet Set, 5 Cut Glass Bottles, Stand, George III, 1768, 9 ¼ In. $750

Rago Arts & Auction Center

Silver-English, Cup, Children Playing, Repousse, Touchmarks, Soloman Houghham, 4 In.
$228

The Stein Auction Co.

Silver-English, Epergne, Garlands, Scrolled Stems, Figures, Barnard, 1890-91, 14 x 20 In.
$9,600

Skinner Auctioneers & Appraisers

Silver-English, Sauce, George IV, Shells, Flowers, Marked, IC, WR, 1820, 6 x 8 In., Pair
$3,949

James D. Julia Auctioneers

Silver-English, Serving Trowel, George IV, Engraved, William Eaton II, 1829-30, 13 ¾ In.
$492

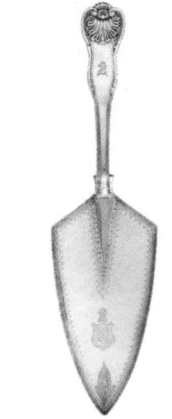

New Orleans Auction Galleries, Inc.

Butter Shell, George III, Coquille Shape, Whelk Feet, c.1796, 4 ¾ x 4 ½ In., Pair	541
Butter, Cover, Oval, Swag, Frosted Glass Liner, c.1885, 5 x 8 In.	354
Cake Basket, Applied Vines Sheaths, Oval, Pierced Handle, E. Romer, 1767, 16 x 12 In.	2006
Cake Basket, Victorian, Pierced, Scrolled, Wing Handle, Sheffield, c.1890, 12 In.	480
Cake Server, George II, Pierced Arabesques, Dolphin Shoulder, Wood Handle, 13 In.	100
Candelabra are listed in the Candelabrum category.	
Candlesticks are listed in their own category.	
Card Case, Embossed Buckingham Palace, Stippled Ground, Scrolls, A. Taylor, 4 In.	1800
Chalice, Waisted, Baluster, Allegorical Scenic Reserves, George III, c.1748, 10 ½ x 5 In.	1875
Cloche, George III Style, Plated, Gadroon Borders, Engraved, Crest, Cast Handle, 20 In.	330
Coffeepot, George I, Lighthouse, Dome Lid, Urn Shape Finial, Engraved Armorial, 10 In.	3000
Coffeepot, George II, Flowers, Scrolls, Treen Handle, c.1758, 9 ¾ In.	814
Coffeepot, George III, Baluster Shape, Wood Handle, Acorn Finial, Gadroon, 13 In.	2100
Coffeepot, George III, Baluster, Crested Double Scroll Handle, Gooseneck, 9 In.	1082
Coffeepot, George III, Chased Drapery, Flowers, Treen Handle, Charles Wright, c.1772, 12 In.	938
Coffeepot, Leaf Repousse, Swan Neck Spout, Treen Handle, Paul Storr, c.1798, 11 In.	4688
Coffeepot, Pear Shape, Flowers, Leaf Scrolls, Wood Handle, 1761, 12 x 9 In.	9440
Coffeepot, Repousse Flowers, Baluster, Wood Scroll Handle, W. & J. Deane, c.1760, 11 In.	1216
Cream Jug, George III, Engraved, Scalloped, Pedestal Foot, 1791, 5 ½ In.	413
Cream Jug, Georgian, Lion Mark, 1700s, 3 ½ In.	148
Cream Pail, Gadroon Rims, Engraved EF, Handle, 1773, 2 ¾ In.	1800
Creamer, Georgian, Melon Shape, Leaf Handle, Rebecca Emes, Edward Barnard I, 4 In.	246
Cruet Set, 5 Cut Glass Bottles, Stand, George III, 1768, 9 ¼ In. *illus*	750
Cup, Children Playing, Repousse, Touchmarks, Soloman Houghham, 4 In. *illus*	228
Demitasse, Spoon, Coffee Bean Finial, Hukin & Heath, Box, 3 ⅛ In., 6 Piece	69
Desk Set, George III, Inkwell, Salter, Taper Holder, Gadroon, 4 Shell Feet, 1825, 8 x 5 In.	649
Dish, Fenestrated Sides, Glass Liner, Mahogany Insert, H. Chawner, London, 1791, 4 x 8 In.	325
Epergne, Garlands, Scrolled Stems, Figures, Barnard, 1890-91, 14 x 20 In. *illus*	9600
Epergne, George V, Trumpet Vase, 3 Branches, Bowls, Scalloped, Gadroon, Baker, 1920, 13 In.	1125
Ewer, Leave, Mythological Figures, Walker & Hall, c.1945, 14 In.	2813
Ewer, Winged Figures, Masks, Lions' Heads, Flowers, Shells, S. Blanckensee, c.1916, 15 x 6 In.	1898
Fish Knife & Fork, Cased, 13 ½ In.	177
Flute, Elizabeth II, Fitted Case, Boosey & Hawkes, c.1962, 26 In.	475
Fruit Spoon, Chased, Gilt Bowl, Marked Richard Crossley, London, 1782, 8 ½ In., Pair	300
Fruit Spoon, George III, Chased, Gilt, Fitted Box, 1782, 8 ¼ In., Pair	300
Goblet, George III, Bell Shape Bowl, Gold Washed Interior, Flared Round Foot, Beading, 6 In.	550
Gravy Boat, George III, Flying Scroll Handle, Gold Interior, 3 Paw Feet, Lion's Heads, 3 In.	325
Gravy Boat, Georgian, Sterling, 3-Footed, Lion's Heads, Paws, Scrolled Handle, 1817, 8 In.	480
Gravy Ladle, Down Turned Handle, Bateman, 1808, c.1824, 6 In.	259
Jug, Hot Water, George III, Lobed, Reeded, Wood Handle, Marked W. Holmes, 1769, 14 In.	2250
Kettle, Henry Holland, Chased Scrolls, Flowers, Pear Shape, Handle, Stand, 1855, 15 In.	1440
Kettle, Stand, Cobweb, Star & Lion's Paw, James Dixon & Sons, 1906, 12 In.	761
Ladle, Stepped Reverse, 1763, 13 ½ In.	472
Letter Holder, Victorian, William Gibson, John Langman, Goldsmith Co., 1897, 4 ½ In.	392
Loving Cup, Repousse Cartouche, Swag, Curved Handles, William Cripps, c.1765, 4 x 6 In.	265
Mace, Ceremonial, Crown, Maltese Cross, Round Boss, Coat Of Arms, Motto, c.1760, 23 In.	8100
Marrow Spoon, Shell, Coat Of Arms, William Eley & William Fearn, c.1819	242
Meat Skewer, Monogram, William Lister Mark, 13 ¼ In.	157
Muffineer, Edward VII, Paneled Body, Octagonal Foot, Stokes & Ireland, c.1905, 8 ½ In.	175
Mug, Repousse Flowers, Scrolls, Flower Capped Handle, Elkington & Co., c.1858, 5 In.	375
Mustard Pot, Engraved Coat Of Arms, Handle, Spoon, 1797, 2 ½ In.	165
Napkin Rings are listed in their own category.	
Nutmeg Grater, George III, Egg Shape, Screw Top, c.1802, 1 ¾ In.	397
Nutmeg Grater, George III, Oval, Hinged Lid, Trap Door, Birmingham, 1799, 1 ⅜ In.	185
Nutmeg Grater, George III, Ribbon Cartouche, Hinged Lid, Oval, c.1785, 2 x 1 ¼ In.	472
Plate, Swirled Repousse Flowers, Green Enamel Triangles, James Deakin, 1907, 4 In., Pair	400
Platter, George III, Gadroon Border, Engraved Crest, Oval, P. Storr, 1815, 17 In.	2006
Porringer, Bombe Shape, Pierced Handle, John Parsons, 1700s, 8 In.	3851
Salt, Gadroon, Flowers, William Reid, 1847, Pair	224
Salt, Georgian, Footed, London, 1757, Pair	153
Salver, Elizabeth II, Round, Gadroon Rim, 3 Scroll Feet, Roberts & Belk, c.1988, 8 In.	225
Salver, Engraved, Shell Edge, Round, 10 ½ In.	826
Salver, George II, Round, Scroll, Shell Engraved Rim, 3-Footed, c.1750, 9 ¼ In.	416
Salver, George II, Scalloped Shell, Scroll Edge, Footed, Putti Heads, Engraved Armorial, 19 In.	4000
Salver, George III, Engraved Armorial, c.1772, 12 ¼ In.	1154
Salver, George III, Round, Gadroon Rim, Applied Shells, Engraved Crest, 3 Scroll Feet	1216
Salver, George III, Shell, Piecrust Border, Footed, Engraved Lions, Flowers, E. Coker	7080

Salver, Triangular, Scrolling, Flowers, Engraved, William Peaston, c.1749, 10 ½ x 10 In.............	2128
Sauce, George IV, Shells, Flowers, Marked, IC, WR, 1820, 6 x 8 In., Pair ....*illus*	3949
Sauceboat, George II, Flower Handle, Etched Shells, 3-Footed, c.1745, 9 In.	944
Saucepan, Brandy, George II, Wood Handle, 3 x 6 ¾ In..	325
Saucepan, Shaped Handle, Bulbous Bottom, Bateman, 1815, 7 ¾ x 11 ½ In...............................	767
Serving Dish, Lid, Gadroon Rim, Hinged Handles, Oval, Benjamin Laver, 12 x 7 ½ In...............	719
Serving Spoon, George II, Back Tipt Handle, Richard Crossley, 13 ½ In...................................	153
Serving Trowel, George IV, Engraved, William Eaton II, 1829-30, 13 ¾ In. ....*illus*	492
Souffle, Liner, R. & Garrard & Co., c.1900, 5 x 7 ½ In., Pair...	1680
Soup, Dish, Gadroon Leaf Border, Crest, Motto, Marked W. Fountain, 1798, 11 In., Pair.............	1125
Spoon, Puritan, Round Bowl, Slip Top, Monogram, 1656, 6 ⅝ In...	1298
Stuffing Spoon, Engraved Dog, Hestor Bateman, 1786-87, 8 ½ In., Pair......................................	118
Stuffing Spoon, Ribbed, Monogram, 14 In.	560
Sugar Basket, George III, Reticulated, Latticework, Burrage Davenport, 3 ¾ x 3 ⅝ In...............	98
Sugar Box, George V, Snake Finial, Leaf Border, 4 Scrolled Feet, 5 In.	800
Sugar Castor, Flared Base, Perforated Top, John Eames, 3 ½ x 1 ¾ In......................................	144
Sugar Castor, Twisted Scroll Design, Pierced, Footed, 1898, 9 ¼ In...	269
Sugar, Lid, Rococo Cartouche, Initials SL, Samuel Taylor, 1772, 5 ½ In.	1800
Tankard, Domed Hinged Lid, Grotesque Mask Spout, Oval Cartouches, Scrollwork, 8 In.............	1900
Tankard, George II, Embossed, Cooke & Gurney, c.1760, 7 ¾ In.	2032
Tankard, George III, Cylindrical, Gadroon Lid, J. Langsland, J. Robertson, c.1760, 8 In.	2816
Tazza, Edwardian, Scrolled Handles, Stepped Base, 1906, 6 x 9 ¾ In.	413
Tazza, Reticulated, Pierced, Raised, 4 Scroll Feet, Goldsmiths & Goldsmiths, c.1900, 5 x 10 In....	608
Tea & Coffee Set, Wood Handle, Gadrooned, Joseph Rodgers & Sons, 8 ¾ In., 4 Piece.................	1400
Tea Caddy, Lid, George IV, Engraved Coat Of Arms, Round, c.1827, 5 ½ In.	900
Tea Caddy, Mask & Paw Feet, Chinese Figure Finial, George III, c.1812, 5 x 5 In........................	1625
Tea Set, George III, Teapot, Sugar, Creamer, Lobed, Ivory Handle, c.1820, 3 Piece.....................	813
Tea Set, Lobed, Angular Handles, Teapot, Sugar, Creamer, J. Deakin & Sons, c.1890, 5 In.	800
Teakettle, Stand, George IV Sterling, Dolphins, Chinese Man Finial, Eagle Spout, 16 In.	8000
Teapot, Embossed Band, Wood Handle, Finial, Bateman, 1801, 5 ¾ x 14 In..............................	365
Teapot, George III, Oval, Wood Handle, Finial, Reeded Foot, 6 ¼ In...	550
Teapot, Oval, Reeded, Wood Handle & Finial, S. Godbehere & E. Wigan, 1787, 7 In...................	644
Teapot, Stand, George III, Faceted, Henry Chawner, 1790, 5 ¾ x 6 ⅝ In. ....*illus*	837
Teapot, Stand, Round, Stepped Rim, Scroll Feet, 1795, 5 ¼ In...	236
Teapot, Stand, Wood Handle, Straight-Up Spout, Ivory Finial, 1785, 7 x 11 In..........................	5664
Teapot, Wood Handle, Finial, Inverted Gadroon, Beading, Round Foot, Victorian, 5 In..............	400
Toast Rack, 6 Slots, Wirework, Scroll Handle, Barnard, 1849-50, 5 x 6 In. ....*illus*	738
Tongs, Sandwich, Pierced, G.W. Adams, 9 ½ In.	266
Tray, 6-Sided Ribbon, Flower Border, Monogram, Handles, Gorham, 20 In.	1121
Tray, George IV, Gadroon, Shaped Oval, Crested, Wm. Bateman, c.1830, 23 In.	3360
Tray, George V, Oval, Pierced Gallery, Cutout Handles, Birmingham, c.1912, 25 In.....................	3125
Tray, Scalloped Rim, Encased Handles, Sheffield, 1897, 26 In..	2520
Trinket Box, Tortoise, Round, Inlaid Lid, Cabriole Legs, E.S. Barnsley, c.1915, 2 ¾ x 1 ½ In.......	150
Tureen, Lid, George III, 8-Sided, Badger Handle, Marked WS, 1797-98, 12 In. ....*illus*	13200
Tureen, Oval, Applied Husk Garlands, Footed, Reeded Loop Handles, c.1945, 13 In.....................	2500
Tureen, Sauce, Lid, Boat Shape, Pedestal Foot, Monogram, H. Bateman, 1782, 8 In...................	2242
Turkey Dome, Sheffield Plate, Handle, Lined, Engraved, Oval Platter, c.1880, 13 x 18 & 22 In...	180
Urn, George IV, Lid, Berry Finial, Acanthus Loop Handles, Ram's Heads, Ball Feet, 16 In.	2100
Urn, Regency, Lion's Mask Ring Handles, Wood Finial, Ball Feet, c.1820, 18 In...........................	472
Vase, Arts & Crafts, Woven Frog Lid, Hammered, 3 Handles, 1924, 5 ½ In. ....*illus*	1020
Vinaigrette, George IV, Scrolled Border, Gold Washed Interior, Flower Grill, 1 ½ In.	250
Wine Funnel, George III, Banded, Shaped Thumbpiece, P. & A. Bateman, 1794, 5 In.	936

SILVER-ETHIOPIAN

Cross, Coptic Shape, 8 ¼ In.	288

SILVER-FRENCH

Asparagus Server, Louis XVI Style, Pierced, Engraved, Scrollwork, c.1915, 11 In. ....*illus*	338
Beaker, Flared, Reeded Foot, Engraved Rene Chesneau, c.1900, 3 ½ In.......................................	330
Berry Server, Gilt, Scalloped Bowl, Reeded Handle, P. Berthier, c.1850, 9 ⅜ In............................	210
Bowl, Fruit, Globular, Wave Band, Waisted Foot, Beaded, Risler & Carre, c.1900, 5 x 7 In.	1230
Bowl, Oval, Wave & Swirl Shape, Scroll Feet, c.1885, 5 x 16 In...	1888
Bowl, Round, Swirl Design, Scalloped Border, 1900s, 2 x 8 ¼ In...	413
Bowl, Scrolled Handles, Engraved, Hearts, Fleur-De-Lis, Louis XV Coin, c.1775, 4 In...................	492
Box, Flowers, Geometrics, Niello, 3 In...	266
Box, Oval, Rocaille, Grisaille Painted, Putti Cartouches, Cobalt Ground, c.1890, 2 x 3 In.............	1408
Castor, Urn Shape, Reed Borders, Overstruck, c.1900, 6 ½ In. ....*illus*	413
Centerpiece, Rococo Style, Oval, Scrolling, Strapwork, Footed, 1800s, 7 x 20 In..........................	7170

Silver-English, Teapot, Stand, George III, Faceted, Henry Chawner, 1790, 5 ¾ x 6 ⅝ In.
$837

Neal Auction Co.

Silver-English, Toast Rack, 6 Slots, Wirework, Scroll Handle, Barnard, 1849-50, 5 x 6 In.
$738

New Orleans Auction Galleries, Inc.

Silver-English, Tureen, Lid, George III, 8-Sided, Badger Handle, Marked WS, 1797-98, 12 In.
$13,200

Skinner Auctioneers & Appraisers

Silver-English, Vase, Arts & Crafts, Woven Frog Lid, Hammered, 3 Handles, 1924, 5 ½ In.
$1,020

Skinner Auctioneers & Appraisers

Silver-French, Asparagus Server, Louis XVI Style, Pierced, Engraved, Scrollwork, c.1915, 11 In.
$338

New Orleans Auction Galleries, Inc.

Silver-French, Castor, Urn Shape, Reed Borders, Overstruck, c.1900, 6 ½ In.
$413

Brunk Auctions

Silver-German, Biscuit Box, Folding, Mechanical, Melon Shape, Cherubs, Paw Feet, 10 ½ x 11 In.
$2.990

Cottone Auctions

Clothes Brush, Art Deco, Silver Plate, J. Despres, c.1930, 3 x 5 In.	406
Coffeepot, Leaves, Buds, Hinged Lid, Shaped Ivory Handle, Maison Cardeilhac, 11 In.	1035
Coffeepot, Oval Shape, Palm Borders, Blossom Finial, Footed, c.1815, 8 ½ In.	590
Gravy Boat, Scalloped Rim, Wide Saucer Foot, Cartier, c.1950, 4 x 9 In.	944
Jewelry Box, Alexander The Great Portrait, Lion Finial, Inscribed L. Oudry, 6 x 8 In.	415
Pitcher, Ladies' Head Medallion, Flowers, Scrolls, Squat, c.1860, 6 In.	325
Platter, Art Deco Monogram, Wood Handles, Henri Lapparra, c.1925, 17 ¾ x 26 In.	3645
Salt Cellar, Double, Cast, Shell Shape Bowls, Gold Washed Interiors, Dolphins, Footed, 4 In.	2300
Serving Dish, Squared, Indented Corners, Applied Handles, Marked, 8 ¾ x 13 In., Pair	1323
Sugar Shaker, Repousee, Flowers, Swags, Scrolls, Monogram, 8 x 3 In.	391
Tureen, Lid, Armorial, Acorn Finial Squared Handles, Footed, c.1820, 10 x 14 In.	1659
Tureen, Urn Shape, Reeded Handles & Borders, Acorn Finial, c.1830, 12 x 15 In.	3068
Wine Cooler, Tulip Shape, Strapped, Satyr Handles, Medallions, 1800s, 15 x 9 In.	6250

SILVER-GERMAN

Basket, Honeycomb, Engraved Monogram, 10 ¼ x 7 ½ In.	184
Biscuit Box, Folding, Mechanical, Melon Shape, Cherubs, Paw Feet, 10 ½ x 11 In. ....*illus*	2990
Bowl, Inverted Bell Shape, Flared Rim, Domed Foot, Putti, c.1900, 8 x 12 In.	1353
Bowl, Oval, Reticulated Sides, Basket, Flowers, Paw Footed, Hanau, 10 ½ x 7 ¾ In.	242
Bowl, Rocaille Pierced, Engraved, Raised Feet, 10 x 4 In.	1150
Coffeepot, Dome Lid, Baluster, Wood Handle, Flared Foot, c.1773, 10 In.	1320
Dish, Condiment, Lid, Liner, Acanthus Border, Glass Insert, 7 x 4 x 3 ½ In.	196
Ewer, Pear Shape, Scroll Handle, Fluting, Cartouches, c.1900, 11 x 5 In.	1045
Goblet, Hunting, Parcel Gilt, Bell Shape Bowl, Gold Washed, Faux Bois Stem, Vine, 14 In.	1900
Jardiniere, Oval, Scroll & Flowers, Footed, Handles, 1900s, 6 x 16 In.	2360
Jardiniere, Seated Cherub, Rocaille Boat Shape, Footed, 13 x 11 In.	3300
Pitcher, Water, Bulbous, Reeded Rim, Wide Spout, High Loop Handle, 8 ¾ In.	600
Soup Ladle, Scroll, Flower Handle, 11 ½ In.	118
Tea Caddy, Repousse Flowers, Simon Rosenau, Bad Kissingen, c.1905	437
Teapot, Strapwork Panels, Engraved, Charlotte Hoffman, c.1865, 6 x 10 In.	443
Tray, Hammered, Handles, Oval, J.D. Schleissner, Sohne, 1900s	1000
Tray, Oval, Chrysanthemum Designs, Cutout Handles, Jugendstil, c.1905, 20 x 11 In.	1280
Trinket Box, Round, Cherubs, Flowers, Hanau, c.1900, 1 ½ In. Diam.	150

SILVER-INDIAN

Bowl, Elephant, Boat, Field Workers, Stamped Ruby House, 3 x 7 In.	768
Bowl, Figures, Fish, Flowers, Openwork Rim, Lobed Body, Footed, 5 In.	384
Fan, Hand, Repousse Flowers, Mythical Woman, Chains, Raised Panel, 14 x 8 In.	1150

SILVER-IRISH

Bowl, Swing Handle, Dragons, Flowers, Repousse, Birds, Leaves, Armorial, 13 In.	2000
Castor, Cylinder, Banded Gadroon, Pierced, West & Sons, 8 In.	649
Coffeepot, Leaf Cap, Fluted Spout, Berry Finial, Michael Cormick, c.1770, 12 In.	2160
Fish Server, George IV, Pierced Design, Engraved Armorial Terminal, 13 In.	425
Goblet, Cylindrical, Pierced Stem, Footed, Royal Irish Silver Co., c.1950, 6 ½ In., 6 Piece	2000
Gravy Boat, 3 Shell Legs, Scroll Handle, Matthew West, Dublin, 1790, 7 In.	702
Ladle, Scalloped Shell Shape Bowl, c.1762, 13 ¾ In.	500
Pitcher, Bulbous Base, Straight Sides, Gadroon Foot, West & Co., Dublin, 7 In.	510
Salver, George II, Oval, Shell & Scroll Rim, Hoof Feet, 1737, 1 x 7 In.	649
Sauceboat, George II, 3 Applied Feet, Scroll Handle, Mark GH, Dublin, 1700s, 4 ½ In.	375
Spoon, Downturned Fiddle Handle, Pointed Fins, 1808, 12 In.	413
Tray, Repousse, Chased, Openwork Rim, J. Moore, Dublin, 1835, 20 In.	10000
Waiter, Round, Gadroon Rim, Nude Man Crest, Charles Townsend, 1775, 7 In.	594

SILVER-ISRAELI

Paperweight, Frog, Figural, Beaded All Over, Lisham Art, 3 ¾ In.	461

SILVER-ITALIAN

Apple, Applied Stem, Leaves Top, Yellow Case Glass Base, A. Buccellati, 5 x 3 ¾ In.	216
Bowl, Hammered, Squat, Lobed, Flared Rim, c.1960, 4 ½ In.	188
Centerpiece, 6 Nautilus Shell Shape, Clamshell Base, Buccellati, 1900s, 14 In.	12000
Conch Shell, Coated, Marked Federico Buccellati, 2 ½ x 4 ½ In.	590
Entree Plate, Stepped Octagonal, Handles, Lid, Underplate, c.1950, 5 x 10 ½ In.	2596
Plate, Marked Allessandria, c.1950, 12 In., 8 Piece	3500
Spoon Warmer, Nautilus Shell Shape, Shell Feet, Ilario Pradella, 4 x 5 ¾ In.	2706
Toothpick Holder, Hedgehog Shape, c.1815, 2 ¼ x 3 In.	338
Tumbler Set, Hammered Rims, Bodies, Buccellati, Italy, 20th Century, 3 ¼ In., 12 Piece	3290
Vase, Grecian Style, Chilles, Ajax, Playing Board Game, 1968, 21 In., Pair	7670
Vase, Telato, Amphora Shape, Leaf Handles, Engraved, Mario Buccellati, 12 In.	5938

SILVER-JAPANESE

Censer, Domed Lid, Chrysanthemums, Enamel, Footed, c.1900, 5 ¼ In. ....*illus*	4612
Coffeepot, Dome Lid, Cylindrical, Tapered, Beetle, Flies, c.1880, 7 ½ In........................	5312
Compote, Openwork Flower Rim, Spread Pedestal Foot, 1900s, 5 x 10 In........................	413
Pitcher, Water, Ring Foot, Scroll Handle, c.1945...	812
Tea Caddy, Lid, Engraved Bamboo, Bird On Branch, Oval, c.1960, 4 In...........................	625
Teapot, Aesthetic Style, Hammered, Lid, Wrapped Bamboo Handle, Hallmark, 6 In............	450
Tray, Oval, Handles, Art Deco Style, Marked, Okubo, 1900s, 29 x 19 In............................	3304
Vase, Long Neck, Filigree, Applied Flowers, Enamel Blooms Panels, Footed, c.1900, 10 In..........	9375

SILVER-MEXICAN

Bowl, Cartouche Shape, Ring Foot, Marked, W. Spratling, c.1942, 2 x 6 In.	708
Bowl, Sterling, Lobed, 4 Ball Feet, Maker's Mark, 1900s, 16 In.....................................	840
Bowl, Swan Form, S Neck, Ribbed Base, Plateria Farfan, 17 x 11 In...............................	1035
Bowl, Wavy Rim, Tane Orfebres, c.1950, 8 ¾ In...	720
Coffeepot, Twisted Body, Wood Side Handle, 10 ½ In.	948
Cordial Set, Glass Cup, Overlay, Stem, Round Foot, Marked ELS Mexico, 3 ½ In., 12 Piece	150
Dish, Stylized Ivy Leaf, Stem Handle, 3 Ball Feet, 6 x 5 ½ In.	98
Ladle, Design On Handle Tip, Wavy Rim, F. Ramirez, c.1950, 6 ½ In.	120
Pitcher, Hammered, Inlaid Azure-Malachite Leaf, E. Castillo, c.1995, 11 ½ In. ....*illus*	2250
Pitcher, Water, Chased Flowers, Oval, Lobed, Scrolled Handle, 12 In.............................	720
Spurs, Inlays, Late 1800s, 3 ½-In. Rowels, Pair ....*illus*	288
Tea & Coffee Set, Bulbous Body, 4 Scrolled Feet, c.1950, 6 Piece	4250
Tea & Coffee Set, Squat, Fluted, Shaped Handles, 31-In. Footed Tray	5175
Teapot, Swan Spout, 6 ¼ In..	830
Tray, Gadroon Edge, Handles, Oval, 25 ½ In..	100
Tray, Handles, Raised Border, 25 In...	1500
Tray, Lobed Oval, Reed & Acanthus Rim, Spatulate Feet, c.1950, 33 x 19 In.	2337
Tray, Oval, 2 Square Handles, Lobed Rim, Marked, Monogram, 27 x 17 In......................	1534
Tray, Raised Border, Handles, Rectangular, 23 ½ In..	1375
Tray, Round, Molded Rim, Marked R.J., 1900s, 15 ¾ In..	560
Vase, Spiral Loved, Green Hardstone Collar, Los Castillo, Taxco, 8 x 6 ¼ In.	246
Wine Basket, 2 Braided Handles, Basket Weave Body, Flared Foot, Taxco, 1900s, 10 In..............	650

SILVER-MIDDLE EASTERN

Utensil, Slotted, Niello, Pierced, Flowers, 10 In.	236

SILVER-NORWEGIAN

Salt & Pepper, Mushroom Shape, Royal Blue Enamel Caps, White Dots, 1 ¾ x 1 ½ In..............	144
Salt & Pepper, Viking Horn Shape, Dolphin Bracket, 2 x 2 In.....................................	132
Tankard, Flower Scroll Medallion, Hinged Lid, Michel S. Refsnaes, c.1800, 6 In....................	750

SILVER-PERSIAN

Cup Set, Libation, Tray, Chased, Blossoms, Leaf Tips, c.1900, 1 ¾ & 10 In., 7 Piece	450

SILVER-PERUVIAN

Beaker, Stippled Ground, Applied Mayan Style Masks, Figures, 2 ¼ x 2 ¼ In.	63
Bowl, Frond Shape, Hammered, Marker's Mark, 24 In.	325
Cake Server, Reticulated Handle, Stamped, 8 ½ x 2 ¼ In..	138
Ice Bucket, Swirl Rim, Applied Handles, Round	325
Serving Bowl, Lid, Round, Hammered, 3-Footed, Handle Over Handle, 11 In.	675
Tray, Hammered, Round, Reeded Shaped Border, Welsch, Lima, 17 In.........................	768

SILVER-POLISH

Basket, Strawberry, Open Design, Swivel Handle, 7 ¼ x 1 ¼ In.	219
Cigarette Case, Enamel, Gilt Icons, Symbols, c.1935, 3 ½ In.	875

SILVER-PORTUGUESE

Basin, Rose Water, Flowers, Stippled Ground, Shaped Rim, Gadroon, c.1880, 2 x 16 In..............	2006
Centerpiece, Swan, Articulated Neck, Glass Eyes, David Ferreira, c.1950, 22 ½ In................	8750
Toothpick Holder, Pig On Openwork Platform, Footed Galleried Tray, Footed	466

SILVER-RUSSIAN. Russian silver is marked with the Cyrillic, or Russian, alphabet. The numbers 84, 88, or 91 indicate the silver content. Russian silver may be higher or lower than sterling standard. Other marks indicate maker, assayer, or city of manufacture. Many pieces of silver made in Russia are decorated with enamel. These prices are based on current silver values. Faberge pieces are listed in their own category.

Basket, Leaves, Blossoms, Lobed, Swing Handle, St. Petersburg, 1856, 11 ½ In............................	875
Basket, Lobed, Swing Handle, Moscow, 1862, 11 ½ In.	875

Silver-Japanese, Censer, Domed Lid, Chrysanthemums, Enamel, Footed, c.1900, 5 ¼ In.
$4,612

Neal Auction Co.

Silver-Mexican, Pitcher, Hammered, Inlaid Azure-Malachite Leaf, E. Castillo, c.1995, 11 ½ In.
$2,250

Rago Arts & Auction Center

Silver-Mexican, Spurs, Inlays, Late 1800s, 3 ½-In. Rowels, Pair
$288

Allard Auctions

S

Silver-Russian, Beaker, Tapered, Chased, Eagles, Branches, Marked, 1700s, 3 ½ In.
$813

Rago Arts & Auction Center

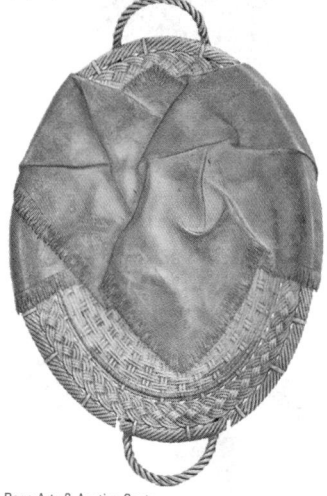

Silver-Russian, Cake Basket, Raised, Chased, Napkin, Gilt, Wire Feet, Khlebnikov, 1885, 15 ½ In.
$8,125

Rago Arts & Auction Center

Silver-Russian, Kovsh, Cloisonne, Beaded Border, Handle, Gold Wash Interior, 4 ½ x 12 ½ In.
$20,700

Humler & Nolan

Basket, Trompe L'Oeil With Folded Cloth, Round, Chased, c.1890, 6 In.	2000
Basket, Trompe L'Oeil, Oval, Handles, Chased Basket, Folded Napkin, Footed, 11 ½ In.	3000
Basket, Wavy Embossed Rim, Twining Handle, Shaped Foot, 1843, 4 x 11 In.	1080
Beaker, Tapered, Chased, Eagles, Branches, Marked, 1700s, 3 ½ In. ....*illus*	813
Box, Pink, Blue Enamel Flowers, 3 In.	1298
Cake Basket, Raised, Chased, Napkin, Gilt, Wire Feet, Khlebnikov, 1885, 15 ½ In. ....*illus*	8125
Cane Handle, Boar Shape, Chased Fur, Erik Kollin, c.1915, 5 In.	875
Chocolate Pot, Cylinder, Beaded Rims, Ebonized Wood Handle, Acorn Finial, 1789, 8 In.	1408
Cigarette Box, Niello, Farmer, Plowing, Geometrics, Flowers, c.1880, 4 In.	531
Cigarette Case, Gilt, Enamel, Scrolling Leaves, Multicolor, c.1890, 3 ½ In.	1320
Cigarette Case, Jeweled Crest, Enameled, Eagles, 2 ½ x 3 ½ x ½ In.	1800
Cigarette Case, Marked K. Faberge, Moscow, c.1900, 3 ¾ In.	4000
Cigarette Case, Moscow, Engraved Scroll, Flowers, c.1910, 4 x 5 In.	832
Cigarette Case, Niello, Kremlin, Arabesques, Medallion, Gold Wash, c.1886, 3 ½ x 3 In.	1440
Cup, Gilded, Niello, Round Medallions, Kremlin, St. Basil's, Strapwork, c.1883, 27 In.	2800
Egg, Enameled, Cloisonne, Imperial Coat Of Arms, Gold Washed Interior, 3 Chicken Feet, 3 In.	1100
Goblet, Laurel Wreath, Flowers, Text, Stepped Foot, c.1888, 6 In.	502
Jug Top, Cockatoo Shape, Nichols & Plinke, c.1900, 5 x 5 In.	1500
Kovsh, Cloisonne, Beaded Border, Handle, Gold Wash Interior, 4 ½ x 12 ½ In. ....*illus*	20700
Kovsh, Cloisonne, Flowers, Leaves, Gold Wash, Marked, 2 ¾ x 8 In. ....*illus*	4484
Kovsh, Cloisonne, Phoenix-Like Bird, Rope Edge, Marked, 3 ½ x 7 ¼ In. ....*illus*	11500
Kovsh, Enamel, Extended Prow, Hooked Handle, Multicolor, c.1900, 5 ¾ In.	6500
Kovsh, Gilt, Enamel, Flowers, Leaves, Multicolor, Spoon, 3 x 2 ⅝ In.	1020
Kovsh, Niello, Flowering Vine, Text, Spout, 1886, 5 ½ In.	3125
Salt Throne, Openwork Back, Flower, 3 ⅜ In.	354
Salver, Scalloped Rim, Faberge, 2-Headed Eagle, Engraved, c.1900, 14 In.	21250
Spoon, Gilt Sterling, Blue Enamel, 7 In.	180
Tea Strainer, Flower Rim, Handle, Marked, St. Petersburg, c.1860, 7 ⅝ In.	81
Teapot, Baluster, Scroll Handle, Spout, Applied Coat Of Arms, Grishin, c.1896, 7 In.	1024
Teapot, Engraved Crown, Ebonized Wood Handle, St. Petersburg, 1811, 9 ¾ In.	1375
Tongs, Maker's Mark Latin IAL, Gold Washed Interior, Tampers To Terminals, 1871, 5 In.	225
Vodka Cup, Enameled, Blue Ground, Leaf Framed Cartouche, Woodland Scene, 1800s, 2 In.	225
Waiter, Stepped Rim, Scrolls, Presentation Inscription, Handles, c.1861, 23 ½ In.	3540

SILVER-SCOTTISH

Bowl, Hand Tooled, Scalloped Rim, Hamilton & Inches, c.1880, 6 x 3 In.	406
Coffeepot, Fruits, Scrolls, Hexagonal Shape, Scroll Feet, Melon Final, c.1867, 9 ½ In.	944
Kettle, Stand, Bulbous, Lions, Dolphins, Coat Of Arms, 1700s, 16 x 10 In.	5850
Vinaigrette, Textured Argyle, Cartouche, Acanthus Grill, J. Nasmyth, 1836, 2 In.	702

SILVER-SOUTH AMERICAN

Cocktail Shaker, Hammered, Marked Arturo Medina, Columbia, c.1940, 11 In. ....*illus*	1599

SILVER-SPANISH

Pitcher, Owl Face, Feet, Swirled Amber Glass Body, Handle, c.1945, 11 In.	1140

SILVER-STERLING. Sterling silver is made with 925 parts silver out of 1,000 parts of metal. The word *sterling* is a quality guarantee used in the United States after about 1860. The word was used much earlier in England and Ireland. Pieces listed here are not identified by country. These prices are based on current silver values. Other pieces of sterling quality silver are listed under Silver-American, Silver-English, etc.

Basket, Flared Scroll Rim, Trumpet Shape, Round Foot, Flowers, 1906, 66 x 10 In.	472
Basket, Fruit, Openwork Rim & Foot, Fruit & Leaf Design, 1900s, 14 x 17 In.	2242
Basket, Repousse, Swing Handle, Grapevine, Marked, c.1910, 5 ¼ x 12 In.	639
Bonbon, Arts & Crafts, M. Carlberg, c.1932, 5 ⅝ In.	149
Bowl, Center, Repousse, Scrolling, Flowers, Scalloped Rim, Dome Foot, 12 In.	1840
Bowl, Grapevine Foldover Border, Red Flambe Base, 1900s, 4 x 13 ½ In.	472
Bowl, Monogram, Flared Rim, Lilies, c.1900, 11 ⅝ In.	300
Bowl, Openwork, Monogram, 6 ½ In.	85
Bowl, Pedestal, Engraved, Anthemion Border, c.1878, 8 ½ In.	299
Bowl, Rococo, Kidney Shape, Chased, Scrolled Legs, Masks, Footed, Unicorn Crest, 9 x 7 In.	518
Bowl, Rope Twist Border, Rolled Rim, 8 In.	240
Bowl, Round, Lion's Mask Handles, Shaped Rim, Putto Masks, Ring Foot, 1916, 6 In.	738
Bowl, Round, Shaped Rim, Reticulated Flower Banding, 1866, 3 ½ x 10 ½ In.	1353
Bowl, Sciarrotta, Stylized Leaves, Scalloped Edge, Ring Feet, Signed, 9 ½ x 4 ¾ In.	777
Box, Hinged, Oval, Relief, Flowers, Rococo Flourishes, Eagle Finial, Footed, 5 ½ x 4 In.	253

Box, Tobacco, Niello, Rounded Edges, Carved Arabesque Scrolls, Hinged Lid, 4 x 3 In.	575
Bucket, Overlay, Glass, Hammered, Multicolor Enamel, Swivel Handle, 5 x 5 ½ In.	207
Candelabra are listed in the Candelabrum category.	
Candlesticks are listed in their own category.	
Centerpiece Basket, Scalloped Rim, Pierced Flowers, Leaves, Vases, c.1900, 13 In.	1000
Centerpiece, Round, Flared, Reticulated Rim, Molded Foot, 12 In.	269
Chalice, Stem Cup, Gilt Wash Interior, Floral Swag, Empire Border, 9 ⅜ x 4 In., 12 Piece	8050
Charger, Armorial, Repousse Banding, Beaded Rim, 1902, 17 ⅞ In.	3585
Claret Jug, Crystal, Angular Handle, Leaves, 1909, 10 In.	492
Claret Jug, Glass, Scrolled Handles, Hinge Lid, Gold Wash, Lion's Mask, 1877, 10 In., Pair	729
Cocktail Pick Set, Crown Finial, Letter A On Shield, Box, 6 ⅛ In., 12 Piece	236
Coffeepot, Demitasse, Tapering Cylinder, Flared Base, Straight Neck, 7 x 3 In.	184
Coffeepot, Pear Shape, Crested Handle, Lid, Gooseneck Spout, 1931, 11 In.	1107
Coffeepot, Urn Shape, Square Pedestal Base, Hinged Lid, 9 ½ In.	185
Compote, Bowl, Medallion, Stirrup Handles, Domed Foot, c.1865, 5 x 11 In.	1230
Compote, Repousse Floral Rim, Hollow Base, Pedestal, 3 ¼ x 6 ¼ In., Pair	276
Compote, Scrolled Border, Gold Washed Interior, Handles, Lotus Leaves, 1900s, 7 In.	720
Creamer, Baluster, Ribbed Borders, Leaf Scrolled Handle, c.1825, 6 In.	210
Creamer, Egg & Dart Rim, Fluted Strap Handle, Squat, Pedestal, c.1800, 4 In.	239
Creamer, George III, 3-Footed, Applied Curved Handle, Engraved S.H., c.1766, 4 x 3 In.	201
Creamer, Georgian, Melon Shape, Leaf Handle, Acanthus Feet, Scroll Base, 1800s, 4 In.	246
Creamer, Oval, Angled Reeded Handle, Banding, Footed, c.1815, 6 ½ In.	540
Cup, Font, Edwardian, Gilt, Lobed Bowl, Trumpet Foot, Banding, c.1906, 5 In.	246
Cup, George II, 2 Scrolled Handles, Medallion, Engraved, Gadroon, 2 ⅝ In.	492
Dish, Condiment, Reticulated Frame, Engraved Flowers, Shell Feet, c.1900, 11 In.	240
Dish, Lid, Oval, Repousse Flowers & Leaves, Flower Loop Handle, c.1900, 8 In.	1800
Dish, Oval, Handles, Lobed, Reticulated, Dolphins, Lizards, Scroll Feet, 1903, 16 In.	660
Dish, Scalloped, Pierced Sides, Stamped Middle Eastern Hallmarks, 6 ¼ In., Pair	98
Dish, Shell Shape, 3 Dolphin Feet, Hammered, 4 ½ x 10 ¼ In.	679
Dresser Set, Tray, 2 Cut Glass Jars, Squat, Monogram, 4 ¼ In. & 6 ½ In.	150
Drinking Horn, Viking Style, Gold Washed Interior, Engraved, Bird Legs, c.1874, 5 In.	1107
Epergne, George V, Trumpet Vase, Reticulated Border, Scroll Arms, 1924, 13 In.	2032
Ewer, Pedestal Foot, Scroll Handle, Flowers, Leaves Repousse, c.1900, 15 In.	2440
Figure, Indian Chief, Seated, Holding Knee, 7 In.	1140
Flagon, Victorian, Domed Lid, Thumbpiece, Scrolled Handle, Ivory, Engraved, 11 In.	3240
Flask, Arts & Crafts, Curved, Hinged Screw Cap, Hammered Finish, 5 ¾ x 4 In.	246
Flask, Woman Smoking, Water Design, 5 ¼ In.	383
Frame, Repousse Birds, Flowers, Velvet Back, 20 x 16 In.	1180
Frame, Repousse, Vining Leaves, Cherubs, Curved Corners, Hinged Leg, 8 x 6 ½ In.	293
Goblet, Bell Shape, Tapered Stem, Stepped Foot, Beaded, 1860s, 6 ¾ In.	1230
Hot Water Urn, Apple Shape, Footed, Shaped Handle, Lid, Finial, c.1900, 16 In.	3540
Jardiniere, Swan Figure, Articulated Neck, Hinged Wings, c.1935, 17 x 22 In.	6150
Kettle, Hot Water, Tripod Stand, Hinged Handle, Wicker Wrapped, Engraved, c.1867, 12 In.	1380
Kettle, Stand, Rococo, Pear Shape, Scroll Handle, Shell Feet, c.1760, 17 x 9 In.	5166
Ladle, Leaf & Thread Design, Monogram, c.1865, 12 ¾ x 9 In.	215
Letter Holder, Leather Clad, Moire Pockets, Printed Blotter, Penholder, 6 ¾ x 10 In.	247
Liquor Decanter Labels, Scotch, Rye, Gin, Bourbon, 2 ¼ x 1 ¼ In.	144
Meat Skewer, George II, Ring To Terminal, Engraved Stag's Head Armorial, 11 In.	185
Menu Holder, Swan Shape, Hinged Flat Base, 3 ¾ x 8 x 8 ½ In., Pair	230
Muffineer, Stepped Base, 8 ¾ In.	124
Mug, Tapering Cylinder Shape, Putti, Dolphins, Scroll Handle, 5 x 4 In.	861
Napkin Rings are listed in their own category.	
Pheasant, Etched Feathers, Removable Heads, 6 ¼ x 17 ½ In., Pair	2124
Pitcher, Baluster, Shell & Leaf Banding, Leaf Handle, c.1835, 10 In.	492
Pitcher, Lobed Baluster, Flower Banding, Scroll Handles, c.1840, 10 In.	570
Pitcher, Martini, Glass Inset, 9 ½ In.	153
Pitcher, Oval, Wide Spout, Loop Handle, Acanthus Design, Marked, 1900s, 10 In.	590
Pitcher, Repousse Flowers, Bulbous, Wavy Spout, Square Handle, c.1910, 5 In.	2280
Pitcher, Water, Art Nouveau, Chased Repousse Water Lilies, c.1900, 9 ½ In.	2625
Pitcher, Water, Baluster, Waisted Collar, Crested Handle, c.1965, 8 ½ In.	584
Pitcher, Water, Bird, Fruit, Leaf Repousse, Monogram, T. Brogan, c.1920, 8 In.	3250
Pitcher, Water, Bulbous, Wide Spout, Acanthus Scrolled Handle, c.1900, 10 In.	660
Pitcher, Water, Paneled Shape, Scroll Handle, Pedestal Foot, 1931, 10 In.	956
Pitcher, Water, Reeded Ring Foot, Loop Handle, Monogram, 1939, 9 In.	480

Silver-Russian, Kovsh, Cloisonne, Flowers, Leaves, Gold Wash, Marked, 2 ¾ x 8 In.
$4,484

Humler & Nolan

Silver-Russian, Kovsh, Cloisonne, Phoenix-Like Bird, Rope Edge, Marked, 3 ½ x 7 ¼ In.
$11,500

Humler & Nolan

Silver-South American, Cocktail Shaker, Hammered, Marked Arturo Medina, Columbia, c.1940, 11 In.
$1,599

Cowan's Auctions

TIP

It isn't always smart to remove engraving from silver. A coat of arms or quality engraving can add to the value of antique pieces. We never remove engraving. If anyone asks we always say the initial belonged to a distant cousin.

Silver-Thai, Bowl, Repousse, Chased, Nobles & Deities, Leafy Scroll, 1800s, 7 x 8 ½ In.
$2,000

Rago Arts & Auction Center

Snow Babies, Figurine, Girl, On Roller Skates, Bunny Costume, Germany, c.1910, 4 ½ In.
$2,166

Theriault's

Snow Babies, Figurine, Girl, White Muff, Blue Coat & Bonnet, Germany, c.1910, 4 In.
$1,026

Theriault's

Pitcher, Water, Wide Spout, Scrolled Handle, Ring Foot, c.1915, 4 In.	390
Plate, Bread, Embossed Rim, 9 ½ In.	147
Plate, Bread, Reticulated Rim, 9 In.	113
Plate, Bread, Round, Plain Rim, c.1950, 5 ¾ In., 11 Piece	1230
Plate, Dessert, Monogram Center, Reeded Rim, 6 In., 12 Piece	540
Platter, Lid, Engraved Leaves & Flowers, Scrolls, c.1900, 13 ½ In.	690
Platter, Meat, George III, Oval, Gadroon, Coat Of Arms, c.1761, 16 In., Pair	4392
Platter, Oval, Serpentine, Scrolled Flower Rim, Monogram, c.1900, 21 x 15 In.	922
Platter, Round, Embossed Banding, Arabesque Cartouches, 13 ¾ In.	922
Powder Box, Tortoise Insert, Wreath, Round, 4 Cabriole Legs, c.1908, 3 ½ x 1 ½ In.	173
Punch Bowl, Ladle, Lid, Melon Shape, Scroll Handles, c.1850, 16 x 16 In.	7995
Punch Bowl, Pierced Rim & Foot, Flower Garland, Scroll, 1900s, 15 In.	4800
Rattle, 2 Bell Rows, Hinged Bail For Suspending, Coral Squiggle, c.1831	374
Salt & Pepper, Buddha, Seated, 2 In.	155 to 173
Salt & Pepper, Flower, Petals, Yellow Pink, c.1950, 5 ½ In.	159
Salt & Pepper, Mt. Fugi, Cherry Blossoms, Pagoda, Birds, Engraved, 3 In.	159
Salt & Pepper, Owl Shape, Enameled, 2 x 1 In.	161
Salt & Pepper, Pagoda Lanterns, Foo Dogs, 1950s, 3 ¼ In.	135
Salver, George III, Gadroon, Shells, Scrolls, Armorial, Ball & Claw Feet, c.1767, 15 In.	1722
Salver, George III, Shell Border, Coat Of Arms, Scrolled Feet, 9 In.	36
Salver, Round, Repousse Flowers, Basket Weave, Monogram, c.1915, 11 ¼ In.	584
Salver, Shell & Scroll Border, Monogram, 3 Scrolled Feet, c.1930, 10 ½ In.	400
Sauceboat, Oval, Scrolls, Shield, Arch Handle, Domed Foot, c.1865, 7 x 9 In.	1107
Sauceboat, Rococo Style, Scroll Rim, Wavy Spout, Footed, c.1910, 5 x 7 In.	418
Sauceboat, Stand, Turtleback Shape, Clover, Flared Edges, 1902, 5 x 9 In.	5166
Serving Bowl, Lobed, Foldover Scalloped Rim, 9 ½ In.	240
Serving Dish, Boat Shape, Leaf Relief Rim, Chased, Monogram, 14 ½ x 9 In.	776
Serving Spoon, Chrysanthemum, Gold Washed Bowl, Monogram, c.1900, 9 In.	196
Sherbet Cup, Saucer Shape, Waisted, Rolled Rim, Footed, 2 ¾ x 3 ½ In., 12 Piece	615
Soup, Dish, George III, Gadroon Border, Engraved Armorial, c.1815, 10 ½ In.	1020
Spoon, Bird's Nest, Gilt, Oval Bowl, Seated Bird, Feathers Splayed, c.1865, 10 In.	418 to 717
Spoon, Leaf Shape Bowl, Fruit Handle, Monogram, Gilt Wash, 1800s, 11 In.	123
Spoon, Souvenir, see Souvenir category.	
Sugar & Creamer, George III, Panel Shape, Grapes, Leaves, 1795, 6 In.	478
Sugar Basin, Spoon, Zodiac, Leaf Bands, Gilt, Fitted Box, Victorian, 1876, 3 x 4 ½ In.	660
Sugar, Spoon, Victorian, Zodiac Design Band, Gilt Interior, Fitted Box, c.1890, 2 x 4 ½ In.	660
Tazza, Victorian, Reticulated, Strapwork, Palmettes, Panther Heads, c.1853, 9 In.	1320
Tea & Coffee Set, Gold Washed Interior, Monogram, c.1920, 6 Piece	2500
Tea & Coffee Set, Plymouth, 9-In. Coffeepot, 5 Piece	1100
Tea & Coffee Set, Plymouth, Monogram, Paneled Urn Body, 13 ½-In. Kettle, 6 Piece	2300
Tea Caddy, George III, Bulbous Oval, Dome Lid, Ivory Finial, c.1800, 6 x 6 In.	1722
Tea Caddy, George III, Navette Shape, Banding, Reeded Handle, Lid, 1796, 7 In.	984
Tea Set, Plymouth, Monograms, Gold Washed Interior, c.1902, 7 Piece	1500
Teapot, Domed Hinged Lid, Vase Shape, Fluted, Flower Finial, c.1850, 11 In.	660
Teapot, George III, Engraved Armorial Crest, Monogram, Marked, SW, 1807, 11 In.	598
Teapot, George V, Gadroon, Elongated Neck, Squat Body, Ball Feet, c.1920, 8 In.	390
Teapot, Oblong, Gadroon Borders, Reeded Banding, Ball Feet, 1818, 9 In.	837
Tray, Asparagus, Monogram, Shell & Scroll Border, Pierced Inset Drain Tray, c.1901, 13 In.	650
Tray, Gadroon & Shell Handles, Scrolls, Flower, 1808, 32 x 19 In.	6871
Tray, George III, Oval, Reeded Rim, Handles, Acanthus Leaves, Mark, c.1793, 28 In.	4305
Tray, Oval, Cartouche, Monogram, Flower Rim, c.1900, 22 In.	1680
Tray, Oval, Chased Border, Handles, Wavy Rim, 26 x 6 In.	1495
Tray, Oval, Pierced Gallery, Cherub Handles, Repousse, c.1850, 20 x 15 In.	2091
Tray, Round, Shaped Rim, Openwork Border, Scroll, 1900s, 16 ¼ In.	885
Tray, Rounded Rectangle, Blossoms, Handles, Reeded Edge, 1900s, 18 x 11 In.	1652
Trinket Box, Repousse, Blossoms, Bamboo, Peonies, Hinged Lid, 1800s, 1 ⅛ x 4 In.	780
Trowel, Faux Handle, Engraved Blade, Presentation Dedication, July 1870, 14 In.	322
Tureen, Lid, Flower Repousse, Loop Handles, Lobed Ball Feet, 1882, 12 In.	1722
Tureen, Oval, Domed Lid, Pedestal, Gadroon Borders, Artichoke Finial, 12 In.	976
Tureen, Oval, Domed, Handled Lid, Oval Foot, Flower Repousse, 17 In.	3750
Tureen, Repousse, Flowers, Bead Rim, Stag Handles, Pedestal, c.1860, 16 x 9 x 11 In.	4062
Vase, Bellflower & Leaf Repousse, Shouldered, Spread Foot, Flared Rim, 24 In.	6435
Vase, Bud, Flared, Tapered, Footed, Presner, 7 In.	62
Vase, Bud, Trumpet Shape, Flared Rim, Cavetto Domed Foot, 6 x 1 ½ In., Pair	153
Vase, Scalloped Rim, Openwork Flower, Shell Base, Trumpet Shape, Monogram, 10 In.	438

Vase, Trumpet Shape, Octagonally Paneled, Cavetto Foot, c.1915, 16 x 3 ½ In.	246
Vinaigrette, George IV, Gold Washed, Monogram, Pierced, Scrolled Liner, 15 In.	780
Wine Cooler, Gadroon Urn, Handles, Masks, Bone Insulators, Pedestal Base, 15 x 10 In.	495

SILVER-SWEDISH

Centerpiece, Shell Flowers, Tree Trunk Standard, 1856, 12 ½ x 14 In.	2950

SILVER-THAI

Bowl, Repousse, Chased, Nobles & Deities, Leafy Scroll, 1800s, 7 x 8 ½ In. ....*illus*	2000
Cigarette Holder, Sterling, Niello, Black, Thai Dancer, Cartouche, Scrolling, 4 x 3 In.	58

SILVER-TIBETAN

Ewer, Design Embossed Reserve, Footed, 1800s, 12 ½ In.	2032

SINCLAIRE cut glass was made by H.P. Sinclaire and Company of Corning, New York, between 1904 and 1929. He cut glass made at other factories until 1920. Pieces were made of crystal as well as amber, blue, green, or ruby glass. Only a small percentage of Sinclaire glass is marked with the *S* in a wreath.

Bowl, Bengal Pattern, Signed, American Brilliant Cut, 3 ½ x 9 In.	325
Bowl, Cornwall, Flared, Singed, American Brilliant Cut, 4 x 10 ¼ In.	207
Bowl, Snowflake & Holly, Signed, 12 ¼ x 9 ½ In.	1400
Goblet, Wine, Engraved Floral Urn, Green Cut To Clear, Signed, Brilliant Cut, 7 In.	413
Teapot, Engraved Flower Garland, Lid, Signed, 5 x 9 In.	350
Tray, Assyrian & Engraved Pattern, Round, Signed, American Brilliant Cut, 10 ¼ In.	1121
Tray, Westminster, Signed, American Brilliant, 11 ½ x 7 ¾ In.	100
Vase, Pedestal, Flute Panels, Greek Key, Laurel Engraved, Signed, 12 In.	71

SKIING, *see Sports category.*

SLAG GLASS resembles a marble cake. It can be streaked with different colors. There were many types made from about 1880. Caramel slag is the incorrect name for chocolate glass. Pink slag was an American product made by Harry Bastow and Thomas E.A. Dugan at Indiana, Pennsylvania, about 1900. Purple and blue slag were made in American and English factories in the 1880s. Red slag is a very late Victorian and twentieth-century glass. Other colors are known but are of less importance to the collector. New versions of chocolate glass and colored slag glass are being made.

Amethyst & White, Pitcher, House, Lake, Canoe, Windmills, 6 ½ In.	36
Amethyst, Pitcher, Ribbed, Sawtooth Panels, Flowers, 5 In.	140
Caramel Slag is listed in the Imperial Glass category.	
Coffee & Cream, Compote, Herringbone Ribs, Scalloped, 8 In.	475
Green, Flower Bowl, Sunburst, Scalloped Edge, 5 x 2 In.	32
Pink, Sauce, Footed, Inverted Fan & Feather, Scalloped, c.1880, 4 x 2 In.	425

SLEEPY EYE collectors look for anything bearing the image of the nineteenth-century Indian chief with the drooping eyelid. The Sleepy Eye Milling Co., Sleepy Eye, Minnesota, used his portrait in advertising from 1883 to 1921. It offered many premiums, including stoneware and pottery steins, crocks, bowls, mugs, and pitchers, all decorated with the famous profile of the Indian. The popular pottery was made by Weir Pottery Co. from c.1899–1905. Weir merged with six other potteries and became Western Stoneware in 1906. Western Stoneware Co. made blue and white Sleepy Eye from 1906 until 1937, long after the flour mill went out of business in 1921. Reproductions of the pitchers are being made today. The original pitchers came in only five sizes: 4 inches, 5 ¼ inches, 6 ½ inches, 8 inches, and 9 inches. The Sleepy Eye image was also used by companies unrelated to the flour mill.

Creamer, Blue, White, No. 1	100
Pitcher, Blue Mountains, Tree, Cream Ground, 4 ¼ x 4 ½ In.	28
Pitcher, Blue Rim, No. 1, 4 In.	210
Pitcher, Blue Rim, No. 4, 8 In.	80
Pitcher, Blue Rim, No. 5, 9 In.	70
Pitcher, Blue, Gray, No. 1, 4 In.	140
Pitcher, Blue, White, No. 4, 8 In.	115
Pitcher, Blue, White, No. 5, 9 In.	110
Pitcher, Brown, Green, No. 4, 8 In.	190
Pitcher, Brown, White, No. 4, 8 In.	875
Pitcher, Tepees, Trees, Cream, Blue, Beaded Rim, 6 ¼ x 6 ½ In.	92
Sugar & Creamer, Blue, Tan, Sugar 3 ¼ x 3 ¼ In., Creamer, 4 x 4 ¼ In.	81

SLOT MACHINES *are included in the Coin-Operated Machine category.*

Snow Babies, Group, Blue Snow Children With Snowman, Incised 4587, c.1910, 5 In.
$1,482

Theriault's

Soapstone, Figurine, Beast, Inscription, Signed, Wu Chang Shou, Chinese, c.1900, 5 ¼ In.
$1,320

Garth's Auctioneers & Appraisers

Soapstone, Figurine, Li Tieh Kuai, Holding Vase, Carved, Stand, Chinese, 1700s, 5 ¼ In.
$1,304

James D. Julia Auctioneers

S

Soapstone, Vase, Phoenix, Chrysanthemums, Carved, Chinese, c.1910, 9 In.
$369

New Orleans Auction Galleries, Inc.

Souvenir, Cup & Saucer, Nassau, Gilt Highlights, Bone China, Royal Standard, England
$15

Ruby Lane, Inc.

Souvenir, Cup, Buick Motor Co., Flint, Mich., Factory, Porcelain, Gilt, Germany, c.1915, 2 ¾ In.
$70

Ruby Lane, Inc.

SMITH BROTHERS glass was made after 1878. Alfred and Harry Smith had worked for the Mt. Washington Glass Company in New Bedford, Massachusetts, for seven years before going into their own shop. They made many pieces with enamel decoration.

Smith Bros. Co.

Biscuit Jar, Cream, Daisies, Silver Plate Lid, 6 ¾ In.	59
Bowl, Melon, Happy Morn, Ribbed, Opal Body, Enameled Blossoms, Gold Accents, 3 In.	86
Fern Pot, Gilt, Enameled Flowers, Lobed, Metal Mount, 6 Feet, c.1885, 5 x 8 In.	219

SNOW BABIES, made from bisque and spattered with glitter sand, were first manufactured in 1864 by Hertwig and Company of Thuringia. Other German and Japanese companies copied the Hertwig designs. Originally, Snow Babies were made of candy and used as Christmas decorations. There are also Snow Babies tablewares made by Royal Bayreuth. Copies of the small Snow Babies figurines are being made today and a line called "Snowbabies" was introduced by Department 56 in 1987. Don't confuse these with the original Snow Babies.

Figurine, Boy & Girl, Blue Outfits, Eating Porridge, Germany, c.1910, 4 In.	1938
Figurine, Boy, Holding Stein, Barefoot, Germany, c.1910, 4 In.	224
Figurine, Children, Pushing Snow Roll, Blue, Germany, c.1910	1938
Figurine, Girl, Birds On Feeder, c.1875, 6 In.	448
Figurine, Girl, Boys, Sledding On Roof, Germany, 2 ⅝ x 2 ¼ In.	65
Figurine, Girl, On Roller Skates, Bunny Costume, Germany, c.1910, 4 ½ In. ....*illus*	2166
Figurine, Girl, Pushing Boy On Sled, Germany, c.1910, 5 In.	855
Figurine, Girl, Tree Stump, Muff, Bonnet, Pastel, Germany, c.1890, 4 ½ In.	616
Figurine, Girl, White Muff, Blue Coat & Bonnet, Germany, c.1910, 4 In. ....*illus*	1026
Figurine, Tinies, Tumbler, Raised Arms, Germany, 1920s, 1 ⅜ In.	45
Group, 3 Musicians, Germany, c.1910, 7 x 5 In.	392
Group, Blue Snow Children With Snowman, Incised 4587, c.1910, 5 In. ....*illus*	1482
Group, Boy, Girl, Pigs On Leash, Eating Clovers, c.1900, 4 ½ In.	672
Vase, Girl, Skiing Down Mountain, Germany, c.1910, 4 ½ In.	392
Vase, Girl, Skiing Through Trees, Germany, c.1910, 5 x 6 In.	448

SNUFF BOTTLES *are listed in the Bottle category.*

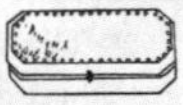

SNUFFBOXES held snuff. Taking snuff was popular long before cigarettes became available. The gentleman or lady would take a small pinch of the ground tobacco or snuff in the fingers, then sniff it and sneeze. Snuffboxes were made of many materials, including gold, silver, enameled metal, and wood. Most snuffboxes date from the late eighteenth or early nineteenth centuries.

18K Gold, Silver Rocaille Urn With Flowers, Gem Set, Hinged Lid, 4 ⅜ In.	5100
Brass, Wrigglework, Anchor, Tavern Accessories, J. Herbert, c.1850, 3 ½ In.	400
Porcelain, Gilt Metal Mounted, Bordered Multicolor Panels, Landscapes, c.1770, 2 ¾ In.	210
Ram's Horn, Mull, Silver Mount Lid, Thistle, Engraved, J. McGlashan Baker, 1800s, 2 ¾ In.	189
Silver, Engraved Flower Lid, Austria, 1 ¾ x 3 In.	70
Silver, Engraved Islamic Designs, c.1800, 3 ⅞ x 2 ¼ In.	480
Silver, George III, John Turner, 1807	179
Silver, Inscribed John Draker, Marked Baldwin Gardner, New York, 2 ¼ x 3 ¼ In.	652
Silver, Malachite, Enameled Insets, Tooled, Applied Star, Inscribed, c.1813, 3 x 2 In.	472
Silver, Repousse, Men Playing Game In Park, Hinged Lid, T. Shaw, 1818, 3 In.	575
Silver, Shoe Shape, Embossed Cherubs, Courting Scenes, Dutch, c.1890, 2 ¼ x 3 ¾ In.	182
Wood, Saddlebag Shape, Rolled Blanket, Hinged, Inscribed, 1882, 2 ¼ x 2 ¾ In.	501

SOAPSTONE is a mineral that was used for foot warmers or griddles because of its heat-retaining properties. Soapstone was carved into figurines and bowls in many countries in the nineteenth and twentieth centuries. Most of the soapstone seen today is from China or Japan. It is still being carved in the old styles.

Bookends, Oval, Carved Guanyin Figure, Lotus Flower, 6 ½ x 4 ½ In.	60
Box, Carved, Bamboo, 20th Century, 2 x 4 ½ x 11 In.	861
Figurine, 18 Luohan Figures, Pine Tree, Dragon In Mountain, Chinese, c.1900, 4 ½ In.	123
Figurine, Beast, Inscription, Signed, Wu Chang Shou, Chinese, c.1900, 5 ¼ In. .....*illus*	1320
Figurine, Buddhist Lions, Playing, Ball, Signed, 2 ⅜ x 2 ½ In.	777
Figurine, Emaciated Luohan, Curly Hair & Beard, Barefoot, Bamboo, 1900s, 6 ½ In.	840
Figurine, Fisherman, White, Standing, Holding Fish, Rockwork, Chinese, 11 In.	96
Figurine, Goddess Of Longevity, Seated On Deer, Mountain, Trees, 1900s, 12 x 8 In.	1230
Figurine, Guanyin, Black, White, Chinese, c.1900, 15 ¾ In.	1058
Figurine, Guanyin, Standing, Lotus Base, Praying Hands, White, Asia, 11 In.	360
Figurine, Li Tieh Kuai, Holding Vase, Carved, Stand, Chinese, 1700s, 5 ¼ In. .....*illus*	1304

Figurine, Seabird, Fish In Mouth, 8 In.	83
Figurine, Woman, Bird, Carved, Signed Tom Huff, 1989, 11 x 14 In.	125
Vase, Lotus Flowers, Leaves, Gray & Russet Color, 7 In.	480
Vase, Phoenix, Chrysanthemums, Carved, Chinese, c.1910, 9 In. ....*illus*	369

SOUVENIRS of a trip—what could be more fun? Our ancestors enjoyed the same thing and souvenirs were made for almost every location. Most of the souvenir pottery and porcelain pieces of the nineteenth century were made in England or Germany, even if the picture showed a North American scene. In the twentieth century, the souvenir china business seems to have been dominated by the manufacturers in Japan, Taiwan, Hong Kong, England, and the United States. Another popular souvenir item is the souvenir spoon, made of sterling or silver plate. These are usually made in the country pictured on the spoon. Related pieces may be found in the Coronation and World's Fair categories.

Badge, Olympics, 1908, London, Victory Profile, Wing, Blue Band, Silver Paint, 2 In.	4912
Badge, Rockaways Play Land, Enamel On Brass, Serial Number 000, 2 ³⁄₁₆ In.	173
Button, Boxer, Max Baer, Earle Week, Portrait, Black & White, 1 ¼ In.	176
Button, Clicker, I Chirp For Columbus, Arch City, Trollies, W&H Backpaper, c.1910, 1 ¼ In.	86
Button, Coney Island, The Great Coal Mine, Miner, Head Lamp, c.1910, 1 ¼ In.	173
Button, James Brown, Portrait, Say It Loud, I'm Black & I'm Proud, 3 ½ In.	115
Button, Rod Stewart, Faces, Concert Button, Red & White, 1971, 2 ½ In.	166
Button, Topeka's Third Annual Carnival, Woman In Sailor Suit, Mask, c.1900, 1 ¾ In.	115
Button, Tourist, Evans Plunge, Hot Springs South Dakota, Woman Diving, c.1960, 1 In.	75
Cup & Saucer, Nassau, Gilt Highlights, Bone China, Royal Standard, England ....*illus*	15
Cup, Buick Motor Co., Flint, Mich., Factory, Porcelain, Gilt, Germany, c.1915, 2 ¾ In. ....*illus*	70
Glass, Los Angeles Olympics 1932, Etched Discus Thrower, 5 ½, 4 Piece	250
Handkerchief, State Of North Dakota, Map, Cotton, Scalloped, 1950s, 13 ¼ x 13 ½ In. ......*illus*	10
Letter Opener, Alaska, Bone, Applied Carved Totem Pole, Painted, 1950s, 7 ⅛ In. ....*illus*	75
Match Safe, Alaska, Indian Totem Pole, Seattle, American Flag, 1 ½ x 2 ¾ In.	180
Match Safe, Loop Bar, Union Station, Seattle, Celluloid, 1 ½ x 2 ⅝ In.	180
Medal, Olympics, St. Louis 1904, Participation, Nude, Leaves, Sun, 8-Sided, Ribbon, 4 In.	30000
Pennant, Coney Island, Luna Park, Felt, Silk Screen, 1930s, 26 In.	185
Pennant, Coney Island, Steeplechase, Parachute Jump, Multicolor, 1920s, Set Of 3	115
Photograph, Aldrin, Autograph, 25th Anniversary Apollo 11 Lunar Landing, 15 x 19 In.	938
Plate, Yellowstone National Park, Scenes, Gold Band, American Ironstone, 10 ¼ In. ....*illus*	21
Spoon, Neil A. Armstrong, Apollo 11, NASA Logo, Stainless Steel, Community, 1969, 6 In.	1400
Torch, Olympics, 1980, Moscow, White, Yellow, Paint, Metal, 22 In.	2251

SPANGLE GLASS is multicolored glass made from odds and ends of colored glass rods. It includes metallic flakes of mica covered with gold, silver, nickel, or copper. Spangle glass is usually cased with a thin layer of clear glass over the multicolored layer. Similar glass is listed in the Vasa Murrhina category.

Basket, Cased Blue, White, Clear, Ruffled, Twisted Handle, 8 ¾ x 7 In.	140
Basket, Cased Cranberry Interior, White Exterior, Ruffled Edges, Twist Handle, 8 ½ In.	60
Bowl, Cased Cranberry Exterior, White & Floral Interior, Boat Shape, c.1890, 11 ¼ In.	277
Condiment Set, Rose Cased, Silver Mica Flecks, Silver Lids & Stand, 5 Piece	720
Cruet, Opaque Black, Gold Mica Flecks, Ruffled Edge, Shaped Handle, Stopper, 6 In.	144
Rose Bowl, Clear Cased Over Cranberry, Opal, Ruffled Rim, 4 In.	75
Rose Bowl, Cranberry, Crimped Edge, 3 ⅝ x 4 ¼ In.	135
Rose Bowl, Dark & Lime Green Cabbage Form, Gold Spangle, Ruffled, 6 In.	139
Rose Bowl, Egg Shape, Blue Opalescent, Ruffled Rim, 3 ½ x 4 ¼ In.	79
Rose Bowl, White Shaded To Pink, Silver Mica, Egg Shape, Ruffled Edge, 7 In.	29
Vase, Pink Over Cased White, Flattened Baluster Bottom, Crimped Edge, c.1890, 4 ⅝ In.	145
Vase, Pink, Green, Tan & Butterscotch Over White, Silver Mica, Ruffled, 12 In., Pair	138
Vase, Ruffled Rim, Melon Shape, c.1890, 7 ¾ In.	115
Vase, Shaded Pink Cased, Mica, Baluster, Swollen Neck, Flared Rim, 9 ½ In.	12
Vase, Yellow Cased, Aventurine, 6 ½ x 3 ½ In.	35
Vase, Yellow, Orange, Applied Floral Rigaree, Continental, 1880s, 6 ¾ x 4 ½ In.	195

SPANISH LACE *is listed in the Opalescent category as Opaline Brocade.*

SPATTER GLASS is a multicolored glass made from many small pieces of different colored glass. It is sometimes called End-of-Day glass. It is still being made.

Basket, Red, Blue, Yellow, Green, Clear Handle, 8-Scallop Foot, 6 x 4 x 7 In.	50
Bowl, Blue & White, Bubble Style Feet, 6 x 10 ½ In.	100

Souvenir, Handkerchief, State Of North Dakota, Map, Cotton, Scalloped, 1950s, 13 ¼ x 13 ½ In.
$10

Ruby Lane, Inc.

Souvenir, Letter Opener, Alaska, Bone, Applied Carved Totem Pole, Painted, 1950s, 7 ⅛ In.
$75

Ruby Lane, Inc.

Souvenir, Plate, Yellowstone National Park, Scenes, Gold Band, American Ironstone, 10 ¼ In.
$21

Ruby Lane, Inc.

Spatterware, Creamer, Cow & Calf, Sponged, c.1800, 7 ⅛ x 6 ¾ In.
$1,440

Skinner Auctioneers & Appraisers

S

Spatterware, Cup & Saucer, Red, 4-Petal
Blue Flower, Handleless Cup, c.1935
$240

Garth's Auctioneers & Appraisers

Spatterware, Mixing Bowl, Pouring
Spout, Multicolor, Spiral Ribs, 4 ¼ In.
$94

Conestoga Auction Co., Inc.

Spatterware, Plate, Peafowl, Paneled,
9 ¾ In.
$177

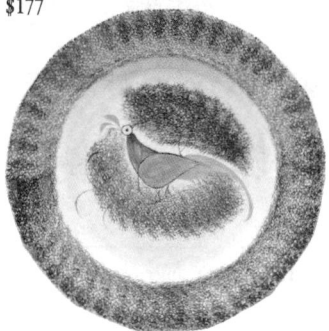

Conestoga Auction Co., Inc.

Spatterware, Plate, Rabbitware, Virginia
Rose, Rabbits In Car Transfer, c.1910,
9 In.
$1,080

Garth's Auctioneers & Appraisers

Bowl, Octagonal Star Shape, Applied Crystal Pincered Trial Rim, c.1890, 8 ½ x 3 ¾ In.	250
Cruet, Ruby, Opal, Tricorn Top, Applied Handle, Faceted Stopper, c.1883, 6 ½ x 3 ½ In.	299
Fairy Lamp, Yellow, Orange, Pink, Ribbed, White Cased Interior, S. Clarke, 5 x 4 In.	175
Pitcher, Cranberry, Clear, Pressed Fan Handle, Crimped Rim, Northwood, c.1890, 8 ½ In.	92
Pitcher, Water, Leaf Mold, Cranberry & Mica, Northwood, c.1900, 8 In.	207
Rose Bowl, Champagne, White, Applied Teal Festoon Rigaree, c.1890, 3 x 4 In.	65
Strawholder, Lid, Pink & White, Cased, Pleated, Northwood, 13 ½ In.	531
Sugar Shaker, Royal Ivy, Metal Lid, Northwood, 4 ¼ In.	235
Syrup, Cranberry, White, Applied Handle, c.1880, 5 ¾ x 4 ¾ In.	75
Vase, Cased Green, Yellow, Pink, White, Swirled Rib, Pulled & Folded Top, 5 ⅜ x 4 ½ In.	60
Vase, Pastel, Pink, Blue, Yellow, Applied Ruffled Rim, c.1910, 9 In.	125
Water Set, Leaf Mold, Canary, Cranberry, Pitcher, Tumblers, Northwood, 8 In., 4 In., 5 Piece	546

SPATTERWARE and spongeware are terms that have changed in meaning in recent years, causing much confusion for collectors. Some say that *spatterware* is the term used by Americans, *sponged ware* or *spongeware* by the English. Spatterware is creamware or soft paste dinnerware decorated with colored spatter designs. The earliest pieces were made in the late eighteenth century, but most of the spatterware found today was made from about 1800 to 1850. Early spatterware was made in the Staffordshire district of England for sale in America. Collectors also use the word *spatterware* to refer to kitchen crockery with added spatter made in America during the late nineteenth and early twentieth centuries. Spongeware is very similar to spatterware in appearance. Designs were applied to ceramics by daubing the color on with a sponge or cloth. Many collectors do not differentiate between spongeware and spatterware and use the names interchangeably. Modern pottery is being made to resemble old spongeware, but careful examination will show it is new.

Bowl, American & French Flags, Red, c.1840, 3 ½ x 6 ¾ In.	360
Bowl, Pitcher, Adams, Peafowl, Blue, Paneled, c.1830, 13 & 11 In.	480
Bowl, Thumbprint, Red, Green, Blue Rainbow, 1800s, 2 ¾ x 9 ¾ In.	415
Charger, Rabbitware, Rabbits, Frogs, Virginia Rose Border, c.1890, 12 ½ In.	180
Charger, Rose Center, Rabbit & Frog Border, c.1900, 13 In.	353
Coffeepot, Red, Blue Rainbow, c.1865, 9 In.	213
Coffeepot, Tulip, Yellow, Blue Stripes, 1800s, 9 In.	8295
Creamer, Black & Purple, 1800s, 4 ½ In.	213
Creamer, Cow & Calf, Sponged, c.1800, 7 ⅛ x 6 ¾ In. ....*illus*	1440
Creamer, Cow Shape, Brown, Black, 1800s, 4 ¾ In.	59
Creamer, Peafowl, Stick Spatter, 4 ½ In.	58
Creamer, Vine & Berry, On Green, c.1830	330
Cup & Saucer, 4-Petal Flower, Red, Blue, c.1865	152
Cup & Saucer, Blue Morning Glory, Handleless, c.1870	120
Cup & Saucer, Dahlia, Blue, Handleless, c.1870	185
Cup & Saucer, Peafowl, Blue, Tan, Red, Handleless	325
Cup & Saucer, Peafowl, Purple, Blue Rainbow, c.1860	334
Cup & Saucer, Rainbow, Red & Green, Handleless, c.1840	123
Cup & Saucer, Red, 4-Petal Blue Flower, Handleless Cup, c.1935 ....*illus*	240
Cup & Saucer, Rose, Blue & Purple, 1800s	207
Cup & Saucer, Shed, Blue Border, Handleless, c.1870	1440
Cup & Saucer, Thistle, Red & Yellow Rainbow, 1800s	516
Cup & Saucer, Tulip, Red, Blue, 1800s	365
Cup & Saucer, Yellow, Red Thistle, Green Leaves, Handleless	413
Cup, 2 Men On Raft, Purple, Handleless, c.1840	330
Mixing Bowl, Pouring Spout, Multicolor, Spiral Ribs, 4 ¼ In. ....*illus*	94
Mug, Red Strawberry, Blue Spattered X, c.1840, Child's	360
Pitcher, 5-Color Rainbow, Alternating Bands, Leaf Scroll Handle, 6 ¼ In.	1416
Pitcher, Adams Rose, Rainbow, Paneled, c.1830, 10 In.	720
Pitcher, Blue, White, Spongeware, c.1860, 9 In.	118
Pitcher, Burgundy, Pink, Blue Swirl, Cased, Crimped Rim, Reeded Handle, 7 ¾ In.	104
Pitcher, Buttermilk, Wild Rose Pattern, Blue, White, c.1920, 8 ¾ In.	92
Pitcher, Milk, 5-Color, Vertical Bands, Scalloped Top, Scrolled Handle, 6 ¼ In.	7080
Pitcher, Milk, Red, Green Vertical Rainbow Bands, Double Bulbous Shape, Loop Handle, 6 In.	295
Pitcher, Rainbow, 5 Colors, Molded Handle, Shell Molded Spout, c.1830, 9 In.	5700
Plate, Blue Border, Dahlia Center, England, c.1840, 8 ¼ In.	241
Plate, Bull's-Eye, Purple & Brown, 1800s, 7 ½ In.	326
Plate, Bull's-Eye, Red, Green Rainbow, 1800s, 9 ½ In.	304
Plate, Dahlia, Blue, 1800s, 9 ⅛ In.	243
Plate, Dahlia, Blue, Paneled, Red & Blue Flowers, Green Sprigs, 9 ¼ In.	295

Plate, Dahlia, Dinner, Purple, 1800s, 10 ¼ In.		668
Plate, Dahlia, Red, Green Rainbow, 8 ⅜ In.		178
Plate, Fort, Blue Paneled Border, c.1830, 9 ¾ In.		123
Plate, Fort, Blue, 1800s, 7 ½ In.		89
Plate, Hollyberry, Blue, 6 ½ In.		154
Plate, Peafowl, Paneled, 9 ¾ In.	*illus*	177
Plate, Rabbitware, Virginia Rose Stick Spatter Center, Rabbits, Frogs, Ironstone, Pair		236
Plate, Rabbitware, Virginia Rose, Rabbits In Car Transfer, c.1910, 9 In.	*illus*	1080
Plate, Rainbow, Red & Green, Alternating Bands, Bull's-Eye, 9 ½ In.		413
Plate, Rainbow, Red, Green, Bull's-Eye Center, c.1810, 8 ¼ In., 2 Piece		362
Plate, Red Peafowl, Blue, Green, Yellow, 9 ⅛ In.		71
Plate, Rose Border, Rabbits Playing Baseball, Eng., Marked, c.1900, 9 ½ In.		823
Plate, Scalloped Edge, Circles Design, Rainbow, Impressed, c.1835, 8 In.		121
Plate, Soup, Blue Peafowl, Blue, Tan, Red, 1 ½ In.		130
Plate, Tulip, c.1850, 8 ¼ In.		296
Plate, Tulip, Red Outline, Paneled Yellow Border, c.1935, 8 ½ In.	*illus*	4920
Plate, Tulip, Yellow & Blue, 1800s, 8 ⅜ In.		1659
Plate, Yellow Acorns, Leafy Branches, Red Border, Shaped Rim, c.1835, 8 In.		1116
Platter, Holly Berry, Blue, Scalloped Edge, c.1830, 12 ¾ x 16 In.		615
Platter, Peafowl, Red, Green, Blue, Oval, 11 ½ x 14 ½ In.		577
Platter, Purple, Octagonal, c.1870, 12 x 16 In.		154
Platter, Rainbow, Blue & Purple, 8-Sided, Marked, 12 x 15 ¾ In.	*illus*	338
Platter, Red Peafowl, Blue, Yellow, Green, Incised Feather Border, 9 ¼ In.		708
Platter, Rose Center, Rabbit & Frog Border, England, c.1900, 10 x 14 ½ In.		529
Platter, Rose, Red, Blue, c.1850, 9 ½ x 12 ¼ In.		356
Soup, Dish, Tulip, Purple & Blue, 10 ⅝ In.		207
Sugar, Lid, Rooster, Purple Band, c.1850, 4 ¾ In.		207
Sugar, Purple, Teal, Green Rainbow, Paneled, Splayed Finial, Open Handles, Flared Foot, 8 In.		561
Teapot, Lid, Handle, Tulip Stick Spatter, 8 In.		29
Teapot, Lid, Vertical Red, Blue Bands, Staffordshire, c.1890, 9 In.		288
Teapot, Red, Green Rainbow, c.1850, 9 ½ In.		356
Teapot, Rose, Blue, 6 ¼ In.		356
Teapot, Schoolhouse, Green Paneled, c.1840, 8 ½ In.		904

SPELTER is a synonym for a zinc alloy. Figurines, candlesticks, and other pieces were made of spelter and given a bronze or painted finish. The metal has been used since about the 1860s to make statues, tablewares, and lamps that resemble bronze. Spelter is soft and breaks easily. To test for spelter, scratch the base of the piece. Bronze is solid; spelter will show a silvery scratch.

Bust, Black Woman, Smiling, Wide Pink Hat, Signed, Ch Masse, c.1905, 26 In.		1920
Card Tray, Seminude Maiden, Brass Poppy Leaves, Flower Base, c.1890, 6 x 9 ½ In.		173
Sculpture, Angel, Winged, Cross, Column, c.1900, 23 x 8 In., Pair		138
Sculpture, Bismarck, Bronze Patina, Stone Base, 5 x 15 In.	*illus*	630
Sculpture, Black Minstrel, Playing Banjo, Cold Painted, c.1910, 8 x 6 In.	*illus*	826
Sculpture, Buffalo, Marble Base, c.1890, 14 x 21 In.		1215
Sculpture, Dog, Hunting, 10 x 22 In.		308
Sculpture, Fisherman Pulling Net, Green Patina, Green Onyx & Black Marble Base, 21 x 25 In.		711
Sculpture, Man, Dancing, Wearing Large Hat, 11 In.		119
Sculpture, Man, Fencer, Sword, Green Patina, Black Pedestal, Ch. Masse, c.1890, 24 x 9 In., Pair		690
Sculpture, Woman, Classical, Standing, Holding Wheat, Olive Branch, c.1900, 32 In.		875
Sculpture, Woman, Holding Snake, Bronze Patina, Wood Base, c.1905, 17 x 6 In.		184

SPINNING WHEELS in the corner have been symbols of earlier times for the past 100 years. Although spinning wheels date back to medieval days, the ones found today are rarely more than 200 years old. Because the style of the spinning wheel changed very little, it is often impossible to place an exact date on a wheel.

Mahogany, Brass, Inscribed S Thorp Abberley Inv., c.1790, 47 ½ In.		1659
Mixed Woods, Blue Paint, Initialed JJW, 1875, 43 ½ In.	*illus*	450
Mixed Woods, Turned Spindles, Signed I. Hook, c.1835, 56 x 45 In.		219
Model, Bone, Jenny, 2 Women, Wheel, Windmill, Prisoner Of War Carved, c.1810, 6 x 3 In.		1652
Niddy Noddy, Maple, Heart Cutouts, 1800s, 17 ¾ In.		92
Oak, Castle Shape, Stamped J. Sturtevant, c.1850, 57 In.		360
Pine, Multicolor Paint, Green, Orange, Red, Rev. Jacob Ariener, c.1850, 50 In.		764
Wood, Ebonized, Bone Finials, c.1850, 46 In.		152
Wood, Yellow Paint, c.1890, 51 x 46 In.		118

Spatterware, Plate, Tulip, Red Outline, Paneled Yellow Border, c.1935, 8 ½ In. $4,920

Garth's Auctioneers & Appraisers

Spatterware, Platter, Rainbow, Blue & Purple, 8-Sided, Marked, 12 x 15 ¾ In. $338

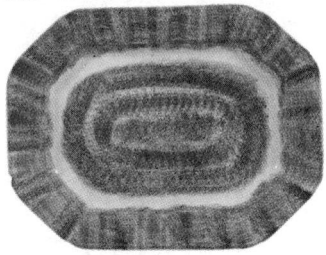

Garth's Auctioneers & Appraisers

TIP
Rub soap on noisy door hinges.

Spelter, Sculpture, Bismarck, Bronze Patina, Stone Base, 5 x 15 In. $630

The Stein Auction Co.

S

Spelter, Sculpture, Black Minstrel, Playing Banjo, Cold Painted, c.1910, 8 x 6 In.
$826

Brunk Auctions

Spinning Wheel, Mixed Woods, Blue Paint, Initialed JJW, 1875, 43 ½ In.
$450

Garth's Auctioneers & Appraisers

Sports, Baseball, Figure, Chalk, Rittgers, 1939, Set of 3, 7 In., 6 ½ In.
$236

Victorian Casino Antiques

Sports, Baseball, Button, Frank Chance, New York Yankees, May 11th, 1913, 1 In.
$350

Hake's Americana & Collectibles

SPODE pottery, porcelain, and bone china were made by the Stoke-on-Trent factory of England founded by Josiah Spode about 1770. The firm became Copeland and Garrett from 1833 to 1847, then W.T. Copeland or W.T. Copeland and Sons until 1976. It then became Royal Worcester Spode Ltd. The company was bought by the Portmeirion Group in 2009. The word *Spode* appears on many pieces made by the factories. Most collectors include all the wares under the more familiar name of Spode. Porcelains are listed in this book by the name that appears on the piece. Related pieces may be listed under Copeland, Copeland Spode, and Royal Worcester.

Cup & Saucer, Red Plants, Cream Ground, 12 Piece	188
Pitcher, Fortuna, Pale Green, 7 In.	34
Plate, Bread & Butter, Stafford Flowers, 6 ⅛ In., 12 Piece	360
Plate, Flowers, Basket, Cobalt Blue Ground, Shaped Gilt Rim, c.1945, 10 ¾ In., 12 Piece	708
Plate, Hunting, Camilla Shape, Plum Border, 11 In., 12 Piece	133
Plate, Thanksgiving, Center Turkey, Orange, Flower, Fruit Border, 10 ¾ In., 12 Piece	325
Tureen, Ancient Rome, Blue, White, Handles, 14 In.	63
Tureen, Lid, Underplate, Feldspar, Houses, Flowers, Branch Handles, c.1830, 13 ½ In.	1250

SPORTS equipment, sporting goods, brochures, and related items are listed here. Items are listed by sport. Other categories of interest are Bicycle, Card, Fishing, Sword, Toy, and Trap.

Baseball, Ball, Autographed, Connie Mack, 1941	160
Baseball, Ball, Autographed, Joe Sewell, 1970s	100
Baseball, Ball, Autographed, Whitey Ford, Case	62
Baseball, Bat, Joe DiMaggio Little League, Louisville Slugger, H & B, 1950s, 32 In.	96
Baseball, Bat, Mickey Mantle Little League, Triple Crown, Wood, H & B, 28 In.	24
Baseball, Button, Bobby Shantz, Philadelphia Athletics, Ribbon, Ball & Bat, 1950s, 1 ¾ In.	104
Baseball, Button, Duke Snider, Brooklyn Dodgers, Ribbon, Celluloid, 1950s, 1 ¾ In.	106
Baseball, Button, Frank Chance, New York Yankees, May 11th, 1913, 1 In. ......*illus*	350
Baseball, Button, Frank Malzone, Boston Red Sox, Portrait, 1960s, 1 ¾ In.	98
Baseball, Button, Gene Woodling, New York Yankees, Ribbon, 1950s, 2 ½ In. ......*illus*	266
Baseball, Button, Geo. Walker, Roslindale Day, Baseball Shape, c.1913, 1 In.	753
Baseball, Button, Gil Hodges, Brooklyn Dodgers, Portrait, Ribbon, Celluloid, 1950s, 1 ¾ In.	86
Baseball, Button, James Gilliam, Brooklyn Dodgers, Ribbon, Ball & Bat, 1950s, 1 ¾ In.	344
Baseball, Button, Mickey Mantle, Batting, Portrait, Black & White, 1950s, 1 ¾ In.	95
Baseball, Button, St. Louis Cardinals, Pennant, Multicolor, 1926, 1 ¼ In.	95
Baseball, Button, Ty Cobb, Tigers, Round, Sepia, Celluloid, Sweet Caporal	210
Baseball, Button, World Series Yankees, Beat Dem Bums, White, Red, Blue, 1947, 2 ⅛ In.	230
Baseball, Figure, Chalk, Rittgers, 1939, Set of 3, 7 In., 6 ½ In. ......*illus*	236
Baseball, Jersey, Bob Turley, Autographed, 1958 N.Y. Yankee MVP Pitcher	107
Baseball, Nodder, Mickey Mantle, Round Base, Box, 1966	592
Baseball, Pennant, Brooklyn Dodgers, Hitter, Cranberry, Yellow, Felt, 1940s, 22 In.	165
Baseball, Pennant, N.Y. Yankees, Sliding Players, Blue, White, Felt, 1940s, 11 x 28 In.	200
Baseball, Pennant, St. Louis Browns, Brownie, Brown, Yellow, Felt, 1940s, 11 x 28 In.	59
Baseball, Photograph, Babe Ruth, Boston Braves, Spring Training, Batting, 1935, 7 x 9 In.	115
Baseball, Photograph, Tampico Alijadores, A. Marsans, Mexican League, c.1946, 8 x 10 In.	1139
Baseball, Pocket Watch, Dizzy Dean, Everbrite Watch Co., Box, 1935	1990
Baseball, Press Pin, World Series, Cleveland Indians, Arrowhead, Enamel, Brass, 1948, 1 ¼ In.	190
Baseball, Program, All-Star Game, Autographed, Babe Ruth, Joe Vosmik, June 2, 1935	1777
Baseball, Roller Skates, Ted Williams, Ted's Picture On Box, Sears, c.1960, 10 x 7 In.	2700
Baseball, Sign, Phil. Athletics 1929 World Champions, Elephant On Ball, Copper, 22 In.	604
Baseball, Stadium Seat, Akron Aeros, Canal Park, Ohio, 20th Century, 33 x 23 x 20 In.	84
Baseball, Stadium Seat, Comiskey Park, Wood, Metal, Paint, Folding, c.1919, 15 x 32 In.	592
Baseball, Watch, Babe Ruth Smiling, Holding Bats, 1949, 1 ¼ In.	153
Billiard, Table, Snooker, Monarch, Brunswick-Balke-Collender, Cherry, c.1900, 5 x 9 Ft. ...*illus*	1824
Boxing, Glove, Autographed, George Foreman, Red, Everlast, Pair	122
Boxing, Glove, Autographed, Muhammad Ali, Red, Everlast	716
Canoe, Fiberglass, Cedar Strip, Cane Seat, Laughing Loon, Maine, 14 Ft. 6 In.	885
Cricket, Bat, Teams Autographed, Eng. Vs. Australia, Wood, Yellow, c.1965, Full Size	81
Football, Helmet, Leather, c.1915	243
Football, Pennant, Detroit Lions, 1950s, 29 In.	85
Football, Program, Harvard Vs. Carlisle, American Indian Image, 1911, 5 ½ x 8 ½ In.	614
Football, Ring, NFL Players Association, Eagle, Helmet, 10K Gold, Green Stone, c.1970, Size 11 ¼	668
Horse Racing, Poster, Turf & Sports Digest, Man & Woman, Racing Forms, 27 x 21 In.	605
Horse Racing, Tumbler, Kentucky Derby, Headless Jockey, 1956, 5 ¼ In. ......*illus*	1661
Hunting, Duck Call, Mallard Head Shape, Glass Eyes, Natural Duck Call Mfg., c.1930, 7 In.	288
Hunting, Poster, Winchester Self-Loading Shotguns, Retriever, c.1907, 15 x 26 In. ......*illus*	3851
Hunting, Whistle, Grizzly Bear Tooth, 1800s, 4 In.	165

Indian Club, Wood, 23 In., Pair		81
Pool, Balls, Numbered, Composition, Paint, In Redware Pan, 21 Piece		180
Pool, Table, Brunswick, Fister, Mahogany, Green Felt, Patented 1893, 9 Ft.		23500
Pool, Table, Mahogany, Turned Legs, Maroon Felt, Fringed Corner Pockets, 8 Ft.		4500
Shooting, Carnival Target, Buffalo Shape, White, Gray Paint, Wood Base, c.1950, 19 x 21 In.		1416
Skating, Ice Skates, Iron, Walnut, Spade Tip, 1800s, 13 In., Pair		150
Skating, Ice Skates, Peggy Fleming, Etched Signature On Blades, Harlick	*illus*	3050
Snowshoes, Wood Frame, Sinew Webbing, Adjustable Leather Shoe Harness, 37 ½ In.		177
Snowshoes, Wood, Leather, Paddle Shape, Pair		150
Snowshoes, Wood, Leather Webbing, Pair		46
Soccer, Ball, 1958 English Football Association Cup Final, Leather, Yellow		8597
Soccer, Program, 1927 English Football Association Cup Final, Daily News		1535
Wrestling, Handbook, U.S. Navy, 1943		70

STAFFORDSHIRE, England, has been a district making pottery and porcelain since the 1700s. Hundreds of kilns are still working in the area. Thousands of types of pottery and porcelain have been made in the many factories that worked and still work in the area. Some of the most famous factories have been listed separately, such as Adams, Davenport, Ridgway, Rowland & Marsellus, Royal Doulton, Royal Worcester, Spode, Wedgwood, and others. Some Staffordshire pieces are listed under categories like Fairing, Flow Blue, Mulberry, Shaving Mug, etc.

Basket, Cream Color, Pierced, Twisted Bail Handle, Scallop Rim, c.1760, 9 In.		1599
Basket, Creamware, Pierced, Handles, 8-Sided, Shorthose & Co., c.1820, 2 x 11 In.		288
Basket, Eddistone Lighthouse, Reticulated, Handles, Blue, 1800s, 3 ½ x 11 In.		1896
Basket, Underplate, Boston State House, Reticulated, Oval, 1800s, 4 x 10 ½ In.		486
Bowl, English Castle Scene, Blue, 12 ¼ In.		357
Bowl, Fence & Peony, Salt Glaze, Round Foot, Interior Rim Border, c.1760, 9 In.		480
Bowl, New York Alms House, Blue, 1800s, 2 x 10 In.		148
Bowl, Peony & Fence Pattern, Salt Glaze, c.1750, 5 ⅝ In.		330
Bowl, Porridge, America & Independence, Blue, Impressed Clews, 1800s, 7 ⅞ In.		122
Bowl, Scratch Blue, Incised, Tasseled Drapery Swags, Salt Glaze, c.1760, 5 In.		2400
Bowl, View Near Philadelphia, Blue, 1800s, 9 ¾ In.		267
Bowl, View Of Albany, Blue, Enoch Wood & Sons, 2 ¾ x 11 In.		4266
Bowl, Windowpane Design, Salt Glaze, c.1770, 9 In.		395
Bust, Fowler's Phrenology, Brown Print, Blue Enamel Trim, Tilted, Inscribed, 1800s, 11 ½ In.		475
Bust, George Washington, Uniform, Square Pedestal Base, 1800s, 8 ¼ In.		150
Bust, Handel, Multicolor Glaze, Stepped Plinth, R. Wood, England, c.1770, 8 ½ In.		1035
Bust, Hercules, Lion Skin To Shoulder, Pink Luster Socle, c.1850, 14 In.		688
Chamber Pot, Lid, Lafayette At Franklin's Tomb, 1800s, 8 x 8 ½ In.		1304
Chamber Pot, Lid, Views Of The Erie Canal, Molded Handle, c.1835, 8 ½ In.	*illus*	2160
Coffeepot, Black Transfer, Tea Party, Shepherd On Reverse, 10 ¼ In.	*illus*	246
Coffeepot, Dome Lid, Flowers, Leaves, Blue Transfer, Pedestal Foot, c.1830, 11 ⅜ In.		104
Coffeepot, Franklin's Tomb, Dark Blue Transfer, Acorn Finial, c.1850, 11 ½ In.		690
Coffeepot, Lid, Eagle, Spread Wings, Blue, 1800s, 11 ½ In.		1304
Coffeepot, Lid, Elongated Pear Shape, Entwined Handle, Reeded Spout, c.1770, 9 In.		600
Coffeepot, Lid, Leaf Handle, Reeded Spout, Relief Fruit Baskets, c.1760, 8 In.		1800
Coffeepot, Lid, Washington At Tomb, 1800s, 11 In.		2015
Compote, Landing Of Lafayette, Blue, Impressed Clews, 1800s, 4 ¾ x 10 In.		1126
Creamer, Agate, Pear Shape, 3 Lion Masks & Paw Feet, Lion Knop, c.1750, 6 ½ In.	*illus*	3120
Creamer, Boston State House, Angled Handle, Blue, 1800s, 5 ⅞ In.		213
Creamer, Calf, Spattered Ocher & Brown, Green Rectangular Base, c.1775, 6 ⅛ In.		861
Creamer, Cow Shape, Standing, Brown Patches, Milkmaid, c.1790, 6 In.		390
Creamer, Cow, Milkmaid, Sponged, Glazed Base, Late 1700s, 6 ⅞ In.	*illus*	800
Creamer, Lid, Pear Shape, Heart Shape Flower Cartouche, Crosshatch, c.1780, 5 In.		492
Creamer, Milkmaid, Black, White, Sponged, Stepped Base, 1800s, 6 ½ In.		180
Creamer, Molded Scrolls, Basket Weave, Strap Handle, c.1765, 2 x 6 In.		431
Creamer, New York City Hall, Blue, 1800s, 5 In.		30
Creamer, New York Hospital, Blue, 1800s, 5 In.		516
Creamer, Peacock Shape, Cream Color, Green, Yellow, Manganese, c.1770, 4 In.		240
Creamer, Pear Shape, Shell, Lion Mask & Paw Feet, Blue & White, c.1750, 3 In.		1020
Creamer, Sponged Black & Magenta, Milkmaid, Raised Octagonal Base, c.1800, 6 In.		390
Creamer, Sponged Black & Ocher, Reclining Calf, Octagonal Base, 1700s, 6 ¼ In.		660
Cup & Saucer, University Of Maryland, Maryland Scenes, Blue & White, c.1830, 2 x 6 In.		1150
Cuspidor, Woman's, Boston State House, Blue Transfer, Handle, Spout, 1800s, 4 In.		7110
Dessert Service, Bagdad, Transfer, Cobalt Blue, Red, Turquoise, 12 Plates, 2 Dishes, 9 In.		330
Dish, Basket Weave, Cartouche, Trellis, c.1770, 11 In.		780
Dish, Game Pie, Lid, Hen & Chicks, Painted, 11 In.		1920

Sports, Baseball, Button, Gene Woodling, New York Yankees, Ribbon, 1950s, 2 ½ In. $266

GENE WOODLING

Hake's Americana & Collectibles

Sports, Billiard, Table, Snooker, Monarch, Brunswick-Balke-Collender, Cherry, c.1900, 5 x 9 Ft. $1,824

Showtime Auction Services

Sports, Horse Racing, Tumbler, Kentucky Derby, Headless Jockey, 1956, 5 ¼ In. $1,661

Cowan's Auctions

S

Sports, Hunting, Poster, Winchester Self-Loading Shotguns, Retriever, c.1907, 15 x 26 In.
$3,851

James D. Julia Auctioneers

Sports, Skating, Ice Skates, Peggy Fleming, Etched Signature On Blades, Harlick
$3,050

Clars Auction Gallery

Staffordshire, Chamber Pot, Lid, Views Of The Erie Canal, Molded Handle, c.1835, 8 ½ In.
$2,160

Garth's Auctioneers & Appraisers

Dish, Leaf, Arms Of South Carolina, Blue, 1800s, 16 x 5 ½ In.	3081
Dish, Lid, Esplanade, Castle Garden Battery, New York, Blue, Lid, 1800, 9 x 11 In.	385
Dog, Spaniel, Seated, Red, White, c.1860, 7 ¼ In., Pair	360
Figurine, Archer, Woman, Holding Arrow, Yellow Target Behind, c.1780, 6 In.	288
Figurine, Ben Franklin, Blue Waistcoat, Tricorner Hat, c.1820, 16 In.	474
Figurine, Blacksmith, Flat Back, c.1885, 16 ½ x 7 In.	492
Figurine, Cat, Speckled, Ocher & Brown Spots, c.1785, 5 ¾ In.	492
Figurine, Cottage, Gothic Design, Tracery Windows, 2 Chimneys, Multicolor, c.1865, 8 ¼ In.	184
Figurine, Cow, Dairymaid, Multicolor, Oval Mound Base, 8 x 8 x 4 ½ In.	40
Figurine, Dog, Pug, Agate, Seated, Rectangular Base, Brown & White, c.1745, 2 ⅞ In.	480
Figurine, Dog, Spaniel, Seated, White, Black Spots, Painted Chain Lead, 11 In., Pair	307
Figurine, Dog, Whippet, Seated, Peach, White, Blue, c.1850, 8 x 4 ¾ In., Pair	68
Figurine, Dog, Whippet, Seated, Tan, Grassy Base, c.1885, 9 ¾ In., Pair	276
Figurine, Gentleman, Seated, Guitar, Spaniel, 1800s, 13 ¾ In.	118
Figurine, Highlander, Fitted As Lamp, 12 In.	84
Figurine, Lion, Standing, Red Brown, Gilt, 11 ½ x 12 ½ In.	1599
Figurine, Little Red Riding Hood, Holding Basket, Wolf By Side, Victorian, 12 In.	110
Figurine, Peacock, Standing, Cream Color, Cobalt Blue Splashes, c.1760, 3 In.	215
Figurine, Scotsman, In Kilt, Blowing Horn, Hunting Dog, Deer, 1800s, 14 ½ In.	58
Gravy Boat, Boston State House, Blue, 1800s, 3 ¾ In.	207
Group, Sailor, Woman, c.1890, 6 ½ In.	177
Jug, Double Puzzle, Ring Center, Acrobat, 3-Nozzle Neck, Leaves, c.1800, 10 In.	863
Jug, King Henry IV, Merry Wives Of Windsor, Purple Transfer, Inscribed, c.1815, 7 ¼ In.	300
Jug, Lid, Cream Color, Reeded Strap Handle, 3 Mask & Paw Feet, c.1760, 7 In.	240
Jug, Lid, Pear Shape, Crabstock Handle & Knop, Flower Sprigs, c.1750, 6 In.	2400
Ladle, Fort Gansevoort, Blue, 1800s, 9 ½ In.	1896
Mug, Black Enamel Painted Joseph, Flowers, White Ground, c.1835, 2 ⅝ In.	219
Mug, Martha, Brown Transfer, 1810-20, Children's, 2 ⅜ In.	660
Mustard Jar, Lid, Catskill Mountain Hudson River, Blue, 1800s, 2 ¾ In.	830
Pastille Burner, Lid, Gothic House, Painted, c.1845, 8 ¼ In.	102
Pitcher, Bulbous, Bearded Mask Spout, Spread Foot, Figure, c.1765, 6 ½ In.	215
Pitcher, Castle, Flag Boats In Foreground, Dark Blue Transfer, J. & R. Clews, c.1830, 10 In.	1080
Pitcher, Dam & Water Works, Philadelphia, Blue 1800s, 6 ⅝ In.	326
Pitcher, DeWitt Clinton Eulogy, Blue, 1800s, 7 In.	237
Pitcher, Deaf & Dumb Asylum, Alms House, Hartford Connecticut, Blue, 1800s, 11 In.	948
Pitcher, Eagle & Shield, Blue, c.1850, 6 ½ In.	425
Pitcher, General Lafayette, Blue, 1800s, 7 ½ In.	415
Pitcher, Landing Of The Fathers At Plymouth, Blue, 1800s, 6 ⅝ In.	273
Pitcher, Seal Of The United States, Blue, 1800s, 5 ¾ In.	1126
Pitcher, View Of The Erie Canal, Blue, 1800s, 6 ⅛ In.	243
Pitcher, Washington, Lafayette, Blue, 1800s, 6 In.	533
Plate, America & Independence, Building, Sheep, Blue Transfer, J. & R. Clews, c.1825, 9 In.	360
Plate, Bear Fishkill, Blue, 1800s, 7 ¾ In.	119
Plate, Cathedral, Clews, R. Hall's Select Views, Blue, England, c.1830, 10 In., Pair	151
Plate, DeWitt Clinton Eulogy, Blue, 1800s, 10 ¼ In.	304
Plate, Dessert, Antelope, Blue Transfer, John Hall & Sons, c.1830, 7 ½ x 8 In., 6 Piece	1080
Plate, Dinner, Lion, Blue Transfer, John Hall & Sons, c.1830, 10 ½ In., 10 Piece	1020
Plate, Entrance Of Erie Canal Into The Hudson At Albany, Blue, 1800s, 10 In.	1007
Plate, Erie Canal, DeWitt Clinton, Blue, 1800s, 8 ½ In.	356
Plate, Franklin With Kite, Blue, Child's Dinner Set, 1800s, 3 ½ In.	89
Plate, Iron Red, Green, Gilt, Cobalt Blue Underglaze, Footed, 9 ¼ In.	23
Plate, Llanarth Court, Blue Transfer, Monmouthshire, R. Hall, 10 In.	94
Plate, Luncheon, Flowers In Cartouche, Cobalt Ground, Gold Trim, Hall, 9 In., 12 Piece	104
Plate, Marine Hospital, Louisville, Kentucky, Blue, Impressed Woods, 1800s, 9 ¼ In.	326
Plate, Mendenhall Ferry, Impressed Stubbs, 1800s, 5 ½ In.	356
Plate, Mt. Pleasant Classical Institute, Blue Transfer, Clews, 1800s, 10 ⅝ In.	21330
Plate, Park Theatre, New York, Blue, 1800s, 6 ⅛ In.	334
Plate, Philadelphia View, Blue, 1800s, 6 ¾ In.	356
Plate, Soup, Fulton Steamboat, Blue Transfer Print, 1815-25, 10 ½ In.	2520
Plate, Transylvania University, Blue, Impressed Wood, 9 ¼ In.	267
Plate, Union Line, Blue, Impressed Enoch Wood & Sons, 1800s, 8 ⅜ In.	304
Plate, Woodlands Near Philadelphia, Blue, 1800s, 6 ¾ In.	122
Plate, Wrights Ferry On The Susquehanna, Blue, 1800s, 9 ⅛ In.	385
Platter, Acorn & Oak, Dark Blue Transfer, Octagonal, England, c.1830, 13 x 17 In.	115
Platter, America & Independence, State Border, Blue, 14 x 16 In.	1560
Platter, Arms Of Delaware, Blue, Eagle Mark, 1800s, 13 x 17 In.	2370

S

Platter, Barley Design, Oval, Reeded Edge, Scalloped Rim, c.1770, 14 ½ In.	400
Platter, Chillicothe, Ohio, Blue, 1800s, 9 ⅜ In.	2607
Platter, Chinese Rail, Basket Weave, Herringbone Border, Mottled, c.1750, 11 In.	720
Platter, Detroit, Blue, Oblong, 1800s, 15 x 18 ¾ In.	3555
Platter, Elephant, Quadrupeds Series, Blue Transfer, John Hall & Sons, c.1830, 18 ⅞ In.	1440
Platter, Farm Scene, Figures, Animals, House, Flower Border, Blue & White, c.1830, 20 ½ In.	230
Platter, Figures, Cobalt Blue, Flower Border, c.1820, 14 ½ x 19 In.	1404
Platter, Highlands Hudson River, Blue, Reticulated, 10 In.	3081
Platter, Landing Of Gen. Lafayette, Blue & White Transfer, 8-Sided, Clews, c.1830, 19 In.	1250
Platter, Landing Of General Lafayette At Castle Garden, Blue, J. & R. Clews, c.1830, 21 In.	1560
Platter, Moose, Quadrupeds Series, Blue Transfer, John Hall & Sons, 1830, 15 ½ In.	960
Platter, New York Heights From Near Brooklyn, Blue, Stevenson, 1800s, 17 In.	1067
Platter, Osborne House, Round, Blue Flower Border, Gilt Rim, Ashworth Bros., c.1850, 15 In.	92
Platter, Peace & Plenty, Blue Transfer, J. & R. Clews, c.1830, 17 In.	1200
Platter, Red, Blue Chinoiserie, Enameled, Oval, c.1820, 18 In.	313
Platter, Rhinoceros, Quadrupeds Series, Blue Transfer, John Hall & Sons, c.1830, 17 ½ In.	1440
Platter, Southwest View Of LaGrange, Blue Transfer, E. Wood & Sons, 1800s, 15 x 19 In.	972
Platter, States Pattern Blue & White Transfer, Oval, Clews, c.1830, 16 ¾ In.	2375
Platter, Tappan Bays, Greenburgh, Impressed Enoch Wood & Sons, 1800s, 8 x 10 In.	4740
Platter, Upper Ferry Bridge Over River Schuylkill, Blue, White, Oval, J. Stubbs, c.1820, 19 In.	1250
Platter, Winter Scene Near Pittsfield, Blue, Impressed Clews, 1800s, 12 ¾ In.	385
Platter, Winter View Of Pittsfield, Massachusetts, Blue, c.1850, 15 ¾ In.	1659
Platter, Yuan, Blue & White, Wood & Sons, c.1900, 16 In.	94
Quill Holder, Whippet Shape, c.1865, 6 x 7 In., Pair	492
Sauceboat, Leaf Shape, Reeded Strap Handles, Cobalt Blue, White, c.1760, 6 In.	510
Sauceboat, Oval, Scalloped Rim, Lion Mask & Paw Feet, Grapevines, c.1755, 7 In.	738
Sauceboat, Press Molded, Translucent Green & Brown, Flowers, c.1765, 7 In.	660
Saucer, American Eagle & Shield, Blue, 1800s, 3 ⅞ In.	1778
Saucer, Castle Garden, Battery, New York, Blue, Impressed Woods & Sons, 1800s, 4 ¼ In.	89
Server, Lid, Gilt Designs, Footed, Center Compartment, 4 Surrounding, Victorian, 11 x 14 In.	58
Serving Bowl, American Villa, Cantered Corners, Blue, 1800s, 3 ½ x 9 In.	237
Serving Bowl, Brooklyn Ferry, Blue, Impressed Stevenson, 1800s, 10 In.	5214
Soup, Dish, Arms Of New York, Blue, Impressed T. Mayer, 1800s, 9 ¾ In.	415
Soup, Dish, Harvard College, Blue, 1800s, 9 ⅞ In.	326
Soup, Dish, Pine Orchard House Catskill Mountains, Blue, Impressed Wood, 1800s, 9 In.	395
Soup, Dish, United States Hotel, Philadelphia, Blue, c.1845, 10 ¼ In.	243
Spittle Cup, Boston State House, Blue, 1800s, 3 ½ In.	770
Spoon Tray, Quatrefoil Shape, Molded Birds & Leaves, Brown, Cream, c.1750, 7 In.	840
Sugar, Dome Lid, Squat, Fruit Basket, Translucent, c.1760, 4 ½ In.	3600
Sugar, Lid, MacDonnough's Victory, 1800s, 4 ¼ In.	456
Tankard, Agate, Cylindrical, Strap Handle, Brown, Rust, Blue, c.1775, 5 In.	2160
Tankard, Cream Ground, Black, Rust, Ale, Leafy Frame, Ring Foot, c.1775, 5 In.	570
Tankard, Cylindrical, Entwined Handle, Woman, Landscape, c.1775, 4 ¾ In.	600
Tankard, Cylindrical, Leaf Handle, Banding, Sponging, c.1765, 5 ¼ In.	1020
Tankard, Strap Handle, Woman, Dress & Cape, Coastal Setting, c.1760, 5 In.	600
Tea Canister, Square Shape, Panels, Flora, Cream Colored, c.1779, 5 In.	1320
Teapot, Almshouse, Blue, Octagonal Base, 19th Century, 8 ¼ In.	8888
Teapot, House, Windows, Salt Glaze, Cobalt Blue Highlights, c.1760, 6 ¾ x 5 ¼ In. ....*illus*	1440
Teapot, Lid, Cauliflower Shape, Cream Florets, Green Leaves, c.1760, 4 x 7 In.	1968
Teapot, Lid, Christmas Eve Scene, Flowers, Dark Blue, Clews, c.1835, 8 ¾ In.	92
Teapot, Lid, Cylindrical, Pinched Neck, Mottled Manganese, c.1755, 4 In.	330
Teapot, Lid, Diamond Shape, Crabstock Handle, Scroll Spout, c.1765, 7 ¼ In.	1353
Teapot, Lid, Flower Basket, Scroll, c.1825, 6 ½ x 10 ½ In.	127
Teapot, Lid, Globular, Acorn Finial, Crabstock Handle, Flowers, c.1760, 4 ⅜ In.	360
Teapot, Lid, Globular, Crabstock Handle & Spout, Grapevines, Gilt, c.1755, 5 In.	420
Teapot, Lid, Globular, Crabstock Handle & Spout, Pink, Flowers, c.1760, 7 ½ In.	2520
Teapot, Lid, Globular, Crosshatched, Crabstock Handle & Spout, Green, Yellow, 5 In.	1920
Teapot, Lid, Melon Shape, Reeded Spout, Green & Yellow Stripes, 6 x 10 In.	5400
Teapot, Lid, Shouldered, Tapered, Leaf Spout, Twist Handle, Flowers, c.1775, 5 In.	780
Teapot, Wadsworth Tower, Blue Transfer, 1800s, 7 In.	178
Toby Jugs are listed in their own category.	
Toddy Plate, Landing Of Fathers At Plymouth, Enoch Wood & Sons, Blue, 1800s, 5 In.	237
Tray, Bank Of Savannah, Blue, 1800s, 6 ¾ In.	1422
Tray, Exchange Charleston, Blue, 1800s, 8 ¼ In.	1007
Tray, Niagara From The American Side, Blue, 1800s, 14 In.	415
Tureen, Cattle By Stream, Fishermen, Blue Transfer, c.1840, 8 ½ x 13 In.	206

Staffordshire, Coffeepot, Black Transfer, Tea Party, Shepherd On Reverse, 10 ¼ In.
$246

Staffordshire, Creamer, Agate, Pear Shape, 3 Lion Masks & Paw Feet, Lion Knop, c.1750, 6 ½ In.
$3,120

Staffordshire, Creamer, Cow, Milkmaid, Sponged, Glazed Base, Late 1700s, 6 ⅞ In.
$800

S

This is an edited listing of current prices. Visit **Kovels.com** to check thousands of prices from previous years and sign up for free information on trends, tips, reproductions, marks, and more.

Staffordshire, Teapot, House, Windows, Salt Glaze, Cobalt Blue Highlights, c.1760, 6 ¾ x 5 ¼ In.
$1,440

Skinner Auctioneers & Appraisers

Stainless Steel, Cutlery Set, Bla Haj, Blue Shark, Svende Siune, Georg Jensen, 1965, 56 Piece
$1,200

Skinner Auctioneers & Appraisers

Stangl Birds

Stangl Pottery birds have been produced since 1939. During the 1940s, hundreds of thousands were made. The figurines were based on illustrations in James Audubon's *Birds of America* and Alexander Wilson's *American Ornithology.*

Stangl, Bird, Scarlet Tanager, Dogwood Branch, 5 ⅝ In.
$431

Humler & Nolan

Tureen, Lid, Bellville On The Passaic River, Blue, Ladle, 11 x 15 In.	1215
Tureen, Lid, White Nesting Hen, Red Comb, Wattles, White Basket Base, c.1860, 7 In.	184
Tureen, Sauce, Lid, Twig Handle, Underplate, Pink, White, Gilt, 1830, 6 x 8 In., Pair	150
Tureen, Soup, Lid, Bellville On The Passaic River, Blue, Enoch & Sons, c.1835, 15 In.	1440
Tureen, Soup, Lid, Dromedary, Quadruped Series, Blue, John Hall & Sons, c.1830, 14 In.	2040
Undertray, Fairmount Near Philadelphia, Blue, Round, 1800s, 14 In.	1659
Vase, Spill, Mother, Reading To Boy & Girl, Multicolor, c.1850, 6 In.	104
Washbowl, Erie Canal, Blue Transfer, Enoch Wood & Sons, c.1825, 11 In.	383
Washbowl, Lafayette At Franklin's Tomb, Blue Transfer, Enoch Wood & Sons, 1830, 13 In.	1020
Washbowl, Upper Ferry Bridge From River Schuylkill, Blue, 1800s, 5 x 13 In.	237
Waste Bowl, Baltimore Court House, Blue Transfer, 1800s, 2 ¾ x 4 ¾ In.	1541

STAINLESS STEEL became available to artists and manufacturers about 1920. They used it to make flatware, tableware, and many decorative items.

Cutlery Set, Bla Haj, Blue Shark, Svende Siune, Georg Jensen, 1965, 56 Piece ....*illus*	1200
Sculpture, Giraffe, Steel, Welded, Handmade, c.1960, 34 x 76 ½ In.	813
Sculpture, Man On Wheel, Steel, Ted Gall, 1993, 13 In.	1063

STANGL POTTERY traces its history back to the Fulper Pottery of New Jersey. In 1910, Johann Martin Stangl started working at Fulper. He left to work at Haeger Pottery from 1915 to 1920. Stangl returned to Fulper Pottery in 1920, became president in 1926, and changed the company name to Stangl Pottery in 1929. Stangl acquired the firm in 1930. The pottery is known for dinnerware and a line of bird figurines. Martin Stangl died in 1972 and the pottery was sold to Frank Wheaton Jr. of Wheaton Industries. Production continued until 1978, when Pfaltzgraff Pottery purchased the right to the Stangl trademark and the remaining inventory was liquidated. A single bird figurine is identified by a number. Figurines made up of two birds are identified by a number followed by the letter *D* indicating Double.

ABC, Dish, Child's, Divided, Oval, 6 In.	86
Amber Glo, Cup & Saucer	8
Amber Glo, Plate, Dinner, 10 In.	21
Amber, Creamer, 6 Oz., 2 ¾ In.	15
Antique Gold, Bowl, Scalloped, 7 In.	14
Antique Gold, Chop Plate, 12 In.	42
Antique Gold, Pitcher, 16 Oz., 5 ⅜ In.	19
Apple Delight, Ashtray, Fluted Verge, 5 ½ In.	8
Aztec, Plate, Dinner, 10 In.	6 to 20
Bird, Bird Of Paradise, No. 3408	300
Bird, Blue Headed Vireo, No. 3448, 4 ¼ In.	60
Bird, Bluebird, No. 3276	50
Bird, Chickadees, No. 3581, 8 ½ x 6 In.	150
Bird, Cockatoo, No. 3584, Stamped Mark, Signed RV, 11 ⅜ In.	94
Bird, Hummingbird, No. 3579, Stamped Mark, 8 ½ In.	94
Bird, Lovebird, No. 3400	95
Bird, Lovebirds, Double, No. 3404D	400
Bird, Oriole, No. 3402, 2 ⅞ In.	45
Bird, Owl, No. 3407, 4 ¼ In.	295
Bird, Rufous Hummingbird, No. 3585, 3 In.	125
Bird, Scarlet Tanager, Dogwood Branch, 5 ⅝ In. ....*illus*	431
Bird, Shoveler Duck, No. 3455, Signed ES, 14 In.	248
Bird, White Crowned Pigeons, Double, No. 3518D, 12 ½ x 7 ½ In.	595
Bittersweet, Chop Plate, 12 In.	16
Bittersweet, Cup & Saucer	6
Bittersweet, Gravy Boat	36
Bittersweet, Pepper, 3 In.	13
Blue Bell, Creamer, 3 ⅜ In.	15
Blue Bell, Creamer, 6 Oz., 3 In.	16
Blue Bell, Cup & Saucer, Footed	14
Blue Bell, Plate, Bread & Butter, 6 In.	7
Blue Bell, Plate, Salad, 8 In.	7
Blue Bell, Salt & Pepper	15
Cabbage, Leaf, Cup & Saucer	8
Carnival, Bowl, Vegetable, Round, 8 In.	38
Carnival, Cup & Saucer	8
Carnival, Plate, Dinner, 10 In.	26
Cosmos, Vase, Pillow, White Matte Glaze, 7 x 3 x 5 In.	25
Creamer, Flowers, Beige Ground, 4 ¾ In.	7

Flora, Cup & Saucer	8
Florentine, Bowl, Vegetable, Round, 8 In.	17
Florentine, Cup & Saucer	6
Fruit, Creamer, 2 ¾ In.	35
Fruit, Sauce, Handle, 8 ½ In.	70
Garden Flower, Creamer, 6 Oz., 3 In.	23
Garden Flower, Cup & Saucer	10
Garden Flower, Pitcher, 24 Oz., 4 ¾ In.	30 to 31
Garden Flower, Plate, Bread & Butter, 6 ⅛ In.	9
Garden Flower, Sugar, Lid, 2 Handles	74
Garland, Bowl, Vegetable, Oval, Divided, 10 In.	44
Garland, Chop Plate, 12 In.	34
Garland, Coffeepot, Lid, 6 Cup, 7 ⅝ In.	84
Garland, Plate, Dinner, 10 ⅛ In.	31
Golden Grape, Bowl, Vegetable, Divided, 10 In.	17
Golden Grape, Chop Plate, 14 In.	25
Golden Grape, Creamer, 3 In.	10
Golden Grape, Cup & Saucer	9
Golden Grape, Dish, Pickle, 10 ¼ In.	16
Golden Grape, Platter, Oval, 13 In.	33 to 34
Golden Grape, Salt & Pepper	18
Granada Gold, Cup & Saucer	12
Granada Gold, Plate, Dinner, 10 ¼ In.	14
Holly, Plate, Dinner, 10 In.	98
Magnolia, Bowl, Vegetable, 2 Sections, 10 ½ In.	59
Magnolia, Casserole, Round, 1 Qt., 7 ⅝ In.	48
Magnolia, Chop Plate, 14 In.	36
Magnolia, Cup & Saucer	11
Magnolia, Gravy Boat	52
Magnolia, Mug	46
Magnolia, Plate, Dinner, 10 ⅛ In.	26
Magnolia, Relish, 11 ⅜ In.	22
Magnolia, Soup, Dish, Lug, 6 ⅛ In.	21
Morning Blue, Cup & Saucer	8
Olde Glory, Plate, Dinner, 10 ⅝ In.	12
Orchard Song, Chop Plate, 12 ⅜ In.	14
Oyster Plate, Pottery, 5 Wells, Shell Shape, White, Blue Ground, 9 In.	186
Paisley, Chop Plate, 12 In.	26
Paisley, Creamer, 8 Oz., 3 ½ In.	16
Paisley, Cup & Saucer	7
Paisley, Gravy Boat, Underplate	42
Paisley, Plate, Salad, 8 ⅛ In.	7
Paisley, Soup, Dish, Lug, 6 In.	6
Prelude, Chop Plate, 12 In.	23
Prelude, Cup & Saucer	9
Prelude, Eggcup, Double, 3 ¼ In.	8 to 9
Prelude, Plate, Dinner, 10 In.	13
Prelude, Sugar, Lid	29
Provincial, Bowl, Vegetable, Divided, Oval, 10 In.	16
Provincial, Casserole, Lid, Round, 1 Qt.	104
Provincial, Casserole, Round, Lid, 1 ½ Qt., 7 ⅜ In.	98
Provincial, Chop Plate, Gold, Burgundy, 12 ¼ In.	20
Provincial, Creamer	14
Provincial, Cup & Saucer	12
Provincial, Pitcher, 24 Oz., 4 ½ In.	37
Provincial, Plate, Bread & Butter, 6 ¼ In.	5
Provincial, Platter, Oval, 13 In.	21
Provincial, Relish, 11 ¼ In.	16
Rooster, Mug, 12 Oz.	36
Rooster, Picher, 16 Oz., 4 ⅛ In.	37
Rooster, Salt & Pepper	21
Sesame, Plate, Dinner, 10 ¼ In.	12
Spun Gold, Bean Pot, Lid	89
Spun Gold, Plate, Dinner, 10 In.	18
Star Flower, Bowl, Fruit, 5 ½ In.	12
Star Flower, Butter, ¼ Lb.	34

Star Wars, Action Ficture, Chewbacca, On Card, Kenner, 1977, 4 ⅛ In.
$356

Hake's Americana & Collectibles

Stein, Character, Gentleman Rabbit, Porcelain, Marked, Musterschutz, Schierholz, ½ Liter
$2,160

The Stein Auction Co.

Stein, Character, Gnome, Pottery, Eckhardt & Engler, ½ Liter
$192

The Stein Auction Co.

S

Stein, Character, Man Holding Cat, Top Hat, Pottery, Diesinger, ½ Liter
$545

Fox Auctions

Stein, Character, Wilhelm I, Porcelain, Schierholz, ½ Liter
$665

Fox Auctions

Stein, Faience, Bird On Tree Stump, Pewter Lid, Footring, Bayreuther Walzenkrug, 1700s, 10 In.
$540

The Stein Auction Co.

Star Flower, Cup & Saucer	6
Star Flower, Teapot, Lid, 5 Cup	148
Stardust, Cup & Saucer	9
Thistle, Cup & Saucer	9
Thistle, Plate, Dinner, 10 In.	24
Thistle, Plate, Salad, 8 In.	14
Vase, Incised Tulips, Marbleized Peach, Scroll Handles, Footed, 5 ⅞ In.	14
Vase, Marbles, Green, Brown, Flared Rim, 12 ¼ In.	59
White Dogwood, Plate, Dinner, 10 In.	19
White Dogwood, Plate, Salad, 7 In.	8
Willow, Soup, Dish, Tab Handles, 5 ½ In.	14

STAR TREK AND STAR WARS collectibles are included here. The original *Star Trek* television series ran from 1966 through 1969. The series spawned an animated TV series, three TV sequels, and a TV prequel. The first Star Trek movie was released in 1979 and eleven others followed, the most recent in 2013. The movie *Star Wars* opened in 1977. Sequels were released in 1980 and 1983; prequels in 1999, 2002, and 2005. *Star Wars: Episode VII* is scheduled to open in 2015, which will increase interest in Star Wars collectibles. The latest episode will include actors from the original cast. Other science fiction and fantasy collectibles can be found under Batman, Buck Rogers, Captain Marvel, Flash Gordon, Movie, Superman, and Toy.

STAR TREK

Belt Buckle, Federation, Star Trek II, Brass, Round, 2 ½ In.	225
Photo, TV Cast, USS Enterprise, Bridge, Glossy, Signed, 8 x 10 In.	587
Spock Ears, Star Trek II, Latex, Frame, 1981, 6 x 4 In.	2750

STAR WARS

Action Ficture, Chewbacca, On Card, Kenner, 1977, 4 ⅛ In. ......*illus*	356
Action Figure, Ben Kenobi, Gray Hair, On Card, Kenner, 1977, 3 ¾ In.	424
Action Figure, C-3PO, Blister Card, Kenner, 1977, 3 ¾ In.	218 to 278
Action Figure, Darth Vader, Blister Card, Kenner, 1977, 4 ¼ In.	1033
Action Figure, Early Bird Set, Luke Skywalker, Princess Leia, Kenner, 1977, 4 Piece	481
Action Figure, Han Solo, On Card, Hang Tag, Kenner, 1977, 3 ¾ In.	386
Action Figure, Jawa, Fabric Robe, On Card, Kenner, 1977, 2 ⅜ In.	475
Action Figure, Luke Skywalker, Posable, Tattoine Desert Gear, Kenner, Box, 1977, 11 ¾ In.	417
Action Figure, Luke Skywalker, X-Wing Pilot, 1983, 6 ½ x 9 In.	196
Action Figure, Princess Leia Organa, Blister Card, Kenner, 1977, 3 ¾ In.	304 to 328
Action Figure, R2-D2, Blister Card, Kenner, 1977, 2 ¼ In.	253 to 314
Action Figure, Tusken Raider, Sand People, Kenner, 1977, 3 ¾ In.	354
Charm, C-3PO, Movable Arms & Legs, Metal, 2 ⅛ x 1 In.	22
Display, Lightsaber, Cardboard, Die Cut, 1977, 15 ¼ x 39 In.	601
Lunchbox, Thermos, Metal, Characters, Box, 1977, 6 ¼ In.	348
Movie Viewer, Crank Style, Advancing Film Strips, Box, Kenner, 7 x 7 x 3 In.	221
Mug, Chewie, Brown, c.1977, 7 x 7 In.	99
Plate, Princess Leia, 24K Gold Rim, Hamilton Collection, 1987, 8 ½ In.	75
Plate, R2D2 & Wicket, 24K Gold Rim, Hamilton Collection, 8 ½ In.	75
Poster, Movie, 20th Century Fox, 1977, 27 x 41 In.	1000
Toy, Swing Set Glider, Jedi Speeder Bike, Empire Strikes Back, Metal, Plastic, 48 In.	60

STEINS have been used by beer and ale drinkers for over 500 years. They have been made of ivory, porcelain, stoneware, faience, silver, pewter, wood, or glass in sizes up to nine gallons. Although some were made by Mettlach, Meissen, Capo-di-Monte, and other famous factories, most were made by less important German potteries. The words *Geschutz* or *Musterschutz* on a stein are the German words for "patented" or "registered design," not company names. Steins are still being made in the old styles. Lithophane steins may be found in the Lithophane category.

Burl, Carved, Lid, Lion Terminal, 4 Reclining Lion Feet, Marked IPSH, Scandinavia, 9 ½ In.	920
Character, Alligator, Standing, Head Lid, Teeth, Porcelain, Musterschutz, 7 In.	754
Character, Apple, Coiled Snake, Porcelain, E. Bohne & Sohne, ⅓ Liter	360
Character, Budman, Stone, Anheuser-Busch, 1976, ½ Liter	144
Character, Cat With Hangover, Hat Askew, Paws Crossed, Porcelain, Musterschutz, 8 In.	551
Character, Drunken Monkey, Musterschutz, Porcelain, ½ Liter	390
Character, Gentleman Rabbit, Porcelain, Marked, Musterschutz, Schierholz, ½ Liter ....*illus*	2160
Character, Gnome, Pottery, Eckhardt & Engler, ½ Liter ......*illus*	192
Character, Gooseman, Porcelain, Pewter, ½ Liter	540
Character, Hunter, Pottery, Inlaid Lid, Marked, J. Reinemann, Munchen, ½ Liter	840
Character, Man Holding Cat, Top Hat, Pottery, Diesinger, ½ Liter ......*illus*	545

S

Character, Munich Child On Barrel, Musterschutz & Pauson, ½ Liter 540
Character, Nick, Stoneware, Tapered, F. Ringer, ¼ Liter.. 1080
Character, Puss-N-Boots, Cat In Shoe, Mouse On Toe, Pottery, ½ Liter...................... 8400
Character, Rich Man, Stoneware, Blue Salt Glaze, ½ Liter 216
Character, Sad Radish, Frowning Face, Inlaid Leafy Lid, Porcelain, Musterschutz, 7 In. 174
Character, Singing Pig, Standing, Pink, Porcelain, Musterschutz, 6 In......................... 435
Character, Snowman, Frowning, Shovel, Inlaid Lid, Porcelain, Schierholz, ½ Liter........ 7865
Character, Turkish Man, Arm Handle, Porcelain, Schierholz, ½ Liter 6240
Character, Wilhelm I, Porcelain, Schierholz, ½ Liter .... illus 665
Faience, Bird On Tree Stump, Pewter Lid, Footring, Bayreuther Walzenkrug, 1700s, 10 In. .. illus 540
Faience, Flowers, Blue & White, Pewter Lid & Footring, Birnkrug, 1700s, 11 In. .... illus 360
Faience, Thuringer Walzenkrug, Pewter Lid & Footring, Late 1700s, 9 In................... 288
Glass, Amber, Thumbprint, Pewter Overlay, Women's Faces, Lid, J. Lichtinger, 2 ½ Liter 252
Glass, Bohemian, Ruby Over Clear, Cameo, Panels, Horses, Dogs, c.1850, ½ Liter 6720
Glass, Grapes, Leaves, Engraved, Franz Paul Zach, ¾ Liter, 8 ¾ In. .... illus 6300
Glass, Ruby Stain, Cut Castle Scene, Bohemian, c.1860, ½ Liter .... illus 194
Mettlach steins are listed in the Mettlach category.
Military, Germania, Iron Crosses, Relief Pewter Lid & Strap, Pottery, ½ Liter.............. 168
Military, Iron Cross, Stoneware, Pewter Lid, Relief Bavarian Coat Of Arms, 1914, ½ Liter ... 204
Military, Third Reich, Komp. J.R. 42, Hof, Stoneware, Pewter Lid, Helmet, Swastika, ½ Liter....... 451
Military, Ulan Uniform, Pewter Lid, Pottery, Prosit Kamerad, ½ Liter .... illus 204
Pewter, Man & Woman, Engraved, Touchmarks, 1834, 1 Liter.................................... 216
Porcelain, Birds, Flowers, Green Glaze, Oriental, c.1750, ½ Liter................................ 2640
Porcelain, Capo-Di-Monte Style, Relief, Painted, Inlaid Lid, 1 Liter, 9 ½ In. .... illus 720
Porcelain, High Wheel Bicycle, Transfer, Enameled, Pewter Lid, 1894, Liter............... 264
Porcelain, Man Playing Bagpipe, Woman, Wreath, Set-On Lid, Child Finial, Dresden, 16 In....... 2040
Pottery, Musical Clowns, Etched Pewter Lid, Toronto, Winnipeg, ½ Liter 168
Pottery, Painted, Hunting Dog, Silver Lid, Marked, Aurelian, Weller, ½ Liter, 7 In. 2400
Regimental, Battr., Feld Artl. Regt. 71, Gaudenz, Reservist Petzold, 1911-1913, 1 Liter ...... illus 840
Regimental, Roster, 6 Comp, Regt. Nr. 9, Helmet Finial, Thumblift, c.1905, ½ Liter, 9 In. 390
Regimental, Roster, 9 Comp, Bayr. Inft. Regt. Nr. 9, Wurzburg, Lithophane, c.1913, ½ Liter ... 432
Regimental, Roster, Battr., Bayr. Feld Artl. Regt. 8, Nurmberg, Thumblift, c.1912, ½ Liter...... 2160
Regimental, Scenic, Bayr., 1 Fahr., Battr., Augsburg, Xaver Faltermeijer, c.1900, ½ Liter...... 216
Stoneware, Enamel Stripes, Hourglass Shape, Pewter Bands, Altenburg, c.1720, 1 ¼ Liter 11400
Stoneware, Lid, Cavalier, Outdoor Scene, Germsheid, 1 Liter .... illus 145
Stoneware, Munich Child, Pewter Lid ½ Liter .... illus 182
Stoneware, Pearl Design, Pewter Lid & Footring, Altenburger Walzenkrug, 1749, 10 In... 1050
Stoneware, Pewter Lid & Footring, Vertical Handle Strap, S. Kugelbauchkrug, c.1700, 7 In....... 3840
Stoneware, Red Stylized Flowers, Transfer, Pewter Lid, Art Nouveau Style, 1 Liter.......... 216
Tankard, Ivory, Bear Hunt, Hound Handle, Gilt Brass, Child Finial, 1800s, 9 In. 3375
Tankard, Ivory, Jewels, Figural Finial, Gilt Silver Mounts, 6 In. 5160
Tankard, Ivory, Romans, Silver Mounts, Centurian Final, c.1875, 8 In........................ 5280
Tankard, Silver, Ear Handle, Horseshoe End, Reeded, 17th Century, 6 ½ In. 1625
Tankard, Silver, George IV, Rocaille, Quilted, Dome Lid, Serpentine Handle, c.1831, 8 In. 1750
Tankard, Viennese Enamel, Drinking Scenes, Relief Mounts, Finial, Figural Handle, 1 Liter....... 16800

STEREO CARDS that were made for stereoscope viewers became popular after 1840. Two almost identical pictures were mounted on a stiff cardboard backing so that, when viewed through a stereoscope, a three-dimensional picture could be seen. Value is determined by maker and by subject. These cards were made in quantity through the 1930s.

4 Black Children, Dog & Pups, Keystone View Co., 1899, 7 x 3 ½ In. 30
Big Trees, Mariposa Grove, Yosemite, California, Universal Photo Art Co., 7 x 3 ½........ 16
Broadway, Grace Church, Stewart's, New York City, c.1860, 3 x 7 In. 18
Cleopatra Terrace, Mammoth Hot Springs, Yellowstone Park, Keystone .... illus 12
Coal Train, Pittsburgh To Conneaut, Ohio, Keystone View Co., 3 x 7 In........................ 10
Feeding Swans, In Park, T.W. Ingersoll, 1898, 3 ½ x 7 In.. 5
French Model Posing, Scantily Dressed, Sepia, c.1855, 7 x 3 In................................... 36
Gems Of Statuary By Eminent Sculptors, Love Tale No. 53, 1867 .... illus 15
Gol Stave Church, Norway, c.1900, 7 x 3 ½ In.. 20
Little Girl With Donkeys, Underwood & Underwood, Comrades 12
Nantucket, Massachusetts, Village Panorama, Freeman .... illus 89
New York City, American Civil War Period, Central Park, 1860s 65
New York City, Broadway, Stewart's Store, Grace Church, 1860s, 3 7/16 x 7 In. ...... illus 18
New York Harbour, Steam Boats, Brooklyn Bridge, Liberty Statue, 1902, 7 x 3 ½ In.......... 12
Perils Of Frontier Life, Giant Of The Forest, Bear, International View Co., 1906.......... 15

Stein, Faience, Flowers, Blue & White, Pewter Lid & Footring, Birnkrug, 1700s, 11 In.
$360

The Stein Auction Co.

Stein, Glass, Grapes, Leaves, Engraved, Franz Paul Zach, ¾ Liter, 8 ¾ In.
$6,300

The Stein Auction Co.

Stein, Glass, Ruby Stain, Cut Castle Scene, Bohemian, c.1860, ½ Liter
$194

Fox Auctions

S

Stein, Military, Ulan Uniform, Pewter Lid, Pottery, Prosit Kamerad, ½ Liter
$204

The Stein Auction Co.

Stein, Porcelain, Capo-Di-Monte Style, Relief, Painted, Inlaid Lid, 1 Liter, 9 ½ In.
$720

The Stein Auction Co.

Stein, Regimental, Battr., Feld Artl. Regt. 71, Gaudenz, Reservist Petzold, 1911-1913, 1 Liter
$840

The Stein Auction Co.

Roosevelt's Rough Riders, Leaving Tampa For Santiago, Keystone View Co., 3 x 7 In.	15
Soldiers, World War I, Letters From Home, Universal Photo Art Co., 3 ½ x 7 In.	15
Trials Of Single Life, Melander, Man Threading Needle, c.1880, 7 x 3 ½ In.	12
Tunisian Jewish Girl, House Costume, 1904, 7 x 3 ¾ In.	35

STEREOSCOPES were used for viewing stereo cards. The hand viewer was invented by Oliver Wendell Holmes, although more complicated table models were used before his was produced in 1859. Do not confuse the stereoscope with the stereopticon, a magic lantern that used glass slides.

Box Form, 2-Sided, Cards, Victorian, 17 In.	1046
Keystone View Co., Wood & Metal, Eye Comfort, 15 x 7 In.	110
Le Taxiphote, Wood, Glass Slides, Fitted Trays, 19 In.	984
Metal, Wood, Underwood & Underwood, Pat. June 11, 1901, 12 ½ x 5 In. *illus*	105
Monarch, Metal, Embossed, Rounded, Glass Lenses, Wood, c.1905, 12 ½ In.	150
Rosewood, Carved, Sliding Easel, Retractable Magnifying Lens, Cards, c.1890, 20 x 12 In.	531
Walnut Veneer, Rotating Belt Mount, Table Top, 1860s, 18 x 10 In. *illus*	775
White Metal & Wood, Square Glass Lens, Tilt Handle, c.1900, 12 ½ In.	125
Wooden, Shaped Handle, Square Lens, c.1885	200

STERLING SILVER, *see Silver-Sterling category.*

STEUBEN glass was made at the Steuben Glass Works of Corning, New York. The factory, founded by Frederick Carder and T.G. Hawkes, Sr., was purchased by the Corning Glass Company. Corning continued to make glass called Steuben. Many types of art glass were made at Steuben. Schottenstein Stores Inc. bought 80 percent of the business in 2008. The factory closed in 2011 and no more of this quality glass will be made. Additional pieces may be found in the Cluthra and Perfume Bottle categories.

Basket, Calcite, Blue Aurene Interior, Crimped, Handle, Swirled Prunts, 7 ½ In. *illus*	2875
Bowl, Amethyst, Vertical Striping, Rolled Rim, Marked, 11 ½ x 4 In.	182
Bowl, Blue Iridescence, Aurene, c.1950, 2 x 10 In.	374
Bowl, Blue, Bulb Shape, Inverted Rim, Aurene, Marked, 8 In.	431
Bowl, Blue, Low, 3 Feet, Aurene, 2 ¾ x 12 In.	472
Bowl, Blue, Wide Rim, Round Pedestal Base, Aurene, 1900s, 4 ½ x 11 In.	590
Bowl, Calcite, Gold, Flared Rim, Aurene, 2 ¾ x 10 ¼ In. *illus*	230
Bowl, Clear, Low, Flared, 6 Ball Feet, Marked, John Dreve, c.1950, 4 ¼ x 15 In.	384
Bowl, Folded Trefoil Rim, Marked, 6 x 9 ½ In.	98
Bowl, Gold Aurene, Calcite Glass, White Opaque Base, Iridized Rim, c.1920, 2 x 13 ½ In.	313
Bowl, Gold Iridescent, Aurene, 4 x 10 In.	326
Bowl, Gold, Blue Veining, Curled Wide Rim, Aurene, 4 x 12 ½ In.	560
Bowl, Gold, Calcite, Onionskin Rim, Footed, Aurene, c.1920, 12 In.	360
Bowl, Gold, Fluted, Crimped Edge, Aurene, 4 ¾ In.	210
Bowl, Jade Blue, Flared, 8 ¼ In.	70
Bowl, Leaves, Wide Flared Rim, Pedestal Foot, 6 ¾ x 8 ½ In.	480
Bowl, Trefoil, Donald Pollard, 3 x 6 In.	60
Bowl, Trefoil, Footed, Engraved Mark, 11 ½ In.	148
Candlestick, Blue, Twist Stem, Round Base, Aurene, c.1910, 8 In., Pair	1140
Candlestick, Cerise Ruby, Baluster Stem, Spread Foot, 10 In., Pair	1035
Candlestick, Flared Cup, Ball Stem, Spread Foot, 10 ½ In., Pair	780
Candlestick, French Blue, Thin Reeded Stem, Footed, 1920s, 14 In., 4 Piece	1375
Candlestick, Gold, Twist Stem, Aurene, Mark, 8 In.	345
Candlestick, Shaped Stem, Spread Foot, Foldover Rim, 9 In.	210
Candlestick, Silver Blue Iridescent, Twist Stem, Gold Aurene, Mark, c.1910, 10 In.	1080
Centerpiece, Florentia, Green Leaf, Satin, Aventurine, Undulating Rim, 12 In.	2300
Centerpiece, Gold, Rolled Rim, 3 Applied Feet, Aurene, Marked, 10 In.	230
Compote, Calcite, Gold, Rolled Rim, 6 x 6 In.	207
Compote, Clear, Round, Flared, Footed, 10 In.	180
Dish, Olive, Scroll Handle, Wide Rim, 3 x 6 In.	180
Figurine, Eagle, Wings At Side, Clear, 4 ½ In.	375
Figurine, Fish, Clear, 7 ½ In.	136
Figurine, Horse, Walking, Head Down, Clear, 7 x 9 In.	290
Figurine, Ice Bear, Polar Bear, Standing On Iceberg, Silver Accents, 5 In.	2125
Figurine, Owl, Big Eyes, 5 x 4 In.	360
Figurine, Snail, Silver Gilt, Clear Shell, 6 ½ In.	1599
Figurine, Trout, Leaping, 18K Gold, Lure, 9 In.	2000
Goblet, Bell Bowl, Long Internal Twist Stem, Clear, 11 ¾ In.	294

Stein, Stoneware, Lid, Cavalier, Outdoor Scene, Germsheid, 1 Liter
$145

Fox Auctions

Stein, Stoneware, Munich Child, Pewter Lid
½ Liter
$182

Fox Auctions

TIP
Wash your hands or wear cotton gloves before handling books, textiles or paper artifacts.

Stereo Card, Cleopatra Terrace, Mammoth Hot Springs, Yellowstone Park, Keystone
$12

Ruby Lane, Inc.

Stereo Card, Gems Of Statuary By Eminent Sculptors, Love Tale No. 53, 1867
$15

Ruby Lane, Inc.

Stereo Card, Nantucket, Massachusetts, Village Panorama, Freeman
$89

Ruby Lane, Inc.

Stereo Card, New York City, Broadway, Stewart's Store, Grace Church, 1860s, 3 ⁷⁄₁₆ x 7 In.
$18

Ruby Lane, Inc.

Stereoscope, Metal, Wood, Underwood & Underwood, Pat. June 11, 1901, 12 ½ x 5 In.
$105

Ruby Lane, Inc.

Stereoscope, Walnut Veneer, Rotating Belt Mount, Table Top, 1860s, 18 x 10 In.
$775

Ruby Lane, Inc.

Steuben, Basket, Calcite, Blue Aurene Interior, Crimped, Handle, Swirled Prunts, 7 ½ In.
$2,875

Early Auction Co.

Steuben, Bowl, Calcite, Gold, Flared Rim, Aurene, 2 ¾ x 10 ¼ In.
$230

Humler & Nolan

S

Steuben, Puff Box, Lid, Gold Ball Finial, Aurene, Paper Label, 5 ½ In.
$805

Early Auction Co.

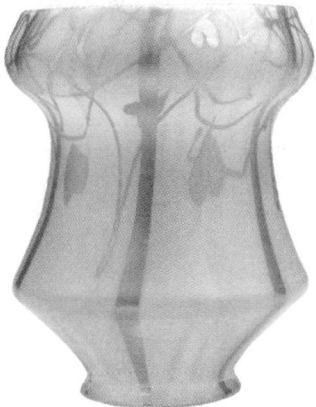

Steuben, Shade, Iridescent, Leaf & Vine, Optic Ribs, Shouldered, 2 ¼ x 5 ¼ In.
$652

James D. Julia Auctioneers

Steuben, Vase, Flowers, Art Deco Style, Godfrey Pattern, Mottled, 3 Tiers, 14 In.
$4,600

Early Auction Co.

Goblet, Jadeite, Flared, Frosted Twist Stem, 5 ½ x 4 ½ In.	92
Goblet, Topaz, Amethyst Feet, Mica Flecks, Cone Shape, 6 ½ In., 4 Piece	288
Goblet, Water, Amber, Undulating Vertical Flutes, Pomona Green Foot, 6 In., Pair	53
Lamp, Electric, Hanging, Leaf & Vine, Blue Aurene Ground, Calcite Interior, 7 x 12 In.	5635
Lamp, Harp, Gold Aurene Shade, Marked Meriden, Conn., 1920s, 54 x 14 In.	1625
Lamp, Luminary, Amber Plaque, Nude Grape Harvester, Bronze Scroll Foot, 17 In.	2300
Mouse, On Cheese, Clear, 18K Gold, James Houston, Box, 1975, 4 x 3 ¾ In.	1980
Paperweight, Apple, Clear Glass, 4 In.	96
Paperweight, Center Bubble, White Latticinio Spiral, Clear, Egg Shape, 3 In.	180
Paperweight, Pear Shape, S On Bottom, 3 In.	106
Perfume Bottle, DeVilbiss, Atomizer, Blue, Footed, Aurene, Gold Fittings, 7 In.	316
Perfume Bottle, Gold, Footed, Blue Jade & Black Flower Stopper, Aurene, 7 In.	2588
Perfume Bottle, Verre De Soie, Melon Ribbed, Blue Teardrop Stopper, 4 ½ In.	288
Plate, Selenium Red, Signed, F. Carder, 8 In.	575
Puff Box, Lid, Gold Ball Finial, Aurene, Paper Label, 5 ½ In. ....*illus*	805
Salt, Brown, Purple Iridescent, Platinum Accent, Bulbous, Aurene, 2 In.	1778
Salt, Gold, Round, Scalloped Rim, Aurene, Mark, 3 In.	150
Sculpture, Aria, Nude Couple Embracing, Clear, Frosted, Engraved, 10 In.	1625
Sculpture, Howl At The Moon, Clear, Frosted, Silver Accents, James Houston, 7 x 7 In.	3900
Sculpture, Mouse & Cheese, Clear, Frosted, Gold Mouse, J. Houston, 4 In.	1625
Sculpture, Planets, Prism, Clear, Frosted, 7 ½ In.	2813
Sculpture, Sphere, Squared, Clear, Box, 6 x 6 In.	1416
Shade, Brown, Calcite Interior, Intarsia Border, Corset, Marked, 2 ¼ x 5 ¼ In.	356
Shade, Calcite, Blue Pulled Feather, Gold Iridescent Tip, Aurene, Marked, 5 ½ In.	403
Shade, Gold Iridescent, Calcite, Green Pulled Feather, Bulbous, 2 ¼ x 3 ½ In., Pair	338
Shade, Iridescent, Leaf & Vine, Optic Ribs, Shouldered, 2 ¼ x 5 ¼ In. ....*illus*	652
Sherbet, Underplate, Calcite, Gold Aurene, 6 In., 6 Piece	288
Sundial, Clear, Round, Stepped Rim, 9 ½ In.	1440
Vase, 3-Bud, Calla Lily, Ivrene, Opalescent, Mark, 6 ½ x 12 In.	427
Vase, 3-Prong Stump, Amethyst, Translucent, Fleur-De-Lis Mark, 6 ¾ In.	518
Vase, Acid Cut Back, Green, Allover Flowers, Leaves, Bulbous, 7 In.	608
Vase, Acid Cut, White Over Green, Flowers, Leaves, c.1920, 14 ½ In.	3000
Vase, Amethyst, White Mottling, Baluster, 8 ½ x 7 In.	995
Vase, Amphora, Green Jade, Oval, Raised Alabaster M-Form Handles, 10 ¼ In.	660
Vase, Black Glass, Stepped Base, c.1925	480
Vase, Blue Iridescent, Aurene, 6 ¼ In.	474
Vase, Blue, Bulbous, Flared Rim, Aurene, Mark, 8 ¼ In.	851
Vase, Blue, Flowers, Vertical Ribs, Inverted Saucer Foot, Aurene, 14 ¼ In., Pair	4740
Vase, Blue, Ruffled Rim, Aurene, c.1910, 2 ½ In.	330
Vase, Blue, Shouldered, Cylindrical, Aurene, 10 In.	660
Vase, Blue, Tapered, Aurene, c.1910, 2 ½ In.	570
Vase, Blue, Tapered, Aurene, Mark, 10 In.	1185
Vase, Blue, Twisted Stem, Spread Foot, Ruffle Rim, Aurene, Mark, 12 x 7 In.	2070
Vase, Boat Shape, Clear, 11 ½ In.	40
Vase, Brown, Organic, White & Yellow Millefiori, Green & Platinum Hearts, Vines, Aurene, 3 In.	2370
Vase, Clear To Blue, Bubbles, Round, Tapered, Ring Foot, c.1935, 7 x 6 In.	1045
Vase, Cluthra, Gold Ruby, Shouldered, 10 ¼ In.	1840
Vase, Cluthra, Green Shaded To White, 2 Applied Clear Handles, 10 In.	1007
Vase, Cluthra, Pink, Eye Pattern, Tapered, Mark, 1920s, 7 ½ In.	1200
Vase, Cornucopia, Selenium Red, Ruffled Rim, Footed, 10 In.	316
Vase, Fan, Clear, Etched Spanish Galleon, Pomona Green Pedestal Base, 8 ½ In.	185
Vase, Florentia, White, Textured, Pink Pulled Leaves, Urn Shape, 12 In.	345
Vase, Flowers, Art Deco Style, Godfrey Pattern, Mottled, 3 Tiers, 14 In. ....*illus*	4600
Vase, Gold Aurene, Cylindrical, Flaring Scalloped Rim, Signed, 7 In.	460
Vase, Gold, Bulbous, Shouldered, Aurene, Mark, 8 ½ In.	518
Vase, Gold, Bulbous, Shouldered, Rolled Rim, Aurene, c.1900, 10 x 9 In.	1200
Vase, Gold, Flared Ruffled Rim, Aurene, c.1910, 9 In.	416
Vase, Gold, Pulled Feathers, Swollen, Aurene, 6 ¼ In. ....*illus*	2300
Vase, Gold, Ribbed, Scalloped Flared Rim, Aurene, c.1910, 5 ½ In.	281
Vase, Green, Translucent, Pulled Leaf & Vine, Gold Aurene, 5 ½ In.	4600
Vase, Jack-In-The-Pulpit, Aurene, 10 ¼ In.	1126
Vase, Jade Green, High Alabaster Handles, c.1910, 12 In.	875
Vase, Jade Over Alabaster, Acid Etched Flowers, 12 x 10 In. ....*illus*	2760
Vase, Jardiniere, Blue, Gold Highlights, Rolled Rim, Aurene, Mark, 7 In. ....*illus*	978
Vase, Red & White Opalescent Stripes, Poppy Shape, Pomona Green Foot, 9 x 8 In.	594
Vase, Stump, 3 Prongs, Thorns, Amethyst, 6 ½ x 4 In.	322

Vase, Thistles, Flowers, Alabaster, Black, Flattened, Round, 6 ½ x 7 ½ In.		644
Vase, Translucent Amber, Iridized Gold, Globular, Aurene, c.1920, 12 In.		1250
Vase, Trumpet, Blue, Diagonal Ribs, Saucer Base, 12 In.		1573
Vase, Trumpet, Gold, Iridescent, Pink, Purple, Aurene, c.1915, 8 x 5 ½ In.		338
Vase, Trumpet, Gold, Onionskin, Scalloped Rim, Footed, Aurene, Mark, 8 ½ In.		720
Vase, Urn, Squat, Flared Rim, 3 Scroll Handles, Aurene, c.1915, 6 In.		625

STEVENS & WILLIAMS of Stourbridge, England, made many types of glass, including layered, etched, cameo, and art glass, between the 1830s and 1930s. Some pieces are signed *S & W*. Many pieces are decorated with flowers, leaves, and other designs based on nature.

Biscuit Jar, Satin Glass, 4 Pinched Sides, Flowers, 9 In.		474
Bowl, Coupe, Rainbow Red, Yellow, Blue Cameo Raspberries, Scalloped Rim, 3 ½ In.		518
Bowl, Flowers, Blue Caramel, Custard, Square Crimped Rim, c.1893, 4 x 5 ½ In.		288
Decanter, Stopper, Green, Rose Cut Overlay, Scrolls, Pinched, Silver Mount, 1898, 8 In.		5750
Dish, Cranberry, Oval, Applied Rigaree Feet, Shell Rim, 7 In.		144
Dish, Sweetmeat, White, Pink Interior, Multicolor Leaves, Silver Plate Cow Finial, 4 x 6 In.		266
Dresser Bottle, Blue Overshot, Amber Flowers, Embossed, Globular, 5 In.		5175
Vase, Blue, Flowers, Cameo, Baluster, Flared, c.1900, 10 ¼ In.		2040
Vase, Bud, Ribbed Melon, Silver Foil, Blue, Gold Accents, c.1910, 7 In.		1500
Vase, Pompeiian Swirl, Green Shaded To Teal Rim, Bulbous, Stick Neck, 9 In.		633
Vase, Pompeiian Swirl, Red Shaded To Purple, Bottle Shape, 9 ½ In.		460
Vase, Stick, Strawberry Diamond Pattern, Rainbow Stripes, c.1900, 5 In.		345
Vase, Trumpet, Opaline, Pink Honeysuckle Vine, Cameo, Footed, 6 ½ In.		259
Vase, White, Pink Interior, Applied Amber Feet, Leaves & Acorns, 9 ½ In., Pair		177

STIEGEL TYPE glass is listed here. It is almost impossible to be sure a piece was actually made by Stiegel, so the knowing collector refers to this glass as "Stiegel type." Henry William Stiegel, a colorful immigrant to the colonies, started his first factory in Pennsylvania in 1763. He remained in business until 1774. Glassware was made in a style popular in Europe at that time and was similar to the glass of many other makers. It was made of clear or colored glass and was decorated with enamel colors, mold blown designs, or etching.

Bottle, Clear, Bird, Flowers, Multicolor Paint, Metal Lid, 5 ½ In.		210
Bottle, Clear, Boy, Holding Goblet, Painted, Metal Top, c.1820, 5 ¼ In.		210
Bottle, Clear, Flowers, Multicolor Paint, Metal Top, 5 ¾ In.		90

STONE includes those articles made of stones, coral, shells, and some other natural materials not listed elsewhere in this book. Micro mosaics (small decorative designs made by setting pieces of stone into a pattern), urns, vases, and other pieces made of natural stone are listed here. Stoneware is pottery and is listed in the Stoneware category. Alabaster, Jade, Malachite, Marble, and Soapstone are in their own categories.

Basket, Birds, Fruit Filled, Carved, 12 ½ In., Pair		300
Bust, Female Buddhist, Carved, Rosewood Stand, Indonesia, c.1900, 14 ½ x 11 In.		472
Figure, Amber, Free-Form, 12 ½ x 4 ⅜ x 5 ¾ In.		142
Figure, Elephant, Trunk Down, Carved, Hardstone, Asian, c.1960, 22 ¾ x 26 In.		313
Figure, Faces, Eagle, Carved, Sticker Marked Cadaha, Some Voice, Onindaga, 8 ½ In.		70
Figure, Foo Dog, Paw On Ball, Red, c.1900, 23 x 33 In., Pair		1912
Figure, Foo Dog, Seated, Carved, 29 ½ In., Pair		1560
Figure, Goldfish, Green Fluorite, Hollowed, Carved Rosewood Stand, c.1900, 6 x 11 In.		615
Figure, Guanyin, Lapis Lazuli, Flowers, Flowing Robe, Carved, 5 ¾ x 4 In.		510
Figure, Guanyin, Rose Quartz, Standing, Flowing Robes, Wood Base, 8 In.		360
Figure, Guanyin, Turquoise, Carved, Long Robe, Flower, Seated, 3 ¾ x 2 ½ In.		150
Figure, Lion, Seated, Carved, Italy, c.1850, 13 In., Pair		861
Figure, Mermaid, Hands Behind Back, Art Deco, Alice Carr, c.1930, 13 ¾ In.		1250
Figure, Monk, Hands Clasped, Lotus, Clouds, Flowers, Chinese, 1800s, 4 In.		3480
Figure, Oval, Pierced, Carved, 3 Cranes, Lotus Flowers, Beige, Brown, Chinese, 3 In.		4200
Figure, Rabbit, Holding Shield, 22 ½ In., Pair		1080
Figure, Seated Goddess, Cherry Amber, Carved, 6 x 4 In.		780
Figure, Toucan, Hardstone, Carved, Red, Black, White Paint, Orange Base, 8 ¾ In.		142
Figure, Turtle, Carved, William Edmondson, c.1935, 6 ½ x 15 In.		2500
Frame, Micro Mosaic, Multicolor Flowers, Copper Backing, Hinged Leg, 8 x 6 ½ In.		483
Lamp, White Paint, Cast, 21 x 22 In.		170
Obelisk, Rock Crystal, Continental, 1900s, 20 ¼ x 4 In., Pair ....*illus*		2440
Obelisk, Rouge Marble, White Marble, Applied Lapis Lazuli Medallions, 35 In., Pair		4484
Plaque, Figures, Limestone, Vines, Bas Relief, Graphics, Asian, 1900s, 58 In.		480

Steuben, Vase, Gold, Pulled Feathers, Swollen, Aurene, 6 ¼ In.
$2,300

Early Auction Co.

Steuben, Vase, Jade Over Alabaster, Acid Etched Flowers, 12 x 10 In.
$2,760

Cottone Auctions

Steuben, Vase, Jardiniere, Blue, Gold Highlights, Rolled Rim, Aurene, Mark, 7 In.
$978

Early Auction Co.

S

Stone, Obelisk, Rock Crystal, Continental, 1900s, 20 ¼ x 4 In., Pair
$2,440

Neal Auction Co.

Stone, Plaque, Pietra Dura, 5 Butterflies, Frame, Italy, 1900s, 4 ¾ x 6 ⅜ In.
$3,776

Brunk Auctions

Stone, Tazza, Rock Crystal, Neoclassical Style, Tall Plinth, 9 ¼ In., Pair
$2,196

Neal Auction Co.

Stoneware, Ashtray, Cobalt Blue Design, Woman, Bust, Robinson Clay, Akron, c.1890, 3 ¾ In.
$86

Crocker Farm, Inc.

Stoneware, Crock, Cobalt Blue Deer, O.L. & A.K. Ballard, Burlington, Vt., c.1860, 5 Gal.
$1,150

Crocker Farm, Inc.

Stoneware, Crock, Cobalt Blue Elephant & Rider, Handles, Ohio, c.1875, 6 Gal., 13 ⅝ In.
$9,200

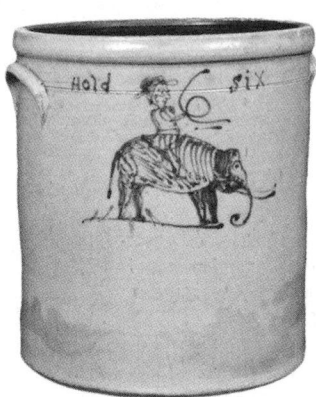

Crocker Farm, Inc.

Stoneware, Cuspidor, Cobalt Blue Design, Greek Key, Albany Slip Glaze, c.1890, 6 x 11 ½ In.
$173

Crocker Farm, Inc.

Stoneware, Flask, Ring, Alkaline Glaze, Lassoed Spout, Stamped J.S. Nash, c.1860, 9 ½ In.
$8,050

Crocker Farm, Inc.

Stoneware, Jar, Cobalt Blue Hand, Lug Handles, N. Clark & Co., Lyons, c.1830, 2 Gal.
$2,760

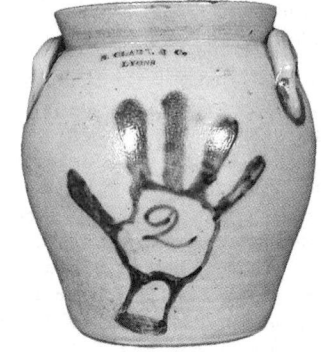

Crocker Farm, Inc.

Healthy Collecting
Ignore doctors and critics unless your collection gets so large there is no room for you in your house. Maybe we have a collecting gene and are storing things for an unknown future. Or, as some experts now claim, finding that "special collectible" sets off endorphins that create pleasure, just like running a race, hearing music, or winning at gambling.

Plaque, Openwork, Child, Lotus, Green, Chinese, 3 In.		120
Plaque, Pietra Dura, 5 Butterflies, Frame, Italy, 1900s, 4 ¾ x 6 ⅜ In.	*illus*	3776
Plaque, Pietra Dura, Figure At Ell, 1800s, 9 ¾ x 5 ½ In.		633
Sculpture, Angel, Winged, Hands Clasped, c.1900, 30 x 9 In.		633
Sculpture, Flamingo, White, 42 ½ In.		374
Sign Post, Mile Marker, Worcester Turnpike, Tombstone Shape, c.1810, 28 x 15 In.		9600
Tazza, Rock Crystal, Neoclassical Style, Tall Plinth, 9 ¼ In., Pair	*illus*	2196

STONEWARE is a coarse, glazed, and fired potter's ceramic that is used to make crocks, jugs, bowls, etc. It is often decorated with cobalt blue decorations. In the nineteenth and early twentieth centuries, potters often decorated crocks with blue numbers indicating the size of the container. A *2* meant 2 gallons. Stoneware is still being made. American stoneware is listed here.

Ashtray, Cobalt Blue Design, Woman, Bust, Robinson Clay, Akron, c.1890, 3 ¾ In.	*illus*	86
Bank, Albany Slip, Incised Knob Handle, Missouri, c.1870, 4 ½ x 4 ½ In.		52
Bank, Cobalt Blue, Spaniel, Seated, c.1850, 9 In.		1185
Batter Jar, Cobalt Blue Flowers, Impressed FH Cowden Harrisburg, Handle, Pa., c.1850, 9 In.		1067
Batter Jar, Tin Lid, Cobalt Blue Flowers, Handle, Sipe, Nichols & Co., Pa., c.1880, 12 In.		326
Batter Pail, Tulip, Wreath, Oval, Spout, Bail Handle, Cowden & Wilcox, Gal.		2300
Bottle, Salt Glaze, Cylindrical, Tapered Neck, Cole & Co., Baltimore, 10 ½ In.		29
Bottle, Square, Pinched Neck, Relief, Iron Glaze, Square Foot, c.1945, 7 ½ x 5 In.		2829
Bowl, Blue Border, White Ground, Rose On Trellis Pattern, 3 ½ x 12 ½ In.		58
Bowl, Wide Shaped Rim, Gray, Richard Devore, 6 x 11 In.		1320
Charger, Portrait, Woman, Brown, Blue, P. Voulkos, c.1952, 18 In.		3000
Chicken Waterer, Brown Glaze, Oval, Turned Finial, Saucer Base, E.A.L. Hyssong, 8 ¾ In.		472
Churn, Clover Decoration, Flaring Collar, Lug Handles, Baltimore, c.1865, 3 Gal.		374
Churn, Cobalt Blue Bird, Oval, Tooled Shoulder, Lug Handles, c.1860, 5 Gal.		144
Churn, Cobalt Blue Bird, Tooled Shoulder, Semi-Rounded Rim, Lug Handles, c.1865, 5 Gal.		374
Churn, Cobalt Blue Decoration, Swan & States, Stonington, Ct., c.1825, 2 Gal.		345
Churn, Cobalt Blue Flowers, 4 Gal., 16 In.		385
Churn, Cobalt Blue Flowers, Tooled Banding Molded Handles		58
Churn, Cobalt Blue Flowers, Urn, White's, Utica, Tooled Shoulder, Lug Handles, 1865, 3 Gal.		2530
Churn, Daisy, Tree, Cobalt Blue, Squared Rim, Lug Handles, Smith & Day, 1840		230
Churn, Impressed Joe Bayer Washington, Missouri, 2 Gal., 11 ½ x 7 ½ In.		196
Churn, Salt Glaze, Flower Design, U.S.A., c.1875, 6 Gal., 19 In.		492
Churn, Wood Lid, Dasher, Joe Bayer, Washington, Mo., 10 ½ x 6 In.		368
Crock, A. Booth's Solid Meat Oysters, Stencil, 5, Lug Handles, c.1880, 13 ¼ In.		345
Crock, Bird, Spotted, Long Neck, Cobalt Blue, Rounded Rim, Lug Handles, 3 Gal.		288
Crock, Blue Flower, Gray & Brown, Salt Glaze, 2 Open Handles, 9 ⅜ In.		460
Crock, Blue Flowers, Lug Handles, West Virginia, 10 Gal., 19 In.		3318
Crock, Butter, Cylindrical, Tooled Shoulder, Squared Rim, Tab Handles, c.1870, Gal.		144
Crock, Butter, Lid, Cobalt Flowers, Squat Cylinder, Pa., c.1855, 5 In.		444
Crock, Cake, Lid, Clover, Swags, Squared Rim, Baltimore, c.1880, 8 x 10 In.		288
Crock, Cake, Lid, Cobalt Blue Feather, Tab Handles, Hickerson, c.1900, 2 Gal., 8 x 10 In.		288
Crock, Cake, Lid, Cobalt Blue Flower, Handles, L.D. Funkhouser, c.1885, 2 Gal., 8 x 10 In.		460
Crock, Cake, Lid, Cobalt Blue Flowers, Leaves, Round, Applied Ear Handles, 7 In.		325
Crock, Cake, Salt Glaze, Stamped Woods & Silber, c.1870, ½ Gal., 5 x 9 In.		403
Crock, Cake, Trailing Vine, Flowers, H. Remmey, Philadelphia, c.1830, Gal.		575
Crock, Cobalt Blue 2-Sided Slip Tulip, Leaves, Ear Handles, 2 ½ Gal., 11 In.		224
Crock, Cobalt Blue 2-Stem Clover, Tooled Shoulder, Stamped P. Herrmann, c.1880		374
Crock, Cobalt Blue Bird, Branch, Incised, Open Handles, Oval, c.1840, 10 ½ In.		180
Crock, Cobalt Blue Bird, Impressed Mark, E.B. Noron, Mass., c.1870, 11 In.		390
Crock, Cobalt Blue Bird, Stump, Stamped Brady & Ryan, Ellenville, N.Y., c.1885, 3 Gal.		259
Crock, Cobalt Blue Chicken, Impressed Fort Edward Stoneware, Co., 4 Gal., 11 ½ In.		425
Crock, Cobalt Blue Chicken, Pecking Corn, Thos. Losee Jr., Handles, 11 ½ In.		738
Crock, Cobalt Blue Chicken Pecking, Impressed Ft. Edwards, 10 ½ In.		540
Crock, Cobalt Blue Clover, Pail Shape, Applied Tab Handles, c.1870, 9 ⅛ In.		403
Crock, Cobalt Blue Deer, O.L. & A.K. Ballard, Burlington, Vt., c.1860, 5 Gal.	*illus*	1150
Crock, Cobalt Blue Design, Handles, Impressed, c.1835, 14 In.		793
Crock, Cobalt Blue Dinosaur, Applied Lug Handles, Fulper Bros., c.1890, 2 Gal.		17250
Crock, Cobalt Blue Double Label Stencil, Eagle, Jas. Hamilton & Co., 20, Handles, 25 In.		1320
Crock, Cobalt Blue Eagle Stencil, Impressed JC Waelde, North Bay, c.1860, 10 In.		1599
Crock, Cobalt Blue Elephant & Rider, Handles, Ohio, c.1875, 6 Gal., 13 ⅝ In.	*illus*	9200
Crock, Cobalt Blue Face, Tooled Shoulder, Lug Handles, William Macquoid, c.1870, Gal.		431
Crock, Cobalt Blue Feather, Flared Shape, Tab Handles, S. Bell, c.1885, 1 ½ Gal., 6 x 11 In.		316
Crock, Cobalt Blue Feather, Incised Ring Handles, Emanuel Suterc, 1880, 3 Gal., 11 x 10 In.		431

Stoneware, Jar, Cobalt Blue Rooster, Lug Handles, C.W. Braun, Buffalo, N.Y., c.1870, 4 Gal.
$18,400

Crocker Farm, Inc.

Stoneware, Jug, Bellermine, Salt Glaze, Bearded Man's Face, Cartouche, Handle, c.1610, 8 In.
$265

Glass Works Auctions

Stoneware, Jug, Cobalt Blue House, Man & Horse, Incised, Handle, c.1810, 2 Gal., 15 ¾ In.
$1,438

Crocker Farm, Inc.

S

Stoneware, Jug, Compliments Of Murdock & Son, Brown Glaze, Black Transfer, c.1900, 3 In.
$242

Glass Works Auctions

Stoneware, Jug, Face, Broken China Teeth, Incised Lines, Stamped, B.B. Craig, 19 ½ In.
$708

Brunk Auctions

Stoneware, Jug, Face, Rock Teeth, Olive Underfired Glaze, Lanier Meaders, 1900s, 9 ¼ In.
$1,180

Brunk Auctions

Crock, Cobalt Blue Feather, Lug Handles, Stamped W.B. Kenner, c.1875, Gal., 7 x 9 In.	196
Crock, Cobalt Blue Feather, Square Rim, Stamped W. H. Lehew, c.1865, Qt., 7 x 5 In.	288
Crock, Cobalt Blue Feathers On Neck, Cylindrical, Stamped J. Keister, c.1865, 9 x 5 In.	489
Crock, Cobalt Blue Flower Basket, Cylindrical, Lug Handles, c.1875, 4 ½ In.	230
Crock, Cobalt Blue Flower, Semi-Rounded Rim, Lug Handles, J. Burger Jr., c.1885, 2 Gal.	144
Crock, Cobalt Blue Flowers, Cylindrical, Semi-Rounded Rim, Applied Lug Handles, 3 Gal.	230
Crock, Cobalt Blue Flowers, St. Pewtress, New Haven, Conn., c.1860, 12 In.	360
Crock, Cobalt Blue Flowers, Impressed Sugar Valley, c.1860, 8 ¾ In.	1304
Crock, Cobalt Blue Flowers, Lug Handles, D. Ack, Montour County, Pa., c.1860, 4 In.	3081
Crock, Cobalt Blue Flowers, Lug Handles, Impressed Lyons, c.1860, 9 In.	356
Crock, Cobalt Blue Flowers, Morgantown, West Va., 2 Gal., 11 ½ In.	889
Crock, Cobalt Blue Leaves, Impressed Evan R. Jones, Pittston, c.1850, 3 Gal., 10 ½ In.	119
Crock, Cobalt Blue Leaves, Lug Handles, Impressed Evan R. Jones Pittston, Pa., c.1865, 14 In.	213
Crock, Cobalt Blue Lettering, E.J. Miller, 4 Gal.	374
Crock, Cobalt Blue Lion, Flower, Impressed F. Stetzenmeyer & Co., c.1850, 6 Gal., 14 In.	7110
Crock, Cobalt Blue Parrot, Semi-Rounded Rim, Lug Handles, F.B. Norton & Co., 1870, 4 Gal.	776
Crock, Cobalt Blue Peacock, Cowden & Wilcox, Harrisburg, Pa., 1800s, 4 Gal., 14 In.	3792
Crock, Cobalt Blue Reclining Deer, Semi-Rounded Rim, Applied Lug Handles, c.1860, 3 Gal.	1955
Crock, Cobalt Blue Shells, Stamped Woods & Silber, c.1870, 2 Gal., 12 x 7 In.	345
Crock, Cobalt Blue Slip Bird, Wreath, Flared Rim, Ear Handles, Cowden & Wilcox, 13 In.	2242
Crock, Cobalt Blue Slip Bowtie Flowers, Leaves, Cowden & Wilcox, 3 Gal., 13 ½ In.	472
Crock, Cobalt Blue Slip Fern, Tulip, Bellflower, Vine, Ear Handles, Cowden & Wilcox, 13 In.	4425
Crock, Cobalt Blue Slip Swan, Water, Bulbous, Molded Lip, Cowden & Wilcox, 8 ¼ In.	3304
Crock, Cobalt Blue Standing Lion, Tooled Shoulder, Applied Lug Handles, c.1865	20700
Crock, Cobalt Blue Starburst, Applied Lug Handles, A.O. Whittemore, c.1865, 5 Gal.	1495
Crock, Cobalt Blue Stencil Label, Dry Goods Store, Hannibal, Ohio, c.1850, 10 In.	705
Crock, Cobalt Blue Tulip, 2-Sided, Impressed John Bell, Waynesboro, Pa., c.1865, 11 In.	8295
Crock, Cobalt Blue Tulip, Leaves, Oval, Flattened Molded Rim, Cowden & Wilcox, 8 In.	118
Crock, Cobalt Blue Tulip, Slip, Oval, Molded Rim, Ear Handles, Wilson & Young, 10 In.	3835
Crock, Cobalt Blue, Oval, Squat, c.1855, 7 x 5 In.	4025
Crock, Cobalt Blue, Scrolls, Cylindrical, Stamped D.H. Henkel, ½ Gal.	1610
Crock, Cobalt Blue, Stenciled, Handles, Rolled Rim, c.1855, 17 In.	558
Crock, Cream, Cobalt Blue Design, Lug Handles, Rolled Rim, c.1890, 31 In.	118
Crock, Cylindrical, Gray, Blue Inscribed Baltimore, Md., 9 ½ In.	554
Crock, Groceries, Notions, Hardware, White Glaze, Banded, 6 ¾ In.	153
Crock, J.B. Leathers, Impressed, Mt. Eagle, Pa., c.1850, 4 Gal., 13 In.	2844
Crock, Lid, Cobalt Blue Leaves, Pa., 1800s, 6 ½ In.	385
Crock, Manganese Flower, Feather, Handles, S. Bell & Son, c.1885, 3 Gal., 12 x 9 In.	546
Crock, Stenciled, Cobalt Blue, 2 Handles, U.S.A., c.1865, 18 ½ In.	331
Crock, Storage, Bulbous, Blue Slip Leaf Shoulder Band, 1 ½ Gal., 10 ½ In.	106
Crock, Swags, Cobalt Blue Over Tan, W.H. Crisman, Strasburg, Va., Gal.	230
Crock, Water, Barrel Shape, Blue & White Stripes, Flower, Lid, Spout, 17 x 12 In.	210
Cuspidor, Cobalt Blue Design, Greek Key, Albany Slip Glaze, c.1890, 6 x 11 ½ In. ....*illus*	173
Cuspidor, Cobalt Blue Feather, Stamped Wm. Moyer, Harrisburg, c.1860, 4 x 8 In.	1955
Feeder, Cobalt Blue Band, Squat, Pa., 5 In.	1896
Feeder, Wide Side Opening, Cobalt Blue Flowers, Pa., c.1845, 14 ¼ In.	948
Figurine, Rooster, Carved, Brown, Tan, White, 28 x 22 ½ In., Pair	600
Flask, Cobalt Blue Tulip, Salt Glaze, Flat Oval Shape, c.1840, 8 x 5 In.	288
Flask, Pig, Cobalt Blue Designs, Copper Cap, c.1850, 6 ¼ In.	1304
Flask, Ring, Alkaline Glaze, Lassoed Spout, Stamped J.S. Nash, c.1860, 9 ½ In. ....*illus*	8050
Flowerpot, Cobalt Blue Flowers, Crimped Rim, 1800s, 9 x 10 ¾ In.	5925
Flowerpot, Cobalt Blue, Tooled Shoulder, Applied Saucer, Slip Trailed Flower, c.1880, 3 In.	201
Gin Cooler, Leaves, Cobalt Blue, Hol. Gin, 2 Handles, Spout, W. Nichols, c.1920, 3 Gal.	2415
Jar, 3 Cobalt Blue Flowers, Applied Lug Handles, c.1835, 15 x 9 In.	2415
Jar, 7 Cobalt Blue Feathers, Salt Glaze, Applied Handles, c.1880, 4 Gal., 14 x 9 In.	374
Jar, A.V. Boughner, Vining, Bands, Stripes, 2, Cobalt Blue, c.1865, 2 Gal.	9200
Jar, Apple Butter, Salt Glaze, Handle, F.H. Cowden, Harrisburg, c.1880, Gal.	29
Jar, Applied Lug Handles, 2, J.W. McCoy, c.1900, 2 Gal., 14 ¼ In.	360
Jar, Basket Of Daisies, Cobalt Blue, Cylindrical, Flared Rim, Cortland, c.1868, Gal.	748
Jar, Brown, Albany Slip Glaze, Impressed, 8X, Stepped Rim, Lug Handle, 4 ¼ In.	201
Jar, Canning, A. Conrad & Co., Stars, Banner, Diamonds, Triangles, Tapered, c.1875	316
Jar, Canning, Salt Glaze, Barrel Shape, J.D. Heatwole, c.1865, 5 x 6 In.	2070
Jar, Cobalt Blue Beehive Flower, Leaves, Molded Rim, Ear Handles, Cowden & Wilcox, 10 In.	1062
Jar, Cobalt Blue Bird, Applied Handles, Shouldered, c.1860, 12 ½ In.	300
Jar, Cobalt Blue Clover, Oval, Applied Lug Handles, 3 Gal., 14 In.	288

Jar, Cobalt Blue Curlicues, Oval, Handles, James River, Va., c.1860, 15 x 8 In.	374
Jar, Cobalt Blue Design, Salt Glaze, Arched Handles, c.1880, 12 ¾ x 9 In.	403
Jar, Cobalt Blue Draped Flowers, Oval, Narrow Opening, Applied Lug Handles, c.1820, 3 Gal.	288
Jar, Cobalt Blue Feathers, Salt Glaze, Lug Handles, c.1835, Gal., 11 x 6 In.	259
Jar, Cobalt Blue Flower, Feather, Oval, Lug Handles, J. Keister & Co., c.1870, 2 Gal, 13 x 8 In.	1725
Jar, Cobalt Blue Flower, Stamped J.M. Hickerson, c.1885, 1 ½ Gal., 10 x 8 In.	374
Jar, Cobalt Blue Flowers, Arched Handles, Andrew Coffman, c.1850, 3 Gal., 13 x 7 ¾ In.	10350
Jar, Cobalt Blue Flowers, Footed Base, Flared Rim, Applied Tab Handles, c.1825, 4 Gal.	518
Jar, Cobalt Blue Flowers, Salt Glaze, Lug Handles, 4 Gal., 14 x 9 In.	374
Jar, Cobalt Blue Flowers, Squat Shape, Cylindrical, Tooled Shoulder, B.C. Milburn, 8 ¾ In.	805
Jar, Cobalt Blue Flowers, Tooled Shoulder, Flattened Rim, Tulip, D.P. Shenfelder, c.1870, Gal.	115
Jar, Cobalt Blue Grape Cluster, Cylindrical, Rounded Shoulder, Gal.	403
Jar, Cobalt Blue Hand, Lug Handles, N. Clark & Co., Lyons, c.1830, 2 Gal. *illus*	2760
Jar, Cobalt Blue Rooster, Lug Handles, C.W. Braun, Buffalo, N.Y., c.1870, 4 Gal. *illus*	18400
Jar, Cobalt Blue Stylized Decoration, Squat Shape, Oval, Lug Handles, c.1850, Gal.	201
Jar, Cobalt Blue Stylized Flowers, Slip Trailed, C. Hart, Sherburne, c.1855, Gal.	230
Jar, Cobalt Blue, H. Lowndes Maker, Petersburg, Va., Lug Handles, c.1840, 2 Gal., 12 x 7 In.	1265
Jar, Cobalt Blue, Salt Glaze, Cylindrical, Handles, S.H. Sonner, c.1875, 3 Gal., 13 x 9 In.	403
Jar, Cobalt Blue, Swag, Oval Shape, Rockbridge Co., c.1845, Gal., 12 x 5 In.	920
Jar, Dome Lid, Cream Glaze, Oval, Matte, Chinese, 3 ¾ In.	777
Jar, Drape, Dots, Tassel, Cobalt Blue, Open Loop Handles, 3 Gal.	115
Jar, Eagle, Banner, Eagle Pottery, Stenciled, Flared Rim, J. Hamilton, Greensboro, Pa., Gal.	2760
Jar, Flowers, 1843, Cobalt Blue, Lug Handles, Smith & Day, Norwalk, Conn., Gal.	518
Jar, Flowers, Henry Lowndes, Applied Rim, Handles, Petersburg, Va., c.1830, 11 ½ In.	2706
Jar, Heart & Drape Decoration, Cobalt Blue, Footed, Open Handles, David Morgan, 3 Gal.	7475
Jar, Honeycomb, Cobalt Blue, Flared Rim, Footed, ½ Gal.	173
Jar, Leaves, C.L. Williams & Co., New Geneva, Pa., Stenciled, 2 Gal.	230
Jar, Lid, Cobalt Blue Feather Under Rim, Stamped Solomon Bell, c.1865, Gal., 11 x 6 In.	219
Jar, Manganese Drape, Oval, Tooled Shoulder, Open Loop Handles, c.1810, 3 Gal.	173
Jar, Manganese Tulip, Flat Rim, Signed George Fulton, c.1870, Gal., 10 x 6 In.	690
Jar, Molasses, Dark Green, Black, Open Handles, c.1900, 3 Gal., 15 x 5 In.	374
Jar, Oval, Wide Rim, Lug Handles, Reeded Neck, c.1810, 9 ½ In.	3900
Jar, Oyster, Wide Mouth, Applied Handle, Robert Pettis, Providence, 11 ½ In.	144
Jar, Pond Lilies, Cold Painted, B.C. Miller, Ohio, 1849, 3 Gal.	316
Jar, Round, Lug Handles, Celadon Glaze, Etched Banding, c.1840, 18 ¼ In.	6490
Jar, Salt Glaze, Incised Sarah Price, 1827, JM	4212
Jar, Salt Glaze, Overhung Squared Rim, Incised Rings, Qt., 5 x 6 In.	184
Jar, Script Writing, Phoenix, Factory, 1840, Thomas Chandler	90000
Jar, Scrolled 2, Vertical Swags, Cobalt Blue, Western Pa., 1860, 2 Gal.	1150
Jar, Star Face, 8 Rays, Cobalt Blue, T. Harrington, Lyons, Lug Handles, c.1860, 12 In.	4600
Jar, Stenciled, Cobalt Blue, Hamilton & Jones, Star Pottery, Greensboro, Pa., c.1875, 8 ¼ In.	1140
Jar, Stenciled Manganese, Cobalt Blue Leaves, Scrolled, Star, Western Pa., c.1875, 6 ½ In.	201
Jar, Stylized Tulips, Wavy Lines, Drape, B.C. Milburn, Alexandria, c.1850, 8 ¼ In.	2530
Jar, Watchsprings, Cobalt Blue, Footed, Loop Handles, Capt. J. Morgan, 3 Gal.	374
Jug, 2 Hearts, Dots, Geddes, N.Y., Cobalt Blue, Sloping Shoulder, 2 Gal.	920
Jug, Albany Slip, Mrs. TG Thompson Scratched Springfield Missouri Co., 1889, 5 x 4 In.	633
Jug, Applied Grape Bunches, Leaves, Vines, Applied Handle, Inscribed, John Meaders, 8 In.	240
Jug, Ball Shape, Wide Loop Handle, Stylized Flowers, Blue & White, 1700s, 13 In.	826
Jug, Batter, Painted Tulips, Leaves, Spout, Bail Handle, Cowden & Wilcox, 8 ½ In.	325
Jug, Bellermine, Salt Glaze, Bearded Man's Face, Cartouche, Handle, c.1610, 8 In. *illus*	265
Jug, Blue, Gray, Impressed Burger Rochester N.Y., 1886, 2 Gal., 13 ½ In.	738
Jug, Brown Glaze, Strap Handle, Mask Design, Inscribed 4, 19 In.	1003
Jug, Bulbous, Strap Handle, Line Design, Olive Mottled Glaze, c.1850, 15 In.	4248
Jug, Case's Pure Cider Vinegar, Clover Hill, Hunterdon, N.J., Bristol Glaze, Gal.	1035
Jug, Cobalt Blue Bird, Branch, N.A. White & Co., Binghamton, N.Y., c.1870, 2 Gal., 13 ½ In.	510
Jug, Cobalt Blue Bird, Branch, Oval, Molded Spout, Loop Handle, N.Y. Stoneware Co., 11 In.	384
Jug, Cobalt Blue Bird, On Branch, 2 Gal., 13 ½ In.	390
Jug, Cobalt Blue Bird, On Branch, Round, Applied Ear Handles, 11 ½ In.	325
Jug, Cobalt Blue E.H. Miller & Co., Danville, Va., c.1900, 2 Gal.	560
Jug, Cobalt Blue Flowers, Gray, Oval, 17 In.	147
Jug, Cobalt Blue Flowers, Impressed Cowden & Wilcox, c.1850, 4 Gal., 15 In.	1304
Jug, Cobalt Blue Flowers, Impressed Cowden & Wilcox, Pa., 11 In.	790
Jug, Cobalt Blue Flowers, Oval, Molded Spout, Loop Handle, John Young & Co., 14 ¾ In.	5610
Jug, Cobalt Blue Flowers, Tooled Shoulder, H. Weston, Honesdale, Pa., c.1860, 2 Gal., 15 In.	201
Jug, Cobalt Blue House, Man & Horse, Incised, Handle, c.1810, 2 Gal., 15 ¾ In. *illus*	1438

Stoneware, Jug, I.W. Harper Nelson Co., Kentucky Whiskey Distillery, Handle, 1880s, 7 ½ In.
$115

Stoneware, Jug, Syrup, Cobalt Blue Birds, Pinched Spout, Fort Edward Pottery, c.1859, 2 Gal.
$1.265

Stoneware, Vase, Carved Flowers, Applied Garland, Salt Glaze, S. Frackelton, 1893, 6 x 8 In.
$10,000

S

Store, Cabinet, Hardware, Wood, Revolving, 80 Drawers, 6-Sided, c.1900, 36 x 23 In.
$1,298

Conestoga Auction Co., Inc.

Store, Case, Display, Curved Glass, Mirrored Back, c.1910, 13 x 33 x 24 In.
$875

Rago Arts & Auction Center

Store, Sign, Arms, Tattoos, Wood, 30 ½ In., Pair
$300

Morphy Auctions

Jug, Cobalt Blue Slip Beehive Flower, Wreath, Loop Handle, T.H. Wilson & Co., 14 In.	443
Jug, Cobalt Blue Slip Tulip, Dotted, Leaves, Loop Handle, Harrisburg, 12 ¼ In.	502
Jug, Cobalt Blue Slip Tulip, Leaves, Oval, Molded Spout, Loop Handle, Harrisburg, 11 ¾ In.	1121
Jug, Cobalt Blue Slip, Geometric Flowers, Leaves, Loop Handle, Cowden & Wilcox, 16 ½ In.	2832
Jug, Cobalt Blue Star, Marked T. Harrington, Lyons, N.Y., c.1850, 2 Gal., 14 ½ In.	630
Jug, Cobalt Blue Stylized Flower, Tan, Cowden & Hubbard, Harrisburg, Pa., 2 Gal.	230
Jug, Cobalt Blue Stylized Flowers, Oval, Molded Spout, Loop Handle, WM. Roberts, 16 In.	266
Jug, Cobalt Blue Triple Flower, Leaves, F.H. Cowden, 2 Gal., 14 ½ In.	325
Jug, Cobalt Blue, Flowers, Impressed Cowden & Wilcox, Pa., 1800s, 2 Gal., 14 ¼ In.	444
Jug, Cobalt Blue, Watch Spring Design, Oval, Loop Handle At Neck, c.1760, 12 In.	960
Jug, Collared Mouth, Strap Handle, Emanuel Suter, c.1885, Gal., 10 In.	80
Jug, Compliments Of C.R. Schilt, Haigler, Neb., Cream, Brown, 3 In.	253
Jug, Compliments Of Junius Bright, Norfolk, Va., Cream, Black Transfer, 3 ⅜ In.	288
Jug, Compliments Of M.J. Leigh, Bloomfield, Neb., Cream, Brown, 3 In.	115
Jug, Compliments Of Murdock & Son, Brown Glaze, Black Transfer, c.1900, 3 In. .... *illus*	242
Jug, Country Fair Scene, Cobalt Blue, 1987, 2 Gal.	374
Jug, D. Goodale, Hartford, Salt Glaze, Handle, 12 ¼ In.	196
Jug, Dean, Foster & Co., 14 Blackstone St., Boston, Gray, Cobalt Blue Bird, 2 Gal.	498
Jug, Etched Church, Stars, Palmyra, Missouri, c.1865, 14 x 9 ¾ In.	3450
Jug, Face, 4-Color Swirl, China Teeth, Loop Handles, B. Craig, 12 In.	502
Jug, Face, Broken China Teeth, Incised Lines, Stamped, B.B. Craig, 19 ½ In. .... *illus*	708
Jug, Face, Handles, Black, White Teeth, Stamped B.B. Craig, North Carolina, 19 ½ In.	480
Jug, Face, Painted African Warrior's Head, Ears, Open Mouth, Incised Teeth, 1920s, 14 In.	1840
Jug, Face, Rock Teeth, Olive Underfired Glaze, Lanier Meaders, 1900s, 9 ¼ In. .... *illus*	1180
Jug, Flowers, Blue, A.J. Butler, New Brunswick, N.J., Oval, Strap Handle, c.1860, 2 Gal.	316
Jug, Grotesque, Applied Handle, Stone Teeth, Jerry Brown Hamilton, c.1991, 9 ½ In.	120
Jug, Grotesque, Pottery Shard Teeth, Glazed, B.B. Craig, Vale, N.C., c.1950, 10 In.	492
Jug, Grotesque, Stone Teeth, Applied Handle, Incised Eyebrows, Facial Hair, 9 ¼ In.	240
Jug, Handles, Cobalt Blue Design, Flat Rim, Oval, Impressed, 11 ½ In.	235
Jug, I.W. Harper Nelson Co., Kentucky Whiskey Distillery, Handle, 1880s, 7 ½ In. .... *illus*	115
Jug, Incised Birds, Tan, Blue, Footed, Spout, Ribbed Handle, D. Morgan, ½ Gal.	1380
Jug, Incised Cobalt Blue Checks, Squares & Initials GR, Westerwald, 10 In.	178
Jug, J. Burger, Jr., Rochester, Cobalt Blue Grapes & Leaves, Salt Glaze, 3 Gal., 16 In.	288
Jug, Levy & Glosking, Distillers, Pure Rye Whiskey, Dover, Del., Bristol Glaze, 3 Gal.	575
Jug, Merchant's, Cobalt Blue Script, 2, Hubert Murray, Buffalo, N.Y., c.1860, 13 ½ In.	240
Jug, Oatmeal, Oval, Strap Handle, Banded Rim, Edgefield, 5 ¼ In.	3744
Jug, Oil, Spout, High Gloss Brown Glaze, Rounded, 1800s, 12 x 9 ¼ In.	127
Jug, Pheasant On Stump, Cobalt Blue, Seth E. Pecker, Boston, c.1855, 2 Gal.	4025
Jug, Pierced Neck Band, 3 Nozzles, Drinkers, Windmill, Tan Glaze, England, c.1830, 8 In.	259
Jug, Reeded Neck, Ocher Stain, Oval, c.1827, 16 ¼ In.	390
Jug, Salt Glaze, Pulled Strap Handle, W.H. Hancock, c.1900, Gal., 11 In.	590
Jug, Salt Glaze, Orange Peel Color, Himer Fox, 1 Qt., 7 ½ In.	770
Jug, Slip Trailed Inscription, Scott & Player, No. 2, Columbia, SC, c.1850, 13 ¾ In.	13200
Jug, Spout Mask Design, Brown, Bellarmine, Germany, c.1765, 17 ½ In.	266
Jug, Squat, Tooled Shoulder, Brown Albany Slip, John B. Caire & Co., Poughkeepsie, Gal.	86
Jug, Stamped W.T. Light, John Stork Pottery, Richland County, SC, c.1880, 12 ½ In.	2880
Jug, Strap Handle, Impressed 3, Sunflower, Cobalt Blue, U.S.A., c.1840, 16 In.	353
Jug, Syrup, Cobalt Blue Birds, Pinched Spout, Fort Edward Pottery, c.1859, 2 Gal. .... *illus*	1265
Jug, Tulip, J. Heiser, Buffalo, N.Y., Cobalt Blue, Swollen Shape, c.1850, 3 Gal.	431
Jug, Whiskey, Blue, White Rings, Phil G. Kelly & Co., Va., 3 Gal., c.1920, 17 In.	196
Lid, Edgefield, Thomas Chandler, c.1845, 8 In.	1200
Milk Pan, 3 Flowers, Cobalt Blue, R.J. Grier, Chester County, Pa., c.1880, 3 Qt.	345
Milk Pan, Swags, Cobalt Blue, Squared Edge, Spout, 2 Ear Handles, 1 ½ Gal.	173
Mixing Bowl, Blue Sponged, Salt Glaze, Double Arch Mold, 13 In.	118
Mug, Blue Bands, Inscribed JA Perkins, Pa., 4 ⅜ In.	474
Mug, Yellow Glaze, Green Slip Blotches, Tapered Applied Loop Handle, 1800s, 3 ¼ In.	130
Pitcher, Blue, Gray, Embossed Indians, Campfire, Ky., c.1925, 8 In.	374
Pitcher, Brown, Impressed J.B. Leathers, Mt. Eagle, 1800s, 9 ½ In.	3081
Pitcher, Cobalt Blue Clover, Impress 4, Circle, Strap Handle, c.1850, 16 In.	780
Pitcher, Cobalt Blue Design, Dry River Shape, J.D. Heatwole, 1860s, 9 x 5 In.	8625
Pitcher, Cobalt Blue Feather, Flower, Flat Glaze, Flat Rim, Strap Handle, Va., c.1785, 13 x 6 In.	575
Pitcher, Cobalt Blue Feather, Round Handle, Joseph Silber, Gal., 10 x 4 ¾ In.	690
Pitcher, Cobalt Blue Flower, Feather, Oval, Stamped J. Keister & Co., c.1870, 2 Gal., 13 x 7 In.	2415
Pitcher, Cobalt Blue Flowers, A.W. Croslee, Dealer, Dry Goods, 7 In.	3402
Pitcher, Cobalt Blue Flowers, Feathers, Salt Glaze, Strap Handle, Maryland, c.1865, 11 x 5 In.	489

Pitcher, Cobalt Blue Flowers, Grainy Brown Ground, Pa., c.1860, 9 In.	711
Pitcher, Cobalt Blue Flowers, Impressed John Bell, Waynesboro, c.1870, 5 In.	3081
Pitcher, Cobalt Blue Flowers, Incised Neck Band, Pa., c.1850, 7 In.	1304
Pitcher, Cobalt Blue Flowers, Maryland, c.1865, 6 ¾ In.	652
Pitcher, Cobalt Blue Flowers, Oval, 1856, Gal., 5 x 5 ½ In.	1955
Pitcher, Cobalt Blue Flowers, Pa., c.1860, 10 ¼ In.	1304
Pitcher, Cobalt Blue Flowers, Shouldered, Maryland, c.1865, 2 Gal., 13 ½ In.	1007
Pitcher, Cobalt Blue Flowers, Shouldered, Pa., c.1860, 9 In.	415
Pitcher, Cobalt Blue Flowers, Squat, Flared Collar, H.C. Smith, c.1835, ½ Gal.	1093
Pitcher, Cobalt Blue Flowers, Stamped R.C.R. Phila., c.1850, 10 ½ In.	1541
Pitcher, Cobalt Blue Pendant Leaves, Heart Shape Blossoms, 1800s, 10 ⅝ In.	660
Pitcher, Cobalt Blue Sunflower, Applied Strap Handle, Oval, H. Smith & Co., c.1825, Gal.	4025
Pitcher, Cobalt Blue Tulip, Pa., 1800s, 7 In.	1067
Pitcher, Cobalt Blue, Salt Glaze, Oval, Stamped S.H. Sonner, c.1875, 9 x 5 In.	1610
Pitcher, Daisy, John Burger, Rochester, Cobalt Blue, Squared Collar, Gal.	920
Pitcher, Incised Leaves, Footed, Tapered Spout, Cobalt Blue Slip, C. Crolius, c.1810, 11 In.	1380
Pitcher, Leaves, Swags, Cobalt Blue, Incised Bands, Philadelphia, 1865, 9 In.	748
Pitcher, Tulip Swags, Cobalt Blue, J. Swank & Co., Johnstown, Pa., ½ Gal., 8 ½ In.	4600
Pitcher, Tulip, Stripes, Cobalt Blue, C.F. Decker, Chucky Valley, Tenn., 3 ½ In.	4888
Pitcher, Wide Neck, Spout, Cobalt Blue Leaves, Heart, c.1890, 9 In.	480
Planter, Cylindrical, Footed, Strawberry Glaze, Rolled Rim, Chinese, 1800s, 8 x 9 In.	237
Plate, Phoenix, Flower Shape, Scroll Rim, Multicolor, Chinese, 1700s, 10 In.	304
Pot, Lid, Cobalt Blue Flower, Script Watermelon, Applied Handles, c.1850, 7 x 6 In.	6900
Puzzle Jug, Brown Salt Glaze, Pierced Neck, 3 Nozzle Collar, Strap Handle, c.1780, 9 In.	288
Puzzle Jug, Pierced 3 Nozzle Neck, Fish, Waves, Motto, Blue, Green, Barum, c.1900, 6 In.	80
Ring Jug, Incised Birds, Spout, Pedestal Base, Daniel Merritt, 10 ½ In.	12650
Statue, Woman, Seated, Bun In Hair, Swollen Belly, Denmark, Signed, 23 x 20 In.	182
Tea Bowl, Geometric Lines, Tan, Ring Foot, Shoji Hamada, c.1960, 3 ½ x 3 In.	2460
Tea Bowl, Wavy Rim, Shaped Ring Foot, Lumpy, P. Voulkos, 1990, 4 x 6 In.	2520
Teapot, Bamboo Handle, Ken Ferguson, c.1968, 7 ½ x 7 In.	1320
Teapot, Black, Brown Glaze, Red Flowers, Bird Finial, Tripod Feet, Eng., c.1765, 5 ½ In.	230
Vase, Black Glaze, Spiral Coiled Shape, Shaped Rim, C. Gustin, 1986, 21 In.	2460
Vase, C. Conover, Round, Elongated, Pinched Neck, Incised, c.1966, 22 x 11 In.	3198
Vase, Carved Flowers, Applied Garland, Salt Glaze, S. Frackelton, 1893, 6 x 8 In. ....*illus*	10000
Vase, Cylindrical, Rounded Bottom, Black Slip, Orange Salt Glaze, 14 x 6 In.	720
Vase, Dome Lid, Flat Rim, Swollen Shoulder, Salt Glaze, c.1984, 6 x 7 In.	800
Vase, Shouldered, Squat, Faces, Words, Multicolor, M. Frimkess, c.1973, 6 In.	780
Water Cooler, Birds In Flowering Tree, Blue, Arched Handles, Morgan, c.1825, 17 In.	230000
Water Cooler, Cobalt Blue Geometric & Scroll Stencil, Ear Handles, F.H. Cowden, 10 In.	1003
Water Cooler, Curly Tulips, Cobalt Blue, Keg Form, Ohio, c.1850, 4 Gal.	403
Water Cooler, E.E. Horton's Apple Juice, Newark, N.J., Bristol Glaze, Strap Handles, 3 Gal.	460
Water Cooler, Flowers, Cobalt Blue, Keg Form, Raised Banding, Stepped Bung Hole, 2 Gal.	748
Water Cooler, Fords Porcelain Works, Cylindrical Shoulder Jug, Hooded Handles, 1919, 26 In.	2300
Water Cooler, Ice Water, Polar Bears, Flowers In Relief, c.1890, 15 x 12 In.	750
Water Cooler, Incised Flowers, Jug Shape, Applied Ribbed Handles, Bunghole, c.1820, 21 In.	3220

STORE fixtures, cases, cutters, and other items that have no advertising as part of the decoration are listed here. Most items found in an old store are listed in the Advertising category in this book.

Apothecary Chest, Pine, 2 Sections, 48 Drawers, Gray Paint, 19th Century, 82 x 87 In.	3916
Bag Holder, Country Store, Cast Iron, Painted, 9 ½ x 30 ¼ x 14 In.	570
Baking Powder Box, Shaped Front, Roll Lid, Multicolor, Metal, c.1890, 11 x 11 In.	180
Bin, Flour, Country Store, Steele-Wedeles Company, Tin, 15 x 18 x 10 In.	1020
Bin, Spice, Country Store, Try Our Spices, 6 Bins, Doors, 33 x 14 x 13 In.	428
Bracket, Figural Cow, For Butcher's Sign, Cast Iron, Painted Black, 24 x 28 In.	2964
Cabinet, Display, Watchmaker's, Oak, 18 Drawers, c.1920, 15 x 33 In.	384
Cabinet, Hanging, Pine, 119 Drawers, c.1890, 19 x 64 In.	1080
Cabinet, Hardware Store, 8-Sided, 72 Drawers, Porcelain Pulls, Revolving Base, 33 x 21 In.	995
Cabinet, Hardware, Wood, Revolving, 80 Drawers, 6-Sided, c.1900, 36 x 23 In. ....*illus*	1298
Cabinet, Portable Wagon Pantry, Tin, Painted, Doors, Fitted Interior, Coffee Mill, 36 x 27 In.	590
Cabinet, Spice, Floor Model, 16 Drawers, Mirror Fronts, 4 Bins, 77 x 48 x 22 In.	1560
Cabinet, Spool, Oak, 8 Drawers, Glass Fronts, c.1900, 16 ½ x 17 ½ In.	431
Case, Display, Curved Glass, Mirrored Back, c.1910, 13 x 33 x 24 In. ....*illus*	875
Case, Display, Etched O.V.B., H.S.B. & Co., Our Very Best, 15 x 28 x 16 In.	627
Case, Display, Gold Plated Collar Button, Decals, Product, J.T. Robin Co., 6 ½ x 7 ½ In.	1824
Case, Jewelry, Oak, Glass, Cast Iron Base, Alliance, Oh., 25 x 66 In.	3300

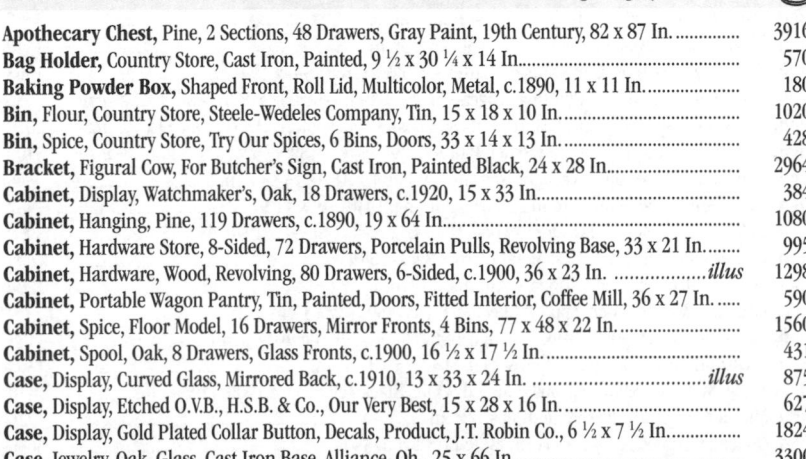

Store, Sign, Arrow Shape, Drive In, 2-Sided, Wood, Painted, c.1950, 20 x 52 In.
$529

Garth's Auctioneers & Appraisers

Store, Sign, Fine Sale Of Umbrellas, 3 Boards, Painted, 1900s, 30 ½ x 23 In.
$1,645

Garth's Auctioneers & Appraisers

Store, Sign, Gypsy Palmist Only 2D, Pointing Finger, Wood, Carved, 1900s, 18 x 8 In.
$5,036

James D. Julia Auctioneers

Store, Sign, Hardware, Padlock Shape, Cast Iron, Raised Bosses & Keyhole, c.1890, 24 x 19 In.
$2,040

S

Skinner Auctioneers & Appraisers

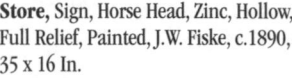

Store, Sign, Horse Head, Zinc, Hollow, Full Relief, Painted, J.W. Fiske, c.1890, 35 x 16 In.
$5,100

Skinner Auctioneers & Appraisers

Store, Sign, Shoe Service, Boot Shape, Sheet Iron, Calligraphy, c.1870, 32 x 20 ½ In.
$1,185

James D. Julia Auctioneers

Store, Sign, Shop, Gold & Blue Paint, Wood, 19 x 80 In.
$480

Cowan's Auctions

Store, Sign, Your Cash Store, 2-Sided, Painted, Wood, c.1900, 17 x 98 In.
$2,115

Garth's Auctioneers & Appraisers

Cheese Cage, Pine, Round, c.1870, 10 ½ x 22 ½ In.	267
Coffee Grinders are listed in the Coffee Mill category.	
Counter, Bean, Oak, 5 Bins, 104 x 34 In.	720
Counter, Country Store, Fir, Diagonal Paneling, 114 x 36 In.	1482
Counter, Display, Country, Pine, 2 Doors, 6 Drawers, Gray Paint, c.1840, 36 x 99 In.	2585
Counter, Pine, 12 Drawers, Stretcher Shelf, Paint, 1800s, 37 x 90 In.	1140
Dispenser, Straws, Plated Metal, Glass Panel, Push Lever, 3 Catch Tabs, 4-Footed, c.1912, 9 In.	333
Display, Buggy Whip Holder, Cast Iron, John H. Best Mfg., Galva, Ill., Patent 1900, 30 x 88 In.	3420
Display, Deer, Mechanical, Bobbing Head, Fur, 43 In.	240
Display, Dress Form, Label, JR Baumn N.Y.C., 52 ½ In.	293
Display, Head, Wax, Glass Eyes, Human Hair, 12 In.	314
Display, Railroad Worker, Billboard, Overalls, Gloves, Lantern, Metal Hook, 9 x 26 In.	382
Egg Carrier, Blue Paint, Stenciled Label, Bail Handle, Lid, Patent 1897, 11 x 14 In.	823
Figure, Man, Colonial Attire, Paint, Gesso, Carved Wood Tobacco Store, 63 ½ In.	4130
Figure, Undergarment, Flexees, Rubber Composition, Wood Base, 1930s, 24 In.	1680
Ice Cream Cone Holder, Glass, Plated Metal Lid & Lift, Holds 4 Stacks, 14 In.	272
Ladder, F.E. Myer's Bros., Ashland, Ohio, 156 x 12 In.	1560
Mannequin, Display, Dress, Great Falls, Montana, c.1900, 61 In.	1083
Mannequin, Young Man, Store Display Papier-Mache, Painted, 50 ½ In.	912
Rack, Comic Book, Spinner, Wire, Metal, Tin Lithograph, Read One Today, 1970s, 11 x 64 In.	528
Rack, Display, Child's Outfit, Nickel Plated, Adjustable	171
Shelves, Butcher, Suspended, Inverted U, Tubular Brass, Glass, Victorian, 52 x 44 x 10 In.	246
Showcase, Cathedral Double Tower, Curved Glass, Oak, Nickel Corners, 72 x 42 In.	10260
Showcase, Countertop, Oak, Curved Glass, 20 x 15 In.	399
Showcase, Oak, Glass, 72 x 38 x 24 In.	798
Showcase, Tombstone, Ebony, Glass, Nickel Plated Corners, 18 ½ x 36 x 20 In.	5700
Sign, 14K Solid Gold Wedding Rings, Round Iron Band, Metal Pendant, 9 In.	178
Sign, 5 Cent Cigars, Cigar Shape, c.1975, 33 ½ In.	450
Sign, All Goods Received In Rear, Pointing Finger, Gilt, Reverse Glass, 7 x 28 In.	1035
Sign, Arms, Tattoos, Wood, 30 ½ In., Pair ....*illus*	300
Sign, Arrow Shape, Drive In, 2-Sided, Wood, Painted, c.1950, 20 x 52 In. ....*illus*	529
Sign, Baker, Rolling Pin Shape, Wood, c.1885, 49 x 6 In.	300
Sign, Beauty Shop, Metal, Glass, Gas Pump Design, Woman's Profile, 26 x 19 In.	834
Sign, Blacksmith, Anvil & Hammer Shape, Tin, Gold Letters, Tafts, c.1890, 33 x 42 In.	3835
Sign, Boot Maker, Boot, Wood, Weathered Red Paint, Iron Hanging Strap, 26 x 16 In.	1337
Sign, Boot, Heeled, Boot Maker, Swelled Calf, Black Paint, c.1890, 17 ⅞ In.	288
Sign, Butcher's, Cow Finial, Gloeklers, Patent June 25, 1889, Cast Iron, 18 x 14 In.	720
Sign, Butcher's, Cow Head, Wood, 17 x 19 ½ In.	230
Sign, Butcher's, Pig Shape, Full Figured, Pine, Curled Tail, 1800s, 16 x 32 In.	4740
Sign, Canoe, Fixed, Sold, Wood, Red Brown Paint, Hanging, Sport Shop, 1800s, 36 In.	1094
Sign, Choice Any Article 10 Cents, Red, Yellow, 36 In.	660
Sign, Clock & Watch Repair, Paint, Zinc, 1800s, 16 x 24 In.	830
Sign, Dry Goods, Cash Grocery, Molded Edge, Painted, c.1885, 13 ¼ x 11 In.	3480
Sign, EAT, Metal Board, Porcelain Letters, 1930s	1200
Sign, Eye, Eye Doctor, Wood, Metal Bezel, Glass Plaque, c.1920, 14 x 14 In.	767
Sign, Fine Sale Of Umbrellas, 3 Boards, Painted, 1900s, 30 ½ x 23 In. ....*illus*	1645
Sign, Fire Hose, Wood, Turned, Painted, Wrought Iron Bracket, 34 In.	652
Sign, Fish Decoys, Fish Shape, Painted Green, Glass Eye, Tine Fins, c.1920, 34 x 12 In.	600
Sign, Fish Market, Wood, c.1910, 77 x 13 ½ In.	3705
Sign, Frog, Wood, Carved, Painted, Tin, c.1950, 23 x 56 In.	1440
Sign, Glovemaker, Leather Glove Shape, Feathers, Flower, c.1885, 40 x 19 In.	1968
Sign, Gypsy Palmist Only 2D, Pointing Finger, Wood, Carved, 1900s, 18 x 8 In. ....*illus*	5036
Sign, Hardware, Padlock Shape, Cast Iron, Raised Bosses & Keyhole, c.1890, 24 x 19 In. ...*illus*	2040
Sign, Horse Head, Zinc, Hollow, Full Relief, Painted, J.W. Fiske, c.1890, 35 x 16 In. ....*illus*	5100
Sign, Horseshoe, Blacksmith, Wrought Iron, Brown Paint, c.1870, 13 x 12 In.	345
Sign, Ice Cream, Wood, White Ground, Black Lettering, 1930s, 49 x 11 In.	1482
Sign, Indian Head, Feather Headdress, Wood, Hooks, Carved, 2-Sided, c.1910, 45 x 25 In.	3960
Sign, Jeweler's, Pocket Watch, Cast Metal, Mirror Back, 26 In.	593
Sign, Key, Tin, Steel, Painted, 3-Hoop Terminus, c.1910, 26 ½ x 8 ½ In.	1800
Sign, Live Bait, Worms, Wood, Applied Sheet Metal, c.1930, 3 ½ x 17 In.	330
Sign, Locksmith, Key, Figural, Iron, Through Tenon Shaft, 19th Century, 23 In.	1185
Sign, Locksmith, Padlock, Steel, Key Inserted, Steel, 13 x 17 ½ In.	1304
Sign, Maple Syrup Warehouse, Wood, Painted White, Black Lettering, c.1900, 11 x 96 In.	1410
Sign, Milliner, Top Hat, Silver Plate, 1800s, 6 ½ In.	720
Sign, Optical, Rimmed Spectacles Form, Blue Eyes Print, 35 In.	3690
Sign, Optometrist, Cast Iron, Colored Glass, Gilt, Wall Mount, c.1890, 11 x 26 In.	3000

S

Sign, Palmist & Clairvoyant, Black, White Paint, 50 In.	5040
Sign, Pig, Head, Zinc, c.1860, 30 ¼ x 15 In.	3900
Sign, Pretzel, Sheet Metal, Carved Wood, Gold & Red Paint, c.1915, 24 x 20 In.	1320
Sign, Read Your Future, Palm Reading, Hand, Paint, Pine, c.1880, 43 ½ x 26 In.	4740
Sign, Report Forest Fire To The Warden By Phone, Porcelain, Flange, 20 x 12 In.	345
Sign, Round Glasses, Blue Eyes, Eye Doctor, Tin, Paint, 33 x 9 In.	776
Sign, Salmon Shape, Full Body, Sheet Iron, Molded Fins, c.1920, 49 ½ x 13 In.	1126
Sign, Saloon, Wood, Paint, 10 Ft. 2 In. x 15 In.	575
Sign, Scissors, Wood, Metal, Painted Silver, Red Sharpening, Iron Hanger, c.1930, 39 In.	920
Sign, Sewing Needle, Brass, Elliptical Eyelet, 19th Century, 34 In.	415
Sign, Shoe Service, Boot Shape, Sheet Iron, Calligraphy, c.1870, 32 x 20 ½ In. ....*illus*	1185
Sign, Shoe, Sneaker, White, Chalkware, Metal, c.1965, 25 In.	210
Sign, Shop, Gold & Blue Paint, Wood, 19 x 80 In. ....*illus*	480
Sign, Stable To Let, Brooklyn, N.Y., White, Black Lettering, Raised Edges, 14 x 14 In.	540
Sign, Stationer, Quill Feather, Figural, Wood, Gilt, 12 ½ In.	59
Sign, Swordfish, Carved, Gray Paint, c.1900, 51 In. x 11 Ft. 7 In.	8295
Sign, Teapot, Sheet Iron, Paint, 43 In.	729
Sign, Tennis, Racket, Wood, Blue, White Paint, 65 In.	4080
Sign, Tobacco Store, Man's Stylized Profile, Cigarette In Mouth, Metal, 1940s, 14 x 21 In.	240
Sign, Top Hat, Red Paint, Silvered Buckle, Band, Sheet Tin, 12 x 19 In.	1185
Sign, Trade, Optometrist, Eyeglasses, Sheet Metal, 1900s, 37 In.	392
Sign, U.S. Post Office, Clear Creek, Calif., Wood, 1-Sided, 86 x 14 In.	4560
Sign, Visit Our Dairy, Cartoon Cow, Tongue Hanging Out, Color, Porcelain, Round, 18 In.	1026
Sign, Your Cash Store, 2-Sided, Painted, Wood, c.1900, 17 x 98 In. ....*illus*	2115
Spice Box, Counter, 2 Mirrors, 8 Drawers, Painted Goose, Reed Scene, c.1880, 16 x 32 In.	1541
Strawholder, Clear Glass, 20 Panels, Pewter Lid & Lifter, Spinning Finial, c.1915, 12 ½ In.	133
Strawholder, Clear Glass, Arched Vertical Panels, Spread Foot, Domed Lid, 12 ½ In.	206
Tobacco Cutter, Embossed, Wood Wheel Handle, Paint, Iron, Germany, c.1865, 21 ½ In.	148

STOVES have been used in America for heating since the eighteenth century and for cooking since the nineteenth century. Most types of wood, coal, gas, kerosene, and even some electric stoves are collected.

Cook, 7 Doors, Flowers, Leaves, Porcelain Tile, Iron, Steel Frame, c.1905, 34 ½ x 45 In.	923
Cook, Quick Meal, Cast Iron, Doors, Shelves, Salesman's Sample, 16 x 17 x 26 In. ....*illus*	2370
Cook, Train Caboose, Cast Iron, Painted Black, Burner Lids, 30 In.	330
Cook, Triumph Range, Cast Iron, Salesman's Sample, 15 x 16 In.	170
Heating, Brass, Tole, Inset Marble Top, France, 1800s, 34 ½ x 20 ½ In. ....*illus*	478
Heating, Cast Iron, Victorian House Shape, Mica Windows, Mansard Roof, c.1865, 30 In.	881
Heating, Wonder Mfg. Co., Potbelly, Oak, Cast Iron, Washington C.H., Ohio, 60 In.	1800
Parlor, Cast Iron, Brass Ball Finials, Paw Feet, Columns, Disks, 1800s, 29 x 34 In.	418
Parlor, Cast Iron, Forest Green, Aubergine, Cylindrical, Dome Top, 4 Legs, Hinged Door, 37 x 13 In.	155
Parlor, Empire, Cast Iron, Black Paint, New Jersey, 1849, 33 x 32 In.	750
Parlor, Gothic, Cast Iron, S.B. Sexton & Co., Baltimore, c.1820, 38 ½ x 27 In. ....*illus*	2074
Parlor, Iris Tile, Marble Top, Cast Iron Base, Pierced Doors, France, 38 x 19 ½ In.	1625
Stove Plate, Dance Of Death, Oval Scrolls, 5 Plates, Pa., c.1749, 24 x 18 In.	11850
Stove Plate, David & Goliath, Cast Iron, c.1790, 23 ½ x 21 ½ In.	652
Stove Plate, God's Well, Cast Iron, 1781, 27 ½ x 25 In.	356
Stove Plate, Heart & Tulip, Cast Iron, George Stevens, York County, 1700s, 22 x 24 In.	1534
Stove Plate, Loggers, Log Cabin, Moose, Cast Iron, c.1900, 13 ½ x 27 In. ....*illus*	1353
Stove Plate, Scrolled Vines, Cast Iron, Berkshire Furnace, 25 x 31 In.	450
Swedish Baroque Style, Yellow, White Ceramic, Gustavian, 4 Sections, c.1890, 64 x 29 In.	1232

STRETCH GLASS is named for the strange stretch marks in the glass. It was made by many glass companies in the United States from about 1900 to the 1920s. It is iridescent. Most American stretch glass is molded; most European pieces are blown and may have a pontil mark.

Bowl, Celeste Blue, Cupped, Fenton, 1920s, 8 In.	70
Bowl, Marigold, Footed, 5 x 2 ½ In.	13
Candleholder, Sky Blue, Tiffin, c.1940, 9 In., Pair	129
Candy Dish, Celeste Blue, Flared, Paneled, Fenton, c.1925, 4 ¼ x 5 In.	18
Compote, Blue, Pedestal, Northwood, 8 In.	35
Compote, Mother-Of-Pearl, U.S. Glass, 1920s, 6 ¾ x 7 In.	115
Vase, Green Iridescent, Venetian, 30 x 10 In.	177
Vase, Red, Square, Iridized, Fenton, 7 ½ In.	104
Vase, Trumpet, Green Iridescent, Pink Accent, Ribbed, Flared, Ruffled Rim, Lundberg, 12 In.	183

Stove, Cook, Quick Meal, Cast Iron, Doors, Shelves, Salesman's Sample, 16 x 17 x 26 In.
$2,370

James D. Julia Auctioneers

Stove, Heating, Brass, Tole, Inset Marble Top, France, 1800s, 34 ½ x 20 ½ In.
$478

Neal Auction Co.

Stove, Parlor, Gothic, Cast Iron, S.B. Sexton & Co., Baltimore, c.1820, 38 ½ x 27 In.
$2,074

S

Neal Auction Co.

Stove, Stove Plate, Loggers, Log Cabin, Moose, Cast Iron, c.1900, 13 ½ x 27 In.
$1,353

Garth's Auctioneers & Appraisers

Superman, Comic Book, No. 6, DC Comics, Sept-Oct 1940
$1,395

Hake's Americana & Collectibles

Superman, Toy, Superman Rollover Plane, Tin Lithograph, Clockwork, Marx, 6 In.
$826

Bertoia Auctions

SUMIDA is a Japanese pottery that was made from about 1895 to 1941. Pieces are usually everyday objects—vases, jardinieres, bowls, teapots, and decorative tiles. Most pieces have a very heavy orange-red, blue, brown, black, green, purple, or off-white glaze, with raised three-dimensional figures as decorations. The unglazed part is painted red, green, black, or orange. Sumida is sometimes mistakenly called Sumida gawa, but true Sumida gawa is a softer pottery made in the early 1800s.

Bowl, 3 Figures, Hanging On Edge, 6 ½ x 3 ½ In.	150
Bowl, Oblong, Man Hanging Over Rim, Orange, 1 ¾ x 6 ¼ x 4 In.	248
Humidor, Man Sitting, Red, c.1900, 6 In.	200
Mug, Girl, Basket, Orange, Green & Brown Glaze, 5 ¼ In.	185
Pilgrim's Bottle, 3 Children, Flambe Glaze, Orange Red, c.1900, 9 x 7 In.	525
Pitcher, Man, Child, Reading, Red, Green & Blue Glaze, 8 ½ In.	475
Teapot, Lid, Snow Leopards, Rocks, Bamboo Handle, Orange, Mottled White, 5 In.	475
Vase, Figures On Sea, 1 Holding Pearl, Black, Red, Tan, Basket Form, Arched Handle, 6 In.	201
Vase, Figures, Holding Shell, Crimped Opening, Orange, Green Glaze, 11 ½ In.	285
Vase, Gawa, Geisha On Shoulder Of Bird, Multicolor Glaze, Signed, 7 ½ In.	29
Vase, Octopus, 2 ¾ In.	472

SUNBONNET BABIES were introduced in 1900 in the book *The Sunbonnet Babies.* The stories were by Eulalie Osgood Grover, illustrated by Bertha Corbett. The children's faces were completely hidden by the sunbonnets. The children had been pictured in black and white before this time, but the color pictures in the book were immediately successful. The Royal Bayreuth China Company made a full line of children's dishes decorated with the Sunbonnet Babies. Some Sunbonnet Babies plates have been reproduced, but are clearly marked.

Baby Cup, Girl, Red Dress, Holding Doll, Boy, Overalls, Loop Handle, 4 ½ x 5 In.	55
Candlestick, Friday, Sweeping, 5 ¼ x 3 ¼ In.	125
Dolls, 2 Mandy, Molly, May, Knickerbocker, 1970s, 6 In., 4 Piece	37
Doorstop, Painted Blue, Gray, Cast Iron, 1920s	85
Lithograph, Little Anglers, Verse, Taber-Prang Art Co., 1902, 12 x 6 ¾ In.	50
Monday, Washing, 7 ½ In.	63
Picture, Lovers, Barefoot Boy Hugging Sunbonnet Baby, Hollyhocks, 7 x 9 In.	75
Plate, Monday, Washing, 7 ½ In.	35
Tea Set, Mending, Washing, Child's, 4 ¼ x 5 ¼ In. Teapot, 3 Piece	575
Vase, Wednesday, Mending, Double Handled, Porcelain, 3 ¾ x 4 In.	125

SUNDERLAND luster is a name given to a special type of pink luster made by Leeds, Newcastle, and other English firms during the nineteenth century. The luster glaze is metallic and glossy and appears to have bubbles in it. Other pieces of luster are listed in the Luster category.

Chamber Pot, Pink Luster, Strap Handles, c.1830, 5 ½ x 8 ½ In.	1550
Mug, 2 Handles, Black Transfer, Mottled Purple Luster, c.1825, 4 In.	480
Mug, Pink Luster, George, c.1830, 2 ½ In.	400
Mug, Splash Luster, Pink, 2 ⅞ In.	135
Pitcher, Pink Luster, Farmers Arms, Transfer, c.1800, 10 In.	895
Pitcher, Pink Luster, Poem, Shouldered, c.1820, 5 In.	372
Plaque, Mate Sound Pump, Morning Noon, Night, Black Transfer, Dixon Co., 1815, 8 x 9 In.	630
Plaque, Ship, Black Lusterware, Scalloped, c.1810, 8 x 9 In.	230
Plate, Commemorative, William Ewart Gladstone, Transfer, 1880s, 8 x 8 ¾ In.	100

SUPERMAN was created by two seventeen-year-olds in 1938. The first issue of Action comics had the strip. Superman remains popular and became the hero of a radio show in 1940, cartoons in the 1940s, a television series, and several major movies.

Bread Card, Hands Across The Sea, Superman Fixing Tower Wires	640
Button, Supermen Of America Club Member, 1947, 1 ¼ In.	95
Cake Tin, Superman, Hands On Hip, Cape, c.1977, 14 x 13 x 2 In.	22
Comic Art, Artboard, Curt Swan, 11 ⅛ x 16 In.	210
Comic Book, No. 6, DC Comics, Sept-Oct 1940 ....*illus*	1395
Comic Book, Superman Over Bridge, No. 15, March-April, DC Comics, 1942	1026
Cookie Jar, Phone Booth Shape, Superman On Phone, c.1978, 13 x 5 In.	375
Figure, Wood Composition, Hands On Hips, 1942, 5 ½ In.	1483
Frame Tray, Superman, Flying, Villains, Capitol Building, Whitman, c.1965, 11 x 14 In.	35
Game, Speed, Superman Leaping Over Buildings, Box, 1940s, 8 ½ x 15 ½ In.	139
Horseshoe Set, Rubber, Wood, Super Swim Inc., c.1954	40
Illustration Board, Classic Pose, Jerry Siegel, Joe Shuster, Mat, Frame, 1941, 35 x 45 In.	11500

S

Lunchbox, Thermos, The Movie, Metal, 1978	266
Movie Poster, Atom Man Vs Superman, Linen, Multicolor, 1950, 27 x 41 In.	2846
Patch, Superman-Tim Club, Felt, Red, Blue, White, 5-Sided, Snellenburgs, 1945, 3 ½ x 4 In.	86
Playsuit, Blue, Red, Yellow, Ben Cooper, Child's, Box, c.1975	40
Print, Lithograph, Passe-Partout, Flying, Raised Arm, Andy Warhol, 1986, 19 x 15 In.	980
Push Puppet, Superman, Ducking, Punching, c.1966, 4 In.	40
Ring, Gold Finish, Red S, Adjustable, DC Comics, 1976	45
Ring, Secret Chamber, Image, S, Superman Defense Club, Ostby & Barton, 1941	4592
Sign, Kellogg's Corn Flakes, Superman Holding Cereal Box, Hanging, 1956, 16 x 36 In.	575
Sign, Superman Und Bateman, Promotional, Germany, 1960s	949
Toy, Kryton Raygun, Film Strips, Box, 10 x 8 In.	510
Toy, Puzzle, Picture, Superman Springs Into Action, 8 ½ x 11 In.	230
Toy, Superman Rollover Plane, Tin Lithograph, Clockwork, Marx, 6 In. *illus*	826

SUSIE COOPER began as a designer in 1925 working for the English firm A.E. Gray & Company. In 1932 she formed Susie Cooper Pottery, Ltd. In 1950 it became Susie Cooper China, Ltd., and the company made china and earthenware. In 1966 it was acquired by Josiah Wedgwood & Sons, Ltd. The name *Susie Cooper* appears with the company names on many pieces of ceramics.

Cheese Dish, Wedge Lid, Rectangular, Jug Handle, Brown, Green, Yellow, c.1935, 5 In.	104
Cup & Saucer, Jockey Pattern, Green Rim, c.1925, 2 ¼ In.	104
Hot Water Jug, Lid, Peacock Feathers, c.1932, 7 ½ In.	92
Pitcher, Jazz Age, Dutch Shape, Blue, Black, Yellow, Orange, Squat, c.1930, 5 In.	138
Pitcher, Jazz Age, Dutch Shape, Green, Black, Orange, c.1930, 4 ½ In.	127
Serving Dish, Orange Circles, Black Dot Design, 3 Indented Wells, c.1932, 8 ⅜ In.	23

SWANKYSWIGS are small drinking glasses. In 1933, the Kraft Food Company began to market cheese spreads in these decorated, reusable glass tumblers. They were discontinued from 1941 to 1946, then made again from 1947 to 1958. Then plain glasses were used for most of the cheese, although a few special decorated Swankyswigs have been made since that time. For more prices, go to kovels.com.

Bustling Betsy, Green, 3 ¾ In.	12
Cornflower Design, Red, Blue, Yellow, 3 ¾ In., 4 Piece	20
Dogs, Roosters, Orange, 3 ¾ In.	8
Lamp, Kettle, Blue, 3 ¾ In.	8
Red & White Stripes, 3 ½ In.	12
Red Tulip, No. 2, White Leaves, 3 ½ In.	20
Spinning Wheel, Bellows, Red, 3 ¾ In.	8
Squirrel, Deer, Brown, c.1940, 3 ¾ In.	10

SWASTIKA KERAMOS is a line of art pottery made from 1906 to 1908 by the Owen China Company of Minerva, Ohio. Many pieces were made with an iridescent glaze.

Ewer, 3 Handles, Swastika Bands, Green, Gilt, 15 In.	265
Ewer, Gold Over Red Over Green Luster Glaze, Bulbous Base, Marked, 13 In.	121
Vase, Peacock, Pine Tree, Pagoda, Flowers, Luster, Marked, 13 In. *illus*	460
Vase, Peacock, Pine Tree, Pagoda, Shouldered, 13 ¼ In.	472
Vase, Trees, Red Abstract Clouds, Gold Round, Luster Glaze, 2 Handles, 10 In.	145
Vase, Water Lily Pads, Green, Gold, Luster Glaze, Tapered, Marked, 8 In.	121

SWORDS of all types that are of interest to collectors are listed here. The military dress sword with elaborate handle is probably the most wanted. A tsuba is a hand guard fitted to a Japanese sword between the handle and the blade. Be sure to display swords in a safe way, out of reach of children.

Artillery, Brass Pommel, Fish Scale Grip, Leather, Brass Sheath, Ames Stamp, c.1845, 25 In.	256
Artillery, Eagle Pommel, France, c.1810, 24 ½ In.	277
Artillery, Officer's, Single Edge, Ivory Grip, Silver, Leather Case, Kucher, Phila., c.1805	10625
Bayonet, Socket, Scabbard, Frog, Belt, Springfield, 1873, 21 In.	110
Broadsword, Steel, Engraved, Pierced Pommel, Germany, 17th Century, 40 In.	1062
Bronze, Basket Hilt, Engraved Blade, Steel Scabbard, c.1900, 40 In.	594
Cavalry Officer, Brass Hilt, Plated Scabbard, 1872, 31 ¾ In.	485
Dress, Engraved Blade, Lion D-Guard, Gem Set Eyes, Germany, 1800s, 38 ½ In. *illus*	500
Hanger, Brass Hilt, Steel Blade, Single Fuller, Cutout Hearts, Walnut Grip, Ball Pommel, c.1780, 32 In.	260
Indian Princess, Mother-Of-Pearl Grip, Spreadwing Eagle, Engraved Leaves, 1830	1673
Infantry, Officer's, Gilt Brass Hilt, Lion Head Pommel, Pierced Guard, 1803, 32 In.	2900

Swastika Keramos, Vase, Peacock, Pine Tree, Pagoda, Flowers, Luster, Marked, 13 In.
$460

Humler & Nolan

Sword, Dress, Engraved Blade, Lion D-Guard, Gem Set Eyes, Germany, 1800s, 38 ½ In.
$500

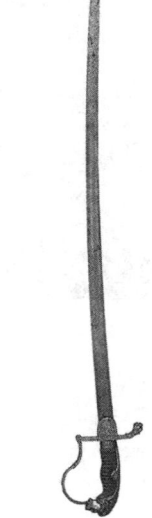

Rago Arts & Auction Center

Tea Caddy, Fruitwood, Apple Shape, Oval Escutcheon, George III, c.1790, 4 ¾ x 4 ¾ In.
$3,585

S

Neal Auction Co.

Tea Caddy, Fruitwood, Pear Shape, Open Interior, Georgian, 1800s, 6 In.
$1,003

Brunk Auctions

Tea Caddy, Fruitwood, Pear Shape, Steel Escutcheon, England, c.1790, 6 ½ In.
$1,440

Skinner Auctioneers & Appraisers

Design Online

The Cooper-Hewitt Smithsonian Design Museum in New York has a new section on its website called "Object of the Day." You'll find a photo of the object and a short history. The objects remain online for a while. On my last virtual visit, I saw early George Washington wallpaper, a modern travel poster, and an antique fan. It's a fun spot to visit. The focus is on design from many centuries.

Kastane, Carved Horn Dragon Head Grip, Gilt Bronze Quillion Hilt, Steel Blade, 27 In.	201
Khanda, Watered Steel Straight Blade, Gold Damascene Guard, Scabbard, India, 1700s, 30 In.	7200
Khyber, Steel, Wood, Brass, T-Shape Blade, Carved Hilt, Sheath, Indo Persian, 1700s, 23 In.	450
Officer's, Medical Staff, Brass Handle, Leather Scabbard, c.1850, 32 In.	2832
Officer's, Saber, Eagle Pommel, Brass Guard, Ivory Grip, Blue, Gold On Blade, c.1820, 33 In.	812
Regimental, Imperial, Cavalry Officer, Model KD 89, Hus. Reg. Konig Wilhelm, c.1900, 38 In.	492
Saber, 4-Slot, Iron Hilt, Spherical Pommel, Acorn Finial, c.1780, 28 In.	2200
Saber, Military, Eagle Head Pommel, Ribbed Bone Grip, c.1835, 34 In.	690
Saber, Military, Horn Handle, Animal Head Pommel, c.1850, 30 In.	431
Saber, Officer's, Symmetrical Guards, Ivory, Copper Bands, England, c.1780, 26 In.	1750
Shashka, Ribbed Grip, Chased, Punched Pommel, Scabbard, Russia, 1945, 38 In.	510
Smallsword, Double Shell Guard, Finger Grip, Urn Pommel, Crescents, c.1725, 29 In.	1675
Smallsword, Silver Hilt, Pierced, Drums, Flags, Cannon, Shell Splay, Rococo, c.1767, 33 In.	3400
Swordfish Bill, Carved, Wood Hilts, Relief Carved Narwhal Whale, Fisherman, 1800s, 39 & 37 In., Pair	460
Tapered Blade, Medial Ridge, Disk Pommel, c.1400, 36 In.	775
Wakizashi, Short, Inlay, Bone, Cloth Grip, Menuki Ornaments, Horse, Bull, Scabbard, 25 In.	360

SYRACUSE is a trademark used by the Onondaga Pottery of Syracuse, New York. The company was established in 1871. The name became the Syracuse China Company in 1966. Syracuse China closed in 2009. It was known for fine dinnerware and restaurant china.

SYRACUSE China

Accent, Bowl, Vegetable, Round, 7 In.	8
Accent, Butter, Cover, ¼ Pound	13
Accent, Cup & Saucer	7
Accent, Plate, Dinner, 9 ¾ In.	9
Accent, Platter, Oval, 12 In.	27
Alpine, Bowl, Vegetable, Oval, 8 In.	41
Alpine, Cup & Saucer	17
Americana, Platter, Blue Eagle, 9 x 8 In.	15
Americana, Platter, Blue Eagle, 11 In.	18
Apple Blossom, Bowl, Cereal, Lugged, 6 In.	16
Apple Blossom, Cup & Saucer	34
Apple Blossom, Plate, Bread & Butter, 6 In.	8
Beacon Hill, Plate, Bread & Butter, 5 ½ In.	4
Belmont, Cup & Saucer	19
Belmont, Soup, Dish, Rim, 8 ¾ In.	71
Berkshire, Gravy Boat, Underplate	36
Berkshire, Relish, 8 In.	18
Bombay, Plate, Bread & Butter, 6 ¼ In.	6
Bombay, Platter, Oval, 11 In.	37
Briar Rose, Gravy Boat, Underplate	102
Briar Rose, Plate, Dinner, 9 ⅞ In.	33
Cadet, Creamer, 8 Oz., 3 ½ In.	14
Caprice, Chop Plate, 14 In.	61
Chester, Cup & Saucer	28
Chester, Plate, Salad, 8 In.	8
Clover, Platter, Oval, 16 In.	82
Clover, Relish, 3 Sections	29
Dorian, Creamer, 6 Oz., 4 In.	12
Dorian, Cup & Saucer	11
Glendale, Platter, Oval, 7 In.	26
Harvest Gold, Bowl, Vegetable, 9 ⅝ In.	25
Jefferson, Bowl, Vegetable, Oval, 10 ⅜ In.	33
Jefferson, Cup & Saucer, Footed	12
Lancaster, Bowl, Cereal, Lugged, 5 ⅜ In.	16
Lancaster, Bowl, Fruit, Rim, 5 ⅜ In.	17
Marlene, Creamer, 3 ⅛ In.	13
Marlene, Cup & Saucer, Footed	15
Millbrook, Cup & Saucer	7
Moonstone, Plate, Dinner, 10 ¼ In.	13
Old Colony, Gravy Boat, Attached Underplate, 6 ½ In.	40
Orchard, Gravy Boat, Underplate	42
Orchard, Plate, Dinner, 10 ½ In.	14
Orchard, Teapot, Lid, 4 Cup, 5 ⅜ In.	138
Pendleton, Plate, Dinner, 10 In.	27
Pendleton, Platter, Oval, 14 In.	36

S

Radcliffe, Bowl, Vegetable, Oval, 10 In.	43
Radcliffe, Platter, Oval, 16 In.	109
Riviera, Cup & Saucer, Footed	21
Serene, Plate, Bread & Butter, 6 ⅜ In.	9
Serene, Platter, Oval, 12 In.	37
Suzanne, Gravy Boat, Attached Underplate, 7 x 9 In.	36
Temple Bells, Bowl, Cereal, Lugged, 6 In.	17
Temple Bells, Cup & Saucer.	16
Temple Bells, Soup, Dish, Rim, 8 In.	11
Westvale, Bowl, Vegetable, Oval, 10 In.	41
Westvale, Plate, Dinner, 10 ⅜ In.	32
Yorktown, Ashtray, 3 In.	13
Yorktown, Cup & Saucer, Footed.	15

TAPESTRY, *Porcelain, see Rose Tapestry category.*

TEA CADDY is the name for a small box made to hold tea leaves. In the eighteenth century, tea was very expensive and it was stored under lock and key. The first tea caddies were made with locks. By the nineteenth century, tea was more plentiful and the tea caddy was larger. Often there were two sections, one for green tea, one for black tea.

Burl, Hinged Lid, Brass Fruit Basket Design, Ring Handles, England, 8 ½ In.	375
Burled Walnut, Brass Paw Feet, Fitted Interior, Blown Glass Bowl, Ring Handles, 6 x 13 In.	413
Enameled, Lid, Yellow, Squared, Canton, 5 In.	182
Faux Tortoiseshell, Black Finial, 9 x 12 In.	492
Fruitwood, Apple Shape, Oval Escutcheon, George III, c.1790, 4 ¾ x 4 ¾ In. *illus*	3585
Fruitwood, Hinged Lid, George III, c.1790, 4 x 4 ½ In.	518
Fruitwood, Melon Shape, Stained Panels, George III, c.1790, 6 x 5 In.	3075
Fruitwood, Pear Shape, Open Interior, Georgian, 1800s, 6 In. *illus*	1003
Fruitwood, Pear Shape, Steel Escutcheon, England, c.1790, 6 ½ In. *illus*	1440
Fruitwood, Pear Shape, Stem On Lid, c.1810, 5 ¾ x 4 ¼ In.	2963
Fruitwood, Pumpkin Shape, 1800s, 5 ¼ In.	2124
Gilt Lacquer, Red, Chinese Battle Scenes, Pewter Liner, Shaped, c.1850, 4 ½ x 9 In.	600
Gilt, Black Lacquer, 6-Sided, Winged Paw Feet, Figural Scenes, c.1815, 4 x 11 In.	1046
Inlay, Octagonal, Draped Leaves, Crossbanded Borders, George III, 1800, 5 x 5 ¾ In.	460
Ivory Veneer, Hinged Lid, Leaf & Flower Border, c.1900, 10 ⅝ In.	5250
Ivory, Tent Top, Gilt Handle, Oval Shield, Reeded Panels, Beading, c.1790, 6 x 5 In.	3107
Lacquer, Gilt, Octagonal, Coffin Shape, Winged Feet, Figural Scenes, c.1815, 5 x 8 In.	956
Mahogany, Bombe Shape, Molded Lid, Bail Handle, Flowers, c.1750, 16 x 10 In.	1195
Mahogany, Bone & Ivory Inlays, Bombe Shape, Fitted Interior, c.1850, 6 x 8 In.	130
Mahogany, Coffin Shape, Lion's Head Handles, Ivory, Brass, 8 x 12 In.	354
Mahogany, Coffin, Tapered Lid, Side Handles, 8 x 13 In.	205
Mahogany, George III, Conch Shell Inlay, Green, Hinged, c.1800, 6 ½ x 12 ½ In.	492
Mahogany, Georgian, Coffin Shape, Lid, c.1860, 7 x 11 In.	296
Mahogany, Hinged Lid, Brass Bail Handle, George III, 5 ½ x 8 ¾ In.	316
Mahogany, Hinged Lid, Brass Ball Feet, 2-Part Fitted Interior, c.1780, 6 x 9 In.	413
Mahogany, Hinged Lid, Inlay, Compartments, England, c.1810, 5 x 8 In. *illus*	600
Mahogany, Inlaid Paterae, Stringing, George III, 4 ½ x 7 ⅝ In.	185
Mahogany, Inlaid, Hinged Lid, Oval Plume, Regency, c.1815, 5 x 7 ½ In.	304
Mahogany, Inlay, Brass Bun Feet, Georgian, 7 ¼ In.	108
Mahogany, Oval Basket Inlays, 2-Part Interior, 5 x 8 In.	384
Mahogany, Quarter Fan, String Inlays, Ivory Escutcheon, Lift Top, Fitted Interior, 7 x 12 In.	325
Mahogany, Quillwork, 6-Sided, Medallions, Cornucopia, c.1790, 5 ¼ x 8 ¼ In. *illus*	1098
Mahogany, Rectangular, Inlays, Brass Bail Handles, Divided Interior, c.1850, 6 x 12 In.	150
Mahogany, Regency, Inlay, Hinged Lid, Fitted Interior, c.1810, 4 ¾ x 5 In. *illus*	356
Maple, Dome Lid, Fitted Interior, 7 ½ x 12 ½ In.	344
Mixed Woods, Lift Lid, Shell Lid Inlays, 2-Part Interior, England, c.1750, 3 ½ x 6 ¾ In.	354
Mother-Of-Pearl, Haliotis, Georgian, Compartments, 1800s, 6 ½ x 10 ¾ x 7 ⅛ In. *illus*	3690
Papier-Mache, Black, Mother-Of-Pearl Designs, Fitted Interior, c.1900, 6 x 8 In.	130
Papier-Mache, Dome Lid, Mother-Of-Pearl Inlay, Coffin Shape, c.1890, 8 x 15 In.	938
Papier-Mache, Mother-Of-Pearl Inlay, Gilt, Shaped Square, c.1850, 5 ¾ x 8 In.	420
Penwork, Coffin Shape, Chinoiserie Image, 2 Interior Compartments, Bone Handles, 9 x 6 In.	1294
Pine, Red Grain Paint, Pa., c.1850, 5 ¾ x 11 ½ In.	326
Poplar, Hinged Lid, Green Paper Interior, Rectangular Shape, c.1820, 4 ¾ x 7 ½ In.	115
Porcelain, Blue & White, Flowers, Butterflies, Chinese Stamp, 5 ¾ In. *illus*	330
Porcelain, Octagonal, Footed, Lid, Cherry Blossom Branch, Chinese, 6 x 5 In.	120

Tea Caddy, Mahogany, Hinged Lid, Inlay, Compartments, England, c.1810, 5 x 8 In. $600

Skinner Auctioneers & Appraisers

Tea Caddy, Mahogany, Quillwork, 6-Sided, Medallions, Cornucopia, c.1790, 5 ¼ x 8 ¼ In. $1,098

Neal Auction Co.

Tea Caddy, Mahogany, Regency, Inlay, Hinged Lid, Fitted Interior, c.1810, 4 ¾ x 5 In. $356

James D. Julia Auctioneers

Tea Caddy, Mother-Of-Pearl, Haliotis, Georgian, Compartments, 1800s, 6 ½ x 10 ¾ x 7 ⅛ In. $3,690

Neal Auction Co.

This is an edited listing of current prices. Visit **Kovels.com** to check thousands of prices from previous years and sign up for free information on trends, tips, reproductions, marks, and more.

T

Tea Caddy, Porcelain, Blue & White, Flowers, Butterflies, Chinese Stamp, 5 ¾ In.
$330

Cowan's Auctions

Teco, Vase, Buttressed, Green Matte Glaze, Stamped, c.1905, 7 x 4 In.
$1,188

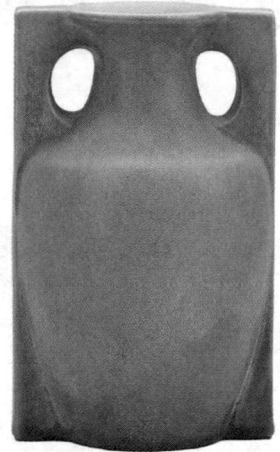

Rago Arts & Auction Center

Teco, Vase, Green Matte Glaze, Buttressed, Marked, c.1905, 6 ½ x 3 ¾ In.
$1,000

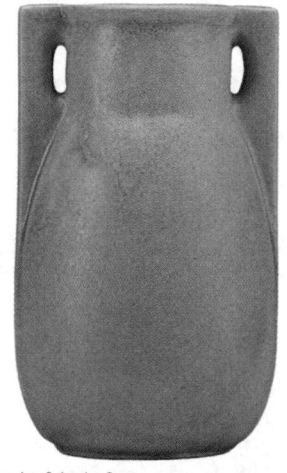

Rago Arts & Auction Center

Rosewood, Brass Inlay, Lion's Head Handles, Footed, 1800s, 8 x 14 In.	531
Rosewood, Coffin Shape, Ivory Ring Handles, 4 Pad Feet, Regency, 7 ½ x 14 In.	225
Rosewood, Geometric Inlay, 2 Lidded Compartments, England, 1800s, 4 ½ x 8 ½ In.	239
Rosewood, Ivory Hinged Interior Boxes, Georgian, 12 x 7 In.	260
Rosewood, Mother-Of-Pearl Escutcheon, Ball Feet, c.1840, 5 x 8 In.	90
Rosewood, Mother-Of-Pearl Inlay, c.1850, 7 ½ x 13 ¾ In.	237
Rosewood, Tunbridge Inlay, Hinged Lid, Victorian, 12 In.	563
Silver, Engraved Leaves, 8-Sided, Middle East, c.1825, 3 ¼ x 4 ¼ In.	432
Silver, Lid, Squared Shoulders, Tapered, Embossed, Dancing Figures, Germany, 5 x 8 In.	362
Silver, Repousse, Figures, Drinking, Eating, Herringbone, Derby Silver Co., 5 x 3 x 3 In.	495
Tortoiseshell, Breakfront, Hinged Lid, Ivory Pulls, Flattened Bun Feet, 5 x 8 In.	840
Tortoiseshell, Coffin Shape, Paneled Sides, Ball Feet, 6 x 7 In.	1521
Tortoiseshell, George III, Coffin Lid, Ball Feet, c.1800, 5 ¼ x 5 In.	1220
Tortoiseshell, Hinged Lid, Tapered, Silver Plaque, Ivory Bun Feet, c.1815, 6 x 8 In.	1140
Tortoiseshell, Ivory, Inner Compartment, Ball Feet, Key, England, 1800s, 3 ¼ In.	1080
Tortoiseshell, Serpentine Front, 2 Compartments, c.1825, 5 x 8 In.	2223
Tortoiseshell, Silver Scroll Overlay, 1800s, 4 ¾ In.	1440
Walnut, Burl, Mother-Of-Pearl, Wood Banded Inlays, England, c.1845, 6 x 10 In.	354

TEA LEAF IRONSTONE dishes are named for their decorations. There was a superstition that it was lucky if a whole tea leaf unfolded at the bottom of your cup. This idea was translated into the pattern of dishes known as "tea leaf." By 1850 at least twelve English factories were making this pattern, and by the 1870s it was a popular pattern in many countries. The tea leaf was always a luster glaze on early wares, although now some pieces are made with a brown tea leaf. There are many variations of tea leaf designs, such as Teaberry, Pepper Leaf, and Gold Leaf. The designs were used on many different white ironstone shapes, such as Bamboo, Lily of the Valley, Empress, and Cumbow.

Bowl, Vegetable, Ladyfinger, Ribbed, Graduated, Alfred Meakin, 5 Piece	60
Butter Chip, Round, Alfred Meakin, 3 ⅛ In., 8 Piece	15
Cake Plate, Brocade, Alfred Meakin, 9 ¼ In.	80
Cake Plate, Hexagon, Anthony Shaw	30
Cake Plate, Woodland, W. & E. Corn	95
Chamber Pot, Moss Rose, Lid, Alfred Meakin	100
Creamer, Cable, Thomas Furnival, 6 In.	55
Creamer, Fern, Wilkinson Maidenhair, 5 ¼ In.	130
Creamer, Pankhurst Rosetta, 5 In.	40
Ewer, Cable, Anthony Shaw, 13 In.	70
Ironstone, Pitcher, Ring O' Hearts, Copper Luster Trim, Jacob Furnival, 10 In.	100
Ladle, Sauce, Square, Ridged, Wedgwood	185
Mug, King Charles, J. & E. Mayer	140
Mug, Lily Of The Valley, Anthony Shaw	55
Mug, Scroll, Alfred Meakin	30
Pitcher, Lily Of The Valley, Anthony Shaw, 7 In.	125
Pitcher, Morning Glory, Portland Shape, Elsmore & Forster, 7 In.	70
Pitcher, Morning Glory, Portland Shape, Elsmore & Forster, 9 In.	70
Soap Box, Lid, Bamboo, Alfred Meakin	25
Tureen, Sauce, Lid, Underplate, Square Ridged, Wedgwood	35
Vase, Brush, Fish Hook, Alfred Meakin, 5 In.	65

TECO is the mark used on the art pottery line made by the American Terra Cotta and Ceramic Company of Terra Cotta and Chicago, Illinois. The company was an offshoot of the firm founded by William D. Gates in 1881. The Teco line was first made in 1885 but was not sold commercially until 1902. It continued in production until 1922. Over 500 designs were made in a variety of colors, shapes, and glazes. The company closed in 1930.

Bookends, Girl Reading, Tan Glaze, 5 x 6 In.	350
Bowl, Green Matte Glaze, Ribbed, Impressed, 8 x 6 In.	438
Jardiniere, Green Matte Glaze, Footed, Ringed Lip, 10 x 15 In.	825
Pitcher, Flowers, Green Matte Over Black Glaze, 2 x 4 ⅛ In.	531
Pitcher, Green Matte Glaze, Pinched Mouth, Bulbous, W.D. Gates, 5 ½ x 4 In.	313
Pitcher, Green Matte Glaze, Whiplash Handle, W.D. Gates, 5 x 9 In.	438
Vase, 3 Organic Handles, Cylindrical, Green Matte Glaze, Impressed Marks, 5 x 11 In.	3660
Vase, 3-Lobe Body, 3 Handles, Green Matte Glaze, W.B. Mundie, 7 x 9 In.	3625
Vase, 4 Buttresses, Green Matte Glaze, c.1905, 17 x 9 ½ In.	13750
Vase, 4-Arm Classical Shape, Green Matte Glaze, Signed, W.J. Dodd, 5 x 12 In.	1000
Vase, Aventurine Glaze, Baluster Shape, Signed W.D. Gates, 4 ½ x 9 In.	976
Vase, Brown Glaze, Stylized Buttress Support, 4 x 9 In.	1063

T

Vase, Buttressed, Brown Glaze, Signed, W.D. Gates, 4 x 9 In.	1063
Vase, Buttressed, Elongated Handles, Stamped, c.1905, 7 ½ x 4 ¼ In.	1875
Vase, Buttressed, Green Matte Glaze, Handles, Stamped, c.1905, 8 ¼ x 6 ½ In.	2125
Vase, Buttressed, Green Matte Glaze, Stamped, c.1905, 7 x 4 In. ....*illus*	1188
Vase, Green Matte Glaze, 3 Organic Handles, Cylindrical, Impressed, W.B. Mundie, 5 x 11 In.	3666
Vase, Green Matte Glaze, 4 Arms, W.J. Dodd, 5 x 12 In.	1000
Vase, Green Matte Glaze, 4 Buttress Shape, Ferdnand Moreau, 5 ½ x 11 ¼ In.	4270
Vase, Green Matte Glaze, Abstract Shape, Wavy Mouth, Ribbed, 7 x 10 ½ In.	1952
Vase, Green Matte Glaze, Bulbous, 4 Flattened Buttressed Handles, 14 ½ x 8 ½ In.	5000
Vase, Green Matte Glaze, Buttress Shape, Signed W.D. Gates, 2 ½ x 7 In.	1200
Vase, Green Matte Glaze, Buttressed, Charcoaling, Stamped, c.1905, 5 ½ x 4 ½ In.	1375
Vase, Green Matte Glaze, Buttressed, Marked, c.1905, 6 ½ x 3 ¾ In. ....*illus*	1000
Vase, Green Matte Glaze, Daffodil Blossoms, Leaves, Cylindrical, 8 ¾ In.	1395
Vase, Green Matte Glaze, Flared, Scalloped Rim, Applied Vertical Leaves, Cutwork, 4 x 12 In.	10980
Vase, Green Matte Glaze, Gray Highlights, Shouldered, W.D. Gates, 5 x In.	563
Vase, Green Matte Glaze, Gray Highlights, Square Rim, Fritz Albert, W.D. Gates, 8 x 16 In.	2196
Vase, Green Matte Glaze, Grecian Shape, Lobed Base, W.J. Dodd, 8 ½ x 13 In.	1708
Vase, Green Matte Glaze, Impressed Reserve Panels, Handles, Cylindrical, 8 x 13 ½ In.	10370
Vase, Green Matte Glaze, Long Angular Handles, Cylindrical, W.B. Mundie, 5 x 11 In.	1200
Vase, Green Matte Glaze, Reticulated, Multiple Leaf Handles, c.1905, 11 ¾ x 4 ½ In.	5625
Vase, Green Matte Glaze, Squared Buttress Handles, 3 ½ In.	776
Vase, Green Matte Glaze, Waisted, Handles, Fritz Albert, 5 ½ x 9 ½ In.	800
Vase, Green Matte, Drip Glaze, 4 Handles, Fritz Albert, c.1905, 14 ⅞ In.	16250
Vase, Oval, Blue Glaze, Incised Lines, Stamped, c.1910, 12 x 7 In.	1250
Vase, Robin's Egg Blue Matte Glaze, Oval, Shouldered Rim, W.D. Gates, 13 x 25 ½ In.	1220

TEDDY BEARS were named for a president of the United States. The first teddy bear was a cuddly toy said to be inspired by a hunting trip made by Teddy Roosevelt in 1902. Morris and Rose Michtom started selling their stuffed bears as "teddy bears" and the name stayed. The Michtoms founded the Ideal Novelty and Toy Company. The German version of the teddy bear was made about the same time by the Steiff Company. There are many types of teddy bears and all are collected. The old ones are being reproduced. Other bears are listed in the Toy section.

Ideal, Mohair, Golden, Cloth Stitching, Shoebutton Eyes, 28 In.	590
Mohair, Apricot, Glass Eyes, Cloth Nose, 19 In.	120
Mohair, Apricot, Shoebutton Eyes, c.1920, 25 In.	180
Mohair, Blond, Shoebutton Eyes, Stitched Nose, Straw Stuffed, Jointed, 15 ½ In.	141
Mohair, Golden, Glass Eyes, Jointed, 20 In.	474
Mohair, Golden, Jointed Head & Limbs, Glass Eyes, Glasses, 24 In.	180
Mohair, Golden, Jointed Shoebutton Eyes, 12 ½ In.	565
Mohair, Honey Color, Linen Paws, Amber Glass Eyes, Germany, 18 In.	180
Mohair, Jointed, Germany, c.1900, 22 In.	61
Mohair, Light Brown, Jointed, Blue Jacket, c.1820, 11 ½ In.	923
Mohair, Shoebutton Eyes, Germany, c.1915, 28 In.	150
Mohair, White, Disc Jointed, Felt Paws, Glass Eyes, Sewn Nose, 15 In.	254
Petz, Musical, Mohair, Blond, Chime Mechanism, Germany, 1920, 15 In.	509
Schuco, Tricky Teddy, Jointed, 14 In.	330
Steiff, Apricot Fur, Felt Pads, 24 In.	5925
Steiff, Jointed, Humpback, White, Ear Button, 3 ½ In.	443
Steiff, Mohair, Blond, Long Arms, Jointed, Shoebutton Eyes, Button In Ear, 12 In.	900
Steiff, Mohair, Chocolate Brown, Jointed, Leather Paws, M. Strong, Box, 1983, 4 Piece	254
Steiff, Mohair, Shoebutton Eyes, Stitched Nose, 1908, 7 In.	540
Steiff, Mohair, Shoebutton Eyes, Stitched Nose, 1908, 10 In.	570
Steiff, Mohair, White, Jointed Head & Limbs, Glass Eyes, Brown Stitched Nose, 5 In.	240
Steiff, Ophelia, White, Ruffled Collar, Ear Button, Jointed, 16 In.	34
Steiff, Panda, Mohair, Jointed Arms, Legs & Head, c.1950, 8 ½ In.	375
Steiff, Shoebutton Eyes, Stitched Nose, Swivel Neck, Hips, Hump, Ear Button, 19 ½ In.	3555

TELEPHONES are wanted by collectors if the phones are old enough or unusual enough. The first telephone may have been made in Havana, Cuba, in 1849, but it was not patented. The first publicly demonstrated phone was used in Frankfurt, Germany, in 1860. The phone made by Alexander Graham Bell was shown at the Centennial Exhibition in Philadelphia in 1876, but it was not until 1877 that the first private phones were installed. Collectors today want all types of old phones, phone parts, and advertising. Even recent figural phones are popular.

American Electric, Chicago, H.I. Burns, Candlestick, Accordion Bracket, 12 In.	330
Association Des Ouveres En Instruts De Precision, Batteries, Wood Case, 1934	300

Telephone, Rotary, Desktop, No. 302, c.1939, Restored
$120

Victorian Casino Antiques

Telephone, Sign, Home Telephone Local & Long Distance, Porcelain, 2-Sided, 17 x 18 In.
$240

Showtime Auction Services

Television, Philco, Predicta, 1950s, 20 x 14 x 27 In.
$720

Victorian Casino Antiques

T I P
Don't leave a voice-mail message at your office or home or a comment on any social media site that indicates you will be out of town.

573

Teplitz, Vase, Fates, Women, Spider Web, Eduard Stellmacher, Amphora, 1902-03, 14 x 7 In. $8,750

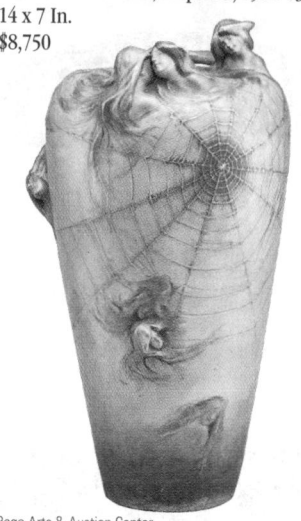

Rago Arts & Auction Center

Teplitz, Vase, Maiden, Calla Lily, Amphora, Riessner, Stellmacher & Kessel, c.1900, 24 ½ In. $3,125

Rago Arts & Auction Center

Cooking Stars

Cooking has become a way of life. Successful restaurant chefs are now stars. Out-of-print cookbooks by memorable personalities like Julia Child sell quickly online. There is even a market for the pamphlets given away by food companies over the past century, even if the instructions don't take into account microwaves or frozen food.

Booth, Built-In, Brass Marquee, Tin Interior, Rotary Phone, Fan, 1920s, 83 x 30 In.	711
Candlestick, French Empire Style, Mahogany, Ormolu, Eagle Finial, France, 18 In.	10200
Candlestick, Western Electric Co., Desktop, Dual Bell Ringer, Box, 1891-1913	240
Pay, Candlestick, Tabletop, Courtesy Coin Box, Local Calls 5 Cents, Stromberg-Carlson	720
Pay, Local & Long Distance, Flange, 2-Sided, Black Ground, White, 10 x 10 In.	171
Pin, Pioneer Telephone, Bell, Woman On Phone, Round, c.1920, 1 ¾ In.	141
Rotary, Black, Quejas 114 Larga Dist. O No. 2-1051, c.1950	120
Rotary, Desktop, No. 302, c.1939, Restored ....*illus*	120
Servant's Caller, Lyman & Schorndorfer, Cleveland, Wood, Spindles, Glass, 23 In.	150
Sign, Bell System Public Telephone, Porcelain, Flange, 2-Sided, 18 x 18 In.	138
Sign, Home Telephone Local & Long Distance, Porcelain, 2-Sided, 17 x 18 In. ......*illus*	240
Sign, Indiana Bell, Blue, White, Porcelain, Flange, 11 x 11 In.	118
Sign, Mt. Vernon Telephone Co., Shield Shape, Porcelain, 20 x 22 In.	311
Sign, Public Telephone, Bell Logo, Blue, White, Porcelain Flange, 11 x 11 In.	207
Sign, Wes-Tex Telephone Co-Op, Stanton, Porcelain, Yellow Ground, Black, Round, 12 In.	330
Switch Board, Samson Electric Co., Canton, Ma., Oak Case, Ear Piece, 26 In.	1046
Telegraph Alarm, Call Box, Clock, E.M. Bryant, Manchester, N.H., Wood, Glass, 33 In.	3075
Utica Fire Alarm Telephone Co., Quartersawn Oak Cabinet, Wall Mount, Utica, N.Y.	660
Wall, Oak, c.1900, 24 In.	115
Wall, Oak, Metal, c.1910, 17 In.	148
Western Electric, Crank, Oak Case, Separate Ear Piece, 2 Bells, 19 In.	119
Western Electric, Model E1, Rotary Dial, Black Handset & Base	270
Wood, Bells, Speaker, Crank, 19 In.	180

TELEVISION sets are twentieth-century collectibles. Although the first television transmission took place in England in 1925, collectors find few sets that pre-date 1946. The first sets had only five channels, but by 1949 the additional UHF channels were included. The first color television set became available in 1951.

Crosley, Model 10-401, Bakelite Case	185
DuMont, Model RA102A, Wood Case, 11-In. Screen	3998
General Electric, Model 803, FM/AM Table Model Receiver, Wood, Metal, 18 x 23 In.	240
General Electric, Model HM 171, Wood Case, 5 Dials, 1939, 14 x 20 In., 4-In. Screen	6000
Guide, First Week Of U.S. Programming, June 30, 1941, NBC-RCA Sticker, 5 ¾ x 6 ⅝ In.	1375
Philco, Predicta, 1950s, 20 x 14 x 27 In. ....*illus*	720
Philco, Predicta, Model 4654, UHF Dial	360
Philco, Predicta, Penthouse, Metal Foot, Blond Console Cabinet	420
Philco, Predicta, Princess, Rounded Screen, Red Metal Base, Swivels, Antenna, 1959	615
Philco, Predicta, Stand, 23 ½ x 24 ½ In.	360
Philco, Safari, Model H 2010 L, Portable, Leather Case, Hinged Handle, 14 In.	180
RCA Victor, Model 621TS, c.1940, 15 x 19 In.	385
RCA Victor, Model CT 100, Wood Console, 1st Color TV Set, 12-In. Screen	1080
Zenith, Model G2355, Wood Case, Porthole Screen	150

TEPLITZ refers to art pottery manufactured by a number of companies in the Teplitz-Turn area of Bohemia during the late nineteenth and early twentieth centuries. Two of these companies were the Alexandra Works founded by Ernst Wahliss, and the Amphora Porcelain Works, run by Riessner, Stellmacher, and Kessel.

Bowl, Sculptural, Maiden Holding Poppy, Tan, Purple, Amphora, Stellmacher, 28 In.	1625
Bust, Man, Art Nouveau, Hat, Tie, Cape, c.1905, 6 In.	600
Bust, Sarah Bernhardt, Blond Hair, Blue Hat, Downcast Eyes, Stellmacher, c.1910, 18 In.	1035
Bust, Woman, Bat In Long Hair, Amphora, E. Stellmacher, 23 x 16 In.	3750
Bust, Woman, Green Dress, Bonnet, 16 In.	1074
Bust, Woman, Lacy Robes, Hat, Rose, Cream, E. Stellmacher, Amphora, 4 ½ x 6 In.	750
Bust, Woman, Ruffled Hat, Dress, Bamboo Fan, Stellmacher, Amphora, c.1900, 20 In.	1495
Ewer, Enamel, Paint, Gilt, Swollen Shoulder, Ruffle Rim, Handle, Arch Feet, c.1900, 13 In.	118
Ewer, Flowers, Pink, Rose, Green, Openwork, Art Nouveau, c.1900, 16 In.	396
Ewer, Mottled Green, Brown Matte Glaze, Organic, Spout, Amphora, 5 x 7 In.	244
Figurine, Dandy, Smoking Cigar, Hat, Green, Blue, Brown, Glaze, Amphora, 11 In.	300
Figurine, Enchantress, Flowing Hair, Garland, Cockatoo On Head, 17 In.	1500
Figurine, Girl On Basket, Feeding Chicks, Pastels, c.1905, 7 x 6 In.	475
Group, Man, 2 Oxen, Brown, Tan, Amphora, 20 In.	249
Group, Satyr, Nymph, Oval Base, Amphora, Austria, c.1905, 14 ½ In.	750
Humidor, Lady's Portrait, Flowers, Mottled Green, c.1900, 6 x 6 In.	325
Jug, Fish, Gilt Fish Scales, Bouquet, Twig Handle, RStK, c.1900, 4 ½ In.	319
Pitcher, Applied Dragon Handle, Berries, Impressed Amphora, Austria, 11 In.	270

T

Pitcher, Birch Trees, Mushrooms, Marked, 6 ⅝ In.	450
Pitcher, Blue, Cream, Orange Glaze, Pinched Rim, Amphora, 9 In.	1020
Urn, Lid, Painted, Flowers, Raised Gilt Scrolls, c.1900, 11 ½ In.	72
Vase, 3 Loop Handles, Oval, Green, Gold Glaze, Squat, 7 In.	590
Vase, Allegory Of Germany, Woman's Profile, Gold, Cream, Bulbous Base, Amphora, 15 In.	10800
Vase, Allegory Of Russia, Woman's Face, Tulip Shape Top, Cinched Waist, Amphora, 6 In.	2700
Vase, Apple Picker, Woman, Reaching Up For Fruit, Sheer Dress, Amphora, 22 In.	3300
Vase, Blue, Mushrooms, Birch Tree Forest, Paul Dachsel, Amphora, c.1906, 15 ¼ In.	10200
Vase, Butterfly, Web, Jewel Inset, Bulbous, Amphora, 11 In.	2700
Vase, Fairytale Princess, Woman's Portrait, Jeweled Flowers, Shouldered, Amphora, 15 In.	3000
Vase, Fates, Women, Spider Web, Eduard Stellmacher, Amphora, 1902-03, 14 x 7 In. ....*illus*	8750
Vase, Fates, Women's Faces, Light Blue, Cream, Gold, Flared, Amphora, 17 In.	3000
Vase, Frog & Fly, Yellow, Flared Cylindrical Red Body, E. Stellmacher, Amphora, 21 In.	10800
Vase, Grape Bunches, Vines, Leaves, Cylindrical, 17 In.	709
Vase, Gres-Bijou, Web Jewel Inset Top, Base, Striated Waist, Amphora, 15 In.	4800
Vase, Iris, Bulbous, Footed, Applied Woman, Bug, Red Dress, Green, Amphora, 17 ½ In., Pair	1400
Vase, Klimt, Coin, Web Designs, Footed, Gold, Brown, Amphora, 8 ¼ In.	1200
Vase, Maiden, Blossoms, Enamel, Amphora, Red Stamp, c.1905, 7 ¾ x 4 ¾ In.	938
Vase, Maiden, Calla Lily, Amphora, Riessner, Stellmacher & Kessel, c.1900, 24 ½ In. ....*illus*	3125
Vase, Maiden, Dragonflies, Iris, Wrapped Stem, Baluster, Amphora, Stellmacher, 18 In., Pair	1125
Vase, Maiden, Flowers In Hair, Trees, Water, Amphora, Red RStK, c.1900, 8 ¼ In.	1500
Vase, Organic, Gourd Shape, Seminude Woman On Leafy Rim, E. Wahliss, Amphora, 8 In.	585
Vase, Parrot, Spread Wings, Cloisonne Style, Amphora, 17 ½ In.	287
Vase, Portrait, Woman, Amphora, Reissner, Eagle Headdress, Marked, c.1900, 15 In. ....*illus*	3120
Vase, Raised Branches, Leaves, Iridescent Metallic Glaze, Ernst Wahliss, Amphora, 8 x 16 In.	375
Vase, Ribbed, Cutout Handles, Green, Tan, Tree, Dragonfly, Paul Dachsel, Amphora, 5 x 6 In.	1464
Vase, Roses, Leaves, Dragonfly, Gilt, Handles, c.1900, 8 In.	195
Vase, Ruffled, Applied Leaves, Vines, Layered Hops, Green, Beige, c.1918, 8 x 8 In.	895
Vase, Shouldered, Metallic Gray, Raised Swirls, Amphora, 5 ½ x 10 In.	915
Vase, Spider Webs, Jewels, Blue, Tapered, Amphora, 15 ½ In.	7800
Vase, Spider, Web, Amphora, Riessner, Stellmacher & Kessel, c.1900, 17 In. ....*illus*	3375
Vase, Stylized Corn, Yellow, Purple, Scrolled Handles, Stellmacher, Amphora, 5 x 7 In.	305
Vase, Stylized Lotus Leaves, 4 Handles, Paul Dachsel, For E.W. Wahliss, c.1911, 9 In.	3900
Vase, Stylized Tree Design, Brown, Tan, Black, P. Dachsel, Amphora, Marked Terex, 5 x 6 In.	732
Vase, Tapered, Footed, Cobalt Blue, Green Butterfly, Brown Ground, Amphora, 13 ½ In.	197

TERRA-COTTA is a special type of pottery. It ranges from pale orange to dark reddish-brown in color. The color comes from the clay, which is fired but not always glazed in the finished piece.

Bust, Black Man, Smoking Cigarette, Impressed Ernst Wahliss Wien, 16 In.	1560
Bust, Classical Woman, Inscribed Italy 78, 15 ¾ In.	334
Bust, French Gentleman, Scarf Around Neck, Sideward Glancing, Pedestal, 18 In.	431
Bust, Griffin, 19 In.	594
Bust, Jeune Femme, Leaves, Flowers, Ruffle, France, Signed, 1880, 24 x 14 In.	738
Bust, Marie Antoinette, Hair Piled High, c.1895, 31 x 16 In.	489
Bust, Paint, Lorenzo De Medici, Breastplate, Faux Bronze Finish, c.1785, 18 x 12 In.	369
Bust, Woman, Renaissance Style, Multicolor, Italy, 1800s, 20 x 23 In.	523
Bust, Woman, Renaissance Style, Paint, Necklace, 1900s, 21 In.	923
Figurine, Bull, Wood Platform, Iron Rod, c.1885, 8 x 10 In.	369
Figurine, Judas Iscariot, Kneeling, Robes, Hand On Forehead, Base, 1800s, 12 ½ In.	118
Figurine, Leda & Swan, Paint, Marble Base, France, 1800s, 17 ½ x 14 ¼ In.	1722
Figurine, Madonna & Child, 10 ¼ In.	313
Figurine, Magi, In Costume, Turban, Robe, c.1885, 17 x 5 In.	369
Figurine, Mother, Hugging Child, Signed E. Mazzolina, c.1926, 17 x 10 In.	413
Figurine, Polar Bear, Prototype, Waylande Gregory, 9 In. ....*illus*	1062
Figurine, Seated Man, Knee Up, Hands On Knee, Looking Up, Italy, 12 x 6 In.	826
Figurine, Standing Harlequin, Arms Crossed, Square Base, 1879, 31 ½ In.	750
Figurine, Warrior, Standing, Armor, Arms Up, Chinese, c.1900, 22 x 9 In.	354
Group, 3 Putti, Playing, Brown Paint, 23 In.	281
Pitcher, Dragon Head Mouth, Rim, Black, Impressed Johann Maresch, 12 ½ In.	480
Plaque, Benjamin Franklin, Portrait, Round, Jean Baptist Nina, Black Frame, c.1777, 6 In.	2375
Plaque, Faith, Charity, Hope, 3 Panels, After Del Sarto, Glazed, France, 1874, 12 x 19 In.	240
Plaque, Flowers, Woman's Profile, Art Nouveau, Marked, 17 x 10 In.	132
Plaque, Madonna, Elongated Octagonal, Praying Hands, 1600s, 21 ¼ x 16 In.	885
Plaque, Middle Eastern Man, Horseback, Leaf Border, Musterschutz, Marked, 1800s, 20 In.	687
Plaque, Renaissance Style, White Mary & Jesus, Seated, Blue Ground, 1800s, 31 x 24 In.	2250

Teplitz, Vase, Portrait, Woman, Amphora, Reissner, Eagle Headdress, Marked, c.1900, 15 In. $3,120

Skinner Auctioneers & Appraisers

Teplitz, Vase, Spider, Web, Amphora, Riessner, Stellmacher & Kessel, c.1900, 17 In. $3,375

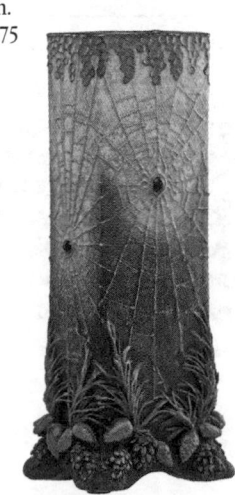

Rago Arts & Auction Center

Terra-Cotta, Figurine, Polar Bear, Prototype, Waylande Gregory, 9 In.
$1,062

Rachel Davis Fine Arts

Textile, Blanket, Hudson's Bay, Point, Stripes, Label, c.1950s, 100 x 108 In.
$196

Allard Auctions

Textile, Flag, American, 24 Stars, Wool Bunting, Cotton, G.H. Gilbert, c.1822-36, 7 x 14 Ft.
$4,200

Skinner Auctioneers & Appraisers

Textile, Flag, American, 36 Stars, Parade, Cotton, c.1865-67, 11 ¼ x 18 In.
$1,410

Cowan's Auctions

Sculpture, Nude, Reclining, Amallioi, Wood Base, 12 x 8 In.	54
Sculpture, Woman, Nude, Embracing Peacock, Classical Pose, Glazed, Italy, 49 In.	2000
Teapot, Lid, Bird Finial, Farm Scenes, Matte Enamel, Flared, Lydia Buzio, 1978, 5 In.	345
Tile, Roof, Arched, Figural Rooster On Top, 18 x 14 ¾ x 13 In.	570
Urn, Amphora Shape, Grand Tour, Metal Base, Mounted As Lamp, 21 In.	861
Urn, Lobed, Fluted, Bud Finial, Grapevines, Handles, Pedestal Base, 94 x 26 In., Pair	4880
Vase, Arts & Crafts, Rolled Rim, Tapered, Oval, 18 x 30 In.	344
Vase, Enamel, Figures, Branches, Swirls, Cup, Bell Shape Base, c.1900, 6 x 5 In.	390
Vase, Woman, Standing By Lily Vase, Partly Draped, E. Wahliss, Amphora, 28 In., Pair	3600

TEXTILES listed here include many types of printed fabrics and table and household linens. Some other textiles will be found under Clothing, Coverlet, Rug, Quilt, etc.

Altar Panel, Silk, Embroidered, Flowers, Gilt, Frame, Italy, 1700s, 48 x 89 In.	1547
Banner, Circus, Giraffe Girl, Alive, Canvas, By Snap Wyatt, c.1930, 113 x 69 In.	2410
Bed Hanging, Woven, Butterflies, Peony Tree, Buddha's Hand, Tassels, c.1900, 76 In.	330
Bible Lid, King, Queen, Trees, Flowers, Silk, Beads, Wool, Labels, England, 7 x 11 In.	5313
Blanket, Hudson's Bay, Point, Stripes, Label, c.1950s, 100 x 108 In. ....*illus*	196
Book Cover, Grenfell Mission, Mixed Fibers, Burlap, 2 Figures, Red Border, c.1930, 9 x 14 ½ In.	492
Diorama, Bird, On Branch, Fruit, Yellow, Green, Brown, Wool, Frame, c.1850, 14 x 18 In.	492
Flag, Admiral Dewey, Hero Of Manila, Image In Wreath, Crossed Flags, Frame, 30 x 31 In.	106
Flag, American, 13 Stars, 13 Stripes, Blue, Red, White, Wood Canton, 1784, 22 x 38 In.	212500
Flag, American, 13 Stars, Banner Shape, c.1890, 24 x 144 In.	560
Flag, American, 13 Stars, Starched Gauze, 1876, 6 ¼ x 4 In.	240
Flag, American, 24 Stars, Wool Bunting, Cotton, G.H. Gilbert, c.1822-36, 7 x 14 Ft. ....*illus*	4200
Flag, American, 34 Stars, Silk, c.1861, 31 x 39 In.	2160
Flag, American, 34 Stars, Wool, c.1862, 17 x 22 ¾ In.	3645
Flag, American, 35 Stars, Cavalry, Guidon, 7 Red Stripes, 6 White, Silk, 28 x 38 In.	27000
Flag, American, 36 Stars, c.1865, 36 x 52 In.	2706
Flag, American, 36 Stars, Parade, Cotton, c.1865-67, 11 ¼ x 18 In. ....*illus*	1410
Flag, American, 37 Stars, 13 Stripes, Silk, Gilt Frame, 1867, 36 x 49 In.	540
Flag, American, 38 Stars, Marking Colorado Statehood, Silk, Printed, c.1890, 12 x 15 In.	2040
Flag, American, 38 Stars, Parade, Stick, Finial, c.1880, 22 x 14 In.	300
Flag, American, 45 Stars, 13 Stripes, Fringe, Silk, Staff, 15 x 16 In.	881
Flag, American, 45 Stars, Mattaposiett, Ma. Label, c.1898, 37 x 71 In.	94
Flag, American, Campaign, Harrison, Grandfather's Hat Fits Ben, Frame, 30 x 22 In.	720
Flag, New York, Artillery Flank Marker, 2nd Artillery, c.1862, 26 x 26 In.	4374
Flag, Silk, 38 Stars, Great Star Pattern, 12 x 17 In.	2350
Hanging, Red Velvet, Dragon, Flaming Pearl, Lotus Flowers, c.1900, 35 x 39 In.	1200
Mat, Grenfell Mission, Mixed Fibers, Burlap, Goose Flying, Pines, Yellow Border, 9 ¼ x 11 In.	240
Mat, Grenfell Mission, Mixed Fibers, Burlap, Husky Dogs, Abrash Sky, 7 ½ x 9 ½ In.	390
Mat, Grenfell Mission, Mixed Fibers, Burlap, Polar Bear, Abrash Sea, Sky, 7 ¼ x 9 ¼ In.	461
Mat, Grenfell Mission, Mixed Fibers, Burlap, Puffins, Abrash Sea, Iceberg, 8 ½ x 9 ¼ In.	677
Panel, Embroidered, Figural Religious Scenes, Metallic Thread, Beadwork, 8 x 13 In.	3360
Panel, Embroidered, Prince, Riding Mythical Animal, Chinese, 1600s, 126 x 80 In.	5904
Panel, Figure, Face, Lizard, African Beaded Council House, 53 x 10 In. ....*illus*	88
Panel, Linen, Embroidered Flowers, Vines, Birds, Metallic, Silk Thread, 1800s, 86 x 48 In.	799
Panel, Patriotic & Fraternal Symbols, Motifs, Dec. 25, 1877, 38 x 40 In.	1320
Panel, Silk & Chenille, Embroidery, Frame, c.1850, 11 ½ x 13 In.	240
Panel, Silk Brocade, Floral Patchwork, Multicolor, Cream Ground, 1800s, 92 x 41 In.	200
Panel, Silk Brocade, Red Velvet Border, Multicolor Leaves, Fountains, c.1900, 53 x 33 In.	300
Panel, Silk Cotton, Ikat, Uzbekistan, c.1890, 95 x 49 In.	538
Panel, Silk, Blue Embroidered, Peach Ground, c.1910, 60 x 83 In.	179
Panel, Silk, Embroidered Kesi Dragon, Yellow, Woven, Qing Dynasty, 1800s, 60 x 53 In.	10762
Panel, Silk, Embroidered, 5 Vertical Panels, Cranes, Frame, 1800s, 57 x 64 In. ....*illus*	4956
Panel, Silk, Embroidered, Charles I, Queen, Metallic Thread, 10 x 11 In.	3600
Panel, Silk, Embroidered, Ferns, Flowers, White, Gray, Orange, Frame, c.1890, 37 x 27 In.	500
Panel, Silk, Embroidered, Figures, Holding Fan, Pine Tree, Monkey, 1800s, 47 x 18 In.	308
Panel, Silk, Embroidered, Flowers, Moths, Dragonflies, Gold Thread, 1800s, 80 x 67 In.	922
Panel, Silk, Embroidered, Guanyu, Brocade Border, Chinese, 1644-1911, 81 x 39 In. ....*illus*	3660
Panel, Woman With Child, Wool, Edwin Scheier, Mexico, 1960s, 72 x 37 In.	1875
Panel, Woman, Standing, Quilted, Painted, Signed Fritts, 54 x 26 In.	1375
Panel, Wool, Needlepoint, Lion & Unicorn, 1923, 32 x 33 In.	120
Patch, Apollo XII Crew, Variant 2, Conrad-Gordon-Bean, 1969, 4 In. Diam.	145
Patch, NASA Logo, Blue, White, Red, 1965, 3 In. Diam.	400
Pillow Case, Appliqued, Floral Wreath, Green, Red, Yellow, Cotton, c.1860, 26 x 20 In.	403

Pillow Case, Patchwork Bear Claw, Red, White Checkerboard, c.1860, 32 x 17 In., Pair		201
Pillow, Crewelwork, Stags, Strawberry Field, Flowers, Wool, Fringe, Linen, 1700s, 14 x 18 In.		5100
Pillow, Raised Strawberries, Vining, Black Ground, Velvet, c.1890, 15 x 15 In.		58
Rank Badge, Embroidered, Egret, Emblems, Frame, Chinese, 1800s, 10 ½ In.	*illus*	790
Runner, Silk Brocade, Rampant Lions, Crowned Eagles, Green, Gold, Tassels, 81 x 22 In.		175
Scroll, Calligraphy, Rows, Black & White, Red, Chinese, 65 x 16 In.		3600
Scroll, Calligraphy, Rows, Black Ground, White, Chinese, 67 x 21 In.		270
Scroll, Calligraphy, White Ground, Black, Signed, Chinese, 12 x 58 In.		420
Scroll, Ink On Paper, Thrush Birds, Crabapple Branches, Signed, Shao'ang, Chinese	*illus*	1094
Shawl, Paisley, Mustard Center, Red, Blue Swirls, France		345
Shawl, Silk Embroidered, Red, Swat Valley, Pakistan, c.1910, 84 x 38 In.		227
Shawl, Sunburst, Moon, Brown, Black, Red, Kashmir, c.1825, 66 x 66 In.		16800
Sleigh Blanket, Gloves, Auburn Horsehair, Victorian, Crosby Tribian Sleigh Co., 60 & 17 In.		29
Spread, Candlewick, Star Medallion, Tulips, Vine Border, Swag, Tassel, 1800s, 94 x 92 In.		230
Table Cover, Flower Baskets, Embroidery, Silk, Chenille, Metallic Thread, c.1900, 98 x 87 In.		1080
Tablecloth, Brussels Lace, Grapes, Leaves, 12 Napkins, Continental, 1900s, 59 x 109 In.		480
Tablecloth, Cotton, Blue Checked Center & Border, Flowers, 1950s, 58 x 45 In.		35
Tablecloth, Flowers, Geometric Shapes, Lace, Handmade, 88 x 70 In.		90
Tapestry, 3 Dragons, Flaming Pearl, Clouds, Coil Pattern, Brocade Border, c.1900		2952
Tapestry, Castle, Bird, Flowers, Flanders, c.1750, 100 x 115 In.		1422
Tapestry, Courting Couple, Autumn Landscape, Leaf Border, Wool, 1700s, 106 x 82 In.		1107
Tapestry, Egrets, Lotus Pond, Standing In Water, Lily Pads, Brocade Border, c.1900		10200
Tapestry, Floating Circles, Jute Fiber, A. Calder, Bon Art, 1975, 72 x 48 In.		10000
Tapestry, Game Birds, Landscape, Trees, Village, Woven Wool, c.1700, 104 x 114 In.		3000
Tapestry, Goodyear, Mohair, Mamosala Mosilili, Masweu Kingdom Of Lesotho, 34 x 59 In.		153
Tapestry, Hunter & Hound Chasing Stag, Flower & Fruit Border, Flemish, 77 x 98 In.		878
Tapestry, Man, Woman, Garden, Fountain, Wool, c.1700, 130 x 103 In.		3480
Tapestry, Medieval Style, Women In Garden, Red Ground, 20th Century, 79 x 52 In.		211
Tapestry, Peasants Under Tree, Sheep, Painted, Silk, Wool, Fringe, c.1830, 75 x 69 In.		1107
Tapestry, Persephone, Pomegranate Vine, Wool, Silk, Muslin, Belgium, 1500s, 108 x 58 In.		6150
Tapestry, Sun, Circles, Red, Blue, Yellow, Maguey Fiber, A. Calder, Bon Art, 1974, 72 In.		9375
Tapestry, Valentine, Wool, Hand Woven, Jim Dine, New York, c.1978, 25 ½ x 35 In.	*illus*	1000
Thanka, Gouache On Cloth, Gilt, Multicolor, Tibet, 1900s, 24 ½ x 16 In.		354

THERMOMETER is a name that comes from the Greek word for heat. The thermometer was invented in 1731 to measure the temperature of either water or air. All kinds of thermometers are collected, but those with advertising messages are the most popular.

American Alliance Insurance, Black, Orange, Porcelain, 27 In.	270
Bake-O-Meter, Good Housekeeping Stamp, Cooper Co., 3 ¼ x 4 x 3 In.	200
Baltimore Cooperage Tank & Tower Co., Illustrated, Corona, N.Y., 24 In.	86
Betsy Ross, Framed Picture, God Bless America, 1940s, 5 x 7 In.	65
Black & White Radio Cabs, Drive Carefully, Paint, Metal, Arched, 16 x 6 ⅜ In.	374
Bubble Up Has Pa-ZAZZ, Tin, Embossed, Die Cut, 5 x 17 In.	*illus*	180
Chew Mail Pouch Tobacco, Metal, 39 x 8 In.	150
Dailey's Ambulance Service, Ambulance, Wood, 11 ⅝ x 3 ⅛ In.	374
Drink Nesbitt California Orange, Black, Yellow, Orange, Tin, 1940s, 27 In.	270
Drink NuGrape Soda, A Flavor You Can't Forget, Metal, 16 x 6 In.	570
En-Ar-Co Motor Oil, Premium Motor Oil, Boy, Slate Logo, Tin, 39 x 8 In.	295
Ex-Lax The Chocolate Laxative, Porcelain, 36 x 8 In.	295
Fine Children's Shoes, Round, Plastic, Metal Glass, 12 In.	150
First National Bank, Aurora, Ill., Porcelain, c.1930, 27 x 7 In.	60
Fleet Wing, Petroleum Products, Flying Bird, Yellow, Metal, 6 ⅜ x 2 In.	184
Gold Medal Motor Oils, Long Life To Your Car, Round, 10 In.	354
Green Spot Soda, Embossed Metal, Hand Holding Bottle, 16 x 4 ½ In.	219
Hires Root Beer, Bottle Form, Tin, Embossed, 28 In.	94
Hull Optometrist, Wood, 24 In.	36
Hygrometer, Wheel, Mahogany, Brass Finial, H. Grimoldi, c.1815, 48 x 14 In.	590
Le Fendrich Cigar, Always A Cool Smoke, Metal, c.1915, 26 In.	62
Lord Stirling Cigars, Cigar Shape, 9 x 47 In.	115
Mail Pouch Tobacco, Porcelain, 8 x 39 In.	485
Mail Pouch Tobacco, Treat Yourself To The Best, Tin, TCA Tru Temp, 8 x 39 In.	*illus*	180
Martin Senour, Pioneers Of Pure Paint, Porcelain, 1930s, 38 x 8 In.	150
Moxie, It's Always A Pleasure To Serve You, Spokesman, Tin Lithograph, 25 ½ In.	518
Moxie, Man, White Coat, Pointing, Tin, Embossed, Cutout, c.1910, 38 In.	3900
NuGrape Soda, Everybody Likes A Change, Metal, 1940s, 16 x 6 In.	600

Textile, Panel, Figure, Face, Lizard, African Beaded Council House, 53 x 10 In. $88

Old Barn Auction

Textile, Panel, Silk, Embroidered, 5 Vertical Panels, Cranes, Frame, 1800s, 57 x 64 In. $4,956

Brunk Auctions

TIP
To untie knots in ribbons, shoelaces, or necklaces, sprinkle a little talcum power on them.

T

Textile, Panel, Silk, Embroidered, Guanyu, Brocade Border, Chinese, 1644-1911, 81 x 39 In. $3,660

Neal Auction Co.

Textile, Rank Badge, Embroidered, Egret, Emblems, Frame, Chinese, 1800s, 10 ½ In. $790

James D. Julia Auctioneers

Obelisk Shape, Tortoiseshell, 9 x 3 In.	795
Orange Crush, Bottle Form, Tin, Embossed, 29 In.	271
Oven, Porcelain, Enamel, 1940s, 5 x 2 In.	45
Pabst Blue Ribbon Beer, At Popular Prices, Man, Strength Game, c.1950, 18 In. ....*illus*	270
Piels Beer, Cream Of Beer, White, Brown, c.1971, 12 In. Diam.	175
Prestone Anti-Freeze, You're Safe & You Know It, Red, White, Blue, 37 x 9 In.	130
Red Crown Gasoline, Polarine, Porcelain	2950
Rislone, Oil Alloy, Red, Orange, Yellow, Tin, 1940s, 26 In.	210
Sauer's Flavoring Extracts, Wood, Paint, Red & White, Bottle, 24 x 7 In.	575
Silver, Fox At Base, E.G. Webster, c.1885, 5 In.	165
Trico Wiper Blades, Red, White, Windshield Shape, 9 x 15 In.	265
Waterman's Ideal Fountain Pen, Gold Nib, Tin, 1920s, 19 ½ In.	3000
Woman, Reaching For Bird, Art Nouveau, Bronze, c.1890, 9 x 3 In.	250
Ya Gotta Have Moxie, Yellow Ground, c.1960, 14 x 6 In.	150

TIFFANY is a name that appears on items made by Louis Comfort Tiffany, the American glass designer who worked from about 1879 to 1933. His work included iridescent glass, Art Nouveau styles of design, and original contemporary styles. He was also noted for stained glass windows, unusual lamps, bronze work, pottery, and silver. Tiffany & Company, often called "Tiffany," is also listed in this section. The company was started by Charles Lewis Tiffany and Teddy Young in 1837 in New York City. In 1853 the name was changed to Tiffany & Company. Louis Tiffany (1848–1933), Charles Tiffany's son, started his own business in 1879. It was named Louis Comfort Tiffany and Associated American Artists. In 1902 the name was changed to Tiffany Studios. Tiffany & Company is still working today and is best known for silver and fine jewelry. Louis worked for his father's company as a decorator in 1900 but at the same time was working for his Tiffany Studios. Other types of Tiffany are listed under Tiffany Glass, Tiffany Pottery, or Tiffany Silver. The famous Tiffany lamps are listed in this section. Tiffany jewelry is listed in the Jewelry and Wristwatch categories. Some Tiffany Studio desk sets have matching clocks. They are listed here. Clocks made by Tiffany & Co. are listed in the Clock category. Reproductions of some types of Tiffany are being made.

Louis C. Tiffany

Ashtray, Match Safe, Adam, Gilt Bronze, Stamped Tiffany Studios New York, 6 x 2 ½ In.	450
Bill File, Bookmark Pattern, Stamped Tiffany Studios New York, 7 ½ x 3 ½ In.	1500
Blotter Ends, Bookmark Pattern, Stamped Tiffany Studios New York, 12 x 2 In.	300
Blotter Ends, Venetian, Bronze, 19 ⅜ x 2 ½ In.	288
Bookends, Adam, Gilt Bronze, Stamped Tiffany Studios New York, 4 ½ x 6 In.	2000
Bookends, Zodiac, Impressed Tiffany Studios, New York, 6 In. ....*illus*	413
Bowl, Intaglio Cut, Gold Favrile Center, Applied Glass Foot, Leaves, Signed, 2 x 8 In.	1007
Box, Bronze, Enamel & Gilt, Ferret Border, Flip Lid, Latch, 2 ½ x 5 ½ In.	2457
Box, Bureau, Pine Needle, Bronze, Green, White Slag Glass, Signed, 2 x 5 ½ x 3 ½ In.	165
Box, Chinese Pattern, Gilt Bronze, Liner, Stamped Tiffany Studios New York, 6 x 5 In.	3000
Box, Glove, Pine Needle, Bronze, Green Favrile Panels, 13 ½ x 3 ½ In.	3245
Box, Pine Needle, Bronze, Green Favrile Glass, 7 x 2 ½ In.	1298
Box, Rubber Band, Bookmark Pattern, Stamped Tiffany Studios New York, 5 x 3 In.	950
Box, Stamp, Bookmark Pattern, Stamped Tiffany Studios New York, 2 ½ x 2 x 1 ½ In.	950
Candelabrum, 2-Light, Bronze, Rosebud, Bulbous Cups, Waby Oval Base, c.1920, 9 In.	1159
Candelabrum, 6-Light, Bronze, Brown Patina, Green & Red Highlights, 15 x 21 In.	6814
Candle, Lamp, Blue, Flared Stretched Shade, Diamond Quilted, Blue Twisted Stem, 12 In.	2015
Candle, Lamp, Ruffled Shade, Twisted Ribbed Trumpet Shape, Favrile, c.1900, 16 In.	677
Candlestick, Art Deco, Blue Enamel, Orange, Green, Yellow, Gold Dore, 7 ½ In., Pair	3555
Candlestick, Bronze, 3-Leaf Clover Base, Reticulated Glass Insert, Signed, 10 In. ....*illus*	3555
Candlestick, Bronze, Cobra Shape, Marked Tiffany Studios, 6 x 7 ½ In.	915
Candlestick, Bronze, Favrile Glass Balls On Cup, Standard, Base, 1906, 15 In.	35400
Candlestick, Bronze, Urn Cup, Flared Foot, Red, Green Verdigris, 19 In.	560
Candlestick, Root Design, 3-Legged Foot, Candle Cup, 3-Finger Mount, 12 ½ In., Pair	2666
Candlestick, Rowfant Club, Standing Groundhog, Open Book, Ernest Seton, 1900s, 8 ½ In.	7110
Chair, Havemeyer, Oak, Silk Upholstery, Open Arms, Slated, Carved, c.1890, 45 x 29 In.	106200
Chandelier, Poinsettia, Red Flowers, Green Leaves, Triangular, Bead Border, 29 In.	306800
Cigar Box, Zodiac, Hinged Lid, Gilt Bronze, Stamped, 2 ½ x 6 In.	625
Clock, Art Deco, Bronze, Panels, Marked, Signed, 3 ½ x 5 ¾ In. ....*illus*	4148
Clock, Carriage, Pine Needle, Caramel Slag Glass Backing, White Porcelain Dial, 5 ¼ In.	5333
Clock, Lyre, Belle Epoque, Dore Bronze, Scrolling Swan Necks, Floral Swag, c.1875, 21 x 7 In.	1783
Clock, Ormolu, Rococo Style, Cupid, Putti, Swags, Porcelain Dial, Breguet Hands, 26 In.	6000
Clock, Venetian, Gold Patina, Black Numerals, Signed Tiffany Studios, 4 x 4 In.	2963
Clock, Zodiac, Cathedral Style, Bronze Gold Dore, Signed Tiffany Studios, 7 x 4 In.	2666
Cross, Altar, Gilt Brass, Topaz, Amethyst, Glass Insets, Raised Base, c.1892, 47 In.	141600
Decanter, Gold Favrile, Iridized Amber, Dimpled, Stick Neck, Stopper, c.1920, 11 In.	563

Desk Set, Bookmark Pattern, Letter Holder, Clip, Blotter Ends, Marked, c.1900, 4 Piece....	881
Dish, Fern, Grape Pattern, Green, Metal Overlay, Copper Liner, Tiffany Studios, 11 x 4 In.	1125
Fire Screen, Opalescent Glass, Grid Panel, Patinated Metal Frame, Stand, c.1910, 39 x 27 In. ...	4688
Frame, Adam, Perpetual Calendar, Gilt Bronze, Tiffany Studios New York, 6 ½ x 6 In....	1200
Frame, Grapevine, Gilt Metal Favrile Glass, Bead Rim, Stamped, 10 x 8 In. ...	1250
Frame, Metal, Chased Vine & Leaves, Scalloped Corners, Hinged Stand, c.1910, 11 In.	861
Frame, Venetian, Bronze, Gold Dore Pattern, Marked Tiffany Studios, 6 ½ x 6 In....	671
Frame, Zodiac, Bronze, Gold Dore Patina, Marked, Tiffany Studios, 4 ½ x 1 ½ In. ...	250
Goblet, Gold Favrile, Purple, Blue, Pink Highlights, Signed L.C.T., 8 ½ In. ...	1180
Inkstand, Bronze, Mosaic Favrile Tiles, Round, 4 ¾ In. ...	12980
Inkstand, Fish Mosaic, Bronze, Favrile Glass Tiles, Impressed Tiffany Studios, 7 x 3 ½ In.	94400
Inkwell, Abalone, Gilt Bronze, 8-Sided, 3 ½ In. ...	307
Inkwell, Adam, Glass Insert, Gilt Bronze, Stamped Tiffany Studios New York, 4 x 3 In. ...	750
Inkwell, American Indian, Bronze, Hinged Lid, Insert, Marked, c.1910, 3 ¾ x 5 ¼ In. ...	338
Inkwell, Bookmark Pattern, Stamped Tiffany Studios New York, 4 ½ x 2 ½ In. ...	1200
Inkwell, Bronze, Openwork Body, Green Reticulated Glass Blown Through Openings, 3 ½ In.....	4740
Inkwell, Bronze, Turtleback Glass Tiles, Casket Shape, Fitted Interior, 4 ¼ x 8 ½ In. ...	47200
Inkwell, Lid, Pine Needle, Bronze Over Green Glass, Signed Tiffany Studios, 4 x 2 In....	688
Inkwell, Ninth Century, Jewels, Strapwork, Insert, Signed, 2 x 2 ½ In. ....*illus*	1185
Inkwell, Paperweight Glass, White Flowers, Yellow, Green, Translucent Green, Silver Lid, 2 x 3 In.	4740
Inkwell, Pen Tray, Bronze, Brown Patina, Round Leaves, Gold Favrile Glass Inkwell, 11 In. ...	5333
Inkwell, Pen Tray, Octopus, Lid, Swirled, Gold Iridescent Glass Insert, c.1910, 12 x 3 In. ...	5100
Inkwell, Pine Needle, Bronze, Glass, Lid, Pierced Overlay, Lavender Slag Glass, 3 ¾ x 7 In.	383
Inkwell, Pine Needle, Brown Patina, Glass Insert, Green Slag Glass, 4 x 3 ½ In. ...	750
Inkwell, Spanish Pattern, Bronze, Gold Finish, Glass Liner, Signed Tiffany Studios, 4 x 6 In. ...	1659
Jewelry Box, Old World, Bronze, Green Velvet Liners, 8 x 3 ½ In. ...	4000
Lamp, 3-Light, Gold Favrile, Bronze, Reeded, Etched L.C.T., c.1910, 16 In. ....*illus*	6600
Lamp, 10 Lily Glass Shades, Iridescent Glass, Gilt Bronze, Tiffany Studios, 18 x 18 x 13 ...	10000
Lamp, Acorn Shade, Geometric Panels, Green, Blue, Yellow, Mottled, Bronze Base, 10 x 53 In...	5925
Lamp, Aladdin, Domed Dore Shade, Cherub, Swan Finial, Tripod Base, 54 In. ...	2596
Lamp, Aladdin, Floor, Bronze, Impressed Mark, 20th Century, 55 In. ...	1560
Lamp, Arabian, Brown Iridescent, Cone Shade, Platinum Zipper, Baluster Base, 7 x 14 ½ In. ...	4740
Lamp, Bronze, Weight-Balance Base, Tiffany Studios, 13 In. ...	1380
Lamp, Candlestick, Gold Favrile, Green Pulled Leaves, Signed, LCT, 12 ½ In. ....*illus*	1380
Lamp, Daffodil, Green, White, Yellow, Signed, 20 In. ...	35400
Lamp, Desk, Carved Leaf Damascene Shade, Adjustable Harp, Bronze Base, 10 In. ...	21240
Lamp, Domed Glass Shade, Yellow Crocus Pattern, Bronze Base, Tiffany Studios, 16 x 22 In....	19520
Lamp, Domed Green Tile Shade, Yellow Band, Bronze, Flared Base, c.1900, 14 x 20 In. ...	8960
Lamp, Domed Peony Favrile Shade, Bamboo Bronze Standard, c.1915, 68 x 25 In. ...	112500
Lamp, Domed Shade, Pulled Gold Waves, Green Ground, Bronze Base, Initialed L.C.T., 16 In.	9480
Lamp, Domed Tulip Pattern, 3-Light, Blown-Out Glass, Bronze Base, 16 x 24 In. ...	36600
Lamp, Favrile Shade, Feathered, Bronze, Tiffany Studios, c.1910, 14 In. ...	1896
Lamp, Geometric, Cone Shape Shade, Yellow, Cream, Butterscotch, 3-Light, 18 x 22 In. ...	14220
Lamp, Geometric, Leaded Domed Shade Green, Blue Mottled Glass, Bronze Base, 14 x 7 In. ...	4428
Lamp, Gilt Bronze, Weight-Balance Base, Dore Patina, 55 ¼ In. ...	1750
Lamp, Lily, 3 Arching Lilies, 1 Tendril, Fluted Shades, Bronze Lotus Base, 8 ½ In. ...	2875
Lamp, Lily, 3-Light, Favrile Shades, Signed L.C.T., c.1920, 13 x 4 In. ...	5625
Lamp, Lily, 3-Light, Gold Iridescent Shades, Tripart Standard, Ribbed Base, c.1902, 13 In....	3360
Lamp, Lily, 12-Light, Amber Favrile Shades, Bronze Stem Base, c.1920, 21 x 5 In. ...	25000
Lamp, Linenfold Shade, Gilt Bronze, 7 ½ x 19 In. ...	5100
Lamp, Linenfold Shade, Green Panels, Bronze Frame, Weight-Balance Base, 10 x 55 In. ...	14220
Lamp, Linenfold, 12-Sided Shade, Green, Ruffled Bronze Edge, Reticulated, 26 x 19 In....	14760
Lamp, Louis XVI, Desk, 2-Light, Acorn Shade, Green Mottled Panes, Bronze, 1900s, 18 In. ...	6150
Lamp, Mosaic, Black-Eyed Susan, 3-Light, Bronze, Tiffany Studios, 18 ½ x 21 In. ....*illus*	30000
Lamp, Mosque, Gold Iridescent Pulled Feather, Platinum Iridescent Trim, 7 ½ In....	7110
Lamp, Mottled Green Turtleback Tiles, Bronze Base, Signed Tiffany Studios, 21 x 30 In....	28060
Lamp, Nautilus, Shell Shade, Bronze Base Standard, 13 x 4 ¾ In. ...	5310
Lamp, Pierced Brass, Slag Glass, Tiffany Studios, c.1905, 17 In. ...	2844
Lamp, Poppy, Favrile Shade, Pond Lily Base, Bronze, c.1906, 25 ½ x 20 In. ...	212400
Lamp, Prism, 3-Light, Bronze, Green Brown Patina, 19 In. ...	13528
Lamp, Pulled Feather Trumpet Shade, Bronze, Weight-Balance, Gold Iridescent, 5 x 11 In. ...	2185
Lamp, Ribbed Green Favrile Shade, Bronze Base, Tiffany Studios, 12 x 55 In. ...	5000
Lamp, Shade, Zipper, Arabia, 1-Light, Marble & Brass Base, 21 In. ...	748
Lamp, Telescopic, Green Favrile Glass Shade, Feathers, Candelabrum Base, 9 x 19 In. ...	8295
Lamp, Weight-Balance, Adjustable, Green Linenfold Favrile Shade, Bronze, c.1905, 15 x 7 In.....	6875
Lamp, Wisteria, Purple, Gray, Blue, Impressed, Footed Bronze Base, c.1902, 27 x 18 In....	283200

Textile, Scroll, Ink On Paper, Thrush Birds, Crabapple Branches, Signed, Shao'ang, Chinese
$1,094

James D. Julia Auctioneers

Textile, Tapestry, Valentine, Wool, Hand Woven, Jim Dine, New York, c.1978, 25 ½ x 35 In.
$1,000

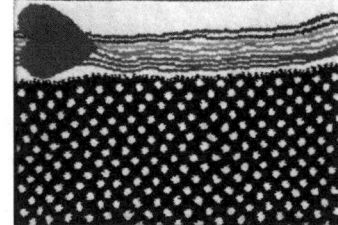

Rago Arts & Auction Center

Thermometer, Bubble Up Has Pa-ZAZZ, Tin, Embossed, Die Cut, 5 x 17 In.
$180

Victorian Casino Antiques

T

Thermometer, Mail Pouch Tobacco, Treat Yourself To The Best, Tin, TCA Tru Temp, 8 x 39 In.
$180

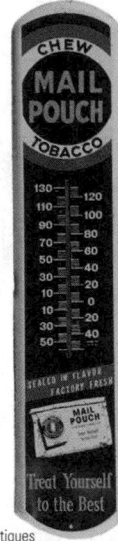

Victorian Casino Antiques

Thermometer, Pabst Blue Ribbon Beer, At Popular Prices, Man, Strength Game, c.1950, 18 In.
$270

Garth's Auctioneers & Appraisers

Tiffany, Bookends, Zodiac, Impressed Tiffany Studios, New York, 6 In.
$413

Humler & Nolan

Letter Holder, Zodiac, Statuary Bronze Dore, Stamped, 6 ¼ x 9 ½ In.	338
Letter Opener, Adam, Gilt Bronze, Stamped Tiffany Studios New York, 9 ½ In.	750
Letter Opener, Bookmark Pattern, Stamped Tiffany Studios New York, 10 ½ In.	750
Letter Opener, Zodiac, Gilt Dore, Signed Tiffany Studios, 9 ½ In.	356
Letter Rack, Pine Needle, Green Slag Glass Etched Metal, Brown Patina, 10 x 6 In.	1200
Magnifier, Bookmark Pattern, Stamped Tiffany Studios New York, 8 ¾ x 4 In.	2500
Pad Holder, Pine Needle, Green, White Glass, Etched Bronze, Tiffany Studios, 4 ½ x 7 ½ In.	549
Paper Clip, Bookmark Pattern, Stamped Tiffany Studios New York, 2 ½ x 3 ½ In.	750
Paper Clip, Spanish Pattern, Bronze, Gold Dore Finish, 2 ¾ x 4 In.	356
Paper Rack, Adam, Gilt Bronze, Stamped Tiffany Studios New York, 9 ¼ x 6 In.	900
Paper Rack, Bookmark Pattern, Stamped Tiffany Studios New York, 9 ¼ x 5 x 2 ¼ In.	1200
Paperweight, Swirled Bronze, Green, Yellow Iridescent Glass, Marked, 3 ¾ x 2 ⅞ In.	5015
Pen Brush, Bookmark Pattern, Stamped Tiffany Studios New York, 3 x 2 In.	750
Pen Brush, Pine Needle, Bronze, Over Green Glass, Signed Tiffany Studios, 2 ½ x 2 In.	469
Pen Tray, Abalone, Gilt Bronze, Rectangular, 3 Sections, 2 ½ x 8 In.	461
Pen Tray, Adam, Gilt Bronze, Stamped Tiffany Studios New York, 9 ¾ x 3 In.	450
Pen Tray, Bookmark Pattern, Stamped Tiffany Studios New York, 8 ½ x 2 ¾ In.	400
Pen Tray, Heraldic, Green Enameled Finish, Signed Tiffany Studios, 9 x 3 In.	119
Pen Tray, Venetian, Bronze, Center Medallion, 4 x 10 In.	259
Photo Album, Pocket, 14K Gold, Rose Gold Stringing, Hammered Finish, 1900s, 2 ½ x 2 In.	1440
Picture Frame, Abalone, Art Deco Grapes, Shells, Signed Tiffany Studios, 11 x 14 In.	2666
Pill Box, Tree Trunk Form, Sterling Silver, Italy, 2 x ¾ In.	264
Pitcher, Leaf & Vine Pattern, Green, Orange, Etch Signed, 4 x 4 In.	1180
Rocker Blotter, Pine Needle, Beading, Brown Patina, Green Slag Glass, 6 x 3 In.	500
Rolodex, Zodiac, Bronze, Brown Patina, Signed Tiffany Studios, 4 ¼ x 3 ¼ In.	2666
Table, Bronze, Orpheus Dish Top, 3 Griffin Standard, Tiffany Studios, 19 x 18 In.	2006
Tray, Bronze Dore, Textured Finish, Stamped, 12 In.	115
Tray, Round, Shaped, Wavy Stepped Rim, c.1880, 13 In.	1375
Utility Box, Pine Needle, Ball Feet, Beading, Brown Patina, Green Slag Glass, 4 ½ x 3 ½ In.	850
Vase, Agate, Green, Orange Pulled Favrile, Bronze Scarab Mount, c.1898, 8 In.	50150
Vase, Aquamarine Glass, Flowers, Pulled Floating Canes, c.1912, 10 ½ In.	88500
Vase, Blue Favrile, 6-Sided, Bronze Holder, Antique Finish, Inverted Saucer Foot, 19 In.	1215
Vase, Crane, Enamel On Copper, Blue, Green, Tan, c.1901, 5 ¾ In.	20060
Vase, Green, Peach, Pulled Feather Design, Metal Base, Signed Tiffany Studios, 12 In.	900
Vase, Sagittaria, Enamel On Copper, Green, Orange, Blue, Inverted Lip, c.1902, 9 ¾ In.	165200
Vase, Toadstool, Green, Enamel On Copper, c.1910, 2 ¾ In.	7080

TIFFANY GLASS

Basket, Favrile, Enamel, Gilt Bronze, Footed Base, Signed LCT Favrile 1925, 7 x 6 In.	850
Bowl, Blue Favrile, Ribbed, Flowing Shape, Signed L.C.T. Favrile, 10 In.	748
Bowl, Blue Iridescent Favrile, Scalloped Rim, Signed, 2 x 7 In.	326
Bowl, Cobalt Blue Iridescent, Lobed, Scalloped Rim, Signed, L.C.T., 3 x 8 In.	325
Bowl, Favrile, Blue Iridescent, Yellow, Wavy Rim, Leaves, Signed, 2 ¾ x 10 In.	1638
Bowl, Favrile, Intaglio Cut Vine, Leaf, Iridescent Gold, Flared Rim, 1925, 3 ½ x 8 In.	750
Bowl, Flower Frog, Favrile, Gold Iridescent, Leaf & Vines, Signed, 4 x 10 In.	2340
Bowl, Gold Iridescent, Green Trailing Hearts & Vines, Bulbous, Squat, Favrile, 6 In.	823
Bowl, Gold Iridescent, Undulating Rim, Signed, 3 ¼ x 8 In.	460
Bowl, Gold, Green, Scalloped Rim, Ribbed, Favrile, 7 In.	390
Bowl, Orange Opalescent, White Ribs, Gold Upper Lip, 2 ¼ x 4 ½ In.	299
Candlestand, Gold Favrile, Swirl Shape, Etched L.C.T., Electric, c.1900, 7 x 4 ¼ In.	253
Compote, Blue Favrile, Iridescent, Crackle Edge, Engraved L.C. Tiffany, 4 x 8 In.	3500
Compote, Blue Favrile, Iridescent, Purple, Green, Platinum, Inverted Saucer Foot, 5 x 4 In.	790
Compote, Blue Favrile, Ruffled Rim, Pedestal Foot, c.1900, 2 ½ x 6 In.	472
Compote, Gilt Iridescence, Quilt Design, Signed, L.C. Tiffany-Favrile, 6 In.	375
Compote, Gold Favrile, Diamond Quilted, L.C.T. Favrile 1726, 6 x 3 ½ In.	1200
Compote, Iridescent Gold Favrile, Flared Rim, Raised Foot, 5 ¾ x 3 In.	885
Compote, Magenta Opal, Crackled Edge, Diamond Quilted, L.C. Tiffany Favrile, 8 In.	1500
Compote, Pastel Glass, Butterscotch To Cream, Crosshatched, Intaglio Cut Butterfly, 3 x 6 In.	356
Finger Bowl, Gold Iridescent, Bulbous, Squat, Raised Ruffled Rim, Favrile, 3 In.	322
Finger Bowl, Underplate, Green Pastel, Gold Iridescent, Signed, 6 In.	460
Goblet, Aquamarine Favrile, Clear, Tapered, Footed, c.1925, 6 In.	813
Inkwell, Ninth Century, Green, Blue Jewels, Animals, Strapwork, Glass Liner, 4 x 3 ¼ In.	1659
Jar, Gold Favrile, Iridescent, Carved Knob Detailing, Engraved L.C.T., 7 ½ In.	2500
Jewelry Box, Grape Leaf Design, Flip Lid, 1 ½ x 4 ½ In.	410
Pitcher, Cut, Lobed Silver Mount, Monogram, Spirals, Faceted Glass Handle, 12 In.	720
Salt, Gold Favrile, Footed, Engraved, 2 ½ In.	325

Salt, Gold Favrile, Master, Ruffled, Engraved, 3 In.	350
Salt, Gold Favrile, Round, Engraved, 2 In..	300
Salt, Gold Favrile, Ruffled Rim, Blue Overtones, 2 In. ....*illus*	201
Shade, Favrile, Platinum On Orange Damascene, Ribbed, Purple Iridescent, 2 ¼ x 4 ¾ In.	3081
Shade, Gold Damascene, Iridescent, Favrile, Signed L.C. Tiffany, 7 x 4 In......	6710
Shade, Green Damascene Pattern, Iridescent Favrile, Signed L.C. Tiffany, 7 x 5 In.	5795
Shade, Lily, Green Pulled Feathers, Purple Highlights, 4 ½ In.	4130
Shade, Tulip, Green Pulled Feather, Gold Over Opal Body, Signed L.C.T., 5 In.	259
Shade, Tulip, Ivory Glass, Vertical Bands, Signed L.C.T., 2 ¼ x 4 ¾ In., Pair........	1778
Vase, Bird-Of-Prey, Enamel On Copper, Brown, Green, Inscribed L.C.T., c.1901, 6 ¼ In.	177700
Vase, Blue Favrile Glass, Green Iridescent Finish, Signed L.C. Tiffany, 4 ¾ In.	237
Vase, Blue Favrile, Thick Neck, Shouldered, Footed, Double Scroll Handles, 8 ¾ In.	4200
Vase, Blue Iridescent Favrile, Green & Bronze Iridescent Hearts, Vines, 2 ½ In.	2607
Vase, Blue Iridescent Favrile, Ribbed Sides, Undulating Rim, 3 ½ In.........	748
Vase, Bud, Blue Favrile, Plum Overtones, Engraved, 10 In.	805
Vase, Bud, Cobalt Blue Favrile, Plum, Yellow, Enameled Metal Base, c.1925, 16 In.	1125
Vase, Bud, Purple, Blue Favrile, Flared Rim, Footed, 8 In.	1888
Vase, Cypriote, Amber, Blue, Purple Iridescent, Textured, Flared Base, 6 ⅜ x 2 ¼ In.	5900
Vase, Cypriote, Applied Metal, Pitted Favrile Glass, Green, Pink, Long Neck, 10 In...................	17700
Vase, Cypriote, Blue, White Mottled, King Tut, Shouldered, Signed, 5 In........	6900
Vase, Cypriote, Gold Favrile, Bulbous, Signed L.C. Tiffany-Favrile, 3 x 3 ½ In.	4375
Vase, Cypriote, Peacock, Green, Variegated Blue, Purple, Reverse Feather, Signed, 22 In.	16100
Vase, Cypriote, Tapered Neck, Iridized Platinum Finish, Signed L.C.T., 7 ½ In.......	2311
Vase, Favrile, Cobalt, Blue, Orange Flowers, Green Stems, Bulbous, c.1921, 8 In........	3125
Vase, Favrile, Flower Shape, Round Base, Tapered, Etched L.C. Tiffany, 1913, 17 ½ x 5 In.	7500
Vase, Favrile, Gold Iridescent, Green Leaf, Flower Shape, c.1900, 9 In.......	1770
Vase, Favrile, Gold Iridescent, Leaves, Swollen Shoulder, Spread Foot, 9 In......	1872
Vase, Favrile, Gold King Tut Design, Iridescent Green, Signed, 9 In. ....*illus*	2185
Vase, Favrile, Green Ivy Leaves, Climbing Vines, Iridescent Gold, 1920s, 13 ½ In.....	615
Vase, Favrile, Green Leaves, Translucent Amber, Oval, Signed, c.1919, 12 In........	5313
Vase, Favrile, Pulled Feather, Flower Shape, Etched L.C.T., 1903, 11 ½ x 4 ¾ In.	3750
Vase, Favrile, Pulled Green, Gold Swirls, Purple, Yellow Neck, L.C. Tiffany, 7 x 7 In.......	8400
Vase, Favrile, Tapered, Footed, L.C. Tiffany, 11 ½ In.	650
Vase, Flower Shape, Wavy Rim, Gold Favrile, Green Feather, Iridescent, L.C.T., 6 x 13 In........	6710
Vase, Gold Favrile, 3 ½ In...	650
Vase, Gold Favrile, Dimpled, Rolled Edge, 5 In.	1800
Vase, Gold Favrile, Flower Shape, Exaggerated Ribs, Scalloped Rim, Signed, 8 ½ In........	805
Vase, Gold Favrile, Green Pulled Feather, Reverse Trumpet Shape, Signed, 7 ¾ In.......	805
Vase, Gold Favrile, Green, White Pulled Feathers, Flower Shape, Signed L.C.T., 4 x 9 ½ In.	3750
Vase, Gold Favrile, Narrow Foot, Vertical Ribs, Gold Iridescence, Pink, Blue, 4 In........	119
Vase, Gold Favrile, Optic Ribs, Oval, Footed, Signed, 6 In...................	1080
Vase, Gold Favrile, Pulled Leaf, Vine, Flared, Footed, Signed, L.C. Tiffany-Favrile, 6 x 10 In.........	2125
Vase, Gold Favrile, Ribbed, 4 In.	750
Vase, Gold Favrile, Vertical Ribs, Iridescent, Platinum Highlights, Intaglio Carved, 9 In......	1778
Vase, Gold Iridescent Interior, White, Green Pulled Feather, Ruffled Rim, 4 ½ In.........	800
Vase, Gold Iridescent, Elongated Oval, Handles, Rolled Rim, Spread Foot, 3 ½ In.......	702
Vase, Green Favrile, Gold Iridescent Pulled Feather, Square Mouth, Blue Foot, 3 ½ x 5 ½ In.	2548
Vase, Green Iridescent, Yellow, Blue, Purple, Bulbous, 4 In....................	3245
Vase, Green Leaves, Vines, Gold Iridescent, Tapered, 13 x 6 In.............	3245
Vase, Green, Blue, Long Neck, Squat Stepped Base, Favrile, Signed L.C. Tiffany, 5 ½ In........	127
Vase, Green, Gold Favrile, Long Neck, Leaf & Vine Design, 6 In............	431
Vase, Iridescent Red, Favrile, Low Waist, Bulbous Base, Signed L.C. Tiffany, 3 x 6 In........	6250
Vase, Jack-In-The-Pulpit, Gray, Green Favrile, Bulbous Base, Signed L.C.T., 9 ¾ In........	11210
Vase, Lava, Brown, Gold Favrile, Bulbous, Tapered Base, 4 ¼ In..............	35400
Vase, Lava, Salmon Iridescent, Brown Ground, Bulbous Base, 12 ½ In........	177000
Vase, Opal Iridescent, Gold Pulled Design, Blue & Green Pulled Feathers, 7 In.	2415
Vase, Paperweight, Cased Blue Favrile, Waves, Oval, Signed L.C. Tiffany, 4 ½ x 2 ¾ In......	4425
Vase, Tel El Armarna, Bulbous, Gold Favrile Body, Smokestack Neck, Footed, 6 ½ In........	3450
Vase, Tel El Armarna, Red, Wavy Design, Blue, White, Squat, Tapered, Favrile, 5 ¼ In........	2375
Vase, Translucent Amber Favrile, Green Leaves, Baluster, Signed L.C.T., c.1804, 9 ½ In.............	1188
Vase, Trumpet, Gold Iridescent, Green Pulled Feathers, Flower Stem, Footed, 14 x 5 In..............	923
Vase, Trumpet, Pulled Feather, Gold, Green Favrile, Pinecone Stem, Foot, c.1905, 15 In..............	2560
Vase, Yellow Favrile, Flower Petal Shape, Signed, c.1925, 5 In................	1500

TIFFANY POTTERY

Vase, Glazed, Inscribed LCT, 10 x 8 In. ....*illus*	3680

TIFFANY POTTERY

Tiffany, Candlestick, Bronze, 3-Leaf Clover Base, Reticulated Glass Insert, Signed, 10 In.
$3,555

James D. Julia Auctioneers

Tiffany, Clock, Art Deco, Bronze, Panels, Marked, Signed, 3 ½ x 5 ¾ In.
$4,148

James D. Julia Auctioneers

Tiffany, Inkwell, Ninth Century, Jewels, Strapwork, Insert, Signed, 2 x 2 ½ In.
$1,185

James D. Julia Auctioneers

T

Tiffany, Lamp, 3-Light, Gold Favrile, Bronze, Reeded, Etched L.C.T., c.1910, 16 In.
$6,600

Skinner Auctioneers & Appraisers

Tiffany, Lamp, Candlestick, Gold Favrile, Green Pulled Leaves, Signed, LCT, 12 ½ In.
$1,380

Early Auction Co.

Tiffany, Lamp, Mosaic, Black-Eyed Susan, 3-Light, Bronze, Tiffany Studios, 18 ½ x 21 In.
$30,000

Skinner Auctioneers & Appraisers

Vase, Mossy Green Glaze, Leaves, Incised L.C.T, c.1910, 11 x 6 In. ....*illus*	8125
Vase, Mottled Green Matte Glaze, Crystalline Accents, Gourd Shape, Signed, 4 x 6 In.	1000
Vase, Scarab, Green, Jeweled Copper Overlay, Long Neck, c.1900, 5 In.	17700
Vase, White Bisque, Impressed Maple Leaves, Signed, L.C.T., 8 In.	2006

TIFFANY SILVER

Asparagus Tongs, English King, U-Shape Handle, Rocaille, 1900s, 8 In.	1250
Basket, Oval, Gadroon Rim, Pierced Bellflowers, Scrolls, Monogram, c.1912, 10 ¾ In.	320
Basket, Quart, Wooden Style Design, 3 ½ x 5 ½ In.	1680
Bowl, 4 Applied Sterling Silver Feet, Stylized Flowers, Marked, 8 ½ x 4 In.	478
Bowl, Art Deco, Exposition Pattern, Bands, 5 Plain Panels, c.1930, 9 In.	2125
Bowl, Chrysanthemum Pattern, 2 x 9 In.	425
Bowl, Cloverleaf Foldover Rim, Repousse, Marked, c.1925, 2 ½ x 9 In.	354
Bowl, Flared Rim, Footed, 6 ¾ In.	360
Bowl, Flared, Round, Stylized Flowers, Footed, 4 ⅜ x 9 In.	2250
Bowl, Flower Holder, Brass Gilt, Flared Rim, Chased, Shells, Leaves, c.1920, 13 ½ In.	1680
Bowl, Flower Vertical Bands, 4 x 9 In.	1875
Bowl, Flower, Engraved Downswept Border, 15 In.	2420
Bowl, Fruit, Round, Shell & Scroll Border, 1892, 9 ¾ In. Diam.	738
Bowl, Leaf Shape, Pierced Handle, Crown & Scroll Design, 10 ¾ In.	531
Bowl, Lobed, Scalloped, Turned Rim, 9 In.	387
Bowl, Olympian, Sterling, Relief Frieze, Putti, Leafy Scroll Foot, c.1891, 10 In.	5000
Bowl, Openwork Base, Branches, Vines, Marked, 4 x 8 ½ In. ....*illus*	1580
Bowl, Reeded Foot, Wide Rim, c.1925, 2 ½ x 5 ½ In.	150
Bowl, Round, Lobed Rim, Shell, Flowers, Leaves, Monogram, c.1930, 3 x 12 In.	576
Bowl, Round, Molded Spread Foot, Wide Rim, Engraved, c.1931, 4 x 11 In.	717
Bowl, Shaped, Flower Rim, 2 ½ x 9 In.	938
Bowl, Sterling, Ribbed Wave Border, Repousse Flowers, Presentation Inscription, 6 ¾ In.	750
Bowl, Wide Rim, Raised Round Foot, c.1920, 2 ¼ In.	2100
Box, Lid, Turtle Shape, Italy, 2 x 7 In.	2415
Cake Basket, Oval, Swing Handle, Greek Fret Border, 12 In.	750
Cake Stand, Sterling, Reticulated, Scallop Shells, Floral Loops, Marked, 5 ¾ x 12 ½ In.	1823
Card Tray, Repousse Leaves, Monogram Center, Rectangular, 6 ½ In.	212
Castor Stand, Egyptian Revival, Parcel Gilt, Cast Sphinxes, c.1866, 10 ½ In.	2375
Charger, Sterling, Enameled, Multicolor, Cherry Branches, Flowers, Butterflies, c.1960, 12 In....	1100
Coffeepot, George II Style, Paul Lamerie Style, Engraved, Monogram, c.1925, 7 ½ In.	723
Crumber, American Indian, Charles Grosjean, Tiffany & Co., 1885, 13 ¾ In. ....*illus*	3444
Cup, Footed, Baluster, Reeded Scroll Band, C-Scroll Handle, Shells, c.1900, 4 ⅛ In.	185
Dish, Leaf Shape, Open Handle, Raised Tip, Ball Foot, Signed, 3 ¼ x 1 ½ In., 4 Piece	293
Dish, Round, Latticework Pattern, Allover Embossed Flowers, Leaves, Footed, c.1930, 7 In.	256
Entree, Lid, Swag & Patterned Borders, Oval, c.1907, 9 x 11 In.	9200
Flask, Hammered, Applied & Chased Grapevines, Parcel Gilt, Marked, 6 In. ....*illus*	2250
Fork Set, 8 Cocktail, 8 Cake, Feather Edge, Sterling, 6 & 6 ¾ In., 16 Piece	472
Gravy Boat, Scroll Handle, Beaded Border, Footed, c.1930, 4 ¼ x 8 ¼ In.	648
Humidor, Rectangular, Stepped Rim, Monogram, 2 x 7 In.	657
Ice Bucket, Sterling, Monogram, Squat, Cylindrical, Dome Lid, Urn Finial, Handles, 10 In.	805
Ladle, Audubon Pattern, Oval Bowl, Bird, Flower Embossed Handle, c.1871, 10 In.	531
Ladle, Renaissance, Shell Shape Bowl, Monogram, 12 ¼ In.	1298
Ladle, Sauce, Renaissance, Monogram, Paulding Farnham, 1905, 7 ½ In.	184
Lipstick Case, Gilt, Satin Finish, Applied Butterfly, Marked Tiffany & Co., 3 ½ x 1 ¼ In.............	179
Nut Dish, Shell Shape, 2 Ball Feet, c.1845, 2 ⅞ x 2 ½ In., 6 Piece	259
Pie Server, Palm Design, c.1885, 11 ¼ In.	390
Pie Server, Strawberry Pierced Pattern, Monogram, Serrated Edge, c.1875	438
Pie Server, Thanksgiving Pattern, Serrated Edge, 2000, 10 ⅝ In.	190
Pitcher, Chased Design, Monogram, Loop Handle, Spread Foot, 34 Oz.	1346
Pitcher, Molded Rim, Collar, Reeded Handle, Faux Bois, Order Of The Garter, 9 ½ In.	1200
Pitcher, Round, Scrolling Flower Band, Lobed, Loop Handle, c.1880, 8 x 8 In.	1652
Pitcher, Water, Engraved Scrolled Leaves, C-Shape Handle, c.1905, 10 In.	1875
Pitcher, Water, Helmet Shape, Etched Swags, Squared Handle, 9 In.	2250
Pitcher, Water, S-Shape Handle, Applied Rim, c.1945, 10 In.	2000
Punch Ladle, Wave Edge Pattern, Shell Bowl, Script Handle, 12 In.	420
Spoon, Lap Over Edge Pattern, Tapered Handle, c.1880, 12 In.	1063
Sugar & Creamer, Reeded Rolled Rim, Triangular Handles, 3 In.	330
Sugar Shell, Shaped Gilt Bowl, Fluted Stem, Acanthus Leaf Terminal, c.1860, 7 ¾ In.................	1625
Sugar Sifter, Olympian Pattern, Pierced, Gilt Bowl, E. Moore, c.1878, 8 In.	406
Sugar Tongs, Hamilton Design, 4 In.	120

T

Table Fork, Wheat Design, Splayed Tines, Edward C. Moore, 8 In.	338
Tea & Coffee Set, Queen Anne, Pear Shape, Ebony Handles, c.1965, 5 Piece	4375
Tea Caddy, Dome Lid, Fern, Flower Repousse, Sunflower Handle, c.1884, 4 In.	1062
Tea Caddy, Monogram, Cylindrical Body, Lid, Palmettes, Scrolls, c.1920, 4 ¼ In.	1400
Tray, Allegorical 4 Season Heads, Scroll Ground, Oval, Handles, Edward Moore, c.1880, 30 In.	6875
Tray, Monogram, Wide Border, Rectangular, 18 In.	1125
Tray, Oval, Molded Rim, c.1950, 13 In.	1000
Tray, Palm & Dart Border, Monogram Center, Marked, 1900s, 20 x 15 In.	295
Tray, Rectangular, Handles, c.1980, 25 x 16 In.	3712
Tray, Round, Flat Rim, c.1925, 12 In. Diam.	600
Tray, Round, Footed, 8 In. Diam.	469
Tray, Scrolled Pattern, 20th Century, 20 ½ In., Pair	3360
Tray, Stepped Rim, c.1945, 13 In.	938
Vase, Art Deco Style, Stepped Domed Foot, Trumpet Shape, 1900s, 12 In.	2000
Vase, Flared Trumpet Shape, Wavy Rim, Round Base, c.1920, 9 In.	236
Vase, Gilt, Trumpet Shape, Fluted Stem, Flared Bowl, Round Foot, c.1915, 9 ½ In.	900
Vase, Trumpet Shape, Tapered Octagonal, B Monogram, c.1930, 11 ½ In.	480

TIFFIN Glass Company of Tiffin, Ohio, was a subsidiary of the United States Glass Co. of Pittsburgh, Pennsylvania, in 1892. The U.S. Glass Co. went bankrupt in 1963, and the Tiffin plant employees purchased the building and the inventory. They continued running it from 1963 to 1966, when it was sold to Continental Can Company. In 1969, it was sold to Interpace, and in 1980, it was closed. The black satin glass, made from 1923 to 1926, and the stemware of the last twenty years are the best-known products.

Cherokee Rose, Bowl, Fruit, 6 ½ In.	25
Deerwood, Server, Pink, Center Handle.	85
Flower Garden With Butterflies, Cheese & Cracker Set, Pink.	120
Flower Garden With Butterflies, Tray, Amber, Rectangular, 7 ¾ x 11 ¾ In.	60
June Night, Bowl, Salad, 10 ¼ In.	65
June Night, Plate, Luncheon, 8 In.	12
June Night, Relish, 3 Sections, 6 ½ In.	32
Line No. 179, Candy Jar, Lid, Pink Satin, Painted.	35
Nymph, Tumbler, Green Foot, 4 ¾ In.	60
Nymph, Wine, Nile Green, Crystal Wide Optic Bowl, 5 ⅞ In., 3 Oz.	36
Persian Pheasant, Plate, Luncheon, Pink, 8 In.	25
Persian Pheasant, Sherbet, Footed, 4 ¾ In., 6 Oz.	15
Psyche, Plate, Luncheon, Green, 8 ³⁄₁₆ In.	35

TILES have been used in most countries of the world as a sturdy building material for floors, roofs, fireplace surrounds, and surface toppings. The cuerda seca (dry cord) technique of decoration uses a greasy pigment to separate different glaze colors during firing. In cuenca (raised line) decorated tiles, the design is impressed, leaving ridges that separate the glaze colors. Many of the American tiles are listed in this book under the factory name.

3 Women, Umbrellas, Asian Attire, Flower Border, Multicolor, Qajar, c.1870, 11 ½ x 15 In.	649
Art Nouveau, Metal Frame, Gilded, Dragonfly, Germany, c.1900, Tile 3 ½ x 10 ¼ In.	625
Bird & Flowers, Glazed, Stamped, Catalina, California, c.1930, 17 ½ x 12 In., 6 Piece *illus*	1750
Carved Medieval Scene, Geometric Border, Tan, Brown, Yellow, Batchelder, 13 ½ x 18 In.	594
Castle, On Hill, Road, Clouds, Over Red Clay, California Faience, 6 ⅞ In. *illus*	345
Dolphin, Red Crown, Orange Ground, Flint Tile Co., 6 x 6 In.	172
Flowers, Arabesques, Blue, Green, Brown, Yellow, Qajar, c.1870, 17 ¼ x 14 In.	944
Flowers, Blue, Cream, Pink Glaze, Hammered Copper, Round, Dirk Van Erp, 1915, 5 ½ In.	540
Flowers, Vines, Hexagonal, Blue, White Glaze, Martin, 7 In.	92
Frieze, Parrots & Dragons, Green, Yellow, Blue, Black, Red Border, 6 Tiles, Malibu, 8 x 16 In.	625
Green Clematis Vines, Black Ground, 6 Sections, Minton, Frame, c.1880, 46 x 6 In., Pair	150
Jack & Jill, Multicolor, Incised Border, Empire Tile Co., Frame, 23 x 23 In.	2250
Jack & Jill, Pail, Muddy Path, Geese, Mosaic, 9 x 9 In.	195
Man On Horseback, Persian, Bird, Yellow, Shaped Edges, Ceramic, 8 ½ x 6 ¼ In.	98
Multicolor Head, Square, Signed, Edition Picasso, Madoura, 1961, 10 In.	4375
Plants, Orange, Green Paint, Incised, Otto & Viveka Heino, 1993, 21 x 13 ½ In.	156
Rampant Lion, Brown, Green Ground, Hartford Faience, Rectangular, c.1905, 6 In.	92
Roof, Arched, Figural Rooster On Top, Terra-Cotta, 18 x 14 ¾ x 13 In.	546
Roof, Curved, Inlaid Rooster, Terra-Cotta, Porcelain Fragments, c.1890, 18 ½ In.	764
Roof, Figure, Horse, Cloud Scroll, Glazed, Wood Stand, 8 ½ x 11 In. *illus*	732
Yellow, Green, Black Glaze, Hexagonal, Martin, Cowan, 6 ¾ In.	92
Cage, Squirrel, Painted, c.1850, 16 x 24 In.	240

Tiffany Glass, Salt, Gold Favrile, Ruffled Rim, Blue Overtones, 2 In.
$201

Early Auction Co.

Tiffany Glass, Vase, Favrile, Gold King Tut Design, Iridescent Green, Signed, 9 In.
$2,185

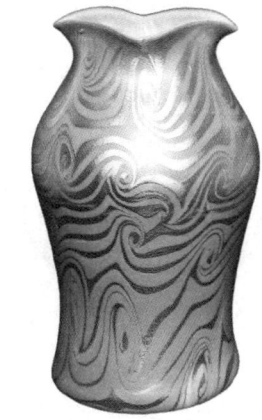

Early Auction Co.

Tiffany Pottery, Vase, Glazed, Inscribed LCT, 10 x 8 In.
$3,680

Cottone Auctions

Tiffany Pottery, Vase, Mossy Green Glaze, Leaves, Incised L.C.T, c.1910, 11 x 6 In.
$8,125

Rago Arts & Auction Center

TIP
Beware! Some of the instant-dip silver polishes contain thiourea, a carcinogen that could be absorbed through the skin.

Tiffany Silver, Bowl, Openwork Base, Branches, Vines, Marked, 4 x 8 ½ In.
$1,580

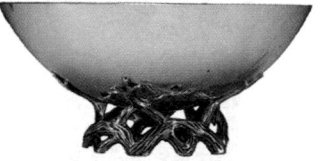

James D. Julia Auctioneers

Tiffany Silver, Crumber, American Indian, Charles Grosjean, Tiffany & Co., 1885, 13 ¾ In.
$3,444

New Orleans Auction Galleries, Inc.

Candlestick, Altar, Tooled Designs, Weighted Base, New Mexico, c.1920, 13 In., Pair	180

TINWARE containers for household use have been made in America since the seventeenth century. The first tin utensils were brought from Europe, but by 1798, tin plate was imported and local tinsmiths made the wares. Painted tin is called tole and is listed separately. Some tin kitchen items may be found listed under Kitchen. The lithographed tin containers used to hold food and tobacco are listed in the Advertising category under Tin.

Candle Box, Shaped Gallery, Cylinder, Loops, Tin, 6 x 10 In.	173
Coffeepot, Lighthouse Shape, Gooseneck Spout, Domed Lid, Flowers, c.1815, 11 In.	1440
Fish Shape, 1800s, 14 ½ In.	130
Food Warmer, Gordon's, Night-Light, Stand, Burner, White Ironstone Cup, Lid, 8 ½ In.	296
Foot Warmer, Punched, Wood Frame, Hearts, c.1850, 6 x 12 x 9 In.	338
Frame, Rope Twist, Fluted Fans, Painted, Engraved, St. Ysidro Labrador, c.1825, 18 x 14 In. *illus*	523
Mold, Candle, 8 Tube, c.1855, 5 ½ x 5 ½ In.	593
Mold, Candle, 12 Tube, Flared Sides, Applied Loop Handle, Arched Base, 11 x 13 ½ In.	177
Mold, Candle, 15 Tube, Wood, Square Nail Frame, Cutout Arch Feet, 19 ¼ x 19 ¼ In.	1416
Mold, Candle, 24 Tube, Wood Frame, 19th Century, 10 ½ x 13 In.	1645
Oven, Reflector, c.1820, 16 ½ x 18 In.	1126
Rattle, Round End, Eagle, ABC Blocks, For A Good Child, Whistle Stem, Black, 5 ¼ In.	65
Tinder Box, Candle Socket Lid, Embossed Stars, Applied Handle, Striker, Flint, Lid	295
Top Hat, Anniversary, Copper Band, Mid 1800s, 7 In.	723
Tray, Peace & Plenty, Boy & Girl Eating Ice Cream, Tin Litho, American Art Works, 13 In.	194
Tray, Punched, Gallery Rim, Loop Handles, Star, Flowers Stamped, Pa., c.1860, 10 x 15 In.	1380
Waiter, Flowers, Garland Border, Red, 2-Sheet, Cantered Corners, c.1825, 12 x 17 In.	11250

TOBACCO CUTTERS *may be listed in either the Advertising or Store categories.*

TOBACCO JAR collectors search for those made in odd shapes and colors. Because tobacco needs special conditions of humidity and air, it has been stored in special containers since the eighteenth century.

3 Elephant Heads, Porcelain, Marked, Austria, 9 ½ In.	390
Bird, Stoneware, Signed Martin Bros., England, c.1908, 12 ½ In.	27600
Bird, Stoneware, Signed, Martin Bros., England, 1907, 9 ¼ In.	26400
Bull Dog, Sitting, Porcelain, 9 ½ In.	240
Cigar, Black Dandy, In Barrel, Painted, Johann Maresch, Austria, 9 ½ In.	210
Man Drinking Beer, Cigar Shape Base, Porcelain, 9 In.	150
Owl Shape, Rocky Perch, Wood, Carved, 20 In.	9375
Smoking Pig, Sitting In Barrel, Tan, Orange, Brown, Marked, Johann Maresch, 7 In.	90

TOBY JUG is the name of a very special form of pitcher. It is shaped like the full figure of a man or woman. A pitcher that shows just the top half of a person is not correctly called a toby. More examples of toby jugs can be found under Royal Doulton and other factory names.

Barnaby, Glass, Clear, Whitefriars, 7 In.	40
Bearded Man, Polka Dot Tie, Occupied Japan, 2 ¾ In.	11
Cavalier, Cape, Boots, Burlington Ware, England, 7 In.	45
Gentleman, Gray Hair, Winking, Occupied Japan, Ucagco, China, 5 ½ In.	35
Jester, Sitting, Red, White, Green, Staffordshire, 9 ¾ In.	425
Man, Clutching Mug, Brown Glaze, Staffordshire, c.1875, 6 In.	65
Man, Seated, Green Chair, Red Coat, Black Hat, H & K Tunstall, England, 5 ½ In.	37
Man, Seated, Holding Mug, Tricornered Hat, Germany, 5 In.	32
Mr. Pickwick, Yellow & White Satin Glass, Paper Label, Kanawha, 1960s, 6 ½ In.	60
Oliver Twist, Pink Hat & Vest, Wood & Sons, Franklin Porcelain, 5 In.	55
Peggotty, Darning Sock, Wood & Sons, 6 In.	59
Portly Gentleman, Hands In Pocket, Blue Delft & White, c.1900, 12 In.	875
Rooster, Tail Up, Multicolor, Germany, 5 x 4 ½ In.	68

TOLE is painted tin. It is sometimes called japanned ware, pontypool, or toleware. Most nineteenth-century tole is painted with an orange-red or black background and multicolored decorations. Many recent versions of toleware are made and sold. Related items may be listed in the Tinware category.

Bathtub, Raised Crossed Arrows, Rondel, Handles, Tin, French Empire, c.1815, 23 x 56 In.	492
Bin, Black Paint, Stenciled Flowers, Leaves, c.1850, 9 x 10 In.	431
Bin, Sloped Top, Ellis In Brass Letters, Asian Scene, England, c.1890, 22 x 20 In., Pair	325

Box, Document, Black, Red Flowers, Gold Leaves, Hammered Handle, 1800s, 7 x 9 In.	123
Box, Document, Painted Green, Stenciled, Flowers, Leaves, c.1890, 9 ¾ In.	115
Box, Document, Yellow, Red, Green, Tin Hasp, Brass Bail Handle, c.1835, 4 ¾ x 8 In.	323
Box, Dome Lid, Red Flowers, Black Ground, Brass Lock, Handle, 7 x 9 ½ In.	652
Box, Dome Lid, Tin, Brass Handle, Pomegranate, Leaves, Japanned, 9 x 10 In. ....*illus*	265
Box, Dome Lid, Yellow Flowers, Black Ground, 6 x 10 In.	563
Box, Dome Lid, Yellow Flowers, Teal Ground, Brass Plate, Handle, c.1860, 6 x 8 ¾ In.	830
Box, Flower, Gold Paint, Black Ground, Handle, 12 In.	360
Box, Flowers, Domed, Bail Handle, Japanned Ground, c.1850, 3 x 6 In.	215
Box, Green, Stylized Flowers, Leaves, c.1890, 9 ¾ In.	115
Box, Mustard Yellow, Hinged Lid, 8 x 9 In.	215
Box, Tea, Painted Black, Flowers, Leaves, Hinged Lid, Wire Ring Handle, 6 ½ x 9 ½ In.	18
Bread Tray, Painted, Handle, Yellow Flowers, Green Leaves, Black Ground, 8 x 13 In.	1020
Bread Tray, Stylized Fruit, Leaves, Red, Green, Yellow, Handles, c.1810, 8 x 12 ¾ In. ....*illus*	441
Bucket, Ash, Gold, Black Trim, Hunter, Deer, Bushes, Bail Handle, Italy, c.1900, 18 In.	150
Candleholder, Orange, Handle, 6 ½ In. Diam.	100
Canister, Coffee, Roll Back Lid, Mirror Front, Painted, S.A. Ilsley & Co., c.1890, 20 In.	750
Canister, White Band, Flower Design, Tin Hasp, Wire Handle, c.1835, 7 ½ x 8 In.	176
Cellarette, Lid, Black, Lion's Heads, Paw Feet, Buildings, c.1865, 22 x 21 In.	5166
Charger, Victorian, Leaves, Shells, Gilt, Painted, 19 ¾ In.	108
Chest, On Stand, Hunt Scene, Black, Gold Paint, 22 x 24 In.	313
Coal Bin, Neoclassical Style, Black, Gold Paint, Bombe Shape, c.1865, 24 x 24 In.	281
Coal Container, Victorian, Painted Scenes, Lid, Handle, c.1890, 25 In.	158
Coal Scuttle, Landscape, Painted, Cutout Handles, France, 12 In.	70
Coffeepot, Black Japanned Ground, Flower Medallions, 1800s, 8 ½ In.	764
Coffeepot, Black, Flower, Leaves, Scrolls, Yellow, Red & Green, Gooseneck Spout, 10 In.	351
Coffeepot, Flowers, Japanned Ground, c.1840, 9 ½ In.	211
Coffeepot, Flowers, Vegetables, Petals, Leaves, C-Scroll Handle, c.1850, 10 In. ....*illus*	1185
Coffeepot, Red & Yellow Flowers, c.1835, 11 In.	572
Coffeepot, Red Flowers, Black Ground, Paint, 8 ½ In.	1060
Coffeepot, Red Ground, Flowers, Red, Yellow Paint, 8 ¾ In.	1560
Coffeepot, Red, Yellow Flowers, Hinged Lid, Ear Shape Handle, c.1810, 9 In. ....*illus*	984
Coffeepot, Red, Yellow, Green Flowers, Gooseneck Spout, Asphaltum, 10 ½ In.	1304
Coffeepot, Stipple Engraved, Flared, Straight Spout, Eagle, Branch, Swag, c.1850, 9 In.	840
Coffeepot, Wrigglework, MB Monogram, Flowers, Pierced Base, Pa., c.1820, 12 ½ In.	1541
Coffeepot, Yellow Red, Green Flowers, Black Ground, Gooseneck Spout, c.1820, 10 ¾ In.	711
Crumb Box, Flowers, Multicolor, Pink Ground, 1920s, 6 x 8 x 2 In.	85
Figurine, Fighting Roosters, Shaped Wood Base, Multicolor, France, 1800s, 15 x 15 In.	1434
Figurine, Grape Harvester, Traditional Costume, Austria, 15 ¾ x 5 ½ In., Pair	478
Figurine, Man, Hats, Long Robes, Vases On Back, Chinoiserie, c.1950, 15 In., Pair	1063
Jardiniere, Hanging, Green, Gilt, Cornucopia Shape, 52 ½ In., Pair..............................	813
Magazine Rack, Stylized Bird, Flowers, Curled Feet & Handle, 1950s, 9 x 15 x 7 In.	64
Monteith, Regency Style, Oval, Red Ground, Painted Figure, Landscapes, 12 In., Pair	813
Pencil Holder, Pink Flowers, Green Leaves, Black Ground, 5 ½ In.	12
Pillbox, Hinged Lid, Yellow Ground, Red Edge, Multicolor Tulip, c.1850, ⅞ x 1 ½ In.............	374
Platter, Turkey, Fruit & Vegetable Border, Multicolor, Oval, 1950s, 17 x 13 In.	38
Shield, Patriotic, Stars, Stripes, Scalloped Top, Red, White, Blue Paint, 17 ½ x 14 In.	600
Tea Canister, Red, Gilt Trim, Gilt Name Plate, Chinese Characters, c.1835, 33 x 8 In.	430
Teapot, Fruit, Flowers, Black Ground, Barrel Shape, c.1865, 5 ¾ In.	652
Tray, Birds, Flowers, Gilt Border, Painted, Rounded Rectangle, c.1865, 23 x 25 In.	923
Tray, Blue Ground, Gilt Flowers, Raised Rim, Round, 1800s, 17 ¾ In.	109
Tray, Classical Figures, Oval, Gallery Rim, Cutout Handles, France, c.1850, 18 x 24 In.	345
Tray, Flower Border, Red Ground, Gold Trim, 19 ½ x 26 ½ In.	201
Tray, Flowers, Multicolor, Pierced Sides, Rolled Edges, Octagonal, 20 x 15 In.	35
Tray, Landscape Roundel, Scrolled Leaves, Painted, Handles, Italy, 14 In.	240
Tray, Oval, Painted Yellow Ground, Round Classical Scenes, France, 30 x 22 In.	1722
Tray, Painted, Man Courting Woman, Gallery, Pierced Handles, Oval, c.1810, 19 x 14 In.	84
Tray, Pierced Lattice Edges, Cutout Handles, Yellow, Fruit Basket, 1800s, 1 ⅜ x 18 In.	472
Tray, Pink Flowers, Black Ground, Pierced Sides, Cutout Handle, 1940s, 12 x 24 In.	95
Tray, Red, Oval Reserve, Ruins, Figures, Pierced Gallery, Handles, England, 21 x 16 In.	108
Tray, Regency, Chinoiserie, Gilt, Mother-Of-Pearl, Black, Figures, Flowers, 20 x 25 In.	240
Trunk, Dome Top, Flowers, Leaves, Berries, Red, Green Yellow, c.1810, 5 ⅜ x 9 x 4 In. ....*illus*	369
Trunk, Dome Top, Red Flowers, Yellow Border, Wire Swing Handle, c.1810, 7 x 9 In. ....*illus*	1134
Umbrella Stand, Dog, Sitting, Bow Collar, White, France, c.1900, 24 x 16 x 7 In.	1900
Urn, Black, Neoclassical Gilt, Lion's Masks Handles, Holland, c.1800, 13 x 8 In., Pair	750
Urn, Regency Style, Parcel Gilt, Gray, Oval, Flame Finial, Lion's Mask Handles, 14 In., Pair	875

Tiffany Silver, Flask, Hammered, Applied & Chased Grapevines, Parcel Gilt, Marked, 6 In.
$2,250

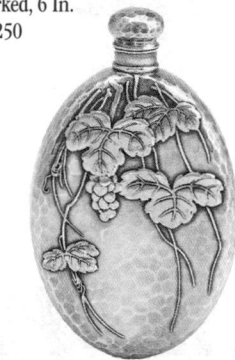

Rago Arts & Auction Center

Tile, Bird & Flowers, Glazed, Stamped, Catalina, California, c.1930, 17 ½ x 12 In., 6 Piece
$1,750

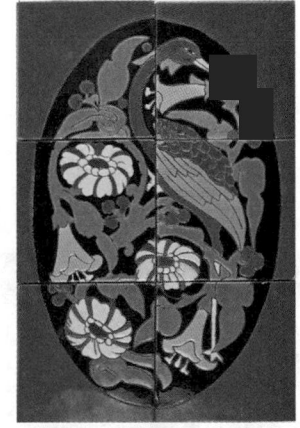

Rago Arts & Auction Center

Tile, Castle, On Hill, Road, Clouds, Over Red Clay, California Faience, 6 ⅞ In.
$345

Humler & Nolan

T

TOLE

Tile, Roof, Figure, Horse, Cloud Scroll, Glazed, Wood Stand, 8 ½ x 11 In. $732

Neal Auction Co.

Tinware, Frame, Rope Twist, Fluted Fans, Painted, Engraved, St. Ysidro Labrador, c.1825, 18 x 14 In. $523

Garth's Auctioneers & Appraisers

Tole, Box, Dome Lid, Tin, Brass Handle, Pomegranate, Leaves, Japanned, 9 x 10 In. $265

Conestoga Auction Co., Inc.

Tole, Bread Tray, Stylized Fruit, Leaves, Red, Green, Yellow, Handles, c.1810, 8 x 12 ¾ In. $441

Skinner Auctioneers & Appraisers

Urn, Regency, Lion's Heads Masks, Ring Handles, Japanned Reserve, Finial, 11 In., Pair	96
Wastebasket, Black, Vines, Alpine Wildflowers, Tapered, Switzerland, c.1890, 15 x 11 In.	2200

TOM MIX was born in 1880 and died in 1940. He was the hero of over 100 silent movies from 1910 to 1929, and 25 sound films from 1929 to 1935. There was a Ralston Tom Mix radio show from 1933 to 1950, but the original Tom Mix was not in the show. Tom Mix comics were published from 1942 to 1953.

Bandanna, Tom Mix, Horse Tony, Best Wishes, Red, White, Brown, 1930s, 17 x 17 In.	21 to 72
Book, Western Songs, 64 Pages, 25 Songs, M.M. Cole Publishing Co., 1935, 9 x 11 In.	39
Boots, Tan, Red, Leather, Pull On, Box, 1930s, Size 3D	128
Button, Tony, Universal Pictures, Yellow, Red Rim, Celluloid, c.1932, 1 ¼ In.	86
Chaps, Batwing, Leather, 24 Conchas, Flower Tooled, Carved, Made For Tom Mix, 35 In.	30250
Decoder Badge, Brass, Embossed, Pistol, 1930s, 2 x 1 In.	50
Film, Tom Mix The Sheriff, Silent, Black Roll, Metal Case, 4 ½ In.	12
Hat, Stetson, Light Gray, Red Interior, Davis, XXXX	17
Magnifying Glass, Plastic, Ralston Straight Shooters, Heart Shape, 2 x 1 In.	25
Medal, Horseshoe, Service Ribbon, Straight Shooters, Ralston Premium, 1945, 3 ½ x 5 In.	115
Paint Book, Portrait, 10 Pages, 1935, 11 x 14 In.	30
Pen Knife, Tom Mix, Gun Drawn, Horse Game On Handle, Closed 3 ½ In.	10
Poster, Green Cross Safety Club, Fold Creases, 1947, 22 x 17 In.	24
Telescope, Logo Transfer, Premium, 2 ½ In.	149
Tin, Red, White, Ralston Straight Shooters' Make-Up, 1930s, 1 ¾ In., Diam.	8

TOOLS of all sorts are listed here, but most are related to industry. Other tools may be found listed under Iron, Kitchen, Tinware, and Wooden.

Bed Wrench, Maple, Turned Post For Tightening Rope Beds, c.1850, 13 In.	323
Bootjack, Wood, Chip Carved Notched Edges, 1800s, 17 In.	29
Box, Carpenter's, Wheels, Wood, Compartments, Metal Handles, Padlock, c.1902, 30 x 15 In.	360
Box, Wood, Divided, Wainscoting, Cutout Heart, c.1900, 8 x 33 In.	58
Bucket, Sugar, Lid, 2 Bands, Blue Paint, Wood Bail Handle, Mid-Atlantic, c.1890, 11 x 10 In.	460
Carpenter's Bench, Vice, Dog Leg Clamp Holders, c.1865, 32 x 50 In.	514
Chest, 3 Drawers, Side Handles, Yellow Grain Paint, c.1890, 20 x 34 In.	360
Chest, Cherry, Lift Top, Drawer, Brass Pulls, Handles, Brass Feet, Tools, 15 x 26 In.	1180
Chest, Wood, Painted, Fitted Interior, 15 x 18 x 32 In.	59
Cleaner, Grain, Seed, Bean, Pine, Iron Crank, A.T. Ferrell Co., Salesman's Sample, 29 In.	711
Cobbler's Bench, Walnut, c.1850, 16 x 45 In.	91
Cobbler's Caddy, Pine, Divided Section, Bootjack Ends, Iron Handle, 1800s, 16 x 24 In.	173
Coffin Lowering Device, Clark, Brass Gear, Vault, Casket, Salesman's Sample, 17 x 18 In.	1215
Coin Changer, Cast Iron, Countertop, Staats, Chicago, 1890	240
Copier Press, Mahogany, Brass, Handles, Tray, James Watt & Co., c.1795, 19 x 12 In.	1800
Corn Husker, Wood, Iron, c.1850, 42 x 24 In.	118
Corn Planter, Automatic, Tin, Wood, Red Paint, Yellow, Stencil Label, c.1890, 35 ¾ In.	185
Cranberry Scoop, Wood, Metal Screen, c.1910, 24 x 22 In.	138
Cranberry Scoop, Wood, Pointed Rods, 16 ½ x 14 ¾ In.	153
Cream Separator, DeLaval Jr., No. 27, Stenciling, Spinner, Bell On Handle, 21 In.	371
Device, Clockmaker's, Brass, Steel, 2 Jaws, Hand Crank, Wood Handle, c.1900, 5 In.	96
Factory Wheel, 6 Spokes, Wood, Metal, Gifford Wood Co., Hudson, N.Y., 40 In.	20
Fog Machine, Challenger Model 5100C, Green, Enamel, Chrome, Z & W Mfg.	90
Grain Elevator, Wood, Metal, Canvas Treadmill, Boggs, Salesman's Sample, 41 In.	1304
Grass Seeder, Wood, Paint, R.C. King, Kentucky, 19 x 10 ½ In.	30
Hacksaw, Metal, Wood Handle, c.1860, 16 In.	60
Hammer, Indian Cap Shooter Top, Cast Iron, Wood Handle, 10 ¾ In.	122
Hand Truck, Barrel, Aluminum, Steel, 2 Wheels, Salesman's Sample, c.1925, 13 In.	369
Hatchel, Hardwood, Chip Carved Board, Red Paint, Wrought Iron Spikes, c.1788, 27 In.	150
Hatchel, Oak, Compass Design, Wrought Iron Spikes, c.1900, 29 In.	120
Hatchet, Splitting, Wood, Grain Painted, Hand Carved, 38 x 15 In.	153
Hay Baler, Nickel Plated Brass, Wood Platform, Spoke Wheels, Salesman's Sample, 19 x 7 In.	8591
Hay Fork, Wood, Stamped M.B. Young, Pa., c.1865, 72 In.	89
Hay Rake, Spoke Wheels, Wood, Curved Tines, Adjustable, Salesman's Sample, 18 In.	2725
Ladder, Orchard, Iron, France, c.1870, 99 In.	456
Ladder, Wood, Folding, Multicolor, Painted, 72 In.	104
Level, Transit, Berger, Model 320, Wood Case	153
Lock, Medieval Style, Octagonal Body, Shaped Dome, Turned Nipple, Flower Bow, 9 In.	1476
Mallet, Circus, Metal, Wood, Inscribed, Ringling Bros., 1898, 31 In.	90
Millinery Wire, Skirt Shape, Adjustable, 48 In.	29

Padlock, Hunchback, Black Paint, Trenton Lock & Hardware Co., 3 In.	889
Pipe Tongs, Iron, c.1750, 22 In.	1610
Plane, Carpenter's, Walnut Block, Whalebone Inlays, 10 ½ In.	561
Plane, Carpenter's, Wood, Cast Steel, Stamped, Isaac Greaves, 10 In.	330
Plane, Combination, Stanley, No. 55, 4 Blade Boxes	118
Plow, Cast Iron, Hillsdale, N.Y., 19th Century, 43 In.	288
Plow, Champion, Horse Drawn, Single Shear, Walnut, 1902 World's Fair, 78 x 36 x 25 In.	10260
Plow, Dual, Triangular, Spoked Wheels, Swivel, Deyrolle, Salesman's Sample, 17 x 9 In.	359
Plow, Horse Drawn, Wood, Iron, Salesman's Sample, c.1890, 4 ¾ x 15 In.	1062
Plow, Planet Jr., Brass, Nickel, Painted, 2 Curved Wood Handles, Salesman's Sample, 16 In.	5629
Pulley, Wood, Iron, Laminated Construction, Patina, c.1910, 36 In.	180
Pump Lid, Well, 2-Story House Shape, Gray, Yellow Paint, c.1910, 45 x 25 In.	267
Reaper, Wood, Canvas, Flat Bed, 4-Part Paddle, Traction, Salesman's Sample, 35 x 15 In.	1778
Scoop, Cranberry, Wood, Branded J.J. Beaton, Cape Cod, Mass., 18 x 21 In.	443
Sector, Brass, Plumb Bob Window, Angle Hinge, ½ King's Rule Scale, Paris, 1700s, 6 ½ In.	246
Seeder, Pine, Black, Red Paint, Wood, Burlap, D.C. Curry & Co., Wooster, Ohio, 1800s, 16 In.	360
Shear Grinder, Economy, Iron, Table Mount, Koken Barbers' Supply Co., 10 ½ In.	1368
Shovel, Wood, Carved, One Piece, 1800s, 46 ½ x 11 In.	115
Square, Bias Cutting & Marking, Patented, George Moore, 1874, 17 In.	83
Square, Whale's Bone, Brass Pins, c.1850, 4 In.	767
Stand, Cobbler's, Iron Shoe Last, 1800s, 8 ¼ In.	36
Strong Box, Wells Fargo & Co. Express, Side Handles, Painted, Red, Black, Gilt, 12 x 9 In.	1140
Threshing Sled, Agricultural, Wood, Stone Blades, 1800s, Continental, 76 x 56 In.	298
Tinder Lighter, Boxlock, Brass Pan, Compartment, Legs, Grip, England, c.1800, 8 ¼ In.	1080
Trammel, Wrought Iron, Punched Design, Initialed, 1765, 37 In.	4700
Trencher, Hardwood, Green, c.1850, 4 x 20 In.	499
Trencher, Hardwood, Rectangular, Painted Blue, c.1860, 4 x 19 In.	646
Wagon Jack, Conestoga, Iron, 1810, 21 In.	385
Wagon Jack, Conestoga, Wood & Wrought Iron, Red Paint, 1811, 26 In.	235
Wagon Jack, Conestoga, Wood, Wrought Iron, Early 19th Century, Pa., 1827, 27 In.	240
Wagon Jack, Conestoga, Wood Body, Iron Hardware, c.1871, 22 In.	142
Wagon Jack, Conestoga, Wrought Iron, Wood, Monogrammed Shaft, 1846, 26 x 8 In. *illus*	277
Wagon Jack, Oak, Wrought Iron, Stamped J. Bryson, 1855, 24 In.	240
Wheel Stop, Conestoga Wagon, Cast Iron, Shaped Sides, Ring, 21 ¼ In.	189
Wheelbarrow, Wood, Blue Paint, Marked, Mich., 66 In.	431
Wheelbarrow, Wood, Iron Wheel, Red Paint	288
Windmill, Star, Wood, Brass, 6 Sections, Derrick Base, 1878, Salesman's Sample, 15 x 12 In.	3851
Wine Corker, Brass, Metal, Standing, Paris, France, 44 x 13 In.	644
Wine Press Screw, Wood, 81 x 10 In.	1170
Work Bench, Tools, Miniature, 17 x 20 x 9 In. *illus*	587
Wringer, Clothes, Stand, Walnut Handle, c.1850, 27 x 27 In.	61

TOOTHBRUSH HOLDERS were part of every bowl and pitcher set in the late nineteenth century. Most were oblong covered dishes. About 1920, manufacturers started to make children's toothbrush holders shaped like animals or cartoon characters. A few modern toothbrush holders are still being made.

Blue Flowers, Ribbed, Footed, Staffordshire, c.1880, 5 ½ In.	64
Dog, Bulldog, Sitting, Black & White, Porcelain, Germany, 1930s, 3 In.	85
Frog, Sitting, Porcelain, Green, Germany, 1930s, 4 ¼ In.	86
Giraffe, Tray Base, Porcelain, Japan, 5 ¾ In.	89
Steeplechase Horse, Jockey, Tray Base, Porcelain, Germany, 4 ¾ x 4 ¼ In.	84

TOOTHPICK HOLDERS are sometimes called *toothpicks* by collectors. The variously shaped containers used to hold small wooden toothpicks are made of glass, china, or metal. Most of the toothpick holders are made of Victorian pressed glass. Additional items may be found in other categories, such as Bisque, Silver Plate, Slag Glass, etc.

Agata, Wild Rose Design, Amber & Purple Staining, New England, 2 ½ In. *illus*	489
Amber, Pig On Flatcar	75
Child, Red Hat, Playing Banjo, Occupied Japan, 3 In.	20
Chrysanthemum Sprig, Pagoda, Turquoise Opalescent, Gilt, Northwood, c.1899, 2 ⅝ In.	127
Czarina, Footed, Fostoria, c.1894	40
Daisy & Button, Top Hat, Colonial Blue, Fenton, 2 ½ x 3 ¼ In. *illus*	10
Derby, Square Base	85
Fan & Feather Custard, Pink & Gilt, Sawtooth Rim, Northwood Glass Co., c.1904, 2 ½ In.	219
Glass, Opalescent, Parker & Davis, Portraits, Eagle, Flags, Gold Accents, 2 ½ In.	209

Tole, Coffeepot, Flowers, Vegetables, Petals, Leaves, C-Scroll Handle, c.1850, 10 In.
$1,185

James D. Julia Auctioneers

Tole, Coffeepot, Red, Yellow Flowers, Hinged Lid, Ear Shape Handle, c.1810, 9 In.
$984

Skinner Auctioneers & Appraisers

Tole, Trunk, Dome Top, Flowers, Leaves, Berries, Red, Green Yellow, c.1810, 5 ⅜ x 9 x 4 In.
$369

Skinner Auctioneers & Appraisers

"Bone" Candlesticks
A dealer we met is collecting jewelry and candlesticks "by Elsa Peretti for Tiffany." He buys them used and brand new. Many are limited editions that have already gone up in price. He's proud of his bone-shaped candlesticks, including terra-cotta and yellow ceramic versions. One set has already gone from $3,000 to $3,700.

T

Tole, Trunk, Dome Top, Red Flowers, Yellow Border, Wire Swing Handle, c.1810, 7 x 9 In.
$1,134

Skinner Auctioneers & Appraisers

Tool, Wagon Jack, Conestoga, Wrought Iron, Wood, Monogrammed Shaft, 1846, 26 x 8 In.
$277

Garth's Auctioneers & Appraisers

Tool, Work Bench, Tools, Miniature, 17 x 20 x 9 In.
$587

Aspire Auctions

T

588

Holly Amber, Golden Agate, Indiana Tumbler & Goblet Co., c.1903, 2 ½ x 2 ¾ In.	403
Idyll, Blue, Scalloped Rim, Jefferson Glass Co., c.1907, 2 ⅝ In.	81
Inverted Fan & Feather Design, Ruffled Top, 4-Footed, 2 ½ In.	35
Nautilus Argonaut Shell, Custard, Green, Gilt Design, Northwood Glass Co., c.1900, 2 ⅞ In.	127
Pomona, Clear, Scalloped Rim, Applied Neck Rigaree, New England Glass., c.1885, 2 In.	127
Rainbow Satin Stripe, Opaque, Pink, Yellow, Blue, Scalloped Rim, c.1950, 2 ¼ In.	81
Reverse Swirl, Cranberry Opalescent, c.1885, 2 ⅛ In.	259
Ribbed Opal Lattice, Blue Opalescent, c.1890, 4 In.	230
Ribbed, Cobalt Blue Opal	70
Shell, Green Opalescent, Sawtooth Rim, National Glass Co., c.1905, 2 ¼ In.	403
Silver Plate, Circus Bear, On Ball, Near Barrel, Marked, Osborn & Co., c.1885, 2 ¾ In.	184
Threaded Glass, Clear, Apple Green, Cranberry, c.1890, 2 ⅛ In.	288
Wild Rose, Satin Finish, New England, 2 In.	259
Windows Swirl, Ruby Opalescent, Oval, Hobbs, Brockunier & Co., c.1888, 2 ½ In.	184

TORQUAY is the name given to ceramics by several potteries working near Torquay, **TORQUAY** England, from 1870 until 1962. Until about 1900, the potteries used local red clay to make classical-style art pottery vases and figurines. Then they turned to making souvenir wares. Items were dipped in colored slip and decorated with painted slip and sgraffito designs. They often had mottoes or proverbs, and scenes of cottages, ships, birds, or flowers. The Scandy design was a symmetrical arrangement of brushstrokes and spots done in colored slips. Potteries included Watcombe Pottery (1870–1962), Torquay Terra-Cotta Company (1875–1905), Aller Vale (1881–1924), Torquay Pottery (1908–1940), and Longpark (1883–1957).

Cheese Keeper, Lid, If You Can't Be Easy Be Easy As You Can, Ships, 6 x 5 In.	46
Creamer, Fresh From The Dairy, Scandy, 3 In.	24
Creamer, From The Old Land, Shamrocks, Sunrise, Mountains, 4 ½ In.	35
Creamer, No Road Is Long With Good Company	35
Hatpin Holder, Sailboat, A Place For Hat Pins, c.1915, 5 In.	100
Pitcher, The Deeds Alone Must Win The Prize, Scandy, c.1920, 6 In.	55
Teapot, Lid, A Thing Of Beauty Is A Joy Forever, 4 ½ In.	86

TORTOISESHELL is the shell of the tortoise. It has been used as inlay and to make small decorative objects since the seventeenth century. Some species of tortoise are now on the endangered species list, and old or new objects made from these shells cannot be sold legally.

Box, Dome Lid, Rectangular, England, c.1915, 2 x 5 x 3 In.	430
Box, Lid, Carved, Figures, Buildings, Wood Base, Chinese, 5 ¼ In. ....*illus*	2318
Box, Necessaire, Paris Views, Continental, 5 ¾ In.	438
Box, Patch, Scroll Engraved Silver, c.1860, 2 ½ x 1 ½ In.	115
Box, Pierced, Squirrel & Grape Design, Brass Mounts, 2 x 3 In.	922
Coin Purse, Mother-Of-Pearl Rondels, Silver Escutcheon, Silk Lined, c.1900, 2 x 3 In.	338
Comb, Reticulated Flowers, c.1890, 4 ½ In., Pair	94
Compact, Brass Inlay, Paste Jewels, Engine Turned Interior, c.1900, 3 ½ x 3 In.	153
Eyeglass Case, Silver Mounts, England, 10 ½ In.	250
Jewelry Box, Bombe Shape, Molded Lid, Window, Paw Feet, c.1850, 11 x 15 In.	2706
Jewelry Box, Edwardian, Nickel Plaque, c.1915, 1 ¼ x 4 ¼ In.	338
Jewelry Box, Ivory, Pierced Panels, Strapwork, Velvet Lined, c.1900, 2 ¼ x 6 In.	369
Lorgnette, Spring Mounted, Scalloped Handle, c.1875, 7 ½ In.	369
Model, Carriage, Tamboured Canopy, Pomegranates, Shell Poles, 9 ⅞ In.	625
Page Turner, Sterling End, George V, E. Bennett, London, 1910, 14 In.	215
Snuff Box, Quilted Pattern, Escutcheon, c.1850, 2 ¼ x 1 ¾ In.	184
Tea Caddy, Silver Plate Escutcheon, Cartouche, Ivory Knobs, c.1915, 5 x 7 In.	861
Writing Box, Boulle Inlay, Maple, Mahogany Interior, c.1750, 6 x 8 ½ In.	344

TOY collectors have special clubs, magazines, and shows. Toys are designed to entice children, and today they have attracted new interest among adults who are still children at heart. All types of toys are collected. Tin toys, iron toys, battery-operated toys, and many others are collected by specialists. Dolls, Games, Teddy Bears, and Bicycles are listed in their own categories. Other toys may be found under company or celebrity names.

2 Black Musicians, Tin, Windup, Red Base, Gunthermann, Germany, 9 x 8 In.	830
Accordion, Gucciolo, Box, 8 x 8 In.	24
Acrobat, Back-Flip, Covered Box, Stepped Platform, Painted, Wood, Paper, 7 In.	1778
Acrobat, Back-Flip, Covered Stairs, Painted, Wood, Paper, 8 ½ In.	1154
Acrobat, On Horse, Pulley Operated, Painted, Metal, Britains, 4 In.	668
Action Figure, Spider-Man, On Original Card, Marvel, Mego, Hong Kong, 1978, 10 In.	84

Air Cab, Amos & Andy, Dog, Multicolor, Tin Litho, Clockwork, 8 In.	649
Airplane, 3-Prop, Painted, Pressed Steel, Marked Kingsbury, 15 In.	240
Airplane, Air Force, Tin Litho, Lights, Battery Operated, Japan, 12 ½ In. ....*illus*	180
Airplane, Biplane, Painted, Tin, Girard, 9 In.	180
Airplane, Biplane, Tail Fin, Marked World Tours, Tin, Windup, Girard, 13 In.	330
Airplane, Bremen, Junker, Green Cast Iron, Propeller, 3 Figures, Hubley, 10 In.	2006
Airplane, Friendship, Yellow Cast Iron, Pontoons, 3 Propellers, Hubley, 13 In.	4130
Airplane, Hangar, Catapult Airplane, Painted, Pressed Steel, Buddy L, 6 x 12 In.	577
Airplane, Lucky Boy, Gray, Red Paint, Iron, Dent, 10 ½-In. Wingspan	395 to 425
Airplane, Lucky Boy, Painted, Aluminum Motor, Embossed, Dent, 1930s, 12 ½ In. ....*illus*	2124
Airplane, Military Transport, 4-Prop, Pressed Steel, Wyandotte, 13 In.	240
Airplane, Monocoupe, Orange, Black Paint, Arcade, 10 ½-In. Wingspan	334
Airplane, National Airmail, Single Prop, Blue, Yellow Paint, Wood, Tin, 7 In.	48
Airplane, Pan Am Super 7 Clipper, Metal, American Flag Decals, Marx, 1940s, 13 x 17 In.	120
Airplane, Pan American, Pressed Steel, Marx, 28 In.	300
Airplane, Pioneer Air Express, Tin Lithograph, Pull Toy, 25 ½ In.	330
Airplane, Question Mark, Blue, Silver Paint, Cast Iron, Dent, 12 In.	830
Airplane, Red, Silver Paint, Cast Iron, Arcade, 5 ¾ In.	61 to 92
Airplane, ROGA, Rising Off Ground Airplane, Flies, Tin, Paper, Box, 12 x 10 In.	266
Airplane, Single Engine, 4 Windows, Decals, Pressed Steel, Turner, 24 In.	330
Airplane, Wire, Wheels, Gray, Black Paint, Tin, 23 In.	186
Airport Hangar, Arcadia, Wood, 1930s, 8 ½ x 12 In.	106
Alabama Coon Jigger, Man, Blue Jacket, Red Pants, Tin, Windup, c.1920, 10 x 5 In.	863
Alphonse & Gaston Car, Cast Iron, Figures Bow When Pulled, Kenton, c.1911, 8 In.	3245
Ambulance, Canvas Top, Cream Paint, Pressed Steel, Buddy L, Box, 14 ½ In.	510
Ambulance, Heavyweights, Purple, Redline, Hot Wheels, Factory Sealed, 1970	175
Ambulance, Painted, Cast Iron, Kenton, 10 In.	770
Amos 'n' Andy, Walkers, Waddle, Eyes Move, Tin Litho, Clockwork, Marx, Box, 11 In.	2124
Andy Gump Automobile, Cast Iron, Red & Green, Arcade, 7 In.	1298
Anxious Bride, Woman In Cart, Driver On Cycle, Tin, Clockwork, Lehmann, Box, 9 In.	4425
Armoire, Doll's, Linens, Arched Crest, Double Doors, Silk Ribbons, France, 25 x 12 In.	2128
Astronaut, Space Explorer, TV Chest, Plastic, Tin Litho, Battery, Japan, Box, 12 ½ In.	210
Astronaut, Tin Litho, Plastic, Battery, Osaka, Japan, Box, c.1993, 13 In. ....*illus*	450
Atomic Energy Lab, No. U-238, A.C. Gilbert, Box, 1951, 25 x 16 ½ x 5 In.	2963
Atomic Pistol, Sparks, Friction, Tip Rotates, Tin Litho, TN, Japan, Box, 1950s, 7 In. ....*illus*	235
Baby On Chamber Pot, Papier-Mache, Fitted Bellows, Baby Bounces, Squeak, c.1875, 7 In.	336
Baby Tractor, Farmer, Graphic Dashboard, Penny Toy, Kellermann, 3 In. ....*illus*	236
Baby, Crawling, Cast Iron, Articulated Arms, Wheels In Knees, Ives, 5 In.	266
Baby, Crawling, Painted, Flock Hat, Clockwork, Germany, 5 ¼ In. ....*illus*	944
Balky Mule, Cart, Tin, Windup, Lehmann, c.1910, 5 x 7 ¾ In.	374
Balloon Vendor, Monkeys, Music Box, Mechanical Arm, Animals, Tin Litho, Kellerman, 6 ½ In. *illus*	472
Banjo Player, Black, Tin, Windup, Painted, Germany, 7 ½ In.	1180
Barnacle Bill, Rowboat, Yellow, Red, Green, Tin Litho, Rubber Band, Emmert Hammes, 9 In.	61
Bears are also listed in the Teddy Bear category.	
Bear, Asian Rider, Composition, Silk Outfit, Pull Toy, 15 ¼ x 14 In.	1094
Bear, Baby, Sleeps, Alarm Clock Rings, Sits Up, Yawns, Cries, Box, Linemar, 9 In.	177
Bear, Brown Fur, Muzzle, Clockwork, 7 ½ In.	593
Bear, Cloth, Pattern Kit, Buttoned Vest, 1930s, 13 ¼ x 10 ½ In.	46
Bear, On Cart, Nickel Plated Metal, 2 Bells Ring, 6 ½ In.	295
Bear, On Wheels, Brown Mohair, Stitched Nose, Leather Collar, Pull Chain, Steiff, 13 x 18 In.	972
Bear, Studio, Tags, Ear Button, Steiff, 1900s, Life Size, 68 In.	360
Bear, Walking, Brown Fur, Clockwork, Martin, 7 ½ In.	334
Bed, Doll's, Iron Canopy, Wood Springs, Steeple Head & Footboards, Coverlet, 24 x 18 In.	448
Bed, Doll's, Rope, Walnut, Shaped Headboard, Turned Posts, Va., c.1835, 16 x 26 In.	690
Bed, Doll's, Shenandoah Valley, Turned Posters, Head, Footboards, c.1850, 13 x 19 In.	1955
Beetle, Red, Green, Yellow Paint, Tin, Windup, Germany, 6 In.	152
Bell Ringer, Boy, Fishing, On Cart, Cast Iron, N.N. Hill Brass Co., 8 ¼ In.	1007
Bell Ringer, Dog, In Suit, Horse, No. 23, Painted, Iron Frame, 6 ½ In.	3600
Bell Ringer, Fire Wagon, Horse Drawn, Driver, Hose Reel, Red, Black Paint, 19 In.	237
Bell Ringer, Girl, Daisy, Holding Doll, Sleigh, Horse, Wheels, Iron, Gong Bell Co., 8 In.	533
Bell Ringer, Goat, Balanced On Metal Frame, Yellow Paint, Tin, 6 In.	474
Bell Ringer, Goat, Tin, Painted, Rocker Base, 7 In.	1094
Bell Ringer, Horse, Trick Pony, Wheels, Painted, Iron, No. 39, Gong Bell Co., 7 ½ In.	593
Bell Ringer, Monkey, On Log, Wheels, Painted, Cast Iron, N.N. Hill Brass Co., 6 In.	182
Bell Ringer, Monkey, On Tricycle, Cast Iron, J. & E. Stevens Co., 7 ½ In.	1126

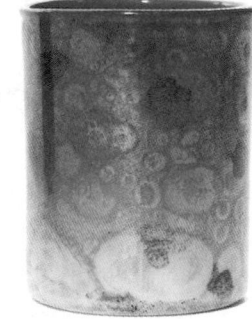

Toothpick Holder, Agata, Wild Rose Design, Amber & Purple Staining, New England, 2 ½ In.
$489

Early Auction Co.

Toothpick Holder, Daisy & Button, Top Hat, Colonial Blue, Fenton, 2 ½ x 3 ¼ In.
$10

Ruby Lane, Inc.

Tortoiseshell, Box, Lid, Carved, Figures, Buildings, Wood Base, Chinese, 5 ¼ In.
$2,318

Neal Auction Co.

TIP

Do not store vintage fabrics or clothing in plastic or cardboard boxes. Natural fabrics like linen or cotton need oxygen and can't be in airtight boxes. White clothes will yellow if kept in plastic.

T

Toy, Airplane, Air Force, Tin Litho, Lights, Battery Operated, Japan, 12 ½ In. $180

Victorian Casino Antiques

Toy, Airplane, Lucky Boy, Painted, Aluminum Motor, Embossed, Dent, 1930s, 12 ½ In. $2,124

Bertoia Auctions

Toy, Astronaut, Tin Litho, Plastic, Battery, Osaka, Japan, Box, c.1993, 13 In. $450

Victorian Casino Antiques

Toy, Atomic Pistol, Sparks, Friction, Tip Rotates, Tin Litho, TN, Japan, Box, 1950s, 7 In. $235

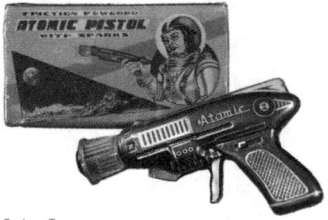

Serious Toyz

T

Bicycles that are large enough to ride are listed in the Bicycle category.

Bicycle, Painted, Rubber, Tin, 10 ¾ In.	296
Billiards Player, Table, Man With Cue Stick, Tin Litho, Clockwork, KiCo, Box, 6 In.	826
Bird, Fan Shape Tail, Dropped Wings, Multicolor, Squeak, Germany, Late 1800s, 7 ¾ In.	144
Bird, In Tree, Tin Lithograph, Windup, Distler, 7 ⅝ x 4 In.	590
Black Man, Tap Dancer, Blue Shirt, Celluloid, Windup, Wood, 5 ½ In.	390
Black Preacher, Leans Forward, Head Turns, Painted Wood Lecturn, Ives, 10 In.	3341
Blocks, Animals & ABCs, Paper, Nested, McLoughlin Bros., Largest 7 In., 7 Piece	319
Boardwalk Delight, Girl, Chair, Tin, Celluloid, Windup, CK, Japan, 8 ½ In. .....*illus*	295
Boat, Barbie & Friends, Blue, Plastic, Irwin, Mattel, Box	396
Boat, Battleship, Columbia, Paper On Cardboard, Lithograph, Wood Guns, Bliss, 26 In.	649
Boat, Battleship, Hillclimber, Wheels, Brown, Tan, White Paint, Tin, 15 In.	119
Boat, Battleship, Maine, Painted, Tin, Marklin, Germany, 20 ½ In.	5103
Boat, Hydroplane, Marilyn, Tin Lithograph, Composition Driver, Windup, Arnold, 14 In.	212
Boat, Motor, Peggy Jane, Mechanical, Tin, Box, J. Chein, 14 ½ In.	428
Boat, No. 1-44, Lionel, Box, 17 ¾ In.	250
Boat, Ocean Liner, 3 Smokestacks, Red, Navy Blue, White, Tin, Clockwork, Bing, 25 In.	4266
Boat, Ocean Liner, 4 Funnels, Black, White, Painted, Tin, Clockwork, 22 In.	431
Boat, Ocean Liner, Burgundy, Yellow Paint, Brass, Tin, Clockwork, 13 In.	213
Boat, Ocean Liner, Red, Black Paint, Tin, Clockwork, Fleischmann, 20 In.	365
Boat, Ocean Liner, Tin Clockwork, Gray, Tin, 17 In.	365
Boat, Ocean Liner, Tin, Clockwork, 3 Black Stacks, Tin, 14 In.	304
Boat, Ocean Liner, White, Blue Stripe Paint, Tin, Clockwork, Germany, 12 ½ In.	273
Boat, Ocean Liner, White, Blue Stripe, Tin, Clockwork, Fleischmann, 20 In.	304
Boat, Paddlewheel, City Of New York, White, Yellow Red Paint, Cast Iron, Wilkins, 14 In.	119
Boat, Paddlewheel, Pilgrim, Paper On Cardboard, Wood, Litho, Whitney Reed, 28 In.	472
Boat, Paddlewheel, Side Wheel, Painted, Cast Iron, Wilkins, 14 ½ In.	122
Boat, Paddlewheel, Union Side Wheel, Pilot Cabin, Paper On Wood, Litho, Reed, 24 In.	1180
Boat, Speedboat, Crank, Sea Hawk, Japan, 1950s, 12 In.	145
Boat, Speedboat, Driver, Tin, Germany, Penny Toy, c.1939, 3 ½ In.	125
Boat, Speedboat, Static, Green, White, Red Paint, Cast Iron, Hubley, 9 ½ In.	1067
Boat, Tankard, Red, Black Paint, Tin, Clockwork, Fleischmann, U.S. Zone, Germany, 20 In.	213
Boat, Tippy Canoe, Original Indian, Tin Litho, Green, Yellow, Windup, Strauss, 9 In.	177
Boat, Torpedo, Tin, Battery Operated, Japan, 1950s	175
Box, For Humpty Dumpty Circus, Teddy's Adventures, Schoenhut, 18 x 30 In. .....*illus*	443
Boxer Rebellion, Chinese Figures, Tossing Figure, Clockwork, Lehmann, 5 x 5 In. .....*illus*	14160
Boxers, Joe Lewis, Max Schmelling, Tin Litho, Clockwork, Einfault, Germany, c.1920, 7 In.	438
Boy, In Cart, Galloping Horse, Clockwork, Althof Bergmann, c.1870, 17 In.	649
Boy, Seated, Waving Flag, Pull Toy, Signed Carol Diefenderfer, c.1890, 8 ¾ In.	533
Brake Carriage, 2-Seat, Horse Drawn, Painted, Motion, Cast Iron, Hubley, c.1910, 17 In.	2916 to 5333
Brake Carriage, 4-Seat, Horse Drawn, 8 Riders, Painted, Cast Iron, 27 ½ In.	2607
Building, Burning, Firemen, Women, Ladder, Wood, Cast Iron, Carpenter, 23 In.	20655
Bulldozer, Farmer Driver, Tin, Windup, Marx, 8 In.	62
Bus, 24 Passenger, Nickel-Plated Bumper, Blue Green, Pressed Steel, Buddy L, 28 In.	6518
Bus, Blue Paint, Red Trim, Pressed Steel, Windup, Kingsbury, 15 ½ In.	474
Bus, Double-Decker, Black, Orange Paint, Cast Iron, Kenton, 7 In.	334
Bus, Double-Decker, Blue Paint, Cast Iron, Arcade, 8 In.	356
Bus, Double-Decker, Cast Iron, Blue, Open Roof, Rear Stairway, 5 Figures, Arcade, 8 In.	1121
Bus, Double-Decker, Driver, Tin Lithograph, Windup, Penny Toy, 3 x 4 In.	271
Bus, Double-Decker, Green Paint, Cast Iron, Arcade, 8 In.	122
Bus, Double-Decker, Green, Orange Paint, Cast Iron, Kenton, 7 In.	334
Bus, Double-Decker, Rear Stairs, Red & Yellow, Tin Litho, Clockwork, Lehmann, 7 In.	1003
Bus, Double-Decker, Red, Green Paint, Cast Iron, Kenton, 10 In.	365
Bus, Double-Decker, Yellow Coach, Green Paint, Cast Iron, Arcade, 13 ½ In.	608
Bus, Double-Decker, Yellow Coach, Orange Paint, Cast Iron, Arcade, 13 ½ In.	486
Bus, Green Paint, Gold Trim, Pressed Steel, Buddy L, 28 In.	2066
Bus, Green, Red Stripe, Doors Open, Pressed Steel, 28 In.	2607
Bus, Greyhound Lines Safety Coach, Fageol, Driver, Painted, Cast Iron, Arcade, 12 In.	1007
Bus, Greyhound Lines, Blue, White, Running Dog Logo, Wood, Buddy L, 18 In.	516
Bus, Greyhound, Americruiser, Tin, Friction, Japan, Box, 8 In.	108
Bus, Greyhound, Blue, Cream Paint, Pressed Steel, Windup, Kingsbury, 18 In.	213
Bus, Inter-City Bus, Green Paint, Pressed Steel, Steelcraft, 24 In.	213
Bus, Inter-State, Tin Lithograph, Windup, Strauss, 11 In.	210
Bus, Lake Shore Line Chicago-Buffalo, Fageol, Painted, Cast Iron, 12 ¼ In.	474
Bus, Mack 6, Red, White Paint, Arcade, 13 In.	1304
Bus, Radicon, Antenna, Bronze Green, Battery, Modern Toys, Japan, Box, 16 x 24 In.	210

Bus, Royal Blue Line, Tin, Red, Gray, Blue, Hercules Balloon Cord Tires, 18 ½ In.	1140
Bus, Safety Coach, Green, Fageol, Gold Paint, Cast Iron, Arcade, 12 ½ In.	237
Bus, Santa Fe Trailways, Cream & Red Paint, Cast Iron, Nickel Grill, Arcade, 9 In.	266
Bus, Sightseeing, Tin, Red, White, Blue, Alps, Japan, Box, 13 In.	195
Bus, Volkswagen, Beach Bomb, No. 6274, Redline, Hot Wheels, Mattel, On Card, 1969 ....*illus*	635
Busy Bridge, 6 Cars, 2 Terminals, Tin Lithograph, Clockwork, Louis Marx, 24 In.	413
Busy Lizzie, Dress, Apron, Mop, Cleans, Tin Lithograph, Windup, Germany, 7 In. .... 413 to 531	
Butcher Shop, Butcher, Hanging Meats, Paper Litho, Wood, Painted, Germany, 8 x 6 In.	790
Butterfly, Wood, Tin, Pegboard, Incised Stripes, Dots, Wheels, Pull Toy, 9 In.	72
Cabinet, Doll's, Oak, 2 Glass Doors, Drawer Over 2 Doors, 31 x 19 In.	270
Camel, On Wheels, U.S. Zone, Germany, Tag, Steiff, 17 ¼ In.	210
Camel, Rider, Bell On Hump, Wheeled Platform, Mustard, Red Paint, Tin, 9 In.	474
Camel, Rider, Tin, Bell On Hump, Wheeled Base, Althof Bergmann, 9 x 9 In.	356
Camel, Rider, Wearing Top Hat, Wheeled Platform, Painted, Tin, Pull Toy, 8 ½ In.	356
Cannon, Cast Iron, Tin, 2 Wheels, Young America, Rapid Fire Gun, 14 In.	108
Cannon, Cast Iron, Wood, 1800s, 5 ½ x 6 x 17 In.	360
Canoe, Birch Bark, Great Lakes Area, c.1950s, 3 ½ x 15 ¼ x 4 In. ....*illus*	52
Canoe, Indian Figures, Oars, Red Cedar, Carved, 1900s, 7 x 29 ½ In.	826
Cap Gun, Black Head, Japanned, Cast Iron, 1887, 4 ½ In.	420
Cap Gun, Chinese Must Go, 2 Men, Walking, On Barrel, Black Paint, Iron, Ives, 4 ½ In.	360
Cap Gun, Hunter, Single Shot, Cast Iron, Embossed, Ives, 1890s	228
Cap Gun, Mountie, Metal, Plastic, Repeating, Kilgore, 1950s, Box.	78
Cap Gun, Sambo Striker, Cast Iron, Patents, c.1890, 4 ½ In.	316
Cap Gun, Shoot The Hat, Mechanical, Man Puts Hat On Man, Explodes Cap, 5 x 5 In. ....*illus*	575
Car, Andy Gump, Red, Silver Paint, Cast Iron, Embossed Sidney Smith Corp., Arcade, 7 In.	593
Car, Armored, Camouflage, Green, Yellow, 6 Wheel, Lineol, 9 ½ In.	1020
Car, Aston-Martin, 1965 Model, Ejects Driver, Battery, Gilbert, Japan, Box, 11 In. ....*illus*	590
Car, Barbie Sports Car, Austin Healey, Pink, Irwin, Mattel, Box, 1960s....................................	198
Car, Benz Racer, Go Stop, Tin Litho, Battery, Japan, Box, c.1950s, 11 In. ....*illus*	390
Car, Cadillac, 1931 Model, Coupe, Trunk Rack, Tin Lithograph, Windup, Marx, 2 In.	563
Car, Cadillac, Convertible, Teal, Gear Shift, Tin Lithograph, Battery, Bandai, Box, 11 In.	413
Car, Cadillac, Electricmobile, 1950, Tin, Friction, Battery, Lights, Nomura, Box, 13 In.	4720
Car, Carriage, Horseless, Hillclimber, Woman Rider, Black, Red Wood, Cast Iron, 7 ½ In............	504
Car, Champion Airflow, Rubber Tires, 6 Windows, Painted, Cast Iron, 7 ½ In.	1560
Car, Chevrolet, Sedan, Black Paint, Cast Iron, Arcade, 8 ¼ In.	1007
Car, Chrysler, Imperial, 1962 Model, Blue, Cream Seats, Tin, Friction, Asahi, Box, 15 In.	26550
Car, Convertible, Assembly Instructions, Plastic, Key, Toy Founders Inc., c.1955, 10 ½ In............	90
Car, Convertible, Flivver, Cloth Top Up, Black, Pressed Steel, Buddy L, 11 In.	273
Car, Convertible, Red, Yellow Paint, Cast Iron, 9 In.	207
Car, Convertible, Slot, Orange Paint, Pressed Steel, Lionel, 8 In.	356
Car, Coo Coo, Bald Driver, Tin Litho, Clockwork, Louis Marx, 1920s, 7 ½ In.	325
Car, Corvette, 1958 Model, Blue, White Roof, Tin, Friction, Yonezawa, 9 ½ In.	207
Car, Coupe, 1922 Model, Driver, Black Paint, Cast Iron, Arcade, 8 ½ In.....................................	415
Car, Coupe, 1926 Model, Red Paint, Cast Iron, Kenton, 10 In.	790
Car, Coupe, Green, Blue Paint, Tin, Windup, Marklin, 14 In..	790
Car, Dodge, Coupe, Driver, Black Paint, Cast Iron, Arcade, 9 In..	273
Car, Driver, Flywheel, Hood Crank, Painted, Pressed Steel, Converse, 9 In.	270
Car, Driver, White, Red, Blue Paint, Clockwork, Germany, 7 ¾ In.	1580
Car, Dump, Flivver, Open, Black Paint, Pressed Steel, Buddy L, 12 ½ In.	474
Car, Easter Rabbit, Chick, Fabric Egg, Moss Covered, 9 In.	652
Car, Farbs Fantastic Car Kooks, Hot Rodney, No. 5854, Redline, Hot Wheels, 1972 ....*illus*	75
Car, Ferrari, 250GT, White, Tin, Flocked Seats, Box, Asahi, Japan, 1960s, 9 ½ In.	767
Car, Fire Chief, Tin, Friction, Louis Marx, 20 In..	171
Car, Flintstones, Rubble's Wreck, Barney Rubble Driver, Tin Lithograph, Linemar, 7 In.	443
Car, Ford, Custom Ranch Wagon, 1956 Model, Tin Litho, Friction, Bandai, Box, 12 In.	1770
Car, Ford, Fairlane, Skyliner, Battery Operated, TN, Japan, Box, 10 x 5 In.	360
Car, Ford, Model A, Sedan, Iron, Decal, Spoke Wheels, Arcade, c.1928, 6 ½ In. ....*illus*	472
Car, Ford, Mustang, 1966 Model, Friction, Wen-Mac, 16 In.	61
Car, Ford, Mustang, Top Opens, Battery Operated, Japan, 1966, 13 ½ In.....................................	275
Car, Ford, Sedan, Brown, Tootsietoy, 1934, 3 In.	135
Car, Ford, Station Wagon, 1961 Model, Orange, Cream, Tin, Battery, Japan, Box, 10 In.	68
Car, Ford, Thunderbird, 1956 Model, Red, White, Tin, Battery, Nomura, Box, 11 In.	413
Car, Horseless Carriage, Black, Red Paint, Tin, Windup, 10 ½ In.	365
Car, Horseless Carriage, Driver, Black Paint, Tin, Windup, Gunthermann, 10 In...........................	2607
Car, Horseless Carriage, Driver, Tin, Windup, Lehmann, 5 ½ In.	577
Car, Irish Mail, Driver, Tin Lithograph, Rubber Tires, Ny-Lint, 8 ½ In.	150

Toy, Baby Tractor, Farmer, Graphic Dashboard, Penny Toy, Kellermann, 3 In. $236

Bertoia Auctions

Toy, Baby, Crawling, Painted, Flock Hat, Clockwork, Germany, 5 ¼ In. $944

Bertoia Auctions

Toy, Balloon Vendor, Monkeys, Music Box, Mechanical Arm, Animals, Tin Litho, Kellerman, 6 ½ In. $472

Bertoia Auctions

This is an edited listing of current prices. Visit **Kovels.com** to check thousands of prices from previous years and sign up for free information on trends, tips, reproductions, marks, and more.

Toy, Boardwalk Delight, Girl, Chair, Tin, Celluloid, Windup, CK, Japan, 8 ½ In. $295

Bertoia Auctions

Toy, Box, For Humpty Dumpty Circus, Teddy's Adventures, Schoenhut, 18 x 30 In. $443

Bertoia Auctions

Toy, Boxer Rebellion, Chinese Figures, Tossing Figure, Clockwork, Lehmann, 5 x 5 In. $14,160

Bertoia Auctions

Toy, Bus, Volkswagen, Beach Bomb, No. 6274, Redline, Hot Wheels, Mattel, On Card, 1969 $635

Serious Toyz

Car, Jalopy, Driver, Slogans, Tin Lithograph, Windup, Marx, 7 In. ....*illus*	89
Car, Komical Kop, Open Top, Beat It Cop, Tin Litho, Clockwork, Marx, 7 ½ In.	266 to 325
Car, LaSalle, Coupe, Nickel Grill, Rubber Tires, Cast Iron, Dent, 4 ½ In. ....*illus*	708
Car, Limousine, Blue, Cream, Tin Lithograph, Windup, Tippco, 10 In....................................	243
Car, Limousine, Canvas Top Down, Driver, Painted, Tin Litho, Windup, Germany, 9 In.	948
Car, Limousine, Citroen, B 14, Black, Yellow, Battery Operated, Brepsomy, France, 20 In.............	851
Car, Limousine, Convertible, Driver, Rider, Painted, Tin, Clockwork, Germany, 12 In.	1778
Car, Limousine, Driver, 2 Riders, Painted, Tin, Clockwork, Carette, 12 ½ In.............................	2370
Car, Limousine, Driver, Blue, Red Paint, Tin, Windup, Fischer, 13 In..	851
Car, Limousine, Driver, Convertible Top Up, Painted, Tin, Windup, Fischer, 10 In.	668
Car, Limousine, Driver, Red Paint, Tin, Windup, Carette, Germany, 12 In..............................	1659
Car, Limousine, Green Paint, Tin, Windup, Bing, 15 ½ In..	1337
Car, Limousine, Hillclimber, Orange, Black, Tin, 12 In..	119
Car, Limousine, Luggage Rack, Passengers, Blue, Yellow, Flywheel, Distler, Penny, 4 In............	384
Car, Limousine, Tin Windup, Germany, 6 In..	326
Car, Lincoln, Continental, Mark V, Retractable Top, Remote Control, Cragstan, Box, 11 In.	207
Car, Lincoln, Touring, Black, Gold Paint, Cast Iron, A.C. Williams, 9 In..................................	474
Car, Lionel, Boxcar, No. 214, Cream, Orange Roof, Brass Trim, Standard Gauge, Box................	192
Car, Lionel, Flat, No. SG 211, Nickel Stakes, Lumber Load, Brass On Wheels, Box....................	156
Car, Lionel, Hopper, No. 216, Dark Green, Brass Trim, Standard Gauge, Box.........................	192
Car, Lionel, Locomotive, No. 42, Green, Standard Gauge...	348
Car, Lionel, Oil Tanker, No. 215, Green, Brass Trim, Standard Gauge, Box............................	228
Car, Mercedes-Benz, 300SL, Red, Tootsietoy, Box, 6 In...	235
Car, MG, Midget, 1950s Model, Convertible, Red, Tin Lithograph, Bandai, Box, 10 In.	236
Car, Moxie, Horse, Rider Driving, Blue, Cutout, Tin, 1917, 9 In..	2700
Car, Pontiac, 1954 Model, Driver, Passenger, Pet, Tin Litho, Friction, Box, Japan, 10 In..............	177
Car, Pressed Steel, Wyandotte, 1930s, 15 In..	245
Car, Purple Sunroof, Redline, Evil Weevil, Hot Wheels, 1971...	675
Car, Racing, Blue, Yellow Paint, Cast Iron, Hubley, 1930s, 7 ¼ In..	406
Car, Racing, Convertible, Green Paint, Pressed Steel, Friction, Wyandotte, 9 ¾ In...................	148
Car, Racing, Driver, Tin Lithograph, Blue, Yellow, Spoke Wheels, Fischer, Penny, 4 ½ In.............	295
Car, Racing, Driver, Yellow & Orange, Disc Wheels, Tin Lithograph, Germany, Penny, 3 In.	148
Car, Racing, Golden Arrow, Driver, Yellow, Red, Black Paint, Cast Iron, Hubley, 10 ½ In.	356
Car, Racing, Green Cast Iron, Driver, Spoke Wheels, Rubber Tires, Vindex, c.1929, 11 In.............	4130
Car, Racing, Indy, Gas-Powered, Velvet Drive, Front Wheel Drive, B.B. Korn, 20 ½ In...............	4444
Car, Racing, Mercedes-Benz, No. 7, Driver, Painted, Tin, Windup, Marklin, 15 In......................	1094
Car, Racing, No. 5, Red, Silver Paint, Cast Iron, Hubley, 9 ½ In..	456
Car, Racing, No. 7, Pressed Steel, Push, Marx, 1930s, 12 In...	295
Car, Racing, Silva Tether, No. 2, Wood, Composition, Aluminum, Painted, c.1958, 17 In.	2370
Car, Racing, Studio 1050, Blue, Red Wheels, Tin, Windup, Schuco, 5 In.................................	45
Car, Radio, Camouflage, Green, Yellow, Driver, Tin, Windup, Tippco, 9 In..............................	600
Car, Red Cross, Bing, Metal, Windows All Around, Red Cross On Top, 1 Gauge, 8 In...............	180
Car, Roadster, Convertible, Red, Die Cast, Faith Mfg. Co., 10 ½ In.......................................	61
Car, Rolls-Royce, Silver Cloud, White, Litho Dash, Tin, Friction, Bandai, Box, 1960s, 11 In.	649
Car, School, 4 Boys, Tin, Windup, Marx, 1950s, 6 In...	195
Car, Sedan, Black, Yellow Paint, Pressed Steel, Schiebels, 18 In..	330
Car, Sedan, Graham, Gold, Green Paint, Pressed Steel, Cor-Cor, 19 ½ In..............................	533
Car, Streamline Roadster, Driver, Blue, Steel, Applied Tin Trim, 1930s, 6 In............................	145
Car, Stutz Roadster, Convertible, Red, Yellow, Silver Paint, Cast Iron, Kilgore, 10 ½ In.	425
Car, Sugar Caddy, Redline Spoilers, Aqua, Factory Sealed, Hot Wheels, 1971..........................	253
Car, Touring, Red Paint, Cast Iron, Kenton, 12 In..	365
Car, Touring, Top Down, Green, Gold, Driver, 3 Riders, Iron, A.C. Williams, 1920s, 12 In............	767
Car, Uhu, Amphibious, Tin Lithograph, Lehmann, 9 ½ In..	578
Car, Uncle Wiggily, Tin Lithograph, Distler, c.1928, 9 ½ In..	2242
Car, Willys-Knight, Sedan, Driver, Nickel, Cast Iron, Kenton, c.1926, 12 In. ....*illus*	374
Car, Woody, Burgundy, Orange, Green Paint, Buddy L, 18 ½ In..	304
Carousel, 3 Riders On Horses, Tin, Ruffled Canopy, Cast-Iron Wheels, Push Stick, 17 In............	212
Carousel, Children, Horses, Airplanes, Tin Lithograph, Windup, Wolverine, 12 In. ....*illus*	501
Carousel, Swan-Go-Around, Painted, Tin, Germany, 6 In...	330
Carriage, Doll's, Fabric Cover, Rubber Wheels, Metal, Red, France, 12 x 9 In..........................	283
Carriage, Doll's, Metal Frame, Handle, Vinyl Hood, Doucet, France, 12 x 10 In.	283
Carriage, Doll's, Tin, Streamline Fenders, Green Paint, c.1903, 23 x 20 In..............................	485
Carriage, Doll's, Wicker, Umbrella, Metal Spoke Wheels, Victorian, 12 x 36 x 33 In.	300
Carriage, Doll's, Wicker, Wire Wheels, 30 x 32 In...	23
Carriage, Lights, Painted, Tin, Germany, 9 ¾ x 24 In..	1458
Cart, Dog Drawn, Black, White Paint, Cast Iron, Harris, 9 ½ In..	122

Cart, Dog Drawn, Cast Iron, 2 Red Spoke Wheels, Seated Driver, Wilkins, 10 In.	885
Cart, Donkey & Clown, Tin, Windup, Germany, Lehmann, 8 In.	186
Cart, Donkey, Driver, Mama Katzenjammer, Spanking Child, Cast Iron, Kenton, 11 ½ In.	790
Cart, Dump, Horse Drawn, Shovel, Burgundy, Silver, Yellow Paint, Cast Iron, Tin, 10 In.	91
Cart, Goat, Pulling Open Carriage, Driver, Silver, Red Paint, Cast Iron, Harris, 9 In.	237
Cart, Horse Drawn, Black Paint, Cast Iron, 10 In.	182
Cart, Horse Drawn, Driver, White, Black, Red Paint, Cast Iron, Pratt & Letchworth, 16 In.	213
Cart, Horse Drawn, Open, Red, Black Paint, Cast Iron, Carpenter, 12 ½ In.	122
Cart, Horse Drawn, Painted, Cast Iron, 10 In.	90
Cart, Horse Drawn, Woman Driver, Painted, Cast Iron, Shimmer, 10 In.	119
Cart, Ice Cream, 5 Cents, Driver, Bell Rings, Tin Litho, Windup, Courtland, 6 ½ In.	424
Cart, Ice, Driver, Horse Drawn, Red, White Paint, Cast Iron, Hubley, 15 In.	365
Cart, Irish Mail, Driver, Tin, 14 ½ In.	770
Cart, Lion Drawn, Girl Rider, Painted, Cast Iron, Pull Toy, 7 ½ In.	213
Cart, Patriotic, 3 Women, Bell, Clockwork, Althof Bergmann, 10 In. ....*illus*	6490
Cash Register, Tom Thumb, Red, Western Stamping Co., c.1945, 7 x 7 x 6 In.	20
Cat, Felix, Black, Cream, On Scooter, Orange, Green, Tin, Windup, 8 In.	395
Cat, Felix, On Yellow Wheel, Wood, Black, White Paint, Push Toy, 13 ½ In.	154
Cat, Felix, Scooter, Tin, Pull Toy, J. Chein & Co., 7 ½ In.	720
Cat, Felix, Speedy, Pull Toy, Schoenhut, Pat Sullivan Copyright 1924, 11 ½ In.	960
Cat, Sitting, Felt, Shoebutton Eyes, Ear Button, Steiff, 1900s, 4 ½ In. ....*illus*	1422
Cat, Velvet, Air-Brushed Stripes, Glass Eyes, Wheels, Steiff, c.1915, 7 ½ In. ....*illus*	2052
Caterpillar, Scraper, Plastic, Revell, 1952, 11 In.	95
Chair, Doll's, Ebony, Spindles, Gilt, Silk Cover, Fringe, c.1885, 12 In. ....*illus*	448
Chair, Doll's, Ladder Back, Red, Gold Paint, 1800s, 7 In.	948
Chair, Doll's, Rocking, Plank Seat, Bird, Fruit, Red Paint, Pa., c.1850, 16 ½ In.	415
Chandelier, Doll's, Crystal, Beads, Prismatic Glass, Teardrops, Wire Frame, c.1875, 11 In.	3808
Charleston Trio, Black Dancer, Fiddler, Dog, Stage, Tin Litho, Windup, Louis Marx, 10 In.	585
Charleston Trio, Black Dancers, Tin Lithograph, Marx, c.1926, 9 ½ In.	438
Chemistry Set, Wood, Test Tubes, Booklet, Chemcraft, No. 2, c.1900	125
Cherub In Shoe, Horse Drawn, Painted, Cast Iron, Kenton, Pull Toy, 8 ½ In.	213
Chest, Doll's, Mahogany, Bowfront, c.1850, 7 ¼ x 6 ½ In.	711
Chest, Doll's, Rosewood, Handles, c.1800, 8 ½ x 15 In.	359
Chest, Doll's, Walnut, Hinged Lid, Va., c.1850, 6 x 14 ½ In.	161
Chest, Doll's, Walnut, Scalloped Backsplash, 3 Drawers, c.1820, 17 x 13 In.	296
Chicken Snatcher, Black Man Holding Chicken, Dog Nips, Tin, Marx, 8 ¼ In.	885
Chicken, Chicks In Cart, Wheels, Multicolor, Cast Iron, U.S. Hardware, Pull Toy, 8 In.	326
Chicken, Pulling Chick, Tin, Windup, German, c.1950, 3 ½ x 9 ½ In.	374
Chicken, Wings Flap, Clucks, Spoke Wheels, Clockwork, Gunthermann, 6 ¾ In.	531
Circus, Flying, Elephant, Balancing Airplane, Tin Lithograph, Windup, Unique Art, 30 In.	472
Circus, Humpty Dumpty, Performers, Accessories, Wood, Painted, Schoenhut, Box, c.1910	3584
Circus, Humpty Dumpty, Tent, Wood, Carved, Schoenhut, Box, c.1925, 27 x 24 In. ....*illus*	2520
Circus, Humpty Dumpty, Trapeze, Ring Master, Clown, Accessories, Schoenhut, 24 In.	1896
Circus, Ring-A-Ling, Ringmaster, Animals, Clown, Tin Litho, Clockwork, Marx, 7 In.	1416
Clicker, PEZ, Boy, Girl, Multicolor, 2 ½ x 3 ½ In.	253
Clown & Monkey, Tin, Penny Toy, 4 In.	354
Clown The Magician, Nose Lights Up, Does Card Tricks, Alps For Cragstan, Box, 11 In.	330
Clown, Bisque, Glass Eyes, Wood, Plays Cello When Pulled, Wheeled Platform, c.1910, 14 In.	1007
Clown, Clarabell, Tin, Windup, Linemar, 4 ¾ In.	350
Clown, On Tricycle, Tin, Windup, Japan, 1950s, 6 In.	195
Clown, Roller Skating, Tin, Felt Cloth, Windup, U.S. Zone, Germany, 8 ½ In.	236
Clown, Roly Poly, Multicolor Paint, Composition, 15 ½ In.	61
Clown, Roly Poly, Musical, Eyes Move Side To Side When Rocked, Germany, 15 In.	36
Clown, Zilotone, Play Xylophone, Tin, Windup, Discs, Wolverine, 9 In. ....*illus*	425
Coach, Tally Ho, Cast Iron, Blue, Cream, 7 Figures, 4 Rearing Horses, Carpenter, 26 In.	3835
Columbus Spiral Block Tower, Paper, Wood, Litho, Flag, Springs, Bliss, Box, 60 In.	8888
Cookware, Enamelware, Pots, Pans, Platter, Funnel, Blue & White, 2 To 4 In., 6 Piece	502
Couch, Fainting, Doll's, Horsehair Stuffing, Fabric, Oak, 20 x 13 In.	68
Counter, Dry Goods, General Store, Rack, Shelves, 9 Drawers, Lift-Top Desk, 14 x 13 In.	652
Cowboy, Behind Pig, Hand Crank, Wood Carved, Willard Watson, c.1980, 12 In.	35
Cowboy, Bucking Bronco, Green Base, Tin, Windup, Lehmann, 7 ½ In.	304
Cradle, Doll's, Pine, Blue Paint, Pa., c.1850, 10 ½ x 21 In.	30
Cradle, Doll's, Pine, Poplar, Shaped Back, Pa., c.1850, 13 ½ x 20 In.	119
Cradle, Doll's, Walnut, Cutout Sides, Ends, Pa., c.1845, 8 ¾ x 16 In.	92
Cradle, Doll's, Wood, Carved, Painted, Pierced Birds, Finials, Monogram, 22 x 25 In.	652
Crane, Mechanical, Magnetic, Decal, Orange, Green Paint, Pressed Steel, Buddy L, 10 In.	207

Toy, Canoe, Birch Bark, Great Lakes Area, c.1950s, 3 ½ x 15 ¼ x 4 In.
$52

Allard Auctions

Toy, Cap Gun, Shoot The Hat, Mechanical, Man Puts Hat On Man, Explodes Cap, 5 x 5 In.
$575

Wm Morford Auctions

Toy, Car, Aston-Martin, 1965 Model, Ejects Driver, Battery, Gilbert, Japan, Box, 11 In.
$590

Bertoia Auctions

Toy, Car, Benz Racer, Go Stop, Tin Litho, Battery, Japan, Box, c.1950s, 11 In.
$390

Victorian Casino Antiques

T

> **TIP**
> *Think about security around outdoor fire escapes, skylights, roof doors, bay windows, and windows under second floor windows.*

Toy, Car, Farbs Fantastic Car Kooks, Hot Rodney, No. 5854, Redline, Hot Wheels, 1972
$75

Serious Toyz

Toy, Car, Ford, Model A, Sedan, Iron, Decal, Spoke Wheels, Arcade, c.1928, 6 ½ In.
$472

Bertoia Auctions

Toy, Car, Jalopy, Driver, Slogans, Tin Lithograph, Windup, Marx, 7 In.
$89

Bertoia Auctions

Toy, Car, LaSalle, Coupe, Nickel Grill, Rubber Tires, Cast Iron, Dent, 4 ½ In.
$708

Bertoia Auctions

Daughter Anne

In 1952 Anne Odel could take a toy to school if it was no larger than a matchbox. Her father made a die-cast steam roller, the first of the famous Matchbox toys.

Crane, Tin, Red, Blue Paint, Wolverine, 19 In.	34
Crash Car, Motorcycle, Spoked Wheel, Rubber Tires, Hubley, 1930s, 12 In. ......*illus*	2666
Crawling Black Baby, Hair Ribbons, Celluloid, Windup, 5 In.	180
Crocodile, Molded, Realistic Painting, Composition, 10 ½ x 44 x 78 In.	861
Cyclist, Kiddy, Boy On Tricycle, Tin Lithograph, Windup, Unique Art, 8 ½ In.	147
Cyclist, Kiddy, Tin Lithograph, Windup, Box, Unique Art, 1950s, 7 ½ x 9 In.	384
Dagwood Aeroplane, Tin Lithograph, Clockwork Driven, Marx, c.1935, 9 In.	1534
Dagwood Driving Car, Tin Lithograph, Clockwork, Marx, 8 In.	649
Dancer On Platform, Tin Litho, Green Embossed Box, Distler, Germany, Penny, 4 In.	354
Dancer, Jigger, Metal Head, Clockwork, Automatic Toy Works, c.1875, 11 In.	813
Dancer, Musician, Tin, Windup, Gunthermann, Germany, 8 x 9 In.	1413
Dancin' Dina, Black Tap Dancer, Wood, Painted, Spring Jointed, Wire Handle	120
Dancing Bears, Black, Yellow Paint, Tin, Wheel Platform, Pull Toy, Germany, 6 In.	356
Dancing Couple, Gnomes, Wheeled Platform, Multicolor Paint, Tin, Pull Toy, 9 ½ In.	593
Dancing Man, Black, Papier-Mache, Metal, Cloth, Wood Base, Clockwork, 1870s, 12 x 8 In.	972
Dancing Sailor, Sways & Kicks, Metal, Cloth Uniform, Clockwork, Lehmann, Box, 7 In.	1652
Dapper Dan, Black Porter Dances On Trunk, Tin Lithograph, Clockwork, Louis Marx, 10 In.	708
Dapper Dan, Coon Jigger, Dancing, Yellow, Green Check Outfit, Tin Litho, Marx, 11 In.	415
Delivery Boy, Pushing Cart, Package, Striped Pants, Tin, Windup, Martin, France, 7 In.	547
Diorama, Butcher Shop, 2 Men, Hanging Meats, Flowers, England, c.1850, 19 x 31 In.	8850
Diorama, Country Store, Grain Painted, Accessories, Germany, c.1900, 12 x 21 In.	189
Ditcher, Buckeye, Orange & Green, Nickel Plated, Cast Iron, Kenton, 6 In. ....*illus*	593
Dog, Boxer, Walking, Kid Leather, Glass Eyes, Painted, Collar, Windup, Barks, 11 In.	1276
Dog, Bulldog, Snapping, Glass Eyes, Wheels, Pull Chain, Head Nods, Growls, 19 In.	2242
Dog, Pug, Brown, Black Eyes, Jointed, Leather Collar, Ear Button, Steiff, 1903, 16 In.	1200
Dolls are listed in the Doll category.	
Dollhouse Furniture, Settee, Chairs, Table, Napoleon III, Paper, Wood, Painted, c.1860	1008
Dollhouse Furniture, Urn, Porcelain, Painted, Landscape, Handles, France, 5 In., Pair ....*illus*	1064
Dollhouse, 4 Rooms, Yellow, Red Roof, Latticework, Panel, Schoenhut, 21 x 22 In.	425
Dollhouse, 12 Rooms, Barbizon, Elevator, Garage, Stucco, Slate Roof, McNeil, 67 x 88 In.	1888
Dollhouse, 2 Story, 6 Rooms, Porch, Tin Lithograph, Red, White, 1950s, 33 x 12 x 19 In.	18
Dollhouse, 2 Story, Lembach House, Wood, Painted, Furniture, C. Hacker, 25 x 25 In.	6720
Dollhouse, 2 Story, Victorian, Porch, Balcony, Carved Trim, Painted, c.1900, 20 x 19 In.	230
Dollhouse, 2 Story, Wood, Porch, Railing, Elevator, Paper Lithograph, c.1890, 22 x 14 In.	1344
Dollhouse, 2 Story, Wood, Sliding Panels, Painted, Windows, Paper Litho, c.1880, 22 In.	1232
Dollhouse, 3 Story, Leaded Skylight, Furniture, Stand, E. Landsdown, 1988, 53 x 22 In.	960
Dollhouse, 3 Story, Wood, Bay Windows Ends, Tan, Brown Paint, c.1880, 24 x 20 In.	720
Dollhouse, Bathtub, Tin, Wood Stand, Blue Paint, 13 In.	153
Dollhouse, Bungalow, 4 Rooms, Wood, Red Roof, Hinged, Stairs, Gottschalk, 20 x 17 In.	547
Dollhouse, Bungalow, Green Roof, Lifts, Side Yard, Picket Fence, Schoenhut, 24 In.	243
Dollhouse, Clothes, Accessories, Fishbowl, Stand, Chandeliers, Frame, Crystals, c.1890, 5 In.	3808
Dollhouse, Deauville, Blue Roof, Openwork Railings, Paper Litho, Gottschalk, 19 x 11 In.	830
Dollhouse, Paper On Wood, R. Bliss, 9 ½ In.	72
Dollhouse, Room, Bedroom Furniture, Szalasi Spielwaren, Germany, 22 x 16 In.	509
Donkey, Bucky Burro, Kicks Back Legs, Paper On Wood, No. 166, Fisher-Price, 12 In.	36
Donkey, Woman Chasing, Wheeled Base, Painted, Wood, Pull Toy, 17 In.	30
Donkey, Woman Rider, Painted, Cast Iron, Pull Toy, N.N. Hill Brass Co., 5 ¾ In.	178
Dresser, Doll's, 4 Drawers, Shaped Mirror, Curled Feet, Wood, 1910, 24 x 14 In.	330
Dresser, Doll's, Mirror, 3 Drawers, Red, Black Paint, Cast Iron, c.1890, 10 x 4 ¾ In.	504
Dresser, Doll's, Mixed Woods, Inlays, Mirror, Candleholders, J. Kilroy, 1888, 16 x 11 In.	920
Dresser, Doll's, Pine, 3 Drawers, Scrolled Columns, Black Paint, Va., c.1845, 15 x 12 In.	1495
Dresser, Doll's, Walnut, 3 Drawers, Scalloped Backsplash, c.1850, 7 x 13 In.	296
Drill, John Deere Van Brunt, Cast Iron, Vindex, 9 ½ In.	1778
Drum Major, Tin Lithograph, Windup, No. 27, Wolverine, 13 ½ In.	96
Drum, Gulliver's Travels, Characters, Tin Lithograph Band, J. Chein, 1939, 13 x 5 In. ....*illus*	115
Drum, Tin, Wood, Painted Rims, Cowboys, Indians, 8 ¼ x 10 ¼ In.	83
Drummer, Black, Vibrates, Plays Cymbals, Beats Drum, Tin, Cloth, Schuco, Box, 5 In.	273
Elephant, Jumbo Bak-Up, Beaded Trunk, Wood, Paper, Windup, Fisher-Price, Box, 10 In.	840
Elephant, Merry-Go-Round, Wheeled Platform, Painted, Tin, Pull Toy, 9 In.	889
Erector Set, Zeppelin, Pressed Steel, Red Case, 27 In.	365
Factory, Steam Plant, Model, Lithograph, Mahogany Base, Germany, 17 In.	365
Farmyard, Fence, House, 5 Animals, Wood, Composition, Elastolin, Germany, 24 x 14 In.	330
Ferris Wheel, 4 Gondolas, Tin Lithograph, Meier, Germany, Penny, c.1920, 2 ½ In.	177
Ferris Wheel, 6 Gondolas, 2 Figures, Cast Iron, Clockwork, Hubley, 17 In.	1534
Ferris Wheel, 6 Gondolas, Clown Face, Tin Litho, Clockwork, Chein, Box, 16 ½ In.	325
Ferris Wheel, 6 Gondolas, Mickey Mouse, Tin Litho, Multicolor, Clockwork, Chein, 17 In.	384

Ferris Wheel, Giant Ride, Tin, Windup, Ohio Art, 16 In.	68
Ferris Wheel, Hercules, Tin, Windup, Painted, Chein, 17 In.	90
Ferris Wheel, Tin Lithograph, Windup, Chein, Box, 17 In.	540
Figure, Butter & Egg Man, Carrying Chicken, Multicolor, Tin Litho, Windup, Marx, 7 ¾ In.	2242
Figure, Hey-Hey, Chicken Snatcher, Dog Chomping At Rump, Tin Litho, 9 In.	2006
Fire Pumper, 2-Man Hand Pump, Friendship 1774, Cast Iron, Colark Ship Model, 15 In.	1121
Fire Station, 2 Story, Faux Stone Exterior, 2 Doors, Painted, Wood, 30 x 37 In.	563
Fire Station, Painted, Cast Iron, Wood, Cloth, Carpenter, 26 In.	3555
Fire Station, Wood, Cast-Iron Facade & Windows, Doors Open, Bell, Ives, c.1890, 12 In.	2360
Fire Truck, Aerial Ladder, No. 79, Keystone, 1926, 30 In.	850
Fire Truck, Aerial Ladder, Red Paint, Pressed Steel, Buddy L, 38 ½ In.	456
Fire Truck, Driver, Wood Ladder, Cast Iron, Red, Gold Trim, Dent, 19 In.	2006
Fire Truck, Extension Ladders, Hose Reel, Wrecker Boom, No. 205, Buddy L, 25 In.	1541
Fire Truck, Hook & Ladder, Pressed Steel, No. 760, Structo, Box, 33 In.	158
Fire Truck, Hook & Ladder, Red, White Paint, Pressed Steel, Tonka, 1950s, 31 In.	68
Fire Truck, Hook & Ladder, Typhoon, Pressed Steel, Structo, Ertl Toys, c.1965, Box, 30 In.	60
Fire Truck, Hose Truck, Packard Fire Department, Painted, Steel, Keystone, 28 In.	334
Fire Truck, Ladder & Hose, Pressed Steel, Buddy L, 1930s, 27 In.	1938
Fire Truck, Ladder, Iron, Bumper, Hood Ornament, Searchlight, Nickel Plate, Hubley, 21 In.	1955
Fire Truck, Ladder, Mack, Driver, Red Paint, Cast Iron, Arcade, 10 ½ In.	547
Fire Truck, Ladder, Mack, Driver, Red, Yellow Paint, Cast Iron, 17 ½ In.	415
Fire Truck, Ladder, No. 2014, Doepke, 1953, 33 In.	395
Fire Truck, Pressed Steel, Kelmut, 1920s, 38 In.	1482
Fire Truck, Pumper, Cast Iron, 20 ¾ In.	486
Fire Truck, Pumper, Christie Transitional, Cast Iron, Boiler, 2 Men, Hubley, 1920s, 14 In.	4720
Fire Truck, Pumper, Driver, Ladders, Red, Silver Paint, Cast Iron, Hubley, 11 In.	948
Fire Truck, Pumper, Driver, Painted, Pressed Steel, Tin, Wood, Windup, Kingsbury, 10 In.	210
Fire Truck, Pumper, Driver, Red, Gold Paint, Cast Iron, Kenton, 11 In.	415
Fire Truck, Pumper, Driver, Rider, Red, Black, Gold Paint, Cast Iron, Carpenter, 18 ½ In.	889
Fire Truck, Pumper, Driver, Yellow, Red, Silver, Tin, Windup, Kingsbury, 11 In.	178
Fire Truck, Pumper, Ford, 1939 Model, Cast Iron, Red, Silver, 6 Men, Arcade, 1940s, 13 In.	708
Fire Truck, Pumper, Hose, Driver, Red, Silver Blue Paint, Cast Iron, Kenton, 14 ½ In.	516
Fire Truck, Pumper, Red, Gold Paint, Pressed Steel, Kingsbury, 23 In.	593
Fire Truck, Pumper, Red, Silver Paint, Cast Iron, 13 ½ In.	243
Fire Truck, Pumper, Red, Tan Paint, Pressed Steel, Kingsbury, Pull Toy, 23 In.	474
Fire Truck, Pumper, Silver, Red Paint, Cast Iron, Hubley, 12 ½ In.	729
Fire Truck, Pumper, Steam, Red, Black Paint, Tin, Ernst Plank, 16 ½ In.	1185
Fire Truck, Pumper, Tin, Windup, Painted, 9 ¼ In.	200
Fire Truck, Snoopy Gus, Wild Fireman, Dog, Ladder, Tin Litho, Marx, Box, 9 In.	885
Fire Truck, Tanker, Driver, Red Paint, Cast Iron, Arcade, 14 In.	296
Fire Truck, Water Tower, American LaFrance, Red Paint, Pressed Steel, Sturditoy, 34 In.	889
Fire Wagon, 2 Horses, Driver, Black, White, Red Paint, Cast Iron, Ives, 25 In.	2133
Fire Wagon, 2 Horses, Driver, Hose Reel, Rider, Painted, Cast Iron, Ideal Toy Co., 24 In.	1067
Fire Wagon, 2 Horses, Driver, Hose Reel, Wheels, Painted, Cast Iron, Shimmer, 13 ¾ In.	385
Fire Wagon, 2 Horses, Ladder, 2 Drivers, Painted, Cast Iron, Carpenter, 24 ½ In.	770
Fire Wagon, Chemical, Horse Drawn, Driver, Painted, Cast Iron, 21 ½ In.	2309
Fire Wagon, Fire Patrol, Horse Drawn, Driver, Painted, Cast Iron, Ives, 21 In.	2844
Fire Wagon, Fire Patrol, Horses, 4 Firemen, Painted, Cast Iron, Carpenter, 16 ½ In.	711
Fire Wagon, Horse Drawn, Chemical, Drivers, Painted, Iron, Harris, 20 In.	1944
Fire Wagon, Horse Drawn, Driver, Firemen, Blue, Gold Paint, Cast Iron, Carpenter, 16 In.	273
Fire Wagon, Horse Drawn, Driver, Hose Reel, Painted, Iron, Carpenter, 14 In.	770
Fire Wagon, Horse Drawn, Fire Chief Driver, Painted, Iron, Hubley, 15 In.	267
Fire Wagon, Horse Drawn, Ladder, Painted, Cast Iron, 30 In.	385
Fire Wagon, Horse Drawn, Water Tower, Driver, Painted, Cast Iron, 30 In.	365
Fire Wagon, Ladder, Horse Drawn, Phoenix, Drivers, Painted, Cast Iron, Ives, 26 In.	395
Fire Wagon, Pumper, 2 Horses, Driver, White, Black, Red Paint, Iron, Carpenter, 18 In.	425
Fire Wagon, Pumper, 3 Horses, Driver, Painted, Cast Iron, Hubley, 21 ½ In.	504
Fire Wagon, Pumper, Cast Iron, Painted, c.1820, 19 ½ In.	563
Fire Wagon, Pumper, Horse Drawn, Cast Iron, 21 ½ In.	326
Fire Wagon, Pumper, Horse Drawn, Driver, Painted, Cast Iron, 15 In.	420
Fire Wagon, Pumper, Horse Drawn, Driver, Painted, Cast Iron, 19 In.	182
Fire Wagon, Pumper, Horse Drawn, Painted, Cast Iron, 24 In.	474
Fire Wagon, Pumper, Horse Drawn, Red, Black, Gold Paint, Cast Iron, Hubley, 22 In.	504
Fire Wagon, Pumper, Horse Drawn, Silver, Red Paint, Painted, Cast Iron, Ideal, 22 ½ In.	2015
Fire Wagon, Pumper, Horses, Rear, Driver, Painted, Tin, Cast Iron, 17 ¾ In.	300
Flintstones, Tank, Rolls Over, Tin Lithograph, Windup, Marx, 3 ¾ In.	354

Toy, Car, Willys-Knight, Sedan, Driver, Nickel, Cast Iron, Kenton, c.1926, 12 In.
$374

Toy, Carousel, Children, Horses, Airplanes, Tin Lithograph, Windup, Wolverine, 12 In.
$501

Toy, Cart, Patriotic, 3 Women, Bell, Clockwork, Althof Bergmann, 10 In.
$6,490

Toy, Cat, Sitting, Felt, Shoebutton Eyes, Ear Button, Steiff, 1900s, 4 ½ In.
$1,422

T

Toy, Cat, Velvet, Air-Brushed Stripes, Glass Eyes, Wheels, Steiff, c.1915, 7 ½ In.
$2,052

Theriault's

Toy, Chair, Doll's, Ebony, Spindles, Gilt, Silk Cover, Fringe, c.1885, 12 In.
$448

Theriault's

Toy, Circus, Humpty Dumpty, Tent, Wood, Carved, Schoenhut, Box, c.1925, 27 x 24 In.
$2,520

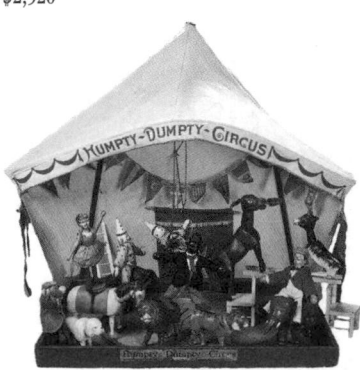

Theriault's

Toy, Crash Car, Motorcycle, Spoked Wheel, Rubber Tires, Hubley, 1930s, 12 In.
$2,666

James D. Julia Auctioneers

Toy, Ditcher, Buckeye, Orange & Green, Nickel Plated, Cast Iron, Kenton, 6 In.
$593

James D. Julia Auctioneers

Toy, Dollhouse Furniture, Urn, Porcelain, Painted, Landscape, Handles, France, 5 In., Pair
$1,064

Theriault's

Toy, Drum, Gulliver's Travels, Characters, Tin Lithograph Band, J. Chein, 1939, 13 x 5 In.
$115

Hake's Americana & Collectibles

Toy, Gnomes, Sawing Log, Tin Litho, Fischer, Germany, Penny Toy, 4 ¼ In.
$265

Bertoia Auctions

Toy, Goose, Witch, Cat, Walks, Tin Litho, Windup, Unique Art, 1930s, 8 ½ In.
$330

Victorian Casino Antiques

Toy, Grasshopper, Painted, Cast Iron, Aluminum, Rubber Tires, Articulated Action, Pull Toy, Hubley, 10 In.
$443

Bertoia Auctions

T

Flying Saucer, UFO-X2, Tin, Battery Operated, Japan, Box, 6 In.	68
Football Player, Press Lever, Kicks Rubber Football, Cast Iron, Painted, 1920s, 8 In.	273
Foxy Grandpa, Flip Toy, Painted, Cast Iron, 3 ¾ In.	89
Fred Flintstone, Riding Dino The Dinosaur, Tin Lithograph, Purple Dino, Marx, Box, 8 In.	502
Freddie Fire Plug, Wood, Take-A-Part, Doepke, Box, 1957, 6 In.	125
Frog, Seesaw, Yellow Wheeled Base, Painted, Tin, Cast Iron, Pull Toy, 5 ½ In.	243
Furniture, Barbie, Wardrobe, Clothes, Vanity, Dresser Set, Bench, Susy Goose	197
Games are listed in the Game category.	
Gamecocks, Fighting On Platform, Tin Lithograph, Windup, Einflat, Germany, 10 In.	354
Gas Pump, Red Paint, Arcade, 6 In.	119
Giraffe, Plush, Ear Button, Steiff, 1980s, 8 In.	1440
Girl, Skipping Rope, Porcelain, Muslin Dress, Japanned Pillar, Clockwork, 6 In.	4252
Giro-Plane, Green, Nickeled, Rubber Tires, Hubley, 3 ¾ In.	295
Glass-Blowing Kit, Tubes, Pump, Booklet, Copyright 1920, A.C. Gilbert, Box, 18 x 10 In.	480
Gnome, Seesaw, Wheeled Platform, Painted, Cast Iron, Pull Toy, Kenton, 7 ½ In.	296
Gnomes, Sawing Log, Tin Litho, Fischer, Germany, Penny Toy, 4 ¼ In. .....illus	265
Goat, Gray, Red Paint, Tin, 6 ½ In.	91
Goat, Mohair, Glass Eyes, Leather Ears, Metal Horns, Collar, Bell, Platform, Wheels, 14 In.	1003
Goat, Riding Toy, Papier-Mache, Pull String, Wood Wheels, 18 x 23 In.	311
Gong Bell, Cast Iron, Cart, Heart Shape Wheels, Black Driver Sways, Rings Bell, 7 In.	2666
Goose, Witch, Cat, Walks, Tin Litho, Windup, Unique Art, 1930s, 8 ½ In. .....illus	330
Grasshopper, Painted, Cast Iron, Aluminum, Rubber Tires, Articulated Action, Pull Toy, Hubley, 10 In. illus	443
Grasshopper, Green, Cast Iron, Pull Toy, Hubley, 9 In.	267
Great Garloo, Remote Control, Plastic, Battery Operated, Marx, Japan, 1962, 23 In. .....illus	455
Greyhound Bus Terminal, Station On Platform, Tin Lithograph, 17 In.	204
Greyhound Rabbit Chase, Tin Lithograph, Windup, Gunthermann, 7 In.	826
Guitar Player, Black, Strums Guitar, Nods, Windup, Gunthermann, 10 In.	1659
Gun, BB, Daisy, 1000 Shot Model B, Patented 1904, 36 In.	240
Gun, BB, Daisy, Patented 1901, 30 ¼ In.	1140
Ham & Sam, Black Piano Player & Dancer, Tin Litho, Windup, Linemar, 1950s, 6 ½ x 5 In.	1416
Hand Car, 2 Me, Girard, USA, Windup, 1920s, 6 In.	245
Hand Car, Moon Mullins & Kayo, Tin Litho, Train Track Wheels, Clockwork, 6 In.	531
Hansom Cab, Black Driver, White Horse, Cast Iron, Kenton, 16 In.	57
Hansom Cab, Black, White, Brown Paint, Cast Iron, Pratt & Letchworth, 13 In.	356
Hansom Cab, Sedan, Red, 2 Lanterns, Driver, Passenger, Iron, Spoke Wheels, Kenton, 9 In.	443
Happy Hooligan, Cart, Donkey Drawn, Painted, Cast Iron, Pull Toy, 10 In.	122
Happy Hooligan, Police Patrol, Driver, Riders, Horse Drawn, Yellow, Black, Iron, 19 In.	1541
Happy Hooligan, Roly Poly, Painted, Composition, Schoenhut, 9 In.	210
Hay Rake, Gray, Green, Yellow Paint, Cast Iron, Arcade, 7 In.	152
Hen Pulling Chick, Gik-Gak, Chick On Wood-Style Crate, Tin Litho, Windup, Eberl, 9 In.	767
High Chair, Doll's, Wood, Carved, Leather Seat, Spindles, Food Tray, c.1860, 20 In.	784
Hobbyhorse, Carved, c.1900, 27 x 48 In.	213
Hobbyhorse, Carved, Painted, c.1860, 22 x 34 ½ In.	267
Hobbyhorse, Carved, Painted, Wheels, Rocker, c.1865, 33 x 46 In.	356
Hobbyhorse, Carved, Red, Brown Paint, 36 x 59 In.	152
Hobbyhorse, Carved, White, Black Paint, Red Wood Base, 1800s, 32 x 40 In.	486
Hobbyhorse, Fabric Head, Yarn Mane, Button Eyes, Amish, Pa., c.1910, 36 In. .....illus	59
Hobbyhorse, Gray, Black Spots, Horsehair Tail, Wood, c.1900, 28 x 51 In.	295
Hobbyhorse, Mobo, Tin, Multicolor Paint, c.1950, 32 In.	72
Hoop, Man Riding Horse, Inside Wheel, Painted, Paper, Wood, Stick Pusher, Gibbs, 33 In.	480
Horse & Wagon, 2 Horses, Transfer, Driver, Painted, Cast Iron, Dent, 17 In.	273
Horse & Wagon, Adams Express, Driver, Barrels, Black, Red Paint, Cast Iron, 17 ½ In.	547
Horse & Wagon, Cement Mixer, Driver, Orange, Red, Black Paint, Cast Iron, Kenton, 14 In.	851
Horse & Wagon, Coal, Driver, Cast Iron, Open Bed, Spoke Wheels, Hubley, 15 In.	236
Horse & Wagon, Coal, Painted, Cast Iron, Dent, 19 In.	334
Horse & Wagon, Dray, Driver, Red Paint, Cast Iron, Wilkins, 20 ½ In.	304
Horse & Wagon, Driver, Barrels, Black, Red, Blue Paint, Cast Iron, Carpenter, 15 In.	243
Horse & Wagon, Driver, Barrels, Red, Yellow, Brown Paint, Cast Iron, 17 ½ In.	830
Horse & Wagon, Driver, Painted, Iron, 14 In.	243 to 385
Horse & Wagon, Driver, Wood, Barrels, Painted, Iron, Steel, 20 ½ In.	510
Horse & Wagon, Dump, Coal, Driver, Painted, Cast Iron, Hubley, 15 ¾ In.	296
Horse & Wagon, Logs On Back, Black, Red Paint, Cast Iron, Shimmer, 25 ½ In.	444
Horse & Wagon, Open, Black Paint, Cast Iron, 12 ½ In.	182
Horse & Wagon, Phaeton, Spider, Cast Iron, Spoke Wheels, 3 Figures, Hubley, 13 In.	1534
Horse & Wagon, Pure Lake Ice, 2 Horses, White, Red, Black Paint, Cast Iron, Harris, 14 In.	593
Horse & Wagon, Riders, Caisson, Ives, 23 In.	1541

Toy, Great Garloo, Remote Control, Plastic, Battery Operated, Marx, Japan, 1962, 23 In.
$455

Serious Toyz

Toy, Hobbyhorse, Fabric Head, Yarn Mane, Button Eyes, Amish, Pa., c.1910, 36 In.
$59

Conestoga Auction Co., Inc.

Toy, Horse & Wagon, U.S. Mail, Tin, Paper Litho, Gibbs Toys, Copyright 1910, 12 In.
$143

Showtime Auction Services

T

Toy, Horse, Rocking, Platform, Wood, Horsehair Tail & Mane, Iron, c.1850, 46 x 53 In.
$2,352

Theriault's

Toy, Indian Brave, Rubber, Painted, Real Feather, Squeeze, Rempel, 1940s, 7 In.
$70

Serious Toyz

Toy, Jeep, Jumpin', Tin Lithograph, Louis Marx Mfg., Box, 6 In.
$171

Showtime Auction Services

Legos

It is estimated that more than 203 billion Lego parts have been made since 1949. You can combine six eight-stud Lego blocks of the same color 102,981,500 different ways.

Horse & Wagon, Stake, Driver, Black, Red Paint, Cast Iron, 16 In.	296
Horse & Wagon, Stake, Driver, Yellow, Red Paint, 15 ½ In.	356
Horse & Wagon, Transfer, Red, White, Black Paint, Cast Iron, 19 In.	334
Horse & Wagon, Trap, 2 Horses, Driver, Top Hat, Painted, Harris, 17 ½ In.	711
Horse & Wagon, U.S. Mail, Tin, Paper Litho, Gibbs Toys, Copyright 1910, 12 In. *illus*	143
Horse Racing, 2 Horses, Jockeys, Wheel Platform, Paper, Wood, Tin, 10 In.	390
Horse, Circus, Rug On Back, Schoenhut, 6 x 9 ½ In.	70
Horse, Mobo, Red Saddle, Brown Spots, White, Reins, Pressed Steel, 1930s, 27 x 31 In.	180
Horse, Oilcloth, Straw Filled, Felt Saddlewood Wheels, Wheels, Pull Toy, Steiff, 16 In.	900
Horse, Platform, Prancing Pose, Composition, Pull Toy, 15 In.	330
Horse, Platform, Stenciled, Painted, c.1900, 44 x 36 In.	424
Horse, Platform, Wheels, Hide Cover, Horsehair Mane, 17 In.	570
Horse, Rider, Black, Blue, Orange Paint, Tin, Platform, 10 ½ x 14 In.	889
Horse, Rocking, Papier-Mache, White, Black, Red Paint, Horsehair Mane, Tail, 12 In.	259
Horse, Rocking, Pine, Carved, Saddle, Horsehair Tail, 1800s, 24 x 46 In.	360
Horse, Rocking, Platform, Wood, Horsehair Tail & Mane, Iron, c.1850, 46 x 53 In. *illus*	2352
Horse, Rocking, Saddle, Springs, White, Red Paint, c.1850, 31 x 42 In.	500
Horse, Rocking, Wood, Carved, Painted, Horsehair Mane, Tail, England, 1800s, 28 x 28 In.	840
Horse, Rocking, Wood, Painted, c.1900, 33 x 25 In.	127
Horse, Rocking, Wood, Yellow Saddle, Black, Red Paint, Green, c.1900, 26 x 43 In.	767
Horse, Saddle, Composition, Gray, Pull Toy, Athco, 20 x 20 In.	308
Horse, Suspended In Metal Frame, White, Red Paint, Tin, Hoop Toy, 5 ½ In.	444
Horse, The Wonder Horse, Riding Platform, Red, Black Paint, 1940s, 32 x 32 In.	34
Horse, Tin, Black, Red Saddle, Bell, Galloping Motion, Wheels, Althof Bergmann, 10 In.	593
Horse, Walking, Wheel Base, Black, Red Paint, Cast Iron, Ives, 6 ½ In.	652
Horse, Walking, Wheels, Cast Iron, Pulling Tin Wagon, Marked Victor, Ives, 13 ½ In.	608
Horse, Wheeled Platform, Gold Paint, Cast Iron, Pull Toy, 7 ¾ In.	326
Horse, Wood, Dappled Paint, Shaped Platform, Wheels, Pull Toy, Meister Line, 16 In.	325
Horse, Wood, Sponged Coat, Tack Eyes, Horsehair Mane, Tail, Pull Toy, 16 ½ In.	259
House That Jack Built, Die Cut Figures, Paper On Cardboard & Wood, Bliss, 11 In.	944
House, Mechanical, Hansel & Gretel, Trees, Figures, Animals, Wood, Carved, 12 In.	660
Hutch, Doll's, Watch, Cherry, Keyhole Window, Pa., c.1810, 8 ¾ x 6 In.	2430
Hutch, Doll's, Watch, Mahogany, Cornucopia, Carved, c.1815, 8 ½ In.	1541
Ice Cream Vendor, Black, Celluloid, Tin, Windup, 1950s	475
Indian Brave, Rubber, Painted, Real Feather, Squeeze, Rempel, 1940s, 7 In. *illus*	70
Irish Mail, Tin Lithograph, Windup, Strauss, 4 ½ x 5 In.	325
Jack-In-The-Box, Pop Goes The Weasel, Metal, Mattel, c.1950, 5 ½ x 5 ½ In.	45
Jazzbo Jim, Black Banjo Player, Cabin, Tin, Windup, Unique Art, c.1940, 10 In.	403
Jazzbo Jim, Black Banjo Player, Dances On Cabin Roof, Tin, Windup, F. Strauss, 10 In.	649
Jeep, Jumpin', Tin Lithograph, Louis Marx Mfg., Box, 6 In. *illus*	171
Jeep, Military, Kubelwagon, 4 Seated Figures, Tin, Clockwork, Lineol, 9 ½ In.	600
Jester, Rolly-Dolly, Papier-Mache, Weighted Base, Schoenhut, c.1915, 10 In. *illus*	1083
Jockey, Cast Iron, Wilkins, Push, 1880s, 6 In.	825
Joe Penner, Duck, Tips Hat, Tin Litho, Windup, Louis Marx, 8 ½ In. *illus*	480
Juggler, Celluloid Head & Hands, Cardboard Legs, Wood Feet, Windup, Irwin, Box, 11 In.	240
Jumping Jock, Elf, Blue, Gold, Articulated, Tug String, Moves, Black Forest, 8 In.	177
Kaleidoscope, Cylindrical, Snowflakes, Multicolor, Cardboard, Steven Mfg. Co., 1950s	30
Keystone Kop, Roly Poly, Blue Uniform, Expressive Face, Germany, 10 In.	266
Kicking Mule, Wheeled Cart, Painted, Iron, Gong Bell Co., Pull Toy, 7 ¾ In.	326
Kid Special Trike, Tin Litho, Pull String, B&R, U.S.A., c.1920s, 6 In. *illus*	205
Kitchen, Tin, Painted, Wood, Lithograph, Window, Furnishings, c.1890, 26 x 12 In.	560
Lady Bug, Riding Toy, Red, Black, Metal, Rubber, Steiff, 1950s, 20 In.	108
Lamb, Fur, Glass Eyes, Brass Bell, Platform, Wheels, Push Pull Toy, Germany, 14 In.	1534
Li'l Abner Dogpatch Band, Unique Art, Box, c.1945, 7 ½ In.	245 to 344
Lincoln Tunnel, Cars, Policeman, Tin Lithograph, Windup, Unique Art, 24 In.	1150
Lion Cub, Plush, Jointed Neck & Legs, Sewn Nose & Mouth, Steiff, 1925, 13 In.	180
Little Bo Peep, Papier-Mache Head, Wool Sheep, Wheeled Base, Germany, 12 In.	1458
Loop-The-Loop, Ride, Car, Tin Lithograph, Windup, Box, Wolverine, 18 ½ In.	413
Louis Armstrong, Tin Lithograph, Japan, Windup, 1900s, 10 In.	281
Lucky Crane, Try Your Skill, Battery Operated, F.J. Strauss Co., Japan, Box, 9 x 6 In.	420
Luggage Trailer, Mullins Red Cap, Green, Arcade, 1936, 3 ½ In.	450
Mammy Pancakes, Holding Up Plate, Walker, Celluloid, Windup, 3 ¾ In.	150
Mammy Sweeping, Apron, Tin, Windup, Lindstrom, 7 ¾ In.	152 to 270
Man Feeding Dog, Man Slides, Dog Jumps To Fetch Sausage, Germany, Penny, 4 In.	207
Man, Face Changing, Striped Suit, Red Top Hat, 3 Faces, Tin Litho, Windup, Distler, 9 In.	1652
Man, On Bench, Smoking, Tin, Painted, Clockwork, Gunthermann, 10 In. *illus*	5605

T

Man, Walking Pig On Chain, Wheeled Platform, Painted, Tin, Pull Toy, 8 x 8 ½ In.	365	
Marble Rolling Ramp, Wood, Red, Orange, Green, 6 Tiers, Catch Box, c.1940, 12 x 26 In.	130	
Marble Shoot, Soccer Player, Orange, Blue, Red, Tin, Clockwork, Gely, Germany, 9 In.	711	
Mary & Little Lamb, Tin, Celluloid, Pull Toy, Box, 6 ½ In.	375	
Men Chopping, Sawing Wood, Steam Toy Accessory, Tin Lithograph, Bing, 10 In.	122	
Merry-Go-Round, Playland, Tin Lithograph, Windup, Bell Sound, Chein, 9 ¾ In.	325	*illus*
Merrymakers Band, 4 Mice, Piano, Marquee, Tin Litho, Louis Marx, Box, c.1929, 7 In.	1416	
Mighty King Kong, Tin, Fake Fur, Windup, Marx, 8 In.	132	
Missile Launcher, Army, Tin Lithograph, Battery Operated, Irco, Japan, c.1950, 8 In.	125	
Monkey, Climbing, Metal, String, Penny Toy, 6 ½ In.	189	
Monkey, On Tricycle, Bell, Painted, Cast Iron, Pull Toy, J. & E. Stevens, 8 In.	1007	
Monkey, On Velocipede, Felt, Glass Eyes, Metal Tricycle, Clockwork, Bing, 1890s, 9 In.	384	
Monkey, On Wheels, Record Peter, Felt, Button Eyes, Fez, Metal, Wood Cart, Steiff, 9 In.	312	
Monkey, Rock & Roll, Rocks, Sways, Plays, Metal, Cloth, Box, Cragstan, 12 ½ In.	142	
Monkey, Yes-No, Seated, Cloth, Jointed, Tail Makes Head Move, Schuco, 8 In.	106	*illus*
Monoplane, Spirit Of St. Louis, Silver, Tootsietoy, c.1930, 2 ½ In. Wingspan	475	
Moon Creature, Tin Lithograph, Windup, Built-In Key, Marx, 1968, 5 ¾ In.	127	*illus*
Moon Express, Red, Blue, White, Plastic, Tin Lithograph, T.P.S., Japan, Box, 15 In.	210	
Mother Goose House, Dormer, Die Cut Figures, Paper On Wood, Litho, Bliss, 15 In.	1416	
Motorcycle, Delivery, Flowers, Say It With, Iron, Blue, Driver, 3 Rubber Tires, 1930s, 4 In.	2950	
Motorcycle, Do-X, Policeman, Sidecar, Nickel Wheels, Cast Iron, Hubley, 5 In.	384	*illus*
Motorcycle, Driver, Tin Lithograph, Friction, Tippco, c.1955, 7 ¾ In.	474	
Motorcycle, Driver, Tin, Windup, Germany, 7 ¾ In.	593	
Motorcycle, Harley-Davidson, Army Green, Gold, Cast Iron, Nickel Plated Wheels, 6 In.	1007	
Motorcycle, Harley-Davidson, Rider, Rubber Tires, Iron, Painted, Hubley, 6 In.	708	*illus*
Motorcycle, Indian, Driver, Cast Iron, Hubley, 8 ½ In.	240	
Motorcycle, Indian, Sidecar, Driver, Orange, Tin Litho, Green Disc Wheels, Marx, 7 In.	1416	
Motorcycle, Parcel Post, Driver, Gold Lettering, Painted, Cast Iron, 9 ½ In.	5700	
Motorcycle, PDQ Delivery, Sidecar, Driver, Red, Blue Paint, Cast Iron, Vindex, 9 In.	1126	
Motorcycle, Policeman Rider, Tin Lithograph, Windup, Marx, 8 ½ In.	240	
Motorcycle, Policeman, Siren, Orange Cycle, Tin Litho, Clockwork, Marx, 8 In.	325	
Motorcycle, Rider, Painted, Tin Litho, Germany, Penny Toy, 3 ½ In.	326	
Motorcycle, RR Rumbler, Road Hog, Blue, Green, Mexico, Hot Wheels, 1972	83	
Motorcycle, Traffic Car, Indian Cycle, Driver, Red, Blue, Cast Iron, Hubley, Box, 9 In.	12980	
Motorcycle, Traffic, Rider, Cart Behind, Blue, Red Paint, Cast Iron, Hubley, 8 ¾ In.	415	
Moxiemobile, Blue Car, Rider On Horse, Tin Lithograph, Die Cut, 6 ½ x 9 x 2 ⅜ In.	1064	*illus*
Mule, Jointed Legs, Black Paint, Ives, 7 ½ In.	243	
Music Box, Square-Dancing Twins, Mattel, 9 In.	45	
Musician, Base Drum, Tin, France, 3 ½ In.	593	
Nanny & Child, Die Cut Feet, Wheeled High Chair, Tin, Windup, Germany, Penny, 3 In.	885	
New York City, Cityscape, Circling Train & Airplane, Tin Lithograph, Louis Marx, 9 In.	325	
Noah's Ark, Wood, Carved Animals, Figures, Germany, 10 x 18 ½ In.	830	
Noisemaker, Couple, Dancing, Tin Lithograph, Wood Handle, Multicolor, 1920s	9	
Oh-My, Black Man, Dancing, Base, Painted, Tin Lithograph, Lehmann, 10 In.	420	
Pail, Nursery Rhymes, Tin Lithograph, Handle, Shovel, Chein, 5 ⅞ x 4 ¾ x 4 ⅞ In.	403	*illus*
Pecking Geese, Coop, 2 Geese, Tin Litho, Yellow, Meier, Germany, Penny, 2 x 2 ¼ In.	325	
Pedal Car, Airflow, Pneumatic Tires, Steelcraft, c.1938, 43 In.	3420	
Pedal Car, Airplane, Fantasy Flyer, Girl's Pursuit, Airflow AFC Collectibles, 45 In.	480	*illus*
Pedal Car, Airplane, Pursuit, Pressed Steel, Silver, Red & Blue Accents, Steelcraft, 48 In.	266	
Pedal Car, Airplane, U.S. Army, Pressed Steel, Gray Fuselage, Steelcraft, 48 In.	472	
Pedal Car, Auburn Super Charge, Pneumatic Tires, Painted, Steelcraft, 1930s, 55 In.	4560	
Pedal Car, Biplane, Roly Toys, Pressed Steel, Tan, Decal, Arden Gun Games, 1920s, 60 In.	6490	
Pedal Car, Blue, Metal, Murray Champion, 33 In.	260	
Pedal Car, Carriage, Tandem, Wood, Tin, Spokes, American National, c.1905, 37 In.	5900	*illus*
Pedal Car, Chrysler, Yellow, Pressed Steel, Murray, c.1940, 37 In.	330	
Pedal Car, Convertible, Green, Steelcraft	2607	
Pedal Car, Dodge, Maroon Paint, White Interior, Steelcraft, 1920s, 36 In.	1596	
Pedal Car, Duesenberg Tandem, Blue, Nickel Details, Gold Trim, 67 In.	1416	
Pedal Car, Fire Captain, Bell, Red, Pressed Steel, Murray, 43 In.	720	
Pedal Car, Fire Chief, German Stigler Model, Red Paint, Bell, 1950s, 41 In.	143	
Pedal Car, Fire Department, Doll In Fire Suit, Dalmatian, Murray, 1950s, 42 In.	285	
Pedal Car, Fire Pumper, Pressed Steel, Nickel Pumper, American National, 64 In.	2655	
Pedal Car, Fire Truck, Water Tower, Steel, Red, American National, 1920s, 87 In.	4956	
Pedal Car, Kidillac, Pink, White Seat, Disc Wheels, Rubber Tires, 1950s, 45 In.	266	*illus*
Pedal Car, Lincoln Limo, Nickel Plated, Battery Headlights, Gendron, 65 In.	2963	
Pedal Car, New York Taxi, Yellow Metal, Gearbox, 34 In.	90	

Toy, Jester, Rolly-Dolly, Papier-Mache, Weighted Base, Schoenhut, c.1915, 10 In. $1,083

Theriault's

Toy, Joe Penner, Duck, Tips Hat, Tin Litho, Windup, Louis Marx, 8 ½ In. $480

Victorian Casino Antiques

Toy, Kid Special Trike, Tin Litho, Pull String, B&R, U.S.A., c.1920s, 6 In. $205

Victorian Casino Antiques

T

Toy, Man, On Bench, Smoking, Tin, Painted, Clockwork, Gunthermann, 10 In. **$5,605**

Bertoia Auctions

Toy, Merry-Go-Round, Playland, Tin Lithograph, Windup, Bell Sound, Chein, 9 ¾ In. **$325**

Bertoia Auctions

Toy, Monkey, Yes-No, Seated, Cloth, Jointed, Tail Makes Head Move, Schuco, 8 In. **$106**

Conestoga Auction Co., Inc.

Pedal Car, Oldsmobile, Pinstripes, Battery Headlights, Steelcraft, 1930s, 42 In.	2133
Pedal Car, Packard, 1933 Model, Tin, Painted, Nickel Details, 45 In.	1416
Pedal Car, Packard, Simulated Ragtop Roof, Spotlight, Steelcraft, 49 In. *illus*	3851
Pedal Car, Racing, Pressed Steel, Blue Paint, Disc Wheels, Rubber Tires, Eureka, 56 In.	384
Pedal Car, Red, Murray Steelcraft, Restored, 1928, 53 In. *illus*	2106
Pedal Car, Runabout, Seat Lifts, Pressed Steel, Red, Keystone, 41 In.	1652
Pedal Car, Speedboat, Pressed Steel, Blue & White, Dolphin Decal, Murray, 45 In.	443
Pedal Car, Sulky, Horsehair Cover, Metal, 56 x 29 In.	480
Pedal Car, Tow Truck, 1938 Model, Yellow, Black, 40 In.	147
Pedal Car, Tractor, John Deere, Green, White Seat, 35 In.	150
Pedal Car, Volunteer Fire Department, Ladder Truck, Ladders, Gearbox, Red, 40 In.	124
Pedal Car, Whirlwind, Brass Light, Metal, Wood, American National, 53 x 31 In.	3278
Pedal Car, Wood Frame, Cream Paint, 1920s, 36 In.	1440
Pedal Car, Wrecker, Pontiac, Cream Paint, Murray, 1940s, 46 In.	513
Pheasant, Mohair, Brown, Cream, Red, Steiff, 15 In.	213
Piano, Cherubs, Trees, 18 Wood Keys, Litho, Lid Opens, Music, Germany, c.1890, 15 In.	112
Piano, Player, Piano-Lodeon, Maroon, 7 Music Rolls, Box, J. Chein	28
Pig, Musical, Natural Pigskin, Glass Eyes & Hoofs, 5 x 2 x 4 In.	275
Pistol, Cap, Plastic, Red, Die Cast Action, Marx	235
Playland Whip, 4 Cars, Tin Lithograph, Windup, Chein, 1950s, 20 x 11 In.	649
Playmobil, Steering Wheel, Driving, Windshield, Wipers Work, Horn Blows, Box, 26 In.	240
Playset, Airport Service, Jeep, Car, Tractor, Trailers, Suitcases, Steel, Box, 1963, 15 x 27 In.	705
Playset, Mt. Vernon, Wood, Paper, Stencils, Outbuildings, Animals, Trees, 12-In. Building	830
Polar Sleigh, 2 Huskies, 2 Riders, Amundsen South Pole Expedition, Tin, c.1906, 10 In.	6490
Policeman, Canadian Mounted, Hat, Saddle, Blanket, Hartland, Box, 8 In.	120
Policeman, Semaphore, Tin, Bradford Co., c.1914, 5 ½ In.	475
Policeman, Traffic Cop, Die Cut, Stop & Go Sign, Tin Litho, 5 ½ In. *illus*	118
Poor Pete, Crying Black Child, Biting Dog, Celluloid, Windup, Japan, c.1930, 5 In.	240
Porky Pig, Holding Umbrella, Tin Lithograph, Windup, Marx, 8 ¼ In. *illus*	207
Porter, Adam, Man Pushes Cart, Luggage, Tin Litho, Clockwork, Lehmann, Box, 8 In.	2655
Porter, Pushing Cart, Trunk, Tin Lithograph, Penny Toy, 3 x 3 In.	224
Porter, Red Cap, Tin, Windup, Marx, 1930s	625
Powerful Katrinka, Jimmy, Tin Litho, Clockwork, Germany, Nifty, c.1923, 5 In. *illus*	1121
Rabbit, Jack, Standing, Mohair, Velvet, Shoebutton Eyes, Steiff, c.1930, 10 In. *illus*	2166
Rabbit, Nodder, Holds Baby Rabbit, Cloth, Papier-Mache, Windup, Mouth Opens, 16 In.	2666
Railroad Car, 2 Men, Tin, Pull Toy, Marx, 1920s, 9 ½ In.	175
Railway, Funicular, House, 2 Coal Cars Go Up & Down, Weighted Balls, Germany, 33 In.	2124
Red Cap Porter, Carrying 2 Suitcases, Black Face, Tin Litho, Windup, Marx, 8 ½ In.	319
Rickshaw, 2 Figures, Tin Litho, Painted, 2 Lead Wheels, Flywheel Mechanism, 5 x 8 In.	1121
Rickshaw, Painted, Tin, 14 ¼ In.	91
Ride A Rocket, Tin Lithograph, Windup, J. Chein, c.1950s, 18 In. *illus*	728
Ring, Cap'n Crunch, Figural, Plastic, C On Hat, c.1975	158
Ring, Cap'n Crunch, Rocket Launching, Red Plastic, c.1975	115
Ring, Flicker, Iron Man, Marvel Super Hero, Gold Luster, Hard Plastic	278
Road Roller, Automatic Reversing, Tin Litho, Windup, Marx, c.1925, 9 In. *illus*	96
Robot, Attacking Martian, Lithograph, Battery Operated, Box, Horikawa, Japan, 11 In.	840
Robot, Big Loo, Giant Moon, Light Bulb Eyes, Battery, Marx, 1963, 37 In. *illus*	4890
Robot, Chime Trooper Astronaut, Tin Litho, Windup, Aoshin Shoten, Japan, Box, 9 In. *illus*	13200
Robot, Laughing, Plastic, Battery Operated, Japan, Box, 14 In.	300
Robot, Lavender, Non Stop, Tin Litho, Battery, Masudaya, 14 ¾ In. *illus*	5100
Robot, Mighty 8, Tin Litho, Painted, Battery Operated, Box, Masudaya, Japan, 12 In.	15600
Robot, R-35, Tin Lithograph, Battery Operated, Linemar, Japan, Box, 7 ½ In.	390
Robot, Radical, Tin, Battery, Yoshiya, Cragstan, Japan, Box, 11 In. *illus*	2700
Robot, Television, Metal, TV Screen In Chest, Battery Operated, Japan, 15 ½ In.	210
Rocker, Fish, Playground Equipment, Foot Stirrups, Metal Frame, Fiberglass, 34 In.	240
Roller Coaster, 2 Cars, Tin Lithograph, Windup, Chein, 19 In.	120 to 300
Roller Coaster, Tin Lithograph, Windup, J. Chein, c.1929, 18 ½ In.	207
Rollo Chair, Boardwalk, Black Man, Tricycle, Tin, Windup, Strauss, 1921, 6 x 7 In.	920
Roly Poly, Papier-Mache, Black Boy Holding Belly, Cream, Blue, Clown Outfit, 9 In.	330
Rookie Pilot, Boy Peeking Out Of Cockpit, Tin Lithograph, Windup, Marx, 8 In.	420 to 440
Rooster, Cart, Chick, Embossed, Tin Litho, Windup, Germany, 8 ½ In. *illus*	374
Royal Circus Farmer Van, Horse Drawn, Driver, Iron, Painted, Green, Hubley, 16 In.	1304
Ruler, Nursery Rhyme, Pussy's In The Well, Tin Litho, Die Cut, 4 x 7 ½ In. *illus*	173
Sailor, Climbing, Oregon, Red, Blue, White Paint, Tin, 8 ¼ In.	122
Salem Witch, Fortune Wheel Spins, Lever, Head Turns, E. Trask, Pat. 1867, 6 In. *illus*	7594
Sambo, Figure Pulls Reins, Horse, Head Moves, Hustler Toy Corp., 1920s, 11 x 5 In.	120

Sand, Busy Mike, Clown Under Funnel, Tin Lithograph, J. Chein, 1930s, 9 In.	57
Sand, Hod Carrier, Tin Lithograph, J. Chein, Box, 1950s, 10 ½ In.	120
Sand, Merry Miller, Sandy Andy, Tin Lithograph, Wolverine, 12 In. ....*illus*	90
Sand, Mike The Monkey, Tin Lithograph, J. Chein, c.1955, 7 ⅜ In.	57
Sand, Rocking Horse, Seesaw, Tin Lithograph, J. Chein, c.1930, 7 ⅜ In. ....*illus*	114
Sand, Seesaw, Never Stop, Tin Lithograph, Gibbs Toy Co., 14 ½ In.	90
Sand, Seesaw, Rabbits, Tin Lithograph, J. Chein, 1950s, 7 ⅜ In. ....*illus*	120
Sand, Seesaw, Tin Lithograph, J. Chein, 1920s, 5 ⅛ In. ....*illus*	29
Seal, Black, Balancing Multicolor Ball, Tin, Windup, Japan, 7 In.	28
Seesaw, Boy & Girl, Gong Bell, Cast Iron, Pull Toy, 7 In. ....*illus*	889
Service Station, Brightelite, Tin Lithograph, Marx, Box, 9 ½ x 4 ¾ In.	660
Service Station, Mobilgas, Tin Lithograph, Windup, Japan, Box, 3 x 6 ½ In.	165
Service Station, Shell, Pressed Steel Cars, Pumps, Gibbs, Wyandotte, 1940s, 16 In.	830
Sheep In Pen, 2 Sheep, Fenced Pen, Palm Tree, Tin, Windup, Penny, 2 x 4 In.	366
Sheep, Curly Beige Wool, Glass Eyes, Bell At Neck, Wheels, Pull Toy, c.1910, 13 In.	1800
Sheep, Curly Fur, Felt, Glass Eyes, Leather Ears, Dresden Collar, Bell, Wheels, 14 In.	1180
Sheep, Fur, Felt, Glass Eyes, Platform, Wheels, Pull Toy, Germany, 18 ½ In. ....*illus*	1652
Shutterbug, Boy With Camera, Snaps Pictures, Tin, Batteries, Nomura, 8 ½ In.	425
Sideboard, Doll's, Biedermeier Style, Upper Cabinet, 3 Drawers Over 2 Doors, 13 x 10 In.	1067
Sled Race, Incline, Riders, Cream Paint, Tin, Windup, Germany, 30 In.	486
Sled, Bentwood, Landscape, Leaf Scrolls, May, Gilt Letters, c.1890, 14 x 37 In.	960
Sled, Double Ripper, 4 Riders, Painted, Cast Iron, Pull Toy, N.N. Hill Brass Co., 8 ½ In.	2844
Sled, Horse Scene, White, Brown, Painted, c.1850, 33 In.	355
Sled, Mixed Wood, Bentwood Runners, Painted Songbirds, c.1900, 35 In.	764
Sled, Painted, Horse, Gipsey, Wood, Jefferson Owen, Turner Bridge, Maine, 33 In.	413
Sled, Painted, Scroll Work, Homer Wagon Co., New York, 1886, 28 In.	295
Sled, Pine, Open Handles, 25 In.	68
Sled, Pine, Painted Flowers, c.1890, 43 x 10 In.	356
Sled, Pine, Running Horse Scene, Red, Black Paint, 1800s, 31 In.	738
Sled, Push, Red, Gold Paint, c.1890, 21 ½ In.	215
Sled, Push, Tufted Upholstery, Red Paint, c.1890, 37 ½ In.	259
Sled, Wood, Green Paint, c.1900, 43 In.	153
Sled, Wood, Iron, Recessed Panels, Painted Flowers, Animals, Russia, 1914, 29 In.	2375
Sled, Wood, Painted, Castle, Stencil Design, c.1900, 34 ½ In.	356
Sled, Wood, Painted, Diamonds, Compass Stars, Germany, c.1885, 12 x 22 In.	584
Sled, Wood, Painted, Wrought Iron Runners, Gooseneck Ends, c.1850, 18 x 38 In.	250
Sleigh, Victorian, Handle, Runner, White Paint, 35 x 41 In.	182
Sleigh, Wood, Runners, Painted, Upholstery, Handle, c.1890, 21 x 35 In.	770
Slipping Sam Fireman, Climbs Ladder, Tin Lithograph, Windup, Louis Marx, 7 ½ In.	266
Soap Bubble Set, Blowing Bubbles, 2 Clay Pipes, Fish Shape Soap, Milton Bradley, Box	54
Soldier, German, Mounted Standard Bearer, Elastolin, 2 ¾ In.	210
Soldier, Kneeling, Shingun No. 2, Celluloid, Windup, Japan, 1930s, 8 In. ....*illus*	207
Soldier, Mussolini, Movable Arm, Lineol, 3 In.	90
Soldier, Take-A-Part, Doepke, Box, 1957, 9 ½ In.	125
Somstepa, Jigger, Red Jacket, Striped Pants, Tin Litho, Marx, 8 In.	472
Space Gun, Planet Patrol G-Man Sub Machine Gun, Marx, Box, c.1940, 21 ½ In.	281
Space Station, Planet-Y, Tin Litho, Battery Operated, Japan, c.1969, 9 In. ....*illus*	259
Spacecraft, Model, Mariner, Metal, 1962, 13 In.	475
Spaceman, Great Garloo, Missile, Balls, Dart, Plastic, Marx, 38 In.	1080
Spacemen, Sealed In Plastic, 10 Men, Painted, Lantoy, Hong Kong, 10 In.	300
Spaceship, Tom Corbett Space Cadet, Tin Litho, Windup, Marx, c.1940s, 12 In. ....*illus*	390
Speed Boy Delivery Cycle, Red, Rider, Blue, Tin Lithograph, Windup, Marx, 9 ½ In.	384
Spic & Span, The Hams What Am, Music, Tin Litho, Windup, Marx, 10 x 6 ½ In.	1121
Spic Coon Drummer, Windup, Tin Lithograph, Marx, 6 In.	1870
Stable, Paper Lithograph, Wood, 3 Arch Opening, Orange, 22 ½ x 33 In.	30
Stagecoach, Tin, Wood, 11 x 16 In.	334
Steam Boiler, Tin, Cast Iron, 14 ½ In.	1033
Steam Coach, Upper Seats, Compartments, Wood, Langedoc, France, c.1900, 38 x 23 In. ..*illus*	11200
Steam Power Plant, Black Paint, Bing, 17 x 16 ½ In.	1033
Steam Roller, Die Cast Metal, Matchbox, No. 11, Box, c.1960, 3 In.	30
Steam Roller, No. 60, Ride 'em, Red & Gray, Keystone, 1930, 20 In.	295
Steam Roller, Painted, Tin, Iron, Fleischmann, 12 ½ In.	334
Steam Roller, Red Paint, Pressed Steel, Buddy L, 18 In.	1185
Steam Shovel, Blue, Red, Yellow, Rubber Wheels, Wyandotte, 1950s, 20 In.	105
Steam Shovel, Caterpillar Treads, Green, Gray Paint, Pressed Steel, Marx, 10 In.	68
Steam Shovel, Good Roads Machry Toys, Red Paint, Iron, Niederst, 18 In.	563

Toy, Moon Creature, Tin Lithograph, Windup, Built-In Key, Marx, 1968, 5 ¾ In. $127

Hake's Americana & Collectibles

Toy, Motorcycle, Do-X, Policeman, Sidecar, Nickel Wheels, Cast Iron, Hubley, 5 In. $384

Bertoia Auctions

Toy, Motorcycle, Harley-Davidson, Rider, Rubber Tires, Iron, Painted, Hubley, 6 In. $708

Bertoia Auctions

Toy, Moxiemobile, Blue Car, Rider On Horse, Tin Lithograph, Die Cut, 6 ½ x 9 x 2 ⅜ In. $1,064

Wm Morford Auctions

T

Toy, Pail, Nursery Rhymes, Tin
Lithograph, Handle, Shovel, Chein,
5 ⅞ x 4 ¾ x 4 ⅞ In.
$403

Wm Morford Auctions

Toy, Pedal Car, Airplane, Fantasy Flyer,
Girl's Pursuit, Airflow AFC Collectibles,
45 In.
$480

Victorian Casino Antiques

Toy, Pedal Car, Carriage, Tandem, Wood,
Tin, Spokes, American National, c.1905,
37 In.
$5,900

Bertoia Auctions

Toy, Pedal Car, Kidillac, Pink, White Seat,
Disc Wheels, Rubber Tires, 1950s, 45 In.
$266

Bertoia Auctions

Pedal Cars

Important pedal car makers
include American National,
Garton, Gendron, Kirk-Latty,
Murray-Ohio (Steelcraft), and
Toledo Metal Wheel Company.

Steam Shovel, Panama, Red, Silver Paint, Cast Iron, Hubley, 13 In.	1944
Steam Shovel, Pressed Steel, Buddy L, 18 ½ In.	61
Steam Shovel, Red, Silver, Green Paint, Cast Iron, Hubley, 6 ¾ In.	356
Steam Tractor, Canopy, Red, Green Paint, Pressed Steel, Structo, 9 In.	425
Store, General Grocery, Children Shopping, Working, Tin Litho, Folding, Box, 13 x 23 In.	1003
Store, Home Town Grocery, Counter, Scale, 2 Cabinets, Tin Lithograph, Box, Marx, 5 In.	620
Stove, Admiral, Cast Iron, Nickel Plated, Vindex, Salesman's Sample, c.1929, 15 In. ....*illus*	325
Stove, Art Nouveau Designs, Earthenware, Green Enamel, c.1890, 8 In.	56
Stove, Cook, Buck's Junior No. 4, Nickel Plated, Below Door Shelf, 22 x 16 In.	2013
Stove, Cook, Fortune Junior, Cast Iron, Thomas, Roberts, Stevenson & Co., 9 x 10 In.	474
Stove, Eagle Brand Ranges, Cast Iron, Nickel Color Finish, 11 ¾ x 12 ½ In. ....*illus*	265
Stove, Godin & Guise, Cast Iron, Enamel, Water Heater, France, c.1890, 13 x 13 In. ....*illus*	1120
Stove, Mt. Penn Stove Works, Black Paint, Cast Iron, 16 x 18 In.	516
Stove, Novelty, Cast Iron, Tin, Scroll & Flower Decoration, Pots & Pans, 12 x 13 In.	425
Stove, Prize, Silver Paint, Cast Iron, J. & E. Stevens, 11 ¾ In.	152
Stove, Tin, Hinged Doors, Chimney, Copper Pots, Black Paint, Bing, c.1900, 14 In. ....*illus*	1120
Street Sweeper, Elgin, Driver, Painted, Iron, Nickel Plated, Hubley, c.1910, 8 In.	2607 to 4740
Strutting Sam, Black Dancer, Table, Hat, Plaid Jacket, Lithograph, Box, Japan, 11 In.	960
Submarine, Green Paint, Tin, Clockwork, Fleischmann, 11 In.	213
Submarine, Model, Gray Paint, Pressed Steel, Wood, 18 ¾ In.	213
Submarine, Wood, Metal, No. R 2, Wilkins Toy Co., Box, 15 In.	132
Surfer Girl, On Surfboard, Cast Waves, Asymmetric Wheels, Iron, Hubley, 8 In.	2950
Surrey, 2-Rail Benches, 4 Men, 2 Women, Horse, Iron, Pratt & Letchworth, c.1900, 15 In.	502
Swan Chariot, Girl Driver, Painted, Cast Iron, J. & E. Stevens Co.	790
Swan, Plush, Windup, 16 ½ x 18 In.	570
Sweeper, Wizard Of Oz, Pressed Steel, Rubber Wheels, Red, Bissell, 1939, 5 x 8 x 2 In.	544
Swing, Pine, Man Profile Sides, Green Paint, Pa., c.1890, 18 x 14 ½ In.	326
Tank, GAMA, Plastic Radar Dish, Tin Lithograph, Battery, Germany, Box, 8 ½ In.	240
Tap Dancer, Black, Tin, Windup, Alps, Japan, Box, c.1950, 8 ¼ In.	281
Taxi, Amos 'n' Andy Fresh Air, Tin Lithograph, Windup, Marx, Box, 7 ¾ In.	444
Taxi, Amos 'n' Andy, Fresh Air, 2 Men, Dog, Tin, Windup, Marx, c.1945, 8 In.	288 to 649
Taxi, Driver, Green, Black Paint, Checker Band, Cast Iron, 7 ¾ In.	1659
Taxi, Driver, Orange, Black Paint, Cast Iron, 9 In.	504
Taxi, For Hire, Open Top, Spoke Wheels, Tin, Die Cut Lamps, Meter, Distler, Penny, 3 In.	354
Taxi, Yellow Cab, Double Stripe, Disc Wheels, Iron, No. 3, Arcade, 1920s, 5 In.	708
Taxi, Yellow Cab, Driver, Black, Orange Paint, Cast Iron, Arcade, 7 ¾ In.	395
Tea Service, Child With Teddy Bear, Germany, c.1920, Child's, 6-In. Teapot, 22 Piece	224
Tea Service, Clowns At Play, Pink Borders, Germany, Child's, 5-In. Teapot, 16 Piece	224
Tea Service, House That Jack Built, c.1900, Child's, 17 Piece	224
Tea Service, Whimsical Fantasy Scenes, Gilt Border, Germany, Child's, 16 Piece	224
Tea Set, Doll's, Ceramic, Teapot, Sugar, Creamer, Cups, Saucers, Box, c.1885, 15 x 11 In. ...*illus*	224
Tea Set, Doll's, Little Hostess, Dragon, Moriage, Box, Japan, 11 In., 21 Piece	96
Teddy Bears are also listed in the Teddy Bear category.	
Thresher, McCormick Deering, Cast Iron, Gray, Chute, Grain Pipe, Blower, Arcade, 12 In.	295
Thresher, McCormick, Cast Iron, Painted, Arcade, Early 20th Century, 9 ½ In.	120
Tiger, Stuffed, Cloth, Wheels, Pull Toy, 14 In.	334
Toonerville Trolley, Cast Iron, Green, Conductor On Back, Dent, Box, 5 ¾ In.	1003
Toonerville Trolley, Rider At Rail, Tin, Windup, c.1922	334
Top, Carousel, Horses, Swan Chariots, Tin Lithograph, 9 In.	270
Top, Carousel, Multicolor Canopy, Tin, Windup, Ohio Art, 6 In.	73
Top, Carousel, Windup, Alps, Japan, 1950s, 5 In.	195
Top, Carousel, Wyandotte, Box, 1930s	275
Top, Multicolor Painted Bands, Landscape, 3 Houses, Square Aperture, 8 In.	720
Tow Motor, Red, Silver Paint, Electric, Urbane Mfg. Co., 14 In.	119
Tractor, Case, Cast Iron, Red, 3 Silver Plows, 3 Spoke Wheels, Vindex, 10 ¼ In.	1534
Tractor, Caterpillar Ten, Cast Iron, Painted, Nickel Driver, Steel Tracks, Arcade, 7 In.	708
Tractor, Caterpillar, Driver, Silver, Yellow Paint, Cast Iron, Arcade, 7 ½ In.	356 to 456
Tractor, Driver, Chains, Silver, Green Paint, Cast Iron, Arcade, 6 ¾ In.	267
Tractor, Driver, Motor, Moving Parts, Plastic, Red, Blue, Yellow, Nosco, 10 In.	265
Tractor, Ford, Red, White Paint, Hubley, 1950s, 12 In.	34
Tractor, Fordson, Bucket Loader, Green Enamel, Red Wheels, Fork, Driver, 9 In.	1718
Tractor, Hough Payloader, Shovel Lifts, Ny-Lint Tool, 1959-61, 17 In. ....*illus*	72
Tractor, McCormick Deering, Driver, Red Gray Paint, Cast Iron, Arcade, 7 In.	243
Tractor, Oliver, Driver, Red, Green Paint, Cast Iron, Arcade, 5 In.	267
Tractor, Sandy Andy, Caterpillar, Pressed Steel, Litho, Windup, Wolverine, 10 In.	118
Tractor, Steam, Brass Boiler, Marklin, 10 ½ In.	334

Toy, Pedal Car, Packard, Simulated Ragtop Roof, Spotlight, Steelcraft, 49 In.
$3,851

James D. Julia Auctioneers

Toy, Pedal Car, Red, Murray Steelcraft, Restored, 1928, 53 In.
$2,106

Showtime Auction Services

Toy, Policeman, Traffic Cop, Die Cut, Stop & Go Sign, Tin Litho, 5 ½ In.
$118

Bertoia Auctions

TIP
Remove small rust spots from old metal with an ink-removing eraser or an old typewriter eraser.

Toy, Porky Pig, Holding Umbrella, Tin Lithograph, Windup, Marx, 8 ¼ In.
$207

Bertoia Auctions

Toy, Powerful Katrinka, Jimmy, Tin Litho, Clockwork, Germany, Nifty, c.1923, 5 In.
$1,121

Bertoia Auctions

Toy, Rabbit, Jack, Standing, Mohair, Velvet, Shoebutton Eyes, Steiff, c.1930, 10 In.
$2,166

Theriault's

Lithographed Tin Toys
Most lithographed tin toys were made between 1870 and 1915, although some were made later. Collectors like animated groups of animals or people, toys that make noise or music, or toys that move. Makers of special interest include Lehmann, Marx, Chein, Unique, Wolverine, and Strauss.

Toy, Ride A Rocket, Tin Lithograph, Windup, J. Chein, c.1950s, 18 In.
$728

Victorian Casino Antiques

Toy, Road Roller, Automatic Reversing, Tin Litho, Windup, Marx, c.1925, 9 In.
$96

Victorian Casino Antiques

Toy, Robot, Big Loo, Giant Moon, Light Bulb Eyes, Battery, Marx, 1963, 37 In. $4,890

Hake's Americana & Collectibles

Toy, Robot, Chime Trooper Astronaut, Tin Litho, Windup, Aoshin Shoten, Japan, Box, 9 In. $13,200

Morphy Auctions

Toy, Robot, Lavender, Non Stop, Tin Litho, Battery, Masudaya, 14 ¾ In. $5,100

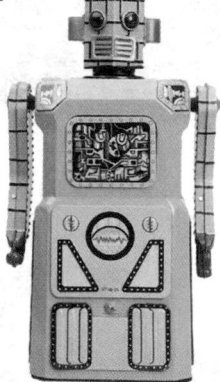

Morphy Auctions

Cleaning Teddy

If you buy an old teddy bear at a garage sale, bring it home and put it in a plastic bag with some mothballs for a few weeks. Don't let the mothballs touch the bear. The fur and stuffing of old bears attract many types of hungry insects.

Tractor, Steam, Brass, Horizontal Boiler, Embossed A, Spoke Wheels, Flywheel, 24 In.	1422
Tractor, Steam, Tin, Iron, 14 In.	456
Tractor, Steel Mule, Embossed Bates Co., Driver, Cast Iron, Vindex, c.1929, 8 In. ......*illus*	5900
Train Accessory, Bascule Bridge, Metal, Plastic, Lionel	150
Train Accessory, Bridge, Double Hell's Gate, Green, Yellow, Lionel, 54 In.	1200
Train Accessory, Bridge, Hell's Gate, No. 300, Standard Gauge, Lionel, 1930s, 11 x 29 In.	484
Train Accessory, Crane, Southern Pacific Intermodal, Plastic, Lionel, Box	150
Train Accessory, Locomotive Backshop, Arched Windows, Domed Cover, Tin Litho	210
Train Accessory, Roundhouse, 2 Sections, 3 Bays, Turntable, Tracks, Buddy L, 33 In.	1003
Train Accessory, Station, Arched Door, Brickwork, Tin Litho, O Gauge, Bing, 1910, 10 In.	325
Train Accessory, Station, Cupola, 2 Arched Ends, Tin Litho, Germany, 15 x 26 In.	600
Train Accessory, Station, Embossed Brickwork, Corrugated Roof, Bing, 15 In.	708
Train Accessory, Station, No. 137, Lionel Town, 1940s-69 ....*illus*	115
Train Accessory, Station, Waiting Room, Brown, Green, 10 In.	61
Train Accessory, Tunnel, Painted Trees, Houses, Bridges, Tin, 14 ½ x 27 In.	851
Train Car, Arcade, Pile Driver, Chain, Orange, Green, Cast Iron, 10 In.	119
Train Car, Arcade, Pile Driver, Chain, Red Paint, Cast Iron, 10 In.	91
Train Car, Bing, Boxcar, Budweiser, Tin Litho, Germany, 1 Gauge, 10 ½ In. ....*illus*	1416
Train Car, Bing, Railroad Crane, Chain, Red, Black, Tin, 12 In.	415
Train Car, Bing, Red Cross, Metal, Windows All Around, 1 Gauge, 8 In.	180
Train Car, Boxcar, New York, New Haven, Hartford, Brown Paint, Pressed Steel, 41 In.	243
Train Car, Buddy L, Caboose, No. 1001, Pressed Steel, Outdoor, c.1930, 18 In. ....*illus*	767
Train Car, Buddy L, Caboose, Outdoor Railroad 3017, Pressed Steel, 19 ½ In.	207
Train Car, Caboose, Penn Valley, Red Paint, Wood, 32 In.	608
Train Car, Caboose, Red Paint, Pressed Steel, 28 In.	395
Train Car, Flatbed, Wood, Brass, Iron, 17 ½ In.	182
Train Car, Flatbed, Wood, Iron, 45 ½ In.	122
Train Car, Gunthermann, Locomotive, Red, Black, Gold Paint, Tin, Clockwork, 10 ½ In.	365
Train Car, Lionel, Boxcar, No. 214, Colored Roof, Brass Trim, Standard Gauge, Box	192
Train Car, Lionel, Boxcar, No. 2954, O Gauge, c.1930	390
Train Car, Lionel, Caboose, Illuminated, Tin Plate, Green, 1930s, 12 In.	150
Train Car, Lionel, Flat Bed, No. SG 211, Nickel Stakes, Lumber, Brass Wheels, Box	156
Train Car, Lionel, Hopper, No. 216, Dark Green, Brass Trim, Standard Gauge, Box	192
Train Car, Lionel, Locomotive, No. 6, Western Maryland Shay Train, Box	390
Train Car, Lionel, Locomotive, No. 42, Green, Standard Gauge	348
Train Car, Lionel, Locomotive, Susquehanna RS-3 Diesel, Box	108
Train Car, Lionel, Tanker, No. 215, Green, Brass Trim, Standard Gauge, Box	228
Train Car, Lionel, Tanker, Sunoco, No. 515, White, Black, 1930s, 12 In.	350
Train Car, Locomotive, America, Red, Black Paint, Tin, Clockwork, 11 ½ In.	1067
Train Car, Locomotive, Cast Iron, Black Paint, 7 In.	48
Train Car, Locomotive, Floor, Black, Red Paint, Cast Iron, 12 In.	119
Train Car, Locomotive, Floor, Black, Red Painted, Tin, Clockwork, 12 In.	1541
Train Car, Locomotive, Riding, Cannonball Express, Tin Litho, Wood, 1950s, 19 x 14 In.	115
Train Car, Locomotive, Tender, Coach, Buffalo, Iron, Pressed Steel, 1890s, 28 In., 3 Piece	413
Train Car, Locomotive, Tender, Floor, Red Paint, Pressed Steel, 27 In.	243
Train Car, Locomotive, Tender, Steam, Cast Iron, Steel, Floor Stand, 43 In.	1823
Train Car, Marklin, Boxcar, Schlitz Beer, Tin Litho, 1 Gauge, Germany, 10 In. ....*illus*	21240
Train Car, Marklin, Locomotive, Crocodile, 1 Gauge, No. 5736, West Germany, Box	900
Train Car, Marklin, Locomotive, Tender, American Profile, Tin, 1 Gauge, 20 In. ....*illus*	8850
Train Car, Pile Driver, Chain, Blue Green, Brown Paint, 10 In.	89
Train Car, Smith-Miller, Boxcar, A.T. & S.F., Orange, Pressed Steel, 33 In., Pair	425
Train Car, Steam Boiler, Cast Iron, Steel, 18 In.	2066
Train Car, Steam Engine, Brass, Iron, 40 ½ In.	972
Train Car, Steam Engine, Cast Iron, Tin, Brass Bell, Stack, 16 In.	2370
Train Car, Steam Engine, Tender, British Railways, Black Paint, Cast Iron, Tin, 32 In.	1580
Train Car, Steam Engine, Tender, Cast Iron, Steel, Green, Red Paint, Floor Stand, 23 In.	3645
Train Car, Voltamp, Locomotive, Suburban, No. 2210, Bell, c.1914, 15 In. ....*illus*	3540
Train Car, Yonezawa, Locomotive, Pennsylvania, Tin Lithograph, Red, Japan, 21 In.	708
Train Set, Hornby, Tin Litho, Clockwork, Engine, 3 Cars, O Gauge, Track, Box, 13 In.	96
Train Set, Ives, Locomotive, Buffet, Observation Cars, Standard Gauge	120
Train Set, Kellermann, Locomotive, Tender, Coach, Tin Litho, Germany, Box, Penny, 6 In.	443
Train Set, Lehmann, Amtrak, Engine, 4 Passenger Cars, G Gauge, Germany, Box	540
Train Set, Lionel, Bicentennial Special, Spirit Of '76, Diesel Seaboard Engine, 3 Cars, Box	108
Train Set, Lionel, Locomotive, 3 Freight Cars, No. 2226, O Gauge	210
Train Set, Marklin, Locomotive, Passenger, 4 Cars, 1 Gauge, c.1905, 5 Piece	767
Train, Bon Ton, Painted, Tin, 10 In.	213

Tricycle, Flintstones, Fred, Holding Club, Tin Litho, Celluloid, Windup, Marx, 4 In.	354
Tricycle, Metal, Rider, Windup, USA, 1930s, 5 ½ In.	295
Trolley, Driver, Yellow Paint, Cast Iron, Windup, 7 ¾ In.	182
Trolley, Green, Tin Lithograph, Windup, Marx, Box, c.1930, 8 ½ x 2 In.	767
Trolley, London, Metal, Drink Peardrax Sweet Pear Juice, Matchbox, No. 56, 2 ⅝ In.	60
Trolley, R.T. Co. 11, Yellow Paint, Hook, Cast Iron, 8 In.	120
Truck, Army Searchlight, Pressed Steel, Buddy L, 14 ½ In.	57
Truck, Atomic Cannon, Pressed Steel, Plastic Radar Dish, Marx, Box, 24 In.	240
Truck, Auto Express, Open Bed, Driver, Red, Gold, Iron, Keystone Emblem, Hubley, 9 In.	708
Truck, Barrel, Stake, Driver, Cream, Black Paint, Jones & Bixler, 14 ¾ In.	326
Truck, Bedford Moving Van, Die Cast, Walls' Ice Cream, Matchbox, No. 2, Box, 4 In.	72
Truck, Borden's Milk & Cream, White, Black, Red Paint, Cast Iron, Hubley, 7 ¾ In.	1067
Truck, Borden's, Milk Bottle Shape, Cast Iron, Arcade, 5 ½ In.	770
Truck, Bulldozer, Driver, Silver Paint, Cast Iron, Hubley, 5 ½ In.	245
Truck, Canvas Top, Pressed Steel, Marx, 16 In.	73
Truck, Car Carrier, 3 Cars, Enclosed Cab, Slant Front Trailer, Iron, A.C. Williams, 10 In.	708
Truck, Car Carrier, 4 Cars, Painted, Cast Iron, Hubley, 10 In.	326
Truck, Carrier, Heavy Equipment, Tandem, Green, Red Paint, Cast Iron, 21 In.	668
Truck, Cement Mixer, Jaeger, Iron, Orange, Aluminum Drum, Scoop, Kenton, 6 ½ In.	325
Truck, Cement Mixer, Jaeger, Painted, Cast Iron, Arcade, c.1920, 6 In.	316
Truck, Cement Mixer, Jaeger, Silver, Red Paint, Cast Iron, Kenton, 7 In.	213
Truck, Cement Mixer, Mack, C-Cab, Red, Extended Rear Body, Rotates, Iron, Dent, 11 In.	3555
Truck, Cement Mixer, Pressed Steel, Buddy L, 13 ½ In.	334
Truck, Cement Mixer, Ready Mix, Red Steel, Yellow Plastic Drum, Structo, 14 In.	135
Truck, Cement Mixer, White, Black Wheels, Pressed Steel, Buddy L, Moline, 20 In.	390
Truck, Cement Mixer, Wonder, Red, Cast Iron, Hubley	175
Truck, Coal, Black, Red Paint, Pressed Steel, Buddy L, 25 In.	729
Truck, Coal, Segmented, Steel Dividers, Crank Body, Sturditoy, 27 In.	3555
Truck, Coal, Side Chute, Tin Wheels, Rubber Tires, Simulated Gauges, Sturditoy, 24 In.	1778
Truck, Compressor, Ingersoll Rand, Driver, Green, Red Paint, Cast Iron, Hubley, 8 In.	5346
Truck, Contractor, Driver, Open Bed, Red Paint, Iron, Kenton, 8 ¾ In.	356
Truck, Delivery, Black, Yellow, Red, Driver, Spoke Wheels, Distler, Penny, 4 In.	266
Truck, Delivery, Borden's Milk, Figural Bottle, Silver Iron, Rubber Tires, Arcade, 6 In.	443
Truck, Delivery, Breyers Ice Cream, Driver, Orange Iron, 3 Doors Open, Dent, 8 In.	565 to 1121
Truck, Delivery, Chad Valley Co. Ltd., Toy Makers To Queen, Green, Tin Litho, 10 In.	533
Truck, Delivery, Driver, Red Paint, Cast Iron, Arcade, 8 In.	1067
Truck, Delivery, Express, Driver, Red Paint, Cast Iron, Jones & Bixler, 14 ½ In.	504
Truck, Delivery, Guernsey Milk, Green, Black Paint, Cast Iron, 7 ¾ In.	385
Truck, Delivery, Hathaway's Bread, Cake, White, Black Paint, Iron, Arcade, 9 In.	851
Truck, Delivery, Heinz 57, White, Decals, Pressed Steel, Metalcraft, 12 In.	60 to 300
Truck, Delivery, National Biscuit Co., Tin, Iron, Arcade, 13 In. ....illus	542
Truck, Delivery, Old Timer, Tin, Friction, Japan, 11 In.	28
Truck, Delivery, Orange Crush, Soda Cartons With Bottles, Buddy L, 28 In.	2006
Truck, Delivery, Peerless, Send Anything Under The Sun, Orange Iron, Arcade, 8 In.	3540
Truck, Delivery, Pressed Steel, Windup, Kingsbury, 9 ½ In.	296
Truck, Delivery, Pure Oil, Pressed Steel, Streamline, Rubber Tires, Fenders, c.1936, 15 In.	652
Truck, Delivery, U.S. Mail, Brown, Green Paint, Pressed Steel, Steelcraft, 22 In.	563
Truck, Digger, Buckeye, Iron, Orange, Green, Open Support Frame, Chain Drive, 9 In.	1180
Truck, Digger, General, Red, Green Paint, Cast Iron, Hubley, 10 In.	152
Truck, Digger, Mack, Iron, Nickel Shovel, Spoke Wheels, Pivots, Hubley, 10 In.	502
Truck, Dump, Army, Red, Green Paint, Canvas, Pressed Steel, 26 In.	486
Truck, Dump, Black, Orange Paint, Pressed Steel, Windup, Kingsbury, 10 ½ In.	360
Truck, Dump, Chain Driven, Black, Red Wheels, Pressed Steel, Buddy L, 24 In.	304
Truck, Dump, Chevrolet, Automatic Release, Friction, Japan, Box, 9 In.	78
Truck, Dump, Construction Co., Green, Red Paint, Pressed Steel, Sturditoy, 27 In.	516
Truck, Dump, Driver, Burgundy, White Paint, Cast Iron, Kenton, 15 In.	948
Truck, Dump, Driver, Red, Green, Silver Paint, Cast Iron, Dent, 15 In.	729
Truck, Dump, Dugan Sand & Gravel, Blue Paint, Cast Iron, Arcade, 10 ¾ In.	444
Truck, Dump, Green, Red Paint, Pressed Steel, Tonka, 11 In.	96
Truck, Dump, International, Blue, White, Pressed Steel, Buddy L, 26 In.	385
Truck, Dump, International, Green, Red Paint, Cast Iron, Arcade, 10 ¾ In.	608
Truck, Dump, Mack, Blue Diamond, White Paint, Pressed Steel, Smith-Miller, 19 In.	385
Truck, Dump, Mack, Driver, Green Paint, Cast Iron, Arcade, 8 ½ In.	365
Truck, Dump, Mack, Lift Bed, Red, Silver Paint, Cast Iron, Arcade, 12 In.	207
Truck, Dump, Mack, Tilt Lever, Driver, Spoke Wheels, Iron, Hubley, 1930s, 7 In.	649
Truck, Dump, Open Cab, Red Paint, Cast Iron, 8 In.	267

Toy, Robot, Radical, Tin, Battery, Yoshiya, Cragstan, Japan, Box, 11 In.
$2,700

Morphy Auctions

Toy, Rooster, Cart, Chick, Embossed, Tin Litho, Windup, Germany, 8 ½ In.
$374

Victorian Casino Antiques

Toy, Ruler, Nursery Rhyme, Pussy's In The Well, Tin Litho, Die Cut, 4 x 7 ½ In.
$173

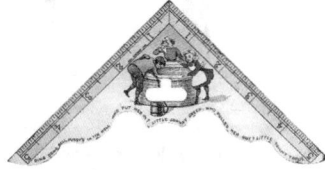

Wm Morford Auctions

Toy, Salem Witch, Fortune Wheel Spins, Lever, Head Turns, E. Trask, Pat. 1867, 6 In.
$7,594

James D. Julia Auctioneers

T

Toy, Sand, Merry Miller, Sandy Andy, Tin Lithograph, Wolverine, 12 In.
$90

Showtime Auction Services

Toy, Sand, Rocking Horse, Seesaw, Tin Lithograph, J. Chein, c.1930, 7 ⅜ In.
$114

Showtime Auction Services

Toy, Sand, Seesaw, Rabbits, Tin Lithograph, J. Chein, 1950s, 7 ⅜ In.
$120

Showtime Auction Services

Truck, Dump, Pressed Steel, Black, Red Paint, Buddy L, 1920s, 24 In.	170
Truck, Dump, Pressed Steel, Blue, Red, Wyandotte, 1930s, 11 In.	130
Truck, Dump, Pressed Steel, Spring Loaded, Black, Red, Wyandotte, c.1930, 15 In.	95
Truck, Dump, Pressed Steel, Sturditoy, c.1926, 27 In. *illus*	627
Truck, Dump, Red, Blue Paint, Cast Iron, Kenton, 8 In.	456
Truck, Dump, Red, Green Paint, Cast Iron, Kenton, 15 In.	911
Truck, Dump, Red, Green, Silver Paint, Cast Iron, Arcade, 7 ¼ In.	243
Truck, Dump, Red, Green, Wyandotte, 1938, 21 In.	175
Truck, Dump, Red, Silver Paint, Pressed Steel, Smith-Miller, 11 ½ In.	152
Truck, Dump, Red, White Paint, Tin, Wyandotte, 13 In.	79
Truck, Dump, Snowplow, State Hi-Way, Orange, Pressed Steel, Tonka, 1950s, 18 In.	170
Truck, Dump, Studebaker, Red, Gray Paint, Pressed Steel, Marx, 18 In.	74
Truck, Dump, White, Pressed Steel, Kelmet, 26 In.	334
Truck, Dump, Yellow Paint, Die Cast, Smith-Miller, 18 In.	215
Truck, Emergency Service, Tin Lithograph, Friction, Marx, Box, 14 ½ In.	270
Truck, Farm, Driver, Mystery Piston, Tin Litho, Battery Operated, Japan, Box, 9 ¾ In.	240
Truck, Ford, Pickup, Dark Blue, Tonka, 1956, 13 In.	125
Truck, Fruehauf Equipment, Orange Paint, Die Cast, Smith-Miller, 26 In.	181
Truck, General Petroleum, Wood, Green Paint, Red Wheels, 9 In.	83
Truck, Green Giant Brands, Giant Holding Peas, Pressed Steel, Tonka, c.1955, 23 In.	472
Truck, Green Paint, Pressed Steel, Buddy L, 26 In.	182
Truck, Green Paint, Pressed Steel, Keystone, 26 In.	304
Truck, Hopper, Side Tipping, Pressed Steel, Disc Wheels, Rubber Tires, Sturditoy, 24 In.	1481
Truck, Ice, Canvas Covering, Glass Ice Cubes, Black, Yellow, Buddy L, 26 In.	3851
Truck, Ice, Driver, Green Paint, Cast Iron, 8 In.	972
Truck, Ice, Enclosed Mack Cab, Rails, Platform, Ice Cubes, Tongs, Blue, Iron, Arcade, 8 In.	443
Truck, Ice, Pressed Steel, Buddy L, 1930s, 26 In.	969
Truck, International Harvester, Pickup, Red Paint, Pressed Steel, Buddy L, 25 In.	593
Truck, Kraft, A Variety Of Cheese For Every Taste, Aluminum, Steel, 7 x 14 In.	248
Truck, Land Rover, Die Cast Metal, No. 12, Matchbox, Box, 2 In.	72
Truck, Log, Studebaker, Die Cast, Orange, Hubley, Box, 6 ½ In.	165
Truck, Log, Trailer, Red Paint, Die Cast, Smith-Miller, 36 In.	316
Truck, Lumber, Black, Red Paint, Pressed Steel, Buddy L, 25 In.	486
Truck, Machinery Hauler, Low Boy, Blue, Yellow Paint, Cast Iron, Kilgore, 12 ½ In.	3888
Truck, Milk Delivery, Borden's, Driver, Door Opens, Cast Iron, Hubley, 8 In. *illus*	1534
Truck, Mobile Clam, Orange Paint, Pressed Steel, Tonka, 17 In.	147
Truck, Moving Van, Allied Van Lines, Yellow Paint, Pressed Steel, 1950s, 24 In.	113
Truck, Moving Van, Harry Dull Moving Storage, Painted, Iron, Ironman Toys, 13 In.	1007
Truck, Moving Van, Heavyweights, Redline, Factory Sealed, Hot Wheels, 1970	75
Truck, Moving Van, Lumar Van Lines, Tin, Marx, 16 In.	147
Truck, Moving Van, Pressed Steel, Green Paint, Fold-Down Gate, 1930s, 21 In.	413
Truck, Moving Van, Red, Black Paint, Pressed Steel, 1920s, 25 In.	203
Truck, Moving Van, Sonny, Green Paint, Pressed Steel, Dayton Toy Co., 26 In.	300
Truck, Moving Van, White, Red, Gold Stripe, Driver, Iron, Arcade, 13 In.	1067 to 3091
Truck, Panel, Iron Wheels, Spares, Green Enamel, Gilt Trim, Arcade, c.1930, 8 In.	2734
Truck, Pickup, Pressed Steel, Painted, Buddy L, 26 In.	540
Truck, Road Grader, Driver, Yellow Paint, Cast Iron, 6 In.	30
Truck, Road Roller, Driver, Green, Red Paint, Cast Iron, Hubley, 13 ¾ In.	1823
Truck, Road Roller, Green, Black, Tin Litho, Windup, Gunthermann, Germany, 10 In.	334 to 456
Truck, Road Roller, Huber, Cast Iron, Green, Red, Nickel Grill, Hubley, 1930s, 14 In.	649
Truck, Sand Loader, Driver, Red Paint, Cast Iron, Arcade, 6 ½ In.	563
Truck, Sanitation, Made Of Real Steel, White, Yellow, Buddy L Jr., Box, 5 x 10 In.	102
Truck, Semi-Trailer, Allied Van Lines, Green, Tonka, 24 In.	182
Truck, Semi-Trailer, Aluminum, Wood, Black Paint, Smith-Miller, 23 In.	124
Truck, Semi-Trailer, British Trailer Co., Die Cast, Matchbox, No. 27, Box.	96
Truck, Semi-Trailer, Express Line, Green, Red Paint, Pressed Steel, Buddy L, 23 In.	365
Truck, Semi-Trailer, Freight, Orange Paint, Pressed Steel, Structo, 1950s, 18 In.	34
Truck, Semi-Trailer, Mack, International Paper Co., Smith-Miller, 26 ½ In.	668
Truck, Sprinkler Tank, Yellow, Green, Red, Steel Discs, Rubber Tires, Keystone, 26 In.	2133
Truck, Stake Bed, 5 Ton, Driver, Yellow Paint, Cast Iron, Hubley, 16 In.	267 to 334
Truck, Stake Bed, 10 Ton, Red, Nickel Stake Rails, Grill & Bumper, Iron, Hubley, 8 In.	708
Truck, Stake Bed, Cast-Iron Fence, Die Cast, Hubley, c.1945, 9 In.	185
Truck, Stake Bed, Driver, Logs, Red, Yellow Paint, Dent, 15 ½ In.	1944
Truck, Stake Bed, International Harvester, Yellow Paint, Cast Iron, Arcade, 9 ½ In.	365
Truck, Stake Bed, International, Nickel Grill, Decals, Arcade, 9 ½ In. *illus*	325

T

Toy, Sand, Seesaw, Tin Lithograph, J. Chein, 1920s, 5 ⅛ In.
$29

Showtime Auction Services

Toy, Seesaw, Boy & Girl, Gong Bell, Cast Iron, Tin, Pull Toy, 7 In.
$889

James D. Julia Auctioneers

Toy, Sheep, Fur, Felt, Glass Eyes, Platform, Wheels, Pull Toy, Germany, 18 ½ In.
$1,652

Bertoia Auctions

TIP
Remove the batteries from a stored toy.

Toy, Soldier, Kneeling, Shingun No. 2, Celluloid, Windup, Japan, 1930s, 8 In.
$207

Victorian Casino Antiques

Toy, Space Station, Planet-Y, Tin Litho, Battery Operated, Japan, c.1969, 9 In.
$259

Victorian Casino Antiques

Toy, Spaceship, Tom Corbett Space Cadet, Tin Litho, Windup, Marx, c.1940s, 12 In.
$390

Victorian Casino Antiques

Toy, Steam Coach, Upper Seats, Compartments, Wood, Langedoc, France, c.1900, 38 x 23 In.
$11,200

Theriault's

Toy, Stove, Admiral, Cast Iron, Nickel Plated, Vindex, Salesman's Sample, c.1929, 15 In.
$325

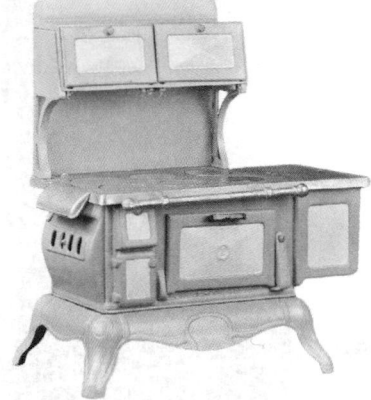

Bertoia Auctions

Toy, Stove, Eagle Brand Ranges, Cast Iron, Nickel Color Finish, 11 ¾ x 12 ½ In.
$265

Wm Morford Auctions

Toy, Stove, Godin & Guise, Cast Iron, Enamel, Water Heater, France, c.1890, 13 x 13 In.
$1,120

Theriault's

T

Toy, Stove, Tin, Hinged Doors, Chimney, Copper Pots, Black Paint, Bing, c.1900, 14 In.
$1,120

Theriault's

Toy, Tea Set, Doll's, Ceramic, Teapot, Sugar, Creamer, Cups, Saucers, Box, c.1885, 15 x 11 In.
$224

Theriault's

Toy, Tractor, Hough Payloader, Shovel Lifts, Ny-Lint Tool, 1959-61, 17 In.
$72

Victorian Casino Antiques

Toy, Tractor, Steel Mule, Embossed Bates Co., Driver, Cast Iron, Vindex, c.1929, 8 In.
$5,900

Bertoia Auctions

Toy, Train Accessory, Station, No. 137, Lionel Town, 1940s-69
$115

Victorian Casino Antiques

Toy, Train Car, Bing, Boxcar, Budweiser, Tin Litho, Germany, 1 Gauge, 10 ½ In.
$1,416

Bertoia Auctions

Toy, Train Car, Buddy L, Caboose, No. 1001, Pressed Steel, Outdoor, c.1930, 18 In.
$767

Bertoia Auctions

Toy, Train Car, Marklin, Boxcar, Schlitz Beer, Tin Litho, 1 Gauge, Germany, 10 In.
$21,240

Bertoia Auctions

Toy, Train Car, Marklin, Locomotive, Tender, American Profile, Tin, 1 Gauge, 20 In.
$8,850

Bertoia Auctions

TIP

If your battery-operated toy stops working, try sanding the terminals and the ends of the batteries. There may be slight corrosion that interferes with the battery connections.

Truck, Stake Bed, Pressed Steel, Blue Paint, Friction Powered, Turner, 22 In.	443
Truck, Stake Bed, Pressed Steel, Red Paint, Turner, c.1925, 16 ½ In.	354
Truck, Stake Bed, Red Paint, Cast Iron, Arcade, 11 In.	385
Truck, Stake Bed, Red, Blue, Wyandotte, 1940s, 12 In.	75
Truck, Stake Bed, Speed, Red, Green, Yellow Paint, Kenton, 11 ½ In.	911
Truck, Sunshine Biscuits, Pressed Steel, Yellow, Metalcraft, 1930s, 12 In.	413
Truck, Tank Line, Sprinkler Bar, Green, Black, Red, Pressed Steel, Buddy L, 27 In.	3555
Truck, Tanker, American Oil Co., Driver, Red, Silver Paint, Cast Iron, Dent,15 In.	1126
Truck, Tanker, American Oil Co., Green, Red Paint, Cast Iron, 10 ½ In.	365
Truck, Tanker, Decals, Doors Open, Chain, Plug Caps, Painted, Steel, Buddy L, 24 In.	2160
Truck, Tanker, Gas, Oil, Green, Gold Paint, Cast Iron, Kenton, 9 ¾ In.	425
Truck, Tanker, Gasoline, Mack, Red Paint, Cast Iron, 13 In.	533
Truck, Tanker, Gasoline, Mobilgas, Tin Lithograph, Friction, Japan, Box, 11 In.	118
Truck, Tanker, Gasoline, Mobiloil, Red, Pressed Steel, Smith-Miller, 19 In.	395
Truck, Tanker, Gasoline, Texaco Fire Chief, Green Paint, Pressed Steel, 1930s, 10 In.	107
Truck, Tanker, Mobilgas, Red, Tin Lithograph, Friction, Japan, Box, 10 In.	106
Truck, Tanker, Mobilgas, Red, White, Tin Lithograph, Friction, Japan, Box, 8 In.	142
Truck, Tanker, Mobiloil, 14 Wheeler, Red, Pressed Steel, Smitty Toys, 6 x 22 In.	288
Truck, Tanker, Oil, Enclosed Cab, Doors Open, Green Tank, Steel, Buddy L, 1930s, 24 In.	2400
Truck, Tanker, Texaco Jet Fuel, Pressed Steel, Plastic, Red, White, 23 In.	24
Truck, Tanker, Texaco, Red, Pressed Steel, Buddy L, 24 In.	71
Truck, Tanker, Tip Top, Die Cast, Rubber Tires, Zinc Wheels, Red, 3 ¼ In.	165
Truck, Tow, Black Cab, Open Yellow Body & Boom, Pressed Steel, Metalcraft, 10 In.	236
Truck, Tow, Ford, 1933 Model, Green, Nickel Boom & Grill, Cast Iron, Arcade, 6 ½ In.	236
Truck, Tow, Mack Wrecker, Blue Paint, Cast Iron, Arcade, 12 In.	770
Truck, Tow, Open Cab, Pressed Steel, Hooks, Cords, Die Cast Gears, Buddy L, 32 In.	2785
Truck, Tow, Red Painted Interiors, Die Cast Gears, Cast Aluminum, Buddy L, 31 In.	2252
Truck, Tow, Red, Green Paint, Pressed Steel, Windup, Kingsbury Toys, 13 ½ In.	122
Truck, Tow, Red, White Paint, Die Cast, 15 In.	79
Truck, Tow, Standard Oil, Pressed Steel, Tonka, 1958, 14 In.	89
Truck, Tow, Yellow, Red Paint, Cast Iron, Dent Hardware Co., 10 In.	711
Truck, Tri-City Express Service, Red, White, Tin, Marx, 14 In.	50
Truck, U.S. Army, Green Paint, Pressed Steel, Keystone, 1920s, 27 In.	424
Turkey, Wings Flap, Push Pull, Tin, Wheeled Platform, Germany, 6 In.	590
Tut-Tut Car, Man, Tin, Windup, Lehmann, Box, 7 In.	1808
Tweety Bird, Warner Bros., Marked TM 80 WB Made In China, 1996, 17 In. ....*illus*	60
Uncle Sam, Drummer, Tin, Windup, Clockwork, Gunthermann, c.1910, 6 x 5 ½ In.	1062
Uncle Wiggily, Tin Lithograph, Windup, Marx, c.1935, 8 In.	531
Van, Delivery, International, Hathaway's Bread, Rear Opens, Arcade, 1930s, 9 In. ....*illus*	3555
Van, Delivery, Red Paint, Smith-Miller, 20 In.	456
Van, Ford, Singer Sewing Machines, Die Cast Metal, Matchbox, No. 59, Box, 2 In.	72
Van, Police Patrol, Blue Paint, Red Wheels, Cast Iron, Dent, 8 ½ In.	1007
Van, Police Patrol, Driver, Black, Silver Paint, Cast Iron, Dent, 8 ½ In.	851
Van, Railway Express Metro, Die Cast, Olive Green, Tootsietoy, 2 ¼ In.	75
Van, Royal Mail, Open Cab, Driver, Rear Open, Tin Litho, Windup, Lehmann, 6 ¾ In.	2950
Van, Volkswagen, Blue, Die Cast, Matchbox, No. 34, Box, 2 In.	72
Van, White, Blue Paint, Cast Iron, Arcade, 8 In.	889
Ventriloquist Dummy, Kayo, Composition, Painted, Ring Moves Mouth, c.1930	70
Vitrine, Doll's, Pressed Metal, Silvered Finish, Silk, Drawer, Glass, France, c.1890, 13 In. ....*illus*	840
Wagon, Auto Cart, Wood, Red Paint, Steel Wheels, Handle, 24 In.	192
Wagon, Boy Driver, Red, Black Paint, Cast Iron, 6 ¾ In.	237
Wagon, Buckboard, Horse Drawn, Driver, Slat Bed, Red, White, Black, Iron, Harris, 13 In.	668
Wagon, Buckboard, Horse Drawn, Red, White, Yellow Paint, Cast Iron, Kenton, 14 In.	119
Wagon, Butcher, Driver, Horse Drawn, Provisions, Tin, Red, Yellow, Spoke Wheels, 11 In.	413
Wagon, Circus, Band, Driver, Musicians, Horses, Painted, Cast Iron, Hubley, c.1915, 23 In.	920
Wagon, Circus, Calliope, Driver, Horse Drawn, Blue, Gold Paint, Cast Iron, Hubley, 16 In.	770
Wagon, Circus, Calliope, Horses, Riders, Red, Open Sides, Iron, Kenton, 13 In.	413
Wagon, Circus, Driver, Cage, Big Show, Lion, Bear, Blue, Orange, Tin, Windup, 9 In.	385
Wagon, Circus, Horse Drawn, Cage, Driver, Elephant, Iron, Tin, Wood, Arcade, 14 In.	178 to 295
Wagon, Circus, Horse Drawn, Cage, Driver, Royal, Bear, Yellow, Iron, Hubley, 12 In.	152
Wagon, Circus, Overland, Band, Driver, Players, Horses, Riders, Iron, Kenton, c.1930, 16 In.	374
Wagon, Circus, Overland, Band, Musicians, Horses, Spoke Wheels, 15 In. ....*illus*	413
Wagon, Circus, Overland, Cage, Driver, White Bear, Disc Wheels, Iron, Kenton, 9 In.	384
Wagon, Circus, Overland, Polar Bear, Horses, Riders, Cast Iron, Kenton Hardware, 6 In.	147
Wagon, Covered, Pike's Peak, Iron, Spoke Wheels, 2 Mules, Driver, Ives, 13 In.	2124

Toy, Train Car, Voltamp, Locomotive, Suburban, No. 2210, Bell, c.1914, 15 In. $3,540

Bertoia Auctions

Toy, Truck, Delivery, National Biscuit Co., Tin, Iron, Arcade, 13 In. $542

Showtime Auction Services

Toy, Truck, Dump, Pressed Steel, Sturditoy, c.1926, 27 In. $627

Showtime Auction Services

Toy, Truck, Milk Delivery, Borden's, Driver, Door Opens, Cast Iron, Hubley, 8 In. $1,534

Bertoia Auctions

T

This is an edited listing of current prices. Visit Kovels.com to check thousands of prices from previous years and sign up for free information on trends, tips, reproductions, marks, and more.

Toy, Truck, Stake Bed, International, Nickel Grill, Decals, Arcade, 9 ½ In. $325

Bertoia Auctions

Toy, Tweety Bird, Warner Bros., Marked TM 80 WB Made In China, 1996, 17 In. $60

Victorian Casino Antiques

Toy, Van, Delivery, International, Hathaway's Bread, Rear Opens, Arcade, 1930s, 9 In. $3,555

James D. Julia Auctioneers

Toy, Vitrine, Doll's, Pressed Metal, Silvered Finish, Silk, Drawer, Glass, France, c.1890, 13 In. $840

Theriault's

Wagon, Delivery, Horse Drawn, Fine Bread, Baker, Wood, Schoenhut, 21 In.	1003
Wagon, Donkey Drawn, Black, Blue, Yellow Paint, Cast Iron, 17 ½ In.	425
Wagon, Dray, Horse Drawn, Driver, Barrels, Multicolor Paint, Iron, Hubley, 22 In.	395
Wagon, Goat, Mixed Wood, Spoke Wheels, Iron Band, Pa., 1800s, 22 x 40 In. *illus*	236
Wagon, Horse Drawn, 2 Horses, Slats, Wood, Paper, Metal, Gibbs, 18 In.	180
Wagon, Horse Drawn, 4 Seats, Figures, Brake, Painted, Cast Iron, 28 In.	5100
Wagon, Horse Drawn, Driver, 3 Riders, Wood, Paint, Gottshall, 9 x 24 In.	577
Wagon, Horse Drawn, Driver, Fairfield Western Maryland Dairy, Crate, Schoenhut, 31 In.	1550
Wagon, Ice, 2 Horses, Enclosed, Red, Green Roof, Spoke Wheels, Iron, Dent, 16 In.	531
Wagon, Ice, Green, Red Paint, Cast Iron, Hubley, 13 ½ In.	182
Wagon, Milk, Blue Paint, c.1840, 23 x 32 In.	152
Wagon, Milk, Borden's, Horse, Wheels, Multicolor, Wood, Tin, Rich Toys, c.1920, 18 In.	154
Wagon, Milk, Jointed Horse, Yellow, Green, Tin Litho, Converse, 8 x 17 In.	708
Wagon, Pony, Painted, c.1850, 29 x 37 In.	830
Wagon, Star Coaster, Iron Wheels, Wood Spokes, Hand Brake, Stencil, c.1900, 43 In.	230
Wagon, Water, Red Paint, Tin, 11 In.	207
Wagon, Western Express, Paper Lithograph Over Wood, Bliss, 19 In.	94
Wagon, Wood, Make Do Brakes, Pull Handle, Spoke Wheels, Stenciled, 1900s	431
Wagon, Wood, Painted, Harvard, Raised Seat, T Handle, Iron-Lined Wheels, 40 In.	881
Waiter, Black Tuxedo, Tray, Bottle, Waddles, Tin Litho, Windup, Germany, 7 In.	1541
Walker, Andy, Amos 'n' Andy, Tin Litho, Clockwork, Marx, c.1930, 11 ½ In.	443
Walking Doll, Pushing Cart, Goodwin's Patent, Pull Toy, 11 x 15 In.	563
Washer Woman, Cloth Dress, Tin Head & Hands, Painted Face, Martin, 7 In. *illus*	6490
Washstand, Doll's, Sarreguemines Basin, Pitcher, Wood, 19 x 19 In.	600
Western Bucking Bronco, Cowboy, Horse, Rocking Motion, Plastic, Marx, Box, 13 In.	72
Wheelbarrow, No. 1, Red, Decal, Arcade, 4 In.	175
Wheelbarrow, Wooden, Salesman's Sample, Inscribed J.W. Marshall, 10 ¾ In.	207
Whee-Whiz Auto Racing Track, Round, 4 Cars, Tin, Windup, Marx, c.1925, 13 In.	1003
Whoopee Car, Flappers, Princeton, Yale Pennants, Tin Litho, Die Cut, Marx, 7 ½ In.	207
Wild Mule Jack, Painted, Cast Iron, Gong Bell Co., 5 In.	237
Workbench, Maple, Pegs, Hammer, 1957, 6 ½ In.	75
Yellow Kid, Goat Cart, Standing, Painted, Cast Iron, 7 ½ In.	182 to 725
Yo-Yo, PEZ Premium, Tin Lithograph, Logo, Germany, 1950s, 2 In.	139
Zeppelin, Los Angeles, Decals, Silver Paint, Tin, Buffalo Toys, 25 In.	273
Zeppelin, Nifty Zep, Side Opens, Silver, Tin, Embossed Gondola, 17 In.	472
Zeppelin, Ride, 3 Dirigibles, Tin Litho, Flag Key, Windup, Germany, Penny, 4 In.	1534
Zeppelin, Tin, Buffalo Toys, 26 In.	150
Zig Zag, 2 Spoked Wheels, 2 Riders, Tin Lithograph, Rolls, Lehmann, 5 In.	885

TRAMP ART is a form of folk art made since the Civil War. It is usually made from chip-carved cigar boxes. Examples range from small boxes and picture frames to full-sized pieces of furniture.

Box, Wood, Hinged, Handle, 10 x 7 In.	74
Cabinet, Mirror Gallery & Shelf, Square Columns, Cutout Skirt, c.1915, 62 x 40 In.	2400
Chalet, Berg Weih Nacht, Christmas Tree, 12 x 7 In.	150
Church, Clock, Arched Door, Windows, Spires, Gray Paint, c.1900, 24 ½ In.	668
Cigar Box, Geometric Designs, Label On Inside Lid, EW 1897, 6 ½ x 8 In.	246
Cigar Box, Round Decorations, Chip Carved, Pyramid Shape Stand, Handle, 9 x 6 x 10 In.	1140
Clock, Shelf, Wood, Tower Shape, French Works, Finish, c.1910, 23 x 17 x 9 In.	677
Compote, Open Pedestal, Painted Multicolor, 12 ¼ In., Pair	189
Drawer, Backsplash, Star Shape, Wood, Carved, 9 ½ In.	1020
Dresser Box, Carved Swans, Birds, Multicolor Paint, Inscribed Charles, c.1890, 6 x 10 ½ In.	1541
Frame, 9 Portrait, Carved, 31 x 16 In.	660
Frame, Cross On Crest, Early 20th Century, 30 x 15 In.	176
Frame, Geometric Lattice Corners, Chip Carved, Stained, 31 x 36 In.	480
Frame, Lucky, Wood, Carved Horseshoe Corners, Hearts, Stars, Painted Gold, 25 x 33 In.	450
Frame, Mirror, Diamonds, Circles, 41 x 31 In.	1920
Mirror, 6 Layers, Ebonized Wood, Shaped Crest, 30 x 16 ¾ In.	813
Mirror, c.1900, 25 x 18 ¾ In., Pair	840
Mirror, Shaped Crest, Applied Stars, Heart, Divided Pane, c.1890, 29 x 20 In.	230
Mirror, Shaped, Carved, Stepped Geometric Segments, Paint, c.1900, 27 x 19 In.	1680
Mirror, Wall Pocket, Carved Love Birds, c.1895, 28 x 16 In.	3080
Shrine, Wood, Carved, Cross Shape, Box, Scalloped Base, Varnish, 12 x 10 x 25 In.	300
Wall Pocket, Double, Grid Design, Wood, Brown, Tan Paint, c.1900, 28 ½ x 12 In.	123
Watch Hutch, House Shape, Round Opening, c.1890, 15 In.	119

TRAPS for animals may be handmade. One of the most unusual is the mousetrap made so that when the mouse entered the trap, it was hit on the head with a mallet. Other traps were commercially manufactured and often are marked with the name of the manufacturer. Many traps were designed to be as humane as possible, and they would trap the live animal so it could be released in the woods.

Animal, Newhouse No. 3	22
Fly, Glass, Dome Lid, Blue Base, 3-Footed, Embossed, Pat. Oct. 28, 1890, 6 ¾ In. ....*illus*	168
Mouse, Metal, Cage, Trap Door, 1800s, 16 x 8 x 7 In.	100
Squirrel, Cage, Pine, House, Wheel, Circles, Red, Yellow Paint, 13 ¼ x 26 ½ In.	711
Squirrel, Cage, Tin, Paint, c.1890, 21 x 23 In.	334

TREEN, *see Wooden category.*

TRENCH ART is a form of folk art made by soldiers. Metal casings from bullets and mortar shells were cut and decorated to form useful objects, such as vases.

Cane, Shell Casings, 8 Interlocking Inert Cases, Horizontal Casing Grip, 34 In.	155
Inkwell, Brass, Shell Nose Cone, 3 Legs, Clover Feet, Hinged, Fleur-De-Lis, WWI, 4 x 4 In.	95
Lamp, Artillery Shell, 2-Light, Signed Capt. Newkirk, Camp Monair, France, 29 In.	30
Lamp, Shell Casing, Wood Base, 1940s, 19 In.	225
Letter Opener, Bullet Shell, Brass, Peace Dove Holding Flower, c.1916, 7 ¾ In.	110
Letter Opener, Bullet, Brass, Silver, 1941, 6 In.	60
Letter Opener, Shell Casing, Engraved Germ-Prisner, 7 ⅜ In.	45
Saltshaker, Machine Gun Casing, Silver, World War II, 3 ¼ In.	20
Vase, Brass, Scalloped Flared Rim, Crimped Sides, Leaves, c.1918, 13 In., Pair	150
Vase, Shell Casing, Brass, Repousse, Eparges, Flowers, World War I, 13 ½ In.	160

TRIVETS are now used to hold hot dishes. Most trivets of the late nineteenth and early twentieth centuries were made to hold hot irons. Iron or brass reproductions are being made of many of the old styles.

Brass, Birds, Floral Urn, Revolving, Pierced Top, Iron Stem, Tripod Base, 1800s, 11 x 12 In.	360
Brass, Flower, Petaled Rose, Repousse, Twisted Rope Border, 1830s, 7 ¾ In.	100
Brass, Hearth, Pierced Top, Masks, Iron Back Legs, England, c.1790, 12 x 16 In.	295
Brass, Iron, Pierced, Scrolled Top, Loop Stretcher, c.1800, 12 x 10 In.	50
Brass, Iron, Turned Wood Handle, Lyre Shape, Stamped, 13 ¼ x 7 In.	47
Brass, Lion, Pierced, Claw Feet, 10 x 5 x 4 In.	75
Brass, Paw Footed, England, c.1850, 12 x 15 ½ In.	90
Cast Iron, Cherubs, Reaching For Wreath, 7 ¾ x 4 In.	15
Cast Iron, Eagle, Griswold No. 1730	28
Cast Iron, Griswold No. 1739	80
Cast Iron, Hearth, Hearts, Thistle, Marked, W. Brimby, Baltimore, 1841, 13 In. ....*illus*	540
Cast Iron, Tree, Griswold No. 1735	15
Iron, Brass Inlaid J. Sellers, c.1830, 11 In.	3318
Iron, Hand Wrought, 18 ½ In.	230
Iron, Shamrock, Pierced Center Diamonds, c.1918, 5 ¾ In.	48
Mahogany, Flame Grain Top, Chip Carving, Cut Out Legs, Pa., 3 ¾ x 8 In.	154
Silver Plate, Etched, Scrolls, Openwork, Expandable, Lunt, 14 x 9 ½ In.	53
Silver Plate, Footed, Flowers, Leaves, Scroll, Oval Wallace, 8 ¾ In.	42
Wood, Anglo-Indian, Carved, Heart Border, c.1850, 8 In.	85
Wrought Iron, Heart Shape, 3 Legs, Pad Feet, 1 ¾ x 6 x 4 ¾ In.	212
Wrought Iron, Wedding, Pierced Date 1852, Marked KW, KE, 13 In.	237

TRUNKS of many types were made. The nineteenth-century sea chest was often handmade of unpainted wood. Brass-fitted camphorwood chests were brought back from the Orient. Leather-covered trunks were popular from the late eighteenth to mid-nineteenth centuries. By 1895, trunks were covered with canvas or decorated sheet metal. Embossed metal coverings were used from 1870 to 1910. By 1925, trunks were covered with vulcanized fiber or undecorated metal. Suitcases are listed here.

Bottega Veneta, Steamer, Black Leather, Brass, Italy, 22 x 39 In.	10455
Camelback, Wood, Metal Strapwork, 3 Latches, Side Handles, 24 x 30 x 19 In.	123
Campaign, Camphorwood, Brass Hardware, England, 40 x 20 In.	3600
Campaign, Leather, Fitted Interior, 49 x 23 In.	1063
Camphorwood, Black Leather Lid, Brass Bound, Handles, China, c.1850, 12 x 29 In.	570
Dome Top, Camphorwood, Handles, 22 ½ x 39 In.	1200

Toy, Wagon, Circus, Overland, Band, Musicians, Horses, Spoke Wheels, 15 In.
$413

Bertoia Auctions

Toy, Wagon, Goat, Mixed Wood, Spoke Wheels, Iron Band, Pa., 1800s, 22 x 40 In.
$236

Conestoga Auction Co., Inc.

Toy, Washer Woman, Cloth Dress, Tin Head & Hands, Painted Face, Martin, 7 In.
$6,490

Bertoia Auctions

T

TIP
Take batteries with you to toy sales if you plan to buy a battery-operated toy. Check to see if the toy really works.

Trap, Fly, Glass, Dome Lid, Blue Base, 3-Footed, Embossed, Pat. Oct. 28, 1890, 6 ¾ In.
$168

Jeffrey S. Evans & Assoc.

Trivet, Cast Iron, Hearth, Hearts, Thistle, Marked, W. Brimby, Baltimore, 1841, 13 In.
$540

Skinner Auctioneers & Appraisers

Trunk, Dome Top, Leather, Embossed, Painted, Iron Hardware, ANO 1796, 42 x 21 In.
$6,000

Skinner Auctioneers & Appraisers

Trunk, Louis Vuitton, Hat, Orange Canvas, Leather, Brass, Stamped, c.1915, 17 x 16 In.
$2,091

New Orleans Auction Galleries, Inc.

Dome Top, Grain Painted, Dovetail Construction, Hinged, Iron Lock, 1800s, 11 x 24 In.	369
Dome Top, Leather, Embossed, Painted, Iron Hardware, ANO 1796, 42 x 21 In. ....*illus*	6000
Dome Top, Leather, Horseshoe Handle, Mexico, 31 x 16 x 21 In.	2450
Dome Top, Pine, c.1820, 12 x 19 In.	267
Dome Top, Tin, Hammered, Iron Strap, Spain, 24 x 55 In.	720
Goyard, Hat Box, Leather Bound, Lift-Out Interior Compartment, 12 x 18 x 16 In.	1680
Goyard, Leather, Monogram, 13 x 39 In.	2500
Goyard, Steamer, Leather Bound, Lift-Out Interior Compartment, Initials, 21 x 28 In.	4320
Gustave Keller, Travel Bag, Men's, 19 x 12 x 11 In.	3800
Harp Steamer, Iron, Steel, Brass, Wood, Canvas Covered, Lyon Healy Inc., 46 x 38 x 75 In.	2500
Hide Lid, Brass Tacks, Leather Straps, c.1805, 10 x 24 In.	154
Leather, Brass Bound, Tacks, Block Print Paper Lining, Chinese, 1800s, 16 x 36 In.	300
Leather, Brass Studs, Straps, Handles, Mattress Ticking Interior, 20 x 46 In.	585
Leather, Brass, 5 Interior Drawers, Hangers, H.W. Roundtree & Bro., 45 x 23 In.	117
Leather, Steamer, 6 Drawers, Initials, 45 x 26 In.	5550
Louis Vuitton, Dog Carrier, Canvas, Monogram, Metal Mesh Window, Lid, 15 In.	523
Louis Vuitton, Flat, Interior Tray, Mrs. Joe Pulitzer Label, 1932, 13 ½ x 44 In.	3800
Louis Vuitton, Hat, Orange Canvas, Leather, Brass, Stamped, c.1915, 17 x 16 In. ....*illus*	2091
Louis Vuitton, Leather, Monogram, 20 x 40 In.	8750
Louis Vuitton, Leather, Monogram, 22 x 30 In.	5938
Louis Vuitton, Set, Soft Sided, Garment Bag, Flight Bag, Overnight Case, Mid 1900s	510
Louis Vuitton, Steamer Bag, 10 x 22 In.	5450
Louis Vuitton, Steamer Bag, Adjustable Leather Closure, c.1945, 14 x 18 In.	1416
Louis Vuitton, Steamer, Asnieres-Sur-Seine Label, c.1910, 13 x 36 In.	2390
Louis Vuitton, Steamer, Black Epi Leather, 21 ½ In.	396
Louis Vuitton, Steamer, Brown Canvas, Early 20th Century, 44 x 22 In.	12900
Louis Vuitton, Steamer, Canvas, Foldover Strap Closure, 22 x 25 In.	1003
Louis Vuitton, Steamer, Cloth, Metal, 24 x 20 In.	2400
Louis Vuitton, Steamer, Leather, 22 x 39 In.	410
Louis Vuitton, Steamer, Logo, 22 x 44 In.	6075
Louis Vuitton, Steamer, Monogrammed Canvas, Wood Straps, Tray, c.1910, 27 x 44 In.	5658
Louis Vuitton, Steamer, Oak Strapping, Leather Edges, c.1910, 22 ½ x 43 ½ In.	8505
Louis Vuitton, Steamer, Wardrobe, Hangers, Drawers, Keys, Monogram, 22 x 44 In. ....*illus*	10935
Louis Vuitton, Suitcase, Brass, Leather, Signed, 16 x 11 In.	1020
Louis Vuitton, Suitcase, Canvas, Leather Trim, Brass Corners, Alzer, 21 x 35 In.	649
Louis Vuitton, Suitcase, Hard Side, Monogram Alzer 70, Leather Handle, S Lock, 18 x 27 In.	2340
Louis Vuitton, Suitcase, Leather Strap, Brass, 16 x 16 In.	900
Louis Vuitton, Suitcase, Leather, Brass, Signed, 28 x 17 In.	1140
Louis Vuitton, Suitcase, Rolling, Monogram, Pegase 55, Double Zip, Padlock, 22 In.	1112
Louis Vuitton, Suitcase, Strato Soft, Leather Lined, c.1950, 9 x 28 In.	207
Louis Vuitton, Toiletry, Men's, 10 ½ x 6 ¼ In.	9900
Louis Vuitton, Train Case, Canvas, Soft Sided, 2 Leather Handles, 1980s, 18 x 13 In.	1121
Louis Vuitton, Travel Case, Monogram, Cowhide Trim, Strap Handle, Striped, 16 x 9 In.	1440
Louis Vuitton, Trunk, Leather Trim, Compartments, Trays, Label, 1930s, 44 x 22 x 22 In.	4800
Louis Vuitton, Trunk, Wood, Leather, Fitted, Red Rondels With Initials, c.1914, 23 x 43 In.	8610
Louis Vuitton, Wood, Metal Bound, Fitted Interior, Lined, Before 1914, 21 x 39 In. ....*illus*	4428
Oak, Hinged Lid, Wrought Iron Handles, Lock Plate, 29 x 14 In.	58
Pine Stave Construction, Rounded Shape, Square Nails, Wallpaper Lined, 1800s, 10 x 24 In.	236
Pine, Paint, Rope Handles, Congressional Correspondence, c.1860, 14 x 24 In.	472
Pine, Patina, c.1900, 33 x 20 In.	1512
Steamer, Pine, Stained, Dome Top, Metal Strapwork, Nail Heads, c.1900, 23 x 34 x 21 In.	307
Suitcase, Goyard, Leather, Wood, France, c.1900, 15 x 18 In.	1845
Travel Case, Leather, Handle, Stickers, Camel Color Interior, Leather Straps, 24 x 15 In.	138
Travel, Expandable Top Compartment, Brass Tacks, Hearts, Bigelow, c.1810, 14 x 24 In.	150
Vellum Parchment, Stand, England, c.1925, 21 x 18 x 19 In.	6900
Wardrobe, Hartmann Co., 6 Drawer, Key, 1920s, 41 x 25 x 22 In.	395
Wood, Brass Inlay, Handles, Hinged Lid, Interior Compartments, 9 ½ x 19 x 12 In.	495
Wood, Carved, Battle Scenes, Deities, Arched Center, Bracket Feet, Chinese, 24 x 40 In.	183
Wood, Leather, Brass Tacks, Buildings Painted Interior, c.1820, 12 ½ x 31 In.	9375

TUTHILL Cut Glass Company of Middletown, New York, worked from 1902 to 1923. Of special interest are the finely cut pieces of stemware and tableware.

Decanter, Grapes, Vines, Paneled, Flat Lip, 12 ½ In.	1239
Nappy, Wild Rose, Signed, American Brilliant Cut, 6 In.	325
Sugar & Creamer, Pedestal, Rounded Handles, Blanks, Marked	400

Sugar & Creamer, Vintage Pattern, Signed, American Brilliant	2655
Tray, Primrose, Signed, American Brilliant, 7 ¾ x 5 ½ In.	350
Tray, Tab Handles, Hobstar Border, Grapes, Leaves, Signed, 13 x 8 In.	1995
Tray, Vintage Pattern, Round, Shallow, American Brilliant, 12 In.	1600
Vase, Oval, Stick Stem, Etched, Flowers, Branches, Footed, Bud, Notched Rim, 12 In.	485
Vase, Wheat Pattern, Corset Shape, Signed, American Brilliant, 10 In.	649

TYPEWRITER collectors divide typewriters into two main classifications: the index machine, which has a pointer and a dial for letter selection, and the keyboard machine, most commonly seen today. The first successful typewriter was made by Sholes and Glidden in 1874.

Corona Four, 1924	175
Corona, Portable, Case, 1917, 10 ½ x 5 ½ x 10 In.	169
Facit, Model 1620, Case, Sweden, 1969	72
Hammond, Ideal, No. 12, Model 53525, Demilune Keyboard, Oak Case	492
Hammond, Multiplex, Oak, Aluminum, 14 Fonts, 1915, 14 x 14 x 7 In.	1100
IBM, Electromatic, Dust Cover, 1940s, 15 ½ x 16 In. .... *illus*	49
L.C. Smith & Corona, Portable, Case, 1920s .... *illus*	189
Oliver, No. 7, Cast Iron, Olive Green, Octagonal Keys, 1914, 14 x 14 x 7 In.	800
Oliver, Printype Model, No. 9, 1912	485
Remington, Model No. 1, Portable, Case, 1921, 11 x 10 x 3 ½ In. .... *illus*	275
Remington, Sticker, 1937 Model, Portable	145
Royal, No. 5, 1911, 15 x 14 x 8 In.	900
Smith Corona, Electra 210, Hard Case, 1970s	59
Smith Corona, Skyriter, Green, 1950s	350
Smith Corona, Super Sterling, Manual, Yellow	59
Smith Premier No. 1, Syracuse, N.Y., Ivory Keys, Rubber Roller, c.1889	308
Tom Thumb Junior, Red, Plastic, Box, c.1960, 10 x 7 x 4 In.	45
Underwood, Leader, Portable, Manual, Green Case, 12 x 11 x 6 In.	150
Valentine, Case, Box, French Instructions, E. Sottsass, Italy, c.1969, 15 x 14 In.	625

TYPEWRITER RIBBON TINS are now being collected. The lithographed tin containers have been used since the 1870s. Most popular with collectors are tins with pictorial graphics.

Beaver Ribbon, Beavers Building Dam, Crystal, M.B. Cook Co., c.1940, 2 ½ x 2 ½ In.	29
Commercial, Blue, White, Woman Sitting Typing, 1940s, 2 ½ In.	24
Elk, Miller-Bryant-Pierce, 2 x 2 In.	20
Keelox Silver Brand, Blue On Silver, 2 ½ In.	11
Panama, Airplane, Ocean, Blue, Green, 1950s, 2 ½ In.	19

UHL POTTERY was made in Evansville, Indiana, in 1854. The pottery moved to Huntingburg, Indiana, in 1908. Stoneware and glazed pottery were made until the mid-1940s.

Boot, Blue, Star, 4 x 3 x 1 ⅞ In.	144
Decanter, Art Deco, Beige, Stopper, 8 In.	35
Mug, Tan, Speckled, No. 16, 4 ½ In.	15
Pitcher, Blue, White Interior, Grapes, Leaves, 9 In.	220
Pitcher, Lincoln Head, Rail Splinter, Embossed, 5 ½ x 5 ½ In.	150

UMBRELLA collectors like rain or shine. The first known umbrella was owned by King Louis XIII of France in 1637. The earliest umbrellas were sunshades, not designed to be used in the rain. The umbrella was embellished and redesigned many times. In 1852, the fluted steel rib style was developed and it has remained the most useful style.

Bakelite Handle, Gold, Burgundy Ombre Cloth, Toledo, c.1940, 17 In.	30
Bubble, Carved Clear Lucite Handle, Clear Vinyl, White Trim, 1960s, 34 In.	95
Burled Wood Curved Handle, Black Silk, 4-In. Lace Trim, Marked Lyoin, Victorian, 36 In.	135
Green Lucite Handle, Mod, Navy Blue, Yellow Dots, White, Yellow Stripes, 1960s, 27 In.	185
Parasol Handle, Ivory, Dragon, Winding Around Bamboo, Signed, 11 ⅛ In.	486
Parasol, Burgundy Silk, Lace Trim, Brass, Wood Handle, Child's, 21 In.	90
Parasol, Carved Ivory Handle, Brown Silk, Child's, 27 In.	165
Parasol, Mother-Of-Pearl, Sterling Handle, Black Fabric, c.1908, 37 In.	127
Parasol, Wood Crook Handle, Red Lace, Over Black, Red Fringe, 1800s, 26 In.	375
Pink Lucite, Silvertone Crook Handle, Pagoda Style, Salmon Pink, Tassel, c.1940, 34 In.	275
Red & White, Stripes, Knob Handle, Red, Plastic, c.1960, 20 In.	125
Wood Dog Head Handle, Movable Mouth Holds Gloves, Blue Cloth, L.U. Co., c.1930, 24 In.	275
Wood Doll Shape Handle, Ducks, Orange, Pink, White, Child's, 17 ½ In.	75
Wood Knob Handle, Red Plaid, c.1930, Child's, 15 In.	45

Trunk, Louis Vuitton, Steamer, Wardrobe, Hangers, Drawers, Keys, Monogram, 22 x 44 In.
$10,935

James D. Julia Auctioneers

TIP

If you are storing a large closed container like a trunk for a long time, put a piece of charcoal in it to absorb odors.

Trunk, Louis Vuitton, Wood, Metal Bound, Fitted Interior, Lined, Before 1914, 21 x 39 In.
$4,428

New Orleans Auction Galleries, Inc.

Typewriter, IBM, Electromatic, Dust Cover, 1940s, 15 ½ x 16 In.
$49

Ruby Lane, Inc.

U
V

Typewriter, L.C. Smith & Corona, Portable, Case, 1920s
$189

Ruby Lane, Inc.

Typewriter, Remington, Model No. 1, Portable, Case, 1921, 11 x 10 x 3 ½ In.
$275

Ruby Lane, Inc.

Union Porcelain Works, Pitcher, Heathen Chinee, Karl Mueller, Stamped, c.1878, 10 x 10 ½ In.
$5,625

Rago Arts & Auction Center

University City, Vase, Crystalline Glaze, Carved, Adelaide Robineau, 1910, 6 x 4 In.
$23,750

Rago Arts & Auction Center

U V

UNION PORCELAIN WORKS was originally William Boch & Brothers, located in Greenpoint, New York. Thomas C. Smith bought the company in 1861 and renamed it Union Porcelain Works. The company went through a series of ownership changes and finally closed about 1922. The company made a fine quality white porcelain that was often decorated in clear, bright colors. Don't confuse this company with its competitor, Charles Cartlidge and Company, also in Greenpoint.

Oyster Plate, 4 Wells, Sea Creatures, White, Blue, Shell Shape, 8 ½ In.	174
Oyster Plate, 4 Wells, Sea Life, 1881, 8 ½ x 6 ½ In.	725
Oyster Plate, 4 Wells, White, Gold Trim, 8 x 6 ½ In.	250
Oyster Plate, 5 Wells, Seaweed, Urchins, Round, c.1879, 9 In.	650
Oyster Plate, 6 Wells, Seaweed, Sea Creature, Green, White, Round, 9 ½ In.	290
Oyster Plate, 6 Wells, Shell Shape, Enamel Painted Sea Life, c.1880, 9 ⁷⁄₁₆ x 6 ⅜ In.	207
Oyster Plate, 6 Wells, Shell Shape, Pink, White, 10 ¼ In.	220
Pitcher, Heathen Chinee, Karl Mueller, Stamped, c.1878, 10 x 10 ½ In. ....*illus*	5625

UNIVERSITY CITY POTTERY, of University, Missouri, worked from 1909 to 1915. Well-known artists, including Taxile Doat, Adelaide Alsop Robineau, and Frederick Hurten Rhead, worked there.

Vase, Crystalline Glaze, Carved, Adelaide Robineau, 1910, 6 x 4 In. ....*illus*	23750
Vase, Gourd Shape, Glazed, Signed, 1912, 6 ¾ x 3 In. ....*illus*	26250

UNIVERSITY OF NORTH DAKOTA, *see North Dakota School of Mines category.*

VAL ST. LAMBERT Cristalleries of Belgium was founded by Messieurs Kemlin and Lelievre in 1825. The company is still in operation. All types of table glassware and decorative glassware have been made. Pieces are often decorated with cut designs.

Vase, Danse De Flore, Cobalt Blue To Clear, Raised Gilt, Frost Band, Footed, 12 In.	357
Vase, Danse De Flore, Ruby To Clear, Gilt Frost Waistband, Footed, 12 In.	327
Vase, Rose To Clear, Flower, Leaves, Gilt Accents, Cameo, Stick Shape, c.1920, 12 In.	489
Vase, Spherical, 4-Sided, Gold Label, Signed, 20th Century, 6 In.	270
Wine, Hock, Berncastel, 1930s	53

VALLERYSTHAL GLASSWORKS was founded in 1836 in Lorraine, France. In 1854, the firm became Klenglin et Cie. It made table and decorative glass, opaline, cameo, and art glass. A line of covered, pressed glass animal dishes was made in the nineteenth century. The firm is still working.

Candlestick, Blue Opaque, Figural Dolphin, 8 In., Pair	150
Candlestick, Figural, Female, Frosted, Scalloped Base, c.1907, 10 In.	140
Dish, Lid, Elephant Shape, Rider, White Opaline, c.1880, 6 x 7 In.	175
Dish, Lid, White Opaline, Grapes, Footed, 6 In.	90
Dresser Bottle, Yellow Opaline, Gilt, Leaves, Bowknots, 7 ½ In.	125
Nut Dish, Amber, Leaf Edge, Zipper & Bead Pattern, Footed, Open Handle, c.1880, 6 In.	40
Toothpick Holder, Glass, Boy, Kneeling, Pack On Back, Amber, 3 ½ In.	60
Trinket Box, Lid, Alligator Shape, Milk Glass, 1880s, 12 In.	3000
Vase, Flared, Blue Opaline, Harvest Design, 1800s, 8 ¼ In.	100
Vase, Frosted Ground, Red Lead & Branch, Signed, 5 ½ In.	708

VAN BRIGGLE POTTERY was started by Artus Van Briggle in Colorado Springs, Colorado, after 1901. Van Briggle had been a decorator at Rookwood Pottery of Cincinnati, Ohio. He died in 1904 and his wife took over managing the pottery. One of the employees, Kenneth Stevenson, took over the company in 1969. He died in 1990 and his wife and son ran the pottery. She died in 2010 and the company closed in 2012. The wares usually had modeled relief decorations and a soft, dull glaze.

Bookends, Dragonfly, Mulberry Glaze, Marked, 5 x 5 ½ In.	365
Bookends, Peacock, Mulberry Glaze, 1920s, 5 x 5 ½ In.	225
Bowl, 4 Buttressed Feet, Mountain Craig Brown Glaze, 1920s, 4 x 7 ½ In.	195
Bowl, Flower Form, Fluted, Flower Frog, Mulberry Matte Glaze, 10 In.	150
Bowl, Green Matte Glaze, Geometric Design, c.1915, 4 ½ x 5 ½ In.	450
Bowl, Mermaid, Ming Turquoise, Marked, 10 ¾ In.	253
Bowl, Oak Leaf & Acorn, Turquoise Matte Glaze, Marked, 3 x 6 In. ....*illus*	75
Ewer, Maroon, Mottled, 8 ½ In.	79
Figurine, Horse, Rearing, Blue Green Glaze, A. Van Briggle, 8 ¾ In.	61
Figurine, Maiden, Kneeling, Blue Glaze, Marked, 8 ½ In.	98
Flower Bowl, Shell Flower Frog, Siren Of The Sea, Figural Mermaid, Fish, Blue, 14 In.	403
Flower Frog, Mulberry Glaze, c.1918, 1 ½ x 4 ¾ In.	35

Flower Frog, Our Lady Of The Lake, Girl, Kneeling, Feeding Goose, White, 1920s, 9 In.	69
Pitcher, Ombre High Gloss Glaze, Abstract Shape, Divided Handle, Art Deco, 9 ½ In..................	61
Planter, Indian Woman Holding Basket, Red & Purple Semimatte Glaze, 8 In...........................	97
Planter, Ming Turquoise, Boat Shape, Marked, 6 ¼ In.	10
Teapot, Brown To Green, Squat, Lug Handles, 5 In..	270
Tile, Landscape, Copper Frame, Colorado Springs, Colorado, c.1907, 6 x 6 In.	1500
Triple Cornucopia, Brown, 4 ¾ x 5 In.	50
Trivet, Stylized Yellow Roses, In Ivory Trefoil, Round, Green Glaze, 4 ½ In.	875
Vase, Blue Green Matte Glaze, Shouldered, Butterfly, 1920s, 7 x 7 In........................	525
Vase, Blue Green Matte Glaze, Tapered, c.1902, 16 ¾ x 8 ¼ In.	3500
Vase, Blue Over Green Matte Glaze, Bears, 1920s, 15 ¼ In.	2875
Vase, Blue To Green, Incised Calla Lily, 10 In.	85
Vase, Bud, Green, 6 In.	57
Vase, Co pper Base, Red, Green Glaze, Colorado Springs, Signed, 1903, 11 ½ x 4 In.....................	27500
Vase, Copper Clad, Stylized Leaves, Garlands, Marked, 3 ¾ In. ....*illus*	944
Vase, Daffodils, Yellow & Light Green Glaze, Marked, 1902, 10 x 4 ¼ In. ....*illus*	2250
Vase, Dark Blue Matte Glaze, Footed, c.1907, 3 x 6 ¼ In.	350
Vase, Dark Blue, Incised Poppy, Round, 4 In..	115
Vase, Deer, Green & Brown Glossy Glaze, c.1955, 4 ¼ x 3 In. ....*illus*	40
Vase, Dragonflies, Ming Blue, c.1924, 6 ⅝ In.	184
Vase, Flower, Leaf Carved, Purple Matte Glaze, Cinched Neck, 1903, 7 x 9 In........................	4375
Vase, Flowers, Red Matte Glaze, Green Highlights, 4 Open Handles, 5 x 5 In.	1000
Vase, Green Matte Glaze, Molded Leaves, Blue Undertones, c.1915, 6 ½ In.	92
Vase, Green Matte Glaze, Vertical Ribbed, Cabinet, c.1930, 7 x 4 In........................	813
Vase, Green, Brown, Rolled Rim, Footed, 4 ¼ In...	104
Vase, Incised Leaves, Mulberry Glaze, c.1925, 8 In.	115
Vase, Lady & Lily, Mulberry, Signed, Marked, 1945, 20 x 12 In. ....*illus*	1500
Vase, Leaves, Blue & Green Glaze, Tapered Neck, Signed, 1904, 11 x 5 In.	1875
Vase, Leaves, Mauve & Green Glaze, Tapered Neck, Signed, 1904, 11 x 5 In.	6250
Vase, Maroon, Moon Shape, Footed, 7 ½ In., Pair	67
Vase, Mulberry, 3 Indian Heads, Tapered, Footed, 1920s, 10 ⅜ In.	173 to 495
Vase, Mulberry, Lobed, Petal Rim, 5 ¾ In...	52
Vase, Mulberry, Swirl Leaf Design, c.1920, 7 ¼ In.	245
Vase, Mulberry, Wide Neck, 1920s, 4 In.	58
Vase, Orchid, Marked, 10 ¼ In.	277
Vase, Peacock Feathers, Mottled Teal & Green Glazes, Shouldered, Flared Rim, 10 In.	1125
Vase, Peacock Feathers, Silver Overlay, Blue Glaze, Signed, 1904, 5 ¾ x 6 ½ In.	10000
Vase, Persian Rose, Flared, Divided Rim, Marked, 10 In.	58
Vase, Poppies, Olive & Verdigris Glaze, Round, Tapered Rim, 1904, 9 ¾ x 8 ½ In.	8125
Vase, Poppy Pods, Celadon & Mauve Glaze, Swollen Neck, 1902, 3 ¾ x 3 ¾ In.	1750
Vase, Purple Flowers, Blue Ground, Flared, Bulbous Base, 5 In.	57
Vase, Raised Flower Heads & Stems, Mulberry Glaze, Squat, Swollen, 1918, 11 In.	489
Vase, Red, Purple, Ribbed, Tapered, 4 ½ In.	96
Vase, Rose, Incised, 5 In.	28
Vase, Stylized Flower, Ming Blue, Cylinder, c.1910, 7 ⅜ In.	127
Vase, Stylized Leaves, Green Glaze, Marked, 1906, 15 x 5 In.	2000
Vase, Tan Matte Glaze, Incised Tulip Design, c.1904, 3 x 8 In........................	1900
Vase, Tulips, Molded, Purple & Maroon Glaze, Swollen Cylinder, 12 x 4 In.	6250
Vase, Turquoise Mottled Matte Glaze, Bulbous, 1905, 7 In.	875
Vase, Virginia Creepers, Pink & Green Glaze, Bulbous, Tapered Neck, 8 x 7 In.	1500
Vase, Yellow Matte Glaze, Organic Design, Shouldered, Incised, Marked, c.1910, 7 x 15 In.	850
Wall Pocket, Tapered, Poppy, Mulberry Glaze, 8 x 4 ½ In..........................	185

VASA MURRHINA is the name of a glassware made by the Vasa Murrhina Art Glass Company of Sandwich, Massachusetts, about 1884. The glassware was transparent and was embedded with small pieces of colored glass and metallic flakes. The mica flakes were coated with silver, gold, copper, or nickel. Some of the pieces were cased. The same type of glass was made in England. Collectors often confuse Vasa Murrhina glass with aventurine, spatter, or spangle glass. There is uncertainty about what actually was made by the Vasa Murrhina factory. Related pieces may be listed under Spangle Glass.

Basket, Applied Clear Twisted Handle, Butterscotch, Red Flecks, 9 x 9 In....................	395
Rose Bowl, Globular, Crimped Edge, White, Peach, 3 ½ x 4 ½ In.	90
Scent Bottle, Laydown, Red, Silver & Gold Flecks, Sterling Cap, 1884, 8 In..................	875
Vase, Jack-In-The-Pulpit, Spatter Glass, Early 20th Century, 11 ½ In..................	180

University City, Vase, Gourd Shape, Glazed, Signed, 1912, 6 ¾ x 3 In. $26,250

Rago Arts & Auction Center

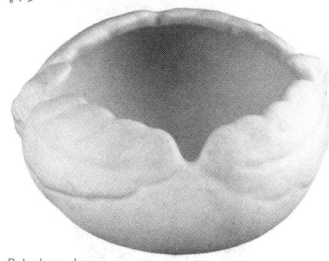

Van Briggle, Bowl, Oak Leaf & Acorn, Turquoise Matte Glaze, Marked, 3 x 6 In. $75

Ruby Lane, Inc.

Van Briggle, Vase, Copper Clad, Stylized Leaves, Garlands, Marked, 3 ¾ In. $944

Humler & Nolan

TIP

Some disciplined collectors have a rule: Add a new piece to the collection only if you can get rid of a less desirable old one. Most of us just keep adding.

U
V

Van Briggle, Vase, Daffodils, Yellow & Light Green Glaze, Marked, 1902, 10 x 4 ¼ In.
$2,250

Rago Arts & Auction Center

Van Briggle, Vase, Deer, Green & Brown Glossy Glaze, c.1955, 4 ¼ x 3 In.
$40

Ruby Lane, Inc.

Van Briggle, Vase, Lady & Lily, Mulberry, Signed, Marked, 1945, 20 x 12 In.
$1,500

Ruby Lane, Inc.

VASELINE GLASS is a greenish-yellow glassware resembling petroleum jelly. Pressed glass of the 1870s was often made of vaseline-colored glass. Some vaseline glass is still being made in old and new styles. Additional pieces of vaseline glass may also be listed under Pressed Glass in this book.

Candlestick, Baluster, Spread Foot With Clear Border, 9 ½ In., Pair	58
Compote, Opalescent, Ruffled Rim, Footed, 7 In.	29
Cruet, Patterned, Gold Band Highlights, 7 In.	89
Dish, Sweetmeat, Nested Ovals, 6-Sided, Scalloped Rim, 6 ½ In.	94
Loving Cup, Barrel Shape, 3 Handles, Enameled Flowers, 4 ¾ In.	118
Vase, Corn Shape, Scoop Rim, 8 ¼ In.	52
Vase, Trumpet Shape, Opalescent, Hobnail, Scalloped, Ruffled Rim, 6 In.	17

VENETIAN GLASS, *see Glass-Venetian category.*

VERLYS glass was made in Rouen, France, by the Societe Holophane Français, a company that started in 1920. It was made in Newark, Ohio, from 1935 to 1951. The art glass is either blown or molded. The American glass is signed with a diamond-point-scratched name, but the French pieces are marked with a molded signature. The designs resemble those used by Lalique.

Bonbon, Molded Butterflies, Lid, Bakelite Handle, c.1942, 2 ¼ x 6 ½ In.	85
Bowl, Chrysanthemums, Raised Base, Marked, 1930s, 10 x 6 x 4 In.	125
Bowl, Fish, Swimming, Frosted, Round, 10 ½ In.	215
Bowl, Frosted Lovebirds, Clear Ground, Boat Shape, Rectangular Base, France, 12 ¾ x 3 ¼ In.	100
Bowl, Lovebirds, Blue Opalescent, Rectangular Foot, c.1940, 6 ½ x 4 ½ In.	140
Bowl, Orchids, Etched, c.1940, 1 ½ x 14 In.	125
Charger, Birds, Bees, Dragonflies, 11 ¾ x 2 In.	165
Platter, Flowers, Opalescent, Round, 3 x 14 In.	130
Platter, Raised Water Lily, Ripples, Bubbles, Opalescent, Round, 14 In.	236
Powder Box, Art Deco, Flower, 1930s, 4 ½ x 1 ½ In.	245
Vase, Berries, Leaves, Frosted Ground, c.1940, 6 ⅝ In.	246
Vase, Blackberry, Opalescent, Tapered, Signed, 6 ¾ x 6 ½ In.	308
Vase, Flared, Smoky Topaz, Metal Base, Etched Designs, 7 In.	325
Vase, Garnitures, Scrolling Vines, Molded, Satin Opalescent, c.1937, 6 ½ x 6 ¾ In.	695
Vase, Mermaids, Sea Life, Smoky Topaz, c.1936, 10 In.	350
Vase, Roses, Acid Etched, Oval, c.1938, 7 ½ In.	225

VERNON KILNS was the name used by Vernon Potteries, Ltd. The company, which started in 1931 in Vernon, California, made dinnerware and figurines until it went out of business in 1958. The molds were bought by Metlox, which continued to make some patterns. Collectors search for the brightly colored dinnerware and the pieces designed by Rockwell Kent, Walt Disney, and Don Blanding. For more prices, go to kovels.com.

Arcadia, Platter, Oval, 13 In.	11
Barkwood, Bowl, Vegetable, Divided, Oval, 11 In.	13
Barkwood, Creamer	8
Barkwood, Cup & Saucer	6
Blueberry Hill, Creamer	12
Blueberry Hill, Plate, Dinner, 10 ⅜ In.	10
Casa California Hermosa, Platter, Marked, 13 ½ In. ....*illus*	23
Chintz, Butter, Cover, ¼ Lb.	219
Chintz, Plate, Dinner, 10 ⅜ In.	21
Del Rey, Chop Plate, 13 In.	24
Del Rey, Gravy Boat, Underplate.	39
Dolores, Bowl, Cereal, Lugged, 7 ½ In.	14
Dolores, Chop Plate, Round, 14 In.	26
Dolores, Cup & Saucer	13
Fantasia, Vase, Pegasus, Resting On Branch, Light Blue, Disney Copyright, 1940, 11 ½ x 8 In. *illus*	348
Harvest, Chop Plate, Round, 12 In.	45
Heyday, Butter, Cover, ½ In.	19
Heyday, Plate, Dinner, 10 ¼ In.	7
Imperial, Cup & Saucer.	8
Imperial, Shaker, Pepper, 3 In.	17
May Flower, Creamer, 3 ⅞ In.	17
May Flower, Plate, Dinner, 10 ½ In.	28
May Flower, Platter, Oval, 13 In.	44
Monterey, Gravy Boat	36

Monterey, Plate, Salad, 7 ½ In.	6
Monterey, Salt & Pepper	13
Organdie, Sugar & Creamer, Lid ....*illus*	25

VERRE DE SOIE glass was first made by Frederick Carder at the Steuben Glass Works from about 1905 to 1930. It is an iridescent glass of soft white or very, very pale green. The name means "glass of silk," and it does resemble silk. Other factories have made verre de soie, and some of the English examples were made of different colors. Verre de soie is an art glass and is not related to the iridescent, pressed, white carnival glass mistakenly called by its name. Related pieces may be found in the Steuben category.

Dish, Sweetmeat, 3 Iridescent Applied Designs, Silver Plate Lid, Bail, Kralik, 5 In.	118
Perfume Bottle, Melon Shape, Ribbed, Flame Stopper, Steuben, c.1910, 7 In.	450
Tumbler, Etched, D, Steuben, 4 In.	150

VIENNA, *see Beehive category.*

VIENNA ART plates are round metal serving trays produced at the turn of the century. The designs, copied from Royal Vienna porcelain plates, usually featured a portrait of a woman encircled by a wide, ornate border. Many were used as advertising or promotional items and were produced in Coshocton, Ohio, by J. F. Meeks Tuscarora Advertising Co. and H.D. Beach's Standard Advertising Co.

Plate, Captain John Smith, Pocahontas, Indians, 1905, 10 In.	100
Plate, Marguerite, Long Hair, Red Cap, Gold, Turquoise, Dark Blue, 10 ⅛ In.	110
Plate, Queen Louise Of Prussia, 1906, 10 ⅛ In.	120
Plate, Woman, Dark Hair, Lowcut Dress, Green, Gold, c.1905, 10 ⅛ In.	115
Plate, Woman, Flowing Hair, Gold, Jade Green, 1908, 10 ¼ In.	100

VILLEROY & BOCH POTTERY of Mettlach was founded in 1836. The firm made many types of wares, including the famous Mettlach steins. Collectors can be confused because although Villeroy & Boch made most of its pieces in the city of Mettlach, Germany, the company also had factories in other locations. The dating code impressed on the bottom of most pieces makes it possible to determine the age of the piece. Additional items, including steins and earthenware pieces marked with the famous castle mark or the word *Mettlach*, may be found in the Mettlach category.

Charger, Virginia, Verse, Multicolor Brushed, Cut Sponge Flowers, Leaves, 12 In.	24
Jardiniere, Scroll Handles, Footed, Leaves, c.1900, 8 x 16 In.	480
Plate, Dessert, Fruit Transfer, 4 Piece	59
Punch Bowl, Underplate, Gnomes, Making Wine, 10 x 16 In.	267
Vase, Satyrs Design, Elongated Oval, Ring Foot, Marked, 10 ¾ In.	413

VOLKMAR POTTERY was made by Charles Volkmar of New York from 1879 to about 1911. He was associated with several firms, including the Volkmar Ceramic Company, Volkmar and Cory, and Charles Volkmar and Son. He was hired by Durant Kilns of Bedford Village, New York, in 1910 to oversee production. Volkmar bought the business and after 1930 only the Volkmar name was used as a mark. Volkmar had been a painter, and his designs often look like oil paintings drawn on pottery.

Jardiniere, Fox Hunting Scene, Footed, Barbotine, Signed, 7 ½ x 15 In.	1268
Vase, Green Glaze, Carved Leaves, c.1900, 14 x 8 In.	1188
Vase, Green Mattte Glaze, Bulbous, c.1911, 10 ½ In.	1230
Vase, Horse Drawn Carriage, Driver, Timber, 4-Sided, Barbotine, 12 x 8 x 3 In.	986
Vase, Leaves, Carved, Green & Tan Glossy Glaze, 4 Extended Tab Feet, 14 In.	1188

VOLKSTEDT was a soft-paste porcelain factory started in 1760 by Georg Heinrich Macheleid at Volkstedt, Thuringia. Volkstedt-Rudolstadt was a porcelain factory started at Volkstedt-Rudolstadt by Beyer and Bock in 1890. Most pieces seen in shops today are from the later factory.

Candlestick, Figural, Children Gathering Flowers, Wheat Sheaves, c.1875, 12 In., Pair	1500
Chocolate Pot, Bouquets, Gilt, Rose Finial, c.1900, 10 In.	250
Cup & Saucer, Roses, Pink, Red, Gold Trim & Interior, Demitasse, c.1960	35
Figurine, Boy, Basket Over Shoulder, Marked, c.1890, 14 In.	450
Figurine, Boy, Girl, Playing Wind Pipe, Marked, 5 In. & 3 In., Pair	245
Figurine, Couple, Dancing, Flowered Outfits, 6 ⅞ In.	309
Figurine, Dog, Scottish Terrier, Gray, 7 x 5 In.	250
Figurine, Gentleman, Bowing, Holding Rose, c.1900, 8 In.	174
Figurine, Girl, Ballerina, Lacy Skirt, Raised Arms, 5 ½ In.	95

Vernon Kilns, Casa California Hermosa, Platter, Marked, 13 ½ In.
$23

Ruby Lane, Inc.

Vernon Kilns, Fantasia, Vase, Pegasus, Resting On Branch, Light Blue, Disney Copyright, 1940, 11 ½ x 8 In.
$348

Hake's Americana & Collectibles

Vernon Kilns, Organdie, Sugar & Creamer, Lid
$25

Ruby Lane, Inc.

Walrath, Vase, Stylized Cattails, Matte Glaze, Signed, 8 ¼ In.
$15,525

Cottone Auctions

U
V

Watch, E. Howard, Open Face, Seconds
Dial, Monogram, Chain, Pocket
$584

Pook & Pook, Inc.

Watch, Elgin, Open Face, Engraved,
Silvertone Dial, 14K White Gold, c.1921,
1 ⅝ In.
$368

Aspire Auctions

Watch, Elgin, Open Face, Gold Filled
Case, 1912, 1 ¼ In.
$83

Manor Auctions LLC

U
V

TIP

*Vintage watches
should be cleaned
regularly, probably
once a year.*

Figurine, Girl, Bonnet, Umbrella, Beige & Gold, 9 In.	180
Figurine, Man, Playing Mandolin, Multicolor, c.1910, 8 In.	136
Group, 3 Girls, Holding Hands, Lacy Dresses, c.1900, 6 ½ x 6 ½ In.	850
Group, Children Playing Chess, Seated At Table, 19th Century, 5 ½ In.	795
Incense Burner, Oriental Style, Foo Dog, 2 Parts, 7 ¾ In.	95
Planter, Figures, Angels, Dolphin, Semi-Nude, Baroque Rim, Sepia, c.1890, 9 x 5 x 4 In.	595
Plaque, Nymphs Swimming, Waves, Deer, Swan, c.1890, 10 x 8 In.	360
Plaque, Seminude, Dolphin, Angels, Baroque Border, c.1895, 10 ½ x 8 In.	695

WADE pottery is made by the Wade Group of Potteries started in 1810 near Burslem, England. Several potteries merged to become George Wade & Son, Ltd., early in the twentieth century, and other potteries have been added through the years. The best-known Wade pieces are the small figurines called Whimsies. They were first were made in 1954. Special Whimsies were given away with Red Rose Tea beginning in 1967. The Disney figures are listed in this book in the Disneyana category.

Figurine, Cairn Terrier, Honey Brown, 1969, 2 ½ x 2 ¾ In.	40
Figurine, Florist Shop, 1 ½ x 1 ⅜ In.	23
Figurine, Humpty Dumpty, 1 ½ In.	12
Figurine, Irish Setter, 2 ½ In.	40
Figurine, Merryweather Farm, 1 ⅞ x 1 ⅞ In.	35
Figurine, Queen Of Hearts, 1 ½ In.	14
Figurine, Why Knott Inn, 1 ½ x 1 ¼ In.	18

WAHPETON POTTERY, *see Rosemeade category.*

WALL POCKETS were popular in the 1930s. They were made by many American and European factories. Glass, pottery, porcelain, majolica, chalkware, and metal wall pockets can be found in many fanciful shapes.

Oak, Rosehead Nails, Molded Front Panel, Incised, 1867, 11 In.	600
Ribbed, Green, Marked Nicodemus, 8 ¼ In.	104

WALLACE NUTTING *photographs are listed under Print, Nutting. His reproduction furniture is listed under Furniture.*

WALRATH was a potter who worked in New York City; Rochester, New York; and at the Newcomb Pottery in New Orleans, Louisiana. Frederick Walrath died in 1920. Pieces listed here are from his Rochester period.

Cider Set, Stylized Grape, Matte Glaze, Pitcher, 4 Cups, 7 x 7 ½ In., 5 Piece	2375 to 2806
Pitcher, Lemon Tree Border, Matte Glaze, 10 x 7 ½ In.	1125
Vase, Orange Flowers, Green Stems, Leaves, Blue Ground, Matte Glaze, Incised, 5 In.	4248
Vase, Stylized Cattails, Matte Glaze, Signed, 8 ¼ In. *illus*	15525

WALT DISNEY, *see Disneyana category.*

WALTER, *see A. Walter category.*

WARWICK china was made in Wheeling, West Virginia, in a pottery working from 1887 to 1951. Many pieces were made with hand painted or decal decorations. The most familiar Warwick has a shaded brown background. The name *Warwick* is part of the mark and sometimes the mysterious word *IOGA* is also included.

Bowl, Blue Trim, Raddison Plaza Hotel, Philadelphia, c.1926, 6 ¼ In.	90
Bowl, Lewis & Neblett Co., Orange Scroll & Flower Border, 6 ½ In.	8
Grill Plate, Tudor Rose, Blue & White, c.1928	25
Plate, 2 Fish, Flower Border, Decal, Marked, 8 In.	85
Plate, Monk, Drinking Out Of Bottle, Transfer, Marked, 9 ⅜ In.	80
Tankard, Elk, Brown Glaze, Decal, Marked, c.1890, 5 In.	75
Tankard, Seafaring Man, Smoking Pipe, Decal, Marked, 4 ¼ In.	55
Vase, Poppy, Oval, Brown Glaze, 11 x 6 In.	59

WATCH pockets held the pocket watch that was important in Victorian times because it was not until World War I that the wristwatch was used. All types of watches are collected: silver, gold, or plated. Watches are listed here by company name or by style. Wristwatches are a separate category.

Borel & Courvoisier, Open Face, 18K Gold, No. 53629, Pocket, 2 ⅛ In.	1680

Cartier, Open Face, Minute Repeater, 18K Yellow Gold, Pocket	10200
Cartier, Open Face, Silvertone Dial, Flower Engraved Back Panel, Swiss, c.1920, 2 ¼ In.	4063
Chronometer, J. Carter, London, No. 697, Silver, Chain Fusee, 2-Day, Fitted Box, 1850, 3 In.	7800
E. Howard, Hunting Case, 18K Gold, Engraved Flowers, Stones, 15 Jewel, c.1875	1560
E. Howard, Open Face, Seconds Dial, Monogram, Chain, Pocket......................*illus*	584
Elgin, Hunting Case, Sterling, Inlaid Yellow, Rose Flowers, White Dial, Signed, c.1900, 2 In.	115
Elgin, Open Face, Engraved, Silvertone Dial, 14K White Gold, c.1921, 1 ⅝ In. ....*illus*	368
Elgin, Open Face, Gold Filled Case, 1912, 1 ¼ In. ....*illus*	83
Elgin, Open Face, Octagonal, 14K Gold, 15 Jewel, Size 8	356
Elgin, Open Face, Porcelain Dial, Goldtone	85
Elgin, Open Face, Silver, 2 In., Pocket	62
Elgin, Open Face, Silver, Key Wind, 2 ¼ In., Pocket	79
Elgin, Rounded Triangle, Indented Corners, Arabic, Gold Filled, Art Deco, Pocket	149
Frederic Lagne, Hunting Case, Stones, 18K Gold, Enamel, Chaux De Fonds, 1 ½ In. ....*illus*	3000
Gilt Brass Case, Painted Horn Back, Hunting Scene, France, c.1800	738
Golay Fils & Stahl, Open Face, White Enamel Dial, Arabic Numerals, 18K Gold, Geneva	960
Gruen VeriThin Co., Open Face, 14K Gold, 17 Jewel	97
Hamilton, 14K White Gold, Open Face, 1 ½ In., Pocket	367
Hamilton, Montgomery Style, Double-Sunk Dial, Blued Spade Hands, Stem Wind, 21 Jewel	270
Hamilton, Open Face, 18K Yellow Gold, Silvertone Dial, Presentation 1937, 1 ¾ In.	886
Hampden Watch Co., Special Railway, 23 Jewel, Porcelain, Marginal Numbers, c.1903, 2 ¼ In. . *illus*	403
Howard, 18K Gold, Double Case, Chain, Mahogany Box, c.1912, Size 16	170
Illinois Watch Co., Bunn Special, Gold Filled, Open Face, Double Sunk Dial, 21 Jewel	300
J. Planche, Pair Case, Gold, Porcelain Dial, Roman Numerals, Gilt Fusee, c.1750	2337
Longines, Enamel Dial, Painted Numerals, Gold Highlights, Silver Case, Woman's, c.1900, 1 In.	150
Longines, Open Face, 14K Gold, 15 Jewel, Black Star & Frost, Pocket, 1 ¾ In.	863
Movado, Hunting Case, Goldtone, Pocket	40
Nicolaus Rugendas, Sun & Moon Dial, Pierced, Punched Case, Repousse, c.1690	3998
Norton, London, Gilt Brass, Enamel, Battle Scene, Chased Flowers, c.1785, Pocket	480
Open Face, 18K Yellow Gold, Enameled Miniature Woman's Portrait, 1 ¾ In.	357
Open Face, Coin Silver, Key Wind, White Dial, Roman Numerals, 2 In. ....*illus*	73
W. Sayer, Pair Case, Gold, Repousse Classical Figures, Scrolls, Brass Dial, Beaded, c.1760	2706
Waltham, 14K Yellow Gold, Engraved Case, Penelope Movement, Woman's	384
Waltham, Ballplayer Hour Mark, Porcelain Face, Pocket, c.1900	1659
Waltham, Hatch, Flower Incised Case, 14K Gold, Pocket, Woman's	242
Waltham, Open Face, Pocket, No. 200060383, Inscribed Captain Hall J. Tibbits, Pocket	120
Waltham, Open Face, Silver, 17 Jewel, 1 ¾ In., Pocket	68
Waltham, Open Face, Swing-Out Style, 14K Gold, 17 Jewel, Size 8	356
Waltham, Premier Colonial, Open Face, 10K Gold, 17 Jewel, 1 ½ In., Pocket	62
Waltham, Skeleton Case, Silvertone, Pocket	68
Zentler & Co., Geneva, 18K Gold, Porcelain Dial, Monogram, Pocket, 2 In. Diam.	4212

WATCH FOBS were worn on watch chains. They were popular during Victorian times and after. Many styles, especially advertising designs, are still made today.

Andale Relay Race, Arrowhead Shape, Indian, Raised Arms, 1930s, 2 In.	15
Art Deco Wings, Goldstone, Moonstone, 1920s, 1 In. Diam.	135
Art Deco, Sterling, Abstract Geometric, Buckle, W. & H. Co., Newark, N.J.	150
Ball, T-Bar, 14K Gold, Black Jet Links, 5 ½ In.	210
Benjamin Franklin, 19th Century, 2 In.	25
Chain, Toggle, Ring Clasp, Lobster Clasp, 14K Yellow Gold, 13 In.	644
Cigar Cutter, Sterling Silver, Flower & Leaves, Germany, c.1900, 3 In.	185
Cleveland Leader, Naps Lajoie, Game Scorer, Leather Strap, Celluloid, c.1910	905
Dart Board, Sterling Silver, Multicolor, Enamel, c.1940, 1 In. Diam.	20
Elks Lodge B.P.O.E., Elk Tooth, White Gold	125
Flowers, Mosaic, Italy, c.1850	155
Formal, Ribbon, 14K Yellow Gold, Lobster Clasp, 5 In.	69
Goldfish, Bulging Eyes, Jadeite, c.1910, 1 ½ In.	135
Knights Of Columbus Seal, Goldstone Setting, c.1900, 1 ⅞ In.	25
Long Mfg., Tractor, Scoop Shovel, Yellow, 1 ½ x 2 In.	20
Ship's Wheel, Ruby Paste Stone, Art Deco, Silver Metal, c.1900, 6 In.	90
Spanish American War Veterans, Cross, Bronze, 1 ⅝ x 1 ½ In.	29
Trout Fly, Brass Frame, c.1900, 1 In. Diam.	95
Turquoise, Sterling Silver, Art & Crafts, 1 ½ x 1 ½ In.	675

Watch, Frederic Lagne, Hunting Case, Stones, 18K Gold, Enamel, Chaux De Fonds, 1 ½ In.
$3,000

Skinner Auctioneers & Appraisers

Watch, Hampden Watch Co., Special Railway, 23 Jewel, Porcelain, Marginal Numbers, c.1903, 2 ¼ In.
$403

Aspire Auctions

Watch, Open Face, Coin Silver, Key Wind, White Dial, Roman Numerals, 2 In.
$73

Cottone Auctions

W

Watt, Apple, Pitcher, No. 16, 3-Leaf
$38

Watt, Arches, Bowl, No. 7, Pumpkin Color, Marked
$16

Wave Crest, Cigarette Jar, Word Cigarettes On Reverse, Shell Pattern Lid, Marked, 3 ¾ In.
$356

Wave Crest, Dish, Sweetmeat, Lid, Panels Of Blossoms, Silver Plate Collar, Handle, 3 ½ In.
$546

WATERFORD type glass resembles the famous glass made from 1783 to 1851 in the Waterford Glass Works in Ireland. It is a clear glass that was often decorated by cutting. Modern glass is being made again in Waterford, Ireland, and is marketed under the name Waterford. Waterford merged with Wedgwood in 1986 to form the Waterford Wedgwood Group. Most Waterford Wedgwood assets were bought by KPS Capital Partners of New York in 2009 and became part of WWRD Holdings.

Bowl, Diamond Cuts, Notched Rim, Acid Stamp, Ireland, 9 In.	60
Bowl, Low, Cutout Rim, Basket Weave Design, 13 ½ In.	330
Candlestick, Clear, Acid Etched Mark, 8 ¼ In., Pair	92
Candlestick, Columnar, Square Stepped Base, Square Cup, 11 In., Pair	150
Candlestick, Seahorse, Clear, Sticker, Acid Etched Mark, 11 ½ In., Pair	115
Champagne Flute, Lismore, 9 In., Pair	50
Decanter, Diamond Pattern, Squat, Narrow Neck, Ball Stopper, 11 In.	96
Decanter, Etched, Bell Shape, Flared Rim, Mushroom Shape Stopper, 11 In.	180
Decanter, Oval, Round Pedestal Foot, Narrow Neck, Stopper, Etched, 15 In.	126
Decanter, Ship's, Lismore, Bulbous Stopper, Acid Etched, 9 ¾ In.	121
Tumbler, Eileen Pattern, 4 ¼ In., 8 Piece	176
Tumbler, Iced Tea, Lismore, 14 Oz., Box, 6 Piece	249
Tumbler, Lismore, 9 Oz., Box, 6 Piece	181
Vase, Acid Stamp, Ireland, 10 In.	90
Vase, Martha Washington Collection, Globular, Ruffled Rim, Acid Etched Mark, 8 x 8 In.	180
Vase, Trumpet Shape, Round Foot, Etched, 10 x 6 ¼ In.	96

WATT family members bought the Globe pottery of Crooksville, Ohio, in 1922. They made pottery mixing bowls and tableware of the type made by Globe. In 1935 they changed the production and made the pieces with the freehand decorations that are popular with collectors today. Apple, Starflower, Rooster, Tulip, and Autumn Foliage are the best-known patterns. Pansy, also called Rio Rose, was the earliest pattern. Apple, the most popular pattern, can be dated from the leaves. Originally, the apples had three leaves; after 1958 two leaves were used. The plant closed in 1965. For more prices, go to kovels.com.

Apple, Bean Cup, No. 75, 3-Leaf, 2 In.	324
Apple, Bean Pot, Lid, No. 76, 3-Leaf, 5 ½ In.	158
Apple, Mug, 3-Leaf, No.121, 3 ¾ In.	165
Apple, Pie Plate, No. 33, 9 In.	92
Apple, Pitcher, No. 16, 3-Leaf ....*illus*	38
Apple, Sugar, No. 89, 3-Leaf, Handles, 4 ¼ In.	195
Arches, Bowl, No. 7, Pumpkin Color, Marked ....*illus*	16
Cherry, Casserole, No. 18, 4 ¼ In.	165
Dutch Tulip, Pitcher, No. 15, 5 ¼ In.	140
Rooster, Mixing Bowl, No. 9, 9 In.	39
Rooster, Mixing Bowl, No. 65, 9 In.	54
Sleeping Mexican, Bowl, No. 601, Ribbed, Brown, 8 ¾ x 3 ¾ In.	35
Starflower, Bowl, Salad, No. 74, 4-Petal, 5 ⅝ In.	45
Starflower, Bowl, Vegetable, No. 60, 5-Petal, 6 ⅛ In.	38
Starflower, Bowl, Vegetable, No. 66, 5-Petal, 7 ¼ In.	48
Starflower, Mug, No. 61, 5-Petal	150
Starflower, Pitcher, No. 15, 4-Petal, 16 Oz., 5 ½ In.	124
Starflower, Pitcher, No. 15, 5-Petal, 5 ¼ In.	80
Starflower, Pitcher, No. 16, 4-Petal, 32 Oz., 6 ½ In.	45
Tear Drop, Pitcher, No. 15, 5-Leaf, 5 ⅜ In.	75
Tulip, Casserole, Individual, Lid, No. 18, 2 ½ x 5 In.	180
Tulip, Creamer, No. 62, 12 Oz., 4 ⅜ In.	96

WAVE CREST glass is an opaque white glassware manufactured by the Pairpoint Manufacturing Company of New Bedford, Massachusetts, and some French factories. It was decorated by the C.F. Monroe Company of Meriden, Connecticut. The glass was painted in pastel colors and decorated with flowers. The name Wave Crest was used starting in 1892.

WAVE CREST WARE

Biscuit Jar, Pink Flowers, Square Shape, Metal Lid & Handle, 8 In.	79
Box, Egg Crate Shape, Mold Blown, Robin, On Floral Branch, Appliqued Brass Wash Feet, 6 In.	593
Box, Helmschmied Swirl Cover & Body, Forget-Me-Nots, Ormolu Feet, 6 x 7 In.	172
Box, Lid, Jamestown, Blue Green Transparent	95
Box, Swirl Molded, Square Top, Metal Hardware, Blue Enamel Flowers, 3 ¼ x 2 ¾ In.	77
Cigarette Jar, Word Cigarettes On Reverse, Shell Pattern Lid, Marked, 3 ¾ In. ....*illus*	356
Dish, Sweetmeat, Lid, Panels Of Blossoms, Silver Plate Collar, Handle, 3 ½ In. ....*illus*	546
Dresser Box, Blue, Pink Enamel Flowers, Raised Design, Round, CFM Co., Nakara, 8 x 6 In.	696

Dresser Box, Blue, Pink Flowers, Cherubs, Wine, Mirror, Round, CFM Co., Nakara, 8 x 4 In.......	754
Dresser Box, Brass Trim, Footed, Square, 6 In..	215
Dresser Box, Daisies, Leaves, Swirled, Paper Label, 4 x 7 In...........................	126
Dresser Box, Pink Flowers, Blue, Enameled, Oval, CFM Co., Kelva, 5 ½ x 4 In...........	242
Dresser Box, Pink Flowers, Egg Crate Shape, Brass, C.F. Monroe, c.1910, 4 x 4 In........	258
Dresser Box, Woman, Pink, Raised White Enamel, Triangular, CFM Co., Nakara, 9 x 5 In........	754
Humidor, Cigar, Flowers, Blue, Lavender Letters, Lid, Gilt Trim, CFM Co., Nakara, 6 x 4 In.	377
Jardiniere, Opal Blue, Flower Reserve, Brass Rim, Footed, C.F. Monroe, c.1910, 9 x 7 In.	259
Jardiniere, Rural Cabin Scene, Round, c.1910, 7 ¾ x 9 In.......................	316
Letter Holder, Flowers, Vines, Purple, Brass Collar, C.F. Monroe Co., 5 ¾ x 4 In........	500
Letter Holder, Green & White, Pink Flowers, 4 ¼ x 6 ¼ In.......................	148
Powder Box, Swirl Lobed, Mauve Flowers, White Ground, Gilt Frame, 3 ½ x 7 In.........	196
Vase, Flowers, Light Green Ground, Metal Dolphin Feet, Handles, 17 In............	522
Vase, White Flowers, Burgundy, Green Enamel, Heavily Scrolled, Metal Handles, 12 In........	928
Vase, Woman, Partly Dressed, Cherubs, Gray Green Ground, Ormolu Handles, Feet, 18 In........	3480

WEAPONS listed here include instruments of combat other than guns, knives, rifles, or swords and clothing worn in combat. Firearms made after 1900 are not listed in this book. Knives and Swords are listed in their own categories.

Armor, Plate Mail, Full Suit, Stand, England, c.1700, 68 In..................................	13750
Armor, Suit, Metal, Wood Base, 1900s, 42 x 14 ½ In. ....*illus*	1375
Ax, Steel, Offset Head, Stamped GB, Wood Handle, 19th Century, 42 In.	382
Battle Ax, Wood Haft, Crescent, Double Point, Crocodile Skin, Sudanese, c.1885, 25 In.	975
Breastplate, Steel Armor, St. George & The Dragon, c.1700, 18 x 15 In............................	360
Gauntlet, Plate Armor, Left Hand, Articulated Pieces, Spain, 17th Century, 10 In........................	441
Gorget, Plate Armor, Pivot, Locking Pins, Red Paint, Spain, 17th Century	512
Gun, Blunderbuss, Walnut Stock, Brass Fittings, Barrel, Ketland & Co., c.1800, 27 ½ In.	2160
Gun, Flintlock Pistol, Belt Hook, Iron, Octagonal To Round End Barrel, c.1790, 8 In.	570
Gun, Grave Robber's, Flintlock Trap, Iron, Stepped Base, c.1810, 19 ¾ In...................	900
Gun, Swivel, Bronze, Cannon Tube No. 1112, Wood Stand, Brass Yoke, c.1800, 23 x 36 In.	3360
Helmet, Cavalry, Steel, Brass, South Salopian Yeomanry, England, c.1900, 14 x 7 In.	1750
Helmet, Close, Fluted, Visor, France, c.1650, 13 x 10 ½ In...................................	7500
Jambiya, White Metal Relief, Embossed Leaves, Stone Handle, Syrian, 5 In........................	135
Pinfire Pistol, Knuckle Knife, Apache, Steel Frame, Blade, 1875, 7 ½ In. ....*illus*	2040
Revolver, Knuckle Duster, My Friend, 22 Caliber, James Reid, c.1865, 4 In.....................	840
Rifle, 1st Model, Walnut Grips, Ethan Allen Grafton Mass, c.1840, 13 ¾ In. ....*illus*	938
Ross Winans Pike, Wrought Iron, Double Edged Blade, Wood Haft, Baltimore, 1861, 80 In.......	1495
Shirt, Chain Mail, England, c.1790, 41 x 29 In.	1000
Signal Cannon, Cast Iron, Wooden Carriage, 34 ½ In..	450

WEATHER VANES were used in seventeenth-century Boston. The direction of the wind was an indication of coming weather, important to the seafaring and farming communities. By the mid-nineteenth century, commercial weather vanes were made of metal. Many were shaped like animals. Ethan Allen, Dexter, and St. Julian are famous horses that were depicted. Today's collectors often consider weather vanes to be examples of folk art, even though they may not have been handmade.

Airplane, Verdigris Patina, 31 x 13 In..	403
Apple, Arrow, Copper, Stand, 30 ¾ x 18 In.	4600
Arrow & Ball, Wrought Iron, Black Paint, U.S.A., c.1865, 63 ½ x 39 In................	430
Arrow, Scrolls, Copper, Patina, 27 x 60 In...	2040
Banner, Arrow, Scrolls, Copper, Signed, 1847, 49 x 75 In............................	6000
Banner, Brass, Directional, 30 In.	840
Banner, Copper, Zinc, Green Patina, c.1850, 24 In.................................	1652
Banner, Pierced E, Scrolls, Copper, Black Stand, 27 In............................	1020
Banner, Sheet Iron, Stand, c.1865, 45 In..	326
Blacksmith Shop, Horse, Anvil, Smoke Rising On Directional, c.1900, 23 x 38 In...........	288
Blacksmith, Black Paint, Sheet Iron, 21 x 35 In......................................	356
Blacksmith, Horse, Sheet Metal, 35 x 21 In.......................................	489
Bull, Full Body, Cutout, Sheet Copper, Wood Stand, c.1885, 16 x 26 In.	1200
Butterfly, Copper, Zinc, Patinated, 30 x 43 In...	2040
Butterfly, Mechanical, Red, Yellow Painted Body, Sheet Iron, c.1915, 22 ½ In.	563
Cockerel, Black, Yellow Paint, Sheet Iron, c.1790, 12 x 15 In.	1304
Codfish, Copper Verdigris, Stand, 25 x 13 In.......................................	575
Codfish, Copper, Green Patina, c.1945, 26 In.	826
Codfish, Full Body, Directionals, Copper, c.1885, 26 x 36 In..............................	5333

Weapon, Armor Suit, Metal, Wood Base, 1900s, 42 x 14 ½ In.
$1,375

Rago Arts & Auction Center

Weapon, Pinfire Pistol, Knuckle Knife, Apache, Steel Frame, Blade, 1875, 7 ½ In.
$2,040

Skinner Auctioneers & Appraisers

Weapon, Rifle, 1st Model, Walnut Grips, Ethan Allen Grafton Mass, c.1840, 13 ¾ In.
$938

Rago Arts & Auction Center

Weather Vane, Grasshopper, Full Body, Copper, Molded, Verdigris, Gilt, c.1885, 15 x 38 In.
$26,730

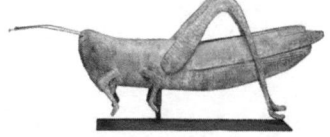

James D. Julia Auctioneers

W

Weather Vane, Horse & Rider, Full Body, Molded, Rod, Copper, c.1925, 29 x 26 In. $1,046

Skinner Auctioneers & Appraisers

Weather Vane, Pig, Full Body, Copper, Verdigris, Gilded, c.1910, 22 x 32 In. $4,444

James D. Julia Auctioneers

Webb, Finger Bowl, Underplate, 3-Color Cascading Flowers, Butterflies, Marked, 4 ½ In. $863

Early Auction Co.

Webb, Ice Bucket, Penguins, Acid Cut Snowy Ground, Signed, 8 ⅞ x 5 ¼ In. $474

James D. Julia Auctioneers

Cow, Full Body, Copper, Zinc Head, 18 x 27 In.	3792
Cow, Standing, Sheet Metal, 27 x 17 In.	4600
Dog, Irish Setter, Brown Paint, Sheet Iron, 20 x 20 ½ In.	316
Dog, Leaping, Copper, Black Stand, 41 x 16 ½ In.	3450
Dog, Setter, Standing, Iron, 32 x 15 In.	6325
Duck, Sheet Iron, Directional, 19 x 27 In.	266
Eagle & Scroll, Directional, Copper, J.W. Fiske, 38 x 58 In.	4500
Eagle, Copper, Verdigris, c.1850, 37 In.	563
Eagle, Full Body, Arrow Directional, Copper, c.1900, 21 x 24 In.	999
Eagle, Full Body, Spread Wings, Copper, Zinc Feet, c.1900, 51 ½ x 35 ½ In.	492
Eagle, On Globe, Directional, Copper, 52 In.	649
Eagle, Spread Wings, 19 x 33 In.	403
Eagle, Spread Wings, Ball & Arrow Mount, Copper, 24 In.	413
Eagle, Spread Wings, Copper, Gilt, c.1845, 13 ½ In.	450
Eagle, Spread Wings, Copper, Gilt, c.1880, 20 x 25 In.	7200
Fire Engine, Horse Drawn, Painted, Arrow, Sheet Iron, c.1885, 16 x 38 In.	3259
Fire Pumper, Horse Drawn, On Arrow, Directionals, Cutout Sheet Metal, Iron, 37 In.	484
Fish, Full Body, Copper, Gilt, Black Metal Stand, 14 x 26 In.	4200
Fish, Wood, Pierced, 46 In.	3600
Fiske Banner, Star Cutout, Copper, Verdigris Patina, 27 x 14 ½ In.	834
Fox, Leaping, Copper, Stand, 28 ½ x 14 In.	4025
Fox, Painted, Carved, Wood, Black Stand, 12 x 25 In.	5520
Fox, Running, Red Paint, Sheet Metal, c.1900, 48 ½ In.	649
Gabriel, Flying, Blowing Trumpet, Holding Bible, Wood, Carved, Mass., 46 In.	9600
Girl, Bloomers, Hoop, Sheet Metal, Black Stand, 18 In.	978
Grasshopper, Copper, Verdigris Patina, 23 ½ x 19 ½ In.	633
Grasshopper, Full Body, Copper, Molded, Verdigris, Gilt, c.1885, 15 x 38 In. ......*illus*	26730
Grasshopper, Steepletop, Full Body, Copper, c.1915, 17 ½ x 24 In.	1422
Hammer, Anvil, Copper, c.1915, 72 In.	1440
Hand, Pointing Index Finger, Wood, Folk Art, 19th Century, 37 In.	953
Horse & Rider, Full Body, Molded, Rod, Copper, c.1925, 29 x 26 In. ......*illus*	1046
Horse & Rider, Full Body, Trotting, Sheet Copper, Stand, c.1885, 18 ½ x 20 In.	11400
Horse & Sulky, Driver, Copper 33 x 9 In.	1750
Horse & Sulky, Driver, Copper, Zinc, 47 In.	49200
Horse & Sulky, Driver, Directional, Copper, Verdigris, 20 x 48 In.	6683
Horse, Full Body, Prancing, Copper, Baluster Shaft, c.1900, 59 x 35 In.	1560
Horse, Full Body, Running, Armature, Copper, c.1885, 28 x 68 In.	3585
Horse, Full Body, Running, Full Mane & Tail, Copper, Stand, c.1885, 22 x 34 In.	1599
Horse, Hackney, Prancing, Molded Copper, J.W. Fiske, New York, c.1890, 21 x 30 In.	1778
Horse, Paint, Sheet Iron, 33 x 24 In.	374
Horse, Prancing, Copper, Cutout Silhouette, c.1915, 32 In.	1200
Horse, Prancing, Sheet Iron, 27 In.	660
Horse, Rearing, Painted Red, Sheet Metal, 24 x 32 In.	468
Horse, Rearing, Sheet Iron, 16 ½ x 15 ½ In.	420
Horse, Rochester Type, Cast Iron, 36 x 27 In.	3450
Horse, Running, Copper, Verdigris, 1800s, 20 x 43 In.	2560
Horse, Running, Copper, Zinc Head, Patina, Wood Post, c.1890, 39 In.	1205
Horse, Running, Copper, Zinc Head, Verdigris, Full Body, Bullet Holes, c.1890, 26 In.	1560
Horse, Running, Directional Stand, Copper, Zinc, 40 In.	1625
Horse, Running, White Paint, Sheet Metal, 18 x 29 In.	720
Horse, Standing, Copper, Zinc Head, Gold Paint, Full Body, Hambletonian, c.1890, 25 x 28 In.	4440
Horse, Standing, Gilt Copper, Zinc Head, Full Body, Ball Finial, c.1890, 19 In.	1265
Horse, Trotting, Full Bodied, Zinc, Copper, J.W. Fiske Co., c.1921, 16 x 38 In.	1230
Horse, Walking, Arrow, White Paint, Sheet Iron, New Eng., 53 x 56 In.	115
Indian, Crouched By Fire, Directionals, Paint, Sheet Steel, c.1890, 44 x 31 In.	2950
Jockey, Horse, Galloping, Copper, Cast Iron, c.1890, 32 In.	2006
Lightning Rod, Arrow Directional, Cranberry Glass Insert, Colored Glass Ball, 42 In.	212
Lobster, Copper, Black Stand, 29 ½ x 19 In.	7763
Pig, Cast Zinc Head & Tail, 12 x 13 In.	6900
Pig, Full Body, Copper, Verdigris, Gilded, c.1910, 22 x 32 In. ......*illus*	4444
Pig, Lightening Rod, 23 x 5 In.	173
Porpoise, Copper, 32 x 25 In.	177
Quill, Copper, 35 x 14 In.	2875
Rod, Directionals, Iron, 126 In.	243
Rooster, 1 Raised Leg, Painted Red, Riveted, Sheet Iron, c.1900, 31 In.	403
Rooster, Arrow Mount, Copper, 23 ½ x 24 In.	1888

W

Rooster, Copper, Gilt, Jewell & Co., 23 x 20 In.	4800
Rooster, Copper, Hollow Body, Sheet Copper Tail, Base, c.1890, 16 In.	900
Rooster, Directionals, Copper, Verdigris, Base, 21 x 63 In.	1725
Rooster, Full Body, Flattened, Weathered Gold Leaf, Wood, Stand, 23 x 16 In.	19200
Rooster, Full Body, Gilt, Copper, 1800s, 22 In.	1188
Rooster, Gilt, Glass Eyes, 22 ½ In.	1888
Rooster, Green, Gold Paint, Zinc, c.1920, 28 In.	504
Rooster, Paint, Copper, 16 x 19 ½ In.	1725
Rooster, Painted Gold, Copper, Molded, 22 x 24 In.	960
Rooster, Painted Red, Sheet Iron, c.1900, 31 ¼ In.	403
Rooster, Sheet Iron, c.1850, 23 x 25 In.	207
Rooster, Standing On Arrow, Copper, Directionals, 24 In.	115
Rooster, Swell Body, Copper, c.1845, 44 ½ In.	326
Sailboat, Sloop, Gold Paint, 34 x 35 In.	1150
Serpent, Sculptural, Sheet Iron, Stand, 50 In.	11400
Sheep, Full Body, Flattened, Copper, Wooly Texture, c.1885, 24 x 29 In.	18000
Ship, 3-Masted, Green, Brown Paint, Wood, Copper, c.1950, 30 In.	225
Ship, 3-Masted, White, Green Paint, Wood, c.1915, 34 In.	384
Smuggler, Running Horse, Flowing Mane, Copper, Molded, Cast Zinc, Harris & Co., 31 In.	288
Soldier, Sheet Metal, 31 In.	230
Sperm Whale, Full Body, Large Head, Copper, c.1915, 21 ½ x 32 ½ In.	6814
Sperm Whale, Wood, Carved, c.1920, 10 x 34 In.	5605
Stag, Leaping, Copper, 29 ½ x 23 ½ In.	4600
Stag, Leaping, Full Body, Gilt Copper, Zinc Antlers, Metal Stand, 18 ¾ In.	4920
Sulky, Copper, Zinc, Full Body Horse, Cast Driver, c.1890, 18 ½ x 31 In.	4440
Sunburst Banner, Inscribed B., 1870, Sheet, Wrought Iron, 35 In.	2844
Surrey, Horse Drawn, Rider, Directional Letters, Copper, Patina, 60 x 16 x 32 In.	584
Tennis Player, Woman, Holding Racket Up, White Paint, Zinc, Copper, 15 x 27 ½ In.	2990
Whale, Copper, c.1900, 56 x 37 In.	660
Whale, Tail Up, Copper, Patinated, c.1915, 37 In.	590
Whirligig, Masquerade Theme, Painted Multicolor, Wood, Carved, 29 In.	72

WEBB glass was made by Thomas Webb & Sons of Ambelcot, England. Many types of art and cameo glass were made by them during the Victorian era. Production ceased by 1991 and the factory was demolished in 1995. Webb Burmese and Webb Peachblow are special colored glasswares of the Victorian era. They are listed at the end of this section. Glassware that is not Burmese or Peachblow is included here.

Webb

Bowl, White Vine, Flowers, Sterling Silver Rim, Foot, Inscription, c.1900, 9 ¾ In.	1320
Cologne Decanter, Cut Glass, Cranberry Panels, Flower Basket, Ferns, Stopper, 11 In.	177
Finger Bowl, Alexandrite, Ruffled Rim, 5 In.	748
Finger Bowl, Underplate, 3-Color Cascading Flowers, Butterflies, Marked, 4 ½ In. *illus*	863
Ice Bucket, Penguins, Acid Cut Snowy Ground, Signed, 8 ⅞ x 5 ¼ In. *illus*	474
Jar, Gorham Silver Rim, Lid, White Over Cranberry, Roses, Inverted Baluster, 4 ¼ In.	1020
Perfume Bottle, Cut Glass, Faceted Stopper, Medallion, Plants, Stuart, 6 ¾ In. *illus*	3450
Perfume Bottle, Mother-Of-Pearl, Spherical, Peacock Eye Body, Enameled Blossoming Branch, 4 In.	1265
Perfume Vial, Laydown, Blue, White Cutback Flowers, 3 ¾ In.	1067
Potpourri Jar, Pierced Lid, Opaque Ivory Ground, Cameo Cut Flowers, Vines, c.1900, 6 In.	720
Vase, Bronze Ware, Multicolor Iridescent, Handles, c.1900, 10 In.	390
Vase, Cabinet, Cased, Amber Shaded To Brown, Pinched Sided, Gilt Gingko Branch, 2 ¾ In.	403
Vase, Cameo Glass, Red, Apple Blossoms, Ferns, Inverted Baluster, Squat Collar, Bands, 8 In.	3000
Vase, Cameo, Frosted Blue Ground, Wheel Carved, Long Billed Bird On Branch, 5 In.	8888
Vase, Flowering Branches, Butterfly, Cameo, Yellow, Molded Mark, c.1890, 10 x 7 In.	2500
Vase, Fruiting Branches, Red, White, Slender Neck, Bulbous, Cameo, c.1910, 14 x 7 ½ In.	1375
Vase, Pink Satin, Gold Enamel Branch, Blossoms, Butterflies, 9 In.	118
Vase, Red, White Roses, Butterflies, Bee, Yellow, Pink Neck, Tapered, Bulbous Base, 8 x 13 In.	6875
Vase, Round, Shouldered, Flared Rim, Acid Cut, Flower Branches, Red, White, 1800s, 5 In.	1840
Vase, Teardrop, Flared Rim, Flowers, Leaves, White On Red, Cameo, Signed, 8 ¾ In. *illus*	2074
Vase, Turquoise, Light Blue Flowering Branch, Butterfly, Shouldered, Cameo, 5 x 9 In.	2500

WEBB BURMESE is a shaded Victorian glass made by Thomas Webb & Sons of Stourbridge, England, from 1886. Pieces are shades of pink to yellow.

Bowl, Flared Rim, Footed, Bird Medallions, Dogwood, 4 ¼ In.	518
Fairy Lamp, Green Leafy Vine, Clarke Base, 4 In.	201
Perfume Bottle, Honeycomb Martele Finish, Globe Shape, Etched, 3 ½ In.	575
Rose Bowl, Hexagonal Rim, Grapes, Leaves, 4 In.	230

Webb, Perfume Bottle, Cut Glass, Faceted Stopper, Medallion, Plants, Stuart, 6 ¾ In. $3,450

Early Auction Co.

Webb, Vase, Teardrop, Flared Rim, Flowers, Leaves, White On Red, Cameo, Signed, 8 ¾ In. $2,074

James D. Julia Auctioneers

Wedgwood, Bottle, Lid, Jasper Dip, Crimson, Classical Figures, c.1920, 6 ¾ In. $1,080

Skinner Auctioneers & Appraisers

W

Wedgwood, Bowl, Fairyland Luster, Dana, Castle, Interior Fairy In Cage, 8-Sided, c.1920, 9 In.
$2,760

Skinner Auctioneers & Appraisers

Wedgwood, Bust, Shakespeare, Black Basalt, Raised Title In Cartouche, Marked, 1964, 10 In.
$400

Skinner Auctioneers & Appraisers

Wedgwood, Group, Bride & Groom, Girl & Boy, Queen's Ware, Arnold Machin, c.1949, 10 ¾ In.
$1,920

Skinner Auctioneers & Appraisers

Wedgwood, Lamp, Oil, Basalt, River Of Life, Gilt Highlights, Stamped, 1800s, 8 ½ x 8 In.
$6,875

Rago Arts & Auction Center

Rose Bowl, Lilac, Crimped Ruffled Rim, Red Berries, Green Leaves, 2 ¼ In.	489
Vase, Egg Shape, 3 Applied Feet, 3 ½ In.	144
Vase, Stick, Gilt Leafy Branches, Bulbous, Paper Label, 8 In.	374

WEBB PEACHBLOW is a shaded Victorian glass made by Thomas Webb & Sons of Stourbridge, England, from 1885.

Perfume Bottle, Amber Shaded To Rose, Branch, Insects, Globe Shape, 5 ½ In.	863
Perfume Bottle, Flask, Amber Shaded To Rose, Blue Rim, Embossed Lid, 9 In.	690
Toothpick Holder, Egg Shape, 3-Footed, 3 In.	325
Vase, Insects, Branches, Enameled, 6 ½ In.	236

WEDGWOOD, one of the world's most successful potteries, was founded by Josiah WEDGWOOD Wedgwood, who was considered a cripple by his brother and was forbidden to work at the family business. The pottery was established in England in 1759. The company used a variety of marks, including Wedgwood, Wedgwood & Bentley, Wedgwood & Sons, and Wedgwood's Stone China. A large variety of wares has been made, including the well-known jasperware, basalt, creamware, and even a limited amount of porcelain. There are two kinds of jasperware. One is made from two colors of clay; the other is made from one color of clay with a color dip to create the contrast in design. In 1986 Wedgwood and Waterford Crystal merged to form the Waterford Wedgwood Group. Most Waterford Wedgwood assets were bought by KPS Capital Partners of New York in 2009 and became part of WWRD Holdings. Some manufacturing will be transferred to Germany, Indonesia, and Slovakia. Other Wedgwood pieces may be listed under Flow Blue, Majolica, Tea Leaf Ironstone, or in other porcelain categories.

Barber Bottle, Lid, Jasper Dip, Lilac, White, Green, c.1866, 10 ¼ In.	431
Biscuit Jar, Jasperware, Lilac, White, Cylindrical, Pewter Lid, Finial, Bail Handle, 8 In.	180
Biscuit Jar, Jasperware, Yellow, Black, Tree, Figures, Shaped Top Handle, 6 x 5 In.	130
Biscuit Jar, Lid, Jasper Dip, Yellow, Black, Muses, Grapevine, Handle, c.1930, 6 In.	600
Bottle, Lid, Jasper Dip, Crimson, Classical Figures, c.1920, 6 ¾ In. ....*illus*	1080
Bowl, Dragon Luster, Fairyland, 3 ¾ x 9 In.	312
Bowl, Fairyland Luster, Asian Scene, Plum, Orange, Green, Footed, 6 x 9 In.	531
Bowl, Fairyland Luster, Castle On Road, Blue Sky, Bird, Octagonal, c.1920, 7 In.	2640
Bowl, Fairyland Luster, Dana, Castle, Interior Fairy In Cage, 8-Sided, c.1920, 9 In. ....*illus*	2760
Bowl, Fairyland Luster, Gilt Dragon Decoration, 8-Sided, c.1920, 3 x 6 In.	205
Bowl, Fairyland Luster, Leapfrogging Elves, Flame Sky, Pedestal Foot, c.1920, 5 In.	2280
Bowl, Fairyland Luster, Willow, Coral Enamel, Stamped, England, 1920s, 4 x 8 ½ In.	3250
Bowl, Fairyland Luster, Willow, Orange Mottling, Coral, c.1920, 10 In.	5400
Bowl, Fish, Inside & Out, Blue Ground, Flared, Footed, 8 ¾ In.	305
Bowl, Jasperware, Cream & Amber, Ring Foot, Rolled-Out Rim, 3 ½ x 8 In.	240
Bowl, Lid, Creamware, Reticulated, Rope Twist Handles, c.1905, 10 In.	489
Box, Lid, Jasper Dip, Crimson, White, Figures, Flowers, Scalloped Rim, c.1920, 4 In.	720
Bust, John De Witt, Black Basalt, 20 x 26 In.	2178
Bust, Shakespeare, Black Basalt, Raised Title In Cartouche, Marked, 1964, 10 In. ....*illus*	400
Candlestick, Basalt, Classical Figures, Flower Border, Cylindrical, c.1850, 6 ¾ In., Pair	472
Cooler, Wine, Barrel Shape, Handles, Mask Heads, Leaf & Berry, c.1850, 10 In.	246
Dish, Game, Lid, Caneware, Molded Game, Grapevine Relief, Hare Finial, Oval, c.1860, 12 In.	250
Ewer, Jasperware, Lilac, White, Tree, Figures, Pedestal, Baluster, Silver Plated Lid, 8 In.	300
Figurine, Aphrodite, Black Basalt, Seated, Rocky Base, Pierced, c.1900, 12 In.	780
Figurine, Bacchante, Faun, Basalt, Round Base, Marked, 16 In., Pair	4270
Figurine, Cat, Tail Up, Black Basalt, Green Eyes, 5 x 3 ½ In.	293
Figurine, Maiden, Seated, Looking At Dog, White Parian, c.1850, 11 ¾ x 6 ¾ In.	403
Group, Bride & Groom, Girl & Boy, Queen's Ware, Arnold Machin, c.1949, 10 ¾ In. ....*illus*	1920
Jam Pot, Jasperware, Metal Cover, Dark Blue Body, Applied Neoclassical Scenes, c.1975, 4 In.	46
Lamp, Oil, Basalt, River Of Life, Gilt Highlights, Stamped, 1800s, 8 ½ x 8 In. ....*illus*	6875
Medallion, Empress Catherine, Blue, White Relief Profile, Oval, Frame, c.1775, 4 ½ In.	4680
Medallion, Princess Margaret, Blue, White Silhouette, Rim, Oval, 4 ½ x 3 ½ In.	36
Muffineer, Jasperware, Blue, White Classical Figures, Pierced Silver Plated Lid, 7 In.	150
Mug, Black Basalt, White, Sports, Loop Handle, 4 In.	60
Oyster Plate, Porcelain, 5 Wells, Mottled Green, Dolphin Dividers, 9 ¼ In.	726
Pitcher, Classical Figures Band, Blue & White, 5 ¼ In.	40
Pitcher, Green & White, Figures, Garland, Bulbous, Loop Handle, 6 In.	360
Pitcher, Jasperware, Blue & White, Squat, Ring Foot, Loop Handle, 1800s, 9 In.	72
Plaque, Nelson, Jasperware, Oval, Frame, 6 ½ x 5 ¼ In.	207
Plate, Blue & White, Harvard Scene, 10 ½ In., 12 Piece	130
Plate, Dinner, Etruria, Farm Scenes, Maroon Bands, 1881, 10 In., 4 Piece	150
Plate, Duke University, Blue Transfer School Scene, Wedgwood, 1937, 10 ⅝ In., 8 Piece	767
Plate, New England Industries, Black Wood Print, Clare Leighton, c.1950, 11 In., 12 Piece	288

W

Platter, Undertray, Jasperware, Powder Blue, White Classical Scenes, c.1820, 8 In.		118
Pot, Fairyland Luster, Candlemas Malfrey, Fairies On Bell Pole, Blue Candles, 8 ¼ In.		5925
Potpourri, Pierced Lid, Ivory Vellum, Globular, Gilt Handles, Flowers, c.1890, 10 In.		369
Tankard, Black Transfer, Children Playing, Cylindrical, c.1775, 6 In.		554
Tray, Jasperware, Lafayette Portrait, Cobalt Blue & White, 2 x 4 ½ In.		48
Umbrella Stand, Argento Majolica, 6-Sided, Molded Prunus Leaves, c.1880, 22 In.		938
Vase, Buff Color Ground, Brown, Rust, Blue, Slip Design, c.1885, 8 In.		180
Vase, Butterfly, Luster, Pearl Ground, Swollen Shoulder, Tapered Foot, c.1920, 10 In.		1560
Vase, Fairyland Luster, Candlemas, Goblins Climbing, Marked, c.1920, 7 ⅝ In.	*illus*	7200
Vase, Fairyland Luster, Figures, Ruby Ground, Fish Border, Trumpet Shape, 8 In.		2040
Vase, Fairyland Luster, Imps On Bridge, Roc Flying, 10 ¼ In.		9480
Vase, Fairyland Luster, Pillar, Paneled Sides, c.1920, 12 In.	*illus*	12000
Vase, Hummingbird Luster, Gilt Birds, Trumpet Shape, c.1920, 11 In.		1320
Vase, Jasper Dip, Green, White, Undraped Figures, Handles At Neck, 1800s, 11 In.		720
Vase, Jasper Dip, Portland, Classical Figures, Marked, 1800s, 10 In.	*illus*	2760
Vase, Lid, Fairyland Luster, Willow Design, Blue Sky, Shouldered, c.1920, 10 In.		9000
Vase, Scallop Lid, Butterfly Luster, Pearl Ground, Swollen Shoulder, c.1920, 11 In.		1320
Vase, Torch, China Blue, White, Slotted Lid, Bird Finial, 7 ½ In., Pair		1526

WELLER pottery was first made in 1872 in Fultonham, Ohio. The firm moved to Zanesville, Ohio, in 1882. Artwares were introduced in 1893. Hundreds of lines of pottery were produced, including Louwelsa, Eocean, Dickens Ware, and Sicardo, before the pottery closed in 1948.

LOUWELSA WELLER

Ardsley, Bowl, Green Glaze, Flared, Marked, 16 ½ In.		127
Baldin, Vase, Apples, Mottled Green Ground, Branch Handles, Bulbous, 9 ½ In.		194
Baldin, Vase, Applied Flowers, Blue Ground, Tapered, 10 x 10 In.		345
Blue Ware, Lamp Base, Dancing Women, Garlands Of Grapes, Hole, Impressed, 13 In.	*illus*	115
Bonito, Flower Frog, Green, Signed N.C., 3 x 6 In.		17
Bouquet, Vase, White, Daisy, Blue, Round, 4 ½ In.		23
Brighton, Figurine, Butterfly, White, Gray, Black, 2 ¼ x 3 ½ In.		126
Bronze Ware, Vase, Tapered, 11 In.		173
Burnt Wood, Jardiniere, Incised Children Playing, Tan, Brown, Rounded Rim, c.1915, 6 ⅝ In.		150
Cameo, Vase, White Flowers, Green Ground, Tapered, Footed, 11 In.		34
Cherry Blossom, Vase, Blue Glaze, Banded Rim, Impressed, c.1935, 7 ⅝ In.		115
Claywood, Jardiniere, Pedestal, School Of Fish, Tan, Loden Green, 25 In.		690
Coppertone, Bowl, Lattice Trim, Green, Marked, 3 ¼ x 11 ¼ In.		218
Coppertone, Flower Holder, Frog Holding Water Lily, Half Kiln Ink Stamp, 4 In.	*illus*	104
Coppertone, Tray, Frog Sitting On Folded Rim, 2 ½ x 6 ½ In.		176
Coppertone, Vase, Green Glaze, 8 ½ In.		104
Coppertone, Vase, Green, Brown, Handles, 14 ¾ In.		431
Cretone, Vase, Black Gazelles, Flowers, Leaves, White Matte Glaze, Round, 6 x 7 In.		390
Dechiwo, Vase, Relief Bacchanalian Scenes, Signed R. Lorber, 13 In., Pair		3000
Dickens Ware II, Humidor, The Captain, Incised, 7 In.	*illus*	69
Dickens Ware, Jug, Monk Playing Flute, Marked, 12 In.		248
Dickens Ware, Jug, Monk, Golden Brown, Zanesville, Ohio, 5 ½ x 5 In.		88
Dickens Ware, Jug, Monk, Green, Tan, Side Handle, Charles Upjohn, 6 In.		127
Dickens Ware, Jug, Monk, Smiling, Flower Stalks, 6 In.		103
Dickens Ware, Umbrella Stand, Hibiscus Blossoms, Artist Signed A.H., c.1900, 21 x 9 In.		240
Dickens Ware, Vase, Golf Scenes, Caddy, Green, Tapered, A. Dunlavy, c.1900, 9 ½ In.		1062
Dickens Ware, Vase, Golf Scenes, Lady Golfer, Green, Tan Ground, c.1900, 12 In.		826
Dresden, Vase, Dutch Girl, Bay, Boats, Windmill, Cylindrical, Levi Burgess, 9 In.		57
Eocean, Vase, Red Berries, Leaves, Ivory To Green Base, Marked, 8 ½ In.		177
Figurine, Fisher Boy, Matte Glaze, Marked, 20 ½ In.	*illus*	531
Figurine, Pop-Eye Dog, Black & Brown Spots, White Matte Glaze, 10 In.		705
Figurine, Pop-Eye Dog, Black Matte Glaze, 4 In.		176
Figurine, Pop-Eye Dog, White, Brown, Black, 9 ¾ In.		3450
Forest, Jardiniere, Pedestal, Orange, Green Incised Designs, 12 ½ x 29 In.		1464
Fru Russet, Vase, Lizard, Mottled, Marked, 4 ½ In.	*illus*	2645
Fudzi, Vase, Painted Lily Of The Valley, Matte Glaze, 3 x 9 ¼ In.		688
Glendale, Vase, Bird, Nest, Flowers, Vines, Cylindrical, 1920, 10 In.		840
Gloria, Bowl, Folded Rim, Red Ground, Marked, 11 ⅞ In.		23
Hudson, Vase, 2 Handles, Robin, Blooming Branch, 7 ¾ In.		2530
Hudson, Vase, Birds, Perched On Branches, Fruit, Mae Timberlake, 29 ⅜ In.	*illus*	10030
Hudson, Vase, Black Throated Warblers, Branch, Marked, 9 ⅜ In.	*illus*	1725
Hudson, Vase, Blue Iris, Yellow, Blue Ground, Signed McLaughlin, 15 ½ In.		518
Hudson, Vase, Blue, Buff, Grapes, Leaves, Rolled Rim, c.1925, 6 ½ In.		104

Wedgwood, Vase, Fairyland Luster, Candlemas, Goblins Climbing, Marked, c.1920, 7 ⅝ In.
$7,200

Skinner Auctioneers & Appraisers

Wedgwood, Vase, Fairyland Luster, Pillar, Paneled Sides, c.1920, 12 In.
$12,000

Skinner Auctioneers & Appraisers

Wedgwood, Vase, Jasper Dip, Portland, Classical Figures, Marked, 1800s, 10 In.
$2,760

Skinner Auctioneers & Appraisers

W

Weller, Blue Ware, Lamp Base, Dancing Women, Garlands Of Grapes, Hole, Impressed, 13 In.
$115

Weller, Coppertone, Flower Holder, Frog Holding Water Lily, Half Kiln Ink Stamp, 4 In.
$104

Weller, Dickens Ware II, Humidor, The Captain, Incised, 7 In.
$69

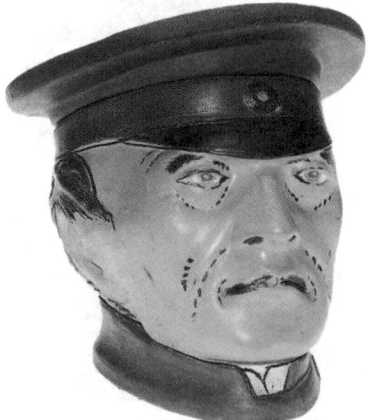

Weller, Figurine, Fisher Boy, Matte Glaze, Marked, 20 ½ In.
$531

Weller, Fru Russet, Vase, Lizard, Mottled, Marked, 4 ½ In.
$2,645

Weller, Hudson, Vase, Birds, Perched On Branches, Fruit, Mae Timberlake, 29 ⅜ In.
$10,030

Weller, Hudson, Vase, Black Throated Warblers, Branch, Marked, 9 ⅜ In.
$1,725

Weller, Hudson, Vase, Dogwood Blossoms, Handles, Sarah Timberlake, Marked, 6 ⅝ In.
$518

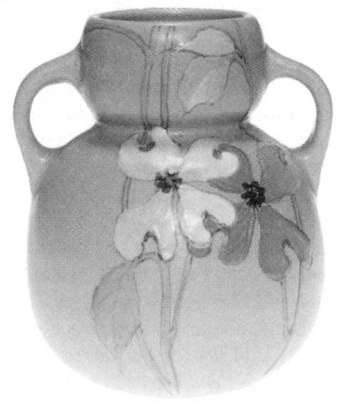

Weller, Lasa, Vase, Palm Trees, Mountains, Lake, 6 In.
$118

Hudson, Vase, Blue, Pink Flowers, Pale Green Ground, Signed LBM, 12 In.		891
Hudson, Vase, Dogwood Blossoms, Handles, Sarah Timberlake, Marked, 6 ⅝ In. ....*illus*		518
Hudson, Vase, Flower Band, Blue Ground, Handles, Hester Pillsbury, 6 ½ In.		196
Hudson, Vase, Painted White Flowers, Blue Ground, Handles, Signed Mae Timberlake, 8 In.		201
Hudson, Vase, Perfecto, Morning Glories, Impressed, 7 ½ In.		189
Hudson, Vase, Perfecto, Yellow Flowers, Signed, 5 In.		115
Hudson, Vase, Pink & White Morning Glories, Blue To Gray Ground, Hester Pillsbury, 11 In.		260
Hudson, Vase, Pink Flowers, Blue, Handles, Round, Signed Walch, 6 ½ In.		299
Hudson, Vase, Pink, White Wisteria, Blue Ground, Bulbous Base, 9 ¾ In.		288
Hudson, Vase, Squared Handles, Signed McLaughlin, 9 ⅜ In.		265
Hudson, Vase, White Flowers, Green Leaves, Tan, Marked, 9 In.		80
Hudson, Vase, White Flowers, Green, Handles, Signed Morris, 7 ¾ In.		365
Hudson, Vase, White Flowers, Light Blue, Loop Handles, Mae Timberlake, 8 x 9 In.		480
Hudson, Vase, White Flowers, Light Green Ground, Cylindrical, 9 In.		115
Hudson, Vase, Windmills, Sailboats, Pink Roofed Houses, Sara Reid McLaughlin, 11 In.		1955
Hudson, Vase, Yellow Iris, Blue Ground, Signed M. Timberlake, 9 ½ In.		173
Hudson, Vase, Yellow, Blue Iris, Cylindrical, Hester Pillsbury, 9 ¼ In.		489
Hudson, Vase, Yellow, Pink Flowers, Blue Ground, Cylindrical, 6 ⅞ In.		242
Kenova, Vase, Flowers, Incised Red Flower Band, Gray Ground, 6 x 7 In.		150
Knifewood, Jardiniere, Squirrel Design, Incised, Green, Brown, 11 ½ x 10 In.		650
Knifewood, Vase, Squirrels, Tan, Brown, Cylindrical, 11 In.		230
Lasa, Vase, Palm Trees, Mountains, Lake, 6 In. ....*illus*		118
Lasa, Vase, Tree, Green Leaf Tree, Multicolor Bands, Golden Ground, 4 In.		90
Lasa, Vase, Trees, Black Body, 11 In.		265
Lasa, Vase, Trees, Mountains, Clouds, Lake, Signed, 7 ⅛ In. ....*illus*		431
Louwelsa, Mug, Painted Dog Portrait, 6 ½ In.		130
Louwelsa, Pitcher, Water, Pineapple, Brown Glossy Glaze, Cylindrical, H. Pillsbury, 17 In.		121
Louwelsa, Tankard, Ears Of Corn, Josephine Imlay, 12 ½ In.		126
Louwelsa, Vase, Chicks Scene, Brown Glaze, Minnie Mitchell, 6 ½ x 12 ½ In.		1125
Louwelsa, Vase, Glossy Red Glaze, Pink Orchid, Mae Timberlake, 7 In. ....*illus*		1062
Louwelsa, Vase, Open Rose, Ball Shape, Signed JF, 7 In.		127
Louwelsa, Vase, Painted St. Bernard, Signed, 11 x 21 In.		1000
Louwelsa, Vase, Pillow, Blue, Poppies, c.1910, 5 ½ x 5 ½ In.		219
Louwelsa, Vase, Red Tulips, Shouldered, 16 ½ In.		1035
Louwelsa, Vase, Yellow Flowers, Deep Purple, Pillow Shape, Footed, 9 ½ In.		63
Mammy, Cookie Jar, c.1935 ....*illus*		48
Matte Green, Jardiniere, One Piece, Lobed Bowl, Twisted Base, 25 In.		604
Matte Green, Umbrella Stand, Raised Flowers, Wavy Rim, 11 x 20 In.		625
Matte Green, Vase, Flared Rim, 8 In.		127
Matte Green, Vase, Lobed, Tapered, Marked, 5 x 8 ½ In.		313
Matte Green, Wall Pocket, Fluted Design, Triangular, 16 x 6 In.		48
Muskota, Flower Frog, Leda & The Swan, 6 ¾ x 7 ½ In. ....*illus*		130
Patra, Vase, Leaf Shape, Marked, 8 In.		92
Patricia, Planter, Duck Shape, 4 ½ In.		35
Pumila, Bowl, Sawtooth Petal Rim, 7 ¼ In.		23
Roma, Bowl, Ivory Yellow, Lily Pad, 2 ½ x 5 In.		30
Roma, Chandelier Bowl, Pink Roses, Green Leaves, Impressed, 17 ½ In.		590
Roma, Jardiniere, Pedestal, Pink Flowers, Leafy Stems, 32 In. ....*illus*		546
Sicardo, Bowl, Clover, Art Nouveau Style, Red Iridescent Glaze, Squat, Folded Sides, 4 ½ In.		726
Sicardo, Box, Lid, Star Shape, 4-Leaf Clovers, 2 ½ x 4 ⅝ In.		316
Sicardo, Vase, Cylindrical, Purple, Platinum Stemmed Iris, Stippling, Signed, 9 ½ In.		863
Sicardo, Vase, Daisies, Signed, 1903-17, 5 ¾ x 7 ¼ In.		1500
Sicardo, Vase, Flared, Metallic Glaze, Stylized Leaf Design, Flared Base, 4 x 7 In.		343
Sicardo, Vase, Flared, Multicolor Metallic Glaze, Stylized Leaves, Marked, 4 x 7 In.		344
Sicardo, Vase, Iridescent Green, Tapered Cylinder, Paper Label, 5 ½ x 3 ¼ In.		276
Sicardo, Vase, Iridescent, Drip Design, Flattened Pillow Shape, Footed, Signed, 3 x 2 ¾ In.		375
Sicardo, Vase, Metallic Glaze, Bowl Shape, 4-Footed, Signed, 4 ½ In.		248
Sicardo, Vase, Mottled Red, Green, Purple, Cylindrical, 3 ½ x 3 ½ In.		313
Sicardo, Vase, Nasturtiums, Embossed, Iridescent, Oil Spots, Swollen, Signed, 11 x 5 In.		5313
Sicardo, Vase, Purple, Blue Metallic Glaze, Stylized Flowers, Flared Base, 9 x 5 In.		427
Sicardo, Vase, Slight Taper, Flat Rim, Gold, Fuchsia, 11 x 8 In.		2808
Sicardo, Vase, Triangular Shape, Teasel Design, Signed, 6 ⅞ In. ....*illus*		354
Silvertone, Vase, Pink Tulip, Tapered, 9 ¾ In.		288
Stellar, Dish, Star Shape, Yellow Interior, Blue, 9 In.		23
Stellar, Vase, White Stars, Blue Matte Glaze, Hester Pillsbury, 5 ½ In.		590

Weller, Lasa, Vase, Trees, Mountains, Clouds, Lake, Signed, 7 ⅛ In.
$431

Humler & Nolan

Weller, Louwelsa, Vase, Glossy Red Glaze, Pink Orchid, Mae Timberlake, 7 In.
$1,062

Humler & Nolan

Weller, Mammy, Cookie Jar, c.1935
$48

Victorian Casino Antiques

This is an edited listing of current prices. Visit **Kovels.com** to check thousands of prices from previous years and sign up for free information on trends, tips, reproductions, marks, and more.

W

WELLER

Weller, Muskota, Flower Frog, Leda & The Swan, 6 ¾ x 7 ½ In.
$130

Humler & Nolan

Weller, Roma, Jardiniere, Pedestal, Pink Flowers, Leafy Stems, 32 In.
$546

Humler & Nolan

Weller, Sicardo, Vase, Triangular Shape, Teasel Design, Signed, 6 ⅞ In.
$354

Humler & Nolan

Sunflower, Jardiniere, Pedestal, Signed Frank Ferrell, 31 x 10 In.	531
Turada, Vase, Crescent, Yellow Bead Design, Footed, 4 ¾ In.	40
Vase, Cat Design, Mae Timberlake, c.1940, 7 In.	972
Vase, Painted Green Leaves, Nuts, Tan Matte Glaze, Signed Hester Pillsbury, 3 ½ x 8 In.	219
Woodcraft, Flower Holder, 5 Stepped Openings, Green, Brown, 6 In.	46
Woodcraft, Hanging Basket, Owl Reserve, Green Ground, 10 In.	173
Woodcraft, Jardiniere, Blackberries, Green, Pink, Marked, 9 ¾ x 8 In.	219

WEMYSS ware was first made in 1882 by Robert Heron, the owner of Fife Pottery in Kirkaldy, Scotland. Large colorful flowers, hearts, and other symbols were hand painted on figurines, inkstands, jardinieres, candlesticks, buttons, pots, and other items. Fife Pottery closed in 1932. The molds and designs were used by a series of potteries until 1957. In 1985 the Wemyss name and designs were obtained by Griselda Hill. The Wemyss Ware trademark was registered in 1994. Modern Wemyss Ware in old styles is still being made.

Figurine, Eagle, Roses, Signed B. Adams, 5 ½ In.	235
Figurine, Rhinoceros, Roses, B. Adams, 6 ¼ In.	314

WESTMORELAND GLASS was made by the Westmoreland Glass Company of Grapeville, Pennsylvania, from 1889 to 1984. The company made clear and colored glass of many varieties, such as milk glass, pressed glass, and slag glass.

Argonaut Shell, Candy Dish, Lid, Green Mist, Frosted, Seashells, Footed, 6 ¾ x 6 In.	59
Bowl, Fruit, Heart Shape, Handle, c.1930, 8 In.	35
Bramble, Candlestick, Red	85
Bramble, Chocolate Box, Lid, Red, 6 ⅝ In.	85
Candleholder, Black, Ribbed, Openwork Foot, 4 ¼ In., Pair	85
Della Robbia, Bowl, Red Flashed, Belled, Footed, 12 In.	125
Della Robbia, Creamer	12
Della Robbia, Sugar, Red Flashed	12
Dish, Camel Lid, Pink, 7 x 5 x 3 In.	80
Dolphin, Candlestick, Green, 9 In., Pair	200
Dolphin, Compote, Amber, Shell Shape, 8 In.	75
Dolphin, Lamp, Green	85
Dolphin, Sandwich Server, Amber, Handle	45
English Hobnail, Coaster	8
English Hobnail, Console, Amber, Rolled, 11 In.	30
English Hobnail, Creamer, Green, Square Foot	55
English Hobnail, Creamer, Hexagonal Foot	10
English Hobnail, Nappy, Square, 6 In.	11
English Hobnail, Plate, Amber, 8 In.	15
English Hobnail, Plate, Amber, 10 ½ In.	18
English Hobnail, Plate, Green, 13 ½ In.	60
English Hobnail, Plate, Luncheon, Round, 8 In.	12
English Hobnail, Plate, Round, 8 In.	10
English Hobnail, Toilet Water Bottle, Stopper, Ice Blue, Wide Mouth	100
Fan & File, Bowl, Fruit, Ruby, Scalloped Foot, 3 ¾ x 7 x 4 ½ In.	75
Forget Me Not, Plate, Black, Girl On Swing, Dog, 8 ½ In.	30
Lotus, Compote, Green, 6 ¾ x 2 ¾ In.	15
Lotus, Plate, Green, 13 In.	50
Lotus, Plate, Pink, 13 In.	50
Marguerite, Cheese & Cracker, Plate, Ebony, 10 ½ In.	20
Milk Glass, Pitcher, Grapes, Leaves, Paneled, Scalloped, Footed, 8 ½ In.	23
Milk Glass, Salt & Pepper, Grapes, Paneled, Chrome Lids, 4 ¾ In.	42
Milk Glass, Vase, Handkerchief, Hobnail, Marked, 5 x 8 In.	75
Milk Glass, Vase, Quilt Pattern, Bell Rim, 9 x 6 In.	24
Octagon, Candy Dish, Lid, Green Frosted, Lb.	55
Stack Set, Green, Sugar, Creamer, Butter Plate Lid	60
Stack Set, Pink, Sugar, Creamer, Butter Plate Lid, 2 Shakers	100
Stack Set, Sugar, Creamer, Butter Plate Lid, Shaker Shelves	40
Teapot, Milk Bottle Shape, Cork Stopper, Crosscut Spout, 1930s, 6 ½ In.	40
Trinket Box, Blue Satin Glass, Coralene, 4-Footed, 2 x 2 In.	20
Wings, Creamer, Amber, Art Deco Decoration	20
Wings, Sugar & Creamer, Green	40
Wings, Sugar & Creamer, Pink	45

WHEATLEY POTTERY was established in 1880. Thomas J. Wheatley had worked in Cincinnati, Ohio, with the founders of the art pottery movement, including M. Louise McLaughlin of the Rookwood Pottery. Wheatley Pottery was purchased by the Cambridge Tile Manufacturing Company in 1927.

Corbel, Brown Glaze, c.1905, 12 ¾ x 5 ½ In., Pair	344
Jardiniere, Brown Matte Glaze, Leaves, Buds, c.1905, 5 ¼ x 7 In.	625
Jardiniere, Green Matte Glaze, Buttressed, 7 x 8 In.	563
Jardiniere, Reeded Leaves & Buds, Brown Matte Glaze, c.1905, 5 x 7 In.	625
Vase, Green Glaze, Bulbous, Leaves, Buds, 1900s, 9 x 7 In.	3750
Vase, Green Matte Glaze, Buds, Leaves, 6-Sided, Marked, c.1905, 17 x 8 In.	2500
Vase, Ocher Glaze, Leaves, Buds, Cylindrical, Marked, c.1905, 19 x 6 In.	2125

WHIELDON was an English potter who worked alone and with Josiah Wedgwood in eighteenth-century England. Whieldon made many pieces in natural shapes, like cauliflowers or cabbages, and they are almost always unmarked. Do not confuse it with F. Winkle & Co., which made a dinnerware pattern marked *Whieldon Ware*.

Creamer, Cabbage Leaf, c.1780, 4 ¼ In.	395
Plate, Molded Rim, Mottled Green, Brown & Amber Glaze, c.1775, 9 In.	180

WILLETS MANUFACTURING COMPANY of Trenton, New Jersey, began work in 1879. The company made belleek in the late 1880s and 1890s in shapes similar to those used by the Irish Belleek factory. It stopped working about 1912. A variety of marks were used, most including the name *Willets*.

Ewer, Long Spout, Violets, Gilt Interior, Belleek, c.1900, 5 ½ In.	69
Vase, Irises, Black Ground, Gold Rim, Marked, Belleek, 17 In. .... *illus*	271
Vase, Peacocks, Flowers, Black, Gold, Florence McLee-Sentacy, Belleek, 10 In. ...... *illus*	649
Vase, Pink Roses, Green Leaves Shaded To Cream, Tapered, Pinched Neck, Belleek, 13 In.	161
Vase, Whooping Cranes, Belleek, Cylinder, 1879-1912, 15 ¾ x 5 ¼ In.	690

WILLOW pattern has been made in England since 1780. The pattern has been copied by factories in many countries, including Germany, Japan, and the United States. It is still being made. Willow was named for a pattern that pictures a bridge, birds, willow trees, and a Chinese landscape. Most pieces are blue and white. Some made after 1900 are pink and white.

Bowl, Vegetable, Lid, Inclined Pines, Orange, Gilt Finial, Handles, Chinese, c.1820, 12 ½ In.	900
Chop Plate, Petrus Regout-Maastricht Holland, 13 In.	149
Creamer, Cow Shape, Stepped Base, Staffordshire, c.1860, 5 ¾ In.	115
Cup & Saucer, England, 1900s	69
Cup & Saucer, Spode Tower Transfer, Pink, Black Back Stamp, Copeland .... *illus*	28
Gravy Boat, Newport Pottery, 7 ¾ x 4 In.	50
Oil Bottle, Stick Neck, Japan, 4 ¾ In.	14
Soup, Dish, Brown, Staffordshire, 8 In.	14
Tea Caddy, Finial, Ringtons, c.1925, 7 x 4 x 4 In.	150

WINDOW glass that was stained and beveled was popular for houses during the late nineteenth and early twentieth centuries. The old windows became popular with collectors in the 1970s; today, old and new examples are seen.

Clerestory, Flashed, Geometric, F.L. Wright, Northome, Frame, c.1912, 23 x 23 In., Pair	15000
Leaded, Arched, Prairie School Design, Multicolor, 39 x 48 In.	344
Leaded, Art Deco, Geometric, Bull's-Eyes, Jewels, Amber Border, Blue, Green, 72 x 36 In.	403
Leaded, Arts & Crafts Design, Linear, Red, Green, Yellow, 22 x 35 In.	226
Leaded, Arts & Crafts, Light Green, Red, Gray, c.1900, 24 x 11 ½ In., Pair	702
Leaded, Flower, Scroll Design, Green, Yellow, Red, Hanging, 34 x 23 In.	210
Leaded, Flowers, Insets, Rippled Wood Frame, Tiffany, 20 ½ x 16 In., Pair	3125
Leaded, Geometric Pattern, Blue, Amber, Rust, 62 x 22 In.	360
Leaded, Painted, Girl, Seated, Pink, White Dress, Stream, c.1920, 39 x 29 In.	1625
Leaded, Painted, Winter Allegory, Woman, Firewood On Head, Frame, c.1895, 19 x 15 In.	750
Leaded, Pendant Panel, Urn, Scrolling, Multicolor, Jewels, Arched Top, c.1910, 28 x 14 In.	561
Leaded, Stained, Annunciation To Shepherds, Continental, c.1875, 35 ½ x 23 ½ In.	390
Leaded, Stained, Arts & Crafts, Farm Landscape, Frame, 1920s, 35 x 28 In.	1875
Leaded, Stained, Exit, Brass Frame, 10 x 24 In. .... *illus*	150
Leaded, Stained, Multicolor, Candle, Scroll, Fleur-De-Lis, 29 ¼ x 25 ½ In.	237
Leaded, Stained, Panels, Religious Scenes, Germany, c.1910, 30 x 25 In.	270
Leaded, Stained, White, Frosted, Flower Design, Lines, 22 x 35 In.	150

Willets, Vase, Irises, Black Ground, Gold Rim, Marked, Belleek, 17 In. $271

Humler & Nolan

Willets, Vase, Peacocks, Flowers, Black, Gold, Florence McLee-Sentacy, Belleek, 10 In. $649

Humler & Nolan

Willow, Cup & Saucer, Spode Tower Transfer, Pink, Black Back Stamp, Copeland $28

Ruby Lane, Inc.

W

629

Window, Leaded, Stained, Exit, Brass Frame, 10 x 24 In.
$150

Window, Stained, 2 Birds, Flowering Branches, Borders, Wood Frame, c.1900, 36 x 40 In.
$900

Wood Carving, 3 Wise Monkeys, Incised, Inlaid Eyes, Japan, 1800s, 2 ⅜ In.
$840

Wood Carving, Club, Root, Head Of Horned Man, Penobscot, Maine, 1800s, 27 In.
$474

Leaded, Stylized Hollyhock, Geo. Washington Maher, 1909, 23 x 52 In.	4375
Leaded, Transom, Arched Panel, Slag, Marbleized, Garland, White Frame, 29 x 118 In.	1003
Louver, Arched Shape, Gray Paint, 27 x 28 ½ In., Pair	593
Oak, Copper Sheet Metal Frame, Round, Scrolled, Green Patina, c.1900, 59 x 72 In.	2360
Stained, 2 Birds, Flowering Branches, Borders, Wood Frame, c.1900, 36 x 40 In. *illus*	900
Stained, 3 Stylized Tulips, c.1910, 28 x 23 In.	180
Stained, Angel, Layered Orb, Leaf Border, Blue, Orange Favrile, Frame, Tiffany, 23 x 40 In.	35400
Stained, Art Deco, Repeating Geometric, Yellow, Green, Red, White, 28 x 22 In., 3 Piece	238
Stained, Arts & Crafts, Flowers, Oval River Scene, Rust, Orange, c.1900, 28 x 28 In.	270
Stained, Fleur-De-Lis, Ribbons, Wreath, c.1900, 34 x 39 In.	390
Stained, Flower Basket, Multicolor, 1900s, 32 x 20 In.	330
Stained, Flowers, Crosshatched Panes, Column Sides, Multicolor, c.1895, 24 x 45 In.	270
Stained, Gothic Style, Window Scene, Flowers, Oak Frame, c.1950, 37 x 32 In., Pair	720
Stained, Prairie School, 2 Chevron Shapes, Green, Yellow, 29 x 33 In.	240
Stained, Prairie School, Arch, c.1910, 42 x 21 In.	210
Stained, Star Of David, Red, Blue, White, Palm, Mahogany Frame, c.1950, 24 x 24 In.	330
Stained, Transom, Shield, Spear, Caramel Slag Glass, Green Border, 71 x 17 In.	288
Stained, Victorian, Geometric, Blue, Yellow, Green, Cream, 35 x 13 In., 4 Piece	238
Stained, Yellow, Green, Peach, Pittsburg, c.1905, 32 ½ x 46 In.	660
Transom, Pine, Carved, Painted, Demilune, c.1855, 17 x 23 ¼ In.	533
Transom, Ranma, Teak, Flowers, Birds, Landscape, Japan, 80 x 10 In.	625
Transom, Scalloped Panes, Wood, White Paint, 13 ½ x 114 In.	115
Transom, Sunburst Style, Flowers, Scroll Top, Beveled Edge, 37 x 68 In.	649
Transom, Sunburst, Pine, White Paint, c.1850, 33 x 58 In.	267
Walnut, Double Hung, Salesman's Sample, 12 ½ x 6 In.	385

WOOD CARVINGS and wooden pieces are listed separately in this book. There are also wooden pieces found in other categories, such as Folk Art, Kitchen, and Tool.

2 Hawks, Walnut, Glass Eyes, c.1950, 23 ½ In.	1534
3 Wise Monkeys, Incised, Inlaid Eyes, Japan, 1800s, 2 ⅜ In. *illus*	840
Abraham Lincoln, Leather Tie, Brass Buttons, Base, Painted, 1900s, 32 In.	5760
Angel, Giltwood, Woman, Hands Folded, Knee Raised, Paint, c.1760, 38 In.	4688
Angel, Parcel Gilt, Robes, Wings, Kneeling, c.1800, 22 x 10 In., Pair	1888
Angel, Praying, Giltwood, Painted, c.1960, 14 In., Pair	938
Angel, Renaissance Style, Oak, Extending Wings, Continental, 20th Century, 22 In.	240
Angel, Winged, Raised Arms, Glass Eyes, Iron Hook, Paint, European, c.1905, 19 x 12 In.	1035
Artist's Model, Jointed, c.1960, 32 In.	554
Basket, Burl, Scoop Shape, Y Handle, Inscribed, 1920, 4 x 5 In.	184
Bellhop, Standing, Arms At Sides, Unpainted, 34 In.	608
Bird Whistle, Painted Bird On Rim, Articulated Beak, 7 ½ In.	593
Bird, Mahogany, Bronze Legs, Inlaid Eye, Hagenauer, c.1950, 4 ½ In.	1047
Bishop, Miter, Robe, Baroque, Germany, 1700s, 40 In.	594
Bishop, Paint, Hand Raised, Holding Book, Branch, 1700s, 16 x 10 In.	738
Blackamoor, Holding Oar, Standing On Gondola, Italy, c.1920, 24 In.	1888
Blacksmith, Black Forest, Germany, 1900s, 16 In.	264
Blue Whale, Plaque, Blue Paint, Signed, C. Voorhees, 1900s, 4 x 19 In.	3075
Bluefish, Pine, Green, Brown Paint, 42 In.	960
Bucket Of Grapes, Tree Stump, Black Forest, c.1885, 7 x 6 In.	538
Buddha, Giltwood, Standing, Lotus Throne, Cloud Mandorla, c.1900, 24 In.	717
Bust, Benjamin Franklin, Pine, c.1880, 18 ¼ In.	972
Bust, Saint Ursula, Square Base, Scroll Feet, Italy, 1700s, 24 x 16 In.	2214
Bust, Soldier, Mexican War Hero, Cinched Base, 31 ½ In.	840
Bust, Woman, Hair Pulled Back, Front Medallion, c.1850, 22 x 18 In.	1840
Bust, Woman, Old, Curled Hair, Flower Headband, c.1900, 12 In.	288
Cannon, Black Paint, 17 In.	1140
Card Receiver, Figural, Monkey, Rockery Base, Wood, Painted, 1900s, 56 In.	300
Card Stand, Monkey, Seated, Wearing Clothing, Holding Tray, Rock Base, 54 In.	1554
Cat, 2 Heads, Lying Down, Wrapped Tails, Green Eyes, Black Paint, c.1950, 17 In.	288
Cat, Seated, White, Black Painted, c.1955, 13 In.	1680
Cattle, Rocky Base, Continental, c.1890, 22 x 30 In.	3750
Cherub, Wings, Draped Clothing, Brown, Green Paint, 19 In., Pair	170
Chinese Man, Standing, Holding Staff, Bird, Root Carved, 19 In.	660
Christ, Good Shepherd, Holding Lamb, Painted, Continental, 38 In.	2000
Club, Root, Head Of Horned Man, Penobscot, Maine, 1800s, 27 In. *illus*	474
Coffin, Pine, Salesman's Sample, 14 ¼ In.	108

Columbia, Blue, Red Liberty Cap, Blue Dress, Shield, Sword, Paint, 1800s, 60 In.	10030
Cowboy, Cactus Desert, Painted, Copper Wire, Mr. Benjamin, c.1935, 10 ½ x 11 In.	510
Crucifix, Spanish Colonial, Stepped Base, Paint, 24 x 12 In.	413
Cup & Saucer, Handleless, Strawberries, Salmon Ground, Joseph Lehn, Miniature	180
Cup, Pussy Willow Springs, Fruit, Flowers, Banding, Pedestal, Joseph Lehn, 1898, 3 ⅝ In.	767
Cup, Saffron, Cover, Poplar, Painted, Turned, Ball Finial, Pedestal, Joseph Lehn, 4 ⅜ In.	708
Dog, Begging, Glass Eyes, Hinged Head, Black Forest, 25 In.	2880
Dog, Black Lab, Painted, Signed Lawson, 1932, 5 ½ In.	492
Dog, Poodle, Standing, Check Design, 6 x 8 In.	1057
Double Faced Man, Hat, Anri	99
Dove, White Paint, c.1920, 14 ½ In.	207
Duck, Black Paint, Stamped M.J. Gray, Maine, 15 In.	240
Duck, Flying, Stand & Base, 1900s, 17 x 18 In.	472
Duck, Preening, Redwood Burl, Olive, Signed Burlingham, c.1983, 10 ½ In.	59
Eagle, American Flag, Banner, Esse Quam Videri, Bellamy Style, 1900s, 96 x 11 In. ....*illus*	2125
Eagle, Federal, Pine, Allover Feathers, On Ball, Gilt, 15 ¼ In.	972
Eagle, Mahogany, Wings At Side, Signed Thomas Head, 1978, 17 In.	570
Eagle, Pilothouse, Carved, Raised Wings, Dome Base, Painted, c.1890, 33 x 23 In.	1150
Eagle, Pine, Spread Wings, Carved, Rodney Boyer, 6 x 11 In.	390
Eagle, Spread Wings, Captured Salmon, Plinth, Leo Moore, 1900s, 40 x 55 In.	750
Eagle, Spread Wings, Clutching Arrows, Giltwood, c.1800, 13 x 43 In.	20912
Eagle, Spread Wings, Flying, Painted, c.1965, 33 x 62 In.	480
Eagle, Spread Wings, Head Turned, Glass Eye, On Log, c.1965, 30 In.	154
Eagle, Spread Wings, Painted, 10 x 19 In.	304
Eggcup, Strawberry, Leaves, Salmon Ground, Yellow Interior, Joseph Lehn, 2 ¾ In.	472
Elephant, Rosewood, Festive Trappings, c.1900, 12 ¼ x 15 ¼ In. ....*illus*	1554
Elephant, Teak, Articulated, Branded Kay Bojensen, Denmark, c.1950, 5 x 2 In., Pair	531
Emperor Penguin, Standing, Marked 1937, 9 ½ In.	502
Farmer, Gleaner, Bundle Of Wheat, Tool, Germany, c.1935, 18 ½ In.	240
Finial, Vase, Leaves, Ball, Paint, 16 In., Pair	840
Fish, Pike, Green, White Paint, 36 In.	403
Fish, Trout, Green Paint, 12 In.	960
Flowers, Yellow, Green Leaves, 2-Sided, Green Base, Elijah Pierce, 5 ½ x 6 ½ In.	706
Foo Dog, Red Paint & Gilt, Seated, Square Footed Base, Chinese, 15 x 10 In., Pair	210
Foo Dog, Seated, Stepped Stand, Red Paint, Gold, Chinese, 1800s, 37 x 25 In., Pair	461
Golfer, Painted, Round Plinth, 1938, 15 In.	3120
Great Blue Heron, Painted, Stand, 31 In.	960
Great Horned Owl, On Perch, Painted, Signed Springer, 33 ½ In.	1560
Guanyin, Bamboo, Holding Bottle, Raised Knee, Chinese, c.1900, 9 In.	480
Hermit Thrush, Rock Shape Base, Jess Blackstone, Signed, 1943, 2 ⅜ In.	70
Heron, Standing, Tan, Cream, Brown Paint, Stand, 54 In., Pair	240
Heron, White Paint, Block Stand Base, 45 ½ In.	360
Homer, Messenger Pigeon, John Fliegerbauer, Pa., c.1973, 11 ¾ In.	540
Hooded Merganser, Brown, Black, White Paint, Round Stand, M.J. Gray, Maine, 14 In.	540
Horse, Artist's Model, Articulated, Fully Jointed, 20 x 21 In.	761
Horse, Model, Glass Eyes, Horsehair Tail, Painted, France, 16 x 20 In.	2596
Horse, Pine, White Paint, c.1850, 22 x 26 In.	356
Indian Chief, Feather Headdress, John Noble, Signed, 20 In.	215
Infant, Baroque, 2 Fingers Raised, Nude, Multicolor, Plinth, Continental, c.1700, 31 In.	1750
Japanese Man, Seated Figure, Court Robes, Sword, Tiered Stand, Painted, 35 In.	5124
Jardiniere, Mahogany, Rococo, Sleigh Form, Serpentine Ends, Scroll Feet, 10 x 23 In.	338
Jardiniere, Octagonal, Bail Handles, Cabriole Legs, 1800s, 15 In., Pair	1169
Knife Urn, Mahogany, Octagonal, Acorn Finial, Ogee Feet, 24 ½ In., Pair	3186
Ladle, Effigy, Bear Handle, Hanging, c.1805, 10 x 5 ½ In.	2340
Ladle, Effigy, Maple, Dog Head, Heart Handle, Shield Shape Bowl, 10 In.	1725
Lion Of Luzerne, Black Forest, Switzerland, Early 1900s, 3 x 5 ½ In.	186
Lion, Seated, Gilt, Stepped Base, 20 x 25 In., Pair	1560
Lion, Tudor, On Hind Legs, Holding Shield, Bearing Teeth, c.1890, 22 In., Pair	1353
Luna & Child, Nude, Arms Raised, Square Base, 1900s, 23 x 8 In.	6274
Madonna & Child, 48 In.	625
Madonna & Child, Queen Of Heaven, Paint, Continental, 37 ½ In.	2700
Male Figure, Artist's Model, Pegged Ball & Socket Joints, Brown Paint, 30 In.	1521
Man, Kneeling, Sword, Painted, Italy, 21 ½ In.	415
Man, Long Robes, Crown, South America, 30 In.	90
Man, Woman Farmers, Boxwood, Dutch, 16 In., Pair	1188
Mask, Helmet, Hardwood, Geometric Design, Africa, 1900s, 29 x 11 In.	240

Wood Carving, Eagle, American Flag, Banner, Esse Quam Videri, Bellamy Style, 1900s, 96 x 11 In.
$2,125

Rago Arts & Auction Center

Wood Carving, Elephant, Rosewood, Festive Trappings, c.1900, 12 ¼ x 15 ¼ In.
$1,554

Neal Auction Co.

Wood Carving, Model, Artist's, Facial Features, Fully Jointed, 31 In.
$1,107

New Orleans Auction Galleries, Inc.

Wood Carving, Plaque, Eagle, Shield, Arrows, Pine, Artistic Company Of Boston, c.1950, 44 In.
$2,460

Garth's Auctioneers & Appraisers

TIP
Don't store wooden bowls and other pieces on their sides. This can cause them to warp.

W

Wood Carving, Saint, Franciscan, Full Robe, Painted, 32 ⅜ In. $717

Neal Auction Co.

Wood Carving, Wall Bracket, Eagle, Spread Wings, Walnut, Fruit, Leaves, c.1900, 15 In. $185

Cowan's Auctions

Wooden, Bowl, Ash Burl, Turned, 1800s, 17 In. $2,400

Cowan's Auctions

Mask, Square Top, Slatted Design, Face, Africa, 36 x 11 In.	90
Mermaid, Upswept Tail, Painted, 48 In.	384
Moai Tangata, Shell Eyes, Oval Base, Easter Island, c.1900, 11 In.	711
Model, Artist's, Facial Features, Fully Jointed, 31 In. *illus*	1107
Monk, Arms Out, Painted, Continental, c.1860, 43 In.	938
Monkey, Standing, Butler Attire, Base, c.1905, 23 ½ In.	1500
Monkey, Teak, Articulated, Seated, Branded Kay Bojensn, Denmark, 1950s, 13 x 15 In.	2500
Monkey, Wearing Topcoat, Hand Out, Black, Red, White Paint, c.1895, 20 In.	395
Mourning Doves, Painted, Lisa Schuler, 1980, 12 In.	720
Muse, Grapes In Hair, Draped Gown, Round Base, c.1885, 27 x 7 In.	1599
Music Stand, Hickory, Cherry, Rosewood, Tripod, Ball Feet, R. Superior, 1980, 59 In.	1500
Night Watchman, Black Forest, Germany, 1900s, 21 In.	280
Nuthatch, Painted, Rock Shape Base, Jess Blackstone, Marked, c.1950, 2 ¼ In.	600
Our Lady Of Guadalupe, Parcel Gilt, Standing On 3 Heads, Painted, 51 In.	522
Owl, Mahogany, Wings Semi-Spread, Signed Thomas Head, 1979, 17 In.	1320
Owl, Painted, c.1900, 8 ¼ In.	652
Owl, Standing, Maple, Black & Yellow Paint, U.S.A., c.1900, 16 x 7 In.	1888
Panel, Archangel Michael, Winged, Sword, 45 x 21 In.	461
Panel, Fruitwood, Blossoming Flowers, Fruit, Continental, 1800s, 26 In., Pair	960
Parrot, Yellow, Green, Red, Blue, Oversize Head, Ohio, c.1950, 11 ½ In.	323
Pen Tray, Boullework, Sloping Surface, Brass Arabesques, Inlaid Tortoiseshell, Ebony, 11 In.	425
Penguin, Black, White Paint, 12 ½ In.	127
Penguin, Painted, Marked Springer, 25 In.	1440
Penguin, Painted, Square Base, Charles A. Hart, c.1950, 2 ⅝ In.	2160
Phoenix, Federal, Spread Wings, Open Mouth, c.1815, 18 ½ x 23 ½ In.	1534
Pilgrim, Gentleman Leaning On Rifle, Mahogany, 19 ½ In.	438
Pipe Fitter, Mustache, Tool Box On Shoulder, Painted, c.1960, 20 ½ In.	59
Plaque, Eagle, American Flag, Shield, Paint, G. Stapf, 1940, 29 x 37 In.	5451
Plaque, Eagle, Arrows, Shield, Painted, 16 ½ x 20 In.	1320
Plaque, Eagle, Shield, Arrows, Pine, Artistic Company Of Boston, c.1950, 44 In. *illus*	2460
Plaque, Eagle, White Paint, John H. Bellamy, c.1910, 38 ½ In.	4200
Plaque, Sailboat, Waves, Landscape, c.1900, 20 ¾ x 34 ½ In.	5451
Plaque, Shield Shape, Eagle, American Shield, Flags, Painted, c.1910, 13 In.	384
Plaque, Winged Putti, Clouds, Molded Rays, Gilt, Italy, c.1815, 51 ½ In.	3690
Portrait, Woman, Dark Skin, Black Hair, William Dawson, 1989, 10 ½ x 20 In.	1200
Pot, Lid, Squat, Bulbous, Footed Base, Grooved Shoulder, Treen, Bail Handle, 7 ½ In.	460
Puffin, Painted, Full Size, Stone Base, Signed C.H. Cord, Jr., 11 ¾ In.	502
Putto, Baroque, Curly Hair, Stepped Plinth, Continental, 1700s, 25 ¾ In.	750
Putto, Flesh-Colored Paint, Gilt Wings, Italy, 23 In., Pair	1694
Putto, Giltwood, c.1910, 22 In.	338
Racehorse, Jockey, Tan, Red, White Paint, 16 In.	243
Robin Snipe, Painted, Rocky Base, Signed L. Johnson, 1962, 7 ¾ In.	474
Robin, Red, Black Paint, Domed Base, A.E. Crowell, 2 x 3 ½ In.	1304
Rooster, On Ball, Carved, 19 x 29 In.	115
Ruffled Grouse, Oval Base, Signed Lisa Schuler, 1984, 21 In.	660
Saint, Franciscan, Full Robe, Painted, 32 ⅜ In. *illus*	717
Salt, Master, Multicolor Flowers, Leaves, Salmon Ground, Yellow Inside, Joseph Lehn, 3 In.	649
Santo, Christ, Multicolor Enamels, Articulated, Fabric Robe, Wood Base, 34 In.	276
Santo, Mary, Gesso, Red, Blue, Black, Brown, 1800s, 17 x 7 ½ In.	161
Santo, Monk, Glass Eyes, Gilt Rope, Robes, Hands Raised, Spain, c.1765, 17 x 9 In.	275
Santo, Standing On Orb, Multicolor Paint, Gilt, Peru, 9 ¾ In.	184
Sea Captain, Holding Instrument, Paint, 61 In.	944
Shovel, Carved From Single Piece, Open Handle, 36 In.	36
Sperm Whale, Bass Wood, Gray, White, Capt. Mike Orbe Brewster, Mass., c.1980, 62 In.	1003
Sperm Whale, Paint, Wood Base, Inscribed, 1900s, 6 ½ x 18 In.	4500
Spirit Chaser, Amish, Figures, Noise Clappers, Clothing, Tin, Umbrella Frame, 55 x 21 In.	300
St. Anthony, Painted, Leading Lost Child, Round Pedestal, c.1815, 12 x 4 ½ In.	461
St. John, Parcel Gilt, Spanish Colonial, c.1850, 36 In.	531
St. Joseph, Painted, Parcel Gilt, c.1900, 41 x 19 In.	676
St. Matthew, Evangelist, Long Hair, Beard, Painted Robes, Germany, 1800s, 24 ¼ In.	2500
St. Patrick, Bishop Hat, Staff, Coiled Snakes, 11 ½ In.	73
St. Sebastian, Half Clothed, Arms Tied, Painted, c.1850, 80 ½ In.	3438
Staff, Ceremonial, Face Terminal, South Pacific, c.1840, 21 In.	6660
Staff, Parade, Paint, c.1905, 77 ½ In., Pair	180
Stag, Bellowing, Black Forest, Signed, Germany, c.1910, 13 In.	180
Stagecoach, 8 Horses, Driver, Painted, Wood Base, 13 x 44 In.	89

Stamp, Bag, Pine, Inscribed John Shott, Pa., 9 ¾ x 11 ½ In.	3888
Swan, Bird's-Eye Rosewood, Polished, Glass Eyes, Signed Grant Millers, 20 x 30 In.	322
Swan, Painted, 10 x 9 In.	380
Swordfish, Painted, c.1900, 51 x 139 In.	8295
Tempietto, Hexagonal Dome, Arches, Fluted Twist Columns, 16 x 11 In.	984
Thrasher, Scratch Feather, Rock Shape Base, Jess Blackstone, c.1965, 2 ⅜ In.	1200
Tiger, Crouched, Male, Female, Striped, Nepal, 1900s, 16 x 29 In.	480
Urn, Neoclassical, Parcel Gilt Urns, Faux Painted, 1800s, 28 In., Pair	5000
Vase, Ash Leaf Maple, Signed Philip Moulthrop, 12 x 8 In.	938
Virgin Mary, Cloud Bank, Winged Masks, Paint, Parcel Gilt, c.1850, 14 In.	2000
Virgin Mary, Deeply Carved Gown, Russia, c.1825, 32 ½ In.	281
Wall Bracket, Eagle, Spread Wings, Walnut, Fruit, Leaves, c.1900, 15 In. ....*illus*	185
Water Buffalo, Child On Back, Glass Eyes, Rosewood, Chinese, 1800s, 10 In.	215
Whale, Black Paint, Base, 12 In.	138
Whistler, Hat, Hands In Pocket, Head Turns, Germany, 13 ½ In.	510
White-Throated Sparrow, Scratch Feather Surface, Jess Blackstone, c.1950, 2 ⅛ In.	720
Wild Boar, Black Forest, Signed, 19th Century, 19 ½ x 23 x 9 In.	6250
Wilson's Snipe, Carved, Painted, Rocky Base, Signed L. Johnson, 1962, 7 ⅝ In.	830
Woman, Holding Goblet, 16th Century Costume, Continental, 1800s, 26 In.	588
Woman, Long Dress, Hand Raised, White, Yellow Paint, 46 In.	20400
Woman, Standing, Parcel Gilt, Paint, Continental, c.1825, 47 In.	2813
Woman, Striped Bathing Suit, Painted, 19 In.	105
Yoke, Ox, 1894, 45 In.	59

WOODEN wares were used in all parts of the home. Wood was used for many containers and tools. Small wooden pieces are called *treenware* in England, but the term *woodenware* is more common in the United States. Additional pieces may be found in the Advertising, Kitchen, and Tool categories.

Barrel, Oak, Brass Bound, Oval, England, 1800s, 24 In.	672
Bed Warmer, Heart Cutout Top, Front Door Carved, CW 1864, 11 x 8 In.	230
Birdhouse, A-Frame, Shingled Roof, 3 Tiers, White Washed, 6 Openings, 1900s, 34 x 28 In.	472
Birdhouse, Church Shape, Stained Glass Windows, Shingle Roof, 15 x 7 x 9 In.	36
Birdhouse, Colonial Style, Lift-Off Roof, Gables, Widow's Walk, Paint, c.1910, 18 x 15 In.	470
Birdhouse, Green, Gray Paint, c.1910, 26 In.	213
Birdhouse, Pine, 2-Story House, Perches, Blue Paint, c.1850, 22 x 24 In.	523
Book Press, George III, Mahogany, c.1780.	360
Book Press, Georgian, Mahogany, Turned Pole, c.1850, 14 ½ x 17 In.	474
Bowl, Ash Burl, Turned, 1800s, 17 In. ....*illus*	2400
Bowl, Ash Leaf Maple, Round, Squat, Inward Rolled Rim, P. Moulthrop, 6 x 10 In.	1404
Bowl, Ash, Ring Turned, Painted Blue, Round, c.1810, 7 x 18 ½ In.	1140
Bowl, Beaded Rim, Painted, c.1850, 18 x 19 In.	288
Bowl, Black Walnut, Turned, Ed Moulthrop, 6 ¾ x 9 ¼ In. ....*illus*	2875
Bowl, Blue, Red Paint, c.1850, 20 ¾ In.	425
Bowl, Burl, c.1850, 2 x 6 In.	948
Bowl, Burl, Handles, New England, c.1850, 6 x 14 ½ In.	948
Bowl, Burl, Maple, Turned, Scrubbed Surface, Rolled Wide Rim, 1800s, 6 x 17 In.	663
Bowl, Burl, Molded Edge, c.1860, 4 x 17 In.	1304
Bowl, Burl, New England, 1800s, 5 ½ x 15 ½ In.	2844
Bowl, Burl, New England, c.1805, 3 ½ x 11 ¾ In.	948
Bowl, Burl, Oval, Hand Carved, c.1800, 4 ⅛ x 13 ¾ x 16 ⅝ In. ....*illus*	3276
Bowl, Burl, Round, c.1800, 11 x 3 In.	435
Bowl, Burl, Turned, 1800s, 9 In.	472
Bowl, Burl, Turned, Molded Edge & Rim, Flared, c.1805, 5 ½ x 15 ½ In.	3159
Bowl, Burl, Turned, Molded Edges, New England, c.1825, 6 x 6 ½ In. ....*illus*	593
Bowl, Burl, Turned, Rolled Wide Rim, Dark Patina, 1800s, 6 ½ x 15 In.	3290
Bowl, Burl, Turned, Wide Rim, 1800s, 2 x 6 In.	588
Bowl, Burl, Wide Rim, 1800s, 4 ¼ x 12 ½ In.	676
Bowl, Crab, Starfish, Multicolor, Signed, Augustus M. Gerdes, c.1913, 11 In.	480
Bowl, Maple Burl, Round, Harry Nohr, 12 x 3 ¾ In.	397
Bowl, Maple, Paint, Trencher Style, c.1815, 4 x 21 In.	230
Bowl, Red Paint, Round, 20 x 7 In.	115
Bowl, Softwood, White Paint, 2 Handles, Wide Rim, 1800s, 9 x 27 In.	176
Bowl, Sycamore, Hand Carved, Notch Handles, Red Wash, 19th Century, 25 In.	511
Bowl, Trencher, Green Paint, c.1840, 18 ½ x 4 In.	230
Bowl, Turned, Beveled Rim, Black Paint, 1800s, 17 In.	125

Wooden, Bowl, Black Walnut, Turned, Ed Moulthrop, 6 ¾ x 9 ¼ In.
$2,875

Rago Arts & Auction Center

Wooden, Bowl, Burl, Oval, Hand Carved, c.1800, 4 ⅛ x 13 ¾ x 16 ⅝ In.
$3,276

Skinner Auctioneers & Appraisers

Wooden, Bowl, Burl, Turned, Molded Edges, New England, c.1825, 6 x 6 ½ In.
$593

James D. Julia Auctioneers

Wooden, Bucket, Clam & Oyster, Handle, Stenciled, H. Edwards, N.Y., 1800s, 9 ½ x 14 In.
$625

Rago Arts & Auction Center

TIP

When cleaning wooden pieces, use the foam from a mixture of 1 tablespoon soap to 1 quart water. Whip the mixture with a beater and clean with the foam.

W

Wooden, Candle Dryer, Pine, Cross Bars On Center Post, 1800s, 26 In.
$338

Garth's Auctioneers & Appraisers

Wooden, Cranberry Scoop, Tin & Wire Mesh, 22 x 9 x 20 In.
$285

Showtime Auction Services

Worcester, Plate, Blind Earl Pattern, Leaves, Flowers, c.1770, 7 ½ In.
$800

Cowan's Auctions

Worcester, Wine Cooler, Enamel, Gilt, Imari Design, Handles, Flight, Barr & Barr, 1800s, 10 x 12 In.
$3,540

Brunk Auctions

Bowl, Turned, Scrubbed Interior, White Over Red Paint, Wide Rim, 1800s, 6 ½ x 20 In.	181
Bowl, Turned, White Paint, 1800s, 18 In.	219
Bowl, Turtle Shell Shape, Head Shape Handle, c.1900, 12 In.	235
Box, Burl, Oblong, Lid, Carved Leaves, U.S.A., 1800s, 2 ¾ x 2 ¾ In.	353
Box, Chip Carved, Scallop Lid, Dovetailed, Staple Hinges, c.1805, 2 x 9 In.	1645
Box, Lid, Treen, Round, 5 ½ In.	124
Box, Scouring, Lid, Divided Interior, 7 ¼ x 11 ¼ In.	150
Brushpot, Bamboo, Tapered, Carved, Landscape Scene, 5 ¼ x 4 ½ In.	9600
Brushpot, Lobed, Hexagonal, Rim Band, Flared Base, Footed, 1900s, 5 x 4 In.	369
Bucket, Apple Butter, Bentwood, Curved Slat Handle, Painted Black, Ritter's, c.1910, 12 In.	86
Bucket, Berry, Red Paint, Brass Bands, Bail Handle, c.1885, 4 x 5 In.	147
Bucket, Clam & Oyster, Handle, Stenciled, H. Edwards, N.Y., 1800s, 9 ½ x 14 In. *illus*	625
Bucket, Kerosene Oil, Painted Red, Staved Construction, Metal Bands, Bail Handle, 11 In.	130
Bucket, Kerosene Oil, Stenciled, Metal, c.1845, 10 ½ In.	118
Bucket, Lid, Rope Handle, Marked Lt. Col. H.C. Grafton Jr., 1943, 8 ½ x 13 In.	1062
Bucket, Mahogany, Beech, Brass Bound, Ribbed, Metal Loop Handle, c.1850, 13 In.	875
Bucket, Maple Syrup, Tin Spout, Wire Bail, 10 x 8 ¼ In.	240
Bucket, Staved, Mustard Graining, Bentwood Swing Handle, c.1890, 10 In.	480
Bucket, Sugar, Bentwood Bands, Gray Paint, Swing Handle, c.1865, 9 ¾ x 13 In.	294
Bucket, Sugar, Lid, Salmon Paint, Yellow, Black Iron Banding, J. Lehn, c.1880, 9 In.	4503
Bucket, Sugar, Stave Construction, Bentwood, Handle, Gray Paint, c.1860, 12 x 12 In.	441
Bucket, Sugar, Yellow & Blue Paint, Banded, Handle, c.1885, 10 x 10 In.	294
Bucket, Vinegar, Pine, Stave, Iron Bands, Oval, New England, 17 ¾ x 7 ½ In.	138
Candle Dryer, Pine, Cross Bars On Center Post, 1800s, 26 In. *illus*	338
Canister, Lid, Turned, Salmon Ground, Red Flowers, Heilig, Pa., c.1880, 7 In.	1007
Canoe, Birch Bark, 28 Rib Interior, 9 x 37 ½ In.	514
Carnival Ride Motorcycle, Silver, Blue, Brown Paint, Inscribed Atha, c.1910, 36 x 50 In.	2640
Carrier, Cutout Handle, Blue Paint, 18 ¾ In.	60
Chopping Block, Shenandoah Valley, 3 Legs, c.1865, 32 x 12 In.	104
Cigarette Dispenser, Red, Black, Maltese Cross, Stepped Lid, Drawers, c.1910, 4 x 7 In.	118
Compote, Japanned, Black Ground, Footed, 11 x 9 In., Pair	115
Container, Vinegar Graining, Barrel Shape, Lid, Treen, 1800s, 6 ½ In.	588
Cranberry Scoop, Tin & Wire Mesh, 22 x 9 x 20 In. *illus*	285
Dummy Board, Young Boy, Hat, Scarf, Huge Brown Pants, Holding Net, Painted, 1950, 37 In.	60
Eggcup, Red Flowers, Leaves, Blue, Treen, Turned, Footed, J. Lehn, Pa., c.1880, 2 ¾ In.	533
Firkin, Crackers Stencil, Gray Paint, Metal Handle, 8 In.	396
Firkin, Green Paint, Handle, 1800s, 12 ¾ x 11 In.	146
Firkin, Lid, Painted Brown, Metal & Wood Bail Handle, Copper Tacks, 6 ⅝ In.	173
Firkin, Lid, Pine Staves, Joint Band, Green, Bentwood Handle, Mass., 1800s, 10 x 10 In.	443
Firkin, Lid, Swing Handle, Black Paint, c.1850, 8 ¾ In.	46
Firkin, Lid, Swing Handle, Gray, Yellow Paint, c.1855, 10 In.	58
Firkin, Painted Blue, Lid, Handle, Staved, 1800s, 11 ½ x 12 ¾ In.	575
Firkin, Painted Green, Staved Construction, Wood Bands, Bent Wood Handle, 13 ½ In.	83
Firkin, Painted, Fitted Lid, Bail Handle, 19th Century, 13 In.	180
Firkin, Painted, Handle, Geometric Design, Zigzag, c.1865, 8 ½ In.	1800
Firkin, Pine, Green Paint, Staved, Bentwood Swing Handle, J. Weeks, c.1830, 15 In.	504
Glove Form, Woman's Hand, Articulated Thumb, Pine, c.1890, 8 ½ In.	150
Grain Bin, Pine, 3 Lift Lids, Compartments, Drawers, Blue, Green Paint, c.1845, 29 x 85 In.	790
Grain Bin, Pine, Blue Gray Paint, Lift Top, c.1850, 28 x 50 ½ In.	395
Jar, Lid, Peaseware, Lathe Turned, Bail Handle, 10 ½ In.	1090
Jug, Staved, Iron Bands, c.1820, 15 x 12 In.	80
Knife Tray, Pine, Divided, Red Pinstripes, Green Paint, 1800s, 3 ½ x 12 ¼ In.	178
Knife Tray, Pine, Painted Blue, Dovetailed, c.1860, 5 x 11 In.	330
Lobster Cage, Wood Slats, Wire, Rope, 16 x 36 x 27 In.	390
Milliner's Head, Woman's Quilted Bonnet, Silk, Painted Face, 1800s, 13 In.	264
Model, Farm Buildings, House, Barn, Chicken Coop, Edwin Nejely, c.1900, 7 ½ x 10 ½ In.	450
Model, House, Green, Cream Paint, c.1930s, 24 x 20 In.	144
Model, Lincoln Hotel, Astor Theater, Painted, L. Butz, Pa., c.1900, 58 x 63 In.	948
Model, Log Cabin, Branches, Shingles, Stone, Cement Chimney, Glass Windows, 12 x 21 In.	92
Model, Log Cabin, Well, Branches, Shingles, Electrified, Twig Fence, c.1960, 12 x 19 ½ In.	120
Model, Sawmill, 2-Story, Painted, Wood, Masonite Shingles, Base, Mechanical Saw, 21 In.	130
Pipe Rack, Cutouts, Carvings, 5 Pipe Slots, Folding Shelves, 10 ½ x 12 ½ In.	79
Powder Keg, Painted Black, Wood Hoops, Powder Grade, F & FF, c.1800, 9 ½ x 6 ¼ In., Pair	540
Reliquary, Mahogany, Continental, c.1800, 41 x 27 In.	326
Salt Cellar, Teak, Metal, Raffia, Extension Handle, Carl Auböck, Austria, c.1950, 6 x 4 In.	625
Salt Dip, Strawberry, Vine Painted, Joseph Lehn, c.1892, 1 ¾ In., Pair	1422
Sculpture, Rocket, Slats, Metal Banding, Tip, c.1920, 118 In.	3068

Sculpture, Soccer Ball, Walnut Panels, Round, Black, Tan, J. Rauth, Stand, c.1980, 29 In.	590
Shipping Box, Pawnee Bill Wild West Show, OK Indian Territory, 15 x 8 x 12 In., 4 Piece	485
Snowshoe Mold, Bentwood, Iron, c.1880, 15 x 37 In.	675
Tankard, Cylindrical, Lion, Hinged Lid, Lion Feet, Scandinavia, 1800s, 10 In.	1140
Tazza, Burl, Saucer Foot, Pedestal, Wide Rim, 1900s, 3 ¼ x 7 ½ In.	118
Tazza, Treen, Inlaid Rose, Scalloped Rim, c.1890, 7 x 11 In.	59
Tool Box, Blue Paint, 20 x 29 ½ In.	230
Tray, Chippendale Style, Mahogany, Round, Carved Border, 20 In.	861
Tray, Cutlery, Walnut, Virginia, c.1840, 5 x 10 ¾ In.	288
Tray, High Wheel Riders, 11 x 14 In.	201
Tray, Knife, Pine, Red, Green Paint, Black Trim, c.1860, 6 x 14 In.	823
Tray, Mahogany, Brass Bound, Oval, Shaped Rim, England, 25 In.	813
Trough, 62 ½ In.	230
Tub, Stave Wrapped, Green, Black Bands, Salmon Interior, Cutout Handles, 1800s, 14 x 10 In....	1888
Urn, Knife, Federal, Mahogany, Inlaid, Turned Finial & Feet, c.1815, 23 x 10 In., Pair	2596
Wagon, Vendor's, 2 Wheels, Handle, Burgundy Painted, Line Detail, Merrimac, 28 x 59 In..........	474

WORCESTER porcelains were made in Worcester, England, from 1751. The firm went through many name changes and eventually, in 1862, became The Royal Worcester Porcelain Company Ltd. Collectors often refer to Dr. Wall, Barr, Flight, and other names that indicate time periods or artists at the factory. It became part of Royal Worcester Spode Ltd. in 1976. The company was bought by the Portmeirion Group in 2009. Related pieces may be found in the Royal Worcester category.

Bowl, Chamberlain, Botanical, Lobed, Oval, Gilt Edge, c.1825, 11 ¾ In., Pair	313
Creamer, Blue, Chinoiserie Landscape, Gilt Rim, Tapered, 2 ¼ In.	75
Dish, Blue Flowers, White Ground, Leaf Shape, 9 In.	688
Jug, Cabbage Leaf, Blue Carnation Pattern, Bearded Mask Spout, c.1775, 7 ¾ In.........................	259
Pitcher, Cabbage Leaf, Mask Shape Spout, Flowering Vines, Bird, 6 ½ In.	188
Plate, Armorial, Blue Rim, Chamberlains, 7 In...	438
Plate, Blind Earl Pattern, Leaves, Flowers, c.1770, 7 ½ In. ....*illus*	800
Plate, Dessert, 3 Flower Bouquets, Blue Band, Gilt, Chamberlain, c.1825, 9 In., 11 Piece............	920
Tea Strainer, Blue, White, Handle, 4 ½ In., Pair	238
Teapot, Dome Lid, Flower Knop, Curved Spout, Multicolor Sprays, c.1770, 5 ½ In......................	311
Wine Cooler, Enamel, Gilt, Imari Design, Handles, Flight, Barr & Barr, 1800s, 10 x 12 In. .*illus*	3540

WORLD WAR I and World War II souvenirs are collected today. Be careful not to store anything that includes live ammunition. Your local police will tell you how to dispose of the explosives. See also Sword and Trench Art.

WORLD WAR I

Album, Aviators, Planes, Barracks, Squadrons, 120 Photographs, c.1918	1652
Lighter, Cigarette, General Joffre, Portrait, Soldier Kissing Baby, 1 ⅝ In...........................	86
Poster, And They Thought We Couldn't Fight, Clyde Forsythe, Frame, 41 x 31 In. ....*illus*	330
Poster, Beat Back The Hun, German Soldier, Foxhole, F. Strothmann, Frame, 30 x 20 In.	180
Poster, Before Sunset, Statue Of Liberty, Flag Ground, 2nd Liberty Load, 1917, 20 x 30 In..........	190
Poster, Daddy What Did You Do During The Great War, Color Lithograph, 29 x 19 In..................	127
Poster, Fight World Famine, Young Man Fighting Vultures, Pitchfork, Frame, 28 x 19 In............	150
Poster, For Victory, Buy More Bonds, Lady Liberty, Shield, Flag, John Williams, 37 x 56 In.	510
Poster, Help Him Buy, Saving & Serving WSS, Frame, 30 x 20 In.	115
Poster, I Want You For U.S. Army, Uncle Sam, James Flagg, 1917, 30 x 40 In.......................*illus*	4253
Poster, Invest In Victory Liberty Loan, They Kept Sea Lanes Open, Ships, 29 x 39 In.	660
Poster, Joan Of Arc Saved France, Buy War Savings Stamps, Color Litho, 1918, 43 x 33 In.	298
Poster, Keep Him Free, C. Bill, Frame, 30 x 20 In...	150
Poster, Remember Belgium, German Soldier Dragging Girl, E. Young, Frame, 30 x 20 In.	150
Poster, See Him Through, Knights Of Columbus Man, Soldier, B. Rice, Frame, 30 x 20 In.	120
Poster, U.S. Marines Recruitment, Spirit Of 1917, Soldiers With Flags, 23 x 31 In.	127
Poster, U.S. Navy Recruiting, I Wish I Were A Man, Frame, 38 ½ x 25 In. ....*illus*	600
Poster, Uncle Sam, I Am Telling You, J.M. Flagg, American Litho., c.1919, 30 x 20 In..................	378
Saddlebag, U.S. Army, Cavalry, Clinton, Leather, 1917	175

WORLD WAR II

Ashtray, Figural, Hitler Phallic Design, Scrotum Base, 1940s, 3 ½ x 6 ½ In.	230
Banner, Reich Chancellery, Embroidered, Red, White, Black Wool, Swastika, 69 x 51 In.	6600
Button, Hitler, Wanted For Murder, Portrait, Swastikas, Black & White, 3 ½ In..........................	127
Button, Make America Strong, Drink More Milk, June 1941, 2 ³⁄₁₆ In. ....*illus*	86
Cup, Metal, Engraved Stylized SS, Oranienburg, Footed, 1940s, 3 ½ In.	83
Cuspidor, Anti-Hitler, Figural, Mouth Is Open, Arrow To Head, 9 x 10 In.	230

World War I, Poster, And They Thought We Couldn't Fight, Clyde Forsythe, Frame, 41 x 31 In.
$330

Morphy Auctions

World War I, Poster, I Want You For U.S. Army, Uncle Sam, James Flagg, 1917, 30 x 40 In.
$4,253

James D. Julia Auctioneers

World War I, Poster, U.S. Navy Recruiting, I Wish I Were A Man, Frame, 38 ½ x 25 In.
$600

Morphy Auctions

W

World War II, Button, Make America Strong, Drink More Milk, June 1941, 2 3/16 In.

$86

Hake's Americana & Collectibles

World's Fair, Compote, 1893, Chicago, Porcelain, Dolphins, Royal Worcester, 6 1/4 x 10 In.

$1,320

Skinner Auctioneers & Appraisers

World's Fair, Figurine, 1936, Cleveland, Ohio, Elephant, Celluloid, Weighted Ball, 3 1/2 In.

$26

Ruby Lane, Inc.

Figurine, Skunk, Hitler Face, Plaster, Painted, Welch Novelty Co., 1940s, 5 In., 2 Piece	115
Game, Bomb A Jap, Target, Dartboard, Tojo Face, Masonite, c.1945, 18 x 25 In.	115
Helmet, U.S., M-1, Front Seam, Fixed Bails, Straps, 11 x 7 In.	48
Magazine Pouch, Canvas, Leather, Nazi Marked W.A. 270, 8 x 8 In.	99
Pin, Vega, Wings, Stars, V, Sterling, 15/16 In.	86
Plaque, Remember Pearl Harbor, Uncle Sam Spanking Japanese Soldier, 8 x 10 In.	115
Poster, Americans, Share The Meat, Rationing, Frame, 28 x 21 In.	60
Poster, Award For Careless Talk, Swastika Ring, Iron Cross, S. Donanos, Frame, 37 x 29 In.	240
Poster, Britain Is Grateful, Mother, Child, Tower Of London, Frame, 22 x 14 In.	120
Poster, Buy War Bonds, Uncle Sam, Holding Flag, Bombers, 1942, 30 x 40 In.	253
Poster, Buy Your Extra War Loan Bonds Here, Color Lithograph, c.1944, 27 x 19 In.	150
Poster, Don't Blab About Train Movements, The Enemy Is Always Listening, Shut Up, 7 x 9 In.	59
Poster, God Help Me If This Is A Dud, Soldier Throwing Grenade, J. Vickers, Frame, 41 x 29 In.	330
Sign, Anti-Axis, Mussolini, Hitler, Tojo, Blame Them, Cardboard, 1940s, 15 x 18 In.	417
Telescope, Kriegsmarine Bridge Mount, 360-Degree Rotating Cradle, Pedestal, German, 61 In.	5040
Ukulele, V For Victory, Wood, Metal Tuning Pegs, Regal Label, 1942, 20 1/4 In.	230

WORLD'S FAIR souvenirs from all of the fairs are collected. The first fair was the Great Exhibition of 1851 in London. Some other important exhibitions and fairs include Philadelphia, 1876 (Centennial); Chicago, 1893 (World's Columbian); Buffalo, 1901 (Pan-American); St. Louis, 1904 (Louisiana Purchase); Portland, 1905 (Lewis & Clark Centennial Exposition); San Francisco, 1915 (Panama-Pacific); Philadelphia, 1926 (Sesquicentennial); Chicago, 1933 (Century of Progress); Cleveland, 1936 (Great Lakes); San Francisco, 1939 (Golden Gate International); New York, 1939 (World of Tomorrow); Seattle, 1962 (Century 21); New York, 1964; Montreal, 1967; Knoxville (Energy Turns the World) 1982; New Orleans, 1984; Tsukuba, Japan, 1985; Vancouver, Canada, 1986; Brisbane, Australia, 1988; Seville, Spain, 1992; Genoa, Italy, 1992; Seoul, South Korea, 1993; Lisbon, Portugal, 1998; Hanover, Germany, 2000; and Aichi, Japan, 2005. Memorabilia of fairs include directories, pictures, fabrics, ceramics, etc. Memorabilia from other similar celebrations may be listed in the Souvenir category.

Award, 1897, Oakland Exposition, Best Piano Manufacturer, Litho, David Smart, 17 x 23 In.	179
Badge, Chicago, 1933, Polish Week, Hospitality, Ribbon, Brass Tone, 3 x 1 In.	35
Bookmark, 1893, Chicago, Columbian Exposition, Ribbon, Washington, Eagle, 10 x 5 1/4 In.	153
Button, 1901, Buffalo, Pan-American, Exposition, Blue, Red, Pinback, 1 1/4 In.	139
Button, 1915, San Francisco, Bear, Tree, Poppies, Building, Blue Sky, 7/8 In.	115
Charm, 1964, New York, Unisphere, Blue, Orange, 1/2 In.	25
Cloth, 1909, Seattle, Alaska Yukon Pacific Exposition, Silk 15 x 10 1/2 In.	23
Coffee Server, 1904, St. Louis, Yale Coffee, 1st Grand Prize, Pottery, 10 In.	95
Compact, 1933, Chicago, Ft. Dearborn, Pearlescent, Enamel, Girey, 3 x 2 In.	60
Compote, 1893, Chicago, Porcelain, Dolphins, Royal Worcester, 6 1/4 x 10 In. _illus_	1320
Cup & Saucer, 1893, Chicago, Flower Shape, Frosted, Gold Writing, Libbey, 2 In.	115
Figurine, 1936, Cleveland, Ohio, Elephant, Celluloid, Weighted Ball, 3 1/2 In. _illus_	26
Handkerchief, St. Louis 1904, Louisiana Purchase Exposition, Silk, 20 In.	35
Match Safe, 1904, St. Louis, Eagle, American Flag, Map, Celluloid, 1 1/2 x 2 3/4 In.	120
Movie Film Viewer, 1939, New York, 3 Rolls Of Film, Multicolor Box, 7 1/2 x 5 In.	84
Mug, 1904, St. Louis, Lithophane, Machinery Hall, Pottery, Here's To Women, 5 1/4 In.	115
Pin, New York Expo, Trylon & Perisphere, White Metal, Rhinestones, Painted, 2 1/8 In.	86
Plate, 1904, St. Louis, Goofus Glass, Gold, 7 In.	25
Poster, 1939, New York, Woman, Arm Raised, Litho, Albert Staehle, 30 x 20 In.	431
Quilt, 1933, Chicago, Century Of Progress, Applique, Black, White, 68 x 82 In.	1920
Show Towel, 1893, Chicago, Wreath, Flags, Recognition To Industry, 45 In.	29
Toy, 1876, Philadelphia, Centennial Exposition, Puzzle, Paper On Wood, 21 In.	177
Toy, 1893, Chicago, Columbian Expo, Landing Of Columbus, Iron, Pull, Bell Rings, 8 In.	130
Toy, 1933, Chicago, Century Of Progress, Truck, Paint, Cast Iron, Arcade, Box, 7 1/2 In.	540
Watch Fob, 1933, Cleveland, Native Americans, Pot Metal, Brass Tone, 1 5/8 x 1 3/8 In.	48

WPA is the abbreviation for Works Progress Administration, a program created by executive order in 1935 to provide jobs for millions of unemployed Americans. Artists were hired to create murals, paintings, drawings, and sculptures for public buildings. Pieces are marked _WPA_ and may have the artist's name on them.

Blasting Machine, Dynamite Detonator, Wood, Leather Strap, Marked, 8 x 13 In.	480
Figurine, Balloon Man, Terra-Cotta, Signed Louise Pain, Chicago, 1930s, 8 x 15 In.	313
Figurine, Mary, Little Lamb, Chalkboard, Blue Dress, Cast, North Dakota, 1930s, 6 In.	1815
Model, Coleshill, English Renaissance Mansion, Plaster, Paint, 9 1/2 In.	30
Painting, Gouache On Board, Cityscape, Blue, White, Allen Stringfellow, Frame, 54 x 24 In.	6000
Painting, Oil On Canvas, House, Trees, Man Hosing Child, R. MacDonald, 1937, 20 x 26 In.	695

TIP

Save your travel souvenirs: the gift shop snowdomes, glasses, key chains, and postcards. They can form the start of a collection.

W

Painting, Watercolor, Houses, Tree, Red, Blue, Brown, Kady Faulkner, 1933, 17 x 22 In.	1150
Puppet, Papier-Mache, Cloth Body, Wood Legs, 1930s, 18 In.	225
Vase, Blue, Rolled Rim, Bulbous, North Dakota, Signed LF, 1937, 3 ⅛ In.	363
Vase, Green, Squat, Incised Arrowhead, North Dakota, 4 ⅞ In.	666
Woodcut, Seamstresses, Vogue Magazine On Wall, Fritzi Brod, 1937, 15 x 12 In.	395

WRISTWATCHES came into use during World War I. Wristwatches are listed here by  manufacturer or as advertising or character watches. Wristwatches may also be listed in other categories. Pocket watches are listed in the Watch category.

Baume & Mercier, 18K Gold, Dual Time, Black, Goldtone, Zone Dial, Case............*illus*	2520
Breitling, Navitimer, Chronograph, Stainless Steel, Black Dial, Batons, 3 Small Dials	1400
Cartier, Date, 14K Yellow Gold, Roman Numerals, Quartz Movement, Link Band	2400
Cartier, Diamond, 18K Gold, Black Band, Woman's, 6 ½ In.	6490
Cartier, Panthere, 18K Gold, Roman Numerals, Brickwork Band, 6 ¼ In.	5400
Cartier, Panthere, Stainless Steel, Quartz Movement, Secret Signature, Box, 5 ½ In.	2091
Cartier, Tank Francaise, Stainless Steel, Squared Dial, Second Hand, Link Bracelet, 6 In.	2813
Cartier, Tank, Square White Dial, Roman Numerals, 18K Gold, Leather Band.	2829
Cyma, 14K Yellow Gold, Round Dial, Link Band, 8 x 1 ½ In.	1170
Endura, Goldtone Face, Bakelite Bangle, Swiss, 1940s, 1 ½ In. ....*illus*	71
Gold Coin, 20 Dollar, Dated 1879, Leather Band	1200
Hamilton, 14K White Gold, Diamonds, 17 Jewel Movement, Woman's, c.1950.	480
Hamilton, White 14K Gold, Oval Face, Diamond Bracelet Style, Woman's.	1016
IWC Schaffhausen, Der Flieger Chronograph, Stainless Steel, Arabic, 3 Subsidiary Dials	3000
Jacques Lemans, Yellow Gold, Sapphire Crystal, 20 Jewel, 1900s, 9 ¼ In.	300
Lucien Piccard, Tutti Frutti, Pearl, Mother-Of-Pearl, Semiprecious Stones, 6 ½ In.	1168
Omega, 18K Gold, Woman's, 6 ¼ In.	605
Patek Philippe, 14K Yellow Gold, Diamonds, Chain Link, Signed, Woman's, 7 In.	2214
Patek Philippe, 18K Rose Gold, Guilloche Dial, Roman Numerals, Seconds Dial	8400
Patek Philippe, Silvertone Dial, Baton Numerals, 18 Jewel, Gubelin Mesh Band	3998
Patek Philippe, Silvertone Metal, Secondary Dial, 18K Gold, 18 Jewel, 1942 ....*illus*	4920
Patek Philippe, White Dial, Roman Numerals, Shaped 18K Gold, Quartz, Leather Band	3600
Piaget, 1897 Liberty Gold Coin Lid, Hinged, Baton Numerals, Black Band	2337
Piaget, 18K Gold Mesh Band, Oval Gold Dial, Diamond Surround, Woman's, 5 ¾ In.	3125
Piaget, Rounded Square Dial, Baton Numerals, Textured 18K Gold, Mesh Band	2040
Rolex, 18K Yellow Gold, Diamonds, Nugget Band, Bezel Set, 8 ½ In.	6457
Rolex, Cellini, 18K Gold, 19 Jewel, Leather Band, Locking Box, 9 In.	2358
Rolex, Cellini, Silvertone Dial, Diamonds, Gold Mesh Band, Woman's.	2640
Rolex, Daytona Cosmograph, 18K Gold, Stainless Steel, White Dial, Batons, 3 Dials	9840
Rolex, Oyster, Nugget, 17K Yellow Gold, Perpetual Datejust, Woman's, 6 In.	2844
Rolex, Oyster, Perpetual, Stainless Steel, Ivory Dial, Teardrop Numerals, Leather, 1960s	1046
Rolex, Silvertone Dial, Baton Numerals, 17 Jewel, Woven Link Band, Woman's	2583
Rolex, Ultrathin, Round Gold Dial, 18K, Baton Numerals, Crocodile Band	3690
Timex, Sterling, Turquoise, Claw, Coral Bracelet, Leaves, Scrolls, Signed LL, 2 ¾ In.	276
Vacheron & Constantin, Square, Arabic & Dot Indicators, Second Dial, 18K Gold	1560
Waltham, Art Deco, 14K White Gold, Square Dial, Diamonds, Silvertone, Woman's, 5 ½ In.	357

YELLOWWARE is a heavy earthenware made of a yellowish clay. It varies in color from light yellow to orange-yellow. Many nineteenth- and twentieth-century kitchen bowls and jugs were made of yellowware. It was made in England and in the United States. Another form of pottery that is sometimes classed as yellowware is listed in this book in the Mocha category.

Bowl, Clover, c.1700, 6 ½ In.	35
Bowl, White Stripe, Marked, 4 ¾ x 8 ½ In.	65
Bowl, Yellow & Green Sponged, Round, Molded Rim, 2 ½ x 6 ½ In.	24
Figurine, Spaniel, Oval Base, c.1850, 10 x 8 In.	345
Humidor, Coat Of Arms, Gothic Fret Border, Whippet Knop, c.1865, 10 x 4 In.	338
Jardiniere, Sponged Multicolor, Beaded Cable & Rib, Scalloped Top, Base, 21 x 11 In.	83
Jug, Rust Slip Ground, Green, Black, Blue Slip Lines, Sprig Inscription, c.1900, 5 ½ In.	142
Mustard Pot, Lid, Blue Seaweed, Cream Band Ground, Applied Handle, 2 ¼ In.	236
Nappy, 1800s, 10 In.	150
Pitcher, Blue Seaweed Banding, Striping, Loop Handle, c.1870, 7 ¾ In.	840
Pitcher, Columbus Landing In New World, Soldiers, Flag, Cross, 7 In.	118
Pitcher, Mask Under Spout, Hexagonal, c.1850, 8 In.	92
Rolling Pin, c.1900, 15 x 3 ¼ In.	399
Serving Plate, Rockingham Glaze, Square, Flared Sides, Brown Mottled, Scroll & Rib, 9 In.	24
Umbrella Stand, Sponge Painted, Cylindrical, c.1910, 21 In.	62

Wristwatch, Baume & Mercier, 18K Gold, Dual Time, Black, Goldtone, Zone Dial, Case
$2,520

Skinner Auctioneers & Appraisers

Wristwatch, Endura, Goldtone Face, Bakelite Bangle, Swiss, 1940s, 1 ½ In.
$71

Manor Auctions LLC

Wristwatch, Patek Philippe, Silvertone Metal, Secondary Dial, 18K Gold, 18 Jewel, 1942
$4,920

Skinner Auctioneers & Appraisers

X
Y
Z

Zanesville, Jug, Ear Of Corn, Handle, Impressed, La Moro, 5 ⅜ In.
$150

Humler & Nolan

Zsolnay, Vase, Giraffe, 3-Footed, Eosin Glaze, Pecs, Hungary, Stamped, c.1900, 9 x 5 ½ In.
$7,500

Rago Arts & Auction Center

Zsolnay, Vase, Red Roses, Gold Trim, Maroon Ground, Marked, 4 ¾ In.
$384

Humler & Nolan

ZANESVILLE Art Pottery was founded in 1900 by David Schmidt in Zanesville, Ohio. **LA MORO**
The firm made faience umbrella stands, jardinieres, and pedestals. The company closed
in 1920 and Weller bought the factory. Many pieces are marked with just the words *La Moro*.

Bowl, Green, Rings, 12 x 6 In.	65
Card Holder, Yellow, Flowers, Leaves, 2 x 2 x 3 In.	11
Jug, Ear Of Corn, Handle, Impressed, La Moro, 5 ⅜ In. .....*illus*	150
Pitcher, Green, Ribbed, Shouldered, 8 ½ In.	60
Planter, Deer, Yellow, Burgundy, Tree Trunk, 7 In.	35
Planter, Duck Shape, Turquoise, 5 x 3 In.	45
Planter, Green, Ribbed, Cylindrical, 5 ¼ x 4 ¼ In.	25
Vase, Black Over Yellow, Tapered, 11 ⅝ In.	58
Vase, Blue Green Gloss, Tapered, 11 ½ In.	40
Vase, Dark Green Matte, Smokestack Shape, 11 In.	81
Vase, Green Glaze, Globular, 5 x 6 In.	18
Vase, Green Matte, 11 ¾ In.	92
Vase, Green Mottled, Black Glaze, Handles, 13 x 22 In.	469
Vase, Green, Embossed Tulips, c.1935, 8 ¼ In.	85
Vase, Rose, Beige, Mottled, Handles, Footed, 6 In.	115
Vase, Tobacco Leaf, Shouldered, Blue, 8 ½ In.	225
Vase, Turquoise, Bulbous, Stick Neck, 7 In.	65

ZSOLNAY pottery was made in Hungary after 1853 and was characterized by Persian, Art
Nouveau, or Hungarian motifs. A series of new Zsolnay figurines with green-gold luster
finish is available in many shops today. Early Zsolnay was not marked, but by 1878 the tower trademark
was used.

Bowl, Blossoms, Purple, Eosin Glaze, Ball Shape, Rolled Foot, 5 Churches Mark, 4 x 6 In.	1750
Bowl, Stylized Landscape, Eosin Glaze, 5 Churches Mark, c.1900, 5 x 6 ½ In.	9375
Candleholder, Flower Shape, Ruby Tulips, Serpentine Stem, Eosin Glaze, 10 In.	431
Coupe, Dimples, Eosin Glaze, Medallion Ghost, c.1900, 7 ¼ x 3 ¼ In.	15000
Decanter, Handle, Double Spout, Melon Swirl Body, Flowers, Blue & Pink Flowers, 10 In.	236
Decanter, Wine, Stopper, Cream, Multicolor Highlights, Flask Shape, Handles, 13 x 11 In.	413
Ewer, Green, Lobed, Allover Confetti Detail, Jug Mouth, 11 In.	120
Ewer, Red Glaze, Gold Accent, Painted Flowers, Dragon Handle, 8 x 10 ½ In.	938
Figurine, Dog, German Shepherd, Sitting, 4 ½ In.	500
Figurine, Girl With Basket, Green, Iridescent, 1950s, 3 In.	167
Figurine, Rabbit, Red, Eosin Glaze, 4 In.	110
Figurine, Snail, On Leaf, Red Luster Glaze, 1900s, 4 ½ In.	46
Figurine, Stylized Rooster, Green Eosin Luster Glaze, Open Body & Tail, 8 In.	646
Figurine, Water Fountain, 4 Spigots, c.1930, 5 ½ In.	220
Figurine, Woman, Cutting Bread, Serving To Little Girl, 12 In.	66
Figurine, Wood Worker, Sitting On Bench, Carving, 13 In.	96
Paperweight, Skull, On Bible, Rosary, Eosin Glaze, 1930s, 3 ⅛ In.	501
Pitcher, Howling Otter, Striated Glaze, Brown, Tan, Blue, Tail Handle, 15 ½ x 6 In.	2625
Tray, Architectural Scene, Yellow Iridescent, 4 ⅜ In.	99
Vase, Angel, Figural, Yellow, Eosin Glaze, Flared Rim, Molded Base, 10 ½ In.	3200
Vase, Bud, 4 Handles, Eosin Glaze, 5 Churches Mark, 6 ¼ x 2 ½ In.	2500
Vase, Cabinet, Leafy Tree, Eosin Glaze, 5 Churches Medallion, c.1900, 3 ¼ x 2 ¾ In.	1875
Vase, Embossed, 4 Women, Grapes, Gold & Green Iridescent, 1900s, 6 ¼ In.	354
Vase, Etched Peacock Feathers, Eosin Glaze, Handles, 5 Churches, c.1900, 9 x 3 ½ In.	12500
Vase, Faience, Red Ground, Flowers, Leaves, Flared Neck, 5 Churches Medallion, 12 x 7 ¾ In.	625
Vase, Flowers, Pink, Purple, Green, Leaves, Bulbous, Signed, 7 ½ In.	150
Vase, Giraffe, 3-Footed, Eosin Glaze, Pecs, Hungary, Stamped, c.1900, 9 x 5 ½ In. .....*illus*	7500
Vase, Lined Pattern, Yellow, Handles, Stick Neck, Ruffled Rim, 4 ⅜ In.	1062
Vase, Ostriches, Cacti, Eosin Glaze, 5 Churches Mark, c.1900, 5 ¾ x 4 ½ In.	2750
Vase, Red Luster, Ball Shape, Marked, 5 ¼ In.	560
Vase, Red Roses, Gold Trim, Maroon Ground, Marked, 4 ¾ In. .....*illus*	384
Vase, Red Stylized Figures, Black Ground, Hungary, c.1955, 12 x 4 In.	125
Vase, Rooster & Hen, Gray Ground, Pink Flowers, Marked, 1880s, 8 ½ In.	531
Vase, Twisted, Bell Flowers, Eosin Glaze, Rippl-Ronai, 5 Churches Mark, c.1900, 9 In.	5313
Vase, Woman Seated, Eosin Metallic Glaze, Bulbous, c.1880, 9 In.	695
Water Jug, Flowers, Double Spouts, Top Ring Handle, c.1870, 5 ¼ In.	950

INDEX

This index is computer-generated, making it as complete and accurate as possible. References in uppercase type are category listings. Those in lowercase letters refer to additional pages where pieces can be found. There is also an internal cross-referencing system used in the main part of the book, so if you look for a Kewpie doll in the Doll category, you will be told it is in its own category. There is additional information at the end of many paragraphs about where to find prices of pieces similar to yours.

A

A. WALTER   1
ABC   1, 552
ABINGDON POTTERY   1
ADAMS   1–2, 176–177, 546,
Admiral Dewey   144, 181, 576
ADVERTISING   2–22, 50, 89, 122, 180, 285, 357, 421
AGATA   23, 587
Airplane   17, 25, 31, 101, 128, 144, 207–208, 370, 519, 589, 599, 613, 621
AKRO AGATE   24, 378
ALABASTER   24–25, 81, 126, 128, 131, 288, 358, 361, 558–559
Album   76, 432, 470–471, 580, 635
ALUMINUM   1, 25, 34–35, 43, 56, 60, 126, 135, 137, 200, 202, 249, 261, 333, 357–358, 361, 363, 503, 586, 606
AMBER GLASS   25, 357, 374, 393, 425, 503, 540
AMBERINA   25–26, 155, 196, 348, 369
Ambrotype   433
AMERICAN ENCAUSTIC TILING COMPANY   26
AMETHYST GLASS   26
Amos 'n' Andy   589, 602
Amphora, see Teplitz
Andirons   201–203, 440
Andiron, see Fireplace; also 559, 705
ANIMAL TROPHY   26
ANIMATION ART   26–27
ANNA POTTERY   27
Apothecary   60, 71, 114, 152, 384, 565
Apple Peeler, see Kitchen, Peeler, Apple
ARABIA   27, 579
ARC-EN-CIEL   27
ARCHITECTURAL   28–31, 128, 533, 638
AREQUIPA   31
ARITA   31
ART DECO   1, 25, 29, 31, 34, 122, 125, 128, 130, 134–135, 144, 147, 160, 168, 189, 191, 213, 218, 223–224, 226, 244–245, 249, 254, 256, 259, 261–262, 265, 267–268, 287, 289, 299, 323, 329, 347, 354, 358, 361, 365, 372–373, 377, 389–390, 401, 410, 412, 438, 457, 461, 467, 469, 474, 509–510, 524–527, 530, 538–539, 558, 578, 580, 582–583, 613, 616, 619, 629– 630, 637
Art Glass, see Glass-Art
ART NOUVEAU   31, 75, 83–84, 88, 90, 92, 97–98, 101, 125, 132, 148, 160, 194, 218, 222–223, 250, 291, 297, 303, 308, 321, 327, 343, 361, 372, 373, 375–376, 379, 382, 387, 389–390, 401, 430, 437, 451, 457, 500, 515, 524–526, 534, 541, 574, 578, 583, 602, 627

Arts & Crafts   29, 31, 56, 78, 93, 99, 122, 126, 128, 148, 201, 203–204, 215–217, 223, 244, 246–250, 254–256, 259–260, 265, 269, 282, 361, 393, 528, 530, 537, 540–541, 576, 629–630
Ashtray   2, 6, 24, 31, 33, 54, 57, 82, 92, 121, 135, 145, 147, 151, 169, 172, 178, 192, 197–198, 208–209, 211–212, 290, 294, 297, 299, 305, 309, 311, 349, 355, 367, 382, 389, 391, 408, 413, 415, 434, 440, 463, 479, 485, 487, 496, 506, 526, 552, 571, 578, 635
Atomizer   159, 214, 283, 429, 558
Aunt Jemima   9, 19, 57, 189
Austria, see Royal Dux; Porcelain
AUTO   13, 20, 31–38, 153, 516–517, 589, 605, 609–610
Automaton   56–57, 140, 181
AUTUMN LEAF   38–39
AZALEA   39

B

Babe Ruth   2, 9, 104, 548
BACCARAT   39–40
Backbar   28, 73, 357
BADGE   9, 33–34, **40**, 55, 80, 88, 104, 120, 132, 545, 577, 586, 636
Banana Boat   156, 214
BANK   28, 40–45, 50, 80, 88, 90, 112, 135, 175, 206, 309, 311, 367, 413, 415, 426, 439, 445, 477, 512, 551, 561, 577, 633
Banner   2, 9, 19, 33, 35, 64, 146, 381, 399, 404, 432, 438, 440, 516, 520, 563, 576, 621–623, 631, 635
BARBER   45–46, 56, 60, 62, 77, 110, 516, 624
BAROMETER   46–47, 424
Basalt   624
Baseball, see Card, Baseball; Sports
BASKET   47–49, 52, 78, 80, 84, 86, 93, 95, 103, 105, 107–108, 117, 134, 137, 139, 147, 153, 155–157, 159, 174, 189–192, 194–198, 206, 208, 214, 218, 286–287, 289–290, 303, 305–307, 309–311, 313–314, 316, 326–327, 334, 337, 341, 349, 367, 371, 375–376, 381, 383, 385, 388–389, 401, 404–406, 409, 412, 419, 423, 434, 436, 446, 457, 467, 470–472, 476, 479, 484–488, 494, 500, 504–505, 510, 513, 515, 523–524, 526–528, 531, 533, 535–541, 545, 548–551, 556, 559, 562, 568–569, 571, 574, 577, 580, 582, 586, 615, 617, 620, 628, 630, 638
BATCHELDER   48
Bathtub   28, 322, 584, 594
BATMAN   49, 144
BATTERSEA   49
BAUER   49–50
BAVARIA   50, 286
Bayonet   569
Beaded Bag, see Purse
BEATLES   50
Bed Warmer   80–81, 147, 633
BEEHIVE   50–51, 63, 121, 390, 513, 562, 564
Beer   6, 8–10, 13–14, 16–17, 19, 23, 51, 62, 92, 119, 122, 382, 383, 406, 441, 486, 503, 517, 578, 584
Beer Bottle, see Bottle, Beer
BEER CAN   51

BELL   28, 37, 51–52, 56–57, 94, 96, 106, 119, 132, 143, 147, 189, 197, 200, 210, 290, 333, 346, 352, 366–367, 398, 400, 402–403, 429, 440, 442, 472, 490, 509, 525–526, 530, 534, 536, 538, 541–542, 552, 556, 562, 571, 574, 589, 591, 597, 599, 601, 620, 638
BELLEEK   52, 59, 629
Belt Buckle   120, 152, 213, 328–329, 346, 526, 554
BENNINGTON   52–54, 99, 378
BERLIN   54
BESWICK   54, 489
BETTY BOOP   54, 138
BICYCLE   16, 55, 175, 207, 292, 308, 394, 433, 555, 590
BING & GRONDAHL   55
BINOCULARS   56, 89, 509
BIRDCAGE   56, 221, 228, 274, 464, 515
Biscuit Barrel   149, 191, 524
Biscuit Jar   96, 154, 156, 291, 328, 368, 389, 392, 396–397, 400, 419, 495, 498, 524, 544, 559, 620, 624
BISQUE   56, 59, 98, 100–101, 119, 146, 179, 180–182, 184–188, 307, 349, 367, 412–414, 438, 495, 508, 582, 593
BLACK   9–10, 17, 19, 20, 23, 43–44, 56–57, 99, 102, 112, 126, 146, 181, 189, 191, 207, 287–288, 321, 382, 409, 419, 427, 438, 474, 547, 555, 575, 584, 588–590, 593–594, 597–600, 602
Black Amethyst   68, 214, 417
Blanket   43, 77, 231–233, 316, 320, 405, 434, 544, 576
BLENKO GLASS COMPANY   57–58
Blown Glass, see Glass-Blown
Blue Glass, see Cobalt Blue
Blue Onion, see Onion Pattern
Blue Willow, see Willow
BOCH FRERES   58
BOEHM   58–59
BONE   46, 56, 60, 79, 101–102, 120, 149, 194–196, 223, 228, 239, 246, 285, 329, 333, 351, 353, 403–404, 462, 503, 515–516, 524, 545, 547, 570–571, 587
Bone Dish   121
Book   49, 54, 59, 76, 80–81, 88–90, 92, 102, 104, 113, 117, 144, 146, 159, 161, 175, 178, 189, 212, 290, 322, 382–383, 398, 401, 415, 419–421, 426, 429, 436, 451, 479, 566, 568, 586, 633
BOOKENDS   10, 59, 151, 178, 212, 214, 346, 370, 405, 411, 428, 479, 485–488, 496, 544, 572, 578, 614
BOOKMARK   60, 135, 152, 578–580, 636
BOSSONS   60
Boston & Sandwich Co., see Sandwich Glass
BOTTLE   2, 6, 8–10, 13–14, 26–27, 33, 52, 57–58, 60–74, 95–96, 110–111, 114, 116, 119–120, 131, 135, 137–138, 157, 163–164, 166, 168, 179, 204, 207–208, 218, 291, 294, 353–354, 356, 377, 381, 389–390, 393, 402–403, 413–414, 423, 426–427, 429–431, 450, 453, 457–458, 472, 480, 486, 496, 499, 503, 505–508, 519, 535, 558–559, 561, 568, 577–578, 605, 614–615, 617–618, 623–624, 628–629, 631

BOTTLE CAP 74, 206, 429
BOTTLE OPENER 74–75
BOTTLE STOPPER 75, 387
BOW 316
BOX 2, 24–25, 31, 49, 57–59, **75**–82, 88–89, 111, 120, 131, 135, 137, 140, 147–148, 151, 157, 159, 164, 178, 194–195, 203, 206, 289, 292, 299, 303–304, 316, 322, 326–327, 330, 348, 352, 355, 381–382, 394, 398–399, 422, 424, 430, 437, 439, 449, 458, 489, 496, 507–508, 510, 512–513, 515–516, 524, 527, 534–535, 537, 540–542, 544, 556, 578, 582, 585–588, 590, 610, 614, 620–621, 624, 628, 634
BOY SCOUT 43, 80
B.P.O.E. 399, 619
BRADLEY & HUBBARD 80, 125, 191, 323, 361
BRASS 6, 16, 26, 28, 31, 43, 46, 51, 52, 56, 59–60, 74–81, 90–91, 97–99, 101–102, 104, 109–110, 120–122, 125–126, 128, 137, 139, 147–149, 153, 159, 164, 175, 179, 190–191, 194, 196, 200–205, 213, 218, 220, 223, 236, 239, 247–249, 253–255, 262, 264, 266, 282, 288, 290, 302, 312–313, 320–321, 330, 334, 338, 347, 350–353, 357–358, 361, 363–366, 368, 372–373, 375, 377–378, 382–383, 393, 399, 402–403, 413–415, 424, 428, 431–433, 445–446, 462, 473–474, 496, 507–510, 513, 544–545, 547, 567, 569, 571–572, 574, 578–579, 582, 584–588, 600, 602, 604, 611–612, 619, 621, 630, 633, 635
Brastoff, see Sascha Brastoff
Bread Plate, see various silver categories, porcelain factories, and pressed glass patterns
Bread Tray 527, 585
BRIDE'S BOWL OR BASKET 81–82, 154, 381
BRISTOL 81–82, 175, 397
Britannia, see Pewter
BRONZE 28, 45, 51, 59, 76–77, 79–80, 82–88, 97–99, 102, 110, 121, 125–126, 128, 131–133, 151, 190, 202–204, 219, 228, 249, 280, 287, 301–305, 321, 324, 346, 357–358, 361, 363–366, 369–370, 377, 379–380, 399, 402–403, 411, 414, 421, 423, 427–428, 437, 438, 446, 449, 470, 483–484, 508, 513, 547, 569, 578–580, 619, 621, 623, 625, 630
Broom 2, 179, 309
BROWNIES 10, 88, 143, 188, 202, 397
BRUSH POTTERY 88–89, 349, 527, 572
Brush-McCoy, see Brush and related pieces in McCoy
BUCK ROGERS 89
Bucket 17, 44, 58, 81, 147–148, 160, 200, 205, 213, 216, 297, 350, 367, 383, 430, 467, 516, 525–526, 541, 585–586, 602, 630, 634
Buckle 120, 152, 213, 316, 328–330, 343, 346, 356, 394, 526, 531, 534, 554, 619
BUFFALO POTTERY 89–90
Buggy 109, 566
Bugle 75, 399
Bunnykins, see Royal Doulton
BURMESE GLASS 90, 110, 196, 364, 397
BUSTER BROWN 90–91
BUTTER CHIP 91, 476, 572
Butter Mold, see Kitchen, Mold, Butter

BUTTON 33, 49–50, 89–91, 103, 117, 137, 161, 213, 290, 308, 372, 440–441, 445, 545, 548, 568, 586, 635–636
BUTTONHOOK 92

C

Cabinet 2, 5, 33, 35, 45, 50, 125, 143, 164, 217–220, 350, 384, 398–399, 424, 432–433, 513, 516, 565, 591, 610, 623, 638
Cake Stand 50, 198, 208, 385, 390, 428, 434, 462–464, 478, 524, 582
CALENDAR 92, 122, 126, 128, 137, 425, 488, 579
CALENDAR PLATE 92
CAMARK POTTERY 92–93
CAMBRIDGE GLASS 93–96, 522
CAMBRIDGE POTTERY 96
CAMEO GLASS 2, 96–97, 110, 154, 161, 166, 196, 292, 353, 366, 396–397, 427, 478, 480, 509, 559, 623
Camera 433, 601
Campaign, see Political
CAMPBELL KIDS 97
CANDELABRUM 52, 93, 97–99, 192, 294, 356, 385, 405, 483, 578
Candlesnuffer 524
CANDLESTICK 25, 49, 54, 80, 88, 93–95, 99–100, 106, 145, 151, 153, 159, 166–168, 170–174, 179, 193, 198, 208–210, 249, 294, 303–306, 309–310, 314, 326, 346, 368, 374, 381–382, 387, 397, 405–408, 411, 413, 415, 417, 419, 429–430, 463, 479, 484–486, 496–497, 502, 505, 556, 568, 574, 578–579, 584, 614, 616–617, 620, 624, 628
Candlewick, see Imperial Glass
CANDY CONTAINER 49, 100–101
CANE 57, **101–103**, 114, 206, 326, 441
Caneware 624
Canoe 156, 214, 316, 402, 548, 566, 590–591, 634
Canteen 80, 120
CANTON CHINA 103, 210, 534, 574
Cap Gun 290, 488–489, 591
CAPO-DI-MONTE 103, 555
CAPTAIN MARVEL 103–104
CAPTAIN MIDNIGHT 104
Car 8, 16, **33**, 35, 37, 113, 119, 139, 140, 160, 175, 179, 300, 351, 517, 577, 589, 591–592, 594, 597–600, 604, 609–610
Carafe 25, 49, 157, 159, 356, 369, 475
CARD 49, **104**–105, **113**, 117, 143, 152, 175, 178, 195, 206, 266, 285, 290, 309, 400, 442, 489, 556
Card Case 426, 527, 536
CARLTON WARE 105
CARNIVAL GLASS 105–109
CAROUSEL 109, 179, 371, 424, 592, 602
CARRIAGE 89, 109–110, 125–126, 128, 361, 366, 588, 591–593, 599
Carte De Visite 433
CASH REGISTER 43, 110, 593
Casserole 39, 199, 211–212, 214, 296, 299, 302, 350, 388, 445, 475, 503, 520, 553, 620
CASTOR JAR 110, 414, 425, 498

CASTOR SET 110, 537–538, 582
Catalog 394, 429
CAUGHLEY 111
CAULDON 111
Cel, see Animation Art
CELADON 72, 96, 111, 288, 328, 348
CELLULOID 5, 10, 17, 19, 54, 57, 60, 91–92, 111–112, 135, 145, 149, 152, 179, 181, 300, 383, 427–428, 440, 442, 445, 474, 515, 594, 598–599
CERAMIC ART COMPANY 112, 368
CERAMIC ARTS STUDIO 112
Chalice 83, 103, 152, 375, 393, 470, 494, 527, 533–536, 541
CHALKWARE 6, 112, 117, 195, 449
Chamber Pot 89, 103, 549, 568, 572, 589
Charger 5, 31, 50, 111, 114, 131, 135, 148, 164, 194–195, 291, 297, 303, 313, 356, 370, 373–374, 375, 383, 385, 389, 407, 430–431, 434, 437, 449, 450, 457–458, 461, 476, 483–484, 490, 496, 507, 527, 541, 546, 561, 582, 585, 616–617
CHARLIE CHAPLIN 113, 515
CHARLIE MCCARTHY 113–114
CHELSEA 114, 116, 125, 176, 403
CHELSEA GRAPE 114
CHINESE EXPORT 114–116
CHINTZ 94, 116–117, 154, 208, 312, 401, 434–435, 471, 522, 616
CHOCOLATE GLASS 117
Chocolate Pot 81, 114, 148, 192, 303, 385, 400, 498, 527, 540, 617
Chocolate Set 407–408, 446, 498
Chopper 350
CHRISTMAS 27, 55, 57, 89, 100, 117, 119, 137, 160, 206, 312, 421, 426, 482, 491, 551, 610
CHRISTMAS TREE 119–120, 160, 420, 426, 610
CHROME 74, 104, 120, 139, 149, 161, 204, 217, 226, 228, 231, 245, 247, 249, 255, 261, 267, 273, 347, 350, 352, 357–358, 361, 365, 405–406, 427
Churn 350, 476, 516, 561
Cigar Cutter 57, 148, 327, 619
CIGAR STORE FIGURE 120
CINNABAR 59, 72, 120
CIVIL WAR 20, 120–121, 191, 382, 438, 555
CKAW, see Dedham
Clambroth 65, 82, 378, 397, 505
CLARICE CLIFF 121
CLEWELL 121–122
CLIFTON POTTERY 122
CLOCK 25, 34, 44, 79, 111, 113, **122**–131, 137, 161, 178, 189, 195, 206, 308–309, 369, 381, 385, 403, 428, 441, 451, 490, 497, 574, 578, 610
CLOISONNE 60, 72, 88, 101, 131–132, 321, 540
CLOTHING 132–134, 396
CLUTHRA 135, 558
COALBROOKDALE 135
COALPORT 135, 320–321
Coaster 135, 165, 168–169, 193, 306, 389, 391, 437, 524, 526, 600, 610, 628

COBALT BLUE   50, 54, 57–58, 63–64, 67–69,
    71, 73, 76, 96, 105–106, 108, 119, 131, 135,
    163, 165, 171, 174–175, 193–194, 196–198,
    209, 214289, 291–292, 294, 296, 302–303,
    306, 313–314, 321–322, 354, 366, 375, 381,
    387, 390, 397, 401–402, 405–406, 408, 417,
    427, 447, 461, 472, 474, 482–483, 488, 492,
    494, 505–506, 512, 551, 561–565
COCA-COLA   117, 119, 135–139
Cocktail Shaker   120, 192, 197, 405, 524–525,
    527, 540
COFFEE MILL   139, 441
Coffeepot   27, 148, 176, 199, 210, 212, 289,
    297, 299, 324, 367–368, 370, 388–389, 431,
    434, 439, 446, 476, 491, 522, 525, 527–528,
    534, 536, 538–542, 546, 549, 582, 584–585
COIN SPOT   25, 82, 106, 110, 139, 411–412
COIN-OPERATED MACHINE   140–144, 400,
    508
Cologne   63–64, 157, 414, 505, 623
Coloring Book   420
Comb   24, 184, 201, 229, 330, 333, 399, 588
COMIC ART   144, 568
COMMEMORATIVE   144, 290, 441–442, 568
COMPACT   144–145, 467, 469, 588, 636
Compass   46, 78, 213, 227, 288, 308, 371,
    402–404, 420, 471–472, 509–510, 586
Condiment Set   150, 489, 545
Console Set   309–311, 314, 488
CONSOLIDATED LAMP AND GLASS COM-
    PANY   145, 364
Contemporary Glass, see Glass-Contemporary
COOKBOOK   1, 146
Cookie Cutter   350
COOKIE JAR   39, 88–89, 146–147, 161, 166,
    170–171, 178, 307–310, 367, 383, 388, 426,
    428, 445, 486, 497, 520, 568, 627
COORS   147
COPELAND   147
COPELAND SPODE   147
COPPER   14, 28–29, 57, 76, 78, 80–81,
    97–99, 122, 147, 178, 194, 200, 203–204,
    220, 249–250, 302, 304, 338, 343, 347,
    350–351, 361, 363–366, 374, 382–393, 399,
    403–404, 462, 477–478, 496–497, 535, 562,
    621–623
Copper Luster, see Luster, Copper
CORALENE   52, 149, 628
CORKSCREW   149, 378
Cornucopia   64–65, 153, 158, 287, 309–311,
    337–338, 371–372, 392–393, 409, 479,
    485–488, 528, 558, 615
CORONATION   149–150, 167, 515
COSMOS   106, 150, 485, 535, 552
COVERLET   150
COWAN POTTERY   151–152
CRACKER JACK   152
CRANBERRY GLASS   81, 110, 149, 152, 292,
    364, 393, 523, 622
CREAMWARE   153, 367, 371, 549, 624
CRIEL   153
Crock   5, 54, 146, 262, 391, 475–476, 512,
    561–562
CROWN DERBY   153
CROWN DUCAL   154
CROWN MILANO   154

CRUET   23, 25, 90, 117, 154–155, 156, 160,
    167, 192, 196–197, 305, 307, 381, 390,
    393–394, 397, 411, 425–426, 445, 467, 472,
    484, 536, 545–546, 616
CT GERMANY   155
Cuff Links   111, 330, 333
CUP PLATE   155, 289
Cupboard   218, 241–243, 245, 466
CURRIER & IVES   14, 92, 155–156
Cuspidor   476, 497, 549, 562, 635
CUSTARD GLASS   156, 164, 197, 384
CUT GLASS   28, 63, 79, 97, 99, 128, 154,
    156–159, 303–304, 321, 358, 361, 364, 369,
    375, 536, 541, 623
CYBIS   159
CZECHOSLOVAKIA GLASS   159
CZECHOSLOVAKIA POTTERY   159

D

Dagger   353
Daguerreotype   433
DANIEL BOONE   159
D'ARGENTAL   159
Darner   425
DAUM   159–161
DAVENPORT   161, 244
DAVY CROCKETT   161, 492
DE VEZ   161
Decoder   104, 586
DECOY   161–163
DEDHAM   163
DEGUE   163
Deldare, see Buffalo Pottery Deldare
DELFT   163–164, 358, 366
DENTAL   164
DENVER   70, 164
DEPRESSION GLASS   165–174
DERBY   82, 146, 174–175, 201, 548, 587
Desk   76, 83, 125, 131, 224, 240, 244–246,
    248, 301, 358, 361, 368, 413, 511, 517, 536,
    579
Desk Set   536
DICK TRACY   175
Dickens Ware, see Royal Doulton; Weller
DINNERWARE   175–177
DIONNE QUINTUPLETS   177
Dipper   132, 205, 352, 511, 516
DIRK VAN ERP   178, 361
DISNEYANA   178–180
Dispenser   5– 6, 9, 137–138, 144, 426, 429,
    445, 566, 634
Doctor, see Dental; Medical; also 58, 64
DOLL   57, 79, 88, 90, 97, 104, 113, 117, 137,
    159, 177–178, 180–189, 194, 308, 316, 349,
    370, 372–373, 415, 420–421, 426, 441, 445,
    515–516, 522–523, 568, 610
DOLL CLOTHES   189
Dollhouse   594
Donald Duck, see Disneyana; also 27, 144, 178,
    179
Doorknob   28
Door Push   6, 81, 137, 356
DOORSTOP   117, 178–179, 189–191, 214,
    445, 512, 568
DOULTON   191, 369
DRESDEN   101, 119, 192, 402, 625

Dresser Box   160, 348, 381, 393–394, 401, 410,
    419, 534, 610, 620–621
Dresser Set   541
Dr Pepper   10
Drum   6, 83, 101, 113, 119–120, 180, 271,
    288, 290–291, 304, 316, 365, 376, 399, 433,
    511, 533, 594, 599
DUNCAN & MILLER   192–193
DURAND   193

E

Earrings   329, 333–334, 337–338, 341
Eggcup   39, 116, 135, 170, 198–199, 289, 306,
    472, 477, 631, 634
ELFINWARE   303
ELVIS PRESLEY   193
ENAMEL   17, 24, 28, 40, 58, 60, 71–72, 74,
    76, 78–81, 91, 113, 121, 125, 145, 160, 178,
    193–194, 280, 283–284, 292–293, 302, 327,
    330, 334, 337–338, 341, 343, 345, 368, 373,
    375, 380, 390, 393, 396–397, 401, 408, 416,
    427–428, 445–447, 449, 469, 483, 498, 506,
    534, 536, 539–540, 542, 545, 550–551, 571,
    574, 576, 578, 580–582, 621, 623, 632, 635
Epergne   90, 152, 198, 209, 291, 364, 369, 525,
    528, 536, 541
ERICKSON   194
ES GERMANY   194
ESKIMO   47, 55, 194–195
Extinguisher   200

F

FABERGE   195, 198–201, 204–206, 208, 540
FAIENCE   164, 195, 366, 373, 461, 491, 555,
    638
FAIRING   195
Fairyland Luster, see Wedgwood
Famille Rose, see Chinese Export
FAN   28, 54, 116, 137, 178, 196, 204, 405, 445,
    486, 488, 558
Federzeichnung, see Loetz
Fence   56, 80, 151,190–191, 292, 308, 323,
    370, 382, 481, 505, 549, 594, 606
FENTON   196–198
Fernery   109
FIESTA   198–199
Figurehead   403
FINDLAY ONYX AND FLORADINE   199–200
Fireback   203
FIREFIGHTING   200–201
FIREPLACE   26, 28–29, 201–204, 425
First Aid   33, 290, 384
FISCHER   204–205
FISHING   10, 13, 44, 49, 76, 155–156, 162,
    205, 290, 323, 327, 418, 511, 589
Flag, see Textile, Flag
Flagon   353, 431, 541
FLASH GORDON   205–206
Flashlight   6, 161, 373
Flask   27, 64–65, 67, 72, 74, 115, 120, 125,
    195, 356, 377, 449, 477, 479, 507, 528, 541,
    562, 582, 624
FLOW BLUE   89, 91, 191, 206, 289, 303, 314,
    482, 488
Flower Frog   151, 163, 214, 380, 408, 412, 429,
    461, 485–486, 488, 580, 614–615, 625, 627

Flowerpot   1, 24, 115, 164, 454, 477, 562
FOLK ART   57, 206–208, 622
Football, see Card, Football; Sports
FOOT WARMER   208, 584
Fortune Teller   140, 304, 326
FOSTORIA   208–210, 587
Frame, Picture, see Furniture, Frame
Foval, see Fry Glass
FRANCISCAN   210–212, 632
FRANKART   212–213
FRANKOMA   218
FRATERNAL   213–214
Fruit Jar   67–68, 305
FRY GLASS   214, 474
FULPER   59, 214–215
Funnel   148, 537, 601
FURNITURE   215–283, 597
FURSTENBERG PORCELAIN WORKS   283

G

G. ARGY-ROUSSEAU   283
GALLE   271, 283–284
GALLE POTTERY   284
GAME   49, 57, 88, 90, 113, 137, 143, 161, 175,
   179, 206, 254, 271, 273, 285–286, 299, 383,
   441, 445, 568, 624, 636
GAME PLATE   286
Garden   29, 287–288, 313, 346, 354, 370, 381,
   435, 577
GARDEN FURNISHING   286–289
GAUDY DUTCH   289
GAUDY WELSH   289
GEISHA GIRL   289, 397
GENE AUTRY   290
GIBSON GIRL   290
GILLINDER   290
Ginger Jar   115, 164, 313, 391, 467, 484, 502
Girandole   128, 158, 250, 252–253, 292, 333,
   365
GIRL SCOUT   290
GLASS-ART   290–291
GLASS-BLOWN   291–292
GLASS-BOHEMIAN   292–293
GLASS-CONTEMPORARY   293
Glass-Cut, see Cut Glass
Glass-Depression, see Depression Glass
GLASS-MIDCENTURY   293–294
Glass-Pressed, see Pressed Glass
GLASS-VENETIAN   294–296
GLASSES   75, 89, 111, 138, 187, 296, 300, 370,
   404, 441, 567
GLIDDEN   296
GOEBEL   296, 382
GOLDSCHEIDER   296–297
GOOFUS GLASS   297
GOUDA   297
Gramophone   516
GRANITEWARE   297, 506
Grater   350, 530, 536
GREENTOWN   117, 298
Grill Plate   39, 168, 170–173, 199, 211, 214,
   618
GRUEBY   298–299
Gun, see Toy
GUSTAVSBERG   299

H

HAEGER   299
Hair Receiver   328
Half-Doll, see Pincushion Doll
HALL CHINA   217, 225, 262, 299, 366
HALLOWEEN   100–101, 299–300
HAMPSHIRE   300–301
HANDEL   301, 549
Handkerchief   80, 149, 228, 270, 294, 296,
   441, 545, 628, 636
Hardware, see Architectural
HARKER   301–302
HARLEQUIN   302
Harmonica   489
Hat   8, 23, 25, 45, 58–59, 64, 76–77, 102,
   113–114, 125, 133–134, 137, 146, 161,
   188–191, 195–196, 201, 207, 213, 294, 304,
   308, 319–320, 322–324, 343, 348–349, 354,
   367, 379, 381–382, 390, 396, 398, 407, 422,
   426, 428, 436, 440–441, 449, 454, 478, 503,
   505, 508, 513, 517, 554, 566, 567, 574, 584,
   586–588, 591, 598, 600, 612, 631–634
HATPIN   107, 302–303, 497–498, 508
HATPIN HOLDER   107, 303, 497–498, 508, 588
HAVILAND   91, 303
HAWKES   91, 303–304
HEAD VASE   112, 304, 346
HEDI SCHOOP   304
HEINZ ART   304–305
HEISEY   305–306
Herend, see Fischer
HEUBACH   182, 184, 307
Historic Blue, see factory names, such as Adams,
   Ridgway, and Staffordshire.
HOBNAIL   81, 152, 192, 197, 307, 370,
   389–390, 393, 499
Honey Pot   121, 213, 346–347
HOLT-HOWARD   307–308
HOPALONG CASSIDY   308
HORN   101, 226, 308, 316, 322, 351, 432, 544,
   570
HOWDY DOODY   308–309, 311–312
HULL   309–311
HUMMEL   311–312
Humidor   57, 88–89, 107, 122, 148, 248, 304,
   348, 355, 376, 380, 390, 393, 408, 454, 568,
   574, 582, 621, 625, 637
HUTSCHENREUTHER   312

I

Ice Bucket   58, 93–96, 119, 148, 197, 209,
   304, 530, 539, 582, 623
ICON   312–313, 320–322, 324
IMARI   153, 313, 382, 447, 492
IMPERIAL GLASS   313–314, 388, 616
Incense Burner   83, 131, 307, 326, 354, 507,
   534, 618
INDIAN   20, 82, 85, 120, 122, 314–320, 516,
   541, 545, 579, 582, 591, 599, 619, 622
INDIAN TREE   192, 320–321
INKSTAND   83, 164, 321, 579
INKWELL   27, 160, 304, 321–322, 346, 356,
   371, 390, 407, 413, 505, 512, 536, 579–580,
   611

IRON   201–207, 322–324
Iron   351
IRONSTONE   91, 206, 324, 474, 572
ISPANKY   324
IVORY   324–327

J

JACK-IN-THE-PULPIT   327, 348, 356, 396, 425,
   470, 558, 581, 615
JADE   50, 72, 102, 145, 174, 195, 214,
   327–328, 330, 333–334, 343, 414
Japanese Woodblock Print, see Print, Japanese
JASPERWARE   328, 346–347, 624–625
JEWELRY   77, 131, 194, 291, 326, 328–345,
   385, 538, 565, 580, 588
Jigsaw Puzzle   104, 285
JOHN ROGERS   346
JOSEF ORIGINALS   346
JUDAICA   346–347
JUGTOWN   347
JUKEBOX   347–348

K

KATE GREENAWAY   348
KAY FINCH   348
Kayserzinn, see Pewter
KELVA   348
KENTON HILLS   348
KEW BLAS   348
KEWPIE   349, 508
Key   37, 45, 143, 206, 305, 323, 329, 354, 400,
   446, 463, 481, 489, 530, 566, 612, 619
KITCHEN   349–353, 598
KNIFE   8, 77, 80, 120, 202, 308, 353, 394,
   519, 530
Knowles, Taylor & Knowles, see Lotus Ware; also
   154, 184–185
KOSTA   353
KPM   353–354
KTK   354
KU KLUX KLAN   354
KUTANI   354–355, 506

L

L.G. WRIGHT   355
Label   8, 17, 19, 49, 70, 73, 93, 146, 161, 200,
   279, 349, 399–400, 402, 408, 424, 445, 511,
   561–562, 566, 610, 612, 614
LACQUER   76, 85, 218–219, 239, 252, 255,
   266–267, 268, 271, 274, 280, 282, 355, 427,
   513, 571
Lady Head Vase, see Head Vase
LALIQUE   355–357
LAMP   24, 55, 74, 80, 90, 115, 117, 139,
   145, 151, 154, 156, 160, 175, 178, 197, 201,
   213–215, 283, 298–301, 304, 307–308,
   347–348, 353, 357–366, 368, 370, 391, 397,
   411, 415, 419, 424, 431, 439, 470, 495, 502,
   503, 505, 512, 546, 558–559, 569, 578–579,
   611, 623–625, 628
Lampshade   25, 172, 196, 209, 353, 366, 470
LANTERN   90, 119, 125, 201, 300, 326,
   364–366, 403, 433, 445, 473–474, 489
Lazy Susan   351
LE VERRE FRANCAIS   366–367

LEATHER   45–46, 49–50, 56, 59–60, 77–78, 91, 102, 109, 132, 134, 161, 178, 180, 200–201, 203–206, 213, 216, 222–224, 226–227, 229, 231, 255, 261, 271, 274, 285, 290, 308, 323, 329, 357, 363, 367, 373, 384, 394, 402, 404, 415, 424, 427, 462, 467, 469, 474, 489, 510, 513, 515, 541, 548–549, 566, 574, 586, 611–612, 630, 636–637
LEEDS   92, 367
LEFTON   367–368
LEGRAS   368
Lemonade Set   25, 412
LENOX   368
LETTER OPENER   83, 323, 368–369, 426, 545, 580, 611
LIBBEY   369
Light Bulb   519
LIGHTER   102, 193, 369, 587, 635
LIGHTNING ROD   369, 622
LIGHTNING ROD BALL   369–370
Li'l Abner   598
LIMOGES   303, 370
Lincoln   8, 59, 82, 84, 143, 346, 365, 390, 420, 440–442, 522, 528, 592, 598–599, 613, 630, 634
LINDBERGH   370
LITHOPHANE   354, 370, 636
LIVERPOOL   153, 370–371, 509
LLADRO   371
Lock   43, 45, 77–78, 323, 586
LOETZ   371–372
LONE RANGER   372–373
LONGWY   262, 373
LONHUDA   373
LOSANTI   373
LOTUS WARE   373
Loving Cup   489, 530, 536, 616
LOW   373
LUNCH BOX   50, 161, 175, 308, 374, 426, 489
LUNEVILLE   374
LUSTER   24, 52, 91, 93, 101, 107, 114, 148, 151–152, 155, 163, 175, 193, 324, 327, 374, 382–383, 407, 409, 416, 426, 430, 470, 474, 498, 502, 568–569, 624–625, 638
Luster, Fairyland, see Wedgwood
Luster, Sunderland, see Sunderland
Luster, Tea Leaf, see Tea Leaf Ironstone
LUSTRES   374–375

M

Maastricht   629
MacIntyre, see Moorcroft
Magnifying Glass   394, 586
Mailbox   29, 148, 323
MAIZE   369, 375
MAJOLICA   58, 88, 91, 321, 358, 375–377, 382, 390, 400, 416, 457, 625
MALACHITE   77, 216, 291, 377, 415, 458, 539, 544
MAP   35, 121, 153, 262, 326, 374, 377–378, 429, 545
MARBLE   286, 378–379, 599
MARBLE CARVING   379–380
MARBLEHEAD   380
MARDI GRAS   192, 380–381, 388

MARTIN BROTHERS   381
Marionette   49, 113, 179, 308, 453
MARY GREGORY   381
Mask   29, 49, 52, 57, 60, 81, 148, 188, 194–195, 215, 286, 287–289, 291, 297, 300, 304, 319, 321, 369, 380–381, 405, 439, 446, 479, 525–526, 537, 540, 550, 564, 631–632, 635, 637
MASON'S IRONSTONE   382
MASSIER   382
MATCH HOLDER   151, 307, 382, 385, 412, 477, 489, 496, 508
MATCH SAFE   80, 159, 213, 382–383, 441, 545, 578, 636
MATT MORGAN   383
MCCOY   146, 383
MCKEE   117, 383
Measure   112, 138, 147–148, 297, 350, 431, 515–516
Mechanical Bank see Bank, Mechanical
MEDICAL   69–70, 384, 433, 533, 570
MEISSEN   385–387
Melodeon   399
MERCURY GLASS   363, 387
MERRIMAC   387
METLOX   387–389
Mickey Mouse   17, 27, 178–180, 419
Microscope   16, 489, 509–510
MILK GLASS   19, 34, 60, 82, 155, 197, 208–209, 308, 322, 363, 365–366, 369–370, 389–390, 421, 462, 474, 484, 507, 628
Millefiori   40, 91, 292–294, 296, 321, 361, 375, 421–422, 431
Minnie Mouse   27, 178–180
MINTON   320–321, 375, 390, 396–397
Mirror   8–9, 29, 52, 80, 83, 90, 131, 144–145, 164, 192, 207, 218–219, 236, 246–247, 249–250, 252–253, 310, 323, 347, 364–365, 391, 420, 431, 441, 453, 473, 507–510, 516, 594, 610
MOCHA   391, 457
Mold   113, 117, 349–351, 498, 546
MONMOUTH   391
Mont Joye, see Mt. Joye
MOORCROFT   391–392
MORGANTOWN   392, 562
MORIAGE   392–393
Mortar & Pestle   81, 83, 147, 351, 511
MOSAIC TILE COMPANY   393
MOSER   265, 393–394
Moss Rose   572
MOTHER-OF-PEARL   46, 77–78, 82, 88, 91, 110, 125, 149, 196, 219, 223, 285, 343, 345, 368, 371–372, 394, 398, 400, 405, 415, 419, 427, 431, 474, 483, 506, 513, 515, 567, 569, 571–572, 588, 613, 623
MOTORCYCLE   34, 394–396, 445, 594, 599, 634
Mount Washington, see Mt. Washington
MOVIE   34, 49, 54, 89, 104, 140, 373, 396, 433, 523, 554, 569, 636
Moxie   2, 5–6, 8–10, 14, 23, 122, 382, 469, 577–578, 592
MT. JOYE   396–397
MT. WASHINGTON   397

Muffineer   197, 200, 375, 536, 541, 624
MULBERRY   92, 95, 324, 397, 478, 520, 614–615
MULLER FRERES   397–398
MUNCIE   398
Murano, see Glass-Venetian; also 20
MUSIC   137, 140, 346, 354, 398–400, 422, 516, 589, 599, 632
MUSTACHE CUP   303, 400
Mustard   2, 8, 40, 67, 93, 111, 379, 391, 410, 457, 489, 500, 536, 550, 577, 585, 634, 637
MZ AUSTRIA   400

N

NAILSEA   400–401
NAKARA   401
NANKING   401
NAPKIN RING   195, 401, 525
Nappy   167–168, 172, 192, 194, 199, 305–307, 314, 463, 612, 628, 637
NASH   369, 401
NATZLER   402
NAUTICAL   138, 161, 402–404
NETSUKE   404–405
NEW MARTINSVILLE   405–406
NEWCOMB   406–408
NILOAK   408
Nickelodeon   399
NIPPON   371, 408, 411
NODDER   9, 119, 409, 426, 548, 600
NORITAKE   409–411
NORSE   411
NORTH DAKOTA SCHOOL OF MINES   411
NORTHWOOD   156, 411–412, 414
NUTCRACKER   412
Nymphenburg, see Royal Nymphenburg

O

OCCUPIED JAPAN   412–413, 584
OFFICE TECHNOLOGY   413, 428
OHR   414
Old Paris, see Paris
Old Sleepy Eye, see Sleepy Eye
Olympics   453, 545
ONION PATTERN   312, 364, 385, 414, 506–507
OPALESCENT GLASS   414
OPALINE   40, 62, 77, 200, 374, 375, 414, 559, 614
OPERA GLASSES   414–415
Organ   44, 191, 398–399
Organ Grinder   191
Ornament   25, 29, 34–35, 57, 81, 88, 119–120, 292, 300, 308, 387, 426
ORREFORS   415
ORPHAN ANNIE   415
OVERBECK   415
OWENS   415–416
OYSTER PLATE   303, 390, 416, 496, 553, 614, 624

P

PADEN CITY   416–417
Pail   9, 19, 81, 101, 119, 180, 297, 516, 536, 561, 583, 599
PAINTING   417–419

PAIRPOINT   16, 419
Palmer Cox, Brownies, see Brownies
PAPER   419–420, 435–437
Paper Clip   580
PAPER DOLL   178, 349, 420–421, 441, 523
PAPERWEIGHT   1, 27, 34, 40, 58, 80, 83, 91, 151, 160, 283, 293, 370, 389, 407, 421–422, 424–425, 441, 445, 480, 492, 512, 538, 558, 580–581, 638
PAPIER-MACHE   6, 8, 88, 100–101, 119, 125, 180, 182, 184, 187–188, 204, 280, 300, 380–381, 409, 422–423, 427, 442, 513, 566, 571, 589, 594, 597–598, 600, 637
Parasol, see Umbrella
PARIS   46, 86, 423, 433, 478, 510, 527, 588
PATE-DE-VERRE   1, 160, 283, 345, 423–424
PATE-SUR-PATE   385, 387, 390, 424
PAUL REVERE POTTERY   424–425, 526
PEACHBLOW   110, 425
PEANUTS   144, 374, 425–426
PEARL   329, 333–334, 338, 345, 426
PEARLWARE   155, 426, 440
PEKING GLASS   72, 426–427
PELOTON   427
PEN   9, 16, 49, 120–121, 179, 321, 393, 400, 413, 427–428, 436, 496, 578–580, 586, 601, 632
PEN & PENCIL   428
PENCIL   27, 54, 89, 113, 178–179, 189, 216, 307, 399, 428, 435–437, 441, 445, 469, 585
PENCIL SHARPENER   113, 179, 428, 445
PENNSBURY   146, 428–429
PEPSI-COLA   429
PERFUME BOTTLE   96, 160, 179, 204, 291, 353, 356, 377, 393, 423, 429, 431, 503, 558, 617, 623–624
PETERS & REED   429–430
PEWABIC   430
PEWTER   59, 100, 139, 150, 190, 195, 243, 288, 320–321, 347, 352, 364–366, 421, 430–431, 441, 462, 524, 555
PHOENIX GLASS   431–432
PHONOGRAPH   140, 348, 432
Photograph   50, 113, 206, 394, 396, 432–433, 442, 519, 523, 545, 548
PHOTOGRAPHY   432–434
Piano   76, 217, 265, 301, 346, 364, 399–400, 426, 516, 597, 599–600
PIANO BABY   434
PICKARD   434–435
PICTURE   104, 442, 525, 568–569, 577, 580
Picture Frame, see Furniture, Frame
PIGEON FORGE   437
PILKINGTON   437
PILLIN   437–438
Pillow   108, 160, 288, 296, 385, 393, 398, 402, 432, 442, 481–482, 487, 495, 520, 552, 576–577, 627
Pin   2, 9, 23, 34, 54, 76, 80, 91, 111, 113, 137, 149, 153, 179, 213–214, 276, 290, 299, 310, 333, 337–338, 341, 343, 348–349, 352, 356, 381, 389–390, 401, 426, 442, 445, 469, 492, 508, 511, 548, 566, 574, 636–637
Pinball   140, 285
Pincushion   326, 513, 515–516

PINCUSHION DOLL   79, 438
Pink Slag, see Slag, Pink
PIPE   6, 8, 10, 20, 57, 76, 78, 113, 189, 195, 254, 319, 354, 367, 390, 400, 413, 438, 445, 454, 534, 587, 618, 632, 634
PIRKENHAMMER   439
PISGAH FOREST   439
Pistol   308, 589, 600, 621
Plane   13, 16, 33, 207, 370, 569, 587, 597
PLANTERS PEANUTS   439
PLASTIC   38, 46, 49–50, 80, 97, 104, 113, 137, 159, 161, 178–182, 184–188, 194, 222, 224, 226, 255, 300, 308, 352, 361, 363, 365, 422, 428, 439, 458, 474, 503, 577, 586, 589, 593, 597, 600–602, 613
PLATED AMBERINA   439–440
PLIQUE-A-JOUR   194, 341, 345, 440
POLITICAL   440–444, 471
POMONA   445, 588
Pontypool, see Tole
POOLE POTTERY   445
POPEYE   27, 144, 417, 421, 445–446
PORCELAIN   10, 13, 17, 34, 51, 60, 72, 74, 77, 97–98, 102, 115, 122, 128, 137–138, 155, 182, 187, 287, 303, 312, 322, 330, 349, 361, 363–364, 382, 384–385, 387, 394, 412, 416, 438, 446–447, 450, 474, 497, 503, 507–508, 512–513, 515–516, 544, 555, 565–566, 571, 574, 577–578, 584, 587, 594, 597, 619, 624, 636
PORCELAIN-ASIAN   447–450
PORCELAIN-CONTEMPORARY   450
PORCELAIN-MIDCENTURY   451
Porringer   164, 274, 391, 431, 531, 536
POSTCARD   245, 290, 442, 451
POSTER   34, 50, 57, 104, 119, 179, 193, 206, 216, 373, 394, 396, 442, 451–453, 523, 548, 554, 569, 586, 635–636
POTTERY   5, 78, 88, 91, 146, 319, 321–322, 382, 400, 426, 431, 454, 458, 477, 503, 512, 553–555, 563–564, 629
POTTERY-ART   454–457
POTTERY-CONTEMPORARY   457–458
POTTERY-MIDCENTURY   458–461
POWDER FLASK AND POWDER HORN   161, 462
PRATT   421, 453, 462
PRESSED GLASS   462–464
PRINT   57, 97, 113, 119, 134, 153, 178, 290, 412, 432–433, 464–467, 469, 471, 523, 549, 569, 612, 624
Projector   433
Puppet   161, 179, 207, 308, 371, 439, 493, 569, 637
PURINTON   308, 466–467
PURSE   9, 48, 104, 113, 145, 179, 194, 334, 441, 446, 467–469, 523, 588
Puzzle   45, 81, 104, 148, 175, 285–286, 327, 413, 426, 442, 478, 550, 565, 569

Q
QUEZAL   426, 470
QUILT   254, 349, 394, 425, 470–472, 499, 580, 628, 636
QUIMPER   416, 472–473

R
RADIO   6, 8, 14, 55, 113, 137, 169, 179, 205, 308, 363, 415, 428–429, 473, 503, 577, 592
RAILROAD   27, 51, 65, 67, 91, 383, 451, 453, 473–474, 519, 566, 600, 604
Rattle   178, 300, 319, 436, 450, 458, 531, 542, 584
RAZOR   6, 46, 474
REAMER   214, 474, 463
RECORD   50, 179, 193, 419–421, 474, 599
RED WING   475–476
REDWARE   43, 57, 208, 321, 350–351, 461, 476–478
Regina   126, 297, 353, 398–399, 434–435
Revolver   621
RICHARD   46, 379, 431, 470, 478, 527–528, 535
RIDGWAY   478
Rifle   621
RIVIERA   478–479, 571
ROBLIN   479
ROCKINGHAM   54, 479, 637
Rogers, see John Rogers
Rolling Pin   75, 352, 390, 401, 511, 566, 637
ROOKWOOD   400, 479–482
RORSTAND   482
ROSE BOWL   58, 90, 93, 105–107, 109, 154, 158, 160, 198, 291, 297, 304–305, 314, 394, 412, 416, 425, 438, 483, 506, 545–546, 615, 623–624
ROSE CANTON   483
ROSE MANDARIN   288, 483
ROSE MEDALLION   483
Rose O'Neil, see Kewpie; also 349
ROSE TAPESTRY   484, 489–490
ROSEMEADE   484
ROSENTHAL   484
ROSEVILLE   484–488
ROWLAND & MARSELLUS   488
ROY ROGERS   374, 488–489
ROYAL BAYREUTH   489–490
ROYAL BONN   490–491
ROYAL COPENHAGEN   491
ROYAL CROWN DERBY   491–492
ROYAL DOULTON   369, 492–494
ROYAL DUX   494–495
ROYAL FLEMISH   495
Royal Haeger, see Haeger
ROYAL HICKMAN   495
Royal Ivy, see Northwood, Royal Ivy
ROYAL NYMPHENBURG   495
Royal Rudolstadt, see Rudolstadt
Royal Vienna, see Beehive; also   192
ROYAL WORCESTER   496, 636
ROYCROFT   217–218, 227, 245, 363, 496–497
Rozane, see Roseville; also 37, 487
ROZENBURG   497
RRP   497
RS GERMANY   497
RS POLAND   497–498
RS PRUSSIA   498
RS SILESIA   498
RS SUHL   498
RS TILLOWITZ   498
RUBINA   82, 95–96, 412, 498

RUBINA VERDE 82, 498–499
RUBY GLASS 369, 393, 499
RUDOLSTADT 499
RUG 26, 179, 308, 319–320, 349, 367, 499–502, 598
Ruler 600
RUMRILL 502
RUSKIN 502
RUSSEL WRIGHT 218, 227, 502–503

S

SABINO 503, 505–513, 515–516, 520, 522, 523–524, 526, 535, 539–540, 543–549, 552, 554–555
Sailor's Valentine 403–404
SALT & PEPPER 39, 50, 93, 112, 116, 147, 156, 167, 169, 171, 175–176, 194, 198–199, 205, 211–213, 296, 306–307, 309–310, 312, 349, 355, 368, 384, 387–388, 390, 393, 397, 400, 406, 412, 439, 458, 466–467, 475, 476, 479, 484, 498–499, 503, 520, 539, 542, 552–553, 617, 628
Salt Glaze 347, 378, 437, 454, 520, 549, 561–565
Saltshaker 173, 393, 397, 410, 611
Samovar 81, 148
SAMPLER 404, 471, 504–505
SAMSON 505, 574
SANDWICH GLASS 505
Santa Claus 44, 101, 117, 119–120, 304, 307, 311, 387, 493–494
SARREGUEMINES 505–506, 610
SASCHA BRASTOFF 506
SATIN GLASS 82, 90, 110, 149, 366, 394, 397, 425, 483, 506, 559, 584, 628
SATSUMA 91, 506–507
Saturday Evening Girls, see Paul Revere Pottery
SCALE 47, 139, 384, 404, 439, 507–508, 513, 569
Scarf 134, 181, 304, 387–388, 442, 446, 575
SCHAFER & VATER 508
SCHEIER 508–509
SCHNEIDER 509
SCIENTIFIC INSTRUMENT 509–510
Scissors 6, 25, 384, 515, 567
Scoop 203, 320, 352, 586–587, 616, 619, 630, 634
Screen 6, 9, 203, 204, 255, 370, 442, 574, 579, 586
SCRIMSHAW 368, 400, 427, 462, 510–511
SEBASTIAN MINIATURES 511
SEG, see Paul Revere Pottery
SEVRES 447, 511–512
SEWER TILE 512
SEWING 13, 16, 48, 228, 277–278, 286, 466, 491, 510, 513–515, 567, 609
SHAKER 25, 64, 69, 96, 120–121, 139, 153, 166, 168–172, 192, 197, 208, 217–218, 221–222, 228, 233, 237, 243, 246–247, 255, 264, 269, 278, 280–282, 291, 381, 390–391, 397, 405, 411–412, 414, 417, 463, 482, 499, 515–516, 524–525, 527, 531, 538, 540, 546, 616
SHAVING MUG 46, 278, 516–520
SHAWNEE 73, 520

SHEARWATER 520
SHEET MUSIC 137, 354, 520–522
Sheffield, see Silver Plate; Silver-English
SHELLEY 522
SHIRLEY TEMPLE 522–523
Shotgun 132, 503
Shriner, see Fraternal
Sideboard 260–261
Sign 9–10, 13–14, 16–17, 19, 35–38, 46, 91, 93, 110, 137–138, 164, 175, 179, 201, 207, 213, 297, 308, 312, 323, 394, 396, 429, 442, 474, 519, 548, 561, 565,–567, 569, 574, 636
Silhouette 137, 394, 436, 487
SILVER DEPOSIT 523
SILVER FLATWARE 523–524
SILVER PLATE 46, 82, 97–98, 100, 110, 113, 148, 154, 178, 250, 252–253, 347, 349, 361, 366, 368, 383, 401, 428, 469, 515, 524–526, 538, 588, 611
Silver, Sheffield, see Silver Plate; Silver-English
SILVER-AMERICAN 526–533
SILVER-ANGLO-INDIAN 534
SILVER-ARMENIAN 534
SILVER-ASIAN 534
SILVER-AUSTRIAN 534
SILVER-AUSTRO-HUNGARIAN 534
SILVER-BOLIVIAN 534
SILVER-CANADIAN 534
SILVER-CHINESE 534
SILVER-CONTINENTAL 534
SILVER-DANISH 534–535
SILVER-DUTCH 535
SILVER-EGYPTIAN 535
SILVER-ENGLISH 535–537
SILVER-ETHOPIAN 537
SILVER-FRENCH 537–538
SILVER-GERMAN 538
SILVER-INDIAN 538
SILVER-IRISH 538
SILVER-ISRAELI 538
SILVER-ITALIAN 538–539
SILVER-JAPANESE 539
SILVER-MEXICAN 539
SILVER-MIDDLE EASTERN 539
SILVER-NORWEGIAN 539
SILVER-PERSIAN 539
SILVER-PERUVIAN 539
SILVER-POLISH 539
SILVER-PORTUGUESE 539
SILVER-RUSSIAN 539–540
SILVER-SCOTTISH 540
SILVER-SOUTH AMERICAN 540
SILVER-SPANISH 540
SILVER-STERLING 540–543
SILVER-SWEDISH 543
SILVER-THAI 543
SILVER-TIBETAN 543
SINCLAIRE 157, 543
Singing Bird 399
Skiing, see Sports; also 126, 147
SLAG GLASS 155, 301, 358, 361, 363, 378–379, 543, 578–580
Sled 23, 119, 500, 544, 587, 601
SLEEPY EYE 17, 146, 543

Sleigh 51, 109–110, 117, 119, 156, 418, 433, 600–601
Slot Machine, see Coin-Operated Machine
SMITH BROTHERS 544
Smoking Set 26, 81
SNOW BABY 544
Snuff Bottle, see Bottle, Snuff
SNUFFBOX 49, 80, 422, 442, 544
Soap 2, 6, 10, 13, 16, 23, 54, 105, 130, 278, 572, 601
SOAPSTONE 368, 544–545
SOUVENIR 156, 545
Sparkler 299–300, 378
SPANGLE GLASS 545
SPATTER GLASS 82, 545–546, 615
SPATTERWARE 546–547
SPELTER 43, 122, 128, 131, 212, 547
Spice Box 347, 567
SPINNING WHEEL 547, 569
SPODE 286, 320–321, 548, 629
Spoon 91, 97, 113, 158–159, 178, 194, 254, 320, 352, 381, 384, 440, 490, 511, 520, 523–525, 527, 531, 533–538, 540, 542, 545, 551, 582
Spooner 156, 200, 463
SPORTS 548–549
Sprinkler 207, 288, 323, 372, 606, 609
STAFFORDSHIRE 1, 153, 155, 321, 426, 453, 559–552, 629
STAINLESS STEEL 552
STANGL 552–554
STAR TREK AND STAR WARS 554
Stationary 148
STEIN 195, 368, 387, 389, 482, 506, 554–555
Stein, Mettlach, see Mettlach, Stein
Stencil 76, 81, 222, 397, 436, 561–563
STEREO CARD 555–556
STEREOSCOPE 556
Sterling Silver, see Silver-Sterling
STEUBEN 293, 556–559
STEVENS & WILLIAMS 559
Stickpin 345, 381, 442
STIEGEL TYPE 73, 559
STONE 194, 254, 278, 286–287, 554, 559–561
STONEWARE 29, 54, 62, 64, 126, 163, 191, 213, 321, 380–381, 436, 457–458, 461, 482, 494, 512, 520, 555, 561–565, 584
STORE 79, 565–567
STOVE 516, 567, 602
STRETCH GLASS 198, 567
Stringholder 19, 57, 138, 308, 323
Sulphide 379
SUMIDA 568
SUNBONNET BABIES 568
SUNDERLAND 568
Sundial 288, 404, 509, 558
SUPERMAN 374, 568–569
SUSIE COOPER 569
SWANKYSWIG 569
SWASTIKA KERAMOS 569
Sweeper 424, 602
SWORD 102, 121, 396, 569–570
Symphonion 398
SYRACUSE 570–571, 613

T

Tapestry, Porcelain, see Rose Tapestry
TEA CADDY   480, 533, 537–539, 542, 571–572, 583, 588, 629
TEA LEAF IRONSTONE   572
TECO   572–573
TEDDY BEAR   60, 573
TELEPHONE   428, 573–574
Telescope   102, 486, 510, 586, 636
TELEVISION   574
TEPLITZ   574–575
TERRA-COTTA   29, 128, 286–288, 454, 575–576, 583, 636
TEXTILE   469, 576–577
THERMOMETER   46–47, 87–88, 138, 404, 429, 577–578
Thermos   308, 374, 489, 530, 554, 569
Thimble   515
TIFFANY   60, 102, 302, 441, 523, 578–581
TIFFANY POTTERY   581–582
TIFFANY SILVER   582–583
TIFFIN   383, 583
TILE   26, 48, 58, 115, 146, 279, 298, 313, 373, 380, 389, 391, 393, 416, 425, 430, 437, 479, 480, 501, 576, 583–584, 615
Tintype   353, 432, 433, 434
TINWARE   584
Toaster   138, 352
Toast Rack   537
Tobacco Cutter, see Store, Tobacco Cutter; also   23
TOBACCO JAR   23, 164, 376, 381, 454, 584
TOBY JUG   153, 494, 584
Toilet   144, 168, 511, 519, 628
TOLE   56, 125–126, 282–283, 358, 361, 366, 567, 584–586
TOM MIX   396, 586
Tongs   203–204, 523, 533–534, 537, 540, 582, 587
TOOL   202–204, 586–587
TOOTHBRUSH HOLDER   179, 587
TOOTHPICK HOLDER   25, 39, 56, 88, 90, 106, 156, 159–160, 195, 197, 200, 210, 305–307, 327, 348, 369, 384, 393, 397, 425, 445, 463, 490, 498, 538–539, 587–588, 614, 624
Torchere   365, 503
TORQUAY   588
TORTOISESHELL   125, 145, 153, 196, 249, 262, 303, 333, 369, 405, 428, 473, 492, 525, 571–572, 578, 588
Towel   14, 46, 636
TOY   50, 89, 113–114, 119, 138–139, 152, 161, 175, 179–180, 206, 290, 308–309, 320, 370, 372–373, 426, 442, 445–446, 489, 506, 554, 569, 588–610, 636
Tractor   36, 517, 589, 600, 602, 604, 619
Trade Stimulator   23, 143, 409
Train   31, 155, 179, 180, 347, 474, 520, 555, 567, 599, 604, 612, 636
TRAMP ART   610
TRAP   34, 424, 611
Tray   1, 9, 23, 38, 52, 56, 81, 84, 88–89, 93–94, 99, 112, 115–116, 119–120, 132, 138–139, 148, 158, 160, 164, 168, 170, 193–194, 206, 208–209, 275, 280, 283–284, 289, 299, 303, 314, 321, 328, 349, 352, 355–356, 367–369, 373, 387, 390, 393, 406,

417–418, 423, 438–439, 442, 447, 449, 463, 473, 475, 478, 483–484, 496–498, 502, 503, 508, 525, 527, 533–535, 537–539, 541–543, 547, 551, 568, 579–580, 582–585, 587, 610, 612–613, 625, 632, 634–635, 638
Treen, see Wooden; also 100
TRENCH ART   611
TRIVET   26, 155, 280, 298, 308, 323, 373, 407, 425, 442, 480, 611, 615
Truck   35–36, 38, 40, 138–139, 201, 445, 516–517, 519–520, 586, 595, 599–600, 605–606, 609
TRUNK   121, 585, 611–612
TUTHILL   612–613
TYPEWRITER   613
TYPEWRITER RIBBON TIN   613

U

UHL   613
UMBRELLA   81, 88, 139, 282, 300, 313, 323, 376, 390, 478, 483, 490, 531, 585, 613, 625, 627, 637
Umbrella Stand   81, 88, 282, 300, 313, 323, 376, 390, 478, 483, 485, 487–488, 490, 585, 625, 627, 637
Uncle Sam   5, 13, 17, 20, 45, 88, 120, 433, 442, 453, 508, 609, 635–636
UNION PORCELAIN WORKS   614
UNIVERSITY CITY   614
University of North Dakota, see North Dakota School of Mines

V

Vacuum Cleaner   353
Valentine   104, 346, 403–404, 437, 577, 613
VALLERYSTHAL   614
VAL ST. LAMBERT   614
VAN BRIGGLE   614–615
VASA MURRHINA   198, 615
VASELINE GLASS   100, 474, 616
Venetian Glass, see Glass-Venetian
VERLYS   616
VERNON KILNS   616–617
VERRE DE SOIE   558, 617
Vienna, see Beehive
VIENNA ART   137, 617
VILLEROY & BOCH   617
Violin   17, 86, 343, 399–400, 472
VOLKMAR   617
VOLKSTEDT   617–618

W

WADE   618
Waffle Iron   353
Wagon   20, 67, 97, 189, 201, 206, 213, 217, 255, 348, 383, 411, 421, 471, 517, 519–520, 526, 565, 587, 589, 591, 595, 597–598, 609–610, 635
Wahpeton Pottery, see Rosemeade
Wallace Nutting photographs are listed under Print, Nutting. His reproduction furniture is listed under Furniture.
Wallpaper   75–76, 79, 255
WALL POCKET   1, 89, 309–311, 380, 404, 430, 457, 473, 482, 484–488, 490, 515, 610, 615, 618, 627

WALRATH   618
Walt Disney, see Disneyana
Walter, see A. Walter
WARWICK   618
Washboard   323
Washbowl   54, 289, 483, 552
Washing Machine   353, 424
Washstand   282–283, 506
Washtub   353
WATCH   49, 91, 104, 144, 161, 180, 206, 290, 337, 343, 415, 446, 548, 618–619
WATCH FOB   213, 442, 619, 636
Watch Holder   88, 327
WATERFORD   174, 620
Watering Can   85, 149
WATT   620
WAVE CREST   620–621
WEAPON   621
WEATHER VANE   177, 621–623
WEBB   131, 623
WEBB BURMESE   364, 623–624
WEBB PEACHBLOW   624
WEDGWOOD   92, 624–625
WELLER   625–628
WEMYSS   628
WESTMORELAND GLASS   628
Whale's Tooth   510, 511
WHEATLEY   629
Wheelbarrow   587, 610
WHIELDON   629
Whirligig   25, 31, 179, 207, 623
Whistle   17, 122, 194, 206, 208, 404, 511, 534, 548, 630
WILLETS   629
WILLOW   89, 177, 554, 624, 629
Windmill Weight   323–324
WINDOW   23, 191, 424, 495, 629–630
Windup   51, 113–114, 432, 442, 445, 588, 590, 592, 594–595, 597–602, 605, 609
Wine Set   406
WOOD CARVING   630–633
WOODEN   112, 200, 259, 556, 610, 621, 633–635
WORCESTER   69, 635
WORLD WAR I   635
WORLD WAR II   635–636
WORLD'S FAIR   34, 126, 144, 636
WPA   636–637
Wrench   586
WRISTWATCH   50, 180, 308, 426, 442, 637

Y

YELLOWWARE   43, 637

Z

ZANESVILLE   69, 74, 488, 638
ZSOLNAY   638

PHOTO CREDITS

We have included the name of the auction house or photographer with each pictured object. This is a list of the addresses of those who have contributed photographs and information for this book. Every dealer or auction house has to buy antiques to have items to sell. Call or email a dealer or auction house if you want to discuss buying or selling. If you need an appraisal or advice, remember that appraising is part of their business and fees may be charged.

Allard Auctions
P.O. Box 1030
St. Ignatius, MT 59865
www.allardauctions.com
406-745-0500

Anderson Americana
P.O. Box 644
Troy, OH 45373
www.anderson-auction.com
937-339-0850

Aspire Auctions
2310 Superior Ave., #125
Cleveland, OH 44114
www.aspireauctions.com
216-231-5515

Auction Team Breker
Otto-Hahn-Str. 10
50997 Cologne, Germany
www.breker.com
703-796-5544 (U.S.)

Bertoia Auctions
2141 DeMarco Dr.
Vineland, NJ 08360
www.bertoiaauctions.com
856-692-1881

Brian Lebel's Old West Show & Auction
3201 Zafarano Dr., Suite C585
Santa Fe, NM 87507
www.codyoldwest.com
480-779-9378

Brunk Auctions
P.O. Box 2135
Asheville, NC 28802
www.brunkauctions.com
828-254-6846

Clars Auction Gallery
5644 Telegraph Avenue
Oakland, CA 94609
www.clars.com
510-428-0100

Conestoga Auction Co.
768 Graystone Road
P.O. Box 1
Manheim, PA 17545
www.conestogaauction.com
717-898-7284

Copake Auction
266 Route 7A
Copake, NY 12516
www.copakeauction.com
518-329-1142

Corkscrews Online
Peter@corkscrewsonline.com
www.corkscrewsonline.com

Cottone Auctions
120 Court St.
Geneseo, NY 14454
www.cottoneauctions.com
585-243-3100

Cowan's Auctions
6270 Este Ave.
Cincinnati, OH 45232
www.cowanauctions.com
513-871-1670

Crescent City Auction Gallery
1330 St. Charles Ave.
New Orleans, LA 70130
crescentcityauctiongallery.com
504-529-5057

Crocker Farm
15900 York Road
Sparks, MD 21152
www.crockerfarm.com
410-472-2016

Dirk Soulis Auctions
P.O. Box 17
529 West Lone Jack-Lee's Summit Road
Lone Jack, MO 64070
www.dirksoulisauctions.com
816-697-3830

DuMouchelles Art Gallery
409 East Jefferson Ave.
Detroit, MI 48226
www.dumouchelles.com
313-963-6255

Early Auction Co.
123 Main St.
Milford, OH 45150
www.earlyauctionco.com
513-831-4833

Fox Auctions
P.O. Box 4069
Vallejo, CA 94590
www.foxauctionsonline.com
631-553-3841

Garth's Auctioneers
P.O. Box 369
Delaware, OH 43015
www.garths.com
740-362-4771

Glass Works Auctions
P.O. Box 38
Lambertville, NJ 08530
www.glswrk-auction.com
609-483-2683

Gray's Auctioneers
10717 Detroit Ave.
Cleveland, OH 44102
www.graysauctioneers.com
216-458-7695

Hake's Americana & Collectibles
P.O. Box 12001
York, PA 17402
www.hakes.com
717-434-1600

Hudson Valley Auctioneers
432 Main St.
Beacon, NY 12508
www.hudsonvalleyauctioneers.com
845-831-6800

Humler & Nolan
225 East Sixth St., 4th Floor
Cincinnati, OH 45202
www.humlernolan.com
513-381-2041

Ivey-Selkirk Auctioneers
7447 Forsyth Blvd.
St. Louis, MO 63105
www.iveyselkirk.com
314-726-5515

Jackson's International Auctioneers
2229 Lincoln St.
Cedar Falls, IA 50613
www.jacksonsauction.com
319-277-2256

James D. Julia Auctioneers
203 Skowhegan Road
Fairfield, Maine 04937
www.jamesdjulia.com
207-453-7125

Jeffrey S. Evans & Associates
P.O. Box 2638
Harrisonburg, VA 22801
www.jeffreysevans.com
540-434-3939

Leighton Galleries
6 Pearl Court, Suite C
Allendale, NJ 07401
www.leightongalleries.com
201-327-8800

Leland Little Auction
620 Cornerstone Ct.
Hillsborough, NC 27278
www.llauctions.com
919-644-1243

Leslie Hindman Auctioneers
1338 West Lake St.
Chicago, IL 60607
www.lesliehindman.com
312-280-1212

Locati Auctions
1425 East Welsh Road
Maple Glen PA 19002
www.locatiauctions.com
215-619-2873

LA Modern Auctions (LAMA)
16145 Hart St.
Van Nuys, CA 91406
www.LAModern.com
323-904-1950

Manor Auctions
2415 North Monroe St.
Tallahassee, FL 32303
www.manorauctions.com
850-523-3787

Martin Auction Co.
P.O. Box 2
100 Lick Creek Road
Anna, IL 62906
www.martinauctionco.com
618-833-3589

Michaan's Auctions
2751 Todd St.
Alameda, CA 94501
www.michaans.com
800-380-9822

Morphy Auctions
2000 North Reading Road
Denver, PA 17517
www.morphyauctions.com
717-335-3435

Neal Auction Co.
4038 Magazine St.
New Orleans, LA 70115
www.nealauction.com
800-467-5329

New Orleans Auction Galleries
801 Magazine St.
New Orleans, LA 70130
www.neworleansauction.com
800-501-0277

Norman C. Heckler & Co.
79 Bradford Corner Road
Woodstock Valley, CT 06282
www.hecklerauction.com
860-974-1634

Old Barn Auction
10040 State Route 224
Findlay, OH 45840
www.oldbarn.com
419-422-8531

Palm Beach Modern Auctions
417 Bunker Road
West Palm Beach, FL 33405
www.palmbeachmodernauctions.com
561-586-5500

Phoebus Auction Gallery
18 East Mellen St.
Hampton, VA 23663
www.phoebusauction.com
757-722-9210

Pook & Pook
463 Lancaster Ave.
Downington, PA 19335
www.pookandpook.com
610-269-4040

Potter & Potter Auctions
3759 North Ravenswood Ave., #121
Chicago, IL 60613
www.potterauctions.com
773-472-1442

Rachel Davis Fine Arts
1301 West 79th St.
Cleveland, OH 44102
www.racheldavisfinearts.com
216-939-1190

Rago Arts and Auction Center
333 North Main St.
Lambertville, NJ 08530
www.ragoarts.com
609-397-9374

Regency-Superior Auctions
229 North Euclid Ave.
Saint Louis, MO 63108
www.regencystamps.com
314-361-5699

Roland Antiques
80 East 11th St.
New York, NY 1003
www.rolandantiques.com
212-260-2000

RSL Auction Co.
295 U.S. Highway 22 East
Suite 204 West
Whitehouse Station, NJ
www.rslauctions.com
908-823-4049

Ruby Lane
381 Bush St., Suite 400
San Francisco, CA 94104
www.rubylane.com
415-362-7611

Seeck Auctions
P.O. Box 377
Mason City, IA 50402
www.seeckauction.com
641-424-1116

Serious Toyz
1 Baltic Place
Croton-on-Hudson, NY 10520
www.serioustoyz.com
866-653-8699

Showtime Auction Services
22619 Monterey Dr.
Woodhaven, MI 48183
www.showtimeauctions.com
951-453-2415

Skinner, Inc.
274 Cedar Hill St.
Marlborough, MA 01752
www.skinnerinc.com
508-970-3000

Stanton Auctions
106 East Longmeadow Road
Hampden, MA 01036
www.stantonauctions.com
413-566-3161

The Stein Auction Co.
P.O. Box 136
Palatine, IL 60078
www.tsaco.com
847-991-5927

Susanin's Auctions
900 South Clinton St.
Chicago, IL 60607
www.susanins.com
312-832-9800

Swann Auction Galleries
104 East 25th St.
New York, NY 10010
www.swanngalleries.com
212-254-4710

Theriault's
P.O. Box 151
Annapolis, MD 21404
www.theriaults.com
800-638-0422

Tom Hall Auctions
4644 Main St.
Schnecksville, PA 18078
www.tomhallauctions.com
610-799-0808

Tom Harris Auctions
203 South 18th Ave.
Marshalltown, IA 50108
www.tomharrisauctions.com
641-754-4890

Treadway Toomey Galleries
c/o Treadway Gallery
2029 Madison Road
Cincinnati, OH 45208
www.treadwaygallery.com
513-321-6742

Victorian Casino Antiques
4520 Arville St., #1
Las Vegas, NV 89103
www.vcaauction.com
702-382-2466

William H. Bunch Auctions
1 Hillman Dr.
Chadds Ford, PA 19317
www.williambunchauctions.com
610-558-1800

Wm. Morford Auction
RD #2 Cobb Hill Road
Cazenovia, NY 13035
www.morfauction.com
315-662-7625

Willis Henry Auctions
22 Main St.
Marshfield, MA 02050
www.willishenry.com
781-834-7774

Woody Auction
P.O. Box 618
317 South Forest St.
Douglass, KS 67039
woodyauction.com
316-747-2694

Wright
1440 West Hubbard St.
Chicago, IL 60642
www.wright20.com
312-563-0020